10/9

THE OXFORD ENCYCLOPEDIA OF
THEATRE & PERFORMANCE

THE OXFORD ENCYCLOPEDIA OF
THEATRE &
PERFORMANCE

EDITED BY

Dennis Kennedy

VOLUME 1 · A–L

OXFORD
UNIVERSITY PRESS

OXFORD

UNIVERSITY PRESS

Great Clarendon Street, Oxford OX2 6DP

Oxford University Press is a department of the University of Oxford.
It furthers the University's objective of excellence in research, scholarship,
and education by publishing worldwide in

Oxford New York

Auckland Cape Town Dar es Salaam Hong Kong Karachi Kuala Lumpur
Madrid Melbourne Mexico City Nairobi New Delhi Taipei Toronto
Shanghai

With offices in

Argentina Austria Brazil Chile Czech Republic France Greece
Guatemala Hungary Italy Japan South Korea Poland Portugal
Singapore Switzerland Thailand Turkey Ukraine Vietnam

Oxford is a registered trade mark of Oxford University Press
in the UK and in certain other countries

Published in the United States
by Oxford University Press Inc., New York

© Oxford University Press 2003

Database right Oxford University Press (maker)

First published 2003
Reprinted 2003, 2005

British Library Cataloguing in Publication Data

Data available

Library of Congress Cataloging in Publication Data

Data available

ISBN-13: 978-0-19-860174-6 (set)
ISBN-10: 0-19-860174-3 (set)

ISBN-13: 978-0-19-860672-7 (Vol. 1)
ISBN-10: 0-19-860672-9 (Vol. 1)

ISBN-13: 978-0-19-860671-0 (Vol. 2)
ISBN-10: 0-19-860671-0 (Vol. 2)

3 5 7 9 10 8 6 4

Typeset in Pondicherry, India, by
Alliance Interactive Technology
Printed and bound in China through
Phoenix Offset

ADVISORY EDITORS

Rustom Bharucha
Writer and director, Calcutta

Jacky Bratton
University of London

Edward Braun
University of Bristol

Marvin Carlson
City University of New York

John Conteh-Morgan
Ohio State University

David Kerr
University of Malawi

Kate McLuskie
University of Southampton

Brooks McNamara
New York University

Kirstin Pauka
University of Hawai'i

J. Thomas Rimer
University of Pittsburgh

Adam Versényi
University of North Carolina

Ronald W. Vince
McMaster University

RESEARCH AND EDITORIAL ASSISTANTS
Mark Patrick Bates, Diane DeVore, Neal Rowland

FOR ANNIE

CONTENTS

VOLUME 1

VOLUME 2

PREFACE AND PRINCIPLES

THIS Encyclopedia is an entirely new work that treats the most important aspects of theatre and performance over time and on a worldwide scale. The volumes offer information and commentary on both general and decidedly specific aspects of the subject for the use of specialist and non-specialist readers. The work attempts to see theatre and performance as human expressions with large cultural significance: what goes on and has gone on in playhouses is the centre of interest but the discussion has been expanded to incorporate key issues in ritual, para-theatrical activities (e.g. tango, parades, public executions), other types of live entertainment (sport, Wild West shows, cabaret, etc.), some aspects of opera, dance and dance-drama, and the relationship of drama and theatre to film, radio, television, and the new media.

There are many different types of performance, each with its historical or contemporary audience. But in a work of this type the most precious resource is space, and it has been impossible to include all the material that it might be desirable to cover. Some readers may be disappointed to find a favourite theatre personality not present, but I hope they will understand that selection of entries has been a difficult negotiation between the ideal and the achievable.

In choosing topics for coverage the editor and advisory editors have been guided by their analysis of the fields of theatre and performance, the outline of which is made apparent in the Thematic Table of Contents. Despite the appearance of detachment in encyclopedias, we recognize that complete objectivity is impossible. We have attempted instead a balanced strategy, encouraging contributors to take positions on issues but indicating when these remain unsettled. In selecting topics and approaches to them, we have been guided by these major principles:

1. A work on theatre and performance should be grounded in contemporary theatre and performance studies. We have therefore included discursive entries on concepts and theories that define the field and its terminology, treat the premises and methods of the subject, and operate as its (sometimes unspoken) foundations. Examples include origins of theatre, theories of drama, theatre, and performance, diaspora, pornography and performance, acting, directing, criticism, politics and theatre, amateur theatre, gender and performance, scenography, comedy, tragedy, puppet theatre, psychoanalytic criticism, performance studies, post-colonial studies, theatre studies, and so on. Thus the factual material contained in the Encyclopedia is expanded by conceptual discussions, written in accessible form.

2. Purely literary matters about drama are handled in many other reference books; here we have emphasized performance-related issues instead. Entries suggestive of this approach include avant-garde, voodoo, interculturalism, performance art, circus, pantomime, sex shows and dances, magic shows, freak shows, applause, audience, and finance.

3. In order to include a large number of biographies (they take up 45 per cent of the text) we have been forced to make some of them fairly short. In general terms we have attempted to make a correlation between the length of an entry and the significance of its topic, whether biographical or otherwise.

4. Summary articles on national traditions of theatre are inevitably shallow and oversimplified. In their place we have commissioned a series of entries on cities and regions that are theatrical centres, focusing on performance as an expression of society and locality, from contributors with deep connections to the area. These include London, Paris, Berlin, Moscow, Algiers, Mumbai (Bombay), New York, Toronto, Mexico City, São Paulo, and many more. In the cases of Asia and sub-Saharan Africa, this policy has been expanded to include linguistic traditions and overviews of countries whose activity will be unfamiliar to many readers. We have been careful not to make these overviews into national theatre histories; rather they are discursive pointers to other more specific entries in the work. They include Africa, India, China, Japan, numerous South-East Asian countries; and more explicit entries on francophone Africa, for example, and Kannada theatre, Manipuri theatre, Telugu theatre, Caribbean theatre, etc. There are 110 city and regional entries, constituting about 10 per cent of the total length of the work.

5. To be fully international, the work includes not only entries on persons, countries, and topics worldwide but also takes account of non-Western concerns when dealing with general and conceptual issues, from applause to directing, from dance to masks and masking. The Encyclopedia is in English, however, and many readers will be interested principally in material from English-speaking regions; though the perspective remains international, more attention has been given to anglophone theatre than to other regions.

ACKNOWLEDGEMENTS

No one knows enough to edit a work like this, least of all myself, and only a very large amount of help has enabled me to complete it. My first and greatest debt is to the Advisory Editors, whose dedication has been remarkable and who have often gone far beyond the boundaries of obligation. In planning the book and locating contributors, in critiquing entries and writing crucial ones themselves, their participation has made the work enormously richer, and I can never sufficiently repay their generosity. A number of contributors made significant interventions with valuable advice, and I must mention in particular Arnold Aronson, Christopher Balme, John Russell Brown, Frances Dann, Victor Dixon, Mark Fearnow, C. Andrew Gerstle, Kiki Gounaridou, Roger Herzel, Pamela Howard, Denis Johnston, Filomena Mesquita, and the late J. R. Stephens. Ric Knowles, Sandra Richards, and Don Wilmeth gave important early assistance, and emergency service was provided by Kazimierz Braun, Sarah Bryant-Bertail, Jae-Oh Choi, Peter Davis, W. D. Howarth, Siyuan Liu, Felicia Hardison Londré, Adrienne Scullion, and Caldwell Titcomb. The research and editorial assistants were dedicated and highly competent, Mark Patrick Bates and Neal Rowland carrying the bulk of the work over lengthy periods. Valuable assistance was also given by Jessica Alexis Kennedy and Megan Kennedy.

At Trinity College Dublin the project has been supported by beneficial grants from the Provost, the Office of Research, and the Faculty of Arts (Letters), and I thank in particular Thomas Mitchell, John Hegerty, and John Scattergood. My colleagues in the School of Drama have been equally supportive, especially Matthew Causey, Ann Mulligan, and Brian Singleton. At Oxford University Press I owe gratitude for the encouragement and faith of Michael Cox and Joanna Harris, as well as to Edwin and Jackie Pritchard, copy editors extraordinaire. Wendy Tuckey deserves a special mention for administering the project from start to finish with efficiency and grace.

Through a challenging, arduous, and seemingly endless task, Ann Tyrrell Kennedy has kept me alive—and happy as well, which is no easy matter.

D. K.

Dublin, September 2002

5 Organizations and institutions

When a venue is primarily associated with a company of the same name, it has normally been listed under category 5.4.

5.1 Performance venues to 1700

5.2 Performance venues 1700–1900

5.3 Performance venues since 1900

5.5 Professional and educational organizations

6 Buildings and material elements

6.1 Architecture of playhouses

LIST OF ILLUSTRATIONS

EDITORS AND CONTRIBUTORS

KEY TO CONTRIBUTOR INITIALS

AA	Arnold Aronson
AB	Annemarie Bean
ACB	Albert Bermel
ACH	Arthur Holmberg
ADW	David Williams
AEM	Anna McMullan
AF	Ann Featherstone
AFJ	Alexandra F. Johnston
AHK	Amelia Howe Kritzer
AJG	Andrew Gurr
AL	Ananda Lal
AlR	Alain Ricard
AMB	Ananda Mohan Bhagawati
AMCS	Anamaría Crowe Serrano
ANG	Arthur Gelb
AP	Ann Pellegrini
AR	Alvina Ruprecht
ARJ	Anthony Jackson
ARY	Alan Young
AS	Adrienne Scullion
ASh	Alison Shell
ATS	Antonio Scuderi
AV	Adam Versényi
AW	Alan Woods
AWF	Adrian Frazier
BB	Birgit Beumers
BBL	Barbara Lewis
BGW	Brian Woolland
BJR	Beatriz J. Rizk
BMC	Bruce McConachie
BNS	Bhabendra Nath Saikia
BRK	Baz Kershaw
BRS	Brian Singleton
BSG	Barbara Gelb
BWFP	Brian Powell
CAG	C. Andrew Gerstle
CAL	Cathy A. Leeney
CBB	Christopher Balme
CD	Charles Davis
CDC	David Cottis
CEC	Claire Cochrane
CFS	Christopher Fitz-Simon
CHB	C. Henrik Borgstrom
ChM	Chris Morash
CJM	Christiane Makward
CJW	Christa J. Williford
CLB	Christopher Baugh
CLS	Christy Stanlake
CM	Cynthia Marsh
CMa	Christine Matzke
CMC	Charlotte Canning
CP	M. Cody Poulton
CPD	Chris Dunton
CPi	Catherine Piola
CPM	Colin Mackerras
CR	Christopher Rawson
CRG	Cobina Ruth Gillitt
CS	Catherine Swatek
CT	Caldwell Titcomb
DaK	David Kerr
DB	David Bradby
DC	David Carnegie
DDP	Dadi Pudumjee
DG	Daniel Gerould
DGM	David G. Muller
DJP	Derek Paget
DK	Dennis Kennedy
DLF	Debra Freeberg
DLR	David Rinear
DM	David Mayer
DMcM	Donatella Fischer McMillan
DR	Dan Rebellato
DRP	David Pellegrini
DT	David Thomas
DWJ	Denis Johnston
DZS	David Z. Saltz
EB	Eckhard Breitinger
EBr	Edward Braun
ECF	Everett Frost
EEC	Eileen Cottis
EEP	Eric Pourchot
EGC	Eric Csapo
EJS	Elizabeth Schafer
EJW	E. J. Westlake
EN	Edna Nahshon
ER	Eli Rozik
ES	Elaine Savory
EW	Eric Weitz
FAK	Fawzia Afzal-Khan
FD	Frances Dann
FHL	Felicia Hardison Londré
FJH	Franklin J. Hildy
FL	Frazer Lively
FM	Filomena Mesquita
GAO	Gwen Orel
GAR	Gary A. Richardson
GB	Günter Berghaus
GBB	Gilli Bush-Bailey
GES	Gretchen Elizabeth Smith
GG	Gerald Groemer
GGE	Gabriele Erasmi
GJG	Greg Giesekam
HD	Hazel Dodge
HFP	Heinrich F. Plett
HJA	Judit Horgas
HMA	Hazem M. Azmy
HNE	Hansel Ndumbe Eyoh
HO	Handan Ozbilgin
HS	Hardja Susilo
IDW	Ian Watson
JAB	John Agee Ball
JAH	Jorge Huerta
JB	John Barnes
JC	Jan Clarke
JCa	Jose Camões
JCC	Juanamaría Cordones-Cook
JCD	Julia Dietrich
JCL	Jane C. C. Lai
JCM	John Conteh-Morgan
JD	John Degen

JDM	Jeffrey D. Mason	LED	Leonard E. Doucette	MRo	Martin Rohmer
JDV	Jozef De Vos	LEM	Lydie Moudileno	MS	Michael Shapiro
JE	John Emigh	LHD	Leslie Damasceno	MSh	Michael Schuster
JEH	Jane E. House	LIB	Liisa Byckling	MWP	Michael Patterson
JF	Joseph Farrell	LK	Loren Kruger	MWS	Matthew Wilson Smith
JG	John Golder	LQM	Lisa Merrill	NC	Noel Carroll
JGJ	Jean Graham-Jones	LR	Lalitha Rajan	NG	Nicholas Grene
JGR	Janelle Reinelt	LRG	Luis A. Ramos-García	NGT	Nicanor Tiongson
JJ	Jan Jansen	LRK	Laurence Kominz	NGu	Nancy Guy
JLRE	José Luis Ramos Escobar	LSR	L. S. Rajagopalan	NHB	Nicholas Barker
JM	Jane Moody	LT	Lib Taylor	NMSC	Neelam Man Singh Chowdhry
JMcC	John McCormick	LTC	Lynne Conner	NW	Nick Worrall
JMG	James Gibbs	LW	Lisa Wolford	OD	Ousmane Diakhaté
JMM	Judith Mossman	MA	Mohd Anis Md Nor	PAD	Peter Davis
JMW	J. Michael Walton	MAF	Mark Fearnow	PBON	Patrick B. O'Neill
JOB	Jose Oliveira Barata	MAK	Michal Kobialka	PCR	Paola Catenaccio Roblin
JOC	Jae-Oh Choi	MAR	Mario A. Rojas	PDH	Peter Holland
JoG	Jose George	MAS	Melissa Sihra	PEC	Paulo Eduardo Carvalho
JP	Jane Plastow	MC	Marvin Carlson	PGH	Peter Hawkins
JR	John Rouse	MCH	Mary C. Henderson	PH	Pamela Howard
JRB	John Russell Brown	MCHM	Marie-Christine	PNN	Pius Nkashama Ngandu
JRS	John Russell Stephens		Hazaël-Massieux	PR	Prasanna Ramaswamy
JSB	Jacky Bratton	MD	Michael Dobson	PS	Patricia Sieber
JSM	James S. Moy	MDC	Matthew Causey	PT	Peter Thomson
JTD	Jim Davis	MDG	Melissa Dana Gibson	PWM	Peter W. Marx
JTR	J. Thomas Rimer	MDS	Michael Slater	PZ	Phillip B. Zarrilli
JuJ	Julie Greer Johnson	MES	Marta Elena Savigliano	RA	Régis Antoine
JWH	John Wesley Harris	MHS	Maria Helena Serôdio	RAA	Richard Andrews
KB	Kazimierz Braun	MJ	Margot Jones	RAC	Richard Allen Cave
KC	Katherine Carlitz	MJA	Mary Jo Arnoldi	RAH	Roger Hall
KF	Karen Fricker	MJB	Maria João Brilhante	RB	Rustom Bharucha
KFN	Kirsten Nigro	MJD	Moira Day	RCB	Richard Beacham
KFo	Kathy Foley	MJK	Matthew J. Kinservik	RCN	Robert Nunn
KG	Keith Gregor	MJW	Martin Wiggins	RGH	Russell G. Hamilton
KGo	Kiki Gounaridou	MKB	Michael Billington	RI	Riad Ismat
KH	Kathryn Hansen	ML	Milan Lukeš	RJ	Russell Jackson
KJ	Kirti Jain	MLa	Maximilien Laroche	RM	Rosemary Malague
KM	Kim Marra	MM	Meg Mumford	RN	Richard Niles
KMC	Kathleen Coleman	MMcG	Moray McGowan	RO	Ranjini Obeyesekere
KMM	Katherine Mezur	MMD	Maria M. Delgado	RV	Rodolfo Vera
KMN	Katherine Newey	MMe	Mohamed Mediouni	RVL	R. Valerie Lucas
KN	Katie Normington	MMH	Made Mantle Hood	RWH	Roger W. Herzel
KNP	Kavalam Narayana Panikkar	MMK	Margaret Knapp	RWS	Richard W. Schoch
KP	Kirstin Pauka	MMu	Magaly Muguercia	RWV	Ronald W. Vince
KPK	Klaus Peter Köpping	MNS	Modali Nagabhushana Sarma	SA	Simon Amegbleamé
KS	Karthigesu Sivathamby	MOC	Marion O'Connor	SB	Sally Banes
KVA	K. V. Akshara	MPB	Mark Patrick Bates	SBB	Sarah Bryant-Bertail
KWB	Karen Brazell	MPH	Marion Peter Holt	SBe	Susan Bennett
LAR	Louis A. Rachow	MPYC	Martha P. Y. Cheung	SBM	Susan McCully
LC	Linda Charnes	MR	Milla Riggio	SBS	Susan Bradley Smith
LCL	Luis Chesney-Lawrence	MRB	Michael R. Booth	SD	Sudhanva Deshpande
LDP	Lois Potter	MRM	Micheline Rice-Maximin	SEW	S. E. Wilmer

EDITOR

DENNIS KENNEDY is Samuel Beckett professor of drama and theatre studies in Trinity College Dublin, and head of the School of Drama. His books include *Granville Barker and the Dream of Theatre* (1985), *Plays by Harley Granville Barker* (1987), *Foreign Shakespeare* (1993), and *Looking at Shakespeare: a visual history of twentieth-century performance* (2nd edn., 2001). He was advisory editor for *The Oxford Companion to Shakespeare* (2001). His essays have appeared in many books and journals and he has lectured around the world, from Los Angeles to Kathmandu. Previously professor of theatre arts at the University of Pittsburgh, he has also held a number of distinguished visiting posts. His own plays have been performed in small theatres in New York and London, and at regional theatres in the USA, and he has frequently worked as a dramaturg. (DK)

ADVISORY EDITORS

RUSTOM BHARUCHA (South Asia; cultural theory). Independent writer, director, and dramaturg based in Calcutta. Combining intercultural theory with grass-roots theatre practice, he has written numerous books including *Theatre and the World* (1993), *The Politics of Cultural Practice* (2000), *The Question of Faith* (1993), and *In the Name of the Secular* (1998). He is a member of the International Advisory Council of the Prince Claus Fund for Culture and Development. (RB)

JACKY BRATTON (Britain and Ireland since 1700; gender issues). Professor of theatre and cultural history, Royal Holloway, University of London. She is joint editor of the Cambridge University Press series Shakespeare in Production and her book on a new historiography of British theatre will be published in 2003. Previous publications include *Melodrama: stage, picture, screen* (1994) and *King Lear: text and performance archive* (CD-Rom, 2000). (JSB)

EDWARD BRAUN (Russia, Soviet Union, Eastern and northern Europe since 1700; theatre and politics). Emeritus professor of drama, University of Bristol. His *Meyerhold on Theatre* appeared in 1969 and was followed by *The Theatre of Meyerhold* (1979), *The Director and the Stage* (1982), and *Meyerhold: a revolution in theatre* (1995). He has also published on Russian drama, futurist performance, contemporary British theatre, and

television drama. His current research is concerned with dramatic representations of history. (EBr)

MARVIN CARLSON (concepts and theory; Western Europe since 1700; North Africa and Middle East). Sidney E. Cohn professor of theatre and comparative literature at the Graduate Center of the City University of New York. He received the ATHE Career Achievement Award in 1995, and is the founding editor of the journal *Western European Stages*. He has published widely in the areas of theatre history, theatre theory, and dramatic literature, including *Theories of the Theatre* (1984), *Places of Performance* (1989), and *Theatre Semiotics: signs of life* (1990). His most recent book is *The Haunted Stage* (2001). (MC)

JOHN CONTEH-MORGAN (francophone Africa and Caribbean). Associate professor of French and francophone literature at Ohio State University. In 2002 he was W. E. B. Du Bois Fellow at Harvard University. His publications include *Theatre and Drama in Francophone Africa* (1994), a translation of Paulin Hountondji's *The Struggle for Meaning: philosophy, culture and democracy in Africa* (2002), and *The Post-colonial Condition of African Literature* (edited with Dan Gover and Jane Bryce, 1999). (JCM)

DAVID KERR (anglophone Africa and Caribbean). Professor of theatre studies at the University of Malawi. He has also taught at the Universities of Botswana, Southampton, and Zambia. His main books are *African Popular Theatre* (1995) and *Dance, Media Entertainment and Popular Theatre in South East Africa* (1998). He is an editorial adviser for *African Theatre* and *Critical Arts* and has also co-authored and directed many plays, films, and videos. (DaK)

KATE MCLUSKIE (Europe 1500–1700). Professor of English and deputy vice-chancellor, University of Southampton. Interested in the commercialization of culture in the early modern period, she is currently editing *Macbeth* for the Arden III series, and has previously edited (with David Bevington) *Plays on Women* for Manchester University Press.

BROOKS MCNAMARA (North America; popular entertainments). Professor of performance studies emeritus in the Tisch School of the Arts, New York University, and director emeritus of the Shubert Archive in New York. He is a specialist in the history of popular entertainment and has written and edited widely in the area. He has been a Fulbright Scholar and a Guggenheim Fellow.

KIRSTIN PAUKA (South-East Asia). Associate professor of Asian theatre, University of Hawai'i. Her areas of expertise and publication include Sumatran Randai theatre, Asian martial arts, and digital technology. She is a member of the Kenny Endo Taiko Ensemble. (KP)

J. THOMAS RIMER (East Asia). Professor of Japanese at the University of Pittsburgh. He has a particular interest in theatre and the Japanese post-war avant-garde and has published numerous essays, books, and translations in those areas, including *Towards a Modern Japanese Theatre: Kishida Kunio* (1974) and *Culture and Identity: Japanese intellectuals during the interwar years* (1990). He has translated Suzuki Tadashi's *The Way of Acting* (1986) and (with Yamazaki Masakuzo) has edited and translated *On the Art of the Nō Drama: the major treatises of Zeami* (1984). (JTR)

ADAM VERSÉNYI (Latin America). Associate professor of dramaturgy at the University of North Carolina and resident dramaturg for PlayMakers Repertory Company. His work in Latin American theatre includes scholarship, translation, and directing. He is the author of *Theatre in Latin America* (1993) and *Theatre of Sabina Berman* (2002), and is regional vice-president of the Literary Managers and Dramaturgs of the Americas, Inc. (AV)

RONALD W. VINCE (Europe before 1500; buildings and material elements). Professor emeritus of drama and English, McMaster University. He has written widely on topics relating to the historiography of European theatre, including *Renaissance Theatre* (1984) and *A Companion to the Medieval Theatre* (1989). He has served on several scholarly organizations and editorial boards, and he now studies ancient Hebrew literature. (RWV)

CONTRIBUTORS

An asterisk in front of a name indicates that an entry in the work is devoted to this contributor.

FAWZIA AFZAL-KHAN, professor of English at Montclair State University, New Jersey, has written *Cultural Imperialism and the Indo-English Novel* (1993) and co-edited *The Preoccupation of Postcolonial Studies* (2000) with Kalpana Seshadri-Crooks. Current research interests include Pakistani alternative theatre. (FAK)

SYED JAMIL AHMED is a theatre practitioner in Bangladesh and associate professor at the University of Dhaka. His publications include *Acinpakhi Infinity: indigenous theatre in Bangladesh* and *In Praise of Niranjan: Islam, theatre and Bangladesh*. (SJA)

K. V. AKSHARA studied theatre at the National School of Drama, New Delhi, and the Workshop Theatre, University of Leeds. He now teaches and directs plays at Ninasam, Heggodu, in south India. He has also published several books on theatre in Kannada. (KVA)

SIMON AMEGBLEAMÉ is professor of African literature at the University of Lomé in Togo. Among his publications are French translations of African novels. (SA)

RICHARD ANDREWS is emeritus professor of Italian at the University of Leeds. He is the author of *Scripts and Scenarios: the performance of comedy in Renaissance Italy* (1993). (RAA)

MOHD ANIS MD NOR is professor of ethnochorelogy and ethnomusicology at the University of Malaya. He has pioneered the study of *zapin* dance and music in South-East Asia and has published widely on the topic. (MA)

RÉGIS ANTOINE is honorary professor and head of course at the University of Paris, Sorbonne. His publications on theatre include *La Tragédie du roi Christophe de Césaire* (1984) and *La Littérature pacifiste et internationaliste française, 1915–1935*. (RA)

MARY JO ARNOLDI is a curator in the Department of Anthropology of the Smithsonian Institute in Washington. She has conducted research on theatre and performance in Mali since 1978. (MJA)

ARNOLD ARONSON is professor of theatre at Columbia University. He is author of *American Avant-Garde Theatre* (2000), *American Set Design* (1985), and *The History and Theory of Environmental Scenography* (1981). (AA)

HAZEM M. AZMY is a comparative literature and Egyptian theatre scholar, dramaturg, and translator. His interests include interdisciplinary humanities and applied post-structuralism, and he has been English editor of the daily of the Cairo International Festival for Experimental Theatre since 1993. (HMA)

JOHN AGEE BALL is a Ph.D. candidate in theatre and performance studies at the University of Pittsburgh. His research interests are twentieth-century American and Czech political theatre. (JAB)

CHRISTOPHER BALME holds the chair in theatre studies at the University of Mainz. He has written on German theatre, intercultural theatre, and theatre iconography, and is associate editor of *Theatre Research International*. Publications include *Decolonizing the Stage: theatrical syncretism and postcolonial drama* (1999). (CBB)

SALLY BANES (University of Wisconsin) writes widely on dance and performance. Her books include *Democracy's Body: Judson Dance Theatre* (1983), *Terpsichore in Sneakers: post-modern dance* (1987), *Greenwich Village 1963* (1993), and *Dancing Women: female bodies on stage* (1998). (SB)

JOSÉ OLIVEIRA BARATA (University of Coimbra) has published extensively on Portuguese theatre. His works include *Estética Teatral* (1981), *António José da Silva. Criação e Realidade* (1985), *História do Teatro Português* (1991), and *O Espaço Literário do Teatro* (2001). (JOB)

NICHOLAS BARKER is a cultural anthropologist based at the University of Hawai'i and the East-West Center in Honolulu. His current research, incorporating fieldwork in the Philippines, examines the revival of religious self-mortification in South-East Asia. (NHB)

JOHN BARNES, formerly of Western State College of Colorado, is a professional writer who has published twenty-five novels. Current interests in theatre include Peircean semiotics, directorless performance spaces, and the origins of French melodrama. (JB)

MARK PATRICK BATES received his Ph.D. in theatre studies from Trinity College Dublin, writing his thesis on the work of Peter Sellars. He now works for BBC television in London. (MPB)

CHRISTOPHER BAUGH is professor of drama at the University of Kent at Canterbury. He has published a book on de Loutherbourg, and articles on eighteenth- and nineteenth-century scenography, Brecht, and stage design. (CLB)

RICHARD BEACHAM is professor of theatre studies at the University of Warwick. Publications include *The Roman Theatre and its Audience* (1992); *Spectacle Entertainments of Early Imperial Rome* (1999); *Adolphe Appia, Theatre Artist* (1987); *Adolphe Appia: texts on theatre* (1993), and *Adolphe Appia, Artist and Visionary of the Modern Theatre* (1994). (RCB)

ANNEMARIE BEAN lectures in theatre at Williams College, Massachusetts. Her work focuses on performance studies and intercultural performance. She is co-editor of *Inside the Minstrel Mask: readings in nineteenth-century blackface minstrelsy* (1996) and editor of *A Sourcebook on African-American Performance: plays, people, movements* (1999). (AB)

SUSAN BENNETT is the author of *Theatre Audiences* (2nd edn. 1997) and *Performing Nostalgia* (1996). She is university professor of English at the University of Calgary, Canada. (SBe)

GÜNTER BERGHAUS is reader in theatre history and performance studies at the University of Bristol. His books include *Theatre and Film in Exile* (1989), *The Genesis of Futurism* (1995), *Fascism and Theatre* (1996), *Italian Futurist Theatre* (1998), and *On Ritual* (1998). (GB)

ALBERT BERMEL has published critical studies of Shakespeare, Molière, and Artaud; on farce and modern theatre; and forty-two translations of French and Italian plays. He is professor emeritus at the graduate programme in theatre in the City University of New York. (ACB)

BIRGIT BEUMERS is lecturer in Russian at the University of Bristol. She is the author of *Yury Lyubimov at the Taganka Theatre, 1964–94* (1997) and *Burnt by the Sun* (2000). She is editor of *Russia on Reels: the Russian idea in post-Soviet cinema* (1999). (BB)

ANANDA MOHAN BHAGAWATI first acted in an *ankiya nat* at the age of 7. Now retired as director of cultural affairs for the government of Assam, India, he continues work on traditional forms through his Institute of Assamese Dancing. (AMB)

MICHAEL*BILLINGTON has been drama critic of the *Guardian* since 1971. He is the author of books on Tom Stoppard, Alan Ayckbourn, Harold Pinter, and Peggy Ashcroft, and a selection of his reviews, *One Night Stands*. He has been visiting professor of drama at King's College, University of London. (MKB)

MICHAEL R. BOOTH is retired and lives in Greece. He is the author and editor of *English Melodrama* (1965), *English Plays of the Nineteenth Century* (1969–76), *Victorian Spectacular Theatre* (1981), and *Theatre in the Victorian Age* (1991). (MRB)

C. HENRIK BORGSTROM is assistant professor of French at Niagara University, New York, specializing in French and francophone African and Caribbean theatre. (CHB)

DAVID BRADBY is professor of drama at Royal Holloway, University of London. His books include *Modern French Drama 1940–1990* (1991), *Beckett: Waiting for Godot* (2001), and, with Annie Sparks, *Mise en Scène: French theatre now* (1997). He has translated Lecoq's *The Moving Body* and plays by Michel Vinaver and Bernard-Marie Koltès. (DB)

KAZIMIERZ BRAUN, professor at the University of Buffalo, has directed more than 130 productions in Poland, USA, Ireland, Canada, and Germany. He has published thirty books including *Theatre Directing: arts, ethics, creativity* (2000) and *Polish Theatre, 1939–1989* (1996). (KB)

KAREN BRAZELL is Goldwin Smith graduate professor of Japanese literature and theatre at Cornell University and director of the Global Performing Arts Consortium. Her most recent book is *Traditional Japanese Theater: an anthology of plays*. (KWB)

ECKHARD BREITINGER, Institute for African Studies at Bayreuth University, has also taught at the Universities of the West Indies, Tübingen, and Kumasi/Ghana. His publications include work on theatre for development, performance in Africa, and African-American theatre. (EB)

MARIA JOÃO BRILHANTE coordinates postgraduate studies in theatre at the University of Lisbon, where she researches Portuguese and French drama and translation issues. (MJB)

JOHN RUSSELL *BROWN edited *The Oxford Illustrated History of Theatre* and has written numerous books on early modern and contemporary theatre. He has held chairs at Sussex, Michigan, and Middlesex Universities; earlier, he founded the drama department at the University of Birmingham. (JRB)

SARAH BRYANT-BERTAIL, associate professor of drama at the University of Washington in Seattle, is the author of *Space and Time in Epic Theater: the Brechtian legacy* (2000). Her essays on European and American theatre have appeared in numerous journals. (SBB)

GILLI BUSH-BAILEY was a professional actress from 1967 to 1992 and currently lectures in theatre history at Royal Holloway, University of London. Her research interests are in female theatre practice in late seventeenth-, eighteenth-, and early nineteenth-century popular theatre. (GBB)

LIISA BYCKLING is a theatre researcher at the University of Helsinki, Finland. She is the author of books on Michael Chekhov and on the Russian theatre in Helsinki. (LIB)

JOSÉ CAMÕES is a researcher and lecturer at the Centre for Theatre Research, University of Lisbon. He edited the complete works of Gil Vicente in 2001 on CD-ROM, and again in 2002 in five volumes. (JCa)

CHARLOTTE CANNING is associate professor in the Department of Theatre and Dance at the University of Texas at Austin. She has written *Feminist Theaters in the USA: staging women's experience* (1996) and numerous articles on feminist history and performance. (CMC)

KATHERINE CARLITZ (Asian studies, University of Pittsburgh) specializes in Ming dynasty fiction and drama and in Chinese conceptions of gender and virtue. She is the author of *The Rhetoric of the Chin p'ing mei* (1986). (KC)

DAVID CARNEGIE is reader in theatre at Victoria University of Wellington, New Zealand. He has worked in professional theatre in Britain and New Zealand, and is a trustee of the New Zealand Theatre Archive. (DC)

NOËL CARROLL (University of Wisconsin) is a philosopher and film theorist. His recent books include *Interpreting the Moving Image* (1998), *Philosophy of Art* (1999), *Theories of Art Today* (ed., 2000), and *Beyond Aesthetics* (2001). (NC)

PAULO EDUARDO CARVALHO is a lecturer in the Faculty of Arts of Oporto University and a researcher at the Centre for Theatre Studies, University of Lisbon. He has published translations of plays by Friel, Crimp, Churchill, and Shawn. (PEC)

MATTHEW CAUSEY is lecturer in drama at Trinity College Dublin. His research interests include digital culture, new media, and experimental performance, and his writing has appeared in a number of journals. (MDC)

RICHARD ALLEN CAVE is professor of drama and theatre arts at Royal Holloway, University of London. He has published on early modern, Victorian, and modern English and Irish theatre, and has a special interest in dance-drama. (RAC)

S. P. CERASANO is professor of English at Colgate University and has written widely on early modern theatre history. She is currently preparing a book on Philip Henslowe's *Diary* and a biography of Edward Alleyn. (SPC)

LINDA CHARNES is associate professor of English and cultural studies at Indiana University. She is the author of *Notorious Identity: materializing the subject in Shakespeare* (1993) and *Hamlet's Heirs: essays on inheriting Shakespeare* (2003). (LC)

LUIS CHESNEY-LAWRENCE, playwright, is the head of graduate studies in arts at Venezuela Central University. He is working on a project concerned with rereading the history of Latin American and Venezuelan theatre. (LCL)

MARTHA P. Y. CHEUNG is professor of translation at the Hong Kong Baptist University. She edited *An Oxford Anthology of Contemporary Chinese Drama* (with Jane Lai, 1997). (MPYC)

JAE-OH CHOI is a Ph.D. candidate in theatre and performance studies at the University of Pittsburgh. Educated in both Korea and the United States, Choi received an MFA in dramaturgy from the State University of New York at Stonybrook and a BA from Chungang University, Seoul. (JOC)

NEELAM MAN SINGH CHOWDHRY is the director of the Indian theatre group The Company, which has performed at major festivals both internationally and in India. He teaches drama at the University of Punjab, Chandigarh. (NMSC)

JAN CLARKE is senior lecturer in French at the University of Durham. Her recent publications include books on *The Guénégaud Theatre in Paris (1673–80)* (1998) and articles on architecture, lighting, repertory, actors, and cross-dressing. (JC)

CLAIRE COCHRANE lectures in drama at University College Worcester, England. Her publications include *Shakespeare and the Birmingham Repertory Theatre 1913–1929* (1993) and *Birmingham Rep: a city's theatre 1962–2000* (2003). (CEC)

KATHLEEN COLEMAN is professor of Latin at Harvard University. She concentrates on poetry of the Flavian period (AD 69–96) and Roman social history, especially arena spectacles and capital punishment. (KMC)

WILLIAM F. CONDEE is director of the School of Comparative Arts and professor of theatre at Ohio University. He received his AB and MA from Vassar College and his Ph.D. from Columbia University. (WFC)

LYNNE CONNER is assistant professor at the University of Pittsburgh. Her publications include *Spreading the Gospel of the Modern Dance* (1997) and essays in, among others, *Crucibles of Crisis* (1996), *Metamorphosis*, and the PBS Great Performances *Free to Dance*. (LTC)

THOMAS CONNOLLY is assistant professor of English at Suffolk University in the USA, and visiting professor at the University of Ostrava. His most recent book is *George Jean Nathan and the Making of Modern American Drama Criticism* (2000). (TFC)

JUANAMARÍA CORDONES-COOK (University of Missouri) is the author of *Poética de transgresión sobre la novelística de Luisa Valenzuela* (1991), *¿Teatro negro uruguayo? Texto y contexto del teatro afro-uruguayo de Andrés Castillo* (1996), and a forthcoming critical anthology of Afro-Hispanic theatre. (JCC)

DAVID COTTIS is artistic director of the Instant Classics Theatre Company in England. He has taught at the University of East Anglia, and was literary manager of the Etcetera Theatre for six years. (CDC)

EILEEN COTTIS is a retired senior lecturer in French at the University of North London. She is joint honorary secretary of the Society for Theatre Research. (EEC)

ERIC CSAPO is associate professor of classics at the University of Toronto. He is the author and editor of books and numerous articles on the history of the ancient theatre, ancient Greek literature, and ancient culture. (EGC)

VALERIE CUMMING was the deputy director of the Museum of London until 1997. She has worked with and advised upon collections of theatre costume. Her publications include six books among numerous articles, catalogue entries, essays, and reviews. (VLC)

SCOTT T. CUMMINGS is associate professor of theatre at Boston College, where he directs and teaches dramatic literature and playwriting. He also works as a freelance arts journalist and theatre critic. (STC)

VASUDHA DALMIA is professor of South and South-East Asian studies, University of California, Berkeley, and taught for many years at the Universities of Tübingen and Heidelberg in Germany. Publications include *The Nationalization of Hindu Traditions: Bharatendu Harischandra and nineteenth century Banaras* (1997). (VDa)

LESLIE DAMASCENO teaches in the departments of Romance Studies and Theatre Studies, Duke University. Her major research and publications are on Brazilian and Latin American theatre, Brazilian cultural theory and cultural politics, and theatre and performance theory. (LHD)

FRANCES DANN teaches at Sheffield Hallam University and is joint honorary secretary of the Society for Theatre Research. (FD)

CHARLES DAVIS (University of Valencia) specializes in archival research on Spanish theatre in the sixteenth and seventeenth centuries. He is director of the series Fuentes para la historia del teatro en España, founded by J. E. Varey. (CD)

JIM DAVIS is associate professor of theatre at the University of New South Wales, Sydney. He has published widely on nineteenth-century British theatre and is co-author of *Reflecting the Audience: London theatregoing 1840–1880* (2001). (JTD)

PETER DAVIS is chair of the MA/Ph.D. programme in theatre at the University of Illinois. He is author of numerous articles, reviews, and book chapters on early American theatre history, and is completing a history of theatre in colonial New York. (PAD)

TRACY C. DAVIS, Barber professor of the performing arts at Northwestern University, is author of *Actresses as Working Women: their social identity in Victorian culture* (1991), *George Bernard Shaw and the Socialist Theatre* (1994), and *The Economics of the British Stage, 1800–1914* (2000). (TCD)

MOIRA DAY is associate professor of drama at the University of Saskatchewan, Canada. She has published extensively on Canadian theatre, with particular focus on women, and served as co-editor of *Theatre Research in Canada*. (MJD)

JOHN DEGEN is associate professor of theatre at Florida State University with speciality in American theatre, particularly in musical theatre. He is a contributor to *The Cambridge History of American Theatre* (1998–2000) and has published widely in journals. (JD)

MARIA M. DELGADO (Queen Mary, University of London) has co-edited *In Contact with the Gods? Directors talk theatre* (1996),

Conducting a Life: reflections on the theatre of Maria Irene Fornes (1999), and *Theatre in Crisis?* (2002). (MMD)

SUDHANVA DESHPANDE, born in 1967, is an actor and director, chiefly associated with street theatre in India. He has been a member of Jana Natya Manch, Delhi, since 1987. He also writes on theatre and film. (SD)

JOZEF DE VOS teaches English literature and theatre history at Ghent University in Belgium. He is the editor of *Documenta*, a journal of theatre studies, and has published extensively on the reception of Shakespeare in the Low Countries. (JDV)

OUSMANE DIAKHATÉ (Université Cheikh Anta Diop in Senegal) is the managing director of the Daniel Sorano National Theatre, secretary-general of the Senegalese office of the International Theatre Institute, and a regional editor of *The World Encyclopedia of Contemporary Theatre*. (OD)

JULIA DIETRICH is professor of English and associate dean for undergraduate education at the University of Louisville. She studies the conflicts that arose when British culture was simultaneously late medieval and early modern, with particular interest in the drama. (JCD)

VICTOR DIXON was professor of Spanish at Trinity College Dublin from 1974 to 1999. His publications include editions and translations of plays by Lope de Vega and over fifty journal articles on Spanish drama. (VFD)

MICHAEL DOBSON is professor of Renaissance drama at the University of Surrey Roehampton, London. His publications include *The Making of the National Poet* (1992), *The Oxford Companion to Shakespeare* (with Stanley Wells, 2001), and *England's Elizabeth* (with Nicola Watson, 2002). (MD)

HAZEL DODGE is Louis Claude Purser senior lecturer in classical archaeology in Trinity College Dublin. Her research on Roman construction has led her to a major interest in the archaeology of Greek and Roman entertainment. (HD)

LEONARD E. DOUCETTE is professor emeritus of French and drama in the University of Toronto. He has published three books and many articles on the history of French and French-Canadian literature, specializing in drama. (LED)

CHRIS DUNTON is professor of English at the National University of Lesotho. He has written a number of books and articles on contemporary Nigerian theatre. (CPD)

VICTOR EMELJANOW is professor of drama at the University of Newcastle, Australia. A theatre historian and professional director, he has published extensively on Victorian popular theatre. His latest book, co-authored with Jim Davis, is *Reflecting the Audience: London theatregoing 1840–1880* (2001). (VEE)

JOHN EMIGH is professor of theatre and English at Brown University, where he has been teaching and directing since 1967. As well as being a performer, he is the author of *Masked Performance* (1996). (JE)

GABRIELE ERASMI is associate professor at McMaster University, Canada. A classicist by training, he teaches Italian literature and Indo-European linguistics. His publications include articles on Italian plays and operas. (GGE)

HANSEL NDUMBE *EYOH is professor of drama and theatre at the University of Yaounde, Cameroon. He is co-editor of *The World Encyclopedia of Contemporary Theatre*, and corresponding editor of *Theatre Research International*. Publications include *Hammocks to Bridges* (1986) and *Beyond the Theatre* (1992). (HNE)

JOSEPH FARRELL is professor of Italian studies in the University of Strathclyde. He has translated plays by Dario Fo, Carlo Goldoni, and Enrico Baricco. His most recent book is the biographical work *Dario Fo and Franca Rame: harlequins of the revolution* (2001). (JF)

MARK FEARNOW teaches in the Department of Theatre at Hanover College, USA. He is the author of two books and numerous articles and chapters on American theatre, with an emphasis on the 1930s. (MAF)

ANN FEATHERSTONE gained a Ph.D. from Royal Holloway, University of London, in 2000, where her research concentrated on nineteenth-century popular entertainment. She has published articles on the *Era* newspaper, freak shows, and fairground entertainments. (AF)

SIMON FEATHERSTONE teaches English at Anglia Polytechnic University in Cambridge. (SF)

CHRISTOPHER FITZ-SIMON was artistic director of the Irish Theatre Company and the National Theatre Society (Abbey and Peacock Theatres) in the 1980s and 1990s. He is the author of *The Arts in Ireland* (1982), *The Irish Theatre* (1983), and *The Boys* (1994). (CFS)

KATHY FOLEY is professor of theatre arts at the University of California, Santa Cruz, and holds the Bhandari Endowed Chair of South Asia Studies. She serves as South-East Asia editor of *Asian Theatre Journal* and performs in Sundanese *wayang golek* puppetry. (KFo)

ADRIAN FRAZIER, director of the MA in drama and theatre studies at the National University of Ireland, Galway, is the author of *Yeats, Horniman, and the Struggle for the Abbey Theatre* (1990) and *George Moore 1852–1933* (2000). (AWF)

DEBRA FREEBERG is professor of theatre and communication arts and sciences at Calvin College in Grand Rapids, Michigan. Her research includes Scandinavian theatre, particularly Olof Molander's productions of Strindberg, and children's theatre, playwriting, and directing. (DLF)

KAREN FRICKER, a Ph.D. candidate at Trinity College Dublin, formerly worked for the New York Shakespeare Festival. She is the editor of *Irish Theatre* magazine and her criticism has appeared in the *Guardian, Variety*, the *New York Times*, and the *Irish Times*. (KF)

EVERETT FROST is professor of radio, television, and film at New York University and is the founder-director of Voices International. Radio productions include the plays of Samuel Beckett and the Hörspiel Project. With Margaret Herzfeld Sander, he is editor of *German Radio Plays* (1989). (ECF)

ARTHUR GELB is the former managing editor of the *New York Times*, having also been cultural and metropolitan editor. With Barbara Gelb he is the author of *O'Neill* (1962; 1973) and *O'Neill: Life with Monte Cristo* (2000). (ANG)

BARBARA GELB is the author of biographies, two studies of the New York police department, and a one-person play, *My Gene*, based on Carlotta Monterey. With Arthur Gelb she wrote *O'Neill* (1962; 1973) and *O'Neill: Life with Monte Cristo* (2000). (BSG)

JOSE GEORGE received his Ph.D. from the School of Drama of Calicut University. He studied in the USA on a Fulbright Scholarship and teaches English at Mar Athanasius College, Kothamangalam, Kerala, India. (JoG)

DANIEL GEROULD is Lucille Lortel distinguished professor of theatre and comparative literature at the Graduate Center, City University of New York. He is editor of *Slavic and East European Performance* (1992); author of *Theatre/Theory/Theatre* (2000), *Guillotine*, and *Witkacy* (1981); and translator of Witkiewicz, Olesha, and Galczynski. (DG)

C. ANDREW GERSTLE is professor of Japanese studies, University of London, and director of the Centre for Asian and African Literatures. Books include *Eighteenth-Century Japan* (1989) and *Chikamatsu: five late plays* (2001). His current project is on Osaka Kabuki actor prints. (CAG)

JAMES GIBBS teaches at the University of the West of England, Bristol. He has recently been involved in editing volumes on African theatre, on Ghanaian culture, and on issues facing African authors. (JMG)

MELISSA DANA GIBSON is assistant professor of theatre at California State University, Fresno. (MDG)

GREG GIESEKAM, senior lecturer in theatre studies, Glasgow University, has written on live art, the Wooster Group, and various British writers and companies. His study of amateur and community theatre, *Luvvies and Rude Mechanicals?*, was published by the Scottish Arts Council in 2000. (GJG)

COBINA RUTH GILLITT is a scholar of Asian performance and Western drama theory, specializing in Indonesian and intercultural theatre. She completed her Ph.D. in performance studies at New York University in 2001. (CRG)

SHANTA GOKHALE is a writer, translator, journalist, and theatre critic. She has written one novel and three plays in Marathi, translated several Marathi plays into English, and published *Playwright at the Centre: Marathi drama from 1843 to the present* (2000). (SGG)

JOHN GOLDER teaches in the School of Theatre, Film, and Dance at the University of New South Wales, Sydney. Currently working on audiences and repertory of the Comédie-Française, he has published extensively on French theatre history and Shakespeare performed in France and Australia. (JG)

KIKI GOUNARIDOU teaches theatre studies at Smith College. She is the author of *Euripides and Alcestis* (1998), *Madame La Mort and Other Plays by Rachilde* (1998), and articles on translation and performance theory, and Greek theatre and film. (KGo)

JEAN GRAHAM-JONES, associate professor of Latin American theatre at Florida State University, is the author of *Exorcising History: Argentine theatre under dictatorship* (2000) and numerous journal articles on colonial and contemporary Latin American theatre and performance. (JGJ)

KEITH GREGOR lectures in English and Irish literature at the University of Murcia, Spain. He is co-editor of *Teatro clásico en traducción* (1996) and the author of numerous articles on early modern and modern drama. He is currently researching the reception of Shakespeare in Spain. (KG)

NICHOLAS GRENE holds the chair of English at Trinity College Dublin and has research interests in Shakespeare and modern Irish drama. Recent books include *The Politics of Irish Drama* (1999) and *Shakespeare's Serial History Plays* (2002). (NG)

GERALD GROEMER is associate professor of Japanese music history and ethnomusicology at Yamanashi University in Kofu, Japan. His publications include *The Spirit of Tsugaru* (1999) and numerous studies of traditional and popular Japanese music and theatre. (GG)

ANDREW GURR is a scholar of Shakespearian theatre. He has published numerous books on Shakespearian stages and staging, audiences, and acting companies. He is also a director of the Southwark Globe. (AJG)

NANCY GUY is assistant professor of music at the University of California, San Diego, with a Ph.D. in ethnomusicology from the University of Pittsburgh. Her research focuses on the music of Taiwan and China. (NGu)

ROGER HALL is professor of theatre at James Madison University in Harrisonburg, Virginia. He is the author of *Performing the American Frontier, 1870–1906* (2001) as well as numerous articles on American theatre in the nineteenth century. (RAH)

RUSSELL G. HAMILTON is professor emeritus of lusophone African, Brazilian, and Portuguese literature at Vanderbilt University. He has conducted research on language, literature, and other forms of cultural expression and has written two books. He is currently updating his two-volume work *Literatura Africana, literatura necessária*. (RGH)

KATHRYN HANSEN is director of the Center for Asian Studies and professor in the Department of Asian Studies at University of Texas, Austin. She is the author of *Grounds for Play: the nautanki theatre of north India* (1992) and numerous articles on the Parsi theatre. (KH)

JOHN WESLEY HARRIS studied at Cambridge, has acted professionally, taught practical theatre, and created the first television course in Britain. He is a lecturer at the University of Hull, where he has published two books on medieval theatre. (JWH)

PETER HAWKINS is senior lecturer in French at the University of Bristol and president of the Association for the Study of Caribbean and African Literature in French. He held a visiting lectureship at the Université de la Réunion from 1994 to 1997. (PGH)

THOMAS HAYS is a lecturer in international intellectual-property law at the University of Aberdeen and a research member of the Molengraaff Institute for Private Law. (TEH)

MARIE-CHRISTINE HAZAËL-MASSIEUX is professor at the Université de Provence, Aix-en-Provence. Her main work concentrates on Creole languages, particularly linguistic and sociolinguistic descriptions in Lesser Antilles. (MCHM)

MARY C. HENDERSON has written five books and many articles on the American stage. She was the curator of the Theatre Collection at the Museum of the City of New York and has taught at New York University as well as other metropolitan area universities. (MCH)

ROGER W. HERZEL is professor and former director of graduate studies in theatre and drama at Indiana University. He is the author of *The Original Casting of Molière's Plays* (1981) and of articles on Molière in various journals. (RWH)

FRANKLIN J. HILDY is professor of theatre history and director of the Ph.D. programme in theatre and performance studies, University of Maryland. He is co-author, with Oscar Brockett, of two editions of *History of the Theatre* (1999 and 2003). (FJH)

TON HOENSELAARS (Utrecht University) has written on Shakespeare and his contemporaries, Joseph Conrad, and James Joyce. He is the president of the Shakespeare Society of the Low Countries, and edits its journal *Folio*. (TH)

PETER HOLLAND is McMeel professor of Shakespeare in the Department of Film, Television, and Theatre at the University of Notre Dame, Indiana. He was previously director of the Shakespeare Institute, Stratford-upon-Avon. His research interests focus on Shakespeare in performance. (PDH)

ARTHUR HOLMBERG, literary director of the American Repertory Theatre, is associate professor of theatre arts at Brandeis University. He is the author of *The Theatre of Robert Wilson* (1996) and the editor of *The Lively ART* (1999). (ACH)

MARION PETER HOLT is professor emeritus of theatre at the Graduate Center of the City University of New York. He is a specialist in modern Iberian theatre and has translated more than twenty Spanish and Catalan plays. (MPH)

MADE MANTLE HOOD has been active in Indonesian music studies since 1988. He was a Fulbright scholar to Germany in 2001–2 and is currently a doctoral candidate in music at the Universität zu Köln. (MMH)

JUDIT HORGAS (Horgas Judit in Hungarian) has been editor of the literary-ecological periodical *Liget* since 1998, where many of her translations and essays have been published. She teaches English drama at the Eotvos Lorand University of Arts and Sciences in Budapest. (HJA)

JANE E. HOUSE is a professional actress and translator. She has taught theatre at the City University of New York, New York University, and Vassar Collage, and edited *20th Century Italian Drama: the first 50 years* (with A. Attisani, 1995). (JEH)

PAMELA *HOWARD is a practising scenographer, theatre director, writer, and teacher. Credits include work for the Royal Shakespeare Company, Royal National Theatre, and English Touring Theatre, as well as original creations for Opera Transatlántica, and a book, *What Is Scenography?* (PH)

WILLIAM D. HOWARTH is professor of French emeritus at the University of Bristol. His books include *Sublime and Grotesque: a study of French romantic drama* (1975), *Molière: a playwright and his audience* (1982), *Beaumarchais and the Theatre* (1995), *French Theatre in the Neo-Classical Era* (ed., 1997). (WDH)

CONTRIBUTORS

JORGE HUERTA holds the Chancellor's Associates endowed chair of theatre at the University of California, San Diego. He is also a professional director and a leading authority on contemporary Chicano and Latino theatre. (JAH)

YVETTE HUTCHISON, senior lecturer in King Alfred's College, Winchester, is assistant editor of the *South African Theatre Journal*. She has co-edited a collection of African plays and has published essays on South African theatre. (YH)

RIAD ISMAT is a dramatist, critic, and director in Syria. Among his eight books of criticism is *Arab Drama: the fall of social masks* (1995). In 2001, he was appointed rector of the Academy of Dramatic Arts in Damascus. (RI)

ANTHONY JACKSON, University of Manchester, specializes in twentieth-century British theatre and theatre as an educational medium. His books include *The Repertory Movement* (with George Rowell, 1984) and *Learning through Theatre* (1980). (ARJ)

RUSSELL JACKSON is director of the Shakespeare Institute and professor of Shakespeare studies at the University of Birmingham. (RJ)

KIRTI JAIN is a stage and television director and professor of Indian theatre history at the National School of Drama in New Delhi, which she headed for seven years. (KJ)

SUSAN PERTEL JAIN, a Chinese opera specialist, holds a Ph.D. from the University of Hawai'i and is associate editor of the *Asian Theatre Journal*. (SPJ)

JAN JANSEN (cultural anthropology, University of Leiden) has translated the Malian epic *Sunjata* (1995) and published *Epopée, histoire, société* (2000), and *The Griot's Craft: An Essay on Oral Tradition and Diplomacy* (2000). (JJ)

JULIE GREER JOHNSON is professor of Spanish at the University of Georgia, USA. Her research interests include women, printing, satire, and theatre in the New World. She is the author of *Satire in Colonial Spanish America* (1993). (JuJ)

ALEXANDRA F. JOHNSTON is professor of English, University of Toronto, and founder and director of Records of Early English Drama. She was previously president of the Société pour l'Étude du Théâtre Médiéval and of the Medieval and Renaissance Drama Society. (AFJ)

DENIS JOHNSTON manages publications and audience education for the Shaw Festival, Canada. He is author of *Up the Mainstream: The Rise of Toronto's Alternative Theatres* (1991) and general editor of the Shaw's Canadian Theatre History series. (DWJ)

MARGOT JONES is a performer and producer. In 1996 she completed her Ph.D., 'Mua Roi Nuoc, the Art of Vietnamese Water Puppetry: a theatrical genre study', at the University of Hawai'i. She lives in Ireland. (MJ)

BAZ KERSHAW holds the chair of drama at Bristol University, and directs, devises, and writes on radical/community-based performance. He is co-author of *Engineers of the Imagination* (1990) and author of *The Politics of Performance* (1992) and *The Radical in Performance* (1999). (BRK)

MATTHEW J. KINSERVIK, University of Delaware, is the author of *Disciplining Satire: the censorship of satiric comedy on the eighteenth-century London stage* (2002). His research interests include censorship, theatre history, and the history of sexuality. (MJK)

MARGARET KNAPP is professor of theatre at Arizona State University. She has published on American theatre in numerous journals, encyclopedias, and collections of essays, and is researching the early twentieth-century non-commercial theatre. (MMK)

MICHAL KOBIALKA, professor of theatre at the University of Minnesota, is the author of *A Journey through Other Spaces* (on Tadeusz Kantor, 1993) and *This Is my Body: Representational Practices in the Early Middle Ages* (1999), and co-editor of *Medieval Practices of Space* (2000). (MAK)

LAURENCE KOMINZ, professor of Japanese language and literature at Portland State University, is currently researching kabuki. Two recent books include *Avatars of Vengeance* (1995) and *The Stars Who Created Kabuki* (1997). (LRK)

KLAUS-PETER KÖPPING (University of Heidelberg) studies Japanese religions, the epistemology of anthropological fieldwork, and theories of ritual actions. His publications include *Adolf Bastian and the Psychic Unity of Mankind* (1983), and *The Games of Gods and Man: essays in play and performance* (1997). (KPK)

AMELIA HOWE KRITZER teaches at the University of St Thomas College of St Catherine. She has published *Plays by Early American Women, 1775–1850* (1995), *The Plays of Caryl Churchill* (1991), and numerous articles. (AHK)

TONIA KRUEGER is completing a Ph.D. at Ohio State University, writing on Jessica Tandy. Her research interests include acting theory and autobiography theory. (TK)

LOREN KRUGER is the author of *The National Stage* (1992) and *The Drama of South Africa* (1999). She is a former editor of *Theatre Journal* and currently a contributing editor for *Theatre Research International*, *Theatre Survey*, and *Scrutiny2*. She teaches at the University of Chicago. (LK)

STEPHEN LACEY is a lecturer in the Department of Film and Drama and director of the Centre for Television Studies at the University of Reading. He writes and publishes on contemporary British theatre and television. (SWL)

JANE C. C. LAI, professor of translation, Hong Kong Baptist University, is a member of Seals Theatre Company. She is the founding member of the Hong Kong Federation of Drama Societies and has translated over twenty plays for performance and publication. (JCL)

ANANDA LAL, professor of English, Jadavpur University, Kolkata, specializes in theatre. His published books include *Rabindranath Tagore: three plays* (2nd edn., 2001), *Rasa: the Indian performing arts* (1995), and *Shakespeare on the Calcutta Stage* (2001). (AL)

WILLIAM RAY LANGENBACH, performance artist, videographer, writer, and curator, has lived and worked in South-East Asia since 1988. He has lectured at Universiti Sains Malaysia, Nanyang Technological University in Singapore, and at present at the Centre for Advanced Design, Kuala Lumpur. (WRL)

MAXIMILIEN LAROCHE, born in Haiti, is professor of French and francophone literature at the University of Laval. His many publications on Haiti, Québec, and the Caribbean include *La Littérature haïtienne* (1981), *La Double Scène de la représentation* (1991), and *Teke*. (MLa)

THOMAS LEABHART, professor of theatre at Pomona College in California, is the author of *Modern and Post Modern Mime* (1989) and editor of *Mime Journal*. He is a well-known practitioner of corporeal mime and a permanent artistic staff member at the International School of Theatre Anthropology. (TL)

CATHY A. LEENEY is lecturer in drama studies at National University of Ireland, Dublin. Research interests include twentieth-century and contemporary Irish theatre, women playwrights, and gender and performance theory. Her practical interests include directing. (CAL)

SAMUEL L. LEITER is Broeklundian professor of theatre at Brooklyn College at the Graduate Center, City University of New York. He has published numerous books on Japanese theatre, American theatre, and the great directors. He is editor of *Asian Theatre Journal*. (SLL)

BARBARA LEWIS, whose research interests are minstrelsy and lynching as performance, has published in several anthologies and journals. She is chair of the theatre department at the University of Kentucky. (BBL)

SIYUAN LIU is a Ph.D. candidate in theatre at the University of Pittsburgh. His research interest is in the modernization of Chinese theatre. (SYL)

FRAZER LIVELY chairs the theatre programme at Wesleyan College in Macon, Georgia. She co-edited and wrote the introduction for *Madame la Mort and Other Plays* (1998) and has published several articles on Rachilde. (FL)

FELICIA HARDISON LONDRÉ, curators' professor of theatre at the University of Missouri-Kansas City, authored *The History of North American Theatre: the United States, Canada, and Mexico from pre-Columbian times to the present* (1998) with Daniel Watermeier. (FHL)

R. VALERIE LUCAS, senior lecturer in drama and theatre studies at the University of Surrey Roehampton, has published in the areas of scenography and representations of race and gender, and directed and designed productions in Europe and the USA. (RVL)

MILAN LUKEŠ, professor of theatre history, theory, and criticism at Charles University, Prague, is the writer and editor of journal *Svět a Divadlo* and chairman of the Festival Committee of the International Festival Divadlo in Plzeň. (ML)

BRUCE MCCONACHIE has written widely on theatre historiography and American theatre history, including *Interpreting the Theatrical Past* (co-edited with Thomas Postlewait, 1989) and *Melodramatic Formations: American theatre and society, 1820–1870* (1992). He teaches at the University of Pittsburgh. (BMC)

JOHN MCCORMICK, puppeteer and historian of European puppetry, has written books on English and French popular theatre of the nineteenth century. He is the founder of the Irish Theatre Archive and was the first director of the Drama Department in Trinity College Dublin. (JMcC)

SUSAN MCCULLY teaches playwriting, drama, and gender studies at the University of Maryland, Baltimore County. She researches lesbian and queer theatre, and her one-woman play *Cyber Becomes Electra* has received multiple performances in North America and Europe. (SBM)

MORAY MCGOWAN, professor of German, Trinity College Dublin, is currently working on German theatre and drama since the 'Wende' of 1989/90. (MMcG)

COLIN MACKERRAS, professor of Asian and international studies, Griffith University, Australia, specializes in Asian, especially Chinese, affairs. He has written widely on Chinese and Vietnamese theatre, both past and present, and on China's minorities. (CPM)

DONATELLA FISCHER MCMILLAN teaches Italian at the University of Strathclyde. Her publications include *A Study of Metadrama in Selected Plays of Edward Bond* and an article on Raffaele Viviani. (DMcM)

ANNA MCMULLAN lectures in the School of Drama, Trinity College Dublin. Her work includes *Theatre on Trial: Samuel Beckett's later drama* (1993) and several articles on contemporary Irish theatre. (AEM)

THERESE MAHONEY received a Ph.D. in ethnomusicology from UCLA. Her dissertation is the first in-depth examination of traditional music in the Lao PDR. She is currently collections curator at California State Polytechnic University, Pomona. (TMM)

CHRISTIANE MAKWARD, professor of French and women's studies, Pennsylvania State University, works on contemporary francophone women writers. Her publications include translated plays, a literary dictionary, and essays on Mayotte Capecia and Corinna Bille. (CJM)

ROSEMARY MALAGUE is a senior lecturer in the theatre arts programme at the University of Pennsylvania. She received her Ph.D. from the Graduate Center of the City University of New York. (RM)

KIM MARRA is associate professor of theatre arts and American studies at the University of Iowa and co-editor of *Passing Performances: queer readings of leading players in American theater history* (1998) and its sequel *Staging Desire* (2001). (KM)

CYNTHIA MARSH is senior lecturer in Russian at the University of Nottingham, specializing in Russian theatre. She has published several books and many articles on Russian literature and drama, particularly on Chekhov and Gorky as playwrights. (CM)

PETER W. MARX, assistant lecturer in theatre studies at the Johannes Gutenberg-University, Mainz, is the author of *Theater und kulturelle Erinnerung* (2002). His research interests include Jewish theatre and theatre in the Weimar Republic. (PWM)

JEFFREY D. MASON is the author of *Melodrama and the Myth of America* (1993) and co-editor of *Performing America: cultural nationalism in American theatre* (1999). He is professor and head of the Theatre Arts Department at the University of Oregon. (JDM)

CONTRIBUTORS

CHRISTINE MATZKE is researching Eritrean theatre for her Ph.D. at the University of Leeds. She teaches in the Department of New Literatures in English at the J. W. Goethe University, Frankfurt am Main. (CMa)

DAVID MAYER is emeritus professor of drama, University of Manchester. His books include *Harlequin in his Element: English pantomime, 1806–1836* (1968) and *Playing out the Empire: Ben Hur and other toga plays and films* (1994). (DM)

MOHAMED MEDIOUNI specializes in the theatre of North Africa, teaching in Tunis and Paris. Publications include *Le Théâtre de Madani et le patrimoine* (3rd edn., 1994), *La Quête d'un théâtre authentique arabe* (1993), and *L'Aventure de l'acte théâtral en Tunisie* (2000). (MMe)

LISA MERRILL teaches at Hofstra University in New York and in the Performance Studies Department of Northwestern University. Her biography *When Romeo Was a Woman: Charlotte Cushman and her circle of female spectators* (1999) was awarded the Joe A. Callaway Prize. (LQM)

FILOMENA MESQUITA is assistant professor at the University of Coimbra and a researcher at the Centro de Estudos de Teatro of the University of Lisbon. She has published essays on Shakespeare and contemporary British women's writing. (FM)

KATHERINE MEZUR holds a Ph.D. in Asian theatre from the University of Hawai'i at Manoa. She has taught at Georgetown University, McGill University, the California Institute of the Arts, and the University of California, Santa Barbara. (KMM)

JANE MOODY is lecturer in English in the Department of English and Related Literature at the University of York. She is the author of *Illegitimate Theatre in London, 1770–1840* (2000). (JM)

CHRIS MORASH is senior lecturer in English at the National University of Ireland, Maynooth. He is author of *A History of Irish Theatre 1601–2000* (2002) and *Writing the Irish Famine* (1995), and consultant editor for the *Encyclopaedia of Ireland*. (ChM)

JUDITH MOSSMAN studied classics at Corpus Christi College, Oxford. After a Junior Research Fellowship at Christ Church, Oxford, she was appointed to Trinity College Dublin, where she is now a fellow and senior lecturer. (JMM)

LYDIE MOUDILENO (University of Pennsylvania) has published *L'Écrivain antillais au miroir de sa littérature* (1997) and numerous articles on contemporary Caribbean and African fiction. Her research interests are in constructions of identity in post-colonial literature and film. (LEM)

JAMES S. MOY is professor of theatre and dance and dean of the College of Fine Arts at the University of New Mexico. He is the author of *Marginal Sights: Staging the Chinese in America* (1994). (JSM)

MAGALY MUGUERCIA's books include *El teatro cubano en vísperas de la Revolución* (1988), *Indagaciones en el teatro cubano* (1988), and *Teatro y utopía* (1998). She teaches at the Instituto Superior de Artes de Cuba in Havana, and in Chile. (MMu)

DAVID G. MULLER is a visiting lecturer in the Department of Theatre and Drama at Indiana University, where he is completing his doctoral dissertation, 'Regarding Racine: the scenography of *tragédie classique* in the modern French theatre'. (DGM)

MEG MUMFORD is a lecturer in the Department of Theatre, Film, and Television Studies at the University of Glasgow. Her research interests include German theatre and dance theatre, feminist and gender studies, and approaches to acting and translation. (MM)

SAL MURGIYANTO, dean of performing arts at Jakarta Institute of the Arts, Indonesia, is a dance critic and performance theorist. He is the director of the Indonesian Dance Festival and lecturer of the dance graduate programme, Taipei, Taiwan. (SM)

EDNA NAHSHON teaches at the Jewish Theological Seminary in New York. She is the author of *Yiddish Proletarian Theatre: the art and politics of the Artef, 1925–40* (1998) and *From the Ghetto to the Melting Pot: Israel Zangwill's Jewish plays*. (EN)

STEVE NELSON teaches musical theatre at New York University's Tisch School of the Arts. He also produces compact discs of Broadway songwriters (Cole Porter, Irving Berlin, etc.) singing their own songs. (SN)

KATHERINE NEWEY is senior lecturer in theatre studies at Lancaster University and publishes widely on British and Australian popular theatre. (KMN)

PIUS NGANDU *NKASHAMA has taught at universities in Congo, Algeria, Limoges, Paris, and the USA, where he is now director of French and francophone studies at Louisiana State University. His publications include novels, plays, and *Théâtre et arts de spectacles* (1993). (PNN)

KIRSTEN F. NIGRO is professor of Spanish at the University of Cincinnati. She has edited six books on Latin American theatre and literature, and is the author of numerous articles and monographs on Latin American and Mexican theatre. (KFN)

RICHARD NILES received his Ph.D. in theatre from the City University of New York Graduate Center. He has taught at Brooklyn College, Columbia University, and is currently associate professor of theatre at Marymount Manhattan College. (RN)

KATIE NORMINGTON, lecturer in drama and theatre at Royal Holloway, University of London, has published on women and medieval drama, devises and directs for freelance companies, and is the co-founder and artistic director of the puppet-theatre company Wooden Tongues. (KN)

ROBERT NUNN, before his retirement in 2000, taught in the Fine Arts Department of Brock University, St Catharines, Canada. He is the author of numerous articles on Canadian anglophone drama and dramatists. (RCN)

RANJINI OBEYESEKERE, anthropology lecturer at Princeton University, teaches South Asian literature and culture. Her books include *Sri Lankan Theatre in a Time of Terror* (1999) and *Portraits of Buddhist Women: stories from the Saddharmaratnavaliya* (2001). (RO)

MARION O'CONNOR has published widely on dramatic revivals and theatrical reconstructions. She is co-editor (with Russell Jackson and Trevor R. Griffiths) of *Theatre Notebook*, the journal of the Society for Theatre Research. (MOC)

PATRICK B. O'NEILL is professor and head of speech and drama at Mount Saint Vincent University, Halifax, Nova Scotia. His

xlvi

primary research interests lie within the fields of Canadian studies and Canadian theatre history. (PBON)

GWEN OREL is literary manager of the Alabama Shakespeare Festival. She is writing on contemporary Czech theatre for her Ph.D. from the University of Pittsburgh. (GAO)

HANDAN OZBILGIN studied theatre at Ankara University in Turkey and Long Island University in the USA. She works in New York as a freelance director and producer. (HO)

DEREK PAGET is reader in drama at University College Worcester, England. He is the author of two books on documentary drama: *True Stories?* (1990) and *No Other Way To Tell It* (1998). (DJP)

KAVALAM NARAYANA *PANIKKAR is an expert on Sanskrit drama and staging. The founder-director of the Sopana Theatre in Kerala in India, he has written twenty-six Malayalam plays and translated many English and Sanskrit texts into Malayalam. (KNP)

MICHAEL PATTERSON, professor of theatre at De Montfort University, Leicester, is the author of several books on German theatre, and is at present preparing a companion volume to this Encyclopedia, *The Oxford Dictionary of Plays*. (MWP)

SIOK SIAN PEK is a journalist based in Bhutan. She has written on children, women, media, and communications for various newspapers, magazines, and broadcast stations. (SSP)

ANN PELLEGRINI, associate professor of drama at the University of California, Irvine, is the author of *Performance Anxieties: staging psychoanalysis, staging race* (1997) and co-author of *Love the Sin: sexual regulation and the limits of religious tolerance* (2002). (AP)

DAVID PELLEGRINI received his Ph.D. from the University of Pittsburgh and now teaches theatre at Eastern Connecticut State University. (DRP)

CATHERINE PIOLA is lecturer in English at University Dauphine-Paris IX. Her work has focused on Irish studies, particularly the Dublin Theatre Festival from 1957 to 1992, as well as sociology and the arts. (CPi)

JANE PLASTOW is deputy director of the Workshop Theatre and of the Leeds Centre for African Studies at the University of Leeds. She has published extensively on African theatre and theatre for development. (JP)

HEINRICH F. PLETT has held the chair of English at the University of Essen since 1972. His work includes *Intertextuality* (1991), *English Renaissance Rhetoric and Poetics* (1995), *Systematische Rhetorik* (2000), and *Rhetoric and Renaissance Culture* (2003). (HFP)

THOMAS POSTLEWAIT, professor of theatre at Ohio State University, publishes regularly on British and American theatre history and historiography. He is series editor of Studies in Theatre History and Culture from University of Iowa Press. (TP)

LOIS POTTER, professor of English at the University of Delaware, is editor of the Arden edition of *The Two Noble Kinsmen* and author of *A Preface to Milton* (1986), *Shakespeare in Performance: Othello* (2002), and many theatre reviews. (LDP)

M. CODY POULTON teaches Japanese literature and theatre at the University of Victoria, Canada, specializing in modern Japanese drama. He is the author of a book on Izumi Kyōka and has translated a number of kabuki and contemporary plays. (CP)

ERIC POURCHOT completed his Ph.D. at City University of New York Graduate Center, where he wrote his dissertation on modern Romanian theatre. He has published articles and reviews on Slavic and East European performance. (EEP)

BRIAN POWELL teaches Japanese theatre at Oxford University and writes on theatre in Japan over the past century. His published work includes a book on a twentieth-century kabuki playwright and translations of plays. (BWFP)

DADI PUDUMJEE is managing trustee of the Ishara Puppet Theatre Trust, New Delhi, vice-president of UNIMA, a member of the National Folklore Support Center Chennai, and of the UNESCO Parsi Zoroastrian Project. He has won the Sangeet Natak Academy award in puppetry. (DDP)

LOUIS A. RACHOW is the director of the Library and Information Service of the International Theatre Institute of the United States. Rachow was formerly librarian/curator of the Hampden-Booth Theatre Library at The Players in New York. (LAR)

L. S. RAJAGOPALAN is one of India's most respected scholars of traditional Sanskrit theatre, primarily *kutiyattam*, on which he has written two books. He has contributed numerous articles to scholarly journals on traditional Indian musicology and performance. (LSR)

LALITHA RAJAN is a Ph.D. candidate in theatre studies at Glasgow University, writing on 'The Poetic Quest for Remembrance: politics in contemporary British performance'. (LR)

PRASANNA RAMASWAMY is a theatre practitioner who directs, translates, and adapts plays for the Indian theatre. She is also the cultural officer for the German cultural centre in Chennai. (PR)

JOSÉ LUIS RAMOS ESCOBAR, playwright, director, and scholar, has won several national and international awards and has published seven books. He obtained his Ph.D. from Brown University and is a professor at the University of Puerto Rico. (JLRE)

LUIS A. RAMOS-GARCÍA teaches Latin American and US Latino theatre at the University of Minnesota. Recent works include *Voces del interior: nueva dramaturgia peruana* (2001), *Miguel Rubio* (2002), and *The State of Latino Theater in the US* (2002). (LRG)

CHRISTOPHER RAWSON is drama critic of the *Pittsburgh Post-Gazette*, member of the English faculty of the University of Pittsburgh, former chairman of the American Theatre Critics Association, and trustee of the American Theatre Hall of Fame. (CR)

SOHINI RAY trained in Manipuri dance with Guru Bipin Singh and received her MA in dance and Ph.D. in anthropology from UCLA, based on research in Manipur. She now lectures in anthropology at the University of California, Irvine. (SR)

DAN REBELLATO is a playwright and lecturer at Royal Holloway, University of London. He is the author of *1956 and All That* (1999). (DR)

JANELLE REINELT is associate dean and professor of drama in the Claire Trevor School of the Arts at University of California, Irvine. She has published widely in the areas of politics and performance, performance theory, and feminism. (JGR)

ALAIN RICARD teaches at the Centre d'Études de l'Afrique Noire, University of Bordeaux. Publications include *Théâtre et nationalisme: Wole Soyinka et LeRoi Jones* (1972), *Livre et communication au Nigeria* (1975), and *L'Invention du théâtre* (1986). (AlR)

MICHELINE RICE-MAXIMIN, from Guadeloupe, is associate professor of French at Swarthmore College and writes on francophone literatures. She is co-editor of *Postcolonial Subjects: francophone women writers* (1996) and *Karukéra: présence littéraire e la Guadeloupe* (1998). (MRM)

GARY A. RICHARDSON, Hunter professor of English at Mercer University, is the author of *American Drama from the Colonial Period to World War I* (1993). He is currently writing on theatrical representations of the Irish in Ireland and the United States. (GAR)

MILLA RIGGIO is James Goodwin professor of English at Trinity College, Hartford, Connecticut. Publications include *Teaching Shakespeare through Performance* (1999), a special issue of *TDR* devoted to Trinidad and Tobago Carnival (1998), and *Culture in Action: Trinidad and Tobago Carnival* (2003). (MR)

DAVID RINEAR is professor of theatre at Trinity University in San Antonio, Texas. He is the author of *The Temple of Momus: Mitchell's Olympic Theatre* (1987) (DLR)

BEATRIZ J. RIZK, Colombian-American scholar and theatre promoter, has written extensively on Latin American and Latino theatre in the USA. Her latest book is *Posmodernismo y teatro en América Latina: teorías y prácticas en el umbral del siglo XXI* (2001). (BJR)

PAOLA CATENACCIO ROBLIN studied in Milan and London and writes on James Shirley, linguistics, and translation theory and practice. She teaches English at the Catholic University of Milan. (PCR)

WILLEM N. RODENHUIS graduated in history (University of Utrecht) and in theatre studies (University of Amsterdam). From 1996 till 2000 he served two terms as secretary-general of SIBMAS, the International Association of Libraries and Museums for the Performing Arts. (WNR)

MARTIN ROHMER works in the Department of Culture for the city of Munich. He studied drama, anthropology, and German literature in Munich and Glasgow and his Ph.D. thesis, *Theatre and Performance in Zimbabwe*, was published in 1999. (MRo)

MARIO A. ROJAS, associate professor of Spanish at the Catholic University of America, Washington, is the author of several publications on Latin American theatre, socio-semiotics of theatre, and narratology. (MAR)

JOHN ROUSE is associate professor in the Department of Theatre and Dance at the University of California, San Diego. He is the author of *Brecht and the West German Theatre* (1989) and articles on contemporary German theatre. (JR)

ELI ROZIK, professor of theatre at Tel-Aviv University, specializes in theatre theory, particularly in non-verbal communication and performance analysis. He has published extensively; among his books are *The Language of the Theatre* (1991) and *The Roots of Theatre* (2002). (ER)

ALVINA RUPRECHT, Carleton University, Ottawa, is co-president of the Canadian Theatre Critics Association and has published numerous articles on Québec and Caribbean theatres. Her latest book is *Le Théâtre francophone et créolophone de la Caraïbe*. (AR)

BHABENDRA NATH SAIKIA obtained his Ph.D. degree in physics from London University in 1961. He has worked in the fields of literature, drama, cinema, and journalism and published twenty-nine books covering short stories, novels, children's literature, essays, and plays. (BNS)

DAVID Z. SALTZ, director of the Interactive Performance Laboratory at the University of Georgia, has published numerous articles exploring the philosophy of theatre and performance art, and the relationship between live performance and interactive media. (DZS)

MODALI NAGABHUSHANA SARMA is a playwright, director, actor, and teacher, the founder and professor of the theatre departments of Osmania and Central Universities in Andhra Pradesh in India. He has written fifteen plays and several critical works. (MNS)

MARTA ELENA SAVIGLIANO teaches in the World Arts and Cultures Department at UCLA. She is the author of *Tango and the Political Economy of Passion* (1995), and has recently completed *Angora Matta: fatal acts of north–south translation*. (MES)

ELAINE SAVORY, director of literature at Eugene Lang College, New School University in New York, has written widely on Caribbean and African literature. She is the author of *Jean Rhys* (1998) and *flame tree time* (poems, 1993), and co-editor of *Out of the Kumbla: Caribbean women and literature* (1990). (ES)

ELIZABETH SCHAFER, senior lecturer in drama and theatre at Royal Holloway, University of London, is the author of *MsDirecting Shakespeare* (1998) and co-author of *Ben Jonson and Theatre* (1999). With Peta Tait she co-edited *Australian Women's Drama* (1997). (EJS)

RICHARD W. SCHOCH teaches in the School of English and Drama at Queen Mary, University of London. He is the author of *Shakespeare's Victorian Stage: performing history in the theatre of Charles Kean* (1998). (RWS)

MICHAEL SCHUSTER works as a professional puppeteer and public folklorist in Honolulu. He has been a student of Asian puppetry since 1974 and trained in India, Indonesia, and Mandalay. He was a founding member of the Train Theatre in Jerusalem. (MSh)

VIRGINIA SCOTT is professor of theatre at the University of Massachusetts at Amherst. Her book *The Commedia dell'Arte in Paris* (1990) won the 1991 George Freedley Award. Her most recent book is *Molière: a theatrical life* (2000). (VS)

ANTONIO SCUDERI is assistant professor of Italian at Truman State University in Missouri. He is the author of *Dario Fo and Popular Performance* (1998) and co-editor of *Dario Fo: stage, text and tradition* (2000). (ATS)

ADRIENNE SCULLION teaches in the Department of Theatre, Film, and Television Studies at the University of Glasgow. Her research interests include Scottish theatre and culture, eighteenth- and nineteenth-century women playwrights, and cultural policy. (AS)

ANAMARÍA CROWE SERRANO obtained a BA in French and Spanish (Trinity College Dublin) and an MA in applied languages (Dublin City University). She is a freelance translator, a reader for the blind, and has published several translations. (AMCS)

MARIA HELENA SERÔDIO lectures on English literature and performance analysis and directs the Centre for Theatre Research at the University of Lisbon. She has published widely on English and Portuguese literature and theatre studies. (MHS)

YVONNE SHAFER is professor of theatre at St John's University in New York. She is a member of the executive board of the Eugene O'Neill Society and author of *Performing O'Neill: conversations with actors and directors*. (YS)

MICHAEL SHAPIRO is professor of English at the University of Illinois at Urbana-Champaign, and also directs the Program in Jewish Culture and Society. He has written on the children's troupes of early modern London and on the disguised heroines in the plays of Shakespeare and his contemporaries. (MS)

TONI SHAPIRO-PHIM is an anthropologist and dance ethnologist who has written extensively on Cambodian dance. She was programme adviser for the 2001 tour of the USA by Cambodia's royal dancers. (TSP)

ALISON SHELL is a lecturer in English studies, University of Durham. She has published *Catholicism, Controversy and the English Literary Imagination* (1999) and is working on a study of English Jesuit drama. (ASh)

PATRICIA SIEBER received her Ph.D. in Chinese from the University of California at Berkeley. Currently an assistant professor at Ohio State University, she is completing a book-length manuscript on the reception of Yuan *zaju*. (PS)

MELISSA SIHRA is lecturer in drama at Queen's University, Belfast, and is completing her Ph.D. on the plays of Marina Carr at Trinity College, Dublin. She specializes in Irish theatre and gender and performance studies. (MAS)

BRIAN SINGLETON is senior lecturer in the School of Drama, Trinity College Dublin. He is editor of *Theatre Research International*, author of *Antonin Artaud: le théâtre et son double* (1998), and co-editor of *Artaud on Theatre* (2001). (BRS)

KARTHIGESU SIVATHAMBY is professor at the International Centre for Ethnic Studies in Columbo, Sri Lanka. (KS)

MICHAEL SLATER is emeritus professor of Victorian literature at Birkbeck College, London. His publications include *Dickens and Women* (1983), the *Dent Uniform Edition of Dickens's Journalism* (1994–2000), and a biography of Douglas Jerrold (2002). (MDS)

WILLIAM SLATER is professor of Greek at McMaster University. His publications have been on Greek poetry, Alexandrian grammar, and aspects of theatre history, especially epigraphy. He is currently working on ancient mimes and pantomimes. (WJS)

GRETCHEN ELIZABETH SMITH is assistant professor of theatre at Southern Methodist University. Her writing focuses on French baroque court performance, women performers of the early modern period, and, as a new project, Parisian actresses of the nineteenth century. (GES)

MATTHEW WILSON SMITH is assistant professor of English at Boston University. His work has appeared in the anthologies *Architect of Dreams* and *Land/Scape/Theater*, as well as several journals. He is at present working on a study of mass culture and the *Gesamtkunstwerk*. (MWS)

SUSAN BRADLEY SMITH's publications include a collection of her own plays, *Griefbox*, and (as Susan Pfisterer) the critical history *Playing with Ideas* (1999) and the anthology *Tremendous Worlds* (1999). She teaches at King's College, University of London. (SBS)

CHRISTY STANLAKE is a Ph.D. candidate at Ohio State University. Her research and publications, including her dissertation 'Mapping the Web of Native American Dramaturgy', are primarily devoted to Native American theatre. (CLS)

VICTORIA STEC, Rose Bruford College, completed a doctoral thesis on 'The Shakespearean Career of Sir Robert Helpmann' at the Shakespeare Institute, University of Birmingham. (VRS)

JOHN RUSSELL STEPHENS (1946–2001) was senior lecturer at University of Wales Swansea. He was a distinguished nineteenth-century theatre historian and author of *The Censorship of English Drama 1824–1901* (1980), *The Profession of the Playwright* (1991), and *Emlyn Williams* (2000). (JRS)

SALIL SUBEDI is a Nepali writer, musician, and performing artist. He has published writing and photography in many newspapers and magazines on arts and culture, heritage, and spiritualism. He is also editor of *Arts Circle* magazine. (SS)

HARDJA SUSILO was born in Yogyakarta, Indonesia, and retired as associate professor of ethnomusicology at the University of Hawai'i. He specializes in Indonesian performing arts, including Javanese music, dance, and theatre. (HS)

CATHERINE SWATEK, associate professor of Asian studies at the University of British Columbia, is the author of *Peony Pavilion Onstage: four centuries in the career of a Chinese drama* (2001). Her research interests are in pre-modern Chinese drama. (CS)

LIB TAYLOR is a senior lecturer in theatre studies at the University of Reading, England. Her research (some of which takes the form of theatre practice) is in women's theatre, gender, and performance. (LT)

DAVID THOMAS is professor of theatre studies at the University of Warwick. Major publications include studies of Ibsen, Congreve, and a documentary history of Restoration theatre. He is currently directing a research project on theatre censorship legislation. (DT)

PETER THOMSON is emeritus professor of drama at the University of Exeter. His books include *Shakespeare's Theatre* (1984 and 1992), *Shakespeare's Professional Career* (1992), *Brecht's Mother Courage* (1998), and *On Actors and Acting* (2000). (PT)

NICANOR TIONGSON, professor at the Film and Audiovisual Communication Department, College of Mass Communication, University of the Philippines-Diliman, has published pioneering books on Philippine dramatic forms and cinema. He edited the ten-volume *CCP Encyclopedia of Philippine Art* (1994). (NGT)

CALDWELL TITCOMB is a theatre and music historian who studied at Harvard University. Professor emeritus at Brandeis University, he is a charter member of the American Theatre Critics Association and president of the Boston Theater Critics Association. (CT)

SIDIBÉ VALY teaches at the University of Abidjan, Côte d'Ivoire. His publications include *Le tragique dans le théâtre de Bernard Dadié* (1999) and (as editor) *Bernard Dadié: conscience critique de son temps* (1999). (SVa)

RODOLFO VERA is resident playwright and co-artistic director of the Philippine Educational Theatre Association in Manila, where he heads the playwriting development programme. He has written approximately twenty plays, and conducts theatre workshops locally and internationally. (RV)

SURAPONE VIRULRAK is professor in the Department of Speech Communication and Performing Arts, Chulalongkorn University, Bangkok. Publications include *Theatre in the Reign of King Rama Ninth 1946–2000, Indonesian Theatre and Dance*, and *Burmese Theatre and Dance*. (SV)

SOPHIE VOLPP is assistant professor of East Asian languages and cultures at the University of California, Davis. Her research interests include late-imperial Chinese theatre. (SYV)

J. MICHAEL WALTON is professor of drama at the University of Hull and director of the Performance Translation Centre. He has published four books on Greek theatre and is general editor of Methuen's Classical Greek Dramatists. (JMW)

IAN WATSON is deputy chair of the Department of Visual and Performing Arts at Rutgers University-Newark in the United States. He is a contributor to numerous journals and has authored and edited several books on Eugenio Barba and performer training. (IDW)

ERIC WEITZ lectures in theatre studies and theatre practice at Trinity College Dublin, University College Dublin, and the Gaiety School of Acting. Also a theatre director, his research interests include humour studies. (EW)

E. J. WESTLAKE is a visiting assistant professor of theatre studies at the University of Michigan. Her book on Nicaraguan and Guatemalan nationalist drama, *Our Land is Made of Courage and Glory*, is due in 2003. (EJW)

MARTIN WIGGINS is a fellow of the Shakespeare Institute and senior lecturer in English, University of Birmingham. He is associate general editor of Oxford English Drama, and publishes mainly on English Renaissance drama and British television drama. (MJW)

DAVID WILLIAMS is professor of theatre at Dartington College of Arts, England, and a contributing editor to *Performance Research*.

Publications include critical anthologies on the work of Peter Brook and the Théâtre du Soleil. (ADW)

SIMON WILLIAMS is professor of dramatic art at the University of California, Santa Barbara. He has published widely in the history of acting, Shakespearian performance, and the theatrical and dramatic aspects of opera. (SJCW)

CHRISTA J. WILLIFORD is an AHRB research fellow in theatre history and information technology at the University of Warwick. Her work applies computer modelling to the study of vanished theatres, most notably Richelieu's Palais Cardinal playhouse. (CJW)

S. E. WILMER is senior lecturer in Trinity College Dublin, specializing in American, Irish, and Finnish drama. Recent work includes *Theatre Worlds in Motion* (co-edited with Hans van Maanen, 1998) and *Portraits in Courage: plays by Finnish women* (1997). (SEW)

LISA WOLFORD teaches theatre and cultural studies at Bowling Green University. She is the author of *Grotowski's Objective Drama Research* (1996) and co-editor of *The Grotowski Sourcebook* (1997). Her research interests include contemporary experimental theatre and performance. (LW)

ALAN WOODS teaches theatre at the Ohio State University and directs the Jerome Lawrence and Robert E. Lee Theatre Research Institute. Widely published, he is internationally known as an advocate for performance accessibility and audio description. (AW)

BRIAN WOOLLAND is a lecturer in the Department of Film and Drama at the University of Reading, and a director and playwright. Publications include articles and books on early modern drama, educational drama, and film. (BGW)

NICK WORRALL is principal lecturer in the School of Humanities and Cultural Studies at Middlesex University. Major publications include *Nikolai Gogol and Ivan Turgenev* (1982), *Modernism to Realism on the Soviet Stage* (1989), and *The Moscow Art Theatre* (1996). (NW)

YONG LI LAN. Dr Yong studied at the universities of Oxford and London and is now senior lecturer in English at the National University of Singapore. Her research interests are Shakespeare, intercultural performance, and film. (YLL)

ALAN YOUNG has published extensively on the Renaissance emblem, Shakespeare, and the tournament. His books include *Henry Peacham* (1979), *Tudor and Jacobean Tournaments* (1987), *The English Tournament Imprese* (1988), and *Henry Peacham's Manuscript Emblem Books* (1998). (ARY)

PHILLIP B. ZARRILLI holds the chair of drama at Exeter University. His books include *Acting (Re)considered* (1995), *When the Body becomes All Eyes: paradigms, practices and discourses of power in Kalarippayattu* (1998), and *When Gods and Demons Come to Play: Kathakali dance-drama in performance and context* (2000). (PZ)

NOTE TO THE READER

Alphabetic arrangement. Entries are arranged alphabetically letter by letter in the order of their headwords, except that 'Mc' and 'St' are treated as if spelled 'Mac' and 'Saint'. The one numerical headword (the company called 7:84) is listed as if spelled out. In order to avoid an unhelpfully long series of entries that begin with a form of the word 'theatre', most such entries are recorded under the next significant word (e.g. theatre of the oppressed is placed under 'oppressed', Théâtre du Soleil under 'Soleil', Teatro Nacional D. Maria II under 'Nacional'). Exceptions include institutions commonly known by their initials (Théâtre National Populaire, Theatre Communications Group) or items that it would be confusing to list otherwise (Theatre Guild, theatre studies, Theatre Workshop).

Names and romanization. Names of persons used as headwords are those the figure is best known by. They follow the form of the relevant country or language; thus Chinese, Japanese, and Korean names, whether in headwords or text, are normally given with the family name first followed by the given name without a separating comma (e.g. Gao Xingjian and Ninagawa Yukio). All accents are included for languages with Roman alphabets. In transliterating other alphabets the standards of the Library of Congress on romanization have been followed and diacritical marks have normally been left out. The major exceptions are Japanese and Korean, where the macron or long mark has been used because of its significance in establishing meaning (e.g. kyōgen and nō in Japanese, *kamyŏngŭk* in Korean). Chinese terms and names in headwords are given first in the *pinyin* system, followed by the Wade-Giles system in parenthesis: *canjun xi* (*ts'an chün hsi*), Gao Ming (Kao Ming).

Dates of plays and translation of titles. Dates of plays are of first production, unless otherwise noted. Foreign play titles follow the most commonly seen version when an English translation of the work is known to exist, but often there is no standard translated title, and more often no translation at all. In such circumstances the contributor has given a translation designed to convey the sense and quality of the original title.

Cross-references. An asterisk (*) in front of a word signals a cross-reference to a relevant entry. Any reasonable form of the referenced headword is marked in the text ('*naturalist' for 'naturalism', '*political drama' for 'politics and theatre'). When the mention in the text is not directed towards the content of the entry by that name, however, the word is usually not marked as a cross-reference ('actor', 'critic', and 'director', which appear very frequently, are tagged only when they refer to the substance of the entries on acting, criticism, and directing). It has seemed unnecessary to mark the many occurrences of the name Shakespeare. Cross-references are indicated the first time they appear in an entry only. '*See*' and '*see also*' followed by a headword in small capitals are used to draw attention to relevant entries that have not been specifically mentioned in the text.

Contributor signatures are given as initials at the end of each entry. A key to these begins on p. xxxv of volume 1, and brief biographies of the editors and contributors begin on p. xxxvii of volume 1.

Thematic contents. All works in dictionary format suffer from the tyranny of the alphabet. As a guide to the entries contained in the work, a Thematic Table of Contents appears in the front of the first volume, offering a topical method of approaching the entries in the Encyclopedia.

Bibliographies. Brief bibliographies have been appended to most longer entries, and a general bibliography ('Further Reading') is placed near the end of the second volume. It should be noted that a number of contemporary theatre institutions have websites, most of them easy to find. We have chosen not to list them in bibliographies, or those of any other Internet reference sources, because web addresses change too frequently to be of long-term use.

Reader's comments. Every effort has been made to ensure that the information in this Encyclopedia is accurate. But minor errors and inconsistencies are inevitable, and readers are invited to call attention to any they discover, or comment on the entries, by writing to:

> Joanna Harris, Trade and Reference Department, Academic Division, Oxford University Press, Great Clarendon Street, Oxford, OX2 6DP, UK

Readers' comments will be passed on to the editor.

·A·

AALBERG, IDA (1857–1915)

Finnish actress, for thirty years the leading actress of the *Finnish National Theatre. From her debut in 1874, she personified a romantic balance of opposites, the period's desire for great actresses coupled with her belief in art as an active sexual force. Her tragic heroines in Shakespeare's and *Schiller's drama were characterized by emotional complexity and intense dynamism. *Ibsen's biographer Gerhard Gran considered her performance as Nora in *A Doll's House* the most perfect of all those he had seen. Besides her native Finnish language, she played in Swedish, Danish, and German in seven countries, in 1905 completing a tour of Scandinavia and Russia. She enjoyed a remarkable triple success as Rebecca West (*Rosmersholm*), Hedda Gabler, and Schiller's Mary Stuart, and became a symbol of Finnish national culture.   LIB

ABBA, MARTA (1906–88)

Italian actress. Abba joined *Pirandello's newly formed Teatro d'Arte in 1925 as a novice but quickly became his leading actress, muse, and (platonic) lover. Their correspondence provides deep insights into an idiosyncratic relationship and into Pirandello's personality and creativity. Under her influence, the female role became dominant in his theatre and from *Diana and Tuda* in 1927 to *When You Are Somebody* in 1933 he wrote parts to accommodate her talents. She lived in America from 1936 to 1953, when she returned to Italy in a vain attempt to revive her stage career.   JF

ABBEY THEATRE

Home of the National Theatre of Ireland, in *Dublin. Theatre-as-building and theatre-as-company are quite distinct. The Irish National Theatre Society (INTS) was created by Frank and W. G. *Fay's National Dramatic Company following its performances of *Cathleen ni Houlihan* (by W. B. *Yeats and Augusta *Gregory) and *Deirdre* (by Æ) in April 1902. The INTS aimed to employ Irish actors and to create a distinctive style: simple staging; fine words finely spoken; and vivid characterization in the small roles. Yeats, the first president of the INTS, fostered a 'theatre of beauty', not of commerce or propaganda. English heiress Annie *Horniman, who 'detested all things Irish' but was fond of Yeats, bought the Hibernian Theatre of Varieties and Mechanics' Institute on Abbey Street, Dublin, and let it rent free and fully refurbished to the INTS. The Abbey Theatre opened on 27 December 1904. The acting area was tight and shallow (7.3 by 4.8 m or 21 by 16 feet). The pit and horseshoe-shaped balcony seated 562. Unlike other Dublin theatres, there was no bar, no easy-come, easy-go from the hall, no sixpenny seats, no *applause until the *curtains, and no house-lights during performance. These conditions made possible artistic use of *light and *sound; they also magnified the effect of disruptions by the *audience, as occurred during the opening of J. M. *Synge's *The Playboy of the Western World* in 1907 (*see* PLAYBOY RIOTS). Frequently, the INTS executive—Synge, Lady Gregory, and Yeats, all authors and all Protestants—quarrelled with the actors, the audience, or their patron Horniman (bought out in 1911) during a period of Catholic nationalist agitation for Irish independence from Britain. At the Abbey every imaginable question about a national theatre was in dispute; the answers changed over time, and still change (*see* NATIONAL THEATRE MOVEMENT, IRELAND).

Periodically unpopular in Dublin, the INTS toured England and the USA for money and fame. After the death of Synge in 1909, the theatre became the home of domestic dramas in a *realist style and of 'kitchen comedies' set in a peasant's cottage. Dozens of playwrights were given a chance to stage plays before Sean *O'Casey arrived with his urban *tragicomedies (*The Shadow of a Gunman*, 1923; *Juno and the Paycock*, 1924; *The Plough and the Stars*, 1926). The acting of Sara *Allgood, Barry

*Fitzgerald, and F. J. McCormick in these plays was a culmination of the Abbey style. With a subsidy in 1925 from the Irish Free State came state appointments to the executive. Following the death of Yeats, Ernest Blythe ran the Abbey from 1941 to 1967. His passion was to make Ireland Irish speaking. In addition to nightly plays in Irish, popular *comedies of 'peasant quality' and O'Casey revivals were the Abbey's staple, not the works of Denis *Johnston, Samuel *Beckett, Brendan *Behan, and the later O'Casey. The Abbey burned in 1951; fifteen years later a new Abbey Theatre opened on the same site, a modernist block of a building (its director Tomás Mac Anna called it 'four walls dead as mutton'), with seating for 628 and a much wider and deeper stage. The *box sets of the old repertoire were now remote from the audience, but by the later 1960s playwrights such as Tom *Murphy, Brian *Friel, and Thomas *Kilroy learned to exploit more open concepts of stage space. The Abbey still reads hundreds of manuscripts annually in search of new playwrights, some of which are produced in its *studio space, the Peacock. The company of state-employed actors has been dissolved. 'Ireland' remains a problem that writers dramatize, but 'national theatre' is now defined as just theatre in Ireland. With the *artistic directors of the 1990s—Garry *Hynes and Patrick *Mason—the performance styles of the past gave way to high production values and overtly theatrical staging. The Abbey showcases the best of the country's directors, actors, and writers, both in Dublin and on *tours to *New York, *London, and elsewhere.   AWF

ABBOTT, GEORGE (1889–1995)

American playwright, director, and producer. In his 106-year lifetime, Abbott was a prime inventor of Broadway as an artistic and commercial enterprise. He attributed his success to principles learned (1911–12) in George Pierce *Baker's playwriting class—dramatic structure, logical *plot and *characters, quick pacing. He directed 113 Broadway shows, many of which he co-authored, adapted, or produced. At the same time, he became a major *film director-writer-producer. As *director, he demanded complete control over actors, often dictating line-readings and specifying exact gestures and timing. After an early career as an actor (1913–25), Abbott turned to playwriting, co-authoring *The Fall Guy* (1925), and the hit *comedy-*melodrama *Broadway* (1926), which he also directed. He helped to create four hit *farces of the 1930s: co-producing and directing *Twentieth Century* (1932), co-writing and directing *Three Men on a Horse* (1935), and producing and directing *Boy Meets Girl* (1935) and *Room Service* (1937). *Jumbo* (1935) was the first *musical he directed, and he dominated that profession into the 1960s: writing and co-directing *On your Toes* (1936); adapting, directing, and producing *The Boys from Syracuse* (1938), *Pal Joey* (1940), and *Where's Charley?* (1948); co-writing, producing, and directing *The Pajama Game* (1954), and *Damn Yankees* (1955); direct-

ing *On the Town* (1944), *High Button Shoes* (1947), *Call Me Madam* (1950), *Wonderful Town* (1954), and *A Funny Thing Happened on the Way to the Forum* (1962). Abbott was working on *New York revivals and new projects until the time of his death.
                                                           MAF

ABDEL-SABOUR, SALAH (1930–81)

Egyptian poet and dramatist, a pioneer since 1957 of the free-verse movement in Arabic poetry. His first play, *Ma'sat El-Hallaj* (*The Tragedy of Hallaj*, 1967), proved far more stageworthy in characterization and language than the work of previous poetic dramatists. The crucifixion of the tenth-century mystic of the title became a powerful metaphor for the troubled relation between contemporary intellectuals and the political authorities. Abdel-Sabour's other four poetic dramas exhibit a mixture of symbolic and *expressionist qualities, sometimes evolving into a Kafkaesque *absurdism, as in *Mosaafer Leil* (*Night Traveller*, 1969).
                                                           HMA

ABDOH, REZA (1963–95)

Iranian-born experimental director and video artist. Hailed by some as an *avant-garde visionary at the time of his death due to AIDS, he began directing at the age of 14 in *London, where he grew up. After settling in *Los Angeles in the early 1980s, his work was seen at various venues, including the *Mark Taper Forum. In 1991 he started an ensemble called Dar a Luz and created a series of large-scale *multimedia *spectacles known for their provocative and enigmatic iconography, aggressive and high-decibel intensity, and concern with moral and social decay. These included *The Hip-Hop Waltz of Eurydice* (1990), *Bogeyman* (1991), *The Law of Remains* (1992), *Tight, Right, White* (1993), and *Quotations from a Ruined City* (1993), which were performed in derelict storefronts, lofts, and warehouses in Los Angeles and *New York. In Europe his work was featured at major arts *festivals.
                                                           STC

ABE KŌBŌ (1924–93)

Japanese existentialist novelist, playwright, and director. The experience of being raised in Manchuria and repatriated to Japan after the war bred in Abe a sense of rootless individualism, an aversion to nationalist ideologies, and an abiding suspicion of authority. His literary and philosophical influences ranged from Dostoevsky and Heidegger to Kafka and *Beckett. Beginning with *The Uniform* (1955), Abe wrote some twenty plays, including *Slave Hunt* (1955), *The Ghost Is Here* (1959; trans. 1993), *You, Too, Are Guilty* (1965; trans. 1979), *The Man Who Turned into a Stick* (1969; trans 1975), and *Involuntary Homicide* (1971; trans. 1993). Abe's most famous play, *Friends* (1967; trans. 1969), became a cult classic in Czechoslovakia and

Poland. A member of the Communist Party, he was expelled in 1957 after criticizing the Soviet invasion of Hungary. His plays feature men thrust into absurd situations in an unjust and hostile social environment; vaguely *allegorical in nature, they defy easy analysis. With his Abe Kōbō Studio (1971–9) he explored forms of theatrical expression that were increasingly anti-literary. His last play, *The Little Elephant Is Dead* (1979), contained almost no *dialogue.

CP

ABELL, KJELD (1901–61)

Danish playwright. Abell trained as a designer in *Paris in the 1920s and the exciting visual experiments he saw there had a lasting impact on his work as a writer. His first play, *The Melody That Got Lost* (1935), was a long-running hit in Copenhagen. Using a mixture of *cabaret sketches and *surreal interludes, the play offered an entertaining critique of the materialist middle class. A similar lightness of tone ran through *Eva Serves her Childhood* (1936). With the threat of imminent war, Abell's critique of middle-class indifference to political issues took on a darker tone. *Anna Sophie Hedvig* (1939) shows a quiet unmarried schoolteacher who is prepared to kill to safeguard her small world. Abell's later plays from *Silkeborg* (1946) to *The Scream* (1961) used visually arresting methods of addressing the same issues that had concerned him from the outset: middle-class indifference and spiritual isolation juxtaposed with the need for individual commitment.

DT

ABHINAVAGUPTA (950–1025)

Sanskrit scholar and aesthetician from Kashmir in *India. His elaborate commentary, *Abhinavabharati*, on *Bharata's *Natyasastra*, the earliest treatise on Indian aesthetics, is considered to be the most clear, comprehensive, and authoritative exposition of this encyclopedic text. Abhinavagupta wrote over 40 treatises on aesthetic and religious experience. Apart from the *Abhinavabharati*, his other outstanding commentary is the *Lochana* on *Dhwanyaloka*, a monumental work on *dhwani* (the aesthetic quality of suggestion) written by Anandavardhana (*c*.840–90).

Abhinavagupta's most important precept treats the theory of *rasa*, which holds that the aesthetic experience is akin to spiritual realization and is the soul of poetry. The word *rasa* draws on a cooking analogy, and in the realm of aesthetics concerns the pleasure of the senses. Abhinavagupta makes a distinction between this experience and that of the bliss attained through universalization, which he holds to be the ultimate goal of art. The aesthetic capacities deepen through a person's accretion of ideas and experience which contribute to spiritual realization. Widely regarded as a seer among India's aestheticians, his views of *rasa* have been applied to philosophy and the visual and auditory dimensions of literature, drama, and poetry.

KNP

ABHINAYA

Acting in the classical *Indian tradition. The prefix *abhi* means 'towards' and the root of *naya* is *ni*, which means 'to lead', thus *abhinaya* signifies leading the spectators towards theatrical pleasure. As delineated in *Bharata's *Natyasastra*, the ancient Sanskrit text on Indian aesthetics and *dramaturgy, the god Brahma combined the elements of *acting from the four Veda (sacred scriptures): recitation from the *Rigveda*, music from the *Samaveda*, mimetic art from the *Yajurveda*, and sentiments from the *Atharvaveda*. Out of a combination of these Veda he created the fifth Veda, the *Natyaveda* or the *Natyasastra*, the scripture or canonical text for dramatic and musical art.

Abhinaya is made up of four components of acting: *angika* (the body), *vacika* (the voice), *sattvika* (mental states), and *aharya* (*costumes, *make-up, *scenery). The interrelationship of these four elements constitutes the Indian concept of acting. Acting with the body is delineated in many chapters of the *Natyasastra*, dealing with *karanas* and *angaharas*. *Karanas* refer to movements in space from one static posture to another, including *angas* (major parts, like the head, hands, chest, and feet) and *upangas* (minor parts, notably the eyes, eyebrows, and nose). There are 108 *karanas* enumerated in the text. *Angaharas* are combinations of five or six *karanas* forming a sequence of movements. There are 32 such combinations. *Hastabhinaya* is acting with hand gestures (*hastas), which are classified as *asamyuta* when they are shown with one palm of the hand and *samyuta* when both hands are used. Bharata has codified 24 single hand gestures and thirteen gestures with both the hands. There are also 29 *nritta hastas* used in dance.

Two distinct modes of acting described in the *Natyasastra* are *lokadharmi and *natyadharmi, by which the style of representation and the delivery of movement and speech are identified. *Lokadharmi*, which draws its inspiration from *loukik* (worldly) situations, is found in diverse forms of *folk theatre incorporating movements, gestures, speech, music, and costumes that relate to real life. Acting in the *natyadharmi* mode, however, is extraordinary, stylized, suggestive, abstract, and graceful, with embellishments of ideas drawn from the dramatic *text. *Lokadharmi* and *natyadharmi* are not contradictory, as their difference in representational acting is merely one of degree. *Sattvika abhinaya* refers to the subtle dimensions of acting that relate to the mind. The ability of the actor to identify with the *character and internalize his or her state of consciousness plays a part in the combining of the psychophysical aspects of acting.

KNP

ABIERTO, TEATRO

Argentinian 'open theatre for a closed country' that staged four festivals between 1981 and 1985. The inaugural *Buenos Aires event had the greatest impact as a collective response to the continuing repression of the military dictatorship. Twenty *one-acts played from July until September 1981, attracting some 25,000 spectators, despite the destruction by 'accidental' fire of the festival's venue.   JGJ

ABINGTON, FANNY (FRANCES) (1737–1815)

English actress, an influential performer on and off the stage. Born into a very poor family in London, she became a rich woman, a wildly popular comic actress, and a leader of fashion in late Georgian Dublin and London. Her contracts at *Drury Lane and *Covent Garden included generous clothing allowances, and she is said to have earned another £1,500 a year as a fashion consultant. On stage, her forte was *comedy, especially young woman roles. She created Lady Teazle in *Sheridan's *The School for Scandal* (1777) and was also popular as Beatrice in *Much Ado* and Millamant in *Congreve's *The Way of the World*. While her range was not wide, her graceful gestures, expertly modulated voice, and skill at ironic pronouncements kept her acting from becoming monotonous. Her value to the Drury Lane company is evident from *Garrick's refusal to dismiss her, despite their perpetual clashes and combative correspondence. Joshua Reynolds immortalized her in his *Mrs Abington as the Comic Muse*, a companion piece to his better-known painting of Sarah *Siddons.   MJK

ABOVE

A standard word in Shakespearian *stage directions, referring to the stage balcony in the centre of the *scaenae frons*. The stage balcony might be used to represent the balcony of a house, a window, a musicians' gallery or a town's walls, with the doorway beneath it (the so-called *discovery space) serving as the town gates. In the hall theatres, and later in the amphitheatres as well, it served as the music room. Commonly it was fronted by a *curtain to conceal the musicians. As an acting space it held few people, who usually served as accessories to those on the main stage.   AJG

ABREU, LUIS ALBERTO DE (1952–)

Brazilian playwright. Abreu works in *São Paulo and is the co-ordinator of Belo Horizonte's *street theatre Grupo Galpão. His work examines interstices between popular and erudite sources, often mixing classical *comedy with Brazilian oral culture in the eight productions of the Brazilian Popular Comedy Project he started in 1995. Among his plays is *O livro de Jó* (*The Book of Job*, Teatro da Vertigem, 1995), since presented nationally and internationally.   LHD

ABSURD, THEATRE OF THE

Term coined by Martin Esslin to describe the work of a number of (chiefly) European playwrights writing in the 1950s and early 1960s. Authors notably connected to the theatre of the absurd include a group of exiles in *Paris, among them Samuel *Beckett from Ireland, Eugène *Ionesco from Romania, the Russian-Armenian Arthur *Adamov, as well as a self-exile, Jean *Genet, who, though French, had spent most of his early life as an itinerant criminal. The first three were not writing in their native languages and brought to the fore an outsider's view of language as constructed and arbitrary, and thus ultimately absurd. Other absurdist writers include Harold *Pinter from England and Edward *Albee from the USA. None was connected in any way to the others and the theatre of the absurd was never more than a convenient critical amalgam of a shared view of the world and human existence. 'Absurdism' never became a theatre movement as such.

Nonetheless the absurdist authors had their shared roots in *modernist theatrical experiments at the end of the nineteenth and the beginning of the twentieth centuries. Significant parallels can be drawn between absurd drama and *Jarry's *Ubu roi* (1896), in which the eponymous antihero (*see* HERO AND ANTIHERO) is motivated only by action, Guillaume Apollinaire's *The Breasts of Teiresias* (1917), in which the constructedness of theatre is displayed, and particularly *Maeterlinck's *symbolist drama *The Blind* (1890), which—like Beckett's *Waiting for Godot*—features a group of people waiting beside a tree for a saviour who never arrives. The *dadaists and *surrealists, with their spontaneous writing, are further predecessors.

The notion of the 'absurd' was first proposed by Albert *Camus in his philosophical essay *The Myth of Sisyphus* (1942). Camus's existentialist notion derives from his experience growing up as a Frenchman in colonized Algeria, and particularly from his research on the effects of pestilence and plague, similar to the investigations conducted by *Artaud. In times of extreme stress, Camus thought, human beings abandon social conventions and morals in an effort solely to survive, and this desire for self-preservation leads to arbitrary and gratuitous actions, which are separated from their consequences. The obvious historical connective between existentialist philosophy and the theatre of the absurd is the Second World War, which provided ample evidence of atrocity on a mass scale. Hitler's industrialization of murder, and the atomic devastation of Hiroshima and Nagasaki, revealed that during the war language was used as an instrument of death, like any other weapon of destruction. The existentialist theatre of Camus and *Sartre, despite its attention to parallel issues, was conventional in its drawing-room settings and articulation of a philosophy in *dialogue form. The theatre of the absurd, on the other hand, has been called the theatricalization of existentialism. No one *character discusses the philosophy; characters exist within it and embody it. Absurd things happen to them and they know not why. They desire to escape but know they cannot. They are chained to their existence and though they struggle they do not leave. They sometimes talk of death but it is usually denied them. They exist in a perpetual state of meaninglessness.

The most celebrated of the absurdist plays is Beckett's *Waiting for Godot*, initially directed by Roger *Blin as *En attendant Godot* (Paris, 1953). It features two tramps on a roadside who wait, passing the time with comic theatrical routines, a self-referential or *metatheatrical tactic common to much absurdist drama. Nothing happens and Godot never comes, denying *plot and *action. In Ionesco's *La Cantatrice chauve* (1950, translated as *The Bald Prima Donna* and *The Bald Soprano*), a knock is heard at the door but there is no one there, and a clock strikes thirteen; Ionesco staged the revolutionary act of disrupting signifier from signified (*see* SEMIOTICS). And in *The Balcony* (1960), Genet shows how existence is created only through its reflection by others.

The unsettling form used in absurdist drama is a reflection and symptom of a society which has lost value and meaning. Stories cannot be told within traditional or recognizable forms; a play's action is in the image or the word; character motivations are, at best, opaque; there is no dramatic conflict. The world of the absurd has lost the unifying factors of logic, reason, and rationality—those qualities so admired in the French tradition deriving from Descartes—which is why the stage cannot present a 'real' world or maintain the standards of *realism. In the absurdist view, everything is possible, and the *dramaturgical mechanics of traditional theatre are exposed as false (Ionesco called *La Cantatrice chauve* an 'anti-play'). Though located historically in the wake of the Second World War, the absurdist tradition lived on into the new millennium and transcended its European borders: postmodern theatre thrives on, and makes a virtue of, disruption and *bricolage*. BRS

BRADBY, DAVID, *Modern French Drama 1940–1990* (Cambridge, 1991)

ESSLIN, MARTIN, *The Theatre of the Absurd* (Harmondsworth, 1961)

GAENSBAUER, DEBORAH B., *The French Theater of the Absurd* (Boston, 1991)

MAYBERRY, BOB, *Theatre of Discord: dissonance in Beckett, Albee, and Pinter* (Madison, NJ, 1989)

ACCESI

One of the more stable and individual of the second-generation Italian *commedia dell'arte* companies, which flourished under the protection of the dukes of Mantua from approximately 1590 to 1623. The troupe was founded and directed by Pier Maria *Cecchini: like others, it toured the northern Italian centres on a regular basis. It made one trip to France in 1600–1, and another very successful one in 1608. Cecchini's difficult personal temperament, and consequent quarrels with colleagues such as Giovan Battista *Andreini, with whom he might have collabor-

ated, probably deprived him and his company of further success in later years. RAA

ACCIUS, LUCIUS (170–after 90BC)

Roman tragic dramatist, whose reputation in antiquity rivalled that of *Pacuvius. Fragments of 46 plays survive, most of them translations or adaptations of *Greek *tragedies, although stamped with Accius' much admired rhetorical style. Accius' scholarly works on literary history and drama are not extant. RWV

ACHURCH, JANET (1864–1916)

English actress. From a *Manchester theatrical family, Achurch appeared at the *Olympic Theatre in *London in 1883, then *toured with the recently formed *Benson company, taking leading Shakespearian roles. She was a tall, golden-haired, statuesque, open-featured actress, independent of mind and interested in the 'New Drama', much admired by *Shaw, for whom she played Candida and Lady Cicely Waynflete in *Captain Brassbound's Conversion*. She and her second husband Charles Charrington are best remembered for mounting the first professional production of *Ibsen in London, *A Doll's House* (1889), in which she played Nora. In *Archer's translation and partly under his direction, the play was highly successful and led to a series of Ibsen productions in the 1890s. *Little Eyolf* (1896) was less well received; in spite of a rapturous review for Achurch by Shaw, she was soon replaced as Rita by Mrs Patrick *Campbell, to Shaw's fury. She retired from the stage in 1911. EEC

ACKERMANN FAMILY

German theatre company active between 1753 and 1767 under the leadership of **Konrad Ernst Ackermann** (1712–71). The troupe performed in numerous towns, basing itself initially in Königsberg (1755) where Ackermann built the first private theatre in Germany. In the turmoil of the Seven Years War the troupe was itinerant, finally settling in Hamburg with its own house (Comödienhaus am Gänsemarkt) in 1765. In 1767 the building, *costumes, and *scenery were leased to the newly formed *Hamburg National Theatre enterprise with which the troupe effectively merged. After the failure of the national theatre Ackermann resumed *touring with a smaller troupe until his death. The troupe occupies an important place in the history of German theatre. Not only did it première many important works (for example, *Lessing's *Miss Sara Sampson* in 1755), but leading members were dedicated to theatre reform and establishing theatre as an artistically and socially respectable institution. Among its members were many of the leading actors of the day such as Sophie Charlotte *Schröder (Ackermann's wife),

Friedrich Ludwig *Schröder (Ackermann's stepson), Konrad *Ekhof, and Sophie *Hensel.   CBB

ACQUART, ANDRÉ (1922–   )

French *scenographer and painter, who studied fine art in Algiers while designing for the university theatre. His first production in *Paris (Montherlant's *Pasiphaé*, 1951) led to work with Michel *Vinaver (*Coréens*, 1957), Roger *Blin (*Genet's *The Blacks*, 1959), and seven productions with Jean *Vilar. Always seeking new ways to enlarge the stage space, Acquart used raw materials—wood, metal, water—often combined with mirrors to abstract reality. To enhance his three-dimensional approach to scenic movement he designed various schemes of folding panels for Roger *Planchon's *Troilus and Cressida* (1964), sliding wooden platforms for his *Bleus, Blancs, Rouges* (*Blues, Whites, Reds*, 1971), and paper screens for Blin's production of Genet's *The Screens* (1966). An instinctive artisan, Acquart trusts his intuition rather than intellect, insists he is not a theoretician, and always visualizes actual materials when making sketches and models. A large retrospective installation exhibition in *Avignon (1986) showed the breadth and sculptural quality of his work.   PH

ACQUAYE, SAKA (1923–   )

Ghanaian artist, composer, and playwright. A trained art teacher, whose sculptures occupy important positions in Accra and whose canvases have been shown in major international exhibitions, Acquaye's extraordinary gifts, which include writing, choreography, and administration, were brought together in a series of productions that included *Obadzeng Goes to Town*. The Ga *folk opera *Lost Fisherman*, which used a *total theatre approach to cut through problems of language, became an almost permanent part of the Ghanaian national repertoire during the 1960s and early 1970s. Acquaye worked with various groups, such as the Dumas Choir and Wulomei, and produced a body of *texts that included *Sasabonsam, Modzawe, TroTro*, and *Scholarship Woman*.   JMG

ACROBATICS

Form of popular entertainment since ancient times. Petronius describes rope *dancers and acrobats at Trimalchio's feast in the *Satyricon*. In thirteenth-century Bourbon, acrobats 'somersaulted on the ground', and by the sixteenth century 'feats of activity' were displayed by troupes at feasts and *carnivals. At the great European fairs, competitions for leaping and balancing were held, and rope dancers, who combined acrobatic balancing with artistic dancing, amazed *audiences with speciality acts, such as Mlle Charini, who danced on the rope with her feet in chains while playing the mandolin. With the coming of the *circus in the late eighteenth century, acrobats found a more permanent home. Leaping—over horses, through balloons of fire—and multiple somersaults were popular, and the Bedouin Arabs were famed for their reverse-pyramid-building act. The Risley act—one acrobat juggling another with his feet—combined adult and child performers and was seen in the circus and in the street. In 1861 Henry Mayhew described the acrobat or 'street-posturer' who worked in a gang of five men on pyramids, and the 'perch', a long pole held by one man, balancing another at the top. Balancing on a rolling globe was made popular in the middle of the nineteenth century by the elegant Signor Ethardo, and the bottle equilibrist, who balanced on the necks of wine bottles, was a frequent sight in the circus. Later circus acrobats tended to utilize apparatus more extensively, though those in the Chinese State Circus, drawing on over 3,000 years of history, still feature stunning feats of foot juggling, ladder balancing, and pyramid building without the aid of technology or nets.   AF

ACT

One of the more or less equal divisions of Western plays, conventionally numbering one to five, usually marked by some combination of (*a*) an interruption of chronological continuity, (*b*) a change of setting, (*c*) a significant change in thought, mood, or *plot development. Possible theatrical markers include the use of a *chorus, a *curtain, *lighting or *music, or entr'acte entertainment. Historically, treatment of act divisions has varied. The five-act structure advocated by *Horace persisted in classically inspired drama through the *early modern period, but it was imposed on Elizabethan drama only with difficulty, and in Spain a three-act structure became the norm. Both three and five acts were treated as 'natural' in nineteenth-century *theory, but in the twentieth century two-act and *one-act plays became frequent. *See also* SCENE.   RWV

ACTING/ACTOR

Acting is the art of performing an *action or of representing human experience on stage or in some other mode of *performance, in which the actor's body and voice serve as the principal tools.

1. Traditional Western acting; 2. Non-Western approaches; 3. Approaches since 1945

1. Traditional Western acting

*Mimesis—the art of imitation, which is embodied by acting—is one of the basic traits of human beings, who replicate the world around them either out of a desire to control their immediate environment, or adapt to it, or laugh at it. Acting is the fundamental art of the theatre and from the earliest days the actor has been its prime interpretative artist. Few records of acting exist until the *Greek theatre of the fifth century BC and even then evidence is scant. Only men acted in ancient Athens. As they played to *audiences of over 15,000 in *open-air *arenas (*see* ANCIENT THEATRES), their gestures were broad and the emotional states they conveyed instantly recognizable. *Masks were worn to establish *character and, in later centuries, massive headpieces and raised boots (*cothornus) were assumed to enlarge the performer's stature. The most prized actors were those who spoke with strength and clarity. In a politicized society like Athens, rhetoric was a valued weapon and actors achieved eminence as purveyors of rhetorical skills to citizens.

For 2,000 years after the heyday of the *Dionysia festivals, actors lived in uncertainty, obscurity, and indigence. Despite the centrality of performance as entertainment in the late *Roman Republic and Empire, actors in plays, *pantomimes, and other *spectacles were slaves and few earned their freedom. There is virtually no documentation of acting for several centuries following the fall of Rome, though the art stayed alive during the Dark Ages and early *medieval period in Europe in the activities of minstrels, *acrobats, comic performers, and storytellers who performed at fairs, taverns, and banquets in the halls of feudal lords. *Liturgical drama was performed solely by those in holy orders and later the *mystery, *biblical, and other *cycle plays were staged mainly by *amateur members of the sponsoring local community, with some participation, perhaps in lead and comic roles, of professional entertainers.

It is in the sixteenth century that we can identify the beginnings of the modern acting profession (*see* EARLY MODERN PERIOD IN EUROPE). There were two formations that actors employed to structure their professional work, which led to different modes of theatre. In Italy, where actors had little access to indoor theatres and few written scripts to perform, from midcentury on they formed troupes which *toured the towns and, whenever possible, the courts of Italy. Their generic name, *commedia dell'arte*, highlighted the professional nature of these activities, but *commedia* is known best to history for *improvisation, a practice whose origins may go back to the *mimes of ancient Rome. Each troupe included between ten or twelve actors who specialized in generic roles, such as romantic lovers, comic old men, comic servants, and braggarts (*see* STOCK CHARACTER); their repertoire was composed of *scenarios in which these characters were involved in a variety of (usually) comic actions. As *dialogue was not written down, actors were free to improvise whenever appropriate, particularly the masked comic old men and servants, whose antics reached heights of prodigious foolery. *Commedia* became noted for the elegance and poetry of its romance as well as for its ribald *comedy. Above all, it catered to the pleasure humans take in playing with appearance; their performances were not so much a literal representation of life but a game that played with it.

By the seventeenth century *commedia* had spread far beyond Italy. Troupes visited Spain, England, Germany, and France; in *Paris it found a permanent home until the late eighteenth century. Improvisation was widely practised in Germany by troupes originating with the *English Comedians but strongly influenced by the *commedia*. *Viennese theatre especially was invigorated by several improvisers from Joseph Anton *Stranitzky's advent in the city in 1705 to the inspired improvisations of Johann Nepomuk *Nestroy in the midnineteenth century. However, even this popular actor was eventually forced to obey the ban on improvisation that authorities had been attempting to impose for 100 years.

Improvisation fell prey to the desire among actors and authorities to make theatre predictable and more respectable, by requiring actors to devote their energies to interpreting a written script. The latter half of the sixteenth century saw the birth of the modern theatre, as permanent companies of actors, who had previously been itinerant, assembled in specially constructed *playhouses, initially in *Madrid, *London, and Paris, to perform a repertoire of scripted drama. In contrast to the improviser who created from the collective imagination of the company, the scripted actor interpreted the invention of another's mind. Fortunately, as the playwrights of Spain and England at this time included Lope de *Vega, Shakespeare, *Calderón, and *Jonson, to mention a few, actors had to develop techniques of in-depth characterization that the earlier, simpler roles in morality plays and *pasos* had not required. In England especially, Edward *Alleyn and Richard *Burbage were noted for their charismatic stage presence.

Acting did not, however, attract attention as a discrete art until the Enlightenment. In the eighteenth century, theatre in England and Europe was employed as one means of cultivating civility in a dangerously violent society. While plays aspired to be morally improving, actors served as models of civilized behaviour, both by the elegance of their demeanour and because the very process of acting required them to feel sympathy for a character other than themselves. The actor became, therefore, an icon of enlightenment. This led to an interest in acting *theory. The little theory from classical times treated acting as a branch of rhetoric and much acting on the eighteenth-century stage reflected this. But more striking was the work of such players as Michel *Baron and *Lekain in France, David *Garrick in England, and Konrad *Ekhof and Friedrich Ludwig *Schröder in Germany, all of whom represented their roles with fullness and elicited empathy from the audience. Garrick, in particular, achieved European fame for the clarity and lightness of his playing and he more than any other actor was a model of Enlightenment humanity. Broadly speaking, these actors generated two schools of thought about the nature of acting. 'Emotionalist' writers such as Sainte-Albine and John Hill considered effective acting to be a product of the emotional sensitivity of the actor, which created a sympathetic bond with the character, while others, notably *Diderot in *The Paradox of Acting* (1773), argued acting was a calculated process and that the actor must not feel with the character, otherwise the performance will fail as it is not subject to any controlling, aesthetic consciousness.

In the course of the eighteenth century, the most prominent actors achieved public respect and social status to a degree previously unequalled. Nevertheless, acting remained one of the least respected of all professions. Suspicion of actors was due in part to the widespread mistrust of the theatre, at times an open hatred, expressed by various denominations of the Christian church. An actor, in assuming personalities different from the one bestowed upon him by God, challenged the very basis of a divinely sanctioned human identity. Furthermore, *women in performance were considered to exercise a profoundly corrupting influence over those audiences gathered to gaze at them. Women had performed with the wandering troupes of Italy, France, and Spain since the late Middle Ages, and they remained once these became permanent companies, but they were not seen on the English stage until the Restoration of 1660. For a good two centuries after this, actresses, being the object of male fantasy, were regularly pilloried from the pulpit and their calling was considered to be identical with that of prostitution (*see* ANTI-THEATRICAL POLEMIC).

Although no actors adopted a theoretical model upon which to develop their art, the dialectic of 'emotionalist' versus 'formal' acting set up in the eighteenth century provides a useful framework for understanding the work of the virtuoso actors who dominated the American and European theatre of the nineteenth century. For example, Edmund *Kean, the volatile English *romantic actor who represented extreme emotions, appealed through his capacity to act with seeming total spontaneity on stage, though there is evidence that he carefully planned each phase of his roles. However, his counterpart in Germany, Ludwig *Devrient, may well have depended primarily upon his instinctual feeling to realize the disturbing undercurrents of his characters. Other prominent romantic virtuoso actors included Frédérick *Lemaître in France, whose prodigious powers of *parody combined with powerful emotionalism provided the most complete embodiment of romantic irony on the European stage, while the American Edwin *Forrest endeavoured to bring the experience of the frontier to the urban stage. However, most great actors of the nineteenth century, such as Sarah *Siddons, William Charles *Macready, *Rachel, Karl *Seydelmann, Edwin *Booth, and Sarah *Bernhardt, several of whom served as *actor-managers of their own companies, achieved national and usually international celebrity for their highly polished, self-conscious interpretations of classic roles.

Although the virtuoso dominated nineteenth-century theatre, ideals of ensemble in which actors worked cooperatively were not entirely absent. From the formation of Garrick's company in *Drury Lane in 1749 and the establishment of the

*Burgtheater in Vienna in 1776, the ideal of ensemble was held up as a desirable alternative to production centred around the star. *Goethe's directorship of the *Weimar Court Theatre (1791–1817) and Charles *Kean's seasons at the *Princess's Theatre, London (1850–9), sustained the ideal of ensemble, but it was not until the Europe-wide *tours of the *Meiningen company (1874–90) and the advent of the *naturalistic drama that ensemble acting was acknowledged as desirable. Among the several ensemble companies that were founded in the final decades of the nineteenth century, the most influential has been the *Moscow Art Theatre under the direction of Konstantin *Stanislavsky, whose great achievement was to develop exercises that allowed actors to explore the psychological depths of their characters while also attending to interplay with other characters. His series of books on acting, notably *An Actor Prepares* (1936), *Building a Character* (1949), and *Creating a Role* (1961), have had a greater influence on modern actor *training than any other texts. Even though the twentieth century has produced a broad spectrum of acting theory, Stanislavsky's commentaries remain basic to the art of representation in the modern theatre. Almost all actors in the Western tradition encounter his work in the course of their training and, in their own way, most incorporate it into performance.

The two other highly influential theorists of acting in the modern theatre have been Bertolt *Brecht and Antonin *Artaud. Brecht's writings on acting have been most useful for staging *historical drama in a Shakespearian tradition. He called for actors to cultivate the 'distancing effect' (*see* VERFREMDUNG), by which they represented their role in a way that engaged the audience but always directed attention to the socio-political forces at work within the character and to the way each character's conduct is formed by deliberate choices rather than by a series of unconscious impulses (*see also* POLITICS AND THEATRE). Brecht rejected the naturalistic-Stanislavskian view of human conduct. He was also ideologically distant from Artaud, who in a series of explosive, brilliant, but often obscure essays, *The Theatre and its Double* (1938), outlined a theatre that revealed the metaphysical universe lying beyond but implicated in human action. Artaud's exhortations to the actor to engage in representations of human action and emotion on a vastly exaggerated plane are perhaps of more use to the *dancer, or even the *opera singer, than to actors engaged in spoken drama. Nevertheless, Artaud's exploration of the realm of poetic theatre expanded the modern actor's awareness of the expressive range of the art (*see* CRUELTY, THEATRE OF).

Until the end of the nineteenth century, most actors trained as apprentices, learning roles and traditional stage business in a *repertory company. In modern times, however, actor training, either in conservatories or universities, has become common. But the prospects of an individual sustaining a lifelong career in live theatre are not at all good. Only in Germany and a few other European countries do resident companies hire actors on long-term (even lifetime) contracts; but with a general decline of government subsidy at the end of the twentieth century (*see* FINANCE), such commitments have become increasingly difficult. Where commercialism reigns, as it does in the United States and increasingly in Britain, actors have few opportunities for extended work with one company. In the USA, Hollywood *films and *television offer more jobs and larger salaries than commercial, *regional, or local theatres, and many actors regard the stage at best as a training ground for more lucrative cinema work.

Nevertheless, the acting profession in live theatre is far from dead. As always, public interest is still centred around the stars of the profession and the modern age has produced a whole array of virtuoso actors as polished and as charismatic as their forebears, from the poetic English virtuoso Henry *Irving, whose career was coming to an end at the start of the twentieth century, through Laurence *Olivier, an actor of unusually heroic stature, who dominated the English-language theatre in the middle decades, to powerful performers such as Helene *Weigel, Vanessa *Redgrave, and Ian *McKellen in the latter part of the century. Yet most major cities in Europe and America are able to support a vigorous theatrical life apart from the flagship theatres. In the United States, for example, the most compelling acting can often be found neither on Broadway nor on the prestigious stages of the regional theatres, but in chamber theatres in city suburbs or smaller communities. Unfortunately it is impossible for actors to earn a living wage under such circumstances; it is sobering, therefore, to consider that much of the finest work is produced by artists who are, at best, semi-professional. But the compulsion to imitate, to play with appearance, and to penetrate and bring to the stage extreme states of mind is so embedded in human nature that the art of acting will always survive.   SJCW

2. Non-Western approaches

Given the association of acting with mimesis and representation in the West, when applied to many non-Western *genres of performance which are non-representational the term is best understood etymologically—from the Latin *actus*, meaning 'to do' or perform. In pre-colonial *Africa, Asia, and the Americas, performance cultures fulfilled socio-cultural needs for *ritual, teaching, as well as entertainment, and ranged across dramas, dance-dramas, ritual dramas, and a variety of orature from storytelling to recitation of epics and delivery of praise poems; therefore, performers were as likely to make use of dance, conventionalized movement, song, mime, or masking, as the spoken word.

Acting can be understood as a culture-specific mode of embodiment and awareness deployed to achieve an aesthetic ideal in performance. Each culture's understanding of acting as a form of embodiment is based on indigenous paradigms of the body in movement (including voicing), the body–mind relation-

ship, and consciousness or awareness. To understand acting in *India, one would need to be informed about several paradigms available in South Asia: vibratory theories of sound, which provide insights into the psychophysical dimensions of voicing and its metaphysical implications; yoga physiology/philosophy, which provides a detailed understanding of what happens during psychophysical practice of exercises of both the physical and 'subtle' bodies; and *Ayurveda* (literally, 'science of life'), the indigenous system of medicine which provides a humoural understanding of the body, physiology, and health. Central to all three of these paradigms is an Indian understanding of the key role that the internal wind humour (*prana vayu*) plays in exercise and voicing. Similarly, to understand *Chinese, *Japanese, or *Korean paradigms of acting, one would have to understand Chinese medicine (or its regional variations), and crucially the concept/principle of *qi* (Japanese and Korean *ki*). As Chinese performers describe it, a good actor must 'radiate presence' (*faqi*), while a poor performer would have no presence (*meiyou qi*). These (usually unarticulated) assumptions about how a performer activates such 'presence' inform and animate the process of acting in training and onstage.

Non-Western acting cannot be limited to 'an' actor interpreting 'a' role. In the Javanese *shadow-puppet theatre (*wayang kulit*), the solo puppeteer (*dalang*) performs all the roles in all-night performances of epic stories, transforming voice and register into easily recognizable characters, managing archaic languages and contemporary dialects, and serving as a conduit for dynamic performative energies bringing alive on the shadow screen everything from refined females to dynamic, rough demons to the bawdy comic byplay of *clowns speaking in the vernacular. In the *kutiyattam* tradition of staging Sanskrit dramas in Kerala, India, a single actor playing a primary character in the drama takes the stage alone for several days in a row as he interprets, narrates, and enacts the stories and all the characters necessary to fill in the background to the action performed by the full company on the final day of performance.

As these examples illustrate, the source and repository of knowledge and authority in most non-Western performance genres lies, not with the *text, but with the actor and his lineage of performing a particular style transmitted across generations. What is most important is not what is performed, but how a story, play, or role is elaborated in performance. The concern with how to perform is evident not only in the lengthy process of training often required, but also in extant written texts about acting, particularly those from India and Japan.

India's *Natyasastra* (perhaps c.200 BC to AD 200) is an encyclopedic work on all aspects of drama (*natya*) attributed to the sage *Bharata, but probably a synthesis of knowledge of the art and practice of acting then current. Its 36 chapters classify and describe in minute detail every aspect of production necessary for an acting company to achieve success when performing the then popular Sanskrit dramas at courts. The *Natyasastra* describes how actors should follow a rigorous training regime including a special diet, seasonal full-body massage, and training in physical exercises, dance postures, and rhythm in order to completely embody each role mentally and physically, thereby 'carrying forward' (*abhinaya) the appropriate state of being/doing (bhava) for the audience to 'taste' (*rasa) within the ever-shifting context of a particular drama. The *Natyasastra* identified eight permanent states of being/doing (sthayibhava) to be savoured by the audience: pleasure or delight, laughter or humour, sorrow or pain, anger, heroism or courage, fear, disgust, and wonder. There are detailed descriptions of how to embody physically each of these states, such as the comic (hasya): 'This is created by . . . showing unseemly dress or ornament, impudence, greediness, quarrel, defective limb, use of irrelevant words, mentioning different faults [etc.; the result is represented] . . . by consequents like the throbbing of lips, the nose and the cheek, opening the eyes wide or contracting them, perspiration, colour of the face, and taking hold of the sides.' The emphasis is on integrating four modes of expression: a complete language of hand gestures (*angika), vocal expression (*vacika), inner expressivity of emotions (*sattvika), and external aspects (*aharya) such as *costumes and *make-up. The ideal, non-conditional state of accomplishment of the actor-dancer able to integrate all four modes of expression is summarized in *Nandikeswara's late Sanskrit text the *Abhinaya-darpana* (c. tenth to thirteenth centuries):

> Where the hand [is], there [is] the eye;
> where the eye [is], there [is] the mind,
> where the mind [is], there [is] the *bhava*;
> where the *bhava* [is], there [is] the *rasa*.

Although the tradition of enacting Sanskrit dramas had, with a few exceptions such as *kutiyattam*, severely declined or died by the ninth or tenth centuries, many of the characteristic features of the approach to acting described above are found in regional genres of performance such as Kerala's *kathakali dance-drama. The *kathakali* actor traditionally begins training at the age of 7 (today more likely at 10 to 12), undergoing a minimum of six years of training through a rigorous annual process of intensive psychophysical exercises combined with full-body massage. He must learn the complete languages of hand gestures and facial expressions, the various rhythmic patterns, set choreographies, and numerous roles in the basic repertory of plays. But the intensive training is only the beginning of the process—onstage experience and the individual's life experience must inform budding virtuosity of techniques, since the actor is not expected to reach artistic maturity until at least the age of 40. It is only as a mature, senior actor-dancer that the *kathakali* performer is allowed to place his individual signature on particular important roles in the repertory within the boundaries of what is considered appropriate.

It is with the twenty or more early fifteeenth-century treatises of *Zeami Motokiyo, the founder with his father *Kan'ami of Japanese *nō theatre, that we encounter the first sole-authored general theory of acting. Zeami's treatises on acting were secret texts, written for exclusive use within his own *family lineage of performers, and were unavailable to the public until 1908 when a collection was discovered in a Tokyo second-hand bookstore. By the age of 36, Zeami had received sufficient court patronage to allow him time to reflect and write on the art of acting. His writings give practical advice on teaching, convey an understanding of the subtleties of the psychophysical process of acting, analyse how to capture the audience's attention, and articulate the way (michi) of nō as a Buddhist path toward enlightenment.

His earliest text, *Kadensho* (*Teachings on Style and the Flower*), was completed when he was 40. It records much of what he learned from his father, and begins to elaborate one of the primary metaphors and principles of acting found throughout his writings—the flower (hana): 'First, look at the flowers in nature and through them understand why we adopt the figure of the flower through all phases of the *noh* play.' The book provides practical advice on teaching youngsters, beginning their training at 7, and on how to approach the role types of woman, old man, bare-faced roles, frenzied people, priests, dead warriors, deities, and demons. Regarding playing an old man, for example, Zeami advises the actor not to be 'too self-conscious of his age and walk with a stoop or shrink of his body', since no flower can be found in playing a stereotype. Emphasizing the need for novelty to keep one's acting fresh and as a means of capturing the audience's attention, he observes, 'There can be no flower which stays forever without decaying. Because the flower decays, it is novel when it blooms again at its own season.'

In one of his later texts, *Kakyo* (*The Mirror of the Flower*), completed in 1424 when he was 61, Zeami identifies three types of performance: the arts of dancing, song, and costume which are visible, easily seen, and therefore appeal to the concrete, physical, and sensual aspect of the audience's experience; the experiential realm aroused by the rhythms of singing and dancing which transcend the material and purely physical, appealing to the ear and hearing; and the highest and subtlest ability of the actor to hold the spectator's attention through the inner dynamism of mental engagement or concentration. Writing at 65 in the *Kyui*, Zeami described the highest level of acting as bearing none of the usual or visible outward signs of achievement. Here the actor achieves the 'Mark of the Miraculous Flower' which transcends dualities and whose mark is 'no-Mark'. The permanent flower is a metaphysical principle in the actor's mind.

In contrast to Zeami's treatises, which are tinged with metaphysical concerns, the flamboyant *kabuki theatre produced at the height of its popularity *Yakusha rongo* (*The Actors' Analects*, 1776), a text which never presumes to be more than a collection of tales, gossip, criticism, advice, and instruction that actors wrote for fellow actors. The best-known item in the collection is 'The words of Ayame', a record of the sayings of *Yoshizawa Ayame, the first great performer of female roles (*onnagata). In contrast to the non-representational approach of the nō actor to playing female roles, Ayame asserts that the onnagata should play his role offstage as well as on by continuing 'to have the feelings of an onnagata even when in the dressing room. When taking refreshment, too, he should turn away so that people cannot see him.'

The question of 'how' to perform revealed in these acting texts continues to be a major preoccupation of many master teachers of non-Western acting, since it is the 'how' that produces the next generation of virtuosic actors within each lineage of performance. But quite in contrast to the traditional genres of performance discussed thus far, throughout the non-Western world the colonial era brought the introduction of Western models of 'spoken drama', especially the plays of *Ibsen, *Chekhov, and Shakespeare, and the concomitant introduction of Stanislavskian character acting. Most early forms of spoken drama were mounted by educated amateurs who performed translations of Western classics, and whose acting often slavishly imitated Western models. The birth of a post-colonial consciousness, especially after the Second World War, brought a critique of this slavish imitation of the West and a search for indigenous aesthetic models and modes of embodiment that could inform contemporary actor training and performance (see POST-COLONIAL STUDIES). PZ

3. Approaches since 1945

Four developments characterize approaches to acting and the actor in the period after the Second World War: the increasing role that stars and *performativity play in shaping popular culture and opinion; consolidation of the role that training plays in developing the contemporary professional actor; the global flow of both training techniques and modes of performance; and the concomitant diversification of paradigms of acting that serve new *dramaturgies and modes.

Although the cult-like status of star actors is a ubiquitous part of many theatre histories, in the post-war period the influence of the global film industries of Hollywood and Bollywood (India), the rise of television, and the creation of voracious popular presses vying for access to the personal life of stars have helped to create the notion of the actor-as-personality in which the lines between private/public and self/character are blurred. Acting has always been considered problematic because it plays with such boundary crossing, and many actors intentionally transgress the boundaries in life and performance. By the end of the twentieth century, however, two developments seemed distinctive: a number of stars had entered political life (in India, the USA, and elsewhere), and the media established performativity as a part of public life. Politicians regularly engage coaches to help shape their public images and rehearse their public performances.

This sociological development runs counter to contemporary trends in acting and actor training around the world. Stanislavsky revolutionized nineteenth-century acting in the West by ushering in a new sense of the actor's work on stage as the product of extensive systematic training and *rehearsal. Emphasizing the long-term development of the actor-as-interpreter, in 1913 Jacques *Copeau, with Charles *Dullin and Louis *Jouvet, retired to the French countryside to prepare a company and a repertoire that would, as Michel *Saint-Denis wrote, free both 'from cumbersome machinery and showy effects' in order to 'concentrate . . . on the development of a new school of acting'. For Copeau training was a period during which the actor should discover an optimal condition or state of 'readiness', a state of 'repose, calm, relaxation, detente, silence, or simplicity'. Following Copeau's philosophy and approach, Saint-Denis later founded three schools of theatre—the London Theatre Studio (1946–52), the *Old Vic Theatre School (1946–52), and the École Supérieure d'Art Dramatique in Strasbourg (from 1954)—all intended to discover new ways of stimulating the creative imagination.

Equally important in the post-war/post-colonial period have been the global tendencies of culture which have internationalized both training and paradigms of performance. In parts of Asia and Africa the increasing importance of modern spoken drama inspired by Ibsen and Chekhov—often used as a means of socio-political critique (see POLITICS AND THEATRE)—as well as the rise of film and television, led to the founding of national theatres and actor-training programmes. The acting courses within the Korean National Academy of the Arts in Seoul and the *National School of Drama in New Delhi immerse students in Stanislavskian approaches as well as indigenous techniques of performance. For example, in Seoul acting students receive regular voice training both in contemporary Western techniques (those associated with Kristin Linklater and Cicely Berry) and in traditional *p'ansori singing.

The transnational flow began earlier in the West. Yoga and Indian philosophy played an important role in the development of some of Stanislavsky's key concepts and approaches to acting—an influence long unrecognized due to Soviet suppression and problems with English translations of Stanislavsky's major books. Subsequent rebellion against body–mind dualism and attempts to find practical ways of better integrating body and mind led to the adoption of non-Western techniques or principles in performer training, such as the use of the Chinese martial art t'ai chi ch'uan to achieve psychophysical integration in the 1960s by Herbert *Blau with his company KRAKEN.

At the *Polish Laboratory Theatre (founded 1959), Jerzy *Grotowski began to develop and articulate an intensive psychophysical pathway for the actor aimed at self-transcendence in which the actor strips the self down to become a living incarnation. Inspired in part by his observations of the intensive training of actor-dancers in the *kathakali*, Grotowski developed an intensive psychophysical process of physical and vocal training aimed at elimination of anything extraneous. His work has been widely influential.

Jacques *Lecoq was another key figure. He founded his own school in Paris in 1956 where the methods and 'laws' of movement are constantly (re-)explored through the use of masks ('neutral' masks, character masks, *commedia* masks), clowning, and practical explorations of the styles of *melodrama, buffoons (drawing on *grotesque fantasy or *parody), or *tragedy. Lecoq training is intended to develop the actor-as-creator: the actor's imagination, improvisation, and kinaesthetic awareness are departure points for creating theatrical performances or for approaching a classical text. Lecoq-based work is fundamental to the methods of Theatre de *Complicité in England, Ariane *Mnouchkine in France, and Théâtre de la Jeune Lune in Minneapolis.

The primacy of collaboration and the notion of the actor-as-creator were simultaneously developed by other practitioners and ensembles during the 1960s and 1970s in order to democratize the theatrical process, moving away from the top-down model of *director's theatre. US and UK ensembles such as *Bread and Puppet Theatre, the *San Francisco Mime Troupe, the *Living Theatre, the *Open Theatre, and *Theatre Workshop developed a variety of collaborative working methods. Reflecting scientific thinking about relativity and indeterminacy, the notions of spontaneity, improvisation, and 'being in the now' were developed through the playing of games by Clive Barker in Britain and Viola Spolin in America. In the UK *devising new work around a social issue, historical period, or incident became the preferred creative method evolved by regional *theatre-in-education companies such as Coventry and Belgrade, socialist touring companies such as *7:84 and Red Ladder, and in some university drama courses. In all such instances the actor is no longer considered an interpreter of a playwright's existing text, but the locus and beginning point of creation.

In addition to shifts in training and working methods, changes in dramatic writing forced the development of new approaches to accommodate the quite different tasks expected of the actor. For example, in many of Samuel *Beckett's later plays, such as *Not I* (1972) and *A Piece of Monologue* (1979), there are no recognizable characters to act, let alone three-dimensional ones, and the physical demands made on the performer are often extreme. In *Not I* all that is visible on the 'stage in darkness' is Mouth—the illuminated lips of a female mouth located about 2.5 m (8 feet) above stage level. Once Mouth, seemingly afloat in a sea of black above the audience, begins her non-stop 25-minute *monologue 'out . . . into this world . . . this world . . . tiny little thing' only her lips move as the text is delivered at breakneck speed 'without colour', that is, without the usual range of vocal inflections used in character acting. As

Beckett said of James Joyce's work, concerns with pattern, form, and detail make such acting 'not *about* something . . . [but] *that thing itself*'. Form becomes content; content is form.

The psychologically whole character was no longer central to many types of theatre after the 1960s, as can be seen in the deconstructive work of the *Wooster Group or Robert *Wilson's spectacular theatre of images in the USA, or the fragmentary, thought-provoking, time-based task performances of Forced Entertainment in Britain. In Japan the psychophysical recreation of Western classics by *Suzuki Tadashi's company, and the dynamic *butoh dance, have dispensed with conventional playing of characters. What the actor or performer does on stage at the start of the twenty-first century ranges from playing a psychologically *realist character to the sequential playing of multiple roles or personae to the enactment of tasks or entry into images without any character implications.

Two of many alternative approaches must serve as examples. Ruth *Maleczech, co-founder of *Mabou Mines in the USA, works with an aesthetic structure more like a musical composition than a playtext. Mabou Mines has developed an approach she defines as a series of tracks: picture, gesture, sound, movement, psychology, pitch, rhythm, music, tableau, *lighting. Any of these elements can be used to carry forward the story, and at any moment the performer can jump from one track to another. This approach is driven not by objectives or desires, but by images—a process Maleczech describes as 'like running a marathon'. Teresa *Ralli of the Peruvian Grupo *Yuyachkani describes a 'thinking actor' as 'multiple', that is, one who sings, dances, and plays musical instruments. The process of the company begins with the body, utilizing *t'ai chi* to investigate the flow of energy in movement and voice, with explorations applied anew in each performance. Ralli approaches each new performance as physical poetry, utilizing images rather than emotions as the entry point.

Alternative approaches to acting and performance have often been inspired by the *modernist theories espoused by Edward Gordon *Craig and particularly Antonin Artaud, whose manifestos of the 1930s helped shape post-war experimentation. He called for a rebellion against 'the subjugation of the theatre to the text' and the 'psychological'. He wanted the actor to be an 'athlete of the heart' who could create and enact a 'metaphysics' 'through the skin', with productions not of written plays but created directly 'around subjects, events, or known words'. These would be productions where space could 'speak' and where the actor, so long denied a voice, would return to a 'physical understanding of images'. Artaud's vision of the actor has been actualized in much contemporary *physical theatre, which intentionally blurs the boundaries between dance, movement, and traditional theatre, as in butoh, Frantic Assembly and DV-8 in the UK, and Pina *Bausch's Tanzteater in Germany.

Many of these developments have led to an emphasis on theatre process rather than the product, establishing the actor as social facilitator, seeking not the development of the virtuosic professional performer but rather the empowerment of the 'spect-actor', to use Augusto *Boal's term. This new actor dramatizes issues of concern in local settings such as schools, day centres, prisons, hospitals, youth clubs, village squares, or on the streets. Theatre games and improvisation techniques are often used in community-based workshops not as a means of training actors but of raising social awareness, developing alternative voices, and assisting in the making and expression of perspectives that are not normally heard in the regular theatres (see also OPPRESSED, THEATRE OF THE; DEVELOPMENT, THEATRE FOR).

The modes of acting in the post-war period outlined here—the actor-as-personality, the actor-as-interpreter, the actor-as-creator, and the actor-as-facilitator—illustrate that acting is no longer dominated by a single perception or paradigm. At the start of the new millennium, the field of acting is characterized by the existence of multiple perceptions, in work that might take place in community halls, the streets, and even in formal playhouses.   PZ

COLE, TOBY, and CHINOY, HELEN KRICH (eds.), *Actors on Acting* (New York, 1970)

DUNN, CHARLES J., and TORIGOE, BUNZO (trans. and eds.), *The Actors' Analects* (New York, 1969)

HODGE, ALI (ed.), *Twentieth Century Actor Training* (London, 2000)

PLASTOW, JANE, *African Theatre and Politics* (Amsterdam, 1994)

RILEY, JO, *Chinese Theatre and the Actor in Performance* (Cambridge, 1997)

ROACH, JOSEPH, *The Player's Passion: studies in the science of acting* (Ann Arbor, 1993)

SONENBERG, JANET (ed.), *The Actor Speaks* (New York, 1996)

WILLIAMS, SIMON, *German Actors of the Eighteenth and Nineteenth Centuries: idealism, romanticism, and realism* (Westport, Conn., 1985)

ZARRILLI, PHILLIP B. (ed.), *Acting Reconsidered*, 2nd edn. (London, 2002)

—— *Kathakali Dance-Drama: where gods and demons come to play* (London, 2000)

ZEAMI, *Kadensho or The Flower Book*, trans. Nobori Asaji (Osaka, 1975)

ACTING COMPANY

American theatre group. Originally called the City Center Acting Company, this group was founded in 1972 by John *Houseman and Margot Harley as a bridge between academic *training and professional work for recent graduates of the drama division of *New York's *Juilliard School. The company, later opened to other young actors, describes itself as 'America's only nationally-touring classical repertory company'. The group specializes in *tours to smaller cities and towns with a repertoire including Shakespeare, *Ibsen, *Molière, *Brecht, *Fugard, *Williams, and commissioned works by American writers. Alumni include actors Kevin *Kline, Patti *LuPone, and David Ogden Stiers.   MAF

ACTION

The two most common meanings of action derive from *Aristotle's *Poetics*, where *tragedy is defined as 'an imitation of an action . . . with persons performing the action rather than through narrative' (see MIMESIS). Action, then, is both (a) the core of meaning, motive, and purpose embodied in the drama, and (b) the actual physical movements and speeches of the actors (dramatic action as opposed to narrative action). Action in its deeper sense was for Aristotle a form whereby reality was made intelligible, and imitated in drama principally by the *plot. Unhappily for this sophisticated notion of action, Aristotle went on to discuss plot as though it were a complete articulation of the action, and thus used the terms interchangeably, a practice that continues. The connection between plot and action is close, but the two are not identical, and their confusion lies behind the mistaken *neoclassical idea that Aristotle insisted on a single plot (see UNITIES). He certainly preferred a single *action*, but he presents no theoretical objection to having a single action imitated by several plots. Since dramatic action represents human behaviour, which is governed by *character (in the sense of predisposition) and thought (perception), it is possible to distinguish an intermediary level of action where the term refers to characters' internal psychological, moral, or intellectual progression. (This action occurs whether character is seen as a function of plot, or plot as a function of character.) But whether identified with dramatic action, character progression, or deep form, action invariably involves a movement—psychic, moral, intellectual—that, often defined in terms of motive, progresses by both logic and irrational means to a new perception.

                                                                                      RWV

ACTOR *See* ACTING/ACTOR.

ACTOR-MANAGER

A leading actor and *manager of his or her own theatre or company. David *Garrick, at *Drury Lane in *London from 1747 to 1776, was the prototypical actor-manager: a leading actor, administrator, investor in his own theatre, he cast, hired, and fired actors, determined their wages, chose the repertory, and oversaw the wardrobe, *costuming, *scenery, scene *painting, *box office, *finances, public relations, and all the multifarious operations of a large business employing several hundred people, among them actors, musicians, *prompters, scene painters, *property men, seamstresses, cleaners, candle-snuffers, box-office keepers, and doorkeepers. Several other candidates provide notable examples of the actor-manager, such as *Molière and Sarah *Bernhardt in France, Eleonora *Duse in Italy, and Edwin *Booth in *New York, but it was in England at the end of the nineteenth century that the actor-manager completely dominated the theatre of the metropolis as well as providing first-class *tours to the provinces and overseas. Henry *Irving at the *Lyceum, George *Alexander at the *St James's, John *Hare at the Garrick, Charles *Wyndham at Wyndham's, Charles *Hawtrey at the Comedy, Cyril *Maude at the *Haymarket, Lillie *Langtry at the Imperial, Mrs Patrick *Campbell at the Royalty, Beerbohm *Tree at *Her Majesty's—and this is not a complete list. They were building on the previous managerial accomplishments of *Vestris, *Macready, Charles *Kean, *Phelps, and Marie *Wilton (the first actor-manager to depend on the *long run), and all took middle-class West End theatres after they had established themselves as leading actors of ability and reputation. Each manager acted in the repertory appropriate to the theatre and to his or her strengths, a repertory carefully composed to mark the theatre's distinctive identity and style in a crowded commercial market and attract a substantial *audience of loyal repeaters. The golden period of English actor-managers ended abruptly with the 1914 war and the subsequent huge demand for light entertainment. After the war, with the old actor-managers retired or dead, and the expenses of production rapidly inflating, theatres and production passed out of the hands of the individual actor and into the hands of speculators and business syndicates. The same thing happened at the end of the nineteenth century in America. There are few modern examples of the actor-manager; Brian *Rix with his *farce company at the Whitehall Theatre in London (1950–67) is one.   MRB

ACTORS' EQUITY ASSOCIATION *See* TRADE UNIONS, THEATRICAL.

ACTORS STUDIO

Workshop founded in *New York in 1947 by *Group Theatre alumni Cheryl *Crawford, Robert *Lewis, and Elia *Kazan. It was intended as a *training institution for professional actors, selected on the basis of intensive auditions, who were given lifetime memberships. The Studio has been in the same West 44th Street space since 1955. Because Lewis and Kazan were too busy to teach, Lee *Strasberg, another Group alumnus, joined in 1949. From the time he took over as artistic leader in 1951 to his death in 1982, Strasberg ran two weekly two-hour sessions, emphasizing his interpretation of the *Stanislavsky acting system, which came to be known as the *Method. This involved exercises aiming at getting actors to 'unblock' their emotional resources. As more and more of America's respected actors of the 1950s, such as Marlon *Brando, James Dean, Geraldine *Page, Kim Stanley, and Shelly Winters, came to be associated with the Studio, its reputation as the home of deeply felt, psychologically authentic *acting was established. However, its many detractors, perhaps confusing the neorealistic *characters played by Studio actors—often in Kazan's *films and plays—with the Method

itself, criticized its proponents for sloppy speech and selfish stage habits in which they put personal expression before the needs of the ensemble, the play, or the *audience. Eventually, the Studio created directors', playwrights', and production units. In 1963–4 the Studio presented a series of productions, including *Strange Interlude* (1963), *Marathon 33* (1963), *Baby Want a Kiss* (1964), *Blues for Mister Charley* (1964), and *The Three Sisters* (1964).   SLL

ACTORS THEATRE OF LOUISVILLE

American *regional theatre and the state theatre of Kentucky. Established in 1964 by Richard Block and Ewel Cornet, ATL came to international renown as a breeding ground for new American plays and playwrights under the leadership of Jon *Jory. In 1969 he became the producing director and in 1976 inaugurated the annual Humana Festival of New American plays, which showcases new works by established and emerging dramatists. Important festival productions include D. L. Coburn's *The Gin Game* (1977), Beth *Henley's *Crimes of the Heart* (1979), and Donald Margulies's *Dinner with Friends* (1998), each of which went on to win the Pulitzer Prize, as well as plays by Marsha *Norman, William Mastrosimone, Richard Dresser, José Rivera, Tony *Kushner, Naomi Wallace, and Charles L. *Mee. ATL has provided sustained support to pseudonymous playwright Jane Martin and experimental director Anne *Bogart. The theatre is also a force in the promotion of short-form playwriting, particularly the 'ten-minute play'. For twelve years (1985–97), an annual Classics-in-Context Festival surrounded productions of classical and modern European plays with lectures, panel discussions, gallery exhibits, and *film exhibitions. After 31 years at the helm, Jory left ATL in 2000 and was replaced by Marc Masterson.

STC

ACTORS WORKSHOP

American *regional theatre in *San Francisco. Created in 1952 by Herbert *Blau and Jules Irving as an experimental studio for professional actors, the theatre was granted the first *Off-Broadway contract outside *New York City in 1955. The company gained a reputation for its anti-establishment attitude and a repertoire that was among the first in the USA to embrace *Brecht, *Beckett, *Pinter, *Genet, and their contemporaries. Important productions included the American premières of *Mother Courage and her Children* (1956), *The Birthday Party* (1959), and John *Arden's *Serjeant Musgrave's Dance* (1962). The company's now-famous performance of *Waiting for Godot* at San Quentin penitentiary led to the formation of the San Quentin Drama Workshop. Despite national attention and significant funding from the Ford Foundation, the Workshop never won solid acceptance in San Francisco. In 1965

Blau and Irving left to take over the Repertory Theatre of *Lincoln Center, and a year later the Workshop disbanded.

STC

ACTOR TRAINING *See* TRAINING FOR THEATRE.

ADAM DE LA HALLE (LE BOSSU) (c.1240–c.1288)

Professional entertainer (*trouvère*). A versatile poet, Adam composed two of the most remarkable vernacular plays of the thirteenth century. *The Play of the Feuillée* (1376), set and performed in his native town of Arras in France, is a blend of fantasy and reality in which local fools and sinners are pilloried. 'Feuillée' can mean leafy bower, but it may also refer to 'la place de la fuellie (folie)' or 'the mad square' in Arras, where executions were held and relics exhibited, and where the play was possibly performed. *Robin and Marion* (c.1283), probably written for Robert of Artois's expatriate court in southern Italy, where Adam spent his final years, is in the tradition of *pastoral dancing-games and features an equally traditional cast of maid, knight, and rustic. The emphasis on singing and *dancing makes *Robin and Marion* an early *musical comedy.

RWV

ADAMOV, ARTHUR (1908–70)

French playwright, born in Russia of an Armenian family who fled to Switzerland and Germany to escape ethnic violence, and finally settled in *Paris in 1924. Adamov was befriended by *Artaud and Roger *Blin and joined their *surrealist circle as a poet. Nearly twenty years of depression, drifting, and a prison term followed, Adamov publishing nothing until *L'Aveu* (*The Confession*, 1946), an account of his ordeal containing a manifesto of what would become the theatre of the *absurd. Also in 1946, influenced by *Strindberg's *Dream Play*, Freud, and German *expressionism, Adamov wrote his first play, *La Parodie* (*The Parody*), staged in 1952 by Blin. Its short scenes, *puppet-like *characters, slowing of time, and shrinking of space were, he explained, 'an outward projection of the mind's sensations'. Other plays combining *dream structure with socio-political critique include *Le Professeur Taranne* (1953) and *Le Ping-pong* (1957). As Adamov's work became more *realistic and historical, he drew on *Brechtian *epic theatre while retaining absurdist elements. *Paolo Paoli* (1956) examines the causes of the First World War, while *Le Printemps '71* (*Spring 71*, 1961) reconstructs the Paris Commune, and *La Politique des restes* (*The Politics of Waste*, 1962) attacks racism in the United States. Adamov's work, and his adaptations of *Büchner, *Chekhov, and *Gorky, have been staged by Blin, *Vilar, *Planchon, and *Mnouchkine. Initially lauded as the equal of *Beckett and *Ionesco, Adamov's bleak plays with their harsh language never gained the same popularity, but with Planchon's 1976 collage *A.A.: le théâtre d'Arthur Adamov*, the playwright regained respect, and is now seen as presciently postmodern (*see* MODERNISM AND POSTMODERNISM).

SBB

ADAMS, MAUDE (1872–1953)

American actress and educator. On stage from infancy, an actress's daughter, Maude Adams appeared in adult roles in 1888, becoming John *Drew's leading lady (1892–6). She starred in her own company from 1897, opening with J. M. *Barrie's dramatization of *The Little Minister*, earning a reputation as Barrie's foremost American interpreter. Adams's low, musical voice, delicate beauty, and slight physique made her especially effective playing young girls and androgynous roles. She was the first American to act in *Rostand's *L'Aiglon* (1900), and in Barrie's *Peter Pan* (1905). Her repertory included Barrie's *Quality Street* (1901), *What Every Woman Knows* (1908), *A Kiss for Cinderella* (1917), and Rostand's *Chanticleer* (1912). Her acting career effectively ended in 1918. In 1937 she founded the drama programme at Stephens College in Missouri, teaching and directing until 1950. Adams was reclusive, rarely appearing in public other than on the stage, and never married.

AW

ADDISON, JOSEPH (1672–1719)

English writer and editor. Although Addison is now mostly remembered for his periodical partnership with Richard *Steele, he was also famous as the author of *Cato* (1713), a play that enjoyed tremendous popularity in both Britain and America for its portrayal of patriotism and stoical virtue. Throughout the eighteenth century, all parties were able to see *Cato* as an endorsement of themselves, ensuring its popularity. His moral *comedy *The Drummer* (1716), loosely based on the last books of the *Odyssey*, was much less successful, as was his effort to capitalize on the vogue for Italian *opera with *Rosamond* (1707).

MJK

ADELPHI THEATRE

A theatre on the Strand, *London, in what is now the West End. Originally the Sans Pareil, it opened as the Adelphi in 1818. Rebuilt in 1858, 1901, and 1930, it is still in existence. Under the *management of Frederick Yates (1825–43) it was one of London's most important *minor theatres, and under Benjamin *Webster (1844–76) it was notable for *farce and *melodrama, a reputation it retained until the end of the century. In the twentieth century it ceased to host a resident company, and its repertory, although eclectic, has been strong in *long-running *musicals.

MRB

ADLER, JACOB P. (1855–1926)

Latvian-American actor, considered the greatest dramatic actor of the *Yiddish theatre. A powerful *actor-manager with a flair for scenic effects, he began his career in Russia, moved to *London, and in 1890 settled in *New York. In 1891 he produced and starred in Jacob *Gordin's drama *Siberia*, a historic event that marked the beginning of the golden age of Yiddish theatre. Other milestone parts were in Gordin's *Yiddish King Lear* (1892) and *The Wild Man* (1905), and Lev *Tolstoy's *The Power of Darkness* (1903) and *The Living Corpse* (1911). Adler left his mark on the mainstream stage when in 1903 he played Shylock in Yiddish with an English-speaking cast. The actor's majestic funeral, attended by tens of thousands, attested to his kingly position in Jewish life. He began a *family theatre dynasty that included his (third) wife Sara and children, the best known of whom was Stella *Adler.   EN

ADLER, STELLA (1901–92)

American actress and acting teacher. The daughter of Jacob *Adler and Sara Levitsky, both major figures in the professional *Yiddish theatre of *New York, Adler was acting from the age of 5. Seeking a systematic approach to *acting, in 1925 she enrolled at the *American Laboratory Theatre, an outpost of the *Stanislavsky system. In 1930 she joined the newly formed *Group Theatre and studied with Lee *Strasberg, her former peer at American Laboratory Theatre. After meeting with Stanislavsky in *Paris in 1934 she returned to challenge Strasberg's emphasis on 'affective memory'. The *Method, she argued, had been rejected by Stanislavsky as both artistically inefficient and psychologically damaging. She offered the Group her own classes, emphasizing 'given circumstances' and 'actions' derived from the play and its context rather than use of the actor's own memories. She left the Group in 1937 to accept a series of *film roles, but returned to New York in 1942 to teach acting, founding her own studio in 1949. Adler quickly became a major force in theatre and film, attracting students such as Marlon *Brando, Warren Beatty, and Robert DeNiro and offering the major rival to Strasberg's Method approach at the *Actors Studio.
                                                          MAF

ADMIRAL'S MEN, LORD

The Elizabethan Lord Admiral, Charles Howard, Lord Effingham, kept a company of players from 1576 until King James made his elder son Henry their patron in 1603, when it became the Prince's Men. Altogether it ran unchanged for 49 years. Its most famous player was Edward *Alleyn, who became Howard's servant in the 1580s. He played at the *Rose in *London from 1592, as a member of *Strange's Men, keeping his Admiral's livery, while the rest of the Admiral's Men *toured the country. In 1594 he formed a new Admiral's Men, one of the two new companies replacing the old *Queen's Men, licensed to play in London exclusively at the Rose. Alleyn had become the son-in-law of the Rose's owner, Philip *Henslowe, in 1592, and the two men ran the company together, as part of the newly authorized 'duopoly' of companies along with the Lord *Chamberlain's Men.

The Admiral's Men had almost all of *Marlowe's plays, and many more produced by a team of collaborative writers, including *Munday, Henry Chettle, *Dekker, *Chapman, *Jonson and others, all of whose dealings are listed in Henslowe's 'diary', the notebook of his playmaking business. The Henslowe papers survive as a unique record of this business in the 1590s, because he passed them on to Alleyn, who gave them to Dulwich College, which he founded in 1620. These papers show that from 1594 the Admiral's staged roughly 30 plays each year, performing a different play each afternoon for six days every week except for Lent.

They played at the Rose for six years, until the other half of the duopoly controlling playing in London built the *Globe just across the road. In 1600 they moved to the other side of the river, where the Globe company had been working, having the *Fortune built for them in Clerkenwell. Under different names they played at the Fortune for the next 25 years. After Prince Henry died they became the servants of the Elector Palatine, husband of Henry's sister Elizabeth.   AJG

ADRIANI, PLACIDO (fl. 1707–40)

Italian author and actor. A Benedictine monk born in Lucca, he both organized and acted in plays within monasteries, surprisingly playing the part of Pulcinella as well as mounting religious dramas. His manuscript the 'Selva' ('Forest; or, Notebook of Comic Conceits', 1734), is a remarkable collection of fragments which could contribute to improvised drama and social performance, many perhaps of his own composition. They include 42 *lazzi, 22 *scenarios, eight *prologues, and nine speeches for a *commedia dell'arte Dottore. The material may have been for the use of *amateurs rather than professionals, but it is still a valuable record.   RAA

AESCHYLUS (c.525–456 BC) *(see opposite page)*

AESOPUS, CLODIUS (fl. mid-first century BC)

Roman actor. Aesopus was the most highly regarded of all the *Roman *tragic actors, although he also appeared in *comedy. He was renowned for the gravity and strength of his characterizations, and his powerful voice. He was a close friend of Cicero, to whom he gave lessons in elocution.   RCB

AESCHYLUS (c.525–456 BC)

Son of Euphorion, Aeschylus was the first great writer of *tragedy and the foundation of our knowledge of *Greek theatre. He fought against the Persians at the battle of Marathon (490 BC), a deed recorded in his epitaph to the exclusion of his dramatic achievements, and which probably suggested aspects of *Aristophanes' *parody of him in *Frogs* as austere and old-fashioned. Of his total of 70 to 90 plays, only seven survive (or six, if *Prometheus Bound* is not his). Aeschylus was extremely successful, gaining thirteen victories in the competitions held at the Athenian dramatic festivals (see DIONYSIA), and his plays quickly became classics, reperformed after his death and winning more victories. Unlike *Sophocles and *Euripides, Aeschylus composed many (though not all) of his plays as connected tetralogies, with three tragedies forming a connected story and a *satyr-play on a more loosely related theme. There is only one such group of tragedies extant, *Agamemnon*, *Libation-Bearers*, and *Eumenides*, collectively known as the *Oresteia*, which deals with the murder of Agamemnon by his wife and her lover, the revenge taken for it by his son Orestes, and Orestes' pursuit by the Furies and trial in Athens. This trilogy was accompanied by a (lost) satyr-play, *Proteus*, whose hero was Agamemnon's brother Menelaus.

This surviving trilogy, first performed in 458 BC, best exemplifies Aeschylus' dramatic genius. *Seven against Thebes* and *Suppliants* are the sole survivors of their tetralogies, and though they are powerful in themselves their part in Aeschylus' original grand design can only be guessed at; *Prometheus Bound* may have been the middle play of a trilogy begun with the theft of fire in *Prometheus Fire-Bearer* and ending with *Prometheus Unbound*, but this is not certain, and the stylistic arguments against Aeschylus being the play's author, or at any rate its sole author, are strong.

Persians (472) was not part of a connected trilogy. Remarkably, it is a historical drama which imagines Persian reactions to their defeat at Salamis (479), where Aeschylus probably also fought. It has some features which anticipate the later *Oresteia*, particularly the role of the *chorus of elders, left behind, like the chorus of *Agamemnon*, too old to fight. The Persian Queen is very different in character from the terrifying Clytemnestra of *Agamemnon*, but her interaction with the chorus is used to set the scene in a similar, if less subtle, manner. Her entry on a chariot, far from being a pointless piece of *spectacle, illustrates for the *audience with beautiful economy the wealth and pride of Persia, so soon to be laid in the dust by Athens (of which she has barely heard), and provides a striking visual contrast with the later entry of the wretched Xerxes, alone and in rags. Agamemnon's entry in a chariot with his captive Cassandra is also outwardly splendid, but only serves to stress his overconfidence and thus his vulnerability to the schemes of his wife and the anger of the gods.

The *Oresteia* uses the myth of the accursed house of Atreus to explore issues of revenge and justice, human and divine. The trilogy shows Aeschylus' technique fully developed and makes full use of the stage resources available in 458, some of which were probably not in use earlier. In particular, the *skene, or background building, with a central door and a solid roof, before which the actors played, is constantly prominent in the *Oresteia* but not in *Persians*. In *Agamemnon* it represents the palace, which is accursed and where horrible things have happened; the play opens with the Watchman placed precariously on the roof, looking out for the signal which will herald the sack of Troy and Agamemnon's return; Clytemnestra controls and dominates its central door, and although others enter the palace, only she leaves it alive. This insistence on the setting was new in Greek tragedy, in sharp contrast with the indeterminacy of place in *Persians*, and is most effective in suggesting the corrupt atmosphere of the house of Atreus. Aeschylus also employed the *ekkyklema, a low wooden platform on wheels which, rolled through the door of the *skene*, was used to show what has been happening inside. In *Agamemnon* the triumphant Clytemnestra stands over the corpses of Agamemnon and Cassandra displayed on the *ekkyklema*; in *Libation-Bearers* that tableau is mirrored, as the matricidal Orestes stands over Clytemnestra and Aegisthus.

Visual as well as poetic imagery is used to bind the trilogy together: red fabric flows out of the house like blood in *Agamemnon* when Clytemnestra lays out tapestries for Agamemnon to tread on as he goes into the house to death; in *Libation-Bearers* Orestes holds up the red bloody robe in which Agamemnon was killed; finally the bloodthirsty Furies are transformed into the awe-inspiring Eumenides when they are clothed with red robes at the end of *Eumenides*. This visual symbol expresses the move from the savage *lex talionis* of the first two plays, enacted without guilt or shame by Clytemnestra and more hesitatingly by Orestes, to the justice system of the Athenian courts laid down by Athena in *Eumenides*, and given further divine authority by the Eumenides' cultic presence. Nothing is perfect; divine vengeance can be as harsh and arbitrary as that of men (and has indeed prompted the atrocities which have bedevilled the house of Atreus); but the final scene of *Eumenides*, with its torchlight procession in honour of the newly named goddesses, seems to illuminate with modified hope the darkness in which *Agamemnon* begins.

In terms of modern adaptation and performance Aeschylus was slower to attain prominence than Sophocles and Euripides. There was no English translation until the eighteenth century, though in the twentieth the *Oresteia* prompted distinguished adaptations: Eugene *O'Neill's *Mourning Becomes Electra* (1931) and T. S. *Eliot's *The Family Reunion* (1939). There was an early production of *Agamemnon* in ancient Greek in 1880 at Balliol College, Oxford. In 1914 *Agamemnon*, in an Italian translation, was the first play produced at the dramatic *festival at Syracuse. A viciously distorted Nazi version of the whole *Oresteia* was produced in *Berlin in 1936; Tyrone *Guthrie adapted it as *The House of Atreus* in 1966; and more recent landmark productions took place in Berlin in 1980, directed by Peter *Stein (revived in *Moscow in 1994), and at the Royal *National Theatre in London in 1981, directed by Peter *Hall, using *masks and an all-male cast, in an adaptation by Tony *Harrison.   JMM

EASTERLING, P. E. (ed.), *The Cambridge Companion to Greek Tragedy* (Cambridge, 1997)

ROSENMEYER, T. G., *The Art of Aeschylus* (Berkeley, 1982)

TAPLIN, OLIVER P., *The Stagecraft of Aeschylus* (Oxford, 1977)

AFINOGENOV, ALEKSANDR (1904–41)

Russian/Soviet dramatist. His best play, *Fear* (1931), staged at the *Moscow Art Theatre, deals understandingly with problems experienced by intellectuals of an older generation in coming to terms with Soviet reality, as well as the fear they lived under during the 1930s. A friend of Pasternak's, Afinogenov had earlier been a prominent member of RAPP (the Association of Proletarian Writers) and editor of the journal *Theatre and Dramaturgy*. His play *Distant Point* about 'the Bolshevik attitude to death', was staged in *London in 1941 and again in 1991. Afinogenov was killed during the first Nazi air raids on Moscow.   NW

AFRICA

This entry summarizes some of the main features of indigenous sub-Saharan African theatre and performance, concentrating on pre-colonial forms. For the syncretic forms which emerged after colonial intervention *see* AFRICA, ANGLOPHONE; AFRICA: ERITREA, ETHIOPIA, SOMALIA; AFRICA, FRANCOPHONE; AFRICA, LUSOPHONE. Africa north of the Sahara, like the rest of the Mediterranean basin, is covered by entries on important cities, forms, and people, but not by national or area histories.

1. Scope and terminology;
2. Indigenous African performance; 3. Aesthetics;
4. Change and modernization; 5. Conclusion

1. Scope and terminology

Cave paintings almost certainly portraying trance-*dances of what are now often called San people can be dated as early as 10,000 BC, but interpreting such ancient performance modes is extremely difficult. This article, therefore, restricts itself to forms which through oral traditions or written records within the last millennium can be more confidently analysed. A general introduction to theatre and performance in sub-Saharan Africa is bound to run into terminological problems. *Theatre is clearly a European term with its own genealogy and associations. Most African languages do have terms roughly parallel to what Europeans call 'theatre', such as *Wasanni* in Hausa, *Michezo* in kiSwahili, *Masewero* in chiNyanja, and so on. The problem is that the individual indigenous terms have subtle differences in tone and semantic frame, and no general term has emerged, accepted even on a regional, let alone a pan-continental level. The catchall 'performing arts' is therefore probably the most useful term, covering what could be narrowly called 'theatre' in the Western sense, but also many other performing arts which overlap with it.

Another heavily contested term is *ritual. The controversy arises from the distinction normally made in occidental analysis between theatre (secular entertainment with clear distinctions between *audience and performers) and ritual (solemn acts incorporating audience participation for spiritual or social regeneration). Wole *Soyinka decries this division on the grounds that 'it is one largely drawn by the European analyst'. Soyinka is right to point to the difficulty in marking a clear dividing line between them, but it is still useful to see performing arts within a frame which has ritual at one end of a spectrum (many rituals being out of the frame completely) and secular entertainment at the other. The distinction, with Soyinka's caveat kept in mind, is particularly useful in examining indigenous or pre-colonial sub-Saharan African performing arts, a topic which necessarily takes on board the issue of African theatre's origins. (*See also* PERFORMANCE; RELIGION AND THEATRE.) Most African thinkers who have theorized about the *origins of theatre in Africa (such as Bakary Traore and Oyin Ogunba) see its genesis in ritual performance, especially masquerade dances. There is an alternative view, however. Owomoyela disputes the very existence

SeZar, an adaptation of Shakespeare's *Julius Caesar* written and directed by Yael Farber, Grahamstown Festival, South Africa, 2001. SeZar (Hope Sprinter Sekgobela) shows his disdain for the Soothsayer's warning about conspiracy by grasping the entrails of the sacrificial goat, an intercultural blending of a European classic text with ritual practice from **Africa**.

of theatre in pre-colonial Africa, and feels that theorists who seek its origins in ritual are simply suffering from mental colonization, attempting to find in African pre-colonial rituals the equivalent of the *Dionysian *dithyramb. It is worth bearing Owomoyela's scepticism in mind while attempting to delineate some modes of pre-colonial ritual performance.

It should be noted that other terms (*'costume', *'stage', and *'actor'), somewhat contaminated by their Western origins, are used here, sanitized by inverted commas. A final caveat is that sub-Saharan Africa is a huge, complex, and diverse continent; the reader must allow for myriad exceptions to the generalizations made.

2. Indigenous African performance

Many modes of African performance, whether we call them theatrical or not, have functions which are pre-eminently spiritual; they are linked to indigenous forms of African religion, sometimes given the rather unhelpful anthropological term 'animism'. Most pre-colonial religions involve the belief in a supreme being who is not normally the object of direct worship or ritual agency. Communication with God is commonly achieved through intervention of ancestral spirits. These spirits have their own hierarchies (dependent partly on the status and achievements of the historical character of the ancestor) and in some cultures, such as the Yoruba, the senior spirits are considered deities, thus constituting a polytheistic religious system. Ritual performances are associated with interaction between spirits and human beings, especially when spirits visit communities at critical moments. Just as the spirits themselves have hierarchies, so do the rituals associated with communication between spirit and human.

Some of the most solemn rituals are masquerade performances, and many can be dated through genealogies to at least the twelfth century AD. Most masquerade theatre forms are found within agricultural economies, but the imagery of their poetry and *masks often refers back to an earlier hunting economy. Politically, some examples, such as *egungun* of the Yoruba people, are associated with fairly centralized royal courts; others, such as *egwugwu* of the Igbo, *nyau* of the Chewa, and *makishi* of the Mbunda, are associated with much less centralized political systems. Masquerades take place at critical times such as funerals of important people, initiation ceremonies, harvest festivals, and installation of chiefs. For danger to be averted communities need to be cleansed of all pollution, a process achievable through a series of rituals, among which masquerades are significant. Masked performers are usually initiates of all-male secret societies, though some all-female masquerade cults do exist. When an 'actor' assumes a mask his whole body is normally covered by the 'mask' (that is, including the 'costume'), thus temporarily extinguishing the human being who hosts the spirit.

The masks and 'costumes' of the masquerades vary enormously, according to the status and character of the spirit. Some masked figures are very solemn with high status, others have low status. Yet others have specialist roles, for example to prepare the way for solemn masks or to control the 'audience'. The tendency is for high-status masks to be abstract in design or to be zoomorphic masks of sacred totemic animals (such as lion, elephant, or python). Lower-status masks are often satirical stereotypes of human physical or psychological frailties (such as the cripple, the syphilitic, the smallpox victim, or the drunkard).

Masquerade performances serve a variety of complex, interlocking functions. At a religious level, the dances reassert the linkages between the community and the world of the dead; they also provide a form of community therapy so that physical, psychological, moral, and spiritual maladies can be purged prior to important events in the human calendar. At a political level the performances reassert the legitimacy of ruling clans or individuals through a celebration of powerful ancestral lineages. The performance becomes a symbolic re-enactment of clan history and hegemony. In some contexts, however, satirical stereotyping in the performances may subvert or even challenge the authority of leaders, if they are not governing in the interests of the people.

It is not always easy to distinguish between political and social functions. At a social level, masquerade performances play an important role in conflict resolution. The ethnic or cultural identity of the group is asserted through the celebration of dominant lineages, but also through *satire directed at ethnic or cultural outsiders. The latter is a complex process which may acknowledge, admire, or even negotiate with the power and skills of outsiders. Social cohesion is also achieved by legitimizing gender and generational hierarchies, namely the power and authority of men over women and older generations over younger. Here too there are ambiguities, as some performances allow the younger generations to lampoon their elders. In *gender relations too, cross-dressing (*female impersonation is almost invariable in male-cult masquerade performances) creates liminal spaces in which gender or hierarchical identities are temporally suspended. Masquerade performances also reinforce moral codes. Antisocial vices such as laziness, drunkenness, theft, adultery, and stinginess can be denounced through the satirical stereotyping of anthropomorphic masked figures.

Though masquerades are the most solemn and spectacular of sub-Saharan ritual performance, there are many others as well. Initiation rites may not seem obviously performance oriented since they largely take place in isolation, with the initiates taken away from the community into the bush for their education. Towards the end of the ceremonies, however, the initiates come out of the forest into the village, and there are usually dances, sketches, or oral narrative performances in public, the function of which is to underline the moral lessons (especially in the sphere of sexuality and adult responsibility) learned by the initiates. Spirit possession rites also have a strong performance aspect. Their primary function is therapeutic. With the help of a spirit medium, men—or more often women—with physical and/or psychological afflictions undertake a series of rituals (such as drinking animal blood) and trance-dances. The medium and sometimes the afflicted assume an ancestral or alien spirit, a process which, if managed properly, helps purge the patient's symptoms. Spirit possession rituals also have a strong political function, helping to provide a popular balance to the power of chiefs. Moreover, during times of political and economic upheaval, they help individuals or even whole communities negotiate the traumatizing impact of social change. The performative aspect of the ritual not only lies in the music and dance associated with the trance, but sometimes also contains mimicry and social satire created in the socially liberated space, the spirit acting through the agency of the possessed, the spirit medium, and all attendants.

There are a large number of other rituals which have performance elements; a varied selection follows. *Carnival-like re-enactments of significant historical events, such as battles, migrations, or the establishment of new towns, provide historical legitimacy to current social structures. Adolescent dances of erotic display, such as athletic agility, provide socially accepted aids to partner selection. Wedding dances not only celebrate the marriage but, through ritualized and choreographed competition between the groom's and bride's relatives, also reduce potential kinship tensions. War dances provide warriors with group building and physical stamina during training, psychological preparation before battle, and celebration of heroism after battle. Funeral songs and dances designed to express the grief of the bereaved praise the dead person's achievements and effect transition from the abnormal state of death back to the normality of the post-grieving period. Oral narratives are performed not simply to entertain audiences, but to allow fantasy relief (for example by audience identification with antisocial trickster heroes) or to give warnings about restricted behaviour. Some performances, such as the *serret* dance of the Tigre people, can be used for many different functions: as wedding celebrations, initiations, and displays of adolescent male courage.

3. Aesthetics

The diversity of performance functions is matched by that of its aesthetic strategies. A few generalized observations, however, are possible, particularly by contrast with Western traditions of performing arts. African performance tends to have a much more flexible time frame than Western counterparts. Since many of the processes outlined above are part of broader rituals, it is not always easy to identify where non-performance rituals (such as beer brewing or cleansing of a dance arena) end and performance specifically designed to entertain an audience begins. Moreover, the performances themselves may go on for a whole night (as is common with spirit possession dances) or even days at a time (as with many masquerades or historical re-enactments). The temporal framing of a performance, which in

a Western context normally entails a clear division between what is and what is not performance, is often blurred in an African context.

The same is true of spatial framing. Whereas most Western genres have cultivated a division between performer and audience through architectural arrangements and audience conventions, African performance tends to encourage a participant audience and fluid spatial arrangements. The use of available *open-air spaces, such as village squares, with in-the-round (*see* ARENA AND IN-THE-ROUND) or flexible audience shapes, tends to encourage a close relationship between spectator and performer. In almost all African performances audiences join in the songs and even sometimes in dances, although there are rules and taboos which restrict audiences from approaching some performers (such as masked dancers). In oral narratives there are participatory devices such as songs or formalized audience responses. In certain types of narrative performance audience members can even assume the narrative function if the original narrator is adjudged to be performing poorly. In others, such as the Fanti *anansesem*, there are quite elaborate orchestral and *mime performances to support the narrative.

A related factor is *genre. Whereas in a Western context, at least from the seventeenth century onwards, genres such as *ballet, orchestral music, choral music, *opera, *drama, mime, and *circus became quite clearly distinguished and labelled, African performing arts (and even visual arts) have tended to rely much more strongly on synaesthesia. A masquerade performance, for example, integrates the arts of costume design (textiles, sculpture, and painting), orchestral and choral music, ballet, opera, mime, drama, *acrobatics, conjuring, and tumbling. In fact, the most useful cohesive factor which distinguishes performance types in the eyes of community audiences may be based not on aesthetic genre, such as masquerade or narrative, but on the functions which they fulfil (war, funerals, installations, initiations, and so on).

4. Change and modernization

A common misconception about African performing arts is that during the pre-colonial period they remained locked into a state of ahistorical immutability, interrupted only by the deracinating impact of colonialism which was imposed by the Portuguese in the seventeenth century and by the British and French in the late nineteenth century at the Treaty of Berlin. Such a theory suggests colonialism introduced new and eventually dominant alien performing arts. Even the terms 'pre-colonial' and 'post-colonial' pander to a 'colonio-centric' and homeostatic model of African culture. The truth is that indigenous African culture has always been dynamic and capable of adapting to change, though obviously some cultures or epochs have been more conservative than others. New performance modes, such as *alarinjo* or *apidan*, emerged among the Yoruba in the seventeenth century as an offshoot of *egungun*, or *kwagh-hir*, a mixture of several different Tiv performance traditions, which became very popular in the twentieth century.

All the performing arts listed above have elements which are capable of adaptation in order to negotiate change. The satirical stereotyping of masquerades, for example, served simultaneously to mock and negotiate the otherness of neighbouring cultures, whether in the guise of invaders, refugees, or traders. Yoruba *egungun* of the nineteenth century, for example, routinely satirized Hausa traders. When European explorers from the seventeenth century onwards, and later missionaries and administrators in the nineteenth century, came to Africa, the masquerade performers introduced 'European' characters. For example, in the Central African Nyau cult, performers of the Gule wa Mkulu dance created characters based on biblical figures, called Simon and Maliya, with pale hues, straight hair, pointed noses, and ungainly walks. These satirical masks helped communities to place the new social phenomenon within a familiar cultural frame, sometimes by way of community adjustment, sometimes resistance. The same was true of spirit possession dances, where Arab or European spirits joined those of other alien African groups whose spirits possessed the afflicted. A whole cult of Arab spirits, *majini*, arose in the early nineteenth century among the Yao of East Africa.

The mimicry involved in the process of absorbing colonial symbolic power gave rise to the commonly held notion that African performing arts (in contrast, for example, with Asian) have an inbuilt tendency towards imitation, a kind of aesthetic dependency. The issue, however, is complex. It is true that many syncretic African performing arts emerged in the early twentieth century which superficially seemed dependent upon colonial culture. A good example is the wave of militaristic dances and mimes which swept many coastal areas at that time. Dances such as *soja* in West Africa and *beni* in East Africa combined elements of indigenous competitive war dances with uniforms and choreography based on marching steps and parade formations copied from colonial armies. These were usually secular performances, though in southern Africa such militaristic mimes tended to be associated with independent Christian churches. The element of imitation may have been strong, but it would be a mistake to see them as purely expressive of cultural dependency. The carnivalesque elements of such dances subverted the solemnity of the colonial originals, but at the same time provided a cultural technique for community negotiation of modernization. In some regions the aesthetic and organizational aspects of such militaristic mime developed into a form of anti-colonial cultural nationalism.

A similar process can be found with performing arts associated with the spread of Islam and Christianity. In some cases, the Islamicized and Christianized performing arts simply allowed Africans to develop indigenous adaptations to these religions. This is true, for example, of the dramatized oral narratives such as *koteba among the Bamana and *wasanni* among the Hausa in Islamic West Africa. In other cases, however, especially with Christianity, performing arts such as nativity plays and operatic moralities developed nationalist elements, for example in early *Yoruba popular theatre, which cultivated forms of Christianity opposed to colonial values.

There is a similar story with literary drama. Its origins lie firmly in colonial culture, either the little theatres built during the late nineteenth and early twentieth centuries in the expatriate enclaves of such cities as Abidjan, Luanda, Nairobi, Salisbury, and *Cape Town, or performance of canonical European *texts (especially by Shakespeare and *Molière) in colonial schools and universities. In the post-colonial period, however (roughly from 1960 onwards), literary drama normally became much more diverse. Educational institutions took an interest in non-canonical European texts, and, even more noticeably, there was an explosion of performance of African literary drama. Some African authors retained close aesthetic and ideological links to European dramatic influences. Many others, however, began to explore indigenous African theatre traditions in order to create a theatre with its own African character, capable of communicating with post-independence African audiences. More radically still, intellectuals engaged in such movements as theatre for *development sought ways not only of linking their skills with indigenous arts, but also of mobilizing such aesthetic and class alliances in a struggle against neocolonialism, exploitation, and injustice.

5. Conclusion

The overall picture of contemporary African performing arts is extremely complex. Indigenous 'pre-colonial' traditions of performance still survive, sometimes with vigour, where their original community functions have been retained, in other cases in a rather artificial manner as tourist *spectacle or public rituals of national pride. Syncretic performances which developed during the colonial and post-independence period also survive. Sometimes these have been reintegrated as an 'invented tradition' into what is often called 'traditional dance'. In other cases, as with the *concert party in Ghana and Togo, Congolese Soukous musical shows, Yoruba popular theatre, or South African *township musicals, the form of entertainment helps audiences negotiate modern urban values within a cultural framework that is still recognizably African. At the same time there are forms such as *drama, which clearly have their origin in Western arts, but have now been adapted for an African environment. All of them respond to transformations in African society and are capable of participating in complex interaction with performing arts from other parts of the world. *See also* POST-COLONIAL STUDIES; RACE AND THEATRE; DIASPORA.   DaK

KERR, DAVID, *African Popular Theatre from Pre-colonial Times to the Present Day* (London, 1995)

OGUNBA, OYIN, and IRELE, ABIOLA (eds.), *Theatre in Africa* (Ibadan, 1978)

OKPEWHO, ISODORE, *African Oral Literature: backgrounds, character and continuity* (Bloomington, Ind., 1992)

OWOMOYELA, OYEKUN, *Visions and Revisions: essays on African literature and criticism* (Washington, 1991)

SOYINKA, WOLE, *Myth, Literature and the African World* (London, 1976)

AFRICA, ANGLOPHONE

This entry treats those parts of sub-Saharan *Africa in which English is the major lingua franca or in which, owing to British colonization, English is the main language of regional communication.

1. Introduction; 2. Literary drama during the colonial period; 3. Syncretic popular theatre; 4. Mainstream art theatre; 5. Mediatized drama

1. Introduction

Theatre in anglophone Africa is an infinitely broader category than anglophone African theatre. It includes not only the latter, but also theatre in a multitude of African languages found in anglophone Africa, theatre in English-based creoles, and even non-English creoles (notably Afrikaans). It also includes various combinations of all these. Inevitably theatre in anglophone Africa is a post-colonial category and thus deals with syncretic modes of performance (*see* POST-COLONIAL STUDIES). Nevertheless, it is important to remember that most of the indigenous or pre-colonial modes of performance, the masquerades, dance *mimes, life passage *rituals, historical re-enactments, praise songs, and dramatized narratives, still continued vigorously after the arrival of colonialism and independence. They also found creative ways of adapting to the forces of modernization. Nor have the syncretic forms been monolithic. The degree and nature of hybridization varies enormously throughout the complex cultures which constitute anglophone Africa, from Nigeria in the west to Tanzania in the east, ranging down to South Africa. Many of these syncretic forms have their origins in the colonial period. They are based on the clashes and interchange between indigenous modes of oral performance and various forms of both literary and non-literary Western performance.

There is some difficulty in defining what is the colonial period in South Africa. According to a legalistic definition South Africa ceased to be a British colony in 1910 with the Act of Union setting up the Union of South Africa. Many would feel, however, that it retained an internal colonialism until democratic all-race elections in 1994. For the sake of easy comparison with other parts of anglophone Africa, most of which started to obtain independence in the early 1960s, I have treated 1961 as the cut-off point for the colonial period; this is when the Nationalist government of South Africa left the British Commonwealth and declared itself a republic (even though based on the racist system of apartheid), after which the apartheid govern-ment ruled 'independently' until the 1994 elections swept in the African National Congress-dominated government. It also needs to be noted that Cameroon in West Africa, owing to unusual historical circumstances, contains both francophone and anglophone sections; references in this article are only to anglophone Cameroon.

The division into mainstream 'art theatre' (with its origins in an elitist colonial literary drama tradition) and a more popular 'syncretic theatre' based on oral traditions, though useful, is somewhat artificial. Several artists in the syncretic tradition have employed literary techniques, including fully scripted plays, and many formally scripted playtexts have relied heavily on indigenous oral traditions in their actual performance.

2. Literary drama during the colonial period

Literary drama had a quite late start in most parts of anglophone Africa. During the early years of the twentieth century those British colonies with sizeable populations of settlers (South Africa, Kenya, and Rhodesia) established 'little theatres' modelled closely on British equivalents. They booked *touring British companies but sometimes also spawned local *amateur troupes. Few of these colonial plays engaged seriously with Africa, preferring to transplant the *pantomimes, *farces, and *vaudeville sketches popular in Britain. The *proscenium-arch stage was also imported as the dominant architectural host for colonial theatre. South Africa was somewhat exceptional, both in the huge scope of the theatrical influence (not only from Britain, but also France and Germany) and in the division of colonial theatre into English and Afrikaans drama, especially after the Anglo-Boer War (1899–1902). English-language theatre, some of which gradually became professional, tended to be dominated by urban escapist entertainment and only rarely engaged with the local context. A notable exception was the comic work of Stephen *Black, popular during the early twentieth century. By contrast, post-war Afrikaans theatre tended to be more serious, more rural, less glitzy, and very nationalistic, promoting Afrikaner culture as a protest against the British values dominant in urban areas. It was only during the 1920s that Afrikaner theatre started to become professional and to join the mainstream of South African theatre. Both English and Afrikaans theatre almost totally excluded black Africans from participation in mainstream theatre, though by the 1920s there were some paternalistic attempts to incorporate them.

Black African participation in Western modes of theatre throughout anglophone Africa started unevenly. Probably the earliest involvement was in Nigeria, where in the 1880s newspaper reports give accounts of plays performed in Lagos in school and community halls by *retournados* (Brazilian ex-slaves who had recently 'returned' to Nigeria under a British scheme). No scripts from this period have survived, but such dramas seem to have been mainly a form of satirical farce aimed at educated black elites. End-of-school concert drama, and entertainment plays for the burgeoning cocoa-growing Fanti elites, also became popular in the early twentieth century in the Gold Coast (later Ghana). The earliest extant script, *The Blinkards* (1915), is a sophisticated *satire written in a mixture of English and Fanti by Ghanaian lawyer Kobina *Sekyi. A generation later in the 1930s, the South African literary and theatre activist Herbert *Dhlomo wrote several plays in English for his own company, the Bantu Dramatic Society, as well as many polemical articles about the need for integration of European and African performance traditions.

Playwriting in indigenous African languages can be traced back to the 1920s, sponsored by the Lovedale Mission in South Africa. In many parts of anglophone Africa, missionaries and later colonial governments encouraged playwriting in local languages, published through mission presses or, after the Second World War, state-sponsored literary bureaux. This was a paternalistic, closely controlled process, in which Shakespeare and the *Greek classics were major influences. The most famous translations of Shakespeare were Solomon Plaatje's versions of *Julius Caesar* and other plays into Setswana in the 1930s. There were translations of Shakespeare into many other African languages as well, including Swahili, Tsongwa, Twi, and Yoruba. The colonial literary agencies also encouraged original *genres, particularly plays about history and African pre-colonial customs. Although some successful authors did emerge through this process, such as Lettle Raditladi in Bechuanaland (later Botswana) in the 1930s and Ferdinand Fiawoo writing in Ewe (Gold Coast) during the 1940s, most of the plays sponsored by the missions and the literary bureaux suffered from a crudely simplistic Christian didacticism which tended to denigrate indigenous culture. Many were also *closet dramas hardly capable of stage performance.

3. Syncretic popular theatre

A far more productive syncretism between indigenous and imported cultural influences emerged in hybrid forms which Africans controlled themselves, strongly rooted in performance. One of the most vigorous forms of oral theatre was *concert party, the origins of which are attributed to a Gold Coast primary school teacher, Master Yalley, who in 1918 adapted existing end-of-term concerts to a form of one-man stand-up comedy, incorporating mime, music, *minstrel show *make-up, and clown-like *costumes. The Axim Trio, led by Bob *Johnson, widened the scope of the stand-up convention into a three-man show which set the pattern for concert party. Axim was an all-male touring group using an improvised *commedia dell'arte technique of music, mime, and stylized costuming and make-up to explore through comedy and stereotyped characterization the conflicts arising through rapid urbanization. Much of their aesthetic was based on indigenous forms such as *anansesem*, a type of satirical performance mixing narrative, music, and mime with a trickster spider as *hero. The plays typically dealt with love,

the impact of money on family cohesion, and witchcraft in an urban context. Occasionally, however, especially during political crises (such as the struggle for national independence), more ideological themes also surfaced. After the success of the Axim Trio hundreds of concert party troupes emerged, their popularity linked to the spread of 'Highlife', an early form of jazz-influenced, urban dance music.

Another major West African form was *Yoruba popular theatre, sometimes called Yoruba opera. The origins of this Nigerian theatre lie in the independent Christian churches which arose in West Africa in the late nineteenth century. These churches, especially the Cherubim and Seraphim, provided urban Yoruba with a form of Christianity which was not bound by the decorum of Western mission-oriented rituals. For a while in the 1920s a type of cantata theatre (*see* KANTATA) emerged in which Bible or morality stories were performed through singing, accompanied by swaying movements, and these became an inspiration for the generation of popular Yoruba theatre practitioners of the 1940s and the 1950s. The great pioneer was Hubert *Ogunde. His first plays (1944–5) were highly Christian, attempting to use Yoruba traditional and syncretic music to tell Christian stories in operatic form. Quite soon, however, he pushed his plays into a more secular direction. Always quick to respond to social and cultural fashions, his awareness of popular anti-colonial sentiments led him to create nationalistic plays which incurred the wrath of colonial authorities. At a later stage he incorporated concert party (1950s), Yoruba populism (1960s), *television (1970s), and *film (1980s). Other pioneers of Yoruba popular theatre were Duro *Ladipo and Kola *Ogunmola, whose first plays date from the 1950s. Both were encouraged by academic enthusiasts in the 1960s to build on indigenous performance modes such as divination chants. By the 1980s Yoruba popular theatre had become both widespread and varied, incorporating wildly popular artists such as Moses Alaiya, who had close links to television and film, and others like Isola Ogunsola, with close links to literary drama.

Just as the coastal towns of Lagos, Accra, and Saltpond provided the cosmopolitan womb for the birth of West African popular theatre, a similar process took place in the coastal cities of East Africa: Mombasa, Lamu, and Dar Es Salaam. *Beni*, a militaristic dance mime, found its origin there after the First World War as a competitive dance which integrated indigenous and Arab spear- and stick-fighting choreography with colonial marching steps, military paraphernalia, and uniforms. After the Second World War it spread to the up-country areas of Kenya and Tanzania, and in its variant forms of *muganda*, *malipenga*, *kalela*, and *fwemba*, then spread to Uganda, Zambia, Malawi, and even parts of Congo. As the mime moved further inland it took on a more traditional form (for example, in the musical instruments and the choreography) and its function became less that of mediating urban factionalism and more that of mediating the modernizing tendencies of returned migrant labourers.

During the period of late colonialism, however, especially in Zambia, it sometimes acquired strong nationalist tendencies. A very different form of syncretic theatre, *vichekesho, also emerged in East Africa. This stylized comic *opera, originating in Zanzibar in the early years of the twentieth century, moved to the mainland of Tanzania, where in the period after independence the ruling party TANU found its system of comic stereotyping and didactic *dialogue useful for campaigns of civic education. TANU made a similar co-option of *ngonjera, a Swahili dialectical, oral, poetic drama.

The coastal cities of South Africa, Durban and *Cape Town, also provided the mix of cultures (Khoisan, Bantu, Dutch, British, Malay, and South Asian), which encouraged the development of syncretic performance. However, the early development of Kimberley and *Johannesburg as mining centres meant that these two inland cities also hosted such synthesis. Examples from the 1890s include the Tickey Drai (threepenny bit) beer party dance and Coon Carnival, a minstrel-influenced street parade. Both of these were originally popular among the mixed race 'Cape coloured' population. Away from the cities, African independent Christian churches such as the Nazarites (founded 1911) and the Zionists (from the 1920s) created militaristic mimes, similar to beni, mixing African choreography and music with Western military regalia and marching steps. Later syncretic musical forms were makwaya (about 1912), a synthesis of Western and African choral music styles, marabi (1920s and 1930s), an entertainment dance associated with illegal drinking houses and prostitution, is'cathelo, a miners' gumboot dance (1930s), tshaba tshaba, a jazz-influenced Johannesburg dance of the 1940s, mbube, popular a cappella music (also 1940s), kwela, a popular jive music dominated by the penny whistle (1950s), township jazz, a mixture of American jazz and African musical traditions (1950s), and mbaqanga, a guitar-dominated music associated with female song and dance groups (1960s).

This long history of eclectic music and dance styles made contributions to South Africa's popular syncretic theatre, the *township musical. By the 1930s theatre activists like Luck Mtetwa and Griffith Motsieloa attempted to blend popular African music and dance forms with concert party dramatic sketches. This tradition, aided (and sometimes controlled) by English-language impresarios or theatre organizations, found occasional prominent expression in such shows as Zonk! (1944) and, most influentially, King Kong (1959). By the 1960s several theatre activists saw the commercial potential of African performing skills. The most prominent of these was Gibson *Kente, who created a flourishing entrepreneurial empire in the 1960s and 1970s through production of musical plays like Singalo, Too Late, and How Long. As with West and East African equivalents, the South African township musical relied heavily on stereotyped characterization, *melodrama, comic set pieces, and powerful music and dance interludes. The music became popular in its own right through record sales.

Although I have tended to describe syncretic popular theatre as a hybrid of Western and African performance traditions, the synthesis is actually much more eclectic. African-American music, such as gospel and jazz, influenced both West and South African popular drama. There were also North African Arab influences on beni and vichekesho, Indian influences on vichekesho, and Malaysian ones on the 'Coon Carnival'.

4. Mainstream art theatre

The first wave of post-independence African dramatists attempting to build a mainstream art theatre (from about 1958 to 1970) were heavily influenced by such European genres as *tragedy, satire, melodrama, and realistic problem drama. The early plays of the great Nigerian Wole *Soyinka from the late 1950s and early 1960s illustrate the process of genre-tasting to some degree. He experimented with *comedy of manners in *verse (The Lion and the Jewel), verse tragedy (The Strong Breed), satirical farce (The Trials of Brother Jero), and poetic melodrama (The Swamp Dwellers). He also wrote satirical farces for television and *radio as well as *agitprop plays for the stage.

Realistic melodrama and comedy were quite popular early genres. Nigerian James Henshaw's plays, such as This Is our Chance (1956) and Companion for a Chief (1964), used melodrama and strong characterization to explore culture clash in a form that was popular for school productions. Sarif Easmon from Sierra Leone used the *well-made play to explore themes of corruption and westernization in Dear Parent and Ogre (1964) and The New Patriots (1965). Ghanaian Joe *de Graft provided a more complex and serious drama in Sons and Daughters (1964) and Through a Film Darkly (1970), where the *naturalism sometimes verged on the *absurd. Ama Ata *Aidoo's Dilemma of a Ghost (1965), while using naturalism to explore culture clash in its Ghanaian *protagonist, works within an African storytelling frame. In East Africa, Ngugi wa *Thiong'o's early plays of the 1960s tended to blend *realism with melodrama.

Many West African dramatists of the period were keen to create tragedies, mixing plots derived from or reminiscent of ancient *Greek models, but incorporating African ritual theatre. John Pepper *Clark-Bekederemo from Nigeria consciously referred to Greek models in the title of his first play, Song of a Goat (1961), which became part of a tragic trilogy with The Masquerade and The Raft (both 1964). Another Nigerian, Ola *Rotimi, created an African version of Oedipus the King in The Gods Are Not to Blame (1971), Soyinka made a Nigerian version of *Euripides' Bacchae (1973), while the Ghanaian Efua *Sutherland adapted Euripides' Alcestis for her Edufa (1967). Even during the early expansion of literary drama, however, African practitioners attempted to find ways of indigenizing the forms, content, staging, and management of theatre.

From the 1970s onwards, this was a theatrical imperative. Authors became dissatisfied with simply providing African versions of European genres and looked instead for African genres. As early as 1960 Soyinka tried to create an epic which incorporated Yoruba masquerade theatre in *Dance of the Forests*. Many authors used traditions of oral narrative as structure, including Aidoo (*Anowa*, 1970), Sutherland (*The Marriage of Anansewa*, 1975), James Ng'ombe (*The Banana Tree*, Malawi, 1977), Asiedu Yirenkyi (*Kivuli*, Ghana, 1980), Femi *Osofisan (*Morountodun*, Nigeria, 1982), and Gcina *Mhlope (*Have You Seen Zandile?*, South Africa, 1988). Other indigenous forms which have inspired playwrights include heroic recitations in Mukotoni Rugyendo's *The Contest* (Tanzania, 1976), ritual theatre in Credo Mutwa's *uNosilemela* (1973), and dance-mime in numerous authors, including Peggy *Harper (1960s), Robert *Serumaga (1970s), Stephen *Chifunyise (1970s and 1980s), and Mbongeni *Ngema (1980s and 1990s). Syncretic popular theatre has also had an impact; Soyinka's *Opera Wanyosi* (1977) was closely influenced by Yoruba popular theatre, Ghanaian Ben Abdullah's *Land of a Million Magicians* (1994) by concert party, and Ngema's internationally successful musical plays, such as *Sarafina 1* (1987) and *Sarafina 2* (1994), by South African township musicals. Several important African choreographers, such as Yaw *Asare and Nii *Yartey (Ghana), Peggy Harper and Akinwumi Isola (Nigeria), Aubrey Sekhabi (South Africa), and Mapopa *Mtonga (Zambia), supported such work through innovative transformations of indigenous performance.

A European genre to which African authors gave a quite radically alternative orientation was that of the *historical drama. Part of this preoccupation was a nationalistic desire to explore local myth and historical heroism, and the integration of indigenous song and dance helped to promote that aim. This motive particularly informs Ebrahim *Hussein's *Kinjeketile* (Tanzania, 1967), wa Thiong'o's, *The Trial of Dedan Kmathi* (with Micere *Mugo, Kenya, 1975), some of Rotimi's plays from the 1970s (*Kurunmi* and *Ovonramwen Ogbaisi*), and Kabwe Kasoma's Zambian plays from the same period (*Black Mamba*). Several authors, however, had an additional reason for exploring myth and history, as allegorical cover for an exploration of politics in regimes, which were too repressive to tolerate overt debate (*see* CENSORSHIP). This might explain the historical interests of authors like Fatima *Dike, (*The Sacrifice of Kreli*, South Africa, 1976) and Steve Chimombo (*The Rainmaker*, Malawi, 1976).

The need to avoid open confrontation with dictatorships parallels pre-colonial forms of oblique criticism of authority in forms like heroic recitation and work songs. Several authors developed skills at creating *allegories which criticized leaders without open confrontation. These include Malawian playwrights during the Banda regime. Innocent Banda (*Cracks*, 1977), Steve Chimombo (*Wachiona Ndani?*, 1984), and Du *Chisiza, Jr., in such plays from the 1980s as *Fragments* and *Papa's Empire*, used absurdism, farce, and allegory as vehicles

for critique. The Idi Amin regime in Uganda was even more repressive. Robert Serumaga survived by employing dance-mime and absurdism to encode political metaphors in *Renga Moi* (1972) and *Majangwa* (1974). The popular Luganda playwright Byron Kawadwa was less lucky. When he revived his historical Christian epic *St Charles Lwanga* (1976), Amin's secret police interpreted the play as an attack on the regime and had the author liquidated.

It was not only through genre that African theatre practitioners explored indigenous traditions, but also through *dramaturgy and theatre organization. One of the major complaints made by many African theatre workers was the inadequacy of the proscenium stage inherited from the colonial tradition. Several attempts were made to create a modern *stage more suited to African traditions of flexible and participatory performance. Two early experiments were Efua Sutherland's Ghana Drama Studio (1960) and Duro Ladipo's arts complex Mbari Mbayo (Nigeria, 1961). Later examples, all fully or partly *open air, include *Chikwakwa Theatre near Lusaka (Zambia, 1969), Chirunga Open Air Theatre, Zomba (Malawi, 1976), Kamariithu Theatre (Kenya, 1977), Ahmadu Bello University Theatre (Nigeria, 1980), and Amakhosi Community Arts Centre, Bulawayo (Zimbabwe 1995). These more Afro-centric performing spaces were accompanied by innovations in stagecraft using locally available materials, designs, and concepts for *playhouse architecture, *lighting, *props, musical instruments, *masks, costumes, and make-up.

In the early 1960s, with the encouragement of drama lecturers, students like Dapo Adelugba at the University of Ibadan helped organize the University of Ibadan Travelling Theatre, based on indigenous models. Ibadan provided a model for several later *university travelling theatre troupes: Makerere (Uganda), UNZADRAMS (Zambia), Chancellor College (Malawi), the University of Botswana, and Maratholi Travelling Theatre (Lesotho). Sharing the scarce intellectual resources of national universities with *audiences away from the metropolis, the troupes in turn provided inspiration for non-academic travelling theatre, ranging from Soyinka's art theatre troupe of the 1960s, Masks, to the commercial troupes performing in Uganda in the 1970s, in Kenya and Tanzania from the late 1970s, and in Malawi from the mid-1980s.

Another key feature of indigenous performance, competitive festivals, found a modern equivalent in schools drama competitions, popular in almost every anglophone country except South Africa. In order to provide equal opportunities, strict rules about length and technical support were enforced. As the chief sponsor was often the British Council, English tended to be the dominant medium, and the institutional links with the educational system created an explicit or implicit censorship of themes. From the early 1970s onwards, however, there was a strong reaction away from theatre modes with conservative or neocolonial influences. This had several manifestations. One was the emergence of national and even regional organizations designed to encourage local rather than imported expertise and theatrical models. Another was a radicalization of theatre themes. A generation of authors who were not content to create 'identity theatre', based purely on essentialist revivals of indigenous theatre techniques, sought to challenge dictatorships and neocolonial regimes. Such authors include Femi Osofisan and Bode Sowande in Nigeria, Bole *Butake in Cameroon, Yulisa Amadu and John Kargbo in Sierra Leone, Francis *Imbuga and Ngugi wa Thiong'o in Kenya, John *Ruganda in Uganda and Kenya, and Cont *Mhlanga in Zimbabwe.

The radicalization of South African theatre proceeded along different lines. The theatre which developed after the Nationalist Party's 1948 victory and the subsequent imposition of apartheid was based on a state-imposed cultural division of the races. State resources poured into Afrikaans theatre through a network of performing arts councils, while English-language theatre could rely on commercial theatre and privately funded foundations. Black theatre, however, at first confined to township musicals, had to rely on the energy of individual entrepreneurs. Some English-language practitioners such as Athol *Fugard and Barney *Simon began to challenge this cultural apartheid from the late 1950s. The Nationalist government, in the wake of the Sharpeville massacre and the withdrawal of South Africa from the Commonwealth (1961), hit back by initiating legislation to prevent interracial casts and audiences.

Afrikaans theatre of the *sestiger* (60s) movement responded by creating a drama which explored Boer family and religious values through the plays of P. G. *du Plessis, Bartho Smit, and Reza *de Wet. After an initially similar reaction some anglophone practitioners, particularly Fugard and Simon, tried to create a liberal protest theatre which addressed apartheid issues. The plays which Fugard *devised with actors John *Kani and Winston *Ntshona, *Sizwe Bansi Is Dead* (1972) and *The Island* (1973), epitomize this movement, and under this pressure the apartheid regime relaxed some of the restrictions on interracial audiences and *casting.

Several black theatre artists from the 1970s onwards, inspired by the Black Consciousness movement associated with Steve Biko, began to resent white liberal intervention and created an autonomous black theatre geared to the urban African townships; these include Matsemela *Manaka of Soyikwa and Maishe *Maponya of Bahumutsi. Yet other black artists (such as Gcina Mhlope and Mbongeni Ngema) resisted apartheid by co-operating with progressive theatre companies such as *Junction Avenue and *Market Theatre in Johannesburg or the Space in Cape Town. The radical theatre of South Africa, owing to its desire to find a common medium of resistance against the Afrikaner-dominated government, tended to use English— though there were exceptions, such as the multiracial and multilingual Workshop 79 group. Several non-Afrikaner theatre groups also began to use multi-language theatre as a deliberate subversion of apartheid policy.

Outside South Africa, there was a renewed interest in African languages from the late 1970s. A major catalyst was Ngugi wa Thiong'o's proselytizing for African language in the wake of his 1977 arrest over Kamariithu Theatre. Some anglophone countries where there was a widespread African lingua franca, such as Tanzania (Swahili) and Botswana (Setswana), had already established African-language theatres, some hosting widely recognized authors like Penina *Mlama. After Kamariithu, however, there was a rapid spread of African-language theatre in Kenya, Uganda, Zambia, Malawi, Zimbabwe, and Lesotho. There was also an increased use of creoles in West Africa, particularly in Sierra Leone and Liberia, where it is the dominant language, but also in Ghana and Nigeria.

Another factor in the increased use of African languages was the rise of theatre for *development after the first experiments with Laedza Batanani in Botswana in the mid-1970s. By the 1980s this methodology, linking theatre to developmental communication campaigns, had spread to every anglophone country. Some practitioners such as Hansel *Eyoh in Cameroon, Chris Kamlongera in Malawi, Ross *Kidd in Botswana, Ngugi wa *Mirii in Kenya and Zimbabwe, Stephen Chifunyise in Zimbabwe, Oga Abah in Nigeria, and Zakes *Mda in Lesotho and South Africa, used it to create major careers, and in some countries—Gambia, Botswana, Swaziland, Lesotho, and Namibia—it had by the 1990s become the dominant form of activity. Increased funding for drama-related AIDS campaigns made international donors with health agendas major patrons for the arts throughout sub-Saharan Africa.

The early 1990s saw several changes of emphasis. The multi-party democratic elections in Namibia, Kenya, Zambia, Malawi, Tanzania, and, most importantly, South Africa, along with ethnic wars in Liberia and Sierra Leone, heightened a post-colonial sensibility which moved away from essentialist assertions of black authenticity. This helped create space for a more pluralist theatre in terms of theme, language, and style. One result was an increased interest in representations of *gender issues. Women such as Efua Sutherland (Ghana), Zulu Sofala (Nigeria), Penina Mlama (Tanzania), Micere Mugo (Kenya), and Rose *Mbowa (Uganda) had already foregrounded women's issues in their work, but audiences became increasingly attentive to positive female messages from authors like Tess *Onwueme (Nigeria) and the South African authors Fatima Dike and Duma Ndlovu. Some male writers also became more sensitive to gender issues.

A pluralist sensibility was also evoked through interethnic and *intercultural theatre. This was particularly noticeable in South Africa where the linguistic divisions encouraged by apartheid began to break down further, with some plays switching fluidly between combinations of the nation's eleven official languages. Similarly hitherto neglected linguistic or cultural constituencies such as the Natal Indians and the mixed-race 'coloureds' found a voice in authors like Ronnie Govender (South Africa) and Freddie Philander (Namibia). Intercultural theatrical experimentation complemented this move by intertextual rewritings of classic European *texts from an African perspective or by synthesizing disparate performance traditions. The trend was seen in practitioners like Soyinka, William *Kentridge (South Africa), and Ibrahim ben Abdullah (Ghana). A similar pluralism was applied to dance-theatre. Although tourist-oriented performance of traditional dances remained popular, several groups attempted an adventurous synthesis of dance traditions, such as Tumbuka in Zimbabwe and a number of modern dance troupes in South Africa.

5. Mediatized drama

From the 1970s onwards there has been a large expansion of drama on the *mass media. Radio drama in African languages dates back to the late 1940s in Zambia and South Africa, and television to the 1960s in Nigeria. By the 1990s nearly all anglophone African countries had some form of drama on radio and television, with widely divergent policies on language, content, commissioning techniques, and technical expertise. Western broadcasting companies such as the BBC and Deutsche Welle have trained artists in the production of scripted radio drama in English. More popular, however, has been a style of moralistic, improvised, comic radio drama in African languages, such as the series *Sewero la Kapalepale* (Chinyanja) in Malawi, *Mahoka* (Kiswahili) in Tanzania, and *Ifyabukaya* (ChiBemba) in Zambia. Both the form and content of these collectively devised plays tend to be based on indigenous traditions of narrative and drama.

Television has given birth to similar semi-improvised comic drama series, such as *Jamaa ya Mzee Pembe* (Kiswahiili) in Kenya and *The Mukudota Family* (mostly Shona) in Zimbabwe. The two giants of television drama in anglophone Africa, however, are Nigeria and South Africa, each with very different policies. Although some sophisticated literary dramatists (such as Soyinka and Ken *Saro-Wiwa) have written for Nigerian television, most of its output is dominated by drama already popular on stage, particularly in the Yoruba popular theatre tradition. Nigerian television drama, like that in much of anglophone Africa, is plagued by limited finance and technical resources, particularly as resources are divided among the various state broadcasting companies. South Africa, by contrast, has developed a technically sophisticated television drama, based largely on Western models. Soap operas like *Generations* and *Isidingo*, predominantly in English but with a peppering of other languages, have become popular not only in South Africa but through satellite exposure throughout southern Africa.

The facility with which African artists have adapted to imported technologies of film, radio, and television, while retaining African cultural forms and sensibilities, points to the strength of the performing arts on the continent. Major socio-economic and political upheavals which have plagued Africa over the last 200 years have deeply affected the performance, but the transformations have often assisted popular resistance to colonial or neocolonial domination—and they have almost always provided a recognizable African identity, necessary for cultural survival in the context of global communication. *See also* AFRICA, FRANCOPHONE; AFRICA, LUSOPHONE; AFRICA: ERITREA, ETHIOPIA, SOMALIA.   DaK

BANHAM, MARTIN, and PLASTOW, JANE (eds.), *Contemporary African Plays* (London, 1999)

BREITINGER, ECKHARD (ed.), *Theatre and Performance in Africa* (Bayreuth, 1993)

DUNTON, CHRIS, *Make Man Talk True: Nigerian drama in English since 1970* (London, 1992)

KERR, DAVID, *African Popular Theatre from Pre-colonial Times to the Present Day* (London, 1995)

KRUGER, LOREN, *The Drama of South Africa: plays, pageants and publics since 1910* (London, 1999)

MDA, ZAKES, *When People Play People: development communication through theatre* (Johannesburg, 1993)

OWOMOYELA, OYEKAN, *African Literatures: an introduction* (Waltham, Mass., 1979)

PLASTOW, JANE, *African Theatre and Politics: the evolution of theatre in Ethiopia, Tanzania and Zimbabwe: a comparative study* (Amsterdam, 1996)

AFRICA, FRANCOPHONE

This entry treats theatre and performance in francophone sub-Saharan *Africa, referring to a diverse group of 21 countries that were formerly part of the French and Belgian colonial empires, and in which the French language is still an importance presence.

1. Introduction; 2. Indigenous performance;
3. Modern francophone theatre;
4. Modern African-languages theatre;
5. Urban popular theatre; 6. Theatre for development;
7. *Théâtre d'animation politique*

1. Introduction

Two major geographic and cultural regions may be distinguished within this huge sweep of territory. The first encompasses the countries of the former Federation of French West African States (AOF) such as Senegal, Mali, and Côte d'Ivoire, whose administrative capital in the colonial era was Dakar in Senegal. Predominantly Islamic, and located for the most part in the savannah and the Sahel, this area is home to ancient polities like the Mali Empire, famous in the early Middle Ages for international trading networks which extended as far afield as the countries of the Maghrib in the north, and Egypt and Arabia in the east. The second comprises the seven French-speaking territories of the Central African and Great Lakes region, including Cameroon, the Central African Republic, and the Republic of

Congo (all members of the then French Equatorial African Federation, AEF), and the former Belgian territories of the Democratic Republic of Congo (formerly Zaire), Rwanda, and Burundi. Unlike the first region, Catholicism and African traditional religions predominate in this one. Because of a Belgian colonial policy that promoted literacy in African languages, Rwanda, Burundi, and Madagascar (whose language was reduced to writing by the London Missionary Society) are the only francophone countries with French and an indigenous language—Kinyarwanda, Kirundi, and Malagasy respectively—as their official languages. A similar dual-language policy exists in Cameroon with French and English, and in Mauritania with French and Arabic.

But in spite of differences, francophone sub-Saharan African is more than just the sum total of these nations. Most countries are bound together by a multitude of institutional, political, and economic links: the franc zone, the Community of West African States (CEAO), the Economic Community of Central African States (ECCAS). Almost all are members of the *francophonie*, an international political organization, rather like the British Commonwealth, created in 1986 to foster economic, cultural, and scientific cooperation between the global community of French-speaking nations. But the most notable symbol of their common identity is the French language and the modern francophone culture that has arisen from its interaction with indigenous African traditions.

Of the various forms this culture has created, the most vital, certainly since the mid-1970s, has been the theatre. Although of relatively recent origin—the first published plays date back only to the 1960s, Séydou Badian's *La Mort de Chaka* (*The Death of Chaka*, 1962), Amadou Cissé Dia's *Les Derniers jours de Lat Dior* and *La Mort du damel* (*The Final Days of Lat Dior* and *The Death of the Damel*, 1965)—theatre has come to be identified with the literature of the *post-colonial period in the same way that poetry was, between the 1940s and the mid-1960s, with that of the nationalist period. In the plays of dramatists such as Sony *Labou Tansi, Werewere *Liking, Tchicaya *U'Tamsi, and Zadi *Zaourou, theatre is prominent in school curricula. It is circulated in many national and continental African francophone *festivals like the *Market of African Performing Arts (MASA) in Côte d'Ivoire, the *Ouagadougou International Puppet Festival (FITMO) in Burkina Faso, as well as in intercontinental ones like the *Avignon Festival and especially the *Limoges Festival of International Francophone Theatres. In the United States, francophone African theatre is an important component of the publishing endeavours of the Ubu Repertory Theatre in *New York, founded in 1984 to present 'contemporary French-language plays in English translation'. In addition to two volumes specifically devoted to plays from the region, others on thematic topics like theatre and *politics and women dramatists also carry francophone African plays. Additionally, the Ubu Bilingual Company, the performance division of the publishing

concern, has organized *Off-Broadway performances and staged readings of plays by such dramatists as Maxime *Ndébéka, Koffi Kwahulé, and Labou Tansi.

In spite of its dominant position, however, which comes from the prestige of its language and the authority of literacy, francophone theatre is far from the only type of performance in francophone sub-Saharan Africa. If anything, it is a minority cultural form, understood and practised only by the French-educated elites who, by the most optimistic figures, account for no more than 30 per cent of the population in the most alphabetized countries (Côte d'Ivoire, Congo, Gabon) and for as little as 5 per cent in states like Guinea and the Central African Republic.

2. Indigenous performance

A variety of forms exist in the region, some overlapping, some distinct. Many of them pre-date colonial rule, and have not only survived it through skilful adaptation but now constitute a fund of techniques and subjects for new drama in French. But unlike the latter, which represents the new nations, these forms are specific to ethnic communities. Two broad categories can be distinguished. The first are ancient but constantly evolving *ritual ceremonies, performed as responses to life crises—sickness or death—or to seasonal and social processes like harvesting, initiation, or marriage. Among the many such documented performances are the *djingo and the *ngué* of the Bassa people of Cameroon, the *do* of the Bambara of Mali, the *kingizila of the Congo, the *bwiti* of the Fang of Gabon, the *n'depp* of the Lebou community in Dakar, and the *sarki of the Hausa of Niger and northern Nigeria.

Highly theatrical, these performances make use of *costumed performers in colourful accoutrements or *masks who, like stage *actors, draw on a range of gestures, body movements, and facial expressions. The ceremonies are enactments of a story (usually symbolic) that has magnitude and is complete, given before a public and in a circumscribed place and using speech, *music, and song. In spite of these similarities, however, performances such as the *ngué* or the *djingo* differ from the modern theatre in French which is based on them (Liking's *Une nouvelle terre* and *Rougeole arc-en-ciel* respectively) in two important respects. First, their objective is not entertainment but is *action oriented: to heal or ensure a bountiful harvest. In other words their effect does not end with the performance, but, in the words of Johan Huizinga in *Homo Ludens*, 'continues to shed its radiance on the ordinary world outside, a wholesome influence working security, order and prosperity for the whole community'. Secondly, although they use the resources of the stage actor, ceremonial performers are not involved, either in their eyes or those of the *audience, in play acting—except, of course, to those modern spectators who have lost faith in the religious premises of the ceremony. They are 'holy actors' who, within the sacred space of their performance, do not *represent* spirit forces, but *are* those forces incarnate. (*See* PERFORMANCE STUDIES; ORIGINS OF THEATRE.)

Side by side with these sacred performances a variety of secular ones exist throughout the region whose context is re-creation and whose purpose is entertainment and instruction, even if their origins, in certain cases, are religious. These include storytelling performances of *folk tales or heroic tales, like the Sunjata or Mwindo epics of the Mandé and Nyanga peoples of Mali and Zaire, or the *mvet* of the Fang of Cameroon and Gabon, works which take on the quality of theatre by virtue of the nature of their delivery. For while the linguistic skills of the *griot* (or narrator) are important, the success of his perform-ance depends on his ability to act the roles of the *characters depicted. The most sought-after oral performers are those whose quality of voice, use of *mime and gestures, not to men-tion talent as a player of the *cora* or *mvet*, make them a delight not just to the ear but also to the eye.

Beyond the lone actor playing several roles and combining narration with action, there exist in francophone Africa more developed theatre forms consisting of several actors whose mode of communication is words and action as opposed to nar-ration. Examples include the *kotèba* of Mali, the *hira-gasy* of Madagascar, the all-female *bena-mambala* of Zaire, and the *sougounougou* of Côte d'Ivoire. Some of these forms like the *hira-gasy* are notable for the way they have evolved with modern circumstances, not only expanding their range of characters to include agents of the colonial and post-colonial states, but also developing new ways of performing. By the eighteenth century, for instance, the *hira-gasy*, once a peasant idiom connected with burial rites, had been taken over by the local Merina monarchy, and transformed into a court entertainment for European vis-itors. As a result of a massive incorporation of European ele-ments, by the nineteenth century the *hira-gasy* had lost many of its original features and become syncretic. Its *dance move-ments, for example, became more militaristic, violins and trum-pets replaced indigenous instruments, and its characters (often the object of *parody, but also a proud symbol of the form's modernity) now were soldiers, conventionalized in broad stripes, missionaries in their regalia, and administrators.

Other widely practised types of theatre that have been secularized over the years include initiation dance events like the *ozila* of the Bulu of Cameroon, the *douga* of the Mandingo of Guinea—performed in celebration of victory (usually) in battle—and the *ntore* of the Banyarwanda of Rwanda (a dance of allegiance to the ruler). The body movements of these dances, together with the performers' costumes, masks, and accom-panying music, weave a complex aesthetic system that tells a story and conveys meaning. But increasingly dislodged from their original ceremonial contexts as a result of modernization, many indigenous dance events are fast becoming commodified articles of folklore, performed by state-subsidized theatre com-

panies like the *Ballets Africains of Guinea, the Ballet National Sambole of Congo (ex-Zaire), the Ensemble de Ballet du Sénégal, and the *Kotèba Ensemble of Côte d'Ivoire. Their work is served up to tourists, as well as to local elites anxious to make a show of 'traditional' culture, or nostalgic about vanishing indigenous cultures.

A final example of traditional performance is *puppet the-atre, such as the *assumbadin* and the *xouss-maniap* theatre found among the Diola and Wolof in Senegal, the *pangwe* com-mon to the Fang of Cameroon and Gabon, or the *konnou-doukili* of the Bambara of Mali. Some puppet traditions are closely connected with religion, but many, like the *konnou-doukili*, are simply public entertainment. The *konnou-doukili* is unique in its performance space: not a building or a public square, but boats on the Niger River. In one boat are musical instruments and a *chorus of singers, and in the other puppets —depicting in a *realistic or non-figurative mode animal or stereotypical human characters—and their manipulators, who are hidden by a screen from the view of the spectators massed on the riverbank. Sculpted in wood, and costumed in grass or cloth, these puppets imitate certain movements and gestures rather than represent an action. Unlike the *konnou-doukili*, the *sogo bò* masquerade puppet theatre, also of Mali, is not an isolated event but part of a well-choreographed new year's festival, the *Tonko*, that brings together the best of the community's plastic and performing arts.

A few general characteristics can be identified. Because of their unscripted nature, indigenous forms emphasize perform-ance: the physical skills of the performer in mask work, song, music, and mime carry more weight than the *text, which (ex-cept in rituals) is no more than a *scenario for improvised *dialogue. Except in rituals, where the performer becomes the character, to the point of being possessed by him, the acting style in recreational forms is non-realistic. Indigenous African theatre is a communal art, depending for its existence on the participation of a live audience, and its playing spaces do not rigidly separate actors from spectators.

3. Modern francophone theatre

The origins and development of modern drama can be div-ided into three phases: from the late 1880s to the early 1930s, from the 1930s to the immediate pre-independence period, and from the early 1960s to the present. The earliest stagings of French drama were in cities with large European communities, such as Dakar and Leopoldville, by visiting French or Belgian troupes, but the new drama was to exert a lasting influence through schools. Missionaries were quick to understand the centrality of performance in African societies, and to use it to propagate the Christian faith and its values. Between 1809 and 1903 the Order of the Ploermel Brothers, and later the mission-aries at St Joseph of Cluny Secondary School in Senegal, made the dramatization of scenes from the Bible part of the activities of important feasts of the religious calendar. In some Catholic schools in Cameroon, missionaries even introduced French *medieval plays like *Le Jeu d'Adam* and *Le Miracle de Théophile*, while in Togo they had their students perform *kantata*, a form that was later to give rise to the Togolese *concert party.

From about 1930 to the late 1950s, public schools and cultural associations became prominent in the diffusion of modern theatre. They emphasized the study and performance of secular drama—especially *Molière's *farces and *comedies—dramatic *monologues, and songs. To one such institution, the *École William Ponty, then the only post-secondary institution for the entire federation, goes the historical credit of having produced in 1933 the first written sketch by a French-speaking African, though the author is anonymous. William Ponty's graduates, among the region's earliest dramatists—Bernard *Dadié, Amon *d'Aby, Cheik *Ndao—set up drama groups in their countries on their return, including the Théâtre Indigène and the *Centre Culturel et Folklorique of Côte d'Ivoire, the Amicale des Fonctionnaires de Niamey in Niger, and Les Tréteaux of Mali. In the former Belgian territories, especially Congo (ex-Zaire), the educated Congolese, the so-called 'évolués', also founded cultural associations whose activities included Western-style drama in French. Unlike the case in West Africa, however, these groups performed as well in local languages like Ciluba, Swahili, and Lingala.

The development of francophone theatre in the post-colonial period, 1960 to the turn of the twenty-first century, has been shaped by a number of factors. These include the establishment of theatre institutes in such cities as Abidjan, Dakar, and Kinshasa, the construction of *playhouses like the Daniel Sorano in Dakar or edifices that contain theatre facilities (usually sports stadiums or legislative assemblies), and the regular secondment of French theatre practitioners and academics to work with aspiring dramatists. Also important is the inter-African *radio drama competition created in 1966 by French international radio, which has seen the submission of hundreds of scripts. Many contemporary dramatists have been contestants in that competition and some, like Labou Tansi, Liking, Senouvo *Zinsou, and Kossi *Efoui, were prizewinners. The establishment of theatre festivals also spurred creativity. But it was a political imperative—the struggle against colonial rule, and its successor local dispensations—that accounts most for the growth and development of the modern theatre. The theatre's ability to communicate unmediated by the unwritten word has made it a weapon of choice in the largely non-literate societies in the region.

Three types of modern play can be identified. The first, the *historical play, is based on a re-creation of events or heroes from Africa's historico-mythical past. Chaka, founder of the Zulu people, Albouri Ndiaye, of the Wolof of Senegal, Gbéhanzin of Dahomey, and Sunjata, founder of the Mali Empire, are among the many figures whose real or imagined exploits have been celebrated in such plays as Séydou Badian's *La Mort de Chaka* (1962), Ndao's *L'Exil d'Albouri* (1967), or Jean Pliya's *Kondo le requin* (*Kondo the Shark*, 1966). Although this *genre became very popular in the immediate pre- and post-colonial periods, it was already present in some William Ponty sketches of the 1930s. But given that these pieces were produced under the watchful eyes of French colonial authorities, they adopted, as in the case of *Assémien Déhylé*, a detached, almost ethnographic point of view, contenting themselves with a presentation of customs and practices connected with the choice and enthronement of traditional rulers rather than with their achievements or encounters with the French. When such encounters were dramatized at all, as in *L'Entrevue du Capitaine Péroz et de Samory à Bissandougou* (*The Encounter between Peroz and Samory*, 1936), or in *L'Entrevue de Bayol et de Béhanzin* (*The Meeting between Bayol and Behanzin*, 1933), they were presented within the prevailing French ideology which characterized the African sovereigns as obstacles to France's civilizing mission. Such a view of history changed dramatically in post-1960s plays, which invariably presented these rulers as nationalists whose heroic defence of the integrity of their territories lives in myth. The reasons for the popularity of the history play are varied, ranging from the nationalist need to reclaim a past obscured by colonial discourse, to that of creating unifying myths for the new nations. The fact that most of the practitioners of this type of play were from the Sahel region is significant. Heirs to ancient and stratified empires with rich historical traditions, they conceived modern drama as a mere extension of the activity of the oral historian or singer whose duty was to preserve and celebrate the past.

Like the historical play, drama dealing with society's manners and customs has been integral to French-language African theatre from the outset. Marriage customs or other social practices inspired such 1930s compositions as *Le Mariage chez les mandégnis* (*Marriage among the Mandingo*) or *Sokamé* (both 1937). Their approach was essentially folkloristic. The social plays of the 1950s, on the other hand, from Côte d'Ivoire and Congo in particular, were critical. They were no longer a *documentary of customs, but a statement on the incompatibility of tradition with modern progress or Christian teachings. Examples include *Kwao Adjoba* (1953) on inheritance in matrilineal societies, *Entraves* (*Shackles*, 1955) on the extended family, both by Amon d'Aby; *Sidi maître escroc* (*Sidi, Master Swindler*, 1960), by Bernard Dadié, on crooks passing for diviners; *Soko Stanley* (1956) by the Congolese Albert *Mongita on the nineteenth-century Welsh explorer Henry Stanley. Very rarely would dramatists satirize aspects of the colonial system, like forced labour in Germain Coffi Gadeau's *Les Recrutés de Monsieur Maurice* (*M. Maurice's Recruits*, 1942).

The concern with social realities and the conflict of values continued in the post-colonial social comedies. But with these plays, no social institution or practice—of European provenance or ancient origin—is spared. The country bumpkin and the city gent, the authoritarian village chief and the status-conscious civil servant, the superstitious rural folk and their culturally alienated and venal urban cousins are all the butt of biting *satire. Examples include *Trois prétendants . . . un mari* (*Three Suitors . . . One Husband*, 1964), *Jusqu'à nouvel avis* (*Until Further Notice*, 1970) by the Cameroonian Guillaume Oyono-Mbia, *La Secrétaire particulière* (*The Confidential Secretary*, 1973) by the Benin dramatist Jean Pliya, *L'Or du diable* (*The Devil's Gold*, 1985) by the Malian Moussa Konaté, *Trop c'est trop* (*Enough's Enough*, 1986) by the Cameroonian Protais Asseng, and *La Marmite de Koka-Mbala* (*Koka Mbala's Pot*, 1966) by the Congolese Guy Menga. Other comedies revolve around issues of greed, moral and political turpitude, and social injustice, as in Dadié's *Monsieur Thogo-Gnini* (1970), Labou Tansi's *Je, soussigné, cardiaque* (*I, the Undersigned Cardiac Patient*, 1981), Birago Diop's *L'Os de Mor Lam* (*Mor Lam's Bone*, 1973), Sylvain *Bemba's *Une eau dormante* (*Sleeping Water*, 1975), *Le Fou* (*The Madman*, 1985) by the Burkina Faso dramatist Jean-Pierre *Guingané, and *La Retraite* (*The Retreat*, 1990) by the Malagasy David Jaomanoro.

While the anti-colonial struggle mostly found expression in historical drama, it also gave rise, sometimes long after that period, to political plays like *L'Enfer, c'est Orfeo* (*Hell Is Orpheus*, 1971), by the Congolese Bemba, and *Tiaroye terre rouge* (*The Red Earth of Tiaroye*, 1981), by the Senegalese Boubacar Boris Diop. But the realities of post-colonial politics—characterized by military dictatorships, single party regimes, neocolonial interference, civil and revolutionary wars, and predatory states—inspired many political farces or *tragicomedies. Plays in this category include Williams Sassine's *Indépendan-tristes* (*Independence Blues*, 1997), U'Tamsi's *Le Maréchal Nnikon Nniku Prince qu'on sort* (*Marshal Nnikon Nninku, Prince Consort*, 1979) and *Le Bal de Ndinga* (*Ndinga's Dance*, 1987), Maxime Ndébéka's *Le Président* (1970), Labou Tansi's *Parenthèse de sang* (*Parenthesis of Blood*, 1981) and *Antoine m'a vendu son destin* (*Antoine Sold Me his Destiny*, 1986), Zinsou's *La Tortue qui chante* (*The Singing Tortoise*, 1984), the Cameroonian Jean Mba Evina's *Politicos* (1974), the Malagasy Michèle *Rakotoson's *La Maison morte* (*The Dead House*), and Kossi Efoui's *Récupérations* (1992).

In spite of the incorporation of elements of oral theatre (the narrative performer, a supple use of space, music), francophone plays up to the late 1970s worked within the conventions of Western drama, with an emphasis on spoken dialogue, plot construction, and a conception of language as 'elevated utterance'. But the years since 1980 have seen attempts by contemporary practitioners such as Liking, Labou Tansi, Zaourou, and Souleymane Koly to break with French-inspired practice and to create a theatre whose format is derived from indigenous modes of performance. In the new style, *collective creation takes precedence over the pre-established script; speech is de-

centred in favour of a theatrical language that appeals to the senses; performance values take precedence over textual ones.

4. Modern African-languages theatre

Although French is the main language of drama in the francophone region of Africa, scripted drama also exists in some indigenous African languages: Ewe in Togo, Ciluba, Swahili, and Lingala in Congo (ex-Zaire), and Malagasy in Madagascar. The work of Protestant and Catholic missionaries in reducing these languages to writing, with a view to translating the Bible, made the emergence of a scripted theatre possible. Some of the early dramatists associated with this type of theatre were F. K. Fiawoo in Togo in the 1930s, Justin Disasi, G. Kitenge, Joseph Kiwele, and Gilbert Mbayi in Congo in the late 1950s, and Justin Rajoro and Naka Rabemanantsoa in Malagasy between 1922 and 1945, and Michèle Rakotoson in the contemporary period.

5. Urban Popular Theatre

Overlapping with oral theatre forms and literate drama, and yet belonging to neither category, is urban popular theatre, which derives from the populace and has wide appeal. Examples of this practice—which is unscripted, relies on *improvisation, and is performed in a medley of local languages and pidginized French—include the concert party of Togo, the theatre of the *Mufwankolo group in ex-Zaire, notable for its radio and *television dramas, and the Hausa-language theatre of various Samariya troupes in Niger.

6. Theatre for development

Theatre for *development, which is widely present in anglophone Africa, is important in certain francophone countries as well. It is practised in Mali by the Nyogolon theatre, in Burkina Faso by the Atelier Théâtre Burkinabé or Le Théâtre de la Fraternité, and in Niger by the Samariya theatre associations. Using indigenous languages and performance techniques, this theatre seeks—in pieces like *Timinandia* (*Perseverance*, 1989) on polio (Nyogolon), or *Papa, oublie-moi* (*Father, Forget about Me*, 1989) on women's and children's rights (Théâtre de la Fraternité)—to communicate, to a mostly rural target audience, development values related to health and agriculture. Unlike urban popular theatre, which is a product of the people even if the values it upholds are not always in their best interest, community theatre for development is produced and sponsored by governmental and international development agencies.

7. Théâtre d'animation politique

The use of theatre by the state for the propagation of party political values became a important feature of several francophone countries in the 1970s, particularly in one-party authoritarian states such as Guinea under the late Sékou Toure, the former Zaire of the late Mobutu Sékou, and Togo under

Eyadema. *Théâtre d'animation politique*, based in part on similar spectacles in communist North *Korea or *China, is a theatricalization of politics, consisting of a crowd of hundreds dressed in the same (usually bright) attire, waving flags, chanting party slogans and songs of praise to the immortal leader, and executing precisely choreographed dances to frenzied drum music. Led by a principal conductor (*animateur principal*) who shouts out slogans that are taken up in chorus, the *théâtre d'animation politique* is organized during important events in the party's calendar. With the emergence in the 1990s of pluralistic political systems across the region this type of theatre is much less in use.

It should be noted that the barriers separating the forms and styles analysed here are not sealed. A constant interpenetration is taking place among them, giving rise to new practices of theatre for the future. *See also* AFRICA, ANGLOPHONE; AFRICA, LUSOPHONE; AFRICA: ERITREA, ETHIOPIA, SOMALIA.   JCM

CONTEH-MORGAN, JOHN, *Theatre and Drama in Francophone Africa* (Cambridge, 1994)

HOURANTIER, MARIE-JOSÉ, *Du rituel au théâtre-rituel* (Paris, 1990)

NKASHAMA, PIUS NGANDU, *Théâtres et scènes de spectacle* (Paris, 1993)

RICARD, ALAIN, 'French-Language Drama and Theater', in Oyekan Owomoyela (ed.), *A History of Twentieth-Century African Literatures* (Lincoln, Nebr., 1993)

SCHÉRER, JACQUES, *Le Théâtre en Afrique noire francophone* (Paris, 1992)

Theatre Research International, special issue on theatre in Africa, 9 (1984)

UPTON, CAROLE-ANNE, 'Words in Space: filling the empty space in francophone theatre', in Patricia Little and Roger Little (eds.), *Black Accents: writing in French from Africa, Mauritius and the Caribbean* (London, 1997)

AFRICA, LUSOPHONE

In pre-colonial lusophone (Portuguese-speaking) Africa—those territories now known as Angola, Guinea-Bissau, and Mozambique—performance was characterized by *music, theatricalized *dance, ceremony, and *rituals that sometimes featured paint-adorned, *mask-wearing performers. In the fifteenth century, when the Portuguese first reached Cape Verde and São Tomé e Príncipe, they found these two archipelagos uninhabited. But with the arrival of slaves from the nearby continent, African cultural rituals were soon transplanted to the islands. Despite the official colonial policy of assimilation, which sought to 'civilize the natives' by suppressing their culture, traditional African performance survived, however hybridized. Fresu and de Oliveira document how African performers frequently parodied Europeans by wearing masks that ridiculed such power figures as colonial administrators, landowners, and even Christian saints. The settlers who witnessed these 'exotically quaint' *spectacles often did not realize when they and their institutions were being mocked.

By the mid-twentieth century, when a black and mixed-race middle class and acculturated intelligentsia had established itself in the urban centres of the lusophone colonies, and when, in the post-Second World War period, independence fervour and nationalist militancy spread throughout the so-called Third World, the colonial authorities increasingly suppressed indigenous cultural expression, especially when construed as a statement of social and political protest. In the early 1960s, with the outbreak of guerrilla warfare in Angola, Guinea-Bissau, and Mozambique, as well as rising opposition to colonial rule in Cape Verde and São Tomé e Príncipe, the authorities imposed strict *censorship and the secret police imprisoned dozens of militants, including many writers. Colonial authorities banned theatre groups and prohibited the staging of plays that celebrated a sense of 'Africanness', transmitted pro-independence messages, or were critical of colonial rule. Dramatic performances, accessible even to the illiterate masses, were deemed especially threatening.

As part of an attempt by writers and musicians to revive Kimbundu-based cultural expression, Domingos Van-Dunem founded Teatro Gesto in the mid-1940s, a Luanda-based experimental group committed to staging dramas based on traditional Angolan stories. Although the authorities eventually banned Teatro Gesto, Van-Dunem himself persisted, and in 1972 he managed to publish and stage his *Auto de Natal* (*Nativity Play*). *Autos*, or *Passion plays, date back to seventeenth-century Luanda, but they were strictly European dramas, often used to proselytize (*see* AUTO SACRAMENTAL). With versions in Portuguese and Kimbundu (one of Angola's principal indigenous languages), Van-Dunem's Africanized *Auto de Natal* played to very receptive, racially mixed *audiences. Presumably the authorities thought it politically innocuous: in a preface to the bilingual edition, Alexandre do Nascimento, a Catholic priest, while praising Van-Dunem's attention to African traditions, also attests to the author's Christian devotion. At the time colonial officials believed that the struggle for political independence, then in its eleventh year, was going badly for the guerrilla forces, and perhaps felt they could relax restrictions on indigenous cultural expression, as a conciliatory gesture to the masses of Africans.

Nearly a year prior to the staging of Van-Dunem's play, something similar occurred in Lourenço Marques. Norberto Barroca, a young Portuguese director recently arrived in Mozambique, staged Lindo Nhlongo's *Os noivos; ou, Conferência dramâtica sobre o lobolo* (*The Newly-weds; or, A Dramatic Discourse about the Bride-Price*—the latter refers to the livestock, goods, or cash paid by the groom to his wife's family). A local reporter noted in 1971 that 'for the first time ever a play written by an African, about African social practices', was staged in Mozambique. It played to a mixed audience of Africans and whites.

Van-Dunem and Nhlongo, who went on to further important work, helped prepare for the theatrical surge that took place immediately after independence in 1974 and 1975. In all five countries the post-colonial period has witnessed an appreciable number of performances, from *radio dramatizations of suppressed short stories to full productions of plays indoors and in the open air. Many post-colonial lusophone African dramas are based on nationalistic themes and are replete with patriotic rhetoric. Their sometimes tendentious ideological cast notwithstanding, some succeed in reviving important aesthetic features of African theatricalized musical and ceremonial traditions. Also worthy of note is Pepetela's *A Corda* (*Tug of War*), a *didactic drama that played to large audiences in Luanda during the late 1970s. Another important *text-based play of that period is Pepetela's *A Revolta da casa dos ídolos* (*The Revolt of the House of the Idols*), a *historical drama. In Mozambique during the late 1970s and early 1980s, FRELIMO, the Portuguese acronym for the Mozambique Liberation Front, which after independence became the ruling party, staged a number of *agitprop plays. The performers of this political and social theatre were often students at the FRELIMO secondary school located in rural, northern Mozambique.

Korda Kaoberdi, creole for 'Awaken Cape Verde', was formed as a 'theatrical nucleus of workers and students' immediately after independence in that country's capital city of Praia. Post-colonial Guinea-Bissau witnessed similar popular initiatives, one of the most successful being the National Theatre Group Okinka Pampa. Meanwhile, in São Tomé e Príncipe independence exuberance led to the founding of theatre groups that regularly perform traditional plays known in creole as *tchilôli*, which translates loosely as *'tragedies'. During the first two and a half decades of political autonomy, in spite of ongoing civil strife, a paucity of resources, and infrastructure problems, theatrical performances have increased in lusophone Africa, especially in Angola and Mozambique.

José Mena Abrantes is one of the most prolific and successful of several playwrights to emerge in Angola. Between the late 1970s and 2001 Abrantes wrote and staged at least seven plays and dramatizations. His award-winning *Ana, Zé e os escravos* (*Ana, Joe, and the Slaves*) set a standard for historical dramas that re-create the colonial past. Abrantes' production of *Sombriluz* (*Shadowlight*), subtitled 'Snapshots of Angolan poetry from the 1950s', first staged in 1997, is a unique dramatization of the works of eight poets of the pioneering literary generation of 1950.

Because of a combination of socio-historical and cultural factors, including a rich tradition of music, dance, masks, and *costumes integrated into dramatic ritual and performance, as well as an ongoing reaction to the legacy of colonialist repression of drama, theatre will no doubt continue to flourish. The growing number of government-sponsored groups, the establishment of relevant departments and courses in Angola's Agostinho Neto University and Mozambique's Eduardo Mondlane University, as well as in other institutions of higher education

and secondary schools, and the attendance rates at public performances, stand as incontrovertible proof of the social, cultural, and aesthetic importance of theatre in lusophone Africa.

RGH

ABRANTES, JOSÉ MENA, *O teatro em Angola, hoje* (Luanda, 1994)
FRESU, ANNA, and DE OLIVEIRA, MENDES, *Pesquisas para um teatro popular em Moçambique* (Maputo, 1982)

AFRICA: ERITREA, ETHIOPIA, SOMALIA

Located in the Horn of Africa, Eritrea, Ethiopia, and Somalia are home to many ancient performing art forms, largely poetry, music, and *dance based, and roughly divided into secular/recreational and religious/spiritual expressions. Generally under-researched and under-theorized, these forms have continued to reflect the distinct cultures of the local peoples, mostly Muslim or Christian nomads and pastoralists belonging to Afro-Asiatic or Nilo-Saharan language groups. Somali theatre arts have been noted for the pre-eminence of their formal, alliterative performance poetry, the main *genres—*gabay*, *geeraar*, and *jiifto*—being reserved for men. Ethiopian and Eritrean highland cultures have been marked by the ecclesiastical performance forms of the Orthodox Church, notably *qene* (double-entendre poetry), *zema* (music), and religious dance, such as *shibsheba*. All required rigid training from early childhood and were the prerogative of the male clergy. Secular professionals, *azmari* (Ethiopia) or *wat'a* (Eritrea), sang praises to the feudal Abyssinian elite or entertained the public as itinerants. Some outstanding female performers were noted in the nineteenth century, though much earlier occurrence can be assumed. As a social group, however, both sexes of *wat'as* and *azmaris* were looked down upon, with women often considered as sex workers.

Western ideas of stage *drama, *musical theatre, and *variety shows came to the region during the heyday of European colonialism at the turn of the twentieth century. From their inception in the late 1880s, Eritrea and the then two Somali colonies had both experienced Italian and British rule, while ancient Ethiopia had never been externally colonized, the dominant Amhara dynasty itself performing the imperialist role. In 1920, the first Italian *opera house, today's Cinema Asmara, was built in the Eritrean capital. Until the early 1940s expatriate entertainment was out of bounds for colonial subjects; but after Italy's defeat in the Second World War indigenous urban theatre in both Eritrea and Somalia started to flourish. Better access to education (school drama), and an increasing politicization—due to the independence movement in Somalia, and Eritrean resentment against the 1952 federation with (and subsequent annexation by) Ethiopia—turned the performing arts into a powerful, if sometimes covert, medium of political expression (*see* POLITICS AND THEATRE). From 1944 to the 1970s, Eritrea saw a succession of urban theatre associations, the most important being Mahber Tewasew Deqabat (1947–56) and Mahber Theatre Asmara (1961 to mid-1970s), which mounted variety shows and plays in the dominant language, Tigrinya. Their most influential member was Alemayo Kahasay.

Indigenous theatre in Somalia is said to have started in the 1930s. The first groups to be noted were Hargeisa Company in the north in 1946, while Kooxda Badda operated in the south. In Ethiopia, modern Amharic drama was introduced by Tekle-Hawariat Tekle-Mariam around 1912–16 with his critical *satire *Yawrewoch Komediya* (*Comedy of Animals*) based on La Fontaine. All drama was subsequently banned (*see* CENSORSHIP) until the 1930 coronation of Haile Selassie, who used theatre as a eulogistic medium controlled by the crown. In 1955 he commissioned the building of the 1,400-seat Haile Selassie Theatre in Addis Ababa. Drama became an oratorical art for aristocratic consumption—the playwright, and not the performers, being significant—while the populace preferred the more physical and long-established variety performance form, *kinet*, as mounted most notably by the Hager Fiqir (Patriotic Theatre Association) since 1935. Ethiopia's most important and often very influential playwrights of modern times have been Tsegaye *Gebre-Medhin, Mengistu Lemma, and Tesfaye Gessesse.

In Somalia and Eritrea, theatre was increasingly used for reformist and revolutionary ends. After independence in 1960, Somalia saw the rise of free companies, such as Horsib, and the 1967 building of the National Theatre in Mogadishu. Plays made extensive use of Somali culture and were noted for their pro-women tenor, such as *Shabeelnaagood* (*Leopard among the Women*, 1968) by Hassan Sheikh Mumin. Following the military takeover by the Siad Barre regime (1969–91), theatre groups were co-opted by the authorities and tended to reflect the government's agenda. In Eritrea, the struggle against Ethiopia engendered cultural troupes in the liberation movements, the ELF and EPLF, which mounted music, dance, and *agitprop in the trenches and liberated areas. In 1981 a professional division of literature and drama was established by the EPLF. While variety shows continued, full-length plays, such as Alemseged Tesfai's *The Other War* (1984), gained new popularity. The Ethiopian military Derg regime also used theatre as a tool for propaganda, its crackdown on freedom of expression from the early 1980s allowing for little else.

The year 1991 was a watershed for all countries. While the civil war in Somalia seemed to have hampered most theatre activities except for occasional theatre for *development projects and *diaspora performances, Eritrea, on independence, counted three major performing arts groups under the state, with some twenty *amateur groups working semi-autonomously until the outbreak of the Ethiopian–Eritrean War (1998–2000). Ethiopia owns five government theatre companies and a promising amateur scene. While spoken drama and *folk performing arts are still divided, the Tigrayan-led government (since 1991) raises hopes for theatre in languages other than the formerly dominant Amharic.   CMa

MUMIN, HASSAN SHEIKH, *Shabeelnaagood: Leopard among the Women*, trans. and introd. B. W. Andrzejewski (London, 1974)
PLASTOW, JANE, *African Theatre and Politics: the evolution of theatre in Ethiopia, Tanzania and Zimbabwe* (Amsterdam, 1996)

AFRICAN-AMERICAN THEATRE

American black theatre entered history literally through a backyard. After the War of 1812, William Henry *Brown offered alfresco amusements for blacks in a tea garden behind his house on *New York's Thomas Street. These became so popular that his fledgling group developed into a company, and by 1821, whites formed much of the *audience at the African Theatre, which presented Shakespeare and contemporary plays incorporating scenes commenting on slavery in the north and south. In 1822 Brown built a 300-seat theatre in Greenwich Village. One of its last productions was his *The Drama of King Shotaway*, reputed to be the first play by an American dramatist of African descent. Two outstanding actors are associated with his *African Company, both excelling in Shakespearian roles: James Hewlett, who *toured America and the Caribbean but is barely remembered, and Ira *Aldridge, who fared far better, lionized on European stages for almost 30 years. It is symbolic that Brown's African Grove started outdoors, since black American performance has always had to push its way inside.

In *Boston in the mid-1800s, a group of free blacks organized the Histrionic Club, which lasted about a decade, giving a dramatic presentation at Chapman Hall in 1858. Its *manager, the historian William Cooper Nell, is said to have written plays, although none has been discovered. That same year, also in Boston, William Wells *Brown published *The Escape; or, A Leap for Freedom*. A former slave, he performed this and an earlier play as *one-person shows on the abolitionist circuit.

Aldridge was not the only African American to seek theatrical freedom abroad in the nineteenth century. Despite the theatrical activity in his home town of New Orleans, Victor Sejour stayed on in *Paris following a run of one of his plays in 1844, and enjoyed an active career there for the next 30 years. J. A. Arneaux, also from New Orleans, went to New York to organize the Louisiana Colored Troupe in 1877, before becoming affiliated seven years later with the Astor Place Tragedy Company, which specialized in Shakespeare, as the African Company had done almost 60 years before.

During the Reconstruction period, segregationist (or 'Jim Crow') legislation placed all black artists under the same *minstrel roof. Comics, dancers, lyricists, dramatists, and *opera singers all participated in this complex entertainment form. Opera singers in particular extended its boundaries, many of them women. From the 1870s to the end of the 1890s, the Hyer

Sisters toured the country as headliners for a musical company, and in 1896 the opera star Black Patti formed the Troubadours, managed for a time by Bob *Cole. African-American composers including Scott Joplin created full-scale operas, although these gained appreciation only in the twentieth century.

Prominent African-American performers at the turn of the century included Ernest Hogan, the Luca family, and Sam Lucas. In 1893 Henrietta Vinton *Davis, known for her Shakespearian recitation, produced a play about Dessalines at the Haitian Pavilion in *Chicago's Columbian Exposition. Written by William Edgar Easton, this play is reminiscent of Brown's *The Drama of King Shotaway* in its focus on a historical theme specific to the Americas. *The Octoroons*, featuring a *chorus of African-American women in contrast to the minstrel show format, was also performed in Chicago during the Exposition. Its director's next show, *Oriental America*, was one of the first all-black *musical productions on Broadway; opening in 1896, it set a standard for later shows and troupes. Successful musical shows by Bert *Williams and George Walker, probably the most popular musical team of the two decades following 1890, included *In Dahomey, The Sons of Ham, Abyssinia*, and *Bandana Land*. After Walker's death around 1912, Williams moved to the *Ziegfeld Follies, where he continued to wear blackface until his death ten years later.

From 1905 to 1911 one of the earliest African-American *stock companies operated in Chicago, where Charles *Gilpin, later famous for his role in *O'Neill's *The Emperor Jones*, was instrumental in attracting a company of former *vaudeville performers to the Pekin, which could accommodate over 1,000 patrons. Other Pekin personalities were Miller and Lyles, a team that paired with *Sissle and *Blake in the 1920s, and Will Marion Cook, a classically trained composer who collaborated with poet Paul Laurence Dunbar on *Clorindy*, an 1898 ragtime *operetta featuring the cakewalk. The cast was received so well that for one heady moment African-American performers believed they had broken the barrier and were on Broadway to stay.

In the same year, Bob Cole wrote and produced *A Trip to Coontown*, with a black director, writer, producer, and performers. Cole also played a key role as resident playwright and director of a New York-based stock company at the Worth Museum. Performers associated with this company appeared in many of the most important shows from the end of the nineteenth to the beginning of the twentieth century, its most prominent star being Aida Overton, who married George Walker and featured in most of the Williams and Walker productions. For a while after her husband's death, she kept the company going, performing cross-*gender roles. Cole and Johnson, the name taken by two legendary performance teams both involving Bob Cole, wrote hit songs for leading Broadway stars, including May *Irwin. *The Red Moon*, one of their last productions, played on Broadway in 1910.

In 1915 Anita Bush founded the *Lafayette Players in Harlem, the most important stock company during the Harlem Renaissance. Karamu House in Cleveland was founded the same year. In 1916 the National Association for the Advancement of Colored People produced *Rachel* in Washington, partially in response to D. W. Griffith's *film *The Birth of a Nation*. Written by Angelina Weld Grimke, *Rachel* is thought to be the first full-length drama to have a black director, black actors, a black producer, and a black playwright. *Shuffle Along*, the Sissle and Blake musical, opened in 1921 and was so popular that it was toured nationally by three companies. Responsible for promoting the careers of Joséphine *Baker, Florence *Mills, and Paul *Robeson, it also established the pattern for black musicals that followed in the 1920s and 1930s, including *Chocolate Dandies* and *Runnin' Wild*, which introduced the Charleston craze. Several smaller theatres also sprang up in Harlem during the 1920s, including the Krigwa Players, the Negro Art Theatre, and the Utopia Players.

Marc *Connelly's *Green Pastures* was a success on Broadway in 1930 with an all-black cast, and a few years later, Gertrude *Stein's *Four Saints in Three Acts* featured black performers. Nonetheless, theatrical prospects for blacks declined during the Depression. Only the vogue of the stage mammy was in the ascendant, exemplified by Ethel *Waters and Rose *McClendon: in 1939 Waters opened on Broadway in *Mamba's Daughters* and McClendon appeared several times as a mammy on Broadway in the 1930s, having first attracted notice in the 1920s. The Negro Unit of the *Federal Theatre Project, with which McClendon was associated, was the leading theatrical venue for African Americans before its closure in 1939, and several black playwrights, including Theodore Browne in Seattle and Theodore Ward in Chicago, were produced under its aegis. The Harlem Unit based at the Lafayette Theatre was one of 22 such units in major cities, presenting plays by *Shaw and Shakespeare under Orson *Welles and John *Houseman. Langston *Hughes, whose play *Mulatto* was produced in 1935, also founded several theatres: the Harlem Suitcase Players, the Skyloft in Chicago, and the Negro Arts Theater in *Los Angeles.

In the summer of 1940 Frederick *O'Neal and Abram Hill motivated a group of dramatic artists to create a permanent black acting company in Harlem: the American Negro Theatre (ANT). In 1945 their *Anna Lucasta* opened on Broadway and toured nationally for two years before being made into a film. Harry Belafonte, Alice *Childress, Ossie *Davis, Ruby *Dee, Roger Furman, Sidney Poitier, Isabel Sanford, and Clarice Taylor are some of the black actors associated with ANT, which lasted ten years. Of the nearly twenty plays produced in the ANT repertory, more than half were original, including works by Countee Cullen, Owen Dodson, and Abram Hill. The actor Canada *Lee also appeared on Broadway during the 1940s in several productions, including a significant lead role in the dramatized version of Richard Wright's *Native Son*, directed by Orson Welles.

While a few plays by black writers were staged in the 1950s, the signal event was the 1959 opening of *A Raisin in the Sun*. Lorraine *Hansberry's play had a black director, Lloyd *Richards, and a stellar black cast, including Dee, Diana Sands, Poitier, and Hattie McDaniel. In the aftermath of the Second World War, African Americans wanted change, and they were not in the mood to wait, as indicated by the play's title, taken from a line in a Langston Hughes poem on the repercussions of deferring a dream.

Finally the dam broke in the early 1960s. Black theatre was never the same after LeRoi Jones (later Amiri *Baraka) wrote *Dutchman* in 1964, followed by his *Slave Ship*, works with an unmistakable, new, and irrepressible voice. It was not a lone voice. In the early 1960s, the actor Douglas Turner *Ward bemoaned in print the dearth of black theatre companies. The foundations listened, and in 1967 he was given a chance to create one, the *Negro Ensemble Company, where playwrights such as Pearl Cleage, Philip Hayes *Dean, Lonnie *Elder III, Gus Edwards, Charles *Fuller, Paul Carter Harrison, and Joseph Walker found a home. *Genet's *The Blacks* had been performed a few years earlier in the same space with Cicely Tyson, Godfrey Cambridge, and Maya Angelou. Within walking distance, Joseph *Papp was giving black actors a greater presence in productions at the *New York Shakespeare Festival, and Adrienne *Kennedy was produced at *La Mama, established by Ellen *Stewart. Uptown in Harlem, Robert Macbeth received a grant establishing the *New Lafayette Theatre; Ed *Bullins would become resident playwright. Further downtown, Woodie *King founded the New Federal Theatre, which subsequently became a central force in black theatre; and around the time that an all-black cast performed *Hello, Dolly!* on Broadway, actresses Rosetta Le Noire, Vinnette *Carroll, and Barbara Ann Teer all founded New York theatres. The decade ended with Charles *Gordone becoming the first black playwright to receive a Pulitzer Prize, for *No Place to Be Somebody*.

The Wiz, a black version of *The Wizard of Oz*, made a big splash in 1975, but the most significant breakthrough of this decade was Ntozake *Shange's *for colored girls*, produced jointly by Woodie King and Papp before moving to Broadway in 1976, where it stayed several years before an international tour. Other notable ventures were Carroll's *Your Arm's Too Short to Box with God* and Dean's *Robeson* (with James Earl *Jones). Within six years of the establishment of the Black Theatre Alliance, over 50 theatres had joined, but when arts funding was cut at the end of the decade few remained. Even NEC, the leading black theatre in the 1960s and early 1970s, fell victim to *finance. White theatres began to receive support for a token number of black shows per season. One black *regional theatre, *Crossroads in New Jersey, came to attention when it produced *The Colored Museum* by George *Wolfe in 1986.

At the beginning of the 1980s, Charles Fuller's *A Soldier's Story* earned a Pulitzer and was made into a film, while a new energy emerged in August *Wilson, whose work was nurtured by Richards at the *Yale School of Drama and at the *Eugene O'Neill Theatre Center. Wilson is a playwright with longevity and epic vision. He launched a cycle of *historical dramas from the perspective of the black community in Pittsburgh, and at the beginning of the twenty-first century saw his eighth play on Broadway. His works have won numerous *awards.

In the 1990s three new women playwrights moved into the limelight: Kia Corthron, Suzan-Lori *Parks, and Anna Deavere *Smith. The last two were nurtured at the New York Shakespeare Festival, now headed by Wolfe. Smith acts in her own *documentary dramas about racial malaise in America. Her two most significant works have been about contemporary race riots: *Fires in the Mirror* (1993) and *Twilight: Los Angeles, 1992* (1993). Parks is interested in revamping African-American history in works such as *The Death of the Last Black Man in the Whole Entire World* (1990), *The America Play* (1995), and *Topdog/Underdog* (2001). Corthron writes contemporary problem plays (*Breath, Boom*, 2000; *Safe Box*, 2001) focused on social maladjustment issues such as drugs, gangs, homelessness, abortion, and suicide. She has been produced at the *Manhattan Theatre Club, the *Goodman in Chicago, and the *Royal Court in *London, among other venues.

The relative lack of foundation support for African-American theatre was the key issue that emerged during a 1997 public debate, which Smith moderated, between August Wilson and the critic and producer Robert *Brustein, in which Wilson called for the establishment of a network of black theatres separate from the dominant regional theatre movement. His proposal underscored the fact that the difficulties of black theatre are primarily institutional. In an environment of protracted struggle, African-American theatre can boast of admirable progress but it still stands outside, in the backyard of the nation, without an established centre where it can develop and sustain itself. Being built up and then falling down, that has been the history of African-American companies in the twentieth century. Longevity and cultural autonomy are the main challenges for the future.   BBL

Hay Samuel, *African American Theatre* (Cambridge, 1994)

AFRICAN COMPANY

Repertory theatre in *New York, founded in 1816 by William Henry *Brown, who in 1822 constructed a 300-seat theatre in Greenwich Village. The actor James Hewlett, whose career outlasted the theatre, was popular in the company's Shakespeare productions, especially *Richard III*. Ira *Aldridge also began his career here. Though spectators were racially segregated, as was the custom at other *playhouses, at the African Company whites tended to be noisy and disruptive, which prompted the police to close the enterprise. Brown's *King Shotaway* (now lost), most likely the first play written by an African American, was a regular feature in the repertory. *See* AFRICAN-AMERICAN THEATRE.   BBL

AFTERPIECE

In the English theatre the afterpiece was introduced in the Restoration period to attract an *audience and to leaven the mainpiece preceding it, especially if this was a *tragedy. Commonly in one act and light of touch, the afterpiece could be a *farce, a *pantomime, or *musical in nature. It remained a fixture of the *playbill all through the eighteenth and early nineteenth centuries; after that a bill could consist of several items.
                                                                MRB

AGATE, JAMES (1877–1947)

English critic and essayist, at his most influential in the period 1923–47 during his long association with the *Sunday Times*. He began his career at the *Manchester Guardian* under the guidance of C. E. Montague in 1907. In 1921 he was appointed to the *Saturday Review*, the position once held by *Shaw and Max *Beerbohm. Although Agate wrote several novels, it was as an essayist covering life in *London, the theatre, and personalities in general that he became most influential. From 1925 to 1935 he was the theatre critic for the BBC. He had much in common with Clement *Scott and A. B. *Walkley. He admired the power Scott had enjoyed on the *Daily Telegraph* during the last third of the nineteenth century, and enjoyed Walkley's elitism and francophilia on *The Times* during the late Victorian and Edwardian periods. Agate sought to position himself in that tradition, and his *criticism consequently is verbose and self-indulgent but hugely entertaining and revealing.   VEE

AGATHON (c.450–c.399 BC)

Athenian tragedian. His elaborately antithetical style (influenced by the sophist Gorgias) and his self-conscious poetic persona were parodied by *Aristophanes and Plato. The first tragedian to compose a play with fictional rather than mythological characters (the *Antheus*), he also introduced the chromatic scale to his musical scores for *tragedy.   JMM

AGITPROP

A form of political theatre which presents urgent social issues from a partisan viewpoint by means of bold rhetorical techniques. Agitprop aims to inform and mobilize its *audience. The term derives from the Russian name for the Department of Agitation and Propaganda established in 1920 by the Soviet Communist Party, but it has been applied retrospectively to similar phenomena from earlier periods. In the inter-war years agitprop was associated with Marxist politics. While So-

viet agitprop theatre troupes promoted state policy, their more Western counterparts addressed issues ranging from industrial action to the legalization of abortion and racial discrimination. The troupes *toured widely, performing at political meetings or more spontaneously in places such as streets and tenement courtyards (*see* STREET THEATRE). Agitprop presentations were structured as a series of punchy and fast-moving sketches containing references to topical and local news. Intelligibility was ensured by sloganistic banners, songs, mass chants, heroic tableaux, stereotyped or satirical characterizations, emblematic *props and *costumes, direct address, and audience participation. Financial restraints and the demands of touring fostered an emphasis on the ensemble, and often groups tried to combine national popular traditions with *avant-garde experimentation. The rise of *fascism and economic stabilization after the Depression contributed to the demise of inter-war agitprop. Since then it has increasingly served political activists, from the anti-Vietnam War and civil rights demonstrators of the 1960s to *feminist and AIDS awareness campaigners. In both developing and affluent countries agitprop continues to provide an educational vehicle at moments of crisis and change. *See also* POLITICS AND THEATRE; OPPRESSED, THEATRE OF THE.   MM

AGON

A Greek term originally meaning 'assembly', especially an assembly to watch athletic events, *agon* came to refer to the competition itself. In the case of dramatic competition, it also referred to the contest between *actors (*agonistes*) and eventually, by association, to the conflict between *characters in a *drama. In *Aristophanic *comedy, the *agon* was a formal part of the play in which characters debated a topical issue. This *agon* at the centre of *Greek drama also pointed to its supposed origins in the myth of the dying-and-reviving god *Dionysus, and in the *ritual combat between the forces of life and death. So seemingly integral was *agon* to the forms and origins of Greek drama that Western dramatic *theory has deemed conflict an essential *dramaturgical principle. The structural analysis of traditional drama has been concerned largely with the development and resolution of dramatic conflict. Usual typologies find the central character (*protagonist) in a drama in conflict with some power or principle beyond human control, with a society that denies individual integrity, with another character over matters ranging from a mutual love interest to philosophical differences, or with opposing thoughts or feelings within him- or herself. Freudian psychology added to internal conflict psychopathological conflict, wherein the conflict is between conscious intention and subconscious impulse (*see* PSYCHOANALYTIC CRITICISM). It has been objected that the agonistic principle is not applicable to all drama, that it is irrelevant, for instance, to the so-called theatre of the *absurd, to *epic theatre, and to much Asian theatre. Nevertheless, so flexible is the notion, and so ingrained in

Western theory, that it persists in both dramatic analysis and *audience expectation.   RWV

AGUIRRE, ISIDORA (1919–)

Leading Chilean playwright and novelist. She became known in 1955 with *Carolina* and her talent was confirmed in *Las Pascualas* (1957), based on a Chilean legend. Her *musical *La pérgola de las flores* (*The Flower Market*, 1960), produced by the Catholic University Theatre Group in *Santiago, became an instant hit and was taken on European *tour. Subsequently, Aguirre's plays have been closely modelled on *Brecht's *epic theatre. In *Los papeleros* (*The Paper Gatherers*, 1963) and *Los que van quedando en el camino* (*Those Left by the Wayside*, 1969: the title is a quotation from Che Guevara), she continued her socio-political concerns with a more explicit leftist ideology. In *Lautaro* (1982), she used an epic fictitious *character to refer to the situation of the Mapuche people, and in *Retablo de Yumbel* (*Yumbel's Altarpiece*, 1986) the victims of the dictatorship are likened to St Sebastian in his martyrdom. Her latest plays are *Manuel* (1999), whose main character is a legendary hero of Chilean independence; and *Marrichiweu* (2000), in which she returns to the Mapuche theme.   MAR

AHARYA

A generic category referring to costumes, make-up, body painting, ornamentation, and the use of stage properties in traditional *Indian performances. The details of jewellery, headdresses, crowns, and garlands are described in ancient treaties like the *Natyasastra* in relation to the status, location, and temperament of specific *characters. Drawing on the primary colours of black, blue, yellow, and red, there are also specific visual codes for the *make-up of gods, noble characters, *villains, demons, and peoples of different regions. In *kathakali*, for instance, the noble characters (*paccha*) have their faces painted green, while demons are painted black (*kari*). There are also different colours of the beard—'red beard' (*chuvanna thadi*) for villainous characters like Duhsasana, and 'white beard' (*vella thadi*) for more venerable figures like Hanuman and Nandikeswara. *See also* ABHINAYA.   LSR/RB

AIDOO, AMA ATA (1942–)

Ghanaian dramatist. *The Dilemma of a Ghost*, premièred at the University of Ghana, Legon (1962), explores the reaction of a Ghanaian family when their son brings home an African-American wife. In both form and theme the play is a trenchant, witty dialogue between Ghanaian and non-Ghanaian theatrical forms and social expectations. All Aidoo's work has an intense oral quality and her short story 'For Whom Things Did Not Change' has been effectively dramatized. Her only other play,

Anowa (1968), stresses the limited opportunities open to women in an episodic form, making use of choric figures to explore ethical issues connected with the slave trade.   JMG

AIKEN, GEORGE L. (1830–76)

American actor and playwright. Born in *Boston, Aiken took to the stage as a child with his actor father. After a three-year period away from the theatre, the 17-year-old Aiken joined his cousin and her *manager husband, George C. Howard, to embark upon a professional acting career. Following them from Providence, Rhode Island, to Troy, New York, in 1851, he was given the task of adapting Stowe's anti-slavery novel *Uncle Tom's Cabin*. Initially, Aiken wrote a three-act version ending with the death of Eva, a role designed for Howard's daughter Cordelia. The play's immediate success upon its 1852 debut occasioned Aiken's adding another three acts that conclude with the death of Tom at the hands of the villain Simon Legree. This melded, six-act version became the definitive adaptation. Aiken's subsequent plays and adaptations were unsuccessful, and he retired from acting in 1871.   GAR

AILEY, ALVIN (1931–89)

American dancer and choreographer. With a background in modern *dance and jazz, Ailey began during the civil rights era to make dances about the lives of African Americans, and the company he formed in 1958 became internationally known as an emblem of black dignity. *Revelations* (1960), his signature work, set to traditional spirituals, was a deeply moving, ultimately exuberant celebration of African-American survival and community. He choreographed dances to music by important black jazz composers, including Duke Ellington and Charlie Parker, and by many other composers, including Leonard *Bernstein, in an emotionally intense style. His works ranged from abstract lyricism to highly theatrical *character studies. His company, directed after his death by former lead dancer Judith Jamison, performs a wide repertory of dances by both black and white choreographers, in the tradition of Ailey's own ecumenical practice and his belief in the power of dance to transcend racial divisions.   SB

AINLEY, HENRY (1879–1945)

English actor, noted for the beauty and musicality of his voice, who first won success playing Paolo in Stephen *Phillips's *Paolo and Francesca* (1902). Though excelling in Shakespearian romantic roles, Ainley was frequently attracted to demanding experimental ventures: Hippolytus (1904), Orestes (1906), Malvolio and Leontes (1912), and the Reader in *The Dynasts* (1914) for Granville *Barker; Young Cuchulain for *Yeats (1916); and J. E. Flecker's Hassan (1923). The intensity of his performances led twice to breakdowns forcing him to retire, the first following his Macbeth of 1926. His late achievements included the husband in *Ervine's *The First Mrs Fraser* (1929) and the Archangel in *Bridie's *Tobias and the Angel* (1930).

RAC

AJOKA

Founded in 1980 by Madeeha Gauhar in Lahore, Ajoka is one of the leading *alternative theatre groups of *Pakistan. The group, whose name means 'dawn of a new day' in Punjabi, began with *street theatre as a protest against the cultural repression of General Zia-ul-Haque's military and Islamist regime. When the former trade unionist, political activist, and playwright Shahid Nadeem joined Ajoka, it developed into a professional company producing plays by Nadeem on social issues like family murders, rape, religious repression, the population explosion, and female education. It has expanded its repertoire to translations and adaptations, especially of the plays of *Brecht, whose themes have major relevance to South Asia. Gauhar has thrived in an atmosphere that is particularly inhospitable to female performers and directors. She and Nadeem (who are now married) are ferociously antagonistic to commercial theatre, which they see as intellectually and artistically bankrupt. Some of Ajoka's most popular plays have been *Barri* (*Acquittal*), *Eik Thi Nani* (*There Was Once a Grandmother*), *Dhee Rani* (*Queenly Daughter*), *Jum Jum Jeevay Jummanpura* (*Population Explosion in Jummanpura*), *Bala King* (an adaptation of Brecht's *The Resistible Rise of Arturo Ui*), and *Dukhini* (*The Abused Woman*), performed bilingually in Urdu and Bengali. Their first English-language production was *Acquittal*, translated from Urdu-Punjabi by Tahira Naqv and performed at the *Los Angeles Biennale (2001). *See also* PUNJAB LOK REHAS.

FAK

AKALAITIS, JOANNE (1937–)

American director and actor. Born in Cicero, Illinois, she studied philosophy at the University of Chicago and Stanford. She *trained in *New York, and travelled with her then fiancé, composer Philip *Glass, to *Paris in 1965, where she worked with other American actors on productions of *Beckett's plays, and studied with Jerzy *Grotowski in 1969. In 1970 with those American colleagues, she formed the theatre *collective *Mabou Mines. The group's early productions at *La Mama in New York caught the eye of Joseph *Papp, who invited them to work at his *New York Shakespeare Festival (NYSF) in 1976. Akalaitis directed and co-created many productions with Mabou Mines, including *Dressed Like an Egg* (1977), based on the writings of Colette, and *Dead End Kids: A History of Nuclear Power* (1981). Beckett disowned Akalaitis's 1984 production of *Endgame* at the *American Repertory Theatre because she deviated from his strict *stage directions. In 1991, Papp named Akalaitis his suc-

cessor at the NYSF, a move that shocked the theatre world because of her lack of administrative experience and specific artistic vision. The NYSF board cited these reasons when they fired her in 1993; it was also said that her gruff manner alienated many. She has since directed many plays and *operas around the USA, and in 1999 became director of the Theatre Department at Bard College. She is the recipient of five Obie *awards and the *National Endowment for the Arts award for sustained artistic achievement.

KF

AKIMOTO MATSUYO (1911–2001)

One of the leading women playwrights of post-war *Japan, Akimoto was a student of the leftist playwright Miyoshi Jūrō (1902–58), and her debut work, *A Sprinkling of Dust*, was published in 1947. She wrote for the major *shingeki* companies and from 1967 to 1970 ran her own company, the Theatre Troupe (Engekiza). Many of her plays, like *Muraoka Iheiji* (1960), *Kaison, Priest of Hitachi* (1967; trans. 1988), and *The Cape of Seven* (1975), are deft critiques of modern Japanese militarism and patriarchy. She also wrote a number of plays based loosely on classical puppet (*bunraku) and *kabuki dramas, the most successful of which, *Double Suicide after Chikamatsu* (1979), was directed by *Ninagawa Yukio and toured Europe in 1989.

CP

AKIMOV, NIKOLAI (1901–68)

Russian/Soviet director and designer. *Artistic director of the Leningrad (*St Petersburg) Theatre of Comedy from 1935 until 1968 (a post from which he was briefly ousted during the 1940s), Akimov is probably best remembered for his 'eccentric' *Moscow production of *Hamlet* (1932), which he designed himself with a paunchy comedian, Anatoly Goryunov, in the title role and with distinctive music provided by Dmitry Shostakovich. The production incurred the wrath of the theatrical establishment and led to Akimov's Leningrad 'exile', where he became especially associated, during the 1940s, with the satirical plays of Evgeny *Shvarts, *The Dragon*, *The Shadow*, and *The Naked King*. As a designer, Akimov's special brand of the colourfully comic *grotesque lent itself well to productions staged in a playfully idiosyncratic style of works by *Sukhovo-Kobylin, Eduardo *De Filippo, *Dürrenmatt, Shvarts, and *Byron (an adaptation of *Don Juan*) during the 1960s.

NW

AKINS, ZOË (1886–1958)

American playwright and screenwriter. Akins first came to wide attention with the drama *Déclassé* (1919) which starred Ethel *Barrymore. She wrote a series of Broadway successes during the 1920s but achieved her greatest fame for the 1935 adaptation of Edna Ferber's novel *The Old Maid*, which starred

Judith *Anderson in a run of 305 performances. A substantial *melodrama about two self-sacrificing women, the play was awarded the Pulitzer Prize; the decision outraged many critics who saw it as sentimental and inferior to *Hellman's *The Children's Hour*. The controversy led to the formation of the Drama Critics Circle, which gives its own annual *award. Akins was screenwriter for such *films as *Morning Glory* (1932) and *Camille* (1937).   MAF

AKSYONOV, VASILY (1932–   )

Russian/Soviet dramatist and prose writer, closely identified with the new youth movement of the 1960s, whose first play, *Always on Sale*, was staged at the popular *Sovremennik (Contemporary) Theatre in 1965. A creative artist in the tradition of satirists from *Gogol to *Bulgakov, Aksyonov fell foul of the Soviet authorities and emigrated in 1980. Settling in the United States, he broadened the scope of his *satire to include ironic commentary on aspects of American culture and society. His *comedies *The Heron* and *The Four Temperaments* were published in English in 1987, the first having been staged in *Paris in 1984. *The Heron*, 'a comedy with intermissions and rhymes', is set in a trade-union holiday home on the Baltic; *The Four Temperaments*, 'a comedy in ten tableaux', is set 'first in the distant future, then outside of space and time, and finally in the present'.   NW

ALARCÓN Y MENDOZA, JUAN RUIZ DE See RUIZ DE ALARCÓN Y MENDOZA, JUAN.

ALBEE, EDWARD (1928–   )

American playwright. Namesake of the American *vaudeville tycoon Edward F. *Albee, into whose family he was adopted, Albee rejected the authority of his wealthy family and any type of school. He turned away from the Albees' patrician pretensions, but throughout his career has subverted the manners and diction of their milieu in his plays. Fleeing to Greenwich Village in the 1950s, he took a series of menial jobs, including delivering Western Union telegrams. He struggled as a poet, but turned to playwriting at Thornton *Wilder's urging. Albee's earliest works were identified as *absurdist, but his later, longer dramas defy categorization. His first play, *The Zoo Story* (1959), was produced in Germany, and the German-speaking theatre world has revered him ever since. *The Zoo Story* is an intense confrontation between two men, ostensibly over a park bench, that touches on emotional and philosophical concerns of modern life. In 1960 both *The Zoo Story* and *The Sand Box* were produced *Off-Broadway and Albee was critically anointed. His next plays, *The American Dream* and *The Death of Bessie Smith* (both 1961), were hailed as further evidence that he was part of the absurdist trend. He responded with a trenchant essay, 'Which Theatre Is the Absurd One?', published in the *New York Times* shortly before *Who's Afraid of Virginia Woolf?* opened on Broadway (1962). Albee's most successful play, and a crucial post-war American drama, it involves a quartet of married 'college-type types', whose witty and searing games dramatize truth and illusion on an intellectual and emotional level. The play's psychic bloodletting has been declared everything from Cold War parable to neo-*Strindbergian *realism.

Albee has frequently adapted non-dramatic literature, but of such efforts, only *The Ballad of the Sad Café* (1963) has achieved measurable success. In 1964 Albee's career turned. Baffled by the complexity of *Tiny Alice*, actors, critics, and *audiences complained that he was deliberately opaque. Always impatient with his critics and never hesitant to chastise them, Albee publicly called the reviewers too stupid and the actors too lazy to understand his play. For the next three decades, in spite of two Pulitzer Prizes (*A Delicate Balance*, 1967; *Seascape*, 1975), Albee seemed to alienate his audience by writing remonstrative and untheatrical dramas. Play after play was rejected by the commercial establishment, and after the debacle of *The Man Who Had Three Arms* (1983) Albee gave up on *New York, though he continued writing and overseeing productions in *Vienna, *London, and in American *regional theatres. Then *Three Tall Women*'s ecstatic critical reception in 1994 reestablished his Broadway reputation. A third Pulitzer for this play, a Kennedy Center lifetime achievement *award in 1996, and the National Medal of Arts in 1997 secured Albee's enthronement as one of the greatest living American playwrights. In 2001 *The Play about the Baby* won acclaim, even as it teased audiences with its seeming reference to the famous non-existent child in *Who's Afraid of Virginia Woolf?* Clearly audiences could now accept Albee's richly allusive *dialogue as well as his challenging symbolism.   TFC

ALBEE, EDWARD FRANKLIN (1857–1930)

American *manager, co-founder of the most successful *vaudeville agency in North America. Albee was a *ticket-seller in a *circus in 1885 when he formed a partnership with B. F. *Keith, and together they opened the *Boston Bijou Theatre, offering continuous vaudeville entertainment for a single price. By maintaining high standards, Albee appealed to the middle-class *audience and deliberately sought to make *variety a respectable, family entertainment. As general manager of the Keith–Albee circuit, he directed operations and oversaw its expansion. By the 1920s Albee's company controlled over 400 vaudeville theatres and employed as many as 20,000 acts annually. With Keith, he formed the United Booking Office in 1906, assuring a virtual monopoly on vaudeville in the USA and Canada. His adopted son is the playwright Edward *Albee.   PAD

ALBERTA THEATRE PROJECTS

Canadian company, founded in Calgary in 1972 by Douglas Riske and Lucille Wagner to develop theatre for *youth, ATP also committed itself to developing the work of regional artists for adult *audiences (1973–83). Under Michael Dobbins (1983–99) and Bob White (1999–), ATP left the 198-seat Canmore Opera House for a new 465-seat facility (1985), rededicated its main stage to high-quality productions of contemporary work, and committed it to new play development through alternative programmes, notably its joint summer writers' colony with the Banff Centre (1997) and annual PanCanadian playRites Festival (1987), the largest Canadian festival dedicated to mounting full mainstage productions of new Canadian plays.

MJD

ALBERTAZZI, GIORGIO (1925–)

Italian actor who made his debut in Florence in plays by Alfred de *Musset, John *Ford, and the *early modern Italian playwright Bernardo Dovizi da Bibbiena. In 1949 Luchino *Visconti cast him as Alexander in *Troilus and Cressida* and subsequently offered him a place in the Compagnia del Teatro Nazionale. Albertazzi's acting was noted for intensity and incisiveness. In 1956 he formed his own company with the actress Anna Proclemer with whom, for over twenty years, he played works by Shakespeare, *Pirandello, *Ibsen, *Camus, and many others.

DMcM

ALBERY, JAMES (1838–89)

English playwright. Influenced by the *comedies of Tom *Robertson, Albery wrote the sentimental *Two Roses* (1870), a success for Henry *Irving as Digby Grant, the comically proud and hypocritical father of two idealized young women. The greatest hit of Irving's career came as the tormented innkeeper Mathias in Albery's version of a French *melodrama, *The Bells* (1871). One of the first adaptations of risqué French *farce, *The Pink Dominos* (1877), for Charles *Wyndham was also successful. The rest of Albery's work was dismissed by his contemporaries as failing to live up to his early promise.

MRB

ALCALÁ DE HENARES, CORRAL DE

Spain's oldest surviving theatre, in Alcalá de Henares near *Madrid, was discovered in 1981, when a disused cinema was found to contain substantial remains of a small *playhouse built in 1601 by a local carpenter, Francisco Sánchez, in a yard behind a house in the market square. Modelled on the Corral de la *Cruz, it had an open-air patio and a roofed *stage, flanked by *gradas* (raked seating), with two tiers of galleries and *boxes and a *tiring house with balcony and machine loft; the stage, the yard and well, numerous timbers, and two boxes beside the stage survive from this phase. In 1769 the yard was roofed and a *proscenium arch installed. In 1831 the venue was converted into a *romantic theatre with elliptical tiers of boxes, called the Teatro Cervantes, and from 1927 to 1972 it was used as a cinema. It was restored in the 1990s, preserving its intriguing combination of structures from three centuries of Spanish theatre history. *See* CORRALES DE COMEDIAS.

CD

ALDREDGE, THEONI V. (1932–)

Greek-American costume designer. Born Theoni Athanasiou Vachlioti in Thessaloniki, in 1949 she embarked on studies at *Chicago's *Goodman Theatre School, where she met her husband, actor Tom Aldredge. For Chicago companies she designed *costumes for seven plays from 1950 to 1957, when she moved to *New York. In 1962 she began a long association with Joseph *Papp's Public Theatre and *New York Shakespeare Festival, which brought her an Obie *award in 1974. Other important *Off-Broadway productions include *Heloise* (1958), *Serjeant Musgrave's Dance* (1966), and *The Basic Training of Pavlo Hummel* (1971). Among her more than 150 Broadway shows are *Who's Afraid of Virginia Woolf?* (1962), the Pulitzer Prize-winning *That Championship Season* (1972), *The Belle of Amherst* (1976), and *Taking Sides* (1996). She has received thirteen Tony award nominations for best costume design—winning for three major *musicals: *Annie* (1977), *Barnum* (1980), and *La Cage aux Folles* (1984). Other musicals include *A Chorus Line* (1975), *Dreamgirls*, and *42nd Street* (both 1982).

CT

ALDRIDGE, IRA (1807–67)

*African-American actor. As a boy in *New York he worked backstage at the Chatham Theatre and studied the performances of major actors at the *Park. He launched his career at the *African Company in *Sheridan's adaptation of *Kotzebue's *Pizarro*, but, convinced he could not have an acting career in America because of race laws and racial bias, he left in 1824 for England, working the *minor and provincial theatres. He acted in a variety of plays about race, including *Othello*, and, taking the abolitionist cause abroad, often concluded his performances with anti-slavery songs. Shortly he was appearing in white roles as well as black in plays such as *Bickerstaffe's *The Padlock, A Slave's Revenge, Titus Andronicus, The Merchant of Venice, King Lear*, and *Richard III*. His reputation increased after he replaced the dying Edmund *Kean as Othello (*Covent Garden, 1833). In 1852 he began the first of several continental tours, performing in *Berlin, *Budapest, *Munich, *Prague, and *Vienna. In 1858 he played Richard III, Othello, and Macbeth in Serbia and *toured Russia. The recipient of many foreign honours, Aldridge was the first African-American theatre artist to receive wide international recognition—though not in his own country. BBL

ALDWYCH THEATRE

*London *playhouse at the eastern end of the Strand, built in 1905 for Seymour *Hicks and Charles *Frohman. Though it saw the first English productions of *Chekhov's *The Cherry Orchard* (1911) and *Williams's *A Streetcar Named Desire* (1949), its history has been undistinguished except for two periods. Between 1924 and 1932 it housed the seasons of *farces mostly written by Ben *Travers and starring Tom Walls, Ralph Lynn, and J. Robertson *Hare, collectively known as the Aldwych farces. From 1960 to 1982 it became the London home of the *Royal Shakespeare Company. During this period significant English premières took place: *Pinter's *The Homecoming* and *Old Times*, *Genet's *The Balcony*, *Brecht's *The Caucasian Chalk Circle*, and Peter *Weiss's *Marat/Sade*. Between 1964 and 1973 the theatre also housed Peter *Daubeny's World Theatre seasons, which brought many European, South African, and *Japanese companies to England for the first time. VEE

ALEGRÍA, ALONSO (1940–)

Peruvian playwright and director, who, as organizer and director of the Popular National Theatre (Lima, 1971–8), accomplished far-reaching aesthetic reforms to government-subsidized work. Affiliated with the Lima Theatre Club (1960) and to dramatists such as Reynaldo D'Amore and Edgard *Guillén, Alegría received a degree from the *Yale School of Drama (1969), taught *directing in the United States, and then joined the Catholic University of Peru. He has staged *Remigio the Grave-Digger* (Peruvian National Theatre award, 1965), *Niagara Crossing* (Cuba's *Casa de las Américas *award, 1969), *The White Suit* (1981), *Daniela Frank* (1984), and *Encounter with Faust* (1999). LRG

ALEICHEM, SHOLEM (SHOLEM RABINOWITZ) (1859–1916)

Ukrainian *Yiddish writer who settled in New York in 1907. Aleichem began to write playlets in 1887, shifting in 1894 to full-length plays, mostly based on his own stories and novels. His first important theatrical success came in 1905 with the *Warsaw production of *Scattered and Dispersed*. His American theatrical career began poorly in 1907 with mediocre productions by Jacob P. *Adler and Boris *Tomashefsky, and he did not live to see his folksy *tragicomedies become the high points of the Jewish repertoire worldwide, with companies as diverse as the *Yiddish Art Theatre, *ARTEF, the *Moscow State Yiddish Theatre, and the *Habima. Aleichem's best-known plays include *People, Stempenyu, Hard to Be a Jew, The Big Win*, and *The Treasure. Tevye the Milkman*, one of Maurice *Schwartz's great roles on stage (1919) and *film (1939), served as the basis for Jerry *Bock's *musical *Fiddler on the Roof* (1964). EN

ALEKSANDRINSKY THEATRE

Named after Nicholas I's consort, Empress Aleksandra, the *playhouse was one of two imperial theatres in *St Petersburg and housed its principal acting company. The original troupe, headed by Ivan *Dmitrevsky, performed plays written by eighteenth-century Russian dramatists in the *neoclassical styles of Western Europe, as well as *melodramas, comic *operas, and Russian *vaudevilles. The company also staged the première of Denis *Fonvizin's *Nedorosl'* (*The Minor*) in 1782. The theatre's present building, designed by Carlo Rossi in magnificent Palladian style with an original capacity of 1,400, stands on Ostrovsky Square off Nevsky Prospekt and opened in 1832. First performances of *Griboedov's comic classic *Gore ot uma* (*Woe from Wit*) and *Gogol's *Revizor* (*The Government Inspector*) were given here in 1831 and 1836 respectively, as well as premières, often delayed by *censorship, of *Lermontov's *Masquerade* (1852), *Ostrovsky's *Thunderstorm* (1859), *Pushkin's *Boris Godunov* (1870), *Turgenev's *A Month in the Country* (1879), and *Tolstoy's *The Power of Darkness* (1895). Outstanding actors at the theatre during the nineteenth century included Vasily *Karatygin, Maria Savina, Vladimir Davydov, and Vera *Komissarzhevskaya, who played Nina in the disastrous première of *Chekhov's *The Seagull* (1896). Between 1908 and the 1917 revolution the theatre was headed by *Meyerhold, who staged twenty productions, including a lavish revival of *Masquerade* in 1917 with Yury Yuriev as Arbenin. In 1919 the Soviet government awarded the theatre 'academic' status and in 1920 it was rechristened the Pushkin Theatre. NW

ALEOTTI, GIOVAN BATTISTA (1546–1636)

Italian architect and engineer in the service of the Estense family who constructed many secular and religious buildings in Ferrara, in the manner of *Palladio. He showed more originality as a designer of theatre machines and stage sets (*see* SCENOGRAPHY), both for dramatic performances and public *spectacles. In 1605–6 he constructed his first permanent *playhouse, in the old granary of Cesare d'Este, followed in 1610 by a temporary stage in the Castello Estense with a *scaenae frons* inspired by the Teatro *Olimpico. In 1612 this structure, with an *auditorium for 4,000, was turned into a permanent theatre. Aleotti's masterpiece was the *proscenium-arch theatre of the Pilotta in Parma, known as Teatro *Farnese (constructed 1618–19).

GB

ALEPH, TEATRO

Chilean theatre company founded in 1969. Their collectively created productions have been a combination of *vaudeville, *musicals, and *Brechtian theatre. Their first works were *Había una vez un rey* (*Once upon a Time There Was a King*, 1972) and *Pasión y muerte de Casimiro Peñafleta* (*The Passion and Death of Casimiro Peñafleta*, 1972), both designed to reflect the cultural policies of the Allende regime. In 1974, because of the explicit references to Allende's fall and the military coup in *Y al principio existía la vida* (*And in the Beginning Was Life*), director Oscar Castro was jailed and then exiled. The group resumed its work in France with *The Incredible and Sad Story of General Peñalosa and the Exile Mateluna* (1976), the story of a dictator and a Latin American exile in *Paris. During the post-dictatorship period the group remained in France, focusing on French racial and immigration problems.   MAR

ALEXANDER, GEORGE (1858–1918)

English *actor-manager. Born George Samson, Alexander first went on stage at Nottingham in 1879, and joined *Irving at the *Lyceum in 1881. He accompanied him to America in 1884 and later distinguished himself as Faust (1885) and Macduff (1888). Alexander managed the Avenue Theatre in 1890 and then embarked upon a long tenure of the *St James's (1891–1918). Here he did his best work, both as an actor and a *manager, producing *Wilde's *Lady Windermere's Fan* (1892) and *The Importance of Being Earnest* (1895), in which he played Jack Worthing. He also staged important plays by *Pinero, such as *The Second Mrs Tanqueray* (1893), *His House in Order* (1902), and *Mid-Channel* (1909). Other dramatists whose plays were seen at the St James's included Stephen *Phillips, Jerome K. Jerome, and Henry *James, whose *Guy Domville* was withdrawn after a rowdy first night in 1895. Alexander's management was socially conservative and solidly upper middle class; the St James's was an attractive, well-run theatre with a loyal *audience. As an actor Alexander was handsome, dignified, and well bred, as successful in romantic, dashing parts as he was in troubled husbands. He was knighted in 1911.   MRB

ALEXANDER, JANE (1939–)

American actress and arts administrator. Alexander headed the *National Endowment for the Arts (1993–7), the first working artist to do so. Her appointment coincided with determined efforts to abolish all governmental support for arts and culture, led by a coalition of political and religious conservatives. Alexander's performance as President Bill Clinton's arts spokesperson received mixed evaluations: the NEA survived, but in a vastly reduced state, and early in her term she often seemed bewildered by political attacks. She eventually proved an effective advocate for the arts with the general public, less so with her determined opponents in Congress and their supporters. Alexander began her acting career in *regional theatres, coming to national attention in Howard Sackler's *The Great White Hope* (1967), first at *Arena Stage in Washington, then in a commercial Broadway transfer. Major roles on stage (*Shadowlands*, 1990; *The Sisters Rosensweig*, 1992), *film (*The Cider House Rules*, 1999; *Brubaker*, 1980), and *television (*Playing for Time*, 1980; *In Love and War*, 1987) followed, with Alexander's patrician appearance and cool emotional power usually featured.   AW

ALFIERI, VITTORIO (1749–1803)

Italy's pre-eminent writer of eighteenth-century *neoclassical *tragedy was born into the French-speaking nobility of Piedmont. After a youth he later called misspent, he turned to literary pursuits and in 1774 staged *Cleopatra*, his first play. He moved to Florence to improve his knowledge of pure Tuscan, and there met the Countess d'Albany, wife of Bonnie Prince Charlie, and the 'worthy love' he had been seeking. Alfieri also wrote several treatises denouncing tyranny and advocating the freedom of the writer, as well as several *comedies, an autobiography, and volumes of verse. Although his hatred of despotism links Alfieri with the Enlightenment, his cult of individualism and portrayal of overwhelming strength of feeling have led to his being seen as a precursor of *romanticism. He accepted unquestioningly the *Aristotelian *unities, eliminated the Racinian *confidant to focus on the *protagonists alone, and stated that his ideal was tragedy 'as dark and fierce as nature permits and with all the fire that is in me'. His tragedies were the fruit of meticulous planning, and all went through three stages—initial conception, prose draft, and versification. The cliché 'titanic' is routinely employed by critics to describe the great, despotic protagonists against whom the younger heroes struggle, even if Alfieri is ambiguous in his depiction of these supposed *villains. In *Filippo* (1780), which pits Don Carlos against his tyrannical father, Philip II of Spain, the struggle is external, but in his finest works, *Saul* (1782) and *Mirra* (1786), his protagonists are at war with themselves.   JF

ALFREDS, MIKE (1934–)

English director. In 1975 Alfreds founded the actor-based story-telling company Shared Experience, having previously worked in the USA (director of Playhouse in the Park, Cincinnati) and Israel. His groundbreaking adaptation of *Dickens's *Bleak House* (1977), with seven actors swapping roles and sharing the narrative, was a precursor to the *Royal Shakespeare Company's production of David *Edgar's *Nicholas Nickleby*. Other notable productions included an adaptation of Evelyn Waugh's *A Handful of Dust* (1982). After leaving Shared Experience in 1987, Alfreds worked briefly as associate director for the Royal

*National Theatre (*Chekhov's *The Cherry Orchard* and an adaptation of Eugène Sue's *The Wandering Jew*). In 1991 he became the *artistic director for the *touring Cambridge Theatre Company (renamed Method and Madness in 1995). He still emphasizes adaptations and classics, and new works by Philip Osment. To promote ensemble *acting, Method and Madness operated as a permanent touring company between 1997 and 2000, almost unique in recent British theatre.   KN

ALGIERS (AL-DJAZAIR)

Capital of Algeria and centre of its political, economic, social, and cultural life. A major port, Algiers was always open to outside influences, and its modern theatre developed, like that of other Arab cities, as a blend of Western culture and nationalism. But theatre did not easily establish a place in the cultural fabric of the city. Based on the Egyptian model of using literary Arabic and making frequent reference to Islamic history, plays of the earlier twentieth century failed to interest *audiences, who after decades of French colonialism were unable to connect with either their language or content. Despite municipal support, Tahar Ali Chérif, founder of the Al-Mouhadiba Company of Arabic Literature and Theatre, managed to present only three Arabic plays: *Recovery after the Trial* (1921), *Perfidy of Love* (1922), and *Badii* (1924). Mohamed Mansali's Attamthil Al-Arabi was no more successful with its two offerings, *For the Fatherland* (1922) and *The Conquest of Spain* (1923).

It was the *musical companies of Algiers that finally created a popular theatre independent of colonial influences. The lead singers and musicians of the Al-Moutribia Company—*Allalou, Rachid *Ksentini, and Mahieddine *Bacheterzi—were responsible for the development of Algerian theatre, Allalou doing comic sketches in the intervals of concerts of the musical company (1923–5), and proceeding to develop the Zahia-Troupe (Merry Company), which presented the first Algerian *comedies. In *Djeha* (1926), co-written with Brahim Dahmoun, Allalou found a subject that finally appealed to spectators, getting inspiration from the daily life of the city and its oral traditions. Other successful comedies dealing with everyday problems followed, including *Bou Akline* (1926), *Abou Al-Hassen* (1927), *The Fisherman and the Genie* (1928), and *The Barber of Grenada* (1931). In 1929 Ksentini and the singer Marie Soussan created a new musical comedy company bearing their names, producing *My Cousin from Istanbul* (1929), *A Hole in the Floor* (1929), *Loundja Andaloussia* (1930), and *Aicha and Bandou* (1932). While the careers of Allalou and Ksentini were relatively short, Bacheterzi worked for more than 50 years. Music and song remained the essential constituents of performance for him, but he also encouraged the Al-Moutribia to evolve into a dramatic company, with comedy as its mainstay. To inform while entertaining was his guiding principle, and his topics were contemporary issues in Muslim Algiers. *The Fake Scholars* (1927), *Not Any Longer* (1934), *The Honour* (1934), *Beni Yes, Yes* (1935), *The Traitors* (1937), *The Algerian Samson* (1937), *Cry Louder* (1937), and *The Liars* (1938) all denounce corrosive elements in society such as alcoholism, drugs, illiteracy, fanaticism, opportunism, and colonialism.

To Bacheterzi also fell the job of organizing the first indigenous producing organization, the Theatre Seasons of Algiers. In 1947 the municipal government, sensitive to the demands of nationalists, made the opera house available to Algerian artists every Friday, granting a modest subsidy to develop a professional company. *Amateur performers were drawn from companies throughout Algiers, and for Bacheterzi this was a powerful opportunity to raise the credibility of the stage. Among those actors and actresses whose talents brought a new theatrical spirit were Mohamed Touri, Sid-Ali Rouiched, Ali Abdoun, Habib Réda, Mustapha Kateb, Keltoum, Latifa, and Nouria. But everything changed with the onset of the war of liberation against France in 1954. The *opera and the Arab theatre came to an end and large numbers of artists joined the National Liberation Front, out of which was born the Théâtre National Algerien, with Kateb as *artistic director. Granted residence in the Opera in 1963, and with a company of more than 60, Kateb redefined theatre in Algiers. The slogans he employed were in tune with the times: theatre of the masses, theatre of awakening, theatre of conscience. Performances echoed current issues. Rouiched's *Hassen Terro*, for example, celebrated the fight for liberation and his *Ogress* dealt with agrarian reform; the housing crisis and rural exodus were the themes of Abdel Kader Safir's *Vacant Property*; Tone Brulin's *The Dogs* dealt with the recurrent topic of racial segregation. *Brecht was also popular. New troupes arose to meet new social circumstances, including *Masrah el Kalaa, founded in 1987 by former TNA member Ziani Chérif Ayad. But the growing instability of the country in the 1990s and the dangers this posed for its artists put brakes on their creativity and threatened even the national theatre. Ayad was called back from his voluntary exile in *Paris to direct the TNA, and planned to stage *A Summer of Ashes* in 2002, a sign perhaps of another new beginning.   MMe

ALIENATION EFFECT *See* VERFREMDUNG

ALKAZI, EBRAHIM (1925–)

Indian director and teacher. Trained at the *Royal Academy of Dramatic Art in *London, Alkazi returned to *India in 1950 and later formed the Theatre Unit in Bombay (*Mumbai), whose productions of *Antigone*, *Medea* and *Oedipus Rex*, all in English, were path-breaking for their energy, aesthetic power, and professionalism. For eight years Alkazi ran a school of dramatic art, and in 1962 became director of the *National School of Drama, New Delhi, and remained at its helm until 1977. With his emphasis on research, production coordination, and strict discipline, NSD productions set new standards, particularly in the Hindustani language. Of the 50 or so plays he directed at NSD, *Andha Yug* (*The Blind Age*, 1963), staged in the Ferozshah Kotla ruins, and *Tughlaq* (1973) in the Old Fort achieved legendary status for their innovative use of space and stunning visual impact. Exemplifying Western standards of professionalism, Alkazi's theatre was sometimes criticized for its lack of connection to Indian realities. His return to theatre in 1991, after a long self-imposed exile, was a disappointment; the productions of his *training and performance group, the Living Theatre, appeared to be in a time warp.   KJ

ALLALOU (SELLALI ALI) (1902–?)

Algerian actor, playwright, and director, one of the founders of modern Algerian theatre. A singer and popular storyteller, Allalou switched to the theatre by creating the Zahia (Merry) Troupe in 1925. The next year he staged *Djaha*, which he wrote with Dahmoun, the first Algerian *comedy. He drew his material and *characters from *The Thousand and One Nights* and popular narratives, such as those found in *Molière. Allalou's plays deal with the daily lives of ordinary people, achieving their comic effect through atmosphere and a series of puns that delighted *audiences in *Algiers. His ironic approach encompassed the heroes of Arab mythology and the venerated caliphs and their symbols. The Caliph Haroun Arrachid (the wise) became in Allalou's hands Arrachi (the corrupted), and his bodyguard Masrour (the merry one) Masroua (the epileptic). Antar Ibnchaddad (the valorous knight) became Antar alhechaychi (the smoker of hashish).   MMe

ALLEGORY

As an attribute of an artistic work, allegory is a form of extended metaphor in which objects and *characters denote meanings beyond the confines of the fiction, usually by presenting abstract ideas in terms of concrete images (although political allegory refers to real persons). In drama, the metaphor takes the form of personification of the idea, a character's allegorical significance indicated by labelling, conventional emblem, or behaviour. Allegorical interpretation is based on the assumption that true meaning lies beneath the fictive surface. Allegory is thus related to parable, which relies on analogy rather than personification, and *exemplum*, which illustrates a meaning already expressed in abstract terms. Allegory is most common in *didactic theatre: the *medieval *morality play, some baroque drama, *expressionist plays, *agitprop theatre. Although they appear two dimensional on the page, allegorical abstractions, embodied in actors, are fully three dimensional on the stage.   RWV

ALLEN, GRACIE *See* Burns, George.

ALLEN, VIOLA (1867–1948)

American actress. After her debut in Frances Hodgson Burnett's *Esmeralda* at the *Madison Square Theatre in *New York in 1882, she appeared with John *McCullough and Lawrence *Barrett before playing Desdemona and Cordelia to Tommaso *Salvini's famous Othello and Lear. In 1893 she joined Charles *Frohman's *Empire Theatre company for five seasons, then became an independent star in 1898 with her definitive vehicle, Hall Caine's *The Christian*, and Shakespearian favourites Hermione and Imogen. Over her 35-year career, much of which was self-*managed and promoted, she projected high ideals of womanly grace, charm, and ethical conviction.   KM

ALLEYN, EDWARD (1566–1626)

English actor, entrepreneur, and founder of Dulwich College. Born in *London, he was the son of a prominent inn holder and porter to the Queen. His older brother, who acted for a short time, was servant to Lord Sheffield. By 1586 Edward was a player with the Earl of Worcester's Men. Two years later, he and his brother were joint owners of playbooks and various theatrical *properties. Though it is impossible to identify his earliest roles, by 1592 Alleyn was lauded as one of the greatest actors of his time, his reputation being largely earned through his performances with the Lord *Admiral's Men in Christopher *Marlowe's plays. Alleyn definitely performed the roles of Tamburlaine and Dr Faustus, and he probably also played Barabas in *The Jew of Malta*, along with a number of other roles. Revered by his contemporaries primarily as a tragedian, Alleyn's style was powerful and charismatic and his exceptional physical stature was an asset for the conquering *heroes he performed; however, no specific details of his *acting are extant. He was described by one of his contemporaries as 'strutting and bellowing' and he became known through some of his eulogies as 'the *Roscius of his age'. By comparison with Richard *Burbage, the leading actor in Shakespeare's company, Alleyn is thought by some historians to have been bombastic and highly stylized, although this is much debated.

In addition to his talents as an actor, Alleyn held many financial investments which were largely (but not wholly) in the entertainment business. Together with his partner and father-in-law Philip *Henslowe (owner of the *Rose Theatre), Alleyn came to own the Rose, as well as the *Fortune and *Hope *playhouses and the Bear Garden. In 1604 Alleyn and Henslowe also acquired the patent for the Mastership of the Bears, Bulls, and Mastiff Dogs (*see* BAITING). By 1606 Alleyn had purchased Dulwich Manor on which he constructed a joint orphanage and pensioners' home now known as Dulwich College. It is due to Alleyn's benevolence that his theatrical manuscripts and those of his father-in-law were preserved at this foundation, where they reside today. SPC

ALLEY THEATRE

American *regional theatre in Houston, Texas, started in 1947 as a *community theatre by a group of ambitious *amateurs led by Nina Vance. The company turned professional in 1954 and became one of the first to benefit from the Ford Foundation's major support of institutional theatres, moving into a large facility in downtown Houston in 1968. Following Vance's death in 1980, the Alley was run by Pat Brown (1981–8), whose tenure was plagued by financial problems, and, from 1989, by Gregory Boyd, who attracted national attention by establishing ties with Robert *Wilson, Edward *Albee, and Vanessa *Redgrave. STC

ALLGOOD, SARA (1883–1950)

The most celebrated of the first generation of *Abbey Theatre actresses, she joined the National Theatre Society in *Dublin in 1903. Her distinctively musical voice (she was a fine singer) was expertly handled, initially under Frank *Fay's tutelage, over a remarkable range of tragic and comic roles: Cathleen Ni Houlihan, Emer, Deirdre for *Yeats; Maurya and the Widow Quin for *Synge; Mary Cahel, Gormleith, Dervorgilla, Mrs Fallon, and Mrs Delane for Lady *Gregory, Mrs Geoghegan for Lennox *Robinson. Allgood had a richly warm stage persona, but she could encompass roles as driven as T. C. *Murray's Mrs Harte and as embittered as his Ellen Keegan. It was, however, *O'Casey who exploited her range to the full with his Juno and Bessie Burgess, the former impersonation being preserved on *film by Hitchcock (*Juno and the Paycock*, 1930). Allgood often toured away from Dublin, notably as Isabella in *Poel's *Measure for Measure* (1908), as First Musician to Mrs Pat *Campbell's Deirdre and as Crysothemis to her Electra (1908), and in J. Hartley Manners's *Peg o' my Heart* throughout Australia (1916–20). After 1940 she lived in Hollywood, performing in over 30 films. RAC

ALLIO, RENÉ (1924–95)

French *scenographer, painter, filmmaker, and architectural consultant. A multidisciplinary artist who managed to combine his many interests throughout his career, Allio was greatly influenced by the work of *Piscator and of the *Berliner Ensemble. Following a period in *Paris, Marseille, and Rennes, he created ten designs for Roger *Planchon from 1957 to 1967, including Shakespeare's *Henry IV*, *Molière's *Georges Dandin*, Planchon's own *La Remise*, and *Racine's *Bérénice*. He designed several productions for the Royal *National Theatre in *London with director William *Gaskill: *Farquhar's *The Recruiting Officer* (1963) and *The Beaux' Stratagem* (1971), and *Arden's *Armstrong's Last Goodnight* (1965). He also designed Molière's *Tartuffe* for Tyrone *Guthrie (1967). His work typically explored all the planes of the stage space, especially exploiting its full depth. He used the *proscenium stage and its techniques as a tool to enhance the narrative visually, following but reinterpreting the principles of *Brecht. His interest in *film extended from the visual to writing and directing, and he made over twelve films between 1962 and 1993. He also continuously painted, exhibiting in Paris 1958 and 1961, and collaborated with architects in reshaping and restoring *playhouses in Paris, Tunisia, and Marseille. PH

ALLOULA, ABDALKDER (1923–94)

Algerian actor and director. At Théâtre National Algérien he staged an adaptation of *Gogol's *Diary of a Madman* (1971) and his own play *El-Khobza* (*The Bread*, 1972), which set a new direction for contemporary Algerian practice. His most important period was at Oran Regional Theatre from 1978, where he created work that intervened in social and *political issues. Attending to popular aesthetics, he found in the tradition of the *gaoual* (reciting poet) the elements of a distinctive *epic theatre form. His *Lagoual* (*The Statements*, 1980), *Lajouad* (*The Generous*, 1983), and *Litham* (*Mask*, 1988) formed a trilogy that defined Algerian theatre in that decade. He was assassinated by the Armed Islamic Group (GIA) as part of a campaign to eradicate Algerian artists, journalists, and intellectuals. MMe

ALMAGRO, CORRAL DE

The surviving *playhouse in the main square of Almagro (south central Spain) dates from 1628 and was discovered in 1953. This fairly small, rectangular *corral de comedia* (14.3 m by 24 m; 47 by 79 feet) has an open-air yard and roofed stage surrounded on three sides by a stone colonnade with two upper galleries. Originally there were *gradas* (raked seating) and benches on the ground floor and the galleries were divided into *boxes, with a women's gallery at the back. The stage, 1.5 m (5 feet) high, occupies the width of the yard and is 4.5 m (15 feet) deep. At the back are wooden posts supporting the *tiring house gallery, which has three balustraded openings; these posts delimit three similar openings at stage level, originally *curtained, with the tiring house wall set nearly a metre further back. The *corral*, always privately owned, was opened by a prosperous local chaplain, Leonardo de Oviedo, in the patio of an inn, and remained in use until the nineteenth century. CD

ALMEIDA THEATRE

Playhouse in north *London that became one of the most exciting and daring producing theatres in Britain under the directorship of Jonathan Kent and Ian McDiarmid from 1990. The former Islington Literary and Scientific Institute, built in 1837, served as a *music hall, wrestling arena, and Salvation Army citadel before being converted by Pierre Audi in 1980 to a theatre for experimental drama and music. Kent and McDiarmid's fare of classic productions included star performances by Cate Blanchett, Ralph Fiennes, Diana *Rigg, and Kevin Spacey, and frequent transfers to the West End or Broadway. The theatre established an *opera season and premièred work by Harold *Pinter and David *Hare. The Almeida's large exposed brick wall gives the ambience of a 'found' space, such as the *Bouffes du Nord in *Paris. After a decade of financial struggle, the theatre received a £5 million refurbishment grant at the turn of the millennium.   KN

ALONSO, JOSÉ LUIS (1924–90)

Spanish director. Alongside Cayetano Luca de Tena and Luis Escobar, Alonso was probably the most important director of the Franco era. He had played a significant role, even while director of the Teatro *Nacional María Guerrero in the early 1960s, in introducing alternative international works to Spain. His role in promoting contemporary *dramaturgy, most visible in his staging of numerous of Antonio *Gala's plays, his productions of forgotten classics like *Valle-Inclán's Romance de lobos (Ballad of Wolves) in 1970 and *Calderón's La dama duende (The Goblin Lady) at the Teatro *Español in 1966, as well as his championing of important trends in international drama—*Cocteau, *Claudel, *Ionesco, *Williams—accorded him a unique role in the modernization of the Spanish stage. A prolific translator and critic, Alonso continued to dominate in the post-Franco era, bringing María *Casares for a landmark production of Rafael Alberti's El adefesio (The Absurdity) in 1976.   MMD

ALONSO DE SANTOS, JOSÉ LUIS (1942–)

Spanish playwright, actor, director, critic, and theorist. After experience with *Madrid's independent collective groups Tabano and the Teatro Libre in the 1970s, he first achieved recognition with an original play in 1975. Hostages in the Barrio (1981) and Going down to Marrakesh (1985) brought him both critical respect and box-office success. These serio-comic plays, dealing with marginal *characters speaking contemporary slang, were appealing to younger *audiences in particular and both were adapted into *films. Other major works are The Last Pirouette (1986), Unhinged (1987), and the *tragicomedy The Generals' Dinner (2000). In 1978 he joined the faculty of the Royal School of Dramatic Arts as professor of *acting and playwriting. He was named *artistic director of Spain's National Company for Classical Theatre in 2000, beginning his new

duties with a revisionist staging of *Calderón's The Phantom Lady.   MPH

ALSINA, ARTURO (1897–1984)

Paraguayan playwright. Born in Argentina, Alsina came to Paraguay when he was 12 and remained for the rest of his life. He founded the Paraguayan Company of Drama and Comedy in 1926. Considered the greatest of Paraguayan national dramatists, much of his work was influenced by *Ibsen. His prolific output includes La marca de fuego (The Firemark, 1926), Evangelista (Evangelist, 1926), El derecho de nacer (Birthright, 1927), Intruso (1928), La llama flota (1940), La sombra de la estatua (The Shadow of the Statue, 1947), and La ciudad soñada (The Dreamed City, 1968).   EJW

ALTERNATIVE THEATRE

A phrase often used to embrace the successive waves of unconventional theatre and performance groups that formed almost everywhere in the second half of the twentieth century, especially following the creative upsurge of the 1960s. 'Alternative theatre' derived from 'alternative society'—a coinage describing the 1960s counter-culture—and gained currency in the 1970s as the number of oppositional theatre companies mushroomed. The associated terms suggest its contested nature. They range from the highly specific *Off-Off-Broadway of *New York to the overly generous 'free theatre' of Europe, but historically four main terms—*fringe, underground, experimental, and independent—have challenged 'alternative' as the key word for practices that were reacting against the aesthetic conventions and ideological orientations of mainstream, establishment, or *legitimate theatre.

'Fringe theatre' was in use in Britain from the late 1950s, initially describing the small groups that performed alongside the official *Edinburgh Festival programme. 'Underground theatre'—on analogy with Second World War resistance movements—emerged in the late 1960s in the UK and USA, indicating sympathy for the revolutionary agendas of the new counter-cultural groups. 'Experimental theatre' was an older term often used to avoid the uneasy political—or hubristic—connotations of 'underground'. 'Independent theatre' reappeared mostly in the conservative 1980s, giving a gloss of respectability to groups that commercial sponsors might find unattractive if labelled more accurately. Towards the millennium's end, 'independent' and 'fringe' fought for prominence, 'underground' was relegated to historical usage, and a further term—'popular theatre'—was increasingly used for 'Third World' *post-colonialist practices that attacked global economic and political inequities. Meanwhile, 'alternative' seemed increasingly passé in the burgeoning diversities of a postmodern world. This is paradoxical, given that the companies labelled in these ways offered alternatives to the mainstream, and often each other—ideologically, aesthetically, organizationally, or otherwise—and so helped to usher in postmodernity itself (*see* MODERNISM AND POSTMODERNISM).

Alternative theatre genealogy includes the great Western traditions of popular, people's, and *political theatre originating in the nineteenth century with *melodrama, *music hall, and *variety shows. Later precursors include the twentieth-century *studio and *Little Theatre movements in Europe and America; the Actresses Franchise League in the UK; the US *Federal Theatre Project; the Workers' Theatre Movement in Russia, Germany (*see* VOLKSBÜHNE), and the UK; the New Theatre movement in Australia; the UK *Unity Theatre movement; the Red Theatres of *China; the companies of the *Indian People's Theatre Association; and the post-war decentralization of theatre in France. These antecedents suggest that conventional critical wisdom that places the start of alternative theatre proper in 1968, aligning it with the international student riots of that year, is an oversimplification. Also there were more immediate portents as early as the late 1950s in many countries. For example, in America the *Living Theatre was founded in 1948, the first *happenings were created in the mid-1950s, the *Caffe Cino became a performance venue in 1958; in Brazil Augusto *Boal staged his first play in 1957 and began working with Arena Theatre in 1961; in Italy Dario *Fo and Franca *Rame started producing satirical popular theatre in 1957; in *Japan the post-*shingeki* movement originated in 1959 with the Youth Arts Theatre (Seigei) and *Kara Jūrō founded Jōkyō Gekijō (Situation Theatre) in 1963; in the UK Arnold *Wesker created the proto-community arts organization Centre 42 in 1962, while John *Arden staged a series of community-based theatre projects between 1960 and 1968. Clearly a movement with international dimensions was beginning to emerge during these years.

By the mid-1960s signs of a youthful and radical revitalization of theatre were fairly common. American groups included the *Bread and Puppet Theatre (1961), *Open Theatre (1963), and El Teatro *Campesino (1965). In France Jérôme *Savary started the Grand Théâtre Panique (1965), in Germany the satirical Reichkabarett (later *Grips) began in 1965, in *India Aloke Roy set up Jagran (1966), in the *Philippines Cecile Guidote created the *Philippine Educational Theatre Association (1967). British groups included the *People Show (1965), CAST (Cartoon Archetypal Slogan Theatre, 1965), and Albert Hunt's Art College students, who staged the Russian Revolution on the streets of Bradford in 1967. But 1968 and 1969 were watershed years. Although the main centres of growth were in Europe and North America—in the UK at least 30 new companies and 13 new venues started in 1968–9—the trend was much broader, and included the creation of Escambray (Cuba), *La Mama (Australia), Bengkel Theatre

(Workshop Theatre, *Indonesia), TPB (Popular Theatre of Bogotá, Colombia), PET and TECON (People's Educational Theatre/Theatre Council of Natal, South Africa), KPAC (Kerala People's Arts Company, India), and Kuro Tento (Black Tent Theatre, Japan).

In the 1960s, paradoxically, wholesale iconoclasm was the order of the day, but three general emergent qualities identified a movement: extreme aesthetic innovation, inventive organizational structures, and cultural and/or social and/or political radicalism. The potent flexibility of this creative mix, coupled to the successive counter-cultures and new social movements that flourished in the final three decades of the twentieth century—feminist, gay/queer, black/ethnic, disabled/impaired, green/ecological, neo-/post-colonial—produced a truly unprecedented explosion of theatre and performance beyond mainstream theatres. *Touring was common, but also thousands of alternative venues were opened, mostly in converted buildings—pub rooms, warehouses, churches, basements, lofts, garages, barns—and performance shrugged off the indoors, as *street theatre and other alfresco genres thrived around the world. The new categories of practice in this astonishing growth are contested and contesting, but they include guerrilla theatre, *environmental theatre, *community theatre, grass-roots theatre, *feminist theatre, women's theatre, *lesbian theatre, *gay theatre, queer theatre, black theatre, *African-American theatre, *Chicano theatre, *Asian-American theatre, Latino theatre, ethnic theatre, *theatre-in-education, theatre in prisons, disability theatre, reminiscence theatre, theatre with elders, celebratory theatre, *performance art, live art, site-specific theatre, visual theatre, *physical theatre, theatre of the *oppressed, theatre for *development, *liberation theatre, and so on. These last types signal major initiatives beyond the so-called developed world, in the popular theatre movements of countries such as Nicaragua, Kenya, Zimbabwe, *Bangladesh, and many more, where alternative performance has aimed to empower the very poor. This international spread of alternative theatres has produced some institutionalization—professional organizations were established, courses created in universities and colleges, state funding schemes made available, development agencies set artistic agendas, and so on—so that, especially in richer countries, accommodations with the mainstream were inevitable, through exchange of personnel, co-productions, residencies, joint funding schemes. Such ideological complexities, though, could not disguise the fact that at the millennium's end alternative theatre and its cousins—fringe, experimental, independent and new kinds of popular performance—were well and truly established as a global phenomenon. BRK

EPSKAMP, KEES P., *Theatre in Search of Social Change* (The Hague, 1989)

HAEDICKE, SUSAN C., and NELLHAUS, TOBIN (eds.), *Performing Democracy* (Ann Arbor, 2001)

SHANK, THEODORE, *American Alternative Theatre* (London, 1982)

ÁLVAREZ QUINTERO, SERAFÍN (1871–1938) AND JOAQUÍN (1873–1944)

Spanish playwrights. Born in Utrera (Seville), the Álvarez Quintero brothers formed a popular literary duo composing for both the stage and, later, the new medium of *radio. The inheritors of nineteenth-century Spanish *naturalism, the Álvarez Quinteros were joint authors of many successful *entremeses, *comedias, and *sainetes, as well as the librettos for several *zarzuelas. The 'golden brothers', as they were known, produced over 200 pieces that filled Spanish theatres for nearly half a century. Their stylized, somewhat episodic depictions of life and customs in Seville and lower Andalusia were especially popular with *Madrid *audiences. Though frequently accused of producing a false and dulcified picture of Spanish rural reality, which sacrificed a vision of actual social hardship for a premeditatedly ingenuous picture of local customs, the Álvarez Quinteros nonetheless won respect from writers such as Azorín, who claimed that they had 'brought to the dramatic art . . . a perfect equilibrium between personal sentiment and collective sentiment, between the individual and society'. In 1920 Serafín was elected a member of the Spanish Royal Academy.

KG

AMALRIK, ANDREI (1938–80)

Russian/Soviet dramatist, prose writer, and dissident. Inspired by the work of Daniil Kharms and the theatre of the *absurd, his plays feature victimized protagonists where a schematic sense of character combines with bizarre and illogical events. His published plays include *Is Uncle Jack a Conformist?* (1964) and *Nose! Nose? Nose!* (1968), based on *Gogol's short story. His best-known works are accounts of his periods of exile, *Involuntary Journey to Siberia* (1970) and the prophetic *Will the Soviet Union Survive until 1984?* (1970, rev. 1981). Amalrik was killed in a car accident in Spain.

NW

AMARAL, MARIA ADELAIDE (1942–   )

Born in Portugal, Amaral migrated to Brazil in 1954 and has worked as playwright, journalist, novelist, and increasingly as a *television writer, where her gift for *dialogue has added depth to miniseries such as the critically acclaimed adaptation of the nineteenth-century Portuguese novel *Os Maias*. Her plays anatomize middle-class *gender relations and family structure, an exception to this theme being her *musical biography of early twentieth-century popular composer Chiquinha Gonzaga called *O, abre alas!* (*Make Way*, 1983). *De braços abertos* (*With Open Arms*, 1984), an intense encounter between ex-lovers, may be her most accomplished drama.

LHD

AMATEUR THEATRE

The word amateur derives from the Latin verb *amare* (to love). The love of performance and the cultural need for both individual expression and collective *play through theatre in its widest sense are worldwide phenomena and as old as theatre itself. Many more people have taken part in communal *rituals or non-professional playmaking, in pursuit of personal and spiritual development or simple pleasure, than have performed as a means of earning a living. Indeed the International Amateur Theatre Association (IATA), which was founded by English director E. Martin *Browne in 1952, coordinates some 100,000 groups in 80 countries spread over five continents. At the beginning of the twenty-first century there are millions of amateur actors. What precisely may be inferred from the designation amateur remains unstable and dependent on value judgements which may shift even within the same cultural context.

In English, the word amateur appears to enter the language towards the end of the eighteenth century, just as professional competence as a means of forwarding the progress of bourgeois individualism within developing capitalism takes on vital economic importance. Thus the amateur is to be regarded as incompetent or inferior in comparison to the professional specialist. Yet the word also referred to one who undertakes a craft or activity from motives akin to love which are not dependent on the economic imperative. And so the skill of the leisured practitioner, at this time almost by definition from the upper class, acquires a special status. This claim to status was appropriated by increasingly affluent members of the middle classes who took up cultural pastimes in the nineteenth century as a sign of growing gentrification. It is possible to trace a strand of amateur theatre from noble amateurs, who might include the sixteenth-century *Japanese aristocrats who practised *nō as taught by revered masters, or the royal *masquers of the English Stuart court in the early seventeenth century, or the aristocratic thespians who entertained in the literary salons of early nineteenth-century Russia. In late nineteenth-century England, when mainstream theatre was concerned to nurture an image of fashionably *costumed respectability, a number of successful actors entered the profession via the route of middle-class amateur theatre clubs. It was also out of this kind of milieu, and dependent on wealthy private circumstances, that radical practitioners like *Stanislavsky emerged. By the late twentieth century, however, the cult of the professional had assumed even greater importance; assumptions that amateur theatre is not only inferior technically, but also irredeemably the preserve of the comfortable and the conservative, have tended to obscure more complex issues of cultural practice.

In *India, which has centuries-old traditions of highly skilled performance, much of its modern theatre could be categorized as amateur because there is little or no financial reward. There are thousands of amateur groups, especially in large urban areas like Calcutta (*Kolkata), playing in virtually all the regional languages. In 1990 the spectrum was wide, ranging from Western-style recreational societies to 'group theatres' in Calcutta modelled on the company organization and serious programmes of Western *repertory theatres, to the cosmopolitan Indian National Theatre in Bombay (*Mumbai) which survived on government grants and dedicated workers, to theatre as just one unit of the Goa Hindu Association which selected and ran productions primarily to raise money for its social services. At the same time highly successful English-language theatre in Bombay coexisted with *avant-garde experimental theatre in Calcutta. Many Indian amateur actors consider themselves to be professional because money-making is not their primary objective.

A frequent tension has existed between the deeply entrenched, transcultural suspicion of the figure of the professional hypocrite-deceiver and the attraction of, and need for, the power of expressive art. In ancient Sanskrit theatre rigorously *trained actors were compared to prostitutes. Actors in the *kote-tlon* of the Bamana people in medieval Mali were condemned as idle drunkards and thieves, despite the fact that their abilities to satirize problematic members of the community were feared and needed as a form of social control. The Christian Church in *medieval Europe could cast opprobrium on professional entertainers while simultaneously promoting the efficacy of Christian theatre. Cultural performance is necessary, as the anthropologist Victor Turner pointed out, as 'a way of scrutinizing the quotidian world'. Either the marginalized and suspect professional artist is required to satisfy the performance expectations of the community *audience or that community must supply the need itself. Thus in early Japanese shamanistic rituals of divine possession, which ideally needed specialist artists, local people in poorer or more isolated communities would undertake the performance themselves and as a consequence modify and dilute the ritual convention. In fifteenth-century Japan when some professional troupes were in decline, a tradition of amateur nō developed, performed by women and boys, which has continued to the present day. In Indian folk drama, it is virtually impossible to distinguish the contributions of professional or semi-professional artists and those of amateur community artists coming together at fixed seasons to perform free of charge.

Where economic or topographical circumstances make professional theatre non-viable, amateur performance will frequently fill the vacuum. *Brecht, discussing amateur theatre in an essay probably written in exile in 1940 when he had access only to amateur actors, noted that there were nearly 1,000 amateur companies in Sweden where the vast distances made professional touring difficult. In Wales, a tiny country where a combination of Calvinist *anti-theatrical bias and mountainous terrain militated against the development of professional theatre, there were hundreds of small amateur groups which flour-

ished in the Depression years between the two world wars. Amateur theatre has remained strong in Northern Ireland despite, or indeed because of, the turbulent political and economic context. In the history of *text-based Western theatre there are many examples of the way communities under stress have performed plays: British troops marooned in *New York during the American Revolution, convicts in Australian penal colonies who built their own theatres, prisoners in twentieth-century Soviet concentration camps.

Playmaking in its diverse forms provides an escape into a separate place which can be actual or imaginative. This can apply equally to a middle-aged suburban housewife and an incarcerated victim of political oppression. The activity can engender collective solidarity and help preserve cultural identity in alien circumstances. So expatriate British communities in colonial *Africa or India would form tight exclusion zones around their leisure pursuits which included English theatre and music. Indeed the legacy of the British love of amateur theatricals is seen in Western-style amateur theatre in modern urban India. MADS (the Madras Amateur Dramatic Society), one of the oldest such English-language organizations in the world, remained strong right up to the 1960s. In Heidelberg in Germany, the Roadside Theater, the US forces community theatre, has been operated by and for American military personnel and civilians for over 40 years.

Group aggrandizement is an equally important incentive. In medieval Europe communities of all sorts would display and celebrate themselves by performance. A vigorously acted play and an extravagantly decorated *pageant wagon could be a splendid advertisement for the health and prestige of a *guild of craftsmen. In the Low Countries in the sixteenth century the Rederijkerskamers or *Chambers of Rhetoric organized big play contests either within one town or between towns. The competitive drama *festival, akin to the civic play festivals (*Dionysia) of ancient *Greek theatre, was developed extensively in the twentieth century. The Welsh Eisteddfod, for example, which has its origins in twelfth-century music and poetry contests and started to award prizes for drama in 1915, creates a pyramid of competitions building up from local to national events. At once festive ritual and *sport for participants and audience, the practice is worldwide. In 2001 the Estonian Amateur Theatre Association promoted 30 local festivals, six international festivals, and four international workshops. Every four years IATA organizes a World Festival of Amateur Theatre in Monaco, as well as World Youth Theatre Festivals and Children's Theatre Festivals.

Brecht pointed out that so many people's concern with art cannot be shrugged off. In the never-ending process of education, which for him was a function of the performative nature of everyday life, theatre was of crucial importance. It meant a good deal that thousands should act to hundreds of thousands and in that multiplicity lay power. The educative role of theatre in the furtherance of religious and ideological interests has for centuries motivated the institutional promotion of amateur performance. The acting of Latin, Greek, and new vernacular drama by pupils in the grammar schools founded in sixteenth-century England is only one *early modern example of countless generations of *university and school performance. Just as the Catholic Church used theatre in the community to reinforce religious faith in medieval Europe, so it also became a tool of imperial expansion. In the sixteenth-century Spanish colonies in what would become Mexico, Franciscan missionary friars systematically involved thousands of the indigenous population in *autos sacramentales which successfully fused Catholic doctrine with native *verse forms (see also EVANGELICAL THEATRE IN LATIN AMERICA). In Canada in the seventeenth century *Jesuit secondary schools for boys, and girls' schools founded by Ursuline nuns, included drama on the curriculum for both evangelical and educational purposes. In West Africa, missionaries attempted to replace indigenous rituals linked to annual agrarian festivals with dramatized biblical stories on the model of *mystery or *morality plays. In elite schools across Africa in the late colonial period, selected young people from the indigenous population were encouraged to perform drama from the European classical repertoire. Future African intellectuals, politicians, and playwrights from the British and French colonies were thus heavily influenced by early exposure to Shakespeare, *Molière, and *Racine.

What evolved out of these Christian educational projects, however, were initiatives by indigenous communities to deploy the same strategies as a means of restoring appropriated cultural identity. The growth in the early twentieth century of independent, African-run churches in Nigeria led to theatrical productions in the Yoruba language which continue to flourish across western Nigeria as popular Bible opera performed by members of church congregations. In the 1940s in the Ewe-speaking area of Togoland, vernacular biblical *kantata plays performed by indigenous religious groups became increasingly secularized plays based on real-life situations or world *folklore. Ewe-language literary drama, which began to appear in the late 1930s, was performed by students in seminaries and religious schools. Since the 1970s, when theatre for *development initiatives across Africa have sought to empower communities through participatory, consciousness-raising performance, many of the initiatives have originated in university student-led projects (see UNIVERSITY TRAVELLING THEATRE).

The boundaries between amateur and professional blurred in radical twentieth-century attempts to make theatre an instrument for artistic and socio-political efficacy. In these cases the amateur becomes a cultural missionary who rejects financial reward along with commercial constraints, and for the most part ultimately seeks legitimacy through state and civic funding. André *Antoine's Théâtre *Libre and Otto *Brahm's *Freie Bühne, the *Moscow Art Theatre and the *Abbey Theatre in *Dublin, all had their origins in amateur companies. Several of the early English *regional repertory theatre companies either started as amateur societies, like the *Birmingham Repertory Company or the Sheffield Repertory Company, or were established within a context where ambitious amateur societies like the Manchester Playgoers' Society flourished. The same pattern may be seen in America in the *Little Theatre movement and in more radical groups like the *Provincetown Players.

Another distinctive strand of reforming socialist amateur theatre emerged out of the late nineteenth-century workers' educational programmes. In the 1920s and 1930s amateur working-class theatre groups developed into an extensive international network, exchanging ideas and techniques with professionals and performing in the *streets and in unconventional playing spaces. The concept of people's theatre, however, which was particularly strong in France and Germany in the early twentieth century, has led in the era of state subsidy to debates about whether empowering theatre should be undertaken for the people or by the people. Community amateur actors directed by professionals often have access to more radical ideas and advanced performance values, but clearly lose artistic autonomy. Doggedly independent 'pure' amateur theatre is seen as inward-looking and artistically inferior. The Little Theatre Guild, founded in Britain in 1946, which in 2001 had 78 member companies, is typical of autonomous amateur theatre found worldwide. Owning or having access to a performance venue, this type of institution is usually run by a number of dedicated individuals who give of their leisure time freely and call upon the commitment of volunteer actors, designers, and technicians. Of necessity financially self-sufficient, they are dependent for their audience on the support of family and friends, or they attract audiences from the wider community with a broadly popular production programme.

In terms of cultural practice such groups are performative communities whose members take time out from a diverse range of day-to-day paid occupations in order to come together in purposeful play, which may well break down other external structural hierarchies. The group plays by itself, with itself, and to itself, laying aside other concerns in the interests of the collective project, while its audience may bring entirely different expectations from those brought to professional performance. To be sure, the practice of amateur theatre is frequently an act of reassurance which is essentially conservative and is not so dissimilar to annual communal rites practised in less technologically developed societies. That said, as advanced capitalism makes such collective 'playtime' increasingly difficult, the work of organizations such as IATA seeks to harness and expand the creative and imaginative potential of non-professional performance.   CEC

BRADBY, DAVID, and MCCORMICK, JOHN, People's Theatre (London, 1978)

BRECHT, BERTOLT, 'Two essays on unprofessional acting', in John Willett (ed.), *Brecht on Theatre* (London, 1964)

HINDLEY, ALAN (ed.), *Drama and Community: people and plays in medieval Europe* (Turnhout, 1999)

HUTCHISON, ROBERT, and FEIST, ANDREW, *Amateur Arts in the UK* (London, 1991)

RICHMOND, FARLEY, *Indian Theatre: traditions of performance* (Honolulu, 1990)

AMERICAN ACADEMY OF DRAMATIC ARTS

Founded in 1884 in *New York, the Academy was the first *acting conservatory in the English-speaking world. Its founding purpose was 'to provide a broad and practical education to those desiring to make acting their profession'. A distinguished list of alumni includes Hume *Cronyn, Colleen *Dewhurst, Ruth *Gordon, Jason *Robards, Jr., and Spencer Tracy. The core of the Academy is a two-year programme with a third-year company consisting of outstanding graduates. *Training combines psychological approaches with physical and vocal technique. A new *Los Angeles facility opened in 2000. MAF

AMERICAN CONSERVATORY THEATRE

US *regional theatre. Founded by William *Ball in 1965, ACT spent six months in Pittsburgh and a year as a *touring company before settling in *San Francisco in 1967 at the Geary Theatre. Early successes included Ball's productions of *Tartuffe* and *Six Characters in Search of an Author*. In leading the company to national prominence, Ball became as well known for his difficult personality, fiscal irresponsibility, and autocratic control as for his exuberant productions and his commitment to a resident ensemble performing in *repertory. In 1986 he was pressured to resign and was replaced by long-time executive director Edward Hastings. In 1989 the company came close to shutting down after a Bay Area earthquake nearly demolished the Geary. The hiring of Carey Perloff as *artistic director in 1991, and the commitment to rebuild the Geary, which reopened in 1996, led to renewed stability. Perloff advanced ACT's long-standing interest in the plays of Tom *Stoppard and broadened its standard repertoire of Shakespeare, *Molière, and *Shaw to include lesser-known works by *Euripides, *Webster, and *Schiller. Throughout its history, ACT has maintained an active conservatory, offering short-term *training to hundreds of students each year, as well as an elite Master of Fine Arts degree programme. STC

AMERICAN LABORATORY THEATRE

Begun as a theatre school in *New York in 1923, the 'Lab' established a *repertory company in 1925. Both theatre and school operated under the direction of *Moscow Art Theatre veteran Richard *Boleslavsky and principal acting teacher Maria *Ouspenskaya, an MAT member who remained in New York after the Russian company's 1923 *tour. The Lab thus became the first *Stanislavsky-based *training programme in the USA and exerted a strong influence over succeeding generations of actors and acting teachers. After moving through five venues in four years, the Lab settled in a former brewery on East 54th Street, where it remained until the theatre disbanded in 1930, the school continuing until 1933. The theatre produced 23 plays in five seasons and the school trained more than 500 students, including key members of the *Group Theatre, such as Harold *Clurman, Lee *Strasberg, Stella *Adler, Ruth Nelson, Eunice Stoddard, and John Garfield. MAF

AMERICAN NATIONAL THEATRE AND ACADEMY

Created in 1935 by the US Congress, ANTA was formulated as a non-profit national theatre, untainted by commercialism or government aid, and devoted to classical revivals and the development of new playwrights and performers. Held back by world conditions, it began producing in 1947. In 1950, Broadway's Guild Theatre became the ANTA Playhouse but it had few successes. From 1948 to 1951, and in 1955, ANTA produced a series of benefits (the 'ANTA Albums') featuring stars enacting popular scenes. In 1963, ANTA built the Washington Square Theatre, first home of the Repertory Theatre of *Lincoln Center. *See also* NATIONAL THEATRE MOVEMENT, NORTH AMERICA. SLL

AMERICAN PLACE THEATRE

Founded in a Manhattan church by Wynn Handman and the Reverend Sidney Lanier in 1963, the American Place Theatre has retained the innovative spirit which accompanied its *Off-Off-Broadway genesis, having mounted premières by dramatists such as Sam *Shepard and Maria Irene *Fornés. In 1971 the theatre was offered a move to a fully outfitted midtown facility. Handman has since overseen the growth of a complex recognized for its commitment to the production and development of new and unconventional works, including precedent-breaking productions by *Asian-American and *African-American playwrights and various *performance artists. The *Women's Project was established by Julia Miles in 1978, and resided at the American Place for a number of years.

EW

AMERICAN REPERTORY THEATRE

Troupe founded by Eva *Le Gallienne and Margaret *Webster in *New York, operating in 1946 and 1947. Its goal of producing classical repertory proved impossible in the face of insufficient funding and negative reviews. The producers originally wanted an arrangement whereby plays produced in three different cities would rotate locations, but financial considerations forced them to settle at New York's out-of-the-way International Theatre. In 1946 they offered *Henry VIII*, *John Gabriel Borkman*, *What Every Woman Knows*, and *Androcles and the Lion*, while 1947 saw *Yellow Jack* and *Alice in Wonderland*.   SLL

AMERICAN REPERTORY THEATRE
(CAMBRIDGE, MASSACHUSETTS)

*Regional theatre. Following his term of office at the *Yale School of Drama, Robert *Brustein founded the ART at Harvard in 1980, bringing many staff and students with him from New Haven. He soon established the company in the vanguard of regional theatres by hiring visionary directors and designers to interpret an ambitious repertoire of Shakespeare, classical *comedies, new plays, and *modernist dramas by *Ibsen, *Chekhov, *Shaw, *Pirandello, *Brecht, and *Beckett. Andrei *Şerban mounted a dozen productions, including a popular version of *Gozzi's *King Stag*, with *costumes, *masks, and *puppets by Julie *Taymor. Other landmark productions include Brustein's adaptation of Pirandello's *Six Characters in Search of an Author* (1984); JoAnne *Akalaitis's controversial treatment of *Endgame* (1984), publicly disavowed by Beckett; and a major section of Robert *Wilson's *the CIVIL warS* (1985), which went on to win the Pulitzer Prize. In the 1990s, David *Mamet premièred several of his plays at ART, including *Oleanna* (1992). Since 1987 ART has operated a *training institute, which formalized a joint programme with the *Moscow Art Theatre School in 1998. In 2002, after 22 years as *artistic director, Brustein stepped down and was replaced by Robert *Woodruff.   STC

AMERICAN SHAKESPEARE THEATRE

Founded as the American Shakespeare Festival Theatre by Lawrence *Langner, the company presented summer Shakespeare productions in an octagonal wooden theatre (capacity 1,550) on the Housatonic River at Stratford, Connecticut, beginning in 1955 with *Julius Caesar* and *The Tempest*, both directed by Dennis Carey. From 1956 to 1959, under John *Houseman's *artistic directorship, attendance grew to 147,000 and artistic quality peaked with a 1957 season featuring Earle *Hyman as Othello, Alfred *Drake as Iago and Benedick, Katharine *Hepburn as Beatrice and Portia, and Morris *Carnovsky as Shylock. Houseman's associate Jack Landau succeeded him at the helm, followed in 1965 by Allan Fletcher. After several years of deficits, 1963 brought another spectacular season with Carnovsky as King Lear. A new era began in 1969 with Michael *Kahn, who dropped 'Festival' from the company name to signal a serious year-round commitment. A ten-week spring season geared to drawing student *audiences proved very successful.

Chronic financial troubles led to Kahn's resignation in 1977 and to that of his successor Gerald Freedman in 1979. Little has been done with the decaying facility since 1982. In its 27 seasons the company presented 27 Shakespeare plays (some revived several times) and twelve plays by other dramatists.   FHL

AMERICAN SOCIETY FOR THEATRE RESEARCH

Scholarly organization, founded in 1967, that supports research in the fields of *theatre studies and *performance studies. Membership is open to all interested scholars worldwide. The Society publishes the biannual journal *Theatre Survey* and the *ASTR Newsletter*, and each November holds a scholarly conference at a North American location. ASTR provides small grants to scholars for research projects and dissertation grants to graduate students. It also administers annual awards for scholarship, including the Gerald Kahan Prize for young scholars and the Bernard Hewitt book award. All officers are selected by the vote of the membership. ASTR is a member of the American Council of Learned Societies.   TP

AMES, WINTHROP (1871–1937)

American director and producer. Harvard educated and independently wealthy, Ames surprised his friends in 1904 by entering commercial theatre—then regarded as a grubby affair dominated by the *Theatrical Syndicate. After producing and directing three seasons in *Boston, Ames toured European art theatres in 1907 and 1908. He returned to become director of the *New Theatre in *New York, and its failure convinced him of the need for smaller venues. He supervised designs for two intimate venues in the Broadway district: the Little Theatre (1912, 299 seats) and the *Booth Theatre (1913, 712 seats). Ames offered carefully prepared and self-financed productions of plays by *Galsworthy, *Shaw, Granville *Barker, and *Gilbert and *Sullivan, as well as American works, such as *Kaufman and *Connelly's *Beggar on Horseback* (1924). Despite many *long-running productions and critical praise, Ames's career slowly decimated his personal fortune.   MAF

AMPHITHEATRE

Literally, 'theatre on two sides', first attested archaeologically in Pompeii about 70 BC after its colonization by war veterans. Its form was normally elliptical, with doors for animals and performers at each end. In the western Roman Empire it largely replaced the public forum as a space for the performance of *spectacles (*munera*), especially *gladiatorial contests, *animal fights, and dramatized public executions (**damnatio*). In the east the classic amphitheatre form is less common, since stadiums, hippodromes, or theatres were adapted, or multipurpose facilities were specially built, but it is found in many centres of Roman influence such as Corinth or Pergamum. Constant improvement led to underground chambers with gangways, trapdoors, and lifts operated by capstans, capable of swiftly elevating beasts, trees, buildings, etc. into the arena. Canvas coverings (*vela*) against the sun could be provided. Aqueducts supplied water in quantity to flush underground rooms or sometimes flood parts of the arena (*see* NAUMACHIA). Front seats were always reserved for dignitaries, even in smaller cities, and the tendency to class-based seating, as in the theatre, grew. The connection of *munera* with the imperial cult gave great ideological importance to amphitheatres, which displayed imperial power through the spectacles given by the chief priests. But the army also constructed wooden amphitheatres for displays of swordsmanship and military skill. So Rome possessed the greatest amphitheatre in the Amphitheatrum Flavium (the Colosseum) built from the spoils from Jerusalem by Vespasian, but also a military version for soldiers, the Amphitheatrum Castrense.   WJS

AMSTERDAM

In its development from a modest fishing village on the banks of the Amstel river in 1300 to the rich mercantile and financial centre of the seventeenth century, Amsterdam benefited from the struggle for independence against the Habsburg monarchy. Over a period of 80 years (1568–1648) the Low Countries were separated into the southern and northern provinces, a process that still can be felt when examining the social, cultural, and religious characteristics of the north (Netherlands) and the south (Belgium). The conquest of *Antwerp in 1585 by Spanish troops led to a large emigration of wealthy merchants, artists, and craftsmen to Amsterdam, who then created fertile ground for the arts. Huguenots fleeing religious persecution in France, and Jews from Spain and Portugal, added considerably to the development. Amsterdam followed the movements of the Low Countries in *medieval theatre: itinerant troupes performed occasionally at fairs in towns, and Rederijkers (*Chambers of Rhetoric), societies of burghers interested in writing and performance, presented plays for one another. The growth and diversity of the population, together with a booming economy, eventually led to the creation of professional theatre. After considerable discussion with the city council and leading Calvinist clergymen, the *Schouwburg (City Theatre) opened in 1638 with a performance of Joost van den *Vondel's *Gijsbrecht van Aemstel*, under the condition that future profits would benefit the city orphanage. Apart from the Cologne-born Vondel, Gerbrant *Bredero and Pieter Corneliszoon *Hooft added their talent to this first flowering of theatre. The Schouwburg was replaced in 1665 by an elegant building fit to stage Italian and French *neoclassical plays, only to be burnt and replaced on two further occasions.

During the eighteenth century the quality of acting was improved by the dedicated work of Marten Corver (1729–94) and Johannes Jelgerhuis (1770–1836), as the declamatory mode of neoclassicism shifted to a more *realistic approach. Jelgerhuis, both actor and painter, provided a vivid theoretical treatise on acting in *Theoretische Lessen over de Gesticulatie en Mimiek* (1827). Nineteenth-century Amsterdam, now exploiting the wealth of the Dutch colonies, embraced artistic influences from abroad. While large *audiences frequented *music halls, *cabarets, and *vaudevilles, the upper classes became acquainted with the *Meiningen troupe, André *Antoine and the Théâtre *Libre, and the works of *Strindberg, *Ibsen, *Maeterlinck, and *Hauptmann. Professional acting was encouraged through the foundation of two *training conservatoires in 1874. Of local artists, the playwright and director Herman *Heijermans appealed to a broad audience with social plays like *Op Hoop van Zegen* (*The Good Hope*), *De Meid* (*The Maid*), and *De Wijze Kater* (*The Wise Tomcat*), while Willem Royaards (1867–1929) and Eduard Verkade (1878–1961) adapted the *modernist international style of *Reinhardt, *Appia, and *Craig.

The Second World War brought deep artistic and social despair with the German occupation, but also delayed the establishment of regular government subsidy for the theatre. After the war the new policy of subvention created the *Holland Festival in 1947, which continues to bring a large international repertoire to Amsterdam. Several new theatre companies encouraged home-grown development, yet in 1969 the system seemed to have failed when theatre students threw tomatoes as a sign of disapproval at the end of a Nederlandse Comedie performance of Shakespeare's *The Tempest*. This so-called Aktie Tomaat focused the widely held notion that the theatre had lost its artistic and social relevance. A thorough examination of the issue led to the reorganization of existing companies, paving the way for new initiatives like the *Werkteater, De Appel, het Onafhankelijk Toneel, and several others that concentrated on educational or political objectives. As a separate development Ritsaert ten Cate (1938–) founded *Mickery Theatre in the mid-1960s, concentrating on *avant-garde theatre from around the world by inviting troupes like Els *Joglars, *Pip Simmons, the *Wooster Group, and Squat Theatre to perform for an expanding audience. The cosmopolitan character of Amsterdam theatre life was underlined in the following decades by *street theatre festivals (where companies like the Doggroep flourished), theatre for *youth, and immigrant theatre (leading to units like De Nieuw Amsterdam and Cosmic), aided by a sophisticated subvention framework for emerging initiatives (*see also* FINANCE). An important addition to the dozens of theatres in the city that have arisen since the 1950s is the Muziektheater (1986). After years of intense discussion about its merits and design, this hybrid building, joined architecturally with the new City Hall, offers the city a major production house for *opera and *dance WNR

BRANDT, GEORGE W., and HOGENDOORN, WIEBE (eds.), *German and Dutch Theatre 1600–1848* (Cambridge, 1993)

GOLDING, ALFRED SIEMON, *Classicistic Acting: two centuries of a performance tradition at the Amsterdam Schouwburg* (Lanham, Md., 1984)

AMUSEMENT ARCADES

Commercial venues of light and often mechanical entertainment particularly popular in the late nineteenth and early twentieth centuries, especially in North America. Amusement arcades have many antecedents. From the sideshows and midways of local *carnivals and fairs to the shopping and panorama arcades of *London and *Paris, novelty amusements were plentiful in the nineteenth century. But in the early 1890s entrepreneurs began to exploit the automatic amusement machines, called in the USA 'nickel-in-the-slots', adapted first from Edison's phonographs and later from his kinescopes. Louis Glass of San Francisco was the first to realize their commercial potential as a form of inexpensive mass amusement. He installed two converted Edison phonographs in the Palais Royal Saloon in 1890, and within six months he owned over a dozen machines in various saloons and waiting rooms, netting an extraordinary $4,000. Nickel-in-the-slot machines were soon installed in hotel lobbies, resorts, and the midways of local and world's fairs.

To attract a wider *audience and a higher class of clientele, entrepreneurs moved their machines into storefront facilities in commercial districts in most major American cities and added other automatic novelty machines, including candy and chewing-gum dispensers, and even early X-ray machines and fluoroscopes. The arcade changed in 1893 with the arrival of Edison's kinescope, the technological forerunner to *film. Thomas Lombard opened the first kinescope arcade in 1894 at the corner of 27th Street and Broadway in *New York. But by 1897 the fad was waning and many owners sold their equipment to 'tenderloin' arcades and shooting galleries. The lurid nature of the arcades' pictures and their attraction for young men drew increased opposition. Still these new 'penny arcades' flourished under new entrepreneurs. Adolph Zukor and Morris Kohn founded the Automatic Vaudeville Company in 1903 and built a number of 'peep-show' arcades in New York as well as Newark, *Boston, and *Philadelphia. By 1905 many arcades had converted to the new nickelodeon format, only to be replaced in 1907 by the one-reel 'screen shows'—the immediate predecessors to movie houses. But amusement arcades never entirely lost their appeal, and made a comeback in the latter part of the twentieth century with the development of games based on computer simulations. *See also* PENNY THEATRES.

PAD

ANAGNORISIS

In *Aristotle's *Poetics*, *anagnorisis* (recognition) refers to a change in the *protagonist from ignorance to knowledge, leading to happiness (*comedy) or misery (*tragedy). In tragedy, *anagnorisis* is often the mechanism whereby *peripeteia* (reversal) is brought about. Taken together, recognition and reversal are central to a complex *plot, revealing the *hamartia* (error) underlying the protagonist's tragic act, and precipitating his suffering. In Aristotle's discussion of the techniques of recognition—made much of in *early modern *criticism—he argues that those dependent on external signs or tokens, or on self-revelation, are inferior to those arising from a logical analysis of the incidents themselves, as in *Sophocles' *Oedipus the King*. Ironically, the inartistic token became the *sine qua non* of *New Comedy and its Renaissance descendants. Late twentieth-century *theory has applied *anagnorisis* to the *audience, either as a sympathetic 'recognition-acceptance' of the situation as perceived by the *characters, or as a detached 'recognition-criticism' of the situation. RWV

ANAGNOSTAKI, LOULA

Contemporary Greek playwright. Though her date of birth is kept secret, she began her career after attending Aristotle University in Thessaloniki. Her first *one-act plays, *Overnight*, *The City*, and *The Parade*, were produced in 1965 by Karolos *Koun's Art Theatre in *Athens. In 1967 the *Greek National Theatre produced her first full-length play, *Relations*, followed by the Art Theatre productions of *Antonio; or, The Message* in 1972, *Victory* in 1978, and Koun's last directorial work, *Sound of Arms*, in 1987. In the 1990s her work included *Deep Red Sky*, *Distant Voyage*, and *Diamonds and Blues*. Her plays have been translated into several languages and performed in Italy, France, England, and Poland. Anagnostaki precisely portrays the influence of historical events on the everyday lives of her contemporaries, especially Greek women. Her main themes range from the failures of the left during the post-war period to individual issues of guilt, loneliness, and lack of communication.

KGo

ANCIENT THEATRES

1. General; 2. Architecture; 3. Theatrical development

1. General

A multi-purpose public theatre, preferably in stone, was considered necessary not only for its religious festivals but also for political assembly by almost every ancient city in the Graeco-Roman world. Cult centres also possessed theatrical buildings, while the later music hall (*odeon) or even an assembly room (*ekklesiasterion*) may look like a theatre. It is important to

Roman theatre at Bosra in Syria, near Damascus. Constructed in the second century AD on a typical Roman plan, this **ancient theatre** was preserved by its conversion into a medieval Arab castle. The steep rake of seating and the semi-circular orchestra are visible, and the background to the stage (*scaenae frons*) is notably grandiose.

acknowledge that political and theatrical space always overlap in the ancient world, so that the Senate of republican Rome could regard a permanent theatre as potentially dangerous. In addition, most theatres, even when required for public festivals and business, could be leased to entrepreneurs to manage and rent out. This not only encouraged a lively irregular theatrical industry, but made space available for such non-dramatic activities as cockfighting, *juggling, and other entertainments without official place in a festival programme.

The theatre has long been construed as a symbol of public order, which derives naturally from its function as a place of assembly, whether spontaneous or formal, most particularly in its seating arrangements. The huge theatre of Megalopolis, the largest known in Greece, was built as an assembly for the Arcadians *c.*300 BC, and inscriptions show that its 'wedges' represent the tribal divisions, and similar markings are common later. The geometry underlying the *Epidaurus Theatre of *c.*330/300 suggests that Pythagorean ideas of mathematical harmony were already creating a philosophy of theatrical order. The culmination of this Pythagorean idea is the Theatrical Law

of Augustus (*c.*20 BC). It specified precisely where not only the senatorial and knightly classes were to sit, but also boys, tutors, civil servants, and other social groupings, and even regulated the clothing to be worn; it is significant that Latin *ordo* means 'social class' or 'order' as well as 'row of seating'. This law was alternately neglected and reinforced, but produced the strange legal consequence that one's class appeared to be determined by where one was seen to sit in a theatre. The concept was applied in varying degrees throughout the empire—though perhaps less so in Greek theatres lacking the requisite barriers—rendering the theatre not only a visible, colour-coded *spectacle of imperial order but also of Roman class distinction.

2. Architecture

Almost all surviving theatres, especially their stages, have gone through several phases of reconstruction, both because of structural damage (*fire, earthquake, or decay) and by necessary upgrading of theatrical facilities to meet a changing demand. Wood would of course be gradually replaced with stone. A typical development of the *Greek classical theatre was to raise the stage about 300 BC to a height of 2.5 m (about 8 feet) with a depth of only 2–3 m (6.5–10 feet) but a length of 20–40 m (65–131 feet). In early imperial Rome it was then lowered to about 1.5 m (5 feet) and possibly expanded forward several metres into the *orchestra to accommodate *dancing and spectacles (*see* ROMAN THEATRE). An early stage might at some point acquire a two-storey pillared stone façade behind the stage proper, and in extreme cases might be connected with the seating in the Roman manner by roofing over the entranceways to the orchestra, as at Pompeii. As a general rule, therefore, the earlier the theatre, the more it will have suffered rebuilding, sometimes partial. Epidaurus is a clear exception. But the extent of reconstruction will depend on the existence of alternative facilities, such as an *odeon* or *amphitheatre, as well as the readiness of sponsors to finance such work. Only good excavation and relevant inscriptions allow us to determine these frequent remodellings with certainty. The great Theatre of Pompey was under major repair for most of its first 150 years; inscriptions show that the theatre at Aphrodisias was altered at least seven times in 500 years. Nonetheless a few later theatres from imperial times survive almost unchanged, as at Bosra in Syria; many were used as fortresses in medieval times.

The Hellenistic theatres with their wooden painted stage decoration and wooden machinery were expensive to maintain. A few such buildings could be dismantled, as at Pergamum, or even rolled aside, as in Sparta, when not in use. Their façade of painted *flats (*pinakes*) was removed and stored in a separate building, as in Delos. Far more expensive were the temporary theatres, the only type allowed in republican Rome, constructed by politicians seeking popular support with their games. These reached absurd levels of wastefulness, with marble pillars, glass, and ivory façades, all to be demolished soon after.

The principal architectural differences between the Roman theatre type, first clearly found in Pompey's theatre but then copied all over the empire, and the classical Greek theatre are seven. (*a*) The Greek theatre did not connect *skene and *theatron. (*b*) As a result of the Roman invention of the arch, the Roman theatre could be constructed not only as an entire edifice but also on flat land, while the Greek *theatron* was almost always built into a hill. (*c*) The perfected Roman theatre had its stage building as high as the *auditorium, with a complex pillared façade of two or three storeys and a stage enclosed by wings at both sides. (*d*) The Roman auditorium was much steeper than the Greek and more conspicuously divided by gangways and barriers into compartments, these being reached by internal stairs from separate outside doors. (*e*) The semicircular orchestra of the Roman theatre provided seating for the elite spectators for theatrical shows. (*f*) The Roman stage was lower and deeper than the Hellenistic. (*g*) The Roman connection between stage building and auditorium bridged over the top of the side entrances to the stage (*iter versurae*) and the side

entrances to the orchestra (*aditus maximus*), and provided a president's box (*tribunalia*) over the right side.

Local traditions, however, often varied and generalizations about development are dangerous. Gaul had a special native tradition of cult amphitheatre-theatres, while the Balkan area preserved elements of the Hellenistic type well into imperial times. The Roman type may owe more than we know to innovations in Sicily. Even the Theatre of Pompey, the first permanent theatre of Rome, with a vast stage *c*.80 by 10 m (262 by 33 feet), built therefore primarily for large spectacles, nonetheless had also been designed to represent the steps of a temple of Venus, which was constructed on the top of the auditorium and dedicated in 51 BC, in the manner of similar cult theatre-temples in Italy. This was solely to avoid, ingeniously, the accusation that it was a theatre, something opposed by the Senate.

3. Theatrical development

Demand for new theatrical effect required constant alterations and improvements to the fabric of theatres. In Hellenistic times, many theatres as at Delos were equipped with one or even two tunnels, known as Charonian steps, leading from the stage building to *traps in the orchestra, and designed for sudden entrances of *ghosts and apparitions. These have been found sealed over in Roman times, as at Argos, obviously having gone out of fashion. The classical theatre had possessed the *ekkyklema* and crane (*mechane*) and could manage ghost appearances and divine epiphanies, as well as thunder, fire, smoke, and earthquake effects. But the Hellenistic theatre, seeking greater *realism, was furnished with wooden machinery, derived probably from siege engineering, which allowed for sudden appearances also on the roof, presumably epiphanies of the *deus ex machina type familiar in *Euripides. The space beneath the raised wooden stage (*hyposkenion*) was used also for *trapdoors which provided similar startling effects, and for the *curtain that could be raised and lowered mechanically to conceal and reveal. While there is almost no archaeological data for these wooden structures, the later Roman amphitheatre clearly represented a further development of such surprise effects with its multiple elevators raising collapsible buildings (*pegmata*) into the arena. Spectator comfort was in Roman times assured by sun awnings which could partially cover the auditorium and stage, by *stoas* and gardens behind the theatre to allow shelter from rain, and, rarely, even the provision of running water and facilities to spray saffron and throw gifts (*missilia*), though seating marked at 41–44 cm (16–17 inches) wide suggests crowding and discomfort.

Gladiators fought in the Theatre of Pompey in 44 BC; in many places thereafter in both east and west, even where there was an amphitheatre, the theatre became adapted for the very popular *animal fights and *gladiatorial contests as well as pantomimic and aquatic spectacles (*naumachia*), and even judicial executions (*damnatio*) often associated with the imperial cult and its festivals. A variety of alterations aimed at spectator protection, for instance by replacing the lower seating with a wall round the orchestra on which was placed a protective net to prevent animals reaching the *audience, as at Macedonian Stobi. At Aphrodisias in Caria, the orchestra was lowered 2 m, and provided with a special entrance for the animals. At Sagalassus the *proskenion* (*see* SKENE) still shows openings suitable only for animals. At Taormina, a tunnel was created under the stage front for animal entrances. In the Theatre of *Dionysus at Athens nets were used and the front seats temporarily abandoned for such spectacles. At Corinth the stage was removed altogether. Many of the surviving theatres of late antiquity had often undergone various functional alterations of this sort before being turned finally into medieval fortresses. *See also* PLAYHOUSES.   WJS

ANDERSON, JUDITH (1898–1992)

Australian actress who enjoyed a highly acclaimed career in the USA. She gained early experience in the Julius Knight company, which *toured Australia during the First World War. Her American work began in 1918, and included Broadway successes such as *Cobra* by Martin Brown (1924), *O'Neill's *Strange Interlude* (1928) and *Mourning Becomes Electra* (1932), and classical roles. She played Lady Macbeth opposite Laurence *Olivier at the *Old Vic in *London in 1937, and opposite Maurice *Evans in *New York in 1941. Anderson was much praised for her Gertrude, against John *Gielgud's Hamlet (1936), and her Medea, (1947), both on Broadway, the latter adapted by Robinson Jeffers from *Euripides. Her talent for heavy *villainesses and emotional acting is clearly on display in her performance as Mrs Danvers in the *film of *Rebecca* (Hitchcock, 1940). In later life Anderson toured the USA in recitals, and was a regular on the *television soap opera *Santa Barbara* (1984–7). She was created Dame of the British Empire in 1960, the first Australian actress so honoured.   EJS

ANDERSON, LAURIE (1947–)

American *performance artist. Born in Chicago and educated at Barnard College and Columbia University in New York, Anderson created pioneering performances during the 1970s that combined *happenings with her training as a classical violinist. She developed her mature performance style during the early 1980s by fusing elaborate technological effects into her performances with short, comically *surrealistic *monologues. Her first major work in this style, *The United States, Parts I–IV*, premièred at the Brooklyn Academy of Music in 1983 (much of this was reprised in her 1986 *film *Home of the Brave*). Besides *avant-garde acclaim, songs from her performances attracted a popular music audience. Warner Brothers released the first of her several albums and music videos, *Big Science*,

in 1982, establishing her as one of the first 'crossover' performance artists in the United States. Anderson *toured extensively in the 1990s and assembled a retrospective, *Stories from the Nerve Bible*, in 1993. She branched out again in 1999 by collaborating with director Anne *Bogart on *Songs and Stories from Moby Dick* (1999).   JAB

ANDERSON, LINDSAY (1923–94)

English stage and film director, documentary filmmaker, actor, and critic. Born in Bangalore, India, Anderson's work across *film, theatre, and cultural criticism demonstrated a fascination with the English working class and a hatred of the British class system. He was a key figure in the Free Cinema documentary movement of the mid-1950s, making short films about working people and their culture (*Thursday's Children* won an Oscar in 1955). In 1957 Anderson became an associate director of the *English Stage Company, which was emerging as one of the principal driving forces behind the new wave of working-class *realist drama. Amongst the works he directed were John *Arden's *Serjeant Musgrave's Dance* (1959) and several plays by David *Storey, including *In Celebration* (1969), *Home* (1970), *The Changing Room* (1971), and *Life Class* (1974). Anderson also directed feature films, including *This Sporting Life* (1962), *If . . .* (1968), *Oh Lucky Man* (1973), and *Britannia Hospital* (1982). He was an early champion of popular cinema (especially the films of John Ford) and an iconoclastic theatre critic and cultural commentator.   SWL

ANDERSON, MARY (1859–1940)

American actress. Anderson trained with George Vandenhoff on Charlotte *Cushman's recommendation, and made her professional debut as Juliet in *Romeo and Juliet* in Louisville in 1875 at the age of 16. She was immediately recognized as an actress of great beauty, and dramatic passion and power. Juliet was the first of her many successes, which included Perdita and Hermione in *The Winter's Tale* and Rosalind in *As You Like It*. Other roles included Parthenia in *Ingomar*, by Maria Lovell, Galatea in W. S. *Gilbert's *Pygmalion and Galatea*, and Clarice in Gilbert's *Comedy and Tragedy*, a role written for her. In 1878 Anderson left the USA for Britain, where she remained, attaining great success throughout the 1880s with repeated engagements at the *Lyceum Theatre, *London, including the first doubling of the roles of Perdita and Hermione (1887). Her marriage to a wealthy American gave Anderson the excuse she needed to retire from the stage in 1889, at the height of her fame. She later wrote in her memoirs (*A Few Memories*, 1896) that like Frances *Kemble, 'the *practice* of my art . . . had grown as time went on more and more distasteful to me'.   KMN

ANDERSON, MAXWELL (1889–1959)

American playwright, the only American writer to see commercial success in the 1930s with *verse dramas, many based on *historical subjects. He was also skilled in prose, collaborating with Laurence Stallings on the *naturalistic war drama *What Price Glory?* (1924). Anderson was regarded in the 1930s as one of America's foremost dramatists, rivalling Eugene *O'Neill in critical reputation, but his work has been little produced since 1960. His verse plays were seen by some critics as pretentious or bombastic. Others disparaged his poetry—a loose blank verse—as only so much prose set in fixed lines. When *Winterset* (1935) was given the first *New York Drama Critics Circle *award (1936) on the fifth ballot, Percy Hammond of the *Herald Tribune* made a speech representing the dissenters, calling the play 'spinach'. When the verse *comedy *High Tor* won the second Circle award (1937) on the eleventh ballot, dissenting speeches were not included in that (or any subsequent) ceremony. *Elizabeth the Queen* (1930) was the first of Anderson's successful verse plays, and *Mary of Scotland* (1933), about the rivalry between Elizabeth I and her cousin, was regarded by many critics as his outstanding work; the 'Tudor Trilogy' was completed with *Anne of the Thousand Days* (1948). Anderson's talents seemed well suited to *musical collaboration. He wrote *book and lyrics for *Knickerbocker Holiday* (1938) and *Lost in the Stars* (1949), both with composer Kurt *Weill. Anderson upheld an *Aristotelian *theory of *tragedy, but one that seemed influenced by *Schiller in its emphasis on the greatness of the human being, heroic in his or her opposition to overwhelming necessity.   MAF

ANDERSON, ROBERT (1917–)

American playwright. Born in New York, Anderson manifested talent as a dramatist while at Harvard and in the navy during the Second World War. Returning to civilian life after the war, he determined to make his way in the theatre. His first full-length play on Broadway, *Tea and Sympathy*, a critical and commercial success in 1953, was a study of a misunderstood and sensitive boy at an elite American prep school, who passes from boyhood to manhood, through the kind ministrations of the headmaster's wife. It was helped by the direction of Elia *Kazan and the appearance of the film star Deborah Kerr in the leading role. A succession of plays on Broadway followed, with varying success: *All Summer Long* (1954), *Silent Night, Lonely Night* (1959), *You Know I Can't Hear You When the Water's Running* (1967); *I Never Sang for my Father* (1968), *Solitaire, Double Solitaire* (1971). *The Days Between*, premièred at the Dallas Theatre Center in 1965 under the auspices of the American Playwrights' Theatre, was subsequently produced at 51 *regional, *community, and university theatres, to prove that dramatic works can survive away from Broadway. Anderson's

plays are sometimes autobiographical but never plot-heavy, and provide telling glimpses into the psychology of the mostly well-bred, intelligent *characters through his graceful *dialogue. He has also written for *film, *radio, and *television; and has taught playwriting at universities throughout the United States.

MCH

ANDRADE, JORGE (1922–84)

Brazilian playwright, best known for his work on the disintegration of the rural society of *São Paulo. The most important play of this cycle, *A moratória* (*The Moratorium*, 1955), dissects the ruin of the coffee aristocracy after the 1929 economic crash. Influenced by Arthur *Miller, Andrade's *characters struggle for moral coherence and ethical direction in the crossfire of tradition and change. His psychologically *realistic dramas experiment with the representation of *action and memory in multiple stage spaces.

LHD

ANDREEV, LEONID (1871–1919)

Russian dramatist and prose writer. A prolific writer, Andreev completed twenty full-length and eight shorter plays in just over ten years between 1905 and 1916. Closely associated with the *symbolist movement, his drama of man's journey from cradle to grave, *The Life of Man* (1906), is more akin to German *expressionism and was famously staged by *Meyerhold in *St Petersburg and by *Stanislavsky at the *Moscow Art Theatre, in 1907. His most famous play, *He Who Gets Slapped* (1915), is set in a *circus and, in a manner anticipatory of Chaplin's *film *The Circus* (1928) and e. e. cummings's *HIM* (1928), dramatizes the problem of the alienated individual in a world where the conflict between bodily spontaneity, physical beauty, and agility is at odds with spiritual ugliness and the destructive power of the intellect. Andreev's own conflicts were reflected in at least three suicide attempts and political vacillation which began with affiliation to Lenin's Social Democratic Party and concluded with outright opposition to the Russian Revolution. A painter, amateur photographer, and author of two strikingly original theatrical essays (*Letters on the Theatre*, 1912–13), Andreev finally settled in Finland where he died of a heart attack.   NW

ANDREINI FAMILY

Italian professional practitioners of *commedia dell'arte* and related *genres. The Tuscan **Francesco** (1548–1624), after military service and Turkish captivity, embarked on a theatrical career in the late 1570s, and married the young Paduan **Isabella Canali** (1562–1604) in 1578. They quickly became a celebrated acting couple, the core of the *Gelosi company, with Francesco playing the part of the braggart Capitano, and Isabella becoming the first professional actress in history to establish a respectable reputation, while playing the part of the Innamorata (*see* WOMEN AND PERFORMANCE). She refuted the accusations of immodesty which were attached to other actresses, composed a *pastoral play and a large number of occasional rhymes, and was fêted in society to the point of being elected as a member of a literary academy. Both of them left behind in print some important pieces of (sometimes disguised) repertoire material from their *arte* improvisations. Their son **Giovan Battista** (1576–1654) followed them into the profession, defended its respectability vigorously in print, and had a long career as *actor-manager with his own troupe called the *Fedeli, which was invited to France five times. He was also a versatile and experimental dramatist. His twenty published plays cover a remarkable range of tones and structures, though the majority keep at least some reference to the mode of *comedy: they include history's first attempt at a comic *opera libretto (*La Ferinda*, 1622, never actually set to music). His first wife **Virginia** was both actress and singer: she premièred the title role in *Monteverdi's *Arianna* in 1608.   RAA

ANDRONICUS, LIVIUS (fl. 240–204 BC)

Founder of *Roman drama. A freed Greek slave from Tarentum, Andronicus presented his translation of a *Greek play in 240, by tradition considered the first dramatic performance at Rome. Titles of twelve works (*comedies and *tragedies) and some 32 words survive. All were probably Latin versions of Greek originals, drawing upon accessible and well-known mythic subjects, in particular the Trojan War. Andronicus both staged and performed in his translations, and was honoured with the right to establish a guild of actors and dramatists. Later critics, including *Horace and Cicero, considered his works crude and makeshift.   RCB

ANG DUONG (1796–1860)

Cambodian king. Acclaimed as the restorer of national unity after centuries of political volatility, he is also credited with spearheading changes to *Cambodia's court dance, basing some of his innovations on carvings of celestial dancers found on the twelfth-century temple of Angkor in north-western Cambodia. Raised in Siam (*Thailand), Ang continued the tradition of cultural interchange by bringing many Siamese to the court, including some dancers. Along with his female dancers, he is reputed to have kept a male troupe at court, which was disbanded following his death.   TSP

ANGELES, ROBERTO (1953–)

Peruvian playwright and director who studied at the Catholic University of Peru and in London. His productions are energy charged, highly rhythmic, vivid in colour and movement, draw-

ing on his experimentation with *dance and martial arts. He has explored controversial issues such as sibling rivalry (*The Cowardly Japanese*, 1999), and AIDS (*Kushner's *Angels in America*, 2000). He also staged *Marité* (1984), *AM/FM* (1985), *Contact* (1986), *Guayasamín in Senegal* (1986), *Do You Want to Be with Me?* (1988), *Metamorphosis* (1993), *Hamlet* (1995), and *Macbeth* (2000). He co-edited *Dramaturgia peruana* (2000) with playwright José Castro-Urioste.   LRG

ANGIKA

Literally 'the body', an inclusive term that refers to all the physical aspects of performance in *Indian classical dance-theatre traditions. As codified in the *Natyasastra*, the 'primary limbs' (*anga*) are the head, hands, breast, waist, sides, and feet, while the 'minor limbs' (*upanga*) include the eyes, eyebrows, nose, and chin. Such are the minutiae of physical acting (*angikabhinaya*) that there are thirteen movements of the head, and as many as 36 glances (*drishti*) to represent emotions in their primary, secondary, and transitory stages. Other components of *angika* include particular stances, postures, walks (*gati*), hand gestures (*hastas*), and specific combinations of hands and feet in dance movements (*karanas*). *See also* ABHINAYA.   LSR/RB

ANGLIN, MARGARET (1876–1958)

Canadian-American actress and producer. Born Mary Margaret Anglin in Ottawa, she made her professional debut in *New York (1894) under the name Margaret Moore in *Shenandoah*, but was soon persuaded to revert to her proper surname. She achieved immediate fame in 1898 as Roxane in *Cyrano de Bergerac*. Her rich voice and highly emotional acting were tempered when she moved into more *realistic plays such as *Moody's *The Great Divide* (1906), which kept her busy for more than two years. Starting in 1908 she appeared in classics around the country and abroad: Shakespeare (Viola, Kate, Olivia, Rosalind, Cleopatra), and the *Greeks (Antigone, Clytemnestra, Medea, Phaedra)—in which she oversaw everything herself including *casting, staging, *costumes, and *lighting. The greatest success in her career was her 1927 Electra in New York. Her final stage appearance came in a *touring production of *Hellman's *Watch on the Rhine* in 1943.   CT

ANGURA

The *avant-garde theatre movement in *Japan, also called the 'post-*shingeki*', or 'little theatre' (*shōgekijō*) movement. *Angura* (underground) rose from a dissatisfaction with the political and aesthetic stance of orthodox modern theatre (*shingeki*); many of its proponents were involved in the nationwide protests over the ratification of the 1960 USA–Japan Security Treaty. The movement centred on work by people like *Kara Jūrō, *Satoh

Makoto, *Shimizu Kunio, *Terayama Shūji, *Suzuki Tadashi, and *Hijikata Tatsumi. The styles of *angura* vary widely, from the carnivalesque to the austere, but some commonalities can be noted. *Angura* eschewed the realism and humanism of *shingeki* in favour of fantasy and myth in an attempt to make sense out of a contemporary world rendered absurd by the war and its aftermath. It typically employed *metatheatrical devices, often in an attempt to recapture the energy and spirit of pre-modern Japanese theatre. It also radically questioned the roles of *text, performance space, actors, and *audience in a performance. Where *shingeki* privileged the text, *angura* tended to stress the physicality of the actor. Even so, some excellent playwrights like Shimizu and Kara have emerged from this movement. Performances were typically held in small theatres (some seating no more than 50 people), in tents, or on the *street. Initially marked by revolutionary roots, *angura* became increasingly apolitical. Some fix its demise around the mid-1970s, but many of its creators are still active, and its stylistic legacy continues in the work of younger artists like *Noda Hideki.

CP

ANIMAL FIGHTS (*VENATIONES*)

The Romans displayed *animals variously as curiosities, to perform tricks, and to engage in combat. Staged hunts developed at Rome during the third and second centuries BC, perhaps stimulated by contact with North African civilizations, and became an integral feature of Romanization throughout the known world. They combined the allure of exotic species with the excitement of the chase. In the late republic the *aediles* (urban magistrates) became responsible for providing regular *venationes*, and competed energetically to acquire animals. There is some evidence that tribesmen from the animals' native habitat were imported to hunt them. Under the empire professional organizations supplied animals and personnel, at least to venues in North Africa, and at Rome a training school for beast-fighters is first mentioned in the reign of Nero (AD 54–68). Republican installations under the Roman Forum indicate that its use as a temporary arena included provision for the display of animals. For massed hunts the largest venue at Rome was the Circus Maximus, while *amphitheatres or converted *Greek theatres and stadia were equipped for spectator protection. Under Augustus (27 BC–AD 14) *venationes* became regularly combined with *gladiatorial contests; sometimes the two halves of the programme would be punctuated by a *damnatio*. The number and type of animals were advertised in advance, and frequently recorded in sponsors' epitaphs. A local community could take pride in an event even if the total number of animals displayed remained in single figures. At Rome, however, the emperors competed in conspicuous consumption. Augustus dispatched 3,500 'African beasts' in 26 displays, Trajan (reputedly) 11,000 animals during his Dacian triumph. Animals were also pitted against one another individually, sometimes chained together to ensure an engagement. Encounters were contrived that balanced the odds: bull versus elephant, rhinoceros versus bison. An animal could also be matched with a beast-fighter who was trained and equipped to outwit it. A theatrical setting sometimes contributed verisimilitude: at the Ludi Saeculares in AD 204 Septimius Severus staged a 'shipwreck' in the Circus Maximus that disgorged a cargo of live animals onto the track. Despite logistical difficulties, *venationes* persisted into the sixth century. *See also* CIRCUS, ROMAN

KMC

ANIMALS

Animals have featured in performance from ancient times. The *Romans had bears and dogs in dramas, elephants who performed rope walking, and built gruesome shows of *animal fights. Throughout Europe, trained animals accompanied itinerant performers to the great fairs—the dancing bear, the tame lion, and the intelligent goat. In *The Winter's Tale,* Shakespeare's famous *stage direction 'Exit, pursued by a bear' is considered by some historians to indicate the availability of trained performing bears, rather than those from the nearby Bear-Pit at Southwark (*see* BAITING). By the seventeenth century animals featured in performances in their own right. At Bartholomew Fair in *London, *fairground booths exhibited animal as well as human performers: the tiger who, in 1701, 'pulled the feathers so nicely from live fowls', the *morris-dancing dogs (who danced before Queen Anne), and an Italian singing pig. It was in the fairs that performing horses established their popularity. Not only were they *animaux savants*, they also demonstrated tricks and feats which formed the basis of the modern *circus. An ape dressed in a soldier's uniform rode a horse, and human riders exhibited trick horsemanship on expertly trained animals in open fields and riding schools.

Astley's Circus opened in London in 1768, and *Astley's Amphitheatre in 1784, featuring mainly equestrian acts. The popularity of the horses encouraged the development of *hippodrama, plays constructed around feats of equestrianism by star performers. Popular themes were *Dick Turpin's Ride to York* (in which the death of Black Bess was the climax) and plays by Shakespeare such as *Richard III* and *Henry V*, where galloping and leaping horses could shine in the battle scenes. By the 1870s dog dramas such as *The Forest of Bondy* and *My Poor Dog Tray* were hugely popular, written to display the talents of well-trained dogs like Sam Wild's retriever Nelson, who would ascend a 12-m (40-foot) ladder, fire a cannon on a perch, and descend on the opposite side. Wild considered Nelson a 'difficult dog to teach', and correspondence in the trade newspaper the *Era* shows that there was much interest in the detail of the practice. Trainers used meat secreted in a pocket or a handkerchief to encourage a dog to 'take the seize', that is, attack or fasten its teeth on an actor's clothing. When such highly trained animals were sold, they took their acts with them: 'For sale, two performing dogs. First dog, twelve tricks; second dog, reader of cards. Suitable for side-show. Professor A Peterson, 27 Mary-street, St George's-in-the-East' (*Era*, 1881).

The exhibition of performing animals continued throughout the nineteenth century. Menageries were extremely popular *touring shows; unlike the circus, they displayed their animals in cages, and many featured novelty shows such as the 'Happy Family'—the caging (and sometimes performance) of disparate and antagonistic animal groups, cats, dogs and mice, for example. In booths, public houses, and exhibition rooms, animal anomalies—the six-legged horse, the two-headed calf, the monster pig ('19 months old, upwards of 60 stone, 9 feet 3 inches long, 3 feet 6 inches in height')—were often challenged by a human-animal, like Jo-Jo the Dog-faced boy, the Leopard or Zebra Child, or Zip (William Henry Johnson) Coon, billed as the 'Man-Monkey' or 'What Is It?' by P. T. *Barnum (*see also* FREAK SHOW). Lion taming was featured in both menageries and circuses. In menageries the performance tended to take place within the cage, and was frequently confined to enraging the animal and then beating it into submission, but in the bigger circuses more skill was needed. A tamer of note was Thomas Batty, who had trained his lions to spring at the bars ferociously as he entered the ring. As he made his way to the cage, a plant in the *audience would plead with him not to go in. His remarkable speed and agility within the cage (and on leaving it) no doubt accounted for his longevity.

Trainers proliferated in the nineteenth and early twentieth centuries as the demand for animal novelties moved from the circus to the *music halls and *variety theatres. M. Permane's Siberian Bears would drink stout from a bottle, don a lady's straw hat, and shake hands. Permane laid claim to radical training methods: 'Catch your bears young,' he said. 'They get untrustworthy as they grow older. It is no use ill-treating them; you must be kind and gentle with them, but you must let them know that you are the master.' The Hungarian M. Nivin was a famed monkey trainer, and his 'Blondin' monkey—who walked, somewhat reluctantly, across a horizontal bar with his head in a sack—was the rage of the London halls during 1894. M. Gris's baboons rode a donkey, jumped through hoops, and turned somersaults on the donkey's back whilst it cantered around the ring.

Animals frequently became stars in their own right. Jumbo, the elephant so coveted by Barnum, was the focus of British outrage when he was sold by the London Zoo to the showman in 1881. Huge sums were offered to Barnum to relent, but he remained resolute. Having shipped him to America, Barnum realized his potential even after the unfortunate animal was killed in a locomotive collision. In Barnum's grand circus parade, Jumbo's skin and the skeleton were mounted on two great wagons, followed by Alice, another elephant from the London Zoo, and a long line of the circus's regular elephants, all carrying in their trunks black-bordered bed sheets and trained to wipe their eyes every few steps.

Convincing animal impersonators are a rare breed. Charles Lauri worked as a famously accurate *pantomime monkey who had trained by observing Sally, a real specimen at London Zoo. He played a *realistic Poodle in the 1888 *Drury Lane pantomime of *Sindbad the Sailor*. He specialized in monkeys, cats, and dogs, and famously walked around the edge of the circle among the audience in animal *character. George *Conquest played a similar range of pantomime animals at the Grecian Theatre, including an octopus and a gigantic ape in the *Grim Goblin* (1876) and a grotesque toad in *Harlequin Rokoko, the Rock Fiend* (1878). A reviewer wrote that 'the Octopus not only looks like the real thing, but in its movements we trace an exact resemblance'. Despite a growing cultural repulsion to performing animals and their human imitators, animal impersonations have not disappeared; in fact they have moved into the mainstream theatre in contemporary *musicals like *Lloyd Webber's *Cats* (1972) and the Disney Company's *The Lion King* (1997), which still realize the human-animal on stage.   AF

ANKIYA NAT

Traditional *dance-drama performed in the north-eastern state of Assam, *India. Attributed to Sankaradeva (1459–1568), a saint-poet and social and religious reformer, who composed as many as six *ankiya nats* for the propagation of Vaishnavism, this form of devotional drama dramatizes the avatars of the Hindu god Vishnu for the spiritual edification of ordinary people. Following Sanakaradeva's first dramatic venture, *Chihnyatra*, which elaborated on the seven *vaikunthas* (heavens), he went on to compose other *nats* (plays) on mythological themes: *Patni-prasada*, *Kali-damana*, *Keli-gopala*, *Rukmini-harana*, *Parijata-harana*, and *Rama-vijaya*. The saint-poet Madhavadeva (1489–1596), continuing Sanakaradeva's spiritual legacy, also composed devotional plays, although most of them are popularly known as *jhumura* rather than *ankiya nat*, because of their short duration.

The performance of *ankiya nat* is known as *anikya bhaona* and begins with a musical prelude from a traditional orchestra, played to the beats of the *khol* (drum) and the clashing of cymbals. After accompanying the *ritualistic preliminaries of the performance, leading into a full-blown musical concert (*guru-ghat*) affirming the divine presence, the *gayana-bayana* is interrupted by the *sutradhara* (director), who introduces the theme of the play, followed by the *nandi* (benediction). Continuing according to the directions of Sanskrit drama as enunciated in the *Natyasastra*, the *nat* then formally begins. Indicating the changes of location and mood in the play with stylized gestures and movement, the *characters are interrelated through the commentary and *dialogue of the *sutradhara*.

Apart from *slokas* (verses) in Sanskrit, the songs, dialogue, and commentary of the different characters are voiced in a vernacular form of Assamese called Brajavali. The performance is highlighted by exquisite dances and simple, yet elegant, *costumes—the *sutradhara* is dressed in an all-white outfit with a decorated waistband, while some of the characters use *masks (*mukha*) and elaborate body-accessories (*cho*) made of bamboo, cane, cloth, and clay. Performed more often than not in a prayer-hall (*namghar*), which is situated within the monastery (*satra*), the *ankiya nat* remains an integral part of Assamese culture today, contributing not only to the rituals of neo-Vaishnavite traditions but to the creation of contemporary cultural practice as well.   AMB

ANNENKOV, YURY (1889–1974)

Russian designer, theorist, and memoirist. Best known for his work with Nikolai *Evreinov at the *Krivoe Zerkalo (Crooked or Distorting Mirror) Theatre in *St Petersburg after 1913, Annenkov graduated from the theatre of satirical 'small forms' to design settings for Evreinov's *mass spectacle in Winter Palace Square, *The Storming of the Winter Palace* (1920). He also illustrated the latter's three-volume *Teatr dlya sebya* (*Theatre for Itself*) and designed productions of *Kaiser's *Gas* (1922) and Aleksei *Tolstoy's *Revolt of the Machines* (1924). He emigrated to *Paris in 1924 but remained active as a stage and *film designer and book illustrator.   NW

ANNENSKY, INNOKENTY (1856–1909)

Russian poet, dramatist, and critic. A leading figure among the Russian *symbolists, he composed modern versions of *Greek drama based on *Euripidean models, the most famous of which was *Famira Kifared* (*Thamira Kitharides/Thamira the Lyrist*) which was produced by Aleksandr *Tairov with designs by Aleksandra *Ekster at the Kamerny Theatre, *Moscow, in 1916. Of the four plays he wrote, this is the only one to have been performed although another, treating of death's defeat through love, was adapted by Fyodor *Sologub and performed during Annensky's lifetime as *The Gift of the Wise Bees* in 1907.   NW

ANOUILH, JEAN (1910–87)

French dramatist. Born in Bordeaux, son of a tailor and a violinist, Anouilh attended school in Paris from 1919. He worked as an advertising copywriter and did military service. Employed as Louis *Jouvet's secretary (1931–2), he wrote his first play, *L'Hermine* (1932), a modest success. Georges *Pitoëff's productions of *Le Voyageur sans bagage* (1937) and *La Sauvage* (*Restless Heart*, 1938) established Anouilh's reputation for slick *dramaturgy with a comic touch and mordant bite. His decade-long collaboration with director André *Barsacq yielded some of his most enduring work: *Le Bal des voleurs* (*Thieves Carnival*, 1938), *Léocadia* (*Time Remembered*, 1940), *Antigone* (1944), *L'Invitation au château* (*Ring round the Moon*, 1947).

Anouilh's plays include reinterpretations of classics by *Sophocles, Shakespeare, and *Wilde, and *historical subjects like Joan of Arc in *L'Alouette* (*The Lark*, 1953) and *Becket; ou, L'Honneur de Dieu* (1959). Social *comedies with risqué overtones include *La Valse des toréadors* (*Waltz of the Toreadors*, 1952) and *L'Hurluberlu* (1959). A frequent *character type is the *gamine*, a self-aware young woman whose obsession with purity enables her to handle would-be seducers with aplomb, as in *La Répétition; ou, L'Amour puni* (*The Rehearsal*, 1950), *Colombe* (1951), and *Cécile* (1954). *Metatheatrical devices abound, for theatre itself is one of Anouilh's persistent themes, its artifice serving to expose falseness in social interactions. Besides his 60 or so plays, Anouilh wrote and directed screenplays. For publication, he grouped his plays under the titles *Pièces roses* (*Pink Plays*), *Pièces noires*, . . . *brillantes*, . . . *grinçantes*, . . . *costumées*, . . . *baroques*, . . . *secrètes*, . . . *farceuses*. Perhaps more than any other French dramatist of the twentieth century, Anouilh found an international *audience: 1955 brought him a Tony *award in *New York for *The Lark*; 1962 saw six of his plays on *London stages.   FHL

ANSKI, SOLOMON (1863–1920)

Russian-Jewish poet, dramatist, historian, folklorist, and prolific writer in both Yiddish and Russian. He is best known for his play of occult possession *The Dybbuk*, staged in Hebrew by the *Habima Studio troupe in *Moscow in 1922, directed by Evgeny *Vakhtangov, and which subsequently *toured the world with great success. The company settled in Palestine in 1932, then in Israel in 1948, staging Anski's *Day and Night* that same year.   NW

ANTAGONIST *See* PROTAGONIST.

ANTHESTERIA

A new-wine festival of *Dionysus celebrated at Athens, 11–13 Anthesterion (February). It included a procession with Dionysus in a wheeled ship, drinking contests, a sacred marriage, ritual abuse, and *rituals to placate ghosts. The statesman Lycurgus (*c*.338–326 BC) added (or revived?) a comic competition.   EGC

ANTHROPOLOGY, THEATRE

A term coined by Eugenio *Barba in the late 1970s which he most recently defines as 'the study of the pre-expressive scenic behaviour upon which different *genres, styles, roles and personal or collective traditions are based'. The term has gone through several incarnations since its inception, but has always been centred on performance. Despite the implications of 'anthropology', it is not concerned with the socio-cultural context or historical origins of particular theatre forms; its focus is the actor on stage. Theatre anthropology is an essentialist or universalist *theory which assumes that performance is based on principles that function across cultures.

Theatre anthropology is inextricably linked to Barba and has its origins in his fascination with 'presence'. Beginning with his studies of traditional Asian theatre forms early in his career, Barba noted that intentional distortion of the body characterized most of them. In *Japanese *nō, *Indian *kathakali, and Balinese *dance-drama, for instance, the performers engage their energies in a way they do not in daily life. This is achieved by altering the normal centre of gravity, the distribution of body weight, and the balance of muscular oppositions in the body. The locked hips and bent knees in nō, the bent knees and open stance on the outer edges of the feet in kathakali, and the open gait with bent knees and toes raised off the floor in Balinese dance-drama are integral to the genres themselves. No matter what *character or situation a nō actor is called upon to portray, underlying it will be the stance that characterizes the form. The stance carries no signification other than identifying the genre, but it calls for a greater expenditure of energy than merely standing or sitting in daily life. This excess energy induces a dynamic state in the performer, that is, the pre-expressive mode (or presence), in which the actor's energies are engaged prior to personal or cultural expression.

In traditional Eastern performance, as well as in the few codified Western performance forms such as *ballet and corporeal *mime, the pre-expressive principles underlying presence are embedded in the codes themselves. But for theatre anthropology, these principles are as important to presence in the *realistic stage conventions of the West or the European classical traditions as they are to codified Asian performance, because the pre-expressive has its origins in the biological body, the distribution of body weight, the opposition of muscular tensions, and the body's centre of gravity, not the cultural setting which spawned and characterizes any one genre.

Theatre anthropology is rooted in the institution it grew out of, the International School of Theatre Anthropology (ISTA), which Barba founded in 1979. ISTA is based at the *Odin Teatret/Nordisk Teaterlaboratorium in Holstebro, Denmark, and arranges conferences in conjunction with sponsors in different parts of the world. As of 2001 there have been eleven conferences throughout Europe and in Brazil, bringing together traditional Eastern performers and their Western counterparts, relatively inexperienced actors and directors from the Euro-American tradition, and teams of theatre scholars, anthropologists, and scientists. The thrust of the meetings has been to examine the performance principles underlying the pre-expressive mode in the various performance forms represented at the particular gathering. Given its narrow focus and the dominant role Barba plays in its construction, theatre anthropology has been frequently criticized, most notably for Barba's authorial posture and research methodology at ISTA, and for his disregard of cultural or personal factors in presence. *See also* INTER-CULTURALISM. IDW

BARBA, EUGENIO, *The Paper Canoe* (London, 1995)
—— and SAVARESE, NICOLA, *A Dictionary of Theatre Anthropology* (London, 1991)
WATSON, IAN, et al., *Negotiating Cultures* (Manchester, 2002)

ANTIQUARIANISM

A method of historically accurate *mise-en-scène. Well before its arrival in late eighteenth-century European theatre, antiquarianism was a widespread cultural movement to preserve, collect, and study historical objects and documents. Through its emphasis on show and display, performance was a natural ally. While novels, paintings, and museums could represent the past, the theatre alone could re-enact it, transforming historical records and monuments into a live, embodied experience.

From the late eighteenth to the early twentieth centuries theatrical antiquarianism meant using historically correct sets (*see* SCENOGRAPHY; COSTUME; PROPERTIES). The series of Gothic architectural designs which William *Capon created for John Philip *Kemble at both *Drury Lane and *Covent Garden between 1794 and 1809 represent the first sustained use of antiquarian scenery in the British theatre. Charles *Kemble and J. R. *Planché's 1823 revival of *King John* at Covent Garden was the first production to feature historically precise costumes. Although contemporary plays such as Edward *Bulwer-Lytton's *Richelieu* (1839) were staged with historical accuracy, Shakespeare's plays became the principal focus of antiquarian propriety. The Shakespearian revivals staged by W. C. *Macready, Charles *Kean, Henry *Irving, and Herbert Beerbohm *Tree all relied upon historically correct—and increasingly elaborate—stage and costume designs. Even plays with no fixed time or setting, such as *The Tempest*, were assigned a precise history and geography in order that they, too, could be staged as historical spectacles. The value placed upon historical accuracy meant that researchers had to track down archival sources and designers had to translate those sources into theatrically effective *scenery or costumes. Thus, Planché's costume for King John was based not upon theatrical precedent, but upon John's actual effigy in Worcester Cathedral. The theatre ranged far in its quest for historical truth, sometimes interpolating re-enactments of documented events into plays which do not dramatize them, such as Henry's triumphal return to London after the victory at Agincourt which Kean added to his 1859 revival of *Henry V*.

For most of the twentieth century, performance historians dismissed antiquarianism as a naive fascination with historical detail which wrongly diverted an *audience's attention from the dynamics of the play itself. Such views reiterate a long-standing prejudice that in the theatre words are more important than pictures. More recent scholarship, however, has shown that theatrical antiquarianism helped to create a popular audience for historical study. *See also* REALISM AND REALITY.   RWS

ANTI-THEATRICAL POLEMIC

In the Western tradition, moral and/or religious objections to the theatre have been raised during most of the periods in which it has enjoyed prosperity and influence and during many in which it has not. Towards the close of the great era of *Greek theatre, Plato (c.428–348 BC) included the theatre centrally in his attack on the mimetic arts in *The Republic*—all poets were to be banished from his ideal commonwealth, not least the playwrights—and while classical Roman writers rarely bothered to follow his example they barely needed to, since by law Roman actors, even celebrities such as *Roscius, were denied citizenship and treated to the kinds of social opprobrium otherwise reserved for prostitutes (*see* ROMAN THEATRE). Plato was eagerly seconded, however, by the early church fathers, who supplemented his view of the theatre as a place of base mimickry calculated to raise our animal passions against our reason by adducing biblical prohibitions against falsity in general and dressing up in particular (Deuteronomy 22: 5, forbidding transvestism, would also be a favourite text with later anti-theatrical polemicists). Tatian's 'Address to the Greeks' (c. AD 160) argued that actors were guilty of inciting the crimes they depicted, and *Tertullian's *De Spectaculis* (c.210) claimed that drama was devised by devils to lure men into idolatry. St Augustine was more ambivalent on the subject: although his *Confessions* (c.400) repent of his youthful addiction to theatregoing, they acknowledge the power of live *tragedy and are themselves highly dramatic. Like Augustine, organized Christianity has been divided ever since between the desire to repudiate the theatre and the desire to appropriate it, which have coexisted uneasily throughout its subsequent history: even during the Church's most spectactular adoption of drama, the *medieval heyday of the *biblical plays, some argued that staging the Passion was innately blasphemous (see, for example, the anonymous fourteenth-century English sermon *A Tretise of Miraclis Pleyinge*). The pendulum swung back against drama at the end of the Middle Ages, and anti-theatrical polemic perhaps enjoyed its European heyday during the *Reformation and Counter-Reformation, when both the courtly and the commercial theatres of England, France, Spain, and Italy (in particular) found themselves under attack from various ecclesiastical factions. In England, though some Puritans (such as *Milton) loved drama and some high churchmen (such as the lapsed play-wright Stephen *Gosson and, more influentially, the Restoration pamphleteer Jeremy *Collier) wrote against it, the theatre's most vociferous opponents, associating drama with courtly corruption and Popish ritual, were Puritans such as Phillip Stubbes (*The Anatomy of Abuses*, 1583) and William *Prynne, who lost his ears for criticizing Queen Henrietta Maria's participation in *masques (in *Histriomastix*, 1633). On the Continent, by contrast, the major campaign against drama was led by senior Jansenists within the Catholic Church, among them the Italian Cardinal Carlo Borromeo and the Frenchmen Armand de Bourbon, Prince de Conti (*Traité de la comédie et des spectacles*, 1669) and Jacques Bénigne Bossuet (*Maximes et réflexions sur la comédie*, 1694). All of these various anti-theatrical attitudes continued to flourish through the nineteenth century, sometimes less visibly in Europe than in the United States—perhaps unsurprisingly given its Puritan heritage and the influence of another man-of-the-theatre turned anti-theatricalist, Jean-Jacques *Rousseau. While the stage has occasionally drawn fire since, it has generally had to be quite strenuously obscene or provocative in order to do so, moralists' attentions having largely transferred to newer *mass media such as *film, *television, and the Internet. *See also* CENSORSHIP.   MD

BARISH, JONAS, *The Anti-Theatrical Prejudice* (Berkeley, 1981)

ANTOINE, ANDRÉ (1858–1943)

French actor and director. His modest beginnings as an employee of the *Paris Gas Company belied the reformative zeal and commitment with which he was to revolutionize stage practice in France. His work was inspirational throughout Europe. In 1887, after experimentation with his *amateur drama group, the Cercle Gaulois, Antoine founded the Théâtre *Libre. His new theatre was funded primarily through subscriptions, a practice which enabled him to avoid the *censor. From the first season he hit on a successful formula of combining unproduced works by known authors with the work of new dramatists, and he refused to rest on the laurels of one playwright's success. His theatre quickly became the refuge for many playwrights rejected by the larger stages; his turnover policy, however, also led to disagreements with authors, as did the emphasis on *realism, which shifted the balance of power away from author and actor to director. His insistence on continuous novelty, often in programmes of short *one-act plays, expanded to include stage adaptations of well-known novels, new prose and *verse drama, and translations of foreign plays. Few indigenous works were to enter the canon of modern French drama during this period, though significant premières of foreign works included *Ibsen's *Ghosts* (1890), *Strindberg's *Miss Julie* (1891), and *Hauptmann's *The Weavers* (1893). Antoine's passion for realism in production linked him falsely with *Zola's project of *naturalism in the theatre, and yet authenticity and exactitude in *costumes, *scenery, and *lighting, and his quest for realistic *acting, did not harm the naturalist cause.

Bankruptcy forced him to cease trading in 1894 but he reopened in the same venue in 1897 under the title Théâtre *Antoine and continued his reformation of theatre practice, although with the same financial difficulties. In 1906 recognition of his success and status came with his appointment to the Théâtre de l'*Odéon, where he was able to put in place what would become standard procedures, such as the abolition of *footlights and darkening of the *auditorium, which increased *audience attention and facilitated more truthful performances from actors. At the Odéon he mounted many notable productions of European classics, including plays by Shakespeare, *Goldoni, *Racine, *Corneille, and *Sheridan, which were characterized by historical realism and scenic exactitude. Ticket receipts during his tenure rose dramatically, but so did production costs. At the Odéon he produced over 360 plays between 1906 and 1914 and was able to carry out some of the architectural changes he had longed for throughout his career. One major hurdle was attracting audiences across the river—by the beginning of the twentieth century most theatres (including his own) were situated on Paris's Right Bank. After the First World War, Antoine, faced with the anti-naturalism of *Copeau and *Jouvet, dabbled in *film and continued to call for reforms in theatre through his dramatic *criticism.   BRS

ANTOINE, THÉÂTRE

*Paris *playhouse, formerly the Théâtre des Menus-Plaisirs, renamed when director and reformer André *Antoine assumed control in 1897 after a seven-year experiment with the Théâtre *Libre (1887–94). Intended as a more successful commercial enterprise than its debt-ridden, *amateur precursor, the Théâtre Antoine played host to its namesake's desire to rid the stage of declamation and *painted *scenery, creating instead 'pointillist *realism'. Antoine left it to work in the Théâtre de l'*Odéon in 1906. Situated on the boulevard de Strasbourg, the theatre continues to produce French classics and modern drama.

BRS

ANTOON, A. J. (ALFRED JOSEPH) (1944–92)

American director. Antoon directed classics, new plays, and *musicals on and *Off-Broadway, and won a Tony *award in 1971 for Jason Miller's That Championship Season. A native of Massachusetts, Antoon enrolled in the *Yale School of Drama, but left before he finished a degree to pursue a professional career. He was championed by Joseph *Papp at the *New York Shakespeare Festival and was noted for his fanciful touch with Shakespeare. His productions for the festival included an Americanized Much Ado About Nothing (1971, which subsequently transferred to Broadway), a Midsummer Night's

Dream set in the milieu of a Brazilian carnival (1988), and a Wild West Taming of the Shrew featuring Tracey Ullman and Morgan Freeman (1990). Antoon's innovative production of the Off-Broadway musical Song of Singapore was still running when he died.   KF

ANTUNES FILHO, JOSÉ ALVES (1929–)

Brazilian director. His 1978 adaptation of Mário de Andrade's novel Macunaíma (1926) brought worldwide attention to Brazilian theatre. Drawing on the legends, *characters, and episodes in Andrade's vision of modernity and national identity, the production became a highly visual *spectacle built on superb *acting and simple *scenography. Antunes has turned his attention increasingly to a minimalist, orientalized theatrical style in directing works by Nelson *Rodrigues and Jorge *Andrade, as well as ancient epics (Gilgamesh, 1995) and *Greek *tragedies (Medea, 2001).   LHD

ANTWERP

Belgian city which, as a crucial port, has long been a major cultural centre of Flanders. There are records of performances on the Market Square as early as the fourteenth century. In the fifteenth and sixteenth centuries Antwerp boasted several flourishing *Chambers of Rhetoric, such as De Violieren, De Goudbloem, and De Olijftak. A highpoint of their existence was the grand 'Landjuweel' of 1561, a *festival in which fourteen Chambers from the Low Countries took part. After the fall of Antwerp in 1585, cultural life went into decline. Willem Ogier, perhaps the only significant playwright in the southern Netherlands in the seventeenth century, had his plays performed by De Violieren, which amalgamated with De Olijftak in a *playhouse set up in the 1660s in the Old Stock Exchange. In 1711 a theatre in the Tapissierspand—a hall for selling tapestries—opened its doors, and remained an important venue during the Austrian and French dominations, though Flemish drama was ousted by French and Italian *opera. On the very spot of the Tapissierspand, the architect Pierre Bourla built a magnificent new theatre in 1834 in *neoclassical style. The Bourla, as it came to be called, was successively the home of the Théâtre Royal Français, the Koninklijke Nederlandse Schouwburg, and, from 1998, the Toneelhuis.

*Amateur companies kept Flemish theatre alive; their perseverance eventually brought about the first professional company, proudly called Nationaal Toneel (1853). First *managed by Victor Driessens, the company set the standard for Dutch theatre in Belgium for more than a century. In its initial period it staged popular *melodramas as well as many original Flemish plays. Towards the end of the nineteenth century it added work from the European classic and modern *naturalistic repertoire, bolstered by guest performances from Tommaso *Salvini,

Ernesto *Rossi, and the *Meiningen Players, which contributed to a growing Shakespeare tradition in Antwerp. From 1922 to 1929 the company was led by J. O. De Gruyter, who improved the standard of the repertoire and stimulated stylized ensemble *acting.

From 1950 till the mid-1970s the Reizend Volkstheater (Travelling Popular Theatre) annually played a Shakespeare production—usually one of the romantic *comedies—in the *open-air setting of the Rubenshuis. Antwerp witnessed a proliferation of small *studio and *alternative theatres in the 1960s and 1970s, which particularly attended to the new *absurdist and *realistic social drama. In the last few decades of the twentieth century the boundaries between centre and margin became more blurred, a trend most apparent in the creation of the Toneelhuis in 1998, merging the Royal Dutch Theatre and *Blauwe Maandag, led by Luc Perceval. Antwerp is also home to the Flemish Opera, which produced a highly innovative *Puccini cycle (1991–7) directed by Robert Carsen. The arts centre deSingel (founded 1980) rapidly became an important international and interdisciplinary home for performance and new forms of *music theatre.   JDV

ANZENGRUBER, LUDWIG (1839–89)

Austrian dramatist and journalist. Anzengruber became famous overnight in 1870 when his first play, Der Pfarrer von Kirchfeld (The Parson of Kirchfeld), was performed in *Vienna. Written in the tradition of *Nestroy's popular theatre with music (Volksstück), this play, and most of the works to follow—such as Der Meineidbauer (The Perjured Peasant, 1871) and Der G'wissenswurm (The Worm of Conscience, 1874)—were set in a peasant milieu. They employed dialect and a critical moral tone which brought the author frequently into conflict with the Church. Carefully delineated *characters and sympathies with *naturalism elevate his work above the usual popular theatre. Despite the local settings and dialect Anzengruber was performed throughout the German-speaking world in the late nineteenth century.   CBB

APOLLO THEATRE

A monument to black entertainment in the twentieth century, the Apollo in *New York was built in 1913 when Harlem was a white immigrant neighbourhood. Reflecting changes in demographics, the theatre abandoned *burlesque and began featuring black talent. In the mid-1930s Amateur Night, an Apollo institution, began with the Schiffman management, which lasted through the 1970s. Some of the legends who have played the Apollo include Anita Baker, Count Basie, James Brown, Nat King Cole, Bill Cosby, Sammy Davis, Duke Ellington, Ella Fitzgerald, Aretha Franklin, Lauryn Hill, Billie Holiday, the Jackson Five, Smokey Robinson, Sarah Vaughn, and Stevie

Wonder. Now publicly owned, the theatre is the setting for a popular *television programme called Showtime at the Apollo. The Dance Theatre of Harlem performed there in 2001.

BBL

APPARAO, GURAZADA (1862–1915)

Pioneer of modern Telugu poetry, short story, and the social problem play in Andhra Pradesh, *India. He is primarily remembered for his classic Kanyasulkam (Bride Price, performed in 1892; first published 1897), a play that mirrored contemporary Telugu society. Among Apparao's several concerns, the most important was his condemnation of the selling of girls by their selfish fathers to old orthodox Brahmans. He laughed at people's idiosyncrasies and hailed the human spirit even among the lowest of the low. The play continues to be popular for its lively characterization. The cynical philanderer Girisam, the miserly old hack Lubdavadhanlu, the cunning village elder Ramappantulu, and above all the humanitarian courtesan Madhuravani—all these dynamic figures have contributed to the popularity of Kanyasulkam, which has been directed by several luminaries of the *Telugu theatre like Govindarajula Subba Rao, Abburi Rama Krishna Rao, K.Venkateswara Rao, and J. V. Ramana Murthy. Apparao also wrote two unfinished plays, Bilhaneeyam (The Story of Bilhana) and Kondubhatteeyam (The Story of Kondu Bhattu), both in colloquial Telugu.

MNS

APPEN, KARL VON (1900–81)

German designer. Appen began his career in 1921 in Frankfurt as apprentice to the *expressionist designer Ludwig Sievert. From 1925 until his arrest and imprisonment in 1941 Appen worked freelance at various German theatres. On his release in 1945 he became chief designer and from 1947 to 1950 *artistic director at the Dresden State Theatre. In 1954 he was appointed designer at the *Berliner Ensemble where he worked in the tradition of Caspar *Neher with *Brecht, Benno *Besson, Peter *Palitzsch, and Manfred *Wekwerth. Notable productions there included The Caucasian Chalk Circle (1954), The Good Person of Setzuan (1957), Arturo Ui (1959), and Brecht's version of Coriolanus (1964). His designs are characterized by stylized *realism and attention to historical detail while avoiding illusionism.   CBB

APPIA, ADOLPHE (1862–1924)

Swiss designer and theorist. Appia has been characterized as the father of modern theatre, the man who provided a complete critique of what he considered to be the disastrous state of theatre practice at the end of the nineteenth century, and then, with prophetic insight, suggested the solutions that would re-establish it upon an entirely different basis. In *Die Musik und die Inscenierung* (*Music and the Art of the Theatre*, 1899), inspired by the staging requirements of *Wagner's *operas, Appia suggested that the musical score should dictate the duration of the performance, the movement of the actors, and the nature of scenic space. Appia built upon this concept what became known as the 'New Art' of the theatre. He called for three-dimensional *scenery, for creative and form-revealing *lighting (developing the concept of the lighting plot), and for settings expressive of the inner reality as art of works of musical drama. Through music all the arts of the theatre could be integrated into a hierarchically ordered, conceptually coherent, and uniquely expressive form.

The actor must perform within a supportive and responsive setting (*see* SCENOGRAPHY). Light, symbolic colouring, and a dynamic sculptured space would be used to evoke atmosphere and psychological nuance, with all these expressive elements harmoniously correlated by the new theatrical artist, whom Appia termed the 'designer-director'. The *audience should no longer be thought of as passive spectators, for Appia believed that experiments along the lines he suggested could involve them in the theatrical act in order both to experience and determine it more directly.

The second phase of Appia's creative career arose from his involvement with the system of eurhythmics devised by his fellow countryman Émile *Jaques-Dalcroze, designed to enhance performers' perception of music through the responsive movement of their own bodies in space. In 1906 Appia encountered eurhythmics for the first time and perceived in it the key to realizing his earlier *theory that the actor must be motivated by music, and through movement determine the nature of the scenic environment. He prepared a series of designs, termed 'rhythmic spaces', which would revolutionize future scenic practice still further. These were essentially abstract arrangements of solid stairs, platforms, podia, and the like, whose rigidity, sharp lines and angles, and immobility, when confronted by the softness, subtlety, and movement of the body, would by opposition take on a kind of borrowed life.

Together with Dalcroze, Appia helped to plan and present a series of extraordinary demonstrations at Dalcroze's institute in Hellerau, Germany, highlighting the potential of eurhythmics for both performance and design. The *proscenium arch was abolished and the lighting, operated from a central 'organ', carefully coordinated with the music and movement as well as the emotional flow of the performance. The *festivals at Hellerau in 1912 and 1913 caused astonishment and admiration and exercised a profound influence upon later scenic practice, as well as directly and indirectly upon the development of modern *dance.

In the last decade of his life Appia developed more radical ideas for the future evolution of what he now termed 'living art'. He realized that what had begun as an analysis and critique of the state of the theatre must end in a fundamental attack on contemporary culture itself. People observed art passively and if it moved them at all it did so artificially, having lost its power to activate emotionally and spiritually an audience that could now only contemplate but no longer enter into it. It was necessary to return to the well-spring of all art, the living experience of the human body, and from there to express and share both the reality of oneself and, simultaneously, one's communal relationship with the rest of society, from which one would no longer be isolated, but reintegrated into living contact. In *L'Œuvre d'art vivant* (*The Work of Living Art*, 1921), Appia detailed the social implications of this new collaborative art. This speculative treatment tends inevitably to be less concrete than his earlier writings but provides a programme and description of many of the developments that have characterized theatrical art in the latter part of the twentieth century. Appia was shy and reclusive, and, despite the eminently practical basis of most of his ideas, found collaborative work difficult and frustrating. His productions were very few, his radical ideas brought him into conflict with traditionalists, and his contribution has been insufficiently recognized. *See also* MODERNISM AND POSTMODERNISM; CRAIG, EDWARD GORDON.   RCB

BEACHAM, RICHARD, *Adolphe Appia: artist and visionary of the modern theatre* (Reading, 1994)

VOLBACH, W., *Adolphe Appia, Prophet of the Modern Theatre* (Middletown, Conn., 1968)

APPLAUSE

Spectators' appreciation for performances has often been demonstrated through the clapping of hands. Applause is part of a larger set of social behaviours intimately related to the reception of performance: approbative signals like cheering, or shouting bravo or encore; disapprobative signals like *booing, hissing, or catcalls; and instinctive emotive reactions like *laughter and weeping. These *audience gestures are not universal; they are culturally specific and have histories just as do the *curtain call and the institution of the *claque. The Romans had an organized series of approbative gestures, ranging from finger snapping to hand clapping (*applaudere* means to strike upon) to waving the flap of the toga or a special handkerchief (*see* ROMAN THEATRE). Roman secular traditions were strong enough to continue not only into Christian times but also into Christian services. In the fourth century Eusebius reports that Paul of Samosata encouraged the congregation to applaud his sermons by waving linen cloths in the Roman manner, and it was apparently the custom in Christian churches in the fourth and fifth centuries to cheer popular preachers. Roman comedians customarily ended a play with 'valete et plaudite' (farewell and applaud), a convention that easily worked its way into the *epilogues of *early modern *comedy throughout Europe, as in Shakespeare's *A Midsummer Night's Dream* (c.1595), which ends with Puck's lines 'Give me your hands, if we be friends | And

Robin shall restore amends.' As a 'tie-sign' applause is a gestural gift that not only makes approbative noise but—as Puck implies—also acts as a substitute for touching, an extension, through raised or outstretched arms, of the spectator's body to the actor's body.

Clapping is considered out of place in some traditional Asian performance modes, especially when they evoke a religious or ceremonial disposition. In the *dance-drama of *krishnattam, for example, performed at the Guruvayur temple in the state of Kerala in the south of *India, no applause will be heard. Similarly, agricultural rites seeking good harvest in some rural areas of India have major dramatic components but clapping would disrupt the observance, just as it might in church ceremonies in the West. What makes applause suspect in churches may be the desire to remove religious events from the taint of secular drama or, as in some *avant-garde secular performances, to suggest that the work is intensely serious. But less conventional churches, particularly those related to the Christian evangelical or charismatic traditions, occasionally encourage applause and other approbative signs during services.

Habits of applause are affected by spectators' class, race, *gender, and nation, since all public gestures are ultimately subject to social order and control. They are affected by time and place as well: the rowdy cheering and jeering that was common in nineteenth-century popular theatre is now welcomed in sporting events but not in the bourgeois *playhouse. Virtuoso displays—in *sport, in *opera, or even in *juggling—seem to generate spontaneous outbursts of applause more readily than the *realistic or spoken theatre, suggesting that spectators take particular delight in the exhibition of skills that are technically difficult and beyond the scope of ordinary people. In India the modern secular traditions of entertainment regularly evoke applause as in the West, though the approbation is usually expressed during or immediately after a particularly pleasing moment in a performance rather than at a final curtain call. In Indian classical dance and music, spectators may use onomatopoeic verbal expressions (clicking of the tongue, or other culture-specific signs) rather than clapping. Thus applause may be considered universal, but it is not universally the same.

In the final analysis, applause in the modern theatre signifies more than approval; it also is the clearest way that spectators, who are otherwise mostly passive witnesses, actively enter the event. When a curtain call is used the audience's formal applause brings closure to the performance more completely than the end of the drama itself, since it is what Erving Goffman calls an 'interaction ritual' that gives the audience some measure of reciprocity with the actors. By signalling that their part in the event is fulfilled, spectators at the curtain call officially recognize themselves as an audience in a group, and thereby acknowledge their ultimate power over the performance. *See also* AUDIENCE DRESS; AUDIENCE CONTROL; RIOTS.

DK

APRON STAGE *See* FORESTAGE.

AQUARIUM

French company, originally a student troupe founded by Jacques Nichet in 1964, it found a permanent home in one of the buildings of the Cartoucherie at Vincennes outside *Paris in 1972. Nichet's vision was a theatre of *collective creation that would respond to contemporary social and political issues, and performances were often *improvisations based upon actual interviews and current documents (*see* DOCUMENTARY DRAMA AND THEATRE). *Marchands de ville* (*The Town Merchants*, 1972) confronted problems of real estate speculation, and *Une jeune lune* (*A Young Moon*, 1976) treated the concerns of striking factory-workers. Since 1986 the theatre has been under the direction of Jean-Louis Benoit and, until 1998, Didier Bezace.

CHB

AQUATIC DRAMA

A specialized form of *melodrama imported to England from the French *circus and theatre in the first decade of the nineteenth century. It glorified English naval achievements and exhibited shipwrecks and battles with pirates on stage. In 1804, following the popularity of naval entertainments at *Covent Garden and the Royal Circus in the 1790s, *Sadler's Wells Theatre installed a large water tank on its stage, called itself the Aquatic Theatre, and for an eleven-year period produced lavish and patriotic marine *spectacles such as *The Siege of Gibraltar* (1804), *The Battle of Trafalgar* (1806), and *The Battle of the Nile* (1815). The battles staged in the water tank, full of dreadful cannonades, drifting smoke, and the smell of gunpowder, were fought by fully rigged model ships which exploded and sank in realistic fashion. Small children, dressed as sailors, struggled in the water. The aquatic drama was the immediate ancestor of the *nautical drama, and from it emerged the notable character of the heroic sailor, the brave and patriotic tar of *melodrama, the common man *in excelsis*. *See also* NAUMACHIA.

MRB

ARABIC DRAMA

Although in much of the Arabic world a performance tradition goes back many centuries and involves such activities as public storytelling, *shadow puppetry, satiric monologues, and many forms of *dance, European-style drama was introduced during the nineteenth century by pioneer dramatists in Syria (which then included today's Lebanon) and Egypt. The first of these was Marun al-Naqqash (1817–55), a Beirut businessman who became fascinated by European theatre on business trips to Italy and France, and who together with his family performed the first modern Arabic play, *al-Bakhil* (*The Miser*, not, however, based on *Molière), in his own house in 1847. The example of al-Naqqash inspired several other members of his family to take up theatrical careers, and their plays and companies spread interest in this activity to Alexandria in Egypt and to Damascus in Syria during the 1870s. In both places they reinforced a theatre interest already being developed by university scholars. In *Cairo, Sheika Rifaa Rafe al Tahtawi (1801–73) of Al Azhaz University translated a number of French classical plays into Arabic, and his efforts were followed by an even more important Egyptian dramatic pioneer, Yacub *Sannu, a Jewish journalist who wrote or translated some 30 plays and founded the first 'national' theatre in Cairo in 1870. In Damascus, Sheik Ahmad Abu Khalil al-Qabbaani (c.1833–1902), a student of languages, began producing plays in 1865. His theatre was closed at the urging of conservative religious leaders in 1881 and al-Qabbaani departed for the more congenial climate of Egypt. Thanks to native theatre leaders like Sannu, and the arrival of other artists from Beirut and Damascus, by the 1880s Egypt had clearly become the leading home of Arabic drama, a position it has maintained ever since.

In many European traditions there has been a struggle between an 'official', 'court', or 'literary' language and one or more popular or colloquial languages or dialects, a struggle that is particularly intense in theatre when it aspires to a literary status through a medium largely composed of spoken *dialogue. Nowhere has this struggle been more fundamental or more complex than in the Arab world, in every part of which there is continual negotiation between formal or classical Arabic (Fusha), the language of the Koran and of Islamic scholarship throughout the centuries (in this respect parallel to Latin in the medieval and *early modern West), and a huge variety of colloquial Arabic languages spoken in different regions. The plays of al-Naqqash were written primarily in Fusha, with a smattering of colloquialisms. Sannu, on the other hand, wrote only in colloquial Arabic, for which he was severely criticized by many literary scholars and critics. Although the language issue remains unresolved to this day, in general the pattern emerged during the late nineteenth and early twentieth century of using Fusha for *historical, epic, serious, and 'literary' plays, including most foreign translations, and using the various colloquial languages for *comedies and plays on local themes. More recently, as the Arabic theatre has become more international, authors seeking only local audiences will normally use the local Arabic, while those hoping that their plays may be presented in other Arabic countries will favour Fusha.

The British occupation of Egypt, lasting from 1882 until 1922, encouraged an interest in European-oriented theatre, both *amateur and professional, but the real flourishing of Egyptian playwriting came during the 1920s when the theatre began to attract a significant public. In this period appeared the pioneer realist Muhammad Taymur (1894–1973), the founder of the Arabic verse play Ahmad Shawqi (1868–1932), and the best-known dramatist of the Arab world, Tawfiq el-*Hakim, whose play *Ahl al Kahf* inaugurated the National Theatre in 1935 and who more than anyone was responsible for making the drama a recognized literary form in Egypt. Under his influence a new generation of dramatists appeared, chief among them in the 1940s Mahmud Taymur (1894–1973, younger brother of Muhammad Taymur) and Ali Ahmad Bakathir (1910–69), and in the 1950s Yussuf *Idris and Alfred *Farag, who like el-Hakim also established European reputations.

Despite continuing religious pressure, a strong theatre interest continued in Syria in the early twentieth century, finally inspiring a golden age of Syrian theatre launched by the founding of a Ministry of Culture in 1958 and a National Theatre in 1960. Among the many actors, directors, dramatists, and critics who came to prominence in the 1960s and 1970s, the most important is unquestionably the dramatist Sadallah *Wannous, who dominates the modern Syrian theatre as Tawfiq el-Hakim does the modern Egyptian. Lebanon, which shared the revival of theatrical interest in the 1960s and 1970s, found this development abruptly stopped by civil war in 1975, from which that country's theatre was beginning to recover as the twentieth century ended. Iraq also had a flourishing theatre in the 1970s which war and international isolation then muted.

Theatrically speaking, the Arab world can roughly be divided into three sections: first, the traditional Middle East, where Egypt, Syria, and Lebanon developed and still dominate the modern, Western-oriented literary theatre; second, the conservative Gulf States, led by Saudi Arabia, Bahrain, and Kuwait, where religion and government have given theatre little encouragement, viewing it as a suspect intruder from the outside world; and third, the Arab states of north-west Africa, known as the Maghrib, the most important of which, Tunisia, Algeria, and Morocco, developed theatre with close ties to their French colonial background. The establishment in 1982 of the Tunisian National Theatre and the Carthage Festival and the founding of that country's first serious theatre journal, all in some way involving the key figure of al-Moncef Souissi (1944–   ), brought that country to the theatrical leadership of the Maghrib.

MC

Landau, Jack, *Studies in the Arab Theatre and Cinema* (Philadelphia, 1958)

Rubin, Don (ed.), *The Arab World*, vol. iv in *The World Encyclopedia of Contemporary Theatre* (London, 1999).

ARBUZOV, ALEKSEI (1908–86)

Soviet/Russian playwright. Arbuzov trained as an actor before turning to dramatic writing in the 1930s. His play *Tanya* (1938) exemplifies the demands of *socialist realism for 'conflictless' drama: Tanya is not allowed to find happiness by devoting herself to her husband and abandoning her career, but only after her transformation into a committed doctor. During the war Arbuzov worked in a 'joint stock' method in his studio for young dramatists. His post-war plays are concerned with the young generation: *Years of Wandering* (1954) deals with the self-centredness of young people, a theme that also dominates *My Poor Marat* (also known as *The Promise*, 1964), where love is placed above duty when Lika marries an invalid although she loves Marat, with whom she is eventually reunited. Arbuzov's plays of the 1970s (*An Old-Fashioned Comedy, Tales of the Old Arbat, Cruel Games*) focus on the disintegration of family life and the difficulty of sustaining relationships, and quickly formed part of the repertoire of *Moscow's leading theatres.

BB

ARCA

Small-scale theatre company in Ghent in Belgium, founded in 1950 as Toneelstudio 50, adopting the name Arca in 1955. The group played a crucial role in introducing to Flanders the theatre of the *absurd and the new *realistic repertoire from Britain, and exploring contemporary drama has remained its hallmark. From 1982 to 1987 directors Herman Gilis and Pol Dehert presented postmodern stagings marked by a 'dialogue' with the *text, often revealing its internal contradictions, and by an overt, ironic theatricality, a project that placed the company at the head of the theatre renewal movement in Flanders. In 2001 Arca amalgamated with the municipal theatre to form the Publiekstheater.

JDV

ARCHER, WILLIAM (1856–1924)

Scottish critic, translator, and playwright. Though born in Perth, Archer spent part of his childhood in Norway and most of his working life in *London. His passion for the theatre and its reform began early, and he spent more than 40 years as a dramatic critic, including 21 years on the *World*. He travelled widely whenever he could afford to, visiting theatres in Europe and all over the world. He constantly campaigned for more *realistic, socially aware, and *naturalistically acted plays, and his fluent Norwegian enabled him to become the leading English-language authority on *Ibsen's work and to translate most of his plays; his faithful though somewhat stiff versions held the stage for many years. He also anonymously helped direct many of the first London performances, including *A Doll's House* (1889), *Ghosts* (1891), and *Little Eyolf* (1896). He was an outwardly austere, high-principled man, a free-thinker and supporter of women's suffrage, an opponent of *censorship, and a lifelong campaigner for a *national theatre, for which he wrote detailed plans with Granville *Barker in 1904. For 40 years he had an argumentative friendship with *Shaw, encouraging him in many ways while constantly criticizing his plays for levity and prolixity. His many publications include collected *criticism, *Masks or Faces?* (1888), and *Play-Making* (1912). He

wrote many unpublished plays, and had an unexpected late international success with a well-constructed *melodrama, *The Green Goddess* (1921). He was completely perplexed by *Chekhov, however, complaining of *The Cherry Orchard* in 1920 that 'nothing whatever happens'.

EEC

ARCHIBALD, DOUGLAS (1919–93)

Trinidadian dramatist, civil engineer, and historian, one of the best known of the 'yard theatre' playwrights whose socially *realist dramas depict life in the urban 'yards'. *Junction Village* (1954) won a Trinidad writers' guild prize. Archibald wrote fourteen more plays, including *The Rose Slip* (1962), with Guyanese actor Wilbert Holder in the Company of Players production, *Old Maid's Tale* (1966), *Anne Marie* (1967), *Island Tide* (1972), and *Defeat with Honour* (1977).

ES

ARCHITECTURE OF THEATRES *See* PLAYHOUSE.

ARCH STREET THEATRE

*Philadelphia *playhouse. Opened in 1826 with William B. *Wood as *manager, it closed within two years due to conflicts among actors and with the owners. Reopening in 1829 under new management, it introduced James E. Murdoch and provided a major venue for Edwin *Forrest. In the 1850s John and Louisa Lane *Drew joined the theatre, Mrs Drew becoming manager in 1860, assembling an outstanding *stock company that performed successfully until the rise of the combination system brought its decline. After Drew retired in 1892, it housed various transient companies until demolition in 1936.

AHK

ARDEN, JOHN (1930–)

British dramatist, theatre-maker, and novelist. Born in Barnsley and trained as an architect, Arden was one of the most political and literate of the post-*Osborne generation. His best-known plays were written between 1958 (*The Waters of Babylon*) and 1963 (*Armstrong's Last Goodnight*), after which time he began collaborating with his wife, the Irish writer and political activist Margaretta *D'Arcy. After an acrimonious row with the *Royal Shakespeare Company over its production of their Arthurian trilogy, *The Island of the Mighty* (1973), Arden and D'Arcy stopped writing for mainstream British theatre. They moved to Ireland, where they have produced political and *community theatre (the six-part *The Non-Stop Connolly Show*, 1974, for example) and have written a number of plays for *radio (including a nine-part epic about early Christianity, *Whose Is the Kingdom*, 1988). Arden has also published some of his critical writing and several novels. He became increasingly committed to revolutionary socialist and Irish nationalist politics after 1968; while his early plays are also political, the politics they proceed from is libertarian and anarchist. There are also continuities between his own work and that written with D'Arcy, chiefly a concern with popular theatre forms and traditions (*The Workhouse Donkey*, 1963), with history (*Serjeant Musgrave's Dance*, 1959, and the *Connolly* plays), and the contemporary world in its historical context (*Live Like Pigs*, 1958). The dramatist Arden most resembles is not *Brecht (as is often argued) but Ben *Jonson, whose work he admires.   SWL

AREITO

An indigenous form of *Caribbean performance banned by Spanish colonizers. Upon their arrival in the Caribbean islands Europeans encountered indigenous peoples engaging in the semi-dramatic form of the *areito*, which employed elements of *costume, *dance, and *music, but was primarily focused on religious and social rites.   AV

ARENA AND IN-THE-ROUND

An ancient form of staging which acquired a new importance in *modernist theatre. The spectators sit in elevated tiers surrounding a central performance space (which may be of any shape, but the geometry of placing as many spectators as close as possible to the *stage tends to favour a circular arrangement). Technically 'arena staging' is any arrangement in which the seating is elevated above, and mostly surrounds, the performance; while 'in-the-round' means that the *audience surrounds the playing area. As a practical matter, nearly all in-the-round spaces have arena seating, and nearly all arena theatres are at least three-quarters in-the-round. Most of the time the distinction reflects no difference. The term 'arena' is from the Latin for 'sand', and originally meant the sand-covered performance area in Roman *amphitheatres (which were used for *sports and combats at least as much as for *dance and theatre).

'Arena' and 'in-the-round' were appropriated by critics and *avant-gardistes of the mid-twentieth century. Arena staging was a refusal of the conventions of *bourgeois entertainment, specifically of theatre as a private, individual dream which *naturalism, the *proscenium stage, and *realistic *lighting and design had fostered. Reaching back to imagined theatrical utopias (mainly *Greek and Elizabethan), the *theorists of the arena stage envisioned theatre as a communal sacrament celebrated in the middle of the spectators, who could neither hide in the dark nor observe from a dispassionate distance. Further, the proliferation of *Stanislavskian technique in *acting, and the experience of *film close-ups, shifted the definition of acting toward a sense of intense reality at the small scale and away from projection and grandiloquence. To provide an experience of 'good acting', it was desirable to get as many people as close to the stage as possible.

The experiments of William *Poel and of various Graecophiles before the First World War are often cited as precursors, but in-the-round genuinely became important in Germany and Russia in the 1920s and early 1930s, with *Brecht and *Piscator's productions in boxing rings in *Berlin, *Reinhardt's stagings in *circuses, and *Okhlopkov's work at the Realist Theatre in *Moscow. The English-language champion of arena staging was Glenn Hughes of the University of Washington, where the Penthouse, the first purpose-built in-the-round theatre, was erected in 1940. In the following decades his experiments were extended by Margo *Jones in Dallas and especially at Zelda *Fichandler's *Arena Stage in Washington, DC. Acceptance in the *New York professional theatre came relatively quickly; after some early experiments at the Hotel Edison, arena staging found acceptance in *Off-Broadway theatre, especially after José *Quintero's successful arena staging of a revival of Tennessee *Williams's *Summer and Smoke* at the *Circle in the Square. Since about 1970 arena has become much more common throughout the world, rivalling the *proscenium for popularity. This may in part be due to the rapid rise in the cost of theatre and the ongoing shrinking of the serious audience. Arena staging provides low cost and great flexibility, and a small audience is able to take much more advantage of the clear visibility and audibility which arena provides. *See also* PLAYHOUSE.   JB

ARENA STAGE

American *regional theatre in Washington, DC. Founded in 1950 by Zelda *Fichandler, Thomas C. Fichandler, and Edward Mangum, it began operations in an abandoned movie house renovated as an *arena theatre in order to keep production costs low. The configuration was maintained in 1956 when the company moved into an old brewery, and in 1961 when a purpose-built *playhouse opened at 6th and Maine in southwest Washington. In the 1970s two further spaces were added, a *proscenium stage (the Kreeger) and a *cabaret (the Old Vat Room). Under the dynamic leadership of Fichandler, and with substantial support from the Ford Foundation, Arena went from pioneer to paragon in the resident theatre movement. Its landmark 1967 production of Howard Sackler's *The Great White Hope*, starring James Earl *Jones and Jane *Alexander, moved to Broadway and won the Pulitzer and Tony *awards, thereby helping to establish regional theatres as breeding grounds for new American plays, and in 1976 Arena was the first to receive the special Tony award for outstanding regional theatre. Living Stage, established in 1965 under the direction of Robert Alexander, became a pioneer of outreach programming with its *improvisation workshops and free performances for non-traditional *audiences. After 40 years at Arena, Zelda Fichandler stepped down and was replaced in 1991 by protégé and associate producing director Douglas C. Wager. In 1998, Molly Smith left Perseverance Theatre in Alaska to succeed Wager as *artistic director, placing a renewed emphasis on American plays in her initial seasons.   STC

ARETINO, PIETRO (1492–1556)

Italian man of letters and dramatist. Born relatively humbly in Arezzo, Aretino established a fearsome reputation as a pamphleteer, satirist, and a man not to be crossed. Non-dramatic writings range from religious treatises to outright *pornography—it was the latter which made his name internationally proverbial. His theatre production consists of one *tragedy, *Orazia*, and five highly original and scurrilous *comedies, written for court and academic circles, dense with linguistic innovation and with overtly judgemental references to contemporary luminaries. The titles are *The Courtier's Play*, *The Stablemaster*, *Talanta*, *The Hypocrite*, and *The Philosopher*. Despite Aretino's initial anti-literary pose, they are all carefully composed, with passages of structured rhetoric and polemic; but some individual scenes are influenced by the techniques of improvised *street theatre, and it is possible that collaboration was envisaged in performance between *amateurs and professionals. After Aretino's works were all placed on the Catholic Church's Index of Forbidden Books, the comedies were reissued after 1600 with false titles and attributions, thus attesting their lasting attraction to readers seeking under-the-counter material.
                                                                RAA

ARGÜELLES, HUGO (1932–)

Mexican playwright, screenwriter, and educator. Considered one of Mexico's major living dramatists, he had his first stage success in 1960 with *The Crows Are in Mourning*, a dark *comedy about black magic, death, and dying in rural Mexico. Many of his other plays have similar settings, such as *The Prodigious Ones* (1961), *The Savage Cocks* (1986), and *Scarabs* (1991), which assume an ironic, often cruel look at the violence born of middle-class hypocrisy, sexual repression, and homophobia. Argüelles is also the author of numerous *historical plays, such as *Royal Eagle* (1992) and *The Rounds of the Bewitched Ones*, which opened the cultural programme for the 1968 Olympics in *Mexico City. The winner of numerous awards for playwriting and for his contributions to Mexican theatre, Argüelles taught playwriting from 1967 to 1973 at the National Institute of Fine Arts, where he has trained some of the finest young dramatists of the 1970s and 1980s.   KFN

ARION (fl. 628–625 BC)

Greek dithyrambist. A native of Lesbos, Arion spent most of his life in Corinth, where he regularized the *dithyramb by

using a trained *chorus and a literary subject. A tenth-century lexicon credits him with the invention of the *tragikos tropos*, probably the musical mode later associated with *tragedy.
                                                                RWV

ARIOSTO, LUDOVICO (1474–1533)

Ferrarese poet and dramatist. As well as the epic masterpiece *Orlando furioso*, Ariosto composed four stage *comedies, plus one more unfinished. *La cassaria* (*The Strongbox Play*) and *I suppositi* (*The Substitutes*) were staged in Ferrara in 1508 and 1509: they were the first original five-act plays in Italian vernacular in the classical mode of *Plautus and *Terence. They thus effectively inaugurated modern European theatre, in the sense of producing scripts which were then published and treated (like classical plays) as high cultural products, rather than as ephemeral texts linked to single performing occasions. They were also the first full-length dramatic scripts ever to be written in prose—though Ariosto may never have intended them to be published in this form, and his later plays (including rewrites of the first two) were in *verse. Like comedies of Plautus, the first two *plots deal with amorous intrigues and conflicts between youth and age in the context of a middle-class urban family. For *I suppositi*, Ariosto moved to a local contemporary setting, rather than the distant neutral locations of *Roman comedy; and his plot details are based more on medieval Italian novella than on Plautus. The later comedies, written in the 1520s, accompany similar stories with greater satirical bite against chosen aspects of contemporary society. *Il negromante* (*The Magician*) attacks charlatan practitioners of the occult, and *Lena* presents a sour view of private sexual exploitation and public administrative corruption. The unfinished *I studenti* gives a more amused account of randy students getting themselves into convoluted scrapes. *See* EARLY MODERN PERIOD IN EUROPE.   RAA

ARISTOPHANES (c.448–c.380 BC)

Greek comic playwright. The work of no other writer of *Old Comedy or *Middle Comedy has survived and this is in itself a tribute to how far the reputation of Aristophanes outstripped that of other comic dramatists of his day. His relationship with the tragic playwrights of his time was ambivalent. *Euripides is satirized as a *character in three plays and is mentioned in fun at least once in all of the others. Though much younger than either *Sophocles or Euripides, Aristophanes did overlap with their careers from 427 BC, the date of the production of his first play, *The Banqueters*, until 406 BC when both the tragic playwrights died. The following year Aristophanes presented *Frogs* at the *Lenaea, the action of which revolves around the god of the theatre, *Dionysus, travelling to the underworld to try to bring Euripides back to save the city. After a

South Italian (Apulian) bell krater, c.370 BC, showing the climactic scene from a local production of **Aristophanes'** *Thesmophoriazusae*. In a parody of Euripides' lost *Telephus*, Euripides' father-in-law (right), an infiltrator to a women-only religious festival, is discovered and threatens to kill the baby of one of the participants, which turns out to be a wineskin dressed with bootees. As if at an animal sacrifice, the mother rushes to collect the 'blood' in what the text calls a ritual basin but appears here as a giant drinking cup for wine. A mirror hangs between the actors, probably a property used in an earlier scene in which the father-in-law is shaved.

competition in Hades in which Sophocles declines to take part, Dionysus brings *Aeschylus back to earth, a decision based more on the older man's political advice than on any superior skill as a playwright. Aristophanes was himself to turn up as a character in Plato's *Symposium*, a dramatic dialogue on the nature of love, to which he is initially unable to contribute because of hiccups. When he recovers, he proposes that mankind was originally a double being, punished by being split into two; and that love is the result of these two being

condemned to spend their lives looking for their other half. This fictional portrait of the comic playwright as a teller of fanciful tales accords well with the whole of his extant output as a comic dramatist. Eleven of his plays survive in all, nine Old Comedies produced between 425 and 405 BC; and two Middle Comedies (sometimes called *New Comedies) written late in his life.

The Old Comedies share a number of common features which suggest similarities with work of his rivals, but also mark him out as the outstanding individual comic talent of his time. The plays are set in locations which are all manufactured stage worlds. *Acharnians* (425), his third play but the first to survive, is set in and around Athens where Dicaeopolis is so upset by the war with Sparta (the Peloponnesian War, then in its sixth year) that he engineers a private peace confined to his own farm. The play won first prize. *Knights* (424) was a concerted attack on Cleon, the most belligerent of the city's demagogues. Three years later, after Cleon's death in battle, Aristophanes returned to the same theme with *Peace* (421), in which an Athenian farmer flies up to heaven on the back of a dung-beetle to rescue Peace who has been thrown down a well by the god of War. Perhaps the best known of his plays is *Lysistrata* (411), where the women of Greece impose a sex strike on their husbands in order to force them to make peace. All these were written and played at a time when the city was committed to this war which his characters refuse to endorse. In other plays Aristophanes' targets were political in a broader sense, dealing with issues of the day: *Wasps* (422), which satirizes the law courts and the enthusiasm of the elderly for jury service; education in *Clouds* (the date is unclear as the surviving version is a later revision), in which Socrates appears as one of the characters swinging in a balloon and indulging in philosophical contemplation of the heavens; *Birds* (414), where two Athenian citizens create a new city in mid-air, undertaking, and winning, a holy war against the gods of Olympus; and *Thesmophoriazusae* (*Women at the Thesmophoria*, also 411) which concerns the attempted revenge of the women of Athens on Euripides for portraying them in such a poor light in his plays.

All these plays posit a stage world in which gods, heroes, contemporary celebrities, and invented characters intermingle. Usually Aristophanes creates some dominant idea which develops through the wildest fantasy into the exploration of all manner of current ideas. Indeed, in the absence of any contemporary social history, and despite his comic and often farcical invention, there is more to be learnt from the plays of Aristophanes about the processes of everyday life in Athens than from any other source. The sheer theatricality is infectious. The *choruses are often animals or unreal creatures, though they can be ordinary Athenians. They and the main characters were *masked and all were played by male actors. Most of them wore exaggerated *costumes, possibly including the *phallus, but the general scurrility and references to sexual and other bodily functions no longer seem as outrageous as in more censorious eras. Amongst the productions that rescued Aristophanes for the stage those of Karolos *Koun in modern Greek were, perhaps, the most influential. Koun began to direct plays by Aristophanes in the early 1930s when he was teaching English at Athens College. He founded the Art Theatre during the German occupation of Greece and later the Laiki Skene (People's Theatre). Amongst his productions, seen all over

the world, were *Birds*, which was banned in *Athens in the late 1950s, *Frogs*, and *Lysistrata*. In all three the chorus was the focal point of the drama and of the *comedy, masked and ever mobile, blending fantasy and sexual *farce with a political hard edge. Spurred by Koun's example other directors have presented most of the surviving plays at one time or another at the Athens and *Epidaurus festivals, and at the *Greek National Theatre in Athens.

Outside Greece Aristophanes has taken longer to establish himself in the repertoire. This has been partly as a result of his earthy humour, partly because of his seemingly parochial politics, though *Wealth* was a popular 'moral' play in the *early modern period, and both *Goethe and *Planché presented versions of *Birds*. More recent attitudes towards translation and production have given licence to directors to stray widely from the given *text and update situations to a modern context. Though this has on occasion resulted in strained parallels, the adaptation of *Frogs* by Burt Shevelove and Stephen *Sondheim gives some indication of how Aristophanes might return to the repertoire. In this *musical version, set in a swimming pool, Aeschylus and Euripides are revived as Shakespeare and *Shaw.

In his last two plays, *Ecclesiazusae* (*Women in Assembly*, 392/1) and *Wealth* (388), Aristophanes marks the transition to a less robust and more parochial kind of comedy. *Ecclesiazusae* raises the prospect of the women of Athens (male actors, of course) taking over the state by disguising themselves as their husbands and then attempting, with conspicuous lack of success, to institute a kind of Platonic communism. *Wealth* follows the efforts of Chremylus to restore the blind god of wealth to sight, and the uncomfortable consequences for a number of characters, including the god Hermes. The war, it appears, had been Aristophanes' source of inspiration. Its ending soon after *Frogs* altered the whole nature of Athenian comedy. *See also* GREEK THEATRE, ANCIENT.   JMW

CARTLEDGE, PAUL, *Aristophanes and his Theatre of the Absurd* (Bristol, 1990)

DOVER, KENNETH, *Aristophanic Comedy* (London, 1972)

MacDOWELL, DOUGLAS M., *Aristophanes and Athens: an introduction to the plays* (Oxford, 1995)

ARISTOTLE (384–322 BC)

Greek philosopher, whose *Poetics* (*c*.330 BC) is the seminal document of Western dramatic *theory. Aristotle studied with Plato and later served as tutor to the young Alexander of Macedon. In 335 he founded a school in Athens, where he spent the last years but one of his life. An indefatigable researcher and collector, and a prolific writer, Aristotle's contribution to theatrical studies represents a small fraction of his output, and that not the most significant. Among his collections of data were lists of victors at the Pythian and Olympic games, and the *Didascaliae*, a record of lyric and dramatic performances at the Athenian dramatic festivals. Fragments of these records survive in stone inscriptions. The cryptic style of the *Poetics* encouraged its interpretation as a collection of precepts, but it is now conceded that the treatise is in fact highly organized.

The *Poetics* was separated from the classic *Greek theatre of fifth-century Athens by nearly a century. Athens could no longer pretend to either democracy or imperial power, and Plato's rational philosophy had replaced the older mythopoeic wisdom. An increasing literacy was making the experience of private reading a valid alternative to the experience of communal performance. Drama had been stripped of the political and religious ideology of its performance at the Theatre of *Dionysus; it was increasingly separated in conception from the *music and *spectacle of its presentation, acquiring as a written *text a new literary status independent of performance. The *Poetics* reflects these changes. Text and *performance, *drama and *theatre are conceptualized as separate phenomena. And Aristotle preferred the literary to the theatrical. The *Poetics* also reflects its author's analytical bent. Poetry is conceived as an art distinguished by its medium (language); drama as a species of poetry distinguished by its manner of presentation (dramatic *dialogue); and *tragedy and *comedy as variants of drama distinguished on the basis of the object imitated (men as better or worse than the average). Aristotle may have intended to include a discussion of comedy, but the *Poetics* as we have it is concerned mainly with tragedy, which is analysable in terms of its constituent parts: *plot, *character, thought, diction, song, and spectacle. Aristotle's listing of the parts in order of decreasing importance is indicative of his choice of the literary over the theatrical. He argued for plot as the 'soul' of tragic art, and dismissed spectacle as belonging to the 'art of staging'. His schematized and problematic 'history' of dramatic *genres, in which tragedy is held to have developed from the *dithyramb and comedy from phallic songs, is similarly devoid of reference to circumstances of performance.

Aristotle provides a lexicon of familiar terms and concepts, at least three of which continue to stimulate thought. While it has proved almost impossible to define unequivocally what Aristotle meant by *mimesis, *catharsis, and *hamartia, taken together they can be seen as providing an answer to Plato's attack on poetic imitation as twice removed from reality, arousing passions dangerous to intellectual health and moral action, and incapable of embodying or communicating knowledge. Aristotle saw poetry as a rational art devoted to the imitation, not of ordinary reality, but of the unrealized possibilities of human action. The learning and pleasure derived from poetic imitation may be linked to the peculiar emotional pleasure associated with tragedy, the arousal and catharsis ('cleansing' or 'purifying') of pity and fear. Ethical action, in drama and in life, requires both an accurate intellectual perception of and a proper emotional response to circumstance. *Hamartia*,

the error that precipitates tragic suffering, can thus be either intellectual or emotional, or both. As slippery as these concepts are, Aristotle's attempt to explain and justify the pleasure produced by poetic imitation, especially tragedy, has not been superseded.

When the *Poetics* was rediscovered by Italian critics at the end of the fifteenth century, it was interpreted in the context of medieval rhetoric and moral philosophy, and, together with the Roman critic *Horace's *Ars Poetica*, provided the ancient authority for 250 years of *neoclassical theory and practice. More importantly, Aristotle and his interpreters have bequeathed two constants to Western theory: (*a*) the idea that the essence of theatre lies in the script, which governs theatrical 'interpretation'; and (*b*) the idea that the forms of drama are to be defined on literary rather than theatrical grounds.   RWV

ELSE, GERALD F., *Aristotle's Poetics: the argument* (Cambridge, Mass., 1967)

HALLIWELL, STEPHEN, *Aristotle's Poetics*, 2nd edn. (Chicago, 1998)

RORTY, AMELIE OKSENBERG (ed.), *Essays on Aristotle's Poetics* (Princeton, 1992)

ARIZA, PATRICIA (1948–)

Colombian actor, playwright, and director. A founding member of Teatro La *Candelaria of *Bogotá (1972), she has acted in most of its productions, playing a wide range of *characters. She was a co-writer in at least six *collective creation works before she wrote and directed *El viento y la ceniza* (*The Wind and the Ash*, 1986), based on the story of a Spanish conquistador who returns old, exhausted, and broke to his fatherland, reversing the Conquest's expected fable of richness and triumph. She was one of the first playwrights in the country to openly explore women's issues in *Luna menguante* (*Decreasing Moon*, 1994), which she wrote and directed for the group La Máscara of *Cali. She was co-director and *dramaturg for *Opera Rap* (1995), which drew upon a group of young rappers from a disadvantaged neighbourhood. Since the 1980s Ariza has been at the helm of the political and artistically active *Corporación Colombiana de Teatro.   BJR

ARJA

Sung, secular *dance-drama from the island of Bali in *Indonesia that developed in the early twentieth century and remains popular today. *Arja* relies on the interdependence of vocal and instrumental music, dance, and drama. The stories are rooted in the fifteenth-century *Panji romances known in Bali as *Malat*, and also portray subjects from *folk tales, the *Mahabharata*, *Ramayana*, and Chinese and Arabian tales. Twelve *stock characters of kings and queens, servants, princesses, and *clowns are depicted in a three-sided *arena with a divided *curtain as the only *scenery. The form's principal feature is its sung *text or *tembang macapat* (poetry sung in fours). Each of the characters sings and dances while making a formal entrance, the singing accompanied primarily by bamboo flutes, the dancing by a highly syncopated and improvised drumming called *kendang krempengan*. Songs and stories often vary in subject matter: the trials and humorous absurdities surrounding romantic love, royal intrigue, religious faith, and spiritual teachings.

MMH

ARLECCHINO (ARLEQUIN) *See* Harlequin; commedia dell'arte.

ARLEN, HAROLD (1905–86)

American composer. Born Hyman Arluck, he dropped out of school to pursue a career in music, working as a dance-band pianist and Tin Pan Alley songwriter during the 1920s. Teaming in 1929 with lyricist Ted Koelher, he wrote his first huge hit, 'Get Happy' (1930). The song's interpolation into a Broadway *revue brought him into the theatre, and he began writing scores for Broadway revues—and, significantly, revues at Harlem's Cotton Club. One of the first white composers to delve seriously into *African-American musical forms, he worked closely throughout his career with black performers. In Hollywood in the 1930s, he first collaborated with lyricist E. Y. Harburg, with whom he would write scores for several *films, including the classic *The Wizard of Oz* (1939), as well as three major stage works dealing with political and racial issues: *Hooray for What?* (1937), *Bloomer Girl* (1944), and *Jamaica* (1957). He also wrote with lyricists Johnny Mercer (*St Louis Woman* for a black cast, 1946) and Ira *Gershwin (the Oscar-winning score for *A Star is Born*, 1954).

JD

ARLT, ROBERTO (1900–42)

Argentinian playwright, novelist, and journalist. Arlt was already an established author when his first play, *300 Million*, premièred in 1932 at Leónidas Barletta's Teatro del Pueblo in *Buenos Aires. Until his death, Arlt continued to write for this pioneer of the independent theatre movement, an alternative to the enervated commercial theatre scene. His eight plays, among which *Saverio the Cruel* (1936) and *The Desert Island* (1937) stand out, display an experimentation also present in his narrative fiction: the creation of a new, modern world through the fusion of quotidian reality with grotesque dreams, illusions, and fantasies.

JGJ

ARMET (MACOUBA), AUGUSTE (1939–)

Martinican playwright and poet. His first play, titled in *creole *Eia Man maille la* (1968), is considered representative of mili-

tant drama in the francophone *Caribbean. Praising political action against colonialism, it is based on a historical moment of Martinican resistance, a three-day popular revolt in Fort-de-France and its bloody repression by colonial authorities in 1959. In addition to its frequent switch between French and creole, the play alternates between intimate tableaux and epic scenes of popular demonstrations, set against a *chorus singing protest songs in creole and the insistent rhythm of Caribbean drums. Its best-known staging was by Roger Robinel with his company Groupe Théâtre Existence.

LEM

ARMFIELD, NEIL (1955–)

Australian director, known for his thoughtful, provocative productions of the classics as well as his challenging productions of supposedly difficult modern Australian playwrights such as Patrick *White. Armfield promotes an ensemble feel at the Belvoir Street Theatre, *Sydney, where he became *artistic director in 1994, but his work is distinguished enough to attract stars such as Geoffrey *Rush and Cate Blanchett to work with him. His theatre has presented work focusing on Aboriginal issues, and Armfield's production of *Cloudstreet*, which addressed the loaded topic of reconciliation in Australia, *toured internationally in 1999 with great success.

EJS

ARMIN, ROBERT (c.1568–1615)

English comic actor and writer. Armin is remembered as the creator of Shakespeare's Jacobean *clowns—among them Feste and Lear's Fool—but he was also a dramatist in his own right, and, according to his own *Quips upon Questions* (1600), a solo performer of improvised comedy. He composed popular ballads during his apprenticeship to a goldsmith in the early 1580s, and he may have attracted the attention of the clown Richard *Tarlton before his term expired: when it did Armin chose jokes over jewellery, joining Chandos's Men as a comedian. His collection of merry tales, *Fool upon Fool*, appeared in 1600 under the pseudonym 'Clonnico de Curtanio Snuffe' (Snuff, the clown at the *Curtain); it was reissued in 1605 under that of 'Clonnico del Mondo Snuffe' (Snuff, the clown at the *Globe) and finally under Armin's own name (as *A Nest of Ninnies*) in 1608. By then, clearly, Armin had made his name, largely because he had taken over as principal clown with the Lord *Chamberlain's (subsequently King's) Men after the departure of William *Kempe in 1599. A less physical performer than his predecessor, Armin's expert singing and his preference for verbal wit over *slapstick have often been cited as reasons for the more cerebral and melodious style in which Shakespeare composed his clown roles after 1599, though Armin's own *comedy *Two Maids of More-Clacke* (printed in 1609, with a title-page illustration which may depict Armin in *costume) is considerably less subtle.

MD

ARNEAUX, J. A. (JOHN A.) (1855–?)

*African-American actor and impresario. Born in Savannah, Georgia, of a white Parisian father and a black mother, Arneaux was trained in languages in New York and Paris. After a brief stint as a song-and-dance entertainer in *New York, he made his legitimate stage debut there in 1876 as a southern planter in *Under the Yoke*, by black playwright John S. Ladue. His major achievements lay in Shakespeare, starting with a highly praised Iago in an all-black *Othello* (1884), which led him to found and *manage the Astor Place Company of Coloured Tragedians. Sporting a wide moustache, he played Romeo, Macbeth, and Othello. His chief triumph was as Richard III, which brought comparisons with the foremost white Shakespearians. His productions moved beyond New York to Providence, *Philadelphia, and Baltimore. In 1888 he went to Paris for further study, intending to resume his American career, but his trail vanishes abroad in 1891.   CT

ARONSON, BORIS (1898–1980)

American scene designer of Russian birth and training. Aronson studied with Aleksandra *Ekster and was deeply influenced by *constructivism and cubism. Arriving in *New York, he was first hired by *Yiddish theatre groups, which allowed him to experiment with bold designs. He eventually caught the eye of *avant-garde groups on and off Broadway. In 1927 he was hired by Eva *Le Gallienne to design $2 \times 2 = 5$ for her Civic Repertory Theatre, then became the designer of several early *Group Theatre plays, notably Clifford *Odets's *Awake and Sing* and *Paradise Lost* (both 1935). His first significant Broadway commissions were for the *revue *Walk a Little Faster* (1932) and J. C. Holm and George *Abbott's *Three Men on a Horse* (1935). Although he was given his share of *realistic settings he always injected a metaphorical abstraction, which led to *opera and *ballet commissions. Aronson's reputation blossomed in the 1940s and 1950s when he designed for emerging playwrights, including Tennessee *Williams's *The Rose Tattoo*, Arthur *Miller's *The Crucible* (1953), and William *Inge's *Bus Stop* (1955). Late in his career, he became renowned as an innovative designer of *musicals, his sets combining his early constructivist leanings with a metaphorical, almost lyrical environment. *Fiddler on the Roof* (1964) was followed by a string of Harold *Prince musicals, most with lyrics or music or both by Stephen *Sondheim: *Cabaret* (1966), *Zorba* (1968), Sondheim's *Company* (1970), *Follies* (1971), *A Little Night Music* (1973), and *Pacific Overtures* (1976).   MCH

ARONSON, RUDOLPH (1856–1919)

American impresario and composer. Born in New York to German immigrants, Aronson showed musical talent early and trained for three years at the *Paris *Conservatoire. In 1880 he built the 3,000-seat Metropolitan Concert Hall in *New York, where for a year he conducted an orchestra and programmed many of his compositions before yielding the *management to others. His major achievement was the building of the Moorish-style Casino Theatre, which he opened in 1882 with a long run of Johann Strauss, Jr.'s *operetta *The Queen's Lace Handkerchief*. The next year he opened the Casino Roof Garden for mild-weather entertainment—a much imitated enterprise. With top-notch performers along with lavish *scenery and *costumes, the Casino became the city's foremost venue for light and comic *opera. His 1886 production of *Erminie* (words by Henry Paulton, music by Edward Jacobowski) ran for 1,257 performances. Aronson published an autobiography, *Theatrical and Musical Memoirs* (1913).   CT

ARRABAL, FERNANDO (1932–   )

Spanish playwright, novelist, and filmmaker. After a traumatic childhood and law studies in Spain, he moved to *Paris, where he became linked with the theatre of the *absurd through French versions of his early iconoclastic plays. Jorge *Lavelli's staging of *The Architect and the Emperor of Assyria* (1967) in Paris and Tom O'Horgan's subsequent production of the play in *New York (1976) presented his work at its best. Arrabal himself directed the New York production of *And They Put Handcuffs on the Flowers* (1972), the most political of his works. New York's INTAR theatre championed his later plays with stagings of *The Red Madonna; or, A Damsel for a Gorilla* (1986) and *The Body-Builder's Book of Love* (1990). Returning to Spain after the demise of the dictatorship, he proved controversial with his frequent pronouncements and a turn to the right politically; but his numerous new plays were as scenically inventive and thematically provocative as his early works. Miguel Narros staged *The King of Sodom* (1983) at the national Teatro *Nacional María Guerrero, and several of his earlier plays were performed in smaller venues. In 2000, a revival of *The Automobile Graveyard* (1958) by the María Guerrero's production team focused new interest on this absurdist piece as it *toured throughout Spain. Critics have not been consistent in categorizing the prolific writer's work, but Arrabal's own terms 'Panic theatre', referring to the mythological god Pan, and 'guerrilla theatre' are generally accepted for specific groupings of his plays.

MPH

ARRIVÍ, FRANCISCO (1915–   )

Puerto Rican playwright, poet, essayist, and arts administrator. In 1958 he helped create the Theatrical Promotion Office at the Puerto Rican Culture Institute; as its director he established the Puerto Rican Theatre Festival (1958), the International Theatre Festival (1966), and indirectly the Avant-Garde Festival

(1967). His playwriting began with poetic dramas such as *Alumbramiento* (*Delivery*, 1945) and *María Soledad* (*Mary Solitude*, 1947), but his main contribution came with *Vejigantes* (*Carnival Masks*, 1958), *Siren* (1959), and the suite *Bolero y Plena* (1956). Published as a trilogy under the title *Máscara puertorriqueña* (*Puerto Rican Mask*, 1971), these plays explore African heritage as an essential ingredient of national identity, and juxtapose it to the racial prejudice that permeates Puerto Rican society. Arriví also experimented with the *absurdist style with *Coctél de don Nadie* (*Cocktail for Don Nobody*, 1965).

JLRE

ARRUFAT, ANTÓN (1935–)

Cuban poet, novelist, and playwright. *El caso se investiga* (*The Case Is under Investigation*, 1957), *La repetición* (*The Repetition*, 1963), *El último tren* (*The Last Train*, 1963), and *Todos los domingos* (*Every Sunday*, 1966) incorporated Cuban speech and situations to the poetics of the theatre of the *absurd. *Los siete contra Tebas* (*Seven against Thebes*, 1968) was publicly rejected by the National Union of Authors and Artists for 'ideological content', thus preventing its première in Cuba, though in 1988 *La tierra permanente* (*The Permanent Land*) was honoured with the National Critics' award. Arrufat has contributed to a reassessment of the *teatro* *bufo* style and of nineteenth-century Cuban playwrights.

MM

ART, THÉÂTRE D'

French company, formed in *Paris in 1890 after the amalgamation of Paul *Fort's Théâtre Mixte, committed to young writers, and Louis Germain's Théâtre Idéaliste, whose aim was to resist *naturalism. Germain swiftly parted company, and much of the work presented in Fort's first year would have found a home at the Théâtre *Libre, but his company quickly became associated with the *symbolist movement. The 1891 version of Shelley's *The Cenci* featured a three-minute silent tableau at the end of each performance, the silent stage which Mallarmé had been advocating. Subsequently Fort declared his theatre symbolist, and premièred some notable plays, including *Maeterlinck's *The Intruder* (1891) and *The Blind* (1892), as well as work by Quillard and Van Leberghe, productions which gave rise to the term 'static theatre'. The curtain came down on the project in March 1892, the result of Fort's inexperience and a programme of limited appeal to an intellectual elite.

BRS

ARTAUD, ANTONIN (1896–1948)

French actor, director, playwright, and theatre *theorist, who shook up the intellectual French elite in his lifetime and whose writings and manifestos came to wield extraordinary influence on post-war theatre. A theatrical jack-of-all-trades, Artaud was master of none. But his powerful legacy came in the form of an immense quantity of epistolary communication with the theatrical *avant-garde, often written in the form of treatises and manifestos with a strident, polemical style, all advocating a revolution in theatre. Artaud's formation of revolutionary ideals was inspired first by the *surrealist movement, whose 'Centrale Surréaliste' he directed in 1925, and it was to the surrealists that he was connected throughout the 1920s. He published a number of significant treatises in this vein, including *Umbilical Limbo* and *The Nervometer* in the same year. His early career was as a man of letters but it was as a *film actor that he made his name. He acted in over twenty films, his most notable roles being Marat in Abel Gance's *Napoléon* (1927), and Brother Jean Massieu in Carl Dreyer's *The Passion of Joan of Arc* (1928). His striking physiognomy was captured vividly on celluloid but the celebrity brought by his cinematic career clashed with his surrealist anti-bourgeois ethic. Although he was to publish many film scenarios and treatments, his creativity in cinema was limited to acting and to one screenplay, *The Shell and the Clergyman* (directed by Germaine Dulac, 1927).

Theatre offered him many more possibilities. After a first flirtation with walk-on parts at the Théâtre de l'*Œuvre he joined *Dullin's Théâtre de l'*Atelier in 1921 and became obsessed with the potential of theatre for breaking with *realism. His treatise 'The Evolution of Set Design' was published by the journal *Comœdia* in 1924, the first of many such writings, culminating in the celebrated collection of essays entitled *The Theatre and its Double* (1938). This book was to become the manifesto for theatre revolutionaries growing up in the political unrest of the 1960s.

Artaud's practical theatre career, after his initial experiments in the companies of the masters Dullin and *Pitoëff, centred on two periods of intense activity around the formation of theatres. The first was entitled the Alfred *Jarry Theatre (in homage to the precursor of surrealism), which mounted four productions in various *Parisian theatres between 1927 and 1929, the most famous of which were *Strindberg's *A Dream Play* and *Vitrac's *Victor; or, Children Take Over* (1928–9). The second was the Theatre of *Cruelty, which survived for only one production in 1935, Artaud's own adaptation of Shelley's *The Cenci*. Uneven in *acting style, it played to poor houses in an inappropriate *music hall for seventeen performances. The demise of his pet project of 'cruelty' (based on a heretical Gnostic belief that the essence of life is cruel and beyond redemption) forced Artaud to reject theatre altogether. It was followed by world travels in search of authentic primitive cultures, and a nine-year period in psychiatric hospitals. Upon his release in 1946 he turned to *radio as a medium for his ideas and recorded three programmes. The last, *To Put an End to the Judgement of God*, was banned in 1948 on the eve of transmission for reasons of blasphemy (*see* CENSORSHIP). Artaud's spirit was crushed; all his performance endeavours had failed, been cut off prematurely, or silenced.

But if his theatrical career let him down, his own life was his true and best performance. His lectures were legendary, and fuelled by psychoses and drug addiction, he acted out his philosophies of affective theatre outside the legitimate media of representation. His entire life was haunted by a series of psychiatric illnesses which both tortured and inspired him. He had a personal relationship with two notable psychiatrists, through whom he encountered much of the inspiration for his revolutionary theatre: research he conducted for them on the psychophysical effects of plague provided for Artaud an *allegory of the psychological affectiveness of what he thought of as 'true' theatre, and even the electro-shock therapy he underwent while incarcerated (although he abhorred its use personally) provided him with opportunity to explore the actor's split between self and other.

After his release into a halfway house in Paris he continued to upset the establishment. At a fundraising lecture called 'Tête-à-tête with Antonin Artaud' in 1947 he tore up his notes and, before a shocked *audience of celebrities, he performed rather than narrated the notion of cruelty. This instance, like so many others, demonstrated that he was far ahead of his time, obsessed with the codification of traditional Asian theatres, the structuring of the unconscious, and the deconstruction of signs and systems of signification. Suffering from cancer in his last year, he was found dead at the end of his bed. *The Theatre and its Double*, and a seemingly endless series of his *Complete Works*, testify to the myth of a living failure and a posthumous revolutionary. BRS

ESSLIN, MARTIN, *Artaud* (London, 1976)

SCHUMACHER, CLAUDE, and SINGLETON, BRIAN (eds.), *Artaud on Theatre*, rev. edn. (London, 2000)

SELLIN, ERIC, *The Dramatic Concepts of Antonin Artaud* (Chicago, 1968)

ARTEF

Acronym for Arbeiter Teater Farband (Workers' Theatre Alliance), a *Yiddish-language left-wing theatre which operated in *New York from 1925 to 1940. ARTEF distinguished itself from other Workers' Theatres by adherence to a consistent artistic style—the poetic *expressionism pioneered by Evgeny *Vakhtangov at the *Moscow *Habima in the early 1920s. ARTEF actors underwent elaborate *training with *artistic director Benno Schneider (a Vakhtangov student) and other teachers. The theatre, governed by a 50-member executive council representing a spectrum of left-wing Yiddish intellectuals and labour leaders, was innovative in the American theatre for its use of tableaux, substitution of song for *dialogue, and conversion of dramatic scenes into *dance. Having acquired in 1937 a large orchestra and a lease on the 1,200-seat Cen-

tury Theatre, ARTEF went bankrupt in 1940 and ceased operation. MAF

ARTISTIC DIRECTOR

A *manager who controls and oversees artistic policy. Though related in function to the German *Intendant* and to the directors of older European *national theatres like the *Comédie-Française, the artistic director arose internationally after the Second World War with the rapid establishment of companies whose *finance was dependent on state or private subsidy (*see also* ARTS COUNCILS). In many countries, but especially in England and North America, the earlier model of theatrical control implied a capitalist form of production in which sharers, a manager, or an *actor-manager owned or leased the *playhouse, chose the scripts, and hired the acting and production company, thus taking the financial risks and reaping the rewards (*see also* COMPANY ORGANIZATION IN EUROPE, 1500–1700). An extension of this model was the development in the early twentieth century of the *producer, a commercial coordinator who controls a production in the interests of profit—the regular pattern still in the West End and on Broadway—but has no long-term investment in a particular playhouse or company. The artistic director, on the other hand, is normally contracted by the board of directors of a stable company and is insulated from the legal and financial responsibility of the institution, which most often is designated as a charitable or non-profit enterprise and thinks of itself as a public service.

The duties of an artistic director can vary considerably, but in most cases involve setting and maintaining standards of production, selecting annual seasons, and supervising *casting, choice of *directors and designers, and maintaining public and governmental relations. Sometimes the artistic director has fiscal, personnel, and material responsibilities as well, though for larger companies these functions fall to a specialist manager without artistic obligations. Artistic directors may be hired for a specified term, as at the *National Theatre in *London, or may remain in post for almost 40 years, as Zelda *Fichandler did at *Arena Stage in Washington. It is a sign of the power structure of contemporary theatre that most artistic directors have been and continue to be stage directors. Almost no designers or *playwrights have been appointed to such posts, and relatively few *actors. Laurence *Olivier at the National in Britain was a highly visible exception to custom; in other cases actors elevated to power have rapidly converted to directing, as Christopher *Newton at the *Shaw Festival did. Notable artistic directors of the post-war period include Jean *Vilar (another actor-director) and Roger *Planchon of *Théâtre National Populaire, Ariane *Mnouchkine of Théâtre du *Soleil in *Paris, Peter *Stein of the *Berlin *Schaubühne, *Suzuki Tadashi of Suzuki Company of Toga in *Japan, and Habib *Tanvir of Naya Theatre in *India. DK

ARTISTS OF DIONYSUS

An organization (*koinon, sunodos*) of free Greek festival performers, first attested *c.*300 BC, which continued until nearly AD 300. It was widespread in all Greek lands, being the most powerful, best-organized, and most enduring of all ancient groups of artisans. Indispensable for Greek religious festivals and for their promoters, the organization gained access to Roman emperors or Hellenistic kings. It swiftly learned how to exact ever greater privileges for members, such as freedom from arrest, freedom of travel, front seating, the right to wear purple, and tax concessions, all confirmed by surviving inscriptions.   WJS

ARTS COUNCILS

The arts council is an institution charged by government with the dispersal of funds to generally non-commercial arts and culture. The arts council normally will maintain a so-called 'arm's length' relationship with government. It is, therefore, not a department of government; it is not a ministry, nor is it an autonomous foundation, nor any other institutional form. The arts council receives funds from government, but government does not determine which arts organizations or artists will receive support. Arts councils are often organized on a national or regional basis, although there are some structures that work internationally. Nevertheless the weight of responsibility in supporting—some might say protecting—national cultures and national cultural flagship institutions remains strong.

The first arm's length arts council was the Arts Council of Great Britain (ACGB), established in 1946 out of the earlier (1943) Council for the Encouragement of Music and the Arts. The British government used the arm's length principle, modelled on existing institutions such as the BBC, as a means of distancing the arts from politics and bureaucracy. It had the twin desires of wanting to empower the arts community itself and to avoid the system of state support that had existed in Russia and Germany before 1945, where official art had been all but imposed by ministers of culture. The ACGB was constituted as a non-departmental public body with a national remit, operating independently of ministers, but for which ministers were ultimately accountable. While John Maynard Keynes, first chairman of the ACGB, described arts patronage in the UK as having come about in a 'very English, informal, unostentatious way', others have described this very British affair as more fatally compromised: the Arts Council in the UK is perhaps the definitive example of that ugly neologistic acronym the 'quango', or quasi-autonomous non-government organization.

The government appoints the members of the ACGB governing board, establishes the overall policies within which the organization works, and determines the amount of funding the organization receives. The Arts Council then determines its own policies and priorities, establishes its own strategic plan, appoints its chief executive officer and other staff, determines the allocation of the budget to various programmes and activities, establishes its various funding programmes, and determines who will receive its financial support. Within this dominant model the Arts Council was utterly dependent on subvention from the UK Treasury; it was supervised by a government department and minister but had a staff who were not civil servants and a council that, while ideally independent of political prejudice, was also appointed by the government of the day; decisions were generally advised by variations on the theme of peer review and evaluation.

An arts council will undertake some or all of the following activities: providing financial support to arts and cultural organizations and individuals; advising the national government on matters related to the arts and culture; developing, implementing, and evaluating national cultural policies; conducting research; promoting public understanding and appreciation of the arts and culture; awarding prizes or honours; and publishing books or magazines. An arts council might also disperse funds for capital projects.

The strength of the arm's length arts council—the model adopted in many anglophone countries, including Ireland and Canada—can also be its particular weakness. Supporting and developing artistic excellence can lead to accusations of elitism, with respect to both type of art produced and *audience served. Support of artistic excellence may result in art that is not accessible to, or appreciated by, the general public. And, of course, even within this framework governments can manage, interpret, and promote culture in significantly different ways: for example, attempting to strike a balance between the twin dynamics of cultural democracy and the democratization of culture. For the contemporary arts council there is, perhaps, a tension between the possibilities of its role as a funding council and that of a development agency. *See also* FINANCE; NATIONAL ENDOWMENT FOR THE ARTS; NATIONAL THEATRE MOVEMENT, BRITAIN; NATIONAL THEATRE MOVEMENT, IRELAND; NATIONAL THEATRE MOVEMENT, NORTH AMERICA; NATIONAL THEATRE MOVEMENTS, EUROPE.   AS

ARTS THEATRE

Always hovering artistically on the fringes of the West End of *London, the 347-seat Arts Theatre opened in 1927 as a club for unlicensed and experimental drama. In its first five years it produced plays by *Galsworthy, *Strindberg, *Ibsen, *Tolstoy, and transferred less risky fare to the West End, including John *Van Druten's *Young Woodley* (1928). Its 1930s repertoire became progressively more random: visiting productions included J. T. *Grein's staging of *Hasenclever's *Marriages Are Made in Heaven* and *And So to Bed* by a Jewish Girl's Club. Alec *Clunes ran it from 1942 to 1952, sometimes with a permanent company in true *repertory plus playwrights on the payroll, premièring, for example, Christopher *Fry's *The Lady's Not for Burning* (1947)—one critic called it 'a pocket national theatre'. Campbell Williams took over in 1953, providing UK premières of *Beckett, *Pinter, and *Albee. *Film producer Nathan Cohen bought it in 1962, giving the *Royal Shakespeare Company a lease for an experimental drama season, followed by Caryl Jenner's Unicorn Theatre. Since then it has hosted London runs of plays by Robert Patrick, *Stoppard, *Godber, Julian *Mitchell, and others.　　　　　　　　BRK

ASAKURA, SETSU (1922–　)

Japanese designer. Born in Tokyo, Asakura began her career as a painter but after study in New York in 1970 took up a theatrical career. She soon became a favourite designer for such important figures in the *avant-garde movement as *Kara Jūrō and *Shimizu Kunio and worked on Japanese productions of Western works, among them a celebrated production of the *Brecht–*Weill *Threepenny Opera* in 1977. Asakura became the best-known Japanese stage designer in Europe and the United States. She designed the sets for a *Medea* seen in Greece and Italy in 1983, and the *scenery and *costumes for Richard *Strauss's *opera *Die Frau ohne Schatten* for the Bavarian State Opera in 1993. In 1985 she designed *Jōruri* by the leading Japanese composer Miki Minoru for the Opera Theatre of St Louis, and returned to do sets and costumes for the world première of Miki's *The Tale of Genji* in 2000. Asakura's goal, in her words, is to express 'the director's image in solid form', but her highly personal use of light, colour, and space invariably provides a sense of innovation and visual surprise.　　JTR

ASARE, YAW (1953–2002)

Ghanaian dramatist and director. His richly textured *Story Ananse Told* (1994), in the Efua *Sutherland tradition of narrative Ghanaian drama (*abibigoro*), aspired to make sharp political points. Following his move from the University of Ghana to the National Theatre in 1994, *Secrets of an Ancient Well* was produced in Accra and at international *festivals, followed by *Desert Dreams* (1999). In 2000 Asare returned to the university, where he founded a theatre group, Dawuro Africa, and directed his play *Sodom and Gomorra*. He was deeply involved in fostering theatrical links with francophone *African countries.　　JMG

ASCH, SOLOMON (SHOLEM) (1880–1957)

Polish-born Yiddish novelist and playwright, whose one-act play *The Eldest Sister* inaugurated the *Moscow *Habima Studio in October 1918. Asch wrote over twenty plays, the earliest of which, *Returned* (1904) and *The Time of Messiah* (1905), deal with the conflict between old and new Jewish lifestyles, a theme also reflected in *God and Vengeance* (1907), staged by Max *Reinhardt at the *Deutsches Theater in *Berlin, which has a lesbian theme combined with a brothel setting. Many of his plays fuse an idyllic romanticism with a sense of harsh realism and express a love for the world of nature.　　NW

ASCHE, OSCAR (1871–1936)

Australian *actor-manager and playwright who made a career on the *London stage. Starting in F. R. *Benson's company (1893–1901) he married the actress Lily Brayton, and in 1904 they joined Beerbohm *Tree at His (*Her) Majesty's Theatre to play a succession of Shakespearian lead couples, which quickly became their trademark. But it was in the realm of popular culture that Asche was to make a mark and a sizeable fortune. Three orientalist spectaculars—*Kismet* (1911), *Chu Chin Chow* (1916), and *Cairo* (1921)—accrued mass appeal in their lavish decors, Arabian Nights fantasies, *dancing orgies, and *costume parades. *Chu Chin Chow* was the most successful, running until 1921 at His Majesty's for 2,238 performances, at that time the longest continuous run in London (*see* LONG RUN). These productions featured the jingoistic claptraps of *melodrama, the oriental settings and *characters of *musical comedy, and the *stock figures and scene transformations of *pantomime, acting as theatrical respite for the fears and anxieties of a nation at war.　　BRS

ASHCROFT, PEGGY (1907–91)

English actress who began her career at the *Birmingham Rep in 1926. In *London in the three years from 1927 Ashcroft appeared in Shakespeare, *Congreve, *Goldsmith, *Shaw, *Strindberg, *Feuchtwanger, *Yeats, and Sidney *Howard, and in the 1930s appeared in *Sheridan, Shaw, *Schnitzler, Goldsmith, *Hauptmann, *Pirandello, *Bulgakov, and Maxwell *Anderson. She played Desdemona to Paul *Robeson's Othello (1930) and Juliet to *Gielgud's and *Olivier's Romeos (1935). At the *Old Vic in the mid-1930s she took on further Shakespearian roles, including Portia and Rosalind, and during the next three decades would play most of the major female parts in Shakespeare except for Lady Macbeth. In the 1940s and 1950s she took the title roles in *Webster's *The Duchess of Malfi* (1945) and *Sophocles' *Electra* (1951), and triumphed in Gielgud's production of *The Importance of Being Earnest* (1942) and in *Hedda Gabler* (1954).

During the 1950s and early 1960s she appeared in Stratford in several roles, including Margaret in the *Barton–*Hall *Wars of the Roses* (1963). She also acted in modern drama, including plays by *Ibsen, *Chekhov, *Pinter, *Albee, and Günther *Grass; her Winnie in *Beckett's *Happy Days* (1975) was particularly remarkable. After reading *Stanislavsky's *My Life in Art* in 1926, she was committed to the principle of *repertory playing. In 1937–8 she joined Gielgud for a season of Shakespeare and

Chekhov; in 1957 she became a member of the *English Stage Company at the *Royal Court; in 1960 she was a founding member of the *Royal Shakespeare Company. Performing on stage in great drama remained her paramount purpose for six decades, though on occasion she also appeared in *film, and won an Academy award as Mrs Moore in *A Passage to India* (1984). She was married three times, most notably to Theodore *Komisarjevsky (1934–6). During her career she received several dozen acting *awards and seven honorary doctorates. She was awarded the CBE in 1951 and made DBE in 1956.

TP

ASHUR, NUMAN (1918–87)

Egyptian playwright. Ashur's major contribution was his faithful depiction of the social shifts and characteristic locales of the Egyptian petite bourgeoisie after the 1952 Revolution, as in *El-Nas Elli Taht* (*The People Downstairs*, 1956), set in a basement, and *Eilet El-Doghri* (*The Family of El-Doghri*, 1963), set in a family house. He identified his mentors as *Sannu, *Hakim, and *Rihany in Egypt, as well as *Chekhov, *Gorky, *Shaw, and *O'Casey, yet the comic and colloquial Arabic of Ashur's plays communicates more immediately than Hakim's philosophical and literary language or Rihany's didacticism.

HMA

ASHWELL, LENA (1869–1957)

English actress, *manager, and writer, born Lena Pocock. Ashwell's most applauded performances were as strong, passionate women in ambiguous moral circumstances, such as Mrs Dane, the woman with a past in H. A. *Jones's *Mrs Dane's Defence* (1900), or the reluctant burglar heroine in *Leah Kleschna* (1905), a part written for her. She managed the Kingsway Theatre, *London, from 1907 to 1909; notable successes included Cecily *Hamilton's *Diana of Dobson's* (1908) with herself in the lead. During the First World War she ran a massive operation to entertain the troops abroad with concerts, extracts from plays, and recitals. From 1919 to 1929 she managed the Lena Ashwell Players, a company which *toured extensively, particularly around London, performing a different play each week and targeting non-traditional *audiences. Ashwell wrote memoirs, an autobiography entitled *Myself a Player* (1936), and a collection of esoteric lectures, *Reflections from Shakespeare* (1927).

EJS

ASIAN-AMERICAN THEATRE

In the late eighteenth century representations of Asia could be found on the American stage, usually offered or performed by non-Asians using racialized *make-up, settings, and *costumes to denote the oriental qualities desired. In 1834, Afong Moy, an authentic 'Chinese Lady', was displayed at the American Museum. Coupled with P. T. *Barnum's similar displays of Chang and Eng, the 'Siamese twins', such performances characterize the earliest performances of Asianness in America. By the 1870s, the large Chinese community in *San Francisco boasted eleven Cantonese opera companies providing entertainment for its mostly Cantonese immigrant population. After the turn of the century, entrepreneurs turned towards the dominant culture, and *cabarets, nightclubs, and especially Chinese restaurants began to exploit the desire for exotica in both cuisine and entertainment.

A discrete Asian-American theatre movement began to emerge in the increasing social awareness of the 1960s. Encouraged by the 'Third World' strikes at San Francisco State University and the University of California in Berkeley, Asian America began to examine the roots of its oppression. Within this context, the acquiescence of Asian-American actors in the perpetuation of stereotypes became the focus of much attention. To address this problem, and to showcase Asian-American talent in the *Los Angeles area, *East West Players, the first socially aware Asian-American theatre company, was founded in 1965. Throughout its history East West Players featured Asian casts in a mix of plays by both European and Asian writers. To encourage plays focused on the lives of Asian Americans, Frank *Chin founded the Asian American Theater Workshop in San Francisco in 1972. Two years later the workshop became the Asian American Theater Company, the first theatre dedicated exclusively to the production of plays by and about Asian America. It is significant that Chin's own *Chickencoop Chinaman* (1972) and *Year of the Dragon* (1974), the first plays by a Chinese American to be produced in *New York, focused on the complexities of Asian identity in America. This issue would become the recurrent theme in the work of later playwrights such as David Henry *Hwang, Rick Shiomi, Chay Yew, Velina Hasu *Houston, and Philip Kan *Gotanda.

The success of these early theatre companies inspired similar organizations across the United States. By the end of the 1970s the Northwest Asian Theatre in Seattle and Tisa Chang's Pan Asian Repertory Theatre in New York had been established, and the mainstream *regional theatres provided additional support. Chin's early workshops received encouragement from San Francisco's *American Conservatory Theatre, and the *Mark Taper Forum in Los Angeles sponsored Chay Yew's Asian Theatre Workshop. At the end of the twentieth century Asian-American theatre companies could be found in virtually every urban centre in the United States. The National Asian American Theatre Company in New York was created to produce classic Western drama with Asian casts. Minneapolis supported both Theatre Mu, established by Rick Shiomi in 1992 with a pan-Asian production programme appealing to mixed *audiences, and the Pom Siab Hmoob Theatre (Gazing into the Heart of the Hmong) which produces bilingual works focusing on Hmong life. Joanna Chan's Yangtze Repertory Theatre Company of America, founded in the early 1970s as the Four Seas Theatre, continues to produce works in Chinese (often with English subtitles) for Chinese Americans in the New York area. *Chicago's Pintig features only Filipino work, while New York's Mi-Ya Theatre Company, established in 1989 to produce works addressing the Filipino experience, has broadened its programme to include new works by other Asian Americans. Sacramento's Asian American Contemporary Theatre, established in 1994 to focus on contemporary plays by Asian Americans, evolved into InterACT in response to the increasingly complex racial mix of that area. A recent directory of Asian-American theatres listed no fewer than 60 companies in addition to at least ten university or college production units.

The existence of Asian-American theatre companies contributed significantly to the growth of their dramatic literature. Where much of the early drama featured one-dimensional attacks on the oppressiveness of Anglo-American stereotyping of Asia, recent plays suggest that playwrights have achieved the confidence to move beyond the details of comparative identity politics. Gotanda's *The Wash* (1985), for example, examines the destructive consequences of a Japanese-American family member's inability to let go of his internment camp experience and to strive for a positive future. Rick Shiomi's *Yellow Fever* (1983) lampoons the *film noir* tradition with an Asian-American detective. Velina Hasu Houston's plays set aside the history of stereotyping to look instead at problems arising from a mixed race childhood. Chay Yew's works discuss the difficulties of achieving the American dream and confront gay Asian life. East West Players presented *Beijing Spring* (1999), a *musical by Joel Iwataki and Tim Dang dealing with the Tiananmen Square tragedy of 1989, and Hwang wrote an adaptation of *Flower Drum Song* to open in 2001 at the Mark Taper Forum in Los Angeles. The recent success of Asian-American comedy troupes like Los Angeles's 18 Mighty Mountain Warriors, Chicago's Stir Friday Night, New York's Slant, and Seattle's Pork Filled Players, suggest a maturing if not assimilation of the Asian-American theatre scene.

JSM

LEE, JOSEPHINE, *Performing Asian America: race and ethnicity on the contemporary stage* (Philadelphia, 1997)

MOY, JAMES S., *Marginal Sights: staging the Chinese in America* (Iowa City, 1994)

ASKEY, ARTHUR (1900–82)

Liverpool-born English comedian of the *music-hall tradition who made his professional debut in 1924. His early career, as the principal comedian in summer season entertainments at British seaside resorts, expanded to a national *audience on *radio, being particularly associated with the innovative BBC show *Band Wagon* which he co-hosted with Richard Mur-

doch from 1938. Askey also appeared—more or less playing himself—in a series of British *films, including the wartime entertainments *The Ghost Train* (1941), *King Arthur Was a Gentleman* (1942), and *Miss London Ltd* (1943). His persona was that of 'Big hearted Arthur', the cheery, but not too cheeky, chappie. Throughout his career Askey was associated with the *Band Wagon* catchphrase of 'Hello playmates!' as well as his piping 'I thank you' and his signature musical number the 'Busy Bee Song'. He was awarded the CBE in 1981. AS

ASPAZIJA (ELSA ROZENBERG) (1868–1943)

Latvian poet and dramatist, wife of the poet Yan Rainis and an early *feminist. Her first play, *The Avenger* (1888), was meant as a protest against serfdom, whilst *The Priestess* and *Forfeited Rights*, both staged in Riga in 1894, were concerned with the struggle for women's rights, as was *The Unattained Goal* (1895). *The Silver Coverlet* (1905) was banned (*see* CENSORSHIP) and one of her later plays, *Aspazija* (1923), had a distinctly autobiographical element. Her career as a playwright was marked by a shift from social concerns towards those of a more personal and psychological nature. NW

ASSUNÇAO, LEILAH (1943–)

Brazilian playwright. Assunçao's work treats the changing condition of middle-class women, the family, and *gender relations in increasing urban chaos. Her most successful play, *Fala baixo, senão eu grito* (*Speak Low or I'll Scream*, 1969), is a *surreal portrayal of a spinster who encounters an intruder who is both real and imaginary. An exception to her usual theme, *The Kuka of Kamaiorá* (1978) is a futuristic *parody of *Latin American dictatorship. LHD

ASTAIRE, FRED (1899–1987) AND ADELE (1898–1981)

American brother–sister *dance team. Born Fred and Adele Austerlitz in Omaha, Nebraska, the Astaires' mother enrolled them in dance school when the family moved to *New York in 1904. The children began appearing in *vaudeville the next year and made their Broadway debut in 1917 with *Over the Top*. The pair were featured in eleven Broadway *musicals between 1918 and 1932, including George *Gershwin's *Lady, Be Good* (1924) and *Funny Face* (1927). The last show in which they performed together was *The Band Wagon* (1931). As a brother–sister team, the Astaires avoided the traditionally sexual basis of male–female dancing, and offered instead an asexual elegance and wit. The critic Brooks *Atkinson called their dancing 'a *comedy of manners' and described their 'droll dance inflections' free of 'showshop trickery'. Adele retired from performing in 1932 when she married Lord Cavendish, the 9th Duke of Devonshire, and moved with him to a castle in Ireland. Fred moved to Hollywood in the same year and began a long *film career.   MAF

ASTLEY'S AMPHITHEATRE

An eighteenth- and nineteenth-century *London circus theatre. Built as an *amphitheatre in 1784 by Philip Astley, a retired cavalryman who invented the modern *circus, it became, after remodelling and rebuilding in 1795 and 1804 (following two *fires), a theatre for *hippodrama, a new form of equestrian *melodrama—and later *pantomime—employing both the circus ring and an attached *stage and using large numbers of trained horses in military *spectacles based upon historical and contemporary battles such as Agincourt, Jerusalem, Waterloo, and the Alma in the Crimea. This kind of spectacle continued through the nineteenth century. After Astley's death the theatre was managed by Andrew *Ducrow, a superb horseman, William Batty, and William Cooke, who equestrianized *Richard III*, *Macbeth*, and *I Henry IV* in 1856–7. Reconstructed and enlarged in 1873 by George *Sanger, it became Sanger's Amphitheatre, with the same kind of repertory. It closed in 1893 and was demolished in 1895.   MRB

ASTON, ANTHONY (c.1682–c.1753)

English actor, playwright, and *manager. 'Tony' Aston was an itinerant player who operated largely outside the *patent theatre system. In between acting and managing with companies of strolling players, Aston travelled widely; he set up as a lawyer in Jamaica and joined the military in the American colonies. His versatility as a performer was recognized in his famous 'Medley', an entertainment written and performed by himself and his family which contained scenes from popular plays, songs, *dances, *monologues, and comical impersonations of animal sounds. Speciality acts were increasingly popular at the patent houses in the eighteenth century but Aston's success stemmed from performing the 'Medley' in taverns and fairs across Britain (c.1710–50). The risk of prosecution for performing without a licence may have led Aston to interrupt his tavern *tours with appearances in the patent companies but these never lasted beyond one season. In 1722 he appeared for John *Rich's company at *Lincoln's Inn Fields, where he used his skill for impersonation to play *characters in the manner of famous actors. His highly personal observations on the particularities of contemporary players were published in *A Brief Supplement to Colley Cibber* (1748).   GBB

ASTOR PLACE RIOT

At the Astor Place Opera House in *New York in 1849, the state militia killed 22 bystanders and wounded over 100 others when rioters protested the performance of English star William *Macready. The 1,800-seat theatre, built in 1847 for elite enjoyment, had adopted pricing policies and dress codes that excluded most of the theatregoing public. Nativist politicians and street gangs used a long-simmering feud between Macready and Edwin *Forrest, the patriotic American star, to organize a *riot protesting the pro-English, pro-elite policies of the theatre and its supporters. The deadly event marked the end of theatre rioting in the USA.   BMC

ASTURIAS, MIGUEL ÁNGEL (1899–1974)

Guatemalan writer. A respected novelist, Asturias also wrote many influential dramas, including *Soluna* (1955) and *La audencia de los confines* (*Tribunal on the Frontier*, 1957). His novel *El señor presidente*, an *allegory of the Cabrera dictatorship, helped him to the Nobel Prize for Literature, and was adapted for the stage by fellow Guatemalan Hugo Carillo in 1974. Asturias's keen interest in Mayan culture and the persecution of contemporary Mayans by the Guatemalan government found its way into his plays.   EJW

ATELIER, THÉÂTRE DE L'

*Playhouse opened in 1922 by Charles *Dullin in the old Théâtre Montmartre in *Paris, originally built for *melodramas in 1822, then converted to a cinema in 1914. As one of the *Cartel des Quatre theatres, the Atelier staged a wide repertoire of classical and modern plays, including the first production in France of a work by *Pirandello (*The Pleasure of Honesty*, 1922). As director of the Atelier, Dullin retained his theatre school, where many notable actors and directors received their *training, including *Artaud, *Blin, *Vilar, and *Barsacq, who took over the Atelier after Dullin moved to the Théâtre Sarah Bernhardt in 1940.   CHB

ATELLAN FARCE

Ancient Italian improvised comic drama. These rustic *farces, named after the Oscan town of Atella, were later performed at Rome in Latin. They featured *masked traditional *stock characters, motivated by some basic appetite (gluttony, lust) or dominant quality (stupidity, anger). These stereotypes were probably used later in Roman literary *comedies, including those of *Plautus, and (controversially) may possibly have influenced Italian *commedia dell'arte*. The farces were lively and crude, with an emphasis on *slapstick and ribald jests. Both their dramatic form, and the simple stages on which they were performed, are likely to have contributed to the development of *Roman theatre.   RCB

ATHENS, MODERN

(for classical Athens, *see* GREEK THEATRE, ANCIENT) During the
*early modern period and the Enlightenment, Greek theatre
flourished in Crete, the Ionian islands, and the Balkans in
two distinct dramatic traditions which also dominated the
Athenian stage in the nineteenth century: 'learned' *texts and
popular plays, the latter mainly inspired by the fight for independence from the Ottoman Empire and written in demotic. In
1840 Constantine Aristias produced the first *tragedy on the
Athenian stage that featured a female actor, Maria Tzivitza.
The theatre company Menander started its performances in
the 1870s, including Shakespeare (featuring Nikolaos Lekatsas
as Hamlet in 1881) and new Greek plays. The 1890s marked the
beginnings of the enormous popularity of the *shadow theatre
Karaghiozis, with its *stock characters and its comic episodes of
resistance to the Ottoman rule (*see* KARAGÖZ). A new type of
popular *musical comedy, *komidilion*, made its appearance on
the Athenian stage in 1889, followed in 1894 by the first
epitheorisis, a *satire of social and political mores. *Realistic
plays by *Ibsen, Kostis Palamas, and others were directed by
Constantine Christomanos for the New Stage (1901–5). The
Greek Actors' Union was founded in 1917, while more attention
was paid to issues of *training with the founding of an *acting
conservatory in 1919 by the Society of Greek Theatre. Fotos
*Politis directed *Sophocles' *Oedipus the King* for the Society
that year, starting a trend for the revival of Greek tragedy later
pursued by Sikelianos in Delphi and by the *Epidaurus Festival.
The *Greek National Theatre was founded in 1932. During the
first half of the twentieth century, two *actor-managers, *Kyveli
and *Kotopouli, dominated the Athenian stage with innovative
productions of classical as well as realist and *bourgeois drama
by *Xenopoulos and others. In 1942 Karolos *Koun founded the
Art Theatre to explore new international styles.

After the Second World War and the Greek civil war, theatre in Athens found itself in a state of ideological confusion.
The legacy of the Resistance against the Nazi occupation and the
revolutionary ideas of the left were not permitted a voice, and
the right-wing post-war government regularly censored, imprisoned, or exiled progressive artists and intellectuals, who
were dealt a second blow during the years of the military dictatorship (1967–74). After 1974, however, *censorship was abolished and theatre in Athens was rejuvenated, aided further in
1985 when Athens became the first Cultural Capital of Europe.
Many new companies were founded, bringing the total count to
over 100 in the 1990s, including children's theatres like Xenia
Kalogeropoulou's internationally known Small Door. New directors, including Minos *Volonakis, Andreas Voutsinas, Roula
Pateraki, Thanasis Papageorgiou, and Lefteris Vogiatzis, and
such actors as Katina *Paxinou, Alexis Minotis, Manos
*Katrakis, Melina *Mercouri, Elli Lampeti, Dimitris Horn,
Jenny Karezi, and Aris Retsos explored new styles for clas-

sical and modern drama. Among the prominent playwrights
were Iakovos *Kambanellis, Loula *Anagnostaki, and Giorgos
Dialegmenos, while composers like Manos Hatzidakis and
Mikis Theodorakis and designers like Yannis Tsarouhis were
important in proposing new interpretations of classical drama.

KGo

ATKINS, EILEEN (1934–)

English actress. Atkins *danced in working men's clubs as a
child, then *trained at the Guildhall School. She played at
Stratford in 1957–8, but was not conventionally attractive
when young and did not come into her own until her thirties.
An intelligent and energetic actress, who chooses her parts carefully, Atkins has done first-rate work for many years in Britain
and the USA, usually outside the subsidized companies. She
won *awards for playing Childie in *The Killing of Sister George*
(1965) and Elizabeth in *Vivat! Vivat Regina* (1970); other favourite roles include Celia Coplestone in *The Cocktail Party* (1968)
and St Joan for *Prospect Theatre Company (1977). She has
often appeared on *television; with Jean Marsh she created
the popular series *Upstairs, Downstairs*. She enjoys playing Virginia Woolf, who was also tall and angular: she adapted *A Room
of One's Own* (1989), and *devised *Vita and Virginia* (1994),
which she performed in *New York with Vanessa *Redgrave.

EEC

ATKINS, ROBERT (1886–1972)

English actor, director, and *manager. Atkins began acting in
1906 at Beerbohm *Tree's His (*Her) Majesty's Theatre, playing
minor Shakespearian roles. Before the war he also acted with
John *Martin-Harvey, Johnston *Forbes-Robertson, and Frank
*Benson. In 1915 he joined the *Old Vic, playing Iago, Richard
III, Macbeth, and Prospero. After serving in the First World
War, he returned to the Old Vic as a director and actor (1920–
5). In 1925 he began to manage his own company, performing
in *London and Stratford-upon-Avon. And he also *toured. During the 1930s and the early 1940s he produced plays at the Open
Air Theatre in Regent's Park and at the *Shakespeare Memorial
Theatre, and after 1945 he presented annual seasons in the Park,
usually featuring Shakespeare. He excelled in comic roles such
as Sir Toby Belch and Bottom. He received the CBE in 1949.

TP

ATKINSON, BROOKS (1894–1984)

Drama critic for the *New York Times* from 1925 to 1960, Atkinson presided over *New York theatre during the era in which
the *Times* review became a make-or-break evaluation for commercial theatre. He avoided most contact with theatre people in
order to retain the perspective of the average theatregoer, his

highest goal being 'to keep things on the level'. A graduate of Harvard (1917) where he studied with George Pierce *Baker, Atkinson evaluated playwrights from *O'Neill to *Albee. Reassigned as a foreign correspondent from 1942 to 1946, his reports on the Soviet Union were awarded a Pulitzer Prize (1947). The first major critic to discover the *Off-Broadway scene of the 1950s, Atkinson saw a gradual decline in Broadway theatre from the 1930s as *audiences moved to electronic media and the creative edge moved to smaller and cheaper venues. When he retired from regular reviewing in 1960, the Mansfield Theatre was renamed to honour him.   MAF

ATY ÑEÉ

Paraguayan company, established by a group of actors and by playwrights Alcibíades González del Valle and Antonio Carmona in 1974. The troupe strove to create a popular theatre committed to *Brechtian practice, and created original pieces for a peasant *audience, including *La fábula de la creación del buey* (*The Story of the Creation of the Ox*) and *Perú Rimá*. One of their best-known Brechtian works is *De la guerra al cabaret* (*From the War to Cabaret*).   EJW

AUBIGNAC, FRANÇOIS HÉDELIN, ABBÉ D' (1604–76)

French dramatist and critic. A member of *Richelieu's household, and sharing the Cardinal's interest in the theatre, d'Aubignac became the most influential of the orthodox *theorists of *neoclassical *tragedy. Developing the views expressed by Chapelain during the 'Querelle du *Cid*' (1637) in his *Pratique du théâtre* (begun in the early 1640s; published in 1657), d'Aubignac found fault with *Corneille over the *unities and on the subject of *le vraisemblable* (what is plausible on stage), and had little sympathy with (or understanding of) the playwright's heroic version of tragedy based on 'admiration'. For d'Aubignac, the point of reference in his vigorous interpretation of the 'rules' is not the authority of the ancients, but an appeal to reason. Corneille's *Trois discours*, published with the 1660 edition of his plays, contains a veiled response to d'Aubignac's attack. D'Aubignac himself composed three tragedies to illustrate his views: *Zénobie* (1640), *La Pucelle d'Orléans* (1640) and *Cyminde* (1641), all written in prose; a most unusual strategy in the neoclassical era.   WDH

AUDEN, W. H. (WYSTAN HUGH) (1907–73)

English writer. Though best known as a poet, he was involved in Rupert Doone's *Group Theatre in *London from 1932, seeing it as a platform for the dissemination of a politicized (left-wing) aesthetic. His first staged play, *The Dance of Death* (1934), broke open the conventional *dance-drama to introduce vibrant social *satire. Subsequent plays, conceived in collaboration with Christopher *Isherwood, were equally eclectic: into a basic *expressionist format were introduced elements of popular *revue and *pantomime in *The Dog beneath the Skin* (1936); social critique, Freudian psychology, and the redemptive metaphysics of *miracle plays in *The Ascent of F6* (1937); *melodrama and Shakespearian tragic *romance in *On the Frontier* (1938). Later Auden became fascinated by the complex demands of creating *operatic librettos, working notably on *Paul Bunyan* for Britten (1939–41), and with Chester Kallman on *The Rake's Progress* for Stravinsky (1947–8), *Elegy for Young Lovers* (1959–60) and *The Bassarids* (1963) for Henze. He wrote incisive *criticism of theatre in performance, the fruit of his invention and thinking about the function of words in drama and opera, included in *The Dyer's Hand* (1962) and *Secondary Worlds* (1968).

RAC

AUDIBERTI, JACQUES (1899–1965)

French dramatist. Born in Antibes, he came to Paris in 1924 and worked as a journalist until the end of the war. He had made his reputation as a poet and novelist, but theatre took precedence with his first produced plays: *Quoat-Quoat* (1946) and *Le Mal court* (*Evil Rampant*, 1947). The latter remains best known of his 30 or so plays, most directed by Georges Vitaly. The force of evil thematically pervades Audiberti's work, arising from his nihilist philosophy of 'abhumanism'. Yet his prolix style has been called 'a feast', incorporating baroque, *surrealist, erotic, fantastic, humorous, and nightmarish elements in loosely structured *plots. Among his darker plays are *La Fête noire* (*The Black Festival*, 1948) and *La Hobereaute* (1956). Some, like *Pucelle* (1950) and *La Fourmi dans le corps* (*An Unscratchable Itch*, 1962), have been classed as historical *'operettas'. Women dominate the action in *L'Effet Glapion* (*The Glapion Effect*, 1959), *La Logeuse* (*The Landlady*, 1960), and others; a ferocious purity is often the source of their mystery and power.   FHL

AUDIENCE

One or more persons assembled to see a performance. The constituency of audiences varies widely according to the social, political, and cultural circumstances of the performance: for the City *Dionysia of the first *Greek theatre, audiences were as large as 14,000; intimate alternative spaces of off-*Off-Off-Broadway in *New York may seat only a dozen people. Since performance assumes the presence of an audience as one of its preconditions, the attraction of spectators to the live event as well as engagement with them during the event is crucial.

Knowledge of who went to theatres at different historical moments and the relative successes of performances they saw tells us much about the values and beliefs of a particular society.

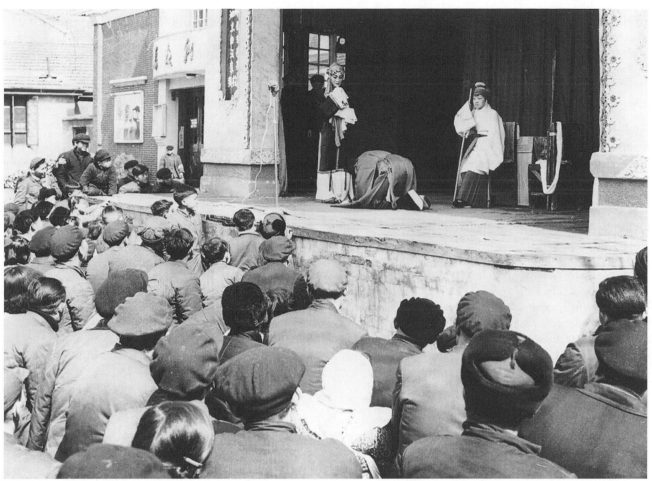

An attentive **audience** of workers at a recreation centre watching an open-air performance in 1959 in Wuhan, the capital city of the Hubei province in central China.

A day at the three-day City Dionysia opened with a ceremony of purification (the sacrifice of a pig), followed by proclamations, three *tragedies, a *satyr-play, a break for dinner, and then a *comedy. This suggests the degree of commitment required as well as the integration of the audience's religious and civic life into the performance (through the ceremonies and proclamations). Here spectatorship elaborates and confirms dominant cultural practices. At the other extreme, *censorship has endeavoured to prohibit audiences from viewing productions that might encourage or incite beliefs or behaviours considered dangerous. In 1980s communist Poland, the Theatre of the Eighth Day (whose productions challenged the government) had to perform surreptitiously in churches, school gymnasiums, and *open-air venues to avoid prohibition and imprisonment. In the 1990s several theatre companies located in North American cities faced threats of defunding and closure for producing Tony *Kushner's openly *gay play *Angels in America*. More typically, the audience for a performance comes together as a result of its collective and individual expectations as well as more general cultural conditions. While much theatregoing is a leisure or entertainment activity, it can also be an expression of faith (such as for audiences in *India for the *ras lila; *see also* RITUAL AND THEATRE).

It is important, then, to consider what place performance occupies since this will shape significantly both the size of the audience and the value spectators attach to their role. Major cities in the Western world have a long tradition of performances in a variety of cultural sites (*playhouses, concert halls, *opera houses, and so on); theatres within these large urban concentrations are often in defined districts where artistic activities predominate. Smaller concentrations of population may have few formal buildings dedicated to the arts, but may rely on multi-use venues and on performances that come from elsewhere. Where performance is inextricably tied to religious practices, sacred spaces such as temples may be used (*see* RELIGION AND THEATRE). Other performances may require no formal venue whatsoever and simply take place wherever the theatre-makers or their audiences are located. Audience expectations and experiences are significantly shaped by interaction with the specificities of location, type, and space of performance.

Many different components of pre-performance inform an audience's attitudes. Foremost among these is the cultural capital afforded to theatre and performance. Is theatre considered a high culture activity? Or a popular form? Are there many opportunities to see theatre? Or is it a rare event? Is theatre considered primarily an 'art' activity or is it tied to other cultural experiences such as religion, politics, tourism, or education? The audience's relation to the generally held concept of theatre, to specific theatre products within their home culture, and to the specifics that inform attendance at an actual performance combine to produce a spectator's attraction to and expectations for the theatrical event itself. A production of *Hamlet* would be outside the theatrical traditions of a *Korean audience, but might draw audiences in Seoul because of Shakespeare's global cultural capital or because of the involvement of a leading Korean theatre practitioner or because of its use of local theatre methods. Further, expectations are likely to be quite different for a theatregoer who has bought a *ticket months in advance for a blockbuster Broadway show than for the *dantai* (groups of workers and their families sent to the theatre by *Japanese companies as an employment perk) or for the tourist audiences of the Mandalay *marionettes in *Myanmar.

The conditions that underlie performance are also relevant. Whether a production relies on some kind of government grant subsidy or the economics of *box office (both of which will impact the selection of play, company, director, actor, and so on), *finance shapes what is available for consumption. Tied to funding is marketing. How a play is advertised or otherwise drawn to the attention of potential audience members will shape the spectator's willingness to buy a ticket or devote time. Reviews, other media reports, discussions, prizes, popularity of an author or actor, scholarship, teachers, and critics all serve to market a performance. Subscriptions and other reasons of habit, as well as word-of-mouth encouragement or tourist guidebooks, might further serve to draw audiences to a particular performance. (*See* PUBLICITY.)

The spectator's arrival at the performance space triggers another level of expectation and preparation. How did the spectator travel to the theatre? Was the journey difficult or easy? Is this part of the spectator's leisure time or is it connected to the workplace or an educational setting? What kind of environment surrounds the performance space? Is it part of an arts district or is it in an isolated and/or unwelcoming neighbourhood? What is the performance space like? Are there foyers, bars, eating places for socializing before the event? Is the spectator alone or with others?

Some elements of the audience-performance relationship will work before the event proper begins: *lighting, *music, presence of actors on- or offstage, visibility of *scenery, programmes or other materials (*see* PLAYBILLS AND PROGRAMMES), availability

and comfort of seating. Particular importance should be accorded to the proxemic relations of performance space (how is the audience positioned in relation to where the action will take place? What hierarchies are explicitly or implicitly established?). Exterior components (both those beyond the space and those within it) provide a broad context for the audience's expectations and understanding. This context informs and interacts with the actual duration and immediacy of the performance itself. Once the performance begins, spectators respond to a combination and succession of visual and aural signs. Some will be fixed (a set that does not change during a show, for example), but the majority will be in flux; all enable an audience to posit the existence of a fictional world with its own dynamic and governing rules.

Visual and aural signs created by an *actor emanate from language, voice, movement, and physical appearance (including *costume, *make-up, and facial expression). Individual performers are linked in their interrelationships within the world of the play and in the context of external signs that derive from the set, *props, lighting, *sound, and music. In the first few minutes of a performance, spectators are likely to focus on all signs so as to establish a context for the fictional world; as the performance continues, some elements will draw less attention unless they are in some way respecified (in the case of a set change) and more spectatorial energy can be devoted to local details (facial expressions, gestures, costume changes of lead actors).

The spectator's experience is one of constant meaning-production, revision, confirmation, and negation within a fixed time period. The only times available for reflection are likely to be determined by performers and not theatregoers (use of intervals, *act or *scene divisions, set changes). Moreover, responses result not only from the interaction between the audience and the represented world of the performance but also from the interaction with the performers as actors. In Western theatre, the presence of a star actor is particularly laden; in some West *African theatres, audience members go onto the stage to stick coins on the foreheads of popular actors or musicians. Responses are also generated from spectator–spectator interaction. A shared collective reaction can be expected (*laughter at the same event), but this can never be guaranteed. Within even the most seeming homogeneity of response, some may be experiencing the performance very differently or may not be paying attention at all. Individual reactions in areas of identification, desire, and fantasy also impact response whether or not an individual expresses these reactions as part of the collective.

Post-performance expressions of *applause or *booing or other signals are an explicit recognition of spectator presence. Devices such as *curtain calls, post-production discussions, receptions and other social events all further contribute to the degree of pleasure experienced. Since theatre audiences tend to comprise varying sizes of groups, their experience often extends to specific social interactions after the performance. Also, reading an available text, reading reviews or other descriptions, seeing another or the same production or a *film version, or discussions with others all have the potential to reconstitute a spectator's understanding and response after the event. In short, the audience is always an interactive and productive part of performance. *See also* AUDIENCE CONTROL; AUDIENCE DRESS; RECEPTION; SEMIOTICS; WOMEN IN AUDIENCES. SBe

BENNETT, SUSAN, *Theatre Audiences* (London, 1997)
BLAU, HERBERT, *The Audience* (Baltimore, 1990)

AUDIENCE CONTROL

Throughout the history of the theatre, practitioners have attempted a variety of physical, psychological, and policing strategies to influence, direct, and regulate the *audience's experience of performance. The positioning of the body of the audience in isolated seats, directed toward the stage, a commonsense function of most *playhouse architecture, serves a multiple purpose of limiting the audience's perception toward the stage while allowing for crowd control and economic restrictions of temporary seat ownership through *tickets. Additional seating positions have traditionally marked social standings and privilege. From the wealthy patrons seated near the European stages of the eighteenth century so as to see and be seen, to the prince's seat in the *early modern *perspective stage *auditorium, to the political and religious hierarchy of Athens seated prominently in the ancient *Greek theatre, audience location has been crucial in marking power, status, and position. To promote a collective indoctrination to Christian teachings, performance in *medieval Europe strove for innovation in spectatorship through experiments in site-specific stagings, theatre-in-the-round (*see* ARENA AND IN-THE-ROUND), and wagon and station street performance. The *avant-garde explored new ways of controlling the audience through methods such as the *environmental theatre of the 1960s *collectives, in which spectators were often encouraged to interact with the performance by a shifting in performance configurations and a rearrangement of the actor–audience relationship.

Crowd control through the design of emergency exit systems has proved tragically essential. Multiple theatre *fires have claimed many lives in world theatres, and *riots in nineteenth- and twentieth-century theatres have likewise forced audience regulation for *safety reasons.

But control of the audience extends to psychological and intellectual cognition. Concepts of *catharsis, the much disputed *Aristotelian notion for manipulating experience toward a moral or therapeutic end, *illusion and the suspension of disbelief, identification, and even the counter-response of alienation (*see* VERFREMDUNG), seek to advance methods in which the theatrical apparatus can direct, hold, and construct the audience's *reception. Asian performance *theory, including *India's *Natyasastra and *Zeami's writing on *nō, discusses the

proper techniques for eliciting emotional responses from the spectator. If one thread of theatre practice undertakes spectator persuasion through representation of illusion and empathic identification (Aristotelian, *realism), the rebuttal had been to distance the audience's reception from emotion toward critical analysis (*Brecht). Interestingly, both theatrical constructions pursue correction of the audience through a soliciting or disciplining perception.

The ultimate audience control through *censorship recurs throughout history in the guise of *anti-theatrical prejudice. Platonic theory argues that physical representations are dangerous to performers, who will assume the attributes of the representation, as well as detrimental to spectators, who will strive to emulate the representations presented. Contemporary media censorship of violence and *pornography makes a comparable argument, suggesting that representations of dangerous, immoral, and antisocial behaviours do not act as a critique but as promotional support of the activity represented. Audience control for safety considerations, performance access and visibility, and economic feasibility, is an inevitable factor in the design of performance and theatre architecture. Yet the disciplining of the audience through physical, psychological, and intellectual policing and censorship expands control into areas that remain a challenge to the creation of new theatre forms and content as well as to spectators themselves. MDC

AUDIENCE DRESS

Codes and practices of audience dress reveal significant information about the role and status of performance in different historical moments and in different cultures. Within a single performance space, different practices of dress provide visual identifiers for social and economic groups. The design of many Western *playhouses has taken into account the significance of social differentiation within an *audience and the most expensive seats often afford the spectator not the best view of the stage, but the best seat from which to be seen by other audience members. The presence of stools on stage in some *early modern theatres, for example, allowed for a fashion display given equal *semiotic value to that of the performance itself. Orazio Busino's account of attending a *masque in *London in 1618 devotes some energy to describing noble and richly arrayed ladies in the audience. In the Restoration period, the presence of the monarch and his entourage at the theatre was a point of reference for all fashion-conscious socialites. This period also saw a trend in women wearing full-face *masks to the theatre, most famously noted in Samuel *Pepys's diary for 1663 where he describes his wife's vizard. Originally adopted by middle- and upper-class women, the practice was imitated by prostitutes. This made a woman's status ambiguous, something that no doubt led to the demise of this fashion for *women in the audience.

Through the eighteenth and nineteenth centuries, spectators in the most costly seats at Western theatres dressed to attract the attention of other audience members, and the development of larger foyer spaces in the nineteenth century was at least in part to afford the expansion of that display so that the middle- and upper-class patrons could show off their stylish dress and jewellery. The practice of wearing formal dress for attending mainstream European and North American theatres continued well into the twentieth century. Popular theatres of the nineteenth century attracted a far less fashion-conscious audience, one with little disposable income. While many accounts of these theatres refer to the working-class audiences putting on their 'Sunday best' clothes to attend a performance, there are also references to workmen in the audience wearing their smocks, and so on. By the end of the twentieth century, audiences rarely dressed formally to attend the theatre. The *opera has been most resilient to this change, with significant portions of audiences at the world's major opera houses still electing to wear formal dress. Another exception is the gala performance (where ticket prices might be especially raised for the evening as a charity benefit) or an opening where formal dress might be expected or even required.

In religious theatres, audiences may have specific dress codes appropriate to the sacred nature of the performance. For the *kutiyattam in *India, spectators are generally expected to take a bath before entering the temple area and many members of the audience will wear white cloth pieces around their waists and carry a smaller white cloth over their shoulders to indicate that they have purified themselves before entering the temple. *See also* RELIGION AND THEATRE. SBe

AUDITION

An actor's opportunity to demonstrate talent, skill, and potential in a sample performance, with the goal of securing a part in a production or a position in a theatre company or school. A routine part of *casting, auditions take various forms. At 'open calls', where directors or their agents screen hundreds or thousands of aspirants, actors often deliver short, rehearsed *monologues. If the field of candidates is narrower, auditioners may instead do 'cold readings' from scripts they have never seen, or 'prepared readings' from plays they have reviewed. The director's goal is to determine the actor's 'rightness' for the part. Criteria vary, but may include intelligence, expressiveness, ability to take direction, and personal 'type'. If special skills are required, as in *musical or some experimental theatre, auditions may also involve singing, *dancing, moving, and *improvising. Although auditions may be rare in some non-Western traditions, such as *kabuki, where many actors are virtually born into their profession, other forms do utilize this test. In *Indian *kathakali, for example, where *training begins early, training schools evaluate young boys for appropriateness of physical

features, sense of rhythm, and sincerity of purpose. In most theatres, auditions are the gateway for actors seeking training and employment. RM

AUDITORIUM

From the Latin 'a place for hearing', since the 1720s 'auditorium' has been used in English to refer to the space in a *playhouse or similar building where the spectators sit or stand while watching the play, often called 'the house'. The form and shape of the auditorium have varied a great deal in history for both performance reasons and social reasons, as the desirable *audience size and degree of class segregation has changed. The contemporary auditorium is generally steeply raked (by the standards of past generations), with considerable attention paid to sight lines and acoustics, thus allowing the spectators to experience the play as individually as possible. It is also highly democratic, with social distinctions reflected by the *box, pit, and gallery, the *stalls and dress circle of past centuries mostly replaced by the single standard of a higher price for the seats with the best visibility and audibility. JB

AUGIER, ÉMILE (1820–89)

French playwright, champion of early *realism, along with *Dumas *fils. Augier first came to prominence in 1844 with his play *La Ciguë* (translated as *The Love of Hippolyta*). Its professed morality was in direct opposition to *romantic drama and heralded a new era in the theatre, beyond the *well-made play, of *bourgeois morals and taste. The contrivance of *plot was replaced by the popular *dramaturgy of the social concerns of the middle classes in Second Empire France, at a time of increasing wealth, unprecedented speculation on the stock market, and the growth of an influential mercantile class. In his large dramatic output, the principal themes of money and class shine out. But although he exposed hypocrisy, he often wrote from within the dominant ideology and failed to see the narrowness of his petty morality, which did not reflect the inequity of society as a whole.

His most notable creation was the 'personnage sympathique', the *character who could right wrong. The best example is the eponymous *hero of *Le Fils de Giboyer* (*The Son of Giboyer*, 1862). The son, Maximilien, is illegitimate, without family connections, and secretary to a businessman and politician, Monsieur Maréchal. Max falls in love with Maréchal's daughter but is rejected in favour of an impecunious nobleman. He resigns his post only to discover that his father's speculation has paid off and he is now a millionaire. But despite losing out in love to his opposite (an illegitimate millionaire to a titled pauper), he still retains highly respectable bourgeois values and remains devoted to his father who, in turn, now has the sole aim of making his son happy. A similar theme occurs in his most successful play, *Le Gendre de M. Poirier* (*M. Poirier's Son-in-Law*, 1854), written for the Gymnase Theatre in collaboration with Jules Sandeau, and revived periodically from 1864 by the *Comédie-Française. *Gabrielle* (1849) won the Prix Montyon, and in 1857, with the assistance of Alfred de *Musset, Augier was elected to the Académie Française. He stopped writing thereafter, though he remained critically celebrated.   BRS

AUJOURD'HUI, THÉÂTRE D'

*Montréal company founded in 1968, devoted exclusively to works by Québec authors. Originally combining three small troupes, it gained prominence when the irreverent Jean-Claude *Germain became *artistic director in 1972. Its offerings, often separatist and anti-colonialist in tone, challenged *dramaturgic and *acting traditions as well, in plays such as Germain's clever *Un pays dont la devise est je m'oublie* (*A Country Whose Motto Is, I Forget*, 1976), alluding to Québec's provincial motto, 'I Remember' ('Je me souviens'). Since 1983 Germain has been succeeded by a series of exceptionally capable administrators, notably Michelle Rossignol (1989–98). In 1991 the company moved to new, larger, and more modern premises.   LED

AUSTRALIAN PERFORMING GROUP
(1968–81)

Australian theatre company. Based in *Melbourne, the APG originated as the La Mama Company at the *La Mama Theatre in 1968 when writers, actors, directors, and designers formed a cooperative dedicated to *devising and performing mostly Australian work. In a time when established companies largely restricted themselves to imported products, the new group established a reputation for local creations with a distinctive style, favouring Australian narratives and with an emphasis on physicality. In 1970 the company became professional, renamed itself the Australian Performing Group, and moved to a new inner-city home, the Pram Factory. The 50-odd members brought radical *politics to the new *collective. Writers such as Jack *Hibberd, John *Romeril, Alex Buzo, and David *Williamson established the APG's reputation for new and exciting theatre, yet its most successful group-devised piece, *The Hills Family Show* (1975), was written by women. APG staged its last performance in 1981, but many plays, such as Williamson's *Don's Party* and Hibberd's *A Stretch of the Imagination*, remain classics of the Australian repertoire.   SBS

AUTO SACRAMENTAL

One-act devotional plays produced in Spain at *Corpus Christi throughout the sixteenth and seventeenth centuries and until late in the eighteenth. For their performance, two floats were drawn up beside a platform at successive points on the route of a procession, which incorporated *street theatre of other kinds, most notably *tarascas* (mechanized dragons). As they came to be financed by rival townships and written and played by professionals, *costumes, *scenery, and mechanical effects grew ever more spectacular. In *Madrid, for instance, though the number of plays was reduced from four to two in 1647, each required four elaborate, two-storeyed floats. After performances over three days, they were played for another fortnight at the *corrales* and especially in nearby villages, for which they usually provided the only experience of drama that year. Since the companies chosen in February and March were well paid, and given exclusive use of the *corrales* for the lucrative post-Lenten season, the contracts to perform them were eagerly sought, and they played a central role in theatrical life.

Sixteenth-century *autos* were often based on stories from the Bible or the lives of saints, and included profaner episodes, but under Counter-*Reformation pressure they became specifically sacramental, celebrations of the festival's message that mankind is redeemed by Christ's body and blood. All the leading playwrights contrived, through *allegory especially, to illustrate that doctrine, but the most accomplished were a specialist, José de Valdivielso, and above all *Calderón. The *auto sacramental* became the supreme example of the fusion of religious and secular life in Golden Age Spain. *See also* MEDIEVAL THEATRE IN EUROPE; BIBLICAL PLAYS; PAGEANTS; EARLY MODERN PERIOD IN EUROPE.   VFD

AVANT-GARDE

A French military term, 'advance guard', became synonymous with progressivism in both art and politics in the later nineteenth century in Europe, and in the twentieth was widely applied to distinguish socially engaged art movements from other strands of early *modernism. 'Avant-garde' still denotes non-commercial and experimentally minded artists, though not necessarily overtly political ones. If the so-called 'historical' avant-garde movements that arose in the inter-war era may be characterized as the 'modernism of modernism', that was mainly the result of their collision with volatile social contexts, a circumstance that has led to an overemphasis on their political rather than their aesthetic goals (*see* POLITICS AND THEATRE). The avant-garde manifesto, itself an emblematic form because of its frequent incorporation in avant-garde performance, more often than not exalted the potential of industrialism at the expense of Western cultural traditions. Like the political tracts from which they borrowed their rhetoric, the avant-gardists' chief target was bourgeois society, particularly the conventions that privileged an art devoid of social consequences. In *constructivism and the *agitprop groups born in the ebullient spirit of the Soviet Revolution, the anti-bourgeois critique appears most organic. *Expressionism and *dada, both of which gained momentum in the aftermath of the First World War, were overtly reactionary; it is no coincidence that the theatrics of disorientation and shock were their favoured performance techniques. Perhaps most reactionary of all, the Italian *futurists made political agitation a staple of their activities beginning with *Marinetti's contentious *serata* in Trieste, which he coordinated with the interventionist political campaign against Austria, and continuing with his lionization of Mussolini, whom he considered the embodiment of the futurist ethos.

The avant-garde was too diffuse geographically and politically to have a cohesive social programme, though many of its artists were affiliated with anarchism or communism; for theorists of the historical movements their broadside against aesthetic autonomy has become paramount. Rooted in the Enlightenment, the doctrine of aesthetic autonomy rationalized the separation of art from the social sphere, reaching its apotheosis in the art-for-art's-sake movements of the late nineteenth century. By contrast, the eradication of the boundaries between art and life became the avant-garde credo, and as early as 1909 Marinetti and the futurists were satirizing traditional representational modes at the same time as they were attempting to incorporate the dynamics of urban industrialism as formal and thematic components in their works. With its brevity, mechanical allusions, and *music-hall conventions, the futurist 'synthetic theatre' was an amalgam of performance forms that heralded the fusion of art and common social experience. Just as the futurists extolled the *variety theatre for its informality and relative lack of artifice, in 1916 the Zurich-based dadaists made the Cabaret Voltaire the cradle of their own performative hybrids of 'simultaneous' poetry, *spectacle, and political *satire. For both groups shock tactics became a performance staple through which they sought to rupture the passivity of their *audiences by encouraging *rioting, *booing, police raids, and, of course, the much welcomed negative *publicity.

Meanwhile the Soviet-sanctioned agitprop troupes, whose chief interest in theatre was its potential for educating the masses, created a host of forms through *collective means that were indictments of the bourgeois individualism traditionally associated with artistic genius. Operating in factories, groups such as the *Blue Blouse collectives, a network of performers that grew to around 100,000 members by 1923, abstracted the new technologies of labour into the physical properties of the performers. Nikolai *Foregger's 'mechanical ballets', which owed more to the *circus than to the *dance establishment, and *Meyerhold's *biomechanics were two examples of new forms that could be mastered by workers as well as dancers, exemplifying the fusion of labour and art. In his collaborations with constructivist designers, many of them architects who turned to theatre to realize their utopian vision of the new Soviet city, Meyerhold's *environmental staging practices were perhaps the most cogent attempts to erode the line separating audience from performance.

What further distinguished the Russian avant-garde was early support by the revolutionary cultural bureaucracy; under the tutelage of the Commissariat of Enlightenment, Soviet avant-gardists enjoyed ideological kinship with the state as well as *financial sustenance. Elsewhere such intersections between the avant-garde and the public sector were never as congenial. Frank *Wedekind, the *Munich-based playwright and *cabaret performer who influenced a generation of younger artists, excoriated bourgeois sensibilities with his political satires and scatological *revues as early as 1901, resulting in *censorship and obscenity charges. The expressionists, whose apocalyptic exaltation of personal suffering in the face of social desolation appeared prophetic in the aftermath of the First World War, consciously placed themselves on the fringe of society and the art market. Tellingly, by the time the dadaists relocated to *Berlin in 1919 they were already excoriating the expressionists for what appeared to be their commodification by the bourgeoisie. Adopting a more radical anti-art agenda, the Berlin dadaists continued contentious cabaret performances but also took them onto the *streets, which in the volatile social milieu following the failed November Revolution served to blur the line between performance and political demonstration.

Perceptions of the radical political nature of the historical avant-garde have been influenced as much by their historical reception as their actual political affiliations. Despite the futurists' allegiance to Mussolini, the dadaists' support of the Spartakist League, and André Breton's increasing association of *surrealism with international communism in the 1920s, the early critical reception of the avant-garde tended to redefine its political meaning. Two initial proponents, Theodor Adorno and Walter Benjamin, placed high value on the organic nature of avant-garde techniques such as *montage and simultaneity, inasmuch as such procedures supported their argument that non-mimetic art was the inevitable expression of advanced capitalism. To Benjamin, the dadaists' penchant for chance construction exemplified his theory about the loss of aesthetic 'aura' as a result of the mechanical reproduction of art. He cautioned, however, that while such techniques served the revolutionary intentions of the dadaists and the Soviet avant-garde, they were also malleable to counter-revolutionary purposes, as the futurists' propaganda for Italian nationalist expansionism had proven.

For other theorists, the politicization of aesthetic theory was the chief avant-garde legacy. Throughout the 1930s Georg Lukács (who subsumed all avant-garde activity under the banner of expressionism) developed the blueprint for the *socialist realist style to which communist artists and arts federations as far away as *China would be forced to subscribe, and which effectively ended the avant-garde impulse in the Soviet Union. In Germany the fate of the historical avant-garde was sealed under National Socialism: the Nazis displayed and vilified expressionist art as 'degenerate', closed the *Bauhaus school, and were still excoriating the dadaists over a decade after the movement had disbanded. And while futurism continued under Mussolini, it achieved neither the widespread acceptance of the Italian public nor the status of 'national-fascist' to which it most aspired.

It is no wonder, then, that the historical avant-garde has become a focal point for scholars attempting to illuminate the mechanisms by which totalitarian arts policies developed in the inter-war years and ultimately were used to legitimize the politics that lay behind them (see FASCISM AND THEATRE). The political spectacles organized by Mussolini's cultural ministers and perfected by the National Socialists aestheticized the military rally, which submerged the individual into the collective and achieved a symbiosis between spectacle and audience that the avant-gardists could only dream of. And the avant-gardists' critique of aesthetic autonomy paved the way for its own demise under Nationalist Socialism, best expressed by Hitler himself, who ironically borrowed their rhetorical attack on expressionism as irrelevant to the German people. Even the return of German art to an archaic *romanticism imbued with the iconography of a worker's revolution can be traced to the avant-gardists' aestheticizing of technology and mechanization. Such phenomena have led some historians to go so far as to posit a causal relationship between avant-garde discourse and techniques and the instruments of fascist legitimization; others emphasize that German, Italian, and Russian forms of totalitarianism were singularly effective in silencing the avant-gardist rhetoric of dissent, even if the first two of those regimes borrowed avant-garde methods.

Historians have often categorized the avant-garde as a subset of modernism, particularly in theatre where the mainstreaming of avant-garde techniques was more evident than in other cultural forms. The avant-gardists themselves recognized their influence over what have become the canonical figures of high theatrical modernism, citing parallels between futurist tactics of audience disruption and *Pirandello's *metatheatre, between dadaist montage and the *epic theatre of *Piscator and *Brecht, as well as the general suffusion of expressionism into early *film. Of such figures, Brecht is perhaps the most contested since he is alternately granted avant-garde status for practices such as collective *dramaturgy and *Verfremdung, or excluded on the grounds that, after all, he laboured within rather than against the institutions of theatre.

Interest in the historical avant-garde was reinvigorated in the 1960s and 1970s through a series of museum retrospectives and by the professed indebtedness of an entirely new generation of socially minded artists, including *collectives such as the *Living Theatre and Théâtre du *Soleil, playwrights such as Peter *Weiss, and directors such as Peter *Stein. The cumulative effect was to galvanize the historical avant-garde as the institutional standard for advanced art production. Concomi-

tantly, scholars and theorists re-examined the legacy of the pre-war avant-garde along aesthetic lines beholden to the social sciences and political theory as much as to traditional art history.

Perhaps the most important of these commentators is Peter Bürger, whose theory of institutions marks off the historical avant-garde from the broader category of modernism on the grounds that by critiquing the bourgeois institutions of art, the avant-gardists revealed once and for all the coordinates by which art was in fact a social institution. Interestingly, despite the pivotal place of the avant-garde in his version of twentieth-century art and aesthetics, Bürger concludes that the avant-garde project was a failure, since it did not escape its own institutionalization and hence fell short of its social and political intentions. While Bürger sidesteps such important issues as the efficiency with which fascism suppressed the politically contentious avant-garde and yet absorbed its means and mechanisms, his critical framework has proven important in subsequent thinking about the socio-political contours of art and aesthetics, and the aesthetic contours of politics. Bürger has also been important in ongoing critical and social debates about the avant-garde and postmodernism, as well as about arts patronage and censorship, which invariably become central topics for both the historical and contemporary avant-garde.

Exactly how the term relates to theatre and performance in the late twentieth and early twenty-first centuries—and whether it should be applied at all—is not settled. In general usage (including in some occurrences of the term in this encyclopedia) 'avant-garde' often merely signifies work that appears formally innovative or is somehow in opposition to mainstream theatre practice. At other times the term is used more critically to designate art and artists attempting to undermine the political and social status quo by inventing or drawing upon subversive content and form, as it often does when applied to *performance art/art performance. But in an age when the novelty sought by early modernism and the historical avant-garde has become a matter for immediate commodification and routine absorption into a throwaway global culture, it is difficult to sustain for long the idea that an 'advance guard' is leading the public or other artists into a new or revolutionary aesthetic condition, much less a social one. In the late 1980s and 1990s the Next Wave Festival at the Brooklyn Academy of Music perhaps best exemplified the contradictions of oppositional art in the postmodern condition, by self-consciously seeking pioneering work and then marketing it to bourgeois audiences according to the best procedures of contemporary capitalism.

At the start of the new millennium the major *festivals anxiously seek the newest and most innovative work of directors like Robert *Wilson, Pina *Bausch, Robert *Lepage, or *Ninagawa Yukio, practitioners who are already established as avant-gardists. Operating on a large and transnational scale, annual events such as the *Avignon Festival and the *Edinburgh

Festival can support the extremely expensive productions of such artists, which are rarely exhibited in regular theatre runs, while an international audience of progressive cultural tourists avidly follow such events as a means of marking their own status. Throughout the world there are numerous examples of companies and artists who create theatre that is both innovative and politically or socially oppositional, ranging from troupes like *Socíetas Raffaello Sanzio in Italy to the *Wooster Group in the USA, from directors like Habib *Tanvir in *India to *Suzuki Tadashi in *Japan, from performance artists like Karen *Finley and Guillermo *Gómez-Peña to playwrights like *Kara Jūrō and Suzan-Lori *Parks. But designating such work as avant-garde, despite the handy properties of the term, in the end only highlights the enormous contradictions that have accompanied its use from the start. DRP/DK

BÜRGER, PETER, *Theory of the Avant-Garde* (Minneapolis, 1984)

GOLDBERG, ROSELEE, *Performance Art: from futurism to the present*, rev. edn. (New York, 2001)

GRAVER, DAVID, *The Aesthetics of Disturbance: anti-art in avant-garde drama* (Ann Arbor, 1995)

AVIGNON FESTIVAL

Annual theatre *festival created by Jean *Vilar in 1947 in the ancient walled city of Avignon in southern France. From its inception, the festival was meant to liberate and popularize a genre which, in Vilar's view, had been relegated to the urban elite. The initial festival lasted one week and consisted of three productions, including the first staging in France of Shakespeare's *Richard II*, performed outside in the courtyard of the fourteenth-century papal palace. For many years the festival was closely associated with the *Théâtre National Populaire (TNP), which Vilar directed from 1951 until 1963, and which played a major role in the decentralization of the French theatre system. Some of the most notable productions of this early period were *Corneille's *Le Cid* and *Kleist's *The Prince of Homburg* in 1951, both featuring the charismatic young actor Gérard *Philipe. Vilar staged *Brecht's *The Resistible Rise of Arturo Ui* in 1960, just as de Gaulle was negotiating with the right-wing factions in the military, and two years later, he presented *Giraudoux's *Tiger at the Gates* in the wake of France's war with Algeria. After he left the TNP, Vilar dedicated himself fully to enlarging the scope, length, and venues of the festival, which by then was attracting upwards of 50,000 spectators. He invited younger directors, like *Planchon and *Lavelli, and added new performance spaces, which allowed for greater diversity in the festival's offerings. In 1968 the *Living Theatre staged a massive protest against the festival, demanding that all performances be free of charge. One year later saw the birth of an independent *fringe festival, as several *amateur troupes began to stage alternative performances in the shadow of the official programme. Over the next few decades this fringe festival, known as 'Avignon Off', rapidly grew to include hundreds of productions, consisting of everything from *mimes and *street performances to period re-creations of the European classics. Today, the festival takes place each year in July and attracts an average of 130,000 spectators to over 500 productions running virtually around the clock. With supplementary *finance provided by the French government and private corporate sponsors, the official festival includes *dance, music, and *film, in addition to theatre, as well as lectures, readings, and discussions with actors and directors. The fringe still dominates the festival, with companies from all over France and Europe, including an increasing presence of francophone *African and *Caribbean troupes. CHB

AVILÉS BLONDA, MÁXIMO (1931–88)

Dominican director, playwright, and poet. After receiving a doctorate from the University of Santo Domingo, Avilés Blonda taught there, directed the University Experimental Theatre, and became Director General of Culture in the Dominican Republic in the last years of his life. His most popular plays include *La otra estrella en el cielo* (The Other Star in the Sky), *Las manos vacías* (The Empty Hands, 1959), *Yo, Bertolt Brecht* (I, Bertolt Brecht, 1968), and *Piramide 179*. EJW

AWANG, USMAN (1929–)

Malaysian playwright, poet, and novelist, whose many pen-names include Tongkat Warrant. He has been widely celebrated as one of the best and most influential modern writers in the Malay language, receiving the title of *Malaysia's National Laureate in 1983. Advocating the concept of art for society, he was a leading figure in *Singapore's 1950s Generation of Writers (ASAS 50) while active in the struggle against British colonial occupation. In the 1960s he held several posts with literary and language councils in Kuala Lumpur. His dramas have typically criticized pre-colonial Malay feudal systems as repressive, while extolling the virtues of the working classes and advocating education for the poor. They include *Matinya Seorang Pahlawan* (Death of a Warrior, 1964), written in *verse and set in the fifteenth century, and *Muzika Uda dan Dara* (Uda and Dara's Music, 1972), based on his 1956 poem 'Gadis di Kuburan' ('Girl in the Cemetery'). CRG

AWARDS IN THE THEATRE

The theatre loves awards. They assist publicity and marketing; in both commercial and subsidized theatres (see FINANCE) they also supply needed signs of approval and celebration, serving *producers, creative and technical staff, performers, critics, *audiences, and readers. Awards occupy the dangerous intersection between art and commerce, and in an intensely collaborative form like the theatre they are often criticized for fomenting destructive competition, glorifying stars at the expense of their less visible (or invisible) colleagues, and sentimentalizing a difficult and often cut-throat profession. But the commercial and psychological value of awards is only enhanced by their tendency toward controversy, whether fuelled by inequity in popularity, *race, *politics, or corporate alliance.

The devil is in the details. Whether the initial intention is to advertise or celebrate, it must be followed by assigning categories, procedures, strategies, and compromises. These details usually cloud the original intention but can be interesting to fans and can even illuminate cultures. In *London, for example, best actor categories are likely to be divided between *drama and *comedy, but less likely to be based on sex, while in *New York, male and female categories are rigorously separated and the *genre division is between *musicals and everything else. Whatever the classifications, winning begets losing. Often there is an attempt to soften loss by multiplying categories or announcing runners-up. But the greater the proliferation of awards, the greater their power to disappoint. A Nobel Prize for Literature given to a playwright, the highest honour available in the theatre, is so rare that few can smart from failure to win. But a Tony award? A suburban best actor award? Fortunately performers have long been inured to disappointment by the ego-bruising competition of *casting.

The model for modern awards was established by those given at the ancient *Greek *Dionysia. Awards may have continued in Europe over the centuries, though the low social status of actors after the Hellenistic period probably ensured that they did not. In *early modern England, even though London lacked the newspaper culture in which awards blossom, marks of official approval such as patronage and licensing fulfilled some of their function. Shakespeare's coat of arms was a conspicuous mark of commercial success, albeit not awarded him by a committee of drama critics. And that symbol was a direct precursor to more official awards, which in England are bestowed by the monarchy on the advice of the government: OBE, CBE, DBE, knighthood. Since Henry *Irving received the first theatre knighthood from Queen Victoria in 1895, there have been handfuls of theatrical knights and dames in each generation—*Gielgud, *Richardson, *Guinness, *Dench, Maggie *Smith, *Ayckbourn, to name only a few—and very occasionally the commercial and cultural weight of theatrical eminence has been rewarded with a peerage: Lord *Olivier, Lord *Lloyd Webber.

More mundane awards derive generally from theatre people, audiences, or critics. In London, the most visible are the Olivier awards, given since 1976 and so named as of 1994. They are administered by the Society of London Theatres, a producers' association, with winners selected by a small mixed panel appointed each year that includes audience members. The Oliviers honour a full menu of creators and performers, with occasional adjustments in categories to keep up with developing practice. There is considerable publicity value in the *Evening Standard* awards, given by that newspaper since 1955, and prestige in those of the London critics, who were previously polled annually by theatre magazines but since 1989 have given awards directly through the Drama Section of the Critics Circle.

In the United States awards have proliferated to an extreme. The current American equivalent of knighthood is the Kennedy Center Honors, given since 1978 to perhaps five artists each year, of whom at least one is usually theatrical. There is a Theatre Hall of Fame located in Broadway's Gershwin Theatre, where more than 300 members are listed on the walls in gold letters, with eight added each year. But the most widely known American theatre awards are three. The first was the Pulitzer Prize for best new American play, founded in 1917 by newspaper tycoon Joseph Pulitzer. He specified that the winning play should show the power of the stage 'in raising the standard of good morals, good taste and good manners', a moralistic straitjacket that inhibited the award until it was removed in 1964 (among other examples, *Albee's *Who's Afraid of Virginia Woolf?*, though recommended by the jurors in 1963, was denied the award). Similar denials in 1934 and 1935 led to the creation of the New York Drama Critics Circle and its annual awards for the best American play, the best foreign play, and the best musical. In 1947 the trio was completed by the Antoinette Perry awards (the Tonys), started by the American Theatre Wing, a service organization, to honour a producer-director who died that year. The Tonys are limited to Broadway productions, though one annual award is given to a theatre outside New York. With a full range of awards for performers and other creators, the Tony ceremony quickly graduated to *television, where it long ranked as the best staged of the many annual awards shows. (The ultimate model for awards ceremonies is Hollywood's Academy Awards. Founded in 1928 and perfected in the glare of TV, the Oscars set an elaborate mould for theatre awards to emulate or avoid.)

The most important other New York awards are those of the Outer Critics Circle (founded 1950); the Drama Desk (1955), which bridges Broadway and *Off-Broadway; and the Obies, Off-Broadway awards selected by critics for the *Village Voice* newspaper (1956). The Tonys are the model for annual awards in other American cities, usually named for theatre notables with local ties. *Boston has its Eliot Norton awards, *Chicago its Jeffs (after Joseph *Jefferson), *Philadelphia its *Barrymores, and Washington its Helen *Hayes awards. In Canada, *Toronto has the Doras, named after Dora Mavor Moore. In Europe, the grandest theatre awards are often connected with *festivals, such as those at Taormina and *Avignon. In Spain the awards are named after Lope de *Vega; in France, after *Molière; Russia gives the Golden Mask; in Germany, *Berlin's *Theatertreffen is a best-of-season retrospective; in Australia, the critics of

*Sydney and *Melbourne give separate annual awards. The major dramatists who have won the Nobel Prize for Literature are *Bjørnson (1903), *Echegaray (1904), *Maeterlinck (1911), *Hauptmann (1912), *Benavente (1922), *Shaw (1925), *Pirandello (1934), *O'Neill (1936), *Beckett (1969), *Soyinka (1986), *Fo (1997), and *Gao Xingjian (2000). Among other Nobel laureates who qualify as part-time playwrights are *Tagore (1913), *Rolland (1915), *Yeats (1923), *Galsworthy (1932), *Gide (1947), *Eliot (1948), *Lagerkvist (1951), *Camus (1957), Patrick *White (1973), and Derek *Walcott (1992). In 1964 *Sartre indicated his disdain for the commercial and political implications of awards by rejecting the Nobel Prize; but awards at levels both high and low can also claim to have rewarded talent and nourished careers.   CR

AYCKBOURN, ALAN (1939–)

English director and playwright. Ayckbourn has been director of productions for the Stephen *Joseph Theatre, Scarborough, since 1971, the company with which he started working as an actor and *stage manager in 1957, and for whom he has written the majority of his plays. A commercially successful writer, he shows the lightness of touch necessary for *comedy but with a strong interest in alternative uses of stage space and narrative and a determination to explore darker areas of human experience. His technical manipulation of narrative was visible in his first major success, the intricately *farcical Relatively Speaking (1967), but he has invented several new formal devices for relating stories. In the trilogy The Norman Conquests (1973), the same events are retold from three different vantage points, a device partially reused in the linked plays House and Garden (1999). In How the Other Half Loves (1969) and Taking Steps (1979) different places are superimposed on one another to giddyingly comic effect. In Sisterly Feelings (1978) and Intimate Exchanges (1982) decisions made by *characters on stage lead to alternative routes for the *action, creating a great variety of possible versions of the plays. In Time of my Life (1992), we begin in the middle of the action and the narrative fans outward to explain the causes and consequences of the opening event.

In the mid-1970s Ayckbourn's work began to take on a wintry tone. Absent Friends (1974) explores the attempt of a group of dysfunctional married couples to cheer the spirits of their recently bereaved friend Colin. A bleakness in suburban marriage is explored alongside the thin horrors of the British class system in Absurd Person Singular (1972). Ayckbourn is rarely an explicitly *political writer but in the 1980s he explored the ethics of political extremism in the *allegorical Way Upstream (1981), and the relationship between entrepreneurial capitalism and family values in A Small Family Business (1987). In A Chorus of Disapproval (1984) and Man of the Moment (1988), he examines the difficulty of being good in an ethically corrupt world. In particular he has been keen to explore the position of women within conventional marriage, most thoroughly in Woman in Mind (1985).

Ayckbourn has also written *musicals, *revues, and several very successful plays for *youth, including Ernie's Incredible Illucinations (published 1969) and Mr A's Amazing Maze Plays (1988). He directs most of his own work, and completed a successful season as a director at the *National Theatre in 1987, where his production of *Miller's A View from the Bridge was widely acclaimed. The design of the new Stephen Joseph Theatre, which opened in 1996, reflects his collaborative view of theatre, with an internal *playhouse architecture that ensures the intermingling of *audiences, backstage crew, and actors, and an in-the-round performance space (see ARENA AND IN-THE-ROUND) that brings the audience together as a collective.   DR

AYLMER, FELIX (1889–1979)

English actor, educated at Oxford, knighted in 1965. Aylmer maintained a long career in West End theatres, from the 1910s to the 1960s. His early roles were in productions organized by Seymour *Hicks, Fred *Terry, Beerbohm *Tree, and Granville *Barker. He also acted with the Birmingham Theatre Company. In *London during the 1920s, 1930s, and 1940s he regularly appeared in plays by *Shaw, *Galsworthy, and Barker. He also acted in a steady run of popular *melodramas and *comedies, occasionally appeared in *New York as well, and after the Second World War he continued to be featured on the London stage. He also appeared in many *films from the 1930s forward, including Henry V, St Joan, The Doctor's Dilemma, Ivanhoe, Exodus, and The Chalk Garden, and by the 1960s he was performing often in *television roles. From 1949 to 1969 he served as president of British Actors' Equity Association (see TRADE UNIONS, THEATRICAL).   TP

AZAR, HÉCTOR (1930–2000)

Mexican playwright and director. The multi-talented Azar combined a rootless sense of the *absurd with the deeply rooted conservatism of Mexican life, in plays such as Olympica (1964) and The Immaculata (1972). His initiative in 1955 created what would later become the Theatre of the University of Mexico, with Azar as its first director. For numerous years he was in charge of the theatre section of the National Institute of Fine Arts. Azar also founded the Centre of Dramatic Art (CADAC) in the colonial suburb of Coyoacan, which he directed until his death.   KFN

AZENBERG, EMANUEL (1934–)

American *producer who has mounted more than 50 productions in 40 years while managing others. Known as a critic of Broadway's methods and power structure, he left the industry trade group, the League of American Theatres and Producers, a path taken by such others as the Disney company. He has produced all 22 of Neil *Simon's plays since 1972, including his best, most autobiographical work—*Brighton Beach Memoirs* (1983), *Biloxi Blues* (1984), *Broadway Bound* (1986), and *Lost in Yonkers* (1991). Other notable productions include *The Lion in Winter* (1966), *Ain't Misbehavin'* (1978), *The Real Thing* (1984), *Sunday in the Park with George* (1984), and *The Iceman Cometh* (revival, 1999). Since 1986 he has taught at Duke University.

CR

·B·

BABANOVA, MARIA (1900–83)

Russian/Soviet actress who began her career with *Komisarjevsky in 1919 before joining *Meyerhold's Actor's Workshop. She appeared as the maligned wife Stella in the groundbreaking *constructivist production of Crommelynck's *The Magnanimous Cuckold* (1922), then as the innocently seductive mayor's daughter in *Gogol's *The Government Inspector* (1926). From 1927 onwards she worked at the Theatre of the Revolution with Aleksei *Popov and then at the *Mayakovsky Theatre under the direction of Nikolai *Okhlopkov. A versatile interpreter of both male and female roles, Babanova excelled as the naive innocent, a talent which endeared her to Soviet audiences.   NW

BABEL, ISAAK (1894–1941)

Russian/Soviet short-story writer and dramatist, born and raised in the Jewish quarter of Odessa. A protégé of Maxim *Gorky, Babel published his first literary efforts in 1916. Gorky encouraged him to acquire experience of real life, which led to his joining Budenny's Cossack cavalry as a Civil War correspondent. The diaries which Babel kept eventually became a group of short stories, *Konarmia* (*The Horse Soldiers*), usually translated as *Red Cavalry*, in which his experiences as a bespectacled Jew—the pseudonymous Lyutov—become a series of laconically related anecdotes full of violent and disturbing incident. A group of these stories was staged in a dramatic adaptation at the Vakhtangov Theatre in the late 1960s, directed by Evgeny Simonov. Babel wrote *film scripts and a play based on life in Odessa, *Sunset* (1927), which recycles some of the earlier short-story material from *Odessa Tales*, and which was staged at the *Moscow Art Theatre in 1928. He also wrote a play based on his experience of city life during the worst days of the Civil War, *Marya* (1935), which is his most

widely available drama in English translation. Condemned by Budenny for the 'false' picture of cavalry life which his stories conveyed, Babel fell silent but was obliged to account for his inactivity at the First Soviet Writers' Congress in 1934. He was arrested in May 1939 and 'disappeared', the full circumstances of his death remaining unclear until the 1990s.   NW

BACHETERZI, MAHIEDDINE (1896–1985)

Algerian playwright, director, and *manager who, with *Allalou and *Ksentini, established modern Algerian theatre. He wrote and directed 70 plays, starting with *comedy (*Yes, Yes, Beni*, 1935; *Perfidious*, 1937; *Liars*, 1939), then dealt with social and *political drama, directing, for example, Tawfiq al-Madani's *Hannibal* (1947). Bacheterzi's talents as a singer and actor added to his flair for management: he was among the first Algerian artists to succeed in provincial and overseas *tours, and in 1947 headed the *opera of *Algiers. By force of personality and example he encouraged a number of artists in his long and diverse career. His memoirs, published in three volumes (1968, 1984, 1986), are a mine of information on Algerian theatre.   MMe

BACON, FRANK (1864–1922)

American actor and playwright. Born in Marysville, California, Bacon first appeared on stage at 14, but worked as a journalist and photographer before making his professional debut in an 1890 San José production of the warhorse *melodrama *Ten Nights in a Barroom*. He won praise for portraying comic oldsters in *San Francisco until the 1906 earthquake led him to move east, where he firmly established himself by playing in *The Fortune Hunter* for three years. From 1892 on, he tinkered with an original play, finally collaborating with Winchell Smith to produce *Lightnin'* (1918), in which Bacon had the title role of the easygoing Lightnin' Bill Jones. The play was *New York's biggest hit of the decade and ran for a record total of 1,291 performances. Bacon was admired for his natural underplaying, admittedly modelled on the *acting style of Joseph *Jefferson. Bacon's autobiography, *Barnstorming*, was eventually published in 1987.   CT

BAGNOLD, ENID (1889–1981)

English novelist and playwright. Primarily known as the writer of the novel *National Velvet*, she wrote the majority of her eight plays towards the end of her life. Formally reflecting the *melodramatic drawing-room traditions of the 1930s, her plays, beginning with *Lottie Dundass* (1941), focus upon independent older women who challenge *gender and class stereotypes. *The Chalk Garden* (1955) was commercially the most successful play in *London of 1956, while *The Last Joke* (1960), *The Chinese Prime Minister* (1964), and *Call Me Jacky* (1968, *A Matter of Gravity* in America) all achieved some popular success.   LT

BAHR, HERMANN (1863–1934)

Austrian dramatist, critic, and director. Bahr's multifaceted career covered the major trends of the *fin de siècle*. While his first full-length drama *Die neuen Menschen* (*The New Men*, 1887) was heavily influenced by *Ibsen, the programmatic essays of the early 1890s ('Zur Kritik der Moderne', 1890; 'Die Überwindung des Naturalismus', 1891) proclaimed the passing of *naturalism and promulgated impressionism and neo-*romanticism. Bahr's work in the theatre included stints as a *dramaturg and director with Max *Reinhardt, as well as a short term as director of the *Burgtheater in *Vienna in 1918–19. Of his many plays only the social *comedy *The Concert* (1909) became an accepted part of the repertory. Bahr's sensitivity to artistic trends made him an important broker between aesthetic developments and the wider public. His essay *Expressionismus* (1913) contributed to the popularization of the term *expressionism.   CBB

BAITING

The goading, torturing, and usually killing of *animals as a form of public or private entertainment. The practice dates from ancient times, and in spite of efforts to curtail or stop it, it continued through the twentieth century. A variety of animals have been baited in a variety of circumstances, from elephants in *Roman *arenas to bulls in Spanish *plazas de toros*, from gamecocks in pits to foxes in the English countryside. Often animals are set on other animals (bear-baiting, dogfights), but humans are also sometimes directly involved as participants (bullfighting, Roman *venationes* or staged *animal fights).

In terms of numbers and varieties of animals baited and slaughtered the Romans exceeded all others. Rhinoceros, ele-

phants, lions, tigers, bulls, and bears were set upon one another in many combinations, often with one or the other restrained by a chain. Other animals, such as deer, were cast as victims (as were criminals or war prisoners; see DAMNATIO). The setting of hounds or lions after deer is a precedent for modern foxhunting. The pitting of armed men against savage beasts developed into a form of *corrida*, in which a single man dispatched an animal that had been goaded into attacking.

Bulls and bears were the animals of choice in traditional English baiting, which flourished from the twelfth to the nineteenth century. An annual bull running, in which the animal was chased to exhaustion and killed, was a feature of several English towns. A royal official in charge of 'bears and apes' was appointed in 1484, and the warrant extended to bulls and dogs in 1573. The position was held after 1604 by Philip *Henslowe and Edward *Alleyn. At least two baiting-rings stood in *London in the mid-sixteenth century, although by 1574 there appears to have been one only, the Bear Garden, rebuilt by Henslowe in 1583 as a three-storey *amphitheatre. This structure, torn down in 1613, was replaced the following year by the *Hope, a dual-purpose *playhouse and baiting arena. Baiting traditionally took place on Sundays. Typically, dogs were set on a chained bear or bull, although there were also lion baitings in the early years of the seventeenth century. The baiting was often accompanied by other diversions: monkeys on horseback, cockfights, dogfights, the whipping of a blinded bear. Parliament banned animal baiting in 1642, but it was revived after the Restoration and persisted in some areas until the late eighteenth century. Baiting was officially forbidden in 1835, although it continued for several years thereafter. On the Continent, baiting continued well into the nineteenth century. At the end of the twentieth century there remained four main forms of baiting, only two of them generally regarded as legitimate. Cockfighting, possibly the most ancient form and a favourite of the leisure classes, is now prohibited in most jurisdictions, although it continues unofficially in many areas. Dog fighting, though less common than cockfighting, is practised surreptitiously in rural areas of North America, among other locations. Bullfighting, enveloped in ceremony and legitimized by 'grace', continues in Spain and *Latin America. Fox-hunting remains a controversial pastime in the United Kingdom, and in some locations in America, Australia, and New Zealand.   RWV

BAKER, BENJAMIN A. (1818–90)

American playwright. A *prompter at William Mitchell's Olympic Theatre in *New York, Baker wrote a series of popular plays depicting Mose, the Bowery B'hoy, a streetwise volunteer fireman, played with great success by Frank S. *Chanfrau. The first, *A Glance at New York* (1848), ran for 70 nights. He followed with *New York as It Is* (1848), *Three Years After* (1849), and *Mose in China* (1850). Despite weak *plots and stilted language, the plays were popular among working-class patrons and provided a palatable perception of New York's lower classes. PAD

BAKER, ELIZABETH (1876–1962)

English playwright. Born and reared in London, she worked as a secretary, writing in her free time. Her most notable play, *Chains*, features a *realistic portrayal of the confining, drab conditions of marriage in lower-class suburbia, and also portrays the monotonous nature of clerical work. After a matinée performance in 1909, it appeared in 1910 as part of the Charles *Frohman *repertory season at the *Duke of York's. *The Price of Thomas Scott* (1913) was performed at Miss *Horniman's *Gaiety Theatre in *Manchester, directed by Lewis *Casson. Baker also wrote *Miss Tassey* (1910), *Beastly Pride* (1914), *Miss Robinson* (1918), *Partnership* (1921), and *One of the Spicers* (1931). She participated in the suffrage movement, for which she wrote the *one-act play *Edith* (1912), but in later life she left London, settling into a comfortable country life with her husband. TP

BAKER, GEORGE PIERCE (1866–1935)

American teacher and theorist. Creator of the first playwriting course in the United States, the list of Baker alumni comprises a Who's Who of American theatre between 1906 and 1950. Playwrights Edward Sheldon, Eugene *O'Neill, Philip *Barry, S. N. *Behrman, and Sidney *Howard; directors George *Abbott and Elia *Kazan; designers Robert Edmond *Jones, Donald *Oenslager, Lee *Simonson, and Stanley McCandless; and critics John Mason Brown and Kenneth *Macgowan, all emerged from Baker's drama courses or workshops offered at Harvard (1905–24) or Yale (1924–33). An advocate of the emotional power of theatre (rather than the prevalent academic emphasis on intellectual content), Baker began at Harvard in 1888 as a teacher of argumentation and public address. Taking over an *early modern drama course in 1890, he insisted the students analyse plays as scripts for performance rather than literary works. The first offering of his playwriting course (English 47) in 1905–6 produced a hit play—Sheldon's *Salvation Nell*—and Baker expanded his work in 1914 to include an extracurricular 47 Workshop to stage student work. Regarded with suspicion by Harvard's administration, the Workshop was evicted from its basement headquarters in 1924, prompting Baker to resign and accept an offer from Yale. There Baker established the first graduate programme in theatre. He retired due to illness in 1933. MAF

BAKER, JOSEPHINE (1906–75)

*African-American performer. She appeared at the end of the *chorus line of *Shuffle Along*, the 1921 hit *musical, and then in *Chocolate Dandies* in 1924. The next year she went to *Paris with *La Revue nègre* and in the finale danced the Charleston wearing only a feathered belt. Remaining in France as a celebrated personality, she seemed the jungle transposed, elegant, tame, and pettable. 'La Baker', as she became known, kept her American passport until her disappointing 1936 trip to the USA to appear in the *Ziegfeld Follies*. During the war she joined the French Resistance. In 1951 she returned to the USA but refused to perform for segregated *audiences, and returned again for the March on Washington in 1963. Ten years later, she toured America for the last time. Her one-woman show, *Josephine*, premièred in Monaco in 1974 and was restaged in Paris in 1975. Her name was synonymous, the world over, with exoticism and libidinal freedom. BBL

BAKST, LEON (1866–1924)

Russian designer. Among the most renowned of the 'World of Art' group centred around the magazine of that name edited by Sergei *Diaghilev, Bakst made his debut in *St Petersburg in 1902 with a production of *Euripides' *Hippolytus*. His collaboration with Diaghilev began in *Paris with designs for *Cléopâtre* (1909) and *Scheherazade* (1910). His interest in the art forms of ancient Greece, stimulated by a visit to that country in 1907, was apparent in his designs for Debussy's *Prélude à l'après-midi d'un faune* and Ravel's *Daphnis and Chloe*, in 1912. He was also influenced by the styles of ancient Egypt and Asia, seen to best effect in *ballets such as *Scheherazade* and Stravinsky's *The Firebird* (1910) and in his designs for *Le Dieu bleu*, a Hindu legend in one act by Jean *Cocteau, staged by Diaghilev in Paris in 1912. His work was seen in *London for a production of *The Sleeping Beauty*, staged by Diaghilev at the Alhambra Theatre in 1921. His designs amazed *audiences by their extravagance of colour, fluidity of line, and transparency of *costume, revealing the dynamic force of the human body and lending it a sensuously erotic power. Some critics objected to the fact that his designs rendered productions too visual, evincing a tendency to over-indulge a taste for exotic lushness of style which, whilst drawing its strengths from the Russian Silver Age, revealed a penchant for the overripe and faintly decadent. NW

BALALINE

Palestinian company founded in Jerusalem in 1970 by François Abou Salem with a dozen young *amateurs. A turning point in the history of Palestinian theatre, the company trained a number of theatre workers and engendered other companies. The founders considered Balaline (which means 'balloons') a theatre of struggle against Israeli occupation, and black humour was the dominant mood of their productions. *Al Atama* (*Darkness*, 1970) and *The Weather News in Enitselap Casino* (1972) were illustrative of this approach. The company ceased operation in 1975.

MMe

BALANCHINE, GEORGE (1904–83)

Russian-American choreographer. Georgi Melintonovitch Balanchivadze was born in *St Petersburg, spent a number of years in Europe with his own company and with *Diaghilev's *Ballets Russes, and emigrated to *New York in 1933 to start (with the critic Lincoln Kirstein) the School of American Ballet, the first step in the eventual founding of the New York City Ballet in 1948. Balanchine's achievement as a choreographer spanned five decades and more than 400 *dance works, including *ballets, *opera ballets, dance sequences for *musicals, *revues, plays, *films, *cabarets, *television shows, and a *circus parade. The trajectory of his career links the old-world concept of a ballet master with the modern concept of a choreographer; no other figure is more closely associated with the development of an American performance style and training tradition in the ballet idiom. Beginning in the mid-1930s, Balanchine moved back and forth between the concert stage and Broadway, choreographing dance pieces for the *Ziegfeld Follies, Babes in Arms, The Boys from Syracuse, Song of Norway, and the groundbreaking 'Slaughter on 10th Avenue', the first dream ballet in musical theatre used to propel the *plot (in On your Toes, 1936). In the late 1930s and early 1940s he travelled to Hollywood to work on several films, including On your Toes and Star-Spangled Rhythm.

LTC

BALDWIN, JAMES (1924–87)

American writer, considered the most insightful and powerful black literary voice during the civil rights era. Best known for his fiction, he also wrote two important plays, Blues for Mister Charlie (1964) and Amen Corner (1967). Both concern the black Church and its leadership role in the *African-American community. In Blues, the son of a southern pastor goes north, but returns home and is murdered, which precipitates an intense moral confrontation between blacks and whites. In Amen, a female minister in a northern church is troubled when her son follows in his father's footsteps and becomes a jazz musician.

BBL

BALE, JOHN (1495–1563)

English playwright, priest, and Protestant polemicist. At various times stripped of clerical office, imprisoned, or forced to flee the country, Bale began playwriting in the early 1530s for the Earl of Oxford, but undertook his most intensive dramatic activity 1538–9 under the patronage of Thomas Cromwell. During Bale's brief tenure in Ireland, several of his anti-papal plays were acted on the occasion of Mary Tudor's coronation, to local outrage.

The best known of Bale's five plays, King John, was probably performed at Archbishop Cranmer's house in 1539 and was revised in 1558, possibly for a performance before Queen Elizabeth.

RWV

BALGANDHARVA (1888–1967)

Legendary actor of the Marathi sangeet natak (music drama) who specialized in female roles. Born Narayan Shripad Rajhans in Pune, he dominated the *Marathi stage from 1911 to 1934. Endowed with a naturally sweet voice, he was taught music from an early age. When he was 10, the political leader Lokmanya Bal Gangadhar Tilak heard him sing in Pune and instantly remarked, 'But here we have a Bal Gandharava' (Little gandharava or celestial singer). The name stuck. Balgandharva joined the Kirloskar Natak Mandali in 1905, where his first female role was Shakuntala in *Kirloskar's Shakuntal, and he achieved stardom as Bhamini in Khadilkar's Manapaman (1911). He set up his own company, Gandharva Natak Mandali, in Pune in 1913, playing in Bombay (*Mumbai) with a repertoire of several popular plays.

Balgandharva's most admired role was Sindhu, an alcoholic lawyer's long-suffering wife in Gadkari's Ekach Pyala (Just One More Glass). Dressed in simple white, he brought the *audience to tears with the pathos of his singing and acting. His melodious voice, expressive diction, feminine gestures, and graceful movements contributed to his phenomenal charisma. With his elaborate hairstyles and specially designed saris, he became a model of fashion for the women of his time, who emulated his mannerisms. The opulence of his productions, which attracted the wealthy communities of Bombay, was such that his production costs far outstripped his income and the company was soon in the red. By the time it became debt free in 1927, Balgandharva had lost his earlier charisma. Modern audiences considered *female impersonation crude, and cinema began to marginalize the theatre. Balgandharva wound up his company in 1934, after he contracted to act in two *films. The first, Dharmatma, in which he played a male role, failed. His only other cinematic part was as the saint-poet Mirabai. He spent his last years in Bombay with Gauharbai, the young singing actress he had married in 1955.

SGG

BALI See INDONESIA.

BALIEV, NIKITA (1877 (1886?)–1936)

Russian cabaret performer who found fame as organizer, in 1908, of the first *Moscow Art Theatre Lenten 'cabbage parties' (kapustniki), which provided the basis for the Fledermaus (Letuchaya mysh) or Bat *cabaret theatre. The cabbage parties were opportunities for the Art Theatre actors to relax after the rigours of rehearsal or performance; an evening's entertainment might consist of *parodies and sketches, often at the expense of members of the company or work in progress. *Stanislavsky was an enthusiast and paid tribute to Baliev in *My Life in Art*. The Bat became independent after 1910, staging comical sketches and parodies of the Russian classics, presided over by a genial Master of Ceremonies, Baliev himself. He emigrated to *Paris in 1920, reconstituting his theatre as the Chauve-Souris at the Théâtre Femina, and continued to play abroad until his death. The theatre experienced a brief American revival in 1943.   NW

BALL, WILLIAM (1931–91)

American director. In 1965 Ball abandoned a successful *Off-Broadway directing career in order to create what he called, in a provocative manifesto of that year, a regionally located 'non-profit, tax exempt educational institution resembling the European concept of Conservatory—adapted so that development and performances are integral and inseparable parts of the professional's creative life'. Though the first incarnation of the *American Conservatory Theatre at the Pittsburgh Playhouse did not last a year, by the 1967–8 season Ball had relocated to *San Francisco and was producing a season of 27 plays in rotating *repertory, using a resident ensemble of actors, a model of the *regional theatre movement. As a director Ball was widely acknowledged for his energetic interpretations of the classics, highlighted in his crisp version of *Tartuffe* originally staged in *New York and then again in both Pittsburgh and San Francisco between 1965 and 1967. Other acclaimed productions from Ball's ambitious first San Francisco season included *Pirandello's *Six Characters in Search of an Author* and *Albee's *Tiny Alice*. In the years following Ball achieved his goal of combining *training and performance by instituting workshops called 'exploratories' that later evolved into a two-year certificate programme for young actors. Though Ball's management style and administrative policies had detractors, he retained a loyal following among members of his ensemble until his resignation from ACT in 1986.   LTC

BALLAD OPERA

A play with songs. Ballad opera flourished after the production in *London in 1728 of John *Gay's *Beggar's Opera*, a wildly popular *satire on Walpole's corrupt government, set among the city's lowlife. The music, based in part on *opera seria*, lampooned that *genre's high seriousness. Although Gay's work spawned scores of imitations, only Henry *Fielding exploited the satirical potential of ballad opera with *burlesques produced at the Little Theatre *Haymarket and *Drury Lane during the late 1720s and 1730s. Its satirical purpose meant the appeal of ballad opera

was purely temporary. Only *The Beggar's Opera* is revived today.   SJCW

BALLARD, LUCINDA (1906–93)

American designer. Born in New Orleans, Ballard, a muralist and fresco painter, turned to theatrical design after assisting Norman *Bel Geddes. She designed both *scenery and *costumes before concentrating on costumes, beginning with a production of *As You Like It* on Broadway in 1937. Her skilful use of colour, drape, and texture, and her insistence that the costume designer assumes the role of full theatrical collaborator, brought her great respect among fellow designers, producers, and directors. Her notable achievements include *I Remember Mama* (1944), *Allegro* (1947), *A Streetcar Named Desire* (1947), *Silk Stockings* (1955), *Cat on a Hot Tin Roof* (1955), *JB* (1958), *The Sound of Music* (1959), and *The Gay Life* (1961).   MCH

BALLET

A term that stands for both a theatrical *dance *genre and a dance technique. The technique, also known as classic dancing or *danse d'école*, developed out of *early modern and baroque (see NEOCLASSICISM) performances in Europe and crystallized in the late eighteenth century. It was related to other bodily disciplines, such as fencing. Serving as a foundational vocabulary and style for the theatrical genre, ballet treats the human body as a machine for beautiful artifice. The diverse national schools of ballet technique are all based primarily on the principles of verticality, five standard positions of the feet, and turn-out (the rotation of the legs and hips so that the feet form an angle approaching 180 degrees). Secondarily, there is a codified use of space (facings of the body that assume the use of a *proscenium stage), of the arms and shoulders, and of various movements, such as turns, jumps, and transitions. At first, male virtuosity reigned in ballet performance, but during the course of the nineteenth century, female performers took centre stage, especially with the development of pointework, or toe-dancing, which began as a tentative, graceful, feathery action but gradually took on a steely strength, vigour, and sense of female agency. Although various academies, often state supported, in France, Italy, and Denmark contributed to ballet's technical development, it is the Russian style, synthesizing all these, that came to dominate the world by the end of the nineteenth century. A strongly athletic Soviet style, using the back expressively, emerged in the mid-twentieth century. And, as Russian émigrés settled in Western Europe and America in the 1930s, two new styles emerged in the West: the British school, characterized by gentle precision, and the American school, stressing speed, expansiveness, and strength.

As a performance genre, ballet has roots in the court entertainments of Renaissance Europe (*see* BALLET DE COUR). The earliest ballets, blending music, dancing, and poetry, involved *amateur performers and social dance movements. But as a professional class of dancers emerged, especially in France in the seventeenth century, a more specialized, refined technique arose. *Allegorical political performances in the Renaissance gave way to grandiose baroque narratives of gods and kings. Some eighteenth-century reformers called for a *ballet d'action*—art dance as an autonomous form of gestural representation in a wordless narrative. But for the most part, until the late nineteenth century, ballets were subsumed within *opera and *variety programmes. In the early nineteenth century, the *romantic ballet focused on themes of *folklore and the supernatural. The late nineteenth-century grand Russian imperial ballet often took fairy-tale themes as a pretext for elaborating evening-length movement spectacles, alternating pantomimed storytelling and pure dance episodes, for example in the ballet *Swan Lake* (1895), choreographed by Marius Petipa and Lev Ivanov to music by Peter Tchaikovsky. During the twentieth century, myriad experiments repeatedly tested the resiliency of ballet, ranging from technical distortions to abstract structures to eschewing music to a synthesis with other genres, such as jazz and postmodern dance. George *Balanchine was the most important ballet choreographer of the twentieth century. Born and trained in Russia, he was part of a generation there who experimented radically with the Russian ballet tradition. After a decade in Western Europe in the 1920s (*see* BALLETS RUSSES), he moved to the United States in 1933 and, as *artistic director of the *New York City Ballet, he specialized in *modernist, abstract, highly musical ballet compositions but also created an enormous, varied repertory in a wide range of styles. Despite its origins in an outmoded Western hierarchical culture, ballet has spread to every corner of the contemporary world and remains one of the most popular forms of dance theatre internationally, both East and West.　　　SB

GRESKOVIC, ROBERT, *Ballet 101: a complete guide to learning and loving the ballet* (New York, 1998)

KIRSTEIN, LINCOLN, *The Classic Ballet: basic technique and terminology* (New York, 1952)

—— *Movement & Metaphor: four centuries of ballet* (New York, 1970)

BALLET DE COUR

Court ballet was a form of *allegorical *total theatre that arose in late sixteenth-century France and flourished until 1670, when Louis XIV quit the stage. Developed by Queen Mother Catherine de Médicis and inspired by Italian *early modern festivals, it combined poetry, music, *dance, and decor, as well as the talents of professional and noble *amateur performers, to celebrate and assert the power of the throne. In *Le Balet comique de la royne* (1581), staged by Balthazar de Beaujoyeulx, the King restored order in the face of Circe's chaos. Louis XIV was an enthusiastic,

skilled dancer; he played the sun, bringing peace after a nocturnal witches' sabbath, in *Le Ballet de la nuit* (1653) and in 1661 established the Académie Royale de la Danse. *See also* MASQUE.

SB

BALLETS AFRICAINS

A performing arts troupe founded in 1952 by Kéita *Fodéba and Facély Kanté to celebrate the 'traditional' performing arts of Guinea, to promote among the population a nationalist sense of pride (especially during the colonial era), and to use them as a vehicle for the serious treatment of social and political topics. Its shows were energetic displays in which percussionists and musicians joined with dancers, *puppeteers, and *acrobats, dressed in traditional *costumes and sporting body decorations, to dramatize events from the historical or legendary past of the peoples of Guinea, or from their contemporary world, in *dance, song, or *mime. After its success at the Festival of Negro Arts in Dakar in 1966, the Ballets undertook regular *tours of several countries in Africa, Europe, and North America. From 1958, when Guinea dramatically declared its independence from France, to 1984, when its first president died, and with him his intensely nationalistic Marxist regime, the Ballets (which still survive, but more modestly) was the country's cultural flagship.　　　PNN trans. JCM

BALLETS RUSSES (DE SERGE DIAGHILEV), LES

*Ballet company that began as a *tour to *Paris in 1909 by dancers and opera singers from the Mariinsky Theatre in *St Petersburg. The company lasted for twenty years, producing some of the twentieth century's most *avant-garde experiments in *dance, music, and visual art. Sergei *Diaghilev had organized Russian art exhibitions, music concerts, and *opera performances in Paris; after 1909 he became the visionary impresario of a world-renowned dance company. At first he exported the collaborative work of Russian dancers, composers, and visual artists to Europe and the Americas. *The Rite of Spring* (1913), choreographed by Vaslav Nijinsky to music by Igor Stravinsky with designs by Nicholas Roerich, was sensational for its antiballetic dancing, polyrhythmic music, and *folkloric images of pagan Russia. After 1917 the company settled in Western Europe (Paris and then Monte Carlo) and became more international; its participants included *Picasso, *Cocteau, Matisse, Ravel, and Satie. Its choreographers included Bronislava Nijinska and George *Balanchine. After Diaghilev's death in 1929, his dancers settled in various countries, founding ballet companies and schools in Europe and the USA. Several subsequent companies known as Ballet Russe (singular) operated with parts of the Ballets Russes repertory until the early 1950s.   SB

BALTAZAR, FRANCISCO (1788–1862)

Filipino poet and playwright. Born in Bulacan, Baltazar was also known as Balagtas, a name he took from his benefactor. He composed a wealth of lyric poems and metrical *romances and became the most famous Filipino romantic poet. His quatrains (called *plosa*) became the standard poetic form until the modern free-verse movement of the 1950s. His most famous romance, *Florante at Laura*, is an *allegory of colonial oppression which—though set in Albania in the Middle Ages— referred to the deplorable conditions of the Spanish colonial *Philippines; he wrote it while imprisoned on unknown charges in 1838. As a playwright Baltazar was just as prolific. His most frequently performed plays are a *sainete* (a short farcical play), *La India elegante y el Negrito amante*, and a *komedya* (a play in *verse), *Orosman y Zafira*. He left a legacy of two trunks filled with his works.   RV

BALUSTRADE, THEATRE ON THE

*Playhouse and theatre company in *Prague, named after the street on which it is located. After informal performances given in the nightclub Reduta in 1957, Jiří Suchý (1931–), Ivan Vyskočil (1929–), and friends established this seedbed of the Czech Little Theatre movement. The loose form of the opening anti-war programme (*If a Thousand Clarinets*, 1958) embraced music, *mime, and drama skits and signified an *alternative to the closed world of the official stages of what was then Czechoslovakia. A process of specialization followed: Ladislav Fialka (1931–91) formed a mime company and Vyskočil developed a specialized performance form called 'author's non-theatre'. Under Grossman's programme of 'appealing theatre' (1962–8), more conventional drama prevailed, with *absurdist texts by *Beckett, *Ionesco, and *Havel, as well as work by *Jarry and Kafka. In the late 1970s and early 1980s the Balustrade was the refuge of director Evald Schorm (1931–88), who after the Soviet invasion was prevented from making *films. Highlights of the period were his productions of Shakespeare, Dostoevsky, and Confortés. In the 1990s the theatre came to the fore again under Petr Lébl's (1965–99) management, especially due to his postmodern productions of *Chekhov.   ML

BANCROFT, SQUIRE (1841–1926)

English *actor-manager. One of the leading figures of the mid-Victorian stage, Bancroft began his acting career at Birmingham. A following engagement at Cork required him to play 40 new parts in 36 nights; then 30 new major parts and some familiar ones in a six-week season at Devonport. Joining Marie *Wilton's new venture at the *Prince of Wales Theatre in *London in 1865, he assumed leading parts in the extraordinarily successful *comedies of Tom *Robertson: Sidney Daryl in *Society* (1865), Angus MacAlister in *Ours* (1866), Captain Hawtree in *Caste* (1867), and Jack Poyntz in *School* (1869). A tall, handsome man, Bancroft acted against *stock company stereotyping and with a polished restraint that matched the restraint of much of Robertson's writing. This restraint also marked his period of management, which he shared with Marie Wilton, whom he married in 1867. In collaboration with Robertson at the Prince of Wales's and later at the larger *Haymarket from 1880 to 1885, they presented a quiet middle-class domestic *realism, in both *acting and production style, which served Robertson well and influenced later playwrights and *managers. At the Haymarket Bancroft introduced the full picture-frame *stage and controversially abolished the pit, replacing it with *stalls (*see* BOX, PIT, AND GALLERY). The Bancrofts retired in 1885 with £180,000, mostly derived from Robertson's plays. As a man of leisure, Bancroft played the role of elegant clubman, appearing in the occasional West End play. He was knighted in 1897, the first actor after *Irving to be so honoured.   MRB

BANDŌ TAMASABURŌ V (1950–)

*Japanese *onnagata* (female-gender role specialist) in *kabuki and *shimpa, and choreographer. He was adopted into the kabuki family of Morita Kanya in 1956, and *Nakamura Utaemon VI, the foremost *onnagata* of the post-war period, recognized his unusual talent and beauty in his early roles such as Hototogisu in *Gosho no Gorozo* (1967) and tutored him. That same year Tamasaburō and the young Kataoka Takao made a sensation in their couple roles in *Sakurahime Azuma Bunshō* (1967). Performing both the young acolyte and the princess in *Sakurahime*, Tamasaburō established his quintessential feature of *gender ambiguity. Known for his aloof beauty and cool sensuality, he excels in the *akuba* (evil woman) parts such as Kirare Otomi and Unzari Omatsu in the plays of those titles. Tamasaburō has worked extensively outside kabuki, choreographing and performing in collaboration with artists such as Maurice Béjart, Andrzej *Wajda, Nuria *Espert, and Yo Yo Ma. Among his Western female roles are Medea, Lady Macbeth, and Queen Elizabeth in Francisco Orrs's *Contradance*. He also directs and performs in *films.   KMM

BANGLADESH

A country of mostly Bengali-speaking people, the tortuous political history of Bangladesh is inseparably linked with West

Bengal in *India; together they constituted greater Bengal until the mid-twentieth century. Bengal was colonized by the British in 1757 and became a province of British India by the first half of the nineteenth century. When India was partitioned along majority religious lines in 1947, the eastern portion became a province of Islamic *Pakistan (known as East Pakistan), while West Bengal became a state in India. After a civil war in 1971 over the question of language-based national identity, East Pakistan emerged as independent Bangladesh. However, the people of this Muslim-majority country have yet to resolve the problem of identity, a fact with deep bearing on all cultural aspects of Bangladesh. British colonial rule left the rural population economically impoverished and its English-educated urban elite estranged from indigenous identity (*see* POST-COLONIAL STUDIES). Consequently theatre in Bangladesh at the end of the twentieth century consisted of two distinct streams: rural-based indigenous forms in the tradition of South Asian theatre, and urban-based forms which arrived with the British.

Of the 70 or more indigenous *genres, about 50 are *religious and nearly twenty are secular. Of the religious performances, about twenty are based on tales of Muslim saints (such as Khizir, Madar, and Gazi) and legendary heroes (the Prophet, Imam Hasan, Imam Hosain, Amir Hamza). Beside a few Buddhist and Natha cult performances, the majority of the rest are brahmanical and are based on tales related to Krishna and Caitanya, Ramachandra, Shiva and Kali, or Manasa. Of the religious performances, those related to Manasa, the Muslim saints, and the Natha cult generally enjoy popularity among both Hindus and Muslims because of their syncretic tendency, and some are even performed by members of both religions. Performances related to Muslim legendary heroes, however, enjoy popularity only among Muslims, and those related to Krishna and Caitanya, Ramachandra, Shiva and Kali, only among Hindus. Secular performances are mostly based on romance and adventure, some of them indigenous, others Persian or Arabian in origin. Important also is the tradition of popular humour in performances such as *sang jatra*, *alkap gan*, and *gambhira gan*, which function as a people's forum for critiquing the ruling elite.

Of all the genres, religious and secular, only *jatra is performed all over Bangladesh and witnessed by members of all communities. Fully professional companies perform few of these genres (*jatra* being the chief one); in most cases, the lead narrators are professionals while the rest must depend on other work for a livelihood. Male performers still dominate and some *female impersonators can still be seen. It is not uncommon, however, for women to take principal roles. In the past all indigenous theatre depended upon sponsorship and offered free admission for spectators, who might be invited to offer a donation, but with the rise of mercantile capital sponsorship began to disappear and many performances now operate on a commercial basis (*see* FINANCE).

A number of distinct types of performance exist in the indigenous theatre, including narrative, dialogic, and song-and-dance forms. (*See*, for example, JARI GAN.) Other forms of note are the processional (large processions with tableaux), the contestual (enacting a contest between two groups of performers; *see* KABI GAN), and those using *masks, *puppets, or scroll painting for representation. Common to all of them, however, are song, music, and *dance. The performances are non-*illusionist, avoid stage settings, and aim at direct communion with the spectators. In general they are performed in pavilions, either temporary or permanent. Temporary pavilions may be created with four corner posts and a slightly elevated ground in the courtyard of rural homesteads, temple premises, or any public space. The performance spaces are normally either circular, where the performers sit in a smaller circle at the centre while the spectators sit all around, or square, where the performers sit in a circle at the centre or along one or two sides while the spectators sit on all four sides. When a permanent performance space (*nat-mandapa*) is used it is always located in front of a Hindu temple sanctum, so that work based on Muslim saints and legendary heroes does not take place there. The most striking example of *make-up can be seen in *sang jatra*, where male *characters paint their faces like masks, not far from the south Indian and the *Chinese practice (although not as developed).

Urban-based European theatre was introduced in Calcutta (*Kolkata) in 1753, but only after the independence of Bangladesh in 1971 did it gain wide currency in its cities, especially Dhaka and Chittagong. State *censorship, originally enforced through colonial legislation (*Dramatic Performances Act, 1876), was finally lifted in 2001. Most work is produced by non-professional groups composed of students, government and non-government employees, and independent professionals, all belonging to the middle class. Of about 300 groups currently active in Bangladesh, around 200 are members of an umbrella body known as the Group Theatre Federation. Ideologically, almost all of them are committed to varying degrees of social change and language-based nationalism (as opposed to the religion-based nationalism of the fundamentalists). Some of the major groups of Bangladesh are Theatre, Nagarik, Aranyak, Dhaka Theatre, and Dhaka Padatik. The groups operate out of meagre *box-office takings, corporate sponsorship, and personal contributions by members; they often perform in ill-equipped and badly constructed *auditoriums more suitable for seminars. Four universities offer courses in theatre but most *training is based in workshops. The original plays of the group theatres, all in Bengali, voice concerns about political and social oppression, injustice, and religious fanaticism. The groups also rely on a significant number of translations and adaptations of European and American playwrights, including Shakespeare, *Molière, *Ibsen, and *Brecht. Playwrights who have followed European *dramaturgy with distinction are Saeed Ahmad, Syed Shamsul

Huq, Mamtazuddin Ahmad, Mamunur Rashid, and Abdullah al-Mamun. Another significant focus is the 'search for roots', where attempts have been made to integrate indigenous theatre idioms with the European; Salim al-Deen, with plays such as *Kittankhola* (*The Fair of Kittankhol*), *Keramat Mangal* (*The Epic of Keramat*) and *Caka* (*The Wheel*), had particular success. Since the late 1970s non-government organizations have relied upon theatre for *development strategies as a part of consciousness-raising, human-development, and solidarity-building programmes with impoverished peoples in rural areas and urban slums. *See also* BENGALI THEATRE; OPPRESSED, THEATRE OF THE.

SJA

AHMED, SYED JAMIL, *Acin Pakhi Infinity: indigenous theatre of Bangladesh* (Dhaka, 2000)

BANGSAWAN

Popular Malaysian and Indonesian commercial urban theatre. *Parsi theatre troupes touring from Bombay (*Mumbai) to *Malaysia in the 1880s are believed to have provided the model. A significant theatrical development, *bangsawan* was Malaysia's (and later *Indonesia's) first purely secular and commercial theatre, characterized by *ticket sales, shameless self-promotion, star appeal, and troupe rivalries. It also introduced indigenous *audiences to the *proscenium stage, *scenery, and *lighting. Flashy and theatrical, *bangsawan* performances appealed across ethnic and class lines. Stories were drawn from popular Middle Eastern, *Indian, and Malay sources as well as from adaptations of Western literary classics and *films. *Dialogue, performed in Malay, was improvised around loose *scenarios—a single play could take several nights to complete if a good rapport with the audience was established.

Because the *plots were commonly known, performances were judged on the basis of the skill and wit of the actors—in particular the young *hero who brought the story to bear on current situations, the heroine whose melodramatics were designed to bring spectators to tears, and the *clowns who excelled in wordplay and sexual innuendo. Spoken scenes were interspersed with song-and-*dance numbers accompanied by orchestras of local and Western instruments. Stage tricks and stunts were central features. In the 1890s Malay *bangsawan* troupes toured to Sumatra and Java where local companies subsequently formed, becoming generally known in Indonesia as *opera melayu* (Malay opera) or *stambul*. *Bangsawan*'s popularity peaked during the 1920s and 1930s and began to decline in the 1940s, as intellectuals from the nationalist movements in both Malaysia and Indonesia criticized it as coarse and unrealistic. The rise in the popularity of film may also have been responsible for *bangsawan*'s demise by the mid-twentieth century, although there have been sporadic efforts to revive it in both countries.

CRG

BANKHEAD, TALLULAH (1902–68)

American actress. Born to a prominent Alabama family, Bankhead moved to *New York in 1917, the winner of a *film role through a magazine contest. Discovered by stage producers as an exotic blonde with a distinctive throaty voice, she *toured 1918–23 in *39 East*. Bankhead was the talk of *London (1923–4) for her uninhibited personal behaviour and stage performance in *The Dancers*. After some film work, she starred in two Broadway productions: *Dark Victory* (1934) and a critically praised revival of the drama *Rain* (1935). One attempt at classical work was the disastrous 1937 production of *Antony and Cleopatra*. Bankhead's outstanding successes were the grasping southern matriarch in Lillian *Hellman's *The Little Foxes* (1939) and the maid/temptress Sabina in Thornton *Wilder's *The Skin of our Teeth* (1942). Her last role was written for her by Tennessee *Williams in *The Milk Train Doesn't Stop Here Anymore* (1964).

MAF

BANKS, JOHN (c.1652–1706)

English playwright. Banks is best known for his *tragedies of suffering heroines drawn from British history, dubbed 'she tragedies'. *The Innocent Usurper* (1683), on Lady Jane Grey, and *The Island Queen* (1684, acted 1704 as *The Albion Queens*) on Mary of Scotland, were initially banned for political reasons. Banks's earlier horror tragedy, *Cyrus the Great*, was either similarly suppressed, or merely refused by the players.   RWV

BANKSIDE

In the sixteenth century, part of *London's suburbs on the south bank of the Thames, opposite St Paul's Cathedral. Set in Surrey, free from the control of the Lord Mayor, it was noted for its resources in entertainment, including *baiting-houses, *playhouses, taverns, and brothels. Bankside was accessible to *audiences from the city either on foot across London Bridge or by ferry. It had three playhouses, the *Rose, built in 1587, the *Swan (1595), and the *Globe (1599). Its bear- and bull-baiting *amphitheatres appeared in the 1560s. A succession of baiting-houses was built on Bankside into the Restoration period.

AJG

BANNISTER, JOHN (1760–1836)

English actor, son of a famous comedian, Charles Bannister (1741–1804). Although Charles encouraged John's talents as a visual artist, after a time at the Royal Academy the son took to the stage. He sometimes acted with his father: the father played Polly Peachum and the son Jenny Diver in George *Colman's transvestite *Beggar's Opera Metamorphosed* at the *Haymarket in 1781. Bannister was an excellent mimic, but he also had a great comic range. Among his disparate roles were Lovewell in *The Clandestine Marriage*, Tony Lumpkin in *She Stoops to Conquer*, and Mother Cole in *The Minor*. He is said to have acted some 450 parts in theatres and towns all over England, Ireland, and Scotland. Bannister usually played at *Drury Lane during the regular season and either at the Haymarket or on *tour in the provinces during the summer.   MJK

BANNISTER, NATHANIEL (1813–47)

American actor and playwright. Born in Baltimore, he began his theatrical career as an actor in *New York and *Philadelphia. Moving to New Orleans in 1834, he married the actress widow of John Augustus *Stone and established his own reputation. He returned to Philadelphia and New York in 1837, playing various houses before becoming an acting regular and resident playwright in 1840 for the *Bowery Theatre. Among the most prolific of nineteenth-century American dramatists, Bannister composed at least 40 plays, generally written to meet the tastes of his *audience. *Putnam: the Iron Son of '76*, his most famous work, premièred at the Bowery Theatre in 1844, ran for 78 performances and was immediately pirated by rival companies. The tone of this spectacular *melodrama is suggested by the 46 m (150 ft) descent Bannister made onto the stage on horseback.   GAR

BARAKA, IMAMU AMIRI (LEROI JONES) (1934–   )

*African-American poet and playwright. As LeRoi Jones, he emerged out of the beatnik era to express the anger and force of black cultural determination. In the 1950s and 1960s he lived and worked on the Lower East Side of *New York, first studying drama in Edward *Albee's playwrights' workshop. He founded the American Theatre for Poets with Diane di Prima in 1961 to promote the work of local writers. That same year his provocative *race play *The Toilet* caught critical fire, and was followed three years later by *The Baptism*, but it was *Dutchman* (1964) that brought him and race issues powerfully to the public eye. Set in a subway car, *Dutchman* pits a cocky black male against a seductive white female in a violent tug of war which ends in the young man's death, and suggests an endless cycle of the same *action. The play seemed to coalesce the latent racial forces about to explode in America. Jones, who was experiencing his own internal struggle in the transition from downtown liberal to uptown revolutionary, changed his name and became affiliated with the Black Arts Repertory Theatre and School in Harlem, which took cultural performance to the *streets. *The Slave* (1964), *A Black Mass* (1966), and *Slave Ship: An Historical Pageant* (1967) confirmed his artistic and political reorientation. He returned to Newark, New Jersey, where he was born, and created the Spirit House Theatre. *The Motion of History* (1975)

shows his rejection of black separatism for a more broadly based international socialism. *The Autobiography of Leroi Jones* was published in 1984.   BBL

BARBA, EUGENIO (1936–   )

Italian director, *theorist, and teacher, based in Denmark. Barba founded the *Odin Teatret in 1964 in Oslo after working with Jerzy *Grotowski for three years in Poland. On moving the Odin to Holstebro in Denmark in 1966, he established the Nordisk Teaterlaboratorium, a research organization modelled loosely on Grotowski's *Polish Lab Theatre. Barba's debt to his mentor culminated in his publishing the first English version of Grotowski's seminal *Towards a Poor Theatre* (1968) and in the Odin arranging Grotowski's initial workshops and performances outside of Poland. Barba is one of the leading figures of the independent group theatre movement that exploded in Europe in the early 1960s and was among the first to realize its relevance through his concept of the 'third theatre'. He was also an early practitioner and theorist of what he terms 'barter', that is, using performance as a means of generating contact between different cultures. His interest in cross-cultural contact and his preoccupation with performer 'presence' led to him to establish the International School of Theatre Anthropology in 1979, a research organization predicated upon what he terms theatre *anthropology, a discipline concerned with investigating performance universals that function across cultures. He has directed more than twenty productions with the Odin and has conducted workshops in many parts of the world. A prolific author, he has written or collaborated on twelve books and more than 80 articles, which have been translated into many languages. *See also* INTERCULTURALISM.   IDW

BARBEAU, JEAN (1945–   )

French-Canadian playwright, the most prolific dramatist in Québec during the 1970s. Barbeau's use of colourful Canadian French, following that of Michel *Tremblay, proved immensely popular, in plays such as *Manon Lastcall* and *Joualez-moi d'amour* (*Speak to Me of Love*, both 1970), the latter a reference to *joual*, a hitherto pejorative term for the language of working-class francophones. Politically committed and savagely parodic of Québec society, Barbeau's black humour entertained *audiences until the election of the separatist Parti Québécois (which he supported) in 1976. His output and influence have declined noticeably since then.   LED

BARBERIO CORSETTI, GIORGIO (1951–   )

Italian director, actor, and author. A leading figure of the 'post *avant-garde', Barberio Corsetti founded La Gaia Scienza in 1976 and the Barberio Corsetti Company in 1984 to perform his original, experimental works. Many of these reflected his desire to seek nourishment in myth and sacred texts and to express ideas through video-theatre (*see* MULTIMEDIA PERFORMANCE). Among the best of them have been *La camera astratta* (*The Abstract Room*, 1987), *Mefistofele . . .* (1995, based on *Goethe's Faust*), *America* (1990) and *The Trial* (1998), both adapted from Kafka, and *Notte* (1998), a mythic meditation on city nightlife.   JEH

BARBICAN THEATRE

The Barbican Centre, the largest arts complex in Europe, was begun as an urban renewal project by the City of *London in 1959. The theatre, which opened in 1982, was intended as the London home of the *Royal Shakespeare Company, which had been leasing the *Aldwych since 1960. The Barbican Theatre was designed in 1965 by Peter Chamberlin, with the RSC designer John *Bury as theatre consultant, using a concept created by Richard Southern. The *auditorium, with a capacity of 1,162, features three levels of shallow balconies that step towards the stage and down along the side walls. Each seating row has its own entrance doors, which are operated by electromagnets. The *stage is a semi-*thrust and exceptionally large at just over 38.2 m (125 feet) wide by 15 m (49 feet) deep. The *proscenium arch has a maximum width of 21.59 m (70 feet). The entire stage was designed to be hydraulically raked and the stainless steel fire *curtain, which follows the outline of the thrust stage, is of a unique two-part design, half coming up through the floor. During the long delays between design and construction much of the specified electronic equipment had become outdated, and the needs of the RSC also changed. The experimental Pit Theatre had to be built out of a planned *rehearsal hall and a lack of on-site construction shops meant increased production costs. Nonetheless for a number of years the RSC transferred its most successful productions from Stratford to the Barbican and later created new shows for the venue. In 1997 the RSC ceased producing a summer season at the Barbican, and in 2001 announced that it would end its twenty-year residency in 2002. The Barbican International Theatre Event (BITE), instituted in 1998, brings productions from around the world for a May to October season.   FJH

BARCELONA

Geography, political upheavals, industrialization, and the periodic suppression of the native Catalan language have all affected the development of theatre in this major Mediterranean city. The city's earliest theatrical activity was the presentation of *medieval *mystery plays in the cathedrals or on floats in the processions at *Corpus Christi. Secular entertainment was limited to *mime shows, *acrobats, and travelling troupes of improvisers. In 1587, when *Madrid was already on its way to becoming a vibrant theatre centre, Philip II granted a theatre monopoly in Barcelona to the Hospital de la Santa Creu, which constructed a theatre at the end of the Rambla and initiated a regular season in 1597, but Madrid, Valencia, and Seville overshadowed the city during the Golden Age.

The support of the city's wealthy mercantile class would prove essential to the development of a distinct Catalan theatre. In the late seventeenth century, a group of burgher intellectuals formed literary circles that included the sponsorship of theatrical performances. Proximity to France and cultural affinities encouraged the translation of *Racine and *Molière, although this took place mainly in monasteries. At the end of the eighteenth century, the local aristocracy became interested in theatre and sponsored private performances in their homes to show off the economic success of the family. Plays by *Voltaire and *Kotzebue were performed in French and shorter pieces of local origin in Catalan. The theatre craze soon spread to the commercial class. One wealthy entrepreneur, Felip Nadal, built a permanent theatre in his villa and employed a private company of actors for several years. Most of the plays performed were *sainetes, short plays about ordinary people which required little stage equipment, and sketches called 'ombres xineses' or 'Chinese shadows' that had been introduced from Italy. Public theatre remained centred at the Santa Creu Theatre, where two companies, one for Italian *opera and one for plays, performed in a season that lasted from Easter to Lent. Destroyed by *fire in 1787, the theatre was rebuilt with seating accommodation for all levels of society and maintained its monopoly until 1833. With the arrival of *romanticism, *acting ceased to be a marginal profession that was handed down from one generation to the next, and the concept of actor *training was introduced, with distinctions between professional and *amateur. After 1850, five regular theatres existed, as well as private gardens and *open-air summer theatres. The avenue known as the Parallel began to be a focus of theatrical activity and the Tivoli Gardens offered *variety shows and *zarzuelas. *Historical plays and *melodramas, following the models of *Hugo, *Dumas *père*, and *Pixérécourt, enjoyed a vogue. The local playwright Víctor Balaguer wrote prolifically both in Spanish and Catalan to supply some of the demand for the popular *genres. Another Barcelonan, Jaume Piquet, rented the Odeon theatre and made it a favourite with unsophisticated *audiences who relished theatrical display.

The rapid expansion of the city in the second half of the nineteenth century was accompanied by a burst of theatre construction and the development of new entertainment areas. By the end of the century, Barcelona became a rival of Madrid for predominance in theatrical activity. Outstanding among a new generation of playwrights was Àngel *Guimerà who launched his career with belated romantic *verse dramas and went on to become a socially committed *realist with *Maria Rosa* (1894) and *The Lowlands* (1897). During the creative ferment of *modernism, the director-scenographer Adrià *Gual established the Teatre Intim, which offered a varied repertory of classical and modern European works while introducing new staging concepts. The panorama of theatrical activity provided a rich mix of elitist and middle-class drama, with variety shows, *cabaret acts, and early 'talking' *film experiments. The period of autonomy that Catalonia enjoyed during the republic was cut short by the victory of Franco's Nationalists in 1939, and Catalan was immediately banned in theatrical performances. Barcelona's theatre would not begin to attract attention again until the formation of *collective groups such as Els *Joglars (1962), Els *Comediants (1971), and La *Fura dels Baus (1979), which specialized in highly visual and *physical performances. With the death of Franco in 1975 and a democratic constitution that granted autonomy to Catalonia, theatre in Barcelona once again began to flourish. The independent Teatre Lliure set high standards for theatrical production, and the Teatro Fronterizo, founded in 1977 by *Sanchis Sinisterra, became the proving ground for a new generation of Catalan playwrights. By the end of the twentieth century, Barcelona rivalled Madrid for the second time in its history and had become increasingly conspicuous in the larger European community.   MPH

FÁBREGAS, XAVIER, *Historia del teatre català* (Barcelona, 1978)
GEORGE, DAVID, and LONDON, JOHN (eds.), *Contemporary Catalan Theatre: an introduction* (Sheffield, 1996)

BARIS

Several types of ceremonial Balinese warrior *dances classified into different categories based on the types of weapons used. *Baris* has been in existence since at least the sixteenth century and was first mentioned in the context of funeral processions. It is customarily performed during temple anniversary festivals (*odalan*) and the dancers are considered the bodyguard of the visiting deities. *Baris* literally means 'line' or 'row', and it is presented by rows of men who perform stylized fighting moves and military drills in pairs. Often two lines face each other and execute complex stylized mock battles in unison. The dancers wear characteristic triangular pointed helmets and use various heirloom weapons (spears, lances, bows and arrows, clubs, shields) depending on the type of dance. *Baris gedé* (grand *baris*) is the most elaborate kind, involving large groups of up to 60 dancers and accompanied by the *gamelan *gong gedé*. Several secular types of *baris* exist as well, such as the *baris melampahan*, which includes dramatic elements. A solo *baris* developed in the late twentieth century as part of the repertoire of tourist performances. *See also* INDONESIA.   KP

BARKER, HARLEY GRANVILLE (1877–1946)

English actor, playwright, director, *manager, critic, and *theorist. Born in *London, he was the son of Alfred Barker and Eliza-

beth Bozzi-Granville, herself a *variety performer. Self-educated, he began acting in 1891, writing plays in 1895, and directing in 1899. As an actor Barker excelled in roles that combined intelligence with romantic dreaminess, and G. B. *Shaw thought his subtle but natural playing particularly suited for lover-poets like Marchbanks in *Candida*, Tanner in *Man and Superman*, Cusins in *Major Barbara*, and Dubedat in *The Doctor's Dilemma*, the last two written with Barker in mind. But *acting did not appeal to him and he gave it up in 1911. At a time when *directing was barely acknowledged in England, Barker built on the models of André *Antoine and Max *Reinhardt and almost single-handedly transformed the quality of production in London. His first assignments were under the limited auspices of the *Stage Society, but at the *Royal Court Theatre from 1904 to 1907 he established himself as the major reformer of the Edwardian stage. With his business manager J. E. Vedrenne, he mounted almost 1,000 performances, mostly of new works (or new translations of *Euripides by Gilbert *Murray); 701 of the performances were of eleven plays by Shaw. Barker collaborated with Shaw in staging his plays, and directed all the others himself. He also acted a number of important roles. In 1906 he married the actress Lillah *McCarthy, soon after they played opposite each other in *Man and Superman*.

Barker's own play *The Voysey Inheritance* (1905), mounted in the second season of the Court venture, remains one of the masterworks of the Edwardian stage. But his other plays, which are highly nuanced in thought, did not much appeal to Edwardian *audiences, who sometimes found them incomprehensible. Unlike his friend and mentor Shaw, Barker was closer in method to Anton *Chekhov, putting *action under the surface. Despite his subtle method, Barker did not avoid important and controversial issues: *Waste* was banned in 1907 because of its twinned subjects of abortion and politics (*see* CENSORSHIP), and *The Madras House* (1910) openly treated the economic domination of women using the embryonic fashion business to analyse contemporary sexual relationships.

The *Vedrenne–Barker seasons established Shaw as a major playwright but did not mean financial stability, and the managers failed when they tried to extend their operation on a more permanent basis at the *Savoy, a larger and more centrally located theatre. A second repertory experiment at the *Duke of York's in 1910, briefly funded by the American impresario Charles *Frohman, reinforced for Barker the need for an endowed *repertory company. In 1904 he had written a book with William *Archer arguing for a national theatre, in the hope that a private benefactor would subsidize such an institution and thus give London what most major cities in Europe took for granted. He continued to champion the cause, both in print and by his example, and his failure to achieve it was the greatest disappointment of his life. His persistent advocacy nonetheless encouraged the growth of the *regional repertory movement in Britain and ultimately influenced the founding of the subsidized English theatres in the 1960s. (*See* NATIONAL THEATRE MOVEMENT, BRITAIN; NATIONAL THEATRE.)

Barker's directing reached its height in three famous productions of Shakespeare at the Savoy: *The Winter's Tale* and *Twelfth Night* in 1912 and *A Midsummer Night's Dream* in 1914. Partly influenced by William *Poel, for whom he played Richard II in 1899, Barker used nearly complete *texts, revoked Victorian pictorial traditions for the sake of *modernist design, and emphasized ensemble acting. The productions moved Shakespeare out of the *realist tradition into the realm of symbol in a lively and contemporary way. But the war changed everything and in the 1920s Barker devoted himself to the study, where he said he always wanted to be. He divorced Lillah McCarthy and in 1918 married a minor American writer, Helen Huntington, who disliked the stage, most actors, and especially Shaw. Her wealth allowed them both the freedom to write. Hyphenating his name to Granville-Barker, he appeared remote and lost the support of his theatrical allies, who believed he had abandoned the battle for a life of luxury. He attended to the stage from a distance, in books like *The Exemplary Theatre* (1922), *The National Theatre* (1930), and *The Use of Drama* (1944). He wrote two more plays—*The Secret Life* (1923) and *His Majesty* (1928)—and with his wife he translated the *comedies of *Martínez Sierra and the *Álvarez Quintero brothers. His most enduring critical work is *Prefaces to Shakespeare* (1927–46), the first major Shakespeare study to attend to practical matters of staging.

In recent years Barker's plays, which now seem prescient in style and theme, have attracted serious attention. In 1975 the *Royal Shakespeare Company produced *The Marrying of Ann Leete*, which in Barker's day had only two private performances by the Stage Society in 1902. In 1985 the RSC mounted *Waste*, which also had been given only two private performances (1907) because of its trouble with the censor. The Royal National Theatre presented a lavish version of *The Madras House* in 1977, *The Voysey Inheritance* was seen there and in many venues in Britain and North America in the late 1980s, and even Barker's difficult late plays were at last given productions, at the Orange Tree Theatre in London, directed by Sam *Walters. Between 1988 and 2002 the *Shaw Festival in Canada undertook to establish Barker as a major playwright by producing most of his plays under the direction of Neil Monro, and the *Edinburgh Festival mounted a major retrospective in 1992 which included productions or public readings of most of his work. At the same time Barker's general contributions have been re-evaluated and his importance for modern theatre securely acknowledged, so that he is now seen as one of the twentieth century's leading innovators. DK

KENNEDY, DENNIS, *Granville Barker and the Dream of Theatre* (Cambridge, 1985)

PURDOM, C. B., *Harley Granville Barker* (London, 1955)

SALMON, ERIC, *Granville Barker: a secret life* (London, 1983)

BARKER, HOWARD (1946–)

English dramatist and director. Barker's early work like *Cheek* and *No One Was Saved* (1970), and *Stripwell* and *Claw* (1975), seemed to place him in the counter-cultural and *political movement of the late 1960s. But soon he evaded neat classification, and his *historical subjects were chosen less for the light they shed on contemporary concerns than for the opportunities they afforded for acts of imaginative speculation in which *comedy and desire could mingle and clash. *The Castle* (1985), for example, is set after the crusades and pits the hierarchical values of the returning male warriors against the spiritual socialism created by the wives they left behind. Barker is unusually prolific: by 2002, he had written close to 90 plays, six books of poetry, and a phenomenal series of dramatic statements and manifestos, many of them collected in *Arguments for a Theatre* (1989, 1997). Through these he articulated a 'theatre of catastrophe' that renounces moral and narrative clarity, and the consequent solidarity of the *audience, in favour of complexity and excess, influenced by the Marxist Adorno as well as by the post-*structuralism of Derrida and Foucault. These goals are realized in *The Possibilities* (1988), based around perverse moral acts, and the hugely ambitious *The Bite of the Night* (1988). Having lost his early champions like the *Royal Shakespeare Company and *Royal Court, who retreated from the difficulty of the new plays, Barker founded the Wrestling School in 1988, which became his main British conduit in pieces such as *Seven Lears* (1989), *Judith* (1995), *Wounds to the Face* (1997), and *A House of Correction* (2001). In his *directing for the company he further developed the theatre of catastrophe in a visual style marked by abrasive austerity and stark beauty, underlining his verbal riches. DR

BARKER, JAMES NELSON (1784–1859)

American playwright, politician, and poet. Son of a prominent *Philadelphia family—has father became mayor—Barker spent his early adulthood writing for the stage. Notable among his early efforts were *Tears and Smiles* (1806), a *comedy contrasting French and American social mores; a pro-Jeffersonian piece, *The Embargo* (1808), that occasioned *riots at the *Chestnut Street Theatre; and *The Indian Princess* (1808), a retelling of the Pocahontas legend with a happy ending. This piece with *music was the first 'Indian play' written by an American to be produced in the United States. He continued in a distinctly nationalistic vein in his 1812 anti-British adaptation of Scott's novel *Marmion*, and in *The Armourer's Escape* (1817). Also in 1817 Barker wrote *How to Try a Lover*, a light comedy unproduced until 1836. After a term as Philadelphia's mayor, Barker penned his masterpiece, *Superstition* (1824), a moving indictment of Puritan fanaticism. Thereafter he became absorbed in politics and confined his literary production to poetry. GAR

BARLACH, ERNST (1870–1938)

German sculptor, graphic artist, and dramatist. After studying art in Hamburg, Dresden, and *Paris, Barlach settled in Güstrow in Mecklenburg in 1910 where he remained until his death. Although primarily known for his expressive sculptures in wood and bronze, Barlach began writing dramas in 1912 with *Der tote Tag* (*The Dead Day*, produced 1917). There followed a series of plays which merged local *realism with abstract metaphysical and religious themes. The most accomplished of these—*Die Sündflut* (*The Flood*, 1924); *Der blaue Boll* (*The Blue Bull*, 1926)—received highly acclaimed productions for which Barlach, despite his expressed lack of interest in theatre, designed the *scenery and *costumes. Defamed by the Nazis as a 'decadent' and 'Eastern' artist, Barlach was forbidden to exhibit or publish. His work achieved a partial rehabilitation on the German stage in the late 1950s. Productions have stressed the metaphysical-religious and, more recently, the local-comic aspects of the plays. CBB

BARNAY, LUDWIG (1842–1924)

German actor and director. Born in Pest (*Budapest) as the son of a Jewish clerk, Barnay worked for ten years as an itinerant actor throughout the Austro-Hungarian Empire before joining the court theatre in *Meiningen in 1874. He toured extensively with them for the next decade. In 1883 he settled in *Berlin where he founded the *Deutsches Theater and then the Berlin Theater, both private enterprises founded on virtuosic *acting styles. He was director of the latter (1887–94), of the *Berlin Royal Theatre (1906–8), and the Court Theatre in Hanover (1908–12). Barnay established the Genossenschaft Deutscher Bühnenangehöriger in 1871, the *trade union of German stage employees.

CBB

BARNES, CLIVE (1927–)

British critic, who has written on theatre and *dance for the *New York Post* since 1977. He was a founding editor of *Dance and Dancers* (1950–97), chief drama and dance critic for the *New York Times* (1965–77), and in Britain wrote for the *Daily Express* (1956–65) and *The Times* (1962–6). Educated at Oxford, his extensive knowledge and enthusiasm for the arts have driven him to consider the critic a teacher who shares his experiences, not a remote arbiter. His books include *Nureyev* (1982) and, as editor, series six, seven, and eight of *Best American Plays*. *See also* CRITICISM. GAO

BARNES, PETER (1931–)

English playwright and director. Born in London, he began his career as a screenwriter. His first stage play, *Time of the Barracudas*, opened in *San Francisco in 1963, but neither this nor *Sclerosis* (1965) received serious critical attention. *The Ruling Class* (Nottingham, 1968, and *London, 1969) was, however, hailed as groundbreaking, an uncompromising mixture of grotesque *spectacle, dark humour, and acerbic *satire on the relationships between the vested interests of Church, state, money, and power. Its examination of how people at all levels collude in submitting to authority has become a continuing theme. Barnes's highly distinctive theatrical voice and determination to write savage comic satires about serious subjects have often resulted in controversy. This was most evident in the mixed critical reception of *Laughter!* (1978), a two-part play which measures Ivan the Terrible's personalized reign of terror against the depersonalized bureaucracy of the Nazi extermination machine.

Barnes has adapted numerous *early modern plays for stage and *radio, directing many of them himself. The influence of writers such as *Jonson, *Marston, and *Middleton can be seen in his major plays which, with the exception of *The Ruling Class*, are all *history plays in the broadest sense, juxtaposing dense neo-Jacobean language with wittily anachronistic allusions to popular culture: *music-hall routines, Gothic horror, *dance, and popular song. Barnes's dislike of *naturalism and love of theatrical spectacle is evident throughout his work, perhaps most notably in *The Bewitched* (1974), which many regard as his finest work. He has won several major *awards, including the Olivier award for best drama (*Red Noses*, 1985). His screenplay for *Enchanted April* (1991) was nominated for an Academy award. BGW

BARN THEATRE

Jamaican *playhouse in a converted garage in Kingston, home of the professional company Theatre 77, which eventually adopted the same name. The venue was founded in 1965 by Trevor *Rhone, George Carter, and Yvonne *Brewster, in the climate of very limited theatrical space before the establishment of the Jamaica Playhouse and the National Theatre Trust. It provided Jamaican practitioners with opportunities otherwise unavailable, and Marina Omowale Maxwell developed her concept of 'yard theatre' there. Rhone's early plays, such as the witty swipe at the tourism industry *Smile Orange* (1970), as well as *Comic Strip* (1973) and *Sleeper* (1974), were produced at the Barn.

ES

BARNUM, P. T. (PHINEAS TAYLOR) (1810–91)

American impresario of commercial entertainment in *freak shows, museums, *variety, theatre, and the *circus. Barnum reinvented his public image and reframed his entertainments several times during his long career. Initially styling himself as a confidence man sympathetic to working-class and slaveholding interests, Barnum presented several exhibits which undermined the values of the emerging middle class, most famously Joice Heth, an elderly slave who Barnum claimed had been the nurse of George Washington. Soon after opening *Barnum's American Museum in *New York in 1841, Barnum changed tactics and began to represent himself and his exhibits as icons of middle-class respectability and a classless America. One of his most successful publicity ventures was the European *tour of the midget Tom Thumb (Charles Stratton), whose performances of democratic energy contrasted with the rigid hierarchies of Europe. In 1850–1 Barnum organized the successful American tour of Swedish singer Jenny Lind; he packaged the business-savvy star as a sentimental nightingale to conform to middle-class notions of proper womanhood. The first edition of Barnum's second autobiography, *Struggles and Triumphs* (1869; five others would follow), announced his rebirth as a post-Civil War Republican. After he entered the circus business in 1871, Barnum's new conceptions of *race and class emerged, especially in the racial exhibitions that dominated his Great Roman Hippodrome of 1874–5. In 1881 Barnum combined his circus interests with those of James A. Bailey to create 'The Greatest Show on Earth', but took little interest in managing it. Barnum virtually invented popular commercial entertainment in the USA; his enormous legacy continues.   BMC

BARNUM'S AMERICAN MUSEUM

The most famous of the proprietary museums in the USA. In 1841 P. T. *Barnum bought Scudder's Museum in *New York City and soon had customers gawking at his natural curiosities, human *freaks, *waxwork tableaux, and *animal menageries. To attract respectable middle- and working-class *audiences, Barnum featured performers and exhibits that underlined the values of Protestantism, temperance, domesticity, and capitalism. Several faked exhibits, such as the 'What Is It' and the 'Feejee Mermaid', also drew on an egalitarian desire to outwit the experts. After expanding his Lecture Room to accommodate an audience of 3,000 spectators for fully staged dramas, he opened in 1850 with a production of *The Drunkard*, the temperance *melodrama. Although known primarily for moral-reform melodramas, including *Uncle Tom's Cabin*, the American Museum company performed a variety of plays, many of which confirmed the whiteness and respectability of Barnum's audience. When the Museum burned down in 1865, Barnum quickly rebuilt, but the second version had little success.   BMC

BARON (MICHEL BOYRON) (1653–1729)

French actor and playwright. While acting in a children's company, the 13-year-old Baron was discovered by *Molière and became his pupil and protégé. On Molière's death he moved, first, to the *Hôtel de Bourgogne, where he created some of *Racine's *jeunes premiers* (young leading men), and then in 1680 to the newly established *Comédie-Française, where he played leading roles in *tragedy and high *comedy. Inexplicably, in 1691 Baron retired from the stage, only giving occasional private and court performances, until 29 years later, aged 67, he returned and not only resumed his former repertoire of *heroes and lovers, including Rodrigue in *Corneille's *Le Cid*, but also created a dozen new roles. Baron had all the attributes of a leading actor—good looks, graceful attitudes, striking presence, and versatility. Apparently, he also had an equal measure of vanity, and *L'Homme à bonnes fortunes* (*The Philanderer*, 1686), the best of the ten comedies he wrote, was a role he played both onstage and off. Baron's *acting was noted for being relaxed and natural, for having 'an art that is so little discernible as art'. These qualities, inculcated by Molière, Baron encouraged in his pupil, the young Adrienne *Lecouvreur, and in the 1720s this unlikely pair proposed an alternative to the highly artificial style of their chanting and roaring contemporaries.   JG

BARONG

Large mythical supernatural beasts (Barong) that appear in Balinese ritual performances and the performances themselves (*barong*). Different types of large *barong* *masks, considered spiritually powerful objects when consecrated, are used in *rituals and performances; they show iconographic features of lions, elephants, dogs, boars, or dragons. Some *barong* masks show similarities to masks used in the *Chinese lion dance. Typically a pair of male dancers play the Barong, one in front animating the large mask and front legs, and one at the back creating the rear part of the beast. *Barong kekek*, the most spiritually powerful and well known, features prominently in ritual processions and performances. The mask has large bulging eyes, a movable jaw with large fangs, a protruding tongue, and a wing-shaped leather collar. It is associated with the animistic spirit Banaspati Raja (Lord of the Forest) as well as with the Hindu deity Shiva; it also shows significant similarities to *wayang wong* masks and to the *bhoma* image above Balinese temple gates. The Barong is considered a guarding spirit and the opponent of the witch-widow Rangda, who is associated with the legendary figure of Calonarang, *leyaks* (witches), and the Hindu deity Durga. Barong and Rangda appear in exorcistic ritual performances that often include dramatic elements from the Calonarang story. Such a performance is intended to reestablish harmony in the community by balancing the super-

Large **barong** beast, manipulated by two dancers and with an elaborate *barong* mask, from Bali in Indonesia, c.1995. In the background another dancer performs part of the *kris* dance.

natural powers of Barong and Rangda, therefore the conflict or battle-dance between them is the central element of the *barong* drama. Other dramatic elements often include *clown scenes with *jauk* characters, *dance scenes performed by the young apprentices of Rangda, and the dramatic *dialogue between Calonarang in her human form and her human opponent, a minister or king. The most spectacular element that made *barong* famous with Western scholars and visitors is the *ngurek*, often referred to as '*kris* dance'. In this section, human followers of Barong go into trance while defending him against Rangda. During this trance, it is believed, Rangda's powerful influence drives them to attack themselves with *kris* daggers; however, the power of the Barong protects them from injuries. The trancers are attended by priests who oversee the whole performance and guide the dancers out of trance at the conclusion of the ritual. Performers of Barong and Rangda also go into trance under the influence of the spiritually powerful masks. The dance of Barong and Rangda, together with the *ngurek* trance-dance, have become famous in tourist performances where they are advertised as 'Barong and *kris* dance' and shortened to an hour-long show in which non-consecrated masks are used. The dancers generally do not go into trance. *See also* INDONESIA.

KP

BARR, RICHARD (1917–89)

American actor, director, and *producer. Born Richard Alphonse Baer in Washington, DC, Barr began as an actor in 1938, and made his directing debut in 1948. His chief importance was as a producer (or co-producer), starting with *At Home with Ethel Waters* (1953). He produced Edward *Albee's *The Zoo Story* in 1960, and went on to produce Albee's subsequent plays, including the Tony *award-winning *Who's Afraid of Virginia Woolf?* (1962) and the Pulitzer Prize-winning *A Delicate Balance* (1966) and *Seascape* (1975). He also produced works by *Beckett, *Ionesco, *Orton, *Guare, and *Sondheim. In 1967 he began 21 years of service as president of the League of American Theaters and Producers.

CT

BARRA, PEDRO DE LA (1912–77)

Director and manager, a pioneer of contemporary Chilean theatre. In 1941 he helped organize the Experimental Theatre of the University of Chile (TEUCH), which he directed until 1957, and thereafter worked to develop other university theatre schools. Granted the National Award of the Arts in 1954, after the coup of 1973 he left Chile for Venezuela, where he died.

MAR

BARRACA, LA

Spanish theatre company. A product of the Second Republic's ambitious cultural programme, La Barraca was formed in 1932 by students of the University of *Madrid with the aim of taking serious Spanish theatre to the provinces and, in the words of the company's manifesto, 'aesthetically renovating the Spanish stage'. Under the *artistic direction of Federico *García Lorca and Eduardo Ugarte, La Barraca drew on innovative Spanish artists for *scenery and *costume design, in a quest for 'plasticity' of dress, *lighting, and movement, with which they revolutionized the performance of plays by authors such as *Cervantes, Lope de *Vega, and *Calderón.

KG

BARRAULT, JEAN-LOUIS (1910–94)

Renowned French actor and director of a wide range of plays, adaptations of novels, and performance events. Eclectic in his choice of repertory, Barrault shifted his *directing and *acting style accordingly, whether *epic, *expressionist, *ritualist, or pantomimic. Opposing 'psychologism', he was a proponent of *total theatre, the synthesis of all performing arts into one expressive symbolic whole, with the bodily arts of *mime, gesture, movement, vocal intonation, and rhythm being primary. Beginning as an extra in *Pitoëff's experimental theatre, in 1931 Barrault joined Charles *Dullin's acting school at the Théâtre de l'*Atelier, where he also studied mime, the field in which he first made his reputation. Influenced as well by *Artaud, *Copeau, and *Decroux, Barrault created his first independent production, *Autour d'une mère* (*Around a Mother/Sea*), in 1935, which he adapted with *Camus from Faulkner's novel *As I Lay Dying*. Surrounded by a swaying, chanting *chorus that evoked the sea and wind was Barrault himself as the 'centaur-horse', creating through movement and vocalization a horse and rider simultaneously, as well as birds of prey overhead. His acting is memorialized in the 1935 *film *Les Enfants du paradis*, in the role of *Deburau, the great nineteenth-century mime. Other early directing successes include *Cervantes' *tragedy *Numancia* (1937), and *Faim* (*Hunger*, 1939), adapted from a Knut Hamsun novel.

After army service, Barrault joined the *Comédie-Française as an actor and director, where he met the distinguished actress Madeleine *Renaud, whom he married in 1940. His major productions at the Comédie-Française include *Racine's *Phèdre* (1942), *Claudel's *Le Soulier de satin* (*The Satin Slipper*, 1943), and Shakespeare's *Antony and Cleopatra* (1945). Barrault shared Claudel's vision of a *tragicomic, epic-lyrical 'holy' theatre and would continue to produce his works over the next four decades. In 1946 Barrault and Renaud left the Comédie-Française to found the private Compagnie Renaud–Barrault, first housed at the Marigny Theatre, then the Théâtre Sarah-Bernhardt and the *Palais Royal. Invited by Copeau, Barrault became *artistic director of the *Odéon Theatre from 1958 to 1968. For his own company and the Odéon, Barrault directed, acted in, or hosted works ranging from *Feydeau, *Marivaux, and Shakespeare to Claudel, *Anouilh, *Genet, *Ionesco, *Fry, *Duras, Kafka,

*Brecht, and *Beckett. Though never a political ideologue, Barrault was attacked by the right for producing Beckett and Genet, and by the left for his 'mystical-ecstatic' productions of Brecht and *Aeschylus.

In May 1968, Barrault, in sympathy with student protesters, allowed them to occupy the theatre, which led to his resignation. At 58 he started anew, found *rehearsal space, and in a year opened triumphantly in a former *sports arena with *Rabelais*, a *carnivalesque creation featuring actors, *clowns, and *bunraku *puppeteers. By fitting coincidence, his *touring *Rabelais* opened at Berkeley, California, just as riots broke out protesting against the National Guard shootings of four Kent State University students at a peace rally. In 1980 Barrault and Renaud settled into the Théâtre du Rond-Point, where they continued to produce classical and modern works, and they died in the same year.   SBB

BARRETT, LAWRENCE (1838–91)

American *actor-manager. Lawrence Barrett became a highly respected star performer of the classic repertory through intense perseverance. Born in Paterson, New Jersey, he ran away from home at the age of 10, teaching himself to read by memorizing a dictionary. Working in *stock companies, he eventually appeared in *New York in 1857. In 1869 he managed the company at the California Theatre in *San Francisco with John McCullough, and was among the first actor-managers to *tour an entire company (1872). He regularly toured in Shakespearian roles thereafter, and in other classic works, successfully reviving George Henry *Boker's *Francesca da Rimini* in 1882, which remained in his repertory for several seasons. Barrett managed the enormously successful final tours of Edwin *Booth (1886–90), playing second leads to the great tragedian. Regarded as an intellectual actor, Barrett's performances were studied and somewhat artificial, and were increasingly regarded as somewhat old-fashioned as theatrical styles shifted in the last two decades of the nineteenth century, although his performances as Cassius, Macbeth, and Othello were recognized as the leading ones of the 1880s.   AW

BARRETT, WILSON (1846–1904)

English *actor-manager. Of powerful voice and physique, Barrett established a reputation playing melodramatic *heroes such as Harold Armytage in George Sims's *The Lights o' London* (1881) and Wilfrid Denver in *The Silver King* (1882) by Henry Arthur *Jones and Henry Herman, *characters wrongfully accused of murder. These plays first appeared under his own management (1881–6) of the *Princess's Theatre in *London; Barrett also undertook provincial management. He enjoyed further success with W. G. *Wills's religious *spectacle drama, *Claudian* (1883), in which he played a profligate and murderous pagan aristocrat

cursed for his sins and unable to die, left untouched even by an earthquake. *Hamlet*, in 1884, was not so well received, although it ran for 116 performances. Other Shakespeare parts included Romeo, Mercutio, and Benedick. In his own enormously popular religious *melodrama *The Sign of the Cross* (1895), Barrett played a dissolute Roman prefect converted to Christianity by the love of a Christian girl, with whom he goes to his death and 'the light beyond' in the jaws of the Colosseum's lions.

MRB

BARRICADA TEATRO

Peruvian *collective, founded in 1976 by Eduardo Valentín in Huancayo. It has committed itself to a *political agenda focusing on the reconstruction of the war-torn Andean regions, advocating a national identity that rejects postmodernity and the by-products of cultural globalism (*see* INTERCULTURALISM). Initially called New Blood, the group first staged *Chile in the Centre of Neruda*, *Two Minutes to Fall Asleep*, and *The One-Eyed*; and as the Rampart Group, *Contracting for Work* and *St Anne of America*. Assuming its present name in 1985, Barricada produced *What Did Mom Give You?*, *The Autopsy*, and *Prelude to the Real Teacher's Day*. As part of the commitment to national reconstruction, the company has organized major *festivals in 1991 and 1994, and performed the ideologically based *Voice of Land That Calls* (1994) and *The Return of Ulysses* (2000).

LRG

BARRIE, J. M. (JAMES MATTHEW) (1860–1937)

Scottish journalist, novelist, and playwright, educated at Edinburgh University. Barrie began his career as a journalist, moving to *London in 1885. Then, in the late 1880s and early 1890s, he began to write novels, including *The Little Minister* (1891), which he later turned into a successful play (1897). In the 1890s he wrote *farces (such as *Ibsen's Ghost*, a parody of *Ibsenism), then soon found his dramatic voice with a series of popular and long-running social *comedies, including *Walker, London* (1892), *The Professor's Love Story* (1894), *The Admirable Crichton* (1902), and *What Every Woman Knows* (1908). He also wrote romantic *costume plays, such as *Quality Street* (1901), and social fantasies, such as *Dear Brutus* (1917) and *Mary Rose* (1920). His greatest success was *Peter Pan* (1904), which starred Nina Boucicault as Peter and Gerald *du Maurier as Hook. It became an annual holiday event, revived each Christmas until 1914. During his lifetime Barrie was celebrated as a genius of the theatre; a series of critical books and biographies proclaimed his importance. Bernard *Shaw praised him as one of the *modernists. Since the mid-twentieth century, however, most of his plays have been dismissed by critics as sentimental and superficial. Except for *Peter Pan*, which remains quite popular as a children's drama, Barrie's plays are seldom revived in the professional theatre (though they continue to be performed regularly by *amateur groups). Yet despite critical reservations about his subject matter, and psychological questions about the sexual implications of his personal life and imaginative world, Barrie's plays reveal an accomplished craftsman of the theatre. His amazingly successful theatrical career, with most productions running a year or more, provides a crucial perspective on the Edwardian theatre and culture. He was knighted in 1913.   TP

BARRY, ELIZABETH (c.1658–1713)

English actress and *manager. Adopted into the household of William and Mary *Davenant, patentees of the Duke's Company, Elizabeth Barry made her first appearance in *Otway's *Alcibiades* (1675). She rose swiftly to become the leading actress in the *patent company and *Dryden, *Lee, Otway, and other prominent playwrights soon wrote parts designed to capitalize on her performance skills. Renowned for her creation of passionate yet sympathetic tragic heroines, Barry also established herself in *comedy. Her early successes included Hellena in Aphra *Behn's *The Rover* (1677), and later *Congreve wrote *Love for Love* (1695) and *The Way of the World* (1700) to capitalize on her eighteen-year acting partnership with fellow leading actress Anne *Bracegirdle. Barry was the first actress to negotiate a personal bonus payment in the form of a *benefit performance and, with Bracegirdle and Thomas Betterton, was instrumental in forming and managing a breakaway company which occupied the theatre at *Lincoln's Inn Fields between 1695 and 1705. For the first time actresses as well as actors shared in the company's profits and under their management the company premièred at least seventeen plays by female playwrights such as Delarivière Manley, Mary *Pix, Catherine *Trotter, and Susannah *Centlivre.   GBB

BARRY, PHILIP (1896–1949)

American playwright, an influential creator of an American *comedy of manners with philosophical and ethical dimensions. *Holiday* (1928) and *The Philadelphia Story* (1939), the most successful and highly regarded of his plays, are animated by conflicting American dreams—the accumulation and enjoyment of wealth versus egalitarian and communitarian ideals. Both plays revolve upon the decision of an intelligent and witty young woman to reject an easy life and socially acceptable marriage to pursue a more adventurous path through marriage with a poor but industrious young man. A thoughtful intellectual, Barry brooded on the incompatibility of money and a moral conscience. Nevertheless, he chose to live among the social elite. A 1919 graduate of Yale, Barry attended George Pierce *Baker's 47 Workshop at Harvard (1919–21) and saw his first Broadway success with *You and I* in 1923. Other major plays are

the *comedies *Paris Bound* (1927) and *The Animal Kingdom* (1932) and the less successful philosophical dramas *Hotel Universe* (1930) and *Here Come the Clowns* (1938).   MAF

BARRY, SEBASTIAN (1955–)

Irish playwright, poet, and fiction writer. Barry, whose mother is the well-known Abbey actor Joan O'Hara, was established as a dramatist by *Boss Grady's Boys* (1988). In this low-key minimalist study of two elderly rural bachelors living together, Barry found his own style of poetic impressionism. Since then, he has produced a series of 'family' plays, *Prayers of Sherkin* (1990), *White Woman Street* (1992), *The Only True History of Lizzie Finn* (1995), taking their origins from sketchy facts about his own ancestors, and imagining them into theatrical existence. Barry's greatest international success in this series has been *The Steward of Christendom* (1995), produced by *London's *Royal Court. The central *character, a senile retired policeman (outstandingly performed by Donal *McCann), meditates on his past as a loyalist Catholic in the period of the Irish revolution. The effect of Barry's work has been to give theatrical expression to forgotten voices from Ireland's history.   NG

BARRY, SPRANGER (1719–77)

Irish actor and *manager. Known as the 'Irish Roscius', Barry was the most serious rival to *Garrick, the 'English Roscius'. Both men began and ended their acting careers around the same time, and reactions to Barry's *acting frequently drew comparisons to Garrick's. Barry was so effective as Othello that Garrick, who acknowledged him as the best lover on the stage, gave up the role rather than force comparisons. The two did compete, however, as rival Romeos in 1750. Barry was strikingly handsome, tall, and graceful. His voice was not strong and expressions of violent rage were beyond his range; he excelled as a dignified, tragic lover. Perhaps his most successful role was Castalio in *Otway's *The Orphan*. When he created the majestic title role in John *Home's *Douglas* in 1757, he was at the height of his powers, performing at *Covent Garden and planning the construction of the Crow Street Theatre in *Dublin. Barry's desire to run his own company was a costly one—in that regard he could not rival the more industrious Garrick. In just nine years he lost great sums of money and property, selling out to his Dublin managerial rival Henry Mossop in 1767 and returning to *London. In his final years frequent bouts of illness and a temperamental nature led him to cancel many scheduled performances. His illness affected his characteristic grace, forcing him into older roles. He left the stage in 1776, playing the elderly Evadner in Arthur *Murphy's *The Grecian Daughter*.

                                                                        MJK

BARRYMORE FAMILY

American acting *family with English roots. In 1876 expatriate English leading man **Maurice Barrymore** (1847–1905) married Georgiana *Drew, herself of a famous stage dynasty. Their children grew up to become the royal family of Broadway.

Maurice Barrymore, born Herbert Blythe in India, came from a middle-class family; he left Oxford—and his title of English amateur middleweight boxing champion—to try a stage career. First appearing at the *Theatre Royal, Windsor, in 1872, he made his way as a provincial player until he sailed for America, making his debut in *Under the Gaslight* in *Boston (1875). His good looks and easy grace attracted both leading ladies and *audiences. His most notable co-star was Helena *Modjeska, for whom he wrote *Nadjezda* (1886), one of his several successful plays. Barrymore found transatlantic fame in a number of contemporary plays such as *Captain Swift*, *The Heart of Maryland*, and *Diplomacy* (in which he appeared with his wife). A noted Orlando and Romeo, his greatest success was as Rawdon Crawley in *Becky Sharp* (1899). Refusing to settle into star vehicles, he insisted on independence, sued *Sardou for plagiarism (*Tosca* is a paraphrase of *Nadjezda*), quarrelled endlessly with *managers, and was reduced to appearing in *vaudeville when paresis ended his career in 1901. His irresponsibility and Georgiana's premature death caused their children to be raised by their maternal grandmother. This made stage careers inevitable for the reluctant trio.

Lionel Barrymore (1874–1954) was hustled on the stage by his grandmother Mrs John Drew as Thomas to her Mrs Malaprop in 1893. Successful from the first, his contempt for *acting almost kept him from stardom. He won great acclaim as Milt Shanks in *The Copperhead* (1918) and when he played harsh *villains opposite the sensitive *heroes of his brother in *Peter Ibbetson* (1917) and *The Jest* (1919). His failure as Macbeth (1921) probably caused him to forsake the stage for the screen. He would make over 200 *films, win an Oscar (for *A Free Soul*, 1931), and, though rheumatic illness left him in a wheelchair, became 'America's most beloved actor' and Hollywood's definitive Grand Old Man.

Ethel Barrymore (1879–1959) first appeared in *The Rivals* with Mrs Drew and in *The Bauble Shop* with her uncle John Drew (both 1894). She then went to *London with William *Gillette's *Secret Service*. Joining *Irving's *Lyceum company prepared her for American stardom, which came in 1901 with her Madame Trentoni in *Captain Jinks of the Horse Marines*. For the next 44 years she was a star whose deep voice, peerless poise, and majestic beauty reigned over the theatre. Most successful in contemporary plays as sympathetic and romantic heroines, her career faltered in the 1930s but revived with her greatest success, the inspiring teacher Miss Moffat in Emlyn *Williams's *The Corn Is Green* (1940). Her final years were spent in Hollywood.

John Barrymore (1882–1942) hated acting even more than Lionel but gained the greater fame. His career began in *Chicago as Max in *Magda* (1903). Reaching *New York the same year, he was content to show off his matchless profile in light *comedies until Edward *Sheldon convinced him to try serious parts. Barrymore electrified Broadway in *Justice* (1916). There followed a series of wrenching portrayals culminating in his magnificent performances in *Richard III* (1920) and *Hamlet* (1922). Though he was the hope of the American theatre and a great *repertory company was planned around him, he proved unable to sustain a part beyond its initial creation. After a triumphant London *Hamlet* he fled the stage for films in 1925. Fourteen years of alcoholism and Hollywood excesses dissipated his talents; he had talked of new Hamlets and even Lear, but his final stage appearance was in a travesty of his own life, *My Dear Children* (1939).

The next generation found notoriety if little fame. John's daughter **Diana** (1921–60) had a fitful stage life but failed to overcome the family curse of alcoholism, which also doomed the career of his son **John Barrymore, Jr.** (1932–). Sundry cousins and collateral relations fought to keep the tradition alive, but only John, Jr.'s daughter **Drew** (1975–) has succeeded. She began as a child star like her great-great-grandmother, appearing in the film *ET* (1982), and, after her own bouts of dissipated living, twenty years later seemed on the road to Hollywood stardom.   TFC

BARSACQ, ANDRÉ (1909–73)

French designer and director. Trained as a visual artist and architect, Barsacq began *painting *scenery for Charles *Dullin, for whom he would later design many productions. His designs for *opera and *ballet, including the first production of Stravinsky's *Perséphone* (1934) at the *Paris *Opéra, were also celebrated. Having been an occasional assistant to Jacques *Copeau, in 1936 he co-founded the Théâtre des Quatre Saisons with Jean *Dasté. He succeeded Dullin as director of the Théâtre de l'*Atelier in 1940, where he enjoyed a significant collaboration with Jean *Anouilh, directing his *Antigone* (1943) with celebrated modern-dress *costumes at the height of the Occupation. Barsacq directed for 30 more years after the war, continuing the tradition of *textual fidelity and scenic experimentation championed by the *Cartel des Quatre.   DGM

BART, LIONEL (1930–99)

English lyricist, playwright, and composer. Bart wrote lyrics for Bernard *Miles's production of *Lock up your Daughters* (1959), and in the same year he collaborated with Frank Norman on the *musical *Fings Ain't Wot They Used t' Be* (1959) for Joan *Littlewood's *Theatre Workshop. A story of small-time criminals in *London's Soho, it established a distinctively English version of the American musical genre, and ran for two years in the West End. Bart pursued the London underworld theme in his most popular work, *Oliver!* (1960), an adaptation of *Dickens's *Oliver Twist*, which had 2,618 performances in London and successfully transferred to *New York. *Blitz!* (1962), a wartime spectacular, and *Maggie May* (1964), the story of a Liverpool prostitute, were also successful, but *Twang!!* (1965), a parody of the Robin Hood story, was critically and commercially disastrous. His later work never recovered the popularity of *Fings* and *Oliver*. It included the short-lived *La Strada* (1969) and the retrospective *Lionel* (1977), and contributions to minor productions, *The Londoners* (1972) and *Costa Packet* (1972).   SF

BARTHÉLÉMY, MIMI (1939–)

Haitian storyteller, director, and writer, who has travelled widely and earned a doctorate in theatre in *Paris. She has issued recordings, published a dozen books, and created her own theatre company, Ti Moun Fou, in Paris. A respected actress, Barthélémy's performances combine singing and traditional Caribbean storytelling using her own creolized French and minimalist settings. *Une très belle mort* (*A Very Fine Death*, *Avignon, 2001), which included an artist improvising designs on stage with white sand, earned special acclaim. *See also* CARIBBEAN THEATRE, FRANCOPHONE.   CJM

BARTIS, RICARDO (c.1946?–)

Argentinian director, actor, and playwright. Already an experienced actor, Bartis made his directorial debut with a restaging of Eduardo *Pavlovsky's *Spiderwebs* in 1985. Closely identified with the post-dictatorship 'new theatre' movement, Bartis's productions (such as the 1988 hit *Argentine Postcards*) are characterized by their deforming of *realistic characters and anti-*naturalist *parodies. In 1992 he premièred a condensed *Hamlet; or, The War of the Theatres*. Outstanding among recent productions is *The Unnameable Sin*, an adaptation of two novels by Roberto *Arlt.   JGJ

BARTON, JOHN (1928–)

English director, one of the most influential interpreters of the classic repertory since he joined Peter *Hall's newly formed *Royal Shakespeare Company at Stratford in 1960. He initially edited playable *texts for the company and began revolutionizing the speaking of dramatic *verse, investigating always the *lived* moment (emotionally and socially) of the performed text. His principles are best demonstrated in his *Playing Shakespeare*, televised and published in 1982. Since *The Wars of the Roses* (1963–4) his many Shakespeare productions have shown a deep engagement with the politics of the plays, exploring the relationship between power and passion. But his work is notable too for its narrative clarity while allowing for psychological nuances of considerable complexity, especially evident in his staging of *Twelfth Night* (1969) and a production of *Richard II* (1971), where the device of actors alternating in the roles of Richard and Bolingbroke enhanced patterns of psychological discrimination. Since 1980 this complex of preoccupations has led to two attempts to stage cycles of plays depicting the Trojan War and its aftermath: the first, *The Greeks* (1979), largely used adapted texts from the *Greek tragedians; the second, *Tantalus* (2001), comprised ten plays of his own devising. Since staging *Pillars of the Community* (1977), Barton has directed key works by *Chekhov (*Three Sisters*), *Ibsen (*The Vikings at Helgeland* and *Peer Gynt* in Bergen and Oslo respectively), and *Strindberg (*Dream Play*), notable for their moral precision and the actor-centred simplicity of their staging, qualities evident too in his chamber production of Granville *Barker's *Waste* (1985).   RAC

BASOCHIENS

Society of Parisian law clerks devoted to comic performance. In 1442 the Basochiens entered into a cooperative arrangement with the *Confrérie de la Passion that continued to the end of the sixteenth century. The Enfants-sans-Souci, who performed in the traditional *costume of the *fool (*sot*), were probably a sub-group.   RWV

BASSERMANN, ALBERT (1867–1952)

German actor. Bassermann first attracted attention as a character actor at the *Meiningen Court Theatre in the early 1890s. In 1895 he settled in *Berlin where he performed successively under Otto *Brahm, Max *Reinhardt, and Leopold *Jessner. For Brahm's *realistic repertoire he played leading roles in plays by *Tolstoy, *Ibsen, and *Hauptmann. After joining Reinhardt he concentrated on the classical repertoire, giving outstanding performances as Shylock, Othello, and as Mephisto in *Goethe's *Faust*. The latter he played as a mixture of cavalier, fallen angel, and *clown. Between 1915 and 1919 he went on extended *tours, including the USA. After 1919 he joined Jessner at the Prussian Staatstheater, performing the title role in *William Tell*. An actor of exceptional range, Bassermann was considered the finest realistic performer of his generation who could distil the realistic essence out of classical as well as contemporary roles. In 1933 he emigrated to the United States with his Jewish wife. He returned to Germany in 1946 but continued to divide his time between that country and America. He died in a plane crash over the Atlantic.   CBB

BASSERMANN, AUGUST (1847–1931)

German actor and director and uncle of the famous actor Albert *Bassermann. After studying law in Berlin and Heidelberg, Bassermann embarked on an acting career that took him to Dresden, *Vienna, *Berlin and included *tours to Hamburg and *New York. In 1895 he was appointed director of the court theatre in Mannheim, which was followed in 1905 by the same position at the court theatre in Karlsruhe. In 1913 he was appointed superintendent of this theatre, a position he held to his retirement in 1916.   CBB

BASURA, TEATRO DE LA

'Garbage theatre', popular movement founded by Honduran schoolteacher Candelario Reyes in the 1980s in response to the political violence spawned by the Nicaraguan *contras* operating in Honduras. Taking its name from the Honduran playwright, poet, and journalist José María Tobias Rosa (1874–1933), whose pen name was Juan Basuro, and recognizing Honduras's position as a literal and figural garbage heap, Reyes created theatre out of the abundant primary materials that surrounded him. *Teatro de la basura* has points of contact with the work of Paulo Freire and Augusto *Boal, using theatre for the *audience's self-development.   AV

BATEMAN FAMILY

Hezekiah Bateman (1812–75), an American theatrical entrepreneur known in England as Colonel Bateman, took *London's *Lyceum Theatre in 1871; it was under his management that Henry *Irving first played in *The Bells* (1871). Bateman had four daughters who went on stage in their childhood. Kate (1842–1917) *toured America as a child with her younger sister Ellen (1844–1936), performing duets from Shakespeare. Ellen retired from the theatre after her marriage in 1860. Kate played several roles at the Lyceum, including Emilia and Lady Macbeth with Irving, and also acted with her sister Isabel (1854–1934), whom Colonel Bateman intended as Irving's leading lady. She did Ophelia to his 1874 Hamlet and Desdemona to his Othello. However, when Irving took over the Lyceum from Mrs Sidney Bateman (1823–81), he quickly hired Ellen *Terry as his leading lady. Isabel went to *Sadler's Wells under her mother's brief management. Virginia Bateman (1855–1940) also appeared at the Lyceum and then, after marrying Edward Compton, with the Compton Comedy Company.   MRB

BATES, ALAN (1934–   )

English actor, who made his *London mark in 1956 as Cliff in the première of *Osborne's *Look Back in Anger* at the *Royal Court. Four years later he was Mick in *Pinter's *The Caretaker*

(1960). Other stage work mixed modern with classical: Simon *Gray's *Butley* (1971), *Otherwise Engaged* (1975), and *Melon* (1987), Pinter's *One for the Road* (1984), *Chekhov's *Ivanov* (1989), and, for the *Royal Shakespeare Company, *The Taming of the Shrew* (1973) and *Antony and Cleopatra* (1999). His stage persona shifted away from youthful certainty and sexual assurance to angry physicality and, in his later career, to a raft of *characters weighted by suffering, anguish, and mourning, such as Fenchurch in David *Storey's *Stages* (1992) and Solness in *Ibsen's *The Master Builder* (1995). Bates has also had a distinguished *film career, appearing in *The Entertainer* (1960), *Whistle down the Wind* (1961), *A Kind of Loving* (1962), *Georgy Girl* (1966), *Far from the Madding Crowd* (1967), *Women in Love* (1968), and *The Go-Between* (1971). His *television work includes *The Mayor of Casterbridge* (BBC, 1978) and *An Englishman Abroad* (BBC, 1982), in which he played a frayed but ebullient Guy Burgess.   AS

BATH

The theatrical associations of this English city date back to *medieval and Elizabethan times. A theatre was first built in 1705, but was demolished in 1738 to make way for the General Hospital; the players then performed in an adapted room under a ballroom. Theatrical performances also occurred at the Globe Inn and at the New Theatre in Kingsmead Street. In 1750 John Palmer opened a new *playhouse in Orchard Street, which in 1768 became the first theatre outside *London to receive the royal *patent. Enhanced by Bath's fashionable status in the late eighteenth century, it also possessed a strong company, nurturing the careers of many actors including Sarah *Siddons. Visiting stars frequently appeared. From 1779 to 1817 the Bath Company also performed at the King Street Theatre in Bristol. A new theatre, designed by George Dance, was built in Beaufort Square, opening in 1805 (the Orchard Street theatre had closed the previous year). By the mid-nineteenth century, however, Bath's reputation as a fashionable resort was in decline, a fact reflected in decreasing attendance from 1820 to 1850. In 1862 the Beaufort Square Theatre was destroyed by fire, but was rebuilt the following year (the architect was C. J. Phipps), reopening with a production of *A Midsummer Night's Dream*. The theatre's fortunes remained in the ascendant for the remainder of the century, although in 1902 modifications were required prior to the patent's renewal. The early twentieth century saw a range of performances, including a visit by *Bernhardt (1911). From 1938 to 1978 the theatre was owned by the Maddox family, noted particularly for *pantomimes. From the 1950s to 1970s it struggled to survive, and in 1977 was purchased by a trust and registered as a charity. It reopened, supported by a consortium of local authorities, in 1982, with the Royal *National Theatre's production of *A Midsummer Night's Dream*.   JTD

BATY, GASTON (1885–1952)

French director and theorist. Baty studied art history in Germany, where he was greatly influenced by the productions of Fritz Erler. His own career began in 1919 in *Paris, working alongside Firmin *Gémier at the Cirque d'Hiver, where he was charged with *lighting the monumental production of *Oedipus, King of Thebes* and where he began to direct his own productions. At the same time he was comprehensively studying theatre history and developed a passion for *puppets. In 1926 he published a series of *theoretical articles, *Le Masque et l'encensoir* (*The Mask and the Censer*), presenting his early ideas about theatre aesthetics, including a controversial polemic against the hegemony of literature and the spoken *text in the theatre. His theoretical and historical writings, including the later testament *Rideau baissé* (*Curtain Down*, 1949), established him as the theoretician of the *Cartel des Quatre (he was the only member who was not an actor). From 1924 to 1928 he took the helm of the Studio des Champs-Élysées, where he produced many contemporary plays, worked to develop lighting as a key element of his *mise-en-scène, and began to champion a French *expressionism based on contemporary German theatre. From 1930 to 1947, Baty headed the Théâtre Montparnasse, where he nurtured the work of young playwrights, created groundbreaking adaptations of novels (for instance *Crime and Punishment*, 1933; *Madame Bovary*, 1936), and produced a wide range of classics, including a celebrated *historicist production of *Racine's *Phèdre* (1940) with Marguerite Jamois.   DGM

BAUER, WOLFGANG (1941–)

Austrian dramatist. After early experiments in the mid-1960s with *absurdist pieces Bauer first came to attention in 1968 with his short play *Magic Afternoon*, which was hailed as an early dramatization of pop culture and remains his most frequently performed work. To combat boredom two young couples indulge in alcohol, drugs, and finally violence. The *'realism' of the play manifests itself in the use of dialect (a feature of most of Bauer's work) but transcends mere slice of life mimeticism to thematicize wider issues of social values and subjectivity. The role of the impotent artist or writer is also a central theme in many works, reflecting Bauer's preoccupation with issues of creativity and self-determination. The author of over twenty plays and *film or *television scripts, Bauer's reputation still rests mainly on the 'pop' plays of the late 1960s, such as *Change* (1969) and *Party for Six* (1967).   CBB

BÄUERLE, ADOLF (OTTO HORN) (1786–1859)

Austrian dramatist. Bäuerle first worked as a theatre journalist—from 1806 to 1809 he was editor of the *Wiener Allgemeine Theaterzeitung*—before joining the management of the Leopoldstädter Theater where he remained until 1828. During this time he established himself as a major author in the tradition of *Viennese local *comedy. His greatest creation is the comic figure Chrysostomus Staberl, who made his first appearance in the patriotic play *Die Bürger in Wien* (1813) and advanced to the status of a *stock character in a series of 'Staberl' plays. The couplets in his comedies (composed by Wenzel Müller) became highly popular tunes. Bäuerle was the most important precursor of *Raimund and *Nestroy.   CBB

BAUERNFELD, EDUARD VON (1802–90)

Austrian dramatist. The author of *well-made plays in the French style with Viennese settings, Bauernfeld was playwright-in-residence at the *Burgtheater in the 1830s. Plays such as *Das Liebesprotokoll* (1831), *Das Tagebuch* (1836), and *Bürgerlich und Romantisch* (1835) are representative of a large output of works favouring witty conversation in upper-bourgeois circles. A supporter of liberal ideas, he became actively involved in politics during the Revolution of 1848, which forced him to give up his government job. In the 1870s he was granted an aristocratic title and made an honorary citizen of *Vienna.   CBB

BAUHAUS

German art school, founded by Walter *Gropius, originally situated in Weimar (1919–25), then active in Dessau (1925–32), where most of the theatre works were created. Due to right-wing pressure the school was forced to relocate to *Berlin (1932–3) and then emigrate to *Chicago. The first phase of the Bauhaus was strongly influenced by *expressionism; during the Dessau years a new *constructivist and technological orientation gave rise to the classic Bauhaus style. The principal aim of the institution was to overcome the division between arts and crafts and to bring different artistic disciplines under the umbrella of architecture. The theatre workshop offered a practical exploration of this philosophy and allowed artists from different backgrounds to collaborate in the exploration and composition of a 'total artwork of the stage'. Initially directed by Lothar Schreyer, and 1923–9 by Oskar *Schlemmer, the workshop investigated the organic and mechanical elements of theatre, the relationship between actor and space, the dynamics of movement, and the contributions made by *light, colour, and *sound. Schlemmer was particularly interested in stripping theatre down to its basic components to reassemble these according to a new 'ABC and grammar' of the stage. The result was a largely abstract form of theatre, presented in the school's studio, at exhibitions and conventions, and on *tour through Germany.   GB

BAUSCH, PINA (1940–)

German dancer, choreographer, and company director. From a young age, Bausch studied with two masters of expressive ballet: Kurt Jooss in Germany and Antony Tudor in *New York. She also studied modern *dance. Bausch succeeded Jooss as director of the Folkwang Ballet in 1969 and in 1973 founded the Wuppertal Tanztheater. Heir to the German *Ausdruckstanz* (expressive dance) movement of the 1920s and 1930s, she has developed a neo-*expressionist form of dance-theatre that often centres on issues of *gender, violence, and, more generally, human angst. Episodic and plotless, her dance-theatre pieces are emotionally intense. Her *mise-en-scène includes extravagant sets (a stage covered with water, a dirt mountain), *props (10,000 artificial carnations), practicables (a construction that turns two dancers into a hippopotamus) and *costumes (at times, *cross-dressing); *animal performers (sheep, fish, dogs); spoken *text (in direct address to the *audience or voiceover); both popular and classical recorded music; *film projections; and dancing that is extremely high energy and virtuosic, though not following the specialized technique of any dance *genre. SB

BAX, CLIFFORD (1886–1962)

English playwright and poet. Bax specialized in sub-*Shavian *historical drama in the vein of Gordon Daviot's *Richard of Bordeaux*. His most successful play was *A Rose without a Thorn* (1932) about the marital tribulations of Catherine Howard and Henry VIII. Similar plays include *Mr Pepys* (1926) and *The King and Mistress Shore* (1936). Bax's forays into other *genres were less successful, although he did adapt Čapek's *The Insect Play* with Nigel *Playfair in 1926. Later in life Bax was a supporter of the *national theatre movement. MDG

BAXTER, JAMES K. (1926–72)

New Zealand poet, dramatist, and literary critic who established his reputation as a poet in the 1940s. His first dramatic work was the *radio play *Jack Winter's Dream* (1958), adapted for the stage in 1960. His twenty subsequent plays were non-*realist dramas that frequently explored autobiographical interests and troubled psychological states, mingling classical themes, *folk ballad influences, and contemporary New Zealand settings. The most notable were *The Wide Open Cage* (1959), *The Spots of the Leopard* (1962), *The Day That Flanagan Died* (1967), and *The Devil and Mr Mulcahy* (1967). SF

BAY, HOWARD (1912–86)

American designer. Bay first came to wide public attention with his innovative designs for the Experimental Wing of the *New York branch of the *Federal Theatre Project. For the public school exposé *Chalk Dust* (1936), Bay designed a gigantic, moving chalkboard, and for *One Third of a Nation* (1938), a *naturalistic tenement, 21m (70 feet) high, capable of burning, partial collapse, and then instant repair. An eclectic designer who worked in styles ranging from flown *painterly *scenery to *environmental staging, Bay's later career included many *long-running Broadway *musicals: *Finian's Rainbow* (1947), *The Music Man* (1957), and *Man of La Mancha* (1965). MAF

BAYLIS, LILIAN (1874–1937)

English *manager and entrepreneur, awarded Companion of Honour in 1929. Trained as a violinist in *London, in 1897 she agreed to assist her aunt Emma Cons, a social reformer who had renovated the Royal Victoria Theatre (later the *Old Vic) as a temperance hall which provided *musical and *variety entertainment. When Cons died in 1912, Baylis took over management, expanding the *opera programme and adding plays and silent *films. She was determined to make the arts accessible to working men and women. To this end, she coaxed donations out of individuals, businesses, charities, and foundations throughout her professional life. Between 1914 and 1923 she presented all of the Shakespeare plays in the First Folio, and also *Pericles*. Among the performers were Sybil and Russell *Thorndike and Robert *Atkins; Ben *Greet directed during the first few years; after the war Atkins returned as actor and director. In the 1920s she added *ballet to her ambitious programme. In 1925 she purchased *Sadler's Wells Theatre, which reopened in 1931 after major renovation. For a few years ballet, opera, and drama were performed in both *playhouses, but soon Sadler's Wells became the home of ballet, featuring the choreography of Ninette de Valois and Frederick Ashton. An ambitious opera programme was also established there, with 50 productions between 1931 and 1937. The Old Vic became the home of drama, under the directorship of Harcourt *Williams (1929–33) and Tyrone *Guthrie (1933–6, 1939–45). Throughout her professional career Baylis struggled with *finance, yet bolstered by religious faith, love of the arts, and fierce willpower, she created the model and rationale for what became the three *national theatres with royal charters: the English National Opera (1956), Royal Ballet (1956), and (Royal) *National Theatre (1963). TP

BAYREUTH FESTIVAL

An annual *festival, founded by Richard *Wagner for the model performance of his own works and other German *operas. It is held in the Festspielhaus (Festival Theatre), on a hill in the suburbs of Bayreuth in northern Bavaria, which opened in 1876 with the first performance of *The Rhinegold*. The theatre is noted for its near-perfect sight lines and acoustics. The *auditorium is wedge shaped so that most *audience members, even those sitting far back, have a clear view of the stage. Because of the size of the Wagnerian orchestra, the orchestra pit is sunken, which has the effect of homogenizing the sound. The double *proscenium is repeated in the architectural abutments that frame the auditorium which creates the *illusion, unique in *playhouse design, that the audience occupies the same space as the singer-actors on the proscenium stage. Wagner intended to equip the stage with the latest technology in *lighting and *scenography. Over the years, his successors have remained true to his intentions and the Bayreuth Festival Theatre is still one of the best-equipped opera houses in Germany today.

The annual festival was held regularly only after Wagner's death, under the direction of his widow Cosima (1838–1930), who limited the repertoire solely to her husband's ten mature music dramas, a restriction that still applies. Bayreuth has acquired a reputation for conservatism, but this is deceptive. It is devoted to preserving Wagner's work, but does so using the most current theatre styles. *Expressionism was introduced under the direction of the composer's son Siegfried (1869–1930). From 1951 on, under the direction of Wagner's grandsons Wolfgang (b. 1919) and Wieland *Wagner, Bayreuth has led the way in innovative design and staging. The Wagner brothers were the first to apply the principles of Adolphe *Appia to all the music dramas. Since then, many leading directors of the German and European theatre have directed at Bayreuth, including Patrice *Chéreau, Dieter *Dorn, Götz Friedrich, Peter *Hall, Werner Herzog, Harry *Kupfer, and Heiner *Müller. Each production is reworked, even redesigned, whenever it is revived.

From the start Bayreuth attracted an international audience and so served as a model for other festivals, such as the *Shakespeare Memorial Theatre in Stratford, *Salzburg, and Glyndebourne, though Bayreuth's reputation suffered immense damage when it became associated with Adolf Hitler. Since then, due primarily to the efforts of Wieland and Wolfgang, the Festival has been restored to its position as one of the prime events in the European opera calendar. SJCW

BEALE, SIMON RUSSELL (1961–)

Penang-born English actor who was a chorister at St Paul's Cathedral and was educated at Cambridge. For the *Royal Shakespeare Company his roles include Oliver in Nick *Dear's The Art of Success (1986), the title role in *Marlowe's Edward II (1991), Konstantin in *Chekhov's The Seagull (directed by Terry *Hands, 1990), the title role in Sam *Mendes's production of Richard III (1992), Ariel in the same director's The Tempest (1993), and Edgar in Adrian *Noble's King Lear (1994). He was hugely successful as the narrator Voltaire and Dr Pangloss in John *Caird's revival of Candide for the Royal *National Theatre (1999). In 2000 he played Hamlet in Caird's production and in 2001 the

stuttering astrophysicist Felix Humble in Charlotte Jones's Humble Boy. He has had relatively few *film roles but was an effective Second Gravedigger in *Branagh's Hamlet (1996), while for *television he was a gentle Charles Musgrove in Persuasion (1995) and a monstrous Widmerpool in A Dance to the Music of Time (1997). AS

BEAR-BAITING See BAITING.

BEATON, CECIL (1904–80)

English designer, photographer, and painter; educated at Harrow and Cambridge University; knighted in 1972. Beaton is equally famous for the wit of his high-society photographs and the grandeur of his *scenery and *costumes for theatre and *ballet. From the 1930s to 1960s he created stylish designs, mainly in *London but also *New York. Best known for the costumes for My Fair Lady (New York, 1956; London, 1958), he also provided set and costume designs for a wide range of productions, from John *Gielgud's revival of Lady Windermere's Fan (1946) to the *musical Coco (1969). He won two Academy awards for production design for the *films Gigi (1958) and My Fair Lady (1964). He also published several volumes of gossipy diaries and an autobiography. TP

BEATTY, JOHN LEE (1948–)

American designer. Beginning *Off-Broadway in the 1970s with the *Circle Repertory Theatre, the *Manhattan Theatre Club, and the *New York Public Theatre, Beatty moved to Broadway as their productions transferred, and has since designed over 53 Broadway productions. His *scenery, usually *realistic and highly detailed, like that for David Auburn's Proof (2000), has a subtle lyricism, though his designs for *musicals are more fanciful. He has done a number of what he calls 'American porch plays', including those of Lanford *Wilson (Tony *award for design for Talley's Folley, 1979) and Beth *Henley (Crimes of the Heart, 1980). Other memorable work includes the musical Ain't Misbehavin' (1978), a revival of Robert *Anderson's Abe Lincoln in Illinois (1993) and Athol *Fugard's The Road to Mecca (Washington, 1990). GAO

BEAUBOUR, PIERRE TROCHON DE (1662–1725)

French actor. Beaubour joined the *Comédie-Française in 1692, replacing *Baron who had retired at the peak of his fame. He played leading roles in works by *Regnard and *Crébillon and was sometimes accused of exaggerated declamation, but enjoyed public support, perhaps because there was no obvious alternative. He retired in 1718 and died seven years later, having been able to observe Baron's triumphant return to the stage in 1720.   JC

BEAUMARCHAIS, PIERRE-AUGUSTIN CARON DE (1732–99)

French playwright. One of the most conspicuous and controversial public figures of his generation, Beaumarchais is best known for his first two Figaro plays, which were soon to reach an even wider public through the *operas of *Mozart and Rossini. However, his career as dramatist began with a series of *parades—short, spicy sketches written for private performance—and in the very different *genre of sentimental domestic drama in which he followed *Diderot's example with *Eugénie* (1767, published with an important theoretical essay) and *Les Deux amis* (1770). The first Figaro play, *Le Barbier de Séville* (*The Barber of Seville*), owes an obvious debt to the author's own *parade Jean-Bête à la Foire*; in his preface he claims to be bringing *laughter back to the French theatre after decades of sentimental and serious *comedy (*see* COMÉDIE LARMOYANTE). *The Barber* was a great success in *Paris at the *Comédie-Française in 1775 with some rewriting after the first night; but *Le Mariage de Figaro* (*The Marriage of Figaro*) was performed in 1784 only after battles with a series of censors extending over several years, and in the face of royal opposition (*see* CENSORSHIP). Advance publicity in the form of readings and private performance led to a wildly successful opening night at the Comédie-Française, quite the most notorious première of the century, which was followed by a record run of over 70 performances. *Parodies abounded, a sure indication of popular success.

While the class-based conflict between Figaro and Almaviva was largely responsible for the success, the disadvantage of hindsight has led many modern biographers and critics, misrepresenting the play's subversive *character, to see Figaro as the herald of the forthcoming revolution. Though a lifelong critic of social abuses, Beaumarchais was no revolutionary: he was a self-made nobleman, and was to suffer exile and loss of civil rights during the revolution. Moreover, *The Marriage of Figaro* was subtitled *La Folle Journée*; and despite the serious issues symbolized by the 'droit du seigneur', the play contains much of the inconsequential, if irreverent, comedy of *The Barber*. Beaumarchais's penultimate work, the libretto for Salieri's opera *Tarare* (performed at the *Opéra in 1787), expresses in a much more indirect way—quite apart from the distancing produced by the operatic medium, the piece is set in an imaginary Eastern country ruled by a tyrant—his commitment to the reform of abuses by constitutional means. Finally, the third play of the Figaro trilogy, *La Mère coupable*, was performed at the *Marais Theatre in 1792, after the return from exile of an older and more disillusioned Beaumarchais. This play reverts to the manner of his early *drames bourgeois*, but it bears the Manichaean imprint of *fin de siècle* *melodrama; while Almaviva could be pardoned in the euphoric finale of *The Marriage*, the *villain Bégearss (based on the lawyer Bergasse with whom Beaumarchais had crossed swords much earlier) must be driven out of any decent society. Figaro, now middle-aged and sententious, does some smart detective work, and achieves this result. A revival at the Comédie-Française in 1797 brought Beaumarchais the final triumph of an onstage reception in front of an enthusiastic *audience.   WDH

HOWARTH, W. D., *Beaumarchais and the Theatre* (London, 1995)

BEAUMONT, FRANCIS (c.1584–1616)

English dramatist. He was the son of a Leicester judge, and, after his education at Broadgates Hall, Oxford, entered the Inner Temple in 1600. He is best known for his collaboration with John *Fletcher: the appearance of a Folio collection of their work in 1647 made the 'Beaumont-and-Fletcher' brand a cultural fixture, even though Beaumont had a hand in no more than ten plays (compared with more than 50 by Fletcher). However, the evidence of revival and publication through the seventeenth century shows that the Beaumont–Fletcher collaborations were always considered the core of the canon.

Already an established poet in *Inns of Court circles, Beaumont began his playwriting career as the solo author of two sharp, satirical *comedies for the *London *boy companies, which show a keen interest in the theatre and a disengagement from downmarket taste: *The Woman Hater* (1606) contains a *parody of Shakespeare's *Hamlet*, and *The Knight of the Burning Pestle* (1607) comprehensively spoofs plebeian preferences when members of the *audience take over the performance and replace the billed play with their own choice (*see* ROMANCE). The first performance of *The Knight* was not a success, but the play was better regarded later in the seventeenth century.

The partnership with Fletcher began in 1609, and produced a run of plays, mainly for the King's Men (*see* CHAMBERLAIN'S MEN, LORD), of which *The Maid's Tragedy* (1611) and the *tragicomedies *Philaster* (1609) and *A King and No King* (1611) are the most significant. The plays are noted for their romantic tone, remote settings, and strong emotional scenes, but also for a politically astute interest in the limits on the power of absolute monarchy, which is often credited to Beaumont (but is also apparent in Fletcher's solo *tragedies). Beaumont was the senior collaborator, and the one responsible for casting the plays into their final form. Their last work together was *The Scornful Lady* (1613), a comedy that kept up its popularity into the eighteenth century but has rarely appeared since. Earlier in 1613 he had scripted the *masque which the Inner Temple and Gray's Inn contributed to Princess Elizabeth's wedding festivities, but thereafter he gave up writing for the theatre, possibly as a result of his marriage to the heiress Ursula Isley.

In the seventeenth century, the Beaumont-and-Fletcher plays appealed primarily to courtly and gentry playgoers, partly because the characters are gentlemen and courtiers, but also because the plays' self-conscious artistry appeals to audiences with a sense of their own cultivation: operating through controlled anticlimax, the *plotting emphasizes the virtuosity of the dramatists as part of the *spectacle. *The Maid's Tragedy* proved Beaumont's most durable stage work: though possibly banned in the 1680s during the Exclusion Crisis, it was frequently revived until the 1740s, latterly with music by Henry Purcell; it also saw through the Victorian era in an adaptation, *The Bridal*, designed as a vehicle for W. C. *Macready. In the twentieth century both it and *The Knight of the Burning Pestle* received intermittent professional productions.   MJW

BEAUMONT, HUGH (HUGHES GRIFFITH MORGAN) (1908–73)

Welsh *producer, who worked for H. M. Tennent management company from 1936 and succeeded Harry Tennent as managing director in 1941. 'Binkie' Beaumont dominated *London theatre for twenty years, famous for lavish productions, star casts, and glamorous settings. But he also produced serious work, including *Priestley's *They Came to a City* (1943), *Rattigan's *The Deep Blue Sea* (1952), and John *Whiting's *Marching Song* (1954), knowing precisely how far to test the limits of middle-class taste. One of his shrewdest moves was to exploit a loophole that exempted 'partly educational' productions from the entertainment tax, by setting up a non-profit subsidiary for classics and new work, including the British première of *Williams's *A Streetcar Named Desire* in 1949. Allegations of a 'gay mafia' dogged Beaumont's reputation. They were unfounded, though his creation of a theatre club in 1956 to present banned American plays on the topic contributed to the abolition of *censorship. Beaumont's empire went into decline in the late 1950s due to a combination of rising *television ownership and the revolutions of the 'angry young men', though he remained on the board of the *National Theatre throughout the 1960s.
                                                                      DR

BECK, JULIAN (1925–85)

American designer, director, actor, and activist. Born in *New York and educated at Yale University, he began his artistic life as a painter in the abstract expressionist school and exhibited at the Peggy Guggenheim gallery. In 1947 he founded the *Living Theatre with his wife Judith *Malina. Under their *artistic direction the company was instrumental in the development of *Off-Broadway in the 1950s, promoting new American and European drama. In the 1960s and 1970s Beck's work combined a radical politics of anarchism and pacifism with processes of *collective creation. He performed in and designed the *scenery for the Living Theatre productions of *Mysteries and Smaller Pieces* (1964), *Frankenstein* (1965), *Antigone* (1967), and *Paradise Now* (1968), which were presented throughout Europe and the USA. His theoretical and biographical text *The Life of the Theatre* (1972) sets forth his political and aesthetic concerns, which he viewed as symbiotic. In the later years of his life, while suffering from cancer, Beck played in several Hollywood feature *films such as *Poltergeist II: The Other Side* (1986) and *The Cotton Club* (1984) and *television series such as *Miami Vice* (1984).
                                                                      MDC

BECKETT, SAMUEL (1906–89)

Irish writer. One of the major innovators of *modernist drama and fiction, Beckett's work also includes poetry and essays on art and literature. Born on Good Friday 13 April into a middle-class Protestant family on the outskirts of *Dublin, Beckett attended Trinity College, Dublin, and taught English at the École Normale Supérieure in *Paris (1928–30), where he first met James Joyce. Returning to Dublin, he taught briefly at Trinity, lived in *London, and eventually settled in Paris in 1937. During the Second World War he was involved in the French Resistance; when their cell was infiltrated, he and his future wife fled Paris for Roussillon in southern France, where they stayed until the Liberation. His return to Paris initiated a particularly creative period during which he wrote in French a trilogy of novels, *Molloy*, *Malone meurt* (*Malone Dies*), *L'Innommable* (*The Unnamable*), and two plays, *Eleuthéria*, begun in 1947, and *En attendant Godot* (*Waiting for Godot*), begun in 1948. Both plays were submitted to the actor and director Roger *Blin in Paris, who chose to produce *Godot*, partly because it had a smaller cast and simpler set. It opened at the Théâtre de Babylone in Montparnasse in January 1953. With these early works Beckett began the practice of translating his own work from French to English (and in reverse when he wrote originally in English).

Between *Eleuthéria* (published in 1995, though performing rights are still unavailable) and *Godot* Beckett developed a radically innovative *dramaturgy, linked thematically to the theatre of the *absurd, and focusing on a formally conceived visual image and a tight, non-linear rhythmic structure. *Waiting for Godot* re-creates on stage the experience of waiting, using *comedy, *metatheatrical commentary, and popular entertainment references to present theatre and life as passing time, diversionary tactics to keep the void at bay. The bare stage, apart from tree and mound, foregrounds the shifting relationships of power and dependency between the tramps Vladimir and Estragon, the landowner Pozzo and his servant Lucky, the mysterious Boy, and the eponymous Godot who fails to appear. The work initially baffled and scandalized *audiences and critics but became one of the most critically acclaimed

Billie Whitelaw as Mouth in the première production of Samuel **Beckett**'s *Not I*, Royal Court Theatre, London, 1973. An example of the punishing demands Beckett often made on actors, this production required that Whitelaw be strapped into an elevated chair and encased almost entirely in black drapes, so that only her mouth would be visible in the fixed spotlight.

plays of the twentieth century and undoubtedly Beckett's best-known work. After *Waiting for Godot* opened in London (directed by Peter *Hall, 1955), Kenneth *Tynan remarked: 'It forced me to re-examine the rules which have hitherto governed the drama; and, having done so, to pronounce them not elastic enough.'

Fin de partie (*Endgame*) was performed in London at the invitation of the *Royal Court Theatre in 1957, directed by Blin. Alan *Schneider directed the English-language première in *New York in 1958. Like the terminal chess moves its title refers to, *Endgame* presents the last stages of the relationship between the *protagonist and storyteller Hamm, his factotum and son substitute Clov, and Hamm's parents Nagg and Nell who, having lost their shanks, are kept in ash cans. Conceived, like *Godot*, within a decade of the Second World War, and set in a shelter after some devastation has apparently destroyed all life beyond its walls, *Endgame* embodies the anxieties of its era: it presents a history and a language in ruins, and yet the performance of

daily life and the consciousness of the performance called life continue until the last moment.

The next two plays were written first in English. *Krapp's Last Tape* (1958) shows an old man on his 69th birthday listening to the voice of his past selves in a series of tape recordings made on previous birthdays; *Happy Days* (1962) features Beckett's first leading female *character, Winnie, buried up to her waist in a mound of earth. Since the visual image and rhythmic structure of his work are as important as the spoken text, from 1966 to 1984 Beckett directed productions of his plays in London, Paris, and *Berlin in order to supervise in precise detail the *mise-en-scène and the actors.

Beckett also relied on a handful of directors who worked with or consulted him, including Blin, Schneider, Donald McWhinnie and George *Devine in England, Pierre Chabert in France, and Antoni Libera in Poland. He was assisted in Germany on various productions for stage and *television by the director Walter Asmus, particularly on the renowned 1975

*Schiller Theater production of *Godot*. In his *rehearsal diary, Asmus reported that Beckett wanted to 'give confusion a shape through visual repetition of themes. Not only themes in the *dialogue, but also visual themes of the body.' Beckett's production notebook describes the patterns of the characters' movements, forming a series of arcs and incomplete circles. Beckett also worked regularly with particular actors, including Jack *MacGowran, Patrick Magee, Billie *Whitelaw, and David Warrilow. Although often flexible in relation to particular directors or companies whose work he admired, Beckett objected to certain productions of his plays which departed from his *stage directions, including the 1984 production of *Endgame* for the *American Repertory Theatre which the director JoAnne *Akalaitis set in an abandoned subway station (*see also* COPYRIGHT; DIRECTING). In 1991 Dublin's *Gate Theatre, under the leadership of Michael Colgan, produced all nineteen of Beckett's stage plays in a festival which *toured to New York (1996) and London (1999).

Beckett's stage works from *Play* (1963) onwards are shorter and meticulously structured. Most of them open in darkness, against which an image emerges, defined by light. The visual focus is almost entirely on the body or body fragments, such as the three heads above urns in *Play* or the suspended Mouth spewing words uncontrollably while observed by a silent, cloaked Auditor in *Not I* (1972). There is little *action, as the drama is interiorized, becoming the scene of a fragmented consciousness struggling with the detritus of body, language, memory, and history: the legacies of post-Cartesian structures of subjectivity and authority. These late plays, including *Come and Go* (1966), *Footfalls* (1976), *Rockaby* (1981), *Ohio Impromptu* (1981), and *Catastrophe* (1982), focus intently on modes of perception, on the efforts to see, hear, and comprehend on the part of *character and audience.

Beckett wrote and was involved in the production of drama for other *media as well. His experiments with the possibilities of sound and camera came at an influential time in the development of his own aesthetic and that of each medium. Between 1957 and 1972 he wrote six *radio plays: *All That Fall*, *Embers*, *Cascando*, *Words and Music*, *Rough for Radio I and II*. Following his one generically titled *Film* (directed by Schneider, 1964)—which uses the camera's eye as agent of self-perception pursuing the fleeing figure of Buster Keaton—Beckett turned to television, investigating the possibilities of space, structure, and the role of the camera in the BBC productions *Eh Joe* (1966), *Ghost Trio*, and *. . . but the clouds . . .* (1977); and the German productions of *Quad I and II* (1981) and *Nacht und Traüme* (1983). He adapted his last stage play, *Quoi ou* (*What Where*, 1983), for German TV in 1985.

Beckett won the Nobel Prize for Literature in 1969. Sometimes described as spanning the aesthetics of European modernism and postmodernism, he rigorously revised the materials and structures of both traditional and new media

in the Sisyphean task of telling, as he put it in a title, 'how it is'.

AEM

KNOWLSON, JAMES, *Damned to Fame: the life of Samuel Beckett* (London, 1996)
—— (ed.), *The Director's Notebooks of Samuel Beckett*, 4 vols. (London, 1992–9)
MCMILLAN, DOUGALD, and FEHSENFELD, MARTHA, *Beckett in the Theatre* (London, 1988)

BECQUE, HENRI (1837–99)

French dramatist who was championed by *Zola. Becque fell between two *dramaturgical movements, the *realism of the *well-made play and slice of life *naturalism. His life was characterized by money worries, a theme which runs through his brief output, which presents a rapacious and amoral picture of middle-class French society. His early play *Michel Pauper* (1870) revealed him as a committed socialist, while *La Navette* (1878) depicted a woman with three lovers, a foretaste of one of his greatest successes, *La Parisienne*. The first of his 'rough' or bitter plays (*comédies rosses*), *Les Corbeaux* (*Comédie-Française, 1882), made his name. The work paints a picture of an idyllic middle-class family whose father dies at the end of the first act, prompting the gradual erosion of the family's wealth and self-respect by the crow-creditors of the title, who were once friends. A harsh and cynical drama of money and class, the *denouement occurs only when a daughter, in a morally ambiguous self-sacrifice, agrees to marry one of the crows. Where *Augier might have recommended thrift and probity for this family, Becque crushes moral and spiritual values and lets greed win the day.

La Parisienne, first performed in 1885 with *Réjane in the leading role of Clotilde, shows a Parisian woman's web of relationships with her husband and two lovers. Her husband is a man of reason, while her first lover is Clotilde's 'husband of the heart'. But her second lover complicates matters greatly, as he makes her first lover jealous and her actual husband professionally successful. Becque presents a woman's sexual life as an economic instrument based on laws of ownership and return on investment. *La Parisienne* entered the repertoire of the Comédie-Française in 1890. It was followed only by a series of sketches, an unfinished work entitled *Les Polichinelles*, and the publication of Becque's memoirs in 1895. He lived out his life on a meagre pension from the *Society of Dramatic Authors.

BRS

BEDFORD, BRIAN (1935–)

English actor and director. After study at the *Royal Academy of Dramatic Art, he arrived in *New York in 1959 with John *Gielgud's production of *Five Finger Exercise* by Peter *Shaffer. Bedford stayed to pursue a sixteen-year career as a Broadway actor. American honours include Tony, Obie, New York Drama Desk, and LA Drama Critics *awards. Persuaded by Robin *Phillips to join the *Stratford Festival company in Canada in 1975, Bedford's long-term association with Stratford has been an important catalyst to his development as a classical actor. An intelligent, charismatic performer with a mellifluous voice, his best work shows a sharp grasp of the comic or ridiculous while communicating a deeper sense of the irrational drives, passions, and pain beneath. Notable roles include Angelo (*Measure for Measure*), Benedick (*Much Ado About Nothing*), the title parts in *Timon of Athens*, *Molière's *Tartuffe* and *The Misanthrope*, and Elyot (Noël *Coward's *Private Lives*) opposite Maggie *Smith and Siobhán *McKenna.   MJD

BEDOYO

A Javanese court *dance from Yogyakarta and Surakarta in *Indonesia performed by nine female dancers. Though *bedoyo* tells a story, the dancers do not have *character roles or recite *dialogue and all dress alike in a trailing batik skirt that confines the body from waist to ankle. *Bedoyo* conveys qualities of patience, calm, and harmony. A sacred version, *bedoyo ketawang*, created during the reign of Sultan Agung of Mataram (1613–45), is still performed once a year to commemorate the anniversary of the Surakarta ruler's accession to the throne. New *bedoyos* continue to be created in a secular theatrical context.   SM

BEERBOHM, MAX (1872–1956)

English critic, author, and cartoonist, knighted in 1939. After *touring as private secretary to his half-brother, the *actor-manager Herbert Beerbohm *Tree, Beerbohm succeeded George Bernard *Shaw as drama critic for the *Saturday Review* in 1898. An associate of aesthetes such as Oscar *Wilde and Aubrey Beardsley, Beerbohm had none of Shaw's polemical purpose, and his reviews displayed a witty, dandyish poise. His subjects were wide ranging and included discussions of *music hall as well as theatrical performances. He left the post in 1910 to live in Italy, where he remained for the rest of his life, except during wartime, and wrote the satirical novel *Zuleika Dobson* (1911). A selection of his *criticism was published as *Around Theatres* (1924). Beerbohm's dramatic work included the *one-act play *The Happy Hypocrite* (1900). From 1935 he made occasional *radio broadcasts for the BBC, often on his memories of Victorian and Edwardian theatre.   SF

BEESTON, CHRISTOPHER (c.1580–1639)

English actor and *manager. Beeston began his career as an actor, appearing with the Lord *Chamberlain's Men in *Jonson's *Every Man in his Humour* (1598). Between 1603 and 1619 he was an actor and sometime business manager of Queen Anne's Men

at the *Rose. In 1617 he built the Phoenix Playhouse (*see* COCKPIT THEATRE), where he housed a series of companies: Queen Anne's (1617–19), Prince Charles's (1619–22), Lady Elizabeth's (1622–5), Queen Henrietta's (1625–37), and the King and Queen's Young Company or Beeston's Boys (1637–42). He was succeeded at his death by his son William *Beeston.

RWV

BEESTON, WILLIAM (c.1606–82)

English *manager. The son of Christopher *Beeston, he probably acted in his father's companies before succeeding him at the head of 'Beeston's Boys' (1638). He was imprisoned in 1640 for staging an unlicensed play with political undertones. Removed from his position, he was succeeded by *Davenant, but was reinstated soon afterwards. During the Protectorate he maintained an active interest in the theatre, restoring the *Phoenix and purchasing the *Salisbury Court, but failed to succeed after the Restoration. A renowned dramatic coach, he was noted for his ability in *training *boy actors.   PCR

BEHAN, BRENDAN (1923–64)

Irish playwright and autobiographer. From a strongly Irish Republican background, he was imprisoned for political offences as a teenager in Britain, an experience recorded in his highly successful memoir *Borstal Boy* (1958), and later in Ireland, where he began to write both in English and in Irish. His first play *The Quare Fellow*, produced by the tiny *Pike Theatre in *Dublin in 1954, after it had been rejected by the *Abbey, shows a day in the life of a prison on the eve of an execution— the condemned man is the non-appearing 'quare fellow' of the title. The freshness of the writing, the unfamiliarity of the subject, and the fierceness of the play's attack on capital punishment made it sufficiently successful to attract the attention of Joan *Littlewood, who staged it with her *Theatre Workshop (*London, 1956). This highly acclaimed production, coming in the same year as *Osborne's *Look Back in Anger*, placed Behan as part of a new political wave in British theatre. Littlewood's 1958 production of his other major play, *The Hostage*, a translated adaptation of the original Irish-language version *An Giall*, brought Behan an international reputation. Controversy has surrounded this *text as to how far it was Behan's own work, how far the product of the Theatre Workshop's *Brechtian house style of ensemble *improvisation. Behan's later years were given over to drunken self-publicizing, and he never completed his last play, *Richard's Cork Leg*.   NG

BEHN, APHRA (1640–89)

English playwright and novelist. Reputed to be the first woman to earn a living by her pen, Aphra Behn has been the subject of several biographies in the twentieth century although details about her origins and life are notoriously unreliable. She was a prolific playwright with at least nineteen plays produced during her lifetime and two more produced posthumously. The first, *The Forc'd Marriage* (1670), was performed by William *Davenant's Duke's Company, which was then under the *management of his widow, Lady (Dame) Mary Davenant. The same company produced sixteen of Behn's plays before uniting with their rivals in 1682. Behn's most popular *comedy, *The Rover* (1677), was frequently revived, with Elizabeth *Barry playing the spirited Hellena, a young woman determined to fulfil her own social and sexual destiny. Behn wrote at least seven leading female *characters for Barry, all of which challenge patriarchal authority, particularly in the realm of love and marriage. Behn was frequently accused of immorality, a charge she defended in her preface to *The Lucky Chance* (1686), vehemently insisting on her rights as a writing woman. The topicality of her plays and her royalist politics attracted fierce criticism but she continued to be commercially successful. Feminist criticism has done much to restore Behn's work: Jules Wright's production of *The Lucky Chance* for the Women's Playhouse Trust was produced at the *Royal Court in 1981 and John *Barton's production of *The Rover* for the Royal Shakespeare Company (*Swan Theatre, 1986) was the first of many revivals of Behn's most successful comedy.

GBB

BEHRMAN, S. N. (SAMUEL NATHANIEL) (1893–1973)

American playwright. From the *Theatre Guild's production of *The Second Man* in 1927 until his last play, *But for Whom Charlie* in 1964, Behrman held a place as the author of serious, humane, and sophisticated *New York *comedies. The author of twenty-six plays or adaptations and one *musical (*Fanny*, with Harold Rome, 1954), Behrman was highly esteemed by critics of his era. Despite his long success on Broadway, Behrman was quickly forgotten during the social and theatrical upheaval of the 1960s. His greatest productivity was in the 1930s, when he faced a special challenge writing social comedy in an era of world economic depression and preparations for war. The east coast drawing rooms and gardens in which his plays took place became, in the words of critic Joseph Wood Krutch, 'realistic substitutes for a spot of enchanted ground upon which deadly enemies can meet'. Major plays of the period revolve around a charming and witty woman contested for by pompous businessmen, fascist sympathizers, idealistic Marxists, and cynical aesthetes. Behrman's plays include *Biography* (1932), *Rain from Heaven* (1934), *End of Summer* (1936), and *No Time for Comedy* (1939). He was a founder of the Playwrights Company in 1938.

MAF

BEIER, KARIN (1965–)

German director. Beier began directing while still a student at the University of Cologne, where she founded the group Countercheck Quarrelsome (CCQ) in 1986. In a short period the group produced radically modernized versions of some nine Shakespeare plays in English. In 1990 she was appointed assistant director at the Düsseldorf Schauspielhaus. Her breakthrough came in 1993 with a production of *Romeo and Juliet* which was invited to the *Berlin *Theatertreffen. Beier's most renowned production is *A Midsummer Night's Dream* (1995) which she directed at Düsseldorf with actors from nine different European countries, all speaking their own languages. Designed to demonstrate both Shakespeare as a 'European' author and the possibility of multilingual theatre, it was followed in 1997 by a similarly multilingual version of *The Tempest* in Cologne. Although best known as a director of Shakespeare, Beier has directed a wide range of plays in both the classical and modern repertoire, including Bizet's *Carmen*.

CBB

BEIJING OPERA *See* JINGJU.

BÉJART FAMILY

Seventeenth-century French actors. This theatre *family of three sisters and two brothers was inextricably linked with the career of *Molière. **Madeleine** (1618–72) was the guiding spirit of the ragtag Parisian troupe that willed itself into existence in 1643 under the name L'Illustre Théâtre; Jean-Baptiste Poquelin, not yet known as Molière, four years her junior and her presumed lover, was one of three actors who rotated the assignment of the *hero, while Madeleine had the contractual right to play any role she chose. She was by all accounts a powerful actress, a talented writer, a free spirit, and a shrewd businesswoman, and after the troupe failed in *Paris she held it together through a thirteen-year exile in the provinces. By the time they returned to the capital her age was beginning to limit the range of roles in which the metropolitan *audience would accept her; still, Molière wrote for her such formidable *characters as Dorine in *Tartuffe* and Uranie in *The Critique of the School for Wives*, and he may well have intended Philaminte in *The Learned Ladies* for her. She died before that play opened, one year to the day before Molière's death.

Madeleine's brother **Joseph** (1616–59) and sister **Geneviève** (1624–75) were also founding members of the troupe, while **Louis** (1630–78) joined it during the provincial years. Joseph played romantic leads, despite his stammer; he died a few months after the troupe returned to Paris, and *La Grange took over his roles. Louis's best feature was his pronounced limp, which was copied by actors playing roles he created and which made him a memorable Mme Pernelle in *Tartuffe*. He retired in 1670 to pursue a military career. Geneviève, acting

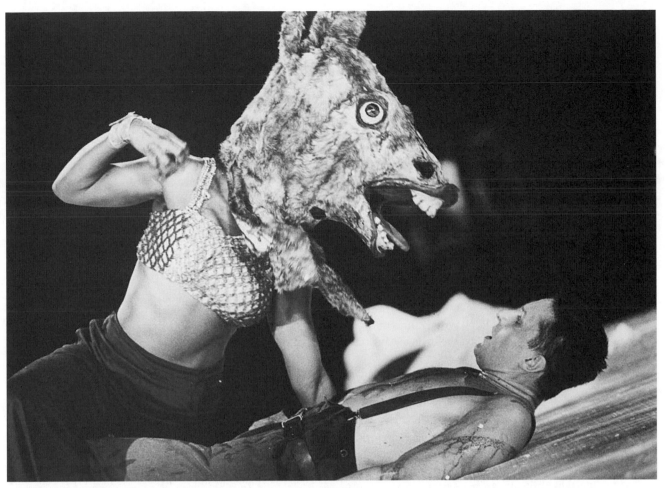

Karin **Beier**'s production of Shakespeare's *A Midsummer Night's Dream*, Düsseldorf, 1995. In a momentary reversal of roles, Titania (Josette Bushell-Mingo, who spoke English in the performance) wears the ass's head that belongs on Bottom (Jacek Poniedzialek, who spoke Polish).

under her mother's name of Hervé, is a mystery: she did almost nothing in the plays of Molière, but continued quietly to collect her pay for 32 years, up to and beyond her death; perhaps she played *confidantes in *tragedy.

The youngest member of the clan was Armande (1642/3–1700), officially registered as their sister but universally believed at the time to be Madeleine's daughter. The controversy, unresolved, has introduced a whiff of scandal into Molière studies to which scholars over the centuries have reliably been drawn. *Montfleury suggested, and some still believe, that her father was Molière. In any case, she married Molière and entered the troupe in 1662, and went on to create a number of youthful roles of considerable liveliness and charm. Her greatest part was Célimène opposite Molière's Alceste, a pairing which has been interpreted implausibly but persistently as evidence of strains in the marriage. She, along with La Grange, held the troupe together after Molière's death. She remarried four years later, to the actor Guérin d'Estriché (1636–1728).

RWH

BELASCO, DAVID (1853–1931)

American *manager, director, and theatrical entrepreneur. The son of English immigrants who arrived in California during the gold rush, Belsaco was born in San Francisco and grew up there and in Victoria, British Columbia, playing occasional roles as a child actor. By 1871 he was *touring West Coast mining camps and towns. He served briefly as secretary and personal assistant to Dion *Boucicault while in Nevada, from whom he may have learned both stage management and playwriting, and he was thereafter appointed *stage manager at Baldwin's Theatre in *San Francisco. Here he began an association with James A. *Herne—together they wrote an adaptation of the *melodrama *Hearts of Oak* (1880)—and eventually caught the eye of the *Frohman brothers, who invited him to *New York as stage manager and dramatist at the *Madison Square Theatre, where he collaborated on the scripts and stagings of a number of productions in 1882–4. His first solo play was the romantic melodrama *May Blossom* (1884). After two years back in San Francisco,

Daniel Frohman hired Belasco to join his company at the *Lyceum Theatre in New York, and in the next four years he and Henry C. *DeMille wrote such hits as *The Charity Ball* and *Lord Chumley*. Belasco also taught at the Lyceum's nascent acting school (*see* TRAINING FOR THEATRE), forerunner of the *American Academy of Dramatic Arts.

His 1890 production of *The Heart of Maryland* started his career as an independent *playwright-*director-*producer. That piece, a popular success in New York, *London, and on tour in the USA, introduced the first of many of Belasco's handmade stars, Mrs Leslie *Carter. Between 1895 and 1902 he produced a string of hits as well as a collection of new stars for the *Theatrical Syndicate. Among his biggest successes were his own *Zaza* (1899) and *Madame Butterfly* (1900), the second famous for its technical innovations, including a twelve-minute *lighting sequence showing the passage of a full evening. Resenting the monopolistic practices of the Syndicate, Belasco leased a *playhouse on 42nd Street in 1902, remodelled it, and named it after himself. For the next fourteen years he successfully challenged the Syndicate by writing, directing, and producing some of the most spectacular shows on the American stage. In 1907 he built an even more remarkable venue on 44th Street, the most technologically advanced facility in the country, renamed the *Belasco Theatre in 1910. This began his most prolific and successful period, writing and producing more than three dozen major hits, including his own *The Girl of the Golden West* (1905) and Eugene Walter's *The Easiest Way* (1909), in which he incorporated the actual contents of a New York boarding house into the set (*see* REALISM; NATURALISM). For his 1912 production of Bradley's *The Governor's Lady*, Belasco built an exact replica on stage of the dining room in Child's Restaurant in New York, and throughout the run Child's catered the production with food and supplies.

During his long career Belasco became the premier director in America, writing or adapting in excess of 100 plays and producing hundreds more. As a director he was renowned for his exquisite adherence to scenic realism and attention to the smallest details. Innovations in lighting and *scenography were his hallmarks. His plays were among the most spectacular ever staged—and two quickly became the basis for *operas by *Puccini, *Madame Butterfly* (1904) and *La fanciulla del West* (1910). Belasco created a stable of stars that dominated the American theatre for years, including Blanche Bates, Ina Clarie, and David *Warfield. Presaging the *film industry, he maintained a tight rein on his actors, carefully crafting their professional personae through sophisticated manipulation of *publicity.   PAD

BELASCO THEATRE

Broadway theatre on West 44th Street in *New York. This approximately 1,000-seat, neo-Georgian-style house, which cost $750,000, opened in 1907 as the Stuyvesant Theatre with *A Grand Old Man*. It became the Belasco in 1910 when an earlier Belasco reverted to its previous name, the Republic Theatre. The best-equipped theatre of its time, it also contained David *Belasco's penthouse living quarters, and his ghost is said to haunt the premises. After a stint as a *radio studio (1949–53), it reverted to theatrical use. Its managements have included Katharine *Cornell, Elmer *Rice, the *Group Theatre, and the *Shubert Organization. Its location near 6th Avenue is considered undesirable.   SLL

BELAVAL, EMILIO S. (1903–72)

Playwright, essayist, and *manager, one of the key figures of Puerto Rican theatre. In his 1939 essay 'What Puerto Rican theatre can be' he outlined the features necessary for a national theatre, asking for plays that merge local perspectives with international standards in production and design. In 1940 he founded Areyto, the first modern producing company of the island, and produced several plays by the new generation of playwrights. His own play *La hacienda de los cuatro vientos* (*House of the Four Winds*) was seen in 1958 in the first Puerto Rican Theatre Festival. In the 1950s he abandoned the stage for politics and law.   JLRE

BELBEL, SERGI (1963–   )

Spanish-Catalan playwright, director, and film scenarist. A major contributor to the resurgence of theatre in *Barcelona in the post-Franco democracy, he quickly gained attention with his first irreverent, postmodern plays that challenged conventional dramatic structure and *dialogue. *Caresses* (1991) has been widely staged in Europe and *Latin America and was *filmed by director Ventura Pons in 1999. *After the Rain* (1993), his most popular play, was staged at *London's *Gate Theatre in 1996 and a production in *Paris received the Molière Prize for the best comic play of 1999. *Blood*, directed by Toni Casares at the Sala Beckett in 1999, was a startling depiction of mindless terrorist brutality. Belbel has directed plays by *Beckett, *Mamet, *Benet i Jornet, Heiner *Müller, and *Koltès.   MPH

BELCARI, FEO (1410–84)

Playwright. The earliest known writer of *sacre rappresentazioni*, Belcari's plays, all composed *c.*1450, were performed in Florence by the leading confraternity, the Vangelista. Belcari's subjects were serious and his treatment *didactic. His best-known play, *Abramo e Isaaco*, stresses human obedience and divine justice, finally resolving into celebratory *music and *dance.   RWV

BEL GEDDES, NORMAN (1893–1958)

American designer. A prolific and influential designer of industrial and household products as well as *scenery, Bel Geddes introduced a smooth grace and elegant functionality into stage sets, trains, and automobiles. A leader in the 1920s movement toward streamlining, his *modernist theatre work was typified by a multiplicity of steps, ramps, and platforms arranged to create the *illusion of having been carved out of solid material as a sculpted and unified mass. His most dazzlingly ambitious work—such as a monumental 1921 design for a staging of Dante's *The Divine Comedy*—was unrealized except as models. An exception was his 1924 design for Max *Reinhardt's *New York production of *The Miracle*. Bel Geddes built out over the seating area and expanded the *stage to the building's rear wall to convert a Broadway *playhouse into a Gothic cathedral. His innovative use of lenses and directional *lighting contributed to the sense of monumental sculptural forms arranged in vast space. His modernist *scenography is reminiscent of *Appia but imagined on a far larger scale, though much of his realized work was *realist scenery for commercial Broadway productions. His set for Sidney *Kingsley's *Dead End* (1935), for example, with its detailed building exteriors and the illusion of the East River into which actors dived and swam, came to epitomize American *naturalism.   MAF

BELL, JOHN (1940–   )

Australian actor and director, leader of the Bell Shakespeare Company, which from 1991 toured the country with energetic and distinctively Australian productions of Shakespeare. In the 1970s Bell was part of the nationalist theatre revival. He co-founded the Nimrod Theatre in *Sydney, promoted the work of David *Williamson, and helped make popular a larrikin, irreverent, Australian theatre, epitomized in the anti-*realistic, *revue-based *Legend of King O'Malley* (1970) which he directed. As an actor Bell is compelling and intelligent with a powerful ability to convince.   EJS

BELLAMY, GEORGE ANN (c.1727–88)

Irish actress, famous onstage and infamous off it. According to legend, in 1744, after a triumphant *Covent Garden debut as Monimia in *Otway's *The Orphan*, James *Quin praised her talents, then warned her against a love of finery and the rascality of men. She heeded neither warning. By the middle of the next decade, she received as much attention for her gaming, love affairs, and *playhouse squabbles as she did for her *acting. Very beautiful, with a plaintive voice and expressive face, and blessed with an ability to cry easily, she was best suited for pathetic roles. Apart from Monimia, she also played such distressed heroines as Indiana in *Steele's *The Conscious Lovers*, Cordelia

(in *Tate's version of *Lear*), Lady Randolph in John *Home's *Douglas*, and Imoinda in *Oroonoko*. She was criticized for attempting Lady Macbeth opposite *Barry's Macbeth; neither had the vocal or emotional range for the roles. Her six-volume *Apology* (1785) created a great stir, but is highly unreliable on points of fact. Hard living took its toll: by 31 she looked old, and despite having had a number of rich lovers, she died poor.   MJK

BELLEROCHE *See* POISSON, RAYMOND.

BELLEROSE (PIERRE LE MESSIER) (c.1592–1670)

French *actor-manager. First documented as apprenticed to Valleran *Le Conte in 1609, he played in the latter's company at the *Hôtel de Bourgogne, in the provinces, and probably in Holland. By 1620 he was leader of a company at Marseille, returning to *Paris to join the *Comédiens du Roi under *Gros-Guillaume in 1622. He became leader of the company in 1638, when he sold this position to *Floridor, though remaining a member of the company until the 1660s. Bellerose figures among the *dramatis personae of Gougenot's *Comédie des comédiens* (c.1633), which shows the democratic governance of a theatre company.   WDH

BELLOTTI-BON, LUIGI (1820–83)

Italian *actor-manager and playwright. Trained in *commedia dell'arte* by his stepfather, the actor and playwright F. A. Bon, he became known as a courtly performer with a quick wit in *improvisation. Through his experience in the 1840s and 1850s with various companies—Gustavo *Modena, Battaglia's La Lombarda, the Reale Sarda, and Adelaide *Ristori (who was his cousin)—he became concerned about the lack of a modern Italian repertory. As actor-manager of the Bellotti-Bon company (1859–73), he commissioned over 70 new plays from prominent authors such as *Ferrari, *Giacometti, and *Giacosa. These Italian works were produced lavishly with fine actors under his meticulous direction. Due in great part to his efforts, Italian theatre from 1860 to 1870 enjoyed a period of prosperity despite the upheavals of the Risorgimento. In expanding to three companies in 1873, he met with artistic difficulties, and a financial shortfall drove him to suicide.   JEH

BELOW

A term with various meanings in Shakespeare's *stage directions. Usually, when opposed to *'above', it meant the main *stage. Where not used in apposition to 'above', it usually meant (somewhat imprecisely) the area beneath the stage. Noises from the understage area, such as the *Ghost's cries in *Hamlet*, or the music of hoboyes (oboes) from under the stage signifying the god Hercules in *Antony and Cleopatra*, and occasionally things made to ascend through the *trap door were said to come 'from below'.   AJG

BELY, ANDREI (1880–1934)

Russian poet, novelist, *theoretician, and dramatist. A key figure in Russian *symbolism, Bely is best known for his experimental *avant-garde novel *Petersburg*, which was adapted for performance by Michael *Chekhov in 1924. A close associate of fellow poet Aleksandr *Blok and a devotee of the anthroposophical school of Rudolf Steiner, his excursions into the theatre include two symbolist plays, *He Who Has Come* (1903) and *The Jaws of Night* (1907), plus stimulating essays on *Gogol, Anton *Chekhov, and *Greek theatre. A stage version of his novel *Moscow* was prepared for *Meyerhold but never staged.   NW

BEMBA, SYLVAIN (1934–95)

Congolese novelist and dramatist. After his studies in Dolisie and then Brazzaville (ex-Belgian Congo), he worked for many years as a journalist, and became political head of the Division of Culture of the Ministry of Information of Zaire in 1973. His writing for the stage began with *radio competition plays such as *L'Enfer, c'est Orféo* (*Hell is Orpheus*, 1970, under the pseudonym Martial Malinda) and *Une eau dormante* (*Sleeping Water*, 1975), and stage plays like *L'Homme qui tua le crocodile* (*The Man Who Killed the Crocodile*, 1973). His work is full of irony created through the distancing technique of the figure of the public entertainer, the buffoon who comments on political events. *Tarentelle noire et diable blanc* (*Black Tarantula and White Devil*, 1976) explores issues of psychological dislocation connected with the slave trade, while *Un foutu monde pour un blanchisseur trop honnête* (*A Bloody Awful World for a Too Honest Laundryman*, 1979) shows the plight of urban communities. One of his last plays, *Noces posthumes de Santigone* (*The Posthumous Nuptials of Santigone*), is a variation on the Antigone theme. Visual elements are strong in Bemba's work, sometimes relegating his parodic intentions to second place. He also wrote four novels and an important study of Zairian music.

PNN trans. JCM

BEN-ABDALLAH, MOHAMMED (1944–)

Ghanaian dramatist and director who has worked in children's theatre, was awarded a Ph.D. in playwriting in America, taught drama, and held a series of cabinet-level posts. In a series of *texts and productions he has made use of local conventions, including oral narratives and oral history (*The Alien King*, 1970). He has explored the languages of *dance and *masks (*Verdict of the Cobra*, 1972), and has come to terms with influential

thinkers and theatre practitioners, including Frantz Fanon and Bertolt *Brecht. His experiments have involved him in work with *puppets (*The Trial of Mallam Ilya*, 1982) and with *concert party musicians (*Land of a Million Magicians*, Accra, 1991). Shortly afterwards Ben-Abdallah returned from government service to university teaching; a play set in Egypt, *Song of the Pharaohs*, has been long expected.   JMG

BEN-AMI, JACOB (1890–1977)

*Yiddish playwright, born in Minsk, Belarus. He joined the Hirshbein Troupe in Odessa, worked with the *Vilna Troupe, and in 1912 settled in *New York. In 1917 he joined Maurice *Schwartz's theatre but left to found the *Jewish Art Theatre (1919–20), a Yiddish company that opposed the star system and was committed to sophisticated scripts and ensemble *acting. In 1920 Ben-Ami began a successful English-language career associated with Eva *Le Gallienne's *Civic Repertory Theatre and the *Theatre Guild. On Broadway he starred in *Samson and Delilah* (1920), *Welded* (1924), *Evening Song* (1934), and *The Tenth Man* (1959); in Yiddish, he performed in numerous plays by Solomon *Asch, David Pinski, Jacob *Gordin, Ossip Dymow, Sholem *Aleichem, and Peretz Hirshbein.   EN

BENAVENTE, DAVID (1941–)

Chilean playwright and filmmaker. *Pedro Juan y Diego* (*Tom, Dick and Harry*, 1976, produced by *Ictus) and *Tres Marías y una Rosa* (*Three Marías and a Rose*, 1979, by the Experimental Theatre Workshop) dealt effectively with the effects of repression and the dictatorship's economic policies on the poor. Benavente's *Tejado de vidrio* (*Glass Roof*, 1981) was also well received.   MAR

BENAVENTE, JACINTO (1866–1954)

Prolific Spanish playwright and recipient of the Nobel Prize in 1922. For more than four decades his plays were staged by the leading theatre companies of Spain and *Latin America, and several reached Broadway and the West End. The complex roles he wrote for female *characters were performed by María *Guerrero, Margarita *Xirgu, and other renowned Spanish actresses. Although his popularity during his lifetime is often attributed to plays with characters of privilege speaking elegant *dialogue, he wrote effectively in a variety of styles from *symbolism and fantasy to *naturalism and *melodrama. One of his most enduring plays, *Witches' Sabbath* (1903), was written early in his career; his international fame derived from *The Bonds of Interest* (1907), with characters based on *commedia dell'arte* prototypes, and *The Passion Flower* (1913), a stark rural *tragedy. Fascinated by American silent *films, he incorporated references to Hollywood in several plays, and in *The Night

Aglow (1927) filmmaking is integral to the *plot, and actors impersonate well-known personalities of the silent era. His professional standing enabled him to resume his career under the Franco dictatorship but his later plays were staged only in Spain and dismissed sight unseen abroad.   MPH

BENAVENTE, SAULO (1916–82)

One of Argentina's two most influential mid-century designers (the other being Gastón Breyer), Benavente designed 100 *films and more than 400 stage productions throughout *Latin America and Europe. Although he often worked in the state-owned theatres, he is associated primarily with Argentina's noncommercial independent theatres. He thought of himself as an artisan, and was known for his beautifully drawn designs and creative use of space and materials, resulting in a *scenography filled with poetic, metaphorical imagery.   JGJ

BEN AYED, ALI (1930–72)

Tunisian actor, director, and *manager who was central to the establishment of modern theatre in the country. In 1962 he was named manager of the Tunisian National Theatre, the only institutional professional theatre. A disciple of Jean *Vilar, Ben Ayed used the post to reform practice in Tunisia by selecting the best *texts, establishing an aesthetic approach, and creating a compatible team of fellow workers. He expanded the company's work beyond Tunis by national *tours, and transformed production in the mode of European *modernism through functional use of *lighting, suggestive *scenography, and stylized *acting. He varied classic and contemporary European plays (*Sophocles, Shakespeare, *Molière, *Goldoni, *García Lorca, *Camus) with those by Arab and Tunisian playwrights (including Izzedine *Madani's *Revolt of the Man on the Ass*, 1970).   MMe

BENE, CARMELO (1937–2002)

Italian actor, director, and playwright. After his debut in 1959 in *Camus's *Caligula*, he directed his own work *Spettacolo Majakovskij* (*The Mayakovsky Show*, 1960), and thereafter made a reputation for subversive, provocative, and often outrageous adaptations of Shakespeare (*Hamlet*, 1975; *Romeo and Juliet*, 1976; *Richard III*, 1977), *Wilde, *Marlowe, and others. His purpose was to create an anti-establishment theatre that questioned traditional repertories, theatrical rules, and the idea of authorship. He promoted an ideological and philosophical actor who created uncertainty and ambiguity of meaning for the *audience, and rejected both the *actor–*character and the actor–*director relationship: in *Romeo and Juliet*, for example, Bene departed from the *text by having Mercutio refuse to die. He moved more and more towards a negative, almost nihilistic concept of the theatre, going so far as to picture a theatre without spectators, where the actor was a lonely and destructive presence, a mere acting machine. His *Manfred* (1989, from *Byron), *Egmont* (1990, from *Goethe), and *Hamlet Suite* (1994, from Laforgue) were examples of Bene's unorthodox and deconstructive view. His *Opera omnia* was published in 1995. *See also* CRUELTY, THEATRE OF.   DMcM

BENEDETTI, MARIO (1920–   )

Uruguayan writer, best known as a journalist and a poet but also closely associated with the work of the Teatro El *Galpón. While some of his dramatic work is poetic, such as *El cumpleaños del Juan Ángel* (*The Birthday of Juan Ángel*, 1971), much of it is politically charged, including *Pedro y el capitán* (*Pedro and the Captain*, 1979). The latter, staged by El Galpón during its exile in Mexico, is set in an interrogation room, dramatizing the encounter between an officer and the political prisoner he tortures.   EJW

BENEDIX, RODERICH (1811–73)

German dramatist and director. Benedix began as an actor with the Bethmannschen Gesellschaft. After the success of his *comedy *Das bemooste Haupt* (1841) he gave up acting, worked as a journalist and as a teacher of literature and elocution, and in 1847 was appointed director of Cologne's municipal theatre. In 1861 he settled in Leipzig and devoted himself to lecturing and writing, producing a large number of successful works in the comic and sentimental vein. With over 120 plays to his credit, Benedix was one of most popular dramatists of the mid-nineteenth century.   CBB

BENEFIT PERFORMANCE

A term used to describe a special theatrical performance intended to benefit financially a playwright, actor, theatrical employee, or philanthropic cause. In English theatre it appears to have been used first in 1681, and Elizabeth *Barry the first performer to have been given the right to an annual benefit in 1686, on the grounds of her immense popularity. Originally such occasions arose in response to special needs. Theatre managements allowed actors in their companies or their families who found themselves in straitened circumstances to solicit public support. By the end of the eighteenth century, however, the system of annual benefits for all members of the theatre, including its minor functionaries, became part of the regular season. It was much vilified on the grounds that *managers were able to depress performers' salaries by the promise of a benefit, and that it forced performers and others who hoped to augment their meagre incomes to become virtual beggars in soliciting *audiences. Nevertheless the system whereby performers and managers negotiated a share of the gross proceeds persisted throughout the nineteenth century, and benefit performances to assist charities have endured into the twenty-first century.

VEE

BENELLI, SEM (1877–1949)

Italian poet, playwright, and screenwriter. After *La Trignola* (1908), a *naturalistic play with existential overtones, Benelli attempted to break with the *realistic tradition and experimented with *verse, writing a series of *historical *tragedies that inspired many imitators: *La cena delle beffe* (1909) and *L'amore dei tre re* (*The Love of Three Kings*, 1910). The first of these, translated as *The Jest*, a drama of *character and intrigue set in fifteenth-century Florence, served as a vehicle for Sarah *Bernhardt in *Paris and John *Barrymore in *New York. Benelli returned to prose in later plays: *Il Ragno* (*The Spider*, 1935), *L'Elefante* (1937), and *L'Orchidea* (1938). JEH

BENET I JORNET, JOSEP M. (1940–   )

Spanish-Catalan playwright and scriptwriter for *film and *television. A leading figure in the post-Franco resurgence of theatre in *Barcelona, he writes exclusively in Catalan; but Spanish translations of many of his plays have been staged regularly throughout Spain and several have been performed abroad. Productions of *The Disappearance of Wendy* (1977), *Description of a Landscape* (1979), and *Witches' Revolt* (1980) focused critical attention on his work. *Legacy*, first staged in 1996 at the Teatro *Nacional María Guerrero, and then directed by Sergi *Belbel for the 1997 Festival Grec in Barcelona, was one of his major successes and was filmed as *Friend/Lover* by director Ventura Pons. *Smells* (2000) completed a trilogy about a decrepit neighbourhood in Barcelona that he had begun in 1964.

MPH

BENGALI THEATRE

Bengali, called Bangla by native speakers, is the mother tongue of 100 million people in *Bangladesh, 70 million in West Bengal, and 2 million in Tripura (both states in eastern *India), and a diasporic population of another 18 million chiefly in the UK and USA. *Jatra, the most popular form of indigenous theatre in Bengali villages, probably originated in *Vaishnava* *religious processions several centuries ago and gradually turned secular by the nineteenth century. Although its heyday has passed and it became corrupted by the influence of commercial *films after the 1960s, *jatra* still entertains crowds in thousands. Several lesser-known folk forms exist in Bengal, such as the *gambhira* *dance, *kathakata* storytelling, and *panchali* songs, all containing significant dramatic content (*see also* JARI GAN; KABI GAN).

British colonizers built the first *playhouse in Calcutta (*Kolkata) in 1753, but *proscenium theatre in Bengali emerged in curious fashion in 1795, when a Russian linguist and musician, Herasim Lebedeff, constructed the 'Bengally Theatre', recruited local actors and actresses, and staged a translated English play, *The Disguise*. A one-off venture, it had no real effect on the growth of a Bengali stage, which had to wait till the 1830s before a couple of wealthy *zamindars* (landlords) put on divertissements in their palatial establishments for the benefit of their guests. By this time English education had infiltrated the Bengali upper-class consciousness; Calcutta intellectuals started emulating Western *dramaturgy and hybridizing it with classical Sanskrit models. A pandit, Ramnarayan Tarkaratna, had the distinction of writing the first original Bengali script to be performed, *Kulin-kulasarbasva* (*All about a Kulin Clan*, 1857). A problem play on the evils of Brahman polygamy, it initiated a major Bengali *genre, the social drama. Productions occurred on an exclusively *amateur basis for invited *audiences. By the 1870s, however, a demand for public theatre arose in Calcutta, and several amateurs felt the need to turn professional. In 1872, a group calling itself the National Theatre opened with Dinabandhu *Mitra's inflammatory *Nil Darpan* (*Indigo Mirror*), whose attack on colonial oppressors made it an immediate success. The following year the first purpose-built playhouse was built, Bengal Theatre, also the first after Lebedeff to hire actresses—a move supported by noted author Michael Madhusudan *Dutt, whose romantic *Sarmishta* inaugurated it. One of the earliest actresses, *Binodini Dasi, rapidly won a devoted following.

From its inception, the public stage began to provoke the British administration with volatile material. Predictably, *censorship was imposed in 1876 by the *Dramatic Performances Act, applicable to all of British India. Undeterred, playwrights like Girish *Ghosh channelled dissent through mythological and *historical drama (*Sirajuddaula*, 1905), dramatizing stories of rebellion against tyranny. Stylistically, Ghosh as *actor-manager typified the commercial formula of spectacular extravaganza and lengthy *melodrama punctuated with songs. Sensitive writers abhorred these methods as escapist. However, except for Rabindranath *Tagore's trailblazing amateur experiments, in a class of their own (like *Raja*, 1911), no one offered an alternative mode. Noticeable changes came in the 1920s, when Sisir *Bhaduri established the idea of *directing in the professional theatre and encouraged a *realistic approach by his own *acting. He managed to bring the alienated intelligentsia back to the playhouse, even receiving praise from Tagore, who gave a few plays to him for staging. But the public theatre soon received blows from three sides: the novelty of *film, India's struggle for freedom culminating in independence but also in Bengal's partition, and the catastrophic Bengal famine in 1943.

The increasing commitment to communist ideology among younger artists led them finally to break with the old-fashioned commercial stage. The turning point, Bijon *Bhattacharya's *Nabanna* (*New Harvest*, 1944) by the *Indian People's Theatre Association, brought the stark economic plight of Bengali villagers before the public eye. Satellite groups from the parent organization, themselves splintering further, gave rise to the 'group theatre' movement after India's independence. The graph of Bengali theatre in the second half of the twentieth century charts the development of these numerous small troupes, which shared amateur status, progressive social ideals, and a predilection for serious drama on class exploitation and political change. The best of these groups displayed technical prowess on a par with professionals. Two made lasting contributions: Sombhu *Mitra's Bohurupee and Utpal *Dutt's Little Theatre Group/People's Little Theatre. Mitra directed several Tagore classics like *Rakta-karabi* (*Red Oleander*) which had a profound impact through nationwide *tours, and brought Mitra renown for his poetic acting and direction. A number of major artists became associated with the Bohurupee company: actors like Tripti *Mitra and Kumar Roy, designers like Khaled Choudhury and Tapas Sen. Actor-director Dutt, an avowed Marxist, wrote many original plays advocating revolution, and often found himself in trouble with the authorities before West Bengal elected a leftist government. His team attracted talented actors like Sekhar Chatterjee and Dutt's wife Sova Sen.

While Calcutta's group theatre boomed in the 1960s and 1970s as the commercial stage declined, an unlikely visionary named Badal *Sircar formulated his concept of 'Third Theatre', rejecting the *proscenium and *ticket sales in favour of open spaces (indoors and outdoors) and voluntary donations from spectators. He composed and directed his own plays for the purpose of social change, earning him a reputation as the foremost contemporary Bengali dramatist. In his attempt to bridge the urban–rural divide, he took his group Satabdi to villages for productions and workshops with local communities. Sircar's ideals inspired many Indian workers to establish similar troupes, like the Living Theatre of Khardah, near Calcutta, and more recent groups following the teachings of Augusto *Boal.

Well-established groups in Calcutta itself include Nandikar, famous for its adaptations of European plays (*Brecht's *Threepenny Opera*, and *The Good Person of Setzuan*; *Pirandello's *Six Characters in Search of an Author* and *Henry IV*) under the actor-director Ajitesh Bandyopadhyay. Later, Rudraprasad Sengupta extended Nandikar's activities to outreach programmes for children and sex workers, apart from conducting an annual theatre *festival. Other group theatres include Sundaram, led by noted dramatist Manoj Mitra, who applies fantasy to humanistic themes, and Anya Theatre under Bibhash Chakraborty, known for his direction of pungent *satire (for instance, Dario *Fo's *Accidental Death of an Anarchist*). At the end of the twentieth century, Bengali groups perse-

vered in their pursuit of 'good' theatre, though beset with problems of dwindling audiences, competition from *television, and a certain insularity of outlook. Ideologically, the fact that most of them have supported the ruling Left Front government since it came into power in 1977 has made their continuing cries for revolution sound paradoxical. Since 1990, many consciously underplayed *politics, sensing the lack of interest of viewers, and turned to domestic or social subjects. On the other hand, group theatre spread to the small towns of West Bengal, resulting in some degree of welcome decentralization from the dominance of Calcutta.   AL

BHARUCHA, RUSTOM, *Rehearsals of Revolution: the political theater of Bengal* (Honolulu, 1983)

RAHA, KIRONMOY, *Bengali Theatre*, 2nd edn. (New Delhi, 1993)

BENNETT, ALAN (1934–)

English playwright, actor, and director. He co-wrote and performed in *Beyond the Fringe* (1960), a *revue that also featured Peter Cook, Dudley Moore, and Jonathan *Miller. Its innovative *satire on English life, institutions, and rhetoric established the concerns and style of Bennett's subsequent work. *Forty Years On* (1968) maintains a revue format in its series of sketches on Victorian values and the decline of empire framed by a minor public school's annual review. *Getting On* (1971) and *Habeas Corpus* (1973) are elegiac *comedies which explore the personal decline of their male *protagonists related to the political decline of post-war England. *The Old Country* (1977) addresses similar concerns through the nostalgia of an English defector to the Soviet Union, a setting Bennett returned to in his *television play about the spy Guy Burgess, *An Englishman Abroad* (1983). Bennett's later work maintains a distinctive comic relish of everyday cliché and an interest in versions of Englishness. *Talking Heads* (1987) is a series of bitter-sweet *monologues for television, the feature *film screenplays *A Private Function* (1984) and *Prick up your Ears* (1987) are studies in provincial repression and rebellion, and his adaptation of *The Wind in the Willows* for the Royal *National Theatre in 1990 a mixture of whimsical fantasy and sharp social observation. These versions of twentieth-century Englishness are counterpointed by work with wider cultural and historical concerns. *Kafka's Dick* (1986) and *The Insurance Man* (1986) are respectively a stage and a television play that examine the relationship of Kafka's creative work and his humdrum life as an insurance man, and the conflicts between privacy and posthumous literary fame. *The Madness of George III* (1991; film version, 1994) is a sympathetic study of an often-derided figure which provides a sceptical version of a formative period of English nation building, as well as pursuing Bennett's concerns with the foibles and failures of professional men—here doctors and politicians.

SF

BENNETT, ARNOLD (1867–1931)

English novelist and playwright. Best known as a social novelist (*The Old Wives' Tale, Anna of the Five Towns*), Bennett also had some success in *London with romantic *comedies (*Cupid and Common Sense*, 1908), and social dramas (*The Great Adventure*, 1911, adapted from his novel *Buried Alive*). In collaboration with Edward *Knoblock he wrote *Milestones* (1912), which starred the popular Henry *Ainley and ran for 607 performances. After the war he wrote two plays on metaphysical questions, *Sacred and Profane Love* (1919, adapted from his novel) and *Body and Soul* (1922). Neither had much appeal, but he had more success with *Mr Prohack* (1927), a social drama, co-written with Knoblock. The play was adapted from one of his novels and starred Charles *Laughton.   TP

BENNETT, MICHAEL (1943–87)

American choreographer and director. A self-described Broadway 'gypsy', Bennett began his career as a show *dancer in the 1960s. His early choreography earned him a series of Tony nominations culminating in *Follies* (1971), the ambitious Stephen *Sondheim *musical that also marked Bennett's debut as a director. In 1974 Bennett began supervising a workshop to create a new musical based on the professional experiences of a group of *New York-based gypsies. Though attribution for the *book of *A Chorus Line* remains a point of dispute, Bennett is credited with guiding its development and contributing a uniquely cinematic look to the staging and the choreography. *A Chorus Line* (1975) is among the most successful musicals of the American stage, running on Broadway for fifteen years and earning nine Tony *awards, including Bennett's for best direction and best choreography. His career continued to flourish with *Dreamgirls* (1981).   LTC

BENOIS, ALEXANDRE (1870–1960)

Russian artist, illustrator, designer, and director as well as an authority on seventeenth- and eighteenth-century French culture. Brought up in *St Petersburg, Benois developed an enthusiasm for drama, *opera, and *ballet and dreamed of becoming a stage designer. His debut was in 1902 at the Mariinsky Theatre with *Twilight of the Gods*. His first major success was *Le Pavillon d'Armide* (Mariinsky, 1907) for which he also wrote the *scenario and which was then staged by *Diaghilev in *Paris in 1909, becoming a key work in the *Ballets Russes repertoire. Benois's trademark was historical detail; in this last case, precise evocation of the age of *Versailles. In 1907 he played a major role in establishing the Starinny Teatr (Theatre of Antiquity) in St Petersburg, where *Evreinov was to leave his mark, and in 1909 Benois became *artistic director of the *Moscow Art Theatre where, working closely with *Stanislavsky, he directed and designed productions of plays by *Molière, *Goldoni, and *Pushkin (1913–15). Closely associated with the 'World of Art' movement and Diaghilev, Benois's career peaked in 1911, which saw the Paris production of Stravinsky's *Petrushka* with designs by Benois derived from Russian *folk art. He emigrated to France in 1926 and continued his work in Paris, Monte Carlo, and at La *Scala in *Milan, where his son Nicholas was resident designer from 1936. Benois was great-uncle to the English actor, travel writer, dramatist, and raconteur Peter *Ustinov.   NW

BENSON, FRANK (1858–1939)

English actor and *manager, educated at Oxford. Most of Benson's career was spent outside *London, either performing Shakespeare in Stratford-upon-Avon during the summers from 1886 to 1919 (except for two years spent driving a Red Cross ambulance during the First World War) or *touring the country during the other months. He also took companies to the United States, Canada, and South Africa. Over the years he performed all of Shakespeare's plays except *Titus Andronicus* and *Troilus and Cressida*. Although Benson brought his productions to London on several occasions for short runs, he never established himself there, though many of the actors he trained became featured performers in the capital. He was an athletic actor, blessed with noble features that served him well in roles such as Henry V and Richard II, but his sometimes awkward gestures and singsong voice hindered his style. His wife Constance acted in his companies and helped with management. Both wrote autobiographies. Benson was knighted in 1916 and received the Croix de Guerre from France in 1918.   TP

BENTHALL, MICHAEL (1919–74)

English director. Primarily but not exclusively a Shakespearian director, in the 1940s and 1950s he produced swift, lucid interpretations with visually appealing stage pictures and a choreographic treatment of ensemble. His *expressionist staging of *King John* (1948) at the *Shakespeare Memorial Theatre was influenced by his partner Robert *Helpmann's *ballet *Adam Zero* (1946), for which he wrote the *scenario; Benthall's other vivid productions at the SMT included *Hamlet* (1948), *Cymbeline* (1949), and *The Tempest* (1951–2). As director of the *Old Vic between 1953 and 1962, he reclaimed the company from financial and artistic decline during his five-year project (1953–8) to present all the plays of Shakespeare's First Folio. His policies provided significant opportunities in repertory theatre for young performers such as John *Neville and Judi *Dench, while star players such as John *Gielgud and Katharine *Hepburn were also accommodated within the company's work in *London and on a series of high-profile overseas *tours. His non-Shakespearian work included *The White Devil* (1947), *The Millionairess* (1952), *The Importance of Being Earnest* (1959), and *Man and Boy* (1963). He also directed a number of *operas, including *Turandot* (1947) and *Queen of Spades* (1950) at *Covent Garden.   VRS

BENTLEY, ERIC (1916–)

Anglo-American critic, translator, and playwright. Educated at Oxford and Yale, Bentley largely introduced *Brecht to America through his translations, his university teaching, and *The Playwright as Thinker* (1946). Bentley worked with Brecht in *Los Angeles in the 1940s, and directed his translation of *The Good Person of Setzuan* in *New York (1956). He preferred what he called the theatre of commitment (in a book of that title, 1967), meaning work that engaged *politics with theatre. Viewed alternatively as elitist and pioneering, Bentley's highly influential *criticism includes *Bernard Shaw* (1947, Shaw's favourite analysis of his work), *In Search of Theatre* (1957), *The Life of the Drama* (1965), the anthology *The Classic Theatre* (1958–61), and translations of *Pirandello and *Büchner, as well as extensive translations of Brecht. Drama critic of the *New Republic* from 1952 to 1956, Bentley 'retired' to playwriting. His plays portray historical subjects battling oppressive institutions, and include *Are You Now or Have You Ever Been . . .?* (1972), *The Recantation of Galileo Galilei* (1973), and *Lord Alfred's Lover* (1979).
                                                                GAO

BERAIN, JEAN (1637–1711)

French designer. Berain was appointed *scenographer to Louis XIV in 1674, responsible for *costumes and *scenery for court entertainments, weddings, and state funerals. Working with Carlo *Vigarani, he was in charge of costumes for *Thésée* (1675), *Atys* (1676), and *Isis* (1677) by *Lully and *Quinault, all first performed at Saint-Germain-en-Laye. In 1680 Berain succeeded Vigarani as designer for the *Opéra in *Paris, being followed in turn by his son Jean Berain II (1678–1726).
                                                                WDH

BÉRARD, CHRISTIAN (1902–49)

French *scenographer. An accomplished painter, Bérard became celebrated during the 1930s and 1940s for designs for *ballet, *opera, and theatre, as well as for *Parisian fashion. After his first ballet work for Michel *Fokine and *Diaghilev he became resident designer at the Théâtre de l'Athénée, embarking on a significant and long-standing collaboration with Louis *Jouvet, for whom he designed several groundbreaking productions including *Cocteau's *La Machine infernale* (1934) and *Giraudoux's *The Madwoman of Chaillot* (1945). Their celebrated version of *The School for Wives* (1936), with a three-dimensional scenic transformation that moved from a Louis XIV interior to a garden exterior amid the overarching

*theatricality of overhead chandeliers—like those found in a seventeenth-century French *playhouse—was said to have revolutionized the staging of *Molière.   DGM

BERGHAUS, RUTH (1927–96)

German director. Initially trained as a *dancer and choreographer at the Palucca-Schule in Dresden, Berghaus began working as a director in the 1950s. In 1954 she married the composer Paul Dessau, whose works she also directed. She was appointed director-in-residence at the *Berliner Ensemble in 1964 and brought out a number of highly acclaimed productions, including Peter *Weiss's *Vietnam Discourse* (1968), *Brecht's *In the Jungle of Cities* (1971), and Heiner *Müller's *Cement* (1973). From 1971 to 1977 she was *artistic director of the Berliner Ensemble. After 1977 she attained an international reputation as a director of *opera with acclaimed productions in Frankfurt (*Wagner's *Ring* cycle, 1985–7), Hamburg (*Tristan and Isolde*, 1988), and *Brussels (Alban Berg's *Lulu*, 1988). Berghaus's productions were renowned for their visual quality and choreographic staging of both singers and actors.   CBB

BERGHOF, HERBERT (1909–90)

Austrian-born actor, director, and teacher. Berghof trained at the *Vienna State Academy of Dramatic Art, making his professional debut in *Don Carlos* (1927). He also studied with Max *Reinhardt and eventually moved to *New York, working with Lee *Strasberg and becoming a charter member of the *Actors Studio. From the early 1940s Berghof appeared in various plays and revivals in his adopted country, including *Ibsen's *The Lady from the Sea* (1950); he played the accused Confederate prison-camp officer in Saul Levitt's *The Andersonville Trial* (1959). His *film appearances include *Five Fingers* (1952) and *Cleopatra* (1963). Among his directorial credits, Berghof staged the first Broadway production of *Beckett's *Waiting for Godot* (1956), which was well received following its miscalculated American première in Florida. He is perhaps best remembered as an *acting teacher, founding the Herbert Berghof Studio in 1945, which he directed with his wife Uta *Hagen.   EW

BERGMAN, INGMAR (1918–)

Swedish director. In his *films Bergman has probed complex patterns of human interaction, often reaching into the darkest recesses of human experience, as in *Cries and Whispers* (1972). He has also explored man's sense of alienation from God, as in *Winter Light* (1962), and the emptiness of a life without overall meaning, as in *Through a Glass Darkly* (1961). In his final film, *Fanny and Alexander* (1982), however, the action concludes with a joyful celebration of art triumphing over darkness and despair. Bergman tended to rely on the same group of trusted actors and his theatre work was distinguished by the passion for clarity and simplicity of technique that characterize his films. He has repeatedly returned to *Molière, *Ibsen, and *Strindberg. His seminal productions of *The Misanthrope* (1973), *Hedda Gabler* (1964), *The Wild Duck* (1972), *A Dream Play* (1970), and *The Ghost Sonata* (1973) were all marked by the same desire to strip away unnecessary visual detail to highlight the complex human issues addressed in the plays. *Hedda Gabler*, acted on a claustrophobic set, used sculpted blocking patterns to show the *characters trapped in an emotional chamber of horrors. His reading of *The Ghost Sonata* was even bleaker. Doubling the role of the Mummy and the Daughter, Strindberg's conciliatory ending was cut to show the characters facing the prospect of endlessly recurring absurdity. During the 1980s Bergman directed disturbing minimalist productions of *King Lear* (1984) and *Hamlet* (1986), both of which showed a world in which all moral values had imploded in the face of anarchy and violence.　　　　　　　　　　　　　DT

BERGNER, ELISABETH (1897–1986)

Austrian actress and director. After *training at the Viennese conservatory she appeared there in 1915. There followed short periods in Zurich, *Munich, and *Vienna before she settled in *Berlin in 1922. She worked mainly for Max *Reinhardt at the *Deutsches Theater but also at the Staatstheater under Jürgen *Fehling. Famous roles during the Berlin period included Miss Julie, Portia, Queen Christina in *Strindberg's play, and Juliet. She quickly established herself as one of the leading actresses of her generation. Her *acting was distinguished by psychological subtlety and vocal finesse, leading to a wide range of roles in theatre and *film, including cross-dressing. In 1933 she went into exile in *London where she successfully continued her acting career; in 1942 she moved to *New York, where she began to direct. She resumed her acting and directing career in Germany in 1954. Her final performance was in 1973 in London's Greenwich Theatre.　　　　　　　　　　　　　CBB

BERKOFF, STEVEN (1937–　)

English director, playwright, and actor. London born to Russian-Jewish parents, Berkoff trained at the Webber Douglas Academy and with *mimes Claude Chagrin (*London) and Jacques *Lecoq (*Paris). In 1968, after six years in *repertory theatre, he began his career as actor-director and playwright, forming the London Theatre Group. Influenced by *Brecht, *Artaud, and the *Living Theatre, Berkoff celebrated the physical inventiveness and primal energy of the actor. 'I want theatre to express those things that go beyond reality into fantasy', he said, 'the dreams and haunting fears beneath the reality.' Berkoff's plays chart the extremes of the human condition, revealing a sensuous love for the spoken word, juxtaposing London slang with Shakespearian-style *verse. His adaptations from Kafka, Poe, and *Strindberg were followed by the quasi-autobiographical *East* (1975) and *West* (1980), savage critiques of the class system in *Decadence* (1981) and of the Falklands War in the *Sink the Belgrano* (1987), and the lyrical *The Secret Love Life of Ophelia* (2001). A theatrical iconoclast, Berkoff remains critical of the British theatrical establishment, despite directing *Salome* (1988) and *The Trial* (1991) at the Royal *National Theatre. Stints as Hollywood *villains and (ironically) as Hitler in the *television epic *War and Remembrance* (1986) bankrolled his own theatre productions, enabling him to retain artistic independence. A key influence upon movement-based theatre of the 1980s and 1990s, he has been mentor to young theatre-makers, notably Deborah *Warner.　　　　　　　　　　　　　RVL

BERLIN

In comparison with other European metropolises, Berlin is young. Founded in the thirteenth century, it was not important until it became the capital of Prussia in 1701, and its history is closely tied to the rise of Prussia as a great power in Central Europe; the traces of *medieval and *early modern theatre traditions are very few. Friedrich the Great (1712–86) instituted the *playhouse Unter den Linden, desiring to create a Prussian equivalent to those at other European courts, concentrating on Italian *opera. In 1789 Friedrich Wilhelm II founded the *Berlin Royal (National) Theatre and appointed August Wilhelm *Iffland as director in 1796. Iffland, already a well-known actor, opened a new building in 1802 and was responsible for the development of Berlin as an important theatrical centre. After his death Carl von Brühl (1772–1837) became director in 1815; influenced by *Goethe's work at the *Weimar Court Theatre, he introduced historicist *costume and *scenography, collaborating with the designer Karl Friedrich *Schinkel, and reformed traditional modes of *casting and *acting.

During the period of the Napoleonic Wars (1806–14) the bourgeoisie gained increasing importance and calls for a democratic people's theatre became more insistent, to supplement the court opera and the Royal Theatre. Friedrich Cerf (1771–1845) received a licence to open a theatre in 1822, but in order to preserve the court theatres' privileges Cerf was not permitted to stage heroic operas or serious dramas; thus he focused on light *comedies in the French tradition of *vaudeville, *Viennese popular theatre, and Italian *opera buffa*. Although the enterprise did not last long, it was an index of the awakening middle-class self-confidence that claimed theatre as an art no longer reserved for the aristocracy.

The population of Berlin grew rapidly, from 172,000 in 1800 to 2 million in 1905, and to 3.8 million in 1920. Under this pressure public entertainment radically changed with a new trade law of 1869, which brought theatre closer to the principles of capitalist production, creating an industry based on commercial success alone. Applying for a theatre licence became easier; most applications were filed by pub owners who converted dance halls into theatres. The number of new playhouses reached its peak after the Deutsches Reich was established in 1871, engendering an economic boom throughout the country. At the same time the idea of a bourgeois *national theatre was revived, and as part of this movement the *Deutsches Theater was founded in 1883 under the direction of Adolf *L'Arronge. Modelled after the Théâtre-Français (1812; see COMÉDIE-FRANÇAISE), and standing in philosophical opposition to the reactionary Berlin Royal Theatre, the theatre's aesthetic was influenced by the *Meiningen troupe, who visited Berlin in 1874, and by the *Munich model performances of 1880 in the tradition of Franz von *Dingelstedt, breaking with the old star system as practised at the court theatres. In subsequent years the Deutsches Theater became the leading stage in Germany, noted especially for its ensemble work.

L'Arronge had emphasized the classics—*Schiller, Goethe, and Shakespeare—but his successor in 1894, Otto *Brahm, who had founded the *Freie Bühne in 1889, was identified with the rise of *naturalism and sought to promote contemporary plays. His emphasis on psychological *realism in acting, and his desire to use theatre as a platform for discussing social change, proved decisive historically, but at the time he had little success. It was left to Max *Reinhardt, who took over the Deutsches Theater in 1905, to balance *audience demand with the ideal of contemporary plays and *modernist production methods. Soon Reinhardt was the most important director in Berlin, greatly outshining the court theatres and rapidly achieving a wide international reputation. Wilhelm II and his court ignored Reinhardt's work: the Royal Theatre became further isolated, and thereafter dramatic art in Berlin was to be driven by the private theatres.

As a reaction to the growing industrialization of theatre and in connection with the rise of socialism, the *Volksbühne (people's theatre) movement was founded in Berlin in 1890. The association aimed to establish a working-class culture and to break the bourgeois privilege of education. Initially the members hired performance venues, until the Volksbühne opened its own theatre of that name in 1914, financed by the voluntary contributions of its members. The repertory consisted of classical dramas as well as naturalistic plays. The Volksbühne was the fourth of the pillars supporting the city's theatre, in addition to the royal houses, the commercial theatres for bourgeois entertainment, and private enterprises like the Deutsches Theater. Together they made Berlin the theatrical centre of Germany.

The Weimar Republic, which replaced the monarchy after the First World War, brought with it a wide-ranging politicization of culture. Public discourse, marked by the confrontation of left-wing parties and right-wing nationalist groups, accompanied by increasingly violent conflicts, affected the four pillars of Berlin theatre in several ways. First, the system of the court

theatres disappeared; the Prussian Royal Theatre became the Staatstheater, though still *financed by the state. Its most important director was Leopold *Jessner, in charge from 1919 to 1930, who offered a radical analysis of the bourgeois heritage from the perspective of a democratic society, most prominently with classic *texts like *William Tell* (1919), *Richard III* (1920), and *Hamlet* (1926). Though Jessner made the former court theatre into one of the most important cultural institutions of the Weimar Republic, he was a constant target of right-wing hostility.

In spite of the economic crisis of the 1920s the second pillar of the system, the popular *bourgeois theatre, gained further importance. With the opening of several new *revue theatres featuring spectacular shows, Berlin now offered a metropolitan culture comparable to *New York, *Paris, or *London, bolstered by the growing importance of jazz and guest performances from international stars like Josephine *Baker, Sam Woodings, and the Tiller Girls. Reinhardt remained the central figure of the third pillar, the private theatre, and went from strength to strength with an elaborate aesthetic that generally avoided political implication, eventually allowing him to extend his enterprises beyond the borders of Germany. In 1919 he opened the *Grosses Schauspielhaus in Berlin, which provided the opportunity for large-scale *spectacles with crowd scenes in work such as *Danton* and *Oedipus the King* (both 1920).

In a heightened political environment, *political theatre became increasingly important. The socialist movement, influenced by Soviet developments, was especially committed, founding a number of *agitprop troupes which performed on *streets as well as in regular playhouses. Berlin also became the locus for an intersection of political agitation and aesthetic experiment, most famously in the work of Bertolt *Brecht and Erwin *Piscator, who sought social reform through *avant-garde means, appealing to the bourgeois intelligentsia as well as the working class. The boundaries between the different types of theatre were not absolute; many theatre workers engaged in projects in several forms, and the developing *film industry in the suburb of Babelsberg provided necessary additional jobs.

Hitler's assumption of power in 1933 meant the end of this vibrant cultural life. Many famous artists who had laid the foundations for the international reputation of Berlin theatre had to leave Germany, their freedom and lives now in danger, including Jessner, Brecht, Piscator, and almost everyone associated with them. The Nazis attempted to gain control of the theatres by appointing directors who were thought to be in sympathy with the new government, most famously Jürgen *Fehling, Gustav *Gründgens, and Heinz *Hilpert, who concentrated on safe versions of the classics and light entertainment. Berlin became isolated and its theatre lost its international importance.

After the Second World War Berlin was divided by the Allies and soon became the front-line city of the Cold War.

Theatre became an agent in the confrontation of rival political systems. East Berlin had the advantage of containing the majority of traditional theatres within its precincts, including the opera Unter den Linden, the Deutsches Theater, and the Theater am *Schiffbauerdamm, which became the home of the *Berliner Ensemble in 1954. Development was determined by returning emigrants like Wolfgang Langhoff (1901–66), who continued the tradition of the Deutsches Theater, and Brecht and Helene *Weigel at the Berliner Ensemble. Though Brecht died in 1956, his attempt to realize *epic theatre was continued by Weigel and disciples such as Benno *Besson, Ruth *Berghaus, and Manfred *Wekwerth. The return of exiles to the new German Democratic Republic was of high symbolic value, signifying a new moral start after the Nazi period. The government wished theatre to become a full participant in the building of a socialist society, and an elaborate system of season tickets was developed, especially for students and working-class citizens. Of course this mandate, and the high levels of subsidy that accompanied it, made theatres subject to political influence and political control. Nevertheless the Deutsches Theater and especially the Berliner Ensemble re-established Berlin's centrality to world theatre.

West Berlin, on the other hand, had lost major parts of its theatrical landscape. The most important playhouse in the 1950s was the Schiller Theater, reopened in 1951, which continued the tradition of bourgeois theatre by offering a repertory of classics and contemporary plays, especially those of Samuel *Beckett. In an attempt to make West Berlin part of West German theatre, *festivals like the Berliner Festwochen (1951) and the *Theatertreffen (1964) were designed to show the best productions of the season from all over Germany. New buildings and new companies arose amid the tense politics of the Cold War: the Freie Volksbühne, in a new building erected for Piscator in 1963, which staged important political work, especially the *documentary theatre of Rolf *Hochhuth; and the *Schaubühne, which became internationally important after the appointment of Peter *Stein in 1970. During the period of its division a double theatrical landscape emerged in Berlin that was based chiefly on state subsidy.

Reunification in 1990 brought an end to the double landscape and a severe reduction in the levels of subsidy. Some theatres were able to survive the tearing down of the Berlin Wall by developing a clear profile. The Deutsches Theater, for example, compensated for the loss of the subscription system by regaining its status as the main bourgeois theatre, while the Volksbühne became an avant-garde theatre under the direction of Frank *Castorf, winning a new kind of audience. But the competition for spectators did not end successfully for all companies; in 1992–3 both the Freie Volksbühne and the Schiller Theater lost their subsidies and were closed. Under the pressure of difficult economic conditions and in competition with other cultural institutions—not to mention film and *television—theatre was forced to renegotiate its status. Though at the start of the new millennium Berlin remains a major theatrical centre, its distinction now must be achieved in the market-place.

PWM

FREYDANK, RUTH, *Theater in Berlin: von den Anfängen bis 1945* (Berlin, 1988)

FUNKE, CHRISTOPH, and JANSEN, WOLFGANG, *Theater am Schiffbauerdamm: die Geschichte einer Berliner Bühne* (Berlin, 1992)

WILLETT, JOHN, *The Theatre of the Weimar Republic* (London, 1988)

BERLIN, IRVING (ISRAEL BEILIN) (1888–1989)

American composer, lyricist, and performer. Berlin personified American popular song and for more than 50 years moved successfully between stage, *film, and commercial songwriting. Born the son of a cantor in Russia, Berlin and family emigrated to *New York where he wrote his first published song, 'Marie from Sunny Italy', in 1907. He had a natural ease with vernacular and with melody that incorporated the feel of ragtime and the rapidly evolving idiom of Tin Pan Alley pop. His career took off in 1911 with 'Alexander's Ragtime Band' and the First World War standard 'Oh! How I Hate to Get up in the Morning', which he performed on stage (and reprised during the Second World War). During the 1920s Berlin produced his own *revues and contributed songs for the *Marx Brothers' show *The Cocoanuts* (1925) and the *Ziegfeld Follies of 1927*. As Thousands Cheer* (1933) was one of the last successful revues of the era, and *Top Hat* (1935) was one of the more popular Fred *Astaire films, with such hits as 'Cheek to Cheek' and 'Let's Face the Music and Dance'. Berlin's stage *musical *Louisiana Purchase* (1940) was a *satire of southern politics, which he followed with the patriotic revue *This Is the Army* (1942). In 1946 Berlin wrote one of the most successful Broadway musicals of all time, *Annie Get your Gun*, and had another hit with *Call Me Madam* (1950), both of which were movie successes (1950 and 1953 respectively). His last Broadway show was *Mr President* in 1962.

SN

BERLINER ENSEMBLE

Company founded in 1949 by Bertolt *Brecht and Helene *Weigel, originally as a group within the *Deutsches Theater in *Berlin, since 1954 at the Theater am *Schiffbauerdamm. Under Brecht's guidance, the company of émigrés and young actors relatively uncorrupted by Nazi theatre developed a version of *epic theatre particularly suited to the post-war situation. The Ensemble's triumphant *tours to *Paris in 1954 and 1955 and to *London in 1956 helped establish its style as a model for performing Brecht's plays and practising such theoretical concepts as *Verfremdung; the production of *Mother Courage* attracted particular attention. Brecht also trained a cadre of young directors who went on to influential careers, including Benno *Besson, Peter *Palitzsch, and Manfred *Wekwerth.

After Brecht's death in 1956, the Ensemble became guided more by his model than his spirit of experimentation. The transition resulted in several famous productions, including Palitzsch and Wekwerth's *Arturo Ui* (1959), and *Coriolan* directed by Wekwerth and Joachim Tenschert (1964). The Ensemble toured these and other productions around the world in the 1960s and 1970s, although it reached North America only in 1986 with a visit to *Toronto. By the late 1960s, however, the company was in danger of becoming a stylistic showcase at a time when theatres elsewhere were moving beyond the Ensemble's original influence. Ruth *Berghaus, who became *Intendant* upon Weigel's death in 1971, resisted this tendency, but several of her projects angered both the East German authorities and Brecht's stylistically conservative daughter, who controlled German-language production rights. Berghaus was replaced by Wekwerth in 1976.

The collapse of East Germany in 1990 called into question the need for a theatre devoted to what had become an epic theatre orthodoxy. Wekwerth was replaced in 1992 by a band of five directors; by 1995, only Heiner *Müller remained as *Intendant*. But the rejuvenated company produced innovative work, including an important Müller production of *Arturo Ui* that year. Müller's sudden death in December threw the Ensemble into a disarray from which it never recovered. In a deal that included replacing the old company, Claus *Peymann took over the Berliner Ensemble am Bertolt Brecht Platz in 1999, finally breaking the historical connection, however problematic, to Brecht's legacy. Ironically, the old company's final tour with *Ui* in summer 1999 was also its first visit to the USA.

JR

BERLIN ROYAL THEATRE

Founded in 1787 by King Friedrich Wilhelm II as a 'national theatre', the first building was erected on the Gendarmenmarkt. The theatre provided a mixture of *opera, *ballet, and drama, achieving European prominence under the artistic directorship of August Wilhelm *Iffland who introduced the aesthetic principles and repertoire of *Weimar classicism with a strong emphasis on *Goethe and *Schiller. A new building designed by Carl Gotthard Langhans was opened in 1801. Iffland was succeeded by Count von Brühl in 1815, who aimed to make it the leading German-speaking theatre. He was aided by a fire which prompted a new building designed by Karl Friedrich *Schinkel (1818–21), which still stands as one of the finest examples of German *neoclassical theatre architecture. After 1820 the Royal Theatre gained increasing prominence as an opera house thanks to its conductor and composer-in-residence Gasparo Spontini. It returned to prominence after the First World War under Leopold *Jessner, renamed the Staatliches Schauspielhaus (State

Theatre). Badly damaged during the Second World War, it reopened in 1984 as a concert hall.

CBB

BERMAN, SABINA (1953–)

Mexican playwright, director, poet, novelist, and screenwriter who has garnered nearly every playwriting *award in Mexico. One of the brightest and most talented contemporary playwrights, Berman belongs to a generation of writers who grew up during what Mexicans call 'the crisis', a protracted period of political and economic instability and corruption which has bred a deeply cynical view of the country's leadership and moral values. The imprint of these years is everywhere evident in Berman's work; for example, in the trio of estranged youths who inhabit an abandoned apartment building in *Sudden Death* (1989); in *Krisis* (1996), a dark, twisted *satire of Mexican politics in the 1990s; in the Kafkaesque world of *The Crack* (1997), where the playwright takes aim at the irrationality and tyranny of Mexican bureaucracies. Berman stands out in Mexico for her continuous record of critical and *box-office successes: *Between Pancho Villa and a Naked Woman* (1993), a *comedy about machismo; *Molière* (1998), notable among other things for its remarkable production which placed the *audience on stage and the actors in the house; *Happy New Century, Doktor Freud* (2000), a *tragicomedy about the repercussions of psychotherapy on its originator and his patients.

KFN

BERNABÉ, JOBY (1945–)

Martinican actor, playwright, and director. Bernabé is the product of theatre experiments in France after the uprisings of May 1968: *agitprop work influenced by *Piscator, the *Bread and Puppet Theatre, *mask techniques, and other forms of *physical theatre. He founded the company Kimafoutésa in 1973, but returned to Martinique in 1976 to pursue research. His own remarkable voice and storytelling ability have been put to good use in vocal experiments in the relationship of theatre, poetic *text, and *Caribbean storytelling.

AR

BERNARD, JOHN (1756–1828)

English *actor-manager. Son of a British naval officer, Bernard abandoned his apprenticeship to an attorney and joined a travelling troupe. After *touring the provinces, he was hired to play comic roles at *Covent Garden in 1787. But his greatest success was found in America where he first performed at the Greenwich Street Theatre, *New York, in 1797. Recruited by *Wignell that same year, he spent six seasons at the *Chestnut Street Theatre in *Philadelphia. He moved to *Boston in 1803 and three years later became a partner and co-*manager at the *Federal Street Theatre. Between 1810 and 1817 Bernard toured the USA and Canada, successfully opening new theatres in several cities, including Albany in 1813. He returned to Boston in 1819 to manage the new theatre at Washington Gardens, but remained less than a year before sailing home to England. Father to playwright William Bayle Bernard, he wrote about his theatrical career in two books published posthumously, *Retrospections of the Stage* (1830) and *Retrospections of America, 1797–1811* (1887). PAD

BERNHARD, THOMAS (1931–89)

Austrian playwright and novelist who did not write his first full-length play (*A Feast for Boris*) until 1970. Until then he worked as a journalist, librettist, poet, and prose author. His collaboration with the director Claus *Peymann was a major inspiration and led to a string of successful stage works, which turned him into Austria's most eminent playwright of the post-war period. At the same time, his critical attitude towards Austrian conservatism and the stifling cultural climate of the country made him an extremely controversial figure in his homeland, where several premières of his plays turned into prolonged altercations with the press and political figureheads. Despite sustained attacks on his work he refused to leave the country and spent the last 24 years of his life as a reclusive figure on a farm in Upper Austria. Regarding his fellow countrymen as incorrigible, he stipulated in his will that none of his works be performed or published in Austria as long as they remain in copyright.

His 21 plays are existentialist studies of the search for a purpose of life in a meaningless universe. The curse of being born forces man into a torturous confrontation with his isolated existence, which the artist and intellectual can survive only by throwing themselves into projects which in the end still turn out to be futile and inane. Bernhard shows a typically Austrian distrust of language as a means of communication. Endless repetition of stock phrases *parodies the banality of life and points towards the senseless patterns of existence. He has often been compared to *Beckett and the theatre of the *absurd, but his bleak world-view is more relentless and rarely offers moments of humour or playful respite. His work shows little concern for *plot and *character development and disregards traditional *audience expectations. Dramatic *dialogues are often interrupted by long, aria-like *monologues of a highly musical quality, delivered by misanthropic, belligerent shrews. They were rendered unforgettable by the actor Bernhard *Minetti, who became a congenial interpreter of these roles in *Die Jagdgesellschaft* (*Hunting Society*, *Burgtheater, *Vienna, 1974), *Die Macht der Gewohnheit* (*The Force of Habit*, *Salzburg, 1974), *Minetti* (Stuttgart, 1976), *Der Weltverbesserer* (*The World Reformer*, Bochum, 1980), *Der Schein trügt* (*Appearances Are Deceptive*, Bochum, 1984), *Einfach kompliziert* (*Simply Complicated*, *Berlin, 1986). GB

BERNHARDT, SARAH (SARAH-HENRIETTE-ROSINE BERNARD) (1844–1923)

French actress. After training at the *Conservatoire, followed by a brief and unremarkable spell at the *Comédie-Française (which she left under a cloud), Bernhardt re-entered the Comédie in 1872 with a triumphant performance as the Queen in a revival of *Hugo's *Ruy Blas*. Her Phèdre in *Racine's *tragedy was equally outstanding in 1874, and she became a *sociétaire* in 1875. While she played virtually the whole of Racine's tragic repertoire, her exceptionally wide range was also to include *Molière, *Marivaux, and *Beaumarchais (she played Chérubin at the age of 29); Shakespeare (Cordelia and Desdemona); Hugo and *Dumas *père* among the French *romantic dramatists; and, among contemporary playwrights, *Dumas *fils*, *Sardou, and *Rostand. Well on the way to becoming the outstanding French actress of the century—if not of all time—but impatient with the conservatism in terms of repertory and *acting style at the Comédie-Française, she resigned in 1880, forming her own company, and later *managing her own theatres (the Renaissance, and later the Théâtre Sarah-Bernhardt). Her enormous international reputation was built up by repeated foreign *tours, especially in England and the USA. A particular feature of the latter part of her career was her fondness for male roles (*see* MALE IMPERSONATION): Hamlet at the Sarah-Bernhardt in 1899 (she had already played Ophelia in 1886); Napoleon's son in Rostand's *L'Aiglon* (1900, followed by frequent revivals); Lorenzo in *Musset's *Lorenzaccio* (1897). This latter play, never performed in Musset's lifetime, was still regarded as *closet drama; it was adapted for Bernhardt by Armand d'Artois, who accommodated the sprawling 'Shakespearian' *text to French *dramaturgical conventions. Her Hamlet won admiring reports from the critics, even in *London; though Max *Beerbohm's article was headed 'Hamlet, Princess of Denmark', and *Punch* suggested that her performance should be followed by Henry *Irving playing Ophelia.

It was while performing one of her favourite roles from the modern repertoire—the heroine in Sardou's *La Tosca*—on tour in South America in 1905 that Bernhardt suffered an injury that was to impose cruel limitations on the remainder of her acting career when, throwing herself off the battlements of the Castel Sant'Angelo, she fell heavily onto a hard floor unprotected by the usual mattresses. The injury remained untreated for too long, and although she was able to conclude her American tour, in which she visited over 60 cities, she was never afterwards free of pain. In 1915, at the age of 70, she agreed to have her right leg amputated; so that for the many stage appearances she continued to make, she was either completely static or had to be carried in a chair. The graceful movements might have gone, but the modulations of the voice were as rich as ever; and by all accounts, it was the distinctive character of her voice that was the basis of Bernhardt's star quality. In the series of performances of Racine's *Athalie* that she gave in 1920, when she was carried on stage as the Jewish Queen in a golden palanquin, this elderly handicapped lady was as spellbinding as ever. She was the archetypal 'monstre sacré' of the French theatre of the *belle époque*, with an extravagant lifestyle and an insatiable need for a vast personal income to support herself and her son Maurice, who, while helping to manage her career, was an inveterate spendthrift. But she was adored by an enormous public, on both sides of the Atlantic: a growing public, once she had begun to experiment with the new medium of *film. Offstage, she fed the appetite of the gossips and scandalmongers with her numerous affairs, but there was no doubt about her devotion to the national cause during the 1914–18 war, when, even after her amputation, she insisted on visiting the front to entertain the French troops. She outshone the two other great actresses of her day, Eleonore *Duse and Ellen *Terry (with Duse, she had a waspish rivalry; with Terry, a genuine friendship built on the latter's admiration); and for those French critics who were of an age to remember *Rachel, there was no doubt that their preference went to 'la divine Sarah', who succeeded, time and again, in bringing poetry to the age of *Zola and *naturalism. WDH

ASTON, ELAINE, *Sarah Bernhardt: an actress on the English stage* (Oxford, 1989)

RICHARDSON, JOANNA, *Sarah Bernhardt and her World* (London, 1977)

BERNINI, GIAN LORENZO (1598–1680)

As well as being the greatest Italian sculptor and architect of his day, Bernini was a dramatist, *amateur actor, and *scenographer in what was in any case the heyday of spectacular stage machinery. He designed apparatuses for the popes in *Rome from 1630, mounted his own plays from 1634; and during a visit to *Paris in 1665 his adverse comments on the *Petit-Bourbon Theatre disturbed the projects and status of the *Vigarani family. As an actor and dramatist, Bernini offered plays in *commedia dell'arte* style (now sadly lost), producing caricatures of current personalities which were sometimes accurate and cutting enough to get him into trouble. As a scenographer, he was capable of enacting floods and fires on stage while avoiding unfortunate side effects. In 1637, for his play *Of Two Theatres*, he constructed a mirror-image set: the *audience was faced from the back of the stage with a representation of itself, with individual portrait *masks, first listening to the *prologue (delivered by two actors simultaneously), then leaving to go home. RAA

BERNSTEIN, LEONARD (1918–90)

American composer, conductor, pianist, lyricist, and educator. Bernstein's talent, versatility, and unflagging energy made him one of the most prominent American musical figures of the twentieth century. As assistant conductor for the *New York Philharmonic in 1943, Bernstein gained sudden renown by stepping in and performing brilliantly for ailing guest conductor Bruno Walter. He served as music director for the Philharmonic from 1958 to 1969. As a Broadway composer Bernstein would bring a classical wit, elegance, and unity to the musical-theatre score. His reputation was established in 1944 with the spirited *ballet *Fancy Free*, choreographed by Jerome *Robbins. It was quickly expanded to Broadway *musical comedy proportions as *On the Town* (1944), with *book and lyrics by newcomers Betty *Comden and Adolph Green, and direction by George *Abbott. Following his score for an adaptation of *My Sister Eileen*, called *Wonderful Town* (1953), Bernstein invested the breadth of his musical savvy and sophistication into an adaptation of *Voltaire's satiric romp *Candide* (1956). Although originally a failure at the *box office, it would gain due recognition in a revised 1974 return to Broadway, imaginatively staged by Harold *Prince. Bernstein and Robbins had long discussed the project which would become *West Side Story* (1957), for which the composer's many indelible tunes—with lyrics by Stephen *Sondheim—include 'Maria' and 'Somewhere'. The show's innovative expression in music and *dance, blended with an up-to-the-minute transposition of Shakespeare's *Romeo and Juliet*, was underpinned by Arthur *Laurents's astute libretto. It burst with critical and popular success upon the New York and *London scenes, and remains a pinnacle of the Broadway musical's golden age. Bernstein's diverse compositional output also included song cycles, symphonies, *opera, a *film soundtrack, and *Mass: a theater piece for singers, players and dancers* (1971). EW

BERRECHID, ABDEL KARIM (1943–)

Moroccan playwright, especially known as the spokesman of Al Ihtifalia (The Ceremonial), a movement for research into authentic Arab theatrical forms. His manifestos of the 1980s called for a break from the dominance of Western theatre and the modern Arab practice that resulted from colonization. The movement seeks an alternative to European influence in the participatory theatricality of popular native fairs. His plays are chiefly *historical dramas with a revisionist twist, his *characters often princes, poets, and statesmen drawn from Arab history who are confronted with modernity. This self-conscious anachronism provides a platform to investigate contemporary social and political questions, as in *Antar in the Broken Mirrors* (1974), *Imruou'ou Alkais in Paris* (1981), *Ibn Arroumi in the Shantytowns, Nimroud in Hollywood* (1990), and *Quaraquch the Great* (1977). His work has been staged in Morocco, *Tunis, and *Cairo. MMe

BERTINAZZI, CARLO ('CARLINO') (1710–83)

Piemontese actor settled in France. He made a speciality of the role of *Harlequin, and was summoned to *Paris from Italy in 1741, specifically to replace Angelo Costantini at the *Comédie Italienne. For his first appearance, uncertain of his French, he used a *scenario where Harlequin remained mute; but his popularity was rapidly established. Praised and admired by *Goldoni and *Garrick, as well as by French intellectuals, he was famed for his expressive bodily elegance and his easy rapport with *audiences. His friendship with the future Pope Clement XIV inspired a number of romantic fictions after 1800.   RAA

BESSON, BENNO (1922–   )

Swiss actor and director. Born in the francophone region of Switzerland, Besson began his theatre career in Zurich in 1943, moved to *Paris in 1945 to work with Roger *Blin, and joined *Brecht in *Berlin in 1949. He directed a number of productions at the *Berliner Ensemble in the 1950s, including *Molière's *Don Juan* (1954), Brecht's *Trumpets and Drums* (1955), and his *The Good Person of Setzuan* (1957). Between 1961 and 1969 he directed mainly at the *Deutsches Theater in East Berlin, producing important interpretations of Greek plays (*Aristophanes, *Sophocles) and contemporary dramatists such as Peter *Hacks. From 1969 to 1978 he was *artistic director of the *Volksbühne, where he continued a repertoire mixing contemporary drama and adaptations of the classics. Besson's directorial style combines a keen analytical, *Brechtian approach with radical, often burlesque exaggeration and witty modernizations. Since 1982 Besson has directed the Comédie in Geneva. His productions have achieved European prominence and been invited to most major *festivals.   CBB

BETSUYAKU MINORU (1937–   )

Manchurian-born *Japanese *absurdist playwright. In 1961 Betsuyaku established the Free Stage (Jiyū Butai) with *Suzuki Tadashi, the precursor to the Waseda Little Theatre. His *Elephant* (1962, trans. 1986), a play in the style of *Beckett and *Ionesco, was instrumental in breaking Japanese drama free from the gridlock of *realism. Both the Free Stage and the WLT produced many of his best plays, like *The Little Match-Girl* (1966, trans. 1992). Betsuyaku left the WLT in 1969 and has since written freelance for various major *shingeki* troupes like Bungakuza (the Literary Theatre) and Gekidan En (Theatre Circle). His style is austere, with spare sets and understated, wry, and enigmatic *dialogue. His plays, which often feature couples—husbands and wives, parents and children, colleagues, masters and servants—often focus on the hidden violence of apparently normal human relationships. Representative works include *The Move* (1973), *The Legend of Noon* (1973), and *The*

Cherry in Bloom (1980). Betsuyaku is also a writer of children's stories and *television and *film scripts.   CP

BETTERTON, MARY (c.1637–1712)

English actress, one of the first women to appear on the English stage, as Ianthe in *Davenant's *Siege of Rhodes* (1661), making such an impression on the diarist *Pepys that he always referred to her by that name. Mary married Thomas *Betterton in 1662 and together they forged a popular and successful acting partnership. Colley *Cibber considered her without equal in Shakespeare, noting that even Elizabeth *Barry could not match her portrayal of Lady Macbeth. Mary was a gifted teacher, coaching the Princesses Mary and Anne in court *masques for which she was rewarded with a pension (which remained unpaid), but imparting her greatest skills to the generation of actresses who succeeded her, notably to Anne *Bracegirdle, who was adopted into the Betterton household as a young child. *See also* WOMEN AND PERFORMANCE.   GBB

BETTERTON, THOMAS (c.1635–1710)

English actor, *manager, and playwright. Traditional histories consider Betterton to have been the greatest figure of the Restoration stage; he certainly was the most prominent and respected of its practitioners. He began as a young actor with Rhodes's company at the *Cockpit but was soon recruited into William *Davenant's Duke's Company where he was the leading player and, following Davenant's death in 1668, manager of the company under Lady Davenant's direction. The highest-paid actor of the time, his contemporaries heaped praises upon his emotional range in *tragedy (his fame as Hamlet was such that he continued to play the part successfully into his seventies) and his versatility made him equally popular in *comedy. Betterton managed the Duke's Company for Davenant's son Charles, and continued as manager when the two *patent companies united in 1682. He employed his first-hand knowledge of French theatrical effects in successful adaptations of Shakespeare and *Fletcher and during the 1690s directed his energies toward producing a number of spectacular *operas. When the theatrical patent passed to Christopher *Rich, Betterton's undisputed rule of the company was challenged. The leading players eventually rebelled against Rich, and by 1695 Betterton, Elizabeth *Barry, and Anne *Bracegirdle had received a royal licence to form their own company at Davenant's first theatre in *Lincoln's Inn Fields. In 1705 Betterton joined forces with *Vanbrugh and the company moved to the Queen's Theatre in the *Haymarket. In 1709 Barry and Bracegirdle came out of retirement to join Betterton for his last appearance in his own retirement *benefit of *Congreve's *Love for Love*. He married the actress Mary *Betterton in 1662.   GBB

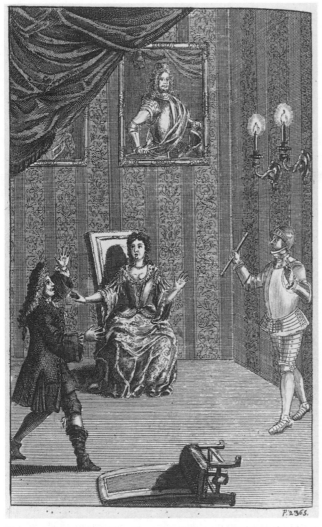

The great Restoration actor Thomas **Betterton** as Hamlet in the closet scene, from the frontispiece to the play in Nicholas Rowe's edition of Shakespeare (1709). The image offers intriguing information about seventeenth-century English staging: the contemporary costumes; the chair, overturned by Hamlet when the ghost of his father appeared; the Ghost dressed in full ceremonial armour; his portrait above the seated Queen; the decorated walls of the scenery; the angled curtain at top left, perhaps suggesting the queen's retiring room; and the fixed candelabra, providing workable lighting on stage.

BETTI, UGO (1892–1953)

Italian playwright. Although once regarded as heir to *Pirandello, Betti's reputation in Italy has suffered total eclipse since his death. He had a healthy distaste for full-time writers but was otherwise the complete man of letters, producing one novel, many critical essays, volumes of poetry and short stories, as well as 25 plays. A magistrate by profession, he proclaimed his disbelief in all legal, earthly justice and set his *characters on a quest for some transcendental, divine standard. His represen-tative character is the person intent on his career and on worldly affairs until some profound inner crisis disrupts his life and causes him to question the hierarchy of values by which he has lived. This was the case of the judge Parsc—Betti's characters were always given strange names to emphasize their universality—presiding over the investigation into the disaster which was the subject of *Accident at the North Station* (1932). Parsc, when required to pronounce on individual responsibility, calls instead for universal compassion. Holders of power invariably turn out to be weak and ineffectual, like the fugitive monarch in *The Queen and the Rebels* (1949) or the statesman in *The Burnt Flowerbed* (1952). These seemingly *political plays advocate no recognizable ideology, but dissolve into the notion that the pursuit of earthly objectives represents surrender to a code of beliefs which is intrinsically mistaken and inappropriate for human beings. The religious element in his work grew increasingly strong, but he never advocated any orthodox Christian creed.   JF

BETTY, WILLIAM HENRY WEST (1791–1874)

Irish child actor, the first in a line of Infant Phenomena on the English stage. Coached by his greedy father and known as the Young *Roscius, Betty stormed *London in 1804–5, playing Hamlet, Romeo, Young Norval in John *Home's tragedy *Douglas*, and other major roles to adoring crowds; Parliament was suspended for one sitting so that members could see his Hamlet. After two seasons the craze expired. Betty attempted a comeback in 1812, then lapsed into obscurity. He was beautiful, graceful, personable, and well drilled, but acted by rote and was quite improbable as a tragic *hero or lover.   MRB

BEVERLEY, WILLAM ROXBY (c.1814–1889)

English scene painter. Beverley started as an actor in *Manchester, but then turned to scene *painting, becoming the chief painter for the *Theatre Royal. He later worked for Madame *Vestris at the *Olympic and Charles *Kean at the *Princess's, settling at *Drury Lane in 1854 until retirement in 1885. His scenes were romantically beautiful, especially for transformations in Christmas *pantomimes. He was also an easel painter and exhibited at the Royal Academy.   MRB

BÈZE, THEODORE DE (1519–1605)

Protestant theologian and polemicist. His *Abraham sacrifiant* was performed by students at Lausanne in 1550. The play bridges medieval and Renaissance *dramaturgy: Satan and an Angel are *characters, but there is also a *chorus. The subject was common in *medieval theatre, but Bèze's treatment stresses Abraham's anguish rather than typologically correct behaviour.
RWV

BHADURI, SISIR (1889–1959)

Bengali director and *actor-manager, often considered the first *modernist director in *India. He resigned a lecturership of English in a Calcutta (*Kolkata) college in 1921 to become a professional actor. His breakthrough came very soon, when he produced two plays titled *Sita* on the heroine of the epic *Ramayana*, the first by D. L. Roy (1923), the second by Jogesh Chaudhuri (1924). The founding that year of his own company, Natyamandir, was the start of a new phase of respectability for *Bengali theatre. Bhaduri directed meticulously, with taste and sensitivity; he acted *heroes *naturalistically and with refinement. The intelligentsia, who had shunned the commercial stage, flocked to his shows and wrote effusively about him, while younger actors emulated his style. Although he introduced writers like *Tagore (*Tapati*, 1929) to his *audiences, they rejected such unconventional drama. Closing Natyamandir in 1930, he formed the first Bengali troupe to travel abroad, staging *Sita* in *New York (1931) to critical acclaim, though a disaster in terms of funding and management, causing his insolvency in 1933. He recovered at the Srirangam Theatre (1941–56), recapturing much of his artistry.   AL

BHAGAVATA

The main singer and narrator in many traditional *Indian theatre forms. Literally 'the one who sings the *Bhagavata Puranas*', epic narratives of the Lord Vishnu, the term was first used for the singer in those forms which present stories from the *Bhagavata*. Later it referred to singer-narrators in other forms including those that depict social and secular themes. The function of the *bhagavata* varies in different forms. In *kuchipudi, for instance, from Andhra Pradesh, he merely sings, whereas in *yakshagana and *sannata* from Karnataka, he intervenes dramatically in the narrative and plays a more active role in the shaping of the performance *text.   KVA

BHAGAVATA MELA

South *Indian traditional theatre performed in the villages around Thanjavur, Tamil Nadu, involving popular plays (*yakshaganas*) by a troupe (*melam*) of Brahman actors trained in *dance, *music, and speech. Originally performed as a part of a *ritualistic offering to Lord Narasimha, an incarnation of Vishnu, the tradition of *bhagavata mela* goes back to the eighteenth century, when Melattur Venkatarama Sastry wrote twelve *yakshaganas* for troupes consisting exclusively of Brahman boys in villages near Thiruvaiyar. Later the performance tradition was consolidated by Venkatarama Sastry, who was responsible for bringing the dance-drama from the court to the street, directly for the entertainment and religious edification of the people. The plays were performed annually during the Narasimha Jayanthi celebrations in front of the temple of Sri Varadaraja Perumal, Melattur. Beginning with an invocation to Lord Ganesha, followed by the entry of the *kattiyakkaran, a court fool, the play would continue with all the major *characters appearing with an entrance dance and song sequence. By far the most popular of Sastry's plays is *Prahlada Charitam*, which has a deep religious content and emotional intensity (*see* PRAHLADA NATAKA). Like the *protagonist Prahlada himself, all the actors in the company are devotees of Lord Narasimha, the presiding deity of the village. Despite some intermittent gaps, the annual performance tradition of *bhagavata mela* has continued since Sastry's time, with Bharatam Natesa Iyer, E. Krishna Iyer, and Balu Bhagavatar contributing to its revival and sustenance. The *bhagavata mela* is increasingly regarded as a rare classical performance art. *See also* TAMIL THEATRE   MNS

BHAMA KALAPAM

*Telugu *dance-drama from Andhra Pradesh, *India, in which Satyabhama, the consort of Sri Krishna, pines for her beloved after being separated from him. *Kalapam* means a collection, and in the context of *Bhama kalapam*, it implies a collection of songs in various metres depicting the varied moods of Bhama (Satyabhama). Apart from Bhama, the *sutradhara*, the director of the performance, takes the role of the second *character, Madhavi, who is Bhama's maid. The story, which is narrated by Bhama herself, dwells on the love-quarrels of her past life, followed by the agony of separation. Recalling several intimate incidents, she portrays the different emotional moods of a *sringara-nayika* (a *heroine suffering from the pangs of love). The *raison d'être* of the *kuchipudi* dance repertoire, *Bhama kalapam* is generally attributed to Siddhendra Yogi (sixteenth century), who is said to have initiated young Brahman boys into the art, making it obligatory for every boy in the village of Kuchipudi to perform the role of Bhama at least once in his lifetime. The representation of changing psychological moods (*sattvika abhinaya*) is widely regarded as one of the deepest artistic challenges of *Bhama kalapam*. From the late twentieth century, Vedantam Satyanarayana Sarma (1935–   ) has been hailed as one of the finest exponents of *Bhama kalapam*, not only as a *female impersonator, but also in his nuanced representation of *abhinaya (acting).   MNS

BHAND

North Indian storyteller, joker, and buffoon. The name derives from the Hindi word *bhanda* (buffooning). *Bhands* were employed by rich landlords or wealthy men, somewhat like the jesters of aristocratic Europe, acting as entertainers and as 'fixers' for their patrons. Now *bhands* are travelling minstrels, roaming the countryside and performing for *street *audiences. Though their position in the social hierarchy is very low, they

The **bhand pather** play *Darj Pathar* performed outdoors in New Delhi, India, 1979, by Gulam Rasool Bhatt and company from Kashmir, seen here standing in front of the canopy.

entertain at weddings and other auspicious occasions. Apart from singing and dancing, they also recite genealogies through gags and double entendres, always working in pairs. They perform stories about avaricious moneylenders, the evils of dowry traditions, and other social issues. Satiric, irreverent, and subversive, they beg forgiveness from their patron before the show, hoping for licence from retaliation.   NMSC

BHAND PATHER

Traditional *folk play from Kashmir. The word *bhand owes its origin either to a humorous play categorized in the *Natyasastra as *bhan*, or to *bhand* (comic actor). *Pather* (or *Pathar*) comes from *patra* (character). The agricultural and largely Muslim community of the *bhands* travel from village to village, particularly in the harvest season, and collect rice paddy, money, and clothes for their performances. An improvised play around social issues, *bhand pather* ridicules invaders and members of the ruling class, like the Pathan Pathar from Afghanistan, the Raja (King) Pathar, and Mala (Priest) Pathar, whose lust, avarice, and deeds of exploitation are exposed. Though there is no written script, the actors use *dance, *music, clowning, buffoonery, and mimicry to create powerful *satires on shared social concerns. The *open-air performances begin with a prelude by six musicians playing the *shehnai* (wind instrument), *naqara*, and *dhol* (both percussion). After this about six dancers perform, followed in turn by four mimics who enter from the *audience encircling the performance area, and then serve as narrators through the performance. Spectacular but simple theatrical devices mark the play, like the transformation of a half-*curtain into a canopy suspended on poles. With the emergence of political insurgency in Kashmir in the late twentieth century, performances of *bhand pather* have become increasingly rare and the survival of its artists is threatened.   KJ

BHARATA MUNI

Traditionally described as the author of the *Natyasastra (c. second century BC–c. second century AD), the ancient *Indian compendium in Sanskrit encompassing all aspects of drama, theatre, and performance. The first chapter of this encyclopedic work narrates the legendary origins of natya (drama), in which Brahma creates the fifth Veda—the Natya Veda—at the request of the other gods, who seek diversion. On Brahma's command, the sage Bharata Muni puts natya into practice with the assistance of his 100 sons. Today it is accepted that while Bharata Muni's authorship cannot be unequivocally assumed for a monumental work that has been compiled over the centuries, the reciters of epic poems in ancient India were called bharatas. Later this word referred to actors in general. LSR/RB

BHARATI, DHARAMVIR (1926–2000)

Indian playwright, novelist, and poet. Bharati was known in the last decades of his life as the editor of the prestigious Hindi weekly Dharmayug, but his enduring reputation rests on two seminal works from the early 1950s. Like Kurosawa's *film Roshomon, the novella Suraj ka satvam ghora (The Seventh Horse of the Sun) portrays a web of triangular relationships, in tales related by a narrator who is involved in the *plot but does not intervene. A similar narrator, implicated in the *action and yet outside it, weaves together the many strands of Bharati's most famous work, the drama Andha Yug (The Age of the Blind, 1954), which blends *folk theatre conventions with those from classic Sanskrit and *Greek drama. It shows the lawless events of the last days of the epic battle of Mahabharata, which signal the coming of a new age of darkness. Questioning the ethical authority radiated by the god Krishna, the play is explicitly concerned with the ethics of war, particularly with the issues raised by the bombing of Hiroshima. Its performance in 1963 under the direction of Ebrahim *Alkazi, in the *open-air setting of Talkatora Gardens in Delhi, was a landmark of modern Indian theatre. VDa

BHASA (probably fl. fourth century AD)

Sanskrit playwright, a precursor of *Kalidasa, whose works were unknown until 1910 when they were discovered by Mahamahopadhyaya T. Ganapathisastri, the first curator of the Trivandrum Manuscripts Library, who published a collection of Bhasa's plays (Bhasanatakachakram) between 1912 and 1924. The thirteen plays attributed to Bhasa contain a variety of themes depicting human character in all its varied dimensions. Bhasa drew from the two Hindu epics, the Mahabharata and the Ramayana, along with the *folk tales of *India constituting the katha tradition. Among his plays based on the Mahabharata, Madhyamavyayoga (The Middle One), Karnabhara (Karna's Task), and Urubhanga (The Broken Thighs) demonstrate great diversity and flexibility of structure with remarkable potential for individual actors to elaborate on the dramatic *action. Bhasa's most popular and best-structured play, Swapnavasavadatta (The Vision of Vasavadatta), is at once a tantalizing love story with a political undercurrent as well as a dream-play interested in the subtle division, and the blurring, of dreams and reality.

Individual acts from many of Bhasa's plays are performed in the temple theatres of Kerala known as *kuttampalam where the traditional cakyar community keeps alive the tradition of Sanskrit plays in *kutiyattam performances. Since 1956 there have been attempts to produce Bhasa in contemporary versions in *Hindi and other Indian languages. Festivals of Bhasa have also been organized by the Madhya Pradesh Natak Lok Kala Akademi in Ujjain, and the Sopanam Institute of Performing Arts and Research in Trivandrum, in which versions of the plays have been staged in the original Sanskrit and in regional languages. These performances have stimulated debate on the challenges of producing Bhasa in India today. KNP

BHATTACHARYA, BIJON (1915–78)

Bengali dramatist and actor. Born and brought up in the countryside of Faridpur district in what is now *Bangladesh, he saw villagers and rural life at first hand, using this knowledge as primary material for his plays. Moving to Calcutta (*Kolkata) in 1930, he became a Communist Party member and co-founded the Bengal unit of the *Indian People's Theatre Association, which staged his first full-length drama, Nabanna (New Harvest, 1944). The prototype of contemporary *Bengali theatre, it showed with stark *realism the disastrous effects of the recent Bengal famine in which millions perished. Bhattacharya directed it jointly with Sombhu *Mitra, and the production was a huge popular success in urban Bengal. Bhattacharya started his own group, Calcutta Theatre, in 1951 with his play Mara Chand (Dead Moon). He wrote fifteen major plays; the others include Gotrantar (Change of Caste, 1959), on east Bengali migration to Calcutta after Partition, Devi Garjan (The Goddess Roars, 1966), which depicts zamindars' (landlords') oppression of peasants, and Garbhabati Janani (Pregnant Mother, 1969), which questions traditional dogmas. In general, his work displays a lack of concern for the conventional *well-made form and a partiality for local dialects and lifestyles. Although a Marxist, he was not a doctrinaire dramatist. As a director he did not attain great heights, but as an actor he flourished, occasionally venturing into *films made by art directors like Ritwik Ghatak and Mrinal Sen. AL

BHAVABHUTI (c. seventh century AD)

Sanskrit poet and dramatist. From a Brahman family of famous Vedic scholars from Padampura in Vidarbha, Bhavabhuti

Jasma Odan at the National School of Drama, New Delhi, India, 1982, written and directed by Shanta Gandhi. This experimental work, first produced in 1968, adapted the **bhavai** folk play *Jasma Vesh* for performance by urban actors. Uttara Baokar as Jasma is centre.

inherited a great legacy of learning from the Sanskrit scriptures. He was a noted poet and scholar in the court of Raja Yesovarman of Kanyakubja, and is famous for three dramas: *Malati Madhava*, *Mahavira Charita*, and *Uttararamacharita*. The first has an invented *plot, while the second is the dramatization of the epic *Ramayana* in seven acts, culminating in Rama's return to Ayodhya, and Sita's 'test through fire' to prove her chastity. Most memorably, *Uttararamacharita* deals in a highly distilled poetic language with the abandoning of Sita in the forest by Rama's brother Lakshmana, her subsequent experiences as she casts herself in the River Bhageerathi, and her recovery by the goddesses of the earth and the River Ganga. Eventually Sita gives birth to two children who remain with her in the hermitage of the sage Valmiki. He is ultimately responsible for bringing Sita back to Rama with her sons, when she is hailed by the people as their queen. Through all these experiences, the dominant sentiment explored by Bhavabhuti is *karuna* (pathos). In contrast to the sensuous love that assumes heightened poetic dimensions in *Kalidasa's plays, Bhavabhuti presents a love which is rooted firmly in spiritual sacrifice.

KNP

BHAVAI

A *folk form from the western state of Gujarat, *India. Though now largely secular in content, it originated in the fourteenth century as a form of *religious worship to the mother goddess Amba. Attributed to Asait Thakur, it is said that as an outcast from his community he associated himself with a subcaste of Brahmans called Targalas, who took to performing *bhavai* professionally in order to comment on larger social injustices. *Bhavai* has become a night-long performance presenting a series of six to ten small plays called *veshas*, each of which has an independent *plot. The *veshas* take their stories from history, mythology, popular legends, or topical issues affecting the community. *Actors represent social character types through stylized movements and different dialects of Gujarati and Marwari, representing the regions of Gujarat. The dramatic form is loosely structured, allowing a considerable amount of *improvisation by the performers and including humour, mimicry, *acrobatics, *music, *dance, and *dialogue. The performance is controlled by the *naik* (narrator) and *ranglo* (jester), who entertain the spectators with ribald comments. All women's roles are played by men, whose art of *female impersonation demands specialized training. Dance and music are an important part of *bhavai*, as with other traditional forms. The dance steps are adapted to the moment of the play, so that they carry a dramatic function in addition to bridging the gap between two *veshas*. The music, incorporating classical *raginis* and folk melodies, also heightens dramatic impact. The chief instruments used in *bhavai* include a long brass pipe instrument called the *bhungal*, the *dholak* and *tabla* (percussion), the flute, and cymbals.

The *open-air playing space, called *chachar* or *paudh*, is circular, around which the *audience is seated with a narrow passage for the exits and entries of actors. No *scenery is required for the performance, which is generally held in the village square. *Costumes signify the social class of *characters, ranging from everyday clothes for the ordinary characters to elaborate attire for kings. The *make-up, using indigenous materials—like lime and sandal paste for the base, saffron and *kumkum* (red) for colour, and soot for the eyes—is simple but heavy. This was suitable when the *lighting source was traditional *kakras* (torch lights) carried by actors or fixed on the performance space, but in the harsh glare of the pressure lamp, the make-up now appears overdone.

Performances are traditionally held during the festival of Navratri, some other Hindu celebrations, and also for specific village occasions. By the end of the twentieth century, with other modes of entertainment available, *bhavai* has lost its earlier charm and is gradually disappearing in rural areas. Valiant efforts have been made by several modern theatre workers to interact with the form in order to rejuvenate it. Most significant among these experiments has been Shanta *Gandhi's *Jasma Odan* (1968), a rewritten *bhavai* script with rich and varied music, aesthetically reworked to suit an urban audience. Two earlier attempts directed by Dina Gandhi deserve mention: *Lok Bhavai* (1945), a *satire on Bombay (*Mumbai) life, and *Mena Gurjari* (1954). KJ

BHUTAN

Isolated for centuries in the Himalayan mountains, the kingdom of Bhutan has tended to preserve its religious, environmental, and cultural heritages despite the inroads of modernity. Inspired by Buddhist mythology, oral history, and the natural surroundings, most performances occur outdoors, associated with local festivals. Though the country's performing arts can be traced to shamanistic *rituals which existed before the arrival of Buddhist civilization in the sixth century, the dominant form is *chham*, *dances performed by Buddhist monks and laymen at annual festivals organized by monastic centres. Most monasteries host an annual *chham* festival—known as the *Tshechu* or *Domchhoe*—and maintain sets of *costumes, *masks, and musical instruments. They also train retinues of

monks as performers, who are sometimes joined by laymen—all religious dances and dance-dramas are performed by men. Choreographed by religious leaders over a long period, the dances are traditional vehicles for edification and enlightenment, and most Bhutanese attend festivals as a form of religious practice. Characterized by elaborate and colourful costumes, headgear, and masks, and accompanied by religious music, the dancers depict different manifestations of deities or representations of the spiritual and animal world. The movements and hand gestures, based on Buddhist rituals and iconography, have symbolic signification that may not be accessible to the non-practitioner. *Chhams* are performed in the courtyards of monasteries on a square flagstone clearing surrounded by the *audience, who sit cross-legged on the ground. The atmosphere is open and interactive. Traditionally, no artificial *lighting or microphones are used. Music is provided by a group of trained monks or laymen, playing cymbals, long horns, clarinets, bells, and drums; sometimes the dancers also work bells and drums.

One of the most popular *chhams* is the tenth-century tantric *Shanag Ngacham* (*Black Hat Dance*), a sacred ritual that portrays the triumph of Buddhism over the forces of evil (which is performed in variant forms by other Himalayan Buddhist practitioners, including the Tibetans). The dancers wear large black hats, assuming the *character of yogis with the power of taking and re-creating life. They prepare for the ritual through prayer and meditation days before the actual performance, a practice that may continue afterwards as well. Bhutanese Buddhists believe that watching the dance dispels mental obstacles to enlightenment. Another typical dance is the *Dramitse Ngacham* (*Dance of the Drums*) from Dramitse monastery in eastern Bhutan, choreographed in the sixteenth century. This *bodchham* (lay) dance depicts the peaceful and terrifying deities in *zangdopelri*, or the celestial abode of the enlightened being. It is performed by lay monks or laymen selected from the community. Also important during the festivals are the traditional dance-dramas, which enact myths as well as the biographies of folk or spiritual heroes; they are performed by laymen and carry a serious moral. A characteristic narrative involves a hunter who abandons his calling when he meets the saint Milarepa, who demonstrates the interdependence of all living things. An important character at the dance festivals is the *atsara*, a jester figure who provides comic relief, known for his bawdy behaviour and sexual humour. Bhutanese believe the *atsara* is a figure of the *archarya* (enlightened being) who teaches by being outrageous. The *atsara* also acts as the stagehand who repairs loose costumes or masks of the performers, and sometimes prompts the dancers. (*See also* RELIGION AND THEATRE.)

Outside the festivals, secular plays were encouraged in the Bhutanese court, often dramatizing local issues and personalities for the entertainment of the royal entourage. These *amateur performances were sometimes staged during public gatherings; with the coming of a modern education system, they were replaced by regular student plays as community entertainment. A royal music and dance troupe has been maintained in the capital since the beginning of the twentieth century, to entertain dignitaries and to promote traditional dance and music. That objective has been furthered by the Royal Academy of Performing Arts, established in 1954 to train traditional performers. The most vibrant of the performing arts in Bhutan is music, which can be categorized into three broad groups: classical (*zhungdra*), folk (*boedra*), and modern (*rigsar*). *Zhungdra* and *boedra* are chiefly songs which express reverence for religious personalities, praise the country and king, or celebrate nature and love. *Rigsar*, popular music that tends to attract young people, surfaced in the 1970s through a variety of influences from Asian and Western pop music.

At the start of the twenty-first century Bhutanese performing arts were undergoing significant change. Some lay *chhams*, plays, and music are now performed on raised platforms or *stages with modern lighting and sound systems, physically distancing the audience from the performance. Secular drama is also gaining popularity, performed by the Royal Academy, independent amateur groups, and students, though the public still prefers plays that treat mythical and *folkloric subjects. The introduction of *television in 1999 has inspired an amateur *film industry in Bhutan, and a growing group of amateur actors, singers, and producers. As might be expected, it has also injected a degree of commercialism into the performing arts.

SSP

BIANCOLELLI FAMILY

Italian *commedia dell'arte* actors settled in France in the seventeenth and eighteenth centuries. They figure in records over four generations, of which the second and third are the most significant. The founders of the dynasty were **Francesco** (d. after 1640) and his wife Isabella Franchini, daughter of a Pantalone. **Giuseppe Domenico** ('Dominique', c.1637–88) was born in Bologna and transferred to *Paris in 1661 after creating a reputation in Italy and *Vienna. He took possession of the role of *Harlequin, and initiated the process by which that mask was transformed from a rough, aggressive, demonic figure into something more refined, balletic, and also protean in its ability to assume *disguises and parody social or theatrical stereotypes. He was on familiar jester's terms with Louis XIV; and he began to introduce passages of French language into the plays of the *Comédie Italienne, in ways then reflected in *Gherardi's published collections of material. He also left a collection of his *scenarios in manuscript: the *texts concentrate selectively on his own role rather than giving an overall picture. His son **Pierre-François** ('Dominique fils', 1680–1734) then became a pivotal figure in the transition between the first and the second Comédie Italienne, as both actor and dramatist. He performed in the French provinces after the expulsion of the Italian

troupe from Paris in 1697, returned to the Paris Foire in 1710, and joined the revived Italian company under *Riccoboni in 1717. He performed as Harlequin, or in the similar servant role of Trivelin, by now entirely in French. A significant aspect both of his performance and his writing involved the current vogue for topical, farcical *parodies of more serious works mounted on other Paris stages: heroic figures would be hilariously caricatured, and impersonated by Harlequin himself. His daughter **Marie-Thérèse de la Lalande** (1723–88) also had a distinguished career as an actress.

RAA

BIBIENA (GALLI DA) FAMILY

Italian painters, architects, and designers. Three generations of Galli da Bibienas were active throughout Europe from the Counter-*Reformation to the Enlightenment, a period spanning approximately 1680 to 1780. Students of the baroque, an age that loved *illusion, they adopted an exuberant style that made use of new architectural forms, ornate columns, *trompe l'œil*, overstatement, and exaggerated modelling (*see* SCENOGRAPHY). Their patrons were emperors and kings, and members of the nobility, as well as the Catholic Church and wealthy merchants in major towns throughout the Italian peninsula, Europe, and Russia; and they spent many years away from the family home in Bologna designing, building, and decorating gardens, palaces, villas, churches; planning and organizing spectacular royal coronations, weddings, and funerals; constructing horseshoe-shaped, many-tiered court *playhouses and modern public or community theatres; designing theatre interiors; creating innovative *scenery; and engineering stage machinery for *operas and *ballets by Scarlatti, Vivaldi, Antonio Caldara, and Carl Heinrich Graun.

Ferdinando (1657–1743), as leading painter and architect for almost 28 years at the Duke of Parma's court, was chief scenographer for the Teatro *Farnese and Piacenza's Teatro Ducale and Teatro Nuovo. In 1711 the German Emperor Charles VI, whose marriage celebrations he had staged in *Barcelona in 1708, appointed him court architect in *Vienna, the imperial seat of the Habsburgs, and gave him command over set designs and decorations for court festivals, opera, and ballet. Ferdinando wrote some important *theoretical tracts: *L'architettura civile* (*Civil Architecture*, 1711) and *Direzioni ai giovani* (*Directions for the Young*, 1731). In these texts he discusses the *scena per angolo*, or sets at an angle, a *perspective technique that he perfected and that became a family trademark. By using two or more vanishing points at either side, *scena per angolo* created a vision that was divorced from the *auditorium in terms of angle and scale. These multiple vanishing points allowed for tremendous variety. Symmetry was no longer necessary, as in *early modern Italian design, and the scale could be altered so that the tops of buildings need not be visible. If the vanishing points were placed extremely low, the set gave a sense of vastness, mystery, and undefined possibility. Inasmuch as only the drawings of these sets remain, it is difficult to say how they were actually executed.

Ferdinando's brother **Francesco** (1659–1739) travelled to *Naples in 1702 to organize magnificent festivities welcoming to the Kingdom of the Two Sicilies its new ruler, King Philip V of Spain, and his Habsburg Queen Maria Theresa. Shortly thereafter Francesco was summoned to Vienna by the German Emperor Leopold I to build Teatro Nuovo (completed in 1704). He built four or five other theatres, including the great theatre at Nancy (1707), *Rome's Teatro Alibert (1720, constructed with his nephew Antonio), and Verona's Teatro Filarmonico (1720), none of which has survived.

Giuseppe (1696–1757), having followed his father Ferdinando to Vienna in 1712, designed over 30 catafalques for the funerals of nobility. Among the splendid court festivities he planned was the 1723 celebration in *Prague of the crowning of Charles VI and his Empress as king and queen of Bohemia. For this he created an *open-air theatre holding 8,000 spectators, a stage 60 m (200 feet) deep, and stage machinery that facilitated startling tricks of transformation during the performance of the opera *Costanza e fortezza*. Giuseppe is best known for his interior of the Opera House in Bayreuth, a prime example of Bibiena court-theatre design which has been faithfully restored. Until the construction of *Wagner's *Bayreuth Festspielhaus it was Germany's largest, best-equipped, and most elaborate theatre. **Antonio** (1700–74), another of Ferdinando's sons, was unrivalled in his time for the number of public theatres he constructed, among which is Bologna's Teatro Communale (1756–63). He also designed the interior of Mantua's Teatro Scientifico (1767–9), renamed the Virgilian Academy, where the 13-year-old *Mozart amazed audiences in 1770. Ferdinando had two other sons, **Giovanni Maria** (n.d.) and **Alessandro** (1687–1769), who were active in Prague and Mannheim, respectively. Francesco's son **Giovanni Carlo** (d. 1760) spent his career in Portugal. The last artist in the family, Giuseppe's son **Carlo** (1725–87), was in demand throughout Europe and in *St Petersburg. *See also* FAMILIES IN THE THEATRE. JEH

Mayor, A. Hyatt, *The Bibiena Family* (New York, 1955)

BIBLICAL PLAYS

Plays that dramatize portions of the scriptures, sometimes embellished with material from the Apocrypha and other sacred legend, were the dominant form of *medieval theatre in Europe. Called variously *Corpus Christi plays, *mystery plays, *miracle plays, *laude*, *Passion plays, Easter plays, Creed plays, or even Pater Noster plays, they have in common subject matter rooted in scripture and performance largely by and for the laity. As a dramatic form they first appear in the mid- to late fourteenth century and seem to have taken their inspiration not from the existing *liturgical drama or the extra-liturgical Latin drama but from *didacticism and personal or 'affective' piety that characterized the religious life of the late fourteenth and fifteenth centuries. Similar types of drama appear all over Western Europe, varying only in their mix of didacticism with emotive response to the events of the Christian story. The proponents of affective piety emphasized the humanity and suffering of Christ to stimulate a closer relationship with him and so enhance faith. The movement had a double thrust. The first was strictly didactic, coming from the decrees of the fourth Lateran Council of 1215 concerning the education of both the clergy and the laity. The other thrust came from St Bernard and the Franciscan mystics who moved beyond simple learning to mystic transformation.

Lateran IV acknowledged a heightening of interest in the cure of souls and initiated a movement to provide a better-educated clergy who could bring the laity to a reasonable understanding of the essentials of Christian belief and practice. The Council was followed by the decree of *Omnis utriusque sexus* which made annual confession to the parish priest and annual communion at Easter obligatory for all Christians. The significance of this decree for didactic vernacular drama was immense. Both the priests and the laity had to have sufficient knowledge of the faith for such confession to have any meaning. The clergy had to be provided with instruction in the elements of moral theology and the laity had to be provided with a rudimentary knowledge of the faith, for, it was argued, only through knowledge of God could man's soul be saved. The 'Lay Folk's Catechism', a fourteenth-century English tract promoting the didactic movement issued in 1357 by John Thoresby, archbishop of York, makes this abundantly clear. Adam and Eve before the Fall had perfect knowledge of God, but in a fallen world knowledge can only be mediated through Holy Church. To reinforce the necessity for such knowledge, the confessional was used not only for penance but also for instruction, as the confessor was expected to cross-examine penitents on their religious knowledge.

Plays that dramatized biblical material, then, were part of a wider movement that included artistic representations in stained glass, wall paintings and alabaster carvings, non-dramatic literary works such as the long didactic poems retelling the Bible stories, and emotive treatments of the material such as Nicholas Love's *The Mirrour of the Blessyd Lyf of Jesu Christ*, based on the Franciscan text attributed to Bonaventure, *Meditationes Vitae Christi*, that had versions in other European languages. The *Meditationes* emphasized the need for the believer to become personally involved in the events of the life and death of Christ, imagining him- or herself present at the key moments of the redemptive act. The plays that appeared all over Europe created just such emotive conditions and can be seen as a major didactic and pietistic tool of the late medieval Church.

Biblical plays had many kinds of sponsors, from individual parishes performing single episodes, such as the play of Jacob and his twelve sons performed at Pentecost in 1481 at Thame in Oxfordshire, to small sequences on the Creation apparently performed in succeeding years by the parish of St Laurence in Reading. The auspices of the single Abraham and Isaac plays that have been located in Northampton and Suffolk cannot be determined, but a 'Play of the Vineyard' based on a parable is mentioned in the records of the York Mercers' Guild and has an analogue among the plays from Lille discovered in 1983. The Lille manuscript contains 73 separate episodes, the majority on quite obscure Old Testament episodes with three (including the Vineyard play) dramatizing parables from the New Testament. The manuscript also includes some plays on classical themes but not the plays on the Passion that we know, from external evidence, were performed in Lille.

Sequences that still retained the shape of the liturgical offices of Easter, beginning with the Deposition at the end of the Good Friday ceremonies and ending with the Resurrection appearances on Easter Monday or Tuesday, were quite common in England. Evidence for such separate Resurrection plays is widespread and exists in records of monastic houses, cathedral chapters, private chapels, and parishes. A similar pattern exists on the Continent. A late example is the early sixteenth-century *Resurrection de Jesuschrist* written by Eloy du Mont for his schoolboys in Caen.

Perhaps the most popular of the biblical dramas were the Passion plays—longer episodic biblical sequences normally performed in 'place and scaffold' (*platea* and *mansion) configurations that added to the Resurrection story the trials, the beating and humiliation, and the Crucifixion itself. This was the most common form of community drama in France. The base *text for many of the French productions was composed about 1440 by Arnoul Gréban, a canon of Notre Dame Cathedral in Paris. Redactions of this text with omissions and additions were performed in many French cities over the next 100 years. French biblical drama tended to be mounted sporadically on a very large scale, sponsored by *confréries* (*see* GUILDS; CONFRÉRIE DE LA PASSION) or simply groups of individuals brought together to mount a single, often multi-day production, rather than undertaken regularly by cities as they were in northern England and the Germanic towns such as Frankfurt, Heidelberg, Marburg, and Zurich. England did have free-standing Passion plays unattached to major cities. The text of one survives embedded in the 'N-Town' manuscript and elaborate records exist for another performed at New Romney in Kent. Passion plays were rare in Italy and only one has been discovered in the Low Countries in Maastricht, but there are surviving examples in Provençal and Spanish. Some of the plays performed in the competitions of the *Chambers of Rhetoric in the Low Countries had biblical subjects.

Biblical plays that dramatize the whole of salvation history beginning with the Creation and ending with the Last Judgement are confined to England and the Germanic areas, including the play from Bozen in the southern Tyrol performed by the craft guilds and the play at Künzelsau, the most complete of the German sequences, performed possibly by the Guild of St John the Baptist. Two surviving English examples are the *cycles of plays from York and Chester. Both were performed in procession by the craft guilds and produced by the city councils. The play in York was performed in one day on the feast of Corpus Christi while the play in Chester was spread over three days at Whitsun (Pentecost). Doubts have been raised about the two other English cycle plays, traditionally called 'N-Town' and 'Towneley'. Modern performances, and new editions that have included detailed palaeographical and codicological study of the manuscripts, suggest that the plays contained in these manuscripts are collections from different sources rather than plays written and revised for performance together in one location as the plays of York and Chester clearly are. The *Towneley Plays* have five episodes that are clearly derived from originals in York and another five written by a single author called by scholars 'the Wakefield Master'. A major clue about the nature of this manuscript comes from the two plays written by the Master concerning the Adoration of the Shepherds. Commonly called the First and Second Shepherds' Play they are called in the manuscript 'Pagina pastorum' ('Pageant of the Shepherds') and 'Alia eorundem' ('Another of the Same'). Each is self-contained and plays very well as a single modern production. The staging requirements for the plays in this manuscript vary from a simple *booth or *pageant wagon set to more elaborate plays (such as the Resurrection) that demand several separate locations. A similar though more complex situation exists with the *N-Town Plays*, where some simple pageant plays are mixed with plays demanding more elaborate 'place and scaffold' sets. Scholarship since the publication of Peter Meredith's *The Mary Play from the N.Town Manuscript* (1987) suggests that these two manuscripts have preserved for us examples of the wide variety of single-episode plays and short sequences. Evidence for the widespread existence of such plays is being collected and published by Records of Early English Drama.

Creed plays, which follow the twelve clauses of the Apostles' Creed, might include scenes based on the Creation, the Nativity, the trials of Jesus (particularly the trial before Pilate), the Crucifixion, the Burial, the Resurrection, the Ascension, and Judgement. A small version of a Creed play in English survives in the Pentecost play in the *Chester Cycle* where, after the descent of the Holy Spirit, the twelve apostles each speak a clause of the Creed. European versions of this form sometimes embellish the formula with figures of prophets to match the apostles, as in Künselsau. A single continental text of a three-day play survives from Eger in Bohemia which covers the biblical events from Creation through to the Appearance to Thomas. During the Last Supper the disciples recite the articles of the Creed.

Material from the apocryphal *Gospel of Pseudo-Matthew* and other Marian material is frequently integrated into the canonical episodes of biblical drama. The story of Anne and Joachim, the birth and early childhood of Mary, and the legends surrounding the betrothal of Mary and Joseph are all treated. One of the separate plays embedded in the *N-Town* manuscript is a four-part play dramatizing Mary's childhood from her conception to the Visit to Elizabeth. Plays using this material are extant in all major European language groups except Spanish. There are, however, several examples of Spanish plays that dramatize parts of the story, originating in the early Church, of the Death, Assumption and Coronation of the Virgin. Assumption plays also survive from Catalonia, France, and the Germanic territories. Scholars have traced the interrelationship between the *Eerste Bliscap*, a Dutch play on the life of the Virgin, the Virgin sequences at Valenciennes, and the plays in the *N-Town* manuscript. Lincoln had plays on both St Anne and the Virgin, a major section of the *York Plays* between Pentecost and Judgement is taken up with plays on the Virgin, and the *N-Town* manuscript contains a fine example of an Assumption play.

Other quasi-biblical stories grew from interpretations of the eschatological passages in Matthew 25, Revelation, and the writings of Josephus. These are sometimes included in biblical play sequences, appearing (as do the plays on the last days of the Virgin) between Pentecost and Judgement, and include treatments of the wise and foolish Virgins and plays on Antichrist. The story of the Destruction of Jerusalem from Josephus was also frequently dramatized. In Arras about 1435 there was a three-day play, the *Vengance Jhesuchrist*, dedicated only to this story, while elsewhere it appears as part of the eschatological scenes of longer biblical sequences.

Finally, a type of biblical drama in England, the Pater Noster plays, bridged the *morality play *genre. Although none of the texts survives, records indicate that there were at least three plays based on the petitions of the Lord's Prayer—one at York, one at Beverley, and the third at Lincoln. In both York and Beverley it is specified that each petition match one of the seven deadly sins. (This matching came ultimately from Hugh of St Victor and was quite common in contemporary English sermons.) In the plays, the biblical text is only part of the pattern, while the *allegorical treatment of the sins provides the other part.

Plays on biblical subjects survived into the Reformation and, indeed, the early reformers adapted the form for their own purposes. New dramatizations of the stories were written from a Protestant perspective by such writers as Théodore de *Bèze and John *Bale. There is evidence in some of the surviving manuscripts of the *Chester Plays* that alternative Protestant and Catholic versions of the same episode were provided. The bib-

lical plays at Coventry ended in 1580 but four years later the city mounted an elaborate play on the Destruction of Jerusalem. In Lutheran towns biblical plays continued while those associated with liturgical practice did not. In 1561 Hans *Sachs wrote a new Passion play and humanists like Nicholas Grimaud wrote Latin plays on biblical subjects. Although in some parts of Eastern Europe the old traditions lasted into the seventeenth century, the medieval form of biblical drama did not survive the religious upheavals of the sixteenth century in the West.

AFJ

BEADLE, RICHARD (ed.), *The Cambridge Companion to Medieval English Theatre* (Cambridge, 1994)

FRANK, GRACE, *The Medieval French Drama*, 2nd edn. rev. (Oxford, 1967)

MUIR, LYNETTE E., *The Biblical Drama of Medieval Europe* (Cambridge, 1995)

Records of Early English Drama, records volumes (Toronto, 1979–)

BICKERSTAFFE, ISAAC (1735–1812)

Irish playwright. Bickerstaffe was, perhaps, the only person in Great Britain to have made a living in the second half of the eighteenth century solely by writing plays. He specialized in short *musical plays and *farces, including *Love in a Village* (1762) and *The Maid of the Mill* (1765). His career was cut short in 1772 when he was accused of attempted sodomy and fled England, never to return. Despite his abrupt and scandalous departure from the *London stage, his plays remained favourites and Elizabeth *Inchbald considered him one of the best farceurs of the eighteenth century.   MJK

BIDESIA

Popular *folk form of western Bihar, *India. Initiated in all probability by Guddar Rai, it gained recognition around the end of the nineteenth century through the legendary writer-actor Bhikhari Thakur. Primarily a musical play, *bidesia* is based on the existing folk and popular music of Bhojpuri, the dialect of the region, noted for its evocativeness and wit. Performed very simply with everyday *costumes and in any available space, *bidesia* requires no more than three or four actors who *double several roles. Soulful songs and situations move *audiences still: the dominant theme is the migration of men from the villages of Bihar to the cities, who must leave their wives and families to find work. At the end of the twentieth century some urban theatre directors made extensive use of *bidesia* elements for new plays on contemporary themes.   KJ

BIEITO, CALIXTO (1963–)

Catalan director. A radical innovator who has embraced a versatile repertoire, equally at home working in *musical theatre

(*Sondheim, Barbieri, *Schönberg), with twentieth-century playwrights (*Shaw, *García Lorca, *Bernhard), and handling classical *texts and *operas. Bieito built up a formidable reputation in the early 1990s working regularly at *Barcelona's Grec Festival, the Mercat de les Flors, the Teatre Lliure, and, more recently, at Catalonia's National Theatre and *Madrid's Centro Dramático Nacional. His reinvention of classics, stripping them of past conventions and imagining them anew for contemporary *audiences, has included contentious productions of *Calderón's *La vida es sueño* (*Life Is a Dream*) produced in both English (1998) and Spanish (2000), and *Valle-Inclán's cruel *Comedias bárbaras* (*Barbaric Comedies*, 2000). He regularly collaborates with *scenery designer Alfons Flors, *costume designer Mercè Paloma, and *lighting designer Xavi Clot, who provide him with conceptual scenic environments where the audience appear as much on display as the performers. As *artistic director of Barcelona's Romea Theatre, his encouragement of innovative companies like Kràmpack has secured a young audience for the venue.   MMD

BIENSÉANCES *See* DECORUM.

BILL-BELOTSERKOVSKY, VLADIMIR (1884–1970)

Russian/Soviet dramatist who spent time as a ship's stoker and farm labourer in the United States before the revolution (hence the prefix 'Bill'). His first plays were *agitprop works designed for *amateur performance and suffered from schematically conceived, poster-like characterization. His Civil War play *Storm*, staged at the *Moscow Trades Union Theatre in 1924, was among the first to introduce a socialist 'positive *hero'. *Life Is Calling* (1934), about the heroic struggles of a Soviet scientist, and his anti-American *Skin Colour* (1949) are typical of the *socialist realist works which became obligatory after 1934.
                                        NW

BILLINGTON, MICHAEL (1939–)

English drama critic for the *Guardian* from 1971. After journalism training in Liverpool he became Public Liaison Officer/Director of Lincoln Theatre Company (1962–4), gaining a tough sympathy for the profession. Often championing *politically challenging drama, his reviews for *The Times* (1965–71), *Birmingham Post* (1968–78), *New York Times* (1978–), and *Country Life* (1987–) became the bedrock of intelligent commentaries across the media. Cheerful eclecticism informs his *television profiles of Peggy *Ashcroft, Peter *Hall, and Alan *Ayckbourn, and his several books, which range from a celebration of the comedian Ken Dodd, *How Tickled I Am* (1977), to

an appreciation of *The Life and Work of Harold Pinter* (1996). *See also* CRITICISM.
                                        BRK

BINODINI DASI (*c.*1863–1941)

Bengali actress, popularly known as Nati (actress) Binodini. Foremost among the earliest group of women to act on the *Bengali stage (previously a male domain), she was born in the community of prostitutes in Calcutta (*Kolkata) which provided the first generation of actresses. Her meteoric career was short (1874–87), but encompassed nearly 100 roles in around 80 productions; an example of her versatility was the six *characters she played in *Meghnad Badh* (*The Killing of Meghnad*), dramatized from Michael Madhusudan *Dutt's epic. Trained by her mentor, the illustrious *actor-manager Girish *Ghosh, she played every kind of character—mythical, realistic, tragic, comic. Her cross-dressed performance as the Hindu religious reformer Chaitanya so overwhelmed the mystic Ramakrishna that he went backstage to bless her—a crucial moment in Calcutta's social history, at a time when the educated public considered theatre immoral. Many respected citizens, *Indian and British, testified to her interpretative versatility. Binodini's memoirs, *Amar Katha* (*My Story*), have a triple significance: as theatre history, as a document for women's studies, and as a record of her own sensitive personality and artistic insight.
                                        AL

BIOMECHANICS

A term associated with the *acting *theories of the Russian director Vsevolod *Meyerhold. A former member of the *Moscow Art Theatre, and familiar with the acting theories of *Stanislavsky, Meyerhold parted company with his mentor in developing a theory based on external mastery of physical movement, rather than on the development of inner emotional states of empathetic feeling. His ideas derived from more physically oriented and popular forms such as the *circus, *pantomime, the 'balagan', and *commedia dell'arte*, but also owed a debt to *acrobatics, eurhythmics (*see* JAQUES-DALCROZE, ÉMILE), and gymnastics, to the 'time and motion' theories of Frederick Taylor, to Japanese acting traditions, to oriental martial arts, and to Pavlovian theories of reflexology. The training courses which Meyerhold instituted immediately after the Russian Revolution eschewed individual expressiveness in favour of a programme of collectivist theatrical action where actors, dressed often in identical acting overalls, performed their stage tasks in the hyper-efficient manner of workers on a production line. Meyerhold devised specific exercises, such as 'Shooting the Bow', 'Dropping the Weight', 'Throwing the Stone', and 'The Leap onto the Chest', in which each movement was prefaced by a dialectical counter-movement, concluding with a synthesizing resolution of oppositions, signalled by a verbal exclamation.

Following practical stage experiments in 1922, the method became largely confined to actor *training and, despite being discredited during the Stalinist period, when Meyerhold became a non-person, was revived during the 1960s and now features prominently, both in Russian acting schools and abroad, alongside the methods of Stanislavsky, *Brecht, and others. *See also* PHYSICAL THEATRE. NW

BIRD, ROBERT MONTGOMERY (1806–54)

American playwright, novelist, and doctor. His 1830 *Pelopidas* won Edwin *Forrest's playwriting contest, but the actor refused to produce it, insisting it lacked sufficient dramatic incident. Bird corrected that in *The Gladiator* (1831), a slave-rebellion play that became a Forrest staple. While the *melodramatic *Oraloosa* (1832) was a theatrical success, Bird's best play, *The Broker of Bogotá* (1834), was a domestic *tragedy in which two children betray their father. After falling out with Forrest over a contracted rewriting of *Stone's *Metamora*, Bird left playwriting, devoting himself to teaching medicine and writing novels. GAR

BIRMINGHAM REPERTORY THEATRE

One of the earliest of the *regional repertory theatres in the UK, the Birmingham Rep was founded and funded by Barry *Jackson, and had its origins in an *amateur group, the Pilgrim Players. Its purpose-built *playhouse opened in 1913 with *Twelfth Night*; Jackson was *artistic director and the playwright John *Drinkwater general *manager. The *stage and *forestage were generous in size, the *auditorium seated 464 in a single sweep of *stalls and raked balcony, and excellent sight lines and acoustics contributed to the intimacy of the space. In the early decades the repertoire was bold, including premières of works by *Shaw (notably *Back to Methuselah*, 1923) and Drinkwater (*Abraham Lincoln*, 1918), and actors included Edith *Evans, Laurence *Olivier, and Ralph *Richardson. Jackson's many Shakespeare productions (credit as director actually goes to H. K. Ayliff) were dominated by a pioneering series in modern dress, of which '*Hamlet* in plus-fours' (1925) attracted particular attention. European plays included *Kaiser's *Gas* (1923), with striking *expressionist sets by the house designer, Paul *Shelving. Unfortunately the repertoire proved too exotic for local *audiences, and in 1923–4 Jackson closed the operation; from 1925 the company's work was seen in a number of *London seasons.

Scene from Meyerhold's production of *The Magnanimous Cuckold* (adapted from *Le Cocu magnifique* by Fernand Crommelynck), Moscow, 1922. This moment, based on the exercise 'The Leap onto the Chest', captures some of the vitality of **biomechanics** as a method of acting and training.

Jackson's protégés in the post-war years included the young director Peter *Brook (*Man and Superman*, *The Lady from the Sea*, and *King John*, all in 1945) and the actor Paul *Scofield. Jackson remained as director until his death in 1961. Among his successors have been Peter Dews, John Adams, Bill Alexander, and Jonathan Church (appointed in 2001), and the tradition of using first-rate actors continued in the 1960s and 1970s with Derek *Jacobi, Brian Cox, and Michael *Gambon. A new 900-seat theatre opened in 1971, with a *studio theatre for experimental work such as David *Edgar's *Mary Barnes* (1978). Mainstage productions have included the British premières of *Miller's *An American Clock* and *Wesker's *The Merchant* (both 1983). In common with most other theatres of its kind, now *financed mainly by a combination of local government and *Arts Council funds, the Rep has long ceased to pursue the early ideal of a *repertory playing with a stable company. RJ

BISHOP, ANDRÉ (1949–)

American *manager and arts administrator. After a brief and undistinguished career as an actor, Bishop became literary manager at *Playwrights Horizons, an active *Off-Broadway company. He became *artistic director in 1981, quickly building an impressive number of commercially viable productions. Under his guidance, Stephen *Sondheim's *Sunday in the Park with George* (1985), Alfred Uhry's *Driving Miss Daisy* (1988), and Wendy *Wasserstein's *Heidi Chronicles* (1989) won Pulitzer prizes. In 1992 Bishop took charge of the *Lincoln Center Theater, the largest and most visible non-profit company in *New York. Following the lead of his predecessor Gregory *Mosher, Bishop managed productions both at Lincoln Center and on commercial Broadway and Off-Broadway stages. Frequently, his larger space, the Vivian Beaumont Theater, was occupied with a long-running success—the Tony-winning *Contact* opened a multi-year run in 2000. Bishop built relationships with several writers, producing most of John *Guare's work, and helped revitalize the *musical through innovative productions (Julie *Taymor and Elliot Goldenthal's *Juan Darien*, 1996; Jason Robert Brown's *Parade*, 1998; Michael John LaChiusa's *Hello Again*, 1994, and *Marie Christine*, 2000). AW

BJØRNSON, BJØRN (1859–1942)

Norwegian actor and director. The eldest son of playwright Bjørnstjerne *Bjørnson, he first made his mark as an actor. Trained in Germany, Bjørnson was the only non-German member of the *Meiningen Players in the early 1880s. In Norway he launched his career as an actor and director at the Christian Theatre in Bergen in 1884, playing the title role in *Richard III*. His Meiningen training was evident in his meticulous direction and rapid dynamic pacing: *audiences were astounded to see crowds turn their backs to them, and hear live *sound effects. Bjørnson's 'authentic' *realism in productions of *The Wild Duck, Peer Gynt, John Gabriel Borkman,* and *Enemy of the People,* among other works, set the national standard for *Ibsen interpretation into the 1930s. The first director of the Nationaltheatret, Bjørnson directed over 120 productions during his tenure there, a repertoire that included his father, Shakespeare, *Holberg, and *Molnár. DLF

BJØRNSON, BJØRNSTJERNE (1832–1910)

Norwegian playwright. The careers of Norway's two greatest writers, Bjørnson and *Ibsen, are closely linked. In particular, Bjørnson first wrote plays in styles that Ibsen later came to adopt. He wrote his national *romantic trilogy *Sigurd Slembe* (1862) the year before Ibsen wrote *The Pretenders.* A decade later Bjørnson wrote plays debating contemporary issues, *The Bankrupt* and *The Editor* (1875), two years before Ibsen turned his attention to contemporary issues with *Pillars of Society.* There were, however, powerful differences between them. In contrast to Ibsen, Bjørnson was an extrovert campaigner and journalist. He fought for women's emancipation, for Norwegian independence, and defended the rights of individuals and groups who were oppressed by others. Many of these issues are reflected in his plays and novels. His play *The King* (1877) challenges the role of the monarchy, the church, and the military establishment in Norway. In *Leonarda* (1879) and *A Gauntlet* (1883) he wrote about marriage and divorce in ways which outraged both the Church and free-thinking radicals, while *Beyond our Powers* (1883) was a powerful attack on dogmatism. His most complex drama, *Paul Lange and Tora Parsberg* (1898), dealt frankly with political issues involved in the suicide of a contemporary politician. At times the artistic quality of Bjørnson's work suffered because of the depth of his social and political conviction. But it was the idealistic temper of his work that brought him the distinction of the Nobel Prize for Literature in 1903. DT

BJÖRNSON, MARIA (1949–2002)

British designer. Born in Paris of Romanian and Norwegian parents, she studied at the Byam Shaw School of Art and Central School of Art and Design. Apprenticeship at *Glasgow *Citizens' Theatre led to collaboration with director David Pountney, and she designed his Welsh National Opera/Scottish Opera Janáček cycle. Awarded the 1983 *Prague Bienniale Prize and Prague Quadrenniale Silver Medal, those expressive, bold designs demonstrate Bjørnson's view that designing 'is about finding out what the problems are by asking the right questions' and offering visual information *audiences 'can't get from the play, but which helps them to understand it'. In addition to spectacular West End productions of *Follies* (1987) and *Aspects of Love,* she is renowned for designing *The Phantom of the Opera* (1987), an opulent Parisian fantasy that captured numerous *awards. Recent work included *Verdi's *Macbeth* (*La Scala, 1997), *The Cherry Orchard* (Royal *National Theatre, 2000), *Plenty,* and *Britannicus* (*Almeida, 1998). RVL

BLACK, GEORGE (1891–1945)

After working in cinema management, Black joined the General Theatre Corporation in 1928 and took control of the *London Palladium, then close to bankruptcy. He revived the theatre by introducing fast-paced and lavish *variety shows to compete with the growth of *film. He brought over American stars to top the bill and changed the style of British *comedy by instigating the anarchic clowning of the Crazy Gang, which regularly played the Palladium during the 1930s. In 1933 GTC absorbed the Moss Empires group and Black became the most influential figure in British variety. SF

BLACK, STEPHEN (1880–1931)

South African playwright, actor, and *mime, born in Cape Town. He wrote two novels (*The Dorp* and *The Golden Calf*) and was a journalist, but is best known as the first South African to write drama in the local context. His first play, *Love and the Hyphen* (Tivoli Theatre, 1908), commented on Cape society. Others include *Helena's Hope Ltd.,* based on his experiences of a Rhodesian gold mine, *Van Kalabas Does his Bit* (1916), based on his war experiences, *The Uitlanders,* and *Outspan.* He also translated French texts into English (for instance, *The Flapper,* 1911). He travelled to *London (1913–15) and France (1918–27), marketing his work, writing, and negotiating foreign rights. Black's satirical plays offer a useful early record of the social mores of early twentieth-century Cape society with its complicated racial interactions. YH

BLACKFACE *See* MINSTREL SHOW.

BLACKFRIARS THEATRE

The pre-eminent indoor *playhouse of Shakespeare's time. A hall theatre built in 1596 by James *Burbage, who planned it to replace the open-air *Theatre, which he built in 1576, Blackfriars was located in a 'liberty', free from the Lord Mayor of *London's control because it had belonged to the Dominican friars. An earlier theatre was established in the same precinct in 1576 by Richard Farrant, the choirmaster of the *Chapel Royal, for commercial performances by his *boy company. Burbage hoped to use his for the same purpose but was stopped by the residents. Shakespeare's company began to use it as their winter playhouse in 1608. Set in a large stone hall 18 by 12 m (60 by 40 feet), its *stage had boxes on each flank, a pit with benches, and galleries curving round the pit (see BOX, PIT, AND GALLERY). Gallants could hire stools to sit on the stage itself. *See also* CHAMBERLAIN'S MEN, LORD.   AJG

BLAKE, EUBIE (1883–1983)

*African-American performer-playwright, who broke into show business in the 1890s playing ragtime piano in a Baltimore bordello. He danced in *minstrelsy and worked in *medicine shows before moving to *New York in 1905. Later he teamed with Noble *Sissle in a *vaudeville act called the Dixie Duo. The two sold their first song, 'It's All your Fault', to Sophie *Tucker, who made it a big hit. With another vaudeville team, Miller & Lyles, they produced and starred in *Shuffle Along* (Broadway, 1921), the first all-black *musical to become a *box-office smash. The *dancing was infectious and the songs unforgettable, including 'Love Will Find a Way' and 'I'm Just Wild about Harry' (which later became the campaign song for President Truman). Blake also wrote *The Chocolate Dandies* (with Sissle, 1924) and *Blackbirds of 1930*. In 1933 and 1952, he and Sissle revived *Shuffle Along*, though without the success of the first version. Retired for some years, Blake was back in the public mind in 1978 with *Eubie*, a Broadway musical celebrating his life and music.   BBL

BLAKELY, COLIN (1930–87)

Irish actor, whose rich stage career in Britain was paralleled by a prolific career as a character actor in *film and *television. After experience as an *amateur, his first professional engagement was with the Group Theatre, Belfast. He progressed to the *Royal Court, *Royal Shakespeare Company, and *National Theatre, where he was a member of the acting company from its earliest days, playing the Norwegian Captain in the company's first production, *Hamlet*, directed by *Olivier (1963). Other early roles there include Kite in William *Gaskill's mounting of *Farquhar's *The Recruiting Officer* (1963), as well as appearances in Lindsay *Anderson's production of Max *Frisch's *Andorra*, Peter *Shaffer's *The Royal Hunt of the Sun* (both 1964), and *Seneca's *Oedipus* (1968). In 1971 he was in Peter *Hall's première of *Pinter's *Old Times* for the RSC at the *Aldwych, and in 1975 in John Schlesinger's National Theatre revival of *Shaw's *Heartbreak House*. In 1985 he appeared in Pinter's *Other Places* in the West End. Blakely died from leukaemia.   AS

BLAKEMORE, MICHAEL (1928–)

Australian director and actor, resident in England. Blakemore's direction is distinguished by attempted self-effacement, attention to detail, and concern for actors. He is particularly known for his work with Peter *Nichols, Michael *Frayn, Arthur *Miller, and fellow Australian David *Williamson. Blakemore worked as an actor for fifteen years in Britain before beginning to direct at the *Glasgow *Citizens' Theatre, where he premièred Nichols's *A Day in the Death of Joe Egg* (1966). He became an associate director at the Royal *National Theatre under Laurence *Olivier, and directed several acclaimed productions there including *Long Day's Journey into Night* (1971), starring Olivier. Unhappy with the new regime under Peter *Hall, Blakemore left the National and pursued a thriving career in commercial theatre. During the 1990s he had great success with *musicals in the USA, and in 2000 he won two Tony *awards, one for *Kiss Me, Kate* and the other for Frayn's *Copenhagen*. Blakemore has produced two autobiographical works: the novel *Next Season* (1968) and the *film *A Personal History of the Australian Surf* (1981).

EJS

BLANCO, ANDRÉS ELOY (1896–1955)

Venezuelan actor, poet, playwright, and politician. Of his large output, only four plays were staged during his life, and his complete works were not published until 1997. His first success came in 1918 with *El huerto de la epopeya* (*The Epic Orchard*). That same year he acted in *Por la patria* (*For the Nation*), adapted by Leoncio Martínez and Luis Roche from Lavadeau's *Servir*, and in 1921 played in *La cena de los cardenales* (*The Cardinals' Supper*), by Julio Dantas. Blanco wrote *El pie de la Virgen* (*The Virgin's Foot*, 1929) while in prison for opposing the dictatorship. *Patria, que mi niña duerme* (*Nation, my Little Girl Is Sleeping*) was first staged in 1937, followed by a *farce, *Venezuela güele a oro* (*Venezuela Smells of Gold*, 1942), written with Miguel Otero Silva, the year that Blanco's lyric *tragedy *Abigail* (written in 1937) also premièred. *Los muertos las prefieren negras* (*Dead Men Prefer Them Black*), written in 1950, reached the stage in 1956 after his death. After a distinguished political career, he was in exile from 1949.   LCL trans. AMCS

BLANK VERSE *See* VERSE.

BLAU, HERBERT (1926–)

American director, *producer, playwright, teacher, and scholar. In 1952 he and Jules Irving started the *Actors Workshop of *San Francisco, where he directed more than 25 productions, including the American premières of *Brecht's *Mother Courage* (1956) and *Arden's *Serjeant Musgrave's Dance* (1962). Blau also directed the legendary production of *Beckett's *Waiting for Godot* that played in San Quentin prison, which also travelled to Seattle, *New York, and *Brussels. In 1965, Blau and Irving took over the Repertory Theatre of *Lincoln Center in *New

York. Within two years, Blau resigned amid much controversy, ending his career in large institutional theatre. In 1971, after three years as a dean and provost at the newly formed California Institute of the Arts, Blau formed KRAKEN, an experimental acting ensemble which developed *physical theatre pieces as a *collective, including *Seeds of Atreus* (1973), *The Donner Party, its Crossing* (1974), and *Elsinore* (1976). After the dissolution of KRAKEN, he concentrated on teaching and scholarship. His prolific writings on performance *theory, Beckett, fashion, and other subjects demonstrate the same qualities that marked his earlier work as a director: intellectual rigour and passion, commitment to experiment, fierce and uncompromising idealism. He has held major appointments at American universities.

STC

BLAUWE MAANDAG COMPAGNIE

Belgian troupe founded in 1984 when actor-director Luk Perceval, in the vanguard of a new generation of theatre-makers, abandoned the conservative Koninklijke Nederlandse Schouwburg at *Antwerp. With Guy Joosten, he launched a new *fringe company with Ghent as its home base, performing mainly at Flemish arts centres and on modest festival stages. With unorthodox productions of *Othello*, *Chekhov's *The Seagull*, and *Strindberg's *The Father*, Blauwe Maandag (Blue Monday) soon became the best known of Belgium's nearly 35 experimental companies. Using a *collective approach, Perceval produced classical plays in a multidisciplinary, deconstructionist, and non-*illusionist, *Brechtian manner, and also commissioned new writing. With the versatile writer and performer Tom Lanoye, Perceval directed *Ten Oorlog* (*To War*, 1997–8), a three-part adaptation of Shakespeare's English history plays twelve hours in length, later mounted in German as *Schlachten!* in Hamburg and at the *Salzburg Festival. To counter the fractured Flemish theatre scene and increase the opportunities for large-scale productions, Blauwe Maandag merged in 1998 with Perceval's former theatre to form a new company, Het Toneelhuis (the Playhouse).

TH

BLEASDALE, ALAN (1946–)

English playwright and screenwriter. In 1982 he achieved overnight success with the *television series *Boys from the Blackstuff*, based on his single drama *The Blackstuff* (BBC, 1980). The play and the series confronted the economic impact of early Thatcherism on working-class Liverpool with mordant irony, pitch-black humour, and a repertoire of startlingly authentic but significantly heightened *characters: Chrissie Todd, reduced to shooting his beloved pet rabbits for food, Snowy Malone, the plasterer who takes pride in his skills but falls to his death trying to escape social services officials, and Yosser Hughes, Bleasdale's angriest and most pitiful symbol of unemployment.

In contrast, his most successful stage play, *Are You Lonesome Tonight?* (1985), focused on the career and mythology of Elvis Presley. His play *On the Ledge* (1993), a savage social documentary about life and death in a block of high flats, returned to a Liverpool setting. Later television work includes the *historical drama *The Monocled Mutineer* (BBC, 1986), the contemporary *satire *GBH* (Channel 4, 1990), and the family drama *Jake's Progress* (Channel 4, 1995).

AS

BLIN, ROGER (1907–84)

French director, actor, and designer who played a crucial role in discovering the works of the *absurdist playwrights. A friend of *Artaud and member of the *Paris *surrealist group in the 1920s, Blin welcomed the brilliant, troubled Arthur *Adamov and produced his first play, *La Parodie* (*The Parody*, 1952). Blin had begun directing in 1949 with *Strindberg's *The Ghost Sonata*. He believed that 'one must always adapt the writing of the *text . . . to the manner in which the author breathes his text', and never overwhelm it with design. Perhaps because of this self-effacing attitude, Martin Esslin scarcely mentions him in *The Theatre of the Absurd*. In the 1930s Blin studied *mime and acted with *Barrault and Artaud, including Artaud's *The Cenci* (1935). He directed the French premières of *Beckett's major plays, and acted in the first two: *Waiting for Godot* at the Théâtre de Babylone (1953) and *Endgame* at the Studio des Champs-Élysées (1957). These were followed by *Krapp's Last Tape* (1960) and *Happy Days* (1963). Blin also directed French premières of *Genet's *Les Nègres* (*The Blacks*, 1959), and *Les Paravents* (*The Screens*, 1966), defending Genet from right-wing attacks. Blin's stagings of Genet were his most visually stunning and theatrical, not to display his virtuosity but because he believed the plays demanded it. At his death he was *rehearsing a new Beckett production.

SBB

BLITZSTEIN, MARC (1905–64)

American composer, lyricist, and cultural critic. At the age of 21 Blitzstein made a traditional concert hall debut as a pianist with the *Philadelphia Orchestra, but later became committed—partly through his exposure to the manifestos of *Brecht and Hans Eisler—to the belief that 'music must have a social as well as artistic base; it should broaden its scope and reach not only the select few but the masses'. During the 1930s he wrote provocative articles on the form and function of socially conscious art while composing his own proletarian pieces, most notably *The Cradle Will Rock* (1937). Though this *agitprop 'play in *music' was ordered closed during *rehearsals by the *Federal Theatre Project, director Orson *Welles managed to open it under now legendary performance conditions. *Regina*, Blitzstein's operatic version of Lillian *Hellman's *The Little Foxes*, appeared briefly on Broadway in 1949 and has since entered the *opera repertoire. His adaptation of *Weill and Brecht's *The Threepenny Opera* was mounted *Off-Broadway in the 1950s, offering Blitzstein some commercial success in his later career.   LTC

BLOCH, WILLIAM (1845–1926)

Danish director. Overshadowed by more famous figures such as *Stanislavsky in *Moscow or *Antoine in *Paris, Bloch nevertheless played a crucial role in establishing a *naturalist approach. Between 1881 and 1893, and again from 1899 to 1909, he worked as a director in the Theatre Royal, Copenhagen, where he directed the premières of *Ibsen's mature plays, from *An Enemy of the People* (1883) to *The Master Builder* (1893). Unlike Stanislavsky, Bloch did not write about *directing, but he did prepare very detailed promptbooks for his productions, which others could consult. *Lugné-Poe, for instance, reviewed Bloch's 1883 promptbook for his own production of *An Enemy of the People* in Paris a decade later. Bloch's approach involved an intensive study of *character and a painstaking attention to detail. He shaped individual roles into a unified performance with the help of an extended *rehearsal process. His delayed production of *Ghosts* in 1903, with Betty Hennings playing Mrs Alving, marked the culmination of his career as a naturalist director.   DT

BLOK, ALEKSANDR (1880–1921)

Russian poet, dramatist, and essayist. The theatre played a crucial part in Blok's life and theatrical themes make frequent appearances in his poems. He took an active interest in the performance of his own plays and after 1917 played a key role in establishing the Bolshoi Drama Theatre in *St Petersburg. In his youth he acted Hamlet, and a series of his lyric verses are concerned with the image of the Dane. His *Balaganchik* (*The Puppet Show/The Fairground Booth*) and *Neznakomka* (*The Female Stranger*) were both poems before they were plays; the first premièred at *Komissarzhevskaya's theatre in St Petersburg in 1906, directed by *Meyerhold, who also played the leading role of Pierrot. The play's conception of life as theatre, which exposes the world as immaterial illusion, is both playful and sophisticated and gained admirers and detractors. Blok's idealized *symbolist concept of the 'Beautiful Lady' takes travestied shape as Columbine, who doubles as 'Death', and who takes a tumble out of a sledge in undignified fashion. Symbolist mysticism and the *mystery play are parodied, as is death itself in the shape of a mortally wounded *clown who declares that he is bleeding cranberry juice. The play was one of a trilogy including *The King on the Town Square* and *The Female Stranger*. In the latter, a poet who sees a falling star discovers that it is the 'Beautiful Lady' of his visions, who has fallen to earth as a prostitute but who then resumes her place among the stars. It was also staged by Meyerhold, alongside a revised version of *The Puppet Show* (1914). *The Rose and the Cross* (1913), set in thirteenth-century Provence, was rehearsed by *Stanislavsky at the *Moscow Art Theatre in the dramatist's presence but was never staged.   NW

BLOOM, CLAIRE (1931–   )

English actress. Early in her career her luminous features and qualities of childlike innocence led to her being cast twice as Ophelia and Juliet. At the *Shakespeare Memorial Theatre (1948) she was Ophelia to the alternating Hamlets of Paul *Scofield and Robert *Helpmann; at the *Old Vic (1953) she played opposite Richard *Burton. Her Romeos, both at the Old Vic, were Alan Badel (1952) and John *Neville (1956). Her work with John *Gielgud included the roles of Alizon Eliot in *Fry's *The Lady's Not for Burning* (1949), Cordelia in *King Lear* (1955), and Sasha in *Chekhov's *Ivanov* (1965). She countered accusations of emotional reserve with strong performances as Nora in *Ibsen's *A Doll's House* (1971 and 1973), and Blanche in *Williams's *A Streetcar Named Desire* (1974). Bloom had a substantial screen career, including the *films *Limelight* (1952) and *The Spy Who Came in from the Cold* (1966) and the *television series *Brideshead Revisited*. Her autobiographies are *Limelight and After* (1982) and *Leaving a Doll's House* (1996).   VRS

BLUE BLOUSE COLLECTIVES

*Agitprop drama groups formed throughout the Soviet Union during the 1920s. Their name derived from the colour of the acting overalls they wore, in preference to conventional theatrical *costume. The first group was formed by Boris Yuzhanin in *Moscow in 1923, and gave performances in workers' clubs and factory canteens. Their vivid style was categorized as *'living newspaper', and utilized a proclamatory and easily assimilable performance mode reminiscent of newspaper headlines, dramatizing events of the day in informative or satirical fashion. They exploited the broad outlines of the propaganda poster, allied to gymnastic agility and aggressive vocal delivery in a non-stop, rapidly rhythmic, agitational-propagandist style. Artists such as Nikolai *Foregger and Sergei *Tretyakov adopted their methods and *Mayakovsky wrote a play for them, *Radio-October*, in 1926. In their heyday, Blue Blouse organizations totalled about 5,000, with some 100,000 members, but their very popularity heralded their downfall, as the dynamism of post-revolutionary enthusiasm ran into the buffers of Stalinist reactionary conservatism and their methods were condemned as both crude and schematic. By the time *socialist realism had become the officially promulgated artistic doctrine in 1934, the Blue Blouse movement had withered to the point of extinction. Nevertheless, their worldwide influence had been felt in America, where the idea of the Living Newspaper grew out of the *Federal Theatre Project; in Germany, among left-wing theatre groups; and in Britain, where the Theatre Workers' Movement adopted comparable agitprop techniques during the 1930s.   NW

BOAL, AUGUSTO (1931–   )

Brazilian theoretician, director, and playwright. After studying with John Gassner in *New York in the early 1950s, Boal became a core member of *São Paulo's Arena Theatre in 1956, where he adapted *Actors Studio techniques to the group's seminars on the development of a national *dramaturgy and theatre practice. As a playwright he is best known as co-author, with Gianfrancesco *Guarnieri, of a series of *musicals about history that contested the Brazilian dictatorship, including *Arena conta Zumbi* (*Arena Narrates Zumbi*, 1965) and *Arena conta Tiradentes* (*Arena Narrates Tiradentes*, 1967). Given the real dangers of artistic protest during the dictatorship, Boal, like a number of other artists, chose exile in 1971. His book *Theatre of the Oppressed* (1974) laid the *theoretical ground for the theatre of the *oppressed, largely developed in periods of exile, a *political theatre movement that remains hugely important worldwide. Boal returned to Brazil in 1986, actively entered politics, and served as a city councillor (1992–6), while continuing his work as a theatrical and cultural activist and teaching and directing for theatre of the oppressed centres internationally. Always interested in *opera and the *Brechtian possibilities of *music, since 2000 he has turned his talents to developing a *genre he calls *sambópera*, producing Brazilianized versions of *Carmen* and *La traviata* with the melodies of Bizet and *Verdi transposed and instrumentalized into the Brazilian rhythms of samba, maracatu, baião, and *carnival marches.
                                                                  LHD

BOAR'S HEAD

Located on the eastern edge of the city of *London in Whitechapel, the Boar's Head was originally a tavern, a square of buildings surrounding an open yard. It was converted into a *playhouse in 1597, once the use of London's *inns for staging plays was prohibited. It was further rebuilt in the succeeding years, as new companies arrived in London, challenging the duopoly of the *Admiral's and *Chamberlain's Men. Worcester's Men, which merged with Oxford's to form the third of the professional companies working in London, had the Boar's Head designated as their regular playhouse in a Privy Council order of 1601. That made it the third licensed place for London playing after the *Globe and *Fortune. As an open-air playhouse it did not have a long life, and Worcester's, now Queen Anne's Men, left it for the *Red Bull in 1604. Prince Charles's Men when newly formed in 1608–9 may have used it for a time. With

only one level of galleries, its capacity was markedly smaller than the other *amphitheatres of the time.   AJG

BOCAGE (PIERRE-MARTINIEN TOUSEZ) (1797–1863)

French actor. Having trained at the Conservatoire, Bocage failed to gain acceptance in *Paris at the *Comédie-Française, but after a few years on the fringe of the company at the *Odéon, he began a successful career at the *Porte-Saint-Martin, where he played in several of the triumphs of the new-style *romantic drama. Lacking the robust stage presence of his contemporary Frédérick *Lemaître, he was ideally suited, in terms of physique and delivery, to the more sombre and melancholy roles in the romantic repertory (though critics were to assert that his voice was like that of Lemaître suffering from a bad cold). The title role in *Dumas *père*'s *Antony* (1831) was his most memorable success. The play received a more enthusiastic reception from its first spectators than any other play of the period, this being due as much to the playing of Marie *Dorval and Bocage—the latter incarnating to perfection the doomed Byronic type—as to the author's dramatic craftsmanship; Lemaître was later to claim that their rendering of the fourth act was unsurpassed in his experience of the theatre. *Hugo's *Marion de Lorme* (also 1831) was only moderately successful, and the triumph was in any case that of Dorval: Bocage's playing of the sombre Didier was judged (by Hugo's wife) to lack variety. In 1832 Bocage played in Dumas's *Teresa*, for once choosing a middle-aged *character with greater psychological nuance; but later in 1832 the same author's *La Tour de Nesle*, a sensational *historical *melodrama, offered him in the role of Buridan what was little more than a caricature of the fatalistic romantic hero.   WDH

BOCK, JERRY (1928–   )

American composer. Showing early talent as a pianist, Bock determined early to write for the stage. Teaming with lyricist Larry Holofcener, he wrote for *television in the early 1950s, honing his skills during summers by writing *revues for adult summer camps. In 1956 they produced their first Broadway score, *Mr Wonderful*, a successful vehicle for Sammy Davis, Jr. Bock then met lyricist Sheldon Harnick, with whom he began a fruitful thirteen-year collaboration with the unsuccessful *The Body Beautiful* (1958). Their next collaboration, however, was a huge success: *Fiorello* won a Pulitzer Prize and displayed Bock's ability to write in period and ethnic styles, which producers would tap again. A failed attempt to clone *Fiorello* with the *musical *Tenderloin* (1960) was followed by the charming pocket *operetta *She Loves Me* (1963), in which Bock managed to insert a *tango, a beguine, and even a bolero. The next year brought the team its greatest hit, *Fiddler on the Roof*, another foray into period ethnicity. An experimental work, *The Apple Tree* (1966), followed, as did *The Rothschilds* (1970), another period, Jewish-flavoured work, this time with a continental sweep. This work marked the end of the partnership, and Bock has remained relatively inactive since, though starting in 1997 he produced some new music-theatre works at the University of Houston. JD

BODEL, JEAN (c.1165–c.1210)

Town clerk of Arras and possibly a professional entertainer (*trouvère*). Bodel was the author of *The Play of St Nicholas* (c.1199–1202). The staging is typically *medieval, requiring five locales among which the *characters move freely. But Bodel invested this serious *saint play with comically realistic tavern scenes. RWV

BOGART, ANNE (1953–)

American director. A native of Rhode Island, Bogart attended *New York University as a graduate student and went on to create original works and direct plays there, including an experimental version of *South Pacific* (1984) which triggered the ire of the *Rodgers and *Hammerstein trust. Her early work was influenced by postmodern *dance and by several stays in Germany, from which she returned intent on exploring American forms, themes, and writers, though not exclusively. She created theatrical collages and dance-theatre pieces for experimental venues until 1989, when she became *artistic director of *Trinity Repertory Company in Providence, a troubled appointment that lasted only one year. In 1992 she directed the world première of Paula *Vogel's *The Baltimore Waltz*, for which she won her second Obie *award. That same year, with *Suzuki Tadashi she co-founded the Saratoga International Theatre Institute (SITI) as a *training ground and laboratory for developing new work rooted in Suzuki's rigorous physical and vocal techniques and Bogart's elaboration of the 'Viewpoints', a stage-movement vocabulary first outlined by choreographer Mary Overlie. With the SITI company she created a number of dense, abstract pieces inspired by twentieth-century culture heroes, including one-person portraits of Robert *Wilson, Virginia Woolf, and Leonard *Bernstein, and ensemble pieces inspired by Marshall McLuhan, Andy Warhol, and Orson *Welles. Several SITI projects, including a *metatheatrical reflection on theatrical convention and the role of the *audience called *Cabin Pressure* (1999), started at *Actors Theatre of Louisville, where Bogart also mounted revisionist versions of William *Inge and Noël *Coward plays. STC

BOGDANOV, MICHAEL (1938–)

Welsh director. A contemporary of Max *Stafford-Clark's at Trinity College, Dublin, Bogdanov worked to make Shakespeare accessible by forming the *English Shakespeare Company with actor Michael *Pennington in 1986. His *touring productions, such as the seven-play history cycle *The War of the Roses* (1987), have been popular successes. His direct, modern-dress ('old clothes aren't living theatre'), socio-political readings are considered 'un-English', and ignore trends for cerebral, *text-based interpretations. Bogdanov has a curious relationship with institutions. The son of a Ukrainian father and Welsh mother, for two years he combined running a Welsh pub with assistant directing at the *Royal Shakespeare Company (including *Brook's *A Midsummer Night's Dream*, 1970). His early reputation for *youth theatre (Phoenix, Leicester, 1973; *Young Vic, 1978) included an *award-winning *Taming of the Shrew* (RSC, 1979). In 1980 Peter *Hall appointed him as associate at the *National Theatre, with a focus on youth and 'breakaway' projects. Here he notoriously faced prosecution under the Sexual Offences Act by Mary Whitehouse for staging gross indecency in *Brenton's *Romans in Britain* (1981). From 1989 to 1992 Bogdanov was *Intendant of the flailing Deutsches Schauspielhaus, Hamburg. His populist productions increased attendance but received mixed critical reception. Since the 1990s he has produced Shakespeare for *film and *television, including the series *Shakespeare Lives* (Channel 4), and directed world *tours for the sporadically funded ESC, and classic and epic texts for the RSC, RNT, and international theatres. KN

BOGOSIAN, ERIC (1953–)

American playwright and actor. Bogosian began creating *characters and performing *monologues while working in a service position at *New York's experimental venue the Kitchen (1976–9). His characters evolved into his first *Off-Off-Broadway *revue, *Careful Moment* (1977). He performed his *one-person shows *Men Inside* and *Voices of America* at the *New York Shakespeare Festival's Public Theatre (1981–2) and achieved wide acclaim for his monologue *Drinking in America* (1986). Bogosian's gritty, serio-comic urban characters evolved into his first multi-character play, *Talk Radio* (1987). His one-man performance *Pounding Nails in the Floor with my Forehead* premièred in 1993 and the plays *subUrbia* (1994) and *Griller* (1998) were presented by major *regional theatres. Bogosian has also appeared in a number of *film and *television productions. MAF

BOGOTÁ

The capital of Colombia, now officially called Santafé de Bogotá. The first secular theatrical performance in post-Conquest Bogotá by a Colombian-born author, Fernando Fernández de Valenzuela (1616–c.1677), was an *entremés (interlude) called *Laurea crítica* (1629). Its aim was to denounce the excesses of the prevailing baroque literary style borrowed from Spain. In the seventeenth and eighteenth centuries other forms like the *loa (usually a curtain raiser), and the *comedia flourished; Comedia nueva: la conquista de Santa Fe de Bogotá (c.1650), by Fernando de Orbea, demonstrating Indian influence, was an early instance. These performances usually took place in private homes or in the primary schools of the elite class. In 1792 the first theatre structure, the Coliseo Ramírez, was erected in Bogotá to house local productions and travelling companies, mostly from Spain. But it was not until independence in the nineteenth century that a truly national author arrived on the scene in the poet and politician Luis Vargas Tejada. His *sainete (short comic interlude) Las convulsiones (1828) had unprecedented success due mainly to its diatribe against the deficient education girls were receiving. Another celebrated writer of the *comedy of manners was the prolific José María Samper (1828–88). His best-known play, Un alcalde a la antigua y dos primos a la moderna (A Traditional Mayor and Two Modern Cousins, 1856), a country versus the big city comedy, was staged by the first recognized national company, headed by Lorenzo M. Lleras (1811–65).

The first half of the twentieth century was largely dominated by two playwrights: Antonio Álvarez Lleras (1892–1956) and Luis Enrique Osorio (1896–1966). Álvarez Lleras was active for 50 years and left behind a massive amount of work. His best-known play is a *historical drama, El virrey Solís (1947), based on the legendary character José Solís, a Spanish viceroy. Osorio, a poet, journalist, *manager, and director, wrote more than 40 plays. Though he used humour and comic devices, his *naturalistic and often *folkloric plays reflect the political turmoil of the times. Osorio also founded one of the more stable theatre companies of the century, the Compañía Bogotana de Comedias (1943). He built his own theatre ten years later, and established the first drama school in the city. Two visits are worth mentioning: the French actor Louis *Jouvet toured Colombia in 1943, prompting a flow of dramas by authors like Jorge Zalamea (1906–69) and Oswaldo Díaz Díaz (1910–67), whose plays were frequently broadcast on *radio. In 1956 a visit by the *Japanese *Stanislavskian director *Sano Seki influenced a generation of theatre artists. In 1946 Bernardo Romero Lozano (d. 1971) founded the first experimental group at the National University, paving the way for the strongly *politicized university theatre movement which lasted until approximately 1973. Its high point was the staging of *Brecht's Galileo in 1965 by Santiago *García, Carlos José *Reyes, Carlos Perozzo, and Carlos Duplat. The play was censured officially; the group disbanded, and García and Reyes went on to found the Casa de la Cultura in 1966, later to become the much praised Teatro de la *Candelaria (1972). Following *Brechtian *epic techniques closely, and relying for the most part on *collective creation to construct a national *dramaturgy, the influential 'Nuevo Teatro' (new theatre) movement was under way.

The groups that would dominate the following decades soon emerged: Teatro *La Mamá (1968) and Teatro *Popular de Bogotá (1970) were formed; Miguel *Torres established El Local (1970); and in 1973 Ricardo Camacho founded Teatro *Libre. In the 1980s the premisses of Nuevo Teatro started to unfold, giving way to a search for aesthetic forms. This resulted, paradoxically, in the arrival of experimental theatre (*Mapa Teatro, but also playwright-directors such as Fabio Rubiano), *dance theatre (Alvaro Restrepo's Athanor Danza), *multimedia performances (María Luisa Hincapié), storytelling performance (Nicolás Buenaventura, Carolina Rueda), and commercial theatre. The last was promoted mainly by the Argentine-born director and actor Fanny *Mikey; as the result of her work, at the beginning of the twenty-first century Bogotá was the site of the largest international theatre *festival in *Latin America. Other important groups that have made the city a continuing site for important work are Acto Latino (1967), led by Juan Monsalve; Teatro de las Marionetas (1967), created by David Manzur; Teatro *Taller de Colombia (1972), under the direction of Jorge Vargas and Mario Matallana; Hilos Mágicos (1974), founded by Ciro Gómez; La Libélula Dorada (1976), directed by Jario Ospina, Iván Darío Álvarez, and César Santiago Álvarez; the Centro Cultural García Márquez (1980), headed by Hugo Afanador and José Assad; Teatro TECAL (1980), founded by Críspulo Torres and Mónica Camacho; and Teatrova (1980), created by Carlos Parada.   BJR

BOILEAU, NICOLAS (NICOLAS BOILEAU-DESPRÉAUX) (1636–1711)

French satirist and critic. Of Boileau's best-known work L'Art poétique (1674), only canto III, in which he discusses the origins and evolution of *tragedy and *comedy, has a direct bearing on the appreciation of dramatic writing. A dogmatic theorist and a trenchant critic, he shows little interest in the medieval origins of the various French literary forms; the criteria for his critical judgement were always common sense and clarity. In formulating the doctrine of the three *unities and its place in the theory of *neoclassical *dramaturgy, he was neatly summarizing the ideas of his predecessors, rather than expressing an original contribution. While praising *Molière for The Misanthrope (and by implication for his other five-act comedies in *verse), he regrets that his friend had not been able to steer clear of the influences of the popular theatre which had shaped his talent. See also THEORIES OF DRAMA, THEATRE, AND PERFORMANCE; CRITICISM.   WDH

BOKER, GEORGE HENRY (1823–90)

American playwright and poet. Born into a wealthy Philadelphia family, Boker embarked on a career as a poet after his graduation from Princeton (1842). He was determined to revive poetic *tragedy, and eventually wrote twelve plays, six of which reached the stage. Samuel *Phelps produced Boker's first tragedy, *Calaynos*, in *London at *Sadler's Wells (1849). *Francesca da Rimini*, with a plot drawn from Dante, proved a starring vehicle for E. L. Davenport in 1855, and was revived successfully by Lawrence *Barrett in 1882 for several seasons, and by Otis *Skinner in 1901. Boker became a respected diplomat in his later years.   AW

BOLESLAVSKY, RICHARD VALENTINOVICH (1889–1937)

Actor, teacher, and director. Born Boleslaw Ryszard Srzednicki in Plock, Poland, Boleslavsky was the vital link between *Stanislavsky and theatre practice in the United States. The young Srzednicki moved with his family to Odessa, where he attended university and became involved in *amateur theatrics. He joined a professional Russian-language troupe in 1904 and was accepted by the *Moscow Art Theatre in 1908. Strikingly handsome, he adopted the name Richard Valentinovich Boleslavsky and quickly became a leading actor. Appointed head of the MAT's First Studio, Boleslavsky quarrelled with Stanislavsky over artistic matters and resolved to leave Russia. He arrived in *New York in 1922 and in 1923 founded the Laboratory Theatre (after 1925 called the *American Laboratory Theatre), the first American school presenting the Stanislavsky approach. Future luminaries of American *acting studied with Boleslavsky and his colleague Maria *Ouspenskaya (who remained after the MAT 1923–4 *tour), most notably Lee *Strasberg and Stella *Adler, instrumental in the *Group Theatre (1931–41) and as rival acting teachers thereafter. Many others were introduced to Stanislavskian techniques through Boleslavsky's *Acting: the first six lessons* (1933). He had a minor Broadway directing career, but moved to Hollywood in 1929 and was an 'A-list' *film director at the time of his death.   MAF

BOLGER, DERMOT (1959–   )

Irish playwright, novelist, poet, and journalist. Born in Dublin, Bolger was one of a number of Irish playwrights in the late 1980s who began to write about a rapidly modernizing Ireland, where life for many young people was dominated by issues of migration or drug addiction, enacted in an urban landscape from which tradition had been erased. His plays include *Lament for Arthur Cleary*, *Blinded by the Light* (*Abbey Theatre, 1990), *One Last White Horse* (Peacock Theatre, 1992), and *In High Germany* (*Gate Theatre, *Dublin, 1990), in which an Irish migrant worker in Germany, watching the Irish soccer team, realizes 'the only country I still owned was those eleven figures in green shirts'.   ChM

BOLGER, RAY (1904–87)

American comic actor and eccentric *dancer, known for his loose-jointed style. After beginning his career in 1922 with a *touring New England *musical repertory company, he played *vaudeville in an act called 'Stanford and Bolger: a pair of nifties'. Bolger made his Broadway debut in *The Merry Whirl* (1926). Following two years in vaudeville on the Orpheum circuit, he returned to Broadway in *Heads Up!* (1929), *George White's Scandals* (1931), *Life Begins at 8:40* (1934), and *On your Toes* (1936), in which he gained renown for the 'Slaughter on 10th Avenue' *ballet, choreographed by George *Balanchine. In the 1940s Broadway saw him in *Keep off the Grass* (1940), *By Jupiter* (1942), *Three to Make Ready* (1946), and *Where's Charley?* (1948), in which he introduced his signature song, 'Once in Love with Amy'. His last two Broadway shows, *All American* (1962) and *Come Summer* (1969), were flops. Bolger also appeared in *film (most notably as the Scarecrow in *The Wizard of Oz*, 1939), on *television, and in a series of *one-person shows.   SLL

BOLSHOI THEATRE

Home of Russia's principal *ballet and *opera company on Theatre Square, *Moscow, built on the site of the Petrovsky Theatre which dated from the 1770s. The present Bolshoi, built in 1824 to designs by Andrei Mikhailov and Osip Bove, burned down in 1850 but rose again from the ashes, retaining the walls and the Ionic colonnade of the 1824 building, but with the interior refurbished in a heavy, neo-baroque style. Since its first opera and ballet performances in 1776 and 1778, the Bolshoi (Big) Theatre has acquired a worldwide reputation, staging first performances of Glinka's *A Life for the Tsar* (1842) and *Ruslan and Ludmila* (1846); Tchaikovsky's *Eugene Onegin* (1881), *Swan Lake* (1887), *The Queen of Spades* (1891), and *The Sleeping Beauty* (1899); Mussorgsky's *Boris Godunov* (1888); Borodin's *Prince Igor* (1898); and several operas by Rimsky-Korsakov. Famous choreographers and *dancers have included Marius Petipa, Michel *Fokine, Kasyan Goleizovsky, and Yury Grigorovich, while singers include Chaliapin, Nezhdanova, and Sobinov. Rachmaninov had a short but fruitful association with the theatre between 1904 and 1906 when he conducted some of his own operas. Works staged during the Soviet period include Glier's *The Red Poppy* (1927) and Prokofiev's *Romeo and Juliet* (1947). The post-Soviet period saw a decline in the theatre's fortunes as it became dogged by both financial and artistic problems following the successful artistic reign of Grigorovich.   NW

BOLT, ALAN (1951–   )

Nicaraguan director and playwright. Bolt was initially supportive of the Sandinista revolution but later openly critical of some of its policies. His play *Banana Republic* (1982) tells the story of Nicaragua's history, from colonization to the revolution, in a *street theatre format that borrows techniques from the *circus. Originally Bolt worked with the university theatre in León, but formed the group *Nixtayolero during the revolution in 1979, living and working with his company on land outside the northern city of Matagalpa. He believes in using theatre for political and social ends, and his company performs *collective works about everything from current events and sustainable agrarian practices to community life and emotional recovery from the trauma of Hurricane Mitch. *See also* OPPRESSED, THEATRE OF THE.

EJW

BOLT, ROBERT (1924–95)

English dramatist and screenwriter. Bolt's first plays were staged in 1957: *The Critic and the Heart*, modelled on Somerset *Maugham, and the successful *Flowering Cherry*, starring Ralph *Richardson as Cherry, a dreamer-salesman. Bolt's plays investigate the individual's moral responsibility in the face of social pressure. Paul *Scofield starred as Sir Thomas More in both the stage (1960) and *film (1966) versions of his best-known work, *A Man for All Seasons*. The use of a *character called the Common Man as narrator, often called *Brechtian, actually reflects the play's origins in *radio (1954). The academic crisis in *The Tiger and the Horse* (with Michael and Vanessa *Redgrave, 1960) mirrors Bolt's involvement with the Campaign for Nuclear Disarmament. Subsequent plays, including *Gentle Jack* (1963), a pointed fairy tale, *Vivat! Vivat Regina* (1970), about rivals Elizabeth I and Mary of Scotland, and *State of Revolution*, written for the *National Theatre (1977), about Lenin and Trotsky, increasingly experimented with form. Bolt's screenplays include *Lawrence of Arabia* (1962), and *Dr Zhivago* (1965).

GAO

BOLTON, GUY (1883–1979)

American librettist and playwright. Bolton, who began as a playwright, was one of the wittiest librettists of his era and an early architect of the American *musical form. He and Jerome *Kern wrote a string of musicals for the Princess Theatre, including the hit *Very Good Eddie* (1915), which was the first of its kind to mine comedy from *character and situation rather than *vaudevillian *clowning. P. G. *Wodehouse joined the team, collaborating with Bolton on a number of librettos to Kern-scored shows like *Leave it to Jane* (1917) and Cole *Porter's *Anything Goes* (1930). Bolton also worked on several shows with George and Ira *Gershwin, joining forces with Fred Thompson for *Lady, Be Good!* (1924) and John McGowan for *Girl Crazy* (1930). Among his non-musical works, Bolton wrote an adaptation for Broadway of *Anastasia* (1954). His contributions for *film include *Easter Parade* (1948).

EW

BOMBAY *See* MUMBAI.

BOND, EDWARD (1934–)

English playwright of working-class background, one of the most sophisticated dramatists of the post-war period. His first plays emerged from the Writers' Group at the *Royal Court, run by William *Gaskill, who directed all his major work until *The Fool* (1975). *The Pope's Wedding* (1962), *Saved* (1965), *Early Morning* (1968), *Narrow Road to the Deep North* (1969), and *Lear* (1971) established Bond's reputation—and he also initiated, through the controversies surrounding *Saved* and *Early Morning*, one of the key battles against *censorship. Bond has been concerned to discuss his methods and *dramaturgy, writing extended prefaces and letters which amount to a body of *theory not unlike Bertolt *Brecht's, whose work Bond's often resembles. He creates what he called 'aggro-effects' of violence, such as the stoning of the baby in *Saved*, to break the limits of rationality and *naturalistic characterization. Similarly he often draws on events long past or projected into the future for his subject matter, sometimes reworking previous sources (*The Trojan Women* became *The Woman* and *King Lear* became *Lear*, for example). His plays offer narratives or parables for our times, interpreting the present in light of the past or future in order to intervene, a move that clearly identifies his work as *epic and politically committed (*see* POLITICS AND THEATRE).

Bond has proved to be a difficult dramatist for English *audiences to appreciate, and, in turn, has become increasingly alienated from his national theatres. His resistance to what he perceives as commercial conventions of *acting, *directing, and, indeed, writing has resulted in an increased desire to control the production of his work. He directed *The Woman* (1979), *Restoration* (1981), and *Summer* (1982) himself, and preferred to direct his own work through the 1980s. He walked out of *rehearsals of *The War Plays* (1985) at the *Royal Shakespeare Company because of frustrations with the actors' stylistic habits and technique. During the late 1980s, as he became increasingly difficult to produce at home, his popularity grew in Europe. This popularity increased in the 1990s as Bond developed a creative relationship with French director Alain *Françon. Beginning with *In the Company of Men* (1992), Bond has enjoyed increased critical appreciation in France, especially in Françon's *mises-en-scène. The production of *The War Plays* at the *Avignon Festival in 1994 achieved what, for Bond, the RSC production lacked. French, not British, productions of *Jackets* (1993), *Coffee* (2000), and *Le Crime du XXIe siècle* (*The Crime of the Twenty-First Century*, 2001) have been particularly striking. *Summer* and *The Sea*, which originated in England decades earlier, received important new stagings by French directors in 1993 and 1998.

JGR

BONDY, LUC (1948–)

Swiss-German director. Bondy received a bilingual education in Switzerland and *Paris before training at the *Lecoq school. His breakthrough in German theatre came in 1974 with a much acclaimed production of *Bond's *The Sea* (*Munich), and thereafter Bondy established himself as a European director, dividing his time between *Berlin, Hamburg, Paris, and *Vienna. From the mid-1980s he worked increasingly at the *Schaubühne in Berlin. His most acclaimed production there was *Marivaux's *Triumph of Love* (1987) in a dazzling set by Karl-Ernst *Herrmann. Bondy has a clear preference for authors of the *fin de siècle* (*Ibsen, *Schnitzler) as well as for contemporary dramatists such as Botho *Strauss, whose plays he has frequently premièred. His directorial style is distinguished by wit, psychological sophistication, and keen attention to *textual nuances in comparison to the confrontational approach frequently prevailing in German theatre. In recent years he has begun to direct *opera with productions ranging from *Monteverdi to Alban Berg. Ten of his productions have been invited to the *Berlin *Theatertreffen.   CBB

BOOING

Typically an expression of disapproval (literally, to imitate the sound of oxen), along with other behaviours such as jeering, hissing, and catcalls. Booing might be used by an *audience to indicate their dislike of a play or of a performance by one or more of the actors and can be expressed either during or at the end of a performance. Customs and practices around such an expression of disapproval vary according to historical period, cultural location, and types of performance. In *Greek theatre, for example, fruit throwing and foot stamping were typical as signs of disapproval and would be expected when plays ran too long or did not engage the attention of the audience. Booing can also be explicitly directed at a particular *character qua character. The *villain of a *melodrama is expected to inspire spontaneous booing by an audience upon his or her appearance on stage.

Popular theatre forms (and perhaps especially theatre for *youth) often expect significant audience participation, and booing would be anticipated in a range of encouraged responses to the dramatic *action. Disapproval can also be explicitly sought during a performance. For example, in the *anansesem* of Ghana, actors often go into the audience to incite responses including boos and jeers. In *pantomimes, placards and other visual or verbal directions from actors are used to build the volume of boos for the show's villain. In such instances, booing is a sign of pleasure rather than disapproval and can contribute to the overall success of the performance. *See also* APPLAUSE.
                                                           SBe

BOOK

(*a*) In *musical comedy, the script exclusive of lyrics; what happens between the *dancing and singing. Some playwrights specialize in this difficult, demanding form; few receive the credit that composers and lyricists do. (*b*) For much of theatre history, the official recorded version of the performance with all blocking and revisions of the *text. Prior to *copyright, the book was usually the only complete script, to prevent plagiarism by competitors, and actors were issued only 'sides', pages containing only their cues and lines of *dialogue. (*c*) 'On book': not yet having one's lines memorized as an actor, carrying a script on stage for *rehearsal; 'off book': memorized (though perhaps still needing *prompting).   JB

BOOTH, BARTON (1681–1733)

English actor and *manager. Along with Robert *Wilks and Colley *Cibber, Booth was part of the triumvirate of *actor-managers who ruled *Drury Lane during the 1710s and 1720s. He achieved his managerial status on the strength of his success as the original Cato in *Addison's play (1713). Before then, he was a hard-working actor who specialized in serious, albeit secondary, roles; after *Cato* he established himself as a leading tragedian. Booth eschewed comic parts, choosing the more stately and impressive parts of the Ghost in *Hamlet*, Oroonoko, Jaffeir in *Otway's *Venice Preserv'd*, Timon, and Brutus. He was exemplary of the 'declamatory' school of acting that *Garrick and *Macklin displaced, though the young Macklin was nonetheless mesmerized by seeing him act. Cibber praised Booth for the musical harmony of his voice. Booth was considered one of the most learned actors of his day, having been educated at the Westminster School in *London.   MJK

BOOTH, EDWIN (1833–93)

American actor. Born in Maryland, Edwin was the second son of acclaimed actor Junius Brutus *Booth and Mary Ann Holmes. Accompanying his erratic and frequently inebriated father on *tour, and occasionally appearing for him, Edwin made his official debut in *Boston in 1849. In 1852 he went with his father to California, where both performed in theatres operated by his older brother, Junius Brutus *Booth, Jr., and until 1856 Edwin toured throughout California, Hawaii, and Australia, acting in companies with Laura *Keene and Catherine Sinclair. He opened in *New York at *Burton's Metropolitan Theatre in 1857 and achieved immediate acclaim, much of which was fuelled by critics Adam Badeau and William *Winter. Booth became one of America's most highly regarded tragedians, particularly in the role of Hamlet; in 1865 he gave 100 consecutive performances, an unprecedented theatrical achievement at the time. Throughout his career, he was noted for emotional intensity, grace, and careful, intellectual study of tragic *characters.

Booth's personal life was itself marked by tragedy. In 1860 he married actress Mary Devlin, who retired from the stage and then died in 1863 at the age of 23 while her husband was on tour in New York (and reputedly too drunk to attend to the telegrams announcing her worsening condition). Devlin's death plunged him into a melancholy that worsened after the assassination in 1865 of Abraham Lincoln by Edwin's brother John Wilkes *Booth. Unlike John Wilkes, Edwin was committed to the Union cause and was instrumental in producing and starring in *benefits for the United States Sanitary Fund. A few months after the assassination Edwin returned to the stage and resumed his theatrical career.

In addition to his acclaim as an actor, Edwin became a co-lessee and *actor-manager of New York's *Winter Garden Theatre, where he mounted distinguished productions of serious plays. The three Booth brothers appeared there together in 1864 in *Julius Caesar*, with Edwin as Brutus, John Wilkes as Mark Antony, and Junius Brutus, Jr., as Cassius, in a benefit to fund a statue of Shakespeare in Central Park. After a *fire destroyed the Winter Garden, Edwin built *Booth Theatre (1869), dedicated to the production of serious drama. Scenic innovations, such as hydraulic machinery for *scene shifting, were well received but costly, and poor financial management led Booth to declare bankruptcy in 1874, though he continued to perform throughout the United States. Noteworthy foreign visits included two seasons at the *Princess's Theatre in *London (1880–2); a number of performances at the *Lyceum (1881), including an Othello against *Irving's Iago; and an extremely successful German tour in 1883.   LQM

BOOTH, JOHN WILKES (1839–65)

American actor. Son of actor Junius Brutus *Booth, John Wilkes Booth was raised in Maryland in an American acting *family that was to become deeply divided over the Civil War. He first appeared on stage under the name J. Wilkes (1857) and joined the Richmond Virginia Theatre company the following year. As a *touring actor, he travelled freely between the northern and southern states, appearing at the *Arch Street Theatre in *Philadelphia and in other cities. His brother Edwin *Booth championed the Union cause, but John Wilkes was an ardent supporter of the segregationist south. His last appearance as an actor was in March 1865 at Ford's Theatre in Washington. Almost a month later, on 14 April 1865, while Abraham Lincoln was attending a production of Tom *Taylor's *Our American Cousin* at the same venue, Wilkes Booth stole into the presidential box, shot Lincoln, and jumped onto the stage shouting, 'Sic semper tyrannis'. He escaped after the assassination but was captured and killed twelve days later.   LQM

BOOTH, JUNIUS BRUTUS (1796–1852)

Anglo-American actor. Son of a lawyer, Booth received a classical education and trained in law. Against the wishes of his father he pursued a stage career, and after several years in the provinces came attention in *London as Richard III at *Covent Garden (1817). Reputed to be of Jewish descent, he incorporated Hebrew into his Shylock (1818). In 1821 he left his English wife and family and emigrated to America with Mary Ann Holmes. Three of their six children became noteworthy performers: Edwin *Booth, Junius Brutus *Booth, Jr., and John Wilkes *Booth, the assassin of Abraham Lincoln. Often described as 'the mad tragedian' and compared to Edmund *Kean, the senior Booth was known for tumultuous *characters such as Richard III and Othello; his knowledge of languages (he performed in French in New Orleans); and his eccentric behaviour and alcoholic binges offstage and on. Walt Whitman claimed that Booth's 'genius was to me one of the grandest revelations of my life'. In later life Booth continued to *tour the United States, often accompanied by his son Edwin; he died returning from *tour in California.   LQM

BOOTH, JUNIUS BRUTUS, JR. (1821–83)

American actor and *manager. The oldest son of Junius Brutus *Booth and Mary Ann Holmes, Junius was originally cast as his father's dresser and companion on *tour, but proved ill suited to the task of watchdog over his erratic parent, and younger brother Edwin *Booth took over. Junius Jr. also pursued a theatrical career, although he never achieved the acclaim afforded his brothers Edwin and John Wilkes *Booth, Lincoln's assassin. After the 1849 California gold rush Junius established theatres in *San Francisco and Sacramento, and in 1852 induced his father to come west for what would be his last tour. In later years Junius assisted Edwin with the management of the *Winter Garden and *Booth theatres in *New York.   LQM

BOOTH, SHIRLEY (1898–1992)

American actress, whose career spanned most of the twentieth century. She began in *stock companies in 1910, making her Broadway debut in 1926 (*Hell's Bells*, opposite Humphrey Bogart), her Oscar-winning film debut in 1952 (*Come Back, Little Sheba*, repeating her *award-winning 1950 stage role), and starred in a hit *television series (*Hazel*, 1961–6). She excelled in *comedy (*Three Men on a Horse*, 1935; *The Philadelphia Story*, 1939; *The Desk Set*, 1955), *musical comedy (*A Tree Grows in Brooklyn*, 1950; *Juno*, 1959), and drama (*The Time of the Cuckoo*, 1952). She played over 600 stage roles, acting into the 1970s on both stage and television; despite high praise for *Come Back, Little Sheba* and Thornton *Wilder's *The Matchmaker* (1958), her *film success came too late for a major career. Throughout

Booth stage, 1608, oil on wood by the Flemish painter David Vinckboons (1576–c.1632). The picture, which emphasizes the rowdiness of the audience, with two boys being driven off the stage, shows the platform mounted on casks and built against the side of an inn. The curtains provide actor access and visual focus, aided by the banners. The stage is high enough to allow the use of a trap, though none is visible here.

her somewhat rumpled, casual appearance and distinctive nasal voice, along with her virtuosity in suggesting concealed heartbreak, endeared her to *audiences. Born Thelma Booth Ford in *New York, she took ten years off her official age early in her career.   AW

BOOTH STAGE

A temporary *stage, outdoors, sized for the space allocated to a vendor in a market-place or fair. Generally it is a simple trestle stage with a rear *curtain to mask a dressing space; the most elaborate might have *traps in the stage floor, a canopy, or sometimes tent seating for the *audience. Booth stages have been used by *touring companies all over Europe from at least late *medieval times, and are possibly much older. In Britain, even professional shows touring the provinces as late as 1910 played on booth stages in a village green, known as 'fit-ups'.   JB

BOOTH THEATRE

Broadway theatre on West 45th Street in *New York, built by Winthrop *Ames and Lee *Shubert, and opened with *The Great Adventure* (1913). It forms a single building with the *Sam Shubert Theatre with which it shares a façade that runs along Shubert Alley. Owned by the Shuberts, it is named for actor Edwin *Booth. With room for 808, it is one of Broadway's most intimate venues and specializes in straight plays and intimate *musicals. Its many memorable productions include *Seventeen* (1918), *The Guardsman* (1924), two editions of *The Grand Street Follies* (1928–9), *You Can't Take It with You* (1936), *The Time of your Life* (1939), *Blithe Spirit* (1942), *Come Back, Little Sheba* (1950), *Visit to a Small Planet* (1957), *Two for the Seesaw* (1958), *Luv* (1964), *The Birthday Party* (1967), *That Championship Season* (1972), *for colored girls . . .* (1976), *The Elephant Man* (1979), and *Sunday in the Park with George* (1984).

SLL

BOQUET, LOUIS-RENÉ (1717–1814)

French designer. Rococo style reached its height in France with Boquet, whose earliest stage work was for the *Opéra and Mme de Pompadour in the late 1740s. After designing for Noverre at the *Opéra-Comique, he succeeded Jean-Baptiste Martin as Opéra costumier in 1758 and worked with *Boucher on designs for *Lully. During the 1760s, as chief costumier for royal spectacles, and after 1770, when he became Inspector General of the Menus-Plaisirs, his *costumes—wide panier skirts, delicate shirts in satins and vaporous gauze—adorned numerous court performances of Rameau, Campra, Trial, and Philidor. In 1778 he created designs for Marie Antoinette's private theatre at *Versailles.   JG

BORCHERT, WOLFGANG (1921–47)

German dramatist. Borchert saw active service on the Russian Front during the Second World War, during which time he was imprisoned for anti-Nazi sentiments, narrowly escaping execution. Borchert is best known for his anti-war play *Draußen vor der Tür* (*The Man Outside*), which marks the beginning of post-war German drama. First broadcast as a *radio play in February 1947, it received its stage première in November of that year at the Hamburg Kammerspiele, one day after the author's death in Switzerland. In short *expressionist scenes, the play tells the story of a soldier's homecoming, dramatizing the inability to readjust in a country physically and mentally ravaged by war.
CBB

BOROVSKY, DAVID (1934–)

Soviet/Russian set designer. Borovsky always starts from the bare stage, filled with functional and authentic *properties. He creates with his set designs a central metaphor, which condenses the literary material in a formal image. In 1969 Borovsky became chief designer for Yury *Lyubimov at the *Taganka Theatre, *Moscow, and began with *Alive: from the life of Fedor Kuzkin* (banned, 1968), *The Mother* (1969), and the famous set for *Hamlet* (1971), consisting of a heavy woven curtain that swept *characters off the stage into an open grave. For the war drama *But the Dawns Here Are so Calm* (1971) he created a variety of settings from the wooden panels of a truck. His sets for Trifonov's *The Exchange* (1979) and *The House on the Embankment* (1980) designate different times to distinct spaces. Borovsky has worked with Anatoly *Efros and Oleg *Efremov, as well as on *opera and theatre productions abroad. He temporarily joined the *Sovremennik Theatre 1984–9 during Lyubimov's exile, and finally left the Taganka in 1999 when Lyubimov stopped working with him.   BB

BORTNIK, AÍDA (1942–)

Argentinian writer. Internationally regarded for her screenplays, Bortnik has also written seven plays, including two for Teatro *Abierto festivals in *Buenos Aires (*Daddy Dearest*, 1981; *One by One*, 1983). Her 1984 *Springtimes*, premièred during redemocratization, traces three generations of Argentines over a 25-year period.   JGJ

BOSTON

The puritan legacy is not the only reason that theatre in this New England city has had such a fitful history. In 1687 John Wing's attempt to operate a theatre in his tavern was suppressed. After the mêlée caused by frustrated spectators at *Otway's *The Orphan* (1750) at the Coffee House on King (now State) Street, plays were forbidden. After the revolution broke out, General Burgoyne organized several performances for the *benefit of his soldiers' widows and children, one of which, *The Blockade of Boston* (1775) at Faneuil Hall, was terminated by news of the battle of Bunker Hill. In 1792 legislator John Gardiner made the first recorded American defence of the theatre. Later that year Joseph Harper opened the New Exhibition Room on Board Alley (near present-day Hawley Street). It had a capacity of 500 and was probably little more than a refurbished stable, featuring rope dancing, singing, recitation, and *ballet in its opening performances. Plays masquerading as 'moral lectures' came afterwards: *Garrick's *Lethe* and Otway's *Venice Preserv'd* were the first.

Five months later agitation arose over the theatre's allegedly foreign and anti-democratic bias. The sheriff tried to close the New Exhibition Room during a performance of *Sheridan's *The School for Scandal* and caused a *riot. The performance was stopped, but this law was never enforced again, and was repealed in 1797. The Board Alley success encouraged the construction of a permanent *playhouse and in 1794 the *Federal Street Theatre was constructed, a well-appointed house seating approximately 1,000. It presented the first professional production of a play by an American woman, *The Medium* by Judith Sargent Murray (1795). During the next 100 years a building boom produced 21 theatres. The *Tremont (1827) was the next significant building; it hoped to cater to fashionable patrons who were unsatisfied by the programme of only one venue. Rivalry between the Federal Street and Tremont closed both by mid-century. The city's two most important playhouses in the nineteenth century were the elegant *Boston Museum and the enormous *Boston Theatre.

*Variety acts were popular from the first. A 'learned pig' entertained Bostonians at Bowen's Columbian Museum (1798) and 70 years later the first human fly act appeared on the ceiling of the Howard Athenaeum. Performers such as the 'Viennoise Children' and the Ravels drew such crowds that in 1853 critic

William Clapp demanded that at least one theatre be reserved exclusively for dramas. When B. F. *Keith and E. F. *Albee began their dime 'show-store' (1883) at the Gaiety Museum, local *stock companies had largely succumbed to the *touring combination companies. By 1894, when the pair opened the Colonial, the first all-*vaudeville theatre, *variety seemed triumphant. Nonetheless the Broadway try-out system, pioneered at the Boston Theatre by playwright Charles H. *Hoyt for *A Trip to Chinatown* (1891), reinvigorated the city's *legitimate theatre through most of the following century.

The *Shuberts gained a monopoly on the downtown houses by 1934, and anything playing in them was either headed for Broadway or on tour from it. They had to contend with the strictest local *censorship in the nation. 'Banned in Boston' became the playwright's bane and the press agent's boon. From 1915 to 1965, a secret rider was attached to every theatrical contract that prohibited everything from lascivious language to 'muscle dancing by either sex'; *O'Neill's *Strange Interlude* was consigned to nearby Quincy (1929), the most notorious banning incident. The system's hypocrisy was transparent: at the 'Old' Howard Theatre strippers muscle danced with impunity (see SEX SHOWS AND DANCES). Meanwhile, the *Little Theatre movement made an impact. Scattered forces from Mrs Lyman Gale's Toy Theatre (1912) and the failed Castle Square Theater, which had presented George Pierce *Baker's Harvard prize plays (1911–17), were marshalled by Australians Henry and Frances Jewett to support a resident company. Jewett built the Repertory Theatre of Boston (1925) but his death in 1930 ended this endeavour.

Through the Depression and war years the New England Repertory and the Tributary Theatre kept local performances alive, and Jerome Kilty's Brattle Theater Company vitalized the local scene (1947–52). A significant *African-American company, the Boston Players, founded in 1930, was taken over by actor Ralf Coleman later in the decade. After the demise of the local *Federal Theatre Project Negro Unit, he gathered its veterans into the Boston Negro Theatre and remained active through the 1940s. In 1957 Michael Murray's Charles Playhouse troupe created the first new performance space in Boston since Jewett's when they converted an old church into a theatre (1957), lasting thirteen years. In the 1960s David Wheeler's Theatre Company of Boston gave the American première of *Pinter's *The Dwarfs* (1966) and presented Al *Pacino in *Richard III* (1973). The 1970s was a transitional decade—by its end the try-out system was gone. There were still artistically successful small theatres, but many efforts of experimental groups seemed increasingly forced. One tiny traditional theatre that prospered was the Lyric Stage, which celebrated its seventeenth season by transferring to a large new theatre (1991). About 50 other small companies still struggle, offering a wide theatrical range. The climax of the post-war era was the nearly simultaneous arrival of two resident companies: the *American Repertory Company (1980) and the Huntington Theatre (1982), sponsored respectively by Harvard and Boston universities. The ART is a technically dazzling *director's theatre, the Huntington reverences the *text above all else.

Theatre critics have been a significant part of Boston theatre (see CRITICISM). The legendary Henry Taylor Parker was a forceful arbiter from 1903 to 1934, and was Brooks *Atkinson's mentor. Elliot Norton was one of the most influential American critics from 1934 to 1982. Numerous producers and directors believed him an infallible guide to the public, frequently consulting with him during try-outs. Norton's successor Arthur Friedman, the 'guru of Harvard theatre' in the 1960s, had written for alternative weeklies before joining the mainstream *Herald* (1982). His wit and integrity raised the standards of both performers and critics. Friedman and his colleagues established the Elliot Norton *awards (1982) for excellence in theatre, a tribute to the doyen of American drama critics as much as a reflection of Boston's rebirth as a *regional theatre centre.

TFC

CLAPP, W. W., *Record of the Boston Stage* (Boston, 1853)
NORTON, E., *Broadway Down East* (Boston, 1978)

BOSTON IDEAL OPERA COMPANY

Founded in *Boston in 1879 by Effie H. Ober to offer an 'ideal' version of *Gilbert and *Sullivan's *HMS Pinafore*. The *long run of this production established the troupe as the pre-eminent American light *opera company. Henry Clay Barnabee was its greatest comedian and its de facto *manager from 1887 (when it was renamed the Bostonians). During the nineteenth century's final decades it set the standard for American comic opera performance, its members and repertoire celebrated for their refined yet lively performances. *Touring extensively throughout the USA and Canada, the company's influence was wide ranging, encouraging local singers and commissioning original works. Important debut compositions included Reginald De Koven's *Robin Hood* (1891) and Victor *Herbert's *Prince Ananais* (1894). The company operated more as a benevolent society than as a business. Barnabee's greatest provincial discovery, soprano Alice Nielsen, deserted after her first season (1898), taking most of the outstanding singers with her. The remaining Bostonians struggled on, disbanding in 1905.

TFC

BOSTON MUSEUM

The most important *playhouse in nineteenth-century *Boston, opened in 1841 by Moses Kimball. At first a 'Museum and Gallery of Fine Arts' in conjunction with a 'concert saloon', in 1843 Kimball started a *stock company. The 100-performance run of *The Drunkard* in 1844 certified the Museum as respectable, and for the rest of the century Bostonians flocked to the inexpensive *tickets for its genteel fare, as successive *managers shrewdly developed one of the finest *repertory companies in the nation. Edwin *Booth made his debut there in 1849, while William *Warren and the beloved Mrs J. R. Vincent (1818–87) were the mainstays. The company disbanded in 1894; the theatre was demolished in 1903.   TFC

BOSTON THEATRE

*Playhouse designed by Henri Nouri and built in 1854 through public subscription after the *Federal Street and *Tremont theatres closed. Dion *Boucicault called it 'the finest theatre in the world'. A technical showplace, its seating capacity of 3,140 made it the largest theatre in the USA. Edwin *Booth first starred there (1857), and Joseph *Jefferson first played Rip Van Winkle there (1869). By 1885 the theatre's well-regarded *stock company operated independently and spent most of its time *touring New England. B. F. *Keith turned the theatre into a *vaudeville and motion picture house after 1909. It was torn down sixteen years later and replaced by the Keith Memorial Theatre.   TFC

BOTTOMLEY, GORDON (1874–1948)

English poet and recluse who aimed to imitate the heroic dramas and *nō-inspired *dance-plays of W. B. *Yeats. His preferred subjects were drawn from *folklore (*Culbin Sands, The Woman from the Voe*), Icelandic saga (*The Riding to Lithend*), and Shakespeare's *tragedies (*King Lear's Wife, Gruach*). Bottomley's ambitions and achievements are ably defined and assessed in his *A Stage for Poetry* (1948), which includes archival photographs of stagings by Terence *Gray, Tyrone *Guthrie, and E. Martin *Browne, at Dartington Hall and Yale. His plays, popular with experimental art theatres, attracted innovative designers like Paul Nash, Edmund Dulac, and Charles Ricketts.   RAC

BOUBLIL, ALAIN (1938–) AND CLAUDE-MICHEL SCHÖNBERG (1944–)

French lyricist and composer team. They first collaborated in 1973 on a 'rock opera', *La Révolution française*, the *Paris success of which led Boublil to suggest in 1978 that they attempt a similar musicalization of Victor *Hugo's *Les Misérables*. Produced in Paris in 1980, it was an even greater success. In 1983 Boublil collaborated with producer Cameron *Mackintosh on *Abbacadabra*, a *musical based on songs by the Swedish pop group ABBA. This led to Mackintosh producing the English version of *Les Misérables* (1985), which became an international hit. Boublil and Schönberg's next collaboration, an adaptation

of the *Madame Butterfly* story in the context of *Vietnam titled *Miss Saigon* (1989), began in England and was similarly successful. A subsequent musical, *Martin Guerre* (1996), has not equalled this success and has been extensively rewritten. Their work is characterized by sweeping melodies used like *operatic leitmotifs, but infused with a rock beat. Schönberg has also had success as a pop composer in France, writing both music and lyrics.   JD

BOUCHARD, MICHEL MARC (1958–)

Québec playwright and actor. His major play is *Les Feluettes* (*Lilies*, 1987), translated into several languages, staged on three continents, with a *film version in English and French. As in most of his work male *protagonists, usually homosexual, challenge the homophobic intolerance of traditional Québec society. A complex drama operating on several linguistic levels while transcending usual concepts of space, time, and *plot, it has been followed by some twenty others, notably *Les Muses orphelines* (*The Orphan Muses*, 1988), *Le Voyage du couronnement* (*Coronation Voyage*, 1995) and *Sous le regard des mouches* (*Watched by Flies*, 1998), the latter a dark drama on the topic of death.   LED

BOUCHARDY, JOSEPH (1810–70)

French playwright. The enormous success of his *melodramas among the popular *audiences in nineteenth-century *Paris earned him the nickname 'King of the Boulevard'. His dramas were resolutely populist in theme and tone, usually concluding with the destruction of a powerful *villain. He acknowledged that he was writing for a generally illiterate public. Often compared with the melodramas of *Pixérécourt, Bouchardy's *plots are infinitely more complex than those of his predecessor. Among his most celebrated works were *Gaspardo le pêcheur* (*Gaspardo the Fisherman*, 1837), *Le Sonneur de Saint-Paul* (*The Bellringer of St Paul's*, 1838), and *Lazare le pâtre* (*Lazarus the Shepherd*, 1840). His last work, *L'Armurier de Santiago* (*The Armourer of Santiago*), was performed at the Châtelet (*Cirque Olympique) in 1868. Although Bouchardy's popularity with Parisian audiences began to wane in the 1850s, many of his plays were translated into Catalan and continued to enjoy great success in Spain.   CHB

BOUCHER, FRANÇOIS (1703–70)

French artist and designer. While he worked at the *Opéra-Comique in 1743 and again in 1752, when he executed decorations and ceiling designs for the refurbished theatre, his most significant contribution was as principal designer at the *Opéra between 1737 and 1739, between 1744 and 1748, and after 1763. During the 1740s he created *scenery for revivals of *operas and *ballets by *Destouches, Rameau, and *Lully. Appointed First Painter to Louis XV in 1765, he designed revivals of Lully, Berton, Trial, and Mondonville. Unfortunately, few of his exquisite rococo designs survive.   JG

BOUCICAULT, DION (1822–1890)

Irish actor, playwright, and *manager who sustained a long career over three continents: Europe, North America, and Australasia. Continual financial problems kept him writing or adapting plays to meet his needs, and he is credited with creating nearly 200 *texts. His English provincial debut in 1838 was under the pseudonym of Lee Morton, when he played many of the standard Irish roles popularized in *London by Tyrone *Power. Early success came with the staging by Madame *Vestris of his *comedy London Assurance (*Covent Garden, 1841), to be followed by over twenty works for Benjamin *Webster at the *Haymarket. During a sojourn in *Paris after 1844 Boucicault studied French techniques of constructing sensational *melodrama, chiefly by translating numerous works for the London stage. By 1852 he had returned to notice in London when Charles *Kean staged The Corsican Brothers and The Vampire at the *Princess's. Boucicault joined Kean's company as actor but became estranged after forming a relationship with the manager's ward and protégée Agnes Robertson.

The couple eloped to America in 1853 with Boucicault initially acting as Robertson's manager. Her acting in the plays he wrote to exploit her considerable talents won them both fame and he began to create for himself a series of roles as lovable, comic, down-at-heel, sentimental rogue, most notably Myles-na-Coppaleen in The Colleen Bawn (1860). This stage persona he abandoned on occasion when a more exotically situated melodrama offered him the chance to play a resplendent but reviled *villain (Nana Sahib in Jessie Brown; or, The Relief of Lucknow in *New York, 1858) or a faithful servant (the devoted but silent Indian Wahnotee in The Octoroon, 1859). In London from 1860 to 1872 the ever prodigal Boucicault veered between financial disaster or great success, especially with Arrah-na-Pogue (1864), Rip Van Winkle (1865), Hunted Down (1866) with *Irving as the villain Scudamore, After Dark (1868), and Formosa (1869). New York, whither the Boucicaults returned in 1872, was to see the launch of his finest play, The Shaughraun (*Wallack's, 1874). In the 1880s the couple became estranged, while Dion lost money in again undertaking management at *Booth's. During a tour of New Zealand and Australia in 1885 he married the youthful Louise Thorndyke in *Sydney, without apparently divorcing Agnes. His final years were spent teaching *acting at a theatre school attached to the *Madison Square Theatre.

As playwright and practitioner Boucicault effected some notable innovations. He created the concept of the provincial *tour independent of a successful metropolitan run; and he campaigned relentlessly for better financial deals for drama-

tists, which resulted in time both in the practice of giving percentage shares of profits and ultimately *royalties on performances. As dramatist, he popularized the locating of romantic or sensation scenes in 'authentic', especially Irish, landscapes. Though he deployed conventional sensational effects (the burning of boats or houses onstage, the onrush of an express train), Boucicault also used current scientific inventions unexpectedly to resolve his melodramatic *plots (a camera as photographic witness to a murder in The Octoroon; the telegraph in The O'Dowd of 1873). In terms of *scenography Boucicault was highly inventive in his quest to realize fresh and surprising effects. He required the supposed fourth wall of one setting to appear and close across the stage like a page turning to reveal the location directly outside, in order to achieve absolute continuity of action in the prison escape in The Shaughraun. Panoramas travelling horizontally across the stage had been in use for some time, but Boucicault devised a means for the device to move vertically downwards in order to allow Shaun credibly to escape his captors by climbing up an ivy-clad tower in Arrah-na-Pogue. Scene constructors had to keep pace with Boucicault's creativity.

Equally inventive was Boucicault's use of melodrama to engage with contemporary political events: slavery and miscegenation in The Octoroon (which was first staged two years before the outbreak of the American Civil War); the motivation behind current political unrest in Ireland and the formation of the Fenian Brotherhood in The Shaughraun. All Boucicault's Irish plays deploy strategies to teach English *audiences about Irish attitudes: even landscape in the plays is politicized and not seen as simply picturesque. At his best he brilliantly used the devices of melodrama to highlight differences between English and Irish modes of perception as shaped by contrasting experiences of colonial power. Boucicault was never afraid to combat the likely political sympathies of his spectators, and in this considerably influenced *Shaw and *O'Casey.   RAC

CAVE, RICHARD ALLEN, 'Staging the Irishman', in J. S. Bratton (ed.), Acts of Supremacy: the British empire and the stage (Manchester, 1991)
McCORMICK, JOHN, Dion Boucicault (Cambridge, 1987)

BOUFFES DU NORD, THÉÂTRE DES

*Playhouse first constructed as a théâtre à l'italienne in 1876 by architect Louis Marie Laménil in the unfashionable 10th arrondissement of *Paris, near the Gare du Nord. During its commercially troubled history as a venue for *melodrama, *café-concert, and drama, in the mid-1890s it was home to *Lugné-Poe's Théâtre de l'*Œuvre, the company that championed *Ibsen and *naturalism in France. Finally abandoned to the elements after a fire in 1952, this 'lost' theatre was found by British director Peter *Brook in 1974 in a state of extreme dereliction. The resonant splendour of its intimate open space, the traces of its past histories, and the patina of its weathered luminosity closely matched Brook's spatial and aesthetic ideals, and it has remained the performance space and base for his *International Centre for Theatre Research into the twenty-first century.   ADW

BOUKMAN, DANIEL (1936–   )

Martinican poet and playwright who lived in *Algiers (1962–81) after refusing to serve in the French army during the Algerian War. His trilogy of anti-colonial plays, produced in Arabic, followed in the wake of the work of Frantz Fanon and Aimé *Césaire. *Chants pour hâter la mort au temps des Orphée* (*Songs to Hasten Death in the Time of Orpheus*, 1967) is a polemic *Brechtian reading of the Middle East conflict, taking the side of the Palestinians. It is composed of *Les Voix dans une prison* (*Voices in Prison*), *Les Voix des sirènes* (*Voices of the Sirens*), and *Orphée nègre* (*Black Orpheus*). Another large-scale work, *Jusqu'à la dernière pulsation de nos veines* (*Until the Last Pulse in our Veins*, 1976), is made up of two tragic *farces, *Les Négriers* (*The Slave Traders*) and *Ventres pleins, ventres creux* (*Full Stomachs, Empty Stomachs*), bearing traces of *Genet's *The Blacks*. After seventeen years in *Paris, Boukman returned to Martinique in 1999 to teach *creole at the Université des Antilles et de la Guyane. His play about the Algerian War, *La Véridique Histoire de Hourya*, written in 1965, was finally published in 2000. *See also* CARIBBEAN THEATRE, FRANCOPHONE.

AR

BOULEVARD THEATRE

At its simplest, 'le théâtre de boulevard' translates as 'commercial theatre': it refers, particularly in the period 1890–1914, to those Parisian establishments which were independent of state control, and developed their own types of play to appeal to a certain class of spectator. It is important to distinguish this development from the earlier 'théâtre du Boulevard (du crime)', as the home of the *melodrama of *Pixérécourt and others was familiarly called in the early decades of the nineteenth century when it catered for a popular *audience of simple tastes. Later *Paris audiences were much more sophisticated, and theatre-going had become an important feature of the social life of the moneyed classes. The limited licence to open new establishments gave way to complete freedom under Napoleon III, and the many new theatres catered for the leisured affluence of the rising middle class, and their increasing mobility in post-Haussmann Paris. An evening at one of the theatres built during the Second Empire—the Châtelet, the *Gaîté, the Lyrique, and the Vaudeville, or the *Porte-Saint-Martin, rebuilt after being destroyed during the Commune—was a match for a visit to *Garnier's new *Opéra: evening dress was obligatory (*see* AUDIENCE DRESS), performances started (late) after dinner, and spectators were there to be seen as well as to watch what was more

often than not an exposé, either serious or light-hearted, of their own mores by playwrights like *Sardou or *Feydeau, or later by Porto-Riche, Courteline, or Bernstein.   WDH

BOURGEOIS THEATRE

A cultural phenomenon which emerged during the rise of the European bourgeoisie in the eighteenth century. In the twentieth century the term has often been applied in a more pejorative manner to dominant forms of theatre culture in capitalist contexts. In Marxist parlance 'bourgeois' refers to the legal owners and, more recently, to the managerial and high state official controllers of merchant, industrial, and money capital who have replaced the aristocracy as the class in control of the means of production. However, bourgeois theatre continues to be created by and appeal to a broader range of social groups, especially members of the diverse middle class, from professionals to clerical, technical, and service workers. Through its assertion of democratic liberalism, bourgeois theatre subversively challenged aristocratic absolutist order. In contrast to the French *neoclassical focus on *plot, the *unities, and the tragic state affairs of royal figures, bourgeois drama emphasized these aspects: characterization, especially of non-aristocratic *protagonists; displays of virtuous civil behaviour, especially by beneficent middle-class patriarchs; treatment of private issues in a manner which invited empathy and appealed to sentiment; and a move towards *realist *illusionism through, for example, the use of mundane prose instead of *verse. In 1757 Denis *Diderot, a prominent spokesperson for the new drama, called for a *genre which embraced both 'serious *comedy'—involving the depiction of the virtue and duties of man—and 'bourgeois *tragedy', which dealt with domestic misfortunes. One of his sources of inspiration was George *Lillo's *The London Merchant; or, The History of George Barnwell* (1731), with its story about a young businessman who steals for a prostitute and is ultimately executed.

Bourgeois theatre's association with pathos-laden subject matter can be related to its assertion of self-expression and sensibility as sources of truth, while its promotion of empathy reflects a humanist emphasis on what is shared by all mankind, regardless of rank. Methods of enhancing the beholder's emotional absorption in *character which gradually unfolded were: the removal of (upper-class) spectators from the stage; the fostering of fourth-wall illusionism; darkening of the *auditorium; and the focusing of concealed stage *lighting upon the actors. These methods, along with a shift from heightened theatricality to realist performance—as fostered by *actor-manager David *Garrick—have been interpreted as a retreat from the public to the private sphere and as an inscription of bourgeois codes of civility. A further display of these codes is to be found in nineteenth-century *playhouse auditoriums, where the introduction of seats in the *stalls as well as increasingly plush decor helped to ensure quiet and disciplined spectatorship. During the nineteenth century bourgeois theatre became an increasingly conservative force, particularly in its manifestation as a spectacular commercial enterprise. While *melodrama may have attracted a considerable number of spectators from the proletariat, such theatregoing was controlled in financial and managerial terms by bourgeois entrepreneurs. It has been suggested that the closed and moralizing narrative structures of melodrama, where vice is punished and virtue rewarded, promoted a form of *embourgeoisement*—the imprinting of bourgeois lifestyle and values. Arguably, even the less commercialized and socially critical dramas written by *Ibsen, *Strindberg, *Hauptmann, and others, and staged by small independent theatres such as *Antoine's Théâtre *Libre, contributed to the process of *embourgeoisement* through their assumption of an educated *audience attuned to the impact of positivist, Marxist, and psychoanalytical thought, and their preference for *naturalist or realist illusionism.

Many *avant-garde and politically engaged practitioners of the twentieth century have defined their work in opposition to bourgeois theatre. *Symbolism and *expressionism rejected the positivist overtones of realism in favour of subjective abstractionism; theatres of *cruelty revolted against the disciplined body of civilized actor and spectator; and left-wing formations such as *agitprop challenged the hierarchical and commodity-oriented structures of commercial institutions. However, very few of these projects can be said to have extricated themselves from the influence of bourgeois capitalist forces, the staging of *Brecht and *Piscator's anti-bourgeois *epic theatre within mainstream institutions being a case in point. As Western theatre has become increasingly characterized by eclecticism in terms of form and content, the label 'bourgeois theatre' has tended to refer more to theatre events dominated by *embourgeoisement* and capitalist modes and relations of production than to specific types of drama and performance. As a descriptor which denotes cultural institutions owned, controlled, and frequented by the bourgeoisie and those who have assimilated its codes and values, 'bourgeois theatre' could be applied to the majority of theatre events in capitalist societies today. *See also* DIRECTING/DIRECTOR; POLITICS AND THEATRE.   MM

BOWERY THEATRE

The Bowery in *New York offered entertainment for popular tastes for 103 years. Opening in 1926, it was the largest *playhouse in America, with seating for 3,000, and the first in New York with gas *lighting. Rebuilt four times after *fires in 1828, 1836, 1838, and 1845, it was most successful under the *management of Thomas B. Hamblin. His eclectic offerings included T. D. *Rice's 'Jim Crow' performances, the spectacle *Mazeppa*, the adaptations of Louisa *Medina, Charlotte *Cushman's stage

debut, the première of *The Count of Monte Cristo*, and a succession of stars, including Edwin *Booth and Frank *Chanfrau.

AHK

BOX OFFICE

Originally referring to the hiring of a box at a theatre (*see* BOX, PIT, AND GALLERY), this term has a broad range of meanings: (a) literally the office where *tickets may be purchased for a performance (either in advance or on the day, either in person or by mail or phone); (b) the staff that runs this office; (c) the financial condition of a performance (total attendance and/or total revenues); or (d) a figure for the appeal or drawing power of some aspect of the performance or a factor affecting that appeal (an *award to a playwright might be described as good box office). A statement of a play's box office can suggest whether a show has been successful in attracting an *audience or not. Whether a performance has been *critically reviewed positively, negatively, or indifferently, box-office success is used as a significant market tool to draw future audiences. The biggest box-office successes are deemed 'blockbusters'. Box office also functions figuratively to suggest the likely boost to ticket sales of a particular play or actor or some other crucial aspect of the production. A star actor might be described, then, as having strong box-office potential. Not surprisingly, there is sometimes conflict between box-office demands and the artistic hopes of a performance: *Shaw said in 1956, 'I dont [sic] want to sacrifice my aim to the box office.'

SBe

BOX, PIT, AND GALLERY

*Audience areas in the *auditorium first established in English indoor theatres of the seventeenth century, such as *Lincoln's Inn Fields and the first *Drury Lane. The highest prices were charged for seats in a box, which might hold up to twenty people. Boxes were at stage level and ran continuously round three sides of the auditorium with at least two boxes situated on the *forestage of seventeenth-century *playhouses. The pit occupied the floor of the theatre at a considerably lower level than the stage and boxes and, unlike the standing pit of earlier *public theatres, contained rows of backless benches set on a raked floor. Seats in the pit were half the price of a seat in the box and attracted a mixed audience of men and women (*see* WOMEN IN AUDIENCES); Samuel *Pepys records that both he and his wife frequently chose to sit in the pit. The activity of the audience in the pit and the behaviour of the occupants of the boxes, especially with the King present, were part of the theatregoing *spectacle. During the eighteenth century onstage boxes were gradually removed as the forestage was brought back to the line of the *proscenium arch in order to accommodate larger audiences. References to the addition of middle and upper galleries in the *patent theatres appear in the 1690s with the

Pit, Boxes and Gallery, 1836, a print by George Cruikshank, depicting the Surrey Theatre, a minor theatre in Lambeth in London. Though this playhouse often catered to the working classes in its choice of action melodrama and nautical melodrama (including Jerrold's *Black Ey'd Susan*, 1829, starring T. P. Cooke), the class divisions typical of the early nineteenth century are nonetheless apparent in audience dress, with a mix of what are probably petty bourgeois seated on pit benches (bottom rank), elegantly attired spectators in the boxes above them, and the rowdiest people at the top in the gallery.

highest gallery level, the 'gods', being first referred to in the 1750s. In the eighteenth century pit benches eventually gave way to rows of seats, with a standing pit at the back of the auditorium, while the last vestige of the early pit, immediately in front of the stage, was replaced by the orchestra pit. In 1849 Drury Lane introduced three rows of orchestra *stalls in front of the orchestra pit and by 1886 all West End *London theatres had introduced stalls and enforced a dress code for stalls, boxes, and dress circle (the first gallery; *see* AUDIENCE DRESS). Social divisions in the auditorium, apparent in the price difference between boxes and galleries in the seventeenth century, became deliberate moves toward social segregation, reflected by the dress codes of the nineteenth and early twentieth centuries. The price difference between the seating areas in traditional theatre buildings was still in force at the start of the twenty-first century, with a stall in London costing about three times an upper gallery seat.   GBB

BOX SET

A *stage set consisting of an interior room open to the *audience side, entirely framed by the *proscenium arch, within which all or most *scenery will be practical. Developed in *Paris for *melodrama and *boulevard *farce between 1800 and 1820, Madame Eliza *Vestris brought the box set to the *Olympic Theatre in *London in 1832. At first the English 'box scene' might have furniture, pictures, and windows painted on, but within two decades the box set would, as much as possible, resemble a real room sectioned by the proscenium. As *realism and *naturalism took hold of the theatre, and as the *Stanislavsky approach to acting made functional *properties more desirable for actors, the box set became the most 'natural' of settings. By 1900 it had largely displaced horizontally sliding scenery (*see* SCENE SHIFTING), for grooves or slots are useless to a box set and actually interfere with its construction. David *Belasco and other Broadway *producers, during the boom years before the First World War, could afford both the materials and the technicians to create spaces in exacting detail, pushing the verisimilitude of the box set yet further. In the years between 1905 and 1920 German designers perfected the *cyclorama, which made possible an apparently real sky beyond an upstage window or door. By 1930 in any substantial professional theatre in any Western country, *audiences expected to be able to experience the scenery as apparently 'real', a kind of vivid hallucination. (This was not the expectation for *lighting, which still tended to be harsh and full-on.) After about 1940, as playwrights and directors began to alloy realism, and with the development of the *open stage, the box set began to seem quaint, static, distant (due to the framing proscenium), and contrived (requiring actors to speak, move, and turn as if they were all conversing with an unmarked windowless wall). *See* SCENOGRAPHY.   JB

BOY ACTOR

In all European theatrical traditions, female roles were regularly played by boys or young men until Italian popular companies introduced actresses in the mid-sixteenth century. Even these companies were not allowed to use actresses throughout Italy, and where actresses were permitted they used male performers to play bawdy female servants (*see* COMMEDIA DELL'ARTE). Gradually, the use of actresses spread across Western Europe, but the English commercial theatre remained an all-male preserve until the enforced cessation of playing in 1642, and only introduced actresses after the Restoration in 1660. Before the 1590s, small itinerant English troupes, accustomed to *doubling roles, often comprised 'four men and a boy', the latter taking all female roles. When larger troupes established permanent *London *playhouses after the 1590s, three or four 'play-boys' in female roles could be on stage at the same time. As virtual if not actual apprentices, these young *female impersonators took female roles until their voices changed, as late as age 18 or 19, and thereafter played young men. Cross-gender *casting was attacked by Puritans and other *anti-theatrical writers. *See also* BOYS' COMPANIES; COMPANY ORGANIZATION IN EUROPE; WOMEN AND PERFORMANCE; GENDER AND PERFORMANCE.   MS

BOYLE, ROGER, EARL OF ORRERY (1621–79)

Irish playwright, soldier, and politician. A favourite of Charles II, Boyle was encouraged by the King to write a play in the 'French fashion'. *The General* (1664), in rhymed heroic couplets, prompted *Dryden to recognize its author as his predecessor in 'the new way of writing scenes in *verse'. Other plays in the *heroic mode followed, including *Mustapha* (1665) and *The Black Prince* (1667). Rigidly formulaic, featuring exalted *characters torn between love and honour and given to interminable philosophizing, Boyle's *tragedies and *tragicomedies

reflect the fleeting fashion their author helped to popularize.
                                                              RWV

BOYS' COMPANIES

Plays performed by boys, in Latin or in English, were a popular element of education at the Tudor grammar schools, an activity extended with academic plays performed by students as a regular feature of university life (*see* UNIVERSITY AND SCHOOL DRAMA). Plays staged by boys were superior in social status to plays by adult groups until well into the seventeenth century. At the Tudor court plays performed by boys were at first favoured over those of the professional adult companies because of their academic associations: in the 1560s boy choristers and schoolchildren played at court 23 times compared with nine plays by adult players. In the 1580s, however, the adults played at court 44 times compared with 23 by the boy companies. At this time two chorister groups were regularly playing: the *Chapel Royal Children at *Blackfriars and Paul's Children at the cathedral. In 1583 they merged into one group under John *Lyly. It was banned from playing altogether at the end of that decade, and by the time they were revived in a different form in 1599 the adult companies were dominant at court.

In 1599 the chorister boys of St Paul's reopened at their tiny *playhouse on the flank of the cathedral. In 1600 an impresario started a second company at the Blackfriars. It was not made up as before of boys officially serving as choristers, although it took its name from the former *Chapel Children and occupied the same complex of buildings in the 'liberty' of the Blackfriars, this time using the playhouse built by James *Burbage in 1596. The social cachet of boy players was a factor in this relocation. In 1596 the residents of Blackfriars objected to the daily noise of the regular playgoers, but they raised no such objections in 1600 to once-weekly performances by the boy company.

Indoor venues inside the city were an advantage in attracting the more gentrified playgoers, and their higher admission prices kept the working class out. Thanks to the ostensibly educational value of boys acting in plays they gave what they called 'private' performances, as distinct from the 'public' playing of the adult companies, who had to be licensed by the *Master of the Revels (*see* PRIVATE THEATRES; PUBLIC THEATRES). This was a freedom the writers for the Blackfriars learned to exploit, but under King James did not last very long. While the Paul's Boys staged new but usually inoffensive 'citizen comedy' plays by *Dekker and *Middleton, the Blackfriars Boys staged *satirical plays mocking citizen values and especially the new crowd of Scotsmen at the *London court (*see* CITY COMEDY). In 1605 the boy cast performed *The Isle of Gulls* in two accents, English and Scottish. In 1606 they staged *Eastward Hoe* by *Jonson, *Marston, and *Chapman, which got the authors and several of the players into prison. Paul's Boys staged plays about more local citizen interests. But they folded in 1606, their plays passing to the Blackfriars group, which lasted two more years until, in a long closure for plague, their impresario surrendered his lease of the playhouse back to the Burbages. A boy company went on playing at the *Whitefriars after that, but the ageing boys then merged into adult groups. Boy companies as such did not resurface, except for the youths of '*Beeston's Boys' at the *Cockpit Theatre in the last five years before the closure of the theatres in 1642. Young players were cheaper and more amenable to impresario control than the adult companies. *See also* BOY ACTOR.   AJG

BRACCO, ROBERTO (1861–1943)

Italian playwright, poet, and critic. An admirer of *Ibsen and *Wagner, Bracco's plays in Neapolitan and in standard Italian were performed by major Italian acting troupes, such as the *Talli-*Gramatica-Calabresi company, and contributed to the renewal of playwriting and dramatic *acting during the *belle époque*. Giovanni *Grasso was memorable in *Sperduti nel buio* (*Lost in the Dark*, 1901), as was Ruggero *Ruggeri in *Il piccolo santo* (*Little Saint*, 1909). Despite his success at home and abroad, Bracco's socialist sympathies led to his marginalization by the *fascists in the late 1920s and critics remained silent at his death.   JEH

BRACEGIRDLE, ANNE (c.1673–1748)

English actress and *manager. Adopted into the *Betterton household, Bracegirdle is named as a member of the United Company in 1688, though she probably performed earlier. Her reputation was as innocent and virtuous as the *characters she played in *tragedy, and she was a regular *prologue speaker and a popular comedienne, particularly in *breeches roles. With Elizabeth *Barry and Thomas Betterton, Bracegirdle co-managed the Players' Company at *Lincoln's Inn Fields (1695–1705) during which time *Congreve wrote *Love for Love* (1695) and Millament in *The Way of the World* (1700) specifically for her. She retired from the stage in 1707, still at the height of her career.   GBB

BRACKENRIDGE, HENRY HUGH (1748–1816)

American writer. Best known for his satirical novel *Modern Chivalry* (1792–1815), Brackenridge's principal contributions to drama were two heroic *tragedies in blank *verse, *The Battle of Bunker Hill* (1776) and *The Death of General Montgomery* (1777). Writing at the start of hostilities, and among the first to write in support of American revolutionary themes, he tried to inspire the American cause by recasting those two recent military defeats into *romantic dramas. He also collaborated

with Philip Freneau on *The Rising Glory of America*, a patriotic commencement ode performed at Princeton in 1772.   PAD

BRADY, WILLIAM ALOYSIUS (1863–1950)

American actor and *producer. Born in *San Francisco, Brady began as a *call boy and fill-in actor in 1882 before heading east and turning to producing in 1888. His *New York production of *Boucicault's *After Dark* (1889) was a big success. He tried out Lottie Parker's sentimental *Way Down East* in *Chicago and New England prior to New York (1898), where it ran for 152 performances and then reaped millions on *tour for two decades. In 1911 he built the Playhouse, where his notable productions included Owen Davis's *Sinners* (1915) and *Forever After* (1918), and Elmer *Rice's *Street Scene* (1929). The last of his more than 260 productions was *Billy Draws a Horse* (1939). As manager-agent, he guided the careers of such stars as Robert B. *Mantell and Helen *Hayes. Brady published two autobiographies, *The Fighting Man* (1916) and *Showman* (1937).   CT

BRAGAGLIA, ANTON GIULIO (1890–1960)

Italian director and journalist. He joined the *futurist movement in 1918 and founded the Casa d'Arte Bragaglia in *Rome, where he promoted the arts through exhibitions and conferences. Between 1916 and 1922 Bragaglia published the arts reviews *Ruota* and *Cronache d'attualità*, and made an experimental *film in 1916 (*Perfido incanto*; *Perfidious Enchantment*). He was committed to the modernization of the theatre through revitalized staging and technology, and in 1922 founded the *avant-garde Teatro degli Indipendenti, which operated until 1930, employing only *amateur actors. In 1931 he staged works by *Strindberg, *Turgenev, *Pirandello, and others. He wrote considerable *criticism and several extended essays on theatre.   DMcM

BRAHM, OTTO (1856–1912)

German critic and *manager. Brahm studied German literature in *Berlin before becoming a theatre *critic in 1881 for the *Vossische Zeitung*. In 1889 he co-founded the *Freie Bühne in Berlin based on *Antoine's Théâtre *Libre (*see* NATURALISM). He also established and edited the periodical *Freie Bühne für modernes Leben* (1890–1), which became the most important organ for propagating the principles of naturalism in Germany. The Freie Bühne, organized as a private society to avoid *censorship, was instrumental in introducing dramatists such as *Hauptmann and *Schnitzler and performing the more controversial plays by *Ibsen. In 1894 Brahm leased the *Deutsches Theater and built up one of the best *acting ensembles in Germany. Although he never appeared as *director on *playbills, he closely supervised all aspects of production and the 'Brahm style' became a synonym for *dramaturgical exactitude and psychological *realism. In 1904 he leased the Lessing Theater, by which time his style was losing popularity against the flamboyant theatricality of his pupil Max *Reinhardt. He stayed with his repertoire but was in dire financial straits at his death.

CBB

BRAITHWAITE, LILIAN (1873–1948)

English actress. Raised in England, Braithwaite began her career in South Africa, performing Shakespeare with her husband Gerald Lawrence. She returned to England in 1900 and acted with the companies of Frank *Benson and George *Alexander, quickly establishing herself in the West End in revivals of Shakespeare and *Wilde. For the most part, her career over the next four decades consisted of roles in popular *melodramas and sentimental *comedies. In the 1920s she had great success in Noël *Coward's *The Vortex* (1924), and she played in a series of Ivor *Novello comedies in the 1920s. For three years in *London during the Second World War she appeared in *Arsenic and Old Lace*. She was made DBE in 1943. TP

BRANAGH, KENNETH (1960–)

Irish actor, director, and *producer. Born in Belfast, Branagh trained at the *Royal Academy of Dramatic Art, made his *London debut in 1982 in Julian *Mitchell's *Another Country*, and joined the *Royal Shakespeare Company in 1984 to play Henry V, Laertes, and the King of Navarre. With such precocious roles, outstanding talent, and adaptable good looks, critics were eager to draw comparisons with the young *Olivier. It was a reputation Branagh seemed to court when in 1987 he cofounded (with actor David Parfitt) the Renaissance Theatre Company, and when he made his *film directorial debut with *Henry V* (1989). For Renaissance he directed *Twelfth Night* (1987), *King Lear*, *A Midsummer Night's Dream* (both 1990), and *Uncle Vanya* (1991); and appeared as Hamlet, Benedick, Touchstone (all 1988), Quince, Edgar (both 1990), and Coriolanus (1992). In 1992 he played Hamlet again, this time for Adrian *Noble in a full *text for the RSC. His film career also focuses on Shakespeare: besides *Henry V*, he has directed and starred in *Much Ado About Nothing* (1993), *Hamlet* (1996, running more than four hours), and *Love's Labour's Lost* (2000). He played Iago opposite Laurence Fishburne in Oliver Parker's *Othello* (1995), and has appeared in a number of other Hollywood movies. *Television roles include Guy Pringle in *Fortunes of War* (1987), based on Olivia Manning's novels, and the title part in *Shackleton* (2001). He directed the West End hit *The Play What I Wrote* (2001) and played Richard III at the *Crucible Theatre in Sheffield (2002). He published an autobiography at age 29, *Beginning* (1989). AS

BRANDO, MARLON (1924–)

American actor. Brando became famous for his *Method *acting style, learned at Lee *Strasberg's *Actors Studio, in his stage and screen performances as Stanley Kowalski in Tennessee *Williams's *A Streetcar Named Desire* (1947, 1951, directed by Elia *Kazan). Though he never returned to the stage he continued to create moody, self-absorbed, and often aggressive *characters in *films such as *The Wild One* (1954) and Kazan's controversial *On the Waterfront* (1954). Other notable films of the 1950s include *Julius Caesar* (1953), *Guys and Dolls* (1955), and *The Fugitive Kind* (1959). After a number of unsuccessful movies in the 1960s, Brando received an Oscar for his performance as Don Corleone in Francis Ford Coppola's *The Godfather* (1971). He remained uncomfortable with Hollywood stardom and continued to work in commercially risky ventures such as Bernardo Bertolucci's *Last Tango in Paris* (1972) and Coppola's *surreal epic about the Vietnam War, *Apocalypse Now* (1979). While he became increasingly reclusive as a person, Brando appeared in mainstream Hollywood movies during the 1980s and 1990s, most notably in a comic parody of Don Corleone in *The Freshman* (1990). JAB

BRATISLAVA

Capital city of the Slovak Republic and centre of its theatre life. There is ample evidence that secular *medieval theatre and *liturgical plays were performed from the thirteenth to the seventeenth century. The first theatre with a permanent stage was built in a Protestant school in 1656, though foreign *touring companies, mostly German and Italian, had been visiting Bratislava since the early seventeenth century. In 1776 the first permanent municipal theatre was built by Count Csaky. A Hungarian theatre company arrived in 1829 and in 1842 an *arena stage was built for it, while the municipal theatre remained in the hands of German *managers. In 1918, when two-thirds of Bratislava's population was German or Hungarian, there was almost no sign of Slovak theatre. The city became the seat of the Slovak National Theatre (SNT) in 1920, shortly after the foundation of Czechoslovakia (1918), though the repertoire, both in *opera and drama, was Czech.

The breakthrough came in 1935 when a Slovak dramatic ensemble was established within the SNT. The first generation of Slovak actors and directors (Jan Borodac, Jan Jamnicky) matured in the 1940s, after many Czech actors and directors (Viktor Sulc, for example) were expelled or decided to leave. In 1946 another repertory theatre, Nova Scena, came into existence and a few years later created a separate company for *operetta and *musical comedy. In the late 1960s another strong generation of actors and directors (Miloš Pietor, Vladimír Strnisko), more cosmopolitan in feeling and less attached to the *realistic style, came to the fore; but their nonconformist Divadlo na

Korze (Corso Theatre) was banned in 1971. Nova Scena and the SNT absorbed most of its actors and directors, and both opera and drama flourished, even in the politically difficult period of the 1970s and 1980s. In the early 1990s, the satirical *cabaret of Milan Lasica and Julius Satinský was revived and some new little theatres emerged, like the provocative Stoka (Ditch), founded by Blaho Uhlar in 1991. There have also been efforts to re-establish the development of Slovak *mime (by Milan Sladek). ML

BRAUN, VOLKER (1939–)

German dramatist, essayist, and poet. Braun grew up in the German Democratic Republic, working as a printer and on construction sites before studying philosophy in Leipzig. From the mid-1960s he worked as a *dramaturg at the *Berliner Ensemble and then at the *Deutsches Theater. During this time he established himself as a dramatist, closely aligned to the ideals of the East German state, while at the same time able to criticize it within acceptable limits. The *characters in his plays are frequently rebels who channel their rebelliousness in a productive way. His best-known work is *Die Übergangsgesellschaft* (*Transitional Society*, 1987), which was premièred in West Germany. Braun received major literary awards in both East and West Germany. CBB

BRAUNSHWEIG, STÉPHANE (1964–)

French director. After studying philosophy at the École Normale Supérieure and theatre at the school of the Théâtre National du *Chaillot under Antoine *Vitez, Braunshweig quickly became one of the most sought after of the younger directors, producing numerous plays and *operas throughout Europe, most notably *Brecht's *In the Jungle of the Cities* (*Paris, 1997), *Measure for Measure* (*Edinburgh Festival, 1997), *The Merchant of Venice* (Paris, 1999), and a revelatory production of Beethoven's *Fidelio* for the Staatsoper, *Berlin (1995). From 1993 to 1998, he ran the Centre Dramatique National for Orléans-Loiret, and in 2000 became the director of the Théâtre National de Strasbourg, where he stood poised to forge that company into an important pan-European theatre. DGM

BRAYNE, JOHN (d. 1586)

English *playhouse owner and entrepreneur. In 1567 he built the *Red Lion *amphitheatre, the first permanent, purpose-designed theatre in England, in the *London suburb of Stepney. In 1576 he established and financed the *Theatre in Shoreditch in an uneasy partnership with his brother-in-law James *Burbage. MJW

BREAD AND PUPPET THEATRE

German sculptor-puppeteer Peter *Schumann moved to *New York in 1961, playing in poor neighbourhoods, baking and distributing bread at performances: his working assumption is that theatre, like bread, is a staple of life. In the 1960s Bread and Puppet began street protests against capitalism and the Vietnam War (*see* STREET THEATRE). They used giant figures—on a scale with the urban environment—*masks, and placards, the whole reminiscent of Soviet *agitprop of the 1920s and the giant festive figures of Iberia. To be more in contact with nature, Schumann moved to a farm in Vermont, establishing an annual 'Resurrection Circus', involving hundreds of participants and huge *audiences. Rich in Christian references, and in a broad range of references to cultural myth, Schumann's work is profoundly humanitarian, and concerned with the false and exploitative values of a post-Cold War consumerism. Discovered at the Nancy Festival in 1968, Bread and Puppet paved the way for the introduction of the *puppet into modern theatre performance, notably with the Théâtre du *Soleil's piece *1789*. JMcC

BRECHT, BERTOLT (1898–1956)

German playwright, director, theoretician, and poet, one of the most influential theatre practitioners of the twentieth century. Born in Augsburg in Bavaria, Brecht began publishing poetry while still in secondary school. He started medical studies in *Munich in 1917, but broke off the next year while working on his first play, *Baal*, to devote himself full time to writing. In 1922 he won the prestigious Kleist Prize for most promising young writer with his second play, *Drums in the Night*. The next year, both *Baal* and a new play, *In the Jungle of Cities*, received productions. All three plays provoked divided, often boisterous spectator response. Brecht rode this wave of notoriety from Munich to *Berlin in 1924, where he took up a nominal position as one of *Reinhardt's *dramaturgs at the *Deutsches Theater while writing *A Man's a Man* (1926); he also worked with *Piscator in 1927–8. Brecht then collaborated with his childhood friend, the designer Caspar *Neher, and the composer Kurt *Weill on *The Threepenny Opera* (1928), which overnight became Weimar Germany's most successful theatre event.

Brecht's three early plays demonstrate both his assimilation of *expressionist technique and a command of dramatic language that helped him develop one of the most significant styles in twentieth-century German writing. They also contain a violent rejection of the bourgeois values with which he had been raised (*see* BOURGEOIS THEATRE) and a developing attack on the Weimar Republic's cold commercialism, an attack that achieved its most exotic expression in the *opera *Rise and Fall of the City of Mahagonny* (music by Weill, 1930). By then, however, Brecht was more interested in creating a new kind of

Bread and Puppet Theatre's *The Convention of the Gods*, an open-air performance in Vermont, USA, 1993, showing the combination of giant puppets, actors, and rapid movement characteristic of the company under the direction of Peter Schumann.

*politically committed theatre, a proletarian theatre performed by workers' groups for worker *audiences. He had begun to study and practise Marxism in the mid-1920s; his initial interests are visible in the somewhat confused exploration of collective identity in *A Man's a Man*. Between 1929 and 1931 he wrote five *Lehrstücke*, or 'learning plays', the best known of which is *The Measures Taken* (also published as *The Decision*, 1930), in which four agitators played by *actors report the story of their mission to China to a 'Control Chorus', played by several large workers' *choruses (and, by extension, by the spectators), to whom the agitators direct their physical demonstrations. Another *Lehrstück*, *The Exception and the Rule*, was not performed until 1938, and became well known only in the 1960s. *The Mother* (1932), one of the finest plays of this period, uses the *Lehrstück* style, as Brecht notes, but is written for professional rather than *amateur actors and does not attempt to break down the difference between performer and spectator.

Brecht directed his first production—the première of his own adaptation of *Marlowe's *Edward II*—in 1924, and he continued to work on productions of his plays, often as *director of

record, often less openly. Until he fled Germany to avoid execution after the Nazis seized power in 1933, his various notes and statements about the theatre involved not abstract theorizing but direct response to a practice. Nowhere is this connection clearer than in the *texts, productions, and notes to the *Lerhstücke*, where Brecht combined a political dramaturgy and a radical rethinking of the productive relationship between performance and spectator to develop fully the *epic theatre he had been experimenting with throughout the decade. Unfortunately, texts of all the *Lehrstücke*, and the many (mostly unpublished) notes, became available in German only in the early 1970s, and in English only in 1997, although the best-known plays were available in the 1960s.

After fleeing Germany, Brecht, his wife and collaborator, the actress Helene *Weigel, and their two children kept just ahead of expanding Nazi hegemony, moving first to Denmark (1933), then Sweden (1939), Finland (1940), and finally California (1941). During this period, he wrote several plays as direct contributions to the fight against Hitler, including the epic *Fear and Misery of the Third Reich* (1938), and the intentionally *melodramatic and hugely successful *Señora Carrar's Rifles* (1937); these were among Brecht's best-known works during his lifetime. In exile, too, Brecht wrote most of the *theoretical essays and plays that first secured his international reputation after his death, including *Life of Galileo* (1937), *Mother Courage and her Children* (1941), *The Good Person of Setzuan* (1943), and *The Caucasian Chalk Circle* (1948). Two political *comedies, *Mr Puntila and his Man, Matti* (1948) and *The Resistible Rise of Arturo Ui* (1958), have met with mixed receptions. They are among Brecht's most frequently performed works in German-speaking Europe, for example, often staged in England, but rarely in North America.

Brecht was unsuccessful in establishing himself as a Hollywood screenwriter and in getting his plays widely produced in the USA. In 1947 he was called to testify before the House Un-American Activities Committee. He defended himself well against charges of being a Communist Party member and writing communist propaganda; indeed, the widely available taped transcript recommends the event as a minor masterpiece of political *street theatre. Brecht left the next month for Switzerland, where in 1948 he directed productions of his own adaptation of *Antigone* at the Stadtheater Chur and of *Puntila* at the *Zurich Schauspielhaus (with Kurt *Hirschfeld as director of record), while working with Weigel towards setting up a new company, the *Berliner Ensemble, at the invitation of the East German authorities. In 1949 he moved to East Berlin. He left unfinished a new play, *Days of the Commune*, and did not complete another. Instead he concentrated on directing and on training a new generation of directors and actors. He developed new variations of his epic theatre, noting once that the post-war, post-Nazi audience simply was not ready for the older, stronger epic theatre of the *Lehrstücke*. He did, however, stage *The Mother* (1951), along with *Mother Courage* (1949), and *Caucasian Chalk Circle* (1954). And he wrote several adaptations for the Ensemble that became influential, including *Lenz's *The Private Tutor* (1950), *Farquhar's *Trumpets and Drums* (1955), and Shakespeare's *Coriolanus*, unfinished at Brecht's early death but staged in 1964.

Brecht's work remained highly controversial in the German Democratic Republic until well after his death. The Berliner Ensemble survived its first few years in part thanks to the European-wide interest the company sparked on *tour, an interest that gradually extended to Brecht's plays. The initial reception took place, however, in the darkest moments of the Cold War; Brecht was boycotted for several years in Austria, for example. Given this climate, it is not surprising that the initial reception gave more value to Brecht's exile plays, making comforting comparisons with the German classics and with Shakespeare, and focusing analysis on their seemingly sympathetic central *characters and their confrontation with large-scale but rather generalized moral dilemmas. Later readings and productions have achieved considerable success in wresting the plays away from this post-war liberalism. But there are still some who agree with Heiner *Müller's 1980 analysis of the exile plays as severely limited by the absence of an audience or a theatre for which Brecht could write, which could provide a system of reference and response as direct as the one that nurtured the *Lehrstücke*.

Several of the *Lehrstücke*, and some of the anti-*realistic staging ideas they embody, had surfaced in the 1960s, when they were championed by *alternative theatre groups such as the *San Francisco Mime Troupe and the *Living Theatre, and the plays received even more attention as additional material became available in the 1970s. This period also saw new interest in Brecht's early plays for their youthful energy and freshness at a time when the later works were beginning to be flattened by a developing Brecht industry. By the end of the twentieth century, most of Brecht's plays could count on periodically finding new champions, even if the champions of one kind of Brecht play frequently despised the others. Adding to the controversy was a highly public flap over the true authorship of some of the plays, prompted by John Fuegi's claims in *The Life and Lies of Bertolt Brecht* (1994) that Brecht had exploited his female collaborators—claims which Fuegi exaggerated far beyond their sometimes legitimate basis in fact. More tellingly, new appreciations frequently refused close reference to Brecht's theory or to the practices of epic theatre, most of which had been absorbed into establishment theatre practice in Europe and America by the 1980s. But Brecht's enormous influence has continued into the new millennium, as his texts and theories still proved useful to populist practitioners and spectators in both the developed and developing worlds. *See also* MATERIALIST CRITICISM; BRECHTIAN.   JR

BRECHT, BERTOLT, *Brecht on Theatre: the development of an aesthetic*, ed. and trans. John Willett (London, 1964)

MARTIN, CAROL, and BIAL, HENRY (eds.), *Brecht Sourcebook* (London, 2000)

THOMSON, PETER, and SACKS, GLENDYR (eds.), *The Cambridge Companion to Brecht* (Cambridge, 1994)

VÖLKER, KLAUS, *Brecht, a Biography*, trans. John Nowell (New York, 1978)

BRECHTIAN

An adjective which attests to the influence of the *dramaturgy, practice, and *theory of Bertolt *Brecht in the twentieth century and beyond. The term has tended to be used in a way that tugs apart two interwoven strands in Brecht's work—*epic theatre and political dramaturgy (*see* POLITICS AND THEATRE). The focus on epic theatre has tended to be stylistic, identifying such devices as self-contained, episodic scene structure or the presentation of the stage as stage (*see* THEATRICALITY) by setting a limited number of permanent or highly mobile set pieces within an open playing space. This use of the term has sometimes been too broad, identifying as Brechtian techniques actually developed by *Piscator or *Meyerhold, for example. The use also reflects the historical assimilation of Brecht's legacy in Western Europe and North America within a Cold War climate that frequently required the separation of various attractive techniques from the goals of Brecht's Marxist theatre (*see also* MATERIALIST CRITICISM). These goals were then made responsible for purported stylistic weaknesses, including flat *characters and an unattractively overt *didacticism.

Such negative use of the term in reference to politics has been overwhelmingly countered by the many practitioners throughout the world who have seen in Brecht's work (and in such concepts as *Verfremdung*) the twentieth century's most sustained attempt create a politically committed theatre. For Brecht, the core of this theatre lay in depicting the world as changeable. Others soon began to rethink this goal and to refashion the practice, but in a way that kept the two strands of Brechtian theatre woven together. The power of such an engagement became quickly visible in the work of innovators such as Roger *Planchon, William *Gaskill, or the *San Francisco Mime Troupe. And the continuing engagement with Brecht has resulted in a legitimately 'Brechtian' moment in the work of stylistically un-Brechtian artists such as Howard *Brenton, Augusto *Boal, or Heiner *Müller.   JR

BRÉCOURT (GUILLAUME MARCOUREAU)
(1638–85)

French actor and playwright. A brilliant and ambitious actor but an unstable personality, Brécourt was a member, but not for long, of every important troupe in *Paris: the *Marais, *Molière's company, the *Hôtel de Bourgogne, and the *Comédie-Française. For Molière he played a clownish servant, a ridiculous philosopher, and a polished courtier; for *Racine he created the role of Britannicus. His greatest success as an author was *The Village Wedding* (1666). Drink, debt, and sword-play kept his career from being better; the indulgent favour of Louis XIV kept it from being worse.   RWH

BREDERO, GERBRANT ADRIAENSZOON
(1585–1618)

Dutch poet and playwright. Like his contemporary P. C. *Hooft, Bredero was influenced by *early modern developments but his works also retain a popular, spontaneous stamp. He saw the English travelling actors (*see* ENGLISH COMEDIANS) in the Netherlands and may well owe something of his keen theatrical sense to them. He was a member of the *Amsterdam Chamber D'Eglantier (*see* CHAMBERS OF RHETORIC) but followed Samuel Coster to the Duytsche Academie. Bredero wrote a number of *romances based on Spanish models, as well as *farces such as *De klucht van de koe* (*The Farce of the Cow*,

1612) which continued the *medieval tradition. More theatrically successful were his *comedies *Moortje* (1615), based on a French translation of *Terence's *Eunuchus*, and *Spaanschen Brabander Jerolimo* (*The Spanish Brabanter*, 1617), the subject matter of which was borrowed from the Spanish picaresque novel *Lazarillo de Tormes*. In this play Bredero created a delightful satiric picture of a destitute but blusterous Antwerp immigrant in Amsterdam. Trained to be a painter, he was particularly effective as a playwright in drawing colourful theatrical pictures of ordinary life in Amsterdam.
                                                          JDV

BREECHES ROLE

A part in which an actress appears in male attire. In English the term has been traditionally applied to parts written for men and performed by women, and has not been used to describe female *characters who begin and end the play in female dress and only temporarily adopt male *disguise. A commercially successful device in the seventeenth and eighteenth centuries, the breeches role began with the arrival of *women on stage in the Restoration. New plays frequently included a female character who adopts male disguise in *plots that ultimately turn on the discovery of her true sexual identity. All-female revivals of stock plays also proved to be financially successful, with actresses Nell *Gwynn, Susannah Verbruggen, and Anne *Bracegirdle receiving popular acclaim in early breeches roles, and Peg *Woffington and Dorothy *Jordan demonstrating the continuing *box-office appeal of the practice in their portrayals of Harry Wildair in eighteenth-century revivals of *Farquhar's *The Constant Couple*. As a device which obviously revealed more of the female body than conventional female dress allowed, the extent to which the cross-dressed actress is an exploited object of the male gaze or active participant in the disruption of female constructs is the subject of ongoing debates. Post-1980s *feminist *criticism has revised and extended the definition of the breeches role and considered the implications of the cross-dressed actress on the public stage in a wider social and cultural context (*see* MALE IMPERSONATION). Aphra *Behn's *The Rover* (1677) is an early example of playwriting by women in which the breeches role is used to disrupt conventional representations of female behaviour and challenge attitudes to female sexual desire. Male playwrights, notably *Southerne in *Sir Anthony Love* (1690), followed Behn's work by creating female characters who adopt male disguise in order to move freely in society and determine their own social and sexual destiny. The breeches role can also provide the actress with an opportunity to satirize male behaviour publicly, clearly demonstrated in a number of plays including *She Ventures and He Wins* (1695) by an anonymous 'Young Lady' using the pseudonym 'Ariadne' for publication.
                                                          GBB

BRENTON, HOWARD (1942–)

English playwright. Many of Brenton's early plays were written for *alternative theatre companies of the late 1960s, including *Christie in Love* (1969), *Fruit* (1970), and *Scott of the Antarctic* (1971). Heavily indebted to situationism, he used a collage of styles to capture the 'society of the spectacle', Guy Debord's term for the superficial and mediatized world of images that Western society had become. Brenton was soon taken up by major theatres: he wrote a pungent intervention on political terrorism, *Magnificence* (1973), for the *Royal Court; *The Churchill Play* (1974, revised 1979), a dystopian vision of Britain under military rule, for the *Royal Shakespeare Company; and *Weapons of Happiness* (1976) for the *National Theatre. His instincts are unusually collaborative; he has worked with many other writers and with collaborative *devising companies like *Joint Stock (*Epsom Downs*, 1977). *The Romans in Britain* (NT, 1980) was the subject of a famous court case for alleged obscenity in a scene which uses homosexual rape as an image of colonialism; the play compares the Roman invasion of Britain with Britain's treatment of Ireland. *Pravda* (co-written with David *Hare, 1985) was a prescient, comic, and unsettling treatment of the relations between politics, industry, and the press.

Along with many of his generation of playwrights, Brenton wrote in the expectation of a final clash between the far left and far right, and his plays debate the ethics of revolutionary activity as well as offering scabrous portraits of the society to be overthrown. The election of Margaret Thatcher's hard-line government in 1979 was an opportunity for rethinking. *A Short Sharp Shock!* (1980) is a gleefully offensive portrait of the new government, but plays like *Sore Throats* (1979), *Bloody Poetry* (1984), and *Greenland* (1988) show an awareness of the increasing remoteness of the socialist utopia, despite a persistent desire to explore its outlines. From the late 1980s Brenton's work has returned in some ways to the immediacy and roughness of his early work, with short *satirical pieces often co-written with another veteran of May 1968, Tariq Ali. *Iranian Nights* (1989) addressed the Salman Rushdie affair, *Ugly Rumours* (1998) lampooned the ideological drift of New Labour, and *Snogging Ken* (2000) satirized the Labour government's intrigues over the election of the first mayor of London. Other plays include *The Genius* (1983), *H. I. D. (Hess is Dead)* (1989), *Moscow Gold* (1990), and *Berlin Bertie* (1992).   DR

BRETH, ANDREA (1952–)

German director. Breth joined the municipal theatre in Heidelberg while still a student. She served her apprenticeship there and in Bremen, and her breakthrough came in 1983 with a production of *García Lorca's *The House of Bernarda Alba* in Freiburg. From 1986 to 1990 she was director-in-residence in Bochum, mounting a number of noted productions, and from 1992 to 1998 *artistic director of the *Schaubühne in *Berlin, where she brought out highly acclaimed versions of *Ibsen and *Chekhov. In 2000 she was appointed director-in-residence at the *Burgtheater in *Vienna. Her directorial style is characterized by psychological subtlety, highly charged atmosphere, and a preference for a slow pace with tension. She has been the recipient of many *awards and invitations to the Berlin *Theatertreffen.   CBB

BREUER, LEE (1937–)

American playwright and director. After studying theatre at UCLA, he co-founded *Mabou Mines performance group in 1970. He adapted and directed three works by *Beckett, *Play, Come and Go*, and *The Lost Ones*, all of which received Obie *awards. Breuer also wrote and directed a triology of what he has called 'performance poetry', inspired by Kafka's animal parables, called the 'Animations' (*The B. Beaver*, *The Red Horse*, and *The Shaggy Dog*, which won the Obie for best play in 1978). In 1980 *A Prelude to a Death in Venice* also received acclaim for its innovative use of actors and *puppets on stage. In the 1980s Breuer collaborated with composer Bob Telson on a series of *music theatre projects; in 1983 they presented *The Gospel at Colonus*, a musical oratorio set in an African-American Pentecostal church in which *Sophocles' *tragedy is the sermon text. The work's première at the Brooklyn Academy of Music was hailed as a model of multicultural performance. Other collaborations include *Sister Suzie Camera* (1980) and *The Warrior Ant* (1986). His work has often been associated with minimalism and the 'theatre of images'. Breuer has taught at Yale and Stanford universities.   JAB

BREWSTER, YVONNE (1938–)

Jamaican actor, director, and producer who is *artistic director of Talawa Theatre Company in *London, which she co-founded with Mona Hammond, Inigo Espegel, and Carmen Munroe. Its inaugural production was C. L. R. James's *The Black Jacobins* (1986). After *training at Rose Bruford College and the Royal Academy of Music, Brewster worked as an actor in London and as a *radio announcer and *television producer in Jamaica. With playwright Trevor *Rhone, she co-founded Jamaica's first professional theatre company, the *Barn Theatre in Kingston (1971). The early 1970s also saw her direct in London: Sally Durie's *Lippo, the New Noah* with an African-Caribbean cast at the ICA in 1971; Derek *Walcott's *Pantomime* in a pub; and a *musical version of Jamaican playwright Barry Reckord's *Skyvvers*. In 1991 she directed *García Lorca's *Blood Wedding* for the Royal *National Theatre. Innovative and challenging productions for Talawa include the first all-black production of *The Importance of Being Earnest* (1989), Wole *Soyinka's *The Road

(1992), Shakespeare's *King Lear* (1994), John *Ford's *'Tis Pity She's a Whore* (1995), the Trinidadian *farce *Beef, No Chicken* (1996) by Walcott, *Flyin' West* (1997) by *African-American playwright Pearl Cleage, and *Medea in the Mirror* (1999) by the Cuban José *Triana. Brewster has served on numerous British boards and advisory committees on the arts. In 1993 she was *awarded an OBE. *See also* CARIBBEAN THEATRE, ANGLOPHONE.

AS

BRICE, FANNY (FANIA BORACH) (1891–1951)

Comic and singer. Brice was already a star in the Ziegfeld *revues when her 'Baby Snooks' *character was introduced in the *Ziegfeld Follies* of 1934. A native of *New York City, Brice was adept at sketch- and song-based comedy (performed in a squawky Yiddish dialect) and at torch songs delivered in a powerful and unwavering alto. She began in amateur contests in 1906 before advancing through the ranks of *burlesque from 1907 to 1910. First hired by Ziegfeld for the *Follies* of 1910, she continued for 1911 but defected to the rival *Shubert brothers in 1912. She appeared on Broadway in *The Honeymoon Express* in 1913, played *London, and returned to New York to appear in two of the Jerome *Kern/Guy *Bolton 'Princess *musicals' in 1915—*Hands Up* and *Nobody Home*. She alternated between *Follies* appearances, Shubert musicals, the Orpheum vaudeville circuit, and Billy *Rose musicals—as well as forays in *film and *radio—until her death from a brain haemorrhage. She was married to confidence-man Nick Arnstein (1919–27) and to composer/*producer Rose (1929–38).

MAF

BRIDGES-ADAMS, WILLIAM (1889–1965)

English director. As director of the *Shakespeare Memorial Theatre (1919–34), his productions were spare but not without pictorial interest. Dubbed 'Unabridges-Adams' for using largely uncut *texts, he nevertheless directed in a fluid manner, unhampered by scenic clutter. After the *fire at the SMT in 1926, he maintained the continuity of the Stratford-upon-Avon Festival by transferring the repertoire to the local cinema. He intended the new theatre, opened in 1932, to be a flexible space for innovative work; guest director Theodore *Komisarjevsky's *The Merchant of Venice* (1932) and *Macbeth* (1933) fulfilled this aim. However, insufficient administrative support for Bridges-Adams's increasingly outward-looking policies led to his resignation in 1934. He later became dramatic adviser to the British Council (1937–44). His writings include *The Lost Leader* (1954), an essay on his early mentor Harley Granville *Barker, and *The Irresistible Theatre* (1957), a history of drama to the mid-seventeenth century.

VRS

BRIDIE, JAMES (OSBORNE HENRY MAVOR) (1884–1951)

Scottish playwright. Mavor wrote under a number of pseudonyms, including Mary Henderson and Archibald Kellock, before he finally settled on James Bridie after his fiftieth birthday. As with his nom de plume, Bridie found his calling as a dramatist late, only after qualifying as a doctor and serving in the Royal Army Medical Corps during the First World War. His first staged piece, *The Switchback* (1922), premièred at the *Birmingham Repertory Theatre. Bridie is most closely associated with Scottish theatre, which he worked hard to promote, founding the *Glasgow *Citizens' Theatre and supporting the Royal Scottish Academy of Music and Drama. His major plays include *The Anatomist* (1931); *Tobias and the Angel* (1932), featuring Tyrone *Guthrie who was later to direct several of his plays; *Storm in a Teacup* (1936), a *satire on Scottish provincialism and local politics; and *Daphne Laureola* (1949), a poetic look at post-war England, directed by Laurence *Olivier and starring Edith *Evans.

MDG

BRIE, MLLE DE (CATHERINE LECLERC DU ROSÉ) (1630–1706)

French actress. She joined *Molière's itinerant company in 1650, remained with it after his death, and retired from the *Comédie-Française in 1685. Although other actresses associated with Molière have received more attention from biographers, Mlle de Brie was the most consistently valuable interpreter of his plays. In the early years she regularly played the *ingénue; the greatest of these roles, which transcends the type, was Agnès in *The School for Wives*, in which she was a popular favourite until her retirement. Molière gradually extended the psychological depth and complexity of her roles, especially after the younger and less experienced Mlle Molière (Armande *Béjart) became available to play conventional ingénues.

RWH

BRIEUX, EUGÈNE (1858–1932)

French dramatist who used the theatre to expose the corruption, malaise, and illnesses of society. The sins of the flesh loom large in his work but he focuses his criticism on the social conditions which give rise to them. Two of his early plays were produced by *Antoine at the Théâtre *Libre, one scoring a huge success (*Blanchette*, 1897), Brieux even taking the advice of critics to write a more positive third act for a revival later that year. Three plays are of particular note: *The Three Daughters of M. Dupont* (1897) portrays the follies and the dangers of marriages of convenience; *Les Avariés* (*Damaged Goods*, 1902) is a teaching play about the conditions which give rise to the spread of syphilis, namely ignorance and fear of exposure; *Maternity* (1903) treats the issues surrounding the legalization of contraception. These three *thesis plays were translated into English in 1909 and championed by Bernard *Shaw, who prefaced their *publication in 1911. *Damaged Goods* had the most effect and Shaw highlighted Brieux as the champion of social reform on the stage. This stark play pulls no punches. Act I, set in a doctor's surgery, uncovers patient Georges Dupont's dilemma regarding his diagnosis of syphilis: he refuses to defer his wedding plans for fear of social scandal and loss of an inheritance. Act II is set in Dupont's new home where he offers to pay a wet nurse to feed his child in the full knowledge that she will contract the disease by doing so. Act III returns to the doctor's study where Dupont's father-in-law, a parliamentarian, requests a certificate of his son-in-law's illness to initiate divorce proceedings. The doctor suggests the creation of a Minister for Health in order to stop the spread of disease through ignorance. Here Brieux linked with *Zola's scientific principles of *naturalism, as the deputy (and the *audience) are shown three case studies. Such was the vehemence of Brieux's attack on society that his plays often suffer *dramaturgically, as *characters give way to sermonizing.

BRS

BRIGHOUSE, HAROLD (1882–1958)

English novelist and dramatist. Associated with the 'Manchester school' of playwrights, he wrote over 50 *one-act and 16 full-length plays, often about contemporary Lancashire life and with a strong bias towards social themes, including *Dealing in Futures* (1910), the *one-act *Lonesome Like* (1911), and *Garside's Career* (1916), all premièred at *Manchester's *Gaiety Theatre. Other notable plays include *The Northerners* (1914) and *Zack* (1916). His most famous work, and the archetypal Lancashire play, *Hobson's Choice*, was ironically given its first performance not at the Gaiety but in *New York before transferring to *London in 1915. A *comedy set in Salford in 1880, challenging conventional expectations of how daughters should behave, it has remained a perennial favourite with repertory *audiences ever since its first performance, and was *filmed in 1954, starring Charles *Laughton and John *Mills.

ARJ

BRISTOL OLD VIC COMPANY

Established in 1945 by the *Old Vic as a residential repertory company at the *Theatre Royal, Bristol, under the direction of Hugh *Hunt, opening in 1946 with *Farquhar's *The Beaux' Stratagem*. Hunt favoured the classics, but after his departure contemporary works were performed, including the British premières of *The Crucible* and *Salad Days* in 1954. From 1962 to 1975 Val May directed the company through some of its most successful years, acquiring a second venue, the Little Theatre, and forming a separate trust in 1963. During the 1960s

several productions transferred to *London, and in 1966 the company celebrated the bicentenary of the Theatre Royal. In 1970 renovations incorporated the adjacent Cooper's Hall, increasing foyer space and creating the New Vic Studio. Richard Cottrell took over as director in 1975. The financial climate became tighter: the Little Theatre was discarded, the Studio used only by external *touring companies. Throughout the late 1980s and early 1990s the company suffered from funding cuts and management crises, although Andrew Hay's appointment in 1992 breathed new life into the venture.

JTD

BRITISH DRAMA LEAGUE

Support organization founded in 1919 by Geoffrey Whitworth (1883–1951) as a focus of theatre revival in the post-war period. Its first chairman was Harley Granville *Barker, and the first issue of the journal *Drama* was published the same year, offering commentary and instruction on all aspects of theatre practice. While not exclusively dedicated to *amateur theatre, by 1923 there were some 360 affiliated societies, and by 1944 there were 5,000. *London headquarters were set up in 1921, together with the nucleus of what became by 2000 the largest specialist drama lending library in the world. The BDL set up *training courses, inaugurated a competitive National Festival in 1927, and was associated with the *national theatre movement, a campaign for school curriculum drama, and a civic theatre scheme submitted to the wartime government in 1942. In 1972 the BDL became the British Theatre Association, but withdrawal of *Arts Council funding in 1986 eventually led to collapse in 1990. The library of more than 200,000 volumes was moved to Cardiff under the auspices of the Drama Association of Wales.

CEC

BRNO

The second largest city in the Czech Republic. Between 1732 and 1735, the Little Tavern at the Cabbage Market was turned into a *playhouse and later named Royal National Municipal Theatre. A modern Municipal Theatre (still in use), designed by Ferdinand Fellner and Hermann Helmer and equipped with one of the first electrical *lighting systems in Europe, opened its doors to the German-speaking public in 1882. A very modest building for the Czech National Theatre opened in 1884; this was pulled down in 1952 and in 1965 replaced by a spacious playhouse bearing the name of Leoš Janáček, most of whose *operas were premièred in Brno. In the late 1920s two young *avant-gardists, Jindřich Honzl and E. F. *Burian, were invited to work in the city, but soon returned to *Prague. In the 1960s, a platform of *political theatre, focusing on *Brecht, developed in the State Theatre's drama company: the productions of Evžen Sokolovský, Miloš Hynšt, and Alois Hajda still stand as the best *Brechtian achievements in the country. Of unique importance in Czech theatre of the 1960s was the Evening Brno, a satirical *cabaret stage. In 1967 a group of young actors, writers, and artists started an experimental theatre programme based on unusual *dramaturgy and physical ensemble *acting (*see* PHYSICAL THEATRE); this Goose on the String (later called Theatre on a String) was soon internationally recognized as the most lively centre in the years of general depression and stagnation. The company is now part of the Centre of Experimental Theatre (CED), which embraces the important experimental company HaDivadlo, which was founded in the nearby city of Prostějov in 1972 and moved to Brno in 1985. Another thriving enterprise is the Municipal Theatre, which divides its activities between standard dramas and *musicals.

ML

BROADHURST, GEORGE HOWELLS
(1866–1952)

Anglo-American playwright and producer. Born in England, Howells emigrated to America in 1886, working as a clerk in *Chicago, *managing theatres in Milwaukee, Baltimore, and *San Francisco, and practising journalism in North Dakota. His first play, *The Speculator* (1896), blended his Chicago experiences with the plot of *Romeo and Juliet*, and did not last long in *New York. He had better luck—especially in *London—with his *farces *The Wrong Mr Wright* (1896), the oft-revived *What Happened to Jones* (1897), and *Why Smith Left Home* (1899). He triumphed with several serious works: *The Man of the Hour* (1906), a *melodrama about political corruption; *Bought and Paid for* (1911); *Today* (1913, co-authored with Abraham Schomer); and a tale of a wife's justifiable murder of her husband, *The Law of the Land* (1914), his last big success. In 1917 the *Shuberts named their new Broadhurst Theatre in his honour, and opened it with the American première of *Shaw's *Misalliance*.

CT

BROADWAY *See* NEW YORK.

BROME, RICHARD (c.1590–c.1653)

English playwright. Nothing is known of Brome's origins and early years, and even his date of birth is conjectural. He became a professional playwright after spending several years in the service of Ben *Jonson, whose influence is often recognizable in his works. He was resident dramatist for the *Salisbury Court *playhouse from 1635 to 1638, afterwards moving to *Drury Lane Theatre. A prolific writer of *comedies and *tragicomedies, his work frequently indulges in *satire and radical political commentary, which recent scholars have learned to appreciate. Among his best-known plays are the comedies *The Northern Lass* (1629), probably his greatest stage success, *The Antipodes*

(1636), which contains a play-within-the-play full of remarks on contemporary theatre, *The Court Beggar* (1640), and *A Jovial Crew* (1641), which enjoyed numerous revivals in the late seventeenth century. The little-known *The Queen and Concubine* (1636), a tragicomedy on the dangers of absolutism, is outspoken in its commentary on contemporary topical issues.

PCR

BRONNEN, ARNOLT (1895–1959)

Austrian dramatist. Influenced by his experience as a soldier during the First World War, Bronnen became a leftist writer whose early dramatic vision tended towards *expressionism. He came to attention with his play *Vatermord* (*Parricide*, co-directed by *Brecht) in 1920. From 1928 to 1933, as a *dramaturg for the *Berlin broadcasting services, he influenced the development of the *radio play in Germany. In the late 1920s he developed right-wing sympathies and became a protégé of Goebbels, but in the late 1930s he returned to communism and joined the anti-Nazi resistance in Austria. In 1955 he moved to the German Democratic Republic, where he worked primarily as a theatre critic. Bronnen was one of the most widely performed and controversial playwrights during the Weimar Republic. Although initially ignored in the post-war period, his work was revived in the 1970s and 1980s. Frank *Castorf's production of *Rheinische Rebellen* (1925) in 1992 was highly acclaimed.

CBB

BROOK, PETER (1925–)

English director, filmmaker, and theorist. Peter Brook's extraordinarily productive career spans more than the half-century since the end of the Second World War, and includes over 70 theatre and *opera productions and a dozen *films. It will be useful to divide this extensive body of work into three periods.

Born in London, Brook was educated at Westminster and Gresham's schools, then Magdalen College, Oxford. The first phase of Brook's work as a *director (1945–63) covers the hyperactive years of his professional apprenticeship in a wide range of performance contexts, forms and styles. At the age of 22, he was already a director at the Royal Opera House, *Covent Garden; and by 1963, when Brook was 38, he had directed over 40 productions, including nine Shakespeare plays and seven major operas. Landmark productions included a luminous and bittersweet *Love's Labour's Lost*, inspired visually by Watteau, for the *Shakespeare Memorial Theatre (1946), a sinisterly erotic and capricious reworking of *Strauss's *Salomé* (1949) with designs and *special effects by Salvador Dalí, a shockingly austere *Titus Andronicus* (1955) with Laurence *Olivier and Vivien *Leigh, and an elemental, absurdist *King Lear* (1962) with Paul *Scofield for the new *Royal Shakespeare Company.

Although best known as a director of classical theatre, Brook also juggled productions of major twentieth-century European playwrights (*Cocteau, *Sartre, *Anouilh, *Genet, *Dürrenmatt) and works by seminal modernists (including *Eliot and *Miller), as well as overtly commercial projects—*boulevard and *musical comedies, *television drama and advertisements. Brook's trajectory reflected his deliberate immersion in a contradictory array of experiences, seeking to find a complex, composite reality through the exploration of opposites. In retrospect, he has referred to this period as a 'theatre of images', informed by an escapist aesthetic of illusionist decoration and artifice—a theatre in which the world of the stage was wholly separated from that of the spectators, and where the director's 'vision' was omnipotent. At the same time, he collaborated with many of the finest performers of his generation, including Alec *Guinness, Orson *Welles, and John *Gielgud.

The second phase (1964–70) constituted a period of reappraisal, maturation, and proactive research. Brook was becoming increasingly disaffected with the existing processes and forms of much contemporary theatre, which he stigmatized as short-sighted, convention bound, and 'deadly'. In his search for theatre languages that could more accurately reflect the complexity of contemporary realities, he questioned the theatrical status quo at every level. This period of work reached fruition in a remarkable series of productions Brook characterized as a 'theatre of disturbance'. An explicit shift in his concerns and processes became evident in an experimental project conducted under the aegis of the RSC, with a group co-directed with Charles *Marowitz. Public 'work-in-progress' showings of this early, tentative research in 1964 were entitled the 'Theatre of *Cruelty' in homage to *Artaud. The culmination of this research occurred with the celebrated production of Peter *Weiss's *Marat/Sade* (1964), a *collectively devised response to the Vietnam War ambiguously entitled *US* (1966), and a choral, *ritualized *Oedipus* (1968) in an abrasive new version (from *Seneca) by the poet Ted Hughes.

This transitional phase was also characterized by a growing awareness of the importance of the *actor within an ensemble. Brook recognized that the creativity of actors would be instrumental in challenging the complacency of prevalent practices and creative hierarchies, as well as in finding theatrical forms as multifaceted as Shakespeare's. Brook took Elizabethan *dramaturgy as his model. He particularly admired its shifts of gear in the mix of *comedy and *tragedy, its vivid language, its spatio-temporal fluidity, and the directness of its forms. Shakespeare became his prototype for a conflation of the 'rough' and the 'holy' into a textured totality he called the 'immediate'. This area of Brook's research reached its apogee with his joyously airborne production of *A Midsummer Night's Dream* (RSC, 1970) which radically dismantled received ideas of the play. In this work Brook and his actor-*acrobats created a counter-image to the harrowing, confrontational tenor of the earlier work of this period with a bright *circus-inflected celebration blurring the divisions between *stage and *auditorium.

Since that time, Brook's ideals and goals have remained constant: the amplification of actors' capacities as instruments attuned and responsive to creative sources, and to an ensemble conceived as 'a storyteller with many heads'; the practice of research as ongoing 'self-research', a process of evolution and individual development in which theatre serves as potent site and means, but rarely as the exclusive end; the act of theatre as affirmative 're-membering', in which a mythical narrative or fable is actualized in the present to create temporary communities of shared experience. Eventually the desire for conditions enabling the pursuit and refinement of such ideals took him from the restrictions of commercial theatre in England to a new base in France.

The third phase comprises Brook's work since 1970 with his international group in *Paris, the *International Centre for Theatre Research (CIRT), with Brook and his multicultural collaborators now cushioned by subsidy from the crippling demands and impositions of the commercial sector (*see* FINANCE). The Centre's focus has ranged from private research behind closed doors, to explorations of theatrical communication between cultures in the field (on journeys to Iran, *Africa, and the USA), to recent forays into the fantastic inner landscapes of neurological disorders and abilities in *The Man Who* (1993) and *Je suis un phénomène* (1998). Core projects have included *Orghast* (1971), a site-specific music-theatre piece performed in the tombs of Persepolis, Iran, in a mixture of dead and invented languages; an adaptation of Colin Turnbull's anthropological study of the demise of a Ugandan tribe, *The Ik* (1975–6); a presentation of a twelfth-century Sufi poem, Attar's *Conference of the Birds* (1979), about the journey of a group of birds in search of their god; a nine-hour version of the sacred Sanskrit epic *The Mahabharata* (1985–8); a spartan staging of Shakespeare's *The Tempest* with the African actor Sotigui Kouyaté as Prospero; and an abridged and physically dynamic version of *Hamlet* (2000–1), with the young black British actor Adrian Lester in the title role.

In addition, as a filmmaker Brook has further developed in cinematic terms his concerns as a theatre director. Major films include *Moderato Cantabile* (1960), *Lord of the Flies* (1963), *Marat/Sade* (1966), *Tell Me Lies* (1968), *King Lear* (1971), *Meetings with Remarkable Men* (1979), and *The Mahabharata* (1989).

While at times Brook has been accused of cultural insensitivity and appropriation, and criticized by Kenneth *Tynan and others for a Eurocentric fatalism perceived to ghost his *intercultural practice, his work with the Centre has remained rigorously syncretic rather than synthetic. Cultural difference has been consistently cherished as a source of creative friction, never erased in a quest for some imaginary theatrical 'esperanto'. Indeed, the make-up of the company itself implicitly offers a paradigm in microcosm of social and cultural coexistence, and of the act of theatre as meeting point. Similarly, throughout this period Brook's dramaturgical model has remained one of narrative, and psychological contradiction within which the poetic, spiritual, political, and carnal can coexist. His characteristically unadorned *scenography at the company's base at the Théâtre des *Bouffes du Nord in Paris has been founded on proximity, openness, and fluidity. Like all popular theatre, it employs eclectic forms of a distilled and mutable simplicity which offer active invitations to imaginative complicity on the part of spectators. The material Brook selects proposes a humanist social critique, suggesting that humankind's greatest threat remains the ignorance and misanthropy of our fellow human beings, and of ourselves. Nonetheless, these fables are ultimately restorative, outlining an itinerary in which fragmentation necessarily precedes reintegration and healing.

Finally, through his own writing Brook has made significant interventions to twentieth-century *theory and practice, especially with *The Empty Space* (1968), *The Shifting Point* (1987), and a memoir, *Threads of Time* (1998).   ADW

HUNT, ALBERT, and REEVES, GEOFFREY, *Peter Brook* (Cambridge, 1995)

TREWIN, JOHN C., *Peter Brook: a biography* (London, 1971)

WILLIAMS, DAVID (ed.), *Peter Brook: a theatrical casebook* (London, 1992)

BROUGHAM, JOHN (1810–80)

Irish-American actor and playwright. Born in *Dublin, Brougham began acting in student theatricals at Trinity College. After his 1830 *London debut, he quickly associated with Madame *Vestris's company, where for a decade he perfected his comic talents, studying company mainstays John *Liston and Charles *Mathews. In 1842 he travelled to the United States where he lived until his death, except for brief *tours of England and Ireland. Although a versatile actor, Brougham specialized in comic roles. He is remembered as a playwright for such *burlesques as *Met-a-mo-ra; or, The Last of the Pollywogs* (1847), a spoof of John Augustus *Stone's Indian *melodrama *Metamora*; *Po-ca-hon-tas* (1855); and his Shakespearian send-up *Much Ado about a Merchant of Venice* (1869).   GAR

BROWN, ARVIN (1940–)

American director. His first professional staging was *O'Neill's *Long Day's Journey into Night* (1965) at New Haven's *Long Wharf Theatre. As the Long Wharf's *artistic director from 1967 to 1997, he was responsible for creating one of America's finest resident companies, and succeeded in moving more of his productions to Broadway and *Off-Broadway than any other *regional theatre director; his revival of *Miller's *All my Sons* (1986) won a Tony *award. He staged mainly modern plays, well known and original, American and European, several *operas and *musicals, and also worked in *film and *television. In 1993 he directed a dramatization of Amy Tan's *The Joy Luck Club* in Shanghai. Although he attempted to expand his range, Brown fostered an 'actor's theatre' that became known for *realistic stagings supported by expert ensembles, an approach perfectly suited to the Long Wharf's intimate surroundings.

SLL

BROWN, JOHN MASON (1900–69)

American critic. At Harvard, Brown was one of George Pierce *Baker's favourites and became a drama critic on his mentor's advice. After reporting on European theatre for the *Boston Evening Transcript* (1923), he wrote for *Theatre Arts* (1924–8), the *New York Evening Post* (1928–39), and the *World-Telegram* (1939–42). Following naval service in the Second World War, he wrote for the *Saturday Review* until he gave up regular theatre reviewing in 1961. A pioneer media critic, both witty and analytical, he often broadcast on *radio and had the first *televised theatre review programme in 1947. He published numerous collections of *criticism.   TFC

BROWN, JOHN RUSSELL (1923–)

English scholar, director, and *dramaturg. Brown followed an academic career, holding important appointments at universities in Birmingham (where he founded the Department of Drama, 1964), Sussex, New York, and Michigan. From 1973 to 1988 he was an associate of the *National Theatre under Peter *Hall, replacing Kenneth *Tynan as script adviser. A leader of the *performance-oriented approach to the study of Shakespeare and *early modern playwrights, his many books have had wide influence; they include *Shakespeare's Plays in Performance* (1966), *Free Shakespeare* (1974), *Discovering Shakespeare* (1981), *The Oxford Illustrated History of the Theatre* (edited 1995), and *New Sites for Shakespeare: theatre, audience and Asia* (1999). He has worked around the world as a director of Shakespeare and modern plays, often experimenting in print and in practice with methods alternative to the *modernist practice of *director's theatre, chiefly by recalling the *actor-led traditions of the Elizabethan stage.   DK

BROWN, WILLIAM HENRY (fl. 1820s)

*African-American playwright and *manager. Brown was a retired ship's steward from the West Indies who founded a pleasure garden for free blacks in *New York in 1816. Called the African Grove, the facility featured occasional outdoor entertainments until officials closed it down in 1821. Undaunted, Brown re-formed his troupe into the *African Company and continued performances indoors. Fearing competition, the nearby *Park Theatre, in cooperation with the city sheriff, had the theatre closed and Brown was forced to perform illegally at various locations until 1823. He also wrote and produced *The Drama of King Shotaway* (1823), the first play by an African-American.   PAD

BROWN, WILLIAM WELLS (1814–84)

American writer, a fugitive slave who wrote and performed two platform plays on abolitionist lecture *tours. *Escape; or, A Leap for Freedom* was the first *African-American play published in the USA (Boston, 1858). Set in Louisiana during the 1830s, it is also one of the first American plays to make reference to lynching. *Experience*, an earlier play about a northern minister who becomes an abolitionist, survives only in a synopsis from an anti-slavery newspaper.   BBL

BROWNE, E. MARTIN (1900–80)

English director. His enthusiasm for poetic and religious drama led Browne to make two remarkable contributions: the promotion of T. S. *Eliot's drama, and staging the York *mystery plays for the Festival of Britain in 1951. Browne toured the USA as an actor, then became director of religious drama for Chichester (1930). He commissioned Eliot's *Murder in the Cathedral*, and performed as the fourth Tempter in Canterbury Cathedral (1935); he later directed all Eliot's plays, and was instrumental in editing his *The Confidential Clerk* (1953). During the Second World War he founded the Pilgrim Players and in 1945, as director of the Mercury Theatre, continued to support poetic drama. He was director of the *British Drama League (1948–57). He subsequently *toured the USA with revivals of Shakespeare, Eliot, and the mystery plays with his first wife, actress Henzie Raeburn.   KN

BROWNE, MAURICE (1881–1955)

English actor, *manager, writer, and champion of the *Little Theatre movement in the USA. Browne was born in Reading and educated at Winchester and Cambridge. There he met Harold Monro with whom he ran the short-lived Samurai Press (1906–8), from which the Poetry Bookshop, *Poetry Review*, and *Poetry and Drama* all grew. Along with Ellen Van Volkenberg, he was founder and director of the *Chicago Little Theatre (1912), which established the parameters of the little theatres in America: mixing professional and *amateur performers, playing in a small venue (their theatre seated a mere 99 people), subscription-based seasons, and a repertoire heavily influenced by European drama. Browne was director of the Ellen Van Volkenberg–Maurice Browne Repertory Company (1918–26), and then a *producer and manager in *London and *New York (1928–37). He presented R. C. *Sherriff's *Journey's End*

at the *Savoy in London in 1929 and then produced it internationally. His autobiography is *Too Late to Lament* (1955).
                                                                    AS

BROWNE, ROBERT (fl. 1583–1620)

English actor. Browne was associated with the Earl of Worcester's company in 1583 and again in 1589; he is named in William *Sly's will in 1608; and he is listed as a patentee of the Queen's Revels company in 1610. But the bulk of Browne's career was spent in Germany, where he played almost exclusively for seventeen years (1590–1607), and where he returned in 1618 as the leader of a company of players, generically known as *English Comedians. He last appears in records in 1620. Records from 1638 and 1639 naming Robert Browne as a *puppet showman may refer to his son.   RWV

BRUCE, LENNY (1925–66)

American comedian, born Leonard Schneider, widely considered to have changed the course of stand-up comedy in the mid-twentieth century, introducing a no-holds-barred cultural criticism. His routines became jagged observational riffs, studiously opposed to the comfortable one-liners and formulaic jokes which previously characterized American comedy. Working in downtown *New York nightclubs in the 1950s, Bruce caught the attention of the establishment with his stand-up assaults on society's soft spots: sex, religion, race, and, most famously, 'talking dirty'. His attempts to deconstruct societal taboos with four-letter language left him vulnerable to prosecution for obscenity. In the 1960s Bruce grew increasingly obsessed with the various court battles which would leave him destitute and virtually unhirable. He died of a drug overdose, and has since been seen by many as a martyr for free speech. His life was dramatized in Julian Barry's 1970 play *Lenny*.
                                                                    EW

BRUCKNER, FERDINAND (1891–1958)

Pseudonym of Theodor Tagger, German-Austrian dramatist and director. Bruckner founded the Renaissance Theater in *Berlin in 1923 and managed it until 1928. During this time he wrote highly controversial social-critical plays typical of the *Neue Sachlichkeit* including *Krankheit der Jugend* (*Malady of Youth*, 1926) and *Die Verbrecher* (*The Criminals*, 1928), before turning to historical themes in the early 1930s with *Elisabeth von England* (1930) and *Die Rassen* (*Races*, 1933). That year he was forced into exile, returning to Germany from the USA in 1951. He was appointed *dramaturg at Berlin's *Schiller Theater, a position he held until his death, but his reputation rests on the works produced during the Weimar Republic.
                                                                    CBB

BRUNO, GIORDANO (1548–1600)

Neapolitan philosopher and dramatist. One of the most original and convoluted thinkers of his period, eventually burned at the stake for heresy, Bruno was also the author of the single *comedy *The Candlestick*, printed in *Paris in 1582. The play takes three farcical victims—a posturing homosexual lover, a would-be alchemist, and a pedant—and has them humiliated by a gang of lowlife jokers, servants, and street criminals. In its tone it owes much to *Aretino, but its scurrilous energy was by then out of fashion for literary *commedia erudita*, and it is unlikely that it was ever performed.   RAA

BRUSSELS

The capital of Belgium, originally a Flemish city that became partly Frenchified over time and rapidly developed into a multicultural and multilingual urban centre towards the end of the twentieth century, an evolution also reflected in its theatrical life. The fifteenth century in Flanders was the age of the *Chambers of Rhetoric, literary and theatrical *guilds that organized competitions and played an important role in society at large. The chamber Het Boek was established in Brussels as early as 1401. From 1448 onwards, the local archers' guild annually organized a performance of one of the seven *mystery plays called *Bliscappen van Maria* (*Blessings of the Holy Virgin*, the *texts of two of which have survived). In the seventeenth century Brussels was much plagued by war, yet in the latter half of the century new Chambers of Rhetoric such as De Wijngaard (the Vineyard) appeared, and in 1650 the first *opera in Brussels, *Ullisse all' isola di Circe* by Zamponi and Amalteo, was performed at the Coudenberg Palace. Opera increasingly became open to the bourgeoisie, which led to the creation in 1700 of the Théâtre de la Monnaie, soon to be one of Europe's foremost opera houses. After the end of the French occupation, the Théâtre du Parc (1782) briefly became an English-language theatre, and, during the short period of the unification of the Low Countries from 1815 to 1830, a Dutch-speaking one.

In the second half of the nineteenth century, Flemish culture, which suffered under the repressive Belgian regime, slowly re-emerged in the city. After the establishment of the first professional company in *Antwerp in 1853, a second Flemish Theatre was created in Brussels in 1887. In its early phrases the company aimed at popular fare but soon also introduced a more sophisticated repertoire. Of particular interest is the period of the 1920s when the Royal Flemish Theatre was led by Jan Poot, who, in collaboration with the author Herman *Teirlinck, staged several highly *expressionist productions. At the same time the Théâtre du Marais was an international centre where the *Vlaamse Volkstoneel gave some of its controversial *constructivist performances.

In 1945 the Francophone National Theatre was founded in Brussels (the Dutch-speaking counterpart had its home base in Antwerp). The post-war period was marked by an expansion of theatre activity, particularly of small theatres. Among these, the Brussels Kamer Toneel (Brussels Chamber Theatre) was one of the most adventurous, introducing many contemporary playwrights. The centenary of the Royal Flemish Theatre in 1977 gave rise to the Kaaitheater Festival, which developed into an important centre of *performance art and contemporary *dance. Kaaitheater stimulated the budding talents of artists such as Jan Lauwers and Anne Teresa de Keersmaeker. In the 1980s the Monnaie National Opera, in the hands of Gerard Mortier, emphasized opera's theatrical dimensions and brought international acclaim to the city.   JDV

BRUSTEIN, ROBERT (1927–)

American critic, director, and playwright. As both pre-eminent cultural critic and influential *artistic director for 35 years, Brustein's career in American theatre is unique. While on the faculty of Columbia University, he became drama critic for *New Republic*, winning the first of two George Jean Nathan *awards in 1963 (*see* CRITICISM). In 1966 he became dean of *Yale School of Drama, where he founded Yale Repertory Theatre and pioneered the partnering of a university-based conservatory with a *regional theatre. In 1979, when his Yale contract expired, he shifted his operation to Harvard and started the *American Repertory Theatre, which he led until 2002. At Yale Rep and ART, he hired inventive directors to stage a high-minded repertoire that mixed classics, *modernist works, and new American plays. He acted in eight productions, directed a dozen others, and produced his own plays as well as his adaptations of *Pirandello, *Ibsen, and others. All the while, he published a dozen books of essays, reviews, and memoirs, including *The Theatre of Revolt* (1962), a study of modern drama; *Making Scenes* (1981), his memoir of Yale; and *Reimagining American Theatre* (1991). An accomplished stylist, fiery polemicist, and vigilant idealist, Brustein campaigned against commercialism, political correctness, and the incursion of popular culture on theatre as a high art, often courting controversy in the process.   STC

BRYANT, MICHAEL (1928–2002)

English actor particularly associated with the *National Theatre, where he demonstrated his versatility over many years. His roles there included the eponymous antihero (*see* HERO AND ANTIHERO) in *Ibsen's *Brand* (1978), Jaques in John *Dexter's *As You Like It* (1979), Bastien, the long-suffering hotel manager in *Feydeau's *A Little Hotel on the Side* (1984), Gloucester, opposite Anthony *Hopkins's Lear, in David *Hare's production

(1986), Prospero in Peter *Hall's *Tempest* (1987), and Enobarbus in Hall's *Antony and Cleopatra* (1987). He also appeared in Michael *Bogdanov's notorious production of Howard *Brenton's *The Romans in Britain* (1980). For his work in 1979 he was nominated for two Olivier *awards: for *Galsworthy's *Strife* (1978) and *Stoppard's version of *Schnitzler's *Undiscovered Country* (1979). AS

BRYCELAND (HEILBUTH), YVONNE (1925–92)

South African actress known for her interpretations of Athol *Fugard's female *characters and for co-founding South Africa's first internationally known non-racial theatre, the Space, in *Cape Town. Despite a professional debut in 1947, Bryceland found her voice reinterpreting Milly in Fugard's *People Are Living There* and especially creating Lena in *Boesman and Lena* and at CAPAB in 1969. Bryceland, Fugard, and Bryceland's husband Brian Astbury opened the Space with Fugard's *Statements after an Arrest . . .*, with Bryceland as Frieda and Fugard as Errol, her coloured lover (1972). Other roles included *Euripides' *Medea* and the definitive (but not the first) Hester in Fugard's *Hello and Goodbye* (1974) at the Space, *Brecht's *Mother Courage* at the *Market Theatre (1976), and the photographic representative of South African English in Robin Malan's comic guide *Ah Big Yaws* (1973). Moving to *London and the Royal *National Theatre, Bryceland played Hecuba in Edward *Bond's *The Woman* (1978) and Emilia in *Othello* (1979), as well as Miss Helen in Fugard's *Road to Mecca* (1985). LK

BRYDEN, BILL (1942–)

Scottish director and writer. Bryden assisted Tony *Richardson (Belgrade Theatre, Coventry), and William *Gaskill (*Royal Court, 1966–8) before becoming director of the Royal Lyceum, *Edinburgh. His tenancy of a resident Cottesloe (*National Theatre) ensemble in 1975 enabled him to produce populist, promenade productions such as *Lark Rise to Candleford* and *The Mysteries*. Bryden's desire to be 'the director of *Mamet in this country' led to premières of *American Buffalo* and *Glengarry Glen Ross*. Although he is 'a director who writes', Bryden's screenplay *Long Riders*, and stage and *television dramas *Benny Lynch* and *Willie Rough* (based on his grandfather, a shipbuilder) have earned him considerable acclaim. His interest in TV was developed by his position as head of drama for Scottish TV (1978) and later for BBC Scotland (1984). In the 1990s Bryden moved to epic productions, directing *The Ship* and *The Big Picnic* in a disused *Glasgow engine shed, and *opera productions such as *Parsifal* (*Covent Garden) and *The Silver Tassie* (English National Opera). KN

BRYUSOV, VALERY (1873–1924)

Russian poet, critic, dramatist, novelist, translator, and editor of *Vesy* (*The Scales*) 1904–10, an influential *symbolist magazine. Best known for his novel *The Fiery Angel* (1907), a tale of supernatural possession set in the Middle Ages and made into an *opera by Prokofiev (1919–23), Bryusov's major impact on the theatre was through his anti-*naturalist essays, especially *Unnecessary Truth* (1902), which argues for a theatre of convention (*uslovny teatr*) in opposition to traditional *realism. Of his twenty or so plays, the apocalyptic *Zemlya* (*Earth*, 1904) and a 'psychodrama', *Putnik* (*The Wayfarer*, 1910), are among the best. NW

BSISSOU, MOUYIN (1927–84)

Palestinian poet, critic, and playwright. Born in Gaza, Bsissou's first collection of poetry (*The Battle*, 1952) already demonstrated a theatrical flair. He realized this promise in *Cairo two decades later with plays such as *The Revolution of the Zenjs* (1970), *Samson and Delilah* (1971), *The Birds Build their Nests between Fingers* (Rabat, 1973), and *The Tragedy of Guevara*, which were staged by the best Egyptian directors. Bsissou was one of the first Arabic poets to use the free-*verse form in drama. In his work the Palestinian cause is indissoluble from questions of social justice, freedom, and truth. MMe

BUCHAREST

The capital of Romania has been a centre of Romanian-language drama since the mid-1800s. By 1800, student and *amateur theatre groups, performing in Greek or German, were active in several cities. Growing nationalism in the mid-nineteenth century saw a focus on Romanian-language education and performance in Bucharest, Iaşi, and Braşov. The predecessor to the National Theatre opened in 1852 in Bucharest with a repertoire of Romanian, French, and Italian drama and *opera. In the 1870s the National Theatre imported German stage machinery and French *acting techniques and organization. Ion Luca *Caragiale's satiric *comedies of the 1880s not only revitalized interest in native drama, but became the most successful of Romanian plays in Europe. In the first half of the twentieth century, six National Theatres operated throughout the country, but private theatres also flourished in Bucharest. Some, such as the Bulandra Theatre and Teatrul Mic (Little Theatre), are still in existence, but many shorter-lived companies introduced foreign works and *avant-garde methods. In turn, Elvira Popescu's company made a highly successful *tour to *Paris in 1923 with Mihail Sorbul's *Patima roşie*.

In 1948 all theatres were nationalized, a situation which led to financial stability for theatres and actors, a high level of state *censorship, and the creation of an extensive rotating *repertory system in which young actors, directors, and playwrights proved themselves in small regional theatres before moving to Bucharest or other urban stages. Rigorous *training academies, annual drama competitions, and the opportunity to hone skills at over 40 professional theatres created the climate for directors such as Liviu *Ciulei, Andrei *Şerban, Lucian *Pintilie, Silviu *Purcărete, David Esrig, Radu Penciulescu, and others to develop international reputations. Despite state control over scripts and performances, the theatre was one of the few places where people could share a glimmer of political and economic protest. To escape censorship, actors and *audiences developed a shared language of symbols and allusions.

After the Revolution of 1989, theatres remained state supported and most actors kept their civil service positions, although economic conditions greatly reduced production budgets. Because *ticket income covered only a small percentage of actual costs, private theatres had little chance of success. A few new independent companies received support for specific projects, including Masca, a *physical theatre group, and Theatrum Mundi, producing work by Romanian playwrights. Many directors took positions abroad as the economy deteriorated.

In addition to at least eleven *youth, *puppet, and drama institutions, Bucharest boasts a *circus, national opera, *musical theatre, and philharmonic orchestra. Other than *folk ensembles, *dance groups have had difficulties gaining audiences and funding. A few playwrights, such as Matei Vişniec (1956–   ) and Marin *Sorescu, have found international success. Freed of state-mandated quotas, most theatres have scaled back production of plays by Romanian authors, and offer a wide repertory of international classics and contemporary works.   EEP

BÜCHNER, GEORG (1813–37)

German dramatist. Born in Darmstadt into a liberal family, Büchner studied medicine and philosophy in Strasbourg and Giessen. At the former he became acquainted with the radical thought of Babeuf and Saint-Simon; at the latter he became involved in political agitation culminating in the pamphlet *Der hessische Landbote* (*The Hessian Country Messenger*). Threatened with prosecution, he fled to Zurich in 1836 where he died of typhus a year later. Büchner wrote only three plays, though his work remained unperformed and largely unpublished in his lifetime. *Danton's Death* (1835) treats a central figure of the French Revolution caught between hedonism and idealism, using techniques prefiguring *documentary drama. The *comedy *Leonce and Lena* (1836) mixes German and French *romanticism, Shakespeare, and *Gozzi to produce a work bordering on the *absurd. The unfinished *Woyzeck* (1836/7) is Büchner's best-known and most performed work. It combines the open, fragmentary style of *Sturm und Drang* *dramaturgy with elliptical, regionally inflected language pres-

aging *naturalism. *Woyzeck* was adapted into an *opera by Alban Berg and *filmed a number of times. Büchner's works were not performed until the turn of the twentieth century when their formal innovation and radical social-critical stance was at last admired. Max *Reinhardt directed important productions of both *Danton's Death* (1916) and *Woyzeck* (1921), while *Leonce and Lena*, although premièred in 1895, has been the least popular of the three works. Since then they have become an integral part of German theatre, and Büchner is one of the few German playwrights to enter the world repertory.

CBB

BUCKINGHAM, GEORGE VILLIERS, 2ND DUKE OF (1628–87)

English playwright and politician. Reared in the family of Charles I, Buckingham shared exile with Charles II during the Commonwealth but after the Restoration became a member of the King's inner circle of ministers known as the Cabal. Given to impetuous action and intrigue, he was imprisoned by the Commonwealth government for illegally returning to England and by the royal government for intrigue. In 1674 Parliament dismissed him from his ministerial post for alleged Catholic sympathies. He also found time to engage in an affair with the widow of a man he had killed in a duel. *Dryden aptly caricatured him in *Absalom and Achitophel* (1681) as 'A man so various, that he seem'd to be | Not one, but all mankind's epitome.' Dryden's *satire was probably payback for Buckingham's portrayal of him ten years earlier as the dramatist Bayes in *The Rehearsal*. The play was originally devised as a satire on William *Davenant and Sir Robert *Howard, but Dryden's appointment as Poet Laureate in 1668, and the production in 1670–1 of his heroic drama *The Conquest of Granada*, made him a more tempting target. *The Rehearsal* presents a *burlesque of a *heroic play in the context of its *rehearsal, with the pompous Bayes explaining his ideas to two critical companions. Although Buckingham had previously dabbled in the theatre, his reputation rests solely on *The Rehearsal*, which became a model for the later burlesque drama of *Fielding and *Sheridan.   RWV

BUCKSTONE, JOHN BALDWIN (1802–79)

English playwright, actor, and *manager. Buckstone began a *London acting career in 1823 at the Surrey Theatre, and for some years wrote and acted for a variety of *minor theatres, especially the *Adelphi, for which in 1826 he wrote and played in an early and important domestic *melodrama, *Luke the Labourer*. Buckstone's dramatic output was eclectic, embracing *burlettas, melodramas, *farces, and *pantomime librettos, over 100 plays altogether. The thematically interesting three-act farces *Married Life* (1834) and *Single Life* (1839), and the melodramas *The Wreck Ashore* (1830), *The Dream at Sea* (1835), *The Green Bushes* (1845), and *The Flowers of the Forest* (1847), represent his best work. In 1853 he assumed the management of the *Haymarket Theatre, retiring from management in 1876. For years his was the best *comedy company in London. As an actor Buckstone was a distinguished low comedian, often performing in his own plays, with irresistibly comic facial expressions and a low chuckle that would send *audiences into fits of *laughter before he reached the stage.   MRB

BUDAPEST

The capital of Hungary. The earliest records of Christmas festivals and revels in the administrative centre of Buda are from the fifteenth century, when King Matthias and his wife Beatrix employed Italian entertainers at court. At the end of the Turkish invasion *Jesuit priests organized several school performances (*see* UNIVERSITY AND SCHOOL DRAMA), a custom lasting until 1771. By the end of the eighteenth century the German company of Felix Berner had two inns remodelled into stages for public shows, and the influence of German companies was overwhelming until the Budai Színésztársaság, a company of actors from Kassa, established the tradition of acting in Hungarian (1833–7). The German-speaking theatre again gained ground until the council of Buda forbade acting in German in 1870. Several theatres were then founded to promote Hungarian acting, including the Budai Népszínház, the Budai Színkör, and the Várszínház.

The Pesti Magyar Színház was built in 1837 in order to support the Hungarian language and Hungarian playwriting. The two most important premières of the nineteenth century took place there: *Csongor és Tünde* (1879) by Mihály Vörösmarty and *Az ember tragédiája* (*The Tragedy of Man*, 1883) by Imre *Madách. The name of the institution was changed into Nemzeti Színház (National Theatre) in 1840, and it has maintained the original goal of staging Hungarian and Transylvanian plays (*Páskándi, *Sütő) alongside a classical repertory of *Sophocles, Shakespeare, *Molière, *Hugo, *Schiller, and the works of twentieth-century playwrights. The theatre reclaimed its original name of Magyar Színház in 2000, as the building of a new National Theatre is to be completed in 2002.

Pest, Buda, and Óbuda were united into the city of Budapest in 1873, but the rapid development of Pest, which began in the 1810s, increased the *audience for new theatres, *music halls, *cabarets, and *variety shows. The Opera House opened in 1884 for the educated elite with a wide repertory of European *opera, while the Király Theatre played the *operettas of young Hungarian composers, and was especially successful with *János vitéz* (*Child John*, 1904) by Pongrác Kacsóh. The Vígszínház was built in 1896 to provide entertainment for middle-class citizens;

seating over 1,000, it developed into a significant venue for contemporary plays from home and abroad, including the premières of a number of works by Ferenc *Molnár. Several generations of directors and actors started their careers there, and in the 1990s it was still going strong, staging popular *musicals.

By the end of the first decade of the twentieth century theatre was flourishing in Budapest. After the First World War many music halls were converted into dramatic theatres, such as the Renaissance Theatre (1921), *managed by the legendary Artúr Bárdos. The inflation during the period from 1944 to 1949 brought immense difficulties, and only two private theatres, the Művész Színház (Art Theatre), managed by Zoltán Várkonyi, and the Fővárosi Operettszínház of Szabolcs Fényes, survived. The Operettszínház performed popular operettas. The Művész Színház was interested in more literary fare, but was often obliged to stage operettas as well for financial reasons.

Theatres were nationalized by the new socialist government in 1949; although this stabilized their financial situation, political influence on the repertory was strongly felt. The Operettszínház successfully combined Soviet operettas, contemporary Hungarian musicals, and classical works. The *avant-garde found its home in Károly Kazimir's Thália Theatre in the 1960s, which was chiefly interested in the theatre of the *absurd, including István *Örkény's first success, *Tóték* (1967). The only independent *studio theatre, the Huszonötödik Színház (1971), struck an independent intellectual and political note in experimental performances, and *toured to remote parts of Hungary. The Játékszín Theatre was created at the end of the 1970s to receive productions from around the country, but by 1983 had begun to present its own productions of contemporary Hungarian plays. The Irodalmi Színpad (1957) was the home of literary evenings for two and a half decades; when transformed into the Radnóti Miklós Színház in 1988 it grew into one of the most popular theatres of the city. Besides professional companies, *alternative groups represent a significant part of the theatrical life of Budapest and have won several *awards at international *festivals. At the turn of the new century they exhibited growing influence on the work of established theatres.   HJA

BUENAVENTURA, ENRIQUE (1925–)

Colombian playwright, director, theoretician, poet, teacher, and painter. He started his multifaceted career with *Cuentos de la selva* (*Jungle Tales*, 1945), a collection of short stories based on indigenous and African legacies. In 1956 he became head of the recently established Escuela Departamental de Teatro of *Cali. His lifelong work at the school, later to become the independent Teatro *Experimental de Cali (1966), established the model for the 'Nuevo Teatro' movement all over *Latin America. Buenaventura painstakingly developed a method of *collective creation for most of his plays, which he also directed. Conceiving of theatre as an experimental laboratory, the method consisted of five phases: research, critical analysis, actor improvisation—considered the backbone of the process—the staging itself, and the final but open-ended performance. His more than 70 dramas are dominated by *A la diestra de Dios Padre* (*At the Right Hand of God the Father*, 1958, an adaptation of a short story by nineteenth-century *folklorist Tomás Carrasquilla), which was rewritten five times in 25 years. Influenced by *Brecht, *Weiss, *documentary, and *historical drama, Buenaventura also produced, wrote, and directed highly successful work such as *Los papeles del infierno* (*Documents from Hell*, 1973), a series of short episodes depicting the 'violent decade' of the 1950s; the *award-winning *Historia de una bala de plata* (*The Story of a Silver Bullet*, 1979), a free adaptation of Eugene *O'Neill's *The Emperor Jones*, a comment on the arrival of neo-liberalism in the Caribbean economies; and *Opera Bufa* (1983), based on the Somoza dynasty in Central America. He has also written numerous *theoretical and historical essays on theatre.   BJR

BUEN CRIOLLO

A character from the nineteenth-century *drama rural* (plays dealing with rural life) of *Latin America. The 'good Creole' (Latin American born but of Spanish ancestry) is an honourable, hard-working, peaceable figure who continues to till his land despite the ever-widening sway of the city and centralized authority. His refusal to corrupt himself dooms him.   AV

BUENOS AIRES

Capital of Argentina, perhaps the most extreme *Latin American example of a megalopolis which defines national cultural production. The port city's historic status as an immigration, commercial, political, and cultural centre, when combined with its rich theatre history, has led to it being regarded as interchangeable with the country's theatrical output. While this is incorrect, per capita Buenos Aires may have more theatrical activity than any other city in Latin America. The earliest documented Spanish-language production took place in the Fortress in 1747. The city's first theatre, the primitive wood-and-straw Ranchería, was built in a patio in 1783 only to be destroyed in a 1792 *fire. By 1804 the Coliseo (which would become the Argentino in 1838) was staging 'universal' plays selected and modified according to the needs of the nascent country. The first 'national' plays—*comedies, *tragedies, and local versions of the Spanish *sainete—were written and staged during the early years of the region's independence movement.

With Argentina established as a nation, Buenos Aires' predominantly *romantic theatre began to mature, but its development was effectively halted during the nineteenth-century dictatorship of Juan Manuel Rosas. (Indeed, the period's best-known authors, such as Juan Bautista Alberdi and Esteban Echeverría, kept Argentine theatre alive in exile by writing plays that would be produced years later.) After Rosas's demise in 1852, the city once more opened itself to the outside world, resulting in numerous visits from European theatrical companies (primarily from Spain, Italy, France, England, and Germany) and the construction of permanent *playhouses on European models, including the first Colón Theatre (1858), the Opera (1872), and the Politeama (1879). By the end of the nineteenth century Buenos Aires had more than 30 functioning theatres. While the majority were booked by European *touring companies, a local theatre was being created for the new *audience of immigrants pouring into the city. Popular tastes were reflected in the huge success of such *circus performers and *pantomimes as José Juan *Podestá, who, in 1886, launched the local *drama gauchesco* with his performance of the *gaucho outlaw Juan Moreira. Yet even as the *one-act *género chico* became the preferred theatre for the masses, European *naturalist theatre exerted its influence on the urban bourgeoisie. The result was Argentine theatre's 'golden age' (1902–10), best exemplified in the rural tragedies of the Uruguayan-born Florencio *Sánchez.

Buenos Aires' theatre was intimately linked to the region's turbulent history. Early in the twentieth centtury, as the city developed its own music, the *tango, it created an accompanying dramatic form, the *sainete criollo*, in which playwrights like Alberto Vacarezza and Nemesio Trejo dramatized the encounters of local creole and immigrant cultures. The 1920s *grotesco criollo* one-act plays centred on the problems encountered by these recent immigrants; playwrights such as Armando *Discépolo and Francisco *Defilippis Novoa wrote biting indictments of poverty and alienation. By 1928, the city had 43 theatres for a population of 2 million. In 1930 Argentina's first military coup of the century coincided with the Great Depression and the birth of the influential independent theatre movement. In response to growing mediocrity in commercial theatre and increasing political repression, independent theatre sought to rejuvenate the Argentine stage through 'theatre in service to art'. Leónidas Barletta's Teatro del Pueblo (People's Theatre) staged plays by new authors (chief among whom was Roberto *Arlt) as well as the latest European and North American plays. Despite great economic and political adversity, the independent theatre movement managed to combine a proletarian commitment with non-naturalistic strategies to probe Argentina's national identity.

By the late 1950s the number of theatres in Buenos Aires had dropped to twenty. Nevertheless, a more critical and ultimately very influential *realism had already taken hold, heralded by Carlos *Gorostiza's *The Bridge* (1949), and soon followed by Augustín *Cuzzani, Osvaldo *Dragún, and Andrés *Lizarraga. Such realism would grow increasingly reflective during General

Onganía's 1960s neo-fascist dictatorship, bringing to the foreground the work of Ricardo *Halac, Roberto *Cossa, Carlos *Somigliana, and Ricardo *Talesnik. At the same time, Buenos Aires was developing a strong *avant-garde performance scene, centred symbolically on the Torcuato Di Tella Institute. Important playwrights like Griselda *Gambaro premièred early works at the Institute while in another part of the city Eduardo *Pavlovsky wrote and performed in his early *absurdist plays.

The 1970s saw the last and most repressive military dictatorship of the century. The theatre, while less overtly *censored than the *mass media, was nonetheless affected, its practitioners subjected to anonymous threats, official bans, unofficial blacklists, performance disruptions, theatre bombings and fires, exile, and, in some cases, disappearance and death. In 1981 the Teatro *Abierto festival responded to a larger community's need for open expression in a still closed society. The first festival stands as a defining moment, the first instance of a massive event bringing together members of Buenos Aires' varied and often contentious theatre community. Later editions of Teatro Abierto helped to cement a new hybrid of realism and avant-garde experimentation. Such experimentation reached its apogee in the late 1980s during redemocratization as an underground theatre movement developed. Unconventional and eclectic, not only in technique and subject matter but also in venues and hours, the 'theatre of rupture' has now become a staple of Buenos Aires performance both at home and abroad, as witnessed in the international success of groups such as De la Guarda and Periférico de Objetos.

At the end of the twentieth century the capital contained some 90 theatres, though many of them could seat fewer than 100 spectators. Proud of its designation as a 'global city', Buenos Aires has sponsored since 1997 a biennial international *festival of theatre, music, and *dance. The global appellation contains more than a touch of irony: while local theatre troupes maintain a precarious existence, many of the most interesting recent productions have been sponsored by and directly exported to international festivals without premiering at home. *See also* CERVANTES, TEATRO NACIONAL; COLÓN, TEATRO; MUNICÍPAL GENERAL SAN MARTÍN, TEATRO.   JGJ

BUERO-VALLEJO, ANTONIO (1916–2000)

Spain's leading playwright of the second half of the twentieth century, whose plays often challenged the official culture of the Franco dictatorship. A young art student and member of the Health Corps of the Republican Army, he was imprisoned for six years at the end of the Spanish Civil War. Upon release he began to write for the stage, and the production of his *Story of a Stairway* in 1949 marked the beginning of a revitalization of post-*García-Lorcan Spanish theatre. During *rehearsals of his second play, *In the Burning Darkness* (1950), he introduced a scenic device that would become fundamental to much of his

subsequent work. In one scene set in a school for the blind, the theatre is plunged into darkness to diminish aesthetic distance and allow the *audience to experience the physical condition of the onstage *characters. The 'immersion effect' is used far more extensively in *The Sleep of Reason* (1970) to convey the isolation of deaf painter Goya, in *The Foundation* (1974) to depict scenically the mental delusion of a young political prisoner, and in many other plays. Musical motifs are used frequently to underscore immersion scenes but rarely for mere mood enhancement. His *opera libretto *Myth* (1967) incorporates an *opera-within-an-opera based on *Don Quixote* into a frame story about a quixotic actor. The first stagings of his plays were usually in *Madrid, but the première of *The Double Case-History of Dr Valmy* (1968) took place in Chester in England after *censorship prevented the play's performance in Spain. Andrzej *Wajda's *Warsaw production of *The Sleep of Reason* in 1976 was instrumental in bringing wider international attention to his work.   MPH

BUFO, TEATRO

Cuban nineteenth-century comic and *musical *genre, reliant on popular *stock characters like *el *negrito* ('the black boy', played by a white actor), *la mulata* (the mulatto woman), *el gallego* (the Gallician), and *el guajiro* (the peasant). *Improvisation played a large part in the performance of the loosely defined script, which contained intrigues spiced with songs and *dances, ending in a final rumba. The *bufo* style was consolidated after 1868, when Francisco (Pancho) Fernández created a troupe of Cuban *bufo* performers. Although rejected by *modernist notions of high art, *bufo* left a deep imprint on Cuban theatrical tradition. The Alhambra Theatre (1891–1936) in *Havana was the home of its major last stand.   MMu

BUGAKU

*Japanese court music, imported from the East Asian mainland, that featured *dance and sometimes included native court dances as well. A sub-genre of *gagaku* (elegant music), the term *bugaku* is often used in contradistinction to purely instrumental pieces (*kangen*, winds and strings) of the larger *gagaku* court music tradition. *Bugaku* is roughly classified into two types, both consolidated and systematized during the Heian period (794–1185): 'dances of the left', accompanied by *tōgaku* ('music-dance of the Tang dynasty', from *China); and 'dances of the right', accompanied by *komagaku* music imported from the *Korean peninsula. *Bugaku* makes use of elaborate *costumes, differing for the *tōgaku* and *komagaku* repertory and for the specific piece to be danced. Simple hand-held *props are sometimes used; *masks, smaller and thinner than those used for *gigaku*, are now and then employed as well. Performances of *bugaku* today contain mostly highly restrained, stylized movements. Solo and pair dances exist, but dances of four performers are most common. Music is provided by the *gagaku* ensemble, including flutes and double-reed winds, mouth organs, percussion, and, in the case of *tōgaku* pieces, zithers and lutes. Some 50 *bugaku* pieces are still in the repertory of the imperial court today.   GG

BUILDINGS *See* PLAYHOUSE.

BULGAKOV, MIKHAIL (1891–1940)

Russian writer. Born in Kiev and trained as a doctor, Bulgakov's obsession with music, especially Gounod's *Faust*, led to him failing the sessional examination. The theme of the pact with the devil and *opera music would influence much of his writing. After the Civil War, during which he served as a military doctor on the side of the Whites (fighting for the independence of Ukraine), he went to the Caucasus, considered emigration, but eventually settled in *Moscow. He began writing satirical sketches, but very soon was drawn to the *Moscow Art Theatre under *Stanislavsky, and adapted his novel *The White Guard* as the play *The Days of the Turbins* (1926). It deals with the life of a White officer's family in *Kiev during the Civil War, and although the *text focuses on the Whites, the production was among Stalin's favourites. In 1925 the Vakhtangov Theatre commissioned a *comedy; Bulgakov found a suitable *plot in the newspaper *Red Gazette* about a gambling den masquerading as a sewing shop, which furnished the basis for *Zoya's Apartment*, completed in 1926. The play turns the world of Moscow in the 1920s into a surreal, phantasmagoric place, while providing a satirical portrayal of the shortage of living space, the degeneration of the former aristocracy, drug dealing, and prostitution. In 1935 he rewrote *Zoya's Apartment* for the Théâtre du *Vieux-Colombier in *Paris, adding some anti-Soviet elements at the request of the theatre. His comedy *The Crimson Island* (1927) was banned in 1929; so was *The Flight* (1928, 1937), consisting of eight dreams about White émigrés, pursuing in a phantasmagoric style the fate of the Whites in the Soviet Union and in emigration.

The *Cabal of Hypocrites* (1929), Bulgakov's stage adaptation of his novel *Molière*, focuses on the conflict between the artist and authority rather than offering a purely biographical portrait. By the end of the 1920s all Bulgakov's plays had been removed from the repertoire after a press campaign against him. Only after Stalin's intervention were some of them restored and Bulgakov offered the post of *dramaturg at the Moscow Art Theatre. Staying safe in his choice of material, he completed a number of adaptations in the 1930s, such as *The Last Days* (1935) about *Pushkin's fatal duel, an adaptation of *Gogol's *Dead Souls* (1932), and *Don Quixote* (1938). His impressions of his work and the atmosphere at the Moscow Art The-

atre fed into his satirical account in *A Theatrical Novel* (*Black Snow*, 1936). Bulgakov's major contribution to world literature is the novel *The Master and Margarita*, written in the last years of his life, but not published until 1966–7. It was brought to the stage by Yury *Lyubimov in 1976.   BB

BULL-BAITING *See* BAITING.

BULLINS, ED (1935–)

*African-American playwright, a seminal figure in the Black Arts Movement. He co-founded Black Arts West and became director of Black House Theatre in Oakland, California, where the revolutionaries Bobby Seale, Eldridge Cleaver, and Huey Newton were affiliated as actors; through them he became minister of culture for the Black Panther Party. In 1967 Robert Macbeth of the *New Lafayette Theatre invited Bullins to *New York after reading *Goin' a Buffalo*, part of a cycle chronicling the lives of ordinary African Americans. Macbeth produced *In the Wine Time* (1968), *The Electronic Nigger* (1968), later done at *Lincoln Center, and *We Righteous Bombers* (1969), written under a pseudonym. Resident playwright at New Lafayette, Bullins also edited the house magazine, *Black Theatre*. When the company disbanded in 1973, Bullins became resident playwright at the *American Place Theatre, and *The Taking of Miss Janie* (1975) won the Drama Critics Circle *award. Bullins's career continued in the 1980s and 1990s, though perhaps without the force that marked his early work. In 1995 he joined the faculty of Northeastern University in *Boston.

BBL

BULOFF, JOSEPH (1899–1985)

*Yiddish actor and director, born in *Vilnius. He joined the *Vilna Troupe in *Warsaw, appearing in its major productions, including *The Dybbuk* (1920). In 1924 he came to the United States with the troupe and developed a distinguished international career on the Yiddish stage, starring in Yiddish classics and translations of world drama, creating a memorable Willie Loman in *Miller's *Death of a Salesman*. He worked on Broadway, where he originated the role of Ali Hakim in *Oklahoma!* (1944), and appeared in several *films, including *Silk Stockings* (1957) and *Reds* (1981).   EN

BULWER-LYTTON, EDWARD (1803–73)

English playwright, politician, novelist, and theatrical reformer, created Baron Lytton of Knebworth in 1866. In Parliament Bulwer chaired the 1832 Select Committee on Dramatic Literature which was responsible for a bill to allow any licenced theatre to play any kind of drama, subject to the authority of the

*Lord Chamberlain. It passed the Commons but was defeated in the Lords. However, the ground was prepared for the Theatres Regulation Bill of 1843 which achieved the same ends (*see* LICENSING ACTS). Already a successful novelist by the 1830s, Bulwer then took up the drama. After the failure of *The Duchesse de la Vallière* (1837), a *romantic *verse drama set in the court of Louis XIV, he had a great success with *The Lady of Lyons* (1838) and *Richelieu* (1839). The former is a drama about the rise of a humble gardener to wealth, military greatness, and the hand of the proud Pauline Deschappelles, the latter another drama of seventeenth-century French court intrigue that provided an attractive role for all Victorian star actors. It was adapted for the stage in collaboration with *Macready, who also produced *The Lady of Lyons*. Its themes of social pretence and ambition, wealth, class hostility, and the conflict between love and pride also distinguish *Money* (1840), a huge success with Macready in the leading role. The most significant *comedy of the century, it influenced much later writing. Eminently playable today, it has been performed by both the *Royal Shakespeare Company and the Royal *National Theatre.

MRB

BUNN, ALFRED (1798–1860)

English *manager and librettist. For two seasons (1833–5) Bunn was manager of both *Drury Lane and *Covent Garden. His taste for *opera and *spectacle rather than *legitimate drama provoked a physical assault from *Macready in 1836 because Bunn forced him to act in a severely truncated *Richard III*. Nobody could make a financial success of the two *patent theatres in the 1830s, and Bunn went bankrupt. He wrote librettos for eleven operas, notably Balfe's *The Bohemian Girl* (1843). His *The Stage: both before and behind the curtain* (1840) is special pleading, but informative about contemporary theatre.

MRB

BUNRAKU

Sophisticated Japanese *puppet theatre. Originally derived from the name Uemura Bunrakuken, the founder of a troupe in *Osaka around 1800, bunraku has become a common term for Japanese puppet theatre (*ningyō jōruri*) which developed out of the medieval storytelling tradition of blind minstrels. Around 1,600 chanters joined with puppets from Awaji and other centres, and various troupes flourished in commercial theatre districts in the cities of *Kyoto, Osaka, and Edo (*Tokyo), as well as in smaller cities and the countryside throughout *Japan until the late nineteenth century. Today the only surviving professional troupe is based in Osaka and performs regularly at the Tokyo and Osaka National Theatres. The three elements of bunraku are chanter (*tayū*), *shamisen*, and puppets. Traditionally the chanter, who voices all the roles and the narration, has been the most prominent figure. The *shamisen* player accompanies him, both of them sitting on a dais stage left near the *audience. The puppets are about two-thirds life size and from 1734 each has been manipulated by three men. The senior puppeteer works the puppet's head with his left hand and its right hand with his own right hand; the second works the left hand with his right hand; the third manipulates the feet. Chanters became sighted performers early in the seventeenth century, but *shamisen* players were usually blind until the mid-eighteenth century.

Because of its origins in narrative, bunraku has always held the story to be of paramount importance. At the time of first performance playbooks were published in full, authorized editions, a situation different from *kabuki, bunraku's rival, which published no full *texts until the modern era. As a result bunraku attracted outstanding playwrights who produced the most famous plays of the popular stage, such as *Chūshingura: a treasury of loyal retainers* (1748) by *Namiki Senryū (Sōsuke), *Takeda Izumo, and Miyoshi Shoraku. The greatest era of playwriting was from 1683 to 1800, when more than 1,000 day-long plays were written. *Chikamatsu Monzaemon, Namiki, Takeda, and *Chikamatsu Hanji all wrote primarily for bunraku. Successful bunraku plays were invariably adapted into kabuki and today form the core of its repertoire. Since famous bunraku plays were kept in print throughout the Tokugawa era (1600–1868), they were widely read and continued to be influential in later kabuki and popular fiction.

Bunraku chanting is based on musical principles, the chanter's art being to vary constantly the style between realistic declamation and various kinds of singing. From the late seventeenth century chanting became an important *amateur activity among men and women, and plays were published with the chanter's code of musical notation. Amateur chanting was popular throughout Japan until the 1940s, and fostered a highly sophisticated audience for bunraku and kabuki. Bunraku theatres were found in all major cities, but Osaka was the creative centre where nearly all of the plays were composed. *Takemoto Gidayū founded the Takemoto-za theatre in 1684, and in the early 1700s his disciple founded the Toyotake-za; this rivalry produced the golden age of bunraku, and the modern art developed from the tradition then established. Indeed *Gidayū* (or *gidayū-bushi*) became the term for bunraku chanting and music. In the eighteenth century bunraku changed from a narrative art to a full dramatic one with the increasing sophistication of the puppetry and *shamisen* music. The nineteenth century saw further development of theatricality as the repertoire coalesced; a *shamisen* notation system led to increasingly complex musical accompaniment.

In performance, the chanter's voice and *shamisen* music infuse the puppets with life. The two junior puppeteers always wear black robes with faces covered by hoods, but the senior manipulator's face is visible in important scenes. Initially the puppets seem to be directed by the three men but as the intensity of *action, voice, and music increases, the puppets appear to lead the puppeteers, as they rush to the fateful climax. The elements of the artifice are obvious to the eye and ear, but the ensemble produces a magical effect of reality that often invokes tears in the audience. A remarkable aspect of bunraku is that the core of virtually every programme, past and present, is *tragedy, perhaps due to its Buddhist and *folk-religious heritage. Takemoto Gidayū described a day of theatre as a cyclical experience, beginning in an auspicious setting, travelling through intrigue, insurrection, and battles, to the impasse of an individual crisis which can only be resolved by death. A tragic action, usually in the middle of a play or programme, ultimately leads to a resolution of the original crisis, which had cast the world into chaos. After the tragic scene, the audience is led through a lyrical dance scene to a final auspicious vision of a world restored to order, with hope for the future. This cyclical structure, originally inspired by *nō drama, is evident today in the orchestration of all bunraku programmes, and has influenced the dramaturgy of kabuki as well.　　　CAG

ADACHI, BARBARA, *Backstage at Bunraku* (New York, 1985)

BRANDON, JAMES (trans.), *Kabuki: five classic plays* (Cambridge, Mass., 1975)

BRAZELL, KAREN (trans. and ed.), *Traditional Japanese Theater: an anthology of plays* (Ithaca, NY, 1998)

GERSTLE, C. ANDREW (trans.), *Chikamatsu: five late plays* (New York, 2000)

KEENE, DONALD, *Nō and Bunraku: two forms of Japanese theater* (New York, 1990)

—— (trans.), *Major Plays of Chikamatsu* (New York, 1961)

BUONTALENTI, BERNARDO (1531–1608)

Italian architect and scenic designer. He entered the service of the Medici in 1547 as a civil engineer and military architect. His inventions of entertaining gadgets, *fireworks, and decorations prepared him for a theatrical career at the side of *Vasari and Lanci. In 1574 he became principal stage designer at the Medici court in Florence, for whom he built the Teatro degli Uffizi (1585) with a capacity of 3,000. Its complex stage machinery and revolving *periaktoi allowed rapid changes of *perspective *scenery, developed to unprecedented height in the 1589 theatre festival, for which Buontalenti also designed the *costumes. *See also* SCENOGRAPHY.　　　GB

BURBAGE, JAMES (c.1530–1597)

English actor, theatre owner, and *manager. A joiner by trade, Burbage became, according to his son Cuthbert, 'in his younger years a player'. Records from 1572 and 1574 name him as a prominent member of the Earl of *Leicester's Men; a court record of March 1576 refers to 'Burbage and his company'. In April of that year he leased property in Shoreditch and proceeded, with the financial backing of his brother-in-law John

*Brayne, to erect the *Theatre, the second purpose-built public *playhouse in England. In 1583 several of Leicester's Men joined the newly organized *Queen's Men, who became the new tenants of the Theatre. Burbage very likely abandoned acting for full-time theatre management at the same time and took up permanent residence in Shoreditch. Between 1583 and 1597, when it was abandoned and subsequently disassembled to provide timbers for the *Globe, the Theatre was home to several *acting companies, including the Lord *Chamberlain's Men (1594–7), reconstituted in 1603 as the King's Men. Burbage's relationship with Brayne was not a happy one, and suits and legal actions over the years suggest that he was an irascible and stubborn man. In early 1597 he purchased one of the houses of Blackfriars and thus initiated an enterprise that would result in the second *Blackfriars Theatre. At his death, Burbage's interest in Blackfriars passed to his younger son Richard *Burbage, and his interest in the Globe to his elder son Cuthbert.　　　RWV

BURBAGE, RICHARD (c.1568–1619)

English actor, the younger son of James *Burbage who built the *Theatre in 1576. He probably acted minor roles as early as 1584, but he was certainly capable of handling more substantial parts by 1590. Around this time he played Gorboduc in the play of that title, and Tereus in *The Seven Deadly Sins, Part II*. During the Christmas season 1594, Burbage was summoned with two other players to perform *interludes before the Queen. From 1595 he assumed a prominent place in the Lord *Chamberlain's Men, remaining with the company when the players obtained a royal patent (1603) to the end of his professional life. He is best remembered for his association with the leading roles in Shakespeare's plays. Burbage's contemporaries stated that he performed Hamlet, King Lear, and Othello; some historians suggest that Richard III, Romeo, Hieronimo (*Kyd's *The Spanish Tragedy*), and Ferdinand (*Webster's *The Duchess of Malfi*) were also his. Doubtless there were many others, largely unknown. Burbage's *acting style has been thought to have been more naturalistic and subtle than that traditionally associated with his contemporary Edward *Alleyn of the Lord *Admiral's Men, who played large, bombastic characters such as Faustus and Tamburlaine. John Davies of Hereford characterized Burbage as one of those actors he loved 'for painting, poesie', and *Middleton wrote an elegy claiming that Burbage's Hamlet seemed so real that 'I would have sworn, he meant to die'. In 1664, Richard *Flecknoe stated that 'he had all the parts of an excellent Orator, animating his words with speaking, and Speech with Action; his Auditors being never more delighted then when he spake'. According to Flecknoe, Burbage never 'fell' in his part 'when he had done speaking, but with his looks and gestures maintaining it still unto the heighth'.

Burbage participated in many performances at court and in public pageants. In 1605 he negotiated with Robert Cecil a performance of *Love's Labour's Lost* (intended for Queen Anne); and in May 1610 he was employed by the city of *London to deliver a speech to Prince Henry in a water pageant on the Thames. Moreover, Burbage was a shareholder in the *Globe and the *Blackfriars *playhouses, and he inherited part of the original Theatre from his father. Surprisingly he excelled as a painter as well. Middleton's epitaph mentions 'painting and playing', and in 1613 Burbage was paid by the Earl of Rutland for painting a heraldic device. A painting of Burbage (Dulwich Picture Gallery) is thought by some to have been a self-portrait. Of the many epitaphs which memorialized his acting talents, the shortest was 'Exit Burbage'.   SPC

BURGOS, JERÓNIMA DE (c.1580–1641)

Spanish actress, married by 1594 to Pedro de Valdés (c.1568–1640), who led his own company with her assistance from 1613 at least until 1637. From 1607 she was closely involved with Lope de *Vega, who provided many plays for her, including *The Dumb Belle* in 1613. But by 1615 intimacy turned to enmity, and Lope wrote for others. That year she created the title role in *Tirso de Molina's *Don Gil of the Green Breeches*, but was apparently too old and fat for such parts.   VFD

BURGTHEATER

Founded in 1741 as the Habsburg court theatre in *Vienna, in 1776 Emperor Josef II designated it as a 'German *National Theatre'. The Burgtheater's first flowering came under Joseph *Schreyvogel (director 1814–32), who favoured classical German drama (*Goethe, *Schiller, *Kleist) and fostered new dramatists (*Grillparzer). Another important reformer was Heinrich *Laube (director 1849–67), who continued the emphasis on highbrow literary theatre but also established a reputation for outstanding *acting. The present *playhouse was built by Gottfried Semper in 1888 in a monumental *neoclassical style. Despite its change from royal to state administration after 1918, the repertoire remained overwhelmingly dominated by the classics. The famous ensemble was severely disrupted between 1939 and 1945 when many actors were forced into exile. A succession of directors rebuilt the ensemble in the post-war years, although none managed to put a distinctive directorial stamp on the theatre until the appointment of Claus *Peymann (1986–99). Under his direction the 'Burg' became an innovative and highly controversial theatre, due chiefly to his preference for contemporary Austrian authors like Thomas *Bernhard, Elfriede *Jelinek, Peter *Handke, and Peter *Turrini, whose work was often critical of Austrian society. Under the director Klaus Bachler, the Burg has been turned into an independent company, *financed but not administered by the state.   CBB

BURIAN, EMIL FRANTIŠEK (1904–59)

Czech director, composer, conductor, playwright, and performer. He started as a musician and performer in the Liberated Theatre (1926), where he introduced his 'voice-band': a highly stylized choral declamation and chant, using actors' voices as sophisticated musical instruments. In September 1933 he opened his own theatre, D34, conceived as a cultural centre (the D stood for *divadlo* (theatre), and the number was changed annually to represent the next year). The opening production (*Life in our Days* by Erich Kästner) qualified Burian as a leftist, but his theatre was essentially poetic, as his adaptations and productions of *romantic poets (*Pushkin, *Goethe, Karel Mácha) indicate. In a similar lyrical vein Burian directed *Wedekind's *Spring's Awakening* (1936) with a new principle of stage design, 'theatregraph', which used non-illustrative *film and slide projection on the backdrop and on transparent front gauze, achieving a dreamy and unrealistic effect. Burian's was a synthetic or *total theatre, where all the elements were of equal importance; the script, frequently non-dramatic or heavily adapted, was treated as a mere libretto for a richly orchestrated production. In March 1941, during the Nazi occupation, D41 was closed, and Burian was later sent to a concentration camp. During the first post-war years, and again in the late 1950s, he made (not completely successful) attempts to catch up with the present and to renovate his programme.   ML

BURK, JOHN DALY (c.1776–1808)

Irish-American playwright and historian. Born in County Cork, Burk emigrated to the United States after engaging in anti-British political activities. The Haymarket Theatre in *Boston produced his play *Bunker-Hill; or, The Death of General Warren* with great success in 1797. Glorifying the American General Joseph Warren, it continued to be produced as a patriotic republican drama well into the nineteenth century. His second play, *Female Patriotism*, featuring Joan of Arc as an ardent republican and staged at the *New York *John Street Theatre during the anti-French 'XYZ controversy' in 1798, proved less successful because of its pro-French republican stance.   SEW

BURLESQUE

In the Restoration and eighteenth-century English theatre the word 'burlesque' was applied to plays like the co-authored *Rehearsal*, *Fielding's *Tragedy of Tragedies*, and *Sheridan's *The Critic*, which were *parodies of contemporary theatrical conventions of writing and staging. This tradition continued into the nineteenth century, with *melodrama and its *villain particular targets of comic *satire. *Jerrold's *Black-Ey'd Susan* and Pocock's *The Miller and his Men*, two popular melodramas, were frequently burlesqued for middle-class *audiences. *Opera and

Shakespeare received the same irreverent treatment in dozens of plays. *Hamlet* was burlesqued at least five times and Shakespeare's *plots and *verse were reduced to the lowest level possible of eccentricity and the grotesque. Burlesque reduced its subject matter, whether drama, myth, or history, to the level of comic and urban domesticity. In stage performance burlesque, which also had roots in the relatively tasteful extravaganzas of J. R. *Planché, the *minstrel show, and the *music hall, was a frothy brew of topical songs, legs, *limelight, puns good and bad, eccentric *dancing, and enormous energy. Increasing middle-class refinement and the growth of *musical comedy killed off the older burlesque at the end of the century. In America burlesque was a non-literary mixture of skimpily dressed women (and eventually strippers) and male low comedians, with dancing, songs, comic patter, and an increasing raunchiness frowned upon by the civic authorities, which began closing burlesque houses by edict, as in *New York in 1942. As a living form, it had virtually expired by the 1950s. *See also* SEX SHOWS AND DANCES.   MRB

BURLETTA

A form of light *comedy on the *London stage in the 1820s and 1830s. The *licensing laws did not permit London's *minor theatres to play *legitimate drama: traditional *comedy, *tragedy, and *farce. However, they were allowed to perform *melodrama and burletta. The word 'burletta' was applied to comic pieces containing a number of songs; the number varied. Even the *Lord Chamberlain seemed uncertain of its meaning; the 1832 Select Committee on Dramatic Literature was offered several definitions. J. R. *Planché believed that a burletta was a piece not played at major theatres, with at least 'five pieces of vocal music in each act'. The heyday of burletta was the 1830s at the *Olympic Theatre under Madame *Vestris; Planché himself was a chief contributor. At the Olympic a burletta was generally a two-act comedy with songs, written with restraint, refinement, and French polish, sometimes known as a *petite comédie*.
                                                      MRB

BURMA *See* MYANMAR.

BURNAND, F. C. (FRANCIS COWLEY) (1836–1917)

English playwright and journalist. He wrote early pieces for the Cambridge Amateur Dramatic Club, which he founded, and became a prolific author of *farces, *burlesques, extravaganzas, comic *operas, and the occasional drama and *comedy. His burlesques for West End *audiences, lively, irreverent, full of puns, *dancing, and singing, were *parodies of *melodramas, history, classical myth, and legend, the most successful being a ver-

sion of *Jerrold's *Black-Ey'd Susan*, which ran for 400 nights. His comic operas included three collaborations with Arthur *Sullivan. Burnand edited *Punch* for 26 years, retiring in 1906. He was knighted in 1902.   MRB

BURNS, GEORGE (NATHAN BIRNBAUM) (1896–1996) AND GRACIE ALLEN (1895–1964)

American comedy team. Burns found *vaudeville success when in 1923 he teamed with Allen, a singer-dancer. They made their debut in Newark, New Jersey, with an act called 'Sixty Forty' in which Allen played straight man to Burns's jokester. *Audiences found Allen funnier, and Burns rewrote their material to feature Gracie's surreal logic delivered cheerily in a childlike voice while Burns asked questions and patiently accepted her twisted statements. This basic act propelled them to stardom on the Orpheum circuit by 1925 and carried them through the next 35 years. Married in 1926, they soon signed a six-year contract for the Keith (later Keith-Orpheum) circuit at $750 per week. Their act translated successfully to *radio (their own show lasted 1933–50), to *film (1934–44), and to *television (1950–8). After Allen's retirement in 1958 Burns continued solo as comic and film actor.   MAF

BURRAKATHA

Popular folk narrative form from Andhra Pradesh, *India. Its name is derived from the percussion instrument (*burra*, also called *dhakki*) that is used in the performance; *katha* means story. *Burrakatha* consists of a three-member team— one primary singer-narrator, who sings to the accompaniment of a simple string instrument, *tambura*, and two accompanists who play on the *dhakki*. Restructured from several *folk ballad forms like *jangam katha* and *jamukula katha* prevalent in Andhra since the fourteenth century, *burrakatha* became an extremely creative medium after its resurrection in 1942 by the members of the Praja Natya Mandali (the Andhra variant of the *Indian People's Theatre Association). Involving the dramatization of a story, with commentary provided by one of the accompanists, a *burrakatha* performance is marked by its pungent humour and timely allusions to everyday life. Used not only for *political propaganda, but also for government publicity campaigns, the stories usually draw on the lives of great patriots and the victims of the political system. Using folk metres like *ragada* and *dwipada*, the three-actor ensemble combines the poetic simplicity of *folk narratives with the intricacies of modern performance techniques. Among several masters of the art, Kakumanu Subba Rao is regarded as one of the earliest exponents of the form, while Sheik Nazar, a master performer, popularized it along with Koganti Gopalakrishnaiah,

Ramakoti, and several women performers like Kondepudi Radha, Tapi Rajamma, and Moturi Udayam. MNS

BURROWS, ABE (1910–85)

American playwright, librettist, lyricist, and director, who broke into show business in the 1930s on the Catskill Mountain 'Borscht Belt'. In 1939 he began a successful career as a Hollywood *radio writer and performer, and was partly responsible for the popular show *Duffy's Tavern*. His Broadway career commenced with his collaboration on the *book of the classic *musical *Guys and Dolls* (with Frank *Loesser, 1950), which earned him a Tony *award. Burrows wrote either the book or lyrics for such later musicals as *Can-Can* (1953), *Silk Stockings* (1955), *Say, Darling* (1958), *How to Succeed in Business without Really Trying* (1961)—a hit for which he shared the Pulitzer Prize and won two Tonys—and *What Makes Sammy Run?* (1964). Also respected as a 'script doctor', Burrows directed some of these shows as well as a number of *comedies. Plays he wrote, or co-wrote, included his hit adaptation of a French comedy, *Forty Carats* (1968). SLL

BURSTYN, ELLEN (1932–)

American actress, born Edna Rae Gillooly. Burstyn had been modelling in *New York when she was cast in *Fair Game* (1957) on Broadway. Following some initial success, she sought *training with Lee *Strasberg and the *Actors Studio, where she has maintained an influential connection. Burstyn has become a figurehead of integrity in the profession with *films like *Alice Doesn't Live Here Anymore* (1974) and diverse stage work, including *Same Time, Next Year* (1975), *84 Charing Cross Road* (1982), and *A Long Day's Journey into Night* (1998). She was the first woman president of Actors' Equity Association (1982–5; see TRADE UNIONS, THEATRICAL). EW

BURTON, RICHARD (1925–84)

Welsh actor whose talent on stage and *film was all but squandered through alcoholism. His reputation as a young actor was won in *Fry's *The Lady's Not for Burning* (1949) and in a series of Shakespearian roles at the *Old Vic, including Hamlet (1953). All but abandoning the stage for an explosive film career, he appeared memorably opposite Elizabeth Taylor in the epic *Cleopatra* (1963) and in Mike *Nichols's film of *Albee's *Who's Afraid of Virginia Woolf?* (1966), the two stars conducting a hugely destructive relationship in public. Other significant film roles included *Becket* (1964), *The Spy Who Came in from the Cold* (1965), and *Shaffer's *Equus* (stage and film, 1977). He also narrated a famous *radio adaptation of Dylan Thomas's *Under Milk Wood* (BBC, 1954). AS

BURTON, WILLIAM E. (1804–60)

Anglo-American actor and *manager. Born in London, Burton was employed by his father as a printer and performed in *amateur theatrics before joining a provincial company in 1825. By 1831 he was a major comic actor in *London, performing with Edmund *Kean and at the *Haymarket. He arrived in the USA in 1834 and joined the *Arch Street Theatre in *Philadelphia where he quickly became renowned at America's top comic actor. Three years later he moved to the National Theatre in *New York and by 1841 was its manager. After *fire destroyed the *playhouse, he returned to Philadelphia and within a short time was managing four houses, the Arch Street and *Chestnut Street Theatres in that city, and two further venues in Baltimore. In 1848 he assumed control of Palmo's Opera House in New York, renaming it Burton's Theatre, and for the next eight years ran one of the best *stock companies in the USA. He produced and performed in a string of highly successful shows, including revivals of Shakespeare and adaptations of *Dickens. PAD

BURY, JOHN (1925–2000)

English stage and *lighting designer. Bury studied chemistry at University College London and served in the Fleet Air Arm (1942–6). After the war he joined Joan *Littlewood's *Theatre Workshop, designing and constructing *scenery and driving the van. His groundbreaking designs there included Shelagh *Delaney's *A Taste of Honey*, Brendan *Behan's *The Quare Fellow*, and the ensemble *musicals *Fings Ain't Wot They Used t'Be* and *Oh! What a Lovely War*, which introduced solid materials and real objects into the then-current artifice of the stage. In 1963 he joined the *Royal Shakespeare Company and created sets and *costumes for John *Barton and Peter *Hall's *The Wars of the Roses* (1963–4), using heavy sheet-metal *periaktoi which allowed transformations on an epic scale, establishing the 'brutalist' style. In 1965 he was appointed head of design at the RSC. Increasing sophistication and developments in light technology came together for Harold *Pinter's *Landscape* and *Silence* (1969), where a divided stage space, enhanced by shadows and reflected light, mirrored the emotionality of the *text. Over ten *operas at Glyndebourne, including the *Mozart–*da Ponte trilogy and Britten's *A Midsummer Night's Dream*, reflected on stage his lifelong love of nature. Following Hall to the *National Theatre, Bury was head of design from 1973 to 1985, where his productions included *Shaffer's *Amadeus* (1979). He was also consultant for new theatres at the Barbican and Glyndebourne. He always began by choosing appropriate materials and lighting for the stage floor, which he considered of primary importance. *See also* SCENOGRAPHY PH

BUSCH, ERNST (1900–80)

German actor. Busch joined *Piscator at the *Volksbühne in *Berlin in 1927. Thoroughly committed to left-wing politics, he performed in important productions such as *Toller's *Hoppla, wir leben!* (*Hoppla, We're Alive!*, 1928), *Brecht's *film *Kuhle Wampe* (also known as *Whither Germany?*, 1932), and participated in political *cabaret. In 1933 he went into exile, served in the Spanish Civil War, and between 1939 and 1940 worked in Belgium, fleeing to France after the German invasion. He was interned in France, and then imprisoned in Germany for treason. After the war he joined the *Berliner Ensemble and played major roles in Brecht's own productions, and came to be recognized as a prototypical *Brechtian actor. The most important theatre conservatory in Berlin, the Ernst-Busch-Schule, is named after him.

CBB

BUSH THEATRE

English *fringe venue above a pub in Shepherd's Bush in the west of *London, opened in 1972. Initially housing work by *alternative companies like *7:84, it has since specialized in new writing, championing Howard *Barker, David *Edgar, Snoo Wilson, John *Arden, Stephen *Poliakoff, and Doug *Lucie. The Bush played a role in the mid-1990s revival of challenging British playwriting with premières from Joe *Penhall, Richard Zajdlic, and Irvine Welsh, and its 1996 'London Fragments' season featured work by Simon Bent, David Eldridge, and Samuel Adamson. In 2000 the notoriously cramped *playhouse upgraded its backstage facilities and installed comfortable seats.

DR

BUSKER

Form of street entertainer dating back to Roman times and subsequently to the goliards, troubadours, minstrels, mountebanks, *acrobats, *puppeteers, and *commedia dell'arte performers of the middle ages. Street performers were prevalent in nineteenth-century *London; for some the work was a last resort before begging or the workhouse. In the early twentieth century buskers entertained queues waiting for admission to the pit and galleries of West End theatres and cinemas, and also performed at markets. They included barrel organists, street boxers, clog dancers, vocalists, boys singing popular *music-hall songs, 'out of work' actors reciting Shakespeare, *Dickens, or popular verses, paper-tearers, and chapeaugraphists. In the late 1930s, kerbside entertainment became more elaborate, with whole companies of buskers presenting regular programmes. Since the 1960s guitarists have been a familiar aspect of busking, while *jugglers, fire-eaters, acrobats, *mimes, and *performance artists busk for crowds throughout the world.

JTD

BUTAKE, BOLE (1948–)

Cameroon playwright whose work, written in English, includes *Shoes and Four Men in Arms* (1984), *The Rape of Mitchelle* (1984), *Lake God* (1986), and *And Palmwine Will Flow* (1990). A professor of African literature, Butake has used the University of Yaoundé Drama Troupe to launch his works, which are chiefly *agitprop in nature.

HNE

BUTOH

At first all modern *dance in *Japan was called butoh (or *butō*), but the term has come to refer almost exclusively to an *avant-garde form created by dancers like *Hijikata Tatsumi and *Ōno Kazuo, who were both students of German expressionist *Neue Tanz*. Around 1960, Hijikata coined the term *ankoku butoh* (the dance of utter darkness) to describe his style; the word *ankoku* has since been dropped. An underground *performance art during the 1960s, butoh's heyday in Japan was in the 1970s. It broke onto the international scene in the 1980s, and in recent years butoh groups have sprung up in Europe and the Americas. Based on the desire to discover a dance form congenial to the Japanese body, butoh's movements often echo *kabuki gestures or traditional agricultural practices. The body is regarded as a repository of repressed cultural memory; the grimaces and tortured gestures typical of this form reflect the dancer's attempts to overcome physical and social inhibitions and to reconnect with a primal energy. Spontaneous expression of the spirit has been considered more important than physical or technical virtuosity, especially in solo or small ensemble performances, but larger groups (like Maro Akaji's Dai Rakudakan, Ohsuka Isamu's Byakkosha, and Amagatsu Ushio's Paris-based Sankaijuku) are highly choreographed.

CP

BYRON, GEORGE GORDON, LORD (1788–1824)

English poet who also had ambitions to succeed as a playwright. For a year (1814–15) he served on the committee of *Drury Lane Theatre, gaining valuable knowledge of current practice. Of Byron's nine plays in *verse only one, *Marino Faliero*, was staged in his lifetime, by *Elliston at Drury Lane in 1821, but it was not the success Byron's letters indicate he hoped for. The plays are based on *historical, biblical, or metaphysical subjects (only one, *The Blues*, is a *comedy); all focus on profound moral choices that have tragic social consequences; the verse is sinewy, spare, and generally undecorated, owing more to the influence of *Alfieri than to Shakespeare, the better to focus attention on the intricacies of the *characters' thinking. The Venetian *tragedies, *Marino* and *The Two Foscari*, arguably his finest, communicate a deepening sense of place to heighten tragic event and deploy stage space to symbolic ends; both sustain a *neoclassical formality far from the conventions of *melodrama. *Macready produced four of the plays (*Werner* continued in his repertoire from 1830 till his retirement); Alfred *Bunn staged a notoriously spectacular version of *Manfred* (1834), and Charles *Kean a pictorial rather than theatrical *Sardanapalus* (1853).   RAC

BYRON, HENRY JAMES (1834–84)

English playwright, actor, and *manager. A very busy author of extravaganzas, *burlesques, *pantomime librettos, *dramas, and *comedies, Byron became popular with his burlesques at the Strand and other London theatres in the 1850s and 1860s. He was the chief punster of the Victorian stage, in both burlesque and pantomime. Byron also wrote a good strong *melodrama in *The Lancashire Lass; or, Tempted, Tried, and True* (1868), in which Henry *Irving played the villain in *London, and several thematically interesting comedies about marital difficulties rather than romantic courtship: *Cyril's Success* (1868), *Partners for Life* (1871), and *Married in Haste* (1876). His most successful comedy, in which he acted, was *Our Boys* (1875); it ran for over four years at the Vaudeville Theatre and was marked by Bryon's love of eccentric comedy, an inheritance from the older Victorian comedy. *Our Boys* concerns the perennial Victorian stage class conflict, this time between a haughty aristocrat and a retired Cockney tradesman, and a romantic relationship between their sons and two women, an heiress and a girl of humble origins. *Our Boys*, too, is inclined to puns. Byron also went into management, unsuccessfully, at Liverpool; more importantly he was initially Marie *Wilton's partner in the new management at the *Prince of Wales's Theatre in 1865 and was instrumental in the acceptance of *Robertson's comedy *Society* in that year. The partnership ended in 1867, Wilton being uninterested in producing Byron's speciality, burlesque; Byron then transferred his managerial energies to Liverpool.

MRB

BYZANTINE THEATRE AND ENTERTAINMENTS

The Byzantine Empire, with its capital in Constantinople, was officially born in the division of the Roman Empire in AD 395, but it continued for nearly 1,000 years after the fall of its Western counterpart, its culture a rich amalgam of Christian religion, Greek language, and Roman imperial politics. The intermingling of civic and religious bureaucracies and courts, of palace personnel and religious leadership, of imperial and ecclesiastical authority, was reflected in the apparent modelling of liturgical dress and conduct after the ceremonial practices of the imperial court, and in the Emperor's habit of blessing the participants at entertainments in the Hippodrome, Constantinople's *circus. There remains too a strong impression that a flamboyant theatricality permeated both courtly and religious ceremony.

Theatrical activities associated with late *Roman antiquity—tragic and comic recitation, *mime, *pantomime, *juggling, variety turns—continued in the Eastern Empire, as did the more spectacular, and violent, of Roman entertainments, both in Roman and Graeco-Roman theatres and in Constantinople's famous Hippodrome, modelled after the Circus Maximus at Rome. An ivory diptych advertising games in 506 depicts *venationes* (*animal fights) in the Byzantine capital. Chariot racing was popular in both Antioch and Constantinople. In the latter city, the races were closely associated with political factions (the 'Blues' and the 'Greens'), and the Hippodrome functioned as a political forum as well as a racecourse. Although there are references to *gladiators in Antioch, there is no evidence that they ever appeared in Constantinople, and all references cease after the mid-fifth century. At the Trullan Synod in 692 Church authorities made a concerted effort to ban these activities, but mimic performance continued unofficially for at least another three centuries.

Indeed, ecclesiastical authorities appear to have found mimes particularly irksome, possibly because Christian practices provided so much material for mimic mockery. Gregory of Nazianzus, a father of the Eastern Church, complained in the fourth century of the depiction of 'comic Christians'; and in a series of decrees and edicts mime actors were deprived of Christian rights unless they repented of their activities. At the same time, Christians were clearly attracted to mimic performance and even appropriated mimic techniques for religious purposes. Arian Christians in particular seem to have been willing to incorporate mimetic gesture and inflection into their liturgy: their opponents referred to their service books as 'stage books'. Even the orthodox Nazianzus was said to follow the model of 'the Syracusan Sophron', a mime writer. Some mime actors in turn apparently became Christians and even earned canonization. Equally significant, the mime Theodora attained royal status when in 523 she married the Emperor Justinian. The Byzantine historian Proclus found this scandalous, but his pupil Choricius of Gaza more charitably defended the respectability and dignity of mimes.

There has been a temptation to find in this ambivalent attitude towards mimes the seed of a *religious theatre in Byzantium. The evidence, however, is not compelling. There are two para-theatrical forms that might have provided a catalyst for a religious theatre: the dramatic homily and the dramatic canticle. By the fifth century the Byzantine sermon included expositions in *dialogue of various biblical episodes, but it is unclear whether they were recited by one or by several members of the clergy. One of the more elaborate of these homilies was *The Encomium to the Mother of God Mariam* by Proclus of Constantinople (d. 447), which features not only the *characters of Mary, Joseph, and the Angel Gabriel, but a council of demons.

Two twelfth-century manuscripts containing sermons by Jacobus Coccinobaphus are illustrated with miniatures that seem theatrically inspired. The *kontakion*, chanted to music and also containing dialogue, had achieved a high level of sophistication by the seventh century when Sophranius, patriarch of Jerusalem, composed a group of twelve canticles intended to be sung during the Christmas service. There are, however, no indications in the *texts of scenic action or gesture, and there is no other evidence to suggest that the dramatic canticle evolved beyond oratorio.

In 949–50 and again in 968–9 Liudprand, bishop of Cremona, visited Constantinople and recorded that the 'capricious Greeks' celebrate the ascension of Elijah with 'scenic plays'; but he indicates no place of performance, and the reference could as easily be to secular mimes as to religious drama. In fact, the texts of only two religious plays have survived from the Byzantine period, both of them highly problematic. *Christos Paschon*, a play on the Passion, death, and Resurrection of Christ composed after the manner of classical *Greek *tragedy, dates from the eleventh or twelfth century, and was very likely never intended for performance. The second text, an outline of a *Passion play in a thirteenth-century manuscript, is more obviously theatrical in that it includes directions for gesture, movement, and *action,

but its immediate provenance was Cyprus, and we have no way of determining its exact date or the circumstances of its performance.

In other words, only wishful thinking can sustain the hypothesis that the dramatic homilies of the sixth century developed by the tenth century into a full-fledged *liturgical drama analogous to that of Western Europe. In a sense, there was no need for such a drama. The ability of a culture intrinsically theatrical in its institutionalized ceremonials to appropriate non-indigenous forms is demonstrated by a description in a manual of ceremonies observed at the Byzantine court (*c.*953) of a battle-play, in which reindeer-clad warriors, chanting in both Gothic and Greek, celebrated Old Testament heroes, praised the Emperor, and invoked Christ's blessing on the empire. In such a culture and in such a place there is no need to 'invent' drama: any *performance can be appropriately theatricized within the courtly-Christian framework.

RWV

BOGDANOS, THEODORE, 'Liturgical drama in Byzantine literature', *Comparative Drama*, 10 (1976)
LAPIANA, GEORGE, 'The Byzantine theatre', *Speculum*, 11 (1936)
STICCA, SANDRO, 'The *Christos Paschon* and the Byzantine theater', *Comparative Drama*, 8 (1974)

·C·

CABARET

Of all theatre forms and styles, cabaret is most clearly and quint-essentially of the modern era, a product of the cities and of the art and the artists of *modernism. It is European in origin but has American variations. It is uniquely mythologized, assuming a patina of the excessive and the decadent, the dangerous and the illicit, the sophisticated and the sexual. It has been imagined and re-created by artists in other media: in the fine art of Tou-louse Lautrec, Otto Dix, and George Grosz; in Christopher *Isherwood's *Berlin novels, *Mr Norris Changes Trains* (1935) and *Goodbye to Berlin* (1939); on stage with John *Van Druten's *I Am a Camera* and John *Kander and Fred Ebb's 1966 *musical *Cabaret*; in cinema in Josef von Sternberg's 1930 classic *Der Blaue Engel*, which along with Bob *Fosse's *film of *Cabaret* (1971) demonstrates that film has been particularly successful in capturing something of the raucous, sexual energy of the Berlin cabaret of the 1930s.

The word cabaret comes from the Spanish *caba retta* and the French *cabaret*, meaning tavern. It came to mean a small entertainment in an intimate setting that might be *improvised in whole or in part with a mixed fare of music, song, sketches, often commenting on social, economic, political, or artistic matters. The term, then, is applied to places of entertainment such as nightclubs as much as to the musical entertainments provided therein. Although it had antecedents in the eighteenth century, modern cabaret begins in *Paris at the time of the Third Republic and the founding of Le Chat Noir in bohemian Mont-martre in 1881. It was at this stage an *avant-garde entertain-ment for an elite and select *audience, but its popularity and audience soon grew. Other cabarets opened across Paris, and by the turn of the century similar venues and entertainments were established in several French and German cities. Le Chat Noir was a small venue seating only 60. It was elaborately designed in the style of Louis XIII and programmes included poetry read-ings and elaborate *shadow plays staged by leading artists. The venue's intimacy was a defining feature of the cabaret and led to the development of a new playing style that emphasized subtlety and preferred everyday and somewhat *naturalistic subjects. French *diseuse* Yvette *Guilbert was at the forefront of this style.

The French tradition remained strong with artists slipping between the intimacy of the cabaret stage and the elaborate, glamorous *revues of the Parisian nightclubs and *music halls such as the Casino de Paris, the *Folies-Bergère, and Le *Moulin-Rouge. From Guilbert to *Mistinguett, from Josephine *Baker to Édith *Piaf, from Maurice *Chevalier to Georges Guétary, Charles Trenet to Jacques Brel, the French tradition of cabaret has been eclectic and distinctively national. Although part of that tradition has been lost to the tourist buses and voyeuristic thrill seekers, the *chanson* and its performers, as well as the elaborate *spectacle of the Parisian revues, are unique contri-butions to popular theatre.

In Germany the tradition of cabaret was championed by the Bunte Bühne, the so-called Überbrettl, which was opened by Baron Ernst von Wolzogen (librettist of *Strauss's *Feuersnot*) and Otto Julius Bierbaum in Berlin in 1901. The same year saw two more developments, with the founding in Berlin of Schall und Rauch by Max *Reinhardt and actors from the *Deutsches Theater and in *Munich of the Elf Scharfrichter, where Frank *Wedekind performed. Munich was also the home of the Kathi Kobus, where the satirical writers and artists of the journal *Simplicissimus* could be seen. These cabarets were rather closer to the aesthetic project of Le Chat Noir than other venues as they tested what was new and experimental in the arts.

Elsewhere in Europe cabaret maintained this mixed econ-omy of popular excess and aesthetic and political experimen-tation, the latter strong at the Zielony Balonik in *Cracow and the Els Quatre Gats in *Barcelona. In Russia cabarets func-tioned as a fringe for the theatre community: Nikolai *Evreinov founded *Krivoe Zerkalo in *St Petersburg in 1908; the Brodyachaya Sobaka (1913–15) was associated with the *futurists; and the Prival Komediantov (1916–19) with *Meyerhold. In Zurich the infamous Cabaret Voltaire (1916–17) provided an appropriate space for Hans Arp and Tristan Tzara to develop *dada.

Within two decades, and despite the impact of the First World War, cabaret was flourishing in the German capital, where it maintained associations with a counter-culture and anti-establishment sentiments. Despite the fact that some German cabarets were subject to heavy *censorship, performers used the cabaret stage, with its mixed bill of sketches, jazz, torch songs, and transvestism, to make a real social statement. Kurt Tucholsky identified *Kabarett* as a socially and politically engaged form, in which a company developed a highly structured programme around a particular theme or themes. *Kabarett* of the period include Trude Hesterberg's Wilde Bühne (1921), the Katakombe (1929), and the Tingel-Tangel (1930). Political *satire was a principal feature of the cabaret of the 1920s and 1930s in Germany, where Kurt *Weill and Hanns Eisler were protagonists. Under the liberal Weimar Republic cabaret achieved mythical status. By 1935, however, all the Berlin cabarets were closed in the aftermath of Hitler's declaration of martial law, reinstating censorship and strict social controls.

In the USA cabaret evolved several interconnected forms, almost all satellites of the nightclub: the shows of the supper rooms of *New York in the 1950s with swing bands, big bands, and lounge singers; the entertainers, composers, and lyricists drawn from Broadway shows; the modern extravaganzas of Las Vegas; and the forms and traditions of *gay culture are none of them cabaret proper but all owe something to the fact and mythology of the form. Amongst the performers of modern American cabaret is Bette Midler, whose first success as a singer came at the cabaret at the gay Continental Baths in New York. Utterly camp, sassy to the limits of brazenness, and dripping satirical wit, 'The Devine Miss M' has spawned myriad cross-dressed imitators (*see* FEMALE IMPERSONATION).

In England cabaret was a rather more genteel form, more like an intimate revue than its French or German counterparts. Nevertheless, something of the *Kabarett* spirit was aspired to by *Auden in *The Ascent of F6* (1936), which included songs set to music by Benjamin Britten. Later Noël *Coward and Marlene Dietrich entertained at elite venues like the Café de Paris, while Peter Cook's the Establishment (1961) attempted to extend the success of the satirical *Beyond the Fringe* revue to a fashionable after-hours club in *London. The sleazier cabaret circuit of Soho evolved in the late 1970s and 1980s into an alternative cabaret scene that re-established stand-up comedy as a popular and vibrant form of entertainment, while more recently the Pizza on the Park and Langans have re-established sophisticated jazz-based cabaret for the metropolitan market.   AS

APPIGNANESI, LISA, *Cabaret* (London, 1984)

BUDZINSKI, KLAUS, *Das Kabarett* (Düsseldorf, 1985)

JELAVICH, PETER, *Berlin Cabaret* (Cambridge, Mass., 1996)

RICHARD, LIONEL, *Cabaret, cabarets: origines et décadence* (Paris, 1991)

SEGEL, HAROLD B., *Turn-of-the-Century Cabaret: Paris, Barcelona, Berlin, Munich, Vienna, Cracow, Moscow, St. Petersburg, Zurich* (New York, 1987)

SENELICK, LAURENCE, *Cabaret Performance: Europe, 1890–1940*, 2 vols. (New York, 1989, 1992)

CABRUJAS, JOSÉ IGNACIO (1937–95)

Venezuelan director, actor, and scriptwriter, one of the most important *Latin American playwrights. He made his debut as an actor with the Teatro de la Universidad Central, and while there wrote *Juan Francisco de León* (1959) and *La sopa de piedra* (*Stone Soup*, 1960). In 1961 he studied at the *Piccolo Teatro in *Milan. On his return he staged his plays *El extraño viaje de Simón el malo* (*The Strange Journey of Simon the Evil*, 1961), *Los insurgentes* (*The Insurgents*, 1962), and wrote or co-wrote a number of works such as *Triángulo* (1962), *En nombre del rey* (*In the King's Name*, 1963), *Días de poder* (*Days of Power*), *Testimonio* (1967), *Profundo* (*Deep*, 1971), and *Acto cultural* (*Cultural Act*, 1976). In 1967 he formed El *Nuevo Grupo together with Román *Chalbaud and Isaac *Chocrón. After 1976 he turned his attention to writing soaps for *television. Other plays include *El día que me quieras* (*The Day You Love Me*, 1979), *Una noche oriental* (*An Eastern Night*, 1983), and *Autorretrato de artista con barba y pumpá* (*Self-Portrait of the Artist with a Beard and Top Hat*, 1990). His last play was *Sonny* (1995), a version of *Othello* about the life of a boxer.   LCL trans. AMCS

CAFÉ-CONCERT

Also known as *cafés-chantants*, *Paris cafés that employed a few singers and musicians and that flourished from the Second Empire to the *belle époque*. At a *caf'-conc'*, a labourer, often accompanied by his family, could relax with a drink while listening to a selection of songs geared to the local clientele, whether melodic musings on daily life, risqué numbers, comic ditties, rousing patriotic songs, or lyrics brimming with political *satire. Some establishments encouraged patrons to join in the refrain, and because customers were expected to continue ordering drinks, the atmosphere could become rowdy. A working-class *caf'-conc'* might be familiarly termed a *beuglant* (bull-roaring). Yet the singers and their pianists were required to wear evening clothes (*see* AUDIENCE DRESS). Large *cafés-concerts* might even hire *poseuses*, well-dressed ladies whose presence among the patrons lent an air of respectability. Around 1900, Paris boasted about 265 *cafés-concerts*. The best known were the Alcazar, the Eden-Concert, the Eldorado, and the Ba-Ta-Clan. These names proliferated on establishments in provincial towns as the phenomenon spread. The popularity of this 'democratized theatre' and its offspring—the more intimate and intellectual *cabaret, the *variety entertainment of the *music halls—was seen as a threat by *legitimate theatre owners. Special issues on *café-concert* were published by both *Paris illustré* (1886) and *Le Figaro illustré* (1896). Though critics deplored the lowering of taste and drunkenness facilitated by *cafés-concerts*, it was only with the rise of *film that the 'temples of song' declined.

FHL

CAFFE CINO

*New York coffee house that became one of the first performance spaces of the *Off-Off Broadway movement. Joseph Cino opened the café in 1958, and simultaneously opened his doors to a variety of poets, musicians, actors, and playwrights who would become the nucleus of New York's *avant-garde in the 1960s. Some of the important playwrights who made use of Caffe Cino's tiny 2.4-m (8-foot) square *stage were Lanford *Wilson, Maria Irene *Fornés, Sam *Shepard, Megan *Terry, John *Guare, and Jean-Claude *Van Itallie. Ellen *Stewart's *La Mama Experimental Theatre Club eclipsed Caffe Cino in importance after the space was destroyed by *fire in 1965.

JAB

CAILLEAU, HUBERT (c.1526–90)

Stage designer and artist. Cailleau was designer of the *Passion performance at Valenciennes in 1547 (*see* BIBLICAL PLAYS). Thirty years later he provided the illustrations for two manuscripts documenting the performance. Each manuscript features a frontispiece depicting the stage, and miniatures illustrating each of the 25 days of performance. Although the pictures must be read carefully (only twelve of the estimated 70 *mansions appear in the frontispieces), Cailleau's art is a precious witness to late *medieval performance. (*See* illustration, p. 831.)   RWV

CAI LUONG

A reformed form of popular *Vietnamese sung drama. It took form by 1918 from ballad traditions mixed with *hat boi* melodies and techniques. The south has always been the focus of activity. The language is mostly colloquial, while the movements, gestures, and *scenery stress *realism much more than the traditional theatre. Actors use their natural voice, not singing falsetto. Due to the large number of southern Chinese in Saigon and other southern cities, the 1920s saw significant *Chinese influence, especially from Cantonese opera (*yueju*), the *cai luong* absorbing elements of such features as its *make-up, *costumes, scenery, and *plots. However, the *dialogue and music were determinedly Vietnamese. The popular love lament 'Vong co' ('Remembrances'), written by Cao Van Lau in 1920, became

absorbed into the *cai luong* and remains prominent to this day. The content of the *cai luong* includes Vietnamese and Chinese historical incidents, but most items are set in the present or recent past and deal with contemporary issues. In the 1930s *cai luong* underwent much Western influence, with adaptations of Western plays such as *Hamlet* and *Mary Stuart*. *Cai luong* items have often been used as *political propaganda, for example against the French during the 1946–54 war.   CPM

CAIRD, JOHN (1948–)

Canadian director who has worked extensively in England for the *Royal Shakespeare Company (as an associate director since 1977) and the Royal *National Theatre. His collaborations with director Trevor *Nunn at the RSC led to the epic productions of David *Edgar's *Nicholas Nickleby* (1980) and the *musical *Les Misérables* (1985). Caird has directed other large-scale productions including Andrew *Lloyd Webber's *Song and Dance* (1982), and a spectacular *Peter Pan* (RNT, 1997) with designer John *Napier. Caird has an interest in Ben *Jonson's work, staging *Every Man in his Humour* (1986), and *The New Inn* (1987) at the RSC's *Swan Theatre. At the RSC he also produced innovative interpretations of *A Midsummer Night's Dream* (1989) and *As You Like It* (1989), strong in directorial and design concepts. In the late 1990s during Nunn's tenure at the RNT Caird demonstrated versatility with new drama: Pam *Gems's *Stanley* (1996) and Charlotte Jones's *The Humble Boy* (2001).   KN

CAIRO

Al-Qahira (the [city] Victorious) in Arabic, the capital of Egypt and the largest city in *Africa. The site Cairo occupies has been settled for more than 6,000 years and has served as the centre of a number of Egyptian civilizations. Its modernity, and the accompanying rise in theatrical activity, was prompted by the Khedive Ismail, viceroy under Ottoman suzerainty (1863–79). Impressed with Baron Haussmann's reconstruction of Paris, Ismail wished to make Egypt a part of Europe. But he also wished to retain the city's connections to its past, which meant that old Cairo was to be kept almost intact while a new city was constructed to the west of it. The juxtaposition of the ancient and modern is at the heart of Cairo's culture, an issue taken up in the theatre through the work of Yacub *Sannu and Naguib el-*Rihany. With the end of British colonization in the 1952 coup and the Suez War of 1956, President Gamal Abdel-Nasser could easily legitimize his own socialist-oriented, Pan-Arab nationalism. Vilifying or erasing earlier social and political orders as either foreign or unpatriotic, Nasser's state deployed its ideological machinery in all sectors, theatre being foremost among the arts chosen to propagate a narrative of progress under a forward-looking nation-state. The period saw the rise of a generation of epoch-making directors, most of them young talents just back from state-funded *training abroad, who introduced *modernist and predominantly *avant-garde stage practices that helped shape the interpretations of the period's major dramatists, including Numan *Ashur, Mahmoud *Diab, Alfred *Farag, Yussuf *Idris, Mikhail *Ruman, Salah *Abdel-Sabour, Ali *Salem, Naguib *Surur, and Saad Eddin *Wahba. Not unexpectedly, this creative collision was instantly hailed as the theatrical renaissance of the 1960s.

The period introduced many of the key issues that still shape contemporary Egyptian theatre. Paramount among them was a struggle over the primacy of the *text. 'Serious' Egyptian playwrights saw themselves as men of letters with a vision—for them popular traditions of performance, not to mention the intrusions of auteuristic *directors, were an unwelcome disturbance. But the humiliating 1967 military defeat at the hands of Israel led Egypt—and, given Egypt's cultural hegemony over the region, the Arab world—to re-examine the cultural assumptions on which its top-down modernizing project had been predicated. Only then was the literary model seriously challenged (though never completely abandoned); indigenous performance traditions, whether deployed experimentally or commercially, were now seen as legitimate alternatives.

Also crucial to the post-1967 transformations was the so-called crisis of the theatre. From the 1970s the private commercial theatres gained the upper hand, driven by the patronage of a new moneyed class, while the bureaucratic government-run theatres were left floundering, treated indifferently by the state and abandoned by an *audience now suspicious of the modernizing movements of the 1960s. Contrary to the literary dramatists' glorification of text, the private theatres' fare tends to avoid clear narrative and sophisticated *dialogue. Making clever, sometimes opportunistic use of indigenous performance traditions, the typical ingredients of a commercial play consist of 'gags, puns, mimicry . . . physical buffoonery, and wild verbal exaggerations that make the most humdrum thing appear droll, fantastic or *grotesque; and, of course, a song or two for every star and lots of *dancing', as Nehad Selaiha put it. After poking shameless fun at almost everything modern or institutional for three to four hours, a play typically concludes with 'the usual, almost mandatory, dose of sentimentality and hypocritical preaching'.

An alternative to the commercial and state-subsidized sectors arose in 1987–8 with the free theatre movement. Consisting of young theatre enthusiasts with varying levels of training and artistic merit, the movement established an independent production model free of state control and the dictates of the *box office. When the 1990 Cairo International Festival for Experimental Theatre (founded 1988) was cancelled in response to the Iraqi invasion of Kuwait, the *fringe troupes organized their own *festival. In addition to the distinctive male voices it has produced (including *directors and *dramaturgs Khaled El-Sawy, Mohamed Aboul-Seoud, and Ahmed El-Attar) the free

theatre movement has given rise to a number of women directors, including Effat Yehia. Though the last free theatre festival was held in 1991, the movement has significantly re-invigorated the state's cultural machinery. The movement leader Khaled Galal (1967–   ) was appointed *artistic director of the state-run Ash-Shabab (*Youth) Theatre in 1997, the youngest person ever to assume such a key position. Yet, with the possible exception of Al-*Warsha company, at the start of the twenty-first century the free theatre faction itself seemed moribund, a development that poses vexing questions about the inevitability of containment through funding (*see* FINANCE) or *censorship.

In the 1960s the alliance between the government and the intelligentsia proved all the more dismal, with the former setting its repressive apparatus to work where the ideological one failed. Many playwrights turned to *historical and mythical settings to hide *political messages. Under Nasser these messages typically blamed the well-meaning head of state for surrounding himself with corrupt advisers and alienating himself from the voice of the people. Such were the themes of Diab's *Bab El-Futuh* (*The Gateway to Conquest*, 1971) and Salem's *Enta Elli Qattalt El-Wahsh* (*You Killed the Beast*, 1970). Similar references became almost a regular fare under Anwar El-Sadat's turbulent and largely authoritarian rule throughout the 1970s. When Hosni Mubarak became president in 1981, he was keen to return to a freer and more democratic atmosphere, which included the relaxation of much official censorship. But the emergency powers installed by Sadat in 1981 remained in place, perhaps as a reminder that the state would always be on guard.

Yet in 2002 the ageing nationalist-modernist discourse contends not only with the drive for globalization but also with an array of traditionalist discourses. These run the gamut from the state-sanctioned, professedly apolitical version of Islam to revolutionary militant Islamism with its embarrassing appropriation of nationalist discourse into one of *jihad* (holy struggle). Similarly conservative voices, typically middle-class ones, regularly forage works of art for the whiff of dissidence, condemning offenders publicly and calling on the censor to ban them on grounds of immorality. *Religion and socio-religious issues, rather than politics themselves, are today's unsafe territory for the theatre.

Whatever the ultimate judgement on the post-1967 cultural transformations, one can argue with Armbrust that they represent facets of Egyptian postmodernity. Like Egyptian modernity, however, this postmodernity may emerge as too complex a phenomenon to lend itself to a simple analogy with its Western counterpart. Indeed, in defying any recognizable closure, postmodern Egypt may be taking after Egypt's metropolis: the new not overlaid on the old, but rather sharing the same space in a tacit and unresolved tension.   HMA

ARMBRUST, WALTER, *Mass Culture and Modernism in Egypt* (New York, 1996)

CARLSON, MARVIN (ed.), *Contemporary Theatre in Egypt* (New York, 1999)

CALCUTTA *See* KOLKATA.

CALDERÓN DE LA BARCA, PEDRO (1600–81)

Spanish dramatist. Born in Madrid, and destined for the Church by his authoritarian father, he studied with the Jesuits and at university in Alcalá and Salamanca, but refused in 1621 to become a priest. He saw his first plays performed in the next few years, and probably wrote more in the 1620s than was previously supposed; three famous works date from 1629, and an early version of *La vida es sueño* (*Life Is a Dream*) now appears to have been written by then. By the mid-1630s he was the dramatist most favoured by the court (and already the leading writer of *autos sacramentales), and in 1637 was made a Knight of Santiago. Having served and been wounded in Catalonia, he wrote far less in the 1640s (when the theatres were often closed), and in 1651 finally entered the priesthood. He ceased to work directly for the *corrales, but produced until his death a stream of spectacular plays and *operas for the court, and monopolized the composition of *auto* for *Madrid. Thus he dominated theatre in Spain for almost half a century, as had Lope de *Vega before him. Altogether he wrote nearly 80 *autos* and more than 100 *comedias, plus a dozen in collaboration and a number of shorter works.

His plays are distinguished by intellectual depth and immaculate craftsmanship. Significantly, he wrote new versions of several of the most famous, and many are reworkings of plays by others. He perfected the *comedia* formula by imposing his own stylization. His *plots are tautly constructed, with relatively few shifts of scene and a limited range of metrics. Though every play is unique, the recurrence of situations, motifs, and symbols is in line with his concentration on characteristic themes: the interaction between the individual and society, freedom and constraint, illusion and reality, and above all passion and reason. Such conflicts both between and within his *characters are very clearly set out, often by the use of patterned exchanges and asides or in extended *monologues. His language is highly wrought, replete with rhetorical devices. His systematized exploitation of images of elemental discord reflects an essentially sombre view of our existence *vis-à-vis* the eternal. Though an orthodox Christian, he offers no complacent solutions to his characters' dilemmas, which are all the more intense for being of their own and others' making.

Life Is a Dream, his most performed play, charts the development of a prince whose father, to avert the acts of violence his horoscope predicted, has imprisoned him in secret from birth, but now has him brought to court for a test of his fitness to rule.

He fails it and is persuaded it was a dream, but learns thereby that all human life is dreamlike. Freed by rebels, he defeats and castigates but then submits to his father, demonstrating that free-willed virtue and prudence can master our baser instincts. His story is both counterpointed and crucially influenced by that of a woman who similarly succeeds in vindicating her identity and honour. Though also concerned with the proper use of power, the play embodies fundamentally a philosophy of life.

Many almost equally famous works are more specifically religious, like *El mágico prodigioso* (*The Prodigious Magician*, 1637), a *Faust*-like *saint-play, *El príncipe constante* (*The Constant Prince*, 1629), a celebration of Christian fortitude, and *La cisma de Inglaterra* (1627), an account of the English schism often compared and contrasted with Shakespeare's *Henry VIII*. Other plays are much more open to diverse interpretation. Three especially in which—as in *El pintor de su deshonra* (*The Painter of Dishonour*, c.1645–50)—a husband murders his wife on suspicion of adultery seem shockingly unchristian. Calderón is traditionally supposed to have seen their *protagonists as exemplary, but today, especially outside Spain, these *tragedies are seen as far more complex works, meant to force their spectators to question ingrained habits of thought. Less disturbing, apparently more *realistic but hardly less controversial, is *El alcalde de Zalamea* (*The Mayor of Zalamea*, 1636). Its protagonist exceeds his civic authority by garrotting the nobly born captain by whom his own daughter has been raped. He persuades the 'Prudent King' Philip II that his action was just and wise, but it can be seen alternatively as devious revenge.

Calderón's best works in lighter vein are his cloak-and-sword *comedies, like *La dama duende* (*The Phantom Lady*) or *Casa con dos puertas* (*A House with Two Doors*, both 1629); in both of these a resourceful girl, confounding attempts to confine her, gets to marry the man she loves. The entertainment they richly provide may be all their author was seeking, but he may have been subtly addressing serious social issues too. By contrast with such *comedias*, his palace plays and operas on mythological subjects exploited fully the use of music and elaborate scenic effects, but within their obligatory celebration of royal power and pomp have been shown to embody careful comments on fundamental (and even specific) matters of state. Perhaps his most remarkable works, however, are his *autos sacramentales*, for many of which his own detailed staging instructions have been preserved. *El gran teatro del mundo* (*The Great Theatre of the World*, c.1633–4) is the one most often produced, but many others are more inventive. Fully versed in theology, he used all manner of *allegories to bring its complexities to life on stage, and thereby gave the *mystery play a range, depth, and dynamism unparalleled elsewhere.

The Golden Age (*see* EARLY MODERN PERIOD IN EUROPE) dramatist most widely known and performed in and since his day, he was hugely influential in nineteenth-century Germany, and is still popular there and in France. *Grotowski's version of *The Constant Prince* won universal acclaim, and other works are played worldwide, especially of course in Spain. Memorable performances in Britain include the *National Theatre's *The Mayor of Zalamea* (1981) and *The Painter of Dishonour* at Stratford (1994). A collaborative production of *Life Is a Dream* was mounted in *Edinburgh, *New York, *London, and Madrid (1998–2000). But much of Calderón's diverse output remains to be revealed.   VFD

CALDWELL, JAMES H. (1793–1863)

American *actor-manager. A pioneering manager in the Louisiana Territory, he came to Charleston as an actor in 1816 but soon embarked on management in developing cities to the west. He established New Orleans's first English-language theatre, and his Camp Street Theatre, opened in 1823, was the first theatre in the country with gas *lighting. Caldwell's interest in gas extended to founding a municipal gasworks, and he retired from theatre management in 1833. Returning in 1835, he built the grand *St Charles Theatre, to compete with Noah *Ludlow and Sol *Smith. The St Charles burned in 1842, bankrupting him.   AHK

CALDWELL, ZOË (1934–)

Australian-American actress and director. Born in Australia, Caldwell made her reputation at the *Shakespeare Memorial Theatre in England and the *Stratford Festival in Canada in the late 1950s, then in the United States, where she understudied Anne Bancroft in *The Devils* (1965). Her career was centred in *New York after her marriage to manager-director Robert Whitehead. Her deep, rich voice and her vivid movements were suited for larger-than-life roles in such plays as *Slapstick Tragedy* (1966) and *The Prime of Miss Jean Brodie* (1968), as well as in *Medea* (1982) and as diva Maria Callas in *McNally's *Master Class* (1996). She received Tony *awards for these sharply contrasting parts. She also acted in McNally's *A Perfect Ganesh* (1995), and directed *Vita and Virginia* (1996), both *Off-Broadway. Caldwell is known for the thoroughness of her preparation and the details in her performances; she used Lillian *Hellman's own brand of perfume for *Lillian* (1985). Despite her reputation as a major actress, she appeared in only one major *film, *The Purple Rose of Cairo* (1985).   AW

CALI

Colombian city with a theatre tradition harking back to colonial times. A *loa* (usually a curtain raiser) was performed in 1760 to commemorate the crowning of the King of Spain, and sporadic performances of *tragedies, *comedies, and *zarzuelas (*operettas) were well received. Cali's Municipal Theatre opened its doors in 1927 with an *opera by the Adolfo Bracale Company.

But Cali entered the national scene with the founding in 1953 of an *amateur group by Octavio Marulanda, affiliated with the Instituto Popular de Cultura. In 1955 the Bellas Artes Institute created the Escuela Departamental de Teatro, bringing Cayetano Luca de Tena from Spain to direct it. A year later the young director and playwright Enrique *Buenaventura took over, and in 1958 gained attention with his *A la diestra de Dios Padre* (*At the Right Hand of God the Father*) at the Second National Theatre Festival in *Bogotá. Buenaventura has remained the director of the group, which in 1966 changed its name to Teatro *Experimental de Cali (TEC), and for more than a generation it was regarded as a model throughout *Latin America, inspired largely by Buenaventura's method of *collective creation, an anti-authoritarian, participatory theatre process designed to subvert traditional concepts of drama. The influence Buenaventura and his group have exercised can be measured by the number of groups created by TEC's former or associate members: Grutela (1970) and Teatro Imaginario (1981), directed by Danilo Tenorio; La Máscara (1974), an all-woman ensemble, directed by Lucy Bolaños; Grupo de Teatro el Taller (1975) by Guillermo Piedrahita; Colectivo de Teatro de Cali (1990) by Aída Fernández; and Barco Ebrio (1994), among others. Another group that has left its mark in Cali is Esquina Latina (1973), founded by Orlando Cajarmarca. Originally a student ensemble, it is now an independent troupe dedicated to developing skills among minorities and to channelling their energy towards social projects. Some of its best-known plays are *El enmaletado* (*The Man in a Valise*, 1986), and *Homenaje a Leo* (1991), celebrating the national poet León de Greiff, both written and directed by Cajamarca.   BJR

CALL BOYS

Familiar from the eighteenth century in European and American theatres, boys were required to call performers on stage from dressing rooms or the *green room and to hand them *properties. They also informed actors needed for *rehearsal the following day. In England they usually summoned actors by name, in America by *character, in France by bell.   JTD

CALLOW, SIMON (1949–)

English actor, director, and writer. After a *London debut in 1975, Callow joined *Joint Stock in 1977 and appeared in *Hare's *Fanshen* and *Brenton's *Epsom Downs*. For the Royal *National Theatre Callow has appeared as Orlando in *As You Like It* (1978), *Mozart in *Shaffer's *Amadeus* (1979), the Little Monk in *Brecht's *Galileo* (1980), and Face in *Jonson's *The Alchemist* (1996). His numerous *films have included *Amadeus* (1983), *A Room with a View* (1986), *Four Weddings and a Funeral* (1994), and *Jefferson in Paris* (1995). In *musical theatre he has directed Johann Strauss's *Die Fledermaus* for Scottish Opera

(1989) and *Rodgers and *Hammerstein's *Carmen Jones* for the *Old Vic (1991), while his debut as a film director was with *The Ballad of the Sad Café* (1991). Unusually articulate and literate, his books include *Being an Actor* (autobiography, 1984), the biographies *Charles Laughton: a difficult actor* (1987), *Orson Welles: the road to Xanadu* (1995), and reminiscences of the agent Peggy Ramsay, *Love Is Where It Falls* (1999). He has also written a short history of the RNT, *The National* (1997).

AS

CALMET, HÉCTOR (c.1946–   )

Argentine scene designer and teacher. After training at the Theatre Institute of the Universidad de Buenos Aires, Calmet designed Abelardo Castillo's *Israfel* in 1966. Since then he has designed myriad productions, served as technical director of both the Teatro *Colón and the Teatro *Cervantes, and taught private students. He has designed Argentine works such as Ricardo *Halac's *Segundo tiempo* (*Second Half*), Roberto *Cossa's *El viejo criado* (*The Old Servant*), and Eduardo *Pavlovsky's *El señor Langsner*, in addition to numerous works from the international repertory.

AV

CALMO, ANDREA (1509–71)

Venetian comic dramatist and performer. He wrote six *comedies in a popular vein for a wide range of performing resources. In each one there is a part for a comic Venetian merchant speaking in dialect, a role which he performed himself: he thus imitated *Ruzante, with whom he may have worked, as a semi-professional practitioner who developed his own 'mask'. This makes him a figure of transition between scripted *commedia erudita* and improvised *commedia dell'arte*.

RAA

CALONARANG See BARONG.

CALVERT, LOUIS (1859–1923)

English actor. Son of English provincial actors, Calvert began acting in South Africa and Australia. Upon his return to England in 1880 he established himself with the companies of Henry *Irving and Beerbohm *Tree, and was also featured with the *Vedrenne–Barker management (1904–7), playing in *Shaw's plays. Calvert was an accomplished Shakespearian actor, and he was widely praised for his Creon in the *Martin-Harvey production of *Oedipus Rex* (1912). He also organized companies that *toured in England and the United States, and proved to be an accomplished *director. He wrote *Problems of the Actor* (1918).

TP

CAMBODIA

In one Cambodian origin myth related in a tenth-century stone inscription, a celestial dancer unites with a sage, together becoming the progenitors of the Khmer. Thus, according to this legend, the mother of Cambodia's people was a dancer. *Dance, music, and drama, in many ways inseparable in Cambodian tradition, have been at the heart of Khmer cultural identity for over 1,000 years. (Ethnic Khmer make up 90 per cent or so of Cambodia's population.) As far back as the early seventh century inscriptions tell of dancers associated with temples. The Khmer Empire of Angkor (ninth to fifteenth centuries), centred in north-western Cambodia, spread over much of what is now mainland South-East Asia, and had a lasting impact on artistic, spiritual, and political life in the region. Intricate and extensive carvings of the heavens, as well as palace and village scenes on the walls of Angkor's great stone temples, attest to the importance of music and dance in idealized and actual existence. The Khmer royalty, which moved its palaces from Angkor to several other places before settling in Phnom Penh in the mid-1800s, has maintained dramatic troupes for communication with the deities, for display of prowess, and for entertainment for centuries, with the *Reamker*, the Khmer version of the Indian Ramayana epic, forming a core part of the repertoire. One of the earliest known literary works composed in Khmer, the sixteenth- or seventeenth-century *text of the *Reamker*, is believed to have been a libretto for performance. A seventh-century inscription mentions dancers and musicians offered to a tree spirit as well as a temple. Indeed, performance is seen as a means of linking the human and the supernatural worlds, whether on behalf of the monarch, a village, temple, or family. The divine, for the Khmer, is found in a rich amalgam of animist, brahmanic, and Buddhist beliefs and practices, with Theravada Buddhism having dominated religious culture since around the fourteenth century.

Village-based theatrical traditions have been commonly associated with Buddhist temples. The temple or a wealthy patron may hire troupes to perform *ayang* (small *shadow puppets), *yikey* (folk opera), *ayai* (improvised, comic repartee singing), or *lakhon bassac* (musical drama with martial arts-like movements). They normally play on makeshift stages in the temple complex on ceremonial occasions. The *Trot*, an itinerant dance in Siem Reap and Battambang provinces that represents a deer hunt, begins at the local temple. Troupes proceed for days or weeks on foot, performing the story of the chase and eventual execution of the deer along the way. The deer is thought to figure danger, and the potential disruption of the agricultural cycle. *Trot* troupes collect money and goods for their temple from onlookers; while the *audience receives religious merit by making such offerings. *Tunsaong* is another example of a village performance rite, one associated with the Peur ethnic group. It enacts the enchantment of a hunter and a tiger by an ox-mating dance they happen upon, and is part of ceremonies held in homage to ancestral spirits.

With dramatic changes in Cambodia's political climate, performance has seen drastic shifts as well. From the royalist days of the mid-twentieth century to the early 1970s when, during the republic, royal words in classical dance-dramas were replaced; to the late 1970s when close to 90 per cent of the country's professional artists perished under the harsh conditions of the Khmer Rouge regime; to the communist rule of the 1980s when *lakhon niyey* (spoken drama) and *lakhon bassac* troupes toured the countryside with messages of support for the government in its ongoing civil war; to the return of the royalty in the 1990s and the beginning of a new millennium, with a princess (and former star dancer of the court), Norodom Buppha Devi, as the Minister of Culture and Fine Arts—in all this the performing artists have created, lost, and created anew bodies of work that mark their heritage and their new circumstances.

Phnom Penh boasts performance troupes of all genres: classical (or court) dance (*lakhon kbach boran* or *lakhon preah reach troap*), folk dance (*robam propeiney*), all-male dance-drama (*lakhon khol*), *folk opera (*yikey*), musical drama with origins among the Khmer in southern Vietnam (*lakhon bassac*), improvised repartee signing (*ayai*), large and small shadow puppets (*sbaek thom* and *ayang*), and spoken drama (*lakhon niyey*), among others, mainly centred at the Ministry of Culture's Department of Arts and the Royal University of Fine Arts. Performance venues are hard to find, however, as theatres were sold or closed in the late 1990s, the majestic Bassac Theatre burned down, and the Chatomuk Theatre became a government conference hall. In 2000, improvements to a theatre at the Royal University of Fine Arts made it the main site of professional performances in the city. *Amateur and professional troupes are found throughout the country as well. But the popularity and low cost of videos (mostly imported) and karaoke, combined with the loss of talented artists in the 1970s, has threatened the survival of many performance troupes, and even forms, for years. The Ministry of Culture and Fine Arts periodically sponsors national festivals, inviting performers from all regions of Cambodia, to encourage perpetuation, appreciation, and revival of traditional performance genres.   TSP

PHIM, TONI SAMANTHA, and THOMPSON, ASHLEY, *Dance in Cambodia* (Oxford, 1999)

CAMBRIDGE FESTIVAL THEATRE

Opened by Terence *Gray in 1926 within the fabric of the *Theatre Royal, Barnwell, which had been built by William Wilkins in 1808 as part of the former Norwich circuit. Though the new design stressed Gray's sympathies with the *expressionist style (it incorporated a *revolve, *cyclorama, and the latest *lighting), the *auditorium retained many of its original Georgian features,

and the playing space its pronounced *forestage (even though the surviving *proscenium arch was removed). Intimacy between actor and spectator was effected by a stepped descent from the forestage to two wide exit aisles through the *stalls, all frequently deployed in performance. Repertory, starting times, and an on-site restaurant catered to students, as did the scheduling of performances into short eight-week seasons matching the university terms. To accommodate a weekly changing programme, Gray, influenced by *Craig, *Appia, and current German production styles, devised architectural design schemes, which, by being built from differently sized pillars and rostra, could be rapidly altered. Mood was created by shifts in the coloured lighting. Till he left the Festival in 1933, Gray established there England's first example of *director's theatre, where every production followed a precise concept, exploring an audacious *metatheatricality to question the nature of performance.   RAC

CAMERI THEATRE

Tel Aviv repertory theatre founded in 1944. Its first major success was Moshe Shamir's *He Walked in the Fields* (1948), an Israeli drama grounded in the reality of kibbutz life and the War of Independence. The Cameri became associated with young Israeli playwrights, notably Hanoch *Levin, and in 1971 was transformed from a *collective run by a council of actors to the Municipal Theatre of Tel Aviv. The theatre stages ten new productions per year in its main *playhouse and in other venues, playing to a socially varied *audience of nearly 500,000 a year. Since its inception it has staged more than 400 productions and has *toured regularly in Israel and abroad. In 2001 the Cameri was under the direction of Noam Semel and Omri Nitzan, who have established it as a socially relevant enterprise.   EN

CAMPBELL, BARTLEY (1843–88)

American playwright. Born in Pennsylvania of Irish stock, Campbell came to the theatre after a failed journalistic career. *Peril* (1871) attracted the actor R. M. Hooley's notice and, working with him between 1872 and 1876, Campbell produced eleven forgettable full-length plays. Striking out on his own, he staged his own work in *London and *Philadelphia but was nearly destitute when *My Partner* opened in *New York (1879) to enormous acclaim. He quickly followed with *The Galley Slave* (1879), *The White Slave* (1882), and *Separation* (1884). He became mentally ill in 1886 and died institutionalized.

GAR

CAMPBELL, DOUGLAS (1922–)

Canadian actor and director, born in Glasgow. He first performed with the *Old Vic company during its 1941–2 *tour of *Medea* with Sybil *Thorndike. A charter-member of the *Stratford Festival in Ontario, he starred in such larger-than-life roles as Oedipus (1955), Othello (1959), Lear (1985), and Falstaff (1956, 1958, 2001), and directed *The Winter's Tale* (1958), *Julius Caesar* (1965, 1998), and *The Country Wife* (1995). Coupled with Tom Patterson, he formed the Canadian Players (1954–66) with Stratford actors who toured Canada during the winter months. Associate director of the *Guthrie Theatre, Minneapolis, in its opening season (1963), he was its *artistic director in 1965.   PBON

CAMPBELL, KEN (1941–   )

English actor, playwright, and director. He founded the Ken Campbell Roadshow in the late 1960s, *touring its anarchic *comedy and clowning around theatres, pubs, and working men's clubs. He wrote the *book for the *musical *Bendigo* (1974), and his Science Fiction Theatre of Liverpool produced *The Great Caper* (1974) and *Illuminatus!* (1976). In 1979 he directed the 22-hour play *The Warp* at the ICA in *London. Campbell became *artistic director of Liverpool's Everyman Theatre in 1980. His idiosyncratic *one-person shows, part stand-up comedy, part eccentric lecture, include *The Bald Trilogy* (1993) and *Ken Campbell's History of Comedy* (2000).   SF

CAMPBELL, MRS PATRICK (BEATRICE STELLA TANNER) (1865–1940)

English actress who *toured with Ben *Greet's company as Rosalind, Viola, and Helena, but then found herself at the *Adelphi in *London in George Sims's *melodramas. She made a sensation in *Pinero's *The Second Mrs Tanqueray* (*St James's Theatre, 1893) and also played the fallen woman in his *The Notorious Mrs Ebbsmith* (1895). She had leading roles throughout the 1890s for George *Alexander and *Forbes-Robertson, and still convinced as the original Eliza Doolittle at the age of 49, opposite Beerbohm *Tree, in *Shaw's *Pygmalion* (1914). In her heyday she was a tall, willowy, Pre-Raphaelite beauty, with large dark eyes, a rich voice, and obvious star quality, but she rapidly became known as capricious and unprofessional. She wished to be taken seriously and to produce uncommon modern plays, but was constantly driven to pot-boilers to pay her frequent debts; however, she did play the Rat-Wife and Rita in *Ibsen's *Little Eyolf* (1896), Mélisande in *Maeterlinck's *Pelléas and Mélisande* in both English and French (1897), Electra (1908), and George Sand in *Bjørnson's *Madame Sand* (1920). Her correspondence with Shaw reveals a fascinating love–hate relationship; he wrote *Caesar and Cleopatra* for her, though she declined it. In later life she became fat and still more capricious, and refused to take supporting roles on stage; but she continued with *radio work, and appeared in several *films.   EEC

CAMPESINO, EL TEATRO

A *Chicano theatre troupe founded by Luís *Valdez and a group of striking farmworkers in Delano, California, in 1965. Under Valdez's guidance, the Teatro members, who had never acted before, collectively created *actos* or sketches intended to educate and entertain. This troupe of farmworkers gave instant visibility to the incipient farmworker's struggle, satirizing the growers and informing workers about the advantages of a labour union. The troupe left the union in 1968 in order to gain autonomy and to address other issues vital to the Chicanos such as the war in Vietnam, police brutality, and poor educational systems. The company moved into their permanent home in San Juan Bautista, California, in 1971, where they have offices and studios and produce a season of plays. An annual highlight is the centuries-old Christmas pageant performed in the eighteenth-century Mission San Juan Bautista.   JAH

CAMPESINO, TEATRO

Literally 'peasant's theatre', a Mexican theatre movement of the 1960s and 1970s that sought to depict the *audience's own experience with injustice and oppression, and that provided a catalyst for social action. Originally begun by students from the national drama school, the movement quickly incorporated the rural people themselves. *Amateur artists and school-teachers received four months' *training in *Mexico City and then returned to their own communities to form theatre groups. Using members of the local population, these groups performed plays about the need for communal organization to solve common problems.   AV

CAMPISTRON, JEAN GALBERT DE (1656–1723)

French playwright. Campistron claimed to be a pupil of *Racine, though his imitations of Racinian *tragedy are universally considered lifeless and uninspired, and he was lampooned by *Boileau in *L'Art poétique*. *Tiridate* (1691) is generally regarded as Campistron's best tragedy, and was successful in the theatre.   WDH

CAMUS, ALBERT (1913–60)

French novelist, essayist, and playwright, born in Algeria. His early student flirtation with the Algerian Communist Party coincided with his first bout of theatrical activity, forming with a group of young intellectuals the Théâtre du Travail in 1936 in *Algiers, with the aim of taking ideologically sound productions to workers. After he was expelled from the party in 1937 for rejecting Marx, he founded the Théâtre de l'Équipe, though maintaining his political and social drives until the outbreak of war. His war years were spent between Algeria and France and he was a member of the 'Combat' resistance. The first of four plays, *Le Malentendu* (*Cross Purpose*), was produced unsuccessfully during the Occupation by the Théâtre des Mathurins, but the Théâtre Hébertot's production of *Caligula* (1945), with Gérard *Philipe in the title role, was well received. Jean-Louis *Barrault directed *L'État de siège* (*State of Siege*) in 1948, and the following year *Les Justes* began a run of over 400 performance at the Théâtre Hébertot. Although he wrote no further plays, Camus was responsible for six successful theatrical adaptations of novels, including Dostoevsky's *The Possessed* at the Théâtre *Antoine in 1959. Sometimes accused of philosophizing more than dramatizing, *L'État de siège* marks an attempt at an experimentation with theatrical form. Camus's thematic focus is on the existentialist notions of the 'absurd' and 'gratuitous action' in tragic situations, which links him back to *Artaud's notion of *cruelty and plague and to the theatre of the *absurd to come.

BRS

CANADIAN STAGE COMPANY

The largest of Canada's regional theatres. It mounts about ten productions a year in four venues in *Toronto, including an *open-air *amphitheatre where 'The Dream in High Park' (usually a Shakespeare play) is performed each summer. As Toronto Arts Productions, it was founded in 1970 to be the resident company for the new St Lawrence Centre for the Arts. In 1983 the company changed its name to CentreStage when the theatre reopened after extensive renovations. In 1987 the Canadian Stage Company was formed when CentreStage merged with Toronto Free Theatre, one of the city's leading *alternative companies. Also known as 'CanStage', the company produces, like most of the country's regional theatres, an eclectic mix of modern classics and recent Canadian and international dramas. It also operates one of the country's most energetic new play development programmes.

DWJ

CANDELARIA, TEATRO LA

Colombian theatre group founded in *Bogotá in 1972 by Santiago *García, Carlos José *Reyes, and other members of the Casa de la Cultura. The new group sought constant experimentation and research through the methods of *collective creation, seen in productions like *Nosotros los comunes* (*We the Commoners*, 1972), based on the first popular resistance movement against Spanish rule in the eighteenth century, *La ciudad dorada* (*The Golden City*, 1974), about urban migration of peasants, and the much-heralded *Guadalupe años cincuenta* (*Guadalupe, the Fifties*, 1976), on the 'decade of violence' of the 1950s. Other notable collective work included *En la raya* (*At the Limit*, 1993), an adaptation of a novel by García Márquez performed with a group of homeless people, while Fernando Peñuela's *La*

trasescena (*Backstage*, 1984) amusingly investigated how theatre reflects the contradictions of the establishment. Influenced chiefly by *Stanislavsky, *Brecht, *Weiss, and *Grotowski, La Candelaria developed its own style of production and has attracted worldwide attention for its application of theatrical elements to pressing social issues.

BJR

CANDLES *See* LIGHTING.

CANJUN XI (*TS'AN-CHÜN HSI*)

An early form of *Chinese drama popular during the eighth and ninth centuries (Tang Dynasty), which consisted of a variety of comic skits. The details of performance are long lost, but scattered references in literary sources indicate that many of the features of the more sophisticated theatre developed in later dynasties were already in place. The origin of the term *canjun xi* (adjutant play) has received various explanations. The rank of adjutant, used in the civil service since the Han Dynasty, was of some importance; in one version of the story, an adjutant during the fourth century was caught in a case of bribery and forced as punishment to exhibit himself at various festivals, wrapped in the cloth he himself had stolen. Another version suggests that a particular actor was so skilful at performing these skits that he was awarded the rank of adjutant by the Emperor. In either case, the humorous content of the plays is apparent.

Literary references show that *canjun xi* were performed in a number of areas in China and so might be considered a national form of proto-drama. The plays involved both singing and *dialogue, an important feature of later classical Chinese theatre, and actresses as well as actors appeared. There is some indication that the plays were performed by groups of strolling players at temple sites for festivals and similar occasions. Actors wore *make-up and were accompanied by a musical ensemble with, at minimum, string and percussion instruments. There are no direct influences of the adjutant plays discoverable in Yuan Dynasty and later forms of drama, but the nature of these entertainments indicates the basic parameters of subsequent Chinese theatre.

JTR

CANO, JOEL (1966–   )

Cuban playwright and novelist. *Fábula de un país de cera* (*Story of a Country of Wax*, 1986), *La fábula de nunca acabar* (*The Never-Ending Story*, 1987), both plays in *verse, *Beatlemania* (1987), and *Timeball* (1989) were presented in Cuba before he left for *Paris in 1994. In France he has premiered *Se vende* (*For Sale*, 1995) and the *monologue *Por culpa de una rusa* (*Through the Fault of a Russian Lady*, 1996), and has published two novels. In 1997 he received Radio France

International's Juan Rulfo award for his story *Los ángeles caídos* (*Fallen Angels*). MMu

CANTINFLAS (1911–93)

Mexican comedian and actor. Born Mario Moreno Reyes, he was once described by Charles Chaplin as the greatest comedian alive. As a youth he became an aficionado of *burlesque and the *political *revues of 'tent theatre' popularized during the Mexican Revolution. At the age of 15, when asked to stand in for an MC at a local show, he suffered a severe case of stage fright that made him speak nonsense, leaving his *audience at first speechless but seconds later howling with *laughter. According to Cantinflas, this was the moment when his life as a comic began. His stage name came from an audience member's jeer: 'En la cantina, tú inflas' (loosely translated, 'in the cantina you puff up'), which Moreno turned into Cantinflas. Appearing in over 25 comic revues in 1936–7, Cantinflas moulded his popular stage personality: with his torn overcoat, drooping trousers, and comic antics, he was the tongue-tied little man who always manages to mock and outsmart powerful people. In 1937 he made his *film debut, and from then on dedicated himself mostly to the cinema. Such was his popularity that in the mid-1950s the Cinema Robles in *Mexico City began to première a Cantinflas movie every first of September. Cantinflas became known to English-speaking audiences with the 1956 film *Around the World in 80 Days* and *Pepe* (1960). Always the comic, Cantinflas insisted on writing his own epitaph: 'It seems like he went, but he hasn't gone'.

KFN

CANTOR, EDDIE (1892–1964)

American singer and actor. With his warbling tenor, his timid persona, and his huge eyes which earned him the nickname 'Banjo Eyes', he began in *vaudeville, typically performing in blackface, before his discovery in the 1916 *Ziegfeld Midnight Frolic*. Promoted to the *Ziegfeld Follies in 1917, he became a *Follies* headliner, appearing in every edition to 1920. He then embarked on a series of *musical comedies crafted to his talents, including *Kid Boots* (1923), *Whoopee* (1928), and *Banjo Eyes* (1941). He made more than fifteen *films between 1926 and 1952, including *Whoopee* in 1930, as well as making regular appearances on *radio and *television. He also recorded hundreds of songs, including such signature tunes as 'If You Knew Susie' and 'Makin' Whoopee'.

JD

CAO YU (TS'AO YÜ) (1910–96)

Chinese playwright, pen-name of Wan Jiabao. Cao's theatrical education began in Nankai Middle School in Tianjin, which had one of the earliest and best-known Western-style theatre pro-

grammes in northern *China. He attended Qinghua University in Beijing where he wrote his first play, *Thunderstorm*, in 1933; initially performed in *Japan in 1935, it is now recognized as one of the greatest of *huajü (spoken drama) plays. In 1936 Cao became a professor at the National School of Drama in Nanjing and wrote two more plays before the Sino-Japanese War: *Sunrise* and *Wilderness* (both 1937). During the war he moved with his school to the Chinese stronghold of south-western China where he wrote *Beijing Man* (1941) and *Family* (1943). Adapted from a novel by Ba Jin, *Family* was staged in Chongqing by the Art Theatre of China with some of the finest actors of the time. After 1949 Cao held several important theatrical positions, including *artistic director of the Beijing People's Art Theatre, the best *huajü theatre in China. He continued writing plays, *Bright Sky* (1954), *Gall and Sword* (1960), and *Wang Zhaojun* (1978) among them, but none reached the artistic excellence of his earlier work.

SYL

ČAPEK, KAREL (1890–1938)

Czech playwright, novelist, and journalist. As a playwright he started in lyrical vein, but it was his post-war *expressionist plays, concerned about the technological future (*RUR*, 1921) and the self-indulgent, greedy, and militant character of man (*The Insect Comedy*, 1922), which drew international attention to him and to Czech theatre. Between 1921 and 1923 he was a *dramaturg in *Prague's Vinohrady Theatre, occasionally directing plays, most notably his own *The Macropulos Secret* (1922), dealing with the problem of longevity, made into an *opera by Leoš Janáček. After *Adam the Creator* (1927) he dropped drama, returning to it as a social weapon in the late 1930s, deeply disturbed by the rise of dictatorship and totalitarianism (*The White Plague*, 1937; *Mother*, 1938), which, after the Munich appeasement, finally broke his spirit. Co-author of most of his earlier plays was his brother Josef (1887–1945), an outstanding painter and scene designer, who died in a German concentration camp.

ML

CAPE TOWN

Theatre in this South African city begins conventionally with French *comedy performed in the Barracks Theatre by officers lodged with the Dutch in the 1780s, rather than the religious ceremonies of the Dutch Calvinist colony (1652–1806) or its predominantly East Indies 'Malay' Muslim slaves. The English African Theatre opened in 1800, while German and Dutch

Karel **Čapek**'s *The Insect Play* in a production at the Czech National Theatre, Prague, 1965, directed by Miroslav Macháček. Josef Svoboda's design increased the busy, insect-like nature of the play's characters through a system of geometrically fractured mirrors.

One of the most notable South African plays of the Apartheid period, *Woza Albert* was written in 1981 by Percy Mtwa, Mbongeni Ngema, and Barney Simon for the Market Theatre, Johannesburg. Pictured here are Zwelibanzi Majola and Zolani Cata in a production at the Baxter Theatre, **Cape Town** (1996), directed by Bo Peterson.

Africaner amateurs performed in the Barracks. Their repertoires included bowdlerized Shakespeare and comedy in English, and patriotic plays in Dutch; *audiences were segregated from 1829, with Muslims and later Africans in the gallery (*see* BOX, PIT, AND GALLERY). Attempts to create professional theatre in classy houses like the Drawing Room Theatre (1855) or the Theatre Royal (1860), at a time when immigration and the railway were increasing the population, were compromised by audiences who preferred ethnic humour, preferably local, as in *Love and the Hyphen* (1908), a *comedy of manners and race by Stephen *Black at the Tivoli Music Hall, hailed by one critic as the 'christening of our National Drama'. Leonard Rayne's Shakespeare Festival at the Opera in 1907 was leavened by fare like Edgar Wallace's *African Millionaire* (about Cecil Rhodes).

Indoor theatre in the nineteenth century competed with outdoor events, from the official Grand Procession celebrating Victoria and Albert's wedding (1863) to the unofficial but regular Emancipation Celebrations held every December since 1834. The latter, now celebrated on New Year's Eve, borrowed techniques of the *minstrel shows from the (white) Christy Minstrels (in Cape Town in 1857) as modified by *African Americans like the Virginia Jubilee Singers who *toured in the 1890s; by 1900 local groups calling themselves Coons and Masqueraders ran the celebrations. White impresarios like Disney Roebuck exploited local popular forms in syncretic shows like *Brown and the Brahmins* (Bijou Theatre, 1875), with 'coloured boys' playing 'Ashanti dancers', while international pageant masters like Frank Lascelles staged the Pageant of South Africa that crowned the celebration of Union and Commonwealth Dominion status in 1910.

While commercial theatre was dominated by African Consolidated (1910–40s), art theatre emerged at University of Cape Town (UCT)'s Little Theatre (1931), which hosted international directors like Leontine Sagan (1891–1974), who grew up in Johannesburg before training with Max *Reinhardt in *Berlin, and Leonard Schach, who later left Cape Town for the *Cameri Theatre in Tel Aviv. Sagan founded the National Theatre Organization with educationalist P. B. B. Breytenbach (1904–84) and actor Andre Huguenet in 1947. While primarily touring, the NTO contributed to the Van Riebeeck Tricentenary with a pageant in Cape Town (1952). Although the Little Theatre included local drama in Afrikaans, its English repertoire favoured European and American imports. Schach's production of Basil Warner's 'miscegenation play', *Try for White* (1959), was performed by his independent Cockpit Players for a mixed audience at the Hofmeyr Theatre. The provincial Performing Arts Councils (PACs) which replaced the NTO (1963) were more conservative, although the Cape Performing Arts Board eventually produced Athol *Fugard's work (in 1972).

Coloured schools and University of the Western Cape taught drama, but a distinctive coloured theatre did not emerge until the 1970s when *Kanna, Hy Kô Hys Toe*, Adam Small's play in Kaaps (the Afrikaans dialect associated with District Six, the emblematic mixed city neighbourhood) was performed, first by UWC's Dramsoc and later by all-white PACs. Dramsoc sponsored a black militant theatre festival in 1972, and later presented anti-apartheid plays on topics like the destruction of District Six. The Space, South Africa's first integrated theatre since Dorkay House closed in 1965, opened in Cape Town in 1972 with Fugard's *Statements after an Arrest under the Immorality Act*. The Space fostered black playwrights, such as Fatima *Dike and Matsemela *Manaka, as well as controversial work by whites, such as Pieter-Dirk Uys's early *gay comedy. The *Market Theatre (1976), and the emigration of founders Yvonne *Bryceland and Brian Astbury (1979), left the Space struggling for funds, although, as Peoples Space under Rob Amato, it offered a strong repertoire until 1981.

Anti-apartheid theatre in Cape Town in the 1980s did not match *Johannesburg's Market Theatre, which adopted Capetonians like Uys or Paul *Slabolepszy. UCT's Baxter Theatre (1977) housed dissident whites like Uys and Charles Fourie, and occasional township groups like the Vuzisizwe women from the militant shanty town Crossroads, but not coloured community theatre in Kaaps like UWC Dramsoc and Cape Flats Players. *Musicals in Kaaps received acclaim in the 1990s, however, with *District Six* (Peterson and Kramer, 1991) and spin-offs. At century's end the Baxter offered a mix of imported hits, local drama, and community festivals, while stand-ups like Mark Lottering moved critical post-apartheid comedy to clubs and cafés. *See also* AFRICA, ANGLOPHONE.   LK

BICKFORD-SMITH, V., et al., *Cape Town: an illustrated social history* (Cape Town, 1998)
—— *Cape Town in the 20th Century* (Cape Town, 1994)

CAPON, WILLIAM (1757–1827)

English designer who provided scenes of Gothic streets, chambers, and Tudor halls for J. P. *Kemble at *Covent Garden. His work and approach correspond closely to those of the fashionable *antiquarian painters, the novels of Sir Walter Scott, and the general romantic enthusiasm for England's medieval and Tudor past. Capon's work coincided with the beginnings of modern, antiquarian scholarship into the nature and historicity

of Shakespeare's plays. The designer's meticulous, detailed, and carefully researched approach earned him the nickname 'pompous Billy'. The size, variety, and the sheer quantity of *scenery became important concerns of the *audience, as did the fact that Capon began to break away from the regularity of the two-dimensional painted wing shutters and back-scenes and introduced quantities of large, three-dimensional scenic pieces. His passion for research gave authority and prestige to the role of scenic artist, but also confirmed the potential that scenery had for becoming the leading performer on stage. His influence in both these areas is clear throughout the nineteenth century. *See* SCENOGRAPHY.   CLB

CAPUANA, LUIGI (1839–1915)

Italian playwright, novelist, and critic. Of Sicilian origin, Capuana studied the works of de Sanctis and Hegel and assimilated the theories of French *naturalists: Flaubert, the Goncourts, and *Zola. As a commentator on contemporary theatre, he promoted Italian *realism or *verismo, and with his and Giovanni Verga's encouragement, regional literature enjoyed a period of growth that produced the dialect theatre of *Pirandello. Capuana's plays in standard Italian and in the Sicilian dialect served as vehicles for *actor-managers such as *Grasso and *Musco. They include *Giacinta* (1888), an adaptation of his major novel; *Malia* (*Enchantment*, 1895); *Il cavaliere Pidagna* (1911).   JEH

CARAGIALE, ION LUCA (1852–1912)

Romanian dramatist. Caragiale's most influential work is the satiric *comedy *O scrisoare pierdut* (*A Lost Letter*, 1884), which was performed by Romanian companies *touring to *Moscow and *Paris in the 1950s and to the USA (directed by Liviu *Ciulei) in 1979. Before 1945 *A Lost Letter* was staged in many European countries as well as in *Japan, *India, and Brazil. Caragiale's plays have remained in the Romanian repertory, despite recurring *censorship of his political *satire. Several of his *characters' names are used as adjectives in Romanian to describe people, and even pets, in everyday life.   EEP

CARBALLIDO, EMILIO (1925–)

Mexican playwright and novelist. A master of the quotidian, Carballido captures the bittersweet realities of simple but significant lives and the oppressive rhythms of provincial life. He is praised for the ability to reproduce the unique speech patterns of his many idiosyncratic *characters and for the gentle, respectful humour with which he censures the serious flaws of Mexico and its people. A prolific playwright, Carballido's method ranges from the *comedy of manners of his first successful play, *Rosalba and the Llavero Family* (1950)—repeated in many subsequent pieces, but with special artfulness in *Photograph on the Beach* (1984)—to works with more political content, many of them under the influence of *Brecht, such as *A Short Day's Anger* (1966), which tells of a small town's brief uprising against a local injustice. Other Carballido plays explore the poetic, the inexplicable, and the twilight zones between the real and the perceived, as in *I Too Speak of the Rose* (1966), where the dramatist's preference for abstract, metaphoric, and pictorial stage settings is much in evidence. Carballido has garnered many *awards and is the author of two of Mexico's longest-running *box-office hits: *Orinoco* (1982) and *The Rose of Two Aromas* (1992), both of which are sensitive to the dilemma of women in a man's world and admire their ability to come out ahead.

KFN

CAREY, HENRY (1687–1743)

English author and songwriter. Carey began writing at a young age and was a protégé of *Addison. Among his most famous early works are the poem 'Sally in our Alley' and the songs in *Vanbrugh's *The Provok'd Husband*. Apart from poetry and music, Carey was a successful playwright, specializing in musical *farces and *burlesques such as *Chrononhotonthologos* (1734) and *The Dragon of Wantley* (1737). He is also credited with having written 'God Save the Queen'. He was the father of the comic actor and playwright George Saville Carey, who was born after Henry hanged himself for unknown reaons.

MJK

CARIBBEAN THEATRE, ANGLOPHONE

The areas of the Caribbean once controlled or colonized by the English, including Jamaica, Trinidad and Tobago, Barbados, Guyana, St Lucia, the Bahamas, Antigua, Grenada, and St Vincent, have vital traditions of theatre and performance which have been expanded in influence by the Caribbean *diaspora in *London, *New York, and *Toronto. Some performative activities, significant in themselves, have also been used as resources for theatre. This is the case with the Caribbean *carnival, which originated in Trinidad and spread over the region and elsewhere. Various religious cults and ceremonies have contributed to the distinctiveness of the Caribbean as well, such as the Pocomania and the Nine Nights Ceremony for the dead in Jamaica, the Shango and Shouters cults of Trinidad, and the secular *ritual of the Landship in Barbados.

Formal staged productions began in the anglophone area with professional *tours from Britain, local *amateur groups, and popular entertainments on the plantations. Two cultural sources fed the creation of plays: the official and visible tradition of European theatre in the eighteenth and nineteenth centuries and the suppressed culture of the majority of the people of the Caribbean, African slaves and their descendants, who maintained whatever African traditions they could in the face of opposition from planters and colonial authorities. For example, the British colonizers silenced the Kalinda drums in Trinidad in 1881, an action which eventually prompted the invention of the steel pan, a musical instrument created in the twentieth century out of discarded oil drums. Other ethnic traditions, such as those of *India, are also significant in Guyana and Trinidad and Tobago, since Indian indentured labour was brought after emancipation to work the plantations. Whereas European theatre initially privileged the well-crafted play on a *proscenium stage, the result of the *rehearsal of a prepared script, African traditions privileged *improvisation, orature, *total theatre (involving words, *dance, *music, *masking, and *costume) in less formal locations. Caught between these two traditions, theme and form were often disconnected in the period of independence in the mid-twentieth century. 'Yard plays', for example, which treated the conditions of the disadvantaged urban and rural populations, often followed conventional European styles and characterization. One of the most celebrated works of this *genre, Errol John's widely successful *Moon on a Rainbow Shawl* (1957), portrays a complex group of people living in poverty in an urban slum yard, and their attempts to sustain hope for the future. John's inventive use of *character and creole language is set in the form of a standard three-act domestic drama.

The African inheritance during colonialism—'the little tradition', as Barbadian poet-historian Kamau Brathwaite has called it—was intensely theatrical. Storytelling as performance is still highly important in anglophone Caribbean culture, and professionals like Louise Bennett (Mis' Lou) of Jamaica, Paul Keens-Douglas of Trinidad, and Alfred Pragnell and the late Bruce St John of Barbados established a tradition of recording and reinventing vernacular performance which has been continued by younger performers like Jamaican 'dub' poets Linton Kwesi Johnson and Mutabaruka, and of course by the long history of calypso and reggae. Calypso originated as satirical songs within the African tradition, taking advantage of the licence of carnival, but has provided wonderfully rich theatrical resources, including extempore performance, inventive wordplay, and clever musical commentary on the words.

The Nobel laureate Derek *Walcott is just one dramatist who has drawn on carnival and calypso, despite his strong commitment to scribal poetics. He worked for years to build an important company, the *Trinidad Theatre Workshop, and plays such as *Dream on Monkey Mountain* (1972), *Pantomime* (1980), and *The Last Carnival* (1986) show a sustained and imaginative use of the carnivalesque. Other playwrights who have used ritual and festival elements include Earl *Lovelace in *Jestina's Calypso* (1978), Dennis *Scott in *An Echo in the Bone* (1970, using the Nine Nights Ceremony), Trevor *Rhone in *Old Story Time* (1979, using storytelling), and Errol *Hill in *Man Better Man* (1985, using stick fighting and calypso). Michael

Gilkes's *Couvade* (1974) draws on the Guyanese *Native American tradition, Roderick *Walcott's *The Banjo Man* (1958) on the St Lucian Lawoz festival, and Rawle *Gibbons's *I Lawah* (*The Warrior-King*, 1986) on carnival and calypso.

There has been no shortage of talent in the anglophone Caribbean, but a general lack of government funding for the arts (*see* FINANCE), and the small size of the theatregoing public relative to the island populations, have meant that professional theatre is nearly impossible to sustain through *box-office receipts. *Playhouses are often inadequate and under-equipped, and *training has been difficult. Through the initial agency of Edna Manley, an artist and wife of Prime Minister Norman Manley, the Jamaica School of Drama proved important, but Derek Walcott had great difficulty sustaining the Trinidad Theatre Workshop, despite his own brilliance and the collective gifts of his actors and technical team. Emigrating north is a common solution, and certainly many professionals, like the late Earl *Warner, expect to spend time in London, New York, or Toronto, or live entirely in those cities, as in the case of the highly successful dramatist Mustapha *Matura in Britain. The Pan-Caribbean Theatre Company, formed to stage Gibbons's *I Lawah* in London in 1986, contained some of the best English-speaking talent but failed financially soon after that first successful production.

Anglophone Caribbean theatre, naturally enough, has responded to changing cultural conditions. Though there is always a threat that surviving African customs like limbo will be reduced for touristic entertainment to a travesty of their original meaning and form, there have also been serious attempts to preserve and adapt traditions for contemporary use. A number of countries, such as Barbados, Jamaica, and Trinidad, have national playwriting competitions, and the great pan-Caribbean cultural festival, Carifesta, has given many performers the chance to show their own work and learn from other Caribbean models. It makes little sense to think of anglophone Caribbean theatre as entirely separate from traditions in French- (*see* CARIBBEAN THEATRE, FRANCOPHONE), Dutch-, or Spanish-speaking Caribbean cultures (*see* LATIN AMERICA). Trinidad's carnival was a French creole festival before it was informed by African and Indian culture, and Spanish elements are quite evident in Trinidadian custom as well. In St Lucia and Dominica, French patois interacts with English. Caribbean culture is a model for thinking creatively across separations and boundaries and for utilizing tradition innovatively. Theatre in the anglophone region is a vital source of such creative energy, despite the problems of material resources. ES

CARIBBEAN THEATRE, FRANCOPHONE

The Republic of Haiti (6 million inhabitants) and the three French departments of Guadeloupe, French Guiana, and Martinique (total population 900,000) shared a common history for two centuries: European settlement, extermination of indigenous Indians, French colonization, enslavement of Africans and creole blacks, plantation economies, and racially hierarchized societies. Since 1802 Haiti has a distinct history born of an anti-slavery war that ended with independence. This event, the subject of considerable heroic drama by Haitians, also exercised a deep fascination on the territories that remained French—thus it is a bit artificial to distinguish plays and performance in terms of geographical or national affiliation. Another shared quality of the region is the African origin of the majority of the population; though this is often obscured, it is apparent in some Haitian plays and in Maryse *Condé's *La Mort d'Oluwémi d'Ajumako*. Finally, a deeply structural poverty afflicts them all, especially Haiti, and that forces economic exile. This situation is masterfully portrayed in *Ton beau capitaine* by the Guadeloupean Simone *Schwarz-Bart, about a Haitian migrant worker in Guadeloupe, and in the highly successful *creole play *Pélin Tête* by the Haitian *Frankétienne, which dramatizes the subhuman life of two labourers living in a *New York basement.

The tradition of *historical drama from the first black republic has continued with Jean *Métellus, who has celebrated the great figures who presided over the birth of Haiti, both its epic feats and its tragedies. An Indian princess is the victim of Spanish conquistadores in *Anacoana* (*Paris, 1988), *Le Pont rouge* (1991) is about the national hero Dessalines, and the 'discoverer' of America is the subject of *Colomb* (1992). Metellus' highly poeticized diction is often reminiscent of the logic and ethic of *Corneille. Among the authors of neighbouring territories, the interest shown towards the 'great blacks' of Haiti is exemplified in the play *Monsieur Toussaint* by the Martinican novelist Édouard *Glissant, while Dessalines has been the concern of the Marxist Vincent *Placoly, the author of fourteen plays, including *Dessalines; ou, La Passion de l'indépendance* (*Dessalines or the Passion of Independence*, 1983) and *La Fin douloureuse et tragique d'André Aliker* (*The Painful and Tragic End of André Aliker*).

In the absence of a history or characters that are as prestigious as Haiti's, radical theatre in the French Caribbean has often sought to stage the aspirations of the ordinary people, to identify conflicts between local conservatives and the French security forces on the one hand, and working-class and peasant activists on the other, in order to foster anti-colonial consciousness. The works of the Martinican Daniel *Boukman, particularly *Les Négriers* and *Ventres pleins, ventres creux* (*The Slave Traders*, and *Full Stomachs, Empty Stomachs*, both 1981), are typical of a current of playwriting of the 1960s and 1970s that was situated at the crossroads between the struggle for identity and internationalist concerns. Further, a rich indigenous culture with performative implications thrives in the region: a strong social life, an oral tradition in a colourful creole language, folk tales and riddles, folk and drawing-room music, rural and city *dances, *rituals like those associated with *voodoo, and *carnivals. The various island dialects themselves, mutually intelligible across the territories, add to the elements which, when staged, enable a community to entertain itself, recognize itself, and define itself. Since the 1970s, especially in the three French departments, this heritage has been preserved and highlighted by government or regional cultural institutions which have funded theatre centres and workshops. But the existence of *amateur or semi-professional troupes remains precarious, for the appeal of the great immigration cities is powerful: Paris for actors from the French departments, Miami, New York, or *Montréal for the Haitians.

Playwrights and performers who draw upon local culture—from the *beguines* of the past to carnival processions and contemporary *zouk* music—have had various success. The imitation of creole speech patterns alone does not make a good creole play, but when a powerful message is included, as in Boukman's work, the local circumstance is given a resonance otherwise unavailable. Such is the case also with the communist play by Georges *Mauvois, *Agénor Cacoul* (1966), about a corrupt mayor and an unemployed man seeking assistance. Here the double use of language, French alternating with creole as instruments of power and cunning, conveys both aesthetic and political worth. *O mayouri* in French Guiana by Elie *Stephenson (1988) works in this way, as do her other plays. In Haiti, where most of the population is illiterate and has no French, fidelity to society and ethnicity has been the major preoccupation of Félix *Morisseau-Leroy and Frank Fouché, who have advocated a theatre in creole as well as creole translations and adaptations of foreign classics such as their *Antigone créole* and *Œdipe-roi*. Frankétienne's experiments with hybrid language and form have also been significant; *Bobomasouri* (1984), *Kaselezo* (1985), and *Totolomannwel* (1986) are plays that call for the deliverance of the teeming numbers of the poor.

Side by side with creole, troupes from France have for some time *toured with *vaudevilles, *operettas, and even *opera. Despite the colonialist implications, these importations have affected local authors. The number of plays written in French is quite high, especially in Haiti: proof of intense assimilation of French culture long after independence. Expanded literary relations with France now enable francophone Caribbean dramatists to build on the traditions of European theatre.

Finally, the four plays of Aimé *Césaire from Martinique, which have been produced all over the world, speak most eloquently of the French Caribbean. Césaire's first play, *Et les chiens se taisaient* (1956, translated as *And the Dogs Were Silent*, 1990), evolves from the lyricism of his poetry. The play concerns a typical rebel, strengthened by *négritude*, who is captured by colonialists; his solitary and sacrificial death will not be celebrated or even noted but 'will cause coral in the depths of the sea, birds in the depth of the sky, stars in the depths of women's eyes to crackle for the instant of a tear'. *La Tragédie du roi Christophe* (1963, *The Tragedy of King Christophe*, 1970) is about a hero of Haiti's independence, a former slave turned head of state with titanic ambitions for his people, obsessed by the desire to see them grow strong, even if it means using forced labour to build the nation. *Une saison au Congo* (*A Season in Congo*, 1965) exalts the African nationalist leader Patrice Lumumba, assassinated through the machinations of Western banks. The most famous of these plays, *Une tempête* (1969), adapts Shakespeare's *The Tempest* to contemporary circumstances, radicalizing the struggle between Prospero, a colonist, Ariel, an idealistic temporizer, and Caliban, a slave determined to recover his confiscated island. Césaire's plays, using an extraordinarily beautiful language, have highlighted history and myths useful in the political and cultural struggles of colonial and post-colonial worlds everywhere. If today francophone Caribbean theatre emphasizes the private sphere, or even pure entertainment, Césaire's legacy is such that it is never entirely without meaning and value.   RA trans. JCM

CARIOU, LEN (1939–)

Canadian actor. Cariou first worked professionally in Winnipeg in summer *musicals (1959) and at the newly established Manitoba Theatre Centre (1961). Between 1962 and 1964 he played roles in *Rostand, *Molière, and Shakespeare at the *Stratford Festival. His *New York debut as Orestes in *The House of Atreus* (1968) led to an expanding classical career at the *Chichester Festival in England (*Love's Labour's Lost*, 1964), the *Goodman Theatre, *Chicago (*Othello*, 1969), the *Guthrie Theatre, Minneapolis (*As You Like It*, 1966; *Twelfth Night*, 1968) and the *American Shakespeare Theatre (*Henry V*, 1969). Cariou's forceful stage presence and powerful voice have also allowed him to interpret effectively such contemporary strong men as Musgrave in John *Arden's *Serjeant Musgrave's Dance* (1968), Stalin (David Pownall's *Master Class*, 1986), and Ernest Hemingway (John de Groot's *Papa*, 1996). An equally gifted interpreter of *musical theatre, and of Stephen *Sondheim in particular, he was nominated for a Tony in *A Little Night Music* (1963), and awarded both the Tony and Drama Desk *awards for *Sweeney Todd* (1979). Active in *film and *television, he has also served as an associate director of the Guthrie Theatre (1972) and the Citadel in Edmonton (1986), and as *artistic director of the Manitoba Theatre Centre (1975–6).   MJD

CARMINA BURANA

An early thirteenth-century manuscript containing a collection of songs (*carmina*), and named after the monastery of Benedicktbeuren in Bavaria where it was found. The songs, in Latin, were written by goliards, wandering students or young ecclesiastics. The manuscript also contains four plays: an Easter play, a Christmas play, and two *Passion plays. The extensive *stage directions, including musical notation, suggest a *liturgical origin and indicate a church setting, but the plays were apparently not attached to the liturgy. Although the plays are in Latin, there is extensive use of the German vernacular in parts of the longer Passion. *See* MEDIEVAL THEATRE IN EUROPE.

RWV

CARNIVAL *see page 226*

CARNOVSKY, MORRIS (1897–1992)

American actor. Born in St Louis, Carnovsky was educated at Washington University. From 1923 to 1931 he acted regularly with the *Theatre Guild in *New York. In 1931, he was a founding member of the *Group Theatre, joining other Guild actors and staff to form a theatre devoted to communal values and their expression through new plays. Carnovsky created key roles for the Group, often playing characters far beyond his actual age, including the grandfather in Clifford *Odets's *Awake and Sing!* (1937) and the father who refuses to let his violinist son become a boxer in Odets's *Golden Boy* (1937). After the dissolution of the Group in 1941, Carnovsky worked on stage and *film, but was blacklisted by Hollywood in the 1950s after his unfriendly appearance before the House Un-American Activities Committee. Carnovsky focused on Shakespeare and other classics for the rest of his life and succeeded in adapting the *Method to classical work. He began a long association with the *American Shakespeare Theatre (Connecticut) in 1956 and later the *New York Shakespeare Festival. His performances of Lear, Shylock, and Claudius established him as a leading Shakespearian actor during the 1960s and 1970s. MAF

CARPA

A nineteenth-century Mexican itinerant *circus. The ancient Quechua term for a covering of interwoven branches, *carpa* came to signify in Spanish a canvas covering or tent and, finally, a circus. The *carpas* were groups of itinerant performers who moved their collapsible stages from town to town, setting up in the main square or the middle of a street, and presenting a programme of song, skits, and comedy that spoke directly to their mixed-class *audience. There was a relaxed, informal atmosphere in these performances in which the audience and the performers engaged each other directly, with audience members giving the performers suggestions, and the performers soliciting the audience for money and cigarettes. The material presented in the *carpas* was highly satirical and frequently *political in nature. The central *character, the *pelado* (naked one), is the Mexican national *clown. A penniless underdog, he brought the popular concerns and spirit ignored by official society into performance. Like Charlie Chaplin, the *pelado* improvised comic routines on such topics as the high cost of living, political

scandals, and treacherous political leaders. Where Chaplin's comedy depended upon his amazing physical abilities, *Cantinflas's comedy was based upon the peculiarly Mexican way of speaking. Cantinflas's verbal dexterity was relentless, although not always making sense, and demonstrated a wry, rascally humour. Cantinflas went on to a hugely successful movie career where, although his linguistic style was maintained, the class-conscious *satire of his earlier performances was largely discarded. AV

CARR, MARINA (1964–)

Irish playwright. Born and raised in County Offaly, her first play, *Ullaloo*, was presented at the *Abbey's Peacock Theatre, *Dublin, in 1991. It and other early works are largely experiments with *absurdist forms, but in the memory play *The Mai* (Peacock, 1994) Carr moved to the combination of lyrical language and idiomatic speech that has become her hallmark. Strongly linked to the Irish midlands landscape, her work centres around the fate of the outsider, aspects of motherhood, and the tendency within families to perpetuate behavioural patterns, usually leading to tragic outcomes. *Portia Coughlan* (1996) was originally written phonetically in the midlands dialect, though *By the Bog of Cats* (Abbey, 1998), a variation on the Medea theme, moved away from strict regional speech. In 2000 *On Raftery's Hill*, her darkest play thus far, opened at the *Gate Theatre, Dublin. MAS

CARRARO, TINO (1910–95)

Italian actor who forged the *acting style of the *Piccolo Teatro in *Milan. Carraro appeared in *amateur companies while studying at the Accademia dei Filodrammatici. Between 1952 and 1962 he was the leading actor of the Piccolo Teatro under the direction of Giorgio *Strehler, playing many memorable roles, both classical and contemporary, in a characteristically understated style. His professional relationship with Strehler reached one of its high points in his 1956 interpretation of Mac the Knife in *Brecht's *Threepenny Opera*. After a falling out with Strehler, Carraro worked with Luchino *Visconti before returning to the Piccolo, first under the direction of Patrice *Chéreau and finally again under Strehler, appearing in the great Shakespeare productions as Lear (1972) and Prospero (1978). He retired from the stage in 1980 with *Pirandello's *I giganti della montagna* (*The Mountain Giants*); in failing health, he was able to act only in the last part of the play. DMcM

CARRIÈRE, JEAN-CLAUDE (1931–)

French playwright, screenwriter, translator, and novelist. In a varied career, Carrière has most enjoyed developing scripts for plays and *films in close collaboration with a director. He wrote

(continued on p. 228)

CARNIVAL

From Italian *carnevale* (earlier *carnelevare*, 'removal of meat'), carnival is a season of celebration associated in Europe and some other Western countries with the pre-Lenten period from Christmas or the feast of the Three Kings (Epiphany, 6 January) to Ash Wednesday. Known in Spanish as *carnaval*, in French as *mardi gras* (or fat Tuesday, the day preceding Ash Wednesday), carnival parallels German *Fastnacht*. More than a festival, carnival is a period of *ritualized conflict and celebration at the crossroads between winter and spring, indulgence and abstinence, death and rebirth, work and leisure, so-called civilization and what is perceived as savagery (wildman *masking). Characterized by masquerading, *dance, *music, drama, *street theatre, *parades, and processions, it licenses the crossing of boundaries—between classes or estates, *genders, *races, ethnicities, and urban neighbourhoods.

Classicizing humanists of the *early modern period assumed carnival to be a Christian Shrovetide appropriation of *Greek and *Roman celebrations, such as the *Dionysia, Lupercalia, and Saturnalia—an attribution that misleadingly lingers on. Though analogous to such pre-Christian celebrations and to a variety of localized seasonal festivities, carnival itself emerged from the Catholic ethos that alternates pre-Lenten excess with penitential abstinence. Its evolution from the twelfth to the twentieth centuries was entangled in the processes of urban expansion and capital development that led to the Industrial Revolution and to the colonial and post-colonial plantation histories of the Americas (*see* POST-COLONIAL STUDIES). By affirming the power of imagination and fantasy against the logic of reason, and by resisting the tyranny of clock time in favour of an organic and seasonal temporal flow, carnival offers what *Goethe called 'der Menschen wunderliches Weben' (the wonderful texture of humanity)—the 'confusion, chaos . . . pushing, pressing, and rubbing' of the market-place as an alternative to the efficiency of the producing, industrializing world. And yet, the festival itself can be fully understood only by considering the demands of carnival production as well as consumption. While carnival both in Europe and the New World retains its link to the pre-Lenten period, variants in the Western hemisphere, which may occur at any time of year, reflect the kinaesthetic cultural memories of *African creole populations, as well as symbolically replaying the struggle between indigenous peoples and their colonizers (*see* DIASPORA).

Carnival is usually categorized as a festival of inversion that reverses social hierarchies during a circumscribed period of release, enthroning, and then scapegoating temporary carnival monarchs. Indeed, in *burlesques, *parodies, and satirical songs or skits, carnival provides a stabilizing vehicle for critiquing social authority and civic pretension. Its masquerades allow revellers both to 'dress down' and 'dress up' and so to play at roles that sometimes reverse their social status and power positions. And though some masquerade balls and exclusive *costume floats separate the elite from the plebeian street fêtes, the amassing of carnival crowds has always allowed for the festive intermingling of the high and the low, the rich and the poor.

Nevertheless, carnival is not just a temporary release from normally restrictive social positions. More invasive than inversive, its revellers joyously appropriate, claim, and protect spaces (streets, city squares, sometimes even private homes). Carnival affirms not only the temporary, restorative value of festivity but also cultural and individual history, seen not as the story of public institutions, centralized governments, systems of law and order, governing economies, or even the conquering or the subjugating of peoples, but as the encoding and imprinting of genetic, cultural, and artistic legacies, of cultural memory embodied in dance, music, fantasy, and at times exotic and threatening images of wildness. Carnival subverts public order, vocation, rules of law, and government by suspending, inverting, or temporarily discarding them ('time out'). But at the same time it affirms art, community, and procreative sexuality ('time in'); it values life defined in terms of genetic continuity and measured by natural cycles and seasons of growth and decay.

Carnival celebrations are individuated by time and place: Venetian masks carry the *commedia dell'arte* spirit; sixteenth-century *Fastnachtsspiele reflect the burgher character of Protestant Nuremberg. Carnivals are both top down (elite French masquerade balls, the New Orleans Mardi Gras Krewe of Comus, civically authorized floats and parades) and bottom up (populist street carnivals, emancipation carnivals of the Americas). Carnival's primary source of energy—and this has much to do with its flexibility—is located in the tension between subversion and affirmation or, put another way, in its dialectic between civilized respectability and vagabondage. By expressing the tension between that which is regarded as respectable, often embodied in civic and urban infrastructures (town hall, corporate centres, policing authorities, the Church as an institution, the workaday world) and community (the family with its many rites of passage, neighbourhoods, carnival-producing societies, krewes, or camps), carnival may be said to affirm the village within the city. By privileging leisure over work, it recalls pre-industrial social rhythms when people lived in the memory of one festival and the expectation of the next.

Carnival is characterized by paradox and contradiction. Historically identified with specific, primarily urban locations, carnival has served through the centuries to exemplify aspects of local nostalgia, even as it inevitably embraces, competes with, but finds a place for that which is new culturally, economically, and aesthetically. Its periods of greatest development (Europe from the fourteenth to the sixteenth centuries and the Americas in the late nineteenth and twentieth centuries) have been periods of urban expansion, intercultural conflict and assimilation, affirmation of local identities framed within a larger geographical context. From Venice, which was in the sixteenth century a cosmopolitan gateway from the East into Europe, to Brazil and Trinidad, post-colonial countries with profoundly multi-ethnic, miscegenated populations, carnival has provided a festival world that both lampoons the pretensions of those with political, social, and economic power and affirms through fantasy an alternative concept of time, order, and basic value. In this sense, though seasonal, carnival is not simply traditional; it invades and embraces, resists and affirms.

The lifeblood of carnival flows from competition; it revels in the potential danger and threatened violence of massing in public places or at sensitive social margins. And yet it manifests community. Its masks reveal identity as much as they conceal it. Indeed, in the Americas the festival itself was often a disguise for emancipation celebrations masked as carnival. By calling basic bodily functions to parodic attention, carnival reaches the human spirit through the flesh, fuelled by food, drink, and sex. Its feasts include rich and fatty foods such as pancakes and sausages—in Königsberg in 1583 butchers carried a 200-kilo (440-pound) sausage in procession. It releases the spirit of intoxication inherent in aesthetic creativity and communion with fellow revellers as much as in its free-flowing alcoholic libations. Though contemporary carnivals are sometimes celebrated in seasons other than spring (particularly in northern climates in mid- or late summer), the festival retains its link with fertility, licensing otherwise forbidden sexual freedom, even as its feasts affirm and reinforce communal sharing.

Carnival violence is ordinarily ritualized and sublimated in informal or organized competitions. However, the festival has periodically provided the occasion for actual violence, sometimes as social protest arising from class or race conflicts (Romans in France in 1580, Trinidad in 1881, Notting Hill in *London in 1976), sometimes as clashes between organized groups of carnival celebrants. Santiago de Cuba, celebrated each July, was used as a cover for an unsuccessful Castro rebellion in 1953, and when Castro came to power in 1959 was officially cancelled (though subversively celebrated) for nearly 40 years. At the same time, the celebration of carnival is typically governed by a process of restraint and a sense of internal decorum—order within licence—even amidst its excesses of consumption and revelry.

Despite nineteenth-century attempts to link carnival to agrarian origins, carnival, though seasonal, is neither agrarian nor rural, even though many of its rituals commemorate harvest practices (slaughtering of fatted cows or pigs, *Caribbean cane-burning ceremonies). Centred in villages (as in Eastern Europe and Spain), towns or settled regions (Bavaria, southern Netherlands, Bahia in Brazil, the island of Trinidad), and cities (Venice, *Rome, *Paris, Cologne, Nice, Nuremberg, New Orleans, *Rio de Janeiro, Port of Spain), it is at base an urban festival. Though it can be celebrated by individuals, its masquerades and even its music are the collective product of groups (*guilds, societies, krewes, 'bands') who often engage in territorial fights or artistic competitions. Fighting to protect urban spaces bounded by city streets, or taking over city squares, 'clashing' or competing for artistic primacy, are—like striking and massing in protest—city activities. Before, during, and after the Second World War Trinidadians converted discarded objects of urban industrialization (wheel hubs, American oil drums) into musical instruments for carnival, thus creating steel drums.

As a season of festivity, carnival has a long and complex evolution. It has analogues, though no verified origins, in the spring rites of many pre-Christian cultures, including Greek, Roman, and Germanic. Its European history (and most would claim its cradle) dates back at least to twelfth-century Italy. Appropriating a term (*carnelevare*) that initially seems to have signified Lent itself, in the early 1140s Canon Benedict of Rome described a ceremony in which animals—a bear, young bulls, and a cock—were sacrificed before the Pope and Roman noblemen on Shrove Tuesday as preparation for the coming period of abstinence. Carnival in *medieval Europe, from the twelfth to the fifteenth centuries, though less well documented than at later periods, expressed the pre-Lenten celebration ethos of feasting before fasting. The carnivals of the European Renaissance (fourteenth to sixteenth centuries) were more often associated with folly, particularly by humanists and Protestant detractors. Carnivals were for the most part authorized events, licensed by the Church and local or state officials. Contemporary commentators such as *Tasso and Castiglione associated Renaissance versions with intoxicated frenzy, sexuality, and feasting, as well as masking.

Carnival traditions were strong in France and Spain, also Catholic countries. In Spain, carnival was primarily a village event. In France, elite aristocratic masquerade parties, especially at the Paris *Opéra, and large public balls often outside the city, had by the eighteenth century set the tone for aristocratic and popular carnival, which maintained a strong tradition of street masking. In Protestant Nuremberg, fifteenth- and sixteenth-century *Fastnacht* celebrations included comic plays.

Carnival as such never fully reached England, which has only scattered records of Shrove Tuesday masquerading (alluded to in Norwich, 1443). But it can nonetheless be linked to the season of masquerade balls and plays that began at Christmas and carried through Shrovetide. In its broader sense, carnival can also be linked to the feast of *fools or the boy bishop and to warm-weather festivities like May Day or midsummer games and St John's celebrations, as times of licence, revelry, masquerading, often associated with the social inversion that is but part of the carnival story.

In the nineteenth and twentieth centuries, carnival emerged in the Americas. Inseparable from the complex colonial and post-colonial history in areas ranging from Cuba to Brazil, Uruguay, and Louisiana (especially the cities of Mobile and New Orleans), American carnivals embedded the processes of cultural resistance in variously submerged hidden transcripts. As in earlier Europe (for instance Ferrara, fifteenth century), masking was often allowed in American plantation cultures only in the days leading up to Ash Wednesday. Thus emancipation festivals of the street—as for example in the cane-burning harvest ritual in Trinidad—were celebrated as carnival rites, often alongside the governor's ball, house-to-house visits, or other European-style celebrations. Contemporary carnivals of the Americas often reflect African influences (the samba schools of Rio, the calinda and calypso of Trinidad, the summer Fiestas de Santiago Apostol *vejigante* processions of Loiza, Puerto Rico) or subtly encode interactive relationships between indigenous peoples and colonial/post-colonial cultures (such as the *Murgas* of Uruguay). As in the development of carnival in Europe, the carnivals of the Americas—positioned in the margin between the past and the future—both resist and at the same time assimilate a broad range of folk traditions and disparate cultural influences reflected in the ethnic intermix-

tures of its celebrants (*Native American and Asian as well as African and European). By developing an urban *diaspora of its own in places ranging from *Toronto, Notting Hill, *Tokyo, Brooklyn, *Boston, Miami, and 40-odd other US cities (with carnival genius Peter Minshall designing the opening and closing ceremonies of the Olympics in *Barcelona in 1992 and Atlanta in 1996, and influencing the Gay and Lesbian Mardi Gras in *Sydney), West Indian carnival has added another chapter to the history of the carnival.

Despite their independent history, carnival masquerades in the Americas involve many of the same traditions and emblems as those of earlier Europe: phallic symbols, mud masking, satirical songs that mock authorities, wild-man masking, and animal masks as well as fancy masquerades. Cross-dressing characterizes both, as does the presence of the *grotesque (Bakhtin's 'laugher of the market-place'). In Caribbean-based carnivals as well as in Rio de Janeiro, playing a royal personage has a more serious, powerful, and often beautiful significance—reflecting African notions of masking and festive play—than the *parody of the carnival king might imply in European festivals. But the essence of carnival remains its inherent capacity to appropriate spaces and transgress boundaries in order to manifest and celebrate aspects of human community.

MR

BAKHTIN, MIKHAIL, *Rabelais and his World,* trans. Helene Iswolsky (Boston, 1968)

BURKE, PETER, *Popular Culture in Early Modern Europe* (1978; Aldershot, 1994)

KINSER, SAMUEL, *Carnival American Style: Mardi Gras at New Orleans and Mobile* (Chicago, 1990)

SCHECHNER, RICHARD, *The Future of Ritual: writings on culture and performance* (London, 1988)

TWYCROSS, MEG, and CARPENTER, SARAH, *Masks and Masking in Medieval and Early Tudor England* (Aldershot, 2001)

the screenplays for six Luis Buñuel films, including *Belle de jour* and *The Discreet Charm of the Bourgeoisie,* as well as for *The Tin Drum, The Unbearable Lightness of Being,* and *Cyrano de Bergerac.* For Peter Brook's *International Centre for Theatre Research in *Paris Carrière successfully adapted *Timon of Athens* (1974); thereafter he became house translator, adapting other Shakespeare plays (*Measure for Measure,* 1978; *The Tempest,* 1990), *The Conference of the Birds* (1979), and other works. He used a very precise and direct French diction, avoiding conscious archaisms and also over-modern vocabulary; he applied the same approach for his and Brook's adaptation of the *Mahabharata* (1985), developed over a period of ten years. He cut many secondary stories and invented others, avoided specifically Christian or medieval words, and reduced the whole to a memorable nine-hour version; he later worked on both the screenplay and the English version of the text. *See also* INTERCULTURALISM.

EEC

CARROLL, PAUL VINCENT (1900–68)

Irish playwright. He began his career as a teacher in Dundalk but he emigrated to Glasgow in 1921. He continued to work as a teacher but began to write plays and short stories. The Peacock Theatre in *Dublin produced his first play, *The Watched Pot* (1930), but it was *Things That Are Caesar's* at the *Abbey Theatre (1932) that launched his career. With the success of *Shadow and Substance* (1937)—it won the *New York Drama Critics Circle *award for best foreign play of 1937–8—he became a full-time dramatist. *The White Steed* received the same award in 1939. In 1943 he was one of the founding board members of James *Bridie's *Glasgow *Citizens' Theatre. His Glasgow plays include *Green Cars Go East* (1937) and *The Strings my Lord Are False* (1942). Later plays include *The Wise Have Not Spoken* (1944) and *The Wayward Saint* (1955).

AS

CARROLL, VINNETTE (1922–2002)

*African-American actress and producer. Carroll was a clinical psychologist when she won a scholarship to the Edwin *Piscator Dramatic Workshop to study with Lee *Strasberg and Stella *Adler, making her debut in *Shaw's *Androcles and the Lion*. She created work for herself by writing and producing a *one-person show that *toured nationally and in the *Caribbean, and in 1956 appeared on Broadway in a revival of *A Streetcar Named Desire*. Eleven years later she founded the Urban Arts Corps in *New York, which promoted the work of black performers, writers, choreographers, and composers. She wrote the *book for *Don't Bother Me I Can't Cope* 1972, which she also directed, making her the first African-American woman to *direct a Broadway *musical. A collaboration with songwriter Micki Grant led to *Your Arm's Too Short to Box with God* (1977), nominated for several Tony *awards. In the 1980s Carroll left New York to found a 250-seat theatre in a renovated church in Fort Lauderdale, Florida.   BBL

CARTEL DES QUATRE, LE

Association of four *Parisian directors and their theatres which led the French inter-war *avant-garde. Created in 1927 by two of Jacques *Copeau's former pupils, Louis *Jouvet and Charles *Dullin, together with Georges (and Ludmilla) *Pitoëff and Gaston *Baty, the Cartel embraced Copeau's aim of respecting the *text. One aim of the association was to increase their *audience base by announcing their programmes in each other's publicity materials. The four directors each had their independent successes: Jouvet discovered a new playwright (Jean *Giraudoux), Dullin *trained a new generation of notable actors in memorable productions of the classics, the Pitoëffs brought a host of foreign plays to French audiences, and Baty experimented with the pictorial elements of theatre. Their work was characterized by high production standards and it rejuvenated the theatre in a period of economic uncertainty.

BRS

CARTER, MRS LESLIE (1862–1937)

American actress. Born Caroline Louise Dudley, she took to the stage after an acrimonious divorce from *Chicago socialite Leslie Carter. Mentored by David *Belasco, Mrs Carter made her acting debut in 1890, but her role as Maryland Calvert in Belasco's Civil War drama *The Heart of Maryland* (1895) made her a star. She followed with triumphs in *Zaza* (1899–1901), *DuBarry* (1901–3), and *Adrea* (1905–6). Her trademark red hair was emblematic of her emotional style, firmly grounded in nineteenth-century *acting tradition. A 1906 break with Belasco began a steady decline in her career.   GAR

CARTWRIGHT, JIM (1958–)

English playwright. Though he draws on the language and attitudes of his industrial Lancashire origins, Cartwright eschews *naturalism in favour of a heightened, poetic style. *Road* (1986) follows the travellers on a road in northern Britain through a night out, elliptically drawing out a landscape of loss and longing in a town devastated by poverty and industrial collapse. His compelling language worked well in a promenade production which took the *audience into and around its characters' lives (*see* ENVIRONMENTAL THEATRE). His next major success was *The Rise and Fall of Little Voice* (1992), a romantic fantasy about a young girl's obsession with her absent father and his record collection, which enjoyed a long West End run and was later *filmed (as *Little Voice*, 1998). *I Licked a Slag's Deodorant* (1996) is comprised of intercut *monologues about a brutal encounter between a loveless man and a prostitute. *Hard Fruit* (2000) continued the investigation of masculinity in its portrait of a closeted gay man and his obsession with wrestling.   DR

CARTWRIGHT, WILLIAM (1611–43)

English playwright. Three of Cartwright's four plays were acted at Oxford, 1635–7. *The Royal Slave* was also acted professionally in 1636 at Hampton Court; and *The Ordinary* and *The Lady Errant* were licensed for performance after the Restoration. Two actors of the same name were together active from c.1598 to c.1675.   RWV

CASA DE LAS AMÉRICAS

Cuban institution created in 1959 to disseminate *Latin American and *Caribbean arts and literatures and to promote exchanges among regional intellectuals and artists. Founded by Haydée Santamaría, in 2001 it was directed by poet and essayist Roberto Fernández Retamar. Its publications include the theatrical journal *Conjunto*, founded in 1964, and its annual *award for drama is perhaps the most important in Ibero-America. It has been received by more than 30 playwrights and troupes from all over Latin America, including Andrés *Lizarraga, Osvaldo *Dragún, Manuel *Galich, Emilio *Carballido, Oduvaldo *Viana Filho, José *Triana, Virgilio *Piñera, Alonso *Alegría, the La *Candelaria group, Enrique *Buenaventura, and Isidora *Aguirre. From 1961 to 1966 Casa de las Américas convened the Latin American Theatre Festival, and continues to organize international meetings and workshops for theatre artists.

MMu

CASARES, MARÍA (1922–96)

Franco-Spanish actress. Daughter of a prominent republican politician who was obliged to flee Civil War Spain for her own safety, Casares and her mother settled in *Paris where, adding a grave accent to her surname to preserve the Spanish pronunciation, she went on to become one of the definitive tragediennes of the post-war era, premièring the dramas of *Camus and *Sartre before forming part of *Vilar's Théâtre *National Populaire (1954–9). Her deep, raspish voice, tinged with a Galician musical lilt, and her expressive almond-shaped eyes and controlled gestural language, were to make her a regular *Avignon performer. With Jorge *Lavelli, a fellow émigré and one of her preferred directors, she was to realize a visceral fiery *Medea* in 1967 which proved a seminal influence on dramatist Bernard-Marie *Koltès. Among *Genet's preferred performers, she undertook the role of the unnamed mother in *Les Paravents* (*The Screens*) both in 1966 under Roger *Blin's direction and in 1983 with Patrice *Chéreau. Casares was to work only sporadically in her native Spain, but her performance of the despotic Gorgo in Alberti's *El adefesio* (*The Absurdity*, *Madrid, 1976) is recognized as a key moment in the Spanish theatre's transition from a climate of dictatorship to democracy.   MMD

CASAS, MYRNA (1934–)

Puerto Rican playwright and director. Casas began her career in 1960 with the psychological play *Cristal roto en el tiempo* (*Broken Glass in Time*), but her main contributions were *Absurdos en soledad* (*Absurdities in Solitude*, 1963) and *La trampa* (*The Trap*, 1964), the first Puerto Rican plays to depict abstract situations without direct links to historical realities. She joined Swan Productions in 1963 and has continued to direct her own plays with that group, including the widely admired *El gran circo eucraniano* (*The Great Eukranian Circus*, 1988), and has also directed the work of other playwrights. She was director of the University of Puerto Rico Drama Department from 1975 to 1980.   JLRE

CASONA, ALEJANDRO (ALEJANDRO RODRÍGUEZ ALVAREZ) (1903–66)

Spanish playwright who chose exile in Argentina during the Spanish Civil War. His plays were characterized by fantasy, poetic undercurrents, and explorations of the role of illusion as an antidote to reality. Although his greatest successes were *The Lady of the Dawn* (1934) and *Trees Die Standing* (1949), his earlier prizewinning *The Stranded Mermaid* (*Madrid, 1933) and *Suicide Prohibited in Springtime*, first staged in *Mexico City (1936), display more theatrical innovation. Several revivals of his plays accompanied his return to Spain in 1963, and a commercial production of *Trees Die Standing* in 1999 proved popular in Madrid.   MPH

CASSON, LEWIS (1875–1969)

Actor and director of Welsh descent. He began his acting career comparatively late, having first considered the priesthood, but then *toured with Ben *Greet, acted at the *Royal Court Theatre under Granville *Barker, whom he greatly admired, and at the *Gaiety Theatre, *Manchester, where he began directing. There he married Sybil *Thorndike in 1908, and they embarked on their 60-year theatrical partnership. He had several periods of management of *London theatres from 1922, and appeared with and directed his wife in London and on many tours. He was a lifelong socialist, drama director of the *Arts Council, and was president of Actors' Equity (1940–5; *see* TRADE UNIONS, THEATRICAL). As an actor he was reliable and intelligent but not first rate, though his voice was very good, owing something to early work with William *Poel. He played a wide variety of main and supporting parts, including Shakespeare's Owen Glendower and Polonius, as well as *Shaw's John Tanner in *Man and Superman*. He was a meticulous director, and supported his wife in a wide variety of serious and experimental productions, ranging from *Greek *tragedy through Shakespeare and *expressionist plays to contemporary drama and *Grand Guignol. He was knighted in 1945.   EEC

CASTELVETRO, LODOVICO (c.1505–1571)

Italian humanist from the duchy of Modena. His importance for theatre history is in issuing an Italian translation with commentary of *Aristotle's *Poetics*, printed in Vienna in 1570. Previous available versions had been either in Greek or in Latin, and a vernacular version immediately made the work more accessible. Although his approach was to resist over-rigorous interpretations of the *text, he was responsible for codifying, some would say for inventing, the three *unities of time, place, and *action which were then accepted as guiding *dramaturgical rules, especially in Italy and France, for the next two centuries. *See also* NEOCLASSICISM.   RAA

CASTILLO, JULIO (1944–88)

Mexican director. An innovative talent of the 1980s, he was much influenced by *film and known for his stunning and often chaotic use of visual imagery. While his first successes were with *texts by *Arrabal, *Ionesco, and *García Lorca, he soon became known as an actor's director whose daring *direction of young Mexican playwrights won him the respect, if not always the understanding, of critics and public alike. He is especially remembered for his gritty rendering of *Of the Street* (1987), Jesús *González-Dávila's play about the street children of Mexico City.   KFN

CASTING

The process of selecting actors to perform roles in plays or other theatrical productions. Historically, *playwrights, *actor-managers, company *managers, and *producers have been among those who carried out this task. In the modern theatre, *directors assume primary responsibility for casting (sometimes collaborating with 'casting directors'), conducting *auditions, and matching actors to roles. In permanent *repertory companies, casts are drawn mainly from within the ranks of company members. Commercial productions (as on Broadway) may be built around well-known stars, with supporting roles cast by audition or invitation. And in ensemble-based or group-*devised projects, casting decisions may be made collectively (*see* COLLECTIVES AND COLLECTIVE CREATION).

Casting is often based on the theory that certain actors are 'right' for certain roles. This sense of 'rightness' may derive from culturally determined attitudes toward *character types and their physical attributes. For example, the *stock characters found in *commedia dell'arte proved widely influential throughout much of Western drama: lovers are often young and attractive, and their comic and *villainous counterparts older and without physical appeal. Directors have frequently sought actors of particular physical, vocal, or personality types; indeed, in some periods (such as eighteenth-century England) and traditions (such as Japanese *nō and *kabuki), casting has been conducted mostly according to 'lines', with actors playing only roles that fall within their predetermined type (*see* LINES OF BUSINESS; STOCK COMPANY). In other eras and styles (such as twentieth-century *Stanislavskian theatre), actors have been prized for physical and emotional versatility. By the late twentieth century, the concept of non-traditional casting was frequently implemented in British and American theatres, partly to redress the limited and often prejudicial ways in which non-white and female actors have traditionally been cast in plays scripted and supervised by white men. 'Colour-blind' and 'cross-gendered' casting expands the numbers of roles available, and provides opportunities for theatrical examinations of racial, ethnic, and sexual politics. RM

CASTORF, FRANK (1951–)

German director. One of the most controversial figures in contemporary theatre, Castorf was born in East Berlin and studied at Humboldt University. Throughout the 1980s he worked at provincial East German theatres before returning to *Berlin in 1988. He first came to national attention after 1989 with productions of *Hamlet*, *Lessing's *Miss Sara Sampson*, and *Goethe's *Tasso*, which radically and notoriously dismantled the *texts. In 1992 he became *artistic director of the *Volksbühne in Berlin and quickly established it as an energetic forum for social debate and a focal point for East German con-

cerns. In his productions he confronts classical scripts with elements of pop culture, textual collage, the aesthetics of *performance art, and the ideology of *dada. His choice of texts is extremely catholic, ranging from the *Greeks to adaptations of *A Clockwork Orange* and *Trainspotting*. CBB

CASTRATO

A castrated male singer with a high voice. In Italy, women could not sing in church choirs, so from the mid-sixteenth century males customarily underwent castration so they could sing the higher parts. Castrati started appearing regularly in *opera at the end of the seventeenth century, and during the eighteenth century they became famed for their capacity to combine the register of a soprano with the strength of a fully trained male voice. As *opera seria* achieved European-wide popularity, castrati became international celebrities. Some, like Nicholas Grimaldi ('Nicolini', 1673–1732) and Carlo Broschi ('Farinelli', 1705–82), were artists of international renown, virtuoso actors as well as singers. Growing controversy surrounding the operation of castration, and the decline of *opera seria*, meant that by the late eighteenth century the supply of castrati was dwindling. Rossini and Meyerbeer wrote for castrati in their early operas, but by 1830 these singers had disappeared from the stage. SJCW

CASTRO, CONSUELO DE (1946–)

Brazilian playwright. Castro's first play, *A prova de fogo* (*Trial by Fire*, written 1968, *censored until 1974), registered student resistance to the military dictatorship installed in 1964. 'My only arm against their violence is theatre,' Castro said, and her best work continued in this vein with *A flor da pele* (*Nerves on Edge*, 1969) and *Caminho de volta* (*The Way Back*, 1974). Although still militant in tone, her plays after the period of redemocratization of 1979–85 focus social critique more specifically on generational conflict and sexual repression. LHD

CASTRO Y BELLVIS, GUILLÉN DE (1569–1631)

Spanish dramatist, an important figure in the *comedia's evolution. Influenced originally by the tragedians of his native Valencia, his plays show an increasingly symbiotic relationship with those of Lope de *Vega. The most famous is his many-faceted *Las mocedades del Cid* (*The Young Cid*), recast by *Corneille as *Le Cid*, but he also wrote many *comedies (including three based on tales by *Cervantes), and dramatized both classical stories and the theme of resistance to tyranny. VFD

CATASTROPHE

Literally 'downturn', the term in classical Greek implies a sudden and serious conclusion to an *action. In modern critical usage catastrophe usually refers to the disastrous unravelling of a *tragedy or to the climactic end of the process. The term has sometimes been used in a more neutral sense. In late antiquity catastrophe was the last of the four rhetorical parts of *comedy. (The others were the *prologue, the protasis or *exposition, and the epitasis or *complication.) In the nineteenth century there were unsuccessful efforts to treat catastrophe as simply the closing action of any *drama.   RWV

CATHARSIS

In the Poetics *Aristotle defines *tragedy in terms of its object of imitation (a serious action; see MIMESIS), its medium (language), and its manner of presentation (by *actors); but he then unexpectedly adds, 'through pity and fear bringing about the catharsis [purgation, purification] of emotions such as these'. This clause presents some interpretative difficulties. It is assumed that Aristotle inserted it in answer to Plato's objection to the deleterious effect of tragedy's arousal of emotion, but the idea is not central to the Poetics, and the philosopher provides no further explanation. Attempts to throw light on Aristotle's meaning by referring to his use of the term in the Politics risk confusing what are probably two different usages. Virtually every word in the catharsis clause is thus doubtfully translated, and there is no consensus on the meaning. The significance of the term for dramatic *theory is more likely to be found in the changing concerns of commentators than in Aristotle.

Among the recurring questions and issues raised over the centuries are the following: (1) Is catharsis a homoeopathic, therapeutic process? If so, are we to assume that spectators come to tragedy in need of a cure? (2) Are pity and fear the only passions involved in tragic catharsis, or are they representative? (3) Are the emotions that are purged in the spectator, or are they located in the play's structure? (4) Is catharsis the end of tragedy, or the means by which tragedy achieves its end? (5) Is catharsis brought about by the direct witnessing of pitiful and fearful events, or by the artistic representation of such events? Although the literature on catharsis is vast, interpretations can be roughly categorized as (a) moral, (b) psychological, (c) intellectual, and (d) structural.

Moral. The view generally held in the *early modern period was that of *Giraldi Cinthio (1543): 'tragedy . . . by means of the pitiable and the terrible, purges the minds of the hearers from their vices and influences them to adopt good morals.' This moral interpretation of catharsis distinguished between the emotions of means (pity and fear) and those purged (avarice, lust, envy, etc.). It ignored the homoeopathic element but did note that artistic imitation provided the delight that in poetry was to accompany instruction. A variation that held that repeated exposure to tragic events inured the spectator to misfortune did account for the homoeopathic element, but downplayed delight. Thus 'health of mind [is] acquired through very bitter medicine' (Castelvetro, 1570). A third moral interpretation saw tragedy purging passions 'by modulating and reducing them to that proper consistency which can contribute to a virtuous habit' (Guarini, 1599). Catharsis was thus related to the Aristotelian mean, and could where necessary involve the increase as well as the reduction of pity and fear.

Psychological. Since the late nineteenth century the most common interpretation of catharsis is that it is a process of emotional, even therapeutic, relief. Jakob Bernays (1880) found support for his view that this process was pathological rather than moral in Politics 8. 7, where Aristotle writes of catharsis as the relief of emotional frenzy. In psychological and sociopsychological writing, *drama, especially tragedy, is often cited together with *ritual as a means whereby debilitating and repressed emotion, the result either of a specific trauma or of collectively held distresses, can be safely confronted and controlled. Tragedy provides an appropriate distance and context for the catharsis of this painful emotion.

Intellectual. In the twentieth century there were several efforts to explain catharsis as an intellectual clarification of the represented incidents, which results in a new perception on the part of the *audience. Once the tragic *protagonist's guilt is properly understood, the spectator is freed from pity and fear. A related notion has it that this intellectual understanding is dialectically related to the emotions that are aroused and that this complex intellectual-emotional response to artistic imitation constitutes tragic catharsis. *Goethe's idea of catharsis as the artistic reconciliation of opposing elements represents an early version of an intellectual interpretation.

Structural. The most controversial interpretation of catharsis treats it as a constituent element of the tragedy, as an emotional element carried forward by the *plot. Gerald Else (1967) argues that catharsis consists of the purification of the initially unclean tragic act through the demonstration of the protagonist's ignorance of its true nature. The spectator is consequently free to pity rather than execrate him. Else's theory has few followers, but it does have the advantage of consistency and the virtue of incorporating catharsis within the nexus of other Aristotelian terminology.   RWV

RORTY, AMELIE OKSENBERG (ed.), Essays on Aristotle's 'Poetics' (Princeton, 1992)

SCHEFF, T. J., Catharsis in Healing, Ritual, and Drama (Berkeley, 1979)

CAVITTU NATAKAM

*Indian performance, literally 'kicking' or 'stamping dramas', traditionally performed in the Malayalam language by

large, all-male companies of Latin-rite Christians on feast days, at weddings, or other major celebrations during the dry season, primarily in the central region of Kerala. The tradition dates from the later half of the sixteenth century, when Jesuit missionaries travelled to the south-west coast of India with Portuguese traders and recruited Catholic converts (in contrast to the early Syrian Christians) to perform anonymous plays based on biblical stories, or lives of the great Christian saints such as St George or the Emperor Charlemagne (*see also* JESUIT DRAMA). Although peculiar to Kerala, the purpose of these performances was similar to the many other forms of Christian drama developed during the period of colonial expansion for celebration and proselytizing: the reconquest dramas of Moors and Christians of the Iberian peninsula, Lenten dramas in the *Philippines (*see* SINAKULO; MORIONES), and New World dramas of conquest by *Native Americans. Performed by all-male companies in front of colourful backdrops, these all-night *dance-dramas derive their reputation for stamping and kicking from the large, wide, forceful leaping and arcing steps, kicks, jumps, and stamps used by the actor-dancers as they perform on raised wooden *stages, or when they enact martial arts-inspired scenes of epic battle. During a performance the group leader serves as visible *stage manager, directing the *action, encouraging the elaborately and regally *costumed performers, *prompting those who are forgetful, and seeing that the long performances maintain a dynamic pace. In a traditional performance the comic *character (*kattiyan*) serves as commentator and often takes roles in the plays. For several centuries *cavittu natakam* performances were as popular at Catholic celebrations and festival days as were *kathakali* dance-drama performances at Hindu temple festivals. Women began to appear onstage in women's roles around 1960. As late as the 1970s, a few new plays were written and companies gave occasional performances, but in spite of attempts to revive interest and patronage in the Catholic communities of central Kerala, performances were rare by the end of the century.

PZ

CECCHI, CARLO (1942–)

Italian actor and director. Cecchi became a prominent figure of the *avant-garde with the performances in *alternative venues of his cooperative group Granteatro (1971–6). Synthesizing the Italian popular tradition with avant-garde ideas—particularly those of the *Living Theatre—he presented works by the Neapolitan A. Petito, *Mayakovsky, *Brecht, *Büchner, *Molière, and *Pirandello. Cecchi went on to explore, as director and performer, the whole spectrum of European drama, including Shakespeare, *Goldoni, *Chekhov, *Beckett, *Pinter, and Thomas *Bernhard. A fine *film actor, he appeared in *Le Mans* (1971), *Death of a Neapolitan Mathematician* (1992), *Steal-*

ing Beauty (1996, directed by Bertolucci), *Hammam* (1997), and *Red Violin* (1998). JEH

CECCHINI, PIER MARIA (1563–1645)

Commedia dell'arte *actor-manager from Ferrara, who created the *Zanni-type mask Fritellino and directed the *Accesi company. Frustrated in his career by quarrels with colleagues and patrons, he expressed his perfectionist vision of improvised theatre in a series of treatises and observations composed between 1610 and 1630. RAA

CELCIT

Centro Lainoamericano de Creación e Investigación Teatral (Centre for Latin American Theatre Creation and Research). Organization founded in 1975 in Caracas, Venezuela, which has branches in several other *Latin American countries including Ecuador and Argentina. Its objective is to build connections among theatre artists of Latin America, Spain, and Portugal, and, secondarily, with those of other European countries and the United States. Perhaps the most prominent of the CELCIT branches opened in Argentina in 1979; it has established several *festivals including La Movida (a festival of new scenic methods) and the annual Encuentro de Teatro Iberoamericano. CELCIT also promotes *training by offering courses through its theatre schools, and publishes theatre journals, including *Teatro/CELCIT*, *Dramática latinoamericana*, and *Teatro: teoría y práctica*. EJW

CELESTE, MADAME (1814–82)

French *dancer, actress, and *mime. A Frenchwoman working in England and America, her passionate depictions of feeling began in thrilling physicality and only slowly moved to spoken English. Her most noted role was the Native American Miami in the *melodrama *Green Bushes* (1845). In *London she *managed the melodrama house the *Adelphi (1844–53), financially supporting her partner Benjamin *Webster's *legitimate dramas at the *Haymarket. They appeared at the Adelphi together for six years more before they split and she moved on to manage the *Lyceum, making a sensation there in her first season as Mme Defarge. JSB

CELLARAGE

A term taken from *Hamlet*, used to describe the understage area. The *Ghost, from underneath the stage, orders Horatio and Marcellus to swear their oath, and Hamlet calls him 'this fellow in the cellarage'. If the Ghost left the stage through the *trapdoor, obviously he would call from under the stage.

AJG

CENSORSHIP

In the theatre, the act of interference, usually by or on behalf of government authority, in the content or representation of a dramatic work or other performance in order to ensure its conformity with prevailing political, moral, or religious norms.

1. Introduction

Plato banned poets from his ideal republic on the grounds that they were subversives. Something of that attitude infuses the censorship of *drama and *performance. Potentially, the act of representing a *text on stage, through *make-up, *costume, gesture, *scenography, style of *acting, or stage business, is as fraught with opportunities for *satire or subversion as the text itself, and in most cases censorships have reserved the right to both pre- and post-performance censorship. Moreover, the very presence of an *audience, disposed to make its opinions evident, has made governments across the centuries aware of the dangers to public order implicit in theatre (*see* RIOTS; AUDIENCE CONTROL).

Awareness of the power of the stage for the promulgation of vice rather than virtue has been present through the ages, as expressed on behalf of the early Christian Church by *Tertullian in *De Spectaculis* at the end of the Roman Empire, through to the Puritans in England, as in Jeremy *Collier's *A Short View of the Immorality of the Stage* (1696), and well into the nineteenth century by evangelicals, mainly in the form of *anti-theatrical sermons like those of Rowland Hill. The view of the last French censor under the *ancien régime*, Jean-Baptiste Suard, was more directly political. Writing in 1789, on the brink of the French Revolution, he argued that 'theatrical performances . . . address themselves to the imagination and the senses; they can excite every passion, and the resulting impressions acquire an extraordinary energy by the simultaneous interaction of all the impressions received by a great multitude in concourse'. Similarly, Robert Southey, with the example of *Hugo's *Le Roi s'amuse* (*Paris, 1832) in mind, emphasized in 1834 the dangers of an uncontrolled stage becoming 'an instrument of popular excitement'. Many governments have adopted similar views. Political concerns have been at the forefront of censorship, but they emerged with virulent effect in the twentieth century when dramatic censorship was used against dissidence in dictatorships in Spain, Chile and much of South America, South Africa, and the Soviet Union. Under rigidly controlled Islamic regimes, such as the Taliban in Afghanistan, no form of theatre is permissible. This entry will trace the major outlines of theatrical censorship by looking at illustrations from around the globe. Since it is clearly impossible to detail all cases, the examples treated here should be taken as representative, not comprehensive. The main story is told with reference to Western Europe, followed by examples from other parts of the globe.

2. Europe

The presiding magistrates or *archons* of the *Dionysia festivals in ancient *Greek theatre may be regarded as embryonic censors in judging the merits of the plays to be offered for public performance, but strictly speaking the first censors were the two elected magistrates in ancient Rome, who organized the census and as a secondary function had responsibility for public morals. This established very early on the link between morality and politics, which almost invariably underpins censorship whatever its expressed intention. Evidence for theatrical censorship in classical times is neither widespread nor reliable, though Cicero makes a few references in *De Republica*. The Greeks and Romans took personal allusion very seriously; *Aristophanes was a victim of censorship over this issue, probably through the influence of powerful families who resented being personal targets, and *Naevius was imprisoned for a time at the behest of the influential Metelli family for this reason. Political satire was generally proscribed in the *Roman era, though *Plautus revelled in jokes and puns and seems to have introduced a degree of topical allusion, occasionally touching on politics.

During the *medieval period, as drama emerged from the confines of the Church and a secular theatre developed, censorships began to be established to control the stage. During the fifteenth century the authorities in France and Spain attempted to control *religious drama (as in Charles VI's licensing of the *Confrérie de la Passion in 1402) and to curtail in mid-century the troublesome activities of satiric troupes such as the *Basochiens and the Clercs. *Mystery plays, often adulterated by secular accretions, were prohibited in France from 1538 and censorship was introduced also for religious reasons in England. The 1543 Act for the Advancement of True Religion was used to underline the changes wrought by the Protestant revolution, but references to the power of the Pope were suppressed in the Chester *cycle plays as early as 1531. Inevitably Catholic doctrine in general was replaced by Protestant, except during the reign of Mary (1553–8), when the process was temporarily inverted. The suppression of the old Catholic feast of *Corpus Christi and its attendant dramatic activity took place in 1548, but a final ban on medieval *biblical plays and *miracle plays was not fully realized until 1581, under Elizabeth I. Early in her reign an Act Prohibiting Unlicensed Interludes and Plays, Especially on Religion or Policy emphasized how concerned the authorities had become over the propaganda power of theatre, and a new system of censorship was instituted which handed the scrutiny of dramatic texts to local authorities (mayors and justices of the peace) throughout the realm. At York, where local records show a fair degree of interference with performances by the *guilds, probably one of the last examples of religious drama in the form of a Pater Noster play was permitted in 1572, after having been suitably 'perused amended and corrected' by the secular authorities.

Medieval and *early modern censorship throughout Europe was conducted in virtual secrecy. But in England from the appointment of Edmund Tilney as *Master of the Revels in 1579, and through his successors in the seventeenth century, such as Sir George Buc and Sir Henry Herbert, censorship acquired a human face and became more firmly established. Tilney's patent of 1581 introduced centralized control, empowering him 'to order and reform, authorise and put down, as shall be thought meet unto himself, or his . . . deputy', anything which he considered injurious to the interests of the state. On the face of it this gave him extensive powers to interfere with the great flowering of Elizabethan drama, but while censorship certainly did operate at this period its true extent is more a matter of conjecture than fact.

One important piece of evidence survives, which may or may not be representative of the wider spread of censorship. Tilney found *Sir Thomas More* (early 1590s) objectionable on a number of grounds, most especially a scene depicting the May Day rioters, who blamed the presence in *London of 'aliens' (immigrants) for the parlous state of the economy. 'Leave out the insurrection wholly and the Cause thereof,' he commanded. Likewise Shakespeare, at work in the potentially dangerous subject of pre-Tudor history in the uncertain years at the end of Elizabeth's reign, may have been the victim of censorship in his plays on Henry IV and Henry V. Most famously, *Richard II* was supposedly given in performance by the *Chamberlain's Men on the night before the Earl of Essex's failed rebellion, which may have occasioned the removal of Richard's abdication scene from the first published version in 1600; it was not restored until 1608. The complete absence of oaths from the Folio text of *Othello* is undoubtedly the effect of the 1606 Act to Restrain Abuses of Players, a Puritan-inspired measure specifically directed at public performances. The law applied retrospectively so that several early seventeenth-century revivals of plays from Elizabeth's reign were similarly expurgated, including *Richard III* and *Dr Faustus*.

At this period censorship usually emphasized the promptbook (*see* BOOK) supplied to the censor and playwrights undoubtedly learned codes or strategies to avoid his attention by seeming to echo politically correct sentiments. While powers of post-production censorship did exist, little account seems to have been taken of the nature of representation, though there were certainly exceptions. Thomas Nashe and Ben *Jonson's *The Isle of Dogs* was staged at the *Swan in 1597 and may well never have existed in a fully written form, which is probably why the censor took some time to register its extreme subversiveness. It may also be that the actors pushed the political satire to more dangerous levels than sanctioned by the authors. In the ensuing controversy Nashe fled and Jonson was imprisoned for a short time for sedition.

Jonson's *Every Man out of his Humour* also suffered performance censorship when it was discovered that the original ending called for the representation of the Queen on stage. This was quickly stopped, initiating a ban lasting several centuries on any representation of the royal family. Prominent personalities generally fell under the same prohibition and in 1624 *Middleton's last play, *A Game of Chess*, an outrageous caricature of contemporary personalities and events, demonstrated the dichotomy that sometimes exists between text and performance. Licensed by Henry Herbert (probably in a much underwritten version), it was discovered in the theatre to refer to the abortive expedition of the future king to Spain to try for the hand in marriage of the Spanish Infanta. It was also audaciously anti-Catholic and anti-Spanish. The play represented with an accuracy that admitted no doubt the personalities of the Duke of Buckingham, the heir apparent Charles, and even the King himself, although Middleton's most merciless caricature was reserved for the Spanish ambassador as the Black Knight. After vociferous protests from the government and from Spain, it was prohibited. In the immediate aftermath Middleton was imprisoned for a short time, while the King's Men were put under temporary restriction until they regained James I's favour and the renewal of their licence. After James's death in the following year the play was printed with an engraved title page boldly reinforcing all the caricatures.

After Cromwell's victory in the Civil War, theatrical representations in England were prohibited from 1642, though the ban was not always obeyed. At the Restoration in 1660 Henry Herbert managed to regain his authority for a short time, though in a diminished form. In licensing the theatrical companies which formed the *patent monopoly, the *Lord Chamberlain reserved powers of censorship over the companies. In a warrant of 1695 the Earl of Dorset reminded *Betterton, Mrs *Barry, and Mrs *Bracegirdle, amongst others, of his traditional authority as Lord Chamberlain, insisting that all performances must 'be always under my government & Regulation, from time to times as hath been Exercised by my predecessors'.

In France censorship was relatively weak during the seventeenth century; it was formally abolished in 1641 by Louis XIII and thereafter serious breaches of decorum by actors or political excess by playwrights were dealt with ad hoc. One prominent victim, who fell foul more of the religious establishment than the secular authorities, was *Molière, whose portrayal of religious hypocrisy in *Tartuffe* (1664) proved too much for the archbishop of Paris, who demanded its prohibition following its première at *Versailles. The play remained interdicted until 1669, when it acquired respectability by being performed before Louis XIV.

That same King was responsible for formal reintroduction of censorship in 1701, reinforced by another edict in 1706 which put in place a structure that existed until the revolution. As in England censorship was largely determined by political concerns, but the French system was limited to the three royal theatres in Paris, especially the *Comédie-Française, which was expected to uphold the best standards of decency and establishment values (*see* NEOCLASSICISM; DECORUM). Authors were at liberty to stage prohibited plays—or those likely to be prohibited, as in the case of *Voltaire, for example—in the provinces, where the powers of local magistrates had very limited effect. At first the work of censor was entrusted to an official in the police with recourse to higher state officials in difficult cases. Responsibility for obtaining a licence rested with the playwright. By mid-century the post was held by writers such as the playwright *Crébillon *père*, who notoriously prohibited Voltaire's *Mahomet* on religious grounds in 1741. On the whole the censorship prohibited anything which might excite discontent or political disruption, interpreted to include personal allusion. Of all banned plays in the pre-revolutionary period the most prominent were those of *Beaumarchais, who enraged the authorities for his political stance on the abuses of the *ancien régime* and for his views on class in *The Barber of Seville* and *The Marriage of Figaro*. Both were prohibited for some years prior to production at the Comédie-Française in 1775 and 1784.

Britain's formal system of censorship, which lasted 231 years, was inaugurated with the Stage *Licensing Act of 1737, replaced by the wider authority of the Theatre Regulation Act of 1843. The original act was a blatant move by Robert Walpole's government to muzzle the political power of the theatre. The satire of *Gay's *Beggar's Opera* (1728) and its sequel *Polly* (1729) troubled authorities, and Henry *Fielding acquired an increasing reputation for perfectly aimed political satire at *Drury Lane (1732–3) and particularly at the Little Theatre in the *Haymarket (1736–7) with *Pasquin, The Historical Register*, and *Eurydice Hiss'd*. Smarting at these and other attacks on corruption and incompetence, the government's case for censorship was strengthened in Parliament by the last-minute appearance of an obscene *farce, *The Golden Rump*, which may well have been written to order from Walpole. It is clear that Fielding was not the only target of the Licensing Act, a broad measure meant to curb the troublesome nature of the stage once and for all. It not only imposed strict censorship but also reasserted the Lord Chamberlain's right to restrict the performance of drama in the cities of London and Westminster to the patent *playhouses, and to exercise pre-censorship by requiring that *managers submit all plays for licensing prior to production.

Opposition to the Licensing Act continued from some playwrights and several scripts were prohibited before 1740, but when Walpole resigned in 1742 the campaign lost its edge and direct political satire had more or less disappeared. An effect of pre-censorship was that audiences became attuned to seek out political allusion, whether or not it was present. James Thomson's veiled references to Walpole under the

cloak of *Aeschylus in his *Agamemnon* (1738) were not picked up by the censor, who interfered only with the *prologue, but spectators saw the parallels immediately. Similarly in a production of *Richard III* in 1738, using a version of the original text rather than *Cibber's adaptation, the audience clapped and cheered at the line 'The King is not himself, but basely led | By flatterers'.

Throughout the century political considerations continued to influence the decisions of the censors, especially at times of political tension. William Shirley's *Electra*, written in 1745, was prohibited when it was announced for first performance at *Covent Garden in 1762, presumably on the grounds that audiences would still recognize the Jacobite parallels. Rather more obvious political satire determined the fate of Charles *Macklin's *The Man of the World* (1770), with its outrageously corrupt *character of Sir Pertinax MacSycophant. Submitted for licensing three times, it was finally allowed in 1781 for performance at Covent Garden by the new Examiner of Plays, John Larpent, who became the longest serving of all examiners (from 1778 to his death in 1824). Larpent was responsible for several notable suppressions, including Joseph Holman's translation (*c*.1799) of *Schiller's *The Robbers*—which in its original form had been censored in the German lands and many other parts of Europe.

In the early stages of the revolution in France censorship was significantly relaxed. *Chénier's *tragedy *Charles IX*, centred on the St Bartholomew's Day massacre of the Huguenots in 1572 and highly anti-monarchist, was suppressed by the royal censorship in 1788 but became a beacon for a new liberty of the stage. Paris was placarded with demands for its performance, and the première took place in November 1789. Dramatic censorship was to all intents and purposes abolished in January 1791 as inimical to the spirit of revolutionary freedom. The new authorities, increasingly aware of its propaganda power, made the theatre serve the interests of the republic by providing lessons in good citizenship. By 1793 censorship was reintroduced discreetly through the agency of the Paris police, who deputed two officers to the task. Their brief was to oversee both new plays and revivals, including all the classical repertoire. Much of their interference was relatively minor, but Molière's *The Misanthrope*, for instance, purged of all references to the royal family, was like many other classic dramas ruthlessly modernized—or, more accurately, republicanized. The formal 'vous' form of address was universally altered to 'tu' (hitherto mainly reserved for addressing children and inferiors), and 'monsieur' and 'madame' were abolished in favour of 'citoyen' and 'citoyenne'. All anti-revolutionary plays were forbidden. After the Reign of Terror and the fall of Robespierre, censorship was reconfirmed and the theatre's function as promoter of morals and promoter of republican principles reinforced. This decree remained in force until the reintroduction of conventional pre-production censorship by Napoleon in the wake of his coup in 1799.

Napoleon often took an interest in new drama, especially tragedies, observing to one victim of his censorship, François Raynouard, who had written a play on Charles I of England, that 'incendiary works have no place in my reign'.

Censorship became more active in Britain during the 1790s in reaction to events in France. Larpent studiously deleted all references to revolution (particularly Irish and French), republicanism, anti-aristocratic or anti-monarchist ideas, whether or not intended, with the result that drama from about 1789 until after Waterloo became detached from the social and political tensions of the period. Thomas *Holcroft was constantly under the censor's attack, and Elizabeth *Inchbald was obliged to defend herself against the charge of sedition in *Everyone Has his Fault* (1793) after *criticism in the newspaper *True Briton*. Larpent interfered in varying degrees in everything from tragedy and *melodrama to *opera and *pantomime: from Richard *Cumberland and James Sheridan *Knowles to John *O'Keeffe and Charles *Dibdin. With the arguable exception of pantomime, much of the material for which was not submitted to the censor, Larpent brought overt political allusion to an end. His policy was continued after his death by George *Colman the Younger, whose first act as censor in 1824 was suppression of Martin Archer Shee's *Alasco*, centred on Poland's struggle for freedom from Russia. Shee published the play with a preface ridiculing the licenser and with all the passages objected to printed in full—another remainder of the contradictory condition of British censorship. As *Shaw would put it later, 'though the stage is bound, the press is free'.

Fear of the theatre as a forum for inculcating revolutionary ideas was common in most of Europe. Under the Habsburgs censorship was directed against anything considered harmful to the state. The Vienna Order outlawed such works in 1794 and censorship was strengthened under Metternich, who by 1819 had imposed a well-disciplined system of spies and censorship police throughout the empire. Franz *Grillparzer's *King Ottakar, his Rise and Fall* fell victim in the early 1820s on the grounds of sedition and his *Thou Shalt Not Lie* was vetoed in 1838. As an expression of his outrage, Grillparzer refused to allow further performances of any of his plays. *Vienna was a particular hotbed of dissent, and Metternich's spies kept careful watch on a group of young radical playwrights known as the Junges Deutschland. Johann *Nestroy's *Freedom Comes to Krähwinkel* was banned several months after its first performance in 1848, as it was seen to respond through ad-libbed allusion to the spate of revolutions throughout the continent. In divided Italy the Austrian censor had control in several areas to the north, while the Pope appointed a board of six *cavalieri* and a prelate to oversee the theatre in *Rome and the Papal States. During the 1820s *Alfieri's tragedies were found to contain subversive allusion and were censored in Lombardy-Venetia. Italian censorship during the 1830 Revolution and throughout the 1840s was as frightened of political allusion as anywhere, a mood that was strengthened considerably by the enthusiastic reaction to *Verdi's operas, especially the chorus of Hebrew slaves in *Nabucco* (*Milan, 1842).

Successive censors in Britain continued to be wary of anything to do with revolution, regicide, or the monarchy in general. George Dibdin Pitt was tempting fate with a drama loosely based on events of 1659, entitled *The Revolution of Paris* (1848). It was immediately suppressed, as were several other of his plays, including *Terry Tyrone (the Irish Tam O'Shanter)* (1847), which referred to the Irish patriot Robert Emmet and the 1798 rebellion. *Boucicault was circumspect enough for his Irish settings to pass muster with the censor, but in general any allusions to patriotism or the unruly state of affairs in Ireland were regularly prohibited throughout the century, as was the singing of patriotic Irish songs like 'The Wearin' o' the Green'. In addition to politics, the British censor was extremely wary of all plays dealing with violent crime, especially burglary and highway robbery, on the grounds of their bad example to the young. The most prominent victim was *Jack Sheppard*, which first appeared in a spate of adaptations following publication of Ainsworth's novel in 1839, and was effectively kept off the stage until the early 1870s.

This move marks a gradual shift in the censor's principal interest from the political to the moral, a change that began in the 1850s and was fully implemented by the 1870s. Political considerations were not abandoned—as in the notorious case of W. S. *Gilbert's *The Happy Land* (1873), when the actors made up on stage as Gladstone and other members of his administration in a bold political satire—but they became secondary to issues of morality, particularly with imports from Paris where risqué elements were more tolerated. Protection of marriage and family life was considered paramount, but the censor's judgement was often poor. *Dumas's *La Dame aux camélias* and *Sardou's *Séraphine*, which treated sexual themes with some seriousness, tended to suffer more serious damage than inconsequential farces. A *burlesque of Boucicault's *Formosa* (*Miss Formosa*, 1871) was, in the words of the examiner, cut to render it 'stupid and passable'. In 1874 the Lord Chamberlain ordered the lengthening of the skirts of *ballet girls in the notorious 'riperelle' *dance in *Offenbach's *Vert-Vert*. With the explicit support of the Queen, the cancan was resisted in London as long as possible into the 1880s. And in an attempt to detect any unwarranted stage business in Offenbach's *The Grand Duchess of Gérolstein* (1868) by Madame Schneider, known for her suggestive gesturing, the examiner was dispatched to the final dress *rehearsal to sit in the front row, equipped with his strongest spectacles.

Opposition to censorship, infrequent and unfocused before 1880, gathered momentum in parts of Western Europe as the nineteenth century drew to a close. It consolidated in the free theatre movement, begun in Paris with *Antoine's Théâtre *Libre in 1887, spread to *Berlin (*Freie Bühne, 1889), and eventually to London (*Independent Theatre Society, 1891), where it was supported by keen anti-censorship campaigners such as William *Archer and Shaw. Censorship inhibited the 'advanced drama' of the period, represented by *Ibsen and others, through its inability to handle serious discussion of moral themes, particularly sexual. One of the most influential dramas of the period, Ibsen's *Ghosts* (written 1881), was banned almost everywhere in Europe for its (quite recessive) treatment of syphilis and marital infidelity, and was seen only in private performances for some years; it remained officially prohibited in Britain until 1914. Shaw's prefaces to his prohibited plays, including *Mrs Warren's Profession* (concerning prostitution as a business, 1893) and the *The Shewing up of Blanco Posnet* (a political satire, 1909), contain virulent attacks on censorship as an institution as well as on the individuals in charge of it. Other works of special merit were banned on grounds of sexual explicitness, including *Wedekind's *Spring's Awakening* (written 1891), *Maeterlinck's *Monna Vanna*, *Brieux's *Damaged Goods*, and Granville *Barker's *Waste*. As a result of pressure from British playwrights, a parliamentary inquiry in 1909 effected some minor modifications to the system, but censorship remained as cautious and conservative as ever.

The drama of the *avant-garde suffered more than most, even those pieces which had attained some international standing. *Pirandello's *Six Characters in Search of an Author* (1921) was suppressed in 1924 for its treatment of incest and dysfunctional family life; one of the Lord Chamberlain's advisers, the octogenarian Squire *Bancroft, described it as 'plain filthiness', and the ban was reluctantly lifted only in 1928. *Strindberg's *Miss Julie* (1888) was refused a licence as late as 1927. In the 1930s the British censor busily deleted references to foreign personalities in case they should give offence. *Rattigan suffered protracted negotiations over his burlesques of Hitler, Gœring, and Gœbbels in *Follow my Leader* (1938) and the play was only allowed after the outbreak of war. Over the same period the fascist regimes of Germany and Italy operated rigorous controls on the drama (*see* FASCISM AND THEATRE). *Brecht and many of his colleagues left for exile on the appointment of Hitler as Chancellor in 1933, and all plays by Jews were banned completely, including those of *Schnitzler. In Italy performances of *Julius Caesar* were suppressed in case they offended Mussolini.

After the Second World War censorship came to an end in West Germany, but in several other countries, including Portugal, it became even more repressive. Under Franco there was a mass exodus of intellectuals from Spain, including a number of influential playwrights, such as Fernando *Arrabal, who exiled himself to France. The climate was inhibiting for those who stayed. Antonio *Buero-Vallejo, even though accused of compromising with the censor by Alfonso *Sastre and others, was imprisoned more than once and his long career punctuated by several conflicts: *The Double Story of Dr Valmy* was interdicted in 1964, followed in 1970 by *The Sleep of Reason*. Franco's cen-

sorship, which lasted until 1975, was manifestly political in nature but Spain was somewhat unusual in that the influence of the Catholic Church was almost as strong. Eastern European countries under Soviet influence, such as Poland and the former Czechoslovakia, also suffered badly: Václav *Havel was a notable victim of the Czech censors, who also banned the work of Milan Kundera and Pavel Kohout. Matters changed quickly in the latter twentieth century, however. France was the first nation to abandon censorship officially, as far back as 1905, though controls remained possible at local level into the 1960s. Censorship collapsed entirely in the European socialist states with the fall of their communist governments in 1989–90, and by 2000 no Western democracy operated any formal control over drama.

But in Britain its abolition was a protracted business. The club device, though untested in law, was used on various occasions to avoid the censor by the *Gate Theatre, the *Arts Theatre, the *Cambridge Festival Theatre, Joan *Littlewood's *Theatre Workshop, and the *Royal Court, which in the 1960s became a haven for several prohibited plays. Although the censor passed *Osborne's landmark *Look Back in Anger* (1956), in general terms by the late 1950s censorship in Britain was regarded as seriously behind what public opinion would tolerate, more particularly after the verdict in 1961 that permitted the publication of the paperback version of D. H. *Lawrence's novel *Lady Chatterley's Lover*. There were many wrangles over 'bad language' which often seemed silly, and an almost incomprehensible ban on homosexuality as a subject remained in force until 1958, so that *Miller's *A View from the Bridge* and *Williams's *Cat on a Hot Tin Roof* had only club performances in 1955.

Several elements led eventually to the abolition of censorship in 1968: the usefulness of the club performances as an escape route, the opposition of powerful institutions like the new *National Theatre, a long campaign in Parliament through the 1960s, and the activities of playwrights who found themselves in conflict with the Lord Chamberlain's office over language, theme, or both. In *Pinter's *The Caretaker* the phrase 'piss off' was removed in 1960, but allowed for a revival in 1965 when it was discovered that the British Board of Film Censors had permitted the same phrase in a *film. John *Arden had a number of difficulties, though none of his plays was ever banned outright, and Joe *Orton escaped a ban on *Loot* (1964), which the authorities found tasteless and unpleasant, only after considerable rewriting, mainly to do with the corpse, which the Lord Chamberlain insisted had to be played by a dummy and not by an actor. Occasional visits to the production by staff from the censor's office ensured compliance. In the final years of British censorship the Lord Chamberlain refused Osborne's *A Patriot for Me* (1964) and Edward *Bond's *Saved* (1965); Bond's *Early Morning* (1967) was also banned and his *Narrow Road to the Deep North* (1968) subjected to heavy cuts. That two major English playwrights, one established, one emergent, could be so thoroughly rejected by what still seemed an arbitrary authority finally tipped the balance, and a new Theatres Act ended formal censorship a few months later. Prosecution under common law is still possible for offences to public standards. But since the failure of a private prosecution in 1982 against *Brenton's *The Romans in Britain* (directed by Michael *Bogdanov at the National, 1980) no major case has been brought before the courts.   JRS

3. Russia and the Soviet Union

From the emergence of Russian drama as a distinctive national school in the 1750s, censorship was a defining factor of theatrical life. Peter the Great's experience during his visit to England in 1698 had convinced him of theatre's power for social and moral improvement, not to mention the glorification of the state. It was inevitable that an autocracy such as imperial Russia would take the necessary steps to control this potential and prevent it from becoming the channel of dissident views. Little was to change until 1985 when Mikhail Gorbachev's policies of glasnost and perestroika irrevocably altered the entire relationship between people and state.

From 1756 the licensing of plays for public performance in the capital *St Petersburg was the responsibility of the director of imperial theatres. Elsewhere, local police authorities were empowered to ban any work that was deemed to offend in word or action against 'the law or morality'. The earliest recorded victim of censorship was Yakov *Knyazhnin, whose tragedy *Vladimir and Yaropolk*, based on *Racine's *Andromaque* and critical of monarchical despotism, was banned after only two performances in 1789, the year of the French Revolution. His *Vadim Novgorodsky* (1793), which dealt with the theme of popular insurrection, was withdrawn from circulation and the Empress Catherine II ordered all copies burnt. A similar fate befell *Slander*, Vasily *Kapnist's satire on the corruption of court officialdom, which was removed from the stage after four performances in 1798.

The accession of Alexander I in 1801 heralded a less paranoid attitude towards artistic expression, though the first codification of censorship soon followed and in 1811 became the responsibility of the newly established Ministry of Police. The relatively liberal regime of Alexander was succeeded by the police state of his brother Nicholas I (1825–55). State security was entrusted to Count Benckendorff, who headed a vast secret police network answerable directly to the Tsar. All artistic activity, including published criticism, became subject to scrutiny, sometimes to that of Nicholas himself. Following the revolutionary events in France and Poland in 1830–1, Benckendorff disseminated a list of proscribed topics, which included the criticism of autocrats or their courts, the depiction of any republican government or national liberation movement, and any manifestation of sympathy for oppressed peoples. No adverse comment on the empire's internal or foreign policy was permissible, and there was to be no depiction of any member of the imperial family or of the leading nobility. Dramatists were exhorted to glorify the acts of the monarchy, to depict the triumph of virtue and the punishment of vice.

With the curious exception of *Gogol's satirical comedy *The Government Inspector* (1836), which happened to appeal to the Tsar's sense of humour, virtually every play of consequence written in the Nicholayan period was banned from performance, including *Pushkin's *Boris Godunov* (1825) and *The Miserly Knight* (1836), *Lermontov's *Masquerade* (1836), *Ostrovsky's *It's a Family Affair—We'll Settle It Ourselves* (1849) and *Turgenev's *A Month in the Country* (1850). The list of banned foreign works is equally lengthy, if unsurprising: *Macbeth* and *Richard III*, Beaumarchais's *The Marriage of Figaro*, Hugo's *Le Roi s'amuse*, *Goethe's *Egmont*, and Schiller's *The Robbers* and *Fiesko*.

The reformist reign of Alexander II (1855–81) finally saw the performance of many of the works banned by his predecessor. In 1865 the responsibility for censorship was transferred to the Ministry of the Interior. Whilst considerably more flexible, it nonetheless baulked at the staging of *Sukhovo-Kobylin's *The Case* (1861) and *Tarelkin's Death* (1869), the last two parts of his trilogy which savagely denounced the tsarist legal system. The Tsar's assassination in 1881 signalled a further era of repression under Alexander III. In 1888 all theatres designated as 'popular' were made subject to separate repertoire restrictions and soon afterwards a ban was placed on any play depicting industrial strife. Inevitably these included *Hauptmann's *The Weavers* (1892) and *Gorky's *Enemies* (1906), neither of which was staged in *Moscow or St Petersburg until after the October Revolution. The rigid morality of the period also led to the proscription of such works as Ibsen's *Ghosts* (1881), *Tolstoy's *The Power of Darkness* (1886), and Hauptmann's *Before Sunrise* (1889).

Following the abortive revolution of 1905 and the reluctant establishment of a constitutional monarchy by Nicholas II, there were repeated demands for the relaxation of censorship which achieved notable concessions. Many of the plays of Ibsen, Tolstoy, Hauptmann, and Gorky were now widely staged, and in 1907 there was even a production by *Meyerhold of Wedekind's sexually explicit drama of adolescence, *Spring's Awakening*, albeit with extensive cuts. However, the imperial censor remained in office and in 1908 barred two attempts to stage *Wilde's *Salome* in St Petersburg.

Immediately following the October Revolution in 1917 all artistic activity was placed under the control of the People's Commissariat for Enlightenment (Narkompros). In 1922 the censorship of all printed matter became the responsibility of the Directorate for Literary and Publishing Affairs (Glavlit), and a year later Glavrepertkom (the Principal Committee for Repertoire Control) was established for the scrutiny of any work intended for public performance. Specifically excluded was anything that was anti-Soviet, affirmative of the old regime, *pornographic, or likely to incite interracial or even religious hostility. Until the late 1920s these regulations were interpreted quite liberally and the repertoire expanded rapidly, but as Stalin's grip on power tightened writers and directors came under increasing pressure to conform to the principles of *socialist realism. After a series of organizational changes, Glavrepertkom was subordinated in 1934 to the Principal Directorate for the Control of Performances and Repertoire (Gurk), whose powers extended to all the republics of the Soviet Union. By now, all texts had to be submitted for final approval at least ten days before performance and Gurk reserved the right to two seats at every performance within the first four rows.

One of the earliest and most distinguished victims of the Soviet censor was Mikhail *Bulgakov. After repeated rewrites, his adaptation of his novel *The White Guard* (under the title *Days of the Turbins*) was finally staged by the *Moscow Art Theatre in 1926, only to be banned in 1929 together with his *Zoya's Apartment* (1926), *The Crimson Island* (1928), and *Flight* (1928). When his newly completed *Molière* was also rejected in 1930, he appealed directly to the Soviet government, with the result that Stalin himself ordered Bulgakov's appointment as an assistant director at the Moscow Art Theatre and the restoration of *The White Guard* to its repertoire. Such interventions from the level of the Politburo were not uncommon. In 1932 the projected première of *Erdman's satire *The Suicide* at Meyerhold's theatre was abandoned after Stalin had deputed his closest comrade Kaganovich to view a run-through. In 1937 Meyerhold's adaptation of Nikolai Ostrovsky's celebrated Civil War novel *How the Steel Was Tempered* was approved by Glavrepertkom, only for its decision to be overruled by the chairman of the Committee for Artistic Affairs which was already planning to liquidate Meyerhold's theatre and could not allow such an indisputably revolutionary production to prejudice its decision.

By this time Stalin's purges were fully under way and all the arts were tightly bound by the dictates of socialist realism, which had been formally adopted as Party policy at the first congress of the Union of Soviet Writers in 1934. Little was to change until Stalin's death in 1953, when Glavrepertkom was dissolved and its functions allocated to the newly created Ministry of Culture. Responsibility for the control and censorship of theatres was divided between a number of bodies, including their own internal artistic councils. In theory this was a more democratic system but in practice it meant that a controversial work would need to negotiate a maze of Party, state, and local authorities, which were sometimes in contention with each other.

The cultural 'thaw' initiated by Khrushchev in 1956 did more to liberalize the publication of literature than the performing arts, though gradually a few writers and directors felt sufficiently emboldened to test the limits of censorship. In 1967 the *Sovremennik Theatre staged a trilogy of new plays devoted to the Russian revolutionary movement, the third of which, *The Bolsheviks* by Mikhail *Shatrov, debated the justification for 'Red terror'. Upon its rejection by the censor, the *artistic director Oleg *Efremov persuaded the Minister of Culture Ekaterina Furtseva to view a rehearsal, after which she gave the production her personal authorization. Yury *Lyubimov, founding director of the *Taganka Theatre, was not so lucky; in 1968 his attempt to stage a version of *Alive*, Boris Mozhaev's contentious short story about collective farm life, was abruptly terminated when Furtseva interrupted a run-through laid on for her benefit. Until Lyubimov's dismissal and subsequent expulsion from the Soviet Union in 1984, the Taganka succeeded time and again in fighting off the censor, due in large measure to the resolve and influence of its artistic council.

Following the years of 'stagnation' under Brezhnev and then Chernenko, Gorbachev was elected General Secretary by the Politburo in 1985. A year later, he met a delegation of leading writers and urged them to participate fully in the process of glasnost. The immediate response was a bitter attack on censorship at the Eighth Writers' Congress, which was soon followed by the publication of such authors as Anna Akhmatova, Boris Pasternak, and Aleksandr Solzhenitsyn, as well as *Sarcophagus*, Vladimir Gubarev's play about the Chernobyl nuclear disaster. The year 1989 saw the premières of Erdman's *The Suicide*, an adaptation of Solzhenitsyn's novel of the gulag, *One Day in the Life of Ivan Denisovich*, and, finally, Mozhaev's *Alive* by the reinstated Lyubimov at the Taganka. By the time of the collapse of the Soviet Union in 1991 the Russian government was far too preoccupied with curbing the power of *television to give serious attention to theatres that were mostly half-empty. Dramatic censorship was no longer worth the trouble.

EBr

4. United States of America

Before the arrival of Europeans, *Native American *rituals, games, and entertainments were often presented as expressions of cultural mores and beliefs. The context for performance obviously varied across time and among hundreds of Native cultures, but censorship existed among them all in the sense of continuous patrolling of established norms. Radical and disruptive performances were in some cases built into cultures as a means of social control. The Sacred Clowns of the Pueblo, for example, were (and are) empowered to mock community members virtually without limit in comic performances. As a result of their uncensored ridicule, the vanity, eccentricity, and self-indulgence of individuals were kept under community control and the offenders brought back within social norms.

European settlers brought with them the theatrical and social limits of their home societies. While seventeenth-century Spanish settlers on the southern and western coasts, and the French in the north-east, were permitted theatrical entertainments, the Protestants who dominated the American colonies strictly controlled or in some cases prohibited all theatre. The English Puritan colonists of New England saw theatre as the devil's lure and a decadence not to be permitted in the purified world. The Dutch Protestants who dominated the New York colony and the English Quakers in Pennsylvania were equally suspicious. The first theatre record in the colonies is a courtroom proceeding against an *amateur actor-playwright (William Darby) who, along with two other actors, was arrested in the Virginia colony in 1665 for performing Darby's short comedy *Ye Bare and Ye Cubb*. The Pennsylvania Assembly outlawed 'stage plays, masks, and revels' in 1700, but this and other outright bans in Pennsylvania were eventually overturned by the English government. The strongest and most long-lived antitheatrical feeling persisted in *Boston. The first attempt to stage a play there was in 1750, when two professional actors headed a company of amateurs in a production of *Otway's *The Orphan* at the Coffee House on State Street. The Massachusetts General Court soon passed a law fining any property owner who provided space for performance, as well as anyone who attended. This law persisted until English troops occupied the city in 1775, but 'banned in Boston' persisted as a reality (and an advertising device) into the 1960s.

The Massachusetts law provided a model that would be employed in *New York, *Chicago, *Los Angeles, and elsewhere into the mid-twentieth century. Other methods were the intervention of police to arrest actors and producers, the prevention of performance by the threat of police action, and—most commonly—by the threat of a municipal government to revoke the licence of a performance venue. The English practice of requiring a government licence for performance venues continued into the late twentieth century, although the use of the licence as a censoring device declined dramatically as the result of key court decisions (and changed social mores) during the 1960s. Before that time, each city and town had a public official responsible for issuing licences for entertainment establishments. In Boston, *Philadelphia, New York, and elsewhere, the licence commissioner developed a small bureaucracy of assistants who took on the role of monitors—reading scripts, demanding omissions or revisions, previewing costumes, and attending performances with an eye toward the maintenance of public standards of morality.

Though outright theatrical bans were reimposed by Massachusetts, Pennsylvania, and Rhode Island after the revolution, these were gradually overturned by 1800 in favour of licensing systems. Smaller New England communities resisted theatre through various other laws. As late as 1833, a group of actors from Boston attempted to open a theatre in Lowell, Massachusetts, and were arrested under a vagrancy law for 'not pursuing an honorable and lawful profession'. New York and the southerly regions were more tolerant, though obscenity laws allowed the closing of theatres and arrest of performers and producers if local officials judged the work unacceptable in terms of exposure of the human body, sexual suggestion, use of language, or, in some cases, the treatment of religion or the clergy. When James *Herne attempted to rent a playhouse for his Ibsenite drama *Margaret Fleming* in 1890, he was unable to find a venue in Boston or New York because the subject matter (adultery in a middle-class family) was considered too shocking. In 1900 a New York performance of Clyde *Fitch's *Sappho* (in which a female character invited a man to follow her upstairs to her bedroom) was raided by police and the play's star, Olga *Nethersole, arrested and charged with the corruption of public morals. She was acquitted in a jury trial. Shaw's *Mrs Warren's Profession* was closed on similar grounds in 1905, and its leading actress and *producer Arnold *Daly arrested, jailed, and later acquitted. When police closed *The Lure* in New York in 1913, the producing *Shubert brothers negotiated cuts and revisions with the grand jury and the show was allowed to reopen. Florenz *Ziegfeld's annual *Follies* were in frequent legal jeopardy due to the near-nudity that was a trademark of these *revues and of their imitators. In 1926 the entire casts of three works were arrested in New York: *The Virgin Man* by William Francis Dugan, *Sex* by Mae *West, and *The Captive* by Arthur Hornblow, Jr. Frustrated by the constant violation of anti-nudity laws (in the revues) and obscenity laws (in plays), legislators in New York state passed the Wales Padlock Law in 1927. This measure, which remained in effect until 1967, allowed the closure for one calendar year of any theatre which housed a work judged to be immoral.

The conservative environments persisted in Boston into the 1960s, with frequent bannings even of plays by *O'Neill or Lillian *Hellman, produced to acclaim elsewhere. With the changing social attitudes of the 1960s, producers and playwrights tested the limits of language, nudity, and sexuality on stage. New York allowed performances of shows featuring total nudity, such as *Hair* (1967) and *Oh! Calcutta!* (1969). Boston officials closed *Hair* in 1969 but the case was appealed to the Supreme Court, which allowed the show to reopen. Only *Che!* (1969) was closed in New York. This show—which satirized politics and religion and featured total nudity and actual sex acts—was closed by police and the cast arrested for public lewdness. The charges were sustained on appeal, the opinion emphasizing the play's lack of artistic merit or other redeeming value.

A 1973 Supreme Court decision clarified the legal situation of obscenity, defining as obscene a work offensive to local tastes regarding sexual content and lacking 'serious literary, artistic, political or scientific value'. Prosecutions on moral grounds became difficult under this language, and moralists shifted focus to government support for the arts. During the 1980s Christian conservatives emerged as the most effective force for this form of control, and their typical target came to be the presentation of homosexual characters and situations, or depictions of Christ or other revered figures in terms deemed blasphemous.

Outstanding cases were those of the 'NEA Four' (four *performance artists whose grants from the *National Endowment for the Arts were withdrawn in the late 1980s) and the punishment (by withdrawal of municipal or county funds) of various theatres around the country which produced Tony *Kushner's *Angels in America* or Terrence *McNally's *Corpus Christi* during the 1990s and early 2000s.   MAF

5. Latin America

Restrictions upon freedom of expression in *Latin America have been endemic from colonial times, but without any particular rationale or pattern. Examples of censorship are multiple. In Paraguay General Alfredo Stroessner ruled the country from 1954 to 1989 with an iron fist, dictating each evening what he wanted to read in the papers in the morning. In Mexico the long-reigning Partido Institucional Revolucionario and the 33 ruling families maintained a stranglehold on the economy, publishing, and the arts, even though freedom of expression was enshrined in the 1917 Constitution. In fact, censorship of the arts in the Americas arguably began with the Conquest in the sixteenth century, when the decimation of indigenous populations by warfare and disease meant that the majority of their forms of performance were lost. Those that did survive in Iberian America were subject to further repression by the Catholic Church as heathen practices, or co-opted by the mendicant orders as a tool for converting the indigenous populations themselves (*see* EVANGELICAL THEATRE IN LATIN AMERICA). During the colonial period, which lasted until the late nineteenth century, theatrical activity consisted primarily of visiting European troupes. Only as wars of independence threw off the colonial yoke did the theatre begin to address local concerns and customs. The new *folkloric or *costumbrismo* dramas were paralleled by plays copying the revolutionary aesthetics of Spanish and French *romanticism. Twentieth-century theatre increasingly focused on questions of political, social, racial, religious, and cultural identity, which often met with official resistance or outright censorship. The following instances are exemplary, but by no means comprehensive.

In Argentina theatre in the nineteenth century laboured under the societal dictum to be 'nationalistic and Catholic'. While outright censorship was infrequent, these strictures limited what was stageable. Juan Perón's dictatorial regime (1946–55), with its rhetoric of 'sandals, yes, books, no', inhibited the arts in general. Matters began to change with the establishment of a number of independent theatre groups in the 1950s and the appearance of a new generation of playwrights in the 1960s, so that by the following decade Argentina possessed a vibrant, varied, and engaged theatre, especially in *Buenos Aires. But its artists were frequently the targets of governmental censorship and right-wing death squads that forced them into exile or, on occasion, murdered them. The situation became more severe after the military coup of 1976, when practically

all direct reference to contemporary events disappeared from the stage. Paradoxically, this increased the sophistication of the Argentine theatre because it developed a metaphoric and subtle theatrical language that provided audiences with a veiled means of opposing the regime, as in plays like Ricardo *Monti's *Visita* and *Marathón*, Roberto *Cossa's *La nonna*, or Eduardo *Pavlovsky's *Telerañas* and *Camaralenta*. The increasingly repressive atmosphere, however, led many practitioners to flee the country, including Pavlovsky and Griselda *Gambaro. In 1981 the playwright Osvaldo *Dragún organized a *festival called Teatro Abierto to demonstrate 'the vitality and strength of the contemporary Argentine theatre', performing three short pieces a day for two months. Since all the participants donated their services, *ticket prices were low, and the event became hugely popular. It continued annually until 1985 and weakened the military junta's stranglehold on freedom of expression. But despite a transition to democracy in 1983, the tenuous nature of democratic rule and habits of mind formed by years of clandestine artistic expression ensured that Argentine theatre of the 1980s and 1990s was marked by self-censorship.

Following the dictatorial regime of Getulio Vargas (1930–45) in Brazil, its theatre of the 1940s and 1950s underwent the same kind of renaissance found throughout the rest of the region. By 1960 companies in *São Paulo and *Rio such as Teatro Arena and Teatro Oficina mounted numerous productions that questioned the nature and fate of Brazil's social classes, but the military coup of 1964, with its slogan of 'tradition, family, and property', quickly made itself felt. The day after the coup censorship was imposed, artists imprisoned, and theatres closed. The regime sought to silence any critical voice, leading to a cat and mouse game between theatres and the authorities between 1964 and 1968, when civil rights were abolished and the country placed under a state of siege. The military leaders systematically employed kidnapping, torture, and 'disappearances'. The director Heleny Guaribe was among the 'disappeared', while other practitioners such as Augusto *Boal and José Celso Martinez *Corrêa went into exile. The little theatrical activity that remained turned to the *grotesque and hyperbole, and discarded *naturalism for metaphor. By the 1970s the Brazilian socio-political and economic situation made permanent theatre companies impossible. Theatre artists banded together in ephemeral groups utilizing *collective creation until the end of the dictatorship in 1980 created a new space for freedom of expression.

Chile followed the same progression from *costumbrismo* to reinvigoration in the 1940s and 1950s. By the 1960s many practitioners began to feel that theatre had become excessively intellectual, unintelligible to the general populace, and lacking in political engagement. Both the role of the *director, seen as excessively authoritarian, and the role of the *playwright, seen as imposing his will on the actor, were increasingly questioned, leading to an emphasis upon collective creation. Governmental support for this kind of work included subsidies and inclusion in the national *mass media. The 1973 military coup, backed by the CIA, overthrew the democratically elected government of Salvador Allende and brought severe political repression, censorship of any sort of dissidence, and economic strangulation of institutions opposed to the regime. The military junta closed all theatre schools and theatre departments at universities under governmental jurisdiction (see TRAINING FOR THEATRE). While independent companies were left relatively free to criticize the regime in their productions (the junta reasoned that their audiences would be the opposition anyway and thus allowed aberration as a method of controlling political unrest), in 1974 the law that had protected Chilean theatres from taxation since 1935 was rescinded. The 22 per cent tax imposed on the gross *ticket sales of all non-governmental theatres forced the majority of them to close.

Political blacklisting and censorship caused many practitioners to seek work in other fields, and one-quarter of theatre professionals went into exile. The example of Teatro *Aleph is instructive: its 1974 production of Al principio existía la vida (In the Beginning Was Life) resulted in the director's lengthy imprisonment and the exile of the company to Paris. While outright governmental censorship was curtailed by the late 1970s, effective censorship was carried out by other means, as when Teatro de la Feria preformed Hojas de Parra (1977) in a *circus tent in *Santiago. Openly alluding to the murders committed by the Pinochet regime, and attracting more than 6,000 people in its first nine days of performance, the affront to the government was ended when persons unknown set the tent alight during the nightly curfew before the tenth day. The decline and subsequent end of Pinochet's power in the late 1980s and 1990s once more opened freedom of expression in the Chilean theatre, though Pinochet's economic policies continue and have created a number of barriers for artistic expression. AV

6. East Asia

In *China, the government attempted in varying degrees to censor the activities of troupes beginning in the Yuan Dynasty (1279–1368), when mature forms of theatre had become established. The authorities, recognizing the power of the theatre to communicate with a vast population, the majority of them illiterate, adopted various stratagems. Some were negative, with bans on certain *genres, themes, and titles; punishments were meted out to authors who overstepped established boundaries. The government of the Manchu Dynasty, the last of the premodern era, was especially suspicious of the power of the theatre over social and religious matters, expressing concern that because 'men and women were mixed together', the theatre had the potential to destroy proper family life. On the other hand, the Ming and Qing governments in the preceding dynasties encouraged theatre to develop its potential as a tool to keep the Confucian value system strong, encouraging plays that enshrined Confucian virtues and condemning those who ventured on the opposite path.

There was little organized censorship in the early twentieth century, but under the communist government of Mao and his successors in the post-war years the same mixture of positive and negative censorship was adopted. During the Cultural Revolution (1966–76) almost all forms of theatre were banned, both foreign and traditional. Mao's wife Jiang Qing led an effort to create 'revolutionary modern drama' (*geming xiandai xi); eight 'model plays' were adopted by troupes everywhere as the only theatrical productions permitted. After Mao's death in 1976 virtually all forms of theatre were restored, although even at the start of the twenty-first century certain plays openly critical of contemporary social injustice have been banned. The plays of the 2000 Nobel laureate *Gao Xingjian have not been permitted on stage in China since the 1980s.

In *Korea, little censorship was employed until the colonization of the country by *Japan in 1910. In a limited sense, the role of the court's Master of Revels (sandae-togam) during the first half of the Chosŭn Dynasty (1392–1912) might be looked on as a form of benevolent censorship, since his organization supervised the kinds of performing arts thought appropriate for court celebrations, but his main function was to encourage the growth of performing arts throughout the country. During the 36 years of the colonial period (1910–45), the Japanese government closely regulated the arts, both traditional and contemporary. When Western-style spoken drama by Ibsen and other progressive playwrights was introduced early in the twentieth century (ironically, via Japan), the Korean intelligentsia believed that this new form (*shingŭk) could provide a means to enlighten the larger population and help create a measure of spiritual independence from Japan. Such efforts, however, were increasingly suppressed by Japanese authorities. Three years after the country's liberation in 1945, the Korean peninsula was divided into two parts, with separate regimes established north and south. As a result, competing ideologies were expressed in the more issue-oriented theatres performing in both countries.

In the case of North Korea, the developments in post-war theatre are largely unknown to the outside world, although it seems clear that the government remains convinced that the theatrical arts are important in promoting the superiority of the socialist spirit. Plays are written under the guidance and control of government organizers; writers and directors are not permitted to change the wording of approved scripts without the permission of the ruling political party and its theatre organization. In South Korea, many playwrights began to treat such issues as the division of the country, the Korean War, and political suppression. In the middle of the 1960s, however, the government organized the Committee for the Ethics of the Performing Arts as an official censoring agency. The committee was highly interventionist in theatre for two decades or more, but since about 1990 its major work has been to rate films and videos.

In Japan, there was no organized theatrical censorship before the Tokugawa Period (1600–1868), although the sponsorship of *nō performances by the aristocracy and Buddhist temples may be responsible, at least to some extent, for the fact that the nō theatre seldom addressed political or social issues directly. With the coming of *kabuki in the seventeenth century, its existence as an urban theatre, dedicated to entertaining a large popular audience, brought its activities under the gaze of the government, which was concerned about questions of public order, morality, and political correctness. The controls imposed by the government were many, ranging from the lavishness of theatrical costume and the salaries of actors to the contents of the plays and a ban on *women performers.

In the modern period, beginning in 1868, the theatre enjoyed increased freedom, although it was customary for kabuki scripts to be checked by government censors before production. Because of its progressive nature, *shingeki, the modern spoken theatre, caused the same difficulties within Japan itself that it caused in colonial Korea. Censorship by the Home Ministry became particularly rigorous after 1937 with the increasing power of the militaristic regime. By 1940 the government had closed down all the progressive modern theatre companies, and a number of prominent directors, writers, and performers were jailed. Only those troupes professing purely artistic goals were permitted to continue.

After the war the American occupation forces, under the direction of General Douglas MacArthur, took over the censorship of entertainment. Many left-wing theatre directors and writers, newly released from prison, became active again, though politically progressive productions did not begin in earnest until censorship was officially lifted in 1950. Kabuki, on the other hand, was examined closely by the occupation authorities because of the supposed danger of its 'feudalistic' elements. Some classic works were forbidden performance. These activities, and all theatrical censorship in Japan, came to an end a few years later. SYL/JOC/JTR

7. South-East Asia

In this vast geographical region, encompassing hundreds of diverse cultures and peoples, censorship has been in place in pre-colonial times, under colonialism, and in the emerging independent nation-states, its targets generally being anti-government sentiments and immorality. Government regulation of content and production, and imposition of aesthetic style, was found in all areas after the establishment of central royal courts, especially those in Burma (*Myanmar), *Cambodia, Java (see INDONESIA), *Thailand, and *Vietnam between the fourteenth and eighteenth centuries. This authority often influenced the content and form of folk performances as well. Court performers as direct subjects of the king acted under the supervision of officials in charge of entertainment and ritual. The artists were often nobles or members of the royal household themselves,

and their performances—including theatre, dance, and *puppetry—were mandated to uphold and glorify the royal status quo. Criticism of the king and the royal family or of court officials was not permitted. The Burmese courts during the Konbaung Dynasty (1752–1885), for instance, instituted a minister called Thabin Wun in 1776, who exercised tight control over every aspect of performing arts within the court, from the selection of the story and *musical accompaniment of dance-dramas to the number and kind of characters allowed in *yokthe pwe puppet plays and the size of the *stages. He even ruled on the correct manufacture of dance costumes and puppets, and oversaw the proper training of performers. His control extended beyond the court as well. All theatre and puppetry troupes in the country had to register with the ministry and prospective patrons were required to obtain permits in order to commission performances. Ministry officials were frequently present to enforce regulations. Violations could result in the revoking of a troupe's licence; in severe cases performers or troupe leaders could be arrested and even executed.

Not all courts needed such strict or detailed regulations. Most performers were fully aware of the proper protocol in the presence of their king, believed to be beyond criticism as a semi-divine being. An outlet for critique was nonetheless possible through *clown characters, both prominent and ubiquitous, and who play a major role in many court genres still. The most famous ones are those appearing in the *wayang kulit *shadow puppetry of Indonesia and *Malaysia. Clown figures may comment on contemporary events and display behaviour that would be considered disrespectful or immoral from other characters.

The various colonial governments vying for power in South-East Asia as early as the 1600s exerted another type of censorship. By the late nineteenth century all regions except Thailand were in the political, administrative, legislative, or military control of Western nations: Malaysia and Burma under English control, Indo-China under French, the Indonesian archipelago under the Dutch and Portuguese, the *Philippines under the Spanish and, in the early twentieth century, the Americans. The colonial administrations, concerned with consolidation and expansion, established strict censorship laws to curb opposing voices. Theatre performances, along with other media, were closely monitored. Similar regulations were imposed by the Japanese occupation during the Second World War, and pro-Japanese propaganda actively encouraged.

After the war and independence, direct and often severe censorship continued, now under native successor governments, paramilitary regimes, and military dictatorships. Some of the most severe cases of censorship and prosecution aimed at theatre artists (and more generally at writers, political activists, and journalists) occurred in Indonesia, the Philippines, Cambodia, Burma, and Vietnam. In Indonesia the fledgling nation under President Sukarno imposed strict censorship laws, ironically inherited from the Dutch colonial government. After the alleged communist coup and the successful counter-coup of 1965, prosecution of any leftist activity was severe and led to the execution or imprisonment of many theatre artists, along with countless other victims. The 'New Order' government under President Suharto kept censorship laws and enforcement in place until the end of his regime in 1998. W. S. *Rendra, Arifin *Noer, and Nano *Riantiarno were some of the more prominent writers and directors who were repeatedly subject to imprisonment or house arrest, their works banned and their theatres closed down. As late as 1998 the playwright and director Ratna Sarumpaet was imprisoned for anti-government activities.

In the Philippines, the rule of President Ferdinand Marcos became increasingly totalitarian, especially from the imposition of martial law in 1972 until the end of his regime in 1986. The Marcos family, the government, and the military were prohibited topics. Severe enforcement, prosecution, torture, and execution continuously imperilled actors and directors. Despite this, theatre continued on the front lines of resistance against the regime for two decades. In Cambodia, the Khmer Rouge under Pol Pot (1975–9) banned all court and urban theatre forms. Playhouses were closed down or demolished, and precious puppet sets and costumes destroyed. Actors and dancers, especially those performing in court traditions, were prosecuted along with intellectuals and writers. Nine out of ten performers were executed, disappeared, died of starvation, or—if lucky—fled into exile. These atrocities severely endangered the passing on of all traditional theatre knowledge, a wound from which Cambodia has still not fully recovered.   KP

8. Francophone Africa

In *Africa the effectiveness of the theatre as a medium of communication, and its capacity to reach and influence a mass audience, especially in non-literate societies, accounts for the suspicion and outright hostility with which it has been greeted by state authorities. Africa in the French-speaking regions (see AFRICA, FRANCOPHONE) may not have the spectacular examples of harsh treatment of practitioners in the anglophone areas, but neither has it been free of censorship, which dates back to the colonial period. In 1942, for example, the French governor of Côte d'Ivoire, Hubert Deschamps, banned Coffi Gadeau's play denouncing forced labour, Les Recrutés de Monsieur Maurice. The same fate befell the dramatized poetry of one of the best-known performers, Kéita *Fodéba, in 1949 in Senegal. Significantly, the publication of his two insurgent poems 'Aube africaine' ('African Dawn') and 'Minuit' ('Midnight') was not banned, since they posed no threat to a largely illiterate audience, but the sale and distribution in the colonies of sound recordings of those poems was forbidden. (Ironically, after independence Fodéba was arrested in 1969 by the Touré regime, and probably murdered in jail.) But cases of direct censorship by France were not widespread. It has been argued by Bakary

Traoré, a former student at *École William Ponty, that French censorship was much less direct. For example, the theatrical activities of students at Ponty were guided towards folklore and away from contentious issues of politics.

Whatever its attitude to government control, France actively encouraged and promoted colonial theatre. It invested material and human resources (and still does in the independent states). But many post-colonial francophone states have been distrustful of the theatre's independence and anxious to bring it into line with official state thinking, using both direct and indirect censorship methods. The latter take the form of benign neglect except when theatres stage harmless folk dances or spread government propaganda. With the exception of the Daniel Sorano Theatre in Dakar, no remotely adequate playhouse exists in any francophone country; halls in *sports stadiums and legislative assemblies are made to double as theatre buildings. But censorship is also more direct. Theatre licensing commissions within ministries of culture have been established in most countries in the region, as in the rest of sub-Saharan Africa. Where dramatists have failed to heed the negative decisions of these commissions (which range from excising portions of plays to refusing them official performance spaces), the police have stopped performances. Such was the case in 1975 in Côte d'Ivoire with the third performance of Zadi *Zaourou's L'Œil (The Eye), accused of endangering public order. Charles Nokan's Les Malheurs de Tchâko (Tchâko's Misfortunes, 1968) suffered a similar fate as did a performance of René Philombe's Africapolis in Cameroon in 1980, a play whose published text had already been censored.

State indifference and occasional harassment has had several effects. Self-censorship often moves writers and directors to trite subjects or improvised texts, as has apparently happened in Cameroon at the turn of the twenty-first century. More subtly, an increasing dependence on foreign patrons may have affected content and form: the turn to *spectacle in recent francophone African drama might well have been shaped in part by the expectations of foreign festival audiences.   JCM

9. Anglophone Africa

In some pre-colonial African communities (such as among the San people) democratic group social control was so sophisticated that there was no need for censorship. In more economically complex groups, especially those involving feudal forms of kingship, performing artists had low status and were subject to control from their royal patron, but at the same time had a measure of poetic licence to criticize official abuses. Variations of this control–licence paradigm applied to societies between the two extremes.

The proselytizing efforts of Islamic imams from the seventh century and Christian missionaries from the seventeenth led to suppression of many indigenous performance modes. These include the banning of the Bori female spirit possession dance by Hausa Islamic leaders, and the attacks by Christian missions on most forms of masquerade theatre. Denigration of African performance continued into the period of formal colonialism in the areas dominated by Britain (see AFRICAN, ANGLO-PHONE). Christian converts were often allowed into church only if they renounced their participation in African dance. A more subtle control was that of co-option or dilution of indigenous performance. For example, in Rhodesia in the early years of the twentieth century missionaries encouraged *Jerusarema* as a sanitized version of the far more erotic popular *mbende* dance. Christian 'kitchen parties' replaced indigenous initiation rites in many parts of urban Africa.

The main colonial method of censoring formal African drama was through control of the schools and printing presses which provided its artistic womb. Formal censorship, however, particularly of films, was introduced in the 1920s, and films already reviewed by the British censorship board had to pass local boards as well. The encouragement of colonial film making was inspired in part by the desire to protect African audiences from the sexuality or violence of Hollywood and European films. Locally appointed colonial committees also began to vet African scripted drama from the 1950s onwards. When plays fell through this net (particularly unscripted or *devised plays) censorship became more heavy handed. In the 1940s, for example, Hubert *Ogunde's *Worse Than Crime, Strike and Hunger*, and *Bread and Bullet* were banned by colonial police officers in various northern Nigerian cities, and Ogunde was arrested twice.

Some of the worst aspects of colonial censorship were reproduced in a far more repressive form by the South African apartheid regime. The old laws were superseded by a series of draconian acts in the 1950s which prevented the racial mixing of actors or audiences in South African theatres. Plays were subject to a large series of hurdles, including letters of approval from the Censorship Board and local licences for each venue and performance. In addition, the police had the power to prevent playhouses from hosting performances, to confiscate assets (such as costumes) of theatre groups, and to arrest actors. Restrictions and banning orders on individuals added further impediments Most of the leading theatre artists from the 1960s to the 1980s experienced some form of censorship or state-sponsored obstruction; these include John *Kani, Gibson *Kente, Winston *Ntshona, Athol *Fugard, Barney *Simon, Mbongeni *Ngema, Maishe *Maponya, and Matsemela *Manaka. Some, like the leaders of People's Experimental Theatre and Theatre Council of Natal, received long prison sentences after their 1975 trials for treason or other serious charges. In Ian Smith's Rhodesia too there was a ferocious censorship system which affected theatre and music. Perhaps more virulent were the attempts to control indigenous rites such as *bira*, which gave support to guerrillas fighting for Zimbabwean independence.

But independent Africa has also suffered from a range of censorship devices, though rarely with racially divisive motives. Instead, post-colonial governments have attempted to suppress criticism of ruling regimes, although other sensitive issues have been ethnicity, religion, and sexuality. Some countries simply retained colonial legislation, as with the Zimbabwe government's refusal to lift the emergency laws passed by the Smith regime. In other countries special legislation was introduced, such as Malawi's 1967 Censorship Act, which gave censors power to cut or ban playscripts and interfere with dances, costumes, programmes, or almost any aspect of performance, authority backed up by a system of police informants and intimidation of performers. Formal censorship was reinforced by bureaucratic measures. In Kenya, for example, each performance had to be granted a licence by the district commissioner, which could be withdrawn at any time. Indirect pressure could be even more effective, such as telephone threats to playwrights or drama competition adjudicators.

The extreme sensitivity of post-colonial governments to theatrical criticism led to the arrest and/or detention of many theatrical activists. These include Wole *Soyinka from 1967 to 1969 in Nigeria, Ngugi wa *Thiong'o for most of 1977 in Kenya for his involvement in the play *Ngahiika Ndeenda*, Yulisa *Maddy in 1977 for *Big Berrin* in Sierra Leone, and John Kargbo in the same country in 1979 for *Poyoh Ton Wahala*. Tragically some playwrights have been killed. Byron Kawadwa was assassinated by Idi Amin's agents in 1977 because of his play *St Charles Lwanga*, and Nigerian playwright and novelist Ken *Saro-Wiwa was executed in 1995 for his ecological activism. Many African theatre workers were forced into exile. These include Soyinka, wa Thiong'o, and Maddy, the Ugandans John Ruganda and Okot p'Bitek, and the Kenyans Ngugi wa *Mirii, Micere *Mugo, and Kimani Gecau. Although democratic reforms of the 1990s have created a more liberal environment in some countries, especially in South Africa, the existence of continued repression and the legacy of past abuses ensure that self-censorship remains a potent instrument in the prevention of free theatrical expression.   DaK

See also POLITICS AND THEATRE; DRAMATIC PERFORMANCES ACT; INTERCULTURALISM; DIASPORA.

CENTLIVRE, SUSANNAH (c.1667–1723)

English playwright and actress. Centlivre had at least nineteen plays performed on the *London stage between 1700 and 1724 and her work was continually revived through the eighteenth and nineteenth centuries; second to Shakespeare, she was the most performed playwright of both centuries. The stories surrounding Centlivre's origins and early life are confused but the notion that she was first an actress may explain why her plays have been of more interest to the performer than the literary critic. *The Wonder! A Woman Keeps a Secret* (1715) was performed at least 250 times by 1800 with at least 65 of those revivals starring David *Garrick, who chose the play for his farewell performance. Centlivre's popularity lay in her ability to capture and reproduce *realistic *characters and *dialogue, a skill that has resulted in accusations that her work lacks 'wit' and literary merit. Her first play, *The Perjur'd Husband* (1700), was performed at *Drury Lane in a season containing plays by fellow female playwrights Catherine *Trotter and Mary *Pix, with whom Centlivre was closely associated. Writing in the heat of the *anti-theatrical polemic headed by Jeremy *Collier, Centlivre did not attach her name to the publication of her next four *comedies, *The Beau's Duel* (1702), *The Stolen Heiress* (1702), *Love's Contrivance* (1703), and her first commercial hit, *The Gamester* (1705). These early plays embrace the move toward sentimental reform comedies but also challenge conventional constructs of virtuous female behaviour. In *The Gamester* the *hero is saved from the vice of gambling by the ingenious actions of a virtuous heroine, and Centlivre exploited the same setting for her less successful comedy *The Basset Table* (1705), in which one woman's socially acceptable obsession with the gambling table is hilariously contrasted with another woman's socially unacceptable obsession with scientific enquiry and experimentation. Centlivre's relationship with London theatres was often turbulent; the players were initially reluctant to perform *The Busie Body* (1709), although it proved to be her greatest success with some 475 performances in the major theatres alone before 1800. *The Wonder! A Woman Keeps a Secret* (1714) and *A Bold Stroke for a Wife* (1718) had repeated *box-office success largely because Centlivre wrote *plots and characters that attracted successive generations of players. Her plays entered the repertoire of strolling companies, fairs, and tavern theatres in Britain and were performed in Australia and colonial America. GBB

CENTRE CULTUREL ET FOLKLORIQUE DE CÔTE D'IVOIRE

Cultural association founded in 1953 in Abidjan by a group of Ivorian writers and professionals including the dramatists F. J. Amon *d'Aby and Bernard *Dadié. Of its four divisions—theatre, public lectures, library/*film, and the press—only the first two were successful. After an early period when its troupe performed the handful of plays available from the *École William Ponty, it expanded to include pieces that encouraged reform of certain social customs and traditions, written for the purpose by such members as d'Aby, Dadié, and Coffi Gadeau. The CCFI is also notable for introducing *women on the Ivorian stage for the first time, and for promoting, through its cultural work, an atmosphere of understanding among Ivorians at a time when the nationalist politics of rival parties (especially the Parti Démocratique de Côte d'Ivoire and the Parti Progressiste) were dividing the nation. JCM

CERVANTES, TEATRO NACIONAL

Although *Buenos Aires possesses two other national theatres (the *Colón and the Teatro de la Ribera), the Cervantes is considered Argentina's theatrical home. As its name suggests, initial ties to Spain were strong. Proposed in 1918 by the Spanish actors Fernando Díaz de Mendoza and María *Guerrero (frequent visitors to Argentina since their 1897 *tour), embellished by Spanish artisans, and with equipment donated by Spain, the Cervantes opened in 1921 with Lope de *Vega's *La dama boba*. By 1936 it was the home of the Comedia Nacional Argentina. It now contains two performance spaces and houses the National Institute of Theatre Studies. JGJ

CERVANTES SAAVEDRA, MIGUEL DE (1547–1616)

Spanish novelist and playwright. Better known today as the author of *Don Quixote* and the *Exemplary Novels*, Cervantes had already gained a reputation as a popular dramatist before turning to prose fiction. The semi-autobiographical *Trato de Argel* (*Trade of Algiers*), based on Cervantes' captivity in North Africa, and *El cerco de Numancia* (*The Siege of Numantia*), a *tragedy mingling historical fact with popular legend and moral abstractions such as Spain, the River Duero, war, and fame, were early proof of his theatrical talent. The reputation, however, was based primarily on the *comedies performed in *Madrid during the 1580s, a small selection of which were published in the *Comedias y entremeses* of 1615. In a much quoted *prologue to the collection, Cervantes defends his decision to reduce the traditional five-act structure of the Spanish *comedia to three and, after acknowledging his debt to writers like Lope de *Rueda, also defends the use of 'moral figures' as in *The Siege*. Though his *entremeses*, with their blend of *realism, subtle characterization, and lively *dialogue, are generally considered to represent the high point of the *genre (*see* ENTREMETS/ENTREMÉS), Cervantes quickly abandoned the stage in self-confessed deference to the superior comic genius of the up-and-coming playwright Lope de *Vega. KG

CÉSAIRE, AIMÉ (1913–)

Martinican writer and politician, considered one of the founders of *African and *Caribbean francophone literature. Césaire was educated in Martinique, and in Paris at the École Normale Supérieure, where he read classics. He achieved prominence in 1939 with the publication of *Cahier d'un retour natal*, a long autobiographical poem that was to launch the movement of *négritude* and establish him as one of its foremost exponents. He published six other acclaimed collections of poetry and two essays. Above all a poet, it was through drama that he eventually sought to bridge the gap between his densely poetic vision and non-literate *audiences, especially in the developing world. Drama was never absent from his poetry: he concluded *Les Armes miraculeuses* (1946) with a dramatic poem, 'a lyric oratorio' that he later rearranged for the stage as *Et les chiens se taisaient* (published as *And the Dogs Were Silent*, 1990). He moved to full-fledged drama with his masterpiece *La Tragédie du roi Christophe* (1963): the philosophical abstraction the figure of the Rebel in *Et les chiens* is given concrete particularity in the historical personage Christophe in Césaire's *tragedy. Through the mirror of the character's experiences as ruler of post-revolutionary Haiti in the early nineteenth century, Césaire reflects on the problems of African decolonization, a question pursued in *Une saison au Congo* (1966) through the tragic career of the leader of Congolese independence, Patrice Lumumba. Césaire's third play, *Une tempête* (1968), rewrites Shakespeare's *The Tempest* to speak to conditions of New World plantation slavery, colonial rule, and the master–slave dialectic.

Like the Rebel in *Et les chiens*, Césaire's central *characters—Christophe, Lumumba, and Caliban—are all possessed of a sense of justice that impels them to rise up against historical conditions that wear the face of an implacable destiny. They invariably fail, but their failure, in the tradition of heroic tragedy, exhilarates rather than depresses. Besides the poetic quality of its *dialogue, and the mythical resonance of its characters and their situations, Césaire's work is especially notable for its combination of *Brechtian and indigenous Afro-Caribbean performance techniques, an effort enhanced by the productions of his plays by the *Brecht-inspired French director Jean-Marie *Serreau. *See also* POLITICS AND THEATRE; POST-COLONIAL STUDIES.

JCM

CÉSAIRE, INA (1942–)

Playwright and ethnologist from Martinique. She studied and taught in France then settled in Martinique, near her sister Michele, a director and playwright, and their famous father, the *négritude* poet-statesman Aimé *Césaire. She has collected traditional tales and women's life-stories, constructing ethnodramas and political *comedies aimed at preserving the Martinican popular heritage. *Mémoires d'Isles* (1985) was first performed in *Paris by the Campagnol troupe and later as *Island Memories* at Ubu Repertory of *New York; *Rosanie Soleil* was staged as *Fire's Daughters* (1992) by the *African-American playwright and director Ntozake *Shange at the same location.

CJM

CHAIKIN, JOSEPH (1935–)

American actor, director, playwright, *producer, and theorist. Born in Brooklyn to Russian émigré parents, he was raised in Iowa and educated at Drake University. In 1955 he moved to *New York and co-founded the Harlequin Players, with whom he acted and directed. Chaikin joined Julian *Beck and Judith *Malina's *Living Theatre in 1959 and performed in such roles as Galy Gay in *Brecht's *A Man's a Man* (1962), for which he won the first of six Obie *awards. He appeared in the Living Theatre productions of *The Connection* (1959) and *In the Jungle of the Cities* (1961). Chaikin founded the *Open Theatre in 1963, an experimental *Off-Off Broadway company, in order to explore new methods of *acting practice and *collective creation. He directed the Open Theatre productions of *Viet Rock* (1966), *The Serpent* (1968), *Terminal* (1969), *Mutation Show* (1971), and *Nightwalk* (1973). Chaikin's *directing strategies proved to be highly influential and included a physical, *improvisatorial, workshop approach developed through notions of the presence of the actor's voice and body. His book *The Presence of the Actor* (1972) sets forth his primary *theories of performance as an organic process based in the actor's body. The Open Theatre disbanded in 1973 and Chaikin went on to found the Other Theatre, where he directed productions of *Van Itallie's *Chekhov translations. In 1976 he founded the Winter Project, an annual twelve-week workshop with actors, musicians, and writers who explored storytelling for the theatre. Chaikin suffered a stroke in 1984 during heart surgery and as a result was rendered aphastic. He has continued to direct, write, and teach, producing collaborations with Sam *Shepard, Van Itallie, and Susan Yankowitz. The Joseph Chaikin papers are housed at Kent State University.

MDC

CHAILLOT, THÉÂTRE DU

*Paris *playhouse, attached to the complex of museums and exhibition spaces in the Palais de Chaillot, built in 1937 on the right bank of the Seine across from the Eiffel Tower. It replaced the old Théâtre du Trocadéro, which since 1920 had been under the direction of Firmin *Gémier and his newly formed *Théâtre National Populaire. The new theatre, with its massive dimensions, doubled as a debating chamber for the United Nations Organization from 1947 to 1951. After Jean *Vilar took over the TNP in 1951, the theatre became a focal point for his vision to popularize and decentralize the arts in France. In 1972 the theatre closed for major renovations, following designs commissioned by Antoine *Vitez, who ran the theatre from 1981 to 1988, and Jack Lang, later the Minister of Culture under François Mitterrand. Jérôme *Savary directed the theatre from 1988 until 2000.

CHB

CHALBAUD, ROMÁN (1931–)

Venezuelan playwright and director. Since *Los adolescentes* (*The Adolescents*, 1951), Chalbaud has written over seventeen plays and directed over 100 plays and sixteen *films. Many of his major works date from the mid-1950s and the 1960s, including *Caín adolescente* (*Cain as an Adolescent*, 1955, filmed 1958),

Sagrado y obsceno (*Sacred and Obscene*, 1964, filmed 1975), *La quema de Judas* (*The Burning of Judas*, 1964, filmed 1974), *Los ángeles terribles* (*The Terrible Angels*, 1967) and *El pez que fuma* (*The Smoking Fish*, 1968, filmed 1976). In 1967 he formed El *Nuevo Grupo with Isaac *Chocrón and José I. *Cabrujas. Recurrent themes are the marginalization of individuals, mother–son relationships, magic and the esoteric, prostitution and homosexuality. His work, fully committed to social justice, criticizes the Church as well as corrupt social and political institutions. He received the National Prize for Theatre in 1984.

LCL trans. AMCS

CHAMBERLAIN'S MEN, LORD

Theatre company in *early modern *London, formed in 1594 as half of a 'duopoly' along with the Lord *Admiral's Men, and created to replace the *Queen's Men as providers of royal entertainment at Christmas. Its membership was drawn from several groups whose patrons had recently died. Most of them came from *Strange's Men and Pembroke's Men via Sussex's. The new company's leading player was Richard *Burbage, son of the owner of the *Theatre, their allocated *playhouse. Shakespeare was a sharer and the company's contracted playwright. They began their long career with a rich repertory of Shakespeare's plays, and at the same time acquired several old Queen's Men plays, subsequently rewritten as *King John*, the *Henry IV* and *Henry V* series, *Hamlet*, and *King Lear*.

The two companies of the duopoly became the longest lived of all the playing companies in the Shakespearian era. The Admiral's Men ran, under different patrons' names, from 1594 until the death of King James in 1625. The Chamberlain's Men, with James as their patron from 1603, ran on as the King's Men until the closure of the theatres in 1642, a total of 48 years. Their staple repertory included all of Shakespeare's plays that have survived, the work of *Jonson, *Middleton, *Massinger, *Davenant, and *Shirley, together with the 50 or more plays by several collaborative authors known as the *Beaumont and *Fletcher canon.

During the duopoly, between 1594 and 1603, they staged more than half the plays given at court for the winter entertainments. That ratio was sustained under the first Stuart kings, especially once the company had the *Blackfriars Theatre for winter playing indoors. Although Shakespeare wrote only one of his plays (*The Tempest*) for the Blackfriars instead of the *Globe, the indoor theatre had been built for them as early as 1596 to replace the old Theatre. Roofed playhouses were always favoured by the gentry and nobility, but in 1596 the company lacked the social cachet they needed to secure a playing-place in the most affluent precinct in the city. Once they had established their name thanks to their Shakespeare plays and had the King as their patron, they had no trouble taking over the Blackfriars in 1608. From then on, using the Globe in summer and the

Blackfriars in winter, they were unchallenged as the foremost playing company in England.

AJG

CHAMBERS, JANE (1937–83)

American playwright. Born in South Carolina, Chambers studied at the *Pasadena Playhouse and Goddard College. She worked as an actress, journalist, and *television broadcaster before she became a full-time writer. *Christ in a Treehouse* (1971) won a Connecticut Educational Television award, and she received a Writers Guild award (1973) for her contributions to the CBS series *Search for Tomorrow*. *A Late Snow* (1974) was her first major play, followed by *The Common Garden Variety* (*Mark Taper Laboratory, 1976), and she received a DramaLogue Critics Circle *award for *Last Summer at Bluefish Cove* (1980). Her other important plays are *Kudzu* (1981), *My Blue Heaven* (1981), and *The Quintessential Image* (1983). Her plays are often set in minority or ethnic subcultures, and her novel *Burning* (1978) is a *lesbian classic. In her name, the Association for Theatre in Higher Education gives an annual award to a *feminist play with strong roles for women.

FL

CHAMBERS OF RHETORIC

Rederijkerskamers were *amateur literary guilds, possibly the descendants of earlier religious confraternities, but similar in their organization to contemporary archers' *guilds. Varying in size from about 15 to 150, the Chambers of Rhetoric dominated dramatic production in the Low Countries in the fifteenth and sixteenth centuries, regularly contributing *tableaux vivants* and dramas, both religious and secular, to public festivities. The *stages used by the Rhetoricians could be very elaborate, featuring several levels and 'inner stages' behind decorated façades. The Chambers also competed with one another in drama, particularly in the *esbattement* (a short *farce), the *factie* (a comic street scene), and the more serious *spel van sinne* (*morality play). The best known among the latter are *The Blessed Apple Tree* (1500), *Man's Desire and Fleeting Beauty* (1546), and *Elekerlijc*, better known in its English translation as *Everyman* (c.1495).

RWV

CHAMOISEAU, PATRICK (1953–)

Martinican novelist, critic, and playwright. Chamoiseau is best known as a novelist, particularly since his third novel *Texaco* received the prestigious Goncourt award in 1992. He is also a key figure of the *créolité* movement fostering *creole language and culture, launched by Martinican intellectuals in 1989. His one play, *Maman Dlo contre la fée Carabosse* (*Mama Dlo against the Wicked Fairy Carabosse*, published 1982), an adaptation for the stage of a creole *folk tale, represents an attempt to bring together theatre and traditional storytelling, in what he calls *théâtre conté* or story theatre. Two of his novels, *Solibo magnifique* and *L'Esclave vieil homme et le molosse*, have also been adapted for the stage (1991 and 1999).   LEM

CHAMPION, GOWER (1921–80)

American choreographer and director. He began his career in the 1930s, *dancing in supper clubs with his partner June Taylor. By the late 1930s, their dancing was featured in Broadway *revues. After the Second World War, he teamed with his first wife Marge, and they danced together on stage and in *films. In 1948 he began directing and choreographing for Broadway, but his reputation as a master director/choreographer was really established in the 1960s with *Bye Bye Birdie*, *Carnival*, and *Hello, Dolly!* While the first two were remarkably clever, the third introduced the Champion hallmark—a polished *spectacle verging on over-production which rarely gave *audiences a chance to catch their breaths. Cleverness was also the mark of *I Do, I Do* (1966), which elevated an intimate two-character *musical to Broadway scale. But Champion's cleverness and tendency to over-production could sometimes harm a show, as in the case of *The Happy Time* (1968) or *Mack and Mabel* (1974). His last success was one of his most opulent: *42nd Street*, produced by David *Merrick, which opened on the day he died.
                                                                    JD

CHAMPMESLÉ, MLLE (MARIE DESMARES) (1642–98)

French actress. Moving with her husband in 1670 from the company at the *Marais Theatre in *Paris to the more prestigious *Hôtel de Bourgogne, Mlle Champmeslé performed with great success in the *tragedies of *Racine (roles of Bérénice, Roxane in *Bajazet*, Monime in *Mithridate*, Phèdre); Racine (whose mistress she became) is known to have coached her in the speaking of his *verse. In 1679 a royal decree transferred the Champmeslés to the *Guénégaud Théâtre, where the enlarged company was to form the Théâtre Français, with Mlle Champmeslé continuing to star in Racine's tragedies. Renouncing her profession on her deathbed, she was given a Christian burial.   WDH

CHANCEREL, LÉON (1886–1965)

French actor, director, and teacher, the champion of *youth and *amateur theatre. A disciple of Jacques *Copeau, Chancerel founded the Compagnie des Comédiens Routiers in 1929. A small, all-male troupe, which was affiliated with the Scouts de France, they *toured throughout the provinces, performing in small venues or in a travelling *open-air tent structure which he called the Theatre of the Four Winds. Conceived as a completely popular theatre, where the repertoire consisted of *medieval *farces, dramatic songs, *commedia dell'arte, and adaptations of Rabelais and *Sophocles, the Comédiens Routiers fashioned their own *costumes and *masks, an activity that became integral to Chancerel's educational goals and amateur aesthetic. At his urging the regional drama centres undertook a teaching mission, each under the direction of an instructor charged with advising an amateur troupe and leading dramatic workshops, culminating in open-air performances for the local community and in a national competition. Chancerel thus became a unique influence on the post-war decentralization of French theatre.   DGM

CHANFRAU, FRANK S. (1824–84)

American actor. Chanfrau won initial fame impersonating Edwin *Forrest, thereafter creating the role of 'Mose, the Bowery B'hoy' in *A Glance at New York* (1848). He indelibly established this stage fireman as an icon in red shirt, turned up trousers, and plug hat, and played the *character for two decades. As age encroached he found two other parts, performed in virtual *repertory until his death. In 1865 he triumphed in *Sam* as a heroic Yankee in England foiling numerous comic *villains (783 performances); and from 1870 he achieved great success as *Kit, the Arkansas Traveller*, a *frontier *melodrama (560 performances).   TFC

CH'ANGGŬK

Korean performance that mixes music, song, and drama. Popular at the beginning of the twentieth century, ch'anggŭk (song and drama) developed from the traditional *folk opera (*p'ansori) under the influence of the Western stage. Inaugurated in the first Western-style indoor theatre in Seoul, the Hyŏpyul Theatre (1902, later renamed the Wŏngak Theatre), the sentimental repertory was based on the five surviving stories of p'ansori. The first ch'anggŭk script, *The Ballad of Ch'oe Pyŏng-tu* (1908), was written for the Wŏngak Theatre; it was based on an actual incident of a provincial inspector who died in prison while on a robbery charge concocted by the Japanese police. This focus on contemporary issues, and the combination of p'ansori stories with Western-style staging, contributed to the sudden popularity of the form.

Modifying the solo p'ansori into a multi-actor Western *opera, ch'anggŭk sought to be a modern performance *genre rooted in tradition. But despite the success of *The Ballad of Ch'oe Pyŏng-tu*, ch'anggŭk lost momentum because of its limited repertoire, giving way to modern commercial theatre (*shinp'agŭk) imported from *Japan. After liberation from Japan in 1945 a women's theatre group continued to perform the genre until the 1960s, and ch'anggŭk performances are occasionally seen today at the National Theatre in Seoul. *See* KOREA.   JOC

CHANLATTE, JUSTE (1776–1828)

Haitian poet and dramatist from Port-au-Prince. As the editor of the *Gazette d'Haiti* in the reign of King Christophe, and of the *Télégraphe* under President Boyer, he put his pen to the service of these two heads of state. Although critics accuse him of excessive flattery of King Christophe in his unpublished play *Nehri* and in *La Partie de chasse du roi* (*The King's Hunting Party*, 1820), they nonetheless recognize his skill in handling plot and his realistic portrayal of *characters in both French and *creole.   MLa trans. JCM

CHANNING, CAROL (1921–)

American actress and singer. A long-legged blonde with peerless comic timing and a remarkably flexible voice that could shift from a shrill squeal to a deep rasp, she began her stage career in the early 1940s. She first attracted major notice in *Lend an Ear*, a 1948 *revue, and became a star as the quintessential gold-digger Lorelei Lee in *Gentlemen Prefer Blondes* (1949), in which she introduced 'Diamonds Are a Girl's Best Friend'. While attempts were made to find a suitable vehicle for her unique talent, none appeared until 1964, when she created the title role in *Hello, Dolly!*, which she would continue to play for twenty years. She worked regularly in nightclubs, on *television, and in *film, earning an Emmy and an Academy award nomination in the 1960s. Recent film work has been confined to voiceovers in animated features. In 1995 she was awarded a special Tony *award for lifetime achievement.   JD

CHANNING, STOCKARD (1944–)

American actress Educated at Harvard, Channing made her debut in *The Investigation* (*Boston, 1966). After briefly appearing on Broadway in 1971, she divided her career between artistically challenging roles on stage and a host of mostly forgettable appearances in *television and *film—with the major exception of her performance as Betty Rizzo in the film version of *Grease* (1978). Her theatre career experienced a rebirth with her *award-winning performance as Sheila in a Broadway revival of Peter *Nichols's *A Day in the Death of Joe Egg* (1985). More critically acclaimed stage work followed, including a revival of *The House of the Blue Leaves* (1986), *Woman in Mind* (1988), and *Love Letters* (1989). She entered the 1990s playing the conscience-stricken New York socialite Ouisa in John *Guare's *Six Degrees of Separation* (1990), which secured her reputation as one of the best actors of her generation, particularly of intelligent, offbeat *characters. Other notable credits

include *Hapgood* (1995) and revivals of *The Little Foxes* (1997) and *The Lion in Winter* (1999).   JAB

CHAPELLE DU VERBE INCARNÉ

French theatre, located in a seventeenth-century former chapel, which showcases productions by actors from the French departments at the *Avignon Festival. It was founded by Guadeloupean actor and director Greg Germain and Marie-Pierre Bousquet in 1998, the 150th anniversary of the abolition of slavery in French territory. Their production company Théâtres d'Outre-mer en Avignon (Overseas Theatres in Avignon) brings artists from Réunion, French Guiana, Martinique, and Guadeloupe to make European *audiences aware of the variety of theatre created by the 'other' French artists from across the seas. *See also* CARIBBEAN THEATRE, FRANCOPHONE.
                                                         AR

CHAPEL ROYAL, CHILDREN OF THE

A company of boy choristers who staged plays at court, and later for the public in the first *Blackfriars *playhouse in *London. The Chapel Royal had choirs at Windsor and Greenwich, and in 1576 Richard Farrant, master at Windsor and a gentleman of the Chapel Royal at Greenwich from 1570, copied St Paul's, where in the previous year a playhouse was built adjoining the cathedral, by opening a playhouse in the nearby Blackfriars. The Children had played regularly at court since 1566, and now, in the year the *Theatre was built for adult players, they extended their offerings to the public. When Farrant died in 1580 the Chapel companies merged, under the Earl of Oxford's patronage, and John *Lyly became their playwright and *manager. Some years later they joined with Paul's Boys, but were banned from playing in 1590. A *boy company playing at a different Blackfriars playhouse from 1600 till 1608 used the same name. *See also* BOY ACTOR.   AJG

CHAPMAN, GEORGE (c.1560–1634)

English dramatist. Born at Hitchin, he was educated at the local grammar school, which had a dramatic tradition, and may have attended university. He emerged as a dramatist in his thirties, later in life than most of his professional colleagues, and quickly established himself as *London's most brilliant comic writer. His first known play, *The Blind Beggar of Alexandria*, was a huge commercial success for the *Admiral's Men in 1596: ostensibly an exotic political romance in the *genre of *Marlowe's *Tamburlaine*, its appeal centres on the multiple identities adopted by the title *character, each one delineated with a distinctive quirk of personality. In Chapman's next play, *The Comedy of Humours* (1597; later printed as *A Humorous Day's Mirth*), this developed into a new technique of comic characterization based on individual idiosyncrasies (*see* COMEDY OF HUMOURS): the play's primary dramatic interest comes from these eccentricities rather than from a sustained, romantic *plot such as had previously been the norm in *comedy. This strikingly original treatment of the *genre was soon imitated by Shakespeare (notably in *Much Ado About Nothing*) and Ben *Jonson.

Chapman continued to write for the Admiral's Men until 1599, but no other plays survive from this period. When the London *boys' companies reopened he transferred his services to them, writing his best-known *tragedy, *Bussy D'Ambois* (1604), for Paul's and a series of polished, sardonic comedies for the *Blackfriars. One of these, the collaborative *Eastward Hoe* (1605, with Jonson and *Marston), led to his imprisonment when its topical *satire offended the King. His interest in recent French history as tragic subject matter, first seen in *Bussy D'Ambois*, had similarly awkward consequences: in 1608, his two-part *Conspiracy and Tragedy of Charles, Duke of Biron* dramatized events of only six years earlier, and its undignified portrayal of living members of the French royal family (including a scene where the Queen slaps a female courtier) resulted in a formal protest from the French ambassador, and the Blackfriars Boys lost their theatre and royal patronage. Chapman stayed with the company in its new form; in 1610 he rewrote *Bussy D'Ambois* for their revival, along with a new sequel, *The Revenge of Bussy D'Ambois*.

Chapman had links with the court, and wrote one of the *masques for Princess Elizabeth's wedding in 1613, but he was unlucky in his patrons: Prince Henry died young in 1612, and the Earl of Somerset's power was eclipsed by scandal in 1615. Chapman returned to Hitchin in debt, and concentrated on non-dramatic writing, including his famous translation of Homer. In 1631 he published another tragedy, *Caesar and Pompey*, but never again wrote for the London stage. His long-term success rested not on his comedies (though *All Fools* and *The Widow's Tears* were produced in the 1660s), but on *Bussy D'Ambois*, which entered the repertory of the King's Men (*see* CHAMBERLAIN'S MEN, LORD) about 1616, with Nathan *Field in the title role. It was among the first plays to be revived after the Restoration, but remained in production only until the 1670s. A revival by Jonathan *Miller (*Old Vic, 1988) was not considered a success.   MJW

CHAPPUZEAU, SAMUEL (1625–1701)

French dramatist and theatre historian. Largely forgotten as a playwright (though he wrote some interesting *comedies of manners), Chappuzeau is deservedly remembered as a pioneer historian of the French theatre. His *Théâtre français* (1674) provides valuable source material for later writers, and in particular offers a sympathetic picture of the life of an actor.   WDH

CHARABANC THEATRE COMPANY

Northern Irish venture, based in Belfast, which *toured some 21 productions extensively during its twelve-year history from 1983. Eighteen of the works were the result of a collaboration by the five co-founders, actors Marie *Jones, Eleanor Methven, Carol Moore, Brenda Winter, and Maureen McCauley, in response to the lack of strong women's roles in Irish theatre. The first production, *Lay up your Ends* (1983), centred around the 1911 Linen Mill Strike in Belfast. Charabanc was noted for its energy, skill, and commitment to voicing the experiences of women within the diverse communities of Northern Ireland.
                                                                     MAS

CHARACTER *see page 253*

CHARIOT AND POLE *See* SCENE SHIFTING.

CHARIOT RACES *See* CIRCUS, ROMAN.

CHARIVARI

In 1841 the British magazine *Punch* borrowed its subtitle from the French daily paper *Le Charivari*, founded in 1832 to ridicule the oddities of society. Meaning 'rough music', it derives from the fourteenth- or fifteenth-century Latin term *chalvaricum*, found in church bans, and referring to a 'tumult' against unpopular marriages, particularly involving widows and unequal matches, which were customarily greeted by a barrage of catcalls. (The German *Katzenmusik* nicely captures its disharmonic pleasures.) The later English version was reserved for the marriage of butchers, when the congregation used marrow-bones and cleavers to create a racket. Noise continued in the eighteenth-century European version, with anarchic processions of *dancers, singers, drummers, and maskers rabble-rousing the night streets. The *masks (or *buffones*) were taken up by the respectable, enjoying the anonymity conferred by devil-masks, demons rattling pots and pans, depraved monks with lions' manes and bare bottoms, and the wild man Hellequin—or *Harlequin.   BRK

CHAURETTE, NORMAND (1954–   )

Québec playwright. His early promise has been amply confirmed in a series of seminal plays that are as impressive for their innovations in *dramaturgy as for their original thematic content, notably *Provincetown Playhouse, juillet 1919, j'avais 19 ans* (*Provincetown Playhouse, July 1919, I was 19*, 1982), now a classic of modern Québécois theatre. Focusing on the onstage murder of a child, it inextricably melds real

(continued on p. 254)

CHARACTER

In narrative generally, a character is a person depicted within a story, either through description or direct speech; in *drama and dramatic *performance specifically, the term usually refers only to the people portrayed by *actors. In either case, characters need not be human beings, but can be any kind of sentient agent: gods, animals, aliens, or even animated plants or household objects. *Aristotle ranks character second only to *plot among the six elements of *tragedy, and in many modern plays, such as *Chekhov's, character is more important than plot. Though character is a ubiquitous term, its meaning has shifted over time and the concept remains highly ambiguous.

One way to conceive of dramatic character is as the representation of an individual person, either real or fictional. Each character has a biography and an array of personal characteristics—physical attributes, mannerisms, desires, objectives, beliefs—that the *text defines only incompletely and that the actor will elaborate on when developing a performance. It follows from this concept of character that when *Aeschylus, *Sophocles, and *Euripides each wrote plays about Electra, they created three distinct characters. It also follows that each actor who plays a role creates a distinct character, so that, for example, Laurence *Olivier's Hamlet was a different character from Mel Gibson's. This concept of character became prevalent toward the end of the nineteenth century as *playwrights such as *Ibsen and *Strindberg created increasingly individuated characters with complex and contradictory motivations and richly developed psychological histories. This kind of psychological *realism encouraged critics and practitioners to analyse dramatic characters as if they were real people. Influential critics of the late nineteenth and early twentieth centuries such as Edward Dowden and A. C. Bradley retroactively applied this concept of character to earlier dramas, especially the works of Shakespeare (see PSYCHOANALYTIC CRITICISM). *Stanislavsky's system, developed during the first decades of the twentieth century, was predicated on a similar concept of character, enjoining actors to flesh out the 'given circumstances' of their characters. This view of character came under attack throughout the twentieth century for various reasons. In the 1930s, New Critics such as L. C. Knights argued that characters have no existence beyond the text that defines them and therefore should be analysed on a purely formal level, as nothing more or less than a particular constellation of words. Marxist critics argued that characters should be understood as representatives of their socio-economic class rather than in terms of individual psych-

ology (see MATERIALIST CRITICISM). In the 1970s and 1980s post-*structuralist theorists suggested that the modern conception of the autonomous subject that underlies this concept of character had not fully emerged during previous periods of theatre history. Jean-Pierre Vernant, for example, makes this argument with respect to *Greek theatre (Myth and Tragedy in Ancient Greece, 1990), and Catherine Belsey with respect to the English *early modern period (The Subject of Tragedy, 1985).

Another way to conceive of character is as a type rather than an individual concept: not as something people are but something they have. For example, a person may have a brave or dishonest character. The ethical connotation of character goes back to the Poetics, where the word Aristotle uses for dramatic character, ethos, is the same he uses in his books on ethics. *Medieval *morality plays explicitly adopt a type concept of character, providing almost no individuating information about characters and giving them abstract names such as Everyman and Vice. Similarly, characters in the Stuart court *masques were almost pure types: aristocrats played idealized fairies, shepherds, and gods that represented the qualities they wished to connect to themselves.

Many theatrical traditions define a limited number of recurring character types. Greek *New Comedy introduced a set of conventional characters, such as the wily servant, the foolish pedant, and the braggart soldier, which carried into *Roman *comedy, resurfaced in the *commedia dell'arte of the Italian early modern period, and persisted throughout the twentieth century in popular *films and *television shows (see STOCK CHARACTER). Many non-Western traditions similarly rely on sharply delineated conventional types. For example, *Indian Sanskrit dramas draw on a set of character types defined in the *Natyasastra, and the texts of the plays indicate the speaker by type name, such as *vidushaka (*clown), rather than an individual character's name. In most theatrical traditions that rely on highly conventional character types, such as the commedia dell'arte or *kutiyattam, actors specialize in the portrayal of a particular type throughout their career (see also LINES OF BUSINESS). In the first half of the twentieth century, performers in the British *music hall and American *vaudeville traditions, such as Laurel and Hardy, Abbott and Costello, and the *Marx Brothers, developed highly identifiable character types that they used to perform a wide variety of individual characters—for example Laurel and Hardy in the Old West or Abbott and Costello on Mars—highlighting the distinction between these two notions of character.

In the 1960s creators of *happenings, *performance artists, experimental theatre groups such as the *Living Theatre, and playwrights such as Peter *Handke tried to remove character from performance altogether. The goal was to produce an unmediated encounter between the *audience and the 'authentic' reality of the performers. Michael Kirby (*A Formalist Theatre*, 1987) described performances without characters or fictional narratives as 'non-matrixed'. The director Jerzy *Grotowski replaced the notion of character with that of the performance 'score': a series of rigorously defined and *rehearsed actions constituting a kind of *ritual. Many theorists, however, came to regard attempts to eliminate character from theatre as quixotic, and Grotowski himself despaired that he stripped away his actors' *masks only to reveal new masks underneath.

As Elinor Fuchs suggests in *The Death of Character* (1996), a key feature of much postmodern theatre is a rejection of traditional notions of dramatic character (*see* MODERNISM AND POSTMODERNISM). Far from trying to expose the true self of the performer, however, the impulse here is to deny the possibility of a true, stable, coherent self either onstage or off. In Robert *Wilson and Philip *Glass's *Einstein on the Beach* (1976), for example, an actor *costumed like Einstein functions as an iconic image in an animated collage, making no attempt to embody the character he signifies, and in plays such as Heiner *Müller's *Hamletmachine* (1979), each speech evokes a dense network of fragmented characters and allusions to previous texts. *See also* THEORIES OF DRAMA, THEATRE, AND PERFORMANCE.

DZS

and solipsistic theatrical time/space, disturbing yet fascinating spectator and reader. *Les Reines* (*The Queens*, 1982), set in London in 1483, explores the offstage world of the female *characters in Shakespeare's *Richard III*, while *Stabat Mater II* (1999) portrays a complexity of attitudes towards death.

LED

CHAUTAUQUA AND LYCEUM

American systems of educational programming. Originating in the nineteenth century with goals of moral and cultural uplift, they both tapped into the American mania for self-improvement but gradually foregrounded entertainment values. The American Lyceum began in 1826 when Josiah Holbrook opened a centre at Millbury, Massachusetts, for exhibits of natural history. Within a decade there were 3,000 lyceums around the country. The range of subjects expanded as prominent platform figures offered lectures and debates; these included Daniel Webster, Frederick Douglass, Henry David Thoreau, Henry Ward Beecher, Oliver Wendell Holmes, Lucy Stone, and Mark Twain. Lyceum, presented indoors during the winter months in population centres, enjoyed the support and participation of college teachers, as James Redpath built his preeminent Lyceum circuit by offering good pay to educators for lecturing.

Whereas Lyceum featured a single presenter in a one-night stand, Chautauqua offered varied programmes that would play a week under brown tents (as opposed to white *circus tents) in rural areas (*see* TENT SHOW). Begun in 1874 as a two-week National Sunday School Assembly on the shore of Lake Chautauqua, New York, by Methodist minister John H. Vincent, Chautauqua brought together the various Protestant denominations in group activities with an intellectual foundation. The enterprise expanded rapidly after 1904 when Keith Vawter began to offer cultural entertainment packages along planned routes in summer. *One-person dramatic performances enlivened the early fare, soon supplemented by musical numbers, scientific demonstrations (hypnotism, electricity, phrenology), chalk talks (sketching in pastels while bantering with the *audience), and stereopticon travel tales. During the First World War, many women were employed as agents travelling independently in assigned territories, often working for both Chautauqua and Lyceum. Circuit Chautauqua peaked in 1923 when it reached 40 million people in 10,000 communities. The rise of *radio and *film eroded public support for the programmes.

FHL

CHAYEFSKY, PADDY (1923–81)

American playwright. A master of *dialogue, he wrote for *television, *film, and stage as his work moved from *realistic romance to socially critical *satire. He helped launch the golden age of live television with eleven plays for NBC (1952–6). Language, not action, drove his *plots about the problems of ordinary middle-class men, drawn from his own Bronx background. *Marty* (1955), originally a television play with Rod Steiger, became a celebrated film with Ernest Borgnine. *Middle of the Night* (1956) travelled from television to Broadway and then to film; the piece shows a young woman and an older man who find love. Tyrone *Guthrie directed Chayefsky's most successful play, *The Tenth Man* (1959), which pits psychoanalysis against the synagogue, as modern sceptics perform a Jewish exorcism. Guthrie also directed *Gideon* (1961), a debate about God. *The Passion of Josef D.* (1964) attempted *Brechtian techniques to dramatize the relationship between Stalin and Lenin. In *The Latent Heterosexual* (1968), an *absurdist piece, an eccentric homosexual succumbs to the lure of the corporate machine. After discord with Zero *Mostel in the leading role, Chayefsky concentrated on film for the remainder of his career. His screenplays include *The Hospital* (1971), *Network* (1976), and *Altered States* (1980).

FL

CHEA SAMY (1919–94)

Cambodian court dancer, teacher, and choreographer. Born in Kompong Cham province to farmers, and raised at the royal palace from the age of 5, she is recognized as the most important figure in post-Khmer Rouge dance in *Cambodia. A star of the court *dance, and a favourite of King Monivong, Chea danced the sacred role of Moni Mekhala. The reverence accorded her as a dancer and teacher before the war and revolution of the 1970s redoubled in the aftermath of the country's trauma. In the 1980s and early 1990s she fought extreme poverty, political interference, and arthritic knees to teach a younger generation the technique and old stories, and to choreograph new pieces, including *Priep Santepheap* (*Doves of Peace*). She also initiated a dance documentation project, still continued by her students.

TSP

CHEEK BY JOWL

British *touring company, founded in 1981 by Declan *Donellan and designer Nick Ormerod. They toured widely at home and abroad with a changing small company of young players, mounting one or two classic plays every year, and usually appearing in *London for several weeks, often at the *Donmar Warehouse. The company's first production, *The Country Wife*, was a great success, which continued with an adaptation of *Vanity Fair*, a good deal of Shakespeare, including a famous all-male *As You Like It* (1991), and foreign plays such as *Racine's *Andromaque* (1984), *Corneille's *Le Cid* (1986), and *Musset's *Don't Fool with Love* (1993). The company's hallmarks were clear and inventive treatment of the *text, fast continuous action, ensemble *acting, and minimal but inventive sets. In 1989 Donnellan and Ormerod produced *Fuente Ovejuna* at the Royal *National Theatre to general acclaim, and since then they have been increasingly in demand elsewhere. For *financial reasons the company was in abeyance from 1998 to 2002.

EEC

CHEKHOV, ANTON (1860–1904)

Russian playwright and short-story writer. Best known for his four major plays, *The Seagull* (1896), *Uncle Vanya* (1897), *Three Sisters* (1901), and *The Cherry Orchard* (1904), Chekhov also produced a corpus of other dramatic works and more than 500 short stories. He began both his literary careers in the 1880s while qualifying as a doctor. The vast apprentice work that is now known as *Platonov* was completed in 1881 but not published until 1923 and first performed (in German) five years later. This was followed by the *one-act plays and *vaudevilles *On the High Road* (1885, published 1914), *Swansong* (*Kalkhas*, 1887), *The Bear* (1888), *The Proposal* (1888), *The Unwilling Tragedian* (1889), *Tatyana Repina* (1889), *The Wedding* (1890), *The Anniversary* (1892), and a dramatic *monologue *On the Harmfulness of Tobacco* (1886, revised 1903). Apart from *Platonov*, his first attempts at full-length plays were *Ivanov* (*Moscow, 1887; revised for *St Petersburg, 1889) and *The Wood Demon* (Moscow, 1889), subsequently reworked as *Uncle Vanya*.

The unsuccessful première of *The Seagull* in 1896 (*Aleksandrinsky Theatre, St Petersburg) almost deflected Chekhov from further playwriting, though the already composed *Uncle Vanya* was performed in the provinces in 1897. Chekhov was persuaded by Vladimir *Nemirovich-Danchenko to allow the *Moscow Art Theatre to restage *The Seagull* in its opening season (1898, directed by him and *Stanislavsky), and the production epitomized the contemporaneity, *naturalistic sets, and *acting style for which the company became famous. *Uncle Vanya* followed in 1899. His reputation firmly established, Chekhov wrote his two final plays for MAT, *Three Sisters* (1901) and *The Cherry Orchard* (1904). He married Olga *Knipper, a leading actress at MAT, and introduced *Gorky to the company. There is little doubt that the partnership of Chekhov, Stanislavsky, Nemirovich-Danchenko, and the designer Viktor *Simov was responsible for the success of MAT in the peak period of 1898 to 1904, the year of the playwright's early death from tuberculosis. Chekhov and Stanislavsky frequently disagreed over interpretation, the playwright insisting his works were social *comedies, the director emphasizing their wistful fragility in order to create mood pieces about a dying way of life. Stanislavsky won this struggle, and the naturalistic productions by MAT set a programmatic style. The collaboration ensured a classic status for Chekhov, both in Russia and when MAT travelled abroad, but led to a constraint on production method which was only questioned in the latter half of the twentieth century. In collaboration with Simov, Stanislavsky captured Chekhov's topography: his sense of landscape and interior and exterior space. Stanislavsky also had an acute ear for Chekhov's innovations in *dialogue, where the uttered *text belied another drama hidden within (the *subtext), contributing greatly to Stanislavsky's understanding of concepts such as 'interior monologue' and 'the inner life of the role' central to his 'system' of acting. Embedded in a repertoire which focused on contemporary drama (*Ibsen, *Hauptmann, Gorky) and Russian classics (*Ostrovsky, *Turgenev), Chekhov's plays echoed and toyed with these other texts.

The MAT monopolized first-rate productions of Chekhov until the revolution, though some competition came from the Aleksandrinsky Theatre, which staged the four major plays between 1902 and 1910. Notable post-revolutionary productions of Chekhov, often seen as out of step with the new times, included *Vakhtangov's *The Wedding* (MAT Third Studio, 1921), the MAT restagings, notably by Nemirovich-Danchenko (*Three Sisters*, 1940), and *Meyerhold's *33 Swoons* (a composite based on *The Bear*, *The Proposal*, and *The Anniversary*, 1935). This latter production was an attempt to adapt Chekhov to a *socialist realist rejection of pre-revolutionary Russia. Aleksandr *Tairov's *The Seagull* (Moscow, 1944) and Georgy *Tovstonogov's *Three Sisters* (Leningrad, 1965) were landmarks in the liberation of Chekhov from the MAT naturalistic house style and in the reassertion of his classic, as opposed to socialist realist, status. Abstract set design and *lighting effects came into their own. Anatoly *Efros (*Three Sisters*, 1967) offered a highly physical *carnival-like interpretation, followed by an equally controversial *The Cherry Orchard* (*Taganka Theatre, 1975) acted out on a single, cemetery-like bleak set. Oleg *Efremov (*The Seagull*, 1970, and *The Cherry Orchard*, 1975, *Sovremennik Theatre, Moscow) combined minimalist sets with the Stanislavskian tradition of emotional impact. Yury *Lyubimov's *Three Sisters* (Taganka, 1981), visually and vocally defiant of convention, made a statement about the brutality of contemporary Russia, and contributed to Lyubimov's swift exodus to Europe. Perestroika was heralded by Efremov's moving, mellow *Uncle Vanya* (Chekhov MAT, 1985) still resting within the traditions of the MAT house style, but capturing the uncertainty of the political moment. Subsequently the performance history is mixed: postmodern or deconstructive productions have appeared, such as those by Yury Pogrebnichko (*Three Sisters*, 1990; *The Seagull*, 1993, Moscow), while at the conservative *Maly Theatre, Sergei Soloviev with the Solomin brothers as Vanya and Astrov returned to Stanislavskian tradition with naturalistic detail and proliferating props (1992).

Exported during the MAT tours, Chekhov's plays have outstripped their Russian beginnings and transcended cultural barriers to reach every corner of the globe. The West, especially Britain, has followed a naturalistic production tradition, regarding Chekhov almost as an untouchable classic. Great actors (*Olivier, *Gielgud, *Ashcroft, *Richardson, *Dench, Michael *Redgrave, *McKellan) have cut their teeth on Chekhov and then returned in later career with mature performances, now regarded as classics of their kind. *Family productions such as those starring the *Cusacks (*Royal Court, 1990) and the *Redgraves (Queen's, 1990) enhanced the ensemble acting style and *realism still seen as quintessential Chekhov. Another thread of production transposed the Russian setting to more familiar territory, for nostalgia and isolation to Ireland (*The Seagull*, adapted by Tom *Kilroy, Royal Court, 1981), or for politics to South Africa (*The Cherry Orchard*, *Birmingham Rep, directed by Janet *Suzman, 1997). Gradually, productions have dropped period and introduced minimalist sets, such as Mike *Alfreds's *The Seagull* (Shared Experience, 1981). Alfreds's *Cherry Orchard* (Oxford Playhouse, 1982) went for the carnival and clownish in an attempt to reach Chekhov's frequently elusive humour. In the British repertoire Chekhov is probably the most performed foreign dramatist; production of his plays is an international industry with landmark productions in the countries of East and West Europe, USA, *Japan, and *China. Like their British counterparts, these productions are as much engagements with cultural transference as they are interpretations of the plays.   CM

ALLEN, DAVID, *Performing Chekhov* (Routledge, 2000)
SENELICK, LAWRENCE, *The Chekhov Theatre* (Cambridge, 1997)

CHEKHOV, MICHAEL (MIKHAIL) (1891–1955)

Russian actor, director, and theorist. The nephew of Anton *Chekhov, Mikhail came to prominence as an actor at the *Moscow Art Theatre Studios after 1912. Here he showed an intense psychological inwardness combined with improvisational brilliance, physical vitality, and plasticity of form in productions directed by *Vakhtangov and *Stanislavsky, including the roles of a mercurial Khlestakov in *Gogol's *The Government Inspector* and a comically lascivious Malvolio in *Twelfth Night*. After the revolution Chekhov played Erik XIV in *Strindberg's play at the Third Studio (1921) in an *expressionist style of febrile intensity, and subsequently indulged his unique brand of psychological expressionism as Hamlet at the Second Studio, which he headed. Increasingly drawn to the anthroposophical works of Rudolf Steiner, Chekhov found theatrical life in the Soviet Union difficult and he emigrated in 1928. After acting and directing in the Baltic states, he settled in England in 1936, opening a theatre studio at Dartington Hall in Devon.

The basis of Chekhov's theory is the 'psychological gesture' which, owing its complex origin to *Stanislavsky, *Sulerzhitsky, Steiner, and others, can be roughly defined as a physical attitude which forms the outline of a role and aids the actor's capacity to think in creative images and radiate feeling in a closed circuit with other performers. Improvisation and inspiration are essential, and need to be given full rein in *rehearsal through work conducted from the outset at maximum physical and emotional pitch. With the onset of the war Chekhov moved to the United States, opening another studio in Ridgefield, Connecticut, in 1939 before moving to Hollywood, where he supported his actor *training with *film work, notably as the psychiatrist in Hitchcock's *Spellbound* (1945). The failure in America of his production of Dostoevsky's *The Possessed*, in the wake of recycled productions of *The Government Inspector* and *Twelfth Night*, meant that the West never saw the best of Michael Chekhov. His major legacy consists of essays on *acting technique and approaches to production: *To the Actor* (1953) and *To the Director and Playwright* (1963).   NW

CHENEY, SHELDON (1886–1980)

American editor, critic, and historian. The author of thirteen books on theatre, art, and architecture, and founding editor of the influential *Theatre Arts* magazine (1916), Cheney was a key intellectual proponent of *modernism in American theatre. A 1908 graduate of the University of California, Cheney studied with Harvard's George Pierce *Baker before writing *The New Movement in Theatre* (1914) and *The Art Theatre* (1916). These, along with *Theatre Arts*, which he edited from 1916 to 1922, encouraged a non-commercial, anti-*illusionistic theatre. A keen historian, Cheney also intended the magazine as a permanent record of the experimental theatre of his time. His book *The Theatre: 3,000 years of drama, acting, and stagecraft* (1929) provided a historical backdrop for the symbolic and even mystical theatre he championed.   MAF

CHENG CHANGGENG (CH'ENG CH'ANG-KENG) (1811–80)

*Chinese Beijing opera (*jingju*) performer. A native of Anhui province, for decades Cheng led the Sanqing (Three Celebrations) troupe, one of the four Anhui troupes that had migrated to the capital in the early nineteenth century. The Anhui companies fused their local music with a number of other regional styles, from the earthy yiyang qiang to the literary *kunqu. In Beijing these regional styles were further melded with northern performance traditions to produce what would, by the twentieth century, be called *jingju* (capital opera). Contemporary sources claim that Chang's musical acumen and high, clear, and melodious voice made him instrumental in the development of the Beijing style, and his probity and refinement served to elevate the profession. He was recognized as the leader of the Jingzhong Miao (Temple of Refinement and Loyalty), the co-operative association of *actors in the capital, and through his troupe's *training academy he fostered numerous younger performers. Chang specialized in the mature male role (*laosheng*). He was famed for his performances as Wu Zixu, the knight errant of the Confucian age; as Yue Fei, the Song Dynasty general martyred for his loyalty; and as Guan Yu, the third-century military hero later revered as a god.   KC

CHENG YANQIU (CH'ENG YEN-CH'IU) (1904–58)

*Chinese actor of the *dan* (female) category in *jingju (Beijing opera). Born into a poor Manchu family, Cheng became an apprentice at the age of 6 and started stage performance at 11. Soon the famous scholar and theatre patron Luo Yinggong discovered him, secured his emancipation, and arranged for him to study with the famous *Mei Lanfang and the respected *dan* teacher Wang Yaoqing. Like many young *dan* actors, Cheng had difficulty regaining an appropriate vocal style after his voice changed, and Wang helped him develop a method of singing with a soft, undulating, and haunting quality. This in part explains the large number of tragic *heroines in his reper-

toire, many written exclusively for him. His singing and delicate gestural acting made Cheng extremely popular, especially among women, and in 1927 he was voted by fans the best *dan* actor on the stage. After a year studying theatre and theatrical education in Europe, Cheng became head of the Chinese Theatre Training Academy in 1933. During the Sino-Japanese War he sold all of his theatrical *costumes in protest and became a farmer. He resumed performing after the war.
                                                SYL

CHÉNIER, MARIE-JOSEPH (1764–1811)

French dramatist. Younger brother of the celebrated poet, Chénier made his name as a writer of *tragedies at the outbreak of the French Revolution. His masterpiece, *Charles IX; ou, La Saint-Barthélemy* (1789), was both *historical drama and topical *allegory, portraying a weak king manipulated by political and religious zealots. Written before the fall of the Bastille and modified afterwards, it led to the abolition of stage *censorship; it also served as launching-pad for the actor *Talma's career. *Jean Calas; ou, L'École des juges* (1791) stands out from the crop of plays inspired by the judicial murder of the Protestant Calas in 1762.   WDH

CHÉREAU, PATRICE (1944–)

French actor and director. Chéreau gained recognition as a director in 1967 with his prizewinning staging of *Lenz's *The Soldiers*, and in 1972 was invited by *Planchon to be co-director of the *Théâtre National Populaire at Villeurbanne, where his hallmark became archetypal *acting and brilliant *scenography created by his designer, the Italian Richard Peduzzi, who still works with Chéreau today. A vast raked wooden stage floor, scant *props and furnishings, and long shafts of light reminiscent of *Appia are typical, creating an abstractly meditative atmosphere that emphasizes the internalized struggles within and between *characters. Chéreau's major productions at Villeurbanne include *Marivaux's *The Dispute* (1973) and *Ibsen's *Peer Gynt* (1981). The most famous work of the Chéreau–Peduzzi team was their Marxist interpretation of *Wagner's *Ring* cycle at *Bayreuth (1976–80), set with massive forms and luminous colour in the nineteenth-century German Industrial Revolution. From 1982 to 1990, as *artistic director of the Théâtre des Amandiers in Nanterre, Chéreau produced, to acclaim and controversy, works by *Genet, Heiner *Müller, *Chekhov, and several new playwrights, including Bernard-Marie *Koltès's *Dans la solitude des champs de coton* (*In the Solitude of the Cotton Fields*, 1987), wherein Chéreau played the Dealer. Since 1990 Chéreau has worked independently in theatre and *film. He has directed five films, including *La Reine Margot* (*Queen Margot*, 1994). Chéreau's aim is both postmodern and *political: to reveal how we construct, through words and images, the reality that we inhabit.　　　SBB

CHESNAYE, NICOLAS DE (fl. 1500)

French playwright, known only as the author of *The Condemnation of Banquet* (printed 1508), a humorous *morality play depicting the deleterious effects of unwise eating, and the subsequent trial, conviction, and execution (by Diet) of the villainous Banquet. The lively scenes of feasting and the attacks of personified maladies, together with the *realistic portrayal of the trial, have fed speculation that Chesnaye had training in both medicine and law.　　　RWV

CHESTNUT STREET THEATRE

*Philadelphia theatre, opened 1794 with a capacity of 2,000, probably designed by John Inigo Richards, the renovator of *Covent Garden (1784), and based on the *Theatre Royal, *Bath. Leased to *actor-manager Thomas *Wignell (and Alexander Reinagle), it had the standard configuration of *box, pit, and galleries, with two *proscenium-arch doors providing access to the apron stage (*see* FORESTAGE). When Wignell retired in 1803, the acting company was considered the best in the USA. Under the management of William *Wood and William *Warren (to 1828), most of the great actors of the age played there, and it was the first theatre in America to be lit by gas (1816; *see* LIGHTING). Severely damaged by *fire in 1820, it was rebuilt by William Strickland in 1822 but burnt down again in 1855. Another theatre with this name was built nearby in 1863; it closed in 1913, and was demolished in 1917.　　　FJH

CHEVALIER, ALBERT (1862–1923)

English actor, *music-hall singer, and lyricist. The son of a schoolteacher, his first success was on the *legitimate stage with the *Bancrofts in 1877. Out of work, he was persuaded to perform character songs and *monologues (many composed by his brother Augustus) on the music halls. His first major appearance was at the *London Pavilion in 1891, where his cocky coster *character, influencing subsequent delineations, was instantly successful. His songs—such as 'My Old Dutch' and 'The Future Mrs 'Awkins'—were subtle characterizations, comically sentimental but always performed with conviction.　　　AF

CHEVALIER, MAURICE (1888–1972)

Debonair French actor, singer, and *dancer whose 50-year career began in the *Paris *cabarets and *music halls, including the *Folies-Bergère, where his partner was the beautiful comedienne, dancer, and singer *Mistinguett. Already internationally known in the 1920s, Chevalier's fame increased enormously

with two Hollywood *film careers: first in the 1930s as a romantic lead in *The Love Parade* (1930), *Love Me Tonight* (1932), and *Folies Bergère* (1935), and again in the 1950s as a character actor playing the avuncular elderly romantic in *Gigi* (1958), *Fanny* (1961), and *In Search of the Castaways* (1962). He became an international icon of Frenchness with his Parisian accent, romantic charm, grace, benign rakishness, and appreciation for women, food, wine, and music. His signature *costume included a tilted straw hat, cane, white spats, and tailcoat. His figure and voice survive as the most popular stereotype of the Frenchman in films, *television, cartoons, and advertising.　　　SBB

CHHAU

Traditional *dance-drama from eastern *India. The three primary styles of *chhau*, Seraikella, Mayurbhanj, and Purulia, are identified by their specific locations in the border regions of Bihar, Orissa, and West Bengal, respectively. While the practitioners of Seraikella and Mayurbhanj *chhau* come from diverse backgrounds—Seraikella's performers include both farmers and the descendants of the royal family of the Sangha dynasty, who used to patronize the form—Purulia *chhau* is more closely identified with the Mundas, a proto-Australoid group of aboriginal people. All three varieties of *chhau* are *ritually linked to the celebration of spring festivals in March or April. Seraikella *chhau* is performed during the Chaitra Parva festival in honour of Ardhanarishvara, the androgynous, composite form of Lord Shiva and his consort Parvati. Purulia *chhau*, on the other hand, is performed as a ritual offering to the sun god, Sing Bonga, whose propitiation is required to ensure an early monsoon for the crops. Agriculture provides the primary source of support for *chhau* dancers today, including the Mundas who were originally nomadic hunters.

The early practitioners of *chhau* were supposedly employed in the infantry (*paik*) of local tribal chiefs and kings. This martial background can be traced in the primary foundations of *chhau* movement, the *parikhanda khela*, or the 'play of shield and sword'. A grammar of combat, including movements of attack and defence, was gradually transformed into different styles of the dance. While Seraikella *chhau* is particularly subtle in its slow, almost hallucinatory movement, with sudden shifts of energy, the Mayurbhanj style is more vigorous and contained within a curvilinear structure, and Purulia *chhau* is positively acrobatic, as the dancers leap and spin in the air, landing on their knees. Apart from drawing on a common pool of exercises, the three modes of *chhau* explore different *chalis* (walks), which include not only the familiar gaits of the tiger and the elephant, but also of the cow passing urine. The more expressive dimensions of *chhau* are to be found in the *upalayas* (patterns of movement), which are very closely linked to everyday household activities, such as pounding and husking paddy, sweeping the floor, and splitting bamboo.

Most of the *chhau* repertoire, particularly in the Purulia tradition, draws on episodes from the *Mahabharata*, the *Ramayana*, and the Puranas. The Seraikella tradition is more lyrical, focusing on seven- to ten-minute vignettes of the *nabik* (boatman), the *prajapati* (butterfly), the *mayur* (peacock), and *shabar* (hunter, which receives a more virile rendition in the Mayurbhanj repertoire). Masks of papier mâché, clay, and muslin are used in the short Seraikella pieces and in Purulia *chhau*, though the Mayurbhanj version is unmasked.

Chhau has made contact with the outer world through the mediation of specific gurus and impresarios. Under the direction of dancer-choreographer B. P. Singh Deo from the royal family, Seraikella *chhau* travelled to Calcutta (*Kolkata) and Bombay (*Mumbai) in 1936, and to Europe in 1937. Purulia *chhau* was widely seen on the international *festival circuit from 1972 onwards through the pioneering initiative of the Bengali academic and anthropologist Dr Ashutosh Bhattacharya. At the beginning of the twenty-first century Mayurbhanj *chhau* provided inspiration for many contemporary dance pieces by choreographers like Chandralekha and the Italian-born Ileana Citaristi. Despite numerous changes in the contemporary performances of *chhau*, which are often justified as 'restoration of behaviour' or the 'invention of tradition', noted gurus like Kedar Nath Sahoo lament the distortions that have diluted its inner strength in the name of modern experimentation.   RB

CHIARELLI, LUIGI (1880–1947)

Italian writer. A novelist and painter, Chiarelli's fame is linked to his plays, particularly *The Mask and the Face* (1916), subtitled 'a grotesque in three acts', which marked the birth of the theatre of the *grotesque in Italy. The play takes an ironic look at the obligations placed on a man whose wife has committed adultery, but at another level it contrasts the inner being and the public persona. The movement influenced *Pirandello and was hailed as liberation from bourgeois convention, but its novelty is now more apparent in its use of *comedy to express sentiments and situations once reserved for *tragedy.   JF

CHICAGO

For most of its history the second-largest metropolis in the USA—a position it lost to *Los Angeles during the 1980s—Chicago has laboured to create a theatre culture distinct from *New York's. The early history of *playhouses was alternately hindered and abetted by a series of major *fires. After J. B. Rice built the city's first theatre in 1847, Chicago became a major site for *minstrelsy, *operetta, and the *variety show. The Great Fire of 1871 destroyed most of the city's theatres, but also brought about a boom in new construction. James H. *McVicker's 2,600-seat theatre was restored for use by the great *touring stars of the era and J. H. Haverly built its rival, the 2,000-seat Columbia

Theatre. Another post-fire venue of consequence was David Henderson's Chicago Opera House (1887). Born an orphan in Scotland, Henderson became the producer of long-running *musical comedies that also enjoyed successful national *tours. He favoured orientalist content, titles like *The Arabian Nights* and *Ali Baba* featuring prominently, and Chicago writers like Will Hough and Frank Adams created a dozen further musicals on similar themes before the First World War.

The inter-war years are sometimes described as a retrograde phase for the Chicago theatre, although other arts, like jazz, flourished. Local *managers, who had preserved a measure of autonomy for the city's theatrical scene, were replaced by the 'road' system of touring shows from New York. Important local talent began migrating eastward, although the newspaper critic Claudia Cassidy remained to scourge the low quality of touring productions. The opening of the *Goodman Theatre in 1925 did little to alter this state of affairs. The Chicago Little Theatre, first organized in 1912, offered an alternative, but to a smaller coterie *audience (see LITTLE THEATRE MOVEMENT). The Great Depression of the 1930s had a chilling impact on the city's commercial theatre, though with the decline of the 'road' non-profit and *community theatre became more prominent. *Hull-House Players, founded in 1897 to help immigrants from Europe and the provinces adjust to the social disciplines of the urban-industrial dynamo, achieved high levels of competence during these years, while the local arm of the *Federal Theatre Project produced a range of work, including social problem plays and the Negro Unit's hit musical *Swing Mikado* (1938).

Viola Spolin, author of *Improvisation for the Theatre* (1983), developed her *acting methods as a city recreation director in the Depression. Through her son Paul Sills, Spolin's *improvisation techniques inspired the creation of one of Chicago's most important post-war contributions to American theatre, Second City (1959). Based on the satirical *revue, Second City's improvisational skits and scenes had enormous influence on comic performance in the United States and Canada. The company opened a highly successful franchise in *Toronto during the 1970s, and the long-running national *television show *Saturday Night Live*, based in New York, was wholly patterned after it. Among the company's best-known graduates are Alan Arkin, Mike *Nichols, Elaine *May, and John Belushi.

Patterned on the *Off-Broadway movement, 'Off-Loop' troupes—located outside the centre formed by the loop of the elevated railway—began to spring up in Chicago during the late 1960s. With funding from the Chicago Community Arts Foundation in 1966, the Body Politic Theatre provided space and production support to a host of emerging non-profit companies, including the Organic Theater, which became a mainstay for local playwrights and performers. The Goodman underwent a major reorganization in 1969 under John Reich and William Woodman that brought it in line with the Off-Loop movement. Gregory *Mosher, who ran the company's Stage 2 programme during the 1970s, achieved national recognition for his commitment to directing new playwrights like David *Mamet (who had himself co-founded the Off-Loop St Nicholas Theater in 1974) as well as classic revivals. The company that best captures the quality of the Off-Loop movement is *Steppenwolf Theatre. Founded in 1974 by recent university graduates, including Gary *Sinise and John *Malkovich, Steppenwolf quickly came to personify a 'Chicago style' of performance emphasizing *naturalistic settings, hard-boiled language, and explosive, physical acting—less kindly described as 'sweaty boy theatre'. Steppenwolf mounted important revivals of Tennessee *Williams and Sam *Shepard in addition to original adaptations of major American novelists, and achieved a national reputation by transferring successful shows to Broadway.

The relaxation of strict city fire codes in the early 1970s, in place since the disastrous Iroquois Theatre fire of 1903, led to a rapid growth in small groups that continue to dominate the city's listings in any given week. Beyond downtown, one of the most important additions to the city's theatrical life during the 1980s was the Chicago Theatre Company (1984). Based on the South Side, the CTC was established to provide a stage for professional *African-American and other minority performers and playwrights. Since its inception, the company has received 20 Joseph Jefferson *award nominations, Chicago's version of the Tony award. After economic gains in the 1990s, the city witnessed a boom in new theatre construction and renovation that was subsidized, in part, to compete with New York for the growing market in urban tourism. Given the commercial theatre's overall dependency on New York for artistic capital, however, it remains to be seen if the city will continue to develop a distinctly Chicago style. Ominously, in 2000 soaring downtown rents forced the Organic Theater to relocate to the suburb of Evanston.   JAB

CHICANO THEATRE

The Chicanos, or Mexican Americans, are the largest Hispanic group in the United States with centuries-old roots, especially in the south-west. Chicano theatre refers to any play or performance that deals with the experiences of the Chicanos in the United States. For some scholars, Chicano theatre has its roots in Mexican indigenous and Spanish colonial *ritual drama. The first play in what is now the USA was performed in 1598 by Spanish and Mexican colonizers near El Paso, Texas. Soon after Spanish missionaries proselytized the natives through religious dramas, plays that can still be seen in Spanish-speaking communities. Secular dramas followed, as did *popular entertainments. Well into the twentieth century, the majority of plays performed in Chicano communities were of Spanish or Mexican origin, performed in Spanish.

With the emergence of the Teatro *Campesino, founded by Luis *Valdez and a group of striking farmworkers in 1965, other young Chicanas and Chicanos began to form student and community-based troupes collectively creating improvisational *actos* modelled on the Teatro Campesino's performances. The themes that these *teatros* explored and exposed dealt with discrimination against the Chicanos in the schools, in the courts, on the streets, and in the military. In the early stages Chicano theatre could be characterized as troupes composed of generally untrained participants who were highly *political, more intent on changing society than on creating 'great art'.

In the 1980s, while Chicano theatre companies continued to evolve and function in many urban centres such as *San Francisco, Albuquerque, San Diego, *Chicago, and San Antonio, individual playwrights began to emerge. As more Chicanas and Chicanos graduated from college and university theatre programmes, the quality of performance standards also advanced. Mainstream theatre companies became interested in the Hispanic *audience and began to commission new plays from Chicanos and other Hispanics, sometimes producing these plays in their theatres. Playwrights such as Josefina Lopez, Cherrie Moraga, Carlos Morton, Milcha *Sanchez-Scott, Octavio Solis, and Edit Villareal began to explore themes and forms beyond the *agitprop *actos* or *documentary dramas: themes of family dysfunction, mostly, as they explored the Chicano condition.

From the first play to the most recent, Chicano playwrights, *collectives, and theatre groups have created non-*realistic theatrical statements that usually revolve around a family in crisis. The enemy forces often come from outside the family circle but can also emerge from within the Chicano community. While docudramas remain popular, many of the plays explore the extraordinary, such as ascensions, *ghosts, and miracles, motivating some critics to label their work 'magical realism'. The search for identity—what it means to be a Chicano in the United States—is a recurring theme, perhaps because the Chicano remains so utterly invisible in the *mass media aside from negative stereotypes.

Chicano theatre includes a wide spectrum of actors, playwrights, directors, performers, and producers; from professional companies to student and community-based *teatros*. Chicano plays are being produced in high schools, universities, and colleges and individual performers are also very active. The issues that concerned Chicanos in the 1960s have not gone away, and Chicano theatre artists still believe in the power of theatre to bring about positive social change. *See also* HISPANIC THEATRE, USA.   JAH

CHICHESTER FESTIVAL THEATRE

English *playhouse in parkland on the edge of a Sussex cathedral city. The design of the building and the stage (by Powell and Moya) was heavily influenced by Tyrone *Guthrie's *Stratford Festival Theatre in Ontario. The theatre opened in 1962 with a ten-week summer season under the direction of

Laurence *Olivier. The large *auditorium seats the *audience on three sides of an *open stage with numerous entrances including two staircases in the *auditorium. The Chichester stage is designed for large-scale productions like *Shaffer's *Royal Hunt of the Sun* (1964) and *Bolt's *Vivat! Vivat Regina* (1970), which premièred in the early years, alongside productions of Shakespeare and *Brecht. Later seasons included revivals of plays written for conventional *proscenium-arch theatres, many of which successfully transferred to *London in the last decades of the twentieth century. The original summer season has been extended for up to five months and the theatre hosts *touring productions. As part of the millennium celebrations a *community project was performed in the main house: *Barchester Chronicles* (April 2000) involved over 250 local inhabitants of all ages. In 1989 the Festival Theatre built a *studio theatre, the Minerva, a more intimate and flexible space that offers a wide range of work from *one-person shows to new *musicals. British and world premières of plays produced in the 1990s included Ronald *Harwood's *Taking Sides* (1995), directed by Harold *Pinter, and William Nicholson's *Retreat from Moscow* (1999), starring Janet *Suzman. GBB

CHIFUNYISE, STEPHEN (1948–)

Zimbabwean playwright, actor, director, musician, and choreographer. In exile in Zambia during the 1970s, his social commentary plays (such as *Blood* and *I Am Not for Sale*) and stylized *dance-dramas (such as *Slave Caravan* and *Mwaziona*) contributed much to the *Chikwakwa Theatre repertoire and style. Other plays, notably *I Resign*, became highlights of Zambian *television in the 1970s. He was a founder of the Zambian International Theatre Institute and national Director of Culture. He returned to Zimbabwe in 1980 and became Director of Culture and later permanent secretary in the Ministry of Education, Sport and Culture, in which posts he did much to decolonize the country's theatre. He published two collections of plays, helped form the *Zimbabwe Association of Community Theatre, and, along with his Zambian wife Tisa, became an ardent advocate for theatre for *development, theatre for *youth, and Zimbabwean performance skills. DaK

CHIKAMATSU HANJI (1725–83)

*Japanese playwright. Born the son of the philosopher Hozumi Ikan, a friend of *Chikamatsu Monzaemon, Chikamatsu Hanji followed tradition in taking the name of his famous predecessor. Hanji began to write for the *Osaka *bunraku *puppet theatre about 1751, and his name appears on 55 works. During his time playwrights worked as a team under a senior author who was responsible for the overall *plot and for writing the climactic *acts. Hanji became senior playwright about 1760 and many of his works are regularly performed today in both bunraku and *kabuki, including *Courtesans and the Straits of Naruto* (1768), *The Omi Genji Vanguard* (1769), *Mount Imo and Mount Se* (1771), *A New Edition of the Osome-Hisamatsu Ballad* (1780), and *A Travel Game while Crossing Iga* (1783). In the third generation of a line of famous playwrights, Hanji is known for his complex plots, music, theatricality, and for exploiting all three elements of bunraku (chanter, puppets, *shamisen*). CAG

CHIKAMATSU MONZAEMON (1653–1725)

Japanese playwright. Born Sugimori Nobumori in Fukui, the son of relatively high-ranking and educated samurai, he was educated in Chinese and Japanese classics. His father left his position for unknown reasons when Chikamatsu was about 14. The family moved to *Kyoto where Chikamatsu served in courtier households; later he worked backstage at *kabuki theatres, performed as a street storyteller, and began writing plays in his late twenties. Experience of samurai, courtier, actor, and merchant life gave him a broad view of the highly stratified society of *Japan. He wrote over 100 plays under contract with *bunraku (*jōruri*) and kabuki theatres in Kyoto and *Osaka, and was considered the 'god of writers' soon after his death. Today he is thought to be one of the most important authors in the Japanese literary tradition, sometimes compared with Shakespeare. Chikamatsu learned his craft as an apprentice to the performers Uji Kaganojō, *Takemoto Gidayū, and *Sakata Tōjūrō. As staff playwright at the Takemoto-za Theatre in Osaka, he produced his most famous plays during the last twenty years of his life, including *The Battles of Coxinga* (1715) and *Love Suicides at Amijima* (1721). His kabuki plays have survived only in summary form, but his nearly 100 bunraku *puppet theatre works survive in complete, authorized editions from the date of first performance. These *texts contain a code of musical notation for the chanters, which was also used by *amateurs who learned to perform the plays from professionals.

Three-quarters of his bunraku plays were set in a historical period before 1600, and were epic five-act dramas that filled a whole day in performance from dawn to dusk. These works (*jidaimono*) have a structure of multiple *plots and contrasts between picaresque, fantastical adventure and intense *tragedy. In 1703, however, after a decade of writing mostly for kabuki, he wrote his first domestic (*sewamono*) tragedy, *Love Suicides at Sonezaki*, a three-scene piece based on an actual incident in Osaka. This three-scene format is comparable to the third act of a period play. After this play's considerable success, Chikamatsu went on to write 23 dramas based on contemporary incidents of love suicide, theft, smuggling, adultery, and murder, works that have been praised in modern times for their powerful *realism and *character portrayal. During these same twenty years, he also produced his most famous period plays. In the last ten years of his life Chikamatsu focused on the nature

Image from a two-sheet announcement for **Chikamatsu Monzaemon**'s *Love Suicides at Sonezaki*, written for the bunraku stage in 1703. The flyer advertises the skill of the great puppeteer Tatsumatsu Hachirobei, who appears on the left manipulating a puppet. (This is a special performance, since it was unusual at the time for bunraku puppeteers to work without a screen.) On the right are the chanter Takemoto Gidayū, his assistant, and the *shamisen* musician, while the man in front of Tatsumatsu is announcing the performance. The three figures in the foreground are spectators.

and consequences of passion, crime, and responsibility, increasingly using similar themes in each of the *genres. For example, over eighteen months he explored the theme of murder in three works, two period and one domestic: *Twins at the Sumida River* (1720), *Lovers Pond in Settsu Province* (1721), and *Woman-Killer and the Hell of Oil* (1721). His mature period plays show two trends: increasingly complex and realistic character portrayal in the context of tragedy in Act III, together with a fantastic theatricality representing the supernatural, particularly in Acts II and IV, achieved by sophisticated stage tricks.

Many of Chikamatsu's plays were revived and revised in the eighteenth and nineteenth centuries. After 1945 a strong movement developed to perform the original texts. The kabuki actor Nakamura Ganjirō III has led a Chikamatsu-za troupe since 1981 with the express intention of reviving the plays,

and today Chikamatsu's work is regularly performed in bunraku and kabuki. CAG

GERSTLE, C. ANDREW, *Chikamatsu: five late plays* (New York, 2000)
KEENE, DONALD, *Major Plays of Chikamatsu* (New York, 1961)

CHIKWAKWA THEATRE

Zambian *playhouse and theatre movement. A group of radical university students and lecturers built this *open-air theatre at a bush site near Lusaka in 1967. The large, grass-covered stage and semicircular *auditorium with seats dug out of the earth, protected by a grass fence, was designed to provide an authentic *African theatre with its aesthetic roots in indigenous artistic and architectural traditions. In the 1970s and 1980s the theatre became a focus for drama which promoted African languages and Zambian performance skills. Its programme of rural, provincial travelling theatre and *training workshops was particularly successful, providing the seedbed for several dramatists and theatre practitioners. It also contributed to Zambian national theatre organizations and to the regional theatre for *development movement. DaK

CHILDREN'S COMPANIES *See* BOYS' COMPANIES.

CHILDREN'S THEATRE *See* YOUTH, THEATRE FOR.

CHILDRESS, ALICE (1920–94)

American playwright who began her career as an actress with the American Negro Theatre, a pioneering *African-American group in the 1940s and 1950s. She began writing in order to counter the tradition of demeaning roles for African-American women. Her plays include *Gold through the Trees* (1952), *Trouble in Mind* (1955), *Wine in the Wilderness* (1969), and *The Wedding Band: a love/hate story* (1966), acted by Ruby *Dee at the *New York Shakespeare Festival in the 1970s. Childress, who once described writing as 'a way to light a candle in a gale wind', was also a novelist. BBL

CHIN, FRANK (1940–)

American playwright and *manager. Chin attended universities in California and Iowa, working as clerk and brakeman for the Western Pacific and Southern Pacific railways to support his education. After graduation he was a writer for King Broadcasting in Seattle and a lecturer in Asian-American studies at the University of California, Davis, and San Francisco State University. In 1972 he established the Asian American Theatre Workshop in *San Francisco to encourage playwriting by *Asian Americans; two years later it became the Asian American Theatre Company, America's first company dedicated exclusively to plays about Asian America. Both his *Chickencoop Chinaman* (1972) and *Year of the Dragon* (1974), which were the first plays by a Chinese American to be produced in *New York, focus on the complexities of Asian identity in America. JSM

CHINA

With a recorded history of more than 4,000 years, China's longevity as a discrete politico-cultural entity far surpasses that of most countries. Though its domain has waxed and waned over the centuries, China is the world's third largest nation in terms of area and the first in population with about one-fifth of humanity residing within its borders. About 92 per cent of Chinese belong to the Han ethnicity; the rest are divided among 55 different national minorities. While students across China are taught to read the same language and to speak the national language (that is, Mandarin, or putong hua, which is based on Beijing dialect), significant linguistic and cultural differences exist from region to region. Even among Han Chinese there are many mutually unintelligible dialects commonly spoken in addition to the national language. Performing conventions and musical styles tend to parallel linguistic groupings.

Much of China's cultural and artistic development occurred in relative isolation, resulting in the evolution of numerous indigenous performing traditions. Due to its integration of speech, singing, *music, *acting, *dance, *costume, and *make-up, among other performative elements, it has become customary in English to refer to traditional Chinese drama as 'opera'. The Chinese term for this genre is *xiqu* (theatre [of] song). Before the twentieth century, dramatic performance without musical accompaniment and the sung delivery of *text was virtually unknown in China. *Huajü* (spoken drama) did not have a presence in China until the early 1900s when young urban intellectuals brought European plays and staging practices to China primarily from *Japan. Before the rise of *Cao Yu and other native playwrights in the mid-1930s, *huaju* performance consisted almost entirely of Chinese translations of European plays.

Due to the lack of extant sources, it is difficult to document with certainty the appearance of the first full-fledged Chinese opera. Elements which became essential features of opera performance, such as song with dance and the use of gesture and costume, were part of religious and shamanistic *rituals from antiquity. The classic *Shujing* (*Book of Documents*) mentions dancing and singing in connection with shamanism during the Shang Dynasty (1600–1027 BC), and ritual practice and dancing occurred in both shamanistic and court dances during the Zhou (Chou) Dynasty (1027–256 BC). The set movements of court dance of this period suggest a narrative quality that may have involved acting, singing, and costumes. Different types of entertainments, including a variety of dances, court jesters' acts, story enactments, and horn-butting games, are mentioned in the records of the Han Dynasty (202 BC to AD 220), but there is no evidence that these had a direct connection to the development of opera *per se*. The Tang Dynasty (AD 681–907) was a time of peace, prosperity, and cultural grandeur, and one from which an abundance of source materials have survived. During this golden age the first signs of widespread play acting appeared. Popular during the eighth and ninth centuries, the so-called adjutant play (*canjun xi) involved acting, speaking, musical accompaniment, singing, costume, and make-up.

There are numerous scattered references from the early and mid-thirteenth century to a variety of performance types, yet there are no full or detailed descriptions of specific performances and there are no extant scripts or musical notations of what could be termed 'opera'. Entertainment falling under

Acrobatic moment in *jingju* (Beijing opera), Beijing, 1981. This play, entitled *White Snake*, is a fairy tale about an ascetic snake who becomes a woman.

the name *zaju* (variety plays) during the Song (Northern Song 960–1127, Southern Song 1127–1279) and Jin (Chin) dynasties (1115–1234) seems to have been highly assorted. A document written around 1280 lists 280 different *zaju* titles. This list indicates several subtypes of plays, ranging from *scenarios that emphasized singing, dancing, or acrobatics to simple comic duos that may have been along the lines of modern *xiangsheng. Xiangsheng*, often translated as 'crosstalk' or 'comedians' *dialogue', is usually performed by two comedians who stand side by side telling stories and jokes, making *parody, and sometimes singing short songs or phrases.

Extant sources allow us to mark the Yuan Dynasty (1279–1368) as the period in which singing, music, costume, and stagecraft were combined dramatically by multiple performers of a detailed story. Sixteen editions of *zaju* texts survive from the Yuan and many more editions were printed during the Ming Dynasty (1368–1644); unfortunately, there are no remaining musical scores or notations. The plays of Yuan *zaju* were usually in four *acts, sometimes preceded by an introduction. Of the several *characters involved in each play, only one would sing

per act and each act was usually performed in only one of nine possible musical modes. It is generally accepted that singing and musical accompaniment were not as integral to Yuan *zaju* as they were in the southern *genre, *nanxi (southern plays), which was contemporary, or in later genres such as *kunqu, or the numerous regional opera forms of the Ming and Qing (Ch'ing) dynasties. Dolby has noted, however, that the structural and spiritual core of the Yuan *zaju* was its songs.

The Ming witnessed the continued popularity of *zaju*, with more than 500 new plays being written, but by the end of the period both its form and music had been radically transformed. The dominant Ming genre was *chuanqi (whose predecessor was the *nanxi). The greatest writer of *chuanqi* is generally considered to be *Gao Ming (Kao Ming, c.1305–70) whose most representative work, *Pipa ji*, has been translated into English as *The Lute*. Perhaps the greatest contribution of the Ming was the development of *kunqu*. (Interestingly, after a period of decline during the Qing dynasty and the early twentieth century, *kunqu* is currently witnessing something of a revival, not only in China but in overseas communities as well.) After about the year 1500, the history of Chinese drama becomes more a history of musical systems than of dramatic types; in other words, music became the most important element in genre formation and identity. An enormous variety of regional opera forms (*difangxi*) took shape during the Ming and continued to thrive and spawn the creation of additional forms during the Qing. Among these is Beijing (or Peking) opera (*jingju*), which began to take form in the late 1700s.

Currently, there are more than 350 different varieties of Chinese opera. Most utilize similar make-up, costuming, and stage conventions; differentiation between forms is made largely on the basis of aural rather than visual content. The dialect used in song and speech and musical materials are key features in distinguishing each form. The name given to a type of opera usually identifies its region of origin or its musical system. For example, *jing* means 'capital' (Beijing) and *ju* means 'drama', while *huangmei* opera is named after the *huangmei* tune, fundamental to its musical system. The regional forms are typically limited to the geographic area where the dialect is understood, though exceptions like *jingju* and *kunqu* transcended boundaries to gain national recognition and popularity.

The stories of traditional operas are often drawn from a common body of well-known legends, myths, novels, historical, and semi-historical narratives. Their themes typically extol Confucian social and moral values such as loyalty, filial piety, chastity, and justice. Single-authored, written scripts exist for elite forms such as Yuan *zaju* and the highly refined *kunqu*, which were patronized and practised by the literati. However, many forms, particularly regional operas, have historically been transmitted without the use of written scripts or musical notation. Typically, troupes work out a general outline of the story before a performance and the actors and musicians improvise their lines and melodies following creative conventions particular to the specific regional form. In the late twentieth century it became increasingly common for troupes to use both written scripts and music notation.

Realistic representation as a guiding aesthetic principle is foreign to traditional Chinese opera. Almost all movements and utterances are highly stylized: the simplest movements and gestures are unlike those seen in life and may carry symbolic meaning. Action is set on a stage that is devoid of properties or may include only a few items such as a table and chairs. Spectators must rely on their understanding of the dramatic situation to fill in the details and to know, for example, that in one situation the table represents a mountain while in another it is a bed or a banquet table. Brightly coloured, patterned, and stylized make-up and costume designs also serve to distance opera from *realism.

All varieties of Chinese opera divide characters into role types (*juese hangdang*). The Tang adjutant plays with their two roles, the adjutant (*canjun*) and 'grey hawk' (*canggu*), show the

beginnings of this convention. The *nanxi* of the Yuan Dynasty established the four categories of roles as still employed today: *sheng* (male characters), *dan* (female characters), *jing* (painted face, male characters), *chou* (comic characters). In practice these categories are further subdivided, thus providing additional insight into a character's age, social status, and level of intrinsic dignity. The finer divisions vary among regional forms.

Role type determines many performative factors including pronunciation, melodic form, voice type (that is, predominant use of either chest voice or falsetto), make-up, costume, and style of movement and gesture. Performers typically train from an early age to specialize in the performance of one role type or type subdivision. Historically, the biological sex of the performer need not match that of the role type in which she or he specialized. There is evidence of cross-gendered performance from as early as the Tang adjutant plays, when actresses performed male roles and were apparently more common than actors. Women frequently acted male roles in Yuan *zaju* and men were also known to perform female roles. Cross-gendered performance was commonly, though not exclusively, practised in China well into the mid-twentieth century. In fact, several of the most important Beijing opera performers of the early century, known as the 'four great *dans*', were male performers of young female roles. Driven by modernist ideology and fuelled by Western-inspired homophobic anxiety, there was a move to train children to perform roles that matched their biological sex, especially after the founding of the People's Republic of China in 1949. There are still performers who specialize in playing roles of the opposite sex, however, particularly in regional opera forms such as Taiwanese opera (*gezai xi*), where the leading male roles are normally performed by women.

In the past, opera was an integral part of ritual life and religious celebration in China. Its performance was often included in the most important occasions of domestic and communal life, such as funerals, exorcism, and temple festivals. Itinerant companies moved from town to town at festival times, performing either on stages that were a permanent part of a temple complex or on temporary stages in front of a temple. Wealthy families sometimes maintained private opera troupes who performed on auspicious occasions such as birthdays and weddings and for guests at dinner parties.

*Puppet theatre performed a role in ritual life similar to that of opera. Because it was much less expensive to hire a puppeteer and his few accompanying musicians than an entire opera troupe, it was not uncommon for a puppet performance to substitute for opera for certain ritual celebrations. Similar to opera, varieties of puppet theatre are distinguished by musical system, dialect, and puppet type. Puppet types include glove puppets (*budai*), *shadow puppets (*piying*), *marionettes (*kuilei*), rod puppets (*zhangtou*), and iron-stick puppets (*tiezhi kuilei*). References to puppetry exist as early as the Han Dynasty and some scholars assert that the varieties of shadow-puppet theatre found throughout *South-East Asia trace their origins to ancient China.

The tradition of itinerant opera and puppet troupes performing on ritual occasions has enjoyed an unbroken practice in Taiwan and some overseas Chinese communities. In the People's Republic of China religious festivals were strongly discouraged for several decades, but are reappearing, and with them has come the revival of ritual opera. Today, most live opera performances are presented in *proscenium-style theatres before paying *audiences. The atmosphere is generally much livelier than that found in theatres in the West with audience members chatting among themselves, spontaneously cheering performers, and, in theatres where it is still permitted, eating snack foods. Besides professional performances, in many areas amateur troupes and opera clubs perform in parks and typically practise weekly.

Theatrical performance has been the subject of official control and *censorship throughout Chinese history. Confucian notions regarding music's power to influence human behaviour have underpinned much of the state's concern. Good and proper music is believed to inspire harmonious human relations; improper music erodes relations and ultimately leads to social and political chaos. Historically official control of the theatre has ranged from the promotion of works which extolled Confucian virtues to the outright banning of entire repertoires and the persecution of writers and performers. With the establishment of the People's Republic of China, drama reform committees were established throughout the country to bring theatrical practice in line with Maoist ideology. Some traditional works were banned, many were revised, and the creation of new works on contemporary and revolutionary themes was encouraged. Opera continued to thrive until 1963, but in the following year the traditional repertoire began to disappear under the influence of Mao Zedong's wife, Jiang Qing. During the Cultural Revolution (1966–76), traditional operas were completely banned. A very limited number of newly written 'revolutionary modern operas' (*geming xiandai xi, also known as geming yangban xi or 'revolutionary model drama'), based on approved contemporary and revolutionary themes with realistic stagings and costumes, comprised the entire repertoire. After Mao's death in 1976 the model operas were temporarily banned and the old repertoire slowly reappeared.

NGu

DOLBY, WILLIAM, *A History of Chinese Drama* (London, 1976)

HSU, TAO-CHING, *The Chinese Conception of the Theatre* (Birmingham, 1985)

MACKERRAS, COLIN (ed.), *Chinese Theater: from its origins to the present day* (Honolulu, 1983)

YUNG, BELL, *Cantonese Opera: performance as creative process* (Cambridge, 1989)

CHINESE REGIONAL OPERA *See* DIFANGXI.

CHINGANA

A form of nineteenth-century Chilean popular theatre. The *chinganas* were inns, restaurants, and cafés bubbling with nightlife and imbued with the spirit of the newly independent Latin American republics. Creole and mulatto singers accompanied traditional Chilean dances while highly irreverent comical *farces flouted all the conventions the colonial authorities had held most sacred. The boisterous and at times dangerous atmosphere of the *chinganas*, with their gaming, drinking, occasional knife-fights, and *satirical performances, raised the ire of the new republican authorities, who saw them as a threat to civic peace and a travesty of legitimate theatre.

The *chingana* resurfaced in the 1970s as part of the *teatro de base* movement during Pinochet's dictatorship. Performed by three to five people, this incarnation might contain *music, song, *dance, poetry, games, audio-visual presentations, and even quasi-*sporting events. All the elements revolved around a central theme, such as working, special skills, or organization of life in the neighbourhood, and sometimes the *chingana* introduced brief training sessions for dealing with social problems, before ending, as always, with food and drink. AV

CHIRGWIN, G. H. (1854–1922)

English *music-hall comedian and musician. Born in *London, he was one of the three Brothers Chirgwin, working street-corner pitches, 'free-and-easies', and seaside resorts. By the 1870s he was 'the White-Eyed Kaffir', sporting a black face and a single diamond-shaped white eye (often reversing the colours), leotard and leggings, or zebra-striped fleshings, and an immense stove-pipe hat. He played the drum, cello, fiddle, and sang in a thin falsetto voice, his most famous songs being 'My Fiddle Is my Sweetheart' and 'The Blind Boy'. He appeared in *pantomime regularly, and at the first Royal *Variety Performance in 1911. AF

CHISIZA, DUNDUZU, JR. (1963–99)

Malawian actor, playwright, and director. In 1983 he founded Wakhumbata Ensemble Theatre and built it into Malawi's only professional troupe. A prolific playwright, several of his over twenty plays have been published in his collections *Barefoot in the Heart* (1983) and *Democracy Boulevard* (1988). His productions were often controversial; the Malawi *Censorship Board banned two early plays, and he learned to use *allegory to criticize the Banda regime in *Fragments* (1988) and *Papa's Empire* (1990). He also explored issues of *gender (*Educating Mwalimu*, 1991), African unity (*Barefoot in the Heart*, 1993), and crime (*Misidi Burning*, 1995). During the 1990s he entered partisan politics, but found his best political medium in *Democracy Boulevard* (1993) and *Da Summer Blow* (1994). As director

Chisiza exercised almost total artistic control of Wakhumbata Ensemble, and was also responsible for *scenery design, actor *training, *publicity, travel logistics, and *finance.　　DaK

CHITTY, ALISON (1948–)

British designer. Trained at St Martin's School of Art and Central School of Art and Design, she became resident designer at the Victoria Theatre, Stoke-on-Trent (1971–7). As resident designer at the Royal *National Theatre, she worked closely with Peter *Gill, and she has designed several Mike *Leigh *films. *Opera design includes contemporary work by Harrison Birtwistle and a long collaboration with Francesca Zambello, for whom she designed a monumental, tiered ship for *Billy Budd* (*Covent Garden, 1994). Her work is characterized by selective detail; discussing *Khovanshchina* (English National Opera, 1994), she argued that 'restraint helps you to guide the *audience towards what you want them to see and what part of the story is important'. Her many *awards include Olivier awards for best opera production (*Billy Budd*) and best *costume designer (*Remembrance of Things Past*). She is director of the Motley Theatre Design School, an international postgraduate course.　　RVL

CHOCRÓN, ISAAC (1930–)

Venezuelan playwright, novelist, and economist. His first play to be staged was *Mónica y el florentino* (*Monica and the Florentine*, 1959) but recognition came with *Asia y el Lejano Oriente* (*Asia and the Far East*, 1965), about the sale of a country. He continued experimenting with the *absurd in *Tric-Trac* (1967), and *Animales feroces* (*Wild Animals*, 1968) dealt with uprooting and loneliness. *La revolución* (*The Revolution*, 1971), a grotesque *parody of the ethical crisis in his country, was followed by *La máxima felicidad* (*Utmost Happiness*, 1974), *Clipper* (1987), *Mesopotamia* (1980), and *Simón* (1983). A co-founder and director of El *Nuevo Grupo with José *Cabrujas and Román *Chalbaud, Chocrón was also director general of the National Theatre Company (1984–92). His dramatic style is based on daring premisses, reflecting an influence from Harold *Pinter. His works have received wide international acclaim, and he was awarded the National Prize for Theatre in 1979.

LCL trans. AMCS

CH'OE IN-HUN (1936–)

Korean playwright. Born in Hoeryŏng in North *Korea, he escaped to the south in 1950 during the Korean War and devoted himself to writing, at first as a novelist. During the 1970s he wrote exceptional plays that are characterized by a fine balance between poetry and prose, by multiple changes of sound and light, and by the adaptation of myths. His theatre work is frequently considered the first to succeed as both literature and drama in Korea, and is chiefly interested in the place of *tragedy and fate in Korean history. *Away, Away, Long Time Ago* (1976), about the birth of a hero who will create a new era, was published in English in *Modern Korean Literature* (Honolulu, 1990). Other work includes *Where We Will Meet as What We Are* (1970), *At Mountain and Field When Spring Comes* (1977), and *Tung Tung Nakrang Tung* (1978).　　JOC

CHONG, PING (1946–)

American director, choreographer, and video and installation artist. A self-described 'artist of the theatre', Ping Chong was trained as a painter but began his *avant-garde performance work after taking a class with the postmodern choreographer Meredith *Monk. He has frequently referred to his early pieces as 'bricolages' in reference to anthropologist Claude Lévi-Strauss's description of the process of assembling 'luminous new worlds' out of bits and pieces of existing, older societies. Chong's cross-cultural, interdisciplinary approach is evident in the well-regarded collaborations with Monk (*Paris*, *Chacon*, *Venice/Milan*, *The Games*), culminating in the mid-1980s, to his experimentation in the 1990s with community-specific pieces, notably in *Deshima*, *Chinoiserie*, *After Sorrow*, and *Pojag*, a quartet exploring East–West relations from a variety of national perspectives. Chong's numerous *awards span several disciplines and demonstrate the range of his achievement.

LTC

CHORUS

A group of singers and/or *dancers who perform in concert; the performance of such a group. A chorus was central to the forms of *Greek performance from which Athenian drama evolved. Choral lyric featured several performance patterns: the chorus often sang and danced in unison, but it could also divide into semi-choruses and, together with the chorus leader, engage in statement and refrain, *exposition and response, or even *dialogue. One form, the *dithyramb, like *tragedy and *comedy a subject for competition at the festivals of *Dionysus (*Dionysia), had a chorus of 50 that sang and danced in a circular formation about the leader. More obviously dramatic were the tragic chorus, originally numbering twelve but raised to fifteen by *Sophocles (the *satyr-play chorus remained at twelve), and the comic chorus, numbering 24. In both cases, the performance included *actors as well. The comic chorus, sometimes fantastically *costumed as birds or animals, was central to *Old Comedy, where, in a section of the play called the *parabasis*, it addressed the *audience directly both in character and as the poet's mouthpiece. The tragic chorus also had both a dramatic identity and an extra-dramatic role as commentator.

Athenian dramatic choruses were rooted in the community from which they were recruited, and their functions reflect their Janus-like status. The chorus could represent *characters, take part in the dramatic *action, and enter into exchanges with the actors. The tragic chorus could also stand outside the main action, offering comment and interpretation either in character, with information and insight limited to that of the characters it represented, or out of character, possessing knowledge denied dramatic characters, even offering an 'official' interpretation of the dramatic events. At other times it was less knowledgeable, but nevertheless sensitive to nuance and could thus function as an ideal audience, guiding the spectator's response. Since it is not always possible to determine whose voice the chorus is using, and since its function could change from *scene to scene, there was no necessary consistency of character. As a continuous presence whose role and function varied, the tragic chorus in particular maintained an artistic integrity mainly through its identity as Athenian citizens.

Dramatic choruses were nevertheless in decline by the end of the fifth century BC. As the theatre became less communal and more professional, less Athenian and more pan-Hellenic, the chorus lost its intimate connection with the audience; and as the emphasis shifted from choral lyric to dramatic dialogue, the chorus became less a part of the action than an interruption of it. In tragedy, *Euripides' chorus retained its dramatic identity but its function was reduced to that of interlude between the episodes. Later, *Seneca's choral interludes were even more loosely connected to the dramatic action. The manuscripts of *Menander's comedies call for the performance of a chorus between the scenes, but this performance was apparently the responsibility of the producer. *Roman comedy dropped the chorus altogether.

Efforts to revive the classical chorus have not been successful. In sixteenth-century Italy and France, humanist authors made half-hearted attempts to include the chorus in their imitations of ancient drama, but had difficulty reconciling it with the *neoclassical demands of verisimilitude. Near the end of the eighteenth century, German writers championed the chorus as an instrument for translating the experience of the sensuous world to an ideal realm, and thereby elevating the spectator to a higher, artistic plane of contemplation. But even Friedrich *Schiller's eloquence in his famous essay 'On the Use of the Chorus in Tragedy' (1803) was insufficient to revive it. In the twentieth century, the chorus was for the most part limited to adaptations or imitations of ancient Greek plays. An exception is T. S. *Eliot's Murder in the Cathedral, which, performed in the communal and ceremonial context of a church festival, endued its Chorus of Women of Canterbury with something of the quality of its ancient counterpart.

The figure called 'Chorus' in some Elizabethan plays is derived, not from classical practice, but from figures developed in *medieval theatre and otherwise known as Presenter, Doctor, or Messenger. These figures typically provided explanatory *prologues and *epilogues, summary sermons, or bridging narrative between dramatized episodes. Thus in Christopher *Marlowe's Dr Faustus the Chorus speaks the prologue and in the epilogue draws the moral. In Shakespeare's Henry V and Pericles the Chorus functions as an epic-narrator, dividing the *acts and connecting the dramatic action.

In the modern theatre, the chorus as an integral part of a larger performance is largely restricted to oratorio, *opera, *musical comedy or review, and classical *ballet. The relative importance of singing and dancing varies: the corps de ballet is devoted exclusively to dance, the oratorio chorus to singing; the chorus in opera or musical comedy is normally required to both dance and sing; in Las Vegas shows the chorus can simply form various spectacular *tableaux, neither dancing nor singing. But whether part of a larger unit or an independent performance, choric performance has continued as part of the Western theatrical heritage, its rhythmic and coordinated sounds and movements expressed in forms as diverse as a massed choir or a military tattoo.

RWV

CHRISTIE, AGATHA (1890–1976)

English crime novelist whose commercial success as a playwright has been phenomenal. The Mousetrap, which began life as a *radio play called Three Blind Mice, opened in *London in 1952 and was still going strong in 2002, its over 20,000 performances probably holding the record for the *longest-running play ever. Christie also had major theatrical hits on both sides of the Atlantic with Ten Little Niggers (1944, or Ten Little Indians and And Then There Were None) and Witness for the Prosecution (1954). She began writing plays seriously because she felt the stage adaptations of her novels had been too respectful of the original *texts, and as a consequence too complex. With her first major play, an adaptation of Ten Little Indians, Christie simplified and radically changed the outcome, although the strength of her playwriting in general is the audacious twisting and turning of the *plot. Though one of the most successful women playwrights in British history, she is rarely considered in depth in dramatic studies. She was made DBE in 1971.

EJS

CHRONEGK, LUDWIG (1837–91)

German actor and director. Chronegk's name is indissolubly linked with the *Meiningen Players. Trained in *Berlin, he had a succession of engagements between Zurich and Königsberg before joining the court theatre in Meiningen in 1866. Initially an actor, the Duke of Meiningen soon recognized Chronegk's artistic and organizational abilities, appointing him director in 1871 and *artistic director (*Intendant) in 1884. Chronegk was the key coordinator in the process of *mise-en-scène, putting into stage practice the Duke's conception and designs. He accompanied the troupe on their extended *tours, where he coordinated the involvement of locally hired supernumeraries. After Chronegk's death, the Duke dedicated a room in the theatre to his memory.   CBB

***CHUANJU* (SICHUAN OPERA)** *See* DIFANGXI.

CHUANQI (CH'UAN-CH'I)

Chinese operas written in the 'southern style' between the southern Sung and the Qing dynasties, often translated as 'romance' or 'southern drama'. *Chuanqi* flourished from the middle of the sixteenth to the end of the seventeenth centuries, roughly coinciding with the golden age of the *kunqu* musical style. *Chuanqi* prevailed on the stage during this period along with northern drama (*zaju*), though the two forms differ markedly in their formal characteristics. Typically, *zaju* are four *acts in length with only one actor in a singing role, whereas *chuanqi* are between 20 and 50 acts in length, with many actors singing. Duets, trios, and *choruses are commonly found in *chuanqi* but not in *zaju*, and northern musical styles are associated with *zaju*, southern ones with *chuanqi*. The distinctions, however, have never been completely firm: some *zaju* had three acts, some eleven, in some all actors were able to sing, and some even used southern tunes. The term *chuanqi* has varied in meaning in Chinese history. Originally it referred to tales written in the classical language during the Tang Dynasty. The phrase literally means 'transmitting the strange' and referred to the supposed motivation for writing such tales, to record unique events. During the Sung and Yuan dynasties, the term suggested both southern and northern drama, both of which frequently took their *plots from Tang tales. During the Ming Dynasty, however, *chuanqi* designated plays longer than the four-act *zaju*, referring to plays of the Song and Yuan in the southern style (*xiwen*) as well as to the long literary dramas of the Ming.

During the *chuanqi* era it was common for gentlemen to be aficionados of the theatre; a number composed *chuanqi* and others owned and trained private troupes. The playwright *Li Yu (1611–80) included a chapter on writing drama in his guide to sophisticated living, *Essays Written in Idleness*, which appears next to chapters on interior decoration and the proper enjoyment of food and drink, suggesting that composing plays was a sign of social distinction. Among the *chuanqi* authors, most worthy of note are Li Kaixian, *Tang Xianzu (especially *The Peony Pavilion*), Ruan Dacheng, Li Yu, *Kong Shangren (*The Peach Blossom Fan*), and Hong Sheng (*The Palace of Eternal Life*). Although *chuanqi* were primarily written by and for the gentry, some were designed for palace performances or for professional troupes. There were two musical styles: *kunqu*, which was popular in the banquet halls of the elite literati, and *yiyang*, a style popular in the outdoor theatres of the common

people. When *jingju (Beijing opera) became enormously popular in the late eighteenth century, it ended the dominance of *chuanqi* in *China, although many individual scenes from the form continue to be performed today.   SYV

CHUNLIU SHE (CH'UN LIU SHE)

The Spring Willow Society, the first Chinese Western-style theatre group. In 1907 a group of Chinese students in *Tokyo performed an act from *The Lady of the Camellias* by *Dumas *fils*. Some of the actors had studied the Japanese *shimpa (new school) theatre and borrowed its techniques; they also received help from the Japanese actor Fujisawa Asajirō. Later that year the group staged *The Cry of the Black Slaves to Heaven*, a five-act play adapted from a Chinese translation of Harriet Beecher Stowe's novel *Uncle Tom's Cabin*. Written purely in *dialogue, it is generally considered the first *huaju (spoken drama) play in Chinese. Chunliu She was active in Japan for a few more years, performing *one-act plays and the four-act *Hot Blood* (1909), adapted from a Japanese translation of *Tosca* by *Sardou. Some of the participants, most noticeably *Ouyang Yuqian and Lu Jingruo, went on to become important forces in the Chinese new theatre movement. After 1910 a number of the group returned to *Shanghai where they started Xinju Tongzhi Hui (the New Drama Society), which used the name Chunliu Jüchang (Spring Willow Theatre) during performance. Between 1912 and 1915, they were considered the most dedicated and best-trained Western-style *wenming xi (civilized drama) group in China. Among the 81 plays they performed about one-third were translations or adaptations of foreign plays or novels, another third came from traditional Chinese themes, and the rest were original creations based on contemporary stories. Following the fashion of *wenming xi* few of these plays had finished scripts; most were *scenarios that relied heavily on *improvisation. But the insistence on European styles, and the high percentage of foreign and tragic plays in their repertoire, distanced Chunliu She from the average *audience. Lu Jingruo, who had become the leader of the group, died of overwork at the age of 30 in 1915, marking the end of Chunliu She as the most important new drama troupe and starting the decline of *wenming xi*.   SYL

CHURCH DRAMA *See* BIBLICAL PLAYS; LITURGICAL DRAMA; MEDIEVAL THEATRE IN EUROPE.

CHURCHILL, CARYL (1938–)

English playwright. She attended Oxford University, where she wrote a number of student plays, but during the mid-1960s she stayed at home with three young children and wrote for *radio. Her first professional stage play, *Owners* (1972), was produced at the *Royal Court Theatre Upstairs in *London, where she became the first woman writer in residence (1974). *Objections to Sex and Violence* and *Moving Clocks Go Slow* were both produced in 1975. In 1976 she began working with two theatre companies, *Joint Stock and *Monstrous Regiment, the latter a feminist socialist troupe. She wrote *Vinegar Tom* for the first and *Light Shining in Buckinghamshire* for the second; both plays, set in the seventeenth century, explore the complex relations between women and other outsiders and structures of law, morality, and religion. *Light Shining* was also her first collaboration with director Max *Stafford-Clark, who has maintained a close working relationship with Churchill throughout her career.

The 1980s consolidated Churchill's prestige as one of the most successful playwrights of her generation. *Cloud 9* (1981), *Top Girls* (1982), *Fen* (1983), and *Serious Money* (1986), all but *Fen* directed by Stafford-Clark, continued the analysis of women and politics, ranging from juxtapositions of colonial and post-colonial culture in *Cloud 9* to dramatic ethnography in *Fen*, to portraits of living in Thatcher's England in *Top Girls* and *Serious Money*. While Churchill was developing a sharp *epic style, she also began to experiment with form and movement, collaborating with choreographer Ian Spink and co-author David Lan on *A Mouthful of Birds* (1986). She became particularly important to a developing feminist performance *theory. Her connections to *Brecht and *materialist analysis of the intersections of economic, racial, and *gender experiences created graphic stagings of great use in answering theoretical questions about how to represent women outside the dominant (male) visual economy of the gaze, and beyond a *realistic *dramaturgy.

Mad Forest (1990) continued her work in the epic mode while several experimental collaborations emphasized movement and music. *Lives of the Great Poisoners* (1991) featured *dance and *music (with Ian Spink and Orlando Gough), and resulted in a production dossier of photographs, musical score, and details of set and projections as well as *text. She continued to work with Spink and his dance company Second Stride on *The Striker* (1994), followed by *Hotel* (1997) in which Churchill's text was sung to music by Gough and danced by Second Stride. Along with these projects emphasizing movement and music, Churchill also pushed the frontiers of language in *Blue Heart* (1997). Her work in this decade took on qualities of the fantastical fable, often nightmarish. In 2000, *Far Away* returned to a more traditional staging, but created an eerie world of threat. *See also* FEMINISM; FEMINIST THEATRE, UK.   JGR

CH'ŎYONGMU, KŎMMU, MUAEMU

Native *dance forms from *Korea containing theatrical elements, originally developed during the long reign of the Silla kingdom (57 BC–AD 935). *Kŏmmu* is a *masked sword dance, inspired by the story of the death of a young warrior who killed an enemy king, while *muaemu* is a dance performed without masks to promulgate Buddhism. *Ch'ŏyongmu*, the most famous

of the three, has dramatic elements that follow the legend of Ch'ŏyong, a son of the Dragon of the East Sea, who used a mask and incantatory song and dance to ward off the spirit of small-pox. *Ch'ŏyongmu* became a two-man dance in the Kory Dynasty (936–1392) and a five-man dance in the early Chosŭn Dynasty (1392–1910). With each revision, the original *ritual purpose was modified for the sake of entertainment, and the dance is still performed today on special occasions. *See* KIAK.   JOC

CIBBER, COLLEY (1671–1757)

English actor, *manager, and playwright. Cibber's prominence in theatre history stems largely from his autobiographical work *An Apology for the Life of Mr Colley Cibber* (1740), written in response to the savage *criticism he received from the satirical pens of Pope and *Fielding. In spite of numerous inaccuracies and the transparent prejudice of Cibber's recollections, his *Apology* offers an invaluable account of seventeenth-century theatre practice and practitioners. Cibber joined the *Drury Lane company in 1690 but remained in small roles until 1695 when the defection of the leading players to *Lincoln's Inn Fields made larger parts available. In his initial work as a playwright, *Love's Last Shift* (1696), he played Sir Novelty Fashion, the first of many 'fop' *characters he successfully created, and in *Vanbrugh's satirical sequel, *The Relapse* (1696), Cibber played Lord Foppington to great public acclaim. As both an actor and playwright, Cibber's strength lay in *comedy and his ability to catch the mood of his *audience. *She Would and She Would Not* (1702) and *The Careless Husband* (1704) reflect the growing trend away from Restoration wit and toward the sentimental comedies which dominated the eighteenth-century stage. As a performer he was less successful in *tragedy but his adaptation of *Richard III* (1700) was the standard acting edition well into the nineteenth century. In 1710 Cibber and fellow actors Robert *Wilks and Thomas *Doggett co-managed Drury Lane in a triumvirate that was successful until the arrival of Barton *Booth, which triggered a number of internal squabbles. Cibber's instinct as a performer led him to choose plays that audiences wanted to see; Mary Porter and Anne *Oldfield were among the company members who prospered under his popular direction. One of Cibber's most successful plays, *The Double Gallant* (1707), was performed over 200 times by the end of the century, though the central *plot was lifted directly from Susannah *Centlivre's *Love at a Venture* (1705), which Cibber had turned down the previous season. Centlivre appears to have ignored this plagiarism but his critics did not. His less contentious version of Vanbrugh's unfinished work *Journey to London*, produced as *The Provok'd Husband* (1728), was well received with Oldfield in the leading role of Lady Townley. Whether it was Cibber's plagiarism or his profession as an actor that rankled his critics, his appointment as Poet Laureate in 1730 was surrounded by controversy.   GBB

CIBBER, SUSANNAH (1714–66)

English actress. Beginning her career as a singer, Susannah joined Theophilus *Cibber's breakaway company at the *Haymarket in 1733 and they married in 1734. Her dramatic debut in the title role of Aaron Hill's *Zara* (1736) brought her public acclaim and she quickly built her reputation as a great tragic actress; her use of a pocket handkerchief to convey emotion was greatly admired, though considered affected and overdone by her critics. Plagued by a scandalous court case, several difficult pregnancies, and repeated illness, Cibber was often absent from the stage. She made several appearances in Ireland and moved between the *London houses. She finally settled in *Garrick's company at *Drury Lane (1753) where she became the highest-paid member of the troupe.   GBB

CIBBER, THEOPHILUS (1703–58)

English actor, *manager, and playwright. The first son of Colley *Cibber, Theophilus joined his father's company at *Drury Lane aged 16. Before he was 20 he was playing leading parts and managing the summer company. His father appears to have blocked his son's succession to the managerial crown at Drury Lane, possibly because of his dissolute reputation offstage. His performance as Pistol in *Henry IV* (1727) and his success as the manager of the *Haymarket company (1733–4) brought him popularity with *audiences but he lost their sympathy as details of his financial and sexual exploitation of his second wife, the actress Susannah *Cibber, were hauled through the courts. He continued to play minor parts and had some success as a hack writer.   GBB

CICERI, PIERRE (1782–1862)

French designer. After study under F. J. Belanger, Ciceri joined the staff of the *Opéra and rose to the post of scenic director (1822–47). He also worked for the *Comédie-Française from 1826, and at other *Paris theatres. His most notable designs for the Opéra included Liszt's *Don Sanche* (1825), Auber's *La Muette de Portici* (1828), and Rossini's *Le Comte Ory* (1828) and *Guillaume Tell* (1829); and at the Comédie-Française, *Henri III et sa cour* by *Dumas *père* (1829), and two major plays by *Hugo, *Hernani* (1830) and *Le Roi s'amuse* (1832). Characterized by elaborate *spectacle, Ciceri's *romantic *scenography earned him Dumas's tribute as 'the father of modern stage design'.   WDH

CIÉSLAK, RYSZARD (1937–90)

Polish actor, best known for his work with the *Polish Laboratory Theatre, of which he was a member from 1961 to its dissolution in 1984. Trained as a *puppeteer, Ciéslak seemed an unlikely figure to become one of the most celebrated experimental performers of the twentieth century, the ultimate realization of *Grotowski's vision of the 'holy actor'. Ciéslak's work in productions such as *The Constant Prince* (1965), in which he performed the role of a political martyr who achieved apotheosis through suffering, was taken as confirmation that Grotowski's vision of the performer's craft as a 'total act', an unveiling of the actor's deepest truth as a confession in the presence of the spectator, could be realized. In the Laboratory Theatre's final production, *Apocalypsis cum Figuris* (1969), Ciéslak performed the role of the Simpleton, an ironic figure for the Second Coming of Christ. His performance was lauded for its extraordinary intimacy, sincerity, and clarity of detail. Thereafter he participated in various para-theatrical projects and directed in Poland and abroad. His last notable role was as the blind King Dhritarastra in Peter *Brook's *Mahabharata* (1985). *See also* ACTING. (*See* illustration, p. 272.)   LW

CINEMA *See* FILM AND THEATRE.

CINTRA, LUÍS MIGUEL (1949–)

Portuguese actor and director, who graduated from Lisbon University in romance philology and studied at the *Bristol Old Vic. Internationally known for acting in Manoel de Oliveira's *films, he is associated with the distinguished theatre company Teatro da Cornucópia, which he co-founded in *Lisbon in 1973 with Jorge Silva *Melo. Cintra has *managed the company with set designer Cristina Reis since the late 1970s. An attractive and brilliant actor, Cintra is also an imaginative director whose work is based on three major principles: the primacy of the literary *text and a passionate belief in the word; the idea that theatre should be an analysis of life 'tortured by the idea of truth and meaning'; and the assumption that theatre should accept and show its own *theatricality. Choosing Portuguese classics (*Vicente, *Silva, and *Garrett), Shakespeare (for instance *Cymbeline*, 2000), or contemporary writers like Edward *Bond (*War Trilogy*, 1987) and Heiner *Müller (*Der Auftrag*, 1984 and 1992), his aesthetic choices rely on Marcuse's idea that great literature can be the spiritual rock against greed, relativism, and the decadence of modernity.

MHS

CIRCLE IN THE SQUARE THEATRE

Non-profit *New York theatre founded by José *Quintero and others in 1951 in a former Greenwich Village nightclub converted to a semi-*arena performance space. Its success with such Quintero stagings as *Summer and Smoke* (1952) launched the post-war *Off-Broadway movement. In 1960 the company moved to Bleecker Street, and in 1972 took over a new

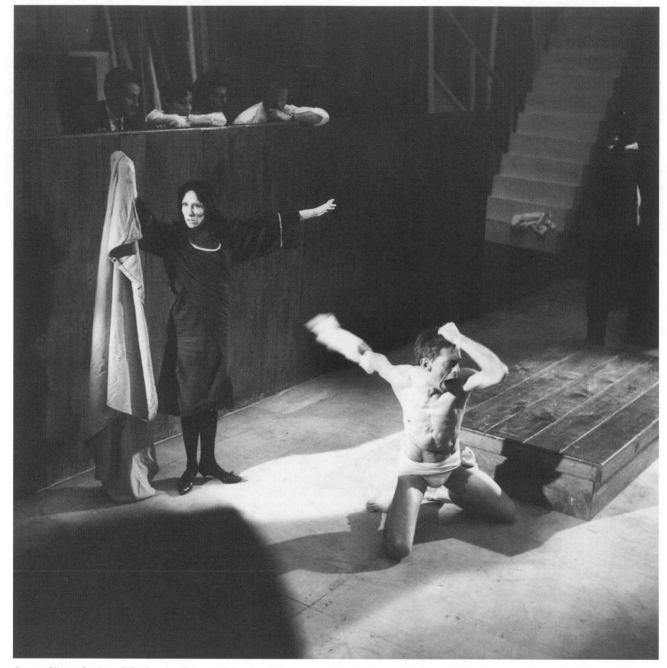

Grotowski's production of *The Constant Prince*, Polish Laboratory Theatre, 1965, with Ryszard **Ciéslak** exhibiting the extraordinary physical control that was one of the hallmarks of the company. The audience (rear of picture), severely limited in size by the design, was arranged in an elevated circle around the playing space, voyeurs peering down at an operating theatre or bull ring (the torturer here has assumed the pose of a matador).

Broadway venue, the Joseph E. Levine Theatre, at Broadway and West 50th Street. Using an oval configuration that allows all 648 spectators a close view of the action, this (often financially troubled) theatre has offered a revival-oriented repertory unusual in Broadway's commercial atmosphere.

SLL

CIRCLE REPERTORY THEATRE COMPANY

American theatre. Founded in a small space on *New York's Upper West Side in 1969 by director Marshall *Mason, playwright Lanford *Wilson, and actors Tanya Berezin and Rob

Thirkield, the Circle Rep became a major force in the 'playwright's theatre' movement of the 1970s and 1980s. Producer Kermit Bloomgarden moved Wilson's *The Hot l Baltimore* to a larger space in Greenwich Village in 1973 (the former *Circle in the Square venue) and as the company's fortunes rose it took even larger quarters a few blocks away on Sheridan Square (1974). Circle Rep's programme featured a complex series of readings and productions of new plays. Among the writers who developed work at Circle Rep were Mark Medoff, Craig *Lucas, Jon Robin Baitz, Jim Leonard, Jr., and William *Hoffman; actors who came to wide attention through the repertoire were Judd *Hirsch, Swoozie Kurtz, Kathy Bates, Alec Baldwin, Christopher Reeve, and William *Hurt. Mason gave control of the theatre to Berezin in 1987 and Austin Pendleton took charge in 1995. The transfers to commercial Broadway productions that sustained the company in its first decades were rare in the 1990s, and the company folded in a *financial crisis in 1996.   MAF

CIRCULAR, TEATRO

Uruguayan company, founded in *Montevideo in 1954 by Hugo Mazza, his brother Eduardo Malet, and others. Two of Mazza's productions propelled the group to prominence: Elsa Shelley's *The Case of Isabel Collins* (1957), seen by 25,000 spectators over the course of its run, and *Osborne's *Look Back in Anger* (1958). The strong direction of the two brothers, and the intense *acting of early company members, helped Teatro Circular develop into one of the most popular independent theatres in Uruguay, mounting an international repertoire that included Ben *Jonson, *Chekhov, and *Pinter. During the dictatorship Jorge *Curi and Mercedes *Rein staged their subversive play *El herrero y la muerte* (*The Blacksmith and Death*, 1981), which ran for five years.   EJW

CIRCUS, MODERN *see page 274*

CIRCUS, ROMAN

Large entertainment building used first and foremost for chariot racing. The most famous of all circuses was the Circus Maximus in ancient Rome. Chariot racing was held as early as the sixth century BC in the area of what became the Circus Maximus in the valley between the Palatine and the Aventine Hills. During the later republic and the early empire the Circus Maximus, to a greater extent than any other circus, also served as the venue for other events. The first structure on the site is said to date back to the sixth century BC (traditionally to the Tarquins), and for a long time all the seating and the starting gates were timber. It was not until the time of Trajan (AD 98–117) that the structure reached its final form. Including the

*arena and seating the structure was 600 m (656 yards) long with an average width of 180 m (197 yards). Estimates of seating capacity vary from 150,000 to 350,000, the latter perfectly possible by the early second century AD.

Games were held throughout the year as part of the religious and political life of the city, and the most popular and exciting events were the *ludi circenses*. On the day of a race, a procession was held that led into the circus. The crowd would cheer and place bets, a trumpet would blow, and the presiding magistrate would signal the start of the race by dropping a napkin. A maximum of twelve charioteers could compete in any one race and they entered the arena simultaneously from the twelve *carceres* or starting boxes at the open end of the circus. It has been possible to reconstruct the starting mechanism from archaeological evidence at Lepcis Magna in Libya. An attendant pulled a lever that operated a catapult system; the catapult jerked out the latches of the gates of each stall, and this enabled the gates to fly open and the race was on. The racers travelled anti-clockwise, normally circling seven times around the *spina*, the 344-m (376-yard) long central barrier along the central axis of the circus. Thus a normal race in the Circus Maximus was of just over 4.8 km (3 miles) (lasting just over eight minutes, incidentally the length of Charlton Heston's race in the *film *Ben-Hur*, 1959) with speeds on the straight reaching 75 k.p.h. (47 m.p.h.); the finishing line was two-thirds of the way down the track. The central barrier was visible to all spectators and thus over time came to be adorned with statues and trophies that had a practical or politico-symbolic function; lap counters in the form of gilded eggs and dolphins counted down the laps and increased the tension of the *spectacle for the crowd.

Crashes were common, especially at the start of a race and at the turns; the charioteers would aim to turn as close as possible to the conical-shaped turning posts. To overtake on the inside as one approached the turn was a tactic particularly admired, as well as extremely dangerous. Each chariot team had a *hortator*, an individual horseman in protective clothing whose job was to ride ahead of the team and act as guide through the dust and confusion of the race. The *hortator*'s job was not as risky as that of the *sparsores*, boys who stood at the edge of the track to provide refreshments to both horses and drivers; a number of reliefs show them going under the wheels of the chariots. By the time of the empire (late first century BC) chariot racing had become a very professional affair, with large stables owned by prominent individuals supplying the horses, chariots, and drivers. All jockeys belonged to teams (*factiones*), and each team had its own colours. From Augustus' reign there were usually four: white worn by the Albata, red by the Russata, blue by the Veneta, and green by the Prasina. The *factiones* were virtual companies or corporations under imperial patronage; they supplied teams to the magistrates giving the games and received money prizes in return. The emperors built

(continued on p. 276)

CIRCUS, MODERN

A quintessentially popular *performance *genre, in which highly skilled performers offer demonstrations of extreme physical virtuosity, precision, and daring. In its traditional form, circus refers to a travelling show, generally comprising a variety of acts, taking place in or above one or more circular stage areas called 'rings', and with the *audience surrounding. The label has been used in a broader sense to evoke a circus-like style which features the performing body at its most astounding. The modern Western notion of circus arose in late eighteenth-century *London as a collective programme for performative displays, emphasizing entertainment, sensation, and *spectacle. Historically, circus acts fall into several general categories: aerial acts (e.g. tightrope and trapeze); ground acts (*acrobatics, balancing, *juggling); clowning (individuals, pairs, groups); *animal acts (equestrian, domestic, wild); and daredevils (knife-throwing, human cannonball). Essentially rooted in the display of physical control, strength, and balance, the spectator's direct access to physical daring surely remains central to the *genre's widespread popularity. The circus act offers a triumph of the human body itself, not a representation—and the spectator's emotional reaction amounts to a 'real-life' response, rather than the empathized feeling of mimetic theatre. Circus may be seen to open itself to audiences across economic and class boundaries. A predilection for the non-verbal makes it readily available to children, and affords travel across cultures.

Most histories trace the origins of the circus to Philip Astley, a former officer in the British cavalry, who in 1768 entertained a crowd of paying customers by displaying his particular skills at handling horses while standing astride them as they galloped around a ring. Astley and his competitors quickly supplemented equestrian demonstrations with the other types of performative skills which have become synonymous with circus (see ASTLEY'S AMPHITHEATRE). Although these 'acts' would have been seen previously on streets and fairgrounds in some form, Astley gathered them within a containable staging area for a single admission price, the spectators encircling the action. The vigour with which Astley and his competitors came to publicize their shows was also elemental to the circus's eventual identity. Charles Hughes, a former employee of Astley's, was chief among his rivals. Hughes gave the circus its name by dubbing his establishment the Royal Circus in 1782 ('circus' being Latin for 'ring'). A ring size of 13 m (42 feet) became the standard, since that diameter can create a centrifugal force that maximizes the speed of the horse while actually assisting in the rider's balance.

The circus spread quickly at the end of the eighteenth century. Astley established an amphitheatre in *Dublin, and built the Cirque du Palais Royale in *Paris in 1787. It was taken over by Antonio Franconi, an exiled Italian noble, when the French Revolution prevented Astley's continued involvement. Franconi and his sons went on to establish many other circus-based amphitheatres, and are considered the fathers of French circus. Hughes, in the meantime, brought the circus to Russia at the behest of Empress Catherine, who commissioned an amphitheatre in *St Petersburg. Jacques Tourniaire, a Frenchman who had been involved with Hughes and the Franconis, assisted further at the birth of the Russian circus, also introducing it to Germany and Scandinavia. John Bill Ricketts, one of Hughes's equestrian stars, established the circus in North America in the 1790s, building permanent venues in *Philadelphia and *New York, and founded the first Canadian circus in *Montréal.

During its first century in Europe, the circus traded primarily on its equestrian roots and theatrical affinities, supplementing horse-riding displays and enactments with other human and animal displays, as well as clowning, *pantomimes, *melodramas, *burlettas, and *dances. The *hippodrama featured equine stars alongside human ones, playing out events with military, mythic, literary, and historic themes. One of the great names in British circus was the Belgian Andrew *Ducrow, an outstanding horseman, who ran Astley's Amphitheatre from 1825 to 1841. He introduced enduring entertainments like 'The Courier of St Petersburg', which presented a fictional messenger standing astride two horses and circling the ring, while other horses, each bearing the flag of a different country, galloped between his legs to join the charge. The act blended the dominant circus elements of the period: a vehicle for the spectacular display of human (and animal) abilities, in which a rousing narrative fed a growing fascination with the foreign. The emphasis on equestrian displays meant that *clowns, too, would explore the comic possibilities of horse and ring. Comic mileage might be derived from the performer's perfect lack of riding competence (the horse making an ideal 'straight man') in contrast to the mastery witnessed in previous acts. It became, in fact, a common clowning strategy to *burlesque whatever 'serious' act had preceded. The English actor-clown Joseph *Grimaldi is considered the progenitor of the Western circus clown, by way of the *commedia dell'arte and pantomime harlequinade.

At first, the circus erected semi-permanent and permanent structures, with major cities in Great Britain, Europe, and the

Americas acquiring elaborate *playhouse-like structures. But in the nineteenth century prospective audiences in the USA were far apart and still moving westward. In 1825 J. Purdy Brown became the first American circus proprietor to take his show on the road with a tent—a portable, constant performance space, custom made for pursuit of a *frontier audience. This new boon to self-sufficiency was the first of several developments which would come to distinguish the American circus from its European counterparts, along with the circus-wagon street *parade, rail travel, and an expansion in the number of rings. With tent in tow, the ability to travel wholly by horse-drawn means led to the rise of the circus wagon. By the second half of the nineteenth century, these wagons, evoking the coaches used by European royalty in previous eras, developed ever more opulent detail and sophistication. The company's arrival in any new town became a grand entrance in the form of a street parade, with wagons, performers, and animals on flamboyant display. The calliope, a steam-powered pipe organ, traditionally took up the rear of the parade, and became the signature sound of the classic American circus.

The European circus remained, for the most part, rooted to the tight-knit family or company tradition, while the American circus was driven by the country's burgeoning entrepreneurial spirit. Perhaps no single name evokes the latter more recognizably than P. T. *Barnum, who, in 1871, combined his existing 'museum' of animal and human oddities with William Cameron Coup's travelling circus. At this time, Barnum and his partners also began to invest in customized railway cars for the transportation of their show, moving to complete train transport in 1890. The larger companies followed suit, with the circus train becoming a defining feature of the American form until the 1930s, by which time motorized road transport had phased in.

Proprietors were trying to stretch their capacities in the 1850s, and it would seem that the one-ring tenting circus had reached a practical limit at upwards of 5,000 spectators. Barnum added two rings, thereby ballooning the performance space and audience capacity, which could eventually accommodate well over 14,000 customers. The additional rings redefined the way circus was performed and received. Displays might be going on simultaneously in all the rings, so there developed a hierarchy among the acts, with the most highly touted taking place in the centre ring. This, of course, made it impossible for a spectator to focus on everything at once, though the overall sensation might be one of unfathomable excitement. The American drive, led by Barnum, for 'more', 'bigger', and 'better' spilled out of the Big Top to greet customers at the very entrance of the circus grounds. The larger American circuses had already begun to offer auxiliary, *carnival attractions in sideshow tents. Adjacent to the main tent one might find the human oddities (see FREAK SHOWS), exotic animals, carnival performers, and animal menageries which had long since begun *touring in tandem with

circuses. Barnum's museum took up residence along a 'midway', an alley of standing attractions which lined the path to the Big Top entrance. Barnum remains an American icon for a spirit of bare-knuckle commercialism, but he was merely extending a circus style and rhetoric established back in Astley's day: a trumpeting call to witness (for the 'modest' price of admission); a willingness to stage elaborate teases and to stretch the definitions of truth in advertising; and a scrappy competitive ethic in trumping the opposition's claims.

Back in Europe, some 200 indigenous circus companies were in operation by the end of the nineteenth century. Well-known performer-proprietors of the time included Ernst Jacob Renz, Giuseppe Chiarini, and Théodore Rancy. George *Sanger, considered Britain's greatest circus showman of the Victorian era, operated Astley's Amphitheatre from 1871 to 1893. By the turn of the twentieth century the American influence could be felt across the Atlantic in an important way: the classic equestrian circus had given way to more extravagant feats of daring and wild-animal acts, both of which became the new stars of the show. Although the Europeans would, for the most part, retain their one-ring tradition, tenting allowed them to spread the seeds of circus near and far. From the middle of the nineteenth century to the beginning of the twentieth, several European companies cut huge swaths across the globe. By such means circus was introduced to Australia in the 1840s, *India, *China, and *Japan in the 1860s, and South Africa in the 1870s. By the twentieth century, *Latin American countries were already building strong circus traditions, generating their own top performers and companies. At the start of the twenty-first century, circus virtually covers the world; the *Moscow and Chinese state circuses have become international operations; South America and India have acquired reputations for healthy circus environments.

It should be recalled that many circus-like acts pre-dated the arrival of the Western institution, having derived from centuries-old performance traditions in countries like Japan, China, India, and Egypt. At the same time, Western circus proprietors have always collected what they considered to be striking acts during their forays abroad. Indian and Asian acrobats, Chinese plate-spinners, and Egyptian contortionists, among others, showed the human body performing new and amazing feats while feeding a fascination for the 'exotic' which circus has always mined (see INTERCULTURALISM). The circus has traditionally played to the audience's orientalist tendencies to enhance a sense of wonder or unique opportunity, and perhaps capitalize on its culture's conceits of superiority. Pageants or speciality acts might be placed somewhere thrillingly 'other' through caricatured *costume and music. American animal-trainer Clyde Beatty, for example, based the costume and conduct of his *character on a stereotype of the African big-game hunter, pushing buttons connected to *gender, *race, culture, civilization, and human domination of the animal world.

Various pressures exerted by the First World War, *music hall, and theatre, the increasing cost of travel, the Great Depression, and, of course, the eventual rise of *film and *television led to an overall reduction and consolidation of companies through the middle of the twentieth century, especially in the USA and Britain. Tenting circuses remained, but many switched to large, standing venues. Some of the best-known names operating into and beyond that period include Ringling Brothers and Barnum and Bailey, and Clyde Beatty–Cole Brothers in the USA; Bertram Mills and sons, the Chipperfields, and the Fossetts in England; and Hagenbeck, Fratellini, Knie, and Krone in Europe. State circuses in the former USSR, China, and Eastern Europe, though untroubled by economic factors, were affected by their political upheavals in the 1980s. By the end of the century, however, European circus was in full bloom, with hundreds of companies of all sizes based in Italy, Spain, France, Germany, and Scandinavia. Ashton's Circus in Australia and the Boswell Wilkie Circus in South Africa also became companies of note.

The circus took another evolutionary turn in the later twentieth century. Many moved away from animal acts, as cultural attitudes changed toward the training, caging, and 'performance' of the once popular beasts, and animal-rights groups became particularly aggressive in their protests. The rise of the circus school meant that training was no longer largely confined to an apprentice-style education. The Russian State Circus School, established in Moscow in 1927, paved the way for the establishment of schools all over the world by the end of the century. On an equally large scale, the teaching of circus skills has been introduced at large as a tool for sociocultural and economic improvement, examples of which have included programmes in Northern Ireland and Ethiopia.

Although 'traditional' circuses have continued to operate into the twenty-first century, a movement called New Circus emerged in the 1970s, applying a born-again interest in circus skills to contemporary performance aesthetics. The New Circus is said to return the genre to its original emphasis on skill and artistry, rather than the spectacle and danger which came to define it in the late nineteenth century. New Circus generally takes a more environmentalist attitude toward animal acts, either avoiding animals entirely or attempting to foster a sense of respect for them on- and offstage. In form, New Circus steers closer to theatre: it features acts based on time-honoured skills but tends to channel them toward theme, narrative, or an *avant-garde aesthetic. Notable New Circus companies have included Circus Oz (Australia), Circus Roncalli (Austria), Cirque de Soleil (Canada), Teatro Circo Imaginario (Chile), Archaos (France), and the Pickle Family and Big Apple circuses (United States). In addition, small circuses from various countries have toured widely, giving performances and skills workshops while bridging cultures. The International Circus Festival of Monte Carlo, established in 1975, has led to a number of festivals and competitions throughout the world for the showcasing and celebration of circus skills.

Circus has held a particular attraction for other art forms and performance genres since the beginning of the twentieth century. As a popular form *par excellence*, it appealed to the *dada and *futurist movements. Antonin *Artaud found a point of contact in its visceral, pre-verbal engagement between mass audience and highly trained performing body. Elsewhere, circus or the circus-like have informed work by playwrights like Frank *Wedekind and Eugene *Ionesco, as well as directors such as V. S. *Meyerhold, Peter *Brook, and Ariane *Mnouchkine. Used as context, the romanticized images of circus life's daily swings from gaudy glamour to sawdust reality, its itinerant, communal lifestyle, its clowns with painted faces, the perceived innocence of a form which serves for many a child as an introduction to live performance: these and other circus themes have served as potent metaphors for theatre, film, dance, music, and *opera.

EW

Loxton, Howard, *The Golden Age of the Circus* (London, 1997)
Speaight, George, *A History of the Circus* (London, 1980)
Stoddart, Helen, *Rings of Desire: circus history and representation* (Manchester, 2000)

stables for each of these teams in the Campus Martius with a full staff of coaches, trainers, blacksmiths, veterinarians, and grooms. The charioteers by this time were mainly professional, drawn from the lower social classes of freedmen and slaves. As with gladiators, those who succeeded were idolized by the public and they could earn enough in prize money of their own to retire as wealthy men. One such charioteer was Gaius Appuleius Diocles, who lived in the first half of the second century AD. A long inscription lists his many victories (over 3,000) and huge earnings before his death at 42.

By the imperial period a full day's programme included 24 races. As well as horse and chariot racing the circus could also be used for other types of spectacle, often put on as part of the entertainment between races. Novelty races might be staged to add variety. Teams of up to ten horses, for example, might be used, or exhibitions of trick riding; athletics displays including boxing, wrestling, and foot races could be put on. *Gladiatorial combat and *animal fights might also be staged. A sixth-century AD papyrus from Egypt preserves the only known circus programme (see PLAYBILLS AND PROGRAMMES) from the ancient world and mentions singing rope dancers as one of the interval entertainments. At the end of the games, the victors received prizes, a victor's palm, crowns, and neck chains of gold. By the late Roman period the circus and chariot racing became increasingly associated with the emperor; the circus was one of the few places where he could be seen by ordinary people. By the sixth century the Blues and Greens had become the dominant factions and attracted fanatical support, illustrated by the Nika *riot of AD 532 which caused much destruction and loss of life in Constantinople. *See also* ROMAN THEATRE.　　　HD

CAMERON, ALAN, *Circus Factions: blues and greens at Rome and Byzantium* (Oxford, 1976)

HUMPHREY, JOHN H., *Roman Circuses: arenas for chariot racing* (London, 1986)

CIRQUE OLYMPIQUE (THÉÂTRE DU CHÂTELET)

*Paris *playhouse, originally an equestrian amphitheatre, established by Philip Astley in 1782 (*see* ASTLEY'S AMPHITHEATRE), then directed by the Franconi family for four decades. It specialized in equestrian *pantomimes and *circus dramas. In 1827 the circus was re-established on the popular boulevard du Temple in a new arena constructed specifically for the performance of elaborate fairy extravaganzas and military 'mimodrames' with titles like *The Republic* and *Jerusalem Delivered*. After the boulevard was demolished in 1862, the theatre moved to the site of the old Châtelet fortress, where it continued its tradition of grand *spectacles and sensation dramas. As the public's tastes changed at the end of the nineteenth century, the Châtelet turned toward more refined musical entertainment and *ballets. Here Parisian *audiences first discovered *Diaghilev's *Ballets Russes in 1909, and Nijinski and Debussy's *Prélude à l'après-midi d'un faune* in 1912. In 1917 *Cocteau staged his controversial *Parade* here, with music by Satie and *scenery by *Picasso. Having undergone acoustic and cosmetic renovations in the 1980s and 1990s, the Châtelet continues to emphasize contemporary *musical theatre.　　　CHB

CISNEROS, ENRIQUE (c.1953–)

Mexican performer associated with leftist *politics of the 1960s and 1970s and the radical Free Centre for Theatre and Artistic Experimentation (CLETA). Cisneros's *monologues and skits denounced the Mexican government's repression of students and labour, as well as the monopoly of performance venues by the official theatre establishment.　　　KFN

CITHARODY

Ancient *Greek performance form in which a gorgeously attired singer, standing on a platform and accompanying himself on a cithar (a stringed instrument), recited heroic stories. Impersonation was required. In Timotheus of Miletus' *The Persians* (c.417 BC), the performer played a dying Persian and a Phrygian who speaks in broken Greek.　　　RWV

CITIZENS THEATRE

Founded in *Glasgow in 1943 by James *Bridie, the 'Citz' took over the Royal Princess's, a Victorian *variety and *pantomime theatre in the Gorbals, a notorious district south of the River Clyde. Although Bridie attempted to develop a national drama, encouraging Scottish writers and actors, under a succession of directors in the 1960s the theatre became indistinguishable from many other British *repertory theatres. Giles *Havergal's arrival in 1969 with Philip *Prowse, a designer/director, heralded considerable change. With translator and writer Robert David MacDonald, they adopted a highly visual and visceral approach to production, presenting neglected Jacobean, Restoration, and European *texts. On Prowse's extraordinary sets, *Webster, *Tourneur, and *Wycherley rubbed shoulders with *Goldoni, *Lermontov, and *Genet, and MacDonald's adaptations of Proust and *Tolstoy. Although a high nakedness count and neglect of Scottish authors originally caused considerable controversy, young *audiences flocked, attracted by cheap seats and a style which seemed to cross punk with *Meyerhold, *Wilde with deconstruction. As critical acclaim and foreign invitations followed, it became regarded as one of Britain's most radical theatres. The triumvirate still ran the theatre in 2002, although the addition of two *studio theatres in 1993 allowed them increasingly to supplement their work with that of new writers and directors.　　　GJG

CITY COMEDY

A term invented by modern scholars to refer to a type of *comedy popular in early Jacobean *London. Set in specific and well-known London locales, such plays addressed, usually *satirically, economic and social tensions caused by the city's recent commercial expansion, increased social mobility, and rapid population growth. While many scenes in a late Elizabethan work like *Dekker's *The Shoemaker's Holiday* (1599) are also set in familiar urban locales, most critics consider that play too romantic or sunny in tone for city comedy. City comedies focus on a cluster of themes, singly or in combination. Some construct class conflict between middle-class shopkeepers and aristocratic gallants as sexual rivalry over women, usually shopkeepers' daughters or wives, as in *Middleton's *Michaelmas Term* (1605). Some explore the cultural friction between miserly and money-grubbing lawyers or usurers on the one hand, and pleasure-seeking penniless upper-class prodigals on the other, as in Middleton's *A Trick to Catch the Old One* (1605) or its later avatar, *Massinger's *A New Way to Pay Old Debts* (1625). Others explore the power differential between master craftsmen and their journeymen and apprentices, as in *Jonson, *Marston, and *Chapman's *Eastward Hoe* (1605). Still others dramatize exploits of criminals or other colourful urban types, as in Middleton and Dekker's *The Roaring Girl*

(1611). Most city comedies were performed by troupes of *boy actors, whose miniaturizing of urban social reality brought out its vice, folly, and absurdity.   MS

CITY THEATRE

This Charleston, South Carolina, venue started in 1794 as the French Theatre, when the second French company in the USA opened with *Rousseau's *Pygmalion*. Under other *managers it was soon called the City Theatre or, because of its location, the Church Street Theatre. Amid a host of largely forgotten plays, *pantomimes, and *operas, it offered well-known works by Shakespeare, *Sheridan, and others. Its stage saw the world première of Audin's *Apotheosis of Franklin* (1796), the American premières of *Dunlap's *Tristram Shandy* adaptation (1795) and Sophia Lee's *tragedy *Almeyda* (1797), and the Charleston première of Sheridan's *Pizarro* (1800), a big hit. In 1800 it was remodelled as a hall for balls and concerts.   CT

CIULEI, LIVIU (1923–   )

Romanian director, designer, and actor. Ciulei completed dual degrees in architecture and theatre in *Bucharest. In 1945 he began acting, directing, and designing for his own company, specializing in the American plays that had been banned during the war years; three years later his *playhouse was nationalized. Under Soviet *censorship, Romanian theatre was dominated by *naturalism, and Ciulei turned to *film. In 1956 Ciulei's manifesto, 'On the Theatricality of Scenery', sparked a turn away from *socialist realism to a rediscovery of the power of *theatricality. During the 1960s and 1970s he developed what would become hallmarks of his *scenography: huge photos within architectural units, which moved in various configurations to suggest locale and mood. At the same time he charted new directions for the Romanian theatre, as with *As You Like It* (1961), which mixed visual elements from various sources. He served as *artistic director of the Bulandra Theatre in Bucharest from 1963 to 1972, when he was dismissed for allowing Lucian *Pintilie's production of *Gogol's *The Government Inspector* to be staged.

*Tours by the Bulandra during the 1970s to Western Europe, Australia, and the United States cemented Ciulei's international reputation, especially with *Büchner's *Danton's Death* and *Leonce and Lena*, I. L. *Caragiale's *A Lost Letter*, *Hamlet*, and *Gorky's *The Lower Depths*. He has worked as a designer and director for *opera and theatre at *Covent Garden in *London and the Birmingham Opera, and in America at the Lyric Opera of *Chicago, *Arena Stage in Washington, and the *New York Shakespeare Festival. He served as artistic director of the *Guthrie Theatre in Minneapolis (1980–5), where he redesigned the *auditorium and mounted a remarkable series of Shakespeare works. Ciulei's *directing style, although eclectic, aims

to distil and comment on the larger social world. In *The Tempest* (Guthrie Theatre, 1981), for example, Prospero's island was surrounded by a sea of blood, in which the detritus of Western civilization floated. As the Players dressed for 'The Mousetrap' in *Hamlet* (Arena Stage, 1986), spectators also saw the courtiers dressing for the evening, and at the same theatre Ciulei emphasized the crushing emotional violence of *Ibsen's *Ghosts* (1997). Although based in New York, Ciulei returned to direct at the Bulandra in 1990 and 2000.   EEP

CIVIC FESTIVALS

Performances that represent a particular place (usually a city), often a particular date (the annual City *Dionysia in Athens, Independence Day in the United States, or the 750th anniversary of *Berlin), and the association of both with commercial as well as community vitality. Engagement with capital, civil society, and secular culture distinguishes civic festivals from *state displays. The latter take their purest form in *rituals of the absolute monarchy or dictatorship, in glorifying the leader and reducing citizens to subjects, but also appear in industrial democracies at liminal moments such as inaugurations, Olympiads, or state funerals. This distinction is not unconditional, since forms like *parades and pageants can under different circumstances qualify as civic festivals or state displays; parades may be more fluid or unpredictable than pageants but, as political manipulation of parades demonstrates to the present, they are not free from state power.

The secular and commercial aspects of civic festivals emerge especially in the Enlightenment, but are present even in festivals associated with *religion. The plays at the City Dionysia in *ancient Greece were sponsored by a *choregus*, chosen from the wealthiest citizens, and included, along with *tragedy, pointed civic *satire. The *mystery *cycles in *York and other medieval cities were the work of the *guilds and reflected commercial interests alongside or in competition with clerical or royal power (*see* MEDIEVAL THEATRE IN EUROPE). The open-air gathering of citizens to celebrate their independent city-states, proposed by *Rousseau in his *Lettre à d'Alembert* (1758), were realized in different ways by the festivals in revolutionary France (1790–2) and the citizens' parades in early US cities; the former may have taken place in *Paris, but ideally represented the central and exclusive authority of the revolutionary state; the latter, such as the Grand Federal Procession in *Philadelphia (4 July 1788), may have 'raised the federal roof' but the roof was supported by Philadelphia artisans and manufacturers asserting their civic and commercial rights. Fortified by 'federal beer' sold along the route, their parade through the city challenged the separation of urban classes. The legacy of this tension between trespass and authorized procession remains in such different events as New Orleans Mardi Gras parades in which black crews have challenged white city control of routes and capital, or the annual Northern Irish Orange parades, whose progress through Catholic areas is hotly contested.

It is against the background of civil strife in urban space that the harmonizing and ruralizing project of the New Pageant movement in Britain and the Commonwealth should be understood. The social tensions underlying the interplay between performance and citizenship, even in the ideal small-scale civic polity of the eighteenth century, erupted in the nineteenth- and early twentieth-century imperial metropolis. As displays of state and of capital from coronations to 'universal expositions' and 'world's fairs' sought periodically to claim public space, their power was challenged by riots and revolutions characterized above all by barricades across public thoroughfares. The emergence of mass socialist parties, especially in Europe, found their performative dimension in rallies, strikes, and especially May Day parades (in France from 1878; officially sanctioned in 1890), which challenged displays of state in such performances as the opening of Parliament, the inauguration of Lord Mayor, or the military parade, and interrupted the flow of capital in regulated industrial labour. From the 'Mother of All Pageants' organized by Louis Napoleon Parker to celebrate the 900th anniversary of Sherbrooke (1905) to 'England's Pleasant Land', by E. M. Forster (1938), antiquarian *spectacle championed England's green and rural past against the perceived evils of urban industrialism. Yet, despite aversion to industrial progress in England, New Pageantry joined forces with industrial *modernism and British imperialism in the colonies. Parker's associate Frank Lascelles went from the New Pageant movement in Britain to act as Pageant Master to the Empire, at the Québec Tercentenary in 1908 and the Pageant of Union in South Africa in 1910. At Empire Exhibitions from *London (1900) to the *Johannesburg Jubilee (1936), the dominions staged their coming of age in national pageants and used the surrounding exhibitions to legitimate their claims to full modernity. Natives contested their exclusion from modernity with counter-festivals, such as the Emancipation Centenary Celebrations (1938).

Pageants, parades, and other civic performances in the post-imperial twentieth century replayed tensions between modern and antiquarian, urban and rural, controversial and communal in the context, not always acknowledged, of the world beyond. Community plays in small towns may be local in the New Pageant tradition, but included not only antiquarian celebrations like The Reckoning (Ann *Jellicoe and the citizens of Lyme Regis, 1978), but also local responses to global issues like nuclear arms and work in Shipyard Tales (*Welfare State and the citizens of Barrow-in-Furness, 1990). The 750th anniversary of Berlin (1987) provoked not only official rivalry between West and East Berlin and thus between West and East Germany, but also unauthorized reminders that Berlin's only other birthday party had been Hitler's (1937). Protests included renaming

'Shakespeare Square' after Benno Ohesorg, who had been shot by police during the Iranian Shah's visit (1967), and displaying of bumper stickers claiming precedence for older East German cities (for instance Leipzig, founded 821) neglected by investment in Berlin. By staging its funeral as a birthday party, including formal and informal performances by Londoners of diverse origins, and a huge 'cake' on the Thames South Bank opposite Whitehall, the populist Greater London Council staged its civic festival to challenge the Conservative state represented by Whitehall, on the eve of its abolition by that government (1986). In this last case, the display of state (of the GLC) became briefly a civic festival, suggesting that the effective state cannot rely merely on display from above and that civility and festivity may, under ideal circumstances, transform the state.

LK

Kershaw, B., The Politics of Performance: radical theatre as cultural intervention (London, 1992)

Kruger, L., The Drama of South Africa: plays, pageants and publics since 1910 (London, 1999)

MacAloon, J. (ed.), Rite, Drama, Festival, Spectacle (Philadelphia, 1984)

Ozouf, M., Festivals and the French Revolution (Cambridge, Mass., 1988)

Schechner, R. (ed.), By Means of Performance (Cambridge, 1990)

CIVIC REPERTORY THEATRE

A rotating classical *repertory in *New York under the direction of its founder, Eva *Le Gallienne. The company *toured extensively but maintained home base at the Fourteenth Street Theatre (an enormous 1866 building) from 1926 to 1933. The theatre specialized in *Ibsen and *Chekhov, but also featured plays by Shakespeare, *Rostand, *Molière, and others. Le Gallienne's vision of 'good plays, good acting and good productions' at the lowest possible prices led to chronic financial shortfalls. Despite a subscription base over 8,000 and near capacity houses, the theatre's democratic prices and lack of subsidy forced it to close in 1935.   MAF

CIVILIZED DRAMA See WENMING XI.

CIXOUS, HÉLÈNE (1937–)

French *theorist, literary scholar, novelist, and playwright, Cixous was born into a Jewish family in Algeria, grew up speaking French and German, and studied English literature at university. She became internationally known in the 1970s as one of four French feminists who developed the theory of écriture féminine (feminine writing), which proposes that representation ('writing') is dominated by the male perspective, and that the female perspective must be liberated (see FEMINISM). Her influential essay 'Laugh of the Medusa' lyrically performs this motif. Her first successful play, *Portrait of Dora* (1976), is a feminist view of Freud's famous case study, a 'writing' of remembered voices and bodies in theatrical space. Since the 1980s, Cixous's major work has been in collaboration with Ariane *Mnouchkine at the Théâtre du *Soleil. First hired as a scholar to consult on the cycle of Shakespeare plays performed in Asian style (*see* INTERCULTURALISM), Cixous was then urged to write original plays with contemporary themes, four of which have been produced, the first two dealing with post-colonialism. *The Terrible But Unfinished History of Norodom Sihanouk, King of Cambodia* (1985) bases its epic structure on Shakespeare to tell, in ten hours, the story surrounding the Cambodian massacre. Using a similar structure, *The Indiade; or, India of their Dreams* (1987) depicts Indian history from 1945 on. In *The Perjury City; or, The Furies' Awakening* (1994), the Furies return as mothers whose children have died from AIDS-contaminated blood. *Drums on the Dyke* (1999) narrates the simple mythic-epic story of a disastrous, preventable flood, with *bunraku-style *puppets manipulated by actors. While Cixous's reliance on myth, parable, and Shakespearian forms is sometimes seen as compromising the historical critique, this critique succeeds when carried by the dialectical force of *text and stage together.

SBB

CLAIRON, MLLE (CLAIRE-JOSÈPHE-HIPPOLYTE LÉRIS DE LA TUDE) (1723–1803)

French actress. Following a triumphant debut at the *Comédie-Française in 1743 as *Racine's Phèdre, she established a formidable reputation in *tragedy, playing the classical repertoire and new work by Buirette de Belloy, Jean-François Marmontel, and especially *Voltaire. Unlike her rival, Mlle *Dumesnil, whose playing was intuitive and inspirational, Clairon was an intellectual actress whose performances were grounded in research and study. With Marmontel's encouragement, and to *Diderot's delight, her *acting underwent a revolutionary mid-career change: she abandoned tendencies towards the vehement and declamatory in favour of a more nuanced delivery and natural manner. Believing that '*realism in stage speech demand[ed] a similar realism in *costume', with the support of her colleague *Lekain she urged that the desire to look fashionable be replaced by the need to look appropriate and historically authentic. As Idamé in Voltaire's *L'Orphelin de la Chine* (*The Orphan of China*, 1755) she adopted 'foreign gestures' and wore 'Chinese' dress, without hoops or cuffs, with bare arms. She retired prematurely at the age of 42 in 1766, following a dispute with the authorities over a colleague who had dishonoured the Comédie, and opened an acting school, where she trained *Larive and Mlle *Raucourt. Between 1772 and 1789 she wrote her memoirs, which offer an insight into her methods and reveal her strong support for the recognition of actors' civil and religious rights.

JG

CLAQUE

A group of people who have been organized or hired, generally to applaud, as part of a theatre *audience. Derived from the French verb *claquer*, the word literally means a clap of the hand. The claque was a most notorious aspect of nineteenth-century French theatre and a Monsieur Sauton is credited as the first (1820) to organize an office in *Paris to provide *claqueurs* for theatrical productions. Claques were both common and influential in European theatre through much of the nineteenth century, but especially so in France. Claque members received free admission (and sometimes a free drink) from theatre *managers, and their leaders (the *chef de claque*) occasionally also received money from the actors. Some of the *chefs de claque* are reputed to have had a sliding scale of charges according to the length and intensity of *applause required.

Claques were so prevalent in Paris during the nineteenth century that several categories of *claqueur* were codified: the *bisseurs* (who had to demand 'bis', asking for a repeat, or encore), the *chatouilleurs* (who were to keep the rest of the audience in good humour), the *commissaires* (who memorized the *text of the play and loudly pointed out its merits), the *pleureuses* (women whose job it was to cry at the tragic turns in a *melodrama), and the *rieurs* (whose job it was to *laugh uproariously at a comic play). The *chef de claque* was an important force in the theatre and often attended *rehearsals to discuss the optimum moments for applause as well as the level at which the applause should take place. In the performances themselves, he would direct the response of the *claqueurs* through a variety of hand gestures. Louis Castel's *Memoirs of a Claqueur* (1829) provides an account of both the theory and practice. By the end of the nineteenth century, however, the claque had all but disappeared in the theatre, although it took somewhat longer to disappear from *opera.

The practice of the claque was not uncommon throughout theatre history and in many geographic settings. The first *Greek theatre was, of course, a competition and groups were organized to applaud enthusiastically so as to influence the judges. In the Edo period (1603–1868) of *kabuki, it was customary for a predetermined spectator to stand when there was a slight pause in the acting and to shout out some encouragement to a particular actor. In some of the *political theatre of the early twentieth century, actors were used as *claqueurs* to encourage the rest of the audience towards the desired message. *Meyerhold, for example, used actors concealed in the audience to guide reactions. The techniques of the claque also take on an explicit form in *television recorded before a live audience where stagehands will hold up placards directing the responses of the spectator, or, in a more mediated fashion, when sitcoms rely on electronic 'laugh tracks' to simulate an audience response.   SBe

CLARK-BEKEDEREMO, JOHN PEPPER (1936–)

Nigerian playwright and poet. Critical attention has focused on the early work of John Pepper Clark rather than the more recent plays published under the name Clark-Bekederemo. His responses to European *tragedy and concern with Delta conventions led to *Song of a Goat* (directed by Wole *Soyinka, 1963) and its sequel *Masquerade* (1965). In Soyinka's production a goat was actually sacrificed on stage, one of the most highly charged moments in the Nigerian theatre, though one which distracted from the poetic *text. Political tensions in newly independent Nigeria prompted *The Raft* (directed by Soyinka, 1964). The large-scale *Ozidi* and *The Ozidi Saga* moved towards a *dance-like style, effectively handled in a groundbreaking production by Odukwe Sackeyfio (1981). Starting in 1982 Clark-Bekederemo threw his energy into establishing a regular theatregoing habit among the Lagos elite by fostering the PEC Repertory Theatre. He also wrote a trilogy, *The Bikoroa Plays*, which follows the fortunes of a Delta family during the first half of the twentieth century. His plays of the 1990s, *The Wives' Revolt* and *All for Oil*, are meditations on the relevance of the past for contemporary society. The second, 'a *history play about the present times in Nigeria', was presented in 2000 at the University of Ibadan, directed by Dapo Adelugba.
JMG

CLARKE, MARTHA (1944–)

American choreographer and director. Trained as a modern *dancer under choreographers Anna Sokolow, José Limón, and Alvin *Ailey, Martha Clarke began developing an idiosyncratic, highly expressionistic theatre of movement and aural imagery that is sometimes given the label music theatre. In 1979 she founded Crowsnest, a chamber movement ensemble dedicated to producing her *auteur*-informed work. During the 1980s her pieces tended to re-envision well-known historical moments with a dreamlike, highly physical and sensual narrative voice. *The Garden of Earthly Delights* (1985), Clarke's version of the painting by Hieronymus Bosch, is among her most famous works of this *genre. In the 1990s Clarke directed *opera in Beijing and for the Glimmerglass Company (Cooperstown, New York), collaborated with Christopher *Hampton on *Alice's Adventures Under Ground* for the Royal *National Theatre, and created *Vers la flamme*, based in part on several short stories by *Chekhov and filled with her signature convolution of longing, grief, and sexuality.   LTC

CLASSICISM *See* NEOCLASSICISM; WEIMAR CLASSICISM.

CLAUDEL, PAUL (1868–1955)

French playwright, poet, and essayist. As a diplomat he served from 1890 to 1935 in the United States, *China, Czechoslovakia, Germany, Italy, Brazil, *Japan, and Belgium, and was elected to the Académie Française in 1946. Many of Claudel's plays were written decades before they were staged, because turn-of-the-century *audiences were not prepared for their complex structure and length, nor for the proselytizing nature of their Catholic world-view of history as a series of cycles in a divine order. In his cosmic dramas, Claudel sought to synthesize history in order to bring out its meaning, which always included *farce as well as epic versions of *tragedy and *comedy. Thus he telescoped time, made every setting both real and symbolic, and used *allegorical *characters and parable *plots. Although his *L'Annonce faite à Marie* (*Tidings Brought to Mary*) was staged by *Lugné-Poe in 1912 and *L'Échange* (*The Exchange*) by *Copeau in 1914, it was not until *Barrault's 1943 production of *Le Soulier de satin* (*The Satin Slipper*) at the *Comédie-Française that Claudel gained wide recognition. Because the dramas accorded with Barrault's vision of a *total theatre synthesizing *drama, *music, *dance, and even *film, he produced many of them over the years, including *Partage de midi* (*Break of Noon*, 1948), *The Exchange* (1951), *Christopher Columbus* (1953), *Tête d'or* (*Golden Head*, 1959), and *Sous le vent des îles Baléares* (*Under the Wind of the Balearic Isles*, 1972).
SBB

CLEVER, EDITH (1941–)

German actress. Clever's career is inextricably connected with that of the *Schaubühne in *Berlin, where she played leading roles in most of the major productions. After *training at the Otto-Falckenberg school in *Munich she worked in Bremen in the 1960s where she joined Peter *Stein. Between 1970 and 1984 she was a member of the Schaubühne ensemble. Since then she has worked almost exclusively with Hans Jürgen Syberberg in his *film and theatre productions, often as a solo performer. In 1994 she played Cleopatra in Stein's *Salzburg Festival production of *Antony and Cleopatra*.   CBB

CLIVE, KITTY (1711–85)

English actress and playwright. Renowned for her singing voice and wry comic ability, Kitty Clive's personal triumph as Nell in Charles Coffey's *The Devil to Pay*, performed at *Drury Lane in the 1730–1 season, doubled her salary and she revived the role throughout her long career. She was a forthright woman who defended her rights against *management moves to reallocate her parts and lower players' salaries. Clive wrote at least six comedies between 1750 and 1765. In her *The Rehearsal; or, Bays in Petticoats* (1750) she played the leading role of a vain female playwright who takes over from the absent leading lady, Kitty Clive.   GBB

CLOSE, GLENN (1947–)

American actress. After graduating from the College of William and Mary, she made her Broadway debut with the New *Phoenix Repertory Company in *Love for Love* (1974). Subsequent stage roles included Mary Tudor in *Rex* (1976), Leilah in *Uncommon Women and Others* (1977), Irene St Claire in *The Crucifer of Blood* (1978), Chairy in *Barnum* (1980), and Yeliena in *Uncle Vanya* with the Yale Repertory Theatre (1981). She won Tony *awards for *The Real Thing* (1984), *Death and the Maiden* (1992), and *Sunset Boulevard* (1995). Her more prominent *film roles demonstrate her unusual versatility: Jenny Fields in *The World According to Garp* (1982), Sarah in *The Big Chill* (1983), Alex in *Fatal Attraction* (1987), and the Marquise de Merteuil in *Dangerous Liaisons* (1988). She also produced and played the title role in the *television movie *Sarah, Plain and Tall* (1991).   JDM

CLOSET DRAMA

A play to be read instead of staged. Although the term sometimes carries a negative connotation, implying that such works either lack sufficient theatrical qualities to warrant staging or require theatrical effects beyond the capacity of most (if not all) theatres, closet dramas through the ages have had a variety of dramatic features and purposes not tied to successful stage performance. They can be Platonic *dialogues, declamatory works (such as *Seneca's plays), *medieval dramas apparently written for a narrator instead of actors (*Hrotsvitha's plays, modelled on *Terence), dramatic dialogues (*Diderot's *Le Neveu de Rameau*), *verse dramas (Shelley's *Prometheus Unbound*), short *jeux d'esprit* (Wallace Stevens's plays), and grand epical works (*Ibsen's *Emperor and Galilean*). Following the invention of the printing press (*see* PUBLISHING OF PLAYS), which brought into being a new culture of readers and a new economics and politics of distribution, the closet drama emerged as a viable dramatic *text without need of performance. For example, Samuel *Daniel's *Cleopatra* (1594), revised and reprinted several times, became popular as a play to read rather than perform; *Milton wrote *Samson Agonistes* (1671) for the reader alone. Moreover, women writers, often refused access to the theatre, wrote closet dramas, and many poets have shared a Platonic ambivalence about the theatre, even an *anti-theatrical prejudice. Unconfined by *actors and staging, the writer is free to create a complex, often philosophical dialogue and conflict in the lyrical mode (such as *Byron's *Manfred*). In the *romantic and modern ages closet dramas often investigate consciousness

and self-identity. This virtual or mental drama locates the *action in a *theatrum mundi* of the imagination of both the poet and the reader. Perhaps the greatest closet drama of this type is *Goethe's *Faust* (Part I, 1808; Part II, 1832). Though its author considered the work unstageable, its vast range over time and space, untrammelled by considerations of nineteenth-century theatre practice, ironically made it an attractive challenge to *directors in the *modernist tradition and numerous successful productions have resulted.   TP

CLOWN

A dramatic *character serving stock comic functions within a theatrical *genre, generally defined by the specific or hypothetical performer for whom the role was intended. The theatrical clown was literally a dim-witted rustic, found definitively on the Elizabethan stage in characters like Costard in *Love's Labour's Lost*. The role was written by Shakespeare for William *Kempe of the *Chamberlain's Men, and the sense of a broadly recognizable comic character, rigged for possibility in time with the performer's specific talents, has become central to the clown identity. As a result, the clown label has sometimes embraced other comic types like *fools and jesters. Above all, the clown signals a predictable source of entertainment. A character for the common spectator, he usually occupies low or marginalized status, commenting upon human imperfection and the individual's place in society, often undermining the dominant discourse through naivety or wit. The clown usually enjoys a privileged relationship with the *audience, and has licence to take comic detours for scripted or improvised turns.

Clown traditions have arisen in cultures worldwide, adapting indigenous, *ritual features to theatrical forms. During the *early modern period, the *Narr* became a stock figure on the German stage, the *gracioso* in Spanish companies. Loosely comparable traits appear in *stock characters of Italian *commedia dell'arte*, *Chinese Sichuan, and West *African theatres. The clown historically has been male, owing to long-standing codes of social propriety. The character's emblematic resonance has been mined by twentieth-century playwrights like *Brecht and *Beckett, while Dario *Fo has explored the subversive possibilities of his own clowning persona.   EW

CLUN, WALTER (d. 1664)

English actor. Clun may have begun his career as a boy at *Blackfriars but he does not appear in records until after the Restoration, when he was briefly a prominent member of the King's company. Samuel *Pepys, who thought highly of Clun, records his murder in 1664.   RWV

CLUNES, ALEC (ALEXANDER SHERIFF DE MARO) (1912–70)

British actor, director, and *manager. Best known for running the *Arts Theatre in *London from 1942 to 1952 and for performing alongside stars such as *Olivier, *Gielgud, and *Scofield, he began his professional acting career with Ben *Greet's company in 1934. Subsequently he acted with major companies of his time, including Tyrone *Guthrie's *Old Vic season in 1936–7 (which premièred Olivier's *Hamlet*), the *Shakespeare Memorial Theatre in 1954 (as Claudius to Scofield's Hamlet), and finally at the *National Theatre in *Hochhuth's controversial *Soldiers* in 1968. His influential Arts Theatre seasons introduced new playwrights and staged forgotten classics.   BRK

CLURMAN, HAROLD (1901–80)

American director, critic, and memoirist. Born in *New York, Clurman was educated at Columbia and the Sorbonne. He worked as play reader for the *Theatre Guild from 1925. In 1930, he began holding weekly meetings in his apartment, attracting young people with his passionate talk of moving beyond the 'art theatres' like the Guild to create a 'real theatre': an artistic expression of its members' ideas on 'the life of our times'. Along with Lee *Strasberg and Cheryl *Crawford, Clurman was made a director of the *Group Theatre when it emerged from the Guild in 1931. He first directed a production with *Awake and Sing!* (1935) by Clifford *Odets, followed by four other Odets plays and two by Irwin Shaw before the Group's collapse in 1941. Clurman worked as a producer in Hollywood during the war, but returned to prominence in theatre in 1945 with the publication of his book *The Fervent Years: the Group Theatre and the 1930s*. His direction of a prizewinning 1950 production of Carson McCullers's *Member of the Wedding* led to his invitation to direct eighteen Broadway productions during the 1950s, including Tennessee *Williams's *Orpheus Descending* (1956). In 1953 he became drama critic for the *Nation*.   MAF

COBURN, CHARLES (1877–1961)

American actor and *manager. Coburn acted with a *stock company in *Chicago, then made his *New York debut in 1901. With his wife, actress Ivah Wills Coburn, he founded the Coburn Shakesperian Players in 1906. The company *toured extensively for several years with a Shakespearian repertoire, bringing classical drama to many parts of the United States. On Broadway, Coburn had leading roles in *The Yellow Jacket* (1916) and *The Better 'Ole* (1918). He continued to act on stage through the 1920s and early 1930s, then enjoyed a long career as a character actor in Hollywood *films.   MMK

COCHRAN, C. B. (CHARLES BLAKE) (1872–1951)

English *manager and impresario. Beginning in the USA as an actor, press agent, and manager, Cochran served as personal secretary to Richard *Mansfield, then as a *producer when he put *Ibsen's *John Gabriel Borkman* on Broadway (1897). He returned to *London in 1902 to become an impresario of everything from *Reinhardt's *The Miracle* (1911) to *circus shows. He produced *ballet as well as popular *revues in the 1910s, the plays of *O'Neill, *O'Casey, and *Coward in the 1920s and 1930s, and *musicals in the 1940s. He was also manager of Royal Albert Hall (1926–38) and a promoter of rodeo and boxing. Everyone called him 'Cockie'. He wrote four autobiographies.   TP

COCKPIT-IN-COURT

Built in 1629 as a permanent replacement for a succession of temporary theatres used at Whitehall Palace to stage plays and *masques for the royal entertainments of the Christmas season, the Cockpit was designed by Inigo *Jones and reflected the distinctive qualities of *Palladio's Teatro *Olimpico at Vicenza (1583), which Jones had studied. An intimate theatre, it had a curved *scaenae frons* with five entry doors, and a complicated balcony area. Jones's drawings survive at Worcester College Oxford. Queen Henrietta Maria had introduced *perspective staging for a play at Somerset House in 1626, and Jones subsequently designed *scenery for several other plays. This experience influenced his design for the new Whitehall Cockpit, although none of the professional company plays staged there in subsequent years made any use of scenery. It lost its function as a *playhouse in 1665, when the Hall Theatre was opened in Whitehall's great hall. *See also* SCENOGRAPHY.   AJG

COCKPIT THEATRE

In 1616 Christopher *Beeston, manager of Queen Anne's Men at the *Red Bull, built a hall *playhouse in Drury Lane in *London, near Lincoln's Inn. Originally named the Cockpit, probably as an extension of an old hall made to stage cockfights, it was sometimes called the Phoenix once it was rebuilt after being burned by apprentices in 1617. Its design, a half-round brick-built *auditorium facing a rectangular stage flanked by *boxes for noble spectators with a square-ended *tiring house behind, might be shown in a set of plans by Inigo *Jones at Worcester College, Oxford. These plans show the *scaenae frons*, heavily decorated with carved figures and pilastering, as an arched central opening with a single door on each side, and a music room above with benches for *audience on each flank. A small structure, the Cockpit was intended to rival the *Blackfriars, and came close to matching it with plays at court in the 1630s.   AJG

COCOLICHE

Latin American *clown from the creole *circus, a foreign *character whose deformed speech liberally intersperses Italian and Portuguese with Spanish to create a nonsensical chatter. Ignorant of cultural customs, he commits endless *faux pas* as he tries to negotiate unfamiliar territory. The character appears in the *sainete, the circus, and the *grotesco criollo*.   AV

COCTEAU, JEAN (1889–1963)

French playwright, author, graphic artist, designer, and film-maker. Son of wealthy parents, Cocteau was born at Maisons-Lafitte, the third of three siblings. His father's suicide when he was 9 occasioned the family's move to *Paris. In a career that embraced virtually all the arts, ranging from classical influences to the *avant-garde, Cocteau called himself 'poet' and chose Orpheus to represent his multifaceted artistry. A personal symbology infuses his preoccupation with death, beauty, and homosexuality: blood, snow, mirrors, glass, horses, tightrope walking. After seeing *Diaghilev's *Ballets Russes in 1909, Cocteau devoted himself to writing *scenarios and designing for *ballet, notably *Parade* (1917) and *Les Mariés de la Tour Eiffel* (*The Wedding at the Eiffel Tower*, 1921). His wry dramatizations of classical mythology include *Orphée* (1926), *Oedipus Rex* (1927, with Stravinsky), and *La Machine infernale* (1934, about Jocasta). Other important plays are *La Voix humaine* (1930, a one-woman *tragedy), *Les Chevaliers de la Table Ronde* (1937), *Les Parents terribles* (1938), and *L'Aigle a deux têtes* (1946). Chief among his seventeen *films are *Le Sang d'un poète* (*Blood of a Poet*, 1930, a compendium of his constant themes), *La Belle et la bête* (*Beauty and the Beast*, 1946, incorporating his *surrealist design elements), *Orphée* (1950), and a virtual artistic farewell, *Le Testament d'Orphée* (1960).   FHL

CODRON, MICHAEL (1930–)

British *producer with a reputation built on supporting the work of new writers in the 1960s. In 1958 he produced plays by John *Mortimer and Harold *Pinter, while later his roster extended to Alan *Ayckbourn, Joe *Orton, David *Halliwell, and Simon *Gray. As co-owner of the Vaudeville Theatre he produced Michael *Frayn's *Benefactors* (1984), while his base at the *Aldwych Theatre has produced a repertoire that includes Tom *Stoppard's *Hapgood* (1988), Ayckbourn's *Henceforward* (1988) and *The Revengers' Comedies* (1991), and Frayn's *Look, Look* (1990). At the end of the century Martin *Crimp and Jim *Cartwright benefited from his expertise.   AS

CODY, WILLIAM FREDERICK ('BUFFALO BILL') (1846–1917)

American *frontier scout, actor, and showman. Cody was born in Iowa, grew up in Kansas, fought in the Civil War, and afterwards took a job killing buffalo to supply meat for railway workers, which established his nickname. When the railway work ended, he rejoined the army as a civilian scout and his exploits made him the subject of a serialized story in 1869 and a play in 1872. Cody took the stage as himself in December 1872 in *Chicago in *The Scouts of the Prairie*, and he continued to act in a series of action-filled *melodramas over the next decade. In May 1883 Cody inaugurated his Wild West Exhibition, a stage show that became a phenomenal success both in America and Europe. Constantly in debt because of bad investments, he continued to perform in *Wild West shows up to the year of his death.   RAH

COE, RICHARD L. (1916–95)

Theatre critic. The reviewer for the *Washington Post* from 1938 to 1978, Coe was a lifelong enthusiast for the promotion and development of the theatre in Washington. Highly regarded for the quality and judgement of his writings, he nurtured the growth of *regional professional theatres, and was instrumental in garnering support for a national cultural centre, which resulted in the Kennedy Center. He fought to desegregate Washington's National Theatre, which finally occurred in 1952. *See* CRITICISM.   AW

COFRADÍAS

Spanish religious associations dedicated to a holy patron. Though initially created for military or chivalric ends, these brotherhoods worked, from the twelfth century on, in close collaboration with Spain's municipal corporations and extended their membership to craftsmen belonging to different trades. Amongst the duties of the *cofradías* was the organization of religious ceremonies, especially the Holy Week processions (a role they still perform today), and of festivities connected with different patron saints. Particularly crucial was their involvement in the performance of *mystery plays. The numerous *cofrades* who made up the brotherhoods were charged with building and preparing the *mansions used in the *parade, as well as playing all of the parts involved. Though the Spanish clergy placed severe constraints on the nature of those parts and banned the participation of women, the *cofradías* were decisive in popularizing and disseminating the *misterios* throughout the Iberian peninsula.   KG

COGHLAN, ROSE (1850–1932)

American actress, born in England. Coghlan began as a child actor; her early adult career was spent in England and the USA, including a *tour with Lydia *Thompson in the 1860s. She settled in the USA in 1877 and became a citizen in 1902, though she returned to *London for short engagements. In the 1880s she was a leading lady at *Wallack's Theatre in *New York, praised for her Lady Teazle (*The School for Scandal*) and Rosalind (*As You Like It*). She sometimes acted with her brother Charles Coghlan. She also acted in plays by *Sardou, *Scribe, *Dumas *fils*, Tom *Taylor, and *Wilde, and in 1907 toured the USA in *Shaw's *Mrs Warren's Profession*. She also performed regularly in *vaudeville.   TP

COHAN, GEORGE M. (1878–1942)

American actor, director, playwright, composer, lyricist, librettist, and *producer. Born to a family of *vaudeville performers, Cohan was on stage before the age of 10. A theatrical jack of all trades, he embodied the brash hustle and vitality of early twentieth-century Broadway. Writing and performing in fast-paced, unabashedly patriotic plays with native *characters and subjects, Cohan gave Broadway its first distinctively American identity. A natural showman with a sure sense of what the public liked, he cut his teeth as writer and director in *The Governor's Son* (1901) and *Running for Office* (1903). His breakthrough came in 1904 with *Little Johnny Jones*, where his cocksure portrayal of an American jockey stopped the show with 'Give my Regards to Broadway' and 'The Yankee Doodle Boy'. His 1906 *musicals *Forty-Five Minutes from Broadway* and *George Washington, Jr.* were also hits, the latter featuring 'You're a Grand Old Flag'. Cohan's prowess as songwriter influenced later greats like Irving *Berlin, who kept Cohan's portrait above the piano in his office. From 1906 to 1920 Cohan formed a highly successful producing partnership with Sam *Harris, which also saw the construction of the George M. Cohan Theatre in *New York. While Cohan's stand against *trade unions during the actors' strike of 1919 alienated him from his profession, his plays continued to find *audiences during the 1920s. Late in his career he had two notable successes as a performer in *O'Neill's *Ah, Wilderness!* (1933) and as President Roosevelt in *Rodgers and *Hart's *I'd Rather Be Right* (1937).   SN

COHEN, ALEXANDER H. (1920–2000)

American impresario. A youthful entrepreneur, Cohen inherited some money and made more. As he wryly described in *Star Billing*, his 1998 solo presentation of barbed theatrical reminiscence, his first Broadway show (when he was 21) bombed, but with his second, *Angel Street*, he was on his way to a lifetime total of 101 in *New York and *London. He

specialized in star vehicles for such as Richard *Burton, John *Gielgud, Maurice *Chevalier, Jerry Lewis, and Marlene Dietrich, the last two among his favourite *villains. His producing taste often ran to English imports—*Beyond the Fringe*, *The Homecoming*, *Home*, Peter *Brook's *Carmen*—but he refused *Cats* and maintained he was glad he did. He devised the *Night of 100 Stars*, an American version of a command performance for charity, and brought similar glamour to Broadway's Tony *awards, which he and his wife, writer Hildy Parks, produced 1967–86. Never shy of controversy, he savoured his role as witty elder statesman and curmudgeon.   CR

COHEN, NATHAN (1923–71)

Leading critic for Canada's largest newspaper, the *Toronto Star*, from 1959 to 1971. Born and educated in Atlantic Canada, Cohen began as a journalist in Nova Scotia and then *Toronto, where he founded a magazine called the *Critic* and later became known as a *radio and *television personality. Like his contemporary Herbert *Whittaker, Cohen was an important figure in the growth of the professional arts in post-war Canada. Though he insisted on high standards from established professional theatres, he also encouraged a number of *alternative ventures in Toronto and beyond.   DWJ

COÏCOU, MASSILLON (1867–1908)

Haitian dramatist and poet who displayed an early passion for theatre. He founded Le Théâtre Haïtien and for it wrote the *historical dramas *Toussaint au Fort de Joux* (1896) and *L'Empereur Dessalines* (1896), socially committed works similar in style to his own collection of verse, *Poésies nationales* (1892). *Liberté* (1904) was performed successfully in *Paris. But it was in *L'Alphabet* (1905), *Féfé candidat* (1906), and *Féfé ministre* (1906) that his social attitudes found their strongest statement. Attempting an 'art for social good', his work fell seriously foul of the Haitian government, who had him shot.

MLa trans. JCM

COLE, JACK (1911–74)

American choreographer. After *training and *touring with the Denishawn Dancers in the early 1930s, Cole invented Broadway 'jazz' *dance by gradually infusing his nightclub-based choreography with a blend of classical technique, acrobatic athleticism, sexual innuendo, and comic timing. In *New York and Hollywood he trained a generation of dance stars, notably Gwen *Verdon and Carol Haney. He was also among the first choreographers to direct his own scenes in Broadway shows and in the Hollywood *musicals *Kismet*, *Gentlemen Prefer Blondes*, and *Some Like It Hot*.   LTC

COLE AND JOHNSON

*African-American performing team, the name of two successive groups instrumental in forging a post-emancipation identity for blacks on the *musical stage. After three years with Billy Johnson, with whom he wrote *A Trip to Coontown* in 1898, **Bob Cole** (1869–1912) teamed with **J. Rosamond Johnson** (1873–1954) in 1901. *A Trip to Coontown* had set the pattern for shows *managed, written, and performed by African Americans, but the second team, which James Weldon Johnson, Rosamond's brother, later joined, was more successful than the first. Two of the Cole and Johnson *New York shows, with superb *dancers in the *chorus, helped break the ban against staging love scenes between black couples: *The Shoofly Regiment* (1906) and *Red Moon* (1908). In addition to their national and international *tours, the team wrote hit songs which were sung by white musical stars of the day, including May *Irwin, Lillian *Russell, and Anna Held. One of them, 'Under the Bamboo Tree', found its way into the musical *Meet Me in St Louis*.   BBL

COLEMAN, CY (1929–)

American composer. Classically trained as a concert pianist, Coleman became interested in jazz, forming a successful trio in the 1950s. He also wrote pop songs with various lyricists, some of which found their way into stage *revues. His first Broadway score, with lyricist Carolyn Leigh, was *Wildcat* (1960), a vehicle crafted for Lucille Ball which established his ability to write for stars. His next two *musicals—*Little Me* (1962), *Sweet Charity* (1966)—were also star vehicles, although he afterwards expanded his horizons. He is notable for his ability to adapt his style to each project, rather than having a characteristic style. Thus the potpourri pop score for *I Love my Wife* (1977) sounded nothing like the sweeping *operetta-flavoured score of *On the Twentieth Century* (1978), nor the jazzy *City of Angels* (1989) like the rock-based *The Life* (1997). He has also written two scores which place a historical figure's life in the musical context of their medium, the *circus-oriented *Barnum* (1980) and the *vaudevillian *Will Rogers Follies* (1991).   JD

COLISEO

The Coliseo del Buen Retiro in *Madrid was the principal court theatre of later seventeenth- and eighteenth-century Spain. Built 1638–40 in the new royal palace of the Buen Retiro in the eastern city, it was designed by the Florentine engineer Cosimo (or Cosme) Lotti, *scenographer to Philip IV since 1626. It opened in 1640 but soon closed again for a decade because of war and theatrical prohibition. From the 1650s spectacular machineplays by *Calderón and others were regularly staged in the Coliseo, initially by another Florentine designer, Baccio del Bianco, as well as many ordinary *comedias. Among the first such productions were Calderón's *La fiera, el rayo y la piedra* (*The Beast, the Thunderbolt, and the Stone*) in 1652 and his *Fortunas de Andrómeda y Perseo* (*Fortunes of Andromeda and Perseus*) the following year; a manuscript of the latter with elaborate scenographic drawings by Baccio himself has survived. Though gala performances were for the royal family and court only, the paying public was regularly admitted at other times. The *auditorium was broadly modelled on Madrid's *playhouses, the *corrales de comedias (though much more luxurious and entirely roofed), but there was a *proscenium arch and a deep *stage equipped for Italianate production with changeable *perspective *scenery and elaborate machinery and *lighting.   CD

COLISEUM

*London *Playhouse built by Oswald *Stoll to designs by Frank Matcham and opened in 1904, seating nearly 3,000. Stoll's seasons mixed high with popular culture: the *Marx Brothers appeared there, but so did *Diaghilev's dancers (from 1918), and *Bernhardt in *Phèdre*. The huge *revolve of three concentric circles was deployed for sensational recreations of horse racing but also for *Reinhardt's *Sumurun* (1911). From 1931 the Coliseum became a stage for lavish *musicals, including *White Horse Inn* and *Annie Get your Gun*, until it became the home of English National Opera in 1968.   RAC

COLLECTIVES AND COLLECTIVE CREATION

Organizational structure for theatre companies and creative process for performance *devising, both emphasizing group dynamics with a non-hierarchical structure of company members. Theatre is at its roots a community and collective effort, and examples of groups of artists and technicians pooling resources and talents to create a company can be found throughout history. *Medieval festival performances produced by trade *guilds, the Asian troupes of *kabuki, *wayang, and *kathakali, the travelling troupes of the Italian *commedia dell'arte, even the early *avant-garde companies such as the Théâtre d'*Art, and the art movements of *futurism, *dada, and *surrealism—all shared some of the organizational strategies of a collective. However, it was not until the social and political changes in the West during the 1960s that the desire for reorganizing theatre production through collectivity became of interest.

Major collectives have included a number of American and European groups. The *Living Theatre (1947–) was led by Julian *Beck and Judith *Malina, whose anarchist and pacifist politics led to experimental productions such as *Mysteries and Smaller Pieces* (1964), *Frankenstein* (1965), *Antigone* (1967), and

Paradise Now (1968), which attempted to engender social revolution and new forms of theatrical experience. The *Open Theatre (1963–73), directed by Joseph *Chaikin, a former member of the Living Theatre, was formed to explore a new aesthetics of theatre based on the actor devising performance through sound and movement explorations; productions included *Viet Rock* (1966), *The Serpent* (1969), *Terminal* (1971), *The Mutation Show* (1973) and *Nightwalk* (1973). Théâtre du *Soleil (1964–), directed by Ariane *Mnouchkine and formed as a social and artistic collective, has created a series of productions such as *1789* (1970), a Shakespeare cycle (1981–4), and *Les Atrides* (1990–3), which developed radical and *intercultural forms of theatre through a borrowing of international performance forms. The *Polish Theatre Laboratory (1957–69) directed by Jerzy *Grotowski and the *Performance Group (1967) led by Richard *Schechner looked to create theatre based in mythological narratives told through physicalized performance. Contemporary collectives such as the *Wooster Group (USA), La *Fura dels Baus (Spain), *Socìetas Rafaello Sanzio (Italy), Theatre de *Complicité (UK), and dumbtype (*Japan) are loosely organized as collectives whose aesthetic concerns continue to explore new configurations of performance, but through a postmodern politics of incorporation as opposed to the earlier modes of confrontation and action.

Although each collective has different objectives and processes, *politics and aesthetics, there are some common aspects. The collectives of the 1960s held a common concern for social activism and personal and group evolution filtered through liberal, leftist, and radical politics. This led to politically informed work that was not only representative of radical thought but strove to embody the principles of cultural revolution within the theatre itself. The process of collective creation sought to reconfigure the traditional structure of an originating writer and a dominant *director whose vision of the *text was realized through subservient actors and technicians. Traditional theatre was understood to constrain the actor's art and disenfranchise the *audience's interaction and critique. The process of collective creation for the companies of the 1960s followed different models but was generally advanced with a company of actors engaged in *improvisation and physically devised *rehearsal. *Text creation included explorations of existing texts (the Performance Group's *Dionysus in 69* from *Euripides' *The Bacchae*), developing new work with resident writers (the Open Theatre's *Terminal* with Susan Yankowitz), or creating work based on specific events or issues (Théâtre du Soleil's *1789* on the French Revolution). Contemporary collectives work in a comparable manner, with texts developed through appropriation (the Wooster Group's *Road to Immortality* trilogy) and adaptation (Théâtre du Soleil's Shakespeare cycle).

Primary in the interests of the collectives of the 1960s was reconfiguration of the audience's experience. The traditional scenic principles of the *proscenium stage, with a clear division between spectators and performers and with specific seating, was often rejected as too restrictive and inhibiting. Experiments in what Schechner and Brooks McNamara termed *environmental theatre explored new audience engagement through physical interaction and individual choice within the performance. Spectators at an environmental performance were placed in patterns surrounding the performance or placed directly within the action. At times the audience was invited to engage directly in the action and given choices that would direct the flow of the performance. In the Living Theatre's *Paradise Now*, audiences were invited to disrobe and take part in a celebratory experience. In the Performance Group's *Dionysus in 69* the audience was again invited to undress and make their way into the streets of *New York to embody a revolutionary spirit. Although the collectives of the 1960s quickly gave way to a return to proscenium staging through the experimental work of Robert *Wilson and Richard *Foreman, in what Bonnie Marranca has called a 'theatre of images', collective creation continues to be viable in contemporary theatre.   MDC

SCHECHNER, RICHARD, *Environmental Theatre* (New York, 1994)
WILLIAMS, DAVID, *Collaborative Theatre: the Théâtre du Soleil sourcebook* (London, 1999)

COLLIER, JEREMY (1650–1726)

English cleric and writer of *anti-theatrical polemic. Unlike his most famous forebears in the genre, Collier was not a Puritan but a high-church monarchist: in 1689, after James II had been driven into exile, he refused to take the oath of allegiance to William and Mary, and in 1696 he publicly absolved two condemned Jacobites who had tried to assassinate them. Though he later became a non-juring bishop, Collier nonetheless achieved less prominence for his politics than for his *Short View of the Immorality and Profaneness of the English Stage* (1698). This long, learned, and intemperate attack on contemporary dramatists, notably *Dryden, *D'Urfey, *Congreve, and *Vanbrugh, singles out in particular their alleged disrespect for marriage and their abuse of the clergy. It provoked an immediate pamphlet war, including replies from Vanbrugh. Ironically, it was the banishment of James, which Collier so deplored, which left the *playhouses vulnerable to his assault: neither William and Mary nor Anne took the same protective interest in the *Theatres Royal as had the earlier Stuarts, and they took no action to defend actors and playwrights from the private prosecutions for blasphemy mounted by some of Collier's supporters, even when the blasphemies in question consisted merely of speaking lines which had been duly licensed by the *Master of the Revels. In the wake of the 'Collier controversy', Societies for the Reformation of Manners were established to uphold public virtue within the playhouses and beyond: the whole furore encouraged a trend away from the graphic dramatic *satire of the Restoration and towards the more sentimental, middle-class morality that would be exemplified by *Lillo (*see* BOURGEOIS THEATRE). MD

COLLIER, JOHN PAYNE (1789–1883)

Dramatic and literary critic. He edited Elizabethan dramas for the new edition of Dodsley's *Old Plays* (1825–7) and wrote a volume on *Punch and Judy. His three-volume history of the stage (1831) was full of new material, much of which he invented. Further falsifications occurred in his editions of Shakespeare and of *Alleyn's and *Henslowe's papers. He made manuscript additions to the Second Folio of Shakespeare, to State Papers, and private collections. In 1859, when the British Museum acquired the Folio, Collier's forgeries were discovered. Despite posthumous proof of his guilt, recent scholarship indicates Collier might have been the victim of a contemporary conspiracy. JTD

COLLINS, LOTTIE (1865–1910)

English *music-hall performer. The daughter of a blackface *minstrel, Collins was performing solo at an early age, and later with her sisters, Marie and Lizzie, in a song-and-dance trio. She was essentially a dancer, 'energetic and agile', with only an adequate voice for her serio-comic songs. It was with 'Ta-ra-ra-boom-de-ay' that she (literally) leapt to fame at *London's Tivoli music hall in 1890. The song was accompanied by a frantic *dance. 'It was', she said, 'the mad rush and whirl of the thing that made it go. I got round a 40 foot circle twice in 8 measures.' AF

COLLINS, SAM (SAMUEL VAGG) (1824–65)

English comic vocalist and *manager, who made his reputation as a stage Irishman. Accounts of his early life are conflicting, but it is certain that he gained a reputation for Irish comic songs in the *London concert rooms and early *music halls of the 1840s. Singing 'The Rocky Road to Dublin' and 'Limerick Races', he was a favourite at Evans's Late Joys and Charles *Morton's Canterbury Hall. He acquired the Rose of Normandy concert rooms in the Edgware Road (later to be renamed the Marylebone Music Hall), and the Lansdown Arms, Islington Green, opened in 1863 as Sam Collins's Music Hall. After his death, the hall retained his name. AF

COLMAN, GEORGE, THE ELDER (1732–94)

English author and *manager. Although encouraged to pursue a career in the law, Colman deviated into theatre as a young man and became a successful playwright, critic, and manager. While at Oxford he collaborated on the periodical the *Connoisseur*. He was called to the bar at Lincoln's Inn in 1757, but spent part of his time writing literary *criticism, including a *parody of Thomas Gray's 'Elegy in a Country Church Yard'. His first dramatic work, *Polly Honeycombe* (1760), was a popular *farce about a girl whose head is turned by novels like *Fielding's *Tom Jones*; ironically, his next and greatest success was *The Jealous Wife* (1761), a full-length *comedy derived from that work. By this time he had become the friend and protégé of *Garrick, with whom he wrote the best *comedy of the mid-eighteenth century, *The Clandestine Marriage* (1766). The next year Colman made the mistake of buying a share of the *Covent Garden Theatre *patent, along with the actor William Powell and two non-theatrical investors, Thomas Harris and Benjamin Rutherford. The four-way partnership quickly foundered, leading to lengthy and costly litigation, and Colman left the management in 1774. His luck improved in 1776 when he leased Samuel *Foote's patent on the *Haymarket Theatre. After Foote died in 1777, Colman was permitted to continue the summer season under annual licences. He expanded the repertory and made many material improvements to the operation, which his son, George *Colman the Younger, took over in 1789. MJK

COLMAN, GEORGE, THE YOUNGER (1762–1836)

English author and *manager, who followed his father's footsteps away from the law and toward the stage. He was an essayist, playwright, manager, and ultimately a zealous Examiner of Plays in 1824, which made him responsible for the review and licensing of dramatic *texts (*see* LORD CHAMBERLAIN). He wrote several short pieces for the *Haymarket as a young man, the most popular being his *musical comedy *Inkle and Yarico* (1787). That work, like his full-length *comedy *The Heir at Law* (1797), became a repertory favourite. Elizabeth *Inchbald's mild *criticism of this play led to a nasty public feud with Colman, which unfortunately prompted her to give up writing criticism for ever. He took over management of the Haymarket in 1789 and ruined the profitable operation left to him by his father. While certainly improvident, recent evidence shows that the Colmans' banker had embezzled huge amounts of money from them, leaving the son in a difficult situation. Although he wrote several successful and lucrative plays, most famously *John Bull; or, The Englishman's Fireside* (1803), the financial problems led him to sell the Haymarket enterprise in 1820. MJK

COLÓN, TEATRO

*Buenos Aires *opera theatre, known for its excellent acoustics, among Argentina's great historical monuments. A prime example of the eclectic style typical of turn-of-the-century opera houses in *Latin America, the Attic exterior contains an interior which combines Italian Renaissance with German and French architectural elements. The first Colón, built in the mid-nineteenth century on a different site, is remembered most as the city's first *playhouse with a metal structure and raised seating. Nearly twenty years under construction, the present-day Colón was inaugurated in 1908 with *Verdi's *Aida*. It now averages ten opera productions annually, and also holds numerous music recitals.

JGJ

COLONIAL, TEATRO

A nineteenth-century theatre form designed to exalt the colonial regimes in *Latin America. Colonial administrations favoured lyric *opera performed by foreign companies, or pieces that bolstered their own popularity. An example of the latter is a one-act *musical comedy from Cuba called *El gorrión* (*The Sparrow*, 1869). Sparrows were brought to Cuba by the Spanish and became associated in the popular mind with colonial rule. *El gorrión* celebrates the loyal service of a sparrow found dead outside the walls of the captaincy general on Holy Thursday. The play became a huge popular success, spawning a series of pro-colonial pieces that used the symbolic *character of the sparrow to play upon *audience emotion.

AV

COLUM, PADRAIC (1881–1972)

Irish playwright. His three major dramas, *Broken Soil* (1903, revised 1907 as *The Fiddler's House*), *The Land* (1905), and *Thomas Muskerry* (1910), create a distinctive *realist style which drew considerably on his childhood experience as son of a workhouse master in Longford. His depiction of the struggles of impoverished rural and small-town societies to earn security and a measure of self-respect and fulfilment resolutely eschewed romanticizing rhetoric or poetry, but not compassion. After emigrating to America in 1914, his stylistic range became more eclectic, embracing fairy-tale *romance in *Mogu the Wanderer* (1917), *Strindbergian *expressionism in *Balloon* (1929), and *nō-inspired dramas of Irish legend (1957–67).

RAC

COMBINATION COMPANY *See* STOCK COMPANY.

COMDEN, BETTY (1915–) AND ADOLPH GREEN (1915–)

American lyricists, librettists, screenwriters, and performers. One of the most productive and enduring creative partnerships of all time, Comden and Green acquired a reputation for their sly wit, irrepressible spirit, and particular affection for *New York. Working together since the 1930s, they had been writing material for their own comic troupe when in 1944 they were asked by Leonard *Bernstein to contribute lyrics and libretto for *On the Town*. They cleverly included roles for themselves, and have since performed individually and together, on stage and screen. Their canon is dominated by a number of collaborations with composer Jule *Styne, beginning with the 1951 *revue *Two on the Aisle*, and going on to *Peter Pan* (1954), *Bells Are Ringing* (1956), *Do Re Mi* (1960), and *Hallelujah, Baby!* (1967), among others. They worked with Cy *Coleman for *On the Twentieth Century* (1978), and wrote the screenplays for *Singin' in the Rain* (1952), *The Band Wagon* (1953), and other *films. Their best-known songs include 'The Party's Over' and 'Make Someone Happy'.

EW

COMEDIA

In Spain, *comedia* was used from the mid-sixteenth to the eighteenth centuries to refer to a full-length secular play, as opposed to *auto sacramental*, which designated a religious play. Modelled on the Italian *commedia erudita*, the Spanish *comedia* was introduced in the early sixteenth century by Bartolomé de *Torres Naharro. Initially structured in five acts, the *comedia* was recast in its more typical three-act form by Lope de *Vega in the early seventeenth century.

RWV

COMEDIA NACIONAL

Uruguayan company founded in 1947 in Montevideo, one of the earliest state-funded professional theatres in South America (*see* FINANCE). Several directors were appointed to oversee its activities, including Carlos Calderón de la Barca, the Spanish immigrant Margarita *Xirgu, and Ruben Yáñez. The Comedia Nacional, which still resides in the Teatro Solís, built in 1856, organized a *training school with Xirgú in charge. Originally dedicated to Uruguayan drama—it opened with Ernesto Herrera's *El león ciego* (*The Blind Lion*)—the directors soon found it necessary to add classic *Latin American and European drama. The Comedia began with a flurry of activity, mounting twelve shows annually in its first five years. After two decades of work it had mounted 176 plays, 50 of which were Uruguayan, and it has continued its repertory policy.

EJW

COMEDIANTS

Spanish company, formed in 1971 (as Els Comediants) as part of the movement for an independent Catalan theatre which rejected the official drama of the late Francoist period. Relying on *collective creation, Comediants avoids *texts and *directors, instead employing actors, musicians, and artists of different styles to create an interdisciplinary performance event that echoes the travelling minstrels of the past. They tend to perform in unusual locales—streets, squares, rivers, meadows, or *sports stadiums—making a provocative 'theatre of the senses' that

assaults the rigid conditions of everyday life. Their work, which ranges from the 'sacred drama' *Non Plus Plis* (1972) to *Maravillas de Cervantes* (*Marvels of Cervantes*, 2000) for the Compañía Nacional de Teatro Clásico, has also adapted and incorporated popular Spanish forms like the *auto sacramental, the *farsa, and the *entremés.
                                                                    KG

COMÉDIE-BALLET

A form of baroque court performance produced in France between 1661 and 1674. Among the artists who created the *comédies-ballets* were *Molière, Jean de La Fontaine, Jean-Baptiste *Lully, Marc-Antoine Charpentier, Pierre Beauchamp, Isaac Bensserade, Giacomo *Torelli, Carlo *Vigarani, Jean *Berain, and Charles Le Brun. While Louis XIV commissioned fourteen of the fifteen *comédies-ballets* for royal festivals, Molière alone participated in the creation of every one. The form drew some of its language and basic structure from *early modern *festival and court *masque: each one combined a full-length play with multiple *intermèdes*, which inserted vocal and instrumental music, *dancing, and *spectacle between the acts of the play, with an elaborate prologue and final *ballet. Both *comédie* and *intermèdes* often incorporated a mixture of styles: *farce, heroic, *pastoral, and *burlesque. Spectacle was lavish and included (but was not limited to) temporary theatres and *scenery, *costumes, *animals, machinery, waterworks and *fireworks (*see also* SCENOGRAPHY). A unique feature was the staging of *comédies-ballets* within the formal gardens of *Versailles, as well as at other royal chateaux. The *genre began with *The Bores*, created by Molière and Beauchamp, which premièred at Vaux-le-Vicomte under the patronage of Nicolas Fouquet in August 1661; the final entry was *The Hypochondriac*, a Molière–Charpentier collaboration performed at Versailles in 1674, seventeen months after Molière's death.
                                                                    GES

COMÉDIE-FRANÇAISE *see page 291*

COMÉDIE ITALIENNE

Name given by the French to the institutionalized presence of an Italian theatre company in *Paris in the seventeenth and eighteenth centuries. To begin with the title had methodological implications—of performing in Italian, and improvising rather than learning a script—and stylistic ones associated with liveliness, physicality, and populist subversive mockery. By the end of its history, however, the Comédie Italienne had merged, in most respects, with native French theatre. Italian actors began visiting France as early as the 1570s, Paris being a more metropolitan venue than their own divided peninsula could provide. The most prestigious were the object of royal invitations,

stemming partly from successive Florentine queens of France, Marie and Catherine de Médicis. Two generations of the *Andreini family visited and influenced between 1603 and 1647. What was to become French *neoclassicism, on the high cultural level, was effectively an importation from Italy, though the French were determined to disguise this fact simply by taking over the dominance of European culture for themselves. On the level of performance the presence of Italian practitioners in the capital was continuously popular, and *Molière himself as an actor was accused of simply aping Tiberio *Fiorilli. From 1653 the company of Domenico Locatelli was recognized by the state, and they shared three successive premises with Molière's French troupe and its inheritors. Then in 1680 theatre in Paris was organized into three monopolies: the new *Opéra, the *Comédie-Française, and the Comédie Italienne. By this time performers from the *Biancolelli, Costantini, *Gabrielli, *Gherardi, and *Romagnesi families were established stars; while in a separate area imported Italian *scenographers such as *Torelli and *Vigarani were contributing to large-scale royal *spectacle. *Texts for the Comédie Italienne began to be partly pre-composed rather than improvised, and partly in French—thus beginning a process of naturalization which attempted nevertheless to retain the perceived exotic character.

Disaster came when the Italians were expelled from Paris in 1697 for an alleged scurrilous attack on Mme de Maintenon, Louis XIV's mistress. Some performers went elsewhere for good: others, such as Pierre-François Biancolelli, played in the provinces for a while and then sneaked back to the less effectively regulated venues of the Paris Foires. In the meantime, Évariste Gherardi's multi-volume printed collection of *Théâtre italien* maintained a nostalgic cultural profile. In 1716, under the Regent for the young Louis XV, a 'new' Comédie Italienne was re-established, still under the autocratic control characteristic of French cultural organization. Direction was entrusted to Louis *Riccoboni, a second-generation immigrant. Under him and his successors it lasted through to 1762, when it lost its identity in a merger with the *Opéra-Comique. In its second phase, in any case, its material had been entirely in French: the company still offered lively and identifiably Italian star performers, but one of its chief playwrights was *Marivaux, the quintessence of purely French *sensibilité*, whose childlike, balletic, sentimental harlequins would have been unrecognizable to the Biancolellis, let alone to Tristano *Martinelli. *See also* COMMEDIA DELL'ARTE.   RAA

COMÉDIE LARMOYANTE

In 'tearful comedy' the noun should be taken in the sense of 'play', for in the purest examples of the *genre the sources of *laughter—extravagant characterization, the antics of comic servants—are absent, and the only feature belonging to traditional comedy is the happy ending. *Steele's *The Conscious*
(continued on p. 293)

COMÉDIE-FRANÇAISE

France's oldest and most celebrated national theatre was created by order of Louis XIV in 1680. The remnants of *Molière's troupe, dispossessed of their theatre at the *Palais Royal, had joined with the 'better' actors of the Théâtre du *Marais and bought the Théâtre de *Guénégaud in 1673, but an effort by the monarch to force the merger of all three French troupes at that time failed because of resentments among the actors. The death of *La Thorillière in 1680 removed the obstacle and the King's scheme was implemented. There were to be three theatrical enterprises in *Paris: the Comédie-Française for French *tragedy and *comedy, the *Comédie Italienne for Italian comedy and *farce, and the Académie de Musique for *opera. Each was to be subsidized by the state, though not generously; in return, each would provide entertainments for Louis's court. The itinerant troupes that had performed throughout France before 1630 were what the critic *Chappuzeau called 'small republics'. Dividing the profits of each performance amongst themselves, the actors managed their own affairs, choosing repertory, selecting new members, voting on extraordinary expenditures. With the introduction of state subventions in 1635, however, the troupes began a long history of loss of autonomy. With the institutionalization of the theatre in 1680, that history accelerated.

When the Comédie-Française was established, the King took a hand in deciding which actors would continue to perform, which would be pensioned, who would play what roles, and how ownership of the theatre, *properties, *scenery, and machines would be settled. The final company consisted of ten men and seven women with full shares and five men and five women with partial shares. The state subvention was to be 12,000 livres. The new company was large enough that one group could perform daily in Paris while another answered calls to court. It opened at the Théâtre Guénégaud on 25 August with *Racine's *Phèdre* and *Les Carosses d'Orléans* (*The Coaches of Orléans*) by Jean de La Chapelle.

In 1684 the King gave authority over the theatres to his daughter-in-law, the Dauphine, who gave her orders to the First Gentlemen of the King's Chamber, four very powerful courtiers. The new *management promptly dismissed four actors, hired a new one, recast the plays, and made clear to the actors that no decisions were to be taken without the consent of *la supériorité*. In 1685 the first of a long series of *règlements* appeared, each authorizing still greater intrusions upon the autonomy of the actors. The most valuable property the actors brought to the new company was the repertory; the union of the troupes meant the union of the works of *Corneille, *Molière, and *Racine. The monopoly awarded to the Comédie-Française, however, also made it alone responsible for finding and developing new playwrights. The first new play produced was *Soliman* by La Tuillière, an actor in the troupe; it was moderately successful. Most of the new plays presented in the early years were comedies, many written by one of the actors, especially *Dancourt. *Campistron was the most active new writer of tragedy, but few of his plays were as successful as revivals of Racine and Corneille. Molière's plays, of course, remained the mainstay of the repertory.

The 'Français' fought long and pugnaciously, but finally unsuccessfully, to defend its monopoly of spoken drama in French. First the Comédie Italienne, which had begun to add scenes in French in the late 1660s, and then theatres at the Paris fairs challenged the French troupe's entitlement. Important comic playwrights—*Regnard, Dufresny, *Lesage, *Marivaux—often turned to the competition. Tragedy remained the private property of the Comédie-Française, however, and after a long fallow period was revived by *Voltaire, who wrote for the troupe for 60 years beginning in 1718. The ambiguous status of the Comédie-Française, part private enterprise, part creature of the state bureaucracy, was first emphasized in June 1687 when the actors learned that they were to be dispossessed of the theatre they owned on the rue Guénégaud because of objections by the Sorbonne, recently awarded tenancy of the nearby Collège de Quatre-Nations (present Institut de France). Given only three months to move house, the actors were blocked at every turn in their efforts to find a suitable plot upon which to build. It was almost two years later that the troupe finally opened its new theatre, designed by François d'Orbay, on the rue Neuve des Fossés, where it was to remain until 1770.

In the eighteenth century the Comédie-Française was an actors' theatre, celebrated for the brilliant Adrienne *Lecouvreur, the tragedy queens *Dumesnil and *Clairon, Voltaire's protégé *Lekain, Lekain's pupil Françoise *Vestris, the dazzling *Molé, Paris's first Hamlet, and many others. These actors, however, found themselves ever more at the mercy of the *supériorité*, especially after the bureaucracy was expanded to include an *intendant* who oversaw the day-to-day management of the royal theatres and served as a buffer between the Gentlemen of the Chamber and the troupes. Administrative procedures became more and more labyrinthine, while actors were treated with contempt. A memo of the period perfectly expresses their plight: 'The First Gentlemen of the Chamber recognize that negligence on the part of the actors to observe the *règlements* to which they are subject was a principal cause of this disorder.' The solution: expand the *règlements* and increase the punishments for ignoring them.

In 1770 the Comédie-Française left Orbay's decaying theatre and occupied a royal venue, the *Salle des Machines in the Tuileries palace, a most unsuitable space, while waiting for a new theatre to be built. They waited for twelve years. Their new Théâtre-Français, on the site of the present Théâtre de l'*Odéon, was finally completed after years of bureaucratic infighting in 1782, but the actors were to enjoy it for only eleven years. In September 1793 the Committee of Public Safety, led by Robespierre, ordered the theatre closed and the actors arrested. The troupe had already experienced a violent schism between the actors who supported the revolution and those who remained loyal to the monarchy. The actor-revolutionaries broke away and moved to a theatre on the rue de Richelieu, originally built for the *Opéra, which they named the Théâtre de la République. The royalists remained at what they called the Théâtre de la Nation until their arrest. Thanks to the intervention of an *amateur actor who was an employee of the Committee of Public Safety, the actors survived their eleven months of captivity, but found no way to re-establish themselves after their release. Finally, in 1799 the Comédie-Française troupe was reunited at the theatre on the rue de Richelieu where it has remained for more than 200 years.

Paris had enjoyed a 'freedom of the theatres' from 1790; by decree of the National Assembly 'any citizen could open a public theatre and produce there plays of any *genre'. The actors of the 'Français' no longer enjoyed special status. In 1807, however, Napoléon re-established theatrical privilege, suppressing most of the new theatres, and granting monopolies to the surviving eight including the Comédie-Française. A decree, signed by the Emperor in *Moscow in 1812, established a new bureaucracy to oversee the actors; an 'imperial commissioner' would report to a 'superintendent of spectacles'. This arrangement gave way in 1850 to the appointment of a general administrator.

Through most of the nineteenth century the actors retained some control over repertory, although successive commissioners and administrators with artistic programmes encouraged certain playwrights to give their new plays to the Théâtre-Français. Baron Tayler, who was appointed commissioner in 1825, scheduled the new plays of *romanticism by Alexandre *Dumas *pere*, Alfred de *Vigny, and Victor *Hugo, including Hugo's infamous *Hernani* (1830). The romantics did not please, however, and the Comédie-Française entered a chaotic period of low popularity and lower receipts. Its salvation was a young actress named *Rachel who first appeared at the age of 17 in 1838 and filled the *auditorium. In 1850 a protégé of Rachel's, Arsène Houssaye, became the first administrator of the Théâtre-Français. When the actors threatened to leave

the company, Houssaye let it be known that he was ready to replace them with stars of the commercial theatre that flourished in spite of Napoléon's effort to restrict the number of theatres in Paris. The disaffected actors remained. Houssaye succeeded in resolving the troupe's delicate *financial situation, and the theatre regained popularity with a cadre of new playwrights including Eugene *Scribe, George Sand, and Alfred de *Musset.

A series of administrators, most from the 'exterior', some chosen from within the troupe, have proposed and imposed a variety of ambitious plans over the last 150 years, while a stream of *règlements* and decrees has shifted the balance of power between administrator and *sociétaires* (or tenured actors). The functions of the various committees have varied as well, sometimes meaningful, at other times ceremonial. What has not changed, at least from the point of view of the actors, is the security of their appointments and their right to a share in the *bénéfices*, the profits.

Few of the leading figures of the twentieth-century French theatre have been members of the Comédie-Française, perhaps because there has never been a provision made for a non-actor to become a *sociétaire*. In 1936 the great actor-director Louis *Jouvet was invited to become the administrator, but rejected the offer. The man who accepted it, Édouard Bourdet, named four 'exterior' artists, Jouvet, Jacques *Copeau, Charles *Dullin, and Gaston *Baty, as stage *directors, the first official notice of the theatre artist who became pre-eminent in the twentieth century. Although some members of the troupe have continued to direct, the trend has been to use outside directors or to appoint French directors as administrators. Among those who have been selected are the Italians *Zeffirelli, *Strehler, and *Fo, the English Terry *Hands, and, as administrators, the French Jean-Pierre *Vincent, Antoine *Vitez, Jacques *Lassalle, and Jean-Pierre Miquel. Several *sociétaires* have also led the troupe since the end of the Second World War, directing and continuing to act. Actors, once elected *sociétaire*, are expected to remain with the troupe, and many do. Others, including such celebrated stars as Jeanne Moreau and Isabelle Adjani, have resigned while they were still *pensionnaires*, probationary actors or actors employed on short-term contracts. *Sociétaires* are restricted professionally, though now permitted to perform in *television and *film.

In 1930–1 the Comédie-Française produced 130 different plays; in the season of 2001–2, it produced 16, down from 19 the previous season. Many factors have led to this decline, primary among them being a shift to *long(er) runs. Although the company maintains a modified *repertory schedule at the Salle Richelieu, with at most three plays sharing the calendar at any given time, at its two smaller theatres each play has a discrete run. Still very much an institutional theatre, the Comédie-Française takes seriously its mission as an 'imaginary museum' of French dramatic art. Five of the sixteen plays advertised for 2001–2 were by *Molière. The remaining plays selected for the

Salle Richelieu were distinctly canonical, although not all of them French. The Comédie-Française is also responsible for two smaller theatres, the restored *Vieux-Colombier, and the Studio Théâtre, opened in 1996 at the shopping mall attached to the Louvre. In these spaces the choice of plays is bolder, although hardly aggressively so. Some new plays, or plays new to France, are performed in these satellite theatres, a return to one of the historical functions of the Comédie-Française, rarely pursued in the late twentieth century. At the Studio, performances begin at 6.30 and last one hour—an aperitif of culture before dinner.

The Théâtre-Français on the rue Richelieu has been restored, remodelled, and rebuilt over the years, most fully after a *fire in 1900, most recently in 1994 to accommodate modern stage technology. The status of the troupe has also been modified to suit modern bureaucratic structures. No longer a 'small republic', the Comédie-Française was declared in 1995 a 'public establishment of the industrial and commercial type' under the authority of the Ministry of Culture.   VS

LORCEY, JACQUES, La Comédie-Française (Paris, 1980)
SURGERS, ANNE, La Comédie-Française: un théâtre au-dessus de tout soupçon (Paris, 1982)

Lovers (1722) had aimed at 'a joy too exquisite for laughter'; and Nivelle de *La Chaussée followed suit in France, achieving considerable success with a formula which subjected a long-suffering *heroine to misunderstandings and other forms of adversity, as in Le Préjugé à la mode (1735) or Mélanide (1741). Although *Voltaire poured scorn on La Chaussée's sentimental moralizing, his own *comedies owe more to sentiment than he would have admitted. The domestic drama of *Diderot and his contemporaries, as well as the fin de siècle *melodrama of *Pixérécourt, can both be seen to invest tearful comedy with a measure of prose *realism.   WDH

COMÉDIENS DU ROI

The earliest documentary evidence of the title 'Comédiens (ordinaires) du Roi' (King's Players in Ordinary)—implying royal protection and *financial support in return for service to the crown—dates from 1598. However, Louis XIII dispensed no annual subsidies until 1629, after which date successive companies at *Paris's *Hôtel de Bourgogne were officially known as the 'Royal Troupe' and given 12,000 livres. The *Marais company, also 'King's Players' from 1634, only received 6,000 livres, as did *Molière's when Louis XIV assumed responsibility for them in 1665. From 1680, Louis's French Players (at the *Comédie-Française) received 12,000 and his Italian Players (at the Bourgogne) 15,000 livres annually.   JG

COMEDY

A *genre in which the ending of a play or *film script proclaims happiness through a love match, a wedding, a triumph over adversity, or a reconciliation. When humour erupts occasionally in a *tragedy or *melodrama, it is more likely to startle theatregoers than to amuse them. Ben *Jonson, Thomas *Shadwell, and other commentators of the 1500–1600s wanted comedy to chastise the folly and villainies of their times, while moralizers before and since have considered such obligations *didactic, inimical to art (see NEOCLASSICISM). But in comedy a tone of optimism sounds during the play's altering relationships. Comedy

toys with such plot devices as coincidences, misunderstandings, and confusions of identity. Its *laughter arises predominantly from clashes of wit and exchanges of 'one-liners'. As opposed to the broader, slow-paced appeal of humour, wit features one or more roles who mean to be funny, preferably at the expense of others. Beatrice strops her wit on Benedick in Shakespeare's Much Ado About Nothing (1599), Mrs Millamant on Edward Mirabell in *Congreve's The Way of the World (1700), and Célimène on Alceste (and he on her) in *Molière's The Misanthrope (1666), while they swap affronts and cannot confess that they love each other. In Lubitsch's film Trouble in Paradise (1932), the leading woman and man, Miriam Hopkins and Herbert Marshall, avoid revealing that they are rival swindlers, mutually attracted. These deceivers spin out delicious wit not to demonstrate what they say but to hide who they innately are—pretenders, charmers, liars: figures *audiences laugh at, rather than with.

1. Origins, Greek and Roman; 2. What is comedy?; 3. Formations

1. Origins, Greek and Roman

Comedy's birth begins, depending on one's sources of information and appraisal, in Attic and Doric Greece and southern Sicily during the 500s–400s BC (see GREEK THEATRE, ANCIENT). Early comedies evidently arose from *rituals in honour of Olympia's pantheon of gods; they mutually strengthened the syntheses of *verse speaking, *clowning, exhibitions of *dance, *music (sung and played), and virtuoso movement. They coalesced over time into troupes that resembled modern *circuses and *revues, like and unlike arts convincingly pulled together, and not from dramatic *texts alone. The pristine forms of comedy, in no definite chronological order, were threefold: first the itinerant *phlyakes of Sicily and Greece during the late pre-Christian era, who put on partly improvised solo turns; these evolved into the fabulae Atellanae (*Atellan farce) when they reached mainland Italy—the foot, Calabria, and the heel, Apuglia—where some individual *acrobats, musicians, singers, *jugglers, conjurors, and *mimes might combine their acts in collective travelling shows displayed out of doors or in halls belonging to wealthy sponsors. Such partly improvised regional productions grew in popularity and geographical breadth all through the *medieval period. By the 1500s acting companies all over Italy in the *commedia dell'arte (professional comics) had stylized their *costumes, *masks, and prose sketches, and had buffed their *acting styles during their circuits within the Italian peninsula to such polished levels that they and their descendants confidently took up invitations, starting with Henry VIII of Britain, to give royal command performances abroad, in the countries to which they would permanently migrate. They eventually grafted their partly improvised *scenarios, staging, and performing skills to national theatre conventions across Europe. Commedia elements remain conspicuous in the dramatic literatures of Russia, the UK, France, Spain, Germany, Sweden, and Italy itself, most strikingly in the plays of Shakespeare, Molière, *Goldoni, *Gozzi, and *Pirandello.

In the growth of a second comic convention, Greek playwrights wrote and directed *satyr-plays. Strung onto tragic trilogies, these strange comedies were played by coarse hairy creatures who liked to burlesque the gods and the revered heroes of myth. The satyr-play may well be a remnant of the *dithyramb, a choral hymn sung to flute accompaniment. Its exalted text and, probably, its performance style ran counter to its salacious lyrics in praise of *Dionysus, god of wine, drama, lust, and other diversions. The Cyclops by *Euripides looks like an example of a satyr-play, a rare survivor of that breed, which had once clung (c.425 BC) to the tail of three linked (but lost) tragedies, among them his grisly Hecuba, in which the *heroine takes revenge on a relative by having him blinded. In the satyr-play some actors wore wreaths, masks, loincloths, and other scanty covering (see PHALLUS). Part-men, part-animals, they talked and acted bawdily, drank plentiful wine in honour of Dionysus, their deity, and followed Silenus, their *chorus leader and, as some say, their common father, if anything resembling these *characters ever existed.

The third source of comedy, the distant forerunner of the modern French and British *well-made play, the comic staple of Broadway and episodic prime-time *television, was less turbulent than either the improvised comedy or the satyr-play. So were comedies written in the early 400s BC, for which *Epicharmus of Sicily has been held responsible on small evidence. Some scholars have ventured that there were playwrights who preceded Epicharmus—although the word *playwright dates back only as far as Ben Jonson in the late 1600s. Theatre can be interpreted as an outgrowth of earlier models but hardly any identifiable supporting documents exist; if they did, this comedy might have run concurrently with the first known tragedies, or even with the epochal production in 534 BC which officially instated tragedy as an Athenian art form at the annual *Dionysia festival. Of the comedies that have come down to us Euripides' Ion (c.408) is probably the first full-length

specimen, so long as his Helen (412) is counted a *tragicomedy, not a true comedy, and so long as previous plays, by *Aristophanes, for instance, are taken to exemplify the characteristics of *farce, not comedy (see OLD COMEDY). In the twentieth century directors and actors delighted in nudging the pliant boundaries between these three sub-genres into unfamiliar shapes.

Authors during the later 400s BC offered their comedies to festivals beyond the spring Dionysia, such as the *Lenaea each winter in Athens. Greek dramatists before Euripides and Aristophanes had already thinned out comic or farcical elements from their tragedies, perhaps to avoid 'tainting' them, despite the Athenian weakness for satyr-plays as relief from tragedies' grim enactments. As Greek comedy exerted a growing influence abroad, it intensified and purified itself. By the succeeding century, satyr-plays had faded out, their possibilities having perhaps been worked dry. Aristophanes' final two plays, Ecclesiazusae (Women in Assembly, late 390s BC) and Plutus (Wealth, 388), are usually termed *Middle Comedy, marking the passage from his politicized farces of Old Comedy to the more domestic bent exhibited in *New Comedy. Only one complete example of Greek New Comedy has come to light, and that recently, during the mid-1900s: *Menander's Dyskolus (The Grumbler or The Bad-Tempered Man), though many fragments of his other works have survived. Menander's drama forms a likely bridge from Greek to Latin New Comic writings which set Roman fathers against their sons and slaves (see ROMAN THEATRE).

Two Roman dramatists of the third and second centuries BC left large samples of comedy. The older artist, *Plautus, made theatrical contributions that would be widely imitated. The Pot of Gold and Pseudolus, for example, incorporated flute-and-percussion music and dancing; they appeared to be close to decorous farce in their own time but turned into out-and-out farcical romp when converted into an American *musical, A Funny Thing Happened on the Way to the Forum (1962), which featured two of the favourite comic complications in Rome: money, which its possessors hate to part with, and the determination of slaves to secure freedom. The younger Roman, *Terence, in such comic plays as The Self-Tormentor and The Twin Brothers (both 160s BC), composed trim and at times haranguing disputes. Mothers are seldom encountered in Latin comedy or farce, women being mostly seen and hardly heard from as young enchantresses stolen in infancy from noble couples, then raised as slaves or sold by pirates or other flesh pedlars. New Comedy's later offshoots passed to innumerable successors after Shakespeare and Molière, down to the creators of television sitcoms.

Much Italian theatre in the *early modern period was breathed out in exclamatory sighs through the lips of softhearted shepherdesses. As an alternative to the productions of commedia troupes, poets who shunned displays of their work in public created the *commedia erudita, 'scholarly' verse for selected audiences, the *closet drama. One exception was the mightily energetic squabbles between duchies in spectacles like the *Orlando furioso* by Ludovico *Ariosto; another exception, *Machiavelli's *The Mandrake*, is a work that toyed with mischievous farce. But indigenous comedy, regional theatre, and *folk dance, especially from *India, *China, *Japan, *Indonesia, Turkey, and the heartlands of *Africa, have usually arisen, like those of ancient Greece, out of mythology and religious ritual. Most of these comedies remain unknown in Europe except through infrequent visits of troupes from Asia, Africa, and Latin America; but film comedies like those of Japan's late Juzo Itami (1933–97), which include *The Funeral* and *Tampopo* (1986), demand comparison, in artistry and impact, with the finest products of the West.

2. What is comedy?

Representatives from all branches of theatre have had ample say. Spokespersons for sects have consulted their gods, or *the* God, and laid down unchallengeable dogma, sometimes joining the procession of zealots who proclaim how (and how not) to write comedies, why (and why not) to purge offensive material; while artistic pragmatists have concerned themselves with extracting noisy laughs in the right places.

In the fifth chapter of *Poetics* *Aristotle observed that comedy dealt with figures of a lower caste than the gods, demigods, and monarchs of tragedy. Bernard Knox has pointed out that as far back as Plautus' plays, two slaves served in each household, one slow, the other smart; vestiges of these opposites survived, he believed, in Caliban and Ariel in Shakespeare's *The Tempest*, in Speed and Launce (*The Two Gentlemen of Verona*), and in Tranio and Curtis (*The Taming of the Shrew*). Most comedies by Molière and his French imitators take place in bourgeois households with servants doubling as valets. A Molière gentleman feels sinewless without his valet. Monsieur Jourdain's daughter seeks counsel from the family maid on how to capture a youth who proves his infatuation by quarrelling with her at every encounter. A male heir looks to his servants to gain him access to a damsel while not damaging access to his inheritance while his father is still alive. In *The Barber of Seville* and *The Marriage of Figaro* by *Beaumarchais the hero, a Molièresque man of the people, outwits his master's rivals in the first play and the master himself in the second. Some historians believe the blatant reversal of master-and-servant power may have helped to incite the French Revolution, which broke out in 1789, five years after the play's first performance. *Mozart and *Da Ponte in their operatic version, *Le Nozze di Figaro* (produced 1786), not only enhanced the comedy with ravishing music and an adroit libretto but also added emotional soundings to Beaumarchais's reformist beliefs. Today almost all television comedy wells up out of suburbs and similar haunts of the self-spoiled middle class, where fractious domesticity reigns, and good-natured bantering gives way—with as short a time as possible wasted between commercials—to family spats that fly between sofas, armchairs, tables, and back fences.

3. Formations

(*a*) **Texts:** One can deduce from Aristophanes' comedies and his peerless farces the main elements of a non-tragic sequence: a *prologue, or introduction, often in Aristophanes as a *parabasis* or direct address by the playwright to his public; then a succession of choral odes divided by episodes spoken mostly by the actors, not sung by the chorus members; and a final epode or *epilogue as the chorus departed. Over time the chorus grew altogether obsolete; in New Comedy and Roman comedy episodes were transmuted scenes; a god (a principal actor) or an unnamed figure delivered the epilogue or the *protagonist summed up. Later still, clusters of *scenes became *acts, whether in the five-act arrangements by Terence, the sprawling five-act but solidly anchored carpentry of the Elizabethans and Jacobeans seventeen centuries later, or the practically motionless five-act masterpieces of French neoclassicism of the seventeenth and eighteenth centuries, declaimed from flights of steps or in front of the wondrous settings and furnishings exported by Italian designers.

(*b*) **Structure:** Modern comedies are as a rule designated short or 'full length' in the theatre world. *Epic plays by *Brecht and his followers are usually broken down, especially for *rehearsals, into scenes. Scenes frequently serve for subdividing costume fittings, sets, swordfights, dances, and singing. Popular musicals favour a two-act format. Act II has roughly half the length of Act I, thereby tightening the suspense and speeding up the ending for the benefit of restless spectators. A solo comic performance or *one-person show, recently welcomed to popular theatre because cheap to rehearse and mount, will often be derived from a memoir. The actor recites it in one non-stop lump so that spectators who wish to walk out inconspicuously before the end are embarrassed into staying.

(*c*) **Roles:** Comic theory has now and then endeavoured to sort roles into sketches of human types and freeze them in place (*see* STOCK CHARACTER). One of the earliest expositions along these lines, the *Tractatus Coislinianus*, is thought by some commentators to have been drawn up by Aristotle. It was introduced to modern readers by Francis Cornford in *The Origin of Attic Comedy* (1914) and again by Northrop Frye in *Anatomy of Criticism* (1957). The author of the *Tractatus* identifies three types (male only) in the plays of Aristophanes. The *alazon* or impostor crashes parties or other celebrations, pretending friendship with the hero; or he retails specialized knowledge such as, say, a medical or scholarly doctor's. Examples of the type include the parasitic priest in Molière's *Tartuffe; or, The Impostor* (1669), Parolles, the show-off in Shakespeare's *All's Well That Ends Well* (c.1602–6), and Sergius in *Shaw's *Arms and the Man* (1898), the latter two being variations of the *miles gloriosus* or cowardly braggart. The second figure from the Tractatus, the *eiron*, or ironic role, may be a self-deprecating type, an intellectual who exposes an impostor or is the prey of an impostor, sometimes the one sensible or unimaginative part in a play, like Horatio in *Hamlet* or most *confidants in the dramatic versifications of *Corneille and *Racine (*see* RAISONNEUR). The third derivation from the *Tractatus* is a poseur, the *pharmakos*, who can tackle a range of parts. Cornford identifies him as an 'antagonist', a leading figure in the *Thargelia* ceremony, associated with wealth and fruitfulness but also with the casting out of hunger, death, and sin. Crow, a mysterious singer (or hoodlum?) who supplants the protagonist in Sam *Shepard's *Tooth of Crime* (1972), is like a professional invader. (*See also* ORIGINS OF THEATRE.)

But there are many parts that are a compound of *eiron* and *alazon*: John Tanner in Shaw's *Man and Superman* (1903), Béralde, the hypochondriac's brother in Molière's *The Hypochondriac* (1673), *Rostand's romantic warrior-hero in *Cyrano de Bergerac* (1897), and Azdak, the scribe suddenly promoted to judge in Brecht's *The Caucasian Chalk Circle* (1944–5). The *pharmakos* may equally play an innocent finally killed or suffering undeservedly, like Chaplin's clown in *The Circus* (1928) and his tramp seeking work in *City Lights* (1931), or the protagonist of *Ghelderode's *Pantagleize* (1929), a tribute to Chaplin, which speeds along as comedy until almost the last line, when it turns into a most poignant moment. Frye remarks that the archetype of an 'incongruously ironic' figure is 'Christ, the perfectly innocent victim excluded from human society'; but it is difficult to see how even a dim-witted treatment of Christ, like that in *Lloyd Webber's musical *Jesus Christ Superstar* (1970), could be convincing as comedy or much else. The disadvantage of overloading these three abstract cubby-holes for comic parts taken from antiquity is that they diminish by comparison comic roles of undoubted consequence like Falstaff, Petruchio, or Helena (*All's Well That Ends Well*), Mrs Millamant, Professor Higgins, Lina Sczepanowska (in *Misalliance*, 1910), and a lavish sprinkling of others, from Winnie in *Beckett's *Happy Days* to his Krapp playing back his last tape.

In his *Comic Theory of the Sixteenth Century* (1950) Marvin T. Herrick discusses five roles mentioned by Terence (in the prologue to his *Self-Tormentor*) and adds another ten listed by Calphurnius, a critic of the 1400s AD. They typify a selection of figures with recognizable quirks taken from varied segments of an average population: the young and aged, male and female, rapacious and indulgent, debauched and delicate. Many, as Herrick points out, are persons one can imagine meeting in a community. But the actors in a play or film or especially a television series often become so intent on mimicking a cast of 'types taken from life' that they speak and behave like lightly animated chess pieces. The bulk of the comedies that visit multiplex cinemas, local *playhouses, and huge home television screens offer a range of stars apparently doing their utmost but most of them working at a level well below capacity. At the start of the twenty-first century, comedies that make heavy demands on actors are not abundant, comedies that producers will put their money behind are even less abundant, and comedies that attach themselves to a spectator's memory will probably stay active there for no more than ten days. Signs of improved comic writing in films, however, have appeared in the development of animated human figures and animals, whose creators have found new devices for mimicking and satirizing live persons in their cartoons.   ACB

BERMEL, ALBERT, *Shakespeare at the Moment: playing the comedies* (Portsmouth, NH, 2000)

CHARNEY, MAURICE, (ed.), *Comedy: new perspectives* (New York: 1978)

JENKINS, RON, *Subversive Laughter: the liberating power of comedy* (New York, 1994)

KERN, EDITH, *The Absolute Comic* (New York, 1980)

SYPHER, WYLIE (ed.), *Comedy* (New York, 1956, essays by Bergson, Meredith, Sypher)

COMEDY OF HUMOURS

Frequently linked to Ben *Jonson's early work, the phrase refers to a handful of plays written and performed in *London around 1600. Like *Every Man in his Humour*, most of them have 'humour' or one of its variants in the title. In *early modern English, a humour could be one of Galen's four bodily fluids regulating human temperament, but it could also be a psychological or emotional tendency, possibly a crotchet, tic, or whim, or, shading into moral deviancy, an affectation. In most *comedies of this type, extensive collections of *characters representing different humours are displayed and sometimes reformed.   MS

COMEDY OF MANNERS

English critical category dating back at least to Charles *Lamb in 1822, and associated particularly with debates about the nature and acceptability of Restoration *comedy. Less parochially it must be seen as analogous to the French term *comédie de mœurs*, used retrospectively to distinguish sub-genres of comedy in the seventeenth and eighteenth centuries. The English term has been succinctly defined (by J. A. Cuddon) as comedy dealing with 'the behaviour and deportment of men and women living under specific social codes'. It is difficult to separate such a category from any form of comic drama which turns a satirical eye on behaviour and motivation in an identifiable society: we might therefore apply the term not only to comedies between 1630 and 1800, but also to *Menander and *Terence, to some *commedia erudita*, to Jacobean *city comedy, and later to Oscar *Wilde—always implying a contrast with sentimental or psychological comedy on the one hand, and with playful fantasy or *farce on the other. Comedies of manners can be attacked as 'superficial' or 'immoral', but such judgements depend on specific cultural or ideological premises which not all critics or ages may share. The *genre may usually involve a disenchanted distance from the *characters depicted, and both *laughter and *satire must be achieved by exaggerating observable social reality; but some reflection of such reality is essential for the desired effect to be achieved. The presence or absence of moral purpose will vary with the play, the production, and the *audience.   RAA

COMMEDIA DELL'ARTE see page 298

COMMEDIA ERUDITA

The name now given to the earliest phase of scripted Italian-language comic theatre produced under the influence of the humanist educational package in the sixteenth century. It was 'erudite' in the sense of being consciously formed with reference to the examples of *Plautus and *Terence which had been studied in the schoolroom; however, it was rapidly and quietly adapted as a performance *genre, though initially just to aristocratic *audiences in courts and academies. Paradoxically, by referring back to classical example this genre set in motion the birth of modern European theatre—by insisting that play scripts were cultural products to be approached on a par with literature, by giving them the social prestige which that implies, and by divorcing them progressively from specific religious or social performing occasions. The first full-length examples were offered by Ludovico *Ariosto in Ferrara in 1508 and 1509. Emulation soon came from other Italian centres—Urbino, Florence, and the Venetian Republic. Plots from *Roman *comedy were merged with those of medieval novellas: the small community of Siena contributed essentially by offering a more emotional romance-based tone, with greater focus on female *characters. In general, however, the comedy of commedia erudita is hard-edged and unsympathetic, based principally on derision. From the 1540s, gentlemen *amateur dramatists and performers were challenged by *commedia dell'arte professionals performing the same material. Scripted comedy in the second half of the century inevitably became influenced by the new genre, while attempting to retain its cultural and social superiority. See EARLY MODERN PERIOD IN EUROPE.

RAA

COMMUNITY ARTS SERVICE

From 1947 to 1962 CAS toured professional low-budget theatre (and small-scale *opera and *ballet) to rural communities throughout the upper North Island of New Zealand. Modelled on the British Council for the Encouragement of Music and the Arts, CAS was funded by the government's new Council for Adult Education, and educational aims included demonstrating how to create high-quality theatre (often in community halls) with the slenderest of stage resources. Although never national in scope, it outlasted the more ambitious *New Zealand Players. CAS *tours included the popular Bruce *Mason, but over-adventurous choices of scripts (including the first New Zealand Waiting for Godot, 1958) contributed to its demise.   DC

COMMUNITY THEATRE

A term much in vogue in the 1970s and 1980s, although the forms of theatre it refers to continue to develop and, in many parts of the globe, expand. It has many functions—it can enable communities collectively to share experiences and retell their own histories; it can encourage participation in political debate; and it can be a tool for social inclusion, embracing sections of society that feel themselves to be marginalized. Community theatre is found in forms as diverse as the functions it serves, but they can be grouped into the following three broad types.

1. Professional theatre devised for its local community, drawing on and retelling its stories, performed in conventional theatre spaces, sometimes by *regional repertory theatres but more usually (as with Cornwall's Kneehigh Theatre Company) on *tour to community centres in the area. Other variations include theatre companies who take their productions to a wider geographical area, playing to 'communities of interest'. Notable examples in the UK have been the work of *Gay Sweatshop (1975–95; see also GAY THEATRE), appealing (though not exclusively) to gay communities throughout the country; and the seminal production by *7:84 Theatre (Scotland) of The Cheviot, the Stag and the Black Black Oil, a lively, provocative celebration of Scottish rural and industrial working-class identity through some 200 years of exploitation, dramatized within the framework of a Scottish ceilidh (an entertainment with songs, traditional *dancing, and storytelling), which toured to rural and town community centres throughout Scotland in 1973–4.

2. Community plays, such as those created under the leadership of Ann *Jellicoe. Stories about the history of a locality are researched, *devised, and enacted, drawing on professional but mainly *amateur resources for the *acting, *directing, *stage management, and backstage work. An example is Entertaining Strangers, commissioned by the Colway Theatre Trust, scripted by David *Edgar and performed by the community of Dorchester, Dorset, in 1985.

3. Community arts centres. Theatres or other venues with performance spaces become a focus for community activity of various kinds, not only drama. The first such centre in the UK was *Inter-Action in north *London, founded by Ed Berman in 1968. More recent examples include East London's Hoxton Hall and *Manchester's Contact Theatre, noted at least as much for their participatory workshop activities for young people (in a range of performance skills from acting to 'hip-hop' dancing) as for their mainstage shows.

(continued on p. 301)

COMMEDIA DELL'ARTE

The term by which we now refer to this form of theatre (which means simply 'professional *comedy') occurs very late in its history. It is first found in a play by *Goldoni of 1750, and it refers to the 'masked comedy', 'improvised comedy' or even simply 'Italian comedy' which had been in existence since the mid-sixteenth century. The fact that the *genre had such a long life still has the effect of confusing popular perceptions of it. A revived interest in commedia dell'arte was taken by French scholars in the *romantic period: this produced studies which rely too heavily on some codifications, and even on some inaccurate legends, stemming from what was believed and recorded by Louis *Riccoboni and the eighteenth-century *Comédie Italienne. To delineate what 'Italian comedy' had become by 1750 is of course crucial to tracing its effect on the 'harlequinades' of later theatre history. However, it is equally important to understand how, and even why, the arte first emerged; and Italian scholars of the late twentieth century have given us a clearer idea of what this genre originally was, concentrating most of all on what is seen as its formative golden age between approximately 1570 and 1630. The effect of these studies has been to correct some entrenched perceptions. First, we now know that the repertoire of arte performers was at least as much verbal as physical: their craft was a form of oral tradition, but it had a close symbiotic relationship with more respectable written culture. (Emphasis on *mime and *ballet may have developed in France, where the Italian *dialogue was not so well understood and needed support.) Secondly, the fact that this was a popular form of theatre does not necessarily mean that it was subversive or anti-establishment: the more famous performers spent most of their time and energy competing for the rich prizes of princely and royal patronage, with a good dose of the conformism and sycophancy which that always implies. It is certainly true, on the other hand, that commedia dell'arte was an 'actors' theatre', in which the performers took ownership of their material and dispensed with the need for a dramatist. Moreover—a fact which has so far been under-stressed by scholars—the professional arte companies introduced the first actresses to Italy and then to Europe. This makes them ultimately responsible for the huge concentration on the female star, or diva, which has characterized Western performing arts ever since. (See WOMEN AND PERFORMANCE.)

The precise origins of this particular form of professional theatre in Italy are not well documented: the earliest surviving company contract dates from 1545, and the earliest record of actresses appearing in public from 1548. By the 1560s there were already Italian *touring companies with female stars; by the 1570s troupes were visiting England, France, and Spain; and in 1589, during the landmark festivities for a Florentine granducal wedding, the improvisations of the *Gelosi company were given equal status with a scripted humanist *commedia erudita. For a couple of generations, the most celebrated performers and troupes won patronage in Florence, Mantua, and Turin, and commercial *audiences in Venice and throughout the peninsula: a military and economic crisis of 1630 is now seen as ending the most glorious period of the genre in Italy. After that the best performers tended to go to France, to the Comédie Italienne. By the eighteenth century, when Goldoni confronted professional theatre practice with his reforms, there were established Italian practitioners who (one deduces) were competent but whose material had got into a rut.

Although there may have been some input into commedia dell'arte from archetypes of *folk narrative and drama (particularly, perhaps, when the mask of Pulcinella came up from *Naples to join an essentially north Italian format), its most important inspiration was the *plot material of recent upper-class commedia erudita, together with its narrative stereotypes. The categorized distribution of roles in a standard company is enough to make this clear. The 'old men' (Vecchi)—usually Pantalone and the Dottore—were the miserly, lustful or pedantic fathers whose intentions were frustrated by the Lovers (Innamorati), and by the latter-day scheming *Plautine slaves (Servi), whose myriad names included Zani, Arlecchino, Brighella, Truffaldino, Pedrolino, and the female Franceschina and Colombina. A blustering but ultimate cowardly Capitano might be a free mover in the plot, usually a 'blocking' character like the old fathers, but sometimes allowed to be a lover. The solution to the intrigue was provided by a mixture of successful trickery and the discovery of lost family relationships. Every one of these elements—taken from *Roman *comedy and from medieval novellas—was first dramatized and made familiar in *neoclassical comedy for courts and academies. The professionals simply stole them, fragmented them, turned them into a repertoire of permutable building blocks, and performed them in their own way. This involved three characteristics in particular: *masks, multilingualism, and *improvisation.

The use of facial half-masks by certain of the stereotypes (Vecchi and Servi, but not Innamorati and not always Capitani)

Harlequin.　　Zany Corneto.　　Il Segnor Pantalon.

O la belle chanſon, Pantalon chantons bien,
Si voulez eſgayer voſtre maiſtreſſe belle,
C'eſt le moyen certain pour en fin ioüir d'elle,
Qu'eſtre muſeau de chien, dy-ie muſicien.

Accordons nous tous trois, ſi bien & proprement
Que puiſſions l'endormir au doux ſon de ma lire,
Encor que comme vous ie n'aye apris à lire,
Ie ne laiſſeray pas de ioüer brauement.

Courage (mes amis) ie chante le deſſus,
De ce plaiſant trio, compoſé pour madame,
La douceur de ma voix luy penetrera l'ame:
Mes paſſages ne ſont ni tortus ni boſſus.　j.

Three stock characters (or 'masks') from **commedia dell'arte**, engaged in a musical scene: from the left, Arlecchino, Zanni the Cuckold, and Pantalone (who is foolishly serenading a lady far too young for him). This engraving is taken from the late sixteenth-century *Recueil Fossard*, and represents Italian players in Paris (*see* COMÉDIE ITALIENNE).

may have helped to dictate an energetic and more visual performing style among the *parti ridicole* (comic roles); and physical comedy, with mime and gesture, clearly helped the genre to be exportable. Even more important, however, is the very concept of a 'mask'—whether actually masked or not—as a permanent theatrical or fictional figure which the genre could constantly reuse, and which acquired a life of its own. In Italy the masks were identified not only by their *costume, but by their language—underlining the fact that this was verbal, as well as visual, comedy. Pantalone had to speak Venetian, the Dottore Bolognese, and the servants a Lombard dialect indicat-

ing up-country Bergamo, the homeland of the original Zanni. (The initially French mask of Harlequin became linguistically assimilated to the other male servants.) A Capitano was usually Spanish; whereas the Innamorati always spoke high-flown literary Tuscan, thus making an important connection with the elitist cultural background from which this material had sprung. Later masks such as Tartaglia and Pulcinella brought in southern Italian dialects. Multilingualism was a feature which inevitably faded when performers went abroad; but within Italy it persisted through to Goldoni's time. Rather than supplying social *realism it rapidly became self-referential, providing an instantly recognizable comic badge for each relevant mask. Initially, the confrontation between Pantalone and Zani had alluded to a north Italian social reality. Later, Pantalone, Arlecchino, Pierrot, and Columbine (in all languages) had become the people's foolish but indestructible *heroes, taking on the fixed imaginative role since usurped by characters from animated cartoon *film. The stories in which they participated often had a cartoon-like implausibility.

The most obvious feature of all, however, was the practice of improvising on an outline *scenario instead of memorizing a written script. This may have been passed down from a first generation of illiterate actors; though its permanent adoption is likely to have been commercially motivated, since it vastly increased the number of apparently different items which a company could offer. The same fragments of material could be recycled in endless permutations, and both performers and companies could retain control of their own repertoire. At all events, the technique won amazement and admiration, and became the defining characteristic of 'Italian comedy'. It is important nowadays to register that it had little to do with the improvisation practised by modern actors and drama students. Rather than a free use of the performer's imagination, aiming at innovation and stretching the creative faculties, it involved the memorization and redeployment of a huge amount of repertoire material. Actors specialized in a single mask, for which they 'learned their part' over a whole career, constantly accumulating in their commonplace books (*zibaldoni*, or *libri generici*) collections of jokes, speeches (comic or serious), and verbal routines in whatever language or dialect was appropriate. Much of this material was taken from written sources, just as the plots to which it contributed were cannibalized and permutated from written plays. Thus the majority of the material delivered in oral performance—details of which, by definition, scholars can never entirely recover—is likely to have been memorized in advance, in snippets and fragments, like the routine of a modern stand-up comedian. Naturally each single entertainment was leavened every time by genuine ad libs, by acknowledgements of the particular place and occasion, and (in the *audience's eyes) by an increase in the element of danger which always underlies live performance. But if this was theatrical acrobatics, it was performed with a safety-net: actors always knew where they were going, within a brief gag or within the plot as a whole. They were guided and constrained by constant mental and physical *rehearsal, and by the directions of the scenario which told them what had to happen, and what had to be mentioned, in each scene. Preconceived *lazzi, on a large scale or small, might figure as self-contained digressions, but also as components which actually advanced the plot. Comparisons have since been offered with the improvisation of jazz musicians, conditioned both by the structure of the song being performed and by immersion in a particular musical style.

All these defining characteristics could have existed for an all-male profession: the historic introduction of female performers was a gratuitous addition, whose acceptance by society remains something of a mystery when one considers the formidable prejudices involved. Women who displayed themselves were assumed to be sexually immoral. It is probable, though not provable, that the earliest actresses were in fact high-class courtesans, who in any case learned a range of verbal accomplishments to entertain clients in their salons, including improvisation both of verse and of music. The rise of the actress may be inseparable from that of the *operatic prima donna. The virtuously married Isabella *Andreini worked hard to dispel the prejudice that she, at least, was a 'public woman'; and the emergence of theatrical *family dynasties, similar to those in other artisan trades or *arti*, did modify the image. However, assumptions about sexual freedom continued in perception and in practice, and in the Papal States female performers of any kind were banned well into the eighteenth century. Nevertheless, their use spread from Italy to the rest of Europe, with England holding out until after the Restoration.

Since the *'texts' of *commedia dell'arte* were indeed oral rather than written, their detailed content and tone remains very much a matter for speculation. Some seventeenth-century playscripts from both France and Italy, including those of *Molière, offer some clues as to how the 'modular' structures of improvised *dialogue, and the stock material of *monologues by individual masks, influenced subsequent comic dramatists who wanted to produce an analogous effect. Scenarios which have survived show that the emphasis of improvised theatre was indeed on comedy, in the hard-edged unsentimental style of *commedia erudita*, leaving *tragedy and *pastoral more often to fully composed scripts. However, the plots of many comedies tend also to draw on the emotionally charged and picaresque formats of mixed genres such as *tragicomedy: this leaves us in some permanent doubt as to how far, and how often, some roles—in particular those of the Innamorati—were played for pathos rather than for laughs. In the end the form must always be seen as existing in a state of permanent overlap, not only between genres, but also between itself and any written theatrical format which had a proven audience appeal. Goldoni's term *commedia dell'arte*, with its reference to a trade guild, implies a 'professional' theatre which therefore also had always to remain 'commercial'. *See also* EARLY MODERN PERIOD IN EUROPE; ACTING/ACTOR.   RAA

ANDREWS, RICHARD, *Scripts and Scenarios: the performance of comedy in Renaissance Italy* (Cambridge, 1993)

FERRONE, SIRO, *Attori mercanti corsari* (Turin, 1993)

FITZPATRICK, TIM, *The Relationship of Oral and Literate Performance Processes in Commedia dell'Arte* (Lewiston, 1995)

RICHARDS, KENNETH, and RICHARDS, LAURA, *The Commedia dell'Arte: a documentary history* (Oxford, 1990)

TAVIANI, FERDINANDO, and SCHINO, MIRELLA, *Il segreto della commedia dell'arte* (Florence, 1982)

In America the term more usually refers to non-professional theatre groups based in local communities whose productions are a focus of heightened community activity at certain times of the year and are frequently a source of local pride. *See* COMMUNITY THEATRE, USA; DEVELOPMENT, THEATRE FOR; OPPRESSED, THEATRE OF THE. ARJ

ERVEN, EUGENE VAN, *Community Theatre: global perspectives* (London, 2000)

COMMUNITY THEATRE, USA

Amateurs gathered to present plays and musical shows as early as the colonial era; such groups began to flourish in the twentieth century and became a significant cultural and economic force. Some colonial authorities (upholding laws that assumed the immorality of theatre; *see* CENSORSHIP) made theatrical presentations difficult if not impossible, but prohibitions eased after the revolution and urban elites in the nineteenth century organized *amateur theatricals for purposes of socializing, intellectual stimulation, and social improvement. In the mid-nineteenth century, the Mormons (members of the Church of Jesus Christ of Latter Day Saints, a religious minority) embraced theatre as a wholesome means of entertainment and education in their remote Western settlements. By the 1890s, American professional theatre was almost completely industrialized via monopoly control by the *Theatrical Syndicate. Spurred by news of amateur art theatres in Europe and by books such as Percy *MacKaye's *The Playhouse and the Play* (1909) and *The Civic Theatre* (1912), the *Little Theatre movement arose around 1911 as an attempt to revive theatre as art and in pursuit of communitarian ideals within a group of like-minded founders. While some of the little theatres (such as the *Washington Square Players, *Provincetown Players, the *Neighborhood Playhouse, and the Cleveland Play House) transformed themselves into professional companies, others remained committed to the ideal of doing theatre for love and not for money. Groups such as the Indianapolis Civic Theatre (founded 1915), the *Pasadena Playhouse (1918), and Le Petit Théâtre du Vieux Carré in New Orleans (1919) grew into complex year-round organizations with sizeable budgets but continued to rely upon volunteers in pursuit of the 'constructive leisure' promoted by MacKaye. Another face of community theatre was seen in the *pageants and *festivals devised by MacKaye, his sister Hazel MacKaye, and others. These scripted mass events, often 're-enactments' of episodes from history, were embraced by communities across the country from 1910 to 1930 as participatory democratic art in the model of ancient Greece. Play-based community theatres survived the era of pageantry and remain a typical feature of American cities and towns. *See also* COMMUNITY THEATRE. MAF

COMOEDIA

A number of twelfth-century *texts, mainly from the Loire Valley, written by clerics partly in narrative and partly in *dialogue, are referred to in the manuscripts and in the texts themselves as *comoediae*; but they owe at least as much to Ovid as they do to *Terence, and their theatricality is suspect. The most 'dramatic' of them could have been performed, but if they were, a semi-dramatic recitation or a *mimed performance was most likely. The best known are Vitalis of Blois's *Geta* and *Aurulario*, Arnulf of Orléans's *Lydia*, William of Blois's *Alda*, and the anonymous *Babio* and *Pamphilus*. RWV

COMPAGNIE DES QUINZE *See* SAINT-DENIS, MICHEL.

COMPANY ORGANIZATION IN EUROPE
(1500–1700)

Professional entertainers, under a variety of names, were active throughout the *medieval period in Europe, generically termed minstrels. Minstrels were primarily musicians and singers, but also storytellers, satirists, jesters, and eulogists. When they formed companies their repertory might also include *dancing, *acrobatics, *magic, *animal acts, *marionettes, and more. By the thirteenth century these professionals were occasionally mentioned in association with secular plays but it is not clear whether they acted, coached *amateur actors, or provided music. The minstrel *Rutebeuf wrote and performed the play *Le Miracle de Théophile* in *Paris in 1261, but it was recited with an assistant, rather than staged, and this may represent the standard approach minstrels took to drama. There are records of individuals and groups, including minstrels being paid for 'playing' in the early fourteenth century, but the term is ambiguous and there are few cases in which it is a clear reference to *acting. By 1427, however, 'interluders' are mentioned as appearing before England's Henry VI and in 1466 *interludentes* appeared at Winchester, suggesting that a distinction, at least in England, between minstrels, who were known first as musicians and variety entertainers and only occasionally as actors, and 'interluders' or players who were known as actors first and variety entertainers second. By the reign of Henry VII, the Players of the King's Interludes (established in 1493) were clearly differentiated from the King's minstrels. Similar distinctions were gradually made throughout Europe but for several decades it is difficult to determine which performers were actors and which minstrels.

Minstrel troupes established the precedents that were followed by the professional acting companies. First, minstrel troupes could be itinerant entertainers or employees attached to noble households. Second, they *toured extensively: some stayed close to their sponsoring household but others chose, or were sent, to travel abroad in search of new styles, ideas, and opportunities. So many minstrels toured that in 1290, when Margaret of England married John of Brabant, 426 arrived to provide entertainment. Third, while minstrelsy was primarily a male occupation, a minstrel company could include women. A woman in a minstrel troupe usually sang and danced but this was not always the case; when Matill Makejoy performed in *London in 1306, for example, she was paid as a comedian. All of these traditions were inherited by the emerging acting companies, who also inherited the increasing number of laws that were devised across Europe to restrict the activities of professional entertainers.

The earliest records of acting companies relate to those attached to noble households. Attached troupes often travelled whenever their lord (or lady) did and provided entertainment along the way. They could also be lent out to other households. When not needed for such duties, or for performances in-house, they were generally free to tour villages, towns, great houses, and monasteries for whatever additional money they could earn, just as the minstrels had done for centuries. In several parts of Europe, being attached to a noble household entitled an actor to wear a household livery or an equivalent identifying emblem, which provided protection from local vagrancy laws. The more important a household was, the more privileges could be secured by wearing its livery. Itinerant minstrels apparently found it easy to get access to such livery. The practice was so common that the London Guild of Minstrels was chartered in 1469 to combat it. Acting companies adopted this ruse and many of the laws relating to acting in the sixteenth century are at least partly designed to stop abuses by demanding that a liveried company also carry a letter of introduction or licence from their lord (or an appropriate governing body); but these too could be forged. This makes it difficult to calculate just how many companies there were in Europe in the early sixteenth century, since a reference to a performance by a known attached company may actually be for an unknown itinerant company touring with stolen livery or forged documents.

The earliest unambiguous records of itinerant companies come from contracts. In 1528–9 Thomas Arthur contracted with George Mayler to be taught acting for one year. After seven weeks, however, Arthur persuaded three of Mayler's bonded servants to form an itinerant company and tour, which they did, earning the sizeable sum of £30. In Spain, six actors were contracted to perform a *farce at the cathedral in Toledo in 1539 and a troupe from Seville, headed by Hernando de Cordoba, was contracted to perform for the Duchess of Osuna in 1543. The earliest existing contract for an acting company in Italy dates to 1545. In it, eight actors agree to form a company to be led by 'Ser Maphio known as Zanini'. There is nothing about any of these documents to suggest that the companies were viewed as new or unusual and there are certainly reports of professional Italian actors performing as early as the 1520s. But reliable records

concerning acting companies do not appear in large quantities until after 1570 in most of the countries of Europe, and not until much later in some.

Attached companies were rare in Spain where the real distinction was between 'titled companies', whose *autor* (*actor-manager) held a licence granted by the Royal Council, and 'companies of the league', who had no such licence and were not allowed to play within a league of the major cities or towns. In 1603 Augustin de Rojas Villandrando identified eight types of touring companies found in Spain. With little alteration, this could serve as a description of the variety of acting companies to be found throughout Europe. The first four types are all clearly holdovers from the days of the minstrel troupes and must often have been mistaken for minstrels in the records. They include the *bululu*, or single performer who can recite parts of a play; the *ñaque*, or two-person company that does the same; the *gangarillo*, with three or four actors (one of whom is the *clown and another a boy to do the women's parts), who can stage short plays; and the *cambaleo*, 'with a woman who sings and five men who lament', who can also do several kinds of short plays. The next four, however, are larger than the minstrel troupes and can perform far more drama than any minstrel troupe would ever have attempted. They are the *garnacha*, with a leading actress, a boy actor, and five or six men who have a repertory of full-length plays, *interludes, and *autos sacramentales*; the *boxiganga*, with two women, a boy, and six or seven men, and an even larger repertory; the *farándula*, with three women and eight to ten men; and the 'company', with '16 persons who act and 30 who eat', among them 'men of much esteem and very respectable women', who have a repertory of 50 or more full length plays and even more of the shorter works. In most countries, the average size of a 'company' was about twelve actors, but a large number of support personnel and family members were additionally involved. Augustin notes that the actors in such companies were overworked by excessive study and continuous *rehearsals. These are the troupes most likely to adopt the strict rules of professionalism we sometimes find in the documents, with fines for tardiness at rehearsals, failing to know lines, being drunk, or misusing the property of the troupe.

England did not allow women players on the public stage until 1658, but women did act elsewhere. Marie Fairet (or Ferré) contracted to act with l'Esperonniere, 'player of histories', at Bourges in 1545, which may well make France the first country to have a professional actress. But actresses did not appear in many French companies before the 1590s and they did not act in Paris until 1607. In Spain, Mariana, wife of Lope de *Rueda, is said to have acted around 1554, but the earliest confirmable appearances of *women on the public stages dates to 1579, and women were not officially licensed to perform there until 1587. The actresses Lucrezia and Flaminia acted in *Rome in 1564 (before the 1588 ban on female performers that lasted for the next two centuries) and it is unlikely that they were the first professional actresses in Italy. Women were found in larger numbers in the Italian troupes than anywhere else. They could achieve great fame, as Vincenza Armani and Isabella *Andreini did, and even *manage companies, as Diana Ponti did starting in 1582.

All companies, regardless of size, toured just as the minstrels had done. The Italian and English troupes travelled the most widely. Italian troupes were in Spain, at Valladolid, by 1548, and in France, at Lyon, the same year. The *English Comedians were at the Danish court in 1579, and were travelling across the Germanic states by 1586. A French company appeared in Seville in 1581 (and one performed in London in 1629). Will *Kempe went to Italy in 1601 but it is not clear if he acted with a company, did solo performing, or worked as a minstrel. The majority of acting companies stayed closer to home. Those fortunate enough to establish themselves in a major city like London, Paris, or *Madrid could tour less often.

The acting companies, like minstrel troupes, had leaders who took responsibility for securing plays, finding work, and organizing tours. Many early companies, and especially those in England, operated on the shares system. Actors took responsibility for a certain percentage of the troupe's expenses in exchange for the same percentage of the profits. When a founding member left a company or the company wished to expand, new actors had to buy the available shares, or sometimes just parts of shares, and contract to hold those shares for a fixed period, generally at least three years. Some sharing companies were remarkably democratic, as the *Chamberlain's Men seem to have been when Shakespeare joined them around 1594. But the company leader owned the most shares and had more decision-making power. On the Continent, especially in Italy where many companies were often *family businesses, the leader was given even more authority. Owning shares in a successful company was quite lucrative, but not every actor who worked for such companies was a shareholder; actors could be hired at a fixed salary when needed.

The impresario-led company was another model of organization copied from the minstrels. An impresario, who owned whatever licence was necessary to allow a company to perform, secured the contracts for engagements and hired the actors and support staff as needed. Actors were generally hired on a fixed salary but percentage-of-profits contracts are not unheard of. This impresario system was used by the *boys' companies in England when they turned professional in 1575–6, and seems to have been used by a number of the *autores* of the Spanish theatre and some actor-managers in Italy. By the 1690s, actors in London came to prefer a fixed salary arrangement over the indefinite income provided by the sharing system (though that system continued to be used in most provincial theatres until the nineteenth century). This may have been the result of the introduction of the benefit system for groups of actors in 1660s

and for individuals in the late 1680s. Under the *benefit performance system a performer received a percentage of the profits of a given performance. A well-attended benefit could produce enormous income, a poorly attended benefit could leave an actor responsible for costs. But at a time when acting companies went bankrupt with alarming frequency, this was preferable to liabilities of shareholding. Most of the major companies adopted this system by the eighteenth century. *See also* EARLY MODERN PERIOD IN EUROPE.   FJH

DUERR, EDWIN, *The Length and Depth of Acting* (New York, 1962)
CHAMBERS, E. K., *The Medieval Stage* (Oxford, 1925)
GURR, ANDREW, *The Shakespearian Playing Companies* (Oxford, 1996)
SERGOLD, N. D., *A History of the Spanish Stage* (Oxford, 1967)

COMPANY THEATRE

A popular theatre movement that inaugurated the commercial possibilities of theatre in late nineteenth-century *India. It is also called *Parsi theatre because the Parsi community in Bombay (*Mumbai) initially sponsored it. Though a pan-Indian phenomenon, it has many regional variants, like the *sangeet natak* in Maharashtra (*see* MARATHI THEATRE) and Company Nataka in Karnataka. During the 1830s and 1840s prominent Parsi businessmen were associated with the management of two theatre buildings in Bombay, the Bombay Theatre and the Grant Road Theatre, and produced plays in English, *Hindi, Marathi, and Gujarati. As the venture succeeded commercially, the movement soon spread to other major urban centres such as Delhi and Calcutta (*Kolkata). By the end of the nineteenth century many companies had become popular in several smaller centres too, including Karachi, Agra, Lucknow, and Hyderabad. The prominent Parsi theatre groups of that time included the Victoria Nataka Mandali, the Elphinstone Dramatic Club, and Madan theatres.

Gradually, several variants of these groups emerged through a synthesis of the Parsi theatre with the existing regional theatre traditions. One such example is the famous *sangeet natak* tradition in Maharastra, which combined local musical traditions with Parsi influences. Between 1880 and 1915, many prominent regional companies attempted their own versions of such a synthesis, including the Great National Theatre (1873), Star Theatre (1883), and Minerva Theatre (1893) in Bengal; Kirloskar Company (1880) and Gandharva Nataka Mandali (1913) in Maharashtra; and the Gubbi Company (1884), Karnataka.

Despite regional variants, the company theatre movement had some common theatrical elements. The most important were the adoption of the *proscenium theatre, the use of *perspective painted scenery, and reliance on melodramatic *acting. The trainers in the Gubbi Company in Karnataka, for example, taught the 'three ps'—*pigure* (figure, the physique), *pose* (the appearance), and *pipe* (the voice). Another element shared by company theatre performances was their use of special effects through new technologies. The figurative descriptions in the epics and fairy tales were translated literally into visuals with these effects—Krishna raising the Govardhana mountain on his finger in the *Bhagavata* episode, for example, or the churning of the ocean in the famous *dashavatar. Finally, songs were included in the structure of the narrative to illustrate, accentuate, and highlight key moments in the *plot. Company theatre borrowed many tactics from Victorian theatre companies visiting from England, often altering or adapting them for the local context. With the advent of cinema in the 1930s the popularity of company theatre began to wane: cinema greatly extended many of its spectacular elements and effects. Though some company theatre groups survived the crisis, the movement was already past its prime by 1950.   KVA

COMPLICATION

Generally, that part of a dramatic *action that follows the *exposition and precedes the resolution (*denouement): the rising action, the equivalent of the rhetorical *epitasis* of late antiquity. More specifically, complication can refer to any factor introduced into the *plot of a play that creates a new or unexpected barrier to the *protagonist's purpose. The accumulation of such complications can result in either a situation too complex for rational choices to be made, or a situation in which there is but a single choice. In either case, complications increase the dramatic tension as the action approaches a *crisis or turning point (*peripeteia).   RWV

COMPLICITÉ, THEATRE DE

*Touring English company founded in 1983 by Simon *McBurney, Annabel Arden, and Marcello Magni, based on the notion of complicity with the *audience. More a loose association of like-minded collaborators with McBurney at its centre than an ensemble, Complicité has been extremely influential since the 1990s, embodying an approach to theatre that owes much to physically oriented European performance traditions (*see* PHYSICAL THEATRE; MIME). The company's work ranges from theatrical adaptations of literary *texts (for example, *The Three Lives of Lucie Chabrol*, 1994, based on a story by John Berger), to reinterpretations of classic texts (for example, *Brecht's *The Caucasian Chalk Circle*, 1996), and *devised pieces (such as *Mnemonic*, 1999). Whatever the source, Complicité's process is constant, and involves a collaborative approach to *rehearsal, the juxtaposition of different media (*sound, *light, *music), and the integration of image, music, and text within an overall production concept. The company tours internationally (by 1999 it had toured 41 countries and won 25 major international *awards), and has pioneered collab-

orations with building-based theatres (for example, *Street of Crocodiles*, 1992, with the Royal *National Theatre in *London). *See also* COLLECTIVES AND COLLECTIVE CREATION.   SWL

COMPUTERS *See* CYBER THEATRE.

CONCERT PARTY (GHANA)

Towards the end of the 1990s the easiest way for many in Accra to watch performances by Ghanaian concert parties was to attend the regular weekend matinées at the National Theatre. Sponsored by Key Soap, these showcases enabled the itinerant concert party companies to perform in opulent surroundings, very different from the cocoa storage sheds and run-down open-air cinemas which were the usual venues. In such places shows often started at 9 p.m. and might, by popular demand, continue until near dawn. The concert party tradition began to coalesce in the 1930s from a variety of ingredients (*see* JOHNSON, BOB). Operated as 'Trios', the popular entertainers were, in effect, small-scale businesses whose fortunes rose and fell with the local economy. Performers criss-crossed the country in unreliable vehicles in pursuit of paying *audiences which expected little in the way of *mise-en-scène and were highly demonstrative in their responses. The pattern that evolved was for an extended 'warm-up' in which contemporary, inherited, and religious music was played, to be followed, once the audience had assembled, by a moralistic drama in which *slapstick, pathos, caricature, *female impersonators, and a wide variety of musical numbers all found a place. During the 1960s, the government of Kwame Nkrumah attempted to give a *political direction to this tradition that had generally resisted ideological orientation. The lasting legacy of the brief 'socialist phase' was the replacement of female impersonators by actresses. Women have become essential to most of the groups that perform at the National Theatre, and experienced actresses, such as Adelaide Buabeng, now lead companies. In the vast auditorium of the National Theatre many of the qualities of the traditional performances are lost, and this distinctive Ghanaian form is being radically reshaped by the constraints of time and space—far more extensively than in the Nkrumah period. *See also* CONCERT PARTY (TOGO).   JMG

CONCERT PARTY (TOGO)

*African popular theatre based on *improvisation. Its actors, freed from the constraints of the written *text, create *dialogue based on a *scenario. The concert party originated in Ghana (*see* CONCERT PARTY (GHANA)) and spread to Togo, where it is widely practised in bars during weekends. Composed of three parts, it starts with a street parade which serves to advertise the forthcoming show. A *prologue of humorous stories and songs is followed by the main performance, which lasts several hours. Comedy, buffoonery, and pathos are the essence of the show. The setting of the concert party is usually simple, and the main *characters are *clowns dressed in rags; and their performance is built on interaction with the spectators and a subtle play of identification and alienation with the characters and *plot. The performance is enhanced by song and *dance, creating a generally festive atmosphere conducive to collective enjoyment: its spontaneous form depends on *audience participation. This festival dimension explains the concert party's social function: as a site of negotiation between prescribed and proscribed social conduct. The characters are defined by their social status, representing social types among the common folk—the houseboy, the idler, the drunk, the unemployed, the prostitute—or embodying noble functions such as chief, company director, rich merchant, or bank executive. Female characters are played by cross-dressed men (*see* FEMALE IMPERSONATION), and each actor plays several roles (*see* DOUBLING).

SA trans. JCM

CONDÉ, MARYSE (1937–)

Guadeloupean writer. Internationally known for her novels (many have been translated into English), Condé is the author of half a dozen plays. *Le Morne de Massabielle* (*The Hills of Massabielle*, 1972) was first performed in France and later at UBU Repertory Theater in *New York (1991). *Pension les Alizes* (1988) was written for the actress Sonia Emmanuel and staged in Martinique and Guadeloupe, with Emmanuel and Jacques Martial in the leading roles. Emmanuel also directed Condé's *An Tan revolisyon*, a grandiose epic of slavery written for the 1989 bicentennial in Guadeloupe. Her other plays include *Dieu nous l'a donné* (1972), *La Mort d'Oluwemi d'Ajumako* (1973), and *Comédie d'amour* (1989). While differing in scope, they all reflect the geographical diversity and the collective struggles and dreams of the *African *diaspora. Condé now resides in the United States, where she directs the Center for French and Francophone Studies at Columbia University. LEM

CONDELL, HENRY (fl. 1598–1627)

English actor, a long-standing member of the companies associated with Shakespeare (*see* CHAMBERLAIN'S MEN, LORD). A shareholder in the *Globe and *Blackfriars *playhouses, he edited the First Folio of Shakespeare's plays with John *Heminges (1623). During Condell's long career he performed in many plays, including *Jonson's *Every Man in his Humour*, *Webster's *The Duchess of Malfi*, and *Marston's *The Malcontent*. Like Shakespeare he was financially successful, and left a sizeable number of properties in London and environs.

SPC

CONFIDANT

As the formal style of French *neoclassical *tragedy developed in the early seventeenth century, the retinues attached to royal or princely *characters tended to be reduced to a single confidant. Such characters were usually passive recipients of the *protagonist's hopes, fears, and projects in affairs of state or matters of the heart; when they offer advice, and particularly when that advice is harmful (for instance the case of Narcisse, Néron's adviser in *Racine's *Britannicus*), the label confidant ceases to be appropriate. WDH

CONFIDENTI

A title which was used by a varied and discontinuous company of Italian *commedia dell'arte* actors between 1574 and 1620, and possibly revived as late as 1639. A variety of leading figures featured in the troupe during this long period, including the early actresses Vittoria Piissimi (who co-directed it, 1579–81) and Isabella *Andreini. Flamminio *Scala directed it in 1612–20, under the more stable patronage of the illegitimate Florentine prince Don Giovanni de' Medici. RAA

CONFRÉRIE DE LA PASSION

A religious and philanthropic fraternity of *Parisian merchants and artisans which in 1402 was granted a monopoly on the production of religious drama. In 1548, its licence to perform *mystères sacrés* was revoked, but it continued to perform secular plays. At the same time it built the *Hôtel de Bourgogne where it staged plays until 1597, when it relinquished the responsibility in favour of acting simply as landlord. Between 1442 and 1597 the Confrérie had a cooperative arrangement with the *Basochiens, who were responsible for comic performances. *See* MEDIEVAL THEATRE IN EUROPE; GUILDS. RWV

CONGREVE, WILLIAM (1670–1729)

English playwright. Born in England, Congreve's early years were spent in Ireland where his father settled after the Restoration, having distinguished himself in the royalist cause during the Civil War. Educated at Kilkenny, then Trinity College, Dublin, Congreve was reputedly a regular visitor to the theatre in *Smock Alley before his first play appeared on the *London stage in 1693. His traditional reputation as the foremost writer of Restoration *comedy of manners rests on his four *comedies and one *tragedy, an unusually small output for a playwright of the period. His first comedy, *The Old Bachelor* (1693), took two years to be brought to the stage and underwent revisions by John *Dryden and Thomas *Southerne before performance by the United Company at *Drury Lane. The performances of the leading players of the day, particularly Anne *Bracegirdle and

Elizabeth *Barry, contributed to the play's huge success and Congreve's subsequent plays were written specifically for them. *The Double Dealer* (1694) was not received with the same enthusiasm but Congreve threw his lot in with Barry, Bracegirdle, and Thomas *Betterton when they broke away from Drury Lane in 1695. The new company at *Lincoln's Inn Fields opened with *Love for Love* (1695), which ran for thirteen consecutive days, a highly successful run at the time. This was followed by Congreve's only tragedy, *The Mourning Bride* (1697), which proved to be another successful vehicle for the Barry and Bracegirdle acting partnership. Congreve's success attracted fierce criticism from the *anti-theatrical lobby, spearheaded by Jeremy *Collier's *A Short View . . .* (1698), which accused Congreve of promoting immorality, charges which the playwright vociferously rebutted in counter-publications. This public war of words may have contributed to the comparative failure of his last comedy *The Way of the World* (1700)—a play that has attracted more revivals in the twentieth century than almost any other Restoration comedy. In 1707 Congreve was briefly involved in the *management of the *Haymarket Theatre with fellow playwright John *Vanbrugh, but wrote no new plays.   GBB

CONJURING *See* MAGIC SHOWS.

CONKLIN, JOHN (1937–)

American designer. Conklin began designing at Yale in the 1950s, where he studied with Donald *Oenslager. Ten summers at *Williamstown Theatre Festival and an early affiliation with *Hartford Stage Company led to a career as one of the USA's most influential postmodern designers for theatre and *opera. Seen at most leading *regional theatres and at major opera houses in the USA and Europe, his abstract sets feature stunning imagery, a dynamic imbalance, quotations from art history, and the incorporation of the random or accidental. He collaborated with such major directors as Mark Lamos, Rhoda Levine, Jonathan *Miller, Francesca Zambello, JoAnne *Akalaitis, and Robert *Wilson. In the 1990s, while still busy as a designer, he took up artistic staff positions at Glimmerglass Opera and City Opera in *New York, working with *artistic director Paul Kellogg on season planning and promoting the migration of leading theatre directors, designers, and even playwrights into opera.   STC

CONNELLY, MARC (1890–1980)

American playwright and director. Connelly amassed a sizeable body of work before writing *The Green Pastures*, for which he was awarded the Pulitzer Prize in 1930. He co-wrote ten plays and *musicals with George S. *Kaufman between 1921 and 1924. Most notable were *Dulcy* (1921) and *To the Ladies!* (1922), both *satires of jingoistic business culture; a *film industry *satire, *Merton of the Movies* (1922); and *Beggar on Horseback* (1924), a dream play which adapted *expressionism as a technique for satire of American business. Connelly's whimsical imagination seemed a suitable foil for Kaufman's biting irony. *The Green Pastures* was adapted from Roark Bradford's *Ol' Man Adam an' his Chillun*, a loose retelling of biblical stories in the supposed idiom of rural *African Americans. Connelly's play, which he directed, interweaves comic scenes with hymn-singing and a serious religious purpose. Despite criticism from African-American intellectuals such as Langston *Hughes, the play was extraordinarily popular, running on Broadway for 640 performances, *touring for three years, then returning to *New York for an additional 71 performances in 1935.   MAF

CONQUEST FAMILY

English actors, *managers, and dramatists whose *family name was originally Oliver. **Benjamin Oliver** (1804–72), a low comedian, managed the ill-fated Garrick Theatre from 1830 until it was destroyed by *fire in 1846. He took over the Grecian Theatre in 1851, establishing a reputation for extravagant *pantomimes. His son **George Augustus Conquest** (1837–1901) was the *acrobatic draw, as the Spider Crab or the Grim Goblin, taking over management from his father in 1872, and in 1881 gaining the Surrey Theatre. There he collaborated with dramatists Paul Merritt and Henry Pettitt in writing highly successful spectacular *melodramas such as *Mankind* (1881). His son **George Benjamin Conquest** (1858–1926) specialized in giant roles, and took over the Surrey until 1904. Sons **Fred** (1871–1941) and **Arthur** (1875–1945) were famous animal impersonators.   AF

CONSERVATOIRE NATIONAL SUPÉRIEUR D'ART DRAMATIQUE

Founded in 1784 as the École Royale de Chant et de Déclamation, the *Paris Conservatoire remains the foremost theatre school in France. Well into the twentieth century the Conservatoire was considered the *training ground for future young *sociétaires* of the *Comédie-Française, and its rigorous curriculum of classical mythology, diction, history, and literature set the standard for the performance and interpretation of the classical repertoire. The great French tragedian (and Bonaparte's favourite) *Talma was a member of the first cohort. Other legendary graduates include Sarah *Bernhardt, María *Casares, and Paul-Émile Deiber. In 1946 the Conservatoire separated from the national conservatory of music to become a specialized drama institute, subsidized entirely by the French Ministry of Culture. Since each cohort is limited to about

Lyubov Popova's **constructivist** set for Meyerhold's production of Crommelynck's *The Magnanimous Cuckold* (1922), showing the vertiginous ramps and moving devices that provided the visual ground for biomechanical acting and a celebration of the power of the machine.

30 students, admission to the Conservatoire is highly selective, and potential candidates face a three-step *audition process before a jury of academics and theatre professionals. In 1994 the curriculum was divided into four distinct departments: history of theatre/theory and practice of language, music and voice, body and space, and cinema. The normal tuition is three years, culminating in public performances and workshops created by students in their final year.   CHB

CONSTRUCTIVISM

An artistic movement which flourished in Soviet Russia during the 1920s, and which sought to bring art into public spaces, linking its materials and processes with those of industrial production and construction. Centred on two institutes founded in *Moscow in 1920, the First Workers' Group of Constructivists included Aleksandr Rodchenko, Varvara *Stepanova, the Stenberg brothers, Aleksandr Vesnin, and Lyubov *Popova. In January 1921 the Group mounted two exhibitions attacking artistic aestheticism and declaring constructivism to be 'the shortest route to the factory'. First attempts to apply constructivist principles in the theatre were made at *Tairov's Kamerny Theatre by the designer Aleksandra *Ekster, with her sets of varying levels for Innokenty *Annensky's *Thamira Kitharides* (1916), *Wilde's *Salome* (1917), and Shakespeare's *Romeo and Juliet* (1921). Vesnin produced an abstract setting of cubist-style

levels for *Racine's *Phèdre* in 1922, and a gantry-style construction with working elevators for *The Man Who Was Thursday* (1926), both at the Kamerny, where the Stenberg brothers also produced constructivist settings for *Ostrovsky's *The Thunderstorm* (1924) and *O'Neill's *Desire under the Elms* (1926).

Meanwhile Vladimir Dmitriev designed a setting of geometrical components for *Meyerhold's production of Verhaeren's *Dawns*, in 1920, and Popova built an 'acting machine' for Meyerhold's famous 1922 production of *The Magnanimous Cuckold*, whose moving parts also exploited the kinetic properties of constructivist work in the manner of Vladimir Tatlin. Another exponent was El Lissitsky, whose tiered theatre-in-the-round structure (*see* ARENA AND IN-THE-ROUND) for Meyerhold's unrealized production of *Tretyakov's *I Want a Baby* in the late 1920s has become a museum exhibit. At the Theatre of the Revolution Viktor Shestakov created a spiral staircase and walkway for Meyerhold's version of Ostrovsky's *A Lucrative Post* (1922) as well as an 'urbanist' construction of moving walkways and working lifts for a production of *Faiko's *Lake Lyul*. At his own theatre, Meyerhold designed a constructivist setting for his production of Ostrovsky's *The Forest*, the principles of which were also applied to the *text, which was taken apart and reassembled in 33 segments like machine components. Rodchenko produced a constructivist setting for *Mayakovsky's *satire *The Bedbug*, staged by Meyerhold in 1929, while his *The Bathhouse*, again in a production by

Meyerhold the following year, had a design by Sergei Vakhtangov for the final scene that was somewhat reminiscent of Tatlin's unrealized Monument to the Third International. By that time constructivist practice was under official attack and was soon supplanted by more orthodox forms of staging. *See also* SCENOGRAPHY   NW

CONTAT, LOUISE-FRANÇOISE (1760–1813) AND MARIE-ÉMILIE (1771–1846)

French actresses. Louise, Mlle Contat the elder, made her debut at the *Comédie-Française in 1776 and quickly made her mark in high *comedy: her nickname was 'Thalie' (the Muse of Comedy). Although notable in *Molière, as Célimène (*The Misanthrope*) and Elmire (*Tartuffe*), she achieved celebrity status as the original Suzanne in *Beaumarchais's *The Marriage of Figaro* in 1784. Later that year, at *Figaro*'s 51st performance, 13-year-old Émilie ('Mimi') joined the cast, as Fanchette. Mimi was formally admitted to the Comédie in 1785. Self-effacingly content to see her elder sister graduate from Beaumarchais to *Marivaux, Mimi remained for 32 years playing *soubrettes. For their royalist sympathies—not only was Louise an intimate of Marie Antoinette, but one of her lovers (and possibly father of her daughter) was Louis XVI's brother the Comte d'Artois— the sisters were imprisoned in 1793. Narrowly escaping the guillotine, they rejoined the reconstituted Comédie-Française in 1799, Louise retiring in 1813 and Mimi two years later.

JG

COOK, MICHAEL (1933–94)

Canadian playwright and critic. Born in *London, Cook emigrated to St John's, Newfoundland, in 1965 to teach at Memorial University where he remained until 1993, at various times also actor, director, adjudicator, theatre and *film critic for the *St John's Evening Telegram*, and, in general, the impetus for the vibrant theatrical culture within Newfoundland in the 1980s and 1990s. While *artistic director of the St John's Festival of the Arts (1970–7), he developed his skill as a playwright and later wrote over 50 popular *radio dramas. Cook's finest works, dealing with Newfoundland's past—*Colour the Flesh the Colour of Dust* (1972), *On the Rim of the Curve* (1977), and *The Gayden Chronicles* (1977)—and its present—*The Head, Guts and Sound Bone Dance* (1974), *Quiller* (1975), *Jacob's Wake* (1975), and *Therese's Creed* (1976)—have also been staged in Germany, Mexico, Poland, Sweden, Switzerland, and the United States. Although playwright-in-residence at the Banff Playwright's Colony (1977) and at the *Stratford Festival (1987), the later plays were not produced during his lifetime.   PBON

COOKE, GEORGE FREDERICK (1756–1812)

English actor, one of the most exciting performers of the *romantic era. Unlike his more famous colleague John Philip *Kemble, Cooke eschewed stateliness and dignity in favour of energy and the powerful expression of malice and duplicity. He was most famous for his *villains, including Richard III, Shylock, and Pierre in *Otway's *Venice Preserv'd*, a role he altered into calculating hypocrite. Even in *comedy he excelled in roles like the combative Sir Pertinax MacSycophant in *The Man of the World* and Sir Archy MacSarcasm in *Love à la Mode*, both by Charles *Macklin. Like Macklin, Cooke favoured a natural style of acting in which he entered into the psychological life of the *character. The apparent ease with which he assumed the whole character belied painstaking research and *rehearsal, as his extant promptbooks show. Cooke's success in *London was great but relatively short-lived. He was known as the 'Manchester *Roscius' and spent the first half of his career mostly on the provincial stage. He began regular London engagements at *Covent Garden in 1800, earning £6 per week, a salary that more than doubled in just two years. A lifelong battle with alcoholism began to affect his work and alienate *audiences. He became the first major British actor to perform in the United States, opening in *New York in 1810. His drinking problem and health worsened, however, and he died in New York two years later, almost certainly from cirrhosis of the liver.

MJK

COOKE, T. P. (THOMAS POTTER) (1786–1864)

English actor. The *hero of *nautical melodramas, and the archetypal British tar, Cooke's most famous roles were those of Long Tom Coffin in *Fitzball's *The Pilot* (1825) and William in *Jerrold's *Black-Ey'd Susan* (1829). As Harry Hallyard in J. T. Haines's *My Poll and my Partner Joe* (1835) he played a Thames waterman in the first act and, after being press-ganged into the navy, a heroic sailor on HMS *Polyphemus*, where he danced a double hornpipe, fought the captain of a slave ship, was heartbroken when he came home, and then made happy again. He took his nautical type *casting very seriously, and frequently went into society in *costume, or at least wearing a naval medal. In a conversation with the Prime Minister, Lord Aberdeen, he was energetic in his opinions about reforms in the navy and suggested, 'If your Lordship likes to see what a real tar was, and what a real tar ought to be, come across the water some night . . . and see me as William in *Black-eyed Susan*'.   AF

COOPER, GILES (1918–66)

Dramatist. Born in *Dublin, Cooper served in the army before becoming a professional actor. His adaptations of the *Maigret* stories for *television won the Writer of the Year *award in

1961; thereafter he wrote 70 original plays for *radio, television, and the theatre. *Everything in the Garden* (1962) was his most successful stage play, but his best work was for radio, with plays like *Unwin, Wittering and Zigo*. He had a facility for unusual *dialogue, 'astringent, sardonic and pared to the bone', and for constructing *plots with unexpected *denouements. Some saw his plays as nihilistic. According to Donald McWhinnie, 'Cooper's fantasies work because they are securely anchored in reality, unlikely though that may seem at first glance; his plainer tales fascinate because they reveal the odd, the eccentric potential of what is seemingly straightforward.' A pioneer of electronic sound effects in radio, six of his radio plays were published by the BBC in 1966.   JTD

COOPER, THOMAS A. (1776–1849)

English-born American actor and *manager. Raised in his cousin William Godwin's circle, Cooper committed to a theatrical career early, *touring with Stephen *Kemble and learning his craft in the provinces before his auspicious 1795 *London debut. Emigrating the next year, Cooper became the pre-eminent actor on the American stage. Touring indefatigably from *New York to New Orleans, Cooper introduced his American *audiences to the formal, declamatory Kemble style. Specializing in dramatic roles such as Macbeth, Hamlet, and Pierre in *Otway's *Venice Preserv'd*, Cooper's handsome good looks made him an audience favourite until he left the stage in 1840.
                                                          GAR

COOPER, TOMMY (1922–84)

Welsh comedian, one of the most popular performers of the final days of the *variety stage in Britain. Cooper's act was a mixture of comic one-liners and *magic, predicated on a façade of apparent incompetence. He teased his *audience with the pretence that he did not know what he had to do next and that his conjuring would go wrong: *props or effects would take on a life of their own, events would spiral towards chaos, and yet somehow the trick would always turn out right. His first *television series, *Life with Cooper*, began in 1957. He continued to parallel appearances on stage and television throughout his life, a regular on *Saturday Showtime* and *Sunday Night at the London Palladium*. His trademark fez was a feature of his stage persona derived from entertaining troops during his war service in Egypt. He died while performing.   AS

COPEAU, JACQUES (1879–1949)

French director, *manager, critic, and man of letters, often considered as the father of modern French theatre. He began his career as author and critic and was co-founder in 1908—along with his friend André *Gide and others—of the influential

Nouvelle Revue française. In 1913 he set up his own company, the Théâtre du *Vieux-Colombier on the Left Bank in *Paris. His primary aim was the renovation of theatre through a rejection of both the spectacular and the *naturalistic, through a focus on a trinity of values: 'the beautiful, the good, and the true'. His reformation required a new actor-centred method with the long-term goal of creating a body of dramatic literature, since the reforms of the end of the nineteenth century carried out by *Antoine, amongst others, had left few plays of lasting merit. But first the company focused on Shakespeare and the French classics. Copeau also set up a model for linking *training to practice through a school connected to his theatre, which wished to broaden *acting beyond mere technique and included study in *masking, gymnastics, and general culture. This model was adopted by directors throughout the twentieth century from Charles *Dullin to Ariane *Mnouchkine, who both acknowledged Copeau's influence.

During the First World War the company decamped to the Garrick Theatre in *New York, bringing its most notable success of the first season, Shakespeare's *Twelfth Night*. Upon return to Paris in 1920 they played again in the Vieux-Colombier, now remodelled to resemble an Elizabethan *playhouse, and designed to purify the theatre in an architectural 'bare boards' approach in which *costume and *lighting were the principal signifiers: little was to impede the work of the actor and the *text. In 1924 a personal crisis—both an illness and a sense of isolation—led Copeau to decamp once again, this time to the Burgundian village of Pernand-Vergelesses, where he and his actors farmed for their sustenance while recouping their artistic and intellectual strength. From their country base during the period between 1925 and 1929, Les Copiaux (as the disciples were known) *toured nationally and internationally to great acclaim, continuing to pursue the aim of artistic purity. Thereafter when Copeau withdrew once more, his disciples continued the same mission under the name of La Compagnie des Quinze (*see* SAINT-DENIS, MICHEL). His subsequent career was mixed and included lectures, a brief spell at the helm of the *Comédie-Française (1940–1), and the publication of his highly influential essay *Le Théâtre populaire* (1941), which provided the *theoretical template for the decentralization movement after the Second World War. Copeau's own move to Burgundy with an internationally successful company had been the prototypical act of decentralization. This 'scenic poet', as his most famous pupil, Louis *Jouvet, once described him, became the icon of truthfulness in performance, and is remembered as a visionary.
                                                          BRS

COPI (RAÚL DAMONTE) (1939–87)

Argentinian playwright, performer, and director. After staging his first play in *Buenos Aires, Copi moved to *Paris in 1962. Known for his irreverent *Le Nouvel Observateur* cartoon strips,

'Montmartre's transvestite' wrote and performed in France, Italy, and Spain. Copi's dozen plays (including his solos, *Loretta Strong* and *The Refrigerator*) take place in a hyperreal space. Their exuberant value inversions were especially amplified by fellow Argentinian expatriate Jorge *Lavelli, who directed five works, including *The Homosexual; or, The Difficulty of (S)expressing Oneself* (1971), *The Four Twins* (1973), and *An Inopportune Visit* (1987). The première of *Eva Perón* (1970) encountered violent response when right-wing Peronist sympathizers attacked cast members, including the male actor playing Evita, outside L'Épée-de-Bois theatre. Although several of Copi's plays have recently been produced in Buenos Aires, *Eva Perón* remains unstaged in its author's native country.　　　　JGJ

COPPIN, GEORGE SELTH (1819–1906)

English-born *actor-manager, at one time regarded as the 'father of Australian theatre'. A son of strolling players, Coppin performed in Britain and Ireland, then in 1842 travelled to Australia with his first wife Maria Watkins Burroughs (1810–48), performing in *Sydney, Hobart, Launceston, Adelaide, and *Melbourne. From 1855, Coppin was a Melbourne public figure as both a theatrical entrepreneur and politician. His policy of importing star actors and lavish productions from Britain and America, including Gustavus Brooke, Charles *Kean, and J. C. *Williamson, remained the dominant practice of Australian theatre until after the Second World War.　　　　KMN

COPYRIGHT

The exclusive legal right to prevent others from reproducing the creations of visual artists, authors, composers, choreographers, *playwrights, *film directors, broadcasters, and recording studios. The right protects literary and artistic expressions as embodied in cultural, entertainment, and informational productions.

1. What copyright protects
2. The scope and duration of copyright protection
3. The formalities of protection and publication

1. What copyright protects

A copyright gives its owner a government-granted monopoly over the copying and performing of protected works. These works may include original creations from a statutory list of forms, regardless of the artistic merit of any particular work. Originality is the fundamental requirement for copyright protection. Thus, different artists, using the same or different mediums of expression, may recast the basic story of Ulysses or of the Nutcracker. Each variation may receive separate copyright protection. Each work does not infringe upon the rights embodied in other works on the same theme, provided that the creator of a particular variant copied only the idea of the story and not another artist's means of expressing that story. This is because copyright protects the original expression of ideas, not the ideas themselves. Though copyright protection is much the same the world over, attention should be given to national variations that may have the effect of increasing or decreasing protection and, inversely, liability in certain circumstances.

The history of dramatic copyright can be traced to ancient *Greece and the *Roman Empire, where writers were outspoken in their concern for receiving credit as the creators of their works. Over the centuries that followed, the emphasis for protection gradually shifted from the artistic or moral interests of creators to the economic interests of those who had invested in the commercialization of a work, aided to a great degree by the invention of the printing press (*see* PUBLISHING OF PLAYS). The commercial interests of publishers first received legal protection under the laws of England in 1534, which later adopted the first copyright statute, the Copyright Act of 1710. Early copyright statutes only protected literary works, but legal protection for the commercial interests in artistic works was firmly established as a general legal principle by the time of the founding of the United States, which expressly acknowledged in its Constitution protection for 'writings', a term that has been expanded to include 'any physical rendering of the fruits of creative, intellectual or aesthetic labour'. The first international treaty seeking to guarantee the rights of authors, the Berne Convention, came into effect after 1886.

Copyright protection has followed the technology by which artistic creations are disseminated to the public. For example, publishers' economic interests were protected after the printing press made the large-scale production of written works possible. By the early nineteenth century, when play scripts and sheet music were being printed for sale to the public in Europe, playwrights and composers were given a 'use' right to control and receive royalties upon each public performance of their works. In the later half of the century—after the invention of photography—paintings, drawings, and photographs themselves were protected by copyright.

In order to be protected, a work must be fixed in some permanent form. A creative work that requires movement, such as a *dance, could not be fixed by a printed illustration or even by still photography. Thus, it was not until after the advent of motion pictures and dance notation in the twentieth century that copyright protection was extended to choreographic works. The same relationship exists between developments in technology and the protection of other elements of theatrical productions, independent of any protection that may exist in an underlying script, lyrics, or music.

Dramatic works, such as a *playwright's script or the written scenario for a *film, must incorporate movement, a story, or action to be included under this category of copyright protection. Thus, a single photograph of a group of performers, which might convey a sense of dramatic effect and which might be protected as part of some other category, is not a dramatic work because it is static. However, a sequence of photographs—if the relevant movement, story, or action can be deduced from the sequence—may qualify as a dramatic work. Like literary works, dramatic works must be original in their expression in order for copyright protection to apply. Unlike literary works, dramatic works must also be capable of being physically performed, a qualification that would exclude an unadapted novel, but which would include a screenplay based on the same novel. Under some national copyright laws, like those of the United Kingdom, dramatic works include those of *dance or *mime. Under other copyright systems, dance is placed in a separate category of copyright protection.

Choreography is the composition of movement in time and space, though the term is not defined in any copyright statute. Until the later half of the twentieth century, choreographed works of pure dance were not protected by copyright. The closest the copyright laws came to protecting choreography was as part of a larger dramatico-musical work, such as the various versions of the *ballet *Swan Lake*, in which the choreography is used to tell a story. Where the choreography was not subordinate to narrative, no copyright protection would apply, though that protection would be available for other components of a performance. For example, in the original stage production of the *musical *Oklahoma!* (1943), Richard *Rodgers's lyrics and Oscar *Hammerstein's music were copyright protectable, but Agnes *de Mille's choreography was not. Amendments to most national copyright statutes and to international treaties now provide choreography with the same protection as literary and dramatic works. Where copyright-protected choreography is set to music, the music is not covered by the same copyright as that in the choreography.

Musical compositions are protected by copyright at both a primary and secondary level. A primary copyright protects a musical creation but not any words, actions, or dance intended to be performed with it. Thus, music composed by Andrew *Lloyd Webber receives copyright protection separate from that of the lyrics written by Tim *Rice, even though the music and the lyrics were intended to be performed together. This is a particularly important point where the *licensing of rights to a musical production is concerned. A licence to perform one aspect of a production, such as the music, does not necessarily extend the right to perform other, independently protected aspects, such as to sing the lyrics or to reproduce the *costumes usually associated with the music or with the performance as a whole. Secondary protection of musical works provides independent copyright for new arrangements of pre-existing compositions, orchestrations, reductions, and the like.

Apart from the categories described above, any original graphic work, photograph, sculpture, collage, architectural work, or work of 'artistic craftsmanship' may be protected by copyright as an artistic work if the creation exhibits a minimum of skill, judgement, and labour, irrespective of the work's artistic quality. Thus a child's finger painting is as potentially protectable as a painting by Jackson Pollock. In the context of theatrical productions, artistic copyrights might apply to backdrops painted by Pablo *Picasso or to *playbill covers painted by Marc Chagall. It should be noted that a photograph of a performance has separate copyright protection from any that may apply to the performance itself. So long as others could not copy the subject of the performance from the photograph alone, the photograph does not infringe any performance-based copyright. This would not be the case where a film is made of a performance. Because the film would be a reproduction of the performance, itself making further reproductions possible, it is capable of infringing the rights embodied in a performance and different rules apply.

Cinematographic film represents the first of the technology-driven variations on copyright protection. The copyright in a film has always been considered distinct from any copyright that might exist in the material portrayed in the film, but until the 1990s the original copyright owner in a film, its 'author' in the context of a dramatic work, was considered to be the film's producer, as representative of the financial and administrative interests involved in film production, rather than the director of the film, the person with artistic control. Now the original copyright protection in a film is shared equally by its producers and directors, a compromise between commercial and artistic considerations. Further to the extreme but of increasing importance are computer-generated works for which there is no immediately identifiable human creator. In such cases, the 'author' is the computer programmer or some other person responsible for making the arrangements that were necessary to induce the computer to perform the creative function.

Broadcasts, cable-casts, and sound recordings are also capable of distinct copyright protection, though that protection is reduced in scope and term in comparison with a comparable live performance. Broadcasts are considered to be by wireless means, such as a radio broadcast of an orchestral performance. Cable-casts are their cable-based counterparts, usually of visual images with accompanying sound. Sound recordings themselves receive specialized copyright protection. A recording of any live sound, without regard to artistic content, is protected by copyright, but the usual ability of a copyright owner to control the public performance of their works does not apply to sound recordings.

2. The scope and duration of copyright protection

Copyright gives a limited amount of protection for a limited amount of time against those who would exploit creative works without the permission of the creator. That protection comes in the form of the legal right to control the reproduction, distribution, first sale, and public performance of a work. For example, copyright ownership allows playwrights to control the copying of their scripts. It also gives film producers or directors the right to control the sales of videotaped copies of their films, and it allows composers to control the public performance of their musical compositions.

This assumes that the creator of a work—the painter, the sculptor, the playwright, the composer—is the owner of the copyright. In most cases, the creator of the underlying work and the owner of the copyright protecting that work, at least at the moment of creation, are the same person. An exception to this rule occurs under limited circumstances when an artist creates something that is intended to be included in a larger work. For example, a photographer might be hired to create illustrations for a book or a painter might be hired to produce specific matt paintings for a film. In such cases, and if the contract commissioning the creation so specifies, the creation will be considered 'a work for hire' and the person commissioning the photograph or painting would automatically be the first copyright owner. This is the usual case, for example, with film scriptwriters, who have been employed by the producers and thus do not own the copyright to their work.

The unauthorized use of another's protected creation is an infringement of the copyright in that creation. Infringement may be of a primary or of a secondary nature. Primary infringement is the unauthorized reproduction, in whole or in part, of the work of another. This misappropriation must be substantial in order for it to be legally actionable. Disputes have raged for years as to what amounts to a substantial taking of someone else's copyright-protected material. For example, a single chord of music is not a substantial part of a musical work. However, four chords together, if widely known and identified with a particular musical composition, such as the opening four chords of Beethoven's Fifth Symphony, might be considered a substantial part of that composition. The prohibition against unauthorized reproduction of a protected work also includes a prohibition against unauthorized adaptations of that work, such as turning a novel into a play, an *opera into a ballet, or translating a work into another language.

Dealing in unauthorized copies of a protected work is a secondary infringement of the copyright in that work if the person doing the dealing knows or has reason to believe that the copies are themselves infringements. This includes any commercial activity that would otherwise be controlled by the copyright owner, such as selling, renting, distributing, or exhibiting the copy to the public. Thus, a person who sells an unauthorized copy of a protected videotape is the secondary infringer of the copyright applicable to that videotape. The primary infringer is the person who made the unauthorized copy. The secondary infringer does not have to know of the illegal status of the goods in order to infringe copyright. All that is required in law is a showing that the secondary infringer knew sufficient facts about the goods to call into question their status.

In some countries, dealing in infringing copies of a protected work is a violation of criminal law and subject to fines and imprisonment.

In addition to protection against unauthorized copying, the copyright in a work allows its owner to control the public performance of the work. The performance rights, inherent in copyright protection, include the broadcasting, cable-casting, live performance, and the playing of a recorded performance of a protected work. Like infringement through copying, the infringement of performance rights may be divided into primary and secondary infringements. Unlike copying, the legal nature of performance-based infringements is highly dependent upon the circumstances and technologies involved, because copyright protection does not cover all of the possible uses for an otherwise-protected work.

As has been noted, musical works are subject to copyright protection. The private performance of such a work is not an infringement of the copyright laws. A public performance of the work would be an infringement if done without the permission of the owner of the copyright in the music. Further, if the public performance were to be recorded, the person doing the recording would infringe both the copyright in the music and the rights in the performance of the music unless done with the permission of both the copyright owner and the performer. If the recorded performance were to be broadcast, the person doing the broadcasting would infringe the copyright in the recording unless the broadcaster had the appropriate permission. If the broadcasted, recorded version of a live performance of copyright protected music were to be played to the public, that playing might infringe the copyright in the underlying music, possibly in the broadcast, but not in the recording. In a similar, equally complicated way, copyrights protect the live or recorded performances of dramatic works.

The secondary infringement of the performance-rights aspect of copyright protection amounts to actions enabling a primary infringement to occur. For example, the owner or *manager of a theatre secondarily infringes the copyright in a dramatic or musical work if they permit the theatre to be used for a primarily infringing performance. The standard for judging what the defendent theatre owner knew or has reason to suspect about the facts of the performance is the same as that applicable to secondary infringement in respect of copies.

There are exceptional uses of copyright-protected material that are not infringements when done without the permission of the copyright owner. A limited number of copies may be made of copyrighted works if those copies are to be used for private study, for instruction, examination, or performance in schools, or for inclusion in the collections of some libraries and archives. Thus, a short passage from a protected screenplay could be copied as part of a performing arts examination. Other exceptions exist, enumerated in the copyright statutes of various countries, for news reporting, use in a *criticism or review of the protected work, copies made under licence from a collective-licensing authority, retransmission by cable-cast of a broadcast, the free public showing of a broadcasted or cable-cast perform-ance, recordings made of a broadcast or cable-cast where the copy is intended for private viewing at a later time, and similar, limited uses.

The copyright protection for new films, literary, artistic, dramatic, and musical works lasts for all of the creator's life and for an additional 70 years in most countries. This is an increase from a term of protection that existed throughout most of the twentieth century of 50 years after the life of the creator. If a work is published anonymously, then the term of protection will be 70 years from the date of creation or, if unknown, the date of first publication. Where more than one creator is re-sponsible for a protected work, the posthumous period begins to run from the death of the last-lived creator. Sound recordings, broadcasts, and cable-casts are protected for 50 years from the making of the recording or its first release or from the date of first transmission. Once the period of copyright protection ends, a work becomes part of the public domain, the cultural resource of society, and may be copied or performed by anyone, as is the case with the novels of *Dickens, the paintings of Caravaggio, and the plays of Shakespeare.

3. Formalities of protection and publication

Under the laws of many countries, particularly those that are signatories of the Berne Convention, copyright protection arises automatically. A creator does not have to complete any formal registration or application requirements before the protection applies to the work. In all countries that have some form of copyright protection, especially those that subscribe to the Uni-versal Copyright Convention, the marking of a published work with the symbol ©, the name of the creator, and the year the work was first published is sufficient to claim copyright protec-tion. Many nations also provide a statutory scheme whereby creators can register their works through depositing a copy in a copyright depository, such as the British Library or the Library of Congress.

Because copyright protects the expression of ideas, as op-posed to ideas themselves, it cannot apply until a work is fixed in a permanent form. The mind of a creator or the memory of performers is not a permanent form. The reasons for this quali-fication are to make works available to society in a reproducible manner and to protect the works themselves from being lost, as was the case with Nijinsky's *Rite of Spring*, a great choreo-graphic work that was never recorded and which died with its creator.

The date of publication is important for determining when the term of copyright protection starts for some types of works. Publication is the act of making authorized copies of a work available by sale, hire, or gift to the public in commercial quan-tities. This includes electronic reproductions in computer data-bases that are accessible to the public. Publication in most countries does not include a performance, broadcast, or cable-cast, nor does it include the distribution of unauthorized copies.

In a commercial sense, the copyright in a work is a collec-tion of divisible rights, each capable of being independently exploited. These fractional rights include the right to publish the work as a whole, to publish it in parts (serialization), to publish the whole or parts in a translation, the film rights, the performance rights in a dramatic work, the right to drama-tize a non-dramatic work, and the right to exploit electronic versions. The copyright owner may exploit each of these rights or all of them together, or, more commonly, the owner may confer them on others, either permanently or for a limited time. A licence of copyright is an agreement in which the copy-right owner gives the licensee permission to exploit some or all of the rights of the owner for a limited time, usually in return for a fee. That fee may be in the form of a single payment or of a portion of the income resulting from the exploitation of the rights, called *royalties. While most licences are in writing, the verbal permission of the copyright owner is effective to extend a licence. An assignment of copyright is a permanent sale of some or all of the rights of the copyright owner. Under most national laws, assignments are only effective if they are in writing. As with other aspects of copyright law, care should be paid to local variation in both the substance of the law and its procedures.   TEH

CORNISH, W. R., *Intellectual Property: patents, copyright, trade marks and allied rights* (London, 1999)

LADDIE, HUGH, PRESCOTT, PETER, and VITORIA, MARY, *Laddie, Prescott and Vitoria: the modern law of copyright and designs* (London, 2000)

NIMMER, MELVILLE, and NIMMER, DAVID, *Nimmer on Copyright* (New York, 1963–)

COQUELIN, CONSTANT-BENOÎT (1841–1909)

French actor. Having trained at the *Paris *Conservatoire, Coquelin made his debut at the *Comédie-Française in 1860, and became a *sociétaire* in 1864, having given an impressive performance as *Beaumarchais's Figaro in 1861. He soon be-came a leading member of the company, not only performing a wide range of *jeune premier* roles in the classical *comedy rep-ertoire, but also creating a number of roles in contemporary plays by *Dumas *fils*, *Augier, and others. The desire to break out of the traditional repertoire at the Comédie, and also to have the freedom to undertake foreign *tours, led him to resign in 1886; and although he returned briefly, he broke permanently with the Comédie-Française in 1892 in order to appear inde-pendently at the *Porte-Saint-Martin. Here he continued to play in a mixed repertoire of classical and modern plays, the peak of his career being the creation of the title role in *Rostand's

Cyrano de Bergerac (1897), a part written for Coquelin, who had praised the playwright's *Princesse lointaine* two years earlier. *Cyrano* was to prove the most successful French play of the century, and Coquelin played the part over 400 times. He was to have performed in Rostand's *Chantecler* (1910) but died of a heart attack during a *rehearsal. Coquelin was the author of two important books on the art of *acting: *L'Art et le comédien* (*The Art of the Actor*, 1880) and *Les Comédiens par un comédien* (*Actors by an Actor*, 1882). His younger brother Ernest (known as Coquelin *cadet*) was also an actor.

WDH

CORNEILLE, PIERRE (1606–84)

French playwright. Born in Normandy and trained as a lawyer, the elder Corneille was the most prolific and versatile of France's major seventeenth-century dramatists. Introduced to the theatre by *Montdory's itinerant company at Rouen, he saw his first play *Mélite*, a *comedy, played with success in *Paris by Montdory in 1629. His *tragicomedy *Clitandre* (1631), a relative failure, was followed by four comedies, including *La Galerie du palais* (1632) and *La Place royale* (1633). Performed by Montdory at the *Marais, these illustrated the *comedy of manners inaugurated by *Mélite*, which Corneille himself later defined as 'the portrayal of social intercourse among persons of good breeding'. This series was followed by his first *tragedy, *Médée* (1635), in which Corneille succeeded in making a sympathetic *heroine of the legendary sorceress Medea. Another sorcerer, Alcandre, presides as surrogate playwright over the comedy *L'Illusion comique* (*The Theatrical Illusion*, 1636, described by its author as a 'strange freak of nature'), helping the hero Clindor, played by Montdory, to demonstrate that an acting career is not a source of shame to his bourgeois family, but of fame and glory. This imaginative work, which illustrates the range of current theatrical styles, regained favour in the twentieth century after lengthy neglect, and now ranks as one of Corneille's most stageworthy plays.

It was followed by the tragicomedy *Le Cid* (1637), deservedly the author's most celebrated. Outstanding among the works of the talented playwrights of the 1630s, it presents the young Spanish hero Rodrigue, who triumphs over the Moors, but is forced to fight a duel in which he kills his beloved Chimène's father, who has insulted his own father. The first version ended happily, implying that Rodrigue will go off to win more victories and return to marry Chimène after a decent interval; however, changes in 1660 (by which time the play was labelled *tragédie*) imply just as strongly that Chimène, despite her love for Rodrigue, will persist in refusing to marry her father's killer. *Le Cid* stands at the very centre of the mid-century debate about *genre (*see* NEOCLASSICISM; UNITIES; DECORUM). The 'quarrel of *Le Cid*' of 1637–40, while it did raise points of critical and theoretical interest, was largely an attack

by vain and envious rivals, fuelled in part by Corneille's own oversensitive pride; Corneille himself had been recruited into the group of five playwrights who were commissioned to further the literary ambitions of *Richelieu but soon left, and the Cardinal's animosity may well have inspired some of the hostile criticism of *Le Cid*. By 1660, however, Corneille's position was much more assured: he had established his reputation as the author of a series of 'Roman' tragedies, notably *Horace* (1640), *Cinna* (1641), *Polyeucte* (1642), *La Mort de Pompée* (1643), and *Nicomède* (1651); and he had been elected to the Académie Française in 1647. A break from the theatre between 1652 and 1659 was largely devoted to writing commentaries on his earlier plays, accompanied by three treatises on the theatre: the *Discours du poème dramatique*, *De la tragédie*, and *Des trois unités*. In part these constitute a further reply to criticism of *Le Cid*, in part a defence of his practice against d' *Aubignac, whose *Pratique du théâtre* had appeared in 1657; but they also offer a positive formulation of his often idiosyncratic ideas about tragic *catharsis, namely that *admiration* is a valid alternative to the *Aristotelian pity and fear. Already illustrated in plays like *Cinna*, *La Mort de Pompée*, and *Nicomède* (as well as contributing to the complex of tragic emotions aroused by the death of the Christian martyr in *Polyeucte*), this notion is central to Corneille's somewhat paradoxical penchant for what he called 'la tragédie heureuse': that is, tragedy with a happy ending.

After *Le Menteur* (1643), judged by many to be his most important comedy, and its inferior sequel of 1645, Corneille wrote no more comedies; however, in 1671 he turned to the spectacle-play, collaborating with *Molière in the 'tragédie-ballet' *Psyché* at the redesigned *Palais Royal. In his last years he was increasingly in competition with *Racine, their rivalry coming to a head in 1670 with simultaneous productions of Corneille's *Tite et Bérénice* at the Palais-Royal and Racine's *Bérénice* at the *Hôtel de Bourgogne. While fashionable opinion favoured Racine, Corneille maintained a following among an older generation of spectators. In his last play, the tragedy *Suréna* (1674)—a neglected masterpiece—the hero's achievements are overshadowed by his resigned acceptance of death.

Throughout the eighteenth century, Corneille maintained his position alongside Racine as representing the outstanding achievement of seventeenth-century tragic theatre, with the acting profession, the theatregoing public, and playwrights like *Voltaire who continued to imitate Corneille's manner. In the nineteenth century, Corneille was championed as a 'reluctant' neoclassical dramatist, temperamentally closer to *Hugo and the other romantics than his rival Racine. More recently, while the *Comédie-Française continues to honour him by mounting an occasional production of *Horace*, *Polyeucte*, or *Nicomède*, much of his work has been mothballed, and enthusiasm tends to be reserved for the 'pre-classical' Corneille. Gérard *Philipe's revival of *Le Cid* at the *Avignon Festival (1951) and Georges Wilson's *Illusion comique* at the *Théâtre National Populaire

(1965) provided two of the outstanding theatrical events of the early post-war period. WDH

BARNWELL, H. T., *The Tragic Drama of Corneille and Racine* (Oxford, 1982)

CLARKE, D. R., *Pierre Corneille: politics and political drama under Louis XIII* (Cambridge, 1992)

HOWARTH, W. D., *Corneille: Le Cid* (London, 1988)

CORNEILLE, THOMAS (1625–1709)

French playwright. The younger brother of Pierre *Corneille, Thomas studied law but turned to the stage in his early twenties. Between 1647 and 1681 he wrote, alone or in collaboration, 46 plays, including four machine-plays (*see* SALLE DES MACHINES) and four *operas. Appointed co-editor with Donneau de *Visé of the periodical *Le Mercure galant* in 1681, and elected in place of Pierre to the Académie Française in 1684, Thomas devoted the remainder of his long life to work as a journalist, translator, and encyclopedist. As a dramatist, he was a follower rather than a setter of fashion, and although he achieved considerable contemporary success, few of his plays escape their historical moment. His most successful play, *Timocrate* (1656), reflected a current vogue for 'romanesque *tragedy', characterized by complex *plots involving *disguise and mistaken identity, and featuring gallant lovers in exotic settings. Later plays of note include *Ariane* (1672), *Le Comte d'Essex* (1678), and *Laodice* (1668). RWV

CORNELL, KATHARINE (1898–1974)

American actress and producer. Known for the dignity, intelligence, and articulation that she brought to her roles, Cornell shared with Helen *Hayes the title 'First Lady of the American Theatre'. Making her debut with the *Washington Square Players in 1916, she played a series of roles in *stock, and emerged as a leading player with a 1919 *London production of *Little Women*. In 1921 she married Guthrie *McClintic, who directed her productions after 1925. She starred in *Shaw's *Candida* in *New York in 1924, a role so well suited that she revived it three times. Her breakthrough to Broadway commercial success was in *The Green Hat*, a 1925 *melodrama directed by McClintic. Elizabeth Barrett in *The Barretts of Wimpole Street* (1931) proved a defining role, revived four times. Critics saw her finest performances in serious work with McClintic: Juliet (1934), Shaw's St Joan (1936), Masha in *Chekhov's *Three Sisters* (1942), Antigone (1946), and Cleopatra (1947). Cornell last appeared as Mrs Patrick *Campbell in *Dear Liar* (1959–60). MAF

CORNISH ROUNDS

*Medieval theatre in Cornwall was performed in 'the round'— the *action took place in an open round space surrounded by several *sedes* (scaffolds or *mansions) representing the location of specific scenes. For example, the stage diagram for the first day of the *Ordinalia* specifies the *sedes* (clockwise from the east) as *Heaven, Bishop, Abraham, Solomon, David, Pharaoh, *Hell (in the north), and Torturers. For the episodes performed on the next two days all but the *sedes* for Heaven and Hell changed according to the requirements of the script. Unlike wagon staging, this convention had the effect of keeping the cosmic struggle between Heaven and Hell constantly before the *audience who sat around the periphery of the *platea* or 'place', a formation similar to the stage design for the fifteenth-century *morality play from East Anglia, *The Castle of Perseverance*. The round structure with a castle in the centre seems to have been created for *Castle* whenever it was performed, but the Cornish practitioners used earthworks, sometimes pre-existing, sometimes custom built, to create *open-air amphitheatres. Two such rounds survive (known in Cornish as *plen an gwary*), measuring between 37 and 49 m (120–40 feet) in diameter, one at St-Just-in-Penwith and the other (the Perran Round) near Perranporth north-west of Truro. The Perran Round is an extraordinary space that despite its size maintains a sense of intimacy and remarkable acoustics. AFJ

CORPORACIÓN COLOMBIANA DE TEATRO

Colombian theatre association, created in 1969 to rally the Nuevo Teatro (New Theatre) movement after the authorities expelled Enrique *Buenaventura and four other Teatro *Experimental de Cali members from the Departmental Theatre School. From 35 groups affiliated in the 1970s, it reached 90 in the 1980s, and it was still very active at the start of the millennium. Now under the leadership of Patricia *Ariza, the Corporación has carried an impressive programme over the years, including several National Theatre Festivals (1975–89), playwriting contests, national *tours, seminars, and even multitudinous walks for peace. BJR

CORPUS CHRISTI PLAYS

The feast of Corpus Christi (body of Christ), which falls on the Thursday of the octave of Pentecost (between 21 May and 24 June), was established as part of late medieval eucharistic devotion. Though Pope Urban IV authorized the feast in 1264, it did not achieve universal acceptance in the Western Church until it was established by Pope Clement V in 1311. The oldest surviving *text of a Corpus Christi play, dated some time after 1360, comes from Orvieto in Italy and dramatizes a miracle of the host. The words 'The plaie called Corpus Christi' are written in a sixteenth-century hand at the beginning of the manuscript of the *N-Town Plays* from East Anglia. The manuscript contains plays covering all of salvation history from Creation to Dooms-day. The most complete records for any English civic drama come from York, where an episodic play dramatizing salvation history was performed in procession. Until the third quarter of the fifteenth century the play and the procession honouring the Real Presence of Christ both took place on the feast of Corpus Christi, which led some scholars of English drama to assume that all *biblical plays depicted salvation history and were performed on that day in procession.

V. A. Kolve's influential book *The Play Called Corpus Christi* (1964) reinforced the idea of a *'genre' of Corpus Christi plays. We now know that such a genre did not exist. The Records of Early English Drama project is demonstrating that, although Corpus Christi was frequently an occasion for dramatic presentations, the nature of the presentations varied widely. Plays performed were frequently episodic biblical plays but more commonly modelled not on salvation history but on the twelve clauses of the Apostles' Creed. A fourteenth-century Innsbruck *Fronleichnamsspiel* survives that combines aspects of a Creed play and a prophet play. The civic drama of Coventry performed on Corpus Christi had no Old Testament sequence and was called a Creed play in the sixteenth century. The Creed play at York substituted for the longer play on salvation history on Corpus Christi every ten years after 1455. All the surviving European texts and records of Creed plays are associated with this feast. The York salvation history play is the only text to survive in England that dramatizes the complete Creation, Redemption, and Judgement pattern that was performed on Corpus Christi day. Such complete sequences were commonly performed on Corpus Christi in the German-speaking countries, however, especially in the southern areas near the Swiss border. But smaller plays on other subjects were also performed on the feast day. For example, in Ashburton in Devon, the presentations varied from short biblical plays to one that involved God and 'St Rosmont'. In Bodmin (Cornwall) the play for the feast seems to have centred on the Passion, while in Bridgwater (Somerset) the play was the Nativity. A play on Corpus Christi is recorded from Perugia in 1450 on the theme of Theseus slaying the Minotaur.

A more universal practice on Corpus Christi was the presentation of intricate *tableaux vivants* as part of the procession honouring the eucharistic host. Elaborate processions with small dramas embedded in them took place in Bologna, Turin, and Toledo. In Britain several towns had processions with *pageants. Among the most elaborate was one at Hereford that had 23 separate scenes depicting biblical events followed by three apparently unrelated tableaux of Pilate, Annas, and Caiphas with Mahound; knights in harness; and St Catherine and her torturers. In Bristol the craft *guilds carried 'pageants' in the Corpus Christi procession, in *Dublin the procession included Arthur and his knights and the Nine Worthies, and the one in Lanark in Scotland included St George and the dragon.

Corpus Christi Day was one of the two favourite summer feast days occasioning various processions and playmaking. Pentecost or Whitsun (which is also a movable feast and falls eleven days before Corpus Christi) was the time for many parish and village festivals and of the processional play in Chester. In Florence, the feast day of St John the Baptist (24 June), the city's patron, was celebrated by a procession and a sequence of plays from the Old and New Testaments, which after 1428 did not include the *Passion. Two more secular feast days filled out the summer festive calendar, particularly in England: May Day and Midsummer. In northern Europe in the period between mid-May and the end of June—after planting and before harvest—the weather would allow outdoor playmaking and revelry. But it is misleading to single out the feast of Corpus Christi for special significance. Different towns and parishes chose different festivals to present their traditional plays and entertainments, and each must be considered a unique event. *See* MEDIEVAL THEATRE IN EUROPE. AFJ

CORRALES DE COMEDIAS

Public 'play yards' or *playhouses of *early modern Spain, also called *patios* or *casas de *comedias. Some 50 at least, and probably many more, were opened all over the country between about 1560 and 1680. Some were short-lived, others were re-built, but a number survived into the eighteenth century. The largest cities, *Madrid and Seville, had two (or three for limited periods). Valladolid possibly had a playhouse by 1560, Seville and Madrid probably before 1570 and certainly in 1574, Toledo from 1576, and at least twenty other cities by 1610. Most were founded by charitable brotherhoods or municipalities and the proceeds were generally used to subsidize hospitals (*see also* GUILDS). Relatively few were privately owned, though a number were leased and run by entrepreneurs. The largest held up to 2,000 people, possibly more. Typically the actors and the *management each collected a standard entrance charge, with further payments to the management for seating. The plays of Lope de *Vega, *Tirso de Molina, and *Calderón, among others, were normally first performed in one of the two Madrid *corrales*, and later in those of other cities and towns.

Unlike the English *public theatres, Spanish *corrales* were virtually never free-standing. Some were wholly purpose built but many exploited and incorporated existing structures. They were usually installed in yards within blocks of houses (as in Madrid), or occasionally in a hospital (Ávila, Guadalajara) or an inn (*Almagro), often near the town centre, with entry through buildings adjoining the yard, which sometimes provided viewing spaces on upper floors. A number, especially after 1600, were built to a coherent, sometimes sophisticated plan (Seville, Valencia, Cordoba, Badajoz), but early *corrales* were often rudimentary and were subsequently modified and developed. All had a roofed *thrust stage projecting from a *tiring house (*vestuario*). The *stage was usually 1.5 m to 1.7 m high (*c*.5 feet, though sometimes lower in theatres with seats in the yard), between 6 m and 9.5 m wide (16 to 31 feet), and between 3 m and 5 m deep (10 to 16 feet). There were often *traps and the understage area was sometimes excavated. The tiring house had three openings at stage level with a gallery or balcony above, and also an upper gallery in Madrid and Seville; the various apertures, normally *curtained, could be opened to reveal *scenery or to extend the performing area. Stage machines were widely used and there was usually a machine loft.

Some semicircular, elliptical, or polygonal playhouses appeared in southern and eastern Spain in the seventeenth century, but most were rectangular. At the sides of the yard, and sometimes also at the back, there was usually raked seating (*gradas*), extending either side of the stage and occasionally adjoining it (as in Madrid); above them, along the sides and back of the yard and beside the stage, were two or three tiers of *boxes or galleries. All these structures were roofed. Sometimes the boxes were rooms in neighbouring buildings. The yard itself was usually open air, though in several cases it was roofed. It was normally occupied by standing groundlings (*mosqueteros*), but there was often some seating and occasionally the yard was largely filled with chairs or benches. Women had a separate entrance and were normally confined to the *cazuela* ('stewpot'), a large gallery usually at the back of the yard. Two *corrales* still survive, in *Alcalá de Henares and Almagro. For other *corrales* see CRUZ, CORRAL DE LA; MONTERÍA, CORRAL DE LA; OLIVERA, CASA DE LA; PRÍNCIPE, CORRAL DEL; see also COMPANY ORGANIZATION IN EUROPE, 1500–1700.　　　CD

ALLEN, JOHN J., *The Reconstruction of a Spanish Golden Age Playhouse: El Corral del Príncipe, 1583–1744* (Gainesville, Fla., 1983)
SHERGOLD, N. D., *A History of the Spanish Stage from Medieval Times until the End of the Seventeenth Century* (Oxford, 1967)

CORRÊA, JOSÉ CELSO MARTINEZ (1937–　)

Brazilian director. Also known as Zé Celso, Corrêa is one of the most creative forces in Brazilian theatre and a founder of Oficina Theatre in *São Paulo (1958, reorganized as Uzina Uzona in 1971). In the 1960s his productions were important cultural responses to the dictatorship. His irreverent, transgressive *O rei da vela* (*The Candle King*, 1967) was a catalyst for cultural protest, as were his fine adaptations of *Brecht (for example, *Galileo*, 1968), *allegories that attacked authoritarian repression. His theatre of aggression reached an apex with *Roda viva* (*Fast Track*, 1968), in which the cast ate the 'live' liver of a dismembered rock star, tossing bits at the public. Although he has been attracted to a wide range of *texts (*Genet, *Artaud, *Euripides, *Chekhov, Shakespeare), his approach has tended to the *carnivalesque, including overtly homosexual pairings, scatology (such as freshly produced faeces), and general sexual euphoria.　　　LHD

CORRIE, JOE (1894–1968)

Scottish socialist playwright and poet whose numerous *one-act and full-length plays emerged out of the radical working-class *amateur theatre movement of the 1920s and 1930s and drew on Scottish traditions of popular entertainment. As a coal miner in Fife, Corrie's first plays, *The Shillin' a Week-Man* and *The Poacher*, were performed by his group of fellow miners, the Bowhill Village Players, during the 1926 General Strike. *In Time o' Strife* (1928), which dramatized the subsequent lockout, was the first full-length play to be staged in a *music hall. It was revived by *7:84 Scotland in 1982.　　　CEC

CORRIERI, SERGIO (1938–　)

Cuban actor and director. His performance in *O'Neill's *Long Day's Journey into Night* (1958) sparked his founding of Teatro Estudio. In 1968 he went on to establish the Escambray group and directed it until 1985, when he took up a series of posts in the Cuban government. He starred in a number of *films, including *Memorias del subdesarrollo* (*Memories of Underdevelopment*, 1968), *El hombre de Maisinicú* (*The Man from Maisinicu*, 1973), *Río Negro* (1978), and in the popular *television serial *En silencio ha tenido que ser* (*It Had To Be Done in Silence*, 1980–2).　　　MMu

COSSA, ROBERTO MARIO ('TITO') (1934–　)

One of Argentina's most important dramatists and screenwriters, Cossa has delved deeply into the failure of the country's middle class. Unlike his early plays, such as *Our Weekend* (1964) and *The Days of Julián Bisbal* (1966), which approached an almost *documentary *realism, the collaboratively written *The Black Airplane* (1970) was a biting socio-political *satire about Perón's anticipated comeback, built upon Argentine cultural models. Cossa returned to the theatre seven years later with *The Granny*, a long-running grotesque whose *protagonist symbolized the blind, destructive forces seizing the nation at the time of its première (see GROTESCO CRIOLLO). In later plays such as *The Old Man-Servant* (1980) and *The Grey of Absence* (1981), Cossa mixed formal experimentation with such concrete cultural elements as the *tango. By the mid-1980s his focus shifted from a general indictment of the middle class to an investigation of the historical and cultural circumstances conditioning middle-class failure. Plays such as *Hand and Foot* (1984), *Gepetto* (1987), the 'socialist *cabaret' *Angelito* (1991), and *The Quack* (1999) presented, one critic writes, 'a lucid social x-ray of our country'. Cossa's plays, purposefully local in dialect, cultural referent, and *character type, defy easy translation; with the notable exception of *The Granny*, few have been produced outside the Spanish-speaking world.　　　JGJ

COSTANTINI FAMILY

Italian actors who built their reputations abroad in the seventeenth and eighteenth centuries. The most famous was Angelo (c.1654–1729), son of the Veronese cloth merchant Costantino who married an actress and then entered the profession, coming to *Paris in the 1680s. Angelo made all his own the liveried servant mask of Mezzettino: on the death of Dominique *Biancolelli in 1688 he eventually preferred to stay with his own role, rather than stepping into Biancolelli's shoes. After the dismissal of the Italian troupe in 1697, he moved to Germany and Poland: his son Gabriele and others of the family performed all over Europe. *See* COMÉDIE ITALIENNE.   RAA

COSTUMBRISMO

*Latin American *folkloric *costume drama. *Costumbrismo* can be any kind of performance presenting *characters, customs, social interactions, style, and local colour peculiar to a region. Particularly strong in nineteenth-century Spain, it became the prevalent form throughout Spanish-speaking Latin America in the late nineteenth and early twentieth centuries. Initially promoted as a way to celebrate the customs, language, and history of the newly independent republics, *costumbrismo* gradually changed from a serious artistic approach to folkloric presentations for touristic consumption.   AV

COSTUME

Distinctive clothing for individuals or groups of performers, a visual presentation of *character or idea through clothed physical appearance.

1. Introduction; 2. Early European; 3. Early modern;
4. Eighteenth century; 5. Nineteenth century;
6. Twentieth century; 7. Non-Western

1. Introduction

Disguising the human form in natural materials—feathers, furs, and vegetation—was the method used by early humans when preparing for ceremonies and *rituals. An individual became extraordinary, or was subsumed into an undifferentiated group, by using costumes, *make-up, *masks, and *wigs. In *performance, costume signified roles, skills, or other identities which conveyed direct or symbolic messages to an *audience. Portable and adaptable, its colours, fabrics, textures, and scale created expectation before *dance, music, and words offered further meaning. In many non-Western countries the complex visual language of stylized costumes is retained. Within European theatre costume evolved differently when pagan, Christian, and *early modern imagery was replaced by reforms and *theories concerning authenticity and *realism. The performer's

control over his or her costume changed according to prevailing conditions—whether there was a patron of a production; the size of the *auditorium and its location (outside in natural light, or inside with *scenery and *lighting); the proximity of the audience; current theories about the significance of costume; the input of a designer or *director; and the cost and availability of appropriate costumes.

2. Early European

Evidence of costume practice between 500 BC and AD 1500 is patchy, anecdotal, and dependent upon limited sources which can be interpreted in differing ways. Interpreting costume, whether theatrical or ordinary wear, is notoriously difficult, and the two are often inextricably linked. The competitive nature of *Greek theatre from the mid-sixth century BC onwards and the large, *open-air *theatron* placed demands upon physical visibility. Surviving Greek pottery and some evidence within the plays identify certain distinctive features. Much of the visual characterization was provided by masks, but costumes had to differentiate between *actors and the *chorus. In *tragedy the latter wore garments which reflected their nationality and/or role; in *comedy a broader style was permissible. Costumes and masks identified birds, clouds, wasps, as in *Aristophanes, for example. Actors in tragedy wore variants of everyday garments, a full-length *chiton* but with the addition of sleeves, not a usual feature of Greek dress, and a long or short cloak. The garments were coloured and patterned so that the overall effect was of reality rendered larger than life; a heroic role was enhanced by costume which was recognizably more impressive than that of the everyday, and identification of character was determined by the colour of a costume and its symbolic associations. An anonymous biographer of *Aeschylus attributed some costume innovations to him, including the sleeved, full-length *chiton* and heightened buskins 'to increase stature'. Comic characters were distinguished by broad exaggeration. Grotesques wore short, loose *chitons* with body padding and a long, protuberant *phallus. A variant of this is depicted on an urn of c.400 BC with two actors in loosely fitted trousers, a long-sleeved *chiton*, and a moulded breastplate with stomach and buttocks padding and a pendant phallus strapped around the waist. Trousers were associated with barbarians and orientals so the urn depicted distinctive characters. The Phylax vases from southern Italy of c.400–320, and a group of terracotta statuettes from Athens of c.380–330 BC, indicated the popularity of comic characters, but by the beginning of the third century BC the grosser features had disappeared.

The Romans assimilated much Greek culture, including some plays and theatrical traditions. Actors wore costume and masks appropriate to character, though with typical grandeur they tended to exaggerate the appearance of tragic actors. The critic Lucian of Samosata (c.AD 125–80) mocked tragic actors of *Roman theatre whose heavily padded garments, raised boots, and masks with wide gaping mouths he found grotesque rather than impressive. The dominant imperial architecture demanded massive, if less mobile performers. There is some evidence of richer, more monumental robes, but there are also images of Roman actors in other styles of costume including long cotton tunics similar to Greek *chitons*. Comedy, *mime, and *pantomime acquired costumes specific to those *genres. Apuleius' second-century account of a pantomime about the Judgement of Paris recorded that Paris was dressed 'after the likeness of a Phrygian herdsman, with barbaric mantle streaming from his shoulders, a fair tunic about his body, and a turban of gold on his head'; Mercury was naked apart from 'the stripling's cloak that covered his left shoulder', and Venus' costume was 'a robe of thinnest silk which . . . clung to her and outlined . . . the charms of her fair limbs'. This description encapsulated Roman interest in and residual fear of the exotic, and delight in scantily clad male and female performers.

The Christian Church denounced this type of decadence as 'the victims of the public lust [who] are brought forward on the stage', but it took several centuries for the old forms of entertainment to disappear. In *Byzantium in the seventh century the Church attempted to ban performances in which there were 'dancing and mysteries performed by men and women according to an ancient custom alien to the Christian life. No man is to wear female dress, nor woman to wear what belongs to a male. No-one is to don the masks of comedy, the *satyr-play or tragedy.' This attempt to ban *cross-dressing was forgotten once the Church realized that *liturgical performances held in church on great feast days could fulfil a public need for instructive entertainment. The clothing of the clergy became as distinctive and, at its highest levels, as sumptuous as that worn by the imperial court in Byzantium. Towering headdresses and layers of richly ornamental robes impressed congregations with their ritualistic *theatricality.

*Liturgical dramas were performed in churches by the clergy and outside churches by secular performers. Religious and secular garments distinguished by emblematic devices and symbolic colours were a feature of this type of drama. This communication of visual ideas is found in *Hildegard of Bingen's late 1140s *allegory *Order of Virtues*. At the outset a character called the Soul is sewing the white garment of immortality (the colour associated with purity), but is tested and covered with painted wounds before ascending to heaven clothed in the 'armour of light'. Colour symbolism drew upon both biblical references and pagan traditions well before Pope Innocent III codified the rules for the colour of vestments in *De Sacro Altaris Mysterio* (1198). In the anonymous twelfth-century *Jeu d'Adam*, Christ was clothed in a dalmatic, Adam in a red tunic (red symbolized the blood of Christ and implicitly truth and justice), and Eve in a 'woman's garment' of white with a white silk headdress. Eve was played by a boy or youth, contrary to earlier prohibitions on cross-dressing. A 'cunningly put together' serpent tempted Eve and once she had tempted Adam the hapless sinner bowed down so the congregation could not see him take off 'his goodly garments' and put on 'poor garments of fig leaves sewn together'.

Such transformations were a feature of liturgical dramas and the later *biblical plays and much thought was given to the problems of nakedness, a religious anathema. Closely fitted garments of some white fabric or even yellow—the symbolic colour for the clay from which the body was formed—were probably worn. Illuminated manuscripts, paintings, sculptures, stained glass, and tapestries provide some evidence of the appearance and content of these plays. The Three Kings and Herod offered opportunities for exotic costumes and headdresses, an orientalism informed by the memories and mementoes of crusaders, merchants, and sailors. Devils and imps developed from frightening into comic figures covered in black hair or feathers, their faces disguised by grotesque masks. Local *guilds kept records of their annual performances. The records for the Smiths' Company in Coventry show that between 1449 and 1585 they regularly bought fabric for costumes, had them repaired, or occasionally hired something fashionable, as with a dress for Pilate's wife in 1490. Emblematic devices of nails, dice, and hammers crowned with thorns identified Christ's tormentors; Caiaphas and Annas wore mitres to signify their exalted religious roles, and both Christ and Peter had gilt wigs. Public expectation required a mixture of familiar and novel costumes. *See* MEDIEVAL THEATRE IN EUROPE.

3. Early modern

The rediscovery of classical art and literature in the *early modern period, and an interest in humanism, found early manifestation in the themes, designs, and costumes for triumphal *entries, *pageants, and courtly entertainments throughout Europe. The first great age of *scenography, dramatic *criticism, and theory was nurtured in the Italian states in the sixteenth century and disseminated by the printing presses. From the plays based upon Latin and vernacular traditions, such as *Calandria* (1514), performed by expensively costumed *amateur male actors for the papal court of the Medici Pope Leo X, to the travelling *commedia dell'arte* troupes of professional players, Italian theatre paralleled Italian art in Europe-wide influence and prestige.

Leone de' *Sommi, who worked at the Mantuan court, wrote about prevailing attitudes to costume in the mid-1560s. These are the views of someone supported by a wealthy patron: 'I make efforts to dress the actors always in as noble a fashion as is possible for me, but in such a manner that there is a sense of proportion, in view of the fact that the rich costume . . . particularly in these times when pomp is at its highest peak, adds much reputation and beauty to comedies and even more to tragedies.' This was theatrical costume as propaganda, one method by which rulers sought to impress visitors with the grandeur of their courts (*see* STATE DISPLAYS). Sommi's major aim was a transformation that rendered the actor unrecognizable. Therefore he suggested that actors must be dressed very differently one from another to beautify and assist understanding of the story. Such differences encompassed styles of costume, accessories, and headdresses, and the use of 'definite colours, light colours', but little black or dark shades. Novelty was essential and he recommended 'stage costumes that are ancient and remote from our fashions', especially Greek costumes for comedies and Roman styles of ceremonial armour. Costume for *pastoral scenes drew upon Homer's description of a Trojan shepherd in short tunic, animal skins, and buskins on the feet. Nymphs wore women's starched smocks 'embroidered and varied', fastened with coloured silk or gold ribbons, and skirts of 'some beautifully coloured and delicate material, short enough to show the ankle', with a 'rich mantle' draped across the body. These styles superimposed elements of the classical past upon contemporary fashions, thereby creating a wholly artificial form of costume which influenced designers and theorists until the early eighteenth century.

*Disguise and transformation in courtly entertainments was not so easily matched in popular plays. The improvisational *commedia dell'arte* with its *stock characters and distinctive regional styles of Italian and Spanish dress infiltrated many European countries, but although the characters and situations were of long-lasting appeal their costumes had less impact on other forms of theatre costume. In France Italian players are depicted in the *Recueil de Fossard* of the 1580s, and some French performers adopted this style of performance and variants of the costumes (*see* COMÉDIE ITALIENNE). From the 1540s, however, as the French moved away from the disparate remnants of religious performance towards a theatre inspired by the drama of antiquity, other sources for costumes became necessary. Professional actors usually provided their own costumes, often acquired second hand. A French verse of *c.*1600 asked a courtier, 'How many times did your silken finery | Clothe the King of Troy, or Amadis and his knights.' (*See* NEOCLASSICISM.)

It was an expensive business acquiring costumes impressive enough to win an audience's approbation. In Spain bands of strolling players ranged in size from a single performer to companies of more than twenty, and their costumes were both stock-in-trade and valuable enough to tempt thieves. A group of five or six men, a leading lady, and a boy to play secondary parts had a chest in which there might be a handful of men's garments, beards, *wigs, and a woman's silk dress. The last, even if secondhand, would be worth more than many months' earnings, but essential to captivate audiences before the wit of the play engaged their minds. Such contemporary fashionable dress was portable wealth—stolen and resold, or pawned if times were hard. The growing knowledge of classical antiquity, its culture, and its potential as a source for costume ideas was interpreted loosely. Most professional performers worked on small budgets and used contemporary styles of dress, investing in novel additions as and when they could afford them.

The proximity of actors to audiences created its own demands. Courtly entertainments and municipal or religious presentations were impressive due to their scale, settings, and the financial investment made in them. They relied on a combination of costume and *special effects to create a sense of awe and excitement. Professional actors had no such luxuries, just their ability to transform themselves in appearance and to amuse, inspire, or terrify with their acting skill. However, even the humblest artisan knew that a king must look the part and actors were, generally, exempted from sumptuary legislation. Sumptuary laws reserved the wearing of certain colours, fabrics, and furs to specific social groups. Avoidance of the usual laws was possible when actors had a powerful patron. In England some late sixteenth-century actors even qualified for household livery, a tangible sign of their protected status. What English actors wore and what significance can be attached to their costumes has led to a good deal of speculative theorizing.

What is known about the appearance of the actors in an original production of a Shakespeare play must, in the main, be based on internal and contextual literary evidence. The only extant illustration is a rough sketch of a scene in *Titus Andronicus*, drawn in 1595. Whether it was done *ad vivum* or from memory is unclear, and although much analysed, it is too slight to be compelling evidence. The six characters wear a haphazard mixture of contemporary, quasi-exotic, quasi-Roman garments, with odds and ends of armour; exactly the mix that might be owned by actors, found in the company *tiring house, with bits borrowed, hired, and bought to give the production a novel appearance, which was what fickle, critical audiences demanded. Although much has been read into Philip *Henslowe's methods of buying, loaning, and pawning costumes, usually at the expense of gullible actors, the look of *Titus*, as with other productions, relied to great extent on the ingenuity of the theatre's wardrobe master and its actors. The inordinately high cost of clothing meant that the costumes for a new play, of which there would be few performances, depended upon ingenuity. The loan or gift of discarded court fashions or their purchase from second-hand clothes dealers was a factor in most performers' lives.

Surviving illustrations of seventeenth-century court entertainments—*ballets, *masques, *operas—demonstrate the powerful influence of Italian designers and performers. The English architect Inigo *Jones visited Italy and on his return designed a series of court masques which were performed between 1605 and 1640. Court patronage and finance allowed him to experiment with costumes, special effects, and staging techniques intended to glorify the new Stuart monarchy, but for the early masques Elizabeth I's wardrobe was ransacked to provide fabrics and robes which could be adapted for costumes. Descriptions of early productions emphasize their exoticism with

Ethiopians, mythological beings such as nymphs and tritons, and imaginary creatures like sea-horses and mermaids. In *Hymenaei* (1606) the male dancers wore costumes supposedly copied from antique Greek statues with breastplates of 'carnation cloth of silver, richly wrought, and cut to expresse the naked, in manner of the Greek Thorax', voluminous silk mantles of various colours, and white plumes as headdresses. Their female partners, cast as celestial beings, wore floating costumes of white and silver. There were numerous variants of these styles but the classical theme was all-pervasive; by 1618 masked cavaliers wore body armour like 'ancient Roman corslets'. The expenditure on visual display, and the emphasis on scenic and costume effects at the expense of the prose and *verse, led to a falling-out between Ben *Jonson, author of the early masques, and Jones. Jonson fulminated against the rise of 'omnipotent design'; he was an early critic of the form which became progressively more dominant.

The exclusivity of this type of performance did not prevent dissemination of these ideas to other forms of theatre. Throughout the capitals of Europe the ingenuity of Italian baroque design swept all before it. Courtiers who performed in such ephemeral productions also attended the theatre and, in a curious development of the mid- to late seventeenth century in *London and *Paris, were sometimes seated at either side of the stage. They were disruptive, badly behaved, and competed for attention, in their fashionable clothes, with genuine performers. This proximity placed pressure on the performers, whose costumes, facial expressions, and acting styles could be scrutinized closely. The apron stages (*see* FORESTAGE) in London theatres added another form of proximity, though Colley *Cibber regretted their passing when writing in the 1740s. He recalled how every element in a performance was more immediate—voice, scene *painting, costume, when 'every rich, or fine-coloured Habit had a more lively Lustre'. Perhaps Cibber had never suffered the criticisms that Spanish courtiers directed at the actors so close to whom they were seated; 'if the player wears a poor costume he insults or hisses him', and, equally disruptive, 'he goes to the dressing-room. There he finds women taking off their street clothes and putting on their theatrical costumes.' Actresses were now found throughout Europe and attracted interest which went well beyond their acting skills. This was exploited by playwrights whose *plots included cross-dressing, *disguises, and scenes which allowed discreetly titillating partial nudity.

Contemporary comedies were played in contemporary clothing, but tragedies displayed some of the stylized features of costumes which had originated in early ballet and opera. Claude-François Ménestrier (1631–1705) gave detailed advice on the appropriate styles of ballet costumes for performers that he described as 'silent actors'. Costumes must be appropriate for the subject matter—history, mythology, unusual locations; colour and texture were important (for instance, 'Winds must be dressed in feathers because of their extraordinary lightness'); there must be group uniformity but some variety for 'diversity always keeps the spectator in suspense'; the costume 'must not be an obstacle, but must leave the body and limbs free to dance'. Ménestrier considered the dress of the 'ancient Romans' the most impressive and described its attributes: 'a cuirass with its scallops, a short cloak reaching to the elbow, and a skirt of pleated silk which serves as a surcoat. A helmet adorned with aigrette and plumes completes this costume.' It was a style which was found in dramatic theatre, as were some of the other characters Ménestrier mentioned—Greeks, Persians, Moors, Turks, Saracens, American Indians, Japanese. As more books and prints depicted different cultures, the range of costumes increased.

4. Eighteenth century

By the end of the seventeenth century there was growing concern about the look of stage costumes and their impact upon audiences. Tragedians thought themselves superior to comedians, and required this to be reflected in the quality of their costumes. Inevitably this caused ill-feeling and the comedian Thomas *Doggett, a collaborator of Colley Cibber's, 'could not, with Patience, look upon the costly Trains and Plumes of Tragedy . . . [which] he thought were all a vain Extravagance'. The critic Joseph *Addison had equal distaste for 'the huge plume of feathers' used to designate the tragic *hero and the 'broad sweeping train' which impeded the movements of the heroine. He acknowledged that 'The tailor and the painter often contribute to the success of a tragedy more than the poet', and that a 'well-dressed play' could draw as large an audience as a well-written one. A desire for reform developed slowly throughout the century. There were practical as well as aesthetic reasons for this. Theatres were being built or rebuilt on a much bigger scale than before, scenic innovations stimulated new ideas about the visual look of a play, and eventually spectators were banned from the stage. At much the same time the interest in antiquity and other historical periods became more rigorous. Books, engravings, paintings, pamphlets fed a growing appetite for historical accuracy.

However, the circumstances of individual performers had not improved much; many were required to provide their own costumes and *properties out of piteously small incomes. Principal performers wore new or specially made costumes, but all actors, whether newcomers or established, had personal preferences, and how they looked was rarely subjected to rigorous scrutiny. The individuality of the performer was unchallenged and encompassed both appearance and acting style. James *Quin first appeared on the stage in 1712 but his long career overlapped with that of David *Garrick. Quin was conservative in his declamatory acting style and his determination to retain the traditional tragedian's costume of short, wide stiffened skirt, full wig, plumed headdress, and marshal's baton. Garrick, a creative and innovative *actor-manager, explored change cautiously. He was a small man and probably knew that the traditional hero's costume would look foolish on him, so he introduced to the stage the Vandyke costume, much used for masquerades throughout the eighteenth century. It hinted at the historic past, and was elegant and easy to wear. His contemporary Charles *Macklin dressed Shylock in a long gabardine coat and red hat, and Macbeth in a quasi-Scottish costume. These were, essentially, principal player innovations which did not extend through the cast of a production.

Garrick owned a 1653 copy of Richard Verstegan's *Antiquities* and may have heard of Aaron Hill's 1731 production of *Aethelwold* which drew upon this source, but he never attempted anything similar. Hill wanted an authentically Anglo-Saxon look for his play, though he hedged his bets by saying that 'beauty must be joined to propriety, where the decoration of the stage, is the purpose to be provided for'. Nevertheless he believed that the use of modern dress for plays set in a specific time in the past reduced the audience's understanding. His sketches and references to Verstegan appear to have been followed, but he was realist enough to propose that many of the subsidiary costumes could be achieved by 'giving new uses, to the old reserves of your [*Drury Lane's] wardrobe'. Perhaps he was disappointed; in 1735 he attacked the haphazard approach to costume in a pamphlet, *The Prompter*, as shabby and subject to 'the Patchwork Inconsistencies' of theatre managements.

The Actor, written in 1750 by a former student of Macklin's, John Hill, asked for a greater realism in costume characterization. He singled out actresses for dressing too finely when playing servants, and both sexes for not seeming to mirror the torments and turmoil of their roles in their appearance. Hill used an analogy which became more significant in the nineteenth century—'the representation of a play is a sort of painting, which owes all its beauty to a close imitation of nature', with the stage having the greater advantage of 'making the *illusion perfect'. Actresses found this type of advice unpalatable because their splendid appearance often attracted admirers and protectors who could look elsewhere for diversion. The ghosted memoirs of Mrs *Bellamy described both stage finery and aristocratic admirers. Dismissive of the stock black velvet and white satin of tragediennes, she acquired a court dress of silver tissue, formerly worn by Augusta, Princess of Wales, for the role of Cleopatra in *Dryden's *All for Love*, improving it with borrowed diamonds. As the Persian Princess Roxane in *Alexander*, revived at *Covent Garden in 1756, she persuaded the theatre management to buy two 'tragedy dresses' from Paris. The eye-catching brilliance of a bright yellow French court dress rendered more splendid with the addition of a purple robe infuriated her co-star Mrs *Woffington. This competitive individuality was one of the reasons why reforms were so difficult to introduce. The other was expense.

By 1790 Tate *Wilkinson's *Memoirs* expressed admiration for current costumes, and recalled that productions in his youth were not as splendidly dressed throughout. The key word is *throughout*, for a few decades earlier only two or three principals were well dressed. The changes that Wilkinson both admired and regretted were, in his words, the transition to 'foil, spangles, beads, interwoven fast embroidery, silks, satin etc. which soon wear', from the reusable velvets, heavy brocades, and metallic laces of earlier in the century. The lighter fabrics reflected a renewed interest in the fluid draperies of neoclassicism which was found in contemporary fashions and on the stage. Principal exponents of this approach were the formidable *Kemble family—John Philip and his sister Sarah *Siddons. The apogee of their careers coincided with Kemble's management of Drury Lane from 1794. He was criticized for preferring dramas which gave opportunity for 'ostentatious *spectacle'. Given the enlarged stage and huge audiences he had to attract and retain, this was perhaps inevitable. He used detailed production books to ensure what Boaden, his biographer, called a 'stage unrivalled for truth of scenic exhibition'. He discarded the Vandyke costume for Hamlet in preference for contemporary court dress in 1783; later, when this seemed inappropriate, he adopted a quasi-sixteenth-century style of billowing white shirt, short black tunic, and long cloak which became the standard dress for Hamlet well into the twentieth century. He was alert to the changes in French theatre and introduced togas and sandals for *Coriolanus* and *Julius Caesar*, and his static acting style was enhanced by substantial draperies. His sister was less susceptible to French innovations, and took time to abandon fashionable wide hoops and towering powdered hairstyles for the simpler lines of neoclassical fashions.

French neoclassicism was linked in the British public mind to the excesses of the French Revolution, and this inspired caution. Well before 1789 there was a move away from the formal heroic styles of French costume, leavened to a certain extent with rococo prettiness, which pervaded ballet, drama, and opera. Adrienne *Lecouvreur's adoption of English court dress and a Garter sash to play Elizabeth I in 1721 indicated a novel if inaccurate attempt at characterization, but the main changes originated with Mlle *Clairon, in the 1750s. Encouraged by her lover Marmontel, she changed both her acting style and her costumes. The abandonment of the hoops under her skirt and the baring of her arms to play Roxane in 'the habit of a sultana' seem modest, but she followed it with an Electra in which she wore 'the simple habit of a slave'. *Diderot applauded the possibilities offered by this approach, exclaiming, 'Ah! What if she dared, one day, to appear on the stage in all of the nobility and simplicity of dress that her parts demand!' He deplored the ornate costumes of the French stage in the late 1750s, asking for 'Lovely, simple draperies, austere in colour . . . not all your tinsel and decorations'. At much the same time as John Hill in England, Diderot told actors to visit art galleries and examine paintings. Clairon agreed that appropriate costume contributed to the illusion created for the spectator, and assisted the player in interpreting a role, but was of the opinion that classical draperies were 'proper only for statues and paintings', because they were too revealing. Clairon's example was matched by her contemporary Mme *Favart, who wore simple costumes for peasant women and Turkish, Indian, and Chinese styles for roles which required them.

The actor who instituted reform was Jean-François *Talma. He was influenced by his friendship with the neoclassical painter David, who encouraged Talma to introduce the toga to the stage for classical roles. Talma also adopted a short, unpowdered hairstyle for the role of Titus in *Voltaire's *Brutus* (1791), which set a fashion for Titus haircuts amongst his young admirers. Talma found costume important to his creation of a role. William *Macready, who met him in 1822, was impressed that Talma dressed for his role well in advance of a performance in order to familiarize himself with the costume's requirements and to use it as an interpretative tool.

The battle between the traditionalists and those who wanted greater realism was found throughout Europe. Two Dutch actors, Marten Corver and Jan Punt, offered the *Amsterdam audiences of the 1760s a choice between a more naturalistic acting style with historically accurate costumes and the formal, heroic French style of acting and appearance. At *Drottningholm, the Swedish court theatre, built in the 1760s, maintained the style, look, and values of conservative Italian designs for costumes, scenic, and mechanical effects. In *Weimar, *Goethe would not present plays which depended upon 'magnificent scenery and a brilliant wardrobe', but relied on well-chosen plays and thoroughly *rehearsed actors. He employed an Italian-trained scenic designer for the court theatre, but the tone of the scenery had to be favourable to the colour of the costumes. His designer's sets of 'more or less of a brownish tinge' allowed the costumes to appear 'with perfect freshness'. Actors who performed within brightly coloured sets were exhorted to wear costumes which did not merge into them.

5. Nineteenth century

The amount of information available about nineteenth-century costume is immense, and from the 1840s surviving evidence includes photographs alongside paintings and engravings. Many more costume designs and provenanced costumes offer information about fabrics, colours, and styles. Costumes had common elements of fantasy, *historicism, comedic overstatement, often similar to the incoherent mix that Frank *Benson recalled buying in 1883. His 30 baskets of costume comprised 'early Venetian doublets, a certain amount of chained or ring armour, a few Roman British costumes, and a little borrowing from the Rob Roy crowd'. With his own additions and adaptations he believed that he matched any elaborate West End or foreign production, not in costliness of material, but in 'artistry, correct archaeology and heraldry'.

Many companies limped along with this curious mixture of styles which had existed for centuries—as long as it looked like stage costume it could be part of the process of convincing audiences of a make-believe world beyond everyday life. However, the seeds of artistry, archaeology, and heraldry which appeared in the eighteenth century blossomed into spectacular flower in the nineteenth century. The over-designed, over-furnished, and overdressed look of society at large was matched by opulent theatrical spectacles which gratified audiences by expanding their knowledge of the past whilst excluding its less pleasant aspects. Benson's 'correct archaeology' extended beyond the results of excavations and research into classical civilization; it encompassed the type of scholarship with which J. R. *Planché underpinned his designs for Charles Kemble's 1823 production of *King John* at Covent Garden. This clothed all of the cast in costumes and armour of the thirteenth century. A similar zeal lay behind E. W. Godwin's 33 articles on *The Architecture and Costume of Shakespeare's Plays* (1875). The belief that there was a correct era, place, and style of costume for Shakespeare's plays was prevalent throughout the century and beyond. Godwin (1833–86) had problems with actors, as Planché had done 50 years earlier, writing, 'The idea of control in the matter of theatrical costume has not yet got into the actor's mind, any individuality or obstinacy I have had to contend with has not been greater than experience led me to expect.'

Actors fought a rearguard action to retain control of how they looked on stage. In Great Britain there were notable adherents to the pioneering work of Planché, a line which stretched from William Macready in the 1820s through to Herbert Beerbohm *Tree in the 1900s. Gradually, in well-established and financially secure companies, the plays of Shakespeare, later classics, new works with historic settings, and *melodramas succumbed to the idea of pictorial splendour. Macready espoused historical accuracy erratically; in the late 1820s a German visitor to London was startled to see his Macbeth wearing 'a fashionable flowered chintz dressing-gown, perhaps the one he usually wears, thrown loosely over his steel armour'. By 1838 his *Coriolanus* was praised for its accurate costumes 'of antique Rome', though a pedantic critic wished that the toga 'wear its natural colour of the wool, in order to make the candidate's gown—a leading point—more conspicuous'.

By the middle of the century public and critics alike expected historical accuracy and pageantry on the stage. It accorded with their knowledge of history paintings and illustrated books on archaeology, history, and literature (*see* ANTIQUARIANISM). Naturally there were mixed views about these costly productions; some critics deplored the meretricious glitter, others praised productions in which the performers 'appear to have stepped out of a Greek vase'. The actor-manager who attracted the greatest criticism in the 1850s was Charles *Kean. His Shakespeare productions at the *Princess's Theatre came with copious programme notes (see PLAYBILLS AND PROGRAMMES) about sources used for costumes and sets, rationalized the choice of location and era in which he had placed the play, and justified his interpolation of hundreds of splendidly clad extras in processions and battle scenes. He defended himself robustly against accusations that the text of a play was 'more like a running commentary upon the spectacles exhibited than the scenic arrangements an illustration of the text', and denied that he had ever allowed 'historical truth to be sacrificed to theatrical effect'. His wife, the actress Ellen *Tree, rejected historical truth by wearing bulky layers of petticoats for all her roles 'in defiance of the fact that classical parts should not be dressed in a superfluity of raiment'. Despite these solecisms Kean's productions were a huge success with the public.

Kean's work was admired by Georg II, Duke of Saxe-*Meiningen (1826–1914), whose court theatre company travelled to *Berlin in 1874, to London in 1881, and to 38 other European cities; the young André *Antoine saw it in *Brussels and *Stanislavsky saw it in *Moscow. Georg II worked closely with his *stage manager Ludwig *Chronegk, but was more like a modern director than the patron and owner of the company. He undertook detailed research, consulted historians, chose and cast the plays, designed the sets and costumes, and, through Chronegk, rehearsed the actors. He required them to work as a coherent unit, and to be familiar with costumes, properties, and sets well in advance of a performance. During their London visit they performed five plays, three of them by Shakespeare. The critic of the *Athenaeum*, whilst full of praise for their ensemble playing, doubted that the costume and scenic effects, much praised in Europe, were superior to those on the English stage. He commented that 'No one would dream of saying that the dresses, Roman and Italian, which are exhibited are handsomer than those to which we are accustomed at the *Lyceum, or that the representation of the Forum in *Julius Caesar* is superior to that of the Temple of Diana in *The Cup*.'

The Lyceum was Britain's most respectable and admired theatre throughout the 1880s and much of the 1890s, and its actor-manager Henry *Irving ruled with autocratic rigour. What he achieved is summarized by the critic E. R. Russell, who wrote of the 1888 production of *Macbeth* that 'By the co-operation of costumiers and scene painters each scene is a very noble picture.' Irving had said much the same about his 1885 *Faust*: 'Each scene is like his picture to a painter. You have to combine colours, group figures, and arrange the mountings.' The *proscenium arch acted as the frame, and the gas and *limelight, the scenery, costumes, properties, the actors and extras conjured up history paintings for an enthusiastic audience. Actors were submerged in splendour and either had to learn how to use these costumes and sets effectively or be overwhelmed by them.

Ellen *Terry, Irving's leading lady, was knowledgeable about artistic trends and their application in the theatre and worked closely with her favourite costume designer Alice Comyns Carr, whose aesthetic tastes coincided with her own. Irving often used a distinguished principal designer, such as Seymour Lucas, Alma-Tadema, or Burne-Jones, but usually let Terry follow her own instincts. In her memoirs she mentions two occasions when he overruled her; once when she suggested that Ophelia should wear black and, later, when he appropriated a blood-red cloak meant for Lady Macbeth and wore it himself. Terry admitted that 'although I knew more of art and archaeology in dress than he did, he had a finer sense of what was right for the scene'. She also understood the importance of the actor inhabiting a costume rather than being inhibited by it; she rejected a crown for Lady Macbeth because it was too heavy to act in, and wrote to her dressmaker about the length, weight, and colour of garments, emphasizing the need for them to be easy to act in and be visually effective even at the expense of archaeological strictures.

Terry noted the major pitfall for any company attempting to recreate a past age by copying its styles of dress. The words were prompted by memories of her youthful apprenticeship with the Keans, 'but then, as now [she was writing in the early 1900s] actors and actresses seemed unable to keep their own period and their own individuality out of the clothes directly they got them on their backs'. Hair, posture, mannerisms, and an unwillingness to adhere to strict period requirements, such as the use of the correct type of corsetry, mitigated against complete authenticity. This can be observed in William *Poel's productions of Shakespeare in the 1890s when he used Tudor and Jacobean buildings as settings, and actors dressed in late sixteenth-century costumes, which in surviving photographs look like jaunty fancy dress. The problem was accentuated by the actors' natural wish to be comfortable in costume, and by the limited understanding about how the dress of the past had been constructed and worn. Artists and designers worked mostly from two-dimensional images, though some owned past fashions as aide-mémoires, but the fabrics and decorations which succeeded best were usually not direct copies of older originals but adaptations to suit lighting and scenic effects. Close examination of surviving costumes confirms this approach.

Actors continued to provide their own clothes, especially for contemporary plays, and Max *Beerbohm identified modern plays which required actors to spend a great deal of money at their dressmakers or tailors. The expense involved meant that late in the century young actresses, such as Mrs Patrick *Campbell and Maud Gill, made their own dresses for the stage but once well established patronized major couture houses in London and Paris. This might offer glamour and individuality but was little different from the competitive bid for attention of eighteenth-century actresses. Naturally this extravagance could only be borne if a play had a *long run. In towns where theatres operated constantly changing programmes, there was a stronger dependence on company wardrobes and performers' personal costumes to dress everything from Shakespeare to modern comedies.

The taste for historical settings and spectacle was found throughout Europe and North America, for Americans had maintained regular contact with British performers and methods from the eighteenth century onwards. Visits by Edmund *Kean, Charles Kemble and his daughter Fanny Kemble, and William Macready in the second quarter of the nineteenth century provided first-hand evidence of traditional and more innovative ideas about costume. Irving's company were regular visitors in the 1880s, and reciprocal visits to Europe by Ira *Aldridge, Edwin *Booth, Charlotte *Cushman, Ada *Rehan, and others allowed them to absorb and adapt British and European costuming techniques to suit domestic circumstances. Cushman was innovative in performing male roles, notably Hamlet and Romeo, dressed in the accepted styles of male costume (see MALE IMPERSONATION), well in advance of Sarah *Bernhardt's similar experiments in France. As in other countries which absorbed European theatre conventions but also developed local traditions, there are distinct national and regional differences which reward further study.

In France the situation was more diverse and experimental, with opportunities for every type of setting and costume from romantic historicism to contemporary social drama. That French standards were as variable as anywhere else in Europe can be judged by Antoine's comments on the Meiningen company, whose work he saw in *Brussels in 1888. He was impressed by the ensemble playing because it was well rehearsed with professional performers who were used to wearing 'bizarre or awkward costumes', unlike their French amateur counterparts. This skill apart, he disliked the costumes for being 'splendidly and ridiculously rich when they are strictly historical' and 'almost always in bad taste' when they were reliant upon a designer who lacked sufficient imagination to produce appropriate effect. Antoine was a disciple of *Zola's naturalistic approach to drama. A programme illustration for the Théâtre *Libre in 1894–5 depicted actors in the rough, ill-fitting clothes of the working classes with a young actress in underclothes. Such an approach was possible in a private theatre club but was not yet permissible on the mainstream stage. Other experiments in Paris included a highly stylized production of Pelléas et Mélisande (1893) for which the playwright *Maeterlinck had suggested designs and colours for the medieval costumes; and *Jarry's Ubu roi (1896) with costumes, designed by the author, caricaturing a childlike world of grotesque *puppets. Experiments with *naturalism, realism, and *symbolism used new subject matter and drew upon interest in oriental theatre whilst rejecting gratuitous spectacle. The work of *Ibsen, *Strindberg, and *Chekhov required ensemble playing of the

highest order and a firm overall conception of how to interpret the writer's intentions with naturalistic costumes and sets.

6. Twentieth century

Although traditional approaches survived, costume in the twentieth century was the servant of philosophical, literary, and artistic interpretations of new works and revived classics. The emergence of the director, the strengthening of the dramatist's input, and the influence of stage designers, some of whom subsumed costume design within their remit, sometimes threatened to bury the performer within a predetermined environment. The appearance of a character became more a matter for tactful negotiation than a performer's choice. Naturalism, realism, *expressionism, *constructivism, and *modernism all imposed physical and visual restraints upon the performer.

The stylized simplicity which characterized the theories of Edward Gordon *Craig and Adolphe *Appia appeared at much the same time that the designers of the *Ballets Russes offered vibrant, sensual interpretations of stock and exotic figures from myth, *folklore, newly discovered foreign cultures, history, and contemporary events. In the 1920s Oskar *Schlemmer, a *Bauhaus designer in Germany, and Vsevolod *Meyerhold in Russia, used geometrical abstractions or didactic uniforms which made performers into illustrative symbols. Dramatists became more closely involved, both describing and sometimes drawing what they required a character to wear. In a 1921 production of Six Characters in Search of an Author, *Pirandello dressed his principals in dark fabrics, rigidly pleated to suggest statues, a look reinforced by their black make-up which resembled 'antique masks of tragedy'. *Brecht experimented with the visual expression of his ideas, and understood that costume could illustrate intellectual and moral transformation. In Galileo the newly elected Pope Urban VIII is ritually vested with the papal habit while a discussion about whether or not to torture Galileo occurs. At the outset Urban is reluctant but as he is physically changed from cardinal to pope his resistance diminishes, until, fully robed in his new persona and inducted into a new role, he permits the Inquisition to proceed with its work. The power of assumed identity and the transformative power of costume are essential elements of the scene.

Competing forms of visual entertainment, notably *film and *television, used some of the spectacular costume effects of nineteenth-century theatre. Films by D. W. Griffith, Abel Gance, Sergei *Eisenstein, and Cecil B. DeMille could not be matched in the theatre, despite Max *Reinhardt's large-scale productions in *arenas and public spaces. Naturalism and realism used the clothes of ordinary life to reinforce the message of the text. Historic costumes were simplified or stylized; and productions in modern dress, or set within periods which added a new resonance to classic texts, became commonplace. Eclectic mixtures of period allusion, timelessness, contemporary and exotic styles taken from Far Eastern and *African traditions created a different visual language. Audiences had a greater visual sophistication than in any previous century, so to capture and retain their attention required imagination and experimentation which drew upon complex sources of visual information.

*Financial restraints had considerable impact on cast size, costumes, and scenery. Costume had to be sturdy to last for a lengthy production, to withstand the rigours of *touring, or to be regularly hired out. Costume hire was standard practice even within large companies from the late nineteenth century, and as early as the 1930s it was noted that few theatres had wardrobe departments, preferring to hire 'from establishments which specialise in these articles'. Costume designers, specialist costumiers, and wardrobes in large theatres drew upon a wide literature aimed at both professional and amateur companies. If historical accuracy or a specific national dress was required, designers and costumiers consulted specialist advisers and *museum collections. The prominence afforded costume designers reduced as modern directors opted for an overall design scheme which incorporated costume and scenery. Directors had definite views on what visually suited their interpretation of a text and, in modern plays, the authors' ideas were influential. Collaboration between director, designer, and author reduced the input of the performer further. The manner in which a costume evolved from discussion to design to actual garment was increasingly arbitrary. Costume was no longer an actor's preferred form of interpretative dress but an element in a process of visual construction.

7. Non-Western

A notable feature of traditional *Indian, *Chinese, and *Japanese styles of theatrical appearance is the complete integration of costume, make-up or mask, and wig or other headdress. Any attempt to divide this physical transformation into categories is to misunderstand its purpose, for each element has a specific, often symbolic meaning. Colours, styles of costume, and its decoration assist in identifying distinct characters, their age, gender, status, state of mind, and role within a performance. Exaggeration, whether in the length of garments, ornamentation of fabrics, choice of colours, in make-up or masks, wigs, or headdress—all define the role but disguise the performer. Interpretation of the meaning of such physical disguise is aided by the stereotypical range of characters. Naturalism is non-existent except in modern forms of theatre.

Indian Sanskrit drama drew upon the encyclopedic treatise *Natyasastra* (c.200 BC–AD 200) for ideas on performance, including the costumes. The style and colour of costumes and the colour of make-up or mask delineated the caste, profession, and regional origins of a character. For instance, elaborately decorated and bejewelled costumes and headdresses, and a reddish-yellow make-up, were reserved for gods, rulers, and Brahmans. This approach to theatrical appearance influenced later folk and dance dramas. In *kathakali, the all-male dance drama of south-

west India, traditional colours of make-up and costumes are found in performances of material taken from the *Mahabharata* and *Ramayana*. Indian films which use historical themes also draw inspiration from traditional costumes. A not dissimilar approach can be detected in the best-known form of Chinese drama, Beijing opera (*jingju). Introduced to Beijing in 1790, this robustly acrobatic and musical style of performance depended upon vibrant costumes, make-up, and properties for its impact. The main character types are *sheng* (male), *dan* (female), *jing* (painted face), and *chou* (clown), with female roles the preserve of young men until the 1930s. The costumes, with the exception of those dealing with episodes from the Manchu Dynasty (1644–1912), are elaborate and somewhat inaccurate derivations of the fashions of the Ming Dynasty (1368–1644).

These costumes are highly ornate, boldly coloured, and accompanied by appropriate accessories or properties—a general is recognized by the long pheasant feathers in his elaborate headdress, a young scholar by the fan he holds, and a supernatural being by his horsehair switch. Colour is important—emperors are dressed in yellow, their senior officials red, and so forth. Black can signify *villainy or, in certain circumstances, invisibility. The rich silks and embroideries of the principals, whether heroic or villainous, are complemented by their painted faces. Such make-up hides the musculature of the face and superimposes the character's personality by application of a brilliantly coloured design; its colour symbolism has changed little since its introduction in the Ming era. White indicates treachery, gold is reserved for gods, and the heavy red and yellow make-up worn by generals and warriors supposedly derives from a Sung Dynasty general who disguised his features in this manner. Facial disguise also includes beards and moustaches, often coloured, all offering more information about the character. In *Vietnam a similar form of opera developed but with costumes and make-up based upon local styles. During the 1920s a new form, in which traditional costumes and modern dress were used together, suggests an early precursor to what happened in China during the Cultural Revolution when new operas introduced the drab uniforms of the Red Guards and the dress of peasants (*see* GEMING XIANDAI XI).

Japanese theatre offers sophisticated examples of the interrelationship between differing types of theatre and the physical manifestation suitable to them. The evolution of *kabuki, the most popular form of traditional theatre, owed much to the traditions of *nō and *bunraku (puppet theatre). A distinguishing feature of nō is the wearing of masks by principal performers. The masks, which cover the face apart from small eye-openings, are carved from paulownia wood and exquisitely painted; many examples, up to 800 years old, survive as national treasures. Make-up is not worn, though masked performers wear wigs; one particular style, *kashira*, a flowing wig worn by demons and spirits, was assimilated into kabuki presentation. Costumes for nō plays were adaptations of official dress which add grandeur and stature to the performer. Made from richly coloured and finely embroidered silks, they consist of outer and indoor garments, the *hakama* (the trailing, loose divided skirts worn by samurai over their kimonos), and head-dresses. Within a play a change of costume can signify a change of rank or position. One test of the principal performer's skill is his ability to move and dance in complicated costume and to speak easily and clearly behind the mask.

The popularity of bunraku was based upon the ingenuity of the makers and the skill of the handlers. By the eighteenth century the puppets were 1–1.2 m (3–4 feet) high, expressive, and clothed in intricate costumes and wigs. Many puppet plays, costumes, and the mannered movements of the dolls were assimilated into kabuki, which was less popular until the 1780s. There is a uniform formality to the handlers and assistants. At the start of a performance a hooded announcer dressed in black appears; his costume is mirrored by that of the assistant doll handlers but with the hood wired away from their faces. A similar costume is worn by stage assistants in kabuki. The leading doll handler's status is signified by the ceremonial dress of the samurai—*kamishino*. This costume is worn also by musicians in nō, bunraku, and kabuki, and consists of a kimono with stiff shoulder pads bearing family crests, and the loose, divided skirt, *hakama*, worn in nō dramas.

The kabuki stage is the most demanding in oriental theatre and its raised gangway, the **hanamichi*, takes performers into the body of the auditorium. This creates pressure on both performance skills and physical appearance, but at its best kabuki provides a larger-than-life entertainment of strongly visual character. Its popularity was based upon spectacle, dance, music, easy manipulation of the ornate costumes, and innovations, either original or drawn from nō and bunraku traditions. One kabuki innovation is the *henge* (variation dance), in which actors dance several characters sequentially or demonstrate a number of moods which involve costume changes. The *hikinuki* requires the actor to wear several layers of costume, sewn loosely together and capable of being swiftly pulled apart to reveal another costume. In *bukkaeri* the upper part of a costume is shed to waist level to display a different garment. All traditional roles have carefully defined styles of costume which have changed imperceptibly in over 200 years. From the mid-seventeenth century all female roles were played by men, and by the late eighteenth century famous female impersonators—**onnagata*—were leaders of fashion, their kimonos and wigs copied by women in Edo (**Tokyo*) society.

The stage kimono—the loose, full-sleeved garment worn by both sexes—is supplied in many different colours, distinguished by embroideries, styles of sash (*obi*), and length of hemline. In the historical *jidaimono* plays the heroine invariably wears a scarlet silk kimono with ornate embroidery whilst the discreet samurai wives are identified by their plain silk kimonos decorated with family crests. Courtesans are distinguished by

excessively ornamental costumes; trailing layers of kimono skirts are turned back to reveal further skirts of differently coloured silks. Manipulating these flamboyant but heavy costumes requires great skill. Actors in male roles, especially those dressed in *suō*, the most formal of samurai styles, wear voluminous sleeved undergarments and loosely trailing divided skirts which require skilful movement. Further skill is required in the use of fans, long silk scarves, the lowering of sleeves, all symbolic expressions of recognizable emotions.

Exaggerated make-up was introduced for certain kinds of plays in the kabuki repertory in the late seventeenth century and was simpler than the Chinese versions from which it may have derived. Red and black are applied to a white base in bold, linear designs which exaggerate the facial angles and features, with indigo and brown used for demons and evil spirits. Warriors, youthful heroes, and humorous monkey faces are among the many variants. In contrast, the *onnagata* roles have plain white faces with delicately delineated brows and mouth, and distinctive wigs. Based mainly upon the complex eighteenth-century styles found on wood prints, the wigs are heavy and intricate, held with combs and other decorative ornaments. Such structures even include a trick wig which, upon the swift pull of threads, collapses into loose hair signifying transformation from a feminine ideal into an evil spirit, or descent into madness. Male wigs, though less cumbersome and diverse in style, are equally significant in their identification of character type.

These complex styles of theatre costume have occasionally inspired Western imitation, as in **Puccini's Madama Butterfly* (1904). More recently Peter **Brook's Mahabharata* (1985), and Ariane **Mnouchkine's Les Atrides* of the early 1990s incorporated certain Eastern styles of costume and make-up in an **intercultural* mode. However, the major impact of the bold colours, rich natural fabrics, and intricate designs found on Indian, Chinese, and Japanese costume has not been on Western theatre costume but on fashionable dress and interior design.   VLC

De Marly, Diana, *Costume on the Stage, 1600–1940* (London, 1982)

Laver, James, *Costume in the Theatre* (London, 1964)

Linthicum, M. Channing, *Costume in the Drama of Shakespeare and his Contemporaries* (Oxford, 1936)

Newton, Stella Mary, *Renaissance Theatre Costume and the Sense of the Historic Past* (London, 1973)

COTHORNUS

A calf-length, loose-fitting boot, often with upturned toes, which by 460 BC had become a standard feature of **tragic *costume* in **Greek* theatre. Flat soled until about 330 BC, cothorni in Roman times raised the actor 20–25 cm (8–10 inches) above the stage and came to symbolize tragedy's 'elevated' style.   EGC

COTTESLOE THEATRE See NATIONAL THEATRE OF GREAT BRITAIN.

COUP DE THÉÂTRE

An unanticipated action in a drama that effects an abrupt change in a dramatic situation. As a technique for bringing about a *peripeteia* or reversal, a *coup de théâtre* is distinguished by its *theatricality, its detachment from the rest of the play. In *realism there is an attempt to disguise the artificiality of the *coup de théâtre*, whereas in non-realistic theatre the effect is prominently displayed. The unexpected appearance in a *melodrama of a *character thought dead may subsequently be accounted for— weakly—in the *plot, but the *deus ex machina of *Euripidean *tragedy remains a completely external device.   RWV

COURT DANCE See BALLET DE COUR; MASQUE.

COURTNEY, TOM (1937-)

English actor. His northern accent and unconventional good looks helped to undermine the gentility of English *acting in the early 1960s. Regional roots inflected his debut performance in *Chekhov's *The Seagull* in *Edinburgh (1960): his Konstantin was doomed both as a romantic and as a provincial. His brilliance as a deadpan comic showed to great effect in *Billy Liar* (1961) when he took over the lead role from Albert *Finney. By 1964 he was with the *National Theatre, as Andrei in *Frisch's *Andorra*. His range widened still further in the 1970s: notable roles included Lord Fancourt Babberly in *Charley's Aunt* (1970), Norman in *Ayckbourn's *The Norman Conquests* (1974), the poet-peasant John Clare in *Bond's *The Fool* (1975), plus Hamlet, Peer Gynt, and the title role in Ronald *Harwood's *The Dresser* during several seasons with the 69 Company at *Manchester's *Royal Exchange Theatre. More classic parts followed with *Molière's *Le Malade imaginaire* (*The Imaginary Invalid*, 1987) and *The Miser* (1991). In 1993–4 he *toured the *one-person show *Moscow Stations*, and in 1996 starred in Yasmina *Reza's hugely successful *Art*.   BRK

COURT THEATRE See ROYAL COURT THEATRE.

COURT THEATRES

From the time of Henry VIII plays were staged to entertain the English ruler and the court during the Christmas season. Under Elizabeth, one or two *masques and six or more plays were the usual supply, performed at first chiefly by groups of boy choristers (see BOYS' COMPANIES), later by the professional men's companies. They usually began with a first play on 26 December, and continued into late February. When James I came to the throne in 1603 the number increased markedly. In most years he saw twenty or more, along with two or three masques, which were considerably more expensive to stage. A variety of venues were set up specially for these shows, chiefly at Whitehall, but also at the palaces at Richmond and Greenwich. Besides the banqueting halls, a series of theatres were built at Whitehall. The forms of entertainment changed over the years, especially in the transition from the Tudor to the Stuart rulers. In the sixteenth century they were constrained by costs and tradition. The Stuart fashion, especially for masques, was more extravagant, and used Italian fashions with staging effects using *perspective and extraordinary devices of *lighting and fire introduced by Inigo *Jones (see SCENOGRAPHY).

Essentially there were four types of entertainment: masques, plays staged by the students of the *Inns of Court, plays by the boy chorister companies and their successors, and plays by the professional adult companies. The masques developed most radically, although the adult plays also changed, between *Gorboduc* in 1566, written by two courtiers and staged by the law students of the Inner Temple, to *Fletcher's *The Scornful Lady* in 1641, the last play staged at court for the early Stuarts. Under the Tudors, masques (sometimes called 'masks' to differentiate them from the more elaborate Inigo Jones creations) were scenic shows, emblematic and colourful, usually designed to teach the monarch, as tactfully as possible, some point of current moral or political concern. Plays staged at court by the Inns of Court, such as *The Misfortunes of Arthur*, written and acted by the students of Gray's Inn in 1588, often had the same underlying purpose. Plays by boy companies such as the *Chapel Royal choristers from Greenwich were chosen by the *Lord Chamberlain's delegate, the *Master of the Revels, solely for their academic and heuristic value. Playing by boys was a standard practice in schools and universities, and was judged to be more respectable than entertainments offered by the professional companies (see UNIVERSITY AND SCHOOL DRAMA). These plays were usually enactments of classical or biblical stories.

The professional adult companies offered the plays that had been hits in the London public theatre through the previous year. The plays chosen to be performed at court were selected by the Master of the Revels on the basis of invited previews, which he watched through the autumn at the Revels office in St John's, Clerkenwell. From the 1590s onwards Shakespeare's plays were a staple of these performances. *King Lear* was chosen for the King at the *Whitehall Banqueting House on 26 December 1606.   AJG

COVENT GARDEN THEATRE

After the success of *Beggar's Opera*, John *Rich had the original Covent Garden Theatre built in Bow Street in *London, near *Drury Lane Theatre, by architect Edward Shephard. It opened in 1732 with a pit (twelve benches), surrounded by three levels of side *boxes, with one level of boxes and two galleries at the rear, and a capacity of 1,397. It had a 3.96 m (13 feet) apron stage (*see* FORESTAGE), a 7.91 m (26 feet) wide *proscenium, and 12.79 m (42 feet) of stage depth. Rich owned the *Davenant *patent, which remained with this theatre until such monopolies were abolished in 1843. *Handel rented the theatre regularly from 1734 to 1737. When Rich died in 1761 Covent Garden became an *opera house until it was sold to playwright George *Colman and his associates in 1767. Thomas Harris had the theatre modernized by John Inigo Richards in 1784 and rebuilt by Henry Holland in 1792, with four levels of horseshoe-shaped tiers supported by cast-iron posts and a capacity of 3,000. George Frederick *Cooke first performed here in 1800, and the first English *melodrama, *A Tale of Mystery*, opened in 1802. John Philip *Kemble became resident *actor-manager in 1803 with Sarah *Siddons as leading actress, and the child prodigy Henry West *Betty made his debut in 1804. In 1808 the theatre was destroyed by *fire.

The second *playhouse, built by John Smirke, Jr., in 1809, was the first major Greek revival building in London and the first public building with central heating. When it opened with a capacity of 2,800, higher ticket prices motivated the *OP (Old Price) riots, which ran for 61 nights. The lobby was illuminated with gas in 1815, the *auditorium in 1817. Charles *Kemble managed the theatre from 1817 to 1832, introducing the fashion for historically accurate *costumes; Fanny Kemble started here in 1829; Edmund *Kean gave his final performance in 1833. William Charles *Macready was its actor-manager from 1837 to 1839, introducing the first *limelight. Charles *Mathews and Madame *Vestris managed it from 1839 to 1842, producing Dion *Boucicault's first play (1841). In 1847 the theatre was redesigned by Benedetto Albano as the Royal Italian Opera House (capacity 4,000), but was destroyed by fire in 1856.

The current theatre was built by Edward W. Barry and opened in 1858 as the Royal English Opera, becoming the Royal Opera House in 1892. In 1946 *Sadler's Wells Ballet became its resident company, and the Covent Garden Opera was added in 1947 (they were designated as the Royal Ballet in 1956 and the Royal Opera in 1968). The theatre was remodelled in 1964 and closed from July 1997 to December 1999 for extensive renovations designed by architects Jeremy Dixon and Edward Jones at a cost in excess of £250 million.   FJH

COWLEY, NOËL (1899–1973)

British playwright, performer, director, and songwriter, as famous for being himself as for any of his varied creative activities. Coward achieved success simultaneously as an actor and playwright in *I'll Leave It to You* (1920) and *The Young Idea* (1923), and *The Vortex* (1924), in which he played the drug-addicted Nicky Lancaster whose mother throws herself at younger men, made a star of its author-leading man. Coward was famously

photographed for the front of the *Sketch* sitting in his bed, surrounded by cigarettes and mysterious bottles, 'wearing a Chinese dressing-gown and an expression of advanced degeneracy'. The iconography was perfect, capturing the moral vertigo of his plays which, inspired by a trip to *New York in 1921 and the wisecracking *dialogue of Broadway, employed fast-talking, smart stichomythia as a powerful motor to leave conventional values standing.

Hay Fever (1925) is typical of the early plays, showing a highly theatrical family running rings around a group of staid outsiders, while *Easy Virtue* (1926) brings the *well-made play into the twentieth century. In *Private Lives* (1930), the pinnacle of the early work, a divorced couple meet on their respective honeymoons with new spouses and elope together; the evasion of moral judgement, and the blur of paradox and witticism, made it a perfect vehicle for Coward and his co-star Gertrude *Lawrence. Through the 1930s and 1940s, alongside classic *comedies like *Design for Living* (1939), *Blithe Spirit* (1941), and *Present Laughter* (1943), Coward wrote *revues, *musical comedies, straight *dramas, and a *historical epic, *Cavalcade* (1931). His work can look flat on the page, the writing defiantly unliterary, yet as a performer he knew how to create dialogue that would release comic momentum. Although he appeared rakishly heterosexual on stage, other meanings could be derived from coded references to homosexuality in his work, which would influence *queer performance companies like Gloria in the 1990s.

Coward cemented his reputation during the Second World War with three successful plays, morale-boosting appearances for the troops, a stirring performance in his own propaganda *film *In Which We Serve* (1942), and several songs of a patriotic or lightly satirical nature. He emerged a very establishment figure, seemingly keen to join the aristocratic and high Tory worlds he had once deflated: *Relative Values* (1951) and *South Sea Bubble* (1956) had little of their author's earlier edge. Not that this mattered to Coward, who had already forged a new career as a *cabaret performer, with celebrated appearances in Las Vegas in 1955. The cover of the resulting record—Coward in the desert in evening dress with a cup of tea, a wittily self-mocking image of his unflappable Britishness—cemented his international fame and as a result he was relatively unscathed by the revolutions taking place in British theatre in 1956. Indeed, many of the angry young playwrights, notably *Osborne and *Pinter, paid tribute to his influence. A great deal of his work continues to be performed worldwide, and the centenary of his birth was marked by a flurry of new productions in Britain and America.   DR

COWLEY, HANNAH (1743–1809)

English dramatist. She wrote her first play, *The Runaway* (1776), out of a dissatisfaction with the new dramas of the time; it was a great success at *Garrick's *Drury Lane, an auspicious beginning to her career. The older Restoration repertory inspired much of her work, including *The Belle's Stratagem* (1780), *A Bold Stroke for a Husband* (1783), and *A School for Greybeards* (1786, from *Behn's *The Lucky Chance*). While Cowley claimed to be indifferent to popular success, her unhappiness with the bad taste of *audiences led her to stop writing plays in 1794.　　　MJK

CRABTREE, LOTTA (1846–1924)

American actress. One of the best-loved performers of the nineteenth century, Crabtree parlayed her banjo-picking, clog-dancing winsomeness into a $4,000,000 fortune. A California gold prospector's daughter, she was spotted by Lola *Montez and taught to sing and *dance. From performing in mining camps and small time *variety shows she stormed *San Francisco in 1858 with *The Loan of a Lover*. By 1864 she was starring in *New York, three years later having her greatest success in the dual title roles of *Little Nell and the Marchioness*, an adaptation of *Dickens's *The Old Curiosity Shop*. Crabtree's popularity never dimmed, and after *touring extensively she retired in 1891.　　　TFC

CRACKNELL, RUTH (1925–)

Australian actor who studied at the Independent Drama School in *Sydney, made her debut in 1947, and has had an immensely varied and successful career. In the late 1950s and 1960s she was known for her appearances in the Phillip Street Revues in Sydney, in the 1960s and 1970s for her professional partnership with Ron Haddick and work at the Old Tote Theatre Company, and in the 1980s and 1990s as a leading actress for the Sydney Theatre Company. Cracknell is best known for the Australian *television comedy series *Mother and Son*.　　　SBS

CRACOW

Until 1600 the royal residence of Polish kings, Cracow is the cultural capital of Poland, containing its greatest art treasures and oldest university. From 1200 a *liturgical theatre existed, and *morality and *mystery plays were staged in market squares. Latin *university and school drama, court *spectacles, and Italian theatre flourished in the *early modern period. With the third partition of Poland in 1795, Cracow became part of the multinational, polyglot Austro-Hungarian Empire. A cultural crossroads more akin to *Vienna, *Prague, and *Budapest than to Russified *Warsaw where harsh *censorship reigned, Cracow was open to the latest European trends and welcomed visiting artists from Italy and Germany.

A small, compact city of only 85,000 in 1900, Cracow's cultural life has always been concentrated around the market square, near which the major theatres are located. Organized at

the end of the eighteenth century, Teatr Stary—Cracow's first permanent professional theatre—still occupies the same building today as in 1799. By the 1860s, when Helena Modrzejewska (*Modjeska) was one of its stars, the Stary achieved eminence through outstanding ensemble *acting and integral staging. Turn-of-the-century Cracow fostered a painterly theatre stressing poetic image and psychological mood. Visual artists like Stanisław *Wyspiański were often playwrights and directors. From 1898 to his death in 1907, he staged seven of his dramas at the Teatr Miejski. Cracow itself was a work of art figuring prominently in Wyspiański's plays and paintings.

After Poland regained independence in 1919, *avant-garde painters established Cricot, where they staged experimental plays, including *Witkiewicz's *Cuttlefish* in 1933. During the Nazi occupation clandestine groups included Tadeusz *Kantor's Independent Theatre and Kotlarczyk's Rhapsodic Theatre, with Karol Wojtyła—the future Pope John Paul II—as actor and theorist. During the Stalinist years from 1949 to 1953 only the new Teatr Groteska of Puppet and Live Actor escaped the heavy hand of *socialist realism. While designing for the *opera and various theatres, Kantor established his own company, Cricot II, in the basement gallery, Krzysztofory, where in 1956 he opened with *The Cuttlefish* to acknowledge his ancestry. In Nowa Huta, a new working-class district, Teatr Ludowy was built as a model socialist theatre, but flourished as an avant-garde theatre with innovative design by Józef *Szajna, later its *manager. In the 1960s, under Zygmunt Hübner's management, Teatr Stary became home to Poland's best directors: Jerzy Jarocki, Konrad *Swinarski, and Andrzej *Wajda. Cracow is also famous for its *cabarets: the turn-of-the-twentieth-century Green Balloon and communist-era Cellar at the Sign of the Rams.　　　DG

'Cracow, European city of culture', *Theatre in Poland*, 1–2 (2000)

CRAIG, EDITH (1869–1947)

English actress, designer, *costume maker, director, and political activist, daughter of Ellen *Terry. Craig directed pageants for the Actresses' Franchise League and devised *A Pageant of Great Women* with Cecily *Hamilton, a suffrage theatre piece remounted by Craig all over the UK with largely *amateur casts during the period 1909–12. While her brother Edward Gordon *Craig *theorized about production, Edy attended to practicalities of *directing, usually away from the commercial mainstream. Her Pioneer Players (1911–25) presented plays largely on Sunday matinées in *London, when friendly commercial theatres were available. The company's repertoire was eclectic and often woman centred: she staged work by *Hrostvitha of Gandersheim, translated by Craig's long-term partner Christopher St John (Christabel Marshall), and later revived Susan *Glaspell's *The Verge*, starring Sybil *Thorndike (1925). Edy

Craig was known for her uncompromising approach, her refusal to suffer fools gladly, and her ability to create spectacular effects on the smallest of budgets. When her mother died Craig established an annual theatre festival in her memory at their home, Smallhythe in Kent.   EJS

CRAIG, EDWARD GORDON (1872–1966)

English actor, designer, and director, the son of Ellen *Terry and E. W. Godwin, architect and scene designer. In 1878, 1885, and from 1889, Craig acted with Henry *Irving's company (he was to write informative memoirs of both Irving and Terry); he left in 1893, partly because, realizing the excellence of Irving's artistry, he could not foresee ways in which *acting might be developed. And Craig wished fiercely to be an innovator. Also in 1893 he had befriended William Nicholson and James Pryde, from whom he learned the art of wood engraving. Craig relished the refinement and simplicity of expression imposed by the medium and in time saw through it the means of revolutionizing the current use of *painted *scenery, which he found artificial. His ideas were first put to the test when with Martin Shaw he staged Purcell's *Dido and Aeneas* (1900), *The Masque of Love* (1901), and *Handel's *Acis and Galatea* (1902) in *London. It was, however, his designs for his productions of Laurence *Housman's *Bethlehem* (1902), and of *Ibsen's *The Vikings* and Shakespeare's *Much Ado About Nothing* for his mother in 1903, which won him wide acclaim. Craig's first *theoretical treatise, *The Art of the Theatre* (1905), defined the importance of the designer-*director in achieving the non-*naturalistic staging he envisaged as the theatre of the future. Count Harry Kessler's and Otto *Brahm's enthusiasm for his work, and offers of commissions in Germany, now enticed Craig to leave England; he was to live and work chiefly on the Continent thereafter.

Craig did not prove an easy partner in collaboration. Only one of three projects for Eleanore *Duse was realized (*Rosmersholm*, staged in Florence in 1906). *Reinhardt, *Diaghilev, and Beerbohm *Tree rejected design schemes. Craig, like Adolphe *Appia, sought to create credible architectural structures on stage, which would be given volume, mass, colour, and mood by angled (electric) *lighting, not by painted effects of chiaroscuro (*see* SCENOGRAPHY). After settling in Florence in 1908 he began experimenting with series of movable screens of varying heights and widths to achieve this effect in practicable terms. Later he envisaged a stage where pillar formations might rise or descend by electronic hoists, singly or in groups, to create stylized scenes. The fruits of this work were published in *Towards a New Theatre* (1913) and *Scene* (1923) with illustrative plates; and throughout the issues of the *Mask*, a magazine which Craig edited (1908–29). This journal, largely written by Craig under numerous pseudonyms, celebrated all manifestations of the arts that comprise performance, historically and internationally.

The chance to test his concepts in practice came first with an invitation from W. B. *Yeats to get involved in design at the *Abbey Theatre in *Dublin, to whom Craig gave plans for a set of screens (first used in 1911). Next, *Stanislavsky (inspired by praise of the designer from Craig's former lover, the dancer Isadora *Duncan) commissioned a production of *Hamlet* (1912) for the *Moscow Art Theatre, although Craig lost the absolute control over the staging that he requested. Disillusioned with both the codification of classical *ballet (when compared with the freedom of Duncan's *dance technique) and the mannerism of contemporary acting styles, Craig evolved over the decade the idea of a new mechanically operated 'performer', which he termed an *Über-marionette. Despite this, he ran for some years after 1913 a school of acting in the Theatre Goldoni, which had become his workplace in Florence (*see* TRAINING). His writings and practice show that a crucial aspect of his agenda was his concern that a director should keep absolute control over all aspects of a production in *rehearsal and in performance, including the acting style.

This theme was restated vigorously in his revised *On the Art of the Theatre* (1911), the tone of which is more emphatic and rhetorical than in the 1905 version. Perhaps aware of Appia's parallel investigations, Craig had become highly defensive of his schemes. This attitude increasingly militated against his receiving that constructive criticism from sympathetic contemporaries which might have tempered his inspiration within the realms of the possible, enabling Craig to achieve in practical stagecraft the revolution he desired. However, Craig's output in books, illustrations, and stage designs after 1918 was prodigious: *The Marionette* (1918), *The Theatre Advancing* (1921), *Woodcuts and Some Words* (1924), *Books and Theatres* (1925), an edition of *Hamlet* for the Cranach Press (1930), all show his theories evolving from his experiences in *Moscow and with Yeats. Designs for two productions were commissioned in this decade: Ibsen's *The Pretenders* for the Poulsens in Copenhagen in 1926, the designs for which were published in *A Production* (1930); and George Tyler's *New York staging of *Macbeth* (1928). While the former re-created Craig's schemes with integrity, the latter felt free in Craig's absence to adapt, truncate, and distort the designer's intentions. Craig spent his final years in France, in *Paris and Vence.   RAC

BABLET, DENIS, *The Theatre of Edward Gordon Craig* (London, 1966)
CRAIG, EDWARD, *Gordon Craig: the story of his life* (London, 1968)
SENELICK, LAURENCE, *Gordon Craig's Moscow Hamlet: a reconstruction* (Westport, Conn., 1982)

CRANE, WILLIAM HENRY (1845–1928)

American actor. Born in Massachusetts, Crane spent his early years in an *opera troupe, making his debut in *Daughter of the Regiment* in 1863, and gaining attention in *New York as the Notary in the première of a *musical version of *Evangeline*

(1874). Leaving music for the straight stage, in 1877 he formed an acting partnership with Stuart *Robson and largely confined himself to *comedy. Their biggest hit was Bronson *Howard's Wall Street comedy *The Henrietta*, which kept them occupied from 1887 to 1889, when they parted. Although admired for his Dromio, Falstaff (*Merry Wives*), Toby Belch, and roles in *Sheridan and *Goldsmith, Crane's overriding passion was comedy by American authors. The role that made him a major star was Hannibal Rivers in *The Senator* (1890), which he played in New York and on *tour for five years and revived thereafter. Most considered his finest creation the title role in *David Harum* (1900). Though his range was limited, he was masterly within it. He left an autobiography, *Footprints and Echoes* (1927).

CT

CRATINUS (fl. 450–422 BC)

Greek playwright whose work survives only in fragments though his reputation in the ancient world was as high as that of any comic writer of the fifth century. He made use of mythological themes but also satirized contemporary figures, including himself in *The Wine Flask*, where he depicts himself as married to *Comedy but chasing after Drunkenness. Though ridiculed by *Aristophanes, Cratinus gave *Old Comedy the overall form that Aristophanes himself adopted. JMW

CRAVEN, HAWES (1837–1910)

English scene painter and designer. Craven learned the craft of scene *painting at the Britannia Theatre, *London. By his early twenties he was working at the major *playhouses, including *Drury Lane and *Covent Garden, and between 1862 and 1864 he served as resident designer at the Theatre Royal, *Dublin. He later joined Henry *Irving at the *Lyceum, and became a leading designer in the 1880s and 1890s, preparing the sets for most of Irving's productions. Toward the end of his career he also designed for Beerbohm *Tree at His (*Her) Majesty's Theatre. Throughout his career he was committed to the principles of *illusionism and historical *antiquarianism. TP

CRAWFORD, CHERYL (1902–86)

American producer. A rising star in the administration of the *Theatre Guild, Crawford broke away to join Harold *Clurman and Lee *Strasberg to found the *Group Theatre in 1931. One of the Group's ruling 'triumvirate,' her main role was to raise funds and mediate between Clurman and Strasberg. Resigning from the Group in 1937, Crawford became an independent *producer while also participating in the founding of the *American Repertory Theatre (*New York, 1946–8), and in 1947 the *Actors Studio. Her commercially successful productions included *Brigadoon* (1947), *Paint your Wagon* (1950), and *The Rose Tattoo* (1951). MAF

CRAZY GANG

British comedians (Bud Flanagan, 1896–1968; Chesney Allen, 1894–1982; Jimmie Nervo, 1897–1975; Teddy Knox, 1896–1974; Charlie Naughton, 1887–1976; Jimmy Gold, 1886–1967; and 'Monsewer' Eddie Gray, 1897–1969). The impresario George *Black first brought together the Crazy Gang at the *London Palladium in 1932, combining well-established *variety solo and double acts. Its fast-paced, anarchic comedy routines, disrupting other acts on the bill and spilling over into the *auditorium, revived the fortunes of the Palladium, where it played 'Crazy Weeks' throughout the decade. The Gang continued the same mixture of *clowning, *burlesque, and *slapstick at the Victoria Palace Theatre from 1947 until 1962. SF

CRÉBILLON, PROSPER JOLYOT DE (1674–1762)

French playwright and dramatic censor. An older contemporary and rival of *Voltaire in the field of *tragedy, Crébillon deliberately staked out the field of sensationalism and horror as a means of arousing tragic emotion, choosing, for example, the fraternal enmity of the *protagonists in *Atrée et Thyeste* (1707)—though substituting a beaker of blood for the human flesh served at the reconciliation feast in the classical source. His masterpiece *Rhadamiste et Zénobie* (1711) also contains its fill of improbable family relationships, ending in assassination. Elected to the Academy in 1731, Crébillon became the official censor in 1735, providing further cause for Voltaire's animosity (*see* CENSORSHIP). WDH

CREOLE THEATRE

In the francophone *Caribbean—chiefly Haiti, Guadeloupe, and Martinique—creole is used alternately with French in daily life, depending on the speaker, circumstance, and purpose. Because creole is a language of orality and proximity, it is useful for *dialogue in the theatre; some plays have been partly or fully written in creole since the nineteenth century, in spite of the difficulties connected to an unstandardized language. It may be that creole theatre has its roots in the evening gatherings of slaves, relaxing by listening to tales and performing sketches. Whatever the origin, today shows are often professionally designed and performed in a variety of spaces. There are four major categories of plays.

1. Those wholly written in creole, modelled on the classics, attempting to demonstrate that the European tradition can be well expressed with creole languages and be entertaining.

Playwrights often accent comic aspects when using creole instead of French: the great *tragedies become *comedies or even *farces. After the famous *Antigone en créole* by Morisseau-Leroi (Haiti, 1953) led the way, we find *Jénéral Rodrig* by Nono Numa (inspired by *Corneille's *The Cid*) or *Mouché Défas* by Lyonel Desmarattes (borrowing the theme of *Molière's *Tartuffe*). More recently, *Don Jan* by George Mauvois (Martinique, 1996) remained loyal to Molière's original *text.

2. Militant *political plays advocating new social order by presenting revolutionary or outrageous events, such as a 1959 murderous repression, the trial of young Martinican nationalists, or the 1967 riots in Guadeloupe. These plays, struggling against alienation and neocolonial repression, were often improvised entirely in creole, and had particular success during the 1970s and 1980s. A few works of this type were written in French by writers such as Auguste Macouba *Arnet, Daniel *Boukman, and Vincent *Placoly.

3. Light fare designed to amuse, regularly using French and creole. The short plays or sketches by Paul Baudot in Guadeloupe in the nineteenth century belong to this category, as does the work of Gilbert de Chambertrand (writing c.1917–1920) and Marie-Thérèse Lung-Fou in the 1950s. The oral popular tradition has prompted further examples, as in the cases of Elie *Stephenson (French Guiana), Ina *Césaire (Martinique), and even Patrick *Chamoiseau (*Maman Dlo contre la fée Carabosse*, 1981).

4. At the end of the twentieth century a new trend dealt with contemporary problems caused by economic immigration, the difficulties of life abroad in France, and the results of coming home. Simone *Schwarz-Bart's *Ton beau capitaine* is a good example, as is *Arivé d'Pari* by Georges *Mauvois. *Dodin* by Jeff Florentiny shows the tension of those torn between their homeland and their adopted country.   MCHM

CRIMP, MARTIN (1956–   )

English playwright. Crimp's transformation of enigmatic, hyper-realistic *dialogue into minimalist stage poetry recalls *Pinter, but the *satire is harsher and the moral ambiguities deeper. First championed by the Orange Tree Theatre in Richmond, who produced *Dealing with Clair* (1988) and *Play with Repeats* (1989), in the 1990s his work was usually premièred at the *Royal Court. The central figure of *The Treatment* (1993) is a *character named Ann, maltreated first by her partner and then by *film producers who want to buy her story. *Attempts on her Life* (1997) splinters her further in seventeen scenes. Showing the influence of some *performance art writing, the *text does not assign lines to characters, forcing every production to intervene further in Ann's story. *The Country* (2000) offers a more conventional narrative, but the riddling complexity of motivations shows the same harsh investigation into human identity. Other plays include *No One Sees the Video* (1990), *Getting*

Attention (1991), and *Face to the Wall* (2002). Crimp has also been acclaimed for translations of plays from French.

DR

CRISIS

A decisive moment, or turning point, in a dramatic *action. In the late nineteenth century Gustav *Freytag identified a traditional five-part pyramidal dramatic structure with a *climax at the apex, and three crises: an initiating action that precipitates the *complication, and action that ends the climax and initiates the *denouement, and an action that brings about the *catastrophe. It has become more common to recognize Freytag's climax as the central crisis, and to use 'climax' to refer to the highest point of *audience interest, which may or may not coincide with the central crisis. William *Archer went further and identified crisis as the essence of *drama. *See also* PERIPETEIA.

RWV

CRISPIN *See* POISSON, RAYMOND.

CRISTI, CARLA (c.1936–   )

Chilean actress. Born in *Barcelona and educated at the Theatre School of the University of Chile, she joined *Ictus in 1958. She became well known for her role in *El cepillo de dientes* (*The Toothbrush*, 1961) by Jorge *Díaz, and has been involved in numerous productions by Chilean companies such as the Catholic University Theatre School, the Municipal Theatre, and the Tunnel. Between 1977 and 1981 she lived and worked in Spain. In 1985 she became one of the founders of the Teatro del Alma in *Santiago.   MAR

CRITICISM/CRITIC

Although there is considerable overlap between the operations of theory and those of criticism, in general theory refers to the articulation of general principles of the phenomenon being studied, and criticism to analysis of a particular case. (*See* THEORIES OF DRAMA, THEATRE, AND PERFORMANCE.) In theatre and drama this usually means the analysis of a particular play or a group of plays or a particular production. An early example of what would today be called criticism was the writings surrounding the appearance of *Corneille's popular and controversial *Le Cid* in 1637 (*see* NEOCLASSICISM). By the mid-seventeenth century regular periodicals in France contained criticism of current theatre. The most important and influential of these periodicals was the *Mercure galant*, edited by Donneau de *Visé from 1672 to 1710.

Theatre and drama criticism first flourished in England in the Augustan age at the opening of the eighteenth century, when Joseph *Addison and Richard *Steele achieved an enormous success with their periodicals the *Tatler* (1709–11) and the *Spectator* (1711–14), both containing reports on all manner of current cultural concerns, including the contemporary theatre, and inspiring many journalistic successors. In Germany, pioneering work in theatre criticism was undertaken by G. E. *Lessing, who was commissioned to write 100 essays to inform the public about the plays offered at the newly formed *Hamburg National Theatre. These collected essays, the *Hamburg Dramaturgy* (1769), formed the critical foundation of the modern German theatre (*see* DRAMATURGY). The reports written back to aristocrats and sovereigns of Eastern Europe on the French theatre between 1753 and 1790 by Friedrich Melchior Grimm, first privately circulated and later collected and published as the *Correspondance littéraire* (1812), also had an important international influence.

The first modern reviews of theatrical productions appeared in France in the wake of the revolution, where a new theatregoing public, unfamiliar with the interrupted tradition, looked to theatrical reviews for a wide variety of information not only evaluative but also descriptive and historical, a guide to understanding the work. This need was answered by the influential critic Julien-Louis Geoffroy, who served as critic for the *Journal des débats* from 1800 until his death in 1814. With Geoffroy the reviewer became a regular feature of the French theatre world, as much a part of it as any actor, director, or playwright, and both the taste and the chronicling of the French theatre of the nineteenth century owed much to Geoffroy's influential nineteenth-century successors, Jules *Janin, Jules Lemaître, and Francisque *Sarcey.

The *romantic movement in the early nineteenth century encouraged the development of elegant, personal essays on Shakespeare, contemporary theatre, and the work of the actors of the time. In France the master of this form, which came to be known as the feuilleton (a term still used in some European newspapers for the review section), was Théophile *Gautier. Germany also produced a number of popular feuilleton authors, headed in the mid-nineteenth century by Theodor Fontane and Paul Lindau. In England the romantic period produced some of the most important dramatic criticism yet to appear in that country, beginning with the essays of William *Hazlitt and Charles *Lamb and continuing with those of Thomas De Quincey and Leigh *Hunt. The deaths of both De Quincey and Hunt in 1859 essentially ended the great tradition of romantic criticism in England, but George Henry *Lewes produced an important body of such writing in the next generation.

British theatre criticism flourished again near the end of the nineteenth century. Bernard *Shaw dominated the field, but he was seconded by a number of other important writers, among them Clement *Scott and William *Archer, who disagreed publicly and bitterly over the worth of the new drama in general and *Ibsen (of which Archer was a translator and

champion) in particular. Shaw's successor as theatre critic for the *Saturday Review* (from 1895 to 1898) was Max *Beerbohm, whose style and wit were very much in the tradition of the European feuilleton.

In Germany, as in England, Ibsen and the new drama encouraged a generation of critics devoted to the development of a serious modern theatre. Julius Hart, Paul Schlenther, and Otto *Brahm were all closely associated with Ibsen and *Zolaesque *naturalism, and their dedication to modern and experimental theatre was carried on by the leading German critic of the early twentieth century, Alfred Kerr.

The rise of the popular press in the nineteenth century, along with the development of the academic study of theatre and drama in the European and American universities (*see* THEATRE STUDIES), created a separation between academic criticism and critical journalism that continued through the twentieth century. In the academy, the dominant tradition became close reading of dramatic *texts with relatively little attention paid to the operations of these texts on stage and with much more concern, especially in the later twentieth century, about dramatic and theatrical theory. The results of this criticism generally appeared in the hundreds of academic journals that flourished during the century, with a primarily academic readership. Critical journalism, in general, carried on the feuilletoniste tradition, often with an overlay of evaluation as theatrical critics became more and more perceived as making significant contributions to the economic success or failure of a production. Such criticism appeared in the popular press, in newspapers and magazines, and later on *radio and *television as well, and its readership was, of course, much more general than that of academic criticism. The two were not entirely separate, since concerns, theories, and from time to time terms of academic criticism filtered into critical journalism, but the two traditions remained essentially separate, and critical journalism produced both feuilletoniste critics who were resolutely anti-intellectual, like James *Agate or W. A. Darlington in mid-twentieth-century *London, and others much involved with current intellectual trends, like Kenneth *Tynan from the 1950s to the 1970s. Among the more recent British critics, only John Elsom, critic for the *Listener*, and Benedict Nightingale of *The Times* have also had close connections with the academy, and neither of their collections of critical writings show much evidence of the style or theoretical orientation of academic criticism of the same period.

A circle of daily critics was established in *New York by the end of the eighteenth century, and such important literary figures as Washington Irving, Edgar Allan Poe, and Walt Whitman all wrote regular theatre reviews, but theatrical criticism could hardly flourish in a culture where theatre itself was not very highly regarded. After the Civil War a number of critics appeared who were dedicated to raising the standards of theatre and theatrical taste in the United States. The leader of these was

William *Winter, who dominated New York theatre criticism for most of the late nineteenth century, to be followed at the turn of the century by Alan Dale. Their efforts were seconded by John Rankin Towse, who wrote for the upper-class readers of the *New York Post* from 1874 to 1927, by Henry Austin Clapp, at the *Boston Daily Advertiser* from 1868 to 1902, and by Henry *James, who brought news of the current European theatre to a number of American papers in the 1860s and 1870s. In America as in Europe the emergence of the new European drama of Ibsen and Shaw called forth critical champions, the most important of whom was James Gibbons Huneker of the *New York Recorder* and later the *New York Advertiser* and the *Sun*.

Huneker's writings were highly influential upon the major new generation of American critics that appeared in the early years of the twentieth century. Closest in spirit to Huneker was the witty and urbane George Jean *Nathan, who wrote for the *Smart Set* from 1909 to 1923, championing, like Huneker, the new European drama and, unlike Huneker, the new American drama, especially that of Eugene *O'Neill. The power of the critic over the success or failure of a play grew markedly during this generation, largely due to the influence of Alexander *Woollcott, the sarcastic and brilliant reviewer of the *New York Herald*, the *Sun*, and the *New York World*. His growing power and cutting style led him into a series of confrontations with the leading New York *producers of the era, the *Shuberts, and his exuberant persona lives on in the outrageous critic based upon him in *Kaufman and *Hart's popular *comedy *The Man Who Came to Dinner* (1939). Although Nathan and Woollcott dominated the critical world of the early twentieth century, they were gradually eclipsed by Brooks *Atkinson, who began reviewing theatre for the *New York Times* in 1926 and remained there (except for a few years in the 1940s) until 1960. He was the first president of the New York Critics' Circle, founded in 1933, and the most influential voice during a generation in which the favourable opinion of the New York critics became more and more essential to the success of a new play. Atkinson carried on the Huneker tradition of encouragement of new experimental work. Unlike Nathan, he looked favourably upon the new *political drama of the 1930s and he, alone among major New York critics, took an interest in the emerging *Off-Broadway movement of the early 1950s, having much to do with the directing of public interest toward that movement.

Atkinson was followed at the *New York Times* by Walter *Kerr, a former professor of drama who inherited Atkinson's position as America's leading drama critic, with even greater power over the success of productions in New York as the number of daily newspapers (and thus the number of readily available reviews of each production) steadily diminished, with only three remaining by 1967. This resulted from time to time in highly public disputes between leading critics like Kerr and theatre directors and producers who resented the power of the critics. One major confrontation of this sort occurred between Kerr and Joseph *Papp, director of the *New York Shakespeare Festival, in 1968–9. The considerable influence that Kerr exercised in the *Times* during the 1970s was continued during the 1980s by his successor Frank *Rich.

The decline in the number of daily New York papers offering theatre criticism meant a rise in the importance of critics who wrote for weekly and monthly magazines. The *Nation* and the *New Republic* have offered a particularly distinguished tradition of such writing, the first with Joseph Wood Krutch and Harold *Clurman, the latter with Stark *Young from 1921 to 1947 and later with Eric *Bentley, Robert *Brustein, and Stanley Kauffmann. Major contributions have also been made to this tradition by writers for the *New Yorker* (among them Edith Oliver and John *Lahr) and *Theatre Arts Magazine* (Kenneth *Macgowan and Rosamund Gilder). A more general public also followed the reviews of Louis Kronenberger or T. E. Kalem in *Time* magazine or Jack Kroll in *Newsweek*. As Off-Broadway developed, the *avant-garde and *alternative theatre developed its own critical tradition, primarily in the pages of the *Village Voice*, with the work of Julius Novik, Alisa Solomon, Michael Feingold, and others.

During the final years of the twentieth century, the *New York Times* remained the most powerful source of criticism in America, though its leading theatre reviewers, David Richards and Ben Brantley, lacked the visibility on the theatre scene of their more famous predecessors. As *regional theatres in America became more important in the later twentieth century, dramatic critics outside New York grew in importance, and although none of them achieved a national reputation, due to the continuing centrality of New York to the American professional theatre, a number of these critics became for their regions as significant in the theatre there as their colleagues in New York were in that city. Among such critics were Richard Christiansen of the *Chicago Tribune*, Kevin Kelly of the *Boston Globe*, Bernard Weiner of the *San Francisco Chronicle*, and in *Los Angeles, Dan Sullivan, who served as a theatre critic for the *Los Angeles Times* from 1969 to 1990 after three years as theatre/music critic at the *New York Times*, and Sylvie Drake, also a theatre critic for the *Los Angeles Times* from 1971 to 1993. *See also* INTERNATIONAL ASSOCIATION OF THEATRE CRITICS.

MC

AGATE, JAMES, *The English Dramatic Critics: an anthology, 1660–1932* (London, 1932)

COMTOIS, M. E., and MILLER, LYNN F., *Contemporary American Theatre Critics* (Metuchen, NJ, 1977)

ENGEL, LEHMAN, *The Critics* (New York, 1976)

CRONYN, HUME (1911–2003)

Canadian actor, writer, and director. While attending McGill University, he appeared with the *Montréal Repertory Company and the McGill Players' Club, and made his American debut in Washington, DC, with Cochran's *Stock Company in *Up Pops the Devil* (1931). After his Broadway debut in *Hipper's Holiday* (1934), Cronyn's roles there ranged from Polonius opposite Richard *Burton's Hamlet to Tobias in *Albee's *A Delicate Balance* (1966). Beginning with Alfred Hitchcock's *Shadow of a Doubt* (1942), he performed in nearly 50 *films, including *Lifeboat* (1944), *Cleopatra* (1963), and *Cocoon* (1988). His marriage to Jessica *Tandy in 1942 provided one of the greatest actor rapports on stage, screen, and *television. 'The first couple of American theatre' performed together at the *Guthrie Theatre (Minneapolis), at the Ontario *Stratford Festival, and in *The Four Poster* (1952), *The Physicists* (1964), *The Gin Game* (1977), and *Foxfire* (1980, which Cronyn wrote with Susan Cooper). For his directorial debut, Cronyn directed Tandy in *Portrait of a Madonna* (1946) at the Actors' Laboratory Theatre, and later directed and *toured with his wife in *Triple Play* (1959). PBON

CROOKED MIRROR *See* KRIVOE ZERKALO.

CROSS DRESSING *See* FEMALE IMPERSONATION; MALE IMPERSONATION.

CROSSROADS THEATRE

American *regional theatre located in New Brunswick, New Jersey, a major producer of *African-American theatrical work. Founded in 1978 by Ricardo Khan and L. Kenneth Richardson, Crossroads offers four productions a year, some of which have *toured nationally and to the *Caribbean, Canada, England, and South Africa. In 1999 it was *awarded a Tony as outstanding regional theatre, and is now affiliated with the Kennedy Center in Washington, the New Jersey Performing Arts Center in Newark, and the New Victory Theatre in *New York. George *Wolfe's highly successful *The Colored Museum* was launched there (1986), as was *Ain't Nothing but the Blues*, which moved to Broadway and was nominated for four Tonys. Crossroads has also featured work by Anna Deavere *Smith, Pearl Cleage, Ntozake *Shange, and August *Wilson, among others. BBL

CROTHERS, RACHEL (1878–1958)

A prolific playwright and skilled director, Crothers was arguably the most prominent woman in the American commercial theatre from her debut with *Elizabeth* in 1899 to her last play, *Susan and God*, in 1938. Thirty-two works were produced on Broadway during this period, with Crothers directing most of them and occasionally acting major roles. Committed to the ideal of a fully professional theatre, earning one's own living, and the value of entertaining while educating a large *audience,

Crothers distrusted the art theatres of her time. Her plays—typically *realistic, serious *comedies—often focused on the double standard by which men and women were judged morally and the seeming incompatibility between modern woman's desire for a career and the demands of husband and children. Her most successful plays were *The Three of Us* (1906), *A Man's World* (1910), *He and She* (1912), *When Ladies Meet* (1932), and *Susan and God*. A talented organizer, Crothers founded the Stage Women's War Relief Fund (1917), the United Theatre Relief Committee (1932), and the American Theatre Wing for War Relief (1940). MAF

CROUSE, RUSSEL (1893–1966)

American librettist, playwright, and producer. Crouse was a journalist and *New Yorker* contributor who began his theatre career with the libretto for *The Gang's All Here* (1931) and served as press agent for the *Theatre Guild. He had his first hit when he helped Howard Lindsay write the *book for the Cole *Porter *musical *Anything Goes* (1934), and thereafter the pair had a highly successful 32-year collaboration. Crouse's gift for wacky nonsense combined with Lindsay's theatre skill in over seventeen *comedies. Their first non-musical, *Life with Father* (1939), ran for eight years, and *State of the Union* (1945), a political *satire, won the Pulitzer Prize. Crouse and Lindsay produced and substantially revised Joseph Kesselring's *Arsenic and Old Lace* (1941), and they wrote the book for *Rodgers and *Hammerstein's *The Sound of Music* (1959). FL

CROWLEY, BOB (1952–)

Irish designer. Trained at Crawford Municipal School of Art (Cork) and *Bristol Old Vic, Crowley is an associate artist of the *Royal Shakespeare Company and the Royal *National Theatre. Interviewed by Michael *Billington (1991), he said the designer's task is to explore 'the arc of the play . . . to uncover its inner logic', offering ambiguities to provoke the *audience's subconscious. For the RSC's *As You Like It* (1985), a forest ambience was created without trees; ladders, rope, and muslin established multiple locations in *The Plantagenets* (1988). Rejecting period correctness, Crowley combined differing periods and conventions within the same design to resonate key themes. His RNT work ranges from a bridge to infinity in *Hedda Gabler* (1990) to the New England-inspired *Carousel* (1994), updated from the 1850s to 1900. With Stephen Rea, he designed and co-directed *The Cure at Troy* (*Field Day Theatre Company, 1990). He designed the *films *Suddenly Last Summer* and *Tales of Hollywood*, and *opera in Britain and abroad. He created a giant pyramid and postmodern fashionable *costumes for Elton John's *Aida* (1998). Among his many honours are the Olivier *award for designer of the year (1990) and the 1994 Tony award and Outer Critics Circle award (for *Carousel*). RVL

CROWNE, JOHN (c.1640–1712)

English playwright. Born in Shropshire, Crowne accompanied his father to Nova Scotia in 1657, and in the same year entered Harvard College, but returned to England in 1660 without taking a degree. In 1671 he began a moderately successful playwriting career, which continued until 1700. His later years were marred by mental illness and he died in poverty in 1712. Crowne was in many respects a typical professional playwright, producing at regular intervals largely undistinguished *tragedies, *comedies, and even a ten-act *heroic drama. He was well connected, enjoying the favour of Charles II and in 1675 devising a *masque for the Duke of York's daughter. Of his seventeen plays, he achieved his greatest successes with *Charles the Eighth of France* (1671), *The Destruction of Jerusalem* (1677), *The Ambitious Statesman* (1679), *City Politiques* (1683), and *Sir Courtly Nice* (1685). RWV

CRUCIBLE THEATRE

English *regional producing theatre in Sheffield. Opened in 1971 and inspired by Tyrone *Guthrie's *open-stage theatres, the Crucible's main *auditorium seats over 1,000 arranged in one semicircular tier around three sides of the large *thrust stage. A flexible *studio space holds 250. Its first director, Colin George, balanced a mainly classical programme with locally oriented work like Alan Cullen's *The Stirrings in Sheffield*. The second director was Peter James, who scored notable successes with the British premières of the American *musicals *Chicago* and *The Wiz*, and introduced the lucrative staging of the annual World Snooker Championships. Clare Venables transformed a financial crisis in 1982 to record surplus in 1987. In 1990 the Sheffield Theatres Company was formed by linking the Crucible with the refurbished Victorian Lyceum Theatre. Since 1999 associate director Michael Grandage has wooed *audiences with star actors like Joseph Fiennes and Kenneth *Branagh in classical roles. CEC

CRUELTY, THEATRE OF

Enterprise launched in *Paris in 1935 by the theatrical visionary Antonin *Artaud, with his adaptation of Shelley's *The Cenci*. The production was the practical culmination of Artaud's long-held plan to revolutionize European theatre by challenging the dominant form of psychological *realism. Adverse critical response and financial difficulties curtailed the run of *The Cenci* to seventeen performances and marked Artaud's last practical experiment with theatre. The production took place in the *music hall Folies-Wagram, an inappropriate venue for *avant-garde theatre, and was acted by wealthy *amateurs and out-of-work professionals who contributed to an uneven stylistic creation. The title derives from a heretical Gnostic belief that the very essence of life (creation and the struggle to survive) is 'cruel' and beyond redemption. Fundamental moments in existence (birth and death) are also considered 'cruel', and moments in Artaud's own experience (such as the administration to him of electro-shock therapy while in hospital) he describes as cruel acts of 'death-in-life'.

This philosophy acted as an analogy for theatrical creation which, Artaud believed, should not be used to narrate or present cruelty but actually to transmit it. The psychophysiological effects of such traumas, rather than the blood, gore, and violence associated with them, were the goals of Artaud's short-lived theatre. 'Cruelty' thus translated into theatrical production centred on the dramatization of moral and social crimes (such as murder, rape, and incest), which were the overriding themes of the Theatre of Cruelty's first production. The notion was expounded in Artaud's celebrated manifesto, *The Theatre and its Double* (1938). Although he never succeeded in successfully realizing the theatre of cruelty himself, the idea acted as a touchstone for a post-war generation of practitioners seeking to revolutionize theatre in a post-totalitarian Europe, in an even more cruel world after the Holocaust. A Theatre of Cruelty season was held in *London in 1964 under the aegis of the *Royal Shakespeare Company, directed by Peter *Brook and Charles *Marowitz. It featured sketches, scenes, *improvisations, a performance of Artaud's playlet *The Spurt of Blood*, and, most importantly, Brook's mounting of Peter *Weiss's *Marat/Sade*. That production and its *film version (1966), coupled with the growing influence of Artaud's *theories in the next decades, greatly affected avant-garde performance worldwide and made the term 'theatre of cruelty' widely current. BRS

CRUZ, CORRAL DE LA

The first of *Madrid's two permanent *playhouses or *corrales de comedias*, the other being the Corral del *Príncipe. Founded by the Brotherhoods of the Pasión and the Soledad, the Cruz opened in rudimentary form on 29 November 1579, and survived, with modifications, until 1736, when it was replaced by a *coliseo* (*proscenium theatre). It was built in a rectangular walled yard (16.7 m by 24.2 m; 55 by 79 feet) within a block, behind a converted house which provided entrances and contained a women's gallery, some *boxes above, and a further gallery in the attic. At the far (south) end was a roofed *stage (8 m by 4.5 m; 26 by 15 feet) projecting from a *tiring house with a lower and upper gallery and a machine loft. Along the sides of the yard, adjoining the stage, were roofed platforms with benches and *gradas* (raked seating); above these were galleries (a distinctive feature of the Cruz). Lateral boxes gradually appeared after 1600 in privately owned buildings on adjoining sites. The yard was roofed in 1703.   CD

CUADRA, PABLO ANTONIO (1912–2002)

Nicaraguan writer. An important poet, Cuadra founded a number of literary and cultural journals and was editor of the opposition newspaper during the Sandinista regime. In the 1930s he promoted a movement that would awaken the sleeping theatre tradition in all parts of Nicaragua, incorporating indigenous performance as well as European models. His play *Por los caminos van los campesinos* (*The Peasants Take the Road*, 1937), set during the American involvement in the country's civil war in the 1920s, heavily criticizes the partisan politics of the time. His other plays include *Satanás entra en escena* (*Enter Satan*, 1948), *Pastorela* (*Shepherd's Play*, 1949), and *Máscaras exige la vida* (*Life Demands Masks*, 1952).   EJW

CUATROTABLAS

Founded by Mario Delgado in 1971 in Lima, Cuatrotablas soon established itself as one of Peru's leading companies, offering 30 local productions and fifteen international *tours to *Latin America, the United States, and Europe. Notable for nourishing several generations of actors, directors, and teachers, Cuatrotablas also organized international meetings in Ayacucho (1978 and 1988), Qosqo (1987), and Huampaní-Lima (1988). Regarded as the foremost Peruvian school for *acting, its members experiment with *improvisation, synaesthesia, and memory techniques, combined with intense physical *training. The company's best-known performances are *Your Country Is Happy* (1971), *Listen* (1972), *The Classics* (1988), *The Town That Couldn't Sleep* (1992), *Listen Again* (1996), *Troilus and Cressida* (2000), and *A Midsummer Night's Dream* (2001). It has won numerous national *awards.   LRG

CUBANA, LA

Catalan theatre company formed in Sitges in 1980. Whilst emerging from the *street theatre tradition of Els *Comedians, the company have forged a particular performance style which embraces *metatheatricality and results in the *audience becoming unwitting *protagonists of the productions. Their wacky street performances have included the episodic sketches of *Cubana's Delicatessen* (1983) staged on alternative stages of *Barcelona. Since the mid-1980s their appropriation of conventional theatre spaces has proved the hallmark of a number of productions, including the *cabaret *revue *Cómeme el coco, Negro* (*Soft Soap Me, Black Man*, 1988), a revisiting of *The Tempest* (1986) in which Shakespeare's play was suspended because of a fierce storm raging outside the theatre, and *Cegada de amor* (*Blinded by Love*, 1994), a theatre-meets-cinema extravaganza which

further blurred the division between life and art. Their most recent production, *Una nit d'òpera* (*A Night of Opera*, 2001), deconstructs the world of operatic excess.   MMD

CUEVA, JUAN DE LA (1550–1610)

Spanish poet and playwright. A prolific writer for the stage, he is distinguished by his blatant disregard for the *neoclassical *unities, his reduction of the traditional number of *acts or *jornadas* from five to four, and his introduction of new metrical forms. With a keen eye for theatrical effect, Cueva often sacrificed theatrical *decorum for the sensationalism of violent death and the supernatural, while in *El infamador* (*The Slanderer*), he created the figure of the libertine who is generally regarded as a model for the Don Juan of *Tirso de Molina.   KG

CUMBERLAND, RICHARD (1732–1811)

English author. Cumberland is usually remembered as a sentimental playwright, attaching to his name all the opprobrium that is directed at that *genre. His best plays, *The Brothers* (1669), *The West Indian* (1771), and *The Jew* (1794), were at once innovative and very popular. Not without humour, they aspire to serious social purpose, particularly the eradication of social prejudice against groups like the Irish, the British living in the West Indies, and Jews. Known at the time as the modern *Terence, Cumberland sought to write morally edifying *comedy that did not stoop to mimicry or topical attacks.   MJK

CUMMINGS, CONSTANCE (1910–)

Anglo-American actress. Born Constance Halverstadt in Seattle, she made her stage debut in a 1926 San Diego production of *Seventh Heaven*. She first appeared on Broadway in *Treasure Girl* (1928), and opened in *London to great acclaim in *Sour Grapes* (1934). Following her marriage to English playwright Benn Levy, the bulk of her career has been in London. Her Shakespearian roles include Juliet (1939), Gertrude (1969), and Volumnia (1971). She has played *Shaw's St Joan and Mrs Warren, and appeared in such classics as *Lysistrata*, *The Cherry Orchard* (twice, 23 years apart), *Who's Afraid of Virginia Woolf?*, *Long Day's Journey into Night*, and *The Glass Menagerie*. A high point came with her portrayal of the stroke victim Emily Stilson in *Kopit's *Wings* (1978–9), bringing her Tony, Obie, and Drama Desk *awards and an Olivier nomination. In 1974 she was made a CBE.   CT

CUMPER, PAT (1954–)

Jamaican playwright. She acted in the production of Trevor *Rhone's *Comic Strip*, studied archaeology and anthropology at Cambridge, and after her return to Jamaica wrote the *award-winning *The Rapist* (1977). Though her second play, *Rufus*, was less successful, *Coming of Age* (1983) won the Prime Minister's award for best play. She has written *radio serials, collaborated with other writers for the Jamaica *pantomime, and her *The Fallen Angel and the Devil Concubine* (1987) was highly thought of. She also has been deeply involved in the work of the Jamaican company *Sistren. ES

CUNNINGHAM, MERCE (1919–)

American dancer and choreographer. Cunningham studied *dance at the Cornish School in Seattle, where he met John Cage. He danced in Martha *Graham's company from 1939 to 1945 and in 1942 began presenting his own work. He developed a distinctive dance technique, synthesizing the verticality, speed, and rapid rhythmic footwork of *ballet with modern dance's flexible use of the trunk and limbs. His characteristic choreographic method since the early 1950s, when he formed the Merce Cunningham Dance Company, has been using chance techniques that decentre space and generate new movements. He has collaborated with numerous contemporary composers and visual artists, including Cage, Robert Rauschenberg, and Jasper Johns. Cunningham's collaborations free dance from its previous dependence on music, although the two elements may share a time structure. A *modernist choreographer, he makes non-representational dances focusing on movement itself. He has co-created several dances for *film and video and since 1990 has worked with computer software to create choreography. SB

CUREL, FRANÇOIS DE (1854–1928)

French dramatist. After inauspicious beginnings as a novelist, and the refusal of his first two plays by the Théâtre *Libre and the *Odéon, Curel made his mark with *L'Envers d'une sainte* (*The Wrong Side of a Saint*) and *Les Fossiles*, both produced by *Antoine at the Théâtre Libre in 1892—this although neither play was in the ultra-*naturalistic mode favoured by that theatre from its inauguration in 1887. Curel's name was in fact to be associated with the 'théâtre d'idées' or problem play (*see* THESIS PLAY), and he has been called the French *Ibsen. He continued to write for the theatre until the 1920s, but never repeated his early success. WDH

CURI, JORGE (1931–)

Innovative Uruguayan director associated with El *Galpón and Teatro *Circular in *Montevideo. Curi uses *Brechtian methods to adapt drama to fit the political situation of Uruguay. His most famous production, which he co-wrote with Mercedes *Rein, was the *politically subversive *El herrero y la muerte* (*The Black-

smith and Death*, 1981) which ran at the Teatro Circular for five years. Other productions include *Los caballos* (*The Horses*, 1992). EJW

CURTAIN

A large movable piece of fabric, used to conceal the *stage from the *auditorium in a *proscenium theatre. Probably because the curtain moves at highly significant moments, it is a general metaphor for the temporal boundary between stage and real life, and thus 'curtain' can mean the last cue, event, or line of a *scene, *act, or play; the start time; the way in which the curtain is moved (fast, slow, interrupted, etc.); or a warning to clear the stage just before the curtain is raised. Curtains are moved by flying vertically, by parting horizontally ('traverse', 'traveller', or 'drawn'), or by being lifted in bunches or festoons ('valances') either vertically ('contour curtains' or 'French valances') or diagonally ('tabs' or 'tableau curtains'). Until about 1900 some curtains were also rolled like window blinds ('oleos').

The *main curtain*, which is part of the house decor rather than the set, has also been called the proscenium curtain, front curtain, house curtain, and by other terms. From the mid-eighteenth century onward, it preserved *illusion by concealing *scene shifting, sets being 'dressed', and machines being prepared. The Restoration's simple green French valance, raised or lowered slowly at the beginning and end of the play, evolved into Henry *Irving's fast, flexible crimson velvet traverse curtain, opened and closed in seconds for every scene change.

The *act curtain*, act drop, or advertising curtain of the nineteenth century was a drop painted with local advertisements or the insignia of the theatre, flown just behind the main curtain. It marked scene and act changes. But Irving's use of the grand drape for all breaks and changes rapidly became the norm in the late century.

The *fire curtain*, safety curtain, 'fireproof', or 'iron curtain' (British usage, pre-dating the Cold War) is two sheets of heavily fireproofed canvas enclosing a few centimetres' thickness of fireproofing material. The fire curtain is flown with a quick release in its connection to the counterweights. If the *stage manager triggers the release, the curtain, weighing several tons, falls instantly into place, cutting through intervening *scenery if necessary, to seal off the stage from the auditorium. This shields the *audience and damps the draught through the flies, giving more time to escape in a *fire. In some major cities, the legal requirement for a fire curtain severely held back development of non-proscenium theatre spaces. Today sprinkler systems and 'water curtains' are gradually replacing fire curtains.

Curtainless spaces (*thrust, *arena, and non-proscenium end spaces) have made the curtain less synonymous with theatre, but as a metaphor for the transformations between everyday and stage life it retains its power. JB

CURTAIN CALL

The appearance of an actor or actors after the end of a performance (literally, to be called back on *stage after the *curtain has fallen) for extended *applause. On the opening night of a theatrical performance, the director may also appear and, in *musical performances, it is customary for the conductor of the orchestra to join the actors for the curtain call. To call the cast back on stage after the dropping of the curtain, through continued applause and perhaps cheering, is a sign of particular appreciation and pleasure at the performance. William Charles *Macready is thought to be the first actor summoned before the curtain at *Covent Garden after his performance in 1888 as Richard III. On opening and closing nights, cast members are often presented with flowers at the curtain call as a further token of *audience appreciation.   SBe

CURTAIN THEATRE

Built in 1577, a year after its neighbour the *Theatre, and located close by it on the main road north out of *London through Shoreditch, the Curtain was probably of similar size and design. An open-air polygon of as many as twenty bays, with its stage built like the Theatre's, it served as an 'easer' to the Theatre, and was used by Shakespeare's company, the *Chamberlain's Men, from April 1597 when the Theatre was closed to mid-1599, when the *Globe opened. John *Marston wrote in 1598 of law students praising and quoting *Romeo and Juliet* and giving it 'Curtain plaudities'. In the early seventeenth century it was one of the *playhouses with the most lower-class clientele, and no company used it for very long. But it did continue to stage plays until at least 1622, making it the longest-serving *amphitheatre of the period in London.   AJG

CUSACK, CYRIL (1910–93)

Irish actor and *manager. He first appeared onstage at the age of 7 with his mother and stepfather's *touring company. He joined the *Abbey Theatre Company in 1932, and over thirteen years played in 65 plays there. He ran his own company from 1946 to 1961, and played at the *Gaiety Theatre (Dublin), throughout Ireland, in *London, and Europe. His best-known roles were in *Boucicault, *Synge, *O'Casey, and *Shaw. His idiosyncratic style of performance could erupt suddenly with intensely powerful passion and vigour. His playing of Christy Mahon in Synge's *Playboy* and Fluther Good in O'Casey's *The Plough and the Stars* was widely acclaimed. He believed his appearance in *Odd Man Out* (1947) established his international reputation as a cinema actor, and his work as a player of screen vignettes spanned 40 years. In 1990 he appeared at the *Gate Theatre (Dublin) as Chebutykin in *Chekhov's *The Three Sis-*

ters with three of his actress daughters, Sinéad *Cusack, Sorcha, and Niamh.   CAL

CUSACK, SINÉAD (1948–   )

Irish actress, the daughter of Cyril *Cusack. She made her stage debut at the *Abbey Theatre in *Dublin before moving to *London in the late 1960s. At the *Royal Shakespeare Company (1979–84) she played leading roles such as Lady Macbeth, Celia in *As You Like It*, Kate in *The Taming of the Shrew*, and Beatrice in *Much Ado About Nothing*. Her provocative and vivid characterizations contributed to the *feminist debate surrounding Shakespeare and representations of women. She said that Kate's 'submission' speech 'isn't a submission speech at all: it's a speech about how her spirit has been allowed to soar free . . . she has made her own rules'. Her work in *television and cinema includes *films with Bernardo Bertolucci and Franco *Zeffirelli. For the *Royal Court Theatre she appeared in *Friel's *Faith Healer*, and for the Royal *National Theatre played Mai in Sebastian *Barry's *Our Lady of Sligo* (1998).   CAL

CUSHMAN, CHARLOTTE (1816–76)

American actress of international fame. Known for her *breeches roles and female grotesques, Cushman often used her muscular body and unusual voice to create a masculine persona on stage (*see* MALE IMPERSONATION). Her sexual orientation as a lesbian probably also contributed to the erotic power of her male *characters. The commanding presence and extravagant expressiveness of her *acting style attracted many female spectators. Cushman first appeared on stage as Lady Macbeth in 1836 and achieved her first notable success with Nancy in *Oliver Twist* in 1839. She worked with William *Macready during his American *tour and followed him to England in 1844 to seek stardom. A sensation in *London, Cushman capitalized on her fame, living in London and *Rome and touring internationally; except for her final years, she rarely returned to the United States. Following her London success, Cushman performed about 35 roles, repeating ten of them with some regularity. Among her most applauded characters were Meg Merrilies in *Guy Mannering*, Queen Katharine and Cardinal Wolsey in *Henry VIII*, Lady Macbeth, and Romeo, which she occasionally played opposite her sister Susan. Suffering from cancer, Cushman retired from the stage in 1869.   BMC

CUZZANI, AUGUSTÍN (1924–90)

Argentine playwright and novelist whose *surreal post-war drama attacked everything from capitalism to technology. One of his first successful plays, *Una libra de carne* (*A Pound of Flesh*, 1954), is a version of the Shylock story. Other work includes *El centro forward murió al amanecer* (*The Centre-Forward*

Died at Dawn, 1955) and *Para que se cumplan las escrituras* (*So That the Scriptures Are Fulfilled*, 1966), which treats God and the computer. EJW

CYBER THEATRE

*Performance created with the aid of new media and computer technologies. The incorporation of advanced media technologies into live performance, and the exploration of *performativity in the virtual spaces of the computer through the technologies of the Internet and the electronic spaces of interactive immersive 'smart' environments, has created the potential for a new theatre language and aesthetic. The technologies of virtual and electronic performativity challenge the most fundamental beliefs concerning performance, including the claims to liveness, immediacy, and presence. The ubiquitous presence of the televisual in contemporary theatre, and the advent of computer-aided performativity, establish a discrete aesthetic category wherein the immediacy of performance and the digital alterability of time and space through technology converge.

Cyber theatre, not unlike *film and *television, does not rely on the presence of a live actor or *audience, and an argument can be made that many examples of cyber theatre might be better described as interactive film/TV, installation art, new media art, or electronic communications. A major theoretical question is posed by these new forms: is it necessary that some live element be present in the performance of cyber theatre to make theatre a useful model? Theatre artists, but also artists working in areas of installations, video and *performance art, and digital technologies, are undertaking the practice of cyber theatre. Research and art areas include:

1. *Digital scenography*: the use of three-dimensional projections with live actors performing before an audience wearing special viewing glasses. Theatres working in this manner include *San Francisco's George Coates Theatre Works and the Institute for the Exploration of Virtual Realities of the University of Kansas.
2. *Televisual* *mise-en-scène: traditional theatre space supplemented with video monitors and projections of live and pre-recorded performers and images, as in the work of the *Wooster Group (USA), Robert *Lepage (Québec), and dumbtype (*Japan).
3. *Telepresent performance*: video conferencing and Internet access, where performance takes place in multiple locations and is presented simultaneously in spaces both real and virtual. Telepresent performance is a common application in business.
4. *Interactive access*: hypertextual databanks, in which audience members, through Internet connections, are able to access and affect the process of a performance, being explored by installation artist Eduardo Kac and California's Survival Research Lab.
5. *Smart environments*: objects, clothing, and the environment itself, through sensoring technology, respond to the presence of actors and spectators, triggering image and sound databanks for projections, or activating stage machinery in some manner. Artists and technicians of the MIT Media Lab and Media Lab Europe are leaders in this field.
6. *Tracking and animation technology*: sensors attached to a performer's *costume and videotaped can process the information of the performer's body to a computer, which in real time can animate a figure to be simultaneously projected upon the actor's body or stage screens. The Interactive Multimedia Technology Centre at Georgia Tech is developing technologies in this area.
7. *Augmented reality*: audiences wearing special glasses are supplied with visual and audio information which is superimposed over a live performance.
8. *Virtual reality*: wearing head-mounted displays and navigation gloves, a spectator is able to pass through virtual environments, interact with synthetic *characters, and create his or her own virtual avatar.
9. *Performance within virtual environments* (MUDs, MOOs): electronic environments (MUDs, multi-user dungeons, and MOOs, multi-user dungeon object oriented) wherein groups of individuals through Internet connections develop characters and *scenarios while forming virtual communities through improvisatorial performance. There were thousands of MUDs and MOOs in operation at the start of the twenty-first century.

The potential of cyber theatre expands with the evolution of new electronic communication technologies. Broad-band communication through fibre-optic connections will allow for such developments as streaming video of live performances with simultaneous interactivity. The next stages of smart and virtual environments with robust interactivity will hold the possibility of creating a theatre not of actors and spectators but of individual interactivity in dramatic scenarios. Not unlike *multimedia performance, which has developed into an element of popular entertainment, cyber theatre, given its high costs of production, will probably find its most active proponents in the mass entertainments of *sports, theme parks, and interactions with film and television. MDC

CAUSEY, MATTHEW, 'Postorganic performance: the appearance of theatre in virtual spaces', in Marie-Laure Ryan (ed.), *Cyberspatial Textuality* (Bloomington, Ind., 2000)
SALTZ, DAVID, 'The art of interaction: interactivity, performativity, and computers', *Journal of Aesthetics and Art Criticism*, 55 (1997)

CYCLE PLAYS

A phrase used by scholars of *medieval theatre to refer to the sequences of episodes that dramatize the sweep of Christian salvation history from Creation to Judgement. These were apparently most common in England, although one continental *text containing a complete sequence has survived from Künzelzau. It was long believed that the normal English medieval play was such a sequence sponsored by city councils and performed in procession on wagons by craft *guilds on the feast of *Corpus Christi. Since 1979, the new evidence being published by Records of Early English Drama is radically altering this view and revealing that English practice had closer affinities to the continental traditions than had been thought.

Texts and records confirming that complete cycles were sponsored by city councils and performed by craft guilds in procession survive for York and Chester. The *York Plays* are preserved in a single fifteenth-century manuscript while there are five complete manuscripts of the *Chester Plays*, all of which post-date the final production of the cycle in 1575. The first references to the plays at York come in the fourth quarter of the fourteenth century. The date of the origin of the plays at Chester is less certain. The early date of 1325 supplied by a civic antiquarian in the seventeenth century is untenable and, although some part of the Passion sequence was performed as early as 1422, the external records of what is clearly the Creation to Judgement sequence do not begin until 1519–20.

The texts of two other English 'cycles' also survive but cannot be precisely located nor do they present the same unity of purpose and tone as the plays from York and Chester. One collection comes from East Anglia and is now commonly called the *N-Town Plays*. Earlier scholarship erroneously identified this text as the *Ludus Coventriae* (the play from Coventry) and it was first published under that title. Other scholars have referred to it as the Hegge Cycle after the family who owned the manuscript. This manuscript is a collection of various kinds of *Biblical plays including a free-standing two-part *Passion play, and a recently recognized and disentangled play on the childhood of the Virgin. The purpose for which the scribe-editor compiled the manuscript some time after 1468 is unclear. The fourth manuscript, the *Towneley Plays*, comes from the West Riding of Yorkshire and was long associated with the town of Wakefield. Since 1974 doubt has been cast on the authenticity of some of the evidence for playmaking in Wakefield. The manuscript contains several groups of plays—for example, five are clearly related to plays from York and a further five have been identified as the work of the 'Wakefield Master'. Like the *N-Town* manuscript, this one, dating from the early sixteenth century, may represent a collection of Biblical plays. A fifth play which ends in the Resurrection, the *Cornish Ordinalia*, survives in Cornish. Under whose auspices it was played is unknown.

External evidence records four other lengthy sequences from Beverley, Newcastle-upon-Tyne, Coventry, and Norwich. The first two, like *York* and *Chester*, were performed under civic auspices by guilds from wagons. Beverley was probably a complete sequence, though the nature of the play at Newcastle is unclear. The other sequences (also civic and processional) were shorter. The play at Coventry began with the Nativity and the one at Norwich ended with Pentecost.   AFJ

CYCLORAMA

A smooth drape or wall used to produce the effect of a sky or of a neutral backdrop at indefinite distance. Though the principle of the 'cyc' was known as early as 1820, it was not until the early years of the twentieth century that European *lighting technicians and scene designers, notably Mariano *Fortuny and Adolph Linnebach, demonstrated the advantages of a backdrop which was perfectly smooth under an even wash of coloured light. The human eye, when it is unable to find any irregularity on which to focus, cannot judge distance, and interprets the surface as infinity; thus the cyc works by mimicking the effect of daylight on the natural sky.

Fortuny had originally hoped that all lighting could be accomplished by reflection from the cyc, and several plaster 'sky domes' were constructed in Germany in the 1920s and 1930s. They worked badly in practice: the dome blocked flown *scenery and cut off much of the wings, and since it was the brightest object in the space it pulled the eye up and away from the stage. Although 'Fortuny lighting' never became important, the cyclorama was immediately adopted by nearly all *scenographers for a wide range of problems. Besides the *realistic effect of sky, it can be used to create a backdrop that is more neutral than black, to suggest mood in impressionistic or *symbolist plays, or to create a feeling that the *action is somehow taking place in eternity, or in a universal space. In its cloth form, the cyc appears almost universal in Western theatres, and has been widely adopted in many non-Western nations as well.   JB

CYSAT, RENWARD (d. 1614)

Director of the Lucerne *Passion play from 1575 to 1614. Cysat's notes on playing stations and his inventory of *costumes, together with detailed sketches of the staging arrangements for the first two days of the 1583 performance in the wine-market, are invaluable for understanding late *medieval open-air theatrical production.   RWV

CZECH NATIONAL THEATRE (NÁRODNÍ DIVADLO)

Though the adjective 'Národní' (national) has been intermittently attached to various Czech theatres, it is permanently connected with a *playhouse and its company. The playhouse was erected on the embankment of the River Vltava in *Prague, and affectionately called the Golden Chapel, the funds for this symbol of national aspiration being raised with the help of a public collection. A *neoclassical building, designed by architect Josef Zítek, was first opened in June 1881, was destroyed by *fire after several weeks, and reopened with more lavish interior decorations in November 1883. Since then it has been used by the National Theatre's resident *opera, drama, and independent *ballet companies, all since 1930 administered and subsidized by the state, performing there in rotating *repertory. In 1920 the Theatre of Estates (built in 1783) was attached to the National Theatre and the three major *genres are also performed there. Between 1948 and 1992 the Smetana Theatre (formerly the German playhouse) was part of the National Theatre complex, and so was the New Scene (built in 1983 and now housing *Laterna Magika) between 1983 and 1992.   ML

·D·

DABUS

A ritual-based traditional martial arts trance-dance found in parts of Sumatra in *Indonesia and in the states of Selangor and Perak in peninsular *Malaysia. Thought to have originated either from the Buginese or Achehnese more than 150 years ago, the performance is centred on the *anak dabus* or *damak*, a short spear-shaped weapon with metal rings attached to the handle. *Dancers rhythmically shake and rattle the weapon to the accompaniment of a number of *rebana* (frame drums), *gendang* (barrel drums), and a pair of hanging gongs. Trance, bloodletting, and miraculous healing of wounds are the trademarks of *dabus*.   MA

D'ABY, FRANÇOIS-JOSEPH AMON (1913–)

One of the founders of French-language Ivorian theatre. An archivist, d'Aby was a founding member of the Théâtre Indigène de Côte d'Ivoire, for which he wrote nine plays between 1938 and 1945. Most of them satirize social customs, notably diviners and other charlatans who are portrayed as merchants of illusions. His Christian education is apparent in some titles: *Noël! Noël! Jésus est né* (*Jesus is Born*, 1943) and *Joseph vendu par ses frères* (*Joseph Sold by his Brothers*, 1945). The nationalist politics of 1953 gave d'Aby an acute awareness of the revolutionary power of theatre to mobilize a people and heighten consciousness. Under the impetus of the *Centre Culturel et Folklorique de la Côte d'Ivoire, he started to write plays that advocated reform: *Kwao Adjoba* (1953) was so successful that it led to a change in the laws of succession based on matriarchy. Its rootedness in local myth and performance traditions made his work an inspiration for contemporary dramatists. His *Le Théâtre en Côte d'Ivoire des origines à 1960* was the first book on theatre in the Ivory Coast.

SVa trans. JCM

DADA

An international art movement created by Hugo Ball and Tristan Tzara in Zurich during the First World War. Their meeting place was the Cabaret Voltaire, where between February and June 1916 they created numerous performances of an experimental nature. In 1917 the group ran a gallery where they organized six dada soirées. The spaces were small and the *audience limited; to convey the ideas and aesthetic principles of dada to the general public they organized three soirées in Zurich guildhalls, which attracted up to 1,000 spectators each. After the war the centre of activities shifted to *Paris and *Berlin, where the dadaists continued the tradition of performing 'sound' poetry, simultaneous poems, movement pieces, and noise music. Audience reactions were often so violent that the actors watched the main action unfold in the *auditorium. In Berlin the dadaists became caught up in the November Revolution of 1918 and the tumultuous events of the early Weimar Republic. Apart from seven soirées they also performed five events in public spaces and undertook a *tour to six other cities. The Paris group produced literary soirées, public exhibits, and seven dada plays. *See* AVANT-GARDE.   GB

DADIÉ, BERNARD (1916–)

Ivorian dramatist, novelist, and politician, the author of three volumes of poetry, three novels (one autobiographical, *Climbié*, 1956), travelogues, and over a dozen full-length plays and dramatic sketches. Dadié was educated in Côte d'Ivoire (1922–33), and in Senegal at the *École William Ponty (1934–6), where he trained for service in the colonial administration. He worked in Senegal as a librarian-archivist until 1947 when he returned to Côte d'Ivoire, where he held various administrative positions before becoming Minister of Education and Culture. He displayed an early interest in the theatre, writing his first play,

Les Villes, in 1933 while still a student. Actively pursuing that interest at William Ponty, he wrote an important article, 'Mon pays et son theatre' ('My country and its theatre', 1937), and a *historical play, Assémien Déhylé, roi du Sanwi (1936), that was performed in Dakar in 1936 and in *Paris in 1937 at the International Exhibition. He co-founded in 1953 the *Centre Culturel et Folklorique de la Côte d'Ivoire, for whose troupe he wrote five dramatic sketches between 1955 and 1960 on social themes. It was not until ten years later that Dadié wrote his first major play, Béatrice du Congo (1970), inspired by Aimé *Césaire's La Tragédie du roi Christophe (1963) and at the suggestion of Jean-Marie *Serreau, who directed it at the *Avignon Festival (1971). Dadié's other major plays include a second *historical work, Îles de têmpete (Islands of Tempest, 1973) on Toussaint L'Ouverture and the Haitian Revolution, Les Voix dans le vent (The Voices in the Wind, 1970), a *tragedy of ambition, and the satirical *comedy Monsieur Thôgô-Gnini (1970) on an arriviste, corrupt businessman. In Papassidi, maître escroc (1975) and Mhoi-ceul (1979) he returned to the vein of *farces that he wrote in the 1950s.   JCM

DALANG See WAYANG KULIT; WAYANG GOLEK.

DALCROZE, ÉMILE-JAQUES See JAQUES-DALCROZE, ÉMILE.

DALDRY, STEPHEN (1960–)
British director. Daldry's deconstructed production of J. B. *Priestley's An Inspector Calls (Royal *National Theatre, 1992; *New York, 1994), with its 1940s air-raid sirens and street urchin, onstage rain, and collapsing Edwardian house, brought him international attention and Olivier and Tony *awards. Daldry likes to use *spectacle and a form of *expressionism with classic, often leftist works (like Sophie *Treadwell's Machinal, 1994, with Fiona *Shaw), and often collaborates with designer and companion Ian MacNeill. After work at the *Gate Theatre and elsewhere in *London, Daldry succeeded Max *Stafford-Clark as *artistic director of the *Royal Court (1992–7). His charismatic and generous leadership fostered an explosion of new playwrights, including Judy Upton, Jez Butterworth, and Sarah *Kane, as well as successful fundraising and building renovation campaigns. Billy Elliott (2000), about a miner's son who wants to dance, was Daldry's successful debut as a *film director, followed by The Hours, David *Hare's adaptation of Michael Cunningham's novel.   GAO

DALIT THEATRE
Theatre of the oppressed castes (dalit) in *India. In the state of Maharashtra the oppressed castes, including the Mahars, Mangs, Chambhars, and Dhors, were once considered polluting and therefore untouchable. They were condemned to live outside the village and were bound to perform menial service jobs. Dr Babasaheb Ambedkar, a Mahar, became their leader and exhorted them to revolt against such work, educate themselves, and fight for human dignity. The earliest dalit theatre took the form of jalsas that were performed to spread Ambedkar's ideas. Mahars and Mangs were traditional performers of *tamasha, which at one time was part devotion and part entertainment. The jalsa writers rejected the religious *ritual of tamasha while retaining the music and making the narrative *didactic. The songadya or *clown was transformed into the chief spokesperson.

Milind College in Aurangabad, established by Dr Ambedkar's People's Education Society, was the centre of dalit theatre after independence. The first principal of the college, M. B. Chitnis, wrote Yugyatra (The Journey of an Age) in 1955 and staged it in Dr Ambedkar's presence on his birthday. The next year it was performed in Nagpur before 600,000 dalits who had gathered to convert to Buddhism. The play is composed of a series of episodes depicting the injustices inflicted on dalits through the centuries. Prakash Tribhuvan's Thamba, Ramrajya Yetay! (Wait, Rama's Regime Is on the Way) and Datta Bhagat's Wata Palwata (Routes and Escape Routes) are two of the many other plays staged in Auragabad. Nagpur, Pune, and Sholapur have been other centres of dalit theatre.

More recently dalit theatre has entered the *proscenium stage in an effort to expand its *audience to the middle class, though the different performance mode has occasionally compromised its political agenda. A dalit theatre conference held in Pune in 1984, and subsequent meetings elsewhere, have highlighted the challenge of sustaining a theatre of the *oppressed in the new commercial and religiously fundamentalist environment of India. Understanding the complexities of contemporary society and politics remains a struggle not only in Maharashtra, but also in other states like Andhra Pradesh and Tamil Nadu where dalit theatre is active.   SGG

DALY, ARNOLD (1875–1927)
American actor and producer. Born in Brooklyn, Peter Christopher Arnold Daly began acting in 1892, making his *New York debut in Pudd'nhead Wilson (1895) and his *London debut in Too Much Johnson (1898). His major importance lies in championing and popularizing in America the plays of *Shaw, a close family friend. In 1903–5 he produced (and often acted in) the US premières of Candida, The Man of Destiny, How He Lied to her Husband (written for Daly), You Never Can Tell, John Bull's Other Island, and Mrs Warren's Profession (which caused his arrest on morals charges and eventual acquittal). He continued acting in plays and *vaudeville until his death.   CT

DALY, AUGUSTIN (1836–99)

American critic, playwright, and *manager. Born in North Carolina and raised in New York, Daly was early captivated by the theatre and began writing plays in his teens. Initially unsuccessful in securing production of his work, he turned to theatre *criticism; between 1859 and 1867, for five different newspapers. Daly's first dramatic success came in 1862 with an adaptation of the German play *Deborah*, as *Leah the Forsaken*. Although there is substantial evidence that he employed several unacknowledged collaborators (most notably his brother Joseph), Daly is generally credited with numerous plays—both original compositions and adaptations, primarily from German and French sources. His more noteworthy original contributions include his great *melodrama *Under the Gaslight* (1867), *A Flash of Lightning* (1868), *Horizon* (1871), and *The Undercurrent* (1888). Daly carefully reworked his adaptations to suit American tastes, a strategy that produced substantial economic successes in *Frou-Frou* (1870), *Divorce* (1871), and *The Lottery of Love* (1888). In addition to his writing success, he owned a succession of *playhouses that were widely recognized for the quality of their productions. In 1879 he reopened *New York's Wood's Museum as Daly's Theatre, quickly establishing it as a venue for elite society. A substantial part of his theatre's appeal was its company's fine ensemble *acting. He established a *stock company of 44 actors—headed by Ada *Rehan, John *Drew, Anne Gilbert, and James Lewis—that excelled at melodrama, light *comedy, and Shakespeare, and provided a training ground for a host of rising American acting talent. Through its English and European *tours of the 1880s (including playing Shakespeare at Stratford-upon-Avon), Daly's troupe secured international recognition of maturing American practice.

GAR

DAMBURY, GERTY (1957–)

Guadeloupean playwright, director, novelist, and poet. Her plays, which she often directs, include *Rabordaille* (1989), *Lettres indiennes* (1993, translated as *Crosscurrents* for UBU Repertory Theater in *New York), *Survols* (1996), all published, and the unpublished *Carfax* (1981), *Bâton Maréchal* (1987), *Camille et Justine* (1992), *Madjaka* (1996), and *Carêmes* (1998). They have been performed in Guadeloupe and in many venues in France. Dambury's *dialogue is sharp, concise, poetic yet *realistic, and she constantly redefines her style. Contemporary women's issues in the Caribbean are her main concern. Her plays have proved popular and culturally important, partly because they represent the history of violence and joy of the *Caribbean people.

MRM

DAME *See* PANTOMIME, BRITISH.

DAMIANI, LUCIANO (1923–)

Italian scenographer who began a long career at the *Piccolo Teatro in *Milan in the 1950s. Under the direction of Giorgio *Strehler he designed a large number of productions, including Bertolazzi's *El Nost Milan* (dialect for *Our Milan*, 1954), *Brecht's *Galileo* (1961), *Goldoni's *Le baruffe Chiozzotte* (*The Chioggian Squabbles*, 1964), and *Chekhov's *The Cherry Orchard* (1973). He also worked as set designer for several *opera productions in Austria and Milan. Damiani considered the visual integral to the dramatic *text. He portrayed emptiness as a poetics of the scene, and he thought of silence as a major part of the *mise-en-scène. He frequently extended the *stage into the *stalls, rejecting the division between playing space and *audience. He has worked with numerous international directors, and in 1996 formed his own company, Teatro Documenti (Theatre of Documents), where the development of the *scenography and theatrical space are recorded through his own preparatory drawings and sketches. He has won many *awards, including the Maschera d'Argento in 1996.

DMcM

DAMNATIO

Public execution at Rome for non-citizens, prisoners of war, and slaves involved 'aggravated' death penalties, singly or in combination: crucifixion, *crematio* (burning alive), and *damnatio ad bestias* (exposure to wild beasts). These penalties were intended to cause the victim prolonged agony and humiliation. Occasionally their potential for spectator appeal was maximized by dramatization. The staging might exploit the miscreant's background or the nature of his crime: a Sicilian brigand in the age of Augustus who was known as 'son of Etna' was brought to Rome to be displayed in the forum on a contraption that 'erupted' and deposited him in a cage of wild animals. A Greek myth or Roman legend might be played out, sometimes with an unusual *denouement: at the opening of the Colosseum in AD 80 a popular *mime that ended in the crucifixion of the *protagonist was combined with *damnatio ad bestias* so that a criminal 'playing' the leading role was actually crucified and simultaneously exposed to a bear. Other myths performed on the same occasion included a version of the story of Orpheus in which, instead of being torn apart by Maenads, he was savaged by a bear; this scenario exploited the standard portrayal of Orpheus as the consummate musician who was able to charm the natural world into submission. A large-scale variant of these displays comprised massed combat involving thousands of participants. In 46 BC in the Circus Maximus, Julius Caesar constructed a 'camp' at either end of the track and staged a battle involving 1,000 infantry, 60 cavalry, and 40 elephants. On the Campus Martius in AD 52, on his return from the annexation of Britain, Claudius re-enacted the storming of a British town and the surrender of the kings, thereby turning the urban populace of

Rome into a vicarious witness of his victory. The most extended form of dramatized *damnationes* was the *naumachia, a staged naval battle based upon a real or imaginary episode from Greek history. *See also* ROMAN THEATRE.   KMC

DANCE AND DANCE-DRAMA *see page 348*

DANCOURT, FLORENT-CARTON (1665–1725)

French actor and dramatist. Born into a good family and destined for the law, Dancourt met and married an actress, daughter of the celebrated actor *La Thorillière, and followed her into the *Comédie-Française company. He performed with distinction in *Molière's plays, and became 'orateur de la troupe', earning the favour of Louis XIV and the Dauphin. He retired from the company in 1718, leaving a daughter to continue the family link with the theatre. As a playwright Dancourt became a master of the *comedy of manners, exploiting topical foibles or abuses: gambling, social climbing, the lottery mania. In *Le Chevalier à la mode* (1687) the central *character is an impudent young adventurer trying to make his way by a rich marriage; *Les Bourgeoises à la mode* (1692) and *Les Bourgeoises de qualité* (1700) both show rich bourgeois wives imitating their 'betters'. Written in prose, Dancourt's plays make their satirical point with considerable *realism.   WDH

DANE, CLEMENCE (WINIFRED ASHTON) (1888–1965)

English playwright. Along with Gordon Daviot and Dodie *Smith, Clemence Dane was one of a handful of women playwrights to achieve West End success between the wars. A multifaceted talent, Dane was a teacher, portrait artist, novelist, and actress as well as a dramatist. Similarly, her plays range widely in *genre, encompassing social problems (*A Bill of Divorcement*, 1921; *The Way Things Happen*, 1924), poetic *historical drama (*Will Shakespeare*, 1921), *musicals (*Adam's Opera*, 1928), religious *cycle drama (*The Saviors*, 1942), children's plays (*Shivering Shocks*, 1923), and adaptations (*The Happy Hypocrite*, 1936). Dane also wrote the screenplays for Greta Garbo's *Anna Karenina* (with Salka Viertel, 1935) and *Fire over England* (with Sergei Nolbandov, 1936). Her most successful work was her first play, *A Bill of Divorcement*, a *melodrama about mental illness and unfair divorce laws. Directed by Basil *Dean, the play ran for over 400 performances in *London and was a hit for Katharine *Cornell in *New York. It was *filmed in 1932, starring Katharine *Hepburn in her first film role.   MDG

DANIEL, SAMUEL (c.1563–1619)

English poet and dramatist. He wrote two *pastorals, *The Queen's Arcadia* (1605) and *Hymen's Triumph* (1615), and two court *masques (1604 and 1610), all for private performances associated with his patron Queen Anne. From 1604 to 1605, he was the licenser of plays for the Children of the Queen's Revels, who performed his *tragedy *Philotas* (1604), but gave up the office after allowing several plays which offended the King. In 1615 he helped to set up an acting company in Bristol. His dramatic writing tends to be delicate and static; some contemporaries found it dull.   MJW

DANIELS, RON (1942–)

Brazilian-born British director. Having founded the Workshop theatre of *São Paulo in 1960, Daniels came to England to train as an actor at the *British Drama League. After a short career as a repertory actor, Peter Cheeseman at Stoke-on-Trent invited Daniels to direct. In 1974 he mounted David *Rudkin's *Afore Night Comes* at the *Royal Shakespeare Company's the Other Place in Stratford, and was put in charge of that small theatre in 1979. At the RSC his interest in social and historical conditions led him to David *Edgar's *Destiny* (1976) and to controversial productions such as Anthony Burgess's *A Clockwork Orange 2000* (1990). His versions of Shakespeare in the 1980s—*Romeo and Juliet* (which he repeated at the *Guthrie Theatre, Minneapolis), *Pericles*, *Timon of Athens*, and *Hamlet*—were directed with simplicity and clarity. In the late 1980s Daniels ran the *Mermaid Theatre in *London. He has directed Shakespeare extensively abroad, including productions of *Hamlet* (*American Repertory Theatre, 1991), *Titus Andronicus* (*Tokyo, 1992), *Henry IV* (ART, 1993), and continues to work freelance in England (Stephen *Poliakoff's *Remember This* for the Royal *National Theatre, 1999).   KN

DANIELS, SARAH (1956–)

English playwright. One of the 'radical *feminist' playwrights of the 1980s, along with Pam *Gems and Caryl *Churchill, Daniels was nurtured at the *Royal Court. Her provocative plays, like *Masterpieces* (1983), which presents *pornography as part of a gynocidal culture, feature women struggling with corrupt patriarchy. *Neaptide* (1986), the first play about *lesbian rights produced at the *National Theatre, was attacked for 'man-hating', loose structure, and *didacticism. Daniels's other plays include *Ripen our Darkness* (1981), *Byrthrite* (1987), *The Gut Girls* (1988), *Beside Herself* (1990), about child abuse, and *Morning Glory* (2000), about the abuse of the elderly.   GAO

(continued on p. 350)

DANCE AND DANCE-DRAMA

Dance may be defined as designed movement, or movement framed to be perceived as designed. Dance-drama implies a spoken *text, and often a story, combined with movement. Both dance and drama seem to be part of every human culture. They occur in myriad *folk, social, *ritual, therapeutic, and theatrical settings; dances may function as games, *sports, combat, psychological and physiological therapy, or social, cultural, and political events. This entry is concerned with dance and dance-drama as part of *theatre and *performance (though in the broadest sense), rather than as part of everyday life unframed as performance.

Because dance is so widespread it is impossible to write a comprehensive overview of its history and implications. However, one way of surveying this vast field briefly is to examine the binary 'dance and dance-drama' as a continuum. Dance and dance-drama may be seen as parallel categories in some ways to symphonic music on the one hand and *opera on the other, or to lyric versus epic poetry, or to non-objective versus objective visual art. The Western terms dance and dance-drama correspond loosely to the threefold South Asian terms, taken from ancient Sanskrit treatises on theatre and dance, *nritta* (pure dance), *nritya* (expressive dance), and *natya* (dance-drama). *Nritta* is devoid of *abhinaya, or expression; it is non-interpretative but exists for the purpose of creating formal beauty. *Nritya* is expressive or mimetic (*see* MIMESIS) dance, interpreting the words of the accompanist's song. *Natya* fully incorporates dancing, singing, and speech by the actor-dancers in a narrative performance. These three distinct concepts in the South Asian tradition begin to suggest that a continuum, rather than a binary opposition, is apt for thinking about these distinctions.

At one end of the spectrum is pure dance: abstract dance that consists only of movement sequences, without other expressive or communicative means, even music. For instance, in *Calico Mingling* (1973), by American postmodern choreographer Lucinda Childs, four dancers walk, in six-step phrases, in similar but not identical paths that consist of circles, semicircles, and straight lines. Despite the simplicity of their basic movements, the slight variations in their paths and patterns result in a highly complex visual and rhythmic pattern of unison, divergence, interweaving, and intersection. Performed in silence, the dance itself seems to become a form of visual music, much as a solo or group tap dance without musical accompaniment creates a percussion piece that seems to occupy a position in the fields of both music and dance. However, other abstract dances, like American postmodern choreographer Yvonne Rainer's *The Mind is a Muscle, Part I* (*Trio A*) (1966), eschew even musical or rhythmic structure, using the medium of dance to explore the movement potential of the human body in pure form.

At the other end of the spectrum is the fully hybrid dance-drama, or *total theatre piece: a theatrical *spectacle that consists of movement, speech, and song in the service of a narrative *plot with *characters and *action. It may also employ other elements of *mise-en-scène, including *scenery, *costumes, *props, *lighting and other visual effects, *music and other *sound effects, *masks, *puppets, performing *animals, machines, and aroma design. In both East and West, the great classical theatres have employed this rich, multi-sensory, multivalent *genre. For instance, in *kathakali, a stylized form of dance-drama that developed in Kerala, *India, in the sixteenth and seventeenth centuries, masked and elaborately costumed actors perform tales from the Hindu epics and Puranas, or traditional stories. They use *mime and dance, a highly codified lexicon of hand gestures, colour coding in costume, mask, and *make-up, symbolic uses of stage space, and music and poetic song to embody tales of heroism and military prowess in a long (traditionally, all-night, although now often shorter) epic performance. *Kathakali*'s roots reach back to earlier traditions, including martial arts, shamanic dances, and Sanskrit drama. Originally created under royal patronage, its training and performance institutions are now funded by the state as well as by private patrons. Its performers include singers, musicians, and dancer-actors (traditionally all male, although now there is at least one female troupe); the songs may provide third-person narrative, sung by the singers, or may engage the characters in *dialogue or *soliloquy; the dances may stop the action to express mood or propel the narrative forward. Like many forms of Indian dance, drama, and music, *kathakali* makes room for virtuoso *improvisation within a fixed structure.

Similarly, *Japanese *nō (dating back to the fourteenth century), *Chinese *jingju or Beijing opera (emerging from older dance-theatre forms in the seventeenth century), Balinese *topeng (arising in the seventeenth century), and ancient *Greek theatre (fifth century BC), as well as *early modern and *neoclassical European operas based on ancient Greek models, merged music, song, poetry, dance, mime, and other elements in order to achieve a totally integrated theatrical effect. In the contemporary world, some of these forms (*kathakali*, nō, Beijing opera, *topeng*, and Western opera) continue, and new forms have arisen. For instance, *musical theatre and *film musicals—whether of the Hollywood or Bollywood (Hindi films, predominantly made in Bombay; see *Mumbai and *Marathi theatre) variety—are two important popular and mass genres that mix song, dance, and story.

In between these two poles are various admixtures of choreography, music, verbal texts, and narrative elements. Much world dance is performed to music, and thus, very close to the end of the pure dance spectrum is a category that contains dances that may be abstract, non-narrative, and non-dramatic, but that have some musical accompaniment, whether spare or full-bodied. Thus these abstract dances, whose performers do not take on the role of characters beyond themselves dancing the dance, may nevertheless have some expressive qualities derived from the music or the choreography. Into this category would fall a genre like *bugaku, the ancient Japanese court dances (dating back to the sixth century AD), which are performed to instrumental music. Although some of the bugaku pieces have stories, most do not—they are non-narrative, non-dramatic dances, slow and symmetrical, prized for their formal beauty and spiritual content. Similarly, *Korean court dance or chongjae (dating back to at least before AD 900) is built on qualities of 'motion within stillness', projecting a quality of beauty and spiritual restraint through subtle formal contrasts.

A modern *ballet like Russian-American choreographer George *Balanchine's Concerto barocco (1941), to Bach's Double Violin Concerto in D Minor, is a dance about the aesthetic, formal tensions of architectural, polyphonic form, not about human drama. And a modern dance like American choreographer Doris Humphrey's Passacaglia (1938), to Bach's Passacaglia and Fugue in C Minor, could be seen as a purely abstract symphonic composition, a visualization of the musical structure, but has also been interpreted metaphorically as a drama of social relations. The dances created at the *Bauhaus in Germany during the 1920s by artists such as Oskar *Schlemmer often experimented, to percussive accompaniment or jazz music, with the geometry of the body and space, as well as with expressive properties of colours in the costumes and lights. Most dance critics and historians call abstract dance with music 'pure dance' or 'absolute dance,' even though the addition of music makes this category step two on the continuum sketched here. On the border between category one, pure dance without music, and category two, abstract dance with music, is the work of American choreographer Merce *Cunningham, whose storyless choreography occupies the same space-time continuum as the music in performance but is neither created nor danced to the music.

Moving from the pure dance end of the spectrum toward dance-drama, the next category might be called imagistic dance. It has more meaning and often more elements of mise-en-scène than pure or abstract dance, and it may even project either the life of characters or a situation or ambience onstage, but it does not have a fully fleshed-out narrative or dramatic conflict. The German modern dance choreographer Mary Wigman, for instance, in her Witch Dance (1926) and Monotony Whirl (1926) created figures somewhere between characters (a witch and a whirling dervish) and states of consciousness (ecstatic possession) through choreography rather than through *acting. In a different manner, the American modern dancer Isadora *Duncan created lyric dances, set to symphonic music, in the first two decades of the twentieth century that embodied emotional qualities such as joy or grief. In many traditional West *African dances, what may look to Western eyes like abstract or formal patterns of rhythmic dancing carry symbolic meaning and serve a moral and spiritual purpose. A dance may celebrate fertility or coming of age; it may promote healing, counter death, or be an act of grieving; it may embody the attributes of gods and ancestors (see also RITUAL AND THEATRE). In the contemporary Japanese genre *butoh (which emerged in the 1950s as a synthesis of Japanese folk and traditional forms, including nō, as well as Western modern and postmodern dance), choreographers such as *Hijikata Tatsumi and *Ōno Kazuo and the group Dai Rakudakan create striking visual images and spiritual or psychological themes through techniques of bodily distortion, fantastic costumes, whitened faces and bodies, and extreme exertion, without overtly telling stories or creating characters.

The late eighteenth-century European debate about the nature, function, and meaning of theatrical dancing casts some light on this discussion of dance and dance-drama. Right at the centre of the continuum is a category that choreographer-theorists such as Jean-Georges Noverre (in France), Gaspero Angiolini (in Italy), and John Weaver (in England) developed, called ballet d'action, or story ballets. Criticizing the danced divertissements in operas that reduced dance to ornament, these theorists advocated a form of expressive dance that could be a serious, imitative art form, telling stories through a medium other than the verbal texts of dramatic theatre—that is, movement and gesture. Thus they argued that dancers could act dramas with strong narratives (and especially *tragedies, which neoclassical theorists considered the highest form of drama), without words. Moreover, the champions of ballet d'action recommended using well-known myths and stories so that even words in the form of programme notes would not interfere with the danced form of the narrative. The ballets created by these choreographers were dance-dramas in the sense that they used choreography as the instrument for dramatic structure, combining mime and expressive dance to convey events and characters. According to Noverre, Roman *pantomime was a precursor to the ballet d'action. This strand of ballet continued, exemplified in the romantic nineteenth-century ballets of the Italian choreographer Filippo Taglioni, the Danish choreographer August Bournonville, and others; the *modernist twentieth-century ballets of the Russian choreographer Michel *Fokine; and later, both the narrative ballets of the English choreographer Frederick Ashton and the psychological dramas of the British choreographer Antony Tudor. However, even the imperial Russian ballets by Marius Petipa and Lev Ivanov in the late nineteenth century, criticized by reformers like Fokine for devoting too much time to ornamental divertissements, were built on the story ballet model. In modern dance, the American choreographer Martha *Graham also created psychologically focused narrative dramas, especially in her dances of the 1940s and 1950s based on Greek myths. While narrative dance-dramas seem to exist in many cultures worldwide, in most non-Western cultures they include verbal storytelling, often in song. This category of mute choreographic storytelling—one result of the artistic specialization and fragmentation that has characterized the arts in Europe and its colonies since the eighteenth century—seems to be a largely Western invention, like absolute music. It has spread from the West to other parts of the world in contemporary performance, but does not seem to characterize non-Western traditional forms.

Edging even closer to dance-drama at the other end of our continuum is the category of dance-theatre. Here the performances are still on the dance side of the dance/theatre divide, rather than existing as *physical theatre or a true marriage of dance and theatre. Movement predominates, but in addition to choreography these events include verbal components as well as dramatic structures (though not necessarily fully fleshed-out narrative plots). Contemporary forms of dance-theatre include the late twentieth-century German Tanztheater of Pina *Bausch; many instances of postmodern dance in the United States, Canada, Europe, and Australasia; and some modern dance. There are also forms of traditional dance-theatre that focus on movement but include songs or chanted poetry, by the performers themselves or by accompanying musicians as part of the performance event, in either an integrated (dance and text are done simultaneously) or compartmented (dance and text alternate) structure. For instance, the north Indian dance form *kathak* embraces both narrative and abstract elements, song and dance. Synthesizing Hindu and Muslim techniques and aesthetics, *kathak* incorporates intricate rhythmic patterns, the whirling of Sufi dervishes, and devotional and narrative songs. Pure dance sections of formal complexity alternate with expressive dance and song.

Although dance and drama are sister arts, the emphasis in the former on the visual and kinaesthetic senses and in the latter on the aural sense, especially in verbal form, at times makes them seem worlds apart. While their different emphases have sometimes led to rivalry and aesthetic competition, especially in the history of dance *theory in the West, in many world traditions pure music and pure dance occur rarely. Rather, the distinctive features of dance and drama complement one another, appearing together in varying proportions in a broad gamut of hybrid forms. SB

BANES, SALLY, *Terpsichore in Sneakers: post-modern dance* (1980; Middletown, Conn., 1987)

COHEN, SELMA JEANNE (ed.), *International Encyclopedia of Dance* (New York, 1998)

COPELAND, ROGER, and COHEN, MARSHALL, *What Is Dance?* (New York, 1983)

DILS, ANN, and ALBRIGHT, ANN COOPER, *Moving History/Dancing Cultures* (Middletown, Conn., 2001)

EMERY, LYNNE FAULEY, *Black Dance in the United States from 1619 to Today*, 2nd rev. edn. (Princeton, 1988)

DANJŪRŌ FAMILY

The Ichikawa *family, whose senior actor usually took the stage name Danjūrō, was the dominant *kabuki acting family in Edo (*Tokyo) from the 1690s until the twentieth century. Other Ichikawa family stage names include Ebizō and Shinnosuke. Danjūrō I (1660–1704) is credited with inventing the bravura *acting style known as *aragoto*. In *aragoto* roles heroic men, and sometimes deities, engage in wild acts of superhuman strength. Danjūrō took his inspiration from *puppet theatre, Buddhist statuary, sutra chanting, and energetic religious *dance, and wrote many of the plays he starred in. *Aragoto kabuki* was a great success and has been passed down through successive generations of actors to the present day. Danjūrō was a man of many contradictions. A dedicated artist and devoted family man, he was prey to the weaknesses of alcohol and bisexual love affairs; a devout believer in his gods, he emulated his samurai ancestors in his ambition to master all competitors. He was murdered on stage by a rival actor.

Danjūrō II (1688–1758) dominated Edo kabuki for half a century. His innovations included striped *make-up for *aragoto* *heroes, and a new, romantic *aragoto* *character with elements of commoner identity, epitomized by the popular hero Sukeroku. He made *aragoto kabuki* essential to the calendar of kabuki events, notably in New Year's plays about the Soga brothers and the heroic 'Shibaraku' scene for the season-opening show. Danjūrō IV (1711–82) added elements of *villain acting to *aragoto* and his son Danjūrō V (1741–1806) played a wider range of roles than any of his predecessors, relying less on the inherited body of family classics.

In 1832 Danjūrō VII (1791–1859) consolidated the authority of the line by establishing the 'Eighteen Great Plays' of the Danjūrō tradition, mainly plays by the first two Danjūrōs. In 1840 he created the *matsubamme* genre (a kabuki dance-drama based on nō staging) but in 1842 was banished from Edo for ten years for breaking sumptuary laws in his productions. He spent most of his exile as a star actor in *Osaka. Danjūrō VIII (1823–1854) blossomed during his father's exile. A beloved actor of romantic male leads, he committed suicide in Osaka for reasons that remain obscure. His younger brother, *Ichikawa Danjūrō IX (1838–1903), was kabuki's great figure in the late nineteenth century; he had no sons and his son-in-law was named Danjūrō X posthumously. From 1903 to 1952 there was no active Danjūrō in kabuki, but **Danjūrō XII** (1946–) became a leading actor and in 2000 his son was preparing to continue the traditions of the line.   LRK

D'ANNUNZIO, GABRIELE (1863–1938)

Italian playwright and director. When D'Annunzio first met Eleonore *Duse in the mid-1890s, she was an internationally renowned actress and he was recognized in Italy and France as a writer of poetry, lyrical works, and novels, among them *Giovanni Episcopo* (*Episcopo and Company*). During a romantic liaison between 1896 and 1904 Duse inspired his major plays. In reaction to *naturalism, and in the spirit of returning to the theatre a sense of *ritual, they dreamed of creating an *open-air theatre, the *Bayreuth of Italy, on the shores of Lake Albano near *Rome where they would produce *Greek *tragedies and the works of worthy modern poets, among them D'Annunzio's modern tragedies. Although funds were raised, the 1899 opening never materialized. Despite Duse's wishes, D'Annunzio promised his first play, *The Dead City* (1898), to Sarah *Bernhardt in a French translation. In 1897 Duse premièred the dramatic poem *A Spring Morning's Dream* in *Paris; and with the *realist actor Ermete *Zacconi, she played in *La Gioconda* (1899), *La Gloria* (1899), and the first Italian production of *The Dead City* (1901).

That same year, under D'Annunzio's direction, she produced and starred in the première of *Francesca da Rimini* (1901), his spectacular medieval tragedy, complete with *chorus. Reviews of these works were mixed, as were the reviews of her purely Dannunzian repertory when she toured the USA (1902–3). The plays were considered too literary; his language, although extraordinarily rich, too rhetorical and formal; his *plots badly structured; and the amorality, distorted passions, and brutality of the plays and their Nietzschean Superman *heroes did not appeal to *audiences. In addition, D'Annunzio, anticipating the role of *director, imposed a formal style of movement and speech on Duse, an actress known for her realistic interpretations. *La figlia di Iorio* (*Daughter of Jorio*, 1904), a *pastoral tragedy in *verse which is set among superstitious peasants in the wilds of Abruzzi and which ends in death by fire, had a dramatic unity missing heretofore and was his only play to meet with resounding success. His decision to allow Irma *Gramatica to première as the earthy prostitute Mila di Codra, a part he had promised to Duse, caused the break-up of their relationship. Facing bankruptcy and the banning of his works in Italy, D'Annunzio lived in *Paris from 1911 to 1915 and wrote in French and Italian for theatre and *film.

Several works starred the Russian dancer Ida Rubinstein: *Le Martyre de saint Sébastien* (1911, music by Claude Debussy, sets and costumes by Leon *Bakst, choreography by Michel *Fokine), was a *total theatre piece in the *symbolist style that used coloured *lights, *sounds, and various aromas and perfumes to stimulate the senses, and combined *music, poetry, *dance, and figurative art, as well as mythic *characters from Graeco-Roman, Judaeo-Christian, and Asiatic legends. *La Pisanelle; ou, La Mort parfumée* (*Pisanelle; or, Perfumed Death*, 1913) had music by I. Pizzetti, and was directed by *Meyerhold with *scenery by Bakst and choreography by Fokine. D'Annunzio became a hero in the First World War, and his mansion on Lake Garda, Il Vittoriale, is a monument to Italian heroism.   JEH

ATTISANI, ANTONIO, 'Gabriele D'Annunzio', in Jane House and Antonio Attisani (eds.), *20th Century Italian Drama* (New York, 1995)

DAO DUY TU (1572–1634)

Vietnamese actor and playwright, the most important writer for the *hat boi* classical theatre. It was probably his influence which spread *hat boi* from north to south *Vietnam and from the court to other social groups. He also Vietnamized *hat boi* both by introducing more *Indian-influenced *music and by writing scripts set in Vietnam itself. His best-known work is *Fort of Son Hou*, which concerns intrigue at the Vietnamese court, resolved through the rightful heir's enthronement. His descendant Dao Tan (1844–1907) was also a major *hat boi* playwright.   CPM

DA PONTE, LORENZO (1749–1838)

Italian librettist, poet, and impresario. Da Ponte's eventful life took him from a Venetian seminary to the theatres of Dresden, *Vienna, *London, and *New York, where he spent the last 30 years of his life, ending up in the unpaid position of professor of Italian literature at Columbia College. A libertine and adventurer, he never established himself in a permanent profession. He is now remembered as the librettist for three of *Mozart's operatic masterpieces: *The Marriage of Figaro* (1786), *Don Giovanni* (1787), and *Così fan tutte* (1790). Each is a model of its kind, marked by a keen theatrical instinct, an acute understanding of the relationship of words to music, and a sense of structure that allows an exceptionally complex *action, normally considered unsuitable for *opera, to unfold with clarity. During his time in Vienna (1782–90), Da Ponte also provided excellent librettos for operas by Salieri and de Soler, among others, but for musical reasons these works are no longer in the regular repertoire.   SJCW

D'ARCY, MARGARETTA (1934–)

Irish playwright. D'Arcy has written a number of plays with her husband John *Arden, beginning with *The Happy Haven* (1960). Their joint work has been controversial and D'Arcy has suffered the ire of critics who blame her for Arden's sharp rejection of mainstream theatre in the early 1970s. Their collaborations tend towards sprawling *epic drama, often on *historical themes. *The Hero Rises Up* (1968) focuses on Admiral Nelson. *The Island of the Mighty* (1972), a reworking of Arthurian legends, gained more attention from the playwrights' quarrels with the director, David *Jones, and for their picketing of the *Royal Shakespeare Company, than for the production itself. *The Non-Stop Connolly Show* (1975) is a mammoth 24-hour play structured like a medieval *mystery cycle. A committed activist for left-wing and Irish republican causes, D'Arcy formed the Galway Theatre Workshop in 1976. Her play *The Pinprick of History* was produced at the Almost Free Theatre in 1977.   MDG

DASHAVATAR

Indian *folk form representing the ten incarnations of Lord Vishnu. It is performed between October and April by itinerant players belonging to the Devali and Gurav communities of the Konkan region of Maharashtra (*see* MARATHI THEATRE), in which men play female roles (*see* FEMALE IMPERSONATION). The first half involves *rituals like invocatory prayers to Lord Ganesh and goddess Saraswati, and the entry of Sankhasur, the evil spirit that Vishnu's first incarnation, the fish avatar, was born to destroy. Sankhasur is dressed in a black robe and a conical black hat with a face flap that has eyes and mouth with a red tongue hanging out. The first half ends with an enactment of the story of the man-lion avatar Narasimha. The second half is a play based on a myth or popular story that is selected in consultation with the patron village. Performed in a declamatory style with improvised *dialogue and songs, it ends only at daybreak when other rituals are performed, involving the entire community.   SGG

DASTÉ, JEAN (1904–94)

French actor and director. Son-in-law of Jacques *Copeau, Dasté was instrumental in the development of decentralized theatre in post-war France, founding the Comédie de Saint-Étienne as one of the first provincial Centres Dramatiques in 1947. His eclectic programming there ranged from an adaptation of a *medieval play, *Un miracle de Notre-Dame*, to the first French production of *Brecht's *The Caucasian Chalk Circle* (1957). An accomplished actor, Dasté appeared in such monumental *films as Renoir's *La Grande Illusion* (1937), Vigo's *L'Atalante* (1934), Truffaut's *L'Enfant sauvage* (*The Wild Child*, 1970), and *Mnouchkine's *Molière*.   DGM

DAUBENY, PETER (1921–75)

English *producer. Peter Daubeny *trained as an actor with Michel *Saint-Denis but turned to *management after the war, during which he lost an arm; in 30 years he mounted more than 200 productions. In the 1950s he introduced many foreign *dance companies to *London, including those of Roland Petit, Antonio, and Martha *Graham, as well as Beijing opera (*jingju*). He presented Edwige Feuillère in *La Dame aux camélias* (1955), and the success of this venture led to the influential first visit of the *Berliner Ensemble in 1956 and of the *Moscow Art Theatre in 1958. From 1964 to 1973 he ran the World Theatre Season for two or three months each year at the *Aldwych, bringing to London the *Comédie-Française, the *Abbey Theatre, *nō and *bunraku, Karolos *Koun's production of *The Birds*, *Barrault's *Le Soulier de satin*, the *Actors Studio, the Theatre on the *Balustrade, Nuria *Espert's company, and many others. He built up a loyal *audience prepared to sit patiently with a translation baton at one ear, and the influx of fine companies had a wider effect on many directors and producers. He was knighted in 1973, but after his early death no successor came forward, to the lasting impoverishment of the British theatre.   EEC

DAVENANT, WILLIAM (1606–68)

English playwright and *manager. Born to the wife of an Oxford innkeeper who later became mayor, Davenant was reputed to have been the godson of Shakespeare and did nothing to scotch the suggestion that the relationship may have been closer. He served as a youth in the household of Fulke Greville, Lord Brooke, and counted John Suckling among his friends. By the early 1630s Davenant had done military service and thus gained royal favour; contracted syphilis, which left him disfigured; married the first of three wives; been convicted of murder (pardoned in 1638); and tried his hand at playwriting. His first acted play, *The Cruel Brother*, appeared in 1627; but the success in 1634 of a *comedy, *The Wits*, and especially of his heroic *tragicomedy *Love and Honour*, settled him on a theatrical career, and over the next five years he wrote at least seven more plays for the King's Men (*see* CHAMBERLAIN'S MEN). Davenant became the principal writer of court *masques after the success of *The Temple of Love* in 1635, and he was appointed Poet Laureate in 1638. In March 1639 he secured a *patent for a large new theatre for the presentation of 'music, musical presentments, scenes, dancing or other the like' by a company that he would assemble. The project was blocked and Davenant agreed not to proceed, but he retained the essentials of the patent. The following year he was appointed governor of *Beeston's Boys, but was soon in the King's service in the Bishops' Wars, for which he was knighted in 1643.

Davenant remained a royalist through the turbulent years of the Civil Wars and the Interregnum. By 1655 he was in *London, planning representations and shows, and in May 1656 began a series of *operatic performances at Rutland House, his London residence, and continued later at the old *Cockpit. These productions were characterized by the music, *dancing, and scenes promised in the 1639 patent. The best known, *The Siege of Rhodes* (1656, revised in two parts 1661), was later cited by *Dryden as the first *heroic play. With the Restoration, Davenant resurrected his 1639 patent, and he and Thomas *Killigrew obtained exclusive rights to the performance of plays in London. Killigrew's King's Company eventually settled the Theatre Royal, *Drury Lane; Davenant's less experienced company at the Duke's Theatre, *Lincoln's Inn Fields, remodelled to accommodate changeable *scenery. While Killigrew inherited rights to the large repertory of the King's Men, Davenant was granted rights only for his own plays and nine by Shakespeare, with the proviso that they be 'improved' and modernized for production. The result was a series of Shakespearian adaptations (including *Macbeth* and *The Tempest*) for which Davenant is sometimes castigated. Other than these, a translation of a French play, and a dramatic medley (*A Playhouse Let*), Davenant contributed no original plays to the Restoration stage. He had found his true calling as an impresario. RWV

DAVENPORT, FANNY (1850–98)

American actress and *manager, daughter of actor E. L. Davenport and English actress Fanny Vining. She began in *stock *soubrette roles, including Carline in *The Black Crook*, at the Louisville (Kentucky) Theatre, moved to *Philadelphia's *Arch Street Theatre, and then to Augustin *Daly's 5th Avenue Theatre in *New York, playing Lady Gay Spanker, Nancy in *Oliver Twist*, and Rosalind, and originating Madge Renfrew in *Pique* (1876). Famously hoydenish in youth, she became picturesquely emotional in maturity, as she successfully managed her own company and starred (after 1883) in numerous *Sardou vehicles: *Fedora*, *La Tosca*, *Cleopatra*, and *Gismonda*. KM

DAVIDSON, GORDON (1933–)

American producer and director. The Brooklyn-born Davidson began his career as a *stage manager and moved west in 1964 to assist John *Houseman at the Theatre Group, an independent theatre at the University of California, *Los Angeles. In 1967 it moved to the *Mark Taper Forum at the new Los Angeles Music Center, with Davidson as *artistic director. Thus began the longest continuing tenure in American *regional theatre, one that made Davidson an influential national figure and the theatrical kingpin in a city dominated by the *film and *television industries. As a producer he pioneered new plays at the Taper with a programme called New Theatre for Now and went on to promote the development of many new works. As a director he attracted early attention on two coasts with his productions of *In the Matter of J. Robert Oppenheimer* (1968) and *The Trial of the Catonsville Nine* (1970). In 1976 he won a Tony *award for his direction of *The Shadow Box*, which started at the Taper before moving to Broadway. In 1989, while remaining head of the Taper, he became producing director for the Ahmanson Theatre, its larger commercial affiliate. STC

DAVIES, HOWARD (1945–)

Welsh director. Davies has been an associate of the Royal *National Theatre, the *Almeida, and the *Royal Shakespeare Company, for which he ran the *Donmar Warehouse in *London. His work emphasizes social context, especially in acclaimed versions of Shakespeare and American drama. At the RSC he directed Edward *Bond's *Bingo* (1976), Pam *Gems's *Piaf* (1978), *Macbeth* (1982), Christopher *Hampton's *Les Liaisons Dangereuses*, and *Troilus and Cressida* (both 1985). At the National Theatre successful productions include *Williams's *Cat on a Hot Tin Roof* (1988), *Boucicault's *The Shaughraun* (1988), Nick Stafford's *Battle Royal* (1999), and *Miller's *All my Sons* (2000). His work at the Almeida includes West End transfers such as *Albee's *Who's Afraid of Virginia Woolf?* (1996) with Diana *Rigg, and *O'Neill's *The Iceman Cometh* (1998) with Kevin Spacey. His Broadway production of *My Fair Lady* (1993) was well received. *Opera productions in Britain include Rossini's *The Italian Girl* (1997), *Mozart's *Idomeneo* (1991), and *Verdi's *I due Foscari* (1993). His *film of David *Hare's *Secret Rapture* (1994) is also notable. KN

DAVIES, ROBERTSON (1913–95)

Canadian writer. Now internationally known as a novelist, Davies was first of all a man of the theatre. A leading actor at Queen's University, Ontario, and then at Oxford, after graduation he worked at the *Old Vic (1938–40) as an actor and *dramaturg under Tyrone *Guthrie. After returning to Canada, in 1942 he became editor of a daily newspaper in Peterborough, where he helped found the Peterborough Little Theatre and directed award-winning productions. He also wrote some widely produced Canadian *comedies such as *Overlaid* (1946), *Fortune my Foe* (1948), and *At my Heart's Core* (1950), which examined the place of art and imagination in a conservative post-war Canada that seemed indifferent to such ideas; another play, *Love and Libel*, directed by Guthrie, toured to *Toronto, Detroit, *Boston, and *New York in 1960. Davies helped in the founding of the *Stratford Festival, and wrote three books chronicling its first years (1953–5). Some of his theatre essays are collected in *The Well-Tempered Critic* (1981) and *Happy Alchemy* (1997); a biography appeared in 1994. DWJ

DAVIS, HALLIE FLANAGAN *See* FLANAGAN, HALLIE.

DAVIS, HENRIETTA VINTON (1860–1941)

*African-American actress and *manager, an elocutionist and orator who specialized in Shakespearian *monologues. Encouraged by Frederick Douglass, Davis made her theatrical debut in 1883. A decade later she founded a theatre in *Chicago where she produced and acted in work by black dramatists, including two plays on the Haitian Revolution by William Edgar Easton (*Dessalines*, 1893; *Christophe*, 1912), and a collaboration with the journalist John Bruce on a drama about the Civil War, *Our Old Kentucky Home* (1898). At the turn of the new century she *toured as an actress throughout the USA, the *Caribbean, and *Latin America, and for a time managed the Covent Garden Theatre in Kingston, Jamaica. She was dedicated to creating an *audience for black performance at a time when African Americans were excluded from the mainstream. Eventually Davis despaired of a full-fledged theatrical career and gave up acting to devote her energies to politics, being especially dedicated to the Marcus Garvey movement from 1919 to 1931.
BBL

DAVIS, JACK (1917–2000)

Australian playwright, actor, and poet. A West Australian stockman and graduate of Perth Technical College, Davis was one of Australia's most influential Aboriginal writers. After writing his first play (*Kullark*, 1979) at the age of 61, his work focused on the experiences of Aboriginal people, dealing with serious themes through comic devices. *The Dreamers* (1982), *No Sugar* (1985), and *Barungin* (1988) were performed as the 'First-Born' trilogy in *Melbourne in 1988, the Australian Bicentennial year, a forceful political comment about the harmful effects of colonization on Aborigines and the need for reconciliation.
SBS

DAVIS, OSSIE (1917–)

*African-American actor of multiple talents, who studied at Howard University with Alain Locke. In 1941 Davis landed a role in *Joy Exceeding Talent* with Harlem's Rose *McClendon Players. Five years later he starred in *Jeb* to great acclaim, and he met his future wife, the actress Ruby *Dee. In 1947 Davis and Dee *toured in *Anna Lucasta*, and Davis was on Broadway again in 1951 in a revival of *Connelly's *The Green Pastures*. During the McCarthy era, when Davis was blacklisted in Hollywood, the pair performed staged readings of a play that Davis wrote about the politics of McCarthyism, *Alice in Wonder* (1953), appeared that same year in *The World of Sholem Aleichem*, and Davis replaced Sidney Poitier in *Hansberry's *A Raisin in the Sun*. Davis wrote and starred in *Purlie Victorious* (1961), a *satire of racial stereotypes, which became the Broadway *musical *Purlie* in 1970. Appearing in many roles in *film and *television, Davis was on Broadway again in 1986 in *Gardner's *I'm Not Rappaport*. His play for young people about Paul *Robeson was produced in *New York in 1998.
BBL

DAWISON, BOGUMIŁ (1818–72)

Polish actor. Born in *Warsaw to a poor Jewish family, he attended the school of drama and acted without success at the Variety Theatre (1838). He was more appreciated in Wilno and Lvov the next year, where he gained the respect of the critics and the love of the public, gradually acquiring star status. Bilingual, he began to perform with the German company as well. At first this hampered his career, since the Polish-speaking public viewed the German theatre as a threat to native culture in Lvov, then under Austrian rule. Frustrated, Dawison moved to Hamburg (1847) and guest-starred in other German cities. He was back in Lvov soon, where he married the actress Wanda Starzewska in 1848. Committing himself more to German, he became the leading actor at the *Burgtheater, *Vienna (1849–53), and the Royal Theatre, Dresden (1854–64). He *toured Western Europe, the United States (1866–7), and his native Poland to great critical acclaim. His penetrating gaze, internal energy, and the ability to imitate were put to excellent use in roles such as Othello, Richard III, Macbeth, Shylock, Mephistopheles, and Franz Moor (in *Schiller's *The Robbers*).
KB

DEAN, BASIL HERBERT (1888–1978)

English actor, dramatist, director, screenwriter, *lighting designer, and *manager. After acting for four years at Miss *Horniman's *Gaiety Theatre, *Manchester, Dean became the director in 1911 of the new Liverpool Repertory Theatre (later called the *Liverpool Playhouse). He acted briefly in *London with Beerbohm *Tree before service in the First World War. In 1919 he became managing director of Reandean, Ltd., a producing syndicate; in 1924 he took a similar post at *Drury Lane. During the 1920s and 1930s he directed regularly in London. In 1931 he founded Associated Talking Pictures, British Film Distributors, and ATP (later Ealing) Studios. He also became a *film director, making a star of Gracie *Fields, among others. During the Second World War he served as director of *ENSA, responsible for entertaining the military forces, and after the war returned to production in London. He wrote two autobiographies, and *Theatre at War* about his experiences in both world wars.
TP

DEAN, PHILIP HAYES (c.1938–)

*African-American playwright. Initially an actor in *New York, he began writing with *The Owl Killer*, which featured Diana Sands in its Harlem première. Another of his early plays,

This Bird of Dawning Singeth All Night Long, was produced at the *American Place Theatre in 1968. His next play, *Sty of the Blind Pig* (1972), was a major critical success and received a number of *awards. Dean has also written *Freeman* (1973), *Everynight When the Sun Goes Down* (1976), and *The American Dixieland Jazz Band* (1980). His *one-person show *Robeson*, which opened on Broadway in 1977 with James Earl *Jones, generated considerable furore when Robeson's son objected to the stage image of his father.

BBL

DEAR, NICK (1955–)

English playwright. Dear gained early success with *Royal Shakespeare Company productions of *Temptation* (1984), followed by his portrait of William Hogarth, *The Art of Success* (1986, also *Manhattan Theatre Club, *New York), which was winner of the Whiting *award and was nominated for the Olivier Award, as was *A Family Affair* (after *Ostrovsky; *Cheek by Jowl, 1988). Playwright in residence at the *Royal Exchange, *Manchester (1987–8), his later plays include *Food of Love* (*Almeida, 1988), *The Last Days of Don Juan* (after *Tirso de Molina; RSC, 1990), and *In the Ruins* (*Royal Court Theatre, 1990). In 1993 *A Family Affair* premièred at the Almeida *Opera Festival as a libretto, as did *Siren Sony* in 1994. In 2001 the RSC staged a co-production *Zenobia* with the *Young Vic. Screenplays include Dostoevsky's *The Gambler* for Channel 4 *television, plus *The Last Days of Don Juan* and an adaptation of Jane Austen's *Persuasion* for Hollywood.

BRK

DE BERARDINIS, LEO (1940–)

Italian actor, director, and author. During the socio-political ferment of the mid-1960s and 1970s, under the influence of *Brecht and the *Living Theatre, this artist of Italian experimental theatre questioned the role of theatre and its form, and with Perla Peragallo and *amateur actors created memorable dialect pieces that incorporated *Neapolitan popular culture and music: *'O zappatore* (*The Farmworker*, 1972), *King lacreme Lear napulitane* (*King Tears, Neapolitan Lear*, 1973), and *Sudd* (South, 1974). After this counter-culture movement failed, he moved to Bologna's cooperative company Nuova Scena to direct *Gelber's *The Connection* (1983), a series of productions based on Shakespeare, and poetic solo works—*Dante* and *Song of Songs*. In 1987 he formed his own company, Teatro di Leo, producing *Macbeth* (1988), *Acts IV and V of Othello* (1992), *King Lear* (1997), and *Strindberg's *To Damascus* (1989). His *multimedia reinterpretations of the classics manipulated slide projections, *film, *dance, *music, and non-traditional *casting. Another solo work, *Come un rivista* (*Like a Variety Star*, 2000), revealed his reverence for the *variety star as a total man of the theatre, a description that certainly applies to him. From 1994 to

1997, he headed *Santarcangelo's summer festival of experimental theatre.

JEH

DEBURAU, JEAN-GASPARD (1796–1846)

French *mime. Memorably brought to life by Jean-Louis *Barrault in Marcel Carné's *film *Les Enfants du paradis* (1945), Deburau was one of the outstanding figures of the French popular theatre during the 1830s and 1840s. Born as Jan Kaspar Dvorak in Bohemia, he came from a family of *acrobats and *circus performers, making his debut at the Théâtre des *Funambules in 1816. Here he developed the mime *character *Pierrot in a long series of sketches which endeared him to the popular *audiences of the 'Boulevard du Crime'. A sad misanthropist, this alter ego was to take on a darker, even a threatening, character after April 1836; out walking with his wife, Deburau was insulted by a young apprentice, who called his wife a whore: he felled the youth with his stick, and the blow proved fatal. Acquitted of unlawful killing, he returned to an enthusiastic welcome from the Funambules audience, but his future performances—and reception—were inevitably marked by the event. A true mime, who never uttered a spoken word during his performances, Deburau occupies a distinctive place in the history of the Pierrot figure, from the eighteenth-century Gilles down to Marcel *Marceau and the *Lecoq school of mime. In his lifetime he was admired by men of letters such as Nodier, *Gautier, and Baudelaire; and Jules *Janin wrote his biography. He was also the subject of a play by Sacha *Guitry in 1918.

WDH

DECORUM

The *bienséances*, an unwritten code of what was fitting or not fitting to be shown on stage, no less powerful than the doctrine of the *unities in determining the character of French *neoclassical drama. While the notion of *vraisemblance* (probability) concerned the representation of customs and events according to ideas generally held about life at the time and place where the action of a play was set, *bienséance* controlled the adaptation of such historical material to the moral ideas—the taste and prejudices—of a modern *audience. A significant change in public taste during the 1630s (no doubt largely due to the growing influence of women in society) may be illustrated by examples from *Corneille. Whereas in *Clitandre* (1632) the heroine had visited her wounded lover in bed, and the pair had enjoyed some fairly suggestive conversation, the fact that in *Le Cid* (1637) Chimène receives the visit of Rodrigue, who had killed her father in a duel, alone at night—and confesses her love for him—was the source of much *criticism during the 'Querelle du Cid' only a few years later. Bloody or violent incidents, which abound in the pre-classical theatre, from the 1640s onwards took place offstage and were reported. Suicide was allowed onstage, but not murder: thus in 1640, Corneille's Horace chases his sister into the wings in order to kill her offstage. Language was similarly sanitized, all overt references to physical functions and to parts of the body such as 'breast' and 'stomach' being replaced by inoffensive circumlocution or ennobled by figurative expression. *Racine is the supreme example of a poet who turned the *bienséances* into a positive advantage; while in *comedy, *Molière in *The Misanthrope* successfully demonstrates the wit and polish of salon repartee. Eighteenth-century successors were less skilful, and the tyranny of the *bienséances* came to be recognized as such. Although *Voltaire denounced Shakespeare's 'Not a mouse stirring' from the beginning of *Hamlet* as incompatible with the dignity of *tragedy, Diderot was soon to complain, 'Cruel *bienséances*! You make our theatre decent but mediocre.' WDH

DECROUX, ÉTIENNE (1889–1991)

French *mime, actor, and *theorist. Inspired by Jacques *Copeau, Decroux invented modern 'corporeal mime' as a reaction against the whitefaced *pantomime of Jean-Gaspard *Deburau and his followers. Corporeal mime emphasizes articulation of the torso and de-emphasizes expressive face and hands, which were of primary importance in Deburau's pantomime. Yet corporeal mime was almost eclipsed during Decroux's lifetime by the performances of his celebrated student Marcel *Marceau, who created his own pantomime form which owed more to Deburau than to Decroux's *modernism. Decroux was also the teacher of Jean-Louis *Barrault and thousands of other students during his 60-year teaching career in *Paris, *New York, *Stockholm, Tel Aviv, and at the *Piccolo Teatro in *Milan. A stage, *radio, and *film actor (best known for his role as Deburau *père* in *Les Enfants du paradis*, 1945), Decroux had a passion for language, politics, and poetry, some of which is apparent in his *Paroles sur le mime* (*Words on Mime*, 1963), which encapsulates his main lines of thought. Eugenio *Barba wrote that Decroux is 'perhaps the only European master to have elaborated a system of rules comparable to that of an Oriental tradition'. TL

DEE, RUBY (1924–)

*African-American actress and playwright, who first appeared on Broadway in 1943 and in the 1946–7 season starred in *Anna Lucasta*. Her career advanced greatly with her performance as Ruth Younger in *Hansberry's *A Raisin in the Sun* (1959), playing opposite Sidney Poitier. She was back on Broadway in *Purlie Victorious* in 1961. At the *American Shakespeare Theatre in Connecticut she was the first African-American actress to appear in leading roles, as Kate in *Taming of the Shrew* and Cordelia in *King Lear* (both 1965). *Off-Broadway she was featured with James Earl *Jones in *Fugard's *Boesman and Lena* (1970;

Obie *award). Her own scripts include *Twin Bit Gardens* (1976), *Take It from the Top* (a *musical, 1979), and *Zora Is my Name*, on Zora Neale *Hurston. Dee's *one-person show *My One Good Nerve: a visit with Ruby Dee* (1998) was based on her life. BBL

DEFILIPPIS NOVOA, FRANCISCO (1892–1930)

Argentinian playwright, *manager, director, and translator. Born in Paraná (Entre Ríos), Defilippis exemplifies the modernization of Argentinian theatre at the beginning of the twentieth century. Although early plays such as *The Little Mother* (1920) are easily categorized as romantic costume drama (*see* COSTUMBRISMO), by the mid-1920s he showed the influence of the European *avant-garde, especially German *expressionism. A translator of *Pirandello and *producer-director of *Strindberg, Defilippis's own *Foolish Mary* (1927) and *I've Seen God* (1930) stand out—the former for its experimentation, and the latter for its mix of *realist humanism, expressionism, and *grotesco criollo*. JGJ

DE FILIPPO, EDUARDO (1900–84)

Italian playwright, actor, and director, known throughout Italy simply as Eduardo. The illegitimate son of the famous Neapolitan playwright Eduardo *Scarpetta and Luisa de Filippo, he made his debut at the age of 4 in his father's play *The Geisha*. After the success of his own *one-act *Sik-Sik l'artefice magico* (*Sik-Sik, the Masterful Magician*) in 1930, de Filippo formed a company with his brother Peppino and sister Titina, opening in 1931 at the Teatro Sannazzaro in *Naples. Among the many admirers of the de Filippo company was the Sicilian playwright Luigi *Pirandello; the next year de Filippo began a collaboration by adapting two Pirandello stories for the stage and translating the novella *Liolà* into Neapolitan. The de Filippo company dissolved after the war, largely due to tension between the brothers. Peppino formed his own company, while Eduardo and Titina incorporated as Il Teatro di Eduardo. The brothers remained estranged for the rest of their lives.

De Filippo had an extraordinarily long and productive career. He wrote 39 plays, several collections of poetry, and many stage adaptations of works by Neapolitan writers. He directed all his plays and acted in most. His mature works, translated and produced widely on international stages, include *Natale in casa Cupiello* (*Christmas at the Cupiellos'*, 1937), *Filumena Marturano* (1946), *Questi fantasmi!* (*These Ghosts!*, 1946), *La grande magia* (1948), *Le voci di dentro* (*Voices from Within*, 1948), *De Pretore Vincenzo* (1957), *Sabato domenica lunedì* (*Saturday, Sunday, Monday*, 1959), *L'arte della commedia* (*The Art of Comedy*, 1964). In *London, Franco *Zeffirelli's productions of *Saturday,

Eduardo **de Filippo**'s *Saturday, Sunday, Monday* at the Old Vic, London, 1973. This highly regarded National Theatre production, directed by Franco Zeffirelli, starred Joan Plowright, Laurence Olivier, and Frank Finlay, all pictured here.

Sunday, Monday (*Old Vic, 1973) with *Olivier and Joan *Plowright, and of *Filumena* with Plowright (1977), were particularly notable. While maintaining links with the theatrical tradition, de Filippo rejected the inflated *acting inherited from the *commedia dell'arte*. He advocated a more *naturalistic mode, devoid of exaggeration, marked by vocal control, where silence was as important as *dialogue.

Most of de Filippo's works were written in a Neapolitan dialect designed to represent the character of ordinary people. Even during the years of *fascism, when the regime imposed standard Italian in the name of nationalism, Eduardo's works were played in dialect. Nonetheless fascist *censorship banned some of his plays, and several remain unpublished. Fascism and the war also affected his outlook: the works composed before 1945 tend to have a positive stance and, with the exception of *Natale in casa Cupiello*, end happily. After that date Eduardo's work became more sombre and more complex. A case in point is *Napoli milionaria!*, which portrays the moral damage perpetrated by the war on ordinary people. In the 1950s and the 1960s his plays reflected major social changes in Italy, such

as the shift in morality and family values in a younger generation eager to free itself from family constraints; *Mia famiglia* (1955) deals with these uneasy relationships. The traditional corruption in Neapolitan politics was attacked in *Il sindaco del rione sanità* (*The Local Authority*, 1960) and *Il contratto* (*The Contract*, 1967). His last play, *Gli esami non finiscono mai* (*Exams Never End*, 1973), written a few years after the legalization of divorce, treats disintegration of the family, betrayal of friendship, and the problem of extramarital relationships. De Filippo also wrote extensively for *film, *television, and *opera, working with major directors such as Zeffirelli and *Pasolini.   DMcM

DE GRAFT, JOE (1924–78)

Ghanaian dramatist, director, and teacher who had a major impact on the School of Music and Drama at the University of Ghana from 1962. His early domestic drama *Sons and Daughters* should be set beside a much more ambitious transposition of *Hamlet* to northern Ghana (*Hamile*) and *Through a Glass Darkly* (originally *Visitor from the Past*, 1962). Clashes within the university led to his move to Kenya where he wrote *Muntu*, a pageant-drama about the experience of *Africa. He also acted with distinction. Back in Ghana during the 1970s, de Graft found inspiration in Shakespeare and radically reworked *Macbeth* to incorporate the experience of politics in post-independence Africa. He also created more roles for female students. *Mambo* was premièred in 1978, by which time he was seriously ill.   JMG

DE GROEN, ALMA (1941–)

Australian *feminist playwright. De Groen's first performed work, *The Joss Adams Show* (1970), enjoyed an international reception. Her plays often represent marginalized women who respond to their entrapment with bizarre behaviour. In *The Rivers of China* (1987) De Groen interweaves the last days of Katherine Mansfield's life with a science fiction narrative. In *Vocations* (1981), women struggle to maintain integrity in the face of patriarchal demands, and *The Girl Who Saw Everything* (1991) is a study of generational responses to *feminism. De Groen has also written for *television, *film, and *radio.

SBS

DEIXIS

Term developed in linguistics and *semiotic *theory, used to describe various performative aspects of human speech, including the ways that speakers locate themselves in reference to listeners and surroundings. Taken up by theatre semioticians, the concept usually refers to the processes by which *characters and objects are located and oriented in time and space by means of the referential signs of language, gesture, and scenic representation. In *dialogue, characters refer to themselves and address one another with pronouns, thus indicating how and where the 'I' and the 'you' are situated. Characters also refer to and gesture toward one another and to objects, thereby indexing and representing the locations for persons and objects within and beyond the visible scene. Thus throughout a play and its staging characters orient themselves—and develop the dramatic *action—by means of deixis, providing a systematic register of orientation for theatrical *mimesis.   TP

DEKKER, THOMAS (c.1572–1632)

English dramatist. He was born in *London, possibly of Dutch extraction, but nothing certain is known of his life until his emergence as a playwright for the *Admiral's Men in 1598. In the next five years he contributed to more than 40 plays, and throughout his career he often worked in collaboration, frequently with younger, less experienced playwrights who went on to become significant in their own right: in 1604 he

wrote with *Middleton, in 1604–5 with *Webster, and in 1621–4 with *Ford. The frantic pace of his work reflects the dominant fact of his professional life, his driving poverty; he was imprisoned for debt at least three times. The longest spell was for seven years from 1612, probably as a result of expenses he incurred in devising that year's Lord Mayor's *pageant; among his creditors was Webster's coach-maker father. When he emerged, white-haired, it was into a different theatrical world: the figures who had dominated it when he went in—*Henslowe, *Burbage, Shakespeare—were all dead, and fashion favoured new, courtlier modes of drama, to which he duly turned his hand. The Dekker plays which have lasted in the repertory, *The Shoemaker's Holiday* (1599) and *The Roaring Girl* (co-written with Middleton, 1611), are notable for their bourgeois London settings and their reliance on racy, demotic vitality more than on complex narrative; but in his own time Dekker was a professional who could master any *genre from tightly *plotted intrigue *tragedy to rollicking *farce. *See* CITY COMEDY.   MJW

DELACORTE THEATRE

Outdoor *amphitheatre in *New York's Central Park, where the *New York Shakespeare Festival stages free outdoor summer Shakespeare productions. The 2,300-seat theatre is named for George T. Delacorte, the philanthropist founder of Dell Publishing, who donated $150,000 towards the theatre's construction (the city of New York put up an additional $250,000). The theatre opened in 1962 with a production of *The Merchant of Venice* featuring George C. *Scott as Shylock. More than a million people saw free Shakespeare in the Delacorte in its first decade alone. In 1971 the Festival renovated the theatre to change its fan-like configuration to a horseshoe form to facilitate a closer connection between actors and performers; Ming Cho *Lee designed the alterations. Among the well-known actors who have appeared in Delacorte Theatre productions are Colleen *Dewhurst, Raul *Julia, Meryl Streep, Kevin *Kline, and Patrick *Stewart. Attending productions in the Delacorte has become a beloved tradition of New Yorkers; for popular productions, *audiences wait in line for hours and sometimes overnight for tickets.   KF

DELANEY, SHELAGH (1939–)

English playwright, best known for *A Taste of Honey* (1958, *filmed 1962), which concerns a pregnant young girl who is thrown out by her slatternly mother. Written with vigour and warmth, under Joan *Littlewood's direction at the *Theatre Workshop its production drew on popular theatre traditions and incidental popular *music that underscored and commented on the action. When it transferred to the West End Delaney was recognized as one of the few 'angry young women' of the British new wave, and the play was instrumental in making regional accents and working-class lives serious dramatic subjects. *The Lion in Love* (1960), a bleak account of a dysfunctional and alcoholic family, was less well received. *The House That Jack Built* (*television 1977, stage 1979) followed a marriage from the drunken aftermath of the wedding through crises to partial reconciliation. All of her plays are remarkable for the affection and resilience of the female *characters, and the tender concern displayed for the broken lives of the *protagonists. Delaney has also written successful screenplays, including *Charlie Bubbles* (1968) and *Dance with a Stranger* (1985).

DR

DELAVIGNE, CASIMIR (1793–1843)

French playwright. The most talented of the dramatists who filled the gap between *neoclassical *tragedy and romantic drama, Delavigne first achieved popularity with *Les Vêpres siciliennes* (1819). *Marino Faliero*, performed at the *Porte-Saint-Martin in 1829, portrays the atmosphere of corruption and intrigues in fourteenth-century Venice in a manner which anticipates *Musset's *Lorenzaccio*; and its use of the alexandrine line, if much less adventurous than *Hugo's, looks forward to *romanticism rather than back towards the stilted versification of eighteenth-century tragedy.

WDH

DEL CIOPPO, ATAHUALPA (1904–93)

Uruguayan director. He began his career in *Montevideo with the theatre for *youth company La Isla de los Niños, where he established himself as a rising artist and began a programme of *training actors which would carry over to his later work. One of his most successful productions, Carlos Dennis Molina's *El regreso de Ulises* (*The Return of Ulysses*, 1948), preceded by a year the merger of La Isla with Teatro del Pueblo to form El *Galpón. Thereafter del Cioppo became an important figure in the independent theatre movement in Uruguay. Although he originally relied on *Stanislavsky to achieve greater *realism and intensity in *acting, with El Galpón he began to experiment with *Brechtian methods and was instrumental in introducing *Brecht to the region through productions such as *The Threepenny Opera* (1957). His mounting of Brecht's *The Caucasian Chalk Circle* at El Galpón in 1959 was well received in Montevideo and *Buenos Aires, and he also staged *Galileo* at the *Comedia Nacional. Del Cioppo's political exile in Mexico helped to form his reputation as the foremost Brechtian director in *Latin America, extending the methods to other *texts for El Galpón such as the collaborative *Artigas general del pueblo* (*Artigas, General of the People*, 1981). Restaged in Montevideo in 1984, it was admired by the public though disparaged by the critics. Before his death del Cioppo put his energy into estab-lishing the Casa Bertolt Brecht, a cultural bridge between artists of Germany and Uruguay.

EJW

DELLA PORTA, GIOVAN BATTISTA (1535–1615)

Neapolitan scientist and playwright. A controversial thinker and inventor, he had frequent brushes with the Inquisition. He wrote at least 29 plays, of which 18 have survived, for performance either in private palaces or in the court to upper-class *audiences in *Naples. The most memorable and influential are his fourteen surviving *comedies. These are based conventionally on sources in *Plautus or in the Italian novella; but they reflect changing tastes in a number of ways. Like much *commedia dell'arte*, they distinguish sharply between parallel strands of *plot and types of *character—sentimental stories alongside farcical buffoonery, high-minded *heroes alongside stereotyped comic victims. Overall, they offer a widening range of emotion and tone which has sometimes been compared, cautiously, to that in Elizabethan drama: in contrast with earlier *commedia erudita*, they constantly blur the previously sharp boundaries between comedy and other *genres.

RAA

DELPINI, CARLO (1740–1828)

Italian dancer, singer, actor, and choreographer, who began his *London career at *Covent Garden in 1776, playing *Pierrot in *Harlequin's Frolics*. Over the next several decades he performed *pantomimes and speciality *dances at *Drury Lane, the *Haymarket, John Palmer's abortive Royalty Theatre, as well as a number of *minor London and provincial venues. He designed *scenery and dances for pantomimes such as *The Norwood Gypsies* (1777) and *Don Juan* (1787). He was a special favourite of George IV, for whom he performed at Brighton in 1790 and gave a masquerade at the Pantheon in the early nineteenth century.

MJK

DELSARTE, FRANÇOIS (1811–71)

French singing teacher and *theorist. After an impoverished childhood, Delsarte studied voice at the *Paris *Conservatoire (1826–9) and performed as a tenor at the *Opéra-Comique. He took exception to the methods he was taught, which he thought impaired his voice, and evolved his own method for teaching voice, expression, and *acting to actors (*Rachel, *Macready), singers (Jenny Lind), composers (Bizet), as well as the clergy, orators, painters, and sculptors. Delsarte's complex system is based on an infinite number of intersecting trinities such as: mind, soul, and body; head, heart, and lower trunk; Father, Son, and Holy Ghost; eccentric, concentric, and neutral. Delsarte's system taught precepts such as 'movement first, then speech', and 'to each spiritual function responds a function of the body. To each grand function of the body, corresponds a spiritual act.' Americans Steele *MacKay, Genevieve Stebbins, and Ted Shawn (*see* ST DENIS, RUTH) were most responsible for the continuation of Delsarte's teachings into the twentieth century. MacKaye founded the first school of acting in *New York after studying with Delsarte; Stebbins popularized Delsarte's teachings through lectures and writings; Shawn, through his many years of lecturing and his book *Every Little Movement*, tried to explain the essence of Delsarte's original teachings. Practitioners as diverse as Mathias Alexander (founder of the Alexander Technique), Jerzy *Grotowski, and Isadora *Duncan attributed primary importance to Delsarte. Much of contemporary performance practice, especially in modern *dance, would be unimaginable without his work.   TL

DE MARÍA, CÉSAR (1960–)

Peruvian playwright. His complex, innovative, and intriguing *satires concern alienation and self-deception, and the conditions ordinary people visit upon themselves. In a world over which his characters have no control, de María's poetic sensibility and technical virtuosity maintain sympathy with the bitter contradictions of 'Third World' politics. One of the most talented and prolific of *Latin American playwrights, and winner of a number of national and international *awards, his major work includes *¡A ver un aplauso!* (*Let's Have Some Applause!*, 1989), *The Black Box* (1992), *Scorpions Looking at the Sky* (1993), and *The Cowardly Japanese* (1999).   LRG

DEMIDOVA, ALLA (1936–)

Russian actress. Demidova trained at the Shchukin School and joined the *Taganka Theatre in 1964. She emerged as a leading actress in the 1970s with her remarkable performance of an intelligent and conspiring Gertrude in *Lyubimov's production of *Hamlet* (1971). She played one of the leads in Abramov's *The Wooden Horses* (1974), endowing her *character with a poetic touch as she remembered the extinction of her family during the purges. She was cast in the part of Ranevskaya in Anatoly *Efros's production of *Chekhov's *The Cherry Orchard* at the Taganka Theatre in 1975, and later played Masha in *The Three Sisters* (1981). She brought the touch of poetry combined with intellect to her roles, and was therefore especially suited for Chekhovian characters. Her Marina Mniszek in *Boris Godunov* (1988) and her Electra (1992) display the calm, reflecting and rational side of her character. In 1988 she played Phaedra in Roman *Viktyuk's production of Marina Tsvetaeva's play, embellishing her role with the recital of the poet's correspondence. She has appeared in a production of *The Stone Guest* directed by Anatoly *Vasiliev (1997). Though she worked in *film

with Andrei Tarkovsky, her fame rests on her roles in the theatre.   BB

DE MILLE, AGNES (1905–93)

American choreographer. The niece of Hollywood director Cecil B. DeMille, Agnes de Mille (family members chose different spellings of the surname) defied the discouragement of an early *ballet teacher and pursued training in *London, where she studied with Marie Rambert, gave solo recitals, and began creating her own work. During the 1930s she travelled between London, *New York, and Hollywood, choreographing for *film, Broadway, and the concert stage. Her association with Ballet Theatre began in the company's initial season (1939) and eventually produced, among others, *Black Ritual* (1940), the first ballet to use black dancers, *Rodeo* (1942), first commissioned by the *Ballets Russes de Monte Carlo but later absorbed into Ballet Theatre's repertory, and *Fall River Legend* (1948). In 1943, de Mille's eighteen-minute dream ballet for *Rodgers and *Hammerstein's *Oklahoma!* considerably advanced the use of movement as an integral element in plotting and characterization in *musical comedy; de Mille wrote the *scenario herself, created the movement, and *cast and directed the ballet, becoming one of the first choreographers to move into a directorial position on Broadway. In the 1950s she launched a distinguished literary career, writing memoirs, dance and cultural histories, and several lively and tart biographies.   LTC

DEMILLE, HENRY C. (1850–93)

American playwright. DeMille collaborated with David *Belasco on a series of highly successful plays, beginning with *The Wife* (1887) and continuing with *Lord Chumley*, a vehicle for E. H. *Sothern (1888), *The Charity Ball* (1889), *Men and Women* (1890), and *The Danger Signal* (1891). Working alone, DeMille adapted Ludwig *Fulda's *Das verlorene Paradies* as *The Lost Paradise* (1891). He founded a performance dynasty: after his sudden death, his widow created the first playwrights' agency run by a woman, and his sons William and Cecil (C. B.) entered motion pictures as a writer and director, respectively, while his granddaughter Agnes *de Mille (the family name was spelt variously) became a noted choreographer.
                                                        AW

DENCH, JUDI (1934–)

English actress, the most distinctively voiced of her generation, who has consistently won acclaim for the psychological veracity, remarkable emotional range, warmth, and fearlessness of her portrayals. In her first *Old Vic seasons (1957–61) she was directed by *Zeffirelli as Juliet. Over 24 roles with the *Royal Shakespeare Company since 1961 include Titania, Isabella,

Viola, Beatrice, Lady Macbeth with Ian *McKellen, Major Barbara, *O'Casey's Juno, Mother Courage, and Helen in *Shaffer's *Gift of the Gorgon*. At the Royal *National Theatre since 1982 she has notably played Lady Bracknell, Cleopatra, Arkadina, Mrs Rafi in *Bond's *The Sea*, and *Pinter's Deborah in *A Kind of Alaska*. In the commercial theatre unexpected successes showing her versatility were Lika in *The Promise* (1967) and Sally Bowles in *Cabaret* (1968). Since 1957, when she appeared in *Talking to a Stranger*, her numerous (often award-winning) *television appearances include the series *A Fine Romance* (with her husband Michael Williams), *Behaving Badly*, *Absolute Hell*, and *Last of the Blond Bombshells*. Memorable *film roles include *Saigon: Year of the Cat*, *Mrs Brown*, *Chocolat*, and *Iris*.

RAC

DENNERY (D'ENNERY), ADOLPHE (1811–99)

French dramatist, author or co-author of some of the most famous *melodramas of the nineteenth century, including *Gaspard Hauser* (1836) and *Les Deux orphelines* (*The Two Orphans*, 1875). He also composed fairy extravaganzas like *Aladin* (1863), and adapted the Jules Verne novels *Around the World in Eighty Days* (1874) and *Michel Strogoff* (1880). He wrote *opera librettos for Adam's *Si j'étais roi* (*If I were King*, 1852) and Massenet's *Le Cid* (1885). CHB

DENNIS, JOHN (1657–1734)

English critic and playwright, who began his career in the early 1690s. *The Impartial Critic* (1693) demonstrated the tolerant *neoclassicism that characterized his best *criticism. *A Plot and No Plot* (1697), his first play, was followed by *On the Usefulness of the Stage* (1698), his contribution to the Jeremy *Collier controversy. Over the next twelve years Dennis wrote seven more plays and produced the bulk of the criticism that was to earn him the title 'The Critic'. After the failure of *Appius and Virginia* (1709), he forsook the stage for ten years, and his career was increasingly characterized by literary quarrels, his criticism fuelled by personal animosity. Dennis abandoned playwriting for good after the failure in 1719 of *The Invader of his Country* and died in poverty. Despite his dramatic failures and the bitterness of his last years, Dennis was an important critic. His neoclassicism was, as he himself said of *Aristotle's *Poetics*, 'Nature and good sense reduced to a method'.

RWV

DENOUEMENT

Literally 'unravelling' or 'untying' in French, in traditional *dramaturgy that part of a dramatic *action which immediately follows the turning point or *crisis, during which the knot of complications created in the rising action is resolved. The na-

ture of the play dictates whether the denouement is a logical outcome of the dramatic action or an artificially imposed solution (*deus ex machina). There are instances of false denouements which ironically introduce fresh complications, and of *absurd denouements which merely bring the action back to its beginnings, resolutions in which nothing is resolved.

RWV

DE PAZ Y MATEOS, ALBERTO (1915–67)

Spanish lawyer and director who moved to Venezuela in 1945. He formed an experimental troupe at a Caracas school (Grupo Experimental de Teatro del Liceo Fermín Toro), which had a modern Hispanic repertoire strongly influenced by Federico *García Lorca. Among his pupils were the playwrights Román *Chalbaud and Nicolás Curiel, director of the Teatro de la Universidad Central. De Paz staged works by Lorca, *O'Neill, *Valle-Inclán, *Cervantes, *Sophocles, Arturo *Uslar Pietri, and Andrés Eloy *Blanco, productions which were the backbone of Venezuelan theatrical renewal in the 1950s.

LCL trans. AMCS

DEPERO, FORTUNATO (1892–1960)

Italian painter, stage designer, and *theoretician, a key member of the *futurist movement. He became a disciple of Giacomo Balla in 1914 and they jointly wrote the influential manifesto *Futurist Reconstruction of the Universe* (1915). His first theatre projects were for dancer-robots, *Mimismagia* and *Colori* (both 1916), which he explained in two theoretical *texts, *Apparition-Like Costumes* (1915) and *Notes on Theatre* (1916). For the *Ballets Russes he designed *Le Chant du rossignol* and *Giardino zoologico* (both 1917, unstaged), and in 1918 he saw his *Plastic Ballets* performed at the Teatro dei Piccoli in *Rome. He also contributed several plays to the Futurist Synthetic Theatre, was actively involved in the Futurist Afternoons at the Galleria Sprovieri, and had some success with his Cabaret Diavolo (1922–4) and the mechanical *ballet *Anihccam del 3000* (1923). Following a stay in *Paris (1925–6), which inspired him to write several *dance scenarios, he moved to *New York (1928–30), but failure to establish himself as a stage designer made him abandon all theatre projects and return to Italy, where he dedicated himself to painting and the applied arts.

GB

DEREVO

Russian *mime group. Derevo (the Tree) was established in Leningrad (*St Petersburg) in 1988 by Anton Adasinsky. A trained engineer, photographer and actor, Adasinsky had made clips for the rock group Avia with Vyacheslav Polunin before joining the latter's company Litsedei, which he left to set up his own group with Tatyana Khabarova and Elena Iarovaya. Initially embedded in Leningrad's *studio movement, Derevo emigrated and worked in *Prague (1990–3), and later in Florence, *Amsterdam, and Dresden. Their early shows include *The Horseman* (1993) and *Fata Morgana* (1994). *Red Zone, Grey Zone*, and the sentimental love story *Once* were shown at *festivals between 1997 and 1999. They use principles of immersion and meditation, strongly influenced by *Ōno Kazu and *butoh, which envisage the revelation of the soul through a meditative approach to theatre. Derevo gained an international reputation, facilitated by the fact that theirs is a non-verbal art.   BB

DERWENT, CLARENCE (1884–1959)

British actor and director. Born in London, Derwent first appeared on stage in 1902 and over five years played 90 roles in Frank *Benson's Shakespearian *touring company. His first directing assignment was *The Merchant of Venice* (1911). From 1915, when he appeared as Stephen Undershaft in the US première of *Shaw's *Major Barbara*, he resided for the rest of his life in *New York, specializing in secondary leads in hundreds of plays and occasional *musicals. In 1945 he established the annual Clarence Derwent *awards in New York and *London for the best performances in supporting roles. He was elected president of *Actors' Equity Association (1946–52), and in 1952 assumed the presidency of the *American National Theatre and Academy. He published an autobiography, *The Derwent Story* (1953).   CT

DESCHAMPS, YVON (1935–)

Québec monologist, perhaps the best-known face and voice on French-Canadian *television, stage, and *radio since his 1968 appearance in the irreverent collaborative 'happening' *L'Osstidicho*. A long, frenetic period of solo appearances followed, which consolidated an almost devout following in a society where the comic *monologue has deep historical roots. His themes have evolved from congenial general topics to a more palpable Québec nationalism, at times tinged with cynicism. This, allied with his unashamedly local idiom and accent, has made his humour virtually impossible to export. Many of his monologues have been published in *Monologues* (1973) and *Six ans d'monologues* (1981).   LED

DESHPANDE, P. L. (1919–2000)

Marathi humorist, essayist, playwright, and *film scriptwriter. Born in Bombay (*Mumbai) he worked as a clerk while studying for his undergraduate degree. He wrote and directed 24 films between 1947 and 1954, often acting in them as well. He also worked in *radio, and when *television arrived in 1972 he was invited to create the inaugural programme. Of his fourteen dramatic works, only *Tujhe Ahe Tujapashi* (*Each to His Own*, 1957) was original, a *satire on the teachings of hypocritical ascetics who deny life itself. The rest were adaptations of plays like *Priestley's *An Inspector Calls*, *Brecht's *Threepenny Opera*, and *Shaw's *Pygmalion*. His *one-person performance of his book *Batatyachi Chaal* (*The Potato Tenement*, 1958) was a landmark in *Marathi theatre, proving that drama could be created without *spectacle and traditional trappings; Deshpande played all the eccentrics of his fictional tenement, changing voice and bearing to suit each *character. His *Vyakti Ani Valli* (*Ordinary People and Eccentrics*, 1966), a collection of sketches of minutely observed characters, was adapted for the stage by Ratnakar Matkari (1998). Deshpande described himself as above all a performer, asserting that his writing too was a form of *performance.   SGG

DESIGN *See* SCENOGRAPHY.

DESIOSI

One of the earliest Italian *commedia dell'arte* companies, first recorded by Montaigne in Pisa in 1581, and probably dissolved around 1600. As with many such troupes, frequent comings and goings of personnel make it unlikely that any continuity or permanent character was established: at one point its star actress was Diana Ponti, who at other times is also listed with the *Accesi and the *Confidenti. Flamminio *Scala may have been director for a time, before he too moved to the Confidenti. The Desiosi performed all round the northern Italian circuit, and also (without their actresses) in *Rome in 1588–90.   RAA

DESMARES, CHARLOTTE (1682–1735)

French actress. Daughter of Nicolas Desmares and niece of Mlle *Champmeslé, she was born in Copenhagen where her father *managed a French troupe. She began her career as a child actress and joined the *Comédie-Française as her aunt's successor in 1699. She excelled in both tragic and comic roles, *understudying and later succeeding Mlle Beauval as the company's leading *soubrette. She retired early, giving occasional private performances in her retirement.   JC

DESTOUCHES (PHILIPPE NÉRICAULT) (1680–1754)

French playwright. Eighteenth-century French *comedy witnessed the steady encroaching of morality and sentiment on the comic process; and Destouches occupies a distinctive position between the comic manner of *Molière and what was to be known as *comédie larmoyante: his plays were moralistic, even sententious, without being unduly sentimental. His masterpiece *Le Glorieux* (1732) portrays an impoverished nobleman, whose arrogance and vainglory are punished by the disclosure that his fiancée's maid is his own sister. His humiliation was to have been completed by rejection of his suit; but Destouches substituted a happy ending to satisfy the actor *Quinault who was to play the part in *Paris, and whose own vainglory was notorious.

WDH

DESYLVA, BUDDY (1869–1950) (LIBRETTIST AND LYRICIST), LEW BROWN (1893–1958) (LYRICIST, LIBRETTIST, AND DIRECTOR), AND RAY HENDERSON (1896–1970) (COMPOSER)

American *musical writing and production team. All three worked with a variety of partners during their careers, but as a trio developed a series of successful musicals, including *George White's Scandals* for 1926 and 1928 and, most memorably, the 1927 college football musical *Good News*, which included such songs as 'You're the Cream in My Coffee', 'The Best Things in Life Are Free', and 'The Varsity Drag'. They teamed again for *Hold Everything* (1928), *Follow Thru* (1929), and *Flying High* (1930). DeSylva was best known of the three, moving to Hollywood in 1932 to produce *films and eventually heading Paramount Studios. All continued to work in theatre through the 1940s, the most notable accomplishment being DeSylva's book for the Cole *Porter musical *Du Barry Was a Lady* in 1939.

MAF

DEUS EX MACHINA

Literally, 'god from the machine' in Latin, the term derives from the ancient *Greek practice of having gods arrive on stage via a *mechane* (crane) to resolve an otherwise insoluble situation. It now means any unexpected resolution by any arbitrary means. *Aristotle restricted use of the device to matters outside the play, noting that it was otherwise inartistic. Its use in *tragedy as an instrument of superior will, or as an ironic commentary on that will (as in *Euripides' *Orestes*), is nevertheless appropriate; and its use in *comedy—usually a sign effecting the recognition (*anagnorisis*)—properly underscores the role of chance in the comic world.

RWV

DEUTSCH, ERNST (1890–1969)

German actor. Born in Prague of Jewish descent, Deutsch achieved prominence as the 'prototypical' *expressionist actor in 1916 in the Dresden première of *Hasenclever's *The Son*. He joined Max *Reinhardt in *Berlin where he was a leading actor at the *Deutsches Theater until 1933. He was particularly noted for playing young rebellious *characters. Between 1939 and 1945

he worked in the USA in both English and German productions. On his return to Germany in 1947, Deutsch worked at leading theatres in West Germany and Austria. His most notable performances were of Jewish characters such as *Schnitzler's Professor Bernhardi, Shylock, and the title role in *Lessing's *Nathan the Wise*, whom he invested with a new dignity in the context of post-war German philo-Semitism.

CBB

DEUTSCHES THEATER

*Berlin *playhouse. Opened in 1883 in the former Friedrich-Wilhelmstädtischen Theater by a group of literary-minded theatre professionals, the 'DT' was designed to provide Berlin with high-quality theatre to combat the flood of commercial offerings then prevailing. The leading personality was the dramatist Adolf *L'Arronge. Although his repertoire was not strikingly progressive, the theatre became an important forum for a new generation of actors such as Josef *Kainz and Agnes *Sorma. A major shift in orientation came in 1894 when Otto *Brahm assumed the lease. For the next decade the DT became synonymous with the 'Brahm style', contemporary drama performed in a *naturalistic mode. In 1905 Max *Reinhardt took charge and added the smaller and more intimate Kammerspiele. This theatre complex became the focal point of Reinhardt's theatrical imperium and one of the premier theatres in the German-speaking world. In 1933 the DT was confiscated by the Nazis and placed under the control of the Ministry of Propaganda. The appointed director, Heinz *Hilpert, managed nevertheless to create an ambitious programme remarkably free of direct political interference until the closure of the theatre in 1945. After the war the DT came under Soviet administration. In 1946 Wolfgang Langhoff returned from exile in Switzerland and was appointed *artistic director (*Intendant*), a position he held until 1963 when he fell foul of the East German authorities. None of his successors was able to make a major contribution, though they included a number of important directors such as Alexander Lang, until the appointment of Thomas *Langhoff in 1991. The theatre then regained national prominence, based on a fine ensemble and a commitment to Germany's dramatic tradition.

CBB

DEVELOPMENT, THEATRE FOR

Widely used term from *Africa to describe instrumental organizations and performances which mobilize *audiences into community development in such fields as health, agriculture, literacy, and conflict resolution. A particularly influential post-independence movement called Laedza Batanani (which means 'the sun is up—it is time to work together'), emerging in Botswana in the mid-1970s, gave theatre for development wide currency. A series of regional and international workshops in the late 1970s and early 1980s spread the Laedza Batanani model, whereby theatre activists researched the problems of a targeted community, created a *scenario through debate, built this into a play through *improvisation, and took the play back to the community for performance, discussion, and follow-up planning. The first and last stages of this process were in close collaboration with social activists such as extension workers or primary healthcare nurses. Discussion after the play led to strategies to improve community involvement and development activities. This model, fuelled by funding from non-government organizations, spread through most of anglophone Africa during the 1980s. In the process several theatre activists critiqued the model for its parochialism, its crudely modernizing ideology, its reinforcement of passive attitudes in communities, and its tendency to isolate development goals from broader issues of political economy. Enthusiasts implemented more participatory and critical methodologies, partly under the influence of Augusto *Boal's *theories and partly by way of a return to indigenous traditions of participatory performance. Theatre for development is now a widely used technique in informal communication in Africa, and has built links with similar movements on other continents, and with *radio and *television. *See also* OPPRESSED, THEATRE OF THE.

DaK

DEVINE, GEORGE (1910–65)

English actor, teacher, director, and *manager. Born in London, Devine was educated at Oxford, where he also acted and became president of the Oxford University Drama Society. On graduating, he acted professionally, and from 1936 to 1939 taught and produced at the *London Theatre Studio, founded by the influential Michel *Saint-Denis, with whom he continued to work at the *Old Vic School after the war. In 1955 he was invited to become the *artistic director of the new *English Stage Company, based at the *Royal Court Theatre, where he remained until shortly before his death. Although the ESC became associated with social *realism in the wake of the phenomenal success of John *Osborne's *Look Back in Anger* (1956), Devine's own theatrical values were broader, embracing the *physical performance style of Jacques *Copeau (championed by Saint-Denis), theatre of the *absurd (the early plays of *Ionesco and *Beckett had a presence at the Court during his tenure), and the work of *Brecht's *Berliner Ensemble (which performed at the Court in 1956). Perhaps Devine's principal achievement was that he both supported new dramatists (even when *audiences were slow to arrive), and provided a means by which they could develop their craft. He encouraged playwrights to become involved in *rehearsal, allowing them to forge close working relationships with directors, and established a writer's workshop. Edward *Bond, John *Arden, Arnold *Wesker, as well as Osborne, owed much of their early success to his energy and clarity of vision.

SWL

DEVISING

An approach to making *performance and theatre that depends crucially on the participation of all the producing group in all or most stages of the creative process, from conception to presentation. Devising often utilizes *collective creation, in which every member of the production team works on an equal footing to the rest, so that the idea of collaboration informs all aspects of a project. It is often contrasted with the 'traditional' sequence of playwright/play—director/production—actors/performance, but this is partly misleading since devising frequently involves all these elements, though not necessarily in that order. It often features unpredictable working methods, such as *improvisation or co-authorship and the exchange or blurring of creative roles, but there are probably as many ways to devise a show as there are groups devising. However, the traditions of devising established in the twentieth century tended to champion democratic participation over a hierarchy of creative jobs, creative experiment over tried-and-tested techniques, and formal innovation and radical themes over established *genres and well-aired topics.

Paradoxically, devising was at the heart of many early *ritual practices, but it was also used by the sixteenth-century *commedia dell'arte* troupes, and probably by the theatre *companies of Elizabethan England (*see* EARLY MODERN PERIOD) and possibly by the Indian *kathakali*'s predecessor form, *ramanattam*. Devising was also crucial to the *dada, *futurist, and *Bauhaus movements in twentieth-century Europe, as well as in the *dance traditions founded by Isadora *Duncan and Martha *Graham. But it was in the second half of that century that devising came into its own in the upsurge of countercultural activity created by the underground, *alternative, *fringe, and independent theatre movements with their roots in the 1960s. The great pioneer company was *New York's the *Living Theatre, founded by Julian *Beck and Judith *Malina, for whom devising was the root of theatrical revolution against the commercialism and bureaucracy of the affluent society. A similarly radical agenda shaped the practice of subsequent devising groups on both sides of the Atlantic. Important early devisers in the USA included the Free Southern Theatre (1963) of New Orleans, El Teatro *Campesino (1965) in California, the *Open Theatre (1963) and the *Performance Group (1967) in New York, and Theatre *Passe Muraille (1970) in *Toronto. In England devising was pioneered by the first *theatre-in-education company at the Coventry Belgrade Theatre (1965), by the *People Show (1965), and the *Pip Simmons Theatre Company (1968), and in mainland Europe by Théâtre du *Soleil (France, 1964), Teater Terzijde (the Netherlands, 1965), Ryhmäyeatteri (Finland, 1967), and others.

Many smaller-scale independent theatre groups followed their example in the late 1960s and through the 1970s and 1980s, as devising was variously used to involve communities (in *community theatre, community plays), to explore and strengthen different identities (in *feminist, *gay, disability, and black theatre), to extend the reach of performance (in theatre-in-education, theatre in prisons, reminiscence theatre), or to create new aesthetic forms and extend existing *genres (in the neo-*expressionism of visual theatre, live art, *performance art). Devising also impacted on more conventional creative processes through the growing power of the *director, as some directors formed partnerships or working groups with playwrights, designers, composers and so on, and as some performers created companies to challenge the dominance of the director or choreographer and to celebrate the power of the ensemble.

These widespread trends in many countries signal the potentially radical force of devising. Besides its challenge to established processes in theatre it has become for some practitioners a rallying call to revolution in society. For example, the Brazilian playwright and director Augusto *Boal in the 1970s and 1980s devised the processes and forms of what he called the theatre of the *oppressed. His image theatre, forum theatre, and invisible theatre were designed for easy access to devising, so that anyone might participate in them as a 'rehearsal for revolution'. Boal's books cleverly codify the exercises to be used in this do-it-yourself devising process, happily risking the making of rules in an approach that was based on the breaking of rules. Boal's influence was enormous, especially in the rapid spread of theatre for *development and for *liberation in virtually all of the poorer countries of the world towards the end of the millennium. Devising became a truly international phenomenon and a small but important factor in the global struggle for democratic rights. BRK

BOAL, AUGUSTO, *Games for Actors and Non-Actors* (London, 1992)

JOHNSTON, CHRIS, *House of Games: making theatre from everyday life* (London, 1998)

ODDEY, ALISON, *Devising Theatre: a practical and theoretical handbook* (London, 1996)

DEVRIENT FAMILY

One of the leading acting *families of the German theatre, of Huguenot origins. The first and greatest member of the family, **Ludwig** (1784–1832), made his name acting leading roles at the Dessau and Breslau court theatres before being called to the *Berlin National (or Royal) Theatre by *Iffland in 1815. He was celebrated for both tragic and comic performances. Although his tragic roles were relatively few—Shylock, Lear, and *Schiller's Franz Moor were the most celebrated—he represented them so strikingly that he quickly acquired a national reputation. He played the unconscious of his *characters, not through the stark contrasts and transitions used by his exact English contemporary Edmund *Kean, but through quietly bringing to the surface impulses, emotions, and fears that undermined the stability of the character and led *audiences to feel, in a deeply disturbing manner, the forces of both pity and fear, for *villainous characters as for tragic *heroes (*see* TRAGEDY). He was equally skilled at *comedy, being one of the first German actors to give a successful representation of Falstaff. His comic speciality, however, was in plays that required him to appear as several different characters in the same evening. So complete was his ability to change himself into a variety of characters that audiences were drawn simply by the wonder arising from his powers of transformation. The call to *Berlin should have initiated an extended period of renown for Devrient, but the peak of his fame passed with his first season at the National Theatre. This was due first to the appointment of Pius Alexander *Wolff as leading tragedian in 1816, hence introducing onto the Berlin stage a style of tragic acting inimical to Devrient's approach. Secondly, his chronic alcoholism began to sap his powers. During his years in Berlin, Devrient gradually acquired a legendary reputation as a romantic *poète maudit*, stemming to a great degree from his mighty nocturnal drinking bouts with the writer, jurist, *opera composer, and theatre director E. T. A. *Hoffmann. Devrient's wild imagination may well have contributed to some of Hoffmann's last stories. After Hoffmann's death in 1822, Devrient's powers went into rapid decline. He continued to tour German theatres, occasionally with success; indeed, a pamphlet describing his guest appearances at the *Vienna *Burgtheater in 1828 suggests he could still act with his old power and concentration. But his powers had left him completely before he died in Berlin. *See* ROMANTICISM.

Ludwig's three nephews all had successful careers in the German theatre. **Carl** (1797–1872), who had a solid career playing roles in the heroic *Fach*, was married for some time to the famous Wagnerian soprano Wilhelmine Schröder-Devrient. **Eduard** (1801–77) was an actor and director at the Royal Theatre in Berlin and later at the *Dresden Court Theatre. As director of the Karlsruhe Court Theatre between 1852 and 1870, he seriously considered but later withdrew from staging the first production of *Wagner's *Tristan and Isolde*. His main achievement was the authorship of the four-volume *History of German Acting* (1848–74), still one of the major sources for the history of the German theatre. The most celebrated of Ludwig's three nephews was **Emil** (1803–72), whose work as an actor was diametrically opposed to that of his uncle. As leading actor of the Dresden Court Theatre between 1831 and 1868, Emil became the model of the virtuoso actor who developed a repertoire of roles, which he then performed throughout the country with little regard for the productions in which he appeared. His polished *acting style and noble demeanour enabled him to serve as the leading purveyor of the Weimar style of acting during the middle decades of the century (*see* WEIMAR CLASSICISM). His lack of response to other actors and excessive vanity earned him much enmity, however, not least that of his brother Eduard. During the latter part of his career much of his energy was taken up in an intense rivalry with Bogumił *Dawison, who adopted a more robust approach to acting and was, from 1852 to 1864, also a member of the Dresden Court Theatre. Devrient and Dawison acted opposite each other on a number of occasions, though little artistic value came from their clashes. After the retirement of Emil the German theatre gradually abandoned its attachment to the Weimar style in favour of *realistic ensemble, so he appeared as the last of the old school. Later generations of the family produced more actors but none achieved the distinction and public recognition of the first two generations.

SJCW

DE WET, REZA (1955–)

South African actress and playwright. Born in Orange Free State, she acted at the *Market Theatre in *Johannesburg and for the Performing Arts Council of the Transvaal. She writes critically about the socio-political realities of Afrikaner society from a personal and *feminist perspective. Her first play, *Diepe Grond* (*Deep Ground*, Market Theatre, 1986), won several awards. It was published in *Vrystaat-Trilogie* with *Op Dees Aarde* (*On this Earth*, 1986) and *Nag, Generaal* (*Goodnight, General*, 1988). She won the Prize for Afrikaans Drama in 1994 for her second trilogy *Trits*, written in the style of magic realism, and again in 1997 for *Drie Susters II* (*Three Sisters II*, 1996). Her English plays include *In a Different Light* (1988) and *A Worm in the Bud* (1990).

YH

DEWHURST, COLLEEN (1926–91)

Canadian-born American actress, president of Actors' Equity (1985–91; *see* TRADE UNIONS, THEATRICAL). A powerful actress with a commanding presence and a deep, resonant voice, at the start of her career Dewhurst was associated with the *Circle in the Square company, and later frequently worked with Joseph *Papp's *New York Shakespeare Festival. Her performance as Josie in *O'Neill's *A Moon for the Misbegotten* (1973) remains one of the greatest in American theatre. She was *awarded her second Tony for this role; her first was for her portrayal of Mary Follett in *All the Way Home* (1960). Other O'Neill plays in which she performed included *Mourning Becomes Electra, Ah, Wilderness!*, and *Long Day's Journey into Night*.

TFC

DEXTER, JOHN (1925–90)

English director. In 1957 John *Osborne introduced Dexter, a former factory worker and actor, to the *Royal Court. Here he subsequently directed an empathetic première of Arnold *Wesker's East End trilogy. As associate director of the *National Theatre (1963–6 and 1971–5), he directed Peter *Shaffer's *The Royal Hunt of the Sun* (1964) and *Equus* (1973); the latter earned a Tony *award on Broadway. Dexter worked as Laurence

*Olivier's assistant on *Othello*, and directed Olivier's final performance, Trevor *Griffiths's *The Party* (1973). His meticulous pre-planning and firm control within the *rehearsal room earned him a large reputation; Osborne admitted that the offstage character of Dexter in *Look Back in Anger* was based upon his friend: 'He's got bite, edge, drive—enthusiasm.' When *directing *opera Dexter demonstrated easy control of *spectacle and crowd movement. His opulent *Benvenuto Cellini* (1966), designed by *Svoboda for *Covent Garden, established Dexter in this form; he frequently directed for the Hamburg State Opera, and was director of production at the *Metropolitan Opera, *New York, from 1974. Here he produced an acclaimed *Aida* (1976), Berg's *Lulu* (1977), and worked with designer David Hockney on *Parade* (1981). His dream of running a company (the *Stratford Festival, Ontario) was shattered when he was denied a Canadian visa. Dexter produced highly acclaimed West End shows in the 1980s: Michael *Gambon in *Brecht's *Galileo* (1980), Diana *Rigg in *Heartbreak House* (1982) and *The Cocktail Party* (1986).

KN

DHLOMO, HERBERT I. E. (1903–56)

South African journalist, playwright, and poet. In 1937 he became the first African librarian at the Carnegie Bantu library in *Johannesburg. After a series of disagreements with his employees he left for Durban in 1941 where he became assistant editor of *Ilanga lase Natal* (*The Natal Sun*). Dhlomo's creative work focused on the *African experience. He wrote at least nine plays (posthumously published as *Collected Works*, 1985) and numerous poems from 1936 onward. His initial play, *The Girl Who Killed to Save* (1936), was the first English-language drama to be published by a black South African. It deals with events surrounding the vision of the Xhosa prophetess Nangquase, which led to a mass cattle killing and famine in 1857. He contributed significantly to early formulation of African perspectives on literature and art.

YH

DIAB, MAHMOUD (1932–83)

Egyptian playwright. Diab's early, predominantly *realistic plays were set mainly in the Egyptian countryside, then a pet locale for writers following Nasser's agrarian reforms. The call by Yussuf *Idris and Tawfiq el-*Hakim for a return to indigenous performance traditions no doubt influenced Diab's *Layali Al-Hasaad* (*Harvest Nights*, 1967), where he revisits a village entertainment form but renders it more theatrically complex by creating three planes of reality. The *Brechtian-influenced *Bab El-Futuh* (*The Gateway to Conquest*, 1971), then banned by the *censor, is described by M. M. Badawi as Diab's 'most outspoken and courageous contribution to the process of political self-examination after the 1967 defeat' by Israel.

HMA

DIAGHILEV, SERGEI (1872–1929)

Russian founder of the *Ballets Russes. After studying law at *St Petersburg university, Diaghilev became acquainted with members of the 'world of art' movement and, in 1898, having published a number of articles on painting, he became editor of the movement's journal. The following year he obtained a post at the imperial theatres but was dismissed in 1901, partly on the grounds of his ill-disguised homosexuality. Between then and 1906 he continued to publish articles, including two on the *Moscow Art Theatre, and mounted six exhibitions devoted to work by members of the 'world of art' group. All his subsequent projects were realized abroad, beginning with an exhibition of Russian art at the *Paris Salon. In 1907 he organized five Russian music recitals and, in 1908, supervised a production of Mussorgsky's *Boris Godunov* at the Paris *Opéra with Chaliapin in the title role. The year 1909 saw the first season of the Russian ballets at the Théâtre du Châtelet (*see* CIRQUE OLYMPIQUE) in Paris with *scenery and *costume designs by Alexandre *Benois, Konstantin Korovin, Leon *Bakst, and Ivan Bilibin. The 1910 season saw five *ballets, including Stravinsky's *The Firebird*, which launched the composer's career. This was followed by *Petrushka* the following year with decor by Benois. These 'seasons' lasted until 1913 and included famous first performances of Ravel's *Daphnis and Chloe* (1912), Debussy's *Prélude à l'après-midi d'un faune* (1912), and the *riot-provoking première of Stravinsky's *The Rite of Spring* (1913), conducted by Pierre Monteux, in which Diaghilev's leading dancer, Vaclav Nijinsky, featured as both soloist and choreographer. Other outstanding performers in the company included Anna Pavlova, Tamara Karsavina, Michel *Fokine, Serge Lifar, and Anton Dolin. Other design collaborators included Natalya *Goncharova, Mstislav Dobuzhinsky, Mikhail Larionov, Aleksandr Golovin, and Nikolai Roerich. During the 1913 season the company *toured widely in *London, *Vienna, *Berlin, and South America. As well as receiving a sound musical education in his youth and acquiring fluency in seven European languages, Diaghilev possessed entrepreneurial flair, acute artistic judgement, and a hypnotic personality which inspired the company with his belief in a composite art form where music, *scenography, and movement coalesced.
NW

DIALOGUE

From the Greek *dialogos* ('words between', or discourse), in the *theatre dialogue normally refers to speech between two or more *characters that conveys information or tone to the *audience. While theatrical *performance is made up of a large number of other elements (*see* SEMIOTICS), and while the *action of a *drama can be accomplished by means ranging from *monologue to actors' movements and gestures to kinetic *scenery and *lighting, it is usually dialogue that is at the centre of a play and

the chief concern of the *playwright. A dramatic *text customarily comprises dialogue and *stage directions—though there are cases where one is used exclusively—and contains at least two characters to be played by different actors who speak, most commonly to one another. What they say and how they say it are functions of a large set of circumstances that are historically contingent, related to dramatic *genre, and dependent on how the spectators routinely construe the purpose of speech. Dialogue may range from extremely artificial and elevated conversation to attempts to capture the rhythms and argot of a current vernacular.

In ancient *Greek theatre, for instance, especially in *tragedy from *Aeschylus on, lengthy exchanges between two characters sometimes occurred in *stichomythia*, the actors each reciting a complete line of hexameter *verse as if they were playing tennis with a live grenade. Frequently one of the actors would have exchanges with the *chorus, an intriguing mixture of a character's speech with group response. The conventions of *neoclassicism, looking back to Greek models, maintained that dialogue should obey the rules of *decorum in *comedy and tragedy, an aristocratic notion of appropriateness that was sustained in French playwriting from the 1630s until the rise of *romanticism 200 years later. The rhyming alexandrines (six-beat lines, like those of the Greeks) of *Racine, *Corneille, and even *Molière, whether in long speeches or in stichomythic interactions, represented an elegant and extremely purified form of the discourse expected in the King's presence at *Versailles, just as the formalized postures and movements of actors (and *ballet dancers) were based upon the body gestures of courtiers. *Early modern English writers, on the other hand, often used highly colloquial and sometimes extremely rude speech, even in tragedy, to develop character and theme. Ben *Jonson's *satires present powerful dialogue from deviant characters that *parodies their own moral status. Shakespeare's mastery of dialogue is a commonplace of dramatic *criticism; it ranged from the *Lyly-influenced formality of *Love's Labour's Lost* (*c.*1594–5) to the flexible blank verse, often close to ordinary speech, of *Twelfth Night* and *Hamlet* (both *c.*1600–1) to the psychotic dialogue of Leontes in *The Winter's Tale* (1609). But in England the French influence eventually proved the stronger in tragedy, and after the Restoration neoclassical principles of dialogue appeared in the heroic couplets of *Dryden and *Otway.

Dialogue has not always been used for direct communication or rational discourse. While the *realist and *naturalist movements tended to rely on stage speech that was immediately comprehensible and in some way mirrored the audience's own utterances, the *avant-garde reactions of the early twentieth century often proposed more abstract modes, using speech in a musical manner or to obscure or deny meaning, as in some works in the *symbolist, *expressionist, and especially *dadaist styles; notable examples include *Jarry's *Ubu roi* (*Paris, 1897), *Strindberg's *A Dream Play* (*Stockholm, 1901), and *Marinetti's *futurist evenings immediately before the First World War. Those experiments, together with *Artaud's *theoretical attempts to lessen the dominance of dialogue, reached a climax with the theatre of the *absurd in Paris in mid-century. In the early work of *Ionesco, language is unstable and thoroughly unreliable. Characters in *La Cantatrice chauve* (*The Bald Prima Donna* or *The Bald Soprano*, 1950) utter nothing but hollow clichés, while the old man and woman in *The Chairs* (1952) prepare for suicide by engaging in banal conversations with invisible guests. *Beckett's dialogic exchanges, particularly in *Waiting for Godot* (1953) and *Endgame* (1957), are masterpieces of *music-hall turns that revolve in comically hideous circles. *Krapp's Last Tape* (1958), a *monodrama in which the character converses through a tape recording with his decades-younger self, prepared the way for Beckett's late research in dialogue *in extremis*, where an onstage figure interacts with electronically mediated speech, as in *Footfalls* (1976), *Rockaby* (1981), and *What Where* (1983).

One result of the *modernist and postmodern experiments that challenged the communicability and virtue of language has been a wide acceptance that stage speech is rarely innocent of ulterior motives. Many of the *acting and *rehearsal techniques developed since *Stanislavsky have relied upon his notion that a *subtext of character desire lies under the written dialogue, and that the actor's job in rehearsal is to delve into the subconscious soup of the text to discover a deeper and somehow 'truer' meaning. Some late twentieth-century writers in the realist mode— *Pinter, *Mamet, *Koltès are good examples, along with Sarah *Kane—have sought a poetry of inarticulateness for their characters, often adapting the coarsest street speech to craft dialogue redolent of menace, sexuality, and vulnerability. On a *political level, the suspicion of language has been central to *feminist and *African-American theatre, where the need to fashion a vocabulary free of patriarchal or racial oppression has led to valuable insights. Caryl *Churchill's overlapping dialogue in *Top Girls* (1982) and her linguistic experimentation in *Blue Heart* (1997) propose woman-centred alternatives to the Western dialogic tradition. Anna Deavere *Smith's use of recorded interviews to generate speech that can be delivered in either monologue or dialogue offers an open-text approach appropriate to her democratic reflections on *race riots in *Fires in the Mirror* (1992) and *Twilight: Los Angeles, 1992* (1993).   DK

DIASPORA

From the Greek *diaspeirein*, meaning 'disperse' or 'scatter', diaspora refers to peoples who have settled, voluntarily or by force, outside their homelands or their traditional or ancestral homelands. Originally referring to the dispersion of the Jews after the Captivity, during the nineteenth century the term became more widely used in the context of Zionism to describe the situation of Jewish people living outside the biblical land of Israel. Today it is applied to numerous exiled communities all over the world.

1. Diasporic theatre; 2. Immigrant theatre; 3. Diaspora as a programme

1. Diasporic theatre

Diasporic theatre is not a fixed concept. It embraces both emigrant culture and *post-colonial structures. In a narrower sense it describes the theatre of people living outside their original homeland, but also can be used to designate a minority group's theatre in opposition to a majority culture. As a consequence diasporic theatre functions as a site of cultural self-reflection and self-assurance, and often becomes a surrogate for the home country and culture. This surrogation can gain an autonomous status, so that the efficacy of diasporic theatre lies less in the reliability of its representation of the original than in the successful presentation of a collective imagination.

The emergence of diasporic theatre is often a symptom of social change. While diaspora originally referred to religious or national groups, diasporic theatre will often signify an increasing loss of the authority of traditional institutions. Not all kinds of culturally displaced theatres can be described as diasporic, however. It is well documented in the history of theatre that people living outside their homeland—especially in imperialist or colonialist circumstances—have imported their theatre to their new home. But the exportation of ancient *Greek and *Roman theatre to far-flung empires, for example, or the introduction of *opera in South America in the nineteenth century, was part of a hegemonic strategy. In these instances theatre functioned as a bridgehead to the motherland for those who were serving abroad and cannot be considered diasporic, since a diaspora is determined not only by geographic distance but also by the exclusion of the immigrants from the dominant culture which surrounds them.

2. Immigrant theatre

The first model for diasporic theatre is a theatre for immigrants. During the huge waves of migration from Europe to America at the end of the nineteenth century new traditions of theatre were established as a reaction to the novel situation. *Yiddish theatre can be regarded as paradigmatic for this development. The invention of an explicitly Jewish theatre was new because religious tradition prohibited any kind of professional theatre. From its beginnings in 1877 in Romania, professional Yiddish theatre was an international theatre of *touring troupes. Abraham *Goldfaden founded the first ensemble to function as a means of enlightenment as well as of entertainment, using Yiddish because it was the common language of most Eastern European Jews. Within a short time centres of Yiddish theatre emerged, in *Vilnius, *Warsaw, *Kiev, and elsewhere. Although Jews thought of their existence in Europe as diaspora, Yiddish theatre in Eastern Europe can hardly be described as diasporic since it was based on a vibrant culture and community. Even inside the majority culture of Russia, Lithuania, or Poland, Yiddish theatre could rely on the Jewish community as a stable social unity; its *audience was familiar with its aesthetics and its language.

At the end of the nineteenth century huge numbers of Jews emigrated from Russia and Eastern Europe to the West due to political oppression and an increasingly violent anti-Semitism. Some of them remained in Germany or Austria, others went to the Americas; between 1881 and 1903, 1,300,000 Yiddish-speaking Jews arrived in the USA. Most of the Jewish emigrants in the USA stayed in *New York City, congregated on the Lower East Side, preserving the culture of their Eastern Europe homelands and speaking their mother tongue. Yiddish theatre thus rose in New York as a diasporic immigrant theatre, its spectators those who spoke a language that marked them as separate. The main purpose of Yiddish theatre was to create an atmosphere of the lost homeland—which was not the Holy Land, but the *shtetl*, the Eastern European ghetto—helping to overcome the cultural displacement and radical alteration in daily life caused by migration. Performances often occurred in a café atmosphere, comparable to *vaudeville or *music hall. Most of the plays concerned the abandoned *shtetl* and used well-known songs; some also addressed the problems of exile and assimilation, offering advice on living in the New World. Though productions were harshly criticized on aesthetic grounds, even detractors admitted the value of the symbiotic community of actors and their audience.

Ultimately the increasing loss of coherence within the New York Jewish community caused a crisis for the Yiddish theatre. In addition to the spread of the Jewish population away from the Lower East Side, identification with an Eastern European Jewish identity primarily determined by the experience of loss naturally ceased with the ageing of the generations of immigrants and the assimilation of their children and grandchildren. A long-term integration into American society erased the diasporic basis of Yiddish theatre, and the *shtetl* became an imaginative place, deriving more from transfiguring nostalgia than from individual experience.

The development of diasporic theatre cannot be removed from the context of the majority culture, as exemplified by the Irish diaspora in the USA. Irish immigration was caused by harsh political and catastrophic economic circumstances, especially during the period of the Great Hunger (1845–51), when very large numbers of people left Ireland. Soon the Irish appeared in the US theatre. In the majority theatre the stage Irishman was one of two popular demeaning stereotypes—the other one being the black slave—and was used as a source of entertainment. This representation was produced by the majority (though the Irish diasporic playwright Dion *Boucicault both exploited the stage Irishman and altered him), whereas the Irish themselves looked for positive images. One such was the figure of Kathleen Mavourneen, imagined as the incarnation of the former homeland of Ireland. When in 1852 the famous Irish singer Catherine Hayes visited New Orleans she was conceived as the embodiment of Kathleen Mavourneen. But this process of symbolic identification was the consequence of an elaborate campaign by her manager, P. T. *Barnum, who understood the need of Irish immigrants for emotional contact with their mother country. As Joseph Roach has pointed out, 'loss creates a hunger that performances like Catherine Hayes's promise to satisfy but merely postpone', opening a space for 'clever impresarios' to manipulate diasporic longing. Thus emigrant theatre is determined by a complex bundle of functions. Primarily it serves the nostalgic desire of representing the abandoned home, yet it also engages in the process of developing or maintaining cultural identity in the face of the demands of the new society. It is intimately tied to migration but depends on the scope granted to immigrants by the majority culture. German immigrants in the USA, for example, had a vivid tradition of German theatre in New York that almost disappeared during the First World War, when German culture was devalued by the majority.

3. Diaspora as a programme

A second type of diasporic theatre emerged in the mid-twentieth century. As a result of the increasing importance of the American civil rights movement and the decline of European colonialism, political discourse about cultural identity changed. In formerly colonized states, especially in *Africa and *India, a post-colonial theatre rose to deal with the sometimes convoluted issues connected to independence and the colonial legacy. At the same time in Western countries, a new kind of diasporic theatre appeared whose paradigm can be considered the black arts movement in the USA (*see* AFRICAN-AMERICAN THEATRE). In the 1960s the long-held ideal of America as a 'melting pot' of numerous cultural groups was increasingly questioned: the concept of an American identity common to all was seen by some radical thinkers and activists as part of a hegemonic strategy of appropriation that refused to recognize the distinctiveness of differing social and ethnic groups. Defining their own situation as diaspora, African-American activists stressed that the immigration of their ancestors was not voluntary, nor forced by economic circumstances and the desire for a better life, but originated in violence, the slave trade, and an oppression that was ongoing.

In contrast to immigrant theatre, which was more or less based on the individual memory of spectators of the former home, or at least on sentiments concerning this home, the black arts movement had to invent its own cultural tradition. The reference point 'Africa' was taken not as a concrete geographic or historic point but rather as an imaginative place, and the theatre operated as an institution of collective memory or collective imagination. A landmark in this development was the Black Arts Repertory Theatre and School in Harlem, founded in 1965 by Amiri *Baraka. Although the group lasted only a few years, it began a search for a theatre with distinctive black American aesthetics. Kimberly Benston has described this process as a curve moving dialectically from 'quasi-*naturalism and a defining obsession with Euro-American institutions toward the shaping of uniquely African-American mythologies and symbolisms, flexibility of dramatic form, and participatory theater *within* the black community'. Baraka's ideal of a revolutionary theatre, as he proclaimed it in a manifesto of 1964, represented an aggressive form of self-assertion by marking itself as separate from white American society. In this case diasporic theatre meant breaking with the concept of integration, which was seen as a disguise for prolonging racial discrimination. While immigrant theatre is situated between the 'old' (the lost home) and the 'new' (the strange home), programmatic diasporic theatre seeks to (re)draw the border between one's own community and the majority in order to redefine the status of the minority.

Programmatic theatre of diaspora is not limited to the African-American case but can be found as a strategy in other subaltern groups. A powerful example in the USA is *Chicano (or Mexican-American) theatre. In 1965 the playwright Luis *Valdez founded El Teatro *Campesino as a theatre company of and for Chicano migrant farm labourers in California, and since 1968 the troupe has been a professional theatre dealing with the Mexican diaspora in the USA. Their style has been a mix of elements drawn from Italian *commedia dell'arte*, Mexican popular theatre, and vaudeville. Its main purpose is to intervene in the negotiation of the status of Chicanos, whose situation in the USA has been shaped by a double experience of exclusion: they have been marked as non-authentic by official political discourse in Mexico, and dominant America has marginalized them as Mexicans. Chicano theatre became a realm to develop a new cultural identity. While other types of diasporic theatres chose their point of reference in the lost or ancestral home, Chicano theatre concentrated on a mythical place, called Aztlán, which in Aztec mythology was the original home of the Aztecs before they came to Mexico. By taking Aztlán as a point of reference, Chicanos can define themselves as descendants of the Aztecs, meaning that not they but white Americans are the immigrants. For Chicano theatre the condition of diaspora became part of a cultural *reconquista*, a process of recapturing an original homeland, no longer an imaginary one. This invented tradition deals with diaspora in a double way: the loss of a homeland becomes the subject of the discourse as well as the status of the Chicanos, who are no longer seen as 'illegal' immigrants but rather as reclaiming their position as the original owners of the land.

The programmatic diasporic theatre is an answer to the challenge of living in a multicultural society. The refusal to embrace cultural integration within a multicultural society might be considered a means of cultural survival. While immigrant theatre disappeared because of the increasing integration of its target group, programmatic diasporic theatre maintains difference in order to improve the cultural status of the minority. The rejection of integration is not so much an act of aggression but rather a strategy for negotiating the conditions of cultural heterogeneity. Remarkably, the emergence of this type of diasporic theatre goes hand in hand with the rise of *avant-garde theatre after the Second World War in many places in the world. Programmatic diasporic theatre can be regarded as the political counterpart of the crisis of representation that the avant-garde foregrounded and attempted to overcome (*see* MODERNISM AND POSTMODERNISM). In the context of diaspora, the renunciation of traditional forms of theatre is an act of rebelling against dominant Western culture which has marginalized subaltern groups. The search for a new aesthetic does not originate in an aesthetic discourse, but from the perceived need to create the group's own aesthetic language, since identity can no longer be achieved by borrowing the methods of the majority culture.

The two types of diasporic theatre sketched above are not mutually exclusive, and at the start of the twenty-first century both kinds can still be observed. Nonetheless in the 1990s an observable increase of interest took place in the dominant Western theatre in specific national and traditional performances, such as Indian *kathakali* or *Japanese *kabuki, in a movement called *interculturalism. Mostly these forms have been part of a process of appropriation that does not consider them within their specific context but rather takes them as parts and signs of a 'world culture'. The diasporic origins of these elements disappear under the veil of social integration, and the elements of foreign culture inscribed in them are always in danger of becoming merely *folkloric window dressing.

Diasporic theatre is mostly an expression of cultural and social change—it may be caused by migration but it can be also a symptom of a vanishing social concept like that of the melting pot in the USA. In the latter twentieth century, diasporic theatre could further be regarded as a counter-concept to the increasing globalization of theatre. While artists like Ariane *Mnouchkine, Peter *Brook, or Robert *Wilson used alien elements to create productions that could be understood all over the world, diasporic theatre remains part of a localization of culture and art—maintaining the importance of the specific in creating and negotiating cultural identity.   PWM

BENSTON, KIMBERLY W., *Performing Blackness: enactments of African-American modernism* (London, 2000)

DHARKWADKER, APARNA, 'Diaspora, nation, and the failure of home: two contemporary Indian plays', *Theatre Journal*, 50 (1998)

JONES, RHETT, 'Place, politics, and the performing arts in the African diaspora', *Western Journal of Black Studies*, 24 (2000)

ROACH, JOSEPH, 'Barnumizing diaspora: the "Irish Skylark" does New Orleans', *Theatre Journal*, 50 (1998)

DÍAZ, JORGE (1930–   )

Chilean playwright, actor, and *scenographer who introduced the theatre of the *absurd in Chile. A member of the *Ictus from 1960 to 1965, that company performed most of his plays, among them *El cepillo de dientes* (*The Toothbrush*, 1961), *El velero en la botella* (*The Ship in the Bottle*, 1962), and *El lugar donde mueren los mamíferos* (*The Place Where Mammals Die*, 1963). They are characterized by the use of the *grotesque, black comedy, human alienation, and loss of identity. *Topografía de un desnudo* (*Topography of a Naked Man*, 1967), based on a mass killing of beggars in Brazil, treats the violence and lack of social justice prevailing in *Latin America. Díaz has written about 100 plays, some for children, and twice received the prestigious Tirso de Molina *award for *Mata a tu prójimo como a ti mismo* (*Kill your Fellow Man as You Would Yourself*, 1967) and *Las cicatrices de la memoria* (*The Scars of Memory*, 1985). His most recent plays deal with such themes as transvestism, exile, and marginality.   MAR

DIBDIN, CHARLES (1745–1814)

English actor, playwright, and musician, the most prolific and popular theatrical songwriter of the late eighteenth century. Self-taught as a musician and singer, Dibdin's big break came in 1765 when he played Ralph in Isaac *Bickerstaffe's *The Maid of the Mill*. He is most famous for his collaborations with Bickerstaffe, writing the *music for such pieces as *The Padlock* (1768) and *Lionel and Clarissa* (1768). Ever short of money, he pursued many theatrical schemes, most notably the founding of the Royal Circus and Philharmonic Academy, which he opened in Surrey in 1782. Soon excluded by his partners, he unsuccessfully attempted to build another theatre, the Helicon, in Pentonville. He found more stability with his Sans Souci Theatres during the 1790s, where he offered musical *revues. Comic and topical in nature, these ephemeral productions were Dibdin's forte. His creative output over his lifetime was enormous, and the bibliography of his songs and shows remains incomplete.   MJK

DICKENS, CHARLES (1812–70)

English writer and performer. In 1832 Dickens, having taken lessons from Robert *Keeley, made an appointment to *audition before Charles *Kemble. Significantly he offered himself in the *line of business of Charles *Mathews, an actor who could write or *improvise his own material and perform solo entertainments in a variety of *characters. Because Dickens had a cold the audition was cancelled, and he made his career in fiction and journalism. He was, however, an outstanding *amateur actor. After the collapse of his marriage in 1858 Dickens undertook to read passages from his books in public. This venture produced

reassuring profits and *applause but the strain probably shortened his life. His friend *Macready equated Dickens's rendering of the murder of Nancy (from *Oliver Twist*) with two Macbeths. Dickens wrote little expressly for the stage but his novels have been a constant inspiration. They were dramatized by numerous contemporary playwrights, including W. T. *Moncrieff, *Boucicault, and *Gilbert. More recently their episodic construction has lent itself to *radio and *television serialization. They have been *filmed with both human and animated performers, and have formed the basis for *musicals and *ballets and the remarkable *Royal Shakespeare Company version of *Nicholas Nickleby* (1980), adapted by David *Edgar. Innumerable fine actors have brought Dickens's fictions to life and occasionally a protean performer such as Simon *Callow has impersonated the characters and their creator also.   FD

DIDACTIC THEATRE

While most theatre contains aspects that can be considered educational, didactic theatre places a discernible emphasis on instruction. In common with *political and therapeutic theatre, of which it can be a subset or close relative, it aims to change or intensify the thoughts and actions of its participants. Typical features of didactic theatre include: (*a*) the foregrounding of ideas and content and their presentation by rhetorical means from a clearly signalled perspective, an approach embodied in *agitprop; (*b*) a stress on codes of behaviour and ethical conduct, as typified by the French *neoclassical stage; and (*c*) attention to the raising of spectators' awareness, the acquisition of practical skills, and teacher–learner relations which characterizes theatre for *development.

Because instructive emphasis is not always overtly signposted or recognized as such, however, the boundaries of didactic theatre are open to interpretation. For example, in periods where theatre was promoted as a tool for philosophical and moral instruction, such as ancient *Greece, teaching was often embodied more covertly in teleological *plot structures. The point at which such forms constitute vehicles of didactic intent rather than aesthetic embodiments of a world-view is difficult to define. Even where instructive intent is clearly signalled, a balanced interplay between instruction and entertainment might mean that a drama or performance event is not received as a pedagogical instance. Although *Aristophanes' humorous *satires on Athenian politics may have a tendentious instructive agenda, whether they are read as didactic drama rather than simply entertaining art will depend on the (historically specific) interpretation of the observer.

Types of more easily identifiable didactic theatre are those whose instructive mode is doctrinal and/or utilitarian. The doctrinal mode is exemplified by the enactment of *biblical narratives in European *medieval theatre or of Hindu epics in the *wayang golek* *puppet theatre of Java. Participants are brought to a conclusion or conviction and a hierarchical, top-down relation between communicator and recipient is common. The utilitarian mode involves the teaching of survival and development skills. Instruction can take the form of the top-down propaganda model, as in the colonial Mass Education Campaign carried out in West *Africa after the Second World War. Alternatively, in post-colonial Africa of the 1970s, development workers fostered a more grass-roots approach of participatory research for and by the target group.

Education through participation is also favoured in didactic theatres which encourage interrogative reflection and action. This exploratory mode may take the form of a drama which incorporates a discussion section—in the manner of the 'problem play' (see THESIS PLAY) advanced by *Shaw in 1895, or the *epic theatre of *Brecht which sought through unresolved contradictions to develop a questioning *audience. At the interventionist end of the exploratory mode are Brecht's *Lehrstücke* (learning plays) and Augusto *Boal's theatre for the *oppressed. The *Lehrstücke* were *texts concerned with social attitudes and conceived as workshop material to be copied, criticized, and, if necessary, altered. Inspired by the *theories of Brecht and the educationist Paulo Freire, Boal extended this model of critique during his work for Peru's national literacy campaign in the early 1970s, encouraging oppressed groups to explore social problems through enacting *scenarios and modifying them through audience intervention.

Brecht and Boal have provided inspiration for movements throughout the world concerned with social change, from Britain's *theatre-in-education to Asia's theatre for liberation. However, didactic theatre also continues to attract much negative *criticism, either in terms of its efficacy as a pedagogical tool or its value as an artistic and relevant form of expression. For those who associate theatre with deception and immorality—the European church fathers of the early Middle Ages being a case in point—theatre is an inappropriate vehicle for sacred or moral instruction. More recently, theatre's role as a primary means of educating a wide and often illiterate audience has been challenged by the rise of the *mass media. For those aesthetes concerned to separate art from life, most famously Oscar *Wilde, didactic theatre is also a compromised art form because it betrays the transcendental goal of art by straying into the realm of ethics. In postmodern capitalist contexts, most instructive theatre proves incompatible with the common opposition to authoritarian meta-narratives, or with the entertainment agenda of a commerce-driven industry (see MODERNISM AND POSTMODERNISM).

Defenders of didactic theatre have argued that its contemporary position as a small and marginal form makes it a democratic counterweight to the hegemonic voice of mass culture. Its power to motivate and raise awareness has been recognized by the numerous constituency groups—ranging from promoters of AIDS awareness to practitioners in the field of community,

heritage, and museum work—who continue to develop the tradition of didactic performance.   MM

DIDASCALIA

Didascalia in Greek means 'teaching' or 'instruction', but it was used by Plato to refer to the *rehearsing of a dramatic *chorus and by Plutarch to refer to the *drama itself. Thus the term had acquired the technical meaning of bringing out or producing a play, and the cognate *didascalus* the meaning of *producer or *director. (The *didascalus* was originally the *playwright himself.) *Didascalia* could also refer to a group of plays consisting of three *tragedies and an unrelated *satyr-play. (If all four plays were related they comprised a tetralogy.) In spite of the promise implicit in the word that it might refer to instructions intended to guide *actors in the performance of plays, extant *didascaliae* consist almost exclusively of theatrical records listing the chorus leaders, poets, actors, plays, and victors at Athenian dramatic festivals (*Dionysia). Most of this material, preserved in stone inscriptions on the Athenian Acropolis and in later editions and treatises, derives from *Aristotle's lost *Didascaliae*, a record of lyric and dramatic performances drawn from official records. Latin *didascaliae*, attached to copies of *Roman *comedies, are confined to brief notes on the plays and a list of the *dramatis personae and the musicians. *Didascaliae* provide a considerable amount of information concerning the chronology of plays and performances, but as the ancient equivalent of modern *stage directions they are a disappointment. In modern *semiotic *theory *didascalia* has assumed the special meaning of the 'nebentext'—those parts of the dramatic *text which are not spoken by actors.   RWV

DIDEROT, DENIS (1713–84)

French playwright and dramatic *theorist. One of the most notable polymaths of his generation, an innovative art critic and the chief editor of the *Encyclopédie*, Diderot pioneered the introduction on the French stage of 'le genre sérieux', in which, drawing on the examples of the English playwrights *Lillo and Moore, he created an intermediate form between the traditional *genres of *tragedy and *comedy (see DRAME). His theoretical writing about the theatre was equally forward looking, and called for important changes both in the staging of a play and in *acting technique. Neither of his plays, *Le Fils naturel* (*The Natural Son*, published 1757, performed 1771) and *Le Père de famille* (*Father of the Family*, published 1758, performed 1761), was very successful in the theatre; however, the *Entretiens sur le Fils naturel* which accompanied the former play was a highly original *text which pointed the way ahead for serious drama by insisting that spectators could be made to take an interest in the detailed representation of their contemporaries in similar walks of life, and that the polished rhetoric of tragedy should give way to the formless incoherence of real-life speech at moments of crisis. The conventional *'characters' of both traditional genres, Diderot argued, should give way onstage to 'conditions'—professions, social milieu and family relationships—so as to bring the realities of life home to spectators. In his own practice he supplemented *realistic *dialogue by the use of *la pantomime*, or dumb show: particularly in *Le Père de famille*, where a protracted scene of silent action precedes the spoken dialogue. Although his ideas anticipated the serious drama of the nineteenth century, Diderot's plays lacked the creative talent shown in his non-dramatic writings; and the idiom of *drame bourgeois* (*see* BOURGEOIS THEATRE) was soon handled more effectively by *Sedaine, *Mercier, and *Beaumarchais. His importance as a theoretician is, however, assured by his *Paradoxe sur le comédien* (*Paradox of the Actor*, not published until 1830), in which he argues cogently (and against current thinking) that the great actor depends on controlled technique rather than on sensibility; and by such occasional writings as his *Observations sur Garrick* (1770), in which he studies the English actor David *Garrick as an illustration of the same thesis. *See also* THEORIES OF DRAMA, THEATRE, AND PERFORMANCE; NEOCLASSICISM.

WDH

DIDIGA

Performance mode of the Bété people of the Ivory Coast, adapted for the modern stage by Bernard Zadi *Zaourou. In its original form, *didiga* narrates the adventures of a mythical hero, Djergbeugbeu, in a fantastic world of monsters and predators. In its modern adaptation, the *hero is an Ivorian Everyman, caught in a world not of mythical beasts, but of rapacious and corrupt human predators. Known as the 'art of the unthinkable', contemporary *didiga* theatre defies everyday logic and rationality. The issues it dramatizes are grotesque to the point of being untenable—in Zaourou's *Le Secret des dieux* (1985), the *character Edoukou signs a pact with the devil to rape his mother in return for absolute royal power—yet they are analogous to the use and abuse of power in the contemporary Ivory Coast. *Didiga* plays rely heavily on symbolism and a densely metaphoric language, accompanied by the *dodo* (a traditional arc-shaped musical instrument) or a panpipe known as a *pédou*.

SVa trans. JCM

DIFANGXI (TI-FANG HSI)

Chinese regional opera. All but two of the over 300 forms of opera constituting the Chinese music-drama tradition known as *xiqu* (theatre [of] song) are classified as regional opera forms. The exceptions are the well-known Kun opera (*kunqu* or *kunju*) and Beijing opera (*jingju*), which are considered national forms, although both have their roots in regional opera. From the sixteenth to the eighteenth centuries *kunqu* was *China's most important theatre form. Beginning in the early eighteenth century, however, its appeal began to decline and gradually urban and commercial theatre came to be dominated by a score of new opera forms that had developed in various parts of China and which embodied regional sensibilities and tastes. The geographic origin of most regional opera can be discovered in the title of the form. In many cases the first one or two written characters of a title refer to the place of origin, while the latter part of the title is generally the word for 'drama' (*ju* or *xi*), or a word indicating the style of music used. For example, *chuanju* means 'drama [of Si]chuan' while *Hebei bangzi* translates as the 'clapper opera [of] Hebei'.

While all regional forms share elements of the *xiqu* tradition, each also has distinguishing elements. The most important factor in determining form identity is aural signature; that is, the dialect and the type of music used in performance. Although Mandarin is now the official dialect of both the People's Republic of China and the Republic of China (Taiwan), local dialects, often incomprehensible elsewhere, are drawn upon for regional opera. Each form also employs one or more musical systems with specific melodic, modal, and rhythmic structures for the vocal and instrumental music of that tradition, along with a unique combination of melodic and percussion instruments for the orchestra. To the Chinese theatregoer a performance that looks in all respects like a Cantonese opera, but which does not sound like it, will not be understood as Cantonese opera. The importance of the aural aspect is reflected in the traditional Chinese habit of talking about listening to theatre rather than watching it.

Common to all regional forms are *character role categories and the four performance skills of song, speech, stylized movement or physical *acting, and martial movement or *acrobatics (*chang, nian, zuo, da*). All opera forms employ stylized *make-up and *costumes, and rely on stories from China's historical, mythological, and religious past, but regional forms draw upon local *folkloric, religious, and social customs for their material to deepen their idiomatic flavour.

Difangxi can be divided into large-scale and small-scale theatre forms based on the size of the dramatic repertoire and the degree of complexity of the form's music and performance practices. Large-scale forms such as Cantonese or Guangdong opera (*yueju*), Han opera (*hanju*), and Hebei clapper opera each employ at least ten different role categories and have dramatic repertoires containing over 500 traditional dramas. Their performance practices are highly developed and require several years of *training to master. In contrast, small-scale forms such as Huangmei opera (*huangmei xi*) and Flower Drum opera (*huagu xi*) developed from folk dance and music sources. Many of the plays in these repertoires use only three role types (young male, young female, and *clown) and depict life in agricultural China. They are frequently performed by *amateur or semi-professional actors and musicians.

SPJ

DIKE, FATIMA (1948–)

South African actress and playwright, born in *Cape Town. Her family was part of the forced removal in the 1930s, the first wave of compelling black and coloured people to move out of the city to townships. From 1972 she worked as *stage manager at the Space Theatre with Brian Astbury but resigned to write *The Sacrifice of Kreli* (1976, English and isiXhosa). Her other plays include *The First South African* (1977), *Glasshouse* (1979), *So What's New?* (1991), and *Streetwalking and Company* (2000). Dike was the first African woman to publish a play in South Africa.   YH

DILIS, JAN (1852–1918)

Flemish actor, who played at the National Theatre in *Antwerp from 1877 to 1917 and was one of the chief exponents of an awakening interest in Shakespeare in Flemish theatres. His *acting combined spontaneity with intellectual alertness. He excelled in several Shakespearian plays but especially in his favourite part of Hamlet, which he studied thoroughly, first performing it in 1886 and reprising the role several times in the following decades. His impressive appearance—tall, buoyant, and with an unmistakably aristocratic touch—almost predestined him for Hamlet, whom he interpreted as a self-confident prince rather than a gloomy dreamer.   JDV

DINGELSTEDT, FRANZ VON (1814–81)

One of the most important directors in nineteenth-century Germany, Dingelstedt's main contribution was in strengthening the position of the *director. Through a succession of important *management positions (Stuttgart, *Munich, *Weimar, *Vienna) Dingelstedt was able to demonstrate that production required the coordination of *textual and visual elements. His style, a *historicist opulence aided by the designer W. von Kaulbach, suited *audience tastes of the mid-nineteenth century (*see* ANTI-QUARIANISM). His greatest successes were Shakespearian cycles in Weimar (1864) and Vienna (1875). Dingelstedt was also known as the author of novellas, satirical verse, and the translator of Shakespeare's collected works (1877).   CBB

DIONYSIA

A generic name in *Greek antiquity for *festivals dedicated to *Dionysus. In Athens the term referred to the 'City Dionysia' or 'Great Dionysia', whereas festivals held in the townships (*demes*) of Attica are now collectively known as 'Rural Dionysia'. Scholars have generally dated the creation of the City Dionysia at 534 BC when, according to tradition, *'Thespis, the poet, who directed a drama in the city, first acted'. Many now place the festival later, soon after 508 in the early years of Athenian dem-

ocracy, in line with a trend to see strong links between drama and democratic ideology. Certainly this later date coincides with the first reliable records for dramatic performances and the earliest archaeological evidence for theatres. Excepting the Panathenaea, the City Dionysia was the most important festival of the Athenian calendar. It took place in Elaphebolion (late March). At the *Proagon*, poets, accompanied by their uncostumed actors and *choruses, 'spoke about their compositions'. Religious festivities began next day with a procession in which the icon of Dionysus was taken from his shrine by his theatre to the Academy, a grove outside the city, and after hymns and sacrifice was returned to the theatre by torchlight. The official festival began two days later when an elaborate parade (*Pompe*) transported hundreds of sacrificial beasts, bread, cakes, and wine from the Dipylon gates to the theatre. A carnival atmosphere was encouraged by drink, satyr *costume, and a series of large, decorated, and sometimes mechanically animated *phallus-poles, carried by men in erect-phallic costumes who *danced under the weight of the pole and sang suitably obscene (and partially improvised) lyrics.

The order of events that followed is disputed and may have varied. Twenty *dithyrambs probably followed the sacrifice (presumably while the meat was cooked and served), performed by choruses of 50 boys and 50 men, all citizen volunteers trained by each of Athens's ten 'tribes'. The following three or four days were given over to competitions for five *comedies (sometimes perhaps three) and three sets of three *tragedies. The tragedies were followed originally by a *satyr-play, later often by a fourth tragedy. Time was also found for lengthy civic ceremonies (purificatory sacrifice, libations, announcements of public honours, parades of war-orphans, and displays of tribute from the empire, not to mention elaborate ceremonies for the selection of the contest judges, the judging, the awarding of prizes, sacrifices and victory feasts in the sanctuary).

The prize was for the production: a single judgement determined the victorious poet (who was usually also the director) and chorus. The prize for the chorus was honorific and given to the *choregus* (a wealthy citizen obliged to organize and pay for the chorus). Victorious poet-directors were crowned with ivy in the theatre but afterwards received substantial honoraria. A comic competition was added to the festival in 486 BC, while prizes for tragic actors, independent of the success of the production, were added around 449. Revivals of 'Old Tragedies', 'Old Comedies', and 'Old Satyr-Plays' preceded the dramatic competitions for the first time in 386, 339, and by 340, respectively, and soon became regular events in the programme and eventually formed separate competitions. By 341 tragedians performed with three tragedies only and no satyr-play. Prizes for comic actors were not included until sometime between 329 and 312 BC. The evidence grows ever sparser with each succeeding century, but tragedy and comedy probably continued to be part of the Athenian Dionysia until the second century of the Christian era.

The Rural Dionysia were possibly celebrated by all 139 Attic *demes*, but we have evidence for only about sixteen. They took place in the month of Posideion (December). Plato speaks of enthusiasts running around to all the Dionysia 'without missing a single one', which suggests some attempt to co-ordinate the festival calendar. Rural Dionysia included phallic processions, sacrifices, and communal drinking and eating, to which other entertainments might be added, ranging from dancing on greased wineskins to dramatic competitions. Six Rural Dionysia attest both tragedy and comedy, four tragedy only, and one comedy only; the full slate of dithyrambic, tragic, and comic competitions is known only from the three largest *demes*. The number of competitors in each *genre was generally smaller than at the City Dionysia: we know of only two competitors in tragedy and three in dithyramb. There is no evidence for the satyr-play at the rural festivals. Despite the common assumption that the rural festivals were derivative and second rate, the evidence regularly attests to the participation of top performers.

EGC

DIONYSUS

A native Greek god, despite frequent representation in myth as a foreigner, later adopted by the Romans as Bacchus. Dionysus embodied liminality as described in Victor Turner's *'rituals of status reversal' (that is, of the *carnival variety). His icon was usually a *mask, a column (sometimes explicitly shaped as an erect *phallus), or a mask or double mask affixed to a column. As god of altered states, Dionysus was associated with disguise, cross-dressing, obscenity, sexual arousal, *dance, drunkenness, madness, ecstasy, exuberant vitality, death, and above all theatre. The earliest known *Greek drama was performed at his festivals (*Dionysia) in Athens.

EGC

DIONYSUS, THEATRE OF

Probably the world's first theatre (c.500 BC), built onto the south slope of the acropolis of Athens, north of the sanctuary of *Dionysus Eleuthereus. Frequent rebuilding in later antiquity, stone-quarrying in the medieval to modern periods, and amateur archaeology in the early nineteenth century have destroyed nearly every trace of the earliest phases. The dating and architectural function of the remains are much disputed. The fifth-century BC *orchestra measured some 30 m (100 feet) across, and an emerging consensus holds that it was rectangular: all other *Greek theatres of that time (perhaps seven) had rectangular orchestras; moreover, the surviving bases for the fifth-century *prohedria* (front-row seats) are designed to join in a straight line. Rectilinearity would have facilitated the rebuilding of the *theatron's (*auditorium's) 50 rows of bleachers which held

10,000 to 15,000 spectators. (Contractors called '*theatron*-sellers' rebuilt the *theatron* regularly from wood, perhaps annually, and presumably dismantled it after each festival season to preserve the wood from damage by the summer sun.) The *skene* (stage building), in existence by 458 BC (the date of *Aeschylus' *Oresteia*), was also wooden, and perhaps also temporary.

The statesman Lycurgus oversaw completion of the first stone theatre (338–326 BC). This *theatron*, which survives, surrounded more than half of a circular orchestra of 20 m (65 feet) in diameter, and sat 15,000 to 18,000 spectators. Revision of the architectural chronology based upon excavations in the sanctuary during the 1960s make it appear that the Lycurgan *skene* was much less elaborate than once supposed, with only one storey, perhaps mainly of wood. The more permanent *skene* with side buildings (*paraskenia*) must be redated to c.300 BC, while the theatre's first *proskenion* (a one-storey building whose roof could serve as a high stage against the backdrop of the *skene*) dates from the second century BC. Later remodelling introduced a *Roman-style deep stage (*pulpitum*), reducing the orchestra to a semicircle (AD 62/1 or c. AD 150). The theatre's demise is signalled by the conversion of the stage into a rostrum in AD 345 and the insertion of a Christian basilica into the *parodos* in the fifth century.

EGC

DIORAMA

A painted scene that offered two views, developed by Louis Daguerre, a scenic artist at the *Opéra in *Paris, during the early 1820s. The technique involved sizing a thin canvas or calico scene drop with rabbit-skin size to provide overall translucency. The first scene was painted with transparent pigments, bound with spirit, on the front surface. The second scene (usually a variation or development of the first) was painted on the reverse of the canvas in opaque pigments. Cross-*lighting from front to rear magically changes the image. Dioramas were popular in their own right in exhibitions and in specially constructed buildings, such as Daguerre's and Charles Bouton's Diorama in Regent's Park, *London (1823). They also had a considerable fashion in the London theatre during the 1830s. Clarkson *Stanfield combined the technique of diorama painting with that of the panorama to create extended, spectacular travelogue scenes. 'Mr Stanfield's Grand Diorama of Venice' for the *pantomime *Harlequin and Little Thumb* (1831) offered its *audience a trip around the city and lagoon. It showed a thunderstorm over the Dogana, a peaceful moonlight over the island of St Giorgio and the lagoon, and a final spectacular sunrise over the Doge's palace and St Mark's Square. Theatre dioramas involved backcloths up to 91m (300 feet) in length unrolling at the back of the stage with dioramic sections interspersed in them. Typical diorama scenes involved transitions from peaceful to stormy landscapes, and daytime scenes to romantic, moonlit scenes.

CLB

DIRECTING/DIRECTOR

Directing is the process of governing preparation for a theatrical performance. In the twentieth century a single person normally exercised this power, now usually called in English the director (formerly called the *producer or the *stage manager, and in other European languages a variety of terms like *metteur en scène* in French, *Regisseur* in German). Theatre in the modern period has assumed that the complexity of production elements demands a final authority who ensures artistic unity and acts as the leader of the production team. In this sense the director is an expressive or enunciatory manager, centring the interpretation of the script and coordinating the many features of production (*scenography, *casting, staging, *acting, *music, and particularly supervising *rehearsal) before the first performance, after which the director's authority normally ceases. Directors vary greatly in the amount of aesthetic control they exercise, and rarely have unfettered dictatorial power; nonetheless they are at the centre of the process of mediation that occurs between the script and the *audience.

In earlier ages in the West theatrical production was generally in the hands of the *playwright or the actors. The ancient *Greek dramatists taught or coached the actors in their *texts, while the training and *costuming of the *chorus were nominally in the hands of the *choregus*, the wealthy citizen who, out of civic duty, financed the performance. In *medieval theatre in Europe a functionary usually called the bookkeeper tempts some historians to conclude that substantial management of rehearsals and performance was practised, especially for the large-scale *biblical plays and *Corpus Christi plays, which used *amateur actors who would presumably need considerable tutoring; similar claims are made for Elizabethan production. But it is unclear what authority such figures exercised, whether they were separate from the writer and actors, and—crucially—how much rehearsal time was allotted. Shakespeare may have taught his actors their parts, but if that chiefly involved learning lines and cues he was not acting in the manner of a modern director. In fact the rise of commercial theatre in the sixteenth century, with the attendant rise of competent and experienced professional actors, suggests a decline in the need for direction. In most periods of Western theatre the task of staging plays was made relatively simple by the existence of cultural assumptions regarding style shared by performers and spectators. New plays were written with the dominant style in mind, and older plays—when they were performed at all—were rewritten to conform to it, as Shakespeare's work was adapted from the seventeenth to mid-nineteenth centuries. During those periods collective theatrical notions were expressed in rigorous conventions of casting, movement, voice, and scenography. Rehearsal time was extremely limited, and actor *training was accomplished by an apprentice system, so that little value was granted to innovation.

Around the end of the nineteenth century in Europe theatrical style became more subjective and more self-conscious. Under the influence first of *realism and thereafter of *naturalism and *symbolism, an *avant-garde arose that favoured novelty of expression and scenic environment, artistic subtlety, and new narrative strategies. Since the techniques needed for naturalist and symbolist production did not exist among the traditional methods, the director emerged as a functionary separate from the playwright and the actor to supervise the particulars and nuances of performance. Much of the subsequent aesthetic experimentation of twentieth-century theatre was at the urging of stage directors, who commonly function as authors of productions. In the early part of the century the growing authority of the *film director, who must arrange actors and scenes into shots for the camera, may have influenced attitudes to stage directors; and there is no doubt that the New Wave in cinema in mid-century, which considered film directors as *auteurs*, further encouraged this development in the theatre.

Madame *Vestris, Charles *Kean, Dion *Boucicault, the *Bancrofts, T. W. *Robertson, Henry *Irving, W. S. *Gilbert, and David *Belasco are examples of *actor-managers or playwrights in nineteenth-century England and America who prefaced the director proper, while the Duke of Saxe-Meiningen (*see* MEININGEN PLAYERS) and his stage manager Ludwig *Chronegk in Germany are often thought of as the first directors who were neither actors nor writers in the production. In *Paris André *Antoine, who founded the Théâtre *Libre in 1887, foregrounded directing by insisting on obsessively detailed naturalistic settings and acting. His free theatre movement spread to *Berlin (Otto *Brahm opened the *Freie Bühne in 1889) and to *London (J. T. *Grein started the *Independent Theatre two years later). Naturalism sought verisimilitude in acting and in scene. It achieved enormous influence through the acting and rehearsal theories of Konstantin *Stanislavsky, whose early work at the *Moscow Art Theatre emphasized elaborately realized *costumes and *scenery and, though relying on nineteenth-century mechanistic psychology, the inward emotional connection between actor and role. In many ways Stanislavsky established the dominant rehearsal practice in the twentieth century by encouraging actors to look beneath the surface of the written lines for a *subtext that was imagined to contain explanations and motivations for the *characters' speech and actions, and the director in the naturalistic tradition has assumed the task of guiding this exploration.

At the same time as naturalism was gaining force, symbolism promoted dreamlike states or abstract visions and had an almost equal influence through the scenographic theories of Edward Gordon *Craig, whose concept of the actor as *Übermarionette* ('super puppet') in the director's control further elevated the director's authority. In the symbolist mode the director, at least in Craig's view, would take direct charge of all elements of production, including design, in order to create a distinctive performance. Many subsequent directors in the modernist tradition have drawn on one or the other of the opposing modes of naturalism and symbolism, adapting them into movements or styles that are associated with directorial intervention (*see*, for example, EXPRESSIONISM; CONSTRUCTIVISM; SURREALISM; EPIC THEATRE; ABSURD, THEATRE OF THE; INTERCULTURALISM). It is clear that the passion for unity, interpretation, and innovation associated with *modernism fortified the belief that only a single arbiter could properly organize a harmonious aesthetic experience. Some of the most notable directors of the twentieth century so operated, from Max *Reinhardt and Vsevolod *Meyerhold to Peter *Brook and Giorgio *Strehler, from Harley Granville *Barker and Leopold *Jessner to Tyrone *Guthrie and Peter *Hall.

In many Asian countries the faithful transmission of performance traditions has been the central feature of style and preparation. A master performer, head of an acting *family, or owner of a troupe might exercise the director's organizational functions, but in *India, *China, or *Japan individualist aesthetic intervention for traditional forms would be considered improper. *Nō masters even today are actors and teachers of acting, not directors in the Western sense. Under Western influence, however, modern theatre in Asia has tended to accept the director as necessary, as in Japanese *shingeki, and powerful directors are now common in many Asian countries: *Ninagawa Yukio and *Suzuki Tadashi in Japan, Habib *Tanvir and Ratan *Thiyam in India, *Ong Keng Sen in *Singapore.

The playwright's relationship to directorial intervention is complex and often problematic. Though the styles mentioned above were in many cases invented or supported by contemporary dramatists (*Zola and *Ibsen for early naturalism, for example, *Maeterlinck for symbolism), many of the most radical or innovative directors of the twentieth century made their marks using classic texts in the public domain, like those of *Aeschylus, Shakespeare, or *Molière. Living authors are a special case and the director's authority has often been challenged by writers or their literary estates, whose *copyright to the words of a play grants them a superior legal position. Most *licences for performance of plays in copyright insist that the text may not be changed without approval, though directors (or actors) sometimes change the words anyway. Dramatic copyright in most countries, however, is ambiguous over matters of staging and thus there are often both legal and practical questions about the director's authority over the text. The case of Samuel *Beckett is instructive: Beckett (and, after his death, his estate) attempted to control not only the words spoken on stage but also significant details of their staging and visuals, claiming that his precise *stage directions had a status equal to the *dialogue. In one sense this position is reasonable, especially for some of Beckett's short plays that consist mostly, or even entirely, of stage directions, yet the Beckett position runs counter to theatre practice in most countries, where even before the rise

of the director it was customary to adapt scripts to fit local circumstances. For their part some contemporary directors have tried to lessen the artistic and financial ownership that playwrights enjoy through copyright law. In certain first stagings of new plays, directors, often supported by the professional societies representing them, have claimed a share in the author's copyright and royalties based on the argument that directors' contributions are so substantial that success or failure of the play itself must be partly ascribed to them.

Actors and critics have also objected to the director's authority at various times and attempted to subvert or bypass it—actors are especially aware of the power relationship they have with the director and can struggle onstage and off with its implications, sometimes in an environment charged with *gender questions or sexual politics. This matter has been intensified by the fact that until the latter part of the twentieth century most directors were men. Authoritarian modes of direction have been challenged through an increasing reliance on collaboration in preparing performances, as proposed by John Russell Brown in *Free Shakespeare* (1974). Other developments have also worked to subvert the peremptory power of the director, especially the autobiographical procedures of *performance art, the *one-person show, and co-directing strategies that to a large extent have emerged from *feminist interventions. The great increase in the number of women directors, and the contributions they have made to notions of directing as well as to the success of specific performances, suggest to some minds that the coercive and aesthetically subjective traditions of the director are waning, an issue that is taken up with conviction by Donkin and Clement. But even under the influence of postmodernism, which retreats from ideas of mastery and unity, directors have retained much of their force; it is a great irony that the diversity, eclecticism, and cultural inclusion of postmodern performance often seem to require even more aesthetic management, as in the productions of Ariane *Mnouchkine, Robert *Wilson, or Robert *Lepage. *See also* COLLECTIVES AND COLLECTIVE CREATION; DEVISING; MANAGER; ARTISTIC DIRECTOR.   DK

BRAUN, EDWARD, *The Director and the Stage* (London, 1982)

COLE, TOBY, and CHINOY, HELEN KRICH (eds.), *Directors on Directing* (Indianapolis, 1963)

DELGADO, MARIA M., and HERITAGE, PAUL (eds.), *In Contact with the Gods? Directors talk theatre* (Manchester, 1996)

DONKIN, ELLEN, and CLEMENT, SUSAN (eds.), *Upstaging Big Daddy: directing theater as if gender and race matter* (Ann Arbor, 1993)

DISCÉPOLO, ARMANDO (1887–1971)

Argentinian playwright, director, and *producer. The author (and co-author) of more than 30 plays in various *genres, Discépolo was most closely associated with the influential *grotesco criollo*, which he defined as 'the art of arriving at the comic by way of the dramatic'. He began writing socially critical plays but gradually turned (alone and collaboratively) to lighter fare before creating the plays he called *grotescos*. His early works include *Between the Steel* (1910), *The Patio of Flowers* (a *sainete from 1915), and the *comedy *Continuous Movement* (1916). They do not share the private misery and unmasking of *protagonists of his later *grotesco criollo* plays like *Mateo* (1923), *Stéfano* (1928), and *Cremona* (1932). *The Little Organ* (1925) is in this category, written in collaboration with his brother Enrique Santos Discépolo, best known for his lacerating *tango lyrics. Armando Discépolo's *grotesco* series closed with *Watchmaker* (1934), after which he ceased writing for the stage.   JGJ

DISCOVERY SPACE

A number of plays written for the Elizabethan *playhouses call for 'discoveries', which seem to have required the drawing back of a *curtain hanging across part of the *scaenae frons* to show something concealed in an alcove. This has come to be called the 'discovery space'. In *Hamlet* Polonius conceals himself behind the 'arras', a cloth used as the curtain, to eavesdrop on the exchange between Hamlet and his mother, and Hamlet stabs him through the cloth when he calls out, drawing it back to reveal the body. A similar cloth was used to conceal the caskets in *The Merchant of Venice*, until Nerissa 'discovered' them to the candidates. The alcove or 'discovery space' in the *scenae frons* may have been quite a substantial room, enough to provide the 'study' where Dr Faustus is 'discovered' at the beginning of *Marlowe's play, although most scenes where *characters are 'discovered' bring them out onto the main stage almost immediately. It used to be thought that the alcove was an inner stage, and that scenes alternated between the inner enclosed space and the outdoor space of the main stage, but the idea is now discredited.   AJG

DISGUISE

When dramatic *characters assume false identities, *audiences are usually but not always aware of the deception, depending on whether the playwright seeks to create dramatic irony or surprise. Disguises are nearly always impenetrable by other characters even when, as in dozens of English *early modern plays, the assumed identity crosses gender boundaries. In drama, as opposed to fiction, disguise has a *metatheatrical dimension, for characters who don disguises are themselves being impersonated by actors.   MS

DISGUISING

An indoor, aristocratic entertainment featuring a *mimed action and *dancing by *masked participants, which appeared in England after the prohibition of the *mumming early in the fifteenth century and which was replaced after 1512 by the *masque. The disguising may have differed from the mumming in its use of a *text and presenter; and the masque was distinguished by its concluding revels, in which the maskers danced with spectators; but there is otherwise little to distinguish the forms. The Italian *maschere* and the Spanish *momeria* were similar court entertainments.   RWV

DISTANCING EFFECT *See* VERFREMDUNG.

DITHYRAMB

A choral song to *Dionysus, originally associated with female devotees of the god. First given regular form by Arion at Corinth *c.*600 BC, it was admitted in 509 BC, as a strictly male affair, to the *Dionysia in Athens. An amalgam of poetry, *dance, and music, the dithyramb featured a circular *chorus of 50, before about 470 BC probably led and accompanied by the poet himself. Later, the poet withdrew, music and dance were elevated over poetry, lyric solo replaced choral song, and *mimetic elements were introduced. *Aristotle's opinion that *tragedy developed from the dithyramb is without warrant.   RWV

DJINGO

A healing or afflictive *ritual of the Bassa people of Cameroon. Its aim is to diagnose and reveal to the patient, his kin-group, or community the root of his misfortune or illness, and to propose appropriate remedial action, herbal or religious. In performance it takes the form of a *dance-drama that follows a clear pattern: an opening scene in which the space is purified and an atmosphere of psychological receptiveness created in the assembly; a processional phase during which the officiant enters the space, followed by his assistants, to the accompaniment of drum music; and a healing sequence proper in which—through shouts, cries, and trance—the healer exhorts members of the community to plumb the depths of their psyches in search of the source of the illness, the premiss being that the transgression of social rules, even if unwitting, is the root cause. The *djingo* has provided the bases of such plays as Werewere *Liking's *Les Mains veulent dire . . .* (*The Purpose of Hands Is . . .*, 1987) and *Rougeole arc-en-ciel* (*Measles, the Colour of a Rainbow*, 1987).   JCM

DMITREVSKY, IVAN (1734–1821)

Russian actor, *manager, and translator, co-founder with Fyodor *Volkov of the theatre in Yaroslavl which is considered the cradle of Russian professional theatre. Dmitrevsky was summoned to *St Petersburg with Volkov in 1752 for the purpose of founding a Russian acting school and in 1756 joined a troupe headed by the dramatist Aleksandr *Sumarokov. From 1780 to 1783 Dmitrevsky was *artistic director of the Knipper Theatre in St Petersburg where, following in the footsteps of Sumarokov, the style of *acting which he fostered was in the Western *neoclassical tradition. He himself was a renowned interpreter of roles such as Alceste in *Molière's *The Misanthrope* and the title role in Sumarokov's *The False Dmitri*. At the same time he acquired a reputation as a translator of Western sentimental dramas. One of his most important contributions to the history of Russian theatre was his staging of the first indigenous *comedy of importance—Denis *Fonvizin's *Nedorosol'* (*The Minor/The Infant*), with its satirical gallery of late eighteenth-century Russian types, one of which, Starodum (Oldthought), Dmitrevsky played himself. He was responsible for *training an entire generation of Russian actors including Aleksei Yakovlev, Ekaterina *Semyonova, Pyotr Plavilshchikov, and Ivan Sosnitsky.   NW

DÖBBELIN, CARL THEOPHIL (1727–93)

German actor and *manager. Döbbelin played leading roles in the most important itinerant troupes of the mid-eighteenth century (*Neuber, *Ackermann) before establishing his own troupe in 1756. Much admired by *Gottsched, Döbbelin was dedicated to performing new German drama. He is best remembered for his productions of *Lessing, *Minna von Barnhelm* (1768), *Emilia Galotti*, and *Nathan the Wise* (1783, with Döbbelin in the title role). In 1767 he established his troupe in *Berlin, where he remained until his death. In 1786 he took over the Komödienhaus am Gendarmenmarkt, which he opened a year later as the Royal National Theatre (*see* BERLIN ROYAL THEATRE).   CBB

DOCKSTADER, LEW (GEORGE ALFRED CLAPP) (1856–1924)

American blackface *minstrel and *vaudeville performer. Born in Hartford, Connecticut, his breakthrough hit was the song 'Peter, You're in Luck This Morning', performed while *touring with the Whitmore and Clark Minstrels. Dockstader joined George Primrose to form the immensely successful Primrose and Dockstader Minstrel Men in 1898, and in 1904 he moved on to form Lew Dockstader's Minstrels, specializing in blackface and whiteface *monologues and characterizations of well-known people. His *film roles include a performance of the song 'Everybody Works but Father' (1905) and a (blackface) slave role in *Dan* (1914). He also worked on Broadway in the shows *Some Party* (1922) and *The Black and White Revue* (1923).   AB

DOCUMENTARY DRAMA AND THEATRE

Plays written, compiled, or even improvised directly from 'documentary' sources became a feature of many theatre cultures during the twentieth century. *Radio, *film, and particularly *television also developed documentary forms of drama, which characteristically deal with contemporary issues. 'Documents' used in such plays include official reports, trial transcripts, newspaper articles, newsreel footage. Although many dramas throughout history have been based on fact (Greek *tragedy of the sixth century BC and Shakespeare's sixteenth-century *history plays among them), documentary plays are much closer to their source material, often incorporating documents themselves directly into performance. The concept of documentary stems from the faith in facts that was a legacy of nineteenth-century positivism. Documents came to be regarded as unproblematical sources of facts and information, and information itself became a component in governments' control and organization of industrial nations. The camera's apparent capacity to record external reality added an important element, and resulted in the associated rise of documentary film and photography from the 1930s.

When the USSR's Department of Agitation and Propaganda employed *Blue Blouse theatrical troupes in the 1920s, the *touring shows they produced were fast-moving entertainments both episodic and flexibly staged that included the *zhivaya gazeta* (*living newspaper). These sketches, presenting facts and information about the progress of the revolution, were the first documentary dramas. The method spread to communist and proto-communist groups in Europe and the USA in the 1920s and 1930s. In Germany, *agitprop groups (like *Berlin's Red Rockets) started to use the political *revue style of the living newspaper following a 1927 Blue Blouse tour. In the largely anglophone cultures of Britain and the USA, far-left political parties held less sway, but British left theatre groups such as *Unity Theatre and Manchester's Theatre of Action produced living newspapers in the 1930s. In the USA, the *Federal Theatre Project (FTP, part of Roosevelt's New Deal) had a Living Newspaper Unit whose plays were researched and produced by unemployed newspaper and theatre workers. Provocative analyses of the Great Depression included shows about agriculture (*Triple-A Plowed Under*, 1935), and housing (*One-Third of a Nation*, 1938). Other documentary dramas were developed through the experiments of major theatrical innovators. The influence in the USSR of Vsevolod *Meyerhold (whose 1924 *Trust D.E.* had living newspaper elements) was matched in Germany by Erwin *Piscator's productions of a series of documentary plays (like *Rasputin*, 1927, a history of the Great War and the Russian Revolution). While Bertolt *Brecht rarely used factual material directly, his use of film, slides, and placards significantly developed the ways documents could be incorporated into stage performance. The Second World War/Cold War period halted a developing tradition of political documentary theatre. Piscator and Brecht went into theatre-less exile, the USSR turned against *modernist 'formalism' in the arts (Meyerhold ending his life in a state security prison). In the USA, the anti-communist investigations of the House Un-American Activities Committee ultimately brought an end to the FTP in 1939.

A new period of heightened political awareness (especially following the 1968 student uprisings) revived the form. In West Berlin, Piscator embarked on a new series of documentary productions, including plays about the Holocaust (Rolf *Hochhuth's *The Representative*, 1963; Peter *Weiss's *The Investigation*, 1965). In Britain, *Theatre Workshop (the pre-war Theatre of Action) produced *Oh! What a Lovely War* (1963), with Joan *Littlewood directing. This *epic theatre analysis of the Great War provided a model for new 1930s-style political theatre troupes like John *McGrath's *7:84 Company, and further inspired a brief spate of 'Theatre of Fact' plays including Peter *Brook's 1966 *US* (about US involvement in Vietnam) and Ariane *Mnouchkine's 1971 *Murderous Angels* (about post-colonial war in the Congo). Documentary forms are still in use both inside and outside the developed world, usually as part of political opposition (in, for example, *Chicano theatre in the USA and via Augusto *Boal's 'arena' and 'forum' theatre methodologies in South America and Asia).

With the rise of television after the war, 'docudrama' became an important TV form. It differs from much documentary theatre in that contemporary social reality is usually portrayed through individual case studies in *naturalistic, not anti-*illusionist, performance and film styles. Periodically, such programmes cause controversy and celebrated examples have raised public awareness of important social and political issues (in Britain and America, for example, *Cathy Come Home* in 1966 and *Brian's Song* in 1971 raised housing and health issues respectively). *See also* POLITICS AND THEATRE.   DJP

ERVEN, EUGENE VAN, *Radical People's Theatre* (Bloomington, Ind., 1988)

LINDENBURGER, HERBERT, *Historical Drama: the relation of literature and reality* (Chicago, 1975)

PAGET, DEREK, *True Stories? Documentary drama on radio, screen and stage* (Manchester, 1990)

DODIN, LEV (1944–)

Soviet/Russian director. Dodin graduated from the Leningrad Theatre Institute in 1965, and began his career as a director at the Leningrad Young Spectator's Theatre. He was appointed chief *artistic director of the *Maly Drama Theatre (now Theatre of Europe) in Leningrad (now *St Petersburg) in 1982, where he has created a fine repertoire, initially adapting prose for the stage. His trilogy based on Fyodor Abramov's rural tales (*The House*, 1980; *Brothers and Sisters*, 1985) caused a stir at the time

because of the outspoken treatment of human suffering during the purges. He adapted William Golding's *The Lord of the Flies* (1986), Yury Trifonov's *The Old Man* (1988), Sergei Kaledin's fiction (*Gaudeamus*, 1990), and Dostoevsky's *The Devils* (1991). His 1987 production of Aleksandr *Galin's *Stars in the Morning Sky* underscored the theatre's role as an advocate of glasnost in staging a play about *Moscow prostitutes. Dodin's productions of the late 1980s resemble those of *Lyubimov in style. In the 1990s Dodin was inspired by a new group of actors he trained at the Theatre Institute for *Claustrophobia* (1994), based on études and improvisations of contemporary prose. *The Cherry Orchard* (1995) shows his skilful psychological exploration of individual scenes and episodes of the play. *Chekhov's *Platonov* (1998) and his adaptation of Platonov's *Chevengur* (1999) displayed his preoccupation with grandiose stage constructions rather than traditional sets, and concentrated on the imagery of water that appears to submerge the individual—actor and man.   BB

DODSLEY, ROBERT (1703–64)

English playwright and publisher. Under the patronage of Alexander Pope, Dodsley staged his first *farce, *The Toy Shop*, in 1735, which proved highly popular. Even more successful was *The King and the Miller of Mansfield* (1737), which inspired a sequel, *Sir John Cockle at Court* (1738). Dodsley also wrote a *masque, *The Triumph of Peace* (1749), and an enormously successful *tragedy, *Cleone* (1758). Venturing into *London publishing in the late 1730s, he became the exclusive publisher of Pope's works after 1737. Dodsley's *Select Collection of Old Plays* (1744–5) is a twelve-volume collection of pre-Restoration plays he wished to save from oblivion.   MJK

DOG DRAMA *See* ANIMALS.

DOGGETT, THOMAS (c.1670–1721)

Actor and *manager. Born in *Dublin, Dogget began his career at *Smock Alley Theatre in 1684, then became a strolling player before joining *Drury Lane in 1691 in *London. His talent for *comedy was first noted in *D'Urfey's *The Marriage Hater Match'd* (1692), and it was as a comedian that he gained public popularity and critical recognition. Contemporary accounts emphasize Doggett's attention to detail in the creation of his *characters, his use of *costume and *make-up complementing his careful observations of mannerisms and speech patterns, particularly in low characters. Doggett's only known attempt at playwriting, *The Country Wake* (1696), was not successful. In between various disputes with London managements, he led companies of strolling players in Norwich, Bartholomew Fair, and Cambridge. He made a permanent return to the *patent company in 1709 when he embarked on a highly successful (although still turbulent) period as co-manager with fellow actors Robert *Wilks and Colley *Cibber. GBB

DOMÍNGUEZ, FRANKLIN (1931–)

Prolific playwright from the Dominican Republic whose work has been translated and performed in *Latin America, the United States, and Europe. He has also written librettos for *musicals. His best plays were composed in the 1970s and 1980s and include *Omar y los demás* (*Omar and the Rest*, 1975), *Lisístrada odia la política* (*Lysistrata hates politics*, 1978), *Los borrachos* (*The Drunkards*, 1983; produced in *New York, 1987), and *Drogas* (*Drugs*, 1986). His production company, Franklin Domínguez Presenta, has been in operation since 1964. EJW

DONELLAN, DECLAN (1953–)

English director. In 1981 Donellan founded *Cheek by Jowl with his partner and regular collaborator Nick Ormerod. A small-scale company with a commitment to *touring classical theatre, Cheek by Jowl included a striking range of European drama in their repertory: from *Calderón to *Lessing, *Sophocles to *Corneille, as well as Shakespeare. Working on Ormerod's spare but effective set designs, the actors were pushed by Donellan to explore social and sexual relationships in a precisely defined milieu. Often exhilaratingly radical in his results, Donellan approached each play through a traditional unremitting attention to the *text. The success of Cheek by Jowl led the duo to the Royal *National Theatre, where they directed a powerful version of Lope de *Vega's *Fuente Ovejuna* in 1989 and the British première of Tony *Kushner's *Angels in America* in 1992. Donellan suspended Cheek by Jowl after disagreements over *Arts Council funding (*see* FINANCE) and he withdrew from work in England, finding conditions in *Moscow more congenial. In 2002 he directed the first production of the *Royal Shakespeare Company's Academy. PDH

DONMAR WAREHOUSE

A banana store in Covent Garden in *London, converted to a 200-seat theatre in 1960 by impresario Donald Albery, who named it after himself and Margot Fonteyn. In 1977 the *Royal Shakespeare Company refurbished it as a *fringe *studio, with seating on three sides to match the layout—and the poor sight lines—of the Gulbenkian Studio in Newcastle-upon-Tyne, which the company had just used for a five-week season. Productions in the three seasons to 1980, when the RSC moved to the *Barbican, included *Brecht's *Schweik in the Second World War*, *Macbeth*, Howard *Barker's *That Good between Us*, C. P. *Taylor's *Bandits*, *Bond's *Bingo*, Barrie *Keeffe's *Frozen Assets*, and Pam *Gems's *Piaf*. BRK

DORN, DIETER (1935–)

German director. Dorn was educated in Leipzig and Berlin before moving to West Germany in 1958. He came to prominence in the early 1970s with a production of Christopher *Hampton's *The Philanthropist*. He was appointed director-in-residence at *Munich's Kammerspiele in 1976 where he worked for 25 years, becoming *artistic director in 1983. Aided by perhaps the finest *acting ensemble in Germany, Dorn developed the theatre into one of the most successful of the last two decades of the twentieth century. As artistic director he found a successful balance between classics and contemporary work by Botho *Strauss, Tankred *Dorst, and Herbert Achtenbusch. His most acclaimed productions are of Shakespeare (*A Midsummer Night's Dream*, 1978; *Twelfth Night*, 1980; *Troilus and Cressida*, 1986; *King Lear*, 1992; *The Tempest*, 1994). Most were recorded for *television; his *Faust I* (1987) was even *filmed. Dorn productions chart a path between striking visual effects and respect for the *text. In 2001 a disagreement with the municipal authorities led to his dismissal and almost immediate appointment as artistic director of the *Residenztheater in Munich. CBB

DORR, NICOLÁS (1946–)

Cuban playwright, whose first plays were produced at the age of 14. *Las pericas* (*The Parrots*) and *El palacio de los cartones* (*The Cardboard Palace*) in 1961, and *La esquina de los concejales* (*The Councillors' Corner*, 1962), revealed a universe of *absurdity, magic, and *dreams. The grotesque mixed with *realism, poetry, and *spectacle, all supported by *music. Other plays include *La chacota* (*The Big Joke*, 1974), *Una casa colonial* (*A Colonial House*, 1981), *Confesión en el barrio chino* (*Confession in Chinatown*, 1984), *Un muro en La Habana* (*A Wall in Havana*, 1994), and *Los excéntricos de la noche* (*The Night Eccentrics*, 1998). MMu

DORSET GARDEN THEATRE

In 1639 the courtier and playwright William *Davenant produced a plan for a theatre providing a wholly new kind of staging. It was to be England's first *operatic *playhouse, offering the wealthier end of the *London public a taste of the grandeurs of court staging, with music and singing and *dancing, set with lavish scenic *perspectives and the costly traditions of the court *masque's spectacles. Sited off Fleet Street, the new theatre was to be much larger than any of the existing playhouses. Although backed by the Earl of Dorset, the project was never realized. After the Restoration, and possibly with the memory of Davenant's grandiose scheme in mind, a theatre was built in Dorset Garden, the most lavish playhouse yet seen, opening with Thomas *Betterton's company in 1671. Like its rival the *Drury Lane Theatre, it was used for scenic staging and operatic shows of the kind Davenant had envisaged 32 years before. It was demolished in 1709, shortly before Betterton died. *See also* SCENOGRAPHY.

AJG

DORST, TANKRED (1925–)

German playwright. In the first phase of his career (1960–7), a strong influence of *absurdist drama is evident, but his major breakthrough came in the late 1960s with a shift to *historical themes and *realist-*documentary plays. The *revue *Toller* (1968) dramatizes the playwright Ernst *Toller's involvement in the socialist *Munich Republic of 1919. Dorst pursued the revue form in *Kleiner Mann, Was Nun?* (*Little Man, What Now?* 1973), based on the work of Hans Fallada, to further explore the history of the Weimar Republic, and his preoccupation with German history continued in the chronicle of the Merz family. This includes *radio and *television drama, theatre plays (*Auf dem Chimborazo*, 1974; *Die Villa*, 1980), and *films (*Dorothea Merz*, 1976; *Klaras Mutter*, 1978) tracing the family during and after the Second World War. The relationship between writing and politics was again explored in *Eiszeit* (*Ice Age*, 1973), a chamber play about the Norwegian novelist and Nobel Prize winner Knut Hamsen, who collaborated with the Nazis. A radical break with both family and political *history came with the monumental drama *Merlin; oder, Das Wüste Land* (*Merlin; or, The Waste Land*, 1981). In 97 scenes, which require two evenings to perform, Dorst dramatizes the Arthurian legends, mixing in an intertextual collage of Celtic myth, medieval epic, *Wagnerian music drama, and even Mark Twain and Tolkien. He returned to a simpler style in his more recent work like *Korbes* (1988), *Fernando Krapp hat diesen Brief geschrieben* (*Fernando Krapp Wrote this Letter*, 1992), and *Herr Paul* (1994). Since 1970 most of his plays have been co-written with his wife Ursula Ehler.

CBB

DORVAL, MARIE (1798–1849)

French actress, who made the most significant contribution to the establishment of *romantic drama on the *Paris stage in the 1830s. Dorval came from a background of itinerant players and the popular *boulevard theatres. Having gained experience by partnering Frédérick *Lemaître, she helped to consolidate the new theatrical idiom at the *Porte-Saint-Martin Theatre, where she played with *Bocage in *Dumas *père*'s *Antony* in 1831: one of the great triumphs of romantic drama, to which Dorval's portrayal of Adèle made a vital contribution, very much in the unrestrained manner of the boulevard *melodramas. This was followed in the same year by success in a *verse play at the same theatre, as Marion in *Hugo's *Marion de Lorme*; but her most memorable triumph was at the *Comédie-Française, where she was admitted to play the tender, demure Kitty Bell in *Vigny's *Chatterton* in 1835, in spite of hostility on

the part of Mlle *Mars and other senior members of the company. The role, an 'almost silent' one (to quote *Gautier), came to life in her cry of agony on discovering the young poet's suicide—followed by the famous 'dégringolade' as, having collapsed at the top of a specially constructed staircase, her lifeless body slid to the bottom, a bit of stage business devised by Dorval herself. Her flexible *acting style, and lack of prejudice against the new drama, made a major contribution to the brief acceptance of romantic authors even at the Comédie-Française. Marie Dorval's personal life was unhappy, and she died in solitude and poverty.

WDH

DOTRICE, ROY (1923–)

English actor. Dotrice began acting in the unlikely surroundings of a German Prisoner of War camp during the Second World War. After the war he worked in *regional repertory until joining the *Shakespeare Memorial Theatre in 1957 and stayed on for the founding of the *Royal Shakespeare Company, for a total of nine years in Stratford. He performed a wide variety of roles, including Father Ambrose in *Whiting's *The Devils* (1962) and the title role in *Julius Caesar* (1963). He doubled as Bedford and Edward IV in *Hall and *Barton's *The Wars of the Roses* (1963), and the following year contributed Gaunt, Hotspur, and Justice Shallow to the RSC's histories sequence. In 1968 Dotrice scored a hit with the *one-person show *Brief Lives*, which *toured internationally. He relocated to America in the 1970s, doing much *film and *television work. He won a Tony *award for his performance of *Moon for the Misbegotten* in *New York in 2000.

MDG

DOUBLING

Standard convention in the history of theatre whereby an *actor plays two or more roles in a production. This was necessary in *Greek *tragedy, for example, with three actors in *masks performing all the *characters. Thus in *Agamemnon* one actor probably played the role of Clytemnestra, and the other two actors played the rest of the characters. Small theatre troupes throughout the ages and around the globe have regularly required double or multiple role playing. Doubling was the norm in most companies in the *early modern period, from *London to *Madrid, *Amsterdam to *Naples. (*See* COMPANY ORGANIZATION IN EUROPE, 1500–1700.) Necessitated by economic constraints, the tradition has also developed into a performance opportunity for actors who can delight *audiences with their versatility. Sometimes actors try to disguise their doubling; sometimes they call attention to each new character. And some plays, such as *Boucicault's *The Corsican Brothers* (1852), are written to feature a dual role for a star actor.

TP

DOUGLASS, DAVID (d. 1786)

Anglo-American *actor-manager. Although little is known of his early life, it seems that Douglass first appeared in Jamaica in the late 1740s as part of an English troupe (see CARIBBEAN THEATRE, ANGLOPHONE). Sometime between 1754 and 1758 he married the widow of Lewis *Hallam, head of the first professional company to *tour British North America. As the company's new actor-manager, Douglass played the Atlantic seaboard in 1758. He built the *Southwark in *Philadelphia, the first permanent *playhouse in the USA, and the *John Street Theatre in *New York. He continued to tour throughout the colonies until forced to leave by an Act of the Continental Congress in 1774, when he returned to Jamaica.   PAD

DOWLING, JOE (1948–)

Irish director. After studies at University College, *Dublin, Dowling joined the *Abbey Theatre acting company where he founded a *theatre-in-education company, Young Abbey. This was followed in 1973 by a three-year directorship of the Peacock, the Abbey's *studio theatre, featuring a programme of largely new writing. After two years as director of the Irish Theatre Company he returned to the Abbey in 1978 as the youngest ever *artistic director. He directed numerous acclaimed productions, and premièred the work of Brian *Friel (Aristocrats, 1979; Faith Healer, 1980). He left the Abbey in 1985 and continued his commitment to *training by founding the Gaiety School of Acting in 1986, as well as assuming managing directorship of the *Gaiety Theatre itself. His sound business sense and an extraordinary ability to capture *audiences' imagination was most visible in his 1996 *Gate Theatre, Dublin, production of *O'Casey's Juno and the Paycock, hailed as definitive by critics in Dublin, *London, and *New York. From the late 1990s Dowling has worked principally in the USA as artistic director of the *Guthrie Theatre in Minneapolis.
                    BRS

DOWNES, JOHN (fl. 1661–1719)

*Prompter and bookkeeper for the Duke's, United, and Players' companies at *Lincoln's Inn Fields in *London, Downes is the author of Roscius Anglicanus (1708), an incomplete but invaluable first-hand account of Restoration theatre between 1661 and 1706. Omissions and inaccuracies have been noted in the most recent edition by Milhous and Hume (1987).   GBB

D'OYLY CARTE, RICHARD (1844–1901)

English impresario, noted for his business partnership with *Gilbert and *Sullivan and his *management of the *Savoy Theatre, which Carte opened in 1881 as a home for their *operettas.

The partnership began with Trial by Jury (1875) and continued with four more at the Opera Comique, including HMS Pinafore (1878) and The Pirates of Penzance (1880). The Savoy, the first theatre in the world to be lit entirely by electricity (albeit with a back-up gas system; see LIGHTING), was inaugurated with a transfer of Patience. After The Grand Duke, Gilbert and Sullivan's last collaboration, Carte relied on revivals and an extensive national and international network of Savoy opera *touring companies. He built the state-of-the-art English Opera House in 1891 as a home for grand *opera, opening with Sullivan's Ivanhoe, but the venture failed; the theatre was sold and became the Palace.
                    MRB

DRAG SHOWS See FEMALE IMPERSONATION; MALE IMPERSONATION.

DRAGÚN, OSVALDO (1929–99)

Argentinian playwright and *film and *television writer. Author of more than 30 plays, Dragún began with the *Yiddish theatre IFT and began to write with the independent Fray Mocho Theatre. One of the first dramatists to introduce *Brecht to *Latin America, Dragún developed his own *epic theatre, exemplified by the *award-winning Eroica of Buenos Aires (1966, unstaged in Argentina until 1984). He also utilized a device he termed 'animalization', '[deformed] man projected onto the reality of animals and things', the best-known example being Stories to Be Told. He effectively created his own theatrical *genre, melding *Brechtian techniques, *grotesco criollo structures, and *absurdist-influenced 'committed' theatre. Onward, Corazón! (1987), perhaps Dragún's most personal play, evokes his Jewish upbringing, and his final play, The Passenger on the Sun Boat, was staged posthumously in the National Theatre in *Buenos Aires in 2000. Dragún also exerted enormous influence on Latin American theatre as a teacher and theatre administrator. He headed *Havana's Playwrights Seminar (1961–3) and returned to Cuba in the 1980s to direct the International Institute for Latin American/Caribbean Theatre. In 1996 he assumed the direction of Argentina's National Theatre, where he remained until his death. But he may have left his greatest mark with Teatro *Abierto. One of the founders of the 1981 festival, he stayed with the project until its demise in 1985 and premièred three plays there: Me and my Obelisk (1981), To the Violator (1982), and Today They Eat Skinny (1983).   JGJ

DRAKE, ALFRED (1914–92)

American actor and singer. Born Alfredo Capurro, he made his professional debut in 1936 in White Horse Inn, followed by Babes in Arms (1937). He acted regularly in small roles until 1943, when his creation of Curly in Oklahoma! made him a star.

From then on, the handsome baritone was the leading man of choice in *musicals for heroic roles requiring bravura *acting as well as excellent singing, notably in *Kiss Me, Kate* (1948) and *Kismet* (1953). An actor as much as a singer, he regularly appeared in non-musicals, from Shakespeare (Claudius in Richard *Burton's 1964 Broadway *Hamlet*) to *Pirandello and *Wilder. In 1990 he was given a special Tony *award for excellence in the theatre.   JD

DRAKE, SAMUEL (1769–1854)

Anglo-American *actor-manager. Born in England, Drake was already an established performer and *stage manager when he moved his family to the United States in 1810. In 1815, while employed as stage manager at John *Bernard's theatre in Albany, he met Noble Luke Usher, an itinerant actor from Kentucky, who persuaded Drake to *tour the newly settled regions west of the Appalachian mountains. With a company of actors consisting of *family members and his friend Noah *Ludlow, Drake established a professional circuit and demonstrated the viability of commercial theatre in the expanding American *frontier, performing throughout the Ohio River valley and as far west as the Mississippi.

                                                                        PAD

DRAMA

A Greek word meaning 'act' or 'deed' used by *Aristotle in the *Poetics* to refer to a presentation of human *action by means of theatrical *performance; thus in modern usage generally, a synonym for *'play'. When Aristotle initially explained the term, however, he suggested that drama is so called because it imitates *drontas*, 'men acting', and thus that it derives from the object rather than the medium of presentation. The passage presents some difficulties, but it does illustrate a potential for confusion that can arise when *actors impersonate *characters, when human action in effect represents human action. The distinction between the imitation and its object, too often blurred, is important for understanding the relationship between drama and *theatre. Although Aristotle elsewhere consistently used 'drama' to refer to a specific medium of representation, modern usage, influenced by the development of new *media, has abandoned theatrical performance as the sole medium for drama, and now includes performance mediated by *radio, *television, video, and *film. Drama necessarily involves performance of some kind, but it need not involve theatre. (Conversely, there are theatrical forms that do not involve drama.)

Nevertheless, the traditional linking of drama and theatre, whether because of confusion or because only dramatic theatre was valued, did not inhibit the notion that drama and performance are separate and distinct entities. Drama is commonly perceived as something intended to be performed, but somehow existing (or pre-existing) independently of its performance, either as an ideal or, more usually, in the form of a script or even a published *text. Theatre clearly need not include such written documents—unscripted or *improvised theatre is common, and even if produced, *texts are sometimes a record of, rather than a blueprint for, performance—but dramatic texts, seemingly permanent and accessible where ephemeral performance is not, have become institutionalized as 'dramatic literature', and 'drama' has come to be defined as a literary *genre, accessible to reading in the same way as are fiction and poetry. Even the caveat that drama is intended to be performed matters little on the printed page, where a *closet drama looks much the same as a drama intended for performance. The argument that it is possible to understand the drama from a study of the written text or script is based on the assumption that the essence of dramatic theatre resides in the text, that the dramatic text is the primary cause of its performance. The assumption is debatable, but there seems little point in denying the validity of the literary experience provided by classic dramatic texts. Finally, drama refers to a form of *bourgeois drama that emphasizes the moral seriousness of everyday life. This form (*le *drame* in French) was first championed in France by Denis *Diderot, but remained common in the nineteenth and twentieth centuries as well. The use of 'drama' in this sense is imprecise, but normally implies a serious play as opposed to a *comedy, but one lacking a *tragic *catastrophe.   RWV

DRAMA GAUCHESCO

A *genre popular in the late nineteenth-century South American River Plate region, when the *gaucho still constituted the quintessential nostalgic symbol of a romantic creole past. The form originated in the Argentinian *circus: in 1886 the performer José *Podestá, following his success portraying the gaucho outlaw Juan Moreira in traditional circus pantomime, presented a spoken version, followed by other popular gaucho plays. When the Podestá family's cycle closed in 1896 with Martiniano *Leguizamón's *Calandria*, performances were moved to theatres, circus performers called themselves actors, and the gaucho was not perceived as an outlaw victimized by urban society but rather as a ranch-hand. In *drama gauchesco* the beginnings of the local *género chico* (*one-act play) can be found, which would reach the height of popularity with the *sainete criollo* and *grotesco criollo*.   JGJ

DRAMA GONG

Secular Balinese theatre created in the 1960s and influenced by a mixture of traditional Balinese theatre and music, modern *genres such as *arja*, *prembon*, and *stambul*, and Western theatre. *Clown scenes feature prominently and typically open

Ingmar Bergman's production of *The Investigation* by Peter Weiss, **Dramaten**, 1965. The play, a documentary drama about the organization of the death camp at Auschwitz, relies on transcripts of the 1964 West German investigation of Nazi war crimes.

the play, which consists of improvised *dialogue, *dance, and *music. Dance numbers and songs are inserted throughout a play for specific events or moods, but spoken dialogue is the core feature. The actors develop the scenes through *improvisation based on prearranged, agreed-on *scenarios. Actors perform in Balinese and *Indonesian, using a *realistic, somewhat *melodramatic *acting style. The scenarios are adapted from traditional stories (*Panji, Ramayana), local *folk tales, or contemporary material. *Costumes and *make-up are semi-realistic and adapted to suit the chosen story. Traditional elements are a *prologue and *epilogue, musical accompaniment provided by the *gamelan *gong* orchestra, certain dances, and ritual preliminaries intended to bless the stage and performers. Western theatre influences are manifest in the acting style and in staging techniques such as painted backdrops and *scenery, set pieces, *lighting, and *sound effects, and the occasional use of electronic instruments. A performance typically lasts from the evening until the early morning hours. Popular with younger Balinese *audiences, *drama gong* has not (yet) been adapted for tourist performances, partially because it favours spoken dialogue over dance and music.

KP

DRAMA SCHOOLS *See* TRAINING FOR THEATRE.

DRAMATEN

Swedish theatre company. Kungliga Dramatiska Teatern, or the Royal Dramatic Theatre, was founded in *Stockholm by royal decree in 1788. King Gustav III was a passionate theatre enthusiast and encouraged the development of native drama. Initially only Swedish plays were performed, but soon the repertoire was extended to include the best of contemporary work from all over Europe. In 1908 the company moved into an impressive art nouveau building on Nybroplan, opening with *Strindberg's *historical drama *Master Olof*, and his plays have continued to occupy a key place in the theatre. Their complex *dramaturgy requires gifted interpreters, and Dramaten has promoted the work of outstanding directors as well as actors. The roll call of directors includes impressive figures such as Alf *Sjöberg, Olof *Molander, and Ingmar *Bergman. At the start of the twenty-first century Dramaten consisted of six different venues ranging from the main house to *studio theatres and a small space dedicated to theatre for *youth. The tradition of an eclectic repertoire has continued.

DT

DRAMATIC AUTHORS' SOCIETY *See* SOCIETY OF AUTHORS.

DRAMATIC PERFORMANCES ACT

British colonial act to control *Indian theatre through a process of *licensing, *censorship, and banning of plays. After 1872, when Dinabandhu *Mitra's incendiary *Nil Darpan* (*Indigo Mirror*) initiated professional *Bengali theatre, the British government grew wary of the new 'entertainment' in Calcutta (*Kolkata). After the Great National Theatre's *Gajadananda o Yuvaraj* (*Gajadananda and Prince*, 1876), blatantly satirizing the Prince of Wales's visit to the women's quarters of a fawning Bengali advocate's house, an ordinance empowered the Lieutenant Governor to prohibit inflammatory plays. But the same company violated this order the next day with two other performances: *Surendra-Binodini* (*Surendra and Binodini*) showed mutiny, defiance of a British magistrate, and his attempted rape of a woman; *The Police of Pig and Sheep* took farcical potshots at Commissioner Hogg and Superintendent Lamb of the Calcutta police. Not surprisingly, Hogg and Lamb arrested the offenders immediately, but a court dismissed all charges. To stop such loopholes the Dramatic Performances Act was passed on 16 December 1876, banning 'scandalous, defamatory, seditious or obscene' productions. Many original scripts in virtually every Indian language fell into its trap over the next 70 years of British rule. Proscribed work included all *political plays, so dramatists resorted to strategic methods, turning to familiar mythical or historical stories of resistance to arouse patriotic feeling in *audiences. Girish *Ghosh's *Sirajuddaula* (1905), on the last independent nawab of Bengal, and K. P. Khadilkar's *allegorical *Kichak Vadh* (*The Killing of Kichak*, 1907), on Rama slaying the demon Kichak, were banned.

Ironically, after India gained freedom in 1947 the Act remained in force, and various states invoked it to suppress communist productions. In Madras, the Congress government banned performances from the opposition Dravida Munnetra Kazhagam; and when the latter party came to power in 1967, it returned the compliment by banning works critical of it. In 1987 Kerala disallowed P. J. Antony's *The Sixth, Sacred Wound of Christ*, for damaging Christian sentiments. While most states repealed the central Act during the 1960s to pass their own (sometimes more stringent) versions, only in West Bengal did the Act lapse entirely, under systematic lobbying from artists.

AL

DRAMATIC THEORY *See* THEORIES OF DRAMA, THEATRE, AND PERFORMANCE.

DRAMATIS PERSONAE

'The persons of the drama'. In published theatrical *texts the list of *characters appearing in the *drama, sometimes including explanatory annotations designed to guide the reader's perception of the characters. In some instances, the actors in the original production are named. Also called 'persons represented' or 'characters' or 'cast of characters'. RWV

DRAMATIST *See* PLAYWRIGHT.

DRAMATISTS GUILD

American advocacy organization for playwrights, composers, and lyricists. First organized in 1912, the Guild began writing contracts for dramatic authors in 1926. It has been continuously outspoken about writers' ownership of their work (*see* COPYRIGHT), regardless of input from *producers, *dramaturgs, and *directors in the production process, and its contracts are responsible for ensuring authors' appropriate billing. Historically tending to focus on *New York and Broadway, the Guild was slow to recognize the importance of the *regional theatre movement for playwrights, but has since become an important advocate for its members regardless of their professional standing. It has regularly critiqued the policies of the *National Endowment for the Arts, and has supported its members during controversies over their work, as with Tony *Kushner's *Angels in America* and Terrence *McNally's *Corpus Christi*. Publications include *The Dramatist*, a quarterly magazine, a newsletter listing members' productions worldwide, and a resource directory for playwrights. GAO

DRAMATURGY/DRAMATURG

Dramaturgy is the study of how meaning is generated in *drama and *performance. It can be understood as an attribute, a role, or a function. As an *attribute* it refers to a particular playwright or play, as in the dramaturgy of *Zola, *Brecht, or *Fornés, and describes the dramatic structure or conventions operating in the work, its *action, *genre, characterization, and implied elements of production such as *costuming, *scenery, or *lighting. Dramaturgy understood in this way intersects with dramatic *theory and must include knowledge of the distinctions between periods, movements, or styles. So conceived dramaturgy might be called the architecture of the theatrical event, involved in the confluence of components in a work and how they are constructed to generate meaning for the *audience (*see* SEMIOTICS). The dramaturgy contained in *Toller's *Man and Masses*, for example, expresses a *political message through visual and aural characteristics designed to heighten emotional content, while the dramaturgy of *Williams's *A Streetcar Named Desire* focuses upon the story and emotional states by placing primary emphasis upon the psychology of the *characters.

But the term dramaturgy need not refer only to *text-based performance. One could speak of the dramaturgy of a *dance piece by Pina *Bausch, the dramaturgy of Buñuel and Dalí's *film *Un chien andalou*, or the dramaturgy of a performance by the Blue Man Group. Analysing the dramaturgy of a play, playwright, or performance enables us not only to discern the manner in which the playwright wrote or how the piece is constructed, but also to understand the ways in which Shakespeare and Guillermo *Gómez-Peña affect their respective audiences. Dramaturgical analysis frequently makes use of dramatic theory, drawing upon thinkers as diverse as Plato, *Diderot, Barthes, or Kristeva and employing their conceptual frameworks to understand the differences inherent in various styles.

Dramaturgy as a *role* describes the person who carries the title 'dramaturg' on a performance *programme or in the institutional setting of a university or an established theatre. Dramaturgs have received *film credit, appeared as characters in *television sitcoms, and been ribbed in *New Yorker* cartoons, illustrating that the function has moved beyond the confines of the theatre into popular consciousness. A dramaturg is a person with knowledge of the history, theory, and practice of theatre who helps a *director, designer, *playwright, or *actor realize their intentions in a production. The dramaturg—sometimes called a literary manager—is an in-house artistic consultant cognizant of an institution's mission, a playwright's passion, or a director's vision, and who helps bring them all to life in a theatrically compelling manner. This goal can be accomplished in myriad ways and the dramaturg's role often shifts according to context, and is always fluid. As there is no one way to create theatre, there is no single model of the dramaturg. Even the profession's spelling is at issue: most people in Eastern and Central Europe, the UK, and the USA prefer the German *dramaturg*, while France and Canada tend to prefer *dramaturge*. In French the word actually means 'playwright', but as the profession has developed the function of the dramaturg is separate from that of the dramatist.

In Western theatre the position of dramaturg is usually considered to have begun with *Lessing's *Hamburg Dramaturgy* (1768). Lessing took issue with the theatrical taste of his audience for French *neoclassicism and for sentimental *bourgeois drama, arguing instead for a national German repertoire, the production of Shakespeare and other older dramatists, and a social function for the drama. While Lessing began the German profession of dramaturgy, the dramaturg in England and the USA only emerged in the 1960s. The tenor of the times caused theatres to look beyond the commercial fare typically offered, and the *regional theatre movement sought to bring theatre to areas far from the traditional theatrical centres of *New York and *London. A renewed interest in the classical repertoire and in the vigorous advocacy of new work for the stage further prompted the development of the dramaturg. Jeremy Brooks with the *Royal Shakespeare Company, Kenneth *Tynan at the *National Theatre, and Jan *Kott's influence on Peter *Brook; Francis Ferguson with the *American Laboratory Theatre, and

Arthur Ballet at the Office of Advanced Drama Research in the USA—all these pioneered the work of the dramaturg by helping to revise and reinvigorate classics or by reading and advocating the work of new playwrights. In Germany, with its much longer tradition of residential theatres, prominent dramaturgs have included *Tieck, *Grabbe, Brecht, Peter *Palitzsch, Botho *Strauss, and Dieter Sturm of the *Schaubühne.

While the modern profession of dramaturg acknowledges Lessing as father, in the anglophone world it is still greeted with suspicion or even outright hostility. Individuals who call themselves dramaturgs grow weary of explaining what they do. Mistrust of dramaturgy derives in part from the largely invisible nature of the dramaturg's work. Unlike a designer or an actor, the dramaturg can rarely point to something tangible as evidence of his or her contribution to a production. In fact good dramaturgy enhances the overall theatrical experience and contributes to the work of everyone involved in the collaborative process. Those most suspicious or dismissive of the dramaturg's role are frequently those who adhere to a *modernist model of theatrical creation in which a single person's vision—usually the director's—is paramount and collaboration is discouraged. For the adherents of this authoritarian model the dramaturg is seen as inevitably threatening their authority instead of seeking to help them realize their vision.

During the eighteenth and nineteenth centuries English *actor-managers such as John Philip *Kemble, Charles *Kean, and Henry *Irving functioned as dramaturgs by reinventing the classical repertory, interpreting plays from the perspective of the times, and adapting texts in ways that would speak to contemporaries. Early twentieth-century innovators, such as Harley Granville *Barker in London, or David *Belasco and the *Theatre Guild in the USA, introduced the dramaturgical concepts of commissioning new plays and producing reinvigorated classics. *Suzuki Tadashi, as he reinvents Western classics for *Japan, and Eugenio *Barba, as he seeks to bridge Eastern and Western performance practices through the International School of Theatre Anthropology, both function as dramaturgs—even though they consider themselves directors. In the twentieth century dramaturgy moved beyond the confines of theatre and dramaturgs can be found working in *film and *television (where they might be called story editors), with dance companies, *performance artists, and *puppeteers.

Dramaturgy as *function* refers to a group of activities necessary to the process of creating theatre. These activities, frequently involving the selection and preparation of material for production, are always being carried out—by *producers, directors, designers, or actors—whether or not someone carrying the title of dramaturg is involved. The functions might include the literary management necessary to select a theatre's season, collaboration with a director to create a new approach to a Shakespeare play, aid to a contemporary playwright in the gestation of a new work, writing programme notes or leading a post-show discussion, preparing a new translation of a play by *Calderón, or providing the visual, textual, or aural tools to stimulate a company's *rehearsal process for *Chekhov. The dramaturgical sensibility begins by questioning received models of production or rehearsal, and seeks to enrich creation with critical, historical, sociological, ideological, and imagistic materials. It addresses itself towards a series of potential communities. Institutionally it helps develop, plan, and implement a theatre's mission. In service to the profession it seeks out, develops, and advocates for new plays, adaptations, translations, or styles of performance. Production dramaturgy looks for pathways into the world of the play and supports the work of the company. Educational dramaturgy enables local teachers to use the theatre to support their curricula and provides outreach to the broader community through seminars and symposia.   AV

CARDULLO, BERT (ed.), *What Is Dramaturgy?* (New York, 1995)
JONAS, SUSAN, PROEHL, GEOFF, and LUPU, MICHAEL (eds.), *Dramaturgy in American Theater: a sourcebook* (Fort Worth, 1997)

DRAME, LE

Generally used to refer to one of two dramatic forms, both of which rejected the conventional polarization into *tragedy and *comedy. In the eighteenth century Denis *Diderot, influenced by English example, created the intermediate *genre of *drame bourgeois*, though his plays *Le Fils naturel* and *Le Père de famille* were less successful than the theoretical writings accompanying them, in which he argued for a serious, moralizing form of theatre, dealing with aspects of contemporary life (*see* BOURGEOIS THEATRE). Diderot was followed by *Mercier and by *Beaumarchais, whose early social dramas were accompanied by a treatise, *Sur le genre dramatique sérieux*. In contrast to this move towards *realism, *le drame romantique* aimed at an imaginative fusion of elements proper to tragedy and comedy—or, to use the terms consecrated by Victor *Hugo in the *Préface de Cromwell*, 'the sublime' and 'the *grotesque' (*see* ROMANTICISM). While Hugo's own plays, notably *Hernani*, *Le Roi s'amuse*, and *Ruy Blas*, successfully exemplify this formula, as does *Musset in *Lorenzaccio*, other leading romantic playwrights—*Vigny in *Chatterton*, *Dumas *père* in *Antony*—demonstrate the abiding influence of Diderot's concept of social drama with a degree of realism (as would the problem plays of *Dumas *fils* and *Augier). For the most successful interpretation of the romantic formula, we need to look forward to *Rostand's *Cyrano de Bergerac* (1897). The two versions of *drame* in France probably helped to cause the decline of 'pure' tragedy and 'pure' comedy in twentieth-century European drama.   WDH

DRAPER, RUTH (1884–1956)

American actress and monologist. Between 1910 and 1956, Draper created an unusual theatrical career by writing and per-

forming *one-person shows staged with only a few *costume pieces and simple *properties. After years of private entertaining and charity performances, she made her professional debut in *London in 1920. Some of her 34 'dramas' required Draper to perform multiple *characters and all involved elaborate interplay with unseen persons. Draper *toured extensively and consistently attracted large audiences in London and *New York. More than portraits, her *monologues are propelled by action and make discernible moral observations.   MAF

DREAMS AND THEATRE

Freud suggests a firm analogy between dream and *theatre, on the grounds of conceiving dream as an ur-theatre in which the psyche is the author, performer of *text, text itself, spectator, referent, and even critic (consciousness). As the dream unfolds, images are flashed within the inner space of the mind, as if on a screen, and watched by inner 'eyes'. But even beyond the analogy, there is an inherent bond between dream and theatre.

The representational level. Freud claims that the final phase of the dream-work, allegedly aiming at distorting the dream-thoughts, is characterized by eventual 'regression' into thinking in images. He assumes that imagistic representation reflects a pre-linguistic and suppressed method of thinking, following Nietzsche's intuition that 'in dreams we all resemble the savage. . . . as man now still reasons in dreams, so men reasoned also when awake through thousands of years.' Plausibly, this phylogenetic phase in human development is also reflected in (ontogenetic) children's thinking. Indeed, Piaget reveals a primeval form of thinking, akin to dreams, in children's imaginative *play, in which they create fictional worlds by imprinting images on their own bodies, similar to the work of theatre. Langer lent theoretical support to the ability of mental images to attach abstractions or meaning (thus contradicting Freud's thesis of distortion), and to create texts, as in theatre.

The fictional level. By means of an imagistic text, dreams describe worlds of *characters and *actions, similar to dramatic fictional worlds. Although a dream rarely features an image of the dreamer, Freud contends that she or he is represented by the dream's entire set of characters. This can be understood in terms of 'self-reference' (the dreamer as object of description) and 'personification' (of various aspects of the dreamer's psyche) and, therefore, in terms of 'metaphor'. Dreams are usually inhabited by images of familiar people, suggesting that these function in a symbolic capacity, focusing an associative load that is activated metaphorically. Theatre too employs ready-made human symbols, such as historical characters (Shakespeare's *Julius Caesar*) and recurrent characters of drama (intertextuality). It can also create such loads by carefully crafted fictional worlds (*Chekhov's *The Seagull*).

Whereas for Freud a dream simply 'deals with the dreamer himself', Jung is more articulate: 'the dream is a spontaneous self-portrayal, in symbolic form, of the actual situation of the unconscious.' A single psyche is represented by a multiple fictional world, which metaphorically describes it. The complete involvement of the dreamer in his dream, and the spectator in drama, is thus hardly surprising, because these are two versions of themselves: being and description.

Psychoanalysis presupposes affinity between dream and myth. Dream structures reflect archetypal wishful and fearful thinking in wish-fulfilling dreams and nightmares respectively. Similar structures may also organize mythical and dramatic actions, which, although more complex and integrating cultural symbols and values, satisfy (or frustrate) spectators' innermost expectations. On the grounds of a perpetual conflict between desire and reality, Frye suggests a closed and complicated fictional system, which arguably accommodates all possible fictional worlds on an axis of gradual displacement from mythical to realist motivation.

The historical level. Dream is a ubiquitous motif in drama. Jocasta's insight in *Sophocles' Oedipus the King* was probably Freud's inspiration: 'As to your mother's marriage bed, don't fear it. Before this, in dreams too, as well as in oracles, many a man has lain with his own mother.' In seventeenth-century drama, 'dream' and 'theatre' are focal metaphors of illusory and ephemeral life, in contrast to the real and eternal salvation or damnation. The most famous examples occur with Segismundo in *Calderón's Life Is a Dream* and Prospero in Shakespeare's *The Tempest*, who insists that 'We are such stuff | As dreams are made on, and our little life | Is rounded with a sleep.' Towards the end of the nineteenth century, playwrights dissatisfied with *realist drama sought to reveal hidden layers of the human experience. *Symbolists like the playwright *Maeterlinck, and directors and designers like *Lugné-Poe and *Craig, aimed at transcending the limitations of apparent reality. Under the spell of psychoanalysis, *surrealists (André Breton) attempted a replication of dream mechanisms by automatic writing, in order to release cognition from the fetters of reason and socio-cultural conventions and reach the alleged insights of the unconscious (Apollinaire and especially *Artaud). *Strindberg's late plays, often called 'dream plays' after the title of one of them, stimulated *expressionists to explore the potentials of *allegory, usually associated with dream, as a rhetorical means for promoting social ideas (for instance *Sorge's *The Beggar*, 1912).

Although this experimentation resulted in drama with a chiefly historical interest, the new concept of theatre as an instrument for a deeper understanding of human nature and social change had a lasting influence on twentieth-century plays and production, from the theatre of the *absurd to the reflections of the shadowy side of optimistic positivism in the work of the director Robert *Wilson. Many texts incorporated nightmarish structures (*Ionesco's *Amédée*) and theatre developed dreamlike elements of *scenography, particularly in *lighting

techniques, for representation of dream-scenes, aiming to distinguish between various modes of human experience, such as 'real' life, memory, and dream.

The ontogenetic level. Freud suggests that in individual growth daydreaming substitutes for imaginative play, and eventually theatre for daydreaming. Indeed, all of them share the same method of representation. However, the imprinting of images on the players' bodies makes play the actual mediator between dream and theatre. Only substitution of the player by surrogate producers and *actors, enacting well-contrived fictional worlds, makes the difference. Consequently, beyond a mere analogy, dreams and theatre share a primeval method of representation and mode of self-description of the psyche. The dream is indeed an ur-theatre in which all the functions are already fulfilled, and theatre is thus a cultural version of dreaming. *See also* ORIGINS OF THEATRE. ER

FREUD, SIGMUND, *The Interpretation of Dreams*, trans. James Strachey (1900; London, 1978)
—— 'Creative writers and day-dreaming', in *Art and Literature*, trans. James Strachey (1907; London, 1990)
FRYE, NORTHROP, *Anatomy of Criticism* (Princeton, 1957)
JUNG, CARL G., *Dreams*, trans. R. F. C. Hull (Princeton, 1974)
LANGER, SUSANNE K., *Philosophy in a New Key* (1942; Cambridge, Mass., 1976)
PIAGET, JEAN, *Play, Dreams and Imitation in Childhood*, trans. C. Cattagno and F. M. Hodgson (New York, 1962)

DRESDEN COURT THEATRE

German *playhouse. The absolutist King August I (the Strong) erected a 'Komödienhaus' in Dresden in 1696 for French drama, which was followed by a large opera house in Italian baroque style (1717). August's successors focused entirely on *opera, which attained European prominence under the composer J. A. Hasse (1699–1783), and a second theatre built in 1755 by Pietro Moretti became the main court theatre. It was rebuilt by Gottfried Semper in 1842 and the theatre attained a certain notoriety during *Wagner's years as Kapellmeister (1843–8). It was reconstructed in 1878 according to Semper's original plans and became famous in the early twentieth century under Ernst von Schuch, who premièred most of Richard *Strauss's operas there. The building was destroyed in 1945 when Dresden was fire-bombed. Rebuilt once again to Semper's design, it reopened in 1985 and is known today as the 'Semperoper'.

CBB

DRESSLER, MARIE (1869–1934)

American character actress, born Leila Marie Koerber in Ontario, Canada. A self-described 'ugly duckling with no promise of swanning', the teenage Koerber discovered that she could help support her impoverished family as a comedienne. Because her father feared tainting of his name, she adopted Marie

Dressler (after an aunt) for her stage name. Arriving in *New York in 1892, she played supporting roles opposite Lillian *Russell before starring as the *music-hall singer Flo Honeydew in *The Lady Slavey* (1896). With successes in *musical comedy and *burlesque, she also triumphed in *vaudeville, playing at Weber's Music Hall (1905–6) and then appearing at *London's Palace Theatre in a 1907 *variety show. Her greatest theatrical success came with *Tillie's Nightmare* (New York, 1910), which featured Tillie Blobbs, the boarding-house drudge who sang 'Heaven will Protect the Working Girl', and launched Dressler into *film with a Keystone Pictures series built around her signature *character. A wartime activist, Dressler then fought to establish Actors' Equity and was founding president of the Chorus Equity Association and a leader in the 1919 actors' strike (*see* TRADE UNIONS, THEATRICAL). Her politics alienated her from theatre *managers, but she returned to stardom with MGM. Later screen successes included Marthy, the waterfront hag in *Anna Christie* (1930), who reportedly stole the film from Greta Garbo, and the Oscar-winning lead in *Min and Bill* (1930) with Wallace Beery. Dressler wrote two autobiographies, *The Life Story of an Ugly Duckling* (1924) and *My Own Story* (1934).

KM

DREW FAMILY

The founder of the dynasty that would become known as the royal *family of the American theatre was Louisa Lane (later **Mrs John Drew**, 1820–97), daughter of a provincial English actor. After her father's premature death Louisa was taken by her mother to America where she flourished as a child performer. In 1827 she played the Duke of York to Junius Brutus *Booth's Richard III at the *Walnut Street Theatre in *Philadelphia and Albert to Edwin *Forrest's William Tell in Baltimore. She made her *New York debut at the *Bowery Theatre as Little Pickle in *The Spoiled Child* (1828). She continued her successful career into adulthood and in 1850 married Irish-born actor **John Drew** (1827–62). They settled in Philadelphia, co-*managing the *Arch Street Theatre from 1853; John Drew also co-managed the National Theatre in Washington shortly before his death.

Mrs Drew was a multi-talented performer, her slight frame augmented by deep-set eyes that cast a piercing gaze. Her parts ranged from Mistress Quickly to Lady Macbeth; her signature role was Mrs Malaprop, which she played throughout her career. Her husband used his Hibernian background to great comic effect in plays such as *The Irish Immigrant*, *London Assurance*, and *The Rivals*. He also played Shakespearian *comedy and was becoming a leading actor in the United States and Britain at the time of his sudden death. In 1861 Mrs Drew took over sole management of the Arch Street and ran it for three decades. Under her strict regime the venue became one of the nation's finest, with a repertoire of classic and contemporary plays acted

with flair and polish. In spite of this, financial reversals forced her to give up management in 1892 and *tour for the final five years of her life.

Two of her children, **John** (1853–1927) and **Georgiana** (1856–93), had important stage careers, while a third, **Sidney** (1863–1919), acted on stage and was also an early screen star. Georgiana quickly established herself as a great favourite; *audiences were consistently enchanted by her effortless charm and lilting voice. She began her career at the Arch Street in 1873, then joined Augustin *Daly's company, and in 1891 went to work for Charles *Frohman; she was rapidly becoming a major star when she died prematurely. In 1876 she had married Maurice *Barrymore, thus starting another acting dynasty. John went on to become one of the most consistently popular stars of the late nineteenth and early twentieth centuries. He was an accomplished classical comedian, frequently playing in Shakespeare and Restoration plays, but also succeeded in contemporary works. His commanding presence carried him from his exciting debut in *The Masked Ball* (1873) to his final triumph in *Trelawny of the 'Wells'* (1927). In 1892 Frohman signed him at the unprecedented salary of $500 a week. During his long career, Drew was idealized by audiences and colleagues alike as 'the first gentleman of the stage'.

TFC

DRINKWATER, JOHN (1882–1937)

English poet, playwright, and director. As a founding member of Pilgrim Players with Barry *Jackson, and later general *manager of the *Birmingham Repertory Theatre Company, Drinkwater was a vital figure in the Georgian revival of poetic drama. Along with fellow poet-dramatist Gordon *Bottomly, Drinkwater criticized Victorian values in plays such as *Rebellion* (1914). He directed Bottomly's *King Lear's Wife* at Birmingham in 1915 and presented a triple bill of his own play, *The God of Quiet*, along with John *Masefield's *The Sweeps of 98* and *Shaw's *The Inca of Perusalem* in 1916. His biggest success came from his *historical drama *Abraham Lincoln* (1918), which transferred from Birmingham to *London, where it ran for a year. Drinkwater scored a late success with his *comedy *Bird in Hand* (1927), featuring Laurence *Olivier and Peggy *Ashcroft.

MDG

DROLL

Although officially banned by Parliament in 1642, theatrical activity in England persisted during the final years of the reign of Charles I and during the Commonwealth. The constant threat of harassment and raids, nevertheless, necessitated offerings that could be quickly opened and as quickly shut down. Thus were born *farces or 'drolls' (from French *drole*, 'imp', 'scamp', 'jester'), short, comic scenes abstracted from full-length plays. Their popularity survived their necessity and they became regular offerings of the Restoration theatre. Two collections of drolls, both titled *The Wits*, were published by Francis Kirkman in 1662 and 1673.   RWV

DROP

A very large flat piece of (usually) painted fabric hanging from a batten to the *stage floor and running the length of the stage, to mask the view backstage and provide a pictorial ground for actors and front *scenery. The painted scenery of the early nineteenth century is thus often called 'wing and drop' scenery (*see* FLATS AND WINGS). Almost all contemporary drops are flown. In past centuries they were sometimes rolled ('oleos'), gathered in bights ('tumble drops'), or raised through the floor ('sloate drops'). *See* SCENE SHIFTING; SCENOGRAPHY.   JB

DROTTNINGHOLM COURT THEATRE

Built in 1766 by Fredrik Adelcrantz for Queen Lovisa Ulrika, at her summer palace on an island 8 km (5 miles) outside *Stockholm, the *playhouse, which still operates, has an unusual T-shaped *auditorium. The King and Queen sat in the front, at the intersection of the T, with five rows of seating for the nobility on either side. The remaining audience sat in the tail, which steps up towards the rear. There are no galleries and only three small *boxes per side, which are screened by lattice grilles. These are the only three-dimensional decorations in the auditorium, the rest being painted (by Adrien Masreliez). The *proscenium is 8.2 m (27 feet) wide and the *stage 17.4 m (57 feet) deep. The theatre still contains the chariot-and-pole system (*see* SCENE SHIFTING) designed by Donato Stopini (which operates six sets of wings and borders and the rear roll *drops), four *traps, and the cloud, thunder, wind, and wave machines (*see* SOUND AND SOUND EFFECTS). *Lighting poles in the wings can be rotated to increase or decrease the illumination on stage. The theatre was at its height in the reign of Gustav III (1772–92), when French designer Jean-Louis Despez created much of the *scenery, commissioned more by Carlo *Bibiena and Johann Pasch (over 30 of these settings still exist), and redesigned the foyer (1791). After the King's assassination (the subject of *Verdi's *A Masked Ball*), the theatre fell into disuse. It was rediscovered almost fully intact in 1921 by Agne Beijer and is now the home of an important theatre *museum and a summer season of early *operas.   FJH

DRUID THEATRE

Irish theatre company founded in Galway in 1975 by the director Garry *Hynes and the actors Marie Mullen and Mick Lally. Druid set a precedent for the development of regional theatres in Ireland, challenging *Dublin's place as artistic centre. Its eclectic early programming included important revivals of Irish classics such as *Friel's *The Loves of Cass Maguire* (1975 and 1996), M. J. Molloy's *The Wood of the Whispering* (1983), and *Synge's *The Playboy of the Western World* (1982 and 1985). The latter *toured to the Aran Islands, *London, and Australia, and marked a renewal of the play's savagery which had been diluted by a tradition of picturesque productions. Playwrights Tom *Murphy and Martin *McDonagh have had major associations with the company, which occupies an important place in the cultural life of Galway and Ireland.   CAL

DRURY LANE THEATRE

Originally known as the *Theatre Royal on Bridges Street in *London, Drury Lane opened 1663 under the *management of Thomas *Killigrew, owner of the first theatre *patent issued by Charles II, who built it as the home of the King's Company of Players. Its design has been variously attributed to John *Webb, Christopher Wren, and Richard Ryder (capacity 650–700). Samuel *Pepys was a regular visitor and Nell *Gwynn made her debut there in 1665. The theatre was destroyed by *fire in January 1672. The second *playhouse opened in 1674, probably designed by Wren. It featured a pit (with ten benches), two levels of *boxes on each side, and one level of boxes surmounted by two galleries at the rear (capacity 2,000). Its apron *stage (*see* FORESTAGE) was 5.5 m (18 feet) deep, and was entered by two *proscenium-arch doors on each side. It closed in 1676 but in 1682 became the home of the United Company under *actor-manager Thomas *Betterton. Christopher *Rich gained control in 1693, beginning a turbulent period marked by the defection of his best actors in 1695, the unpopular reduction of the forestage in the renovations of 1696, and ending with his final expulsion in 1709. A triumvirate of actors (Colley *Cibber, Robert *Wilks, and Thomas *Doggett, replaced in 1713 by Barton *Booth) gained control in 1711 and managed it effectively until 1733, after which the theatre went into decline. David *Garrick opened here in 1742 and returned in 1747 as actor-manager with his partner James Lacey; together they made important innovations in *acting and design.

In 1775 the theatre was renovated by Robert Adam (capacity 2,300), and Richard Brinsley *Sheridan became *manager when Garrick retired in 1776. Demolished in 1791, it was rebuilt by Henry Holland on Sheridan's orders in 1794 (capacity 3,611), and opened with a production of *Macbeth* starring John Philip *Kemble, Sarah *Siddons, and Charles *Kemble. Though it had the world's first fire *curtain and was advertised as 'flame proof', it nonetheless burned to the ground on 24 February 1809. A fourth theatre was built in 1812 by Benjamin Dean Wyatt for Samuel Arnold (capacity 3,060), modelled on the Grand Theatre, Bordeaux. Edmund *Kean made his debut here in 1814, and his son Charles *Kean in 1827. In 1817 Drury Lane joined *Covent Garden in introducing gas *lighting. A portico was added in 1820, a colonnade in 1831. The interior

Theatre Royal, **Drury Lane**, after the rebuilding of 1797. The growing vastness of the patent theatres in London is well represented in this aquatint of 1808, in which every space seems crowded in the boxes, pit, and stacked galleries, demanding a declamatory mode of acting and gesture. The chandeliers throughout the auditorium remind us that the audience and actors shared the same lighting.

was remodelled many times, the present one being created by F. Emblin-Walker and F. Edward Jones in 1922 (capacity 2,283). Since 1947 it has been primarily known for its *musicals; Andrew *Lloyd Webber bought this theatre, along with nine others, in 2000. FJH

DRYDEN, JOHN (1631–1700)

English poet, critic, translator, and playwright. A product of Westminster School and Trinity College, Cambridge, Dryden was probably employed by the Commonwealth government, but was quick to seize the opportunities offered by the Restoration of 1660, including the demand for new plays in the reopened theatres. Some of his first successes were collaborations: *The Indian Queen* (1664) with Sir Robert *Howard; an adaptation of Shakespeare's *Tempest* (1667) with William

*Davenant, now the patentee of the Duke's Company; and (probably) *Sir Martin Mar-all* (1667), based on two French comedies, with William Cavendish, Duke of Newcastle. Though he claimed to dislike *comedy as a form, Dryden was a successful writer in the 'Spanish' style, which balanced a central *plot dealing with court intrigue against the sexual warfare of a witty couple. The success of *Secret Love* (1667), with its subplot featuring Charles *Hart and Nell *Gwynn, led to a contract with the King's Company (1668–78). The subplot of his best comedy, *Marriage à la Mode* (1671–2), both exemplifies and ridicules the comedy of infidelity: two friends, each in love with the other's wife or fiancée, make various attempts at adultery, but finally decide that their mutual obsession must mean that their original partners have something to recommend them after all. His later comedies included the anti-Dutch propaganda of *Amboyna* (1673), the satiric *Mr Limberham* (1678), and, at the height of the Popish plot, the anti-Catholic *The Spanish Friar* (1680).

The *heroic play, with its distinctive use of the rhyming couplet (*see* VERSE), was a form that he made still more his own. In Dryden's hands, this short-lived experiment was a curious mixture of extravagant heroism, complex love intrigue, and intellectual discussion. Preferring plots about the conflict of cultures and religions, he created situations (like the Christian priest's attempt to convert Montezuma under torture in *The Indian Emperor*, 1665, or in *Tyrannic Love*, 1669, the debate between St Catherine of Alexandria and the Egyptian priests) where serious religious debate was inherent to the plot. The heroic couplet lent itself to the debate structure, and Dryden defended it effectively in his *Essay of Dramatic Poesy* (1667) and elsewhere (his critical writing often took the form of prefaces, *prologues, and *epilogues to his own works). The form was never altogether accepted: *The Rehearsal*, a collective burlesque of heroic plays by the Duke of *Buckingham and others, focused particularly on Dryden ('Mr Bayes')—a natural target since in 1668 he had succeeded Davenant as Poet Laureate. Dryden's two-part *Conquest of Granada* (1670–1), with its noble savage hero Almanzor, came in for particular ridicule.

Whether or not affected by *The Rehearsal*, the prologue to Dryden's last heroic play, *Aureng-Zebe* (1675), expresses weariness with rhyme in drama and in the 1670s he turned toward different models. In 1677 he produced his most Shakespearian adaptation, *All for Love*, and published an adaptation of *Paradise Lost*. Though John Aubrey says that he got *Milton's permission to turn the epic into an *opera, *The State of Innocence and Fall of Man* seems never to have been set to music or performed (except as a *puppet show in 1712). *All for Love*, however, was his most successful work for the theatre: it largely replaced Shakespeare's *Antony and Cleopatra*, to the point where it was sometimes performed under that name in the eighteenth century. Sometimes the two plays were conflated, to take advantage of the expanded role that Dryden had given Octavia. In 1977, Dryden's play, directed by Frank Hauser with Barbara *Jefford and John Turner, was performed alongside Shakespeare's at the *Old Vic and the *Edinburgh Festival, and actually had the better of the comparison.

Dryden did not write for the theatre during James II's short reign; having declared himself a Roman Catholic, he became heavily involved in religious controversy, which made it inevitable that he would lose his court appointments after the Revolution of 1688. Despite his disgrace, some of his subsequent plays—*Don Sebastian* (1689) and an adaptation of *Molière's *Amphitryon* (1690)—were highly successful, as was *King Arthur* (1691), his 'semi-opera' written for the composer Henry Purcell. In the last months of his life he contributed *The Secular Masque* to *Vanbrugh's *The Pilgrim*, an adaptation from *Fletcher. The sheer variety of his theatrical works, like that of his better-known poems and critical essays, is perhaps their most impressive feature, but their rare revivals (as in his native Northampton) have been successful enough to suggest that he deserves more theatrical attention.   LDP

DUBÉ, MARCEL (1930–   )

Québec playwright. Few dramatists have marked their era as indelibly as Dubé did French Canada in the 1950s and 1960s. Innovative, prolific, and popular, he saw his first play produced in 1950. Over the next 25 years he added some 40 others, along with many *television and *radio scripts. Among them are some of the seminal works of the period. *Zone* (1953) was the first to attract national attention, especially in its TV adaptation. Dubé was in fact the first Québec playwright to realize fully the potential of the new medium, and all of his subsequent work is profoundly influenced by it, notably *Un simple soldat* (*Private Soldier*, 1957), and *Les Beaux Dimanches* (*Fine Sundays*, 1965; *film version 1974). Critics point out that Dubé's own upward socio-economic evolution is closely reflected in the *plots and *characters to which he turned thereafter. Mainly tragic in inspiration and middle class in setting, plays such as *Bilan* (*The Accounting*, 1960) and *Au retour des oies blanches* (*The White Geese*, 1966) have now become part of the canon of Canadian theatre.   LED

DUBLIN

Founded as a ninth-century Viking settlement on the River Liffey, Dublin became the administrative centre of Norman Ireland in the early thirteenth century and continued in this role for successive waves of colonizers—a factor that would shape the history of performance in the city. The earliest recorded Dublin drama was a Latin *liturgical play, the *Visitatio Sepulcri* (*see* QUEM QUERITIS TROPE), probably performed in the church of St John the Evangelist (located behind the larger Christchurch Cathedral) about 1400. The text of the Dublin *Visitatio* play is extant, as is the script for an early fifteenth-century *morality play, *The Pride of Life*, probably performed on an outdoor scaffold stage in the city. By the end of the fifteenth century, Dublin was home to a large civic *Corpus Christi pageant, and by the end of the sixteenth century there were private performances of plays in Dublin Castle, the seat of colonial government. The first Dublin theatre was an appurtenance of the viceregal court of Thomas Wentworth, built *c.*1635 behind Dublin Castle in Werburgh Street. Although it was home to the playwright James *Shirley for several years, the Werburgh Street Theatre was destroyed in 1640 in the warfare that lasted until the early 1660s. In 1662, its former manager, John Ogilby, returned to Dublin to build the *Smock Alley Theatre, once again situated at the epicentre of power, in the middle of a rectangle bounded by Christchurch Cathedral, Dublin Castle, the Law Courts, and Trinity College.

Smock Alley played a pivotal role in Irish theatre history. In the 1660s, it had close ties to Dublin Castle, and many of the theatre's early actors—including Robert *Wilks—were commissioned officers in Castle regiments. It was in Smock Alley that George *Farquhar, Thomas *Southerne, and William *Congreve had their first experiences of theatre, and in the 1730s, *tours by the Smock Alley company spread the culture of professional theatre throughout Ireland, visiting Cork, Limerick, and Belfast. Peg *Woffington, Thomas Sheridan, and Spranger *Barry all made their debuts at Smock Alley, and it was on this stage that David *Garrick first played Hamlet. But its existence remained precarious, largely because the close proximity of *London always threatened to draw away new talent. When new Dublin theatres opened in Aungier Street (1734) and Crow Street (1760), the competition almost ruined everyone concerned, and it was generally agreed that Dublin could support only one large theatre.

Smock Alley closed in 1788, just as Irish political life was becoming dangerously volatile. Since the 1660s, the patronage of Dublin Castle had been a commercial necessity, attracting fashionable society to the theatre in its wake; however, in the decades surrounding the rebellion of 1798, close ties to the colonial administration threatened to alienate a growing segment of the potential *audience. Hence, although the next major Dublin theatre, the Hawkins Street Theatre Royal (1821), had a separate viceregal entrance and *box, state visits to the theatre dwindled after a series of *riots in the late 1820s, and during the middle decades of the nineteenth century Dublin's stages were largely filled with either *opera or *variety entertainments. It was not until after Dion *Boucicault's triumphant return to his home city in 1861 with *The Colleen Bawn* that touring and an expanding middle-class audience re-established the theatre's commercial viability. New theatres began to be built, including the *Gaiety (1871) and the Queen's, constructed in 1844, but reopened as the 'Home of Irish Drama' in 1884. The decision to offer Irish *melodrama at the Queen's was indicative of the heated culture of nationalism in Dublin during the late nineteenth and early twentieth centuries. With one eye on this new passion for all things Irish, and another on the small art theatres opening in London and *Paris in the 1890s, W. B. *Yeats, Lady Augusta *Gregory, and Edward *Martyn established an indigenous Irish company, the *Irish Literary Theatre, opening with Yeats's play *The Countess Cathleen* in 1899. By 1904, with a subsidy from A. E. F. *Horniman, they moved into a converted *music hall. Taking their name from their new home—the *Abbey Theatre—the company had premièred 68 new Irish plays by 1910.

Most major Irish plays of the early twentieth century were written for the Abbey. Some, such as John Millington *Synge's *Playboy of the Western World* (1907) or Sean O'Casey's *Plough and the Stars* (1926), erupted in riots (*see* PLAYBOY RIOTS). In the decades after Irish independence and the Irish civil war of the early 1920s, the cultural ferment behind the Abbey's remarkable initial burst of innovative writing and production had dissipated. Dublin theatre languished somewhat in the 1930s and 1940s, brightened only by *Gate Theatre productions (established 1928), whose founders Micheál *MacLíammóir and Hilton *Edwards mixed *modernist staging techniques with traditional showmanship. However, the real impetus behind the revival of Dublin theatre in the final decades of the twentieth century came with the *Dublin Theatre Festival (established 1957), which provided the double stimulus of bringing world theatre to the city and creating a showcase for new Irish writers, such as Brian *Friel.

In spite of the emergence of a generation of talented writers, actors, and directors in the 1960s, Dublin theatre suffered from an ageing infrastructure and a lack of state subsidy throughout the 1970s. The opening of the new Abbey Theatre in 1966 helped somewhat, but it was not until the early 1980s, when Irish Arts Council funding for theatre increased, that Dublin theatre began to expand and diversify. After a decade of unprecedented economic growth in the 1990s, there were ten professional venues in the city by the year 2000, including a dedicated children's theatre. Although the number (and quality) of regional Irish companies has increased rapidly since 1980, Dublin retains its place as the major centre for theatrical activity in Ireland. ChM

FLETCHER, ALAN J., *Drama, Performance and Polity in Pre-Cromwellian Ireland* (Cork, 2000)

MORASH, CHRIS, *Irish Theatre, 1601–2000: a history* (Cambridge, 2001)

DUBLIN DRAMA LEAGUE

Founded in 1918 by Lennox *Robinson, James Stephens, Ernest Boyd, and W. B. *Yeats to offset the prevailing style of the *Abbey Theatre's repertory by staging examples of innovative continental and American drama. Performing at irregular intervals on Sunday and Monday nights when the Abbey was generally closed, the League allowed members of the company to attempt *directing or undertake roles which extended their conventional technical skills. After 1928 (when the *Gate Theatre was founded in *Dublin with a similar manifesto), the League's endeavours, having staged some 52 productions, became increasingly spasmodic, ending with *Büchner's *Woyzeck* in 1941. RAC

DUBLIN THEATRE FESTIVAL

Created in 1957, this annual Irish event was fraught with controversy in its early years. Protests and arrests surrounded Alan Simpson's production of Tennessee *Williams's *The Rose Tattoo* at the *Pike Theatre in the first year, and in 1958, when Sean *O'Casey's *The Drums of Father Ned* was to be premièred, the

entire festival was cancelled in the face of objections from the Catholic Church. Thereafter it matured rapidly, incorporating exhibitions, public debates, *dance, *puppet theatre, *mime, and *cabaret. Its original intention, to expose the somewhat insular Irish *audiences to international influences, has been maintained, from two Jean *Vilar productions in 1957 to Robert *Wilson's *Woyzeck* in 2001. It has also contributed to the success of Irish dramatists: many of Hugh *Leonard's plays were written for the festival, and the world premières of Brian *Friel's *Philadelphia Here I Come!*, Tom *Murphy's *The Gigli Concert*, Thomas *Kilroy's *Talbot's Box*, and Frank *McGuinness's *Carthaginians* took place under its auspices. Although it has played an important role for tourism in Ireland's capital, the festival's *financing is limited and it relies heavily on corporate sponsorship.
CPi

DU BOIS, RAOUL PÈNE (1914–85)

American designer. Born in New *York, Du Bois became known for his colourful sets and gaudy *costumes, especially in *musicals. His first Broadway assignment was the costume design for the *Ziegfeld Follies of 1934*. He also costumed *Carmen Jones* (1943), *The Music Man* (1957), and *Gypsy* (1959). He designed both *scenery and costumes for *Du Barry Was a Lady* (1939), *Call Me Madam* (1950), *Bells Are Ringing* (1956), and *Irene* (1973). He was nominated for a Tony *award six times, winning in 1953 for *Wonderful Town* and in 1971 for *No, No, Nanette*.
CT

DUBOIS, RENÉ-DANIEL (1955–)

Québec playwright, actor, director. Trained in *Montréal and *Paris, he first captured public attention with *Ne blâmez jamais les Bédouins* (*Don't Blame the Bedouins*, 1984), a brilliant, solo *tour de force* comprising twenty different roles in different languages and accents, all played by Dubois. *Being at Home with Claude* (1985, same title in French), a disturbing portrayal of murder perpetrated in the name of absolute (homosexual) love, was another critical success, in its stage and *film (1992) versions. A controversial figure at the heart of Québec theatre, Dubois has also directed major stage and *opera productions.
LED

DUCHESNOIS, MLLE (CATHERINE-JOSÉPHINE RAFUIN) (1777–1835)

French actress. Protégée of Napoleon's wife Joséphine de Beauharnais, she was admitted to the *Comédie-Française on the same day in 1802 as Mlle *George, mistress of Napoleon. As ill-favoured as Mlle George was beautiful, Mlle Duchesnois was transfigured into a fine tragic queen by a sensibility and spon-

taneity reminiscent of Mlle *Dumesnil's. The press fuelled a bitter rivalry between the two actresses until, in 1808, Mlle George left for Russia. From then until her retirement in 1829, Mlle Duchesnois, who partnered *Talma for over twenty years, created a number of contemporary *tragedies, including Luce de Lancival's *Hector* (1809) and Étienne de Jouy's *Sylla* (1821).
JG

DUCIS, JEAN-FRANÇOIS (1733–1816)

French playwright. Ducis was the first to put Shakespeare on the French stage, adapting *Hamlet* (1769), *Romeo and Juliet* (1772), *King Lear* (1783), *Macbeth* (1784), and *Othello* (1792) according to a hybrid aesthetic that combined the decorous regularity of *neoclassical *tragedy with the mawkish sentimentality of eighteenth-century *drame bourgeois*. Having no English, his principal source was the reading translations of Pierre-Antoine de La Place (1745–9). Ducis's own most successful plays were *Oedipe chez Admète* (1778), which won him *Voltaire's chair in the Académie Française, and *Abufar; ou, La Famille arabe* (1795), which gave *Talma one of his finest roles.
JG

DUCLOS, MLLE (MARIE-ANNE DE CHASTEAUNEUF) (1668–1748)

French actress. She began her career at the *Opéra with only moderate success, joined the *Comédie-Française in 1693, understudying Mlle *Champmeslé from 1696. She was the company's leading tragic actress for over 40 years. Her declamation was considered to be unnatural but affecting, but by 1730 fashions had changed and she was compared unfavourably with Adrienne *Lecouvreur. In 1725, aged 55, she married her 17-year-old colleague Duchemin. Avisse's *Réunion* is supposedly based on the couple's marital difficulties. She retired from the stage, some said too late, in 1733.
JC

DU CROISY (PHILIBERT GASSAUD OR GASSOT) (1626–95)

French actor, creator of the role of Tartuffe. After playing romantic leads in the provinces, he joined *Molière's troupe in 1659, shortly after its installation in *Paris. He was noted for a ponderous, overemphatic style of speech, which Molière exploited in a series of important cameo roles such as the poet Oronte in *The Misanthrope* and the philosophy master in *The Would-Be Gentleman*. Tartuffe was his only leading role. He retired from the *Comédie-Française in 1689. His wife and daughter also acted, with little success.
RWH

DUCROW, ANDREW (1793–1848)

Belgian-English *circus entertainer who was an outstanding *mime, *acrobat, and equestrian. His great speciality was miming activities from life at sea or impersonating Greek statuary while standing on a galloping horse. Much of his early career was spent in France, though he came to fame in *London in 1814 at *Astley's Amphitheatre, where he returned in 1824 and was *manager from 1830 to 1841. He staged *melodramas such as J. R. *Planché's *Mazeppa* (1831), but particularly promoted spectacular shows and *hippodramas such as *The Battle of Waterloo* (1824).   JDV

DUFF, MARY ANN (1794–1857)

American actress. Though born in England, Duff lived in the United States permanently after 1810, acting primarily in *Boston and *Philadelphia theatres. Often referred to as 'the American *Siddons', she is considered, in Garff Wilson's words, 'the first great actress of the American stage'. Trained as a *dancer, she initially relied on her grace and natural beauty to win *applause, but steadily improved her acting until, by 1821, she was able to hold her own opposite a visiting Edmund *Kean in Shakespearian *tragedies. Kean's tributes enhanced her reputation. She retired from the stage in 1838.   AHK

DUFRESNY, CHARLES-RIVIÈRE (1648–1724)

French playwright and novelist. As a writer of traditional *comedy in the period following *Molière's death, Dufresny has always trailed in third place behind *Dancourt and *Regnard: compared with these contemporaries, he seems to have felt more keenly the difficulty of finding an original style in the shade of Molière. However, he also wrote for the *Comédie Italienne, and here he was more successful, attracting the admiration of *Marivaux.   WDH

DUKE OF YORK'S THEATRE

Located in the centre of *London's West End, the *playhouse opened in 1892 as the Trafalgar Square Theatre, changing its name in 1895. Designed by Walter Emden for Frank Wyatt and his wife Violet Melnotte, it remained in their family until 1935. Its most celebrated period occurred during the *management of Charles *Frohman (1897–1915) which saw a remarkable series of new plays and revivals performed. Most of J. M. *Barrie's plays were premièred there, notably *The Admirable Crichton* (1902) and *Peter Pan* (1904). Although short-lived, the attempt by Frohman to mount a *repertory season in 1910 saw performances of *Galsworthy's *Justice*, *Shaw's *Misalliance*, and Granville *Barker's *The Madras House*. Subsequently the theatre became identified with the plays of Noël *Coward (especially 1923–6) and as a venue for Nancy Price's efforts to launch a People's National Theatre (1933–6). With its seating capacity of a modest 650, it is especially valued as a West End venue for transferring successful out-of-town productions or for trying out riskier commercial ventures.   VEE

DUKES, ASHLEY (1885–1959)

Complete man of the English theatre, being by turns a *critic (*New Age*, *Star*, and *Illustrated London News*), dramatist, translator, *producer, and *manager. He championed the more innovative work of his contemporaries while acting as English editor for *Theatre Arts Monthly* and worked zealously to get staged in *London the best of continental playwriting, translating extensively to that end from French and German drama, especially work in the *expressionist style. His own plays, notably *The Man with a Load of Mischief*, are characterized, remarkably for the 1930s, by their thematic focus on social and racial tolerance. In 1933 he created the Mercury Theatre in Notting Hill, providing a platform for experimental *verse drama; by bringing *Murder in the Cathedral* to London he launched T. S. *Eliot's theatrical career. Dukes consistently supported his wife Marie Rambert in working to establish her *dance company from 1931, also at the Mercury.   RAC

DULLIN, CHARLES (1885–1949)

French actor, director, and teacher who worked briefly with Jacques *Copeau but left his company in 1918 to join Firmin *Gémier in a quest for a popular theatre. Dullin set up the Théâtre de l'*Atelier in 1922 along the lines of Copeau's *Vieux-Colombier, combining a company with a *training school. In his renowned revivals of the classics, Dullin starred in plays by *Aristophanes, *Molière, and Shakespeare, and he also championed the work of *Pirandello. He was influenced by *physical and popular forms of theatre, among them *commedia dell'arte* and *kabuki, making him the one director of the *Cartel des Quatre to come close to the notion of *total theatre. He had many notable disciples who had a significant impact on theatre in the twentieth century, among them Jean-Louis *Barrault and (briefly) Antonin *Artaud. He gave up the running of the Atelier in 1940 to one of his disciples, André *Barsacq, but continued to direct, produce, and influence future generations. His interest in *audience development resulted in a commissioned report for the Front Populaire government in 1937 which became the template for post-war decentralization of theatre and the arts in France.   BRS

DUMAS, ALEXANDRE (DUMAS *FILS*) (1824–95)

French novelist, playwright, and pamphleteer. Illegitimate son of the prolific dramatist of the *romantic generation, *Dumas *père*, the son came to be regarded as leader of the 'école du bon sens': writers who showed a firm moral tone in dealing with subjects from contemporary society, especially relations between the sexes. His first play, however, had much more in common with romantic drama, with its theme of passionate love defeated by the conventions of a hostile world. This was *La Dame aux camélias*, (*The Lady of the Camellias*, sometimes known as *Camille*), adapted from the author's own novel, and based on his liaison with the courtesan Marie Duplessis. Initially banned by the *censor as an offence to public morality, the play was phenomenally successful at the Vaudeville in *Paris in 1852, and was immediately adopted by *Verdi to provide the libretto for *La traviata* (1853), which faithfully reproduces both the *plot and the emotional appeal of Dumas's play.

Thereafter, the moralist in Dumas progressively took charge, and a series of plays including *Le Demi-monde* (1855), *Le Fils naturel* (*The Natural Son*, 1858), and *L'Ami des femmes* (*The Friend of Women*, 1864) show an increasingly didactic approach to problems of sexual morality. The best of his later plays is perhaps *Les Idées de Madame Aubray* (1867), in which dramatic action is persuasively linked to moral thesis. In *La Femme de Claude* (*Claude's Wife*, 1873), however, despite the powerful impact of his message—a warning of the need for moral regeneration after the national collapse in the Franco-Prussian War—Dumas's crusading fervour caused *realistic characterization to be subordinated to crude symbolism. In terms of dramatic craftsmanship, Dumas was content to endorse the views of *Scribe and other contemporaries who championed the *well-made play; he himself emphasized the qualities he required in a plot in the following terms: 'the *denouement must be the inexorable consequence of the *characters and events presented during the *action.' However, his ideas about a 'useful theatre', expressed in prefaces and pamphlets, show him to be a much more original thinker; as early as the preface to *Le Fils naturel* he had denounced 'art for art's sake' as a completely meaningless phrase: 'any literature that does not promote the moral improvement of humanity is an unhealthy monstrosity.'   WDH

DUMAS, ALEXANDRE (DUMAS *PÈRE*) (1802–70)

French novelist and playwright. Of the four names commonly linked in any account of the *romantic movement in French nineteenth-century drama—Victor *Hugo, Alfred de *Vigny, Alfred de *Musset, and Dumas—it was only the last who possessed a genuine innate sense of theatre. This was stimulated by the visit to *Paris of the English actors under J. P. *Kemble and

Edmund *Kean in 1827; and like Berlioz (who was to marry Harriet *Smithson) Dumas recorded in his 'How I became a playwright' a lyrical account of the impact of Shakespeare on a young French *audience. Having begun by writing *vaudevilles, Dumas now aimed at success in a literary theatre. His *Christine; ou, Paris, Fontainebleau, Rome*, a *historical drama, though accepted at the Théâtre-Français (see COMÉDIE-FRANÇAISE) in 1828, was only performed in 1830 at the *Odéon; his prose play *Henri III et sa cour* thus became the first romantic drama to be staged at the Théâtre-Français. *Napoléon Bonaparte* (Odéon, 1831) was written to a very different formula: with six acts and 23 *tableaux, it aimed at an 'epic' presentation of history rather than a conventional dramatic construction; though its success was probably due to Frédérick *Lemaître in the title role and to spectacular scenic effects (the Beresina crossing, the burning of *Moscow) rather than to dramaturgical innovation. *La Tour de Nesle* (*Porte-Saint-Martin, 1832) was also written for Lemaître as Buridan, but it was in fact *Bocage who created the role in what is little more than a sensational *melodrama.

Though Dumas continued to choose historical subjects—for instance *Catherine Howard* (1834) or *Lorenzino* (1842, with the same subject as Musset's *Lorenzaccio*, published in 1834 but not performed)—his repertoire of historical plays was to become a list of dramatizations of his own successful historical novels, especially after he acquired his own theatre, the Théâtre-Historique, in 1847. He had already produced *Les Mousquetaires* with the help of Auguste Maquet, his collaborator in many of these works, at the Ambigu-Comique in 1845; *La Reine Margot* (*Queen Margot*, 1847), *Le Chevalier de Maison-Rouge* (1847), *Monte-Cristo* (1848), and *Les Girondins* (1848) were among plays created by the same collaboration in Dumas's own theatre. However, it is to his plays on contemporary subjects that one should look for the best representation of the romantic aesthetic. *Antony*, in which Bocage played the Byronic *hero and Marie *Dorval the sympathetic heroine torn between love and duty, was outstandingly successful in its appeal to spectators at the Porte-Saint-Martin in 1831 as well as in frequent reprises later in the century: its melodramatic *coups de théâtre* are not such as to cheapen the genuine emotional effect. *Richard Darlington* (Porte-Saint-Martin, 1831), on the contrary, is pure melodrama; but *Kean; ou, Désordre et génie* (*Kean; or, Disorder and Genius*, Variétés, 1836), as well as offering a sincere tribute to the great English actor (who had died in 1833), provided a magnificent vehicle for a virtuoso performance by Lemaître as a convincing representation of a flamboyant if unruly genius. Dumas's *Kean* was reworked by *Sartre in 1954 as a vehicle for Pierre Brasseur.   WDH

DU MAURIER, GERALD (1873–1934)

English *actor-manager. The son of George du Maurier (the author of *Trilby* and an artist), Gerald was better educated than most performers of his generation and became the quintessential gentlemanly actor. He *toured with *Forbes-Robertson in 1895, and later with Beerbohm *Tree (playing Dodor in *Trilby*); he then took a variety of largely upper-class parts, avoiding anything controversial, preferring undemanding contemporary plays for a fashionable *London *audience. He was popular as Raffles (1906) and Bulldog Drummond (1921), and was much praised in the plays of J. M. *Barrie. His Captain Hook in *Peter Pan* (1904), greatly enjoyed by his novelist daughter Daphne, was much larger than life, and more effective for being the antithesis of his usual relaxed *acting style, which tended to conceal his careful preparation and skilled vocal technique. He was co-manager of Wyndham's Theatre (1910–25) and of the *St James's (1925–9), and was knighted in 1922.　　EEC

DUMB SHOW

In sixteenth- and early seventeenth-century English drama, a passage of silently *mimed *action, often quasi-symbolic, within a work otherwise couched in *dialogue. The dumb show was originally an *allegorical survival from the *morality play, and examples in Tudor *interludes feature personifications of abstract virtues and vices who contend in ways which foreshadow and moralize the fortunes of the play's *characters. In early Elizabethan *tragedy, however, spectacular dumb shows featuring the characters themselves serve narrative as much as *didactic purposes, sometimes carrying most of a play's action in between dialogue passages confined to static debate. The dumb show achieved its most sophisticated development in the professional theatre of the 1580s and 1590s, allowing playwrights such as *Peele (in *The Old Wives Tale*, printed 1595) and *Kyd (in *The Spanish Tragedy*, c.1589) to depict important and thematically resonant events outside the framework of narrative verisimilitude or chronological sequence (anticipating cinematic devices such as the flashback). The most famous dumb show occurs in a play influenced by *The Spanish Tragedy*, Shakespeare's *Hamlet* (c.1600), but by then the device already seemed antiquated, and Shakespeare's most elaborate dumb shows are reserved for a work deliberately composed in a mock-medieval dramatic idiom, *Pericles* (1608). Dumb shows survived, however, as an element of the *masque, and as such feature in masque-within-the-play episodes in the Jacobean tragedies of *Webster and *Middleton.　　MD

DUMESNIL, MLLE (MARIE-FRANÇOISE MARCHAND) (1713–1803)

French actress. She made her debut at the *Comédie-Française in 1738 in passionate 'noble mother' roles such as *Racine's Phèdre and Clytemnestre (*Iphigénie en Aulide*)—a *line of business she was to make her speciality. Rival of the more intellec-

tual Mlle *Clairon, she relied on intuition and inspiration to give performances in which 'half the time she has no idea what she's saying, then she'll create a sublime moment' (*Diderot). One such moment occurred in *Voltaire's *Mérope* (1743), when, as the eponymous *heroine, she broke with conventions of tragic dignity and ran across the stage. Her *acting, by turns pathetic and terrifying, excited *audiences for over 40 years, until she retired in 1776.　　JG

DUNCAN, ISADORA (1877–1927)

American dancer and choreographer. A key forerunner of modern *dance, Duncan repudiated the artificiality of nineteenth-century *ballet, creating a new form of dance which she claimed was natural and would free women's bodies. She danced barelegged and barefoot in a neoclassical tunic. Drawing eclectically in her dance and writings from ancient Greek art, Nietzsche, and French and Russian revolutionary thought, Duncan influenced dress reform and inspired artists in every medium. She was both lyrical and powerful as a solo dancer, although she also created group dances. While her choreography was often simple—she skipped, walked, ran, paused, and gestured—her charismatic emotional power and profound musicality were intensely affecting to *audiences. She shared a spare, evocative aesthetic with Edward Gordon *Craig (one of her lovers), whom she introduced to *Stanislavsky. She opened a series of schools for children in Europe, the last of which was in *Moscow, where she lived for several years after the communist revolution.　　SB

DUNLAP, WILLIAM (1766–1839)

American playwright, *manager, painter, and historian. Born in New Jersey, Dunlap studied painting in England before returning to *New York to work at the *John Street Theatre. His early dramatic work, *The Father; or, American Shandyism* (1789) and *Darby's Return* (1789), a short piece based on John *O'Keeffe's *Poor Soldier*, proved popular, but his major play *André* caused controversy in 1798. Because of its favourable portrayal of the British soldier Major John André, who conspired with Benedict Arnold during the War of Independence, and its critical treatment of George Washington, the work was hissed at its opening performance. Dunlap made some emergency modifications to get it through its three-day run, and later rewrote it as a popular patriotic piece called *The Glory of Columbia: Her Yeomanry* (1803), portraying Washington as well as an ordinary American soldier as heroic figures. Dunlap became the manager of the newly opened *Park Theatre from 1798 until he went bankrupt in 1805, then helped to manage it under the actor Thomas *Cooper. He wrote numerous adaptations of *Kotzebue's *melodramas, including *The Stranger* (1798), *False Shame; or, The American Orphanage in Germany* (1799), and *Pizarro in Peru*

(1800). He also adapted French plays, for instance *The Wife of Two Husbands* (from *Pixérécourt, 1804) and *Thirty Years; or, The Life of a Gamsester* (1828), and continued to write original dramas about domestic subjects like *A Trip to Niagara; or, Travellers in America* (1828). Considered the first major American dramatist, he completed more than 50 plays. He also published the important *History of the American Theatre* (1832), a biography of the actor George Frederick *Cooke (1813), and *History of the Arts of Design* (1834).

SEW

DUNLOP, FRANK (1927–)

English director and *manager, best known for founding the *Young Vic in *London and for running the *Edinburgh International Festival for almost ten years. He trained at the *Old Vic, formed the Piccolo Theatre (1954), was director of the Nottingham Playhouse (1961–4), and subsequently was *Olivier's assistant at the *National Theatre. At the Young Vic he directed populist productions such as *Molière's *Scapino* (1970), and fought the *Arts Council for better funding. His reputation as a tyrannical director did not deter media stars such as Jim Davidson, Spike Milligan, and Richard *Burton from working with him. His appointment to Edinburgh in 1983 was unexpected. His energetic productions (such as *Treasure Island*, 1990) were sometimes thought lowbrow but were broadly appealing, though his inexperience in programming music at the festival was often criticized. Dunlop resigned in 1991 after a festival of Eastern European work highlighted funding problems and ideological differences.

KN

DUNNOCK, MILDRED (1901–91)

American actress. A schoolteacher, Dunnock studied acting with Maria *Ouspenskaya at the *American Laboratory Theatre, and made her *New York debut at the age of 30 in *Life Begins* (1932). She was acclaimed for her supporting role in the 1940 Broadway production of Emlyn *Williams's *The Corn Is Green* and as Lavinia in Lillian *Hellman's *Another Part of the Forest* (1946). But it was the role of Linda Loman in Arthur *Miller's *Death of a Salesman* (1949) that became a trademark. Her sensitive and dignified characterization was repeated in the Laslo Benedek *film (1951) and in the *television production (1966). A favourite actress of Elia *Kazan (who directed the 1949 *Death of a Salesman*), Dunnock created the role of Big Mama in Kazan's staging of *Cat on a Hot Tin Roof* by Tennessee *Williams (1955) and she appeared in the Kazan films *Viva Zapata!* (1952) and *Baby Doll* (1956). Dunnock acted into her seventies, winning a Drama Desk *award for her performance in Marguerite *Duras's *A Place without Doors* (1970).

MAF

DUNSANY, LORD (EDWARD PLUNKETT) (1878–1957)

Anglo-Irish dramatist, poet, and novelist, associated with the Irish Literary Revival. His early plays at the *Abbey Theatre included *The Glittering Gate* (1905) and *The Laughter of the Gods* (1919). Like *Yeats and *Maeterlinck, his writing is often ornate and quasi-mythic, and his short plays were popular with the *Little Theatre movement in America. In the late twentieth century he was best known to devotees of science fiction.

GAO

DU PARC, MLLE (MARQUISE-THÉRÈSE DE GORLA) (c.1633–1668)

French actress. She began by singing and *dancing in her father's *medicine show in Lyon; there, in 1653, she met and married René Berthelot, known as Du Parc or Gros-René, a *farce player in the itinerant troupe headed by *Molière. A famous beauty but a declamatory and inflexible actress, Mlle Du Parc was more valuable to the troupe in *tragedy than in *comedy. In 1667, by now a widow and the mistress of *Racine, she defected to the *Hôtel de Bourgogne where, drilled by Racine 'like a schoolgirl', she created the role of the faithful widow Andromaque.

RWH

DU PLESSIS, P. G. (1934–)

South African playwright and literary scholar. His plays, including *Die Nag van Legio* (*The Night of Legio*) and *'n Seder val in Waterkloof* (*A Cedar Falls in Waterkloof*, 1977), use social dialects to explore different cultural groups within Afrikaner communities. He is best known for *Siener in die Suburbs* (*Seer in the Suburbs*, 1971) which treats poor whites in suburbia. The seer is trapped by social and economic pressures of a poor Afrikaner life, and is manipulated by powerful shadowy agents. Du Plessis was director of the Institute for Language, Literature, and Arts in Pretoria from its formation in 1971.

YH

DURANG, CHRISTOPHER (1949–)

American playwright and actor. Durang gained attention as a playwright in the late 1970s, with *regional and Broadway productions of *A History of the American Film*. *Off-Broadway, *Sister Mary Ignatius Explains It All for You* earned a 1979 Obie *award while stirring protests about its anti-Catholicism. A humanist rage animates Durang's anarchic cartoon worlds, with their screwball debasements of religious dogma, psychobabble, and America's precious ideals of the nuclear family and its heterosexual inscription. Literary *parody and pop-culture *satire also have figured strongly in his work. The savage thrust and crackpot logic of Durang's comic vision has acquired a certain mainstream following with plays like *Beyond Therapy* (1981) and *The Marriage of Bette and Boo* (1985), which is widely considered his most sustained full-length effort. His output since *Laughing Wild* (1987) has been more sporadic, but includes *Sex and Longing* (1996) and *Betty's Summer Vacation* (1999). Possessed of an affinity for performing since his university days, Durang has appeared in *cabaret, *revues, stage works (including his own), *film, and *television.   EW

DURANTE, JIMMY (1893–1980)

American comic actor and singer. Durante worked as a ragtime piano player in *New York saloons from the age of 17. In 1923 he opened a club in the Broadway district and—teamed with actor-dancer Lou Clayton and singer Eddie Jackson—became a favourite among club acts. The trio moved into *vaudeville, starred in a *film (*Roadhouse Nights*, 1930), and were prominently featured in the 1930 Herbert Field/Cole *Porter stage *musical *The New Yorkers*, after which Durante began a successful solo career. With a comic personality built around his large nose, gravelly voice, and an underlying warmth and charm, Durante became a star of musical comedies and *revues in the 1930s and 1940s, including the spectacular Billy *Rose *circus musical *Jumbo* (1935) and Cole Porter's *Red, Hot, and Blue* (1936). Aside from nightclub appearances, most of his work after 1940 was on *radio, *film, or *television.   MAF

DURAS, MARGUERITE (1914–96)

French novelist, playwright, screenwriter, and director, who often transformed her novels into plays and her plays into *films. Duras was born and spent her childhood in Indo-China and a *post-colonial consciousness is evident throughout her work, as is her interrogation of representation itself: memory, time, history, and identity as voice, *text, and image. Taken together, Duras's works are intertextual, often revisiting the same material but continually reweaving it. Her first play, *The Square* (1955), concerning the impossibility of true communication, is typically *absurdist. During the 1950s and 1960s her plays were often staged by *Barrault, notably *Des journées entières dans les arbres* (*Days in the Trees*, 1965), but in the 1970s she turned to director Simone Benmussa, whose spatial poetry accommodated Duras's search for ways to represent the feminine voice, and her rejection of a patriarchal style marked by rising suspense, climax, and Oedipal power struggles. *L'Amante anglaise* (*The English Lover*, 1968) and *L'Éden cinéma* (*Eden Cinema*, 1977) replay themes from her childhood in Indo-China, while her film scripts *Hiroshima mon amour* (directed by Alain Resnais, 1959) and *India Song* (which Duras directed, 1972) are also set in a remembered Asia, and reveal memory as unreliable and identity and time as fluid. Other plays include *Les*

Viaducts de la Seine-et-Oise (*The Viaducts of the Seine and Oise*, 1963), *Véra Baxter; ou, Les Plages de l'Atlantique* (*Vera Baxter; or, The Atlantic Beaches*, 1985), and *La Musica deuxième* (*Musica Second Version*, 1985). Duras herself successfully directed *Savannah Bay* in 1983, wherein a daughter and grandmother relate their memories to each other, together reconstructing the life of their dead daughter and mother and completing a portrait of three generations of women. Duras was awarded the Goncourt Prize for literature in 1984.   SBB

D'URFEY, THOMAS (1653–1723)

English playwright. Though later neglected, D'Urfey had at least 33 plays produced on the *London stage between 1676 and 1721, most of which were *comedies. His satirical *farces and songs were popular with Charles II and James II and he continued to receive royal favour from subsequent monarchs and commercial success with the merchant *audience of the early eighteenth-century theatre. D'Urfey earned his living by writing. His plays are overtly theatrical pieces, written for the leading performers of the day and their audience; thus they sit uncomfortably in the literary tradition attributed to contemporaries, such as William *Congreve. D'Urfey's three-part adaptation of *Don Quixote* (1694–5) attracted the unwelcome attention of the *anti-theatrical lobby, headed by Jeremy *Collier, but was frequently revived until 1785. *The Marriage Hater Match'd* (1692) and *The Richmond Heiress* (1693), written for the acting partnership of Elizabeth *Barry and Anne *Bracegirdle, are typical D'Urfey comedies, containing a strong social commentary which reflects the shift toward the sentimental *comedy of manners that dominated the eighteenth-century stage.   GBB

DUROV FAMILY

A Russian troupe of *circus *clown and *animal trainers, consisting of the brothers Vladimir Leonidovich (1863–1934), Anatoly Leonidovich (1865–1916), and their children and grandchildren, Anatoly Anatolevich (1887–1928), Vladimir Grigorevich (1909–72), Yury Vladimirovich (1910–71), and Anna Vladimirovna (1900–81). The two founders were unusual in incorporating political *satire into their acts in which donkeys and pigs performed the roles of bureaucrats or policemen. They also trained performing seals and elephants. Vladimir conducted research into animal training in the 1920s and believed that the transformation of the world would result from a better understanding of reflex activity. They *toured widely abroad.   NW

DÜRRENMATT, FRIEDRICH (1921–90)

Swiss playwright and novelist. Together with Max *Frisch the most important Swiss dramatist and one of the best-known

German-language playwrights of the twentieth century. Born the son of a pastor near Berne, he studied philosophy and theology there and in Zurich. He began his career as a draughtsman and theatre *critic. His early plays reflect his religious education, most notably *An Angel Comes to Babylon* (begun 1948, premièred 1953). Thereafter he began to adopt a lighter tone, as in *Romulus the Great* (1949), in which the Roman Emperor is more concerned about his chickens than about the invading barbarians from the north. Dürrenmatt achieved international fame with *The Visit* (1956), a characteristically grotesque 'tragic comedy' (*see* TRAGICOMEDY), in which an old woman, Claire Zachanassian, constructed almost entirely from prostheses, returns to her home village. The village has been forgotten by time but not by Claire, who uses her colossal wealth to exact revenge on the man, significantly named Ill, who abandoned her in her youth. In an echo of the Nazi past, the villagers are gradually corrupted and conspire together to murder Ill. In 1960 Peter *Brook directed *The Visit* in London and in 1963 Dürrenmatt's other major play, *The Physicists* (1962). Set in a mental hospital housing three homicidal inmates who claim to be famous physicists, the action reveals that they are actually a scientist and two agents pretending to be mad. They agree to keep up their pretence, so that potentially dangerous discoveries cannot be exploited by an evil world. However, the manager of the asylum is genuinely mad and has already stolen the nuclear secrets. Dürrenmatt shows how the world may be in the grip of barbarian forces, of ruthless capital, or of the insane application of scientific discoveries, but set against this is the quiet courage of Romulus, Ill, and the three 'physicists', which provides the only hope in a grotesque world. Dürrenmatt's further work for the stage included adaptations of Shakespeare's *King John* (1968) and *Titus Andronicus* (1970), and domestic pieces, such as *Play Strindberg* (1969). The last is a schematic adaptation of *Strindberg's *Dance of Death*, presenting the struggle between Alice and Edgar as the twelve rounds of a boxing match. The *dialogue is stripped to a minimum, the action sharpened and exaggerated, with Edgar descending into babbling infantility and Kurt revealed as a master criminal. After the 1970s Dürrenmatt concentrated on prose writing.   MWP

DUSE, ELEANORE (1858–1924)

Italian *actor-manager. Born into a poor company of errant actors, Duse captured critical attention with her interpretation of Juliet on a makeshift wooden stage in Verona's *amphitheatre (1875), and as the tormented Thérèse in *Zola's *Thérèse Raquin* (1879) at the Fiorentini Theatre, *Naples. Over the next six years (1880–6), she achieved fame in Italy as a member of Cesare Rossi's company which performed at the Teatro Carignano in Turin during the winter, and the Teatro Valle in *Rome during the summer. Her fame was primarily due to the psychological *realism of her interpretations in French *well-made plays (*Sardou, *Scribe and Legouvé, *Dumas *fils*) and in new Italian works, among them the première of Verga's first *verismo play, *Cavalleria rusticana* (1884). She also proved herself a superb comedienne in *Goldoni's *Pamela nubile* and *La Locandiera*.

When Rossi disbanded his company after an 1885–6 South American *tour, Duse, assisted by the actor and director Flavio Andò, became actor-manager of Compagnia Drammatica della Città di Roma (1887–94). She added to her repertory *Giacosa's *Tristi amori* (*Sad Loves*, 1887), Arrigo Boito's adaptation of *Antony and Cleopatra* (1888), *Praga's *Ideal Wife* (1890), *Ibsen's *A Doll's House* (1891, making her the first to present the Norwegian author in Italy), and *Sudermann's *Heimat* or *Magda* (1892). Between 1889 and 1894 the company toured Egypt, Spain, Russia, *Vienna, Germany, the USA, and England. Her international renown led to comparisons with Sarah *Bernhardt, and in 1895 both performed Camille and Magda in *London. Bernard *Shaw, in a famous review, concluded that after seeing Duse's restrained *acting in these roles, her lack of *makeup, her unobtrusive entrances, and her believable and rich emotional life (including blushing at will), Bernhardt's performances seemed false, albeit charming. Other reviewers characterized Duse's acting as spiritual or mystical because of her small gestures, her silences, and her pauses.

By the early 1890s the *symbolist movement was in the ascendant; Duse, who loved to read and challenge her intellect, was tiring of her realistic, popular, and mostly French roles as noble *heroine or sophisticated wife. She wanted to find poetic material that would engender respect for Italian playwriting. For seven years she devoted herself to promoting the plays of the Italian poet, and her lover, Gabriele *D'Annunzio, an artistic decision that *Pirandello, among others, deemed misguided. After premièring his dramatic poem *Spring Morning's Dream* in the role of the Madwoman in 1897 in *Paris, during a famous competition with Bernhardt that attracted all of fashionable society, she toured Italy and the USA with *Francesca da Rimini*, *La Gioconda*, and *The Dead City*. Although mostly unsuccessful, the presentational style of these plays reputedly enriched her voice and taught her to achieve more physical weight on stage. As part of their dream for a golden age of Italian theatre, the couple wanted to create an *open-air theatre on the shores of Lake Albano, near Rome, for the presentation of D'Annunzio's works, *Greek *tragedies, and worthy modern poets, but the 1899 opening never materialized. She broke from D'Annunzio when he allowed Irma *Gramatica to première *Daughter of Jorio* (1904) and, although she would continue to perform his work, she found new material in *Maeterlinck's *Monna Vanna* (1904), *Gorky's *Lower Depths* (1905, with Virgilio *Talli), and particularly Ibsen. To the *Hedda Gabler* which she first presented in 1898, she added *Rosmersholm* (1906, with sets by Gordon *Craig), *John Gabriel Borkman* (1908), and *Lady from the Sea* (1908). Aurélien *Lugné-Poe of Paris served as director and impresario for some of her many tours between 1905 and

1909 throughout Europe, South America, and Russia. In January 1909 Duse formally retired from the stage but continued to pursue projects and acted in her only *film, *Cenere* (*Ashes*, 1916), an adaptation of Grazia Deledda's novel. Facing financial difficulties, she returned to the stage in 1921 with the help of Ermete *Zacconi and continued to be innovative. When she fell ill and died in Pittsburgh during her fourth US tour, her repertory included *The Dead City*, *Ghosts*, *Lady from the Sea*, Praga's *Closed Door*, and Gallarati Scotti's *Thy Will Be Done*. She was mourned internationally and remains a legend to this day.

JEH

BASNETT, SUSAN, 'Eleonora Duse', in *Bernhardt, Terry, Duse* (Cambridge, 1988)

PIRANDELLO, LUIGI, 'Eleanora Duse: actress supreme', *Century Magazine* (June 1924)

SHAW, GEORGE BERNARD, 'Duse and Bernhardt', in *Our Theatre in the Nineties*, vol. iii (London, 1932)

DUTT, MICHAEL MADHUSUDAN (1824–73)

Bengali dramatist. An ardent lover of Western literature as a college student in Calcutta (*Kolkata), he converted to Christianity and spent several years in Madras before returning to devote his energies to writing in his mother tongue. He made major contributions to Bengali poetry, while for *Bengali theatre he invented an influential variety of blank *verse and successfully combined classical Sanskrit *dramaturgy with European techniques. Dutt became involved with *amateur theatricals, composing several scripts which later were permanent fixtures in the professional repertoire, among them the romantic *Sarmishta* (*Sermista*, 1859) and the satirical *Ekei ki Bale Sabhyata?* (*Is this Called Civilization?*, 1860). As the translator of these plays, he may have been the earliest playwright of *Indian theatre in English. He also translated Dinabandhu *Mitra's revolutionary *Nil Darpan* (*Indigo Mirror*) in 1861— anonymously, because of its anti-British theme depicting colonial planters' exploitation of Indian peasants. A liberal thinker, Dutt encouraged the movement to introduce *women on the stage in Bengal.

AL

DUTT, UTPAL (1929–93)

Bengali dramatist, director, and actor. He participated in English-language college theatricals in Calcutta (*Kolkata), founded his own Little Theatre Group (LTG) to stage English drama, and was associated with Geoffrey Kendal's *touring Shakespeariana company where he learnt a professional approach based on discipline and punctuality. Later he became a convert to Marxism. Dutt changed LTG's medium from English to Bengali, took up *management of the commercial Minerva Theatre to reach a wider public, and began writing plays.

Angar (*Coal*, 1959), about a mining catastrophe, overwhelmed *audiences with the enormity of the disaster by *spectacle supported by *lighting and *sound effects. The Royal Indian Navy mutiny of 1946 provided the subject matter for *Kallol* (*Waves*, 1965), LTG's longest-running production. Dutt invented the Bengali *documentary drama with *Manusher Adhikare* (*People's Rights*, 1968), on the 1931 trial of black youths in Scottsborough, Alabama, specifically to encourage revolution among his working-class spectators.

Around this time he grew interested in the *folk genre of *jatra because of its potential of communicating to an even larger rural population. He prepared nineteen *jatra* shows with communist messages, which he took to villages. He also created what he called the 'poster play': *street-corner *agitprop in which the group read out and theatricalized factual accounts of class oppression. He wrote fifteen such scripts. At the same time he continued to work in the *proscenium theatre. In 1969, after leaving Minerva, he renamed LTG the People's Little Theatre and staged some of his finest works with that group: the richly *metatheatrical *Tiner Taloyar* (*Tin Sword*, 1971); *Barricade* (1972), on Nazism, thinly disguising electoral corruption and the murder of a judge in Bengal; and *Duhswapner Nagari* (*Nightmare City*, 1974) on police brutality, a production immediately labelled seditious.

Dutt laboured incessantly till his death, after which his wife Sova Sen, who had acted with him from the early days, assumed charge of PLT. In his remaining years, he directed, in addition to his 22 full-length proscenium plays, another 40 or so productions, including work by Shakespeare, Michael Madhusudan *Dutt, Girish *Ghosh, and *Tagore. He translated Shakespeare and *Brecht into Bengali and wrote essays prolifically for his journal *Epic Theatre*, as well as books such as *Towards a Revolutionary Theatre* (1982). He maintained a parallel career in *film, acting in art and commercial movies in both Bengali and Hindi, though he tended to be typecast as the *villain or older buffoon. His stage *acting featured a fine comic sense and perfect timing, but in an almost *Brechtian manner, he always played himself as well as the *character. For all his ideology, his directorial hallmark remained grand theatricality and biting *satire. *See also* BENGALI THEATRE.

AL

DUVAUCHELLE, MARÍA ELENA (c.1945–)

Chilean actress and director. From 1964 to 1973 she performed a number of important roles in the groups Los Cuatro and *Ictus. After the military coup she went into exile in Venezuela where she was actively involved in theatre and television and received several *awards. After returning to Chile in 1984 she was one of the founders of El *Nuevo Grupo, and acted in their production of Antonio *Skarmeta's *Ardiente paciencia* (*Burning Patience*), based on the life of the Chilean poet Pablo Neruda and the downfall of the Allende government.

MAR

DUYM, JACOB (1547–1612 or 1624)

Flemish-born playwright. After serving in the army of William of Orange and spending some time in captivity, he settled in Leiden in the Netherlands, where he became a leading member of the immigrant Flemish *Chamber of Rhetoric called d'Oraigne Lelie (the Orange Lily). He was the author of two collections of six plays each, *Spiegelboeck* (*Book of Mirrors*, 1600) and *Ghedenckboek* (*Book of Memory*, 1606). As the title of the first suggests, Duym's work is in the *allegorical, moralizing style typical of the Rhetoricians but at the same time also shows *early modern features such as the five-*act structure and the use of alexandrine *verse. The plays in *Book of Memory* are political and propagandist, recalling great episodes from the struggle against Spain. Duym's elaborate *stage directions are an important source for knowledge of the early Dutch stage, which still retained *medieval characteristics.   JDV

DYBWAD, JOHANNE (1867–1950)

Norwegian actress. Johanne Dybwad (née Juell) made her acting debut in Bergen, the city of her birth, in 1887. The next year she moved to the capital to begin work at the Christiania Theatre, where she became famous for a number of popular *ingénue roles. She also played the younger female roles in *Ibsen's plays, including Hedvig (*The Wild Duck*), Solveig (*Peer Gynt*), Hilde (*The Master Builder*), and Frida (*John Gabriel Borkman*). In 1899 she and her colleagues moved to the newly created National Theatre, and after a slow start she gradually became established as one of Norway's leading actresses. She excelled in complex roles such as *Bjørnson's Tora Parsberg, Ibsen's Rebecca West (*Rosmersholm*), and Shakespeare's Rosalind. She went on to develop a distinguished career as a director, mounting a wide range of productions, including plays by Ibsen, *Schiller, and Shakespeare.   DT

DYER, CHRIS (1947–)

English designer. From 1975 to 1986, he was resident designer at the *Royal Shakespeare Company; in addition to *scenery and *costume design, he was part of the RSC team which designed the Elizabethan-style stage for the 1976 season, and the stages and seating for the Other Place, the *Donmar Warehouse, and the Pit. His work on Shakespeare with Michael *Bogdanov at the RSC and the *English Shakespeare Company was particularly notable. He was joint winner of the Golden Troika *award for theatre design at the 1979 *Prague Quadrenniale. He teaches at Central St Martin's College of Art and Design in *London, and he is also director of research for Virtual Stages, an interactive model of performance spaces.   RVL

·E·

EARLY MODERN PERIOD IN EUROPE
(1500–1700)

1. Introduction; 2. Shared qualities; 3. Italy; 4. England;
5. Spain; 6. France

1. Introduction

The early modern period includes overlapping epochs that have
been variously called the Renaissance, the *Reformation, the
Restoration, the Enlightenment, the Age of Reason, and the
Age of Revolution. Each of these terms designates specific intellectual, artistic, religious, economic, political, and scientific
developments in Western culture. Influential cultural historians
of the late twentieth century, such as Christopher Hill, William
Bouwsma, Norbert Elias, and Natalie Zemon Davis, have long
used the term early modern to describe Europe and England
from the fifteenth to the eighteenth centuries. For historians it
encompasses a totality of cultural practices including, but not
limited to, aesthetic production. Phenomena as diverse as *guild
memberships, plague effects, the formation of cities, enclosure
acts, demographic migration, child-rearing practices, and material production are considered crucial to understanding the social history of the period. More recently, literary scholars, who
until twenty years ago talked about the 'Renaissance', have become interested in the wider cultural intertext that was hitherto
the province of historians. By the 1970s and 1980s, literary
movements such as formalism, *structuralism, and the New
Criticism gave way to more interdisciplinary scholarly approaches, including post-structuralism, cultural *materialism,
the new *historicism, and *feminist theory, practices which utilized the methods of social historians, Marxist and post-Marxist
political philosophers, and cultural anthropologists.

In the last decades of the twentieth century, the term
Renaissance became the target of historicist and materialist cri-

tiques for its implied elitism, privileging of humanism, and
narrow concern with purely aesthetic values. Consequently it
is now used with some degree of discomfort and defensiveness,
as it is regarded in some scholarly circles as a naive or uncritical
term that celebrates the revival of classical learning and the
flowering of the arts at the expense of what was happening
among the peasantry, the lower classes, and in women's lives.
This viewpoint has accompanied the more general critique
levelled at the humanist educational regime, which had gradually supplanted the scholasticism of the Middle Ages. Anthony
Grafton and Lisa Jardine, in *From Humanism to the Humanities*
(1986), acknowledge that humanism helped to secularize the
educational process; but argue that it better suited the ruling
elites of fifteenth- and sixteenth-century Europe, and did not
exactly provide a blueprint for radical individualism. However
accurate their claim, it is nonetheless the case that the humanist
agenda, furthered by the advent of mechanical printing in the
later half of the fifteenth century, provided the basis for an
education that would eventually become available to a much
broader lay constituency than medieval scholasticism ever
had. Humanist education may have led, as Grafton and Jardine
propose, to centuries of mystification of the arts, but its
emphasis on the mastery of languages and rhetorical skills
led to some of the most brilliantly subversive writing of the
time, from Rabelais's *Gargantua and Pantagruel* (1532–4) and
*Cervantes' *Don Quixote* (1605–15) to *Milton's *Areopagitica*
(1644).

Certainly much has been gained by the widening of a field
once known simply as Renaissance studies. If 'Renaissance'
makes us think of the brilliant sculptures of Michelangelo,
the fabulous wealth of the Medici, Elizabethan poetry, and New-
tonian physics, 'early modern period' conjures the emergence
of mercantile capitalism, the troubled politics of Divine Right,
the embattled status of women and younger sons in a patriarchal culture, and the appearance of the 'new man' who

would eventually gain a toehold for a nascent middle class: the first in European history.

However, as welcome as escape from the aesthetic parochialism of 'the Renaissance' may be, the more politically correct 'early modern period' carries its own fundamental assumptions and biases worthy of examination. The very notion of something called 'the modern' is itself field specific and field invented, and includes different applications and widely, if not wildly, divergent time frames. Consequently, as an umbrella term 'early modern' is not, nor should be, uncontroversial. Douglas Bruster has observed that 'seemingly a simple phrase, "early modern" betrays some of its complexity even in the understated tension between its components: "early", which takes time in one direction, and "modern", which leads it in another'. Since there is no universal consensus on what constitutes the chronological totality called 'modernity', the early part of the modern period is as ideologically loaded a concept as the Renaissance: it is just one that appropriates the institutional authority and language of historians. The cultural bias that holds that history is more objective than literary or theatre study still persists; and scholars who have persuasively deconstructed the descriptivist veneer of historiography nonetheless continue to rely on its veil of legitimacy for their own historicist readings. The current academic preference for the term 'early modern' derives from the same empiricist bias as the ideology of 'the Enlightenment', and draws on the same authority granted to the New Science to rescue the humanities from charges of subjectivism, frivolity, and elitism. Reproducing the scientific bias of the general public, as well as academic administrations, scholars who critique humanism have not in fact escaped its purview: they are simply privileging one branch of humanism over another.

The concept of modernity implies something that has been updated and improved, or even detached from what has come before. With its implicit basis in science and its explicit reference to progress, the term early modern bespeaks a notion of history that comes perilously close to historical positivism—a view few scholars would directly endorse, since such essentialism underwrites colonialist ideology and the 'manifest destiny' approach to history. The most serious criticism to be made of the term early modern is that it advances a strictly Eurocentric and Western vision of historical development, a view determined by the emergence of capitalism and increasingly industrialized modes of production in England, France, Spain, Italy and, in the eighteenth century, America, and reinforced by the use of categories such as 'First World', 'developing countries', and 'Third World'. As long as the word 'modern' remains the linchpin of our chronology, contemporary critical thinking, however updated, remains tethered to Eurocentric assumptions and epistemological and ethical foundations that are now over 400 years old.

LC

2. Shared qualities

It is apparent that the combined effect of these changes generates something considerably different in the realm of *performance in Europe after 1550. Traditionally, aesthetic expression of the sixteenth and seventeenth centuries has been associated with a 'renaissance'—a 'rebirth'—of classical learning, which led to a new humanism based upon the art and thinking of antiquity. This notion, forcefully promulgated by J. C. Burckhardt at the end of the nineteenth century (*The Civilization of the Renaissance in Italy*), has coloured many treatments of the theatre of the early modern period. Historians might point to the rapid rise across Europe of royal and commercial *playhouses, some of them clearly based on classical models; to the ostensible changes in modes of *acting and theatre production, which abandoned the frequently *amateur, occasional, and festival-based methods of the *medieval theatre for a more regular and professional approach that could be commercially exploited; and to the introduction of the new *scenography in Italy, based on the principles of *perspective and *illusion and often involving *scene shifting by complicated machines to create effects that astonished the eye. Most especially, historians might notice the new *playwrights of *comedy and *tragedy—like *Marlowe, Shakespeare, Lope de *Vega, *Calderón, *Corneille, and *Racine—who evoked *characters and narratives, usually in highly sophisticated *verse, concerned variously with individualism, *gender roles, mercantilism, nationalism, the legitimacy of authority and *religion, or the adventure of global imperialism.

All those matters are relevant in attempting to introduce the age. At the same time, however, it is crucial to note that in no one country of Europe did every one of the artistic trends exist simultaneously. Nor did they spread like wildfire: their dissemination across the continent and to the island of Britain was shaky, erratic, and lengthy, so that it was not until the latter part of the seventeenth century that the theatres of the major countries of Europe could be considered fully *neoclassical. Further, unlike medieval theatre, which shared certain features across a Europe united by a common religion and the Latin language, playwriting and production in the early modern period had to contend with the Reformation, embattled notions of kingship, the rise of capitalism, and the gradual destruction of the feudal order. Theatre in Renaissance Italy, Elizabethan *London, Golden Age Spain, and the *Paris of the Sun King developed along national lines, suiting notions of national identity in the themes of the plays and in the methods of *company organization.

Two separate strands of *management developed, the royal and the popular. In Italy and France the former predominated, and gave rise to the most obvious novelties of early modern practice: playhouses and scenography designed for the pleasure of the court. In these cases theatrical production was usually *financed by the king or the local duke, even if the subsidy was often insufficient and required performances for general *audiences in order to meet expenses and make a profit. It was the tastes of the monarch and of the aristocracy that set style in motion, and it is not surprising that the scenic effects of the *proscenium stage and the sophisticated modes of *opera and *ballet were inaugurated under this dispensation. In England and Spain, on the other hand, the popular or *public theatres drove the expansion of performance, though here as well the most successful troupes were commanded to perform at court, and in England were officially protected by noblemen (like Shakespeare's *Chamberlain's Men). Companies were usually run by actors (though some of them like Shakespeare and *Molière could be magnificent dramatists as well), and plays were commodities for hire that once purchased could be used indefinitely without the author's further consent or dispensed with entirely after one performance. The need for a constantly changing bill, under the conditions of *repertory playing that obtained in most countries, meant that writers had to work fast, hit the mood of the moment, and construct playable *dialogue and engaging *characters. Shakespeare wrote (or co-wrote) about 40 long plays that still are read and performed, an extraordinary achievement, but his output pales beside that of Lope de Vega. Working in Spanish conditions that expected shorter plays, Lope may have written as many as 600 or 700 *comedias and numerous *autos sacramentales; of the two types a total of about 400 survive. These are conditions that do not encourage great originality and usually depend on conventionalized structures, narratives, and borrowed *plots. Actors had little time to prepare and *rehearse. Their skill at learning lines and inhabiting many roles had to be superb—well beyond what was required in the theatre after *Stanislavsky—which suggests a dominant concept of acting that relied upon *stock characters and physical presence rather than psychological subtlety. That so many competent dramatists across Europe flourished under these conditions, and that so many great actors appeared to give breath to their creations, is the period's greatest shared characteristic, and its most enduring legacy.   DK

3. Italy

It was the humanist revolution in Italy which pioneered major European transformations in terms of how theatre was conceived and managed, both in terms of the structure and content of plays and as regards the social and physical organization of theatres themselves. Italian humanists insisted dogmatically that classical models should be followed and medieval ones obliterated, the latter being seen as totally lacking in cultural and (just as importantly) social prestige. On the one hand, this transformed *dramaturgy by introducing sharply delineated *genres of comedy and tragedy, with *pastoral as a later and more innovative addition; and eventually by inflicting on dramatic *theory the constraints of the three *unities (time, place, and action) allegedly derived from *Aristotle. These rules were

adopted rigorously in France (see NEOCLASSICISM); but taken with much greater pinches of salt in England and Spain, where there was more continuity with the imaginative and poetic insights of pre-Renaissance drama. More generally accepted was the promotion of playwriting to the rank of high artistic creation, worthy of being preserved in print like the masterpieces of Greece and Rome—an attitude accepted in Italy long before Ben *Jonson was derided in England for publishing his dramatic Works. This rise in status also aided the progressive transformation of performance into an autonomous cultural activity, abandoning the strictly occasional character of medieval religious and courtly drama. The humanists, wedded as they were to gentlemanly amateurism, probably never intended the inevitable corollary, that theatre should become a commercial enterprise.

In practice, the introduction of classical models was carried out initially in relation to comedy, with the genre now categorized as *commedia erudita being inaugurated by *Ariosto in Ferrara in 1508 and 1509. Close and exclusive imitation of the content, as well as the style, of *Plautus and *Terence soon proved too constricting. Bibbiena, in 1513, recognized that audiences already had their expectations formed by the medieval comic novella, particularly Boccaccio's Decameron, and such sources soon came to influence both plot conventions and verbal style. Then, in the 1530s, the Sienese Accademia degli Intronati, in its collectively authored comedies, made the crucial step of introducing elements from medieval *romance and associated pre-humanist drama. By paying more attention to the sentiments and predicaments of young lovers, which included granting more autonomy and stage time to female characters, the Sienese completed the blueprint for European comedy, and laid the ground for links with other more emotional genres of drama.

Experiments with classical-style tragedy took a little longer. From 1515, with *Trissino's Sofonisba, *texts were circulated and discussed on paper; but it was only in 1541 that Giovan Battista *Giraldi Cinthio organized the first actual performance, again in Ferrara, of his tragedy Orbecche. Tragedy was probably never as popular with audiences as other genres; but its prestige in ancient times meant that examples continued to be written if not always to be performed. Giraldi also tried to revive the third known classical genre of the *satyr-play, with his Egle in 1545; but the pastoral mode of drama (which is not quite the same thing) was already known to, and liked by, courtly audiences through a tradition of brief ephemeral 'Eclogues'. The 'regular' five-*act play which truly established a format and humanist credentials for Renaissance pastoral was Il sacrificio (1554) by Agostino Beccari. Once again, by coincidence or not, the venue for this piece of pioneering was Ferrara, under the patronage of the Este dukes.

The desire to resurrect ancient modes of *dramaturgy was naturally associated with attempts to understand and re-create ancient theatre architecture, at a time when the notion of a building dedicated to performance and nothing else was a total innovation. Intense study was devoted to such archaeological evidence as was available, and to *Vitruvius' *De Architectura* of the first century AD. In the meantime, however, makeshift venues were needed quickly, and independent ideas on scenography were developing out of Renaissance achievements in perspective painting. Real venues thus developed in a pragmatic, piecemeal (and cheaper) way, and the archaeologists were overtaken by events. The first dedicated theatre building in Italy, the Teatro *Olimpico at Vicenza, was not opened (with a production of *Sophocles) until 1585, nine years later than James *Burbage created the *Theatre in *London.

Productions of the new genres of drama took place in existing indoor locations adapted for performance. These were either public rooms in rulers' palaces, spaces in private houses, or the premises of academies. Eventually some such rooms were refurbished as permanent performance spaces. An early attempt in the Ferrara ducal palace, supervised by Ariosto, was destroyed by *fire almost immediately; but the Medici theatre inside the Uffizi palace in Florence (by Bernardo *Buontalenti, 1585–6) became an example of what rulers thought was appropriate and affordable. Seating plans varied; but they always involved segregation of the sexes (*see* WOMEN IN AUDIENCES), and frequently the place of honour for the prince or principal host had the status almost of a second stage. The performing area itself was a raised platform at one end of the room, closed by *curtains but not initially framed by a proscenium arch. The picture-frame effect was nonetheless implicit; because the static scenography dictated by the unity of place involved from the very earliest productions (probably from Ariosto's *Cassaria* of 1508 in Ferrara) the use of an illusionistic perspective backcloth depicting a townscape or other suitable panorama. This was a satisfactory union of classical dramaturgical practice and the most up-to-date resources of the visual arts: it must have helped to convince an audience that these ancient formats could provide an art for their own times.

Scenographic practices which had probably been current for nearly 40 years were then codified by Sebastiano *Serlio in his architectural treatise of 1545, which offered descriptions and illustrations of standard sets for Comedy, Tragedy, and Pastoral. Whether or not these structures and designs really had anything to do with what could be deduced about *Greek or *Roman theatre became increasingly irrelevant, though claims for their authenticity continued to be made. By the time the Teatro Olimpico did open, its semicircular shape and its elaborate architectural *scaenae frons* were at least partly authentic, but no longer reflected general practice. The Teatro *Farnese in Parma (1618) was the real model for the future: it offered flexible stage space, proscenium, *stalls, and rising tiers of seats in an elongated horseshoe. Later Venetian theatres added the vertical tier of *boxes which became standard. Meanwhile, the

demand for pure *spectacle, contrasting with the static constraints of neoclassical drama, was producing radical innovations in scenography. For *pageants and *interludes, and then later for the *operas which developed out of them, stage engineers began to create elaborate movable and moving *scenery, able to produce miraculous effects and transformations: they were in fact building on experience gained in the fifteenth century in religious dramas mounted in churches. The Florentine *intermedii* at the Uffizi, for a granducal wedding in 1589, were an internationally famous event, establishing for all Europe that Italians were the leaders in scenographic development, and leading to bids from other countries after 1600 to hire their expertise.

These technical advances coincided with a quite separate development in the human organization of performance. During the 1540s and 1550s, in a process which is relatively undocumented and hard to reconstruct, performance by gentlemen amateurs was being both paralleled and rivalled by the appearance of professional troupes. The content and conventions of *commedia erudita* seem to have been hijacked—initially, it is thought, in the territory of Venice—by actors who increasingly made theatre a full-time artisan activity. In response to the taste of paying audiences, but also moved by commercial demands, they switched the emphasis of their shows from scripts which looked tidy on paper to texts which gave opportunity to virtuoso performance. This had an inevitable tendency to fragment dramaturgical structures into separate performable, and movable, 'numbers'. Eventually they dispensed with scripts and dramatists altogether, and used outline *scenarios on which they *improvised (though the word needs to be used with some care): this method was most often classed at the time simply as 'Italian comedy', but we now know it as *commedia dell'arte*. At the same time, they made another staggering innovation by introducing *women on stage in the more romantic roles, in the teeth of enormous social and religious prejudice. Dates for this revolution, which was crucial for the whole of European or Western performance, are frustratingly hard to identify. The hiring in Lyon of an Italian company including women in 1548 suggests that at that date the phenomenon already existed. By the 1560s there were established troupes in northern Italy, including actresses and even directed by actresses, playing a full range of material both comic and sentimental, probably both scripted and improvised. From the start such companies operated via an uneasy mixture, which caused constant tension, between strictly commercial organization and a post-feudal dependency on the patronage of princely rulers of the various Italian states and centres.

Meanwhile, commercial use of space for theatre performance developed first of all in Venice. As early as 1517 there had been records of *tickets being sold there for shows in private houses. Full *public theatres developed in the same city in the

1580s, as enterprises conceived by noble merchant families: rooms in their palaces, and then whole buildings, were re-designed for permanent theatre use. As the seventeenth century progressed, it was Venice which led the way for the rest of the Italian peninsula in developing venues, and promoting commercial theatre and opera, in ways which might still be recognized in the twenty-first century.   RAA

4. England

Choosing the exact dates for any period is an arbitrary exercise, and is sure to invite bickering. However, the early modern period in England is generally considered to be 1500–1700. Although changes in commerce, agriculture, architecture, law, religion, printing, demographics, literacy, artistic production, politics, natural philosophy, physics, medicine, and family life rarely develop in tandem, during the early modern period these fields—each in different throes of transition in different principalities—begin to display a legible set of patterns that continue to the present day. Jean-Christoph Agnew character-izes this period as one in which 'an identifiable market culture' emerged during the 'transition to capitalism'. The changing fi-nancial economy transformed aesthetic values as well. Com-modity exchange, credit, and cash profits increased the mobility and instability of the market process, rendering it more fluid and less marked by pre-existing class boundaries. Most historians regard the effects of nascent capitalism as key to the emergence of a middle class; but 'middle' in this context does not so much mean financially comfortable as upwardly mobile, particularly intergenerationally, due to the new possi-bilities of acquiring wealth. This sense of possibility, more than its realization, generated heightened expectations among the non-nobility and anxiety about the loss of prerogative among the aristocracy.

The up-and-coming 'new men' were often perceived as a direct threat to feudal entitlement. To this social restlessness, the Reformation added an emphasis on individual conscience, an increase in literacy among the laity, and a focus in general on the importance of fashioning selves and manipulating them as a mode of social performance. In England between 1550 and 1700 the growing participation of the non-nobility in a public and political economy heightened their visibility in the cultural marketplace. To be sure, landed gentry continued to reap the greatest benefits; English society remained firmly hierarch-ical during this time, and patriarchy based on primogeniture continued to govern social behaviour, inheritance laws, and sexual and family life. Advances in gender equality lagged far behind other developments and would continue to do so until the twentieth century: the increasing social mobility en-joyed by men was largely denied to women, who in legal status remained the chattel of fathers and husbands. However it was now possible for a self-made man such as, say, William Shake-speare to earn enough money from his labours to purchase a coat of arms for his family, leaving behind his lowly status as a glover's son.

But as Shakespeare understood so well, social mobility comes at a psychological cost. Boundaries—physical, commu-nal, social, and even cosmological—were collapsing, as William Bouwsma explains (*A Usable Past*, 1990): 'no objective system of boundaries could now supply either security or effective guid-ance.' The upheavals of early modern culture gave rise to one of the signal psychological characteristics of modernity: 'the need of the individual to adapt to unpredictable circumstances and the changing expectations of others.' The heightened emphasis on *performativity in everyday life, combined with the anxieties provoked by rapid change, helped to fuel the explosion of popu-lar interest in theatre in England during this period.

English theatre in the Middle Ages was not centralized in playhouses. Usually linked to civic and religious holidays and festivals, performances, often haphazard and cobbled together by amateurs, took place in town halls, private houses, churches, *streets, courtyards, and on temporary scaffolds erected during market fairs and *pageants. While a variety of entertainments were provided during such occasions—music, *juggling, *dan-cing, storytelling—the drama of the late fifteenth and early six-teenth century consisted mostly of *mystery, *morality, and *miracle plays (*see also* BIBLICAL PLAYS), which undertook to il-lustrate biblical episodes and dilemmas, as well as more general *allegories of religious conflicts between Good and Evil. In the later sixteenth and early seventeenth centuries, drama began to incorporate more secular material and to focus on the social and political fates of characters that were increasingly individual-ized. The highly popular *stock characters of earlier *cycles still circulated as thinly disguised representations of Vice and Virtue (Shakespeare's Richard III, *Webster's Flamineo in *The White Devil*, Marlowe's Jew of Malta, Jonson's Volpone are notable examples); but playwrights also demonstrated a thriving and, in the case of Marlowe and Shakespeare in particular, an even urgent interest in individual motivation.

As medieval patronage of private players gradually dimin-ished, the building of public theatres proliferated in London after 1576, when James *Burbage built in Shoreditch what Fran-ces Yates has called the 'prototype' of the new playhouse, the Theatre. This fuelled a spate of building, including the *Curtain; and the *Rose, built on *Bankside in 1587, started a fashion for playhouses on the south bank of the Thames. Theatres like the *Swan were followed by the most famous of all, the *Globe, where Shakespeare staged many of his plays. Building con-tinued with the *Fortune, the *Red Bull, and the *Hope, repre-senting the best known of the *public theatres, just as *Blackfriars is the best known of the *private theatres. Unlike those in Italy and France, English public playhouses were not for the most part built and financed by royalty: Burbage came from the same artisan class as Shakespeare, but financed the building of the Theatre himself. In keeping with the new and growing spirit of entrepreneurship, then, theatrical productions were aimed not at small coterie audiences but at a broad and varied public; and many if not most productions were financial successes.

Consequently, theatre companies and troupes, such as the Earl of *Leicester's Men, the Lord Chamberlain's Men (later the King's Men), as well as several *boys' companies, became profitable and highly competitive enterprises. Different companies fought to attract audiences, and competition—like all forms of free enterprise—generated ever more variegated genres, such as *revenge tragedy, *city comedy, *tragicomedy, *historical drama, pastoral drama, *Senecan drama, variations of the comedies of Terence and Plautus, and various combinations of the above. Of special interest were plays about history and court life. England's history, once the province of churchmen, court-supported propagandists, and hired chroniclers, was disseminated to the theatre audience, many of whom were illiterate. English theatre also presented cutting *satires of other aspects of the new market, and of the types of people who profited by it. Those with aspirations above their stations understood that theatricality, or 'acting the part', could help lay the foundation for upward mobility; and countless plays lampoon the affectations and ambitions of the wannabes and the parvenus. Jonson's plays are particularly virulent in their critique of the social crassness of the 'new men'.

By the late 1590s, the theatre was subject to royal *censorship and, increasingly, Puritan attack. Despite the fact that the plays frequently critiqued the perceived immorality of the growing commodity culture, the theatre was still condemned as a convenient site for whoring, gambling, and improper mingling of men and women of different classes, making it as controversial as it was popular (see ANTI-THEATRICAL POLEMIC). Nothing aroused as much Puritan indignation as the cross-dressing required in the theatre. Since all female roles were played by men and pubescent boys, androgyny was a fundamental condition of the early modern English stage; the homoeroticism and multiple sexualities it conjured were frequently thematized (see FEMALE IMPERSONATION). Rigid gender distinctions were insisted upon outside the theatre, as a function of patriarchy; but the fact that audiences so willingly embraced the 'heterosexual' relations presented to them on the stage by cross-dressed male actors suggests that early modern audiences may have recognized gender roles as fundamentally performative (see GENDER AND PERFORMANCE). If they did, they may, indirectly, have been authorized to do so by the undisputed master of gender theatricality, Queen Elizabeth, who brilliantly manipulated codes of gender in her own histrionic and rhetorical performances. Her ability to play all parts to her people seemed to inspire a fascination with the imaginative possibilities of gender-crossing in the drama of the time. But it probably also triggered a widespread backlash against the threat of individualism in women. The punishment of independent, domineering, or headstrong women, daughters, and wives is brutally violent in the tragedies, and humiliating in the comedies, throughout the period.

Thus the theatre became both the mirror and the scourge of English society—and was blamed for everything from taking the poor man's living out of his pocket to spreading the plague. The Puritans offered the greatest assault on what they perceived to be the excesses and bad examples proffered in the playhouses. Stephen *Gosson's The School of Abuse kicked off a spate of pamphleteering against the theatre that may even have been commissioned by the city fathers. Puritan Parliament and the English Civil War would bring the theatres to a close in 1642, and early modern English theatre would remain in suspended animation until the Restoration in 1660, when it would undergo an uneasy and highly censored resurrection, during which plays had to be approved both for performance and for *publication. By the time the *Master of the Revels insisted, in 1663, that even old plays enjoying a revival be 'recensored', the formidable and potentially transformative power of English theatre had been fully acknowledged. The English theatre was the indisputable media giant of its age, a showcase in which gender roles, political authority, official versions of history, and class boundaries were represented, challenged (even if only to be reinforced), and dangerously subverted. LC

5. Spain

Except in Catalonia, which kept pace with much of Europe in developing a *liturgical drama, medieval Spain had little true theatre. At the dawn of the fifteenth century, however, three Hispanic Renaissance men proved exceptionally adept at devising entertainments for aristocratic courts: Juan del *Encina at Alba (near Salamanca), Gil *Vicente in Portugal, and Bartolomé de *Torres Naharro in Italy. This remarkable first generation of dramatists had, sadly, few able successors; but the Church was now increasingly active in promoting plays for its feast days; the best that survive are 47 by Diego Sánchez de Badajoz. At the universities of Alcalá and Salamanca, moreover, Roman comedies (and vernacular imitations) were sometimes performed, and masters at the *Jesuit schools first founded in the 1540s wrote edifying plays (in Latin, mostly) for their students to enact (see UNIVERSITY AND SCHOOL DRAMA). By mid-century, however, professional companies, like one led by Lope de *Rueda, were also playing widely, and these would be rivalled for decades by visiting Italian troupes. Both of course needed venues to which they could charge admission, and when the charitable brotherhoods who ran hospitals for the poor found providing these an important source of funds, the result was the establishment, all over Spain, of permanent *corrales, which both fuelled and accompanied an upsurge in demand for drama at every level of society. That demand would determine to a large extent both the nature and the quantity of the following century's theatre. It would thwart for instance attempts by moralists to prevent either acting by women (who were no less important than men on the Spanish stage; *see* WOMEN AND PERFORMANCE); and the spread of performances (except in Lent) to almost every day of the year. By the end of the century drama was flourishing in every sizeable town, especially in Valencia, Seville, and Toledo, but above all in *Madrid, which coincidentally had been the birthplace, a year after becoming the capital in 1561, of a playwright sufficiently productive, popular, and proficient, if not to create unaided a national drama, to determine for a century both its content and its form.

The 'new comedy' (*comedia) established by Lope de Vega and his coevals is a play in three acts, each comprising about 1,000 lines of verse, mostly but not exclusively octosyllabic, with frequently changing patterns of assonance or rhyme. Its tone may be light-hearted or serious, and is often both by turns; for seventeenth-century Spaniards a rigid division between comedy and tragedy was alien to the variety of nature and human life. Some earlier writers, especially toward the end of the sixteenth century, like the Valencians Andrés Rey de Artieda (1544–1613) and Cristóbal de Virués (1550–1609), had tried the Senecan tragic style, but even they had mostly been willing to compromise or experiment, and Cervantes and Juan de la *Cueva had done so even more. The public, moreover, not only demanded increasingly a constant stream of new plays, so that playwrights could neglect no possible source of plots, but expected to see whole stories, 'from Genesis to Judgment'. Thus while unity of action was generally maintained (though multiple or parallel plots were common), *comedias* might comprise as many as twenty *scenes, and accommodate large leaps in time and place. Many, however, did not; the formula was flexible. For instance, 'cloak-and-sword' comedies, including those that featured a *figurón* (caricatured *protagonist), were usually confined to three or four days and a single city, while *comedias palatinas*, set in the faraway world of romance, were less neoclassical still. Such simply comic plays were common, but very many others (religious, mythological, more or less historical, or even journalistic) were fundamentally serious. Pure tragedies were rare, and even in these the public expected at least one clownish *gracioso*; but Golden Age dramatists were by no means precluded by their Christian faith in ultimate justice from evoking terror and pity by their depiction of human guilt and anguish.

Nor were they unconcerned, as is often suggested, with the exploration of character. Many *comedias* centre on one or more individuals very carefully portrayed. These may be types, or even archetypes, but some playwrights showed a profound understanding of motives and behaviour, and the whole-story formula permitted both complexity and development. A pervasive idea or message is often present; the best *comedias* strike a balance between story, persons, and theme. But that message is by no means always conventional or clear-cut. The

playwrights, like their public, may never have questioned the fundamental structures of their monarchical state, but they were never establishment lackeys. The theatre was the principal forum and focus for debate, and though some plays were promoted as propaganda many others reflect dissent on various issues: the conduct of government, the nature of honour, the scope of social mobility, or the social role of women. The dozens of dramatists who together wrote several thousand *comedias* always strove for originality, but inevitably their plays were broadly homogeneous. Reworkings and collaborations were common, especially as the century wore on. Considerable uniformity was imposed, moreover, by the structure of the companies that performed them. The *autor* (*actor-manager) who led each bought plays outright (expecting meaty parts for himself and his wife), and adapted them as he saw fit. Early each year he hired supporting actors for specified types of role, including above all male and female specialists as his indispensable comics. He had to value complementary skills, for every show was a whole afternoon of non-stop entertainment. The *comedia*, preceded by *music and sometimes a *prologue, might itself include songs and dances, and both intervals were filled with *farces, *jigs, or the like. In practice, though, several companies changed comparatively little, and playwrights frequently wrote with specific casts in mind.

In Madrid, only a limited number of *autores* were licensed to perform by the council of Castile, one of whose members, the Protector of Hospitals, controlled their operations. Every new text had to be submitted to his censors, and constables attended every performance to impose his regulations and keep the various sectors of the audience (especially the common women) apart. Even early in the century, the *corrales* could provide a number of mechanical effects, but their style of staging was always primarily non-illusionistic and dependent on the public's imagination. The *comedia*, replete with imagery, rhetoric, irony, and wit, perhaps made most impact via the ear, but relied too on spectators conversant with the exploitation of emblematic visual signs (especially *costumes), and with a wide range of conventions. Many plot complications, for instance, relied on transparent *disguises (especially cross-dressing by women, which always deceived all on stage) or on errors occasioned by darkness (though the stage was always sunlit). The spectators must have been aware that the play was simply play, aware that the mirror held up to nature showed a poetic distortion of life, which itself in their age was commonly described as a deceptive *dream or drama.

This 'poor' theatre, however, was increasingly invaded and eventually eclipsed by a spectacular style of staging, emanating mainly from Italy and fostered by the court. From early in the century, and above all in the reign of Philip IV, royalty and the nobility participated far more than before in the promotion of drama. Their palaces, especially the Alcázar, saw extremely frequent command performances by the professional companies, and newly commissioned productions began to proliferate. Significantly, the scenery for one of three plays performed by courtiers at Aranjuez in 1622–3 was designed by an Italian engineer, and in 1627 another, Cosimo Lotti, astonished Spain with the hidden *lighting, perspective settings, and transformation scenes he had devised for its first attempt at opera, *La selva confusa* (*The Loveless Forest*). Lope de Vega, as the librettist, was forced to confess that such effects made 'the ears defer to the eyes'. Many further productions by Lotti consolidated the triumph of spectacle in the works performed at an increasingly spectacular court; especially elaborate, for example, were his stagings of two mythological plays by Calderón (1635–6). More importantly still, he planned the state-of-the-art *Coliseo that completed in 1640 the new palace of the Retiro, which itself had been created far less as a royal retreat than as the performance space for a show in which the Planet King was unquestionably the star.

The following decade, during most of which wars and royal mourning kept the theatres closed, was crucial in this transition. At its end, court theatre revived with the arrival of another Italian designer, Baccio del Bianco, who in 1652–3 staged extremely lavish productions, full of transformations and aerial effects, of two more Calderón plays. The popular *corrales*, by contrast, would never fully recover, especially since the Coliseo, which in addition to its spectaculars could accommodate simpler plays, also admitted the paying public, and always required the professionals to give its demands priority. The Retiro, however, was not the only palace to house elaborate productions in which music, song, and ballet were playing an increasingly prominent part. Others, apart from the refurbished Alcázar, were those at El Escorial, El Pardo, and La Zarzuela. The last gave its name to a combination of spoken dialogue, *recitative, and arias (the *zarzuela), but some works were fully-fledged operas, like *La púrpura de la rosa* (*The Purple of the Rose*, 1660). The librettist, as for many such total theatre productions, was Calderón; by mid-century the undisputed master of the *comedia*, he would continue for three decades to ride with no less success the tide of illusionistic display that had swamped it.

VFD

6. France

In France the years 1550 and 1650 are convenient bookends for the transition between 'medieval' and 'modern'. Theatre transformed from religious to secular, from amateur to professional, from nomadic to established. The sixteenth century saw the beginnings of literary drama in France and the development of a theoretical discourse. The early seventeenth century was characterized by the recognition of dramatic genres as legitimate forms of literary expression. Physical theatres and physical production also changed in response to the literalness of neoclassical theories of drama about time and place and to the importation of Italian scenic practices.

Although performance of plays with religious subject matter continued in the provinces throughout the sixteenth century, the conflict between Catholics and Huguenots that ravaged the country motivated other towns to follow the lead of Paris and abolish a possible source of controversy. The Parlement of Paris, in 1548, forbade any further performance of religious drama by the *Confrérie de la Passion, the organization charged with the production of *mystères* (*see* MYSTERIES) in Paris, while granting in exchange a monopoly of secular theatrical production. Any actors who proposed to play in the capital were obliged either to rent the Confrérie's newly built theatre, the *Hôtel de Bourgogne, or to pay a fine.

Itinerant troupes of farceurs roamed France from at least the fourteenth century, but in the 1540s actors began to band together in legal associations. Six men signed a contract at Chartres in 1549, joining together to 'see the country and perform farces, moralities, and other shows'. Another agreement of the same year obliged Robert d'Escosse to assist in the performance of histories, moralities, and farces. Also of interest is a contract signed at Bourges in 1545 engaging a woman, Marie Ferré, to play 'antiquailles' of Rome. Only a few women had participated in the performance of religious plays, but by the end of the sixteenth century many professional troupes included women on stage.

Literary genres gained favour in the second half of the sixteenth century with the educated elite. Theatres in the schools (*see* UNIVERSITY AND SCHOOL DRAMA) produced Roman comedies as well as neo-Latin plays inspired by Roman models but seasoned with Christian moralizing and religious politics. At the same time, French humanists began to study Latin theoretical writings on drama. Although many of the poets who constituted the Pléiade experimented with drama, Étienne *Jodelle is credited with the revival of classically based tragedy in France. His *Cléopâtre captive* was performed at court and at the Collège de Boncourt in Paris in 1553. The French court also introduced the Italian style of tragedy with a production of a translation of Trissino's *Sophonisba* in 1556.

The nascent literary drama and the nascent professional troupes should have found each other before the last decade of the sixteenth century, but the continuing crisis of the Wars of Religion, the monopoly of the Confrérie de la Passion in Paris, and the royal preference for the Italian *commedia dell'arte* retarded the development of established professional theatre. The most illustrious playwright of the century, Robert *Garnier, published seven tragedies and one *tragicomedy between 1568 and 1583. His plays were frequently republished and widely imitated but were produced only by amateurs, privately or in the schools, until late in the century. Tragedy was not seen at court after the accident that killed Henri II in 1559. His superstitious wife, Catherine de Médicis, feared that the performance of *Sophonisba* had somehow predestined the catastrophe. The Valois monarchs preferred ballet to theatre; when actors were summoned to court they were usually brought from Italy. The emerging professional French players were left to fill with farces and moralities the gap caused by the prohibition of religious plays. Only gradually did professionals adopt the literary repertory, but once a play was in print nothing prevented its performance by anyone, and by the end of the century troupes were performing plays by Jodelle and Garnier.

The first professional playwright in France was Alexandre *Hardy, who contracted with various itinerant troupes to provide them with new plays. His career began about 1595 and by 1628, according to Hardy himself, he had written 600 plays. The most celebrated and long-lived of the troupes that employed him was that of Valleran *Le Conte, also known as the *Comédiens du Roi. Valleran is first heard of in Bordeaux in 1592, co-starring in tragedies and tragicomedies with a beautiful actress. In 1599 he rented the Hôtel de Bourgogne, establishing the pattern that endured for the next 30 years as troupes formed and reformed, playing briefly in Paris, then roving the provinces.

The French provincial theatre is known largely through contracts of association, rental agreements, and town records. Since purpose-built theatres did not exist outside Paris, most performances took place on platforms set up on trestles or barrels, often within a *jeu de paume* (covered *tennis court) or a room in the town hall, although provincial towns did not always welcome actors. After Louis XIII became patron of the royal troupes, other nobles offered protection and occasionally subventions, but in the early period only the Prince de Condé appears to have given a troupe the right to use his name. Nonetheless the actors persisted, and when all the information about provincial performance in the reigns of Henri IV, Louis XIII, and Louis XIV is mapped, the result shows that, with the exception of the Massif Central, actors found their way to every corner of France. After 1630, however, the Paris theatres became dominant.

In December 1629, with the intervention of Louis XIII, the Confrérie de la Passion lost the right to rent its theatre to itinerant companies and was directed to lease it to the Comédiens du Roi. At almost the same time, another troupe opened a second theatre at the Jeu de Paume de Berthaud. Paris finally had not one but two established theatres. The Comédiens du Roi, at odds with their former poet Hardy, made a new arrangement with the promising Jean *Rotrou, while the other company presented the first play of a young poet from Rouen, Pierre *Corneille. After several moves, this troupe settled into the Jeu de Paume du Marais and became known as the Théâtre du *Marais.

A typical roster of actors in the 1630s would include six or seven men and four or five women. While Hardy's plays include only a few roles for women, the new generation of playwrights could feature actresses. Women were especially strong at the Marais, where Mlle Villiers became the first female star of the French theatre, playing Chimène in Corneille's *Le Cid*. At the Hôtel de Bourgogne, a change in the composition of the troupe signalled a new repertory. At the beginning of the decade, the troupe relied heavily on three elderly farceurs: *Gros-Guillaume, *Gaultier-Garguille, and *Turlupin. Four years later, all were dead, and the troupe was attracting a more refined *audience with tragedies and society comedies. The 1630s also saw the beginnings of state control of the newly established Paris theatres when the King—who granted royal subventions in 1635—and his cardinal-minister *Richelieu began to wield both the stick and the carrot, and the actors, accustomed to governing what *Chappuzeau called their 'small republics', found they had traded away some of their freedom. Six actors were forcibly transferred by the King from the Marais to the Hôtel, while the Cardinal found ways to discourage baroque tragicomedy, based, like Corneille's *Le Cid*, on Spanish models, and encourage drama that was regular and French. Richelieu also commissioned a theatre in 1641 at his Palais Cardinal in the modern style, suited for perspective scenery, later to be known as the Théâtre du *Palais Royal.

As late as 1634 the Hôtel de Bourgogne still performed plays with multiple settings in the medieval style of simultaneous staging. As theorists insisted on the unities of time and place, however, most plays began to require a single setting, and the taste of the moment wanted that setting to be executed in perspective. The dilapidated Hôtel de Bourgogne and the converted tennis court in the Marais no longer suited either the new French drama or the elite Paris audience. The Marais was rebuilt after a fire in 1644 with new boxes and provisions for scenes and machines, while the Hôtel was remodelled in 1647 with 38 boxes instead of 12 and a new stage that was higher, deeper, wider, and raked to enhance the perspective.

By the middle of the seventeenth century, then, the characteristics of the 'classical' French theatre were in place, exhibited so magnificently by *Racine in the 1660s and beyond. To assume, however, that French theatre in the second half of the seventeenth century consisted merely of approved comedies and tragedies written in *verse and declaimed in a pretentious style by actors lined up in front of a single setting would be a mistake. Farce was played for years with great success by an Italian *commedia dell'arte* troupe at the *Comédie Italienne, also subvented by the King, and was reintroduced into the French repertory by Molière. Acting style was a matter of controversy. Scenic spectacle was so popular with the Paris audience that it became the salvation of several troupes. Subventions were granted, to be sure, on the assumption that the actors would support the royal agenda, but subventions were inadequate and could be revoked. The actors had also to be responsive to the pressures of the marketplace. Their struggle for balance between the opposing powers of patronage and commerce became the continuing story of French theatre until the revolution.

VS

GENERAL

AGNEW, JEAN-CHRISTOPH, *Worlds Apart: the market and the theatre in Anglo-American thought, 1550–1750* (Cambridge, 1986)

HILL, CHRISTOPHER, *The Century of Revolution, 1603–1714* (New York, 1980)

GRADY, HUGH (ed.), *Shakespeare and Modernity: early modern to millennium* (London, 2000)

ITALY

PIERI, MARZIA, *La nascita del teatro moderno in Italia tra XV e XVI secolo* (Turin, 1989)

PIRROTTA, NINO, *Music and Theatre from Poliziano to Monteverdi*, trans. K. Eales (Cambridge, 1982)

ZORZI, LODOVICO, *Il teatro e la città* (Turin, 1977)

ENGLAND

GURR, ANDREW, *Playgoing in Shakespeare's London* (Cambridge, 1987)

—— *The Shakespearian Playing Companies* (Cambridge, 1996)

THOMSON, PETER, *Shakespeare's Professional Career* (Cambridge, 1992)

YATES, FRANCES A., *Theatre of the World* (Chicago, 1969)

SPAIN

ARELLANO, IGNACIO, *Historia del teatro español del siglo XVII* (Madrid, 1995)

McKENDRICK, MELVEENA, *Theatre in Spain 1490–1700* (Cambridge, 1989)

RUANO DE LA HAZA, J. M., and ALLEN, JOHN J., *Los teatros comerciales del siglo XVII y la escenificación de la comedia* (Madrid, 1994)

FRANCE

HAZARD, MADELEINE, *Le Théâtre en France au XVIe siècle* (Paris, 1980)

HOWARTH, WILLIAM D. (ed.), *French Theatre in the Neoclassical Era, 1550–1789* (Cambridge, 1997)

EAST WEST PLAYERS

The first *Asian American theatre company in the United States. Founded in 1965 to showcase the theatrical talents of Asian Pacific Americans, the company now features the work of some 600 ethnically diverse artists each year. To date it has produced over 100 plays and musicals featuring Asian-American cast members. Artists associated with East West Players include Mako, John Lone, B. D. Wong, David Henry *Hwang, Frank *Chin, Chay Yew, Philip Kan *Gotanda, Rick Shiomi, Wakako Yamauchi, Amy Hill, Nobu McCarthy, Lauren Tom, Tsai Chin, and Nancy Kwan. In 1997 East West Players moved into the David Henry Hwang Theatre, a newly renovated space located in the Little Tokyo area of *Los Angeles.   JSM

EBB, FRED *See* KANDER, JOHN.

ECCENTRISM

A brainchild of the *St Petersburg *avant-garde, who in July 1922 published 'The Eccentric Manifesto'. Proclaiming that they stood for 'art without a capital letter, a pedestal or a fig leaf', they declared in favour of 'the present', denoted by 'Factories, Workshops, Dockyards', rather than 'Museums, Temples and Libraries'. Eccentrism was to be 'hyperbolically crude, stupendous, nerve-wracking, openly utilitarian, mechanically-precise, momentary, rapid', and sought to celebrate 'The Theatre of Chance' and 'Bullshit!' Their art was to be like 'a tireless ram shattering the high walls of habit and dogma' favouring the 'Americanization of the Theatre' and 'a cinema of demystification'. In fact, the movement's impact was felt largely in *film, via the 'Factory of the Eccentric Actor' (FEKS), founded by the movement's leading lights, Grigory Kozinstev and Leonid Trauberg, who went on to make avant-garde films during the 1920s. The impact of their iconoclasm was also felt at *Foregger's 'Mastfor' Workshop, in *Eisenstein's 'eccentric' productions for *Proletkult, and in his film *Strike* (1924), as well as in *Terentiev's ostentatiously outrageous productions of Russian classic plays in the mid-1920s. *See also* FUTURISM.

NW

ECHEGARAY, JOSÉ (1832–1916)

Spanish playwright, mathematician, and politician. His plays ranged from the effective social drama *The Great Galeoto* (1881) to neo-*romantic works with excessive passions. *Ibsen's *Brand* was an influence on his *Madman or Saint* (1876), and *The Son of Don Juan* (1892) echoed the theme of *Ghosts* in a Spanish setting. Although his plays are seldom revived, he enjoyed immense esteem in Spain for three decades and was popular throughout Europe. In 1904, in the twilight of his career, he became the first dramatist to receive the Nobel Prize for Literature, an *award that inspired protests in Spain.   MPH

ECKENBERG, JOHANN CARL (1685–1748)

German *manager. Eckenberg began his career as an *acrobat and strongman with itinerant troupes. He arrived in *Berlin in 1717 and impressed Friedrich I, who permitted him to perform throughout Prussia. He also *toured extensively, visiting Königsberg, Denmark, Sweden, and *Vienna in the 1720s. Having settled in Berlin in 1731, he dominated theatre there on and off until 1741. More impresario than man of the theatre, Eckenberg staged acrobatics, *puppet theatre, and *ballet, as well as *farces. He lost his dominant position in 1742 to J. F. *Schönemann.   CBB

ÉCOLE WILLIAM PONTY

College founded in 1903 in Senegal, designed to train an elite cadre of colonial subjects for service in teaching and administration for what was then known as the Federation of French West African countries (AOF). It also became the nursery for theatre, producing the first wave of francophone *African

413

playwrights. An innovation in the curriculum asked students to write down *folkloric material (myths, social customs, rites) collected as a summer vacation assignment. Originally intended to improve the students' French writing skills, the exercise soon expanded by dramatizing the best compositions and performing them during school events. The earliest written dramatic piece in French by an African, the anonymous *La Dernière Entrevue de Béhanzin et de Bayol* (1933), was the first product. A significant number of student pieces followed, all anonymous, including *Un mariage au Dahomey* (1934), *Entrevue de Samory et du Capitaine Péroz* (1936), and *Un mariage chez les Mandégnis* (1937). The high point of theatrical life in the college was the Fête d'Art Indigène, an annual event from 1935, and attended by the Governor-General of AOF and other French colonial officials. The highly successful 1937 plays, *Les Prétendants rivaux* and *Sokamé*, represented AOF's contribution later that year to the International Exhibition in *Paris. A reform of its curriculum in 1945 ended significant theatrical activity at the École William Ponty.　　　JCM

EDGAR, DAVID (1947–)

English playwright, writer for *radio, *film and *television. Edgar grew up in Birmingham, where he continues to live. He started as a journalist, and became part of the generation of socialist playwrights who emerged in the 1960s. He continues to write political columns and book reviews for various publications, and for ten years he ran an MA course in playwriting at Birmingham University (1989–99). His best-known work is an adaptation of *Nicholas Nickleby* (1980) for the *Royal Shakespeare Company, directed by Trevor *Nunn. Many of his plays have been large-scale epics, seeking to capture a wedge of history or a socio-political contradiction in its unfolding. *Destiny* (1976), *Maydays* (1983), *The Shape of the Table* (1990), and *Pentecost* (1994) are representative. Working with smaller casts and more intense psychological scenes, *The Jail Diary of Albie Sachs* (1978), *Mary Barnes* (1978), and *That Summer* (1987) nevertheless take up critical *political questions—from apartheid in South Africa, to R. D. Laing's controversial treatments for schizophrenia, to the 1984–5 miners' strike. In 2000, his adaptation of Gitta Sereny's book on Albert Speer opened at the Royal *National Theatre, also directed by Nunn. *Albert Speer* featured more than 25 actors and an elaborate *multimedia setting, showing that Edgar's dramatic imagination remains epic in scope and style. He has also published several books of essays and collections including *The Second Time as Farce* (1988) and *State of Play* (1999). Perhaps because he has trained many playwrights in his course, he is exceptionally cogent in his understanding of *dramaturgical structures and their relationship to both staging and history.　　　JGR

EDINBURGH

Little regular public theatrical activity occurred in the capital of Scotland before the eighteenth Century. David *Lindsay's *A Satire of the Three Estates* was performed on Calton Hill in 1554, and in the late sixteenth century the court witnessed various *masques. Visits by 'Inglis comedians' in 1593 and 1599 provoked fierce criticism by the Kirk, setting the tone for two centuries following the removal of the Scottish court to London in 1603. The Tennis Court Theatre at Holyrood House hosted occasional productions from the 1660s onwards, including *Marciano* (1663), a *tragicomedy by Edinburgh lawyer William Clark, and a visiting English company's *Macbeth* in 1672. The Presbytery issued decrees against a company performing *Macbeth* and *The Beaux' Stratagem* in 1715 and against Anthony *Aston's activities in Skinners' Hall during 1726–8. Productions by the Edinburgh Players between 1730 and 1736 included Allan Ramsay's *pastoral *The Gentle Shepherd*, but their attempt to establish a theatre in Carruber's Close was thwarted by the 1737 *Licensing Act.

The Act was subsequently evaded by advertising free theatrical performances after concerts, as Sarah Ward did at Canongate Concert Hall, which in 1747 became the city's first purpose-built theatre. The venue for John *Home's controversial *tragedy *Douglas* (1756), it was refitted as the Theatre Royal in 1767. The patent transferred to a new *Theatre Royal in Shakespeare Square in 1769. Under *managers including Stephen *Kemble, Henry Siddons, and W. H. Murray, this was the leading Edinburgh theatre for almost a century, with the Circus (1793, renamed the Adelphi in 1830) being its main rival. Sarah *Siddons and John Philip *Kemble played there and it championed the work of Scots such as Joanna Baillie and Walter Scott, adaptations of whose novels formed the core of a 'national' drama in nineteenth-century Scotland. Robert Wyndham ran it from 1853 to 1859, employing Henry *Irving as leading juvenile. With J. B. Howard he opened the Royal Lyceum in 1883, laying foundations for the Howard and Wyndham chain of theatres. The Moss Empires chain also originated in Edinburgh; having first acquired a *music hall in 1877, Edward Moss opened the Empire Palace in 1892 (a Frank Matcham building, which underwent reconstruction in 1994 and reopened as the Festival Theatre, offering one of the largest stages in Britain for *dance and lyric theatre).

During the late nineteenth and early twentieth centuries theatres such as the Lyceum, the Kings, and the Playhouse mostly received *touring productions, although repertory seasons of classics, modern drama, and *comedy were presented from 1933 to 1955, first by Jevon Brandon-Thomas and then by Wilson Barrett (grandson of the Victorian *actor-manager Wilson *Barrett). In 1953 the Gateway opened as a year-round repertory theatre, doing much to encourage Scottish writing and acting. The Gateway was superseded by the Civic Theatre

Company which took over the Royal Lyceum in 1965. Their work has been complemented by the more experimental offerings of the *Traverse Theatre, founded in 1963, and Theatre Workshop, which since 1965 has played a strong role in developing community theatre in the city. Since 1947, for three weeks in August the city hosts the *Edinburgh International Festival and its accompanying Fringe Festival, when almost every public building is turned into a venue for thousands of performances.   GJG

EDINBURGH INTERNATIONAL FESTIVAL

One of the world's leading arts *festivals, held annually in the Scottish capital. For three weeks in August *Edinburgh hosts a selection of the best international theatre, *opera, *dance, orchestral and other music in the city's major theatres and concert halls and other prestige venues. The festival was founded in 1947 as a symbol of post-war European reconciliation, a parallel to the *Avignon Festival of the same year. It aimed to present a programme of work that would be representative of the highest possible artistic standards, presented by the foremost artists in the world. As with many international events the organizers have to balance the needs of Scottish *audiences with those of the significant tourist market drawn to the festival. Significant Scottish companies and artists that have been featured include the *Glasgow *Citizens' Theatre, Scottish Opera, and *Traverse Theatre. The Festival is programmed by an *artistic director, and artists and companies perform on invitation. Since the founder, Rudolf Bing, there have been seven directors, Sir Ian Hunter (1950–5), Robert Ponsonby (1956–60), Lord Harewood (1961–5), Peter Diamand (1966–78), John Drummond (1979–83), Frank *Dunlop (1984–91), and Brian McMaster (from 1992).

From its beginnings the festival also attracted to the city many more *amateur and professional groups than those invited to the official events. It was not long before this peripheral activity was formalized as the Edinburgh Festival Fringe Society, and now many hundreds of shows are presented in its programme. Although there is a director, any company or individual who wants to perform, can locate a venue, and pay the appropriate fee can find a spot on the fringe. The range of work presented in this context is extraordinarily wide, from prestige productions by leading companies to the opportunistic one-off, from the work of established talent to the eclectic and the bizarre. A criticism of the contemporary fringe has been the proliferation of stand-up comedy in its schedule—Edinburgh is now an event of huge significance for this sector—though this has proved important for showcasing emerging performers. The fringe in turn has spawned a series of satellite festivals, including the Military Tattoo, the International *Film Festival,

the Book Festival, and the Jazz and Blues Festival. Against this backdrop the 'festival city' has capitalized on its reputation with Edinburgh's Hogmanay, the Edinburgh Science Festival, and the Scottish International Children's Festival benefiting from association with the August events.   AS

EDUCATIONAL THEATRE

While all theatre might be construed to be 'educational' in the broadest sense (just as many have claimed that all theatre is *political), the term is generally used (especially in Britain) to encompass three specific dvelopments.

1. *Theatre-in-education. TIE began in England at the Belgrade Theatre, Coventry, in 1965, when a team of 'actor-teachers' was established to take work into local schools, combining performance and participatory drama techniques. Funded by a partnership of local authority and the theatre, the team became the first of a series of such groups to be set up at various theatres across the country, some becoming independent companies in their own right, and the TIE movement went on to play an influential part in the development of progressive education, *community theatre, and theatre for *youth in Britain. TIE has spread widely beyond the UK, evolving in diverse ways in response to differing cultural needs. Companies such as TEAM in *Dublin, Graffiti in Cork, Arts in Action in Trinidad, and the Creative Arts Team in *New York have established significant reputations beyond their own shores.

2. *Theatre in health education*, a branch of TIE that emerged during the 1990s in direct response to the growing need for innovative approaches to educating young people in matters of sexual health, AIDS awareness, and drug abuse. The formats are similar to TIE programmes (for instance a play followed by interactive workshop) but the funding normally comes from health promotion agencies and the work must meet specific briefs and criteria. The best work tries to offer young people a rich dramatic experience rather than merely a vehicle for an all-too-predictable message.

3. *Theatre in museums*. During the last two decades of the twentieth century, as directors of museums and heritage sites endeavoured to find new and more appealing ways to interpret their collections, historic locations, and reconstructions, the use of theatre, TIE techniques and 'first-person interpretation', or *costumed role play, has gained increasing popularity. Notable examples are the extensive use of first-person interpretation at Colonial Williamsburg and Plimoth Plantation (USA), theatre-in-education programmes produced by the National Trust (UK), cameo performances presented as a regular feature of daily programming at *London's Science Museum, the Royal Armouries in Leeds, the Science Museum of Minnesota, and a diverse array of site-specific performances at historic locations across Europe, from battle re-enactments to the intensive role-play days for schoolchildren

in the nineteenth-century Apprentice House at Quarry Bank Mill in Cheshire.

A further term, coined in the 1990s, applied theatre, denotes a closely related, overlapping field to educational theatre. It encompasses techniques which, while having their own artistic validity, are deployed to meet the requirements of agencies or organizations that lie outside conventional theatre, serving social agendas such as education, the rehabilitation of prisoners, social inclusion, and the empowerment of marginalized communities (youth at risk, inner-city housing estates, the rural poor, street children). While the term is often used to include TIE, theatre in museums, and theatre in health education, applied theatre has become particularly associated with three additional activities.

1. *Theatre in prisons.* Work in this area includes interactive drama workshops conducted with prisoners, probation groups, or at-risk youth over a number of days or weeks, culminating in the presentation of a show *devised and performed by the participants; and the presentation by professional companies of plays with direct or indirect relevance to the *audience's lives. Specialist companies and facilitating organizations include: Geese Theatre (founded in the USA in 1980 but with branch companies now in a number of other countries, including the UK and Romania); Clean Break (a women's theatre company for prisoners and ex-offenders, London); and the TIPP (Theatre in Prisons and Probation) Centre, *Manchester. Notable work on an occasional basis has been done by the outreach units of professional theatres such as the *Royal Shakespeare Company; and Timberlake *Wertenbaker's play *Our Country's Good* was inspired in part by the *Royal Court Theatre's activities in prisons.

2. *Theatre for *development*, meaning the use of theatre in the developing world to convey information and promote awareness of health and other issues to do with improving the condition of impoverished or disadvantaged communities, funded by either government or non-governmental organizations. The theatre of the *oppressed techniques developed by Augusto *Boal, such as forum theatre, are commonly employed.

3. *Outreach theatre.* A term much used in the USA, outreach refers chiefly to performances or workshops by building-based companies taken to audiences for whom theatre is inaccessible, beyond their financial means, or outside their normal social horizons.

In the USA, 'educational theatre' is often extended to include theatre for *youth and other forms of dramatic activity with young people inside and outside the school curriculum, involving training in theatre skills and the production of school plays. In many other countries, especially in mainland Europe where the tradition of professional theatre for children is strong, the term 'educational theatre' does not translate well, having connotations for many directors and actors of an infer-

ior form, compromised by a supposed requirement to teach. Since good theatre for children will of itself be educational (for instance in inducting children into the classics, stimulating and enriching their imaginations, widening their horizons, challenging preconceptions in its tackling of social problems), it is argued that education does not, and should not, have to be the primary goal. ARJ

JACKSON, TONY (ed.), *Learning through Theatre: new perspectives on theatre in education* (London, 1993)

SCHUTZMAN, M., and COHEN-CRUZ, J. (eds.), *Playing Boal: theatre, therapy, activism* (London, 1994)

THOMPSON, JAMES (ed.), *Prison Theatre: perspectives and practices* (London, 1998)

EDWARDES, GEORGE (1852–1915)

English *manager, *producer, director, and impresario. Born of an Irish father and English mother, Edwardes began his *London career in 1878 when Richard *D'Oyly Carte hired him as *box-office manager for the *Gilbert and *Sullivan *operettas. In 1881 he became manager of the new *Savoy Theatre, and in 1885 John *Hollingshead, who ran the *Gaiety Theatre, hired him as co-manager; a year later Edwardes took control. For several years he continued to stage popular *burlesques that featured Nellie *Farren, Edward Terry, Kate *Vaughan, Edward Royce, and Fred *Leslie. He also produced a *variety show at the Empire Theatre. With *A Gaiety Girl* (1893), he developed a new kind of *musical comedy that came to dominate the London stage for two decades. Edwardes—called the 'Gov'nor' by his associates—oversaw an empire of writers, composers, designers, musicians, performers, and several hundred staff members who helped him to produce an almost unbroken string of *long-running musicals. Expanding beyond the Gaiety Theatre, which featured the alluring 'Gaiety Girls' in fashionable *costumes, he began to use Daly's Theatre in 1895, purchasing it in 1899 when Augustin *Daly died. In 1903 he opened a new Gaiety Theatre, with King Edward VII and Queen Alexandra in attendance. Sometimes Edwardes had to lease or purchase a third, fourth, or fifth *playhouse to accommodate new shows or the transfer of long-running ones. Throughout this period his productions *toured Britain, the USA, Canada, Australia, South Africa, and elsewhere in the British Empire. Among his most successful shows were *An Artist's Model* (1895), *The Geisha* (1896), *San Toy* (1899), *A Country Girl* (1902), *The Cingalee* (1904), and *The Quaker Girl* (1910). His star performers included Marie *Tempest, Seymour *Hicks, Ellaline Terriss, Ada Reeve, and the beloved Gertie Millar. TP

EDWARDS, GALE (1954–)

Australian director. Edwards is known for her energy, her bold, unapologetic, and challenging interpretations of the classics, and her work on musicals, particularly those of Andrew *Lloyd Webber for whom she has directed revivals of *Aspects of Love* (1992), *Jesus Christ Superstar* (1996), and *Whistle down the Wind* (1998). Edwards's international career took off after working as Trevor *Nunn's associate director on the Australian production of *Les Misérables* in 1987. Her directing at the *Royal Shakespeare Company includes a controversial *Taming of the Shrew* (1995), which had a strong *feminist bite at the end, and critically acclaimed productions of *Don Carlos* (1999) and *The White Devil* (1996, redirected for the *Sydney 2000 Olympic Arts Festival). Edwards stresses clear storytelling and thrives in big spaces, filling large stages confidently and spectacularly, particularly when working with designer Peter J. Davison. Her use of violence onstage is also uncompromising, particularly notable in *The White Devil* and in a savage and critically acclaimed *Coriolanus* for the Sydney Theatre Company (1993).

EJS

EDWARDS, HILTON (1903–82)

English actor and director. After seasons with Charles Doran and the *Old Vic, Edwards met Micheál *MacLíammóir in 1927, with whom he established the *Gate Theatre, *Dublin, a year later. He was a full-blooded, energetic performer with a studied concentration on stage that nicely offset his partner's romantic fervour. Edwards, a remarkably inventive director, took full advantage of current international innovations in *expressionist and presentational techniques of staging to bring a hugely diverse repertoire, classical and modern, to Ireland. This ensured that the Gate became a leading experimental art theatre, staging the best of new continental and American drama alongside works by Irish playwrights (Denis *Johnston, Mary Manning, Maura Laverty) who favoured non-*naturalistic *dramaturgy. Edwards vividly described his productions and *rehearsal techniques in his autobiography *The Mantle of Harlequin* (1958). He excelled at establishing a precise dynamic rhythm for a production, choreographed crowd scenes to achieve ensemble sequences of great power, and placed his actors spatially within a design scheme to achieve effects of *total theatre unique in Irish practice.

RAC

EFFENDI, RUSTAM (1903–79)

Indonesian playwright, whose *Bebasari* (1926) was the first Indonesian scripted drama. Dutch educated, he learned that drama in Europe could express *political ideas, then took the kidnapping of Sita in the *Ramayana* for his theme. The title character Bebasari ('sweet freedom', that is, *Indonesia) is a princess held captive by the demon Rawana (the Dutch), and is released by Bujangga (Indonesian youth). The *text used the emergent language of Indonesian at a time when writing in what was a merchants' argot was considered a revolutionary

act; Effendi and other nationalists abandoned ethnic languages to argue for a politically and linguistically unified nation-state. Performance was blocked by the Dutch and the self-published play was banned, but Effendi's model of political activism set the course for modern Indonesian drama.

KFo

EFOUI, KOSSI (1962–   )

Togolese dramatist. An anti-conformist playwright, Efoui gained public attention with his plays *Le Carrefour* (*The Crossroad*, 1989) and *Récupération* (1993). He uses his work as a weapon in the struggle for democracy, dramatizing issues of liberty and human rights. His plays are notable for subtle use of the technique of *mise en abyme*, in which *characters engage in joyous and profuse discussions about the theatre (*see* METATHEATRE).

SA trans. JCM

EFREMOV, OLEG (1927–2000)

Soviet/Russian actor and director. Efremov began as an actor during the early 1950s at the Central Children's Theatre, and soon became the prototype of the rebel hero of the 1960s, both through his roles and through his activity as the founder of the *Sovremennik Theatre in *Moscow (1957). As a director of that brilliant company he combined stylized or abstract sets with grounded and *realistic performances in the *Stanislavsky tradition, as in *Rozov's *Alive Forever* (1956, 1961), *Volodin's *Five Evenings* (1959), and *Shatrov's *Bolsheviks* (1967). In 1970 he accepted the most prestigious position in Russian theatre: chief *artistic director of the *Moscow Art Theatre. The MAT had ossified after 30 years without genuine artistic leadership. Efremov faced a huge challenge, which he surmounted by introducing the work of young dramatists which addressed the concerns and conflicts of contemporary *audiences. His main interest as a director lay with ethics and the individual conscience. He was the first to offer successful interpretations of the complex plays of Aleksandr *Vampilov: *The Duck Hunt* (1979) remains a landmark for the subtle investigation of the *hero's psychology. His interpretations of *Uncle Vanya* (1985) and *The Three Sisters* (1997) set new standards for staging *Chekhov with Stanislavsky's method. Alongside his work as a stage actor and director, Efremov played numerous roles in *film.

BB

EFROS, ANATOLY (1925–87)

Soviet/Russian director. Efros graduated from the State Institute of Theatre in 1950 and joined Maria *Knebel at the Central Children's Theatre, *Moscow, in 1954, where he excelled with a production of Viktor *Rozov's *In Search of Happiness* (1957). In 1963 he was invited to head the Theatre of the Lenin Komsomol, where he created a repertoire largely based on contemporary drama. In the 1960s he provoked political controversy with a number of productions, including Edvard *Radzinsky's *104 Pages about Love* (1964) and *A Film Is Being Shot* (1965), criticized by the *censoring body for their sexual explicitness. *Arbuzov's *My Poor Marat* (1965), placing love above duty, did not please the authorities either. Serious objections were also levelled at Efros's interpretations of *Chekhov: *The Seagull* (1966) and *The Three Sisters* (1967) were condemned as unorthodox in that they saw Chekhov as a precursor of the theatre of the *absurd. Efros was sacked from the Lenin Komsomol Theatre and transferred to an inferior post at the Malaya Bronnaya Theatre, where he staged classical plays, enhancing the tragic dimensions in comic *texts (such as *Gogol's *The Marriage*). Efros developed a method of structural analysis to externalize *character psychology and a concept of stage movement that made inner psychological changes visible (psychophysics). In 1984 he was appointed chief *artistic director of the *Taganka Theatre after *Lyubimov had been exiled. Efros had to face an ensemble only partly willing to cooperate, while trying to preserve his own style with productions such as *Gorky's *Lower Depths* and continuing Lyubimov's device of prose adaptations. He retained this post until his death.   BB

EGURZA, TITO (c.1945–)

Argentinian designer who has designed nearly 100 productions since 1975, including some landmark stagings. His other career as an architect is evident in his all-encompassing *scenography. *Marathon* (1980) and *Hopscotch* (1994, both directed by Jaime *Kogan), refashioned the stage and *auditorium and seemed to enter into dialogue with the playtext itself. Egurza has directed the remodelling of several *Buenos Aires theatres, including the Teatro del Pueblo and the Payró.   JGJ

EGYPTIAN PERFORMANCE *See* ORIGINS OF THEATRE.

EISENSTEIN, SERGEI (1898–1948)

Russian/Soviet stage and *film director and designer. He began his career with travelling theatre groups during the Civil War before joining *Proletkult in 1920, where he designed and part-directed a version of Jack London's *The Mexican*. He then moved to *Foregger's Workshop, where he experimented in *music hall and *circus techniques before becoming assistant to *Meyerhold at the latter's Moscow State Directors' Workshop. In 1922 he assumed *artistic directorship of the Proletkult Theatre and staged a famous *avant-garde production of *Ostrovsky's *Na vsyakogo mudretsa dovol'no prostoty* (*Wise Man*) as a '*montage of attractions', breaking the play down into episodes staged as turns in a circus ring with actors dressed as *clowns, and incorporating *acrobatic stunts and a high-wire act. There followed productions of two works by Sergei *Tretyakov: his 'agit

guignol' *Are You Listening, Moscow?!* (1923) and his *melodrama *Gas Masks*, given six performances in a *Moscow gasworks in 1924. Eisenstein also planned productions of *Shaw's *Heartbreak House*, *Tieck's *Puss in Boots*, a dramatized version of Zamyatin's dystopian novel *We*, and a cubist *Macbeth*, all to his own designs. His rejection by the Proletkultists caused him 'to drop out of the theatre into the cinema', as he put it. His first film, *Strike* (1924), put the theories advanced in his 1924 essay 'Montage of Attractions' into cinematic practice and also revealed his debt to Meyerhold's acting theories of *biomechanics. Throughout his career, Eisenstein remained devoted to Meyerhold and during the period of Meyerhold's suppression as a 'non-person' helped to store and preserve his archive secretly. Eisenstein held classes in *acting and film directing during the 1930s; among the applicants was Samuel *Beckett, who apparently received no reply. Eisenstein also directed *Wagner's *opera *The Valkyrie* (1940).   NW

EKHOF, KONRAD (1720–78)

German actor. One of the most respected performers of the mid-eighteenth century, Ekhof's *acting was analysed by *Lessing in *Hamburg Dramaturgy*. He worked with the finest troupes of the period (*Schönemann, *Ackermann, Seyler) and was the first German actor who tried to systematize his craft, founding a short-lived acting academy in 1753. He was admired particularly for his rich use of gesture and subtle speaking voice, creating important roles in Lessing's plays such as Odoardo in *Emilia Galotti* and Tellheim in *Minna von Barnhelm*. He was *Intendant of the first permanent troupe at a German court theatre, in *Gotha (1778).   CBB

EKKYKLEMA

A large wheeled platform pushed onto the stage from the central doors of the stage building (*skene*) in *Greek theatres. In *Sophocles and *Euripides the device normally presented interior scenes, particularly tableaux of murder victims, as if seen through opened doors. *Comedy used the device for tragic *parody and mock heroics.   EGC

EKSTER, ALEKSANDRA (1884–1949)

Russian designer who began her career at *Tairov's Kamerny Theatre with the designs for Innokenty *Annensky's *Thamira Kitharides* (1916), which sought to represent the Nietzschean conflict between Apollonian and Dionysian forces. The following year her concept of 'dynamic' or 'kinetic' staging was deployed in Tairov's production of *Wilde's *Salome*. Ekster believed that *costume materials, such as silk or brocade, possessed uniquely expressive qualities and that stage space needed to be organized so that setting and costume played complementary and equal roles, serving to integrate the movement of the costumed actor within an organically conceived design (*see* SCENOGRAPHY). These ideas were further developed in her designs for Tairov's production of *Romeo and Juliet* (1921), where costume merged with a setting of steps, arches, and bridges over which the actors swarmed at speed, especially in the fight scenes. For a time Ekster worked in *film, designing futuristic costumes for Protazanov's *Aelita* (1924) before emigrating to *Paris. She continued to experiment and in 1925 invented 'epidermic costumes' for a *ballet project where the dancers wore body paint and minimal costume. An admirer of Adolphe *Appia, whose influence was apparent in *Thamira Kitharides*, Ekster also used *lighting in original and distinctive ways. NW

ELDER, ELDON (1921–2000)

American designer and teacher who studied with Donald *Oenslager, and designed *scenery, *lighting, and *costumes for more than 200 Broadway, *Off-Broadway, *opera, *regional, and foreign productions. His first notable Broadway success was *Legend of Lovers* (1951), but his assignments more often came from opera and theatre companies throughout the country. In *New York, he created the *Delacorte Theatre in Central Park for the *New York Shakespeare Festival, for which he also designed many productions. Author of *Will It Make a Theatre?*, he was consultant on many theatre design projects both in North America and abroad. MCH

ELDER, LONNIE, III (1927–96)

*African-American playwright, an early member of the Harlem Writers' Guild. He started as an actor, and studied with Alice *Childress, with whom he performed in summer *stock. In the 1950s he roomed with Douglas Turner *Ward, who steered him toward playwriting. Elder appeared on Broadway in *Hansberry's *A Raisin in the Sun* (1959; national *tour, 1960–1), and in 1965 took the role of Clem in Ward's *Day of Absence*. Elder's first play, *A Hysterical Turtle in a Rabbit Race*, has not been published or performed but focuses on his recurrent theme of the black family. *Charades on East Fourth Street* was produced in Montréal in 1967. His major work, *Ceremonies in Dark Old Men*, was produced by the *Negro Ensemble Company in 1969 and won the Drama Desk *award. Elder has written a number of successful *films about the African-American experience, including *Sounder* (1972) and its sequel, *Sounder, Part II* (1976). BBL

ELIOT, T. S. (THOMAS STEARNS) (1888–1965)

Anglo-American poet, dramatist, and critic. Born in the USA, he studied at the universities of Harvard, the Sorbonne, and Oxford, before settling in London in 1915, the year he married Vivien Haigh-Wood. His first dramatic work, *Sweeney Agonistes: Fragments of an Aristophanic Melodrama* (1932), directed for the *Group Theatre by Rupert Doone, was also his most innovative. Its rejection of *naturalist *dialogue in favour of the theatrical vitality of a drama indebted to the *music hall and *minstrel show suggested possibilities which Eliot never fully pursued. In 1934 he provided *text for a religious pageant, *The Rock*, to an outline by E. Martin *Browne, who directed all of Eliot's subsequent dramatic work. The theatrically effective spoken *chorus in *The Rock* anticipated Eliot's *Murder in the Cathedral* (1935). First performed by *amateur actors in the chapter house of Canterbury Cathedral, this *historical *verse drama was produced professionally at the Mercury Theatre in *London (1935), and later on Broadway (1938), with Robert *Speaight as Becket.

Eliot's religious preoccupations and sense of guilt stemming from his unhappy marriage pervaded his writing. Issues of conscience were central to his next play, *The Family Reunion* (1939), featuring Michael *Redgrave at the Westminster Theatre. Based on *Aeschylus' *Oresteia*, the play's classical-style choric passages and the presence of the Eumenides were at odds with its conventional drawing-room setting. Eliot's remaining plays, all premièred at the *Edinburgh Festival, also had classical models, but their mythic *subtexts were hidden by a *comedy-of-manners format, and the metre of the verse moved towards naturalistic prose. *The Cocktail Party* (1949), based on *Euripides' *Alcestis*, featured Alec *Guinness and Irene *Worth; *The Confidential Clerk* (1953), based on Euripides' *Ion*, and *The Elder Statesman* (1958), based on *Sophocles' *Oedipus at Colonus*, both featured Paul Rogers. The warmer tone of the latter play was thought to reflect Eliot's more contented circumstances following his second marriage to Valerie Fletcher in 1957. Eliot's life and work have themselves spawned pieces of theatre: the play about his first marriage by Michael Hastings, *Tom and Viv* (1984), and Andrew *Lloyd Webber's musical *Cats* (1981), based on the poems from *Old Possum's Book of Practical Cats* (1939). Successful revivals of *Murder in the Cathedral* (1993) and *The Family Reunion* (1997) were mounted by the *Royal Shakespeare Company at the *Swan Theatre. VRS

ELIZABETHAN STAGE SOCIETY

*London play-producing society like the *Independent Theatre. Founded by William *Poel, according to the programme for its second production (*The Comedy of Errors* at Gray's Inn Hall, 1895), the society was formed to serve 'the principle that Shakespeare's plays should be accorded the conditions of playing for which they were designed'. This meant Shakespearian playing spaces (imitated on fit-up *stages and/or revisited in buildings where Shakespeare's company once played), *early modern *costume, cross-sex casting (usually females playing males, an inversion of Shakespeare practice), and Poel's notion of period pronunciation. Across ten years from its inaugural production, Shakespeare's *Twelfth Night* (1895), the society presented a total of 33 productions, counting revivals. Although most of these were of Elizabethan *texts, plays from other periods were also staged: indeed, the only productions which did not incur losses were *Milton's *Samson Agonistes* (1900) and the *medieval *morality *Everyman* (1901). In 1905 the Elizabethan Stage Society was wound up, and its stages, costumes, and *properties were auctioned. Some of this equipment remained in Poel's control, to be used, along with the society's name, by him in productions which he directed under other auspices before the First World War.   MOC

ELIZABETHAN THEATRE *See* EARLY MODERN PERIOD IN EUROPE.

ELKUNCHWAR, MAHESH (1939–   )

Marathi playwright. Born in the Vidarbha region of Maharashtra in *India, Elkunchwar contributed to the new turn in *Marathi theatre in the 1970s. His short play *Holi* (1970) was an aggressive exposition of the disillusionment of the younger generation with the world. Since then he has written seventeen plays in every form except *folk drama, which he rejects as alien to his urban sensibility. Compassion entered his work with *Raktapushp* (*Flower of Blood*, 1980), and reached a peak in *Wada Chirebandi* (*The Stone Mansion*, 1985), a finely nuanced *naturalistic play about the crumbling feudal order in rural Maharashtra. Two sequels followed—*Magna Talyakathi* (*Pensive by a Pond*) and *Yuganta* (*End of an Age*)—to complete a trilogy, staged in 1994. The versatility of Elkunchwar's dramatic imagination is testified by *Pratibimb* (1987), a witty fantasy that deals with a man's loss of his mirror reflection.   SGG

ELLIOTT, DENHOLM (1922–92)

English actor who *trained at the *Royal Academy of Dramatic Art after war service with the Royal Air Force and three years in a prisoner of war camp. He made his *London debut in 1946 in *The Guinea Pig*. Early successes included *Fry's *Venus Observed* and *Anouilh's *Ring round the Moon* (both 1950), and the *films *The Cruel Sea* (1952) and *They Who Dare* (1953). In *New York in 1964 he was Trigorin in *The Seagull* and Hale in *The Crucible* in Eva *Le Gallienne's productions, with subsequent Broadway appearances in *The Imaginary Invalid*, *A Touch of the Poet*, and *Still Life*. By the time of *Come as You Are* (London, 1970) he had found his stage and screen persona playing seedy lowlifes, louche rogues, poignant losers, and struggling underdogs. Film appearances of particular interest include *Alfie* (1966),

Trading Places (1983), *A Private Function* (1984), *Defence of the Realm* (1985), and *A Room with a View* (1985).   AS

ELLIOTT, MICHAEL (1931–84)

English director. A superb craftsman, Elliott's productions of *Ibsen were highly respected. He began his career in *London by founding the 59 Theatre at the *Lyric Hammersmith, directing Vanessa *Redgrave in *As You Like It* at Stratford in 1961, and running an acclaimed season in 1962 at the *Old Vic (*Peer Gynt*, *Merchant of Venice*, *Measure for Measure*). His production of *Little Eyolf* for the *Edinburgh Festival in 1963 was particularly lauded. He joined the *National Theatre in 1965, but refused to be *Olivier's assistant and instead founded the 69 Company in *Manchester, which became the *Royal Exchange. His in-the-round productions (*see* ARENA AND IN-THE-ROUND) of *naturalist drama and Shakespeare in the old Corn Exchange building were often commended, and he managed to establish the Royal Exchange as a flagship *regional company. He directed extensively for *television, most notably his award-winning *King Lear* (1984) with Olivier.   KN

ELLISTON, ROBERT WILLIAM (1774–1831)

English actor and *manager. After two years on the York circuit, Elliston joined the *Bath Theatre Royal in 1793, appeared at the *Haymarket in *London, and arrived at *Drury Lane as a leading actor in 1804. Five years later he went enthusiastically into management, leasing successively the Royal Circus, the Surrey, the Olympic, Drury Lane (1819–26), and the Surrey again. He also leased provincial theatres. Handsome, dashing, elegant, and softly sentimental and romantic when required, Elliston was the prince of light comedians and stage lovers, much admired by Charles *Lamb, Leigh *Hunt, and George III. Charles Surface and Captain Absolute in *Sheridan's *comedies, Duke Aranza in Tobin's *The Honey Moon*, and the Rover in *O'Keeffe's *Wild Oats* were among his finest parts. He played *tragedy and Shakespeare, but not so successfully, with the exception of a superb Falstaff. Elliston was also a significant manager, tastefully renovating theatres, insisting upon adequate and disciplined *rehearsals, and—at the *minor theatres—challenging the monopoly of the *patent theatres with *burletta versions of Shakespeare and the *legitimate drama.   MRB

ELTINGE, JULIAN (WILLIAM DALTON) (1883–1941)

American *female impersonator. Eltinge first appeared in women's clothing at the age of 10 and made his professional debut in 1904 in the Jerome *Kern *musical comedy *Mr Wix of Wickham*. Especially popular with female spectators who admired his elaborate *costumes, Eltinge became a *vaudeville headliner; a 1907 *Variety* review of his act at *New York's Alhambra Theatre declared that 'The *audience was completely deceived as to Eltinge's sex until he removed his wig after the second song.' In 1911 he appeared in a dual role as man and woman in *The Fascinating Widow*. So successful was the show on *tour that *producer Al Woods named his new Broadway theatre on 42nd Street after Eltinge (1912). He appeared in a series of silent *films (1915–19) and one sound film (*Maid to Order*, 1931). His career suffered under the harsher moral standards of the 1930s, and his final performance, at a *Los Angeles nightclub in 1940, was sparsely attended and ruined by the city's prohibition of cross-dressing: Eltinge was only permitted to stand next to his costumes while offering the matching impersonations. MAF

EMPIRE THEATRE

*New York *playhouse designed by J. B. McElfatrick for Charles *Frohman, completed in 1893 at Broadway and 40th Street, heralding the theatre district's move uptown. Featuring electric *lighting and a 1,099-seat *auditorium in the era's finest decor (upgraded to Louis XIV style in 1903), it was the permanent home of Frohman's *stock company, nerve centre of the *Theatrical Syndicate he spearheaded in 1896, and housed the offices of agent Elisabeth Marbury. After Frohman's untimely death on the *Lusitania* in 1915, the theatre retained its high reputation as a *legitimate house until demolition in 1953. KM

ENAD (ESCUELA NACIONAL DE ARTE DRAMÁTICO)

Colombian theatre school founded in *Bogotá in 1959 by the director Victor Mallarino (1912–67). During the directorship of Santiago *García (1976–80), through an agreement with the National University, the school was authorized to grant degrees and has *trained numerous actors and directors. Its productions have been seen at several national and international theatre *festivals, and it publishes a theatre magazine, *Gestus*, and collections of plays. BJR

ENCINA, JUAN DEL (1469–after 1529)

Spanish dramatist, whose eight dramatic eclogues, performed before the court of Alba *c.*1492–6, are among the earliest examples of secular Spanish drama. Four feature lovesick shepherds speaking a rustic dialect, whose presence in the ducal hall implicated their aristocratic *audience in the dramatic fiction. Four other eclogues, intended for Easter or Christmas, were possibly acted in the Duke's private chapel. Following a visit to *Rome *c.*1500, Encina abandoned his use of dialect,

although the best known of his later plays, *Placida and Victoriano*, acted in Rome in 1513, retained the basic features of the eclogue. RWV

ENGEL, ERICH (1891–1966)

German director. Initially trained as an actor, Engel soon switched to *directing, first in his home city of Hamburg, and then in 1922 in *Munich, where he met *Brecht and the designer Caspar *Neher. Their collaboration was to be crucial for the development of *epic theatre. In Munich Engel directed Brecht's *In the Jungle of Cities* (1923) before joining Max *Reinhardt in *Berlin in 1925. Important productions there included *Coriolanus* (1925), which stressed the individual scenes as self-contained entities and decisively influenced Brecht's *theories on episodic structure. Of Brecht's work, he directed the premières of *The Threepenny Opera* and *A Man's a Man* (both 1928), among others. During the Nazi period he worked at the *Deutsches Theater with Heinz *Hilpert, and after the war he was *artistic director of the Munich Kammerspiele before joining Brecht at the *Berliner Ensemble, which he co-directed with Helene *Weigel after Brecht's death in 1956. In keeping with the principles of epic theatre, Engel's productions were marked by analytic clarity and a distrust of all extraneous effects.

CBB

ENGLISH COMEDIANS

Itinerant English theatre companies which *toured throughout Germany from the late sixteenth to early seventeenth centuries. In many ways similar to the *commedia dell'arte* troupes, the Englische Komödianten differed from the Italians in two important respects; they performed in German as well as English and they quickly included local actors. For this reason they were important in the development of professional German theatre. They were renowned for an exaggerated *acting style which may have been necessitated by language problems. They adapted English *clown *characters into the famous figure of Pickelhering, a mainstay of German itinerant theatre until the eighteenth century. This figure acted as a guide and commentator for the *audience who sometimes had to follow a play in English. They also introduced the Elizabethan and Jacobean repertoire to Germany, including the first performances of Shakespeare (probably), *Marlowe, and *Kyd on the Continent, albeit in crude adaptations. A troupe consisted of ten to fifteen actors plus several musicians. They were largely dependent on aristocratic patronage but also performed for local people in towns. The first troupe arrived in Germany via Denmark in 1586; the second, the famous ensemble of Robert *Browne, came in 1592, possibly because of Puritan opposition to the theatre in England, more likely because of the closing of the *London theatres for the plague. The troupe played at various courts before splintering off into rival ensembles. The outbreak of the Thirty Years War in 1618 severely curtailed the English Comedians' activities. Although some returned after 1648, notably a troupe led by Joris Joliphus, they never regained their former dominance. Nevertheless, their structure and organization formed the basis of the German itinerant companies of the second half of the seventeenth century.   CBB

ENGLISH SHAKESPEARE COMPANY

Troupe formed in 1986 by the director Michael *Bogdanov and the actor Michael *Pennington, chiefly in disillusion with the work of the *Royal Shakespeare Company and the *National Theatre. Seeking to make Shakespeare again the centre of a popular tradition, and resisting the high-cultural assumptions that Shakespeare should be depoliticized (that is, moved towards a rightist *political position) and solemn, they *toured *1 and 2 Henry IV* and *Henry V* to the largest provincial theatres in England and Wales as well as to Germany, France, and Canada. Aggressively eclectic in style, the productions relished stirring up contemporary resonances, with Henry V's invading army as a bunch of football fans chanting ''Ere we go, 'ere we go'. Further tours extended the cycle of histories to include *Richard II* and a three-part version of the first cycle, until by 1989 they were performing seven-play cycles amounting to 23 hours of theatre to excited *audiences largely new to Shakespeare. Subsequent productions of Shakespeare and *Jonson were less successful. The withdrawal of *Arts Council funding (*see* FINANCE) led to virtual collapse except for schools work.
                                                           PDH

ENGLISH STAGE COMPANY

Founded by George *Devine, Tony *Richardson, and the dramatist Ronald Duncan, the ESC became synonymous with the *Royal Court Theatre and the renovations in British theatre begun in 1956. With Devine as *artistic director, the first season was dominated by the success of *Osborne's *Look Back in Anger*, which set the agenda thereafter for challenging, urban, socially engaged new British writing. The list of important playwrights championed by the ESC is enormous, from Osborne, *Wesker, and *Arden in the 1950s to *Ravenhill, *Kane, and *Crimp in the 1990s. Under William *Gaskill, who succeeded Devine in 1965, the company developed a socialist and *realist programme, with a fine series of revivals of D. H. *Lawrence's plays, directed by Peter *Gill, and the premières of most of *Bond's early work. It also presented the Come Together Festival in 1970, bringing in a large number of *performance art companies. In the early 1970s the ESC fostered the new wave of left-wing political dramatists, including Howard *Brenton and David *Hare.

In 1980 Max *Stafford-Clark took over the company and remained until 1993, when he was succeeded by Stephen *Daldry. Under Stafford-Clark, the ESC championed women playwrights like Louise *Page, Timberlake *Wertenbaker, Sarah *Daniels, and pre-eminently Caryl *Churchill. Daldry's tenure saw a broader range of plays and production styles, with the company's tradition of radical new writing revived through the discoveries of Sarah Kane, Jez Butterworth, Joe *Penhall, and Nick Grosso. Daldry converted the space into a theatre-in-the-round (*see* ARENA AND IN-THE-ROUND) for a revival of Wesker's *The Kitchen* (1994), and companies like DV8 and Gloria were brought in to widen the range. He also saw the Court through its renovation in 1997–2000, during which time he was replaced by Ian Rickson.   DR

ENNIUS, QUINTUS (239–169 BC)

*Roman poet and playwright. Originally Oscan, he was awarded Roman citizenship and was admired and supported by leading politicians. Titles of twenty *tragedies survive (and about 400 lines), mostly on *Euripidean themes and subject matter. He emphasized pathos and rhetorical effects, as well as everyday problems and ethical questions.   RCB

ENSA (ENTERTAINMENTS NATIONAL SERVICE ASSOCIATION)

Formed by Basil *Dean in 1938–9 to provide entertainment for British and Allied military personnel and war workers, ENSA presented some 2.5 million shows for *audiences of over 300 million for the duration of the Second World War. This huge logistical exercise was coordinated from *London's *Drury Lane Theatre, sending artists to all the fronts across the world, as well as to British hostels and factories. Bernard *Miles once performed on a platform slung between destroyers in the Orkneys, while Donald *Wolfit *toured Shakespeare to garrison theatres and army camps.   CEC

ENSAYO (ASOCIACIÓN DE ESTUDIOS Y PRODUCCIÓN TEATRAL)

Peruvian research and production association founded in Lima in 1983 by Luis *Peirano, Jorge *Guerra, and Alberto *Isola. Their commitment to research in *directing and to *training methods sought to raise artistic standards in Peruvian theatre and to stage carefully selected plays and classical adaptations. The group's major productions included José Ignacio *Cabrujas's *The Day When You Love Me* (1983), Isaac *Chocrón's *Simón* (1986), Sławomir *Mrożek's *Émigrés* (1986), *Brecht's *The Good Person of Setzuan* (1986), *Euripides' *The Bacchae* (1987), Roberto *Cossa's *Yepeto* (1991), Ariel Dorfman's *Death and the Maiden* (1992), Mario Vargas Llosa's *Pretty Eyes, Ugly Pictures*

(1996), and Arthur *Miller's *Broken Glass* (1997). Ensayo ceased active work in 1998.   LRG

ENTREMETS/ENTREMÉS

Entremets (French) and *entremés* (Spanish), literally food served between main courses, or a side dish, came to indicate any diversion between courses, and in the late *medieval period referred to elaborate entertainments, usually performed by professionals, during a formal banquet. In Spain, *entremés* could also designate *biblical scenes in *pageant processions. Like its English equivalent, *interlude, the Spanish *entremés* had by the sixteenth century become a common term for any short play of the popular repertory, an alternative to *paso*.   RWV

ENTRIES, ROYAL

The ceremonial entry of a royal personage or occasionally some other eminent person into a city. During the *medieval and *early modern periods, the celebration of coronations, royal weddings, visits of foreign royalty, the return of monarchs from exile, and the military victories of a royal commander frequently included a processional entry into one or more important cities. Typically, entries were civic events, financed and organized by local governments and trade *guilds. The mayor (or his equivalent), accompanied by other civic officials, would meet the person to be honoured outside the city before escorting him or her in procession through city streets decorated with hangings and thronged with spectators. Along the processional route at suitable locations such as gateways, conduits, and entrances to major streets, there might be a series of *pageants as complex and costly as any courtly entertainment. Elaborately constructed arches that distantly echoed the Roman triumphal arch, scenic devices, and *stages (often multi-tiered) then offered the city's guest a series of *spectacles involving some combination of emblematic images, banner-texts and mottoes, *tableaux vivants*, speeches, and even dramatic scenes. Subjects tended to derive from history, heraldry, mythology, or religion and were selected both to honour the person whose virtues were being celebrated and on occasion express particular concerns of the citizenry. Such civic pageantry has been recognized since at least the 1960s as having played an integral role in the development of early modern drama and the theatres built to accommodate it.   ARY

ENVIRONMENTAL THEATRE

A term coined by the American Richard *Schechner in 1968 to refer to the non-frontal, spectator-incorporative theatre he was then creating with the *Performance Group. Although the term was new, the concept could be traced to the processional and church-based productions of *medieval theatre in Europe, as well as many forms of traditional Asian theatre and various *folk performances. Whereas most representational theatre creates a frontal or oppositional relationship between the *stage and *auditorium—and creates an aesthetic distance through an implicit or explicit separation of performer and spectator space—environmental theatre seeks to incorporate the spectator in some way within the performance and to diminish the sense of aesthetic distance. As a general rule, environmental theatre can be defined as any form of theatre in which a spectator cannot apprehend the total performance space within the normal frontal lines of vision.

*Audience incorporation may be achieved in several ways and in varying degrees. The stage or *scenery may partially or completely surround the audience. Such approaches may range from the merely atmospheric, as when an auditorium is decorated to enhance mood but the relationship to the stage does not change; to the structural, as with ring-like stages that surround the audience, or projecting stages such as the *hanamichi* of *kabuki theatre, or the futuristic projects of artists such as Jacques Polieri, Frederick Kiesler, or Walter *Gropius which placed audiences in the midst of spherical theatre; to totally enveloping environments as in some *happenings and some of the work of Jerzy *Grotowski, Tadeusz *Kantor, and others in which all the space is potentially available to actors as well as spectators. Similarly, processional performances which move through a city, civic structure, or sacred or festival space—such as the medieval *mysteries and *biblical plays of England or Spain, royal *entries, the *Ram lila* of *India, or contemporary *parades and pageants—are environmental in that they traverse great distances that cannot be completely observed by a single stationary spectator, while at the same time implicitly transforming the urban architecture into a scenographic space. (*See also* CIVIC FESTIVALS; STATE DISPLAYS.)

Whereas *religious, *folk, and traditional performances around the world have evolved environmental strategies with little *theory, much twentieth-century Western theatre has self-consciously experimented with non-frontal staging either as an attempt at greater *naturalism (as with the productions in *Moscow of Nikolai *Okhlopkov's Realistic Theatre or the *Living Theatre's staging of Jack *Gelber's *The Connection* in *New York). More often artists have used environmental staging as a means of thwarting conventional *illusion, as in various productions of *Meyerhold, Eugenio *Barba, Ariane *Mnouchkine, the *Bread and Puppet Theatre, and others. Of more recent vintage is 'site-specific performance' in which a production is staged not in a purpose-built *playhouse but in an existing structure or natural environment that is chosen either because of its theatrical qualities or its appropriateness for the theme of style of the production. In such cases the site becomes the theatrical environment and the spectator is surrounded by the *scenography whether the entire space is used for the performance or not. Several *performance artists, postmodern *dancers, and production organizations such as En Garde Arts (USA) and

Brecht's *Schweik in the Second World War* in a production by Richard Eyre at the National Theatre in London, 1982, costumes by Lindy Hemming, scenery by William Dudley. The giant Hitler figure dwarfing the soldier, and the map suggesting the episodic nature of the play, derived from Brecht's theory of **epic theatre**.

Forced Entertainment (UK) have presented works on beaches, railway stations, hotels, art galleries, city streets, factories, and the like. In site-specific work, as in much environmental theatre, the environment itself often becomes the central aspect of the performance and incorporates performer and spectator equally.

AA

ARONSON, ARNOLD, *The History and Theory of Environmental Scenography* (Ann Arbor, 1981)

EPICHARMUS (fl. 485–467 BC)

A pupil of Pythagoras who wrote comedies for King Hieron of Syracuse. Only small fragments of some 30 plays survive, but the titles suggest mythological backgrounds, and perhaps a *parody of *Aeschylus. *Aristotle in *The Poetics* refers to him as the originator of the fully worked-out *plot. JMW

EPIC THEATRE

The term coined by Erwin *Piscator and Bertolt *Brecht to describe their innovative theatrical principles, developed both collaboratively and independently from the 1920s until Brecht's death in 1956 and Piscator's in 1966. Piscator located the germane idea for epic theatre in his experience as a draftee in the German Front Theatre, where he acted in a production of *Charley's Aunt* amid bombed ruins, with shells exploding in the distance, a real-life 'estrangement effect': the juxtaposition of escapist entertainment on the stage framed by mass destruction and death. Brecht contrasted epic theatre with 'dramatic' or 'Aristotelian theatre', which he identified with *Aristotle's ideal climactic structure, noble *characters, and his rejection of the Homeric epic's representation of history in favour of *Greek *tragedy's representation of fate as beyond human control. More immediately, Brecht and Piscator were reacting against the conventions of *naturalism and *expressionism: neither naturalism's restricted slice-of-life picture nor expressionism's focus on the psyche of one individual could register, much less critique, the larger social, political, and historical realities beyond the theatre. Thus neither movement could comment on its own production of signs.

Although Brecht and Piscator worked together frequently in *Berlin, from the days of *dada in 1918 to the productions of

Hoppla, We're Alive! (1927), *The Good Soldier Schweik* (1928), and *Tai Yang Awakes* (1931), their concepts and practice of epic theatre differed. Piscator established the 'big picture' through a wealth of documentation via the old media of *actors and *dialogue and the new media of *film, slides, loudspeakers, and life-size *puppets. Brecht, on the other hand, began with the parable as a microcosm of the social and economic system, through which the *audience could imagine and understand the larger world. Although Brecht also used projections, documentation, titles, and a *revolving stage reminiscent of Piscator's conveyor-belt stage, and juxtaposed these mechanical media with live actors, his focus remained on the characters' relations with each other. Both men followed the principle of the *Verfremdungseffekt* (which has been variously translated as the alienation, estrangement, or defamiliarization effect); for them, the greatest power of art lay in its ability to challenge our habitual modes of perception and presumptions about what is normal in social relationships. Epic theatre became a medium for a Marxist-based *materialist critique of capitalism's economic and social power structure, insisting that the world can be changed. The other key concept of epic theatre is the *Gestus*, a term coined by Brecht which combines the senses of 'gesture' and 'gist'. The *Gestus* materializes the social attitudes and relationships of the characters on every level of the play, from the actors' handling of an object to the overarching design of the story (or *Fabel*, to use Brecht's term). Marxist dialectic is effected by the radical separation of theatrical elements: 'words, *music and setting must become independent of each other', Brecht insisted, rather than being fused into the 'muddle' of the *Wagnerian *Gesamtkunstwerk*, or 'total work of art', where 'all elements are equally degraded' (*see* TOTAL THEATRE).

The influence of epic theatre was spread first by the *Berliner Ensemble's *touring production of *Mother Courage* in *Paris in 1954, directed by Brecht. Documentation of this and other Brecht stagings was published in the next decade or so as an example for future directors. In contrast to Brecht's extensive publications, Piscator's major account of his work, *The Political Theatre*, was originally published in 1929 but not translated into English until 1978. Notwithstanding its influence, epic theatre has met with resistance from theatre practitioners and critics who insist that art should be without overt *politics. It has also sparked support or controversy among intellectuals as diverse as Walter Benjamin, Roland Barthes, Theodor Adorno, and Jacques Derrida. And though it arose in the highly charged political atmosphere of Germany between the wars, the principles of epic theatre have been taken up and adapted by succeeding generations of socially critical artists, first in Europe and North America, and then in *Latin America, Asia, and *Africa. *See also* BOURGEOIS THEATRE; BRECHTIAN; DOCUMENTARY DRAMA AND THEATRE; ILLUSION; REALISM AND REALITY; THEORIES OF DRAMA, THEATRE, AND PERFORMANCE. SBB

EPIDAURUS, THEATRE OF

The best-preserved *ancient theatre in Greece, frequently used for modern performances, seating about 11,000. Unlike the Theatre of *Dionysus in Athens, it was a cult theatre and not a city theatre, built before 300 BC for the pilgrimage sanctuary of Asclepius, the god of healing, and designed for its *ritual performances. Its high narrow stage was remodelled later but the present two tiers of seating probably represent the original design. While its general form may have been indebted to the Athenian theatre, which had been recently remodelled, its architectural mathematics are unique, being based on the so-called Pheidonic cubit, the pentagon, and the ratio known as the golden mean. As a result it seems likely that this 'most harmonious' theatre (so called by the ancient writer Pausanias) owed its form to advanced Pythagorean ideas of mathematical-musical harmony, designed to provide a healing environment. (*See* illustration p. 426.) WJS

EPILOGUE

A speech or very occasionally a short *scene at the conclusion of a play that comments on or draws conclusions from the presented action, offers reasons for deserving the *audience's approbation, or simply asks for *applause. Epilogues can therefore be either integral to the play or dissociated from it. They are commonly spoken by one of the *dramatis personae, although in some instances this is a mediating figure such as 'Chorus' or 'Doctor'. Because they are outside the fiction epilogues serve to connect the world of the play with the world of the audience. Unlike the *prologue, the epilogue was not formally recognized in classical *theory; like the prologue, it ran counter to the conventions of the *realistic theatre. RWV

EPITHEORISIS

Modern Greek popular *revue with skits and songs that satirize current social and political mores. Its beginnings were in 1894 when, according to the critics, a 'new type of *musical comedy', influenced by *komidilion*, made its appearance on the Athenian stage with M. Lambrou's *A Little Bit of Everything*. Between 1905 and 1921 the new *genre achieved great popularity. In 1905 Evangelos Pantopoulos's company presented *Here and There*; following that productions of *epitheorisis*, such as *Panathenaia* and *Cinema*, were presented annually in *Athens. During the Balkan wars and the Greek civil war of the 1940s and 1950s, the content of the performances changed to include patriotic and partisan skits. The 1960s were triumphant years for *epitheorisis* with such leading actors as Orestis Makris and Anna Kalouta taking part in the form. Political *satire was largely replaced by expensive *scenery and *costumes as well as *dance numbers in the next two decades, but in the

The remains of the Theatre of **Epidaurus** in the Peloponnese, which achieved its final form c.160 BC. The original theatre, built in the late fourth century BC, served as a model for many Hellenistic theatres and might have been the first to contain a circular *orchestra*. Even today its acoustics are remarkable. This photo was taken in the 1950s before the contemporary wooden stage was constructed over the ruins of the *skene* (right); the venue is now used in the summer to present a festival of ancient Greek plays.

1990s politics made another comeback on the *epitheorisis* stage. KGo

EQUESTRIAN DRAMA *See* HIPPODRAMA.

ERDMAN, NIKOLAI (1900–70)

Soviet/Russian playwright. Erdman was a co-founder of the Theatre of Satire, *Moscow, for which he wrote (with others) the opening *revue *Moscow from a Point of View* (1924). He composed sketches and interludes for the classical repertoire for the Vakhtangov Theatre, and his first full-length play, *The Mandate* (or *The Warrant*), premièred at the Meyerhold Theatre in 1925. In this *satire on the petty bourgeoisie, the Gulyachkin family only pretend to accept Soviet values. For the sake of securing the marriage of his sister to a former aristocrat, Pavel Gulyachkin claims to have joined the Party and soon realizes the power that comes with Party membership, using his forged mandate to tyrannize everybody around him. The Meyerhold Theatre commissioned *The Suicide*, which was completed in 1931 and rehearsed both by *Meyerhold and by *Stanislavsky before the *censorship board stopped *rehearsals in 1932. In the play the unemployed Podsekalnikov is mistakenly suspected of wanting to commit suicide and visited by representatives of different social groups who want him to die for their cause: the intelligentsia, women, Marxists, tradesmen, and the clergy. The play was not published in the Soviet Union until 1987, and received further attention through *Lyubimov's production of 1990. During the 1930s Erdman wrote a number of *film scripts, including those for the *musical comedies *Jolly Fellows* and *Volga-Volga*. He was arrested in 1933 for anti-Soviet propaganda and exiled to Siberia. After his return to Moscow he wrote mainly scripts for animation and prose adaptations for the stage. He was formally rehabilitated in 1990, twenty years after his death.

BB

ERMOLOVA, MARIA (1853–1928)

Russian actress. Daughter of a *prompter at the *Maly Theatre, Ermolova first studied *ballet before becoming one of the outstanding tragic actresses of the Russian theatre. Her chance came in 1870 when Glikeria *Fedotova fell ill before a benefit performance of *Lessing's *Emilia Galotti* and Ermolova was invited to take her place in the title role. Her success was instantaneous and she became a member of the Maly Theatre company the following year. In 1873 she acted Katerina in *Ostrovsky's *The Thunderstorm* and, in 1876, the role of Laurentia in Lope de *Vega's *Fuente Ovejuna*, where her interpretation of a common girl who becomes an inspired leader of a popular uprising was so powerful that the authorities rapidly removed it from the repertoire (*see* CENSORSHIP). Ermolova also scored successes as Shakespeare's Ophelia (1878) and Lady Macbeth (1896), *Schiller's Joan of Arc (1884) and Mary Stuart (1886), and as *Racine's Phèdre (1890).

NW

ERVINE, ST JOHN (JOHN GREER ERVINE) (1883–1971)

Irish playwright and critic. Ervine briefly and contentiously *managed the *Abbey Theatre in *Dublin (1915–16), where most of his plays also premièred, beginning with *Mixed Marriage* in 1911. Many of his plays concern Northern Ireland, including *The Magnanimous Lovers* (1912), *The Orangeman* (1914), *John Fergusson* (1915), and *Friends and Relations* (1941). Ervine also had several light *comedies staged in *London, including *Anthony and Anna* (1926) and *The First Mrs Fraser*. His most successful play was *Robert's Wife* (1937), which provided a memorable role for Edith *Evans. He served as theatre *critic for the *Observer* between the wars.

MDG

ESCOBAR, RUTH (1935–)

Portuguese *manager and impresario working since 1951 in *São Paulo, Brazil. In the 1960s she promoted daring *Artaudian *spectacles that tested the limits of *censorship during the dictatorship of 1964–79. The eight international *festivals she organized at her own theatre from 1974 to 1999 emphasized experimentation and interchange between the political *avant-garde and ethnic theatre, and introduced Robert *Wilson, *Grotowski, *Mabou Mines, and Els *Joglars to Brazilian *audiences.

LHD

ESCOFET, CRISTINA (c.1945–)

Argentinian playwright, novelist, and essayist. Since *Aunties' Teatime* (Teatro *Abierto, 1985), Escofet has combined humour with a committed *feminism and interest in archetypes to create bitingly witty and highly theatrical plays. *Señoritas in Concert* (1993) has been widely staged throughout the Americas, as has the one-woman *All Alone in the Den* (1988).

JGJ

ESCUDERO, RUTH (1945–)

Peruvian actress and director. As the head of the National Theatre (1995–2001), she conducted an aggressive campaign to decentralize Peru's theatre by organizing regional conferences and establishing international networks in Minnesota, *New York, *Havana, *Madrid, *Paris, and Sofia. She worked for a higher standard of *acting through rigorous *training and high-quality productions. Starting in 1973 Escudero's own *directing work has explored women, *gender, *race, and social milieu in productions such as *Three Marías and a Rose, Isabel, Three Ships and One Actor, Scorpions Looking at the Sky, The Garden of the Cherries, The Day of the Moon, A Toy*, and, more recently, *Qoillor Ritti* (1999) and *The Rupertos* (2000). She is the editor of a number of books on Peruvian theatre.

LRG

ESPAÑOL, TEATRO

Built in 1745 as the Teatro del Príncipe on the site of a former *corral de comedia*, the *Madrid *playhouse was renamed in the reign of Isabel II and rebuilt and modernized in the mid-nineteenth century. Formerly the home of *opera and symphonic music, it stood for decades as Spain's main dramatic theatre. It sprang to particular prominence in the years after the Spanish Civil War, when it went some way to fulfilling the Francoist dream of 'restoring the theatres to their rightful owners . . . people of a recognized political decency'. With the nationalization of the theatre and its incorporation in the network of so-called 'national theatres', the post-war diet of light *comedies and *zarzuelas was replaced in 1940 with a solid repertoire of classics by Spanish and foreign playwrights, a tendency which has persisted to the present. To this classical repertoire should be added weekly performances for schools and colleges by the Compañía de Teatro Infantil Municipal and the holding of the annual award of the Lope de *Vega prize for theatre. The theatre has also included seasons by the Teatro Nacional de Cámara y Ensayo, with experimental pieces by contemporary authors alternating with classical work. Following a *fire in 1975 which destroyed most of the interior, the theatre was extensively refurbished and reopened in its present form in 1980.

KG

ESPERT, NURIA (1938–)

Spanish-Catalan stage and *film actress, and director. From her student days in *Barcelona, she performed roles in both Spanish and Catalan from *Greek *tragedy to modern European and American playwrights. International attention came in 1971 when she portrayed *García Lorca's Yerma in a dynamic production directed by Víctor *García. In 1986 she made her directorial debut with a *London staging of Lorca's *The House of Bernarda Alba*. Important roles in her career were Medea (1954) and Shen Te/Shui Ta in *The Good Person of Setzuan* (1967), in the first production of *Brecht's play in Spain during the Franco period. In 1999 she appeared in *McNally's *Master Class*, followed by *Albee's *Who's Afraid of Virginia Woolf?* in 2000.

MPH

ESSLAIR, FERDINAND (1772–1840)

German actor. His debut in Innsbruck in 1795 set him up for a successful career, which led him to *Prague (1798), Nuremberg (1801–6), Mannheim (1809–12), Karlsruhe (1812–14), Stuttgart (1814–20), and *Munich (1820–37). He was one of the greatest heroic actors of his time, comparable only to *Garrick, *Devrient, and *Talma. His *acting style came close to the principles of the *Weimar school; his resonant voice and sophisticated rhetoric made him an ideal interpreter of tragic roles, but he also convinced in the more 'natural' idioms of the *bourgeois drama of the period. *See* ROMANTICISM.

GB

ESSON, LOUIS (1879–1943)

Australian playwright and journalist. Inspired by the examples of W. B. *Yeats and J. M. *Synge, Esson abandoned the wit and style of his play *The Time Is Not Yet Ripe* (1912) for serious national drama, grounded in a vision of working-class life as heroic, as in *The Drovers* (1923). With his wife Hilda Bull, his friend Vance Palmer, and the Pioneer Players (founded 1922), Esson worked hard to promote Australian drama. Never commercially successful, his career was subsidized by Bull, a director, social worker, and doctor, who published Esson's plays in 1946.

EJS

ESTORINO, ABELARDO (1925–)

Cuban playwright and director. *El robo del cochino* (*The Theft of the Pig*, 1961) opened Cuban drama to issues emerging from the revolution after 1959, and *La casa vieja* (*The Old House*, 1964) showed for the first time on stage the contradictions generated by socialism. *Los mangos de Caín* (*Cain's Mangoes*, 1965) marked Estorino's first incursion into a non-*realist aesthetic, to be expounded later in *La dolorosa historia del amor secreto de Don José Jacinto Milanés* (*The Sorrowful Tale of the Secret Love of Don José Jacinto Milanés*), about the fate of a nineteenth-century Cuban poet. Though written in 1974, official political doctrine prevented its production until 1985. The country's crisis of values following the disappearance of the international socialist bloc was the reference point of *Parece blanca* (*She Does Look White*, 1994). His other plays include *Las vacas gordas* (*Times of Plenty*, 1962), *Las penas saben nadar* (*Regrets Do Not Drown in Alcohol*, 1989), *Vagos rumores* (*Vague Rumours*, 1992), and *El baile* (*The Dance*, 2000). Estorino usually directs his own plays.

MMu

ETHEREGE, GEORGE (1635–91)

English playwright. The son of a royalist who died in France, Etherege probably spent time in that country before appearing in *London in 1664 as the author of *The Comical Revenge*. The play's great success procured his entry into the inner circle of court wits, which included *Buckingham, Rochester, and *Wycherley. Following the production of *She Would If She Could* (1668) Etherege spent three years in Turkey as secretary to the English ambassador. Five years after his return he produced his masterpiece, *The Man of Mode* (1676). Knighted in 1679 and married the following year to a wealthy widow, he was posted to Bavaria in 1685. He did not return to England after the 1688 Revolution. Etherege was in many respects a typical Restoration figure, variously libertine, poet, courtier, and diplomat. His *comedies are similarly protean, brilliantly exploiting changing theatrical fashion. *The Comical Revenge* combines four distinguishable dramatic modes in its four *plots: *heroic play, *comedy of manners, intrigue comedy, *farce. *She Would If She Could* focuses on love and courtship among members of London's upper class, forgoing plot in favour of *character and wit. *The Man of Mode* reflects the development of sex comedy in the 1670s, presenting in the rake Dorimant's efforts to change mistresses and woo a country maid an unblinking examination of how the sexual game is played. In Sir Fopling Flutter, Etherege created 'the pattern of modern foppery'.

RWV

ETHERTON, MICHAEL (c.1944–)

Irish director and educator who has worked extensively in *Africa. At the University of Zambia in 1968 he helped conceive and design *Chikwakwa Theatre near Lusaka, contributing much to its ideological and artistic rationale. He also helped establish the *university travelling theatre provincial *tours and directed two very influential productions, Mario Fratti's *Che Guevara* and Andreya Masiye's *Kazembe and the Portuguese* (1971). Deported from Zambia in 1972, Etherton later joined the University of Ahmadu Bello in northern Nigeria and implemented theatre for *development projects. In the early 1980s his colleagues adapted Augusto *Boal's ideas to create participatory theatre for several communities in Zaria.

Etherton also adapted Ferdinand Oyono's novel *Houseboy* for the stage, edited two collections of African plays, and is the author of a scholarly text on African drama, *The Development of African Theatre* (1982).   DaK

EUGENE O'NEILL THEATRE CENTER

Founded in 1964 in Waterford, Connecticut, the Center is known primarily for the National Playwrights Conference, a highly selective workshop that develops new plays and was directed by Lloyd *Richards for 30 years from 1969. Writers associated with the Conference include John *Guare, Wendy *Wasserstein, and especially August *Wilson, whose *Ma Rainey's Black Bottom* Richards encouraged at the Conference before directing it at the Yale Repertory Theatre in 1984. Other programmes include a festival of work written by residents of south-eastern Connecticut, the National *Puppetry Conference, the National Critics Institute, the National Music Theatre Conference, and the Cabaret Symposium, all involving artists and writers engaged in workshops with experienced mentors.

JDM

EULJ, AHMED TAIEB AL- (1928–)

Moroccan songwriter, actor, playwright, and director, a highly visible figure in theatre since the 1950s. He was a member of the Moroccan Theatre Company from 1956 and its co-*manager from 1959, and remained important after its reorganization as Al-Maamoura. Among the 50 plays which constitute the repertory of that troupe, more than twenty were written or adapted by him. In his career he composed hundreds of songs, wrote about 50 plays, and adapted more than twenty. As an actor he created the majority of the roles in the *Molière plays he adapted, including *The Imaginary Invalid* (1958) and *Walyallah* (*Tartuffe*). Although he was versatile in a number of *genres, and used formal Arabic in many of his plays, light *comedies remained his speciality, the Moroccan Arabic dialect his particular medium.   MMe

EUPOLIS (fl. 429–411 BC)

Greek playwright, a contemporary of *Aristophanes and rival in the presentation of *Old Comedies in Athens. About 200 lines have been found of *Demes*, in which former statesmen come back to life. He also wrote several savage attacks on contemporary politicians, including Alcibiades, but no complete plays survive.   JMW

EURIPIDES (c.480–407/6 BC)

Athenian *tragic dramatist. The youngest and most problematic of the three great tragedians of *Greek theatre, Euripides wrote about 90 plays. He won only four victories at the *Dionysia, for reasons which are wholly uncertain, but which scholars usually link to comic portrayals of him as *avant-garde and amoral. Many more of his plays survive than of his rivals: nineteen in all, though *Rhesus* is probably not his. One group (*Alcestis, Medea, Hippolytus, Andromache, Hecuba, Trojan Women, Phoenician Women, Orestes, Bacchae*, and *Rhesus*) was preserved by selection; the other (*Helen, Electra, Children of Heracles, Heracles, Suppliant Women, Iphigeneia at Aulis, Iphigeneia among the Taurians, Ion*, and *Cyclops*) seems to be part of an alphabetical collection of all his plays, and therefore represents a more random sample of his work.

Perhaps as a consequence of this, his work appears more varied than either *Sophocles' or *Aeschylus'. His surviving plays include the only extant complete *satyr-play, *Cyclops* (a late work, from around 408 BC), and the extraordinary *Alcestis* (438), performed fourth in its tetralogy instead of a satyr-play and apparently of intermediate *genre. Among the *tragedies there is also considerable variety: some have seemed to critics more *melodramatic than tragic, like the 'escape' plays *Helen* and *Iphigeneia among the Taurians*; others have been criticized because they have more complex structures than most tragedies, like *Hecuba* and *Heracles*. The later plays are seen as most problematic, both in thought and in form. While there is no reason to endorse the old view of Euripides as an *enfant terrible* alienated from his society, it is true that in some respects, notably the manipulation of tragic conventions, Euripides genuinely (and not only in the imagination of *Aristophanes) seems to have been a compulsive innovator throughout his career. He delights in unexpected and theatrical entrances, as when Medea, having killed her children offstage, re-enters, not through the central door, but high up in the chariot of the Sun, represented by the crane (*mechane*). This shockingly transposes the infanticide to the usual location of the divine and emphasizes the abasement of Jason. Other (lost) plays like *Bellerophon* also used the *mechane* to striking effect, as Aristophanes' *parody in *Peace* testifies.

Euripides has often (and sometimes angrily) been said to use his stagecraft parodically: his Electra, married off to a peasant in a striking mythological innovation, enters bearing an urn in which she is fetching water, a 'realistic' action rather than a tragic one. This has been seen as a parody of the libation urns borne by Electra and the *chorus in Aeschylus' *Libation-Bearers*, which deals with the same story, and perhaps also of the urn in Sophocles' *Electra*, which she is falsely told contains Orestes' ashes. Certainly this is very different from Sophocles' connected use of significant *properties—the urn is used to characterize Electra and her situation at her first appearance and then is discarded—but Euripides is not so much parodying other treatments of the myth here as marking out his own approach to the well-known story of Orestes' revenge. He sometimes does adopt a more Sophoclean use of significant objects when it suits him:

in *Hippolytus*, a script framed by the appearance of two warring goddesses, Artemis and Aphrodite, the stage is similarly framed by their statues. The visual motif of veiling and unveiling is also used with great subtlety to underline the terrible choice between speech and silence faced by Phaedra, Hippolytus' hapless stepmother, whose unrequited love for him, imposed by Aphrodite, precipitates the *catastrophe. Phaedra, in other versions of the story a *villainess, is here a neurotic but infinitely pitiable victim of divine cruelty, one of a whole range of sympathetically drawn, and thus controversial, female tragic *characters for which Euripides was famous (Aristophanes travestied his interest in female psychology in *Women at the Thesmophoria*).

Especially in his later plays, Euripides does seem to have enjoyed pushing tragic convention to its limit, but only in order to make a tragic point. *Orestes* (408) has been called a play of extremes, and so it is, but for a reason: the grotesque internecine struggles of the house of Atreus and the mythological deformations they undergo in this version are made more grotesque still by the revolutionary staging. When Orestes, sentenced to death for killing his mother, attacks Helen inside the house, the outrage is described by a Phrygian slave who enters apparently by climbing over the *skene* and dropping down onto the stage (that this was a dangerous feat is demonstrated by the addition of some lines in the fourth century which are designed to cover the actor's entrance by a more normal route). The abandonment of normal tragic *decorum is compounded by the actor's monody, a splendid example of the radical New Music of which Euripides was the most admired exponent and which was so splendidly parodied by Aristophanes in *Frogs*. The breakdown of the tragic conventions mirrors the breakdown of mythological norms, and of the family and the city in the play. And yet when we turn to *Bacchae*, it becomes very clear that novelty for Euripides was a tool, not a disease: nothing could be more conservative, not to say archaic, than his handling of the chorus in this posthumously performed play.

Euripides was very popular in later antiquity, partly because his characters often (sometimes highly ironically) utter lofty sentiments which were suitable, when taken out of context, for anthologies. But there is also good evidence of frequent reperformance. Perhaps the most bizarre of these revivals took place at the Parthian King's court in 53 BC, with the actor Jason of Tralles playing Agave in the final scene of *Bacchae*, where the crazed woman realizes that she is carrying the head, not of a lion she has killed, but of her son Pentheus. Jason was paid the enormous sum of a talent; the severed head of the defeated Roman general Crassus featured as the head of Pentheus.

In modern times Euripides was highly popular in the *early modern period, but in the seventeenth and eighteenth centuries his innovative approach and his intellectualism made many of his plays lose popularity, first in the face of the *neoclassical taste for the *unities, then through *romanticism's distaste for rhetoric and for highly coloured Euripidean violence. Some re-

mained popular, though, especially *Medea*. *Corneille's *Médée* (1635) combined elements from Euripides and *Seneca; both Charpentier (1693) and later Cherubini (1797) wrote *operas called *Médée*; and *Medea* continues to be performed and adapted frequently. Notable modern productions include Robinson Jeffers's adaptation with Judith *Anderson and John *Gielgud as Jason (and initially as director), which ran for 214 performances in *New York (1947); a remarkable all-male Japanese production directed by *Ninagawa Yukio, seen at the *Edinburgh Festival in 1986; a more traditional but extremely powerful version directed by Jonathan Kent with Diana *Rigg in the title role (*London, 1992); and an intense production by Deborah *Warner with Fiona *Shaw (*Dublin and London, 2000–1). The combined tensions between *genders and *races which fuel *Medea* look set to ensure its continued prominence in the repertoire: apart from a number of productions with white Medeas and otherwise black casts, a recent Irish adaptation, Marina *Carr's *By the Bog of Cats* (Dublin, 1998), used the play to explore tensions between the settled and traveller communities in modern Ireland. From having been popular in the seventeenth century as a play about love, *Medea* has become a *political play, in its own way as timely as Euripides' *Trojan Women* (set the morning after the Sack of Troy) seemed during the inter-war years of the twentieth century.

JMM

CONACHER, D. J., *Euripidean Drama* (Toronto, 1967)
EASTERLING, P. E. (ed.), *The Cambridge Companion to Greek Tragedy* (Cambridge, 1997)
HALLERAN, MICHAEL R., *Stagecraft in Euripides* (London, 1995)

EUROPE, THÉÂTRE DE L'

Organization founded in *Paris in 1983 by François Mitterrand's Minister of Culture Jack Lang and Italian director Giorgio *Strehler, as a means to revitalize the production of classic and contemporary works by European playwrights. Housed permanently in the *Odéon Theatre, which it shared with the *Comédie-Française from 1986 to 1990, the Théâtre de l'Europe is a focal point for European theatrical production. Under the direction first of Strehler, then of Georges Lauvadant, who took over in 1996, the Théâtre de l'Europe has staged classic and modern plays by French authors as well as French translations of works by *Brecht, *Pirandello, and *Chekhov, to name a few. The theatre also maintains active partnerships with several other European companies, such as the *Piccolo Teatro of *Milan, the Düsseldorf Schauspielhaus, the *Royal Shakespeare Company, *Stockholm's *Dramaten, *Cracow's Teatr Stary, and the Katona Jozsef Theatre of *Budapest, who regularly stage productions at the Odéon in their native languages. The season also includes non-text-based productions from countries outside Europe, such as a Balinese *dance *spectacle in 1998, and a presentation of music from Iran in 2000. In addition to the productions on the main stage, the adjacent black-box theatre, le Petit Odéon, produces work by contemporary dramatists, including Heiner *Müller, Edvard *Radzinski, Lars Nören, Hélène *Cixous, and Marie Brassard. Since 1997 the theatre has published collections of essays, interviews, and directorial commentaries to accompany theatre projects, under the title *Les Cahiers de l'Odéon*.   CHB

EVANGELICAL THEATRE IN LATIN AMERICA

Theatrical activity in the new world by various religious orders, including the Franciscans, Dominicans, Augustinians, and Jesuits, was designed to convert the indigenous population after the Conquest, starting as early as the arrival of Franciscans in Mexico and Central America in 1524. Lacking any knowledge of the local languages, the mendicant friars turned to a visual and aural one, and saw at once the theatrical possibilities of the *rituals of indigenous society. They communicated in order to convert, and the method of communication was the theatre. As the early Franciscan friars moved from province to province constructing churches and monasteries with the Indians' aid, they also invoked their prerogative of control over education, founding schools as they went along. In doing so they discovered the existence of trained indigenous professionals and lost no time in incorporating their skills into the theatrical forms they established. (In Mexico these professionals were composers, *dancers, musicians, singers, and other artisans trained in Aztec schools.) By creating a theatre of pageantry and display similar to the native rituals and ceremonies they had observed, the friars sparked the enthusiasm of the professionals and awed the populace, reactions that hastened the conversion of the people.

The friars adapted portions of native theatrical forms to carry out their missionary work. The Church subsidized the arts, paying singers and dancers for their services in a manner virtually identical to the Aztec partial support of singers, dancers, actors, and artisans. A highly developed *spectacle emerged from the confluence of indigenous forms and European *medieval drama familiar to the friars. The events were on a huge scale, frequently employing thousands of performers, relying on spectacle, and tending to blur the lines between actor and role, and between drama and spectator. An actor portraying the role of an infidel would at the end of the performance be baptized both as the *character and as himself. Such a baptism would be part of a mass celebrated for actors and *audience as the conclusion of the performance. The actor–audience relationship was fundamentally different from that in Western theatre after the Middle Ages. In these works the spectator, having assisted in the production in some way (made things for it, contributed a little money, made the food, or provided the *cos-

tumes for the festival), bought no ticket and witnessed the event in the religious, social, and economic centre of the town. The saint depicted in the performance was the same saint seen on the altar at mass. The performance itself surrounded and invaded the audience's space, to the point where the spectators had to avoid being hit by the actors or becoming the butt of their jokes. The performance did not end with *applause but with a communal meal or drinking party, and it would have been common for an actor to be a member of the spectator's family. *See also* RELIGION AND THEATRE.   AV

EVANS, EDITH (1888–1976)

English actress; made DBE in 1946. After beginning her career with William *Poel and then *touring with Ellen *Terry, she established herself in the 1920s as a distinguished *London actress capable of a wide range of roles. For over five decades she performed in the canonical repertory, including Shakespeare, *Dekker, *Dryden, *Congreve, *Wycherley, *Farquhar, *Goldsmith, *Sheridan, *Ibsen, *Chekhov, *Wilde, *Shaw, *Kaiser, *Maugham, and *Coward. She often appeared at the *Old Vic in the 1920s and 1930s, and starred regularly in the West End theatres, often in modern plays by such dramatists as Edward *Knoblock, Elmer *Rice, Emlyn *Williams, James *Bridie, Christopher *Fry, and Enid *Bagnold. During the Second World War she toured widely to entertain the military. She also appeared in *films, including *The Importance of Being Earnest* (1952), *Tom Jones* (1963), and *The Chalk Garden* (1964). Sybil *Thorndike, a great actress herself, called Evans 'our greatest actress'. In *comedy she was peerless.   TP

EVANS, MAURICE (1901–89)

English actor and director, who became an American citizen in 1941. After starting his career in 1926 as Orestes in *The Oresteia* at the *Cambridge Festival Theatre, Evans achieved his first *London success in *Sherriff's *Journey's End* (1928). In the 1930s he appeared in Shakespeare, *Shaw, and Granville *Barker at Lilian *Baylis's *Sadler's Wells, where both his Hamlet and Richard II received praise. In 1935 he moved to the USA, where he settled for the rest of his career. He first *toured with Katharine *Cornell in *Romeo and Juliet*, then he appeared in Shakespeare productions directed by Margaret *Webster. During the war he entertained troops with his *GI Hamlet*. For the next three decades he performed in Shakespeare and Shaw, on tour and in *New York. He also had a Broadway success in *Dial M for Murder* (1952). He appeared occasionally in *film, including *Planet of the Apes* (1968) and *Escape from Planet of the Apes* (1969). In 1987 he published a memoir, *All This—and Evans Too*.   TP

EVELING, STANLEY (1925–)

English playwright. Born in Newcastle upon Tyne, Dr Eveling spent his working life teaching moral philosophy at the University of *Edinburgh. Many of his plays first appeared at the *Traverse Theatre, and they are all suited to small *alternative venues. He is sometimes referred to as a dramatist of the *absurd, but he writes in many styles, often combining provocative moral questioning with wry humour and a sense of comic despair; in the early 1970s several of his plays dealt with suicide. His most *naturalistic work, *Come and Be Killed* (1967), dealing with abortion, transferred to the Open Space Theatre in *London, as did the more *surreal *The Lunatic, the Secret Sportsman and the Woman Next Door* (1968). *Dear Janet Rosenberg, Dear Mr Kooning* (1969), directed by Max *Stafford-Clark, became his one major West End success, and also went to *New York.

EEC

EVERYMAN THEATRE

Norman McDermott founded this small theatre in Hampstead, *London, as a showcase for experimental work in 1920, during the next six years producing plays by *Shaw, *Chesterton, and *Coward—most notably *The Vortex*, starring the Master himself (1924)—and introducing *O'Neill, *Bjørnsen, *Chiarelli, and *Pirandello to the English stage. Raymond *Massey and Malcolm Morley continued this tradition up until 1929, when *Ostrovsky's *The Storm* had its first UK production. Various small companies subsequently used the building, including the *Group Theatre (1932 and 1934). It was converted into a cinema in 1947, appropriately specializing in foreign and non-commercial films.

BRK

EVREINOV, NIKOLAI (1879–1953)

Russian theatre director, dramatist, theorist, and theatre historian. In the spirit of *Meyerhold, Evreinov was drawn to pre-Renaissance non-realistic theatre (see REALISM) and to popular forms such as *commedia dell'arte*. At the Starinny Teatr (Theatre of Antiquity), which he founded in *St Petersburg, he staged *mystery and medieval *romance plays but his real impact was felt at the satirical 'theatre of small forms', the *Krivoe Zerkalo (Crooked or Distorting Mirror) Theatre in St Petersburg, where between 1910 and 1917 he staged roughly 60 productions, including his own *Theatre of the Soul*, 'a *monodrama in one act' (also staged in *London by Edith *Craig, 1915). Evreinov simultaneously published works of theatrical *theory: his *An Introduction to Monodrama* appeared in 1909, followed by *The Theatre as Such* (1912), and *The Theatre for Oneself* (three volumes, 1915–17). Deriving its impetus from German *expressionism, monodrama conceives stage reality entirely in terms of the subjective consciousness of a single *protagonist who draws the spectator into the mental realm of the *action; the spectator, in turn, perceives the other participants in the drama reflected through the consciousness of the central figure. Initially enthused by the events of the Russian Revolution, Evreinov staged a *mass performance, *The Storming of the Winter Palace* (1920), as an example of 'theatre in life', a *film of which survives. He emigrated to *Paris in 1925, where he wrote an idiosyncratic history of Russian theatre (1946). Some of his plays appeared in English in 1973.

NW

EXECUTIONS, PUBLIC

From Roman crucifixion (*see* DAMNATIO) to contemporary Muslim fundamentalist beheadings, the agonies of death in public have assumed a para-theatrical significance. Although it might be seen as an emotional, or even an aesthetic experience, the public execution is also a gruesome *performance, incorporating all the elements of staging, *costume, *text, *actors, and *audience. The death platform provides the *stage: *London's Tyburn Tree (now the site of Marble Arch) and *Paris's Place de la Révolution (now the Place de la Concorde) became notorious and were often compared to the theatre. It is said the scent of blood was so strong in the Place de la Concorde after the guillotining of almost 3,000 people between 1793 and 1795 that a herd of cattle once refused to cross the grounds. Costume is particularly important for public executions. For beheading in England, the condemned were required to wear only enough to preserve their modesty: Mary Queen of Scots is reported to have said, with a smile, that she had 'never put off her clothes before such a company'. Before the passing of the Murder Act in 1752, the doomed could sell their bodies to a surgeon in advance so that they might buy presentable clothes for death.

The public demeanour of the condemned is a significant part of the performance as well, the reported cheerfulness of Mary Queen of Scots comparing alarmingly with the abject terror of some of America's death-row inmates. Charles I requested thicker underwear so that he would not shiver from cold and cause spectators to mistake this for fear. Timothy McVeigh's silence before his execution in 2001 for the Oklahoma bombings was regarded with surprise, given his unrepentant stance. Pamphlets recording death-row confessions, moralizings, or pleas of innocence survived well into the nineteenth century. Anne Boleyn ironically commended Henry VIII ('for a gentler nor a more merciful prince was there never'), while Mary Wilson, condemned to hang for the murder of her fiancé, wrote honestly and directly to her parents ('locked up in my solitary cell, I am rather glad than sorry, for I never could have lived to see him the husband of another'). Spectators have always been plentiful, witnesses to the state's ultimate power over its people. For the last public execution in Leeds in 1864, as many as 100,000 congregated around Armley Jail to see the hanging of James Sargisson and Joseph Myers, and some states

Execution of Charles I, London, 1649, in an anonymous seventeenth-century painting. The scaffold strongly resembles a booth stage; though the king's head is held aloft, the picture makes the spectators' reactions central to the event. The inset of the executioner with axe and head at top right clearly makes him the equal and worthy antagonist of the king at top left.

in the USA in the early twenty-first century still permit close relatives of the victims to observe the execution of their murderers, a terrible and ghastly indicator that vengeance remains a powerful rationale for capital punishment in those countries where it survives.

The death venue and the means of execution change according to cultural norms, from the overt *theatricality of horror in the Roman Colosseum to the religious function of the medieval burning at the stake, from the personalized nature of hanging to the industrial efficiency of the guillotine, from the pseudo-scientific electric chair to the self-contradictory medical trappings of lethal injection. But the analogy to the theatre is hard to escape. *Dramaturgically speaking, a public execution is an *agon between the *protagonist (the condemned) and the antagonist (the executioner); the *plot moves implacably towards *tragedy, even though it may have comic elements; the *catastrophe and *denouement are predetermined. Some hangmen in Britain have even become popular celebrities, notably William Marwood (1820–83) and Albert Pierrepoint (1905–92), actors on the great stage of death. In turn the theatre has often drawn upon the scaffold for material. John *Gay's *The Beggar's Opera* (1728), as well as its descendant, the *Brecht–*Weill *Threepenny Opera* (1928), both rely on last-minute reprieves for their *heroes, *parodies on the gallows of the *deus ex machina ending. Courtroom and police dramas, from *Aes-

chylus' *Eumenides* (458 BC) to numerous American *television shows about lawyers and cops, often secure narrative intensity from the threat of capital retributive justice, while the photo-*realism of cinema has encouraged a subgenre of prison execution *films. The theatre has tended to place execution offstage (Cawdor's reckoning in *Macbeth*, for instance), though there have been powerful representations of *characters' final moments: Peter *Sellars staged the dual execution in *Handel's oratorio *Theodora* as an American-style lethal injection (Glyndebourne, 1996). *See also* GLADIATORIAL CONTESTS; NAUMACHIA.

AF/DK

EXPERIMENTAL DE CALI, TEATRO

Colombian theatre group. Founded in 1955 as a drama school by the Bellas Artes Institute of *Cali, Enrique *Buenaventura took over its direction in 1956. It gained immediate recognition at the National Theatre Festivals in *Bogotá where it obtained the best play and best ensemble awards in 1958 for *A la diestra de Dios Padre* (*At the Right Hand of God the Father*) by Buenaventura; and again in 1959 for an adaptation of *Oedipus the King*, which was memorably played on the steps of the neoclassical National Congress building. TEC had staged more than 50 plays from the classical and modern repertory by 1966, when it split from the school and became an independent troupe. Relying on methods of *collective creation, TEC was a fully participatory theatre. It concentrated thereafter on Buenaventura's highly political plays, written in collaboration with the group. Starting around 1990, most of the original members left, either to enter the *television market or to found new groups, and a new TEC was formed under the direction of Buenaventura and his wife Jacqueline Vidal.

BJR

EXPOSITION

The presentation of information necessary for the *audience's understanding of the dramatic situation and *action in the *performance of a play. In traditional *dramaturgy, the exposition is identified with the introductory *scenes preceding the rising action. In less rigidly prescribed dramaturgy, the exposition might be scattered and extended throughout the play. Information is commonly presented through *dialogue, often among minor *characters, or between a *protagonist and *confidant; but it can also come through *soliloquy or narration, or through a *prologue-*chorus. In a wider sense, exposition is also a function of *scenography and *costume, and of *publicity, reviews (*see* CRITICISM), and *programmes.

RWV

EXPRESSIONISM

A broad aesthetic term that has been applied to any portrayal of intense emotion, especially in the visual arts, but in the theatre it refers more usefully to a specific movement originating in Germany in the early twentieth century. Reacting against the limited and untheatrical nature of *naturalism, the defining characteristics of expressionist theatre are, in addition to the depiction of powerful emotions: the rejection of individual psychology in order to penetrate to the essence of humanity; a concern with the contemporary social situation; episodic structures (*Stationendramen*); generalized, often nameless *characters; strongly visual incidents in place of scenes dependent on linguistic exchange; a highly charged, often abrupt language (telegraphese); symbolic stage sets (*see* SCENOGRAPHY), *lighting, and *costumes; and powerfully theatrical performances. Major forerunners of expressionism were August *Strindberg, especially in *To Damascus* (1898) and *The Ghost Sonata* (1907), and Frank *Wedekind, notably in his social drama *Spring's Awakening* (1906), in which episodic scenes reveal how young people are crushed by a repressive older generation, many of whom are caricatured in the play. Another pre-expressionist piece, *Murderer Hope of Womankind* (1909) by the Austrian painter Oskar *Kokoschka, in which a Greek 'He' and an Amazonian 'She' encounter each other in sexually charged combat, develops by means of violent incidents rather than through its ecstatic language. The first truly expressionist play to be staged was Walter *Hasenclever's *The Son* (1916),

in which an oppressed and nameless son rebels against his father and goes off to an ill-defined freedom. Max *Reinhardt staged a similar piece in 1917: Reinhard Johannes *Sorge's *The Beggar* (written in 1912). Here the *protagonist, a young poet, actually murders his technologically crazed father.

The best dramatist of the movement, and the only one to win *Brecht's respect, was Georg *Kaiser, who succeeded in harnessing ecstatic emotion and despairing insights in a series of monumentally constructed dramas, 'the molten becoming rigid in form': *The Burghers of Calais* (1917) about an individual self-sacrifice for the sake of humanity; *From Morning to Midnight* (1917), which traces the progress of a nondescript bank clerk through the stations of one day, as he discovers that the money he has stolen cannot bring him fulfilment and so shoots himself; the *Gas Trilogy* (1917–18), the second two plays of which are prophetic pieces about a devastating gas explosion, the failure of a visionary to replace the factory with an idyllic rural existence, and an invasion by dehumanized figures. The other major expressionist playwright was Ernst *Toller, who wrote a number of impassioned *political pieces with a socialist bias: *Transfiguration* (1919), in which a young Jewish protagonist, after experiencing the horrors of the First World War, leads a revolution of 'worker/prisoners'; *Masses and Man* (1920), in which a female revolutionary refuses the chance of escape from prison when she learns that a guard will have to be killed; *The Machine Wreckers* (1922), a mystical account of the Luddite uprising; and *Hinkemann* (1923) about a man driven to suicide after being emasculated in the war. Some expressionist writers pushed the theatre to its limits, such as August Stramm in *Happening* (written 1915) and Hasenclever in *Humankind* (1920), where the *action takes on the quality of a *dream, and whole scenes consist of one-word exclamations and questions. Apart from Kaiser and occasionally Toller, few plays survive in the repertoire, owing to the complexity of their staging, their political vagueness and naivety, and their imprecise and over-inflated language.

The true legacy of expressionism is to be found in the challenge the playwrights threw out to theatre practice. Using architectural sets, influenced by *Appia and *Craig, the new lighting technology, and the kind of vast ensembles which Reinhardt had been employing for years, the theatre once again became a place of visual excitement and *spectacle. *Acting, which in naturalism had limited itself to accurate imitations of reality, once more became a mode of artistic expression. 'Let the actor throw his arms wide, and speak as he has never spoken before,' urged the playwright Paul *Kornfeld. While there were imitators elsewhere, most notably in America—such as Eugene *O'Neill's *The Emperor Jones* (1920) and *The Hairy Ape* (1922), Elmer *Rice's *The Adding Machine* (1923)—the biggest debtor to expressionism was the political theatre of the Weimar Republic that superseded it. From 1919, the Berlin director Leopold *Jessner employed expressionist methods in his political

Richard **Eyre**'s production of the American musical *Guys and Dolls* by Frank Loesser, National Theatre, London, 1984. John Gunter's design created a dingy Broadway by day and a glorious imaginary one out of neon light by night. Filling the large Olivier stage, *Guys and Dolls* was one of the National's most successful attempts to popularize its repertoire through large-scale spectacle and accessible offerings.

adaptations of classics like *Schiller's *William Tell* (1919) and Shakespeare's *Richard III* (1920). The episodic construction, generalized characters, and bold theatricality of expressionism laid the foundations for the theatre of Brecht.   MWP

PATTERSON, MICHAEL, *The Revolution in German Theatre 1900–1933* (London, 1981)
WILLETT, JOHN, *Expressionism* (London, 1970)

EYOH, HANSEL NDUMBE (1943–)

Playwright from Cameroon. Eyoh gained his Ph.D. from Leeds University, and served as academic administrator and ministerial Director of Culture. He co-founded the anglophone Yaoundé University Theatre, and organized the international theatre for *development workshop in Kumba, which led to *Hammocks into Bridges* (1984). *The Magic Fruit* (1990) deals with a self-enriching village chief, while *The Inheritance* (1993) speaks of a diplomat who inherits a traditional chieftaincy title, meeting stiff opposition from the villagers. *Munyenge* (1990) recreates the *folk tale of the village belle who insists on marrying a

husband of her choice, who happens to belong to the spirit world.   EB

EYRE, RICHARD (1943–)

English director. Eyre's appointment as successor to Peter *Hall at the Royal *National Theatre in 1988 caused some concern, but he was to prove his detractors wrong. His theatrical training (the Phoenix, Leicester, and Royal Lyceum, *Edinburgh, in the early 1970s, and Nottingham Playhouse 1973–8) shaped much of his nine-year tenure in *London. Eyre's passion for new writing, shown through his association with left-wing playwrights David *Hare, Howard *Brenton (*Brassneck*), and Trevor *Griffiths (*Comedians*) at Nottingham, and as director for BBC *television's *Play for Today* (1978–80), spilled into the National Theatre, most memorably through Hare's 'state of the nation' trilogy, a biting assessment of the Anglican Church, British law, and the Labour Party. Eyre's policies supported the production of *musicals (*Guys and Dolls*, 1982), encouraged internationalism (hosting Robert *Lepage), and enabled special projects (an in-the-round season (*see* ARENA AND IN-THE-ROUND) in the Olivier Theatre, 1997, with Theatre de *Complicité). He promoted new directors like Stephen *Daldry, Declan *Donellan, Nicholas *Hytner, and Sam *Mendes, and writers like Patrick *Marber and Martin *McDonagh. His own directing was often acclaimed, especially for Granville *Barker's *The Voysey Inheritance* (1989), *Richard III* (1991), and *King Lear* starring Ian *Holm (1997, televised 1998). Eyre's other work includes the *films *The Ploughman's Lunch* (1983), the highly acclaimed *Iris* (2002), and the controversial Falklands *television drama *Tumbledown* (1988). Since leaving the RNT Eyre has combined the role of public figure (Report into the State of Opera, governor of the BBC since 1995); and freelance directing of new plays. He wrote and presented a TV history of British theatre, *Changing Stages* (2000), and was knighted in 1997.   KN

EYSOLDT, GERTRUD (1870–1950)

German actress. The original Lulu in *Wedekind's *Earth Spirit* (1903), Eysoldt was one of the most acclaimed actresses in *Reinhardt's troupe from 1902 to 1933, performing the part of Puck between 1905 and 1921 in his five productions of *A Midsummer Night's Dream*. Other important roles were the title parts in *Hofmannsthal's *Elektra* (1903) and *Wilde's *Salome* (1903). In her youth Eysoldt fascinated *audiences with her erotic presence; in her mature years she convinced with a clear, analytic approach to roles. The Eysoldt Ring, an annual *award for actors, is named after her.   CBB

·F·

FABBRI, DIEGO (1911–80)

Italian playwright and scriptwriter who was also a judge, Fabbri once wrote that he would not hesitate to call all his plays 'trials' whose main purpose was to lay bare some moral sore. A prolific writer, whose work sometimes collapses under the weight of the intricate dilemmas he devises, he created a drama founded on a quintessentially religious vision. But his insistence on sin, especially sexual sin, when combined with the onstage nudity common in the 1960s, displeased believers and attracted those indifferent to all creeds. His concern was both with individual guilt and with deviance of Church and state, apparent in works like *Inquisition* (1950) or *A Thief in the Vatican* (1973).

JF

FABRE, JAN (1958–)

Flemish theatre and *performance artist, born in Antwerp. As a visual artist, author, choreographer, theatre and *opera director, Fabre represents the shift towards *performance and the blurring of *genres. His often enigmatic productions, which are reminiscent of Robert *Wilson, seem to be built on the tensions between reality and imagination, between order and chaos. His work is characterized by sheer and often extreme physicality of *acting as well as by repetitive elements. *Het is theater zoals te verwachten en te voorzien was* (*This Is Theatre Like It Was Expected to Be and Foreseen*, 1982), for instance, was an eight-hour production in which the actors performed with utmost precision activities such as dressing and undressing, or licking up yoghurt from the stage. Mere duration and repetition allowed reality (*see* REALISM AND REALITY) into the theatrical world. In *De macht der theaterlijke dwaasheden* (*The Power of Theatrical Madness*, 1984), which earned him international renown, the falsity of theatrical *illusion was the central theme. Fabre's most ambitious work is the opera trilogy *The Minds of Helena Troubleyn*, two parts of which were produced in 1990 and 1992. It deals with a woman who lives in the world of her own imagination.

JDV

FABULA

The ancient *Roman term for a play. The genres of Roman drama were named and classified according to their subject matter. A *fabula palliata* was a play composed in Latin, but based upon Greek models and subject matter, and notionally set in Greece. The actors wore *costumes similar to those worn by Greeks, including the *himation*, which in Latin was called a *pallium*. The works of *Plautus and *Terence were of this type. A *fabula praetextata* was a play using subject matter drawn from Roman legend and history, and took its name from the coloured stripe adorning the togas of Roman magistrates. *Fabula togata* referred to a fictional play that used Roman subject matter and settings; the name was derived from the Roman garment called the toga. *Atellan farces (rustic unscripted plays) were termed *fabulae atellanae*.

RCB

FACTORY THEATRE

Canadian company, the first *alternative theatre in *Toronto to produce only Canadian-written plays. It was founded in 1970 by director/playwright Ken Gass, who proclaimed it the 'home of the Canadian playwright' and pursued an energetic but underfunded production schedule. After losing its first venue in 1973 because of fire-code violations, the company produced in various locations until 1984 when it moved to a Victorian building that contains two spaces seating about 200 and 110 respectively. After Gass resigned in 1979, subsequent *artistic directors continued to focus on new Canadian plays, and Gass himself returned in 1996 to help resolve a financial crisis. The playwright most closely associated with the Factory is George F. *Walker, who has premièred twenty plays there since 1971.   DWJ

FAGAN, J. B. (1873–1933)

Irish producer, director, and author. He worked with *Benson, *Tree, and Granville *Barker, and wrote plays for George *Alexander and Mrs Patrick *Campbell. He is best remembered, however, for running the Oxford Players (1923–9), paralleling the work of Terence *Gray at the *Cambridge Festival Theatre, but in a cramped theatre with few facilities. He put on a term-time repertory of *Congreve, *Ibsen, *Strindberg, *Shaw, *Sophocles, Shakespeare, *Pirandello, and Emlyn *Williams, with young actors including Tyrone *Guthrie, Flora *Robson, and John *Gielgud (in his first leading part in *Love for Love*). His groundbreaking *Cherry Orchard* (1925) transferred to the *Lyric Hammersmith, and encouraged *Komisarjevsky's *Chekhov productions.   EEC

FAIKO, ALEKSEI (1893–1978)

Russian/Soviet dramatist whose plays were staged in experimental style by *Meyerhold in the early 1920s. *Lake Lyul*, a *melodrama on the theme of capitalist decadence, was mounted on *constructivist working lifts and walkways. *Bubus the Teacher*, about the intelligentsia's difficulty in coming to terms with revolution, used a background of bamboo rods, a thickly carpeted stage, plus piano accompaniment and a style known as 'pre-acting', based on techniques of anticipatory *mime preceding speech that the young Meyerhold had seen A. P. Lensky deploy as Shakespeare's Benedick in the previous century.
    NW

FAIRGROUND BOOTHS

Early booths in Britain were simply temporary trading places, arranged in 'streets' and offering more substantial accommodation than straw or canvas stalls. As the entertainment aspect of fairs began to predominate in the seventeenth century, booths were adapted to house performances and exhibitions. A makeshift *stage might be erected with a simple *forestage and a *curtained area at the rear, or more elaborate structures could be built with an open parade and an indoor venue behind. Richardson's theatrical booth, reputedly one of the largest, was said to be 30 m (100 feet) long and 9 m (30 feet) wide, with an *audience capacity of about 1,500 people. According to *Dickens it offered 'a *melodrama (with three murders and a *ghost), a *pantomime, a comic song, an overture, and some incidental *music' (*Sketches by Boz*, 1835). At Bartholomew Fair in the eighteenth century, engagements in theatrical booths such as Hippisley and Chapman's or Bullock's provided *training for young performers and employment for regular actors when

the *London *playhouses were closed. Booths gave both *dramas and *farces, such as the *History of Judith and Holophernes* and *The Dragon of Wantley* ('to be performed by the Lilliputian Company from D. L.'). Elsewhere fairground booths accommodated exhibitions of freaks of nature, *puppets, *operas, wrestling, and what Dickens called 'The Crown and Anchor'—a temporary ballroom, complete with refreshment area and orchestra. The vast and elaborately carved show fronts of booths built by firms such as Orton and Spooner of Burton-on-Trent were marvels in their own right. The heyday of the fairground booth was the nineteenth century, and the decline of booth shows was rapid during the twentieth century as the increased mechanical sophistication of fairground rides provided the main attraction. Though the *freak show and novelty booth continued into the 1950s and 1960s, the demise of the booth was soon almost complete. At the start of the twenty-first century Ronnie Taylor ran the last boxing booth to travel the English fairs. *See also* BOOTH STAGE.   AF

FALCKENBERG, OTTO (1873–1947)

German director and dramatist. Falckenberg spent his entire career in *Munich, first as a writer for the *cabaret the Eleven Executioners (with *Wedekind), then as a freelance director, and finally as *artistic director of the Munich Kammerspiele which he *managed from 1917 to 1944. His first major successes were a cycle of *Strindberg plays and Wedekind's *Spring's Awakening* in 1915. Under his direction the Kammerspiele became an important forum for new drama. Important premières included *Bronnen's *Parricide* (1922), *Brecht's *Drums in the Night* (1922), and *Barlach's *The Dead Day* (1926).   CBB

FAMILIES IN THE THEATRE

A frequently essential element of the organizational structure of the theatre has been the family. At the lowest and most durable economic level of theatrical activity, the strolling troupe, the family had always been the core unit. A nucleus of husband and wife, perhaps a sister and brother, and one or two children was sufficient to cope with many of the essential character parts of their repertory, without the necessity of sharing revenue with too many outside actors. At a more sophisticated organizational level, the family also provided strength in a company. The first professional company to *tour America arrived in Virginia from England in 1752 and was dominated by the *Hallam family, including three children. Lewis Hallam, the son of a *London actor, was the *manager, and when he died in 1755 the company was taken over by David *Douglass, who had married Hallam's widow; its leading man was Hallam's son. Seventy years after the Hallams arrived in America, another English theatrical emigrant, Junius Brutus *Booth, formerly a leading actor at *Drury Lane and *Covent Garden, appeared in Richmond, Virginia, as

Richard III. Booth established a major American theatrical dynasty: his sons Edwin *Booth, Junius Brutus *Booth, Jr., John Wilkes *Booth, and his daughter Asia all went on the stage, as did two sons of the younger Junius Brutus. The corresponding English theatrical dynasties were the *Kembles and the *Terrys, the former supplying the two supreme tragic actors of the late eighteenth and early nineteenth centuries, after the death of *Garrick and before the advent of Edmund *Kean, John Philip *Kemble and his sister Sarah *Siddons. There were three more Kembles of distinction: Charles *Kemble, his daughter Fanny, and his brother Stephen. Kemble siblings and descendants are found on stage well into the twentieth century. The Terry family, whose most notable member was Ellen *Terry, was likewise extensive. Her mother and father were actors; three of her sisters and her brother made considerable stage careers. A succeeding generation of Terrys—Dennis, Phyllis, Mabel Terry-Lewis—appeared on the twentieth-century stage, all overshadowed by Ellen's son Edward Gordon *Craig, and John *Gielgud, Ellen's grand-nephew. The 'Hereditary Theatrical Families' entry in *Who's Who in the Theatre* (1952) covers, for England alone, 88 pages and lists 121 such families.

The significance of the dynastic family in the structure of the theatre is indisputable. Family connections could ensure young members entering the profession a secure position in a good company, with advancement coming much sooner than it might with a novice from an obscure background. Actors from established families gravitated naturally toward leading roles and management; they could also count on favourably disposed *audiences with pleasurable memories of their illustrious mother, father, uncle, or aunt—or all of them together. On a lower level families now forgotten, whose members all went on stage, were well represented in innumerable small companies which would have struggled mightily without them. Though less significant in the latter twentieth century, dynasties in theatre and *film in the West have continued with such examples as the *Redgraves in Britain, the *Cusacks in Ireland, the *Fondas in America, and the *Scarpetta-*de Filippo family in Italy.

In Asia the family unit has often provided the foundation for traditional performance. Sometimes the lengthy physical and mental *training required for many forms has encouraged a parent–child relationship. Although there is no conclusive evidence that such was the case in various forms of traditional *Chinese theatre, in *Japan the troupe which gave rise to the first significant form subsequently referred to as *nō was created and sustained by the father–son bond of *Kan'ami to *Zeami. After Zeami's time, the five main schools of nō, the Komparu, Hōshō, Kanze, Kongō, and the Kita troupes, were sustained through such hereditary relationships. The same patterns prevailed among male *kabuki actors. A variety of families, among them those of *Ichikawa, *Ono, *Nakamura, and Sawamura, passed along acting and other related theatrical traditions from father to son, although the occasional possibility remained of adoption into these families in the case of talented outsiders not directly in the family line, particularly when the head of the family in a particular generation was not considered sufficiently skilled or magnetic as a stage performer.

In *India, the widespread phenomenon of families in the theatre cannot be separated from the realities of hereditary professional occupations determined by the institution of caste. Even at the start of the twenty-first century there are itinerant performers, impersonators, *acrobats, *puppeteers, balladeers, and storytellers from traditional families of performers and musicians, generally from low-caste backgrounds, who wander through the villages and small towns. Some oral epic traditions like *Pabuji ki parh* from Rajasthan are made up of husband–wife teams. The acrobats (*nats*) and puppeteers, however, travel with large families, most of them originating from the same district. The *folk traditions of performance are also linked to families from specific caste groups—the Purulia *chhau, for instance, is associated primarily with the aboriginal group of the Mundas, while *tamasha was associated for a long time only with low-caste Mang and Mahar communities.

Some classical performance traditions are even more determined by the expertise controlled by a few families in a particular caste group—for example, until the end of the twentieth century the lineage of *kutiyattam going back ten centuries was monopolized by six families from the *cakyar* community in Kerala. The temple-based *krishnattam tradition has long histories of particular families from the Nair community who are permitted to *dance but not sing, while the Brahmian and temple-serving *ambalavasi* communities provide the narration and *music. In the more secular and popular traditions of twentieth-century theatre, the family has continued to feature through travelling companies like the *Surabhi theatres from Andhra Pradesh, which in the 1960s had almost 36 companies from the same family and the same village of Surabhi performing in different parts of the state. In more metropolitan centres like *Mumbai (Bombay), Prithvi Theatres, directed by the legendary Prithviraj *Kapoor, whose sons Raj, Shammi, and Shashi became stars of the commercial Hindi cinema, was another family-dominated theatre. Shashi in turn married Jennifer Kendal, whom he met while performing in the travelling theatre company of Shakespeariana, another family theatre company, directed by the Englishman Geoffrey Kendal, where the communist Bengali director and actor Utpal *Dutt received his first professional training. Dutt in turn went on to foster his own family tradition in the Little Theatre Group and People's Little Theatre with the active participation of his wife-comrade and daughter, a phenomenon duplicated in yet another husband–wife–daughter team in the Bengali group Bohurupee, directed by Sombhu *Mitra. Other such partnerships are common in different contemporary Indian theatre traditions, notably in groups like Kalakshetra Manipur in Imphal, where the director *Kanhailal's vision has been primarily embodied by his actress-wife Sabitri. Even when there are no biological family links between individual members of Indian theatre companies, the structure of the company and the hierarchies and loyalties attached to it remain strongly, and in some cases uncompromisingly, familial.   MRB/JTR/RB

FARAG, ALFRED (1929–)

Egyptian playwright. Farag's experimentation with different forms and styles makes him difficult to categorize. His plays generally exhibit a blend of Western representational and *folk-inspired performance strategies. He emulated his mentor *Hakim but wrote *dialogue in Fus'ha (literary Standard Arabic) that is more theatrically successful, as in *Halaq Baghdad* (*The Barber of Baghdad*, 1964). His *El-Nar wel Zaytoun* (*Fire and Olives*, 1970), written on a visit to Germany to study *Brecht and his successors, was the first Egyptian *documentary drama. Though written in prose, the poetic and tragic nature of his plays like *Sulayman el-Halabi* (*Sulayman of Aleppo*, 1965) suggests Shakespearian influence.   HMA

FARCE

A dramatic *genre in which most earlier works (some of *Molière's excepted) had happy endings, not unlike those of *comedy. But farces generally rely less than comedies do on wit; they often specialize in broad, and at times cruel or crude physical antics, skits on pretentious verbosity, and zany science fiction. The *protagonist of a farce is a born victim of bad luck and ill-treatment. As a *clown, he lacks protective skills. The *laughter that greets and sustains him onstage springs from the wit of others and his own verbal ineptitude. Yet his *audience quickly shows affection towards him because he means them no harm. He knows he is in the theatre to give them a good time. And from its infant days farces have supplied highly—at times, wildly—popular entertainment. They appeal to both intellectual circles and marketplace consumers pausing between shopping bouts. The most thoroughgoing farceur in theatre history, *Aristophanes, mercilessly taunted his fellow Athenians for wasting their youthful limbs and capacities on the Peloponnesian War when they could have been feasting, drinking, dancing the merry *kordax*, and making love. In *Peace* (421 BC) one of Aristophanes' madcap science fiction creatures flies to Olympian heaven on the back of a dung-beetle to beg any gods who will listen to bring an end to the military hurly-burly and launch a new, tranquil future. In *Lysistrata* (411 BC) a brash Athenian matron induces her neighbours to withhold sexual favours until their men stop the fighting. *The Frogs* (405) humiliates Aristophanes' rival, *Euripides, by judging him the loser in a debate with the dead *Aeschylus, now, as a presumed ghost, a revered

dramatist. Aristophanes' eight surviving plays ridicule strong men and pompous leaders from Socrates to the tyrant Cleon. Performing his own *prologues, Aristophanes proved himself a powerful actor-rhetorician.

After Aristophanes, farces can be shuffled into five superimposed groups:

1. *Knockabout*, in which servants and other menials are humiliated: with a *slapstick, consisting of two wooden lengths bound together at one end and giving out dangerous-seeming but harmless cracking sounds. Slapsticks probably originated in Sicilian theatres set outdoors in the 400s–300s BC. Knockabout seems unrelentingly brutal, but is harmless. *Plautus, the most renowned Roman dramatist, introduced local Roman jokes to farce, using names spelled in pig Latin and in outlandish Greek (Polymachaeroplagides). In the 21 Plautine plays that have reached us, smart slaves manipulate events; foolish and gullible older men misinterpret whatever they see and fail to hear; and lovesick youths ache for lovely girls. Nagging wives, ever hungry parasites, and obliging courtesans strut across the stage, a wooden platform with three front doors for *scenery. Plautus refurbished stories and roles which became staples for *commedia dell'arte* or professional performers during the following millennium. On their wanderings through Italy the comic actors became identified with their *costumes, roles, moulded leather *masks, and quickly recognizable characteristics, such as age, work, regional dialects, and place of origin: doctors came from Bologna, merchants from Venice, pedants from Padua (*see also* STOCK CHARACTER). Some knockabout material from distant farces borrowed from *folklore had already shown up in European dramas and on far continents, some of it hardly more than brief sketches, some inserted into lengthier plays, such as the gigantic Sanskrit epics from *India, the *Mahabharata* and the *Ramayana*, the Beijing opera's (*jingju*) acrobatic *wu* roles for men—soldiers, bandits, tiger-killers, and 'painted face' parts—and the *Japanese *kyōgen which softens an otherwise stately *nō performance.

2. *Verbal farce*. Numerous playwrights, benefiting from a caustic sense of humour and a scholarly upbringing, had by the later eighteenth century shown up farce's most conspicuous (and beloved) shortcoming: its spasms of crudeness and platitude. An array of wits brought forth *Volpone* (1606) from Ben *Jonson, *La locandiera* (*The Mistress of the Inn*, 1753) from *Goldoni, *Il re cervo* (*The King Stag*, 1762) from *Gozzi, *She Stoops to Conquer* (1773) from *Goldsmith, *The School for Scandal* (1777) from *Sheridan, and *The Barber of Seville* (1775) from *Beaumarchais. They gave new zest to many *dialogue exchanges that had grown worn from overuse. The innovators traded in comedy and its positive *heroes as readily as they slipped in and out of the attitudes of farce. Through the nineteenth century farce became the staple of playwrights such as Eugène *Labiche (for instance

An Italian Straw Hat, 1851: a misplaced hat almost ruins a wedding) and William S. *Gilbert, with the composer Arthur *Sullivan (for instance *The Mikado*, 1885: Victorian artists put an oriental gloss on British *opera). The twentieth century yielded British farceurs by the score, the more celebrated including Peter *Barnes, Caryl *Churchill, Michael *Frayn, Harold *Pinter, Joe *Orton, N. F. Simpson, and Ben *Travers. *Boulevard playhouses in *Paris, *London's West End, and on Broadway in *New York swallowed a generous share of the commercial farce. Paris acquired a reputation for farce, as Courteline and *Feydeau drove dupes through tangled *plotting in bourgeois homes and hideouts. The physical torture these quarries endured is an obverse of Aristophanes' wish-dreams of unending sex and delight.

3. *Nightmares.* These make us think of attacks of unreal horrors, perhaps borrowed from the unconscious, rather like insanity, and enacted all out. In *Cops* (1922) Buster Keaton accidentally bumps into a gathering of police. They determine to punish him. He is chased along a street by the horde of faceless men: freeze the frame momentarily and you have a still life of a nightmare image. Another nightmarish farce shows Buster trying to dodge a threatening tornado. Courteline's hero in *Boubouroche* (1893) finds himself one evening in a closet sheltering a man living there with Boubouroche's mistress, whose apartment rent has always been paid by the same Boubouroche. His nightmare is a revelation—not a foretaste of shivers about the future but a retrospective of his last eight years steeped in deception. Less directly expressed nightmares illustrate some of farce's versatility: Jules *Romains's memorable *satire of a doctor as a dictator in *Knock; or, The Triumph of Medicine* (1923) shows a dictator who operates over his patients' private lives in their private lodgings.

4. *Tragi-farces.* Alfred *Jarry, with his *Ubu roi* (1896) and his other Pa and Ma Ubu plays, led poets like André Breton into some of the recesses of automatic writing and the twisted artistic logic of *surrealism. The new century inaugurated a host of farcical novelties, among them the sad plotting and laugh-soaked *tragedies of *Pirandello (*Henry IV* and *Six Characters in Search of an Author*, both 1922), *Ionesco's *The New Tenant* (1957), a theatre of the *absurd piece in which furniture blocks every street in Paris, and *Beckett's two brief *mime pieces, *Acts without Words I and II* (1958–9). Mixing the serious with the hilarious, playwrights taught themselves to squeeze mirth from cruelty, to accentuate the discomfort of a laughing stock, such as a prisoner. Many authors dipped freely into farce's new guises on *film, beginning with the silent comedies of Mack Sennett's Keystone Kops and in some of the cleverest screenplays in film farce's heyday by Chaplin, Keaton, Fatty Arbuckle, Harold Lloyd, and Ben Turpin. Film gave them new vehicles to conquer and be defeated by. Machines! Cars, trams, buses, boats, lawnmowers, scooters, bicycles (not forgetting 'penny-farthings'), and aeroplanes, which all have touchy temperaments and may decide to travel at high speeds through crowded places or to shut down when most desperately needed, as they do in life. Film farce also made a fetish of another danger, heights, specifically tall trees, skyscrapers that virtually beg to be climbed, and lofty bridges that span immeasurable depths.

5. *Farcical interruptions.* At the end of the sixteenth century Shakespeare compiled what must be the most striking series of farcical roles in the two pairs of twins in *Comedy of Errors*, Bottom in *A Midsummer Night's Dream*, Dogberry in *Much Ado About Nothing*, Sir Andrew in *Twelfth Night*, and, most weightily, Falstaff in *1 Henry IV*. But long before Shakespeare appeared in the theatre, farce benefited from an air of corruption, sedition, and conspiracy. In the second half of the twentieth century farce episodes took over the entire content of *radio shows (*The Goon Show*), and then did the same in some *television programmes (*Monty Python's Flying Circus*). In the last example farce continually interrupted itself when a segment of dialogue, played by the actors, cut in on one of Terry Gilliam's weird illustrations, which itself ended when an oversized bare foot stamped the latest image out of existence. Anton *Chekhov, whose youthful farces enhanced his early reputation as a short-story writer, was followed by some of Russia's most accomplished (and rebellious) writers, directors, and actors: *Mayakovsky, *Meyerhold, Isaac *Babel, and Yury *Olesha, some of whom saw their work suppressed and themselves, as their plays had metaphorically foreseen in farcical forms, imprisoned, executed, or driven to suicide or silence.   ACB

BENTLEY, ERIC, *The Life of the Drama* (New York, 1964)

BERMEL, ALBERT, *Farce: A history from Aristophanes to Woody Allen*, 2nd edn. (Carbondale, Ill., 1992)

DAVIS, JESSICA MILNER, *Farce* (London, 1978)

FARNESE, TEATRO

In 1618 Ranuccio I, Duke of Parma, commissioned a theatre on the first floor of the Palazzo della Pilotta (after the game 'pelota'), and named it after his Farnese dynasty. The architect, Giovan Battista *Aleotti, was probably instructed to rival the indoor granducal theatres which Ranuccio had seen in Florence: this brief led to a firm division between *stage and *auditorium by means of a *proscenium arch, diverging from the models of the Teatro *Olimpico and *Sabbioneta, which were otherwise influential. Behind the proscenium was a huge stage, 40 m deep and 12 m wide (131 by 39 feet), giving ample space for the elaborate concealed machinery which could produce the multiple surprise effects of baroque theatre. The horseshoe-shaped seating for the *audience also foreshadowed the structures of modern theatres; though since *tournaments and even naval battles were to be mounted on the 'orchestra' floor, there were also elements of an *amphitheatre in the design. The elaborate integrated decoration of the hall, involving architectural design, sculpture, and a richly painted ceiling, was more in the humanist tradition of attempts at classical imitation (*see* NEOCLASSICISM). The audience was seated on raked steps around the horseshoe, with a prominent central place for the Duke and his guests. Vertical tiers of *boxes were still to come; nonetheless, the Teatro Farnese is seen as an important step towards the baroque theatre blueprint which became standard throughout Europe. Very few spectacles were staged there, however, the last one in 1732. Bombed in 1944, the Teatro Farnese can now be seen in a restored form. RAA

FARQUHAR, GEORGE (1678–1707)

Irish playwright, the best comic dramatist of the eighteenth century in Britain. His plays achieved unprecedented runs, and two of them continue to be performed today, *The Recruiting Officer* (1706) and *The Beaux' Stratagem* (1707). Born in Derry (Londonderry), he studied in Trinity College, Dublin, and started his career as an actor at *Smock Alley in 1696, where he met Robert *Wilks. They became lifelong friends, and Wilks was the leading man in many of Farquhar's plays. On Wilks's advice, Farquhar left for *London, where he had the good fortune of staging his first play, the semi-autobiographical *Love and a Bottle* (1698). Real success awaited Farquhar's next work, *The Constant Couple* (1699), which featured Wilks as Sir Harry Wildair, a good-natured, nonchalant, and exuberant *hero. The play was an incredible success, running 53 nights in its first season and remaining in the repertory throughout the century, reviving the fortunes of Christopher *Rich's *Drury Lane company.

Success on the scale of *The Constant Couple* breeds envious detraction, and Farquhar was not immune. He responded to charges that the play was generically irregular and farcical by claiming that as a playwright he was beholden to no rules of *genre or *criticism (*see* NEOCLASSICISM). In his *Discourse upon Comedy* (1702), he asserted that the rules of *comedy are given by the *box, pit, and gallery. Although *Sir Harry Wildair* (1701), the sequel to *The Constant Couple*, was unsuccessful, Farquhar scored another hit with *The Stage-Coach* (1701), a *farce whose success helped to popularize the genre of the *afterpiece. He adapted John *Fletcher's *The Wild Goose Chase* as *The Inconstant* (1702) and tried to respond to Jeremy *Collier's criticisms of the morality of the stage in the surprisingly earnest *Twin Rivals* (1702; *see* ANTI-THEATRICAL POLEMIC). But his greatest successes came after a hiatus from the stage, during which he served in the army as a recruiting officer. *The Recruiting Officer* and *The Beaux' Stratagem*, huge and enduring successes, exemplify the originality and good-natured humour characteristic of Farquhar's best work and mediate between the caustic

*satire of the Restoration and the benevolent comedy of the eighteenth century. MJK

FARR, FLORENCE (1860–1917)

English actress, gifted but untrained, associated with experimental ventures (1890–1912) after appearing in Todhunter's *A Sicilian Idyll*. *Shaw encouraged her to play Rebecca in *Ibsen's *Rosmersholm* (1891) and offered her *Arms and the Man* to salvage her ailing management of the Avenue Theatre (1894). W. B. *Yeats, considering her musicality in *verse-speaking unrivalled, invited her to illustrate his lectures on the subject; she staged his *Countess Cathleen* for the inauguration of the *Irish Literary Theatre (1899) and played Dectora in his *Shadowy Waters* (1905). Critical opinion was divided over her mannered Herodias in *Wilde's *Salome* (1906) and her Clytemnestra to Mrs Pat *Campbell's Electra (1908). RAC

FARRAH, ABDELKADER (1926–)

Algerian-born designer, teacher, and self-taught painter. In 1949 he was commissioned to paint a 100 m (330 feet) square mural for the Carmelite College at Fontainebleau, which was seen by various directors and resulted in his first theatre design, Saint-Saëns's *Samson and Delilah* (*Amsterdam, 1953). He became head of design at the National Drama Centre in Strasbourg, working with the director Michel *Saint-Denis (1955–61), who brought him to the *Royal Shakespeare Company as associate designer, with special responsibility for the RSC experimental studio which Saint-Denis conducted (1962–4). With Tom Fleming, Farrah launched the Royal Lyceum Company, *Edinburgh, and promoted the participation of thousands of children as designers (1965–9). He collaborated with Jan *Kott on the *Mrożek double bill *Out at Sea* and *Police* and designed the Edinburgh Royal Gala performance of *Brecht's *Galileo* (1966). As head of theatre design at National Theatre School of Canada (*Montréal), Farrah was awarded first prize at the Theatre Training in Americas Festival. Between 1962 and 1991 he designed over 50 RSC productions, including the première of Edward *Albee's *Tiny Alice* (1971) and Jean *Genet's *The Balcony* (1972). His vision of England in the RSC's *Henry IV* and *Henry V* (1976–7) was created in a strong but simple emblematic style, without cumbersome scene changes. Colours and treated fabrics gave a painterly impression to the dramatic landscape. Farrah has been the recipient of numerous international and British design awards and honours. PH

FARREN, ELIZABETH (1762–1829)

English actress. Farren began performing in the provinces during the early 1770s, and made her *London debut as Miss Hardcastle in *Sheridan's *She Stoops to Conquer* at the

*Haymarket in 1777. The following season she secured her first engagements at the winter theatres and played almost exclusively at *Drury Lane until her retirement in 1797. One of the most beautiful and fashionable women of her age, she succeeded in genteel comic roles such as Clarinda in *The Suspicious Husband* and Charlotte Rusport in *Cumberland's *The West Indian*. She left the stage in 1797 to become the Countess of Derby. MJK

FARREN, NELLIE (1848–1904)

English actress, a member of a long-established theatrical *family. She played boys' parts in *melodrama and *burlesque from 1864 to 1868 and then joined the *burlesque company at the *Gaiety Theatre in *London, which under John *Hollingshead's *management became the last home of English burlesque. Charming and vivacious, with a great deal of personality, she acted, sang, and *danced as a member of the famous and durable Gaiety quartet, whose other members were Edward Royce, Kate *Vaughan, and Fred Leslie. Nellie Farren retired prematurely in 1891, ill and exhausted from her unremitting labours on stage. MRB

FASCISM AND THEATRE see page 444

FASSBINDER, RAINER WERNER (1945–82)

German *film director and dramatist. Best known for his internationally successful films, Fassbinder first came to attention as the co-founder of the small *Munich theatre group Antitheater, which he ran as a *collective together with Hanna Schygulla, Peer Raben, and Kurt Raab from 1967 to 1971. During this period he wrote and directed a number of controversial plays, such as *Katzelmacher* (*Cock Artist*, 1968), *The Bitter Tears of Petra von Kant* (1971), *Pre-Paradise, Sorry Now* (1969), and *Bremen Coffee* (1969), which dealt with racism, lesbianism, and mass murder respectively. Classical authors such as *Gay, *Goethe, and *Goldoni were presented in radically truncated *textual collages. In the season 1974–5 he was appointed director of the Theater am Turm in Frankfurt but resigned when his play *Der Müll, die Stadt und der Tod* (*The Refuse, the City, and Death*) was banned over charges of anti-Semitism. CBB

FASTNACHTSSPIEL

Shrovetide play and the earliest form of German secular *drama, performed *c*.1430–*c*.1600 as part of pre-Lenten festivities. The even earlier spring rites that underlay the *carnival atmosphere are reflected in the *Schembalaufen* (revels) of the butchers' *guild as well as in the ribald subject matter of the *Fastnachtsspiel*. At Nuremberg, from which the bulk of the 144 surviving *texts come, the *Fastnachtsspiel* was associated with the guild of Meistersingers. The most prominent writers were Hans Rosenplut (fl. 1450), Hans Folz (1450–1515), and especially Hans *Sachs. A later contributor, Jakob Ayrer, is credited with the invention of the stage *clown *Hanswurst (Hans Sausage). RWV

FAUCIT, HELEN (1817–98)

English actress. She was thoroughly tutored by the older William Farren, and rose to prominence playing opposite *Macready during his *Covent Garden (1837–9) and *Drury Lane (1841–3) *managements, and at the *Haymarket in 1840. She conceived an affection for Macready, a solid family man, which made professional relations between them a little difficult. Faucit was a beautiful, poised, and elegant actress, admirable as Portia, Cordelia, Desdemona, Imogen, and Rosalind. She was not up to the great tragic parts like Lady Macbeth, which she played, but excelled in portraits of romantic love and tenderness; Pauline in *Bulwer-Lytton's *The Lady of Lyons* was one of her best parts. Her powers of pathos were considerable. Her career was relatively short, since she married the well-connected writer Theodore Martin in 1851 and became Lady Martin when he was knighted. She returned to the stage infrequently, and published *On Some of Shakespeare's Female Characters* in 1892, a sympathetic study of characters' lives, as was the fashion in this especially Victorian type of commentary. MRB

FAVART, CHARLES-SIMON (1710–92)

French dramatist and theatre administrator. The stage-struck son of a *Paris pastrycook, Favart made his debut as a playwright at the age of 22 with an anonymous *parody of *Destouches's *Le Glorieux*, but was soon writing prolifically under his own name, chiefly comic *operas and *vaudevilles for the fairground theatres and the *Opéra-Comique. He became *stage manager of this theatre and married a young actress who was to act in many of his plays. On the closure of the Opéra-Comique, Favart became director of the company of Maurice, Maréchal de Saxe, who took Mme Favart as his mistress; when husband and wife absconded, they were imprisoned by *lettre de cachet*, being released only on the Maréchal's death in 1750. Thereafter, until her death in 1772, the couple enjoyed a highly successful theatrical partnership, Favart himself becoming director of the amalgamated Opéra-Comique and Théâtre-Italien in 1762. Much of his output was ephemeral, but the best plays are his first, *La Chercheuse d'esprit* (*The Adventuress*, 1741); *Les Amours de Bastien et Bastienne* (*The Loves of Bastien and Bastienne*, 1753), a parody of *Rousseau's *Devin du village*; *Les Trois sultanes* (*The Three Sultans*, 1761) and *L'Anglais à Bordeaux* (*The English at Bordeaux*, 1763). This latter, commissioned

(continued on p. 445)

FASCISM AND THEATRE

A discussion of fascist theatre needs to distinguish between theatrical performances in countries ruled by fascist regimes and performances conceived and produced by fascist artists with the intention of promoting the ideology and political tenets of the fascist movement. The term 'fascism' is used here generically to cover several ultranationalist and anti-liberal movements in the twentieth century that established dictatorial regimes, where their ideology of regeneration was translated into a variety of performative media. This was achieved on a large scale in Italy and Germany, and to a minor degree in Spain and France.

1. Theatre under fascist regimes;
2. Fascist theatre aesthetics

1. Theatre under fascist regimes

Mussolini's seizure of power in 1922 in Italy had little immediate impact on the theatre, which was almost entirely commercial in orientation and adhered to the *actor-manager system until the 1930s, providing the same type of entertainment as in previous decades. Attempts from within the Fascist Party to use the theatre to propagate their political ideas and world-view did not lead to any success. Plays written for this purpose came mainly from *amateurs and were of such low standard that presenting them as examples of fascist drama was considered detrimental to the reputation of the regime. Suggestions that the state, together with local authorities, might provide funds for the creation of a national theatre were regularly turned down on *financial grounds (see NATIONAL THEATRE MOVEMENTS, EUROPE). Mussolini's vague concept of a theatre for the masses did little to alleviate the crisis in the theatre, which had caused serious concern since the early 1930s, when *box-office receipts for cinema became five times as high as those for theatre. In 1930 Mussolini created a Corporation of Spectacles, promulgated a new *censorship law in 1931, and in 1935 instituted an Inspectorate of Theatre and Music in the Ministry for Press and Propaganda (later the Ministry for Popular Culture). Although Mussolini's functionaries reorganized the structures and economy of Italian theatre, authors, directors, and actors continued to produce shows with few signs of political engagement. In August 1943 the theatre journal *Comoedia* diagnosed the complete failure to create a professional fascist theatre: 'It is abundantly clear now that the theatre desired in the higher political spheres of the country, i.e. a theatre that expressed the politics and propaganda of the regime, has never seen the light.' State intervention was more successful outside traditional playhouses. In 1929 the *Carri di Tespi* (itinerant theatre companies) were instituted and reached an *audience that had rarely seen the inside of a theatre building. But their lack of enthusiasm for fascist drama meant that the repertoire was soon dominated again by *comedies and lightweight plays. Similarly, the *open-air mass theatre (*teatro di ventimila*), which Mussolini opened in 1938 in the Terme di Caracalla in *Rome and which was copied in 38 other cities, soon reverted to a traditionalist, mainly *operatic, repertoire. Most plays with a decidedly pro-fascist message were performed by amateur companies (*filodrammatici*). Their numbers increased from 113 in 1923 to 2066 in 1938, when 6 million spectators saw 20,000 performances, but again only a fraction of these were dedicated to fascist drama.

The situation was markedly different in National Socialist Germany. Immediately after coming to power, Hitler ordered a reorganization of all cultural institutions and established the Reich Ministry for Enlightenment of the People and for Propaganda (13 March 1933). A theatre section in the ministry came into being a month later, followed in September 1933 by the Reich Chamber for Cultural Affairs, whose guild-like structure also contained a section for theatre artists. These new institutions and the Reich Theatre Act of May 1934 ushered in a draconian surveillance and censorship system, which ensured that every cultural activity was closely scrutinized and every artist vetted before exercising his or her profession. The result was a mass exodus of some 4,000 theatre artists and 420 dramatists into exile. Although the new authorities had achieved complete control over the personnel and repertoire of 291 theatres, they were less successful in finding ways and means of creating the desired 'drama of the Third Reich'. In the second half of the 1930s new authors came to the fore who delivered plays that complied with Nazi political objectives, but they were extremely unpopular with audiences. The same can be said about the *Thingspiel* movement, another Nazi attempt at invoking (or inventing) ancient Teutonic culture. Some 400 open-air theatres were planned, but by the time 40 of the *Thingstätten* had actually been constructed and seen 30 *Thingspiele* performed on them, the complete failure of the costly initiative had become apparent and received official disapprobation after 1938. Consequently the repertoire of German theatre throughout the Nazi period was vastly dominated by classical plays and innocuous *farces and comedies.

2. Fascist theatre aesthetics

In the course of the 1920s and 1930s a number of critics, dramatists, and artists sought to develop a fascist aesthetic of theatre and to create performances that translated these ideas into practice. Although their specific dramatic and performative means drew heavily on national traditions and were therefore different from country to country, one can still discern certain fundamental features that pertained to most *theories and practical realizations. Attempts to stage fascist theatre in traditional *playhouses with conventionally trained actors were, on the whole, unsuccessful. However, the large-scale *spectacles of a cultic nature that gave symbolic representation to fascism as a secularized religion attracted mass audiences and proved to be a captivating force unequalled by propaganda in the print media (*see* MASS PERFORMANCES). They shared with other *rituals the creation of communities out of isolated individuals, turning everyday anxieties into inner peace, providing desolate souls with self-confidence and a place of belonging. Whilst fascist mythology furnished the *plot and *politics furnished the dogma, the ritual celebrations became the liturgy and produced consensus and universal adherence to the New Order.

The great pageants and mass rallies were dramatically structured, narrating events with an overpowering emotive force that elicited profound responses and acted as an effective tool for binding the masses to the fascist leader. The series of celebrations in the National Socialist festival year began on 30 January, the day of the seizure of power, and ended on 9 November, commemorating the martyrs of the movement. In between came a wealth of remembrance hours, consecration feasts and demonstrations. The most important and most spectacular of these were the Nuremberg Rallies. The ban on Hitler's public appearances in Bavaria had been lifted in 1927, and the National Socialist Party held the first rally there in 1929, which became an annual event. The Nuremberg festival alternated mass rallies and hours of commemoration, appeals and parades, military show-manoeuvres and public entertainment, and lasted at first four, then seven, and finally eight days. The heroic style and *dramaturgy of the rallies were fixed on celluloid by Leni Riefenstahl in her *film *Triumph of the Will* (1934), which more or less provided a model for subsequent outdoor rallies until 1939. Some of these experiences could be recaptured in cultic drama and choric plays written for political gatherings and open-air festivals. However, when these were performed by professional actors for a passive audience, they shared the fate of other fascist dramas performed in playhouses.

GB

---

to mark the end of the Seven Years War, was the only play of Favart's to be performed at the *Comédie-Française. Favart's published correspondence provides valuable information for theatre history. WDH

FAVART, MARIE-JUSTINE (1727–72)

French actress. Married to the playwright and *manager of the *Opéra-Comique, Mme Favart acted in many of her husband's plays, their collaboration making a popular contribution to the lighter forms of *comedy. Her most notable legacy concerns *costume design, where she—like *Lekain and Mlle *Clairon at the *Comédie-Française—is credited with a move away from the performer's own fashionable town dress to authentic period costume. WDH

FAY, FRANK (1870–1931)

Irish actor and director. He established with his brother William *Fay, several *amateur companies in *Dublin (including one associated with Maud Gonne's Daughters of Erin), which staged plays in Irish and English. While theatre reviewing for the *United Irishman* (he vaunted the superiority of French *acting, especially *Coquelin's, over English), Fay evolved *theories of performance which he deployed successfully in practice after joining (1901–8) the various enterprises aiming to establish an Irish *national theatre, realized in 1904 with the founding of the *Abbey. The style developed inner focus in performers, quiet but precise delivery, and disciplined, functional movement. As an actor he excelled in poetic drama and heroic roles, especially in *Yeats's plays, notably the Wise Man (*The Hour Glass*), Seanchan (*The King's Threshold*), Cuchulain (*On Baile's Strand*), and Forgael (*The Shadowy Waters*). After seceding from the Abbey in 1908 he performed in America and England, returning to Ireland in 1918 to teach elocution. RAC

FAY, WILLIAM (1872–1947)

Irish director and actor who deployed his slight build to excellent effect in *comedy. After performing with various *touring companies throughout Ireland, he directed several *amateur ventures but came to general notice performing in Irish in Douglas Hyde's *Casadh an tSugain* in the final programme for the *Irish Literary Theatre's season in 1901. Fay became *manager of the *Abbey company (1904), directed many of their subsequent productions, and won popularity for his versatile range of comic roles for Lady *Gregory, *Synge (Christy Mahon in *The Playboy of the Western World*), and *Yeats (the Fool in both *The Hour Glass* and *On Baile's Strand*). After disagreements with Annie *Horniman, sponsor of the Abbey enterprise, Fay seceded in 1908, subsequently acting in America, then in England for *Poel, *Barker, and *Tree. After chairing the

Actors' Association (1914), Fay held directorial appointments at the Nottingham Repertory Theatre (1920–3), *Birmingham Rep (from 1926), and with the Scottish National Players.

RAC

FECHTER, CHARLES ALBERT (1824–79)

French actor and *manager. Fechter acted in English, with a strong accent, as well as in French, in both England and America. He first appeared with the *Comédie-Française in 1840 and rapidly became a leading actor in *Paris. In 1860, at the *Princess's Theatre in *London, he played the brave, handsome, and impetuous *hero in an English version of *Hugo's *Ruy Blas*. This was followed in 1861 by an unconventional new Hamlet, in which the Prince was the perfect Parisian gentleman, dignified, elegant, and courteous, with taste, breeding, and intellect, who thought deeply and was capable of romantic tenderness. In 1862 Fechter undertook Othello in London, and then Iago, receiving more praise for the latter than the former, which was considered too close to French *melodrama. This kind of drama was indeed Fechter's strong point in his management of the *Lyceum from 1863 to 1867, and in it he was the nonpareil of the dashing Gallic hero. He rebuilt the Lyceum *stage according to modern French practice, abolishing wings and grooves, incorporating the chariot-and-pole system, and installing labour-saving machinery (*see* SCENE SHIFTING). Fechter was a great success as Claude Melnotte in *Bulwer-Lytton's *The Lady of Lyons*, and, at the *Adelphi in 1867, as the villain Obenreizer in *No Thoroughfare*, by *Dickens and Wilkie Collins. From 1870 to 1879 he was mostly in America, *touring and managing the Globe Theatre in *Boston, which he renamed the Fechter. He retired in 1876 and died in America.

MRB

FEDELI

Of the second-generation Italian *commedia dell'arte* companies, the Fedeli were the most stable and long standing, simply because they can be identified with the career of their founder and director Giovan Battista *Andreini. The troupe was established in 1601 and taken into the patronage of the dukes of Mantua in 1604. The war which devastated Mantua in 1630 deprived Andreini and many other theatre professionals of their principal support; and after that date it is likely that he was only intermittently able to assemble groups to which the name Fedeli could be attached, though the title was resurrected as late as 1652, two years before Andreini's death. In their director's prime, and despite tensions and quarrels with leading figures such as Tristano *Martinelli and Pier Maria Cecchini, the company won notable successes all over northern Italy, were summoned to *Paris no fewer than five times, and visited *Vienna and *Prague in 1628.

RAA

FEDER, ABE (1909–97)

American *lighting *designer. Trained as an architect at Carnegie Institute, Feder was a prime inventor of the art of lighting design. He devised lighting for 300 Broadway shows, including landmark productions—*Four Saints in Three Acts* (1934), the *Federal Theatre Project productions of *Macbeth*, *Dr Faustus*, and *The Cradle Will Rock* directed by Orson *Welles between 1935 and 1938; and the *musicals *My Fair Lady* (1956) and *Camelot* (1960). A noted architectural lighting designer, Feder illuminated Rockefeller Center, the United Nations, and St Patrick's Cathedral in *New York, and the John F. Kennedy Center in Washington, DC.

MAF

FEDERAL STREET THEATRE

The first *Boston *playhouse, erected in 1794 by Charles Bulfinch and holding 1,000 spectators, it was a stately brick building with stone facings fronted with an arcade. It burned in 1798, but was rebuilt by Bulfinch the next year. Though it survived a vicious rivalry with the Haymarket Theatre (1796–1803), the onslaught of *variety entertainments, and the construction of other venues, the Federal Street was undone by inconsistent *management. Converted into a block of stores in 1853, it was finally destroyed in the Great *Fire of 1872.

TFC

FEDERAL THEATRE PROJECT

Large-scale government-funded producing organization active in the United States 1935–9. The FTP represented a comparatively small part of the Works Progress Administration (WPA), a massive system of public works instituted by the Roosevelt administration as a means of restarting the Depression economy by providing short-term employment to the jobless (who would then buy goods and services) and through direct government purchase of materials, payment of rents, etc. While other WPA workers built bridges, schools, post offices, planted forests, or cleaned streets, the FTP employed actors, designers, directors, writers, technicians, ushers, and other theatre personnel to stage shows for free or at low cost to *audiences across the nation. The FTP employed more than 10,000 persons and operated in 40 states, offering more than 60,000 performances to nearly 30 million spectators. The FTP was organized in multiple 'units' that shared material, designs, and staging ideas across wide geographical separations via a central office in Washington. *Touring outside one's own region was discouraged, the purpose being to create and provide theatre by local people for local audiences. Units were organized by type of shows presented and included a broad range of material and styles, including serious drama, classics, foreign language drama, *circus, 'Negro' theatre, *puppet shows, children's theatre, *musical theatre, and *opera. A separate Federal Dance Project emerged in 1936 but was folded into the FTP in 1937. The first large-scale experiment in government-subsidized theatre in the United States, the FTP was from its beginnings a target of political criticism, and was shut down by Congress in 1939, disappointing many who had seen the Project as the best hope for a permanent, government-subsidized national theatre for the United States.

The FTP was directed by Hallie *Flanagan, head of the Experimental Theatre at Vassar College. Because the purpose of the FTP was based in Keynesian economics more than in cultural aspiration, the government's charge to Flanagan had little to do with art: her main responsibility was to employ as many jobless persons as possible and to spend her entire allotment. Flanagan set out energetically and the Project helped to launch many careers, including designers Abe *Feder and Howard Bay; directors John *Houseman and Orson *Welles; actors Joseph Cotton, Will Geer, John Huston, and Arlene Francis; and writers Arthur *Miller and Mary Chase. Though proclaimed as 'uncensored', FTP productions were closely scrutinized by conservatives who suspected the Roosevelt administration of using the Project as a political weapon. Though the vast majority of FTP productions had no discernible political bias, a persistent left-wing perspective was noticeable in some of the productions with highest visibility—especially *Living Newspapers such as *Triple-A Plowed Under* (1936) and *One-Third of a Nation* (1938) and Sinclair Lewis's *It Can't Happen Here* (1936), an anti-fascist play produced simultaneously in 22 locations across the nation. Called to testify before Congress, Flanagan was unable to defuse conservative attacks on the supposed neutrality of the FTP and, its funding unrenewed, the FTP ceased operations on 30 June 1939. *See also* FINANCE; CENSORSHIP; POLITICS AND THEATRE.

MAF

FEDOTOVA, GLIKERIA (1846–1925)

Russian actress. Orphaned at an early age, Fedotova's first stage appearances were under the name of her adopted parents before she married the actor and director Aleksandr Fedotov, who was *Stanislavsky's teacher at the Moscow Society of Art and Literature. Associated throughout her life with the *Maly Theatre, *Moscow, and the great acting legacy of Pavel *Mochalov and Mikhail *Shchepkin, Fedotova first appeared there in 1858, becoming a permanent member of the company in 1863 and playing leading roles from the outset. The Maly Theatre being known as the 'House of *Ostrovsky', it was not surprising that Fedotova's fame was associated primarily with central roles in his plays, a total of 29 in all, including Katerina in *Groza* (*The Thunderstorm*) and the Snow Maiden in the play of the same name (*Snegurochka*). Fedotova also acquired a considerable reputation in Shakespearian roles, performing nineteen in all, the most notable being Beatrice (1865), Katherine (1871),

Portia (1877), Lady Macbeth (1890), Mistress Ford (1890), the Queen in *Cymbeline* (1891), and Volumnia in *Coriolanus* (1902). In 1886 she acted opposite another great Maly Theatre actress, Maria *Ermolova, as Queen Elizabeth I to the latter's Mary, Queen of Scots in *Schiller's *Mary Stuart*.

NW

FÉERIE

A dramatic presentation of a story of the supernatural in which the prime attraction is visual *spectacle. The *féerie* is associated almost exclusively with popular French theatre of the nineteenth century. Originating in the eighteenth-century fairground theatres, *féeries* shared the same black and white approach to morality as did *melodrama, though while melodrama remained within the human sphere, the *action of the *féerie* invariably involved *magical effects, which were executed by the increasingly versatile stage machinery, and it extended into realms beyond the purely human. *Féeries* could be seen in most of the major *Parisian theatres, including the *Porte-Saint-Martin and the *Cirque Olympique, though the *genre, by its very nature, defied clear definition and was often aligned with other popular modes such as the *pantomime and *operetta. Early *féeries* included Cuvelier de Trie's *Tom Thumb; or, The Orphan of the Forest* (1801), the same author's *Puss-in-Boots* (1802), and a spectacular *comedy with magic effects by Alphonse Martainville, *The Sheep's Foot* (*Gaîté, 1806). But the most celebrated of all *féeries* was probably Anicet Bourgeois and Laurent's *The Pills of the Devil* (Cirque Olympique, 1839), in which the unfortunate *hero, or more correctly victim of the action, is subjected to every trick that the imagination of the scenic mechanist could devise. Toward the end of the century the *féerie* came to be regarded as suitable mainly for children and as a genre it disappeared into other modes of spectacular performance. *See also* PANTOMIME, BRITISH.

SJCW

FEHLING, JÜRGEN (1885–1968)

German director. Fehling's breakthrough came in 1921 with acclaimed productions of *The Comedy of Errors* and *Toller's *Masses and Man*. He joined Leopold *Jessner at the Berlin State Theatre (*Berlin Royal Theatre), which remained his base until 1944. Strongly influenced by *expressionism, Fehling's productions were also marked by sensitivity to psychological nuances. In a sense he blended *Brahm's *naturalism and expressionism to find a new synthesis which enabled him to direct the whole gamut of dramatic literature as well as *opera. He directed over 100 productions at the State Theatre. Noteworthy were the premières of Ernst *Barlach's work in the 1920s and his Shakespeare productions, particularly *The Merchant of Venice* in 1927 with *Kortner as Shylock and *Richard III* in 1936 with Werner *Krauss. Fehling's career as a director ended in 1944. He was unable to re-establish himself in the post-war period. CBB

FELIPE, CARLOS (1914–75)

Cuban playwright who—together with Virgilio *Piñera and Rolando Ferrer—modernized national drama. Self-taught, an insatiable reader of classical and contemporary playwrights, his works adapted the methods of the *avant-garde: *dreamlike atmospheres, ambiguities of identity, interplay of the *real and the imaginary, and a frequent resort to *metatheatre. His *characters, self-centred and solitary, pursue unachievable dreams in an environment marked by a lack of authenticity. When the revolution occurred in 1959 he had staged *El chino* (*The China-man*, 1947), *Capricho en rojo* (*Whim in Red*, 1950), and *El travieso Jimmy* (*Mischievous Jimmy*, 1951) on a small scale for few performances. He later attained critical and popular success with his *comedy *De película* (*Like in a Film*, 1963). His most important play, *Réquiem por Yarini* (*Requiem for Yarini*, 1965), is a well-structured *tragedy in a popular setting, inspired by a mythical pimp with political connections who reigned in *Havana's brothels in the 1920s. Other works include *La bata de encaje* (*The Lace Robe*, 1962), *Los compadres* (*Buddies*, 1968), and *Ibrahim* (1968). MMu

---

FEMALE IMPERSONATION

With origins in *folklore, mythology, and shamanism, female impersonation was often associated with religious *ritual. It was also a feature of saturnalia and *carnival, as witnessed in Italy by *Goethe: 'Young men dressed in the holiday attire of women of the lower classes, exposing an open breast and displaying an impudent self-complacency, are the first to appear' (1786). Female impersonation has also been a significant feature of theatre, East and West. Men played female roles in *Greek *comedy and *tragedy. Female impersonation features dramatically in *Euripides' *The Bacchae*, in which Pentheus *disguises himself as a woman to observe the celebrations of the Maenads. In *Aristophanes' *Thesmophoriazusae* female impersonation is used for comic and vulgar ends, although the pivot of the *plot is again the clandestine presence of a disguised male at a women's festival. During the *medieval and much of the *early modern periods female impersonation occurred in many theatrical entertainments. In England *boy actors in *boys' companies played female roles until the closing of the theatres in 1642, although female impersonation continued after their re-opening in 1660, despite the introduction of actresses. Popular boy actors included Nathan *Field (probably the first Ophelia), Richard *Robinson, Alexander Cooke, and Edward *Kynaston, whose performance of female roles after the Restoration was praised by *Pepys. (The tradition of female impersonation in Shakespeare has recently been re-established in all-male produc-

tions of *As You Like It* by the Royal *National Theatre, 1967, and *Cheek by Jowl, 1991.) Female impersonation as a plot device occurs in Ben *Jonson's *Epicene*, and both Falstaff in *The Merry Wives of Windsor* and Sir John Brute in *The Provok'd Wife* (1697) resort to female disguise. In *Rome the laws banishing women from the stage were not repealed until 1797. Goethe praised Roman actors in female roles in a *Goldoni play, because he had enjoyed 'not the thing itself, but its imitation, to be entertained not through nature but through art, to contemplate not an individuality but a result'. He also admired the effectiveness of Italian *castrati in female roles.

Female impersonation was and still is a feature of various classical forms of Asian theatre. In *Japanese *nō male actors play female roles, their femininity specifically defined by a *mask. *Kabuki was created by women, but after a ban on female performers in 1628, *wakashū* kabuki developed, in which young men played female roles, to be replaced in 1652 in *yaro* kabuki by more mature actors. A crucial aspect of the form was the *onnagata*: male actors devoted their lives to playing female roles and were expected to live as women in everyday life also. Strict rules for dress, *make-up, gesture, and deportment suggest the performance of the *onnagata* communicates a highly constructed notion of femininity (*see* GENDER AND PERFORMANCE; FEMINISM). In *China women were banned from the stage in the mid-eighteenth century and the *tan* actor developed. The Beijing opera (*jingju*) featured female impersonation, most famously in the twentieth century in the person of *Mei Lanfang, an innovative performer whose technique was much admired by *Brecht and *Stanislavsky. In *Indian *kathakali* *dance-drama, a highly stylised form of female impersonation is the norm.

Female impersonation in eighteenth- and nineteenth-century Europe often tended towards the grotesque, particularly in England. Charles Bannister as Polly Peachum (*The Beggar's Opera*), various comic actors as Moll Flagon (*The Lord of the Manor*), singing witches played by men in *Macbeth*, contributed to a tradition from which developed the grotesque middle-aged females of nineteenth-century *burlesque and the *pantomime dame. Female impersonation often occurred in the harlequinade (Samuel Simmons played Mother Goose in *Harlequin and Mother Goose* in 1805), but by the late nineteenth century comedians such as Dan *Leno and Herbert Campbell were playing female roles in annual pantomime, a tradition continued through the ensuing century in the performances of George *Robey, George Lacey, Douglas Byng, Arthur *Askey, and Clarkson Rose. Female impersonation sometimes figures as a plot device in *farce, most famously in Brandon *Thomas's *Charley's Aunt* (1892), in which Lord Fancourt Babberly assists his friends by impersonating a wealthy aunt.

Female impersonation also featured in *music-hall, *minstrel, and *pierrot shows, *variety, and even the *circus. *Acrobats such as Lulu and Barbette delighted *audiences, many of whom were taken in by their disguises. Performers such as Fred

Foster, 'the Girl of the Period', played the halls in the 1870s, while in the United States in the early 1900s Julian *Eltinge's skills as an impersonator won him immense popularity and a strong female following. Even spectators were sometimes female impersonators, as with Ernest Bolton's and Frederick Park's predilection for attending theatres in female attire, which led to their 1871 trial.

Female impersonation was common in armed services entertainment during the First and Second World Wars. Some all-male troupes continued to perform in peacetime *revues and variety shows, one such being the subject of Peter *Nichols's *Privates on Parade* (1977). Female impersonation also had its detractors: Mae *West's *Pleasure Man*, which included impersonators among its *characters, was banned in 1928, while the phenomenon virtually disappeared from the homophobic Britain and Ireland of the 1950s.

From the late 1960s and 1970s female impersonation re-emerged in many guises. In the United Kingdom Danny *La Rue's combination of comedy and glamour proved effective in several shows, commencing with *Come Spy with Me* (1966), and re-established drag as potential family entertainment. In the 1970s *The Rocky Horror Show* broadened the parameters of female impersonation, as did Charles *Ludlam as Camille and in other roles at the *Ridiculous Theatrical Company in *New York, and Lindsay *Kemp in *Wilde's *Salome* (1977) and *Onnagata* (1992) in *London. All-male revues featuring female impersonators attracted audiences from the 1950s in some countries (Le Carrousel in *Paris and Les Girls in *Sydney). 'Radical drag' emerged in the 1970s through *gay groups such as Hot Peaches, Cycle Sluts, and the Fabulous Cockettes, while social and political *satire informed the performances of the South African Pieter-Dirk Uys as Evita Bezuidenhout and Barry *Humphries as the Australian Dame Edna Everage. The boundaries of female impersonation have been further extended by the cult *musical *Hedwig and the Angry Inch* (1998) and by the transsexual performer Kate Bornstein. *See also* MALE IMPERSONATION; LESBIAN THEATRE; QUEER THEORY.   JTD

BAKER, ROGER, *Drag: a history of female impersonation in the performing arts* (London, 1994)

FERRIS, LESLEY (ed.), *Crossing the Stage: controversies on cross-dressing* (London, 1993)

SENELICK, LAURENCE, *The Changing Room: sex, drag and theatre* (London, 2000)

FEMINISM

Political discourse which examines the power relationships between women and men, and promotes women's struggle for self-determination against patriarchy and sexism. It had a major influence on late twentieth-century and early twenty-first-century Western theatre concerned with identity politics, and its precepts have defined many of the issues significant for this work. Feminism encompasses doctrines which promote sexual, social, and political equality for women, the emphasis of its principles depending upon the particular theories and methods of analysis adopted by specific feminist ideologies. Its definitions depend upon race, sexuality, nationality, and class, as much as upon ideology or philosophy.

The first publications to examine women's social position in society (as distinct from men's) appeared in the eighteenth century, such as Mary Wollstonecraft's *A Vindication of the Rights of Women* (1792). It was not until the nineteenth century with the rise of the suffrage movement in Europe and America that organized feminism emerged as a political force campaigning for female emancipation and universal suffrage. Connecting with the suffrage movement, and with concerns for social reform and the material position of woman in the family and society, were the women writers of the early twentieth century who comprise first-wave feminism, for example Olive Schreiner and Virginia Woolf. First-wave feminists fought for universal suffrage and struggled for women's rights to self-determination, education, and social welfare. In *A Room of One's Own* (1929) Virginia Woolf analysed the financial, social, and educational disadvantages under which women writers work, arguing that financial independence and self-determination are essential for women writers to achieve their potential. Woolf's experimental *modernist fiction foreshadowed the concerns of second-wave feminism by questioning gender assumptions and challenging patriarchal literary discourses.

The figure who acts as a bridge between first-wave and second-wave feminism is Simone de Beauvoir (*The Second Sex*, 1949), who coined the phrase 'One is not born, but rather becomes, a woman', showing that woman is that which is 'Other' and negative to the male's positive. Thus she delineated a major concern of late twentieth-century feminists (Hélène *Cixous, Luce Irigaray) who identify the central problem for women as their positioning as the binary opposite of men. The second wave of feminism grew out of the protests of the 1960s: civil rights, the anti-Vietnam movement, CND, the students' movements. It focused on reproductive rights, issues of inequality, women's access to education, and equality in the workplace. Betty Friedan's *The Feminine Mystique* (1963) revealed 'the problem with no name', the alienation and dissatisfaction felt by American housewives confined to the home. Germaine Greer's *The Female Eunuch*, Kate Millet's *Sexual Politics*, and Eva Figes's *Patriarchal Attitudes* followed in the 1970s and defined how patriarchy functions in contemporary society. All three books discuss literature as part of the culture which constructs 'woman'. Since the early 1970s feminism has developed into a complex of critical discourses which affect every aspect of life and have been one of the major motors of change in the late twentieth century. Its influence has spread beyond social and political inequity into personal relationships and sexual identity. It has redefined the analytical modes by which we examine cultural and historical products, and promoted forms of cultural, historical, and political representation which are inclusive of women.

Developing from de Beauvoir's work, a resistance to the notion that it is 'natural' for women to be passive and subservient is central to feminism: characteristics of femininity are socially determined. Feminism separates biological sex from definitions of gender derived from norms of masculine and feminine behaviour. If feminine behaviour is not intrinsic to women but rather developed through a process of socialization, then the notion that gender power structures are rigidly and indisputably fixed is contested, and a transformation of gender relationships is possible. Differences in ways of defining and countering sex-role stereotyping have resulted in a diversity of feminist theories and practices which emphasize that women have been circumscribed by a rigid classification which limits their sphere of influence within patriarchy.

Although women have not achieved full equality, feminism has had a substantial impact upon social and working practices, particularly in the Western world, advocating not only equal opportunities for women but also changes in the working environment. At the same time, forms of feminist criticism have infiltrated most academic disciplines, and theories of feminism, sex, and gender have explored the historical roots of women's oppression, the development of gender roles in social, psychological, and emotional development, and gender stereotyping in forms of cultural representation such as theatre.

Work on language has been crucial to rethinking gender in cultural terms. Dale Spender's *Man Made Language* (1980) explored the gender prejudices embedded in apparently gender-neutral language. She detected discrimination in the negative connotations of words describing women and their activities, while epithets connected to men implied authority and strength. Spender's analysis revealed that language does not transparently describe, but through a process of binary opposition privileges masculine over feminine, constructing differences between men and women where women are subordinate. Women lack an 'authentic' voice and are required to speak and write in a language which is alien to and unrepresentative of them. Spender's work resulted in a call for new formations of language in which women could define themselves and their concerns. History writing was also examined for the insidious patriarchy hidden within its methodologies, and new historical perspectives revised conventional histories, revealing possibilities for change in women's position in society. Histories of and for women were developed, and this also impacted on conventional approaches to historical research.

Psychoanalysis has offered very significant developments in feminist theories since the 1970s (*see* PSYCHOANALYTIC CRITICISM). Freud's description of women as 'castrated men' and his male-centred analysis of child development define women as inadequate and inferior. French, British, and American feminists have refocused psychoanalytic perspectives in order to draw attention to the sexism of Freudian theories and outline alternative readings of psychic development. Feminists accepted the significance of Freud's theory of undifferentiated infant sexuality and psychoanalytic explanations of the acquisition of sexual identity through repressing socially unacceptable desires. But feminist psychoanalysis repudiates Freud's implication that sexual identity is predestined by the body's sexual organs. Freud's model of the development of the child defines sexual difference as culturally acquired, and feminist theory has developed this insight into a tool of resistance. Drawing on Jacques Lacan's language-centred reading of Freud, feminists such as Juliet Mitchell and Jane Gallop have appropriated psychoanalysis. Lacan defines language as a culturally constructed order which positions women linguistically and sexually as subservient to men under the 'Law of the Father'. Lacan's work can reinforce gender difference and male superiority, but its insistence on the cultural construction of language opens a space for resisting cultural norms. French feminists such as Hélène Cixous, Luce Irigaray, and Julia Kristeva have developed connections between language, psychoanalysis, and subjectivity further. Cixous has championed a linguistic process called *écriture féminine* as a way of subverting masculine language and resisting the binary oppositions which define woman as the Other. Luce Irigaray in *Speculum and the Other Woman* (1974) and *This Sex Which Is Not One* (1977) contends that women are absent from representation since they can only mimic men's language and cannot speak autonomously. Julia Kristeva is similarly concerned with the relationship of writing, culture, and subjectivity, defining the female *'semiotic' (the pre-linguistic, instinctual level) as devalued in relation to the masculine symbolic (the conscious, socialized, rational level). All three of these theoreticians have had a significant impact on the development of feminist criticism.

In theatre the number of women occupying positions of responsibility has increased since 1970, with more female directors and producers (Ariane *Mnouchkine, Deborah *Warner, Anne *Bogart, JoAnne *Akalaitis), and a greater number of female playwrights in Europe, America, and Australasia (Pam *Gems, Caryl *Churchill, Ntosake *Shange, Paula *Vogel). This has resulted in a far more positive theatrical representation of women. Theatre became a forum for exploring social and political inequality and for raising awareness of equal opportunity issues in education, the workplace, and the home (Simone Benmussa's *The Singular Life of Albert Nobbs*, Franca *Rame's *Female Parts*, Sarah *Daniels's *Gut Girls*). Responding to Spender's analysis of language as exclusive rather than inclusive of women and to psychoanalytic feminism's linking of language and identity, writers and directors have developed forms of representation more appropriate for depicting women. Cixous's *Portrait of Dora* (1976) is an example of a play which in its recasting of a Freudian case study attempts both

Top Girls by Caryl Churchill, Royal Court Theatre, London, 1982, directed by Max Stafford-Clark. Set in a London restaurant, the opening scene brings together famous women from history and art to celebrate the promotion of Marlene as managing director of an employment agency called Top Girls. In a series of contemporary sketches that follow, the play becomes a **feminist** investigation of the cost of women's success in Thatcher's England.

to expose the sexism of Freud's model of sexuality and liberate Dora's desire from the male circumscription. By deconstructing traditional forms of theatre and systems of representation, playwrights and theatre practitioners have found ways of positioning the woman as the subject rather than object of performances. *See also* FEMINIST THEATRE, UK and USA; GENDER AND PERFORMANCE; LESBIAN THEATRE; WOMEN AND PERFORMANCE; WOMEN IN AUDIENCES; QUEER THEORY; THEORIES OF DRAMA, THEATRE, AND PERFORMANCE. LT

ASTON, ELAINE, *An Introduction to Feminism and Theatre* (London, 1995)

CASE, SUE-ELLEN, *Feminism and Theatre* (London, 1988).

CIXOUS, HÉLÈNE, and CLÉMENT, CATHERINE, *The Newly Born Woman*, trans. B. Wing (Manchester, 1986)

MOI, TORIL, *Sexual/Textual Politics* (London, 1985)

FEMINIST THEATRE, UK

Feminist theatre in the UK developed as part of the 1970s Women's Liberation Movement (WLM; *see* FEMINISM). Demonstrations against female discrimination and sexism in the late 1960s and early 1970s used performance as a means of protest.

The first public displays of women's dissatisfaction took the form of theatrical interventions in the Miss World competition in *London in 1970 and 1971, staged to make points about stereotyping women as sex objects. Using theatre as a means of highlighting women's position was not without precedent. During the nineteenth century, plays by *Ibsen and *Shaw drew attention to the subordination of women and in 1908 the Actresses Franchise League was formed to promote women's suffrage. Feminist theatre in the 1970s had two main objectives: to raise consciousness of the social and political issues which concerned women and to improve the conditions of women working in the theatre. Taking the WLM slogan of 'The personal is political' as the central tenet, it aimed to educate *audiences about discrimination, working conditions, and equal rights, as well as explore relationships between private and public spheres of experience. Furthermore, women wanted to hold more authoritative positions in the institutions of theatre, and encourage positive and diverse representations of women on stage.

Early women's theatre adopted *agitprop styles of performance. In 1972 the Women's Street Theatre Group, formed in

1970, produced *The Amazing Equal Pay Show* and the Bolton Octagon *Theatre-in-Education company devised *Sweetie Pie*, both of which aimed to raise ordinary women's awareness of their rights. In 1974, Red Ladder, a socialist theatre company, performed *Strike While the Iron Is Hot*, which traced a working woman's change from naivety to independence. In 1973 Ed Berman organized a season of women's work at the Almost Free Theatre, after which a series of feminist companies were set up, notably the Women's Theatre Group, an all-female company whose first play was *My Mother Says* (1974), and *Monstrous Regiment, a socialist-feminist company whose first play was *Scum: death destruction and dirty washing* (1976) by Claire Luckham and Chris Bond. In 1975 *Gay Sweatshop was founded as a company of lesbians and gay men. *Any Woman Can* (1976) by Jill Posner and *Care and Control* (1977) by Michelene Wandor were two plays which focused directly upon lesbianism (*see* LESBIAN THEATRE). While these companies accounted for much of the work produced late in the decade, a number of women playwrights began to have plays produced in other areas of subsidized theatre: Caryl *Churchill worked with the *Royal Court and *Joint Stock Theatre Group, while Pam *Gems had *Dusa, Fish, Stas and Vi* (1977) presented at the *Hampstead Theatre Club and *Queen Christina* (1977) produced by the *Royal Shakespeare Company.

British feminist playwrights of the 1980s focused upon materialist feminism and the examination of historical contexts (*see* MATERIALIST CRITICISM). Caryl Churchill's *Cloud Nine* (1979) and *Top Girls* (1982) analyse relationships between class and *gender by juxtaposing past and present, while Timberlake *Wertenbaker's *The Grace of Mary Traverse* (1985) examines women's oppression through the lens of the eighteenth century. This emphasis has supported feminist revision of history and the reclamation of a hidden past. Alongside the production of new plays, there have been significant rediscoveries of work by past women writers, for example Aphra *Behn and Githa *Sowerby. Furthermore, women actors and directors have reworked classics in order to expose the sexism of the dramatic canon.

Much black feminist theatre, like Jacqueline Rudet's *Basin* (1985) and Winsome *Pinnock's *Leave Taking* (1987), has originated in *studio spaces. Founded in 1982, the first black company devoted to the work of black women was the Theatre of Black Women, which presented Jackie Kay's *Chiaroscuro* (1986). The most successful black women's theatre has been Talawa, founded in 1985 and directed by Yvonne *Brewster.

The influence of feminist theory in the 1980s has directed women's theatre towards the development of new representational aesthetics which cross the boundaries of *dance, live art, and theatre (*see* PERFORMANCE ART). Influenced by the work of women performance artists such as Bobby Baker and Rose English, experimental theatre has attempted to release the representation of women from theatrical conventions. Feminist

reworkings of *psychoanalytic theories have led to the exploration of memories, *dreams, and the unconscious by, for example, Deborah Levy in *Clam* (1985) and *The 'B' File* (1992). In the twenty-first century, postmodernist theatre is looking to models of feminist theatre for new forms of expression. *See also* MODERNISM AND POSTMODERNISM; GAY THEATRE AND PERFORMANCE; QUEER THEORY.   LT

GOODMAN, LIZBETH, *Contemporary Feminist Theatre: to each her own* (London, 1993)

WANDOR, MICHELENE, *Carry on Understudies: theatre and sexual politics* (London, 1986)

FEMINIST THEATRE, USA

Performance as an articulation of feminist politics has been an important constituent of theatre in America, never more so than in the last 30 years of the twentieth century. In early manifestations, women used theatrical performance as well as theatricalized street protest as, for example, during the suffrage movement. While this early activity was highly significant and paved the way for what followed, it was not until the late 1960s and early 1970s that feminist theatre—that is performance for, by, and about women as a political and cultural category—emerged. New Left political movements, the *alternative theatre scene, and the larger feminist movement (*see* FEMINISM) contributed to the manifestation of feminist theatre. The *Open Theatre, *San Francisco Mime Troupe, and *Bread and Puppet Theatre are examples of companies that provided women with crucial exposure to techniques and performance but also frustrated their attempts to create from and perform a feminist politic. Founders of groups including the Women's Experimental Theatre (WET), *Spiderwoman Theater (ST), At the Foot of the Mountain (AFOM), Lilith, and Interart left experimental theatres to found feminist theatres. Feminists came together across the country in a grass-roots movement in order to convey women's experience both individually and collectively. Lacking an elite leadership, definitive manifestos, and national models, feminist theatre groups were not centralized.

Women sought to create performance from actual lived experience. These stories were absent from the stage, feminists believed, and the only way they would appear was for feminists to create them. Topics of plays focused tightly on women's experiences overlooked by the larger culture—women's friendship and sexuality (*Voz de la mujer*, Valentina Productions, 1980; *Split Britches* by *Split Britches, 1981), mothers and daughters (*The Daughters Cycle Trilogy*, WET, 1976–80; *The Story of a Mother*, AFOM, 1978), violence against women (*Rape-In*, Westbeth Feminist Playwrights Collective, 1971; *The Mountain Is Stirring*, It's Just a Stage, 1980), *race (*Chicana*, Las Cucarachas, 1974; *Winnetou's Snake Oil Show from Wigwam City*, ST, 1987), history and myth (*Persephone's Return*, Rhode Island Feminist Theater, 1974; *Daughters of Erin*, Lilith, 1982), and spirituality (*Antigone Prism*, Women's Ensemble Theater, 1975–6; *Snake Talk: urgent messages from the mother*, A Traveling Jewish Theater, 1986). Feminist groups were heavily invested in acknowledging the presence of the community as *audience in order to serve larger feminist concerns. Groups usually preferred to perform for all-women audiences. Most spectators experienced feminist theatre as affirming and supportive, although there were often lively, sometimes rancorous, debates about definitions of feminism and issues raised by the plays.

Production was also completely reinvented. A high value was placed on collectivity and collaboration, with power shared equally in decision making on questions ranging from creative material to managerial issues. The emphasis on collective collaboration came from the feminist belief that the personal is political. Participants wanted to re-examine modes of creation, especially traditional theatre hierarchies, though each group found its own articulation of *collective creation and *management. While many workers heavily invested in these collective modes as feminist models, some objected that they gave too much power to timid voices.

Connections among women and companies were crucial. Several groups collaborated on projects as well as on festivals. One of the most productive was the Women's One World Festival in *New York in 1980. This led to the founding of the *WOW Café in 1982, a performance space that has launched and supported the careers of many feminist performers and groups, including Carmelita Tropicana, Holly *Hughes, and the Five Lesbian Brothers.

Race and sexuality were both divisive and uniting. As feminism was dominated by white heterosexual women, so too was feminist theatre. That is not to say that lesbians and women of colour were not influential and central participants, but that the problems of racism and homophobia were present in theatre companies. Women struggled to make coalitions across these divides, however, and plays often reflected these experiences (*Cycles*, Womanspace Theater, 1972; *Exit the Maids*, Lilith, 1981). Playwrights Ntozake *Shange (*for colored girls who have considered suicide/when the rainbow is enuf*, 1975) and Cherrie Moraga (*Giving up the Ghost*, 1986) were heavily influenced by the feminist theatre around them and brought many of those ideas into their influential work on race (*see also* AFRICAN-AMERICAN THEATRE; HISPANIC THEATRE, USA).

While most feminist theatre groups had disbanded by the late 1980s due to decreased funding, member burnout, and changes in the feminist movement, many members went on to create theatre in other ways. There has been a proliferation of solo performers in the 1980s and 1990s (Marga Gomez, Robbie McCauley, Peggy Shaw, and Marty Pottenger, for example) and, in the twenty-first century, an explosion of plays performed in a variety of venues that have emerged from this work. *See also* FEMINIST THEATRE, UK; LESBIAN THEATRE. CMC

CANNING, CHARLOTTE, *Feminist Theaters in the USA: staging women's experience* (London, 1996)

CHINOY, HELEN KRICH, and JENKINS, LINDA WALSH (eds.), *Women in American Theater* (New York, 1983)

MARTIN, CAROL (ed.), *A Sourcebook of Feminist Performance: on and beyond the stage* (London, 1996)

FENICE, LA

The initiative to build Venice's opera house, originally intended as a venue for drama as well as *opera, came from a group of disaffected box-holders who had lost control of the San Beneto Theatre. The project was entrusted to the architect G. A. Selva, whose interior design, stalls plus five levels of *boxes, and uninspired façade aroused much satirical comment. The Fenice (Phoenix) was opened in 1792, burned to the ground in 1836, reopened the following year, and was radically restructured in 1854 to become exclusively a home for opera. It was again destroyed by *fire in 1996 and is again being rebuilt according to the original plans. While lacking the renown of La *Scala, it has always been a prestigious home of opera and has seen the première of masterpieces from *Verdi's *Rigoletto* (1851) to Luigi Nono's *Intolleranza* (1960). JF

FENN, EZEKIAL (fl. 1635)

English actor. As a *boy actor with Queen Henrietta's Men at the *Cockpit, Fenn in 1635 played the role of Sophonisba in Thomas Nabbes's *Hannibal and Scipio*, and probably acted the part of Winifred in a revival the same year of *The Witch of Edmonton*. He subsequently joined *Beeston's Boys in 1637, but his career after 1639, when he apparently switched to male roles, is a blank. RWV

FENNARIO, DAVID (1947–)

Canadian playwright, born David Wiper in *Montréal. His plays, most of which premièred at Centaur Theatre, Montréal, reflect his commitment to the working-class anglophone district of Pointe Saint-Charles where he grew up, and to revolutionary socialism. Beginning with *On the Job* (1975), he wrote a series of plays using fourth-wall conventions, most notably *Balconville* (1979). Convinced that the form could only reflect but not change social conditions, he turned to a presentational *agit-prop style, exemplified in *Joe Beef* (1984), performed by and for his own community. In the 1990s he performed the autobiographical *one-person shows *Banana Boots* (1994) and *Gargoyles* (1997–8). RCN

FENNELL, JAMES (1766–1816)

English and American actor. Born in England, Fennell came to the United States in 1793, as an actor in *Wignell's company.

453

Tall and attractive, he excelled in tragic roles and became one of the most popular actors in early America. He was closely identified with the role of Hamlet. Quarrelsome and restless, he broke with Wignell, after which he appeared intermittently at both the *Park Theatre in *New York and the *Chestnut Street. He also staged independent performances, including one-man dramatic Bible readings and dramas with other cast members recruited from the Park. In a review of his 1810 farewell performance as Richard III, one critic wrote: 'As a correct and classical player he has never found an equal on the American boards, and is perhaps surpassed but by one man living', probably meaning either G. F. *Cooke or Edmund *Kean. In his later years, Fennell made several unwise investments, including a scheme for salt manufacture. He was arrested and imprisoned for debt, after which he attempted a return to the stage, but alcoholism and illness impaired his ability to perform.

AHK

FERBER, EDNA (1885–1968)

American playwright. Ferber began writing plays in 1915 with *Our Mrs McChesney*, a collaboration with George V. Hobart and starring Ethel *Barrymore. Ferber preferred collaboration, *The Eldest* (1920) being her only solo play. *Minick* (1924) began a successful collaboration with George S. *Kaufman which resulted in three admired *comedy-dramas concerning the lives of actors—*The Royal Family* (1927), *Dinner at Eight* (1932), and *Stage Door* (1936). Two later works with Kaufman were poorly received. Ferber's novel *Show Boat* (1927) formed the basis for the *Hammerstein–*Kern musical.

MAF

FERNANDES, (CARLOS) AUGUSTO (c.1935–   )

Argentinian actor, director, and teacher who was instrumental in developing Argentina's 1960s generation of playwrights such as Ricardo Halac. Considered a pioneer of *Stanislavskian actor *training, Fernandes nonetheless escapes easy categorization as a *realist; he also directed the original 1968 production of Griselda *Gambaro's *The Camp*.

JGJ

FERRARI, PAOLO (1822–89)

Italian playwright. Ferrari resided in *Milan for 30 years as a professor, leaving frequently to stage his plays and staying briefly in *Rome (1883–4) while serving as director and poet of the prestigious National Dramatic Theatre. Skilled in delineating *character and expert in structuring *plot, he often rewrote his plays in *verse or adapted them from various dialects (Massese, Modenese, Venetian) into standard Italian for production by major troupes (*Bellotti-Bon, *Ristori). While his repu-

tation rests on *Goldoni e le sue sedici commedie nuove* (*Goldoni and his Sixteen New Comedies*, 1852), he wrote additional *comedies based on the lives of Italians (Dante, *Alfieri) and patriotic *historical dramas such as *La Satira e Parini* (*Satire and Parini*, 1856) and *Fulvio Testi* (1888). Of particular note are his *thesis plays, forerunners of *realism, that address current social problems: *Il duello* (1868), *Causa ed effetti* (1871), and *Il suicidio* (1875). He also wrote sparkling adaptations of works by Goldoni and contemporary French dramatists (Pailleron, *Augier), *farces for young students, and lively dramas for the child actress Gemma Cuniberti.

JEH

FERRER, JOSÉ (1912–92)

Puerto Rican-born American actor, producer, and director. He made his stage debut in 1934 performing *nautical melodramas on *showboats cruising Long Island Sound, and appeared on Broadway a year later as a policeman in *A Slight Case of Murder*. He played in a number of important works in *New York, including *Spring Dance* (1936), *Brother Rat* (1936), *Missouri Legend* (1938), *Mamba's Daughters* (1939), *Key Largo* (1939), *Charley's Aunt* (1940), and the title role in *Cyrano de Bergerac* (1946). With his acclaimed performance of Iago to Paul *Robeson's Othello in 1943, Ferrer entered a new phase of his career as an actor and producer of classical drama. In 1948 he was appointed director of the New York Theatre Company at the City Center, where he appeared in *Volpone*, *The Alchemist*, and *Richard III*, in addition to plays by *Chekhov, *Čapek, and *O'Neill. Other notable productions for City Center include *Stalag 17* (1951) and *The Shrike* (1952), in which he performed the role of a husband wrongly committed to a mental asylum by his unscrupulous wife. In 1963 he created the role of the Prince Regent in the *musical *The Girl Who Came to Supper*. His extensive *film career included *Moulin Rouge* (1953), *The Caine Mutiny* (1954), *Ship of Fools* (1965), and an Academy award for *Cyrano de Bergerac* (1950).

JAB

FERRON, JACQUES (1921–85)

Québec dramatist and novelist. A physician by training, he began writing *comedies in the 1950s but turned more towards socially committed theatre during the turbulent 1960s. The plays of the latter period are his best known, such as *Les Grands Soleils* (*The Sunflowers*), completed in 1958 but not performed until 1968, offering a radically revised view of the Patriot Rebellion of 1837, and *La Tête du roi* (*The King's Head*, 1963), centred on the destruction of a statue of Edward VII but evoking other confrontations with colonialism. A lifelong political activist, he founded the *Ionesco-inspired Rhinoceros Party in 1963 to protest Canada's electoral system.

LED

FESTIVALS OF THEATRE

The term 'festival' derives from 'feast', and refers to a periodic series of performances tied to a certain place or season. The roots of the festival tradition are found in the West in the *Greek *Dionysia, a holiday honouring *Dionysus in the fifth century BC. A combination of religious *rituals and the performance of *comedies, *tragedies, *satyr-plays, and *dithyrambs, the Dionysia were held annually in Athens and were the occasion for celebration and entertainment. Theatrical performances were merged with a contest of playwrights, leading to a prize for the best tragedy. The combination of theatre and ritual can also be found in *medieval religious plays in Europe, from *Quem Quaeritis tropes of the tenth century, the *liturgical drama of the twelfth century, and on to the vast *cycles of *mystery and *biblical plays lasting in some locales to the sixteenth century, all generally tied to important ecclesiastical holidays. While the relationship of ritual to the theatrical continues to be contested, it is clear that in ancient Greece and medieval Europe the spheres of *religion and art were not strictly separated.

A new phase in the development of the festival arose in the *early modern period. Under monarchical absolutism and the rediscovery of classical learning and art, the festival was detached from a religious context and put into a secular frame. As the realm for the demonstration of royal power, these festivals, which lasted for several days, had a high visual impact and used many performative elements like water games, *fireworks, *tournaments, *ballets, *parades, royal *entries, and theatre and *opera productions. The *neoclassical festival became an opportunity for staging the court, whose members were actors and spectators at the same time (*see also* MASQUE; BALLET DE COUR; STATE DISPLAYS).

The rise of the bourgeois class and the ideas of the Enlightenment profoundly affected theatre production, especially in Central Europe. The great festivals and events of the aristocracy began to be replaced by notions of a *national theatre which belonged to the people (or at least to the middle class); the control of the festival moved from noble hands to the hands of entrepreneurs serving the interests of the bourgeois *audience. In England, where theatre had remained in the seventeenth and eighteenth centuries almost entirely a commercial affair without royal or public subsidy, the actor David *Garrick arranged a celebration in Stratford-upon-Avon in 1769 in honour of Shakespeare. Though the affair was not a success, it can be considered the first of the new tradition of festivals, starting the sequence of Shakespeare festivals that continue today there and around the world.

The revival of festivals did not merely continue the traditional connection of theatre and festive occasion, but also appropriated it in the new *romantic cult of genius. Celebrating a single great figure, art was proffered as a surrogate for religion, and educated spectators were granted social markers of distinc-

tion, of self-assertion, and self-representation. At the end of the nineteenth century, as nationalism gained further importance for the bourgeois ideology, the festival responded: the *Bayreuth Festival, founded in 1876 by Richard *Wagner, was conceived as a realm for his *operas that would express the inner impulses and aspirations of national myths. Attending the festival thus became a kind of national pilgrimage and part of nation building. A similar type of festival occurred as a site-specific event, turning *ancient theatres or ruins into a venue for celebration of historical continuity. A prominent example is the festival in the Roman theatre in Orange in the south of France, founded in 1869. Such festivals increased enormously in the latter part of the twentieth century, when the choice of spaces became linked to cultural tourism.

Max *Reinhardt's founding of the *Salzburg Festival in 1920 was a fusion of the site-specific festival, the bourgeois concept, and the backdrop of the Middle Ages. Even today the festival is opened by staging Hugo von *Hofmannsthal's adaptation of the medieval *morality play *Everyman*, contextualizing the event with a reminder of the history of European theatre. After the Second World War a number of festivals were founded for new or experimental work. The most famous ones are the *Avignon Festival (1947), the *Edinburgh International Festival (1947), a ballet and opera festival in Aix-en-Provence (1948), and the *Berlin Festwochen (1951). These festivals can be no longer considered as rituals of self-assertion for the bourgeoisie—they have in part become an institutional realm for *fringe or *alternative performance. Their programmatic aim is closely connected with the emergence of *avant-garde theatre forms that go beyond the traditional bourgeois theatre, though the middle class might well attend them. The festivals also offer the opportunity for large-scale comparisons and thus contribute to the internationalizing of aesthetic trends. Festivals also provide a scope for neglected kinds of performance like *puppet theatre, or for projects of different art forms; examples include the Venice Biennale (1951) and the Adelaide Festival of Arts (1960). Since the 1970s a number of festivals have emerged with the purpose of promoting an artistic analysis of electronic media, like the Ars Electronica in Linz (Austria, 1979).

The effects of festivals on the theatrical landscape are twofold. First, they favour the emergence of 'global players', famous directors, actors, and international troupes that concentrate mainly on these events (*see* INTERCULTURALISM); second, they give small companies and excluded ethnicities the opportunity of self-representation. Shevtsova has called this later aspect 'festivalization', which she sees as a decentring force because even small, out-of-the-way towns can create events of considerable note. Festivals, she says, have become central to the expansion and 'dissemination of theatre, not least because they provide opportunities for struggling groups, as well as to mavericks whose appearance on the scene is vital to its health overall'. While the nineteenth-century tradition of bourgeois rituals continues, festivals also provide scope for the emergence of experimental aesthetics and new troupes outside the system of institutional theatres. *See also* CIVIC FESTIVALS. PWM

SHEVTSOVA, MARIA, 'Bells and alarm clocks: theatre and theatre research at the millennium', *Theatre Research International*, 24 (1999)

FEUCHTWANGER, LION (1884–1958)

German novelist and dramatist. Better known as a novelist, Feuchtwanger's connection with theatre is mainly through his collaboration with *Brecht: he contributed to *Edward II* in the 1920s and to *The Visions of Simon Machard* in the 1940s. His considerable dramatic output is largely forgotten, although many of his novels have been dramatized for theatre, *film, and *television, especially *Jud Süss* (1925), *Erfolg* (*Success*, 1930) and *Die Geschwister Oppenheim* (*The Family Oppenheim*, 1933).
CBB

FEYDEAU, GEORGES-LÉON-JULES-MARIE (1862–1921)

French dramatist. Son of the Second Empire novelist Ernest Feydeau, Georges Feydeau made his name both in France and abroad as a writer of well-crafted, swift-moving, farcical *comedy. Taking over where Labiche had left off, Feydeau soon developed a distinctive formula, which he was very ready to acknowledge: 'When I sit down to write a play', he said, 'I identify those *characters who have every reason to avoid each other; and I make it my business to bring them together as soon, and as often, as I can.' If not unique—it can be seen at work in *Beaumarchais's comedies, for instance—this formula was exploited more openly and systematically by Feydeau than by any of his predecessors; and the result is a superior form of literary *farce: for the dominance of a fast-moving *plot should not be taken to mean that his characters are mere ciphers. Indeed, he insisted that his characters are recognizable as inhabiting the same world as his spectators, with the same hypocrisies, marital infidelities, and sham respectability; and through the latter part of his career, he was moving towards a more serious exposé of the whole institution of bourgeois marriage.

As for his plots, he suggested that these should be seen as the intrusion of a nightmare sequence of events into the otherwise unremarkable lives of his very ordinary characters. A typical plot establishes in Act I the need for secrecy on which the subterfuge and duplicity of the leading characters will depend; in Act II we move to a public meeting place—most notoriously a hotel of not very savoury reputation, as in *L'Hôtel du Libre-Échange* (*A Little Hotel on the Side*, 1894), or *Une puce à l'oreille* (*A Flea in her Ear*, 1907); while Act III restores things to a somewhat precarious status quo. The nightmare quality of Feydeau's middle acts is given visual expression not only by the frenzied comings and goings, but also by mechanical stage accessories such as the revolving bed in *Une puce à l'oreille*, which delivers characters on stage and whisks them off again, apparently with a will of its own—a device of which Feydeau, as its inventor, was extremely proud. His plays were all produced outside the national theatres; and from the success of *Tailleur pour dames* (*A Gown for his Mistress*), produced at the Renaissance Theatre in 1886, he was to be accredited provider for this theatre, the Nouveautés, and other *boulevard houses. Apart from a series of *one-act plays written as *curtain raisers, production at the *Comédie-Française had to wait until after the Second World War, when *Le Dindon* (*Sauce for the Goose*, originally performed at the *Palais Royal in 1896) confirmed Feydeau's established status as a classic. In Britain, it was Noël *Coward who first took up Feydeau, when *Occupe-toi d'Amélie* (1908) was presented as *Look after Lulu* in 1959; while other successful adaptations into English are those of John *Mortimer for the Royal *National Theatre (*A Flea in her Ear*, 1966; *The Lady from Maxim's*, 1977; *A Little Hotel on the Side*, 1984). WDH

FIALKA, LADISLAV (1931–91)

Czech *mime, choreographer, and director. Fialka devoted most of his time to his troupe based in the Theatre on the *Balustrade, one of the few fully professional *repertory mime companies in the world. He choreographed and directed thirteen different productions there, ranging from a loose series of sketches (*Mime on the Balustrade*, 1959; *Études*, 1960) to attempts at coherent drama (*Button*, 1968; *Caprichos*, 1971) based upon his own *texts. Most of his productions were kept in repertory for years and *toured abroad extensively. Impressed since his youth by French mime from J.-G. *Deburau to Marcel *Marceau, Fialka created his modern version of *Pierrot, close to Marceau's Bip, showing a great variety of expression, from a tender melancholic to a tormented soul. At the same time he gave prominence to ensemble performance and technical ability. In the 1960s Fialka's mime was one of the highlights of Czech theatre and a prestigious International Mime Festival was held in *Prague in 1969 and 1971. Thereafter a new generation of 'black mime' emerged, represented by Ctibor Turba and Boris Hybner, who were encouraged by Fialka, though they opposed his traditional whiteface mime. ML

FICHANDLER, ZELDA (1924–)

American director and *manager. Along with Tyrone *Guthrie and Margo *Jones, Fichandler was the visionary of America's *regional theatre movement. In 1950, in an abandoned cinema in Washington, DC, she founded *Arena Stage, the first racially integrated theatre in that city. She was Arena's *artistic director from 1952 to 1990, when she stepped down to be the director of New York University's graduate acting programme. Her interests in psychoanalysis, political activism, and Russian literature were evident in her directing, in Arena's repertoire, and in her philosophy that 'not-for-profit theatres do exist to generate a profit of a social nature, and a profit that is earned from the examination of reality by means of theatrical art'. Under her leadership, Arena won the first regional Tony *Award in 1976, became the first American theatre to tour the USSR (1973), and, with her production of Howard Sackler's *The Great White Hope* (1968), starring Jane *Alexander and James Earl *Jones, the first regional theatre to transfer a show to Broadway.   GAO

FIELD, NATHAN (1587–1620)

English actor and dramatist. As a boy Field was a member of the Children of the *Chapel and the Queen's Revels. He seems to have been Ben *Jonson's scholar, and later appeared on stage in several Jonson plays performed by the Lord *Chamberlain's Men: *Cynthia's Revels* (1600), *The Poetaster* (1601), and *Epicene* (1609). Many of Field's roles are unknown although scholars suggest that he performed female *characters early in life. It is possible that he played Humphrey in *Beaumont's *The Knight of the Burning Pestle* (c.1610), and he was much celebrated in the title role in *Chapman's *Bussy D'Ambois* (published in 1607). He may also have played Littlewit in Jonson's *Bartholomew Fair* (1614). By 1613 he had joined Lady Elizabeth's Men, but by 1616 transferred to the King's Men. Field wrote two plays under his own name and collaborated on others with *Massinger and *Fletcher. Jonson compared him to Richard *Burbage, the most prominent actor in Shakespeare's company.
                                                                  SPC

FIELD DAY THEATRE COMPANY

Northern Irish enterprise, founded in 1980 by playwright Brian *Friel and actor Stephen Rea. The Derry-based company aimed at creating a hypothetical fifth province of Ireland committed to exploring history, language, and identity both north and south of the border. From 1980 to 1991 Field Day *toured the island every year with a new Irish play, the first being Friel's *Translations* (1980). Other work included Thomas *Kilroy's *Double Cross* (1985) and Stewart *Parker's *Pentecost* (1987). Field Day also published a series of pamphlets, books, and anthologies of Irish literature.   MAS

FIELDING, HENRY (1707–54)

English playwright, novelist, and magistrate. Fielding is now known almost entirely for his novels, but before turning to that *genre he was the most successful dramatist of his generation. Beginning in 1728, his ten-year career as a playwright and occasional *manager was marked by conspicuous success. He wrote 26 plays, all but five of them premièring before 1737. His early efforts were unremarkable genteel *comedies, but he scored his first hit with *The Author's Farce* (1730), a high-spirited *farce that ridiculed the *patent houses and their rapacious managers. *Tom Thumb* followed (1730), a *burlesque of contemporary *tragedy, later revised as *The Tragedy of Tragedies*. Fielding produced these and many other works at the *Haymarket Theatre, a venue that had no permanent company and no manager, granting great freedom of expression. This freedom came at the cost of production quality, and Fielding sought productions at the patent theatres whenever possible. A gifted farceur, he nevertheless wanted to write five-act comedies of serious social purpose, something that only the skilled patent house performers could handle. He had some success in this genre, notably with *The Modern Husband* (*Drury Lane, 1732), but in general his patent house hits were the farces he wrote for Kitty *Clive, like *The Intriguing Chambermaid* (1734), or his adaptations of *Molière.

After the failure of *The Universal Gallant* (Drury Lane, 1735), Fielding turned again to the Little Haymarket, where with James Ralph he established a more formal troupe of actors that he styled 'The Great Mogul's Company'. The theatre became a venue critical of both the Walpole ministry and the patent theatres, scoring Fielding's most impressive triumphs, including *Pasquin* (1736) and *The Historical Register of the Year 1736* (1737). Partly in response to Fielding's *satire, the Walpole government engineered the 1737 theatre *Licensing Act, giving complete *censorship authority to the *Lord Chamberlain, and putting Fielding out of business because he did not have a royal patent. He wrote a few more plays and briefly operated a *puppet show in the 1740s, but left the theatre entirely to write his great novels: *Joseph Andrews* (1742), *Tom Jones* (1749), and *Amelia* (1751). He also read for the law and had a simultaneous and effective career as an anti-corruption magistrate, attacking some of the same abuses that had provoked his dramatic satires.   MJK

FIELDS, GRACIE (GRACE STANSFIELD) (1898–1979)

English *variety artist, singer, and actress. From humble beginnings in Lancashire, 'our Gracie' achieved international celebrity on stage and *film. As a child she sang in local *music halls, juvenile troupes, and Pierrot shows in Blackpool and St Anne's. She met her first husband, comedian Archie Pitt, while *touring the *revue *Yes, I Think So* in 1915. In 1918 Pitt produced his own revue, *Mr Tower of London*, which, after touring the provinces with Gracie in the lead, achieved huge success at Oswald Stoll's Alhambra Theatre in *London. Stardom followed both in revues and variety shows, as well as films such as *Sally in our Alley* (1931). During the Second World War Gracie entertained British troops with songs like 'Wish Me Luck as You Wave Me

Goodbye', and raised considerable funds for the war effort. Her extraordinary ability to move from comedy to pathos, *slapstick to sentiment, was demonstrated in songs such as 'Walter', 'The Biggest Aspidistra in the World', and 'Sally'.   AF

FIELDS, LEW *See* WEBER, JOSEPH.

FIELDS, W. C. (WILLIAM CLAUDE DUNKENFIELD) (1880–1946)

American comic actor whose gravel voice, vitriolic wit, and deadpan mutterings expressed disdain for authority, children, animals, and teetotallers. Born in *Philadelphia, Fields ran away from home as a child and learned to *juggle, his old-fashioned, frayed *costume saving him money. He became a famous tramp juggler on the *vaudeville circuit in the USA and Europe, receiving top billing at the *Folies-Bergère in *Paris and the *Hippodrome in *London, and starred in several editions of the *Ziegfeld Follies between 1915 and 1925. Fields patented his best skits, such as the failed golf lesson and the fiasco of packing a car for a vacation. As Eustace McGargle in *Poppy* (1923), his first speaking role on stage, he developed the *character of the disreputable huckster he would repeat on *film. He appeared in *The Earl Carroll Vanities of 1928* and as Q. Q. Quayle in *Ballyhoo* (1930). He acted in several cinema gems, most of which he wrote himself.   FL

FIERSTEIN, HARVEY (1954–   )

American actor and playwright whose plays address *gay men's search for love and acceptance. Fierstein performed in nightclubs as a *female impersonator and played a corpulent lesbian in Andy Warhol's *Pork* (1971). The semi-autobiographical *Torch Song Trilogy* (1981) links three *one-act plays, originally performed at *La Mama Experimental Theatre Club before moving to Broadway. Fierstein played the leading role, Arnold, a comic drag queen whose lover deserts him for a woman (*The International Stud*, 1976); who joins this couple in bed with Alan, his new lover (*Fugue in a Nursery*, 1979); and who mourns Alan's murder and raises their adopted son (*Widows and Children First*, 1979). In *La Cage aux Folles* (1983) a mature homosexual couple try to gain a son's approval; the commercially successful *musical entertained without arousing controversy. *Safe Sex* (1987) gave Fierstein's reactions to the AIDS crisis. He has acted in over 70 stage productions, and his other plays include *Freaky Pussy* (1976), *Spookhouse* (1983), and *Forget Him* (1988).   FL

FILIPPO, EDUARDO DE *See* DE FILIPPO, EDUARDO.

FILM AND THEATRE *see page 459*

FINANCE

Theatre has always been more than a performance by people for people: someone has to pay for the activity, with cash or its equivalent in gifts of time and labour. When itinerant actors perform in a public place, a hat will be passed around during or after the show for the *audience to show its appreciation and contribute to costs. For more elaborate productions financial arrangements are far more complex, less direct, and usually completed long before an actor steps in front of an audience. Only the most popular theatres have been financed entirely by their audiences, notable among them *kabuki of *Japan in its original forms, *commedia dell'arte*, and *early modern Spanish and English theatres, including the company and theatre in which Shakespeare was a sharer, the Lord *Chamberlain's Men. Only theatres producing *melodramas and popular *comedies have continued this direct dependence on the public at large through the nineteenth and into the twentieth centuries. Often they have had to go on prolonged *tours to find their audiences: for example, the *jatra theatres that still thrive in *India today. Comedies written by *Noda Hideki, who is also both actor and director, were exceptional when they filled *Tokyo theatres for months on end in the 1980s and 1990s; this was a sophisticated and technically ambitious theatre able to sustain itself solely by public support and its own efforts. Towards the end of the twentieth century, a number of mega-*musicals originating in *New York or *London could also show profit. Their producers ran the risk of huge losses but, once acclaimed as popular successes, the spectacular shows could be reproduced in the biggest theatres around the world and make millions of pounds and dollars for their producers, directors, composers, designers, authors, and, to a lesser extent, a few of their performing artists.

Down the centuries, the largest and most reliable sources of income for theatre have been the patrons, sponsors, state and municipal governments, and, occasionally, religious, ideological, or communal organizations that have made it their business to pay for the public to see theatre. Plays written for *festivals at Athens during the fifth century BC were part of official civic and religious celebrations and a manifestation of the wealth and culture of the city-state. Individual productions were paid for by leading citizens and prizes given to those judged the best in any one year (*see* GREEK THEATRE, ANCIENT). Throughout early modern Europe, princely courts supplied both finance and the theatres in which to perform; in France, Louis XIV (1643–1715) spent huge sums on productions that would boost his public image as the Sun King and at the same time gratify his own taste for splendour, music, *dancing, and fine writing (*see* VERSAILLES). In Italy especially, learned academies and other public bodies followed this lead while to this day, throughout Europe, government and municipalities have helped to finance theatre companies. On occasion, they subsidize tours

(continued on p. 465)

FILM AND THEATRE

The intricate and spasmodic relationship between motion pictures and the live stage requires consideration of two separate subjects. The first is the lengthy attempt to articulate a reliable *historiographic approach which, without favouring either theatre or film, effectively describes how the two media have interacted. The second is the actual history of how two different but related means of entertainment, sometimes sharing the same or similar material but employing different technologies to reach different but related *audiences, have interacted for more than a century.

1. Historiography; 2. Theatrical background;
3. Theatre into film; 4. Convergence; 5. The sound era;
6. Two industries?

1. Historiography

The previous—and still deeply entrenched—model for depicting the relationship between the live theatre and narrative film was established in 1949 by Nicholas Vardac and elaborated thereafter by a succession of film historians who, as a subtext to their accounts, sought to distance film from its theatrical sources and describe it as an independent art. Vardac, recognizing in silent film elements of theatrical method and subject matter which filmmakers had adapted from nineteenth-century American, British, and French entertainments, noted that Victorian stage machinists and scene *painters, in depicting environments and moments of high peril and excitement in the *sensation scenes of *melodrama, strove for but (in his view) failed to achieve *illusions of absolute *realism. In contrast, he assumed that motion picture photography effortlessly achieved reproductions of the material world which lay beyond the skill of scenic artists. Vardac concluded that the late nineteenth-century stage had exhausted its resources for depicting, on the one hand, the realism which was the scenic objective of melodrama and, on the other hand, elements of fantasy and magic which were the province of English *pantomime and the French *féerie. He thus declared that the Victorian stage had surrendered its artistic and popular pre-eminence to the vitality and specificity of film. For Vardac and Vardac's adherents, the relationship between stage and cinema was unidirectional, continual, and inevitable: primitive theatrical material evolving—and thus progressing—into sophisticated cinema.

Vardac's successors took a further step in citing optical and additional narrative sources which prepared the way for film, introducing the teleological concept of 'pre-cinema' which re-sulted in nominating theatrical, non-theatrical devices, and narrative forms which further distanced film from theatre. These included a variety of optical toys (such as the zoetrope and praxinoscope), such narrative media as strip cartoons, and extended in a megalomanical embrace to include pyrodramas (large-scale *fireworks plays) and other outdoor *pageants. Concurrently another film historian, Tom Gunning, drew parallels between cinema and theatre by describing early film as a 'cinema of attractions', likening the heterogeneous subjects on view to the *variety stage and *music hall.

Since the 1990s the Vardac paradigm has been challenged by accounts which indicate that, far from theatrical material undergoing unidirectional transmutation into film, there has been a constant, if irregular, record of exchanges in both directions: not merely a vigorous predatory cinema devouring the resources and subject matter of theatre, but live theatre exploiting cinema technologies and strategies in mixed-media productions (*see* MULTIMEDIA PERFORMANCE). In neither direction has there been a constant flow; each event of interchange is random and isolated from others. The borders between live performance and film have been—and continue to be—irregular, fluid, and mutually permeable. At the start of the twenty-first century significant stage shows, frequently located in large amusement parks which attract numerous international visitors, interleave stage and film illusions, sometimes fusing older and current technologies, to the astonishment and mystification of spectators. And it has been thus since the early days of silent film.

2. Theatrical background

Conditions which were to make theatres suitable venues for the exhibition of films and, eventually, locales in which to seek adaptable theatrical material are to be found in the music halls and variety theatres of Europe and America. This is especially the case of the British music halls, where the Theatre Regulation Act of 1843 and subsequent legislation (*see* LICENSING ACTS), and tacit agreements between licensing authorities and theatrical and music-hall proprietors, underscored differences between the variety theatres and *legitimate houses. The Act, giving music halls the right to sell and consume alcoholic beverages in the *auditorium, also stipulated that material performed was to be chiefly non-dramatic or, if dramatic, of such brevity that it did not impinge on the legitimate houses' privilege of presenting full-length dramas. The privilege was guarded assiduously by theatre *managers and reinforced by punitive legal actions. In consequence, music halls—offering varying bills mixing music, *dance, *magic shows, comics, performing *animals, *circus skills, and such mechanical novelties as incubators and parachutes—introduced drama into their programmes in the guise of the 'dramatic sketch'.

The importance and nature of the sketch has been underemphasized in most histories of the variety theatre. It was a narrative drama, but by a tacit agreement reached in the late 1880s between theatrical and music-hall proprietors was limited to casts of no more than six actors, sparse in the amount of spoken *dialogue, confined to one or two *scenes, and restricted in duration to eighteen minutes. Expository narrative was provided in the printed *programme or, as frequently, sung by a narrator who remained outside the dramatic *action. Like most music-hall variety turns, the sketch was accompanied by incidental orchestral music. A notably successful dramatic sketch was John Lawson's *Humanity* 'in 18-minutes' (1897). Lawson, a former *acrobat, undertook the role of Silvani, a wealthy Jew who befriended a gentleman—a Gentile—who in turn seduced his wife and attempted to elope with her. Detected by Silvani, who intercepted a note from the seducer describing him as 'only a Jew', the couple were confronted. Lawson stepped out of *character to sing 'Only a Jew', then returned to his role to engage in a fierce battle with his rival. The fight destroyed the apartment, setting fire to the staircase down which the two struggling adversaries fell to their deaths. *Humanity*, and numerous sketches of similar brevity and action, as well as comic and romantic sketches, none fettered with excessive language and all understandable in *mimed action, *toured the variety theatres of the world, introducing spectators to brief silent dramas. The sketch was a well-established form when, in 1896, motion pictures were exhibited in these same theatres.

A further development came in the late 1870s. The introduction of electric stage *lighting gradually brought to an end the long practice of leaving the auditorium illuminated during performances. Now audiences sat in semi-darkness and gazed at an illuminated stage, and in these darkened variety theatre auditoriums audiences first saw motion pictures. The 'kinematograph' or the 'biograph'—the projector and an assortment of exceedingly brief motion pictures—was introduced as a mechanical novelty: the opportunity to observe photographs which actually moved as they depicted current events, native and foreign celebrities, railway journeys, domestic scenes and industrial labour, animals, military and state processions—all animated, but few purporting to offer dramatic *plots. If there was a narrative, it was brief: boys stealing the clothing of women bathing in a river, a gardener soaked with his own watering hose. As with other variety entertainments, each of these films was accompanied by orchestral or piano music. It was general variety house practice to place the film programme immediately preceding or following the dramatic sketch. By 1905, the sketch had expanded to a maximum 30 minutes, but at this date narrative (that is, dramatic) films, introduced

about 1903, were likely to run for 10 to 15 minutes, and they were to lengthen further before being shown in venues other than variety theatres. Additionally, other films in the bioscope segment exhibited stage entertainments especially reproduced for the camera. Thomas Edison's studio in Fort Lee, New Jersey, regularly persuaded touring stage acts to visit and permit their acts to be filmed. By 1907 Edison's cameramen had filmed Streator's Zouaves, a military drill and wall-scaling troupe from Illinois, Japanese acrobats performing a 'Risley' act, American and European acrobats and *jugglers, comic barbershop sketches, dancers whose choreography had been inspired by Loïe *Fuller, various rapier and broadsword combats lifted from Broadway hits, and an anonymous touring production of *Macbeth*.

Seizing on the novelty, the growing popularity of the kinematograph programme, and the awe that this new medium inspired, showmen from various quarters of the profession attempted to exploit its possibilities. Perci Honri's 'Mr Moon' illusion (c.1900) utilized a moving image of this musical performer projected upon the 'face' of the man-in-the-moon. A *puppet's body affixed to the screen plucked at a banjo, whilst Honri, from the wings, sang the Moon's serenade to the earth, synchronizing his song to his projected facial expressions.

Conjurors and illusionists were amongst the earliest stage artists to appreciate the possibilities of film. The English conjuror David Devant introduced around the same time rear-projection and tinted film in an illusion-sketch called *The Magic Mirror*. The 'mirror' was a motion picture screen, by turns opaque and capable of reflecting Devant's image or, alternately, translucent and able to display a sequence of projected images of a diabolic figure, a bride, and the conjuror himself. Devant then attacked his screen image and, apparently tearing garments from the screen, tore at its clothing to reveal a second impostor-image of Mephistopheles.

Another conjuror to turn to film and to have considerable impact on motion picture content, form, and methods was Georges Méliès. Fascinated with the stage illusions, Méliès had become by 1891 a leading figure amongst French *magicians. Purchasing the theatre of the conjuror Robert-Houdin as a venue where he might exhibit his skill, Méliès became intimately familiar with the *trap-work and numerous illusion devices of the late Victorian stage. When Méliès turned to film in 1896 as a means of furthering illusions, he rebuilt the apparatus of the Théâtre Robert-Houdin in his studio at Montreuil-sous-Bois, adding further technical effects of his own devising. Méliès's films sometimes have the structure and appearance of the *féerie*, sometimes of the *commedia dell'arte* as practised at the *Funambules in *Paris, at other times are more rigidly narrative and less improvisatory, but especially in his earlier work there is a reliance on stage machinery. His films remain an invaluable source for observing nineteenth-century trap-work of all sorts: falling-flap and sink-and-rise *scenery, doors which pivot and spin, and various illusions propelled and operated by concealed stagehands.

Film also held attractions for the legitimate theatre. Bruce 'Sensation' Smith added the movements of filmed fish projected onto scenery in *Drury Lane's 'autumn' drama *The White Heather* (1897). In an episode in which two suited and helmeted divers fought over treasure on the sea's bottom, the fish were intended to add verisimilitude to the underwater effect. In America, Lincoln Carter's 1899 Civil War melodrama *Chattanooga* featured a scene in which a locomotive appeared to race at great speed before a back-projected image of moving countryside and passing villages.

3. Theatre into film

Whereas these events reflect a growing but piecemeal exchange between stage and film, two motion pictures, both made in 1903 by Edwin Porter at the Edison Studios, foreshadow an altogether new and enduring relationship: stage plays quarried to supply narrative material for motion pictures. An unknown combination company (*see* STOCK COMPANY) of white actors and *African-American dancers was then touring the eastern seaboard with a version of *Uncle Tom's Cabin* (*see* TOM SHOW). Persuading them to remount their production before the Edison cameras, Porter shot the key episodes of the play, using the actors' practised gestures and stage business and the dancers' routines in front of the company's own scenery. Each episode was linked by inter-titles (captions explicating the action), and the entire drama was released as a twelve-minute film. Only months later, Porter took the further step of adapting and reshaping a stage play for the screen. Choosing Scott Marble's 1896 *The Great Train Robbery*, popular for seven years on eastern and Midwest circuits, Porter stripped the play of its several main plots, understandable only with dialogue, and focused on the train robbery and its aftermath. He also included a portion of Marble's *cabaret scene so as to introduce, as was expected in combination melodrama, an episode of music and dance. These two Porter achievements created a widespread taste for complete narrative films. Original screenplays would account for many subsequent films, but the live theatre would also be ransacked for other screen-worthy dramas, and the existing repertoire of European and American plays popular on the smaller circuits would contribute to the need for drama understandable through action and occasional inter-titles.

Apart from the exhibition of films in variety theatres, music halls, *waxworks, and travelling *fairground booths, theatre and film people and their audiences inhabited different worlds. Established stage actors were reluctant to compromise their reputations by appearing in movies. Audiences who attended stage plays complained that the flickering light-beam from the projector caused headaches, and that storefront cinema theatres ('nickelodeons') were unclean, unsavoury, and patronized by the poor and immigrant classes. It is against this hostility toward motion pictures, their makers, and their audiences that we must view a key attempt at adapting a stage vehicle for the screen. Aware of the undiminished popularity of William Young's stage version (1899) of Lew Wallace's novel *Ben-Hur* (1880), the Kalem Company of *New York attempted in 1907 to bring the drama to the screen. Hiring chariots, horses, and drivers from New York firefighting companies, renting *costumes from the *Metropolitan Opera House, engaging supernumeraries from the same source, and renting scenery originally used in James Pain's outdoor fireworks *spectacle *The Last Days of Pompeii*, Kalem established an open-air studio on a Long Island racetrack.

His company filmed *Ben-Hur* in 'seven tableaux', each one a scene from a major incident in Young's six-act adaptation. As with Porter's *Uncle Tom's Cabin*, the plot and incidents from *Ben-Hur*—at that date the most read novel in the world—were so well known as to make dialogue or inter-titles unnecessary; audiences could be expected to piece together narrative from the brief scenes. Once completed and exhibition announced, Kalem was halted by legal action by the theatrical entrepreneurs Klaw and Erlanger, who insisted that this inferior and unauthorized version of a stage play vulgarized the original and infringed on the author's rights. Klaw and Erlanger's case was upheld by the court, Kalem fined a substantial $25,000, and the film ordered to be destroyed. Fortunately, not all prints were destroyed, but the New York Federal District Court's decision remains the cornerstone of American intellectual property law (*see* COPYRIGHT).

Despite Kalem's setback, studios continued to adapt dramatic material for film, often disguising their adaptations under variant titles so that they were less recognizable, or adapting scenes or incidents rather than entire dramas. David Wark Griffith was particularly proficient at this kind of development. An unemployed stage actor, Griffith sought work at the American Mutoscope and Biograph Company in New York. He was soon supplementing his acting wages with money earned as an author of 'photoplays' (*scenarios), and soon thereafter as a director filming them. In the period of his association with Biograph between 1907 and 1912, Griffith directed more than 500 films, often at the rate of 2.7 per week. Many of his films refer to or reproduce—almost inevitably abridging—the stage repertoire of the period. Some, such as *The Barbarian Ingomar* (1908), a truncated version of Maria Lovell's long popular *Ingomar, the Barbarian*, take the setting of the early acts out of doors, but *A Drunkard's Reformation* (1909) combines a modern version of a temperance melodrama with scenes from Charles *Reade's *Drink*, a hit in *London from 1879. Griffith insisted that his leading actor make up as the late Charles Warner—who had on several tours performed *Drink* in North America—and coached him in Warner's mannerisms and stage business. As homage to Warner's remarkable playing, the production placed stage *acting within a film and, perhaps for the first time, depicted the differences between theatrical and film performance.

Equally significant are some thirteen Biograph films which Griffith made between 1909 and 1911 on the subject of the American Civil War. When he started work the American stage had been offering numerous professional melodramas on the subject since 1877. Although many were written for audiences with sympathies to the Union, such plays conceded hardship and loss on both sides. The devastation and, to some lesser extent, the humiliation of the south were openly acknowledged and regretted. Both Confederate and Union forces were shown to have men of valour and principle; women were celebrated for their bravery and loyalty. The war, the national tragedy and the national epic, was depicted as a temporary division, viewed from final acts which saw this wound closed and healing.

In such films as *In Old Kentucky* (1909), *Swords and Hearts*, and *The Rose of Kentucky* (both 1911), Griffith adopted the strategies of stage melodramas—such as Bronson *Howard's *Shenandoah* (1888), Augustus *Thomas's *Alabama* (1891), David *Belasco's *The Heart of Maryland* (1895), and William C. DeMille's *The Warrens of Virginia* (1905)—to show families and pairs of lovers with opposing ideologies and sectional loyalties fractured and separated by the war, their isolation and miseries compounded by renegade *villains who are loyal to no cause but their own self-interest. With or without these stage and film dramas, the American Civil War has never been a stable field with an agreed history and harmonious interpretation. The war remains an evolving, contested event which is host to vehemence, disruption, and difference What is observable in this large cluster (some 60 or more plays and nearly 30 films) is the extent to which both theatre and film became active participants in a long-running and continuing debate about the impact and meaning of the war, not merely asking fresh questions about a receding past, but also ameliorating lingering hurt, reconciling difference, and soothing memory.

Many silent films, but especially those from the period before 1920, raise questions in the modern spectator's mind about actors' performances and the techniques used in realizing them. Not only are there numerous acting styles rather than a single approach to performance, but silent film acting often strikes the modern viewer as needlessly extravagant in the use of gesture and facial expression to depict emotional states and enact simple narrative. Especially in Protestant middle-class cultures, where displays of intense emotions are discouraged and are customarily contained, actors' emotive gesticulations appear excessive. In response to modern misgivings about 'large' performances, several points may be raised: there was no model for screen acting, nor, until the close-up shot enlarged the face well beyond life size, was there concern that acting was excessive for the circumstances. Moreover, all models for acting are initially derived from the stage. Sometimes actors with stage experience appear in films, but many of the performers in early

film are persons who have witnessed but not experienced stage performance and are attempting to act as they have seen others do. These persons had numerous and very different models to choose from. New York audiences regularly observed actors from Scandinavia, Britain, France, Germany, Hungary, and Italy as well as those trained on the American stage. European audiences similarly experienced varieties of actors and performances. But all actors of the period, irrespective of nationality, were accustomed to performing to incidental *music, which encouraged them to sustain and elaborate gestures. Musical accompaniment—a piano, a violin, a small trio—actually supported film actors as they emoted before the camera, and later, when films were exhibited in small nickelodeon cinemas or major 'picture palaces', they were accompanied by house musicians playing from the side of the screen or from an orchestra pit. Thus large gestures were backed by music, just as stage melodrama had been, and continued to be well into the 1930s.

4. Convergence

Films continued to précis stage dramas until 1912, when a series of disconnected events converged to bring theatre and motion pictures into closer alignment. First, the film industry began to woo middle-class spectators, who had previously been resistant to cinema and somewhat dismissive of its allure for working-class audiences. Second, British, and French filmmakers attempted to induce well-known actors and actresses to perform before the camera. And third, Italian and French filmmakers deliberately sought to raise film to the status of literature. The immediate results of these separate developments were films of considerably greater length and far richer in production values than the twenty-minute features formerly produced.

In Italy, Carlo Guazzioni's *Quo Vadis?* (1912) brought Sienkiewicz's 1896 novel to the screen, followed the next year by Arturo Ambrosio's *The Last Days of Pompeii*, a film which owed more to previous Victorian theatrical versions than to *Bulwer-Lytton's novel. The dramatist Gabriele *D'Annunzio collaborated on an original screenplay, *Cabiria*. Simultaneously in America, Adolph Zukor and the theatrical *producer Charles *Frohman formed the Famous Players company, persuading Sarah *Bernhardt to appear in *La Reine Élisabeth* (1912), subsequently adding full-scale dramas and performances by such popular favourites as James *O'Neill (*Monte Cristo*, 1916) and Arthur *Schnitzler (*The Affairs of Anatol*, 1893, filmed 1921). In Britain Beerbohm *Tree was induced to perform his 1895 role of Svengali in a restaging of *Trilby* (1913) for the screen. Frank *Benson restaged his *Richard III* (1915), and John Lawson produced an hour-long version of his *Humanity* sketch for the Magnet Film Company (1913). Maurice Elvey, Britain's leading film director of the 1920s, brilliantly adapted both W. P. Drury's 1908 popular melodrama *The Flag Lieutenant* (1926) and Stanley *Houghton's 1912 *Hindle Wakes* (1928). American screen fare included such full-length plays as Wilson *Barrett's 1895

The Sign of the Cross (1914) and, notably, two American plays which, appearing on Broadway within a few years of each other, had disputed the status of the Native American and his or her place in white American society: William C. DeMille's 1904 success *Strongheart* (1914) and Edwin Milton Royle's 1907 *The Squaw Man*, directed on film by DeMille's nephew Cecil B. De Mille (1913, again in 1918, and a sound version in 1931; members chose idiosyncratic spellings of the family name).

Outstanding adaptations of stage plays for motion pictures were made by D. W. Griffith. Beginning in 1913 with Thomas Bailey Aldrich's 1904 vehicle for the actress Nance *O'Neil, *Judith of Bethulia*, Griffith moved on to Thomas Dixon's viciously racist *The Clansman* (1905) to produce an equally divisive *The Birth of a Nation* (1915) and thence, superbly, to Lottie Blair Parker's 1898 *'Way down East* (1920), again to the Kate Claxton version of *Two Orphans* (1875) to realize *Orphans of the Storm* (1921), and—with notably less success—Dorothy Donnelly's 1923 *Poppy*, retitled *Sally of the Sawdust* (1925). Many actors and actresses in Europe and America participated in translating their stage successes into motion pictures. From 1912 to the arrival of sound in 1927, the 'silent' screen was no barrier to intelligent and moving adaptations of stage dramas.

In this period of expanded films, the major New York and regional theatrical producers, such as the J. J. *Shubert, Klaw and Erlanger, and Edwin Thanhauser organizations formed motion picture divisions to realize on film their own theatrical successes and extend the drawing powers of their dramatic properties. The former two producers' choices included 'autumn dramas' from Drury Lane—such as Henry Hamilton's and Cecil Raleigh's *The White Heather* (1897), *The Great Ruby* (1898), and *The Whip* (1909), adapted and Americanized by the young film director Maurice Tourneur in 1915–16—and popular favourites from the Continent which these theatrical entrepreneurs had successfully brought to the New York stage and sent on national tours. The melodramas and other Drury Lane favourites were also adapted, sometimes without permission, by such British firms as the London Film Company and, in America, by Sigmund Lubin. Regrettably, all but Tourneur's *The Whip* have perished. Thanhouser, meanwhile, began by adapting 'combination' melodramas popular on his Midwest circuits and from 1916 turned to making original films.

If 1912 marks the beginning of longer motion pictures and of adapting full-length plays into films, it also signals the origin of a standing division between 'feature-length' films and 'short subjects'. Since a number of the shorts derived directly from music-hall sketches, it is small wonder that so many rising figures of the American screen were British or European. It is in this context that the two-reel films of the French Max Linder, and the English Charlie Chaplin and Stan Laurel, may be understood. Some of Chaplin's early screen comedies were extended sketches taken from the halls and, in particular, from the comic repertoire of the Fred Karno troupe with whom Chaplin had

toured. Stan Laurel, born Stanley Jefferson, adapted for Laurel and Hardy some of the sketches written and performed by his father Arthur Jefferson. Between 1915 and 1919, the English comic Fred Evans, under the name of 'Pimple', transformed a music-hall act into a series of comedy shorts in which Pimple performed *burlesque versions of current West End and touring stage melodramas.

5. The sound era

Because motion pictures had already expanded in duration, the advent of sound films in 1927 did not bring radical changes to the adaptation of stage pieces for the screen, apart from the obvious fact that actors now spoke the dramatists' lines rather than having speech rendered by inter-titles which, interrupting scenes, disrupted dramatic action. At the same time, the film industry became more aware of the playwright, and more dramatists were encouraged to adapt their work for the camera. Earlier successes were revived. Leonid *Andreev's 1914 *He Who Gets Slapped*, first shot as a silent film in 1924, was remade in an early sound version (1928). So too were the Broadway hits *Abie's Irish Rose* (1928) and *What Price Glory?* (1929). Current British dramas, Frederick *Lonsdale's 1925 *The Last of Mrs Cheney* (1929) and R. C. *Sherriff's 1928 *Journey's End* (1929), were soon adapted for motion pictures and featured players who had appeared in the stage productions.

The Shakespearian repertoire, popular with silent film-makers courting respectable audiences and attempting to counter local Watch Committee accusations that films were immoral, finally came into its own as silent stars, eager to prove their credentials, made sound versions. The Mary Pickford–Douglas Fairbanks *The Taming of the Shrew* (1929), Max *Reinhardt's *A Midsummer Night's Dream* (1935), Irving Thalberg's *Romeo and Juliet* (1936) with Norma Shearer and Leslie Howard, and Laurence *Olivier's 'Battle of Britain' *Henry V* (1944) and *Hamlet* (1948) were among the better of numerous Shakespeare-with-sound productions. It also became evident that films might manage some effects more skilfully than earlier stage versions. The clumsy transformations, with errant dentures, grotesque wigs, and prosthetics, which had bedevilled Richard *Mansfield's and Daniel Bandmann's 1887 stage version of *The Strange Case of Dr Jekyll and Mr Hyde* were skilfully and frighteningly managed in John *Barrymore's silent film (1920) and even more so when Fredric *March appeared in the remake (1932). Plays by Eugene *O'Neill, Arthur *Miller, Tennessee *Williams, John *Osborne, David *Hare, August *Wilson, and David *Mamet—dramas which, if not *naturalistic, nevertheless offer a link with pictorial *realism—have translated well into motion picture versions, while Bernard *Shaw, Tom *Stoppard, Sean *O'Casey, Thornton *Wilder, Harold *Pinter, and other dramatists whose works call for more imaginative environments, and whose concepts and language require more attentive theatre audiences, have been less well served in film adaptations.

If the translation of stage dramas into film was not immediately and directly affected by the addition of sound, sound films nevertheless made it possible to bring musical entertainments—light *opera, *musicals, *revues, and variety turns—to the screen. Although some stage successes were effectively remounted as films complete with their stars (such as *Rio Rita* with Bebe Daniels and Bert Wheeler, 1926, filmed 1929), original film musicals or compilations of existing acts in such films as *Broadway* (1929) and *Broadway Melody* (1929) were the option preferred by most studios. Major stage musicals, such as *Hammerstein and *Romberg's 1926 *The Desert Song* (1926, 1943, 1953), Franz Lehár's 1907 *The Merry Widow* (1925, 1934, 1952), and Hammerstein and *Kern's 1930 *Show Boat* (1936, 1951), might sufficiently retain their public appeal to encourage remakes. Most stage musicals, however, irrespective of their popularity, were represented by a single expensive film adaptation, usually made within a few years of the Broadway opening. Examples include the *Berlin–*Crouse–Howard Lindsay 1947 *Call Me Madam* (1953), Sidney Sheldon and Berlin's 1948 *Annie Get your Gun* (1950), and the *Loesser–*Burrows–Joe Swerling 1951 *Guys and Dolls* (1955). Numerous *Rodgers and Hammerstein musicals were great film successes—the 1943 *Oklahoma!* (1955), the 1946 *Carousel* (1956), the 1948 *South Pacific* (1958), the 1951 *The King and I* (1956), the 1964 *The Sound of Music* (1965)—as were the *Bernstein–*Laurents–*Sondheim 1957 *West Side Story* (1961), Meredith Willson's 1958 *The Music Man* (1962), and *Kander and Ebb's 1966 *Cabaret* (1972). But for each adaptation of a stage musical to film, as many as half a dozen original musicals issued from motion picture studios.

6. Two industries?

Although sound films initially emphasized that motion pictures were products of national culture, each with its own national vocabulary, national musical style, and regional accent, and not immediately marketable beyond national or cultural frontiers, these limitations were short-lived. The practice of dubbing local voices and the use of subtitles—as well as the comparative cheapness of a film print relative to a full stage production—established the cinema as the vast international industry recognized today. As motion pictures inexorably gained economic ascendancy over the theatre, drawing audiences away, paying higher wages, and bestowing more prominence on performers, writers, designers, and directors, theatrical occupations became more precarious. In any Western country, film work normally pays more than corresponding—and often harder—work in the theatre. Dramatists have particularly noted the economic discrepancy and retain screen rights over their plays (*see* COPYRIGHT) in the event of interest from the film industry.

Nevertheless, theatre work continues to hold its attractions for film people, chiefly actors, who seek opportunities to develop roles and to collaborate with other performers over the duration of a sustained run. Some actors speak of these periods as 'getting back to their roots', acknowledging that film praxis is still informed by basic theatrical skills. Such diverse stage and film performers as Lillian *Gish, Danny Kaye, Josef Schildkraut, Olivier, Vivien *Leigh, Henry *Fonda, Ingrid Bergman, W. C. *Fields, John *Malkovich, Fredric March, Amy Irving, Lauren Bacall, Gérard Depardieu, Nicole Kidman, and Dustin *Hoffman have all moved between live stage performances and film roles, and audiences were and are drawn to their live performances by the desire to observe screen stars in the flesh.

Although at the start of the twenty-first century theatre and film are discrete industries employing separate personnel and, especially as digital processes increasingly enhance film illusion, relying upon largely different technologies, there are again areas where theatre and film intersect. Such confluences are most readily observable at theme parks, but also within modern museums and at heritage sites with interactive displays. Honri's 'Mr Moon' illusion from the start of the twentieth century is currently widely used again. It may be recognized in Disneyland's 'The Haunted House' illusion, where a woman, mysteriously shrunk to diminutive size and imprisoned in a glass bottle, pleads for her release. The 'woman' is merely a white plaster or fibreglass figurine—a three-dimensional 'screen'—upon which, from a concealed source, a film is projected. The figurine, whose projected garments and limbs are shown in motion, thus appears to move, and the illusion is enhanced by the actor's voice issuing from a hidden speaker nearby. Elsewhere the illusion is found on mannequins dressed in period costume topped with a three-dimensional white-painted fibreglass face, the face and head framed by a wig. As a film is projected upon the face, the mannequin explicates history to museum visitors. A further variant is the fairground mechanical 'gypsy fortune-teller' which, in exchange for a coin activating its hidden projector and voice-recording, appears to read the customer's palm. In this instance, it is the customer's own hand which conceals the projector's beam as a film plays upon the gypsy's whitened face-like screen, and the voice-recording issues a prophetic statement.

Another trick returns us to the first theatrical interest in film, when the screen was made permeable to performers and solid objects. By 1910 the illusion of someone appearing in a film and then suddenly bursting through the screen was contrived by placing the live actor in a fold or pocket in the screen, the fold pinched shut by vertical rollers. When the actor broke through the screen, the concealing pocket was pulled taught against the rollers and, helped by pyrotechnic distractions and appropriate sound effects, itself became the screen. This technology, with further development of a screen cut into strips, was subsequently elaborated by the *Laterna Magika theatre company of *Prague, founded in 1958 by Alfréd *Radok and the *scenographer Josef *Svoboda. The most recent manifestation of unified stage and film technology is employed in the

1999 'Terminator' show at the several Universal Studios theme parks, where a motorcycle appears to break through its projected image and to become, abruptly, solid and three dimensional. Mobile screens, which can be instantly raised and lowered upstage and downstage of the motorcyclist, and which deprive the spectator of a sense of changing depth whilst fostering the illusion of sudden change in dramatic media, also tacitly inform the spectator that an unspoken link has been forged between filmed and live performance.

See also CYBER THEATRE; MEDIA AND PERFORMANCE; RADIO; SPECIAL EFFECTS; TELEVISION. DM

GUNNING, TOM, 'The cinema of attractions: early film, its spectator, and the avant-garde', in Thomas Elsaesser (ed.), *Early Cinema* (London, 1990)

MAYER, DAVID, 'Acting in silent film: which legacy of the theatre?', in Peter Kramer and Alan Lovell (eds.), *Screen Acting* (London, 1999)

—— *Playing out the Empire: Ben Hur and other toga plays and films, a critical anthology* (Oxford, 1994)

—— and JOHNSON, STEPHEN, *Spectacles of Themselves: popular melodramas which became significant silent films* (Westport, Conn., 2002)

VARDAC, A. NICHOLAS, *Stage to Screen: theatrical method from Garrick to Griffith* (Cambridge, Mass., 1949)

to other countries and visits of productions from abroad. This support lends authority and a degree of permanence to a precarious profession.

Some governments resist this responsibility. Almost all theatre performances in Japan are self-financing, from *ticket sales and sponsorship. In the United States of America, theatre has no supportive *arts council, as in Britain and numerous Commonwealth countries, and no Ministry of Culture, as in Eastern Europe. The *National Endowment for the Arts does give grants to individual artists and short-term projects, but takes no permanent responsibility for theatre companies or theatre buildings. Yet tax relief is given for donations made to theatres as charitable, 'not-for-profit' organizations and this, in effect, means that the state donates a very large subsidy that indiscriminately finances only those companies that please rich corporations and those citizens who have money to spare and give away. By the end of the twentieth century, except for the few shows that appeal to large audiences and can be often repeated, theatre had become dependent on financial support from various external sources. Frequently ticket sales account for less than half of a company's yearly income, perhaps only 40 or 30 per cent; in Germany, where municipalities are traditionally generous, it may be as little as 20 per cent. In Turkey, the state has accepted responsibility for 'making art available to all citizens'; tickets are priced very low—always less than £3—so that, although theatres are usually full, *box-office receipts are not a significant source of income.

In other than the very smallest scale, the cost of creating and running theatre productions has escalated because of increased labour costs and the large number of special skills involved, both big factors in the pricing of one-off, hand-crafted products in a mass-oriented consumer society. New and lavish buildings, provided by public funds, and the maintenance or modernization of old theatres have added to financial difficulties. So has recent technical elaboration in staging, often undertaken in an effort to rival the attractions of the spectacular and easily disseminated products of the *film industry. Further costs have been incurred in pursuit of sponsorship: by the turn of the century, the fundraiser for a theatre company had often

become the second highest-paid person, after the *artistic director.

The financial burden on a medium-sized theatre that produces its own plays is evident in the staffing requirements of the Huntington Theatre in *Boston. At the head are both a producing director and managing director; under them are separate departments for administration, marketing and public relations, development (that is, fundraising), education and outreach services, subscriptions and box office, production, building maintenance, and security. In the administration department, leading staff members are the business manager, house and company managers, executive secretary, information systems manager, accounts analyst, and literary associate. The production department is even larger, with its technical director, master carpenter, *prop master, scenic artist, *costumier, head draper, costume craftsperson and dyer, wardrobe coordinator, master electrician, production electrician and board operator, *sound engineer, together with numerous assistants. In many theatres today, administration and production costs are greater than the combined salaries of all the artists.

One way of making theatre more financially viable has been to adopt ancient *Greek precedent and organize *festivals in which productions share *publicity costs, a holiday and communal spirit is encouraged, and audiences may more easily be lured from one show to another. In Australia, for example, over 1,300 festivals had been established by 1996, after attracting over 2.2 million paid attendances in the previous season. While promoting civic pride, the concentration of many exceptional events means that festivals are especially attractive to state organizations and commercial sponsors. For the first *Edinburgh Festival in 1947, the city corporation gave £22,000, the government-funded Arts Council £20,000, and donors £19,791; there was a deficit of £20,776. For the festival of 1995, the Edinburgh District Council contributed £950,000, the Lothian Regional Council £350,000, the Scottish Arts Council £747,000, and sponsors and donors £1,041,678; the deficit was £34,440.

By the turn of the century, few self-financed productions were to be seen on Broadway in New York, in the West End of

London, or in commercially viable theatres around the world. By this time it was clear to everyone that films and spectator *sports, supported by exposure on *television, were attracting by far the greater crowds and raising far wider interest. At the same time, finance from government and municipal sources had become less forthcoming because calls on the public purse from health, education, and pensions were all, simultaneously, increasing rapidly. In 1999 the Arts Council for England commissioned the latest in a number of official inquiries and the following year circulated a paper called 'The Next Stage: towards a national policy for theatre in England'. Almost its first words announced what everyone concerned knew from their own experience: theatre 'is an art form in crisis'. In the state-subsidized theatres fewer and smaller productions were being staged and these were attracting smaller audiences. Companies were going bankrupt or amassing crippling debts. The medicines prescribed by the Arts Council were bigger government subsidy and new effort by theatres to widen audiences, take educational initiatives, and give preference to innovation in playwriting, staging, direction, and technology. In effect, the government-funded Arts Council was pressurizing theatre companies to move in certain culturally and socially desirable directions. In the name of sound finance, this state organization, intended to be 'quasi autonomous' and supportive, had become an instrument for intervention according to a *political agenda.

Although the programmes of most *regional or experimental theatres in the United States print a list many pages long of private and corporate sponsors, behind this façade of prosperity a company's financial health is often precarious. Here, too, theatres have gone bankrupt and a professional organization, the *Theatre Communications Group, regularly chronicles the situation. By 1991, half of the 184 theatres surveyed were posting operating deficits: 25 theatres had closed in the past five years and, for the first time since records began in 1973, attendance had declined. The sudden reversal seems to have been 'caused by curtailed performance activity, reduced marketing resources, [and] rising ticket prices'. All this had led to 'a precipitous decline in the number of full-time and full-season employees'.

The financial difficulties of theatre are long-established and endemic. In one of his 'open letters' to members of the *Intima Teatern, back in 1908–9, August *Strindberg had warned that, despite a conspiracy of silence, theatre attendance was poor and performances were being cancelled. Both the Swedish and the Royal Dramatic Theatres were in trouble; when the latter's building became badly run down, 'the authorities condemned it but allowed the theatre to continue its activity in the biggest firetrap in town'. At the same time, however, Strindberg and his associates were starting a new theatre: time and again theatre has continued to outface financial difficulties with new artistic developments and new investment, loans, and donations.

Theatre history since the last decades of the nineteenth century is full of the names of independent innovators who started from nothing rather than attempt to reinvigorate existing establishments that were in financial trouble and set in their ways. Annie *Horniman, the heiress of a tea merchant, funded a season of innovative plays at the Avenue Theatre in London in 1893; subsequently, with W. B. *Yeats and his associates in *Dublin, she was instrumental in founding the *Abbey Theatre. In *Moscow in 1897 *Stanislavsky, an *amateur actor with private means, met with *Nemirovich-Danchenko, an actor-teacher, and together they founded what would become the *Moscow Art Theatre. Barry *Jackson both financed and directed the Birmingham Repertory Theatre that opened in 1913. The *Provincetown Players in the United States was started by a group of unpaid amateurs in 1915; later the company moved to New York, where it premièred works by Eugene *O'Neill and new translations of European classics.

Finance, for all its importance and necessity, is neither the source nor heart of theatre and, in many ways, a process of renewal continues. In 1964 Ariane *Mnouchkine and a few friends from university days started the Théâtre du *Soleil, a theatre cooperative that by 1970 had developed a distinctive style and in future years would tour productions around the world. In the 1990s, Simon *McBurney, again with some university friends and scarcely any money, started a very small company, Theatre de *Complicité, and within a few years it was performing in London at the Royal *National Theatre and commercial venues. Increasingly, an alliance with educational institutions has provided the basis for new initiatives. In the USA, for example, several of Anne *Bogart's early productions were staged by New York University's Experimental Theater Wing.

At the end of the twentieth century, the theatre most successful financially was started almost single-handedly by the actor Sam *Wanamaker, who had dreamed of rebuilding Shakespeare's *Globe on *Bankside in London. Slowly, over a period of 30 years, money was given, much of it by individuals more enthusiastic about Shakespeare than endowed with riches, authoritarian objections were removed, and, at length, construction started. In 1999, only a few years after the theatre had opened, the new Globe performed Shakespeare's *Julius Caesar* to 95 per cent capacity, *The Comedy of Errors* to 93 per cent, and *Antony and Cleopatra* to 91 per cent. For all productions that year, including those of Elizabethan and Jacobean plays that no other theatre would dare to produce and some by visiting companies, more than a quarter of a million tickets were sold. This is a theatre that is proud to be 'self-financing in operational terms and does not depend on public subsidy': even in adverse conditions, not all theatre is in crisis.

JRB

ALLEN, JOHN, *Theatre in Europe* (Eastbourne, 1981)
REID, FRANCIS, *Theatre Administration* (London, 1983)

FINLAY, FRANK (1926–)

English actor. After *training at the *Royal Academy of Dramatic Art, Finlay was a member of the *English Stage Company at the *Royal Court from the late 1950s, appearing in the premières of *Wesker's *Chicken Soup with Barley* (1958) and *Chips with Everything* (1962), and a member of *Olivier's *National Theatre, playing the First Gravedigger in the company's first production, *Hamlet* (1963). Subsequent appearances in that company included a celebrated Iago opposite Olivier's Othello (1964) and Dogberry in *Zeffirelli's *Much Ado About Nothing* (1965). In the 1970s, balancing the stage with the screen, he appeared at the National in Trevor *Griffiths's *The Party* (1973), Howard *Brenton's *Weapons of Happiness*, and in Michael *Blakemore's revival of Ben *Travers's *Plunder* (both 1976). Finlay reached a huge *audience through his roles in the *television series *Casanova* (1971) and *A Bouquet of Barbed Wire* (1976), and as a flamboyant Porthos in Richard Lester's *films *The Three Musketeers* (1973) and *The Four Musketeers* (1974). At the Palace Theatre, Watford, he appeared in Ronald *Harwood's *The Girl in Melanie Klein* (1980) and in the West End in Jeffrey Archer's *Beyond Reasonable Doubt* (1988). He was the monstrous patriarch Astley Yardley in Simon Nye's black sitcom *How Do You Want Me* (1998–9). AS

FINLEY, KAREN (1956–)

American *performance artist. Trained as a visual artist, Finley began performing in 1979 after her father's suicide, staging works in *cabarets and alternative spaces. She married and collaborated with Brian Routh of the Kipper Kids, a performance art duo known for its transgressive and scatological work. Finley's solo performances, which examine the objectification and abuse of women in patriarchal culture, are characterized by nudity, graphic language, and explicit imagery. Performed in a trance-like state, her pieces are neither directly autobiographical nor *character based, comprised of disparate *monologues in both male and female voices, often directly political in focus and assaultive in tone. Food is a recurrent symbol, as in *The Constant State of Desire* (1986) and *We Keep our Victims Ready* (1989), in which she covered her nude body with substances such as raw eggs and melted chocolate to symbolize the culturally ascribed abjectness of women's bodies. One of four artists singled out by the *National Endowment for the Arts on charges of indecency, Finley became a central figure in the 'culture wars' of the 1990s. As a playwright, her works include *The Theory of Total Blame* (1988) and *The Lamb of God Hotel* (1992). LW

FINNEY, ALBERT (1936–)

English actor. One of the young, rough-edged regional actors of the English new wave theatre, Finney has proven to be a versatile performer in classical and comic roles. After work at the *Birmingham Repertory Theatre and the *Shakespeare Memorial Theatre, Finney achieved widespread recognition in the title roles of Hall and *Waterhouse's *Billy Liar* (1960) and *Osborne's *Luther* (1961). He joined the *National Theatre with notable roles in *Arden's *Armstrong's Last Goodnight* (1965) and Peter *Shaffer's *Black Comedy* (1966). His production company, Memorial Enterprises, presented Peter *Nichols's *A Day in the Death of Joe Egg* (1967), with Finney playing the lead in *New York. After a stint as an associate director at the *Royal Court (1972–5), Finney became vital to the early years of Peter *Hall's tenure at the National Theatre, playing Hamlet, Macbeth, and Tamburlaine. In 1996 he formed part of the original *London cast of Yasmina *Reza's *Art*. Finney has had a lengthy *film career, performing memorably in *Saturday Night and Sunday Morning* (1960) and *Tom Jones* (1963). MDG

FINNISH NATIONAL THEATRE

The first professional company in the language of the dominant people of Finland was founded in *Helsinki in 1872 by Dr Kaarlo Bergbom, designed to promote Finnish plays and to produce classical and modern world drama. The first great native *comedy, Aleksis Kivi's *The Heath Cobblers*, was played in 1875. Influenced by developments elsewhere in Europe, especially Germany, Bergbom's production styles ranged from *romanticism to *realism, often with Ida *Aalberg in the leading roles. A new building in the national romantic mode was constructed in 1902, when the company assumed the name of the National Theatre. Under Eino Kalima (director, 1917–50), a style based on *Stanislavsky's and *Copeau's psychological method became prevalent, while Arvi Kivimaa (director, 1950–74) was active in building international contacts, which led to foreign *tours by Finnish companies. Modern *absurd drama was introduced on the small stage, opened in 1954. Kai Savola (director, 1974–92) promoted young playwrights, opened two experimental stages, and invited well-known foreign directors, such as Yury *Lyubimov and Lev *Dodin, to work at the theatre. Maria-Liisa Nevala has been director since 1992, presenting a yearly repertory of twelve productions on four stages. LIB

FIORILLI, TIBERIO (c.1608–1694)

Neapolitan actor performing in France and abroad. One of the most celebrated actors of the century, and object of a picaresque and partly inaccurate biography, he perfected the mask of Scaramuccia (Scaramouche), a cross between a *Zanni-type servant and a braggart Capitano. He had an international career, but gravitated most often towards *Paris, where he was favoured by Louis XIV and was alleged to have a major influence on the acting style of *Molière. See COMMEDIA DELL'ARTE; COMÉDIE ITALIENNE. RAA

FIORILLO FAMILY

Italian seventeenth-century theatre family: a connection with Tiberio *Fiorilli is both claimed and disputed. **Silvio** (fl. 1584–1634) brought the Neapolitan mask of Pulcinella to northern *commedia dell'arte, and also played Capitano Matamoros. He wrote several full-length plays, most notably *Faithful Lucilla* (1632), which offers a verbal confrontation between his own two masks, Policinella and Matamoros. His son **Giovan Battista** (n.d.) played the mask of Trappolino in Italian venues during the seventeenth century.   RAA

FIRES IN THEATRES

Fire was the chief threat to a *playhouse and its *audience, particularly in the nineteenth century. Fires did occur earlier: the first *Globe Theatre in *London burned in 1613, and before gaslight and flown *scenery there was still a danger from candles and oil lamps (*see* LIGHTING); for instance, 70 people died in a Richmond, Virginia, theatre fire in 1811. The incidence of fire increased dramatically in the nineteenth century, especially the second half of it, with the introduction of gas into battens over the stage, wing lights, and portable stage lights, as well as the use of closely packed flown scenery instead of sliding wings and back shutters (*see* SCENE SHIFTING). The destruction of *Covent Garden in 1808, and *Drury Lane in 1809, was by pre-gaslight fires caused by carelessness; they occurred without an audience present. During the gaslight period there were many fires without fatalities, or fires in which only a few workmen, passers-by, or theatre staff died.

However, there were also disastrous fires with a great loss of life that occurred during performances with, of course, an audience present: 800 dead at Lehmann's Theatre in *St Petersburg (1836), 175 at the Nice Municipal Theatre (1881), 450 at the Ring Theatre, *Vienna (1881), 170 at the Baquet Theatre, Oporto (1888), and 570 at the Iroquois Theatre, *Chicago (1903, in a theatre lit by electricity). There were many more without such fatal consequences. In London between 1841 and 1865, the *Adelphi, the Garrick, the *Olympic, the Pavilion, Covent Garden, and the Surrey were completely, or almost completely, destroyed by fire; in the provinces at least 26 theatres were so destroyed between 1839 and 1880. Deaths also occurred when audiences panicked and rushed for the exits because of a false alarm of fire, as in the *Theatre Royal, *Glasgow (1849), when 65 died, and the Liverpool Coliseum (1878), with 37 deaths.

Such fires and their deadly consequences had several clearly explainable causes. Firstly, every theatre lit by gas had hundreds of gas jets burning above and around the stage, and hundreds of feet of tubing on the stage itself. Gas could leak from ill-fitting joints and perished tubing and ignite, or flame from unprotected jets could ignite the *costumes of *dancers, scenic cloths, *drop curtains, and borders. The heat of gaslight above the stage was so intense that everything—wood, fabric, canvas—was utterly desiccated and reduced to tinder; it could catch at the slightest spark. Captain Shaw of the London Fire Brigade reported in 1882 that in several London theatres the temperature above the stage on the *grid during performances exceeded 38°C. The second cause of fire and death was, until near the end of the century, the almost total lack of *safety regulations, as regards both fire prevention and audience overcrowding. After 1850, in some civic jurisdictions theatres were regularly inspected, reports written, faults indicated, and recommendations made, but there was little legal machinery to enforce compliance upon *managers, who did their best to avoid the cost of safety improvements. Thirdly, attractive and beautifully designed *auditoriums were too often provided with too few and badly designed exits (especially from the gallery), and often had poorly built staircases with sharp right-angled turns as they descended to the street. Fourthly, audience panic in a rush for badly marked, overcrowded exits, sometimes in pitch darkness as theatre lighting failed, greatly increased the number of deaths.

This is what happened in the Exeter fire, most of the deaths occurring on the single exit stairway from the gallery, where people stumbled and fell on top of each other, and within a very few minutes were choked to death by poisonous gases flowing out of the auditorium. In Vienna and Chicago and other cities the same thing happened. The most dangerous place in case of fire was the gallery, the pit and *stalls the safest, since exit to the street was quick and relatively easy (*see* BOX, PIT, AND GALLERY). The progress of a theatre fire was extremely rapid. In setting a scene, a stagehand might accidentally ignite a gauze *curtain or a flown scenic cloth. If the burning fabric was not immediately cut down and extinguished—and this was often done satisfactorily—the flames would spread at once to more scenery: literally tons of it hung over the stage. Unable to control the fire, stage staff, actors, and musicians would flee out of backstage exit doors, leaving them open and thus creating a rush of oxygen from auditorium to stage which fed the fire. The enormous pressure of the air onstage pressing outward would have prevented a safety curtain from being fully lowered, if there was one at all. Within two minutes hot and noxious fumes would have poured into the auditorium, rising quickly to the dome and then, accompanied by great bursts of flame, forcing their way to the gallery, the balconies, the exits there, and finally the boxes and stalls. Within five or ten minutes from the initial outbreak of fire, everybody remaining in the auditorium or trapped in the passageways would have been dead. The Iroquois Theatre was brand new and entirely electrified; nevertheless the above course of events was followed in a full house of 1,800 spectators when an electric carbon arc began to spark and ignited a border. Seventy per cent of the gallery audience perished.

These terrible fires prompted the development of safety measures over the next generation: fireproofing scenery, redesigning exits, substituting iron for wood, installing sprinkler systems, modernizing and automating vents above the stage to release gases. Civic and national authorities everywhere adopted and enforced fire and safety regulations, and reduced seating in auditoriums. The electrification of stage lighting, however, was the most important single factor in making theatres safer.   MRB

REES, TERENCE, *Theatre Lighting in the Age of Gas* (London, 1978)
WILKINSON, HUGH, 'Fatal theatre fires in nineteenth century Britain', *Theatrephile*, 3 (1990)

FIREWORKS

When gunpowder became available, fireworks became an expected part of the *medieval *cycle plays, particularly for the *hell mouth. *Stage directions before 1400 refer to fireworks. During the late Middle Ages and the *early modern period, four basic effects were possible: flames; smoke; 'squibs' (or 'fizzgigs' or 'serpents', tubes of gunpowder open at one end, which could either be released as rockets or held to spray sparks and flame); and firecrackers and bombs (enclosed gunpowder that made a report when it burst its container). As Butterworth notes, modern notions of *safety were not a factor and many stunts would be unthinkable today—fireworks thrown into the *audience, worn on clothing, held in bare hands, and carried in the mouth. Burning, sparking devils emerging from a smoky, flaming hell were crowd-pleasers, and many plays until about 1680 incorporated fireworks. Technical improvements appeared throughout the early modern period. Small smoke-and-flame bombs in front of a *trap, to cause actors to appear and disappear in a roar and flash, occurred as early as 1501 in France. Rockets and flame pots guided on wires, commonly signifying lightning, were in use in the 1550s in Italy. By 1600 the combination of flash-and-boom effects with the transformation trap, so that one *character could explosively become another, was standard stagecraft.

More controllable fireworks developed in Italy during the early sixteenth century. Adding a dash of the salts of certain metals to the powder could produce vivid colours. Small quantities of inert materials could make it somewhat more certain that a squib would burn rather than explode. With the general movement of theatre indoors, theatrical fireworks focused more on quality of effect than on sheer volume, whereas outdoor displays, with no specifically theatrical component, continued to grow bigger, louder, and more elaborate. This divorce between pure fireworks and stage pyrotechnics has continued to the present. By the early eighteenth century, the great rage for fireworks on stage was clearly over; only the *Comedié Italienne in *Paris regularly featured indoor displays.

The early French *melodrama revived fireworks. The invention of a reasonably safe indoor cannon aided a vogue in the rue de Temple theatres in the 1790s for battle scenes, amplified with firecrackers and smoke bombs. *Féeries advertised new and improved fireworks, and the fashion spread rapidly across Europe. Technical improvements resumed: gas burners for flames on cue, composite materials for indoor fire fountains, and smokeless powders so that technicians could choose rather than accept how much smoke should occur. By 1840 audiences had become accustomed to this new round of technical improvements, and fireworks again fell out of fashion (the always-popular battle scenes excepted). In the twentieth century most technical improvements in stage fireworks were in safety. Concerns about injuries, hazardous substances, and *fire predominated; the only significant innovation was electric firing. The most common firework effects in recent theatre have been simple fires, clouds of smoke, and bomb explosions. But should the demand ever reappear for gaudier, more elaborate displays, modern materials science could rapidly bring many new and interesting effects to the stage.   JB

BUTTERWORTH, PHILIP, *Theatre of Fire: special effects in early English and Scottish theatre* (London, 1998)

FISHER, CLARA (1811–98)

Anglo-American actress and singer. On the stage from the age of 6, when she appeared at *Drury Lane as Richard in a 'Lilliputian' version of *Richard III*, she performed in other *breeches parts throughout her childhood in *London. Her family emigrated to the United States in 1827, where she was a success in melodramatic fairy-tale roles, and as Lady Teazle, Viola, and the Fool in *King Lear*. In *Boston in 1834 she married Scottish singer and musical director James Meader, and thereafter starred in his *opera productions throughout the United States.   LQM

FISKE, HARRISON GREY (1861–1942)

American editor, *critic, playwright, director, and *producer. As editor of the *New York Dramatic Mirror*, Fiske exposed the business tactics of the *Theatrical Syndicate in 1897, leading to a protracted libel case and the Syndicate's banning of any productions featuring Fiske's wife (married 1890) Minnie Maddern *Fiske. H. G. Fiske acquired the Manhattan Theatre in 1901 and produced and directed a series of successful vehicles starring Mrs Fiske. They formed the Manhattan Company in 1904, *touring extensively in North America with plays such as Langdon *Mitchell's *The New York Idea* (1906) and *Ibsen's *Rosmersholm* (in 1907). The Syndicate's ownership of most theatre buildings in the United States made touring a heroic hardship and the Manhattan Company was disbanded when Fiske declared bankruptcy in 1914. He emerged soon after to produce additional works until the death of Mrs Fiske in 1932.   MAF

FISKE, MINNIE MADDERN (1865–1932)

American actress, director, *manager, and playwright. Fiske's influence on American theatre was threefold: she introduced the plays of *Ibsen to the American public, developed an analytic approach to *realistic *acting, and emphasized the importance of ensemble. Born into a theatrical family in New Orleans, she played numerous juvenile roles before graduating to adult parts in *melodrama and light *comedy. When she married Harrison Grey *Fiske in 1890, she retired from the stage for several years, but returned to perform in and promote serious, intellectually challenging, and socially conscious drama. Garff Wilson describes her innovations as 'a clean break with the traditions of the nineteenth century'. In addition to Nora, Hedda, and other major Ibsen characters, she created the title roles of *Tess of the d'Urbervilles*, *Becky Sharp*, *Mary of Magdala*, *Leah Kleschna*, and *Salvation Nell*. For most of these productions she selected and trained the company, encouraging psychological truthfulness, concentration on inner feeling with simplified external action, and fidelity to the dramatist's purpose. She established the Manhattan Theatre Company as a permanent ensemble in 1904. As a manager, Fiske fought the *Theatrical Syndicate and was forced by the monopoly to use run-down halls and even skating rinks for her productions. Alone among managers, she remained defiant to the end, but suffered great financial loss for her independence. In addition to work in theatre, Fiske performed in *film, primarily in roles she had already made famous on the stage. She also wrote a number of *one-act plays.   AHK

FITCH, CLYDE (1865–1909)

American playwright and director. Astoundingly successful, Fitch wrote 60 plays from 1890 to 1909, 36 original, the remainder adaptations. During the 1900–1 season he had ten plays in *New York and on the road. *The City* (1909) was his greatest success (shocking *audiences with the line 'You're a God damn liar!'). Critic Walter Prichard Eaton said of him, 'Fitch's works correctly illustrated, would give future generations a better idea of American life than newspapers or historical records.' Most of Fitch's plays are conventional *melodramas; in 1899 he wrote one of the first cowboy dramas, *The Cowboy and the Lady*. His *Captain Jinks of the Horse Marines* (1901) made Ethel *Barrymore a star. Fitch's industry made him a hero to the public. He was seen as the ideal American writer: productive and primarily interested in his public, the embodiment of the Broadway 'show shop' playwright.   TFC

FITZBALL, EDWARD (1792–1873)

English playwright, who added his mother's maiden name, Fitz, to his own surname, Ball. A prolific author for a wide variety of major and *minor theatres, Fitzball did his best work before 1840, especially in *nautical, criminal, and supernatural *melodrama. *The Floating Beacon* (1824), *The Pilot* (1825, an adaptation of a Fenimore Cooper novel), *The Inchcape Bell* (1828), and *The Red Rover* (1829, another Cooper adaptation) are good examples of his nautical vein. Fitzball also knew about staging; he insisted on a setting for his popular crime melodrama *Jonathan Bradford; or, The Murder at the Roadside Inn* (1833) that would reveal *action in four rooms of the inn simultaneously. For *The Flying Dutchman* (1827) he suggested the back projection of magic lantern slides for the approach of the Dutchman's ship, rather than the usual costly building of a stage ship. Fitzball acted as reader of plays for both *Drury Lane and *Covent Garden, and his autobiography, *Thirty-Five Years of a Dramatic Author's Life* (1859), while deficient in chronology, is informative and entertaining.   MRB

FITZGERALD, BARRY (WILLIAM JOSEPH SHIELDS) (1888–1961)

Irish actor, born in Dublin, brother of the actor Arthur Shields. Fitzgerald began acting in popular Irish *melodramas about 1914, joining the *Abbey Theatre in 1916. Projecting a roguish charm on stage, his broad *acting was in stark contrast to the static, incantatory style of the previous generation of Abbey actors; however, it was precisely what Sean *O'Casey was looking for, casting him as Captain Boyle in *Juno and the Paycock* (1924). This led to a long association with the playwright, including Fluther Good in *The Plough and the Stars* (1926), and Sylvester Heegan in the original *London production of *The Silver Tassie* (1928). In 1929 Fitzgerald formed his own company to tour the United States with O'Casey's work. He moved to Hollywood in 1937, and acted exclusively in *films from 1941, winning an Oscar for *Going my Way* (1944).   ChM

FLANAGAN, HALLIE (HALLIE FERGUSON FLANAGAN DAVIS) (1890–1969)

American teacher and administrator. Flanagan became a national figure in the 1930s as director of the *Federal Theatre Project (FTP), a Depression-era programme designed to employ theatre people and provide free or low-cost entertainment to the masses. A theatre instructor at Grinnell College, Flanagan studied with George Pierce *Baker at Harvard (1922–4). Inspired by European and Soviet theatre seen during a tour in 1926—and by her meetings with Vsevolod *Meyerhold, E. Gordon *Craig, and others—she built an innovative and respected theatre programme at Vassar College. Flanagan was appointed by Roosevelt aide Harry Hopkins in 1935 to head the FTP, and she succeeded in organizing a massive national theatre system that produced more than 1,000 plays, *operas, and other performances for more than 30 million spectators before its funding was withdrawn by Congress due to political pressures in 1939.   MAF

FLANDERS, MICHAEL (1922–75)

English lyricist and performer, best known for his *revues with Donald Swann (1923–94) at the piano, *At the Drop of a Hat* (1956) and its sequel. Their witty and gently satirical songs usually dealt with domestic British matters (the weather, workmen, interior decorating), with an occasional distinctly sharp touch ('The Reluctant Cannibal', 'All Gaul'); the one most remembered is 'The Hippopotamus Song'. Ian Strachan revived some of the songs at the *King's Head in *London as *Under their Hats* (1994), with reasonable success. Despite his confinement to a wheelchair, Flanders played the Storyteller in *Brecht's *The Caucasian Chalk Circle* (*Royal Shakespeare Company, 1962).
                                                                                          EEC

FLATS AND WINGS

A flat is a large flat vertical surface forming part of a scene, kept rigid with a frame, supported by braces, jacks, poles, or fly lines. A wing is a flat whose offstage edge is beyond *audience sight lines, thus masking the backstage; or it may be a drape serving the same purpose. From the sixteenth century until the mid-nineteenth, many wings were movable on trucks or wheels in slots or grooves for very rapid *scene shifting. After 1840 the flat was the basic unit out of which *box sets were constructed. In 1950 flats were still the fundamental medium of the scenic artist; 50 years later, despite more three-dimensional *scenery and *cyclorama effects, they remained important. For centuries the paintable surface was canvas or muslin, which was light, took paint well, and improved with repainting, but was prone to waves and tears. Better, cheaper particle boards are replacing the traditional (or 'soft') flat with a fabric-surfaced board on a reinforcing frame ('hard flats'). Hard flats, though heavier, are tougher and not subject to ripples or waves. *See also* SCENOGRAPHY; PAINTING OF SCENES.   JB

FLAW *See* HAMARTIA.

FLECK, JOHN (1951–)

American actor and *performance artist. Born in Cleveland, Fleck put aside his early aspirations to the Catholic priesthood and became a stage, *film, and *television actor. He has tried to do a play every year, appearing in *Ludlam's *The Mystery of Irma Vep* in 1999 and winning acclaim in 2001 for his performance in Charles *Mee's *The Berlin Circle*. But he is best known for his highly successful solo performance art pieces, which in

1990 won *awards from the *Los Angeles and San Diego Critics Circle. Among these offerings are *Mud in your Eye*, *Blessed Are All the Little Fishes*, *Psycho Opera*, and *I Got the He-Be-She-Be's*. Openly *gay, he views his work as healing social injustices by addressing normally taboo subjects such as homosexuality, alcoholism, violence against women, and religion—even appearing as a mermaid, urinating on stage, and creating an altar out of a toilet bowl. In 1990 he achieved notoriety as one of a quartet of performance artists denied grants by the *National Endowment for the Arts (the 'NEA Four') for alleged affronts to 'general standards of decency'.   CT

FLEISSER, MARIELUISE (1901–74)

German playwright. A contemporary of *Brecht and *Horváth, her reputation rests mainly on two *folk plays, *Purgatory in Ingolstadt* (1926) and *Pioneers in Ingolstadt* (1928). Both deal with the oppressive structures of her Bavarian home town but the issues—religion, sexual repression, and exploitation—have interest that goes beyond the local. Brecht promoted and directed her work (the *Berlin production of *Pioneers* in 1929 caused a notorious scandal). She was rediscovered in the late 1960s in the context of the *Volksstück* revival associated with R. W. *Fassbinder, Martin *Sperr, and Franz Xaver *Kroetz.
                                                                                          CBB

FLETCHER, JOHN (1579–1625)

English dramatist. He was born in Rye, the son of a clergyman (later a bishop), and educated at Corpus Christi College, Cambridge. He had a hand in more than 50 plays in a sixteen-year theatrical career. His first, the *pastoral *tragicomedy *The Faithful Shepherdess* (1609), was modelled after *Guarini's *Il pastor fido* and illustrates the interest in recent European literary movements which is a recurrent feature of his work. An overtly formal play, it was unsuccessfully produced at the *Whitefriars Theatre, though a King's Men revival in 1634 met with more approval. Fletcher may already have made minor contributions to Francis *Beaumont's *The Woman Hater* (1606), and from 1609 they began to collaborate on a regular basis. The partnership lasted until Beaumont's retirement in 1613. During this period Fletcher also wrote his solo *comedy *The Woman's Prize* (1610): following a fashion for plays which countered, and apologized for, the misogyny of some earlier drama, it was a sequel to *The Taming of the Shrew* (the two comedies later played back to back in the King's Men's repertory), and it may have drawn him to the attention of Shakespeare. The fact that Shakespeare wrote his last three plays, the lost *Cardenio*, *Henry VIII*, and *The Two Noble Kinsmen*, in collaboration with Fletcher suggests that he was grooming the younger man as his successor as the King's Men's principal dramatist, a role he assumed when Shakespeare retired around 1613. Fletcher's notable early contributions include two Roman tragedies about constructions of masculine honour, *Bonduca* (1613) and *Valentinian* (1614).

In 1619 a regular collaboration with Philip *Massinger began with their *censorship-troubled *tragedy about Dutch current affairs, *Sir John van Olden Barnavelt*. The two men worked mainly together, producing well-made plays in all *genres, until Fletcher's death in the plague of 1625, though Massinger's contribution was effaced when the plays were published in 1647 under the 'Beaumont-and-Fletcher' trademark, to be rediscovered by scholars in the twentieth century. Some of their plays, notably *The Sea Voyage* (1622), illustrate the dead Shakespeare's growing imaginative dominance in the work of his younger colleagues.

Some twentieth-century writers saw Fletcher as a complacent monarchist: his recurrent attention to aristocratic and gentry codes of behaviour, his interest in other world cultures in plays like *The Custom of the Country* (1620) and *The Island Princess* (1621), and his slick management of *action in comedies like *The Pilgrim* and *The Wild Goose Chase* (both 1621) were all interpreted as a retreat from political seriousness. Others, however, saw a pervading political unease beneath the polished surface of his writing; attention has also been called to the strength of his female *characters as agents of *denouement. The plays held the stage through the eighteenth century, but have been rarely produced since. *The Chances* (*c*.1625), often considered Fletcher's best comedy, was revived for *Chichester Festival Theatre's inaugural season in 1962, but its commercial failure put the black spot on Fletcher for several decades. Several smaller theatre companies rediscovered his plays at the end of the twentieth century.   MJW

FLETCHER, LAURENCE (fl. 1595–1603)

Scottish actor. Fletcher's precise connection to the theatre remains unclear and none of the roles he performed are identifiable. First sited as an actor in Scotland (1595, 1599, 1601), he was later included in the patent for the King's Men (1603; *see* CHAMBERLAIN'S MEN, LORD), leading historians to hypothesize that he came to *London with King James. Fletcher lived near the *Globe and was buried in St Saviour's parish where a fee book describes him in 1608 as 'a player, the King's servant, buried in the church, with an afternoon's knell of the great bell'.   SPC

FLEURY (ABRAHAM-JOSEPH BÉNARD) (1750–1822)

French actor. Fleury, whose father had managed King Stanislas of Poland's court theatre, joined the *Comédie-Française in 1778. A natural elegance and courtier's polish equipped him well for leading roles in classical *comedy and his forte, *petits maîtres* (fops). His most successful role was that of Frédéric II in Ernest de Manteufel's *Les Deux pages* (1789). Director of Marie Antoinette's court theatre at *Versailles, he was imprisoned in 1793 for anti-patriotic activities. He escaped the guillotine, however, and in 1799 returned to the reconstituted Comédie-Française for a further nineteen years, the last of the courtier-actors.   JG

FLIES AND FLOWN SCENERY

The flies—plural with no singular—is the space above the *stage, concealed from the *audience, to and from which *scenery is shifted, and in which there are usually many *lighting positions for top, back, side, and *cyclorama light. Scenery which is suspended on, and movable by, ropes or cables is said to be 'flown'. The advantages of flown scenery over scenery standing on the floor—rapid *scene shifting, fewer hands, clear floor space in the wings, relative *safety from crushing injuries, and the elimination of slots, grooves, and tracks from the acting and dancing surface—were well known to *early modern stage machinists; some scenery was flown in the latter sixteenth century in Italy. But until about 1830–40, most movable scenery in most Western theatres was shifted from the wings, for physical reasons:

1. wooden pulleys, rollers, and cogwheels jam frequently;
2. a floor strong enough to support a mass in compression is easier to design than a truss strong enough to support the same mass in tension;
3. the high vertical walls required for full flies were difficult to build and prone to collapse.

As better iron parts (adapted from sailing ships) and stronger construction became available, the change to flown scenery was rapid after about 1840.

The *pinrail*, copied from the system for handling sails, was the first major system for flying scenery. The line supporting the scenery is tied off to a pin passed through a heavy wooden rail in the wings. Workers shifted scenery by pulling out the pin and moving the line, then repinning and tying at the new height. Sandbags tied to the line on the rail side of the pulley supplied some counterweighting, but the movement was accomplished primarily by human muscle. A few pinrail theatres persist, especially in *Latin American provincial cities. Beginning about 1910, with substantial completion by 1950, theatres in the West moved to the *counterweight* system. The several lines supporting each batten are tied to a set of iron weights on a steel rack (the 'arbour') which runs vertically on a track or cable backstage. A separate control line is used to move the arbour. Properly counterweighted scenery has an effective weight of zero and can be moved by a single operator. Since the 1950s, electrical *winches* have come into use in wealthier theatres in industrial nations. Winches have significant advantages over counterweights in both operation and safety, though for many theatres the winch is still prohibitively expensive. JB

FLIMM, JÜRGEN (1941–)

One of the most influential German directors of the 1980s and 1990s, Flimm is a leading exponent of director's theatre (*see* DIRECTING/DIRECTOR). As *artistic director of the city theatre in Cologne (1979–85) and the Thalia Theater in Hamburg (1985–99), he created productive environments for other directors (such as Jürgen *Gosch). Under Flimm the Thalia became the German home for Robert *Wilson, originating many important productions. In his own productions Flimm ranges widely over the classical repertoire with a clear preference for Shakespeare and *Kleist. His best productions (Kleist's *Käthchen von Heilbronn*, 1979; *Chekhov's *Platonov*, 1989; *King Lear*, 1992) are characterized by bold visual metaphors as interpretative keys to the *texts. Since 1990 he has directed *opera as well, including *Wagner's *Ring* at *Bayreuth (2000). In 1999 he was elected president of the Bühnenverein, the organization of German theatres. CBB

FLORENCE, BILLY (1831–91)

American actor. Born in Albany as Bernard Conlin, in 1849 he made his stage debut in Richmond, Virginia, playing Tobias in *Dunlap's *The Stranger.* His *New York bow came the next year in *Brougham's *Home*—the first of his many Irish parts (often starring with his wife). He was especially lauded for his ability to submerge himself in a role by altering his appearance and changing his voice. Notable vehicles included the American première of Tom *Taylor's *The Ticket-of-Leave Man* (1863), in which he had the title role of Bob Brierly; and *Dickens and Collins's *No Thoroughfare*, in which he played the *villainous Obenreizer. His supreme characterization was the Hon. Bardwell Slote in Woolf's *The Mighty Dollar* (1875). In 1890 he joined the famous Joseph *Jefferson to play Sir Lucius O'Trigger in *Sheridan's *The Rivals* and Zekiel Homespun in *Colman's *The Heir at Law.* CT

FLORIDOR (JOSIAS DE SOULAS, SIEUR DE PRIMEFOSSE) (1608–71)

French actor. Son of a minor aristocrat, he served in the army before taking up acting. He led a troupe to *London, and also played briefly in the French provinces, before making his debut in 1638 at the *Marais, where he soon established himself as troupe leader and a worthy replacement for *Montdory. In 1642–3 Floridor probably created the leading roles in Pierre *Corneille's *Cinna, Horace, Polyeucte*, and *La Mort de Pompée.* In 1647, perhaps by royal command, he transferred to the rival

*Hôtel de Bourgogne, buying from *Bellerose his position as troupe leader. At the Bourgogne he rose to new heights, reviving Marais successes and adding new repertoire by both Pierre and Thomas *Corneille. His greatest triumphs in his latter years were in *Racine's *tragedies: as Pyrrhus (*Andromaque*) and Titus (*Bérénice*). It was no accident that when *Molière lampooned the Bourgogne tragedians' exaggerated posturing and bombastic delivery, he made no mention of Floridor. As Donneau de *Visé wrote, 'his gestures, manner and posture are somehow so natural that he attracts universal admiration'. Floridor appears to have been as highly regarded off the stage as on it, and in 1668 obtained a King's Council decree stating that a nobleman could be an actor 'without derogation'. JG

FLOTATS, JOSEP MARIA (1939–)

Catalan actor and director. Flotats trained at the Strasbourg theatre school before forging a career in *Paris. He worked with Georges Wilson at the *Théâtre National Populaire, Jean Mercure at the Théâtre de la Ville, Jean-Louis *Barrault at the Théâtre d'Orsay, and had a two-year stint with the *Comédie-Française. He returned to his native *Barcelona in the mid-1980s to establish the hugely influential Companyia Josep Maria Flotats at the Poliorama Theatre, introducing French plays there and subsequently. As the founder-director of the Teatre Nacional de Catalunya he has gone on to play a crucial role in reshaping the Catalan theatrical landscape. A meticulous director and versatile actor, Flotats's professionalism and *training acquired in France has assisted in the building up of Barcelona's status as Spain's de facto theatre capital. With a staging of Yazmina *Reza's *Art* (1998) in which he performed alongside Josep Maria Pou and Carlos Hipolito, Flotats consolidated his position as one of Spain's most versatile theatre artists. MMD

FLYING ACTORS

The *illusion of a flying human being has been part of Western *spectacle since the *mechane of the ancient *Greek theatre. The greatest visual and emotional impact is achieved when a person appears to rise and fly completely unaided, and most of the history of flying actors is a history of erasure: for centuries technicians have sought to make the machinery invisible, inaudible, and inexplicable. So far as we know, the Greek (and *Roman) machine was a simple crane on top of the *skene, from which flying cars or harnessed actors could be lowered and raised on a rope. In the *medieval and *early modern theatre, enough pictures survive that we can be reasonably certain that flown actors were simply raised or lowered on a rope. In Renaissance Italy the cloud machine effect, the first real progress since ancient times, allowed an actor to ride the piece of painted *scenery (a cloud, a swan, a chariot) up into the *heavens or

Three **flying** fairies in *Mr Kirkby's Flying Ballet*, London, 1943, with hidden suspension and flying devices.

down from the heavens to the *stage. Aided by nearly silent hydraulics and *lighting that conceals the necessary slotting, this trick remains effective (for example the helicopter and the flying Cadillac in the *musical *Miss Saigon*, 1989).

In the nineteenth century, many techniques emerged for the effect of flying unaided—that is, without any car or cloud beneath the feet. By 1800 it was well understood that if the supporting wires or cables are thin enough, and if the actor is not backlit, the means of support can be almost entirely concealed. But the *illusion depends upon the path of the flight not resembling any simple machine—not straight up and down (explicable as a pulley), nor in symmetrical arcs (a pendulum), nor in a straight and level path (an overhead carriage). By combining simple machines, the technician can complicate a flight path to conceal the underlying machinery from the viewer. The earliest such trick was simply to swing the actor on a line while the fly crew pulled the line in or paid it out, to produce effects like flying down from a balcony or up into a tree. Using a carriage to catch and raise the line attached to the actor's harness can produce a much more sophisticated and better controlled

effect; this was the basis of the flying tricks of W. P. Dando and Mlle Aenea in their immensely popular *touring acts in the 1890s, and is still the technique used to make Peter Pan fly in *Barrie's play. More recently, electric winches and motorized, computer-controlled carriages have made extremely *realistic human flight possible.   JB

FO, DARIO (1926–   )

Italian playwright, actor, director, and designer, who uses traditional Italian forms and *stock characters to produce powerful contemporary *political theatre. His dedication to theatrical tradition has baffled both fellow activists and theatre *critics, since Fo has simultaneously espoused revolutionary politics and theatrical conservatism. He has always despised the *avant-garde as elitist; the *farce, reshaped to combine *didacticism with *slapstick, has been the favoured *genre throughout his career.

He made his debut with *one-person *radio pieces, *Poer Nano*, in 1950, before moving into *variety theatre in *Milan, where he met and subsequently married the actress Franca *Rame. After a brief sortie into *film, in 1958 the couple staged two programmes of *one-act *farces by Fo with such success that they were invited to perform his longer, more complex, satirical *comedies in the main theatres of Italy. During what he called the 'bourgeois period between 1959 and 1968', Fo attacked the holders of power in Church and state with vehemence and wit, but grew increasingly dissatisfied with the compromises forced on him. In 1968 he and Rame broke with *bourgeois theatre to establish a theatrical cooperative, Nuova Scena, with the purpose of performing popular, political theatre in an *alternative circuit of venues provided, initially, by groups close to the Communist Party. *Mistero buffo* (1969), the main work from this time, is a series of revised medieval sketches performed solo by Fo in the style of the medieval jester (*giullare*). The *satire of the thirteenth-century Pope Boniface VIII was also aimed at the contemporary pontiff and at the institutional Church as centre of power, but the work disconcerted comrades who demanded a more directly militant theatre.

He moved to the left of the Communist Party, and in 1970 established a second cooperative, La Comune, which produced *Accidental Death of an Anarchist* (1970), Fo's most successful venture in the style of hard-hitting but madcap political farce. In 1974, with the dissolution of La Comune, Fo and his associates took over the Palazzina Liberty in Milan, which became his base for the next decade. With the ending of the age of mass protest, he turned his attention to social problems, such as drugs (*Mum's Marijuana Is Best*, 1976), and, under the influence of *feminism, to the dilemmas of women (*All Bed, Board and Church*, 1977). In the 1980s and 1990s, while continuing to write and act, he directed productions of writers like *Molière and *Ruzante, whom he regards as predecessors. He was awarded the Nobel Prize for Literature in 1997.　　　　　　　　　　　　　　　JF

FODÉBA, KÉITA (1921–71)

Guinean dramatist and choreographer who founded an African *dance and music company in 1950, using drum music as gestural language. In his productions of *Le Maître d'école* (1952) and the poem *Aube africaine*, he relied on storytelling and *griot* musical techniques. In 1958, at the time of independence, he founded the *Ballets Africains ensemble and mounted large-scale performances of *total theatre. Shortly after his return from France in 1956, he went into politics, serving among other capacities as Minister of Defence. In 1969 he ran foul of the regime of Ahmed Sekou Touré, who had him arrested and, it is believed, murdered in jail.　　　　　PNN trans. JCM

FOKIN, VALERY (1946–)

Soviet/Russian director. Fokin trained at the Shchukin School before joining the *Sovremennik Theatre (1971–85) in *Moscow,

where he directed numerous contemporary plays. In 1986 he became *artistic director of the Ermolova Theatre, where productions such as Ovechkin's *Speak!* (1986) and Nabokov's *Invitation to a Beheading* (1990) underscored his commitment to Gorbachev's reforms. After a split of the Ermolova Theatre (1991) he set up the Meyerhold Centre, where he organized independent projects, such as Kafka's *Metamorphosis* (1995), and *A Room in a Hotel in the City of N* (1994, based on *Gogol's *Dead Souls*), set in the space of a small hotel room.　　　BB

FOKINE, MICHEL (MIKHAIL FOKIN) (1880–1942)

Russian *ballet dancer, choreographer, and *costume designer. He began his career at the Mariinsky Theatre in *St Petersburg performing a range of roles with the distinctive grace and lightness which characterized his *dancing style. His first ballet was *Acis and Galatea* (1905), followed by Cherepnin's *Le Pavillon d'Armide* (1907) and Arensky's *Egyptian Nights* (1907–8), which revealed his talents as a reformer and innovator. He was generally opposed to traditional ballet and in tune with the *modernist impulses of designers such as *Benois, *Bakst, Roerich, Golovin, and Dobuzhinsky, with whom he collaborated. His fame abroad began in 1909 with the first seasons of the *Ballets Russes, when his major successes as a choreographer included *Daphnis and Chloe*, *Petrushka*, *Prince Igor*, and *Le Spectre de la rose*. In 1919 he settled in *New York, where he worked for the next ten years. *Drury Lane and *Covent Garden in *London hosted some of his ballet productions in 1925, 1937, and 1938, including *Le Coq d'or*, based on a *Pushkin fairy tale, with designs by Natalya *Goncharova.　　　　　　　　　NW

FOLIES-BERGÈRE

*Paris *music hall, opened in 1869 for productions of *operetta and *pantomime. The first *manager, Léon Sari, operated the hall until 1885; by allowing prostitutes into the large indoor promenade, he made the area a popular destination for young men and the venue became a fashionable spot. Between 1885 and 1918 various speciality acts appeared, and *audiences saw major performers such as Loïe *Fuller, Maurice *Chevalier, and Yvette *Guilbert. Paul Derval became manager in 1918 and created the internationally famous image of the Folies-Bergère as a showplace for naked or slightly clad women with huge plumed headdresses and sequinned trains. Although the *stage was fairly small, Derval staged opulent *revues with grand staircases and tableaux. Additional acts included *jugglers, *acrobats, singers, *dancers, and comics. The Folies-Bergère still drew tourists at the start of the twenty-first century, both foreign and French, but its appeal has faded since its lush heyday between the world wars. *See also* SEX SHOWS AND DANCES.　　　FL

FOLK AND FOLKLORE

An important theme in Western thought about culture; the assumed *origin of dramatic art among scholars of some schools; the body of collected and recorded oral tradition from which many theatre practitioners in various cultures have drawn. Western culture is deeply originalist; the peoples of Europe have always been obsessed with where things and ideas came from. As democracy spread through European culture, critics came reflexively to attribute the origins and 'vitality' of artistic traditions to their roots in the oral tradition of the communal folk. Despite the poverty of evidence on any side of the question, drama was said to begin either in a primitive phase of undifferentiated classless society, or among peasants, shepherds, and illiterates, from whom it gathered its energy and meaning—certainly not among kings, warriors, or scholars.

This pro-folk bias can be seen beginning with *romanticism, both in the works of artists (for instance the *closet dramas of Walter Scott, *Schiller's *William Tell*, 1804) and in the focus of scholarship (the interest in *mummers' plays and in the *mystery plays). In early *realism, the interest in folk matters was strengthened and the depiction of scenes among the common folk became a standard trope, very often co-opting and sentimentalizing their real struggles, as in *Boucicault's *The Colleen Bawn*. Scholars began to look for sources for Shakespeare and other cultural icons in the oral tradition; the rude mechanicals in *A Midsummer Night's Dream* assumed an importance they had not previously had, as evidence of the popular performance tradition.

By the early twentieth century, the reaction against the modern industrial world (*see* MODERNISM AND POSTMODERNISM) had spawned both Marxist (*see* MATERIALIST CRITICISM) and reactionary movements, and unsurprisingly Marxists found evidence of resistance to oppression in the *medieval *Second Shepherd's Play* (*see* BIBLICAL PLAYS; CYCLE PLAYS) at about the same time that *Wagner and his followers were reconstructing a German racial mythos from the merest fragments of a pagan tradition. Theatre scholarship was slowly becoming an organized discipline with a tradition and methods of its own, and the great division between elite (or court or classical), popular (or mass), and folk drama was applied anthropologically to many cultures around the globe, most especially to *India and *China. According to this division, folk drama is oral, local, based in its community, *amateur, so tightly rooted in *ritual that the roots are still visible, simple, intimate, emotional, and participatory. Since these are matters that in general the past three generations of theatre scholars have approved of, the ideological circle closed perfectly, and folk theatre was taken to be successful and enduring because the observers recognized its excellent qualities.

In the late 1990s the issue of folk drama, folklore, and what is meant by folk reopened, with some scholars and movements reasserting the primacy of folk drama and folk sources (*see*, for example, ANTHROPOLOGY, THEATRE) at exactly the same time that others began to deconstruct the concepts in hopes of seeing beyond them. The tendency to essentialize the primitive, so often apparent in the orientalizing narratives associated with Western colonialism, has been attacked from a number of fronts, and this has certainly affected thinking about folk and folklore (*see* INTERCULTURALISM; POST-COLONIAL STUDIES). Whatever else the folk idea may have done in its two centuries of dominance, it motivated ethnographers to collect performance traditions before they were hopelessly contaminated or extinct; the resulting body of ethnographic work is impressive, and though much was lost, much was preserved.

Whether the older concept of 'folk' can continue to serve theatre research and practice well, with so few communities untouched by modernity, is an open question. Steve Tillis's wide-ranging and cross-cultural *Rethinking Folk Drama* (1999) argues for an emphasis on actual performance practices within living communal traditions, and for special attention to the way that variation occurs within repetitive, self-conscious tradition. This is very different in spirit from the old approach of explaining a people's drama by looking at the *dances, games, and skits of the peasants. But with its emphasis on observation of actual practice, and its final divorce from issues of originalism, it may well reinvigorate the folk idea.   JB

FOLK PLAY (MEDIEVAL)

Folk drama appears a worldwide phenomenon, characterized by seasonal performance in rural communities by *amateur actors who enact a *plot and recite lines that have been passed down through generations. Commonly the performers wear traditional *disguise and conclude their performance by demanding coins or drinks. We have no texts of *mummers' plays in English before the eighteenth century, but the appearance of *folk elements in other forms of *medieval drama, such as the *morality play *Mankind*, suggests that they were familiar at least in the late middle ages and probably much earlier. Textual references to plays about Robin Hood go as far back as the thirteenth century. Sword plays and *morris dances are also forms of folk drama with late medieval textual documentation.

Folk plays, with some common dramatic elements such as wooing or combat or a martial display, appear in a wide variety of cultural settings across the globe, including *China, Iran, Turkey, Russia, and Brazil. The earliest scholars of the folk drama, influenced by Frazer's *The Golden Bough*, theorized that all the folk plays that enacted a death and a resurrection were devolutions from a seasonal *ritual intended to ensure the return of spring and fertility after the winter's dying-back (*see* ORIGINS OF THEATRE). The Cambridge anthropologists, writing in the earliest years of the twentieth century, therefore emphasized the elements of the drama that appeared most easily traceable to a ritual origin (for instance, a symbolic beheading) and concentrated their scrutiny on the mummers' plays. Beginning in the 1970s, however, scholarly interest turned from questions of origin to those of function, and scholars began to investigate the role played by various kinds of folk drama in building or maintaining community, preserving or undermining social hierarchy, or channelling social disruptions into socially acceptable bounds. The continuing appearance of successive volumes of the Records of Early English Drama has provided more descriptions of more types of folk drama and a better understanding of the dramatic venues.

A *Robin Hood play, for example, seems to have been a not uncommon feature of church ales, fundraising fairs that flourished in England in the late Middle Ages. The theme of assisting the poor by taking from the wealthy would have lent itself well to an event that was raising money for community charity. Its anti-authoritarian elements, such as Robin's humiliation of the Sheriff of Nottingham, have prompted scholars to explore the challenge to political and religious interference by the central government and the containment of that resistance. Whereas it was once believed that such plays simply lost popularity, it is now widely accepted that the plays and the church ales that sponsored them were outlawed by episcopal decree, making the plays themselves outlaws and thus changing their social meaning.

Performance traditions of folk plays differ by type and venue, but overall it appears that *costuming, *scenery, delivery, and movement tended to be non-naturalistic, emphasizing the performance not as a simulation of *reality but as a disruption of the status quo. Performances appear to have been more likely to announce themselves than to take place at an expected hour; mummers' troupes visited private and public houses during the Christmas season and demanded entrance whenever they arrived. Some surviving mummers' troupes use *naturalistic clothing but the majority wear costumes of multicoloured fabric or paper ribbons, simply a 'disguise' rather than a *character costume. Disguise also figures in the action of several Robin Hood plays. The prominence of disguising in sixteenth-century England may well be connected with an anxiety about the basis for identity, as the feudal and manorial hierarchy confronted merchant wealth and urban anonymity. Likewise evidence suggesting that the players may have declaimed their lines with more volume than subtlety suggests the importance of common men gaining a voice through their roles in folk plays, just as they gained the right to demand payment from assembled spectators of any class. We may surmise that 'Turkey Snipe' is an incorrectly transmitted version of 'Turkish Knight' from the crusading era, and from the nonsense substitution we may further surmise that the play itself was not nearly so important as its playing. *See also* FOLK AND FOLKLORE   JCD

FOLKSBIENE

The oldest surviving *Yiddish theatre company. It was established in *New York in 1915 as an *amateur troupe under the auspices of the Workmen's Circle, a leading Jewish fraternal organization with close links with the American labour movement. The company has always maintained its amateur status, its actors being working-class men and women. From 1925, however, it also maintained close ties with the professionals of the Yiddish stage, employing its directors, designers, choreographers, and actors as guest artists. The first Folksbiene production was *Ibsen's *An Enemy of the People*, and its first major success came in 1917 with Peretz Hirshbein's innovative *Forsaken Nook*. The company has staged many Yiddish classics by I. L. Peretz, Solomon *Asch, Abraham *Goldfaden, and Sholem *Aleichem, and in its early years also mounted Yiddish translations of plays by Maxim *Gorky, Eugene *O'Neill, and Upton Sinclair. In response to the decline of Yiddish, in recent years the company has added simultaneous translations in English and Russian.   EN

FONDA, HENRY (1905–82)

American actor, known for his understated performances of decent American men. Fonda began acting at the Omaha Community Playhouse in 1925, *stage managed at the Cape Playhouse, Falmouth, Massachusetts, and joined the University Players, which included other future luminaries. He achieved recognition in *New Faces of 1934* on Broadway, and found stardom in *The Farmer Takes a Wife* (1934), whose Hollywood version provided the beginning of his illustrious *film (and later, *television) career. A rare movie star who often returned to the stage, his most memorable Broadway roles were in *Mister Roberts* (1948), which earned him a Tony *award, *Point of No Return* (1951), *The Caine Mutiny Court Martial* (1953), *Two for the Seesaw* (1958), *Generation* (1965), and *Clarence Darrow* (1974). His final stage work was *Last Monday in October* (1978).

SLL

FONTANNE, LYNN *See* LUNT, ALFRED.

FONVIZIN, DENIS (1745–92)

Russian writer of satirical prose and plays. Born into the gentry, Fonvizin worked as a translator in the Foreign Office and then as secretary to a cabinet minister. His first plays were translations from French originals by *Voltaire (*Al'zira; or, The Americans*, 1762) and Gresset (*Korion*, 1764), but Fonvizin is best known for two original plays, *Brigadier* (written 1766–9, first produced in *St Petersburg, 1780) and *The Minor* (or *The Infant*, 1782). One further play, *The Selection of a Tutor* (1790), has been eclipsed by the other two. Contributing to the new trend of the mid- to late eighteenth century, both major plays are *didactic *satires set in Russia yet conform to the rules of *neoclassical *comedy by sticking closely to the three *unities and maintaining clear divides between the virtuous and vicious *characters. The language of *Brigadier* is strikingly contemporary to its period, discarding the rigid, elevated conformity of neoclassicism. A situation comedy, it targets the transparent morality and excessive Francomania of the provincial gentry, taking sideswipes at the corrupt Russian judicial system. The satirical tone is harsher in *The Minor*, which attacks the low moral and educational standards of the provincial gentry, in particular their maltreatment of serfs. The 1782 première occurred in St Petersburg with Dmitrevsky directing and playing the moral spokesman (Starodum). His delivery of the attack on social injustice ensured a controversial start for a play which, along with the marginally less successful *Brigadier*, has scarcely left the Russian repertoire since. Unusually for the late eighteenth century, the *realistic content of this dark comedy prompted *naturalistic standards in *costume and the stage setting was modest and simple. Fonvizin's satire is regarded as an important precursor of Aleksandr *Griboedov and of *Gogol's social comedies.   CM

FOOL

A comic entertainer, sometimes physically deformed, whose behaviour is the product of real or pretended mental deficiency. An Egyptian record of about 2200 BC mentions such a figure, and fools have been recorded in many cultures, variously associated with luck, religious sacrifice, poetic power, clairvoyance, and wisdom. In Europe, professional fools or jesters flourished from about 1300 to about 1500 as official household or court fools, or more generally as entertainers in taverns and brothels, or as civic functionaries. The conventional dress of a medieval fool consisted of a motley coat, often chequered red and green, a cowl-shaped hood with ears or coxcomb, and a sword, bladder, or bauble (called a marotte) carried in the hand. The fool also functioned as a theatrical creation, appearing as a *character type in ancient *mime and *farce (Bucco, Stupidus, Herakles), as a mask in the *commedia dell'arte (Arlecchino), as a *clown on the Elizabethan stage, as the German *Narr* and the French *sot*. The stage fool has replaced the motley fool, continuing in a number of guises, ranging from the Three Stooges to Chaplin's Little Tramp.   RWV

FOON, DENNIS (1951–   )

Canadian playwright, director, and screenwriter. He co-founded Green Thumb Theatre for Young People (*Vancouver) in 1975, and until 1987 was its *artistic director. He has written scripts for Green Thumb and other Canadian companies. His plays, which have won numerous *awards, address serious themes such as racism and abuse through a playful theatricality incorporating presentational *acting, *masks, and *puppetry. Among his plays are *New Canadian Kid* (1981), *Liars* (1986), *Skin* (1987), *Bedtime and Bullies* (1987), *Mirror Game* (1991), *War* (1994), *The Short Tree and the Bird that Could Not Sing* (1995), and *Chasing the Money* (1999).   RCN

FOOTE, SAMUEL (1720–77)

English actor, *manager, and dramatist who became known as the English *Aristophanes for his satirical portraits of eighteenth-century personalities. As a young man Foote played Othello to *Macklin's Iago at the *Haymarket. In 1747 he published two pamphlets on *acting: *A Treatise on the Passions* and *The Roman and English Comedy Considered*. After the passing of the *Licensing Act of 1737, Foote evaded the new restrictions on the performance of drama by staging a satirical *revue entitled *The Diversions of the Morning; or, A Dish of Chocolate* (1747), in which *audiences were invited to tea at the Haymarket, and then offered a performance by the way; a similar event took place in 1748 called *The Auction of Pictures*. Foote's plays include *The Author* (1757), later suppressed by the *Lord Chamberlain for its portrait of an eccentric Welshman called Aprece (*see* CENSORSHIP), and *The Minor* (1760), a controversial *satire on Methodism in which Foote impersonated Dr Squintum (the famous evangelical preacher George Whitefield). He also wrote a three-act *comedy entitled *The Liar* (1762), followed by *The Patron* (1764), and *The Mayor of Garratt* (1764), a highly successful satire on corrupt electioneering. After falling from the Duke of York's horse in 1766, Foote was compelled to have his leg amputated. As partial compensation, the Duke obtained for him the *patent of the Haymarket Theatre. Foote remodelled the *playhouse and managed it until 1776. Several of Foote's later plays, including *The Devil upon Two Sticks* (1768) and *The Handsome Housemaid; or, Piety in Pattens* (1773), a satire on Richardson's *Pamela* and the conventions of sentimental comedy, cleverly transformed the actor's wooden leg into a source of laughter. Other plays included *The Nabobs* (1772) and *The Trip to Calais*, a mischievous satire on Elizabeth Chudleigh, the infamous Duchess of Kingston, which was refused a licence in 1775.   JM

FOOTLIGHTS

Upward-pointed, lensless lights on the *stage or below it, usually with a trough-shaped metal reflector, often called 'foots' or (especially in Britain) 'floatlights' or 'floats', since floating candles were used for *fire *safety and better reflection. Footlights were in use in Europe from *c*.1620 and throughout the West until early in the twentieth century, normally placed at the spectator edge of the *forestage or in line with the *proscenium. Since no natural light sources shine on the human face from below, footlights create an effect that can be variously unattractive or eerie. But until electric lighting became practical, footlights remained crucial elements of *lighting because they were easy to reach, conceal, and dim (by lowering into the footlights *trap). They are rare today except in evocations of earlier theatrical styles, and in the received language of newspaper *critics.

JB

FORBES-ROBERTSON, JOHNSTON (1853–1937)

English actor and *manager; knighted in 1913. Equally successful in *melodrama and Shakespeare, Forbes-Robertson was an elegant, handsome performer with excellent elocution and graceful movement. In the 1870s he acted with Samuel *Phelps (his mentor), Ellen *Terry, Geneviève *Ward, and the *Bancrofts. In the 1880s he appeared with Madame *Modjeska, Wilson *Barrett, the Bancrofts again, and *Irving's *Lyceum company, and also performed Shakespeare with Mary *Anderson in the USA and *London. In the 1890s he continued to act with Irving and Terry, but in 1895 he created a company with Mrs Patrick *Campbell, featuring *Romeo and Juliet*, *Sudermann's *Magda*, and H. A. *Jones's *Michael and his Lost Angel*. His *Hamlet* was especially well received, but so too was his *Othello* (both 1897). In 1900 he appeared on *tour in *Shaw's *The Devil's Disciple*; Shaw admired Forbes-Robertson's *acting and wrote *Caesar and Cleopatra* (1906) for him. In 1908 he played the Stranger in Jerome K. Jerome's *The Passing of the Third-Floor Back*, a popular play that he revived often during the next five years, despite growing tired of the role. From 1900 forward his company, which also featured his wife Gertrude Elliott, balanced London performances with tours, including trips to America. He retired in 1913, publishing an autobiography in 1925.

TP

FORD, JOHN (1586–c.1639)

English playwright. Born in Lincolnshire, he was a member of the Middle Temple and involved in the legal profession in some capacity. But his main interest was the theatre. His early work was non-dramatic, and included both poems and prose pamphlets. He began his theatrical career collaborating with Thomas *Dekker on a number of plays, the best known of which is *The Witch of Edmonton* (1621, with William *Rowley). He worked in close association with some of the most prominent dramatists of his time, including *Massinger, *Shirley, *Brome, and *Webster, all of whom published plays with commendatory verses by Ford. He cultivated a large circle of powerful patrons, most of them actively involved in contemporary politics.

Ford's best-known solo works are the two *tragedies *'Tis Pity She's a Whore* and *The Broken Heart* (printed in 1633), which portray impossible moral dilemmas that oppose self-asserting individuals against the conventions of society. A gory story of incestuous passion, often branded as morbidly sensational and a sign of the decline of the stage under Charles I, *'Tis Pity* was nonetheless successfully revived in the late nineteenth century and was by far the most successful of Ford's plays in the twentieth, regularly performed in academic and major venues. Notable productions include Alan *Ayckbourn's for the Royal *National Theatre (1988), JoAnne *Akalaitis's for the *New York Shakespeare Festival (1992), and David Lan's at the *Young Vic (1999). It has also been adapted for *film (1973) and *television (BBC, 1980).

Together with Ford's other works, it became the object of renewed critical interest in the 1990s, when the moral and ideological challenges portrayed began to be appreciated more thoroughly. Politically oriented criticism is likewise responsible for the reappraisal in the 1990s of Ford's *historical drama *Perkin Warbeck* (printed 1634), a 'chronicle history' of the events leading to the defeat of the Yorkist pretender to the throne at the hands of Henry VII in 1495. The play provides a commentary on the ideology of kingship, especially in the theatricalized treatment of the performance of power.

PCR

FOREGGER, NIKOLAI (1892–1939)

Russian/Soviet director and *ballet master. His work in experimental *dance technique, based on functionalist, mechanical principles, was influenced by *futurism and *constructivism and drew upon the work of *Meyerhold and *biomechanics. In 1918 Foregger established his Theatre of Four Masks, where he experimented with *circus-style entertainment before setting up the MASTFOR Workshop (Masterskaya Foreggera) in *Moscow, where a programme of revolutionary and satirical 'machine dances', based on industrial production processes and circus *acrobatics, were performed in a colourfully eccentric style using jazz and popular music, deriving partly from *film techniques. *Eisenstein worked as a designer at MASTFOR during the 1922–3 season. The theatre also staged productions in styles which satirized those of the *Bolshoi, the *Moscow Art Theatre, *Tairov, and Meyerhold. Foregger's theatre burned down in 1924 and he subsequently worked at *opera and ballet theatres in Kharkov, *Kiev, and Kuibyshev.

NW

FOREMAN, RICHARD (1937–)

American experimental director, writer, *theorist and *manager. Born in *New York, he received an MFA in playwrighting from *Yale School of Drama (1962). He founded the *Ontological Hysteric Theatre in 1968 in New York and has staged his plays under that banner at several different venues there and in *Paris. Productions have included *Bad Boy Nietzsche* (2000), *Perminant Brain Damage* (1996), *I've Got the Shakes* (1995), *Film Is Evil, Radio Is Good* (1988), and *Rhoda in Potatoland* (1975). His *dramaturgical strategies have been influenced by Gertrude *Stein and her notion of a 'landscape play', which structures a continuous present beginning again and again. Traditional *action, narrative, and *character are elided and thus *audience identification and empathy are resisted in favour of performative moments which foreground the *text's and the theatre's apparatus for producing meaning. The ontological structure of the *text in performance in dialogue with the cognitive processes of audience and performer is the subject of his plays.

In addition to his work with the Ontological Hysteric Theatre, Foreman has written and directed works for the *Wooster Group and has directed other writers' works such *Brecht and *Weill's *Threepenny Opera* at the *New York Shakespeare Festival, *The Fall of the House of Usher* by Philip *Glass at *American Repertory Theatre, and *Strauss's *Fledermaus* at the Paris *Opéra. Foreman has published four collections of plays and theory.   MDC

FORESTAGE

Also called the 'apron', the forestage extends the *stage into the *auditorium of a *playhouse, beyond the imaginary line of the *proscenium. In the seventeenth and early eighteenth centuries the forestage was the main acting area since it had better light and audibility; this practice also kept actors at a distance from forced-*perspective painted scenery. As *realism and *naturalism took hold in Europe in the nineteenth century, and as *lighting, acoustics, and scenic technique improved, the acting area moved upstage and the forestage shrank to a vestigial curve holding the *footlights and *prompter's box. In the twentieth century, especially as fashions changed in Shakespeare revivals, many new stages were constructed with large forestages, temporary aprons were constructed in older houses, and the *thrust stage came into wider use. *See also* OPEN STAGE.   JB

FORNÉS, MARIA IRENE (1930–   )

American playwright and director. Born in Cuba, she emigrated in 1945 with her mother and a sister to *New York, where she was eventually caught up in the bohemian subculture of Greenwich Village. Fornés helped to define the *Off-Off-Broadway movement of the 1960s with a series of short, madcap plays, the most successful of which was *Promenade* (1965, music by Al Carmines). In the 1970s she began to direct the initial productions of her plays, developing a precise, austere, formalist style. In 1977 she wrote her most significant and widely produced work, *Fefu and her Friends*, a landmark in *feminist drama which also revealed her interest in site-specific theatre (*see*

ENVIRONMENTAL THEATRE). Fornés's most prolific period came in the 1980s, during which she wrote and directed such plays as *Mud* (1983), *Sarita* (1984), *The Conduct of Life* (1985), and *Abingdon Square* (1987). Each uses a series of short, snapshot-like *scenes to trace a female *protagonist's wrenching passage from innocence to experience. Of Fornés's many prizes and commendations, the most telling are her nine Obies *awards over 35 years, more than anybody except Sam *Shepard. The quintessence of Off-Off-Broadway's insouciance and resourcefulness, she was affiliated over the years with Judson Poets Theatre, Theatre for the New City, INTAR, Padua Hills Playwrights Festival, and Signature Theatre, which devoted its 1999–2000 season to her work. Despite neglect by the mainstream theatre, she is perhaps the most important American woman dramatist of the twentieth century.   STC

FORREST, EDWIN (1806–72)

The first native-born star of the US stage. Acclaimed for his patriotic heroics, Forrest's acting centred on his muscular build, booming voice, and strenuous *realism. His charismatic appeal and Jacksonian populist persona induced hero worship from male working-class spectators in US cities. Following several supporting roles with Edmund *Kean in 1825, Forrest gained stardom with his performance of Othello in 1826. To increase the number of his leading roles, Forrest organized several play contests and performed some of the winners throughout his career, adding *Metamora*, *The Gladiator*, *The Broker of Bogotá*, and *Jack Cade* to his mostly Shakespearian repertory. US critics celebrated King Lear and Metamora, a Native American *hero, as his best roles. Forrest blamed his lukewarm success with *London critics on the intervention of William *Macready and persecuted the English actor in the press, a rivalry that contributed to the *Astor Place riot in 1849. When Forrest and his English-born wife sued each other for divorce in 1851, the trial served as another lightning rod for social antagonisms, dividing the pro-English US elite from nationalistic working-class Americans who favoured traditional patriarchal values in marriage. Forrest amassed millions during his long career, which he prolonged as a platform speaker in the years before his death.   BMC

FORSSELL, LARS (1928–   )

Swedish poet, playwright, and lyricist. One of the most important literary voices in post-war Sweden, Forssell committed himself to an eclectic mix of serious and popular literary styles. He has written popular verse, song lyrics, political ballads, and erudite poetry, the mix sometimes published in a single collection. A translator as well, Forssell introduced Ezra Pound to Swedish readers, and recast French *cabaret songs into national equivalents. His plays, including *The Jester Who Belonged to his Bell*,

Mary Lou, *The Madcap*, and *The Sunday Promenade*, investigate *mask, role playing, and identity. His *politically conscious *Sweden, Sweden, the Farce of the Bourgeoisie*, *The Bourgeoisie and Marx* (a retelling of *Molière's *The Would-Be Gentleman*), and *The Hare and the Vulture* expose the emptiness of class-conscious social climbers. *Street-Lasse; or, Pirates* features *music, free *verse, and rhymed couplets, while *The Dynamite Blaster and his Daughter Eivor* is a *naturalistic *tragedy. He was elected to the Swedish Academy in 1971.   DLF

FORT, PAUL (1872–1960)

French director and poet, most famous for his support of the *symbolist movement. While still at school he formed the Théâtre Mixte (1890), which was committed to the work of young people. Later that year he joined forces with Louis Germain's Théâtre Idéaliste, which opposed *naturalism as a poor reaction to the *well-made play, to found the Théâtre d'*Art. Their early material surprisingly would have found a home at *Antoine's Théâtre *Libre, which Fort strongly opposed, but over the course of some eighteen months between November 1890 and March 1892—the lifetime of the Théâtre d'Art—he produced some of the most important symbolist dramas, most notably *The Intruder* and *The Blind* by the Belgian Maurice *Maeterlinck. But Fort's programming was eclectic, and a mixture of short plays, poetry recitations, and silent *tableaux (along with gauze *curtains, smells, and inaudible *acting) led to both the incomprehension and outright hostility of critics. Fort's limitations as a *manager, together with poor programming and a narrow appeal of the repertoire, led to the theatre's demise. While the symbolist and *avant-garde baton immediately passed to *Lugné-Poe and the Théâtre de l'*Œuvre, Fort continued his creative output as a poet.   BRS

FORTUNE THEATRE

A *London *playhouse built in 1600 to replace the *Rose, when it acquired a new neighbour, the *Globe. *Henslowe and *Alleyn, its financiers, used the carpenter who had just completed the Globe. Located in Golding Lane in St Giles, the Fortune site was square, putting the building in contrast with the round features of the Globe. The builder's contract, which survives amongst the Henslowe papers, specifies that it should be 24 m (80 feet) square, making the open yard a 17-m (55-foot) square, with three levels of surrounding galleries in twenty bays, and two stair towers for access to the galleries, and should have a stage 13 m (43 feet) wide reaching into the middle of the yard. Initially it housed the *Admiral's Men, half the duopoly formed with Shakespeare's company, until in 1603 they became the Prince's Men. The Fortune burned down in December 1621, at night-time, when—unlike the occasion when the Globe burned—nobody was around to save the *properties and playbooks. Its company of players paid to replace it, possibly in brick, and it continued in service as what Thomas Wright called 'a citizen playhouse', catering to the less affluent and still staging the famous old plays of the 1590s, until the general closure of the theatres in 1642.   AJG

FORTUNY, MARIANO (1871–1949)

Painter, photographer, and designer. Born in Granada, he studied painting in Paris and moved to Venice in 1899. Greatly influenced by the Arts and Crafts movement, Fortuny dedicated his career to all aspects of design. For the theatre he created the 'Fortuny dome', designed to give the optical *illusion of *light from the sky on *stage. The first model of the dome was demonstrated in *Paris in 1902, and successfully installed at the Théâtre de l'Avenue Bosquets in 1906 (*see* CYCLORAMA). He also designed *playhouses and concert halls, and created new fabric dyeing and pleating techniques, put into effect at his factory in Venice. His dress designs were inspired by ancient Greek garments and became highly fashionable among the wealthy.   DMcM

FOSSE, BOB (1927–87)

American choreographer, director, and dancer. Fosse's choreography exuded a slouching sexuality; his *dances, precise to the raise of an eyebrow or the tip of a hat, appeared almost anti-balletic in their angles and isolations but were capable of show-stopping *spectacle. Fosse had performed on Broadway and in Hollywood *musicals by the early 1950s, when he was given a chance at Broadway choreography by director-writer George *Abbott. His staging for *The Pajama Game* (1954), and particularly for the 'Steam Heat' number, became the talk of the town, defining his seductive, razzle-dazzle style. Fosse soon began directing as well as choreographing, and gained acclaim with, among others, *Sweet Charity* (1966) and *Chicago* (1975). The latter cast a cynical look at celebrity, which resonated anew in a hugely successful 1990s Broadway revival, spawning a number of international offshoots. Fosse directed several *films, including *Cabaret* (1972) and *All That Jazz* (1979), a thinly veiled autobiographical rumination about an overdriven, chain-smoking, womanizing choreographer, which ironically foresaw his own death by heart attack.   EW

FOSTER, GLORIA (1936–2001)

*African-American actress. Foster first appeared *Off-Broadway in 1963 in the *documentary drama *In White America*, for which she won an Obie *award, and later took roles in *New York in the world repertoire not tied to her *race, including *Medea* (1965) and *Yerma* (*Lincoln Center, 1966). At the *New York Shakespeare Festival she performed with Morgan

Freeman in *Coriolanus* (as Volumnia, 1979), in *Mother Courage* (1980), in Bill Gunn's *The Forbidden City* (1989), and as the mother in *Blood Wedding* (1992). On Broadway she played in Emily Mann's *Having our Say*, about the centenarian Delaney sisters. She appeared on *television and in *film, including the role of the oracle living in the projects in *The Matrix* (1999).

BBL

FOURCADE, GEORGES (1884–c.1967)

Réunionese creole singer-songwriter and dramatist. He is best known for his prolific output of songs, including 'P'tite Fleur aimée', an anthem familiar to all Réunionese, and for his collection of creole stories, *Z'histoires la caze* (1928). He collaborated with many of the island's popular musicians of the mid-twentieth century, such as Jules Fossy ('Ah! Nénère', 'Mon Doudou') and Jules Arlanda ('Séga piqué'), as well as adapting traditional tunes ('P'tit Paille-en-queue', 'Laisse à moin marier'). Many of these use the local Séga rhythm, and originally formed part of short comedy sketches in creole.

PGH

FOX, GEORGE W. L. (1825–77)

American actor, pantomimist, and *manager. George Washington Lafayette Fox was born in *Boston, the eldest of six children. Making his stage debut at 5, he received his first *playbill listing in 1832. He was one of a family troupe ('The Little Foxes') that performed around New England and then moved to Troy, New York. Gaining renown especially in *burlesques of Shakespeare and *Sheridan, Fox in 1850 moved to *New York City, where over the years he managed a series of theatres. In 1853 he scored a huge success by importing his family from Troy and presenting an adaptation of *Uncle Tom's Cabin* (fashioned by his cousin George *Aiken), which ran for 325 performances (*see also* TOM SHOW). A series of money-making *pantomimes (1864–7) led to the peak of his career when he premièred in 1868 Clifton Tayleure's *Humpty Dumpty*, the first full-evening pantomime on Broadway (1,286 performances), which he would *tour for sixteen months (1874–5) to 26 states. His grimacing and *slapstick clowning caused many to consider him the funniest performer of his day; and for some time he was the highest-paid entertainer in America. Insanity ended his career.

CT

FOY, EDDIE (1856–1928)

American actor and singer. Foy was born Edwin Fitzgerald in *New York, where he was a sidewalk entertainer from the age of 8. At 16 he changed his surname and embarked on a series of jobs as singer, *dancer, and *acrobat. Teaming with James Thompson in 1877, he spent six years in *minstrel and *variety shows, mostly in western states. From 1888 to 1894 he worked for David Henderson in *Chicago, starring in *The Crystal Slipper*, *Bluebeard Jr.*, *Sinbad*, and *Ali Baba*. From 1898 to 1912 his comic talents enchanted New York *audiences in ten *musicals, including *Hotel Topsy Turvy*, *The Strollers*, *The Wild Rose*, *Mr Hamlet of Broadway*, and *Over the River*. His final years were largely spent with his children ('The Seven Little Foys') on the *vaudeville circuit, where he died on tour in Kansas City. He published an autobiography, *Clowning through Life* (1928).

CT

FRANÇON, ALAIN (1946–)

French director. After mounting several noteworthy productions of plays by Michel *Vinaver in the 1970s and 1980s, Françon became director of the Centres Dramatiques Nationaux in Lyon (1989–92) and Annency (1992–6). In 1996 he succeeded Jorge *Lavelli as the second director of the Théâtre National de la Colline, the newest of France's national theatres, noted for its attention to contemporary drama. There, after staging Edward *Bond's *War Plays* at the *Avignon Festival (1992), he continued to champion the later work of the English playwright, directing *In the Company of Men* (1994, 1997) and *The Crime of the Twenty-First Century* (2001).

DGM

FRANKÉTIENNE (FRANCK ÉTIENNE) (1936–)

Haitian writer and painter. In the wake of the success of *Dezafi*, a novel written in creole, he switched to drama in that language. *Twou foban* was successfully staged in 1978. *Pèlen tèt* was banned the same year and enforced a break from the theatre. Frankétienne returned to the stage in 1983 with *Zago Loray*, followed in quick succession by *Bobomasouri* (1984), *Kaselezo* (1985), *Totolomannwèl* (1986), *Minwy mwen senk* (1987), *Kalifobobo* (1987), and *Foukifoura* (1999). These small-cast plays rely on a *doubling of roles that recalls the ceremonies of *voodoo where a subject can successfully be possessed by several *loas* or spirits. Frankétienne's accessible symbolism from traditional culture is counterbalanced by *Brechtian distancing techniques and a playful organization of *action.

MLa trans. JCM

FRASER, CLAUD LOVAT (1890–1921)

English painter and designer. Fraser first impressed critics and the public with his elegant designs for *As You Like It* and *The Beggar's Opera* at the *Lyric Theatre Hammersmith in 1920. Commissions for theatre and *ballet quickly followed, but his sudden death a year later cut short a promising career. His designs drew upon the colours and moods of rococo painting and *romantic landscape.

TP

FRAYN, MICHAEL (1933–)

English playwright and novelist. Frayn began writing plays and screenplays after ten years as a successful journalist. His commercial success derives from a deft sense of comic *character and construction, yet his philosophical training at university underpins all his work. *Alphabetical Order* (1975) farcically explores the relationship between order and chaos in the office of a provincial newspaper, while *Clouds* (1976) is set amongst journalists writing on Cuba after the revolution. On one level a comic *satire on the media, it also engages with the philosophical question of our relationship to sensory experience, how we organize and interpret the world around us. *Make and Break* (1980) and *Benefactors* (1984) are more socially engaged, critiquing the values of commerce and community. *Copenhagen* (1998) investigates a mysterious encounter between two great nuclear physicists, Niels Bohr and Werner Heisenberg, during the Second World War, finally uncovering what might be the most significant misunderstanding of the twentieth century. His most famous play, *Noises Off* (1982, revised 2000) is a meticulously constructed *metatheatrical *farce, which depicts a disastrous production of a crude sex farce, *Nothing On*, at its inept technical *rehearsal, then backstage on its first night, and finally on stage again late in its *tour, when the relationships and production have deteriorated beyond repair. Yet even here, the play addresses the relationship between chaos and order, using the metaphor of *acting to consider what happens to our sense of purpose and identity when the scripts of our lives fail us. Frayn is a fluent Russian speaker and his translations of *Chekhov's plays are widely acclaimed.

DR

FREAK SHOW

Public exhibition of the extraordinary body for pleasure and profit. Since the *medieval period, the 'othered' body has been displayed, particularly at *carnival occasions such as *London's Bartholomew Fair. Henry Morley's *Memoirs of Bartholomew Fair* (1859) reveals the freak show as part of the theatrical, anarchic, and bizarre *spectacle. Dwarfs and giants were present in the royal courts of Europe; *fools and jesters and 'innocents' were royal companions. The cheapest freak shows in seventeenth-century England were in street or *fairground booths and rooms in coffee houses. Advertised on handbills with 'true likenesses' to whet the appetite, conjoined twins and dog-headed men were *toured and exhibited throughout the seventeenth and eighteenth centuries. By the nineteenth century the freak show, informed by the medical respectability of teratology, often assumed a proto-scientific status. Showmen such as P. T. *Barnum exhibited their 'specimens' in 'museums', though at the same time parading them theatrically: General Tom Thumb (Charles Stratton) performed imitations of Napo-

leon Bonaparte, singing and reciting material specially devised for him by Barnum. Less fortunate was Joseph Merrick, the Elephant Man; exploited by unscrupulous showmen, he was rescued and again exhibited for the medical establishment by Sir Frederick Treves. On *film Tod Browning's *Freaks* (1932), the tale of the love of a *circus midget for a 'normal' trapeze artist and featuring actual sideshow performers, was banned in the United States until 1962, though it now enjoys academic cult status. As late as 1984, Otis the Frog Man, born with under-formed limbs, was earning his living in a sideshow in America.

AF

FRÉCHETTE, LOUIS-HONORÉ (1839–1908)

French-Canadian poet and playwright. His poetry displays more talent than his drama, although his *Félix Poutré* (1862) was the most popular play in Québec in its time, until the memoirs it is based upon were proven false and its titular hero shown to have been a paid spy for British colonial authorities. Other plays are problematic as well: *Le Retour de l'exilé* (*The Exile's Return*) plagiarized from a French novel, and *Véronica* written for him by another French author. Despite its lack of originality, Fréchette's drama brought new themes and modern techniques from France to Québec's nascent stage.

LED

FREIE BÜHNE (FREE STAGE)

German theatre society. The Freie Bühne belonged to the European movement of 'free theatre' societies that began with André *Antoine's *Théâtre Libre in *Paris, established to promote the progressive drama of *Ibsen and others by avoiding direct *censorship through performances that were technically private. Set up in 1889 by Otto *Brahm with a group of like-minded writers and actors, the Freie Bühne staged Ibsen's *Ghosts* in September 1889 and *Hauptmann's *Before Dawn* a month later. Other playwrights included *Tolstoy, the duo Arno Holz and Johannes Schaf, and *Anzengruber. The society's periodical *Die Freie Bühne für modernes Leben* became an influential literary journal. The Freie Bühne never had its own theatre but contributed significantly to establishing *naturalism in Germany. Its activities came to an end when Brahm took over the *Deutsches Theater in 1894.

CBB

FREJKA, JIŘÍ (1904–52)

Czech director, one of the three leading figures of the Czech inter-war *avant-garde. Fascinated by *commedia dell'arte, French *surrealism, and Russian *constructivism, he rejected *realism utterly and advocated lyricism in drama and spontaneity in *acting. He founded the Liberated Theatre with Jindřich Honzl, which opened in *Prague with an adaptation of *Molière's *Georges Dandin* in 1926. After a split with Honzl, Frejka founded the *Dada Theatre in 1927 and the Modern Studio in 1929. K. H. *Hilar invited him to establish a studio that year at the *Czech National Theatre, and Frejka's artistry developed in spectacular productions of Lope de *Vega's *Fuente Ovejuna* (1935) and *Julius Caesar* (1936), both designed by František *Tröster. Between 1945 and 1950 he was in charge of the Vinohrady Theatre, where his productions of Shakespeare were again the most memorable. Unable to comply with *socialist realism, he was dismissed and transferred to an *operetta theatre, and he soon ended his own life.   ML

FRENCH, DAVID (1939–)

Canadian playwright. CBC-TV produced his first play, *Beckons the Dark River* (1962) and French became associated with the *alternative theatre movement of the 1970s to promote and develop Canadian playwrights, especially at the *Tarragon Theatre, *Toronto. In Tarragon's Bill Glassco, French found the ideal director for *Leaving Home* (1972), and the subsequent plays, *Of the Fields, Lately* (1973), *Salt-Water Moon* (1984), and *1949* (1988), that form a tetralogy dealing with the complex problems of economic oppression and marginalized cultural values that afflict the Mercer family on their move from Newfoundland to Toronto. Other works directed by Glassco include *Jitters* (1979), a backstage *comedy which was French's greatest commercial success, *One Crack Out* (1975), a translation of *Chekhov's *The Seagull* (1977), *The Riddle of the World* (1981), and *Silver Dagger* (1993). French has received many major Canadian awards, and his works have been produced across North and South America, Europe, and Australia, in English and in translation.   PBON

FREYER, ACHIM (1934–)

German designer and director. Known principally for his work with *opera, Freyer trained and worked as a scene designer in East *Berlin before emigrating to the West in the early 1970s. He designed for Claus *Peymann in the 1970s (*Faust I and II*, 1978) before turning to directing in the 1980s. Important productions for the dramatic stage include an adaptation of Ovid's *Metamorphoses* (1987) and *Büchner's *Woyzeck* (1988) at the *Burgtheater. Like all his productions, these were characterized by strong colour, slow rhythm, *mask-like *make-up, and exaggerated *costumes, all intended to create *surreal, *dreamlike worlds.   CBB

FREYTAG, GUSTAV (1816–95)

German dramatist, novelist, and critic, remembered today chiefly for his influential treatise on dramatic writing *Technik des Dramas* (*The Technique of Drama*, 1863). It remained current well into the twentieth century and was translated into many languages. He constructed a five-part model of dramatic *action consisting of *exposition, build-up, climax, *peripeteia, and *catastrophe, which formalized rules for writing *well-made plays. His best-known play is the *comedy *The Journalists* (1854), an insightful exploration of the relationship between journalism and politics.   CBB

FRIEL, BRIAN (1929–)

Irish playwright and short-story writer. The son of a teacher from Omagh, County Tyrone, he himself taught until success with short stories allowed him to become a full-time writer. He first came to prominence as a playwright with *Philadelphia Here I Come!*, produced in *Dublin in 1964, and subsequently to enormous acclaim on Broadway where it became the longest-running Irish play on the *New York stage. The play used a relatively conventional small-town setting, but with the formal innovation of casting two actors for the central character of Gar O'Donnell, one his Public persona, the other his Private unvoiced self. The theatrical interplay between the two allowed for a lively *comedy invigorating the drabness of the village setting, and a poignant, lyrical meditation upon Gar's situation on the eve of emigration to America. Friel's characteristic preoccupation in succeeding works, *The Loves of Cass Maguire* (1966) and *Lovers* (1968), remained with the personal life of emotion and memory, often rendered theatrically with framing narrators. These concerns and stylistic preferences are notable also in his family plays *Living Quarters* (1977) and *Aristocrats* (1979), the latter heavily influenced by *Chekhov. One of his greatest plays, *Faith Healer* (1979), consists just of four remembering *monologues. However, events in Northern Ireland forced Friel into *political drama with the polemic *The Freedom of the City* (1973), a fictionalized version of the Derry shootings of Bloody Sunday (1972), concerned with the misrepresentations of the action's accidental victims.

Together with the actor Stephen Rea he founded the *Field Day Theatre Company in 1980 as a theatrical means of exploring issues of national identity behind the political crises in the North. Field Day opened in Derry with a triumphant production of Friel's play *Translations* that went on to tour in both parts of Ireland, and was received with equal acclaim in Dublin and *London. The setting of a hedge school at the time of the British Ordnance Survey mapping of Ireland, the convention by which the English *dialogue of the Irish-speaking *characters is supposed to be unintelligible to the English speakers, made of *Translations* an evocative theatrical expression of the colonial process. Although through the 1980s Friel devoted to Field Day much of his energy and several of his plays, including *The Communication Cord* (1982) and *Making History* (1988), it was at the *Abbey that Friel had his next major success with *Dancing at Lughnasa* (1990, directed by Patrick *Mason). Set, like virtually all his work, in the imagined small town of Ballybeg, it was based on Friel's own 1930s memories of his mother's Donegal family. The theatrical vitality of the five unmarried sisters' *dance in the play's first act, the resonance of dancing with its associations of Ireland's pre-Christian past, elements of period nostalgia, all contributed to the critical and popular acclaim won by the play in London and New York. If later plays, *Wonderful Tennessee* (1993), *Molly Sweeney* (1994), and *Give Me your Answer Do* (1997), have been less successful, Friel, with the lyricism of his dramatic style, remains Ireland's most eminent contemporary playwright.   NG

FRIGERIO, EZIO (1930–)

Italian designer. In 1955 Frigerio began a long and productive association with Giorgio *Strehler, serving as his designer for many plays at *Milan's *Piccolo Teatro over the next four decades, including *House of Bernarda Alba*, *Threepenny Opera*, *Mountain Giants*, *King Lear*, *Servant of Two Masters*, *de Filippo's *Grand Magic*, *Strindberg's *Storm Weather*, and *Mozart's *Così fan tutte*. He was Strehler's designer for *operas at La *Scala as well, including *Simon Boccanegra*, *Falstaff*, *Lohengrin*, *The Marriage of Figaro*, and *Don Giovanni*, and his designer at Théâtre de l'*Europe in *Paris for *Illusion comique*. Frigerio's international reputation took him all over Europe and to the United States for work in theatre, opera, *ballet, *television, and *film. His sets for Rudolf Nureyev's productions of Prokofiev's *Romeo and Juliet* and Tchaikovsky's *Sleeping Beauty* were typical: monumental in scale, with stable architectural elements that enabled different levels and planes of action, and movable pieces such as baroque columns (his signature), gates, *curtains, painted backdrops, and chandeliers, which together created an atmosphere of magical beauty. Frigerio was nominated for an Academy award for his production design of *Cyrano de Bergerac* (1990).   JEH

FRIML, RUDOLF (1879–1972)

American composer. A Czech-born piano prodigy who studied with Antonín Dvořák, he emigrated to America, performing his own compositions in concert halls by 1906. Hired by Arthur Hammerstein in 1912 to write the score for a new *operetta, he composed *The Firefly*, his entrée to musical theatre. Hammerstein made him a staff composer, asking him to write overblown *musical comedies completely inappropriate to his training. He toiled in relative anonymity until 1924, when his score for *Rose Marie* (abetted by Herbert Stothart) was a huge success. It was followed by several more full-throated, romantic operettas, including *The Vagabond King* (1925) and *The Three Musketeers* (1928). Unable to adapt his style, Friml's success did not outlive the age of 1920s operetta.   JD

FRINGE THEATRE

The origin of the term is customarily placed at the *Edinburgh Festival in the 1950s, when a number of smaller temporary companies performed on the 'fringes' of the official events. It was well enough established by 1960 for the Cambridge Footlights group to appear there with a satirical *revue called *Beyond the Fringe*, which then transferred to *London. Often coupled with the *Off-Off-Broadway theatre of *New York and the 'free theatre' of Europe, 'fringe theatre' has usually been used promiscuously to refer to the proliferating ranks of experimental, underground, *alternative, and independent theatre companies which flourished in the liberating wake of the 1960s. In this sense it has tended to carry an implicit negative charge, as fringes are fripperies, though many theatre critics and historians also acknowledge that the fringe creatively feeds the mainstream. It would be foolish to try to pin down such a slippery history completely, but it may be helpful to use it mainly with reference to theatre and performance that is most clearly linked to mainstream sectors of the cultural industries, such as commercial theatre, *national or state theatres, major *regional theatre systems, and so on.

In Britain, the expatriate American bookseller Jim Haynes is usually credited with creating the first fringe theatre proper, when he opened the *Traverse Theatre Club in *Edinburgh in 1963. As well as hosting key groups from abroad, such as New York's *La Mama troupe and *Grotowski's 13 Rows from Opole, the Traverse gave Tom *Stoppard and C. P. *Taylor their start. In *London, early fringe ventures made links back to the between-wars Little Theatre movement through their venues: at the Jeannette Cochrane Theatre in 1966, Haynes and another American, Charles *Marowitz, set up the London Traverse, while Ed Berman and Naftali Yavin used the Mercury Theatre for community-oriented events. In 1968 Marowitz went on to found a new fringe venue in a converted basement in Tottenham Court Road: the Open Space opened with John Herbert's *Fortune and Men's Eyes*, which transferred to the West End. In the same year the Theatre Upstairs opened at the *Royal Court Theatre, and the ICA (Institute of Contemporary Arts) moved to its current premises in the Mall. Even at this early stage some fringe venues were not in opposition to the mainstream, in the ways that, say, Peter Oliver's Oval House (1967) and Jim Haynes's Arts Laboratory (1968) were. But there were probably few, if any, fringe *groups* which had ambitions to work in mainstream theatres at this time—or if they had they dared not admit it.

The phenomenal growth of fringe and alternative theatre in Britain in the 1970s, plus the advent of monetarist culture in the 1980s, ensured interactions with the mainstream that grew inevitably more complex. Many new fringe venues were opened in the major cities, some in unlikely places, others as part of mainstream institutions. In London, for example, a synagogue was converted to create the Half-Moon Theatre (East End, 1972), while the *King's Head (Islington, 1970), the *Bush Theatre (Shepherds Bush, 1972), and the Orange Tree (Richmond, 1972) were all in pubs, and in 1977 the *Royal Shakespeare Company opened the Warehouse (see DONMAR WAREHOUSE) in Covent Garden while the Cottesloe opened as the fringe in the *National Theatre itself. As the 1970s progressed some fringe playwrights—David *Edgar, Howard *Brenton, David *Hare—shifted into mainstream theatres to gain a voice for opposition on larger stages, but it was not until near the end of the decade that a number of fringe productions used fringe venues as stepping stones to more established theatres.

A watershed was passed with the transfer in 1979 of Belt and Braces' production of Dario *Fo's *Accidental Death of an Anarchist* to the West End, closely followed by Pam *Gems's *Piaf* from the Warehouse. In the 1980s growing numbers of fringe companies part-mirrored the mainstream, with programming devoted to new plays, *musicals, or the classics. Notable among the last were Deborah *Warner's Kick Theatre (1980) and Declan *Donellan's *Cheek by Jowl (1981). In the 1990s especially successful fringe groups—such as Theatre de *Complicité and *Tara Arts—and fringe directors—including Donellan and Warner—were invited to stage work at the National Theatre. But these were just the tip of an iceberg of accommodations between the fringe and mainstream theatres. What had started out as a movement of resistance had become mainly a conduit for filtering the best talent into the most privileged parts of theatre as a cultural industry.   BRK

CRAIG, SANDY (ed.), *Dreams and Deconstructions: alternative theatre in Britain* (Ambergate, 1980)

SHANK, THEODORE (ed.), *Contemporary British Theatre* (London, 1996)

FRISCH, MAX (1911–91)

Swiss novelist and dramatist. Frisch studied and worked as an architect before becoming a full-time writer in 1954. His work owes much to Thornton *Wilder and *Brecht, both of whom were staged in Zurich where Frisch lived. His first play, *Now They Are Singing Again* (1945), grapples with the problems of guilt and war. *Don Juan; or, The Love of Geometry* (1953) revisits the mythical hero as a study of constructed identity; the great lover is forced to assume the masks and behaviour that society projects onto him, although he wants nothing more than to study geometry. His internationally best-known works are the parables *Biedermann und die Brandstifter* (*The Fire Raisers*, 1958) and *Andorra* (1961). In the former, a respectable bourgeois manufacturer called Biedermann takes in a trio of doubtful *characters despite his anxiety about a series of suspicious fires in the neighbourhood. Although the arsonists blatantly prepare their materials, Biedermann remains oblivious to the danger, despite warnings from a Greek *chorus of firemen. This *absurdist 'cautionary tale' gave rise to a plethora of *political readings with the arsonists being seen on both sides of the Cold War divide. Explicitly ethical is the situation analysed in *Andorra*, where the inhabitants of a small town ostracize an inhabitant whom they consider to be Jewish. Although received as a study in anti-Semitism against the background of post-Holocaust Europe, the play is a much more generalized study of prejudice and xenophobia.   CBB

FROHMAN, CHARLES (1860–1915)

American *manager. After a series of show business jobs, Frohman and his brothers Daniel and Gustave took over Steele *MacKaye's *Madison Square Theatre in 1877. They devised a production system that changed American theatre, sending out full *touring companies with versions of successful *New York shows. In 1883 Frohman's own producing career started with *The Stranglers of Paris*, but fame only came with his production of Bronson *Howard's *Shenandoah* (1889). After taking over Proctor's Theatre and running his own *stock company there in 1890, Frohman built the Empire Theatre in 1893. By the century's turn he had co-founded the *Theatrical Syndicate (1896) and was the leading *producer in New York and in *London, introducing plays by *Barrie, *Pinero, *Wilde, and *Maugham. Frohman's ruthless reputation belies the fact that he died penniless and that stars such as Margaret *Anglin, Julia *Marlowe, Otis *Skinner, Billie Burke, John *Drew, and Ethel *Barrymore were fiercely loyal to him throughout their careers. Maude *Adams was the emblematic Frohman performer: he had Barrie adapt *Peter Pan* as a vehicle for her. Frohman successfully manipulated his theatrical system for over two decades, creating stars who created *audiences for the works of his own playwrights, and ultimately produced over 500 plays. He went down on the *Lusitania*.   TFC

FROHMAN, DANIEL (1851–1940)

American *producer and *manager. Born in Ohio, Daniel—like his younger brothers Gustave and Charles *Frohman—made his mark in theatre management. After jobs at several *New York newspapers starting in 1864, Frohman spent four years (1874–8) as agent for the all-black Callender's Georgia *Minstrels. In 1879 he joined the management of the *Madison Square Theatre in New York, moving in 1885 to the *Lyceum Theatre. He developed a *stock company that contained such future stars as Henry *Miller, Maude *Adams, E. H. *Sothern, and Annie *Russell. He presented plays by such important British writers as *Wilde, *Barrie, *Jones, and *Pinero. He also produced Hollywood *films (1912–18). From 1903 to 1940 he served as president of the Actors' Fund of America. His autobiographical works are *Memories of a Manager* (1911), *Daniel Frohman Presents* (1935), and *Encore* (1937).   CT

FRONTIER THEATRE

Theatrical productions on and about the American frontier, where the encroaching European culture confronted native populations and natural elements. When Europeans settled the American colonies in the late seventeenth century, the towns along the seacoast were themselves the frontier, and survival the primary concern. Theatre appeared first in the south, which enjoyed warmer climate and fewer *religious restrictions. A theatre opened in Williamsburg in 1718, and the Dock Street Theatre in Charleston began operations in 1736. Early companies such as those of Walter Murray and Thomas Kean beginning in 1749, and the *Hallams from 1752, brought theatre to seaboard cities.

As settlement moved west to the Allegheny Mountains and beyond, theatre followed: along the Ohio and Mississippi rivers as, beginning in Pittsburgh in 1815, Samuel *Drake and his company played emerging river towns in Ohio and Kentucky. Noah *Ludlow, a member of Drake's original contingent, established his own company (1817), brought theatre to Nashville and St Louis, and laid claim to the first English-speaking company to play in New Orleans. Also important to the growth of theatre along the rivers was Sol *Smith, who started his own company in 1823 and, in partnership with Ludlow from 1835, controlled theatre on the Mississippi for nearly twenty years. Both Ludlow and Smith wrote important accounts of early frontier theatre. The most prominent theatre *manager on the lower Mississippi was James H. *Caldwell, who opened the Camp Street Theatre in New Orleans in 1824, complete with the first gas *lighting in America. Over the next decade Caldwell expanded his operation upriver to Nashville, St Louis, and Cincinnati. In 1833 in New Orleans he inaugurated the *St Charles Theatre, one of the finest in the country, but financial setbacks in the late 1830s ruined his theatrical empire. In contrast to New Orleans, the first theatre building in *Chicago was not opened until 1847.

One American institution that plied the rivers in the nineteenth century was the *showboat. Although Ludlow had occasionally presented plays on his keelboat, William Chapman and his family of performers launched their Floating Theatre in Pittsburgh in 1831 and became regulars on the rivers until 1847. Other showboats, such as the Spalding and Rogers Floating Circus Palace (1851), which could seat over 3,000 patrons, soon followed. The Civil War interrupted river traffic, but showboats resumed their trade after the war and continued into the twentieth century.

After gold was discovered in California in 1849, miners rushed to the Pacific coast and again theatre followed the settlements. The Spanish in California had sanctioned some religious drama, but in 1849 the first professional English-speaking company performed in the only theatre in California, the Eagle Theatre in Sacramento. Within two years, *San Francisco had three theatres. The leading theatrical entrepreneur in San Francisco was Thomas Maguire, who managed a circuit of theatres in California and Nevada (1850–84). Brigham Young, who led the Mormons to Salt Lake City, had a keen interest in theatre and in 1861 erected the lavish Salt Lake Theatre, which supported a permanent company and served as an oasis for travelling *stock companies on the long trek to the west coast.

In the second half of the nineteenth century theatre filled in the areas between the Mississippi River and the west coast, especially after the transcontinental railway was established in 1869. Most of the important performers played seasons in California and the west coast became a breeding ground for theatrical talent. Lotta *Crabtree developed her singing and dancing skills in mining camp performances. David *Belasco, a San Francisco native, cut his teeth as a writer and manager in California before moving to *New York. Although born in *Boston, Frank *Mayo learned his acting craft in San Francisco before achieving star status playing the backwoods hero Davy Crockett.

The frontier also provided uniquely American material for numerous plays that entertained eastern audiences. *Metamora* (1829) by John Augustus *Stone provided Edwin *Forrest with the opportunity to play a noble Wampanoag chief. Joaquin Miller's *The Danites* (1877) featured tales of Mormon revenge. Buffalo Bill *Cody starred in a series of action-filled *melodramas between 1872 and 1884. By the turn of the century, with Augustus *Thomas's *Arizona* (1899), drama about the fast-vanishing frontier became common in New York theatre, culminating in such plays as Edwin Milton Royle's *The Squaw Man* (1905), David Belasco's *The Girl of the Golden West* (1905), and William Vaughn *Moody's *The Great Divide* (1906).

RAH

BERSON, MISHA, *The San Francisco Stage* (San Francisco, 1989)
LUDLOW, NOAH, *Dramatic Life as I Found It* (St Louis, 1880)

FRY, CHRISTOPHER (1907–   )

English playwright, the most commercially successful writer in the revival of poetic drama in the mid-twentieth century. Unlike T. S. *Eliot, Fry pushed poetic language to the foreground, delighting in spiralling metaphors and verbal abundance. *The Lady's Not for Burning* (1948) is a romantic medieval *burlesque, set amongst witch-burners and satirically drawn petty officials. The lightness of his tone and the freedom of the *verse proved an attractive antidote to the austerities of post-war *London, and the darker themes of the play—which prefigure the themes of the *absurdists—are offset by a final affirmation of life and love. The poetic drama revival began in the 1930s, largely through the efforts of Canon George Bell at the Canterbury Festival, but Fry's non-doctrinaire Christianity was always worn lightly, even in the more overtly religious pieces like *The Boy with a Cart* (1938) and the pacifist *A Sleep of Prisoners* (1951). *The Dark Is Light Enough* formed the 'winter' corner of a seasonal tetralogy and showed a welcome gravity and probing ethical sense. The theatrical revolution at the *Royal Court in 1956 held no place for Fry, and apart from the sober *Curtmantle* (1961) and *A Yard of Sun* (1970) his theatrical writing appeared to slow down. His linguistic exuberance has never entirely come back into fashion, but revivals of *Venus Observed* (1950), and of his adaptation of *Anouilh's *L'Invitation au château* called *Ring round the Moon* (1950), have proved the continuing theatrical strengths of his work. DR

FUCHS, GEORG (1868–1949)

German journalist, dramatist, and theatre reformer. The product of a strictly pious upbringing, Fuchs found his spiritual father in Nietzsche while a student in Darmstadt. His move to *Munich in 1894 brought him into contact with the *symbolist circle of Stefan George and the burgeoning art nouveau movement. His radically aesthetic understanding of theatre was nurtured in these years. It found its first practical manifestation in the festival play *Das Zeichen* (*The Sign*, 1900), a homage to Nietzsche, staged for the artists' colony in Darmstadt. He first summarized his ideas on theatre reform in *Die Schaubühne der Zukunft* (*The Stage of the Future*, 1904). Fuchs dreamed of a theatre free of commercial considerations in which the theatrical experience could be closer to *ritual and able to invoke a mystical union of spectators and performers. He radically redefined the art in terms of its inherent theatricality. In Fuchs's *theory the performer would assume centre stage, together with generalized concepts such as rhythm, light, and space. A cornerstone of the theory is the 'relief stage'. Anti-*realistic in conception, the relief stage, with stylized backdrops, was intended to frame the performer like a bas-relief. The theory was given architectural form in the *Munich Art Theatre (1908), for which Fuchs worked until its closure in 1914. After this his ideas became increasingly nationalistic: during the First World War he promulgated the notion of national theatre *festivals with *Passion plays as propaganda. His own contribution, *Christus* (1919), marked the end of his theatrical activity. CBB

FUDDA, ASAAD (1938–)

Syrian director and actor. After study at Cairo University, he became *artistic director of the National Theatre in Damascus, then director general of theatre and music in Syria. He directed over 23 productions, including Dostoevsky's *Brothers Karamazov*, *Molière's *Don Juan*, *Pirandello's *It's So (If You Think So)*, *García Lorca's *Blood Wedding*, Evgenyi Schwartz's *The Dragon* and *The Naked King*, and *Mrożek's *Tango*. He collaborated with several Syrian and Arab playwrights, especially Sadallah *Wannous, for whom he directed three plays, including a revival of *Mughamaret Raes'l-Mamlouk Jaber* (*The Adven-*

ture of Slave Jaber's Head) in Weimar. A renowned actor, he has performed in *Death of a Salesman*, *St Joan*, *Oedipus the King*, *The Visit*, *The Optimistic Tragedy*, and *Diary of a Madman*. He also starred in 38 *television serials and seven feature *films, and is currently president of the Syrian Syndicate of Artists. RI

FUGARD, ATHOL (1932–)

South African playwright, actor, and director, born in the Eastern Cape. His father was a handicapped immigrant of Irish Catholic descent and his mother was from a prominent Calvinist Afrikaner pioneer family. Fugard first encountered *amateur dramatics in Port Elizabeth in 1935, and on a scholarship to the University of Cape Town he developed a fascination with *Camus, T. H. Huxley, and Darwin. Two months before his final examinations he hitch-hiked up Africa, signed on as a deckhand on a British steamer in Sudan, and began writing on board. He returned to Port Elizabeth within the year and freelanced for the *Evening Post*. Fugard became involved in theatre through actress Sheila Meiring, whom he married in 1956, and they formed the Circle Players at the Labia in Cape Town. In 1958, while working as a clerk in a Native Commissioner's Court in *Johannesburg, where pass offenders were tried, he made his first contacts in the black townships. The Fugards started the African Theatre Workshop in Sophiatown (1958–9), where they created *No-Good Friday* (Bantu Men's Social Club, Johannesburg, 1958) and *Nongogo* (1959). *The Blood Knot* (1961) established Fugard as a playwright, and using his moderate fame he initiated an international writers' boycott of South Africa in 1963 to protest segregation legislation. From 1963 he worked with the Serpent Players, directing local adaptations of established plays, creating new work like *The Coat* (1967), and collaborating on plays that he, Winston *Ntshona, and John *Kani would later take to the Space. His Port Elizabeth plays include *Hello and Goodbye* (1965), *People Are Living There* (*Glasgow, 1968), and *Orestes* (1971).

The day after a performance of *The Blood Knot* on British *television in 1967 his passport was withdrawn 'for reasons of state safety and security'; it was not returned until 1971. In 1972 he opened the Space/Die Ruimte/Indawo, a theatre in a converted warehouse near the Cape Malay quarter, with Brian Astbury, Yvonne *Bryceland's husband. There they premièred the plays he, Ntshona, and Kani had workshopped: *Statements after an Arrest under the Immorality Act* (1972), *Sizwe Bansi Is Dead* (1972), and *The Island* (originally entitled *Die Hodoshe Span*, 1973). After the Black Consciousness movement made collaboration with black artists even more difficult, Fugard shifted to internal themes in *A Lesson from Aloes* (*Market Theatre, 1978), and *Dimetos* (*Edinburgh Festival, 1975). In 1982 he returned to engaged work with *Master Harold and the Boys* (Yale Repertory Theatre, 1982; Market, 1983). Later plays,

Athol **Fugard**'s *Boesman and Lena*, Theatre Upstairs, Royal Court Theatre, London, 1971, directed by the author. Pictured here as Lena is the South African actress Yvonne Bryceland, who played the role in the original production in Cape Town in 1969.

which have been widely performed internationally, include *Road to Mecca* (Yale and Market, 1984), *A Place with the Pigs* (Yale, Market, *Grahamstown Festival, 1987), *My Children! My Africa!* (Market, 1989), *Playland* (Market, 1992), *My Life* (1994), *Valley Song* (*Royal Court Theatre, *London, 1996), *Cousins* (an autobiographical memoir, 1994), *The Captain's Tiger* (1997), and *Sorrows and Rejoicings* (2001). Fugard often directs his own work. YH

FUKUDA TSUNEARI (1912–94)

Japanese dramatist, translator, and literary critic. Shortly after the Second World War Fukuda became established as a dramatist through such plays as *Kitty Typhoon* (1950), *The Man Who Stroked a Dragon* (1957), and other *satires of post-war intellectual life. In 1954 he and other prominent playwrights of the period, such as *Kinoshita Junji and *Mishima Yukio, joined the staff of the influential new magazine *Shingeki* (*New Theatre*), through which Fukuda's reviews and commentaries were widely disseminated. He long remained a leader in several prominent theatre companies which were devoted to artistic rather than political ends. Some of Fukuda's plays have been successfully produced in English translation in the United States, notably at the Milwaukee Repertory Theatre. Fukuda held a lifelong interest in English literature and translated the entire dramatic works of Shakespeare into Japanese. His translations have often been performed, replacing those created in the late nineteenth and early twentieth centuries by *Tsubouchi Shōyō. JTR

FULDA, LUDWIG (LUDWIG SALOMON) (1862–1939)

German playwright. A co-founder of the *Freie Bühne, Fulda belonged to the *naturalistic movement in *Berlin, but his socially committed plays were far less successful than his *comedies. Best known are *Der Talisman* (*The Talisman*, 1893) an anti-monarchist *satire in the form of a fairy tale, and *Die Seeräuber* (*The Pirate*, 1912), which was later *filmed with Gene Kelly and Judy Garland and music by Cole *Porter (1948). Several others were filmed in Germany. Fulda was a

highly respected literary figure who was driven to suicide by the Nazis.
CBB

FULLER, CHARLES (1939–)

*African-American playwright. *The Perfect Party* (1969) was Fuller's first play to attract critical attention, followed by *Off-Broadway productions of *In the Deepest Part of Sleep* (1974), *The Brownsville Raid* (1976), about black soldiers in a Texas town early in the twentieth century, and *Zooman and the Sign* (1980), about the accidental shooting of a young girl in a black neighbourhood. His most important work, *A Soldier's Story*, concerns the murder of a hated black sergeant in Louisiana in 1944, was performed by the *Negro Ensemble Company in 1981, and became the second play by an African American to win the Pulitzer Prize; it was adapted into a *film three years later. In the 1980s Fuller wrote *Sally*, which premièred at the National Black Arts Festival, *Prince under the Umbrella*, and *We. Jonquil* was produced in 1990, and a short play about Vietnam, *The Badge*, was seen on cable *television in 1998.
BBL

FULLER, LOÏE (1862–1928)

American actress, *dancer, and choreographer. In 1891, while performing a small role in a *burlesque-circuit *melodrama, Mary Louise Fuller created the Serpentine Dance by manipulating her silk skirt in and out of the gas stage *lighting. Encouraged by *audiences and reviewers, Fuller continued to experiment with the expressive possibilities of her own moving body by wearing layers of draperies, using wands to extend her limbs, and inventing coloured slides and gels to enlarge the lighting palette. In *Paris her appearances at the *Folies-Bergères caught the attention of *symbolist poet and theorist Stephane Mallarmé, who called her 'La Loïe' and famously described her dancing as 'the dizzyness of soul made visible by an artifice'. Fuller remained based in Europe for the rest of her career, where she patented her lighting and *costume innovations and in 1908 founded her own school.
LTC

FUNAMBULES, THÉÂTRE DES

Built as a showplace for *acrobats and tightrope dancers on the famed boulevard du Temple in *Paris in 1813, it was taken over three years later by Michel Bertrand for the production of situational *farces and harlequinades. Its well-appointed stage allowed for rapid set changes, ideal for popular *spectacles and fairy extravaganzas such as *L'Œuf rouge et l'œuf blanc* (*The Red Egg and the White Egg*). The then unknown Frédérick *Lemaître played there, and in the 1820s and 1830s the theatre attracted enormous crowds with Jean-Gaspard *Deburau's performances in *pierrots by Champfleury and *pantomimes by Charles Nodier. After the Revolution of 1830, Bertrand added *vaude-

villes to his repertoire. His nephew Charles Louis Billion took over the direction of the theatre some years later, adding nearly 300 seats to the house. It was demolished in 1862, along with the rest of the boulevard, during Haussmann's urban reconstructions.
CHB

FUNDADORES, TEATRO DE LOS

*Playhouse built in Manizalez, Colombia, in 1965, reputedly the best-equipped theatre in *Latin America at the time, with a *revolving stage and a seating capacity of 1,257. It became the home of the Latin American University Theatre Festival (1968–73), and from 1984, with the event renamed the Manizalez International Theatre Festival, Teatrode los Fundadores continued to be its annual focal point.
BJR

FURA DELS BAUS, LA

Catalan theatre company founded in 1979. Although emerging from the same *street theatre tradition as Els *Comediants and Els *Joglars, La Fura embraced the language of urbanism in their fiercely paced, aggressive interdisciplinary *spectacles which reinvented the language of performance for the postmodern era. Working in abandoned or alternative urban spaces like morgues or abandoned warehouses, their visual and visceral productions like *Accions* (*Actions*, 1983) and *Suz/o/Suz* (1985) merged the languages of *acrobatics, rock, painting, and *dance to create fast and furious stagings which denied narrative cohesion in favour of episodic treatments of space that ruptured *audience/actor boundaries (*see* ENVIRONMENTAL THEATRE). Organizing the opening ceremony of the *Barcelona Olympic Games in 1992, the company secured a wider audience. More recently they have made excursions into *opera with *El martiri de Sant Sebastià* (*The Martyrdom of St Sebastian*, 1997) and *DQ* (2000), a collaboration with architect Enric Miralles which reinvisaged the myth of Don Quixote for Barcelona's refurbished Liceu opera house.
MMD

FURTTENBACH, JOSEPH (1591–1667)

German architect. After travelling in Italy for ten years (c.1610–20), where he studied architecture and scene design with Guilio *Parigi, Furttenbach took up his career in Ulm where, as city architect, he designed numerous structures, including a theatre, and wrote several architectural treatises. In *Civil Architecture* (1628), *Recreational Architecture* (1640), and *The Noble Mirror of Art* (1663), he provided the most extensive accounts we have of *early modern stage machinery and scenic practices. Although some of the practices he describes (such as the use of *periaktoi) were out of date by mid-century, his ideas on *lighting were in advance of Italian practice.
RWV

FUTURISM

Italian art movement founded in 1909 by F. T. *Marinetti, originally with a literary orientation but soon expanding into other disciplines. Marinetti was a man with considerable stage experience and employed performance to disseminate his artistic and political creeds. Futurism's entry into the theatre began with a series of controversial *serate* (evenings dedicated to the reading of manifestos, declamations of poetry, and presentations of paintings and musical compositions), followed in 1913 by a *tour by a professional Italian company that included several plays by futurist authors. In 1914 a second troupe toured a repertoire of exclusively *avant-garde and futurist plays. The central problem of the early futurist theatre was that none of the actors belonged to the movement and they did not find an adequate scenic language for the work. Marinetti and his colleagues soon realized that they would be unable to renew Italian theatre simply by writing innovative plays. They formulated their concepts of a new dramatic and theatrical style in a number of tracts: *Manifesto of Futurist Playwrights* (1911), *Variety Theatre Manifesto* (1913), *Manifesto of Futurist Synthetic Theatre* (1915), *Dynamic and Synoptic Declamation* (1916), and *Futurist Dance* (1917). Amongst the writers in the movement there was a tendency to seek inspiration from the popular traditions of theatre (*music hall, *circus), which led to several collaborations with stars of the *variety stage.

A different approach was taken by artists in *Rome (Giacomo Balla, Fortunato *Depero, Enrico *Prampolini), who proposed a mechanization of the stage, principally making use of three models: the *marionette, robot, and automaton; *costumes that imitated machines; and a mechanized body language aided by appropriate costume. Some of their ideas came to be realized in collaboration with the *Ballets Russes and the marionette company Teatro dei Piccoli. A third line of development was explored in the *pomeriggi futuristi*, semi-public performances presented in the permanent futurist gallery of Giuseppe Sprovieri in Rome.

Marinetti, Emilio Settimelli, and Bruno Corra confronted the problems of a futurist *acting style on both theoretical and practical levels, but their proposals were not realized until the 1920s when the Futurist Mechanical Theatre produced a number of shows in which the performer was little more than the motivator of a machine-like costume. Prampolini again pursued a different route, in which the *dancer's body imitated the kinetic properties of a machine. These experiments led to the futurist pantomimes, first presented in *Paris in 1927, and the 'aerodances' of the 1930s. In the course of the 1920s futurism entered mainstream theatre and made an impact on both stage design (*see* SCENOGRAPHY) and dramatic writing in Italy and abroad. In the 1920s Marinetti and company were no longer interested in the scandals, shock effects, and avant-garde gestures that had characterized the early performances. But the futurists had cleared the ground for other artists who were now becoming their competitors, among them *Chiarelli, *Betti, and *Pirandello, a clear sign that futurism had a profound effect on the Italian cultural scene. At the same time it introduced ideas from the international avant-garde (*expressionism, *surrealism, *constructivism) into the otherwise stale theatre of fascist Italy (*see* FASCISM AND THEATRE).　　GB

·G·

GABRIELLI FAMILY

Italian actors in the sixteenth and seventeenth centuries. **Giovanni** (d. between 1603 and 1611) played the servant's role of Sivello, and was renowned for his controlled non-scurrilous tone and his ability with *mime and bodily gesture. His son **Francesco** (1588–1636) played the liveried servant Scapino, which was later used as Scapin by *Molière. He was acclaimed by Niccolò Barbieri as 'the best *Zanni of his times', and was an accomplished singer and musician. Francesco's daughter **Giulia** played an Innamorata role as Diana. There is debate about whether later performers with the Gabrielli surname belong to the same family.   RAA

GAIETY THEATRE (*DUBLIN)

Designed by C. J. Phipps, the Gaiety Theatre was opened in 1871 by John and Michael Gunn. Located just off fashionable St Stephen's Green, it was built as a *touring house, targeting the upper end of the market, although in 1900 and 1901 it hosted early productions by the *Irish Literary Theatre (later the *Abbey Theatre company). Its tiered, 1,124-seat *auditorium (divided into private *boxes, dress circle, stalls, and gallery) facilitated the transition to *variety and musical recitals in the 1920s. However, by 1940 the Gaiety was once again offering theatre and *opera, and was used by the *Gate Theatre company of Micheál *MacLíammóir and Hilton *Edwards from 1940 until 1968; it was in the Gaiety that they premièred Brian *Friel's *Philadelphia Here I Come!* (1963). The Gaiety's annual Christmas *pantomime is a fixture of the Dublin theatre scene, produced every year since 1871.   ChM

GAIETY THEATRE (*LONDON)

A theatre dedicated to light entertainment on the Strand. Opened in 1869 by an ex-journalist, John *Hollingshead, it presented a repertory consisting mainly of *burlesques, which were energized by the famous singing/dancing quartet of Nellie *Farren, Kate *Vaughan, Edward Terry, and E. W. Royce. In 1886 Hollingshead sold his interest in the theatre to his partner George *Edwardes, who maintained the burlesque repertory for several years and then replaced it—thus snuffing out Hollingshead's treasured 'sacred lamp of burlesque'—with a new kind of popular entertainment, *musical comedy. The first was *In Town* (1894), followed by *The Shop Girl* (1894) and *The Circus Girl* (1896). These musicals possessed a notable performance feature, the carefully selected and beautiful Gaiety Girls who comprised the female *chorus. The Gaiety disappeared in a road-widening scheme in 1903, and Edwardes built another one in the new Aldwych development. Distinguishing the later Gaiety musical comedy were the *dancer and singer Gertie Millar and the comedian Leslie Henson, by the 1930s the last Gaiety star. Edwardes died in 1915; the last performances were given in 1939, and the theatre was finally demolished in 1957.   MRB

GAIETY THEATRE (*MANCHESTER)

English *playhouse, built in 1884 by Alfred Darbyshire, remodelled by Frank Matcham in 1908 to a capacity of 1,350, and demolished in 1959. It flourished under Annie *Horniman's *management from 1908 until 1917, as the first and perhaps the most successful English *regional repertory theatre. Ben Iden *Payne, the first *artistic director, established a careful ensemble with Lewis *Casson, Sybil *Thorndike, and some local actors, including Charles Bibby and Basil *Dean; Casson became artistic director from 1911 to 1913. The theatre's repertoire included William *Poel's *Measure for Measure* (1908) and *costume plays at Christmas, but is best known for serious local plays, including Stanley *Houghton's *Hindle Wakes* (1912) and Harold *Brighouse's *Hobson's Choice* (1916), both still regularly revived. Other plays by Allan *Monkhouse (*Mary Broome*, 1911), Elizabeth *Baker (*Chains*, 1911), and St John *Ervine (*Jane Clegg*, 1913), all with strong women's parts, are worth reviving.   EEC

GAÎTÉ, THÉÂTRE DE LA

The oldest *playhouse on the boulevard du Temple in *Paris, the Gaîté began life in 1759 as the Théâtre de Nicolet, the home of *fairground actor-entrepreneur Jean-Baptiste Nicolet's troupe of *acrobats, rope dancers, and pantomime artists. Rechristened the Théâtre des Grands Danseurs du Roi in 1772, it finally became the Gaîté in 1791. In 1807 Napoleon decreed that it confine its repertoire to 'spectacular *melodramas, *pantomines without *ballets, harlequinades and *farces'. In 1808 the theatre was rebuilt by Antoine-Marie Peyre, with a capacity of over 1,800. Between 1825 and 1835 it was managed by *Pixérécourt and staged many of his plays. Rebuilt after a *fire in 1835, it became celebrated in the mid-century when Frédérick *Lemaître performed there. The Gaîté was finally demolished in 1862, a consequence of Baron Haussmann's urban redevelopment.   JG

GALA, ANTONIO (1936–   )

Spanish poet, novelist, and playwright. A popular author, Gala has had a love–hate relationship with the theatre. Berated by many critics for their sentimentalism and, in the Francoist period, persecuted by the *censors, Gala's plays have nonetheless drawn large *audiences which, in general, have responded favourably to their blend of social critique and emotional and lyrical intensity. His first success was *Los verdes campos del Edén* (*The Green Fields of Eden*), often associated with the 'poetic' wing of the new Spanish *realism, which earned its author the Premio Nacional Calderón de la Barca in 1963. The popularity of the play was matched a few years later by that of *El sol en el hormiguero* (*Sunshine in the Ant's Nest*), a variation on the theme of the great theatre of the world, and *Noviembre y un poco de hierba* (*November and a Bit of Grass*), a daring indictment of the Spanish Civil War. After winning the Premio Nacional de Teatro in 1972 for *Los buenos días perdidos* (*The Good Days Are Gone*), which ran for over 1,000 performances, Gala retired briefly from the stage only to return in 1979 with *Petra Regalada* and, six years later, *Samarkanda*, a semi-autobiographical piece which deals with the theme of repressed homosexuality.   KG

GALICH (GINZBURG), ALEKSANDR (1919–77)

Soviet/Russian writer and bard. Galich *trained as an actor, but emerged as a playwright after the war. In 1957 Oleg *Efremov intended to open the *Sovremennik Theatre in *Moscow with Galich's *Matrosskaya tishina* (*Seamen's Silence*), but the production was banned for its treatment of Jews: their contribution in fighting fascism during the war was deemed unsuitable for the stage. The final *rehearsal is recounted by Galich in his autobiographical sketch 'The Dress Rehearsal'. He wrote numerous poems and sang them to the guitar. He emigrated in 1974, and died in Paris in an electrical accident.   BB

GALICH, MANUEL (1913–84)

Guatemalan playwright from a theatrical *family. Galich began his career writing *costumbrismos (*costume dramas) with a political edge. His *Papa-Natas* (*The Gullible*, 1938) is often called the beginning of modern Guatemalan theatre. He was instrumental in the overthrow of the Jorge Ubico regime in 1944 and subsequently served as Minister of Education, Minister of Foreign Affairs, and ambassador to Argentina. Several of his plays, including *El tren amarillo* (*The Yellow Train*, 1957), deal with the economic imperialism of the United States. He supported the Castro revolution and helped establish the model for new political theatre in Cuba, where he lived for many years.
                                                                    EJW

GALIN (PURER), ALEKSANDR (1946–   )

Soviet/Russian playwright. Galin emerged as a popular playwright during glasnost and perestroika, when his plays were staged by the leading theatres and *avant-garde directors in *Moscow: *The Eastern Tribune* (directed by Leonid Kheifets, *Sovremennik Theatre, 1983); *The Roof* (Tabakov Studio Theatre, 1986); *The Wall* (directed by Roman *Viktyuk, Sovremennik Theatre, 1987), *The Toastmaster* (directed by Kama *Ginkas, *Moscow Art Theatre, 1986). His play *Stars in the Morning Sky* (1982, published and staged 1988) was directed by Lev *Dodin at the *Maly Drama Theatre in Leningrad (*St Petersburg) and became a landmark of new writing. Galin tackled head-on the façades created by the Soviet system to present the country in a favourable light, using the case of the evacuation of prostitutes from the city centre during the Olympic Games (1980). He has directed several of his own plays, including *A Czech Photograph* at the Lenin Komsomol Theatre (Moscow, 1996).   BB

GALLAGHER, ED (1873–1929) AND AL SHEAN (1868–1949)

American *vaudeville team. Edward Francis Gallagher was born in San Leandro, California; Albert Schönberg was a native of Germany who emigrated to *New York in 1876. After working with their own partners for some years, Gallagher and Shean met in *Chicago in 1910 and performed for four years as a vaudeville team, Gallagher as the straight man and Shean as an English-mangling pseudo-foreigner (their 1912 appearance in the Broadway *musical *The Rose Bird* was a departure). After a six-year rift, the pair reconciled in 1920, and created a sensation in the *Ziegfeld Follies of 1922* with their ever-varying song-sketch 'Mr Gallagher and Mr Shean in Egypt' (which they recorded the next year). The refrain—'Positively, Mr Gallagher?' 'Absolutely, Mr Shean'—became a catchphrase for decades. After the *Greenwich Village Follies* (1923–4), the pair separated for good. Shean was the maternal uncle and mentor of the celebrated *Marx Brothers.   CT

GALLEGOS, DANIEL (1930–)

Costa Rican playwright, director, and teacher. After studying at the *Actors Studio in *New York with Lee *Strasberg, Gallegos began to teach *Method *acting at the University of Costa Rica. He wrote several controversial plays modelled on the European *avant-garde, including *La colina* (*The Hill*, 1968), *Los profanos* (*The Profane Ones*, 1960), and *En el séptimo círculo* (*In the Seventh Circle*, 1982).   EJW

GALLIARI FAMILY

Italian designers, commencing with **Bernardino** (1707–94) and his brother **Fabrizio** (1709–90) and ending with **Gaspare** (1761–1823), who worked in many European cities (Innsbruck, *Berlin, *Vienna, *Paris) but primarily in Turin and *Milan. They were sensitive to the new trends in *scenography—*scena per angola*, creation of mood through *lighting—and saw a rise in demand for domestic and rustic settings to meet the growing interest in comic *opera. They created settings depicting classical ruins, sparked by the rediscovery of Herculaneum (1709) and Pompeii (1748). The family also designed royal weddings and royal *entries.   JEH

GALPÓN, EL

Uruguayan *collective, established in *Montevideo by members of Teatro del Pueblo and La Isla de los Niños in 1949. Among the founders were writers, actors, and directors such as Atahualpa *del Cioppo, Ugo *Ulive, Rubén Yáñez, and Jorge *Curi. The name ('storage shed') was chosen when the group erected their first stage at a construction site, though they opened a permanent space in 1951. The approach was eclectic, but El Galpón ultimately found its focus in the ideas of Bertolt *Brecht, and its early repertoire included Brecht's *The Caucasian Chalk Circle*, *Chekhov's *The Three Sisters*, and *Ibsen's *An Enemy of the People*. After a successful funding campaign, the company and its theatre schools moved in 1969 to a converted cinema with 650 seats and up-to-date *lighting and *sound equipment.

The 1973 military coup installed a dictatorship which clamped down on dissent (*see* CENSORSHIP); El Galpón was seriously harassed on numerous occasions, culminating in the imprisonment of several members in 1975. Most were freed in 1976 and fled the country, and the theatre operated in exile in Mexico until the end of the dictatorship in 1984. Upon return to Uruguay the company remounted *Artigas general del pueblo* (*Artigas, General of the People*), which had been developed in Mexico in their familiar *Brechtian style, directed by del Cioppo. They continue to produce the plays of Brecht, *Molière, *Pirandello, *Albee, and Lope de *Vega, as well as work by Uruguayans such as Yáñez, Mauricio *Rosencof, and Milton Schinca.   EJW

GALSWORTHY, JOHN (1867–1933)

English playwright and novelist. Along with contemporaries *Shaw and Granville *Barker, Galsworthy was a force for the New Drama in Edwardian England. He infused the *well-made play format with *realistic *dialogue, producing *thesis dramas that attacked the injustices of the English class system. In his breakthrough year of 1906, Galsworthy published *The Man of Property* (the first instalment of his Forsyte novels) and had his first play, *The Silver Box*, produced at the *Royal Court Theatre under the *Vedrenne–Barker management. A critical rather than commercial success, *The Silver Box* is a morality tale of the inequities of the legal system: a Member of Parliament's alcoholic son steals a purse from a prostitute but escapes punishment while his servant's husband gets hard labour for taking a silver cigarette case in exchange for helping the drunken son home. His next play, *Strife* (1909), about a strike at a tin works, was a minor success. Galsworthy claimed that it was less a play about labour relations than about fanaticism, and this lack of commitment works to the play's detriment. In 1910 Galsworthy produced his most historically important play, *Justice*, a plea for prison reform. The *protagonist, Falder, is sentenced to solitary confinement after illegally altering a cheque from his employer. Galsworthy depicts the horror of Falder's solitary confinement with an *expressionist intensity in a nearly wordless scene. *Justice* had the unusual distinction of actually affecting policy when it prompted Home Secretary Winston Churchill to restrict the use of solitary confinement as punishment.

After the war Galsworthy achieved his greatest commercial success with *The Skin Game* (1920) and *Loyalties* (1922), which both deal with social caste, and *Escape* (1926). While popular at the time, these post-war plays faded rapidly from critical esteem and his reputation as a playwright came to rest on his Edwardian dramas. Although his plays receive occasional revivals, he has not been rediscovered as a great Edwardian dramatist in the way Barker was in the late 1970s and 1980s. As a result Galsworthy, who won the Nobel Prize for Literature in 1932, is better known for his novels, especially *The Forsyte Saga*.   MDG

GAMBARO, GRISELDA (1928–)

Argentinian playwright and novelist. Gambaro's first play, *The Blunder* (1965), premièred at *Buenos Aires's *avant-garde DiTella Institute. Dismissed by the theatre establishment as apolitical and aestheticist, Gambaro's plays written before her political exile to Spain in 1977 dramatize Argentina's escalating social crisis. The *protagonists of *The Siamese Twins* and *The Camp* (1967) are passive, silent victims of a surrounding terror. Several plays were not staged until the junta's decline (including 1973's *Saying Yes*, premièred during the Teatro *Abierto festival, 1981), and the much discussed *Information for Foreigners* (1973) has still to be performed in her homeland. Gambaro's post-dictatorship works exhibit important changes: in *Bitter Blood* (1982), *From the Rising Sun* (1984), and Alberto *Ure's 1984 restaging of *The Camp*, the female *characters, once relegated to passive or non-existent roles, rebelliously take centre stage; and the *texts began to experiment with classical models and intertextuality. *Antígona furiosa* (1986) and *It's Necessary to Understand a Little* (1995) demonstrate a continued interest in the causes and consequences of authoritarianism, but with even more fury. *Antígona* follows the *Sophoclean structure while distinguishing two Antigones: one, the democratic artistic product of Athens; the other, totalitarian Argentina's tragic *heroine. The theme of the disappeared informed the 1992 chamber *opera *The House Not at Peace*. Staged by Laura *Yusem at the Teatro *Municipal San Martín, the production exposed an Argentina 'without memory, where silence and oblivion have been imposed'. In *A Mother by Profession* (2000) a woman attempts to come to terms with her lesbian mother's earlier rejection. Gambaro has always written for an Argentine *audience, hence her inability to write plays during exile. 'One cannot confess alone,' she said.   JGJ

GAMBOA, FEDERICO (1864–1939)

Mexican novelist and playwright who wrote *melodramatic critiques of the social and economic inequities during the reign of Porfirio Díaz (1894–1911). *The Revenge of the Soil* (1904) depicts the rigid and cruel caste system which contributed so heavily to the explosive violence of the Mexican Revolution.   KFN

GAMBON, MICHAEL (1940–)

Dublin-born actor whose career has been predominantly in *London and in a series of hugely successful *television roles, peppered with appearances in Hollywood *films. Gambon joined the *National Theatre for its inaugural season in 1963 and has played regularly for both it and the *Royal Shakespeare Company. He has had a long association with *Ayckbourn, appearing in *The Norman Conquests* (1974), *Just between Ourselves* (1977), *A Chorus of Disapproval* (1985), *A Small Family Business* (1987), and *Man of the Moment* (1990). Rather different work includes *Pinter's production of Simon *Gray's *Close of Play* (1979), John *Dexter's production of *Brecht's *Galileo* (1980), and *Miller's *A View from the Bridge* (1987). In London in 1995 he appeared in the title role in Ben *Jonson's *Volpone* and as a middle-aged restaurateur attempting to reunite with his mistress in David *Hare's *Skylight*. He most celebrated television role is Philip E. Marlow in Dennis *Potter's *The Singing Detective* (1987), but he also appeared in the title role of *Maigret* (1992). He was a monstrous thief in Peter Greenaway's film *The Cook, the Thief, his Wife and her Lover* (1989). Gambon was knighted in 1998.   AS

GAMBUH

Oldest surviving *dance-drama genre of Bali (*Indonesia). It originated during the late Majapahit era (1293–1520) under influence from classical Hindu-Javanese court culture and performing arts. *Gambuh* is considered the cradle of most classical Balinese performing arts, and for several hundred years constituted one of the main court-supported dance-dramas. It went into decline in the early twentieth century due to the sudden loss of court patronage during conflicts with the Dutch colonial forces. In 1906 this collision culminated in a ritual mass suicide (*puputan*) by the members of the eight royal houses of Bali. Following the demise of the courts, *gambuh* found a new system of support in village communities in the context of *odalan* or temple festivals. However, the high level of sophistication and large repertoire from the court could not be preserved entirely and *gambuh* today is performed in simplified and shorter versions. A *Gambuh* Preservation Project was founded in the 1990s to retain this theatre tradition in Bali.

Gambuh consists of a synthesized form of dance, drama, language, and *music. The dramatic material (*lakon*) is drawn from the *Malat*, episodic poetic stories about the mythical eleventh-century Javanese Prince Panji and his romantic and adventurous quests. Besides Panji, the main *characters are mostly known by their titles or functions, such as the opponent king (Prabu Keras), the princess (Raja Putri), her lady-in-waiting (Condong), ministers (Patih), royal retainers (Kakan-kakan), and clown-servants (Semar, Togog). These type characters all have specific standardized movements and speaking styles, ranging from highly refined (*alus*) to coarse (*kasar*). Refined characters speak in ancient Javanese Kawi, which is translated into contemporary Balinese for the *audience by attendant and *clown characters. Core melodic and rhythmic instruments of the *gambuh* orchestra consist of two to six flutes (*suling gambuh*), a set of paired drums (*kendang*), and a two-stringed fiddle (*rebab*). Additional punctuating and rhythm instruments include gongs (*kempur, kajar*), chimes (*kelenang*), metallophone (*kenyir*), cymbals (*rincik, kangsi*), metal cylinders (*gumanak*), and a bell tree (*gentorag*).   KP

Contemporary medium-sized **gamelan** orchestra in Bali, Indonesia, showing some of the percussion instruments that create its distinctive sound. Gamelan ensembles are used to accompany *wayang kulit* and other Balinese and Javanese performances.

GAMELAN

A unified court or folk musical ensemble comprised mostly of gongs and slabs (percussion instruments commonly made of bronze, brass, or iron). Although similar ensembles are found in other parts of South-East Asia, gamelan has developed into a large orchestra primarily in Bali and Java (*Indonesia) that constitutes the principal musical accompaniment in all traditional and several contemporary theatre *genres. A complete Javanese gamelan consists of ten to 50 instruments, including double-headed laced drums (*kendang*), a double-string spiked fiddle (*rebab*), xylophones, plucked zithers, and flutes. There are two basic tunings—the seven-tone *pelog* and the five-tone *slendro*—and though musical notation is available, musicians generally rely on aural practice. In the theatre the gamelan ensemble must abide by the need of the play by starting and stopping, shortening and lengthening phrases, or changing dynamics as the drama demands. Some gamelan are considered sacred and treated with considerable reverence.   HS

GANASSA, ZAN

The Italian *actor-manager Alberto Naseli (*c.*1540–84) adopted the stage role of 'Zan Ganassa', one of the earliest *Zanni roles in *commedia dell'arte*. The troupe which he managed for over twenty years was known by his name, rather than by a more allusive title. His first recorded appearance is in 1568 in Mantua. After a visit to France in 1571, the company worked in *Madrid for ten years from 1574, where they played a crucial role in acquainting Spanish theatre with Italian models. The *gracioso* role in Spanish drama is said to be influenced by Zan Ganassa as well as by Arlecchino.   RAA

GANDHI, SHANTA (1917–)

Actress and director from Gujarat, *India. After training as a *dancer, Gandhi became one of the founders of the *Indian People's Theatre Association, a cultural wing of the Communist Party of India. Here she performed in *dance-dramas like *Voice* of Bengal, Spirit of India, and India Immortal, and came into contact with eminent artists like Shanti Bardhan and Ravi Shankar. In the early 1950s a chance involvement with tribal communities of southern Gujarat compelled her to create a method for educating underprivileged peoples and children by using their traditional expressions. After 1960 she was a faculty member at the *National School of Drama in New Delhi, where she taught production techniques and classical Indian drama. Her direction of *Bhasa's Sanskrit play Madhyam Vyayoga (1965) was the first major step towards recovering the classical Indian *texts and methods for their performance. Through her landmark production of Jasma Odan (1968), a play adapted to the Gujarati traditional theatre form of *bhavai, and her experiment with professional *nautanki artists in a reinvented version of Amar Singh Rathor (1968), she foregrounded the issue of the preservation of traditional forms and their adaptation in urban Indian theatre.   KJ

GANZ, BRUNO (1941–)

Swiss-born German actor. As the current bearer of the high *award of the Iffland-Ring, Ganz can be officially considered the most important living German stage actor. He came to attention in 1969 in Peter *Stein's Bremen production of *Goethe's Torquato Tasso, where he played the title *character as an 'emotional clown'. Throughout the 1970s and 1980s he was one of the leading actors at the *Schaubühne in *Berlin, appearing in title roles in *Kleist's The Prince of Homburg (1972), Empedokles (1975), Hamlet (1982), and as Orestes in Stein's Oresteia (1979). His most recent stage appearance was as the older Faust in Stein's monumental production of Faust I and II (2000–1). He has also worked extensively in *film (Knife in the Head, 1978; Nosferatu, 1979; Wings of Desire, 1987).   CBB

GAO MING (KAO MING) (c.1305–70)

Chinese playwright and native of Wenzhou, Zhejiang, the birthplace of southern drama (*nanxi). Gao wrote Pipa ji (The Lute), a foundational nanxi, sometime after he retired from service to the Mongol (Yuan) Dynasty in 1356. By 1368 Zhu Yuanzhang, founder of the Ming Dynasty, considered the work equal in importance to the Confucian classics. Gao substantially elevated the artistic level of nanxi in this play about a filial son, Cai Bojie, caught between the desire to care for his ageing parents and the duty to serve his ruler. The Lute reflects a preference for country life but also endorses orthodox Confucian values. In this respect Gao broke with earlier nanxi that portrayed callous officials who abandon family for life in the capital. Performances typically consisted of excerpts from the play's 42 scenes. Scenes depicting Cai Bojie's opulent life with his second wife Madam Niu in the capital might be performed at banquets, while arias sung by his first wife Zhao Wuniang, as she journeys there in search of him,

were adapted for performance as tanci, a form of storytelling accompanied by lutes. At lineage-sponsored performances in ancestral halls, scenes of Zhao Wuniang's struggles to care for starving in-laws at home, or of Cai Bojie's homesick thoughts in the capital, were likely favourites.   CS

GAO WENXIU (KAO WEN-HSIU) (fl. 1270)

Chinese playwright. With over 30 *zaju operas to his credit, Gao was popular and prolific enough to earn the nickname 'Little Hanqing' after the recognized master of the genre, *Guan Hanqing. Many of Gao's opera titles feature *heroes from the Shuihu zhuan, a popular story cycle about noble bandits fighting for loyalty, justice, and political legitimacy. One of only 30 cheaply printed, fourteenth-century zaju texts, Gao's Zhao Yuan the Drunkard Meets the Emperor embodies some of what might have appealed to Yuan audiences: robust humour, flawed yet likeable *characters, and a playful disregard for customary reverence and decorum. Yet for all their popularity in the Yuan Dynasty, Gao's operas were poorly transmitted. In dramatic and novelistic adaptations of the Shuihu cycle in the Ming period, the portrayals of the bandits became more overtly polarized and moralistic, militating against the earlier, less predictable alignments of male virtue, valour, and beauty.

PS

GAO XINGJIAN (KAO HSING-CHIEN) (1940–)

Chinese playwright and novelist. After studying French at university, Gao became a pioneer in experimental theatre in the early 1980s. As resident playwright for the Beijing People's Art Theatre, he wrote Absolute Signal (1982), Bus Stop (1983), and Wilderness Man (1985), *avant-garde plays that marked both a formal and thematic breakaway from the official *realistic theatre, bringing him critical and popular acclaim and official distrust. The Other Shore was banned from public performance in 1986 and the next year Gao went into exile in France, where he resides now. Exile (1990), about three people running from government pursuit after the 1989 Tiananmen incident, put him at odds with both the Chinese government and the exiled Democracy Movement. His other dramas, including Hades (1987), Between Life and Death (1991), Dialogue and Rebuttal (1992), Nocturnal Wanderer (1993), Weekend Quartet (1995), and Snow in June (1997), have often been called modern Zen plays. Banned from production in China since 1990, his work has been staged in *Hong Kong, Taiwan, *Japan, the USA, and many European countries. His painting, done chiefly in black ink, has been much admired in France, and his philosophical novel Soul Mountain has achieved wide international recognition (Chinese edition, Taiwan, 1990; English translation, 2000). In 1992 he was named Chevalier d'Ordre des Arts et des Lettres by the French government, and was awarded the Nobel Prize in Literature in 2000 for his 'bitter insights and linguistic ingenuity, which have opened new paths for the Chinese novel and drama'.   SYL

GARCÍA, SANTIAGO (1929–   )

Colombian director, playwright, actor, theoretician, and teacher, who trained under Seki *Sano and co-founded the group El Búho in 1959. García was part of the university theatre movement until his staging of *Brecht's *Galileo* in 1965 prompted the authorities to remove him from the National University. This led to the foundation of La Casa de la Cultura, which eventually established the prestigious Teatro la *Candelaria (1972) under his direction, where García's masterly use of *Brechtian techniques, his creative designs, and his attention to detail in *props and *costumes have created memorable work. His playwriting alternates between adaptations of the classics and new social and political material. His works include *El diálogo del rebusque* (*The Dialogue of a Rogue*, 1982), based on a picaresque *character by the seventeenth-century Spanish author Quevedo; *Maravilla estar* (*Wonderful to Be*, 1986), a parable about the transition from utopianism to scepticism as neo-liberalism failed to alleviate the economic and social crisis in *Latin America; and *El Quijote* (1999), a version of *Cervantes' masterpiece. From 1976 to 1980 he was the director of *ENAD (the National School of Dramatic Art) and restructured its curriculum, and he has continued to teach through a workshop he established at the *Corporación Colombiana de Teatro. He has written extensively on the theatre; some of his essays are contained in *Teoría y práctica del teatro* (1983).   BJR

GARCÍA, VÍCTOR (1934–82)

Argentine director. Born in Argentina of Spanish parents, García began studies in medicine and architecture before moving to *Buenos Aires where he gave up formal schooling in favour of the theatre. In his late twenties he went to *Paris, studying alongside fellow Argentine Jorge *Lavelli. With a non-*naturalistic repertoire including *Claudel, *Valle-Inclán, *García Lorca, and *Arrabal, García soon demonstrated an architectural understanding of theatre space. Abandoning *realistic decor in productions like Arrabal's *The Automobile Graveyard* (Dijon, 1966) and *Genet's *The Balcony* (*São Paulo, 1969), he created baroque imagery which juggled the *ritual with visceral impact. From 1968 to 1976 he directed three seminal productions with Nuria *Espert's Spanish company: *The Maids* (1969), *Yerma* (1971), and *Divine Words* (1975). Critics who had previously expressed unease at the dwarfing of actors in García's giant architectural structures were won over by the expressive physicality of the performers. Each production was dominated

by a strong conceptual image—what the director referred to as the 'metallic spittoon' of *The Maids*, the womb-like trampoline of *Yerma*, the portable organ pipes of *Divine Words*—that undermined conventional ideas about the works. García's bold scenic creations paved the way for some of the most radical experiments in Spanish and French theatre in the latter decades of the twentieth century.   MMD

GARCÍA LORCA, FEDERICO (1898–1936)

Spanish poet, dramatist, and director, born into a wealthy Andalusian family. Although he entered the University of Granada in 1914, he largely shunned academic study in favour of music and literature. His first volume of travel writings (*Impressions and Landscapes*, 1918) was followed by early success as a poet with his *Libro de poemas* (*Book of Poems*, 1921). His first play, however, *El maleficio de la mariposa* (*The Butterfly's Evil Spell*), which premièred at the Eslava Theatre, *Madrid, in 1920, directed by Gregorio *Martínez Sierra, was poorly received by critics and *audiences. Although he continued writing for the theatre, it was only in 1927 that the most famous actress of the day, Margarita *Xirgu, chose to present his second full-length play, *Mariana Pineda*, a study of the nineteenth-century Granadine martyr, during the difficult years of the Primo de Rivera dictatorship. Xirgu encouraged García Lorca's directorial aspirations—he was credited as director for the production and assisted Cipriano de Rivas Cherif in *La zapatera prodigiosa* (*The Shoemaker's Prodigious Wife*, 1930), with Xirgu in the leading role. In his statement that 'theatre is, above all, a good director', García Lorca recognized the importance of the *rehearsal process in shaping his *dramaturgy.

During the 1930s he served as *artistic director of the student theatre company funded by the Second Republic, La *Barraca, taking the Golden Age canon to rural villages where it could be revised and restaged for the demands of the age. These years were to produce his best-known works, the rural *tragedies *Bodas de sangre* (*Blood Wedding*, 1933), *Yerma* (1934), and *La casa de Bernarda Alba* (*The House of Bernarda Alba*), written in 1936 but not performed until 1944. All these plays, crafted within the register of poetic *realism, use the rural Andalusian landscape of his birth as the backdrop to a series of social dramas which investigate the claustrophobic frustration experienced by women in an environment of stifling constraint and oppressive surveillance.

In the late 1920s and early 1930s García Lorca travelled to the United States, Cuba, Argentina, and Uruguay. He also juggled the lyrical realism of the rural trilogy with a more elliptical dramaturgy in work that went unstaged in his lifetime. Incomplete works like *Comedia sin título* (*Play without a Title*, written 1936) and *El público* (*The Public*, c.1930), which present the interaction of differing linguistic and dramatic registers and celebrate sexual and political difference, suggest the directions he wished to pursue. During the 1980s revelatory productions by director Lluis *Pasqual demonstrated this 'alternative' García Lorca, indicating a dramatist whose theatrical versatility defied attempts to pigeonhole him as a *folkloric writer.

The historical, cultural, and physical landscapes of Andalusia nonetheless had a profound influence on García Lorca's dramatic world, which is undeniably rooted in a rural environment where characters make reference to pastoral images in revealing their angst and desperation. But whilst it shaped his pictorial and literary imagination, García Lorca's work cannot be reduced to that arid milieu. Although infused by his native Granada, the richness of his writing comes as much from the traditions of earlier generations of poets like Góngora and Garcilaso, his period at Madrid's Oxbridge-like Residencia de Estudiantes in the 1920s—with the two *enfants terribles* of twentieth-century *surrealism, Luis Buñuel and Salvador Dalí— his travels to *New York and Cuba in 1929–30, and the pioneering work of his contemporaries like Ramón del *Valle-Inclán and Manuel de Falla.

García Lorca was an early martyr of the Franco regime, shot by nationalist troops soon after the outbreak of the Civil War. His name has stood as a potent symbol of a liberal era brutally brought down by an illegitimate alliance of repressive elements keen to curb the changes begun by the (elected) left-wing Popular Front government. He now stands as a potent *gay icon as well, and a symbol of Spain's theatrical renaissance during the 1920s and 1930s which was to provide the framework for many of the cultural policies of the socialist government during the 1980s.
MMD

GARDNER, HERB (1934–)

American playwright. A lifelong resident of *New York, the setting of all his plays, he began at the age of 19 as a syndicated cartoonist, then graduated to novels and drama. His career-making success was *A Thousand Clowns* (1962), which starred Jason *Robards, Jr., and was made into a popular *film. *The Goodbye People* (1968), set on Coney Island and starring Milton Berle, failed, as did his one *musical, *One Night Stand* (1980, music by Jule *Styne). *Thieves* (1974), starring Marlo Thomas, did better, but his biggest hit, played widely since, was *I'm Not Rappaport* (1985), a dark *comedy about ageing set in Central Park and starring Judd *Hirsch as an elderly Marxist Jew and Cleavon Little as his black companion. *Conversations with my Father* (1992; *London, 1995), which also starred Hirsch, is an unsentimental study of an unbending Lower East Side immigrant bar owner. Gardner's best *characters are cantankerous, principled free spirits or throwbacks who wage spirited war with the present. He has a streak of anger and grit missing in the more fluent work of Neil *Simon, which may explain why the latter is more popular.
CR

GARDZIENICE

Polish experimental company devoted to cultural anthropology, created by Włodzimierz Staniewski (1950–). Staniewski studied at the Jagiellonian University, worked with the experimental STU Theater in *Cracow (1968–71) and the *Polish Laboratory Theatre in Wrocław (1971–6). In 1977 he organized his own company in the village of Gardzienice near Lublin. The founding members included Mariusz Gołaj, Tomasz Rodowicz, and Anna Zubrzycka. The company live in simple accommodation, perform manual work, and follow a rigorous physical and vocal regimen (*see* COLLECTIVES AND COLLECTIVE CREATION). Their productions included *Gargantua and Pantagruel* (1978), *Sorcery* (1980), *The Life of the Archpriest Avvakum* (1983), *Carmina Burana* (1989), and *Metamorphoses* (1997), which *toured Poland, Europe, America, and elsewhere, attracting great interest from *audiences, critics, and scholars. Gardzienice's work is founded on two major concepts: 'the expedition' and 'the gathering'. 'The expedition' is both a real journey and a model of the human condition. Travelling on foot from place to place, the actors carry necessary equipment in backpacks and a small cart. Arriving in a village, they invite local people to a meticulously staged, expressive performance built around actions, songs, and *dance. A communal encounter follows: 'the gathering'. Lasting several hours, it includes exchanges of stories, songs, *dances, and food. Gardzienice treats theatre as an integral part of culture, able to shape the lives and spirits of the people involved in the theatrical process. In addition to its theatrical and paratheatrical activities, Gardzienice hosts conferences, workshops, and training sessions for students and specialists from all over the world. *See also* ANTHROPOLOGY, THEATRE.
KB

GARIN, ERAST (1902–80)

Russian/Soviet actor who spent the 1920s working for *Meyerhold and became a skilled exponent of *biomechanics—a *theory of *acting which he memorably applied in productions of *Give Us Europe* (1924), as Gulyachkin in *Erdman's *The Mandate* (1925), as Khlestakov in Meyerhold's 1926 production of *Gogol's *The Government Inspector* (a film clip of which survives), and as Chatsky in *Griboedov's *Gore ot uma/Gore umu* (*Woe from Wit*, 1928). He subsequently worked at the Leningrad (*St Petersburg) Theatre of Comedy and the *Moscow Film Actor's Studio. Among many *film roles, his bridegroom in Isidor Annensky's film of *Chekhov's *The Wedding* (1944) is outstanding.
NW

GARNEAU, MICHEL (1939–)

Québec dramatist, director, actor, translator, musician, and poet. Brilliantly eclectic, his career began in *radio at the age of 15. His plays (more than 40 to date, many written to order) are characterized by intense social and political commitment (he was briefly imprisoned during Quebec's October Crisis in 1970), allied with an irreverence for everything previous generations considered sacred. They are usually in blank *verse, and in popular Québécois idiom, yet they have had broad international success, notably *Quatre à quatre* (*Four to Four*, 1973), dealing with four generations of Quebec women, performed in more than a dozen countries, and his *Émilie ne sera plus jamais cueillie par l'anémone* (*Emily Will Never Again Feel the Breath of the Delphinium*, 1981), a loose depiction of the life and works of the American poet Emily Dickinson. Garneau's translations/adaptations of Shakespeare (*Macbeth* and *The Tempest*, in particular) have been acclaimed by critics in their *Montréal performances.   LED

GARNIER, ROBERT (1545–90)

French dramatist, whose career as lawyer and poet spanned the turbulent years of France's religious wars. His three *tragedies based on Roman history were possibly intended as warning commentaries on political strife. Garnier also wrote three tragedies based on Greek myth, one on biblical history, and a *tragicomedy. His tragedies, rhetorical and lyrical, are filed with emotional *monologues and lamenting *choruses. Although two of his plays may have been acted at the *Hôtel de Bourgogne, Garnier was apparently indifferent to theatrical performance. English translations of *Antony* (1590) and *Cornelia* (1594) were *closet dramas.   RWV

GARRETT, JOÃO BAPTISTA DE ALMEIDA (1799–1854)

Portuguese poet, novelist, and playwright. The leader of Portuguese *romanticism and the founder of modern Portuguese prose, one of Garrett's chief preoccupations as Inspector-General of Theatres was the professionalization of the national stage and the creation of a distinctly Portuguese dramatic repertoire. The first performances of the newly created Teatro *Nacional D. Maria II (1846) included a selection of his own work, encompassing five *comedies, two *historical dramas, and the groundbreaking *Um auto de Gil Vicente* (1838), a celebration of the *early modern Portuguese playwright *Vicente. In 1850 came *Frei Luís de Souza*, widely regarded as the most important play of Portuguese romanticism. Based on the true story of a Portuguese nobleman who, presumed dead in battle, returns to his homeland to the dismay of his daughter and wife, who has since remarried, this patriotic *tragedy was the most performed play of the first 100 years of the Nacional's existence.   KG

GARRICK, DAVID (1717–79)

English actor and *manager who dominated the eighteenth century. From his first season to his last (1741–76), his pre-eminence was never seriously questioned. His first performance in *London was as an anonymous actor at an illegal *playhouse, and his last was as the 'English Roscius' at a *Drury Lane that his three decades of management had transformed into the best theatre in Europe. Raised in Lichfield, Garrick took a famous walk to London with Samuel *Johnson in 1737. After a half-hearted attempt at the wine business, Garrick began acting with Henry Giffard's company at Ipswich in summer 1741, taking on a number of major roles, including Sir Harry Wildair in *Farquhar's *The Constant Couple* and Chamont in *Otway's *The Orphan*. In October 1741 he made a legendary London debut as Richard III at *Goodman's Fields, his success immediate and immense. The naturalness of his performance style contrasted markedly with the more formal, declamatory method of veterans like James *Quin.

When Goodman's Fields was forced to close, Garrick gave his first performance at Drury Lane in 1742 and quickly became the company's chief performer. After leading the failed actors' rebellion of 1743, Garrick left Drury Lane for *Dublin in 1745–6 and *Covent Garden in 1746–7. In April 1747 he signed articles to become co-manager of Drury Lane with James *Lacy, beginning a 27-year partnership that, while sometimes uneasy, was amazingly profitable for the partners and the London stage. Garrick was responsible for the stage business, and he made improvements to the theatre immediately by banishing gentlemen from going behind the scenes during a performance. In the 1762–3 season he banished spectators from the stage during *benefit performances, though he was unsuccessful in his attempt to abolish the custom of charging half price to those who arrived after the third act. In 1765–6 he installed wing lights similar to those he had seen on a recent trip to France, vastly improving the illumination of the stage.

While Garrick liked to think of himself as the guardian of Shakespeare's sacred name, he nonetheless made concessions to the public appetite for *spectacle. In the 1770s he hired the Alsatian painter and scenic wizard Philip de *Loutherbourg, who combined scene *painting, *lighting, and other media into a more compelling visual presentation. While Garrick could bemoan Lacy's unilateral decision to hire a rope dancer as a degradation of the house of Shakespeare, the spectacular effects of Loutherbourg were acceptable. Similarly, he could deride Covent Garden for its reliance on *pantomime while regularly bringing out pantomimes by Henry *Woodward at Drury Lane—including Garrick's own *Harlequin's Invasion* (1759), which denounces pantomime in a pantomime. Garrick's instincts for song and spectacle were generally sound, although he badly miscalculated when he brought in French dancers to perform the *Chinese Festival* in 1755, on the eve of the Seven

Years War, when anti-French sentiment was running high. *Rioting broke out, and the venture cost the theatre £4,000. Another costly fiasco was the Great Shakespeare Jubilee of 1769, which was Garrick's pet project. The multi-day celebration in Stratford-upon-Avon featured a horse race, *fireworks, torrential rains, and Garrick's 'Jubilee Ode', but no performances of Shakespeare plays. Garrick was roundly criticized for this exercise in vanity, and he reportedly lost £2,000 for his pains, but he began the vogue of bardolatry still flourishing in Stratford.

As Garrick's correspondence shows, in dealings with actors and playwrights he was always diplomatic. For instance, he established a warm relationship with the volatile Kitty *Clive and was able to employ the mercurial Spranger *Barry and Ann (Dancer) Barry for several seasons. As for authors, he politely dealt with the many entreaties he received to stage new plays, though he wrangled repeatedly with Arthur *Murphy and alienated John *Home after refusing his surprisingly popular *tragedy Douglas (1756). An author himself of light *farces and of dubious alterations of Shakespeare plays like Hamlet and Macbeth, Garrick was sometimes accused of stifling other playwrights while forcing his own work on the public.

He played an enormous variety of roles. In tragedy he had no rivals for Macbeth, Lear, and Richard III. Francis *Gentleman praised Garrick's dizzying range of emotions in Macbeth, whom Garrick played as a sympathetic *hero-*villain, complete with a pathetic death speech of Garrick's invention. In letters he frequently complained about the physical demands of the role, which he considered his most demanding. His portrayal of Lear avoided bombast and abstraction, emphasized a characteristic modulation of emotions, and exploited opportunities for pathos. But Hamlet was the *audience's favourite, and Garrick played it 90 times, from his second season to his last. Commentators were impressed by his melancholy demeanour and claimed that his skin actually grew paler upon seeing the *ghost. His great non-Shakespearian tragic roles included Lothario in *Rowe's The Fair Penitent, Jaffeir and Pierre in *Otway's Venice Preserv'd, and Lusignan in Aaron Hill's Zara.

In *comedy Garrick's most popular role was Abel Drugger in *Jonson's The Alchemist, a low comic role that he skilfully underplayed, making it all the more convincing. Far different was his portrayal of the suave, rakish, but good-hearted Ranger in Benjamin Hoadly's The Suspicious Husband (1747). Although Quin scoffed at the young Garrick playing Sir John Brute in *Vanbrugh's The Provok'd Husband, the part became a mainstay of his repertory. Other great comic roles included Benedick in Much Ado and Don Felix in *Centlivre's The Wonder, the *character Garrick played for his final performance on 10 June 1776. Knowing that the emotion of actor and audience would be overpowering on the occasion, he wisely closed his unparalleled career on a comic note. And sensing that a rhyming *epilogue would detract from the dignity of the moment, he made a mod-

est and emotional address in prose, bowed to all corners of the house, and walked slowly off the stage.　　　MJK

Burnim, Kalman A., David Garrick, Director (Pittsburgh, 1961)
Stone, George Winchester, Jr., and Kahrl, George M., David Garrick: a critical biography (Carbondale, Ill., 1979)
Woods, Leigh, Garrick Claims the Stage (Westport, Conn., 1984)

GARRICK CLUB

*London gentlemen's club. It owes its origin to the Duke of Sussex, who 'recognized the need for furthering the literary industry in England by the formation of a Club on less formal lines than the Athenaeum, recruited from the most active caterers for public taste with pen and pencil, in the studio and on the stage' (T. H. Escott). The first committee meeting was held in January 1831 and the club opened in November of that year under the patronage of the Duke, moving to premises in King Street in 1832. The present clubhouse opened in July 1864. The club, which has numbered many leading *actors among its members, has been no stranger to disputes, including one between *Dickens and Thackeray over Edmund Yates's membership, and in 1992 another dispute over female membership. It houses a major collection of theatrical works of art, comprising 972 paintings and drawings and 56 pieces of sculpture, based on its acquisition of Charles *Mathews's collection of paintings in 1835. A new catalogue of the entire collection was published in 1997.　　　JTD

GARRO, ELENA (1920–98)

Mexican playwright and novelist. Best known for her magical realist novels Remembrance of Things Past (1963), Garro began writing plays in the 1950s as a member of Poetry Out Loud. Known for her lyrical, often magical plays, she combined childhood memories with images of Mexico's indigenous culture and history. A Solid Home (1957) tinkers with the pre-Columbian belief that death is an extension of life by bringing together various generations of a Mexican family, all of them dead and buried in the same crypt. Other plays are *surrealistic, often violent encounters between men and women (The Trace, 1984), the rich and the poor (The Tree, 1983), the dead and the living (The Lady on her Balcony, 1966). While her plays have not always had the productions they deserve, her *historical drama on the revolutionary hero Felipe Angeles (1979) won *awards and enthusiastic *audiences.　　　KFN

GAS See LIGHTING.

GASCON, JEAN (1921–88)

French Canadian actor and director. After working with Émile *Legault's troupe he studied theatre in France 1946–51 and on his return helped found the Théâtre du *Nouveau Monde, becoming its *artistic director and leading actor. Notable for his performances of *Molière, he was responsible for introducing that author's work to the *Stratford Festival. He was Stratford's artistic director from 1968 to 1974 and was a major contributor to its national and international success, with tours of the USA, Europe, the Soviet Union, and Australia. Active in *film and *television, Gascon also served as director of *Montréal's National Theatre School and of the National Arts Centre in Ottawa.   LED

GASKILL, WILLIAM (1930–)

English director. After early experience as a *regional repertory actor and *stage manager, Gaskill became assistant director to George *Devine with the *English Stage Company at the *Royal Court Theatre from 1957 to 1959. The promotion resulted from his staging of N. F. Simpson's *absurd concoctions *A Resounding Tinkle* and *The Hole*. He established a reputation for forging strong ensemble work in productions of plays by Donald Howarth, *Osborne, and *Wesker, attracting invitations to direct at the *Royal Shakespeare Company and to be associate director at *Olivier's new *National Theatre in 1963. Notable productions in this period included the RSC's *Richard III* (1961), *Cymbeline* (1962), and *Brecht's *The Caucasian Chalk Circle* (1963), and even a West End *Baal* (1963) starring Peter *O'Toole. In the National's first season he staged *Farquhar's *The Recruiting Officer* (1963), followed by Brecht's *Mother Courage* (1964) and *Arden's *Armstrong's Last Goodnight* (1965). He became *artistic director of the Royal Court Theatre from 1965 to 1972, producing some highly influential seasons. He directed *Bond's early plays *Saved* (1968), *Early Morning* (1969), *Lear* (1971), and *The Sea* (1973), as well as opening the *studio Theatre Upstairs (1969) and hosting a *festival of *alternative theatre, Come Together (1970). In 1972 he went freelance, and in 1973 with Max *Stafford-Clark he founded the cooperative *touring company *Joint Stock, making it one of the leading *fringe theatre groups in England, with premières of scripts by *Hare, *Brenton, *Churchill, and Stephen Lowe. Gaskill continued to work in the major subsidized theatres in the UK, mainland Europe, and further afield into the 1990s. His productions included *The Barber of Seville* (Welsh National Opera, 1977), *Oedipus the King* (Dubrovnik, 1976), *Hamlet* (*Sydney, 1981), *Women Beware Women* (Royal Court, 1986), Osborne's *The Entertainer* (*New York, 1983), *Shaw's *Candida* (Minneapolis, 1985), and *Pirandello's *The Mountain Giants* (Royal National Theatre, 1993).   BRK

GASSMAN, VITTORIO (1922–2000)

Italian actor and writer. Born in Genoa, Gassman made his theatrical debut in 1943 and worked with the finest directors of his time, including in the 1940s Luchino *Visconti (*A Streetcar Named Desire* and *Troilus and Cressida*) and in the 1950s Luigi *Squarzina, his co-director in the Teatro d'Arte Italiano. Gassman's first *film role in Italy came in 1946, but he did not find success in cinema until Mario Monicelli's *I soliti ignoti* (*Persons Unknown*) in 1958 when he appeared alongside the Neapolitan actor Totò. He moved to Hollywood, joined the MGM stable, and shot films with King Vidor and Joseph H. Lewis, and in the 1970s with Robert Altman (*Quintet*, *A Wedding*). In 1974 he won the best actor prize at Cannes for his performance in *Profumo di donna*. A charismatic actor who felt his real métier was theatre, he was also successful as director, translator, especially of Shakespeare, and latterly as author of novels and autobiographical works.   JF

GATE THEATRE (*DUBLIN)

Opened in 1928 under the joint *management of Micheál *MacLíammóir and Hilton *Edwards, playing initially at the Peacock in the *Abbey Theatre before moving in 1930 to a theatre within the Rotunda. The founders aimed to provide classic and contemporary international plays to complement, not rival, the work of the Abbey. Edwards directed, MacLíammóir designed, both acted. To relieve accumulating creative and financial pressures on them, a patron, Lord Longford, ran a second company, Longford Productions (1936–60), to share the theatre on a six-monthly exchange. Since the founders' retirement (1978), Michael Colgan has maintained their policy as *artistic director.   RAC

GATE THEATRE (*LONDON)

Opened by Peter Godfrey in 1925, first in a loft in Covent Garden and, after 1927, in a one-time *music hall under Charing Cross Station. It was one of London's first *fringe theatres: experimental, contemporary, challenging (especially for the *Lord Chamberlain's office, given Godfrey's taste for daring *expressionist work). Over nine years he staged some 300 plays (*Strindberg, *Wedekind, *Toller, *Kaiser, *O'Neill, *Rice, *Feuchtwanger), occasionally exchanging productions with *Gray's *Cambridge Festival Theatre. Norman *Marshall, succeeding in 1934, pursued a more conservative policy but continued staging only new writing. The theatre was bombed in 1941.   RAC

GATTI, ARMAND (1924–)

French dramatist, journalist, poet, and director. Gatti was born in Monaco of a poor Italian immigrant family, and at 17 was deported to a labour camp in Germany; the image of the concentration camp (and of the Resistance) appears in several of his works. An ebullient self-styled anarchist, he had considerable success in the decentralized French theatre of the 1960s, starting with the semi-autobiographical *La Vie imaginaire de l'éboueur Auguste Geai* (*Imaginary Life of Auguste Geai*, 1962), which showed his father at five different ages, played by five actors on seven stages, sometimes simultaneously. He wrote plays on the Chinese Civil War, the Guatemalan struggle for independence, the execution of Sacco and Vanzetti, and Vietnam, often presenting fragmented *characters and events, but reflecting his belief that the theatre could effectively raise the political consciousness of his *audiences. After the banning of *La Passion de Général Franco* (*The Passion of General Franco*, 1968, finally played 1976), he turned to a more directly 'engaged' form of *community theatre on politically sensitive subjects in France and abroad, involving whole communities for several months in events where the result was liable to appear in a wide variety of media rather than a published *text. He was invited to Derry in 1984 by John *Arden, and his *film *The Writing on the Wall* used Catholic teenagers to play Protestants and vice versa. He has also made documentary films, and currently arranges events in Seine-Saint-Denis, the most recent being *L'Internationale* (2001), on the Spanish Civil War.   EEC

GAUCHO

Symbol of Argentine and Uruguayan independence in poetry, theatre, and the *circus. The gaucho *character is characterized by a fiercely rural lifestyle, the picturesque nature of his speech, and larger-than-life personal exploits. He demands justice against the arbitrary exercise of power, and acts in proud, insolent silence. *See* DRAMA GAUCHESCO.   AV

GAULTIER-GARGUILLE (HUGUES GUÉRU) (1572/3–1633)

French actor. His earliest known affiliation was in 1606 with Valleran *Le Conte's troupe, which *Gros-Guillaume later joined; these two plus *Turlupin were a notable *farce team at the *Hôtel de Bourgogne for nearly two decades. He played the old man, wearing a black *costume, large spectacles, and a *mask with a long, pointed beard; he had long legs and was extremely thin, in contrast to Gros-Guillaume. He was said to be a serious student of his art, to have perfect control of his limbs, and to move like a *marionette. He published a collection of his songs in 1632. In *tragedy he acted under the name of Fléchelles.   RWH

GAUTIER, THÉOPHILE (1811–72)

French man of letters, playwright, and *critic. As a 19-year-old art student Gautier helped to mastermind the defence of *Hugo's *Hernani* against the opposition of certain traditionally minded members of the *Comédie-Française cast, in the tumultuous atmosphere of the first few performances (*see* RIOTS). His *Histoire du romantisme* (1874) looks back on this experience as 'the outstanding event of the century': though Gautier himself had long since moved on to a career as journalist, art critic, and novelist, and was a leading figure in the mid-century art for art's sake movement, he retained a nostalgic memory of the idealism and excitement of the *romanticism of the 1830s. His major contributions to the theatre were the *scenarios for the ballets *Giselle* (1841) and *La Péri* (1843); and in contrast, a deliberate throwback to the *melodrama of *Pixérécourt in *La Juive de Constantine* (1846).   WDH

GAY, JOHN (1685–1732)

English playwright, most famous for *The Beggar's Opera* (1728). The unprecedented run of that *ballad opera (it ran for 63 nights in its first season) and its experimental nature made it the most important and successful play of the eighteenth century, and became the basis of *Brecht and *Weill's *The Threepenny Opera* (1928). His first produced work was *The Wife of Bath* (1713), a loose adaptation of Chaucer's *Canterbury Tales*, and his first success came with *The What D'Ye Call It* (1715), a *burlesque *afterpiece which held the stage throughout the eighteenth century. *Three Hours after Marriage* (1717), which Gay co-wrote with fellow Scriblerians Alexander Pope and John Arbuthnot, probably suffered from hostility to Pope and was unsuccessful. Gay's happy-ending *tragedy *The Captives* (1724) had a short run at *Drury Lane and brought the patronage of Princess Caroline. While nothing Gay did could compare with the triumph of *The Beggar's Opera*, the blend of burlesque, *farce, and compelling *music that characterizes that play was the culmination of the components of his earlier works. Not merely an attack on opera—after all, Gay wrote the libretto to *Handel's *Acis and Galatea* (1718)—the ballad opera simultaneously exploited and ridiculed *musical theatre. That the play was seen as an attack on Sir Robert Walpole's ministry was perhaps inevitable, given Gay's Tory friends and patrons, chiefly Pope and the Duke and Duchess of Queensberry. The political firestorm that erupted over its interpretation led to the suppression of the sequel, *Polly* (1729).   MJK

GAY SWEATSHOP

British company founded in 1975 which emerged out of the *gay liberation movement. Initially the five-strong company was all male, including Alan Pope and Drew Griffiths, who wrote the first *touring play, *Mr X*. In 1976 two autonomous gay and *lesbian groups were formed run by a mixed *collective. Despite periodic funding crises, and the controversial Section 28 which forbids the promotion of homosexuality by local authorities, the company, reintegrated in 1984, survived until

1997 when funding was withdrawn. Writers included Martin Sherman, Edward *Bond, Noël Greig, and Bryony Lavery, while actors included Antony *Sher and Simon *Callow.　　CEC

GAY THEATRE AND PERFORMANCE

Various forms of theatrical production conceived and performed by gay men for gay *audiences. By the 1990s, as 'queer' became the conventional term to signify non-normative *gender or sexual identities (*see* QUEER THEORY), 'gay' began to refer specifically to homosexual men. Antecedents of gay drama can be found from the late part of the nineteenth century onward, notably in the work of Oscar *Wilde.

The gay theatre movement itself had its origins in the United States and soon afterwards England in the 1970s. In America, the movement is usually linked to the establishment of *Off- and *Off-Off-Broadway as locales for experimental theatre in the 1960s. In *New York, *Caffe Cino, founded by Joe Cino in 1960, often showcased gay playwrights, including Robert Patrick, Lanford *Wilson, Tom Eyen, H. M. Koutoukas, Ronald Tavel, Jeff Weiss, and Doric Wilson. The Judson Poets Theatre, established by Al Carmines, and Ellen *Stewart's *La Mama Experimental Theatre Club soon followed. Charles *Ludlam and his *Ridiculous Theatrical Company (1967) began to mount a series of plays that helped popularize a new gay aesthetic: drag, exaggerated *acting, 'cheap theatrics', and camp treatment of production values. This highly *metatheatrical and anti-*naturalistic treatment of theatrical performance and design was taken up by other gay companies: the Ballet Trockadero de Monte Carlo, La Gran Scena Opera Company, Hot Peaches, and Bloolips (in England).

In 1968 Mart Crowley's *Boys in the Band* become an Off-Broadway commercial hit. Although it hardly presented a positive image of gay life, Crowley gave mainstream heterosexual audiences the first opportunity to observe gay men interacting with each other, uncensored and without apology. Gay theatrical activity intensified in the 'post-Stonewall' decade of the 1970s. Political activism generated by the gay and lesbian liberation movement led to a wider, more visible community of gay men, thus creating a new audience, less closeted and eager to see itself portrayed on the stage. Newly formed companies dedicated to presenting exclusively gay and *lesbian theatre included Doric Wilson's TOSOS (1974) and John Glines's the Glines (1976). Gay theatre companies sprang up across the country: *San Francisco (Theatre Rhinoceros), *Los Angeles (Celebration Theatre), Houston (Diversity), *Boston (Triangle Theatre), and *Chicago (Lionheart Theatre). In 1978, Terry Helbing formed the Gay Theatre Alliance to help develop and promote gay and lesbian theatre.

Comparable activity surrounded *London's gay theatre, particularly after the Theatres Act of 1968 abolished *censorship. The *Gay Sweatshop, founded in 1975, sought to present positive images of gays and lesbians in contrast to the repressed and homophobic identities that had often been shown in the past. In 1979, Martin Sherman's *Bent*, a play about the Nazis' brutal treatment of gays, opened in the West End, became a hit, and transferred the following year to Broadway. Gay activists soon appropriated the pink triangle as a recovered emblem of gay liberation. In 1981 the Glines' production of Harvey *Fierstein's *Torch Song Trilogy* moved to Broadway, where it ran for several years, winning the Tony *award for best new play. The AIDS epidemic, while decimating the ranks of gay artists and audiences alike, stimulated work that reflected the anger, frustration, and loss felt by the community. *As Is* by William M. *Hoffman and *The Normal Heart* by Larry *Kramer, both produced in 1985, were two early examples of the many plays that dealt in differing ways with the epidemic.

By the 1990s gay plays began to sound the call for integration and empowerment rather than opposition and separatism. Tony *Kushner's two-part *Angels in America* (Broadway, 1992–3), while ostensibly dealing with familiar topics such as the AIDS crisis and internalized homophobia, made a prediction that 'we will become citizens'. Kushner won the Pulitzer Prize and the Tony for best play two years running for both parts of *Angels*. With a heightened awareness of ethnicity, *race, and class within gay communities, the 1990s also brought more diverse voices in gay theatre production, such as Guillermo Reyes (*Hispanic), Chay Yew (*Asian American), and Pomo Afro Homos (*African American). The work of *performance artists like Tim *Miller, Ron Athey, James Lescene, and Eddie Izzard attested to the variety of identities and concerns that gay men possess beyond sexuality. By the early years of the new millennium, gay plays were being developed and mounted in theatres across the United States, Canada, Australia, and Great Britain. Many crossed over to the mainstream commercial theatre and moved from one country to another, giving gay theatre an active international presence.　　RN

BRECHT, STEFAN, *Queer Theatre* (London, 1986)
CLUM, JOHN M., *Still Acting Gay* (New York, 2000)
SINFIELD, ALAN, *Out on Stage* (London, 1999)

GEBRE-MEDHIN, TSEGAYE (1936–)

Ethiopia's most famous and prolific dramatist. A playwright from early youth, he studied theatre in Britain and France in 1959–60 and became director of the Haile Selassie Theatre on his return. Work such as *Ye Kermasow* (*A Man of the Future*, 1965), a play in support of the ordinary people, was supplemented by translations of Shakespeare and *Molière into Amharic and four original plays in English. Gebre-Medhin supported the overthrow of Haile Selassie in 1974 with his play *Ha Hu Ba Sidist Wore* (*ABC in Six Months*), but later alienated theatre personnel and lost control of the National Theatre. Under the military Derg regime he suffered from increasing *censorship; after overthrow he wrote *Ha Hu Wayim Pa Pu* (*ABC or XYZ*) as a rebuttal of his earlier play.   JP

GEJU (*KO-CHÜ*)

Chinese song-and-*dance dramas. The term can be applied to any full-length musical drama, and can even be used to denote Western *opera, but in the People's Republic of *China *geju* normally connotes the communist-inspired, ideologically driven musical shows of the 1940s to the 1970s. *Geju* are still performed by government-sponsored troupes, but the *genre itself, a product of a time when art was explicitly harnessed to the government's social objectives, lost focus in the more pluralist atmosphere at the turn of the twenty-first century (*see* POLITICS AND THEATRE).

Geju have two main roots, *yangge* (rice-planting songs) and traditional Chinese opera. 'Rice-planting songs' were actually short musical dramas, part of village religious *ritual in northeast China. When Mao Zedong and his followers settled in at Yenan in Shensi province in the 1930s, *yangge* presented themselves as a perfect ideological vehicle. Infused by Mao's cultural workers with new content, *yangge* could teach the masses, and since they relied on authentic peasant music, contact with *yangge* could purify the thought of the cultural workers. As early as 1943 'new *yangge*', such as *Xiongmei kai huang* (*Brothers and Sisters Open up Wasteland*), were being performed by the Lu Xun Academy of Arts in Yenan, and the far more famous tale of struggle against an evil landlord, *Baimo nü* (*The White-Haired Girl*), developed the *folk-inspired form into a full-length *musical play. By 1964 *Dongfang hong* (*The East Is Red*) was a nationally famous *spectacle staged by more than a thousand performers. Traditional opera had conditioned the masses to expect musical forms of drama, and *geju* provided an alternative to the rigours of operatic training and the dubious ideological content of most opera *plots (*see* GEMING XIANDAI XI). The government thus found *geju* an attractive vehicle for furthering the state's agenda, from cultivating wasteland to encouraging literacy. Moreover, *geju* could serve as a means of cultural integration by incorporating the music and dances of the various national minorities and disseminating them nationwide.

Geju were group productions. Some originated in village troupes, others were presented by government-sponsored companies, and a system of local, regional, and national *festivals allowed plots and styles to travel on a national level. After the Cultural Revolution, as the government ceased using approved artistic creations as models for mass behaviour, the festival system declined and with it the popularity of *geju*.   KC

GELBART, LARRY (1923–)

American writer for *radio, stage, *film, and *television. One of the top comedy writers of his generation, Gelbart has for dec-

ades proven an astute gag writer with an instinct for the satiric kill. He began writing comedy for the radio while still in his teens and in the 1950s joined the creative staff of television's legendary *Your Show of Shows*. Gelbart tried his hand at playwriting in the 1960s; along with co-librettist Burt Shevelove he distilled *Plautus' surviving canon into the *plot for *A Funny Thing Happened on the Way to the Forum* (1962). His other stage works include a contemporization of Ben *Jonson's *Volpone* as *Sly Fox* (1976), the Reagan-era lampoon *Mastergate* (1989), and the book for the *film noir* *musical spoof *City of Angels* (1989). Gelbart's screenplays include *Tootsie* (1982); he was creator, *producer, and frequent writer for the long-running television series *M*A*S*H*.   EW

GELBER, JACK (1932–)

American playwright and director. Gelber burst onto the *New York scene in 1959 with the *Living Theatre's production of his first play, *The Connection*. Set to live jazz, this *naturalistic drama about a group of heroin-addicted musicians waiting for their drug dealer ran for 778 performances and received three Obie *awards, including best new play. His screen adaptation appeared two years later. Gelber's subsequent work is characterized by a persistent exploration of dramatic form and theatrical presentation. *The Apple* (1961) experiments with *audience perspective as it portrays the life of a supposed madman. Other plays include *Square in the Eye* (1965), *The Cuban Thing* (1968), *Sleep* (1972), and *Rehearsal* (1976). Gelber became a full-time professor at Brooklyn College in 1972, where he founded a graduate programme in playwriting. The following year he received an Obie for his direction of Robert Coover's *The Kid*.   JAB

GÉLINAS, GRATIEN (1909–99)

French-Canadian playwright, actor, director. His contributions to Canadian culture span seven decades, from *radio drama in the early 1930s through comic *monologues, sketches, and *revues, to social dramas for the stage, *film, and *television. For the revues he created Fridolin, initially an endearing street urchin, evolving into a good-humoured critic of social norms and individual foibles, then into the darker title roles of his two best plays, *Tit-Coq* (1948), a social drama from which the advent of modern theatre in Québec is usually dated, and *Bousille et les justes* (*Bousille and the Just*, 1959). *Bousille*, generally considered his best work, is a stinging indictment of Québec society just before its Quiet Revolution, while *Hier les enfants dansaient* (*Yesterday, the Children Were Dancing*, 1966) deals with the stresses caused by that movement. Both were performed at La Comédie-Canadienne, founded by Gélinas in 1958, a much needed venue for home-grown *texts and players.   LED

GELLERT, CHRISTIAN FÜRCHTEGOTT
(1715–69)

German playwright and poet, whose sentimental *comedies typified the *bourgeois taste of the Enlightenment period. Their success was less determined by their dramatic form than by their moral content, which emphasized middle-class values and elevated them to universal guidelines of human behaviour. He defended the sentimentality and exemplary behaviour of his model characters in the treatise *Pro Comoedia Commovente* (1751). *See also* NEOCLASSICISM.   GB

GELMAN, ALEKSANDR (1933–   )

Soviet/Russian playwright. Gelman is best known for his 'production dramas' of the 1970s and 1980s, which set industrial themes against the psychological investigation of *characters. *Minutes of a Meeting* (1976) investigates a factory's refusal to accept a bonus after having forged the figures. *Alone with Everyone* (or *A Man with Connections*, 1982) explores a crisis between husband and wife after an industrial accident in which their son loses both hands and for which the father is responsible. Oleg *Efremov, who shared Gelman's concern for truth, directed his work at the *Moscow Art Theatre, but so far Gelman has not written plays since perestroika.   BB

GELOSI

Probably the earliest named troupe of Italian *commedia dell'arte* actors, first recorded and identified in 1568. (Their name translates as 'Zealous', rather than 'Jealous'.) They visited France as early as 1571, and then later in 1603–4, thus beginning the process whereby *Paris became a magnet for the best Italian theatre practitioners. In 1578 (it is thought) they were joined by Francesco and Isabella *Andreini, who together became a star attraction and provided the company's identity, to the extent that when Isabella died and Francesco retired in 1604 that identity became unsustainable. However, they also attracted other leading actors such as Vittoria Piissimi, whose star presence was alternated with that of Isabella at the famous Florentine wedding interludes of 1589. The Gelosi were renowned particularly for their ensemble teamwork and their versatility: whether or not they were the first performers of *Tasso's *Aminta*, their repertoire included all *genres, both scripted and improvised. *See also* COMÉDIE ITALIENNE.   RAA

GÉMIER, FIRMIN (1869–1933)

French actor and director. Acting extensively at the Théâtre *Libre before creating the title role in *Jarry's *Ubu roi* at the Théâtre de l'*Œuvre (1896), Gémier began to direct in the footsteps of *Antoine, finally taking the directorial helm of the Théâtre *Antoine from 1906 to 1922. Strongly committed to the idea of a people's theatre, he embarked on several eclectic and influential projects that would lay the groundwork for a popular and decentralized theatre in France. The founder of the Société Shakespeare, his production style for plays such as *The Merchant of Venice* (1916) and *The Taming of the Shrew* (1918) prefigured that of later innovators. Foreshadowing the architectural innovations of *Copeau and *Jouvet at the *Vieux-Colombier, Gémier restructured the Théâtre Antoine to admit greater performer–*audience interaction. For two years he made a bold (and financially disastrous) attempt to create a Théâtre Ambulant outside *Paris, for which a 1,650-seat tent theatre travelled from city to city. He briefly took over the operation of the Cirque d'Hiver, which he saw as a model for the communal ethos of ancient *Greek theatre, put to the test in his popular production of Saint-Georges de Bouheliér's *Oedipus, King of Thebes* (1919). During the 1920s, in addition to directing the *Odéon, Gémier directed the newly created *Théâtre National Populaire at the Palais de Trocadéro, an underfunded and impractical venture that would not be fully realized until after the Second World War.   DGM

GEMING XIANDAI XI (KO MING HSIEN TAI HSI)

'Revolutionary modern drama', Chinese plays with revolutionary themes, the only theatrical repertoire permitted during the Cultural Revolution. Despite the performance of modern plays, Mao was not pleased to see 'many Communists enthusiastic about promoting feudal and capitalist art instead of socialist art'. In 1963 Mao's wife Jiang Qing, a former *film star in *Shanghai, took an interest in developing revolutionary plays that 'help the masses to propel history forward'. Faced with resistance from the Cultural Ministry and the mayor of Beijing, Jiang found allies in younger *jingju (Beijing opera) actors and the mayor of Shanghai, who enthusiastically endorsed her plan in his opening speech to the East China Drama Festival in Shanghai that year. Although the two sides struck a temporary balance in 1964, Mao and Jiang did not win final victory until after the start of the Cultural Revolution.

Also called *geming yangban xi* (revolutionary model drama), the original eight model plays, performed in Beijing in 1967 to celebrate the 25th anniversary of Mao's *Yan'an Talks*, included five *jingju* (*The Red Lantern*, *Shajia Bang*, *Raid on the White Tiger Regiment*, *Taking the Tiger Mountain by Strategy*, and *On the Docks*), two *wujü or *dance-dramas (*Red Detachment of Women* and *The White-Haired Girl*); and the symphonic music from *Shajia Bang*. In the early 1970s several other revolutionary *jingju* received permission for performance, including the *Hymn of Dragon River*, *Battle on the Plain*, *The Dujuan Mountain*, *Red Detachment of Women* (a play based

Performance of *Raid on the White Tiger Regiment* in China, 1967. One of eight *geming xiandai xi* or 'revolutionary modern dramas' permitted during the Cultural Revolution, this text was in the *jingju* (Beijing opera) style, despite the proletarian scenery and costumes. A portrait of Mao is prominently hung upstage centre.

on the earlier *wujü* version), and *Panshi Wan*. These works were also adapted locally by inserting different tunes into the original scripts. The model drama departed radically from traditional Chinese theatre. Aside from the revolutionary subject matter and highly simplified heroes of 'workers, peasants and soldiers', the model plays used Beijing dialect, much plainer *make-up and *costumes, more complicated *scenery and *lighting, *act and *scene divisions, and a symphonic orchestra. Banned from performance after the Cultural Revolution, *geming xiandai xi* were revived in the late 1980s and early 1990s as an attempt to boost the image of the Communist Party after the Tiananmen incident and the fall of communism in Europe and the former Soviet Union. They were received with a mixture of suspicion and cynicism, but also with a sense of nostalgia by the generation who had grown up with them as their sole entertainment.

SYL

GEMS, PAM (1925–)

English playwright. Gems came to playwriting relatively late in life, at 47, after having raised a family. Establishing herself with

Ed Berman's Almost Free Theatre in the early 1970s, she found success with *Duse, Fish, Stas and Vi* (which premièred at the *Edinburgh Festival as *Dead Fish*) in 1976. Although the work solidified her reputation as a *feminist playwright, Gems was criticized in some feminist quarters for writing the suicide of her politically active *protagonist, Fish, after a failed romantic relationship. *Guinevere* (Edinburgh Festival, 1976) inaugurated an approach that was to become her hallmark: a biographical drama that is also a feminist reworking of a well-known myth or novel. She continued in this vein with *Queen Christina* for the *Royal Shakespeare Company in 1977. The RSC also produced *Piaf* (1978) about the French singer, which garnered its star, Jane Lapotaire, both an Olivier and a Tony *award for best actress. Through the next decade, Gems continued to revision stories of women in plays such as *Camille* (1984), *La Pasionara* (1985), and *The Blue Angel* (1991), as well as writing adaptations such as *Przybyszewska's *The Danton Affair* (1986) and *Chekhov's *Uncle Vanya* (1991). She had another hit with the Royal *National Theatre production of *Stanley* (1996) about painter Stanley Spencer, which won the Olivier award for best play and best actor (for Antony *Sher). In 1999 Sian

Phillips starred as the elderly Marlene Dietrich in Gems's *Marlene*.   MDG

GENDER AND PERFORMANCE *see page 510*

GENÉ, JUAN CARLOS (1928–)

Argentinian actor, director, and playwright. Author of eight plays, Gené has worked in theatre since the 1950s. *The Blacksmith and the Devil* (1955) is the best-known product of his independent theatre years. During the 1960s he worked on stage and *television with the group Theatre People. In 1977 he was exiled to Venezuela, where he co-founded Grupo Actoral 80 in 1983. The group has staged several of his plays, including *Knocks at my Door* (1984, later a *film) and *Memorial of a Murdered Lamb* (1986). Gené returned to Argentina in the 1990s, serving briefly as director of the Teatro *Municipal General San Martín.   JGJ

GÉNERO CHICO

A nineteenth-century popular form imported to Argentina from Spain. A number of short pieces fall into this category, including *operettas and *revues, which presented various familiar *character types. Boulevard sketches depicting life on *Madrid's central avenue, for example, were quickly adapted to the *Buenos Aires milieu.   AV

GENET, JEAN (1910–86)

French playwright associated with the theatre of the *absurd. After the troubled early life of an orphan, spent in reformatories and as an itinerant and petty criminal, Genet's literary career began while in prison, where he wrote novels in a homoerotic and poetic language, focusing on themes of crime, homosexuality, and the marginalized in society. His subsequent plays present life as a series of transactions between masters and servants; the drama resides in the tensions between images of self and the fragility of their construction. Genet's work exposes the roles we play as illusions by relying on overt *theatricality. *Ritual, transformation, and the interchangeability of identity are all characteristics of his drama; so too is his rejection of *plot and *character psychology. His first play, *Haute Surveillance* (*Deathwatch*, not performed until 1949), features

Jean **Genet**'s *The Balcony*, a Royal Shakespeare Company production at the Aldwych Theatre, London, 1971, directed by Terry Hands, designed by Farrah. In an exaggerated and enlarged *costume, the General (Philip Locke) plays out fantasies of dominance and submission with one of the prostitutes.

the tensions and battles for supremacy of three prisoners in one cell, while another watches. *Les Bonnes* (*The Maids*, directed by *Jouvet, 1947) shows two servants acting a mistress-and-servant ritual, exposing their hatred of their oppression and of themselves for participating in it. Self-loathing carried on to *Le Balcon* (*The Balcony*, directed by *Brook, 1956), which features pillar-of-society characters (bishop, judge, general) being 'enacted' in master-and-servant ritual games in various fantasy rooms in a brothel, while a revolution is raging outside to topple those very characters in real life.

Genet's final two plays *Les Nègres* (*The Blacks*, directed by Roger *Blin, 1959) and *Les Paravents* (*The Screens*, written 1961; directed by Blin, 1966) added *race to his theatrical ritual of power and domination. In the former, a troupe of black actors perform the ritualistic murder of a white woman before a jury of blacks wearing white masks. The play is not so much concerned with the representation of a race crime but with the *performativity of race. *The Screens*, Genet's most adventurous work, is a long investigation of the Algerian conflict—screens are used to point out how reality can never be essentialized, and that the images of a reality reflected on screens are always only images. These last two plays show how the imperialist legacy is a mentality that persists long after colonial systems have been dismantled. Genet's work was vilified in its day by the far right, and considered by many to be subversive. An outsider in his early life as a criminal, and throughout his life as homosexual, he was championed by the intellectual left, who secured a presidential pardon from a sentence of life imprisonment for recurrent theft. The greatest tribute was *Sartre's major study, *Saint-Genet, Actor and Martyr* (1952), in which Genet's appropriation of the label of *villain placed upon him by society is seen as an act of resistance and defiance: an appropriation which would later be termed 'queer' (*see* QUEER THEORY). From the mid-1960s he virtually gave up writing but continued to lecture and support radical causes, including the Black Panthers and Palestinian liberation groups. Numerous companies and directors have returned to Genet's work, from the *Living Theatre's *Maids* (1965) and Víctor *García's *The Balcony* (1969) to *Chéreau's *Screens* and *Stein's *Blacks* (both 1983).   BRS

GENRE

The four traditional genres supplied a typology for basic criticism of *drama, defining outlines and the broad distinctions among them. But continual rebellions and enlargements forced them to keep admitting exceptions to the old definitions. A *tragedy* once portrayed the defeat or downfall—not necessarily the death—of a figure of high standing, because of stupidity or stubbornness. But the mid-nineteenth century introduced *protagonists created by Friedrich *Hebbel, Henrik *Ibsen, August *Strindberg, and other middle- and lower-class roles to which the adjective 'tragic' applies more accurately when the roles in

(continued on p. 511)

GENDER AND PERFORMANCE

A concern with identity politics has made issues of gender fundamental to late twentieth- and early twenty-first-century culture. The significance of gender in determining social behaviour and in defining power relations between men and women has been a major part of cultural debates since the 1970s. Theatre, like other cultural practices, has developed ways of engaging with *theories of gender and has devised critical approaches to performance which foreground gender identity and offer critiques of narrow representations of masculine and feminine ways of being. The term 'gender' refers to the socially constructed division between the sexes. It is concerned with the culturally determined group of attributes, including emotional and psychological characteristics, which differentiate masculinity and femininity. 'Sex', on the other hand, designates the biological and physiological differences between male and female. Culture ascribes particular gender qualities to maleness or to femaleness, and expectations of masculine or feminine social behaviour are assigned to the male and female child. Theories of gender, deriving from *feminism and studies of masculinity and sexuality, aim to unravel the patriarchal and heterosexual hegemonies which dominate culture. They attempt to clarify the distinction between sex and gender, enabling an analysis of the cultural formation of gender roles and opening up possibilities for change. From the separation of sex and gender comes the notion that although the child is biologically defined as male or female at birth, it is society, rather than a process of nature, which shapes women and men.

From its early history, questions of gender have been significant for theatre. Theatre performance depends upon the construction of fictive roles which are separate from the actors' identities. In many historical forms, such as ancient *Greek, *Japanese, and English *early modern theatre, where women were prohibited from appearing on stage, female roles were created by male actors. The female role was produced through a set of coded visual signs (gesture, *costume, *mask, etc.) designed to convey 'woman' to the *audience. Whether the audience was made aware of the distinction between actor and role as in Japanese *nō theatre, or the male/female distinction was blurred as in *kabuki where the *onnagata actor aimed to impersonate the female in every detail, there was a tension between masculinity and femininity in the performance. In many of Shakespeare's plays, for example *Twelfth Night* and *As You Like It*, this tension was developed to create a critique of gender and sexuality dependent upon the ironic aware-ness of the gender split between *character and *actor, cross-dressing, and confused identities.

In modern theatre questions of gender have been raised in several ways. First, there have been revisions of Western theatre history and a reworking of the theatrical canon to re-assess historical gender roles and to critique gender relationships in dramatic literature. The application of contemporary theories of gender and sexuality to canonical *texts has produced radical performances which challenge traditional interpretations of texts. Furthermore, there have been rediscoveries of 'forgotten' writers, such as the seventeenth-century woman playwright Aphra *Behn, whose life and work challenge received notions of the ways women lived and were portrayed in theatre.

Second, issues of gender—historical, social, and political—have become major themes in the work of many late twentieth-century playwrights and theatre practitioners, exemplified by feminist playwrights Megan *Terry and Pam *Gems, whose plays examine the role of women in society, and by Martin Sherman and David *Rabe, whose plays focus on questions of sexuality and masculinity. Forms of theatre and performance have been developed which enable the deconstruction of gender roles in history and contemporary society. Drawing on models of practice developed by *Brecht, writers such as Caryl *Churchill in *Cloud Nine* (1979) and Simone Benmussa in *The Singular Life of Albert Nobbs* (1978) have used the separation of actor and role to foreground the social construction of gender as separate from sex, and developed strategies of alienation (*Verfremdung) to draw attention to the political implications of the cultural construction of gender.

Third, using Lacanian *psychoanalytic theory and feminist approaches derived from the French theoreticians Hélène *Cixous, Julia Kristeva, and Luce Irigaray, playwrights and performers have experimented with new forms of theatre aesthetics which dismantle traditional representational modes and offer new ways of delineating gender subjectivity. Marguerite *Duras in *India Song*, Caryl Churchill in *A Mouthful of Birds*, and Tony *Kushner in *Angels in America* disrupt traditional narrative structures and character coherence in order to foreground fluid gender identities. One effect of this emphasis is to focus on the body, for example in strategies of drag, cross-dressing, and *male and *female impersonation. The work of German choreographer/director Pina *Bausch and the British *physical theatre company DV8 crosses the boundaries between *dance and theatre, using the physical skills of dancers in theatrical performances which centre on corporeal inscriptions of socially determined gendered behaviour.

Issues of gender have been a priority for live *performance artists such as Rose English, Annie Sprinkle, Orlan, Karen *Finley, and Holly *Hughes, who are interested in examining questions of subjectivity. Rather than focusing on theatrical role play, this work uses the body of the artist as a site for exploring how sexual and gender identities are 'performed'. Postmodernism, feminism, and psychoanalysis have all theorized gender identity as performative. Developing the work of J. L. Austin, Judith Butler has described gender construction as proceeding through an endless process of citation and reiteration. She does not ally this notion of *performativity with theatre. Gender performativity is not a self-conscious perform-

ance involving the voluntary adoption of patterns of behaviour but a process whereby models of gender conduct are unconsciously absorbed. Nevertheless, Butler's theories of performativity have had an impact on the theory and practice of live art and theatre, since self-conscious performance can reveal the functioning of unconscious performativity. *See also* FEMINIST THEATRE; LESBIAN THEATRE; GAY THEATRE; QUEER THEORY; MODERNISM AND POSTMODERNISM; STRUCTURALISM AND POST-STRUCTURALISM.   LT

AUSLANDER, PHILIP, *From Acting to Performance: essays in modernism and postmodernism* (London, 1997)
GOODMAN, LIZBETH, *The Gender Reader* (London, 1999)
HARRIS, GERALDINE, *Staging Femininities: performance and performativity* (London, 1999)

question undergo a severe, self-inflicted downfall. In a *melodrama the downfall comes about because of opposition from a foe or more than one; the loser, whether *hero or *villain, becomes a victim, or even a society's scapegoat. A *comedy takes a positive direction: the protagonist wins a lover, marriage partner, perhaps wealth and acclaim, and *laughter from onlookers. A *farce also ends on an upward note for its heroic roles and disgrace or confusion (or worse) for the antagonists, but its stage movements may rely on physicality and be more troubling to watch than comedy.

Overlapping genres: what of a play or *film, a western, say, or a thriller, in which a private eye, an honest cop, a husband or mother bent on revenge defeats enemies? Strict interpretation might stamp this mixture a comedy, but it *feels* like a melodrama (*see also* REVENGE TRAGEDY). Similarly, *Euripides' Medea, a tragedy for the protagonist who kills her own children, is also a sober comedy since her murders enable her to triumph over her unfaithful husband. Italian and French critics of the fifteenth and sixteenth centuries (*see* NEOCLASSICISM) tried to attach more precise labels to such cases by coining *'tragicomedy' for a comic structure with a tragic ending (Shakespeare's *Troilus and Cressida*) or a tragic structure with a comic ending (Ingmar *Bergman's film *Ansiktet* (*The Face* or *The Magician*), 1958). As for a tragicomedy in which the texture throughout is simultaneously funny and sad (Ibsen's *The Wild Duck*, 1885, or *Chekhov's *The Cherry Orchard*, 1904), J. L. Styan's term 'dark comedy' is sometimes appropriate. As a further complication, tragedy is widely considered the noblest of the genres and implicitly the finest. But if tragedy is a true genre, it cannot also serve as a mark of superiority, any more than farce can be accepted as a cheap term of abuse.

Many critics frequently qualify the basic genres to narrow or amplify a description: a *historical melodrama, an epic tragedy, a spectacular comedy, a balletic farce. Without mandates from official academies such as the French, which gave Pierre *Corneille a difficult time when *The Cid* (1637) did not meet the

membership's stern standards, pure genres stand little chance of holding on to approval while theatre continues to take advantage of surprises and happy discoveries. By the later twentieth century some genres had almost given way to sub-genres, stimulating bookfuls of dramatic discourse. Under the influence of post-*structuralism, the entire concept of genre has become critically embattled. *See also* THEORIES OF DRAMA, THEATRE, AND PERFORMANCE; MODERNISM AND POSTMODERNISM.   ACB

BENTLEY, ERIC, *The Life of the Drama* (New York, 1964)

GENTLEMAN, FRANCIS (1728–84)

Irish actor and author, who began his career performing in Thomas Sheridan's *Smock Alley company in *Dublin in 1749. Like Sheridan, Gentleman went on to be both an actor and an elocutionist. He acted in Dublin and *Bath before going to *London in the 1750s. Never a success, he nonetheless found some stability at *Foote's summer theatre in the early 1770s, performing mostly comic roles. But he is best known for his *farce *The Tobacconist* (1760, rev. 1771), and for his *criticism in *The Dramatic Censor* (1770), which the *Biographical Dictionary* calls one of the 'most considerable and extended critical commentaries on both plays and performers written by an actor until the nineteenth century'. And although John Bell's edition of Shakespeare does not bear Gentleman's name, in 1772 Bell commissioned Gentleman to annotate the plays and write introductory material.   MJK

GEORGE, MLLE (MARGUERITE-JOSÉPHINE WEIMER) (1787–1867)

French actress. Born into an acting family, she came to the notice of Mlle *Raucourt, who secured her entry to the *Comédie-Française. Making her debut in 1802, she partnered *Talma in many of the classical roles for which her queenly beauty and regal manner fitted her; a different kind of partnership was her liaison with Napoleon. After a successful spell in Russia, followed by a further period at the Comédie, she helped to ensure the success of some of the more *melodramatic plays of the *romantic repertory. As the mistress of Harel, who *managed the *Odéon and then the *Porte-Saint-Martin theatres, she created the roles of Marguerite de Bourgogne in *Dumas *père*'s *Tour de Nesle* (1832) and the eponymous *heroines of *Hugo's *Lucrèce Borgia* and *Marie Tudor* (both 1833). Ending her career at the Comédie-Française, she gave her farewell performance as Rodogune in *Corneille's play of that name in 1853.

WDH

GERMAIN, JEAN-CLAUDE (1939–)

Québec playwright, director. In 1969 he founded the anti-establishment Théâtre du Même Nom, a parodic anagram (TMN) of Québec's conservative Théâtre du *Nouveau Monde (TNM), which presented some of the liveliest theatre of the 1970s, featuring home-grown talent, preferably iconoclastic, and generally in Québec's homely popular speech. Here many of his own works were staged: about 30 to date, most with untranslatable titles, such as the historically revisionist *A Canadian Play/Une plaie canadienne* (1980) punning on the homonym meaning 'wound' in French. Germain has taught at the National Theatre School since 1972.

LED

GERMANOVA, MARIA (1884–1940)

Russian/Soviet actress who began her career at the *Moscow Art Theatre. From 1902 to 1919 she appeared there in a range of roles including Grushenka (*The Brothers Karamazov*), Agnes (*Ibsen's *Brand*), and the eponymous Ekaterina Ivanovna in *Andreev's play, in all of which her emotional intensity shone through. Her exceptional height and facial expressiveness contributed to a powerful stage presence, which could be seen on *tour with the Art Theatre Prague Group from 1919 to 1930, when she retired from the stage. She also appeared as Ekaterina Ivanovna and as Anna Karenina on *film.

NW

GERSHWIN, GEORGE (JACOB GERSHVIN) (1898–1937) AND IRA (ISRAEL GERSHVIN) (1896–1983)

American composer and American lyricist. The Gershwin brothers were two of the most gifted and popular songwriters in *musical theatre. Ira was reflective and bookish, a genial intellectual who loved wordplay and avidly read W. S. *Gilbert, P. G. *Wodehouse, and *Shaw. George was a torrent of restless energy, talent, and drive—he was playing piano by ear at the age of 10 and began serious instruction at 12. Their early musical and theatrical influences included Irving *Berlin, ragtime, and Jerome *Kern's Princess Theatre musicals. In 1914 George became a song plugger for the Remick publishing company. His piano playing soon drew admiration from such established figures as ragtime great Eubie *Blake, Berlin, and Kern, for whom Gershwin was often *rehearsal pianist. In 1919 he wrote his first hit song, 'Swanee' (lyrics by Irving Caesar), and his first Broadway score, *La La Lucille* (lyrics by Howard Jackson and Buddy *DeSylva). From 1920 to 1924 George wrote such songs as 'I'll Build a Stairway to Paradise' (1922) for George *White's annual *revue, *Scandals*. Up to 1924 Ira wrote lyrics under the pseudonym Arthur Francis (the first names of another brother and a sister), but subsequently he worked under his own name and almost exclusively with George.

Their first hit show, *Lady, Be Good* (1924), carried forward Kern's style of light-hearted, witty musical shows and infused it with a solid jazz feel and snappy, conversational lyrics. Gershwin musicals up to 1930, including *TipToes* (1925), *Oh, Kay!* (1926), *Funny Face* (1927), and *Girl Crazy* (1930), showcased the premier talents of the musical stage, including Fred *Astaire, Ethel *Merman, and Gertrude *Lawrence. When the Great Depression arrived, the frivolous musical comedies of the 1920s lost much of their appeal. The Gershwins responded with *Strike up the Band* (1930), an anti-war *satire, and *Of Thee I Sing* (1931), a political spoof that won the Pulitzer Prize. Its integration of *music, song, and *dialogue revealed a sophistication of technique and content then rare on Broadway. The sequel, *Let 'Em Eat Cake* (1933), had an even stronger satiric tone. George considered it his finest work to date. The Gershwins' theatrical career culminated in the ambitious *Porgy and Bess* (1935). Since the mid-1920s, George had wanted to create an *opera based on Dubose Heyward's short novel *Porgy*, which was set in a black neighbourhood in Charleston. Despite some confusion as to whether it was opera or musical theatre, the show's stature has grown in the intervening years, and it is now considered one of the Gershwins' masterpieces.

George's untimely death cut short one of the century's great musical talents. No other American composer more successfully straddled the worlds of 'serious' and popular music or more completely embodied the spirit of the Jazz Age. From *cabaret to the world's concert halls, the Gershwins made American popular music the world's popular music. Ira went on to write lyrics with Kern, Kurt *Weill, Harold *Arlen, and other noted songwriters. The last show on which he worked, *My One and Only*, opened in *New York in 1983 and ran for 762 performances. Ed Jablonski's *The Gershwin Years* (1996) is one of many treatments worth attention.

SN

GERSHWIN THEATRE

*New York *playhouse located on Broadway between 50th and 51st Streets. Designed by Ralph Alswang, and opened as the

Uris in 1972, it was Broadway's first new theatre since 1931. This large theatre, seating 1,900, and intended for *musicals, was considered an architectural eyesore with poor acoustics, and the tall office building into which it was incorporated was criticized for ruining the area's low-rise look. Inside the theatre is a wall of names called the Theatre Hall of Fame. Among the theatre's relatively few notable shows was *Sweeney Todd* (1979). The Uris was renamed the Gershwin in 1983.   SLL

GHELDERODE, MICHEL DE (ADEMAR MARTENS) (1898–1962)

Belgian playwright. Though he wrote in French, Ghelderode's work is markedly Flemish in spirit, characterized by a combination of popular, *folkloric, fantastic, and strongly visual elements. His early work did not appeal to French-speaking *audiences but matched the style of the *Vlaamse Volkstoneel, the popular modernist Flemish company, which from 1924 developed a highly *expressionist code. Ghelderode's plays written for the company include *Images de la vie de Saint-François d'Assise* (*Pictures from the Life of St Francis*, 1927), a *burlesque *spectacle; *Escurial* (1927), in which the Spanish sovereign and his Flemish *fool exchange roles; and *Barrabas* (1928), a *Passion play seen from the point of view of an anarchist. Of particular interest is *Pantagleize* (1929), whose eponymous (anti-)*hero becomes unknowingly involved in a revolution and is executed. Pantagleize represents the little man in the jungle of city life as well as the poet who is unable to adapt to modern society.

Ghelderode considered *Mademoiselle Jaïre* (1934) his most characteristic work, a quasi-*mystery play in which a young girl is resuscitated from death but continues to long for the other world. Integrating biblical materials in a local context, the play contains a striking mixture of religious elements, popular humour, repressed eroticism, and macabre tone. It was not until the late 1940s and early 1950s that Ghelderode's work was discovered in France. The post-war *avant-garde recognized him as a kindred spirit, sharing elements with the theatre of the *absurd and the theatre of *cruelty. He created a *total theatre, invoking all the senses and making use of *masks, *clowns, *mime, *magic, and *ritual, with *characters who are often *allegoric and symbolic.   JDV

GHERARDI FAMILY

Italian actors residing in France. **Giovanni** (d. 1683), born in Spoleto, took his own mask of Flautino to France around 1675: he had a talent for imitating musical instruments with his voice. His son **Evaristo** (1663-1700) was a great Arlecchino/*Harlequin, taking formal possession of the role in *Paris after the death of *Biancolelli in 1688. After the 1697 expulsion he performed privately, and died from a fall sustained on stage. In his volumes of *Théâtre italien*, published from 1694 onwards, he recorded and codified the contributions of the *Comédie Italienne to French theatre. His son **Jean-Baptiste** (1696–?) continued into the eighteenth century.   RAA

GHOSH, GIRISH CHANDRA (1844–1912)

Bengali *actor-manager and dramatist. Starting his career as a composer of theatre *music, he acted on the *amateur Calcutta (*Kolkata) stage before leaving his desk job to turn professional, managing the National Theatre from 1880. Although he organized companies well, he could never stay tied to one for long. He established the popular idiom for *Bengali public stage by combining spectacular entertainment and stylized declamatory acting, equally influenced by *folk and Western models. He trained his actors intensively, winning fame as the 'father of Bengali theatre'. The author of approximately 80 plays, Ghosh tried his hand at many *genres: mythological, historical, social, nationalistic, *musical, and comic. Many of the mythological works, like *Bilwamangal Thakur* (1886), proved commercially successful, but critics rank the social *melodrama *Praphulla* (1889) as his best. In the final decade of his life, some of his patriotic plays, all of which did well at the box office, brought him into conflict with the British administration, who banned *Sirajuddaula* (1905), for example, about the last nawab of Bengal (*see* DRAMATIC PERFORMANCES ACT). Ghosh also translated or adapted classics by Shakespeare and *Molière. His prose writings on Bengali theatre throw some light on his *acting methods.   AL

GHOST

Stage figure of *revenge tragedy, who predicts or demands retribution for a past wrong. Rare in *Greek *tragedy, the figure was firmly established by *Seneca, whose bloodthirsty shades were models for *early modern dramatists, especially in Italy. Brilliantly exploited by Shakespeare in *Hamlet*, the figure was a staple of Jacobean tragedy as well.   RWV

GIACOMETTI, PAOLO (1816–82)

Italian playwright. Influenced by *romanticism, Giacometti believed in a national, popular theatre with humanitarian and educational goals. From 1848 to 1852 he was resident poet of Turin's prestigious Reale Sarda Company. Thereafter his works—numbering over 80, many of them *melodramatic *historical dramas—served as vehicles for prominent *actor-managers (*Bellotti-Bon, *Ristori, *Salvini, *Zacconi, *Novelli). *La Morte civile* (1861), considered his finest problem play, addresses the theme of divorce when the husband is a convicted murderer. It afforded actors the opportunity to horrify *audiences with *realistic portrayals of a man suffering the agonies of suicide by poison.   JEH

GIACOSA, GIUSEPPE (1847–1906)

Italian dramatist and librettist. Best known as the librettist, with Luigi Illica, of *Puccini's *operas *La Bohème* (1896), *Tosca* (1900), and *Madama Butterfly* (1904), Giacosa also enjoyed significant success as a dramatist. His early plays, including the popular *Game of Chess* (1871) and *Triumph of Love* (1872), are late *romantic works with poetic charm but little dramatic vigour. After several *historical dramas and light *comedies, Giacosa came under the influence of *realism in the work of *Ibsen, *Zola, and *Becque. His finest *verismo dramas are *Unhappy Love* (1889), a tense and tautly structured play on an adulterous triangle, which avoids easy moral judgements, and *Like Falling Leaves* (1900), in which a rich family falls upon hard times, during which their life of luxury is shown to have undermined their capacity to survive. Giacosa, who wrote 32 plays in all, was never an original dramatist, but he introduced into the Italian theatre *naturalistic themes from northern Europe that did much to prepare for its revival in the early twentieth century.   SJCW

GIBBONS, RAWLE (1950–)

Trinidadian director and playwright influenced by *Brecht, the Nigerian Femi *Osofisan, and the Jamaican Dennis *Scott. As an undergraduate at the University of the West Indies in Jamaica, Gibbons founded the Caribbean Theatre Workshop with Tony Smith. Since his Master's thesis on traditional Trinidadian performance, he has been interested in *ritual theatre which expresses strategies for the liberation of *Caribbean culture from colonial influences (*see* POST-COLONIAL STUDIES). He has directed for *Sistren in Jamaica, as well as directing Derek *Walcott's *Ti-Jean and his Brothers* and *Dream on Monkey Mountain* (1984), C. L. R. James's *The Black Jacobins* (1979), and Dennis *Scott's *Dog* (1980). Gibbons's own plays include *Mano* (1973) and *Shepherd* (1981). *I Lawah* (*The Warrior-King*, 1984), a brilliant articulation of the importance of Caribbean tradition, takes Errol *Hill's advice to use *carnival for inspiration, and portrays the community of Hell Yard in Trinidad during the Canbouley riots in 1881. *A Calypso Trilogy* (published 1999, including *Sing de Chorus*, *Ah Wanna Fall*, *Ten to One*) shows a further commitment to carnival and *audience participation.   ES

GIDE, ANDRÉ (1869–1951)

French novelist, critic, and playwright. Gide was educated in Paris but vacations in Algeria led him away from the strictures of his Protestant upbringing, and he openly advocated homosexuality in his treatise *Corydon* (1920). His plays had less crit-ical success than his other works, but they paved the way for *Camus and *Sartre through an original style with little connection to *symbolist, *neoclassical, or *naturalist theatre; thoughtful and ambiguous, they lack climactic *plots and emphasize ideas over *action. *Saul* (produced 1922, written 1903) concerns a love triangle among King Saul, David, and Jonathan. In *Le Retour de l'enfant prodige* (*The Return of the Prodigal Son*, 1928; written 1907), the prodigal persuades his brother to run away with him. *Oedipe* (1932) changes *Sophocles' play to a battle between individuality and submission to religious authority. Gide translated *Antony and Cleopatra* (1920), and his *Hamlet* (1946) opened the *Renaud–*Barrault company's first season. He also wrote an adaptation of Kafka's *The Trial* for Barrault. Other plays include *Philoctète* (1919), *Persephone* (1934; later a Stravinsky *opera, 1950), and *Robert; ou, L'Intérêt général* (*Robert; or, The General Interest*, 1946).   FL

GIEHSE, THERESE (1898–1975)

German actress. Born in *Munich, Giehse balanced throughout her career the popular Bavarian with the intellectual *Brechtian tradition. Forced into exile by the Nazis, she emigrated to Zurich where she founded a political *cabaret and played the original Mother Courage (1941), a role she repeated in a number of productions. She joined *Brecht at the *Berliner Ensemble from 1949 to 1952, and thereafter divided her time between Zurich and Munich. Her last major role was in Peter *Stein's production of Brecht's *The Mother* (1970), a living link with the Brechtian tradition that the *Schaubühne endeavoured to demonstrate in its inaugural production.   CBB

GIELGUD, JOHN (1904–2000)

English actor and director. Longevity as well as achievement made Gielgud into the icon of traditional values in English *acting in the twentieth century. But his respect for the *text and for the skills he epitomized often overshadowed critics' understanding of the quirky brilliance of his performances, his fascination with new forms of theatre, and his surprising ability to remake himself to suit successive models of performance. Gielgud came from a strong theatre *family: Ellen *Terry was his great-aunt (*see also* TERRY FAMILY). Family connections did him no harm in his early career as, after training at the *Royal Academy of Dramatic Art, he made his debut as the English Herald in *Henry V* (1921) and began to be recognized as prodigiously talented. By 1924 he was playing leading roles in *London, including Romeo (the first of four times) but also in *Ibsen, *Chekhov, and *Shaw. With his Richard II (1929) and Hamlet (1930, a role he would play in over 500 performances in six different productions up to 1946), he was established as the greatest lyric actor of his generation, his voice praised for its musicality and its romantic potency: as he mockingly commented later, 'I spoke

Ralph Richardson as Jack and John **Gielgud** as Harry in David Storey's *Home*, Royal Court Theatre, London, 1970, directed by Lindsay Anderson. A pairing of two of Britain's best-loved actors, repeated in Harold Pinter's *No Man's Land* in 1975.

rather well, but rather too well, and fell in love with my own voice.' Above all, he spoke with an overwhelming awareness of the *verse line, rejecting *naturalism in delivery while never losing sight of his *characters' reality. His Hamlet was cynical and witty as well as a poet prince, and his performances always worked through minutely controlled variations of pace. Moving in *tragedy, Gielgud also proved himself the consummate master of classical *comedy in *Congreve, *Sheridan, and especially as John Worthing in *The Importance of Being Earnest* (1930, 1939, 1942, 1947). What for many was the exhibition of exquisite taste and for a few was an excess of fastidiousness defined his supreme authority within the limits he prescribed for himself.

In the 1930s he used his prestige as an actor to become a director, working frequently with the three then unknown designers who formed *Motley to find a new style for Shakespeare production that used permanent sets to bring speed to the flow of *scenes. At the New Theatre (1934–7) and the Queen's Theatre (1937–8) in London, Gielgud found a new *managerial style, creating a genuine ensemble of superb actors to explore the classical repertory, a combination of what he sought in Shake-

speare and had learned from Chekhov. His own performances continued to gain almost unstinting praise, especially as Richard in Daviot's *Richard of Bordeaux* (1932), which made him even more of a popular star. His roles included Shylock, Romeo, Mercutio (when *Olivier took over as Romeo), an icily manipulative Joseph Surface in *Sheridan's *School for Scandal*, and Benedick in *Much Ado About Nothing*, often playing opposite Peggy *Ashcroft. His 1934 Hamlet, which later went to *New York, probably his finest performance of the role, may have been strongly aware of tradition but his staging was also influenced by the experimental *Moscow Art Theatre version (1912) directed by *Stanislavsky and his second cousin, Edward Gordon *Craig. No dry traditionalist, Gielgud was excited early by the work of Granville *Barker and *Komisarjevsky and would encourage Michel *Saint-Denis and Peter *Brook.

The first years after the war were difficult. Gielgud was less admired than Ralph *Richardson and Olivier (then running the *Old Vic), but in 1950 his work at Stratford, including Angelo (his first role for Brook), Cassius, and Leontes, showed how his understanding of a role—especially when encouraged by a great director—could lead to simplicity and shocking power in exploring neurotic emotions. He was knighted in the coronation honours list of 1953 (and arrested the same year for homosexual importuning) but his career seemed to have lost direction. A disastrous King Lear (1955, his fourth attempt at the role) increased the sense that he was on the wane. In 1957 he began ten years of *touring a *one-person Shakespeare show, *The Ages of Man*, which was admired but also seemed irrelevant to English theatre culture.

In Brook's production of *Seneca's *Oedipus* for the *National Theatre in 1968, Gielgud looked like a relic from a lost theatrical world; yet his fear of Brook's new methods was balanced by his awareness of how necessary it was for him to work in a radically different kind of theatre. As the Headmaster in *Bennett's *Forty Years On* (1968), Harry in *Storey's *Home* (1970), Shakespeare in *Bond's *Bingo* (1974), and Spooner in *Pinter's *No Man's Land* (1975), Gielgud showed an unexpected sympathy for new forms of drama and wholly new ranges in his own performance style. He played Prospero in 1974, looking deliberately and remarkably like Shakespeare, and Caesar in 1977, but, barring a brief return to the West End in 1988, he left the stage. He had often acted in *films but in his last years he appeared in an inordinate number (100 from 1970 until his death), gaining an Academy award for his very English butler in *Arthur* (1981). In 1991 he played Prospero again, over 60 years after his first *Tempest*, in Peter Greenaway's film *Prospero's Books*, where he spoke all the parts and became explicitly the playwright and director as well. In this merging of roles and unique act of ventriloquism, Gielgud became the embodiment of Shakespearian theatre, the centre of tradition in an experimental film (and brave enough to be naked on screen at 86). He was made a Companion of Honour in 1977 and appointed to the Order of Merit in 1996 but perhaps the most significant honour was that London's Globe Theatre, where he had often performed, was renamed the Gielgud Theatre in 1994. Of his six books and memoirs, *Early Stages* (1939), *Stage Directions* (1963), and *An Actor and his Time* (1979) are notable. PDH

CROALL, JONATHAN, *Gielgud: a theatrical life* (London, 2000)
MORLEY, SHERIDAN, *John G: the authorised biography of John Gielgud* (London, 2001)

GIGAKU

An ancient Japanese *genre of *masked *dance, pantomime, and music, of a comic and often erotic nature, also sometimes known as *kuregaku* or in ancient times as *kure no utamai* (dance-music from Wu). Though originally a Chinese art, *gigaku* was transmitted to *Japan from *Korea. According to the *Nihon shoki*, in AD 612 Mimashi of Paekche (Korea), who had studied *gigaku* in Wu, emigrated to Japan and taught this art to young people there (*see* KIAK). A large number of painted wooden *gigaku* masks, most dating from the Nara Period (710–84), are preserved at the Hōryūji and Tōdaiji temples and the im-

perial treasure house (Shōsōin), all in Nara. Many of these masks depict semi-mythical beasts, legendary warriors or kings, gods, or other *stock figures. Nara-period *gigaku* dancing was accompanied on hand gongs, hip-drums, and flutes; later cymbals apparently replaced the hand gongs. After the thirteenth century, *gigaku* declined rapidly in popularity, becoming more or less extinct in the following centuries. *Gigaku* masks may, however, have influenced the development of the *nō mask.

GG

GILBERT, JOHN (1810–89)

American comedian and *manager. Gilbert began his stage career at the *Tremont Theatre in his home town of *Boston in 1828 and worked the *frontier circuit until his debut in *New York in 1839. After an early start as a tragedian, he switched to comic roles and joined *Wallack's company in 1862, staying until the troupe folded in 1888. During that time he became one of America's most popular *character comedians, best remembered for his portrayal of Sir Peter Teazle in *Sheridan's *The School for Scandal*, a part he continued to play throughout his life. PAD

GILBERT, MRS GEORGE H. (ANNE HARTLEY) (1821–1904)

American actress, born in Lancashire. Apprenticing in the *corps de *ballet at *Her Majesty's Theatre and *Drury Lane, she married George Henry Gilbert with whom she emigrated to the USA in 1849. She played supporting roles in the Midwest before signing as 'first old woman' (*see* LINES OF BUSINESS) at the Olympic Theatre in *New York. From 1869 to 1899 she was associated with Augustin *Daly, becoming a permanent fixture in the company (after he opened his new theatre in 1879) as Grandma Gilbert, the character actress in the 'Big Four' of high *comedy with Ada *Rehan, John *Drew, and James Lewis. KM

GILBERT, W. S. (WILLIAM SCHWENCK) (1836–1911)

English playwright and librettist. Gilbert began as a barrister in 1863, but found it more interesting and profitable to write verse for comic periodicals like *Fun* and *burlesques for the stage, especially *operatic burlesques such as *Dulcamara; or, The Little Duck and the Great Quack* (1866) and *Robert the Devil; or, The Nun, the Dun, and the Son of a Gun* (1868). His comic verse was first collected under the title of *Bab Ballads*—'Bab' being his *Fun* pseudonym—in 1869, and by then Gilbert had begun an interesting series of 'fairy' *comedies, including *The Palace of Truth* (1870) and *The Wicked World* (1873), which dealt satirically, but also pathetically, with themes of truth, falsehood, enchantment, deceit, pretence, and the failure of love. Some of the same ideas appear in Gilbert's best and controversial comedy, *Engaged* (1877), a revolutionary and anti-idealistic play in which his powerfully developed sense of irony deals destructively with Victorian stage icons: romantic love, friendship, filial and paternal affection. Every *character is ruthlessly and hypocritically selfish and mercenary.

By 1877 Gilbert was well embarked upon his collaboration with Arthur *Sullivan, leading to their business partnership with the impresario Richard *D'Oyly Carte. Thirteen works, representing collectively the very best of English comic opera (*see* OPERETTA), were the fruit of this collaboration, of which the first, *Thespis* (1871), is now lost. The last eight were produced at the *Savoy Theatre. The collaboration was busy and fruitful; the list comprises *The Sorcerer* (1877), *HMS Pinafore* (1878), *The Pirates of Penzance* (1879), *Patience* (1881), *Iolanthe* (1882), *Princess Ida* (1884), *The Mikado* (1885), *Ruddigore* (1887), *The Yeomen of the Guard* (1888), *The Gondoliers* (1889), *Utopia Limited* (1893), and *The Grand Duke* (1896). Gilbert's wit is playful, but also mocking; his somewhat bilious view of mankind and his satirical fantasies are transformed by Sullivan's music into something softer, kinder, more charming. Only the last two operettas are not in the repertory today; the rest are the mainstay of innumerable *amateur operatic societies all over the English-speaking world. Of the plays, only *Engaged* is now performed; it is a unique Victorian comedy, and Gilbert, influenced as he was by the extravaganzas of J. R. *Planché and the Victorian burlesque, is nonetheless a unique Victorian playwright, a true original in an age when so many dramatists were imitators and hurried caterers to a mass market. Gilbert was knighted in 1907.   MRB

GILFORD, JACK (1907–90)

American actor and comedian. Born Jacob Gelman to immigrants on Manhattan's Lower East Side, he was raised in Brooklyn by his mother, who bootlegged whiskey. Starting as a mimic, he grew into a *vaudeville and café comic who *toured with stars like Milton Berle and Jimmy Dorsey, his famous routines including a day in the life of a golf ball and pea soup coming to a boil. Refusing to answer questions on communist sympathies in 1956 resulted in a decade-long blacklist from much *television and *film work, but his sad eyes, malleable face, and quick wit made him a tragicomic stage favourite in *The World of Sholem Aleichem* (1953), *The Diary of Anne Frank* (1955), *Cabaret* (1966), and the *Metropolitan Opera's *Die Fledermaus* (often). He did his last comic solo in 1988.   CR

GILL, PETER (1939–   )

Welsh director and playwright, who established his reputation with productions in 1968 of three little-staged D. H. *Lawrence

plays at the *Royal Court Theatre, where he had acted since 1959. The Court premièred two of his plays in 1969, *The Sleepers' Den* and *Over Gardens Out*, and in 1976 *Small Change*, which captured the textures of everyday life with impressionistic lyrical grace. He left to run the *Riverside Studios in 1977, directing productions of *Chekhov's *Cherry Orchard* (1978), *Middleton and *Rowley's *The Changeling* (1978), and *Measure for Measure* (1979), and making the Studios into an important *alternative venue for new dramatists and experimental companies. Peter *Hall made him associate director at the *National Theatre (1980–97), where he was founder director of the Theatre Studio (Cottesloe). At the National he continued to champion new writing, with a notable season in 1985, and to stage impressive productions such as *Turgenev's *A Month in the Country* (1981) and Büchner's *Danton's Death* (1983). Later work includes directing his own *Cardiff East* (1997) and *Friendly Fire* (1999), a play for *youth theatres.   BRK

GILLETTE, WILLIAM HOOKER (1853–1937)

American actor and playwright. Born into a prominent Connecticut family, Gillette showed a histrionic inclination while still in school. He struck out in 1873 to pursue a stage career, acting over the next few years in small roles in New Orleans, *Boston, Cincinnati, and Louisville. His first acting and writing success came when he took the lead in his own play, *The Professor* (1881). Subsequently his original plays provided him with a series of notable parts: Blane in *Held by the Enemy* (1886), Billings in *Too Much Johnson* (1894), and Thorne/Dumont in his Civil War spy *melodrama *Secret Service* (1895). His signature role, one he played more than 1,000 times over 30 years, came from his adaptation of Arthur Conan Doyle's stories as *Sherlock Holmes* (1899). His impersonation of the famous detective defined the *character for generations of American and English theatregoers. When his own writing no longer found public favour, Gillette still enjoyed acting success in many plays, including J. M. *Barrie's *The Admirable Crichton* (1903) and *Dear Brutus* (1918). While limited in range, Gillette perfected a cool, detached *acting style that perfectly matched the characters he assumed. His physical movements were sparse and his enunciation clipped, a stark contrast, especially at the beginning of his career, to the *romantic acting approach that dominated American theatres in his era. He presented his views on acting in a famous 1913 lecture that was later published as *The Illusion of the First Time in Acting*.   GAR

GILPIN, CHARLES (1878–1930)

*African-American actor who originated the title role of *O'Neill's *The Emperor Jones* (1920). A founding member of the

Pekin Company and the *Lafayette Players (he worked again with them in 1924 in *Roseanne*), to sustain his career he took a series of ordinary jobs including printer, barber, janitor, porter, and elevator operator. He came to attention on Broadway as the minister in *Drinkwater's *Abraham Lincoln* (1919), and was cast in O'Neill's play the following year. O'Neill considered Gilpin a brilliant actor, one of the best to appear in his plays. But when Gilpin objected to some of the lines he changed them in performance, part of the reason why Paul *Robeson was chosen to replace him later, on stage and in the *film (1933). Gilpin suffered from racial prejudice and the difficulty of sudden fame, and he drank his career away.   BBL

GIMÉNEZ, CARLOS (1946–93)

Venezuelan director, born in Argentina. Winner of many international *awards, Giménez was for a time director of the Teatro Bellas Artes in *Mexico City. In 1971 he formed *Rajatabla in Caracas, where most of his work was carried out, created the International Theatre Festival of Caracas, was founder of the Directors' Centre for New Theatre (1986), and was instrumental in starting the National Youth Theatre (1990), a *training institution. He staged works by over 70 authors from around the world, directing in Argentina, the United States, Mexico, Peru, Spain, Russia, Italy, and other countries. Notable among his productions were *El señor presidente*, a version of the novel by Miguel Ángel *Asturias, *Bolívar* and *La muerte de García Lorca* by José Antonio Rial, and *El coronel no tiene quien le escriba* (*No One Writes to the Colonel*), his own adaptation of the novel by García Márquez. He was awarded the National Prize for Theatre in 1990.

LCL trans. AMCS

GINGOLD, HERMIONE (1897–1987)

English actress and singer. Having studied under Rosina Filippi, she made her debut in Beerbohm *Tree's *The Merry Wives of Windsor* (1909). Although she continued to play serious roles at the *Gate Theatre, she began her long association with *revues as a singer-comedienne in 1936. Especially noteworthy was her wartime series at the Ambassador's Theatre, beginning with *Sweet and Low* (1943). More at home on stage than in *film, her trademark was her husky voice and her expert double entendres. Kenneth *Tynan commented that 'no actress commands a more purposeful leer, and in nobody's mouth do vowels sound more acidly curdle' [*sic*].   VEE

GINKAS, KAMA (1941–)

Soviet/Russian director. Born in Kaunas, Ginkas graduated from the Leningrad Theatre Institute. He worked in Krasnoyarsk (1970–2) before returning to Leningrad (*St Petersburg),

where his production of *Pushkin and Nathalie* (1979) defined his genuinely innovative approach to theatre, perceiving the actor as a figure who 'plays' with the character. Since 1980 Ginkas has worked in *Moscow, and his productions at the Young Spectator's Theatre (headed by his wife Genrietta Yanovskaya) have established him as one of the city's leading directors with work such as *Notes from the Underground* (1989), *We Play Crime* (1991), *K.I. from Crime* (1994), *Room for Laughter* (1998), and *The Black Monk* (1999).   BB

GIRALDI, GIOVAN BATTISTA ('CINTHIO') (1504–73)

Ferrarese humanist, author, and dramatist. The plots of his short stories, or *Hecatommithi* (published 1565), became an important source for European drama and literature, including Shakespeare. However, his most important and seminal work for the theatre was as a dramatist and dramatic theorist. Giraldi's *Orbecche* was the first original classical-style *tragedy performed in Italy, in 1541: its *plot was related to Boccaccio's *Decameron* IV. 1, but its theatrical inspiration was the bloodthirsty tragedies of *Seneca. After two more plays, Giraldi began to put theoretical ideas on paper, and his *Discourses on Composing Romances, Comedies, and Tragedies . . .* was published in 1554. In this work, and in most of his nine tragedies, he struck a balance between *Aristotelian precepts and real contemporary demands. His most striking decision was that the ferocious Senecan *catastrophe should be replaced by something more emotionally and morally satisfying; so his plays after *Orbecche* are 'tragedies with happy endings', in which virtuous *heroes and heroines, although severely threatened, emerge unscathed, and lurid punishments are reserved for the *villains who deserve them. In this way Giraldi reconciled classical *catharsis with Christian poetic justice and paved the way for the *genre later designated as *tragicomedy. His views inevitably aroused opposition, particularly from the rival tragedian Sperone Speroni, with whom he conducted a partially anonymous debate. Giraldi also mounted a *'satyr-play', *Egle*, in 1545; but his chosen formats (based on *Euripides, and involving gods and woodland deities rather than human characters) were not those ultimately canonized for the *pastoral genre. *See also* THEORIES OF DRAMA, THEATRE, AND PERFORMANCE; EARLY MODERN PERIOD IN EUROPE.   RAA

GIRAUDOUX, JEAN (1882–1944)

French dramatist and novelist. A career diplomat until 1940, Giraudoux published carefully polished short stories and novels in his spare time. He did not turn to theatre until he was 46, but became generally regarded as the leading French dramatist between 1928 and the Second World War. This was largely due to his collaboration with the actor and director Louis *Jouvet, who reworked and cut the plays extensively in *rehearsal, and staged them inventively in fashionable *Paris theatres with leading actors and little or no subsidy. Giraudoux was essentially a literary dramatist, with a distinctive, subtle, poetic style; his *characters use complete sentences, long speeches, and *monologues, and his success depended on a regular *audience of well-educated, middle-class Parisians. In his first play, *Siegfried* (1928), the *protagonist is a French soldier who lost his memory and was re-educated as a German, reflecting Giraudoux's recurring preoccupation with relations between the two countries, shown most clearly and pessimistically in the debates on war in his greatest success *La Guerre de Troie n'aura pas lieu* (translated by Christopher *Fry as *Tiger at the Gates*, 1935).

Other plays treat twentieth-century preoccupations through Greek myth (*Amphitryon 38*, 1929; *Électre*, 1937) or biblical sources (*Judith*, 1931); *Intermezzo* (1933) has a lighter and more fairy-tale atmosphere; and the posthumous *La Folle de Chaillot* (*The Madwoman of Chaillot*, 1945) is a whimsical attack on capitalism. *L'Impromptu de Paris* (1937), in the tradition of *Molière's *Impromptu de Versailles*, shows Jouvet and his leading actor Pierre Renoir discussing the function of the theatre, and paradoxically deciding that a play should appeal to the senses and imagination of the audience rather than to its understanding. Giraudoux's plays were frequently produced in *London until the 1950s, but fashion has moved against them. *Amphitryon 38* was successfully revived by the *National Theatre in 1971, with Geraldine *McEwan in the strong part of Alcmene, but Harold *Pinter's production there of *The Trojan War Will Not Take Place* in 1983 (Fry's translation, but reverting to the original title) was criticized as static and wordy.

EEC

GIROUX, CAROLINE (MRS SEARLE) (1799–c.1855)

Born into an extensive *family of *dancers and dancing-masters, she made her debut aged 3 at the Royal Circus, performing in a family troupe. After several seasons there, and acting as well as dancing under Jane *Scott at the Sans Pareil, she completed her training in *Paris. Her importance is in the transmission of skills both within, and outwards from, theatrical dance: she and at least two of her sisters became teachers, and by the 1820s she had an extensive list of private pupils as well as 31 professional apprentices.

JSB

GISH, LILLIAN (1893–1993) AND DOROTHY (1898–1968)

American actresses. Born in Ohio, the Gish sisters were both on stage from 1902, *touring in separate *melodrama companies as the last resort of their financially straitened mother after her alcoholic husband abandoned them. The lively Dorothy, known as the 'dimpled darling', earned excellent reviews for her scenes of pathos, one of which involved her being thrown into a cage of lions. The more introspective Lillian enjoyed her only formal schooling, some months at an Ursuline convent, as a respite from the travails of touring. From their appearance together in the Biograph one-reeler *An Unseen Enemy* (1912), the sisters worked in silent *film for over fifteen years before returning to the stage. Lillian's long collaboration with director D. W. Griffith included *Birth of a Nation* (1915), *Broken Blossoms* (1919), and *Way Down East* (1920)—she titled her 1969 memoir *The Movies, Mr Griffith, and Me*. She directed Dorothy in *Remodeling her Husband* (1920) while supervising the remodelling of a Long Island studio for Griffith. Dorothy's comic genius blossomed as 'the little disturber' in Griffith's *Hearts of the World* (1917). The sisters starred together in his *Orphans of the Storm* (1922). From 1928 to 1956 Dorothy performed in about twenty Broadway productions, several with the *Theatre Guild. Lillian's Broadway career spanned 1930 to 1975. The sisters made their last stage appearance together in *The Chalk Garden* (1956). Both also worked in live *television drama. Lillian's deeply ingrained work ethic kept her active in film and *television until 1987, after which she toured with her lecture on the silent film era.

FHL

GLADIATORIAL CONTESTS

Gladiatorial displays originated at aristocratic funerals at Rome in the third century BC to honour the deceased. The funerary context persisted throughout the republic, but politicians began to exploit this practice as an opportunity to buy popularity by staging memorial games in honour of relatives some years dead. The first such opportunist was Julius Caesar; as aedile in 65 BC he staged a gladiatorial show (*munus*, or *munera* in the plural) in honour of his father, who had died twenty years previously. The transition from memorial to entertainment was completed by Caesar's heir Augustus. As Rome's first *princeps* (emperor) he established the *munus legitimum*, combining beast-hunts or *animal fights (*venationes*) and *munus*. To keep potential rivals from cultivating popularity by staging *munera* he passed legislation requiring the Senate to authorize each *munus* and limiting sponsors to two *munera* annually. The imperial cult that he established was staffed in every municipality by priests who were responsible for staging gladiatorial displays on the Emperor's birthday. Gladiators originally competed in the local forum, which continued to be used ad hoc in communities where no *amphitheatre was ever built. The oldest known amphitheatre is at Pompeii (c.80 BC). Amphitheatres are largely confined to the west; in the east, Greek theatres and stadiums were usually adapted for gladiatorial shows and beast-hunts (*see* ANCIENT THEATRES).

Gladiators were trained combatants comprising two broad categories: slaves, and freeborn persons who had sworn to subject themselves to physical coercion, thereby acknowledging a servile relationship with their owner/trainer (*lanista*). Freeborn gladiators forfeited their social status and were technically *infamis* (unspeakable); in exchange they received a cash payment. Gladiators were highly trained and well fed. They fought in numerous distinctive styles characterized by special equipment that may originally have been associated with specific ethnic groups. Most wore helmets and heavy armour. Opponents might fight in the same style, or else advantages and disadvantages might be balanced in a mixed pair. One example of such pairing was the contest between the *retiarius* (netter) and the *murmillo* (sporting the emblem of a fish on his helmet). The *retiarius* was fast but vulnerable, unprotected except for a shoulder-guard and equipped with a net, trident, and dagger. The *murmillo* was heavily armed, hence well protected but encumbered. The different styles attracted loyal supporters. At Rome it was politic for emperors to share their subjects' enthusiasms, and individual emperors were known for supporting their favourite style. The capacity to fight in more than one style was a prized accomplishment. Left-handed skills were also vaunted; since all gladiators were trained to fight right-handers, a left-hander usually had an advantage over his opponent. Female gladiators are occasionally attested.

A *lanista* might put on a show himself and charge admission. More often he rented gladiators to a magistrate sponsoring a gladiatorial show, or a private individual commemorating a deceased relative. The number of pairs was advertised in advance, and sponsors often recorded in their epitaphs how many they had displayed. In small communities in Italy and the provinces as few as three or four pairs might fight on a single occasion. At Rome under Augustus (27 BC–AD 14) the Senate passed legislation making 60 pairs the limit for one *munus*, although Augustus himself displayed 10,000 pairs in eight *munera*. The pairs fought separately. An umpire presided over the fight, a band supplied musical accompaniment, and spectators chanted slogans. Though a contest often ended in unambiguous victory or defeat for the participants, gladiators were seldom killed in combat. A defeated party could appeal for a reprieve, and spectators indicated their verdict by gesturing with the thumb. In the case of a draw, both opponents were declared 'reprieved standing'. Gladiatorial schools recorded the performance of individual gladiators, and these details reappear in gladiators' epitaphs commissioned by their relatives or fellow gladiators. Gladiatorial combat survived the advent of Christianity and did not cease until early in the fifth century.

KMC

VILLE, GEORGES, *La Gladiature en occident des origines à la mort de Domitien* (Rome, 1981)
WIEDEMANN, THOMAS, *Emperors and Gladiators* (London, 1992)

GLASGOW

While *folk and *liturgical plays appeared in Glasgow during the *medieval period, the seventeenth century witnessed increasing attacks by Kirk and magistrates on theatre as 'a temple of Beelzebub'. *Touring productions occasionally visited in the early eighteenth century and Burrel's Hall housed rope dancing and tumbling in the 1750s, but an attempt in 1752 to establish a regular theatre was defeated by mob violence. In 1764 John Jackson built a theatre which was promptly set on *fire, but the famous Irish actress Mrs *Bellamy persevered in opening it, appearing in borrowed *costumes. After a subsequent fire, in 1782 Jackson built the Dunlop Street Theatre, which played host to Mrs *Siddons, the *Kembles, and William *Betty. Edmund *Kean became a regular performer at the Theatre Royal, Queen Street (1805), which in 1818 became the first British theatre to use gas *lighting. While both theatres employed regular *stock companies, the repertoire was mostly English.

The nineteenth century saw a boom in theatre building, from popular halls such as Mumford's Geggie (1835), housing *melodramas and adaptations of Walter Scott, to grander theatres such as the Royalty (1879), which hosted visiting companies such as *Irving's *Lyceum Company. By 1906 there were 29,000 theatre seats in Glasgow, mostly presenting various forms of popular drama, especially *variety and *pantomime. The Glasgow Repertory Theatre (1909–14; *see* REGIONAL REPERTORY THEATRES, UK) was established by Alfred Wareing to encourage Scottish drama but is better known for its British première of *Chekhov's *The Seagull* (1909). Its legacy was revived by the Scottish National Players, which toured many new Scottish plays between 1921 and 1948. In the 1930s–1940s their work was supplemented by small theatre clubs such as the Curtain and the Park, and a thriving *amateur movement including Glasgow Unity Theatre.

In the post-war period many theatres were either converted to other use or demolished, although the *Citizens' Theatre has established a strong reputation since its foundation in 1943, as has Scottish Opera (founded in 1962, based since 1974 in the Theatre Royal). Glasgow's other theatres include the Pavilion (1904), which houses popular entertainments, the King's (1904), frequently used by amateurs and visiting *musical productions, the Tron, a converted church (1978), which mostly hosts medium-scale touring theatre, and Tramway, a former tramshed converted into a performing space in 1988 to house Peter *Brook's *Mahabharata*. It has since hosted many international productions, including work by Robert *Lepage, the *Maly Theatre of *St Petersburg, and the *Wooster Group. The city has also been home to many touring companies, such as the *political theatre groups *7:84 and Wildcat, and new writing companies Clyde Unity and Lookout.

GJG

GLASPELL, SUSAN (1876–1948)

American playwright. An Iowa journalist and fiction writer, Glaspell had published two novels and a collection of stories when she married poet George Cram Cook in 1913 and they moved to *New York's Greenwich Village. Spending the summer of 1915 with a group of artists, writers, and political radicals in Provincetown, Massachusetts, Glaspell and Cook staged *Suppressed Desires*—their short *comedy on the fad for Freudianism. Glaspell's *Trifles*, a deftly structured short play in which two women cooperate in concealing evidence to assist an absent woman, was one of eight works staged the second summer, when the group formalized as the *Provincetown Players. Soon beginning a winter operation in Greenwich Village, the Players would stage nine more Glaspell plays, including the full-length works *Bernice* (1919), *Inheritors* (1921), and *The Verge* (1921). Glaspell and Cook moved to Greece in 1922, where she returned to fiction writing, but experienced a period of low creativity after Cook's death in 1924. She won the Pulitzer Prize for her last produced play, *Alison's House* (1930), but *Trifles* has been most widely produced and *The Verge*, which uses *expressionist and *symbolist techniques, rediscovered by critics as a formally innovative work. MAF

GLASS, PHILIP (1937–)

American composer. Graduating from the University of *Chicago at 19, Glass moved to *New York to study *modernist musical composition at *Juilliard. Afterwards, he moved to *Paris to study under Nadia Boulanger. His encounter there with non-Western music led him to renounce his previous efforts in favour of minimalist composition techniques. In 1970 Glass co-founded *Mabou Mines, an *avant-garde performance *collective that included JoAnne *Akalaitis and Lee *Breuer. This event signalled the beginning of a series of collaborations with performing artists in the fields of theatre, *dance, *opera, *film, and *performance art. Glass is probably most famous for his work with American avant-garde director Robert *Wilson. *Einstein on the Beach* (1976), a four-hour opera that combines the trance-inducing repetition of musical phrases with Wilson's non-narrative collage of *texts and *dream imagery, is a landmark of twentieth-century avant-garde performance. Other notable musical-theatre creations with Wilson include *White Raven* (1991), *the CIVIL warS* (1994), *Monsters of Grace* (1997), and an adaptation of *Büchner's *Woyzeck* (2001). Glass has also written *music for dance choreographers Twyla Tharp and Susan Marshall. JAB

GLEICH, JOSEPH ALOIS (1772–1841)

Austrian dramatist. Gleich belongs to the trio of dramatists (together with *Bäuerle and *Meisl) who dominated the Viennese popular theatre before the golden age of *Raimund and *Nestroy. Although his main occupation was as a civil servant, Gleich still managed to write some 200 plays in various *genres, specializing particularly in the 'magic play'. He is best remembered for *Die Musikanten vom hohen Markt* (*The Musicians from the Upper Market*, 1815) and its sequel, *Herr Adam Kratzerl von Kratzerlfeld* (1816), which saw the first major success of his son-in-law Ferdinand Raimund in the role of Adam Kratzerl. CBB

GLISSANT, ÉDOUARD (1928–)

Martinican poet, critic, and playwright. One of the most prominent and prolific francophone authors, Glissant began as a poet in the 1950s. His major contribution to theatre is *Monsieur Toussaint*, a *historical *tragedy based on the hero of the Haitian Revolution, Toussaint L'Ouverture. Particularly noteworthy performances have been a *radio broadcast with actors Douta Seck and Toto Bissainthe (1971) and two productions by Benjamin Jules-Rosette (1977 and 1985). LEM

GLOBE RECONSTRUCTIONS

The idea of building replicas of the Elizabethan theatres started with Ludwig *Tieck in Leipzig in the 1830s. Having visited *London, met Edmund *Malone, the first scholarly excavator of information about the early theatres, and seen the contract for the *Fortune Theatre in the Dulwich College papers, he conceived with the Shakespeare translator A. W. *Schlegel the idea of building a new Dresden Opera House modelled on the Fortune. It was never built, but it reflects an ambition re-energized when de Witt's drawing of the *Swan interior was found in 1888. In London William *Poel and his *Elizabethan Stage Society mounted plays in versions of the Fortune and the *Globe, and promoted the idea of a national theatre modelled on the Globe. In 1912 an exhibition at Earl's Court put on show a reduced-scale model of the Globe designed by Edward Lutyens.

The national theatre idea came to nothing, partly because it was backed by George Bernard *Shaw, whose controversialist stance never won his causes rich friends (*see* NATIONAL THEATRE MOVEMENT, BRITAIN). In the 1930s the 'Mermaid Shakespeare Society' planned a Globe on *Bankside, modelled on Claes Visscher's engraving of the Globe as a tall octagon. It was backed by important figures including major Shakespeare scholars. The war stopped that project, and despite further moves in London during the 1951 Festival of Britain it was not until 1970 when Sam *Wanamaker resurrected the idea that it regained its impetus. His Bankside Globe opened in 1997. In the meantime other countries made their own attempts, in San Diego, at the Folger Shakespeare Library in Washington, DC (using a Cranford Adams design based on Visscher's octagon), elsewhere in the USA, and in *Japan, where a Fortune Theatre was created some years before the Panasonic Globe was built in *Tokyo in 1988.   AJG

GLOBE THEATRE

Shakespeare's Globe was a second-best option as a *playhouse, built out of the old timbers of the open-air *Theatre in 1599 to stand in for the *Blackfriars, an indoor playhouse built for the company to use in 1596. Its builders, the brothers Cuthbert and Richard *Burbage, lacked enough money to complete it, since their inheritance from their father James *Burbage was locked up in the Blackfriars, which they could not use. Consequently they had the Theatre, their former playhouse, dismantled and took its timbers for the new theatre, cutting in five of the players in the company to help finance the construction. Thus the Globe became the first playhouse owned by an actors' cooperative. Six of the playing company's eight sharers became landlords to themselves as players.

In the next ten years, staging Shakespeare's new plays along with his existing repertoire, the Globe became the most celebrated playhouse in *London. In 1608 the Burbages retrieved the Blackfriars. They made shares of it on the same basis as the Globe, and after a long closure because of plague they started the practice of using the Globe through the summer and retreating to the indoor Blackfriars each winter. This was an elite version of the practice all London-based companies had followed up to 1594, using the city's *inns with their large upper rooms in winter. No other company was able to follow this practice. The King's Men (formerly the *Chamberlain's Men) were sufficiently affluent to leave one playhouse empty while they used the other, even though some London companies were without a home.

This affluence was put to the test in 1613 when the first Globe burned down, thanks to a smouldering wad from a cannon which lodged in the thatch roofing the galleries. The company rebuilt it more lavishly than before, this time with a tiled roof, on the same foundations. It continued to serve as the King's Men's summer playhouse until all the theatres were closed in 1642. In 1644 the second Globe was pulled down to make way for tenement housing.

In 1970 Sam *Wanamaker, an American actor, conceived the idea of rebuilding the Globe in Southwark. His first concept was a modern structure, with a glass roof, electric light, and other conveniences, on the original site. He soon saw the value of constructing as exact a replica of the first Globe as scholarship could devise, in order to replicate the conditions in which Shakespeare and his fellows performed. Using the original site proved impossible, since it would have destroyed the original foundations, some of which were excavated nineteen years later. A site alongside the Thames was secured from Southwark Council, and building commenced in 1986. The discovery of sections of first the *Rose and then the Globe by archaeologists in 1989 caused some modifications to the design, which was completed in 1997. Plays at the Globe staged in authentic dress and properties have since become an extremely popular attraction. *See also* GLOBE RECONSTRUCTIONS.   AJG

GŁOWACKI, JANUSZ (1938–   )

Polish writer. A student of Jan *Kott's in *Warsaw, Głowacki worked as a journalist before publishing short stories and novels, and wrote screenplays for important *film directors including Andrzej *Wajda. *Adultery Punished* (1971) began his playwriting career. In London when martial law was imposed in Poland in 1981, he chose not to return and moved to *New York. He occasionally lectured at Yale, Cornell, Columbia, and elsewhere, and was writer-in-residence at the *New York Shakespeare Festival and the *Mark Taper Forum in *Los Angeles. *Hunting Cockroaches* was produced *Off-Broadway (1984) and had a successful life in American *regional theatres. *Antigone in New York*, a version of *Sophocles' *tragedy in which the *characters are immigrants from Puerto Rico, Poland, and Russia, had major productions in Washington and New York. His works were again published and produced in Poland after the changes of 1989; *Antigone in New York* opened in Warsaw in 1993, and soon was staged in six other theatres. Głowacki's other plays include *Cinderella* (1979), set in a girls' correction home, *Fortinbras Gets Drunk* (1986), a footnote to *Hamlet* full of *political allusion, and *The Fourth Sister* (1999), an ironic continuation of *Chekhov. In general his work combines *realism with the *grotesque, creating a dark but hilarious pastiche.   KB

GLUCK, CHRISTOPH WILLIBALD (1714–87)

Bohemian-Austrian composer. Early in his career Gluck proved himself to be a skilled composer of conventional operatic *genres, but several years after settling in *Vienna in 1752 he composed three 'reform' *operas for the *Burgtheater that would have a major impact upon future composition, *Orpheus and Eurydice* (1762), *Alceste* (1767), and *Paris and Helen* (1770). Gluck, with his librettist Ranieri di'Calzibigi, proposed to restore theatrical life to *opera seria* by achieving a 'beautiful simplicity'. They did this by paring down the *action and having the music serve the poetry, by avoiding all ornamentation and any music designed solely to display a singer's voice. These acclaimed reforms were drawn in part from Gluck's experience with French lyric *tragedy, so when he began to compose operas for the *Paris *Opéra in 1774, he encountered sympathetic *audiences. His major works for this theatre included *Iphigenia in Aulis* (1774), *Armide* (1777), and *Iphigenia in Tauris* (1779). His popularity in Paris led to a public controversy between his supporters, who favoured drama as the prime element of opera, and those of the Italian composer Niccolò Piccinni, who favoured the purely musical aspects of the genre.　　SJCW

GODBER, JOHN (1956–　)

English playwright and director. A Yorkshire miner's son, in 1984, after a string of *award-winning *youth plays, he gave up teaching to run Hull Truck Theatre, a *touring company based in Hull. In 1993 he was the third most produced playwright in Britain, according to *Plays and Players*. His first production at Hull Truck, the Olivier *award-winning *Up 'n' Under*, typifies his style. The play is accessible to northern working-class oral culture, utilizes a small ensemble who play multiple *characters, has physical gags, and mocks the establishment. Other work includes *Bouncers* (1985), *Teechers* (1987), *Salt of the Earth* (1988), and *On the Piste* (1990). Godber's detractors—mainly from the south of England—claim that his plays are stereotypical and shallow, but he reached the *Guinness Book of Records* in 1982 when 47 *amateur companies simultaneously performed *Happy Families*, commissioned by the Little Theatres Trust. Godber fuelled debate in 1998 when he said 80 per cent of theatre productions were tedious.　　KN

GODFREY, THOMAS (1736–63)

American playwright. A *Philadelphian, Godfrey wrote *The Prince of Parthia* (1759), a *neoclassical *verse *tragedy in the style of *Addison's *Cato*. Performed by David *Douglass's American Company in 1767, the work was the first tragedy written by a native-born playwright to be professionally produced in America.　　GAR

GOERING, REINHARD (1887–1936)

German dramatist. An influential *expressionist, Goering turned his war experiences as a medical officer into a series of plays. Most successful was *Seeschlacht* (*Sea Battle*, 1917) which depicts seven nameless sailors 'imprisoned' in the gun turret of a battleship. The form of *verse *tragedy stands in strange contrast to the modern technological warfare represented—combat is heard but not seen. Goering was responding to reports of the battle of Skagerrak (1916) which took place without the ships ever sighting one another. The use of types rather than *characters, the interweaving of *dream and reality, *action and vision, and the extensive use of *monologues all belong to the repertoire of expressionist technique. *Reinhardt's production in *Berlin (1917) was an important breakthrough for expressionist theatre. Goering's only other success was *Die Südpolexpedition des Käpitans Scott* (*Captain Scott's Expedition to the South Pole*, 1930) directed by *Jessner. Both plays explore the notion of fate in a modern world.　　CBB

GOETHE, JOHANN WOLFGANG VON (1749–1832)

German dramatist, poet, novelist, scientist, director, and court official, the major literary figure in the German language. Born in Frankfurt am Main, he became acquainted with the theatre, especially in the form of *puppets, at an early age. Influenced by *Lessing's admiration for Shakespeare, he became a leading exponent of *Sturm und Drang*, notably in *Götz von Berlichingen* (1773, translated by John *Arden as *Ironhand*), a sprawling epic piece in prose about a charismatic medieval knight in revolt against corrupt political rulers. Premièred in a heavily shortened version in 1774, it established a vogue for *Ritterdramen* (knight-dramas). In 1775 he was invited to the court of Weimar, where he became involved with the flourishing *amateur theatre, writing and directing plays and *Singspiele*. In 1780 he was appointed privy counsellor and was ennobled two years later. By now he had left behind his wild youth and was committed to moderation and renunciation, not least because of his unconsummated love for Frau von Stein, the wife of a fellow courtier. Significantly, his *Iphigenia on Tauris* reveals the humanizing quality of a noble woman in a rewriting of *Euripides' play. In Goethe's version Iphigenia and her brother Orestes do not steal the statue of Diana but trust in the nobility of the barbarian king to set them free. Premièred in 1779 in prose by the Amateur Theatre, with Goethe playing Orestes, it was first performed in *verse in 1800. There followed *Egmont* (1789), a prose *tragedy perhaps most familiar from Beethoven's overture. Egmont, a leader of the revolt by the Netherlands against Spanish misrule, is captured and executed mainly as a result of his blind conviction in his own invincibility.

In 1791 Goethe became director of the newly founded professional court theatre at *Weimar, where he undertook to reform the state of German theatre. Goethe introduced a respect for the *text and worked with his actors as a disciplined ensemble in place of the self-indulgent attitudinizing he described in his novel *Wilhelm Meister's Apprenticeship* (1796). He trained his actors in the skills of verse speaking and had a painter's eye for pleasing visual arrangements on stage. He insisted on careful read-throughs and *rehearsals, where his cast worked in a disciplined and committed manner. He demanded that his actors be word-perfect in performance, unusual for the period. Such firmness gave rise to scurrilous attacks that 'Goethe played chess' with his actors. In fact, his *Rules for Actors* (written 1803) are full of pragmatic advice about good vocal delivery, verse speaking, positions on stage, gesture, and *costume. He treated his actors well, and they became accepted members of court society, a remarkable change from the common eighteenth-century perception of performers as vagabonds. Far from promoting his own work (performances of his plays represented only 7 per cent of the total repertoire), Goethe, together with a majority of lighter theatrical fare, presented Shakespeare, the *operas of *Mozart, and the great verse tragedies of *Schiller. Too easily dismissed as a throwback to *neoclassical theatre on the French model, and clearly in opposition to the prevailing trend in *Berlin theatres towards more natural performance, Goethe and Schiller's work (see WEIMAR CLASSICIAM) made it possible for the first time for fine verse tragedies to be performed on the German stage (when Schiller's *Don Carlos* had been premièred in Hamburg in 1787, the actors could cope only by 'translating' Schiller's verse into prose). In 1807 the court theatre staged Goethe's other major verse play, *Torquato Tasso*, dealing with the court poet at Ferrara finding himself torn between his creative passion and the demands of court life, similar to Goethe's experiences as a young arrival in Weimar. As in *Iphigenia*, Goethe avoids a tragic outcome, here through Tasso's collapse and submission to the social order. In 1969 in Bremen the young Peter *Stein revealed the continuing relevance of the piece by directing *Tasso* as a reflection on the role of the hired performer in the entertainment industry.

The avoidance of the tragic is also at the core of Goethe's major drama, his reworking in two parts of the Faust legend. His *Faust*, more a long dramatic poem than a piece for the stage, was begun in 1773 and not completed until 1831. The core of the legend is retained: the learned doctor who, anxious to live life to the full, pledges his soul to Mephistopheles. In Part I he woos and impregnates an innocent young girl, Gretchen, and abandons her when she faces execution for the murder of her baby. In Part II his adventures range far wider, including a liaison with Helen of Troy. Finally, when Mephistopheles comes to claim Faust's soul, Faust is saved by the 'Eternal Womanly', with the angels declaring that 'Whoever strives endlessly can be saved.' Usually only Part I of *Faust* is performed, although *Reinhardt staged both parts (1909 and 1911). It was famously directed by Gustav *Gründgens, who also played Mephistopheles, throughout the 1930s and 1940s, and can now be read as a metaphor for Gründgens, like Faust, allying himself with the forces of Nazi evil. *Brecht adapted Goethe's original version, the *Urfaust*, in 1952, but it was performed only privately. In 2000 Peter Stein directed both parts with success, with Bruno *Ganz as Faust. In 1817, when the Duke's mistress insisted on having a performing dog in a court theatre production, Goethe resigned from his directorship. Though his dramas lack the theatricality of Schiller's plays, they remain a staple of the German repertoire. Goethe's contribution to theatre practice, while tending towards heavy formality, helped to make it possible for verse tragedy to become established in Germany, and his ensemble ideal laid the foundation for the work of the *Meininger.   MWP

CARLSON, MARVIN, *Goethe and the Weimar Theatre* (Ithaca, NY, 1978)

PATTERSON, MICHAEL, *The First German Theatre* (London, 1990)

GOGOL, NIKOLAI (1809–52)

Russian playwright and prose writer. Early success came with his short stories, eclipsing his first dramatic efforts, which were the unfinished *Vladimir Medal of the Third Class* (1833) and a play about Anglo-Saxon England, *Alfred* (1835). Gogol's theatrical reputation rests primarily on his masterpiece *The Government Inspector* (1836, *Aleksandrinsky Theatre, *St Petersburg, and *Maly Theatre, *Moscow, with *Shchepkin as the Mayor), with *Marriage* (Aleksandrinsky, 1842) a strong but lagging second. A final play, *The Gamblers* (*Bolshoi Theatre, Moscow, 1843), has not had the same success. His two major plays respond to Gogol's desire, expressed in articles on the theatre, to create a national repertoire. *The Government Inspector* brought him notoriety, evoking wildly differing reactions. The play turns on the dignitaries of a small town mistaking the identity of a passing adventurer, Khlestakov, for a government inspector; its splendidly comic treatment of the serious theme of state corruption and oppression sets it apart from most other *satires. It also exploits *acting and the *theatre as thematic metaphors, as Khlestakov creates and performs a fantasized version of himself and the officials perform ideal versions of themselves, but reveal their true personalities through exaggeration and corruption. A *tableau closes the play as the officials are visibly petrified into anguished poses at the arrival of the real inspector. *Marriage* comically satirizes the matchmaking market, but the twist is that the *hero Podkolyosin, disturbed by the concept of marriage itself, escapes betrothal by leaping through a window at the climactic moment.

In these plays, as well as in the stories and his novel *Dead Souls* (1842), the inexplicable and the unexpected lurk just beneath the *comedy and social comment: in *The Government Inspector* the Mayor puts on a hatbox instead of his hat, plaintiffs' hands are thrust through windows, or dejected derelicts stand in an empty landscape. Gogol's vitality as a dramatist was maintained in the Soviet period and after, and abroad as well. *The Government Inspector* has attracted major directors and landmark productions, including those by *Meyerhold (Moscow, 1926) and *Tovstonogov (Leningrad, 1972). Anatoly *Efros's *Marriage* (Moscow, 1975), Yury *Lyubimov's composite portrait of Gogol's work (*Inspectorate Fairy Tales*, *Taganka Theatre, 1978), various adaptations of *Dead Souls*, including the *Moscow Art Theatre's (1932) and another composite by Efros (*Road*, 1979), are signs of his continuing significance.

CM

GOLDEN AGE *See* EARLY MODERN PERIOD IN EUROPE.

GOLDENBERG, JORGE (1941–)

Argentinian playwright and screenwriter. Among his plays are *Changing of the Guard 1923* (1975), *Knepp* (1983), and *Krinsky* (1986). *Cleaning House* (1984) incorporates a series of *monologues written for the 1983 Teatro *Abierto festival.   JGJ

Gogol's great satire of small-town, small-time corruption, *Revizor* (*The Government Inspector*), in Meyerhold's landmark production, Moscow, 1926. Ninety years after its first showing, Meyerhold used the text as a critique of the entire pre-revolutionary way of life in Russia.

GOLDFADEN, ABRAHAM (AVROM GOLDFADN) (1840–1908)

Ukrainian dramatist and composer, considered the father of the modern *Yiddish stage. In 1876 he joined forces with two Yiddish folk singers in a tavern in Jassy, Romania, imposing a simple dramatic framework on their material and relying on a style similar to *commedia dell'arte* in its combination of a fixed *scenario with *improvised *dialogue and stage business. Goldfaden then mounted full-fledged *operettas, some of which—*The Witch* (1879), *The Two Kuni-Lemls* (1880), and *Shulamith* (1880)—became Jewish classics, with the names of their characters—Schmendrik, Kuni Leml, Hotzmakh, and Bobbe-Yakhne—entering the Yiddish lexicon. He wrote, composed, directed, and designed his productions, which by 1880 were *touring throughout Russia. But wandering troupes had little regard for *copyright laws, so that his popular plays and

tunes were stolen and plagiarized and soon Goldfaden's work was the mainstay of numerous Yiddish companies. He came to *New York in 1887, hoping to capitalize on his fame, but returned to Europe after a cold welcome. He was back again in America in 1903 but he never regained his earlier position. Goldfaden wrote about 60 *musical plays; his last work, the Zionist-inspired *Ben-Ami* (*Son of my People*), premièred in New York a few days before his death.   EN

GOLDONI, CARLO (1707–93)

Italian playwright. Goldoni boasted that he was 'born under the star of *comedy', but the reputation as 'Papa Goldoni', writer of good-hearted comedies, has long been an obstacle to an adequate appreciation of this complex figure whose importance in the history of Italian theatre can scarcely be overstated. He was born in a Venice which had lost its empire and discovered a role as the Las Vegas of the age. Theatre was big business, with old and new money poured into private and public theatres and talent as eagerly sought as in contemporary Hollywood. The city had sixteen theatres when *London had four. Goldoni reflected the life of the city he loved in its period of transition before the Napoleonic invasion, after which, in Browning's words, 'the kissing had to stop'. He was a sharp, critical observer, too genial to jeer but too intelligent to fail to chronicle and mock the vice, folly, and hypocrisy of his own time.

Goldoni studied law and his work in theatre was interspersed with periods of practice as lawyer or criminal prosecutor in several cities. In 1731 he fled to *Milan to escape an unwished-for marriage, and there underwent the embarrassment of seeing his first theatrical work, a *melodramma* (a *musical drama in heroic style) entitled *Ammalasunta*, derided by actors and salon intellectuals for its failure to comply with the rules which in his century had the status of dogma (*see* NEOCLASSICISM). Perhaps that episode convinced him of the need for the reform he later implemented. He was brought back to Venice by the *capocomico* Giuseppe Imer, the first of the theatrical professionals who employed Goldoni. His wife, whom he married in 1736, was Genoese and he acted as Genoese consul in Venice. He returned to the law in Pisa in 1745, although he wrote *The Venetian Twins* and *Servant of Two Masters* during this period. He was enticed back to Venice and its theatre three years later, remaining there until, nauseated by the endless disputes with fellow playwrights Carlo *Gozzi and Pietro Chiari, he accepted an invitation to move to *Paris and the *Comédie Italienne. His life there was made difficult by recalcitrant actors who abominated his reform programme. He wrote his *Memoirs*, dedicated to Louis XIV, in 1784 and died in poverty in Paris after the revolution.

Goldoni represents a kind of artist who emerged only in the eighteenth century, one who aspired neither to the position at court sought by classical artists nor to the lofty independence of the later *romantics. He settled for the position of hired hand, producing goods as required by contract, not in accordance with the promptings of some demiurge. Classical *heroes, subjects from myth or religion, were not for him, and like the painter Roberto Longhi, with whom he recognized an affinity, he preferred domestic or social themes. His creativity was boundless: he produced around 150 comedies as well as *melodrammi*, *tragedies, *tragicomedies, and *opera librettos, in addition to the occasional writing his contract required him to produce for the company's social occasions. In 1750, for a wager, he turned out sixteen plays, including such masterpieces as *The Coffee House* and *The Liar*. His writing was designed for that evening's performance, not for posterity, and he adapted his work to meet public taste and the requirements of a contracted cast. For *The True Friend* (1750), a dramatization of the clash between friendship and love, he intended to have one of the two men loved by the sister of the other, but since the company did not have an actress of the correct age, he converted the sister into an aunt.

Goldoni preferred *realist drama and had no truck with fantasy, but when the public taste demanded exotic work set in far-off lands he turned his hand to *The Persian Woman* (1753) and *Ircana in Julfa* (1755). For all his surface bonhomie, there was a dark side to Goldoni, sometimes hidden by the reworking of his plays for publication. *The Coffee House* started life as an *intermezzo* (*see* INTERMEDIO) with overtly erotic passages which were smoothed away in a successive dialect version and totally eliminated in the final, standard Italian version. This darker side was never completely absent, and has been brought to the surface by twentieth-century directors like Giorgio *Strehler.

Goldoni's output and development were closely tied to the successive companies he worked for. The years with the Imer company at San Samuele Theatre were years of apprenticeship and of growing dissatisfaction with the restrictions placed on the writer by actor-dominated *commedia dell'arte*, and of irritation with the virtuosity or coarseness and ribaldry to which the *genre had declined. He achieved his reform in Sant'Angelo, with the Medebac company. The play *Il teatro comico* (1750) can be regarded as a manifesto for a multifaceted programme which involved conferring on the author that primacy in theatre which had previously been the privilege of the actor, compelling the actors to learn parts rather than rely on *improvisation and the recall of standard situations, removing the *masks, and converting the *stock characters of *commedia dell'arte* into individuals with a psychological structure of their own. The stock characters did not disappear entirely: the reformed Pantaloon, no longer lecherous buffoon but respected counsellor and tradesman, was central to his vision. The positive hero of his theatre was the industrious, morally irreproachable bourgeois, such as the coffee-house owner, or Mirandolina of the *Inn Keeper* (1752), and the butt of his humour often the socially redundant nobleman. The reform programme encountered the opposition of the *acting profession, and both his hostility to traditional Italian theatre and his allocation of the central role to bourgeois characters aroused the enraged bile of Gozzi, who saw Goldoni as the proponent of Enlightenment ideas. But Goldoni was not an ideas playwright, and espoused no explicit programme. He consolidated his reforms with his output at Antonio Vendramin's San Luca (1753–62), where he staged such late works as *The Lovers* (1759), a dissection of love and jealousy worthy of *Chekhov, and *Il campiello* (1755) and *The Chioggia Quarrels* (1761), the only works in which working people feature. Work with the Comédie Italienne required him to abandon his reforms and return to *commedia* styles, but his reforms of Italian theatre endured.   JF

GOLDSMITH, OLIVER (c.1730–1774)

Irish playwright, poet, novelist, journalist, biographer, and historian. Born in County Longford and educated at Trinity College, Dublin, he settled in *London and became an astonishingly prolific writer, turning out a continuous flow of journalism, biographies, and histories in an ineffectual struggle to order his ramshackle financial affairs. 'No man was more foolish when he had not a pen in his hand', commented Samuel *Johnson, 'or more wise when he had.' Goldsmith's major writings for the theatre are few in comparison to his prodigious output: two plays and an essay. However, those two plays—*The Good Natur'd Man* (1768) and *She Stoops to Conquer* (1773)—and the essay 'A Comparison between Laughing and Sentimental Comedy' (1773) were to have a lasting influence on English theatre. '*Comedy', Goldsmith argued, 'should excite our *laughter by ridiculously exhibiting the Follies of the Lower Part of Mankind'; it should not, he insisted, 'expose the Virtues of Private Life' by making us applaud *characters with 'an abundance of Sentiment and Feeling'. *She Stoops to Conquer*, a comedy of confused class identities, puts this *theory into practice. It was an immediate success when first staged at *Covent Garden, and has held the stage ever since.   ChM

GOMBROWICZ, WITOLD (1904–69)
Polish novelist, playwright, and essayist. In 1939 he left Poland never to return, first for Argentina, then for France in 1964. Most of his work was banned in Poland until the 1980s. He attracted attention with his first play, *Ivona, Princess of Burgundy* (1938); *The Wedding* (1953) and *Operetta* (1968) followed. His novels include *Ferdydurke* (1937), *Trans-Atlantic* (1953), *Pornography* (1960), and *Cosmos* (1965). Gombrowicz wrote about the psychological, intellectual, social, and national structures and conventions that identify, shape, and limit individual freedom, emphasizing that what he called 'immaturity' is a source of beauty, curiosity, and rebellious energy. The plays have been widely translated and produced internationally.   KB

GOMES, ALFREDO DIAS (1922–99)
Brazilian playwright. Gomes's existential-political plays of the 1960s and 1970s were set mainly in the north-east of Brazil. His most popular work, *O pagador de promessas* (*Payment as Promised*, 1969), which won a Golden Palm for its 1962 *film adaptation, treats the clash of rural values with urban corruption, religious intransigence, and political and media opportunism. During the last decades of his life Gomes wrote for Brazilian *television, creating *satirical-*absurdist *comedies focusing on regional social hierarchies.   LHD

GÓMEZ DE AVELLANEDA, GERTRUDIS ('TULA') (1814–73)
Spanish playwright, poet, and novelist. Born in Cuba, she emigrated to Spain and became that nation's best-known woman dramatist of the nineteenth century and a staunch defender of women writers as well. After the *Madrid première of *Munio Alfonso* in 1844, she wrote fifteen other full-length plays that usually reflect *romantic motifs and focus on religious sentiment or conflict. Two of her greatest successes were the biblical drama *Saul* (1849), staged in lavish settings at the Teatro *Español, and the pseudo-historical *Baltasar* (1858). A different side of her talent was revealed in the equally popular *The Daughter of the Flowers* (1852), a three-act *verse *comedy that dealt more with middle-class social values than romantic passions.
                                                  MPH

GÓMEZ-PEÑA, GUILLERMO (1955–   )
*Performance artist and cultural *theorist. Born in *Mexico City, he began working in the United States in 1978, and came to international attention in 1989 as a result of his solo performance *Border Brujo*, a bilingual, narratively fractured piece in which he embodied various archetypal *characters associated with the US–Mexican border. His performance projects include poetic *monologues, interactive gallery installations that subvert the colonial format of the living diorama, experimental *opera, and large-scale *multimedia works for the *proscenium stage. Gómez-Peña's publications include *Warrior for Gringostroika* (1993), *The New World Border* (1996), and *Dangerous Border Crossers* (2000), as well as *The Temple of Confessions* (written with Roberto Sifuentes). He has also published two books of experimental fiction. Recipient of numerous *awards, including a MacArthur Fellowship (1991) and an American Book award (1999), Gómez-Peña epitomizes the role of the artist as citizen diplomat and public intellectual, using performance as a tool to initiate dialogue on a range of issues, including immigration, global capitalism, and Anglo-American attitudes toward Latinos and indigenous peoples.
                                                  LW

GONCHAROVA, NATALYA (1881–1962)
Russian/Soviet painter, illustrator, designer, and lifelong companion of the futurist artist Mikhail Larionov, with whom she founded Bubnovy Valet (the Jack of Diamonds Group) in 1910, and Osliny Khvost (the Donkey's Tail Group) the following year. After 1912, she moved from a neo-primitivist style, influenced by Russian folk art, to one influenced by *futurism and rayonism. Her first significant works for the theatre were designs in 1914 for *Tairov's production of *Goldoni's *The Fan* at the Kamerny Theatre, and for *Diaghilev's production in *Paris of *Le Coq d'or*. For the second she supplied sumptuous backdrops and *costumes in stylized colour combinations which drew on traditional peasant costume, handicrafts, and ornaments. She later produced plain designs in white and maroon for Stravinsky's *Les Noces* (Paris, 1923), with costumes based on

the *dancers' own work clothes. Her designs for a refurbished production of *The Firebird* (1926), first seen at the *Lyceum Theatre in *London, were in a style reminiscent of ancient Russian icons. Her association with the *Ballets Russes continued in Monte Carlo but she also worked with *Baliev's Chauve-Souris, in *New York in 1933, and in London during the 1950s.

NW

GONZÁLEZ-DÁVILA, JESÚS (1940–2000)

Mexican playwright. Relentlessly pessimistic, González-Dávila's plays capture the sordid reality of a lost generation, as in his highly successful *Of the Street* (1987), which gives an unsentimental but sympathetic look at street urchins surviving in the underbelly of *Mexico City. Many of his plays are pieced together with episodes that move the *characters from one seamy urban space to another. In other plays the dramatic world is claustrophobic, enclosing families and lovers in rooms with no exit except violence, such as the shabby hotel rooms and apartments of *A Delicious Garden* (1984) and *Amsterdam Boulevard* (1986). KFN

GOODBODY, BUZZ (1946–75)

English director. Goodbody (born Mary Ann) joined the *Royal Shakespeare Company in 1967 and became the first woman to direct for the company. A committed *feminist and communist, she worked with Theatregoround, the RSC's educational outreach programme, and did much to develop the *fringe venue the Other Place in Stratford. Her controversial 1970 *King John*, featuring Patrick *Stewart, was unashamedly *political, *farcical, and irreverent, though her mainstage *As You Like It* (1973), which included rock songs and hippie *costumes, received a critical mauling. In 1974 Goodbody became *artistic director of the Other Place, where she directed *King Lear* (1974) and a modern-dress, fast-paced *Hamlet* (1975). Starring Ben Kingsley, *Hamlet* gained stunning reviews but Goodbody had committed suicide before it opened. Her work was always politically engaged, bold, energetic, and full of risk. Her influence on the RSC can be seen in the large number of Other Place Shakespeare productions in the years following her death, which successfully exploited the intimate space as her *Hamlet* had done. EJS

GOODMAN'S FIELDS THEATRE

A *minor theatre in the East End of *London, which opened in 1729 against fierce opposition from the *patent *managers and their city backers. *Actor-manager Henry Giffard rebuilt the theatre in 1733 but it was temporarily closed down by the 1737 *Licensing Act. With only three theatres in London licensed to perform plays, Giffard circumvented the law by mounting a musical evening during which a play was performed free of charge. The success of *Garrick's appearance there in 1741–2 led to both Giffard and Garrick accepting jobs at *Drury Lane, and Goodman's Fields closed. Opened again briefly for speciality acts, it closed in 1751 and was destroyed by *fire in 1802.

GBB

GOODMAN THEATRE

American *regional theatre. Founded in 1925 at the Art Institute of *Chicago, the Goodman housed a *repertory company until 1930 and a respected School of Drama. In 1969 a resident professional theatre was revived, and in 1977 the link to the Art Institute ended. Under *artistic directors Gregory *Mosher (1978–85) and Robert Falls (since 1986), the Goodman came to national prominence, partly by promoting the work of David *Mamet and August *Wilson and reviving American classics by *O'Neill, *Williams, and *Miller. In 2001 operations shifted to a brand new facility in Chicago's North Loop theatre district.

STC

GOODWIN, NAT C. (1857–1919)

American actor. An enormously popular light comedian, Goodwin apprenticed in *stock companies in *vaudeville, and on *tour with *Harrigan and Hart before gaining stardom on the *New York stage and in touring companies, appearing in a *farce, *Hobbies* (1877). He succeeded in Augustus *Thomas's *In Mizzoura* (1893), a local colour *melodrama. Later he turned briefly to the traditional repertory, joining an all-star revival of *The Rivals* in the mid-1890s, and touring in *The Merchant of Venice* with his third wife, actress Maxine Elliott (1898). He continued in contemporary light *comedy, ending his career with a return to vaudeville. AW

GORDIN, JACOB (1853–1909)

Ukrainian *Yiddish playwright. Immersed in Russian culture, Gordin arrived in *New York in 1892 and was soon commissioned by the actor Jacob *Adler to write *Siberia*, a *melodrama that marked the beginning of serious Yiddish drama. He wrote dynamic plays with strong parts for Yiddish stars, including Adler, David Kessler, Bertha Kalich, and Keni Liptzin. Much of his best-known work was inspired by Shakespeare, *Tolstoy, and *Goethe, and focused on themes such as intergenerational conflict, the rights of women, and the pursuit of wealth. His plays—*The Jewish King Lear* (1892), *Mirele Efros* (1898), *God, Man and Devil* (1900), and *The Kreutzer Sonata* (1905)—have been revived, translated, and *filmed, and have earned a permanent place in the Jewish dramatic canon. Gordin was instrumental in introducing a more *natural stage language and insisted on strict adherence to a playwright's written *text.

EN

GORDON, RUTH (1896–1985)

American actress and playwright. After years of *touring in stock productions (often in the roles performed on Broadway by Helen *Hayes, with whom she was frequently compared), Gordon became a Broadway star when cast by Guthrie *McClintic in Maxwell *Anderson's *Saturday's Children* (1927). In *They Shall Not Die* (1934), she shattered her usual type by playing a prostitute. She was invited by Tyrone *Guthrie in 1936 to play Mrs Pinchwife in *The Country Wife* at *London's *Old Vic, in a cast including Michael *Redgrave and Edith *Evans. Major roles followed in London and *New York, including Nora in *A Doll's House* (1937) and Natasha in McClintic's 1942 production of *Three Sisters*. Thornton *Wilder adapted the role of Dolly Levi for her in *The Matchmaker*, an international success in 1954–5. Married to writer Garson *Kanin in 1942, the pair wrote numerous plays and screenplays, including *Adam's Rib* (1949).

MAF

GORDONE, CHARLES (1925–95)

*African-American actor and playwright. His *New York career began with *Climate of Eden* (1957). Two years later he joined an illustrious cast in *Genet's *The Blacks*, performing along with Maya Angelou, James Earl *Jones, and Cicely Tyson. He *managed the Vantage Theatre in Queens, and also worked in a Greenwich Village bar named Johnny Romero's, which became the setting of his play *No Place to Be Somebody*. Produced in 1969 at the *New York Shakespeare Festival, *No Place* was transferred to Broadway by Ashton Springer, a black producer, and became the first play by an African American to win the Pulitzer Prize. For the next seven years Gordone was occupied with national *tours, and in the 1980s he co-founded the American Stage in Berkeley, California. He joined the faculty at Texas A&M University as distinguished lecturer in 1987.   BBL

GORELIK, MORDECAI (1899–1990)

American *designer and *theorist. Born in Russia, Gorelik emigrated to New York with his parents and attended school in Brooklyn. He graduated from Pratt Institute in 1920, having studied with designers Serge Soudeikine, Norman *Bel Geddes, and Robert Edmond *Jones. Gorelik focused on the production's effect on the *audience's way of thinking. In contrast to the poetic interests of contemporaries Jones or Jo *Mielziner, Gorelik showed the influence of *constructivism and *epic theatre. He called the production 'a machine-for-theatre'. His industrial, collage-like setting for *Processional* (*Theatre Guild, 1925), the sliding panels and wagon stage for the *Group Theatre's *Men in White* (1933), and the room suggestive of a boxing ring for the Group's *Golden Boy* (1937) typified Gorelik's technique. Exposed to *Brecht through reading and while designing *The Mother* in 1935, Gorelik's book *New Theatres for Old* (1940) introduced Brecht's theories into the United States.   MAF

GORKY, MAXIM (ALEKSEI PESHKOV) (1868–1936)

Russian dramatist, prose writer, and publicist. He was persuaded to write for the theatre by *Chekhov and *Nemirovich-Danchenko; the first two of his sixteen plays, *Philistines* and *The Lower Depths*, were staged by the *Moscow Art Theatre (MAT) in successive seasons in 1902. *Philistines* is an attack on the capital-driven bourgeoisie, while in *The Lower Depths*, his best-known play internationally, Gorky portrayed the down-and-out inhabitants of a doss-house. Both were addressed to a largely intellectual *audience from the boards of a middle-class institution, and a similar political antagonism colours all Gorky's plays of the pre-revolutionary period. Ironically the bourgeoisie provided his most memorable *characters, while his fledgling revolutionaries often failed to appear credible. Apart from *political themes, his work treats the meaning of art, the status of women, the destructiveness of vengeance, and the dynamics of the family. Gorky wrote plays about different social groups: *Summerfolk* (*St Petersburg, 1904), *Children of the Sun* (MAT, 1905), and *Barbarians* (Riga, 1906) are about the intelligentsia; while *Enemies* (*Berlin, 1907) is about the class struggle.

Exiled after his involvement with the 1905 Revolution, most of his later plays were written in Italy. A work about police corruption, *The Last Ones* (1908), was followed by *Eccentrics* (1910) and by two about the rapacity of the merchant class, *Vassa Zheleznova* (1910, awarded the Griboedov Prize for drama) and *The Zykovs* (1918), then another about the bankruptcy of the urban petty bourgeoisie, *Counterfeit Coin* (begun in 1913). Gorky returned to Russia under amnesty that year, completing a play about revenge before the revolution, *The Old Man* (produced 1919), and three-quarters of another, *Yakov Bogomolov* (1916–17). The comic treatment of political, verbal diarrhoea in the *one-act *Workaholic Slovotekov* (1920) irritated the Party leaders. Gorky again went into exile in 1921, ostensibly for his health. To recapture the heroic spirit of the 1917 Revolution, in the late 1920s he wrote the masterly *Egor Bulychov and the Others* (*Moscow, 1932), followed by *Dostigaev and the Others* (Leningrad, 1933), with some characters appearing in both plays. *Somov and the Others* (1928), found only after Gorky's death, concerns the 1928 show trials of bourgeois technical experts accused of wrecking Russian industry. The antagonism of the early plays was replaced by engagement with the new Bolshevik *hero, but this character is not convincing when compared to his studies of the former bourgeois. Gorky finally returned to Russia in 1933. Fêted as a master of literature, engaged in the formulation of *socialist realism (1934), he remodelled two plays apparently to fit the new requirements. With Gorky's changes, *Enemies* was restaged (MAT, 1935), and he rewrote *Vassa Zheleznova* as a punishing indictment of the amorality of the merchant class (1936). Was Gorky free to speak as he wished in the last years of his life? He protected as many people as he seemed to betray by his closeness to Stalin, but it is almost certain he was poisoned on Stalin's orders.   CM

GOROSTIZA, CARLOS (1920–)

Argentinian playwright, novelist, and director. Gorostiza has been a constant presence in *Buenos Aires theatre for nearly 50 years, from his early days as *puppeteer and independent theatre actor to his service as national Secretary of Culture (1983–5), and especially for his nearly 30 plays. Gorostiza's realistic theatre has evolved over the years, beginning with *The Bridge* (1949, heralding a national *realism on a par with US and European theatre), continuing with *Our Fellow Men* (1966), and finally the more theatricalized realism of *The Accompaniment* (1981) and *Aeroplanes* (1990).   JGJ

GOROSTIZA, CELESTINO (1904–67)

Mexican playwright, director, and translator, a pivotal figure in the development of the modern professional stage. In 1932 Gorostiza created the Teatro de *Orientación, which for three years was an energetic site of experimentation and renovation, mounting plays by established European playwrights and, more importantly, by contemporary Mexicans who did not have easy access to production. Gorostiza began by writing plays in the manner of *Cocteau and *Lenormand, but is best remembered for *The Color of our Skin* (1952), a powerful, *realistic study of the subtle but destructive forces of racism in Mexico.   KFN

GOSCH, JÜRGEN (1943–)

German director. Gosch trained and worked in East *Berlin before shifting to the West in 1978. As director-in-residence in Cologne under Jürgen *Flimm in the early 1980s, he gained a national reputation with *Molière's *The Misanthrope* (1983), which was staged on a long sweeping staircase, and *Oedipus the King* (1985), which utilized *masks. A short-lived period as director of the *Schaubühne (1988–89) ended after disastrous reviews and protests from the company. In 1993 he joined the *Deutsches Theater in Berlin as director-in-residence, where he has established a solid reputation for productions of the classics, particularly Shakespeare and *Kleist.   CBB

GOSSON, STEPHEN (1554–1624)

English pamphleteer and sometime playwright. Gosson in his youth wrote several plays, but in 1579 attacked the stage in *The*

School of Abuse. The revival of two of his plays prompted *Plays Confuted in Five Acts* (1582). Gosson's pamphlets, with those of Anthony *Munday, make the main Puritan case against the theatre. *See* ANTI-THEATRICAL POLEMIC.   RWV

GOTANDA, PHILIP KAN (1951–)

American playwright. Born in Stockton, California, Gotanda graduated from the University of California, Santa Barbara, in 1974 and received a degree from Hastings School of Law in 1978. While working for North Beach Chinatown Legal Aid in *San Francisco, Gotanda wrote his first play, *The Avocado Kid* (1980), a *musical inspired by the Japanese children's story 'Peach Boy'. *The Avocado Kid* premièred at *East West Players, the first *Asian-American theatre company. His second play, *A Song for a Nisei Fisherman* (1981), examines the life of a physician who is mentally damaged by the internment of Japanese Americans during the Second World War. Subsequent plays include *Bullet Headed Birds* (1981), *Dream of Kitamura* (1982), *American Tattoo* (1983), *The Wash* (1985), *Yankee Dawg You Die* (1988), *Fish Head Soup* (1991), *Day Standing on its Head* (1994), and *Ballad of Yachiyo* (1996). Throughout his career as *filmmaker, director, and playwright Gotanda has remained steadfast in his attempts to provide sensitively written, realistic alternatives to the Asian stereotype.   JSM

GOTHA COURT THEATRE

A key institution in the growth of the German theatre. Between 1775 and 1778, under the direction of Konrad *Ekhof, the first *repertory company staffed purely by German actors under royal patronage was installed at the court theatre of Gotha in Thuringia. Ekhof attempted to introduce measures that would improve the professional status of German performers. The company that he trained included August Wilhelm *Iffland, Heinrich Beck, and Johann David Beil, who, after Ekhof's death and the subsequent dissolution of the company, went on to form the nucleus of the *Mannheim Court Theatre.   SJCW

GOTTSCHED, JOHANN CHRISTOPH (1700–66)

German dramatist and critic. While professor of literature in Leipzig he formed a close acquaintance with Caroline *Neuber

Andrei Şerban's production of *King Stag* by Carlo **Gozzi**, American Repertory Theatre, Cambridge, Massachusetts, 1984. The scenography, including the design of the large animal puppet held aloft, was by Julie Taymor.

and her acting troupe in the 1730s. Together they vigorously opposed the improvisational practices and taste for low *comedy that characterized most German itinerant troupes. In his influential work *Versuch einer Critischen Dichtkunst vor die Deutschen* (*Critique of Poetry for the Germans*, 1730) he laid down rules for drama based on French *neoclassical principles. His *tragedy *Der sterbende Cato* (*The Dying Cato*, 1732) is an attempt to follow them and had some success when performed.

CBB

GOW, MICHAEL (1955–)

Australian playwright, actor, and director. Gow's best-known play is *Away*, about three dysfunctional families going away for the Christmas (summer) break. Another international success was *Sweet Phoebe* (1995), a yuppie *comedy originally starring Cate Blanchett. Whether writing or directing, in commercial theatre or in theatre for *youth, Gow's work often deals with problems of communication and tensions within families. After directing several successful productions for the *Sydney Theatre Company, Gow became *artistic director of the Queensland Theatre Company in Brisbane in 1999.

EJS

GOZZI, CARLO (1720–1806)

Italian writer. Gozzi was born into the ancient Venetian aristocracy which Carlo *Goldoni, his lifelong adversary, satirized as a set of impecunious drones. His brother Gasparo became an essayist of note, but also a supporter of Goldoni. Carlo entered the army, fought in Dalmatia, and devoted much of his energy to endless legal cases over the family inheritance. In 1747 he helped establish the Accademica dei Granelleschi, a facetiously semi-obscene title for a quintessentially eighteenth-century body whose stated purpose was the preservation of the purity of Italian against French influences. The Academy became a conservative citadel opposed to innovations of all sort, especially those proposed by Goldoni. Gozzi's *Useless Memoirs* (1797) are a surprisingly dull document, particularly since their prime purpose was to defend the author against gossip concerning his complex relations with the actress Teodora Ricci.

Gozzi was author of many verses and pamphlets, mainly polemical in purpose, and from them he emerges as a bilious defender of the nobility, Church, and state against the encroachment of Enlightenment thought, and indeed as an opponent of reform of all types, literary, philosophical, moral, or political. He was every inch the patrician, dilettante man of letters, out of sympathy with the new breed of professional artist emerging in the proto-capitalist Venice of his day. His main *bêtes noires* were the two leading playwrights of the time, Goldoni and the abbé Pietro Chiari, whom he identified as exponents of reform and spokesmen for the newly empowered bourgeoisie. He attacked

them both in *La tartana degli influssi per l'anno bisestile 1756* (*The Logbook of Influences for Leap Year 1756*), and was repeating the same theme in his *Marfisa bizzarra* (*Marfisa the Marvellous*, 1772), a mock chivalric epic, anti-Enlightenment in outlook, where the two appear as caricature knights. By then Goldoni, tired of the endless polemics, had left for *Paris and Chiari had abandoned the stage.

Gozzi made himself champion of *commedia dell'arte*, eviscerated by Goldoni's reform programme. It was a spirit of rivalry and bravado which drove him to compose the ten fables (1761–5) which were intended to restore traditional Italian drama to its pristine vigour. These fables represent a world of fantasy, magic, and *illusion which stands at the opposite extreme from Goldoni's theatre of *realism and observation, but Gozzi incorporated into his fables, especially *The Beautiful Green Bird* (1765), his continuing struggle against the new philosophy. He had a role for the *stock characters of *commedia* alongside freshly created *characters, but he deluded himself over his ability, or willingness, to restore *improvisation to Italian *comedy and to undo Goldoni's reforms. His Pantaloon was the same wise counsellor who appeared in Goldoni's reformed theatre, not the lecherous goat of late *commedia*, and only the first play, *L'amore delle tre melanrance* (*The Love of the Three Pomegranates*, 1761) was written as a *commedia* script affording actors the old freedom to improvise *dialogue and *action. From *The Crow* (1761) onwards, Gozzi produced fully written scripts, including *The Stag King*, *The Serpent Woman* (both 1762), and *The Green Bird* (1765). *Turandot* (1762), a hauntingly exotic tale with elements of the misogyny which recurs in his work, remains his most powerfully imagined work (and the basis for *Puccini's *opera, 1926). Gozzi's taste for fantasy has attracted unexpected admirers from *Goethe to *Brecht, but it is no accident that his work has had most success when adapted for *ballet and opera. (*See* illustration p. 531.)

JF

GRABBE, CHRISTIAN DIETRICH (1801–36)

German dramatist. The author of *historical dramas on a grand scale, Grabbe remained largely unperformed in his short lifetime. Works such as the two-play cycle *Die Hohenstaufen* (*The Hohenstaufens*, 1827), *Napoleon; oder, Die hundert Tage* (*Napoleon; or, The Hundred Days*, 1831), and *Hannibal* (1835) focus on great military leaders and historical figures in an epic form that was considered unproduceable. In his fascination with the failure of great leaders Grabbe outlines a pessimistic view of history, occasioned by the restoration of the monarchy after 1815. *Don Juan und Faust* (1829), the only work he saw performed, explores the two figures as indicative of the principles sensuality and spirituality. Best known today is the *comedy *Scherz, Satire, Ironie und tiefere Bedeutung* (*Joke, Satire, Irony, and Deeper Meaning*, 1827) in which he takes issue with the literary pretensions of his fellow *romantic writers and the small-town provincialism he suffered. Grabbe's work became influential after 1900 when he was seen as a precursor of both *expressionist and *epic drama.   CBB

GRAHAM, MARTHA (1894–1991)

American dancer, choreographer, teacher, and company director. A pioneer of American modern *dance, she developed a technique of contraction and release that was angular and percussive, stressing the body's weight and giving in to gravity with falls to the floor. She taught at her own school and also for many years *trained actors at the *Neighborhood Playhouse in *New York. Her choreography was dramatic and expressive, making use of modern literary and cinematic techniques such as flashbacks and interior *monologues. Graham frequently collaborated with Isamu *Noguchi, whose stark, symbolic sculptures captured the essence of her dramas, and with American composers, including Aaron Copland. Though she choreographed for nearly 70 years, she is best known for her *Greek *tragedies of the 1940s, often told from the point of view of a sexually anguished mythical *heroine, such as Jocasta in *Night Journey* (1947), Graham's adaptation of the Oedipus story.
                SB

GRAHAMSTOWN FESTIVAL

The largest arts *festival in South Africa. Originally established by the 1820 Settlers' Foundation to promote English theatre and culture, it moved towards embracing resistance theatre, with English as the 'language of liberation' which would oppose the government's insistence on separate development of South Africa's people, which meant keeping cultural forms separate. The festival includes visual art, *dance, music, *film, theatre, and a winter school. For two weeks in July established artists are commissioned to present work for the Main Festival, while the Fringe provides venues for experimental and student work. Since 1990 the festival has become more multilingual and diverse in its range, and important work from the *Market Theatre Laboratory has premièred there.   YH

GRAMATICA, EMMA (1872–1965) AND IRMA (1867–1962)

Italian actresses. Emma played Sirenetta in *D'Annunzio's *Gioconda* (1899), acted in top *touring companies with *Duse, *Ruggeri, and her sister Irma, and formed her own troupes. She helped introduce *Hauptmann, *Ibsen and *Shaw to Italy. Irma was a lyrical performer with an excellent voice, and made her name in the popular French repertory of the 1890s, especially in *Zola's *Nana* and *Thérèse Raquin*. She then became lead actress for *Zacconi and *Talli. In her vast repertory—Shakespeare, *Schiller, *Pinero, *Sardou, *Hauptmann, *Giacosa, *Praga, *Sudermann—she originated many roles, including Mila in D'Annunzio's *The Daughter of Jorio* (1904).   JEH

GRAN CIRCO TEATRO

Chilean troupe founded by Andrés Pérez in 1988. Its main objective was to reach a mass *audience; to this end it incorporated elements of Chilean popular culture that had been prohibited by the dictatorship. It used theatrical innovations Pérez had learned from Ariane *Mnouchkine at Théâtre du *Soleil, such as *nō and *kabuki *acting styles and orchestral accompaniment. Extensively relying on *melodrama, light humour, and Chilean festive traditions, Gran Circo became one of the most successful theatres in Chile in the late twentieth century. *La Negra Ester* (1988), based on Roberto Parra's poem about his love affair with a beautiful prostitute, became an instant hit. Other successful works produced collectively by the group are *Allende-Epoca 70* (1990), *Popol-Vuh* (1992), *Nemesio Pelao* (1999), and *Mishima Yukio's *Madame de Sade* (1998). *La huida* (*The Flight*, 2001) treated the persecution of homosexuals during the dictatorship of Carlos Ibáñez del Campo (1929–31).   MAR

GRAND-GUIGNOL, THÉÂTRE DE

*Paris *playhouse dedicated to portrayals of dread and torture. Oscar Méténier founded it in 1895; in 1899, under the direction of Max Maurey, it moved to a building that had been a convent (and kept its wooden angels). Aficionados claimed they heard ghosts of nuns moaning above the 285-seat theatre. At first *naturalist slices of life were interspersed with *comedies, but the *genre changed to horror, especially under the direction of André de Lorde, known as the 'prince of terror'. He wrote over a hundred thrillers modelled upon the stories of his idol Edgar Allan Poe. Although de Lorde favoured psychological distress, he also wrote shockers with believable depictions of ripped skin, gouged eyeballs, burning flesh, and other disasters. Actors judged success by the number of spectators who fainted or vomited. Evenings began with a comic curtain raiser, showed two horror plays, and ended with a sex *farce. By the 1940s detective stories dominated the offerings, and in the 1950s *audiences found the plays camp rather than chilling. The theatre closed in 1962.   FL

GRAND MAGIC CIRCUS

After collaborating on a performance of *Le Labyrinthe* in 1967, director Jérôme *Savary and playwright Fernando *Arrabal founded a theatre *collective, which they called the Grand Théâtre Panique. The company changed its name to the Grand Magic Circus a year later, and produced a series of highly successful and distinctly unconventional shows. Combining his interest in *musical theatre, decorative arts, and American jazz, Savary used a *circus-like *cabaret format to stage biting social *satires. His 1970 production of *Zartan* employed a comic-strip style to present a picaresque anti-Tarzan demolishing various images of institutional authority. Similarly his *Robinson Crusoe* in 1972 attacked myths of colonial supremacy. In the 1980s Savary turned away from iconoclastic message-driven theatre and began to direct *comedies and light *operas, notably *Molière's *The Would-Be Gentleman* (1980), and *Kander and Ebb's *Cabaret* (1987), faithfully maintaining the popular festive style that marked his earlier work. CHB

GRAND OPERA See OPERA.

GRANDVAL, CHARLES-FRANÇOIS RACOT DE (1710–84)

French actor. Admitted to the *Comédie-Française in 1729 as *Quinault-Dufresne's understudy, Grandval had graduated to leading roles by the 1740s: his comic specialities were fops and men of the world, and in *tragedy he created several major roles for *Voltaire (from *Mahomet*, 1741, to *Sémiramis*, 1748). After 1750 he yielded the leading tragic roles to *Lekain, retaining for himself the high comic repertory—roles in which he was unequalled. JG

GRANVILLE BARKER, HARLEY See BARKER, HARLEY GRANVILLE.

GRASS, GÜNTHER (1927–)

German novelist, graphic artist, and playwright. The Nobel Prize-winner for literature and world-famous novelist had only a passing interest in the theatre. A number of short pieces in an *absurdist mode (*Flood*, 1957; *The Wicked Cooks*, 1961) were followed by his only full-length play (*Plebians Rehearse the Uprising*, 1966), which discusses in a play-within-a-play format *Brecht's part in the 1953 uprising of workers in East *Berlin and debates the options of reform or revolution. CBB

GRASSI, PAOLO (1919–81)

Italian *manager, born in Milan, who worked as critic, director, and company manager in the fascist years. He was active in the Resistance, and after the Liberation he and Giorgio *Strehler founded the *Piccolo Teatro in *Milan. The two divided responsibility, with Strehler becoming *artistic director and Grassi taking on the role of administrator. 'I preferred to occupy first rank as cultural operator rather than second or third rank as director,' he wrote. The two men shared a common vision of theatre as a

public service, accessible to all and with a social and moral function. Grassi was on hand for Strehler's productions of *Goldoni, *Brecht, and *Pirandello which brought the theatre international renown. He remained at his post when Strehler left in 1968, and ceded sole control to Strehler when he returned in 1972. Grassi moved on to become superintendent at La *Scala, charged with reshaping the image of the *opera house in turbulent times and with restoring artistic standards. In 1977 he was made chairman of RAI, the state broadcasting company. JF

GRASSO, GIOVANNI (1873–1930)

Italian actor, who began his career in Sicilian *verismo plays with his friend Angelo *Musco. Grasso's style was marked by a raw earthiness, and admirers included *D'Annunzio and *Meyerhold. He became a leading figure of Sicilian dialect theatre, and starred in Nino *Martoglio's *film *Sperduti nel buio* (*Lost in the Dark*, 1914). ATS

GRASSO, OMAR (1940–)

Argentinian director. After working with Uruguay's *Galpón Theatre, Grasso returned to Argentina where he became known for his unconventional, ideological productions of the classics. In the 1980s and 1990s he staged many of his compatriots' plays, often going beyond *naturalism into the realm of the poetic. JGJ

GRAY, JOHN (1946–)

Canadian playwright and composer. His best-known play, *Billy Bishop Goes to War* (1978), is a two-person *musical that examines the ambiguous attitudes of Canada's most famous flying ace of the First World War. It premièred in *Vancouver, went on two national *tours, and appeared on Broadway in 1980. Other major musicals include *18 Wheels* (1977), about long-distance truckers; *Rock and Roll* (1981), about a small-town Canadian rock band; and *Don Messer's Jubilee* (1985), about a one-time cultural icon of Gray's native Nova Scotia. Another musical, *Health* (1989), was not so well received. Gray's novels include *Dazzled* (1984), *A Gift for the Little Master* (2000), and *The Fiend in Human* (2002), and he has written regular columns for Canadian newspapers. DWJ

GRAY, SIMON (JAMES HOLLIDAY) (1936–)

English playwright. Educated in Canada, Gray began an academic career in Vancouver and continued it as a lecturer in English at Queen Mary College, London (1956–85), while his writing career flourished. His plays frequently reflect the quixotic and sometimes exclusive worlds of academia and publishing and tell stories of the so-called 'chattering classes' of the south-east of England. In fact his plays are much less safe than this might suggest: they contain violent and abusive sexual relations, emotional betrayal, and complex relationships, often concerning men forced to the edge of society and into destructive isolation by confused sexual identity or crippling shyness. His first West End play set the tone: the central male *character of *Wise Child* is a transvestite, played by Alec *Guinness (1967). The theme featured again in *Butley* (1971), in which Alan *Bates appeared as the savagely witty but appallingly self-destructive eponymous *hero, a university lecturer whose affair with a male student hastens the collapse of his sham marriage.

The Common Pursuit (1984) follows a group of university friends over twenty years, though with a structural device that has the last scene set only fifteen minutes after the first one. The play builds towards the reported suicide of one of the characters, another common motif in Gray's imagined world. *Melon* (1987) again provided Bates with a meaty and complex role of a successful literary publisher flailing to recover his true self in the face of psychological collapse, similar to the character Bates played in *Otherwise Engaged* (1975). *Quartermaine's Terms* (1981), with its *Chekhovian overtones, and the *television play *After Pilkington* (1987), are perhaps Gray's most assured and complete works of emotional regret, intellectual failure, and social alienation. While his contemporaries *Ayckbourn and *Stoppard may be more prolific and more critically successful, Gray's plays remain poignant and at times acerbic accounts of educated England and the masculinities it restrains, excludes, and ultimately destroys. Gray's account of the *rehearsal process of *The Common Pursuit* (*An Unnatural Pursuit*, 1985), is something of a cautionary tale for all those enamoured of West End glamour. His 1995 play *Cell Mates* (about the spy George Blake and the petty criminal Sean Bourke) attracted significant *publicity when the actor Stephen Fry suffered stage fright and quit the cast.   AS

GRAY, SPALDING (1941–)

American actor and writer. The surface simplicity of Spalding Gray's autobiographical *monologues belies a complex investigation of the postmodern sense of self. A Rhode Island native, Gray attended college in Boston and moved to *New York in 1967 with his then-girlfriend, the director Elizabeth *LeCompte. His mother committed suicide that year, an event that became material for some of his and LeCompte's theatrical experiments with the *Wooster Group. He and LeCompte formed that company in 1980 after having worked with the *Performance Group, where Gray became interested in using his own self, rather than mimicking make-believe emotions on stage. The Wooster Group created *Three Places in Rhode Island*, multi-*character pieces in which Gray played himself and used his own experiences as material. His best-known monologue is

Swimming to Cambodia (1985), which concerns his experiences acting in the *film *The Killing Fields* (1984). When performing Gray sits behind a desk in street clothes with a notebook and seems to talk quite casually, but his monologues are in fact closely scripted and continually reworked over many years. His subsequent pieces have charted his life in detail, including his experiences of writing a book (*Monster in a Box*, 1990), suffering illness (*Gray's Anatomy*, 1993), leaving his wife for another woman (*It's a Slippery Slope*, 1996), and fatherhood (*Morning, Noon, and Night*, 1999).   KF

GRAY, TERENCE (1895–c.1987)

Irish director and *manager. An avid experimental practitioner, Gray, while working with *toy theatres to create *Craig-inspired illustrations for two volumes of his own plays, evolved a system akin to building blocks for easily movable architectural scenic units. Acquiring a theatre, which he renamed the *Cambridge Festival, he put his experimenting into practice (1926–33) in a series of iconoclastic productions, inspired by continental anti-*naturalistic innovations. Gray proved how readily adaptable the *expressionist staging methods deployed by *Jessner and *Fehling in *Berlin were to the repertoire of classics. He staged *Aeschylus, *Sophocles, *Aristophanes, *Terence, Shakespeare, *Wilde, *Yeats, *Shaw, *Strindberg, *Čapek, *Pirandello, and contemporary German and American *political drama, proving the remarkable adaptability of his scenic system (only *Ibsen defeated his staging method). Gray appreciated that a markedly expressionist stagecraft required significant changes to *lighting design (he worked with Harold Ridge, installing a *cyclorama and the latest Schwabe-Haseit system); and that the resulting style of performance necessitated changes in actors' modes of delivery, stance, and movement too. To meet this last need, Gray brought in his cousin Ninette de Valois as movement director, offering her in return a stage for her choreography. Endlessly experimenting, he discovered how to deploy a *revolve to give rhythmic, visual interest to an otherwise permanent set for *early modern drama. Gray's achievements (many now common practice) were discussed and illustrated in contemporary journals as offering a lead to other small-scale 'art' theatres; but it was his predominantly undergraduate *audiences that made Gray's iconoclasm possible.   RAC

GREBAN, ARNOUL (c.1420–1470)

Playwright and choirmaster. Greban's *Passion*, the most celebrated French *Passion play of the fifteenth century, was performed at least three times before 1473, and, together with the *Passion* of Jean *Michel, provided an interdependent *text for many performances during the fifteenth and sixteenth centuries, including those at Mons (1501) and Valenciennes (1547). Greban also collaborated with his brother Simon to write

The Play of the Acts of the Apostles, performed at Bourges in 1536. RWV

GREEK NATIONAL THEATRE

Following in the footsteps of the Greek Royal Theatre, the Greek National Theatre was founded in *Athens in 1932 with the purpose of recruiting the most talented theatre artists and presenting the best of the national and international repertory. Its first building, on St Constantine's Street off Concord Square, was demolished in 1938 and a new theatre was built in the same location. Under the leadership of Ioannis Gryparis, its first directors, Fotos *Politis and Dimitris Rondiris, presented Greek *tragedy, Shakespeare, *Ibsen, as well as new Greek and international plays. The National Theatre inaugurated the *Epidaurus Festival in 1955 with cutting-edge open-air productions of *Euripides' *Hecuba* (1955) and *Aristophanes' *Lysistrata* (1957). In 1961 the State Theatre of Northern Greece, an offshoot of the National Theatre located in Thessaloniki, began offering quality productions from the international repertory. Aimilios Hourmouzios and Nikos Kourkoulos were among the most innovative of the National Theatre's *artistic directors, and Aimilios Veakis, Katina *Paxinou, Alexis Minotis, Antigone Valakou, Jenny Karezi, Dimitris Horn, and Manos *Katrakis were among its finest actors. The theatre's memorable productions included *Chekhov's *Three Sisters* directed by Karolos *Koun (1951), *O'Neill's *Long Day's Journey into Night* directed by Minotis (1965), and Alan *Bennett's *The Madness of George III* directed by Andreas Voutsinas (1993). Attached to the National Theatre are its conservatory which offers tuition-free *training to selected young actors; the New Stage, founded in 1968 to develop experimental performances and new Greek plays; and its *touring company, which brings critically acclaimed productions to international *audiences.

KGo

GREEK PLAYHOUSES *See* ANCIENT THEATRES.

GREEK THEATRE, ANCIENT

1. Origins of theatre in Greece;
2. Late Archaic and Classical Greek theatre (508–317 BC);
3. Hellenistic theatre (317–86 BC);
4. Greek theatre under the Roman Empire (86 BC–AD 692);
5. Greek dramatic literature

1. Origins of theatre in Greece

*Aristotle argued for an *origin for *drama in three *genres of Dionysiac song and *dance: he derived *tragedy from 'those who led the *dithyramb' and from 'a *satyr-play like performance'; *comedy he derived from 'leaders of the phallic songs'. So far as we know drama in Classical Athens was performed only at festivals of the god *Dionysus, but this was not true elsewhere or in later periods. Outside Athens, even in the fifth century, theatres were built in the sanctuaries, and dramas performed at festivals, of other gods. In later centuries drama's link with Dionysus appears still more tenuous. One might then freely doubt that drama originated in exclusively Dionysiac *ritual, especially as *costumes, *masks, and mythological pageants are also attested for the cults of the goddesses Artemis and Demeter, and minor mystery gods, called the Cabeiri. But the evidence we possess shows that Aristotle's claim is in outline correct, if over-schematic. Drama's most immediate antecedent was ritual entertainments at festivals of Dionysus, and particularly those entertainments in which a *chorus interacted with a 'leader', singing refrains, to what, in origin, was probably improvised *verse.

The material remains of Archaic Greece offer three types of iconographic evidence which in part corroborates, and in part modifies, Aristotle's assertion. Well over 1,000 vases depict groups of dancers known as 'komasts'. 'Komast vases' appear first in Corinth around 630 BC, then in various parts of Greece and Italy until the end of the sixth century BC. As depicted, the dance has typical lively gestures, and is performed to pipe music. The dancers may dance in procession, or in scattered disunity around a wine jar, or in a sacrificial or convivial setting. Dancers often hold ritual drinking horns or wine cups. Sometimes they wear costumes very much like those worn by comic *actors in the historical period, consisting of padded body suits with enlarged breasts, bellies, and buttocks, and less often a *phallus ranging in size from decently petit to grotesquely large. The komasts' gestures are frequently obscene and they sometimes pursue women, who are usually scantily clad, like the idealized female companions of Dionysus called nymphs. In a few cases inscriptions show that the komasts are playing roles. In others, the dancers participate in a procession or mummery with implied narrative contents. The emphasis upon wine, sexuality, and obscenity is typically Dionysiac.

Beginning at the same time as komast vases are vase paintings showing satyrs (more properly *silens*), mythological male companions of Dionysus, half-horse and half-human in form. They are also associated with wine, sex, and group dance and use gestures comparable to those of komasts, together with whom they sometimes appear. Satyr iconography became popular in Athenian art in the mid-sixth century when komast iconography began to decline. The satyrs' movements are more often coordinated than those of komasts, suggesting that the artist took some inspiration from choreographed performances, and the paintings more often contain narrative elements, especially from myths which involve processions. A favourite subject is the 'Return of Hephaestus', when Dionysus persuaded the recalcitrant Hephaestus to return to Olympus by giving him wine and escorting him, drunk, on the back of his donkey.

Some vases show the advent of Dionysus in his wheeled ship, or satyrs in a phallic procession.

About twenty Athenian pots from 560 to 480 BC depict a third group of dancers, men with regular choreographed movements dancing in procession or in a circle to pipe music. They wear elaborate masks and costumes, of animals, exotic foreigners, women, or mythological creatures, such as are often found in the choruses of *Old Comedy (for instance *Aristophanes' *Birds* and *Knights*), but there is nothing more to suggest that the vases depict drama. One vase shows a 'leader' improvising song and interacting with the chorus, as do two komast vases.

Our earliest literary attestation of dithyramb is contemporary with the first appearance of komasts and satyrs in art. A fragment of the earliest Greek lyric poet, Archilochus, boasts, 'For I know how to lead off the beautiful dithyramb song of the lord Dionysus, my mind blasted by wine.' At the same time, in Corinth, the semi-mythical *Arion is said to have first formally organized a dithyrambic chorus. A close association between drunken processional dance and early dithyramb is indicated by the use of the archaizing word *komos* (drunken procession) to designate dithyrambs in official decrees and inscriptions relating to the Athenian theatre. In the historical period, at any rate, grand processions were a regular feature of Dionysiac festivals, and they usually involved men dressed in satyr costume, phallic processions, or processions for sacred marriages.

2. Late Archaic and Classical Greek theatre (508–317 BC)

Ancient scholars claimed that one *Thespis first performed a tragedy in Athens around 534 BC, during the reign of the tyrant Pisistratus. But the first certain evidence of drama comes from the earliest years of the Athenian democracy which ousted the Pisistratid tyranny in 508 BC. A fragmentary inscription (*Fasti*), thought to rely on official archives, begins a list of productions from this date. The end of the sixth century BC also saw the building of the first Theatre of Dionysus in the city and the earliest *deme* theatre (at Thorikos). Many scholars now think that, despite ancient tradition, drama was a creation of the Athenian democracy.

Clearly the democracy found theatre suited to its ends. The occasions for theatrical performance soon multiplied and spread through the territory of Athens (Attica). Originally, drama may have been performed only at the urban festival of Dionysus (City *Dionysia). From about 508 BC there were competitions for dithyramb and for tragedies (followed by satyr-plays). In about 486 BC a contest for comedy was added. A second major festival, the *Lenaea, assumed competitions for both tragedy and comedy in about 440 BC. At this time the larger village festivals (Rural Dionysia) began to incorporate dramatic competitions, and the *Anthesteria added comedy by 326 BC. Before the collapse of the democracy in 322 BC, there were at least fourteen annual dramatic festivals in Attica, all crammed into the four winter months, some lasting several days.

One democratic (also Dionysiac) feature of the theatre was its inclusivity. The earliest Athenian theatre held perhaps 10,000 to 15,000 spectators, and, like later theatres, it constituted the largest place of assembly in the state (*see* ANCIENT THEATRES). The figure represents only 3 to 5 per cent of the estimated total population of mid-fifth-century BC Athens, but indicates a spectatorship rivalled only by the athletic games of the large pan-Hellenic sanctuaries. Slaves, foreigners, and children were freely admitted in the *audience, and probably women (though their attendance is still debated).

A second democratic feature was drama's openness to citizen participation. By law membership in the dramatic chorus was restricted to Athenian citizens, though the Lenaea and lesser festivals admitted also resident foreigners (*metics*). Chorus members received maintenance and probably monetary compensation for the *training period. The chorus was officially identified with the production and the competition was notionally for the best chorus. The chorus was the focal point of audience sympathy both in the drama and in the festival competition: in the narrative the chorus generally represented a group of ordinary citizens, relatively disempowered in contrast to the *characters played by the actors; in the theatre competition chorus members, insofar as they were ordinary citizen *amateurs, were personally known to many in the audience. A great many in the audience had performed in choruses at some times in their lives—a very conservative estimate of the annual demand for dramatic chorus members in Athens by the later fourth century BC is 1,332, and probably closer to 6,000 if we include dithyramb (about 17 per cent of the estimated citizen male population, or indeed closer to 50 per cent of all eligible male citizens, since chorus duty was considered too strenuous for anyone over 30). This also helped make the chorus a focal point of audience identification. Public participation was also encouraged by the judging process. Although a panel of judges was selected from the audience, in the final instance by lottery, our sources make it clear that judges were expected to take audience reaction into account—we even hear of the people prosecuting judges at the Dionysia for 'incorrect judgement'. The notion that the audience determined the outcome of the competition was at least shared by the comic poets who make frequent appeals for audience support, and who eventually developed *claques to stimulate audience response. Athenian audiences were anything but passive. They drove many plays out of the theatre by prolonged clucking, heel banging, and whistlings.

A third democratic feature, mainly affecting comedy, was poetic outspokenness. Old Comedy, and especially the comedy of the 'radical democracy' (430–405), freely abused politicians and prominent public figures, or was outspoken in its ridicule of social and *political policy. The public encouraged such behaviour, and libel laws, prosecutions, and attempts at *censorship had little or no effect, not only because comedic licence was consistent with the licence of the Dionysiac festival, but because it conspicuously affirmed the rights of equality and free speech which were fundamental to the democracy.

A fourth democratic feature was strict financial and administrative control of theatre by public officials. The chief responsibility was assumed by the 'Eponymous Archon', an ordinary citizen, selected by lot. In addition to general *management of the festival, the archon appointed sponsors (choregi), selected poets, and, by the later fifth century, made contracts with actors and probably pipers. The large scale of theatrical festivals at Athens required a complex mixture of private patronage, volunteer and paid labour, user fees, private enterprise, and public money. Wealthy elites were appointed by the archon to serve as choregi, which meant they were compelled to pay for the costuming, training, and maintenance of the chorus. In return they received a purely symbolic prize on behalf of the chorus, together with considerable prestige if they were successful. Private entrepreneurs called 'theatron-sellers' bought contracts from the state to manage the theatres, and in particular to rebuild the wooden benches in the *theatron for each festival season. In return they received not inconsiderable entrance fees (charged for the first time at any religious festival in Greece). Since entrance fees excluded many poorer citizens, the public treasury distributed a 'festival-dole' (theorikon) to all citizens to defray entrance costs sometime between 450 and 343 BC. Public funds also went to sacrifices for the festival and fees and prizes for the professional performers. The result of this complex arrangement was to make production far less sponsor directed than other traditional forms of music that normally relied on aristocratic patronage, but also to create a financial stake for all parties (other perhaps than the choregi) in the creation of a mass entertainment industry on an ever larger scale.

Greek drama was not, however, uniquely Athenian nor inherently democratic (though it would certainly have appeared in a different form, if at all, in a less democratic age). Other cities claimed to be the birthplace of tragedy, comedy, and satyr-play. Moreover, an independent comic tradition developed in Syracuse in mainland Megara, and its colony, Sicilian Megara. Indeed, far from adapting Athenian drama, the influence seems to have run in the other direction: Aristotle claims that Athenian comic poets learned to 'write *plots' from the Sicilian *Epicharmus. The costs and organizational complexity of dramatic festivals, were, if anything, better handled by Greek states governed by 'tyrants', while the prestige and populism of theatre festivals made drama especially attractive to these self-made autocrats. Under the tyrants Gelon and Hieron (490–466 BC), Syracuse became a centre for the performing arts, attracting among others the Sicilian comic poets Epicharmus and Phormis, and the tragedian *Aeschylus, who visited twice (471–469 and 458–456 BC).

We have little evidence for the spread of theatre beyond Syracuse and Attica until the last decades of the fifth century BC, when the Macedonian tyrants Perdiccas and Archelaus collected dithyrambic and dramatic poets, including *Euripides and *Agathon, and instituted a dramatic festival. Artefacts or remains of theatres make drama probable for at least half a dozen other cities in southern Italy and mainland Greece. In the fourth century tragedy and comedy in the Attic style were disseminated rapidly through the Greek world. Within the first two decades an active trade in terracotta figurines of actors demonstrates interest in theatre from the Greek colonies on the Black Sea to as far away as North Africa and Spain. By the 370s BC poets and actors come from all parts of the Greek world. By 350 theatres in Greece are plentiful, and by 300 ubiquitous. The fourth-century Macedonian monarchs emulated Archelaus' lavish patronage of theatre, buying the friendship and allegiance of theatre performers of every description. Actors were adroitly employed as ambassadors and negotiators. Philip conspicuously cultivated theatre in order to assert Macedon's (otherwise dubious) place within Greek culture. Alexander punctuated his voyage of conquest across Asia by producing massive theatre festivals which attracted thousands of artists from all over the Greek world. His policy in doing so was to attract the attention of the refractory Greek states to his unbroken string of conquests, while at the same time advertising his growing empire as a triumph for 'Greek' (not 'Macedonian') culture. The theatre industry was indeed Alexander's principal beneficiary.

The large-scale economics of the theatre industry permitted a degree of specialization and professionalization never before seen in Greece. In the early fifth century most aspects of dramatic production were firmly in the control of the poet: he took the role of *music director, dance instructor, and even *actor, all functions which belonged to separate specializations by the fourth century. We are also told that in early drama the poet himself hired the actors and the piper. Official recognition of the importance of the acting profession comes first in about 449 BC with the creation of a tragic actor's prize independent of the success of the performance, and a decade later with the creation of both tragic and comic actors' prizes at the Lenaea.

From the 420s BC theatre artefacts indicate a shift in popular interest from a nearly exclusive focus upon the (volunteer) citizen chorus, to a nearly exclusive focus upon the (professional) actors and pipers. Theatre pipers began to achieve wealth, fame, and stardom by developing a new level of virtuosity and expanding the range and dexterity of their instrument through technical innovation. In the later 420s Euripides began to incorporate their more complex music into his tragedies and to transfer the burden of musical delivery from the amateur chorus to the professionally trained voice of the actor. Comic poets and elite philosophers condemned the more liberated, professional, emotional, and, frankly, more musical 'New Music' as decadence caused by mercenary interests catering to the tastes of vulgar audiences. The same sources indicate that actors too had begun to develop the power of their voice and gestures to reach much higher standards of mimetic *realism. The more popular the new styles in music and acting became, the more vehemently elitist critics decried them as affronts to traditional tragic dignity and propriety.

With just such reactionary gloom Aristotle observed that actors in the fourth century were more important than poets. The rapid spread of theatre created the conditions for the emergence of professional superstars. Organizers were forced to advance huge deposits to encourage actors to appear at their festivals, and to levy huge fines when they failed to do so. Even the Athenian Dionysia might be passed by, as it was by the actor Athenodorus in 331 BC. By 341 BC star actors so completely determined the success of a performance that the archon was forced to require each team of actors to perform in one play of each competitor. Over the century the income of top actors rose from large to legendary: Theodorus, the most famous tragic actor of his day, was able to contribute four times more to the rebuilding of the temple of Apollo at Delphi than any other private individual; Neoptolemus could afford to give substantial monetary gifts to Athens in exchange for public honours; Aristodemus and Polus are said to have charged 'appearance fees' of a talent or five talents (roughly 6,000 to 30,000 times the average daily wage for even a skilled labourer). An inscription shows that Polus charged so much for an appearance that the medium-sized state of Samos, desperate in 306 BC to celebrate its new kings with due magnificence, heaped fulsome honours upon him when he agreed to accept reduced fees and deferred payment in exchange for all the *box-office proceeds.

In 322 BC Antipater, the Macedonian viceroy, crushed a Greek revolt stirred up by the Athenian democracy. He exiled or disenfranchised the poorest Athenians and in 317 BC instituted an oligarchy under the regency of Demetrius of Phaleron. Demetrius abolished the festival dole and the choregic system. Drama was now organized, in the city, by an 'Arranger of Contests' (agonothetes). This wealthy functionary continued to sponsor dramatic competitions, though now for poets and actors, not choregi and choruses. He made large contributions from his own pocket, but it was a very different form of public munificence from the choregia, as it put total control over drama into the hands of the wealthiest few. Demetrius had merely implemented the recommendations of his teacher Aristotle that financial obligations be attached to the chief magistracies 'so that the common people will gladly have no part in them and show indulgence to those in office, who pay a great deal for the privilege', and that when they have enjoyed some public benefit at the magistrates' expense 'the commoners will be glad to see the [oligarchic] constitution remain in place'.

The institution of the agonothesia probably brought the first professional choruses to the Athenian *orchestra. Public participation came to an end. In the plays of *Menander (mostly after 317 BC) choral entertainments were mere entr'actes with no connection to the drama. Thus, while the drama of the democracy was a drama of symbolic inclusion focused on the chorus, *New Comedy sooner expressed the community's exclusion. Where once Old Comedy invited the world of the theatre into the drama (so often that some scholars reject the utility of the word *'illusion' altogether), New Comedy erected a 'fourth wall' that was rarely breached. Where once Old Comedy offered radical solutions to political problems, New Comedy's problems were private, deliberately trivialized, morality plays. Aristophanes' lower-class *heroes, whose triumphs over the establishment satisfied the wish-fulfilment fantasies of the powerless, were now replaced by Menander's naive, ironically distanced, well-meaning, upper-class heroes, all struggling to maintain their proper niche within a given social order.

3. Hellenistic theatre (317–86 BC)

The conquests of Alexander brought with them an immediate dissemination of theatre to all corners of his empire, where new theatres, along with gymnasia, could be regarded as one of the central elements of the Hellenization of non-Greek peoples. Only among some parts of the population of Judaea was there strong opposition to heavy-handed implementation of the new cultural policies. The dominance of the theatre was undoubtedly supported both by the creation of an educational system in which Greek Classical drama was studied and even acted, and also by the well-organized association of the *Artists of Dionysus; these had both close personal connections to the Hellenistic rulers, and the ability to staff the festivals that sprang up in the newly prosperous cities of Asia Minor, Syria, and Egypt, not only celebrating the old gods but also the new semi-divine members of the ruling families. Regrettably, we have almost no surviving evidence for these dramas, after Menander, other than in epigraphy, archaeology, and anecdotes.

The programmes of these festivals, known to us from many victor lists and other inscriptions, show remarkable consistency in their dramatic components, following the fashion at Athens with its dramatic prizes. First, even at small festivals there could be prize competitions for the writers of new comedy, new tragedy, and surprisingly sometimes even new satyr-play. By 'new' is meant 'contemporary', 'recently written', and a prize therefore went to the poet of these genres, but also to the best overall actor of new tragedy and new comedy, but very rarely of new satyr-play, perhaps because the choral performance was its principal attraction. It is important to emphasize that such contemporary dramatic writing, despite its almost complete disappearance, flourished in Greek festival culture until c. AD 200 at the local and international level, and many of its writers and actors are known by name to us. Some held public office and were people of substance.

The other division of drama, the performance of Classical plays, was undoubtedly more prestigious, as we can tell from the prizes awarded. Of course prizes in this 'old drama' category were limited to the actor-producer, known now formally as the *tragoidos* and *komoidos*. Old satyr-plays were produced, but they were rare and not in a regular prize category. We must beware of assuming that these revivals of Classical plays, with the favourites being Euripidean tragedy and the New Comedy of Menander, were acted with an eye to historical accuracy. On one hand, they were undoubtedly exposed to the technological tricks of the Hellenistic theatre and its actors, with corresponding emphasis on the demands of the contemporary audience for the sensational and rhetorical, and this might have led to minor insertions of modernizing material or even an ambitious re-organizing of the Classical *text by creative Artists of Dionysus. On the other hand, changing taste, especially in music, could mandate major changes in performance, whereby the original speeches were adapted for operatic singing, or choral odes removed. Our evidence for this now comes largely from accusations by the grammarians who sought to purify the texts from such suspected alterations. On a practical financial level, the great chorus of Classical drama would not be normally possible, and we may assume that on those occasions where the chorus was not entirely removed, a smaller professional chorus sufficed.

On the whole, despite the consistency of the festival programme—a feature that should be connected with the conservative traditions of the Artists' associations, and the need to preserve the regulations for competitive festival categories—we should recognize the potential for innovation, variety, and development inside and outside contemporary and classic drama during the years 300 BC to AD 100. The mechanical snail trailing slime which led the procession through the Theatre of Dionysus in 308 BC gives us a telling early example of the spectacular new effects that were now possible and popular; at this same time the new ruler of Athens, Demetrius of Phaleron, also introduced the first known *mimes on the Athenian stage, and soon we find performers of quasi-dramatic genres appearing in festivals outside of formal competition, and even a female entertainer at Delos. A dancer is later listed as belonging to the Egyptian Artists. In some places, such as Boeotia, there was clearly a strong and consistent local tradition; but in other areas, especially under Roman or non-Greek influence, adaptation was welcomed. An excellent example is the biblical story of Exodus 1–15 dramatized as a Greek tragedy *Exagoge* by the (otherwise unknown) Jewish writer Ezechiel, probably in second-century BC Alexandria; it is the longest surviving fragment (269 lines) of Greek tragedy after Euripides, but we cannot tell whether it was ever acted. We have evidence for boldly operatic and musical adaptations of Classical drama, which would have fallen outside the scope of the strictly controlled festival prize categories of drama, but would be increasingly popular as irregular entertainment. Some of these could make their way into the festival programme too, either under the old categories of arias sung to the lyre or pipe (*kitharoidia, aulodia*), or in a new category of

'chorus with piper'. Already in 100 BC we can find decrees honouring men not only for paying for festivals, but for providing irregular entertainments 'at the demand of the people'. Among many puzzles, it is notable that neither in tragedy nor comedy did the chorus entirely disappear, whether in contemporary or classic genres, as was often assumed; oddly one group of chorusmen seemed to serve different dramas at the same festival, and sometimes was paid directly by the festival organizers. Yet the term 'tragic chorusman' was never used, while 'comic chorusman' is frequent in the records, and even 'satyr chorusman' is found. Apparently 'chorusman' without qualification implies 'tragedy' as the choral genre *par excellence*.

It is impossible to generalize about this long and little understood phase in the history of drama. While the conservative Artists of Dionysus in their own interest sought to maintain a relatively stable festival programme and to encourage festivals generally, concluding contracts with several cities simultaneously for the staffing of their performances and even supplying their members under favourable conditions to cities in financial straits, at the same time dramatic and musical innovation was proceeding apace. One clear sign is the breakdown of the earlier strict division between the genres, so that we find the first named actors of both comedy and tragedy in the late second century BC; writers became players and vice versa. Of great importance for the history of drama is the rise of mime, by which we mean broadly a polymorphous type of *music-hall *farce, which was not usually masked. This immensely popular genre was nowhere allowed into the formal programme of Hellenistic prize competitions but, like dancing, led a marginal life. The title of the Artists' associations can now sometimes add 'and their synagonists', and we could perhaps understand by this a concession to the popularity of the professional mimes and dancers, who did not qualify for official prizes but were paid to appear as fringe groups.

It was probably the unifying effect of the actors' associations that introduced and maintained consistency of clothing and masks, though even here steady change can be distinguished. The formalized categories of comic masks made many of the character-types universally identifiable, but required that any changes be slowly introduced. Tragic masks became more artificial and even grotesque, while eventually high shoes (*cothornus) and bright clothing added imposing stature, but suggest more static performance. This period is also distinguished by expensive construction and sometimes novel reconstruction of theatre buildings to accommodate the hundreds of new festivals that provided steady work for the Artists of Dionysus. We find their associations in dispute with one another over staffing of the Pythian games at Delphi, a quarrel which required the repeated intervention of the Roman Senate, and their Asian branch was repeatedly in conflict with civic authorities in the second century BC; but more productively they were engaged in the foundation of new or expanded games, volunteering for religious festivals, and especially for processions, where they were conspicuous in their gold and purple. They had their own ceremonies and temples in major cities, with funds coming at least partly from endowments; their organization had its priests, ambassadors, secretaries, and managers, who could bargain on behalf of its members, or pass formal decrees to honour them. Whether they had their own festivals, as they later did, is uncertain.

Theatre and political life had always overlapped, and spontaneous democratic gatherings could be held in the *deme* theatre of the Peiraeus even in the fifth century. We find in many theatres from the fourth century onwards specific and more frequent inscriptional indications that the seating represented civic divisions, very often by tribe, and usually in the form of a vertical division by 'wedges'. In addition the old honour of front seating continued, thus making a further horizontal division. These divisions could be employed for voting by acclamation, or for ensuring order during distributions of sacrificial meat, as well as for seating during performances. Not surprisingly the theatre was the scene of important political events: real tyrants making their own dramatic appearances, victorious generals addressing the people, or life and death debates. At Athens we can document the use of political invective and eulogy in comedy even after Menander, and it is tempting to assume that Greek theatre never entirely lost its ability to be politically relevant. Regrettably, almost nothing survives of the lively and inventive drama of the greatest Greek Hellenistic city, Alexandria in Egypt, a multicultural metropolis with a Greek elite insistent on imposing its cultural hegemony, but also one riven with violent ethnic and religious rivalry. Not surprisingly Alexandria was notorious for *riots in both the theatre and *circus.

But the chief connection of theatre to politics was that between the Artists of Dionysus and the powerful. As they had been associates of Alexander and his successors, of the Ptolemies of Egypt, and many others, so now the Artists helped the Roman generals with their celebrations. The culmination came with their profitable employment by Mark Antony, the self-styled 'New Dionysus', whose fatal war with Augustus established the empire and ended any hope of Greek autonomy.

4. Greek theatre under the Roman Empire (86 BC–AD 692)

Already before the first century BC there had been numerous Greek festivals in honour of Rome, and festivals for Roman generals were founded. As the Greek world under Augustus recovered from the ravages of Roman armies, cities and provinces naturally established formal worship of the emperors with attendant local and provincial festivals. These were celebrated by local magnates who had been appointed chief priests of the imperial cult, both in the east and west, and who helped to establish the hierarchy of empire and ties with Rome. Such festivals, therefore, some linked to older celebrations, soon become significant as a visible representation of Roman power,

and as such were early distinguished by the additional appearance of Roman entertainments given in the name of the emperor. These consisted not only of the expensive Roman programme of *gladiators, *animal fights, and even judicial execution (*damnatio), which were associated in the east only with the imperial cult, but also of mimes and *pantomime spectacles, which were especially popular in imperial Rome (see ROMAN THEATRE). But these mimes and dances were not prize competitions, and so they appear only very rarely in the programmes of regular Greek prize festivals after AD 170. Soon after AD 200 our real inscriptional evidence for imperial drama disappears, though mimes and pantomimes certainly continued for several centuries in the chief cities, especially Antioch, Alexandria, and Constantinople.

The actors of Greece were all free citizens, but their associations found it easy to adapt to the installation of the warlords who followed Alexander, whose pro-theatrical views they could only encourage. Greek Artists had assisted in Macedonian Amphipolis at the Greek festival with which Aemilius Paulus celebrated his Macedonian victories in 167 BC, and in Rome itself at the triumphal festivities of Anicius Gallus the next year. The adjustment to the arrival of the Romans was not without difficulty, and their headquarters in Athens was destroyed by Sulla in the siege of 86 BC. Nonetheless the Artists took care to have their privileges confirmed by Sulla soon after, and since the Emperor Claudius is known to have confirmed the privileges of the Artists, it is likely that earlier emperors had done the same, and assured their patronage (and perhaps eventually control) of the association. Claudius' successor Nero was certainly a strong supporter of Greek theatre, and under Hadrian there was a well-endowed chapter of the Artists in Rome itself. The fundamental difference between Rome and Greece is that acting for money on the public stage was never officially acceptable to Roman society, though private acting probably was. As a result the Greek Artists did not have a Latin-speaking branch, and festivals with programmes of the Greek type were very rare in the west save in the Greek areas of Africa and Gaul.

The influence of Greek Egypt was famously in scholarship and science, but almost certainly also in political mime and pantomime dance. Scurrilous nicknames for emperors, originating in Egypt, were soon known in Rome. The art of rhythmic handclapping (see APPLAUSE) came from Alexandria to Rome under Nero, and from there and Syria the great pantomimes arrived in Augustan Rome. From Alexandria too we have our most detailed description of the organization of theatre claques for the purposes of acclamations and even rioting, both of which played such an important role in Rome itself. The Greeks of Alexandria chose the theatre to carry out publicly an ugly persecution of the Jewish minority. Obviously the Greek theatre continued to maintain its social significance, while its influence via Alexandria on Roman theatre behaviour must have been considerable.

Theatres had always been places for the people to see their leaders. The people soon learned to express their opinions not only of the performance but of these leaders by concerted rhythmic shouting and clapping. Theatre claques, or paid supporters of actors, which Greeks called choruses, are first known from *Plautus in c.200 BC, but must be earlier in Greece; soon afterwards the theatre was the place for any well-known figure to discover if he was popular or not. Naturally emperors and their officials sought to control these expressions, not always successfully, by placing soldiers and police in the theatre, but especially by their own claques, organized in quasi-military manner; Nero's numbered 4,000. The shouts of the theatre were formally noted from the beginning of the empire as a political statement, since indeed there was no other place for popular expression, just as the silversmiths of Ephesus protested in the theatre against the visit of St Paul (Acts of the Apostles 19), or the people of Antioch protested there against high taxes to the annoyance of the Emperor Julian. None of this was necessarily spontaneous, and we know that the main professional claque in Antioch in the third century AD was 300 strong, and did not respond even to emperors unless paid; in Christian Alexandria it was 500 in number. The repeated shouting was accompanied by complex handclapping and the waving of banners and clothing. The *agonothetes* of the Greek world expected to be applauded formally by the theatre crowd for their generosity, just as the victors in competition were for their skill.

Apart from some mime fragments, nothing of Greek drama from this period survives, and it may never have left the hands of the professional Artists. But inscriptions demonstrate that it was still performed after AD 200, and Classical drama continued to be studied in schools and performed privately for centuries afterwards. But a deconstruction of Classical tragedy into solos and choral works is also evident; these artists 'sing tragedy' in imperial times. As mime replaced comedy, so tragedy was replaced by danced pantomime, and its Greek artists called themselves not 'pantomimes' (that is, 'all-mimes') but 'actors of tragic rhythmic movement', which makes evident their claim to be cultural descendants of tragedy and the gymnasium. They 'danced tragedy', and they were by far the most popular artists of late antiquity, becoming attached to the powerful circus factions of Constantinople. Thus Greek myth continued to maintain its cultural appeal even in the multicultural world of early Greek Christianity, while scenes from Menander's comedies decorating the living room floor of a fourth-century gentleman still served as a sign of antique taste. As Plutarch had said 200 years earlier, a dinner would be as incomplete without Menander as without wine.

5. Greek dramatic literature

Thanks to a continuous copying tradition, 44 ancient Greek plays survive virtually complete, including 32 tragedies, eleven comedies, and one satyr-play. Six of the tragedies are by Aeschylus, seven by *Sophocles, seventeen by Euripides, and two by unknown authors (*Prometheus Bound* and *Rhesus*, though attributed to Aeschylus and Euripides). The eleven comedies are by Aristophanes and the satyr-play (*Cyclops*) by Euripides. Drama is the best-represented Greek literary genre before the late fourth century BC, yet the remains constitute only 13 per cent of the total output of the four named dramatists, and a minuscule fraction of the drama performed at antiquity's major festivals.

Papyri and ancient quotations add fragments of about 2,000 plays and another 470 playwrights. The fragments vary in size from mere titles to nearly complete plays. They particularly enhance our knowledge of antiquity's two most popular playwrights: another sixteen Euripidean tragedies are represented by substantial fragments, while papyrus finds since 1896 have restored several large fragments of Menander, including one virtually complete comedy (*Dyscolus*), and extensive fragments of another six. The papyri also permit us to make reasoned judgements about the extent to which the Roman comic poets followed Greek models, and so add the evidence of 27 surviving Roman comedies to our information about Greek New Comedy. The comedies of *Plautus and *Terence adapt plays by at least six or seven Greek authors, all of the late fourth and early third centuries BC.

Papyrus fragments of some two dozen subliterary Greek mimes survive entirely by chance. But ancient selection had something to do with the survival of most other remains, leaving our knowledge of Greek dramatic literature spotty and uneven. Our texts and fragments come mainly from tragedies of 480–330 BC, and especially 430–405 BC, and from comedies of 430–388 and 317–263 BC. Because considerations other than quality or theatrical success sometimes played a determining role in the formation of the ancient canon, we cannot assume that our preserved texts are typical or representative of dramatic production in their respective periods.

The subject matter of tragedy is normally heroic legend: tribulations of noble families, set in a quasi-historical time (within two generations on either side of the Trojan War) when gods took a more direct interest in human affairs. Exceptionally, four or five historical dramas (including Aeschylus' *Persians*) were produced from about 492 to 460 BC, all dealing with the relatively recent Persian Wars or their immediate prehistory (historical tragedies are also known from the fourth century). A far more unusual type of tragedy—uniquely attested, but by the excellent authority of Aristotle—told no traditional tales, but was entirely fictional. Unfortunately, though Aristotle speaks of an entire class of fictional tragedies, he cites only the example of *Agathon's *Antheus* (416–401 BC). The world's first experiments in serious fictions have thus vanished without trace, 'deselected' by ancient tradition, and perhaps for no better reason than their failure to satisfy Aristotle's specification that the best plots deal with legendary heroes.

At a crucial stage in the tradition, it appears that an important criterion for the formation of the comic canon was the capacity of certain authors and plays to exemplify a particular *theory of comic evolution. According to this theory (Aristotelian in inspiration), comedy originally sprang up in democracy and served as a tool of the common people to check the power of the political and social elite. Sometime after the Athenian 'radical democracy' (425–405 BC), fear of the oligarchs induced poets to express themselves *allegorically, using myth, or tragic *parody. Finally Macedonian repression voided comedy of political content altogether. It is unlikely to be a coincidence that the remains of Old Comedy (486–404 BC) are dominated by the most political plays of the most political poets (especially *Cratinus, Aristophanes, and *Eupolis), while the selection from New Comedy (after 320 BC) is dominated by the gentle, ethical, and philosophical comedy of Menander and Philemon. These authors best exemplify the standard ancient theory of comedy's evolution. Yet the evidence of fragments and titles indicates that, despite ancient theorists, myth parody was more typical of Old Comedy than of *Middle Comedy (404 to c.320 BC). Moreover, our fragments give abundant evidence of fifth-century BC domestic comedies in a New-Comic style, and of virulent political *satire continuing well into Hellenistic times. The survival of a few non-canonical authors and works would permit a very different impression of the development of Greek comedy. But that is precisely why they did not survive.

Though the remnants are fewer, we have a good impression of what constituted the typical themes of satyr-play, thanks to a large number of vase paintings depicting satyrs and frequently influenced by drama. Satyr-play mainly uses myth, in the strict sense of tales set in a more remote past, when divinities, strange beasts, and ogres wandered freely on earth, and when the rudiments of human culture found their origin. Typically plots involve the satyr chorus's (frequently first) confrontation with the (newly invented) symbols of culture (like fire, the first musical instruments, wine, *sports, the first woman), or conversely the release and liberation of the satyrs from some more unpleasant aspects of civilization (especially bondage or serfdom). Heroic legend is freely adapted to admit a chorus of satyrs together with satyr-play's typical themes. But here too ancient quotations indicate a variety which our manuscript and papyrus texts would not have led us to expect. In the fourth century BC, satyr-play seems to have grown increasingly comic, sometimes involving satire, literary parody, and invective against contemporary figures.

Greek dramatic poetry in all genres alternates between spoken verse and verse that is chanted or sung. The former was never accompanied by music, the latter normally accompanied by pipes. Chanted verse was accompanied by marching, sung verse by dancing (both choreia, 'dance'). All spoken verse is written in iambic trimeter (a flexible verse rhythm approximating natural speech). Iambic trimeter was assigned almost exclusively to the actors, or the coryphaeus (chorus leader), while the chanted and sung verse was normally delivered by the chorus all together.

While the iambic lines are the principal vehicle for the development of the plot, it is primarily choral song and dance which articulates dramatic structure. The ancient terminology divides tragedy into the part before the entrance of the chorus (prologos, *prologue), the entrance of the chorus (*parodos), the episodes (epeisodia, literally perhaps 'the entry that follows') which are divided by songs sung by the chorus in the orchestra (stasima, literally choral performance 'in station'), and the exit of the chorus (exodos) which ends the play. Not all tragedies have prologues and the number of episodes normally fluctuates between four and six. It is sometimes difficult to decide whether a choral song is an interlude or structurally significant (that is, a stasimon): the best criterion is that a song divides episodes if actors depart before and/or arrive afterwards.

The structural function of choral song is most evident in Aristophanic comedy. All extant comedies begin with a prologue, followed by the parodos. Then normally follows a highly structured 'debate' (*agon), followed by the departure of the actors and the performance of a still more elaborate complex of alternating recitative and song during which the chorus march up to the first rows of the theatron and address the audience directly (parabasis, 'the walking up alongside'). After the parabasis the structure resembles tragedy's episodes, divided by much shorter choral songs, though many comedies have a second (less elaborate) agon and/or parabasis. The final departure of the chorus normally takes the form of a komos, a drunken, festive procession, in real life normally associated with weddings, victories, or Dionysian revels, and in Aristophanes often a confusion of all three.

Rather than merely articulating the plot structure, as in tragedy, the choral pieces are the backbone of the comic narrative. The questing hero, who embodies the plot's political and social concerns, requires little more than the support of the chorus to establish his or her new political order. Aristophanes' loose and minimal plots merely serve to motivate the progress from one choral set piece to another: the chorus obstructs the hero (parodos), is persuaded (agon), comments on the benefits of the new political regime (parabasis), witnesses its consolidation ('postparabatic' episodes), and celebrates the hero's victory (exodos). Other writers may have structured their comedy differently. Cratinus and Eupolis, at least in some plays, appear to have merged the parabasis or 'parabatic' elements with the parodos, presumably to avoid interrupting the progress of their more elaborate plots with a choral address to the audience in mid-drama. Aristophanes' set choral pieces, and especially the parabasis, show signs of formal disintegration in the later plays. Of the last five complete plays, the earlier three have defective parabases, the last two have none.

The demise of the Aristophanic chorus replicates a general pattern of choral decline in Classical drama. Aeschylean tragedy is 42 to 51 per cent choral, but Sophoclean and Euripidean tragedy is less than 30 per cent choral and goes as low as 10.5 per cent in Euripides' *Orestes* (408 BC). In qualitative terms the tragic chorus is reduced from full participation in the action (Aeschylus' *Suppliants*, *Eumenides*) to a group of chance bystanders whose presence is all but ignored by the main characters (Euripides' *Iphigenia at Aulis*). New Comic choruses serve only to divide the '*acts'. Their songs were completely separable from the action and are, in fact, omitted from the manuscripts. The decline of the chorus is generally ascribed to the growth of dramatic *realism.

Our extant texts attest a shift of interest in the themes of drama from the heroic to the familiar, from theology to psychology, and from the political to private life. In form, fantasy, and expression, the otherworldly grandiosity of early drama succumbed to a new aesthetic canon based on ordinary, everyday experience. Within this realist aesthetic, the illusory world of the drama merged more fully with the real world of the performance. The fluidity of tragic space, for example, which permitted Aeschylus five or six changes of scene in *Women of Aetna*, yielded, after Sophocles' *Ajax* (c.445 BC), to a strict *unity of place. The comic stage of Aristophanes, which a word sufficed to convert into Olympus or Hades, was in New Comedy so realistically presented that it typically represented a street in Athens with the precise compass coordinates of the *skene of the Theatre of Dionysus. With regard to time, it is again the earlier authors, Aeschylus and Aristophanes, who were least concerned to synchronize dramatic with real time. By Menander's day, however, the correspondence was close enough to give the impression of five fifteen-minute extracts from a single day, evenly spaced between sunrise and sunset, while unrealistic time-lapse was entirely confined to the choral entr'actes. New Comic dramatic time was, moreover, always contemporary with the production: poets studiously avoided any historical reference which might suggest otherwise.

In matters of delivery, form, language, or characterization, the literary history of Greek drama is inseparable from the history of theatre production. Though clearly affected by the great sweep of change from the religious and mythical Archaic mentality to the secular and rationalistic mentality of later Classicism and Hellenism, the poets were more immediately motivated by a concern to maximize the available resources of production. The decline of the chorus is in large part a result of the poets' eagerness to take advantage of the new virtuosity of the rising auletic (piper's) profession. By the last quarter of the fifth century BC, the dramatic festivals were of a scale and frequency that permitted, for the first time, the development of specialized and highly competitive professional musicians (*see* section 3 above). The 'New Musicians' made and maintained their reputations through conspicuous innovation and virtuos-

ity. As a result dramatic music and dance acquired a complexity better suited to the professionally trained actor than to the amateur citizen chorus. The decline in the volume and importance of choral music is therefore not evidence of a decline in dramatic music, but, on the contrary, a massive shift of the burden of musical performance from chorus to actor. The amount of song in Euripidean and Sophoclean tragedy actually increases over time. After about 425 BC the actors carried an ever larger proportion of tragic song and recitative (in *Orestes* nearly 73 per cent). By the time of New Comedy, the chorus was entirely professional, and probably arranged its performance independently of the poet.

In much the same way the movement towards literary realism reflects an increasing professionalism among actors. Dramatic language grew more natural, and increasingly mimetic (*see* MIMESIS), taking advantage of the actor's developing skill in portraying emotion and character. A new generation of actors looked to the familiar empirical world for their models. As early as the 420s BC, the actor Kallippides was condemned by his elder colleagues for 'going too far' in imitating gesture, because he mimicked the behaviour of non-aristocrats and especially lower-class women. Tragic masks grew less idealized; tragic costume less invariably magnificent. Euripides, in particular, was much mocked for presenting his beggared heroes in rags.

It was as part of this general movement towards realism in production values that Euripides abandoned the decorous and undifferentiated grandiloquence of early tragedy. He is credited with lowering the social and literary register of tragic diction, so as to make his heroes speak 'like ordinary human beings' (so the character of 'Euripides' boasts in Aristophanes' *Frogs*), and Aristotle credits Euripides with being the first writer to compose from the vocabulary of ordinary conversation. The effect, as both critics agree, was to make performance more 'persuasive', and to strengthen the illusion. Euripides also loosened the rhythm of spoken verse to bring it closer to the irregular patterns of natural speech (the trend to freer iambics increases so steadily in later Euripides that 'iambic resolution' is a fairly accurate index of the chronology of undated plays). At the same time as Euripides served the actor by providing opportunities to portray a familiar and more compellingly illusory world, he took full advantage of the actor's developing art by increasing the intensity, variety, and volubility of the tragic emotions displayed on stage.

By the last quarter of the fourth century BC traditional comic costume with its undifferentiated Dionysiac body-padding, exaggerated phalluses, and grotesque masks was abandoned for a much greater variety of costumes and masks portraying a large set of familiar, 'empirical', *stock characters. At the same time the texts abandoned the undifferentiated loquacity of early comedy for precise mimicry of the vocabulary, syntax, sociolect, speech tones, and expressions of characters distinguished by age, *gender, social status, and profession. Menander was justly famous in antiquity for 'adapting his language to all manner of emotions, dispositions, and character' (Plutarch). EGC/WJS

BLÄNSDORF, J. (ed.), *Theater und Gesellschaft im Imperium Romanum* (Tübingen, 1990)

CSAPO, E. G., and SLATER, W. J., *The Context of Ancient Drama* (Ann Arbor, 1995)

EASTERLING, P. E., and HALL, E. (ed.), *Actors and Acting in Antiquity* (Cambridge, 2002)

GREEN, J. R., *Theatre in Ancient Greek Society* (London, 1994)

LE GUEN, B., *Les Associations des Technites dionysiaques à l'époque hellénistique*, 2 vols. (Nancy, 2001)

MORETTI, J.-C., *Théâtre et société dans le Grèce antique* (Paris, 2001)

PICKARD-CAMBRIDGE, A. W., *The Dramatic Festivals of Athens*, 2nd edn. rev. J. Gould and D. M. Lewis (1968), reissued with supplements and corrections (Oxford, 1988)

GREEN, ADOLPH *See* COMDEN, BETTY.

GREEN, PAUL (1894–1981)

American playwright. Green invented a style of '*folk play' intended to capture the reality of common people and rendered in terms that were poetic, yet simple, direct, and accessible to an unsophisticated *audience. Beginning with *The Lost Colony* in 1937, he pioneered the 'symphonic drama', blending play, *pageant, and regional lore in *spectacles intended for large-scale production in outdoor *amphitheatres. After the First World War and university, Green returned to North Carolina, which—despite frequent trips to *New York and Hollywood—he maintained as home for the rest of his life. He came to wide public attention in 1926 when the *Provincetown Players produced *In Abraham's Bosom*, a *tragedy about an African-American teacher lynched by the Ku Klux Klan, and the play was awarded the Pulitzer Prize. New York intellectuals developed a fascination with Green's work, leading to a series of Broadway productions of his plays in the 1930s and 1940s. The *Group Theatre selected *The House of Connelly* as their first production (1931) and they commissioned Green's collaboration with composer Kurt *Weill on *Johnny Johnson* (1936), an anti-war *musical. In 1941 Green's adaptation of Richard Wright's novel *Native Son* was produced by the *Mercury Theatre, directed by Orson *Welles. Green was unenthusiastic about New York success and spent the majority of his career developing regional pageant-dramas based on *historical or legendary materials. In addition to *The Lost Colony* (produced annually on Roanoke Island in North Carolina), Green was commissioned to craft outdoor dramas for sixteen sites ranging from Virginia to California. Several, such as *Trumpet in the Land* (New Philadelphia, Ohio) and *The Stephen Foster Story* (Bardstown, Kentucky), continue annual performances to large audiences. MAF

GREENE, GRAHAM (1904–91)

English novelist and playwright. The exotic settings and formal innovation of his novels were not reflected in his plays, which were *well made in form even when their content was mysterious in nature. Greene's recurring theme was the tension between divine law and human desire in a Roman Catholic context. In *The Living Room* (*Stockholm, 1952) an orphaned girl (Dorothy *Tutin in *London, 1953) is driven to suicide by the guilt of an adulterous affair. In *The Potting Shed* (with John *Gielgud and Irene *Worth, 1958) an atheistic family deals with a terrifying miracle. *The Complaisant Lover* (with Ralph *Richardson in London, 1959, Michael *Redgrave in *New York, 1961) provocatively explores marriage conventions. Greene's reputation as a playwright suffered by comparison to John *Osborne and the Angry Young Men school after 1956; Harold *Hobson relegated him, along with Terence *Rattigan and T. S. *Eliot, to the individualistic past. Greene's screenplays include *The Third Man* (1949, adapted into a novel, 1950) and *Our Man in Havana* (1959, based on his 1958 novel). GAO

GREENE, ROBERT (1558–92)

English playwright and pamphleteer. As a graduate of both Cambridge and Oxford, Greene was one of the so-called *university wits whose dramatic experiments dominated the *public theatres in the 1580s. Greene was, according to his own accounts, a particularly dissolute specimen, but he was also a prolific writer of *romance fiction and a talented playwright. His contribution to the theatre has sometimes been overshadowed by his unflattering reference to Shakespeare in *Greene's Groats-worth of Wit* (1592) as 'an upstart crow', and by Gabriel Harvey's report that his death resulted from a surfeit of Rhenish wine and pickled herring. The five plays attributed to Greene exhibit considerable variety. *Alphonsus* (*c*.1587) and *Orlando Furioso* (*c*.1591) imitate, or *parody, *Marlowe's *Tamburlaine*. *A Looking-Glass for London and England* (*c*.1590) dramatizes the biblical story of Nineveh as a warning to London. *James IV* (*c*.1591) unites Italian *romance and Scottish *history. *Friar Bacon and Friar Bungay* (*c*.1589), Greene's finest play, successfully integrates sorcery and *farcical *comedy with a story of true love. RWV

GREEN ROOM

The English-language term for an offstage room where actors wait for cues and rest during performances and *rehearsals. Since the green room is normally a centre of the company's social life, many expressions refer to it: in Britian 'to talk green room' means 'to gossip'; in America 'save it for the green room' means 'do not conduct personal business during rehearsal'. Admission to the green room for a fan indicates a connection more intimate than meeting at the stage door, though less intimate than meeting in the dressing room. The origins of the term are obscure and no etymology is well supported; we know only that it first appeared in print in 1678 and has been in use ever since.   JB

GREET, BEN (1857–1936)

English actor, *manager, and director. Reputedly born on a training ship on the Thames and destined for a naval career, Greet became a schoolmaster, then joined J. W. Gordon's *stock company at Southampton. He performed in Sarah Thorne's Margate company, and in *London at the *Lyceum with Mary *Anderson and Lawrence *Barrett. He formed his own provincial *touring troupe, and by 1907 had between ten and fifteen companies travelling in England and America. His *open-air productions of Shakespeare at Kew Gardens were paralleled by his promotion of the Shakespearian repertoire in America. With William *Poel he revived the *morality play Everyman (1902), touring it successfully in England and America. At the *Old Vic he was a prominent director of over twenty Shakespeare productions between 1915 and 1918. He was knighted in 1929.   AF

GREGORY, ANDRE (1934–)

American director and actor. After studying acting in *New York at the *Neighborhood Playhouse and the *Actors Studio, Gregory began his directing career with a popular *Off-Broadway production of Jean *Genet's The Blacks (1962). By the late 1960s he was closely associated with the Polish director Jerzy *Grotowski, and in 1968 founded the Manhattan Project, a *collective dedicated to creating 'poor theatre'. Although the Project produced plays by *Beckett, *Chekhov, and Our Late Night (1975) by Wallace *Shawn, the group's best-known work was their adaptation of Alice in Wonderland (1968) set in a mental asylum, which they *toured for five years. During the late 1970s, Gregory left theatre production altogether to explore para-theatrical experiments in the Grotowski manner. This formed the background to his return in a *film co-written with Shawn, My Dinner with Andre (1981); a second film, Vanya on 42nd Street (1994), began as a theatre workshop; both were directed by Louis Malle. Gregory directed the American première of Shawn's The Designated Mourner (1999).   JAB

GREGORY, AUGUSTA (LADY) (1852–1932)

Irish playwright, theatre *manager, translator, *folklorist, and leading figure in the Irish cultural renaissance. Born into the Anglo-Irish ascendancy class, in 1880 she married Sir William Gregory (aged 63), a former Member of Parliament, Governor of Ceylon, and owner of Coole Park. While married she travelled widely, returning to Coole on the death of her husband in 1892. She established the house as a meeting place for writers and activists in the nationalist cultural project. 'I would like to leave a good memory and not "a monument of champagne bottles" ', she wrote. With W. B. *Yeats and Edward *Martyn she conceived in 1897 the idea of a national theatre, which in 1904 became the *Abbey Theatre (see NATIONAL THEATRE MOVEMENT, IRELAND). She wrote prolifically for the Abbey stage in a wide variety of theatrical styles. Her work includes skilfully constructed *comedies like Spreading the News (1904), The Workhouse Ward, and The Rising of the Moon (both 1907), folk history plays like Dervorgilla (1907), Kincora (1904 and 1909), Grania (1911), and 'wonder' plays. She made translations of *Molière, *Sudermann, and *Goldoni. The Gaol Gate (1906), a brief tragic threnody, is a masterpiece of condensed form. She was a dynamic manager of the Abbey Theatre, confronting and quelling powerful opposition to *Synge's Playboy on the company's *tour to the USA in 1911–12, and defending *O'Casey's The Plough and the Stars (1926) against cuts and public outcry. After her death several of her plays were performed at the Abbey in Irish-language translation, and An Fear Siúil (The Travelling Man) was at the Peacock in 1985.   CAL

GREIG, DAVID (1969–)

Scottish dramatist. Greig has been a leading figure in the 1990s renaissance in Scottish playwriting, marking a shift away from *naturalism and *melodrama in favour of global and *historical themes, and placing traditional questions about Scottish national identity in a much wider European context, in pieces like Europe (1994) and The Cosmonaut's Last Message to the Woman He Once Loved in the Former Soviet Union (1999). His early plays dealt with subjects like war guilt (And the Opera House Remained Unbuilt, 1992), the collapse of the communist bloc (Stalinland, 1992), and German reunification (One Way Street, 1993). He displays the influence of Michel *Vinaver in his playfulness with narrative, particularly in work for his own company, Suspect Culture, such as Timeless (1997) and Mainstream (1999). He has written for national companies like the *Traverse Theatre (Europe, 1994; The Architect, 1996; The Speculator, 1999) and the *Royal Shakespeare Company (Victoria, 2000). His work is deeply, if inexplicitly, *political, displaying an acknowledgement of the damage caused by a society of consumerist individualism, and a yearning for utopian forms of connection.   DR

GREIN, J. T. (1862–1935)

Dutch journalist, playwright, and *manager, born in Amsterdam but later a British citizen. An ebullient and optimistic man, largely self-educated, Grein spent 50 years promoting the cause of English drama and tirelessly writing dramatic *criticism. His main strengths were his knowledge of European languages and theatre. The highlight of his long career was the founding of the *Independent Theatre Society in *London in 1891 as a subscription theatre, on the model of *Antoine's Théâtre *Libre in *Paris, to produce worthwhile non-commercial plays, some of which had been banned by the *Lord Chamberlain (*see* CENSORSHIP). The first production, *Ibsen's *Ghosts*, caused such a scandal that no manager would thereafter risk an unlicensed play; but in seven years' existence Grein's society mounted two plays by Ibsen, two by *Zola, one by *Brieux, and thirteen new English works, including *Shaw's first play, *Widowers' Houses* (1892). Unlike Antoine, Grein was not a director, never had a permanent company or theatre, never acted himself, and rarely attended *rehearsals; and his hopes of a stream of new English plays were dashed. During the rest of his life he supported many causes, including the *Stage Society and a German Theatre in London. *See also* BRAHM, OTTO; FREIE BÜHNE.

EEC

GRENFELL, JOYCE (1910–79)

English actress and entertainer, born in London, who made her debut in *The Little Revue* (1939). She *toured hospitals in concert parties during the Second World War and continued to appear in *revues until the early 1950s when she began her *one-person show *Joyce Grenfell Requests the Pleasure*. Her métier was the comic *monologue in which she described and gently mocked the habits and foibles of middle-class English spinsters, schoolmistresses, and other assorted eccentrics: the very type of role she played in several British *films directed by Frank Launder, including *The Happiest Days of your Life* (1950), *The Belles of St Trinians* (1954), and *Blue Murder at St Trinians* (1957). Her autobiographies are *Joyce Grenfell Requests the Pleasure* (1976) and *George Don't Do That* (1977). From 1988 Maureen *Lipman revived Grenfell's monologues in her show *Re: Joyce*.

AS

GRÉVIN, JACQUES (1538–70)

French poet, physician and dramatist. A friend of Ronsard and member of the Pléiade, Grévin contributed one *tragedy, *La Mort de César* (*The Death of Caesar*, 1561), to the mid-century stock of humanist drama; this was derivative and declamatory, and though it was played at the Collège de Beauvais, scholarly opinion holds that the performance must have been a rhetorical recital. Grévin wrote two *comedies, *La Trésorière* (*The Treasurer*, 1552) and *Les Esbahis* (*Taken by Surprise*, 1560), the latter also being performed. Soon afterwards he abandoned literary pursuits to devote himself to medicine. He converted to Protestantism and twice took refuge in England, before dying at Turin at the early age of 32.

WDH

GRIBOEDOV, ALEKSANDR (1795–1829)

Russian dramatist and poet whose reputation, unusually, rests on a single play *Gore ot uma*, variously translated as *Woe from Wit*, *The Misfortune of Being Clever*, *Wit Works Woe*, *'Tis Folly to Be Wise* and, more simply, *Chatsky* (after the name of the play's central figure). The play owes an obvious debt to *Molière's *The Misanthrope* and concerns the return to Moscow, after a sojourn in the West, of a young rebellious nobleman, Chatsky. The play then charts the course of his disillusionment with his unfaithful girlfriend and her father. Chatsky's outspokenness, reminiscent of Molière's Alceste, leads to rumours of his madness, and the play ends with his abandoning Muscovite society for good. The reputation of the play rests not only in its notoriously untranslatable *verse, but also in the wonderful opportunities it offers character actors. *Shchepkin and *Stanislavsky were famous Famusovs and *Meyerhold staged two productions of a play whose language has become part of everyday Russian expression. A commissioned officer in the Hussars, Griboedov transferred to the Russian Foreign Office, studied Arabic and Persian, and was posted to Tehran in 1819 as a diplomat. Following a religious dispute a crowd of Islamic fanatics invaded the Russian legation and slaughtered the entire staff, including Griboedov. His play was banned before being performed in a heavily *censored version in 1833 and published in its entirety in 1861.

NW

GRID

The exposed framework of beams and rafters over the stage, from which *lights, *scenery, and the *fly system are suspended; short for 'gridiron'. In converted spaces the grid is usually anchored to the frame of the building and suspended from the rafters, so that access must come from below; while in most purpose-built *playhouses since the nineteenth century the grid can be united with the frame of the building, with catwalks providing much easier access.

JB

GRIEVE FAMILY

English scene *painters. The Grieve dynasty, pre-eminent among nineteenth-century stage designers, spanned three generations: the scion, **John Henderson** (1770–1845); his sons **Thomas** (1799–1882) and **William** (1800–44), and **Thomas Walford** (1841–82), son of Thomas. For almost a century they were principally associated with *Covent Garden, where John Henderson created picturesque designs under John Philip *Kemble's *management and where Thomas and William began their careers assisting their father. In 1835 William joined the rival *Drury Lane but returned to Covent Garden in 1839 under the new management of Madame *Vestris and Charles *Mathews. Thomas is best remembered as one of the principal scenic artists for

Charles *Kean's lavish *antiquarian stagings of Shakespeare at the *Princess's Theatre in the 1850s. His son Thomas Walford first served as an apprentice to his father at the Princess's. Given the diversity of the nineteenth-century theatrical repertoire, the Grieves created *scenery for everything from Shakespeare to *ballet to *pantomime. Like Clarkson *Stanfield, they incorporated the *diorama into theatrical scenery, thus linking performance even more closely with the prevailing popular culture of *spectacle and display. They excelled in picturesque, evocative landscapes—the haunting Gothic ruin, the desolate mountaintop, the dreamy moonlit sky—rather than full-scale architectural settings. Thomas's historically accurate designs for Kean were the major exception to careers specializing in virtuosic stock scenery. Hundreds of the original watercolour elevations for their designs are preserved in the University of London Library and the Victoria and Albert Museum. *See also* SCENOGRAPHY. RWS

GRIFFERO, RAMÓN (1954–)

Chilean playwright, director, and sociologist. In 1983 he formed Fin de Siglo, an underground movement whose postmodern productions (*see* MODERNISM AND POSTMODERNISM) had a great impact in *Santiago. In *Historias de un galpón abandonado* (*Stories of an Abandoned Warehouse*, 1984), *Un viaje al mundo de Kafka* (*A Trip to Kafka's World*, 1985), *Cinema Utoppia* (1985), and *La morgue* (1986), he used a metaphorical language and *expressionist *scenography to depict the ominous world of the dictatorship. In 1985 he received a major *award for his work as a director. His more recent plays deal with Chilean subculture, marginality, drugs, and abuse of power. MAR

GRIFFIN, HAYDEN (1943–)

South African designer. In his prolific career as a designer of theatre, *ballet, and *opera, Griffin has been associated with England's flagship institutions. Beginning in the late 1960s he worked with the *Royal Court Theatre, designing the premières of Edward *Bond's *Narrow Road to the Deep North* (1968) and *Bingo* (1974). In the mid-1970s Griffin began working with the *National Theatre, particularly with director Bill *Bryden, for whom he designed *Playboy of the Western World* (1975), *The Plough and the Stars* (1976), *The Madras House* (1977), *The Crucible* (1981), *Don Quixote* (1982), *A Month in the Country* (1994), and *The Good Hope* (2001). Other National Theatre designs include *Watch It All Come Down* (1976), *Weapons of Happiness* (1976), and *Plenty* (1978). Griffin has also worked for the *Royal Shakespeare Company, *Joint Stock, the Birmingham Royal Ballet, the *Chichester Festival Theatre, and the *Metropolitan Opera in *New York. MDG

GRIFFITHS, TREVOR (1935–)

English playwright and director. During the 1960s and 1970s Griffiths developed a *political theatre that drew upon European models—especially *Brecht and *Chekhov—but used specifically British inflections. *Occupations* (1970) establishes his main concerns in its analysis of the *politics and morality of a revolutionary moment, and of the relationship between political conviction and private behaviour. Set in Turin in 1920, the play presents a political debate between a pragmatic Soviet envoy and the idealistic intellectual Gramsci. The issue is never resolved, but, as Griffiths's next play suggests, Gramsci's emotional politics is a powerful corrective to emergent Stalinism. *Thermidor* (1971) is set in a Soviet interrogation room during the 1930s purges and returns to the relationship between conscience and revolutionary commitment. *The Party* (1973), produced at the Royal *National Theatre and starring Laurence *Olivier, is a British political debate between fashionable radicals against the backdrop of the French insurrection of 1968. Griffiths's next stage play, *Comedians* (1975), dramatizes the possibilities and betrayals of post-war working-class politics through the performances of would-be stand-up comics as they are forced to choose between artistic integrity and the demands of commercial success.

Griffiths was given wider exposure in his work for *television and *film. His first TV play, *All Good Men* (1974), deals with familiar themes of the struggles and betrayals of post-war socialism, but is also attentive to the role of television in British culture. *Bill Brand* (1976) developed these concerns in an eleven-part serial, and *Country* (1981) returns to an examination of a revolutionary moment, here the 1945 general election. *The Last Place on Earth* (1985) is a study of nationalism through the story of the Arctic explorer Captain Scott, and the screenplay *Reds* (1981) is set during the Russian Revolution. Griffiths's later work has again been for the theatre and includes *Real Dreams* (1984), which returns to *The Party*'s interest in 1960s radicalism, *The Gulf between Us* (1992) about the 1991 Gulf War, and *Thatcher's Children* (1993), which considers the effect of Thatcherite politics on different ethnic groups. SF

GRILLPARZER, FRANZ (1791–1872)

Indisputably the most important Austrian dramatist of the nineteenth century, Grillparzer managed to synthesize the legacy of Spanish baroque drama and the practice of *Viennese popular theatre with German *neoclassicism and *romanticism. The director of the *Burgtheater, Joseph *Schreyvogel, encouraged Grillparzer and arranged premières. His first success was *Die Ahnfrau* (*The Ancestress*, 1817) an exercise in the fate tragedy (*Schicksalstragödie*) popular at the time. It was followed by a classical *tragedy, *Sappho* (1818), which dramatized the poet's life as a conflict between life and art. An important work is the

Golden Fleece trilogy (1821) exploring the Jason and Medea story as a clash of cultures and sexuality. In the final part, *Medea*, the conflict is manifested in contrasting speech rhythms: the Greek *characters speak measured blank *verse while Medea and the inhabitants of Colchis speak in staccato free verse. *Des Meeres und der Liebe Wellen* (*Waves of the Sea and Love*, 1829) dramatizes the story of Hero and Leander and proved his most popular play. Grillparzer's interest in the Spanish baroque tradition led to a reformulation of *Calderón's *La vida es sueño* as *Der Traum ein Leben* (*A Dream of Life*, 1832), a dramatic fairy tale in the Viennese popular style. The failure of his *comedy *Weh dem, der lügt!* (*Woe to Him Who Lies!*, 1838) led Grillparzer to forsake the theatre. Other major works, such as *Bruderzwist in Habsburg* (*Family Strife among the Habsburgs*) and *Die Jüdin von Toledo* (*The Jewess of Toledo*), were performed posthumously in 1872.   CBB

GRIMALDI, JOSEPH (1778–1837)

English *pantomime *clown. Grimaldi was from a family of Italian dancers, though born in London; his father was a Pantaloon. After Grimaldi, clowns were called 'Joey', and it was Grimaldi who devised the *make-up that became traditional; a white face with a red half-moon (or spot in later clowns) on each cheek. The talented Joey was performing at *Sadler's Wells when he was little more than an infant, and became a regular member of that company, appearing also at *Drury Lane and then settling at *Covent Garden, with regular visits to Sadler's Wells. He was a huge success at Covent Garden in 1806 in *Harlequin Mother Goose*, which was acted 92 times, and gave further notable performances in *Harlequin and Padmanaba* (1811) and *Harlequin and the Red Dwarf* (1812). Worn out and crippled by extreme exertions on stage—at one time or another he broke almost every bone in his body—he retired in 1823, making two brief farewell appearances, with great difficulty, at Sadler's Wells and Covent Garden in 1828. Grimaldi's Joey defined the nineteenth-century clown and took the focus away from the previously dominant *Harlequin. He was a gluttonous thief, a terror to the watch, shopkeepers, servant girls, and babies, with a voracious enjoyment of life and fun. Additionally, Grimaldi was a trained *dancer and *acrobat, a superb singer of comic songs, a parodist of contemporary dress and behaviour, and an ingenious inventor of trick scenes and stage transformations.   MRB

GRINGO

Beginning in the nineteenth century the gringo appeared as a character in a variety of theatrical forms in *Latin America. Variously portrayed as a ridiculous or predatory *character, always a foreigner from outside Latin America, he was the quintessential outsider incapable of comprehending local society.   AV

GRINGORE, PIERRE (1475–1538)

French playwright. Gringore was a prominent member of the Enfants-sans-Souci, a Parisian society devoted to the performance of *sotties (fool plays), with the attendant right to compose sotties, *moralities, and *farces. His *Prince des sots* (*Prince of Fools*) was performed at Shrovetide in 1511, with Gringore acting the role of Mother Fool. Between 1502 and 1517 Gringore devised several *mystères mimes* (*dumb shows) for official *entries into *Paris, including one in 1514 for Mary Tudor.
                                    RWV

GRIPS THEATER

*Berlin-based theatre for *youth. The name is Berlin slang equivalent to the British 'nous' (meaning native intelligence or cleverness). The theatre was founded as part of the left-wing *cabaret Reichskabarett in 1966 by Volker Ludwig, who is still the director and author of most of its plays. The first children's plays (*Stokkerlok and Millipilli*, 1969; *The Mugnog Kids*, 1971) combined social themes with strong anti-authoritarian sentiments. Grips itself was officially created in 1972 when the cabaret was dissolved. The theatre has been hugely successful and expanded its repertoire to include work for teenagers and adults (*A Leftish Story*, 1980; the hit *musical *Line One*, 1986). Its plays have been translated and adapted throughout the world in over 500 productions and more than 30 languages.
                                    CBB

GROCK (CHARLES ADRIEN WETTACH) (1880–1959)

Swiss *clown. The 'king of clowns' was born in France, the son of an *amateur *acrobat, and already performing professionally at 14. His own speciality was as a musical clown, a routine he learnt while on an extended tour to South America in 1903. By 1907 he had a successful solo programme in which he played a multitude of musical instruments 'badly'. As his numbers grew in length they became unsuitable for *circuses and he performed in *music halls and *cabarets throughout Europe. In a career spanning 60 years he became the most successful (and probably the richest) clown of the twentieth century. His trademarks were a white face, bald head, and ill-fitting clothing. He often appeared with a comic foil whose only function was to highlight Grock's own zaniness. Towards the end of his career he owned his own travelling circus (1951–4).   CBB

GROPIUS, WALTER (1883–1969)

German artist and architect. As director of the *Bauhaus in Weimar from 1919 to 1928 Gropius was indirectly connected with the important theatrical experiments conducted there by Oskar

*Schlemmer. His most famous theatre project, the so-called 'Totaltheater' for Erwin *Piscator, was never realized. A multi-purpose, elliptically shaped *playhouse with different *stage configurations and flexible seating, it was designed to vary spatial relationships between performers and *audience. It could be changed from a conventional *proscenium stage to a *thrust stage and to a theatre-in-the-round (see ARENA AND IN-THE-ROUND). A domed ceiling could be used for projections. Although never built, the design ideas influenced post-war theatre architecture.   CBB

GROS-GUILLAUME (ROBERT GUÉRIN)
(d. 1634)

French actor. A member of various troupes that acted at the *Hôtel de Bourgogne as early as 1598, he headed the *Comédiens du Roi (King's Players) from 1622 until his death. For nearly two decades he, the rail-thin *Gaultier-Garguille, and the knavish *Turlupin formed an inimitable trio in *farce. He played rustic and naive *characters, dressed in a flat cap, striped trousers, and a loose tunic; his impressive belly was set off by two belts above and below, and his open, trusting moon-face was heavily floured, in contrast to his two companions who wore *masks. His persona was also incorporated into *pastorals and *tragi-comedies; when performing *tragic roles he used the name La Fleur. A favourite of Henri IV and of the general public, his popularity did much to establish the viability of commercial theatre in *Paris.   RWH

GROSSES SCHAUSPIELHAUS

*Playhouse erected in *Berlin by Max *Reinhardt in 1919 as a forum for large-scale productions. The architect Hans Poelzig redesigned a former *circus (Zirkus Schumann) in the form of a Greek theatre (see ANCIENT THEATRES) with *orchestra for the crowd scenes or *chorus, a raised forestage for the main actors, and an upper stage. The 3,000 spectators were seated around the stage in a semicircle. Reinhardt's idea was to bring highbrow theatre to the masses, and he opened with *Aeschylus' Oresteia (1919). It was followed by Romain *Rolland's Danton and Hamlet (both 1920). After Reinhardt moved to *Salzburg in 1920, the theatre was used increasingly for *popular entertainment.   CBB

GROSSMAN, JAN (1925–93)

Czech director and critic, for the greater part of his life ostracized and persecuted by the communist regime. First esteemed for his intelligent *criticism (including influential interpretations of *Brecht), he later turned to practical theatre work. He was *artistic director of the Theatre on the *Balustrade in

*Prague (1962–8 and 1989–93), where he developed a programme of 'appealing theatre', which was close to the ideas of Brecht but also affected by the *grotesque, existentialism, and the theatre of the *absurd. Productions of *Jarry (Ubu roi), Kafka (The Trial), *Havel (Memorandum), and *Molière (Don Juan) were sharply intellectual and based upon thorough analysis of script.   ML

GROTESCO CRIOLLO

An early twentieth-century form, popular in Argentina and neighbouring countries. Evolving from the earlier *sainete criollo and influenced by European *tragicomedy, the grotesco criollo was far more critical and grim. The form is associated with playwrights such as Armando *Discépolo and Francisco *Defilippis Novoa, while actors like Luis Arata developed an appropriate performance style which unmasked the external characterization conventional in the sainete. Most grotescos centred on the problems encountered by New World immigrants: poverty, alienation, identity, and disillusionment at the loss of the American dream. Anguish was the prevailing emotion, and verbal, even physical, violence frequent. As the focus switched from the collective to the individual, the action tended to move from the patio setting of the sainete to the interior spaces of private dwellings. The grotesco was intimately tied to the changing fortunes of the Argentinian middle class. Following its initial success during the 1920s and 1930s, the form's popularity declined as middle-class optimism grew (1935–55). The neogrotesco appeared in the late 1960s amid growing pessimism and economic decline. In plays such as Roberto Mario *Cossa's The Granny (1977), the neogrotesco evoked the earlier form even as it *parodied its ideological discourse.   JGJ

GROTESQUE, THEATRE OF THE

A term derived from the Italian 'grotta' (cave) and alluding to a kind of decorative painting found on the walls, or sculpture contained within such places, and characterized by fantastically extravagant, bizarre representation of human and animal forms often interwoven with foliage and flowers. The term then came to characterize a work of art produced in this style. These grotesque frescos, discovered in ancient ruins during the *early modern period, had an impact on dramatic literature and dramatic representation, although the term 'theatre of the grotesque' did not gain currency until the twentieth century. The grotesque can be linked with the *comedy of *masks of *Greek and *Roman times and subsequently resurrected by the Italian *commedia dell'arte. The grotesque draws attention to discrepancies between the ideal and the real, mind and body, the surface and what lies below, and often relies on a marriage between incompatible elements. It is especially susceptible to deployment in a post-Renaissance, *bourgeois world characterized by smooth, unruffled appearances on the surface and turbulent emotional (especially sexual) feelings beneath. In his preface to his play *Cromwell* (1827) Victor *Hugo defended the grotesque in art as a means of contrast, especially when injected into a classic play where nobility of tone is monotonously dominant. In the twentieth century, G. Wilson Knight famously described *King Lear* as 'a comedy of the grotesque'. Ruskin saw the grotesque as a feature of Gothic architecture, where the heavenward trajectory is constantly interrupted by grotesque reminders of hell in gargoyle shape. This idea was developed by *Meyerhold in one of the best essays on the significance of the theatrical grotesque, *The Fairground Booth* (1912). The actual 'teatro grottesco' was an Italian dramatic movement which emerged during the First World War and derived from a play by Luigi *Chiarelli, *La maschera e il volto* (*The Mask and the Face*), a 'grotesque in three acts' which explored the contrast between public and private role playing. Others who exploited this vein include Luigi *Pirandello, especially in plays like *Henry IV* where past and present, sanity and madness, appearance and reality, theatre and life are all treated as aspects of a grotesque world. NW

GROTOWSKI, JERZY (1933–99)

Polish director and acting theorist. Grotowski's father fled Poland during the Second World War; his mother, a schoolteacher, introduced him to Eastern religions at an early age. Grotowski studied directing in *Moscow under the tutelage of Yury *Zavadsky, and completed his education at the theatre school in *Cracow, where his earliest productions displayed traces of *constructivism. In 1959, *dramaturg Ludwig Flaszen was given charge of a small theatre in Opole, Poland, and invited Grotowski to work with him as *artistic director. Grotowski established a stable company with a commitment to ongoing *training and rigorous research into the fundamental bases of *acting. He was assisted in early productions by Eugenio *Barba, who played a crucial role in disseminating the *theories and principles of what became known as the *Polish Laboratory Theatre. The company eventually gained international renown for its highly unconventional stagings, which emphasized the encounter between actor and spectator as the core of the theatrical exchange, stripping away extraneous elements of *costume and *scenery in order to focus on the actor's ability to create transformation by means of craft alone. Grotowski's contributions to performance, as detailed in his manifesto *Towards a Poor Theatre* (1968), include an investigation of the possibilities of *environmental staging, an approach to *textual montage that posited the *director's role as *auteur* rather than executant, and an emphasis on the performer's obligation to daily physical and vocal training, as well as the methodical investigation of a performance technique rooted in the principles of *Stanislavsky's 'method of physical actions'.

Grotowski rejected theatre as entertainment, seeking to revitalize the ritualistic function of *performance as a site of communion. Central to his precepts was the notion of the 'holy actor', one able to use the dramatic role as a surgical instrument, peeling away the daily mask of social behaviour. Grotowski believed that this act of testimony could serve as a provocation for the spectator, inviting the viewer to conduct a similar act of self-penetration. Keenly aware that such an intimate confession could only be received and understood by the spectator if clearly articulated through signs, Grotowski emphasized the need for a combination of discipline and spontaneity, pushing his actors to construct a precise and repeatable score of actions and associations in order to create the necessary structure to support the more elusive and ineffable aspects of the performer's craft.

The first of the Laboratory Theatre's productions to gain critical attention outside Poland was *Dr Faustus* (1963), an adaptation of *Marlowe's text that unfolded during the final hour of the *protagonist's life, with spectators seated around a table on which the action took place. Grotowski's staging of *Wyspiański's *Akropolis*, a play which celebrates the achievements of human civilization through depiction of classical and biblical vignettes, was starkly recontextualized in a concentration camp. This was perhaps the most formalist of the Laboratory Theatre's productions, with the actors working with the construction of rigidly exaggerated facial expressions and delivering their lines in a rhythmic manner that resembled song or litany more than daily speech. *The Constant Prince* (1965), departing from Julius *Słowacki's adaptation of *Calderón, positioned the spectators as voyeuristic observers of a process of torture and martyrdom. Ryszard *Ciéslak's performance in the central role was viewed as the complete realization of Grotowski's vision of the 'total act' and the pinnacle of the Laboratory Theatre's achievement. The company's final production, *Apocalypsis cum Figuris* (1969), cast Ciéslak as a village idiot/Christ figure, rejected by the modern world. During the run of the production, the company worked to minimize all traces of theatricality and moved toward a progressively more intimate spatial relation between actors and spectators.

With his staging of *Apocalypsis* Grotowski felt that he had accomplished everything he could within the realm of theatre. From 1969 to 1978 the Laboratory Theatre investigated a range of para-theatrical activities. Using simple theatrical elements such as song, movement, and interaction with an outdoor environment, Grotowski began to explore circumstances in which a fuller and more authentic meeting between actors and spectators could occur, seeking to minimize or erase the boundaries between them. Beginning in 1976, he shifted his attention to examining *ritual performance practices of various world cultures, a project he described as 'theatre of sources'. His intent was to discern whether these performative elements could exert a tangible, psycho-physical impact on participants, regardless of culturally conditioned structures of belief. This line of investigation proved fruitful for subsequent stages in Grotowski's research.

Grotowski fled Poland in 1982 following the declaration of martial law. He received political asylum in the USA, and was eventually given the opportunity to continue his research at the University of California–Irvine. Diagnosed with leukemia in the early 1980s, his awareness of mortality became more urgent after he suffered two strokes in the early 1990s. He became preoccupied with questions of transmission, how to pass on the knowledge required for an investigation he identified as simultaneously artistic and esoteric, combining his work involving culturally traditional performance techniques with an extension of Stanislavsky's research on psychophysical action.

Beginning in 1986, Grotowski took up residence at a secluded centre in Pontedera, Italy, where he initiated 'art as vehicle', the culmination of his life work. Built around performance of traditional songs, primarily from the African *diaspora, art as vehicle examined the potential of ritual instruments to trigger a process of energetic transformation in the doers. Work with the songs was pursued in the context of a simple narrative/theatrical structure. While the work was conceptualized as a form of embodied meditative practice that exists for the doers rather than observers, the performance structures have been made accessible to spectators in small groups and can be received and appreciated as theatrical events. Thomas Richards and Mario Biagini, long-term leaders in the work, continue to explore this line of research.   LW

KUMIEGA, JENNIFER, *The Theatre of Grotowski* (London, 1985)
SCHECHNER, RICHARD, and WOLFORD, LISA (ed.), *The Grotowski Sourcebook* (London, 1997)

GROUND ROW

A piece of low, *flat, *painted scenery, often indicating shrubbery or other garden foliage, with its top edge exposed as a scenic effect. Originally ground row referred to strip lights on the stage which illuminated upstage *scenery, but the term transferred to the masking scenery in front of them.   JB

GROUP THEATRE (*LONDON)

Company founded by Rupert Doone in 1933 at the Westminster Theatre. As a private company it produced an impressive array of aesthetically experimental, *politically radical, and commercially hopeless shows before the outbreak of the Second World War. Doone, clearly at home with major poetic drama, directed the first staging of *texts by T. S. *Eliot (*Sweeney Agonistes*,

1935), W. H. *Auden (*The Dance of Death*, 1935), Auden and Christopher *Isherwood (*The Dog beneath the Skin*, 1936; *The Ascent of F6*, 1938; *On the Frontier*, 1939—all written for the Group), and Stephen Spender (*Trial of a Judge*, 1938). Nugent Monck and Michel *Saint-Denis were guest directors in 1936 for, respectively, a modern-dress *Timon of Athens* and Jean Giono's now forgotten *Sowers of the Hills*. The style overall was pared-down serious-cheap: bare stage, little or no *props or *scenery, interesting occasional use of *masks. Melodic stiffening was often provided by incidental *music specially composed by Benjamin Britten. The company closed down during the war, but reopened briefly in 1950–3, when it revived its earlier political purpose by staging the UK première of Jean-Paul *Sartre's *The Flies*.   BRK

GROUP THEATRE (*NEW YORK)

Ensemble active from 1931 to 1941. Asked in 1931 by the Board of Managers of the *Theatre Guild about the rebel 'Group' that he was leading among the Guild's younger staff, Harold *Clurman answered, 'We want to establish a theatre, not merely a production organization.' A true theatre, Clurman continued, 'is a homogenous body of craftsmen to give voice to a certain point of view which they share with the dramatist, whose works might be described as the most clearly articulated and eloquent expression of the theatre's conscience'. The Guild responded by giving money, two salaries, and their option on Paul *Green's *The House of Connelly* to launch the Group on its first summer retreat. Influenced by his contact with Jacques *Copeau, who emphasized dialogue between theatre and *audience, and the *Moscow Art Theatre, with their shared artistic language, Clurman was the intellectual inventor who 'talked the Group into being'. *Managed by a triumvirate of Clurman, Cheryl *Crawford, and Lee *Strasberg, its initial membership included 27 actors, among them a few well-known performers such as Stella *Adler, Franchot Tone, Mary Morris, and Morris *Carnovsky. Crawford took charge of business affairs and was a valuable mediator between Clurman and Strasberg, whose *acting *Method was to provide an ensemble unified by technique as well as philosophy. The opening of *The House of Connelly* in 1931 was a sensation, the Group praised as the inheritor of the ensemble tradition of the Moscow Art Theatre.

Severing connections with the Guild, they began their continual search for plays which, according to Clurman's founding idea, had to be new, American, and optimistic. Their early hope in this regard was John Howard Lawson. The Group produced *Success Story* in 1932 and *Gentlewoman* in 1934, but Lawson's abilities waned with his defection to Hollywood. The Group's peak year was 1935, when Clifford *Odets, a minor actor in the Group, brought forward two plays he had written specially for its actors. *Waiting for Lefty* and *Awake and Sing!* ran simultaneously in packed Broadway theatres. By 1937, the Group had suffered multiple *financial failures, Strasberg had resigned, and Odets had followed Lawson and Group actors such as Franchot Tone and Jules (renamed John) Garfield in accepting lucrative offers from Hollywood. The Group reorganized during the late 1930s under Clurman and Elia *Kazan, but the original Group idea of shared consciousness ended in the winter of 1937. Reasons offered for the Group's dissolution were the financial stress of operating an art theatre on a strictly commercial basis, the non-existence of a stream of new high-quality plays meeting the Group's criteria, and the emotional strain of working and living so closely together in so intense and idealistic an environment. The Group's influence would be felt for many years in American theatre and *film—through the *Actors Studio (founded by Kazan and Crawford), the teaching there of Strasberg, and through the acting studios of Stella Adler, Morris Carnovsky, Robert *Lewis, and Sanford *Meisner.

MAF

GRÜBER, KLAUS MICHAEL (1941–)

German director. Grüber, who began as an assistant to Giorgio *Strehler, is one of the most uncompromising and idiosyncratic contemporary German directors, his intense personal vision creating radical readings of classical *texts. Highly controversial was his *Faust I* at the *Berlin Freie *Volksbühne (1982), which he reduced to just three *characters: Faust, Mephisto, and Gretchen, the latter played by an *amateur. In Germany he has worked almost exclusively at the *Schaubühne. Important productions include *Horváth's *Tales from the Vienna Woods* (1972), which he staged as the nightmarish recollections of one of the characters; *Euripides' *The Bacchae*, as part of the *Antikenprojekt* (1974); and *Winterreise*, a staging of Hölderlin's epistolary novel *Hyperion* in the Berlin Olympic stadium. During the Schaubühne's early political phase Grüber insisted on aesthetic autonomy for the theatre. Seven of his productions have been invited to the Berlin *Theatertreffen. In the 1990s he directed mainly *opera.

CBB

GRUMBERG, JEAN-CLAUDE (1939–)

French playwright. One of the most successful and popular French dramatists of the 1970s, Grumberg's *Amorphe d'Otten-berg* (1971), a *farcical *satire on the Nazi rise to power, was produced by the *Comédie-Française in 2000. Often concerned with themes of racial intolerance, anti-Semitism, genocide, and the legacy of the Occupation, his best-known plays are *Dreyfus* (1974), *L'Atelier* (1979), and *Zone libre* (1990), each using a different format and style, ranging from *Jarry-esque *absurdism to hyper-*naturalism. Grumberg also writes extensively for *film and *television, and collaborated with François Truffaut on the screenplay for *The Last Métro* (1980).

DGM

GRÜNDGENS, GUSTAF (1899–1963)

German actor and director. Arguably the most famous German stage actor of the mid-twentieth century, his astonishing versatility defies easy categorization. From 1923 to 1928 he acted and directed at the Hamburg Kammerspiele where he came to the attention of Max *Reinhardt. He joined the *Deutsches Theater in 1928 and rapidly became one of *Berlin's leading actors. Apart from dramatic roles, Gründgens directed *comedies, performed in *cabaret, *opera, and *film (for instance the ruthless underworld boss in Fritz Lang's thriller *M*, 1931). In 1932 he moved to the Staatstheater where his Mephisto in *Faust I* was, according to the critic Herbert Ihering, a composite of '*cabaret singer and Charley's Aunt, cavalier and coy lady: a hundred variations on the theme Mephisto but never the theme itself'. In 1934 Hermann Göring appointed Gründgens director of the Staatstheater. Thus began the most controversial period in his career, as he tried to balance connivance with and resistance to the Nazi regime. This balancing act is analysed by Klaus Mann in his novel *Mephisto* (1936) and was dramatized by Ariane *Mnouchkine for the Théâtre du *Soleil in 1979. After his denazification in 1946 his most important posts were the directorships of the Düsseldorf Schauspielhaus (1951–5) and the Hamburg Schauspielhaus (1955–63). Here he directed *Faust* and performed Mephisto once again (1957; filmed in 1961). In his final years Gründgens vociferously opposed the emergence of director's theatre (*see* DIRECTING/DIRECTOR) and defended the pre-eminence of the author.

CBB

GRUNDY, SYDNEY (1848–1914)

English playwright. From 1869 to 1876 Grundy was a barrister in Manchester, where he was born and educated. His first play, a *farce, *A Little Change* (1872), appeared at the *Haymarket in *London, and he wrote some 60 more, including many adaptations from French and German. Grundy's most popular play was the fairy-tale *comedy, from the French, *A Pair of Spectacles* (1890), which ran for 335 performances at the Garrick Theatre and provided a fine part for John *Hare, the *actor-manager, as the philanthropist Benjamin Goldfinch, who takes on his brother's flinty and miserly *character when he breaks his spectacles and borrows his brother's. All is well, and his brother reformed into the bargain, when his mended spectacles are restored. Grundy was a social conservative and a bitter opponent of both *Ibsen and *feminism; his comedy *A New Woman* (1894) reflects some of these prejudices.

MRB

GRYPHIUS, ANDREAS (1616–64)

German dramatist and poet. A native of Glogau (Glogow), Gryphius in his youth travelled widely in the Netherlands, France, and Italy before taking up an administrative post in his home town. Although his plays were not performed professionally in his lifetime, they are regarded as important contributions to German baroque drama. His 'martyr *tragedies' are classically structured examinations of earthly vanities and human wretchedness, stoic variations on the theme of illusion and reality. A similar theme informs his far livelier *comedies, of which *The Beloved Thorn-Rose* (1660) and *Mr Peter Quince* (1663) are the most accessible.   RWV

GUAL, ADRIÀ (1872–1943)

Catalan playwright and director. The author of several pieces which oscillated between rampant *modernism and the strictest theatrical *realism, Gual is perhaps better recognized as a director who revolutionized the stage in his native *Barcelona. The founder of the Teatre Íntim, marked by its resistance to the hegemony of popular *bourgeois drama, he directed in Catalan the work of *Goethe, *Lesage, *Molière, *Ibsen, *Aeschylus, and Shakespeare, as well as that of contemporary local authors such as Joan Maragall, Ignasi Iglésias, and Àngel *Guimerà. Gual was also instrumental in the creation of what is now called the Instituto del Teatro, under the auspices of the Catalan local government.   KG

GUAN HANQING (KUAN HAN-CH'ING) (c.1240–c.1320)

Chinese playwright. The most versatile and prolific Yuan Dynasty dramatist, Guan has traditionally been considered the originator of *zaju as a literary form. Neither a landed scholar nor a court-appointed official, Guan represented a new breed of writer. Nearly a third of his more than 60 known *zaju* are extant and exhibit a prodigious imagination. Using military, political, courtroom, domestic, romantic, and lyrical themes, Guan's range was wide and his lively vernacular rich. Such thematic and linguistic breadth did not endear him to the Ming court and to the Ming literati, but did grant him pre-eminence with modern critics. Even in their redacted incarnations, the resourceful women *protagonists of Guan's five romantic *comedies, including *Rescuing One of the Girls*, defy the clichés of female virtue and vice. Of the courtroom plays, *Injustice to Dou E* entered the Qing Dynasty operatic repertoire and became recognized in the early twentieth century as a *tragedy. In the early decades of the People's Republic of *China, Guan gained a new reputation as an articulate spokesman for the oppressed. His plays were enlisted in the service of political campaigns, biographical details were invented, and he became known as the Chinese Shakespeare.   PS

GUARE, JOHN (1938–)

American playwright. A native New Yorker, Guare is a prolific playwright with a distinctive voice. Many of his plays deal with *characters distanced from an affluent society and their ways of reconstructing reality, a theme present in his first major success, the *Off-Broadway *The House of Blue Leaves* (1971, revived 1986), in his most popular later play, *Six Degrees of Separation* (1990; *film, 1993), and in the *Lydie Breeze* trilogy tracing the failure of a nineteenth-century utopian experiment. Other plays explored familial relations (*Bosoms and Neglect*, 1979; *Lake Hollywood*, 1999). Guare experiments with dramatic structure, often purposefully shattering the conventions of *realistic theatre, and frequently employing direct *audience address. He developed strong connections with the non-profit theatre: his libretto for a rock *musical version of *Two Gentlemen of Verona* was produced by the *New York Shakespeare Festival, and many of his plays after 1986 premièred at the *Lincoln Center Repertory Theatre. The Signature Theatre Company (*New York) devoted its 1998–9 season to a retrospective of his work. Although *Two Gentlemen of Verona* and the revived *The House of Blue Leaves* appeared in Broadway theatres, the productions were non-profit; Guare had not, by 2001, ever been presented by a commercial *management. A screenplay for Louis Malle's *Atlantic City* (1980) was highly praised, but Guare has written little for *film or *television, focusing his energies on the live theatre. Many of his plays were published as *The War against the Kitchen Sink* (1996).

AW

GUARINI, BATTISTA (1538–1612)

Ferrarese courtier, teacher, and playwright. He was the author of the internationally successful *pastoral play *Il pastor fido* (*The Faithful Shepherd*), first drafted in the 1580s and published in Guarini's own definitive edition in 1602. This work established a model for the pastoral *genre of theatre all over Europe, and was translated and imitated for many generations. Equally important were his own glosses to the play and other theoretical writings which argued for the legitimacy of pastoral drama, and for the mixed genre of *tragicomedy, despite the absence of both from the standard classical authorities such as *Aristotle and *Horace.   RAA

GUARNIERI, GIANFRANCESCO (1934–)

Brazilian playwright, actor, and leftist activist. Guarnieri began his career as actor and playwright in *São Paulo's Teatro de Arena in 1956. Arena's production of his *Eles não usam black-tie* (*They Don't Wear Black-Tie*, 1958), on working-class solidarity, strike politics, and generational conflict, marked a turn in Brazilian drama toward addressing the economic conditions and cultural life of the urban poor. A prolific author, his *musicals, dramas, and *television scripts have always targeted the social and economic injustices of capitalism.   LHD

GUBENKO, NIKOLAI (1941–)

Soviet/Russian actor and director. Gubenko trained at the State Institute for Cinematography and joined the *Taganka Theatre in 1964. He played a number of lead roles before he turned to *filmmaking, but returned to the Taganka in 1980, where he played the main part in *Boris Godunov* (banned 1982, produced 1988), giving a most powerful portrayal of the conscience-stricken Tsar. Gubenko took over *artistic directorship of the Taganka (1987–91) and revived several previously banned productions. From 1988 to 1991 he was the Soviet Minister of Culture; since then he has headed the theatre called Comradeship of Taganka Actors, which broke away from *Lyubimov.

BB

GUÉNÉGAUD, THÉÂTRE DE

On *Molière's death in 1673, a royal decree reduced the theatre companies in *Paris from three to two: the long-standing *Comédiens du Roi at the *Hôtel de Bourgogne, and a new company bringing together Molière's surviving colleagues and actors from the Théâtre du *Marais. This was known as the Compagnie de Guénégaud, from the location of their theatre, where they successfully continued the speciality of the Marais company in a series of spectacular machine-plays. In 1680 these two companies were merged to form the *Comédie-Française: with the Guénégaud company as link, France's *national theatre can claim direct descent from Molière.

WDH

GUERRA, JORGE (1952–)

Peruvian playwright, director, and designer who works in the United States. A founding member of the *Ensayo group (1983), Guerra has had broad international *training and experience. Influenced by Augusto *Boal and Atahualpa *del Cioppo, his *directing is balanced between the formal and the innovative with productions such as *Brecht's *Mr Puntila and his Man, Matti* (1983), Nigel Williams's *Class Enemy* (1985), *Euripides' *The Bacchae* (1987), and *Goethe's *Faust* (2001), all performed in Lima.

LRG

GUERRERO, MARÍA (1868–1928)

Spanish actress. Following her theatrical debut in 1886 in *Echegaray's *Sin familia* (*No Family*), and an early career which was confined to parts in *género chico*, Guerrero trained in *Paris under the guidance of Constant *Coquelin and went on to act alongside Sarah *Bernhardt. In 1896 she married Fernando Díaz de Mendoza, with whom she formed a successful company which acted in Spain, France, Italy, and South America, and was instrumental in the construction of the Teatro Nacional *Cervantes in *Buenos Aires. Her repertoire included plays by classical and modern Spanish authors such as Lope de *Vega, *Calderón, *Moreto, Echegaray, Pérez Galdos, *Guimerà, and *Benavente, but also a number of foreign playwrights, notably *Rostand, *Schiller, and *Maeterlinck. A graceful and highly expressive actress, Guerrero specialized in the role of the witty and resourceful woman, performing in more than 150 plays over a 40-year span. *Madrid's Teatro *Nacional María Guerrero is named after her.

KG

GUIGNOL

Generic name for a glove *puppet in France. The *character was invented in Lyon around 1808 by Laurent Mourguet. With his drunken cobbler friend Gnafron, Guignol delighted drinkers in cafés. The first Guignol repertoire was purely oral, with *scenarios based on well-known plays, but social and satirical comments attracted the attention of the *censors in 1852. In 1878 Pierre Rousset, at the Café Condamin (Lyon), created a new repertoire of dramatic and *operatic *parodies. By 1900 puppets were perceived as children's entertainment, and the character of Guignol became younger and politer.

JMcC

GUILBERT, YVETTE (c.1867–1944)

French singer and *cabaret *monologist (*diseuse*). Guilbert began her career in *Paris as a model, actress, and singer, and became the rage in the 1890s, singing at the Chat Noir, the Divan Japonais, and the *Moulin-Rouge, and inspiring many lithographs and *posters by Toulouse-Lautrec. She performed witty, mildly risqué songs (such as 'Madame Arthur', the lady with the famous 'je ne sais quoi'), presented as mini-dramas, some written especially for her by Aristide Bruant. She was tall, red-haired, and angular, with a slightly raucous but mobile voice and clipped clear diction, and wore trademark long black gloves. In a long career she appeared in *London, many European countries, and *New York. After 1900 she developed a larger repertoire of historical songs, both secular and religious; she also appeared in *revues and plays and in Murnau's *film of *Faust* (1926).

EEC

GUILDS

The responsibility for much of the production of late *medieval drama in Europe was taken by groups of people, both lay and clerical, who formed organizations known as guilds, confraternities, or *confréries*. These took several forms. First there were the strictly professional 'craft' or mercantile guilds whose primary purpose was industrial or commercial. In some cities, particularly in the German-speaking countries and in England, the craft guilds undertook to perform individual sequences in long episodic or *cycle plays. The *texts of two such plays survive from *York and Chester in England and a German text with a list of the craft guilds that performed it survives from Bozen in the southern Tyrol (now part of Italy). In Brussels, the town guild of archers (*boogschutters*) undertook plays in honour of the Virgin from 1448 to 1556. The Goldsmiths' Guild of *Paris also had a confraternity associated with it, the Puy des Orfèvres, that for much of its life was associated with playmaking.

Although some scholars have tried to make thematic connections between the episodes performed by the craft guilds and the essence of their crafts, most connections seem to be based on more practical considerations. The episodes of Noah and the Ark, for example, were performed by the shipwrights, fishmongers, and mariners in York, the waterleaders and drawers of Dee in Chester, and the shipwrights in Newcastle-upon-Tyne. All of these crafts had access to boats or the necessary skills to make a *pageant ark. Props and special effects can also be linked to craft ascription. The goldsmiths performed the Adoration of the Magi in York while in Chester it was the spicers. The butchers of York, with easy access to blood, undertook the Death of Christ. Many of these essentially commercial guilds, with the addition of their womenfolk and chaplains, functioned as a form of a religious confraternity. For example, the Mercers' Guild of York was also the Guild of the Holy Trinity.

Second, there were community lay and clerical guilds or confraternities devoted to the veneration of a particular saint (such as St George, St Denis, or St Anthony), to the eucharist (such as the *Corpus Christi guilds or the French guilds of the *Saint Sacrament*), the Pater Noster, or the Passion. One such guild, the Gonfalonieri di Santa Lucia (the Bannerbearers of St Lucy) was formed in *Rome from several different groups of *disciplinati* to stage a *Passion play in the Colosseum from c.1460 to 1540. Another, the *Confrérie de la Passion of Paris, was a civic and *amateur group that performed regularly in a fixed indoor location.

Third, there were civic or parish-based guilds often established to honour the patron saint through the dedication of a shrine or altar in a parish church or perform a play in the saint's honour, such as the Confréries de Saint-Georges, Sainte-Barbe, and Saint-Jacques in Mons. Sometimes, as with the Guild of the Holy Cross in the parish of St Helen's, Abingdon, south of Oxford, such guilds became central to the governance of a town, serving as a surrogate town council.

Finally, there were confraternities that were also literary societies or *Chambers of Rhetoric, especially in France and the Burgundian Low Countries, where the societies held annual contests to determine the best new plays. Competitors from other towns often took part: the Crossbowmen of Mons won in Ghent in 1498. Each guild had a unique structure and relationships to the society in which it was embedded and must be studied in its own context.

The guilds' involvement in playmaking varied widely and is still not entirely understood. It is clear, however, that although guild members often took part in their plays, a high degree of professionalism had developed, with paid actors and other entertainers taking key directorial and acting roles. The productions depended, it appears, on a mix of amateur and professional personnel dedicated to the seemly performance of the work. Some confraternities, such as the Pater Noster Guild of York, were narrowly focused—in that case to the production of the Pater Noster play and the maintenance of the tablets containing the prayer in English that hung in York Minster. Others, such as the York Corpus Christi Guild, had a wider social function with numerous charitable endeavours not unlike a modern service club. Its playmaking activity was limited to the production of the Creed play every ten years. The major function of most confraternities all over Europe was to provide social services such as hospitals, orphanages, hostels, poor relief, and much else that made life in the major cities tolerable. They also conducted regular religious observances such as funeral masses for members and maintained chantry chapels. The mimetic or ceremonial activity—a large episodic *biblical play or a smaller play for a patronal feast, an annual procession or 'riding' representing the patron saint (such as the St George Ridings popular all over England), or the entry into an annual play competition in Paris or Bruges—was only part of the life of a confraternity. Similarly, the contributions of the craft guilds to larger civic productions were incidental to the professional purpose of what were essentially closed shops of master craftsmen and their journeymen.
AFJ

GUILLÉN, EDGARD (1938–)

Peruvian actor, one of the finest *Latin American classical actors. He is internationally acclaimed for his solo performances (*Solo Guillén Solo*) and for his playing (often through *female impersonation) in *Identification Card* (1966), *Sarah Bernhardt and my Memories* (1984), *Domestic Shakespeare* (1984), *A Glance from the Cherry Garden* (1985), *Isadora* (1989), *Federico-Federico* (1993), and *The Human Voice* (1994). Guillén writes and stages his *one-person shows, which include *Unknown Whereabouts* (1994), *Richard III* (1995), *Emily* (1995), *Faust* (2000), and *Good Morning, Gabo* (2000).
LRG

GUILLOT-GORJU (BERTRAND HARDOUIN DE SAINT-JACQUES) (1600–48)

French *farce player. Son of a prominent Paris physician, he practised medicine for a time before going on the stage. In 1634 he joined the *Hôtel de Bourgogne to replace *Gaultier-Garguille, performing briefly alongside *Turlupin and *Gros-Guillaume, the two remaining members of the famous farce trio. He played the ridiculous doctor, ranting in Latin and wearing a black robe and an oversized wig; he always wore a *mask, though he was said to be so ugly that he did not need one. Guillot-Gorju left the stage in 1642 and joined the medical faculty at Montpellier.   RWH

GUIMERÀ, ÀNGEL (1845–1924)

Catalan poet and playwright. Already a prizewinning poet, Guimerà turned in the late 1870s to his true vocation, the theatre. *Gala Placídia* (1879) and *Judith de Welp* (1883) were his first incursions into the *genre of *verse drama; they revitalized the outmoded mode of historical *romanticism. This romantic phase was soon superseded by a more *naturalistic theatre, exemplified in the immensely popular and frequently revived *Mar i cel* (*Sea and Heaven*, 1888), *Maria Rosa* (1894), and the internationally acclaimed *Terra baixa* (*Lowlands*, 1897). A confirmed Catalanist, Guimerà's love of his local language was crystallized in the dramatic *monologues of the 1890s, *Mestre Oleguer* (*Master Oleguer*) and *Mort d'en Jaume d'Urgell* (*Death of Jaume d'Urgell*). His unsuccessful flirtation with psychological drama was followed by a return, at the very end of his career, to the historical plays of his youth.   KG

GUINAND, RAFAEL (1881–1957)

Venezuelan playwright, actor, and journalist. Like Rafael Otazo, Guinand was one of the most productive writers in the *costumbrista* style, the *costume drama of manners popular throughout *Latin America. Recognition of his acting came in 1914, the year of his first work, *El pobre Pantoja* (*Poor Pantoja*), followed by *Amor que mata* (*Love that Kills*, 1915, a comic *opera), *El rompimiento* (*The Break-up*, 1917), *El dotol Niguin* (*Doctor Niguin*, 1919), *El boticario* (*The Chemist*, 1923), a *monologue, *Los apuros de un torero* (*The Trials of a Bull Fighter*, 1929), and *Yo también soy candidato* (*I'm a Candidate Too*, 1939). His pieces were short, tailored to popular and Creole *audiences. They were critical pieces injected with humour, always with a keen social vision.   LCL trans. AMCS

GUINGANÉ, JEAN-PIERRE (DAOGO) (1947–   )

Dramatist and critic from Burkina Faso who has created a social theatre in the national languages. His work, rooted in the storytelling tradition, shatters traditional performance space and relies on *masks and other overtly theatrical elements, opening the stage to spectators who are sometimes invited to replace the actors. *Le Fou* (*The Madman*, 1984) denounced politicians for their demagoguery and deception. He is best known as the founder and the director of one of his country's two troupes, Le Théâtre de la Fraternité (established 1979). His work seeks its inspiration from pre-colonial performance forms, and his productions are non-*realistic.   PNN trans. JCM

GUINNESS, ALEC (1914–2001)

English actor and director. After initial difficulties at the *Old Vic, struggling to meet the expectations of John *Gielgud and Tyrone *Guthrie, he developed into an accomplished actor in the 1930s, notably as Aguecheck in *Twelfth Night* (1937) and, somewhat less convincingly, as Hamlet in Guthrie's modern-dress production (1938). During the Second World War he served in the Royal Navy, after which he excelled on stage and screen for the next five decades. He continued to act in a wide range of plays, from *King Lear* (the Fool, 1946) and *Gogol's *The Government Inspector* (1948) to T. S. *Eliot's *The Cocktail Party* (1949) and Simon *Gray's *Wise Child* (1967). He also adapted Dostoevsky's *The Brothers Karamazov* for the stage (1946), directed occasionally (*Twelfth Night*, 1949; *Hamlet*, 1951), and starred in the initial season of the *Stratford Festival in Canada. In cinema he played comic and serious roles with equal brilliance. He starred in the famous Pinewood Studios *comedies *Kind Hearts and Coronets* (1949, in which he played eight roles), *The Lavender Hill Mob* (1951), and *The Lady Killers* (1955), while his serious *films included *The Bridge on the River Kwai* (1957, Academy Award), *Tunes of Glory* (1960), *Lawrence of Arabia* (1962), *A Passage to India* (1984), and *A Handful of Dust* (1988). He achieved cult standing for his portrayal of Obi-Wan Kenobi in *Star Wars* (1977). He also acted on *television, notably in adaptations of John Le Carré's spy novels (1979, 1982), and he regularly did *radio programmes, including *Dr Faustus*, *Richard II*, *Antigone*, *A Christmas Carol*, *King Lear*, and a reading of *The Waste Land*. He was knighted in 1959. His autobiographies are *Blessings in Disguise* (1985) and *My Name Escapes Me* (1996).   TP

GUITRY, SACHA (1885–1957)

French actor, writer, *filmmaker, and boulevardier. Born to French parents in *St Petersburg, he was the son of France's finest *fin de siècle* actor, Lucien Guitry. Sacha made his stage debut at 5 in a court performance with his father for Tsar Alexander II. After his parents' divorce, Sacha was raised in France, ardently patriotic and obsessed with theatre. From the 1910s to 1930s, Guitry had at least two *comedies of sexual intrigue playing each season in *Paris. He also wrote bio-dramas, including *Pasteur* (1919), which featured his father's commanding presence in the title role. Guitry directed most of his 125 plays, usually playing the leading role opposite his current wife. He married five times, notably Yvonne Printemps (1919–32). His stage *character was usually a bon vivant or a detached seducer, but later he enjoyed playing multiple roles with *make-up changes. His frequently revived *N'écoutez pas, mesdames!* (*Do Not Listen, Ladies*, 1942) heartened French *audiences during the Paris occupation. He also wrote and directed 30 films, and published about twenty books of memoirs and sketches.

Legendary for his ready wit, Guitry is often compared to *Molière in impact on his time. FHL

GUNTER, JOHN (1938–)

English designer. Trained at the Central School of Art and Design, he was head of theatre design at Central St Martin's, *London, for eight years. He has designed for the *Royal Court, *Royal Shakespeare Company, the Peter *Hall company, and the West End. Gunter maintains that stage design should be 'evocative, suggestive of ambience' to set *audiences 'off on a visual journey that they complete for you'. Head of design at the *Royal National Theatre under Richard *Eyre, he won Olivier *awards for *Guys and Dolls* (1982) and *Wild Honey* (1984). He has designed for *opera in Europe, Australia, and the Americas. RVL

GUO MUORUO (KUO MO-JO) (1892–1978)

Chinese playwright and scholar. One of the most prominent literary and cultural figures in twentieth-century China, Guo's playwriting career falls into three periods. At the time of his return from *Japan in 1923, he was already well known for his poetry, translations, and romantic historical plays. In the following years he wrote three plays with historical heroines that advocated women's liberation: *Zhuo Wenjun* (1924), *Wang Zhaojun* (1924), and *Nie Ying* (1925). In 1937, after ten years of self-exile in Japan to avoid government persecution, Guo returned to *China to lead the literary resistance movement in the Sino-Japanese War, completing six *historical plays in eighteen months between 1941 and 1943. Four of them were about tragic *heroes of the era of the Warring States (770–221 BC), and again utilized a thematic correspondence to the present. After the communist victory in 1949 Guo held a series of high-ranking government posts relating to the arts. He wrote two highly influential historical plays in his last period: *Cai Wenji* (1959), about a great woman poet, and *Wu Zetian* (1960), about the only empress in Chinese history. SYL

GURIK, ROBERT (1932–)

Québec playwright. Born in France, trained as an engineer, he emigrated to *Montréal in 1950. He first attracted attention with the cleverly parodic *Hamlet, prince du Québec* (1968), lampooning the principals in the heated confrontation between Ottawa and Québec caused by the visit of Charles de Gaulle in 1967. Thereafter his plays reflect growing concern for the marginalization of individuals in modern mechanized, consumerist society. Typical is *Api 2967* (1971), portraying a sterile, Orwellian future where human values no longer exist. *Le Procès de Jean-Baptiste M.* (*The Trial of Jean-Baptiste M.*, 1972), based on a real-life occurrence, presents an individual who, pushed to the limit,

decides to murder all three of his capitalist employers 'on principle'. *La Baie des Jacques* (*Jacques' Bay*, 1976), inspired by *Brecht's *Mahagonny* and set in Québec's remote north, develops similar themes. Many of his twenty-odd plays have been translated and staged in several languages. LED

GURNEY, A. R. (ALBERT RAMSDELL, JR.) (1930–)

American dramatist. Educated at Williams College and *Yale School of Drama, Gurney has become identified with the northeastern affluent culture where he locates most of his plays. His wry *comedies foreground wit and social form, while he presents time as fluid and personality as fragmentary. In both *The Wayside Motor Inn* (1977) and *The Dining Room* (1982), vignettes overlap in the same space while the *characters are oblivious to each other. Gurney explored *theatricality more topically than structurally in such plays as *The Perfect Party* (1986), where putting on a party becomes analogous to mounting a theatrical production, and *The Fourth Wall* (1992), which involves a dramatist asking his family's permission to base a play on their experiences. He took unusual approaches to character in *Sweet Sue* (1982), *doubling each of the two roles in order to sketch them from multiple perspectives, and in *Sylvia* (1995), whose title role is ostensibly a man's pet dog but played as (and by) a witty, alluring young woman. Perhaps the quintessentially disengaged Gurney play is *Love Letters* (1988), an epistolary romance in which interaction is limited to correspondence and the seated actors read the *text to the *audience. JDM

GUTHRIE, TYRONE (1900–71)

Anglo-Irish actor and director. He began his career with J. B. *Fagan's Oxford Repertory Theatre but gave up acting when the chance was offered to direct for Anmer Hall at the *Cambridge Festival Theatre (1929–30), which Hall ran while Terence *Gray took a fifteen-month sabbatical, and at Hall's new Westminster Theatre after 1931. Guthrie was appointed director at the *Old Vic in 1933 and 1936, and administrator of the Old Vic and *Sadler's Wells theatres (1939–45), when he earned a reputation for staging *opera as well as drama. His notable productions over these years included *Tobias and the Angel* (1930) and *The Anatomist* (1931) by James *Bridie, *Hamlet* with Laurence *Olivier (1937), and *Peer Gynt* with Ralph *Richardson (1944). After 1948 his career became increasingly international, largely in consequence of his staging *Lindsay's *A Satire of the Three Estates* in the old Assembly Hall at the *Edinburgh Festival. This non-theatrical space allowed him to develop his interest in non-*proscenium venues. Gray's theatre in Cambridge had introduced him to the special challenges of *directing and *acting in unconventional performer–spectator configurations. This experience had been an invaluable aid when in 1937 a projected performance of *Hamlet* at Elsinore Castle had, because of storms, to be redesigned in-the-round (*see* ARENA AND IN-THE-ROUND) within a nearby hotel ballroom.

The years in which Guthrie directed the *Stratford Festival (Canada, 1953–7) allowed him the opportunity with the designer, Tanya *Moisewitsch, to develop a form of *thrust stage which carried the action right into the body of spectators. Aisles and vomitoria allowed for the rapid entrance and dispersal of actors. The thrust emerged from a permanent structure allowing for the use of an upper and a lower playing area with multiple entrances in a design scheme reminiscent of both the *skene* of ancient *Greek theatres and the *tiring house wall backing Elizabethan *public theatres. It was an epic theatre space, ideal for performance of the classic repertoire. The concept was further refined with the creation of the *Guthrie Theatre in Minneapolis in 1963, a stage which became the prototype for many built in England in the ensuing decade: Sheffield's *Crucible Theatre, the Leeds Playhouse, and the *Chichester Festival Theatre.

In later years Guthrie's directing focused almost entirely on *Greek or *early modern plays, though his approach was never orthodox. Several times he essayed modern-dress productions (*Hamlet* with Alec *Guinness and Ben *Jonson's *The Alchemist* at the Old Vic), while in *Volpone* with Colin *Blakely at the newly formed *National Theatre he experimented with movements inspired by the creatures after which the *characters are named. His excellence at choreographing crowd scenes was seen at its best in his staging of *Marlowe's *Tamburlaine the Great* with Donald *Wolfit for the Festival of Britain (1951). His several books, notably *Theatre Prospect* (1932), *A Life in the Theatre* (1960), and *Tyrone Guthrie on Acting* (1971), record his thinking about directing, the demands facing actors in particular roles, and the strengths and limitations of particular kinds of *stages.   RAC

GUTHRIE THEATRE

American *regional theatre in Minneapolis. Conceived in 1959 by Tyrone *Guthrie, Oliver Rea, and Peter Zeisler, it opened in 1963 as the Minnesota Theatre Company in a new *playhouse, originally called the Tyrone Guthrie Theatre, adjacent to the Walker Art Center. To achieve actor–*audience intimacy, the facility featured a steep *auditorium and a deep, asymmetrical *thrust stage designed by Tanya *Moisewitsch, based on her experience with Guthrie at the *Stratford Festival Theatre in Ontario. In its commitment to establish a permanent resident theatre that brought a classical repertory to America's heartland, the company became a flagship of the regional theatre movement. Guthrie stepped down as *artistic director in 1966 and was replaced briefly by Douglas *Campbell (1966–7), and eventually by Michael *Langham (1971–8), both close colleagues at

Stratford. Other artistic directors include Alvin Epstein (1978–80), Liviu *Ciulei (1980–6), Garland *Wright (1986–95), and Joseph *Dowling (from 1995), former head of *Dublin's *Abbey Theatre. Dowling spurred a major increase in attendance as the company prepared to move into a new three-theatre complex on the Mississippi River, slated to open in 2004.   STC

GUTZKOW, KARL (1811–78)

German dramatist, journalist, and critic. One of the leading representatives of the liberal movement Junges Deutschland, Gutzkow, like Heinrich *Laube, criticized reactionary tendencies in post-1815 Germany in his numerous novels and plays. He fell foul of the *censor in 1836 and was imprisoned. His plays range from *historical dramas to *comedies; best known are the *tragedy *Richard Savage* (1839), and the comedies *Pigtail and Sword* (1844) and *The Original Tartuffe* (1844). The only play to have survived the test of time is *Uriel Acosta* (1846), which dramatizes the conflict between enlightened and orthodox Judaism.   CBB

GUZMÁN, DELFINA (c.1936–   )

Chilean actress and director. For several years she was one of the leading actresses of *Ictus, and participated actively in the reorganization of the group that gave priority to *collective creation and to seeking a larger *audience. She also played a vital part in the production of plays intended to resist the military dictatorship, such as *La mar estaba serena* (*The Sea Was Calm*, 1976), *Cuántos años tiene un día* (*How Many Years Are in One Day*, 1978), and *Lo que está en el aire* (*Up in the Air*, 1986). She has worked on *television and in *films directed by Chileans Raúl Ruiz and Silvio Caiozsi. *Este domingo* (*This Sunday*, 1990), produced by Ictus, and *Cuarteto* (*Quartet*, 1996), written by Guzmán with Alfredo Castro, have been among her most successful recent acting work.   MAR

GWOKA

Guadeloupean *dance of *African origins (*n'goka* in Sango). Accompanied by a low-pitched and two high-pitched drums, all made of oak barrels tied together with ropes and topped with goatskins, the form has seven rhythms expressing different emotions: *toumblack* (joy, love), *léwoz* (fight, melancholy), *graj* (spirit of work), *roulé* (work), *kaladja* (suffering, sadness), *mendé* (collective escape), and *padjanbèl* (joy, freedom). The *boulayè* (accompanists), sitting astride their drums, set a cyclical, continuous tempo and rhythm for the *vokal* (singer), the *répondè* (choir), and the dancer(s). Most importantly, the *makéyè* (marker or improviser) uses his fingers, hands, elbows, and feet to conduct the ensemble and the dancers through refined improvisations, while the overlapping rhythms of the three drums link the *audience to the performers. During the period of slavery, *gwoka*, sung in creole, expressed resistance, revolt, joy, suffering, solidarity, and encouragement—and it still does today for people of African descent, particularly in the cities.

MRM

GWYNN, ELEANOR 'NELL' (c.1642–87)

English actress and *dancer. Nell Gwynn's fame for her offstage role as Charles II's mistress has largely obscured her onstage success as an accomplished comedienne. She first joined the King's Company at *Drury Lane around 1663 and by 1665 was playing leading roles opposite the *actor-manager Charles *Hart, reputed to be one in a line of influential lovers. The rags-to-riches story of Nell, the orange girl, rising to become a popular *prologue and *epilogue speaker who attracted the attentions of the King, epitomizes traditional notions of the actress as whore. Samuel *Pepys's *Diary* includes several references to Nell's offstage attractions but also praises her onstage performances, particularly as Florimel in John *Dryden's *Secret Love* (1667), a comic *breeches role in which she excelled. Nell retired from a relatively short acting career in 1670, following the birth of her first son by the King. She maintained her connections with the *playhouse and in 1679 Aphra *Behn dedicated *The Feign'd Curtizans* to 'the fair, witty and deserving' Nell Gwynn.

GBB

·H·

HABIMA THEATRE

Israel's national theatre since 1958. Established in *Moscow in 1917 by Nahum *Zemach, the theatre's Zionist ideology emphasized the centrality of modern Hebrew in the formation of a national Jewish culture (Habima is 'the stage' in Hebrew) . It became an independent *studio of the *Moscow Art Theatre, led by Evgeny *Vakhtangov, who assisted the company with its best-known production, *Anski's *The Dybbuk* (1922). Habima left Moscow in 1926, *touring Europe, America, and Palestine with *The Dybbuk* and plays by Pinski, *Leivick, and *Aleichem, among others, and in 1931 it settled permanently in Tel Aviv. In the 1930s and 1940s half of the repertoire was European and half Jewish drama, mostly Hebrew translations of *Yiddish plays by Aleichem, Leivick, *Gordin, and Peretz Hirshbein, some of its actors (notably Hanna *Rovina) becoming cultural icons. After a difficult period in the 1980s and 1990s, by the start of the new century the company presented a mixed repertoire of original Hebrew plays and translations of classic and modern works. It played 41 productions in *repertory in 1999, sixteen of them new, before a total *audience of almost three-quarters of a million. *See also* DIASPORA.   EN

HACKETT, JAMES H. (1800–71)

American actor and *manager. Born in *New York, Hackett embarked upon an acting career in 1826. Drawing upon personal knowledge gained in upstate New York, he perfected a *realistic Yankee *character that endeared him to his countrymen, although it was unappreciated by *Londoners in 1826 when he became the first American to appear in such a role. A gifted comedian, he was known for his Nimrod Wildfire in James Kirke Paulding's *The Lion of the West* (1831) and Rip Van Winkle. On both sides of the Atlantic, he was considered one of his era's finest Falstaffs.   GAR

HACKS, PETER (1928–)

German dramatist. After studying at *Munich University, Hacks moved to East *Berlin in 1955 where he worked as a *dramaturg at the *Deutsches Theater until 1963. His first plays and theatre essays were heavily influenced by *Brecht and analysed contemporary concerns with wit and historical distance. In *Anxieties and Power* (1960) he examined problems of production in the German Democratic Republic, and in *Moritz Tassow* (1965) the debate between pragmatic and idealistic versions of communism. His indirect, ironic style did not always find the approval of East German authorities, which led him to turn to translations and adaptations. Particularly successful were *Peace* (*Aristophanes, 1962), *Helen of Troy* (*Meilhac and Halévy, 1964) and *Polly* (John *Gay, 1966), in congenial productions by Benno *Besson. In the 1970s he treated a number of literary subjects and achieved a major success with the witty *monodrama *A Conversation in the Stein Household about the Absent Herr von Goethe* (1974). Although considered the most important GDR dramatist after Heiner *Müller, with the exception of his plays for *youth he has been much less performed.   CBB

HADAD, ASTRID (1957–)

Mexican *performance artist. Of Lebanese descent, Hadad is internationally known for her subversive cantina-cum-*cabaret routines that combine *dance, song, stand-up comedy, and *parodies of every sacred cow in Mexican society, especially politics, machismo, and religion. A performance hallmark are the outrageous and kitsch *costumes she uses to poke fun at the icons of Mexican identity; in *Heavy Nopal* (1990), for example, she wears the typical *charro* or Mexican cowboy hat, a Madonna-like halter top, and a skirt adorned with stone skulls and hands, with a bow made of enormous cactus leaves at the back.   KFN

HAGEN, UTA (1919–)

American actress and teacher. Born in Germany, Hagen made her debut as Ophelia in Eva *Le Gallienne's *Hamlet* (1937) and her first Broadway appearance as Nina in the *Lunts' production of *The Seagull* (1938). She played Desdemona opposite Paul *Robeson's Othello (1945). Through director Howard *Clurman and actor-teacher Herbert *Berghof, Hagen learned the *Stanislavsky system and began to teach in 1947. Despite acclaim for her performances of Blanche in *Williams's *A Streetcar Named Desire* (1948), Georgie in *Odets's *The Country Girl* (1950), Natalia in *Turgenev's *A Month in the Country* (1956), and especially Martha in *Albee's *Who's Afraid of Virginia Woolf?* (1962), Hagen subordinated her *acting career to teaching. As a performer, she was clear and understated, with a strong presence and deep voice. In her teaching, she supported the *Method but opposed its tool of emotional memory. Former students include Jack Lemmon, Geraldine *Page, Matthew Broderick, and Jason *Robards. Her *Respect for Acting* (1973) and *A Challenge for the Actor* (1991) offer pragmatic and *theoretical advice. *Sources* (1983) is a personal memoir.   FL

HAKAWATI, EL-

Palestinian company founded in East Jerusalem in 1977 by François Abou Salem, the son of a French artist and a Hungarian doctor. The theatre (the name means 'the storyteller') has had three phases. Initially it was itinerant, *touring Palestinian cities, villages, and refugee camps, offering a 'theatre of consciousness' that mixed popular imagery with material drawn from the harsh daily lives of Palestinians. The work included *In the Name of the Father* (1978–9), *Mahjoub* (1980), and *The Thousand and One Nights of a Stone Thrower* (1982). The second phase began in 1983 when the company created El-Hakawati Theatre in a burnt-out cinema in Jerusalem. Now more secure, the group directed its attention widely, creating *The History of Kufur Shamma* (1987), about disappearing Palestinian villages, and performing adaptations of *Brecht's *The Exception and the Rule* (1986) and Dario *Fo's *Mistero buffo* (1988). The third phase began with an international tour (1988–9), which led to the central members of the company settling in France. *The Search for Omar Khayyâm* (Toulon, 1991) questioned the division of Self and Other, while *Motel* (1997) related the story of Jean Baptiste, 'a French-Hungarian who becomes Abu Ghazaleh the Palestinian' and who is forced to make a life-or-death decision.   MMe

HAKIM, TAWFIQ EL- (1898–1987)

Egyptian playwright. Hakim's *Ahl Al-Kahf* (*The People of the Cave*, 1933) was the first original Egyptian dramatic *text—as distinct from translated or adapted ones—to be considered ser-

ious literature. He subsequently drew on various indigenous and French traditions, as well as on Egyptian social themes. He also undertook daring experiments in language and *genre. These include *Al-Safqa* (*The Deal*, 1958), which uses a third language halfway between colloquial Egyptian vernacular and the more literary Standard Arabic (Fus'ha); *Ya Tali Al-Shagarra* (*The Tree Climber*, 1963), an attempt at an Egyptian formula of *absurd theatre; and *Bunk Al-Qalaq* (*Bank of Anxiety*, 1968), a combination of novelistic and dramatic forms. His tendency to foreground *dialogue and philosophy suggest that his work is intellectual *closet drama, but many of his plays have been successfully staged at home and abroad.   HMA

HALAC, RICARDO (1935–)

Argentinian playwright. Author of sixteen plays, Halac inaugurated 'reflexive *realism' in *Buenos Aires theatre with *Loneliness for Four* (1961). Under the 1970s dictatorship his work became more critical, interspersing quasi-realistic scenes with grotesque short 'cuts' (as in *Second Half*, 1976, and *The Weaning*, 1978). By 1980 (*A Fabulous Job*) the *grotesque and the real fused. Outstanding among recent work is *A Thousand Years, One Day* (1993), a fictionalized account of Spanish Queen Isabella's Jewish physician.   JGJ

HALL, OWEN (JAMES DAVIS) (1853–1907)

English librettist who began his professional life as a solicitor and journalist. Notorious for his acid journalistic *satire, it was as the librettist of a series of highly successful *musical comedies that he made his name in the late Victorian and Edwardian periods. Together with composers like Ivan Caryll, Sydney Jones, and Leslie Stuart, he helped shape a new direction for English musical comedy after *Gilbert and *Sullivan. His most enduring contributions were *A Gaiety Girl* (1893), reputedly the first work to be called a musical comedy, *The Geisha* (1896), *Florodora* (1899), and *The Girl from Kay's* (1902).   VEE

HALL, PETER (1930–)

English director and *manager. Energetic in directing undergraduate productions at Cambridge, Hall soon became director of the *Arts Theatre in *London where, among other work, he mounted the first British production of *Waiting for Godot* (1955). After the success of his productions at the Stratford *Shakespeare Memorial Theatre (such as *Cymbeline* in 1957), he was invited to become its *artistic director in 1960. Backed by the board of directors, he transformed the company into the *Royal Shakespeare Company in 1961 as a permanent ensemble playing both in Stratford and at the *Aldwych Theatre in London, offering actors two- or three-year contracts. The company's repertory reflected Hall's interests: not only Shakespeare but also other *early modern drama rescued from neglect, major European and American plays, and a firm commitment to new work. The RSC became the major national company and its Shakespeare productions, including Hall's own, were marked by a powerful and often politicized modernity balanced by scrupulous attention to the *text and to *verse speaking. Hall's best work at this time included *The Wars of the Roses* (1963) which made the neglected *Henry VI* plays and *Richard III* into a trilogy investigating power-politics, and *Hamlet* (1965), in which David *Warner played a contemporary student prince. Hall also directed the premières of a number of *Pinter's plays.

Resigning from the RSC in 1968, Hall briefly became director of productions at the Royal Opera House, where he had first mounted a spectacular version of Schoenberg's *Moses and Aaron* in 1965. He complained about *Covent Garden's extravagant budgets (though he continued to direct *opera there and elsewhere, including *Wagner's *Ring* at *Bayreuth in 1983). He succeeded *Olivier as director of the *National Theatre in 1973, though Olivier was not consulted about the appointment. There Hall survived strikes, boardroom battles, and perennial fights for sufficient funding (see FINANCE). He supervised the company's move from the *Old Vic to its own home on the South Bank and programmed its three theatres with an immense range, epitomized by his own productions of *Marlowe's *Tamburlaine* (1976), *Shaffer's *Amadeus* (1979), and a *masked, all-male version of *Aeschylus' *The Oresteia* (1981) in Tony *Harrison's translation. He was knighted in 1977. Leaving the National in 1988 (after productions of three of Shakespeare's late plays), he established his own company to direct the same vast variety to which he has always been committed, using West End theatres, the Old Vic, and also playing in *New York.

A powerful presence in British theatre, often its staunchest advocate against the parsimony of successive governments, Hall has never directed popular *musicals, keeping to classical theatre and opera and to new writing (by Shaffer, Pinter, *Ayckbourn, and others) and often returning to rethink a play he has explored before (for instance *Hamlet* in 1965, 1975, and 1994). His productions of *Greek drama, including *Lysistrata* (1993) and the Oedipus plays (RNT, 1996), have kept it vital in Britain and led to his flawed but bold adaptation of the *Tantalus* sequence by his colleague from Cambridge onwards, John *Barton. If his productions occasionally lack daring, they show a deep commitment to the *text and to the importance of theatre to national culture.   PDH

HALL, ROGER (1939–)

British-born New Zealand playwright. The spectacular success of *Glide Time* (1976), an office-based civil service *comedy of circumscribed middle-class lives, launched Hall's career as the most performed playwright in New Zealand. It also secured a place for locally written plays in theatres which had until then relied on *London and *New York hits. *Middle-Age Spread* (1977) had a similar success in New Zealand, won the London Comedy of the Year *award for its long West End run, and was subsequently *filmed. *Audiences revelled in Hall's *Chekhovian *satire and sharp one-liners reflecting the small triumphs and despair of their own lives. Twenty years after *Glide Time* almost all its original cast appeared in *Market Forces* (1996) to show how the same *characters (now household names from Hall's *radio and *television series) were coping (or not) with a restructured public service in a deregulated economy. In addition to his many comedies, Hall has written *musicals, *pantomime, children's shows, *revues, serious drama, and British television sitcom. He is a major force in teaching and supporting young playwrights.   DC

HALLAM FAMILY

English actors who were the first professional performers to *tour the British North American colonies successfully. The first Hallam to gain a measure of repute was **Thomas** (d. 1735), whose greatest fame came as the fatally impaled victim of Charles *Macklin's rage in a *green room dispute over a missing wig. The Hallams were a well-known theatrical *family in early eighteenth-century *London, making their reputations on the stages of licensed *playhouses and *fair booths prior to the *Licensing Act of 1737. Adam Hallam regularly maintained a booth in Bartholomew Fair and appears as a character tumbling from a platform in Hogarth's 1733 painting *Southwark Fair*. Adam's two sons **William** (d. 1758) and **Lewis** (1714–55) continued the family tradition, though the decade following the Licensing Act was difficult for the brothers, as their endeavours were under constant surveillance and subject to arbitrary imposition of the law. In 1751, after a financially disastrous turn as *manager of the *Goodman's Fields Theatre, William took the extraordinary step of sending part of his company to the New World.

Led by Lewis, the troupe arrived in Williamsburg, Virginia, in June 1752 and opened their eleven-month season in September with performances of *The Merchant of Venice* and *The Anatomist*. For the next two years, they toured the colonies, building theatres and playing an ambitious repertory of English standards, including *Lillo, *Congreve, *Gay, and Shakespeare. While public reaction was mixed, and even hostile in places, they carried their tour to *New York, *Philadelphia, and Charleston before retreating to Jamaica as the French–Indian War expanded (see CARIBBEAN THEATRE, ANGLOPHONE). Lewis died in Jamaica; his widow married David *Douglass, an itinerant actor of uncertain origin. **Mrs Hallam** (d. 1773) had been a performer of some note on the London stage before accompanying her husband to America, where she continued to play leading roles. With Douglass in charge, the American Company, as it was now known, returned to the northern colonies in 1758. Lewis's son **Lewis Jr.** (1740–1808) was elevated to his father's leading roles while his mother and sisters (**Nancy** (fl. 1770s–1780s) and **Helen** (fl. 1750s)) joined him on stage.

From then until 1774, when the Continental Congress attempted to ban theatre, the Hallam/Douglass company remained the dominant professional troupe in the colonies. Among their many accomplishments was the first professional staging of a script by an American playwright, Thomas *Godfrey's *The Prince of Parthia* (1767). Lewis Jr. also holds the distinction of being the first actor in America known to have performed Hamlet. He and his mother were also the first to play Romeo and Juliet. After waiting out the Revolutionary War in the West Indies, Lewis Jr. returned to reorganize the company, assuming full management after Douglass's death in 1786. Eventually joining forces with John *Henry, John *Hodgkinson, and William *Dunlap, Lewis Hallam rebuilt the *Southwark Theatre in Philadelphia and the *John Street Theatre in New York. Although he relinquished his managerial duties in 1798, he continued to act and occasionally to tour the major east coast cities until his death. PAD

HALLE, ADAM DE LA *See* Adam de la Halle.

HALLIWELL, DAVID (1936–   )

British playwright. Halliwell is mainly known for a single play, *Little Malcolm and his Struggle against the Eunuchs* (1965, US title *Hail Scrawdyke!*), a comedy about a group of Huddersfield fantasists who form a pressure group against the 'castrated' status quo. After an unsuccessful West End production with John Hurt as the megalomaniacal Malcolm Scrawdyke, it was rescued by the *National Youth Theatre. Seen in the 1960s as a study of rebellious youth, it was revived with Ewan McGregor in 1998, when it seemed like a comment on that period's crisis in masculinity. Halliwell's other plays share *Malcolm*'s ebullient, word-drunk style, though none has been as successful. *K. D. Dufford Hears K. D. Dufford Ask K. D. Dufford How K. D. Dufford'll Make K. D. Dufford* (1969) uses several subjective versions of each scene (a device also found in *Muck from Three Angles*, 1970) to portray the multi-eponymous child-murderer. *The House* (*Joint Stock, 1979) is set in a stately home used as a military hospital, and shows the class conflict of the First World War through interior *monologues. CDC

HAM

A pejorative term applied to a kind of 'coarse acting', generally denoting an overblown vocal style and excessive broadness of gesture and movement. Ham *acting, now rarely encountered anywhere except in *parody, is a debased form of nineteenth-

century *melodramatic acting, which itself had its roots in tragic acting and the *mime technique of English *dumb show theatres of the 1790s. However, a direct correspondence between the intensely physical and vocal techniques required by melodrama and the hugely enlarged emotions and extreme moralities of its content meant that melodramatic acting was actually the perfect vehicle for the expression of the plays. MRB

HAMARTIA

Literally 'a missing of the mark', *hamartia* could in ancient Greek range in meaning from innocent mistake to wilful evil. *Aristotle's tragic *protagonist is somehow responsible for an act he performs in ignorance of its true nature; and in some *tragedies he undergoes a change in fortune (*peripeteia) because of some *hamartia*. The traditional debate about *hamartia* as moral flaw or intellectual error makes it an attribute of *character, but it is equally possible to see it as part of the *plot, an *action rather than a character flaw. We might also see it as ignorance itself, the human condition that renders the act tragic. RWV

HAMBURG NATIONAL THEATRE

A short-lived but influential undertaking, the Hamburg National Theatre operated from 1767 to 1769 in the Komödienhaus am Gänsemarkt using *Ackermann's troupe of actors. Established as a permanent theatre, financial backing was provided by a consortium of Hamburg citizens who appointed a board of four including the writer Johann Friedrich Löwen (1727–71). The theatre was dedicated to providing a highbrow dramatic repertoire with minimal reliance on foreign drama. Although the performance of German-language plays was explicitly encouraged, the repertoire still remained heavily reliant on translations of French and English works. Competition from a visiting French troupe was so intense that the theatre had to close its doors temporarily, and financial problems forced final closure. Despite its failure the experiment was immensely influential in Germany and provided the model for many other theatres. Its other important legacy was the series of critical articles written by its *dramaturg, G. E. *Lessing, during the first year of operation and published as the *Hamburgische Dramaturgie* in 1769. CBB

HAMILTON, CECILY (1872–1952)

English playwright, actress, and suffragist. Hamilton began as a writer of *one-acts, and first achieved success in 1908 with *Diana of Dobson's*, a social play about working women, performed by Lena *Ashwell's company. She was co-founder of the Women Writers' Suffrage League and the Actresses' Franchise League.

In 1909 she produced two suffragist plays, *How the Vote Was Won* and *The Pageant of Great Women*, and in 1911 acted in *Shaw's *Fanny's First Play*. During the First World War she worked as a hospital administrator in France; her later plays include *The Human Factor* (1925), though none received commercial success. She also wrote novels and worked as a journalist. With Lilian *Baylis she compiled a history of the *Old Vic (1926), and in the late 1920s and 1930s wrote a series of travel books. Her autobiography is *Life Errant* (1935). TP

HAMMERSTEIN, OSCAR I (1846–1919)

American impresario and *manager. Born in *Berlin, Hammerstein ran away and emigrated to *New York in 1863. A series of patented inventions enriched him sufficiently to build eight theatres: the Harlem Opera House (1889), the Columbia Opera House (1890), the Manhattan Theatre (1892), the Olympia Music Hall (1895), the Victoria Theatre (1899), the H. B. Harris Theatre (1904), and the *Belasco Theatre (1904). These culminated with the Manhattan Opera House (1906), where he introduced such *opera stars as Mary Garden, Nellie Melba, and Luisa Tetrazzini. The Victoria was a venue for straight plays, but switched to *vaudeville in 1904. In 1908 Hammerstein opened the *Philadelphia Opera House, and then the *London Opera House in 1911. He wrote several *musicals himself, notably both words and music for *Santa Maria* (1896). His most successful Broadway show, however, was Victor *Herbert's *Naughty Marietta* (1910). He was the grandfather of the renowned lyricist Oscar *Hammerstein II. CT

HAMMERSTEIN, OSCAR II (1895–1960)

American lyricist, author, and *producer. Along with composer Richard *Rodgers, Hammerstein revolutionized the *musical theatre form. Hammerstein came from a theatrical background—his grandfather, Oscar *Hammerstein I, was an *opera impresario and his father a *vaudeville theatre *manager—and studied law at Columbia University. His first experience writing lyrics was for Columbia Varsity shows, on which he collaborated with Lorenz *Hart and the man who was to become his most productive partner, Rodgers. But before he and Rodgers began working together professionally, Hammerstein worked primarily in *operetta, breathing new life into this near moribund *genre with composers Rudolf *Friml (*Rose Marie*), Sigmund *Romberg (*The Desert Song*, *The New Moon*), and George *Gershwin (*Song of the Flame*). He then worked with Jerome *Kern on a number of musicals including their epochal masterwork about the American south, *Show Boat* (1927). Hammerstein also wrote the acclaimed 1943 musical *Carmen Jones*, an all-black retelling of Bizet's opera *Carmen*.

Rodgers and Hammerstein's first collaboration, *Oklahoma!*, was a huge success and won a special 1943 Pulitzer Prize for drama. Their shows combined accessible and entertaining music with involving, often serious stories, and broached such difficult subject matter as domestic abuse (*Carousel*, 1945), *racism (*South Pacific*, 1949), and Nazism (*The Sound of Music*, 1959). Hammerstein is noted for his simple, heartfelt lyrics. The partners formed their own music publishing firm in 1949 and from that year on produced their own works as well as those of many others, including John *Van Druten's *I Remember Mama* (1944) and Irving *Berlin's *Annie Get your Gun* (1946). The duo wrote one musical directly for *film, *State Fair* (1945), and one for *television, *Cinderella* (1957). Hammerstein's personal honours included two Pulitzer prizes, two Academy awards, and five Tony *awards. The last song that Hammerstein wrote was 'Edelweiss' for *The Sound of Music*, written during that show's *Boston try-out in 1959. KF

HAMPDEN, WALTER (1879–1955)

American actor and *producer. Born in Brooklyn and educated at Harvard, Hampden apprenticed in England with Frank *Benson's company, where he learned Shakespeare roles in the grand heroic style. He also performed under Henry *Irving and Granville *Barker, and appeared in America in 1907 opposite Alla Nazimova in her *Ibsen repertory. He played Manson, a reincarnation of Jesus, in Charles Rann Kennedy's *The Servant in the House* (1908), a role which fed his Shakespearian ambitions; in 1918 he *financed a series of Shakespeare matinées on Broadway. Hampden triumphed in 1923 with *Rostand's *Cyrano de Bergerac*, which ran for over 1,000 performances. He assumed *management of the Colonial Theatre and led his own company there (1925–30), frequently reviving *Cyrano* to boost *box-office receipts, but focusing on Shakespeare. His romantic *acting style and script choices failed to keep the theatre afloat during the Depression, though he performed Shakespeare on *tour. As a member of the *American Repertory Theatre in *New York, he played Cardinal Wolsey in *Henry VIII* (1946). His final role was Danforth in *Miller's *The Crucible* (1953). FL

HAMPSTEAD THEATRE CLUB

This north *London club became a classic upmarket *fringe theatre. It opened in the multi-purpose Moreland Hall in 1959, producing London premières of plays by *Pinter and *Ionesco. In 1962 it occupied a prefabricated hut in Swiss Cottage, whose simple end-on *stage and 150-seat *auditorium proved effective for adaptations, including Laurie Lee's *Cider with Rosie* (1963) and Aubrey's *Brief Lives* (1967), both transferring to the West End. Relocating in 1970 to a nearby bigger, steeply raked theatre, successive directors—including James Roose Evans, Michael *Rudman, and Michael Attenborough—created risky programmes of new plays and visiting companies. Playwrights premièred included Michael *Frayn, Pam *Gems, Brian *Friel, and James *Saunders, ensuring that it continued to serve the West End.   BRK

HAMPTON, CHRISTOPHER (1946–)

English playwright. Hampton's long, successful career began even before he graduated from Oxford when the *Royal Court produced his first play, *When Did You Last See my Mother?*, in 1966. *Total Eclipse* followed (1968), then *The Philanthropist* (1970), *Savages* (1973), and *Treats* (1976), all for the Royal Court. Hampton's urbane, witty style (best exemplified in his hit *The Philanthropist*, a response to *Molière's *The Misanthrope*), made him an unlikely writer for the Court, where the emphasis was on *political theatre; Hampton may be the most 'continental' of his English contemporaries considering his extensive work translating European authors. Such works include *Chekhov's *Uncle Vanya* (1970), *Ibsen's *A Doll's House* (1973) and *An Enemy of the People* (1997), Molière's *Don Juan* (1972) and *Tartuffe* (1983), Yasmina *Reza's *Art* (1996), and Choderlos de Laclos's novel *Les Liaisons dangereuses* (1985), which was a huge success for the *Royal Shakespeare Company. Hampton also promoted the work of Ödön von *Horváth, translating *Tales from the Vienna Woods* (1977) and *Don Juan Comes back from the War* (1978). Horváth inspired Hampton's *Tales from Hollywood* (1982), about the émigré literary community in California during the war. Hampton contributed another tale of Hollywood, with the book for Andrew *Lloyd Webber's musical version of *Sunset Boulevard* (1993), for which he won a Tony *award. Since winning an Academy award for the screenplay of the (retitled) *Dangerous Liaisons* (1988), Hampton has written a number of *films including *Total Eclipse* (1995), *Carrington* (1995), which he also directed, and *The Secret Agent* (1996).   MDG

HANAMICHI

The 'flower path' in Japanese, a characteristic feature of the *kabuki stage, is a platform a little less than a metre (3 feet) long, the same height as the stage, running from stage right to the back of the *auditorium. (A similar, temporary *hanamichi* from stage left is used for a few plays.) The audience is seated on both sides of this ramp, which is used primarily to give impact to entrances and exits. Important action usually takes place seven-tenths of the way from the back of the auditorium at a spot known as the *shichi-san* (seven-three), where a *trap is located for magical appearances and disappearances. Most contemporary kabuki theatres have a motorized cable system rigged to allow *flying exits from the *shichi-san*, over the *hanamichi*, to an exit at the rear of the top balcony. The origins of the *hanamichi* are in dispute, but the term may have referred originally to the place where fans could step onto the stage and present gifts to the actors (*hana* means 'flower' and thus 'gift'). During the seventeenth century kabuki was most often presented on a stage

resembling that of the *nō theatre, with entrances and exits played on the *hashigakari* bridgeway parallel to the stage at the right. But beginning in the 1680s the bridgeway was gradually expanded, eventually resulting in a much wider main stage with no room for lateral runways. Various temporary runways and *thrusts perpendicular to the main stage were experimented with, until by the 1730s the permanent *hanamichi* came into common use.

Beginning in the 1680s the *hashigakari* bridgeway of early nō performances was gradually expanded to the width of the main stage, and various temporary runways and thrusts were used in experimental forms. By the 1730s the permanent *hanamichi* was in common use in kabuki.   LRK

HANCOCK, SHEILA (1933–)

English performer. An assured comedienne and fine dramatic actress, Hancock first made her name in *television in the sitcom *The Rag Trade* (1961–3). She appeared in the West End in *The Anniversary* (1964), on Broadway in the US première of *Orton's *Entertaining Mr Sloane* (1965), was a wicked Miss Hannigan in the West End revival of *Annie* (1978), an ebullient Mrs Lovett in the *London première of *Sondheim's *Sweeney Todd* (1980), a spurned Lady Wishfort in *The Way of the World* at the *Lyric Theatre Hammersmith, and the brittle murderer in Neil Barlett's *operatic adaptation of Ruth Rendell's novel *A Judgement in Stone* (both 1992). In 1985 she directed Ian *McKellen in *Sheridan's *The Critic* at the *National Theatre. She was Anne, a middle-aged teacher awakening to love, in David Eldridge's *Under the Blue Sky* at the *Royal Court (2000) and appeared with Corin Redgrave in Barlett's *In Extremis* at the RNT (2000).   AS

HANDEL, GEORGE FRIDERIC (1685–1759)

German composer. After several years in positions at court theatres in Italy and Germany, Handel settled in *London in 1712. Between 1720 and the late 1730s he wielded power and influence as the director of various *opera companies, which performed at the King's Theatre (*Haymarket) and, after 1734, at *Covent Garden. His 42 operas, many of which were *opera seria*, were neither musically nor theatrically innovative, but his bounteous melodic gift which he used to create vivid and compelling *characters meant his work stood out from his contemporaries'. Among his finest operas are his international success *Agrippina* (Venice, 1709), and in London, the spectacular *Rinaldo* (1711), the dramatically arresting *Giulio Cesare in Egitto* (1724), his masterpieces *Ariodante* and *Alcina* (both 1735), and the comedy *Serse* (1738). In the latter part of his life, Handel turned to oratorio and established the basic features of that particularly English *genre. His operas disappeared in the nineteenth century, but underwent substantial revival in the twentieth. The period instrument movement did much to further their cause, but recently they have been taken up by theatre directors (like Peter *Sellars) who find in Handel's now somewhat arcane stage world much to exercise their imagination.   SJCW

HANDKE, PETER (1942–)

Austrian playwright and novelist. After studying law in Graz he established a literary career with his prose works *Die Hornissen* (1966), *Der Hausierer* (1967), and *Begrüßung des Aufsichtsrats* (1967). His controversial *Publikumsbeschimpfung* (*Offending the Audience*, 1966) became one of the most widely performed 'anti-plays' of the 1960s. The *plotless, *characterless torrent of offensive sentences went far beyond the confines of *absurd theatre, which had done much to inject new energy into post-war drama. Handke rejected overtly *political drama of the *Brechtian mould and instead sought to uncover the deficiencies of society by critiquing its language. His interest in Wittgenstein informed his 'speech plays' *Weissagung* (*Prophecy*, 1966), *Selbstbezichtigung* (*Self-Accusation*, 1966), and *Hilferufe* (*Calling for Help*, 1967). In *Kaspar* (1968) the language of the civilized world imposed on a 'wild child' foundling is a tool of both socialization and victimization, which pushes the boy from a state of natural existence into madness. However, for the actors the 'speech-torture' has a liberating effect as it shifts the emphasis away from word-centred drama to the performative language of *physical theatre. In the play without words *Das Mündel will Vormund sein* (*My Foot my Tutor*, 1969), a ward and his guardian are locked in a power struggle, but the precise description of their actions is regularly interrupted by the indeterminable movements of a cat on stage. Chance and improvisation provide a refreshing counterbalance to the otherwise rigid *scenario. *Quodlibet* (1970) abolishes the role of author and focuses on the process of reception in the theatre. Handke's *text suggests situations and topics of conversation, which are left up to the actors to develop, yet certain key phrases and fragments of sentences are predetermined and establish through the *audience's associations the meaning of the play. Handke considered it a draft version of or prelude to *Der Ritt über den Bodensee* (*The Ride across Lake Constance*, 1971) where the same characters, now given the names of famous actors of the Weimar Republic, engage in highly cryptic *dialogues. This and his latest plays, *Die Unvernünftigen sterben aus* (*They Are Dying Out*, 1974), *Über die Dörfer* (*Across the Villages*, 1982), *Das Spiel vom Fragen* (*A Play about Questions*, 1990), and *Die Stunde da wir nichts voneinander wußten* (*The Hour We Were Ignorant of Each Other*, 1992), are large-scale works for major *playhouses and have not seen many productions.   GB

HANDS, TERRY (1941–)

English director. After Birmingham University and the *Royal Academy of Dramatic Art, Hands co-founded the Liverpool Everyman Theatre in 1964 but moved in 1966 to run the *Royal Shakespeare Company's small-scale *touring company Theatregoround. For the main company, his *The Merry Wives of Windsor* (1968) showed the town world of Windsor with comic affection. Hands extended the RSC's repertory with *Genet (*The Balcony*, 1971) and other new work, and he directed Shakespeare at the *Comédie-Française (for example, *Richard III*, 1972), becoming a consultant director there in 1975. More aware of European theatre than any other director at the RSC, he shared the populist vision of Jean *Vilar. His versions of *1 and 2 Henry IV* opened the *Barbican Theatre, the RSC's purpose-built *London base, and he directed the other cycle histories with Alan *Howard as the kings. In 1978 he became joint *artistic director with Trevor *Nunn and sole artistic director from 1986 to 1991. Ambition could outreach itself: his production of *Nichols's *political *pantomime *Poppy* (1982) had little bite and his attempt to emulate Nunn's success in *musicals with a musical version of *Carrie* (1988) was an abject failure, doing nothing to alleviate the *financial crisis at the RSC which it was intended to solve. But at his best, in *Much Ado About Nothing* (1982) and *Cyrano* (1983), both starring Derek *Jacobi, he could create a subtlety and individuality rarely seen in his larger-scale productions. He became artistic director of Theatr Clwyd in 1997.   PDH

HANG TUN HAK (1926–75)

Cambodian playwright. Upon returning to *Cambodia in the 1950s following theatre studies in France, Hang was key in the development of *lakhon niyey* (spoken drama), in the establishment of a National Conservatory of Performing Arts, and in bringing theatre to the general public through national *tours. He was called 'Cambodia's *Molière' by colleagues and students for pieces such as *The Sun Is Rising* and *Our Elders* that explore social tensions. He served as rector of the Royal University of Fine Arts in the 1960s, and as the country's Prime Minister in the early 1970s.   TSP

HANKIN, ST JOHN (1869–1909)

English playwright and journalist. Hankin began his career writing dramatic *criticism, and then wrote four major plays between 1905 and his suicide. They were produced in *London by the *Stage Society or at the *Royal Court Theatre, and were popular with the provincial *repertory theatres before 1914, but were overshadowed by the fame of other Court dramatists and did not reach the West End until John *Gielgud mounted *The Return of the Prodigal* in 1948 (originally directed by Granville *Barker, 1905). Hankin's plays, *well made but unsentimental and deterministic, have a disillusioned humour that found favour with *Shaw. *The Cassilis Engagement* (1907) was successfully revived at the Orange Tree Theatre in 1999.   EEC

HANLON-LEES BROTHERS

English aerialists and comedians. Originally **Thomas** (1836–68), **George** (1840–1926), and **William** (1842–1923) appeared at the *London *Hippodrome in 1847 as *acrobats; **Alfred** (1844–86), **Edward** (1846–1931), and **Frederick** (1848–86) were recruited later. The Lees surname was a tribute to their trainer, John Lees, who died of yellow fever while on *tour with his protégés. The brothers toured Europe and America extensively, notably at *Niblo's Gardens in *New York in 1860, where they amazed the *audience with trapeze stunts. They split up briefly in 1866, re-forming in 1868. During the 1870s they devoted themselves to comic sketches and *pantomimes. Their ever changing repertoire reflected their diverse individual talents, ranging from stunts to *acrobatics and *slapstick comedy.   AF

HANSBERRY, LORRAINE (1930–65)

*African-American playwright who broke the Broadway colour line for women with *Raisin in the Sun* (1959). After witnessing a *rehearsal of *O'Casey's *Juno and the Paycock* as an undergraduate, Hansberry realized she had found the medium for her message. Taking its title from a line in Langston *Hughes's poem 'Harlem', *Raisin* won the Drama Critics' Circle *award and launched a new era in African-American theatre. Directed by Lloyd *Richards, the cast, all unknowns at the time, included Diana Sands, Ruby *Dee, Louis Gossett, Douglas Turner *Ward, and Sidney Poitier. (Because white audiences flocked to see *Raisin*, several black militants charged that her work was racially conciliatory.) *The Sign in Sidney Brustein's Window*, about a Jewish couple, also premièred on Broadway (1964). In 1960 NBC commissioned Hansberry to write a *television drama honouring Abraham Lincoln, but declined to produce it because of its strong racial position. *To Be Young, Gifted and Black*, completed and arranged by her former husband, was produced in 1969 after the playwright's early death from cancer. The next year, *Les Blancs*—the title an inversion of *Genet's *Les Nègres* (*The Blacks*), the play about the ending and after effects of European colonialism in Africa— was produced at the Longacre (revived in *San Francisco, 1986). *Raisin* was been frequently revived, and a television version with Esther Rolle and Danny Glover was broadcast in 1989. Hansberry's last published play was *What Use Are Flowers* (1972).   BBL

HANSWURST

A generic *character in *improvised *comedies in German-speaking Europe. Although his name dates from the sixteenth century, the figure of Hanswurst (literally, 'John Sausage') emerges early in the eighteenth century as an amalgam of the comic types of Pickelhering from the *English Comedians, and *Harlequin from *commedia dell'arte. An invention of *Stranitzky, Hanswurst was a coarse and roguish peasant from Salzburg, always attired in a red jacket, yellow trousers, white ruffle, and conical hat. When Stranitzky moved to *Vienna, Hanswurst acquired Viennese characteristics; in later, sentimentally influenced interpretations by *Prehauser and *Kurz-Bernadon he became a more sympathetic character. For much of the eighteenth century throughout Germany Hanswurst was iconic of *improvised *comedy and was reviled as an enemy by *Gottsched, who contrived to have him 'expelled' from a performance by the *Neuber troupe in Leipzig in 1737, and by *Sonnenfels, who attempted to suppress improvisation in Vienna in 1768. Nevertheless, the energies of Hanswurst could not be curbed and he returned to the stage, under different names and different guises. Although he was incorporated into the milder *bourgeois comedy of the nineteenth century, the astringently brutal commentary he provided on the affectations and foibles of privilege has survived wherever *satire flourishes.   SJCW

HAPPENINGS

A performance *genre developed by Allan *Kaprow towards the end of the 1950s. Starting off with action paintings, action collages, assemblages, and then environments, Kaprow began to add flashing *lights and audible elements, and finally integrated visitors as mobile components into the structure of his exhibitions. This led in 1959 to *18 Happenings in 6 Parts*, performed at the Reuben Gallery in *New York. Parallel developments took place in *Paris by the Nouveau Réalisme group organized by Pierre Restany, in *Vienna amongst a group of painters who later became known as Viennese Actionists, and in the Rhineland amongst the Zero group. These artists worked entirely independently of each other and were only united by their interest in exploring time-based structures in their works and introducing aspects of everyday life into art. The integration of materials not commonly associated with high art extended to the use of human beings. Some of the resulting 'events' were *improvised, but usually happenings were premeditated or even scripted. This structuring and planning aimed at offering a concentrated experience of life and focused attention on aspects of reality usually considered unworthy of artistic attention. A more minimalist version with stronger musical direction was advocated by the Fluxus movement directed by George Maciunas, active chiefly between 1962 and 1966 in various European locations and in New York. *See also* PERFORMANCE ART.   GB

HARBACH, OTTO (1873–1963)

American lyricist, librettist, and playwright. Harbach (Hauerbach before 1917) collaborated with composer Karl Hoschna on *Three Twins* (1908) and its success encouraged him to give up journalism and work full time in *musical theatre. He would have more than 50 works produced on Broadway and become a legendary 'script doctor'. He collaborated with composers Rudolf *Friml and Herbert Stothart and lyricist Oscar *Hammerstein II on *Rose Marie* (1924); with Hammerstein and composer Jerome *Kern on *Sunny* (1925); with Hammerstein, Frank Mandel, and composer Sigmund *Romberg on *The Desert Song* (1927); with Mandel, Irving Caesar, and composer Vincent Youmans on *No, No, Nanette* (1925). Harbach wrote both *book and lyrics for what were perhaps his outstanding artistic accomplishments, both collaborations with Kern: *The Cat and the Fiddle* (1931) and *Roberta* (1932). Harbach also wrote nonmusical plays, the most successful being the *farce *Up in Mabel's Room* (with Wilson Collison, 1919).   MAF

HARDWICKE, CEDRIC (1893–1964)

English actor, knighted in 1934. After beginning with Frank *Benson's company, Hardwicke moved to the *Old Vic in 1914. After the war he joined the *Birmingham Rep, then shifted to *London in 1925, appearing in several of *Shaw's plays in the next ten years. He also acted at the *Malvern Festival. In the late 1930s he performed in *New York, then he moved to Hollywood and *films. In 1948 he returned to the Old Vic, taking roles in *Chekhov, *Marlowe, and Shakespeare. In 1958 he once again shifted to New York, which became his base for the rest of his career. His autobiography was published in 1961.   TP

HARDY, ALEXANDRE (c.1570–1632)

French playwright. Almost certainly France's first full-time professional dramatist, Hardy supposedly began his prolific writing career in about 1592. He was attached to Valleran *Le Conte's itinerant troupe, possibly from 1598, as salaried author, and later to the *Comédiens du Roi under *Bellerose, at the *Hôtel de Bourgogne in *Paris, from 1622 to 1626. In 1627, in exchange for a company share, he contracted to supply 36 plays over six years to the troupe of Claude Deschamps de Villiers. As *Mahelot's *Mémoire* reveals, fifteen figured in the Bourgogne's repertory in the 1630s. Of the '600 plays and more' Hardy estimated he wrote, only 54 are known. Forty-one survive in print, mostly *tragicomedies, though he drew little *generic distinction between *tragedy, tragicomedy, and *pastoral. Composed with total disregard for the *neoclassical unities, Hardy's structurally chaotic dramas were intended for a simultaneous staging system. He plundered sources as disparate as Homer and Heliodorus, Lucian and Lope de *Vega, Cinthio (*Giraldi) and *Cervantes, to devise plays whose titles betray the extravagant baroque subject matter his *audiences enjoyed: *Le Ravissement de Proserpine* (*The Rape of Proserpine*, 1626), *Lucrèce; ou, L'Adultère puni* (*Lucretia; or, Adultery Punished*, 1628), *La Folie de Turlupin* (*Turlupin's Madness*, 1621/32). *Melodramatic *texts of physical and emotional violence involving gods and *ghosts, shepherds and satyrs, Turks and Christians, these have a spectacular theatrical energy. While his obscure, elevated *early modern *verse style makes them inaccessible today, Hardy helped effect a transition from the stilted, *Senecan academic drama of the sixteenth century to the lively professional theatre of the seventeenth.   JG

HARE, DAVID (1947–)

English playwright, writer for *film and *television, director, and essayist. Hare grew up in Sussex, attended Cambridge University, and then quickly established himself as one of a group of *political theatre practitioners, founding Portable Theatre (1968) with Tony Bicât and *Joint Stock Theatre (1973) with Max *Stafford-Clark and David Aukin. His early plays include *How Brophy Made Good* (1971) for the Portable, *Slag* (1971), and *The Great Exhibition* (1972), *Knuckle* (1974), and *Fanshen* (1975) for Joint Stock. He also directed plays by colleagues Howard *Brenton, Snoo Wilson, and Trevor *Griffiths, including such collaborative efforts as Hare and Brenton's *Brassneck* (1973) and the multi-authored *Lay-By* (1975).

The year 1975 brought further recognition for Hare's writing and *directing, and his first televised work. That year Hare wrote and directed *Teeth and Smiles* starring Helen *Mirren. Produced at the *Royal Court, both it and *Brassneck* were also televised by the BBC, and *Knuckle* was televised in America. Over the next five years, Hare enjoyed sustained productivity and wide recognition as one of the most important writers and directors of his generation. He directed Brenton's *Weapons of Happiness* as the first new play to be staged at the *National Theatre on the South Bank in *London in 1976, and wrote and directed *Licking Hitler* (1978) and *Dreams of Leaving* (1980) for television. Perhaps the best play of the decade, *Plenty* (1978), directed by Hare and starring Kate Nelligan, opened at the National.

Through the 1980s Hare continued to write and direct for multiple media, frequently featuring a woman *protagonist who negotiates issues of personal ethics and agency against a complex *political backdrop. His best-known works include *A Map of the World* (1982), *Pravda* (1985) with Howard Brenton, and *The Secret Rapture* (1988). He also wrote and directed the films *Wetherby* (1985), starring Vanessa *Redgrave, and *Paris by Night* (1989), starring Charlotte Rampling. Fred Schepisi's film version of *Plenty* with Meryl Streep was released in 1985. During the 1990s Hare conceived of a trilogy of plays on national institutions for Richard *Eyre, then *artistic director of the National. *Racing Demons* (1990) about the ministry and religion was extremely successful; *Murmuring Judges* (1991) and *The Absence of War* (1993) were only slightly less so. Except for *Strapless* (1990), there were no more films during this decade; however, Hare continued to write and direct highly successful plays such as *Skylight* (1995), *Amy's Room* (1997), and *The Blue*

Room (1999), appearing himself in a solo piece about the Middle East (*Via Dolorosa*). Except for the last, these plays increasingly telescoped their action to domestic and psychic interiors where personal struggles with disillusionment took primary focus. In 2000 *The Zinc Bed* joined the first season of the remodelled Royal Court Theatre, proving that Hare, at 53, was still mid-career.   JGR

HARE, JOHN (1844–1921)

English actor and *manager. Hare obtained a position in 1865 with Marie *Wilton at the *Prince of Wales's in *London, playing in all six *Robertson *comedies produced there and specializing in old men. In 1875 he assumed management of the *Royal Court, with a strong company containing Ellen *Terry and the *Kendals. He then joined the Kendals in the management of the *St James's in 1879, taking over the new Garrick Theatre in 1889, the Globe in 1898, and *touring extensively. He was knighted in 1907. Hare was a polished actor in refined comedy and society drama, like *Pinero's *The Profligate* (1889) and *The Gay Lord Quex* (1899) which he first produced, and one of the leading West End *actor-managers of the day.   MRB

HARE, J. ROBERTSON (1891–1979)

English actor, who first appeared as a torch-bearer in *Reinhardt's *Oedipus* (1912). His *London career and his enduring partnership with Ralph Lynn began with the *farce *Tons of Money* (1922). Thereafter the two of them became identified with the *Aldwych farces—for example, *A Cuckoo in the Nest* (1925), *Rookery Nook* (1926), *Thark* (1927), and *Turkey Time* (1931)—written by Ben *Travers. Hare played often indistinguishable comic *characters who epitomized the small, respectable man doomed to be victimized by his disreputable but suave companions. He continued to play these roles on *film and *television.   VEE

HARISHCHANDRA, BHARATENDU (1850–85)

Indian playwright, poet, and publicist. The son of a rich merchant, based in the holy city of Banaras, Harishchandra devoted his wealth and energies to the creation of a literary public sphere and a corpus of literature in modern Hindi. It was for his services in this last cause that he was awarded the title 'Bharatendu', Moon of *India, by his contemporaries. He edited and wrote prolifically for two literary journals, perfecting the art of short satirical sketches, engaging with the social reform issues of the day such as polygamy and the effects of high-handed colonial legislation. He translated the classical Sanskrit political play *Mudrarakshasa* (*The Minister's Ring*) and the nineteenth-century *Bengali play *Vidyasundar*, in addition to the plays of Shakespeare, seeking a synthesis of technique and presentation that could link classical Indian aesthetics to a political and socially engaged *dramaturgy. He experimented with a wide variety of forms and conventions through the late 1870s and early 1880s. He wrote religious-romantic plays in the style of the *ras lila, such as *Chandravali*, but, for the most part, his plays were fiercely patriotic, often bitingly satirical.

Nildevi is the only explicitly *historical drama, concerned more with constructing figures and notions of authority than with demolishing them. *Vishashya Vishaumaushadham* (*Poison as the Antidote of Poison*) is concerned with contemporary *politics. A *soliloquy by a traditional insider, the house priest of a native chief, it relates the exploits of the unscrupulous Chief as manipulated by the British for their own political purposes. *Andher Nagari* (*Lawless Town*) *satirizes the arbitrariness and lawlessness of British rule. A wandering mendicant, who enters the town with the permission of his guru, discovers that all goods cost the same, regardless of quantity or quality. The guru takes to his heels when he hears of this dangerous state of affairs, advising the young mendicant to follow suit. The Raja puts in an appearance and then follows one grotesque error of judgement upon another, ending with the Raja declaring that he himself be hanged. Harishchandra's full-length plays were written to be performed, but in late nineteenth-century north India, there was no secular urban stage apart from the itinerant *Parsi theatre, which was considered barely respectable. Consequently, most of Harishchandra's plays were performed only on the *amateur stage in his lifetime. There has been renewed interest in his works since the 1980s, and *Andher Nagari* has been successfully performed.   VDa

HARKER, JOSEPH C. (1855–1927)

English scene painter, particularly associated with the productions of Henry *Irving at the *Lyceum Theatre from 1888 and those of Beerbohm *Tree at *Her Majesty's from 1898. Renowned for his spectacular, *illusionistic scene *painting, Harker's services were in constant demand by West End *managers. He worked extensively for George *Edwardes at the *Gaiety and Daly's theatres in productions like *San Toy* and *A Country Girl*, for Oscar *Asche (notably *Chu Chin Chow* at Her Majesty's in 1916), and from 1918 to 1923 for Marie Lohr, when she and her husband Anthony Prinsep managed the Globe Theatre.   VEE

HARLEQUIN

Also known as 'Arlechino', 'Arlecchino', 'Harlechino', a *stock character of *commedia dell'arte said to have originated in Bergamo. *Riccoboni states that before the seventeenth century Harlequin was a proficient tumbler and an inveterate trickster.

Tristano *Martinelli was the earliest acclaimed Harlequin, while Dominique, in Louis XIV's reign, developed the *character's wit. Always undertaking intrigues for his master and getting into scrapes, by the second half of the seventeenth century his *costume consisted of patches of blue, red, and green triangles joined with yellow braid, later replaced by diamond-shaped lozenges. He wore a short jacket, a double-pointed hat, and a half-*mask and black chinpiece: his arched eyebrows and beard were bushy with stiff bristles; his forehead lined with wrinkles; and tiny holes represented eyes. He often commented on topical events and parodied the serious drama. In English *pantomime he was a silent character, a *dancer, and tumbler, leaping through *traps to evade Pantaloon and *Clown, and empowered by a magic bat.

JTD

HARLEQUINADE See PANTOMIME, BRITISH.

HARPER, PEGGY (1923–)

South African dancer and choreographer. As director of the School of Dance at the University of Ibadan during the 1960s, Harper was convinced of the need to record existing forms. She conducted extensive research into the *dances of Nigeria, paying particular attention to the role of innovation and the way dance reflected changing circumstances. She used her findings in a series of workshops and strikingly original productions that shifted the emphasis from what she termed 'ethnic dance' to 'theatrical dance'. She collaborated with the actor Kola *Ogunmola on a sequence that was *filmed by Frank Speed, and her influence spread internationally through the Igbo dance elements incorporated in *Danda* (Dakar Festival, 1965).

JMG

HARRIGAN, EDWARD (1844–1911) AND TONY HART (1855–91)

American playwright and actors. Together Harrigan and Hart were the most popular American stage comedy team from 1871 to 1885. Born in *New York, Harrigan was a ship caulker when he took to the stage in *San Francisco as a *minstrel performer in 1867. Originally from Worcester, Massachusetts, Hart, born Anthony Cannon, also received his theatrical grounding in minstrel shows. Meeting in *Chicago in 1871, Harrigan and Hart formed an act whose *character songs, *dancing, and *clowning soon propelled them to the heights of the *variety circuit. Opening Manhattan's Theatre Comique in 1875, they initially replicated their variety act, but eventually Harrigan began writing longer pieces or reworking earlier material. For example, working in 1872 with his future father-in-law, composer David Braham, Harrigan wrote 'The Mulligan Guard', a song that achieved international fame. By 1873 the song had evolved

into a ten-minute sketch of the same name satirizing New York's pseudo-militias called 'target companies'. By 1878 the original idea had become *The Mulligan Guard Picnic*, the first of several full-length plays dealing with Irish, German, and Italian immigrants and the *African Americans who shared the lower rungs of New York life. Harrigan and Hart's antics in multiple roles, combined with carefully rendered city types and appropriately tailored songs, made the Mulligan series phenomenally popular with both critics and *audiences. Harrigan and Hart served as a bridge between minstrelsy and American *musical theatre.

GAR

HARRIS, AUDREY See MOTLEY.

HARRIS, JED (1900–79)

Austrian-born American director-*producer. Harris came to prominence in the 1920s when he produced a series of Broadway *melodramas and fast-paced *comedy hits, including *The Royal Family* (1928) and *The Front Page* (1928). His shows were known for their smooth pacing, expert *casting, psychologically truthful *acting, and tasteful decor. Even when not credited as director, Harris participated closely in the staging and script revisions. He often quarrelled with dramatists over his claims to co-authorship, and had an abusive disposition that helped foster his image as a ruthless tyrant. His first credited Broadway directing job was a revival of *Uncle Vanya* (1930). Despite many flops, Harris maintained a reputation with the homosexually themed *The Green Bay Tree* (1933), a revival of *A Doll's House* (1937) starring Ruth *Gordon, and, most notably, *Our Town* (1938), for whose famed minimalist staging Harris claimed responsibility. His later successes included *Dark Eyes* (1943), *The Heiress* (1947), and *The Crucible* (1953), although this last was marred by artistic differences with playwright Arthur *Miller. Harris's Broadway career ended in 1956.

SLL

HARRIS, MARGARET See MOTLEY.

HARRIS, ROSEMARY (1930–)

Anglo-American actress who made her *New York debut in *The Climate of Eden* (1952) and appeared the following season in *London in *The Seven Year Itch*. She worked at the *Bristol Old Vic and the *Old Vic in London, returning to New York as Cressida in the Old Vic's *Troilus and Cressida* (1956). She has been a prominent member of numerous transatlantic companies: the *Chichester Festival Theatre, the *National Theatre, *Lincoln Center, the *American Shakespeare Festival, and the *Williamstown Festival. Stunning and graceful, she has achieved distinction in classical and contemporary roles, making the transition from youthful to mature and older roles with elegance and ease. TFC

HARRIS, SAM (1872–1941)

American *producer. Harris began producing *melodramas in 1900 in partnership with Al Woods. From 1904 to 1919 he co-produced with George M. *Cohan, including such Cohan-authored successes as *Forty-Five Minutes from Broadway* (1905) and *Seven Keys to Baldpate* (1913). Though the two remained close (their wives were sisters), the partnership collapsed during the actors' strike of 1919, when Cohan refused to accept *Actors' Equity. Known for his honesty and fairness as well as his business acumen, Harris was sought out by leading writers and performers. He joined with Irving *Berlin in building and *managing the Music Box Theatre, where a series of *revues (1921–24) introduced numerous Berlin standards. Harris's association with Berlin and George S. *Kaufman led to his producing *The Cocoanuts* (1925), wherein Harris introduced Margaret Dumont into the *Marx Brothers' orbit. Other Harris successes include *The Jazz Singer* (1925), *Animal Crackers* (1928), *Of Thee I Sing* (1932), *You Can't Take It with You* (1937), *The Man Who Came to Dinner* (1939), and *Lady in the Dark* (1941). MAF

HARRISON, REX (1908–90)

English actor, knighted in 1989, who began in 1924 at the *Liverpool Playhouse. Harrison appeared in *London from 1930, quickly establishing himself as a stylish comic actor, adept in the plays of *Rattigan and *Coward. In the 1930s he also appeared regularly in *films. During the war he served in the Royal Air Force, then resumed his career in England and the USA. On stage he performed in *Van Druten's *Bell, Book and Candle* and *Fry's *Venus Observed*, but his major stardom was achieved as Henry Higgins in *Lerner and Loewe's *musical *My Fair Lady* (1956) in *New York and London; he also played the role in the film version (1964). For the rest of his career he alternated between stage and screen. On stage in London or New York he appeared in *Anouilh, *Chekhov, *Pirandello, Rattigan, and *Shaw. He was married six times, and wrote two autobiographies: *Rex* (1974) and *A Damned Serious Business* (1991). TP

HARRISON, TONY (1937–)

English dramatist, poet, and director. His first dramatic work was a translation of *Molière's *The Misanthrope* (1973). Its success initiated a long relationship with the *National Theatre which produced *The Oresteia* (1981), a translation of *Aeschylus' trilogy, and *The Mysteries* (1985), a version of medieval *mystery (or *biblical) plays. Both are large works that rely on a diction inflected by speech from the north of England. Harrison's interest in the relationship of classical and contemporary culture, and his commitment to a demotic poetic drama, have marked his theatrical work which expanded in scope and reference during the 1990s. *The Trackers of Oxyrhynchus* (1990) is a version of *Sophocles' *satyr-play, whilst *Square Rounds* (1992) is a mordant account of the inventors of the machine gun and poison gas using *mime and *clowning. Harrison's later work experiments with modes and locations. *Black Daisies for the Bride* (1993) is a *television *documentary drama concerning Alzheimer's disease, and *The Kaisers of Carnuntum* (1995) and *The Labourers of Herakles* (1995) were written for production in *amphitheatres in Austria and Greece. Harrison wrote and directed the epic *film *Prometheus* (1999) which again blends classical myth and contemporary locations. SF

HART, CHARLES (c.1628–83)

English actor. Charles Hart's relationship to William Hart, an actor active with the King's Men in the 1630s, is not clear, but it is clear that neither actor can be associated with the William Hart who was Shakespeare's nephew. As a *boy actor Charles played *female roles at *Blackfriars, but his fame rests on his distinguished Restoration career at *Drury Lane under Thomas *Killigrew, where he excelled in both *tragedy and *comedy. RWV

HART, LORENZ (1895–1943)

American lyricist. With composer Richard *Rodgers, Hart contributed to many successful *musicals from 1925 to 1943. Noted for bittersweet love songs, he was one of Broadway's most gifted lyricists. Hart's talent first emerged at Columbia University where he and Rodgers wrote college shows. Their first hit song, 'Manhattan' (in *The Garrick Gaieties*, 1925), was followed by a string of popular shows, including *Dearest Enemy* (1925) and *A Connecticut Yankee* (1927). After writing for Hollywood musicals in the early 1930s, Rodgers and Hart returned to Broadway with such distinguished shows as *On your Toes* (1936), with an innovative *ballet by George *Balanchine, and *Babes in Arms* (1937), which included the songs 'My Funny Valentine' and 'The Lady Is a Tramp' (two numbers that found their way into the 1957 *film of *Pal Joey* starring Frank Sinatra). In its original stage version, *Pal Joey* (1940) departed from romantic musicals with its cynical main *character and shady nightclub setting. Though vastly talented, Hart was a troubled man. His descent into alcoholism ended both his partnership with Rodgers and his life, but the breathtaking dexterity of his rhymes and lyrics has seldom been equalled. SN

HART, MOSS (1904–61)

American playwright and director. Hart achieved fame when he collaborated with George S. *Kaufman on Hart's draft of the

Hollywood *satire *Once in a Lifetime* (1930). Among his eight collaborations with Kaufman were the *comedies *You Can't Take It with You* (1936, Pulitzer Prize) and *The Man Who Came to Dinner* (1939), as well as the *musical satire of F. D. Roosevelt *I'd Rather Be Right* (1937, music by Richard *Rodgers and lyrics by Lorenz *Hart). Hart wrote the *book for and staged the innovative musical on psychoanalysis *Lady in the Dark* (1941, music by Kurt *Weill, lyrics by Ira *Gershwin). Hart's outstanding solo work was the backstage comedy *Light up the Sky* (1948). As a director Hart created some of the most admired stagings of twentieth-century Broadway, especially the unified visual palette and balletic crowd scenes in *My Fair Lady* (1956), a production which ran for nearly 3,000 performances. Hart's memoir of his career up to 1930, *Act One* (1958), has endured as an archetypal rags-to-riches theatrical story.   MAF

HART, TONY *See* HARRIGAN, EDWARD.

HARTFORD STAGE COMPANY

American *regional theatre in Hartford, Connecticut. Founded in 1963 in the self-proclaimed insurance capital of the world, HSC was first led by *artistic directors Jacques Cartier (1963–8) and Paul Weidner (1968–80). Mark Lamos took over in 1980 and brought the theatre to national attention with a greater emphasis on contemporary plays and spectacular productions of Shakespeare and such epic pieces as Kenneth Cavender's *The Greeks* (with Mary B. Robinson as co-director) and *Peer Gynt* (with actor Richard Thomas). Lamos stepped down in 1998 and was replaced by Michael Wilson, whose plans included a long-term investigation of the Tennessee *Williams canon.   STC

HARWOOD, JOHN EDMUND (1771–1809)

Well-educated English actor. Recruited by *Wignell to perform at the *Chestnut Street Theatre in *Philadelphia, he began his American engagement in 1794 as Tripplet in *Garrick's *Lying Valet*, playing more than twenty roles that year. He soon became one of Philadelphia's most popular actors, but in 1803 moved on to William *Dunlap at the *Park Theatre in *New York. There he established himself as the country's leading comic actor, though he was often criticized for his lack of preparation. His signature role was Falstaff, which he first performed in 1806. He retired early from the stage, having become both indolent and corpulent. He became a bookseller, resumed his interest in poetry, and married Miss Bache, the granddaughter of Benjamin Franklin.   PAD

HARWOOD, RONALD (1934–)

South African playwright. Harwood moved to Britain in the early 1950s and joined Donald *Wolfit's company as an actor,

an experience which would inform his best-known play, *The Dresser* (1980, *filmed 1983), which centres on the relationship between a barnstorming *actor-manager, known only as 'Sir', and his quietly efficient dresser. The play shows a wry fondness for the world of the theatre also found in *After the Lions* (1982) and *Reflected Glory* (1992). Harwood's career has mostly unfolded in the commercial sector, which has contributed to his being critically underrated. Plays like *J. J. Farr* (1987), on the meaning of religious faith, and *Taking Sides* (1995), exploring the charges of collaboration made against the German conductor Wilhelm Fürtwangler, are serious and complex pieces. Their themes of resistance and oppression, and of faith and politics, are explored further in his autobiographical work like *Tramway Road* (1984) and *Another Time* (1989), and the overtly political *The Deliberate Death of a Polish Priest* (1985), based on the murder of Father Jerzy Popieluszko.   DR

HASENCLEVER, WALTER (1890–1940)

German dramatist. The première of *The Son* (1916) marked the beginning of *expressionism on the German stage. The play's exalted language, episodic structure, and eponymous figure who rebels against a tyrannical father are prototypical of the movement. *Antigone* (1919) displays a typically expressionist utopia of a new society. Hasenclever changed track in the mid-1920s and wrote sophisticated *comedies. *Ein besserer Herr* (*A Man of Distinction*, 1927), featuring a marriage swindler, was a runaway success, while *Marriages Are Made in Heaven* (1928), a widely performed *succès de scandale*, attracted charges of blasphemy. His exile plays *Münchhausen* (1934) and *Scandal in Assyria* (performed in *London in 1939) were less successful. He committed suicide after the German invasion of France.
   CBB

HASHMI, SAFDAR (1954–89)

Communist playwright, actor, director, lyricist, and *theorist, chiefly associated with *street theatre in *India. He was a founding member of Jana Natya Manch (Janam) in 1973. Initially performing open-air *proscenium plays for mass *audiences, Janam took to street theatre in 1978 with *Machine*, which was written collaboratively, with Safdar (as he was generally called) making a large contribution. His contribution grew in later plays, though none is attributable entirely to him. He was the de facto director of Janam, which gave about 4,000 performances of 24 street plays until his death. In 1979 he married his comrade and actress Moloyashree. Hashmi's output includes two proscenium plays—an adaptation of *Gorky's *Enemies* (1983), and *Moteram ka Satyagraha* (with Habib *Tanvir, 1988)—many songs, a *television series, poems and plays for children, and documentary films. While committed to radical, popular, and left-wing art, Hashmi refrained from clichéd portrayals and was not afraid of formal experimentation. Janam was attacked by political hoodlums while performing *Halla Bol* (*Attack!*) in an industrial area near Delhi on 1 January 1989. Hashmi succumbed to his injuries the following day, and became for many a symbol of cultural resistance against authoritarianism.

SD

HASTA

Hand gesture, as delineated in the diverse vocabularies of classical *dance-theatre traditions in *India. The different gestural ideograms created through the fingers and the hands constitute one of the most highly codified sign languages in world theatre. Depending on the direction of the palm (up, down, slanting), the particular positioning of the fingers, the elevation of the gesture, and the speed with which it is represented, *hastas* are divided into different categories. The *Natyasastra* specifies 64 *hastas*, 24 of which are shown by a single hand (*asamyuta*), though sometimes both hands show the same gesture. There are thirteen *hastas* shown by both hands (*samyuta*), and 27 are specifically delineated for dance (*nritta*). Drawing on treatises like the *Abhinayadarpana* and the *Hastalakshanadeepika*, the actors of *kathakali* have refined their storytelling skills through their elaborate use of *hastas*. In *kutiyattam, hand gestures are used to convey grammatical shifts in registering the tense, number, and case of particular sentences in the dramatic *text. In their more iconographic usages, particularly in sculpturesque poses, *hastas* are also referred to as *mudra*.

LSR/RB

HAT BOI AND HAT CHEO

The two traditional forms of sung drama in *Vietnam, *hat* meaning 'sing'. *Hat cheo* is a popular form, using vernacular language and possibly originating in funeral music. Its performance probably included *mime, singing, *dancing, and poetry by the tenth century. *Hat boi* originated as court theatre about the eleventh century, but spread throughout society by about the eighteenth. It used educated language, which was a Sinicized Vietnamese, or even just Chinese. Until modern times there were no *texts for *hat cheo*, the plays being handed down orally. However, *hat boi* texts are numerous, the Vietnamese theatre archives still housing many hundreds of scripts.

Hat cheo focuses on rural society and the lives of the poor. Many items are amusing skits, but include serious commentary on life and society, even *political *satire. The choreography is feminized, most of the main *characters are female, and the characterization and *plot show women in a favourable light. The content of the *hat boi* is quite Confucianized, meaning that themes focus on Chinese or Vietnamese history and feature loyal generals or ministers, filial piety, and patriotism. Many plays deal with the imperial family's struggle against traitors, who invariably come to a bad end. From very early days, *hat boi* was heavily influenced by Chinese theatre, including in its *costumes, gestures, *make-up, movements, and *music. *Hat boi* does, however, have its own identity. While the musical instruments which accompany it also take their origin from *China, the actual mix is quite different. For instance, the double-reeded wind *ken* dominates *hat boi* music, whereas most forms of Chinese sung drama feature fiddles or flutes. Both *hat cheo* and *hat boi* still exist in Vietnam today. The government especially favours *hat cheo* as a distinctively indigenous mass-based theatre.

CPM

HAUPTMANN, GERHART (1862–1946)

German playwright, poet, and essayist. Born in Silesia, he studied sculpture in Breslau and *Rome before coming to *Berlin, where he wrote his first play, *Before Dawn* (1889), a *naturalist piece with brutish peasant *characters, which caused an uproar at its première at the *Freie Bühne. Precipitated into becoming the leader of the German *naturalist movement, Hauptmann continued to write plays about ordinary people. Originally written in Silesian dialect, his best play, *The Weavers* (1894), describes the weavers' Luddite revolt against their paymasters in 1844. Together with *Büchner's *Woyzeck*, it is the most powerful social drama in German and is distinguished by the fact that the community of weavers forms a collective *hero. In *Rose Bernd* (1903) a desperate young girl, like Gretchen in *Goethe's *Faust*, strangles her newborn baby, and *Carter Henschel* (1898) and *The Rats* (1911), a 'Berlin *tragicomedy', both end in suicide. The latter contains a scene parodying Goethe's work with actors, in which Spitta utters the naturalist credo: 'Before art as before the law all men are equal.' At the same time as Hauptmann was writing these desolate pieces about individuals crushed by their environment, he was writing *comedies, most notably *The Beaver Coat* (1893), set in a Berlin suburb with a larger-than-life washerwoman as the central character, and a *historical piece, *Florian Geyer* (1896), set during the Peasants' Revolt. He was also gradually turning more and more towards *symbolism, most successfully with *The Sunken Bell* (1896), a fable exploring the relationship between the artist Heinrich (once played by *Stanislavsky) and the real world of nature, and in *And Pippa Dances* (1906), a magical piece about a monstrous giant from the woods, a noble young suitor, and a sensitive young girl who expresses herself through *dance. Awarded the Nobel Prize for Literature in 1912, Hauptmann's prolific output of later plays, including a reworking of the *Atridean Tetralogy* (1944), never quite matched the excitement of his early naturalist work. He died at the age of 84, just in time to witness the defeat of Germany, where he had remained under the Nazi regime.

MWP

HAUPT- UND STAATSAKTION

Generic term for the drama performed by travelling troupes in Central Europe during the seventeenth and eighteenth centuries. Literally 'head and state action', it was usually a form of political *melodrama. Based originally upon bastardized versions of Elizabethan plays brought to Europe by the *English Comedians, *Haupt- und Staatsaktion* dramatized the exploits of popular *heroes and feudal rulers alongside the buffoonery of the common people. Surviving manuscripts give no indication that the *dialogue possessed literary merit; *tragedy was packed with rant and hyperbole, while *comedy, probably obscene and basic, was largely *improvised. Nevertheless, performers of *Haupt- und Staatsaktion* were seasoned professionals. As their repertoire expanded with material taken from German, French, and Spanish tragedy and *opera, *audiences were drawn by the versatility of their *acting and the resourcefulness of their spectacle. In the early eighteenth century, *Haupt- und Staatsaktion* formed the backbone of the nascent *Viennese theatre, where productions were noted for *spectacle and comic effect. Nevertheless, in other parts of German-speaking Europe, accounts suggest that *Haupt- und Staatsaktion* frequently remained rudimentary in performance until it finally disappeared with the founding of permanent *playhouses. SJCW

HAUSSMANN, LEANDER (1959–)

German director. After training at the Ernst Busch academy in East *Berlin, Haussmann worked first as an actor at regional theatres. His breakthrough as a director came in 1990 with a production of *Ibsen's *A Doll's House* in Weimar, and he was voted best new director in 1991. From 1991 to 1995 he worked freelance at major German theatres and established a reputation for unorthodox productions, especially of Shakespeare. Perhaps most successful was his *Romeo and Juliet* (*Residenztheater, *Munich, 1993). Haussmann is particularly renowned for mixing classics with elements of contemporary pop culture. From 1995 to 2000 he was *artistic director in Bochum, and most recently has worked as a *film director. Particularly successful is the film *Sonnenallee* (2000), a nostalgic look at youth in East Germany. CBB

HAVANA

Although its first *playhouse was not built until 1775, Havana had enjoyed theatrical performances since its founding by the Spanish in 1519. On the Plaza de Armas, *Corpus Christi festivities with performances of *autos sacramentales* had preceded a variety of *carnival *parades and informal entertainments, especially those of black slaves, now freed, who gradually became Cuban without surrendering their *African performance heritage. The history of theatre in Havana is woven out of conflict and compromise between these influences, the Cuban-African and the European, and it is rife with colonial repression and *censorship. By 1800, when the Teatro Circo opened, Havana was entertained with *opera, *ballet, *tragedy, *comedy, *circus,

and *puppet shows. But by the time the elegant Teatro Diorama was inaugurated in 1829, anti-Spanish sentiment was running high, and the tragedy *Tiberio* by Cuban poet José María *Heredia, denouncing the King's despotism, was being circulated, if not performed. When the even more ostentatious Teatro Tacón was inaugurated in 1838, its première of José Jacinto Milanés's (1814–63) tragedy *El conde Alarcos* sparked a scandal for its pro-Cuban, anti-monarchist implications. For the next few decades, such Cuban authors were rarely produced, and European works and companies predominated, reinforcing colonial rule. Exceptions were the playwrights Getrudis *Gómez de Avellaneda and Joaquín Lorenzo Luaces (1826–67), whose *Mendigo rojo* (*The Red Beggar*, 1859) did much to establish a tradition of Cuban theatre.

The only Cuban form to flourish during this period was the *teatro *bufo*, a popular entertainment developed by the legendary Franciso Covarrubias (1775–1850), inventor of the *stock character of the *negrito, a blackface caricature, and consolidated in 1868 with the creation of the company Bufos Habaneros. Although *bufo* was derived from the Spanish *sainete* (*one-act *farce), it incorporated Cuban *dance, creole comedy, and plantation stereotypes, and ridiculed Spanish *melodramas. It supported the 1868–78 War of Independence against Spanish rule, produced the significant author Ignacio Sarachaga (1855–1900), and gained its own playhouse in 1891, the Teatro Alhambra, before finally declining in popularity in the 1930s. By this time another national *genre had gained the devotion of Havana's inhabitants: the Cuban *zarzuela, a musical melodrama fostered by local composers.

The 'cultured' repertory remained in the hands of European companies, and was challenged only in 1936 when Luis Alejandro Baralt founded La Cueva, which opened with the Cuban première of *Pirandello's *Tonight We Improvise*, establishing an art theatre movement. Between 1940 and 1950 art theatre was promoted by the first drama *training school, ADADEL, and by new theatres including the Teatro Universitario, Prometeo, and Las Máscaras. But these, based on a subscription system, could give only one or two performances a month, offering fleeting exposure for Cuban playwrights such as Virgilio *Piñera and Carlos *Felipe. The situation changed abruptly in 1954 when, due largely to a campaign by the critic Rine Leal, a production of *Sartre's *The Respectful Prostitute* by Erick Santamaría ran for 102 consecutive performances, starting an irreversible trend to full-time performance. By the time Vicente *Revuelta opened the Teatro Estudio in 1958 with *O'Neill's *Long Day's Journey into Night*, at least ten small playhouses were operating regularly in Havana in addition to the traditional *bufo* and *vaudeville companies.

Following the revolution led by Fidel Castro in January 1959, hundreds of theatrical events took place with government, military, and union support. Revuelta directed the first Cuban production of *Brecht's work *The Good Person* of *Setzuan*, while the Teatro Martí alternated a show about combat with a *musical comedy fundraiser for aeroplanes and arms. Between 1959 and 1960, 53 Cuban plays opened, and by 1965 Havana had seven theatre groups supported by state subsidy (*see* FINANCE), staging new works by Piñera, Felipe, Antón *Arrufat, Gloria Parrado, and others. A new generation of playwrights emerged, including José *Triana, Abelardo *Estorino, Nicolás *Dorr, and Héctor *Quintero, marking a shift to a more nationalistic repertory. One production serves as an example of Cuban theatrical synthesis. In 1962, José Ramón Brene's *Santa Camila de la Habana Vieja* (*St Camilla of Old Havana*), directed by Adolfo de Luis, combined the highbrow and the popular by applying *Stanislavskian techniques to a *bufo* play, and performing to 20,000 spectators in under a month.

But ideology brewed its own tensions. In 1964 the theatre tackled the contradictions generated by socialism for the first time in Estorino's *La Casa Vieja* (*The Old House*); Revuelta's 1966 production of Triana's *La Noche de los Asesinos* (*Night of the Assassins*) was seen as embodying foreign and elitist influences; and in 1967 Eugenio Hernández Espinosa's popular *María Antonio* was attacked for its lack of class vision. The resulting crisis provoked a restructuring of the theatrical movement: Teatro Estudio broke up; Revuelta founded Los Doce, a group that took its inspiration from *Grotowski; and Sergio *Corrieri created the *collective Teatro Escambray, taking it into the mountains to integrate theatre into rural life. During the 1970s official dogma dominated the theatre world, and it was not until the creation of a Ministry of Culture in 1976 that the theatre could gently begin to function again as a mouthpiece for social dissatisfaction. The transition to ideologically critical work, albeit only in metaphor, was apparent in productions like Teatro Escambray's *Molinos de Viento* (*Windmills*, 1983), Estorino's *Morir del Cuento* (*Death from Storytelling*, 1983), Revuelta's new version of *Galileo* (1985), and Victor Varela's *La Cuarta Pared* (*The Fourth Wall*, 1988).

Throughout the 1990s *audiences shocked by the collapse of the European socialist bloc crowded Havana's playhouses in search of debate. In the absence of other public forums, theatre offered a discussion of the conflict between individual and nation. Varela's *Ópera ciega* (*Blind Opera*, 1991), Piñera's *La niñita querida* (*My Darling Little Girl*, 1993) directed by Carlos Díaz, Alberto Pedro's *Manteca* (1993), directed by Miriam Lezcano, *Parece blanca* (*She Does Look White*, 1994), written and directed by Estorino, and Marianela Boán's dance-theatre all enabled actors and audience to share views of their future. By the second half of the decade, the exodus of many artists to other countries, the scarcity of resources, and the lack of state support created difficulties for the theatre, although audiences remained faithful, and at the start of the twenty-first century a total of 30 professional theatre groups were still operating in Havana.

MMu trans. AV

GONZÁLEZ FREIRE, NATIVIDAD, *Teatro cubano (1927–1961)* (Havana, 1961)

MUGUERCIA, MAGALY, *El teatro cubano en vísperas de la Revolución* (Havana, 1988)

HAVEL, VÁCLAV (1936–)

Playwright, essayist, politician, and statesman; President of the Czech Republic since 1989. His first professional contact with theatre was as a stagehand in the ABC Theatre in *Prague (1959–60). In 1962 he was finally allowed to enter the Prague Academy of Performing Arts, graduating in 1967. At the same time, he was assistant director and *dramaturg of the Theatre on the *Balustrade, where his plays *The Garden Party* (1963), *Memorandum* (1965), and *The Increased Difficulty of Concentration* (1968) were premièred. Although he was no longer as fascinated by *Ionesco as in his earliest (unproduced) *texts, these plays were nonetheless labelled *absurdist. With considerable justification: they indeed exposed the absurd distortions of human behaviour and communication under the communist regime. On a deeper level the subjects of human manipulation, the relationship between the individual and a dehumanized system or institution, and of freedom and the temptation to give up freedom in exchange for material welfare or collectivist ideology, remained Havel's preoccupation. In the late 1960s, he was increasingly explicit on these issues; after the Soviet invasion of 1968, Havel was persecuted and later repeatedly jailed. In the 1970s and 1980s his work—including *Largo Desolato* (1984), *Temptation* (1985), and *Urban Renewal* (1987), the three highlights of his dramatic career—was banned in Czechoslovakia but published and staged abroad. In November 1989 Havel was the architect of the Czech Velvet Revolution and a month later was elected President.

ML

HAVERGAL, GILES (1938–)

English director, writer, and actor, *artistic director of the *Glasgow *Citizens' Theatre since 1969. With director-designer Philip *Prowse and playwright Robert David MacDonald, Havergal created a 'people's theatre' with low-priced *tickets and equal billing for actors. His fare of literary adaptations (for example, a version of *Nicholas Nickleby* in 1969), classic and twentieth-century drama, and extravagant campy *pantomimes has been highly popular. He directed, wrote, or acted in a number of striking productions, most notably accomplishing all three functions in *Travels with my Aunt* (1989). He also guest directed for Shared Experience (1985–7).

KN

HAWTREY, CHARLES HENRY (1858–1923)

English *actor-manager who began his acting career in 1881 at the *Prince of Wales's Theatre and his long managerial career with the lease of *Her Majesty's in 1885. Although extraordinarily active in both capacities (he managed more than sixteen *London theatres), his range as a performer was narrow. He preferred to identify himself with *characters that reflected aspects of his own personality and were palatable and recognizable to his late Victorian and Edwardian society *audiences. In this he was eminently successful, playing a sequence of likeable upper-class rogues with effortless ease within a *farcical framework. He was especially noted for his performances in *The Private Secretary* (1883), *A Message from Mars* (1899), *The Man from Blankley's* (1901) and the plays of H. V. Esmond, Charles Brookfield, and Comyns Carr. He *toured the United States extensively (1901, 1903, 1912) with equal success. As a personality actor in *comedy he inherited the mantle of Charles *Mathews and anticipated the qualities with which Noël *Coward and Rex *Harrison were later associated—charm, knowing detachment, and elegance.   VEE

HAYES, HELEN (1900–93)

American actress, sometimes called 'the First Lady of the American Theatre'. Discovered at the age of 5 among a Washington, DC, *stock company, Hayes performed in numerous Broadway plays and *musicals for producer Lew Fields. Her small physical stature and wide-set eyes gave her an appearance that, as Hayes said, led people to 'coddle and care' for her. During the years 1917–23, she personified the plucky *ingénue, performing in a series of light *comedies. She broke this pattern in 1924, playing Cleopatra in *Shaw's *Caesar and Cleopatra*. During the long run of *Coquette* (1927–9), she married playwright Charles *MacArthur. Hayes was admired for her transformative *illusion from youth to old age in the long-running *Victoria Regina* (1935–9) and, though the playwright disliked her performance, *critics praised her Amanda Wingfield in the 1948 *London première of Tennessee *Williams's *The Glass Menagerie*. Withdrawing from public view only briefly after the deaths of her daughter and husband, Hayes acted almost continuously until 1985.   MAF

HAYMARKET, THEATRE ROYAL

Located in the centre of the West End, the Theatre Royal, Haymarket, remains one of the oldest and most successful *playhouses in *London. This can be attributed to its lengthy periods of *managerial stability, its relative intimacy (888 seats in 1994), and its close identification with the performance of *comedy and revivals of established period pieces. The first theatre was built in 1720. The *political *satires of Henry *Fielding produced there led directly to the passing of the *Licensing Act of 1737, which brought about the *censorship of English theatre and the monopoly of *legitimate drama in London by the *patent theatres, *Drury Lane and *Covent Garden. In 1766, the

Haymarket's *manager, Samuel *Foote, obtained a patent licence to run the theatre during the summer months, which remained the basis of operation until the Theatre Regulation Act abolished the monopoly in 1843. The venue's identification with comedy was continued by the *Colman family from 1776 to 1817.

The second theatre opened in 1821 immediately adjacent to the old site. Benjamin *Webster managed it from 1837 to 1853; he had it lit by gas (one of the last London theatres to abandon candlelit performances; *see* LIGHTING) and introduced orchestra *stalls. The house's nineteenth-century heyday coincided with the management (1853–78) of John Baldwin *Buckstone, himself a 'low comedian'. Squire and Marie *Bancroft it took over for five years from 1880 and transferred many of their successful productions, consisting largely of the plays of T. W. *Robertson; their management introduced the first complete picture-frame stage to England. Beerbohm *Tree's tenure (1887–96) was marked by the first performances of Oscar *Wilde's *A Woman of No Importance* (1893) and *An Ideal Husband* (1895), while Cyril *Maude and Frederick Harrison bought the theatre's lease in 1896 and produced the plays of Henry Arthur *Jones, J. M. *Barrie, and Sidney *Grundy. In 1904 the theatre was given a major refurbishment, including the re-establishment of the pit (*see* BOX, PIT, AND GALLERY), and from 1905 to 1981 remained in the hands of Harrison and the trustees of his estate. The lease was then acquired by the Louis Michaels company and in 1994 the Haymarket was completely redecorated at a cost of £1.3 million. *See also* THEATRES ROYAL.   VEE

HAYMARKET THEATRE

*Playhouse at one time located in the Haymarket, *London, but not to be confused with the existing Theatre Royal, *Haymarket. Originally the Queen's Theatre, it was built by John *Vanbrugh and opened in 1705. Destroyed in 1789, it was rebuilt and became identified with *opera and *ballet throughout most of the nineteenth century. Renamed Her Majesty's in 1837, it was destroyed by *fire in 1867; again rebuilt in 1872, it was finally demolished in 1892. The existing *Her Majesty's Theatre (1897) occupies much of the original site. The theatre housed many distinguished premières: the first English oratorio (*Handel's *Esther*, 1732), and the first productions in England of *Mozart's *La clemenza di Tito* (1806), *Verdi's *Ernani* (1845), Beethoven's *Fidelio*, (1851), and *Wagner's *Ring* cycle (1882). Plagued by the exorbitant costs of visiting celebrities, the theatre had rare periods of financial success despite its high-society reputation.
                                                    VEE

HAZLEWOOD, COLIN (1823–75)

English playwright. Hazlewood was a prolific purveyor of *melodramas to the Britannia Theatre in the East End of

*London and to working- and lower-middle-class neighbourhood London theatres. The Britannia gave him about £5 a script, not, apparently, a weekly wage. Between 1863 and 1875 he wrote at least 125 plays for the Britannia, taking his material from crime reports in newspapers, magazine stories, novels, and prints of popular narrative paintings. Such titles as *Cast on the Mercy of the World; or, Deserted and Deceived* (1862), *The Mother's Dying Child; or, Woman's Fate* (1864), *Alone in the Pirate's Lair* (1867), and *Pure as Driven Snow; or, Tempted in Vain* (1869) indicate the character of Hazlewood's melodramas. Many centre on the suffering of women in humble circumstances. His most famous play, and one occasionally revived today, is *Lady Audley's Secret* (1863), from Mary Elizabeth Braddon's novel.   MRB

HAZLITT, WILLIAM (1778–1830)

English writer, one of Britain's greatest theatrical critics. Hazlitt wrote for a variety of *London newspapers including the *Examiner*, the *Champion*, the *Morning Chronicle*, and *The Times*, as well as producing a series of dramatic *criticisms for the *London Magazine*. Many of these reviews were later collected into two seminal volumes: *Characters of Shakespeare's Plays* (1817) and *A View of the English Stage* (1818). Hazlitt was fortunate enough to work during an age of celebrated performers such as Sarah *Siddons, John Philip *Kemble, John *Liston, and especially the leading *romantic tragedian, Edmund *Kean. For Hazlitt, Siddons was quite simply the personification of *tragedy; by contrast, he interpreted Kean as a 'radical' performer, brilliantly original (though often disturbingly erratic) as an interpreter of Shakespeare in particular. Hazlitt brought to his reviews a fierce and judicious intelligence, and a searching fascination with the *politics of Shakespearian *character. He was the first critic to describe Iago as an actor ('an amateur of tragedy in real life'). In his essay on *Coriolanus*, Hazlitt made a now famous argument about the way in which theatre spectators tend to collude with the interests of the powerful (Coriolanus) against those of the powerless (the plebeians). Such views were highly controversial: the literary establishment was horrified by Hazlitt's critique of Isabella, not to mention his praise for Barnadine, in the essay on *Measure for Measure*. It is a mark of Hazlitt's genius that many of the questions he raised remain central to critical debate in our own time.   JM

HEATH, THOMAS *See* MCINTYRE, JAMES.

HEAVENS

A *mansion structure or 'house' representing heaven often appeared in the simultaneous settings of *cycle plays in *medieval theatre, and was traditionally located to stage right in opposition to *hell mouth on stage left, or to the east of any open acting area. It could be crowned with rings of painted angels surrounding a heavenly throne, and Christ sometimes ascended into it by means of a concealed pulley and tackle. It could also be found on some of the *pageant wagons, where it took the form of a small upper balcony where angels stood, and from which God could descend.

In the Elizabethan theatre the 'heavens' was an upper room located above the rear part of the stage, supported by pillars resting on the stage (as at the *Swan Theatre) or by beams running forward from the roof (as at the *Hope). It contained a winch for lowering actors and objects to the stage, and its lower surface was usually decorated with paintings of the sun, moon, and stars. *See also* PLAYHOUSE.   JWH

HEBBEL, CHRISTIAN FRIEDRICH (1813–63)

German dramatist, poet, and novelist. Arguably the most important German dramatist of the mid-nineteenth century, Hebbel draws on the Old Testament, Roman history, ancient myth (*Gyges und sein Ring*, 1856), Germanic saga, the Middle Ages (*Genoveva*, 1843; *Agnes Bernauer*, 1852), and his own time. The plays employ both *verse and *realistic prose. The *tragedy *Judith* (1841) brought Hebbel his first success. He provides the Judith–Holofernes story with an original psychological motivation that anticipates Freudian theories of the unconscious. Mistrust and sexual conflict also motivate the blank verse tragedy *Herodes und Mariamne* (1849), which combines individual psychology, *historical setting, and *religious overtones (the play ends with the appearance of the Three Kings). Hebbel's most popular work in his lifetime was the *Nibelungen* trilogy (1855–60), which was seen in the nineteenth and early twentieth centuries as a nationalistic epic dramatizing the transition of the German nation from a mythic to a Christian world view. Recent revivals (*Heyme in Stuttgart, 1973, *Flimm in Hamburg, 1988) have concentrated on the mythic world and the *character conflicts. His most successful play remains the *bourgeois tragedy *Maria Magdalene* (1846), which marks an important step towards the social drama of *Ibsen and *Hauptmann. In the foreword to the play and other dramatic essays ('My Word on Drama', 1843) Hebbel argues for a redefinition of tragedy, claiming that tragic conflicts reside ultimately in the individual subject and are not dependent on religious or class factors.
                                                                        CBB

HECHT, BEN (1894–1964)

American playwright. Most of Hecht's notable work in theatre was written in collaboration with Charles *MacArthur, with whom he shared a background as a *Chicago newspaperman. *The Front Page* (1928), a *melodrama-*farce about the newspaper business, was a major success for the pair and was followed by another successful collaboration, *Twentieth Century* (1932), a similarly antic- and *plot-driven play about theatre. Hecht and MacArthur wrote the *book for the *musical extravaganza *Jumbo* (1935, music and lyrics by Richard *Rodgers and Lorenz *Hart) and collaborated intermittently up to *Swan Song* in 1946. Both turned mostly to screenwriting after 1933. Hecht wrote or co-wrote more than 60 Hollywood *films (including such classics as *Nothing Sacred*, 1937, and Hitchcock's *Notorious*, 1946), published fifteen novels and fourteen volumes of short fiction, and a biography of his former collaborator.

MAF

HEIJERMANS, HERMAN (1864–1924)

Dutch playwright and drama critic. Although Heijermans's early plays were influenced by the *naturalism of *Ibsen and *Hauptmann, he found their determinist philosophy too pessimistic. His tragic dramas, set among the working and middle classes of the Netherlands, have frequently been compared to the Dutch domestic paintings of the seventeenth century. Heijermans's socialist beliefs in the possibility of utopia on earth endowed his plays with some optimism. *The Good Hope* (1900), about the loss of a fishing vessel at sea, is generally acknowledged as his masterpiece, but *Ghetto* (1889), *Ora et Labora* (1902), *The Maid* (1908), and *The Devil to Pay* (1917) powerfully dramatize class tensions in Dutch society and display compassion for the underprivileged, even when they engage in acts destructive of the happiness of wealthier people. Heijermans was the only Dutch playwright of the twentieth century whose plays were regularly staged outside his native country.

SJCW

HEIREMANS, LUIS ALBERTO (1928–64)

Chilean playwright and novelist whose most important plays were produced in the 1960s by the Catholic University Theatre School in *Santiago. His symbolic and poetic work was a departure from the *naturalistic trend that then prevailed in Chilean theatre. His trilogy *Versos de ciego* (*Verses of the Blind*, 1961), *El abanderado* (*The Outlaw*, 1962), and *El tony chico* (*The Little Clown*, 1964), in which he endeavoured to project a universal meaning without neglecting Chilean cultural roots, are considered his best plays. *The Outlaw* interestingly combines elements from religious *medieval theatre and *Brechtian *epic theatre.

MAR

HELLENISTIC THEATRE *See* GREEK THEATRE, ANCIENT.

HELLMAN, LILLIAN (1905–84)

American playwright and memoirist. Often ranked with *O'Neill, *Williams, *Miller, and *Wilder as one of America's outstanding playwrights, Hellman built an impressive body of serious *realistic drama over the course of three decades. A native of New Orleans, educated at New York University and Columbia, Hellman began work as a journalist and then script reader. Influenced by the advice of writer Dashiell Hammett, with whom she had a long romantic relationship, Hellman turned to playwriting in 1934 with *The Children's Hour*, based on a Scottish libel case concerning a female student's accusation of lesbianism against two teachers. The painstakingly crafted play, reminiscent of *Ibsen in the taut contingencies of its *plot and the communication of a moral message through a *catastrophic conclusion, ran for 691 performances and countless revivals. After the failure of the labour drama *Days to Come* (1936), Hellman returned with *The Little Foxes* (1939), in a production featuring Tallulah *Bankhead. This play, considered by many Hellman's finest work, is at once a realistic depiction of the power struggle within an antebellum southern white family and a parable about the corrosive effects of capitalism on moral character. The play ran for 410 performances and has seen numerous revivals. Evaluation has spawned bitter controversy, some praising its rhetorical power and artfully ambiguous conclusion, others dismissing the work as a commercial *melodrama. Hellman's string of realistic, family-centred dramas continued with the anti-fascist *Watch on the Rhine* (1941); *The Searching Wind* (1944), a morality tale about the causes of the Second World War; *Another Part of the Forest* (1946), a prologue to *The Little Foxes*; *The Autumn Garden* (1951), a diffuse and comic work about a southern boarding house; and *Toys in the Attic* (1960), a drama about incestuous desire and race consciousness. After the failure of a 1963 adaptation, Hellman withdrew from theatre and focused on her memoirs. These three slender volumes—*An Unfinished Woman* (1969), *Pentimento* (1973), and *Scoundrel Time* (1976)—were bestsellers and aroused accusations of self-serving misrepresentation of the past, especially concerning Hellman's depiction of her own behaviour and that of others during the 1930s and the House Un-American Activities Committee investigations of the 1950s. As a result of those investigations, Hellman was blacklisted and unable to work in Hollywood for nearly a decade from 1952.

MAF

HELL MOUTH

A *mansion structure or 'house' representing hell often appeared in the simultaneous settings of *cycle plays in *medieval theatre, and was traditionally located to stage left in opposition to heaven on stage right, or to the west or north-west of any open acting area. It took the form of a monstrous dragon's head with gaping jaws, inside which the damned could often be seen being boiled in a cauldron.

JWH

HELPMANN, ROBERT (1909–86)

Australian *dancer, choreographer, and actor. He began his career assisting Pavlova on her *tour of Australia (1926) and later Margaret Rawlings who, encouraging his coming to *London in 1931, introduced him to Ninette de Valois in whose *Sadler's Wells Ballet he starred (1933–50), rapidly proving a worthy partner to Markova and Fonteyn and a brilliant *mime, a quality de Valois exploited when creating Tregennis (*The Haunted Ballroom*), the Rake (*The Rake's Progress*), and the ailing Red King (*Checkmate*), a role he was still playing six weeks before his death. Helpmann's own choreography was narrative based and theatrical: *Comus* and a *surreal *Hamlet* (both 1942), *Miracle in the Gorbals* (1944), *Adam Zero* (1946), *Elektra* (1963). During this period he also acted, chiefly in Shakespeare (Oberon, Hamlet, Shylock, King John, Richard III) and directed (*Antony and Cleopatra, Madame Butterfly, The Soldier's Tale*). From 1965 to 1976 he was director of the Australian Ballet, for whom he created *The Display, Yugen*, and a revised *Elektra*.   RAC

HELSINKI

Finland was ruled by the kingdom of Sweden until 1809, when it became an autonomous grand duchy of Russia with Helsinki as the capital. The first *playhouse was opened in 1827 to host companies from Sweden and Germany; later called the Arkadia Theatre, it became the home of the first native company until the *Finnish National Theatre was built in 1902. The Alexander Theatre was opened in 1880 to receive productions from *St Petersburg. Until 1918 three distinct theatre cultures coexisted in the city—Finnish, Swedish, and Russian—but they seldom converged, even though their productions shared the features of European *realism. When Finland achieved independence in 1917, the country was offically declared bilingual, and the Helsinki Swedish Theatre took on the status of a second national theatre. A further alternative was offered by workers' venues like the People's Theatre, which offered plays about the social conditions of workers and peasants, often influenced by the styles and themes of German *expressionism. Theatres in Finland existed on modest subsidies from municipalities and the state (*see* FINANCE), but popular taste prevailed and towards the end of the 1920s a wave of *operettas swept over Helsinki.

A remarkable artistic renaissance occurred after the Second World War. The Helsinki City Theatre, formed from the union of two smaller companies, inherited a repertory of *folk drama and *musical theatre. It moved into a palatial new building in 1967, and became noted for innovative productions by Jouko *Turkka, Ralf *Långbacka, and Kalle *Holmberg. The Swedish-language Little Theatre was radically transformed by Vivica Bandler into one of the most adventurous in Scandinavia. In the 1970s independent democratic groups were established to serve *audiences not reached by the institutional theatres. The most important was the left-wing KOM Theatre, founded by the composer Kaj Chydenius and Kaisa *Korhonen, which continues to mount new Finnish drama. In general terms Finnish plays amount to about half of the performances given each year in the country. Other small companies dot the city, including the Group Theatre, which performed a six-hour spectacular *Lord of the Rings* on the fortified islands of Suomenlinna in the summers in the 1990s; the Swedish-language Viirus Theatre; the Mars Theatre, which presented a four-hour family chronicle *Glorious is the Earth* (1995), written and directed by Joakim Groth; and Kristian Smeds's Forge Theatre, dedicated to *physical theatre.

In 2001, Helsinki, with a population of little more than half a million, had fourteen state-subsidized and thirteen partly subsidized theatres, most of them repertory companies. In addition there were three theatres without subsidy, a few *amateur theatres, and several *puppet theatres and theatres for *youth. Artistic standards are high, and the accent tends to be on seriousness and emotional impact rather than intellectual coolness. *Revues and *satire have a recognized place on the Finno-Swedish stage, but are rare in Finnish-language productions. Recently *street theatre, cross-disciplinary events, and communal experiments have made significant inroads. The country as a whole boasts 54 subsidized theatre companies. In 2000 almost 3 million tickets were sold—an amazing figure for a total Finnish population of 5 million.   LIB

HEMINGES, JOHN (1556–1630)

English actor. Heminges probably began his career in the late 1580s with the *Queen's Men, but moved fairly soon to *Strange's Men and then to the *Chamberlain's Men. He remained with them when they became the King's Men although it is unclear how long after 1611 he continued to perform. Heminges's roles as an actor are unknown, even though he is listed in many cast lists for *Jonson's plays. He held many business interests, theatrical and non-theatrical, and apparently served as the company's business *manager and payee for court performances. With Henry *Condell, Heminges was responsible for the compilation of the First Folio of Shakespeare's plays (1623), and was appointed trustee for Shakespeare's property in the *Blackfriars (1613).   SPC

HENDERSON, JOHN (1747–85)

English actor, the 'Bath Roscius'. He gained fame in *Bath from 1772 and did not appear on the *London stage until 1777, when George *Colman engaged him at the *Haymarket. He subsequently acted at *Drury Lane and *Covent Garden. Although short, chubby, and lacking an expressive face and strong voice, Henderson was a great favourite, praised for his comprehension of roles and his great judgement.   MJK

HENDERSON, RAY *See* DeSylva, Buddy.

HENLEY, BETH (1952–)

American playwright. Mississippi-born Henley's first full-length play, *Crimes of the Heart* (*Actors Theatre of Louisville, 1979), was the first play to win a Pulitzer Prize before a Broadway run (1981), and the first Pulitzer given to a woman since 1958. It signalled the arrival of a new generation of women playwrights, including Marsha *Norman and Wendy *Wasserstein. The play typifies Henley's use of the southern idiom, quirky *comedy, female perspective, and movement towards understanding instead of resolution. Frank *Rich said it captured truth 'like lightning in a bottle'. Other plays include *The Miss Firecracker Contest* (1980), about a dark horse in a southern beauty pageant, *Abundance* (1990), about mail-order brides in the Old West, *L-Play* (1995), made up of six *scenes in six styles, all titled with L-words, *Impossible Marriage* (1998), and *Family Week* (2000). Henley wrote the screenplays for Hollywood *films of *Crimes of the Heart* (1986) and *The Miss Firecracker Contest* (1998). Often classified as southern Gothic, Henley has sometimes been compared to *Chekhov and *Williams.   GAO

HENRÍQUEZ, CAMILO (1769–1825)

Chilean friar, journalist, and playwright who believed that sentimental drama was a suitable means to educate common people and transmit ideas of liberty. Ironically his own *Camila o la patriota Sud América* (*Camila; or, The Patriot of South America*, 1817) has never been performed.   MAR

HENRY, JOHN (1738–94)

Irish actor. Despite a promising debut at *Covent Garden in 1762, Henry soon left *London for Jamaica where he married Helen Storer and perhaps acted. In 1766 he joined David *Douglass's company at *Philadelphia's *Southwark Theatre and performed both comic and leading roles. After American independence, Henry joined *Hallam's American Company as co-*manager and leading comic actor. In 1792 he secured a contract for John *Hodgkinson, who eventually replaced him as both actor and manager. Henry became one of the most popular actors in early America, though his tumultuous personal life, involving his late wife's three sisters, was often the fodder for critics and opponents of the stage.   PAD

HENRY, MARTHA (1938–)

Canadian actor and director, born Martha Buhs in Michigan. She moved to Canada in 1959 to work at the Crest Theatre, and then appeared at the *Stratford Festival in 1961 as Miranda in *The Tempest*. During twenty seasons at Stratford, she portrayed women of strong convictions, such as Cordelia (1964), Titania (1968), and Lady Macbeth (1999). She made her directorial debut at Stratford with *Brief Lives* (1980), and abandoned *acting in 1986 to focus on *directing. Henry served as the *artistic director of the Grand Theatre, London, Ontario (1988–95). Since returning to Stratford in 1994, she has acted Mary Tyrone in *O'Neill's *Long Day's Journey into Night* (1994) and Linda in *Miller's *Death of a Salesman* (1997), and directed Timothy Findley's *Elizabeth Rex* (2000) and *Ibsen's *Enemy of the People* (2001). She has also acted in *London's West End, at *Lincoln Center in *New York, and in theatres across Canada.   PBON

HENSEL, SOPHIE FRIEDERIKE (1738–89)

German actress. A member of many prominent troupes, Hensel is best known for her roles in the *Hamburg National Theatre where she was much admired by *Lessing. She was most successful in tragic roles, espousing the new *realistic style of the mid-eighteenth century. After a short-lived marriage to Johann Gottlieb Hensel she married the actor and theatre director Abel Seyler and performed in *Vienna, Leipzig, and again Hamburg under F. L. *Schröder.   CBB

HENSLOWE, PHILIP (c.1555–1616)

English *manager, financier, and courtier. Originally a dyer by trade, Henslowe became part-owner of the most successful theatre entrepreneurship in *early modern *London. Born of an old Sussex family, Henslowe's father was Master of the Royal Game in Ashdown Forest, and Philip eventually held several court positions as well: first a Groom of the Chamber (1593), later Gentleman Sewer, and finally a Gentleman Pensioner (1603). With his son-in-law, the prominent actor Edward *Alleyn, Henslowe jointly held the patent to the Mastership of the Bears, Bulls, and Mastiff Dogs. During his early years in London Henslowe invested in a variety of businesses, including starch making and moneylending. In 1587 he decided (for reasons that are unclear) to build the *Rose Theatre in Southwark. In 1592 he undertook substantial renovations on the same structure, and in the same year his stepdaughter married Alleyn. The two men formed a partnership that eventually included three playhouses (the Rose, *Fortune, and *Hope), and the Bear Garden, a *baiting arena rebuilt as the Hope in 1613.

Many players and several companies performed in Henslowe's theatres, but he was primarily connected to them as a financier, for which he collected a portion of the profits from performances. He and Alleyn also arranged for dramatic contracts with playwrights, paid for *licences for the performances of plays, and authorized payments for *costumes and other necessities. Henslowe's well-known 'diary'—a memorandum book recording many of his financial dealings—is one of the most significant documents of the early modern theatre. The book spans the decade between 1593 and 1603, and in it Henslowe noted payments to dramatists, the titles of plays and the days on which they were performed, costume purchases, loans to actors, performance receipts, and contracts with players. In addition the diary provides the material to study the dramatic choices that made up the repertory of the Lord *Admiral's Men and the scheduling of particular plays. Henslowe lived his adult life in Southwark in the shadow of the Bankside *playhouses. His estate passed on to his stepdaughter and Alleyn, much to the consternation of Henslowe's disgruntled relatives. His manuscripts also passed to Alleyn, who preserved them, along with his own papers, at Dulwich College.   SPC

FOAKES, R. A., and RICKERT, R. T. (eds.), *Henslowe's Diary* (Cambridge, 1961)

HEPBURN, KATHARINE (1907–2003)

American actress. Born to a wealthy family, Hepburn began her professional acting career after graduating from Bryn Mawr College. Her 1928 *New York debut, *These Days*, closed after eight performances. Following a series of firings, she succeeded with *The Warrior's Husband* (1932), in the same year acting her first major *film role—in *A Bill of Divorcement*, initiating a long film career. Returning to Broadway in 1933 in *The Lake*, she was excoriated by *critics. Hepburn's appearance in Philip *Barry's *The Philadelphia Story* re-established her stardom in 1939–40. She played Rosalind in a Broadway production of *As You Like It* (1950), and appeared at the *American Shakespeare Festival as Portia in *The Merchant of Venice* (1957), Beatrice in *Much Ado About Nothing* (1957), Viola in *Twelfth Night* (1960), and Cleopatra (1960). Her final stage appearance before retirement was in *West Side Waltz* in 1981.   MAF

HERBERT, JOCELYN (1917–)

English designer, who has designed over 70 productions for drama, *opera, and *film since she joined the staff of the *English Stage Company at the *Royal Court in 1956. Influenced by *Brecht's designer, Caspar *Neher, she rapidly devised an innovative minimalist style, remarkable for its concise but poetic functionalism, achieving atmosphere and place by sculptural rather than painterly means. Dramatists with whose work she showed a profound affinity are *Ionesco (*Exit the King*), *Beckett (*Krapp's Last Tape, Happy Days, Not I, Footfalls, That Time*), *Wesker (*Roots, I'm Talking about Jerusalem*), *Osborne (*Luther, A Patriot for Me*), and *Storey (*Home, The Changing Room, Life Class*). For the Royal *National Theatre she designed Brecht's *Mother Courage* and *Galileo* and many of Tony *Harrison's stage works, notably his translation of *The Oresteia*. Opera designs include Berg's *Lulu* and Birtwistle's *The Masks of Orpheus*, while in film she has worked for Tony *Richardson, Karel Reisz, and Lindsay *Anderson.   RAC

HERBERT, VICTOR (1859–1924)

American composer. Irish born, trained in Germany as a cellist, he came to America in 1886, playing in the pit of the *Metropolitan Opera and serving as a part-time military bandmaster. He soon became an American citizen and set out to learn the popular American musical idiom. All of these influences would affect the style of the man who was America's first theatre composer of lasting note. In 1894 he began writing *music for the stage, and in 1898 he had his first hit, the gypsy-flavoured *The Fortune Teller*. Now in demand, he cranked out stage works with rapidity until he scored a huge success with *Babes in Toyland* (1903), a spectacular children's story bathed in music ranging from marches to ragtime to the Irish-flavoured 'Toyland'. A series of popular *operettas followed, culminating in *Naughty Marietta* (1910), a work which essentially set the standard for American operetta. He wrote the music for more than 40 stage works, becoming the grand old man of American theatre music. He was also a founder of ASCAP, the music licensing firm protecting songwriters' *copyrights.   JD

HEREDIA, JOSÉ MARÍA (1803–39)

Cuban poet. The author of the ode *Al Niágara* (*To the Niagara*), he wrote *neoclassical *tragedies such as *Tiberius* (1827) and two 'indigenous epics', *Moctezuma* (1819) and *Xicotencatl* (1823). The first Cuban to denounce Spanish colonial oppression in his plays, he was sentenced to death but lived out his life in exile, dying in Mexico.   MMu

HER (HIS) MAJESTY'S THEATRE

Located in the Haymarket, *London, the *playhouse was built by Beerbohm *Tree in 1897 from the profits of his production of *Trilby*, and remained in his control until his death in 1917. Decorated with flamboyant lavishness to reflect Tree's ostentation, the theatre included a penthouse where he often stayed and entertained. He staged spectacularly *realistic Shakespearian revivals as well as the poetic plays of Stephen *Phillips and *Shaw's *Pygmalion*. The sheer scale of the theatre made it particularly suitable for large productions: Oscar *Asche's *Chu Chin Chow* (1916), *West Side Story* (1958), *Fiddler on the Roof* (1967). *See also* HAYMARKET THEATRE.   VEE

HERMAN, JERRY (1933–)

American composer and lyricist. With no formal musical training, he taught himself to play piano. During the 1950s he wrote words and *music for several *Off-Broadway *revues, cracking Broadway in 1961 with *Milk and Honey*, a tuneful romance set in Israel with a featured performance by *Yiddish theatre veteran Molly *Picon. This focus on an older central *character would mark Herman's next several *musicals, notably his greatest hit, *Hello, Dolly!* (1964), and its successor, *Mame* (1966), both exuberant, highly traditional, but irresistibly appealing scores with songs that repeatedly emphasized the shows' titles. A more adventurous score still emphasizing older women, *Dear World* (1969), was less successful, as were his next two shows, *Mack and Mabel* (1974) and *The Grand Tour* (1979). But in his next musical, the highly successful *La Cage aux Folles* (1983), he effectively re-established his formula of an energetic traditional score framing an untraditional situation, with the first *gay-themed Broadway blockbuster. Since then Herman has seen several revues of his popular tunes—*Jerry's Girls* (1985), *The Best of Times* (1995)—and written a *television musical, *Mrs Santa Claus* (1996).   JD

HERNÁNDEZ, GILDA (1912–89)

Cuban director, playwright, and actress. Founder of the Taller Dramático and Escambray groups, she directed the first staging of Carlos *Felipe's *Requiem for Yarini* (1965) and *The Crucible* (1968). A major organizer within the Escambray, her play *El juicio* (*The Trial*, 1975) marked the summit of the group's achievement.   MMu

HERNÁNDEZ, LUISA JOSEFINA (1928–   )

Mexican playwright, novelist, and educator. The first woman to achieve an equal place in the male-dominated Mexican theatre world, Hernández has guided generations of aspiring playwrights through her professorship at the National Autonomous University of Mexico. *The Fallen Fruit* (1957), written when she was a student of Rodolfo *Usigli and directed by the Japanese émigré Seki *Sano, who introduced *Method acting into Mexico, established Hernández as a master of psychological *realism with a keen insight into the hypocrisy of the middle class, especially in relation to sexuality. Her *History of a Ring* (1967) and *The Mulato's Orgy* (1970) are *Brechtian critiques of political corruption and economic oppression. Hernández also has written *historical plays such as *Popol Vuh* (1967), based on the holy Mayan text, as well as numerous short plays for a variety of student activities. Translated into English and various European languages, Hernández has won important national *awards for playwriting, although her works are not often given professional stagings in Mexico.   KFN

HERNANI RIOTS

Performance of Victor *Hugo's *Hernani* in 1830 gave rise to sustained disorder in the theatre. Foreseeing opposition from the traditionalist patrons of the *Comédie-Française, Hugo had dispensed with the paid *claque, and for three performances managed to pack the theatre with his own band of young supporters—students and artists—thereby ensuring a relatively trouble-free reception. When the supply of complimentary tickets ceased, however, turbulence in the *audience became the norm, and for the remainder of a record-breaking 39 performances the long-suffering cast, whether or not loyal to Hugo, were obliged to play in conditions of serious unrest, close to *riot. (*See* illustration p. 584.)   WDH

HERNE, JAMES A. (1839–1901)

American *actor-manager and playwright. With no formal education past the age of 13, Herne built a lifelong career as a popular performer in romantic *melodrama, after several years with barnstorming troupes on America's east coast. He eventually settled in *San Francisco, becoming *stage manager at the New San Francisco Theatre in 1874, moving to the Baldwin Theatre in 1876, where he began writing plays with David *Belasco. With *Hearts of Oak* (1879) and *Drifting Apart* (1888), Herne developed a strength for rural dramas, with *dialogue reflecting the actor-playwright's growing interest in the work of *Ibsen and other early *realists. The plays remained recognizably melodramatic in *plot and structure. Herne attempted a serious realistic social drama with *Margaret Fleming* (1890). The work and its performance by Herne and his wife Katharine Corcoran were highly praised by the literary establishment in *Boston, where the play was presented as a private club performance, but it never gained popular acceptance. Herne's major popular success was *Shore-Acres* (1892), which remained his signature role for the rest of his life. Although a romantic melodrama with a rural Maine setting, it features such realistic elements as the preparation, serving, and eating of a Thanksgiving dinner on stage, and an astonishing ending, performed entirely in silence, with Herne on stage puttering about closing the family home for the evening, while reflecting on events, the first clear use in American drama of what *Stanislavsky would later call *subtext.   AW

HERO (HEROINE) AND ANTIHERO

Terms used to denote the *protagonist of a dramatic *action. In drama prior to *romanticism, hero described a figure in either *tragedy or *comedy. Heroes were distinguished by admirable personal qualities, by the sense that they often had access to sources of energy and insight denied the common man, and by their status as representatives of the social community. Romanticism, however, posited the hero as one who was alienated from society and highly critical of it. The 'antihero', as this figure could be called, often stood at the centre of the action in the *realistic dramas of *Ibsen, *Strindberg, *Chekhov, and *Shaw, and became the icon of the 'angry young man' English drama of the 1950s. From a post-*structuralist perspective, several of the central *characters in tragedies by playwrights as diverse as

LES ROMAINS ÉCHEVELÉS A LA 1re REPRÉSENTATION D'HERNANI.

Si le drame avait eu six actes, nous tombions tous asphyxiés.

*Euripides, Shakespeare, and *Calderón now appear to be more antiheroic than heroic. Yet nineteenth-century *melodrama, and its numerous descendants on stage and in Hollywood action *films, relied on the heroic qualities of the protagonist for the successful resolution of the action, usually pitting him or her against an evil *villain in order to clarify the hero's morally superior status.   SJCW

HEROIC TRAGEDY

A form of serious drama which flourished briefly in England during the Restoration. Heroic tragedy, in rhymed couplets, featured a titanic *protagonist, spectacular action in an exotic setting, bombast and overwrought emotion, and themes of love and honour. It had affinities with *Corneille's *tragedies, but its immediate progenitor, according to its most prominent advocate, *Dryden, was *Davenant's *Siege of Rhodes* (1656). Dryden, with Sir Robert *Howard, inaugurated the vogue with *The Indian Queen* (1664), but after *Aureng-Zebe* (1675) he turned to blank *verse tragedy and by the early 1680s heroic tragedy had run its course. The form is sometimes called heroic drama in that a tragic *denouement is not a requisite.   RWV

HERON, MATILDA (1830–77)

American actress. Born in Ireland, Heron came to the United States at an early age. She made her stage debut in 1851, at *Philadelphia's *Walnut Street Theatre, then *toured California and appeared at the *Bowery in *New York. Her greatest success came in the role of Camille, in the *Dumas play she adapted and virtually made her own. Heron's version ran for 100 nights at *Wallack's in New York, in 1857, after which she toured it with phenomenal success. Her style of *acting, which was noted for its emotional *naturalism and what William *Winter called 'elemental power', greatly influenced other actors of the late nineteenth century. Aspects of her style that were new to American *audiences included using a conversational tone for *dialogue, turning her back on the audience, and portraying illness and suffering without refinement or sentimentality. Her career also established a pattern for later stars.   AHK

HERRMANN, KARL-ERNST (1936–)

German designer and director. One of the most important stage designers of the post-war period, Herrmann began his career as assistant to Wilfried *Minks. In 1969 he began an association with Peter *Stein and was a founding member of the *Berlin

*The **Hernani** riots. Supporters of romanticism attack neoclassical traditionalists at the Comédie-Française during the run of Victor Hugo's *Hernani*, 1830. The final scene is shown on stage; note the prompter's box lightly sketched downstage centre.

*Schaubühne, where he worked on practically all of the best-known productions. Most notable were *Peer Gynt* (1971), where he constructed a square *arena stage with the *audience on both sides; *Gorky's *Summerfolk* (1974) featuring real birch trees; the *environmental staging in *Shakespeare's Memory* (1976); and *Chekhov's *Three Sisters* (1984) with a reconstruction of the set of the original *Moscow Art Theatre production. Since 1982 Herrmann has worked as a director and designer of *opera. Important productions (especially for the Brussels National Opera) include *Mozart's *La clemenza di Tito* (1982; *Salzburg Festival, 1992), *La finta giardiniera* (1986), and *Don Giovanni* (1987); Verdi's *La traviata* (1987); and *Gluck's *Orpheus and Eurydice* (1988). Herrmann's designs are characterized by innovative spacial experiments in conjunction with a keen awareness of the *dramaturgical and historical requirements of the *texts. Most importantly, after decades of allusive abstractionism Herrmann reintroduced *realism as well as *environmental staging into German *scenography.   CBB

HEWES, HENRY (1917–)

American *critic. Writing for the news weekly *Saturday Review* (1951–79), Hewes was the first influential *New York critic regularly to review the nascent *Off-Broadway and *regional theatre movements and the only one to cover all four posthumous premières of Eugene *O'Neill in Sweden. A main mover in the founding of the American Theatre Critics Association, Theatre Hall of Fame, Drama Desk, Theatre Wing Seminars, and Maharam (now Hewes) *awards for design, he also chaired the Margo *Jones awards and edited *Best Plays*. He most memorably said, 'I'm sorry for every nasty thing I wrote. The fact that I was always right is no excuse.'   CR

HEWETT, DOROTHY (1923–2002)

Australian playwright, poet, and novelist. One of the country's most acclaimed playwrights, Hewett studied at the University of Western Australia and first came to notice with *This Old Man Comes Rolling Home* (1966), a drama of *Sydney working-class family life. A controversial and distinctive writer, her partly autobiographical and intensely personal style emphasized sexual and family relations in plays such as *The Chapel Perilous* (1971). Later work, such as *The Man from Muckinupin* (1979) and *The Fields of Heaven* (1982), chronicled the need to value cultural heritage and cherish landscapes. A radical writer with a free-ranging style, Hewett remains a figure who polarizes *audiences and critics.   SBS

HEYME, HANSGÜNTHER (1935–)

German director. After first studying architecture, then German literature and philosophy, Heyme became assistant to Erwin

*Piscator in *Berlin and Mannheim in 1956. From 1958 to 1963 he was director-in-residence in Heidelberg where he directed among other works Ernst *Toller's *Hinkemann* (1959) and *Camus's *The Possessed* (1960). Heyme's first production to attain national recognition was *Weiss's *Marat/Sade* in Wiesbaden, where he was director from 1964 to 1968. As *artistic director of Cologne's municipal theatre (1968–79), he experimented remarkably with *Greek *tragedy and *comedy. The central focus, however, was the German classical tradition of *Goethe, *Schiller, and *Hebbel, and a number of productions were invited to the *Berlin *Theatertreffen. His farewell production in 1979 was a controversial *Hamlet* designed by the *performance artist Wolf Vostell which made extraordinary use of *television monitors and other electronic mediation of the stage events. Heyme succeeded Claus *Peymann as artistic director in Stuttgart in 1979 and he continued his predecessor's predilection for controversial productions. From 1985 to 1992 he was artistic director in Essen. During this time he also assumed the directorship of the Ruhrfestspiele in Recklinghausen, a position he still held at the start of the twenty-first century. Heyme is an important representative of German *director's theatre, which established itself as the dominant aesthetic trend in the 1960s and 1970s. His productions are based on intensive cooperation with *dramaturgs and fuse scholarly research with radical reinterpretations of the classics.   CBB

HEYWARD, DOROTHY (1890–1961) AND DUBOSE (1885–1940)

American husband and wife playwriting team. Though they occasionally worked apart, as in Dorothy's *Cinderelative* (1930) or Dubose's *Brass Ankle* (1931), the Heywards' major stage works were written as a team. The creative process typically involved field research, the creation of a novel by Dubose, which was then dramatized by Dorothy and polished together. Their three successes were based upon research into folkways of African Americans in South Carolina. Rouben *Mamoulian's *ritualistic and semi-musical staging of *Porgy* (1927) contributed to the interest in *folk drama in the 1920s seen also in plays by Paul *Green, who—like the Heywards—was a sympathetic white intellectual observing black culture. When *Porgy* was reworked as the folk *opera *Porgy and Bess*, with *music by George *Gershwin, book by Dubose Heyward, and lyrics by Heyward and Ira *Gershwin, it was hailed as a masterpiece and has seen major revivals. The Heywards' other success was *Mamba's Daughters* (1939), a violent and eventful *tragedy which featured Ethel *Waters in the central role.   MAF

HEYWOOD, JOHN (1497–c.1579)

English playwright, musician, and poet. From 1520 Heywood was active at the court of Henry VIII as a 'singer and player of virginals' and later as master of an acting troupe of boy singers. He apparently continued to produce *pageants and entertainments during the reigns of Edward VI and Mary Tudor. In 1564 he fled to Flanders, where he died. Five of Heywood's six plays (which were all written before 1533) take the form of comic debates, which poke fun at academic chop-logic while simultaneously making a didactic point: *The Play of Love, Witty and Witless, The Play of the Weather, The Four PP, The Pardoner and the Friar*. The scatological humour and *farce in the last two is central to Heywood's best play, *John John, Tib, and Sir John*, a brilliant translation/adaptation of a French farce. Heywood wrote for his *boy actors, but his more ribald plays were also suited to the popular repertory.   RWV

HEYWOOD, THOMAS (c.1574–1641)

English playwright, actor, and pamphleteer. Heywood was an industrious participant in the *London theatrical world for over 40 years. In 1598 he was contracted as an actor with the *Admiral's Men, for whom he also wrote a couple of plays. About 1600 he began a twenty-year association as actor, playwright, and shareholder with the Earl of Worcester's (later Queen Anne's) company at the *Rose (1602–3), the *Curtain (1603–c.1606), and the *Red Bull (c.1606–17). By 1612 the company was apparently in decline; Heywood wrote no plays for them after 1614, and ceased to act by the end of the decade. Between 1624 and 1634 he wrote plays for Christopher *Beeston's companies at the Phoenix or *Cockpit. In 1631 he produced the first of seven *pageants for the annual Lord Mayor's Day. Of the more than 220 plays that Heywood claimed to have written or collaborated on, approximately two dozen are extant. *A Woman Killed with Kindness* (1603), a domestic *tragedy, is his finest play, but several others are worthy representations, not only of Heywood's career, but of Elizabethan popular taste: *If You Know Not Me, You Know Nobody* (two parts, 1605–6), on Queen Elizabeth's early years; or *The Fair Maid of the West* (two parts, 1610, c.1630), a romantic tale of adventure. One of Heywood's last plays, the *masque-like *A Challenge for Beauty* (1634–6), was a great success at court as well as at the Phoenix. Heywood's defence of players in *An Apology for Actors* (1612) is good natured and informed, and may mark the growing respectability of the profession.   RWV

HIBBERD, JACK (1940–)

Australian playwright. He studied medicine at the University of Melbourne and practised as a physician from 1964 until 1973, when he resigned to devote himself to the theatre. Until 1977 he was closely associated with the *Australian Performing Group in *Melbourne, who presented ten of his early plays, including *White with Wire Wheels* (1967). Hibberd's work presents distinctly Australian attitudes in an extravagant theatricality, demonstrating an increasing distancing from *realism, with *music and song reminiscent of *Brecht. *Dimboola* (1969) is typical, seeking *audience involvement and requiring the serving of food. Others, such as *A Toast to Melba* (1976), ironically celebrate famous Australians, and *The Stretch of the Imagination* (1972) is the best known of his *monodramas. Hibberd returned part time to medical practice in 1986 but has also published novels, translated poetry, and continued writing for the theatre.   SBS

HICKS, EDWARD SEYMOUR (1871–1949)

English *actor-manager and dramatist. He first appeared at the Grand, Islington (1887), subsequently *toured America with the *Kendals, and co-produced *Under the Clock* (1893), the first *revue staged in *London. Early successes included *Walker London* (1892) and J. M. *Barrie's *Quality Street* (1904). He wrote light *comedies and Christmas plays (such as *Bluebell in Fairyland*). He built the *Aldwych Theatre (1905), the Globe (1907)—opening both with his own plays—and took over Daly's (1934). Awarded the Légion d'Honneur in 1931, he was knighted in 1935. During both world wars he took performers to France. He was married to the actress Ellaline Terriss.   JTD

HIGHWAY, TOMSON (1951–   )

Canadian playwright. Born to a Cree family in northern Manitoba, like many First Nations children he was taken from his parents to a Roman Catholic residential school where he learned English. After attending high school in Winnipeg and then training as a classical pianist, he worked with James *Reaney in play-development workshops in London, Ontario, and in Native community services there and in *Toronto. Highway became a major new voice in Canadian theatre on the strength of two *award-winning plays, *The Rez Sisters* (1986) and *Dry Lips Oughta Move to Kapuskasing* (1989). The plays, both set on the fictional reserve of Wasaychigan Hill on Manitoulin Island in Lake Huron, are structured as a diptych: the former with seven female *characters plus a male Nanabush (the traditional Native 'trickster' figure), the latter with seven male characters plus a female Nanabush. Essentially a crossover artist, Highway sprinkles Cree and Ojibway *dialogue, often untranslated, in these mostly English-language scripts. The plays draw heavily on both Native and Christian religious imagery; and though one is a *comedy and the other a *tragedy, both mingle the comic and tragic in ways that Highway describes as characteristically Native. Both plays premièred in Toronto, where each won a Dora Mavor Moore award as the year's best new script. The third play of Highway's 'Wasy' trilogy, a *musical entitled *Rose*, has been in workshops with three professional companies in Canada but as of 2001 had not been produced professionally. *See also* NATIVE AMERICAN PERFORMANCE.   DWJ

HIJIKATA TATSUMI (1928–86)

Japanese dancer and choreographer, one of the originators of *butoh. His *Forbidden Colours* (1959), a *dance based on *Mishima Yukio's novel of homosexuality, was a *succès de scandale*, and is generally acknowledged to be the first genuine butoh performance. A seminal figure in the cultural ferment of 1960s *Japan, Hijikata was friend and collaborator with major writers, artists, and composers. He worked extensively with *Ono Kazuo and Ono's son Yoshito on dances such as *Notre Dame des fleurs* (1960) and *Rose-Coloured Dance* (1965). His own work demonstrated a taste for the decadent, the violent, and the anarchic—*Genet, Sade, Lautréamont, and Beardsley were early influences—but *kabuki and the *folkways of his native Tōhoku were instrumental in creating his unique style. Representative pieces include *Revolt of the Flesh* (1968) and *A Tale of Smallpox* (1972). For the last decade of his short life, Hijikata worked chiefly as director and choreographer for large dance ensembles.   CP

HIJIKATA YOSHI (1898–1959)

Japanese director. In 1920 Hijikata met *Osanai Kaoru and became one of his most ardent disciples. Living in *Berlin in 1922, Hijikata then fell under the influence of such *expressionist playwrights as *Toller and *Kaiser. On his way back to *Japan immediately after the 1923 *Tokyo earthquake, while waiting in *Moscow for rail connections, he first saw *Meyerhold's productions and was deeply impressed by the ideals and accomplishments of Soviet theatre. Hijikata was active in the establishment of the *Tsukiji Little Theatre in *Tokyo, directing plays by Reinhard *Goering, Romain *Rolland, and others. After Osanai's death in 1928, Hijikata formed Shin Tsukiji Gekidan (the New Tsukiji Troupe), dedicated to the principles of *socialist realism. In 1933 he was invited to the Soviet Union where he remained until 1941; on his return he was immediately arrested and jailed until 1945. In the last decade of his life he was permanently in poor health, but managed to direct occasionally. Hijikata has remained a hero of the Japanese theatrical world for his resistance to *fascism and for helping to create the Tsukiji Little Theatre.   JTR

HILAR, KAREL HUGO (1885–1935)

Czech director, critic, and poet. He was the *dramaturg, then director of the Vinohrady Municipal Theatre, *Prague, from 1911 to 1921; between 1921 and 1935 he was head of the *Czech National Theatre's drama company. An early admirer of *Reinhardt, his later style was closer to *Jessner's, sometimes even anticipating him. Hilar used the script to present a vision of contemporary world, with original *scenography, commissioned music, and stylized *acting as instruments. In the National

Theatre his style changed to sober matter-of-factness, close to *neue Sachlichkeit*, the German 'new seriousness' of the same period. Amongst his Shakespearian productions, his antiheroic *Hamlet* (1926) was acclaimed by the young generation. His version of *expressionism well suited *The Insect Play* (1921) by Karel and Josef *Čapek. His last significant production was *Mourning Becomes Electra* (1934) by Eugene *O'Neill. Though a leading figure of the official stage, he was also highly respected by the young radicals of the 1920s and 1930s. ML

HILDEGARD OF BINGEN (1098–1179)

Benedictine abbess and mystic, founder of the Abbey of Rupertsberg near Bingen, Germany. Hildegard's religious visions and insights are recorded in three major works: *Scivas* (*Knowledge*), *Liber Vitae Meritorum* (*Book of a Life of Merit*), *Liber Divinorum Operum* (*Book of Divine Works*); her theology in two treatises; and an unexpectedly sophisticated knowledge of the human body in two medical texts. She also wrote 77 *carmina* (songs) besides a number of songs incorporated into *Scivas* and used in her musical play *Ordo Virtutum* (*c.*1155). The *Ordo* is an early example of a *morality play. Based on Prudentius' *Psychomachia* (fourth century), it features a struggle between sixteen personified virtues and the forces of the devil for the Christian soul. The play was possibly intended to be played by the nuns of Hildegard's convent. Certainly the success of performances and recordings since 1980 attests to its theatricality. *See* MEDIEVAL THEATRE IN EUROPE. RWV

HILDESHEIMER, WOLFGANG (1916–91)

German essayist, dramatist, and artist. Born in Hamburg, the son of a Jewish chemist, Hildesheimer emigrated to Palestine with his parents in 1933. After the war he served as a simultaneous translator at the Nuremberg trials. In 1950 he settled in Germany, moving in 1957 to Switzerland. In the late 1950s and early 1960s Hildesheimer wrote many plays for stage and *radio, establishing himself as Germany's major exponent of *absurdist theatre, a position reinforced by a famous lecture in Erlangen of 1960 'On Absurd Theatre' in which he developed the notion of a 'philosophical' theatre in which the alienation and estrangement of the modern condition should be made manifest on stage. This goal was perhaps best achieved in the *one-act play *Nachtstück* (*Night Play*, 1963). Hildesheimer is best remembered as a novelist and for his innovative *Mozart biography (1977). CBB

HILL, ERROL (1921–)

Trinidadian playwright, director, scholar, and long-time professor of drama at Dartmouth College in the USA. Hill founded the Whitehall Players in 1946, wrote *Brittle and the City Fathers* the

next year, began to experiment with local speech rhythms with *The Square Peg* (1949), and in *The Ping Pong* (1950) created an early 'yard play' with a clear Trinidadian identity. He studied on scholarships at the *Royal Academy of Dramatic Art in *London (1950–1) and the *Yale School of Drama (1958–62), His work from 1953 as drama officer of the University of the West Indies allowed him to travel throughout the *Caribbean investigating new theatre companies, and from 1954 he published a series of West Indian plays. His most important play is probably *Man Better Man* (first seen at Yale, 1960), which centres on stick-fighting traditions in Trinidad and incorporates calypso music and songs. This helped formulate his *theory of the *carnival as the basis for a national theatre, expressed in his book *The Trinidadian Carnival* (1972, 1997). *The Jamaican Stage 1655–1900* (1992) is a key resource; it pays close attention to colonial theatre and to aspects of orature, performance, and *ritual among former slaves, which laid the foundations for future Jamaican theatre. ES

HILL, GEORGE HANDEL ('YANKEE') (1809–40)

American actor. Born in *Boston, Hill was affected in his youth by an itinerant *African-American *variety performer named Potter, though his greatest influence was the English comedian Charles *Mathews, upon whom he consciously modelled himself. Hill's theatrical apprenticeship began in 1825 in *New York. He became a star in 1832 as Jonathan Ploughboy in *Woodworth's *The Forest Rose*, and he continued triumphantly in a series of Yankee roles in the 1830s and 1840s, becoming the greatest performer of that *stock character with the dry sense of humour and wry perspective. Eventually performing in *London, *Dublin, *Edinburgh, and *Paris, Hill retired from the stage several times. TFC

HILL, JENNY (1851–96)

English *music-hall performer, 'the Vital Spark' of the first generation of stars of the halls. She excelled in *characterizations of women of her own working-class background, moving over time from rude acrobatic *dancing in songs like 'The Coffee-Shop Gal' to sympathetic and caustic representations of abused wives 'determined no longer to stand it'. Her *male impersonations included a version of 'Arry' the flashy cockney stereotype who asserted his superiority to idle upper-class men. In later years she used brief *melodramas with elaborate *scenery and supporting casts to ease the demands of solo work. A prominent member of music-hall society, known for her readiness to speak up for herself from the stage and at celebratory dinners and formal functions, she repeatedly tried and failed to break into the male monopoly of music-hall *management. In 1875 she invested in the Star Music Hall in Hull; in 1882 she took the lease of a *London pub, the Albert Arms; and in 1884 bought the Rainbow Music Hall in Southampton. None of these ventures succeeded.

JSB

HILLER, WENDY (1912–)

English actress. After starting her career in 1930 with the *Manchester Repertory Theatre, Hiller became a success in *London in 1935 in Love on the Dole, adapted by her future husband Ronald Gow from Walter Greenwood's novel. In 1936 at the *Malvern Festival she played the title role in *Shaw's St Joan and Eliza in Pygmalion, then did the *film versions of Pygmalion (1938) and Major Barbara (1941). After the war she featured in Shakespeare at the *Old Vic and in several plays adapted from the novels of Henry *James, Thomas Hardy, and H. G. Wells. Additional roles included Josie in *O'Neill's A Moon for the Misbegotten (*New York, 1957), Carrie Berniers in *Hellman's Toys in the Attic (London, 1960), and Queen Mary in Royce Ryton's Crown Matrimonial (London, 1972). In 1975 she appeared with Peggy *Ashcroft and Ralph *Richardson in *Ibsen's John Gabriel Borkman at the *National Theatre. Selectively, she continued to do films, including A Man for All Seasons (1966) and The Elephant Man (1980); she won Academy awards for Pygmalion (1938) and Separate Tables (1958). She was made DBE in 1975.

TP

HILPERT, HEINZ (1890–1967)

German director. One of the leading directors in Weimar Germany, Hilpert began his career as an actor in 1919 but soon switched to *directing, making his debut in 1922 at the *Berlin *Volksbühne. After a period in the provinces he joined Max *Reinhardt at the *Deutsches Theater, where he was appointed head director. A specialist in social drama, his breakthrough came in 1928 with Ferdinand *Bruckner's Die Verbrecher (The Criminals). He also directed the première of *Horváth's Tales from the Vienna Woods (1931) and many plays by Gerhart *Hauptmann. After a short period as director of the Volksbühne (1932–4), he took over Reinhardt's theatres in Berlin and *Vienna when Reinhardt was forced into exile. After the war Hilpert became director of the Deutsches Theater in Göttingen from 1950 to 1966, establishing it as a major venue. His *directing was noted for attention to psychological detail. Often seen as a pupil of Reinhardt, he thought of himself more in the tradition of Otto *Brahm.

CBB

HINDI THEATRE

Performance in the Hindi language is concentrated in the northern states of *India, including Himachal Pradesh, Haryana, Uttar Pradesh, Madhya Pradesh, Rajasthan, and Bihar. In these cul-

turally and linguistically diverse regions, both religious and secular forms have emerged which have some continuity with the Sanskrit tradition, though with regional variations. *Religious forms like *Ram lila, *ras lila, and bhagat, and popular secular forms like *nautanki, *khayal, *mach, nacha, and swang, draw on mythology and legend, adopting a flexible presentational mode of performance replete with song, *dance, and *spectacle. With exposure to the colonial models of British theatre in the nineteenth century, the indigenous traditions became increasingly identified with the rural areas and small towns.

Meanwhile two types of urban theatre developed under the influence of the educated elite—the commercial *Parsi theatre and the 'serious' *amateur theatre. Parsi theatre, popular roughly from 1860 to 1930, was a highly eclectic form of entertainment, based primarily on Victorian *melodrama, and initiated by the Parsi merchant community as a business enterprise. Though it was not based as such in the Hindi-speaking region, it was popularized through *touring companies from Maharashtra and later from Calcutta (*Kolkata). Significant playwrights in *Urdu and Hindi were Agha Hashr Kashmiri, with plays like Yahoodi Ki Ladki (The Jew's Daughter, 1913) and Rustom Sohrab (1929); Narayan Prasad Betab with Ramayana (1916) and Mahabharata (1913); and Radheshyam Kathavachak with Veer Abhimanyu (The Brave Abhimanyu, 1914) and Shravan Kumar (1916). Amateur theatre was pioneered by the playwright-actor Bharatendu *Harishchandra, who in his short life of 35 years almost singlehandedly created a vibrant amateur theatre with a strong sociopolitical statement in a language that pulsated with the music of regional dialects. Subsequently, the poet-playwright Jaishankar Prasad (1889–1937), with his *historical plays in the Shakespearian mode like Skandagupta (1928) and Chandragupta (1931), handled the conflict between the public and private with sensitivity and a *modernist sensibility. Plays from the 1930s and 1940s remained more or less confined to the page, except those by Upendra Nath Ashq and Laxmi Narayan Mishra, based on *Ibsen's *realist model, which found an occasional platform in the university theatre.

In the mid-1940s the anti-imperialist and anti-fascist *Indian People's Theatre Association encouraged a number of intellectuals and artists to write plays about social and *political issues. One serious attempt at creating a professional theatre, after the Parsi companies wound up with the advent of the talkies in 1931, was made by Prithviraj *Kapoor when he launched his Prithvi theatre in Bombay (*Mumbai) in 1944. In its span of sixteen years it produced several plays like Deewar (Wall), Gaddar (Traitor), and Pathan (1948), which, albeit in the Parsi theatre mode, stood out for their idealism, commitment, and professional standards.

Only after independence did Hindi theatre provide significant drama. Jagdishchandra Mathur's Konark (1951) and Shardiya (1959) explored delicate human relationships in a markedly contemporary idiom; Dharamvir *Bharati's Andha

Yug (*The Blind Age*, 1954), a bold anti-war play in *verse, reinterpreted mythology; Mohan Rakesh's *Asadh Ka Ek Din* (*A Day in Asadh*, 1958), *Lehron Ke Rajhans* (*Swans of the Waves*, 1963), and *Adhe Adhure* (*Halfway House*, 1969) explored the relationship of men to women in the context of larger issues like the search for identity in a fragmented world. Important directors also emerged in this period as interpreters of new Hindi plays, like Habib *Tanvir with Naya Theatre in Delhi, who amalgamated Chhattisgarhi tribal artists and traditions with an urban sensibility; Satyadev Dubey with Theatre Unit in Bombay; and Shyamanand Jalan with Anamika (Calcutta).

Hindi theatre flourished in the 1960s and part of the 1970s with several theatre groups emerging in different regions: Dishantar and Abhiyan in New Delhi, Rupantar in Gorakhpur, Darpana in Kanpur, and Kala Sangam in Patna. Important directors included B. V. *Karanth, Rajindernath, Om Shivpuri, Girish Rastogi , Mohan Maharishi, Ranjit Kapoor, B. M. Shah, Bansi Kaul, M. K. Raina, Satish Anand, Bhanu Bharti, Dinesh Thakur, Satyendra Sharad, and Raj Bisaria. Apart from Rakesh, the significant playwrights of the time included Surendra Verma and Shanker Shesh, who carried on the realistic tradition; Laxmi Narayan Lal, Giriraj Kishore, and Mudra Rakshas, who wrote in the *absurdist idiom; and Sarveshwar Dayal Saxena and Mani Madhukar, who incorporated elements of the traditional theatre to make contemporary social comments.

Despite large potential, Hindi theatre has not consolidated itself. There are several reasons for this. First, the entire Hindi-speaking region has low industrial growth and a slow growth of the middle class, who are the primary spectators and promoters of urban theatre in India. Similarly there has been little business initiative in promoting theatre as a commercial enterprise. Then, with the advent of Indian *film, largely in Hindi though based in Bombay, the Hindi-speaking *audiences have been exposed to a large body of entertainment in their language, and consequently they do not miss theatre in any significant way. The politics surrounding Hindi as the national language have also affected the perception of its theatre practice. On the one hand, the official version of the language, artificially created and propagandized, has alienated even the people of the Hindi-speaking region from their own language; on the other hand, there has been much opposition to the imposition of Hindi from non-Hindi speaking groups.

Yet Hindi theatre has played a crucial role in the development of the Indian theatre as a whole. For almost half a century most of the significant plays written anywhere in the country have been translated and performed in Hindi, giving them national exposure and allowing further translations into regional languages. Further, the Hindi stage, quite unlike other linguistic regions, has constantly provided a platform to non-Hindi directors like B. V. Karanth (Karnataka), K. N. *Panikkar (Kerala), Shanta *Gandhi (Gujarat), Prasanna (Karnataka), and Ratan *Thiyam (Manipur), who have contributed to the pan-Indian

aura of Hindi theatre. Though the region is marked for its conservatism, particularly with regard to the role of women in society, it is here that a large number of women directors has emerged, like Amal Allana, Anamika Haksar, Anuradha Kapur, and Tripurari Sharma. Their work has shifted focus towards collaboration, resulting in experimental perspectives on *gender and power equations, the questioning of female stereotypes, and the deconstruction of patriarchal narrative structures. They could well provide the direction for Hindi theatre in the future.   KJ

HIPPODRAMA

A theatrical form employing specially trained horses as major performers, dating from the beginning of the nineteenth century in both France and England. The *Cirque Olympique in *Paris and *Astley's Amphitheatre in *London produced *spectacle *melodramas in a space that evolved into a strong, large *stage connected by ramps to a *circus ring. The *action could take place in both areas and frequently involved large numbers of horses and hundreds of performers. Patriotic military spectacle was the principal material of hippodrama. At Astley's, for example, *The Battle of Waterloo* was given four times, as well as many battles from the Napoleonic and later wars, including the Crimean War. In France there were a great number of Napoleonic war battles at the Cirque Olympique, all with a magnificently heroic Napoleon. Hippodrama was also staged at other venues, like *Vauxhall Gardens in London and the Roman *amphitheatre at Nîmes, and was even welcomed at *Drury Lane and *Covent Garden. The notorious Ada Isaacs Menken flaunted her curvaceous figure in *Mazeppa*, and there was a brief vogue for equestrianized Shakespeare at Astley's in 1856 and 1857, with *Richard III* (containing a spectacular battle of Bosworth Field), *Macbeth*, and *Henry IV*. *Sanger's Circus, late Astley's, closed in 1893 after a long series of equestrian performances, and Paris turned away from the hippodrama to essentially non-equestrian spectacles. Racing melodramas and the chariot-filled *Ben-Hur* (*New York, 1899; London, 1902) were the last refuge, outside circus, of equestrian drama.   MRB

HIPPODROME (*LONDON)

Located at the corner of Cranbourn Street and Charing Cross Road in the West End, the theatre was designed by Frank Matcham and opened in 1900 as a venue for *circus and large shows. The huge water tank built into the stage allowed the performance of plays like *The Earthquake* and *The Typhoon*. The circus arena was replaced by *stalls in 1909, and until 1912 the *playhouse was a venue for *ballet and *variety. Albert de Courville made it known as a *revue theatre (1912–25), a reputation it retained when it became London's version of the *Folies-Bergère (1949–51) and in its final incarnation as a *cabaret-restaurant, *The Talk of the Town* (1958). It closed in 1982.   VEE

HIPPODROME (*NEW YORK)

Theatre on the west side of 6th Avenue between 43rd and 44th Streets. It opened in 1905 with *A Yankee Circus on Mars*. The world's largest and best-equipped theatre, with 5,200 seats, it specialized in *spectacle. Its stage could hold 600 people and contained a gigantic tank for aquatic effects; the *lighting system used over 25,000 bulbs. Shows cost so much to produce that the theatre struggled to survive, and E. F. *Albee converted it to a *vaudeville house in 1923. It was closed from 1930 to 1933, then reopened with the hit extravaganza *Jumbo*. It was torn down in 1939.   SLL

HIRIART, HUGO (1942–   )

Mexican playwright, director, and novelist. Known for his playful approach to theatre, Hiriart has gained attention at home and abroad for works in which he combines *puppets which seem real with *actors who appear to be *marionettes. Two plays stand out for this technique, *Minotastas and his Family* (1981) and *Around the World in Eighty Days* (1992). Other plays explore traditional themes, for example, femininity in *Gynocomaquia* (1972) and couple relationships in *Intimacy* (1984), but always in an experimental manner and most often staged in small, *alternative venues with minimalist sets.   KFN

HIRSCH, JOHN (1930–89)

Canadian director. Born in Hungary, Hirsch emigrated to Winnipeg in 1947 after losing all his immediate family in the Holocaust. After working in theatre for *youth, *community theatre, and *television production, in 1957 he founded his own company, Theatre 77, which the next year merged to form the *Manitoba Theatre Centre. As its first *artistic director (1958–66) he staged several acclaimed productions, most notably *Mother Courage* with Zoë *Caldwell (1964). In 1965 he directed *The Cherry Orchard* at the *Stratford Festival, beginning his long association with that company; other celebrated productions there included *Richard III* with Alan *Bates (1967), *The Three Musketeers* with Douglas Rain (1968), *A Midsummer Night's Dream* with Christopher *Newton and Martha *Henry (1968), and *The Three Sisters* with Maggie *Smith (1976). In 1967 he was named associate artistic director of the festival, but left two years later following his controversial production of a new *musical play *The Satyricon*. In the ensuing years he directed and taught extensively in the USA, including seven productions at *Lincoln Center in *New York, and won an Obie *award for directing *AC/DC* by Heathcote Williams. He also served as head of CBC television drama (1974–7) and as consultant artistic

director for the *Seattle Repertory Theatre (1979–80). Hirsch returned to Stratford as artistic director from 1981 to 1985, mounting several memorable productions including *The Tempest*, *As You Like It*, and *Tartuffe*. Besides his demanding and inspirational leadership, he is best known for bringing contemporary imagery and European edginess to productions of classic plays by Shakespeare, *Brecht, and especially *Chekhov.
                                                                                            DWJ

HIRSCH, JUDD (1935–   )

American actor. He created the roles of Bill in *The Hot l Baltimore* (1973) and Matt in *Talley's Folly* (1980), both for Lanford *Wilson, and he won Tony *awards for *I'm Not Rappaport* (1985) and *Conversations with my Father* (1991) by Herb *Gardner. He also appeared in *Scuba Duba* (1968), *Knock Knock* (1976), and *Art* (1998), and he played the role of Murray in *A Thousand Clowns* (1996). He won two Emmy awards as cab driver Alex Rieger in the *television situation *comedy series *Taxi* (1978–83); other television credits include John Lacey in *Dear John* (1988–91). His *film roles include Dr Berger in *Ordinary People* (1980) and Julius Levinson in *Independence Day* (1996).   JDM

HIRSCHFELD, KURT (1902–64)

German *dramaturg and director. Hirschfeld is remembered chiefly for his contribution to the *Zurich Schauspielhaus during the Nazi period and after, working in 1933–4 and again from 1938 to 1960 under Oskar *Wälterlin. After Wälterlin's death he became *Intendant of the theatre in 1961. During the years when many German theatre artists in exile found a home at the theatre, Hirschfeld developed a repertoire of contemporary German drama and German-language premières of plays by *Wilder, *Claudel, *García Lorca, *Eliot, and *Sartre. He was also instrumental in maintaining relations with *Brecht, and directed the première of *Puntilla* in 1948. After the war Hirschfeld fostered close ties between the Schauspielhaus and the Swiss dramatists Max *Frisch and Friedrich *Dürrenmatt, who saw much of their work premièred there.   CBB

HIS MAJESTY'S THEATRE *See* HER MAJESTY'S THEATRE.

HISPANIC THEATRE, USA

The term 'Hispanic' is used to refer to those people living in the United States who were either born in a *Latin American country or who were born in the USA of Latin American parents. The three largest Hispanic communities are the Chicanos (or Mexican Americans; *see* CHICANO THEATRE), the mainland Puerto Ricans, and the Cubans. Hispanic theatre therefore refers to playwrights, performers, producers, and theatre companies that identify themselves as Hispanic and usually address issues related to the Hispanic experiences in the USA. The majority of Hispanic plays and performances are presented in their respective communities, often ignored or overlooked by mainstream *critics and scholars. Thus, with the exception of a few notable performers, companies, playwrights, and directors, Hispanic theatre remains largely of and by the people for whom it is created.

Hispanic performances can be traced back to 1598 when Spanish and Mexican colonizers entered what is now the United States and performed a (lost) play about their adventures. Initially the Spanish missionaries produced *religious plays, plays that continue to be produced by Spanish-language churches and theatre groups throughout the country. Secular performances and popular entertainments could also be found in public spaces. By the mid-nineteenth century plays were being performed in major centres of Spanish-speaking population in *New York, California, and Texas. Spanish-language plays were popular in Florida from the 1890s onward and professional Spanish-language companies were performing from San Antonio to New York City to *Los Angeles in the 1920s.

The 1960s were a period of regeneration of Hispanic theatre throughout the country. In New York professional theatre companies began to form, producing Spanish classics in Spanish as well as plays by Puerto Rican and other Latin America playwrights. The most notable pioneering New York companies are INTAR (International Arts Relations), the Puerto Rican Travelling Theatre, and the Repertorio Español. In other parts of the country, student and *community-based theatre troupes such as Teatro de la Esperanza in California, Su Teatro in Colorado, or La Compañía de Teatro de Albuquerque, in New Mexico, were forming. Initially, many companies focused on plays and performances that reflected their particular communities. Chicanos addressed Chicano issues, Puerto Ricans dramatized their experiences, and Cubans focused on their community. Much of the Cuban theatre was in Spanish only, written by exiles addressing their displacement and longing to overthrow Castro and return to Cuba. Similarly, Puerto Rican performances addressed their neocolonial status. By the 1980s, however, companies began to present plays from any of the Hispanic communities as they reached beyond their own experiences. Hispanic performances are sometimes produced in Spanish, but more often bilingually, expressing the linguistic patterns of the *audiences.

Those companies that produce plays in Spanish, such as Repertorio Español in New York and the Bilingual Foundation for the Arts in Los Angeles, generally rely on native-speaking immigrant actors. Conversely, the companies that produce plays about Hispanic experiences often employ US-born Hispanic actors who might be more comfortable in the bilingual setting. By the end of the twentieth century *gay and *lesbian *performance artists and other performers gained recognition through pieces about their further marginalization as homosexuals. Hispanic theatre artists continue to address issues such as identity, social injustice, and domestic dysfunction in a variety of *genres and modes, from *documentary dramas to domestic dramas, from magical realism to *one-person performances.

JAH

HISTORICAL DRAMA

Any dramatic *genre—*tragedy, *comedy, *melodrama—loses coherence upon close scrutiny, but historical drama seems to lose the most. The term is often arbitrarily applied (Shakespeare's *Richard III* is labelled one of his history plays, but *Antony and Cleopatra* normally is not) and definitions usually raise more questions than they answer. Is any play set before the playwright's time a history play? Must history plays contain historically real *characters (*Marlowe's *Edward II*), or will composite or typical characters suffice (Lope de *Vega's *Fuente Ovejuna*)? Must dramatists present history 'the way it really happened' (*Bolt's *A Man for All Seasons*), or may they utilize poetic licence (*Schiller's *The Maid of Orleans*)? Is historical accuracy a matter of dramatizing verifiable facts (Heinar *Kipphardt's *In the Matter of J. Robert Oppenheimer*) or of capturing the historical *Zeitgeist* (*Lawrence and Lee's *Inherit the Wind*)?

Given such indeterminacy, there are a number of ways to analyse historical drama. A commonly constructed binary, often unconsciously employed, distinguishes between what might be called plays of history and historical *costume dramas. Plays of history, such as Shakespeare's *Henry V* (1599), *Shaw's *St Joan* (1923), and *Brecht's *Galileo* (1947), examine history itself as part of their topic. Historical costume dramas, on the other hand, such as *Bulwer-Lytton's *Richelieu* (1839), Gordon Daviot's *Richard of Bordeaux* (1932), or *Shaffer's *Amadeus* (1979), use history as local colour to spice up a melodramatic tale. Of course, plays of history often employ *spectacle and costume dramas do hold a philosophy of history. This distinction, however, has formed the basis of a canon of historical drama which embraces the plays of history and rejects the often commercially successful costume drama. Cinema's appropriation of the latter has probably reinforced this phenomenon.

Historical drama has sought respect by nominating *Aeschylus' *The Persians* (c.472 BC) as the first history play. Classical notions of history, myth, and their representation differ so significantly from modern ideas, however, that *The Persians*, something of an anomaly in extant *Greek drama, is really only an honorary member of the genre. Historical drama is most commonly viewed as a by-product of *early modern political historiography and is particularly associated with the vogue for historical chronicle plays in England in the 1590s. Elizabethan chronicle plays borrowed their *dramaturgy from medieval *cycle plays, turning the *mystery cycle's episodic, cosmic history into a national drama that shifts between providentialism and humanist politics. Elizabethan dramatists shared with their contemporary historians an energetic willingness to experiment with the representation of history—such as in the question of Perkin Warbeck's identity in John *Ford's play, or the cause of the death of Arthur in *King John* (1596). Modern critics tend to see the Shakespearian model of historical drama as the pinnacle of achievement in the genre, judging the worth of subsequent plays by their resemblance to the Shakespearian ideal. By the eighteenth century, the expansive chronicle play had contracted into domestic tragedy on a historical theme in response to both the widespread influence of *neoclassicism and the emergence of *bourgeois morality. Such melodramatic underpinnings signalled the emergence of the historical costume drama, in which the politics of the chronicle play were pushed aside for pathos and moralizing.

The nineteenth century was perhaps the golden age of historical drama, as it was for historical novels and genre painting. Fuelled by *romanticism's idealizing of the past, and the increasing sophistication of stage technology (*see* SCENOGRAPHY), grand historical *spectacle thrived. Costume drama capitalized on *antiquarian interest in historical accuracy, re-creating the trappings of history before the eyes of the *audience. Testaments to the historical authenticity of the costumes, heraldry, and weapons sometimes featured on advertising bills (in the productions of Charles *Kean, for example), while the authenticity of the historical events rarely received such attention. Survivors of this trend in the twentieth century include *opera, which relies heavily on historical themes, and the Hollywood epic *film, which took over the goal of historical accuracy on a grand scale.

Plays of history also found new life in the age of history-inflected philosophies. The dramaturgy of the nineteenth- and twentieth-century history play has largely rested on Hegelian notions of history as stable historical epochs punctuated by moments of crisis that bring forth great men. As a result, one of the primary issues addressed in sophisticated drama was that of historical agency. Schiller devoted an entire play to discussion of his absent eponymous *hero, Wallenstein, delaying the character's appearance until the second play of his trilogy. *Büchner fills *Danton's Death* (composed 1835) with theatrical allusions that foreground role playing and agency in ways that were to become common in the twentieth century.

Brecht became the most important later playwright for historical drama, taking up Marx's theories of collective historical agency by frequently employing typical characters (*see* MATERIALIST CRITICISM). Part of Brecht's significance lies in reviving a Shakespearian dramaturgy that explores multiple *historiographies; for instance, Brecht simultaneously provides and critiques a worm's-eye view of the Thirty Years War in *Mother Courage* (1941). Brecht's techniques influenced the Brit-ish *epic theatre playwrights, informing plays such as David *Hare's *Plenty* (1978) and David *Edgar's *Maydays* (1983). Epic historical drama also lies behind Tony *Kushner's *Angels in America* (1991). Brecht (and his one-time colleague *Piscator) also influenced a form particularly powerful in the second half of the twentieth century, the *documentary drama, which relies upon the direct use of historical records in the creation of a *text. These documents, which might range from newspapers and court records to interviews and visual materials, are often incorporated directly into the performance, lending an aura of fact and truth despite the obvious selection, organization, and editing they have undergone. The *agitprop work of the *Blue Blouse troupes in the early Soviet Union, the *living newspapers of the *Federal Theatre Project in the USA, the work of dramatists as diverse as Rolf *Hochhuth and Anna Deavere *Smith, all have extended the scope of what constitutes history on stage.

While exploration into issues of historical agency continues to be an important theme in plays of history, there has been a shift since the 1980s from dramatizing crises *in* history to dramatizing the crisis *of* history. Works like Suzan-Lori *Parks's *The America Play* (1994) question whether history can be dramatized at all when the nineteenth-century dictum to tell it 'the way it really happened' is equated with the erasure of alternative histories by oppressive forces. Ultimately, such historiographical concerns go right to the heart of the history play genre's dilemma: just as notions of what properly constitutes history were radically destabilized in the late twentieth century, notions of what properly constitutes a history play have always been unstable. *See also* HISTORICISM.   MDG

LINDENBERGER, HERBERT, *Historical Drama: the relation of literature and reality* (Chicago, 1975)

WIKANDER, MATTHEW, *The Play of Truth and State: historical drama from Shakespeare to Brecht* (Baltimore, 1986)

HISTORICISM

One answer to the ancient question of whether historical explanation is nomothetic, concerned with the pervasive and universal, or idiographic, concerned with the specific and the individual, modern historicism was conceived at the end of the eighteenth century in reaction to the Enlightenment assumption, based in the new scientific discipline, that historical truth was abstract and universal. Historicism stressed instead that such truth was to be found in a particular object or event, which is explicable only in terms of the idiosyncratic context of its own time and place. There were hints, even during the Enlightenment, of a historicist perspective that recognized the variety of human institutions, and realized that those who lived differently must also have thought differently. Giambattista Vico, for example, asserted that the real events of history were the large-scale changes in the collective frame of mind;

and Gottfried Wilhelm Leibniz denied that historical enquiry could establish general laws. In Germany, where it originated, historicism is most closely associated with Johann Gottfried von Herder (1744–1803) and Leopold von Ranke (1795–1886). In *Also a Philosophy of History* (1774), Herder argued that comparisons among cultures or periods were inappropriate and that, consequently, notions of 'progress', which involved comparisons, were invalid. Ranke, most famous for his comment that the proper concern of history was with the past 'as it actually was', similarly abjured the judgement implicit in comparison, and championed a positivistic 'documentary imperative' by which the historian is precluded from reasoning beyond the document. And since every world-view, including that of the historian, is historically determined, every view and every history is limited and relative. Wilhelm Dilthey (1833–1911), equally abjuring historical generalization and the divine providence that had comforted Ranke, denied any objectively understandable reality at all. Theodore Lessing (1872–1933) went even further, arguing that history was an act of myth making designed to impose meaning on the meaningless flux of human existence. The philosophical dilemma posed by the ontological and ethical relativism of historicism, although significant, does not detract from its central tenets: that each period or culture is unique and incomparable, and must be understood in its own terms; that all social and cultural phenomena are historically determined; that, as an idiographic enterprise, historical study finds reality in the particular and the local; that the criteria for judgement too are local and temporal, not universal; and that historical writing is itself culturally and historically conditioned.

German historicism did not survive the Third Reich: indeed, several aspects of historicism—its denial of continuity, its reluctance to judge, its focus on the state as the locus of stability—have been cited as factors contributing to the rise of *fascism. Certain of its features, however, appear in two late twentieth-century movements, the 'new history' and the 'new historicism'. These movements are not specific about any debt to the older historicism, and in fact may simply reflect the fact that in a broad sense historicist thought has become part and parcel of the contemporary mindset. The new history and the new historicism designate a variety of historiographical and critical practices that share some common tendencies:

1. History, no longer confined to politics, is conceived as the study of *all* past human activity, thought, and institutions. These are in turn conceived as culturally or socially constituted and thus subject to change. Since everything has a history, there are no privileged historical concerns: the previously ignored or marginalized have an equal claim on the historian's attention.
2. Written documents no longer constitute the historian's sole evidence. New sources include visual and artefactual evidence, as well as oral discourse.
3. Disciplinary and sub-disciplinary compartmentalization is rejected.
4. Statistics and long-term measurement are central to the conception of history as less a narrative of events than an analysis of structures wherein collective movements are as significant as individual actions.
5. Above all, both the new history and the new historicism take seriously the idea implicit in the older historicism that historical writing is as culturally and historically determined as its subject matter, that the historian has no choice but to examine the past from the point of view of the present.

The new historicism is something of an anomaly in that it arose, not among professional historians, but among students of *early modern literature, many of them associated with the University of California at Berkeley, who were interested in reconstructing literary texts as historically determined objects. Although they pay occasional lip service to Ranke and Dilthey, the practitioners of the new historicism developed their methodologies in the context of the *structuralist and deconstructive theories of Michel Foucault and Paul de Man, and are primarily concerned with the intertextuality and interaction of institutionalized discourse, both elitist and popular, in a particular historical moment. A literary text, then, has no trans-historical status; aesthetic value is similarly seen as a matter of cultural convention, the product of a political hegemony. Like German historicism, the new historicism eschews judgement, and is thus distinguishable from the politically engaged cultural *materialism which otherwise shares many of its presuppositions.

Theatre *historiography has also been influenced by these ideas. The privileging of literary theatre and its treatment as high art have given way to the serious study of previously marginalized and ephemeral forms. Visual and artefactual evidence has no longer to be justified as, or limited to, support for understanding the literary theatre. The quantitative tools of the social sciences are central to the social and economic analysis of theatre as an institution.   RWV

BURKE, PETER (ed.), *New Perspectives on Historical Writing* (University Park, Pa, 1992)

POSTLEWAIT, THOMAS, and McCONACHIE, BRUCE (eds.), *Interpreting the Theatrical Past* (Iowa City, 1989)

VEESER, H. ARAM (ed.), *The New Historicism* (New York, 1989)

HISTORIOGRAPHY

Historians practice the craft of historical research and writing according to some basic procedures and models that exist within the scholarly discipline. In varying degrees of attention and self-criticism, historians also reflect upon the historical methodologies, guiding assumptions, established practices, pedagogical approaches, and theoretical principles that define and shape their disciplines. This abiding condition of historical self-consciousness goes by the general name and concept of historiography. The concept thus encompasses the philosophy of history, the logic of historical thought, the rules of evidence, the semantics of key historical concepts, and the rhetorical modes and narrative styles for writing history.

It also refers to the history of history. Thus, various scholarly studies, such as Ernst Breisach's *Historiography: ancient, medieval, and modern* (1983), provide a survey of the development of historical writing. Other studies, such as Peter Burke's *New Perspectives on Historical Writing* (1991) and Georg G. Iggers's *Historiography in the Twentieth Century* (1997), describe and analyse the contending approaches to historical study in modern times, while Paul Ricœur's *Time and Narrative* (1984–8) and David Novick's *That Noble Dream: the 'objectivity question' and the American historical profession* (1988) focus on specific problems in historical methodology and philosophy.

Necessarily, then, the field of *theatre studies has its own history and its own historiographical dimensions. It is possible to chart and study the emergence of the writing of theatre history in each language or nation. In this way, for example, a historian could study the development of the field of British theatre history between 1650 and 1900. To do so, she might examine the contributions of various theatre historians from Richard Flecknoe (1653) and Gerald Langbaine (1691) to John Genest (1832) and John Payne Collier (1831, 1879). A comparative study of some or all of the works by these early historians of the field would be an exercise in theatre historiography.

There are many possible projects in theatre historiography. Historians might chart the changing historical ways that a specific dramatist has been studied, as Samuel Schoenbaum did in *Shakespeare's Lives* (1991), which examines the numerous biographical approaches to Shakespeare since Nicholas *Rowe's short memoir in 1709. They might investigate how the field of theatre history, which emerged in the eighteenth and nineteenth centuries, became an academic discipline during the twentieth, a project taken up by R. W. Vince in a series of books and essays (outlined in Postlewait and McConachie). Historians could focus on the development of *Theaterwissenschaft* (theatre science) in Germany, then trace its spread into American academic training, as Michael Quinn succinctly did. Or they could take the measure of how scholars within theatre and *performance studies have defined and developed their disciplinary practices, from manuals on historical methodology to guidelines on teaching. More specifically, historians could consider how the issues of *gender or *race operate not only in the history of the theatre but in the historical assumptions and practices of scholars as they attempt to write their histories.

In the late twentieth century theatre historiography increasingly became a regular feature of scholarly conferences and publications, and academic courses in the subject were developed, especially in graduate programmes. Theatre scholars, like their colleagues in the other historical disciplines, have come to recognize that in order to operate they need to reflect upon the developmental nature, theoretical assumptions, and operational principles of historical study. The merit of historical scholarship depends, at least in part, upon an understanding of the historiographical issues and problems that theatre historians face. *See also* HISTORICISM. TP

ARNOTT, JAMES, 'An introduction to theatrical scholarship', *Theatre Quarterly*, 39 (1981)

HUME, ROBERT D., *Reconstructing Contexts: the aims and principles of archaeo-historicism* (Oxford, 1999)

POSTLEWAIT, THOMAS, and McCONACHIE, BRUCE (eds.), *Interpreting the Theatrical Past* (Iowa City, 1989)

QUINN, MICHAEL, '*Theaterwissenschaft*' in the history of theatre study', *Theatre Survey*, 32 (1991)

HOBSON, HAROLD (1904–92)

English drama *critic who studied at Oxford and became an authority on French *avant-garde theatre. As the influential drama critic of the *Christian Science Monitor* (1931–74) and the *Sunday Times* (1947–76), Hobson championed many new playwrights, including *Beckett (he was one of the first to celebrate the 1955 British première of *Waiting for Godot*), *Pinter, and *Stoppard. His books include *French Theatre since 1830* (1978), an autobiography, *Indirect Journey* (1978), and *Theatre in Britain: a personal view* (1984). He was knighted in 1977.

AS

HOCHHUTH, ROLF (1931–)

German playwright. Hochhuth came to international prominence in 1963 with the *documentary drama *Der Stellvertreter* (*The Representative* or *The Deputy*) in a production by Erwin *Piscator, subsequently widely produced internationally. This controversial play, in which the relationship between Pope Pius XII and the Nazis is critically examined, provided Hochhuth with his overriding theme, the exploration of moral responsibility and *political action, and his formal approach, historical debate based on extensive documentary research. In *Soldaten* (*Soldiers*, 1967) he accuses Churchill of the unnecessary bombing of German cities and other war crimes. *Guerillas* (1970) departs from the documentary approach in its fictional story of an idealistic US senator who stages a *coup d'état* in order to break the power of the military-industrial complex, the first of a number of plays in which individuals go beyond the law for moral reasons. In *Die Hebamme* (*The Midwife*, 1972) a young woman resorts to illegal means in order to publicize the plight of the homeless; in *Judith* (1984) an assassination attempt on Ronald Reagan is morally justified as 'rebellion of the powerless'. In *Juristen* (*Lawyers*, 1979) Hochhuth returns to documentary drama in his exposé of a leading German politician's Nazi past, and in *Ärztinnen* (*Women Doctors*, 1980) his target is the pharmaceutical industry. Hochhuth's last play *Wessis in Weimar* (*Westies in Weimar*, 1993) critically examines reunification and the sell-out of East German industry by the state-run trust company. In a controversial move, Hochhuth gained control of the *Berliner Ensemble in 1997 under the auspices of the Ilse Holzapfel Foundation which he founded.   CBB

HOCHWÄLDER, FRITZ (1911–86)

Austrian dramatist. Hochwälder's plays are traditional in form, adhering almost slavishly to the three *unities. The themes revolve around complex moral questions against historical or biblical backdrops. His most successful work, *Das heilige Experiment* (*The Strong are Lonely*, 1943) depicts the violent end of the Jesuit state in Paraguay as a conflict between the realpolitik of the Catholic Church and the utopian idealism of the Jesuits. In *Der öffentliche Ankläger* (*The Public Prosecutor*, 1947) the idealistic and ruthless sides of the French Revolution are given equal treatment.   CBB

HODGKINSON, JOHN (c.1765–1805)

Anglo-American *actor-manager. Born John Meadowcroft in Manchester, he was a self-taught musician, singer, and actor who ran away from home at 15 and became a star of the Bristol stage. Ever ambitious, he played a wide range of parts and was known as the 'provincial *Garrick'. He changed his name to Hodgkinson after running off to *Bath with the wife of his *manager. It was there that he was recruited by John *Henry to perform in *New York. By 1794 he was the manager of the *John Street Theatre, a position he held until 1798. Though possessing a powerful voice and extraordinary memory, he preferred comic roles and was never a great leading man.

PAD

HOFFMAN, DUSTIN (1937–)

American actor. Born in Los Angeles, he took classes at the *Pasadena Playhouse before studying with Lee *Strasberg in *New York, where Hoffman made his debut in Steven Gethers's *A Cook for Mr General* (1961). After acting for the Theatre Company of *Boston (1964), he was assistant director for a revival of *A View from the Bridge* with Robert Duvall (1965). He played Immanuel in Ronald Ribman's *Harry, Noon and Night* (1965) and Zoditch in Ribman's *Journey of the Fifth Horse* at the *American Place Theatre (1966). He won *awards for his performance of Valentine Bross in Henry Livings's *Eh?* (1966) and for Murray Schisgal's *Jimmy Shine* (1968). A brilliant *film career followed, starting with Mike *Nichols's *The Graduate* (1967). Hoffman returned to Broadway to direct Schisgal's *All over Town* (1974) and to co-produce and star as Willie Loman in an acclaimed performance of *Death of a Salesman* (1984). He also

played Shylock in Peter *Hall's *Merchant of Venice* in *London and New York (1989–90).   FL

HOFFMAN, WILLIAM (1939–)

American playwright and librettist. Born in *New York, he graduated from City College with a degree in Latin. For eight years he worked as a publisher's editor, and later edited several volumes of new plays. He acted and directed occasionally in the 1960s and 1970s, but his main concern has been playwriting, beginning with the *monologue *Thank You, Miss Victoria* (1965). His work covers a broad range: poetic *naturalism (*Spring Play*, 1967), musical *revue (*Uptight!*, 1968), *pantomime *scenario (*From Fool to Hanged Man*, 1972), *opera libretto (the best known being Corigliano's *The Ghost of Versailles*, mounted by the *Metropolitan Opera in 1991). Openly gay, Hoffman has dealt with homosexuality in several works—most notably *As Is* (1985), which won Drama Desk and Obie *awards *Off-Broadway and then moved to a long Broadway run, receiving three Tony nominations. Although not the first AIDS play, it was the first to reach Broadway. *See also* GAY THEATRE.

CT

HOFFMANN, E. T. A. (ERNST THEODOR AMADEUS) (1776–1822)

German poet, novelist, composer, and *manager. A multi-talented artist and writer (today he is remembered for his romantic short stories), Hoffmann composed *operas and set other works (by *Goethe and Clemens Brentano) to music while still a Prussian civil servant in *Warsaw. In 1808 he was appointed music director in Bamberg, where he developed closer connections to opera; his most famous work from this period is the opera *Undine* (1814). He also tried to create staging techniques congenial to *romantic *theories emphasizing realms of experience beyond the mundane. On his return to *Berlin and the Prussian civil service in 1814, he applied himself to prose. Perhaps his most lasting legacy to theatre is the novella *Princess Brambilla* (1814), which attempts to capture Callot's *commedia dell'arte* etchings in prose, and provided inspiration for *Meyerhold and *Tairov.   CBB

HOFMAN, VLASTISLAV (1884–1964)

Czech scenographer, architect, and painter. K. H. *Hilar engaged him in 1919 to design the sets for Arnošt Dvořák's drama *The Hussites*, a milestone in the history of European stage design (*see* SCENOGRAPHY). Afterwards he worked chiefly for the Vinohrady Municipal Theatre and the *Czech National Theatre, *Prague, where his designs for *Coriolanus* (1921), *Queen Kristina* (1922), *Hamlet* (1926), and *Richard III* (1934) were particularly impressive. Hofman was the co-author of Hilar's directorial vision. His sets and *costumes were highly expressive and markedly subjective: not a cool background for the play, but a very personal statement about its meaning.   ML

HOFMANNSTHAL, HUGO VON
(1874–1929)

Austrian poet, playwright, and librettist. Hofmannsthal first came to attention as a teenager with his *verse play *Gestern* (*Yesterday*, 1891) and quickly became an important figure in *Viennese literary circles, particularly the neo-*romantic movement. Although he wrote several verse dramas in the 1890s, his first performed work was *Die Frau am Fenster* (*The Woman at the Window*, 1898), a verse *tragedy set in Renaissance Italy. He grew increasingly fascinated by the theatre and formed a close acquaintance with Otto *Brahm and Max *Reinhardt. The latter staged Hofmannsthal's *one-act play *Elektra* in 1903, which formed the basis for the *opera by Richard *Strauss (1909). Their collaboration intensified with *Der Rosenkavalier* (1911), *Ariadne auf Naxos* (1912), *Die Frau ohne Schatten* (1919), and others. Few of his stage plays have stood the test of time. His *comedy of manners *Der Schwierige* (*The Difficult Man*, 1921), loosely based on *Molière's *The Misanthrope*, is a sophisticated analysis of pre-First World War Viennese society. His most famous play remains *Jedermann* (*Everyman*, 1911), an adaptation of the *medieval *morality play, which is still performed every year during the *Salzburg Festival. The idea for the *festival was developed by Hofmannsthal in 1917, together with Reinhardt and Strauss, and in the 1920s became a major European cultural event.   CBB

HOLBERG, LUDVIG (1684–1754)

Danish dramatist. Born in Bergen in 1684, Holberg became a gifted academic and from 1717 occupied a succession of professorial appointments at the University of Copenhagen. As a student he travelled widely in Europe; his prodigious talent as a writer enabled him to make good use of the ideas he had encountered on his travels. Throughout his life he published a series of philosophical works stressing the importance of human reason as a central value. He also demonstrated a gift for addressing more light-hearted topics, as in his *Satires* (1722) and his *parody of Virgil, a mock epic called *Peder Paars* (1720). Because of his success as a satirical poet, Holberg was invited to write *comedies for Denmark's first public theatre, which was established in Copenhagen in 1722. In great haste, he wrote five volumes of comedies for the enterprise between 1722 and its closure six years later. All offer larger-than-life *satires of contemporary individuals who have forsaken the light of reason out of obsession or brute stupidity. In *The Political Tinker* Holberg mocked the political arrogance of ordinary folk; in

Erasumus Montanus he satirized a bumptious undergraduate; in *Jeppe of the Hill* he drew a satirical portrait of a drunken peasant; and in *Jean de France* he satirized a local lad aping French fashion. The theatre reopened in 1746, when Holberg provided it with further plays. Although influenced by *Molière, Holberg's comedies are distinctively Danish in tone and content.   DT

HOLBROOK, HAL (1925–)

American actor. Holbrook developed a *one-person show on the writings of Mark Twain while a college student. The result, *Mark Twain Tonight!*, became his professional debut in 1954; by 2001 he had performed Twain over 2000 times, and spawned a virtual industry of solo performers re-creating historic figures. Holbrook's success was due to the skill with which he wove together Twain's writings, and his ability to play convincingly, in his late twenties, a man in his seventies. Holbrook created a series of effective performances on Broadway and in *regional theatres, also appearing frequently on *film and *television. He played major roles in *Miller's *After the Fall* (1963) and Robert *Anderson's *I Never Sang for my Father* (1968), *King Lear* (Cleveland, 1990), and in Wendy *Wasserstein's *An American Daughter* (1997). Holbrook's Midwestern roots and commonsense approach allowed him to play *characters ranging from honourable politicians (*The Senator*, television series, 1970), to a less honourable financier (the *film *Wall Street*, 1987), and martyred presidents (*Abe Lincoln in Illinois*, 1963 on stage; *Sandburg's Lincoln*, television, 1976).   AW

HOLCROFT, THOMAS (1745–1809)

English actor and author. Holcroft began his stage career as a comic actor and singer at Foote's *Haymarket Theatre in 1770, then played in *Dublin and the provinces before his debut at *Drury Lane in 1777. His greatest contributions are his plays. His first was a comic *opera, *The Crisis* (1778), and he produced a popular translation of *Beaumarchais's *Le Mariage de Figaro* called *The Follies of a Day* (1784). His most important plays, however, are spoken dramas of serious moral purpose. Treading the line between sentiment and strong social commentary, works like *Duplicity* (1781) and *Seduction* (1787) chastise the bad habits of social elites, such as gaming and sexual promiscuity. *The Road to Ruin* (1792) characteristically exposes the vices of the rich but ends in repentance and sentimental reconciliation. In the 1790s, Holcroft's radical sentiments required that some of these plays be published anonymously, for fear of a backlash, and in 1794 he was briefly imprisoned on charges of high treason (he was released without trial). His memoirs, finished by *Hazlitt, are a good source of information on the theatre during his lifetime.   MJK

HOLLAND, GEORGE (1791–1870)

British comic actor. Born in London, Holland was a physical, low comedian who perfected an exaggerated style of *farce. Though popular at home, he went to *New York in 1827 and first worked at the *Bowery Theatre in a role which required him to wear seven male and female *disguises. After *touring the south, he became a member of William E. *Burton's acting company in 1853, and from 1855 to 1869 he was a member of James *Wallack's. He did work with the blackface *minstrel troupe Christy Minstrels in 1857 as a *female impersonator in their *burlesque of Burton's *comedy *The Toodles*. In 1869 he became aligned with Augustin *Daly until his death.   AB

HOLLAND FESTIVAL

Founded in June 1947 (a few months earlier than the *Edinburgh and *Avignon *festivals) to import internationally acclaimed events to *Amsterdam, Rotterdam, The Hague, and the smaller Dutch towns. Now concentrating on the major cities, the festival offers some 200 theatre, music, *opera, and *dance productions, with a growing preference at the beginning of the new century for contemporary, experimental, and controversial works. The festival has hosted major foreign companies from *La Mama Experimental Theatre Club and the Martha *Graham Dance Company to the *Berlin *Volksbühne and *Mnouchkine's Théâtre du *Soleil. It has also proved fertile soil for the native theatre scene. One influential product was *Reconstructie: een Moraliteit* (1969), created by five Dutch composers, two librettists, and an architect, who seized the opportunity of state subsidy to mount an engaged tribute to Che Guevara, meant to shock the Dutch establishment and the capitalist world. The festival enjoys municipal and state subsidy but also requires corporate sponsorship (*see* FINANCE). An estimated 100,000 spectators attend each year.   TH

HOLLINGSHEAD, JOHN (1827–1904)

English *manager. In 1868 Hollingshead abandoned journalism, and with £500 of his own money and a borrowed £5,000 took over the newly built *Gaiety Theatre in *London. He presented a popular repertory based on *burlesque, keeping 'the sacred lamp of burlesque', as he put it, burning brightly until 1886, when he disposed of the theatre to George *Edwardes. It was Hollingshead who assembled the famous burlesque quartet of singers and dancers: Edward Royce, Kate *Vaughan, Edward Terry, and Nellie *Farren. By 1880 Gaiety burlesques had a three-act structure, a greater elegance of dress and decor, and more *music than previously. Hollingshead also staged the occasional serious work, such as the first English version of an *Ibsen play, by William *Archer: *Quicksands; or, The Pillars of Society* (1880). He also wrote an entertaining account of his

management, *Gaiety Chronicles* (1898), and an autobiography, *My Lifetime* (1895).   MRB

HOLM, CELESTE (1919–)

American actress and singer. Holm, who was working professionally with a *stock company by the age of 17, made her Broadway debut in William *Saroyan's *The Time of your Life* (1939). Eventually she was cast as the irresistibly naughty Ado Annie in the original production of *Oklahoma!* (1943), which led to her first starring role in *Bloomer Girl* (1944). Holm soon had a Hollywood contract, appearing in a few *films before her Oscar-winning performance in *Gentleman's Agreement* (1947). She returned to *New York to star in productions of *She Stoops to Conquer* (1949) and *Anna Christie* (1952), remaining connected to the stage in Broadway productions like *Candida* (1970) and *I Hate Hamlet* (1991), while occasionally appearing on *television and film.   EW

HOLM, HANYA (c. 1898–1992)

German-American choreographer. Born Johanna Eckert in Germany, she was a student of Mary Wigman, whose hallmark was dark *expressionistic shapes and tension between dancer and space. Arriving in America in 1932, Holm studied the diversity of American culture, incorporating it into the *expressionistic idiom in which she was trained. Her chief concern was visual imagery, with a strong sense of *costume and awareness of the space to be filled. Between 1948 and 1960 she choreographed six Broadway *musicals, in all of which she emphasized regal bodily shapes in period costume. Her debut was *Kiss Me, Kate* (1948), her first great success. Subsequent shows included *The Golden Apple* (1954), *My Fair Lady* (1956), and *Camelot* (1960), after which she devoted herself to her school and concert *dance, which were always her primary focus.   JD

HOLM, IAN (1931–)

English actor who trained at the *Royal Academy of Dramatic Art, and after national service joined the *Shakespeare Memorial Theatre in 1954. In 1956 he made his *London debut in *Love Affair*, and *toured Europe with *Olivier in *Brook's *Titus Andronicus* in 1955. From 1957 to 1967 he was a member of the *Royal Shakespeare Company, where he played Hal, Henry V, and Richard III in the *Hall–*Barton *The Wars of the Roses* (1963–4), as well as Romeo (1967). In the modern repertoire he appeared in *Pinter's *The Homecoming* (1965; *New York, 1967) and *Bond's *The Sea* (1973). Famously, in 1976 he left the theatre after suffering stage fright during *rehearsals for *O'Neill's *The Iceman Cometh*, only returning to stage *acting in 1993 in a production of Pinter's *Moonlight*, subsequently appearing as Lear in Richard *Eyre's production at the Royal *National

Theatre (1997). His repertoire of screen roles is substantial and hugely diverse: *Alien* (1979), *Chariots of Fire* (1981), *Dance with a Stranger* (1984), and *The Sweet Hereafter* (1997). Holm was knighted in 1998.   AS

HOLMBERG, KALLE (1939–)

Finnish director. At the Turku City Theatre (1971–7) with Ralf *Långbacka, he triumphantly directed classic *texts, including an adaptation of Aleksis Kivi's novel *The Seven Brothers*. In the 1980s at the Helsinki City Theatre he directed *Schiller's *The Robbers*, *Macbeth*, and *Pushkin's *Boris Godunov*. Continuing with adaptations, he turned to Dostoevsky's novels and the epic *Kalevala*, dramatized by his wife Ritva Holmberg. His work with actors accentuates physicality as the means of textual analysis. He also works in *opera.   LIB

HOME, JOHN (1722–1808)

Playwright and churchman, the theatrical favourite son of Enlightenment Scotland. His romantic *tragedy *Douglas* (1756) was rejected by *Garrick and had its première at the Canongate Theatre, *Edinburgh, to a wildly rapturous *audience. The play was considered in its time to have Shakespearian dignity, and has been called a blend of 'she-tragedy' sentimentality and Gothic *romanticism. Home was a moderate clergyman with strong ties to Enlightenment thinkers like David Hume and Adam Ferguson, friends who helped polish *Douglas* and promote it at home and in *London. The play elicited a strong rebuke from conservative elements of the Kirk, and equally spirited defences by Home's friends, Ferguson and Alexander Carlyle. It appeared at *Covent Garden in early 1757 and was equally successful. Garrick, duly chastened for rejecting the work, produced Home's *Agis* (1758), *The Siege of Aquileia* (1760), and *Alonzo* (1773), but none matched the success of *Douglas*.   MJK

HOME, WILLIAM DOUGLAS (1912–92)

English playwright. From the 1940s to the 1970s, Home crafted a number of comic star vehicles for the West End stage, which took little notice of the new wave theatrical revolution of 1956. He drew on his family life (son of an earl and brother to Prime Minister Alec Douglas-Home) to write sentimental *satires of upper-class political manoeuvrings, notably in his first hit, *The Chiltern Hundreds* (1947), which featured A. E. Matthews. Other *comedies in a similar vein include *The Manor of Northstead* (1954), *The Reluctant Peer* (1964) with Sybil *Thorndike, *The Jockey Club Stakes* (1970) with Alastair *Sim, *Lloyd George Knew my Father* (1972) with Ralph *Richardson and Peggy *Ashcroft, and *The Kingfisher* (1977) starring Richardson again. Home occasionally approached other dramatic styles in plays such as

Now Barabbas . . . (1947), a drama about a condemned man awaiting execution, and *The Thistle and the Rose* (1949), a *historical drama about the battle of Flodden.   MDG

HONG KONG

A British colony, later called British territory, until its return to *China as a Special Administrative Region in 1997, Hong Kong enjoys the theatrical heritage of China and the West. The dominant form up to the 1970s was Cantonese opera (*yueju*), a provincial version of traditional Chinese opera (*see* DIFANGXI). With the retirement from the stage of various masters of the art form, there was a lull in its activities with only sporadic highlights. In the 1990s frequent visits of Chinese opera troupes from different provinces and support from local arts grants brought new interest in the traditional Chinese opera scene. In rural areas, villages continue the tradition of hiring opera troupes to perform during festivals.

Western speech drama (*huajü*) was introduced to China in the first decades of the twentieth century and brought to Hong Kong by the waves of refugees from the mainland. Those fleeing the Japanese invasion brought propaganda plays. The establishment of the People's Republic of China in 1949 brought to Hong Kong writers and dramatists like Xiong Shiyi and Yao Ke whose period *costume adaptations of historical romances and literary masterpieces stimulated local interest in drama. In the 1950s the colonial government of Hong Kong tried to maintain a delicate balance between the communist and the nationalist elements which coexisted in the territory. A *censorship system was set up to vet acting scripts before approval for performance. Delving into the past was less politically sensitive, which encouraged period plays.

The development of Western drama in the late 1950s also made its impact, and those plays did not touch on immediately sensitive issues. Drama enthusiasts performed plays by *Ionesco, *Pinter, Thornton *Wilder, *Dürrenmatt, *Beckett, *Brecht, Tennessee *Williams, and many others, ranging from *Aeschylus and *Sophocles to Shakespeare to Sam *Shepard and other *Off-Broadway plays. In translation this work became the mainstream on the Hong Kong drama scene, moving from the universities and colleges to the popular stage. Between 1980 and 1990, 130 Western plays were translated and performed in Hong Kong, and the trend continued into the early 1990s. Experimentation followed exposure. Familiarity with Western forms facilitated self-expression, especially when the 1997 *political change necessitated cultural repositioning. Hong Kong troupes adapted older plays to new settings and ideologies, linked modern forms with traditional culture, and broke from reliance on narrative and words.

Drama in English appeared in Hong Kong first as ventures of *amateur clubs and in academic circles, then became popular with English-educated locals, some of whom produced it for the

Chinese public. In the 1980s, a couple of amateur American groups began to emerge as British groups left the stage. Annual offerings of drama in English during the arts *festivals or sponsored by the British Council still enjoy strong support from a sector of the community. *See also* YUNG, DANNY.   JCL

HONG SHENG (HUNG SHENG) (c.1646–1704)

Chinese author of *Changshengdian* (*Palace of Lasting Life*), a Kun opera in 50 *scenes. Equated with *Kong Shangren as an influential Qing Dynasty playwright, Hong, like *Liang Chenyu a century earlier, historicized a traditional love theme and examined how love and *politics become entwined. In the play, the infatuation of the Tang Emperor Xuanzong (ruled 712–56) with his 'Precious Consort' Yang Guifei leads to the usurpation of his throne by An Lushan and his barbarian allies. Despite its veiled references to the turbulent early Qing period, the Kangzi Emperor enjoyed *Changshengdian* when it was performed in Beijing in 1689. Hong was later imprisoned for attending a performance of it during a period of national mourning, but the play remained extremely popular. It took three days and nights to perform all 50 scenes, and a 28-scene abridgement was made by Hong's friend Wu Shufu (c.1657–?), whose commentary on the *text addresses aspects of performance. *Changshengdian* was most commonly performed as *zhezixi* (highlights), though it is now sometimes staged in a version consisting of eight to ten scenes. *See* CHINA.   CS

HOOFT, PIETER CORNELISZOON (1581–1647)

Dutch playwright, poet, and historian. As the son of an important merchant, he attended the Latin school in his home town and travelled widely in France and Italy. Hooft was a typical *early modern artist who joined Samuel Coster when he established the Duytsche Academie in *Amsterdam (1617), the forerunner of the *Schouwburg (1638). Hooft wrote a number of *tragedies in the classical style. *Achilles and Polyxena* and *Theseus and Ariadne*, both published in 1614 but written earlier, show features of *Senecan drama. *Geeraerdt van Velsen* (1613) is a classical tragedy about the conspiracy against Count Floris, the national *historical episode which Joost van den *Vondel was to dramatize in his famous *Gijsbrecht van Aemstel* (1637). Hooft also wrote a *pastoral play, *Granida* (1605), partly inspired by the Italian examples of *Guarini and *Tasso. The play for which Hooft is best known and which still holds the stage is his *comedy *Warenar* (1617), an adaptation of *Plautus' *Aulularia*. First performed at the Duytsche Academie, *Warenar* far surpasses Hooft's other dramas in lively language and theatrical vigour.   JDV

HOPE THEATRE

Built by Philip *Henslowe in 1614, when there were more playing companies in London than licensed *playhouses, the Hope was designed to double as a theatre and a bear-*baiting arena for Henslowe's other main business. Plays were to be staged on Mondays, Wednesdays, Fridays, and Saturdays, and bears were to be baited on Tuesdays and Thursdays. It was built as a playhouse, like its neighbour the *Swan, but its stage had no posts, the *heavens covering the stage being supported from the gallery roofing. This allowed the stage itself to be removed to make more space when the *animals had to use it. The players, however, objected to the smells and rubbish produced by the bears and dogs. In *Jonson's *Bartholomew Fair*, one of the first plays staged there, they claimed that it was 'as dirty as Smithfield, and as stinking every whit'. From 1616 the only entertainment offered was the bears.   AJG

HOPGOOD, ALAN (1934–)

Australian actor and playwright. In 1963 the Union Repertory Theatre, *Melbourne, staged his first major play, *And the Big Men Fly*, which focuses on Australian Rules football (the major *sport in Melbourne), and which became a huge success. Later plays include *The Golden Legion of Cleaning Women* (1964), and *Private Yuk Objects* (1966), which looks at Australia's involvement in Vietnam. Thereafter he turned chiefly to *television and *film, playing Dr Reed in the Australian Broadcasting Corporation's series *Bellbird* for six years and writing the Alvin Purple sex comedy films.   EJS

HOPKINS, ANTHONY (1937–)

Welsh actor. Perhaps the most internationally recognized British performer of his generation, Hopkins's success on screen has come to overshadow his earlier career on the stage. He initially studied at the Cardiff College of Music and Drama before, in 1961, he won a scholarship to the *Royal Academy of Dramatic Art. His first professional role was in a 1964 *London production of *Julius Caesar*, and in 1965 he joined the *National Theatre, where he achieved great successes, playing in *Strindberg's *Dance of Death* (1967, initially *understudying *Olivier), and *Shaffer's *Equus* on Broadway (1974). Later roles at the National include the quintessential 1980s media monster Lambert LaRoux in *Brenton and *Hare's *Pravda* (1985), and the lead parts in *King Lear* (1986) and *Antony and Cleopatra* (1987). In 1991 Hopkins won an Academy award for his performance as Hannibal Lecter in the *film *The Silence of the Lambs*. Its critical and popular success established him as a major star and led to a series of high-profile, critically praised film roles, including Henry Wilcox in *Howards End* (1992), Stevens in *The Remains of the Day* (1993), C. S. Lewis in *Shadowlands* (1993), and the title role in Julie *Taymor's *Titus* (1999). In 1996 he made his film directorial debut with *August*, an adaptation of *Chekhov's *Uncle Vanya*. He received a knighthood in 1993.   AS

HOPKINS, ARTHUR (1878–1950)

American director and producer. Influenced by the writings of Richard *Wagner and Edward Gordon *Craig and productions of Max *Reinhardt, Hopkins was instrumental in introducing the 'New Theatre' and—in his collaborations with designer Robert Edmond *Jones—the 'New Stagecraft' onto the Broadway stage in the 1910s and 1920s. Hopkins's *theory of 'Unconscious Projection' saw the stagework communicating directly with the unconscious mind of the *audience. He sought a simple, unified stage and clear, unmannered performances to still the conscious mind and open the pathways to the unconscious. His first Broadway production, *Poor Little Rich Girl* (1916), employed *symbolist techniques of fantasy and suggestion. His 1922 collaboration with Jones on *Macbeth* shocked *New York as the first major *expressionist production seen there. Equally adept at *realism, Hopkins's productions of *Holiday* (1928) and *The Petrified Forest* (1935) were among his many commercial successes. His last production was *The Magnificent Yankee* (1946).   MAF

HOPKINS, PAULINE (1859–1930)

*African-American writer, a pioneer in *musical comedy. At the age of 18 she wrote *Colored Aristocracy*, a work performed by the black troupe the Hyer Sisters during the 1880s. *Peculiar Sam; or, The Underground Railroad* (*Boston, 1880), written for Sam Lucas (and with the author in the cast), includes sixteen songs; the *plot ends in Canada during the post-Civil War Reconstruction period. Hopkins later wrote a third play, about Daniel in the lions' den. Like her later prose works, her musical plays recorded the heroism and achievements of her race.   BBL

HOPPER, DE WOLF (1858–1935)

American actor and singer. Born in *New York, he began his acting career in *Conscience* (1876) and *Our Boys* (1878). With an inheritance he financed a *tour of *One Hundred Wives* before bringing it to New York in 1881. Tall and lanky, he realized that his fine bass voice would be best channelled into *musical comedy. His first starring vehicle was *Castles in the Air* (1890). Starting in 1911, he popularized *Gilbert and *Sullivan by appearing in half a dozen of their comic roles. He also appeared as Falstaff in *The Merry Wives of Windsor*, making his final Broadway bow as the mad doctor in *The Monster* (1933). He was famous for reciting Ernest Thayer's mock-heroic ballad 'Casey at the Bat', which he first delivered in 1888 and repeated thousands of

times in succeeding decades. Hopper published an autobiography, *Once a Clown, Always a Clown* (1927).   CT

HORACE (QUINTUS HORATIUS FLACCUS) (65–8 BC)

Roman poet and critic. His *Ars Poetica* (*Art of Poetry*), probably composed *c.*19 BC, was, together with *Aristotle's *Poetics*, central to the development of *neoclassicism. Horace was influenced by Neoptolemus, a follower of Aristotle, but there is no evidence of a direct knowledge of Aristotle. Two principles governed Horace's comments on drama: (*a*) the necessity for *decorum or appropriateness (no mixing of *genres; traditional and consistent *characterization); (*b*) the purpose of poetry as instruction or delight. Several 'rules' supported these principles: plays must have five *acts, the offensive and marvellous must be kept offstage, gods should appear only if absolutely necessary, actors are restricted to three, the *chorus should be morally exemplary. *Early modern *theorists used *Ars Poetica* as a key to Aristotle's *Poetics*. The two documents were compared and conflated, fused and confused until they were barely distinguishable.   RWV

HORDERN, MICHAEL (1911–95)

English actor born in Hertfordshire, who studied at Brighton College and performed as an *amateur before making his professional debut in *Othello* at the People's Palace in 1937. After the war he worked at the *Shakespeare Memorial Theatre (1952), and at the *Old Vic (1953–4) he appeared in a range of classical roles including Polonius, King John, Prospero, and Malvolio. He was later in *Pinter's own production of *The Collection* (1962), was a touching and closely realized Lear for Jonathan *Miller at the *National Theatre (1969), was in *Stoppard's *Jumpers* (1972), Howard *Barker's *Stripwell* (1975), and played Sir Anthony Absolute in *The Rivals* (1983). He specialized in ageing eccentrics, sometimes amiable and slightly dotty, sometimes dark and manipulative. Extensive *film credits include *Passport to Pimlico* (1949), *A Funny Thing Happened on the Way to the Forum* (1966), *The Slipper and the Rose* (1976), and *The Missionary* (1981). He made many *television appearances, including John *Mortimer's *Paradise Postponed* (1986), and was also a memorable narrator for the animated series of Michael Bond's *Paddington Bear* (1975). Hordern was knighted in 1983.   AS

HORNIMAN, ANNIE E. F. (1860–1937)

English *manager. The daughter of a Quaker tea merchant, she studied art and then spent much of her modest fortune on the emerging *regional repertory movement. She helped to finance

Florence *Farr's 1894 season at the Avenue Theatre, which presented *Yeats's *Land of Heart's Desire* and *Shaw's *Arms and the Man*; she greatly admired Yeats's work, and later offered to buy the Irish National Theatre Society its own building (*see* NATIONAL THEATRE MOVEMENT, IRELAND). This opened as the *Abbey Theatre in December 1904, and she continued to support it financially until 1907, in spite of strained relations. She was much happier with her next venture, at the *Gaiety Theatre, *Manchester, which she bought in 1908, taking Ben Iden *Payne with her from *Dublin as *artistic director. Here she stayed until 1917, establishing a company committed to short runs, *naturalistic *acting, and serious plays, including those of the 'Manchester school' (*Brighouse, *Houghton, *Monkhouse). She mounted more than 200 plays between 1908 and 1917, over half of them new writing, and encouraged *tours to *London, Canada, and the USA.   EEC

HOROVITZ, ISRAEL (1939–   )

American playwright, screenwriter, and founder *artistic director of the Gloucester Stage Company. A prolific and Procrustean playwright, Horovitz focuses on betrayal, passion, and violence. These themes were apparent from the start of his career; he achieved national prominence in 1968 with his *Off-Broadway double bill of *The Indian Wants the Bronx*, in which a Bengali is gratuitously mugged, and *It's Called the Sugar Plum*, wherein a Radcliffe student allows her fiancé's killer to seduce her. He continued to find success with short plays such as the *absurdist *Line* (1968), still running in *New York in 2002, and an uncharacteristically uproarious *comedy, *The Primary English Class* (1976). Horovitz's later, longer works evince a stern proletarian work ethic. Outstanding are *Henry Lumper* (1985), a reworking of Shakespeare's *Henry IV*, and *North Shore Fish* (1986), a gritty survival drama of working women. These are part of a cycle about the fishing community of Gloucester, Massachusetts. He has won numerous *awards and is one of the most frequently produced American playwrights in France.
                                                                TFC

HORVÁTH, ÖDÖN VON (1901–38)

Austrian playwright. The son of an Austro-Hungarian diplomat, Horváth was educated in Budapest, Vienna, and Munich. Although officially a Hungarian citizen, he received a German education and wrote exclusively in that language. Arguably the most important twentieth-century German playwright after *Brecht, Horváth's fame and influence rest essentially on four plays written between 1929 and 1932: *Italienische Nacht* (*Italian Night*, 1931), *Tales from the Vienna Woods* (1931), *Kasimir und Karoline* (1932), and *Glaube, Liebe, Hoffnung* (*Faith, Hope, and Charity*, produced 1936). In these works Horváth unmasks the consciousness of the German petty bourgeoisie towards the

end of the Weimar Republic. He analyses *characters through their language—a mixture of half-understood literary quotations, proverbs, dialect, and media clichés. All four plays are termed *Volksstücke*, a *genre more associated with nineteenth-century peasant *comedy than with critical analysis of social problems. This deconstruction of genre expectations is a crucial part of his *dramaturgical strategy. In 1933 Horváth was forced into exile and his writing shifted to more 'universal' themes as he struggled to find an *audience. His most important works from this period, *Don Juan kommt aus dem Krieg* (*Don Juan Comes back from the War*, 1936) and *Figaro lässt sich scheiden* (*Figaro Gets Divorced*, 1936) both explore the predicament of exile. After his death in *Paris (he was struck by lightning), Horváth was forgotten, but in the mid-1960s a renaissance began which focused on the social critical plays of the Weimar period. More recently lesser-known works such as *Zur schönen Aussicht* (*Bellevue*, 1926) and *Der jüngste Tag* (*Judgement Day*, 1937) have been successfully revived.   CBB

HÔTEL DE BOURGOGNE

The first public theatre in *Paris was built by the *Confrérie de la Passion in 1548, on property once owned by the dukes of Burgundy. That year, to compensate for a Parlement de Paris edict banning them from performing *religious plays, the Confrérie were granted a monopoly on all drama in Paris. They turned to *farces and other secular pieces, until in about 1570 they gave up acting and concentrated on *management, leasing their theatre to various itinerant and foreign companies. From 1629, the *Comédiens du Roi, led successively by *Bellerose, *Floridor, and Hauteroche, became the Confrérie's permanent tenants. The Confrérie was dissolved in 1677, whereupon ownership of their theatre passed to the Hôpital des Enfants-Trouvés. In 1680, when the *Comédie-Française was established at the Hôtel *Guénégaud, Tiberio *Fiorilli's Italian troupe was granted occupancy of the Hôtel de Bourgogne. From then until its final closure in 1783—except for the period 1697–1716, when it stood dark—the *Comédie Italienne, as it became known, remained the Italians' home in Paris.

The theatre's original design was probably inspired as much by the great hall of the Hôpital de la Trinité (where the Confrérie had played until 1539) as by the traditional *tennis court, to which its dimensions bore a marked similarity. Eighteenth-century plans show that the *playhouse was a parallelogram, with internal measurements of 13.8 m (45 feet) by 32.2 m (106 feet). In the early seventeenth century the *stage was 10.7 m (35 feet) deep, with a smaller, practicable upper stage projecting from the rear wall. The *auditorium was dominated by a pit for standing spectators, on three sides of which, parallel to the walls, were two tiers of *boxes, seven along the side walls and five facing the stage, plus an open *paradis*. Rising sharply above and behind the boxes opposite the stage was an *amphithéâtre* of tiered benches.

The Hôtel de Bourgogne was refurbished many times during its long life: in 1647 the stage was extended by 3.3 m (11 feet), a front *curtain installed, and the auditorium modified; in 1686 the *paradis* was converted into discrete boxes and stage boxes were built over the *forestage; in 1691 new machinery was installed in the stage house; in 1760 *proscenium columns were erected, a *parquet* built behind the orchestra pit and the *amphithéâtre* (by this time moved to the rear of the pit) reshaped, and in 1765 the columns were removed and additional private boxes installed over the forestage. JG

HOUDINI, HARRY (EHRICH WEISS) (1874–1926)

Hungarian escape artist. Starting as a magician in American dime museums in the early 1890s, his first major illusion was a substitution trunk called 'Metamorphosis'. In 1899 Martin Beck booked him on the Orpheum *vaudeville circuit as an escape artist, and he was soon known as 'The King of Handcuffs'. In 1900 he executed his first jail cell escape, and in 1906, he first leapt from a bridge into deep water and freed himself from manacles before surfacing. Responding to challenges, he escaped from a submerged crate, an iron boiler, a rolltop desk, a diving suit, a mail pouch, a titanic rope-fibre manila envelope, a gigantic football, an oversized milk can, a coffin, and the innards of a dead creature reported as a 'whale-octopus'. In 1912 he introduced the Water Torture Cell, escaping from a small cabinet filled with water after being suspended from his ankles and locked in, and in 1916 he first released himself from a straitjacket while hanging upside down over a city street filled with spectators. Spending most of his career in the United States, Houdini combined meticulous skill with showmanship and a keen eye for publicity, responding to the public fascination with crime and playing on spiritualist expectations even while debunking the tricks of mediums and psychics. *See also* MAGIC SHOWS. (*See* illustration p. 604.) JDM

HOUGHTON, NORRIS (1909–2001)

American *producer, director, designer, and writer, influential proponent of non-profit and *regional theatre. He began his career as undergraduate designer at Princeton University, and worked as a director and designer on Broadway between 1932 and 1957. He co-*managed the *Phoenix Theatre, where he staged over 70 plays *Off-Broadway between 1953 and 1964. His six books include *Moscow Rehearsals* (1936), *Advance from Broadway* (1941), *Return Engagement* (1962), and *Entrances and Exits* (1991). Among his academic posts, he headed theatre departments at Vassar College and the State University of New York, Purchase. FL

HOUGHTON, STANLEY (1881–1913)

English dramatist, one of the 'Manchester school' of playwrights closely associated with Annie *Horniman and her pioneering *regional repertory company at the *Gaiety in *Manchester. His plays include the *one-act Lancashire *comedy *The Dear Departed* (1906), *Independent Means* (1909), *The Younger Generation* (1910), and most famously *Hindle Wakes* (1912), a *satiric comedy about a working-class girl who causes a scandal by refusing to marry the son of the wealthy local mill owner, believing that a mere fleeting affair should not condemn her to marrying a man she does not love. This controversial twist gained the play rapid notoriety and popularity. First presented by the company in *London, it soon transferred to the Gaiety and was taken on successful *tours in both Britain and America. Its fame helped ensure the financial success of the Gaiety, advanced the cause of the UK repertory movement, and paradoxically marked the beginning of the Gaiety's decline. ARJ

HOUSEMAN, JOHN (1902–88)

American *manager and director. Born in Bucharest as Jacques Haussmann, he was educated in Europe and worked throughout the 1920s as an international grain-trader in Argentina, London, and beginning in 1926 as a travelling representative based in New York. His long-standing interest in theatre increased with his marriage in 1928 to actress Zita Johann. When business collapsed in 1929, Houseman attempted playwriting, but found success as a director when he staged the Gertrude Stein–Virgil Thomson *Four Saints in Three Acts* (1934). This cryptic '*opera to be sung' in Hartford, Connecticut, was a major event for the American *avant-garde and transferred to Broadway. In 1935 Houseman was named director of the 'Negro Theatre' unit of the *Federal Theatre Project (FTP) in Harlem. A skilled organizer, Houseman here began his collaboration with the director-actor Orson *Welles. Their acclaimed production of a Haitian-inflected *Macbeth* launched a sustained collaboration, with Houseman *producing and Welles directing. In 1936 they founded a classic-based unit for the FTP, staging inventive productions of *Horse Eats Hat* (from *Labiche's *An Italian Straw Hat*) and *Marlowe's *Dr Faustus* (1937). Political pressure over their production of the left-wing opera *The Cradle Will Rock* (1937) forced Houseman and Welles to leave the FTP and found the Mercury Theatre. Their modern-dress *Julius Caesar* (1937) set in a fascist state was a landmark in reinterpretation.

Splitting with Welles after the 1941 production of *Native Son*, Houseman worked as a *film producer in California and continued as stage director in projects such as *O'Neill's *Anna*

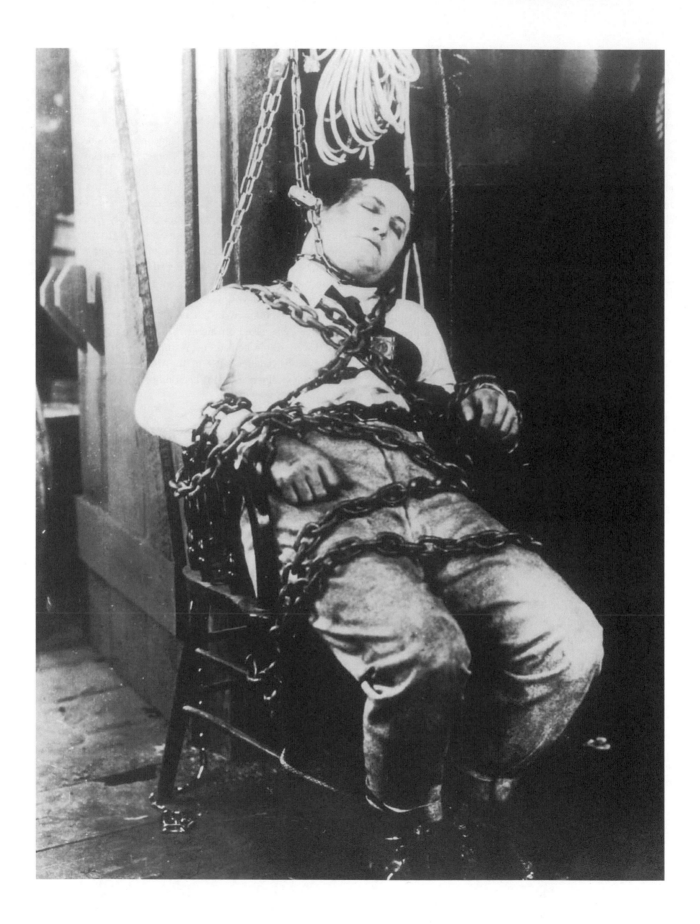

Christie starring Ingrid Bergman. Houseman's later career centred around classical theatre and training of young actors. He was *artistic director of the *American Shakespeare Festival (1956–9) and the Theatre Group at the University of California at Los Angeles (1959–64). Along with Michel *Saint-Denis, Houseman founded the drama division at the *Juilliard School of the Performing Arts (1968) and the *Acting Company, a *touring company of Juilliard graduates, in 1972. His four volumes of memoirs are *Run-through* (1972), *Front and Center* (1980), *Final Dress* (1983), and *Unfinished Business* (1989).　　　MAF

HOUSMAN, LAURENCE (1865–1959)

English playwright. An unlikely figure in the struggle against theatre *censorship, Housman frequently found his quaint, reverential plays banned for depicting sacred or royal figures on stage. Refused by the *Lord Chamberlain, *Nativity* (1902) was staged by Edward Gordon *Craig in a private performance. Housman collaborated with Harley Granville *Barker on *Prunella; or, Love in a Dutch Garden* (1904), in which Barker played Pierrot. Banned from public performance, his best-known works, often chronicle plays, initially appeared as *closet dramas. *Little Plays of St Francis*, first published in 1922, became a Christmas staple of *amateur theatre. His most famous piece, *Victoria Regina*, was a selection of ten vignettes (out of an eventual 50) on the life of Queen Victoria. Its first professional production was in *New York, starring Helen *Hayes (1935). It would wait for a public *London production until 1937.　　　MDG

HOUSTON, VELINA HASU (1957–)

American playwright. The child of a Japanese mother and a father of mixed African-American and Native American heritage, Houston attended universities in Kansas and California and eventually became head of the playwriting programme at the University of Southern California. Her first three plays, *Asa Ga Kimashita* (*Morning Has Broken*, 1981), *American Dreams* (1984), and *Tea* (1987), which examine the *politics of multiracial life in America, established her as a unique voice. She has since written over twenty plays, including *Necessities* (San Diego, 1991) *The Matsuyama Mirror* (Washington, 1993), and *Kokoro* (*True Heart*, *New York, 1994). She has also written numerous screenplays. Her work questions the myth of solidarity among racial groups in America, creating a complex and troubling view of *race relations.　　　JSM

The great escape: Harry **Houdini** bound to a chair in chains and shackles somewhere in America, c.1925, shortly before his death.

HOWARD, ALAN (1937–)

English actor who made his *London debut at the *Royal Court in *Wesker's *Roots* (1959). Howard began a long association with the *Royal Shakespeare Company with Lussurioso in *The Revenger's Tragedy* (1966). He rose rapidly to play Edgar in *King Lear* and Benedick in *Much Ado About Nothing* (both 1968), Hamlet (1970), and the remarkably *doubled Oberon and Theseus in *Brook's famous *A Midsummer Night's Dream* the same year. He was Hal and Henry V in 1975, beginning a fruitful association with Terry *Hands, who directed him in most of Shakespeare's history plays including *Henry VI* (1977), *Richard II*, and *Richard III* (both 1980). He played Halder, a liberal professor whose cowardice leads him to join the Nazi Party, in the première of C. P. *Taylor's *Good* (1981). Following a break from stage work he appeared in *The Silver King* and *Scenes from a Marriage* at *Chichester (both 1990). At the Royal *National Theatre he was Higgins in *Pygmalion* (1992) and George in *Cocteau's *Les Parents terribles* (1994). For Peter *Hall he was Vladimir in *Waiting for Godot* and Lear (both 1997). Howard's *film career has been less prolific but includes the eponymous lover in Peter Greenaway's *The Cook, the Thief, his Wife and her Lover* (1989).　　　AS

HOWARD, BRONSON (1842–1908)

American playwright. Born in Detroit, Howard came to playwriting after stints as a drama *critic for Detroit and *New York newspapers. His first major success was *Saratoga* (1870), a satiric examination of the stylish resort. After a series of lacklustre plays, Howard next caught the public imagination with *The Banker's Daughter* (1878). The evolution of this play became the subject of an 1886 Harvard lecture, later published as *The Autobiography of a Play* (1914). With his next major success, *Young Mrs Winthrop* (1882), Howard moved toward a more *realistic examination of contemporary American society. He continued in this vein in *The Henrietta* (1887) and *Aristocracy* (1892), both of which examined an emerging American type, the business tycoon. Howard's greatest popular triumph was *Shenandoah* (1888), a spectacular Civil War *melodrama. He sought to elevate playwriting in America to a profession, and to that end he helped found the American Dramatists' Club in 1891. With others he also successfully lobbied for revisions in the *copyright laws to prevent script piracy.　　　GAR

HOWARD, EUGENE (1880–1965) AND WILLIE (1886–1949)

American comedians. Their early experience was in *vaudeville; after teaming up in 1903, they were particularly known for their turn 'French Taught in a Hurry' and a spoof of *Rigoletto*. Their first appearance together on the legitimate *musical stage was in

The Passing Show of 1912. They appeared in further *Passing Shows* and in other *Shubert *revues before returning to vaudeville. From 1926 they appeared in several editions of *George White's Scandals*, as well as *Ballyhoo of 1932*, the *Ziegfeld Follies of 1934* and *The Show Is On* (1937). Eugene was the straight man; Willie was the sad-faced comedian (and a talented mimic) who got the laughs. Both possessed good singing voices, as demonstrated in their *parodies of grand *opera. Eugene retired in 1940, but Willie continued, although less successful as a solo performer.　　　　　　　　　　　　　　　　JTD

HOWARD, PAMELA (1939–)

English designer. Born in Birmingham, she trained at Birmingham College of Arts and Crafts and at the Slade School of Fine Art. She designed a Venetian-inspired *Othello* (*Royal Shakespeare Company, 1979), an intriguing set of torn and crumpled shrouds, sails, and projected images for Ted Tally's *Terra Nova* (*Chichester, 1980), and a bleak version of *Shaw's *On the Rocks* (Chichester, 1982). Howard's *scenography plays with manipulating space, as in the site-specific set for *Border Warfare* (*Glasgow, Old Museum of Transport, 1988), where the forest primeval later metamorphosed into a football pitch. For *The Rose Tattoo* (Theatre Clwyd, 1995), a 'wall of memories becomes an altar of dreams' as past merges with future. Her design for *Hedda Gabler* received the best *touring production *award. She has also designed *Yerma*, *The School for Wives*, and *Happy Birthday Brecht* for the Royal *National Theatre, and a fascinating touring production by Di Trevis of *The Taming of the Shrew* for the RSC (1985). She co-directed *Concierto barroco* (1999) for Opera Transatlantica, for which she is *producer. At Central St Martin's College of Art and Design in *London, she developed the international MA in scenography and was appointed professor in 1996. She has advanced the critical debate on theatre design through Scenofest (an international scenography festival), work with the international organization OISTAT and the Prague Quadrenniale, and through publications, the most recent being *What Is Scenography?* (2001).　　　RVL

HOWARD, ROBERT (1626–98)

English playwright and politician. Howard was knighted early in his life for bravery as a soldier and he died a successful politician, but between 1660 and 1670 he was a well-known contributor to *London theatre as a playwright and as an intimate of playwrights. His brothers Edward and James were dramatists, and his sister married *Dryden. Together with *Davenant, Howard was *Buckingham's initial target in *The Rehearsal* (1671); and he was caricatured as Sir Positive At-al in *Shadwell's *The Sullen Lovers* (1668). He collaborated with Dryden on *The Indian Queen* (1664), the first *heroic drama, but later engaged in a protracted critical controversy with his brother-in-law concerning the use of rhyme in drama. (Howard appears as Crites in Dryden's *Essay of Dramatic Poesy*, 1668.) Howard's other plays include three *comedies, *The Committee* (1662), *The Surprise* (1662), and *The Country Gentleman* (1669, banned); and two *tragicomedies, *The Vestal Virgin* (1664, provided with an alternative tragic ending) and—his greatest success—*The Great Favourite* (1668). After 1670, he concentrated on his political career.　　　　　　　　　　　　　　　　RWV

HOWARD, SIDNEY (1891–1939)

American playwright. A veteran of the First World War who became a committed pacifist and socialist, Howard developed American social drama along pragmatic and rational lines in the 1920s and 1930s. His accidental death cut short a productive career. He studied playwriting with George Pierce *Baker at Harvard (1915–16) and achieved wide recognition in 1924 with the *Theatre Guild production of *They Knew What They Wanted*. This drama about an older man's pursuit of a younger woman was admired for its maturity and rationality: the *characters avoid *tragedy by rejecting obsession with sexual love and choose instead security, stability, and personal loyalty as surer roads to happiness. This success was followed by such dramas as *The Silver Cord* (1926), in which a son rejects his mother's possessiveness, and *Yellow Jack* (1934), a *documentary *historical drama about the fight against yellow fever. Howard was a skilled adapter of the work of others, crafting *The Late Christopher Bean* (1932) from a French source and *Dodsworth* (1934) from the Sinclair Lewis novel, and as a screenwriter won Academy awards for *Arrowsmith* (1931) and *Gone with the Wind* (1939). The critic Joseph Wood Krutch saw in Howard's drama 'a daylight world, in which common sense is still the standard by which everything is judged'.　　　MAF

HOWARD-FOX FAMILY

American acting clan. When Canadian George Cunnabell Howard (1815–87) married Bostonian Caroline Emily Fox (1829–1908) in 1844, the result was a fusing of two theatrical *families that, between them, over four generations, contained 26 members with some connection to the stage. In 1846 Howard established the Howard-Fox Dramatic *Stock Company, which took numerous works on *tour throughout the east and later Midwest, with periodic stops in *New York. Caroline's four brothers were all performers: George W. L. *Fox, James (1827–1900), Charles (1833–75), and Henry (1836–44); and three of her eight children were actors: Cordelia Howard (1848–1942), John (1851–63), and Walter (1868–1945). The troupe's biggest success was the adaptation of *Uncle Tom's Cabin* commissioned in 1852 from Caroline's cousin George L. *Aiken—with Caroline as Topsy, her husband as St Clare, the playwright as George Harris, and little Cordelia (who had made her stage debut at 2½) as Eva. CT

HOWE, TINA (1937–)

American playwright. Her anarchic sources are *Ionesco, *Beckett, and the *Marx Brothers, but her plays are *feminist comic fantasies that deal with food, art, family, and loss. The savage *Birth and After Birth* (published 1973, produced 1995), dives into the turmoil of motherhood, with a hairy adult toddler who dominates his parents. When *producers rejected the script, Howe turned to public settings fraught with ludicrous mayhem: an art gallery in *Museum* (1976), a restaurant in *The Art of Dining* (1979), a fitting room in *Appearances* (1982). Carole Rothman directed premières of the later, richer plays. In *Painting Churches* (1983), an artist faces the decline of her ageing parents, while *Approaching Zanzibar* (1989) follows a fractious family road trip toward a dying aunt. *One Shoe Off* (1993) reveals a house devoured by indoor vegetables as five adults attack each other with literate quotations. *Pride's Crossing* (1998) travels through time, seven actors playing twenty *characters in the life of an aristocratic old woman, a former Channel swimmer. Other work includes *Coastal Disturbances* (1986) and *Swimming* (1991). Howe teaches playwriting at Hunter College and New York University. FL

HOWELLS, WILLIAM DEAN (1837–1920)

American novelist, editor, and playwright. Born in Ohio, Howells worked as a newspaper reporter and editor before his campaign biography of Lincoln earned him appointment as United States consul to Venice. By 1866 he had become assistant editor of the *Atlantic Monthly*, where his duties exposed him to a wide range of politically and aesthetically progressive thought. In his book reviews in the *Atlantic*, his subsequent 'The Editor's Study' column in *Harper's Magazine*, and later articles in *Harper's Weekly* and the *North American Review*, Howells was an indefatigable proponent of a new *realism in art, singling out in American drama the works of Edward *Harrigan and James *Herne for particular praise. He was also an early and consistent advocate of Henrik *Ibsen. Howells produced only two full-length realistic plays: *A Counterfeit Presentment* (1877) and *Yorrick's Love* (1878), both of which were successfully mounted by Lawrence *Barrett. Many of his other 34 plays he published in *Atlantic* and *Harper's*, earning him a devoted, if predominately *amateur, following. See also CRITICISM. GAR

HOYT, CHARLES (1860–1900)

American playwright, director, and *manager. Charles Hale Hoyt was born in Concord, New Hampshire. While a *Boston newspaper columnist, Hoyt began writing for the stage in 1881,

and had penned some twenty stage works by his early death. Employing large casts, these were chiefly *satirical *farces in which he addressed many contemporary issues: hotel management (*A Bunch of Keys*, 1883), city life (*A Tin Soldier*, 1885), railways (*A Hole in the Ground*, 1887), fetishism (*A Brass Monkey*, 1888), rural life (*A Midnight Bell*, 1889), political corruption (*A Texas Steer*, 1890), baseball (*A Runaway Colt*, 1895), women's suffrage (*A Contented Woman*, 1897). Some of his works contain so many songs that they fall between the *genres of play and *musical comedy—such as *A Milk White Flag* (1894) and *A Stranger in New York* (1897). He normally directed his own shows, sometimes in his own theatre, and they frequently went on to *tour for many years after their *New York runs. His biggest hit was the musical *A Trip to Chinatown* (1891), whose run of 657 performances held the Broadway record for nearly three decades; it toured the country for more than twenty years. CT

HROTSVITHA OF GANDERSHEIM (c.935–973)

German poet and playwright. Hrotsvitha was a member of a religious community of women, 'secular canonesses', at the Abbey of Gandersheim in Saxony. Such communities were usually restricted to the nobility and did not require the renunciation of private property. Hrotsvitha's body of written work, discovered by the humanist Conrad Celtis in 1494 and published in 1501, reveals an author well versed in classical literature as well as scripture and the Christian fathers. Her writings, in Latin, included eight saints' legends, six plays, and accounts of the deeds of Otto I and the history of Gandersheim Abbey. The three categories are closely interrelated, with complex structural and thematic parallels. By her own account, Hrotsvitha modelled her plays on those of the *Roman playwright *Terence, 'so that in that self-same form of composition in which the shameless acts of lascivious women were phrased | The laudable chastity of sacred virgins be praised'. Constancy, conversion, and martyrdom are the themes of *Gallicanus, Dulcitius, Calimachus, Abraham, Pafmutius*, and *Sapienta*, but Hrotsvitha extends the emotional range with *scenes of *burlesque (*Dulcitius*) and of homoeroticism and necrophilia (*Calimachus*). There is a considerable amount of stage *action, the *dialogue is lively, the settings varied and specific—all evidence of their performability, although semi-dramatic recitation is the most likely mode of any original performance. There have been a number of successful modern productions. RWV

HUAJÜ (HUA CHÜ)

'Spoken drama', the Chinese term for Western-style drama with *realistic *dialogue. In 1957 *Tian Han, one of *China's best-known playwrights and then president of the All-China

Dramatists' Association, defined *huajü* as 'a new dramatic form imported from Europe together with capitalist civilization half a century ago, or created with strong foreign influences. It portrays contemporary life struggles and historical stories, using language and movement as major means of expression, as well as modern playwriting techniques with *act and *scene divisions, realistic *makeup, *costumes, sets, and *lighting.' In 1907 in *Tokyo a group of Chinese students, calling themselves *Chunliu She (the Spring Willow Society), performed *The Lady of the Camellias* and *Uncle Tom's Cabin*, marking the beginning of Western-style theatre in Chinese. The first form of new drama was *wenming xi* (civilized drama), which flourished in *Shanghai in the 1910s. Most of the *wenming xi* were *mubiao xi* (outline plays), *scenarios that relied heavily on *improvisation. The performance style was a mixture of Japanese *shimpa* and traditional Chinese theatre.

To counter the commercial tendencies of the *wenming xi*, *aimei jü* (*amateur drama) became popular in the 1920s, emphasizing direct translations of modern European plays. At the same time plays by Chinese playwrights, mostly educated in Japan, Europe, and the USA, were beginning to draw national attention. The term *huajü* was first adopted by Tian in 1927 and the form had matured by the next decade, with a repertoire of quality plays and diversified performance styles as more directors returned from abroad. During the Sino-Japanese War (1937–45), *huajü* became a powerful propaganda weapon, with almost all theatre people enthusiastically involved in the anti-Japanese effort. In the 1950s the close Sino-Soviet relationship ushered in the *Stanislavsky system, even though the idea of the 'self' was eliminated because of its bourgeois individualism. Banned as a capitalist 'poisonous weed' during the Cultural Revolution, *huajü* later returned and remains one of the major theatrical forms in China. SYL

HUBERT, ANDRÉ (1624–1700)

French actor. Hubert played at the Théâtre du *Marais, which his mother owned, from 1659 to 1664, when he joined *Molière's company. A versatile actor and good mimic, he took a variety of roles including the excitable young men Damis in *Tartuffe* and Acaste in *The Misanthrope*. On Louis *Béjart's retirement in 1670, Hubert took over the parts of elderly women such as Mme Pernelle in *Tartuffe*; he was much acclaimed in this speciality, and subsequently created the more nuanced roles of Mme Jourdain in *The Would-Be Gentleman* and Philaminte in *The Learned Ladies*. He retired from the *Comédie-Française in 1685. RWH

HUBRIS

In ancient Greece hubris was originally a legal term denoting an illegal action, one overstepping the boundaries of justice. It later came to include the religious notion of trespassing the boundary between human and divine. It could also refer to the human attribute that causes the transgression and thus came to mean the presumptuousness or arrogance that leads to the overstepping of legal or divine boundaries. Hubris, sometimes rendered less pejoratively as 'pride', has often been seen as the *sine qua non* of the *tragic *protagonist, whose presumptuousness in pursuing his own destiny provokes an inevitable retribution.

RWV

HUGHES, BARNARD (1915–)

American actor. A *New Yorker by upbringing, Hughes made his professional debut in 1934, becoming a solid Broadway supporting actor in *The Teahouse of the August Moon* (1956), *Advise and Consent* (1960), *Gielgud's *Hamlet* (1964), and *Hogan's Goat* (1965). Maturing into a powerful character actor with a burly, gravel-voiced intensity and eyes that could twinkle or glower, he excelled as Dogberry, Serebriakov, and Falstaff. Stardom and many *awards came with his signature role, first in New York (1978), later in *Dublin, as the irascible title *character in Hugh *Leonard's *Da*; T. E. Kalem described him as 'an expansive field marshal of lifelong defeat who acts with the authority of an uncaged lion'. Later Broadway leads included *Angel's Fall* (1983), *The Iceman Cometh* (1985), and *Prelude to a Kiss* (1990). He and actress Helen Stenborg celebrated their 50th wedding anniversary in 2000, fêted on stage by Lauren Bacall and Rosemary *Harris, while they were all appearing in the New York première of Noël *Coward's *Waiting in the Wings*. CR

HUGHES, DUSTY (1947–)

English playwright, who has also been assistant director at the *Birmingham Repertory Theatre (1970–2), theatre editor for the magazine *Time Out* (1973–6), *television script editor for the BBC's *Play for Today* series (1982–4), as well as joint *artistic director (1976–9) of the *Bush Theatre. Hughes's early plays *Commitments* (1980) and *Heaven and Hell* (1981) were precursors to his successful adaptations of two neglected Russian classics for the *Royal Shakespeare Company: *Bulgakov's *Molière* (1982) and *Gorky's *Philistines* (1985). The world of Russia and Eastern Europe recurs in his play for the *National Theatre, *Futurists* (1986), set in a Petrograd café in 1921 and peopled by poets, artists, and politicos caught up by revolutionary fervour, and also in *A Slip of the Tongue* (1992), in which a series of sexy girls try to wheedle secrets out of a reluctant dissident, played in both *Chicago and London by John *Malkovich. AS

HUGHES, HOLLY (1955–)

American playwright and *performance artist. Her plays such as *The Well of Horniness* (1983) and *The Lady Dick* (1985), darkly comic ensemble pieces that foreground *lesbian sexuality and *parody conventions of *film noir*, were developed at *WOW Café in *New York. After writing *Dress Suits to Hire* (1987) for Peggy Shaw and Lois Weaver of *Split Britches, Hughes shifted to solo work. Her solo pieces are primarily autobiographical, recounting memories of her mother, her sexual identity, and her suburban childhood. While she celebrates women's sexuality, her style is by no means graphic. Nonetheless she was one of four artists singled out by the *National Endowment for the Arts on charges of indecency. Ironically, the piece for which funding was denied, *World without End* (1989), had only peripheral lesbian content and little that could reasonably be construed as indecent. Hughes fought lengthy court battles challenging the constitutionality of the Endowment's efforts to control the content of funded work, ultimately losing her appeal in the Supreme Court. This experience provided the point of departure for *Preaching to the Perverted* (1999), in which she examines how queer identity is excluded from constructions of American citizenship (*see* QUEER STUDIES). LW

HUGHES, LANGSTON (1902–67)

*African-American writer, considered the poetic voice of the Harlem Renaissance. His play *Mulatto* (1935), the story of the white patriarch and the long-suffering maid who bears his children, was the first full-length drama by an African American to appear on Broadway. Prior to this Hughes had collaborated with Zora Neale *Hurston on a *folk play called *Mule Bone*, based on her short story; the partners quarrelled, and the work was not produced until 1991. Hughes worked with Cleveland's Karamu House in 1936, then founded the Suitcase Theatre in Harlem, which staged his *Don't You Want to Be Free*. In the 1940s he collaborated with Kurt *Weill and Elmer *Rice on *Street Scene*, and with William Grant Still on *Troubled Island*, an *opera set in Haiti. In 1957 Hughes wrote the libretto for *Simply Heavenly*, and his *Tambourines to Glory*, a gospel *musical, was on Broadway in 1963. BBL

HUGO, VICTOR-MARIE (1802–85)

French poet, novelist and dramatist. Hugo was the outstanding exponent of *romanticism in French drama, a fashion in dramatic writing which lasted a mere fifteen years, leaving no works with a firm place in the national repertoire, but which succeeded in its day in providing a focal point for the cultural and political aspirations of a generation. Hugo achieved early distinction as a poet and a novelist; his fascination with the theatre is said to have been set going by repeated visits to a *Pixérécourt *melodrama, and he had tried his hand at dramatic composition as a schoolboy. His first mature play, published in 1827, was a vast, unplayable historical verse drama. *Cromwell*, however, was accompanied by a forceful preface, in which the young poet and would-be dramatist set out the most important manifesto for a vital new form of theatre with which to challenge what Hugo and his friends saw as an effete and outdated dramatic form. The impact of the *Préface de Cromwell* was tremendous: the main characteristics of the revitalized drama it envisages are the abolition of the crippling *unities of time and place; a rounded approach to *character, involving both 'sublime' and '*grotesque' elements in the human make-up; and a *versification freed from *neoclassical constraints on metre and vocabulary.

The theoretical challenge received practical shape in *Hernani* (1830), whose innovations of form and content provoked the famous 'battle' in the *auditorium of the *Comédie-Française night after night (*see* HERNANI RIOTS; RIOTS). *Marion de Lorme* had a less turbulent reception at the *Porte-Saint-Martin in 1832, running for 68 performances, with Marie *Dorval and *Bocage as the ill-starred romantic couple; while *Le Roi s'amuse* (*The King's Pleasure*, Comédie-Française, 1832) was suspended by government order after the first night, to receive its second performance exactly 50 years later. *Ruy Blas* was the most successful of Hugo's plays both at the Renaissance Theatre in 1838 with Frédérick *Lemaître in the title role and when taken into the national repertoire (*Odéon 1872, Comédie-Française 1879 with *Bernhardt playing the Queen). In the meantime, Hugo had tried his hand at romantic drama in prose, with mixed success, in *Lucrèce Borgia* and *Marie Tudor* (1833) and *Angelo* (1835). The first of these was the most successful; *Marie Tudor* was taken off by the *management while still running because of arguments, largely due to Hugo's stubbornness in *casting his mistress Juliette Drouet; while *Angelo*, a study of passion and jealousy that in verse might have produced a masterpiece, was instead written in a banal prose which reduced it to the level of popular melodrama.

Les Burgraves (1843) is conventionally regarded as marking the end of romantic drama; and although it ran for over 30 performances at the Comédie-Française, Hugo's genius had by now moved away from the manner of his early plays towards an epic and visionary imagination ill-fitting a stage drama. The middle-aged Hugo, disappointed in his political ambitions after the 1848 Revolution, went into exile in Jersey, spending most of the rest of his life in Guernsey, where he wrote the verse *satires *Les Châtiments*, the philosophical collection *Les Contemplations*, and composed poems for *La Légende des siècles*, as well as writing the novels *Les Misérables* (1862), *Les Travailleurs de la mer* (1866), and (much less successful) *L'Homme qui rit* (1869). The only drama *texts of note to have survived from this period are *Torquemada*, a powerful verse play indicting religious fanaticism, and in quite a different vein *Mangeront-ils?* (*Shall They Be Fed?*), an *allegorical fantasy with something of the lightness and spontaneity of Shakespearian *comedy. The latter play was taken into the repertory of the Comédie-Française in 1919, joining *Les Burgraves* (admitted in 1902) and the outstanding survivors from the 1830s.

The stage history of Hugo's drama in the twentieth century did very little to restore his fortunes after the lack of success and neglect that his plays suffered in the second half of the nineteenth; and the much praised production of *Ruy Blas* at the Comédie-Française in 1954, with Gérard *Philipe in the title role, stands out as a reminder of what French romantic drama at its best might be able to offer. None of Hugo's verse plays of the 1830s—*Hernani, Marion de Lorme, Le Roi s'amuse*, and *Ruy Blas*—ever achieved major success in the theatre; and Hugo's lasting legacy was to remain the *theoretical challenge of the *Préface de Cromwell*, whose most successful realization was to be seen not in his own plays, but in *Rostand's *Cyrano de Bergerac* of 1897. It should not be forgotten, however, that *Hernani* and *Le Roi s'amuse* do still flourish in the theatre, thanks to *Verdi, as *Ernani* and *Rigoletto*.   WDH

> AFFRON, CHARLES, *A Stage for Poets: studies in the theatre of Hugo and Musset* (Princeton, 1971)
> HOWARTH, W. D., *Sublime and Grotesque: a study of French romantic drama* (London, 1975)

HULL-HOUSE THEATRE

Jane Addams founded Hull-House as a social settlement establishment in *Chicago in 1889. Believing that theatre could teach social and moral values to her immigrant neighbours, Addams established a 'dramatic section' in 1893, in 1899 an *auditorium was completed, and in 1901 actress Laura Dainty Pelham was appointed to head the Hull-House Players. In its first years the company focused on *realist and *naturalist writers, including *Ibsen, *Shaw, *Galsworthy, and *Hauptmann, and the Players acquired a national reputation as a company dedicated to serious drama. The company continued through a number of artistic and organizational changes until 1941, and was revived in the 1960s.   MMK

HUME, SAMUEL (1885–1962)

American designer. One of the first Americans to disseminate the works of *Craig and *Appia, Hume was an early leader in the New Stagecraft and *Little Theatre movements. He studied at Harvard with George Pierce *Baker, and in 1914 organized the first exhibition of innovative European stagecraft. As director of the Detroit Arts and Crafts Theater he employed a Craigian system of adaptable pylons and platforms. He is co-author of *Twentieth-Century Stage Decoration* (with W. R. Fuerst, 1929).   WFC

HUMPHRIES, BARRY (1934–)

Australian performer who first unleashed his most famous cross-dressed creation, Edna Everage, in 1955. The *character of this mousey suburban housewife, who satirizes the middle-

class *Melbourne environment of Humphries's upbringing, evolved into a flamboyant *television megastar famous for her ability to humiliate people, and for her surreal wardrobes and spectacle frames. Humphries moved to *London in 1959 and since then has made a career out of ridiculing Australian lifestyles. His strip-cartoon character Barry McKenzie, the innocent Australian abroad, appeared in *Private Eye* and resulted in two Barry McKenzie feature *films. Other famous Humphries characters include the slob Australian cultural attaché Sir Les Patterson, and Sandy Stone, a faded, Melbournian suburban man, later a ghost. Humphries continues to combine an international TV career with the cut and thrust of live performances, where he is willing to say the unsayable, and to insult anyone and everyone. *See also* FEMALE IMPERSONATION.   EJS

HUN

*Puppet theatre from *Thailand, divided into three types. (*a*) *Hun luang*, or royal puppets, only on display in museums, are human figures about half a metre (about 1½ feet) tall. They are manipulated from below by strings passing through the hollow figure. (*b*) *Hun krabok*, influenced by Chinese and Lao puppets, were introduced in 1893. Of the same height as *hun luang*, and also *costumed in the style of Thai classical theatre, these puppets are detailed only in the head and hands, the body being replaced by three rods covered by a cloth bag. A single puppeteer controls the head with his left hand, the hands with his right, and simultaneously sings and dances to the accompaniment of *pipat* music. The repertoire is based on local plays. (*c*) *Lakon lek* are dressed and performed in similar style; somewhat larger than the other two types, one puppet has three operators, one for the head and right arm, a second for the left arm, a third for the feet. They move in time with offstage singers and *pipat* music. *Audiences have steadily declined, and since 1990 efforts have been under way to popularize the form.   SV

HUNT, HUGH (1911–73)

Welsh director. After Oxford a production of *King John* (1933) at the New Theatre, *London, gained him appointments successively at the Maddermarket Theatre, Norwich, the Croydon Repertory Theatre, and the Westminster Theatre. From 1935 to 1938 he was *producer at the *Abbey Theatre, *Dublin, where he directed 33 productions, among them the premières of St John *Ervine's *Boyd's Shop*, Teresa Deevy's *Katie Roche*, George *Shiels's *The Passing Day*, P. V. *Carroll's *Shadow and Substance* and W. B. *Yeats's *Purgatory*, all revived many times. At the Abbey he collaborated fruitfully with the designer Tanya *Moisewitsch and the author Frank O'Connor. Following military service, he became director at the *Bristol Old Vic in 1945, working mainly in Shakespeare and other established playwrights. In 1949 he moved to the *Old Vic in London, consolidating his reputation as a Shakespearian interpreter, and was appointed professor of drama at Manchester University in 1961. He returned to the Abbey as part-time *artistic director, when his most memorable productions were revivals of *O'Casey's The Silver Tassie and Red Roses for Me.   CFS

HUNT, LEIGH (1784–1859)

English critic and essayist. Hunt's early theatrical essays for the News were later published as Critical Essays on the Performers of the London Theatres (1808). His dramatic *criticism appeared in the Examiner, a leading political and theatrical newspaper which he founded in 1808, and later in the Tatler. He also published an edition of Restoration dramatists and a number of plays including the *tragedy A Legend of Florence, which was performed at *Covent Garden in 1840. Hunt inaugurated the tradition of independent theatrical criticism in England. His willingness to chastise performers and to expose the arrogance of the *patent *managers at *Drury Lane and Covent Garden transformed the tone and conventions of the stage review. He was fascinated by changing theatrical tastes and gave a cautious welcome to the transformation of dramatic *genres and theatre institutions taking place in the 1820s and 1830s. Nevertheless, he remained implacably opposed to the performance of Italian *opera, which he regarded as a form of cultural prostitution.
                                                                                                                                                                JM

HUNTER, KATHRYN (1957–   )

Dynamic and versatile English actor and director who came to prominence with Theatre de *Complicité. Celebrated appearances include *Dürrenmatt's The Visit (1991) for that company, Lear in Helena Kaut-Howson's production at the Leicester Haymarket and *Young Vic (1997), and Galactia in Howard *Barker's Scenes from an Execution (1999). One of her more extraordinary roles came in Spoonface Steinberg (1999). Lee Hall's drama, originally a *radio play, was adapted for stage with Hunter as the eponymous *opera-loving, autistic, Jewish child of 7, struggling to come to terms with cancer. Hunter's directing credits include *Brecht's Mr Puntila and his Man Matti (1998), Thomas *Bernhard's Destination, and Rebecca Gilman's The Glory of Living at the *Royal Court (both 1999).
                                                                                                                                                                AS

HUNTER, N. C. (NORMAN CHARLES) (1908–71)

English playwright. Although he had been writing plays since the 1930s, Hunter found commercial success in the West End only in 1951 with Waters of the Moon. Chosen for the Festival of Britain, the play served as a vehicle for Sybil *Thorndike,

Wendy *Hiller, and Edith *Evans. Its success spurred similar star-studded productions, like A Day by the Sea (1953) with John *Gielgud, Ralph *Richardson, Irene *Worth, and Thorndike, and A Touch of the Sun (1958) with Michael and Vanessa *Redgrave. Hunter's genteel plays are mood pieces whose bittersweet melancholy prompted comparisons at the time to *Chekhov, a plaudit they hardly seem to warrant in hindsight. Like Terence *Rattigan's work, Hunter's plays have come to represent the glamorous, 'quality' West End drama of their producer, Binkie *Beaumont, that was supposedly rendered obsolete by the new wave drama issuing from the *Royal Court and *Theatre Workshop.
                                                                                                                                                                MDG

HURRY, LESLIE (1909–78)

English designer who first turned to stage design when commissioned for *scenery, *props, and *costumes for *Helpmann's *ballet Hamlet (1942). This led to his twice designing Swan Lake for de Valois's company (1943 and 1952), and Turandot (1947) and *Wagner's Ring (1954) for *Covent Garden. A long association (1950–69) with the *Shakespeare Memorial Theatre encompassed designs for King Lear, Hamlet, Troilus and Cressida, and The Duchess of Malfi. Hurry's *surrealist interests resulted in epic, rhythmical settings which created dynamic social and psychological environments for performers, most notably in Tamburlaine for Tyrone *Guthrie (1953) and his many stagings from 1964 for the *thrust stage at the *Stratford Festival, Ontario.
                                                                                                                                                                RAC

HURSTON, ZORA NEALE (1891–1960)

*African-American writer, best known for her fiction. She began writing plays at Howard University; Color Struck took second prize in an Opportunity magazine contest judged by Fannie Hurst and Eugene *O'Neill (1925). From 1930 to 1935 Hurston tried to establish a theatrical career, writing over a dozen works, including The Great Day (Broadway, 1932). In 1931 she began a dramatic adaptation of one of her short stories with Langston *Hughes, but the collaborators fell out and Mule Bone did not see the stage until 1991 (at *Lincoln Center). Thereafter she wrote for Fast and Furious, a Broadway *revue with comedian Moms Mabley and Hurston herself in the cast, and coached actors at the Harlem unit of the *Federal Theatre Project, but was unsuccessful in achieving productions of her plays. Ten Hurston plays were discovered at the Library of Congress in 1997; one of them, Polk County, was produced at *Arena Stage in Washington in 2002.
                                                                                                                                                                BBL

HURT, WILLIAM (1950–   )

American actor. Hurt graduated from Tufts University, studied at the *Juilliard School, and made his professional debut in the

1976 *New York Shakespeare Festival production of *Henry V*. He worked with the *Circle Repertory Company (1977–82), creating the role of Ken Talley in Lanford *Wilson's *The Fifth of July* (1978), and playing Hamlet in 1979. He made his Broadway debut in David *Rabe's *Hurlyburly* (1984). His *film roles range from the understated to the flamboyant, including Ned Racine in *Body Heat* (1981), Arkady Renko in *Gorky Park* (1983), Tom in *Broadcast News* (1987), Macon in *The Accidental Tourist* (1988), and the award-winning Luis Molina in *Kiss of the Spider Woman* (1985).   JDM

HUSAIN, SHAHAROM (1919–   )

Pioneering playwright of modern drama in *Malaysia. Dedicated to promoting Malay language and literature, he was a central figure in its growth and development, especially during his tenure at Sultan Idris Training College in Kuala Lumpur. His plays were engaged with the social realities of the time—particularly the Malay struggle for independence from the British—although the majority of his plays (*sandiwara*) were set in feudal times and were not historically accurate. His best-known work, *Si Bongkok Tanjung Puteri* (*The Hunchback of Tanjung Puteri*, 1956), tackled the theme of loyalty versus personal freedom.   CRG

HUSSAIN, FIDA (1899–2000)

Indian singer, actor, and director in the *Parsi theatre tradition. Born in Muradabad, Uttar Pradesh, as a young man Hussain joined the famed New Alfred Theatrical Company of Bombay (*Mumbai). Under the directorship of Sohrabji Ogra, who strictly opposed the introduction of actresses onstage, the morally conservative New Alfred became the most popular company in the 1910s and 1920s and performed all over *India. 'Master Fida Hussain', as he was known, played *female roles for many years, achieving particular popularity as the melodious *heroine in *Parivartan*. He assumed the male role in *Laila Majnun* in 1930, and after the break-up of the New Alfred in 1932 joined the *film industry in Calcutta (*Kolkata). In the 1930s and 1940s he continued his theatrical work as a member of several companies, including the Kajjan Theatre, the Shahjahan Theatre, and Hindustan Theatre. In 1939 he received the stage name 'Narsi' for his portrayal of a devotee in the play *Bhakt Narsi Mehta*, just one of his many portrayals of Hindu gods and saints. In 1950 he joined the Moonlight Theatre of Calcutta where he worked as lead actor and director until his retirement in 1968. With his deep voice, artful enunciation of *Hindi and *Urdu, and commanding physical presence, Hussain became a mentor to young actors at the *National School of Drama. He received countless *awards in his long career, and in 1985 he was presented with the *Sangeet Natak Akademi award for acting by the government of India.   KH

HUSSEIN, EBRAHIM (1943–   )

Tanzanian playwright and poet. His first play, *Kinjeketile* (1969), is a deep and original meditation on power and on traditional religion: can magic repel guns? After a successful performance at home it was chosen to represent Tanzania at African *festivals abroad, and was translated from Swahili into English by the author. His other plays, *Mashetani* (*Devils*, 1971), *Arusi* (*Wedding*, 1980), and *Kweneye ukingo wa thim* (1988, translated as *At the Edge of Thim*, 2000), were published in Nairobi and became set books for exams, but were considered too sophisticated and too complex by Tanzanian *critics. Hussein received a Ph.D. in the mid-1970s in *Berlin and became the first professor of drama at the University of Dar es Salaam. He resigned in 1986 and withdrew from theatre work.   AlR

HUSTON, WALTER (1884–1950)

Canadian-born American actor. After a false start as an entertainer in the early 1900s, Huston was back on the *vaudeville circuit by 1909. He made his Broadway debut in *Mr Pitt* (1924), followed in the same year by an acclaimed performance as Ephraim Cabot in *O'Neill's *Desire under the Elms*. Known for his unaffected honesty and emotional dynamism, Huston was snatched by Hollywood to play opposite Gary Cooper in *The Virginian* (1929). He appeared in many *films—including *The Treasure of the Sierra Madre* (1948), which was directed by his son John—but still found time for theatre, giving notable performances in *Dodsworth* (1934) and *Othello* (1936). In his first Broadway *musical, Huston was cast as the autocratic governor of New Amsterdam in *Knickerbocker Holiday* (1938); the show's most enduring number, 'September Song', was custom-written for him by Kurt *Weill and Maxwell *Anderson.   EW

HUTT, WILLIAM (1920–   )

Canadian actor and director. Born in Toronto, Hutt received the Military Medal while serving with the Canadian Light Field Ambulance in the Second World War. A passion for the theatre was aroused while a soldier in *London; later he enrolled at the University of Toronto and acted in Hart House productions. He established his career in regional summer *stock at Bracebridge (1948) and Niagara Falls (1950–2) and worked with the Canadian Repertory Theatre, Ottawa (1952–4), during the winter. A member of the inaugural *Stratford Festival company in 1953, he was greatly influenced by Alec *Guinness, who starred in that season. With the Canadian Players between Stratford seasons, Hutt performed such major roles as Macbeth (1955), Hamlet (1956), and King Lear (1960), and earned his first major role at Stratford as Prospero in *The Tempest* (1962), where he has since played King Lear (1972, 1988, 1996), *Wilde's Lady Bracknell (1975, 1976, 1979), Falstaff (1978, 1995), the Fool opposite Peter

*Ustinov's Lear (1980), Titus Andronicus (1980), and James Tyrone in *O'Neill's *Long Day's Journey into Night* (1994). Although he has performed on Broadway and in *London's West End, he remains a bulwark of the Stratford stage, 'the great Canadian actor who stayed in Canada', playing more Shakespearian roles than *Olivier and *Gielgud combined. The first member of the Stratford company to direct at the festival, his *Waiting for Godot* (1968) was followed by *Much Ado About Nothing* (1971), *St Joan* (1975), and *Hamlet* (1976). Although he served as the *artistic director of Theatre London (Ontario) between 1976 and 1980, Hutt never achieved this post at the Stratford Festival.

PBON

HWANG, DAVID HENRY (1957–)

American playwright. The son of a Los Angeles Chinatown banker, Hwang wrote *FOB* ('fresh off the boat') in 1978, while still a student at Stanford University. It was produced *Off-Broadway in 1980. He subsequently wrote *The Dance and the Railroad* (1981), *Family Devotions* (1981), *House of Sleeping Beauties* (1983), and *The Sound of a Voice* (1983). These early plays featured *characters of Asian ancestry, and established Hwang as an important voice in the emerging genre of Asian-American literature. His most important work to date, *M. Butterfly* (1988), won numerous *awards including the Tony award for best play. Based on a true story of a French diplomat's relationship with a Chinese opera performer, who was later revealed to be a man, the play reworks the Madame Butterfly myth and attacks Western stereotypes of Asia. Since then, Hwang has written two *musicals (*One Thousand Airplanes on the Roof*, 1988, music by Philip *Glass; and *The Silver River*, 1997, music by Bright Sheng), an *opera (*The Voyage*, 1992, music by Glass), *Bondage* (1992), *Face Value* (1993), *Golden Child* (1996), and new adaptations of *Ibsen's *Peer Gynt* (1998) and *Rodgers and *Hammerstein's *Flower Drum Song* (2001). *See* ASIAN-AMERICAN THEATRE. JSM

HYMAN, EARLE (1926–)

American actor, who may have undertaken more Shakespearian *characters than any other contemporary *African-American actor. One of his earliest roles was the young boy in *Anna Lucasta* (1944), an American Negro Theatre production that started in the basement of the Schomburg Library in Harlem and travelled to Broadway and *London. In the 1950s, when he was also studying at Howard University, he was cast primarily in classical roles, including *Hamlet* and *Othello*, which he has played many times; in Oslo he was knighted when he performed *Othello* in Norwegian. He has also played Macbeth and King Lear. In 1988 Hyman was the solicitous chauffeur in the stage version of *Driving Miss Daisy*. Despite his classical work, he is more widely known for his cameo role on *The Cosby Show* as Russell Huxtable, Cosby's father. BBL

HYNES, GARRY (1953–)

Irish director. She graduated from University College Galway and co-founded *Druid Theatre Company in that city in 1975. Her work with Druid was interrupted when she became *artistic director of the *Abbey Theatre (1991–4), and she has also directed for the *Royal Shakespeare Company and the *Royal Court Theatre. Her compelling productions of Tom *Murphy, Martin *McDonagh, and Marina *Carr established the reputations of these writers. Her revivals of *Synge's *Playboy* and of *O'Casey's *The Plough and the Stars* challenged received opinions of *audiences and *critics, proposing new performance energies in the Irish canon. She won the Tony *award for best direction (for McDonagh's *The Beauty Queen of Leenane*) in 1998. CAL

HYTNER, NICHOLAS (1956–)

English director. Hytner's exuberant, moving, clear, and visually rich productions secured his reputation as an outstanding young director. His highly acclaimed debut for the *Royal Shakespeare Company (*Measure for Measure*, 1989), and in the ensuing year for the Royal *National Theatre (Joshua *Sobol's *Ghetto*), followed regional directing and work in *opera. His productions demonstrate considerable versatility: *musicals such as *Miss Saigon* (*Drury Lane, 1989) and *Carousel* (RNT, 1992); *operas such as *The Turn of the Screw* (*Sadler's Wells) when he was 20, and *Mozart's *La clemenza di Tito* (Glyndebourne, 1991 and 1995). An associate director of the RNT since 1989, his direction there of Alan *Bennett's *The Madness of George III* (1991) led to Oscar nominations for the subsequent *film. Other film credits include *Miller's *The Crucible* (1997). Hytner returned to the stage with productions of Shakespeare, Tennessee *Williams, and new writers Mark *Ravenhill and Martin *McDonagh. His interest in high art and showbiz is unusual. In 2001 he was appointed to succeed Trevor *Nunn as *artistic director of the RNT. KN

· I ·

IBSEN, HENRIK (1828–1906)

Norwegian playwright. Born in Skien, Ibsen was the son of a wealthy merchant, Knud Ibsen, whose business empire collapsed in 1835. Ibsen left home in 1843 to work as an apothecary's assistant in Grimstad, where he drafted his first play, *Catiline* (1849). When he left Grimstad in 1850 to enrol as a student in the capital (then called Christiania), he paid his last visit to his parents. Though he never contacted them again, refracted images of his parents appear in several of his later works, notably *The Wild Duck* and *John Gabriel Borkman*.

In Christiania Ibsen wrote *The Warrior's Barrow*, which was performed by the Christiania Theatre in 1850. In 1851 he gave up his studies to accept the post of assistant director at the newly founded National Theatre in Bergen, and during his six years there learnt how to make effective use of stage space. He continued writing plays in a national *romantic tradition, the most important being *Lady Inger of Østraat* (1855) and *The Feast at Solhaug* (1856). In 1857 Ibsen left Bergen to become *artistic director of the Norwegian Theatre in Christiania, and in the following year married Suzannah Thoresen. His years in the capital were a time of poverty and despair. His own theatre went bankrupt in 1862, after which he eked out a living as a literary adviser for a rival theatre. Despite these setbacks, he managed to write a light-hearted *satire, *Love's Comedy* (1862), and the last of his national romantic plays, *The Pretenders* (1863).

With the help of a state grant, Ibsen left Norway in 1864 to spend a year in *Rome, the beginning of a period of exile that was to last 27 years. The sense of relief he felt in leaving behind him a country and a life that had brought personal defeats unlocked his creative energies. In swift succession he wrote two magnificent *verse plays that brought him international recognition: *Brand* (1866) and *Peer Gynt* (1867). Both plays explore issues that were to become recurring concerns in Ibsen's later work: the tension between environmental determinism and human agency, and the demands of vocation juxtaposed with those of love. In 1868 Ibsen moved to Dresden, where he completed an edition of poems and a lengthy philosophical play, *Emperor and Galilean* (1873), in which he attempted to dramatize the clash between Christian and pagan thought centred around the *character of Julian the Apostate.

During the late 1870s he embarked on a new and decisive phase in his playwriting, aiming to address contemporary social issues in his work (*see* REALISM; NATURALISM). The first of these plays, *The Pillars of Society* (1877), is a caustic critique of contemporary capitalist entrepreneurs. In *A Doll's House* (1879) and *Ghosts* (1881) Ibsen subjected middle-class marriages to a remorseless process of deconstruction. He denied that he was a *feminist but he nevertheless highlighted the exploitation of women in a society that deprived them of any legal, property, or democratic rights. In response to the outrage these plays caused, Ibsen offered an ironic portrait in *An Enemy of the People* (1882) of an individual who, like himself, is hounded for telling the truth.

With *The Wild Duck* (1884) he began to exploit *symbolist techniques. The central symbol of the wild duck is associated with a number of the characters in the play, but above all with the young adolescent girl Hedvig who is driven to shoot herself by the selfish and inadequate behaviour of her father Hjalmar. After a brief visit to Norway in 1885, Ibsen wrote *Rosmersholm* (1886) and *The Lady from the Sea* (1888). *Rosmersholm* is arguably his most complex and subtle work and traces out the thwarted and lethal passion of two central characters who drive each other to suicide in a mill race. The last play Ibsen wrote during his exile, *Hedda Gabler* (1891), caused consternation to Ibsen's contemporaries by its use of comic effects to treat the serious issue of a woman responding violently and destructively when she finds herself trapped in a stifling middle-class marriage.

Ibsen's *Peer Gynt* in a Kannada adaptation called *Gundegowdana charitre*, Rangayana Theatre, Mysore, India, 1995, directed by Rustom Bharucha. Peer (Hulugappa Kattimani) in white suit encounters an Indian folk version of the Button Moulder (Manjunatha Belakere), a messenger of Yama, god of death, who appeared as a locksmith jangling his keys.

In the final group of plays, which Ibsen wrote after his return to Norway in 1891, he embraced elements of *expressionism in order to subject his own life as a creative artist to critical scrutiny. In *The Master Builder* (1892), *John Gabriel Borkman* (1896), and *When We Dead Awaken* (1899), he explored the conflicting demands of art and life, vocation and personal happiness, in ways which brought together realist and *dream-play techniques. All three express his own harsh judgement of himself as a man and artist. In 1900 Ibsen suffered the first of two strokes, which left him unable to write and increasingly paralysed and helpless.

Ibsen's characters create meaning or absurdity for themselves by the quality of their interaction. Often they succumb to environmental pressures, but he shows that human beings can use their will power to act freely. Nora leaves her doll's house marriage to find her real self, whereas Ellida Wangel in *The Lady from the Sea* decides to remain with her husband to make their marriage work. His plays do not provide neat solutions, and often leave questions provocatively unresolved. They are full of hidden resonances and richly layered *subtextual meanings, but a moral framework is implied in the *action and *audiences are invited to judge the behaviour of the characters by responding thoughtfully to the subtle and complex issues that are developed. Ibsen's plays have had a profound impact on twentieth-century playwrights concerned with social issues, notably Arthur

615

*Miller, but also writers as diverse as Edward *Bond and David *Hare.

Ibsen's plays effectively launched the naturalist movement in the theatre. William Bloch at the Theatre Royal, Copenhagen, André *Antoine in *Paris, and Vera *Komissarzhevskaya in *St Petersburg were just some of the outstanding directors who first presented detailed naturalist readings of his work. In 1906, a new generation of directors presented symbolist and expressionist readings: *Meyerhold in St Petersburg (*Hedda Gabler*), *Craig in Florence (*Rosmersholm*), and *Reinhardt in *Berlin (*Ghosts*). In these productions, stages were stripped of all naturalist detail to bring out the hidden resonances or inner symbolism of the plays. Productions in the inter-war years were marked by outstanding *acting performances rather than notable examples of director's theatre, but from the 1960s leading European directors offered a series of challenging interpretations. Ingmar *Bergman's 1964 *Stockholm production of *Hedda Gabler* used stark expressionist minimalism to bring out the anguished state of mind of the *protagonist. Peter *Stein presented a provocative Marxist version of *Peer Gynt* in Berlin (1971), and Peter *Hall presented a restrained emblematic reading of *John Gabriel Borkman* in *London (1975). In the 1980s and 1990s there have been postmodern productions based on ironic deconstruction of Ibsen's *texts (particularly in Germany), juxtaposed with some finely judged acting performances of a more traditional kind (notably in England and the USA). In particular, productions of *A Doll's House* have occasioned outstanding performances by actresses as diverse as Liv *Ullman (*New York, 1975), Cheryl Campbell (London, 1982), and Janet McTeer (London and New York, 1997). DT

MEYER, MICHAEL, *Ibsen* (Harmondsworth, 1974)
THOMAS, DAVID, *Henrik Ibsen* (London, 1983)

ICHIKAWA DANJŪRŌ IX (1838–1903)

*Kabuki actor, the fifth son of Danjūrō VII (*see* DANJŪRŌ FAMILY) and the leader of kabuki during the Meiji Period (1868–1912) in the transition from feudal to modern *Japan. An actor impressive in both voice and stature, he played a wide range of roles. In early Meiji he became a leader of kabuki reform, particularly with the Living History Play movement, for which he applied notions of psychological *realism to the interpretation of *characters. Later he and Onoe Kikūgorō V formed a popular acting combination and in 1887 they starred in the first kabuki plays to be seen by an emperor, part of Danjūrō's campaign to improve the social status of the art. From the late 1880s he emerged as a leader of a conservative movement, successfully preserving the authority of old families over upstart actors. When Living History Plays proved unpopular Danjūrō returned to the classics and enjoyed great success in both *dance pieces and dramatic plays, establishing his own 'New Eighteen Great Plays'. LRK

ICTUS

Chilean troupe created in 1955 which became the most important private theatre in *Santiago. The group's first works were experimental, such as *El velero en la botella* (*The Ship in the Bottle*, 1962), and dealt mainly with psychological and existentialist themes. At the end of the 1960s, in response to changes taking place in *Latin America, Ictus started to produce plays with socio-political overtones, such as *Díaz's *Topografía de un desnudo* (*Topography of a Naked Man*, 1967), and to develop *collective works that reflected Chile's cultural and social context. After the military coup of 1973 the group was obliged to reorient its style in order to avoid *censorship, and began producing metaphorical and *allegorical plays that referred obliquely to military repression. Works from this period include *Pedro Juan y Diego* (*Tom, Dick and Harry*, 1976, written in collaboration with David *Benavente), *¿Cuántos años tiene un día?* (*How Many Years Are in One Day?*, 1978), *Primavera con una esquina rota* (*Spring with a Broken Corner*, 1985, an adaptation of a novel by the Uruguayan Mario *Benedetti), and Carlos Cerda's *Lo que está en el aire* (*Written in the Wind*, 1986), which touches on the theme of the 'disappeared'. For several years Ictus produced a popular series called *La manivela* (*The Crank*). Since 1962 the company has had its own theatre, La Comedia, in the centre of Santiago. Many important theatrical figures have worked with Ictus, among them Carla *Cristi, Delfina *Guzmán, Jaime Zeledón, Claudio di Girolamo, and Nissim *Sharim. MAR

IDRIS, YUSSUF (1927–91)

Egyptian writer. Originally a physician, Idris is regarded today as the Egyptian short-story writer *par excellence*. Outstanding among his eight plays is *Al-Farafir* (*The Flipflaps*, 1964). With it and a series of articles entitled 'Towards an Egyptian Theatre' he rejected *illusionist European drama in favour of 'authentically Egyptian' performance traditions with more vigorous performer–*audience interaction. As alternatives Idris proposed *shadow theatre, *Karagöz, *folk *rituals, and *al-sāmir* (a peasant theatre-in-the-round (*see* ARENA AND IN-THE-ROUND) consisting of *acting, *music, and *dance). Though it now seems that *Al-Farafir* owes as much to *avant-garde European models as to any exclusively Egyptian tradition, Idris's contribution nonetheless paved the way for the post-1967 trends in Egypt that sought to rediscover indigenous art forms. *Al-Farafir* also occasioned the first Egyptian public dispute between a playwright and a director over the artistic control of production. HMA

IFFLAND, AUGUST WILHELM (1759–1814)

German *actor-manager and dramatist who began his career at the *Gotha Court Theatre under the tutelage of Konrad *Ekhof.

He moved to Mannheim in 1779 where he came to prominence as a major exponent of *realistic *acting (the 'Mannheim school'). During this time he began writing highly successful moralistic *comedies and *melodramas which rivalled those of *Kotzebue in popularity. In 1796 he assumed the directorship of the *Berlin Royal Theatre which he managed until 1813. He oversaw the building of the new Theater am Gendarmenmarkt (1802) and established *Berlin as a centre for German-speaking theatre, rivalling *Vienna's *Burgtheater. Following *Goethe's example at *Weimar, he performed a mixture of classical (Goethe, *Schiller, *Molière, *Voltaire, Shakespeare) and popular drama. He involved himself in all aspects of production from *dramaturgical adaptation to supervision of *rehearsals. As an actor he was particularly renowned for his Shakespearian roles, as a director for his productions of Schiller's plays.   CBB

IKHLASI, WALID (1935–)

Syrian writer. He established his reputation with a collection of short stories in 1963, followed by his first novel in 1965. In that same year he published two plays which pioneered *surrealistic and *absurdist techniques in the Syrian theatre. Thereafter he has written more than twenty other plays in a wide variety of styles, but is best known for his search for a drama rooted in Syrian culture in such work as *The Path* (1976) and *The Shrine of Ibrahim and Saffia* (1980).   MC

ILINSKY, IGOR (1901–87)

Russian/Soviet actor who began his career in *Moscow with *Komisarjevsky and *Foregger before joining *Meyerhold, with whom he worked, on and off, until 1935. A great comic actor, Ilinsky was an expert interpreter of Meyerhold's *acting techniques, seen to startling effect as the frenetically jealous Bruno, in Crommelynck's *The Magnanimous Cuckold* (1922), as the comic actor Schastlivtsev in *Ostrovsky's *The Forest* (1924), as the naive, bourgeoisified Prisypkin in *Mayakovsky's *The Bedbug* (1929), and as the pathetic Raspluyev in *Sukhovo-Kobylin's *Krechinsky's Wedding* (1933). The rest of his career was spent at the Moscow *Maly Theatre, where in his 80th year he gave a three-hour performance as *Tolstoy. Ilinsky was an actor of extraordinary versatility, charm, and energy. Whether playing Byvalov, in the *film comedy *Volga-Volga* (1938), or the tragic role of the peasant Akim, in Tolstoy's *The Power of Darkness* (1956), his talent was inimitable and uniquely Russian.   NW

ILLUSION

The aesthetic experience which is generated when a representation has the appearance of being true or real and when recipients respond to it as such. Illusion is thus the product of an interaction influenced by a range of variables, including the artistic media and social context involved. Renaissance (*early modern) architects fostered pictorial illusion by means of optical tricks such as *perspective settings, borders, *flats and wings, and the *proscenium arch which masked the offstage space and its machinery (*see* SCENOGRAPHY). Due to the development of a materialist conception of reality, embodied in nineteenth-century *realism, illusion became increasingly characterized by an emphasis on historically accurate replication and the further removal of features, including visible *footlights and spectators, which drew attention to the artifice of the stage event.

Despite its prominence in the age of reproductive technology, empiricist replication is not the only mode of illusion. According to the *neoclassical idea of *vraisemblance*, believable drama represented what ought and what was normally (or socially) expected to happen. In line with *romanticism, S. T. Coleridge gave greater emphasis to the role of imagination, famously claiming that illusion requires 'a willing suspension of disbelief', the recipient voluntarily relinquishing the impulse to judge and compare with external reality. By contrast, commentators such as *Diderot have regarded the spectator's participation as an involuntary response to sensory and emotional arousal. The spectator's identification with *character is a major source of such arousal, one supposedly enhanced when the actor maintains the illusion of a fourth wall by performing as if sealed in the character's world and unaware of the *audience beyond the playing space.

Since the advent of realism, there have been numerous challenges to the modes of illusion associated with it. While the *symbolists replaced detailed attention to surface appearance with abstract expression of an ideal essence, *Brecht used *Verfremdung* (distancing) to expose imitation and fourth-wall illusionism as tools for preserving the bourgeois status quo (*see* EPIC THEATRE; BOURGEOIS THEATRE). Brecht argued that a focus on character-centred identification and linear *plot encouraged a passive self-indulgent spectator with a fatalist outlook, one whose ability to reflect critically on social reality was inhibited. While his self-reflexive use of *Verfremdung* is sometimes described as anti-illusionist, to draw attention to the process of illusion making is itself an attempt to give the appearance of being true or real. Whenever makers of representation engage with conceptions of reality and art's relation to it, they by definition contribute to the constitution of illusion. *See also* POLITICS AND THEATRE; VISION AND THE VISUAL.   MM

IMBUGA, FRANCIS (1947–)

Kenyan director and playwright. Trained in Nairobi and Iowa, Imbuga started writing *television scripts in the 1970s, and his early plays like *The Fourth Trial* (1972) and *The Married Bachelor* (1973) maintained a TV style of domestic *comedy. With

Betrayal in the City (1976), *The Successor* (1979), and *Man of Kafira* (1984), he turned to *political issues of social unease, crisis of leadership, and corruption. His work is based on current events and well-known political figures, designed 'to tell the truth laughingly', as the director John Ruganda has said. Imbuga has taught theatre at Kenyatta University in Nairobi and now works for the UN in Rwanda.   EB

IMITATION *See* MIMESIS.

IMMERMANN, KARL LEBERECHT (1796–1840)

German director, dramatist, and novelist. As a Prussian official in Düsseldorf, Immermann established the first municipal theatre there, pursuing a literary repertoire based on *Goethe's model at the *Weimar Court Theatre. Preferred dramatists were Shakespeare, *Calderón, Goethe, *Schiller, and *Kleist. Although this undertaking was short-lived (1835–7) and closed for financial reasons, Immermann's philosophy of theatre was influential. His approach to production called for a cohesive vision unifying *textual and *scenographic exigencies, which enhanced the status of the director. He stressed ensemble playing over virtuoso *acting and insisted on extensive *rehearsals. In 1840 he mounted *Twelfth Night* on a stage built to his specifications that combined elements of the Elizabethan *open stage with an Italian pictorial one. His dramatic output is largely derivative; only *Merlin* (1832), and *Andreas Hofer* (1834) have been revived.   CBB

IMPROVISATION

Unscripted *acting in which the performers collectively make up the story or situation as they go, or collectively try to carry out a specified difficult performance in the presence of the *audience. There have been many kinds of improvisational theatre through the centuries. *Commedia dell'arte* is probably the best known among the Western traditions, but most comic or *clown traditions have allowed the performer to establish rapport through improvised jokes and patter, as Hamlet complains in his instruction to the Players to speak only what he wrote for them. Almost any performance involving direct interaction with the audience must have an improvisational content. But improvisation as a separate form of theatre was formalized through acting exercises in the United States and Britain in the mid- and later twentieth century, especially as popularized by Viola Spolin's *Improvisation for the Theater* (1963). In general the form relies on structuring the *action into games or conventionalized rules that somewhat resemble *commedia* *scenarios or the old *lines of business. For example, actors may be required to begin all lines of *dialogue with successive letters of the alphabet, working from a specified A to a specified Z, while trying to maintain a coherent story; or a *scene may start with two *characters, with more added progressively, each character bringing some additional *exposition or *complication for the others to cope with. The audience's interest is not in the improbable situation but in whether or not the actors will carry it off with panache and grace, making it look easy. Some companies have specialized in improvised performance, such as Second City in *Chicago.   JB

INBA

Spanish acronym for the National Institute of Fine Arts of Mexico, established in 1947. Its creation marked the post-revolutionary government's first coherent programme to fund the arts and was a recognition of the need to transform *Mexico City, then with less than 1 million inhabitants, into a major cultural centre. With INBA's largesse, playwrights and directors could experiment without the pressure of the *box office. During its early years INBA promoted then-unknown playwrights such as Emilio *Carballido and Sergio *Magaña, who would go on to become major figures. While INBA continues to play an important role in theatre, it has become progressively more bureaucratized, subject to political and economic fallout, and has lost its centrality to other agencies such as the National Council for the Arts and Culture. While it still produces plays, it does not own a variety of suitable venues.   KFN

INCHBALD, ELIZABETH (1753–1821)

English actress and author. Despite a lifelong stutter, at the age of 19 Inchbald began acting on the provincial stage, establishing a large and diverse repertory of roles, such as Fanny in *Colman and *Garrick's *The Clandestine Marriage*, Hermione in *The Winter's Tale*, and Louisa Dudley in *Cumberland's *The West Indian*. She acted at *Covent Garden throughout the 1780s, adding important roles like Mrs Fainall in *Congreve's *The Way of the World* and Imoinda in *Oroonoko*. She was tall, beautiful, and (although self-taught) highly intelligent. Realizing that she could not achieve great fame on the *London stage, she left off acting at the age of 37 and devoted herself to writing. Her original plays, such as *The Child of Nature* (1788) and *Everyone Has his Fault* (1793), and her translations of *Kotzebue, often explore important social issues, eschewing easy sentimentality while expressing great sympathy for the oppressed. She edited collections of plays, Bell's *British Theatre* (25 volumes, 1806–9), and *The Modern Theatre* (10 volumes, 1809).   MJK

INDEPENDENT THEATRE

Private society founded by J. T. *Grein in *London in 1891. Its name advertised imitation of André *Antoine's Théâtre *Libre

The washerwomen in a Punjabi translation of García Lorca's *Yerma*, staged by the Company at Bharat Bhavan, Bhopal, **India**, 1993, directed by Neelam Man Singh Chowdhry. Crossing borders with vibrant reinventions of European classics, the Company (based in Chandigarh, Punjab) includes actors from urban backgrounds and *naqqals* (traditional ballad singers and female impersonators), who are featured in this picture.

(1887) in *Paris and Otto *Brahm's *Freie Bühne (1889) in *Berlin. Like Brahm, the Independent Theatre chose *Ibsen's *Ghosts* for its inaugural production, a single performance at the Royalty Theatre in March 1891. The society's 22 productions included English premières of two further plays by Ibsen (*The Master Builder* in 1893, *The Wild Duck* in 1894) and also *Shaw's first play (*Widowers' Houses*, 1892). Aiming 'to give special performances of plays which have a *literary* and *artistic*, rather than a commercial value', the Independent Theatre was organized as a producing society: membership subscriptions, paid in advance of production, both provided capital and permitted performances to be deemed private and thus disregarded by the *Lord Chamberlain's Examiner of Plays. After a *financial crisis in 1894, the Independent Theatre survived through 1898 by incorporating and thereby limiting the liability of its members. With or without this protective modification, similar organiza-

tion was adopted by others determined to present plays which, being restricted in appeal or controversial in subject matter, were unlikely to be staged in a commercial theatre economically driven by *long runs and legally subject to pre-*censorship. *See also* STAGE SOCIETY.
MOC

INDIA

Any attempt to encapsulate the prodigious diversities of the Indian subcontinent has to take into account its multilingualism, consisting of eighteen constitutionally recognized languages from at least four families of languages—Indo-European, Dravidian, Tibeto-Burman, Austro-Asiatic—and eight scripts. India also has numerous religions, including Buddhism, Hinduism, Jainism, and Sikhism, that originated in India, along with religions from outside the country like Christianity, Islam, and Zoroastrianism, which have been indigenized over centuries. Above all, India's vast population of more than 1.3 billion people incorporates numerous communities, castes, sects, and indigenous peoples, all of which have contributed to the scale and range of its diverse cultural legacies.

Along with these diversities, however, there are also considerable differences that need to be acknowledged in any cultural study of India. At the linguistic level itself, there have been considerable tensions whereby the politics of individual languages precipitated the formation of distinct regional states from the late 1950s onwards, so that *Tamil, for instance, is identified with the state of Tamil Nadu, *Marathi with Maharashtra, *Kannada with Karnataka, and so on. The acceptance of *Hindi as the 'national language' of the country is still a matter of considerable dispute, while English, spoken by less than 5 per cent of the population, continues to be used as an official link-language, along with Hindi, in Parliament and the courts. The disparities are even more marked when one considers that India commands an increasingly powerful role in the global market of information technology, even as a large percentage of the population remains illiterate. With the intensification of sub-national and secessionist movements, particularly in the northern and north-eastern borders of the country, India's nationalist credo of 'unity in diversity' has been increasingly challenged in recent years, thereby provoking new readings of its 'imagined community'.

Within the contradictions of *post-colonial India, it becomes obvious that the attempt to uphold a unitary or synoptic vision of 'Indian theatre' is bound to fail, or succumb to the worst kind of reductionism and simplification. Without the necessary qualification, 'Indian theatre' can be perceived as a monolithic category, with an all-encompassing capacity to subsume the traditional, devotional, *folk, and contemporary traditions of Indian performance over three millennia. Not only does this risk essentializing a vast spectrum of practices independently of their distinct social, economic, and political contexts, it also elides the specific mutations of intersecting and diverse historical processes.

In this regard, one of the traps in mapping Indian theatre has been to duplicate the notorious colonial division of Indian history into three distinct periods—Hindu, Muslim, British. Within this framework, the first period inevitably connotes a nationalist affirmation of Indian cultural authenticity; the second suggests the communal implications of foreign invasion and the subsequent diffusion, dilution, and distortion of 'Indian' identity; and the third gets equated with the dubious benefits of modernity. It is not uncommon, therefore, to come across readings of Indian theatre in which the authentic past is associated with *Sanskrit drama, a legacy that was disrupted by the 'Muslim invasion' around the tenth century AD, only to be replaced by a colonial *dramaturgy instituted by the British from the late eighteenth century onwards. Even within the crudities

of such a chronology, there are empirical inconsistencies, not least because the so-called living traditions of Indian theatre and performance, in both the classical and folk sectors, have survived over centuries. Indeed, they have coexisted and interacted in diverse ways with the processes of modernization, industrialization, and secularization that are far from being uniform in all parts of the country.

Countering the restrictive chronology of Indian performance traditions, therefore, it is more accurate to acknowledge the multiple times embodied in the individual traditions themselves. Take, for example, the highly refined Sanskrit performance tradition of *kutiyattam in Kerala, which has a continuous tradition of more than ten centuries, whose transmission has been more or less regulated until very recently within the confines of the cakyar community. Far from being a relic from the past—a mere affirmation of the 'intangible' world heritage status that it received from UNESCO in 2000—kutiyattam is a dynamic and highly tangible performance tradition that is performed on a regular basis. Likewise, there is concrete evidence of performance traditions from the fifteenth and sixteenth centuries as well, including different manifestations of theatre as a form of worship (bhakti). Drawing on the lives of Hindu gods like Rama and Krishna, popular theatrical forms like *krishnattam (Kerala), *ankiya nat (Assam), and *dashavatar (Maharashtra) continue to reach out to vast sections of the population. While the devotional content in celebrations like *Ram lila, *ras lila, Krishna lila in the northern parts of India continues to be strong, other popular *genres like *yakshagana (Karnataka) have become increasingly more secularized in their retelling of stories from the Mahabharata and Ramayana.

Not only is the evidence of these performance traditions intrinsically related to specific techniques and conventions, it is also closely linked to the lives of communities and the social organization of festivals and *rituals. Krishnattam, for instance, is staged every night at the Guruvayur temple in Kerala for pilgrims, while the Ram lila is unfailingly celebrated every year during the Dussehra festival with massive community support in small towns like Ramnagar near Banaras. Yet another source of textual evidence put forward by scholars for the continuities of Indian performance traditions relates to the *Natyasastra (c. second century BC–second century AD). This ancient Sanskrit encyclopedia of dramaturgy, *acting, *dance, *music, and *spectacle is sometimes regarded as providing Indian theatre with an overall conceptual framework. To a large extent this is true when one considers the generic categories defined in this monumental text attributed to the sage *Bharata (but more likely to have been compiled over the centuries by a body of scholars). Traditionally viewed in orthodox circles as the Natyaveda, an additional scripture to the four existing Vedas, the Natyasastra advocated the use of natya (a composite form of dance, drama, and music) as an emotional diversion. Far from being didactic or exclusionary, it was regarded as a form of entertainment accessible not only to the gods but to all people, regardless of their class or caste.

Despite the highly mythologized *origins of natya, the actual contribution of Bharata's text lies in its meticulous codification not only of dramatic structure (which is *Aristotle's point of emphasis in the Poetics), but of the most highly crystallized categories of performance (which Aristotle does not address). In effect, one does not consult the Natyasastra merely to verify details of dramaturgy in the plays of Sanskrit playwrights like *Bhasa, *Kalidasa, *Sudraka, *Bhavabhuti, *Visakhadatta, and *Mahendravikramavarman, one turns to Bharata's text to seek discriminations of *angika (body), *vacika (voice), *sattvika (inner emotional states), *aharya (*costumes, *make-up), all of which constitute the crucial art of *abhinaya (acting). Supplemented by the minutiae of *hastas (hand gestures), among other physical (and psychophysical) manifestations involving the eyes, eyebrows, neck, and facial expressions, the codification of acting in the Natyasastra contributes towards a reading of *rasa (literally, 'flavour, taste'), the aesthetic pleasure of a performance in which the spectator and actor participate at a heightened imaginative level. (See ABHINAVAGUPTA and NANDIKESWARA for elaboration on rasa.)

The Natyasastra elaborates primarily on the *natyadharmi (stylized) dimensions of acting, while the *lokadharmi elements (which refer specifically to loka, the world) are left uncodified. Inevitably, the so-called *'realistic' dimensions of acting involving *improvisation, horseplay, grotesquerie, buffoonery, and allusions to real life, so evident in the rich repertoire of folk theatrical forms—*bhavai (Gujarat), *mach (Madhya Pradesh), *bidesia (Bihar), *karyala (Himachal Pradesh), *khayal (Rajasthan)—cannot be said to draw on the Natyasastra directly. At a broad level, however, it could be argued that almost all traditional performances in India follow a certain format set forth in the Natyasastra: the ritualistic preliminaries of the purvaranga (introduction), the entrance of the *sutradhara (literally, 'string-holder', the *director-like figure who coordinates the entire performance through his commentary), his recitation of the nandi (invocation), announcement of the play, and so on. But considerable regional, linguistic, and histrionic variations exist within these conventions—for instance, the jester-like *character of the *vidushaka, so prominent in Sanskrit drama, has numerous avatars in the folk drama of India, such as the *kattiyakaran (in the *terukkuttu, literally 'street theatre' performances of Tamil Nadu), the ranglo (the *clown-like character in the bhavai of Gujarat), the *bhands and *naqqals of Punjab. Not only do these comic characters display a vastly different repertoire of satirical idioms, directed at contemporary society and *politics, they also have highly localized caste loyalties, which counter the implicitly brahmanic discourse of the vidushaka.

The problem of categorizing the 'folk' (which is itself a European invention that cannot be separated from the gradual disappearance of traditional artisan communities in Europe following the Industrial Revolution) has much to do with the fact that folk cultures are still alive in India today. Far from exemplifying antiquarian and revivalist notions of dying indigenous skills, the 'folk' have interacted with contemporary art forms and practices so much so that it is difficult at times to determine whether the folk is not another version of the contemporary. Thus, *jatra, the *Bengali folk opera that is said to have originated in religious processions of the fifteenth to sixteenth centuries, has been secularized over the years, through the nationalist political interventions of writers/composers like Mukunda Das in the early decades of the twentieth century, followed by more revolutionary manifestations in the 1960s when jatra stars like Shantigopal played Lenin and Stalin, followed in turn by new icons of global capitalism as transmitted through recent narratives like Jurassic Park. Today jatra (in West Bengal at least) is more accurately described as a form of rural and mofussil (small town) entertainment, not unlike the enormously popular spectacles of *mobile theatre in Assam, whose narratives, drawing on the *film Titanic, among other blockbusters, draw vast crowds in the remotest of villages.

Just as some traditions of the folk have been contemporized through a process of secularization, it could be argued that the *proscenium theatre, branded as a colonial importation, has also been indigenized since it was first introduced by the maverick Russian bandmaster and linguist Herasim Lebedeff, who is said to have collaborated in Calcutta (*Kolkata) on a Bengali adaptation of an English play in 1795. Ostracized from entering British *playhouses like the Playhouse in Calcutta, the first proscenium theatre built exclusively for the British in 1753, the Indian elite staged spectacles in their own homes—for example, the Bengali aristocrat Nabin Chandra Basu staged a lavish production of Bidya Sundar in 1835; the ruler of Awadh, Wajid Ali Shah (1822–87), had his own musical dance-drama Radha Kanhaiya ka Qissa (The Tale of Radha and Krishna, 1843) staged in his court. These exclusive private entertainments continued till the 1850s, when Vishnudas Bhave, the author of the first Marathi play Sita Swayamvar (The Wedding of Sita, 1843), staged the first ticketed show of Marathi theatre in Bombay (*Mumbai) in 1853 at the Grant Road Theatre. In that very year, Ram Narayan Tarkaratna won a competition in Calcutta for Kulin-kulasarbasva, a social play on the evils of polygamy practised by Kulin Brahmans—a new kind of work which indicated the growing interest in theatre as a site for social and political debate.

From the 1850s onwards, there is evidence of an emergent secular consciousness in theatre in different parts of India, as in the anti-traditionalist Bengali social satires of Michael Madhusudan *Dutt, like his highly irreverent *comedy Ekei ki Bale Sabhyata (Is this Civilization?, 1860). In Madras (Chennai) as well, there were plays focusing on social realities like Thashildar Natakam (The Drama of the Village Officer, 1868) and P. V. Ramaswamy Raj's Prathapa Chandra Vilasam (The

House of Prathapa Chandra, 1879). By 1872, the Bengali theatre staged its first ticketed performance in Calcutta of a somewhat radical play featuring the plight of Indian peasants oppressed by British indigo planters—Dinabandhu *Mitra's *Nil Darpan* (*Indigo Mirror*, translated by Madhusadan Dutt and published by Revd James Long in 1861). In a more literary register, some highly original plays in Hindi by Bharatendu *Harishchandra like *Vishashya Vishaumaushadham* (*Poison as the Antidote of Poison*) and *Andher Nagari* (*Lawless Town*) were written, even though they were not staged professionally.

The reason often given for the dearth of staged performances of Harishchandra's plays is the commercial dominance of the *Parsi theatre, a phenomenon that had emerged in the 1850s through the enterprising leadership and *financial patronage provided by the mercantile Parsi community in Maharashtra and Gujarat, who promoted an unabashedly entertainment-oriented theatre, full of song, dance, and spectacle inspired by the proscenium conventions and stage effects of *melodramas and *pantomime performed at *Drury Lane and *Covent Garden in late nineteenth-century *London. An all-India phenomenon, the Parsi theatre inspired the emergence of similar companies in different parts of the country like the famous Gubbi Company in Karnataka masterminded by Gubbi *Veranna, resulting in many variants of Company Natak (*Company Theatre) in different Indian languages.

While Parsi theatre was flourishing in the nineteenth century, it influenced any number of derivations like the *sangeet natak* (musical theatre) of Maharashtra, which was initiated through an 1880 musical version of *Shakuntala* by Annasaheb *Kirloskar. This resulted in the phenomenon of singer-actors, most notably the legendary *female impersonator *Balgandharva, based in Pune, Maharashtra, who was a model of femininity for Indian women in the early twentieth century, along with a lesser known but no less subtle impersonator from Gujarat, Jaishanker *Sundari. In a more realist register, the musical folk form of *sannata* from Karnataka was used to dramatize highly explosive contemporary events, such as adultery and murder, in plays like *Sangya Balya* (c.1880), which is often regarded as the first modern Kannada play. The social and historical inputs of the Bengali playwright-actor-producer Girish Chandra *Ghosh are also significant. His nationalist historical play on *Sirajuddaula* (1905) was banned by the British government under the *Dramatic Performances Act of 1876. In Maharashtra, K. P. Khadilkar's *Keechaka Vadh* (*The Killing of Keechaka*, 1907), which critiqued the Bengal partition through an allegorical treatment of an episode from the *Mahabharata*, was also banned in 1910. Such blatant acts of *censorship indicate that the British colonial administration regarded theatre as a potentially volatile political force.

With the advent of the talkies in the early 1930s, the seductive lure of Parsi theatre was greatly reduced. New *amateur theatre groups emerged, exploring regional and social issues within the contexts of specific languages. (*See* individual entries on BENGALI THEATRE; HINDI THEATRE; KANNADA THEATRE; MANIPURI THEATRE; MARATHI THEATRE; PUNJABI THEATRE; TAMIL THEATRE; TELUGU THEATRE.) Inevitably, the intensification of the nationalist movement from the late 1930s, accompanied by affiliations to anti-fascist and anti-imperialist struggles worldwide, led to the creation of India's first national cultural movement through the organization of the *Indian People's Theatre Association in 1943. Sponsored by the Communist Party of India in different regional centres, IPTA coordinated and directed the talents of a broad section of democratically inclined artists, including budding composers like Ravi Shankar and choreographers like Shanti Bardhan, who *toured the villages and cities of India with people's *ballets ('patriotic pageants'). The more radical theatrical interventions involved the politicization of folk forms like the ballad tradition of *powada* in the working-class districts and factories of Maharashtra, and the *burrakatha* in Andhra Pradesh. For its advocacy of critical realism, IPTA is best remembered for its landmark production of Bijon *Bhattacharya's *Nabanna* (*New Harvest*, 1944) on the man-made famine of Bengal, which killed more than 3 million people. Bhattacharya's co-director was Sombhu *Mitra, who broke away from IPTA to form one of the pioneering amateur theatre companies in post-independence India, Bohurupee, famous for its productions of *Tagore's masterpieces *Raja* and *Rakta-karabi* (*Red Oleander*).

These amateur theatre groups spread all over India from the mid-1950s through the 1960s. They included the Little Theatre Group (later, the People's Little Theatre), headed by the actor-director-playwright Utpal *Dutt, and Nandikar in Calcutta; Rangayan (directed by Vijaya Mehta in Bombay), from which Arvind and Sulabha Deshpande split to create Awishkar; and the Naya Theatre founded by Habib *Tanvir in collaboration with tribal actors from the Chhattisgarh region of Madhya Pradesh. Apart from Dutt, who specialized in staging his own plays, most of these groups experimented with adaptations of European plays, notably by *Brecht, *Ionesco, *Pirandello, *Sartre, *Beckett, in addition to the plays of contemporary Indian playwrights like Badal *Sircar, Mohan *Rakesh, Vijay *Tendulkar, and Girish *Karnad. While the last three are remembered for their dramaturgical breakthroughs, Sircar is valued for his plays and his initiation of the Third Theatre movement. Committed to 'poor theatre', not only in its elimination of *scenery, *lights, costumes, make-up, but in its advocacy of a free theatre performed in open public spaces, this movement has clearly inspired a vast number of *street theatre groups in India, of which Janam in New Delhi is one of the most prominent, not least because its communist director Safdar *Hashmi was murdered following the disruption of a performance in 1989.

Countering the political immediacy of street theatre and Third Theatre, there have been other theatrical interventions sponsored by established cultural institutions, like the *Sangeet Natak Akademi (founded 1953). Prominent among these initiatives has been the attempt to revive and reinvent traditional Indian theatre and folk forms, ostensibly inspired by the *Natyasastra*, within the framework of the 'theatre of roots'. While the names of prominent directors like B. V. *Karanth (Rangayana), Kavalam Narayana *Pannikkar (Sopanam), and Ratan *Thiyam (Chorus Repertory Theatre) are often included in this category, they have staged their productions primarily in proscenium theatres, adapting their affinities to traditional narratives and acting traditions, folk music, and martial-arts training within specifically *modernist approaches to Indian theatre. All these directors have been closely associated with the *National School of Drama which has produced a large number of India's most prominent actors and directors, but criticized for continuing to focus on acting exclusively in the Hindi language, thereby marginalizing other languages (and cultures) of the country. Some new theatre schools like the *Ninasam Theatre Institute, based in the village of Heggodu in Karnataka, and drama departments like the School of Drama in Trissur (Kerala) and Thanjavur (Tamil Nadu) have attempted to counter this 'Hindi nationalism' by offering *training in other languages.

Apart from the absence of adequate training programmes for contemporary urban theatre practitioners across the country, unlike established training centres for traditional performances like *kathakali at the *Kerala Kalamandalam (1930), there is also an acute dearth of professional repertory companies where contemporary actors can hone their skills and earn a living by making theatre. Regional companies like Bharat Bhawan in Bhopal (Madhya Pradesh) and Rangayana in Mysore (Karnataka) have been plagued with administrative and political problems. Most theatre workers in India function as amateurs, which means that theatre remains essentially a part-time activity, restricted to evening *rehearsals after a day's work in an office or school or bank. Yet it is still possible for a commercial house like Shivaji Mandir in Mumbai to run three different productions a day, seven days a week.

The internationalization of Indian theatre has been largely restricted to a few impresario figures, notably Ratan Thiyam, who is sometimes accused of catering to an international *festival aesthetic with his allegedly exotic use of martial arts (*thang-ta) and neo-Vaishnavite spectacle. Indian performance techniques drawn from traditional forms like *kathakali* have also been adapted over the years by European directors like Jerzy *Grotowski, Eugenio *Barba, and Ariane *Mnouchkine. More recently, the Kerala martial arts tradition of *kalarippayattu and the underlying martial principles of the dance-theatre tradition of *chhau from Orissa have also been adapted by scholar-practitioners like Phillip Zarrilli and choreographer-dancers like Chandralekha, Daksha Sheth, Ileana Citaristi, and Maya Rao for intercultural workshops and *training programmes. The adaptation of traditional Indian narratives, not-

ably the *Mahabharata* directed by Peter *Brook, has also opened critical issues on the politics and ethics of *intercultural exchange, its relationship with cultural tourism and the global economy. Most Indian theatre workers are unaware not only of what is happening outside the country—there are, as yet, no international theatre festivals held in India—but, more critically, of what is going on within and across the linguistic regions of different states.

Beyond a few national theatre festivals in New Delhi and the state capitals, the Nandikar theatre festival in Kolkata, and very poorly organized regional festivals administered by the Zonal Cultural Centres, there is no sustained infrastructure for intracultural exchanges both within and across the borders of regional states. Translations of plays across Indian languages remain restricted. Knowledge of traditional forms remains increasingly limited to specific regions. A performer of *teyyam from Kerala may never have heard of, still less seen, a performance of ankiya nat from Assam; a bhand (clown) from Punjab could be totally unaware of *bhand pather from Jammu and Kashmir, itself a state under political siege where traditional performances are almost disappearing. In contrast, the ubiquity of the army and the seething intertribal tensions in border states like Manipur have not undermined the sheer vitality of its diverse theatre culture, including the spectacles of Ratan Thiyam, the intensely lyrical performance pieces of Heisnam *Kanhailal, the reflective mythic-historical productions of Lokendra Arambam, *shumang lila performances, and the ancient festival of the *lai-haraoba, whose ritual genealogy can be traced back to more than two millennia. In Manipur alone, there is evidence of the range and depth of all the diversities that constitute Indian theatre, even though this state is politically estranged from the rest of India. Rather than a nationalist monolith, 'Indian theatre' is better understood as a spectrum of differentiated practices, cutting across time, language, and context.   RB

Bharucha, Rustom, *Theatre and the World: performance and the politics of culture* (London, 1993)

Byrski, M. Christopher, *Concept of Ancient Indian Theatre* (New Delhi, 1974)

Jacob, Paul (ed.), *Contemporary Indian Theatre* (New Delhi, 1989)

Japan Foundation, *Dance and Music in South Asian Drama* (Tokyo, 1983)

Lal, Ananda, and Dasgupta, Chidananda (eds.), *Rasa: the Indian performing arts in the last twenty-five years*, vol. ii (Calcutta, 1995)

Schechner, Richard, *Performative Circumstances from the Avant Garde to Ramlila* (Calcutta, 1983)

Vatsyayan, Kapila, *Traditional Indian Theatre: multiple streams* (New Delhi, 1980)

INDIAN PEOPLE'S THEATRE ASSOCIATION

Society of performing artists formed at communist initiative in 'defence of culture against Fascism and Imperialism', in the organization's own words, and to make art 'at once the expression and organizer of our people's struggle for freedom, cultural progress and economic justice'. The name was inspired by Romain *Rolland's book *People's Theatre*. IPTA's Bangalore unit was formed in 1941, Bombay (*Mumbai) in 1942, and the all-India organization in May 1943. Its immediate antecedents were the European anti-fascist movements and the Progressive Writers' Association (formed 1936) in *India. IPTA provided a model of organized cultural activism that combined an emphasis on *realism, in the footsteps of *Gorky, with the need to revitalize traditional *'folk' arts. Many theatre persons, music composers, singers, dancers, and filmmakers came into IPTA, and in the 1940s its membership was a virtual Who's Who of the Indian cultural scene. IPTA's best-known productions were Bijon *Bhattacharya's play *Nabanna* (*New Harvest*, co-directed by the playwright and Sombhu *Mitra, 1943), and Jyotindra Moitra's song series *Nabajibaner Gaan* (*Song of the New Life*, 1944). There was also considerable *agitprop theatre in urban working-class areas and the countryside. IPTA's influence was strongest in Bengal, Maharashtra, Andhra Pradesh, Punjab, Kerala, Assam, and Orissa. It provided a galaxy of talent for the Mumbai *film industry, and produced the feature film *Dharti Ke Lal* (*Sons of the Soil*, 1946). IPTA's decline began in the mid-1950s, and in spite of its network of units, which still exist in some states, and despite a short-lived revival at the time of its golden jubilee (1993–4) when many new units arose, the decline has continued. In retrospect, perhaps IPTA's greatest achievements were to make current the idea that (as IPTA put it) 'art forms . . . should cater to the needs of the toiling and suffering people', and to inspire *politically committed cultural groups.

SD

atre's production of *Tagore's *The Post Office* (*Dublin, 1913), probably the world première in English of an Indian play: the Bengali original was not staged till 1917. Among the many Indian students in England, Niranjan Pal founded the Indian Players, who performed his English scripts in *London during the 1920s; and T. P. *Kailasam, after returning to India, wrote drama both in *Kannada and English.

After independence, *closet drama in English increased greatly, much of it composed in *verse, until Asif Currimbhoy pioneered contemporary Indian-English drama in the 1960s with nearly 30 diverse plays on domestic, social, historical, and *political themes, among them at least a dozen major works. His *The Doldrummers* (1961) was banned in Bombay for vulgarity of language and a too-candid portrayal of frustrated youth. The epic sweep of his later plays, treating China's annexation of Tibet or the liberation of Bangladesh, was too difficult technically for Indian-English theatre and they were not staged. Most English-language groups were content to serve the complacent tastes of the metropolitan upper crust by offering standard Western fare. Only a handful experimented with original drama in English: the Theatre Group in Bombay under Alyque Padamsee; the Madras Players, who had in their ranks the playwright Girish *Karnad (who translates his own work into English); the Oskars in Calcutta who staged Currimbhoy; and Yatrik in Delhi. Yet at the end of the century in Bombay, a proliferation of bedroom comedies in a patois of Hindi and English made English-language theatre commercially viable. And Mahesh Dattani won the Sahitya Akademi *award, India's most prestigious literary prize, for *Final Solutions* (1993), on the Hindu–Muslim riots, certifying that English drama had found official recognition.

AL

INDIAN THEATRE IN ENGLISH

Theatre in *India in the English language pre-dates all the *proscenium traditions in the Indian languages. The British constructed the first modern *playhouses for their own communities in the fortified port towns: the Playhouse (Calcutta, 1753; *see* KOLKATA) and the Bombay Theatre (1776; *see* MUMBAI), playing *amateur versions of Shakespeare and English Restoration and eighteenth-century *comedies. Possibly the first Indian to publish a play in English was Krishna Mohan Banerji, whose *The Persecuted* (1831) depicted 'the Present State of Hindoo Society in Calcutta'. After English became India's official medium of education in 1835, Indian students began to act *scenes from English drama in college, but Indians did not break the *race barrier until 1848, when a Bengali gentleman, Baishnab Charan Auddy, acted a 'real unpainted nigger Othello' in an otherwise British production. In 1859 the eminent *Bengali playwright Michael Madhusudan *Dutt translated his own *Sarmishta* into English, which might qualify as original drama in English. Milestones outside India included the *Abbey The-

INDONESIA

The Republic of Indonesia consists of more than 17,500 islands, populated by over 300 different ethnic groups, each with its distinct language, culture, and uniquely regional characteristics. Indonesian theatre *genres reflect these diverse cultural traits: regional theatre forms utilize regional languages, such as Balinese, Javanese, Sundanese, and Minang, while Indonesian modern theatre and *film employ the national language, Bahasa Indonesia. Throughout its history Indonesia has gradually assimilated aspects of many outside cultures, in particular those of *India, *China, Arabia, Portugal, the Netherlands, *Malaysia, and, later, America. For centuries prior to colonization by the Dutch, the patronage of the royal courts on the islands of Java and Bali helped cultivate indigenous theatre, music, and *dance into elegant performing arts, while the symbiotic relationship between *folk forms and court entertainments immensely enriched the overall traditions of the islands.

Traditional performance. Foremost among the traditional performing arts are the different types of *wayang* theatres, particularly the *wayang kulit. Employing the native ensemble called *gamelan for musical accompaniment, wayang kulit has survived for over a millennium, primarily in Bali and Java. It has accommodated changing belief systems, tastes, politics, technologies, and the onslaught of Western culture. Employing dozens of carved and painted flat leather *puppets, it is traditionally illuminated by a single coconut-oil torch which casts shadows of the puppets on a tightly stretched white screen. Depending on the nature of the performance, wayang kulit may be considered a simple entertainment, a court, folk, or governmental celebratory event, or an adjunct to *religious and *ritual acts. The primary sources of stories for wayang kulit theatre are the Hindu epics Ramayana and Mahabharata. However, the original epics have been thoroughly localized and expanded to include many uniquely Javanese or Balinese creations. In Java these epics are also performed in *wayang wong, a dance-drama with spoken *dialogue. In Bali wayang wong recounts the events of the Ramayana, and as many of the *characters are either demons or animals, the dancers wear appropriate topeng (*masks). In Java and Bali wayang wong is never referred to as *topeng theatre, however, as that term is reserved for a dance-drama depicting characters and *historical figures of the period of the east Javanese and Balinese kingdoms, which extended from the thirteenth to the sixteenth centuries (the Majapahit Empire). In topeng all characters, animals or otherwise, wear masks. South of Jakarta in Priangan, a rod wooden-puppet theatre, the Sundanese *wayang golek, relies upon the Mahabharata. As in traditional wayang kulit, the manipulation of all of the puppets, as well as the vocal characterization, the dramatic singing, and the creation of *sound effects, are accomplished by a single puppeteer called dalang. A different type of wayang golek prevails in central Java. Drawing from an Islamic epic known as the Menak cycle, this form demonstrates the influence of yet another culture on the multi-layered wayang tradition. Various experimental wayang forms are found in Bali and Java, and Bali in particular supports dozens of other types of theatre, including *arja, *baris, *barong, *drama gong, *gambuh, *kecak, *legong, and *sanghyang. Beyond Bali and Java, the highly popular *randai dance-drama theatre of the Minangkabau people of west Sumatra employs martial arts movements and uses stories from Minang folklore.

Western influence. The use of the *proscenium arch and painted *perspective backdrops in such commercial and popular regional theatres as *ludruk, ketoprak, and wayang orang (or wayang wong panggung) points to the early influence of Western theatre. And as in much of Asia, the spirit of Indonesian modern plays is clearly indebted to *modernist Western playwrights. Major twentieth-century theatre artists such as Arifin *Noer, W. S. *Rendra, and Nano *Riantiarno shaped a uniquely Indonesian modern theatre movement responding to rapidly changing socio-political circumstances after independence.

In response to tourism, in 1961 the Indonesian government commissioned a dance-drama recounting the Ramayana, to be called Ballet Ramayana, a designation which later was changed to Sendratari Ramayana. Based on wayang wong dance movements, this new theatre replaced dialogue with physical gesture in the hope that it would be more widely appreciated. In its later development *sendratari draws its stories from wider sources, including mythological figures and historical events. Simultaneously Indonesian modern dance theatres gradually emerged, greatly influenced by the Martha *Graham school as well as by indigenous dance traditions, with Sardono *Kusumo and Gusmiati *Suid emerging as two of the most influential choreographers. See also BEDOYO; PANJI; SIDJA, I MADE; SRIMPI; EFFENDI, RUSTAM; SUNARAYA, ASEP SUNANDER.　　HS

INGE, WILLIAM (1913–73)

American playwright. A native of Kansas, Inge was working as drama *critic for a St Louis newspaper in 1944 when he interviewed Tennessee *Williams, whose Glass Menagerie Inge had promoted during its *Chicago run. Williams encouraged Inge to complete a play he was writing, and with Williams's recommendation, Farther off from Heaven was produced in 1947 by Margo *Jones at Theatre 47 in Dallas. When staged on Broadway in 1950 as Come Back, Little Sheba, this drama chronicling the private suffering of an alcoholic chiropractor and his depressive wife secured Inge's position as a talented *realist to join Williams and Arthur *Miller. Three more successful plays of small-town Midwestern life followed: Picnic (1953), about the effects of a sexually charismatic male outsider on five women; Bus Stop (1955), about a cowboy's pursuit of a lounge performer during a Kansas snowstorm; and The Dark at the Top of the Stairs (1957), a family drama set in Oklahoma. Inge was awarded the Pulitzer Prize for Picnic and an Academy award for his screenplay for Splendor in the Grass (1962). He wrote three more full-length plays but after the critical and commercial failures of A Loss of Roses (1959), Natural Affection (1963), and Where's Daddy? (1966), he grew increasingly depressed and struggled with alcoholism, and committed suicide in Los Angeles. With the growth of the *regional theatre movement in the 1970s, Inge's four successful plays from the 1950s became staples of the American repertory.　　MAF

INGEGNERI, ANGELO (1550–1613)

Italian poet and dramatist who led a peripatetic life at a variety of Italian courts. He was a member of the Olympian Academy in Vicenza, for whom he directed a magnificent production of Oedipus the King (1585), which inaugurated the Teatro *Olimpico designed by *Palladio. Ingegneri's *pastoral drama Danza di Venere (Dance of Venus) was produced at the court of Parma in 1583, though the *tragedy Tomiri (1607) remained unperformed. From 1586 to 1592 he served as theatrical adviser of Ferrante Gonzaga at the court of Guastalla. He is best known for his two treatises *On Dramatic Poetry* and *How to Produce Stage Plays* (Ferrara, 1598). GB

INGÉNUE

A term from the French theatre denoting a youthful actress who played significant parts. In the English theatre 'female juvenile lead' meant the same, and she would have played opposite her *stock company counterpart, the male juvenile lead. *Heroines fell into this category, if they were young and not played by the company's leading lady. Qualities of innocence and simplicity, qualities abundant, for instance, in the heroines of *melodrama, were essential. From the Shakespearian repertory, Ophelia, Desdemona, and Cordelia are examples of parts that would have fallen to the ingénue; from the French, Mariane in *Tartuffe* and Aricie in *Phèdre*. See also LINES OF BUSINESS. MRB

INNER STAGE *See* DISCOVERY SPACE.

INNS AS PLAYHOUSES

From medieval times until the first custom-built *playhouses were created in *London in 1567 and 1576, players in England used any venue with enough capacity to hold a paying *audience. Itinerant players performed in market-places, in any large indoor room such as a schoolhouse, the great hall in a country house, even a church or a churchyard. Under Elizabeth many guildhalls were used for a visiting company's initial performance in front of the mayor, before he would allow them to be seen by the people, whether in the same hall or elsewhere around the town. Above all the biggest inns provided space both outdoors and indoors for plays. The most common place for a play at an inn seems to have been in the central courtyard. At these inns the accommodation and drinking rooms were built in a square around the yard, usually with galleries on each inner face which gave extra viewing room, and shelter in poor weather to the spectators positioned underneath. The other kind of inn, obviously preferable in winter, was a building positioned on the main street of a town, with no yard but with a large room on the upper floor, which might have a seating capacity comparable to the town's guildhall or a schoolroom.

In London throughout the sixteenth century the travelling companies of professional players performed at inns. This was tolerated only reluctantly by the city fathers, chiefly because performances normally took place in the daytime, when a citizen's employees were supposed to be at work. Once professional playhouses started to appear in the suburbs in 1576, in areas outside the control of the city fathers, that hostility intensified; it focused on the inns because citizen rule applied

to them and was being flouted. For twenty years the Lord Mayor of London campaigned to have all playing stopped. The Privy Council made some concessions, for instance in 1584, once the *Queen's Men had been created, when it allowed no other companies to play and specified which city inns they could use. In 1594 the Council licensed two suburban playhouses, the *Theatre and the *Rose, for two companies to use and forbade any further playing at inns in London.

Up to this decision the main city inns used for playing outdoors included the Bel Savage on Ludgate Hill, the Bull in Bishopsgate Street, and several others originally built to house the wagons and coaches that brought food, goods, and people in from the country. Their open yards made them suited to daytime performances; their large capacity and ample natural *light meant they were appropriate for stinging 'prizes' (fencing matches), as well as plays. The Bell and the Cross Keys in Gracechurch Street appear to have provided indoor venues. In October 1594 the Lord *Chamberlain's Men asked for the use of the Cross Keys for their winter performances in preference to the *open-air Theatre. The *Boar's Head in 1597–9, and possibly the *Red Bull in 1604, were inn yards converted into permanent playhouses once the Privy Council, bowing to the years of pressure from the Lord Mayor of London, finally banned all playing at the city's inns. AJG

INNS OF COURT

Students of the law of the four major and three junior Inns always provided a substantial element of playgoing *audiences. In 1628–9 Edward Heath of the Middle Temple, who kept meticulous accounts, recorded 49 visits to plays and the purchase of ten playbooks. Gray's Inn and the Middle Temple in particular had a strong tradition of playgoing and of staging their own plays and even mounting *masques and plays at court. They also invited professional players to perform in their dining halls. Gray's Inn had Shakespeare's company, the *Chamberlain's Men, perform *The Comedy of Errors* at Christmas 1594, and John Manningham recorded his attendance at *Twelfth Night* in February 1602 in the Middle Temple hall.

In the Tudor period plays written by Inns of Court men were performed occasionally by the 'gentlemen' of the Inns as part of the Christmas season of festivities at court. The Inner Temple put on *Gorboduc* for the Queen in 1562; Gray's Inn staged *The Misfortunes of Arthur* in February 1588. Such events did not recur in the Stuart years, when the plays were almost entirely provided by the professional and *boys' companies, though in February 1618 Gray's Inn gentlemen took part of their annual Christmas 'Prince of Purpoole' entertainment to court. On several occasions under the early Stuarts students of Oxford or Cambridge brought their plays to court, but the Inns did not.

Masquing at court in Tudor times sometimes included offerings from the Inns. The gentlemen of Gray's Inn staged 'A Mask of Satyrs and Tilters' before Elizabeth in March 1565, and that same month another called 'Proteus and the Adamantine Rock'. In January 1598 the Middle Temple put on 'The Mask of the Passions'. *Chapman wrote a masque for the Middle Temple and Lincoln's Inn to stage jointly in February 1614, and one by *Beaumont was done a week later by Gray's and the Inner Temple. All the Inns had to combine to *finance *Shirley's lavish 'The Triumph of Peace' in 1634. Mostly in the Jacobean period the Benchers of the Inns just paid the cost of the staging, using professionals for the speaking parts. It could be expensive. Francis Bacon paid over £2,000 for a Gray's Inn masque presented as part of the wedding celebrations of Frances Howard and James's favourite, the Earl of Somerset, in 1614.   AJG

INOUE HISASHI (1934–)

Japanese playwright and novelist. A graduate in French literature from Sophia University in Tokyo, Inoue began his career at a striptease parlour as a comedy skit writer for the popular actor Atsumi Kiyoshi, moving in the 1960s to *radio and *television drama. His first stage play was *The Japanese Navel* (1969); he has since written dozens of plays and novels that have won both popular and critical acclaim. His best-selling 1981 novel, *The Kirikirians*, won the Yomiuri Literary Prize. Many of his best dramas, such as *Dōgen's Adventures* (1971), *Kobayashi Issa* (1979), and *Headache, Stiff Neck, Higuchi Ichiyō* (1984), are satirical biographies or *parodies of *historical events. Inoue's plays demonstrate considerable verbal and *dramaturgical dexterity. His light, comedic approach to serious subjects, such as social or regional discrimination, has injected new energy, wit, and inventiveness into contemporary mainstream Japanese theatre. Since 1983, his own theatre troupe, Komatsuza, has staged most of his plays. *The Great Doctor Yabuhara* (1973) and *Make-up* (1982) have been well received in Europe and North America.   CP

INTENDANT

*Artistic director in German theatre. The *Intendant* has extraordinary power in *repertory theatres, as he or she fulfils the function of both managing and artistic director. In recent years the success of a theatre has frequently depended on the stature of its *Intendant*, often referred to as the 'the star of the German theatre'. Prominent *Intendanten* of the late twentieth century include Peter *Stein at the *Berlin *Schaubühne (1970–85) and Claus *Peymann, who was *Intendant* at Stuttgart, Bochum, and the *Vienna *Burgtheater, prior to taking over the *Berliner Ensemble in 1999. *Intendanten* also direct *opera companies, most notably Götz Friedrich at the Deutsches Oper, Berlin.   SJCW

INTER-ACTION

A *London-based community arts umbrella organization founded by expatriate American director Ed Berman in 1968. It started with the Ambience in Queensway, a lunchtime theatre that staged plays by many new playwrights, including early works by *Stoppard and Ed *Bullins, then in 1972 moved to the Almost Free in Piccadilly, so named for its *ticket pricing policy: people paid what they could afford. Berman's entrepreneurial energy spawned an array of small companies, which were eventually housed in 1977 in a highly functional, purpose-built structure in Kentish Town. Determinedly *multimedia, they included the double-decker Fun Art Bus, a Community Media Van, an inventive *street theatre group (Professor Dogg's Troupe), the transatlantic British American Repertory Theatre, a small printing outfit (Imprint), a *film production unit (Infilms), and the first City Farm in the UK. Subsequently a branch was opened in Milton Keynes, to further spread the not-so-cheap but cheerful message that art should be for everyone.   BRK

INTERCULTURALISM *see page 628*

INTERLUDE

In the *early modern period an interlude was a short *farce or a light-hearted moral piece which was 'played between' (its Latin meaning) the courses of a meal, or at its end. In other contexts it can mean a piece played between the *acts of another drama or *opera, like the Italian *intermezzo* (see INTERMEDIO). In sixteenth-century England the term often meant simply a short play. *See also* MORALITY PLAY; MEDIEVAL THEATRE IN EUROPE.   JWH

INTERMEDIO (*INTERMEZZO*)

A musico-dramatic piece performed between the *acts of full-length dramas. *Intermedi* were a regular feature of dramatic performances at the courts of Italian princes, especially the Florentine Medici, during the sixteenth century. They could be brief instrumental pieces, *choruses, or spectacular *allegorical *actions. An evening's entertainment might include up to six *intermedi* interwoven with the five acts of the mainpiece; sometimes they were thematically linked and they often exceeded the mainpiece in interest. The *intermedio* is one of the *genres from which *opera developed, and the practice of *intermedi* continued into the seventeenth century after the establishment of opera; full-length operas themselves were punctuated by *intermedi*. In eighteenth-century Italy, comic *intermezzi*, as the *intermedi* came to be called, were inserted between acts of *opera seria*. The practice was abandoned by mid-century

(continued on p. 631)

INTERCULTURALISM

Interculturalism and *performance is perhaps the most talked about and controversial cultural practice of the late twentieth and early twenty-first centuries, characterized at best by a sharing and mutual borrowing of the manifestation of one theatre practice by another. At worst it features the appropriation and annihilation of indigenous, pre-modern practices in traditional societies by a rapacious 'First World' global capitalism. Interculturalism has its roots in orientalism, a term used to describe a European art movement of the mid-nineteenth century obsessed with both *realism and a fascination with the unknown, the tribal, non-Christian, and seemingly unregulated societies at the far side of the Mediterranean, from Morocco to the Near East. This artistic practice came at a time of European colonialism and expansion into the Far East. New trade routes permitted the shipping back of foreign goods and artefacts, as well as an obsession with what was not understood or not permitted for the Westerner, namely the harem and the temple or mosque.

In the first half of the twentieth century *modernist European theatre practitioners, from W. B. *Yeats to Antonin *Artaud, sought to overhaul their work and produce ever stimulating novelty by seeking out oriental practices and holding them up as templates for the theatre of the future. Yeats's plan for a new indigenous Irish theatre looked to Ireland's pre-colonial myths and legends for his subject, but also to the classical *nō plays of *Japan for his *dramaturgical construction. For example, *Cathleen Ní Houlihan* (1902) features the restless soul of an Old Woman who is ritually transformed into a young girl by the blood sacrifice of Ireland's volunteer revolutionaries; like the *shite *protagonists of nō she is appeased through *ritual performance. Artaud's experience of oriental cultures was in tourist versions of Balinese (*see* INDONESIA) and *Cambodian *dancing, but the codified movements he saw as unleashing mystical powers and their formalism came to represent for him a template for European theatre of the future. The interculturalism of these two major figures was abetted by geographical distance, as they lived in a colonial world that separated them from the cultural Other. Their experience of other cultures came from imported and sanitized versions brought to Europe in the Great Exhibitions as triumphalist trophies of European dominion. *Orientalism* (1976), the seminal work by the Palestinian cultural historian Edward Said, mapped out the politics of this cultural practice, particularly the hegemonic imperialism inscribed within it, and has been used as the theoretical touchstone for the analysis of Western intercultural theatre.

A post-1960s generation of directors—Peter *Brook, Ariane *Mnouchkine, and Eugenio *Barba, among others—came under the spotlight as they sampled the cultures of *Africa and Asia in their search for a form to break with realism. Brook's version of the Hindu epic *The Mahabharata* (1985), featuring actors from the four corners of the globe in a production which *toured the world, set alight the debate on the ethics of such practice. The social, cultural, and most importantly *religious context of the work was deemed by some to be lost in an aestheticized package for global consumption. Removed from its religious and devotional context and placed in a new European setting of non-believers, the *text lost its third dimension, namely its *audience of the gods.

Mnouchkine's intercultural work of the 1980s and 1990s largely escaped the critical wrath directed at Brook, since her direction was an imagined oriental practice layered on the textual heritage of Europe. The most famous of her productions, three plays by Shakespeare (1981–4), and four ancient *Greek texts called *Les Atrides* (1990–3), featured multinational troupes of actors who had trained in the forms of oriental theatres and from that *training had imagined and created their own form. Mnouchkine thought that the surviving classical theatres of the Far East were suitable templates for constructing new forms for the presentation of ancient or medieval histories of Europe, given that European theatre has no such equivalents. *Costumes were eclectic mixes of both European heritage and oriental samples, while the *mise-en-scène (like its Eastern models) broke all the bounds of realism.

This brand of interculturalism feeds into the practice of modernist orientalism in its nostalgic search for a formalism with which to reinvigorate theatre practice and to produce novelty. It seems to suggest that European theatre has been exhausted and that the classical forms of oriental cultures are to be quarried for the Western palate. Alongside these productions of European classics Mnouchkine also worked with playwright Hélène *Cixous in productions of contemporary Asian history. *The Terrible But Unfinished History of Norodom Sihanouk, King of Cambodia* (1985) pitted *Brechtian distancing (*see* VERFREMDUNG) against very familiar images of Pol Pot's killing fields and disastrous US foreign policy decisions in the region. *The Indiade; or, India of their Dreams* (1997) similarly charted the struggle for independence in India. The proximity, and familiarity through media representation, of these histories and the real-life figures meant that a theatrical formalism could not be applied; the productions faltered with images of a white

French actor playing King Sihanouk and Ghandi. Mnouchkine's production of Cixous's *Drums on the Dyke* (1999), however, presented an imagined version of a real event, namely the flooding of a valley in China in order to create a dam, thus wiping out communities and cultures. It was a groundbreaking experiment of live actors being manipulated as *bunraku puppets, challenging Western notions of *character.

Perhaps Eugenio Barba's *Odin Teatret of Denmark comes closest to the concept of interculturalism in its strictest sense, in that he and his actors, though touring the world, engage in a bartering process with the other culture, as hosts and guests present work to each other. But this kind of exchange is forever lopsided, as the traditional theatre forms that Odin Teatret encounters have a history and a constituency within their cultures and societies. That is not true of Barba's troupe, which can be seen as a band of high-art experimenters attempting to establish an essentialism of performance in order to discover the commonalities of all cultures (*see* ANTHROPOLOGY, THEATRE).

The liberal humanist American scholar and director (and Hindu convert) Richard *Schechner set the agenda for the practice and *theory of interculturalism, and gave value to Western experimentation with Asian culture as a quasi-anthropological exercise, in a series of articles published in the early 1980s and later in books such as *Between Theatre and Anthropology* (1985) and *By Means of Performance* (1990). In these he dichotomized West and East, modern and pre-modern, the aesthetic and the ritual, entertainment and efficacy, and by so doing came to create a cultural division of the world mirrored by the split between traditional societies and 'First World' capitalism. By discussing his traditional 'others' he was accused of misunderstanding, appropriating, and even speaking for them. The Calcutta (*Kolkata) critic and director Rustom Bharucha forcefully argued against such appropriating practices.

But interculturalism quite clearly does not operate solely on a unidirectional East/West, Asian/European axis. Throughout the twentieth century Asian practitioners have sought inspiration in European practices. For instance, the Japanese *shingeki* movement modelled itself on the new drama of Europe, inspired by the plays of *Ibsen, while the popular female *musical-theatre form *Takarazuka has always invested heavily in pastiches of Western culture, from nineteenth-century *opera to classical Hollywood *film. Further, the post-*shingeki* *dance form *butoh, though it draws on pre-modern mysticism, owes a debt both to Artaud's Theatre of *Cruelty and the choreography of Mary Wigman. More recently, directors such as *Japan's *Ninagawa Yukio and *Singapore's *Ong Keng Sen have sought not to reinvigorate their own national theatre practices but to reject authenticity and embrace hybrid multiple realities. Thus one of the reasons why First World interculturalism has become a global phenomenon is that it purloins the surfaces of other cultures in order to attain the greatest market share, by reaching out for the largest common denominator of mythologized cultural icons. Ninagawa and Ong are very much part of the transnational circus of the supra-cultural *festival circuit (joining Western directors such as Brook, Robert *Lepage, and Robert *Wilson), whose constituency has no real national or social hinterland other than the globalized community of high-art consumers, many of whom experience theatre as cultural tourists.

What place then for the local and indigenous? One of the more sinister aspects of recent cultural imperialism by multinational companies and First World practitioners is an obsession with native cultural traditions which are appropriated into the signification of global capitalism. This ensures that the transnational product achieves a degree of popularity by dint of it recognizing, assimilating, and valorizing the local. This type of practice is often referred to as 'glocalization'. Thus, at the opening ceremony of the Nagano Winter Olympics (1998), for example, a familiar transnational icon of Japanese *sport, a sumo wrestler, localized by his presence the cultural experience for global consumption, and a soprano in kimono sang 'Un bel dí' from *Puccini's orientalist opera *Madame Butterfly*. Instantly recognizable and mythologized intercultural icons are being used in popular culture for transnational communication, in order to ensure the greatest coverage to the biggest possible market. In theatre, the elite band of directors use various eclecticisms to soak up recognizable cultural icons, used as a language to communicate transnationally in world tours. Their productions belong nowhere other than the virtual space of a First World cultural hegemony, traversing the globe, speaking to and for all nations, representing none.

Points of resistance to such practices can be found in various national and post-colonial agendas. Instead of relying on the method of global iconicity to fill the void left by colonial policies which erased indigenous culture, in many locations practitioners seek a rediscovery and reassembly of pre-colonial practices. The asymmetric power relations between colonizer and colonized can now sometimes give way to indigenous (and some might say nativist) discourses within globalized cultural markets, which treat the pre-modern local traditions as raw materials to be repackaged for export, rather than as historical entities to be respected and protected. Ghana's Efua *Sutherland, Nigeria's Wole *Soyinka, and *India's Kavalam Narayana *Panikkar are representative post-colonial playwrights who have imagined and reconstructed indigenous performances which resist the transnational trends of interculturalism. These practices are known as 'intracultural': the pre-colonial cultural practices are first recognized as temporal, though not cultural, 'others', and then are mastered and assimilated into a contemporary idiom. In many respects this 'nativist' practice shares the same characteristics as interculturalism in its binary opposition of two cultural practices. However, the politics of such practices (permitting indigenous artists to imagine and reconstruct their own cultural past for present consumption) ensures that they do not fall into the trap of First World cultural imperialism, at a time when political leaders are often encouraged to westernize and join the mêlée of a one-world, global society.

As the world increasingly breaks down its borders and the virtual world of telecommunications challenges our notions of national cultures, the potential and the possibilities of indigenous cultures come into sharp focus. Performance is under pressure for survival as an expression of a cultural, societal, or even national need. The practices of global capitalism divide up the world into Wests and Easts, not according to their geographical location but to where economic and political power reside. Interculturalism, like its precursor orientalism, positions desired cultures everywhere east of the West, and proceeds to imitate, perform, purchase, and eventually own them in processes of assimilation. All that interculturalism quite often leaves behind in traditional societies is a desire to transform indigenous performance in order to suit the palate of the Western consumer. The intercultural Western project swapped the material produce of empire for its own ideologies of capitalism and Christianity. Interculturalism thus becomes a means by which everything which is wished for in Western or First World culture can be fantasized, created, and played out. The quest for appropriation is fuelled by a vision of the Orient as a nostalgic space of lost ritual, formalism, and religion, a nostalgic space for the authentically pure, sometimes barbarian, for everything the Westerner is not: his or her opposite in cultural fixity, morality, devotion, tradition, and belief. Whether the interculturalist is in *Tokyo, *London or *New York, she or he is performing from a single ruling perspective that defines itself as West.

Interculturalism thus is paradoxical, since it stems from both a self-belief and an anxiety. Nevertheless, it provides a framework and a guiding set of principles for the representation of traditional cultures by others whose only shared cultural practice is that of the hybrid: cultural heritage, then, is replaced by cultural choice. Ruling the empires from the sixteenth to the mid-twentieth centuries (orientalism), and controlling the markets in late twentieth-century performance culture (interculturalism), share a dominant characteristic: treating the Orient as exotic material to be incorporated in the cultural expression of self. Interculturalism is a means of imagining culture as a landscape which, when occupied, produces, transmits, and substitutes for a once authentic culture. Rather than a mutual meeting in a space between cultures, intercultural performance is most often a practice of the desire, imagination, and anxieties of the one cultural system which looks to the other culture for formalist or aesthetic templates for the renovation of itself. Intercultural theatre thus operates in the space between two or more cultures, but those cultures themselves rarely, if ever, meet, let alone interact.

But not all intercultural practices operate within a dichotomized structure of cultural exchange, where one dominant First World practice feeds off its Third World other. Some movements in Asia, for example, such as the Indian *Parsi the-

atre, modelled themselves on the performance practices of their nineteenth-century colonial masters, a sign of the practitioners' aim to single themselves out as a home-ruling cultural elite. Many of the aforementioned practices of both modern and postmodern Western theatre, what is more, although seemingly rooted in orientalist drives for self-regeneration, in fact exist less on a material plain and more on a theoretical level or within only one geographical region and economic system. Such trajectories of exchange break down the East–West dichotomy and were not mediated by colonialism at all.

Yeats's borrowings of nō dramaturgy, for example, though rooted in modernism's obsession with novelty, were formulated at a philosophical level and from a desire to create a new Irish idiom beyond available contemporary realities. Thus his interculturalism did not replicate the surface of an Asian culture, since there was no actual exchange of anything, but was simply a means of imagining a new drama, with a medieval oriental ritual theatre (such as nō) providing the *allegorical and dramaturgical framework for revolutionary political drama for which realism was inappropriate. Similarly, the influence of the Beijing opera (*jingju) performer *Mei Lanfang on *Brecht's notion of Verfremdung represents more of a conceptual borrowing of a theatrical form for political reformation than an orientalist appropriation.

So, although rooted in the drives of orientalism, many modernist innovations differ from the late twentieth-century's obsession with speaking for and materially representing their desired Asian others. Complicating the interculturalism of early modernism further is the knowledge that intercultural influences roam intercontinentally, beyond the trade routes of cultural exchange. For example, Yeats also acknowledged a debt to the Indian poet *Tagore, who himself was influenced by Japanese philosopher Okakura Tenshin; and the form of nō that provided Yeats with his template had its roots in rural ritual songs and dances with origins in China. This ideational interculturalism is a less problematic form of exchange than the materiality of colonial and/or imperialist representation. Further, the digitized possibilities of new technologies (*see* MEDIA AND PERFORMANCE; CYBER THEATRE) in the twenty-first century abet ideational roaming, but also call into question the notion of culture as a property, of the nation with confined borders, and the old intercultural binaries of self/other, colonizer/colonized, and West/East. *See also* POLITICS AND THEATRE; POST-COLONIAL STUDIES; DIASPORA; RACE AND THEATRE.   BRS

BHARUCHA, RUSTOM, *Theatre and the World: performance and politics of culture* (London, 1993)

FISCHER-LICHTE, ERIKA, RILEY, JOSEPHINE, and GISSENWEHRER, MICHAEL (eds.), *The Dramatic Touch of Difference: theatre own and foreign* (Tübingen, 1990)

MARRANCA, BONNIE, and DASGUPTA, GAUTAM (eds.), *Interculturalism and Performance* (New York, 1991)

PAVIS, PATRICE (ed.), *The Intercultural Performance Reader* (London, 1996)

as the *intermezzo* developed into *opera buffa*, and *seria* abandoned any admixture of *comedy in its *action. SJCW

INTERNATIONAL ASSOCIATION OF THEATRE CRITICS

Founded in 1956 at the Festival of *Paris, the IATC is a non-profit non-government organization under the distant umbrella of UNESCO. To foster theatre *criticism, protect critics' interests, and increase understanding among cultures, it holds world congresses every two years, twice-yearly young critics' seminars, irregular symposia, and frequent executive committee meetings worldwide. Its official languages are English and French and its legal domicile is Paris. The membership is mainly some 50 national critics' groups, such as the American Theatre Critics Association and the Critics Circle of *London, but critics in countries without national organizations join individually. During the Cold War IATC provided a forum in which critics from East and West could easily meet. Since then it has been called upon to mediate between adversarial critics' groups, such as those formed in some Eastern European countries after control by government arts ministries lessened. CR

INTERNATIONAL CENTRE FOR THEATRE RESEARCH

Company founded in *Paris in 1970 by British director Peter *Brook and French producer Micheline Rozan as Centre International de Recherche Théâtrale, a multicultural research and production agency. Usually referred to as 'the Centre', the acronym CIRT properly refers to the organizational umbrella for research work conducted between 1970 and 1973 in Paris and overseas by Brook with an international group of artists. This initial research phase was funded by the French government through the Ministry of Culture, and by a host of international foundations (Ford, Gulbenkian, Anderson, UNESCO, etc.). A subsequent change of name in 1974 to Centre International de Créations Théâtrales signalled a shift of focus from research to public performance, coinciding with the Centre's move to the Théâtre des *Bouffes du Nord. Since that time the Centre has produced and *toured sixteen major productions directed by Brook, in French and some in English: *Timon d'Athènes* (1974), *Les Iks* (*The Ik*, 1975), *Ubu aux Bouffes* (*Ubu*, 1977), *Mesure pour mesure* (1978), *La Conférence des oiseaux* (*Conference of the Birds*, 1979), *La Cerisaie* (*The Cherry Orchard*, 1981), *La Tragédie de Carmen* (Bizet's *opera, 1981), *Le Mahabharata* (1985), *Woza Albert!* (1989), *La Tempête* (1990), *Impressions de Pelléas* (1992), *L'Homme qui* (*The Man Who*, 1993), *Qui est là?* (1995), *Oh! Les Beaux Jours!* (1995), *Je suis un phénomène* (1998), *Hamlet* (2000).

The Bouffes du Nord remains the company's *rehearsal and performance space and administrative base, although there has never been a permanent company *per se*. The Centre is most usefully perceived as a loose alliance of actual and potential collaborators constellating around Brook. Some of these alliances have been long-standing. The performers *Oida Yoshi and Bruce Myers, for example, have remained integral to Brook's work since the inception. Other long-term collaborators include writer Jean-Claude *Carrière, designer Chloé *Obolensky, performers Maurice Bénichou and Sotigui Kouyaté, and assistant director Marie-Hélène Estienne. The Centre continues to use both its acronyms, CIRT and CICT, interchangeably. This dual identity perhaps reflects slightly different emphases at different moments in Brook's evolution, in the continuum between the two poles of his interrelated activities: private research and public performance. ADW

INTERNATIONAL FEDERATION FOR THEATRE RESEARCH

Founded on the initiative of the British *Society for Theatre Research in 1955 to promote collaboration and the exchange of information between individuals and organizations connected with the emerging discipline of *theatre studies. Representatives from 21 countries convened at the British Academy, *London, where IFTR was conceived. A bilingual organization (English and French), its financial base is in Berne (the Swiss franc being the most stable currency in Cold War Europe), and its principal activities include an annual conference, a quadrennial congress, and a noted journal, *Theatre Research International*. Members are invited to join working groups of thematic and generic interest. The Federation is headed by a president, two vice-presidents, and an executive committee, elected every four years, and is administered by two secretaries-general. BRS

INTERNATIONAL THEATRE INSTITUTE

Under the auspices of Julian Huxley, the first director-general of UNESCO, J. B. *Priestley, Jean-Louis *Barrault, Rosamond Gilder, and Lillian *Hellman, the International Theatre Institute was chartered in *Prague in June 1948. Ratified by eight countries, its purpose was to promote international cooperation and exchange of ideas among theatre artists as well as to protect the theatrical rights of practitioners. The governmental policies and activities of the organization, headquartered in *Paris, are now carried out by over 90 centres, each representing a country or a major cultural population. Through the workings of eight committees (communications, cultural identity and development, *dance, dramatic theatre, *music theatre, new projects, *playwrights, and *training) ITI weaves a network of global communication by means of conferences, *festivals, workshops, exchanges, and world congresses. In the aftermath of the Second World War, through the Cold War years, and in current trends toward world democratization, ITI has continued a policy of introducing colleagues to theatre life in other nations, advising and consulting on international initiatives, promoting artistic awareness, and protecting the rights of performing artists.   LAR

IN-THE-ROUND *See* ARENA AND IN-THE-ROUND.

INTIMA TEATERN (INTIMATE THEATRE)

Swedish company, founded by the playwright August *Strindberg and the actor August Falck, who leased a warehouse in central *Stockholm and converted it to a *studio theatre with seating for 161 spectators. The stage was small but the building was equipped with the latest electric *lighting. Intima Teatern opened on 11 December 1907 and, until it closed in December 1910, presented a repertoire of plays written exclusively by Strindberg. Some of these (his 'chamber plays') he wrote for the theatre, but most popular were earlier works such as *Miss Julie, Easter,* and *The Father*. Strindberg also wrote a series of letters to the ensemble with advice on *acting and staging (*Open Letters to the Intimate Theatre*, 1909). Initially, Falck used *naturalist *scenery, but increasingly moved towards visual simplicity to focus attention on the *acting. Mounting economic difficulties and disagreements between its founders brought the enterprise to an end.   DT

IONESCO, EUGÈNE (1912–94)

Born in Romania, Ionesco became a major playwright of the French *absurdist theatre, rejecting *realism, psychologism, causal action, and the Marxist theatres of *Brecht and *Sartre. Sharing the absurdists' existential themes and the *surrealists' use of *dreams, he attempted to create verbal and visual language to express a reality beyond the objective. Like the *dadaists in his satiric humour and disillusionment with art, he sought through 'anti-plays' to 'give the lie to each spoken word by taking it apart, making it explode, and transforming it', through vivid concrete images and in *dialogue. In Ionesco's view, society uses language not to communicate meaning but to bury it in clichés, propaganda, and banalities. His *characters are often puppet-like and live in a present from which they cannot escape. The cultural alienation in Ionesco's characters was also present in his life: when he was 1 year old, he moved with his Romanian father and French mother to Paris, but upon their divorce when he was 13, he was sent back to Romania to live with his domineering father. Refusing to study law as his father wished, he chose French literature instead, and in 1938

left to study in Paris, where he stayed permanently. His lifelong sense of being split between two cultures infused all of his plays, beginning with *La Cantatrice chauve* (1950, known in English as *The Bald Prima Donna* and *The Bald Soprano*), which he described as 'a *tragedy of language' until the *audience reacted to it as a powerful *comedy. Several more *one-acts followed, including *The Lesson* (1951) and *The Chairs* (1952), for which his term 'tragic *farce' is appropriate. In *The Lesson* a timid professor is transformed into a knife-wielding tyrant who threatens his student, while in *The Chairs* an old couple wait for their guests, play word games, and pull so many empty chairs onto the stage that they become trapped. The early plays appeared in small experimental theatres in the Latin Quarter, often playing to nearly empty houses. Yet *The Bald Soprano* and *The Lesson* have played continuously since 1957 in La Huchette, a living museum for generations of students and scholars.

The next plays were full-length, including *Amédée* (1954) and *Tueur sans gages* (*The Killer*, 1959), and drew larger audiences as Ionesco's reputation rose to the point where *Rhinoceros* was directed by Jean-Louis *Barrault at the *Odéon Théâtre (1960). Here the character Bérenger, who also appears in *The Killer*, *Le Piéton de l'air* (*A Stroll in the Air*, 1962) and *Le Roi se meurt* (*Exit the King*, 1962), struggles in vain against an 'epidemic' of ideological conformity. As Ionesco became the most produced modern French author in *Paris, and indeed in the world, Brecht's *epic theatre was gaining adherents, including Kenneth *Tynan of the *London *Observer*, who called Ionesco 'the king of the surrealist conjurors' and charged him with undermining reality itself. In their famous debate, Ionesco countered that Tynan recognized 'only one plane of reality: the "social", which [is] the most superficial', supported by the 'fossilised language' of ideologies. Brecht remained Ionesco's nemesis, appearing as a caricature, alongside Sartre, in *L'Impromptu d'Alma; ou, Le Caméléon berger* (*Improvisation; or, The Shepherd's Chameleon*, 1955) and again in *La Soif et la faim* (*Hunger and Thirst*, 1966), the latter directed by Barrault at the *Comédie-Française.

Ionesco came to see his anti-leftist plays of the late 1960s as too politically explicit, but soon effectively combined *politics with *slapstick, dream, and *Artaudian violence in *L'Épidémie; ou, Jeux de massacre* (*The Killing Game*, 1970) and *Macbett* (1972), a *Jarryesque *parody of Shakespeare. Even more autobiographical than the Bérenger plays is *L'Homme aux valises* (*The Man with the Luggage*, 1974), wherein First Man searches for his identity in a strange country, surrounded by Freudian suitcases, dolls, and disguises, and finally capitulates to the authoritarian father figures. Ionesco drew on the same material for his last play, *Voyages chez les morts* (*Journeys among the Dead*, 1983), achieving the hallucinatory quality of his early works. Its première at the *Théâtre National Populaire in Villeurbanne was directed by Roger *Planchon, who retitled it *Ionesco* and included other writings by the author, transforming it from

Ionesco's personal journey into a monumental production of his life and times. Responding to the controversy this caused, Planchon argued that Ionesco's work and life should be re-evaluated as part of the 'chronicle of damage' done to Western humanism by the Cold War. Besides his twenty major plays, Ionesco published poetry, *film scripts, short stories, literary criticism, memoirs, and children's tales, and in 1970 was elected to the Académie Française.   SBB

GAENSBAUER, DEBORAH, *Ionesco Revisited* (New York, 1996)
IONESCO, EUGÈNE, *Fragments of a Journal*, trans. Jean Stewart (New York, 1990)

ION OF CHIOS (c.480–c.421 BC)

Uniquely versatile ancient *Greek author of *tragedies, *satyr-plays, and perhaps *comedies, as well as lyric poetry, history, and personal reminiscences. The dramatic fragments remaining are elegant, but too scanty for Ion's reputation, great in his own day, to have survived antiquity.   JMM

IRELAND, WILLIAM HENRY (1775–1835)

English author, the forger of the legal documents supposedly bearing Shakespeare's signature (1795). Their 'discovery' generated great excitement in Shakespeare-mad eighteenth-century *London, but after initial acceptance Ireland's forgery was definitively exposed by the century's greatest Shakespeare scholar, Edmund *Malone, in 1796, just before the *Drury Lane première of *Vortigern*, which Ireland passed off as a newly discovered Shakespeare play. It was a failure, and Ireland's other spurious Shakespeare play, *Henry II*, was never performed. He also forged manuscripts of *King Lear* and *Hamlet*, but eventually admitted his deception in *An Authentic Account* (1796) and in *Confessions* (1805).   MJK

IRISH LITERARY THEATRE

Founded in *Dublin by *Yeats, Lady *Gregory, and Edward *Martyn (1899–1901) with the intention of challenging English theatrical taste and dramatic forms with plays specifically on Irish subjects. The most significant venture proved to be not the founders' works but Douglas Hyde's *Casadh an tSugain*, given in Irish by the *Fay brothers' *amateur company. *See also* ABBEY THEATRE.   RAC

IRONS, JEREMY (1948–   )

English actor. Irons's brooding appeal first came to international attention in the BBC *television mini-series *Brideshead Revisited* (1981), followed by his passionate, enigmatic performance opposite Meryl Streep in the *film of *The French Lieutenant's Woman* (1981; screenplay by *Pinter). Sometimes known as 'the thinking woman's sex symbol', Irons won a Tony *award for his role in *Stoppard's *The Real Thing* (1984, opposite Glenn *Close). He trained with the *Bristol Old Vic before joining their *touring company; his first West End role was John the Baptist in *Godspell* (1971). The characters Irons chooses are usually internally conflicted and often disturbed, including twin gynaecologists in David Cronenberg's film *Dead Ringers* (1988), Humbert Humbert in Adrian Lyne's screen adaptation of *Lolita* (1991), and Scar in Disney's animated *The Lion King* (1994). He won an Academy award for his portrayal of accused murderer Claus Von Bulow in *Reversal of Fortune* (1990). He has performed in several seasons with the *Royal Shakespeare Company, including a commanding portrayal of Willmore in John *Barton's production of *Behn's *The Rover* (1986). He is married to actress Sinéad *Cusack.   GAO

IRVING, HENRY (1838–1905)

English actor and *manager. Born John Henry Brodribb in Keinton Mandeville, Somerset, his father a travelling salesman of Somerset farming stock, his mother from a Cornish Methodist background, Brodribb took the name of Irving for his professional stage debut in *Richelieu* at Sunderland in 1856, having turned down an offer from *Phelps at *Sadler's Wells. Previously he had been a clerk in an East India merchant's office, and much given to *amateur theatricals. After Sunderland, Irving moved to two theatres in *Edinburgh, assuming the extremely heavy workload of the beginning provincial actor; in his first three years he played a total of 451 different parts. Following a brief appearance at the *Princess's Theatre in *London in 1859, he returned to the provinces: Edinburgh, *Dublin, *Glasgow, Liverpool, *Manchester—where he played his first Hamlet in 1863—Oxford, Edinburgh, Manchester, Douglas, Birmingham, Liverpool, Manchester—the endless plodding around the country was no more than the ordinary life of Victorian actors.

Eventually, however, from 1867 Irving played in several London theatres until his Digby Grant in *Albery's *Two Roses* at the Vaudeville in 1870 led to a *Lyceum engagement as leading man with Colonel *Bateman. In 1871 Irving was immediately propelled into the front rank of actors by his extraordinary performance of the haunted Burgomaster Mathias in Albery's *The Bells*, a good family man who twenty years before had robbed and murdered to lay the foundations of his prosperity. Irving played Hamlet again in 1874; it ran for an astonishing 200 performances. In 1879 the Batemans' star actor took over the Lyceum himself as *actor-manager, and immediately engaged Ellen *Terry as his leading lady. Irving stayed at the Lyceum until 1902, still with Ellen Terry by his side. Since 1899 he had been working, without much recompense, for a syndicate to which he was forced to relinquish control because of the

Irving in his most famous role, *The Bells*, Lyceum Theatre, London, 1871. The Burgomaster Mathias sees a vision of the man he killed two decades earlier. Created by illuminating the upstage scene behind a scrim or gauze curtain, the picture shows how psychological melodrama in the nineteenth century depended on spectacular effects, engineered in this case by Irving's sophisticated lighting techniques.

Lyceum's precarious financial position and the loss of most of its scenic stock in an 1898 warehouse fire.

During his 23-year tenure at the Lyceum, Irving made it a place of pilgrimage for the famous and the artistic, splendidly entertaining leading figures from the arts, politics, the Church, the law, royalty, and aristocracy. He gave the Lyceum an immense social as well as artistic cachet; it was both popular and fashionable. Eight company *tours to North America extended his reputation across the Atlantic, and regular provincial touring made him a household name in Britain. His repertory was principally Shakespeare (twelve plays) and poetic, *romantic, and *historical drama, and his company was remarkably stable. Besides Terry, John *Martin-Harvey stayed with him for fourteen years, and lesser actors, his stage and business managers, and his *prompter from start to finish. The Lyceum was a large theatre, holding 1,700–1,800 spectators, with a backstage staff

of well over 100; during *Faust* (1885) it employed, altogether, over 350, for *Robespierre* (1899) over 600. Thus it required a grand style of production and big *acting. Neither Irving nor Terry were modern psychological actors, and Irving, much to the disgust of *Shaw, was not interested in the modern experimental repertory. As the Lyceum's chief, Irving controlled and supervised everything: employment of actors, wages, the *music, the repertory, *rehearsals, and the *limelight. The stage *lighting system was his personal creation, and his productions were pictorially beautiful in the best Victorian tradition.

Years of overwork, poor health, a declining *box office (except for touring), the *scenery fire, and the failure of the syndicate combined to push Irving out of the Lyceum in 1902, and except for an unsuccessful production of *Sardou's *Dante* (1903) at *Drury Lane and a farewell London season in 1905, he spent his last years traversing the provinces once more, old, sick, and weary. He died in Bradford, after a performance of *Becket*. His funeral in Westminster Abbey was appropriately theatrical and on a grand, Lyceum-like scale.

As an actor Irving took a long time to reach greatness; once there, he easily dominated his profession and the English theatre as a whole, despite the cavils of a few contemporaries. Having played hundreds of roles in such a long apprenticeship to stardom—he had, for instance, played seven parts in *Hamlet* before he played the prince—Irving brought both enormous experience and a discriminating intelligence to the art of acting. Despite physical faults in speech and movement, he was an intense, magnetic, haunted actor who could almost hypnotize an *audience. He was equally powerful at playing nobility and goodness on the one hand, and malignity and evil on the other. The gentle vicar Dr Primrose in *Wills's *Olivia* which he played in 1885, the saintly king in the same author's *Charles I* (1872), the holy Becket in Tennyson's *Becket* (1893), were within his powers as much as were Iago, the malevolent king in *Boucicault's *Louis XI* (this he first acted in 1878), and Mephistopheles in *Faust*. As a young lover he was not really credible, and his Romeo was a failure. Both Shylock and Cardinal Wolsey were noble in their ruin. Irving's Hamlet, also noble and injured, was a revelation: rejecting all tradition and conventional 'points', and combining psychological insights with modern domesticity, it was a new, contemporary Hamlet, one of the finest Victorian stage performances. Irving was knighted in 1895, the first actor to be so honoured.   MRB

IRVING, LAWRENCE, *Henry Irving* (London, 1951)

IRWIN, BILL (1950–)

American *clown, *dancer, actor, and director. Irwin's singular marriage of physical virtuosity and postmodern mischief-making has appealed to critics and mass *audiences alike. His self-effacing persona and seemingly boneless body have served as comic centrepieces for several full-length shows, including *The Regard of Flight* (1982) and *Largely New York* (1989). These *surreal concoctions drew on traditional clowning strategies in satirizing hi-tech culture, the *avant-garde, and other contemporary targets, serving to associate him with the *New Vaudeville movement. A trademark routine saw Irwin struggling haplessly against unseen forces which threatened to suck him into the wings. *Fool Moon*, his clown *revue with David Shiner, merited several incarnations in the USA and Europe from 1993 to 2001. Irwin has been as likely to show up on children's *television (among other TV and *film appearances) as in stage roles like Galy Gay in *Brecht's *A Man's a Man* (directed by Robert *Woodruff in 1985). He has also appeared in plays by *Fo, *Molière, and Shakespeare. His direction for the stage includes his own *one-person performance of *Beckett prose pieces, *Texts for Nothing* (2000).   EW

IRWIN, MAY (1862–1938)

American actress, born Georgia Campbell in Ontario, Canada. Beginning as the younger of 'May and Flo, the Irwin Sisters', she played the *variety circuit and reached Tony *Pastor's in *New York; moved to *Daly's company in 1883, excelling in comic servant roles with lead actors Ada *Rehan and John *Drew; returned to *vaudeville; then joined Charles *Frohman's company in 1893. Her greatest stardom came as a 'coon shouter' in *farce with *The Widow Jones* (1895), which introduced 'The Bully Song'. She continued in similar vehicles into the 1920s, also earning wealth in real estate and dairy farming.   KM

ISAACS, EDITH (1878–1956)

American *critic and editor. A reporter and editor for the *Milwaukee Sentinel* before moving to *New York in 1904, Isaacs's major work began when she joined *Theatre Arts* in 1918. Editor from 1922 to 1946, she expanded the quarterly magazine to a monthly in 1924 and pursued its mission of promoting an American theatre based on art rather than commerce. A longtime champion of a *national theatre for the United States, Isaacs was instrumental in founding the National Theatre Conference (1925), the *American National Theatre and Academy (1935), and in conceiving the *Federal Theatre Project (1935).   MAF

ISHERWOOD, CHRISTOPHER (1904–86)

English writer. Best known as novelist and writer of short stories, he collaborated (1934–8) with W. H. *Auden on three plays to be staged by the *Group Theatre in *London: *The Dog beneath the Skin* (1935), *The Ascent of F6* (1937), and *On the Frontier* (1938). Precisely who was responsible for which elements in the composition is not clear, but presumably Isherwood conceived the overall *scenario and then developed the *plot and (somewhat thin) characterization of each of these works in the *expressionist manner required. Isherwood had experienced expressionist drama during his lengthy stay in Germany (1930–3); none of his fictional writings of the time demonstrates the profound moral and social *satire found in the plays, nor the developed Marxist *political critique that underpins them. The plays are remarkable for their vigour, lively and surprising invention, and eclectic fusing of varied elements of performance, high culture, and popular art. Yet beneath all three lies a deep-rooted anger and disgust, doubtless the product of Isherwood's time in *Berlin, with a Europe mindlessly succumbing to *fascism while pursuing a seemingly endless round of fun.   RAC

ISOLA, ALBERTO (1953–)

Peruvian actor, director, and member of *Ensayo in Lima (1983). He studied at Peru's Catholic University, *Milan's *Piccolo

Teatro School, the Drama Centre in *London, and Eugenio *Barba's workshops. Commanding a range of styles, Isola's powerful stage presence is well suited to difficult roles such as Hamlet, Lear, *Goethe's Faust, and *Brecht's Galileo. As a director, he modified the principles of *epic theatre, particularly in *The Red Sauce* (1984), *The Good Person of Setzuan* (1986), *La Nonna* (1993), *Real Numbers* (1994), and *Quintuplets* (1995).

LRG

ISTANBUL

Despite the existence of ancient forms of performance, modern Turkish theatre began with the introduction of Western-style plays in the nineteenth century. During the *Tanzimat* (the Ottoman reformation) period between 1839 and 1876, French theatre groups brought Western plays to Beyoglu, a district of Istanbul mostly comprising minorities, and young performance groups immediately translated these plays into Turkish. Gullu Agop, a young Armenian Ottoman artist, founded a company and directed plays in Turkish. He was followed by Ibrahim Sinasi, the author of the first Western-style Turkish play, *The Marriage of the Poet*, and Ahmet Vefik Pasha, who adapted *Molière to Turkish *characters. Theatrical *criticism began in this period, and was often concerned with a debate between Western and traditional forms.

The opening of the Darulbedayi (House of Beauty) National Conservatory in 1914 was the first step toward institutionalizing the new forms. Muhsin Ertugrul, often called the founder of modern Turkish theatre, was its driving force, and his success was such that Darulbedayi became the first government-subsidized theatre in 1931, changing its name to the Istanbul Municipality Theatre. The first Turkish private theatres opened in the 1950s and the movement expanded after the 1961 constitution, which created a freer environment for all the arts. New playwrights and theatre groups were increasingly concerned with social and political issues, influenced chiefly by *Brecht's *epic theatre, and the 1960s and 1970s were a time of provocative work.

This *politically charged environment was abruptly halted by the 1980 military coup which brought major constraints on the freedom of speech and expression. Political theatres were banned, severe *censorship was applied against other work, and some theatre workers were charged with offences. At the same time, government-subsidized and depoliticized theatres spread through the country. In the 1990s the municipal and state theatres of Istanbul continued to produce conventional work, mostly classical and modern plays by Turkish and foreign playwrights. Experimental groups emerged, seeking alternative forms of performance, influenced by exposure to international trends seen at the annual International Istanbul Theatre Festival.

HO

IVANOV, VSEVOLOD (1895–1963)

Russian/Soviet dramatist and prose writer, one of whose early occupations was as a *circus *clown, his experiences being later recorded in the autobiographical *We're Going to India* (1960). Influenced by Maxim *Gorky, Ivanov became a member of a Proletarian Writers' group, the Cosmists, in 1921, before joining the Serapion Brotherhood, named after E. T. A. *Hoffmann's hermit who had a liking for fantasy. Ivanov's own subject matter, couched in an ornamental style, tends to be grim and rather brutal. He adapted his novel about Siberian partisan activity, *Armoured Train 14–69* (1922), as a play for the *Moscow Art Theatre (1927). The production, which was directed by Ilya Sudakov, listed *Stanislavsky as an adviser and its optimistic, if melodramatic, revolutionary message became a turning point in the Art Theatre's relationship with the Soviet regime. It also gave *Kachalov as Vershinin (not to be confused with *Chekhov's colonel in *Three Sisters*) the opportunity to play a peasant role, although other members of the company, such as Olga *Knipper, did not relish the change from their normal *casting. Ivanov's play about the Kronstadt sailors' rising of 1921, *Blockade*, was also staged at the Art Theatre (1929).

NW

IVANOV, VYACHESLAV (1866–1949)

Russian poet, dramatist, theoretician. Whilst in *Paris, during the 1890s, Ivanov became interested in medieval *mystery plays and in Nietzsche's *theory of *tragedy. In 1905 he settled in *St Petersburg where his apartment, the Tower, became an artistic meeting place and theatrical venue. He is important as a theorist who sought, in the spirit of the *symbolist movement, to resurrect the religious ecstasy and theatrical forms of *Greek theatre as aspects of communal experience. He wrote two tragedies, *Tantalus* (1903) and *Prometheus* (1919), which express his religio-philosophical views, as does his essay 'The Essence of Tragedy' (1912).

NW

IZENOUR, GEORGE CHARLES (1912–   )

American theatre consultant, inventor, educator; a leader in modernizing theatre technology. Izenour's most significant contribution came through his work at the Electromechanical Laboratory at Yale, of which he was the founder (1939–77); he also taught at the *Yale School of Drama. He invented many important *lighting, rigging, and computer control systems for theatre and *television, and served as design and acoustical consultant for over 100 theatres around the world. He is primarily known for his advocacy of adaptable, multiform theatres designed for optimal sight lines and acoustics. His books include *Theater Design* (1977) and *Roofed Theaters of Classical Antiquity* (1992).

WFC

IZUMI KYŌKA (1873–1939)

Japanese novelist and playwright. Starting in 1894, much of his early melodramatic fiction was adapted for the *shimpa stage, but Kyōka (he was usually known by that assumed 'art' name) became increasingly dissatisfied with adaptations of his work. In contrast to the *shimpa* *melodramas, his own plays were more fantastic and *surrealistic in style, like his best fiction. His 1907 translation (with the German scholar Tobari Chikufū) of Gerhart *Hauptmann's fairy play *The Sunken Bell* was a guide for the *dramaturgy of fantasy, but he also had *nō and *kabuki for models. Ahead of their time, his best plays—*The Sea God's Villa* (1913), *The Castle Tower* (1917), and *The Wild Rose* (1923)—were not staged until after his death. Kyōka's works have enjoyed something of a revival since the 1960s, thanks largely to adaptations by *Kara Jūrō, *Terayama Shūji, *Suzuki Tadashi, and *Ninagawa Yukio. The popular kabuki *onnagata *Bandō Tamasaburō V frequently stars in *shimpa* productions of his plays, and has directed two *films based on Kyōka's work, *The Surgery* (1990) and *The Castle Tower* (1995).

CP

·J·

JACKSON, BARRY (1879–1961)

English director and *manager. Trained as an architect, Jackson was heir to a fortune derived from one of the leading grocery firms in the Midlands. In 1907 he founded an *amateur group in Birmingham, the Pilgrim Players, which went professional in 1913 as the *Birmingham Repertory Theatre, one of the first examples of the *regional repertory movement. Jackson funded a new *playhouse that year, and despite a number of *financial crises maintained the venture out of his own pocket for 22 years. (After 1935 the theatre was administered by a trust, with support from subscription holders.) A close associate of *Shaw's, Jackson was also the prime mover of the *Malvern Festival, which he directed from 1927 to 1939. In 1945 he succeeded Robert *Atkins as director of the *Shakespeare Memorial Theatre in Stratford, where he attempted to break out of the provincialism that had bedevilled the annual *festivals. Among his successes were Peter *Brook's productions of *Love's Labour's Lost* (1946) and *Romeo and Juliet* (1947) and Michael *Benthall's *Hamlet* (1948) with Robert *Helpmann and Paul *Scofield alternating the lead. But Jackson's cosmopolitan orientation, and his policies of higher spending and more adventurous productions, did not accord with the conservatism of the governors, and he was replaced in 1948 by Anthony *Quayle. He was knighted in 1925, and continued to direct the Birmingham Rep Theatre until his death.
RJ

JACKSON, GLENDA (1936–)

English actress. Jackson first came to critical notice with her participation in Charles *Marowitz and Peter *Brook's Theatre of *Cruelty season in *London (1964). She impressed spectators with her transformation in one sequence from a Christine Keeler figure performing a striptease to Jackie Kennedy in mourning. This led to a much-praised starring role as Charlotte Corday in Brook's production of Peter *Weiss's *Marat/Sade* (1965), a sexually knowing Ophelia to David *Warner's angry young Hamlet in Peter *Hall's controversial production for the *Royal Shakespeare Company (1965), and Masha in the *Royal Court Theatre production of *Chekhov's *The Three Sisters*, directed by William Gaskill (1967). Other notable stage performances include *Mortimer's *Collaborators* (1973), the RSC's *Hedda Gabler* (1975), Hugh Whitemore's *Stevie* (1977), *O'Neill's *Strange Interlude* (1984), and Charles *Wood's *Across from the Garden of Allah* (1986). Having appeared in over 30 movies, Jackson's *film career has been more consistent than her stage work. She garnered two Academy awards for her performances in *Women in Love* (1969) and *A Touch of Class* (1973). She reached a popular *audience playing Elizabeth I in the *television mini-series *Elizabeth R* (1971), a role which exploited her ability to project a powerful intelligence and sexuality. Jackson retired from acting in 1992 and was elected to Parliament. She was appointed Under-Secretary of State for Transportation in the Tony Blair government, and later campaigned (unsuccessfully) to be the Labour Party candidate for Mayor of *London.
MDG

JACOBEAN THEATRE *See* EARLY MODERN PERIOD IN EUROPE.

JACOBI, DEREK (1938–)

English actor. After beginning his professional career at the *Birmingham Repertory Company, Jacobi joined the fledgling *National Theatre in 1963, playing Laertes to Peter *O'Toole's Hamlet. He also appeared in *Othello* with Laurence *Olivier (1964), Noël *Coward's *Hay Fever* (1964), Peter *Shaffer's *Black Comedy* (1966) and Clifford *Williams's all-male production of *As You Like It* (1967). In 1972 Jacobi joined the *Prospect Theatre Company, notably playing the leads in *The Lady's Not* for *Burning* (1978) and *Hamlet* (1977), which *toured internationally. From 1982 to 1985, he worked with the *Royal Shakespeare Company, playing Peer Gynt, Prospero, Benedick, and Cyrano, for which he won an Olivier *award. In 1986 he originated the role of Alan Turing in Hugh Whitemore's *Breaking the Code*. Jacobi also appeared in a number of starry West End revivals including *Richard II* and *Richard III* (1989), *Kean* (1990), and *Becket* (1991). He served for two seasons as *artistic director of the *Chichester Festival Theatre, playing the lead in *Uncle Vanya* there in 1995. Jacobi is best known for playing the title role in *television's *I, Claudius* (1976).   MDG

JACOBS (RICH), SALLY (1932–)

English designer. London born, she studied at St Martin's School of Arts and the Central School of Arts and Crafts. Her first job was for British Feature Films, but she became Peter *Brook's favourite designer at the *Royal Shakespeare Company, collaborating on the Theatre of *Cruelty season (1964), *The Screens* (1964), *US* (1966), and the *film and stage versions of *Marat/Sade* (1964), where inmates in grubby white tunics cavorted like Daumier caricatures in a brick-walled asylum littered with sunken pits. For Brook's *A Midsummer Night's Dream* (1970), Jacobs created a galleried white cube with iron ladders, trapezes, and scarlet-feathered trampoline; stilt-walking, plate-spinning fairies stalked woodland glades of coiled wire, which dropped upon the unwary lovers. In 1973, following Brook's research tour of West Africa, she designed *The Conference of Birds* and his film *Meetings with Remarkable Men* (1976). In 1982, four years after her husband's death, Jacobs returned to *London; her 1984 collaboration with director Andrei *Şerban on the orientalist *opera *Turandot* gave rise to a flourishing career with the Royal Opera at *Covent Garden, Paines Plough, and the *Royal Court.   RVL

JAHNN, HANS HENNY (1894–1959)

German novelist, dramatist, music publisher, and organ builder. Jahnn established his name as a major writer with *Pastor Ephraim Magnus* (1919), a controversial play dealing with homosexuality and incest which brought him the coveted Kleist Prize. His best-known play is *Medea* (1926), in which the title figure is explicitly cast as a 'Negress' in order to draw parallels with European *racism. Other plays include *Die Krönung Richards III* (*The Coronation of Richard III*, 1922) and *Thomas Chatterton* (1956). His style was highly idiosyncratic, bearing the influence of *expressionism as well as an eclectic personal mythology. In both his writing and life he rejected social norms and institutions, championing instead a heathen, pan-erotic return to the deeper strata of mythology, where Western dualisms are transcended.   CBB

JAKARTA

Located in western Java in *Indonesia, Jakarta is a sprawling harbour metropolis founded in 1527 as Jayakarta (City of Victory). As the Dutch East India Company's administrative centre for over 350 years, it was known internationally as Batavia until 1945 when Achmad Sukarno—Indonesia's first president—declared the country's independence and established Jakarta as the nation's capital. With over 12 million mostly immigrant residents in 2001, Sundanese (from west Java), Javanese (from central and east Java), and ethnic Chinese comprise Jakarta's major ethnic groups. The city's indigenous inhabitants, *orang Betawi* (Batavia people), and their theatrical traditions were gradually marginalized until the 1970s when *lenong* (popular drama), as well as the *shadow-puppet *wayang kulit Betawi* and the *masked *dance *topeng Betawi* were 'rediscovered' through government and private efforts. Many Betawi revivals have been staged at Taman Ismail Marzuki in central Jakarta. TIM, supervised by the Jakarta Arts Council, has mounted domestic and international theatre, *dance, and music in its four *auditoriums and arts college since 1968. Much of its programming was a reflection of Mohamed Suharto's New Order government (1966–98) mandate to develop a national identity by promoting the 'peaks' of Indonesian culture while assimilating the best of Western culture.

Jakarta has been the centre of Indonesian-language theatre (*sandiwara*, *tonil*, *drama*, *teater moderen*) since the 1920s when Rustam *Effendi and other Western-educated nationalist intellectuals were active. In 1955, in response to prevailing theatrical conventions, the National Theatre Academy was founded to *train actors in the *Stanislavsky system. However, after W. S. *Rendra's groundbreaking experimental piece *Bip Bop* (1968) at the Balai Budaya (Cultural Pavilion), a new generation of theatre practitioners working at TIM—including director-playwrights Arifin C. *Noer, Putu *Wijaya, and Nano *Riantiarno—were inspired to delve into their own cultural roots rather than adhere to Western *realism. Despite years of strict government *censorship, their plays have shaped the direction of Indonesian theatre as a whole for over 30 years.   CRG

JAMES, HENRY (1843–1916)

American novelist. Hoping also for a career as playwright in *London, the expatriate completed some fifteen plays, though only four of these were staged: *The American, Guy Domville* (a *historical *tragedy written for George *Alexander which met a hostile reception in 1895), *The High Bid*, and *The Saloon*. James, profoundly observant of the *acting techniques of French theatre, which he deemed superior to English styles, became a shrewd critic of performance; his collected reviews were published in *The Scenic Art* (1949; see CRITICISM). These and his detailed advice about her roles to Elizabeth *Robins (chiefly in *Ibsen's plays) offer considerable insight into turn-of-the-century practice. *The High Bid* (1907), revised from a *one-act drama (*Summersoft*) created for Ellen *Terry in 1895, shows James's *dramaturgical principles at their best. The *dialogue teems with directions, determining not movement but the meticulous tonal placing of words and phrases. James's was to be a drama of psychological, not physical, *action.   RAC

JANIN, JULES-GABRIEL (1804–74)

French journalist. The foremost dramatic critic of his generation, Janin started his journalistic career at *Le Figaro*, before moving to the *Journal des débats*, where he produced the weekly theatre feuilleton for 40 years. Disapproving of Victor *Hugo, and generally hostile to the *Comédie-Française, he was never afraid to express trenchant *criticism of plays he disapproved of: his comments on *Dumas's *Caligula* (1837) provoked the author to challenge him to a duel. He championed François Ponsard's revival of the *neoclassical manner, and was enthusiastic in his support of the young *Rachel.   WDH

JANNINGS, EMIL (1884–1950)

German actor. Jannings began his career in Görlitz and various provincial theatres before moving to *Berlin in 1914. His breakthrough came in 1918 in Max *Reinhardt's production of *Kleist's *The Broken Jug*, in which he played the magistrate Adam. From 1920 he acted predominantly in *film, working with Ernst Lubitsch and F. W. Murnau. Between 1926 and 1929 he was in Hollywood with Joseph von Sternberg, receiving the first Oscar for best actor for his leading role in *The Last Command*. He returned to Germany in 1930 to play Professor Unrat in Sternberg's *The Blue Angel* opposite Marlene Dietrich, and divided his time between stage and cinema. Under the Nazis he played a dominant role as actor and representative of the film industry, and received various awards culminating in 1940 with his appointment as director of UFA, the state-controlled film company. Jannings effected a successful transition from a highly *expressionistic style in stage and silent film roles to a more controlled *realism for the talkies.   CBB

JAPAN

The performing arts have a long history in Japan, stretching back to shamanistic rituals in pre-Buddhist times before the fourth century. *Kojiki* (*The Record of Ancient Matters*), compiled in 712, already indicates the presence of older Shinto propitiatory ceremonies and dances that may be considered early manifestations of theatrical expression. With the coming of Buddhism and Chinese culture to Japan in the sixth century and after, proto-theatrical forms were imported from *China and performed at court. *Bugaku*, 'dance entertainment', accompanied by *gakgaku* (Chinese-style court music), was introduced in the eighth century and is still performed today. Related forms called *gigaku* preserve music and *dances from Buddhist *rituals. These early forms included the use of *masks and other elements later incorporated into indigenous Japanese theatre, which grew from this base of imported forms mixed with *folk elements. Two unusual aspects stand out. First, difficulties of travel were such that Japanese theatre developed virtually independent of foreign models from the period of these early cultural contacts until the end of the nineteenth century. Secondly, patronage—whether from the court or a more general public—continued to support theatrical families in various types of theatre; as a result, most major varieties of traditional performance have persevered, providing important influences on newer forms.

The earliest major Japanese theatre was the *nō, brought to its first great peak of excellence in *Kyoto, the imperial capital, by *Kan'ami (1333–84) and his son *Zeami (1363–1443). Nō, which normally uses one masked performer in the leading role (*shite), is a form of total theatre involving dance, pantomime, chanting, singing, and declamation. The use of a *chorus and small musical ensemble, and the high literary and spiritual value of its *texts, have sparked comparisons with ancient *Greek theatre, which shares many of the same devices. Performers are male. The nō began as a popular theatre and remained the central theatrical form patronized by the educated as well as the popular classes down to the end of the medieval period. After 1600, urbanization created new *audiences largely drawn from a growing merchant class. The nō, now reserved almost exclusively for aristocrats and higher government officials, was seen less often by ordinary audiences but because of its prestige continued to serve as a source of *plots, *characters, and general cultural authority.

Two new forms of theatre became central in the Tokugawa Period (1600–1867). The first of these was the *puppet theatre or *jōruri* (since the nineteenth century referred to as *bunraku), which began in the Kyoto–*Osaka area even before 1600. The puppets of bunraku are worked from below, unlike Western *marionettes. They were used in the late medieval period to illustrate the musical narratives of itinerant chanters who roamed the country performing sections of such well-known texts as *The Tale of the Heike*. The new urbanism brought about both fixed theatres for such performances and playwrights to provide the chanters with fresh material. The greatest of these writers was *Chikamatsu Monzaemon, whose dramas, both contemporary and historical, were and are deservedly popular, particularly his love suicide plays.

*Kabuki, the actors' theatre of the period, first developed in Kyoto, supposedly with the suggestive dances of *Okuni and her female troupe in the first decade of the seventeenth century. Concerned about civic order, the new Tokugawa government banned these performances and eventually those of the troupes of young boys which soon took their place. Kabuki as an art form began when adult male actors developed a set of aesthetic principles for it. Men now played women's roles, as in Shakespeare's time, and these so-called *onnagata brought performances to a high level of elegance and beauty. The troupes borrowed thematic material from the nō and bunraku theatres in order to elevate their artistic status, but in the eyes of the public kabuki did not reach a satisfying level of accomplishment until the mid-eighteenth century. Many of the great plays in the kabuki repertory, such as *Chūshingura*, began as bunraku plays, quickly appropriated by companies of live actors. Despite social strictures against actors in Tokugawa Japan, the great performers were as popular as rock stars today, imitated and written about.

In the early nineteenth century it became clear to the Japanese government that the country, closed since the 1630s, must face the growing presence of Europe and the United States in Asia. Japan was officially opened by the young Emperor Meiji in 1868, and the first generation of young Japanese artists and intellectuals who travelled abroad were fascinated by the theatre performances they attended in Europe. That fascination was to lead to a whole set of new developments. In the latter decades of the nineteenth century, bunraku and kabuki were still contemporary theatres, staging new plays with only an occasional revival. With the continuing inroads of Western culture, however, audiences began to find the melodramatic stories and, in particular, the use of men playing women's roles clumsy and unrelated to the changing culture of the time. By the turn of the century, these two forms of Tokugawa theatre joined the nō in becoming iconic and classical forms. All three remained widely performed and appreciated, but are now understood as explorations of the general human condition, and few modern or contemporary dramas utilizing their methods have found any success.

Two important new forms of Japanese theatre developed from the late nineteenth century onwards. The first of these, *shimpa (new school drama), attempted to modernize kabuki and make it more responsive to social and personal issues at the turn of the century, mixing actresses with *onnagata*, using more colloquial language, and commissioning plays from contemporary writers. Nevertheless, the form lost its cutting edge after a decade or two. Troupes and performances still continue today, but the productions seem sentimental and outmoded. Nevertheless, playwrights such as *Izumi Kyōka and *Mishima Yukio were attracted to *shimpa* and found genuine artistic success in its style. The second development was *shingeki, 'new theatre', a spoken theatre created along Western lines. Japanese admiration for three European playwrights—Shakespeare, *Chekhov, and *Ibsen—helped bring this about, and the work of *Tsubouchi Shōyō and *Osanai Kaoru was crucial in the development of the form. Japanese intellectuals were attracted to Western theatre, among other reasons, because spoken *dialogue allowed for discussions of contemporary issues, both personal and political. Left-wing *political theatre, particularly in Germany during the Weimar Republic, brought similar developments in Japan as well. In this inter-war period, some gifted writers and directors, such as *Kishida Kunio, continued to work for what they considered to be artistic ends, while others, such as *Kubo Sakae, saw theatre as a means to enlighten their public on the nature of social evils. Such social concerns flew in the face of continuing repression in Japan by the militaristic government; by 1940 most of the theatre companies were closed down and many left-wing artists and intellectuals were jailed.

In the post-war period the theatre of the left, now free from government interference, continued to express a strong sense of social concern. A number of superior playwrights worked in the first two decades after 1945, in particular *Kinoshita Junji, but the models employed were still European in nature. With the coming of the 1960s, however, and the debates over Japan's involvement with the US Security Treaty and the Vietnam War, a new generation of playwrights, performers, and directors took little interest in the *realistic forms imported from abroad and sometimes went back to pre-modern Japanese forms such as kabuki or shamanistic ritual to find inspiration. Such contemporary directors as *Suzuki Tadashi and *Ninagawa Yukio began their work during this period, as did playwrights like *Shimizu Kunio, *Kara Jūrō, *Terayama Shūji, *Betsuyaku Minoru, and others. In the 1990s, however, Japan entered a quieter political period and the theatre, as in the United States and Europe, often became more introspective and self-conscious, bringing *metatheatrical and metaphysical elements to the fore. Representative of these trends is the work of director and writer *Ōta Shōgo, whose plays, often located in such unlikely settings as a garbage dump or a public water station, examine the nature of contemporary Japanese society through non-verbal techniques.

In addition to these ambitious forms, other entertainments have taken over the function served by kabuki in the Tokugawa Period. Japanese versions of foreign *musicals, as well as musicals written by Japanese composers, have become increasingly popular, and skits and commercial dramas are widely performed around the country, both in the theatre and on *television. The institution that has drawn the most attention from foreign observers is the *Takarazuka revue, an all-girl troupe with companies in *Tokyo and the Osaka area. The actresses who play the *heroes and heroines are made into important stars, and the audiences are largely female. The Takarazuka performers, as well as someone like *Bandō Tamasaburō, the brilliant actor who plays female roles both in kabuki and in special adaptations of Western plays like *The Lady of the Camellias* by *Dumas *fils*, are far more popular with the public than the distinguished artists in the post-war *avant-garde.   JTR

BRAZELL, KAREN (ed.), *Traditional Japanese Theater: an anthology of plays* (New York, 1997)

ORTOLANI, BENITO, *The Japanese Theatre: from shamanistic ritual to contemporary pluralism* (Princeton, 1990)

POWELL, BRIAN, *Japan's Modern Theatre: a century of change and continuity* (London, 2000)

JAQUES-DALCROZE, ÉMILE (1865–1950)

Swiss teacher and composer who invented eurhythmics, a method of music education. Fauré and Bruckner were among his teachers in *Paris and *Vienna (1884–91), and he observed the intersections between rhythm and movement in *African music while conducting in Algiers. As professor at the Geneva Music Conservatory (1892–1910), he found that his students could read music but lacked listening skill, so he developed an innovative approach that used the human body to appreciate music. From the basic elements of walking, singing, breathing, and beating time, he turned to bolder methods: barefoot skipping, running, lunging, jumping, cooperating with partners. From 1911 to 1914 he taught in the model garden city of Hellerau ('on a high plateau') near Dresden. There he attracted international interest in a college where students learned *solfège* (ear training), gymnastics, improvisation, music theory, and *dance. *Appia designed the performance space, an enormous hall seating over 700 in movable raked seats; steps and platforms could be changed easily, and fabric hid banks of electric lights that dimmed and brightened. Among the artists who visited Hellerau were *Reinhardt, *Stanislavsky, *Shaw, *Claudel, Ernest Bloch, *Diaghilev, *Laban, Mary Wigman, and Marie Lambert, some of whom witnessed an influential student recital of *Gluck's *Orpheus* (1913) which used Appia's stage and *lighting designs. The First World War ended the Hellerau experiment, and Jaques-Dalcroze returned to Geneva to teach until just before his death. By 1935 he had published 25 volumes on his technique. His two most important books are available in translation as *Rhythm, Movement, and Education* (1921) and *Eurhythmics, Art, and Education* (1930). Eurhythmics continues to be taught around the world. FL

JARDIEL PONCELA, ENRIQUE (1901–52)

Spanish playwright and novelist. After an early success with a clever but traditional *comedy, *A Sleepless Spring Night* (1927), he developed a personal style of *absurdism in *plot and language that is often described as 'jardielesco'. During the period of the Spanish Republic and the early years of the dictatorship, he became Spain's most innovative comic writer and reached his peak of popularity with *A Round-Trip Husband* (1939) and *Eloise Is under an Almond Tree* (1941). In 1933–4 he worked as a scriptwriter in the Spanish division of Fox Studios and later based one of his most ambitious plays, the darkly parodic *Love Only Lasts 2000 Metres* (1941), on his impressions of Hollywood. Renewed interest in his plays came with a new production of *Eloise* at Spain's National Theatre Centre in 1984 and a major revival of his *operetta spoof *Carlo Monte in Monte Carlo* (1939) at the Teatro *Español in 1996. MPH

JARI GAN

A number of performances in *Bangladesh bear the generic name *jari*. Though varied and divergent in form, most are based on legends relating to Muslim heroes Imam Hasan and Imam Hosain, grandsons of the Prophet. The most renowned is *jari gan* from eastern Mymensingh, which commemorates the death of Hosain at Karbala. The performers, who are male Sunni Muslims, work chiefly as farmers. From the evening of the new moon of Muharram, villagers conduct austere rites and make offerings in the local *dargah* (shrine) or *mukam-ghar* (consecrated house) constructed in honour of Imam Hasan and Imam Hosain. They also form processions carrying the *tabut* (imitation coffin), *tazia* (a replica of the tomb of Imam Hasan and Imam Hosain), and horses (live as well as effigies), accompanied by musicians and armed devotees. *Jari gan* is usually performed in the daytime from the first to the tenth of Muharram, in the courtyard of the houses of devotees. The performance space is a large circle, about 9 m (30 feet) in diameter, with spectators standing or sitting around it, the *mukam-ghar* at one end of the courtyard. The lead narrator (*bayati*) performs in the circle while choral singer-dancers (the *khedual*), colourfully dressed and wearing ankle-bells, provide vocal and rhythmic accompaniment in an inner circular arrangement. No other musical instruments are used. The *texts concern events leading to the death of the two Imams, the rescue of the family of Hosain by Hanifa, their stepbrother, and the slaying of Yazid. The performance usually begins with religious salutations. The *bayati* then delivers short passages of an episode in song, moving in rhythm around the circle of *khedual*, who sing a refrain and dance at the end of each passage. *Jari gan* is one of the few indigenous performances of Bangladesh which ends in pathos. SJA

JARRY, ALFRED (1873–1907)

French playwright, most famous for *Ubu roi* (Théâtre de l'*Œuvre, *Paris, 1897), performed when Jarry was 15 years old by the champion of the *symbolists, *Lugné-Poe. The play, which began life as a schoolboy send-up of Jarry's physics teacher, caused a scandal in the theatre with its scatological and theatrical irreverence. The play essentially is a *satire on *Macbeth* and features a *Punch-and-Judy-like king and his wife who are motivated by avarice or whim. The *plot is a series of spontaneous murderous events which are quite often illogical. Accused of puerility, the play broke every convention of nineteenth-century theatre with its anti-*realism and *metatheatrical self-consciousness. It features one of the most notorious opening lines of the theatre: 'Merdre!' ('Crrrap!'). Jarry invested heavily in the production, dictating everything from *scenery to actors' delivery. From then on Ubu became his obsession and in his personal life he took on Ubuesque characteristics which led to some extreme antisocial behaviour. He wrote three further unsuccessful Ubu plays (*Ubu cocu*, *Ubu enchaîné*, and *Ubu sur la butte*). But his influence spread right throughout the twentieth century: *Ubu roi* was accepted as a precursor of *surrealism and the theatre of the *absurd, Jarry's name headed Antonin *Artaud's first theatrical enterprise, and his spoof philosophy, 'Pataphysics' (described as upsetting 'the balance of waking logic'), inspired a literary movement after the Second World War. Alcoholism contributed largely to his premature death.

BRS

JATAKA

Stories of Buddha's previous births. All *jataka* tales are centred on the doctrines of *karma* (deed) and *samsara* (cycle of birth and death), and include, in their prose forms, animal fables, *folk tales, and adventures or romances of Bodhisattva kings and princes. *Jataka* stories are popular in traditional theatres of mainland South-East Asia, especially in the Thai theatre form called *lakon*.

MA

JATRA

Bengali theatre form performed by itinerant companies travelling to distant villages and small towns. A *jatra* troupe in *Bangladesh is comprised of seven to ten musicians, eight to ten female dancer-singers, about twelve actors, four or five actresses, a director, *prompter, and stagehands (who might serve as cooks as well as supernumeraries); in West *Bengal in *India the troupes are even larger. *Jatra* is usually given in the open under a temporary canopy, the musicians sitting on opposite sides of an elevated stage, the spectators arranged on three sides. In urban areas of West Bengal, *jatra* is also performed on *proscenium stages with scenic projections and recorded *sound effects. Often disdained by the urban middle class, *jatra* enjoys immense popularity among ordinary people of all religions and castes.

Jatra (literally, 'act of setting out on a journey') performances are based on written *texts, composed mostly in prose interspersed with a few lyrical passages. The plays fall into three broad categories: social, *historical, and biographical. Common to all are heightened conflict and highly charged displays of emotion. In social plays, which have the widest popularity, the *characters and stories are drawn from contemporary life. Historical plays enact fictional accounts of past events in order to promote heroism, patriotism, nationalism, or harmony between Hindus and Muslims. Biographies of important personalities such as Gandhi, Hitler, Ho Chi Minh, and Che Guevara have recently become important materials for a third

variety of *jatra* plays. In addition, a few devotional plays use religious legends drawn from the *Ramayana*, the *Mahabharata*, and various Puranas. No matter the category, the plays are eventful and fast moving, built on principles of European *dramaturgy, and tend to rely on type characters who are clearly divided into the virtuous and the vicious. A distinctive figure, Vivek, is a personification of conscience who urges the *protagonist(s) on to the path of truth and virtue and warns the antagonist(s) of the fatal outcome of vice. The Vivek replaced an earlier convention known as the Juri, a group of four to ten singers who sang for the characters.

A *jatra* performance in Bangladesh usually commences around eleven in the evening. The musicians begin with the 'opening concert', the tune of which is the signature piece of the form. Then comes a patriotic song by a group of female singers, followed by a variety show of song-and-dance numbers and comic interludes (which are inserted again at the end of each *act or section of *scenes). Around midnight, a fast-paced overture ensues, followed by the play proper. The performance is mostly *dialogic, interspersed with occasional *soliloquies and *monologues. The music and songs seek a heightened emotional intensity. Similarly, a competent *jatra* performer is much larger than life in both body and speech; she or he can hold a few thousand spectators spellbound, moving them to tears and *laughter. The performance ends by daybreak. In West Bengal, however, *jatra* performances are often only three hours in duration and are given mostly in the evenings.

Jatra evolved from ancient Buddhist processions with subsequent layers of acculturation by Tantric Shaivite, Vaishnavite, and other indigenous cults. The process of secularization began in the first quarter of the nineteenth century in the urban areas of Bengal, especially Calcutta (*Kolkata). In the early twentieth century, when Bengal was deeply immersed in nationalist Swadeshi movement against British colonialism, a popular *jatra* actor-director, Mukunda Das, evolved a *political variant called *swadeshi jatra*, which attained great popularity. The partition of Bengal in 1947 had a tremendous impact on the form. Since Calcutta was the artistic and economic centre, companies based there lost the market of eastern Bengal, which became a province of *Pakistan (and later became Bangladesh). *Jatra* in West Bengal made a tremendous economic recovery starting in the early 1960s by incorporating *illusionist stage techniques. Since the mid-1970s it has become a sizeable entertainment industry superseding even the commercial theatre of Calcutta, and many renowned actors and directors have succeeded with the form. On the other hand, in post-1947 eastern Bengal *jatra* suffered from subtle ideological intervention from the Islamic state, causing gradual erosion of Hindu religious elements. With the emergence of Bangladesh in 1971 the form attracted renewed interest; 50 companies were performing *jatra* in 1972, over 200 in 1987, though the government of Bangladesh continues to be suspicious of *jatra*'s moral status.

SJA

JAVA *See* INDONESIA.

JEFFERSON FAMILY

Anglo-American actors. **Thomas Jefferson** (1732–1804), patriarch of the *family, was a minor actor under *Garrick at *Drury Lane, *toured the provinces, and became a *manager in Plymouth. His son **Joseph I** (1774–1832) began his career with his father, but was brought to the USA by John *Hodgkinson to join the *Park Theatre in 1795. Jefferson remained there until 1803, when he moved to *Philadelphia and the *Chestnut Street Theatre. He was considered one of the best comic performers on the American stage. His son **Joseph II** (1804–42) was less regarded as an actor than as a scenic artist. He worked at both trades in *New York (1835–7), first at William Dinneford's Franklin Theatre and then at *Niblo's Garden. After 1837 he toured the west with his family, playing many of the same venues as Noah *Ludlow and Sol *Smith.

His son **Joseph III** (1829–1905) became the most famous comic actor on the nineteenth-century American stage. His first theatrical experience was at the age of 4 when he performed with T. D. ('Jim Crow') *Rice. After his father's death, he toured the south with his mother and soon was playing supporting roles for such leading stars as Junius Brutus *Booth and Edwin *Forrest. For a short time he managed theatres in Baltimore and Richmond before joining Laura *Keene's company in *New York. His comic talents were quickly recognized, and he gained popular acclaim for his portrayals of Dr Pangloss in *The Heir at Law* and Ase Trenchard in Tom *Taylor's *Our American Cousin*. He moved to the *Winter Garden Theatre in 1858 where he began a pivotal association with Dion *Boucicault. After a failed attempt at playing the title role in his own version of *Rip Van Winkle* in 1859, Jefferson convinced Boucicault to revise the play. In 1865, while in *London, Jefferson perfected the *character that would define his life and career for the next 40 years in America. Although he played other comic leads on occasion, Rip Van Winkle remained his primary role until his retirement in 1904.   PAD

JEFFORD, BARBARA (1930–   )

Accomplished English actress, born in Devon, who trained at the *Royal Academy of Dramatic Art and played almost all of Shakespeare's *heroines at the *Shakespeare Memorial Theatre (1950–4), *Old Vic (1956–62), and *Prospect Theatre (1977–9). At Stratford her roles included Isabella, Desdemona, Rosalind, and Helena in *A Midsummer Night's Dream*, while at the Old Vic she appeared as Imogen in *Cymbeline*, Beatrice, Portia, Viola, Ophelia, Lady Anne in *Richard III*, Queen Margaret in *Henry VI*, Isabella, Regan, Ophelia, Rosalind, and Lady Macbeth. At the *National Theatre she was Gertrude (1976) and, returning to Stratford for the *Royal Shakespeare Company, was Volumnia

in *Coriolanus* (1989), the Countess in *All's Well That Ends Well*, and Mistress Quickly in *The Merry Wives of Windsor* (1992).

AS

JELINEK, ELFRIEDE (1946–   )

Austrian novelist, dramatist, poet, and essayist. Initially a writer of *avant-garde prose and poetry, Jelinek first came to attention as a dramatist with *feminist-inflected pieces about *Ibsen's Nora (*Was geschah, nachdem Nora ihren Mann verlassen hatte oder Stützen der Gesellschaft, What Happened after Nora Left her Husband*, 1979) and Clara Schumann (*Clara S*, 1981). The latter abandons *characters and *plot for a collage of voices, a device which became typical for her writing. Despite an expressed dislike of theatrical representation, Jelinek has become one of the most celebrated and controversial writers in the German-speaking world.   CBB

JELLICOE, ANN (1927–   )

English playwright and director. In the early 1950s, Jellicoe founded the Cockpit Theatre Club for experimental work, while teaching at the Central School of Speech and Drama. After her play *The Sport of my Mad Mother* placed third in the 1956 *Observer* drama competition, Jellicoe became the only woman in the *Royal Court's stable of angry young men, co-directing her play with Keith Johnstone in 1958. *The Sport of my Mad Mother*, a *surrealistic fantasia on violence with striking visual imagery and rhythmic *dialogue, broke from the Court's typical *kitchen sink *realism and was coolly received. Her next play, *The Knack* (1962), was her one true commercial and critical success. This lightly *absurdist piece with its free-wheeling *plot about youthful sexual games looks forward to Swinging *London later in the decade. After spending several years in the early 1970s as the literary manager for the Royal Court, Jellicoe founded the Colway Theatre Trust and concentrated her energies on *community theatre, writing and directing the massive *history play *The Reckoning* (1978). In 1985, Jellicoe resigned from the Colway in protest at budget cuts.

MDG

JENKIN, LEN (1941–   )

American playwright and director. Born in New York, Jenkin received BA, MA, and Ph.D. degrees at Columbia University. He is the author of many stage works, which he occasionally directs himself. These began with *Kitty Hawk* (1972) and *Grand American Exhibition* (1973). *Limbo Tales* (1980) won him an Obie *award for both writing and directing. Another Obie came his way in 1984 for the *New York production of *Five of Us* (Seattle, 1981), an unsettling play about the attempted burglarizing of a retarded epileptic. He has a fondness for bizarre *characters and incidents. His work includes some adaptations of prose tales, such as *Voltaire's *Candide* (1982) and Kafka's *A Country Doctor* (1983). His plays have received productions throughout the USA, Europe, and *Japan. Since 1980 he has been a professor in the dramatic writing programme at New York University.

CT

JERNIDIER, JOSÉ (1959–)

Guadeloupean director, playwright, actor, and co-founder (with José Egouy, 1987) of Théâtre, Tradition et Culture + Bakanal, a semi-professional company performing popular French and creole theatre in Guadeloupe and *Paris. The troupe arose from *improvisational techniques, *street theatre, storytelling, popular *farce, *carnival, and Lewoz *rituals. Jernidier directed its best-known work, *La Mort d'Oluwemi d'Ajumako* (*The Death of Oluwemi d'Ajumako*, 1986) by Maryse *Condé, the *devised *Moun Koubari* (*The Koubari Neighbourhood*, 1991), and the première of Condé's *Comédie d'amour* (1993).

AR

JERROLD, DOUGLAS (1803–57)

English dramatist and journalist. Born into a family of strolling players, he served for two years in the navy as a boy and subsequently became a printer's apprentice in *London. He wrote many *farces and *melodramas for the *minor theatres from 1818 to 1832, working for a few months in 1828 as a much exploited house dramatist at the Coburg (see OLD VIC THEATRE). He scored a huge success with a *nautical melodrama, *Black Ey'd Susan* (Surrey Theatre, 1829), which held the stage for the rest of the century but made him no money. His first success in the *legitimate theatre was a domestic drama, *The Rent Day* (*Drury Lane, 1832); this also entered the repertory and was frequently revived. He continued to write plays for the next two decades but moved away from the radical themes found in several of the early melodramas, notably in another nautical play, *The Mutiny at the Nore* (Pavilion Theatre, 1830), and concentrated on *satirical high *comedies palely reminiscent of *Congreve (without the sex) and *Sheridan. These plays (for example *Bubbles of the Day*, *Covent Garden, 1842; *Time Works Wonders*, *Haymarket, 1845) were often favourably noticed, especially for the sparkle of their *dialogue, and Jerrold was constantly praised for his efforts to 'revive the drama', but his weakness in dramatic structure and his cardboard *characters condemned them to speedy oblivion. Increasingly disillusioned and disgusted by contemporary theatrical conditions, and especially by the meagre financial rewards that were the lot of most dramatists of the period (see ROYALTIES), Jerrold channelled his energies more and more into journalism, especially in his work for *Punch*. His career as a playwright came to a dismal end with a bitter wrangle with Charles *Kean over the production of Jerrold's last play, *A Heart of Gold* (*Princess's Theatre, 1854).

MDS

JESSNER, LEOPOLD (1878–1945)

German director who began in a *naturalistic style in Hamburg and Königsberg, but came to prominence in 1919 as the first director of the newly reformed Staatliches Schauspielhaus (see BERLIN ROYAL THEATRE) in *Berlin, the former court theatre of the Kaiser. He welcomed the new Weimar Republic by opening his programme with a production of *Schiller's *William Tell*, a celebration of republican freedom. In place of traditional Alpine *scenery, he performed this classical *verse drama on a construction of wooden ramps, stairs, and bridges. Each location was defined by the simple addition of a tree or a cross, in a manner that anticipated *Brecht's minimalist use of the stage. So incensed was the *audience at this treatment of a beloved classic that the lead actor Albert *Bassermann reprimanded the hecklers, and the police had to be called. *Tell* established Jessner's method of appropriating the classics for *political ends and, in the manner of *expressionism, using symbolic settings and *lighting in place of *realistic scenery (see SCENOGRAPHY). His next production, of *Wedekind's *The Marquis von Keith* in 1920, was a piece of *physical theatre which reflected *Meyerhold's influence. Jessner's version of Shakespeare's *Richard III*, a prophetic warning of the danger of a tyrant seizing power, possessed the clarity of a *morality play. As Gloucester the actor Fritz *Kortner was costumed in black, then as King Richard in red, while his noble opponent Richmond was dressed in white. Played once again on an almost bare stage, this production introduced a flight of steps, for which Jessner became renowned (the *Jessnertreppe*). In 1921 he directed *Othello*, again using a permanent architectural set with different levels. Other striking productions nearly all contained a political theme: Schiller's *The Conspiracy of Fiesco in Genoa* (1921) and *Don Carlos* (1922); Christian Dietrich *Grabbe's *Napoleon* (1922); *Hamlet* (1926), which he set in the court of Kaiser Wilhelm; *Hauptmann's *The Weavers* (1928); and Georg *Kaiser's *Gas I* (1928). Under increasing pressure from right-wing elements, Jessner resigned his directorship in 1930, and, as a Jew and a socialist, was forced into exile by the Nazis in 1933. He first emigrated to *London, but ended his life in the USA. (*See* illustration p. 646.)

MWP

JESUIT DRAMA

School drama performed in educational institutions run by members of the Jesuit order; the term is sometimes more generally used as a designation for Catholic *university and school drama across Counter-*Reformation Europe from the sixteenth to the eighteenth centuries. Having much in common with the broader tradition of humanist *religious drama, Jesuit drama nevertheless maintained a distinctive emphasis on Catholic proselytism, especially in areas where non-Catholics were likely to be in the *audience, such as parts of Germany. Its

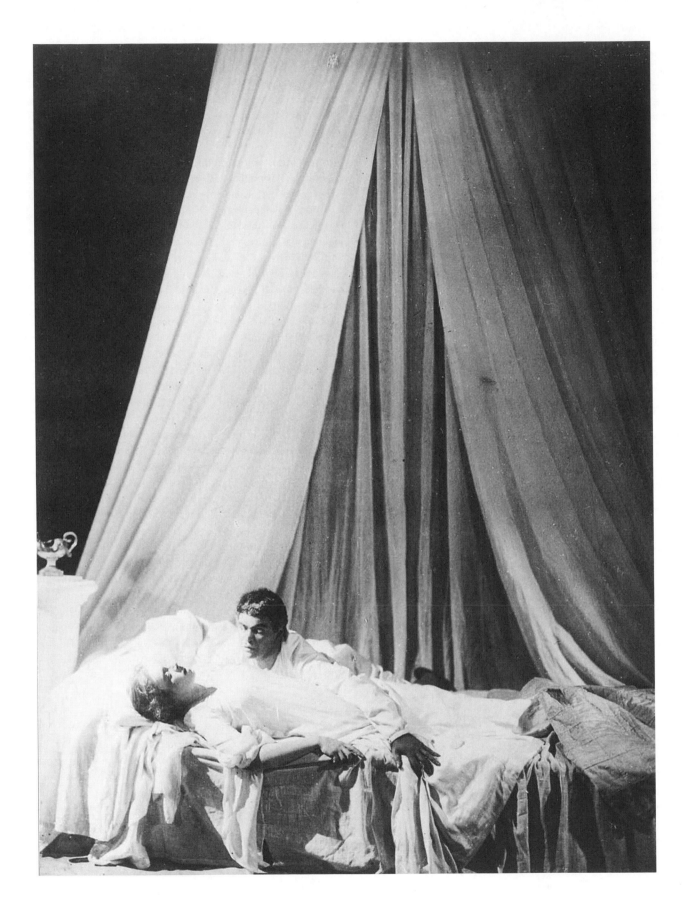

concentration on shaping the mental and spiritual attitudes of its youthful actors by means of role playing, and on empowering them to perform exemplary actions, is often visible in exhortatory *prologues and *epilogues.

The range of subject matter dealt with by the dramatists is wide, including biblical stories and martyr dramas drawn from a range of historical periods, from early Christianity to the Reformation. Many plays have both a literal and an *allegorical significance, pointing up such didactic themes as worldly transience and the inevitability of divine judgement. The Jesuit *Ratio Studiorum* of 1598 forbade the representation of *women on stage, though in practice this rule was widely disregarded. However, the prohibition did encourage a focus on non-sexual emotional issues such as friendship, betrayal, and the tutor–pupil relationship. Writers often exploited the youth of the performers by choosing stories where children played a central or leading role.

Jesuit dramatists, where they can be identified, were most often schoolmasters (perhaps with intervention from pupils). Some—most famously Jacob Bidermann with *Cenodoxus* (1602)—achieved the status of print and had their plays performed at several institutions. More usually the plays were anonymous and occasional, often surviving only in manuscript. They were produced to mark high points in the school year or to honour visiting dignitaries, and long remained an important means for the schools to foster civic goodwill. Though the plays tended to be in Latin, they were made generally comprehensible and attractive by the distribution of a vernacular *plot synopsis, and the prominence given to *musical interludes, *dumb shows and *dance; Jesuit drama has been identified as among the precursors of *opera.   ASh

---

JEWISH ART THEATRE

*Yiddish repertory company located at the Garden Theater in *New York, founded in 1919 by Jacob *Ben-Ami and other dissidents from Maurice *Schwartz's *Yiddish Art Theatre. The troupe, ideologically opposed to the star system and commercialism, was organized as an actors' *collective and was the first Yiddish company to employ a professional director, Emanuel Reichler, a student of *Reinhardt's. Devoted to literary plays, its critically acclaimed productions included works by leading Yiddish playwrights Peretz Hirshbein, Solomon *Asch, Sholem *Aleichem, David Pinsky, and Ossip Dymow, as well as Yiddish translations of Gerhart *Hauptmann, Lev *Tolstoy, and Sven Lange. Considered the finest of the Yiddish art theatres, it

Jessner's production of Shakespeare's *Othello*, Berlin, 1921, scenography by Emil Pirchan. Fritz Kortner as Othello, Joanna Hofer as Desdemona. The monumental white canopy and bedclothes contrast with Kortner's black make-up, and diminish the human figures in an expressionist manner.

could not maintain itself *financially for more than two seasons and closed in 1920.   EN

JEWISH THEATRE *See* JUDÍO, TEATRO; YIDDISH THEATRE.

JIG

The English jig was a sprightly *dance, related to the hornpipe, that featured heel stamping and rapid footwork with little movement of the torso. As an element of Elizabethan stage entertainment it became associated with *clowns such as Richard *Tarlton and Will *Kempe. Four of Kempe's jigs were entered in the Stationers Register (1591–5), but are now lost. There is, however, some music extant for his and Tarlton's jigs. The jig was introduced to the Continent by the *English Comedians. Robert Reynolds, known in Germany as Pickelhering, performed 'Nobody's jig' in *Nobody and Somebody* (c.1592). While the jig could be incorporated into the performance of plays, it was more popularly performed as an independent afterpiece. Words and farcical *action were added to the dance to provide a broad and bawdy entertainment. (An Order of 1612 refers to the 'violence or outrage' that accompanied the performance of jigs.) The singing of doggerel *verse to popular tunes, interspersed with lively dances, anticipated the later *ballad opera.   RWV

JINGJU (CHING CHÜ)

Beijing (or Peking) opera, an indigenous Chinese theatrical form. Its beginnings are popularly traced to 1790 when actors and musicians from around *China gathered in Beijing for the celebration of Emperor Qianlong's eightieth birthday. Troupes from Anhui province, who specialized in *xipi* and *erhuang* music, provided the basis for the new musical system; *jingju* was first known as *pihuang* opera, a name combining characters from *xipi* and *erhuang*. Its current name means literally 'capital drama', referring to Beijing. As with other *genres of Chinese opera, *music gives Beijing opera its unique identity—the primacy of music is captured in the expression for theatregoing, *ting xi* (listening to theatre). The traditional orchestra is made up of two parts. The melodic portion (*wenchang*) consists primarily of bowed and plucked string instruments; the percussion portion (*wuchang*) includes a large and a small gong and hand-held cymbals, led by the player of a small single-headed drum and clappers. Starting in the mid-twentieth century the orchestra was gradually expanded with additions from Chinese *folk and classical instruments, but it was not uncommon to hear cello, double bass, and timpani in late twentieth-century productions.

The performative elements of *jingju* are highly synthesized: the story is told through song, stylized speech, pantomime,

Beijing opera (*jingju*) performers in full costume, Beijing, 1982. *Jingju* ('capital drama'), which developed in the late eighteenth century, has for some time been the most popular of indigenous forms in China, a vibrant musical theatre which appeals in part because of the type of colourful and extravagant costumes and make-up, represented in this scene from one of the many versions of *The Militant Yang Family*. The warrior character Jiao Zan (left) traditionally has a red beard and carries an axe. Both he and his friend Meng Liang, whose beard is black, are *jing* or painted-face roles.

*dance, and sometimes *acrobatics. Beijing opera singers frequently dance, perform complicated *mime routines, or even engage in combat while singing. The traditional stage is sparse, with only a carpet, a table, several chairs, and no backdrop. The form makes use of a rich vocabulary of convention and symbolism; a stylized whip held in a performer's hand, for instance, signals the presence of a horse. Dance-acting movements communicate whether the character has mounted or dismounted, or if the horse is stuck in mud. Meaning is also encoded in percussion patterns and certain melodies: the pattern played when a character enters may reveal whether he is dignified or unscrupulous.

Imperial patronage from the mid-1800s promoted *jingju*'s status, drawing the interest of wealthy patrons and talented performers. Its golden age was in the first several decades of the twentieth century, when it was the most pervasive and popular of all entertainments in China. The work of actors, musicians,

and librettists of the early republic period (*c.*1911–49) remains unsurpassed in terms of volume, innovation, and frequency of performance. Among the many important works from this period are *Mei Lan Fang's *Farewell my Concubine*, *Cheng Yanqiu's *Snow in Midsummer*, and Zhou Xinfang's *Four Advancing Officials*.

Mao Zedong's ideology became the guiding principle for Beijing opera reform with the founding of the People's Republic of China in 1949. New operas on contemporary themes were composed and traditional operas were revised to emphasize themes such as equality between the sexes and patriotism. Changes made in the early 1950s to *The Butterfly Dream* provide an example. In the opera the Taoist philosopher Zhuangzi feigns his own death to test the chastity of his wife Tian Shi. A student comes to mourn and Tian Shi immediately falls in love. She marries the young man, who is Zhuangzi in disguise, but he falls ill on their wedding night and the only cure can be found in the brain of a fresh corpse. When Tian Shi opens Zhuangzi's coffin to fetch his brain, he sits up and accuses her of adultery. In the traditional opera she has no choice but to commit suicide; in the revised version she refuses suicide and proclaims that wives have equal status in the New Society.

During the Cultural Revolution (1966–76), traditional Beijing opera was banned and numerous top performers were tortured or killed. 'Revolutionary modern drama' (*geming xiandai xi), whose themes were revolutionary and presented with *realistic *costumes and staging, was the only form permitted on stage. The traditional repertoire and performance style slowly returned after 1976. In the late twentieth century jingju's future as a living tradition was uncertain. Following its economic reform policy, the state has withdrawn substantial funding from professional companies and *training schools; some talented performers have turned to more profitable professions; and young people's interest in the traditional arts is waning.

NGu

JOAQUIN, NICK (1917–)

Filipino writer. His plays, written in English and set in various *Philippine historical eras, have been the most frequently produced dramatic works in the country. In *A Portrait of the Artist as Filipino*, set in pre-war Intramuros, two impoverished spinster sisters guard an old painting by their sick father as they reminisce about bygone grandeur and desperately attempt to cope with the loss of Manila's innocence. First staged in 1955, it has been translated into Filipino (1969), adapted for *film, and turned into a *musical. Other plays include *The Beatas*, *Tatarin* (1978), *Fathers and Sons* (first produced in Filipino, 1976), *Camino Real*, and a domestic drama set in the Marcos years, *Pinoy Agonistes* (both 2001). He has also written fiction, essays, and a considerable amount of journalism. RV

JODELET (JULIEN BEDEAU) (c.1600–60)

French actor. A member of *Montdory's troupe on its arrival at the *Marais in 1634, Jodelet was transferred to the *Hôtel de Bourgogne for a few years but returned to the Marais and was the mainstay of that theatre for most of his career. He arrived in *Paris just as the period of *Gros-Guillaume and the other great *farce players was coming to an end, and died just as *Molière's career was beginning; for an entire generation he was the one performer who kept the farce tradition alive. He created the role of Cliton, the valet in *Corneille's *comedy *Le Menteur* (1643), and played scheming, cowardly, or naive valets named Jodelet in comedies by *Scarron and others. His trademarks were his floured face and his nasal voice. He joined the newly arrived company of Molière for the last year of his life. His brother François, known as L'Espy, acted with him throughout his career. RWH

JODELLE, ÉTIENNE (1532–73)

French poet and dramatist. A member of the Pléiade, Jodelle is considered the most important of the mid-sixteenth century humanists who initiated the emancipation of French drama from the declamatory models of *Senecan *tragedy. He pioneered the writing of tragedy in French, and prepared the way for *Garnier and *Montchrétien, who had a better-developed sense of stage presentation and conflict of *character. His tragedy *Cléopâtre captive* and *comedy *Eugène* made history in 1552 when they were played by the 20-year-old author and his young friends at the Collège de Boncour and before Henri II at court, earning a payment of 500 crowns. Though static and lacking in dramatic structure (Jodelle's five *acts correspond to Act V of Shakespeare's *Antony and Cleopatra*), and though bearing the mark of its academic origins, *Cléopâtre captive* was an important first response to Du Bellay's call in 1549 for an indigenous French tragedy. *Eugène*, though put forward in Jodelle's *prologue as turning away from *medieval dramatic forms towards the models surviving from antiquity, clearly in practice still bears the mark of medieval *farce tradition; its subject matter—the cuckolding of a simple-minded husband and a satirical portrayal of the clergy—owes little to classical influence. Jodelle's other surviving tragedy, *Didon se sacrifiant* (1558), is almost as static as *Cléopâtre*, consisting largely of lament over a predictable outcome. Its merit is that it was written entirely in alexandrines (*Cléopâtre* had been in a mixture of verse forms), thus establishing a model for nearly the whole of *verse tragedy to come. *See also* EARLY MODERN PERIOD IN EUROPE.

WDH

JOFFRÉ, SARA (1935–)

Peruvian playwright, director, editor, and founder of Homer–Teatro de Grillos in Lima (1963). Joffré is particularly recognized for her work with theatre for *youth, her dynamic organizational skills, and her contribution to the creation of the Peruvian Theatre Festival (1974–2000). She also played a significant role in the development of regional and *avant-garde playwriting by editing ten volumes of *Teatro peruano* (1974–85) and the journal *Muestra* (2000). Joffre's numerous plays fall into several categories: broad, expansive works on social, *political, or *historical themes; urban domestic plays, often with ingenious *naturalistic detail; and emotionally charged *monologues for women. Most of her plays explore ethical, economic, and social issues with disturbing frankness and harsh solutions. Her best-known works are *In Monica's Garden* (1962), *The Drummers* (1976), *An Obligation* (1976), and *There Is Room at the Back of the Van* (1984). Adaptations include *The Mother* (1994), *Dreaming about Camille* (1999), and *Lope's Daughter* (1999).

LRG

JOGLARS, ELS

Catalan theatre company formed in 1962 by Anton Font, Carlota Soldevila, and Albert Boadella, influenced by their *training in *Paris with *Lecoq. Moving away from conventional theatre, the company (the name means 'jesters') embraced *mime to form a theatrical vocabulary which was able to defy the Francoist *censor. Under Boadella's *artistic direction since 1966, Els Joglars were at the forefront of the cultural fight against Francoism, collaborating with innovative designers like Iago Pericot on *Mary d'Ous* (*Egg Mary*, 1972) and Fabià *Puigserver on *Àlias Serrallonga* (1974). In the post-Franco era they have continued experimentation with a series of productions which have interrogated contemporary myths. These include *Yo tengo un tío en América* (*I Have an Uncle in America*, 1991) and a corrosive trilogy on Catalonia which began in 1995 with the audacious *Ubu president*, an acerbic critique of the extreme Catalan nationalism promoted by President Jordi Pujol, and concluded in 1999 with *DAAALÍ*, a delicious *spectacle on the painter's extraordinary life and death.   MMD

JOHANNESBURG

South African city, which began as a mining camp in 1886 and became a boom town by 1890. Before the Anglo-Boer War (1899–1902), most entertainment for miners and magnates meant *variety shows in saloons that earned Johannesburg the epithet 'Monte Carlo on top of Sodom and Gomorrah'. Offerings at the first commercial theatre, the Standard (1891–1959) in Market Street, included *Helena's Hope Ltd.*, a gold-mine *melodrama on the occasion of Union (1910) by local writer-*manager Stephen *Black, but most productions were *London imports, from melodrama like *The Girl Who Lost her Character* to suffragist Cecily *Hamilton's *Pageant of Great Women*.

White theatre in the Union period (1910–1940s) was dominated by African Consolidated (Mines, Film, and Theatre), which hosted *tours, but a few non-profits like the Library Theatre housed *amateurs like Johannesburg Repertory Company (1927–69), which offered European drama and some local plays, such as Lewis Sowden's *Red Rand* (1936), about the 1922 miners' strike. Segregation, previously unenforced in working-class districts, became the norm, forcing black elites to attend white theatres at *managers' discretion and to establish, with liberal patronage, separate venues like the Bantu Men's Social Centre (1924–59) in central Johannesburg, where *Dhlomo's Bantu Dramatic Society performed plays from *Lady Windermere's Fan* to his own *Moshoeshoe* (1938). Impresarios like Griffiths Motsieloa (1896–1950) produced programmes of gags, nationalist songs, and plays on racial uplift to elites at the BMSC as well as to newly urbanized Africans in peripheral townships like Orlando. The townships also housed mixed entertainment, from the Lucky Stars' 'tribal sketches' to gangster-dominated

marabi concerts and other *ingoma ebusuku* (night music; that is, indoors, urban, for cash, as against rural *ritual). In union halls in Fordsburg, the communist-affiliated African National Theatre (1940–1) depicted *African dispossession in plays like the Sotho-language *Tau*, based on an actual case. In the mining compounds, migrants, mostly Zulu, performed *indlamu*, 'war-dances', for their own and tourists' entertainment. Excepting *marabi*, all these forms, and a Pageant of South Africa, appeared at the Empire Exhibition celebrating Johannesburg's 50th anniversary in 1936.

Apartheid legislation in the 1950s and 1960s, especially after South Africa left the Commonwealth (1961), removed blacks to the townships (consolidated as Soweto in 1963) and curtailed mixed-race theatre, but some central venues housed integrated ventures like jazz *opera *King Kong* (1959; at Witwatersrand-Wits-University) by Todd Matshikiza, who also wrote the Peace Cantata for Johannesburg's 70th anniversary (1956), or Athol *Fugard's *No-Good Friday* (1958) and Barney *Simon's *Phiri* (1964, at Dorkay House). Commercial managements continued with hits from London and, after the British playwrights' boycott (1961), *New York, while the subsidized Performing Arts Council of the Transvaal (PACT, 1963) produced European classics from Shakespeare to *Brecht and local, mostly Afrikaans plays first in Pretoria headquarters, then in Johannesburg at the Alexander Theatre. In the townships, the Soweto Ensemble produced classics, but *musicals predominated, produced above all by Gibson *Kente, whose combination of hymns, jazz, sentimental stories, and a pretty *chorus line mined the African variety vein opened up by Motsieloa.

Resurgent student and union dissent in the 1970s facilitated a return to integrated theatre at Wits (the Nunnery and the Box), while black activists like People's Educational Theatre worked Soweto. The Market Theatre, supported by mining conglomerates (especially Anglo-American) and local and international foundations, opened in a renovated market in Newtown near Fordsburg in June 1976, just before the Soweto Uprising. It became South Africa's most successful anti-apartheid cultural venue and, under Barney Simon's direction (1976–95), the crucible for its distinctive *genre, the work-shopped testimonial play, such as *Woza Albert!* (1981) or *Born in the RSA* (1985). Around the Johannesburg Centenary (1986), the Market Foundation also spawned renewal projects that attempted unevenly to revive the inner city. In the absence of township venues, other than the Funda (Learn!) Centre in Soweto (1984) and community halls and churches, the Market hosted township groups, but, apart from bussing in spectators, could not easily reach blacks compelled by law to vacate the centre at night.

In the 1990s blacks moved into the inner suburbs, especially high-rise Hillbrow, but short-sighted city governance before and even after the first post-apartheid local elections (1996) missed the opportunity to involve local social and cultural organizations in urban renewal and job creation. The consequences of this neglect included, alongside the rise in crime and the flight of capital to affluent northern hubs like Sandton, an uncertain future for venues like the Market and the Civic Theatre. Commercial performance moved out of specialized central theatres into multi-purpose for-profit spaces like casinos or theme parks, while community theatre appeared at *festivals, schools, and other public institutions. *See also* AFRICA, ANGLO-PHONE; CAPE TOWN.

LK

KRUGER, LOREN, *The Drama of South Africa* (London, 1999)
TUCKER, P., *Just the Ticket* (Johannesburg, 1997)

JOHNSON, BOB (1904–85)

Ghanaian entertainer. Born in Saltpond, Gold Coast, Johnson and some friends established the Versatile Eight in 1930, building on tradition and the cinema to create *comedies of domestic discord. The group eventually shrank to become 'The Two Bobs and their Carolina Girl', with E. K. Dadson as the *female impersonator and Johnson as the bizarrely dressed, mischief-making houseboy, the joker, or 'Bob'. Their work, which incorporated *satires of recognizable types and a medley of musical interludes, was extensively *toured and highly popular. During the 1930s the patterns of *publicity, business practice, and performance emerged for what became known as *concert party, and continued evolving for three decades. Johnson grew with the tradition, the pioneer and father-figure of a form closely wedded to popular taste. The demands on him as a stage instructor in Nkrumah's socialist propaganda group were curiously at odds with the capitalist ethos of the concert parties.

JMG

JOHNSON, SAMUEL (1709–84)

English writer. Though Dr Johnson was the literary arbiter of Britain, he never found the fame as a playwright that he desired. He carried his *tragedy *Irene* on his famous walk to *London in 1737 with his pupil David *Garrick. The play was ultimately produced at *Drury Lane in 1749, but only because Garrick was co-*manager of the theatre. Although it ran for a respectable nine nights, it could not be considered a success. Garrick's *management was inaugurated in the autumn of 1747 with Johnson's famous *prologue that declared

> The drama's laws, the drama's patrons give,
> For we that live to please, must please to live.

This attitude toward the rules of drama found even more famous expression in the preface to Johnson's edition of Shakespeare (1765), in which he attacked the *neoclassical *unities and eloquently defended Shakespeare's 'irregular' *dramaturgy. A revised edition of Shakespeare was published by Johnson and George Steevens in 1773.

MJK

JOHNSTON, DENIS (1901–84)

Irish dramatist, actor, and *radio and *television director. Deeply impressed by the potential of the *expressionist manner, Johnston conceived a number of plays adhering to that style: *The Old Lady Says, 'No!'* (1928); *A Bride for the Unicorn* (1933), and *The Dreaming Dust* (1940), all staged by Hilton *Edwards at the *Gate Theatre in *Dublin. Other works pursued a strict attention to *realism, making them of greater appeal to the *Abbey directorate: *The Moon in the Yellow River* (1931), situated in the aftermath of the civil war, and *The Scythe and the Sunset* (1958). This tackles the same territory as—and engages in a moral and political dialogue with—*O'Casey's *The Plough and the Stars*. It is not surprising that, having trained as a barrister, Johnston devised two plays which criticize the inadequacy of legal processes: *The Golden Cuckoo* (1939) and *Blind Man's Buff* (1936). Interestingly, this drama, a creative adaptation of an expressionist play by Ernst *Toller, was later reworked in the realist mode as *Strange Occurrence on Ireland's Eye* (1956). His plays are notable for their games with time, style, verbal register, and dramatic form, rigorously designed to disconcert *audiences out of overly conventional patterns of thinking.

RAC

JOHN STREET THEATRE

Built by David Douglass in 1767, as part of a chain of theatres for the American Company, it was *New York's leading *playhouse for 30 years. Located near Broadway, it was constructed of wood and painted red. Its *auditorium contained two rows of *boxes, a pit, and a gallery, and its entrance had a covered walkway extending to the street. As its *manager, Douglass encountered financial trouble when religious opposition suppressed attendance. After the hiatus enforced by the revolution, the American Company returned under the management of Lewis *Hallam and John *Henry, and later John *Hodgkinson and William *Dunlap. The John Street identified itself with American patriotism through premièring Royall *Tyler's *The Contrast* in 1787, hosting visits by President George Washington in 1789, and producing many works of the American dramatist William Dunlap. It closed in 1798, with the opening of the new *Park Theatre.

AHK

JOINT STOCK

English company largely devoted to *touring, founded by William *Gaskill and Max *Stafford-Clark in 1974 with the express agenda of making the creating of a play a wholly collaborative act. Actors, director(s), designer, and playwright would research a chosen theme. In workshops they would *improvise extensive material from this shared experience, which the dramatist would then shape into a *text to be further rehearsed corporately for performance. Notable achievements were *The Speakers*,

Fanshen (with David *Hare), a dramatization of *The Ragged Trousered Philanthropists*, *Cloud Nine*, and *A Mouthful of Birds* (both with Caryl *Churchill). RAC

JOLSON, AL (1886–1950)

American performer. Born Asa Yoelson in Lithuania, Jolson was one of the most popular stars in America in the 1920s and 1930s; George *Burns famously said, 'there was no greater entertainer than Jolie!' The son of a rabbi, Jolson ran away from home in Washington at the age of 13 to *tour in *vaudeville and *burlesque, becoming known for his blackface performances with Lew Dockstader's Minstrels (*see* MINSTREL SHOW). His first Broadway *musical, *La Belle Paree* (1911), began a thirteen-year association with the *Shuberts, who built Jolson's 59th Street Theatre in 1921. Jolson's warmth and sentimentality endeared him to *audiences; his charismatic performances introduced such songs as 'Mammy', 'Sonny Boy', 'Swanee', and 'Toot, Toot, Tootsie'. In *The Jazz Singer* (1927), the story of a cantor's son who goes on the stage, Jolson became the first speaking actor in a feature-length talking *film with the words 'you ain't heard nothing yet'. *Hold on to your Hats* (1941) was his final Broadway show. He entertained troops during the Second World War and the Korean War, and the film *The Jolson Story* (1946) resurrected his recording and broadcasting career. GAO

JONES, DAVID (1934–)

Anglo-American director whose career in stage, *television, and *film has been divided between Britain and the United States. His work is characterized by a self-effacing directorial style—he cites Keats's 'negative capability' as a central credo—and a close association with certain playwrights, notably David *Mercer, Maxim *Gorky, Harold *Pinter, and Richard *Nelson. Jones joined the *Royal Shakespeare Company in 1964, later becoming company director for *London, directing Shakespeare, Gorky, and Mercer, as well as Graham *Greene's theatrical swansong, *The Return of A. J. Raffles* (1975). Less happy was John *Arden and Margaretta *D'Arcy's Arthurian trilogy *The Island of the Mighty* (1972), a famously troubled production that was picketed by its authors. In 1979 Jones became *artistic director of the Brooklyn Academy of Music theatre company in *New York, appointing Richard Nelson as his literary manager (*see* DRAMATURGY/DRAMATURG). Jones went on to direct several of Nelson's plays in Britain and the USA, and to collaborate with him on *Making Plays* (1995), a book on the author–director relationship. CDC

JONES, HENRY ARTHUR (1851–1929)

English playwright. Jones was born in Buckinghamshire of Welsh working-class descent; he worked from the age of 12, largely as a commercial traveller. He was a determined autodidact, and in spite of his religious dissenting background he attended the theatre avidly and wrote unpublished plays. After the production of *A Clerical Error* at the *Royal Court Theatre in 1879, he intrepidly became a full-time playwright. He wrote nine plays in the three years before his first real success, *The Silver King* (1882), written in collaboration with Henry Herman for Wilson *Barrett. It was less sensational and more natural in *dialogue than most *melodramas, and it withstood revivals in the 1990s at *Chichester and the *Shaw Festival in Canada. William *Archer called Jones a rising playwright in *English Dramatists of Today* (1882), even before *The Silver King*, but Jones was a natural anti-Ibsenite, and he and Herman wrote a version of *Ibsen's *A Doll's House* called *Breaking a Butterfly* (1884) in which Nora recognizes the error of her ways and returns to her family.

Jones's writings and lectures on the theatre were extensive and often advanced. He thought the stage should be free to treat important questions, and he wished to raise the status of the author and the actor at the expense of the *actor-manager. Some of his earlier writings are collected in *The Renascence of the English Drama* (1895), and he later attacked *censorship and advocated a *national theatre. Unfortunately his many serious plays suffer from his own conventional morality. In a move that was unusual for the time he used *religion as a theme, depicting the dissenters he was brought up with, treating faith healing, and even staging a church service in work such as *Saints and Sinners* (1884), *Judah* (1890), and *Michael and his Lost Angel* (1896). But he satirized the New Woman in several plays, and often seemed to accept the double standard of morality. Some of his *comedies were successfully revived in the latter twentieth century, such as *The Liars* (1897) at Colchester in 1973 and *The Case of Rebellious Susan* (1894) in *London in 1994. Both plays deal with marital difficulties but end with a return to the status quo, and both have peculiarly irritating *raisonneurs*, but also present satirical pictures of high society and have fast and intricate *plots. *Mrs Dane's Defence* (1900), his last real success, has a fine interrogation scene in Act III, though, as usual, the fallen woman has to pay. EEC

JONES, INIGO (1573–1652)

English architect and designer. The son of an impoverished London clothworker, Jones designed *scenery and *costumes for many of the major Jacobean and Caroline court *masques. His first such commission, probably won through connections in Queen Anne's household, was in 1605 for the Queen's Twelfth Night masque, *The Masque of Blackness* (libretto by Ben *Jonson); he continued to work on these entertainments until they ended in 1640 with *Salmacida Spolia* (libretto by William *Davenant). Jones was appointed successively Surveyor of the Works to Prince Henry (1610–12) and to the crown (from 1615), and in this capacity he designed a new *Whitehall Banqueting House (1622) and converted Henry VIII's Whitehall cockpit into a *playhouse, the *Cockpit-in-Court (1630); these two buildings were the regular venues for Charles I's court performances. In 1616 he may also have designed the *Cockpit Theatre in Drury Lane for Christopher *Beeston.

Jones was already 'a great traveller' by 1605, and he spent an extended period on the Continent in 1613–15. His work was heavily influenced by Italian sources, notably the paintings of Giulio *Parigi and Jacques Callot, and his study of the theatre designs of Sebastiano *Serlio revolutionized English stage technology. *The Masque of Blackness* saw the first use of *perspective *scenery in England, and later in 1605 he incorporated *periaktoi* for scene changes when he redesigned the college theatre at Christ Church, Oxford, for a series of performances associated with a royal visit. At court he developed scenery which would transform itself on a revolve or pivot (*machina versatilis*), and in *Oberon the Fairy Prince* (1611, libretto by Jonson) successive scenes were *painted on movable shutters (*scena ductilis*). His masques were also notable for their extensive use of *flying *characters.

Jones's creativity as a designer of *spectacle was sometimes inhibited by the circumstances of production. In 1618, for example, the King found it difficult to find the money to pay for *Pleasure Reconciled to Virtue* (libretto by Jonson), and the budget was finally assigned less than a week before; in consequence the designs were less elaborate than expected, and Jones was said to have 'lost in his reputation'. However, his creative tension with Jonson, his principal literary colleague until the early 1630s, was valuable, until it provoked a bitter personal quarrel after the production of *Chloridia* (1631). Jones won: Jonson was never again employed at court, and took revenge by *satirizing Jones on stage in *A Tale of a Tub* (1633) and *Love's Welcome at Bolsover* (1634), while Jones became the dominant force in court theatre, his poet-collaborators now conceived merely as contributors of *'verses'. In consequence, during the 1630s the masques' non-literary elements became central to their *allegorical meaning: separated from their design and performance, the surviving *texts often seem abstruse, disjointed, and obscure. *See also* SCENOGRAPHY.   MJW

ORGEL, STEPHEN, and STRONG, ROY, *Inigo Jones: theatre of the Stuart court* (London, 1973)

ORRELL, JOHN, *The Theatres of Inigo Jones and John Webb* (Cambridge, 1985)

PEACOCK, JOHN, *The Stage Designs of Inigo Jones: the European context* (Cambridge, 1995)

JONES, JAMES EARL (1931–)

*African-American actor, one of the most popular black performers of the twentieth century. The son of the actor Robert Earl Jones (they played together at the Harlem Suitcase Theatre in *Moon on a Rainbow Shawl*, 1962), James *trained at the University of Michigan and the *Actors Studio. He first appeared on Broadway in *Sunrise at Campobello* (1958) and made an impression at the *New York Shakespeare Festival in the early 1960s in a number of varied roles. It was Howard Sackler's *The Great White Hope* (1968), however, that brought him fame and a Tony *award as the black boxer Jack Jefferson who becomes heavyweight champ in 1910 but is ruined through an affair with a white woman; Jones magnificently repeated the part in Martin Ritt's *film (1970). He has appeared frequently in Shakespeare, powerfully assuming the tragic *heroes (Lear, Coriolanus, Macbeth, Othello opposite Christopher *Plummer in 1982), and in a parallel modern role as Paul *Robeson in Philip Hayes *Dean's controversial play of that title (1979). In 1987 Jones was awarded another Tony for his portrayal of the might-have-been baseball star Troy Maxson in August *Wilson's *Fences*, and he appeared in a number of Athol *Fugard's works directed by Lloyd *Richards. He has become a Hollywood fixture in such films as the *Star Wars* sequence (as the voice of Darth Vader), *Field of Dreams* (1989), and those based on Tom Clancy's novels (*The Hunt for Red October*, 1900; *Patriot Games*, 1992; *Clear and Present Danger*, 1994).   BBL

JONES, JOSEPH S. (1809–77)

American actor, *manager, playwright, and doctor. The quintessential Jacksonian era playwright, Jones wrote well over 100 plays encompassing a wide range of subjects and styles. At the start (*The Liberty Tree*, 1832) and at the end (*Paul Revere and the Sons of Liberty*, 1875), he held an abiding interest in patriotic themes. On the other hand, he was also adept at *character portraits, often of Yankees or rural innocents, such as those found in *The Green Mountain Boy* (1833), *The People's Lawyer* (1839), and his most successful play, *The Silver Spoon* (1852). Finally, he wrote numerous *melodramas, including *The Surgeon of Paris* (1838) and *The Carpenter of Rouen* (1840). He managed *Boston's *Tremont Street and National theatres, but, except for brief periods, retired from the stage when the Tremont was forced to close in 1843, the same year he received a medical degree from Harvard.   GAR

JONES, LEROI *See* BARAKA, IMAMU AMIRI.

JONES, MARGO (1913–55)

American *producer and director. Jones achieved national celebrity as the founder and *artistic director of Theatre '47 (later the Margo Jones Theatre) in Dallas. The theatre and her book *Theatre-in-the-Round* (1951) offered fresh models for the successful *management of a *regional theatre and emphasized the artistic and economic advantages of *arena staging. Closely associated with Tennessee *Williams, she co-directed the original production of his *The Glass Menagerie* (1945) and in Dallas directed the première of *Summer and Smoke* (1948), pioneering the regional theatre as a venue for new play development. She went on to direct the *New York production of *Summer and Smoke* as well as works by other writers before her early death.

MAF

JONES, MARIE (1951–)

Irish playwright and actor. Co-founder of *Charabanc Theatre Company, Belfast, her work as actor and resident writer from 1983 to 1990 included *Somewhere over the Balcony* and *Girls in the Big Picture.* She co-founded the company DubbelJoint in 1991. Her plays use vibrant humour to challenge forms of discrimination and prejudice. *A Night in November* (1994), *Women on the Verge of HRT* (1997), and *Stones in his Pockets* (1999) *toured Ireland and transferred to *London and *New York in commercial productions. She has written for *radio, *television, *theatre-in-education, and *community theatre.

AEM

JONES, ROBERT EDMOND (1887–1954)

American designer and *theorist. Primarily responsible for the introduction and proliferation of the 'New Stagecraft' in the United States, Jones's designs, teaching, and ideas were central to movements toward *modernism in American theatre between 1915 and 1930. Graduating from Harvard in 1910, where he studied with George Pierce *Baker, Jones taught in the university's Fine Arts Department for two years, then spent a life-changing year in Germany, studying with Max *Reinhardt at the *Deutsches Theater. In *New York in 1914 he became involved with the newly forming 'art theatres', designing *Dunsany's *The Glittering Gate* and *Maeterlinck's *Interior* for the Washington Square Players (1914–15) and two short plays for the *Provincetown Players (1915). Jones's first mainstream attention was for his starkly simple and non-representational design for Anatole France's *The Man Who Married a Dumb Wife* (1915), directed by Harley Granville *Barker. Jones's major collaborator became Arthur *Hopkins, an artistically driven, experimental *producer-director working—most unusually—in the Broadway environment; Jones would design 40 Hopkins productions in twenty years. His designs for Hopkins's production of *Macbeth* in 1920 featured gigantic *masks above the stage, suggesting their omnipresence, and comprising the first major *expressionist production in New York.

The centrality of Jones in the movement toward American modernism was reinforced with the publication in 1922 of *Continental Stagecraft* by Jones and the critic Kenneth *Macgowan. Jones's 40 illustrations of theatres and settings reinforced the text's advocacy for an American theatre that eschewed a material idea of *realism and built itself instead upon a spiritual reality, to be evoked through techniques of *Appia, *Craig, Reinhardt, *Stanislavsky, *Jessner, *Copeau, and *Jouvet. At the same time, Jones's designs for *O'Neill's *The Hairy Ape* (1922), *The Emperor Jones* (1924), and *Desire under the Elms* (1924)—originated in the Provincetown's tiny theatre and expanded when the plays transferred to Broadway—demonstrated Jones's creative use of scrims, empty space, shadow, and *light. The designs enabled O'Neill to see fulfilled his vision of transparent 'walls', hypnotic delusions, and trees imbued with the presence of a protective mother. Between 1923 and 1925 Jones formed part of a triumvirate (also including O'Neill and Macgowan) which revived the Provincetown (then threatened with extinction) under the title the Experimental Theatre, Inc. After 1930 Jones was seen as a talented and creative mainstream designer, producing satisfying work for Broadway, the *Metropolitan Opera, and the *Theatre Guild, designing such projects as O'Neill's *comedy *Ah, Wilderness!* (1933), Stokowski's *The Crucifixion of Christ* (1943), and O'Neill's *The Iceman Cometh* (1946). Jones's 1941 *The Dramatic Imagination* exerted wide influence in its call for the self-abnegation of the designer in service to the universal and eternal truth in the play. He was in high demand in his later years as a university speaker and mentor to design students.

MAF

JONGLEUR

French term that began to be used in the ninth century to designate a versatile entertainer in the tradition of the earlier *mime and scop. Other terms for the same figure include *tregatour* (England), *Minnesinger* (Germany), and *joglar* (Spain). In the eleventh and twelfth centuries, troupes of jongleurs were organized under the leadership of poet-entertainers called troubadours or *trouvères*; by the early fourteenth century they had achieved *guild status in France. As poets and musicians, *dancers and actors, *acrobats and *jugglers, the jongleurs were an important conduit for narrative and dramatic *texts at a time when printing was unknown and manuscripts scarce.

RWV

JONSON, BEN (1572–1637)

English dramatist and poet, born in London, the posthumous son of a minister. He was educated at Westminster School, but had to leave when his stepfather decided he would be better set to work as a bricklayer. He began his long theatrical career as a *touring actor, and by 1597 he was back in *London writing plays for Pembroke's Men; from this period there survives only his *Plautine *comedy *The Case Is Altered.* In the later 1590s he worked for both the major adult companies, the *Chamberlain's Men and the *Admiral's Men, though he abandoned the latter (and chose not to preserve anything he wrote for them) when the *boys' companies reopened at the turn of the century. One strand of Jonson's career was a model of progressive success, affluence, and social standing. He came to the Chamberlain's Men with *Every Man in his Humour* (1598), a *comedy of humours which remained in their repertory for decades, and after their elevation as the King's Men he wrote them two more long-term bankable classics in *Volpone* (1605) and *The Alchemist* (1610). The move to the Children of the *Chapel, with their indoor theatre and elite *audiences, was also a step up, and 1605 saw the first of his court *masques, *The Masque of Blackness*. Throughout James I's reign he was a prominent contributor to the dramatic entertainment offered at high-profile state occasions (37 of his scripts are extant), which brought him recognition, status, and, in 1616, a royal pension which enabled him temporarily to give up commercial stage writing.

However, there was also an underside of failure and misjudgement, driven by his difficult personality, his fussy sense of his own literariness, his equivocal attitude to authority, and partly also by sheer bad luck. In 1597 he was imprisoned after the Privy Council took exception to satirical material in his collaborative play with Thomas Nashe, *The Isle of Dogs*; the incident led to the collapse of Pembroke's Men as a *London operation. It was the first of many occasions when his pen landed him in trouble: later brushes with power concerned, among others, his stage representation of Queen Elizabeth I in *Every Man out of his Humour* (1599), the inclusion of a piece of gossip about Lady Arabella Stuart in *Epicene* (1609), and offence taken by an unknown courtier at *The Devil Is an Ass* (1616). In 1600–1 he engaged in the 'War of the Theatres': when John *Marston, probably intending a compliment, represented him on stage, he took offence and retaliated with the devastating personal *satire of *Poetaster*. If he gave the King's Men *box-office success with his comedies, his *tragedies were less fortunate: vocal audience displeasure forced the players to abandon both *Sejanus' Fall* (1603) and *Catiline's Conspiracy* (1611) in the middle of their first public performances, and Jonson was questioned by the Privy Council about the *political content of *Sejanus*. If in 1605 he pleased the court with his Twelfth Night masque, only months later he was back in jail, having offended the King with anti-Scots satire in his collaborative comedy *Eastward Hoe* (written with *Chapman and Marston).

Jonson was difficult because, for all his success, he was insecure: the premature end of his formal education made him the more proud of his scholarly attainments and anxious for his work to be adjudged worthy by the accepted standards of *neoclassical aesthetics. This meant that he would often downgrade the theatrical side of his work. It is typical that in the 1630s he quarrelled with Inigo *Jones, the producer of his court masques, over the relative status of his scripts and Jones's designs (*see* SCENOGRAPHY). Characteristically, Jonson was the first English dramatist to assert the literary value of his plays by including nine of them alongside his poems and masques in a Folio collection of his *Works* in 1616.

The publication of the Folio also marked the start of the middle-aged Jonson's sense of his place in literary and dramatic history: print made that place secure, giving his plays access to the future, transcending the ephemerality of the stage. Only a few years earlier, in the induction to *Bartholomew Fair* (1614), he had proclaimed a straightforward modernity for his work, drawing a contrast with the old-fashioned barnstormers *Titus Andronicus* and *The Spanish Tragedy*. Now he saw himself in a broader context. For him, England, like ancient *Greece, had its 'Old Comedy' and its 'New', the former being the sixteenth-century *morality play, and in his next two comedies, *The Devil Is an Ass* and *The Staple of News* (1626), he explored the differences and continuities between the two. Jonson spent his final years out of circulation and confined to one room. Some contemporaries assumed that he had died; in fact, he had suffered a stroke in 1628 and the following year, annoyed by the failure of *The New Inn*, resolved to give up writing for the stage. It was a promise he was unable to keep for long, and he completed two more plays, *The Magnetic Lady* (1632) and *A Tale of a Tub* (1633); a *pastoral, *The Sad Shepherd*, remained unfinished.

Jonson's core comedies were regularly in production after the Restoration and through the eighteenth century: David *Garrick made notable appearances in *The Alchemist* (from 1743) and *Every Man in his Humour* (from 1751), in roles later taken by Edmund *Kean (1814 and 1816 respectively). By then, however, the plays had begun to lose their popularity: 'coarse' elements were removed from *Volpone* when it was staged in the 1770s, and it dropped from the repertory altogether, along with *Epicene*, in the 1780s; only *Every Man in his Humour* reached the Victorian stage, with notable productions by W. C. *Macready (1838) and Charles *Dickens (1845). The plays returned to production at the end of the nineteenth century, rediscovered by theatrical antiquarians like William *Poel, and the twentieth saw a wider range of his work on the stage; in 1987, the *Royal Shakespeare Company even revived *The New Inn*, and made a modest artistic success of it. MJW

JORDAN, DOROTHY (1761–1816)

English actress. 'Dora' Jordan was the most famous comic actress of the late eighteenth and early nineteenth centuries. She began at the Crow Street Theatre, *Dublin, in 1779 as Dorothy Bland, and remained in that city for three years, fleeing in 1782 when pregnant by the unscrupulous *Smock Alley *manager Richard Daly. She acted in Tate *Wilkinson's company for several seasons, establishing a wide comic repertory under her new name, Jordan, given by Wilkinson because she had 'crossed the water'. Her *London debut came in 1785 at *Drury Lane. She quickly became a favourite, and throughout her long career she was especially praised for her rich voice, her engaging laughter, and her pathos. Among her most famous roles were Viola, Ophelia, and (improbably) Young Pickle in Isaac *Bickerstaffe's

The Spoiled Child (1790). Her long affair with the Duke of Clarence inspired a great deal of gossip, but it did not prevent her acting throughout Great Britain. She was a national institution by the time of her death in Paris.   MJK

JORY, JON (1938–)

American director and *producer. The son of Victor Jory and Laura Innes, veteran *stock company actors who went on to Hollywood, he was born to the stage. Following stints at the University of Utah, Cleveland Playhouse, and the army, Jory studied playwriting at the *Yale School of Drama but left in 1965 to found the *Long Wharf Theatre with Harlan Kleiman. He moved on after two years and in 1969 became the producing director of *Actors Theatre of Louisville. Over the next three decades he fashioned ATL into one of the USA's pre-eminent *regional resident theatres. He brought a pragmatist's common sense and an impresario's bravado to his position, forging ties with civic and business leaders and creating programming that drew national and international attention to a city better known for its alcohol and tobacco industry. His most important initiative was the Humana Festival of New American Plays, but he also created *festivals around short plays, solo performances, and modern classics. Jory is widely assumed to be the pseudonymous playwright Jane Martin, all of whose plays premièred at ATL under his direction. After 1,500 productions, 141 of which he directed, he left ATL in 2000 for a professorship at the University of Washington.   STC

JOSEPH, STEPHEN (1927–67)

British director, actor, lecturer, *regional theatre enthusiast, and champion of theatre-in-the-round (*see* ARENA AND IN-THE-ROUND). Son of flamboyant actress Hermione *Gingold and publisher Michael Joseph, after Oxford he became *producer for the Lowestofte Repertory Theatre. He gained a drama degree from the State University in Iowa and *trained at the Central School of Drama in *London. In 1955 Joseph founded the Studio Theatre Company in London to promote theatre-in-the-round, soon after moving to the Yorkshire seaside town of Scarborough. From there he *toured to theatreless towns, mostly in the north, eventually settling in 1962 in Stoke-on-Trent, where the old Victoria Cinema was converted to create the UK's first permanent theatre-in-the-round. He was appointed (1962) to the first fellowship in the Drama Department at Manchester University, beginning an influential, but sadly short, career in teaching and research. Sometimes mistaken for a monomaniac for commitment to the cause of theatre-in-the-round, his books, both published in 1968—*New Theatre Forms*, and *The Story of the Playhouse in England* (for children)—demonstrate unpretentious and generous learning.   BRK

JOUVET, LOUIS (1887–1951)

French director and actor. Jouvet began his career, together with Charles *Dullin, in Jacques *Copeau's first company of the Théâtre du *Vieux-Colombier as *lighting designer and actor (most notably Sir Andrew Aguecheek in a famed *Twelfth Night*, 1914). He left Copeau in 1922 for the Comédie des Champs-Élysées, where one of his earliest critical and commercial successes was as director of Jules *Romains's *comedy *Knock*, and in which he played the lead role in over 1,400 performances. In 1927, together with Gaston *Baty, Georges *Pitoëff, and Charles Dullin, Jouvet formed the *Cartel des Quatre, a loose association of four theatres designed to share costs and protect common interests against the mainstream commercial theatre. His greatest triumph, however, was another association, this time with playwright Jean *Giraudoux, and the names of both author and director were celebrated far beyond *Paris. At the end of his lease Jouvet moved to the Athénée, where he staged with enormous success Giraudoux's *La Guerre de Troie n'aura pas lieu* (1935, translated by *Fry as *Tiger at the Gates*). Jouvet maintained his *film acting career up to and beyond the Second World War but kept his theatre dark during the Occupation and *toured to South America. Upon his return he directed notable premières, including Giraudoux's last play, *The Madwoman of Chaillot* (1945), *Genet's *The Maids* (1947), and *Sartre's *The Devil and the Good Lord* (1951), and continued to tour the world.   BRS

JUANA INÉS DE LA CRUZ, SOR (JUANA RAMÍREZ DE ASBAJE) (1651–95)

Mexican poet and dramatist. Self-educated, she became an illustrious lady-in-waiting at the viceregal court of New Spain and later entered a convent of the Order of St Jerome as Sor Juana. Writing on both religious and secular themes, a matter of contention among her ecclesiastical superiors, she composed three-act *comedias, *autos sacramentales on the sacrament of the Holy Eucharist, a variety of shorter sketches, and dramatic poems to be sung in church that incorporated roles for Africans, Aztecs, Moors, and Basques. Sor Juana's plays, which were performed at court in *Mexico City and in churches throughout New Spain, generally conform to the style of *early modern Spain, showing particular similarity to the work of *Calderón, but she often arranged *plots and reversed roles to emphasize *gender issues and the circumstances of the New World. *Los empeños de una casa* (*The House of Trials*, 1683), a traditional Spanish *comedy of love triangles, honour, and mistaken identity, presents the difficulties of a noblewoman who was much like Sor Juana herself. *El divino Narciso* (*The Divine Narcissus*, 1689), considered to be her masterpiece, transforms myth into a *pastoral love story with theological significance in which Christ is Narcissus, Echo is the Devil, and Human Nature represents all of humanity. An unusual *prologue presents the Aztec *ritual of the god of the seeds as prefiguring the Christian sacrament of communion.

JuJ

JUDÍO, TEATRO

Argentinian dramatic form about Jewish life. The Jewish immigrant first emerged as a *character type in the regional *sainete criollo, in plays by non-Jewish authors, after the waves of immigration at the end of the nineteenth century. Thereafter *Yiddish theatre flourished in *Buenos Aires until about 1940. In 1932 the IFT (Idisches Folks Theater) was founded in Buenos Aires, a *collective proletarian troupe that was one of Buenos Aires's first independent theatres. Contemporary Jewish authors such as Samuel Eichelbaum, Osvaldo *Dragún, Ricardo *Halac, Germán *Rozenmacher, Jorge *Goldenberg, Hebe Serebrisky, and Diana *Raznovich have continued to dramatize the Argentine Jewish experience.

JGJ

JUGGLER

In Massenet's *opera Le Jongleur de Notre Dame (1902), derived from the *medieval *mystery play called (among variant titles) The Juggler of God, an old and impoverished juggler, having nothing to offer the Virgin and Christ Child but his skill, performs before their statues, which are miraculously animated. The almost supernatural skill of juggling—'the dextrous manipulation of objects'—was probably recognized before the time of the ancient Egyptians, but around 2000 BC they were the earliest to depict (women) jugglers, in the Beni-Hassan tombs. Juggling figures later appeared on Greek pottery and Roman wall reliefs. Tagastus Ursus (AD 53–117) claimed to have been the first to juggle with glass balls, and had this feat inscribed on his gravestone. References to juggling in ancient stories are not infrequent. The fifth-century Irish hero Cuchulain juggled nine apples and, more spectacularly, Tulchinne, the jester at the court of King Conaire, is described as juggling nine swords, silver shields, and balls of gold. The juggling of large numbers of objects is not unusual; the world record in 2001 was twelve rings, eleven balls, and eight clubs. Juggling is an indigenous skill amongst many *Native Americans, and in Tonga young girls still juggle limes, gourds, or tui tui nuts.

The association of juggling with *magic and sleight of hand is of long standing. The Roman term praestigiator referred to the trickster-magician as well as the juggler, and in the West suspicion has always been mixed with admiration. For the ancient *Chinese, on the other hand, juggling was allied with the skills of hunting and fighting. The 'Hundred Entertainments' of the Han Dynasty combined the exhibition of jugglers with *acrobats, *animal tamers, equestrians, and other *circus trades now familiar in the West. In the nineteenth-century popular mind, juggling was located in the East, particularly in *India and *Japan, and overlaid with the exoticism of fire-walking and sword-swallowing; to attract an *audience the German juggler Karl Rappo was forced to wear a turban and appear as an Indian. William *Hazlitt's essay on the 'Indian Jugglers' (Table Talk, 1828) records his admiration for their skill in juggling with four brass balls, though the talent, he believed, was turned 'to little account'. The *music hall claimed many jugglers from the circus. Paul Cinquevalli juggled billiard balls and caught a cannon ball on his neck. Kara, who performed in evening dress, juggled a hat, a cigar, gloves, a newspaper, matches, and a coffee cup. It was not until the first part of the twentieth century that the specialized talents of jugglers such as Enrico Rastelli and Bobby May were appreciated. Whilst balancing on a board, itself on a rolling cylinder, Rastelli juggled seven balls, twirled three rings on one leg, and spun balls on a mouthpiece.

AF

JUILLIARD SCHOOL

Located at *Lincoln Center in *New York, the Juilliard School is one of America's leading performing arts conservatories. It originated as the Institute for Musical Art in 1905, affiliated with the Juilliard Graduate School to become the Juilliard School of Music in 1926, added *dance in 1951, drama in 1968, and was renamed the Juilliard School in 1969. Juilliard's drama division, founded by John *Houseman and Michel *Saint-Denis, is renowned for its rigorous and comprehensive four-year actor-training programme. Under Michael *Kahn's leadership in the 1990s, the drama division developed graduate-level programmes in *playwriting and *directing. See TRAINING.

RM

JULIA, RAUL (RAFAEL CARLOS JULIA Y ARCELAY) (1940–94)

Puerto Rican actor. Julia played five roles in San Juan before he appeared in *New York in a Spanish-language production of *Calderón's La vida es sueño (Life Is a Dream, 1964). From 1966 onwards he performed with Joseph *Papp and the *New York Shakespeare Festival, winning praise for Proteus in the *musical adaptation of Two Gentlemen of Verona (1971), Osric in Hamlet (1972), and Orlando in As You Like It (1973), and appearing twice as Othello (1979 and 1991). He had success as Mack the Knife in the *Weill–*Brecht Threepenny Opera (1976) and as Charles Wykeham in the *Loesser–*Abbott musical Where's Charley? (1974). He played Lopakhin in *Chekhov's Cherry Orchard (1977) and Jerry in *Pinter's Betrayal (1980). In addition to over 100 stage productions, Julia also played in *films such as Kiss of the Spider Woman (1985) and gained popular renown for The Addams Family (1991). He won a posthumous

657

award for a *television movie about Brazilian martyr Chico Mendez, *The Burning Season* (1994).   FL

JUNCTION AVENUE THEATRE

South African *collective troupe formed in the mid-1970s in *Johannesburg. Originally its members were almost exclusively young, university-educated whites—Malcolm Purkey, William *Kentridge, Pippa Stein, Astrid von Kotze, Ari Sitas, and Patrick Fitzgerald—but broadened when several of Workshop '71's township members joined in 1978. The focus has always been on personal and communal histories. *The Fantastical History of a Useless Man* (Nunnery Theatre, 1976) was JAT's first piece, followed by *Randlords and Rotgut* for a history workshop at Witwatersrand University (1978), with Ramolao Makhene, Siphiwe Khumalo, and Arthur Molepo. Other work includes *Will of a Rebel* (1979, about Breyten Breytenbach), *Security* (1979), and Dikitsheng (1980, about employment exploitation). A collaboration with workers in *The Sun Also Shines: Ilanga Lizo Phumela Abasebenzi* (1982) led to the development of the Worker Theatre movement in Natal. *Marabi* and *Sophiatown* (Upstairs at the *Market, 1986) focused on forced removals of blacks to the townships, while *Tooth and Nail* (Market, 1989) presented fragments of alternative South African histories. The *musical *Love, Crime and Johannesburg* was a great success in 1999. The company has also produced theatre for *youth and *educational projects. Their *film *Howl at the Moon* (1981) received awards at American film festivals.   YH

JUVARRA (JUVARA), FILIPPO (1678–1736)

Italian architect and designer. Born in Messina, he studied architecture in *Rome with Carlo Fontana. Juvarra's architectural works can be seen in Italy, Spain, and Portugal. The sets he designed for *operas include *Giunio Bruto*, commissioned by the Emperor Josef I of Austria, and *Ciro*, scored by Alessandro Scarlatti. Juvarra's theatre designs influenced his buildings, and the definition of space in his later works is marked by a theatrical fluidity and elegance, exquisite examples of early Italian rococo.   ATS

JUVENILE THEATRE *See* TOY THEATRE.

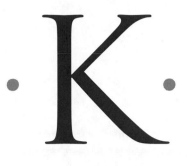

·K·

KABI GAN

A secular form of contestual performance in *Bangladesh, normally performed outdoors under a canopy usually in the dry season. Two professional minstrels (*kabiyal* or *sarkar*) and their troupes of singer-musicians present an argument on important social and religious issues in extemporaneous Bengali *verse and song, with musical and choral accompaniment. Regardless of their faiths, the *sarkar*s assume any one of a number of conventional opposing roles (such as Hindu and Muslim, Science and Philosophy, or Capitalism and Socialism) and debate the issues in sequential sessions. The performance begins with salutations to Hindu deities (and also to Allah and the Prophet if the performers are Muslims). The first troupe opens the debate by posing questions, the rival troupe tenders reply, and the arguments and counter-arguments continue. A final session, with both troupes occupying the performance space together, shows the *sakars* resolving their differences. *Kabi gan* remains popular all over Bangladesh, though it has flourished most in Mymensingh, Jessore, Faridpur, and Khulna. It is also popular in West Bengal in *India. It is significant that Hindus, Muslims, men, and women perform, in public *puja* celebrations (mostly for Hindus), or village fairs (for Hindu and Muslim spectators). In most cases *kabi gan* troupes, usually composed of six to eight performers, are not fully professional and depend on alternative sources of income, such as farming.

SJA

KABUKI

Lavish Japanese stage performance that includes *dance, music, and dramatic *acting, now the nation's most popular form of classical theatre. Kabuki was founded in *Kyoto around 1600 by the female temple dancer Izumo no *Okuni. At that time 'kabuki' referred to persons or styles that were chic, suggestive, or eccentric. Okuni often dressed on stage in men's clothing and wore a rosary and items of European dress. Okuni's kabuki included dances by women, playlets about contemporary dandies and prostitutes, and sideshow acts. Her kabuki was soon imitated by troupes of prostitutes who added the three-stringed *shamisen* to the *nō flute and drums used in Okuni's musical ensemble. Travelling troupes created a kabuki boom that swept the country. The lawlessness and social inversion that accompanied kabuki performances led to numerous local prohibitions and finally to a national ban of women's kabuki in 1629. Early kabuki was also performed by young men (*wakashū*), many of whom were homosexual prostitutes. When *wakashū kabuki* was banned in the 1650s, mature men became the main performers and kabuki began its development away from *vaudeville-like performance into drama. Producers looked to the more highly developed *puppet theatre for inspiration in this endeavour. Actors began to specialize in role types—there were women's role specialists (*onnagata*), male leads (*tachiyaku*), *villains (*katakiyaku*), and so on.

In the late seventeenth century great actors turned kabuki into an art of breadth and sophistication. Permanent licensed theatres were located in Kyoto, *Osaka, and Edo (*Tokyo). In Kamigata (Osaka and Kyoto) *Sakata Tōjūrō I perfected the art of the romantic male lead (*wagoto*) and was kabuki's first stage idol, attracting women fans to the theatre in record numbers. He experimented with psychological approaches to acting. Kamigata was the breeding ground for great *onnagata*. *Yoshizawa Ayame advocated living offstage as a woman so that the slightest onstage gesture and nuance might be convincingly feminine even to women in the audience. Actors in Edo took a different approach. Ichikawa *Danjūrō I (1660–1704) created the bravura style (*aragoto*), featuring superhuman feats by martial *heroes who are given their powers by the gods they revere. Danjūrō wrote his own plays, and made the deities he worshipped heroes in many of them. His

Kabuki performance, woodcut triptych by Toyokuni I, Edo (Tokyo) Ichimura Theatre, 1800. The varied populist audience is on three sides and on three levels, engaged in conversation, selling, and eating, as well as watching the show. The two young women standing on the extreme left seem to be displaying themselves while searching for seats. The *hanamichi* runway cuts through the auditorium in front of them, while the stage contains simple scenery, male characters in aggressive postures (the central figure is the actor Ichikawa Danzō IV, 1745–1808), and delicately rendered *onnagata* actors upstage. The artist created a series of similar triptychs, replacing only the middle panel with the play being advertised; this is probably *The Two Images of Shunkan*, a derivative of Chikamatsu's *Heike and the Island of Women* (1719).

descendants dominated kabuki in Edo for the entire Tokugawa Period.

By the early 1700s kabuki's calendar of events was set. Most important was the *kaomise* (face-showing) production in the Eleventh Month, which showcased actors hired by the theatre for the subsequent year. Festive New Year's productions (in Edo, always about the Soga brothers' revenge), spring plays about romance, and summer productions featuring ghosts and monsters were other seasonal favourites. When plays drew poorly, they were quickly replaced by new ones. From the outset kabuki was commercial theatre, intended primarily for urban commoners. From the 1690s on kabuki relied on published plays and actor critiques, and *ukiyo-e* posters, prints, and advertisements to publicize its actors and shows. By the mid-1700s leading actors, especially *onnagata*, supplemented their already generous salaries by endorsing products decorated with their personal crests and designs. Product placement in plays began in the 1710s.

Until the late 1600s playwriting was relatively unimportant in kabuki. Plots were chosen by leading actors and lines were written down, but actors were free to change them. By the 1680s it was clear that long, integrated scripts were necessary to stage successful plays. *Chikamatsu Monzaemon (1653–1724) became the first specialist playwright, and by the 1700s

teams of staff playwrights worked under a leading actor-producer (*zamoto* or *zagashira*), crafting plays that would be star vehicles for leading actors. Plays were divided into two broad categories: *history plays (*jidaimono*) about samurai conflicts of the pre-Edo era, and domestic plays (*sewamono*) about the contemporary commoner class.

Initially kabuki was performed on nō stages, but over the years the bridgeway expanded into an extension of the main stage. The *hanamichi* runway leading from the stage to the back of the *auditorium came into use in the early 1700s. Today this feature distinguishes the kabuki stage from any other variety. Around the late 1600s painted backdrops started to appear and large *properties were employed. Various *traps, lifts, revolves, and *flying harnesses were devised for *special effects scenes, and the full-stage *revolve was in use by 1758, long before it was introduced into Europe. In the mid-eighteenth century actors began to eschew narrow role specialization in favour of broader acting skills. Dance-dramas, hitherto the speciality of *onnagata*, were written to include *tachiyaku*. Many new dances featured magical transformations by spirits and required one performer to dance multiple roles. In the early nineteenth century the playwright *Tsuruya Namboku IV pioneered a new *genre, the 'raw domestic play', featuring heroes from Japan's lowest classes—criminals and outcasts—and more brutality, violence, and terrifying scenes of the occult than in previous plays. Later in the century *Kawatake Mokuami created a new genre of plays about gallant outlaws. Other innovations were pioneered by actors. In 1832 Ichikawa *Danjūrō VII (1791–1859) canonized his *family's *aragoto kabuki* heritage by publicizing the 'Eighteen Great Plays', inspiring others to do the same with their family acting traditions. In 1840 he devised a new genre of dance-drama based on nō and *kyōgen plays; the first and most popular of these is the *aragoto* classic *The Subscription List*.

In 1840 the central government ordered Edo's theatres torn down and relocated to a north-eastern suburb and in 1842 it banished Danjūrō VII from Edo for infraction of sumptuary laws. These were among the more drastic measures taken by the shogunate in its two-and-a-half-century-long battle with kabuki. The government attempted to suppress the baleful influences of the form by restricting attendance, theatre size, and design, the sumptuousness of productions, actors' salaries, and housing. After a major scandal in 1714 involving a love affair between a senior lady-in-waiting and a leading actor, the government permanently liquidated one of Edo's four theatres. Nevertheless, no government policy ever managed to deter the commoners' beloved kabuki theatre. Japan's modernization presented greater challenges. In the Edo period kabuki had set fashion trends and enacted contemporary issues and scandals, but *buyō* dance-based acting made no sense when performers wore Western clothes. After several fruitless modernization attempts in the late 1800s ('living history plays', 'cropped-hair plays'), kabuki found its niche in modern Japan as classical drama. Productions were redesigned to present great acts from unrelated master works. Certain twentieth-century innovations did succeed, including 'new kabuki'—historical dramas featuring psychologically complex *characters delineated through *dialogue and modern, *realistic acting. Fine playwrights emerged to write new works, *Mishima Yukio among them. In 1986 Ichikawa Ennosuke III (b. 1939) created Super Kabuki—spectacular, hi-tech plays with scripts in modern Japanese. They have enjoyed great commercial success. Today the Shōchiku Corporation runs kabuki as a profit-making venture in Japan's major cities. The federal government assists with productions in Tokyo's National Theatre. Acting remains very much a family business—the great names pass from father to son—but supporting actors are trained by the National Theatre and by Shōchiku. Some leading actors work to revive lost plays, and others use their kabuki skills in *television, *film, and experimental dance and drama.

LRK

BRANDON, JAMES (trans.), *Kabuki: five classic plays* (Cambridge, Mass., 1975)

——, MALM, W., and SHIVELY, D., *Studies in Kabuki: its acting, music, and historical context* (Honolulu, 1978)

BRAZELL, KAREN (trans. and ed.), *Traditional Japanese Theater: an anthology of plays* (Ithaca, NY, 1998)

ERNST, EARLE, *The Kabuki Theatre* (Honolulu, 1974)

HALFORD, AUBREY, and GIOVANNA, M., *The Kabuki Handbook* (Rutland, Vt., 1956)

LEITER, SAMUEL L., *New Kabuki Encyclopedia: a revised adaptation of 'Kabuki Jiten'* (London, 1997)

KACHALOV, VASILY (1875–1948)

Russian/Soviet actor who joined the *Moscow Art Theatre in 1900 and became the company's romantic lead. Possessing superb vocal qualities, Kachalov was a natural tragedian but also proved extremely successful in *Chekhov roles. He played Tuzenbach in *Three Sisters*, inheriting the part from *Meyerhold, Trofimov in *The Cherry Orchard* (1904), and the eponymous Ivanov (1904). He starred as Hamlet in the *Stanislavsky–*Craig production (1911) and performed leading roles in productions directed by *Nemirovich-Danchenko, appearing as the Baron in *Gorky's *The Lower Depths* (1902), as Julius Caesar in 1904, as *Ibsen's Brand in 1906, and Ivan Karamazov (1910).

NW

KAHN, MICHAEL (1937–)

American *producer, director, and educator. *Artistic director since 1986 of the Shakespeare Theatre in Washington, DC, Kahn has also been head of drama since 1992 at the *Juilliard School in *New York. In directing on Broadway, *Off-Broadway, in *regional theatre, and *opera, he specializes in the classics, wielding an eclectic vigour that has attracted many important actors (such as Susannah York, Brian *Bedford, Morris *Carnovsky, Eva *Le Gallienne, Glenn *Close, Max *Von Sydow, Eileen *Atkins, José *Ferrer). At the Shakespeare Theatre, his stars have included Fritz *Weaver, Hal *Holbrook, and Pat Carroll, who played both Falstaff and Volpone, certainly a professional first for a woman. Kahn's directorial freshness and use of stars has expanded American interest in Shakespeare, and he has been a key figure in the growth of non-commercial theatre, having previously led the *American Shakespeare Festival in Connecticut, the McCarter Theatre in Princeton, and the *Acting Company in New York.

CR

KAHN, OTTO (1867–1934)

Banker and patron of the arts. Having left the Deutsche Bank to join a New York firm in 1893, Kahn became chief adviser to Edward Harriman in the reorganization of the railways. Kahn became the outstanding American arts patron of his time, directing millions of dollars to theatre, *opera, and *dance companies as well as to individual artists, providing support to the *New Theatre, the *Washington Square Players, the *Provincetown Players, and the *Civic Repertory Theatre, among others. Open minded and politically liberal, Kahn often supported

KAILASAM. T. P.

radical companies—such as the New Playwrights Theatre—that challenged the basis of his wealth.   MAF

KAILASAM, T. P. (1884–1946)

Playwright and director from Karnataka in south *India. A student of geology in Madras and London, he developed an intense interest in theatre through his exposure to *modernist plays as well as to *music-hall performances in *London between 1908 and 1915. After his return to Bangalore, he wrote his first play *Tollu Gatti* in 1918. It inaugurated his typical theme, the tension between the brahmanical tradition and the modernity of the emerging upper middle class in southern Karnataka. He wrote twenty plays in *Kannada (for example, *Poli Kitty*, *Home Rule*, *Nam Kampni*) and four in English (including *Karna* and *Purpose*). All feature a highly stylized range of *characters, representing the two contending social classes of his times, the traditional and the upwardly mobile. To represent this new class Kailasam invented a hybrid composite of English and Kannada that is both witty and farcical. He vehemently opposed the standard *melodrama of the professional theatre of the time; in fact *Nam Kampni* (*Our Company*) parodies such overblown *theatricality. Kailasam wanted his *audience to think. Although he has had several imitators in Kannada theatre, because of their intricate language his plays have largely remained inaccessible to *amateur theatre groups outside southern Karnataka.   KVA

KAINZ, JOSEF (1858–1910)

Austrian actor. The most acclaimed German-speaking actor of the late nineteenth century, Kainz left school at 15 to join a *touring company in Austria. From 1877 to 1880 he performed leading roles for the *Meininger; he left to join the *Munich Court Theatre, where became a favourite of King Ludwig II. His international fame began after 1883 when he moved to *Berlin, performing first at the new *Deutsches Theater, then with Ludwig *Barnay at the Berlin Theatre, where he soon broke contract. This resulted in a ban at all theatres belonging to the German Stage Organization, which he overcame with extended tours in Europe and the USA. In 1892 he returned to the Deutsches Theater and performed for a short time with Otto *Brahm, but virtuosic style was incompatible with Brahm's *realism. In 1899 he had his debut at the *Burgtheater in *Vienna, where he remained until his death. Kainz retained throughout his career a youthful appearance and dynamism which electrified *audiences. His greatest asset was his voice, which he used in an almost operatic manner.   CBB

KAISER, GEORG (1878–1945)

German playwright. Although the best dramatist of German *expressionism, his reputation rests primarily on only six of his 70 plays. After working in South America as a shipping clerk, he began writing in 1905 when malaria forced him to return to Europe. After a few light *comedies, he achieved a breakthrough with *The Burghers of Calais* (written 1913, premièred 1917). The victorious English demand the sacrifice of six burghers of Calais. When one of them sets an example by taking his own life, the English King frees the others and kneels in homage. The play is characteristically expressionist: there is no attempt at historical authenticity, the action is generalized and depersonalized, the language is strongly rhetorical, above all there is the optimistic conclusion that individual sacrifice can lead to universal regeneration. Kaiser discovered a means of containing his passion within well-constructed plays: 'The scream [*Schrei*] must become a voice. The molten must become rigid in form.' In *From Morning to Midnight* (written 1912, premièred 1917) a nondescript clerk steals money from his bank, tries to buy excitement, and, disillusioned, throws it all away at a Salvation Army meeting. Betrayed by greed, he shoots himself, his dying words being 'Behold the man!' From this indictment of capitalism, Kaiser passed on to attack industrialism in the *Gas Trilogy* (1917–20). The central play, which is the best, *Gas I*, describes how a devastating gas explosion in a factory might be used as the opportunity to turn away from technology to create an idyllic rural lifestyle, but the visionary *hero, the Millionaire's Son, is defeated by the workers' resistance to change. In *Gas II* the manufacture of poison gas can be stopped only by setting off a bomb that will destroy the human race. Compared with *Gas*, which strongly influenced Fritz Lang's *film *Metropolis* (1926), most of Kaiser's later dramas seem either trivial (for instance, *Side by Side*, 1923), or reflect his obsession with his own privileged status as an artist, as in his reworking of *Pygmalion* (1944). In 1933 the Nazis banned his plays, and in 1938 he emigrated to Switzerland.   MWP

KAKUL, I NYOMAN (1905–82)

Balinese performer and teacher, the leading *topeng* (masked dance) performer of his generation. By the age of 13 he had joined a travelling *dance-theatre troupe. Studying wherever he could, he became known as an exceptionally versatile performer and was employed as a dance master by several regional courts. In 1953 Kakul toured Europe and America as featured performer in an all-star troupe. Upon his return, he won further renown as a solo performer of remarkable grace, knowledge, and humour; started a *topeng* troupe; and helped revive the venerable form of *gambuh*. When formal conservatory programmes were established in the late 1960s, Kakul became a master teacher of *topeng*, profoundly influencing the next generation of Balinese artists and teachers and introducing several Western performers and scholars to the rigours and beauty of Balinese dance-drama.   JE

KALARIPPAYATTU

The martial art of Kerala, *India. Dating from at least the twelfth century, every village had its own *kalari* (place of training) for the exercise/training (*payattu*) of local fighters under the guidance of a *gurukkal* (honorific plural of 'guru'). *Kalarippayattu* was practised primarily by Hindu Nayars who pledged themselves to serve their rulers to death, but also by some Christians, Sufi Muslims, Cattar Brahmans, and Ilavas known as *chekor* who were hired to fight duels (*ankam*) to the death to settle legal disputes. Some young girls also received training until puberty, and a few achieved expertise. Training takes place in specially constructed and sanctified *kalari*. After initiation the student, having oiled the body, learns a vigorous array of 'body preparation' exercises including poses, kicks, steps, jumps, and leg exercises performed in increasingly complex combinations back and forth on the *kalari* floor. Most important is mastery of basic animal poses comparable to yoga *asanas*. Repeated practice of the exercises, combined with full-body massage, renders the external body flexible, and 'awakens' the internal subtle yogic body. Ideally a master's body 'becomes all eyes', that is, provides the practitioner with an intuitive ability to respond, animal-like, to his environment. Students are eventually introduced to combat through training weapons (long staff, short stick, curved stick or *otta*), and then to combat weapons including dagger, sword and shield, mace, spear, and flexible sword. Masters finally learn Ayurvedic physical/massage therapies for muscular problems, conditions affecting the 'wind humour', and setting broken bones.

Kalarippayattu influenced many performance traditions in both content and technique, including *folk dances, *teyyam *ritual performances where deified heroes are worshipped, *kathakali *dance-drama which enacts stories of India's epic heroes and uses *kalarippayattu* techniques and massage to train its actors, and the Christian dance-drama *cavittu natakam*, which uses *kalarippayattu* techniques to display the prowess of Christian heroes like St George and Charlemagne. *Kalarippayattu* is used in contemporary performer training both inside and outside India by Kavalam *Panikkar (Sopanam Theatre, Trivandrum), choreographer/dancer Daksha Seth (Trivandrum), Soogi Kim (Korean National Academy of the Arts, Seoul), and Phillip Zarrilli (director/actor-trainer, UK). PZ

ZARRILLI, PHILLIP B. *When the Body Becomes All Eyes: paradigms, practices and discourses of power in kalarippayattu* (New Delhi, 1998)

KALIDASA

The greatest Sanskrit poet and playwright of *India. His dates are controversial (suggestions range from the first century BC to the fifth century AD), but it is widely accepted that he was among the nine 'jewels' in the entourage of King Vikramaditya of Ujjain. It is also believed that he was an unlettered cowherd by birth, who by the grace of the goddess Kali was transformed into a great literary figure. Hence the name Kalidasa (the devotee of Kali).

His long narrative poems (*mahakavyas*)—*Meghaduta*, *Raghuvamsa*, and *Kumarasambhava*—are regarded as gems of Sanskrit, excelling in the use of metaphor, and his genius as a dramatist is equally acknowledged. Three plays are ascribed to Kalidasa. *Malavikagnimitra* is a court *comedy depicting the love of King Agnimitra for a maid in the service of one of his Queens. Although the Queen attempts to obstruct his amorous strategies, he finally succeeds in his venture with the help of his friend, the *vidushaka (jester). In the second play, *Vikramorvasiya*, based on an ancient legend in the *Rigveda*, the mortal king Pururavas falls in love with the celestial nymph Urvasi. The most mature work is *Abhijnanashakuntala*, which is adapted from an original story contained in the epic *Mahabharata*. Kalidasa's play focuses on the meeting between King Dushyanta and Shakuntala at the sage Kanva's hermitage; Dushyanta's infatuation for Shakuntala and their subsequent consummation of love; his loss of memory due to the curse of the sage Durvasa; the birth of a child to Shakuntala while she is abandoned; and the developments leading to Dushyanta's reunion with Shakuntala. These stages in the loss and retrieval of memory all evoke the transcendence of love. The poet has reinvented the original myth by introducing the symbol of a signet ring. The word *abhijnana* (prefixed to Shakuntala) signifies the King's recognition on seeing this ring, which he had earlier presented to Shakuntala as a token of his love.

Shakuntala has inspired theatre practitioners all over the world. The *text has been translated into many Indian languages. Since 1960 productions based on Sanskrit plays, including Kalidasa's masterpieces, have been presented at the Kalidasa Samaroh in Ujjain and at national theatre *festivals by contemporary Indian directors like K. N. *Panikkar and Vijaya Mehta. Adaptations have also been produced, like K. V. Subbanna's *Lokashakuntala*, which questions the assumptions of authority and property in Kalidasa's world.

Kalidasa was first introduced to Europe through George Forster's 1791 German translation of *Abhijnanashakuntala* from the earlier English translation by Sir William Jones. *Goethe openly acknowledged his poetic debt to Kalidasa's work in his *prologue to *Faust*, while the German *romantics envisioned in Shakuntala the very embodiment of femininity. At the outbreak of the First World War, Aleksandr *Tairov opened his season at the Kamerny Theatre in *Moscow with a *symbolist translation of *Shakuntala*. In 1960 *Shakuntala* received yet another *avant-garde interpretation by the Polish theatre director Jerzy *Grotowski, who sought to create new psychophysical models of gesture and behaviour in European theatre, which could provide an understanding of oriental theatre. Through the centuries *Shakuntala* has remained identified with a mythical 'India', compelling Western spectators to respond to its ethos in diverse ways. KNP

KAMABOLON CEREMONY

A five-day event in Kangaba (south-western Mali), first reported in 1954 but much older. Normally held every seventh year, the ceremony is part of the initiation rite of young men. It consists of the restoration of the Kamabolon, an ancient sanctuary in the traditional form of a round mud hut. On Monday the old roof is removed, then the walls are restored, painted, and (on Friday afternoon) a new roof is raised by young men of pure noble descent. The ceremony owes its particular fame to the recitation on Thursday night of the 'authoritative' version of the *Sunjata* epic by renowned *griots* (traditional bards) from Kela, a village south of Kangaba. The version used in the Kamabolon Ceremony is secret; no outsiders are allowed to approach the sanctuary during the five days of the ceremony, and those who do are severely beaten or even killed. The *Sunjata* epic is recited all over West Africa, its origins traceable to the fourteenth century. Based on *rehearsals observed among the Kela *griots*, however, it appears that their version resembles variants recorded elsewhere. JJ

KAMBANELLIS, IAKOVOS (1922–)

Greek playwright. Born in Naxos, he grew up in *Athens and his first play, *To Dance on Wheat*, was produced by the innovative company of Adamantios Lemos in 1950. *The Seventh Day of Creation*, produced by the *Greek National Theatre in 1956, was the first of a trilogy that continued with *Yard of Wonders* (1957), directed by Karolos *Koun for the Art Theatre, and ended with the Art Theatre's *The Age of Night* (1959). Kambanellis's trilogy marked the beginnings of a new era for modern Greek theatre. He took the *realistic tradition of the nineteenth and early twentieth centuries a step further, not only by re-creating the everyday reality of post-war Greece, but also by criticizing this reality and attempting to explain its complex social structure. His other plays include *Tale without Title* (1959), *Odysseus, Come Home* (1966), and *Our Dad the War* (1980). KGo

KAMBAR, CHANDRASEKHAR (1938–)

Playwright, poet, and folklorist who writes in *Kannada, a south Indian language, recognized as one of the foremost contemporary dramatists in *India. Born at Ghodageri in north Karnataka, he began writing short *modernist plays before his first major poem *Helatena Kela* (*Listen, I Will Narrate*, 1964) established him as an indigenous poetic talent. This led him to explore idioms of *folk theatre such as *sannata*; he also compiled and co-edited the *text of *Sangya Balya*, a popular Karnataka folk play, which became the prototype for most of his own work.

His first success was *Jokumaraswami* (1973), about a rebellion against a feudal lord; interspersed with the *ritualistic slaying of the phallic god Jokumara, it relies on song, *dance, and witty *dialogue. Its huge success prompted a number of imitations. Kambar continued to explore folk themes as metaphors of contemporary experience in plays such as *Alibaba* (1980) and *Huliya Neralu* (1988). Since then his work has shifted towards a more symbolic exploration of folk mythology, the best example being *Sirisampige* (1992), about a prince who divides himself into a serpent and a human self. Kambar's plays have been translated into several Indian languages and into English.

KVA

KAMERNY THEATRE *See* TAIROV, ALEKSANDR.

KAMIŃSKA, IDA (1899–1980)

*Polish actress and director, born to an illustrious theatrical *family including her father Abraham Kamiński (1867–1918) and her mother Esther-Rokhl Kamińska (1870–1925), the 'Yiddish *Duse'. Ida began in her father's *Yiddish company in *Warsaw as a child, later rising to a major actress in the *Warsaw Yiddish Art Theatre (VYKT). Her family fled to Soviet-controlled areas in 1939, but after the war Kamińska returned to Warsaw and, against all odds, organized a company and obtained for it the status of the Yiddish State Theatre. Kamińska directed, translated, and starred in plays by *Gordin, Sholem *Aleichem, *O'Neill, and *Brecht, and *toured extensively. In 1968, following Poland's official anti-Semitic campaign, she left for America. She appeared in several *films and was hailed for her role in the Czech *The Shop on Main Street* (1965).

EN

KAMMERSPIELE

*Playhouse built by Max *Reinhardt in 1906 in *Berlin as an addition to the *Deutsches Theater, with the express purpose of providing a suitable space for intimate works (literally, 'chamber plays'). It seated only 200 and dispensed with an orchestra pit in order to bring *audience and *stage closer together. It opened on 8 November 1906 with *Ibsen's *Ghosts*, designed by Edvard Munch. The success of the theatre resulted in a number of imitations, most notably the Kammerspiele in *Munich. Both buildings owe much to art nouveau in their architectural philosophy and interior decoration. CBB

KAMYŎNGŬK

A term that covers all versions of *masked *dance-drama in *Korea, the country's most pervasive form of traditional performance. Probably developed from ancient religious ceremonies, its ceremonial aspect gradually disappeared as theatrical possibilities were exploited. Regardless of origin, *kamyŏngŭk* can be classified into two main types: various masked dance styles, collectively known as *sandaegŭk* (mountain play); and village-festival masked dance forms. Major *sandaegŭk* types are regional and include *pyŏlsandae* (special mountain) plays of Yangju and Songp'a; *t'alch'um* (masked dance) plays of Pongsan, Unyul, Haeju, and Kangnyŏng; *ogwangdae* (five elements) plays of T'ongyŏng, Kosŏng, Kasan, and Chingu; and *yaru* (field pleasure) plays of Tongnae, Suyŏng, and Pusanjin. The village-festival masked dramas include the *pyŏlsingŭt* (special god festival) play of Hahoe, the lion dance play of Pukch'ŏng, and the *kwanno* (government slave) play of Kangnŭng.

In rural villages, masked dance-dramas are still performed at festivals at the New Year, Tano (5 May), and other special occasions of the lunar calendar. Of the village festival masked dramas, the *pyŏlsingŭt* play of Hahoe is the best known. The performance traditionally occurs on the Tano festival, supplicating the prosperity of the village, expulsion of evil spirits, and the prevention of demons. The structure of the performances is orally transmitted from generation to generation. The play does not have an overall *plot but consists of independent *scenes held together by themes: *satires of transgressing monks, for example, or of corrupt upper classes or insensitive local officials. Twelve masks were used in the past, though only the nine most delicate wooden masks remain in use. Masks were traditionally housed in the village shrine because villagers regarded them as protective gods. The nine original masks are now kept at the National Museum in Seoul.

Despite regional differences, performance elements common to all *sandaegŭk* styles include masks, dance, song, music, pantomime, and *dialogue. The plays are anonymous and transmitted orally, though since the 1960s performances have been recorded, transcribed, and published. Content varies according to region, but most plays can be divided into the following scenes: the nobleman (*yangban*) scene, which reveals the conflict between a nobleman and a servant; the old woman scene, which portrays an argument between an old woman and her husband about his concubine; an old monk scene, which deals with an argument between a monk struggling with worldly desires and a troublemaker hanging around the markets. The *characters tend to reflect the villagers' point of view, and the dialects used are regional. Performances are traditionally held at night in an outdoor space, lit by torches, with the *audience sitting in a circle. *Costumes for servants and women are bright and gaudy. The masks, made from gourds, paper, and other materials depending on region, were traditionally burned at the end of each performance. Comic, *grotesque, and exaggerated, they have established standard features, though the performers add characterization through gestures and dance. In the course of the dance, the dancers often speak to the audience or the musicians. The musical ensemble is generally made up of two fifes, a flute, a barrel drum, an hourglass-shaped drum, and a gong, and uses three types of tunes having twelve-beat or six-beat patterns. The songs, which are interlaced with dance and dialogue, are mostly derived from folk songs and shamanistic incantations. *Kamyŏngŭk* has been the source of the modern open-space theatre (*madangŭk*). Performances of *kamyŏngŭk* today are presented as government cultural events or as tourist entertainments.   JOC

CHO, HO-KON, *Traditional Korean Theatre* (Berkeley, 1988)

KAN'AMI (KANNAMI, KANZE KIYOTSUGU) (1333–84)

*Japanese *nō playwright, *manager, and actor, the father of *Zeami. Kan'ami headed the Yūzaki troupe (renamed Kanze) in Ise. Later he moved to Yamato, where he won the patronage of the shogun Ashikaga Yoshimitsu in 1374. Despite his success in the capital, however, Kan'ami continued to *tour the countryside and died after a performance at Sengen temple in Suruga (modern Shizuoka). He combined the best elements of various *sarugaku* performers and adopted the rhythms and materials of *kusemai* (a medieval song-and-dance form) into nō, thereby helping to transform it into a highly successful theatrical form. Zeami writes admiringly of Kan'ami's *acting skills and musical abilities and claims that his own earliest writings express his father's ideas. As Zeami reworked most of Kan'ami's plays, it is difficult to evaluate the father's skills as a dramatist, but many plays connected with him are still considered masterpieces, including *Matsukaze*, *Motomezuka*, *Sotoba Komachi*, *Kayoi Komachi*, and *Eguchi*.   KWB

KANDER, JOHN (1927–   ) AND FRED EBB (1932–   )

American composer and American lyricist. Kander and Ebb first collaborated on popular song hits in 1962. Kander, for nearly a decade a *rehearsal pianist and *dance arranger (notably for *Gypsy*), had just seen the failure of his first Broadway score, *A Family Affair*. Ebb had been writing lyrics for club acts and *revues. Under the aegis of Harold *Prince, who had directed *A Family Affair*, they collaborated on *Flora, The Red Menace* (1965), and *Cabaret* (1966), scores which displayed their ability to combine traditional Broadway sounds with an evocation of a historical period. The extraordinary success of *Cabaret* established Kander and Ebb as a major team in *musical theatre, and they proved extremely enduring, maintaining an exclusive collaboration that has continued for more than 35 years and eleven Broadway (or Broadway-bound) musicals, in addition to club acts for specific performers, notably Liza Minelli, who starred in both *Flora* and the *film version of *Cabaret* (1972) and for whom they wrote the award-winning *television special *Liza with a Z*. Their work has regularly included both traditional and innovative shows; among the latter are the geriatric musical *70 Girls 70* (1971) and *The Rink* (1984), a Broadway-sized musical with three principals and a *chorus of six men who play all the other roles, male and female. They have demonstrated the ability to write for stars—as in the case of *Woman of the Year* (1981), a vehicle for Lauren Bacall—and for conceptualist directors such as Bob *Fosse, with whom they wrote *Chicago* (1975). In addition to *Cabaret*, their films include *Funny Lady* (1975) and *New York, New York* (1977), the title song of which has become a standard.   JD

KANE, SARAH (1971–99)

English playwright. *Blasted* (1995) brought Kane to attention in a disturbing way. A middle-aged journalist and a young girl spend the night in a British hotel room; an explosion rips the room apart, and the *characters endure a horrific series of violent encounters and sexual violations. That this disorienting structure mimicked the uprooting of life during the Bosnian genocide was lost on the *critics, but its influence was strong. Her subsequent plays, notably *Cleansed* and *Crave* (both 1998), continued to investigate the extremes of human experiences, the second a delicate, elliptical piece that affirms suicide as an act of liberation. Feeling herself sinking once again into profound depression, Kane took her own life. Her final play, *4.48 Psychosis* (2000), was posthumously performed at the *Royal Court, where most of her other work had been seen. It is a bleak piece of scattered poetry, with almost no *textual indications for staging, tracing the contours of a mind in the deepest state of despair.   DR

KANHAILAL, HEISNAM (1942–   )

Director and writer from the north-eastern state of Manipur, *India. A drop-out from the *National School of Drama in New Delhi, Kanhailal formed the group Kalakshetra Manipur in his home town of Imphal in 1969. Identified in his early years with the 'Third Theatre' tradition of Badal *Sircar, Kanhailal has explored non-verbal, *physical, ensemble *acting in numerous theatre pieces, steeped in the indigenous myths and conventions of Meitei culture. After experimental plays like *Tamnalai* (*Haunting Spirits*) and *Kabui-Keioba* (*Half-Man, Half-Tiger*), Kanhailal created a sensation with his sharp and lyrical retelling of a popular *folk tale *Pebet* (1975), in which Mother Pebet, a mythical bird, succeeds through subterfuge in reuniting her children, who have been abducted by the Cat. Thinly disguised as an *allegory of neocolonial domination, with the Cat masquerading as a Vaishnavite monk, the play was condemned as 'anti-Hindu' and 'anti-Indian', even as it was hailed as a theatrical masterwork.

Seeking a less ethnically determined idiom of protest to depict the violence of everyday life in Manipur, Kanhailal dramatized L. Samarendra Singh's poem *Africagee Wakhanda Gee* in another memorable evocation of the survival of the human spirit in *Memoirs of Africa* (1985). His wife, the actress Sabitri, was central to both productions, performing with the power of a contemporary shaman. More recently, Kanhailal has attempted to deepen the communitarian and *ritualistic dimensions of his theatre in the context of suffering. His plays have also begun to move outwards from their inner lyrical resilience towards a more verbal, layered, and ironic reading of myth and history, as in his reinterpretation of *Karna* (1997), the tragic warrior from the *Mahabharata*, and his adaptation of Mahasweta Devi's story *Draupadi* (2000). *See also* MANIPURI THEATRE.   RB

KANI, JOHN (1943–   )

South African actor and producer, born in Port Elizabeth. He was a janitor in the Ford factory when he joined the Serpent Players (1965), acting Creon in *Antigone*. His first major production was *Camus's *The Just* (retitled *The Terrorists*, *Cape Town, 1972), after which he and Winston *Ntshona became full-time artists. Within months they collaboratively produced *Sizwe Bansi Is Dead* (1972) and *The Island* (1973) with Athol *Fugard. Kani originated the lead roles in a number of other Fugard plays, locally and abroad, including *Statements after an Arrest . . .* (1972) and *Master Harold and the Boys* (1982), and appeared in a revival of *The Blood Knot*. He has played a number of *racially controversial roles: he was the first black Othello opposite a white Desdemona in South Africa (in Janet *Suzman's 1987 production, *Market Theatre, *Johannesburg), and was the servant Jean in *Strindberg's *Miss Julie* opposite Sandra Prinsloo (Baxter, 1985). He also acted in the *film *Marigolds in August*, written by Fugard (1979). He became director of the Market Theatre after Barney *Simon's death in 1995, and chair of the board of the Performing Arts Centre of the Transvaal in 1999.   YH

KANIN, GARSON (1912–99)

American actor, playwright, director, and screenwriter. Kanin dropped out of high school in *New York to pursue a career in acting. He studied at the *American Academy of Dramatic Arts and appeared in such Broadway productions as *Little Ol' Boy* (1934), directed by George *Abbott. Kanin left acting to become Abbott's assistant, working on such productions *Room Service* (1937), and made his directing debut with *Hitch your Wagon* (1937). Discovered by Samuel Goldwyn, he moved to Hollywood to direct *films, and continued making films during his war service (1941–6). Kanin's greatest stage success came with his hit *comedy *Born Yesterday* (1946), a Pygmalion-like story about a young man hired to tutor a tycoon's girlfriend. Kanin married actress-writer Ruth *Gordon in 1942, and together they wrote a series of successful film comedies in the 1940s and 1950s, most directed by George Cukor—among them *Adam's Rib* (1949) and *Pat and Mike* (1952). In addition to his direction of *Born Yesterday*, Kanin staged other Broadway productions, including *The Diary of Anne Frank* (1955) and *Funny Girl* (1964).

MAF

KANNADA THEATRE

Kannada is a language spoken by the majority of people in Karnataka, a region in south *India. Though the Western notion of theatre arrived only in the nineteenth century, varieties of theatrical forms have existed in Karnataka over several centuries. *Yakshagana*, for example, is a popular form that has a history of at least 300 years. Other forms of traditional performance include *ritualistic *genres like the *bhutaradhane*; semi-*religious forms like the *Srikrishnaparijata* and *doddata*; and secular forms like the *sannata*. Many of these traditional performances, which have continued to evolve over the years, coexist with the modern Kannada theatre and have often influenced its practice.

The formative phase of the modern Kannada theatre, between 1870 and 1900, was marked by a new kind of dramatic writing supplementing the emergence of secular and commercial companies. During this period Kannada theatre searched for its identity by borrowing from tradition and opening to Western influences. Translations and adaptations of Shakespeare in the 1880s coexist with revivals of classical Sanskrit drama. Important plays of this period include *Iggappa Hegade Vivaha Prahasana* (1887), the first play to depict a contemporary social theme in Kannada, and *Sangya Balya* (*c*.1880) based on a contemporary incident of murder and extramarital love composed in the traditional *sannata* form. After 1900 theatre in Karnataka gradually branched into two directions, the professional and the *amateur. The professional theatre had A. V. Varadachar (1869–1926) in the south and the Konnuru and Shirahatti companies in the north as its pioneers. If Varadachar individuated the type *characters of the epics with a new sense of *realism, the northern companies used extravagant *scenery and equipment for presenting epic themes. A blend of the northern and southern styles of professional theatre soon became popular as Company Nataka, and reached its peak with the Gubbi Theatre Company, which travelled extensively in Karnataka and reigned over the popular theatrical imagination for more than two decades. With such competition, the more prosaic and wordy amateur theatre struggled to exist in the urban centres like Bangalore, Mysore, and Dharawad. Though it had a limited elite support, the amateur movement produced remarkable actors like Bellary Raghava (1880–1940). It

also stimulated playwrights like *Samsa (1898–1939), *Kailasam (1884–1946), and Srinivasa (1891–1986) in the 1920s, and, somewhat later, *Sriranga and G. B. Joshi (1904–93), who dealt with contemporary social issues.

As elsewhere in India, during the 1930s and 1940s Kannada professional theatre was almost entirely eliminated by the widespread popularity of sound *film. The urban amateur theatre, however, continued to hold on to its limited base, but because of its distaste for the popular it could not expand. It came out of this deadlock only in the early 1970s when directors like B. V. *Karanth came on the scene. His productions, which revelled in exuberant *music, stylized movements, and crowd scenes, created a new theatrical energy which spread to different parts of Karnataka. Soon Karanth became an exponent of the 'theatre of roots' which proposed to reinvent an indigenous and authentically Indian theatre, in contrast to the realistic style of its colonial heritage. The upsurge in activity in the late 1960s and early 1970s coincided with the emergence of new playwrights such as Girish *Karnad (*Tughluq*, 1964; *Hayavadana*, 1971) and Chandrasekhar *Kambar (*Jokumaraswami*, 1972). Both writers began with *modernist plays but soon aligned themselves with the indigenous movement to employ traditional dramatic structures and idioms to explore contemporary themes, like the dialectic of mind and the body and the dilemmas of the self.

The 1970s was also a period of social awareness and activism. Countering the Karanth wave, a troupe like Samudaya asserted the need to take theatre to the masses through its statewide street performances, and for a while *street theatre became an important vehicle for *political and social issues. Theatrical activities spread to all the urban and rural areas of Karnataka, with directors like Prasanna (1953–   ) introducing young theatre workers to Marxism. A new professionalism emerged with the opening of the *Ninasam Theatre Institute (1980) and with several travelling theatre companies like Ninasam Tirugata (1985) and Rangayana (1989). A crop of younger directors, trained at the *National School of Drama, also made their presence felt: B. Jayasree (*Lakshapati Rajana Kathe*), C. R. Jambe (*Aa Ooru Ee Ooru*), Raghunandan (*Etta Haride Hamsa*), Basavalingaiah (*Kusumabale*), and others. There were some discernible shifts in playwriting too, as younger dramatists like H. S. Shivaprakash came on the scene. At the beginning of the new century Kannada theatre has remained intensely active and is more decentralized than other Indian-language traditions.

KVA

KANTATA

A popular form of theatre on the West *African coast, the *kantata* is sung drama with stories and themes drawn from the Bible. Staged in churches, its performance style derives from both African and Judaeo-Christian traditions. Music is an essential part of the show, while the choreography is a mixture of stylized *Indian hand movements (*mudra*) and Togolese animist *dances. The form depends upon interaction between performers and *audience. SA trans. JCM

KANTOR, TADEUSZ (1915–90)

Polish director, designer, visual artist, and *theorist. Born in Wielopole, he studied painting and stage design at the Academy of Fine Arts in *Cracow (1933–9), where he became interested in *symbolism, *constructivism, and the *Bauhaus. In 1938 he founded the Ephemeric (Mechanic) Theatre and during the Nazi occupation founded the experimental Independent Theatre, for which he directed *Słowacki's *Balladyna* (1942) and *Wyspiański's *The Return of Odysseus* (1944), a production instrumental for his concepts of an autonomous performance space, the poor object, the *actor as object, and 'reality of the lowest rank'. After the war Kantor worked as a designer. In 1947 he received a scholarship for a year in *Paris, where he saw the works of Kandinsky, Klee, Miró, Ernst, and Hans Hartung. Upon his return to Poland he organized the first post-war exhibition of modern Polish art. In 1949 he publicly refused to participate in the official culture of *socialist realism; his professorship at the Cracow Academy (to which he had been appointed the previous year) was revoked, though he continued to work as a designer and painter.

At the end of the Stalinist period Kantor co-founded CRICOT 2, named after the 1930s theatre created by visual artists, Cricot. The opening event was his production of *Witkiewicz's *The Cuttlefish* (1956), which developed his notions of Autonomous Theatre (independent of any external reality) and Annexed Reality (reality which could not be appropriated by the prevailing conventions or assigned a cultural use-value). Subsequent productions of *texts by Witkiewicz marked the stages in Kantor's development: *The Country House* (1961: 'Informel Theatre'), *The Madman and the Nun* (1963: 'Zero Theatre'), *The Water Hen* (1967: 'Theatre-Happening', an outgrowth of his experiments with *happenings from 1965), and *Dainty Shapes and Hairy Apes* (1973: 'Impossible Theatre'). All these sought to depreciate the value of reality by exploring its unknown, hidden, or everyday aspects (matter, marginalized objects, degraded objects, self-enclosed actions) and challenged traditional notions of representation. 'The Theatre of Death' manifesto (1975) marked a major shift, and productions which followed explored notions of memory, history, myth, artistic creation, and the artist as the chronicler of the twentieth century. *The Dead Class* (1975), presented memories taking place behind an impassable barrier, and other productions dealt with similar themes—*Wielopole, Wielopole* (1980) introduced the concept of the room of memory; *Let the Artists Die* (1985) explored a place where memories are superimposed upon each other, using the theory of negatives; *I Shall Never Return* (1988) put forth the concept of the inn of memory, which existed beyond the confines of time and space, where Kantor encountered his own past creations; and *Today Is my Birthday* (1990) focused on the crossing of a threshold between the world of illusion and the world of reality. A characteristic feature of Kantor's performances was his presence on stage observing, and often correcting, his actors. *See also* SYMBOLISM; MODERNISM AND POSTMODERNISM. MAK

KANTOR, TADEUSZ, *A Journey through Other Spaces: essays and manifestos, 1944–1990*, ed. and trans. with a critical study by Michal Kobialka (Berkeley, 1993)

KANZE HISAO (1925–78)

*Japanese actor. The eldest son of Kanze Gasetsu, the seventh Tetsunojo (1898–1988), Kanze Hisao was the most influential *nō actor and *theorist of the mid-twentieth century. His talent as a performer was recognized in his youth, and after the Second World War he helped reinvigorate nō, giving new life to old ideas and practices without resorting to the fashionable lure of *realistic drama (*see* SHINGEKI). In 1962 he went to France where he studied theatre with Jean-Louis *Barrault, and in the 1960s and 1970s he participated in various forms of modern theatre. He also founded study groups for *Zeami's theories. A superb, traditional nō actor, Kanze was interested in new approaches to staging plays, exemplified in his *music and choreography for *Takahime* (*Hawk Princess*), a 'new' nō play based on *Yeats's *At the Hawk's Well*. His collected writings were published in Japanese in four volumes and continued to exert influence after his early death. KWB

KAPNIST, VASILY (1757–1823)

Russian dramatist and poet. His major claim to fame is the *satirical *comedy *The Slanderer* (1796) which, with its themes of bureaucratic jerrymandering, bribe-taking, and general inefficiency, is in the tradition of *Fonvizin and anticipates the world of *Gogol's *The Government Inspector*. Given its first performance in 1798, *The Slanderer* was banned after four showings and was not staged again until 1805. It has since provided an excellent vehicle for actors, the leading role of president of the Civil Court Krivosudov (Lawbender) proving popular with *Shchepkin later in the century, and is the one play of Kapnist's to have continued to prove stageworthy. His *tragedy *Antigone* was performed in 1814 for the *benefit of E. S. *Semyonova, a leading tragic actress of the day, and in 1806 he translated *Molière's *Sganarelle*. NW

KAPOOR, PRITHVIRAJ (1906–72)

Scion of *India's leading *film family, actor in over 50 silent and sound films, and *actor-manager of Prithvi Theatres, a professional *Hindi-*Urdu drama company. Born into a middle-class family of Peshawar, Kapoor began acting while in high school in Lyallpur and at Edwards College in Peshawar. He left law school for Bombay (*Mumbai) and appeared in nine silent films. He next *toured India with the Grant Anderson Theatre Company, performing Shakespeare in English. Between 1933 and 1944 he returned to cinema and starred in the epic *Sikandar* and other early sound films. In 1944 he established his own repertory theatre group and *toured India extensively for sixteen years. Prithvi Theatres was known for its *naturalistic stagecraft and the *political thrust of dramas such as *Deewar* (*Wall*), *Pathan*, and *Gaddar* (*Traitor*), which opposed Partition and promulgated communal harmony. A commanding personality with a handsome appearance, Kapoor always played the lead and took responsibility for *finances. Travelling with a company of 100, Kapoor sought to establish a national theatre movement in India on the tumultuous eve of independence. The company launched the acting careers of Kapoor's sons Raj, Shammi, and Shashi, as well as fostering Ramanand Sagar, Shankar-Jaikishen, and Ram Ganguly, key members of Raj Kapoor's film crew. In the 1950s and 1960s, Prithviraj Kapoor made many well-known films, including *Mughal-e Azam*, *Dahej*, and *Awara*. He was posthumously given the Dadasaheb Phalke award for his contribution to Indian cinema, and his son Shashi Kapoor revived Prithvi Theatres in his honour.   KH

KAPROW, ALLAN (1927–)

Painter, critic, and performer, the inventor of *happenings. Inspired by Jackson Pollock's Action Paintings he developed a technique of 'action-collage' in the mid-1950s. When he introduced flashing *lights, audible elements, and thicker chunks of material, these assemblages turned into *environments, which could incorporate viewers as part of their structure. This led to *18 Happenings in 6 Parts* at the Reuben Gallery in *New York (1959). The gallery space had been divided into three compartments, where six sequences of events occurred simultaneously. The *actions had been fixed in a *scenario and *rehearsed by friends of the artist. Visitors at the exhibition were given precise instructions that allowed them to carry out actions within clearly defined parameters of time and space. In the following years he organized over twenty major happenings. After 1970 he focused on much simpler events, activities, and self-performances, which became barely distinguishable from occurrences in everyday life. *See also* PERFORMANCE ART/ART PERFORMANCE.   GB

KARAGÖZ

Popular Turkish *shadow puppet, which once covered an area from Romania to the Maghrib. The show centres on the solo puppeteer's improvised comic and topical repartee between

Karagöz (Black Eye) and his friend Hacivat. A series of familiar social types also appears. Performances occurred mainly during Ramadan and in cafés, with special shows at court or for circumcisions or marriages. The figures are made out of translucent dyed camel skin. Jointed at the neck or waist (Karagöz also has a jointed arm), they are held against the screen with horizontal rods. In Egypt the name passed to the glove puppet Aragoz. In nineteenth-century Greece Karagöz evolved into Karaghiozis and rose on a tide of nationalism, holding his own until the last quarter of the twentieth century. He was also popular as a strip-cartoon figure. *See also* PUPPET THEATRE.

JMcC

KARA JŪRŌ (1940–)

Japanese playwright, director, actor, and novelist. With *Terayama Shūji he was one of the spearheads of the underground (*angura) theatre movement in *Japan. The productions of his Situation Theatre (Jōkyō gekijō, established 1963) in a red tent were a symbol of 1960s counter-culture and a tribute to the carnivalesque spirit of early *kabuki. Like *Hijikata Tatsumi, Kara attempted to revive the native, erotic energies of traditional Japanese theatre by emphasizing the actor's physical presence. His complex plays are lyrical, *surrealistic, shocking, funny, even baffling. He came into his own as a playwright with such 1970 works as *John Silver* and *The Virgin's Mask*, and *toured *Korea with *A Tale of Two Cities* (1972), *Bangladesh with *Bengal Tiger* (1973), and Palestine with *Matasaburō of the Wind* (1974). He disbanded the Situation Theatre in 1985 and founded a new company of younger actors, the Kara Gang (Kara-gumi), in 1987. Later plays include *Invisible Man* (1990). In 2000 he continued to tour Japan with his red tent.   CP

KARANTH, B. V. (1928–2002)

Prominent Indian director and composer. Born in Karnataka in south *India, Karanth joined the famous Gubbi Theatre Company (*see* VERANNA, GUBBI) as a child actor. He studied literature and music at Banaras and trained at the *National School of Drama, New Delhi. After graduation, he began to direct and compose *music for plays in Delhi and Karnataka. Between 1967 and 1972 he produced a phenomenal number of plays in the *Kannada language, often at a feverish pace, and soon established himself as a major director. His vigorous celebration of *music, *dance, and visual theatricality inspired the *amateur theatre movement in Karnataka, and by 1978 he was known widely in India for his experimentation with indigenous theatrical forms in a contemporary idiom. From the late 1970s he headed a number of important theatre organizations in India, including the National School of Drama, Bharat Bhavan in Bhopal, and the Rangayana Repertory at Mysore. His major productions include *Evam Indrajit* (1969), *Jokumaraswami* (1972), *Hayavadana*

(1973), *Sattavara Neralu* (1975, all in Bangalore), *Barnam Vana* (an adaptation of *Macbeth*, New Delhi, 1979), *Ghashiram Kotwal* (Bhopal, 1982), and *Gokula Nirgamana* (Heggodu, 1993). He received many important *awards.   KVA

KARANTH, SHIVARAMA (1902–97)

Playwright, scholar, and director, a prominent cultural figure in Karnataka in south *India. Though theatre was only one of his varied interests, his contribution to the reformation of the traditional *yakshagana* form was seminal. He began his exploration of theatre during the 1920s with operatic *ballets for children in educational experiments. Soon he was drawn to *yakshagana* and undertook extensive research on its history and theatricality. Concluding that the tradition was losing its artistry under commercial pressure, he began to explore ways of creating a new form in a lyrical mode. In the 1970s he established a *yakshagana* school at Udupi and later a repertory company which travelled with his productions in India and abroad. These 'yakshagana ballets' departed from the conventional form in a number of ways, including the elimination of spoken word. While his interventions made *yakshagana* accessible to the outside world, his work was sometimes criticized at home for abandoning the rough and earthly qualities of the *folk tradition. Karanth also wrote several *verse plays and *farces, including *Garbhagudi* (*Sanctum Sanctorum*, 1932), *Somiya Soubhagya* (*Somi's Fortune*, 1936), *Yaro Andaru* (*Somebody Said So*, 1938), and *Jambada Janaki* (*Janaki's Vanity*, 1957).
                                                        KVA

KARATYGIN, VASILY (1802–52)

Russian actor. Raised in the tradition of *neoclassicism, his *acting style was always contrasted with that of the more *romantic Pavel *Mochalov, the Edmund *Kean of his day, and engaged the polemical partisanship of writers as diverse as Belinsky and Herzen. A highly intelligent actor, Karatygin moved in artistic circles which included *Pushkin and *Griboedov. His stylized deportment and declamatory style lent themselves well to roles such as *Corneille's Le Cid (1822) and Hippolyte in *Racine's *Phèdre* (1823), and when the *Aleksandrinsky Theatre opened in *St Petersberg in 1832, Karatygin became the company's leading tragedian. Here he performed leading roles in *neoclassical works by Russian dramatists but also made his mark in Shakespeare, following first translations of the latter's work by Nikolai Polevoy in the 1830s. Chief among his Shakespearian roles were Othello (1836), Hamlet (1837), and King Lear (1838). He appeared as Karl Moor and as Ferdinand in *Schiller's *The Robbers* and *Love and Intrigue* respectively, and was the first to perform the roles of Chatsky in Griboedov's *Woe from Wit* (1831) and Arbenin in *Lermontov's *Masquerade* (1852).
                                                        NW

KAREDA, URJO (1944–2001)

Canadian *critic, *dramaturg, and director. Born in Estonia, Kareda grew up in *Toronto where he developed a passion for theatre, *film, and *opera. After graduate studies at Cambridge University, he returned home to write for the *Toronto Star*, Canada's largest newspaper, and was its lead drama critic from 1971 to 1975. His passionate, literate reviews contributed to the rise of Toronto's *alternative theatres in that period. In 1975 Kareda became literary manager of the *Stratford Festival and, for a few months in 1980, the company's co-artistic director. From 1982 to 2001 he was *artistic director of *Tarragon Theatre, and although he rarely directed, he gained a national reputation as a broker of new plays and as a leading intellectual in Canadian theatre.   DWJ

KARGE, MANFRED (1938–)

German actor, director, and playwright. Karge trained in East *Berlin and worked first at the *Berliner Ensemble, then at the *Volksbühne. He is known chiefly for productions co-directed with Matthias Langhoff. In the 1970s the duo became known in the East and West for radical reinterpretations of the classics, particularly *Ibsen and *Chekhov, which they stripped of *realist trappings and placed in stylized settings. They also directed premières of Heiner *Müller's *The Battle* (1975), *The Mission* (1983), *Desolate Shore* (1983), and *Medeamaterial* (1983). As a dramatist Karge is best known for his *monodrama *Jacke wie Hose* (*All the Same*, 1982).   CBB

KARNAD, GIRISH (1938–)

Playwright, *filmmaker, and actor from Karnataka in south *India. A Rhodes Scholar at Oxford, Karnad first worked in Indian publishing. Though his early plays were inspired by existential *modernist drama, the themes focused primarily on Indian myths, history, and *folklore. His first play, *Yayati* (1960), for example, recounts the story of a king who borrows youth from his son. His second, *Tughluq* (1964), is concerned with the fourteenth-century king Muhammad-bin-Tughluq, who in his apparent madness becomes increasingly more violent in order to bring about an ideal state; critics noted the oblique similarity to Nehru's dreams of an ideal India. *Hayavadana* (1971) is based on a folk story about the exchanging of heads between two friends, and dramatizes the modernist opposition between mind and body. The play relies upon several conventions from folk performance, and the advocates of the 'theatre of roots' movement soon regarded it as a key *text. Karnad's other important works include *Nagamandala* (*The Serpent Ritual*, 1980), *Taledanda* (1990), and *Agni Mattu Male* (*Fire and the Rain*, 1994). Many of his plays have been translated and performed in other Indian languages and in English, and he is regarded as one of the foremost modern Indian playwrights. *See also* KANNADA THEATRE. KVA

KARTUN, MAURICIO (1946–)

Argentinian dramatist, actor, and director whose work exposes the cultural contradictions of his own childhood (*Bye Misterix*, 1980) and Argentina's history (*Pericones*, 1987). He has adapted and transformed theatrical traditions (*Jump to the Sky*, 1991, is based on *Aristophanes' Birds*), especially the *sainete criollo* (*The Partner*, 1988). JGJ

KARYALA

Prominent *folk performance of Himachal Pradesh, *India. It is traditionally performed at the Dussehra festival (around October) for sixteen nights continuously, or on invitation by those who have made a promise to the gods for the fulfilment of a wish. An all-night performance of several small, unscripted sketches usually begins with the *karyala taal* (rhythm) played on the drum, followed by the *chandravali nritya*, a *ritual *dance to consecrate the performance space. The various playlets follow, and portray *characters from everyday life through music, poetic couplets, and *dialogue (often improvised) replete with witty local proverbs. The popular play of the *bairagi* (mendicant), for example, contains sketches between different types of beggars, some knowledgeable, others frauds. The rest of the play is full of *satire, buffoonery, and double entendre in free *verse, punctuated by popular regional melodies. KJ

KASPER (KASPERL, KASPERLE)

A traditional role of the old *Viennese popular theatre and the German *puppet theatre, derived from the Italian Arlecchino (*see* COMMEDIA DELL'ARTE) and the German *Hanswurst. After Caroline *Neuber's symbolic expulsion of *Harlequin *farces from the German stage in 1737, the comic figure found a new home in the Austrian theatre and was performed under different guises by *Stranitzky and Gottfried *Prehauser. Towards the end of the eighteenth century, Kasper was given a 'classic' form by Johann Laroche, and his main stage, the Leopoldstädter Theater, was thereafter referred to as 'Kasperletheater'. The coarse humour of this proletarian figure particularly appealed to the tastes of lower-class *audiences, and around 1800 he entered the repertoire of German puppet theatres, where he expressed the children's hatred of the regimented world of adults. Franz Graf von Pocci elevated him to a literary status, but also romanticized the figure and defused his oppositional quality. In the twentieth century various authors rediscovered the figure's anarchic, subversive quality and gave his cudgelling and anti-authoritarian rebellion a distinctly *political character. GB

KATAEV, VALENTIN (1897–1986)

Russian/Soviet dramatist and prose writer. His first notable work was the novel *The Embezzlers* (1927), an adventure story set during the New Economic Policy period and concerning two corrupt Soviet officials in search of 'high society'. It was adapted and performed at the *Moscow Art Theatre in 1928, directed by Ilya Sudakov. *Squaring the Circle*, an engaging *comedy about the accommodation shortage facing young people in 1920s *Moscow, was also staged at the Art Theatre in 1928, directed by Nikolai Gorchakov, and proved popular with English and American *audiences during the 1930s. Kataev also dramatized his Five-Year Plan novel *Time, Forward!*, which depicts the construction of a metallurgical plant, where a group of workers set a world record for pouring concrete (Moscow Drama Theatre, 1932). Other stage adaptations of his work include *I Am the Son of Working People* (Vakhtangov Theatre, 1937) and *For Soviet Power* (MAT, 1954). Kataev also made stage versions of his books for children *A White Sail Gleams* (1937) and *Son of the Regiment* (1945), both produced at the Central Children's Theatre in Moscow. NW

KATHAKALI

Literally, 'story play', *kathakali* emerged as a new *genre of performance in the late sixteenth and early seventeenth centuries in Kerala, *India. Under the patronage of regional rulers, it was created from a confluence of arts including the martial art (*kalarippayattu*) whose Nayar practitioners provided the first actor-dancers, Sanskrit temple drama (*kutiyattam*), the devotional *dance-drama sacred to Lord Krishna (*krishnattam*), and *ritual performances (*teyyam*, *mutiyettu*).

A highly physical dance-drama staging stories written in Sanskritized Malayalam and based on Indian epics (*Ramayana*; *Mahabharata*) and Puranas, *kathakali* is performed on a bare stage with only stools and occasional *properties, by three groups of performers: actor-dancers, percussionists, and vocalists. With a few exceptions, all-male companies of actor-dancers use a highly physicalized performance style embodied through years of training to play kings, *heroines, demons, demonesses, gods, animals, priests, and a few *characters drawn from everyday life. Each role is easily identifiable to a local *audience as a particular character type. Roles are created by using a repertory of dance steps, choreography, a complex language of hand gestures (*hastas*) for 'speaking' their character's *dialogue with their hands, and a pliable use of the face and eyes to express the internal states (*bhava*) of the character. The percussion orchestra includes three drums, each with its own distinctive sound, and brass cymbals, which keep the basic rhythmic cycles around which the dance-drama is structured. Two onstage vocalists keep the basic time patterns on cymbals and sing the *text, including both third-person narration and first-person

One of the best-known contemporary *kathakali* actors, Gopi Asan, performs King Rugmamgada in Killimangalam, Kerala, India, 1995. A 'heroic' role in *kathakali*, Rugmamgada is here in a state of transformative fury.

dialogue, in an elaborate, repetitious vocal style. Performances traditionally begin at dusk, and end at dawn.

Kathakali playtexts consist of third-person metrical *verses (*slokas*) which, often composed completely in Sanskrit, narrate what happens in the ensuing dialogue or soliloquy sections of the text. *Padams* (songs) are composed in the first person in a mixture of Sanskrit and Malayalam, and are interpreted onstage by the actor-dancers. *Slokas* and *padams* are set to specific musical ragas appropriate to the mood and context; *padams* are also set in specific rhythmic patterns (*tala*) and tempos (*kala*). Successive generations of performers have modified *kathakali* playtexts by handing down techniques and styles of performance for specific plays. In keeping with the *rasa aesthetic, which encourages elaboration of all performative modes to enhance the pleasure of aesthetic delight, performative interpolations (*ilakiyattam*) are added to the performance. Lasting up to an hour, the best known are opportunities for senior performers to display one or more aspects of their virtuosic abilities, such as the choreographic *tour de force* of Arjuna's interpolation in *Kalakeya Vadham*, in which he describes the sights of the heav-

enly abode, Devaloka, or the histrionic display of inner emotional turmoil demanded of the actor playing Nala in *Nala Caritam*, when he enacts the wrenching turmoil of his decision to leave his beloved Damayanti at the mercy of the wild forest. What distinguishes interpolations from the literary text is that they are not sung, but simply enacted without repetition by the actor or actors, through action and hand gestures.

Many plays still in the active repertory have been 'edited' to shorten them to three- to four-hour performances. It is commonplace for an all-night performance to include three shortened plays focusing on scenes of most interest to connoisseurs. Since 1930 when the best-known Malayali poet, Mahakavi Vallathol Narayana Menon, founded the now well-known Kerala State Arts School, the *Kerala Kalamandalam, *kathakali* has been adapted both by practitioners from within the tradition and by artists and entrepreneurs from without. These experiments have included *kathakali* for tourist audiences, writing and staging new plays based on traditional epic/puranic sources, transforming *kathakali* techniques and choreography into modern forms of Indian stage dance and/or dance-drama, and writing and staging new plays based on non-traditional sources and/or current events, such as the 1987 leftist production of *People's Victory* which pitted the personified hero (World Conscience) against the personified *villain (Imperialism). Non-Hindu myths or non-Indian plays have also been adapted for *kathakali* style productions, such as the stories of Mary Magdalene, the Buddha, Faust, as well as the *Iliad* and *King Lear*.   PZ

ZARRILLI, PHILLIP B., *When Gods and Demons Come to Play: kathakali dance-drama in performance and context* (London, 2000)

KATONA, JÓZSEF (1791–1830)

Hungarian actor, translator, and playwright. In 1808, while still a student, Katona joined the company of the celebrated actress Madame Déry, with whom he was in love, using the stage name Békesi. He translated several plays for the company and adapted prose works for the stage. The performance of his masterpiece, the *historical drama *Bánk bán* (*The Viceroy*, written 1815), was banned (*see* CENSORSHIP). Published in 1820, it was presented posthumously in 1833. Katona had been influenced by the *Sturm und Drang* movement and his play is full of the national ardour of *romanticism; it was revived at the National Theatre of *Budapest on the eve of the Hungarian Revolution of 1848. Ferenc Erkel, the composer of the Hungarian national anthem, transformed *Bánk bán* into an *opera in 1861, and his version has remained in the Hungarian repertoire. Katona returned to his home town, Kecskemét, in 1826 and worked as a district attorney. He attempted unsuccessfully to establish a theatre there, after which he retired from artistic activity.   HJA

KATRAKIS, MANOS (1908–84)

Greek actor, whose career began in the 1927 silent *film *The Banner of 1821* followed by a stage debut the next year. After performing with the *Greek National Theatre, he starred in Shakespeare's *Tempest* and *Schiller's *Don Carlos*, both directed by Takis Mouzenidis for the Curtain Theatre company during the 1945–6 season. After imprisonment for his leftist politics he was back on stage in 1952 to play *Prometheus Bound* in Delphi to international acclaim for his stage presence, voice, and artistic sensitivity. In 1955 he founded the People's Theatre in *Athens where he produced numerous plays, including Lope de *Vega's *Fuente Ovejuna* and *Kambanellis's *Yard of Wonders*. Katrakis also starred in several films, including George Tzavella's *Antigone* and Theo Angelopoulos's *Voyage to Cythera* (1984).

KGo

KATTIYAKKARAN

The narrator and commentator of *terukkuttu*, a traditional *dance-theatre form from Tamil Nadu in the south of *India. Originating from *kattiyam* (announcement) and *karan* (liter-

ally, the one who makes the announcement), the *kattiyakkaran* is a regional variation of the pan-Indian convention of the *vidushaka*, the jester-like *character in Sanskrit drama, who provides satirical humour as the trusted *confidant of the *protagonist. Making the first entry in the *terukkuttu* performance with a vibrant dance movement, the *kattiyakkaran* greets the *audience, announces the play, and performs *rituals invoking the Hindu god Ganapati, who is believed to remove all deterrents. The irreverence of his performance is evident in the way that he worships and mocks the gods at the same time. Apart from introducing all the primary characters, he also deflates their heroic stances with witty *dialogue and barbed asides in colloquial Tamil. In dazzling and improvised wordplay, the *kattiyakkaran* draws on topical references, linking the mythical narrative of *terukkuttu* to contemporary politics.   PR/RB

KAUFMAN, GEORGE S. (1889–1961)

American playwright and director. Known as 'the great collaborator', Kaufman wrote only one solo play, *The Butter and Egg Man* (1925). Between 1917 and 1930 he was drama editor for the *New York Times* and between 1921, with the success of *Dulcy* (with Marc *Connelly), and 1953, with a comeback hit, *The Solid Gold Cadillac* (with Howard Teichmann), he was among the most prolific and sought-after comic writers and directors in the United States. Kaufman collaborated with Connelly on ten plays (some of them *one-acts) between 1921 and 1924, including *Merton of the Movies* (1922), which ran for nearly 400 performances, and *Beggar on Horseback* (1924), an *expressionistic *satire of business culture. He collaborated on six plays with Edna *Ferber, including the dark *comedy *Dinner at Eight* (1932), and with other writers such as Dorothy Parker, Ring Lardner, Herman Mankiewicz, Morrie Ryskind, and the composers George *Gershwin, Arthur Schwartz, Richard *Rodgers, and Cole *Porter. Kaufman's enduring comic successes came with Moss *Hart: *Once in a Lifetime* (1930), *You Can't Take It with You* (1936, Pulitzer Prize), and *The Man Who Came to Dinner* (1939). Kaufman was in high demand as a play doctor during the 1930s, called in by producers to rework *plot lines and add jokes to plays by other authors. He directed most of the plays he wrote as well as other work, including *The Front Page* (1928) and *Of Mice and Men* (1937). The satire *Of Thee I Sing* (1931, with Ryskind and the Gershwins) was the first *musical to be awarded the Pulitzer Prize.   MAF

KAWATAKE MOKUAMI (1816–93)

Japanese *kabuki playwright. Mokuami (his stage name) worked with, but subordinate to, actors in the kabuki theatre all his creative life, but the range of his production has elevated him with the very few playwrights who have left their mark on the form. He came into his own in the 1870s and 1880s, when kabuki took some hesitant steps towards modernization; he wrote for all the most famous actors of his day and was chief playwright at the Shintomi-za, a theatre which reformed many aspects of kabuki theatregoing. Not a natural innovator himself, Mokuami raised the general artistic level by judicious and sustained use of musical background, by paying much more attention to *dialogue than his predecessors had done, and by adapting *nō plays for kabuki. He responded to calls for plays more in tune with the age by writing *katsurekigeki* (plays of living history), in which there was some observance of historical fact, and *zangiri-mono* (cropped-hair pieces), featuring characters from contemporary Japan.   BWFP

KAZAN, ELIA (1909–)

American director. A veteran of the *Group Theatre and co-founder of the *Actors Studio (1948), Kazan's direction of plays by Arthur *Miller and Tennessee *Williams epitomized the *naturalistic *acting and poetic staging associated with serious American theatre in the post-war period. Of Greek heritage, Kazan emigrated with his family from Turkey at the age of 4. Graduating from Williams College in 1930, he studied at *Yale School of Drama (1930–32) but left to accept an unpaid apprenticeship with the Group Theatre. The Group's social consciousness, *Method acting, and emphasis on ensemble left indelible marks. Kazan became adept at the close reading of *texts and psychological analyses of *character. 'Direction', he later said, 'finally consists of turning psychology into behavior.' He emerged as a viable actor in the Group in *Odets's *Waiting for Lefty* (1935) and as director with two plays by Robert Ardrey: *Casey Jones* (1938) and *Thunder Rock* (1939). After the Group's collapse (1941), the collaborations with Miller and Williams seemed a fortuitous meeting of the director's talents and the literary strengths of the playwrights. His productions of Miller's *All my Sons* (1947) and *Death of a Salesman* (1949) and Williams's *A Streetcar Named Desire* (1947), *Camino Real* (1953), *Cat on a Hot Tin Roof* (1955), and *Sweet Bird of Youth* (1959) were inflected by a poetic delicacy derived partly from Kazan's frequent collaboration with designer Jo *Mielziner. Despite Kazan's artistic sympathy with Miller, their relationship was put under great strain by Kazan's 1952 testimony before the House Un-American Activities Committee, during which Kazan named as communists eight former Group Theatre associates. Kazan served as director of the *Lincoln Center Repertory Company in New York from 1962 to 1964, but thereafter devoted his energies to his other careers in *film direction and writing.
                                                           MAF

KAZANTSEV, ALEKSEI (1945–)

Soviet/Russian playwright who emerged during perestroika (notably with *And the Silver Rope Snaps*), but built his reputation in the 1990s. *This Other World* (1993), staged in both *Moscow and *St Petersburg, comments on the medium of cinema: *film is more real than life, and only when life is treated like a film is self-recognition possible. *Running Wanderers* (1996) deals with the change of times and people. With Mikhail *Roshchin, Kazantsev established a centre for young playwrights and directors; he is editor of the journal *Dramaturg*, which he launched in 1993.   BB

KAZANTZAKIS, NIKOS (1883–1957)

Greek playwright and novelist. Born in Heraklion in Crete, he spent many years travelling in Europe and Asia. Best known for his novels, particularly *Zorba the Greek* (1946), and for his 33,333-line epic poem *Odyssey* (1938), he also wrote several *tragedies, some in *verse, whose *characters were largely based on Greek myth and history. His first play, *It Is Dawning* (1907), was followed by *Comedy* (1908, notable for its existential and *absurdist content), *Christ* (1921), *Odysseus* (1922), *Nikiforos Fokas* (1927), *Melissa* (1937), *Julian the Apostate* (1939), *Prometheus* (1943), *Capodistria* (1944), *Sodom and Gomorrah* (1948), *Kouros* (1949), *Christopher Columbus* (1949), *Constantine Paleologos* (1951), and *Buddha* (1956). His work was philosophical in nature and greatly influenced by his teacher Henri Bergson, Nietzschean theory, and Buddhism. Kazantzakis emphasized poetic elements and often disregarded the practical demands of staging. There were, however, several productions of his plays worldwide, including the *Greek National Theatre's *Capodistria* (1976) and *Buddha* (1978), both directed by Alexis Solomos.   KGo

KEACH, STACY (1941–)

American actor. Keach studied at the University of California, Berkeley, Yale University, and the *London Academy of Music and Dramatic Art. He won an Obie *award for the title role of *Macbird!* (1967) and went on to play the title role in *Ibsen's *Peer Gynt* (1969), Buffalo Bill in *Kopit's *Indians* (1969), and Jamie in *O'Neill's *Long Day's Journey into Night* (1976). He also took the leading role in the *New York première of *The Kentucky Cycle* (1993). Most often cast in tough guy parts, his screen appearances include Abraham Wright in *Brewster McCloud* (1970), Bad Bob in *The Life and Times of Judge Roy Bean* (1972), and Frank James in *The Long Riders* (1980). On *television he played the title roles in the Mike Hammer series and *Hemingway* (1988), and he directed *Incident at Vichy* (1973) and *Six Characters in Search of an Author* (1976).   JDM

KEAN, CHARLES (1811–68)

English *actor-manager. The son of Edmund *Kean, he was raised to be a gentleman but became an actor against his father's wishes. He made his debut at the age of 16 as Young Norval in *Drury Lane's production of John *Home's *Douglas*. Garnering sympathetic but not encouraging notices, Kean set out to learn his craft in provincial theatres. He returned to Drury Lane as Hamlet in 1838, receiving triumphant reviews and the princely sum of £50 per night. Throughout the 1840s Kean played leading roles at *Covent Garden, Drury Lane, and the *Haymarket. In 1842 he married the actress Ellen *Tree. Kean's celebrity was enhanced in 1848 when Queen Victoria asked him to produce private theatricals at Windsor Castle, a task which he undertook for the next ten years. In 1850 Kean assumed joint *management of the *Princess's Theatre with the comedian Robert *Keeley. He became sole lessee after two years, supervising productions of Shakespeare, *melodrama, *comedy, and *pantomime. Despite its moderate size and unassuming shop-front exterior, the Princess's became one of *London's most fashionable *playhouses, patronized by such celebrities as Queen Victoria and Prince Albert, Charles *Dickens, and William Gladstone. Kean relinquished the managerial reins in 1859 and spent the remaining nine years of his life performing throughout Britain, America, and Australia.

Never widely praised as a tragedian, Kean nonetheless excelled in cape-and-sword melodramas. The critic G. H. *Lewes complained that Kean 'detonated' his way through Shakespeare yet praised the actor's 'gentlemanly demeanour and drawing-room manner' in Dion *Boucicault's *The Corsican Brothers* (1852) and *Louis XI* (1855). In these plays Kean offered mid-Victorian *audiences what they wanted in a stage *hero: restraint, not magnificence; detail, not oratory; and decorum, not passion. As a theatrical manager he is remembered for staging lavish *historical spectacles. Between 1852 and 1859 he re-created not merely the medieval and Tudor England of Shakespeare's chronicle plays, but also Assyria (*Byron's *Sardanapalus*, 1853); Peru (*Sheridan's *Pizarro*, 1856); Periclean Athens (*A Midsummer Night's Dream*, 1856); and Renaissance Italy (*The Merchant of Venice*, 1858). Kean's antiquarian revivals were celebrated—and censured—for their sets, *costumes, and *properties of unprecedented historical precision; re-enactment of events not dramatized by Shakespeare (such as the return of Henry V to London after the battle of Agincourt); interpolation of *dialogue and music of presumed authenticity (such as insults hurled at the captive Richard II); and *playbill essays on his historical research. (*See* ANTIQUARIANISM.) So fastidious was Kean's insistence upon authentic stage accessories that *Punch* dubbed him not the 'Upholder' of Shakespeare, but the 'Upholsterer'. For more than a century after Kean's death, theatre historians complained that his productions sacrificed Shakespeare on the altar of spectacle. But scholars in the 1980s and 1990s have explored the ways in which these performances—and the socially inclusive audiences which they attracted—were a vibrant part of Victorian historical culture and its nationalistic political agenda. RWS

SCHOCH, RICHARD, *Shakespeare's Victorian Stage* (Cambridge, 1998)

KEAN, EDMUND (c.1787–1833)

English actor, the leading tragedian of the *romantic age. His violent *acting style, full of energy and passion, displaced the cold, declamatory *neoclassicism of John Philip *Kemble. Kean's most famous roles also played a crucial part in transforming established critical views about Shakespearian *characters, notably Richard III, Iago, and Shylock. Kean was the illegitimate son of a minor actress; as a young man playing the provincial circuit, he was acclaimed for his performances as *Harlequin and in noble savage roles. He and his family were in a state of abject poverty when he finally secured an engagement at *Drury Lane Theatre. On 26 January 1814, a night so cold and misty that the theatre was almost deserted, a short, undistinguished man, with a sallow complexion and thick black hair, made his debut as Shylock in *The Merchant of Venice*. Kean astonished his fellow actors by wearing a black wig and beard in place of the traditional red one; moreover, his sympathetic portrayal boldly challenged convention. William *Hazlitt, one of the few *critics present, commented, 'His style of acting is, if we may use the expression, more significant, more pregnant with meaning, more varied and alive in every part, than any we have almost ever witnessed.'

Kean's unprecedented popularity saved the ailing Drury Lane from bankruptcy. His performances were celebrated for their frenzied, tempestuous emotion and for sudden, unexpected transitions between contrasting moods. In Richard III, perhaps his finest role, Kean was full of ironic contempt and sardonic humour; as Hamlet, he famously returned at the end of the nunnery scene to press his hand tenderly to Ophelia's lips. Other roles included Macbeth and a leaden Romeo (both 1815), a bitter, sceptical Timon, and the *villainous Sir Giles Overreach in *Massinger's *A New Way to Pay Old Debts* (both 1816). Kean also portrayed the wild and yet pathetic Oroonoko in Thomas *Southerne's eponymous drama (1817), as well as King John (1818), Coriolanus (1819), and King Lear (1820).

Kean became one of the great celebrities of the Romantic era. As well as numerous engagements in the provinces, he visited America twice and performed in *Paris. But the actor's dissipated lifestyle and notorious addiction to alcohol rapidly destroyed both his health and his career. In 1825 he was successfully prosecuted by Robert Cox, a member of the Drury Lane committee (Kean had been conducting a long and scandalous affair with Cox's wife Charlotte). Violent opposition greeted Kean's appearance at Drury Lane in the aftermath of this conviction; when he visited America soon afterwards, outraged *Boston *audiences hounded him from the stage. On his return to *London, Kean gave only occasional performances. In March 1833, he played Othello to the Iago of his son Charles *Kean, but collapsed on stage during the third act and died a few weeks later. JM

KEANE, JOHN B. (1928–2002)

Irish playwright. Born in County Kerry, after a period in England in the 1950s he returned to Ireland, where his first play *Sive* caused a sensation at the 1959 All-Ireland Drama Festival. At once a *realistic and *ritualistic drama of rural cruelty and hypocrisy, *Sive* was declined by the *Abbey Theatre. Subsequent plays were produced by Theatre of the South in Cork and Gemini Productions in *Dublin. The Abbey produced *Hut 42* in 1962, by which time Keane's work had entered the national repertoire. The land and people of north Kerry, with their idiosyncratic customs and language—in which pithy Gaelicisms abound—are at the centre of Keane's work. Among his best plays are *Sharon's Grave* (1960), *Many Young Men of Twenty* (1961), *The Year of the Hiker* (1963), *The Field* (1965), and *Big Maggie* (1969). Ben Barnes's resourceful productions of *Sive*, *The Field*, and *Big Maggie* at the Abbey in the 1980s put an end to the metropolitan perception of Keane as a 'talented provincial'. He also wrote short stories, novels, and reminiscences.

CFS

KECAK (CAK)

*Indonesian *dance-drama created in the Gianyar province of Bali in the 1930s by Balinese performers, in collaboration with Western artists and anthropologists Walter Spies and Beryl de Zoete. With the steep increase in tourism since then, *kecak* has become a popular and standardized entertainment component of tourist performances, also advertised as 'Monkey Dance'. *Kecak* is famous for its large male *chorus of over 100 chanters, seated in dense concentric circles surrounding a small playing area illuminated by a single, large oil lamp. While chanting highly complex, interlocking rhythmic patterns of 'cak cak cak', directed by the lead chanter, they wave their arms and torsos in time to the chanting. This chorus originated in the *sanghyang* trance-dance traditions in which the chorus induces trance in the dancers, signalling that the ancestor spirits or deities have taken possession of them. The chorus in *kecak*, however, is divorced from its original religious function and involves no trance-dance. Instead the dance sequences are based on episodes from the *Ramayana* epic and resemble the Balinese *wayang wong* in most of their performance convention, including dance style, *acting, and *costuming. No *masks are used. The leading refined *characters, such as Rama, Sita, and Laksmana, use Kawi (the ancient Javanese court language), while less refined characters and clown servants use colloquial Balinese.

KP

KEDROV, MIKHAIL (1893–1972)

Russian/Soviet actor and director who joined the *Moscow Art Theatre in 1924, performing roles in productions of plays by *Bulgakov, *Beaumarchais, and Vsevolod *Ivanov. During the 1930s he was involved in prolonged *rehearsals with *Stanislavsky of the roles of *Molière's Tartuffe and *Gogol's Manilov in *Dead Souls*. Kedrov's work as a director dates from the 1930s when he became the appointed legatee of Stanislavsky's *acting *theories, which he sought to promote in plays in the mode of *socialist realism. He was a respected teacher, who numbered Yury *Lyubimov as one of his admiring, but more independent-minded, pupils.

NW

KEEFFE, BARRIE (1945–)

English playwright. One of Britain's 1970s political playwrights (*see* POLITICS AND THEATRE), Keeffe was the miniaturist, drawing sharp pictures of frustrated working-class youth in *Gimme Shelter* (1977) and *Barbarians* (1977). Coming home to find a Borstal runaway ransacking his flat, Keeffe, instead of calling the police, had a beer with the boy and wrote about him in *Frozen Assets* (1978). His plays are often named after 1960s rock songs; he collaborated with the Kinks' Ray Davies on *Chorus Girls* (1981), and wrote about a British Janis Joplin figure in *Bastard Angel* (1980). *A Mad World, my Masters* (1977) attempted to re-create the mood of *Middleton's Jacobean *city comedy in modern *London. *Sus* (1979), set in a police station on the evening of Margaret Thatcher's election, was one of many plays, including *King of England* (1988) and *Not Fade Away* (1990), in which Keeffe created convincing black *characters. He struck a blow for integrated *casting by writing on the director's script of *My Girl* (1991) that 'either character could be either colour'.

CDC

KEELEY, ROBERT (1793–1869) AND MARY ANN (1806–99)

English actors. By the time Miss Mary Ann Goward made her *London debut Robert Keeley was established as a player of comic old men and country boys at *Covent Garden. She began as a singing actress, performing the Mermaid's song in the first production of Weber's *Oberon* in 1826. They regularly appeared on stage together as supporting players in Shakespeare and classic *comedies or leading the cast in *farces. They *toured America in 1836–7 and from 1844 to 1847 *managed the *Lyceum Theatre in London. In accordance with the prevailing custom that ugly old women should be played by men and adolescent boys by women (*see* FEMALE IMPERSONATION; MALE IMPERSONATION), Keeley was a ripe Sairey Gamp and his wife a heart-rending Smike in adaptations from *Dickens. Her most striking *breeches role was Jack Sheppard in Buckstone's 1839 version of Ainsworth's novel. The Keeleys frequently played servants; Robert was the first and best Jacob Earwig in Charles Selby's *Boots at the Swan* (1842) and Mrs Keeley excelled as the sprightly maid in many comic pieces. She retired from the stage when her husband died but never lost touch with it. In 1891 she delivered a *prologue at the opening of the new Lyceum Theatre in her home town of Ipswich. In 1895 Queen Victoria expressed a wish to meet her and they exchanged reminiscences of performances 50 years before.   FD

KEENE, LAURA (1826–73)

American actress and *manager. Born in England, she went on the stage after an early marriage failed, apprenticing with Emma Brougham and Madame *Vestris before emigrating to the United States in 1852. She achieved immediate success playing romantic roles opposite Lester *Wallack at the Lyceum, but conflicts with Wallack prompted her to lease and manage a Baltimore theatre. She subsequently *toured California and Australia with the young Edwin *Booth and managed the American Theatre in *San Francisco before returning to *New York. In 1855 she opened Laura Keene's Varieties, moving to a new theatre in 1856. Though her own magnetism as a performer was an element in the theatre's popularity, she also built a strong ensemble, used publicity well, and closely supervised all aspects of production. She toured with her ensemble after 1863. At her performance of Tom *Taylor's *Our American Cousin* at Ford's Theatre in 1865, Abraham Lincoln was assassinated by the actor John Wilkes *Booth.   AHK

KEITH, B. F. (BENJAMIN FRANKLIN) (1846–1914)

American *vaudeville *producer. Living the American boy's dream, Keith ran away from his family's New Hampshire farm to join the *circus, working for several major companies including P. T. *Barnum's. By the mid-1880s he was *managing the *Boston Gaiety Musée, where he claimed he developed the form of continuous entertainment that would become known as vaudeville. He formed a partnership with Edward F. *Albee in 1885 and opened the Bijou Theatre in Boston, beginning the great Keith–Albee vaudeville chain. For the small fee of ten cents, they offered a non-stop line of performers, comics, singers, and *dancers that ran from 10 a.m. to 11 p.m. Within three years the firm had expanded to *Philadelphia and Providence, growing to a national chain of more than 400 houses by 1920. While Albee handled the business side, Keith focused on day-to-day management and insisted on maintaining a moral code on stage that forbade profanity or innuendo, striving to appeal to the Victorian sensibilities of a middle-class *audience.   PAD

KELLAR, HARRY (1849–1922)

America's most popular magician from 1898 to 1908. He learned *magic in his teens, and later worked for Davenport Brothers and Fay, a spiritualist show. In 1873 Kellar and Bill Fay established their own production, a mix of magic, escape, and spiritualist acts. After years of *touring around the world, Kellar opened his own full show in 1884 in *New York and quickly became the rival of Alexander Herrmann, then the most popular. The two competed for the greatest illusions and best bookings until Herrmann's death in 1898. Kellar was a perfectionist, with every word and movement carefully prepared. At the end of his final tour (1907–8), he turned his show over to Howard Thurston. Kellar performed one last time in 1917 in a benefit organized by Harry *Houdini, after which he was showered with roses and chrysanthemums amidst a standing ovation.   WFC

KELLY, FANNY (1790–1882)

Irish pioneer of theatre *training, who founded an *acting school and theatre in *London's Dean Street. She financed the venture by *touring a solo show of her *Dramatic Recollections* (1832). Her previous career had been as a much loved actress in *legitimate *comedy: she was the original Annette in S. J. Arnold's *The Maid and the Magpie*. She remained independent all her life, having rejected offers of marriage from, amongst others, Charles *Lamb, who adored her 'divine plain face'. Mystery surrounds the failure of 'Miss Kelly's Theatre' (the Royalty), but she survived to be pensioned as a grand old lady of the theatre.   JSB

KELLY, GEORGE E. (1887–1974)

American playwright and director. Beginning as a writer-performer in *vaudeville in 1912, Kelly made his name as a playwright with *The Torchbearers* (1922), a *satire of the *Little Theatre movement. His most admired and successful play was *The Show-Off* (1924), an incisive *satire of a back-slapping small-town businessman, which ran for 575 performances. Kelly turned away from *comedy with the Pulitzer Prize-winning *Craig's Wife* (1925), about a woman obsessed with running an orderly home. He wrote seven more plays between 1927 and 1946, but their increasingly bleak and even cynical outlook—Joseph Wood Krutch called them 'dour and frost-bitten'—disappointed critics and failed to attract *audiences.   MAF

KELLY, HUGH (1739–77)

Irish *critic and playwright. His critical work *Thespis* (1766), an imitation of Charles Churchill's *Rosciad* (1761), analysed the merits and demerits of the *Drury Lane company. His first play, *False Delicacy* (1768), was a great hit; often criticized as a mawkishly sentimental *comedy, in fact it ridicules excessive (or false) delicacy. Nevertheless a benevolent impulse did animate Kelly's playwriting, as can be seen in works such as *A Word to the Wise* (1770) and the very popular *School for Wives* (1773). His one effort at *tragedy, *Clementina* (1771), was unsuccessful.

MJK

KEMBLE FAMILY

English actors, *managers, and writers. **Roger and Sarah Kemble**, itinerant actors, had twelve children, the eldest of whom was Sarah *Siddons; other members of the *family to succeed in *London included **Stephen** (1758–1822), who was to make his career chiefly in management.

The next child after Sarah, **John Philip** (1757–1823), received a classical education but opted for the stage, having played juvenile roles in his father's company. After improving his skills on the well-respected York circuit, he made his London debut as Hamlet at *Drury Lane in 1783 shortly after his sister's triumph. He soon established himself not only as an effective leading man supporting Mrs Siddons but in his own right as a specialist in pensive and tragic roles. His appearance fitted him for classical *characters, such as Shakespeare's Brutus and *Addison's Cato, but he could also embody romantic *heroism, as the picture of him as Rolla (in *Sheridan's *Pizarro*) by Thomas Lawrence attests. The leading roles in the so-called 'German' drama of the 1790s suited him well, and his *impersonations of Penruddock in *Cumberland's *The Wheel of Fortune* and Count Waldbourg in *Kotzebue's *The Stranger* made good use of his remarkable gift for conveying the effects of past experience. He was a studious actor, a buyer of books, and an editor and adapter of plays. Some *laughter was excited by his insistence upon unusual pronunciations, but apart from this he had no gift for *comedy.

Not being inclined to mimicry and gossip proved a decided advantage when he mingled socially with well-born men who like himself had a traditional education, polished manners, collecting habits, and a formidable capacity for drink. His skill in declamation was also particularly admired in these circles at a time when oratory was a real force in public life. While he was manager of *Covent Garden Kemble's high connections intensified the hostile feelings aroused in the *audience by a rise in seat prices and in the number of private *boxes. His dignity, prestige, and private fortune suffered as a result of the *OP (Old Price) riots which disrupted performances from September to December 1809. From 1814 Kemble's *acting was insistently contrasted with that of the newcomer Edmund *Kean, and the *neoclassicism of the older actor described as either a standard of excellence from which the *romanticism of Kean had deviated or a pompous stateliness which had had its day. At his best Kemble had ample power to play the most taxing roles,

but he was increasingly troubled by asthma and gout and in 1817 gave his last performance in his favourite character of Coriolanus.

He made over his share in Covent Garden to his brother **Charles** (1775–1854), who shared the good looks and good manners of his siblings. He found success in less weighty Shakespearian parts such as Mercutio, Cassio, Benedick, Faulconbridge, and Mark Antony (in *Julius Caesar*). He was for many years London's leading fine gentleman in comedy, renowned for his insinuating charm and the elegance of his demeanour. His status as the younger Kemble brother, together with his unflagging energy, extended his hold on youthful roles well into middle age. He was the obvious choice to play Icilius in Sheridan *Knowles's *Virginius* (1820) but his Romeo to his daughter Fanny's Juliet in the 1830s gave rise to jokes such as 'Why is Charles Kemble like an old coquette? Because he plays too much with his Fan.' He retired in 1836 and became Examiner of Plays (*see* LORD CHAMBERLAIN) but three years later played four leading roles by royal command so that Prince Albert might see him act. Increasing deafness eventually made even readings impossible. He gave the edited *texts he had used for these to his daughter and ceded his appointment to his son **John Mitchell Kemble** (1805–57), a pioneering scholar in the field of Old English studies.

Charles married **Marie-Thérèse De Camp** (1774–1838), a *dancer and actress of unblemished reputation who specialized in the important mimed roles of early *melodrama. She wrote and adapted a number of plays. Her brother **Vincent** (1779–1839) was active on the London stage and as a provincial manager.

Frances Anne ('Fanny') (1809–93), daughter of Charles and Marie-Thérèse, emerged from a comparatively secluded girlhood to play Juliet at Covent Garden in 1829 as a desperate measure to save her father from bankruptcy. She was successful, and went on to play many of the parts associated with Mrs Siddons, some of them exceedingly old-fashioned by then but still regarded as essential tests for aspirants to the tragic crown. In new plays she was the first Julia in Knowles's *The Hunchback* (1832) and a fine Bianca in Henry Hart Milman's *Fazio*. She followed her father into high comedy in roles such as Lady Teazle and Kate Hardcastle, and continued the family's literary tradition by writing plays, memoirs, and poetry. In the course of a triumphant *tour of America in 1834 she met and married Pierce Butler, who expected her to dwindle into a wife. After strenuous attempts to ameliorate the living conditions of his slaves and to convert him to her views, Fanny returned to her English family. Her younger sister **Adelaide** (1815–79) enjoyed a brief but glorious career as an *opera singer and performed for Queen Victoria, at whose court Fanny was presented. In 1842 Adelaide married Edward Sartorus and became the hostess of a distinguished European social circle always open to her sister even after her divorce from Butler. Fanny made some stage appearances in the 1840s but enjoyed great success thereafter with readings of Shakespeare plays, which gave full scope to her splendid voice.

The importance of the Kembles in the history of the stage depends to a great extent upon there having been a tribe of them. When Covent Garden was a Kemble stronghold and various other theatres were run by relations and allies they were occasionally denounced as clannish, haughty, and overbearing. Nevertheless their influence tended to strengthen the stage's connections with literature, scholarship, the fine arts, and family values. Conspicuous and mostly well-regulated lives, which included making influential friends, giving readings to select gatherings, and speaking up for their profession, counteracted the exploits of the more raffish kind of entertainer and led towards the esteem in which great performers have come to be held when they combine histrionic power with public spirit.

FD

KEMP, LINDSAY (1938–)

Scottish *mime, dancer, actor, and director, whose company, founded in the early 1960s, has throughout fifteen productions explored the boundaries between the media for live performance, incorporating influences from *ballet (Kemp studied at the Rambert School), *nō, *butoh, and *kabuki, Weidman-inspired modern *dance, *Marceau-trained mime, *opera, and *physical theatre. Kemp's productions include the much revived *Flowers* (1974–94), based on themes from *Genet's novels; a version of *Wilde's *Salome*; *Mr Punch's Pantomime*; *A Midsummer Night's Dream*; *Duende*; *Nijinsky*; *The Big Parade*; *Onnagata*; and *Cinderella*, staged as a Gothic *operetta. All Kemp's stage work is notable for its powerful imagery, achieved by innovatory *lighting, *scenery, and *costume design, which together create an erotic visual poetry. For Ballet Rambert he created *The Parade's Gone By* (1975) and *Cruel Garden* (1978) inspired by *García Lorca's life and works. Some seven *film appearances include *Savage Messiah* (1971) and *Valentino* (1977) for Ken Russell and *Sebastiane* (1974) and *Jubilee* (1977) for Derek Jarman. For David Bowie he directed the 'Ziggy Stardust' concerts in 1972.

RAC

KEMPE (KEMP), WILLIAM (d. 1603)

English comic actor. Kempe, a highly physical performer celebrated for his *dancing, was perceived as the natural successor to the *clown Richard *Tarlton, whom he may have replaced as principal comedian with *Leicester's Men as early as 1583: his style was sufficiently non-verbal for his popularity to have extended to the Continent, which he *toured in the 1580s and again around 1601. He joined *Strange's Men in 1592 and then served with the Lord *Chamberlain's Men between 1594 and 1599, where he created the role of the servant Peter in

Shakespeare's *Romeo and Juliet* in 1595. After this his Shakespearian roles increased in prominence, from Bottom in *A Midsummer Night's Dream* (probably) via Lancelot Gobbo in *The Merchant of Venice* (probably) to Dogberry in *Much Ado About Nothing* (certainly) and Falstaff in the *Henry IV* plays and *The Merry Wives of Windsor* (probably). For whatever reasons, however, Kempe went solo (and was replaced by Robert *Armin) soon after the company moved to the *Globe, performing a marathon *publicity-stunt *morris dance all the way from *London to Norwich (described in his pamphlet *Kempe's Nine Days Wonder*, 1600). Hamlet's attack on clowns who speak more than is set down for them has suggested to many that Shakespeare and Kempe had quarrelled over his ad libbing; certainly Kempe's comic business is criticized as intrusive and vulgar in the Cambridge student play *The Return to Parnassus* (1597), which speaks of his pulling crooked faces, sawing up cheese with a dagger, and lapping up puddles.

MD

KEMPINSKI, TOM (1938–)

London-born playwright who was educated at Cambridge and was an actor for part of his career (1960–71). His plays usually deal with individuals (often artists) who are in some way cut off from mainstream life. This is a key theme in his first major work, *Duet for One*, which was produced with huge success at the *Bush Theatre in 1980. The play, loosely based on the life of cellist Jacqueline du Pré, focuses on a concert violinist suffering from multiple sclerosis and in psychotherapy. The nature of the artist and the nature of communication are at the root of *Separation* (1987), which enacts an odd long-distance relationship between a reclusive writer in London and an ailing (perhaps dying) actress in New York. The theme of analysis, Freudianism, and a structure based on conversation and even interrogation lie at the heart of *When the Past Is Still to Come* (1992), which reworked his own experiences of therapy in attempting to deal with family memories of the Holocaust.

AS

KENDAL, MADGE (MARGARET ROBERTSON) (1848–1935) AND WILLIAM HUNTER (1843–1917)

English husband and wife actors, active from 1874 until 1908. Before their marriage in 1869, Madge Robertson's theatrical career had been considerable. She had *trained at the *Theatre Royal, Bristol, before making her *London debut as Ophelia in 1865. She subsequently played Desdemona to Ira *Aldridge's Othello (1865), Edith in the spectacular *Drury Lane *melodrama by Andrew Halliday, *The Great City* (1867), and Lilian Vavasour in Tom *Taylor's *New Men and Old Acres* (1869). She had already established her signature style: a combination of arch vivacity in *comedy and dignified pathos in adversity. She herself was a paragon of middle-class respectability, a quality which influenced her choice of roles and ultimately made her an overly dignified arbiter of good taste. By contrast, William Kendal had little theatrical background. He developed his abilities as part of the *Haymarket comedy company (1866–74), playing roles like Harry Lester in *Lewes's *The Game of Speculation*, Charles Surface in *Sheridan's *The School for Scandal*, and Orlando in *As You Like It*. His performances were regarded as agreeable but unexciting. After their marriage he undertook secondary roles while proving himself to be an astute *manager. Between 1875 and 1888 he was involved in the management of the *Royal Court Theatre and the *St James's together with John *Hare. The Kendals made five consecutive *tours of North America (1889–96), where they introduced *Pinero's *The Second Mrs Tanqueray*. Often compared with the *Bancrofts, they epitomized the respected position to which Victorian actors aspired. VEE

KENNEDY, ADRIENNE (1931–)

*African-American playwright. Participation in Edward *Albee's playwriting workshop at *Circle in the Square led to the production in 1964 of her first play, *Funnyhouse of a Negro*, and her involvement in the *Off-Off-Broadway movement. Her plays of that period, which include *The Owl Answers* (1965) and *A Movie Star Has to Star in Black and White* (1976), are quasi-autobiographical explorations of a troubled consciousness, both female and black, divided against itself and at odds with the world around it. The imagery is private and visceral, the form subjective and fragmented, and the situations often violent. On the surface, her later work is more serene and narrative in form but just as concerned with racial injustice and identity. Her plays are more widely studied than performed, but in 1992 Great Lakes Theatre Festival in Cleveland premièred *The Ohio State Murders* as part of a festival in her honour. The 1995–6 season of the Signature Theatre in *New York was devoted to her work and included the world première of *Sleep Deprivation Chamber*, written with her son Adam and directed by Michael *Kahn, who also staged many of her earlier plays. She is the recipient of three Obie *awards. STC

KENNY, SEAN (1932–73)

Irish designer who first worked in *London with Joan *Littlewood on *The Hostage* (1958) and Lindsay *Anderson on *The Lily-White Boys* (1960), and ultimately designed over 35 West End productions. Trained as an architect, Kenny's aim was to create a dynamic, three-dimensional stage environment where materials like wood, steel, and rock were important for their sound, movement, and texture. The timber unit set for Lionel *Bart's *musical *Oliver* (1960) shifted and *revolved to form different

configurations for each *scene. For Bart's *Blitz* (1962), there were two giant motorized towers. Eager to break down the artificial divisions of traditional theatres, he worked on the unified *stage and *audience relationship in the *Mermaid Theatre, where he was first resident art director, and redesigned the *Old Vic *auditorium for the *National Theatre's 1963 inaugural production of *Hamlet*, though his cumbersome, revolving, spiral rock and metal ramp set was over-dominant. In 1968 he designed and directed *Gulliver's Travels* at the Mermaid, using projected *film sequences to create shifts in perspective. CEC

KENTE, GIBSON (1932–)

South African actor, composer, and producer of *township musicals. Originally from Grahamstown, he worked in Soweto, initially with Union Artists. His early productions, which he wrote, directed, and played in, include *Manana, the Jazz Prophet* (1963) and *Sikalo* (1966). He broke with Union Artists to form his own company with Sam Mhangwane, creating *Lifa* (1968) and *Zwi* (1970), and by 1974 he managed three companies, in which the performers earned four times a factory worker's wage. Although not overtly political, Kente's work was influenced by the Black Consciousness movement; his *film *How Long?* (1974) and the plays *I Believe* and *Too Late!* (1975) were banned (*see* CENSORSHIP). Later productions that he wrote and directed include *Can You Take It* (1977), *La Duma* (1978), and *Mama and the Load* (1980). Kente's use of narrative, *mime, movement, voice, *music, and *dance has blended established forms of theatre with traditional African oral performance to create 'township *melodrama', relying on urban experience and culture. YH

KENTRIDGE, WILLIAM (1955–)

South African director, designer, and artist. Born in *Johannesburg, where he continues to live, he has created animated *films and videos that are often used in theatre and *opera productions. His collaborative scripting and *devising with members of the *Junction Avenue Theatre includes *Fantastical History of a Useless Man* (1976), *Randlords and Rotgut* (1978), *Security* (1979), and *Dikhitsheneng* (1980). His collaborative work with the Handspring Puppet Company includes *Woyzeck on the Highveld* (1992), *Faustus in Africa!* (1995), *Ubu and the Truth Commission* (1998), and *Monteverdi's *Il ritorno d'Ulisse* (1998). He has made nine animated films and had many exhibitions of his drawings. His work, both visual or dramatic, looks at abuse, suffering, guilt and confession, subjugation and emancipation. He uses classic texts (*Goethe, *Jarry) or art from the past (*Büchner, Goya, Hogarth, *Berlin *dada, *expressionism) to frame ongoing *post-colonial issues. YH

KERALA KALAMANDALAM

Indian *training academy which gives instruction in the major Kerala classical arts: *kathakali, *kutiyattam, mohiniyattam (a classical *dance form), thullal (storytelling in dance), and panchavadyam (a musical ensemble of five instruments). Kalamandalam was founded in 1930 by the Malayalam Poet Laureate Vallathol Narayana Menon, with the assistance of Mukunda Raja, to promote the indigenous arts of kathakali and mohiniyattam which faced decline because of the disappearance of feudal structures of patronage. Vallathol liberated these two traditional art forms from the narrow boundaries of regional culture by exposing them to an international *audience. He institutionalized their training systems in a democratic manner, and popularized them outside of the Indian subcontinent by consciously working against prevailing social and religious stigmas. Unable to sustain Kalamandalam as a private institution, Vallathol transferred it to the government of Cochin in 1941; when the state of Kerala was formed after independence, the academy became a grant-in-aid institution financed directly by the state government. In 1971 it moved to a new location with modern facilities but it continues to retain its traditional gurukula system of training, based on direct interaction between teacher and student.   JoG

KERN, JEROME (1885–1945)

American composer. Kern's pioneering insistence on *musicals that fully integrated *dialogue, *character, song, and staging had a profound impact on the development of twentieth-century musical theatre. His masterpiece, Show Boat, is arguably the most important and influential stage musical ever written. Born in *New York, Kern first achieved notice when his song 'They Didn't Believe Me' (lyrics by Herbert Reynolds) was interpolated into the 1914 New York production of The Girl from Utah. Between 1915 and 1918 Kern wrote a series of musicals with lyricist P. G. *Wodehouse and librettist Guy *Bolton at the intimate Princess Theatre that set a new standard for the integration of their elements. In 1927, Show Boat (*music by Kern, lyrics and libretto by Oscar *Hammerstein II) achieved a more complete unification of song and story. Touching on sensitive social issues (interracial marriage, spousal abuse, abandonment, and alcoholism), it was a far more serious treatment of such material than had previously been attempted in musical comedy. With a rich score and the first racially mixed cast on Broadway, Show Boat was a major advance. Kern also composed for Hollywood, including two *films for Fred *Astaire (Roberta, 1935; Swing Time, 1936) and a bevy of standards such as 'Smoke Gets in your Eyes', 'The Way You Look Tonight', and 'Long Ago and Far Away'. Kern died in New York while preparing to write music for Annie Get your Gun (1946), a project ultimately undertaken by Irving *Berlin.   SN

KERR, WALTER (1913–96)

American critic, playwright, and director. Walter Kerr was one of the most influential theatre critics of his generation, and also an accomplished theatre artist—a rare balance. Born in Evanston, Illinois, he was educated at Northwestern University and took a teaching job at Catholic University in 1938. A number of plays and *musicals which Kerr wrote, co-wrote, or adapted transferred to Broadway, including Count Me In (1942), Stardust (1943), and Song of Bernadette (1946, with his wife Jean Kerr). He moved to *New York in 1949 to become theatre critic for Commonweal; in 1951 left that publication for the New York Herald Tribune; and moved on to the New York Times from 1966 to his retirement in 1983. Kerr was noted for the intelligence of his *criticism and his strong sense of principle: he never attacked a production on moral grounds. In 1990 the Ritz Theatre on Broadway was renamed in his honour.   KF

KETOPRAK

An operatic theatre form of Javanese origin, evolved from the early ketoprak lesung, the name taken from the use of a grinding mortar struck with long poles to produce a rhythm that accompanies *dances and *improvised *acting. Ketoprak eventually included spoken *text, improvisation, stereotyped *characters, more *naturalistic acting, dance, and music, relying on *plots based on the Ramayana, the Mahabharata, or historical and modern topics. During the early decades of the twentieth century, ketoprak went through further refinements when temporary *stages were replaced by *proscenium stages, dances were better choreographed, tembang (singing) techniques were borrowed from traditional Javanese music, and dagelan (comic skits) were enhanced. While Javanese *gamelan ensembles were incorporated in ketoprak gamelan, Western musical instruments such as the violin, mandolin, and drum-sets were adopted for the ketoprak tobong and ketoprak panggung (as the form is known when played in proscenium theatres). Staging techniques changed in the 1920s and the 1930s in terms of settings, blocking, musical arrangements, and style of presentation; painted backdrops became common, depicting scenes similar to those regularly featured in other popular theatre such as *bangsawan and even *wayang wong. During this period ketoprak became popular among new patrons from the middle and upper classes, and it is still played today. See INDONESIA.   MA

KHAYAL

Traditional theatre form from Rajasthan, *India. Derived from khel (play), khayal probably took shape as a musical *dance-drama in the early eighteenth century. It is based on mythological, historical, or popular romantic tales, emphasizing qualities of heroism, self-sacrifice, and nobility. There are several

A **khon chak** performance at the National Theatre in Bangkok, Thailand, c.1990. Phra Ram (Rama) and Phra Lak (Laksmana) arrive by carriage to do battle with Ravana, attended by the monkey army in masks.

types of *khayal*, identified by the kind of stage used or the musical variations selected. The Turra Kilangi *khayal* is performed on an elaborately decorated stage, while the Kuchamani *khayal* is simpler in presentation but has specific music and *dance steps. Highly *improvisatory in nature, with loosely structured *plots and witty *dialogue, *khayal* requires an intimate *audience–actor relationship. Its primary attraction is its soulful singing, accompanied by the *nakkara* and *dholak* (both percussion), *sarangi* (bowed instrument), and sometimes *shehnai* (wind instrument).   KJ

KHMELNITSKY, NIKOLAI (1791–1845)

Russian dramatist. Having fought for his country against Napoleon in 1812, Khmelnitsky entered *St Petersburg literary circles. Before long he turned to the composition of *comedies involving love intrigues which played variations on a number of familiar themes, such as matchmaking and procrastination (the themes of *Gogol's *Marriage*), and in which his *heroes were usually idle talkers or dreamers. His first successful play was *The Chatterbox* (*Govorun*, 1817); others that followed tended to rework French models with the addition of a distinctive Russian flavour, which

matched the talents of *vaudeville actors especially well. He also wrote *historical dramas and translated *Molière.   NW

KHON

Masked *dance-drama of seventeenth-century *Thailand, which began as a royal pageant in the fifteenth century. Deriving from the *nāng yai* *puppet theatre, *khon* borrowed many elements from its predecessor including story material, dance style, narrative structure, and musical accompaniment. The play was originally performed by male dancers who portrayed four type *characters—*hero, heroine, demon, and monkey—each wearing a different *mask. Today, however, female roles are usually played by women and only the demons and monkeys wear masks. *Khon* begins with a musical homage to teachers and deities that asks them to bless the performance. The play proper, taken from an episode in the *Ramayana*, represents the battle between Ravana and Rama through dance. It normally ends with the defeat of Ravana's general, though the death scene is never portrayed. There are three distinct styles of presentation. (*a*) Performed to celebrate auspicious state ceremonies, *khon klang plaeng* is an outdoor performance on a vast field, which usually depicts a mythical battle scene. (*b*) *Khon na jaw* is performed outdoors in front of a *nang yai* white screen on a raised wooden platform with a door on each end. A bench stage right symbolizes Rama's camp, stage left is designated as Ravana's territory, and the large central area is reserved for military troop dances and battle scenes. (*c*) *Khon chak* is performed indoors on a *proscenium stage with realistic sets, and with a large apron stage for the dances.   SV

KIAK

Ancient Korean music and *dance, originally designed for Buddhist religious services. *Kiak* probably originated from simple dances performed before the statue of Buddha in *India and was brought into *China where it was shaped into a broader art form. At about the start of the seventh century it reached *Korea where it was again altered and was performed at Buddhist temples as a didactic *masked dance-drama for a general *audience. *Kiak* travelled from Korea to *Japan where it was called *gigaku*. Though the dance became extinct in Korea and Japan around the thirteenth century, the Japanese *Kyōkunshō* (1223) describes an actors' procession, a lion dance, a priest, an old woman, a nobleman, and a story of a love triangle. *Kiak* was performed with large masks entirely covering the performers' heads. It is possible that it influenced the Korean masked dance-drama (*kamyŏngŭk*) which survives today.   JOC

KICH

The spoken drama of *Vietnam, which originated through French influence. Although a translation of *Molière's *The Miser* was performed in Vietnamese in 1907, the first truly Vietnamese spoken play was *The Cup of Poison* by Vu Dinh Long (1901–60), published and premièred in 1921. It concerns a civil servant whose family sinks into poverty through debauchery and dependence on fortune-tellers; about to drink the poison of the title, he is saved by a friend and a rich brother's money. *Kich* is *realistic in its movements, gestures, *scenery, and *dialogue. Its themes are social and contemporary, with many items strongly moralistic or propagandistic. Its strongly French flavour did not prevent its being used as propaganda against French colonialism, and it still carries socialist content under the communist government. From the start the main *audience for *kich* was the intelligentsia, which is still true today.   CPM

KICHENAPANAÏDOU, MARC (1943–)

Réunionese dramatist. His contribution to the culture of his Indian Ocean island was to lead a revival of the use of creole in the Réunionese theatre, usually mixed with standard French, in *realist and *didactic social dramas such as *L'Esclave* and *Le Père Lafosse* (*The Slave Woman* and *Father Lafosse*, both 1977),

La Demande en mariage and *L'Ivrogne* (*The Proposal of Marriage* and *The Drunkard*, both 1980).   PGH

KIDD, MICHAEL (1919–)

American director and choreographer. Born Milton Greenwald, he began in *ballet, working with several companies marked by an interest in stylized Americana, which drew him to Broadway. His first assignment was to choreograph *Finian's Rainbow* (1947), featuring energetic country *dancing as well as the balletic dances of Susan the Silent. Other major assignments followed, including *Guys and Dolls* (1950) and *Can-Can* (1953). He also choreographed for *films, including *Seven Brides for Seven Brothers* (1954). In all of these he featured his special brand of dance—highly athletic and so technically demanding that it required a special stable of dancers capable of executing it. In 1956 he became a director/choreographer for *Li'l Abner*, a practice he would continue throughout the rest of his stage career, although without great success. He continued to choreograph for film (*Star!*, *Hello, Dolly!*), as well as acting occasionally in films, notably *Smile* (1975).   JD

KIDD, ROSS (1945–)

Canadian adult educator who later took Botswana citizenship and became a zealous and influential proselytizer for theatre for *development in the 1970s and 1980s. Taking Paulo Freire's ideas about 'conscientization' as a starting point, Kidd led a group of Botswana adult educators promoting the project called Laedza Batanani, using theatre as a method of communication with rural communities about social issues. He initiated a series of important workshops at Molepolole (Botswana, 1977), Chalimbana (Zambia, 1979), Koitta (*Bangladesh, 1983), and Murewa (Zimbabwe, 1984) in order to strategize how theatre for development could be implemented and disseminated. A major achievement in the mid-1980s was a critique of his own earlier practices in an endeavour to encourage theatre for development workers into more radical and participatory methodologies. He also did much to link *African practitioners with their counterparts in Asia and elsewhere.   DaK

KIEV

Religious capital of ancient Russia and capital of the Ukraine. Kiev lagged behind *Moscow and *St Petersburg in terms of its theatrical development and the first theatre of consequence, seating less than 900, was not constructed until 1856. It became a venue for foreign performers such as Ira *Aldridge, Ernesto *Rossi, Sarah *Bernhardt, Eleanore *Duse, and others during the 1880s and 1890s. A Literary Artistic Association was set up in the 1890s which included the dramatist Lesya Ukrainka and, in 1903, Nikolai Lysenko organized a musical-dramatic school which became a *training conservatoire in 1913. In 1891, Nikolai Solovtsov organized the Society of Dramatic Artists, who staged plays to a high artistic standard, but a good deal of theatrical activity was hampered by the tsarist *censorship laws. After the Revolution of 1917, the cultural situation in Kiev was as chaotic as the political one and is well characterized in *Bulgakov's play *Days of the Turbins* (1926), which deals with the several changes of leadership during a series of power struggles between Ukrainian nationalist forces, occupying Germans, and the Bolsheviks. Inspired by an upsurge of experimental activity in Moscow during the early 1920s, Kiev saw a burgeoning of theatre groups embracing *modernist forms, led by the Berezil Theatre, founded in 1922 by Les *Kurbas and inspired by the example of *Meyerhold and others. In order to curb some of this enthusiasm and to encourage *realist tendencies, the Ivan Franko Theatre, with an established reputation for performing classic plays in a realist manner, was transplanted from Kharkov to Kiev as a model to imitate. By the end of the Second World War, the Ivan Franko and the Lesya Ukrainka theatres were established as the main focus of Ukrainian theatrical life but their repertoire, with the occasional concession to indigenous drama, tended to follow Moscow's example. Productions of *Trenyov's *Lyubov Yarovaya* (1927) and Vsevolod *Ivanov's *Armoured Train 14–69* (1928) followed Muscovite precedent as did productions of *Vishnevsky's *Optimistic Tragedy* and *Gorky's *Enemies* (in 1933), a pattern which was suspended during the wartime German occupation but resumed subsequently. The Ivan Franko Theatre, by contrast, sought to promote the work of Ukrainian dramatists, including Shevchenko, Ukrainka, Franko, *Korneichuk, Dmiterko, and Minko, and with a leavening of Western classics, managed to sustain a distinctively Ukrainian repertoire less subservient to Russian example.   NW

KILLIGREW, THOMAS (1612–83)

English playwright and *manager. Samuel *Pepys reports that as a child Killigrew volunteered to play devils at the *Red Bull in order to see plays for free. Later, as a page at the court of Charles I, Killigrew was a member of Queen Henrietta's literary circle (he married a maid of honour) and continued his interest in the drama. Two of his courtly *romances, *The Prisoners* (1632–5) and *Claracilla* (1636), were acted at the Phoenix by Queen Henrietta's Men. A third romance, *The Princess* (c.1636–7), and a *comedy, *The Parson's Wedding* (1639–40), were probably played by the King's Men at *Blackfriars. Killigrew spent the Interregnum on the Continent in the service of the royal family. *The Pilgrim* (c.1646) may have been intended for performance by English actors in exile, but three long, two-part *romances, written between 1649 and 1654, are clearly *closet dramas. (Aphra *Behn based *The Rover*, 1677, on *Thomaso the Wanderer*.) At the Restoration in 1660, Killigrew, together with William *Davenant, was granted a monopoly on the *London stage,

and Killigrew launched an unsuccessful career as manager of the King's Men at the *Theatre Royal and then at *Drury Lane. Unable to adapt to changing theatrical tastes, and lacking business sense, by 1676 he had ceded control of the company to his son Charles. He succeeded Sir Henry Herbert as *Master of the Revels in 1673 and held the post until 1677.   RWV

KILROY, THOMAS (1934–)

Irish playwright, novelist, literary critic. Born in County Kilkenny, Kilroy has had an academic as well as a writing career. His play *The Death and Resurrection of Mr Roche*, staged in *Dublin in 1968, was significant as the first explicit exploration of homosexuality in Irish theatre. Kilroy has often been drawn to historical settings and biographical material. One of his most innovative plays, directed by Patrick *Mason at the *Abbey's Peacock Theatre in 1977 with a transfer to *London's *Royal Court, was *Talbot's Box*. In this, the inner psychology of Dublin's worker saint Matt Talbot, and the political context of his times, were dramatized by just five actors within an all-purpose stage box that figured at once mind and society. *Double Cross*, produced by *Field Day in 1986, evoked the lives of Irishmen Brendan Bracken, British loyalist, and William Joyce, the traitor Lord Haw-Haw, both played by the actor Stephen Rea. Kilroy's capacity for combining conceptual rigour with dramaturgical innovation was again displayed in his most recent play *The Secret Fall of Constance Wilde* (Abbey, 1998).   NG

KIM U-JIN (1827–1926)

Korean director, producer, theorist, and playwright. Despite his brief career, Kim had a remarkable influence upon modern theatre in *Korea (*see* SHINGŬK), writing five plays, numerous essays on Western theatre and drama, and three translations of foreign plays. As a student at Waseda University in *Tokyo, Kim saw Japanese modern theatre (*shingeki*), and in 1921 he used the Tongwuhoe (Society of Comradeship) to introduce Western theatre in Korea. He was the first Korean playwright to be influenced by the work of *Ibsen, *Shaw, *Strindberg, and *O'Neill, and through his essays also introduced Lord *Dunsany, *Čapek, and *Pirandello to Korea. He experimented with *realism, *naturalism, and *expressionism, writing about conflict between old customs and new ideas, including the difficulties women endured under the old ways. His representative plays, written between 1924 and his suicide, are *High Noon*, *Yi Yŏng-nyŏ*, *The Disillusion of Poet Tudugi*, *Shipwreck*, and *The Boar*.   JOC

KING, THOMAS (1730–1805)

English actor and *manager, the foremost comic actor during the *Garrick era. He created such roles as Lord Ogelby in the Garrick–*Colman *Clandestine Marriage* and Sir Peter Teazle in

*Sheridan's *The School for Scandal*. Discovered by Garrick in 1748, King spent the majority of his career at *Drury Lane, though he acted and *danced in many provincial theatres and had a managerial interest in Bristol and *Sadler's Wells. He was also Sheridan's *stage manager at Drury Lane.　MJK

KING, WOODIE, JR. (1937–)

*African-American *manager. *Artistic director of Concept East in Detroit (1960–3), King moved to *New York in 1964 and was picked by the legendary black politician Adam Clayton Powell to head a community arts programme called Mobilization for Youth. King founded the New Federal Theatre in 1970, which he has continued to direct, giving unparalleled exposure to African-American theatre artists. His successes include playwrights Amiri *Baraka, Ed *Bullins, and Ntozake *Shange, and *film actors Morgan Freeman and Denzell Washington.　BBL

KINGIZILA

Ancient form of theatre of healing which, along with the *lemba*, *nkoloba*, and the *milako*, has been made popular by itinerant performers (*bisi kwim*), an important group in the history and culture of the kingdom of Congo. The ceremony, structured like a well-organized play, and characterized by song and *mime, aims at containing and destroying sickness through the use of specific therapeutic gestures executed by highly skilled performers. It is generally staged in public every three days over a 40-day period, at the end of which the possessed (*yeza*) is deemed cured. More difficult cases call for repeated performances.　PNN trans. JCM

KING'S HEAD

Opened in 1970 by Joan and Dan Crawford in Islington, the King's Head continues as one of the leading pub theatres in *London. Seating 100 in an informal layout, it started with evening shows, then introduced lunchtime theatre in 1971. Early successes included Athol *Fugard's *Hello and Goodbye* and Tom Gallacher's *Mr Joyce is Leaving Paris*. Robert Patrick's *Kennedy's Children* and Martin Sherman's *When She Danced* both went on to the West End. Longevity was secured through a mixed programme of downmarket *cabaret, small-scale *musicals, and *fringe plays which appealed to wining and dining mainstream *audiences.　BRK

KINGSLEY, SIDNEY (1906–95)

American playwright and director. Kingsley's dramatic output was small—only nine plays over 30 years—but his works were exceptionally well crafted and raised the standard for social drama in the United States. A native of *New York, Kingsley was educated at Cornell University, worked briefly as an actor and script reader, and won the Pulitzer Prize for his first play, *Men in White* (1933). A tautly constructed *melodrama that dealt almost matter-of-factly with issues such as abortion and racial prejudice, it was exquisitely staged by Lee *Strasberg for the *Group Theatre and set the tone for much of Kinglsey's work. *Dead End* (1935), a *naturalistic drama set outside a New York tenement and featuring Humphrey Bogart as a ruthless killer, ran for nearly 700 performances. Kingsley directed that production and all his later plays with the exception of *The Patriots* (1943). *Detective Story* (1949) and *Darkness at Noon* (1951, from Arthur Koestler's novel) were admired by *critics and saw long Broadway runs and *film adaptations.　MAF

KING'S MEN *See* CHAMBERLAIN'S MEN, LORD.

KINGSTON, GERTRUDE (1866–1937)

English actress, *manager, and playwright. Beginning with Sarah Thorne's company at Margate in 1887, she settled in *London the following year, acting with many of the leading *actor-managers during the 1890s and 1900s. In 1910 she built the Little Theatre, opening with *Aristophanes' *Lysistrata*. In 1912 she played Lady Cecily in a revival of *Captain Brassbound's Conversion* by *Shaw, who then wrote the role of the Empress in *Great Catherine* for her (1913). Over the following decade she appeared often in Shaw's plays, in London, *New York, and Birmingham. Kingston wrote a few plays and an autobiography, *Curtsey While You're Thinking* (1937).　TP

KINOSHITA JUNJI (1914–)

Japanese playwright. Active in the *shingeki* (new drama) movement since 1939, Kinoshita has both written within the prevailing *realistic mode of that movement and consciously moved outside it. His search for dramatic form appropriate to modern *Japan has focused on language, consciousness of sin, and fate. *Yūzuru* (*Twilight Crane*, 1949), the most famous of his *folk tale plays, makes innovative use of language to suggest different moral and ideological worlds. An underlying recognition of ineradicable sin is an organizing concept in several plays about recent Japanese *history, such as *Okinawa* (1961). Kinoshita's greatest work is *Shigosen no Matsuri* (*Requiem on the Great Meridian*, 1978). In this monumental play the rhythmic language of a thirteenth-century war tale is blended with Kinoshita's contemporary version of it in seamless transitions from group chanting to *dialogue between individuals. *Characters step out of the group, thus symbolizing collective historical consciousness; cosmic forces and fate, the latter recognized clearly by the *hero, bring about his and his clan's destruction.　BWFP

KIPPHARDT, HEINAR (1922–82)

German playwright. Kipphardt's name is synonymous with the *genre of *documentary theatre to which he (together with Rolf *Hochhuth) made a decisive contribution. His play *In the Matter of J. Robert Oppenheimer* (1964) relied heavily on the trial transcripts of the eponymous nuclear physicist during the 1950s, which *Piscator's *Berlin production further visualized with slide projections and film clips (*see* MULTIMEDIA). It was an international success with productions in *Paris by Jean *Vilar and in *Milan by *Strehler, both in 1964. *The Story of Joel Brand* (1965) draws on documents to dramatize a deal made between Eichmann and Hungarian Jews. Both plays were originally written for *television. Other successful plays include *März* (also a novel and TV play, 1980) and the posthumous *Brother Eichmann* (1983), a complex collage of scenes which draws parallels between the Vietnam War, the Baader-Meinhoff terrorists, and the Adolf Eichmann trial.   CBB

KIRLOSKAR, ANNASAHEB (1843–85)

Indian writer, director, and actor. Born Balwant Pandurang in Gurlhosur in north Karnataka, Kirloskar was drawn to theatre during his student days in Pune. As a schoolteacher in Belgaum he wrote several plays in the form made popular by Vishnudas Bhave, considered the father of *Marathi theatre. In this form of drama, the *sutradhara* (narrator-manager), accompanied by a group of musicians, sang while the actors *mimed, occasionally supporting action with impromptu speech. By the 1870s, however, influenced by university education and the popularity of *Parsi theatre, *audiences sought a more refined form of theatre. In this context Kirloskar adapted *Kalidasa's Sanskrit *verse play *Abhijnanashakuntala* into spoken Marathi, calling it *Shakuntal*, rendering parts as prose *dialogue and the rest as songs performed by the actors themselves, and reducing the *sutradhara*'s contribution to singing the opening invocation and introducing the theme of the play. The tunes were drawn from every source, from *folk and women's songs to *lavanis* from *tamasha* and classical music. Kirloskar staged four *acts in Belgaum in 1875 prior to the full version in Pune in 1880. Acclaimed by patrons, critics and discerning audiences alike, this new form, the *sangeet natak* (music drama), dominated the Marathi stage for the next 50 years. Kirloskar wrote one further play, *Sangeet Saubhadra*, which has become a classic of Marathi theatre.   SGG

KIRSHON, VLADIMIR (1902–38)

Russian/Soviet writer who became known in the West when his first play, *Red Rust* (1926), was performed in *New York by the *Theatre Guild (1929), as well as elsewhere. The play centres on social problems of post-revolutionary Soviet youth, just as *Bread* (1930) centres on the problem of the kulaks (rich peasants) during collectivization, and *The Rails Are Humming* on the 'heroic task' of industrialization. His *comedy *The Miraculous Alloy*, about research in the aircraft industry, proved extremely popular. Kirshon fell foul of the regime and became a victim of Stalin's purges.   NW

KISHIDA KUNIO (1890–1954)

Japanese playwright, director, and critic. Kishida's love of French literature led him to *Paris in 1919, where he studied with Jacques *Copeau at the *Vieux-Colombier. Back in *Japan in 1923, he determined to create a modern Japanese theatre with high artistic standards. Kishida's interests remained with the poetic and psychological, for which his early *one-act plays provided a congenial format, and he took no interest in the socialist theatre then in the ascendancy. Of his longer plays, the strongest is *The Two Daughters of Mr Sawa* (1935), which chronicles complex and nihilistic personal family relations. In 1938 Kishida and others formed a new troupe entitled Bungakuza (the Literary Theatre), which upheld literary rather than political ideals. Kishida joined in the war effort and was severely treated afterwards by his colleagues. His few post-war plays are subdued but effective.   JTR

KITCHEN SINK

Term applied to the wave of *naturalistic, working-class plays that emerged in Britain during the 1950s, notably in *London from the *English Stage Company and the *Theatre Workshop. 'Kitchen sink drama' was initially used rather dismissively, to suggest disdain for the mundane subject matter and dreary settings of plays which contrasted with the grand drawing rooms and country residences of the earlier period. Soon it became a positive term to denote the aggressive *realism of *Osborne's *Look Back in Anger* (1956), *Delaney's *A Taste of Honey* (1958), and *Wesker's *Roots* (1959), though only the last actually uses a kitchen sink.   DR

KI-YI, VILLA

Côte d'Ivoire artists' commune founded in Abidjan by Werewere *Liking in 1983. Complete with a theatre, modest exhibition space for *African arts, and art-training facilities, the villa is home to between 80 and 100 artists and has a company, the Ki-Yi Mbock ('Ultimate Knowledge' in Bassa) Theatre, formed in 1985. As a private enterprise, Ki-Yi Mbock is *financed through gate fees to cultural events and gifts from individuals and foreign governments. Theatrical performances are the mainstay of its activities, but it also organizes art exhibitions, especially of its rare collection of *masks, *puppets, and beads. A notable aspect of its troupe, in addition to elaborate use of masking and puppetry, is its pan-African outlook. Its members and performance styles are drawn from a variety of *African countries and cultures, as are its songs: in eight different languages in *Berceuses d'éveil*, for example, and thirteen in Liking's *Un touareg s'est marié à une pygmée* (1992), a play whose geographical sweep stretches from the Sahel to the equatorial forests of Congo.   JCM

KKOKTUKAKSI NORŬM

Traditional *puppet theatre of *Korea. Also known as *Pak Ch'ŏmji norŭm* (old Pak's play) or *Hong Tongji norŭm* (Hong Tongji's play), its precise origin is unknown, though it may have come to Korea from the Asian continent in the seventh century. The central *characters (Pak Ch'ŏmji, Kkoktukaksi, and Hong Tongji) enact familiar tales that deal humorously and satirically with the corruption of Buddhist monks, domestic problems, and the malfeasance of the ruling classes. Traditionally *kkoktukaksi norŭm* was performed by three or four puppeteers on a simple portable stage in any open space, with three or four musicians in attendance. The puppets, called *kkoktu*, were of two main types: those representing human beings and Buddha, given central roles, and those delineating animals such as serpents, birds, and dogs, which served as supporting characters. A puppeteer manipulated a single puppet at a time, speaking the *dialogue and singing songs to music, while the musicians took their place in front of the stage, sometimes talking with the puppets in response to promptings from the *audience. The music, created by a small gong, an hourglass-shaped drum, and a Korean oboe, was generally improvised. *Kkoktukaksi norŭm* is still performed today as government cultural events or tourist entertainments.   JOC

KLEIST, HEINRICH VON (1777–1811)

German writer of plays, novellas, and essays, the finest tragedian of the romantic period (*see* ROMANTICISM). Born in Frankfurt an der Oder, Kleist was destined for a military career but in 1799 began to study philosophy. From 1800 he travelled restlessly. In Paris in 1803 he burned his manuscripts and tried to join the French army to fight against England. He was deported to Germany, where he had a breakdown. His first extant drama, *The Schroffenstein Family* (1804), is a dark *Schicksalstragödie* in *verse, in which two lovers from rival families are destroyed. After settling in Königsberg, he began three of his best-known plays: *Amphitryon* (1807), in which *Molière's theme of Jupiter's seduction of Alcmene is used to show a woman whose unerring belief in her own innocence is vindicated; *Penthesilea* (1808), a sexually charged encounter between Achilles and the Amazonian princess Penthesilea, ending in her crazed murder of him and her own suicide; and *The Broken Jug* (1808), one of the few classic German *comedies that survives in the repertoire. In this

work the judge Adam is himself found guilty of breaking a jug when he made a hasty exit from the house where he had been forcing his attentions on a young girl. The judge's name, and the theme of the guilty judge, as in *Sophocles' *Oedipus the King*, point to deeper themes than the comic situation at first suggests. In 1807 Kleist was arrested in Berlin by the invading French forces and taken to France, unsettling him even further. In 1811 he shot himself. His plays met with little success in his own lifetime: *Amphitryon* was not performed until 1898, *Penthesilea* in 1876, *The Broken Jug*, after an unsatisfactory première at the *Weimar Court Theatre in 1808, was first successfully staged in 1820. His best work, *The Prince of Homburg*, was not published and performed until 1821. A young Prussian officer wins a battle by defying orders. In order to remind him of the need for discipline, he is sentenced to death and undergoes a mock execution. The play reflects Kleist's ambiguous relationship with Prussian militarism, and casts doubt on his former trust in inner certainty. Kleist was also the author of a seminal essay, 'On the Marionette Theatre' (1810), which argues that the *puppet is graceful because it is free of self-consciousness, a prototype of *Craig's deindividualized *Über-marionette*.   MWP

KLINE, KEVIN (1947–)

American actor. He graduated from Indiana University and completed further studies at the *Juilliard School, making his Broadway debut in 1972 as a founding member of John *Houseman's *Acting Company. With the *New York Shakespeare Festival he has played various roles, including two renditions of Hamlet, first directed by Liviu *Ciulei (1986) and then under his own direction (1990), and also Trigorin in *Chekhov's *The Seagull* (2001). He won Tony *awards for Bruce Granit in *On the Twentieth Century* (1978) and the Pirate King in *The Pirates of Penzance* (1981); other Broadway credits include *Loose Ends* (1979), *Arms and the Man* (1985), and *Ivanov* (1997). He made his *film debut as Nathan in *Sophie's Choice* (1982) and went on to play Harold in *The Big Chill* (1983), Paden in *Silverado* (1985), Douglas Fairbanks, Sr., in *Chaplin* (1992), the title role in *Dave* (1993), Howard in *In & Out* (1997), and Bottom in *A Midsummer Night's Dream* (1999). His work ranges from the seriously thoughtful to the zany nonsense of Otto in *A Fish Called Wanda* (1988; Academy award for best supporting actor) and Jeffery in *Soapdish* (1991).   JDM

KLINGER, FRIEDRICH MAXIMILIAN VON (1752–1831)

German poet and dramatist who came to prominence in 1776 with the publication of his play *Sturm und Drang*, which gave the literary movement of the 1770s and 1780s its name. Together with J. M. R. *Lenz, Klinger was the movement's most important representative. Strongly influenced by *Rousseau, his dramas are characterized by highly expressive, exaggerated language with *protagonists usually in conflict with the social order. After a short period as an actor and dramatist Klinger had a highly successful career as an army officer, retiring in 1802 at the rank of major general. In his later years he wrote a number of philosophical novels. CBB

KNEBEL, MARIA (1898–1985)

Russian/Soviet actress, director, and teacher. She trained in Michael *Chekhov's Studio before joining the Second Studio of the *Moscow Art Theatre in 1921, then worked at the main MAT from 1924 to 1950, playing numerous roles. She began to direct in 1935, first at the Ermolova Theatre. In 1950 she gave up acting and 1955–60 was chief *artistic director of the Central Children's Theatre where she helped the careers of a number of young directors, including Anatoly *Efros and Oleg *Efremov. She began teaching in 1932, was with the Shchepkin School (1940–8) and then at the State Theatre Institute (GITIS). Her pupils include Anatoly *Vasiliev (School of Dramatic Art), Iosif Raikhelgauz (School of Contemporary Plays), and Boris Morozov (*Maly Theatre). Her importance as theatre theorist and teacher is often underestimated. She greatly influenced directors who adhered to the *Stanislavsky tradition but who were seeking to modify and develop it along the lines of Michael Chekhov, whose works were not published in the Soviet Union until 1986. Her chief contribution to drama *theory consists of her 'action analysis' of the play and the role. BB

KNIPPER-CHEKHOVA, OLGA (1868–1959)

Russian actress, who married *Chekhov in 1901. Having studied under *Nemirovich-Danchenko from 1895, Knipper was one of several prime candidates for the *Moscow Art Theatre which Nemirovich-Danchenko set up with *Stanislavsky in 1897. Knipper created a remarkable series of classic roles, beginning with Chekhov's major heroines: Arkadina (*The Seagull*, 1898), Elena (*Uncle Vanya*, 1899), Masha (*Three Sisters,* 1901), Ranevskaya (*The Cherry Orchard*, 1904), and Sarah (*Ivanov*, 1904). She also played major roles in MAT productions of plays by *Hauptmann, *Ibsen, and *Gorky, and was significantly instrumental in creating the core of the MAT repertoire. Her style of playing suited these contemporary works in *naturalistic productions, and she was recognized for her ensemble skills, her penetrating and detailed study of *character, her natural grace on stage, her discipline, and her exacting standards. Knipper's lifelong career at MAT called for adaptability: after the revolution she continued to play the favourite roles but also created memorable characters in a vastly different political situation, notably Polina in Gorky's *Enemies* (1935). Her devotion to the theatre was rewarded by two of the highest Soviet accolades:

she was made a People's Artist of the USSR in 1937, and awarded a state prize in 1943. CM

KNOBLOCK (KNOBLAUCH), EDWARD (1874–1945)

American playwright, educated at Harvard; he settled in England and became a British subject. Knoblock wrote popular plays, some derived from French sources, and his major successes came from adaptation, usually of novels. He often worked in collaboration with performers and writers, including Oscar *Asche (*Kismet*, 1911), David *Belasco (*Marie-Odile*, 1915), J. B. *Priestley (*The Good Companions*, 1931), and Vicki Baum (*Grand Hotel*, 1931). With Arnold *Bennett he adapted *Milestones* (1912), *London Life* (1924), and *Mr Prohack* (1927), and he translated *Maeterlinck's *Sister Beatrice* in 1910. He also worked in *film, providing screenplays for Douglas Fairbanks and Mary Pickford (such as *The Thief of Baghdad*, 1935). TP

KNOWLES, JAMES SHERIDAN (1784–1862)

Irish playwright. Knowles was immensely popular in his time, and hailed as a second Shakespeare for his *tragedies and *comedies written in blank *verse and prose imitative of the Elizabethan manner but thoroughly imbued with the domestic spirit of the nineteenth century. Starting in Ireland as an actor, Knowles attained fame with *Virginius* (1820), a tragedy staged at *Covent Garden by *Macready, who played a Roman patrician who kills his own daughter to keep her out of the *villain's clutches. *Virginius* provided star actors with a leading role for the rest of the century. The father–daughter and father–son relationship is also the heart of other dramas such as *William Tell* (1825), *The Daughter* (1836), and *The Rose of Aragon* (1842). *The Love-Chase* (1837), reminiscent of *Much Ado About Nothing*, is his most stylish and witty comedy. Knowles was fortunate in having the best actors of the day in his principal *characters, but his work, now unplayable, represents the last twilight of the legitimate Elizabethan-influenced verse tragedy and comedy. MRB

KNYAZHNIN, YAKOV (1740–91)

Russian dramatist. One of the outstanding *neoclassicists of the late eighteenth century, Knyazhnin wrote his first *tragedy, *Dido*, in 1769. He also wrote satirical *comedies which targeted serfdom and the francophilia of the Russian aristocracy. His best comedy is *Khvastun* (*The Braggart*) 1786, whose central figure anticipates the character of Khlestakov in *Gogol's *The Government Inspector* (1836). Knyazhnin's tragedy *Vadim Novogorodsky* (1789) unfortunately coincided with the French

Revolution and its anti-despotic subject matter led to his arrest and torture. When published in 1793, Catherine the Great ordered that copies of the play be burned. NW

KOCH, GOTTFRIED HEINRICH (1703–75)

German actor and *manager. Koch began with the *Neuber troupe, where he also worked as a scene *painter. From 1749 to 1756 he managed his own company based in Leipzig, and was joined in 1756 by Konrad *Ekhof and the remainder of the *Schönemann troupe. Between 1758 and 1764 Koch was in Hamburg, and returned to Leipzig in 1766 to open the new Schauspielhaus. Later he took over the Theater in der Behrenstrasse in *Berlin and premièred *Goethe's *Götz von Berlichingen* (1774). Koch is remembered chiefly for having introduced light *opera (*Singspiel*) to Germany in 1772 and for his reform of *costume: he avoided conventionalized French *neoclassical dress and adapted the costume to the play.

CBB

KOGAN, JAIME (1937–96)

Argentinian director of theatre and *opera. A renowned *lighting designer as well, Kogan was master of the total production. Trained in the independent theatre, he co-founded the Equipo Teatro Payró in 1968, his home base until his death. Although responsible for such landmark productions as Eduardo *Pavlovsky's *Mr Galíndez* (1972) and *Brecht's *Galileo* (1984) and *Mahagonny* (1987), Kogan is most frequently associated with Ricardo *Monti, five of whose plays he staged. JGJ

KOKKOS, YANNIS (1944–)

Greek *scenographer and director whose work has been chiefly in France. Kokkos studied at the École Supérieure d'Art Dramatique in Strasbourg, after which he collaborated on many productions with noted directors including Jacques *Lassalle and Antoine *Vitez, for whom he designed at Théâtre d'Ivry, the Théâtre National du *Chaillot, the *Comédie-Française, and the *Avignon Festival. Instrumental in Vitez's deconstructive visions of plays such as *Racine's *Britannicus* (1981), *Hugo's *Hernani* (1985), and *Claudel's *The Satin Slipper* (1987), Kokkos often presented a stark minimalism and experimented with reverse *perspective and other techniques designed to reorient spectators' perceptions of space. He has designed *operas and *ballets at many of the world's great houses, including the *Paris *Opéra, the *Vienna Staatsoper, *Covent Garden in *London, La *Scala in *Milan, the Grand Théâtre in Geneva, the *San Francisco Opera, and the Hamburg Ballet. His directing credits include Racine's *Iphigénie* (1991) and *La Thébaïde* (1995) at the Comédie-Française, as well as

several ambitious opera productions for which he served as both director and designer. DGM

KOKOSCHKA, OSKAR (1886–1980)

Austrian painter, graphic artist, designer, and dramatist. Although Kokoschka is best known as a painter and major exponent of German *expressionism, he was also actively involved in the theatre around the time of the First World War. His best-known play is *Mörder, Hoffnung der Frauen* (*Murderer Hope of Womankind*, 1910), a prototypical expressionist work in its combination of sound, colour, and expressive language. Other plays are *The Burning Bush* (1913), *Job* (1917), and *Orpheus and Eurydice* (1919), some of which he directed and designed at the Albert Theater in Dresden. Kokoschka returned to the theatre in his later years, working mainly as a designer. CBB

KOLIADA, NIKOLAI (1957–)

Soviet/Russian actor, director, and playwright. Koliada was an actor at Sverdlovsk (Ekaterinburg) Drama Theatre before completing studies at the Literature Institute. His plays reveal an interest in *dream worlds, in the fairy-like quality of another reality into which his *characters escape from the dull existence in post-Soviet Russia. *The Catapult* (1989) deals with a homosexual relationship, realized only in dream sequences. In *Oginski's Polonaise* (1994) a Russian émigré returning to *Moscow is unable to face reality. Koliada uses colloquial language, while beautiful images counterbalance everyday life in his own stage productions of *Ship of Fools* and *Leave, Leave*. BB

KOLKATA (CALCUTTA)

One of four megalopolises in *India, and capital of West Bengal state. Allegedly established in 1690 by the English trader Job Charnock on the site of three small villages, Calcutta rapidly grew into the chief business centre of the British East India Company and, subsequently, the capital of British India. As the biggest city in Bengal during the nineteenth century, Calcutta gave birth to the so-called Bengal Renaissance, of which the theatre was a vital expression. Even though the Raj shifted the capital to Delhi in 1911 for strategic reasons, Calcutta remained in the limelight as the second city of the British Empire. The British erected the first *playhouses in the eighteenth century for themselves, but the first *proscenium theatre in which a Bengali play was staged appeared as early as 1795. *Amateur endeavours for invited *audiences in makeshift halls and aristocratic mansions continued till 1872, when a troupe calling itself the National Theatre went public. After that, the Bengali professional stage held sway, catering to (but also creating) the tastes of a large middle-class clientele right up to the late twentieth century. In any given year, playhouses for Bengali theatre never numbered more than seven, though a complete list of companies would seem huge. Playhouses changed hands at a brisk rate, owners moving premises, renaming them, and floating new troupes every few years like musical chairs.

By the mid-twentieth century several factors forced changes in Calcutta's theatre. Independence, its violent prelude, and its aftermath of Partition brought a new artistic agenda. Young, amateur, left-wing groups drew committed spectators away from the commercial houses, and the glamour of *film forced some playhouses to be converted into cinemas. Others commercialized their offering further, appealing to a lower-class population with progressively more sleazy productions. While professional theatre faded, 'group theatre' assumed leadership under Sombhu *Mitra's Bohurupee company and Utpal *Dutt's Little Theatre Group, aimed at the educated section of society. In the year 2000, Kolkata (now the official Bengali name) had over 2,000 registered theatre groups—perhaps the largest number in the world—though these do not own performance spaces, usually booking *auditoriums for each show; as early as the 1970s, Badal *Sircar and his disciples introduced non-proscenium theatre at *street corners and in found spaces.

Kolkata's culture is multilingual. English performances by Bengali college students followed local British theatre in the eighteenth and nineteenth centuries, ultimately developing into a parallel—even if elitist—movement after independence. One of the few significant Indian dramatists in English, Asif Currimbhoy, worked in Calcutta during the late 1960s and 1970s (see also INDIAN THEATRE IN ENGLISH). A professional theatre in Hindi/Urdu for the migrant population developed in the early twentieth century, epitomized by the spectacular *musicals of Fida *Hussain's *Parsi theatre company; and after 1947, *Hindi theatre grew to earn national respect through the work of the amateur groups Anamika, Padatik, and Rangakarmee. Less theatrical activity exists in Kolkata in Gujarati, Tamil, and Malayalam than in Hindi, but the city regularly plays host to visiting productions from around India and from abroad. At the close of the twentieth century, theatre faced decreasing attendances for the first time, as audiences switched to *television. The commercial stage became virtually defunct, and many groups moribund, though enough survive to ensure continuity and quality. See also BENGALI THEATRE. AL

MUKHERJEE, SUSHIL, The Story of the Calcutta Theatres: 1753–1980 (Calcutta, 1982)

KOLTAI, RALPH (1926–)

Designer, born in Berlin, who emigrated to England in 1939. In 1945 he was attached to British Intelligence at the Nuremberg trials and subsequently to the War Crimes Interrogation. Thereafter he studied theatre design at the Central School of Art in *London, his first production being the *opera Angélique (1950). He has since designed over 200 productions of opera, *dance, *musicals, and drama in Britain, Europe, Canada, Australia, and *Japan. As associate artist of the *Royal Shakespeare Company he designed over 27 plays from Shakespeare and *Beckett to Solzhenitsyn and *Brecht, including the world première of *Hochhuth's The Representative. Koltai directed and designed La traviata and The Flying Dutchman for the *Hong Kong Arts Festival (1987), and Tennessee *Williams's Suddenly Last Summer for Nottingham Playhouse. In 1997 a major retrospective of his work was seen in London, Beijing, Hong Kong, Taipei, and *Prague. He is acknowledged as an innovator in the use of materials, notably mirrors, but he sets out to focus on the actor, 'without whom', he said, 'the stage is dead'. PH

KOLTÈS, BERNARD-MARIE (1948–89)

French playwright and novelist. After training at the Théâtre National de Strasbourg school under Jean-Pierre *Vincent, Koltès abandoned theatre in the 1970s. But he came to prominence with his play Combat de nègre et des chiens (Struggle of the Dogs and the Black, 1983) directed by Patrice *Chéreau, who thereafter staged most of his plays at the Théâtre des Amandiers in Nanterre. Koltès's work features multiracial *characters and narratives in marginal, contested territories such as colonial West Africa and an abandoned American docklands warehouse. Most famous are Quai ouest (Quay West, 1985), Dans la solitude des champs de coton (In the Solitude of the Cotton Fields, 1986), and Roberto Zucco (staged posthumously by Peter *Stein at the *Schaubühne, *Berlin, 1990). In these works Koltès combined the antithetical ideologies of rich and poor, natives and immigrants, the collective and the individual, transnational capitalism and community, creating dramas of violence, crime, fear, and racism. His characters are presented without apology, but with an intense compassion that matches the playwright's hatred of the establishment. His plays quickly received international attention and continue to be performed all over the world. BRS

KOMEDYA

Play in *verse from the *Philippines depicting the Christian saints, real events, or imaginary kingdoms. The last, also called moro-moro, dramatizes the conflict between medieval Christian kingdoms and the Moorish empire and ends in the triumph of the Christians over the Moors. Komedya scripts are usually adapted from metrical *romances involving European heroes, such as Gonzalo de Cordoba, Rodrigo de Villa, or Charlemagne and the twelve peers of France.

Indebted to the Spanish *comedia, the typical Filipino komedya unfolds in three parts and takes about three days or nights to perform. Sponsored by landlord families and the blessing of the curate, this community play is mounted during the town fiesta on an *open-air stage with one set, the tiered façade of a palace. A passage for the Christians (in black or dark colours, with princesses in pastel gowns) is on stage right, and another for the Moors (in fiery red) is on the left. Christian royals—civilized, loyal, and noble—are fair-skinned like Europeans; Muslim princes—uncouth, selfish, and cowardly—are dark like Filipino natives. All actors exhibit the same stylized approach to verse, choreographed battles, and marches for entrances and exits. From 1598 to 1898 *komedya* contributed in no small measure to colonization by converting Filipinos to Spain's religion, by teaching them to obey authorities, by imposing European standards of beauty, and by fomenting enmity between Christianized natives and the Muslims of the southern Philippines who resisted colonization to the end of the Spanish regime. Since then *komedya* has gradually declined and now survives only in a few rural towns where a Hispanized feudal culture continues to hold sway.   NGT

KOMIDILION

Type of Greek *musical comedy in prose with inset songs, at its peak between 1889 and 1896, which treated everyday themes and *characters. Although the practice of adding songs to plays started in 1888, it was Dimitrios Koromilas who in 1889 wrote *Maroula's Fate*, an original *comedy with music and songs. Its production was seen by *critics as an important moment in the development of the new Greek theatre because it depicted the lives of common working people and 'spoke their everyday language', demotic Greek. This trend continued with Dimitrios Kokkos's *The Lyre of Old Nicholas* in 1891 and with the very successful three-act 'comedy with songs' *The General Secretary*, by Elias Kapetanakis. The play dealt with such themes as the blind imitation of foreign customs by Greeks and the political corruption of state officials. In 1891 *komidilion* influenced the creation of the dramatic *idilion* and the pastoral *idilion*, like Dimitrios Koromilas's *The Shepherdess's Lover* which adopted the fifteen-syllable verse common in popular folk songs.
                    KGo

KOMISARJEVSKY, THEODORE (FYODR KOMISSARZHEVSKY) (1882–1954)

Russian director, designer, half-brother to Vera *Komissarzhevskaya, and son of an *opera singer who gave *Stanislavsky singing lessons. 'Komis', as he became known in England, began his career at his sister's theatre in *St Petersburg (1906) and in collaboration with *Evreinov at the Merry Theatre for Grown-Up Children (1909) before moving to *Moscow, where he worked at a number of theatres, including his own, the *Maly, and the *Bolshoi, directing both plays and operas. He emigrated to England in 1919, staging Borodin's *Prince Igor* at *Covent Garden that year and *The Government Inspector* with

Claude Rains (1920). Komisarjevsky's productions of *Chekhov proved revelatory for British *audiences, his first (*Uncle Vanya*) staged at the *Royal Court Theatre in 1921, followed by *Ivanov* at the *Aldwych Theatre in 1925. But his tenure of the Ranelagh, a tiny theatre in Barnes (1925–6), produced the greatest impact. Here he staged productions of *Uncle Vanya*, *Three Sisters*, and *The Cherry Orchard* with casts which included Robert Farquharson, John *Gielgud, Charles *Laughton, Peggy *Ashcroft, and Jean Forbes-Robertson. Hitherto English productions had tended to stress Chekhov's mournful and lyrical side; Komisarjevsky brought out the lightness and sense of the absurd in the plays, in a manner highly original for the time. Alongside productions of *Pirandello, *Andreev, Dostoevsky, *Faiko, and *Pushkin at other venues, he also found time to direct *Ibsen's *Pretenders* in Welsh (Holyhead, 1927).

The next important phase of his work began in 1932, at the *Shakespeare Memorial Theatre in Stratford, where he staged groundbreaking productions of *The Merchant of Venice* (1932), *Macbeth* (1933), *The Merry Wives of Windor* (1935), *King Lear* (1936), *The Comedy of Errors* (1938) and *The Taming of the Shrew* (1939). *Antony and Cleopatra* (1936), however, with Eugenie Leontovich and Donald *Wolfit, received a *critical mauling and Komisarjevsky's exodus was already on the cards. During the 1930s he was also closely associated with Sidney Bernstein, for whom he designed a number of cinema interiors, his *pièce de résistance* being the Granada in Tooting. Having settled permanently in the USA in 1939, Komisarjevsky opened a drama school in *New York which he ran until his death. He staged professional productions of his own play *Russian Bank* (1940), a version of *Crime and Punishment* with John Gielgud and Lillian *Gish (1947), and, in *Montréal in 1950, Shakespeare's *Cymbeline*. He became a British citizen in 1932 (though he died an American) and married Peggy Ashcroft in 1934 (annulled 1936).   NW

KOMISSARZHEVSKAYA, VERA (1864–1910)

Russian actress and *manager, half-sister of Theodore *Komisarjevsky, who made her professional debut in 1893, having acted as an *amateur at *Stanislavsky's Society of Art and Literature. She made her mark as the first interpreter of Nina in *Chekhov's *The Seagull*, at the *Aleksandrinsky Theatre, *St Petersburg (1896), giving a memorable performance in an otherwise ill-fated production. She founded her own theatre in St Petersburg in 1904, where she appeared in productions of Chekhov—*Ivanov* and *Uncle Vanya*—and as Desdemona, Ophelia, and Nora (in *Ibsen's *A Doll's House*). Convinced of theatre's idealistic role, and tired of theatrical routine and the dominant *naturalistic trends, Komissarzhevskaya boldly extended an invitation to the young *Meyerhold to join her company, fresh from his unsuccessful attempts at Stanislavsky's behest to stage *symbolist plays at the *Moscow Art Theatre.

Meyerhold proved to be more interested in staging methods than in providing vehicles for a great actress and, apart from appearances as Hedda in an experimental production of Ibsen's play, and as Sister Beatrice in a stylized version of *Maeterlinck's play (both in 1906), the collaboration proved unfruitful. Meyerhold failed to cater for her *acting style, which combined intense emotional sensitivity with high theatrical seriousness, and he was dismissed in 1907. The remainder of Komissarzhevskaya's career was spent *touring, but her fame was such that when she died of smallpox in 1910, her funeral was attended by vast crowds of mourners.   NW

KOMPAORÉ, PROSPER (1950–)

Director from Burkina Faso. Born in Côte d'Ivoire, he was educated in Burkina Faso and Paris, where he took a degree in *theatre studies. In 1978 he founded the Atelier Théâtre Burkinabé, a troupe specializing in theatre for *development campaigns (an average of 50 a year), aimed mostly at rural communities. Its subjects range from good health practices in *Halte à la diarrhée* (*Stop the Diarrhoea*) to family planning in *Fatouma; ou, La Machine à créer des enfants* (*Fatouma; or, The Child-Breeding Machine*, both 1989). The company relies on a participatory approach, involving the *audience in the making and critique of theatre projects, inspired by Augusto *Boal's 'forum theatre'. In 1989 Kompaoré founded the International Festival of Theatre for Development, an event that brought to Burkina Faso Boal himself and many troupes from around the world. *See also* OPPRESSED, THEATRE OF THE.   JCM

KOMPARU ZENCHIKU (UJINOBU) (1405– c.1470)

*Japanese *nō playwright, actor, *manager, and theorist, active mostly in the Nara region. Disciple, son-in-law, and artistic successor of Zeami, Komparu headed the Emman'i troupe (modern Komparu school) and was in competition with On'ami, head of the Kanze troupe. He composed over ten poetic nō plays that are still admired today, including *Bashō, Kamo, Tamakazura, Teika, Ugetsu*, and *Yokihi*. His critical treatises, such as *Rokurin ichirō* (*Six Circles, One Dewdrop*, 1455) and *Kabuzuinō* (*The Essence of Song and Dance*, 1456) combine Buddhist and Confucian philosophy, poetics, musical theory, and nō aesthetics.   KWB

KONGELIGE TEATER, DET

The Theatre Royal, Copenhagen, founded in 1748, is one of Europe's oldest *national theatres. By the 1770s it had become firmly established as a court theatre open to the public, presenting a repertoire of plays, *operas, and *ballets. The sound performing traditions established by the company led to an exceptional blossoming of *dance and *music theatre in the nineteenth century. From 1830 August Bournonville established a ballet troupe that was widely admired in Europe. The *naturalist era saw premières of *Ibsen's major plays in a new *playhouse opened in 1874. In the twentieth century, a strong ensemble of outstanding actors, including Poul Reumert and Bodil Ipsen, gave memorable performances that impressed even *Brecht during his exile. The Danish Royal Ballet has continued its pioneering work as one of Europe's leading ballet companies. In June 2001 plans were announced for a new building to house the company.   DT

KONG SHANGREN (K'UNG SHANG-JEN) (1648–1718)

*Chinese dramatist, best known as the author of the *chuanqi* drama *The Peach Blossom Fan* (1698). The play deals with the last days of the Ming Dynasty, directly addressing the literati who still mourned its end. The most *metatheatrical of Chinese plays, Kong relied on the metaphor of the world as stage to propose that all worldly attachments, including those to family and nation, are but illusion. Although *The Peach Blossom Fan* is a tribute to Ming loyalism, it was popular at the Qing court. Soon after its performance, however, Kong was demoted in rank, which some interpreted as a sign that the Emperor was not as pleased with the play as he seemed. Kong Shangren's own attitude was paradoxical: he had great sympathy for loyalist recluses and interviewed many as research for the work, yet he was also a devoted servant of the new dynasty. His pedigree as a linear descendant of Confucius (Kong zi) in the 64th generation granted him the opportunity to lecture upon the Confucian classics to the Qing Emperor Kangxi and act as guide when the Emperor toured Qufu, the site of the national shrine to Confucius. Kong was also an expert in *ritual, and wrote several treatises on the subject.

The Peach Blossom Fan was his only success. Although of great literary merit, the play demonstrates little concern for performance values and was seldom staged after the initial stir. It was revived by the early twentieth-century reformer Liang Qichao, who wrote a preface to a new edition in the hope that the play's nationalism would inspire patriotic sentiment. Since then the work has been firmly ensconced in the Chinese literary canon as the last of the great *chuanqi* dramas.   SYV

KÖNIG, MICHAEL (1947–)

German actor. König was trained at the Otto-Falckenberg-Schule in Munich. He made his debut at the *Munich Kammerspiele in 1966 where he met Peter *Stein and appeared in his production of *Bond's *Saved* (1967). He followed Stein to Bremen, playing Ferdinand in *Schiller's *Kabale und Liebe*

(1968), and was a founding member of the *Berlin *Schaubühne. His most notable roles there include the young Peer Gynt (1971), Alfred in *Tales from the Vienna Woods* (1972), Dionysus in *The Bacchae* (1973). Orlando in *As You Like It* (1977). He also directed Achtenbusch's *Ella* (1978) and *Büchner's *Woyzeck* (1981) at the Schaubühne. A tall blond actor, König moved from youthful leads to mature roles within the ensemble system of the Schaubühne. He left in 1999, one of the few members of the original ensemble to remain so long.   CBB

KOONEN, ALISA (1899–1974)

Russian/Soviet actress and wife of Aleksandr *Tairov, with whom she established the Kameny (Chamber) Theatre in 1914 and where, for the next 30 years, she performed leading roles in productions directed by her husband. Excellent in both *tragedy and *comedy and blessed with physical beauty, grace, and an expressive voice, Koonen numbered among her outstanding roles *Kalidasa's Shakuntala (1914), *Wilde's Salome (1917), *Scribe's Adrienne Lecouvreur (1919), *Racine's Phèdre (1922), *Shaw's St Joan (1924), Abbie in *O'Neill's *Desire under the Elms* (1926), Ellen in Sophie *Treadwell's *Machinal* (1933), the woman commissar in *Vishnevsky's *Optimistic Tragedy* (1933), Cleopatra (Shaw/Shakespeare, 1935), and Emma Bovary (1940).   NW

KOPIT, ARTHUR (1937–   )

American playwright. A prolific writer of *absurdist *satires while an undergraduate at Harvard, Kopit was 25 years old when he scored his first *Off-Broadway success with the extravagantly titled *Oh Dad, Poor Dad, Mamma's Hung You in the Closet and I'm Feelin So Sad* (1962). This Oedipal tale about an overbearing woman who keeps her husband's corpse in the closet and tyrannizes her son became characteristic of Kopit's early enthusiasm for madcap *characters and situations. Kopit entered his maturity as a playwright with *Indians* (1968), a *tragicomedy about the nineteenth-century American frontier scout and showman Buffalo Bill *Cody. By depicting Buffalo Bill's slide from friend and protector of Native Americans to killer and exploiter, he cleverly historicized the United States' military campaign in Vietnam as the repetition of an older, discredited project of genocide and empire building. *Wings* (1978), the least characteristic play of Kopit's oeuvre, depicts a woman who struggles to reclaim her ability to speak—and the coherence of her identity—over the course of suffering two debilitating strokes. After writing the *book for a successful *musical adaptation of Federico Fellini's screenplay for *8½* (1981), Kopit returned to satire as his *genre of choice. *End of the World* is a semi-autobiographical work about a dramatist who is commissioned to write a play about the dangers of nuclear proliferation (1984). His next work, originally entitled *Bone-the-Fish*, is a blis-

tering and controversial spoof of David *Mamet's satire on Hollywood, *Speed-the-Plow*. Revised as *The Road to Nirvana* (1991), Kopit exploited the irony of the original Broadway production of Mamet's play, which starred the pop singer Madonna (she had never acted on stage before). *Y2K* is an anti-technology parable that portrays a couple whose privacy is invaded by a computer hacker (1999).   JAB

KOREA

The home of over 60 million homogeneous Koreans, who share one culture and speak a single language. The long history of the Korean people has been marked, first, by the continuing influence of *China and Chinese culture, and since the nineteenth century, by the political and cultural inroads of *Japan and the Western powers. After the Second World War, only a short period after Japan was forced to surrender Korea as a colony, the Korean War forced the division of the country into two political states, the Republic of Korea with Seoul as its capital south of the 38th parallel, and to the north the Democratic People's Republic of Korea, with P'yŏngyang as its capital, a split that still continued into the twenty-first century.

Broadly speaking there have been four major cultural periods in Korean history, each providing a different cultural setting for the development of theatre. The first dominant culture, spanning the epochs from the prehistoric period to the time of the Three Kingdoms (Kogury, Paekche, and Silla, 57 BC–AD 667), was dominated by shamanistic religious impulses connected to agricultural life. *Rituals constituted the main cultural events of this early society, consisting of the performance of *dances, singing, and *acrobatics. Some scholars trace the origins of Korean theatre to these entertainments, some of which reveal certain proto-theatrical elements.

With an increase of Chinese influence, Korean culture gradually became more complex. During the Three Kingdoms period, the Chinese language itself was imported and the use of Chinese characters became widespread. Adaptations of written Chinese characters were also used to transcribe the Korean language, which brought about a literate culture among the aristocratic classes. At a later phase in the Three Kingdoms period Buddhism, also imported from China, became widespread, encouraging the growth of *kiak, a simple, didactic *masked dance for Buddhist ceremonies. During the long reign of the Silla kingdom (57 BC–AD 935), which absorbed the other two kingdoms in 667, a number of important dance forms developed that contained theatrical elements.

The second phase of Korean culture came about through the growing influence of Buddhism, which reached its height during the Koryŏ Dynasty (936–1391) and became an official national religion. Forms of entertainment were now related to religious festivals. The *yŏndunghoe* (lantern festival), a national religious festival in honour of the Buddha, was held in the first lunar month, while *P'algwanhoe* (festival for heaven), largely ritualistic in nature, honoured indigenous Korean deities. In these festivals, the amusements offered included *acrobatics, *puppet plays, and various forms of masked dance-dramas. Since both religious traditions continued to exist, it is highly likely that, under the influences of Buddhist culture, some shamans became professional performers, as they were adept at dancing and music. *Narae*, a ritual of this period used to expel devil spirits, was performed in public by *kwangdae* (clowns), doubtless the first professional actors in Korean theatre.

The third phase is associated with the Chosŭn Dynasty (1392–1912), in which Confucianism, also imported from China, heavily influenced most cultural activities. During the early centuries of the dynasty, the Master of Revels (*sandaetogam*) at the royal court organized the performing arts throughout the country. Theatrical performances now served an official function and were promoted at court celebrations. After the position of Master of Revels was abolished in 1634, however, court performers were amalgamated with village folk performers, contributing to the formation of various regional masked dance-dramas (*see* KAMYŎNGŬK), some of which have been handed down until the present time. During the latter part of the Chosŭn Dynasty, *p'ansori*, a kind of solo folk opera, was developed by professional performers. *P'ansori* contributed to the development of a Western-style *opera (*ch'anggŭk*), popular in the early twentieth century.

Korean traditional culture changed dramatically when Western culture was abruptly introduced at the end of the nineteenth century. The Korean government, alarmed by these incursions, initially attempted to close the nation to outside influences, but failed to do so. Soon after the opening of the nation, Korea became a colony of Japan. During this colonial period (1910–45), much traditional Korean culture was suppressed by the Japanese, and performances of traditional Korean theatrical arts were drastically decreased, creating the most abrupt change to the country in some 2,000 years. The urban intelligentsia of the country, however, became interested in spoken, Western-style drama introduced to Korea via Japan. They thought that the creation of such a drama in Korea, based on the model of *Ibsen and similar progressive playwrights, might provide a useful means to teach and enlighten the larger population, thus serving to create a measure of spiritual independence from Japan. Although many members of the intelligentsia did become involved in this new theatre movement both through the modern commercial theatre (*see* SHINP'AGŬK) and Western-style drama (*see* SHINGŬK), such theatrical efforts were increasingly suppressed in the latter years of the colonial period, eventually creating a kind of cultural vacuum.

Even after the establishment of the Republic of Korea after the Second World War, Koreans underwent new political and economic upheavals because of the Korean War. In this vortex of rapid change, many found the adoption of Western values a useful means to deal with the problems of South Korean culture. During this period, contemporary theatre imitated the Western *realistic and *naturalistic models. Traditional forms of theatre risked becoming mere museum pieces, as little effort was made to revive them. Korean post-war theatrical culture now seemed cut off altogether from its traditional roots. The economic growth of the 1970s, however, brought about a reawakening of Korean culture and identity, and traditional *folk theatre joined modern culture. Many playwrights, such as *Ch'oe In-hun and *O T'ae-sŏk, combined ancient legends, shamanistic rites, and various elements from traditional folk performances.

The nature of North Korean post-war theatre remains largely unknown to the outside world, although it seems to be characterized by a strict adherence to communist ideology, which is directed at propagating a sense of the superiority of the socialist spirit. In 2000 the two Korean presidents met and issued a joint declaration intended to serve as a milestone that could lead to reconciliation, cooperation, and reunification. At some point in the future it may again be possible to speak of a unified Korean theatre. JOC

CHO, OH-KON, 'Korea', in James R. Brandon (ed.), *The Cambridge Guide to Asian Theatre* (New York, 1993)

KARDOSS, JOHN, *An Outline History of Korean Drama* (New York, 1966)

KOREAN NATIONAL COMMISSION for UNESCO (ed.), *Traditional Performing Arts of Korea* (Seoul, 1975)

KORHONEN, KAISA (1941–   )

Finnish director, trained in *political theatre, who has combined deep analysis of the *text with powerful emotion. In *Helsinki in 1969 she co-founded the left-wing theatre KOM where her production of *Chekhov's *The Three Sisters* (1979) was memorable for an internalized *acting style and bare setting. She often works with small, closely knit groups where the actors' personalities are allowed to emerge. As a director of the Swedish-language Little Theatre (1981–4) she produced *The Cherry Orchard* and Hagar Olsson's *The Snow War*. Her interest in psychological *realism and strong female *characters has led her to direct *Gorky's *Vassa Zheleznova* and Dostoevsky's *Crime and Punishment* at the Helsinki City Theatre. LIB

KORNEICHUK, ALEKSANDR (1905–72)

Ukrainian/Soviet dramatist best known for his wartime play *Front* (1942), which stresses the need for new and youthful military leadership at a time, ironically, when Stalin had already decimated the ranks of experienced senior officers. In his *satirical *comedy *Mr Perkins' Mission to the Land of the Bolsheviks* (1943), an American millionaire discovers the virtues of the Soviet Union, an interesting anticipation of future dealings between Soviet communism and capitalist magnates. Other notable plays include a drama about heroic sailors during the revolution, *The Wreck of the Squadron* (1933), and a play about a young Soviet surgeon, *Platon Krechet* (1935).   NW

KORNFELD, PAUL (1889–1942)

German dramatist. Kornfeld grew up in *Prague where he was associated with the writers Franz *Werfel, Max Brod, and Franz Kafka. Kornfeld first came to prominence during the First World War with *expressionist dramas (*Die Verführung* (*The Seduction*), 1918), and essays such as 'The Man of the Soul and the Psychological Man' (1918), a central manifesto of the expressionist movement. His greatest success was the *tragedy *Himmel und Hölle* (*Heaven and Hell*, 1920) at the *Deutsches Theater in *Berlin. He then turned to psychological *comedies (*Killian; or, The Yellow Rose*, 1926) and *historical plays (*Jud Süss*, 1930). In the 1920s he worked as a *dramaturg for Max *Reinhardt, and returned to Prague in 1933. After the German invasion he was deported to Łódź in Poland, where he was killed in a concentration camp.   CBB

KORTNER, FRITZ (1892–1970)

German actor and director. Kortner trained at the Viennese Academy of the Performing Arts from 1908 to 1910, followed by numerous engagements at various German and Austrian theatres. He quickly established himself as a major talent and divided his time between *Berlin and *Vienna. He played the main role in *Toller's *Die Wandlung* (*Transfiguration*, 1919), his breakthrough in Berlin, and joined Leopold *Jessner to play the title roles in many of Jessner's most important productions. Particularly noteworthy were his performances in *Schiller's *William Tell* (1919), Shakespeare's *Richard III* (1920), and *Wedekind's *Marquis von Keith* (1920). In this period he came to be regarded as the prototypical *expressionist actor, a style which he introduced into both contemporary and classical plays. At the same time he established himself as a major *film actor. His performances in the late 1920s were informed by a more restrained, *realistic style. His Shylock in *Fehling's production of *The Merchant of Venice* (1927) introduced new complexity to the *character in a time of growing anti-Semitism. In 1933 Kortner was forced into exile, moving from Vienna to *London, *New York, and finally to Hollywood, where he established himself as an actor and scriptwriter. In 1949 he returned to Germany and worked mainly as a director. In protracted, intensive *rehearsals he demanded absolute precision from actors, developing a distinctive style characterized by a search for realism in contrast to the prevailing abstract classicism. His interpretations of classical plays were often accompanied by controversy.   CBB

KOSSAMAK, NEARYRATH (1904–75)

*Cambodian queen and patron of court *dance. Great-granddaughter of King Ang Duong, her marriage to Norodom Suramarit united the two branches of the Cambodian royal family. Her son Norodom Sihanouk became king in 1941. While he held power (1941–70), she tailored royal dance performances to fit the requirements of a *proscenium stage and the time frame of Western theatrical tradition by featuring episodes from *dance-dramas rather than full plays. She commissioned discrete non-narrative dance pieces that have continued as staples, including *Tep Monorom*, *Chuon Po*, and *Apsara*. The latter featured *costuming based on ancient stone carvings of celestial dancers. Inspired by village performers, she recruited boys to take the monkey roles in court dance, which had been exclusively female for at least a century.   TSP

KOTÈBA

A *satirical drama performed in local languages by troupes of young men in Mali. Associated primarily with Mande-speaking peoples, it is a pre-colonial form that probably originated in rural Mali but was adopted by other ethnic groups in Burkina Faso, Ivory Coast, and Senegal, especially in those regions that have historically come under the influence of Mande cultures. In Mali it flourished during the colonial period and continues to be a vital and popular drama in both rural and urban settings. During an evening's event, a troupe performs a series of *improvised skits, many based on traditional themes. Older subjects include satires on marriage, on local family and community relationships, and on neighbouring ethnic groups. Skits also provide ribald commentary on the nature of power whether defined as economic, political, or esoteric. New themes which highlight changing social conditions are regularly incorporated into the existing repertoire, and more recent subjects satirize urbanites, the school experience, civil servants, and politicians. Certain themes, however, are deemed inappropriate for *kotèba*, including the lives of cultural heroes and men's initiation rites. Since the late 1960s Malian national arts festivals have featured *kotèba* dramas, and today they are performed on national *television. *See also* KOTÈBA ENSEMBLE.   MJA

KOTÈBA ENSEMBLE

Ivorian troupe founded in 1974 in Abidjan by the Guinean director Souleymane Koly. It derives its name from an ancient but still lively idiom of theatre practised by the Bambara people of Mali, the *kotèba*. The Kotèba Ensemble stages *satirical *dance-dramas somewhat like the Mali original, and addresses a wide, popular *audience. It pointedly avoids French-language *African drama, considered unrepresentative of the nation, and prefers its own *collective productions, *improvised around a *folk tale or around topical concerns such as urban migrants and the corruption of the new elites. Works are created to suit the particular acting or singing talents of the performers and are produced mostly in the popular West African trade language, Dioula, and the pidginized French of Abidjan, referred to as the 'français de Moussa', or 'langage nouchi'. A typical Ensemble show, like *Adama Champion* (1979), *Didi par-ci, Didi par-la* (*Didi This Way, Didi That Way*, 1979), or *Waramba, opéra mandingue* (1991), combines sung and spoken sequences and frequently relies on physical expression, partly to cater to the linguistically diverse *audience. In 1993 the Kotèba Ensemble was invited to the *Avignon Festival with *Funérailles tropicales* (*Tropical Funerals*), its only piece by a literary dramatist, William Sassine, though he wrote it after he had spent time observing the troupe's style and methods.   JCM

KOTOPOULI, MARIKA (1887–1954)

Greek actress and *manager. Born in a family of actors, Kotopouli made her stage debut at the age of 7. She performed for the Greek Royal Theatre (1902–8) and managed her own theatre company from 1906. Her roles ranged from *vaudeville to *tragedy and she was praised for her unique vocal technique and dramatic expression. Among her most notable performances were Ellida in *Ibsen's *Lady from the Sea* (1907), Elizabeth in *Schiller's *Mary Stuart* opposite *Kyveli's Mary (1932), *Sophocles' *Electra* (1939), and Clytemnestra in *Aeschylus' *Oresteia* (1912 and 1949).   KGo

KOTT, JAN (1914–2001)

Polish scholar and critic who studied law and literature in *Warsaw and *Paris. He was professor of romance languages at Wrocław University (1949–52), of Polish literature at Warsaw University (1952–65), and held visiting professorships in the USA, Belgium, and Israel. His major work, *Shakespeare our Contemporary* (1961), interprets Shakespeare's plays as emblematic of the modern world. Other works include *The Eating of the Gods* (1973), *The Theatre of Essence* (1984), and *The Memory of the Body* (1992). Greatly affected by Cold War conditions in Eastern Europe, Kott converted historical knowledge into living experience, reading old literary works with contemporary consciousness. His famous analysis of *King Lear* as an example of the theatre of the *absurd compares it to the comic grimace of *Beckett's *Endgame*. *Shakespeare our Contemporary* was enormously influential in *criticism and production, most notably affecting Peter *Brook's production of *King Lear* for the *Royal Shakespeare Company in 1962. 'Kott is undoubtedly the only writer on Elizabethan matters', Brook wrote, 'who assumes that every one of his readers will at some point or other have been awoken by the police in the middle of the night.'

KB/DK

KOTZEBUE, AUGUST FRIEDRICH VON (1761–1819)

German dramatist. Kotzebue began writing for the stage while still a law student in Duisburg, where he founded an *amateur theatre. In 1781 he went to St Petersburg to work in the Russian state service; he held a variety of appointments and was eventually granted a title before returning to Germany. Napoleon's invasion of Germany in 1806 forced him to flee to Russia again, where he re-entered the Tsar's service and published anti-Napoleonic periodicals. His staunchly monarchist stance led to tension with liberal students in the post-Napoleonic period, and he was assassinated by one in 1819. His sentimental drama of adultery *Menschenhass und Reue* (*Misanthropy and Repentance*, 1789) made him famous overnight and established the basic formula he varied across *genres approximately 200 times: skilfully constructed dramatic tension, mixed with comic relief, sentimental endings, and moral didacticism. Like many of his works, this play was widely translated into other languages. In England Benjamin Thompson adapted it as *The Stranger* (1798), one of the most successful plays of the nineteenth century. Kotzebue particularly favoured exotic settings, which he combined with love interests in *Pizarro: the death of Rolla; or, the conquest of Peru* (1794, adapted in English by *Sheridan, 1799) and *La Peyrouse* (1797), a topical treatment of the lost French expedition to the South Seas, which was adapted into a *pantomime (*London, 1799), a *ballet (*Naples, 1822), and a drama (*Paris, 1859).

Kotzebue was acutely aware of social issues, not afraid of controversy, and part of his success lay in the ability to present current social questions. *Kind der Liebe* (1796, known in English as *Lovers' Vows*, a performance of which is banned in Jane Austen's *Mansfield Park*) was castigated for sexual and political frankness. Nevertheless, the overwhelming success of his plays made them a mainstay of theatre for over 30 years, and his successful *dramaturgical formula had a seminal influence on the development of Anglo-American *melodrama. Hugely prolific, his plays featured prominently throughout Europe and America until the mid-nineteenth century, though few have remained in the repertory. *See also* ROMANTICISM.   CBB

KOUN, KAROLOS (1908–87)

Greek director. He taught English at the American College in *Athens for several years before founding the People's Stage in 1934 with the artist Yannis Tsarouhis, where Koun directed a critically acclaimed production of *Euripides' *Alcestis*. He founded the Art Theatre in 1942 in order to explore international dramatic styles using a psychological method. Among his most innovative productions were *Ibsen's *The Wild Duck* (1942) and *Rosmersholm* (1943), *Chekhov's *The Cherry Orchard* (1945), Tennessee *Williams's *A Streetcar Named Desire* (1949),

*Brecht's *The Caucasian Chalk Circle* (1957), *Kambanellis's *Yard of Wonders* (1957), and *Ionesco's *Rhinoceros* (1963). Koun made his mark on the staging of *Aristophanic comedy as well, emphasizing *expressionist elements of Greek popular culture in the *characters and situations. He also directed for the *Greek National Theatre and *toured Europe with several of his productions, including *Birds* (*Paris, 1962; *London, 1964).

KGo

KOUŘIL, MIROSLAV (1911–84)

Czech architect and designer. Fascinated by Russian *constructivism, Kouřil began designing *sets for E. F. *Burian's theatre in *Prague in 1934, first with four other students of architecture and between 1935 and 1941 as chief designer. Exploring the effects of *light on stage, in the late 1930s he was one of the creators of Theatregraph, the most important precursor of the *Laterna Magika system. Between 1957 and 1963 Kouřil was in charge of the National Theatre Scenographic Laboratory, which under his leadership expanded into the Scenographic Institute, where he engaged in research in *scenography on both the *theoretical and technical levels.

ML

KRAMER, LARRY (1935–)

American writer and AIDS activist. One of the first to predict the spread of the disease, Kramer postponed a successful screenwriting and fiction career to agitate for immediate solutions. He co-founded Gay Men's Health Crisis (1981) and founded ACT UP (AIDS Coalition To Unleash Power, 1987). *The Normal Heart* (1985) describes his angry crusade for AIDS treatment, and was the longest-running production in the history of *New York Shakespeare Festival/Public Theatre; it also broke *box-office records at the *Royal Court in *London (with Martin Sheen), and has had over 600 productions worldwide. A sequel, *The Destiny of Me* (1993), explores the troubled past of the same *protagonist as he confronts family and doctors. In *Just Say No: a play about a farce* (1988), Kramer excoriates the Reagan administration for allowing AIDS to become a plague. *Reports from the Holocaust* (1989) is a collection of Kramer's political journalism.

FL

KRAUS, KARL (1874–1936)

Austrian writer. Kraus is best known for the periodical *Die Fackel* (*The Torch*), which he founded in 1899 and wrote in its entirety after 1912. His main concern was the decline of language under the influence of *mass media. Linguistic decay was nowhere more apparent than on the contemporary stage, which he castigated mercilessly, sparing neither Max *Reinhardt nor Erwin *Piscator. His remedy was to adapt classical dramas for solo recitation, and he performed works by Shakespeare, *Nestroy, and *Offenbach to great acclaim. In 1918 he published a monumental anti-war drama, *The Last Days of Mankind*, first performed in 1964 in an abbreviated version.

CBB

KRAUSS, WERNER (1884–1959)

Austrian actor who began his career at various provincial theatres before joining Max *Reinhardt in *Berlin in 1913. His breakthrough came in 1914 in Reinhardt's cycle of *Wedekind plays. Krauss's virtuosic style and uncanny ability to change appearance made him a prototypical 'new actor' for *expressionism, and he is best remembered for his title role in the expressionist Robert Wiene's *film *The Cabinet of Dr Caligari* (1919). In the 1920s Krauss worked for both *Jessner and Reinhardt in Berlin, playing Macbeth, Richard III, Julius Caesar, Lear, and modern roles. He attained notoriety under the Nazis for his racist rendition of Shylock at the *Burgtheater in 1943 and for his part in Veit Harlan's anti-Semitic propaganda film *Jud Süss* (1940), which got him banned from work after the war until 1948. Krauss was made an honorary member of the Burgtheater in the 1950s.

CBB

KREJČA, OTOMAR (1921–)

Czech actor, director, and *manager. In 1940 he began acting in provincial companies; in 1945 E. F. *Burian engaged him at his D46 theatre in *Prague. The next year Jiří *Frejka brought him to the Vinohrady Theatre to play the lead in his production of *Macbeth*. Krejča left after Frejka was forced out, and entered the *Czech National Theatre in 1951, becoming the head of its drama company between 1956 and 1961. The highlights of his acting career were Don Juan in 1957 and Malvolio in 1963, both based upon a thorough analysis close to the *Brechtian model, although Krejča was never a partisan of *Brecht. In these years, however, he was already an established director devoting himself mainly to modern Czech drama (Hrubin, Topol, Kundera, *Havel) and exploring, with Josef *Svoboda as scene *designer, the possibilities of simultaneous *action, kinetics, and *light on stage. In the Theatre beyond the Gate, established for him in 1965, the emphasis on the actors' performances became more prominent, and the lyrical line (*Chekhov, Topol) prevailed within a broader and more sophisticated repertory (*Schnitzler, *Nestroy, *Musset, *Sophocles) in which the playwright's scripts were sometimes dismantled and rearranged. In 1972 the Theatre beyond the Gate was closed and Krejča banished to a suburban theatre; between 1976 and 1989 he was permitted to work only abroad. Shortly after the Velvet Revolution in November 1989, the Theatre beyond the Gate was re-established, though it closed again in 1994. In 1997 Krejča's adaptation of *Goethe's *Faust*, with Svoboda's ingenious sets, opened at the National Theatre.

ML

KRISHNATTAM

A *religious *dance-drama in eight parts celebrating the life of Lord Krishna, performed in the Guravayur temple in the south-western state of Kerala, *India. Inspired by the 'play' of Krishna (as the word *attam* suggests), this form is generally attributed to Prince Manaveda, the Zamorin of Calicut between 1655 and 1658, who apparently saw the child Krishna dancing in the temple courtyard with a peacock feather stuck in his hair. Through almost 350 years of a slowly evolving *dramaturgy and choreography, which remains almost entirely undocumented, *krishnattam* has emerged as an intimate dance-drama representation of Manaveda's chaste Sanskrit composition of *Krishna-geeti*. Inspired by the narrative of Vyasa's *Bhagavata Purana* and the devotional rhetoric and music of Jayadeva's *Geeta Govinda* and Melpattur Bhattatiri's *Narayaneeyam*, *Krishnageeti* is the first composition in Kerala in which the *raga* (melodic line) and *tala* (rhythmic beats) have been prescribed by the composer. To date this *text is sung in the *sopanam* style by two upper-caste singers, accompanied by two *maddalam* drums, cymbals, and gong, punctuated by a conch shell for particularly auspicious moments in the performance. The dancer-actors, who do not sing, are primarily from the Nair community, originally employed as soldiers in the Zamorin's court.

In earlier times a solitary troupe of *krishnattam*, based in Calicut, would travel to Guruvayur every year, performing at various temples *en route*. This tour would culminate in the performance of all the eight plays in the *krishnattam* cycle. Since it was considered inauspicious to end the cycle with Krishna's death in *Swargarohanam* (ascension to heaven), it was obligatory to follow this performance with the opening play of *Avatharam* (incarnation), which deals with Krishna's birth. The other six plays in the cycle deal with Krishna's love-play with the *gopis* (milkmaids) in *Rasakreeda*; the celebration of marriage in *Swayamvaram*; and the defeat of arrogant and *villainous *characters like Kamsa, Banasura, Vivida, and the snake Kaliya in *Kamsavadham*, *Banayuddham*, *Vividavadham*, and *Kaliyamardanam* respectively. Each of these plays is performed as a *ritual offering every night between 9 pm and 3 am in the north-eastern courtyard of the Guruvayur temple. The pilgrims who pay for each performance select the play on the basis of specific desires and needs—for instance, if one seeks blessings for a child, then one can sponsor a performance of *Avatharam*; likewise, *Swayamvaram* is offered for marriage.

Less elaborate than the performance traditions of *kutiyattam and *kathakali, to which it bears close resemblance in its use of hand gesture and *costumes, the more lyrical performative idiom of *krishnattam* is highlighted by *folk elements and a highly imaginative use of *lokadharmi*, or the so-called 'realistic' dimensions of performance. The intimacy of the performance contributes to the immediacy by which it enhances the *bhakti* (devotion) of thousands of pilgrims. And yet this consolidation of *krishnattam*'s practice within the ritualistic and religious framework of Guruvayur has also restricted its accessibility to larger *audiences. Though it does travel outside the temple precincts to secular performance forums in India and abroad, it has not been internationalized like *kathakali*, and consequently its artists sometimes feel that they have been denied due recognition. Moreover, there has not been any significant change in the repertoire over the years, resulting in a certain mechanization and lassitude in the daily performances.

LSR/RB

KRIVOE ZERKALO

The Russian name for the *satirical 'Crooked [or Distorting] Mirror' Theatre of Small Forms in *St Petersburg. Co-founded by the literary editor and theatre critic Aleksandr Kugel and his actress-wife Zinaida Kholmskaya in 1908, the theatre provided a daily diet of theatrical *parodies and political *satire, *pantomime, and *musical comedy. Kugel and Kholmskaya had been influenced by Western *cabaret and managed to attract the diverse talents of Nikolai *Evreinov, Ilya Sats, Yury *Annenkov, and Boris Geier. One of their first successes was a *parody of Italian *opera, *Vampuka, the Italian Princess*, with the result that the theatre made a speciality of parodying theatrical conventions of one kind or another. In his time there Evreinov reckoned he staged about 100 productions, including his own *monodramas, such as *The Theatre of the Soul*. His most famous was a version of *The Government Inspector*, staged in parodic styles ranging from Edward Gordon *Craig to Max *Reinhardt and silent *film comedy, including an especially malicious lampoon of *Stanislavsky's methods. The theatre was closed in 1918, only to reopen in *Moscow in 1922, before returning to Leningrad where it ran from 1925 until 1931.

NW

KROETZ, FRANZ XAVER (1946–)

German playwright. After training as an actor in *Munich and *Vienna, Kroetz came to attention in the late 1960s as one of a group of Bavarian and Austrian playwrights dedicated to regenerating dialect and local themes. Heavily influenced by Marieluise *Fleisser and Ödön von *Horváth, Kroetz was perhaps the most radical in terms of his *political commitment. In plays such as *Heimarbeit* (*Work at Home*, 1971), *Wunschkonzert* (*Request Concert*, 1972), and *Stallerhof* (1972), Kroetz portrays both petit bourgeois and rural existence in brief *scenes. The language of the characters (the unemployed, tradespeople, shop assistants, farmworkers) is an impoverished artificial dialect punctuated by pauses—communication is primarily non-verbal. During the 1970s Kroetz was the most performed playwright in Germany after *Brecht. He obtained notoriety when he joined the German Communist Party in 1972 and remained an active member until 1980. During this period, plays such as *Nicht Fisch nicht Fleisch* (1981) and *Der stramme Max* (*Max Strong*, 1980) examined the effects of unemployment and technological change on the personal lives of skilled workers. In this and later works like *Der Drang* (*The Urge*, 1994), which include *surrealistic scenes and highly explicit sexual language and actions, Kroetz tested the last taboos in German theatre. Although he has written over 30 plays, his output in recent years has declined. He became a household name in Germany playing the society journalist Baby Schimmerlos in Helmut Dietl's satirical *television series *Kir Royal*.   CBB

KRYLOV, IVAN (1769–1844)

Russian dramatist and fabulist. His early *tragedies based on classical models did not achieve recognition, and Krylov turned his attention to theatrical *criticism. However, in 1802, his *comedy *The Pie*, satirizing the current vogue for sentimental drama, gained admirers. After the Napoleonic invasion, he turned librettist for a patriotic *opera *Ilya the Warrior Knight* and also wrote two comedies *satirizing the Russian aristocracy's taste for French manners, *The Fashionable Boutique* and *A Lesson for Daughters*. None of his plays was staged during his lifetime, and after 1807 he increasingly devoted himself to the writing of animal fables.   NW

KSENTINI, RACHID (1887–1944)

Algerian actor, singer, playwright, and director. He began his career acting in *Allalou's Zahia Troupe in 1926 and finished it in 1944 with *Bacheterzi's company; between these two dates he created a company that produced his own plays. A wide traveller, Ksentini viewed Algerian society with a satiric eye. He recorded more than 200 comic songs, composed and played about 30 sketches, and wrote and directed 25 *comedies (including *Hole in the Ground*, 1931; *Hold Tight*, 1935; *What Was Said*, 1938). He ridiculed the conservatism and superstition prevalent in Algerian society through typically Algerian comic *characters, in plays such as *Bouborma* (1928) and *Bousebsi* (1932).   MMe

KUBO SAKAE (1900–58)

Japanese playwright and director. While studying German literature at Tokyo University, Kubo became a disciple of *Osanai Kaoru at the *Tsukiji Little Theatre. After Osanai's death in 1928, Kubo, now a committed Marxist, chose to work with *Hijikata's New Tsukiji Troupe. Both as a director and as a writer Kubo became a respected spokesman for the importance of historical *realism in the theatre. His most fully accomplished work, the lengthy and much revered *Land of Volcanic Ash* (1937), remains a masterpiece of modern socially committed Japanese drama.

Drawing on his childhood knowledge of the difficulties of colonizing *Japan's cold northern island of Hokkaido, Kubo created in his nuanced portrait of the protagonist Amamiya a tragic figure who attempts to combine his humanism with his scientific knowledge. Under house arrest during the Second World War for his left-wing politics, Kubo never fully recovered his health and committed suicide in 1958 after several episodes of nervous exhaustion.   JTR

KUCHIPUDI

A classical *dance-drama tradition of Andhra Pradesh, *India. It derives its name from the village Kuchipudi in the Krishna district. The Machupalli *kaifiat* (revenue record) of 1502 refers to the *kuchipudi* male actors performing in Veeranarasimharaya's court. The village was initially gifted to the families of actors by Abul Hasan Tanasha, a gift confirmed by a revenue order dated 17 April 1795.

In earlier times, *kuchipudi* belonged to the *natya mela* (theatrical troupe) tradition in which a male troupe enacted the story through dance, *music, and drama, as opposed to the *nattuva mela* tradition in which women, generally from the *devadasi* caste, performed solo items. For a long time the major performances of *kuchipudi* centred around the *Bhama kalapam*, which provided enormous scope for portraying the varied emotions of the *sringara nayika*, the *heroine afflicted by love. In the course of time, *kuchipudi* performers included *golla kalapam* and *pagati veshams* in their repertoire. *Golla kalapam* is a philosophic treatise on the birth of the universe, which is addressed through an intellectual discussion between a Brahman and a female cowherd. *Pagati veshams*, on the other hand, are humorous *character studies; they are enacted during the day, more often than not in the off-season of *kuchipudi*. The characters in these plays are drawn from the everyday rural life of Andhra in the nineteenth century, including familiar figures like the orthodox Brahman, the miserly tradesman, the authoritative community leader, the old husband, and his young wife. Of late, with the increasing popularity of solo performances (and the growing embarrassment of going from house to house for donations), *kuchipudi* performers have stopped enacting *pagati veshams*.

In addition to the *Bhama kalapam* and *pagati vesham*, the *kuchipudi* performers started performing *yakshaganas, song-and-dance plays, in the latter part of the nineteenth century under the leadership of Chinta Venkataramaiah (1886–1945). Soon there were many family troupes performing *yakshganas* with a devotional content. By 1956 all the groups amalgamated under one banner, Venkatarama Natyamandali, directed by Chinta Krishna Murthy (1912–69). Like other *yakshnagana* traditions as in Karnataka, *kuchipudi yakshaganas* also contain an elaborate *poorvaranga* (introduction), followed by the entry songs (*pravesa daruvus*) of important characters. As in *Bhama*

Scene from the **kunqu** play *Strange Double Reunion,* a production in Taipei, 1993. The actors are Hua Wenyi and Kao Hui-lan.

kalapam, male actors play female roles, and the actors render their speeches and sing their *dialogue-songs themselves, a tradition unique to all the performing arts of Andhra.

In the second half of the twentieth century, Vedantam Laxminarayana Sastry (1886–1956), a great teacher of *kuchipudi*, started a new trend by choreographing solo dance numbers with trained female dancers. Sastry arranged more than 100 such items and was responsible for incorporating songs into the *kuchipudi* solo repertoire. The choreography of new dance-dramas in the *kuchipudi* style has also become popular since the 1960s, primarily through the initiative of Vempati Chinna Satyam (1929–), who has inspired several young *kuchipudi* gurus to continue and extend his experiments.

MNS

KUKOLNIK, NESTOR (1809–68)

Russian dramatist and poet. A reactionary *romantic, Kukolnik's first play, *Torquato Tasso*, consists mainly of verbose speeches of inordinate length. He followed this with one of the most famous 'hurrah-patriotic' plays of the nineteenth century, *The Almighty's Hand the Fatherland Hath Saved*, staged for *Karatygin's *benefit in 1834 and celebrating the arrival on the scene of the Romanov dynasty in the early seventeenth century. So significant was the play that when, in 1866, an unsuccessful assassination attempt was made on the life of Alexander II, the fifth act was performed in *Moscow as a rallying cry and act of thanksgiving for preserving the Tsar's life. Of the many other dramas Kukolnik composed, almost all have been forgotten, with the possible exception of *Prince Mikhailo Vasilevich Skopin-Shuisky* (1835). Set during the same period as *The Almighty's Hand*, the play is partly an attempt to create a Russian Lady Macbeth in the person of one Katerina, who poisons a prince but who is then herself forcibly poisoned with the drink she has administered. The *hero who turns the tables is Prokopi Lyapunov, whose thunderous exclamation, 'Drink under the knife of Prokopi Lyapunov', became the watchword of any aspiring *melodramatist.

NW

KUMMER, CLARE (c.1873–1958)

American playwright. Born Clare Rodman Beecher, she came to prominence as a songwriter under her first husband's name (Frederick Arnold Kummer), which she retained professionally throughout her longer marriage to Arthur Henry. Her playwriting career began with the 1912 adaptation of a German *operetta into an American *musical libretto, which Arthur *Hopkins produced in 1916 as a straight play. This first effort, *Good Gracious, Annabelle!*, remains the best known of her twenty or so produced works. Kummer's fresh, buoyant whimsy and amusing *characters compensated for weak *dramaturgy. Her hits included *A Successful Calamity* (1917), *Be Calm, Camilla* (1918), *Rollo's Wild Oat* (1920), and *Her Master's Voice* (1933).

FHL

KUNQU (K'UN-CH'Ü)

One of the dominant musical styles of Chinese opera of the late imperial and modern periods. Traditional Chinese theatre is essentially *opera with lyrics that can be sung in any number of musical styles. Considered particularly elegant and subtle, *kunqu* was most popular among the gentry from the late sixteenth to the late eighteenth centuries. It originated in the Kunshan area of Wenzhou, and is a refinement of the regional style of singing popular there during the fifteenth century. The scholar *Wei Liangfu is credited with combining the northern and southern musical styles to create *kunqu* (the term condenses the words *kunshan quiang*, 'music of Kunshan'). Aided by local teachers of the Kunshan style and by a musician from the north named Zhang Yetang, Wei based the new style on Kunshan's regional music that blended the flute, reed pipes, small drum, and clapper. In Wei Liangfu's time *kunqu* was used only for song suites or for art songs (*sanqu*). The writer *Liang Chenyu, after experimenting with setting northern *zaju plays and art songs to *kunqu* music, wrote the first *kunqu* play, *Huan Shaji* (*Washing Silk*), around 1579, a sensational success that popularized the *kunqu* style.

In fact *kunqu* is better suited to the performance of individual songs than to the stage. A particularly slow style, it lends itself to great clarity of pronunciation, as the labial and final of each word are distinctly enunciated. The music is also softer and more delicate than that of the other styles popular during the late imperial period; its most important instrument is the flute, and it uses no big drums or gongs. For these reasons, *kunqu* lent itself to performances in enclosed, intimate settings, such as the banquet halls of the scholarly elite. The other dominant style at the time, *yiyang*, which originated in Jiangxi, was faster and noisier, incorporating drums and cymbals, and thus better suited to the *open-air performances favoured by the common people. The growing popularity of Beijing opera (*jingju) in the eighteenth century, and the devastation wrought by the Taiping rebellion upon southern China in the mid-nineteenth century, contributed to the end of *kunqu*'s dominance of the Chinese stage. It is kept alive today by professional troupes in *China and Taiwan and *amateur singers the world over. The current repertoire consists mainly of plays from the late imperial period, though in the last decades of the twentieth century a divide opened between traditionalists and reformers. The Nan-

jing *kunqu* troupe, for example, sought to preserve traditional staging, while the *Shanghai troupe implemented contemporary choreography and visual effects in order to attract younger audiences.

SYV

KUPFER, HARRY (1935–)

German director, born in Berlin. His first engagement was in Halle (in the German Democratic Republic). From 1973 to 1980, he was *opera director in Dresden, and in 1981 became *artistic director of the Komische Oper, *Berlin. His 1978 production of *The Flying Dutchman* in *Bayreuth—his debut in the West—brought him international acclaim. His production of the *Ring* there in 1988 with Daniel Barenboim conducting was considered the most important since *Chéreau's version in 1976. Eschewing all operatic conventions, Kupfer approaches both *text and *music in novel ways, which results in surprising interpretations and fresh perspectives.

CBB

KURAVANJI

A *dance-drama from Andhra Pradesh, *India, derived from *kura-vanji*, a woman of the Kurava or Erukala tribe. This form, whose central *character is a Kurava tribal fortune-teller, has evolved through the interaction between the classical performance traditions and the *folk elements of religious *ritualistic performances. During the reign of the Nayaka kings (1565–1673) and the Marathas (1674–1855) at Thanjavur, many of the *desi* (regional, local, folk) elements were included in the *marga* (classical, canonical) *texts. Romantic in its narrative content, *kuravanji* represents a princess suffering from the pangs of love. On seeing a local deity in human form, or a king, she loses her heart to him. While she continues to suffer for her lost love, the Kurava woman appears, invokes the mother goddesses, and predicts that the woman's wishes will be fulfilled. Structurally, this dance-drama is no different from the *kuchipudi yakshaganas* from which *kuravanji* evolves. The dramatization of the Kurava woman's appearance on the stage has added a new dimension to the *yakshagana* tradition, forging a synthesis between the classical and folk elements.

Many court poets of Thanjavur wrote *kuravanjis*—for example, Darbha Giriraja Kavi, a court poet of Shahaji (1684–1712), the Maharashtrian king at Thanjavur, and Kanthirava Narasarju (1704–13), who was himself the ruler of Mysore. Along with these *Telugu compositions, *kuravanjis* also became increasingly popular in *Tamil, not least because a large Kurava population interacted with local communities. Testifying to its multilingual possibilities, *kuravanjis* were also written in *Kannada and *Marathi during the Maratha period (1674–1832). Several modern *bharatanatyam* gurus and dancers like Rukmini Devi, Balasaraswati, Kamala, Vyjayanthimala, Padma

Subrahmanyam, and Chitra Visweswaran have also produced *kuravanjis* as part of their repertoire.   MNS

KURBAS, ALEKSANDR (LES) (1887–1937)

Ukrainian/Soviet director whose career began as an actor in 1912. His first directorial experiments were in *Kiev (1917), where he anticipated the *avant-garde innovations of *Meyerhold in *Moscow. The establishment of the Berezil Theatre in 1922 was part of an attempt to unify the proliferating *studio groups inspired by Kurbas's example, the fourth and most radical of which described itself as 'a new type of revolutionary theatre'. The range of Kurbas's work, at both the studios and the Berezil, included *constructivist versions of *Kaiser's *Gas* (1922) and *Jimmy Higgins* (1923, after Upton Sinclair, which Meyerhold invited to Moscow), a version of *Macbeth* as *grotesque Grand Guignol (1924), highly *expressionistic versions of Prosper Mérimée's *Jacquerie* (1925), and *Sadie Thompson* (after Somerset *Maugham, 1927). He also directed plays by Shevchenko, Kulish, and Mikitenko in Ukrainian *folkloric style. A production of *Korneichuk's *The Wreck of the Squadron* (1933) was heavily influenced by *Tairov's example. The constant attempt of the authorities to exert control over Kurbas led to the Berezil Theatre being relocated from Kiev to Kharkov in 1926. Kurbas's last work was as assistant to *Mikhoels and *Radlov on *King Lear* at the *Moscow State Yiddish Theatre, before he was arrested in 1934 and 'disappeared'.   NW

KUROCHKIN, MAKSIM (1970–)

Russian playwright. Kurochkin studied history at *Kiev University and his plays are dominated by the theme of war, which haunts civilization from past to future. He uses language skilfully, with local dialects underscoring historic authenticity. *The Fighter 'Medea'* (*Vilnius, 1995) portrays a war between an international male force and their female counterparts. In *Steel Will* (1999) the Polish gentry fight with the help of a computer control station. *The Kitchen* (*Moscow, 2000), exploring the Nibelungen myth, was commissioned and directed by Oleg *Menshikov.   BB

KURZ-BERNADON, JOSEPH FELIX VON (1717–84)

Austrian actor and dramatist. The author of 300 *comedies and creator of the comic *character Bernadon (related to *Hanswurst and *Harlequin), Kurz was a member of various acting troupes in the German-speaking world, most notably in *Vienna, *Prague, and Wrocław. From 1772 to 1781 he was director of a permanent German troupe in *Warsaw (Die Deutsche Komödie) and the owner of a paper factory.   CBB

KUSHNER, TONY (1956–)

American playwright. Born in New York and raised in Louisiana, Kushner had been writing plays for a decade when the success of *Angels in America* catapulted him to international fame. Its two separate parts—*Millennium Approaches* and *Perestroika*—were developed and premièred in phases at the Eureka Theatre in *San Francisco and the *Mark Taper Forum in *Los Angeles in the early 1990s. *Millennium Approaches* opened in *London in 1992 and on Broadway in 1993, where it won the Tony *award and the Pulitzer Prize. *Perestroika* opened in London and New York in 1993 and won the Tony. Subtitled 'A Gay Fantasia on National Themes', the two parts form an epic *comedy that sets the millennial anxiety of the AIDS epidemic against the backdrop of the Reagan era and a more general American restlessness. Its frank yet amusing depiction of a spectrum of homosexual *characters, from a drag queen to an AIDS sufferer to a closeted Mormon to the historical figure of Roy M. Cohn, constituted a significant step in mainstreaming gay subjects and themes. Kushner followed *Angels in America* with a 'coda' about the collapse of the Soviet Union, *Slavs!* (1995); several shorter, occasional pieces; adaptations of *Brecht's *The Good Person of Setzuan* and *Anski's *The Dybbuk* (both 1997); and a book of essays, *Thinking about the Longstanding Problems of Virtue and Happiness* (1995). Earlier works include *A Bright Room Called Day* (1987) and a popular adaptation of *Corneille's *L'Illusion comique* (1988). *Homebody/Kabul* (2001), his first original full-length play after *Angels in America*, took up the subject of Afghanistan; written before the attacks on the USA of 11 September 2001, it gained timeliness when it premièred at the New York Theatre Workshop at the height of the USA-led war against the Taliban regime and al Qaeda. *See also* GAY THEATRE; QUEER THEORY.   STC

KUSUMO, SARDONO (1946–)

*Indonesian choreographer-director. Trained in Javanese classical *dance and with Martha Graham, his work combines visual aesthetics and a strong movement base and crosses ethnic boundaries. *Samgita Pancasona* told of two monkey brothers in the *Ramayana* who struggle over a kingdom and a wife, while *Story of Dirah* showed a witch-widow spreading pestilence and used Balinese *kecak (monkey chant), *shadow plays, and *masks. *Plastic Forest* used dancers from Kalimantan to explore issues of the ravaged rain forests. The controversial *Meta-ecology* had dancers wallowing in enormous pools of mud to highlight environmental issues. In the 1990s he created a choreography based on the *bedoyo court dance of Solo (the city of Surakarta) to explore the anachronism of sacralized traditions in a secularized world.   KFo

KUTIYATTAM

A highly elaborate performance tradition of *Sanskrit drama. In an unbroken tradition of more than ten centuries, it is enacted by the temple-serving caste of the Cakyar community in the south-western state of Kerala in *India. Originally called *kuttu* (drama), *kutiyattam* literally means the combined acting of more than one person. Other participants in this rarefied tradition controlled by approximately six families include the Nambiars, who provide the rhythmic background for the performance by beating on a large pot-drum (*mizhavu*), and the Nangyars—the women of the Nambiar community—who enact the female roles in *kutiyattam* apart from singing and beating time with cymbals. As a Hindu temple-based art, which is more often than not performed either in specially built temple theatres (*kuttampalam*), or in the inner hall of the temple complex itself, the performance of *kutiyattam* begins with *rituals drawn from the *purvaranga*, the introductory section to Sanskrit drama as delineated in the *Natyasastra*. Along with these invocatory rites on the first day of the performance, a *character is introduced from behind a hand-held half-curtain, his painted face and stylized *cutti* (rice-flour facial border) bearing a close resemblance to the more elaborate *kathakali* conventions of *costume and *make-up that have clearly been influenced by *kutiyattam*. While the introduction lasts around two to three hours, a *kutiyattam* performance can stretch to eight hours, extending over several nights.

After the introduction of the character, on the second day of the performance the same actor recalls the story of the play leading to the point of his character's entry. This intricately stylized flashback (*nirvahana*) is improvised entirely by physical and gestural means. Using codified hand gestures (*hastas*) drawn from the manual of the *Hastalakshandeepika*, the actor elaborates on each word in his *text, embodying the nuances of his character's inner state of being with close attention to the grammatical details of voice, tense, mood, and punctuation. Countering this virtuosic physical enactment that could last several nights, the *vidushaka* (the *clown or jester in Sanskrit drama) proceeds to entertain the spectators with vocal improvisations on the joys of food, sex, deception, and good living. Translating (and, in the process, parodying) the heightened rhetoric of Sanskrit and Prakrit into the local language of Malayalam, the *vidushaka* also uses a Sanskritized form of Malayalam or Manipravalam for comic effect.

While the duration of the *nirvahana* and the role of the *vidushaka* vary according to the circumstances and occasion for each performance, the dramatic text used in *kutiyattam* is always enacted in the final days of the performance. However, the focus is invariably on one *act rather than the entire play. Drawing from a rich repertoire of Sanskrit classics (including the plays of King Kulasekharavarman, the earliest patron and reformer of *kutiyattam*), the repertoire draws extensively on *Bhasa, whose plays existed in the acting and production manuals of *kutiyattam* long before they were discovered as dramatic texts in the early decades of the twentieth century.

Despite its literary inputs, the fundamental challenge in the performance of *kutiyattam* is not merely to tell the story of the play, which is already known to its relatively small coterie of spectators, but to elaborate on the character's innermost feelings and sentiments through subtle tremors of the lip, the eyes, the eyebrows, and even the cheek. This histrionic regimen, which demands a psychophysical understanding of breathing and energy, is nurtured through hereditary modes of *training which continue to be imparted at schools such as the Ammannur Gurukulam (Irinjalakuda), Margi (Trivandrum), and the *Kerala Kalamandalam (Cheruthuruthy). The outstanding modern *kutiyattam* performers include Ammannur Chachu Cakyar, Ammanur Madhava Cakyar, Pynkulam Narayana Cakyar, Rama Cakyar, and Mani Madhava Cakyar. While shortly after India's independence in 1947 *kutiyattam* was on the verge of extinction, it has received a new lease of life through the patronage of cultural institutions like the *Sangeet Natak Akademi and the dedicated and passionate intervention of scholars and connoisseurs like K. R. Pisharoti, K. P. Narayana Pisharoti, Appukuttan Nair, and Venu G. Increasingly studied by foreign artists, *kutiyattam* has been seen in diverse cultural forums. Some of its artists, like Madhu Margi, have participated in inter-Asian productions such as *Dragon Bond Rite* (1997) and *Desdemona* (2000), directed by *Ong Keng Sen of Theatreworks in *Singapore. *Kutiyattam* has now been recognized by UNESCO as part of the world's 'intangible heritage'.

LSR/RB

RAJA, KUNJUNNI, *Kutiyattam: an introduction* (New Delhi, 1964)

KUTTAMPALAM

Temple theatre of Kerala, *India, used for performances of Sanskrit drama (*kutiyattam*) and *monologues (*kutu*) on the Puranas. This rectangular performance structure is situated in the courtyard of the temple on the front right of the main shrine. Meticulous *rituals for the consecration, construction, and maintenance of ritual purity in the temples apply to *kuttampalams* as well. Following the spatial directions of the *Natyasastra along with other texts on architecture, the structure of the *kuttampalam* is adapted to the environmental and climatic conditions of Kerala. For example, its pyramid-like roof, reinforced with copper sheets or terracotta tiles, is always sloped at an angle of 45 degrees to facilitate the drainage of water during heavy monsoon showers. This construction also contributes to the fine acoustics of the *kuttampalam*, in which no sound amplification is needed.

The inner space of the theatre is divided almost equally into the stage pavilion (*ranga-mandapa*) and the *auditorium (*prekshagriha*). Behind the raised square stage is the dressing room (*nepathya*), which has two doors—the left is used for the entrance of the *characters, the right for their exit. Between these two doors are placed two large copper pot-drums (*mizhavu*), which are held in wooden stands. The only other stage *properties are a wooden stool and a half-*curtain (*yavanika*), which is held by two stagehands for the entry of different characters. Dominating the stage with its ornate wooden ceiling and roof, framed by pillars, is a 1.2 metre (4-foot) bell-metal oil lamp (*nilavilakku*), which highlights the subtle facial expressions of the actors. The spectators sit in front or on the sides. Some portion of the auditorium is slightly raised where in earlier times the upper-caste spectators would sit. Economic yet aesthetic in its intricate fretwork of wooden trellises, brackets, and battens, the *kuttampalam* is an architectural joy, as can be discerned in the well-maintained temple theatres at Irinjalakuda, Guruvayur, Haripad, and most splendidly, at the Vadakkunnathan temple in Trichur.   LSR/RB

PANCHAL, GOVERDHAN, *Kuttampalam and Kutiyattam* (New Delhi, 1984)

KVAPIL, JAROSLAV (1868–1950)

Czech director, playwright, and poet, the librettist for Dvořák's *opera *Rusalka*. As a *dramaturg and director, he was the leading artistic personality of the *Czech National Theatre in *Prague between 1900 and 1918, and from 1921 to 1928 of the Vinohrady Municipal Theatre. At first he favoured the psychological and symbolic plays of *Ibsen; later, impressed by the *Moscow Art Theatre, he turned to *Chekhov; and he produced a cycle of fifteen Shakespeare plays in 1916. He also revelled in Czech *historical drama, celebrating the heroic past of the nation particularly in the plays of Alois Jirásek. He respected the integrity of the script and the individuality of actors.   ML

KYD, THOMAS (1558–94)

English dramatist. He was born in London, the son of a professional scribe, and educated at the Merchant Taylors' School, whose headmaster, Richard Mulcaster, encouraged school drama as a pedagogic and money-making activity. Kyd's only surviving plays are *The Spanish Tragedy* (*c*.1586) and *Cornelia* (1594), the latter the first in a projected series of literary translations from French *neoclassical *tragedy which he undertook near the end of his life. He may also have written a lost play based on the Hamlet story, and there have been over-optimistic attempts to trace his hand in other extant plays of the time. In 1593, heretical writings were found amongst his papers and he was arrested; he later claimed that the documents belonged to Christopher *Marlowe, with whom he had shared accommodation a few years earlier. Though he was eventually released, his prison experiences left him emotionally exhausted, and may have hastened his death.

In the late sixteenth century, people regarded *The Spanish Tragedy*, along with Marlowe's *Tamburlaine*, as marking the beginning of 'modern drama'. Set in a fictitious modern European court, it is striking for its intricate, layered architectonics and its use of intrigue and dramatic irony as tragic devices, but sixteenth-century *audiences found it most compelling for the stark, powerful rhetoric which expresses the leading *character Hieronimo's psychological disintegration after the murder of his son. The play was frequently performed in 1590s England (notable actors of Hieronimo included Richard *Burbage and the young Ben *Jonson), and generated several spin-offs extending or retelling the story; it was also adapted by Jonson for a revival in 1601, bringing it into line with newer, sophisticated modes of dramatic characterization. In its original version, it inaugurated English *early modern tragedy's preoccupation with the social, ethical, and political dilemmas of revenge which were ultimately addressed in *Hamlet*; its bleak sense of human subjection to destiny also influenced Shakespeare in *Romeo and Juliet*. Its stage life continued well into the seventeenth century, and twentieth-century productions by the *National Theatre (*London, 1982) and the *Royal Shakespeare Company (1997) demonstrated the durability of its raw dramatic power. *See also* REVENGE TRAGEDY.   MJW

KYIN U, U (1819–53)

Burmese playwright. Along with U *Pon Nya, he is considered one of the best nineteenth-century court dramatists. *Mahaw, Waythandaya, Daywagonban*, and *Parpahein* are the four extant plays out of six attributed to him in a list compiled during the reign of King Mindon (1853–78), although it is believed he wrote many more. Prepared in outline form, his works were *improvised by a troupe of professional actors. The stories were based on or inspired by *jataka* tales about the incarnations of Buddha, and portrayed *characters with mistaken or hidden identities. Composed between the first and second Anglo-Burmese Wars (1824–6 and 1852–3), U Kyin U's dramas reflected Burma's power struggles and defeat by the British by recounting stories of political intrigue, deception, torture, and murder. Brutal and aggressive acts were not staged but described in emotional 'weeping songs', or *ngo-chin*, which showed off the virtuosity of the performers. *See also* MYANMAR.   CRG

KYLE, BARRY (1948–)

English director. Kyle was an associate director of the *Royal Shakespeare Company from 1978, and was made honorary associate director in 1991 after directing nearly 40 plays for the company. His fascination with Jacobean *texts led him to produce, with John *Barton, John *Ford's rarely staged *Perkin*

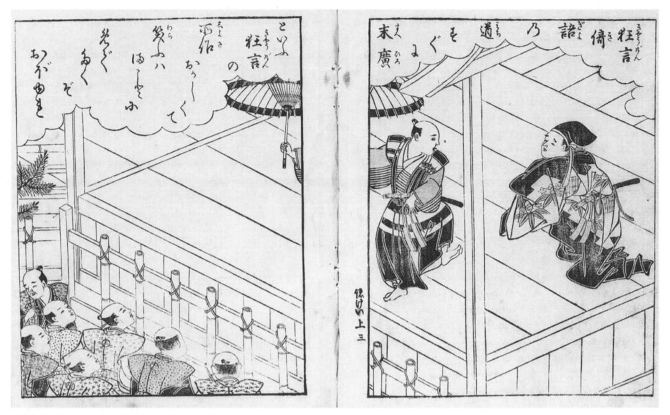

Kyōgen on a nō stage, from a Japanese woodcut by Harunaka, 1763. Traditionally these short comic plays are presented in intervals between nō performances.

Warbeck (1975). He also collaborated with Barton on *King John* (1974) and *Cymbeline* (1974), and wrote and directed *Sylvia Plath* (1973). His socialist views were exemplified in productions like *Brenton's *The Churchill Play* (1988). Kyle's other productions for the RSC include *The Taming of the Shrew* (1982), *Love's Labour's Lost* (1984), and Louise *Page's *The Golden Girls* (1984). In the 1990s he directed Shakespeare abroad (Australia, France, Germany, Poland), though was most successful in *New York with *award-winning productions of *Henry V* (1994, with Mark Rylance), and *Henry VI* (1996). He holds a professorship in theatre at Louisiana State University, where in 1992 he founded Swine Palace Productions. He still directs freelance in England, including *King Lear* (2001) for the *Globe Theatre.   KN

KYNASTON, EDWARD (1643–1712)

English actor. One of the few *boy actors to continue playing female roles after the Restoration, Kynaston's offstage performances extended to appearances in Hyde Park, where fashionable women vied to be seen with the cross-dressed actor in full female *costume. A sharing member of the King's, United, and *Lincoln's Inn Fields companies, Kynaston's talent for mimicry made him some enemies but brought him success in a variety of leading male roles.   GBB

KYŌGEN

Short *farces performed between *nō plays; also, actors who play kyōgen roles; also, a term used after the 1650s for *kabuki performances and/or *texts. The characters *kyōgen* mean 'mad words'. Kyōgen farces are *Japan's oldest *dialogue drama. Humorous skits were part of early *sarugaku* (*see* NŌ), and kyōgen plays were differentiated from nō plays by the mid-1300s. Medieval kyōgen actors were members of nō troupes, but in the seventeenth century they left to form three kyōgen schools: Okura, Izumi, and Sagi. Pre-seventeenth-century kyōgen plays were simple *plots performed extemporaneously, and the names of authors are unknown. Full playtexts were first published in 1623, and the first treatises on the art were written by Okura Toraakira in the 1630s.

Kyōgen actors perform two primary functions. First, they play minor roles in nō plays, often during the interval when the *shite* changes *costume; such intervals are called *ai-kyōgen*. Second, they perform in discrete kyōgen plays (*hon-kyōgen*), which present humorous conflicts between *stock characters:

masters and servants, lords and retainers, samurai and commoners, husbands and wives, deities and mortals, etc. Usually the socially inferior party emerges victorious, and many plays *parody authority figures such as samurai, priests, and gods. While dialogue is central, many examples contain short dances and/or songs which resemble nō in rhythm and timbre, but are light-hearted in semantic content. The posture and gait of kyōgen actors closely resemble their counterparts in nō. Speech in kyōgen is much livelier, however, and contains substantial amounts of onomatopoeia. Contemporary *audiences easily understand kyōgen speech.

Today's leading kyōgen actors are members of *families that have been performing for many generations. Training begins within their families at about 5 years of age, and actors pass through a series of progressively more difficult graduation pieces during the course of their careers. Almost all professional kyōgen actors are men. Kyōgen *masks are used for deities, demons, and animals, and exhibit grotesque, exaggerated expressions. They are also sometimes used by human characters to disguise themselves. Most kyōgen costumes are made of relatively inexpensive materials and feature large, bold, earthy designs. Today the major acting families among the two surviving schools (Okura and Izumi) stage all-kyōgen shows in addition to performing in nō productions. Since the Second World War a few new kyōgen plays have been written and staged, based on sources as diverse as French farce, Shakespeare, and Japanese folklore.

LRK

KYŌKA *See* IZUMI KYŌKA.

KYOTO

In AD 794 the royal family of *Japan moved to Heian-kyō (now Kyoto), which remained the seat of the imperial court until 1868, although ruling military families had their headquarters in Kamakura (1185–1333) and Edo (*Tokyo; 1600–1867). Early performing arts (such as *bugaku and kagura) moved to Kyoto with the aristocrats, and new arts arose; performances took place in and around Kyoto, in aristocratic mansions and palaces, at temples and shrines, and in the dry riverbeds running through the city. In the mid-fourteenth century, dengaku, a predecessor of *nō, which combined song, *dance, and *music, was enthusiastically supported by the first Ashikaga shogun, Takauji (1305–58). He attended a riverbed performance in 1349 during which the *audience rose up, stamping their feet in approval, and caused the stands to collapse, killing and injuring scores of people and inciting others to loot and *riot.

In the following two centuries, *Kan'ami, *Zeami, Zenchiku, On'ami (1398–1467), Zenpo (b.1454), Nobumitsu (1453–1518), and others flourished with the support of Kyoto leaders, creating the nō theatre and most of its standard repertory.

In 1603 a woman known as *Okuni, depicted dancing in Portuguese-style trousers, wearing a foreign-style hat, with a gong in her hand and a Christian cross around her neck, performed the first recognized *kabuki dance on the Kamo riverbed. Later in that century *Chikamatsu Monzaemon moved to Kyoto and begin writing kabuki and *puppet plays (*see* BUNRAKU), some for the famous kabuki actor *Sakata Tōjūrō, who helped develop the 'soft' (wagoto) Osaka-Kyoto style of *acting. By the mid-eighteenth century, however, Kyoto had been eclipsed by Edo as the major theatrical centre. The 'official' nō actors had moved to Edo with their shogunal patrons, the puppet theatre's attraction had waned, and kabuki's centre of gravity also shifted eastward. At the beginning of the twenty-first century, several nō and *kyōgen families reside and perform regularly in Kyoto both in nō theatres and at the more popular outdoor, torchlight performances. The Minami-za Theatre presents a kaomise (literally, 'face-showing') kabuki performance each December, in which local dignitaries sometimes play small roles, and other theatrical and musical arts the rest of the year. Mibu kyōgen (*mime), kagura, bugaku, geisha, and maiko dances and other performing arts can be seen at temples and shrines and during festivals. Productions of modern theatre are brought to Kyoto or Osaka, and in addition, there are several small but active *avant-garde companies that often gain national attention for their innovative productions.

KWB

KYVELI (ADRIANOU) (1887–1978)

Greek actress and *manager. Kyveli made her debut in 1901 with Constantine Christomanos's New Stage, where she acted in plays by Shakespeare, *Ibsen, and *Sophocles until she formed her own company in 1906. She played the leads in *Ibsen's *A Doll's House* and *Strindberg's *Miss Julie* to critical acclaim, and in 1908 she appeared as Lord Byron in Spiros Potamianos's play of that title. After acting in a large number of Greek and European dramas, in 1932 she was notable as Mary Stuart in *Schiller's play, opposite Marika *Kotopouli's Elizabeth. Her third marriage was to the politician George Papandreou in the late 1930s. In 1958, at the age of 70, she gave one of her most memorable performances in *Brecht's *Mother Courage*.

KGo

· L ·

LABAN, RUDOLF (1879–1958)

German choreographer, dance theorist, and educator. Laban was a key influence upon European *modernist *dance in the 1920s and 1930s. His schools in Germany emphasized improvisation and expressive plastic rhythms, as demonstrated in his 'movement choirs', which involved amateur and professional dancers. At the height of his popularity, his *Vom Tauwind und der neuen Freude* was performed at the 1936 *Berlin Olympics, but Goebbels's disapproval ended his career in Germany. His former pupil Lisa Ullmann enabled him to continue his work in England, where Laban analysed the organizing principles of human movement: space, time, weight, and flow. Employed by Frederick Lawrence to work on time–motion efficiency, Laban adapted his methods to serve the war effort. His Labanotation system enabled precise recording of choreography. His principles have been extended by former pupils: Mary Wigman and Kurt Jooss founded their own dance companies; Jean Newlove worked with Joan *Littlewood's *Theatre Workshop; Yat Malmgren developed a Laban-based system of actor *training. Valerie Preston-Dunlop has detailed his remarkable career in *Rudolf Laban* (1998). RVL

LABERGE, MARIE (1950–   )

Québec playwright, actress, and novelist. She was an accomplished actress before her much acclaimed *C'était avant la guerre à l'Anse à Gilles* (1981) was staged in English as *Before the War, down at L'Anse à Gilles*, revealing Québec's hypocritical, patriarchal society of the 1930s. A score more plays followed, several acclaimed internationally. Notable are *L'Homme gris* (1984), performed more than 300 times in France and Belgium, and, under the title *Night*, in *Toronto and *New York; *Oublier* (*Forgetting*), first staged in *Brussels (1987), presenting four sisters reunited around their mother's deathbed; *Le Faucon* (*The Falcon*, 1991), in which a family deal with murder by one of their own; and *Pierre; ou, La Consolation* (1991) dealing not with Québec but with the famous, tragic love of Héloïse and Pierre Abélard. A recipient of national and international theatre *awards, Laberge has since 1991 turned almost exclusively to prose fiction, with considerable success. LED

LABICHE, EUGÈNE (1815–88)

French playwright. Taking over from *Scribe and his contemporaries the well-established formula of *comédie-vaudeville*, Labiche began by retaining the 'airs de vaudeville' set to music, which interrupt and comment on the spoken *dialogue, but he gradually dispensed with this feature. He wrote most of his plays in collaboration with other talented dramatists, his most regular partners being Marc-Michel and Martin. Fifty-seven of his 175 plays are included in the ten-volume edition of his *Théâtre*, published in 1879; and the playwright *Augier, in a foreword to this edition, complimented Labiche on the fact that his plays gain enormously by being read as well as seen. The blend of fast-moving *farce and literary *comedy makes plays like *Un chapeau de paille d'Italie* (*An Italian Straw Hat*, 1851), *Le Misanthrope et l'Auvergnat* (*The Misanthrope and the Man from Auvergne*, 1852), *Le Voyage de Monsieur Perrichon* (1860), or *La Poudre aux yeux* (*Dust in the Eyes*, 1862) such a joy to read as well as to see on stage. In *Un chapeau de paille* it is action which predominates over characterization. On the morning of Fadinard's wedding, his horse eats the straw hat belonging to an unknown lady, who cannot return home and face her husband until it has been replaced (she was keeping an assignment with a military lover). Each *scene adds more absurd complications and misunderstandings, as the wedding party (who have to remain in ignorance, lest the bride's father call off the wedding) chase around Paris until all is resolved, as a problem that need never have existed. Everything depends on chance, and the role of *character is minimal. In *Monsieur Perrichon*, however, *action does depend on character. Of the two suitors for Perrichon's daughter, one is constantly helpful, even saving his life, while the other allows Perrichon to save *his* life, recognizing that certain people feel more gratitude towards those they have helped. The *action is equally swift moving, even if its mainspring lies in fixity of character rather than in the apparent randomness of chance. *See also* WELL-MADE PLAY.

WDH

LABOU TANSI, SONY (NTSONI ZA BUTA MARCEL) (1947–95)

Dramatist and novelist from ex-Belgian Congo, who went to university in Brazzaville and taught English in secondary schools in Pointe à Pitre. He later worked at the Ministry of Culture of Zaire where he founded the *Rocado Zulu Theatre with his friends. A writer of important works of prose fiction, Labou Tansi is best known for his fourteen plays, leaving several more in manuscript form. His interest in the theatre is present even in some of his novels, like *Les Sept solitudes de Lorca Lopez* (1985), where the actor Sarngata Nola is an important figure and a source of inspiration for the peasants. Labou Tansi's plays, which include *Conscience de tracteur* (1979), *La Parenthèse de sang* (1981), *La Résurrection en rouge et en blanc de Roméo et Juliette* (1990), and *Antoine m'a vendu son destin* (1997), are mostly concerned with the dictatorial abuse of power and are notable for their ferocious *satire, their use of fantasy and the grotesque, and their nightmarish atmosphere. To him the modern theatre should aspire to the condition of the *mbongi*—the public space in Congolese villages where meetings and feasts are held and the affairs of the community transacted. To this end he often took his troupe to traditional, rural occasions like the *matanga*—feasts of remembrance of the dead—where his contribution, in the midst of a liberal flow of alcohol, took the form of a performance of a piece entitled 'A Legend on the Invention of Death'. His troupe was well known for innovative productions in Congo and France, especially at the *Limoges Festival.

PNN trans. JCM

LA CHAUSSÉE, PIERRE-CLAUDE NIVELLE DE (1692–1754)

French playwright. La Chaussée's name is firmly linked with the *genre of *comédie larmoyante*, which he pioneered in the 1730s and 1740s: a form of sentimental drama not unlike that championed in England by *Steele in *The Conscious Lovers* (1722), to whose aim, to produce 'a joy too exquisite for *laughter', La Chaussée could well have subscribed. La Chaussée shared *Destouches's view that *comedy, however amusing, must have a clear moral end—though it seems that playing on an *audience's sensibility was a calculated appeal to contemporary fashion rather than a reflection of his own temperament. La Chaussée's career met with early success, his first play *La Fausse Antipathie* (*False Antipathy*, 1733) being followed by *Le Préjugé à la mode* (1735), in which the 'modish prejudice' was an aristocratic scorn for the marriage tie. Next came his masterpiece, *Mélanide* (1741). These plays were all strongly supportive of conjugal love, with *heroes—and more particularly heroines—surviving the challenge of prejudice and adverse circumstance in order to win a happy ending in a welter of sentimental clichés (the idiom of these *verse plays often reflecting that of *Corneille's heroic *tragedies rather than the more robust language of *Molière). La Chaussée was the butt of constant criticism from *Voltaire, who scornfully dismissed *comédie larmoyante* as 'the tragedy of chambermaids', but he occupies an influential place in the development from *character comedy to the sentimental *drame bourgeois* of *Diderot and his followers. His later plays include *Paméla* (1743), based on Richardson's novel.

WDH

LACY, JAMES (1696–1774)

Irish actor and *manager, the original Robin of Bagshot in *Gay's *The Beggar's Opera*, Fustian in *Fielding's *Pasquin*, and Sourwit in Fielding's *Historical Register*. Lacy was the first person imprisoned under the Stage *Licensing Act of 1737 for his unlicensed 'oratories' critical of Walpole's Spanish policy. In the early 1740s he was a planner of Ranelagh Gardens, and is reputed to have designed the famous Rotunda. In 1744 he bought into the *Drury Lane management, and in 1747 persuaded *Garrick to join him as co-manager.

MJK

LACY, JOHN (c.1615–81)

English actor and playwright. Lacy was apprenticed as a dancer and acted with *Beeston's Boys at the *Cockpit before the closing of the theatres. After the Restoration he achieved prominence as a member of Thomas *Killigrew's company at the Theatre Royal (*Drury Lane); his acting and dancing were much admired by Samuel *Pepys. Besides major roles in revivals of *Jonson, *Fletcher, and *Shirley, Lacy created the role of the Irishman Teague in Robert *Howard's *The Committee* (1663). Lacy also adapted *The Taming of the Shrew* as *Sauny the Scot* (1667), and wrote three successful but undistinguished *comedies.

RWV

LACY, THOMAS HAILES (1809–73)

English *publisher and playwright. Lacy wrote a handful of plays of no distinction for *London's *minor theatres. In 1851 he set up as a play publisher at 89 Strand, establishing a series entitled Lacy's Acting Editions. Together with other series such as those issued by Dolby, Cumberland, Duncombe, Oxberry, Richardson, and the later Dicks, all unbound on cheap paper with small print, Lacy's represented almost the only way that plays were published after about 1830, when the market for the bound octavo play at 3 shillings or 5 shillings disappeared. Lacy bought the author's copyright for a small sum, sometimes as low as £5 or £3, and then collected acting fees from both *amateurs and professionals for all plays on his lists, except for those whose copyright had expired (*see* LICENSING OF PLAYS). Lacy's series was taken over by Samuel French in the 1860s and French continues to this day.　　　　　MRB

LADIPO, DURO (1931–78)

Nigerian performer and playwright. After some early plays, he founded the *Mbari Mbayo Club in Oshogbo (1962) with his friend and mentor Ulli Beier. Ladipo was soon performing there with his travelling theatre group, later known as the Duro Ladipo Players. Moving away from Christian sources and from the preoccupations and 'glees' of Hubert *Ogunde, Ladipo selected episodes from the history of the Oyo kingdom as the basis for plays, which were sometimes called Yoruba folk operas. Productions of *Oba Koso* (*The King Did Not Hang*), *Oba Waja* (*The King Is Dead*), and *Moremi* were enriched by extensive research and proved popular on *tours to *Berlin (1964) and Britain (1965). A performer with an imposing stage presence, Ladipo generally played the charismatic central roles that were a feature of his *dramaturgy. During the 1970s his plays and productions moved closer to the populist style appreciated by the paying public in western Nigeria. *See also* YORUBA POPULAR THEATRE.　　　　　JMG

LAFAYETTE PLAYERS

*African-American troupe in *New York. Harlem's first *stock company, it was founded in 1915 by actress Anita Bush, who had performed with Bert *Williams and Walker. Charles *Gilpin, the original Emperor Jones in *O'Neill's play, Evelyn Preer, Lawrence Chenault, and Edna Thomas were among the actors who honed their craft with the group. Popular enough to warrant national *tours, the Lafayette Players did not survive the Great Depression of the 1930s.　　　　　BBL

LAGERKVIST, PÄR (1891–1974)

Swedish writer who received the Nobel Prize for Literature in 1951. The quest for existential meaning preoccupied him as a young poet, as it did in his late novels. His *expressionist play *The Secret of Heaven* (1919) showed a group of grotesque figures living isolated lives on a huge blue sphere; it was given a striking production at Nya Intima Teatern. *The Man Who Lived his Life Over Again* was a less abstract *morality play, reflecting the new *realism of the period; Per Lindberg's production at *Dramaten was warmly received in 1928. As the Nazis swept to power in Germany, Lagerkvist expressed passionate opposition to totalitarian violence. His anti-Nazi play *The Hangman*, directed by Lindberg in 1934 with Gösta Ekman in the lead role, was warmly received in Norway but caused some embarrassment in a Sweden that had many Nazi sympathizers. Lagerkvist's remaining plays were mainly concerned with terrorism, *The Man without a Soul* (1936), and the struggle between democracy and Nazism, *Victory in the Dark* (1939).　　DT

LA GRANGE (CHARLES VARLET) (1635–92)

French actor. The most important of *Molière's colleagues, he joined the troupe shortly after it arrived in *Paris, held it together after Molière's death, published his last plays, and was a mainstay of the *Comédie-Française. His *Registre*, a day-by-day accounting for 26 years of the troupe's repertory, receipts, expenditures, and personnel actions, is an unparalleled source of information. His gracious, charming, self-assured stage image destined him initially for young-lover roles, but this image soon became the essential foil to Molière's own comic performance: Molière played far more scenes with La Grange than with any other actor, and the list of the pairs they undertook—Alceste–Philinte, Arnolphe–Horace, Sganarelle–Don Juan, Jourdain–Dorante—suggests how essential La Grange was to the development of Molière's comic vision.　　　　　RWH

LA GRANGE-CHANCEL, FRANÇOIS-JOSEPH DE (1677–1758)

French dramatist and satirist. One of a group of worthy but undistinguished writers of *tragedy in the generation following *Racine, he adopted Greek subjects in (for example) *Oreste et Pylade* (1697), *Méléagre* (1699), *Amasis* (1701), *Alceste* (1703), and *Ino et Mélicerte* (1713). His innovations generally emphasize *plot at the expense of *character.　　　WDH

LAHR, BERT (1895–1967)

American comic actor. Born Irving Lahrheim in *New York, Lahr entered burlesque at 15. Commentator Alistair Cooke would call him 'the last and most marvellous of the American *clowns cradled by *burlesque'. He began in a series of 'Crazy Kid' acts and stepped into *vaudeville in 1921 with a sketch featuring his wobbly, mock-heroic singing and rubbery physical presence. The 1927 Broadway revue *Harry Delmar's Revels* led to featured casting in *Hold Everything* (1928) and his first *film appearance in 1930. Despite international success as the Cowardly Lion in *The Wizard of Oz* (1939), Lahr was rarely used effectively by Hollywood. His greatest stage success was also

1939 in the Cole *Porter *musical *Du Barry Was a Lady*, playing a men's room attendant who dreams he is Louis XV. In addition to roles in musicals, *revues, and classical *comedies, Lahr played Estragon in the American première of *Beckett's *Waiting for Godot* (1956).   MAF

LAHR, JOHN (1941–)

American critic, biographer, and author. John Lahr is the only person to have won the George Jean Nathan *award for theatre *criticism twice. He was raised in the *New York theatrical milieu and pursued graduate study at Oxford. He has written sixteen books of criticism, biography, and interviews, among them *Notes on a Cowardly Lion* (1969, about his father Bert *Lahr, the famed comedian) and *Prick up your Ears: The Biography of Joe Orton* (1986) which was made into a *film (1987). He has been theatre critic of the *New Yorker* since 1992 and is noted for the unusual form of his essays, which often combine critique of productions with interviews with theatre artists.   KF

LAI, STAN (1954–)

Taiwanese playwright, director, and producer. After obtaining his Ph.D. in dramatic art from the University of California, Berkeley, Lai returned home and since 1983 has been teaching at Taiwan's National Institute of the Arts. In 1984 he founded his own theatre group, Performance Workshop, and since then has consistently staged what the *Far Eastern Economic Review* called 'the most exciting theatre in the Chinese-speaking world'. He makes extensive use of *collective *improvisation and is particularly adept at *comedy. His innovative blending of high art and popular Taiwanese culture makes his productions—mostly about life in contemporary Taiwan—attractive even for the international *audience. In addition to over 200 episodes of a groundbreaking *television comedy that revolutionized television in Taiwan, Lai has created nineteen original plays, some of which have gone on overseas *tours, and directed many more. Especially popular are *Plucking Stars* (1984), and *Pining. . . In Peach Blossom Land* (1986). The latter was made into the award-winning *film *The Peach Blossom Land* (1992), with Lai as director. The new millennium witnessed a more reflective mood in Lai, as he explored the themes of death, compassion, and religion, most movingly in his seven-hour production *Dream-like Dream* (2000).   MPYC

LAI-HARAOBA

A religious festival of the Meitei community in the northeastern state of Manipur in *India, belonging to a pre-Hindu tradition. The word *lai-haraoba* is derived from *lai hoi lauba* which literally means 'shouting of the word *hoi* by the gods' in the Meitei creation myth. Though there are four regional modes of celebrating *lai-haraoba*, the *kanglei haraoba* (performed in major parts of Manipur) is the most common. Celebrated any time between April and June, *lai haraoba* may last from a day to a month depending on the enthusiasm and finances of the community. The festival is dedicated to the local pre-Hindu deity, and is officiated by *maibas* (male priests), *maibis* (priestesses), and the *pena-khungba* (the player of the *pena*, a stringed instrument).

The mythological basis of *lai-haraoba* is very complex, contained in handwritten manuscripts known as the *puyas*. It is commonly believed that it originated in the Koubru hills with all the gods of the Meitei pantheon taking part in the *rituals. *Lai-haraoba* begins with the waking of the deity from water on the first day (*lai-ikouba*). The morning ceremonies continue with the awakening of the deity by singers with *pena* accompaniment (*lai-yakaiba*), followed by the prediction of the future by the *maibis* (*laiman-phamba*). The evening rituals consist of offering flowers to the deity by the common people (*lei-langba*); the singing of the *maibis* (*hoi-laoba*); a *dance to invoke the deity (*thougal-jagoi*); yet another dance of the *maibis* with expressive movements (*laiching jagoi*); and the dance of creation (*laibou-chongba*). All these sequences end with *leiren mathek*, in which the participants indicate the movement of a snake in a single line that symbolizes the snake god Pakhangba. Finally, there are the closing rituals (*wakol*), when all the cultic objects are returned to the temple, with a concluding song to lull the deity to sleep.

The *lai-haraoba* ceremony also includes *lai-lamthokpa*, in which the deity is paraded in a palanquin, and the *kanglei-thokpa*, when the *maibi* chooses the bride of the deity. On the last night of *lai-haraoba*, the *pena*-player and the *maibis* enact the mythological story of Tangkhul and Nurabi in an all-night performance known as *lairoi*. This highly ritualized tale symbolizes the nurturing of fertility in Meitei society. Apart from affirming the pre-Hindu cultural identity of the Meiteis, *lai-haroba* provides the foundations for the dance and theatrical traditions of Manipur. See also MANIPURI THEATRE.

SR

PARRAT, SAROJ N. ARAMBAM, and PARRAT, JOHN, *The Pleasing of the Gods: Meitei lai-haraoba* (New Delhi, 1997)

LAKHON

Cambodian term for drama or theatre. Major theatrical forms in *Cambodia include *lakhon preah reach troap* or *lakhon kbach boran* (court or classical *dance, including short dance pieces and lengthy dance-dramas, some of which are part of ceremonies staged to ask the deities for blessings), *lakhon khol* (all-male *masked dance-drama associated, in Kandal province, with magic powers connected to the performance of certain episodes of the *Reamker*), *lakhon bassac* (musical drama with origins among the Khmer population in what is now southern

*Vietnam, incorporating Chinese and Vietnamese influences), *yikey* (*folk opera with stylized movement), *lakhon niyey* (Western-influenced spoken drama), *sbaek thom* (large *shadow puppets manipulated by dancers), *ayang* (small shadow puppets), *ayai* (improvised repartee singing between a man and a woman), *apee* (akin to *ayai*, with an extended storyline), and *lakhon mohori* (folk musical most often exclusively featuring animal characters).   TSP

LAKHON FON

*Dance-drama from *Laos, part of a shared cultural tradition with *Thailand and *Cambodia. *Costumed dancers with elaborate headpieces, and sometimes *masks, act out a story through dance and *mime, accompanied by a classical music ensemble. *Lakhon fon* was formerly cultivated at the palace in Luang Prabang: the Lao King commissioned episodes from the sacred epic *Phra Lak Phra Lam* (the Lao *Ramayama*) for special festivals and diplomatic events. The *marionette theatre in Luang Prabang also enacted *Phra Lak Phra Lam* accompanied by a classical music ensemble. Today taught at the national school, *lakhon fon* is promoted for the international community. Short dance-dramas are performed for diplomats and tourists in major cities of Vientiane and Luang Prabang and at international festivals, though appeals for international funding to support *lakhon fon* and to restore the marionette theatre in Luang Prabang have met with mixed success.   TMM

LAKON

*Dance-drama from *Thailand, first appearing in the early fifteenth century. There are four main styles. (*a*) *Lakon chatri* is the oldest and simplest dance-drama form with links to animistic practices and spirit worship, traditionally done by an all-male troupe. Today it is performed with four main *characters: *hero, heroine, *villain, and *clown; all save the clown are performed by women. *Costumes are in traditional Thai theatre style, with a cone-shaped crown, a tight embroidered jacket, knee-length trousers wrapped with a loincloth, pendant, belt, bracelets, and anklets for the male clown, and a shawl and pleated long skirt for the women. The repertoire is based on *jataka* (tales of Buddha's incarnations) and local stories. Throughout the performance, the troupe master narrates the text to the accompaniment of a *pipat* orchestra. Singing and dancing alternates with improvised *dialogue from the actresses. The stage, about 5 m (16 feet) square, is covered with mats. The performers sit on a bench to one side facing the *pipat* ensemble; when not engaged in the *action they sing in *chorus, sounding wooden clappers. *Lakon chatri* is traditionally offered as a show of appreciation to the gods. The performance starts in the morning with a musical prelude, an invocation to the deities, a dance of offering, followed by the play proper. After a noon break, the play continues until late afternoon; a musical conclusion sends the gods back to their heavenly abodes. (*b*) *Lakon nok* developed as a refinement of *lakon chatri*. While the performers do not sing, they still improvise dialogue and dance to lyrics from offstage singers. The stage is a raised wooden platform with a bench upstage centre for the performers, in front of a painted backdrop; the *pipat* ensemble is stage right. *Lakon nok* also begins with an invocation to deities but its play lasts only two hours and is given in a theatre. *Lakon nok* went into decline in the early twentieth century and is now rarely performed. (*c*) *Lakon nai* developed around the early eighteenth century from court *ritual dances and short dance-plays which were combined with elements from *khon and *lakon nok*. Similarities to Khmer court dance forms are apparent, but the extent of the influences is disputed. It is considered the finest form of Thai theatre as it incorporates literature, music, dance, and costume, and uses dancers who were once ladies at court. Now presented only by women, in the past it was performed by men as well. Based on the Javanese legend of *Inao*, *lakon nai* is chiefly dance with a few *verse dialogue lines. The performance consists of a musical prelude, a dance overture, and the play proper, which presents one or two episodes from *Inao*. Each episode features a main character who dances a long solo suite, considered its main attraction. (*d*) *Lakon pantang*, emerging in the mid-nineteenth century, is a *variety theatre whose stories, characters, songs, and dances were greatly influenced by the mosaic of cultures brought by early migrants to Bangkok. Seen as a departure from earlier traditions, it is clearly a derivation of *lakon nok* and relies upon the same structure as the traditional form.   SV

LA MAMA, TEATRO

Colombian group, founded in Bogotá in 1968 by a group of artists who counted on the support of Ellen *Stewart of *La Mama Experimental Theatre Club in *New York. The group has staged more than 50 productions. Notable are the *collective creations under Eddy Armando's direction, including *El abejón mono* (*The Fair Drone*, 1971), based on a text by Arturo Alape on the guerrilla movement in the 1950s, *Joselito Carnaval* (1980), and *Los tiempos del ruido* (*Bygone Times*, 1985).   BJR

LA MAMA EXPERIMENTAL THEATRE CLUB

La Mama was founded in *New York by Ellen *Stewart in 1961 as a basement gallery by day and shoestring performance venue by night, and within five years was at the centre of the *Off-Off-Broadway movement. La Mama's first production was an adaptation of a Tennessee *Williams short story about a male prostitute in New Orleans entitled *One Arm* (1962). After a short period of plays by *O'Neill, *Pinter, *Arrabal, *Ionesco, and other established playwrights, La Mama began nourishing most of the important *avant-garde American theatre artists of the 1960s. Stewart helped launch the careers of a generation of American playwrights, including Lanford *Wilson, Tom Eyen, Sam *Shepard, Megan *Terry, Jean-Claude Van *Itallie, Ed *Bullins, and Charles *Ludlam. Wilson's *Balm at Gilead* (1966), a hyper-*realistic portrait of the emergent New York counter-culture, quickly established La Mama at the forefront of controversial, 'hip' theatre. The following year wider *audiences could see the *film *Three Plays from La Mama* (1967) which showcased Van Itallie's *Pavane*, Shepard's *Fourteen Hundred Thousand*, and Paul Foster's *The Recluse*.

La Mama also fostered the work of innovative directors and actors. Tom O'Horgan, who directed many of the company's early productions, including an all-male version of *Genet's *The Maids* (1964), transplanted the La Mama style to Broadway with the *musical *Hair* (1968). Joseph *Chaikin's *Open Theatre staged several productions, including Megan Terry's *Viet Rock* (1966), and the company created shock waves with the first American showing of Jerzy *Grotowski's *Polish Laboratory Theatre in 1969. Since then, La Mama has supported pioneering work by Andrei *Şerban, *Mabou Mines, *Spiderwoman Theater, the Pan Asian Repertory Theatre, *Split Britches, Ping *Chong, Trockadero Gloxina Ballet Company, Ubu Repertory Theatre, and others. Despite dwindling support from the *National Endowment for the Arts after the culture wars of the 1990s, by the end of the decade La Mama had staged almost 2,000 productions and received numerous *awards for its development of playwriting and performance.   JAB

LA MAMA THEATRE

Australian theatre established by Betty Burstall in *Melbourne in 1967 after she experienced the informal intimacy and innovation of *alternative *New York theatre, particularly the *La Mama Experimental Theatre Club. Burstall leased an inner-city factory, opening with Jack *Hibberd's *Three Old Friends*. The *playhouse provided writers with a supportive environment without the pressure of *box office in which to develop their work. The La Mama Company and the *Australian Performing Group were among famous occupants. With more than 75 per cent of its programming Australian, La Mama continues to play an important role in the country.   SBS

LAMARCHE, GUSTAVE (1895–1967)

French-Canadian playwright, director, poet. A Catholic priest, his vast *pageant plays on biblical themes, such as *Jonathas* (1933), *La Défaite de l'enfer* (*Hell Defeated*, 1938), *Notre-Dame-des-Neiges* (*Our Lady of the Snows*, 1942), and *Notre-Dame-de-la-Couronne* (*Our Lady of the Crown*, 1947), involved hundreds of actors, musicians, and choirs and attracted scores

of thousands of spectators to their outdoor performances, thereby validating live theatre in a Catholic society where it had long remained suspect. His *Œuvres théâtrales* (1972–5) contains 35 plays, and he is the subject of a monograph by René Pageau, *Gustave Lamarche: poète dramatique* (1976).

LED

LAMB, CHARLES (1775–1834)

English essayist, whose dramatic *criticism includes fine descriptions of contemporary performers such as George Frederick *Cooke, Joseph *Munden, and Fanny *Kelly. His most memorable essays are 'Stage Illusion' and 'On the Artificial Comedy of the Last Century', a provocative argument about how the public's censorious morality had destroyed the imaginative pleasures of watching Restoration *comedy. Lamb's scepticism about performance—as seen in 'On the Tragedies of Shakespeare' (1812)—can be explained in part by the unfavourable conditions of the contemporary stage. Nevertheless, Lamb was fascinated by the different experiences we have as readers and as spectators of plays. For him, 'the plays of Shakespeare are less calculated for performance . . . than those of almost any other dramatist whatever'. Lamb compiled *Specimens of English Dramatic Poets Who Lived about the Time of Shakespeare* (1808), a significant text in the critical revival of Elizabethan and Jacobean drama and, together with his sister Mary Lamb, the children's classic *Tales from Shakespeare* (1807). He wrote several plays including a *farce, *Mr H*, which was hissed off the stage at *Drury Lane Theatre, and a *tragedy entitled *John Woodvil*.

JM

LAM LUANG

Syncretic musical theatre from *Laos. It grew from the Lao *molam* (expert singer) tradition, in which a performer gestures expressively while singing semi-improvised poetic stanzas. Its origin can be directly traced to a form popular in the 1930s in which a solo *molam* enacted several roles accompanied by a *khene* (free-reed mouth organ); in the 1940s this developed into *lam mou* (song with props), with a group of *molam* singing different roles. Subsequently renamed *lam luang*, the form then incorporated staging conventions and *costumes from the Thai *likay*. A popular rustic tradition that can last an entire evening in performance, *lam luang* features *molam* in gaudy costumes and *make-up singing with both traditional and amplified Western instruments and surrounded by extravagant *scenery. Risqué humour, topical references, and male–female repartee singing combine in a colourful pastiche of semi-improvised vignettes loosely based on Lao myths, epics, and history. In contrast to the many troupes performing *lam luang*, the Central Troupe is the only group that performs *lakhon lam*, a didactic, *socialist realist form. Here singers in modern costumes enact

Lao revolutionary narratives accompanied by a mixed traditional and Western orchestra, costumes, and framed by a naturalistic backdrop. TMM

LAMPE, JUTTA (1943–)

German actress. After training in Hamburg she joined the Bremen Theatre in the late 1960s. Here she met Peter *Stein, playing Leonore in his legendary production of *Goethe's *Torquato Tasso* (1969). She was a founding member of the *Berlin *Schaubühne and became one of its most important actors. Significant roles in Stein productions include Solveig in *Peer Gynt* (1971), the Doctor in *Gorky's *Summerfolk* (1972), Rosalind in *As You Like It* (1979), Masha in *The Three Sisters* (1984), and *Racine's Phèdre (1987). In 1990 she played the title role in Robert *Wilson's production of *Orlando* (after Virginia Woolf), for which she was voted best actress of the year (for the second time). Cinema work includes two *films with Margarete von Trotta, *Schwestern; oder, Die Balance des Glücks* (1979) and *Die bleierne Zeit* (1981). Lampe's *acting ranges from finely observed psychological *realism to highly stylized classical declamation. CBB

LAMPS *See* LIGHTING.

LANG, MATHESON (1879–1948)

English *actor-manager. Although he came to be identified with exotic *characters like Wu LiChang in *Mr Wu* (1913) and Huan Sing in *The Chinese Bungalow* (1925), Lang was also a fine Shakespearian actor. He played with the F. R. *Benson company (1898–1905), Ellen *Terry (1903), at the *Old Vic under Lilian *Baylis (1914), and was particularly admired for his performances as Benedick and Othello. He *toured extensively in North America, Australia, South Africa, and *India and from 1916 was one of the first English serious actors to have a successful *film career. VEE

LÅNGBACKA, RALF (1932–)

Finnish director. Influenced by *Brecht, he was a leading figure of the leftist generation in the 1960s when he worked at the *Finnish National Theatre. The Turku City Theatre reached a high point when he and Kalle *Holmberg worked there as directors (1971–7). His finest work includes classics (*Büchner's *Danton's Death* and *Leonce and Lena*) and modern drama (*Weiss's *Marat/Sade* and Brecht's *Galileo*). As *artistic director of the City Theatre in *Helsinki (1983–7) he mounted a *Peer Gynt* in which the old Peer existed side by side with the young *hero, while his *Chekhov productions were based in the tradition of psychological *realism. He has directed over 100 pro-

ductions of theatre and *opera, and is well known for his work in Gothenburg and *Stockholm. He published books of essays on Brecht (1981) and Chekhov (1986). LIB

LANGE, HARTMUT (1937–)

German dramatist and director. Lange trained in East *Berlin before fleeing to West Berlin in 1965, where he worked as a *dramaturg and director. Heavily influenced by *Brecht, his early plays such as *Marski* (1966), a parable-like exploration of East German land reform, were founded in a dialectical view of social change. His most successful play, the *comedy *Die Gräfin von Rathenow* (*The Countess of Rathenow*, 1969), is an adaptation of *Kleist's novella *Die Marquise von O*, and reveals the absurdities underpinning the Prussian code of honour. In recent years he has written mainly prose. CBB

LANGHAM, MICHAEL (1919–)

English director who began his directing career while a prisoner of war in Europe. After the war he directed with the Midland Theatre Company (Coventry), where his work attracted the notice of Tyrone *Guthrie, and he served as *artistic director of the *Birmingham Rep and the *Glasgow *Citizens' Theatre. Freelance assignments included *Julius Caesar* at the *Shakespeare Memorial Theatre (1950) and *Othello* at the *Old Vic (1951). In 1955 Guthrie invited Langham to Canada's *Stratford Festival, and the next season Langham succeeded him as artistic director. Though lacking Guthrie's personal magnetism, Langham gradually won the company's admiration, built its reputation internationally, and became an important director of Shakespeare. His productions there, admired especially for their mastery of movement on Stratford's *thrust stage, included *Henry V* (1956), *Romeo and Juliet* (1960), *Coriolanus* (1961), *Love's Labour's Lost* (1961), *Cyrano de Bergerac* (1962), *Timon of Athens* (1963), *King Lear* (1964), and *The Government Inspector* (1967). Langham later served as artistic director of the *Guthrie Theatre in Minneapolis (1971–7), where he restored that company's flagging fortunes, and headed the drama division of *New York's *Juilliard School (1978–92). His busy freelance career has included productions with the *Chichester Festival, *Royal Shakespeare Company, and Royal *National Theatre. DWJ

LANGHOFF, THOMAS (1938–)

German director. Born in Zurich, the son of director Wolfgang Langhoff, he grew up in East *Berlin where his father was *Intendant of the *Deutsches Theater. After a period as an actor and *television director, Langhoff's breakthrough came in the mid-1970s at the Maxim-Gorki-Theater with important productions of *Hauptmann, *Chekhov, and Shakespeare. From the 1980s he also worked in West Germany establishing a reputation as specialist in psychological *realism with a keen eye for *textual nuances. In 1991 he was appointed *artistic director of the Deutsches Theater, which he developed into one of the leading German-speaking ensembles. CBB

LANGNER, LAWRENCE (1890–1962)

American producer. A founder of three major theatre companies, Langner maintained a remarkable double life, working by day as an internationally known patent lawyer. Emigrating from London in 1911, he became involved with an artistic and political social set in the Greenwich Village section of *New York. This circle, which gathered at the Liberal Club, launched a dramatic society in 1914, and from those origins Langner organized the *Washington Square Players, a *Little Theatre committed to the artistic renaissance of American theatre. The Players achieved remarkable success (1915–18) but disbanded due to overwhelming debts and loss of personnel to war duty. Langner expertly reorganized the group with a new set of principles and a new name (thus avoiding indebtedness) in late 1918 and the *Theatre Guild—managed largely by Langner and Theresa Helburn—would become the model of an American art theatre surviving in a commercial environment throughout the 1920s and 1930s. In 1951 Langner founded the American Festival Theatre (later the *American Shakespeare Festival) in Stratford, Connecticut. MAF

LANGSNER, JACOBO (1927–)

Uruguayan playwright and screenwriter. Born in Romania, raised in Uruguay, and a *Buenos Aires resident since the 1960s, Langsner is best known for *Waiting for the Hearse* (1962), one of the region's most biting and popular *comedies about local middle-class family life. In the 1985 *film version, the missing grandmother was played by the male actor Antonio Gasalla (in keeping with *neogrotesco* tradition of such plays as Roberto *Cossa's *The Granny*; *see* GROTESCO CRIOLLO). Outstanding among Langsner's other plays are *Other Paradises* and *Una Margarita llamada Mercedes* (*A Daisy Called Mercy*), both from 1997. JGJ

LANGTRY, LILLIE (1853–1929)

British actress. The daughter of the dean of Jersey, Langtry moved to *London with her first husband and established herself as a noted society beauty. In 1881 she separated from her husband, and in the same year became one of the first society ladies to appear on the professional stage when she played Kate Hardcastle in *Goldsmith's *She Stoops to Conquer*. She briefly joined the *Bancroft company, after which she founded her own company and made her *New York debut in 1883 in Tom *Taylor's *comedy *An Unequal Match*. She *toured America with

great success. Although a limited actress, Langtry was a shrewd entrepreneur and self-publicist. Her role as Mrs Trevelyan in Sidney *Grundy's *The Degenerates* (1899), a story of scandal in high society, reflected her personal life which involved a number of public love affairs, including a long-standing liaison with the Prince of Wales, the future Edward VII. Langtry's other celebrated roles included Rosalind in *As You Like It* and Lady Teazle in *Sheridan's *The School for Scandal*. SF

LANGUICHATTE (THÉODORE BEAUBRUN) (1918–98)

Haitian playwright, director, and actor. Out of a varied 57-year career, he is best remembered for his comic portrayals on *radio and *television. On radio in 1941 he created the *character Languichatte Débordus, who reappeared in most of his subsequent work. A huge success with the public, Languichatte played him with masterful sensitivity: as a *clown, who spoke a hilarious mixture of French and creole, and as a stunning psychological combination of the traits of two of the most popular figures of Haitian *folklore, Bouki the fool and Malis the trickster. Of the many *comedies Languichatte wrote, only two have been published: *Anna* (1962) and *La Haine au service de l'amour* (*Hate in the Service of Love*, 1963).

MLa trans. JCM

LANGUIRAND, JACQUES (1931–)

Québec playwright, author, and director. He is best known for the absurdist plays he wrote and produced in the 1950s and 1960s, after an extended stay in *Paris where theatre of the *absurd was much in vogue. *Les Insolites* (*The Weirdos*, 1956) shows evident *surrealist influence in its self-destructive use of language, while *Le Roi ivre* (*The Drunken King*, 1970; broadcast on *radio in France, 1950), *Les Grands Départs* (*Great Departures*, 1958), and *Les Violons de l'automne* (*Violins of Autumn*, 1962) evolve towards more accessible *plot and structure. After experimenting with *multimedia work, such as the *musical *Klondyke* (1971), he abandoned theatre for live *television. LED

LANSBURY, ANGELA (1925–)

Anglo-American actress. English born, sent to America to escape the Blitz, she began her acting career with the *film *Gaslight* (1944), for which she received an Academy award nomination, her first of three. She made 21 films before her 1957 Broadway debut in *Hotel Paradiso*, followed by *A Taste of Honey* (1960). She reached stage stardom in a series of *musicals in the 1960s and 1970s—*Anyone Can Whistle*, *Mame*, *Dear World*, *Gypsy*, and *Sweeney Todd*—winning Tony *awards for the last four. In 1984 she began a twelve-year run as Jessica Fletcher in the *television series *Murder, She Wrote*, all the while continuing her film work. In a career stretching from ingénue to dowager, from elegant *heroine to depraved *villainess, she has displayed durability and flexibility, as well as a highly admired work ethic.

JD

LAOS

'Land of a million elephants and the white parasol', this small nation was once a sprawling kingdom with territory that encompassed much of modern Thailand. Today its fertile river valleys and rugged mountain ranges are home to diverse ethnic groups whose language families include Lao-Tai, Mon-Khmer, Sino-Tibetan, Tibeto-Burman, and proto-Malay. Bordering five nations—*China, *Thailand, *Myanmar, *Cambodia, and *Vietnam—Laos has a population of 5.4 million and is governed by the lowland Lao (the ethnic majority at 50 per cent), who retain close ties to the Lao in north-east Thailand and to the Thai. During the era of French colonization, royal *dance troupes and musical ensembles as well as theatrical singing traditions existed in the kingdom of Laos. Cold War politics and the Vietnam War, however, influenced the performing arts in Laos: both sides appropriated the arts to further their political agendas. The USA established a Lao School of Music and Dance (Lao Natasin) in the 1950s and provided scholarships for accomplished performer-teachers to study *lakhon fon* (dance-drama) in Bangkok. The United States Information Service commissioned *molam* (expert singers) from Thailand to perform anti-communist versions of *lam luang* (sung story/folk opera) in Laos. On the revolutionary side, the Pathet Lao adapted the *lam luang* tradition in 1969 by creating an official socialist folk opera, *lakhon lam* (sung drama), in Houaphan province.

When the Lao People's Democratic Republic was established in 1975 it continued to promote social and political agendas through the arts. Today the government directs and supports the central *lakhon lam* troupe, the central dance troupe (*kom Silapakom*), the National School of Music and Dance (formerly the Lao Natasin School), and the departments of spoken drama (*lakhon vow*) and *puppet theatre (*lakhon tuthakah*). A *marionette theatre that existed in Luang Prabang foundered during the Cold War era and may have become extinct. Scholarly research has thus far touched on only a few of the many *genres found in the country.

TMM

LAO SHE (1899–1966)

Chinese novelist and playwright, pen-name of Shu Sheyu. By the time Lao She turned to plays he was one of the best-known writers of novels and short stories in *China, having started his career in 1926 while teaching Chinese at the University of London. After the Sino-Japanese War broke out in 1937, Lao was elected the head of the All-China Anti-Japanese Writers' Federation, a position he held until after the war. His first play, *The Remaining Fog*, was written in 1939 as a *satire of the corruption in the Chinese-controlled south-west during the war. Although somewhat immature in its dramatic technique, the play received wide acclaim for its *dialogue and satire, trademarks Lao had exhibited in his novels. This was followed by about ten more plays written during the war. Between 1946 and 1950 he lived in the USA, where he wrote and supervised the translation of several of his novels. His best plays, including *Dragon Beard Ditch* (1951) and *Teahouse* (1957), were written after his return to China. Using a teahouse as the backdrop to life in Beijing between 1910 and the 1940s, the latter has become a classic of modern Chinese theatre.

SYL

LARIVE (JEAN MAUDUIT) (1747–1827)

French actor. In 1778 Larive succeeded *Lekain, not only as the *Comédie-Française's leading tragic player, but also in his efforts to introduce greater authenticity into Graeco-Roman *costume, where he dispensed with full wigs, hair powder, and hip-pads. A handsome, if emotionally cold actor, he triumphed as *Voltaire's Œdipe in 1790. In retirement he devoted himself to teaching, and published his *acting classes as a two-volume *Cours de déclamation* (1804–10).

JG

LARIVEY, PIERRE DE (c.1540–1619)

French playwright. Italian by birth—his name is a pun on the family name Giunto, 'the newly arrived'—Larivey was the most significant comic dramatist before Pierre *Corneille and the author who acclimatized Italian *commedia erudita* to Gallic culture. Inspired by performances of the *touring *Gelosi troupe, he published a collection of six *comedies in 1579 and a further three in 1611. Translating and adapting Italian models, Larivey relocated the setting of these plays in France, gave the *characters French names, and created an original colloquial Gallic comic prose style for them. Whether his work reached the public stage in its own day is uncertain, but it was widely read: five new editions of the 1579 collection appeared during his lifetime. In his best-known comedy, *Les Esprits* (*The Ghosts*, 1579), Larivey transposes to a contemporary bourgeois *Paris context Lorenzino de' Medici's comedy about avarice *Aridosia* (1536), a play in turn adapted from two Plautine comedies *Aulularia* (*The Pot of Gold*) and *Mostellaria* (*The Ghost Play*), and *Terence's *Adelphi* (*The Twin Brothers*). There is evidence of both Larivey and *Plautus in *Molière's *L'Avare* (*The Miser*, 1668), as there is in Jean-François *Regnard's *one-act comedy *Le Retour imprévu* (*The Unexpected Return*, 1700). In an adaptation by Albert *Camus, *The Ghosts* was staged in Angers, south-west of Paris, in 1953.

JG

LAROQUE, PIERRE REGNAULT PETIT-JEAN (c.1595–1676)

French actor. Laroque began his career in the provinces, but performed regularly with the *Marais company from 1637 onwards, eventually succeeding *Floridor as orator. He was considered a poor actor but an excellent administrator. In 1673, he and most other Marais actors transferred to the *Guénégaud, where they joined the remaining members of the late *Molière's troupe. Laroque retired in March 1676 and died three months later.   JC

L'ARRONGE (ARONSOHN), ADOLF (1838–1908)

German *manager, conductor, and dramatist. L'Arronge trained initially as a musician and worked as a composer and conductor at various provincial and metropolitan theatres. In 1881 he purchased the Friedrich-Wilhelmstädtische Theater in *Berlin, which he managed from 1883 to 1894. Under the name *Deutsches Theater he established it as a leading forum for dramatic literature, both classical and contemporary, with star actors such as *Kainz and *Sorma. L'Arronge was also a highly successful author of sentimental *comedies, the best known of which is *Mein Leopold*.   CBB

LA RUE, DANNY (DANIEL PATRICK CARROLL) (1927–)

Irish *female impersonator and popular entertainer. He began performing in troop entertainments whilst serving in the Royal Navy before working in British *regional repertory and *variety theatre. He made his *London debut in *revue at the Irving Theatre, and by 1955 was a *cabaret star at Winston's Club. In 1964 he opened his own nightclub, the Danny La Rue Club, in Hanover Square. On stage he appeared in *Danny La Rue at the Palace* (1970), as Dolly Levi in *Hello, Dolly!* in the West End and on Broadway, and as numerous *pantomime dames, notably in *Queen Passionella and the Sleeping Beauty* (1969). Bob Hope described him as 'the most glamorous woman in the world'. He was awarded the OBE in 2002.   AS

LASSALLE, JACQUES (1936–)

French director. After a long career of directing classical and contemporary plays and running the Théâtre National de Strasbourg (1983–91), Lassalle became director of the *Comédie-Française from 1991 to 1993, staging *Marivaux, *Molière, and *Goldoni, as well as opening the company's current second theatre, the renovated Théâtre du *Vieux-Colombier, with a production of two plays by Nathalie Sarraute. He has taught at the *Conservatoire in *Paris from 1994, during which time he worked in France and around the world on plays by *Euripides, *Racine, *Chekhov, *Hofmannsthal, *Pirandello, Véronique Olmi, and David *Hare.   DGM

LA TAILLE, JEAN DE (c.1540–1608)

French playwright, an outstanding member of the generation of humanist writers of *tragedy, chiefly of Protestant background, which flourished in the mid-sixteenth century. La Taille was also among the first, in his *Art de la tragédie*, to give a coherent account of the 'rules' of tragedy and to formulate an aesthetic interpretation of the *genre. Although neither of his tragedies (*Saül le furieux* and *La Famine: ou, Les Gabeonites*) was written for performance, there is evidence of the staging of both in colleges around the end of the century. La Taille's two *comedies, *Le Negromant* and *Les Corrivaux*, both seem to have remained unperformed. *See also* NEOCLASSICISM.   WDH

LATERNA MAGIKA

Czech performance organization, a *multimedia combination of theatre and film rhythmically organized and synchronized. Relying on a complex structure of music, sound, and visual images, and the interaction of the bodies of performers with their ephemeral images, it was conceived by the director Alfréd *Radok and the designer Josef *Svoboda. The first Laterna Magika programme was shown at the Expo 58 in *Brussels as an entertaining piece of state publicity. A more ambitious second programme was banned and Radok forced out. Self-supporting now and headed by Svoboda after 1973, Laterna Magika was one of the *Czech National Theatre companies between 1973 and 1992. Its live performers are *dancers. *See also* SCENOGRAPHY; MEDIA AND PERFORMANCE.   ML

LA THORILLIÈRE (FRANÇOIS LE NOIR) (1626–80)

French actor. After two years at the *Marais, he joined the company of *Molière, where he played a range of roles, from kings to *clowns, and created the *character of the society poet Trissotin in *The Learned Ladies*. After Molière's death he moved to the *Hôtel de Bourgogne; his own death weakened that troupe and hastened the merger of the two rival companies into one. His three children and three grandchildren all had acting careers at the *Comédie-Française.   RWH

LATIN AMERICA

The history of theatre and performance in Latin America takes on forms as diverse as the countries that span the region. Prior

The fairies in *A Midsummer Night's Dream* set in an Amazonian rain forest, in Werner Herzog's adaptation of Shakespeare's play, Teatro João Caetano, Rio de Janeiro, 1992.

to the Conquest indigenous *ritual and warfare contained many performative elements. The Aztecs in Mexico conceived of themselves as a warrior mystic race whose divine mission was to take sacrificial victims in battle. Such battle was highly *ritualistic, in a format largely composed of elaborate announcements of hostilities prior to any actual fighting. When they did fight, they fought with obsidian blades, wore splendid *costumes, and carried brilliant standards. Since the point was to capture prisoners for subsequent sacrifice, they avoided killing their opponents, and if their leader was slain or their standard taken, they surrendered, with both sides deciding between them the amount of tribute to be paid by the losers. So necessary to the continuance of Aztec society was human sacrifice, in fact, that in times of peace an artificial form of warfare, called 'Flowery Wars', was devised to provide the necessary victims. Battles were staged between the Aztecs and their closest tribute-paying neighbours, the Tlaxcaltecas. Since sacrificial victims could not come from the Aztec community itself, Tlaxcala was kept in a state of perpetual limbo, never fully vanquished, never free, in order to provide a steady source of sacrificial victims.

Ritual warfare and sacrificial offerings are not theatre in the normal sense, of course, but the *spectacle of these Aztec actions contained numerous para-theatrical elements. The same elements can be found in the Maya and Quechua civilizations further to the south with the Mayan *Rabinal Achí as the only extant indigenous script. The subsequent European *evangelical theatre would skilfully use those elements to its own advantage as it undertook its task of Christianizing the New World. What the evangelical theatre retained and developed were the spectacular and transformational aspects of ritual performance, wedding them to Christian theological and political concerns.

By the seventeenth and eighteenth centuries European colonial and ecclesiastical authority was firmly established in Latin America. Theatrical activity during this period was largely ceremonial; the plays were those of the great Spanish baroque dramatists Ruiz de *Alarcón, Lope de *Vega, *Calderón de la Barca, *Tirso de Molina, and their Iberian and colonial imitators. There were also instances of indigenous theatrical activity such as the anonymous Nicaraguan play *El güegüense* that *satirizes civil authority, or the works of the Mexican nun Sor *Juana de la

Cruz, with their incipient nationalism. That nationalism found its theatrical expression in the late eighteenth and early nineteenth centuries with the construction of lavish colosseum theatres from *Mexico City to *Santiago de Chile, which were built for the self-aggrandizement of the colonial authorities (whose names they frequently bore) and to demonstrate that the colonies could create theatrical spaces as beautiful as anything Europe could produce.

Such theatres quickly became the site of *political discourse with works performed both by those who yearned for independence and by those who strove to maintain colonial domination. While the authorities sought to dazzle and divert the *audience with the opulence of the theatres and a series of harmless entertainments, a number of *neoclassically oriented, journalistically formed, and politically astute creole playwrights saw the theatre as a powerful weapon for Latin American independence. One instance of theatre linked to political ambition was the Teatro Tacón in *Havana, built at the beginning of the nineteenth century by the island's governor whose name it bears. Desiring to build the most impressive theatre in Latin America, Tacón levied a seventeen-peso tax on every slave imported into Cuba. The money collected, according to contemporary records with their marked tendency to overstate the theatre's grandeur, not only enabled him to construct a theatre containing 4,000 seats and 150 boxes, but left him sufficient funds to build the first railway across the island and erect drinking fountains throughout the capital. The introduction of African slaves into Cuba and elsewhere in the region would affect not only the physical design of the Teatro Tacón, but the theatrical content of subsequent performances as well, with the incorporation of African tribal rituals and *dances, and type *characters such as the *negrito.

Alongside the neoclassical theatre for the creole elite blossomed a series of popular theatre forms such as the *sainete, *costumbrismo, the teatro *gaucho, the *chingana, the teatro *bufo, and the drama rural that converted the inns, squares, and *circus tents of the popular classes into theatrical spaces presenting characters and events that reflected the *audience's own experience. These new forms reflected the growing gap between the creole elite now in power after independence and the masses who remained as politically and financially disenfranchised as they were under colonial rule. The gap between rich and poor was exacerbated at the turn of the twentieth century by a flood of immigrants from around the world into Latin America. Between 1871 and 1920 immigrants to *Buenos Aires alone numbered 4.5 million. The influx of new cultures, forms of speech and dress, and political ideas led to significant social and political unrest. This situation is reflected theatrically in the Argentine *grotesco criollo in the early twentieth century, as well as in the various forces that combined to create Juan Moreira, the seminal play of the teatro gaucho in the late nineteenth century.

Despite independence, the peoples of Latin America often perceived the region as economically and aesthetically inferior to Europe and North America, which remained the centres of power. Such perceptions began to change in the theatre in the 1920s. Following the Mexican Revolution the teatro de *masas movement sought to validate the new Mexican society through the creation of a performance style reminiscent of indigenous ritual and a celebration of the mixture of Spanish and indigenous cultures that formed the contemporary Mexican state. Elsewhere throughout the region a series of university-affiliated and independent theatre groups were formed. The organizational structure of these groups and the production style they adopted differed greatly, but their central concern was the forging of a specifically Latin American theatrical consciousness capable of speaking to and for the various countries in the region. This can be seen in the work of playwrights as varied as Elena Álvarez, Mauricio *Magdaleno, and Rodolfo *Usigli in Mexico, Germán Luco Cruchaga in Chile, or Samuel Eichelbaum in Argentina. The Mexican independent and university-affiliated groups such as the Grupo de los Siete, Teatro de *Orientación, Teatro de *Ulises, and Teatro de Ahora, or the Chilean Teatro Experimental were matched by the Argentine Teatro del Pueblo and Teatro B. Justo, the Cuban Teatro Adad, and numerous university-affiliated groups in Puerto Rico. From their ranks came playwrights such as Isidora *Aguirre, Egon *Wolff, Emilio *Carballido, Osvaldo *Dragún, Virgilio Piñera, and René *Marqués. These artists, along with a host of actors, directors, and designers, sought to build a socially conscious Latin American theatre through a radical restructuring of history, ritual, and mythology.

The critique of the political and social context continued into the 1960s and 1970s with the appearance of various forms of *liberation theatre throughout the region. Springing from the conditions caused by the immense disparity between rich and poor, based upon the consciousness-raising techniques of the Brazilian educator Paulo Freire, liberation theatre attempted to discover the needs and interests of a given community rather than impose external notions of what was important upon it. Sharing the daily lives and tribulations of their audience, these theatre practitioners sought to discover theatrical forms that allow their communities to find their own voices, rather than speaking to them in a way that mirrored the patronizing attitude of centuries of colonial oppression. Some of the best known of these practitioners are Santiago *García and Enrique *Buenaventura in Colombia, Alan *Bolt in Nicaragua, Candelario Reyes in Honduras, and Augusto *Boal in Brazil.

In the latter half of the twentieth century Latin America entered a period of political upheaval. From the CIA-sponsored overthrow of Jacobo Arbenz in Guatemala in 1954 to the Cuban Revolution in 1958, from a series of brutal civil wars in Central America during the 1970s and 1980s to a series of military coups d'état in South America during the same period, a number of events combined to alter the relationship between theatre and society. Latin American theatre increasingly engaged with *politics, with direct consequences for the livelihood and lives of its artists. As the theatre sought to place its mark upon society, its practitioners incurred governmental wrath in the form of *censorship, imprisonment, and forced exile. The Uruguayan playwright and Tupamaro guerrilla leader Mauricio *Rosencof and the Brazilian director and playwright Augusto Boal were imprisoned and tortured. Important companies such as Uruguay's El *Galpón or Chile's Teatro *Aleph were forced into exile. Numerous theatre artists from across the region destroyed their personal records and libraries in order to erase trails of association as they fled the region.

Under such conditions theatre artists fought to maintain the artistic quality and political and social relevance of their work. Metaphorical representations of contemporary events were presented in productions that emphasized simplicity and aesthetic beauty. Classical texts such as Lope de Vega's *Fuente Ovejuna* were reworked as critiques of totalitarian regimes. Theatrical expression frequently made use of encoded forms of speech or images immediately comprehensible to both actor and audience in order to evade censorship and to comment upon contemporary events. Demanding an end to military repression in Argentina the playwright Osvaldo Dragún organized a host of Argentine theatre artists in a celebration of theatre and life, as opposed to dictatorship and death, called Teatro *Abierto. Representative of these strategic approaches is the work of Argentinian playwrights such as Ricardo *Monti, Griselda *Gambaro, and Eduardo *Pavlovsky, as well as Chilean playwrights Isidora Aguirre and Juan *Radrigán.

The late 1980s and early 1990s were a period of disorientation and dislocation. With the decline of dictatorship throughout the region, theatre practitioners were left searching for themes, forms, and techniques appropriate to the new context. No longer conceiving itself as a site of resistance to dictatorship, the theatre seemed confused about its identity, and a veritable explosion of performance styles and theatrical forms resulted. In very general terms these styles and forms can be linked to the cultural history of the region itself. Three main groups emerged that could be broadly defined as (*a*) those countries formed by a shared heritage in the great pre-Columbian civilizations such as the Aztec, the Maya, and the Inca; (*b*) those countries—largely in South America—with a historically significant history of European immigration; and (*c*) Brazil and the Caribbean countries where active trading in black African slaves during the colonial period has greatly influenced the nature of society.

These categories were reflected in theatrical investigation of historically important figures in the separate countries, or of popular forms such as the *tango in Argentina, the *murga* in Uruguay, or *African aesthetics, religion, and philosophies in Cuba and Brazil. By the early twenty-first century such investigation displayed a greater anthropological understanding of Latin America itself. A new sense of an established identity en-

abled the theatre to borrow from global theatrical forms in order to raise the level of its own practice. While the political orientation of the latter half of the twentieth century was not discarded, its doctrinaire qualities were abandoned as the theatre incorporated a greater sense of magic, sacrament, and just plain fun. Consequently the most prevalent tendency in Latin American theatre at the start of the new millennium was an emphasis upon experimentation with scenic space intimately connected to Latin American culture and society. Examples are as varied as the Colombian company Barco Ebrio's production *Crápula mácula*, that explored contemporary Colombian society through a performance style drawing upon Japanese *nō and *bunraku, the Mexican Grupo Espiral's *Nahui Ollin* (*The Fifth Sun*), which blended South-East Asian *shadow puppetry with indigenous codexes, or the Cuban Teatro Escambray's *Paloma Negra* (*Black Dove*), with its sophisticated theatre of images. All clearly demonstrated the continued vibrancy of theatre throughout the region.   AV

ALBUQUERQUE, S., *Violent Acts: a study of contemporary Latin American theatre* (Detroit, 1991)

DE COSTA, ELENA, *Collaborative Latin American Popular Theatre: from theory to form, from text to stage* (New York, 1992)

TAYLOR, DIANA, *Theatre of Crisis: drama and politics in Latin America* (Lexington, Mass., 1991)

VERSÉNYI, ADAM, *Theatre in Latin America: religion, politics, and culture from Cortes to the 1980s* (Cambridge, 1993)

WEISS, JUDITH, et al., *Latin American Popular Theatre* (Albuquerque, N. Mex., 1993)

LAUBE, HEINRICH (1806–84)

German dramatist, critic, and director. Laube first came to prominence as a journalist and member of the radical writers' group Junges Deutschland. He was imprisoned in 1837 for political activities and his writings were banned. By the time he became a member of the 1848 Frankfurt National Assembly, his political views had mellowed and his interests were chiefly focused on the stage. From 1849 to 1867 he was *artistic director of the *Burgtheater in *Vienna, where he was a proponent of *realistic staging and paid utmost attention to textual fidelity. He combated virtuoso *acting, encouraging actors to play to each other rather than the *audience. He discouraged the opulent *scenery popular at the time, considering it a distraction from the *text. He also wrote many plays, the most interesting of which is *Die Karlsschüler* (1846), dealing with *Schiller's school years and the writing of *The Robbers*. His writings on the theatre were also influential, especially the *Briefe über das deutsche Theater* (1846–7) and his history of the Burgtheater (1868).   CBB

LAUDA

A medieval poem in praise of God and the saints, set to music and sung in *chorus. The earliest examples date from thirteenth-century Umbria and were performed by lay religious *confraternite*. It developed into the *lauda drammatica*, conceived in the form of *dialogue, which lent itself to theatrical performances.   GGE

LAUDER, HARRY (1870–1950)

Scottish actor. Born in Edinburgh, Lauder became the highest-paid performer of his time as an international *music-hall star. After working in a flax mill and in coal mines, he created a sensation in *London in 1900, perfecting *monologues, and a wide variety of broadly drawn Scottish caricatures, and singing Scottish songs. Some of the songs he wrote himself, including his signature tunes 'Roamin' in the Gloamin' ' and 'I Love a Lassie'. Knighted in 1919 for his part in organizing troop entertainments during the First World War, Lauder's act appealed not just to the domestic market but to the Scottish *diaspora and beyond, and he *toured to the USA, Canada, and Australia almost annually from 1907. He wrote three volumes of autobiography: *A Minstrel in France* (1918), *Between You and Me* (1919), and *Roamin' in the Gloamin'* (1928).   AS

LAUGHTER

Indication, by sound or action, of amusement. Laughter is the expected response of the *audience to a comic moment or *scene and evidence that the *comedy has been successful. Dramatic *theories of comedy have necessarily paid attention to laughter as one of the *genre's key objectives. Cicero provides considerable discussion of the rhetorical strategies that might stimulate laughter in the hearer through particular uses of language. Theorists of the theatre add the effects of dramatic action to those of language as the causes for laughter. The *Tractatus Coislinianus* (a tenth-century document but generally believed to be a work of late Greek or early Roman origin) considers laughter to be the cathartic effect of comedy, purging the emotions. Laughter at the expense of the wrongdoer or fool is the means of restoring appropriate social *decorum in a comedy.

Early eighteenth-century dramatic theorists debated the specificities of laughter following from Thomas Hobbes's claim that comic pleasures came from a sense of intellectual security relative to the experience of others. Thus comedy was seen as morally bankrupt and laughter merely the result of ridicule. Instead of the ridicule of comic *characters, Richard *Steele argued for more sober and polite 'mirth'. With the comedies of *Terence as his examples, Steele suggested a reform of comedy that would take as its goal sympathy and admiration rather than ridicule, sentiment rather than laughter. George Meredith's essay 'On the Idea of Comedy' (1877) categorizes the 'powers of laughter' into various sub-groups: *satire, irony, and humour. Satire is the cruellest because it affords so little sympathy with the object of the laughter, whereas humour is the kindest and

the pity it can evoke may even be strong enough to dispel laughter altogether. Meredith claims that the most successful comedy 'shall awaken thoughtful laughter'.

Philosopher Henri Bergson's discussion of laughter in 'Le Rire' (first published in the *Revue de Paris* in 1900) has been particularly influential. Bergson claims, 'To understand laughter, we must put it back into its natural environment, which is society, and above all must we determine the utility of its function, which is a social one. . . . Laughter must answer to certain requirements of life in common. It must have a *social* signification.' In Bergson's analysis, laughter is a weapon used by society to intimidate others and he concludes by describing it as 'a froth with a saline base'—initially pleasurable but ultimately bitter-tasting. Laughter occasionally takes place on stage as a reaction to moments of extreme *tragedy and horror (what Freud might describe as a defence mechanism). Some of the most famous examples appear in *early modern plays—in Shakespeare's *Titus Andronicus*, confronted with the severed heads of two of his sons, the rape and mutilation of his daughter, as well as his own severed hand, Titus responds to his brother's threats with the line 'Ha, ha, ha!' Asked by Marcus (his brother) why he laughs, Titus responds, 'Why, I have not another tear to shed.' *See also* APPLAUSE.   SBe

LAUGHTON, CHARLES (1899–1962)

English actor and director. Identified principally with *film, he had a distinguished stage career especially in the period from 1926 to 1936. He worked with Theodore *Komisarjevsky in his groundbreaking seasons of Russian plays at the Barnes Theatre in 1926, and made his first appearance in *New York in 1931 as Hercule Poirot in an adaptation of Agatha *Christie's *The Alibi*. He returned to England in 1933 to act at the *Old Vic under Tyrone *Guthrie, playing Angelo in *Measure for Measure*, Prospero in *The Tempest*, Macbeth, and Canon Chasuble in *Wilde's *The Importance of Being Earnest*. From 1932 he spent most of his time in America creating the roles on film for which he became famous, including Bligh in *Mutiny on the Bounty* (1935) and Quasimodo in *The Hunchback of Notre Dame* (1940). In later life his most distinguished stage contributions were his collaboration with *Brecht on the first production in English of *The Life of Galileo* (*Los Angeles, 1947) and his own production of *The Caine Mutiny Court Martial* (New York, 1954). Laughton revelled in fleshy, often cruel parts which allowed him to demonstrate his abilities as a *character actor oscillating between sensuality and vulnerability.   VEE

LAURENTS, ARTHUR (1918–   )

American playwright, librettist, and director. After a half-hearted career as a salesman, Laurents reached Broadway with his first play, *The Home of the Brave* (1945). Subsequent successes included *The Time of the Cuckoo* (1952) and *A Clearing in the Woods* (1957). At the same time he was writing screenplays for Hollywood *films, including *Rope* (1948) and *Anastasia* (1956). His career took yet another direction when he wrote the libretto for two successful *musicals: *West Side Story* (1957) and *Gypsy* (1959). As he continued writing plays and screenplays, he also began to direct, starting with his own play, *Invitation to a March* (1960). In 1962 he began directing musicals with *I Can Get It for You Wholesale*, continuing with *Anyone Can Whistle* (1964), for which he also wrote the libretto. Further screenplays include *The Way We Were* (1973) and *The Turning Point* (1977), while additional plays are *The Radical Mystique* and *My Good Name* (both 1997).   JD

LAUTENSCHLÄGER, KARL (1843–1906)

German stage technician. Following in the footsteps of his father Karl Brandt, Lautenschläger worked as a stage machinist in Darmstadt, Riga, and Stuttgart. In 1883 he joined the *Munich Court Theatre as head stage technician, where he remained until retirement in 1902. Here he introduced electric *lighting in 1883, the first such installation in Germany. His most famous invention was a *revolving stage powered by an electric motor (*Drehbühne*). A large disc set into the existing stage was divided into segments which could be changed out of sight of the *audience, and within seconds a new setting could be brought into view. First demonstrated in 1896 at the *Residenztheater, the system effectively replaced *scene shifting by sliding *flats. Lautenschläger also developed a Shakespearian stage together with Jocza *Savits, which was first presented in 1889.

                                                         CBB

LAVELLI, JORGE (1931–   )

Argentinian director. Trained as an actor in *Buenos Aires' independent theatre movement, Lavelli went to *Paris on a scholarship in 1960, winning recognition three years later for his staging of *Gombrowicz's *The Wedding*. His name has since been associated with highly visual, *ritualistic productions of plays by *Arrabal, *Ionesco, Shakespeare, and *Goethe, but also the works of fellow Argentinian expatriate *Copi (including *Diary of a Dreamer*, 1967, and *An Inopportune Visit*, 1988). In the 1970s Lavelli began staging *operas. He relies on an aesthetic closer to *Beckett than *Brecht, privileging situations over words, truth over verisimilitude, and *theatricality over *text. After 25 years of nomadic freelancing, Lavelli directed France's new Théâtre Nationale de la Colline from 1987 until his retirement in 1997. He continues to work in Buenos Aires and other major cities and to direct his long-lived troupe Méchant Théâtre.

                                                         JGJ

LAWLER, RAY (1921–   )

Australian playwright, actor, and director. Lawler started writing plays as well as acting and directing with the *Melbourne Union Theatre Repertory Company. He is best known for the ninth of his sixteen plays, *The Summer of the Seventeenth Doll* (1955), which was an enormous success in Australia before transferring to *London's West End. Later *filmed and staged as an *opera, this work is a *realistic, *well-made play famous for its Australian story, *characters, and vernacular. Lawler eventually wrote two prequels, *Kid Stakes* and *Other Times*. He was director and *dramaturg for the Melbourne Theatre Company until 1987.   SBS

LAWRENCE, D. H. (DAVID HERBERT) (1885–1930)

English novelist, dramatist, and poet. Only two of Lawrence's eight plays were produced in his lifetime, *The Widowing of Mrs Holroyd* (1910, produced 1920), a *realist study of a mining community, and his last play *David* (1927), a biblical epic. Five of the other plays were written before 1914 and explore concerns similar to his autobiographical novel *Sons and Lovers* (1913), while *Touch and Go* (1919) drew upon and anticipated the publication of his novel *Women in Love* (1921). Lawrence's plays were revived after a successful performance of his first play *A Collier's Friday Night* (1906) at the *Royal Court in *London in 1965. Two years later the same company produced *The Daughter-in-Law* (1912), and in 1968 presented a season of these two plays with *The Widowing of Mrs Holroyd*. The *comedies *The Merry-Go-Round* (1910) and *The Fight for Barbara* (1912) were first performed in 1973 and 1967 respectively.   SF

LAWRENCE, GERTRUDE (1898–1952)

English singer, dancer, and comedy actress who had a glittering career, chiefly in the USA. She appeared in *musicals, plays, and minor *revues in *London before she joined André Charlot's revues in 1916, making her Broadway debut in 1924 in one of these. In 1926 she starred in George and Ira *Gershwin's *Oh, Kay!* (1926), which transferred to London the next year, and in 1928 appeared in their *Treasure Girl*. Her signature performance was as Amanda in Noël *Coward's *Private Lives* (1931), a role written for her, which she played opposite Coward's Elyot and *Olivier's Victor. Her greatest triumph was as Liza Elliot in the Moss *Hart–Kurt *Weill musical *Lady in the Dark* (1941). Her last stage role was in *The King and I* (1951). She appeared in a handful of *films, including a memorable performance as Amanda Wingfield in *The Glass Menagerie* (1950).   AS

LAWRENCE, JEROME (1915–) AND ROBERT E. LEE (1918–94)

American playwrights and educators. Lawrence and Lee formed a writing partnership in 1942. Prominent in dramatic writing for *radio, they made their Broadway debut with the *musical *Look, Ma, I'm Dancin'!* (1948). Their next theatrical work was *Inherit the Wind* (1955), presented at Margo *Jones's Theatre '55 in Dallas and quickly produced on Broadway. They scored another success in their adaptation of *Auntie Mame* (1956), and a major triumph in 1966 with the musical *Mame*. Their anti-war play *The Night Thoreau Spent in Jail* (1970) was widely produced across the United States through the American Playwrights Theatre, founded by Lawrence and Lee in 1966 as an alternative to the commercial theatre. Their final success was *First Monday in October* (1978). A strong social consciousness is apparent in all Lawrence and Lee plays: freedom of speech and thought in *Inherit the Wind* and *The Night Thoreau Spent in Jail*, *censorship issues as the driving force in *First Monday in October*. Both taught playwriting at universities in *Los Angeles in the last three decades of the twentieth century. AW

LAWSON, JOHN HOWARD (1895–1977)

American playwright and *theorist. Lawson's *Processional* (1925) was a left-wing 'political *vaudeville' set during a West Virginia coal miners' strike. The successful *Theatre Guild production introduced *epic theatre techniques to the mainstream *audience. His *Loudspeaker* (1927) and *The International* (1928), written for the radical New Playwrights Theatre, continued his experiments with theatrical form and socialist ideology. *Success Story* (1932), *The Pure in Heart*, and *Gentlewoman* (both 1934) were *realistic plays produced by the Group Theatre and written under the influence of Communist Party directives toward *socialist realism. Lawson refused to testify against others before the House Un-American Activities Committee and served a one-year prison term, 1950–1. His *Theory and Technique of Playwriting* (1936) emphasized the conflict between a *protagonist and his or her society. MAF

LAYA, JEAN-LOUIS (1761–1833)

French dramatist. Laya emerged from the decent mediocrity of his previous works, the *tragedy *Jean Calas* (1789) and the *drame *Les Dangers de l'opinion* (1790), to produce, in his *didactic *comedy *L'Ami des lois* (*Friend of the Law*, 1793), a play which had the greatest impact of any written during the revolutionary period. Adopting the *plot structure of *Molière's *Femmes savantes*, it features two Jacobin impostors, Nomophage (= Robespierre) and Duricrâne (probably Marat). This pro-Girondin attack led to the closing of the theatre and the arrest of the actors; Laya, who had the courage to defend his play before the Paris Commune, escaped punishment. WDH

LAZARENKO, VITALY (1890–1939)

Russian/Soviet *circus artist renowned for his *acrobatic skills and eccentric political *satire, whose career began in 1898. His *Moscow debut was in 1914, and he later performed with his own troupe at the Civil War front. A friend of *Mayakovsky's, Lazarenko made a guest appearance in 'the first Soviet play', Mayakovsky's *Mystery-Bouffe*, directed by *Meyerhold in *St Petersburg in 1918. Lazarenko also starred in a play for circus performance, *The Universal Class Struggle Championship*, which Mayakovsky wrote especially for him. He took part in political demonstrations, usually with a loud hailer and mounted on stilts, and he made *film appearances. NW

LAZZO (PLURAL: *LAZZI*)

Italian jargon term from *commedia dell'arte*, possibly derived from a word meaning a 'lace' or 'link': its meaning might be rendered in English as 'gag', 'number', 'act', or 'routine'. The word emerged during the seventeenth century, and is found in manuscript collections of *scenarios denoting some form of pre-prepared joke—its details will rarely be explained in the scenario *text, because it is assumed that the performers know already what any given *lazzo* involves. Either a particular mask is given the opportunity to come up with material from his/her own repertoire (for instance '*Zanni does his *lazzo . . .*'); or else a brief shorthand reference (such as 'the *lazzo* of the sponge . . .') is enough to remind performers of what is involved. Such evidence as we possess suggests that a *lazzo* could be anything from a one-line gag to a complex physical or verbal routine involving many players, which would need separate *rehearsal; but all cases would have implied drawing on a stock of items already stored in the memory, rather than inventing something from scratch while on stage. Attempts by scholars, at a distance, to distinguish *lazzi* rigorously from material which advanced the stage *plot can sometimes be exaggerated. No doubt there were many separate routines, transferable from one play to another; but *dialogue which contributed to the narrative could also be composed of well-tried and well-memorized units. Composition by and around *lazzi* simply confirms the fragmentary nature of much performed *comedy, which *commedia dell'arte*, constructed from stock repertoire, tended to emphasize. RAA

LEADING MAN AND LADY

In England and America, the actors who played the most important male and female *characters in a play in a *stock company. Frequently these actors, especially in *touring and provincial companies, were husband and wife. Hamlet, Richard III, and Shylock would have been taken by the leading man; Lady Macbeth, Beatrice, and Jane Shore by the leading lady. These two did not specialize in *character types as did the rest of the stock company; their prominence was such that they assumed the leading roles, irrespective of age or the nature of their parts. *See also* LINES OF BUSINESS.   MRB

LEBEAU, SUZANNE (1948–)

Québec playwright and director. The foremost author of drama for *youth in French Canada (much of it translated and staged abroad), she was trained in Québec, in *Paris, and Poland (studying *mime and *puppet theatre) before co-founding in 1975 *Montréal's Le Carrousel, devoted specifically to children's theatre. There all her plays have been staged, including *Une lune entre deux maisons* (1979), translated and performed in English (*A Moon between Two Houses*, 1981), Spanish, Portuguese, Catalan, Flemish, and Polish. Her *characters recreate the wonder of childhood as they explore the risks and rewards of the real and imaginary worlds.   LED

LECOMPTE, ELIZABETH (1941–)

American director. As *artistic director of the *New York-based *Wooster Group, LeCompte is a major figure in international theatre practice. She was born in New Jersey and studied painting at Skidmore College; she says that she still considers herself as much a visual artist as a theatrical one. After college she became involved with Spalding *Gray. They moved to New York where Gray's connection with the *Open Theatre under Joseph *Chaikin spurred LeCompte's interest in theatre; in 1970 both joined Richard *Schechner's *Performance Group. LeCompte was heavily influenced by Schechner's use of multiple materials and sources, from books and *films to the actors' own experiences, to create his performance pieces. Growing disillusioned with Schechner, in 1974 LeCompte, Gray, and other Performance Group members started creating their own work; in 1980 when the Performance Group disbanded LeCompte and her company formed the Wooster Group. Non-linear and sensorially dense, LeCompte's productions emphasize process over a finished product—she banned reviews of Wooster Group shows until the late 1990s—and have generated significant controversy. *Route 1 & 9* re-enacted blackface *minstrel routines against passages from Thornton *Wilder's *Our Town* and resulted in the company being censured by the New York State Council on the Arts for their 'harsh and caricatured portrayals of a racial minority', even though the group insisted that part of their project was to expose *racism.   KF

LE CONTE, VALLERAN (fl. 1590–c.1628)

French *actor-manager. Perhaps the best documented of the early French player-managers, he played biblical *tragedy, dramas by *Jodelle, and Italianate *farce—he was accounted a good lover—mainly in north-eastern France, before leasing the *Hôtel de Bourgogne in *Paris for the first time in 1599. He played intermittently at the Bourgogne until at least 1628, probably offering a repertory of tragedy and *tragicomedy by house playwright Alexandre *Hardy, whose new literary drama he had championed since the 1590s. Valleran was succeeded as troupe leader by *Bellerose, who had trained as his apprentice.   JG

LECOQ, JACQUES (1921–99)

French teacher and *theorist. Beginning as a teacher of physical education, Lecoq became one of the world's most influential theatre teachers in the second half of the twentieth century. Continuing the work of Jacques *Copeau's École du *Vieux-Colombier (which he learned from Jean *Dasté), Lecoq emphasized the use of *masks in actor *training. He taught for eight years in Italy, first in Padua, where he studied masks with Amleto Sartori, and later in *Milan, where he founded (with Giorgio *Strehler) the school of the *Piccolo Teatro. Lecoq's school in *Paris was a magnet for students of *mime, *physical theatre, and masks from 1956 until his death. There he developed the use of the 'neutral mask', a concept he learned from Dasté, and, still following Copeau's example, brought the *clown back into the theatre. While not primarily a performer, Lecoq's work demonstration entitled 'Everything Moves' was considered by many to be a brilliant piece of theatre. His influential students included Ariane *Mnouchkine of Théâtre du *Soleil, Simon *McBurney of Theatre de *Complicité, and the Swiss masked troupe Mummenchanz. His widow and long-time collaborator Faye Lecoq continues the school in Paris.   TL

LECOUVREUR, MLLE (ADRIENNE COUVREUR) (1692–1730)

French actress. Spotted in an *amateur production by the actor-dramatist Marc-Antoine Legrand, Mlle Lecouvreur played in the provinces and at the court of the Duc de Lorraine, before being admitted to the *Comédie-Française in 1717. She turned her slight build, frail constitution, and limited vocal range to advantage, developing a playing style in which emotional sincerity and simplicity of expression supplanted the traditional sing-song artificiality and howling. Seeing in her a kindred spirit anxious to emphasize the emotional content of a *text rather than form, Michel *Baron emerged from retirement in 1720 to act with her for eight years. But while he was occasionally charged with familiarity, she 'never descended below heroic grandeur'; she was also commended for her 'silent *acting' and 'ability to listen onstage'. Although she played regularly in *comedy—for example, in *Molière, *Marivaux, and Alexis *Piron—her real talent was for the *tragedies of *Racine, Pierre *Corneille, and contemporaries *Crébillon and *Voltaire. Her most frequently performed role was that of Constance in Houdart de La Motte's *Inès de Castro* (1723). She died in the arms of *Voltaire, a fervent admirer whose Artémire (1720) and Mariamne (*Hérode et Mariamne*, 1724) she had created, and the Maréchal-Comte Maurice de Saxe, who had been her lover since 1720. Despite her celebrity, since she had not renounced her profession she was refused Christian burial by the curé of Saint-Sulpice and her body cast into a Seine-side lime-pit. An appalled Voltaire compared her treatment to that of Anne *Oldfield, whom the English buried the same year—in Westminster Abbey.   JG

LEE, CANADA (LEONARD CONEGATA) (1907–52)

*African-American actor, who was a boxer and musician before turning to the stage. While leading a band in 1934, he auditioned for a Harlem production of *Brother Mose*, and later played Banquo in Orson *Welles's *'voodoo' *Macbeth* for the Harlem Unit of the *Federal Theatre Project (1936). Several other *New York roles followed, including one in *Stevedore*, as the Emperor Christophe in *Haiti* (1938), and, on Broadway with Ethel *Waters, in *Mamba's Daughters* (1939). Two years later he achieved great critical success as Bigger Thomas in the stage version of Richard Wright's *Native Son*, a role that stands as an indicator of Lee's commitment to *political theatre and social causes. In classical works he was Caliban in Margaret *Webster's production of *The Tempest* (1945) and Bosola (in whiteface) in *The Duchess of Malfi* (1946). His last great role was on *film, as the lead in *Cry the Beloved Country* (1951).
                                                                    BBL

LEE, EUGENE (1939–   )

American set and *lighting designer. After an early affiliation with Andre *Gregory in *Philadelphia, Lee began a career-long partnership with director Adrian Hall as resident designer at *Trinity Repertory Company, at Dallas Theatre Centre, and elsewhere. Among their dozens of collaborations was Amiri *Baraka's *Slave Ship* (1969) at Chelsea Theater Center in *New York. Lee pioneered an iconoclastic and innovative approach to design that rejected *illusionistic *scenery in favour of rough-hewn environments that emphasized the intimacy of the actor–*audience relationship. His designs use raw, natural materials—unpainted wood, scrap metal, dirt—and ramps, catwalks, scaf-

folding, and platforms to create multiple playing areas that penetrate or surround the *auditorium. For Peter *Brook, he designed *Orghast* (1971) at the Shiraz Festival in Iran and *Handke's *Kaspar* (1980) in *Paris. He won Tony *awards for the Broadway productions of *Candide* (1974) and *Sweeney Todd* (1979), both directed by Harold *Prince. In *television, Lee created the trademark industrial set for NBC's *Saturday Night Live* and served for many years as the show's production designer.   STC

LEE, HUGH (1955–   )

Taiwanese playwright, director, and actor. After a successful early career as a stage performer and *television comedian, Lee founded the Ping-Fong Acting Troupe in 1986 and started writing and directing his own work. He had written close to 40 plays and 100 television scripts by the year 2000. Most of his plays are *satirical *comedies about urgent social and *political issues. Zany in argument, irreverent in tone, stirring in effect, and with the *dialogue and *action criss-crossing the realms of *farce and the *absurd, Lee's productions—at once prizewinners and *box-office successes—have popularized the theatre in Taiwan. With the profits thus made, Lee set up Ping-Fong branches outside Taipei and runs training courses in order to help 'lay a strong foundation for Taiwan theatre'. Lee has taken his productions on overseas *tours since 1992. Particularly well received have been *National Salvation Corporation Ltd.* (1991), *The Classified* (1992, in which he played 22 *characters), *West of Yangkuan* (1994), and *Shamlet* (1994, 1996), a *parody of Shakespeare.   MPYC

LEE, MING CHO (1930–   )

American designer. Born in Shanghai, Lee entered America on a student visa in 1949, eventually moving to *New York as apprentice and later as assistant in Jo *Mielziner's studio. His first credits were in *regional theatre and *Off-Broadway. In 1962 his work was introduced on Broadway in *The Moon Besieged*, but he was able to develop his own style when he became resident designer for the *New York Shakespeare Festival in the same year, a position he held for more than a decade. With low budgets for *scenery, Lee created sets that were sculptural and textural, using natural materials consciously and forcefully, avoiding the painted pictorial in favour of *environmental settings. He placed the actor in stage space rather than against or before *illusionistic scenery. His style broke new ground, particularly in classic plays, Shakespeare, and *opera. Lee has moved easily from Broadway to noted regional theatre companies (*Arena Stage, *Guthrie Theatre, *Oregon Shakespeare Festival, *Seattle Repertory Theatre, *Long Wharf Theatre, *Mark Taper Forum), and important opera companies in America and Europe. As a teacher since 1968 at the *Yale School of Drama, he has influenced a generation of young American

designers. Among the high achievements of his career have been his designs for *Little Murders* (1967) and *K2* (1983) on Broadway; *Electra* (1964) and *Hair* (1967) for the New York Shakespeare Festival; *Angels in America* (1996) for the Dallas Theatre Center; and *Khovanschchina* (1985) for the *Metropolitan Opera.
MCH

LEE, NATHANIEL (c.1648–1692)

English playwright. After a brief acting career (1672–3), Lee turned to playwriting and between 1674 and 1683 produced, besides two plays in collaboration with *Dryden, eleven *tragedies marked by rapid and bloody *action, emotional tension, and spectacular stage effects. Failures were equally interspersed with popular successes. *Lucius Junius Brutus* (1680), arguably his finest play, was banned on political grounds after six performances. *The Princess of Cleve* (1680–3) was a savage attack on *heroic drama and sex *comedy. *The Rival Queens* (1677), Lee's greatest success, is a relatively restrained blank *verse tragedy whose contrasted female *characters, acted among others by Elizabeth *Barry and Anne *Bracegirdle, were echoed in Dryden's *All for Love* (1677), and became a dramatic stock-in-trade. Lee spent four of his last six years insane and died in obscurity.
RWV

LEE, ROBERT E. *See* LAWRENCE, JEROME.

LE GALLIENNE, EVA (1899–1991)

American actress, director, producer, and translator. Born in London (the daughter of the poet Richard Le Gallienne) and trained at Beerbohm *Tree's *acting academy, Le Gallienne went to the United States in 1915. She achieved fame starring in the *Theatre Guild production of *Molnár's *Liliom* (1921) and continued as a leading Broadway actress until founding the *Civic Repertory Theatre in 1926. She disliked the serial quality of commercial theatre, which she compared to an 'Indian totem pole, never growing in stature but merely gaining in the number of new grimaces carved on its surface'. This ambitious company, often featuring Le Gallienne in leading roles, her *direction, or her translations of *Ibsen and *Chekhov, presented 37 plays between 1926 and 1936 when its chronic financial shortfalls forced closure. Le Gallienne went on to co-found two other short-lived *repertory companies, to act in *regional productions and *tours, and to perform on Broadway in star vehicles such as the 1961 revival of Maxwell *Anderson's *Elizabeth the Queen* (1930). Her last appearance was in a 1982 revival of her adaptation of *Alice in Wonderland* (1932). She wrote a biography of Eleanore *Duse and two volumes of memoirs. She was *awarded a special Tony for lifetime achievement in 1964 and the National Medal of Arts in 1986.
MAF

LEGAULT, ÉMILE (1906–83)

French-Canadian director and *manager, founder of the most influential troupe in Québec, Les Compagnons de Saint-Laurent (1937–52). Profoundly influenced by the ideas of *Copeau, *Dullin, *Baty, Ghéon, and others while studying in *Paris (1938–9) he resolved to implement their *theories and techniques on his return to Canada. With Legault as catalyst, the Compagnons—initially an *amateur troupe—became the central source of renewal for French-Canadian theatre, providing *training for most of the professional actors, directors, and technicians who would enrich francophone theatre for the next two generations.
LED

LEGIDO, JUAN CARLOS (1923–)

Uruguayan playwright, poet, and professor of art and theatre history. He achieved a high intellectual profile in the 1950s but was eclipsed during the repression of the military dictatorship when he went into exile to Argentina and Spain (1973–80). His work is chiefly *realistic with elements of the poetic, exploring national identity, social responsibilities, and cultural traditions, including the *tango and the Jewish experience of exile in Uruguay after the Second World War. A sample of his plays ranges from *La lámpara* (*The Lamp*, 1952) to *Veraneo* (*Summer Holiday*, 1961) and *Historia de judíos* (*The Story of the Jews*, 1968).
JCC

LEGITIMATE DRAMA

A term applied in the first half of the nineteenth century to English 'traditional' *drama. The 1737 *Licensing Act specified that only *Drury Lane and *Covent Garden could perform spoken drama. By the late eighteenth and early nineteenth centuries other *London theatres had sprung up which were permitted to play 'illegitimate' drama: *dumb show, *melodrama, *musical pieces, *burletta. The 'legitimate' meant, in contrast, Shakespeare, *Jonson, and the older dramatists, and new *tragedies, *comedies, and *farces, all 'regular' forms going back to the sixteenth and seventeenth centuries. Conservative *critics considered it to be the true English drama, and the 'illegitimate' was decried as debasing the heritage of Shakespeare, Jonson, and *Sheridan. After 1843 and the Theatres Regulation Act, whereby any theatre could play any kind of drama it wished, subject to the *censorship powers of the *Lord Chamberlain, the distinction between 'legitimate' and 'illegitimate' ceased to have any meaning. *See also* PATENT THEATRES; MINOR THEATRES.
MRB

LEGONG

Classical Balinese dramatic *dance performed by two or three pre-pubescent girls. According to court chronicles, it was created by royal commission in the late eighteenth century. It combines elements of older traditions, taking music, choreography, and story material from *gambuh, and movement vocabulary from the trance-dance *sanghyang dedari. The story typically centres on an episode of the *Panji tale in which Princess Rangka Sari is kidnapped by King Lasem. The dancers do not speak; the *text is delivered by singers, accompanied by the *gamelan pelegongan orchestra. Dancers are dressed in tightly wrapped skirts and elaborate headdresses. Outstanding features are expressive eye movements and the use of fans with the fast, precise dance movements. A full *legong* performance consists of a complex introductory dance by the maid *character (*condong*), followed by the dramatic dance between Princess and King, and an abstract closing dance. Originally a court tradition, it became popular in the villages in the twentieth century and is performed during temple festivals. Shorter versions of *legong*, often performed by adult women, have become popular for tourist entertainment. *See also* INDONESIA. KP

LEGUIZAMO, JOHN (1964–   )

Latin American actor and *performance artist. Born in Colombia, his family moved to *New York when he was 3. Overcoming difficulty in school he enrolled in *acting classes and eventually *trained at New York University. He worked in acting and stand-up comedy (his hero is comedian Richard Pryor) and gained recognition for his highly energetic *one-person shows *Mambo Mouth* (1991), *Spic-O-Rama* (1992), and *Freak* (1998), which send up stereotypes of America's minority cultures. Leguizamo has appeared in over twenty *films, including *To Wong Foo, Thanks for Everything, Julie Newmar* (1995), *William Shakespeare's Romeo and Juliet* (1996), and *Moulin Rouge* (2001). KF

LEGUIZAMÓN, MARTINIANO (1858–1935)

Argentinian playwright. Born in Entre Ríos, Leguizamón moved to *Buenos Aires to study law and work as journalist and educator. The author of many books, Leguizamón wrote only four plays; the best known is *Calandria* (1896), a picaresque *comedy tracing a gaucho's transformation from outlaw to ranch-hand. JGJ

LEICESTER'S MEN

The Earl of Leicester ran a company of *touring players from the late 1550s, using them to advertise his rising status in England. In 1574 the company's six sharers, who included James *Burbage and Robert *Wilson the clown, secured the first 'patent' or royal licence to travel the country. Their quality was evidently good. They received higher payments than other groups from the towns they visited, and three of the six were taken in 1583 to help form the new *Queen's Men. Burbage was not one of the three. By then he had built his *London *playhouse, the *Theatre, which may have housed the company when in London. The 1570s were their best time, if performances at court are any indication. When Leicester went to the Netherlands as Lord Governor and general, some of his players accompanied him. The English company ceased to exist when he died in 1588. AJG

LEIGH, MIKE (1943–   )

English dramatist and director. Leigh is particularly famed for his *improvisatory work with actors. The son of a doctor, he grew up in Salford, Lancashire. His first original play, *The Box Play*, grew out of improvisations at the Midland Art Centre in Birmingham. His *television plays for BBC include *Hard Labour* (1973), *Nuts in May* (1975), *Grown Ups* (1980), and *Four Days in July* (1984). He has made several *films for Channel 4, including *High Hopes*. An earlier feature film, *Bleak Moments*, was developed from a play originally performed at the Open Space Theatre, *London; other stage plays include *Babies Grow Old* (*Royal Shakespeare Company, 1974), *Abigail's Party* (1977), *Ecstasy* (1979), *Goose-Pimples* (1981), *Smelling a Rat* (1988) and *Greek Tragedy* (*Sydney, 1989). Other films include *Life Is Sweet* (1990), *Naked* (1993), *Secrets and Lies* (1995), *Career Girls* (1997), and *Topsy-Turvy* (1999), in the last of which Leigh's recurrent themes of repression and non-communication are placed in a historical milieu, for which late Victorian performances of *Gilbert and *Sullivan *opera are painstakingly reconstructed. JTD

LEIGH, VIVIEN (VIVIAN MARY HARTLEY) (1913–67)

English actress. Best known for winning an Academy award for her role as Scarlett O'Hara in *Gone with the Wind* (1939), and for her troubled marriage of two decades to Laurence *Olivier, Leigh was born in India, and briefly studied *acting in *Paris and at the *Royal Academy of Dramatic Art. Her first major success, which brought her instant fame, was her portrayal of Henriette in the première of *The Mask of Virtue* in *London. She subsequently performed in numerous productions with the *Old Vic company, as Ophelia in *Hamlet* (1937), Titania in *A Midsummer Night's Dream* (1937), Lady Teazle in *The School for Scandal* (1949), and Lady Anne in *Richard III* (1949). In 1949 she also appeared as Blanche Dubois in the London version of *A Streetcar Named Desire* and won her second Academy award for the Hollywood *film version (1951). Her performance as Lavinia in Peter *Brook's production of *Titus Andronicus* at Stratford (1955), opposite Olivier, was striking and unforgettable. TK

LEIGHTON, MARGARET (1922–76)

English actress who had a successful career as a leading lady in stage plays and *films and later easily adapted to roles of older eccentric and utterly knowing women. Trained for the stage from teenage years, in the 1940s Leighton joined the *Old Vic under *Olivier and *Richardson. She was in their première production of *Priestley's *An Inspector Calls* and part of the company that performed *Henry IV, Uncle Vanya, The Critic,* and *Oedipus* on Broadway, all in 1946. Later she returned to Broadway to appear in *Rattigan's *Separate Tables* (1956) and *Williams's *Night of the Iguana* (1961), winning Tony *awards for each production. Again on Broadway she appeared in *Slapstick Tragedy*, two *one-act plays by Williams (1966), and in Mike *Nichols's revival of *The Little Foxes* (1967). Leighton married three times: first to Max *Reinhardt, then to Laurence Harvey, and finally to Michael Wilding. Her screen career began in 1948 with *The Winslow Boy* and she was nominated for an Oscar for *The Go-Between* (1971).   AS

LEISEWITZ, JOHANN ANTON (1752–1806)

German dramatist. Leisewitz belonged to the *Sturm und Drang* movement, had close ties with *Lessing and *Goethe, but is remembered today for his *historical drama *Julius von Tarent* (1776), one of several plays of the period dealing with fratricide. Although no longer performed, it was highly regarded in the German repertoire in the 1770s and 1780s, influencing many dramatists including *Schiller, in his *The Bride of Messina*.   CBB

LEIVICK, H. (LEIVICK HALPERN) (1886–1962)

Russian-American poet and dramatist. After seven years in the Tsar's prisons for revolutionary activity, Leivick escaped in 1913 to settle in *New York, where he became a leading *Yiddish writer. He sympathized with labour, and two of his major plays are situated in the garment district: *Rags*, first produced by Maurice *Schwartz (1921), and *Shop*, produced by Jacob *Ben-Ami (1926), both of which became classics of the Yiddish stage. His plays on revolutionary themes include *Hirsch Leckert* (1928) and *Chains* (1930), but his best-known work is *The Golem*, about a medieval clay robot made by a Prague rabbi, which premièred in Hebrew translation at the *Habima Theatre (*Moscow, 1925). Plays written after the Second World War include *In the Days of Job, A Wedding in Fernwald,* and *The Miracle in the Warsaw Ghetto*.   EN

LEKAIN (HENRI-LOUIS CAIN) (1729–78)

French actor. Lekain was *Voltaire's protégé: his first and last performances, as a young *amateur in 1748 and as the century's leading tragedian in 1778, were in plays by the philosopher-playwright. During a 28-year career at the *Comédie-Française he played 178 roles in plays by 65 different authors. But Lekain—short, bow-legged, unattractive, with a harsh voice—was neither shaped for heroic or romantic roles, nor particularly inclined to comic ones. Rather his passionate, gestural playing style, marked by powerful pauses and eloquent business, drew him towards Voltaire's *melodramatic *tragedies, and he played in twenty of them, scoring spectacular successes as Gengis-Kan (*The Orphan of China*, 1755), Arsace (*Sémiramis*, 1748), and Orosmane (*Zaïre*, 1732). In the 1750s, with Mlle *Clairon's support, Lekain pioneered the introduction of a 'new *realism' in several aspects of stage production. He sought to replace conventional tragic skirts, *wigs, and gloves with *costumes that offered novel hints of local colour. Having urged the removal of spectators from the Comédie-Française *forestage in 1759, he explored a more spectacular *mise-en-scène and more dynamic use of stage space. He also insisted on orchestral interval music that was appropriate to the mood of the play being staged. Nor were Lekain's indefatigable and meticulous energies confined to work onstage. In 1756 he was the first to argue a case for the establishment of a national *acting school (*see* TRAINING). And in the 1760s he was the driving force behind the implementation of wholesale reforms of the Comédie-Française's internal administration, from service on a new management committee to the drafting of duty statements for the theatre's numerous salaried employees.   JG

LEMAÎTRE, FRÉDÉRICK (ANTOINE-LOUIS-PROSPER LEMAÎTRE) (1800–76)

French actor. After training at the *Conservatoire and failing to gain acceptance at the *Odéon, Frédérick (from early in his career he simply used the single name) started by performing in the *boulevard theatres, where he contributed hugely to the success of popular *melodrama. He did this by turning *L'Auberge des Adrets* (1824) from a vehicle for conventional sentiment into a *burlesque *parody of the *genre, each performance being liable to contain ever more outrageous extempore variations. Banned by the government after 85 performances for its subversive character, the play was revived in 1832; and in 1834 Frédérick was the co-author of a phenomenally successful sequel, *Robert Macaire*, which made the *hero, an amoral criminal, into a cult figure. He did, however, have higher aspirations, and was keen to play a significant part in the more literary theatre of the *romantic dramatists. Joining Harel at the Odéon, and later at the *Porte-Saint-Martin, he created the roles of Napoleon in *Dumas *père*'s *Napoléon Bonaparte* (1830), Concini in *Vigny's *La Maréchale d'Ancre* (1831), Richard Darlington in Dumas's play of that name (1831), and Gennaro in *Hugo's *Lucrèce Borgia* (1834), before undertaking the two roles which—apart from that of Robert Macaire—constitute the peak of his achievement. In 1838 he played the title role in *Ruy Blas*, the most successful of Victor Hugo's plays; but although the valet loved by the Queen of Spain provided plenty of scope for Frédérick in terms of temperament, he was probably less happy with the alexandrine *verse medium than with prose. The success of *Ruy Blas* was compromised by a quarrel between the co-*managers of the Renaissance Theatre, and the play was taken off after 50 performances. In 1836, however, at the Variétés, he had been able to create, in Dumas's *Kean*, the part of the great English actor who had died only three years earlier, a part written specifically for him, and in which he was to score an unqualified triumph. Dumas's play is subtitled 'Disorder and genius', a label which is just as appropriate to the French actor's life as to that of the Englishman he was portraying. If a life of disorder is more apparent to the reader of Dumas's play than evidence of artistic genius, it is not difficult to imagine the theatrical effect of the extravagant tirades the author put into the mouth of *Kean, declaimed with fitting panache by the most flamboyant actor of his time. *Gautier praised Frédérick's performance by saying that Kean 'couldn't have played his own part any better'. And a different kind of tribute was provided by the equally flamboyant twentieth-century actor Pierre Brasseur, who was to play Frédérick most memorably in the film *Les Enfants du paradis*. However, the decline in popularity of romantic drama on one hand, and of old-fashioned melodrama on the other, by the middle of the century signalled the decline of Frédérick's success in the theatre, and he died in poverty. WDH

LEMOINE, JEAN-RENÉ (1959–)

Haitian writer who left his native country for Zaire at a very young age. In his novel *Compte-rendu d'un vertige* and his plays *Chimères, ecchymose, l'odeur du noir* (1996), and *Ode à Scarlett O'Hara* (1997), he explores absence and presence and the power of death in the midst of life. He now works as an assistant at the Union for European Theatres in *Paris, where most of his works have been performed. MLa trans. JCM

LENAEA

Festival of *Dionysus at Athens celebrated in Gamelion (late January). To this ancient *festival (dated to before 1000 BC) competitions for *tragedy, *comedy, tragic actors, and comic actors were added around 440 BC. The programme included two or sometimes three sets of two tragedies, and five (sometimes possibly three) comedies. EGC

LEÑERO, VICENTE (1933–)

Mexican writer. A major figure in contemporary letters, Leñero began with *documentary plays which combined his back-ground in journalism with lucid criticism of Mexico's social ills; for example, *Rejected People* (1968) censures religious intolerance and *The Trial* (1971) looks at political assassination and judicial corruption. *The Martyrdom of Morelos* (1982) is a critique of official historical discourse that passes as truth. *The Night of Hernan Cortés* (1992) is a hallucinatory trip back to the horrors of the Spanish Conquest of Mexico as remembered by the conquistador on the eve of his death. Consistently inspired by current events, Leñero took a cue from the 1994 Zapatista Indian rebellion in Mexico's southern state of Chiapas for *We Are All Marcos* (1995). In *The Move* (1979) Lenero focuses on the materialism and self-absorption of a young middle-class couple blind to the poverty and misery surrounding them. One of his most discussed works, *Nobody Knows Anything* (1988), is a *political thriller that was staged simultaneously in nine contiguous spaces, an example of what Leñero has called hyper-*realism. In addition to his original *texts, Leñero has adapted Dostoevsky and Dante, as well as his own award-winning novel *The Bricklayers* (1963). *How Quickly It Becomes Late* (1997) and *As the Years Pass* (2000) are bittersweet explorations of ageing. At the turn of the century, Leñero announced his retirement from the theatre in order to concentrate on *film work.

KFN

LENO, DAN (1860–1903)

British comedian, actor, and *dancer. Victorian England's most feted *music-hall comedian and best-loved *pantomime dame, billed as 'the funniest man on earth', was born George Galvin and started his performing life at the age of 4 as 'Little George the Infant Wonder Contortionist and Posturer'. By 9, he was a seasoned performer appearing as part of the family troupe run by his stepfather William Grant, whose stage name was Leno. His first adult successes were as a dancer, winning the title of 'Champion Clog Dancer of the World' in 1883, and he continued dancing throughout his career. He became associated with comic songs incorporating large amounts of patter, and strongly reliant on the creation of *characters: 'The Grass-Widower', 'The Shopwalker', 'The Recruiting Sergeant', 'The Huntsman', a Beefeater in 'The Tower of London', and the determined woman of 'I'll Marry Him', one of his many *female impersonations.

He first appeared in pantomime as Dame Durden in *Jack and the Beanstalk* (1886), and starred every Christmas at *Drury Lane between 1888 and 1903, usually as the dame, opposite performers like Marie *Lloyd, *Little Tich, Vesta *Tilley, and his most frequent accomplice, Herbert Campbell, whose Falstaffian frame contrasted with the 1.6 m (5 feet 3 inches) Leno. Scripts were written by the theatre's *manager, Augustus *Harris, and later by J. Hickory Wood, who created Leno's most famous vehicle *Mother Goose* (1902), essentially a comic reversal of the Book of Job, in which Demon King and Fairy Queen make a poor woman wealthy to see if she will lose her virtue. Leno also appeared in the comic plays *Orlando Dando* (1898), *In Gay Piccadilly!* (1899), and *Mr Wix of Wicknam* (1902). In 1901 he played a command performance at Sandringham, after which he was referred to as 'the King's Jester'. His last years were affected by ill-health and alcoholism, leading to a premature death. His comic skills were ill-served by recording technology, and he is mainly known now through the recollections written by admirers like Charlie Chaplin, Harley Granville *Barker, and Max *Beerbohm. CDC

LE NOIR, CHARLES (d. 1637)

French *actor-manager. From itinerant beginnings, he moved to *Paris in 1622 join the Prince d'Orange's company, becoming their leader in 1624. By the 1630s he was joint leader with *Montdory at the *Marais; but this company suffered a serious setback in 1634, when Le Noir and five colleagues were transferred by royal command to the *Comédiens du Roi at the *Hôtel de Bourgogne. The inventory made on his death bears witness to the richness of a player's wardrobe. WDH

LENORMAND, HENRI-RENÉ (1882–1951)

French playwright. Strongly influenced by the psychological dramas of *Strindberg, *Pirandello, and *Chekhov, Lenormand felt theatre should elucidate the mysteries of the 'inner life'. He owed much of his success to Georges *Pitoëff, who introduced his work to Parisian *audiences, including *Le Temps est un songe* (*Time Is a Dream*, 1919) and *Les Ratés* (*The Failures*, 1920). His *Confessions of a Playwright* (1953) explores the dramatic profession of his period. CHB

LENSKY, ALEKSANDR (1847–1908)

Leading Russian actor at the *Moscow *Maly Theatre. The illegitimate son of Prince Gagarin by an Italian woman, Lensky joined the Maly company in 1876 after a successful career in the provinces, and acted in a diverse range of plays from Russian classics to Shakespeare, *Sudermann, and *Ibsen. He was also an excellent teacher and extremely skilled at *character analysis—specific examples being his approach to the role of Figaro in *Beaumarchais's two plays, Famusov in *Griboedov's *Woe from Wit*, and Falstaff—all of which were anatomized in his *Notes of an Actor*. *Meyerhold based his *theory of 'pre-acting' on Lensky's performance as Benedick in Shakespeare's *Much Ado About Nothing*, in which the actor gave a masterly display of *mimed reaction to the false disclosure of Beatrice's love for Benedick. He also proved to be an excellent *director of plays by Shakespeare and *Ostrovsky, as well as a successful *manager. NW

LENYA, LOTTE (1900–81)

Austrian actress and singer. Born Karoline Blaumauer in Vienna, the daughter of an alcoholic cabby, she moved to *Berlin in 1927 where she met and later married the composer Kurt *Weill. Her breakthrough came in 1928 with the role of Polly in Weill's collaboration with *Brecht, *The Threepenny Opera*. She advanced to significant acting roles in major productions such as *Oedipus* (1929) and *Danton's Death* (1931) at the Berlin Staatstheater, and a major success was Jenny in the Brecht–Weill *opera *Mahagonny* (1931). Her career in Germany ended in 1933 when she accompanied Weill into exile, performing Anna in the Brecht–Weill *Seven Deadly Sins* in *Paris (1933). They divorced shortly afterwards but reunited in 1938 when Weill emigrated to the United States. Lenya launched a second career after Weill's death in 1950 when she devoted herself to popularizing her husband's work in the USA and Europe in concerts and recordings. She also performed in many *films (most curiously in the second James Bond adventure, *From Russia with Love*, 1963) and on Broadway (*Cabaret*, 1968). With her highly expressive, if not particularly melodic voice, she defined the tradition of performing Brechtian songs. CBB

LENZ, JAKOB MICHAEL REINHOLD (1751–92)

German dramatist. A key figure in the *Sturm und Drang* movement, Lenz's first efforts were adaptations of *Plautus which remained unperformed in his lifetime. More important are his plays *Der neue Menoza*, a grotesque *comedy (1774); *Der Hofmeister; oder, Die Vorteile der Privaterziehung* (*The House Tutor; or, The Advantages of Home Education*, 1774); and *Die Soldaten* (1776). His reputation rests mainly on the latter two works, of which only *Der Hofmeister* was performed in his lifetime. Both are critical of aspects of the feudal system: private tutors in the one, and the officer caste in the other. Formally, the plays reveal the influence of Shakespeare in the use of short *scenes, indifference to the *neoclassical unities, and rich characterization. His 1774 essay *Anmerkungen übers Theater* (*Notes on Theatre*) is an important manifesto of the *Sturm und Drang* movement, particularly in its espousal of individual genius over rationalism and an anti-*Aristotelian preference for *character over *action. Lenz was an important influence on dramatists such as *Büchner, *Grabbe, *Wedekind, and *Brecht. *See also* ROMANTICISM. CBB

LEONARD, HUGH (1926–)

Irish playwright and journalist. The adopted son of a gardener in Dublin's suburb of Dalkey, Leonard (pseudonym of John Byrne) has had a prolific career writing for *television as well as the theatre, in Britain as well as Ireland. He has been a notably skilful adapter, for example in *Stephen D*, his 1962 version of Joyce's *A Portrait of the Artist*. Breaking with the Irish dramatic tradition of rural or small-town settings, Leonard has concentrated on the urban and suburban middle classes, as in his *satiric *farce *The Patrick Pearse Motel* (1971). His major international success came with *Da* (1973). Autobiographically based, it centres on the remembered figure of the father who haunts the mind of the returning Irish writer, played on stage both in his older and younger selves. This split time and double casting were repeated in the sequel *A Life* (1979), produced at the *Abbey with a notable central performance by Cyril *Cusack.

NG

LEONIDOV, LEONID (1873–1941)

Russian/Soviet actor whose career began in his native Odessa. After spells at the Solovtsov and Korsh theatres, he joined the *Moscow Art Theatre in 1903. An intelligent actor of volatile temperament, he appeared as Vaska Pepel in *Gorky's *The Lower Depths* (1903), as Lopakhin in *Chekhov's *The Cherry Orchard* (1904), Solyony in *Three Sisters* (1906), the Man in *Andreev's *The Life of Man* (1907), as Dmitry Karamazov (1910), as Peer Gynt (1912), as Cain in *Byron's play (1920), and as Othello in *Stanislavsky's 1930 production. He also played the miser Plyushkin in Stanislavsky's production of *Gogol's *Dead Souls* (1932).

NW

LEONOV, LEONID (1899–1994)

Russian/Soviet novelist and dramatist whose literary career began in 1922 with some short stories. His first play, *Untilovsk* (1928), about a Siberian scientist's conversion to Bolshevism, was staged at the *Moscow Art Theatre in 1928, whilst a dramatization of his novel *The Badgers*, about the ideological contrasts between city and village, had been staged at the Vakhtangov Theatre in 1927. Following a further dramatization of a novel about another scientist, *Skutarevsky* (*Maly Theatre, 1934), Leonov composed a Soviet response to *Chekhov's *The Cherry Orchard* in the shape of his quasi-symbolic play *The Orchards of Polovchansk,* in which the sounds of approaching war are heard (Moscow Art Theatre, 1939). The same year saw his play *The Snowstorm* banned for ideological incorrectness. His best-known play outside Russia is the war drama *Invasion*, about a released political prisoner who becomes a staunch defender of the Soviet Union (Maly Theatre, 1943). *The Golden Carriage*, set in post-war Russia, was staged at the MAT in 1957, and his novel *The Russian Forest* (1953) was adapted for the stage in 1959. Another play, *An Ordinary Man*, was *filmed by Mikhail Romm that year.

NW

LEPAGE, ROBERT (1957–)

Canadian (Québécois) director, writer, performer, and filmmaker. Lepage's productions combine *physical and visual elements with *text and *performance and are rich in imagery and sensory appeal. Born in Québec City and *trained as an actor there, Lepage joined the experimental troupe Théâtre Repère in 1982, which created its productions collaboratively through *improvisation. Lepage became one of the troupe's leading lights and in 1985 spearheaded the creation of what became an epic, six-hour-long production, *The Dragon's Trilogy*, which depicted life in three Canadian Chinatowns over the span of 70 years. The show was highly successful in Canada and internationally. Lepage went on to create a number of original *devised pieces, including *Polygraphe* (1988), a thriller for three actors about a real-life murder case in which Lepage was briefly a suspect; and *Tectonic Plates* (1988), a collaboration between Québécois and Scots actors that used continental drift as a metaphor for the movements of whole populations as well as individuals around the world. Lepage's work also includes solo pieces for himself, such as *Vinci* (1986), about a young Quebecker on his first, soul-searching trip to Europe, *Needles and Opium* (1991), which drew on the work of Miles Davis and Jean *Cocteau, and *Elsinore*, a version of *Hamlet* (1995). Lepage's productions involve concepts of searching and connecting: his *characters are often on quests for personal identity and for systems, ideas, and experiences which will give them a sense of connectedness to the world. As his career has developed his subject matter has become increasingly international and cross-cultural (*see* INTERCULTURALISM).

Having left Théâtre Repère in the late 1980s, Lepage served as *artistic director of the National Arts Centre of Canada from 1990 to 1992. He formed a company to develop and produce his work, Ex Machina, in Québec City in 1994. Ex Machina's projects have included *The Seven Streams of the River Ota* (1994), seven interconnected, hour-long *acts which focused on the ideas of devastation and rebirth; *Geometry of Miracles* (1998), about the unlikely overlapping of ideas in the careers of architect Frank Lloyd Wright and mystic Georgi Gurdgieff; and *The Far Side of the Moon* (2000), a solo piece which sets the story of two Québécois brothers forced to confront their differences when their mother dies against the back-story of the space race. Lepage has directed *operas and plays in many international venues and *festivals, and has made several *films, including *Le Confessional* (1995) and *Possible Worlds* (2001). *See also* POST-COLONIAL STUDIES.

KF

LERMONTOV, MIKHAIL (1814–41)

Russian poet, novelist, and playwright. Best known as a lyric poet and for his novel *A Hero of our Time*, Lermontov wrote five plays, none of which was staged in his lifetime. At the point where he might have developed theatrical contacts he was exiled to a serving army unit in the Caucasus for his poem *Death of a Poet* (1837). Like *Pushkin, the subject of that poem, Lermontov was killed in a duel. Early attempts at playwriting show strong influence of Shakespeare and *Schiller: *The Spaniards* (1830), *People and Passions* (1830), and *The Strange Man* (1831). His best-known work, *Masquerade* (1835–7), retains these early influences reflecting Shakespeare's *Othello*, while Schiller's *romantic approach to *character and setting is placed within a *melodramatic framework. Lermontov's swansong in drama was the unfinished *Two Brothers* (1836) based on autobiographical material concerning his long-term relationship with Varvara Lopukhina. Set in *St Petersburg high society, *Masquerade* charts the mounting jealousy of Arbenin towards his innocent wife Nina. Suspecting her of infidelity at a masked ball, he poisons her and gloats as she writhes in agony. Nemesis comes in the form of a mysterious stranger who confronts Arbenin with his evildoing and declares that his wife was innocent. The only one of the plays to achieve a stage life, *Masquerade* was finally performed in 1852 (*Aleksandrinsky Theatre, Petersburg), though only in extracts (also see at the *Maly, *Moscow, 1862). *Meyerhold provided the key production in 1917 on the eve of the February Revolution, with richly decorated sets and *costumes creating a unified effect by the artist Aleksandr Golovin, and music by Aleksandr Glazunov. The production turned the enigmatic personality of the *hero and the nightmarish world he inhabits into a metaphor for the uncertainty of the times. Other notable twentieth-century performances retained the richness and controversy which seemed attached to this play: the Vakhtangov Theatre production in 1941 (directed by Ruben *Simonov) had music provided by Khachaturyan, and Anatoly *Vasiliev's version for the *Comédie-Française (*Paris, 1993) caused a storm of controversy. Some works by Lermontov have reached the stage in other forms (Anton Rubinstein's *opera *Demon*, 1875) and Laputin's *ballet *Masquerade* (1956), while *A Hero of our Time* was an early production by Yury *Lyubimov at the *Taganka Theatre (Moscow, 1964).

CM

LERNER, ALAN JAY (1918–86) AND FREDERICK LOEWE (1901–88)

American lyricist and librettist, and American composer. *Rodgers and *Hammerstein, whose collaboration covered virtually the same years, and Lerner and Loewe were the pre-eminent *music-theatre songwriting teams of the post-war era. Loewe, born in Germany, the son of an *operetta tenor, was a classically trained piano prodigy who moved to *New York in 1924 and learned English (and the American popular musical idiom) while playing piano in clubs. He first reached Broadway in 1938 when he wrote the music for *Great Lady*, a flop that

sent him back to the clubs. A few years later he met Lerner, a wealthy New Yorker who was himself a competent pianist; having written show songs at Harvard, he had a yen to write for the theatre. They first collaborated on *What's Up?* (1943), a conventional old-fashioned *musical that quickly failed. Their next effort, *The Day before Spring* (1945), was far from conventional; a *critical success, it investigated the psychology of nostalgia. Encouraged, the team struck gold with *Brigadoon* (1947), a fantasy of a 200-year-old Scottish town that comes to life for one day every hundred years. With a chance to work in both a contemporary and an old-fashioned idiom, Loewe had found his stride.

In a pattern which would haunt their collaboration, Loewe, unused to wealth, took time off to enjoy success. Lerner, however, wanted to work, and he teamed with Kurt *Weill to write the extremely innovative *Love Life* (1948). When Loewe was ready to resume, they turned to period Americana with *Paint Your Wagon* (1951), set in the old west. Loewe was not as comfortable with this idiom, and the show was less successful than *Brigadoon*. Not so their next effort, *My Fair Lady* (1956), whose early twentieth-century setting and swirling waltzes suited Loewe perfectly, while Lerner, basing his libretto on *Shaw's *Pygmalion*, had a ready-made structure. *My Fair Lady* was the biggest hit of the 1950s, setting a *long-run record, and Loewe would collaborate with Lerner only twice more. The *film *Gigi* (1958) offered Loewe another opportunity to write in the idiom with which he was most comfortable, but *Camelot* (1960) was an unpleasant experience for all concerned, and Loewe retired to enjoy his wealth.

Lerner would continue writing musicals with a string of other collaborators, including Leonard *Bernstein, but he would never again find the success he had with Loewe. Only one of his six subsequent musicals—*On a Clear Day You Can See Forever* (1965)—could be called a hit. But their partnership was legendary, and *My Fair Lady* is still held as one of the finest examples of musical theatre. Like Lerner and Loewe, it contributed little that was new, but it was a splendid example of how the traditional devices can be adeptly applied by masters of the form.

JD

LERUS, ARTHUR (1949–)

Guadeloupean actor, playwright, director, and co-founder (with Harry Kancel, in 1973) of Théâtre du Cyclône. The company is named after *Siklon*, its emblematic play in which a tropical storm signifies an all-consuming political protest that will transform the island. Lerus's *politically committed theatre is based on phyical training, *improvisation, breathing exercises, storytelling, and the use of a repertoire of typical stage gestures. Most of the work has been created *collectively, based on observation and research, and includes *Férié Mawon* (1987) and *Bwabam* (1991).

AR

LESAGE, ALAIN-RENÉ (1668–1747)

French playwright and novelist. Orphaned in his teens, Lesage went to *Paris about 1690, where he embarked upon a writing career with *comedies adapted from Spanish plays by *Rojas and Lope de *Vega. His first real successes, however, came in 1707, with the publication of *Le Diable boîteux* (*The Devil on Crutches*), a satirical novel aimed at contemporary French society, and a *one-act comedy for the *Comédie-Française, *Crispin rival de son maître* (*Crispin, Rival of his Master*). His next play, *Turcaret* (1709), is a comic masterpiece, in which the eponymous *hero, a nouveau riche tax farmer, finds himself exploited as heartlessly as he exploits others. It is a cynical *satire exposing the self-obsessed materialism of Regency society. *Turcaret* met with powerful political opposition and was quickly suppressed; reinstated in 1730, it remains a fixture in the repertory. A quarrel with the actors, however, caused Lesage to forsake the Comédie-Française for the Paris fairground theatres of Saint-Germain and Saint-Laurent, and between 1712 and 1737, either alone or with collaborators Louis Fuzelier and Jacques-Philippe d'Orneval, he penned over 100 pieces for them. In the preface to the fifteen-volume anthology of these works—typically *opéras-comiques*, placard-plays, and *vaudevilles, liberally spiced with sexual innuendo, physical buffoonery, song, and *dance—Lesage wrote that the very title, *Théâtre de la foire*, 'carried a notion of lowness and vulgarity'. Throughout this period Lesage continued to produce his own fiction, especially the work that constitutes his claim to fame as a novelist today, *Gil Blas* (1715, 1724, 1735).   JG

LESBIAN THEATRE

Although the history of theatre contains many examples of women who displayed homoerotic attachments both on and off the stage, the social category 'lesbian' did not emerge until the late nineteenth century. Theatre created by self-identified lesbians and intended primarily for lesbian, *feminist, or *gay *audiences dates to the early 1970s in both the United States and Britain, following the second wave of feminist and gay liberation movements (*see* FEMINISM; QUEER THEORY). The form and content of early lesbian theatre reflected the consciousness-raising practice that Canning suggests in her study of feminist theatre in the United States: it was a concurrent, geographically fragmented *community theatre, rather than an organized or centralized movement. Groups in this period included Medusa's Revenge in *New York, Front Room Theatre Guild in Seattle, the Lesbian-Feminist Theater Collective of Pittsburgh, the Lavender Cellar in Minneapolis, Red Dyke Theater in Atlanta, the Theatre of Light and Shadow in New Haven, and the Lesbian Feminist Theatre Workshop in *Chicago. Performance *texts were largely autobiographical, first-person narratives of the author's struggle to overcome op-

pressive gender and sex roles. Another popular narrative included a performer's 'coming out' story. In most instances performers assumed an intimate audience of lesbian, gay, or feminist spectators, and the object was to project positive representations of lesbians on stage.

Lesbian theatre in Britain followed a similar trajectory, rising out of the *fringe theatre movements of the 1960s. Women played a significant role in founding and sustaining *London's *Gay Sweatshop during the early 1970s, which can be seen as a critical moment in this history. Although decentralized and poorly funded, lesbian troupes have maintained a fringe presence in Britain through the 1990s; major groups include Siren, Sadista Sisters, Women's Theatre Company, *Monstrous Regiment, the Character Ladies, Shameful Practice, Outcast, and Cunning Stunts.

The American equivalent of Gay Sweatshop was the seminal *WOW Café. After the founding *collective began the Women's One World international performance *festival in the summer of 1980, this tiny performance community in New York's East Village became a centre for lesbian performance. Operating on spartan resources, the self-producing artists of WOW included Holly *Hughes, Five Lesbian Brothers, Carmelita Tropicana, Reno, and *Split Britches. The members of Split Britches (Peggy Shaw, Lois Weaver, and Deb Margolin) became the bellwether for feminist and lesbian performance in the late twentieth century. The notoriety surrounding Split Britches is due largely to the lesbian-feminist performance scholars who have claimed WOW Café and its artists as a paramount site of progressive lesbian representation. These academic writers, including Sue Ellen Case, Kate Davy, Teresa de Lauretis, Jill Dolan, Lynda Hart, Peggy Phelan, and Alisa Solomon, have defined lesbian theatre not only as a performance practice but also as a lesbian viewing practice where the audience creates a politicized reading of the *texts. Performance practices include butch/femme role playing, campy formal elements such as lip-synching *satire and *vaudevillian shtick, an aesthetic shaped by marginalized, cash-poor conditions, and content drawn from current lesbian and feminist politics.

Belle Reprieve, a queer deconstruction of Tennessee *Williams's *A Streetcar Named Desire*, represents a defining moment. Peggy Shaw and Lois Weaver of Split Britches joined Bloolips, a gay male company, to perform a gender-bent send-up of the American classic. Butch-lesbian Shaw played Stanley to drag-queen Bette Bourne's Blanche; while Bloolips' Precious Pearl played Mitch as a 'sissy' and Weaver performed Stella as a femme dyke in love with her lesbian husband. The *characters and *plot were based not only in Williams's text, but also in the cultural iconography of Marlon *Brando and the *film version of the original play. Shaw's bellowing Stanley in a ripped T-shirt and padded jeans performed a *parody of Brando's machismo. The resultant Stanley became a farcical masquerade of hypermasculine behaviour. The script is also rife with *Brechtian interventions that disrupt the well-known narrative, such as a scene in which all four actors attempt to escape Williams's heterosexist script.

At the start of the twenty-first century lesbian representations have become more widely available in mainstream venues. A number of openly lesbian playwrights write plays with identifiable lesbian characters, which are produced in America in *regional and *Off-Broadway theatres, starting with Jane *Chambers's *Last Summer at Bluefish Cove* (1985) Off-Broadway. Other contemporary lesbian playwrights include Paula *Vogel, Joan Schenkar, Susan Miller, and Carolyn Gage. *See also* GENDER AND PERFORMANCE. SBM

CANNING, CHARLOTTE, *Feminist Theaters in the U.S.A.: staging women's experience* (London, 1996)

FREEMAN, SANDRA, *Putting your Daughters on the Stage: lesbian theatre from the 1970s to the 1990s* (London, 1997)

LESCARBOT, MARC (c.1570–1642)

French historian and minor poet, of interest primarily as author of the first dramatic *text in French composed and performed in the New World. This verse playlet, *Le Théâtre de Neptune en la Nouvelle-France* (*The Theatre of Neptune in New France*), was performed in November 1606, near Port-Royal in the newly founded colony of Acadia, to welcome the safe return of the tiny colony's founders. This function identifies it as a traditional *réception*, a short ceremonial drama marking the arrival or departure of an important dignitary, a *genre destined to endure in French Canada. LED

LESLIE, FRED (1855–92)

English actor who made his name in *burlesque roles at the *Gaiety Theatre. He first appeared in *London in 1878 in a burlesque version of Poole's *Paul Pry*. From 1885 he was principally associated with Nellie *Farren at the Gaiety, with whom he played in *Little Jack Sheppard*, *Monte Cristo Junior* (1886), and *Ruy Blas* (1889). His last burlesque, which he co-wrote, was *Cinder Ellen up-to-Date* (1892). He *toured America and Australia with the Gaiety company and was much admired for his physical inventiveness, his ability to imitate prominent actors, and his singing of popular songs. VEE

LESSING, GOTTHOLD EPHRAIM (1729–81)

German dramatist and *critic. He was drawn to the theatre by the famous *Neuber acting company, whom he saw as a student in Leipzig in 1746 and for whom he wrote his first play, *Der junge Gelehrte* (*The Young Scholar*, 1748). In *Berlin he became one of the first German writers to make a living from his pen. In 1750 he published with Christlob Mylius the quarterly *Beyträge zur Historie und Aufnahme des Theaters* (*Contributions to the History and Reception of the Theatre*). Friendship with the philosopher Moses Mendelssohn caused him to write the play *Die Juden* (*The Jews*, 1775). In *Theatralische Bibliothek* (*Theatrical Library*, 1754–8) he developed the concept of a 'domestic *tragedy' which advocated the use of middle-class *characters as tragic *heroes, and with *Miss Sara Sampson* (1755) he produced one of the most successful examples of this new *genre.

His *Letters Concerning the Latest Literature* (1759–65) attacked the French *neoclassical interpretation of the *Aristotelian *unities and *Gottsched as its chief exponent in Germany. By using Shakespeare as a role model for German theatre, he suggested replacing rigid French aesthetics with a more natural language and freer *dramaturgy, which would focus on the *audience's emotional responsiveness and moral improvement. In 1760 he published *Das Theater des Herrn Diderot* (*The Theatre of Mr Diderot*), which introduced the innovative French dramatist and critic *Diderot to the German stage. His 'Laokoon' essay of 1766 was one of the most important formulations of an Enlightenment aesthetics internationally. In 1767 he became literary adviser of the *Hamburg National Theatre, a short-lived *repertory company, which caused him to write an influential collection of reviews and essays, *Hamburgische Dramaturgie* (1767–9, usually translated as *Hamburg Dramaturgy*). The loose structure of these reflections underscores the fact that Lessing had no intention of establishing a new 'book of rules' for playwrights, but rather wanted to stimulate debates on the creation of a new national drama and its realization on stage. For this purpose he offered an original interpretation of Aristotle's *Poetics*, set the concept of genius against neoclassical dogma, discussed the latest trends in French and English *bourgeois drama, and redefined many central categories of theatre. His critical *theories were put into practice in *Minna von Barnhelm* (1767), *Emilia Galotti* (1772), and *Nathan the Wise* (1783), which became his most enduring plays. The lead roles have been interpreted by some of Germany's greatest actors and still enchant *audiences through their wit, deep humanity, and passionate defence of the values of tolerance and mutual understanding. *See also* ROMANTICISM. GB

LEVIN, HANOCH (1943–99)

Leading Israeli dramatist whose plays are characterized by biting *satire and vivid *theatricality. Recurrent themes in his *absurdist *tragicomedies are the shabbiness of everyday life and the vulgarity of human existence; his *characters, either oppressors or oppressed, are mostly stupid, inept, and cruel. Levin wrote 50 plays, 34 of them originally staged from 1969 on, mostly directed by him. Much of Levin's work is associated with the *Cameri Theatre, where he served as resident playwright. His best-known work includes *You, I, and the Next War* (1970), a sharp *political satire that stirred enormous controversy, *Yaacobi and Leidental* (1972), *The Rubber Merchants* (1978),

The Passion of Job (1981), *The Suitcase Packers* (1981), *The Labour of Life* (1988), *Murder* (1998), and *Funeral* (1999), which he directed from his hospital deathbed.   EN

LEWES, GEORGE HENRY (1817–78)

English playwright and *critic. Lewes was a polymath whose professional interests extended to philosophy, physiology—he was professor of physiology in the University of London—sociology, and psychology, as well as biography and literature. From 1854 until his death he was the partner of the novelist George Eliot. A grandson of the eighteenth-century comedian Charles Lee Lewes, he acted with the *Dickens *amateurs and in his own *tragedy *The Noble Heart* (1849). He was the drama critic of the *Leader* in the 1850s and wrote essays on the drama for the *Pall Mall Gazette*. His *On Actors and the Art of Acting* (1875) is the best book in English on nineteenth-century *acting. Lewes wrote thirteen plays, most of them for the *Vestris–*Mathews *management at the *Lyceum. The most interesting is *The Game of Speculation* (1851), adapted from the French and containing the popular Victorian dramatic themes of money, social ambition, speculation, and ruin. It provided a star part for Charles Mathews, Jr., as the cunning and scheming speculator Affable Hawk.   MRB

LEWIS, MATTHEW GREGORY (1775–1818)

English writer, usually called 'Monk' Lewis after his most notorious novel, *The Monk* (1796). Lewis was the author of several plays and his verse and fiction were freely pillaged by other dramatists. His most successful piece was *The Castle Spectre* (1796), a five-act drama which combines influences from Shakespeare with many elements of Gothic. His *romantic *melodrama *Timour the Tartar* (1811) is an equestrian *spectacle (*see* HIPPODRAMA) for which horses are not indispensable, best remembered as a favourite script for *toy theatre. Lewis's emphatic and highly coloured diction came to be an essential component of popular melodrama.   FD

LEWIS, ROBERT (1909–97)

American actor and director. After working with the *Civic Repertory Theatre, Lewis joined the *Group Theatre, becoming known for his eccentric roles. He advocated *Stanislavsky's *acting *theories, shifting from Lee *Strasberg's emphasis on emotional memory to Stella *Adler's when circumstances warranted. Eventually he became a leading acting teacher, and with Elia *Kazan and Cheryl *Crawford founded the *Actors Studio in 1947. He also created the Robert Lewis Acting Company in Westchester, New York. His *directing style was often called

'poetic *realism', first noted in *My Heart's in the Highlands* (1939). He directed many plays and *musicals, on Broadway and elsewhere, but rarely attempted classical material. His best-remembered Broadway shows are *Brigadoon* (1947), *The Happy Time* (1950), Arthur *Miller's version of *Ibsen's *An Enemy of the People* (1950), *Teahouse of the August Moon* (1953), *Witness for the Prosecution* (1953), *Jamaica* (1957), and *On a Clear Day You Can See Forever* (1965).   SLL

LEYBOURNE, GEORGE (1842–84)

English *music-hall singer. Born in Stourbridge in the Black Country, Leybourne's early life is obscure. He had some success as a 'buffo' singer in the north-east, but it was Billy Holland at the Canterbury Hall in *London who exploited his magnetic appeal. With songs such as 'Champagne Charlie' and 'Moet and Chandon', Leybourne was the archetypal 'lion comique', handsome, debonair, with Holland insisting that he drive between halls in a carriage drawn by four white horses. Already ill, he made his last appearance in 1884 at the Queen's, Poplar, dying soon after, alcoholic and impoverished.   AF

LIANG CHENYU (LIANG CH'EN-YÜ) (1520–c.1593)

*Chinese playwright, author of *Huansha ji* (*Washing Silk*), the first southern drama (*chuanqi*) written for the newly refined Kunshan musical style. Though he did not enjoy the same high regard as his teacher *Wei Liangfu, Liang broadened Kunshan's appeal by using it in a work that was staged, not simply sung to musical accompaniment. Set in Suzhou in the fifth century BC, *Huansha ji* links its love theme to the theme of national survival, drawing on historical accounts of rivalry between the ancient kingdoms of Wu and Yue to allude to contemporary events, in a manner subsequently imitated by the early Qing playwrights *Hong Sheng and *Kong Shangren. Liang's poignant depiction of the beauty Xi Shi and her lover Fan Li, who forgo personal fulfilment out of devotion to king and country, remained popular onstage until the modern era. *Huansha ji* is second only to *Gao Ming's *Pipa ji* (*The Lute*) in the number of highlights preserved in Qing miscellanies. Its lush settings and elegant artifice offered striking contrasts to the arid northern setting and atmosphere of *The Lute*, making *Huansha ji* a fitting vehicle of this new southern style.   CS

LIBERATION THEATRE

*Latin American theatre, particularly of the 1960s and 1970s, that is socially aware and *politically conscious. Related to 'liberation theology' and frequently inspired by Paulo Freire's

Pedagogy of the Oppressed, liberation theatre attempts to enable the *audience to speak for itself, rather than to use theatre to speak to the audience in a patronizing way that mirrors centuries of colonial oppression. Under these policies theatre is seen as another force for liberation from inherited social, political, or aesthetic structures. Internationally, the best known of these approaches is Augusto *Boal's theatre of the *oppressed (his book *Theatre of the Oppressed* was published in English in 1979). Boal called for the creation of a new theatrical system with two main components: everyone can and should be an actor; and the themes encountered should cut across class barriers and affect everyone within a given social, cultural, or economic milieu. Potential solutions to a personal, political, or social problem should be suggested by actors and audience alike and then enacted by both in an effort to find the best solution. The solutions should then be taken out of the theatre into the larger world. By altering the aesthetic image of their oppression, Boal argues, participants will create the tools necessary to change social reality.

Numerous other theatre practitioners shared Boal's central perception that Latin American theatre has historically reflected the concerns of the region's colonial and neocolonial oppressors (*see* POST-COLONIAL STUDIES). Enrique *Buenaventura and Santiago *García, for example, part of the New Theatre movement in Colombia, saw the international repertory as the artistic equivalent of a colonial government oppressing the indigenous population; liberation from colonial authority could be achieved only by finding a specifically Latin American *dramaturgy. Thus Latin American short stories, poetry, popular myths, and songs were frequently used as the basis for productions, and the actors' improvisational responses to the material shaped the collectively created piece. The actor is theoretically freed from the tyranny of the playwright, and the productions themselves are always tested against the perceptions of an audience responding out of its own experience, bringing spectators into the *collective process.

The emphasis upon process was also evident in the work of Nicaraguan Alan *Bolt during the late 1970s and early 1980s. Bolt's group would live with a community, research its problems, and create theatrical pieces that directly addressed its needs. A village's lack of a sewage system or a factory's abusive foreman would be depicted along with potential solutions for the audience's discussion. The goal was to create not a theatre product but a process of investigation. At Bolt's home base, a farm called La Praga in Matagalpa province, community groups were encouraged to employ theatrical expression to identify problems and act upon them. After the Sandinista revolution this theatre work had direct consequences: ineffectual labour leaders, for example, could be removed from their posts. In a sense liberation theatre uses theatre in an attempt to eliminate theatre: even the process is worthless unless it contributes to building a better life.   AV

LIBRE, TEATRO

Colombian company founded in 1973 by Ricardo Camacho and other members of *Bogotá's Los Andes University Faculty of Philosophy. Germán Moure has shared its direction with Camacho since 1975. The company has run a school for actor *training since 1988, as well as a dramatist's workshop. Operating from two different *playhouses, Teatro Libre has specialized in the classics, presenting work (often in adapted form) by *Aeschylus, *Sophocles, Shakespeare, *Molière, *Pirandello, *Valle-Inclán, *Brecht, and *Miller. The theatre also produces original work by Colombian writers such as Jairo Aníbal *Niño, Piedad Bonnet, and two of its founding members, Esteban *Navajas and Jorge *Plata.   BJR

LIBRE, THÉÂTRE

Private French company opened in 1887 by the director and reformer André *Antoine. The Théâtre Libre (Free Theatre) became the home and testing ground of Europe's new drama and the model for independent theatres elsewhere, such as Otto *Brahm's *Freie Bühne in *Berlin (1889), J. T. *Grein's *Independent Theatre in *London (1891), and *Yeats's and Lady *Gregory's *Abbey Theatre in *Dublin (1904). More by accident than design, Antoine's theatre became associated with *naturalist drama, although the director himself was more concerned with *realism. He was inspired by the work of the *Meiningen company, particularly in their ensemble *acting and historical exactitude. Antoine's artistic policy was eclectic, and included *verse drama, naturalism, *symbolism, and the translation of foreign works (including plays by *Strindberg, *Ibsen, *Bjørnson, and *Hauptmann). New writers and new plays by established writers featured heavily but Antoine was unwilling to give authors a second chance, such was his desire for the production of novelty. The company's trademarks included the darkening of the *auditorium, the abolition of *footlights, overhead and side *lighting, three-dimensional *scenery, authentic *costumes, and truthfulness of *acting. From the outset Antoine's company was privately funded through subscriptions to avoid *censorship. But the rapid turnovers, the burdens of realism, *touring, and the lack of a permanent home (the company moved three times in seven years, crossing the Seine with each move) led to *financial collapse, leaving the company stranded in September 1894 on tour in *Rome. *See also* ANTOINE, THÉÂTRE.   BRS

LIBRETTO *See* BOOK.

LICENSING ACTS

The Stage Licensing Act (1737) transformed the regulation of theatre in Britain and established a system for dramatic *censorship which lasted until 1968. Before this Act, *Masters of the Revels had exercised some authority over the licensing and correcting of plays. This authority, however, was compromised by the granting of theatrical *patents for *London to Thomas *Killigrew and William *Davenant at the Restoration because the patents allowed the holders to censor those plays performed by their own companies. During the early 1730s, moral, religious, and economic opposition to theatres intensified: commentators and pamphleteers denounced *playhouses as nurseries of vice and debauchery which encouraged indiscipline and distracted the lower classes from their work (*see* ANTI-THEATRICAL POLEMIC). In 1735 Sir John Barnard introduced a bill to limit the number of playhouses in London. Although the bill was defeated, many of its measures were incorporated into the Licensing Act. But the most immediate catalyst for the Licensing Bill was the determination of Robert Walpole, the Prime Minister, to quash the political *satires being performed at the Little Theatre in the *Haymarket by Henry *Fielding and his company. At a time of great anxiety over public disorder and fears of impending revolution, playhouses became an immediate and easy target. Nevertheless, the Licensing Bill met considerable opposition in Parliament. The most eloquent spokesman against the Bill was Lord Chesterfield, who drew attention to the absence of any mechanism for appealing against the *Lord Chamberlain's decisions.

The Licensing Act sought to control theatre in Westminster by limiting performances to those theatres acting under the authority of letters patent or licence from the Lord Chamberlain. In practice, this meant that performances became restricted to the London patent theatres and to the provincial *theatres royal in cities such as Bristol, Norwich, and York. Performers at unlicensed playhouses were now treated in accordance with the stipulations of the Vagrancy Act, that is, as rogues and vagabonds. The new legislation effectively outlawed theatres such as *Goodman's Fields and Fielding's Little Haymarket: Fielding soon gave up theatrical management and decided to write novels instead.

The Lord Chamberlain and the Master of the Revels had traditionally possessed the authority to suppress unauthorized companies of players and to prevent offensive performances. But the most striking feature of the Licensing Act was the comprehensive system it introduced for the censorship of playscripts. The Act stipulated that all new plays had to be submitted for censorship to the Lord Chamberlain's office at least fourteen days before the date of their first performance. (In practice, the reading of scripts was undertaken by the Examiner of Plays and his deputy; the Lord Chamberlain was consulted only in the case of a controversial submission.) *Managers who failed to submit plays according to the provisions of the Act were fined £50 for each offence. The Licensing Act allowed the Lord Chamberlain to forbid 'as often as he thinks fit' any dramatic piece acted 'for hire, gain or reward' anywhere in Great Britain. Successive Lords Chamberlain did indeed ban some plays outright; in many cases, the Examiner insisted on the deletion of particular speeches or entire *scenes. Despite periods of protest and rebellion against stage censorship, especially during the 1890s and early 1900s, the Lord Chamberlain and the Examiners of Plays continued to exercise a powerful stranglehold over the British stage until the second half of the twentieth century.

The Stage Licensing Act had a profound and long-lasting effect on the development of British theatre. As Chesterfield had predicted, some managers became adept at discreetly circumventing this attempt to rid the stage of *politics: old plays, for example, were exempt from the provisions of the Act. Crafty impresarios like Samuel *Foote bypassed the prohibition on acting for hire, gain, or reward by inviting his *audiences to pay for a dish of chocolate or cup of tea: dramatic performances were then offered gratis. During the late eighteenth century, new places of entertainment began to open on the south bank of the Thames and around the East End. These establishments were regulated not by the Lord Chamberlain but rather by annual licence from local magistrates, according to the provisions of the Disorderly Houses Act of 1752. The Theatrical Representations or Sixty-Day Act of 1788 also permitted local magistrates to license dramatic performances in the provinces. This system unwittingly created a legal loophole which enabled the *minor theatres beyond Westminster to stage plays without submitting their playtexts for censorship. The freedom from censorship became a notable feature of late Georgian theatre in London and was not addressed in law until the Theatre Regulation Act of 1843.

By the late 1820s the legislative division enshrined by the Licensing Act between the patent theatres, which effectively possessed a legal monopoly over spoken drama in London, and the minor playhouses, had all but collapsed. Moreover, several controversial productions had drawn attention to the freedom enjoyed by the uncensored theatres beyond Westminster. In 1843, the Theatre Regulation Act, which superseded the Licensing Act of 1737, abolished the patent theatres' monopoly over spoken drama. It gave legal recognition to all the London minor theatres, which were henceforth required to submit playscripts for censorship to the Lord Chamberlain's Office, a condition that continued until the abolition of censorship in 1968. JM

CONOLLY, L. W., *The Censorship of English Drama 1737–1824* (San Marino, Calif., 1976)

LIESENFELD, VINCENT J., *The Licensing Act of 1737* (Madison, 1984)

MOODY, JANE, *Illegitimate Theatre in London, 1770–1840* (Cambridge, 2000)

LICENSING OF PLAYS

The licensing of a play is the giving of permission by those who have legal rights in the play to others to exercise those rights.

The licensed rights may be some or all of those owned by the *copyright owner, including the right to copy the written form of a play, to perform the play, to record a performance, to broadcast a performance, and to adapt the play to some other form of expression, such as using the play as the basis for a *ballet or *opera. An exercise of any of these rights without permission is an infringement of those rights. Permission is usually given by means of a formal, written agreement, but there is no legal requirement that a licence be in writing. Licences are often limited as to time and place. For example, the owner of the rights in a play (the licensor) might give permission for a theatrical company (the licensee) to perform the play for a year within the territory of a specified country. A performance of the play after the designated year or in another country would infringe the exclusive rights of the play's owner. In return for a licence, the licensee usually promises to pay the licensor a fee. This fee may be in a single amount, a variable amount (such as a percentage of *ticket sales), or a combination of both. Because the copyright protection of dramatic works lasts for 70 years after the death of the playwright, the licensing of plays is often handled by organizations specifically created for that purpose, such as copyright-royalty collecting societies. Where a licence is given for an *amateur performance of a play, the licensing fee may be given at discounted rate.

Licences of the same rights may be granted to more than one licensee. Because of the potential for conflict between licensees attempting to exploit the same play at the same time in the same place, one licensee may insist upon an exclusive licence, which gives the licensee the sole right to perform a play in a certain place for a certain time in a certain way. To avoid competition for the same *audience, licensing agreements must be carefully drafted to exclude potential conflicts. In most countries, in order to be enforceable against other performers an exclusive licence must be in writing.

A licence to perform a play does not grant licence to some other protected aspect of a performance. For example, where music is involved in a performance, the copyright in the music is separate from the copyright in the play itself, and the copyright in any words sung with the music is subject to still other copyright protection. A licence to perform one aspect of a performance does not necessarily include a licence to perform other aspects of the same performance. Separate design-right protection may also apply to *lighting, *costumes, and *scenery.

TEH

LIERA, OSCAR (1946–90)

Mexican playwright, director, and actor. Born Jesús Cabanillas Flores, he gained notoriety with his anticlerical *satire *Cúcara and Mácara* (1981), which incited violent protests by groups who (erroneously) read into it a defamation of the Virgin of Guadalupe. Beginning as a *realist, Liera ended as a visual and playful playwright whose *characters often travel seamlessly from the real to the magical. In the trilogy *The Horseman of the Divine Providence* (1984), *The Perverse Fables* (1985), and *The Red Road to Sabaiba* (1986), history, legend, and myth function as an effective means of escape from social injustice.

KFN

LIGHTING *see page 738*

LIGIER (1796–1872)

French actor. Famous as much for his strong voice as for his small stature, Ligier specialized in sinister roles, making his debut as Néron in *Racine's *Britannicus* at the *Comédie-Française in 1820. Because of personal differences with the company, he broke with the Comédie in 1824 to perform at the *Odéon and the *Porte-Saint-Martin, where he created *Delavigne's Marino Faliero in 1829. He eventually returned to the Comédie-Française as a *sociétaire* in 1832 and continued playing the darker *characters in classical *tragedies and *romantic dramas. Among the roles he created were Triboulet in *Le Roi s'amuse* and Frédéric in *Les Burgraves* by Victor *Hugo, Glocester in Delavigne's *Les Enfants d'Édouard*, Savoisy in *Charles VII chez ses grands vassaux* by Alexandre *Dumas père, and Antoine in Jules Lacroix's *Le Testament de César*. He retired in 1851, although he refused the Comédie pension so that he could continue to play at the Porte-Saint-Martin and the Odéon. After 1856 he returned to his native Bordeaux where he appeared in local performances until his death at the age of 75.

CHB

LIKAY

A popular form of spoken drama from *Thailand, blending *pipat* music, classical dance, and modern *folk songs, which arose in the late nineteenth century. Actors improvise *dialogue and song lyrics in line with a scenario provided by a storyteller, who is usually the troupe master and *director. The repertoire is dominated by stories from the past but includes a few modern tales, all treated as light romantic *comedies, usually derivatives of a standard *plot. Short, action-filled scenes flow in rapid succession, played in front of wing and drop *scenery. The male *costume is an elaboration of court theatre dress, whereas actresses are dressed in traditional Thai style. The performance, which begins about 8 p.m., contains a musical prelude, an introduction, and the play proper, which ends around midnight. A long and elaborate *clown scene is always presented towards the end of the play, much appreciated by *likay*'s predominately female, urban, lower-middle-class *audiences.

SV

(continued on p. 747)

LIGHTING

The very word *theatre, a 'seeing place' (*theatron), implies that a stage will be lighted, for the *audience cannot see without light. Stage lighting began with simple visibility, but a complex interaction of technical advance, theatrical convention, and aesthetic *theory has made light a fully plastic medium, and lighting an art.

1. Pre-optical lighting;
2. Early modern discovery of light, 1500–1680;
3. The enlightenment discovery of optics, 1680–1820;
4. Gas and controllable light, 1790–1890;
5. Electricity and controlled light, 1840–1950;
6. Art of controlled light, 1950–present;
7. Contemporary practice

1. Pre-optical lighting

The pre-industrial scripted performance traditions about which we know anything—*China, *India, *Greece, *Rome, *medieval Europe, *Korea, *Japan, *Indonesia—contain many usually brief accounts of mostly unsuccessful experiments in stage lighting: colouring with reflectors or media, *fireworks, use of natural light (such as the sunrise in *Agamemnon*), rear-projected shadows, and chiaroscuro. But until very recently in theatre history, the main issue regarding light was visibility. Plays were performed during the daytime, outdoors or in covered spaces with large windows. If social circumstances forced theatre indoors or into the night, plays were performed with candles, torches, and lamps as close to the stage as possible. Theatre *historiography about light in these periods is about what the stage probably looked like, not intention, and about how performance adapted to the light, not about how light was designed for performance. For example, the cresset, a pole-mounted open cage for burning material, was sometimes used for stage light on the Tudor stage, so reconstructing the stage picture requires knowing that a cresset's light was dim orange-red and flickered severely, but it was a method of visibility, not a tool for representation. Though the cresset itself may have communicated as a *prop (for example, carried by the revellers in *Romeo and Juliet*), its light said nothing.

For almost all of human history, a good day for a play was a bright, sunny one, because the performance was outdoors. The world seems more 'alive' in sunlight; when sunlight comes in at about a 45-degree angle, the eye sees most clearly, and in bright sunlight our colour vision is closest to true. Naturally show times tended to be set for when the audience could see best.

In temperate Europe and China, where the sun is always far south of the zenith, outdoor performances tended to begin in the early afternoon; in tropical India, Africa, and Mesoamerica, performances began later (often needing to be finished by firelight).

Sunlight has drawbacks. It is not reliable in many locations. Daylight may be too valuable to use for the theatre. And from the actor's standpoint, sunlight is far too democratic; it also falls on the audience, who may find each other more interesting than the performance, and it is found mainly outdoors where hecklers and drop-ins are more likely (because it is harder to keep them out). In general a dark *auditorium with restricted entrances is a relatively more quiet and attentive auditorium; outdoor audiences are rowdier and less attentive.

Thus, because the weather was bad, because the local lord wanted his theatre before bed, or because a better-behaved audience was wanted, theatre sometimes moved indoors and into the night. When it did, the performance adapted to the way it was lighted; light could not be designed when it could not be controlled. In the *kathakali theatre of south India, performers who needed to be seen had to stay near the oil lamp at centre stage; many entrances were by figures emerging from the dark beyond, and this became part of the drama. In the *Bengali *jatra, with its strings of lamps overhead, the dim downlight created a theatre in which speaking *characters normally stood, and in which disguisings and unveilings were common.

The source of light can greatly influence performance. For example, *shadow puppets are found in many places and eras, but the lamp that casts the shadow on the screen determines, to a great extent, what the theatre can and cannot do. The dim, flickering *blentjong* that lighted the traditional *puppet stages of Java with a single big flame compelled that the shadow puppets be pushed as close to the screen as possible, created a bright blurry spot on the screen, and made magical effects of sudden appearances and disappearances relatively easy to achieve, since a puppet more than a few centimetres away from the screen effectively vanished (*see* WAYANG KULIT). The brighter banks of lights, further away from the screen, used in Hunan, meant that shadow puppets could be translucent and painted, clearly showing colour through the screen and providing half-tones by the relative coarseness of their lacework, but had to make entrances and exits from the wings or below. In the Greek *karagiozis* (*see* KARAGÖZ), strips of lights above and below created a very bright screen on which shadows were only

An excellent representation of eighteenth-century European **lighting** techniques, for Ludvig Holberg's *Jeppe of the Hill* in Copenhagen in the 1740s. The two chandeliers drop from the proscenium, while the footlights at the edge of the forestage are attended by a snuffer to the right, necessary for safety purposes. The illumination made the audience in the front of the auditorium, whether in boxes or on pit benches, almost as visible as the actors and the wing flats on the stage.

activated by objects extremely close to it; this allowed for extensive covered movement and sudden appearances.

Usually wherever modern Western lighting becomes available, it displaces the older system. The oil lamp is still lighted in *kathakali*, but the stage is often in a general wash; the downlight of *jatra* has been mellowed with frontlight in more recent decades. But the effective playing area of *kathakali* is larger and the performers' whole bodies can be clearly seen; the *jatra* downlight still shapes and sculpts the body, but the overall shape of the body is more clearly perceptible. These and many more examples seem to indicate that audiences everywhere are willing to see something different from what they have traditionally seen, as long as they can see it more clearly. Shadow puppets around the world are now more commonly lighted by a slide projector or other source of strong directional light. There are exceptions: Indonesian shadow plays rely so heavily on effects that can only be achieved in non-directional unfocused light that the light bulb has been substituted for the *blentjong* with little else changed, and the dimly firelit Olua festival night

*dance (*see* SPECIAL EFFECTS) has kept its traditional lighting in order to preserve its traditional effects. But for the most part, human beings go to the theatre to be able to see, and the workings of the eye and brain trump culture; lighting is largely transcultural because vision is. Thus to a great extent the history of European lighting, which has become nearly universal lighting, is the development of methods to produce sunlight-like light indoors and on demand.

Perhaps the most remarkable feature in the development of modern Western stage lighting is the co-evolution among aesthetics, technology, and theory that appears to take on the character of the inevitable. There are many false starts and failed experiments in the development of lighting from the *early modern period to the present, but almost no turnings or reversals; furthermore no other Western practice has been adopted more quickly, thoroughly, and easily by non-Western theatres. This apparent convergence is so unusual in any sort of cultural history that it requires some explanation. Unlike almost any other area of enquiry in the history of the theatre, the history of stage lighting does not seem to be either an intra-cultural issue (one with multiple answers which only make sense in some cultures, like the *unities or the proper role of visible stagehands), nor a multicultural issue (one with different answers in different cultures, like audience–performer relationship or the tension between *illusion and convention).

Lighting seems to be transcultural—something with the same answer in most or all cultures, like avoidance when possible of hunger, cold, pain, or fear. This is rare but not unknown in cultural history; a simple related example is that few spectators anywhere voluntarily choose to have a pillar or a wall between themselves and the stage if a place with a good sight line is available. In the theoretical and aesthetic development of modern Western stage lighting, visibility was gradually discovered to be composed of several different elements, variously optical, neurological, psychological, and cultural. One of these elements, which is almost entirely optical/neurological, is acuity, the relation between the size of a detail and the distance at which it can be distinguished (usually expressed as a ratio between the performance of the observing eye and a standard or normative eye). In the past 500 years, nearly all lasting changes in stage lighting, both technical and customary, have resulted in improvements in acuity. It seems likely that acuity is a genuinely transcultural value, probably because it is entirely physiological.

2. Early modern discovery of light, 1500–1680

The early modern period was fascinated with light. *Perspective illustrates the geometry of light: objects in the field of vision have their apparent shapes and sizes because light travels in straight lines through the tiny aperture of the iris. Renaissance painting famously developed the means to depict light, proposing that the kind of light striking an object strongly influenced what it looked like, and noting the visual implications resulting from the fact that sunlight is naturally highly collimated. The collimation of a beam of light is the extent to which its rays form parallel lines. The sun is so far away that for practical purposes all light coming from it to the earth is parallel. The results are familiar: sharp, unidirectional shadows in uniform proportion. Throughout the early modern period alchemists, painters, scientists, and artisans experimented with manipulating the light around a subject, just as they experimented with depicting the effects of light in perspective and chiaroscuro; at the time, the need for strong collimated light could be met only with windows or with mirrors reflecting them.

Collimated beams are also highly useful in stage lighting: brighter at greater distances; strongly directional, so they can be aimed through openings and cast shadows like those seen in sunlight; less prone to scatter and glare; narrow at the source, and thus easy to colour. Although the late Renaissance scene *painters did not know how to make bright collimated beams that would mimic sunlight, they understood their desirability.

In a fashion analogous to Leonardo's flying machines for which no engines existed, scene painters between 1545 and 1595 wrote about and drew what stage light ought to be, imagining light for accent, contrast, time of day, and mood, and providing an analytic technique for imitating natural light, for focused and directed coloured beams, the darkened house, concealed sources, dimming, translucent gauze effects, and shuttering in the manner of a modern spotlight.

In his *Second Book of Architecture* (1545), *Serlio not only discusses the use of *bozze*—hollow glasses flat on one side and curved on the other, filled with coloured water or oil, crude versions of the plano-convex lens—but even describes the placement of a torch between a polished barber's basin and *bozze*, very similar to the mid-twentieth-century plano-convex spotlight. Angelo *Ingegneri described a flying batten of lamps, that is, the borderlights of a century after; *Sabbatini proposed a system for lowering and raising open-ended cylinders over candles for dimming at a distance. *Bozze* were common in Italian theatres; the surviving *bozze* at the Teatro *Olimpico are hemispheric, about 7 cm (2.75 in) in diameter, and are mounted on the backs of painted wings to illuminate *scenery further upstage. *Bozze* give dim, slightly collimated light. Effective light barely reaches 2 m (6 feet) away, which explains why they are found on wings and not in borders. Often they were used as oil lamps, which are brighter than candles, but the position of the flame meant that it could neither be coloured nor focused.

Ultimately the early modern dreams of stage lighting could not be realized because to collimate light, whether with a lens or a reflector, it must be passed through a very small focus. A flame at the end of a wick was too dim and too large. Even some critical experiments were unperformable: the role of contrast for acuity went undiscovered, and important theorists like Serlio and Joseph *Furttenbach taught that stage lighting should be as even as possible, a notion that persisted for centuries until brighter sources exposed it as an error.

3. The enlightenment discovery of optics, 1680–1820

The lens-grinding industry developed in the seventeenth century, but lenses were small, and thus gathered little of the light around a flame, particularly until conic-section reflectors were invented. Theatre lighting practice remained oriented almost entirely toward visibility. It is often asserted that in the Restoration theatre, audience and actors were in equal light. This is an exaggeration; stage to house ratio was smaller than a modern or even Victorian audience might expect, but still significant, and increased during the period. The basic source, a chandelier over the *forestage which could be moved on a pulley, was closer to the backcloth than to the galleries when lowered for performance, making the stage somewhat brighter than the house.

This effect was increasingly enhanced with *footlights, borderlights, and scene ladders, vertical columns of candles or oil lamps attached to the inside edges of the wings to light the playing area and the wing or drop (*see* FLATS AND WINGS) immediately upstage. By the 1720s many scene ladders were equipped with scene blinds, reflector shades consisting of two nested rotating partial cylinders, usually of tin, surrounding the candle or lamp. The cylinder created an opening which could be aimed, narrowed, or widened, allowing crude direction and dimming. Often all the scene blinds on a scene ladder were controlled by a common rod running through them.

Because self-consuming wicks had not yet been developed, candles required constant snuffing (wick cutting) while they burned, to prevent guttering, in which a too-long wick fell over and melted through the lip, sending the molten wax running uselessly away into a dangerous flammable puddle. Snuffers were vital personnel in a candlelit theatre, and took priority over everything for *safety's sake, and guttering candles provoked loud shouts of 'Snuffers!' during performance. While the play continued, snuffers walked onto the stage to trim footlights or to reach for borders and chandeliers with long-handled tools, and crossed between wings upstage as they tended scene ladders and sconces.

The major innovations of the period were the work of scientists in general illumination. Two centuries of effective household and workplace lighting have obliterated the memory, but before Murdoch's gaslights (see below), all artificial lighting—not just stage lighting—was difficult, expensive, and inadequate. The problem became more urgent after 1760, because the Industrial Revolution was making it necessary for people to work indoors and after dark. Much of the scientific and technical talent of Europe was engrossed in trying to solve the problem of illumination. Antoine-Laurent Lavoisier (1743–94), best known now for his basic work in chemistry, spent much of his life on the problem of illumination. He demonstrated that in an unsnuffed candle, only about 10 per cent of the wax or tallow was actually consumed for light, which shifted lighting research toward better oil lamps (and eventually to the Argand burner), but his direct contribution to stage lighting was the *réverbère*, the first conic-section reflector.

The conic sections (they are the circle, ellipse, parabola, and hyperbola) by definition relate points to other points (foci) and to parallel lines. Thus, Lavoisier pointed out, light coming from a source placed at the focus of a reflector whose shape is the rotation of a conic section can be focused into a small point or collimated into a beam. Those used as reflectors in stage lighting are the ellipsoid, sphere (rotation of a circle), and paraboloid. *Réverbères* were semi-ellipsoidal, with the flame of an oil lamp placed at the internal focus so that all rays in the wrong direction would be redirected to the external focus, doubling the delivered light of any one source. Developed originally for street lighting, *réverbères* were quickly adapted to stage use, particularly in borders. Lavoisier noted that scattering of light could be further reduced by putting a paraboloid outer reflector around the opening of the *réverbère*, but this does not seem to have been put into practice before the twentieth century.

Trough-shaped *réverbères*, installed as footlights and borders, considerably brightened the stage, especially relative to the house, and would later form the basis for many of the safety footlights of the gas era. Their other important influence was in bringing the attention of scientists and engineers to bear on what became the central technical problem in stage lighting: because the foci of conic sections are infinitely small, to produce perfectly collimated beams, the source would have to be infinitely small. Much of the history of subsequent stage lighting concerns the search for smaller, brighter sources. In 1780 Aimé Argand introduced a burner consisting of a hollow metal ring pierced with tiny holes on the top, through which oil was brought by a permanent, never-consumed wick. The central column of air created a leaner fuel–air mixture for a higher-temperature flame. The Argand lamp was a threefold improvement in brightness, enough to allow the first real experiments in designed light.

Though *Garrick did not, as is sometimes claimed, introduce footlights to the *London stage (they preceded him by decades), he did emphasize footlights by not lowering the chandelier, and introduced float lights for safety. But Garrick's most important contribution to stage lighting was that he brought Philip James de *Loutherbourg to London in 1771 as a scene painter. In 1781 Loutherbourg struck out on his own with a display he called the *Eidophusikon*, a series of painted scenes presented under controlled light on a roughly one-third-scale stage in a darkened room, with Argand lamps in overhead front-of-house lighting, ellipsoidal and parabolic reflectors, and mechanical dimming. The *Eidophusikon* depicted changing light, including a dawn over Greenwich Park, a sunset/moonrise, and a storm. As a remarkable *succès d'estime*, it influenced stagecraft and scene painting for generations afterward.

4. Gas and controllable light, 1790–1890

The Argand burner for oil lamps was introduced less than two decades before coal gaslights first appeared on the outsides of theatres; some spectators who saw *Beaumarchais's *comedies by candle saw *Scribe's by gas. The difference in less than one long generation must have been about a tenfold increase in brightness. Gaslight, in turn, enabled big strides toward fully designed light. Nineteenth-century coal gas, distilled by heating bituminous coal in a sealed retort, was a varying, dirty mixture of three flammable gases (hydrogen, methane, and carbon monoxide) plus the flammable hydrocarbons that released the soot that incandesced to make the flame a bright, ruddy yellow. Coal gas smelled variously like modern petrol or paint thinner, deposited greasy black carbon in streaks above the burner, and was usually contaminated with sulphur and ammonia, which corroded pipes and burners dangerously. It also burned eight times more brightly than oil, and could be shut off from a distance in an accidental *fire. Best of all from the standpoint of the intensely market-oriented theatre of the day, its already low price was subsidized by the sale of coke and coal tar, the other products of coal distillation.

In the early 1790s, James Watt's chief assistant William Murdoch demonstrated that coal gas burned brightly and (relatively) cleanly in an Argand burner. By 1797 Murdoch had lighted the Birmingham works of Boulton & Watt with coal gas. A major public display in 1802 attracted investors and in 1804, Frederick Albert Winsos, founder of London's first gaslight company, delivered a lecture at the *Lyceum Theatre, lighted by gas. Theatrical possibilities were seen at once, but realization waited on two innovations with confusingly similar names. The gasometer was a constant-pressure tank, one that put out gas at the same pressure regardless of how full the tank was. This was important so that lights would neither flare dangerously when the tank was full nor backfire as it emptied. The ordinary gas meter was also important because prior to it, buildings were charged by the burner, and stage lighting required numerous burners, making the cost of gas prohibitive. Both the gasometer and a practical and reliable gas meter were invented in 1817, and gas lighting was in use on theatres, if not yet in them, within weeks of their availability.

Penzel notes that new stage lighting rarely begins on stage, because lighting, still less lighting development, rarely holds priority in theatre budgets. New lighting technology tends to appear on the exteriors and in the house, to attract the *ticket buyer, and some of the first 'gas lighted' theatres in London and *Philadelphia were lighted on the outsides or in lobbies. For this reason some uncertainty remains as to the exact date and place at which the performance itself was routinely lit entirely by gas. In any case, exterior gaslights required gas equipment to serve them, and gas stage lighting always followed quickly once theatres had access to coal gas and a gasometer with which to handle it safely. Gasification of stage lighting was complete in London by early 1822, and spread to every other city, worldwide, as soon as there was a gasworks.

At first gas burners simply replaced oil lamps in the same fixtures. By 1830 instruments specific to gas were manufactured, and before 1840 they had nearly reached their final forms. Gasified foots, borders, lengths (gas scene ladders), and *ground rows were trainées or trough lights, rows of burners enclosed by a long elliptical-cross-section reflector. New gas instruments included side lamps (permanent trees of multiple burners in the wings); bunch lights (mobile multiple-burner floor lamps, often with a réverbère); and conical reflector floodlights. Though the simple metal cone reflectors of these last instruments had no focal point, and were not nearly as effective a reflector as a conic section, they could be made by any tinsmith and allowed some of the first experiments with a *cyclorama.

The gas era was also the era of *limelight. Though much brighter than ordinary gaslight, it was still a flame, and not a good approximation to a point source. Nonetheless enough light passed through the focus to permit the experiments with lensed instruments, and limelight was bright enough to shine through coloured media, enabling colour mixing. Limelight was expensive, however, and the limes required much maintenance by skilled labour, sharply limiting its use.

Gaslight's brightness allowed for a wider range of contrast, so that gauzes, *Pepper's ghost, and other such devices worked well. One of the paradoxes of visibility is that how well the audience sees is physiological, but what they want to see and how well they want to see it are cultural. A rough rule is that the audience will want to see, as clearly as possible, what they are supposed to see, which is not always what is actually happening. To fool the eye, detail must sometimes be sacrificed, but the sacrifice is generally minimal and the illusion is better if the visibility of the intended *spectacle is clearer. For example, Pepper's ghost, J. R. *Planché's famous 'witch trick' in Macbeth, and Henry *Irving's gauze in The Bells all worked their wonders because the ghostly or imaginary figures, though blurred, were seen in great detail, clearly alive and real, however obscured; the difference in acuity was an icon of the way we see when we *dream, or when our mind is playing tricks on us. Gas provided the first light intense and collimated enough to make acuity a matter of choice. The audience's default preference for high acuity means that whenever lower acuity is chosen, it is always read in some way as meaningful or symbolic (even if it is only an index of an incompetent designer or an inadequate budget).

By the 1840s it was well known that blue light for night was highly effective, because in strongly blue light, even if it is very bright, colour vision vanishes. The brain interprets this colour suppression as dimness, even when light is ample, and thus blue light looks like night on stage. Brighter light led to many other experiments with effects. Though they went unremarked at the time, J. E. Dove's experiments (*Edinburgh, 1845) demonstrated that collimated light from plan angles increased acuity and footlights reduced it. (Two instruments are at plan angles if they are 45 degrees off the centre line and 90 degrees off each other.) Using a complex and carefully choreographed mixture of scene and lighting effects, Frederick *Lloyds was able to produce strikingly *realistic sunrises and sunsets.

The availability of lighting effects, even the very simple ones of the time, required fading from one set of gaslights to another, which prompted the first unified control systems. Up to a limit, gaslights are brighter depending on how much gas they receive; thus a valve that partially closes a line can be used to dim a light, and for effects, it was most convenient if all the valves were in a central location backstage, called the gas table. By the mid-1860s, new theatres were built with centralized gas tables, but control was difficult and unsophisticated. For safety's sake, no light could be dimmed to black and then reused. Operators had to rely on hand signals or speaking tubes to know what was happening on stage, and synchronization by multiple operators depended on simultaneously watching the position of each other's valves and a glass bubble tube. The same central main, with a single valve, usually fed all the side lamps, foots, and borders. Few gas tables had sub-valves; even an advanced gas table of the 1870s had only nine valves, three dedicated to the house—in effect, six dimmers. At the very end of the gaslight era, the *actor-manager Henry Irving experimented with having all lights of the same colour on a single valve, and the *Paris *Opéra constructed an 88-valve gas table.

Gas lighting required large numbers of operators. The *Vienna *opera had a standing staff of eighteen gasmen, and for a major production like *The Corsican Brothers* in London, 30 gasmen were required every night. Although oil was much more expensive than gas, in the French theatre most *rehearsals were conducted with oil lamps because it was too expensive to pay gasmen to attend. Technical advances accelerated, with several significant inventions per decade. Until about 1875, these were primarily concerned with safety; after that time brighter sources and better optics were the focus of attention. Two major innovations late in the period briefly kept gas competitive with electric light. The Siemens regenerating burner (1879) used heat from the flame to preheat a gas–air mix, so that incoming gas did not cool or choke the flame, which burned much hotter. Siemens burners went into almost immediate use. The mantle was introduced in 1885, so late that many houses were already electrified: a fine net of heat-resistant, easily incandesced material supported in the flame made the light much brighter, more even, and less flickery.

Beginning in 1878 at the Lyceum, Irving, with his assistant Bram Stoker, introduced a very modern look: a fully darkened house, selective area lighting, routine (some would say excessive) use of gauzes, colour media, and mixing in limelight, masking by the use of black velvet hung in the dark, colour grouping of footlights, and lacquered glass colour media. A single gas table cued by the *prompter, and much brighter light everywhere from the new Siemens burners, gave Irving more control over light than anyone had had before. The Lyceum productions were extremely influential in the development of lighting; in particular the production of *Faust* (1886), with its use of cyclorama and of some isolations, pointed the way to the future. Already, too, some critics complained that Irving's use of light for emphasis primarily emphasized Irving, and that his designs often represented kinds of light that would never occur in nature, while others praised the heightened effects he achieved. Just at its end, gas had finally achieved controllable light.

5. Electricity and controlled light, 1840–1950

From its first practicality in 1879, the electric incandescent filament was superior to gas. Electricity was intrinsically cleaner (coal gas did not illuminate if it did not emit soot), and had a far better light-to-heat ratio than either gas or limelight. It was also far safer. An overload could not flash back to detonate the gas-

ometer, the risk of fire was far less, and the danger of leaks nil. Safe electric cable was cheap and easy to manufacture, whereas even the best gas hoses of the 1890s, rubber-coated leather in jointed steel-mesh tubes, were expensive and yet still prone to leaks and punctures.

In October 1881 Richard *D'Oyly Carte reopened the *Savoy in London as the first theatre with all-electric lighting. There were immediate complaints that electric light was 'harsh' or 'cold'. But since the light was also much brighter than gas, it could be 'cut down' with red or yellow media without making the stage too dark. Coloured media, either gelatine or glass, thus became much more important, and by 1920 it was rare to see an uncoloured instrument; with electricity colour went from optional to mandatory. Gas lingered in some small provincial houses until the First World War, but lost ground rapidly after 1890. When 1,000-watt electric lamps became commercially available in 1913, limelight too vanished. But the habits of gas lingered longer; at first electricity was used mainly to provide a cheaper and brighter version of what had been done with gas. As Jean *Rosenthal wrote, 'The electrified theatre was burdened with gaslight traditions. Positions for lighting remained the same and the lighting was limited to floodlighting in borders and footlights and to spots and arcs elsewhere. Spotlights— casting the pools of light which are the true beginning of modern lighting design—could be hung in relatively few and severely regimented places . . . Comedies were bright; dramas were uncheerful. Day was yellow; night blue. Effects were naïve (storms, fires, clouds).'

Until electricity, sources had always been inadequate. Candlelit stages were probably at a brightness ranging from one-quarter of a foot-candle upstage to one foot-candle on the apron, barely enabling colour vision. Argand lighting roughly tripled those levels, to half the brightness of a modern movie screen. Gas lighting at the Paris Opéra was probably between 25 and 50 foot-candles, similar to a living room today. Electric lighting made an even brightness of 200 foot-candles easy and cheap; it was finally possible to make every part of the stage brilliant and shadowless. Electricians of the generation which began with gas gave priority to an even brightness; shadows were undesirable accidents. The discovery that contrast mattered more than brightness, and that deliberate shadows enhanced vision, was strongly resisted by many designers, despite Dove's decades-old demonstrations, the observations of reviewers as early as 1882, and numerous experiences with the vividness of colour-mixed limelight. Even after 1900, Mariano *Fortuny created his skydomes (or cycloramas) deliberately to bathe the stage in shadowless bright light; the indirectness of cyclorama produced decollimated light of uniform colour that went where it was supposed to, providing a pleasant, even glow. Critics noted, however, that everything in that glow looked slightly blurry and muddy. Fortuny lighting was beautiful in the abstract, controllable and flexible in execution, and not inherently more expensive than plan-angle direct lighting, but it was thoroughly decollimated and it was of a uniform colour rather than colour mixed. Thus it reduced acuity rather than increased it, and ultimately acuity proved to be the deciding issue.

Adolphe *Appia, in *Die Musik und die Inscenierung* (*Music and the Art of the Theatre*, 1899), stated that colour mixing and contrast were the keys to improved visual acuity, and gave a detailed example applied to *Tristan and Isolde*, the first true lighting concept in published form. Appia was more right than he knew. Though the neurology of sight would not be understood for decades, experiments by Stanley McCandless in the 1920s revealed that an object surrounded by darkness and lighted by differently coloured collimated beams at plan angles is perceived with greater acuity than in real life; an eye with 20/20 vision sees at about 20/15, perhaps as well as 20/12 under ideal conditions. The crossing, coloured beams create thousands of tiny coloured shadows at right angles on fabric, skin, and every textured surface. The visual cortex responds to difference rather than to absolute brightness, both for colour and for shape, and the number of visible differences created is orders of magnitude greater than that occurring in natural sunlight. Visual acuity will be optimal where difference is maximized, that is, where the instruments are at plan angles and gelled in complementary colours at different saturations. Such light, blended by adding a top light, is called 'McCandless lighting', and is used in nearly all theatrical productions worldwide today. The struggle between evenness and contrast persisted, but the evidence was on McCandless's side; people go to the theatre to see, and under McCandless lighting they saw better. Nonetheless, Fortuny and the other 'evenness' designers had given us the cyclorama, and its striking beauty to a generation raised on painted skies, and the 'common-sense' argument that shadows must interfere with, not enhance, vision, carried great force. Even just before the Second World War most new theatres were built with electrified footlight traps, and new plaster skydomes and elaborate systems to use them for indirect lighting were still being constructed in Germany.

The debate went on even within McCandless himself. Though he had established experimentally that visual acuity was about as good in 5-50 foot-candles of plan-angle lighting as it was in 150-250 of smooth even light, still, in the first two editions of *A Method of Lighting the Stage* (1932 and 1938), he advocated striking a balance between contrast and brightness. Many early electric lighting instruments were therefore designed for evenness and shadow killing. In addition to electric foots, borders, and striplights, standard equipment included 'border floods' and free-standing boom-mounted floods called 'olivettes'. Though these were almost entirely obsolete in the last quarter of the twentieth century, the ellipsoidal reflector floodlight (ERF or 'scoop'), the last in the lineage of the *réverbère*, persisted for cyclorama washes.

Other early electric instruments were highly specialized directional instruments, and were superseded by the ellipsoidal reflector spotlight (ERS). Beam projectors, arc followspots, the plano-convex spotlight (PCS), and the Linnebach projector have mostly been replaced by the modern ERS, developed just before the Second World War. The ERS places a filament at one focus of an ellipsoidal and focuses a plano-convex lens on the other focus, thus organizing the light into a smaller-than-the-filament virtual source and projecting an extremely well-collimated beam. A telescoping lens mounting allows partial decollimation as needed, and there are shutters and slots between the virtual source and the lens, for controlled shadowing and the insertion of gobos (metal cut-out slides used to project light patterns on the set or stage floor). Two other instruments developed between the wars persist to the present. In the Fresnel light a lamp backed by a hemispherical reflector slides on a track behind a Fresnel lens (a flat transparent plate cut into concentric curved ridges which focus light less precisely than a plano-convex lens, but with much less weight for the same refraction). Moving the slider can collimate the light to a good approximation of a PCS, or decollimate it almost as much as a scoop.

The PAR (parabolic aluminized reflector) lamp has, as a reflector, a coating of aluminium on the inside of the parabola-shaped envelope. Because nothing further is needed to shape the light, which is intermediate in collimation between a Fresnel and an ERS, PARs are generally mounted in simple black metal tubes called 'PAR cans'. Fresnels, scoops, and PARs are all much cheaper and usually more robust than ERSs, and when they are used within their optical limits, their effect is not significantly worse. So although Fresnels, scoops, and PARs could theoretically be replaced by decollimated ERSs, it seems likely that they will remain in use.

Besides collimated front light, the new lighting required many quick cue changes. In 1900 the only practical form of dimming available was to put lamps in series with a variable resistor. The first commercial dimmers were small tanks of salt water within which resistance was varied by changing the distance between upper and lower electrodes. Hence the valves of the gas table were at first succeeded by the cranks of the tracker wire regulator. The cranks pulled tracker wires that ran through a pulley system to position the moving electrode. It took several seconds to crank an individual dimmer between 'off' and 'full', and the largest tracker wire regulators operated 120 dimmers. To speed up the process, cranks could be locked together with a submaster wheel, and the submasters with a master. A crank could be controlled by only one submaster, and the same submaster could not bring two different lights to full and half simultaneously. Nonetheless, with a gigantic tracker wire regulator, a small team of technicians could produce the smooth and graceful transitions and seemingly infinite flexibility of *Reinhardt's seminal *Midsummer Night's Dream* at the Neues Theater (*Berlin, 1905), which, with its very large number of smooth light

cues, front-of-house lighting, and cyclorama, was a visual wonder to audiences and finally established the superiority of electricity, for an army of gasmen could not have accomplished
anything like it.

The wire-wound resistance dimmer, in which a lever
moved an electrode along a resisting coil, was safer and easier
to work than the salt-water dimmer, and because handles could
be locked together, it preserved mastering and submastering.
These dimmers were large and awkward (a travelling 'road
board' with eight dimmers was as large and heavy as a kitchen
range, and a permanent array of about 100 dimmers was 10 m
wide by 2 m high by 1 m deep, or 33 by 6.5 by 3.3 feet), but the
eye–hand feedback of the lever was superb. For the first time,
the timing of a cue was determined by what looked right on
stage and not limited by how long it took to set a valve or turn a
winch.

Extensive experimentation in dimming in the 1920s and
1930s introduced features which became goals and priorities of
the next generation of engineers. Frederick Bentham's lighting
console in 1934 demonstrated the advantages of assigning any
dimmer to any channel on the console. The all-electric board
built by General Electric for *Radio City Music Hall in 1933 used
saturable-core dimmers, in which the AC power passing
through is controlled by a very small DC voltage. With no moving parts, and DC regulated by simple slider resisters which
moved just a few centimetres from off to full, the board was
no bigger than a large desk. The Radio City board also introduced presetting. Five complete sets of sliders on the console
could each control all the lights. A technician could set up
four cues ahead, transferring control from one set of sliders
to another at each cue point. Even very complex transitions
of hundreds of instruments simultaneously changing tens of
levels in a few seconds could be accomplished by a single
operator.

6. Art of controlled light, 1950–present

Ultimately, psychophysics and the eye trumped tradition
and the installed base, and the generation that grew up
with 'McCandless lighting' abandoned evenness as a goal.
McCandless's advocacy, and the example of the generation
that followed him, established contrast-based lighting, with visual acuity, expression of emotional atmosphere, and realism as
its goals, as the basis of contemporary lighting. The transformation to modern practice was nearly complete by 1960. Jean
Rosenthal, one of the artistic leaders of that new generation,
noted that the American theatres of the 1930s, from whom
McCandless lighting was widely copied—the *Federal Theatre
Project, and the *Mercury Theatre, *Group Theatre, Theatre
Union, and Phoenix Theatre—had little money for scenery
and inadequate *scene-shifting equipment, but performed plays
written in cinema-like short scenes. A properly coloured and
angled pool of light can isolate two actors in a convincing

environment much more cheaply, effectively, and quickly than
flying in a painted drop (see FLIES AND FLOWN SCENERY). Furthermore, by manipulating angle and saturation in McCandless
lighting, one could imitate natural latitude, time of day, temperature, dustiness, apparent depth of field, and humidity, and
audiences adapted easily and naturally to reading this information from the light around the actors rather than from a painting
behind them.

After the Second World War, the rebellions and experiments of the 1930s became the foundation of the restored theatre. Works like *Miller's *Death of a Salesman* and *Williams's *A
Streetcar Named Desire* relied upon lighting to make a realistic
unit set flexible. Other plays were written to have lighting
designs, and the lighting designer was no longer 'a bloody electrician with notions', as Rosenthal was called early in her career,
but a necessary artist among artists.

Though technical innovations were more numerous than
ever, most of those outside the control booth had only minor
effects. The variable focal length ERS, in which the lenses in the
lens train can be moved relative to each other, proved popular
for projections, but its higher cost and fragility made it an adjunct, not a replacement. Cheaper and more durable coloured
media became available. Some low-voltage high-intensity instruments made it possible to conceal instruments in smaller
and more enclosed spaces than ever before. Tungsten-halogen
lamps burned brighter, lasted longer, and did not dim with age.
Perhaps the most important recent innovations will turn out to
be movable instruments, which can reaim, refocus, and recolour
themselves on remote command between a large number of settings. As of 2001 they are still much too expensive to be used
routinely in theatre productions and the market for them is
primarily for pop music concerts. But they allow one instrument
to do the work of a dozen, and the audience for large *musicals
enjoys the effect of beams suddenly changing in direction and
colour.

The real revolution was not in the instruments but in how
they were controlled. Though a technician of 1950, if transported to a theatre 50 years later, would recognize nearly everything hanging overhead, the control and dimming system
would be an utter enigma, both in what it can do and how it
does it. In 1947, Yale University introduced the first electronic
board, a 44-channel board with multi-scene presetting, which
used the new thyratron tube. Like all vacuum tubes, thyratrons
were expensive, cranky, and prone to burn-out, and few
thyratron boards were built. But in 1959 silicon-controlled rec-
tifier (SCR) dimmers appeared—solid-state thyratrons, also
known as thyristors. They had all the advantages of the
thyratron but were relatively rugged, long-lived, and cheap,
and became almost universal by the end of the century.

The limit of human dexterity was to manage presets
of about 50 sliders, cross-fading between two presets while
also operating one or two independent submasters. If more

instruments needed to be controlled, then more than one instrument went into a common dimmer, or more than one dimmer into a common channel. Yet artistically interesting designs might require many more instruments than 50 to act independently (though in coordination). This problem led in 1964 to Thorn Electric's development of programmable memory at the BBC studios; one could program the cues before the show, at a speed a good deal slower than real time, to be activated by the operator's recalling them from machine memory at the proper time. In 1967 Electronics Diversified in the USA introduced the first true computer board, at the *Shubert Theatre on Broadway. This first board, which remained in place through the long run of *A Chorus Line*, cost $100,000 in 1967, and could operate 125 channels for 100 cues.

The interfaces of early computer boards were computer models of familiar light boards, and inherited their limitations. Most copied preset and cross-fade all-electric boards, so that each cue had to be written anew rather than modified from the previous one. Some boards copied wire resistance dimmers, so that only the specified channels changed; these often left the operator with 'orphan' instruments still lighted during supposed blackouts. In 1980 Strand Century introduced the Light Palette, a light board that could read a cue sheet, and could thus be told that a given cue was a modification of or return to another, or a blackout, or a full up. The computer 'thought' in a language similar to the one the designer used. In 1986 the DMX512 standard was promulgated, allowing any console to communicate with any dimmer, and the process of making the operation of the lights completely transparent to the designer was complete.

7. Contemporary practice

Like all design, lighting design is a mixture of art and craft; uninspired but serviceable designs which merely follow the rules abound, but the best modern designers are able to step far beyond, based on a grasp, sometimes intuitive, of space, light, script, and production. Ideally the designer takes extensive notes during *rehearsals to identify acting areas and special cues, acquires and analyses copies of the set and *costume renderings for colour, and accumulates extensive pictorial research on the appearance of the light in the locations and times in which the play is set. The designer then draws 'keys', diagrammatic plans for imitating the real light while modifying it to support visibility, actor and director choices, and set and costume designs. Normally each key has:

1. a key light, a more saturated light of the same hue as the real light, coming from about the same angle, but cheated toward 45-degree angles whenever possible;
2. a fill light, relatively unsaturated light in a complementary colour at right angles to the key;
3. a top light gelled, in a colour which erases the double coloured shadow produced by the key and fill, and puts a bright high-

light around the edges of actors to 'pop' them against the background.

The designer then works out a colour distribution for the cyclorama to create an appropriate sky, as needed, and works out boosters for practicals (such as a ruddy glow by a fireplace) and director specials (such as an isolated spot for a *soliloquy).

Normally actor movement patterns are analysed into areas about 2 m (6 feet) across (the approximate width of a beam at the stage) and a list is prepared of the keys needed in each area. On a scale paper map, the instruments necessary to accomplish each key are geometrically projected outward from the centre of each area to find the nearest feasible position for hanging an instrument; this eventually produces a complete map of the positions of the instruments, their assignments to circuits, and their colours, which is called a light plot. The master electrician and the crew follow the light plot to hang, circuit, aim, focus, and gel the instruments.

The designer marks the script, noting which set of keys should be brought up to which levels at what times, along with accompanying cyclorama, booster, special, and practical lighting; each arrangement of power levels, together with decisions about how fast it should be faded up or down, is called a cue (somewhat confusingly, since the signal to activate it is also called a cue). The cue sheet is programmed into the light board (or, in older systems, written out in a form to be easily read and executed by the board operator). The operation of the completed plan is practised during technical and dress rehearsals, and extensive revision is normal, as what was worked out on paper is adjusted to the physical theatre.

There is still much remaining to be accomplished. Stage lighting rarely reaches perfect acuity and never does so over the whole area of a stage; colour mixing still is mostly worked out in trial and error after a first rough guess; many cues are still sharply limited by what control systems can accomplish. True perfect lighting over the whole area of a stage, so that the designer's keys were executed exactly at every point and acuity was maximal, would require the replacement of large instruments with many thousands of tiny, aimable apertures, covering much of the ceiling of the theatre, each producing a coloured collimated beam; colour mixing by splitting a beam into its component wavelengths and routing them to different apertures, thus automatically producing perfect mutual complementarity between key, fill, and top; and a micro-supercomputer in the lightboard, equipped to read video input from cameras focused on the stage, to control, fade, and mix applied keys on the stage, and to do such simple things as reaim the light for actors who fail to hit their marks and tweak keys to optimize them for a given costume or set piece (so that, in effect, each actor would always be in perfect light). Interestingly enough, the hardware for all of this existed at the beginning of the twenty-first century, either in industrial laboratories or off-the-shelf. Perhaps the lighting revolution that has been nearly continual since 1550 is far from over, and we are merely in a pause, waiting for the moment when enough capital becomes available to the next generation of innovators—a development which, because of the transcultural nature of stage lighting, could come at any time, in any tradition, in any country. *See also* MEDIA AND PERFORMANCE; MULTIMEDIA PERFORMANCE; SCENOGRAPHY. JB

GILLETTE, J. MICHAEL, *Designing with Light: an introduction to stage lighting*, 3rd edn. (Mountain View, Calif., 1998)

HAYS, DAVID, *Light on the Subject*, 5th edn. (New York, 1989)

KELLER, MAX, *Light Fantastic: the art and design of stage lighting* (London, 1999)

McCANDLESS, STANLEY, *A Method of Lighting the Stage*, 4 edns. (New York, 1932, 1939, 1947, 1957)

PENZEL, FREDERICK, *Stage Lighting before Electricity* (Middletown, Conn., 1978)

REES, TERENCE, *Theatre Lighting in the Age of Gas* (London, 1978)

ROSENTHAL, JEAN, and WERTENBAKER, LAEL, *The Magic of Light* (New York, 1972)

SANDSTRÖM, ULF, *Stage Lighting Controls* (London, 1997)

SIMONSON, LEE, *The Art of Scenic Design* (New York, 1950)

LIKING, WEREWERE (NICOLE NGO NJOCK) (1950–)

Cameroonian dramatist and novelist. Based in Côte d'Ivoire for the past two decades, Werewere Liking is one of francophone *Africa's most innovative and prolific writers. She has published three novels, including *Orphée-Dafric* (1981), two volumes of art criticism, including *Marionnettes de Mali* (1987), three collections of short stories, one of which is *Contes d'initiation féminine du pays bassa* (1982), and a volume of poetry. But she is best known as a dramatist, director, and head of the *Ki-Yi Mbock artists' commune that she founded in Abidjan. Liking's eight published plays eschew the *realist techniques of the French-derived dominant theatre in Cameroon in favour of an *Artaud-like method of *dream and narrative non-linearity. Her work is more psychological than social, promoting self-knowledge rather than heightening *audience awareness of issues of *politics and society. Finally, unlike the mainstream theatre, her plays are rooted in indigenous performance idioms. Her early work was rooted in the ceremonial practice of healing, funeral, and investiture *rituals, in such plays as *La Puissance d'Um* from 1979 and *Une nouvelle terre* from 1980 (published in English as *The Power of UM* and *A New Earth*, 1996), while the later phase is secular, consisting of dramatized epics, *dance-dramas, and *folk tales, as in *Singué Mura* (1990), *Un touareg s'est marié à une pygmée* (*A Tuareg Weds a Pygmy*, 1992), and *Héros d'eau* (*Water Heroes*, 1993). In spite of accusations of hermetic *avant-gardism, Liking's work, an example of *total theatre at its best, is widely performed in francophone Africa and, through the international *festival circuit, in France and Québec. JCM

LILL, WENDY (1950–)

Canadian playwright, screenwriter, and politician. Lill's career-long advocacy of social justice is reflected in her plays. *The Occupation of Heather Rose* (1986) deals with the destruction of northern native culture, *All Fall down* (1994) with a doubtful child molestation incident, *The Glace Bay Miners' Museum* (1998) with workers' battles, and *Corker* (1998), with government responsibilities to persons with disabilities. Elected as Member of Parliament for Dartmouth, Nova Scotia, in 1997, she was (in 2001) the New Democratic Party's critic on culture and communications. PBON

LILLIE, BEATRICE (LADY ROBERT PEEL) (1894–1989)

Canadian comedienne. Born in Toronto, Bea Lillie made her English stage debut in 1914 and her American debut in 1924, dividing a career of some 50 shows between the two countries. Her forte lay in the *revue and solo *cabaret, with a handful of *musicals and plays. Slender and short, she had a long, expressive face, and enjoyed a widespread reputation as the funniest woman in the world. In the 1950s she *toured her *award-winning *An Evening with Beatrice Lillie* around the world for several years. Her triumphant stage farewell came on Broadway in 1965 as Madame Arcati in a musicalized version of *Coward's *Blithe Spirit*. She wrote an autobiography, *Every Other Inch a Lady* (1972). CT

LILLO, GEORGE (1693–1739)

English author, most famous for his *bourgeois *tragedies *The London Merchant* (1731) and *Fatal Curiosity* (1736). Although far from being the first playwright to write a domestic tragedy, Lillo is routinely credited with revolutionizing the *genre by eschewing royal courts for the bourgeois world of masters and apprentices in *The London Merchant*, the story of a good apprentice gone bad. The play was a runaway success during the eighteenth century (it inspired Hogarth's *Industry and Idleness*) and for its psychological power. Criticized more recently for its pious morality and faith in the virtues of bourgeois capitalism, the play expresses widely held beliefs of its day and became a favourite of *London masters, who sent their apprentices to the theatres to see its annual performances. *Fatal Curiosity* was not a great success initially but became very popular later in the century, adapted by George *Colman the Elder in 1782 and Henry Mackenzie in 1784. It is the story of impoverished parents who kill a lodger for money, only to discover that he was their rich son, returning home incognito. These works reveal

Lillo's interest in promoting Christian morality. Even when working in *genres like the *ballad opera (*Silvia; or, The Country Burial*, 1730), *historical play (*The Christian Hero*, 1735), and Shakespearian *romance (*Marina*, 1738), his interest in temptation and Christian fortitude are evident. *See also* DRAME, LE; VOLTAIRE. MJK

LIMELIGHT

When calcium oxide (lime) is heated to incandescence, it gives off bright, almost perfectly white *light. Instruments designed to project that light, the light they cast, and the attention thus created were all called limelight. Invented in England in 1816, it was in standard use in the West by about 1855. Though the light could not be sharply focused, its brilliant, warm glow was flattering to most actors and was sentimentalized when replaced by the colder, bluer electric spotlight. JB

LIMOGES FESTIVAL OF INTERNATIONAL FRANCOPHONE THEATRES

French *festival (Le Festival International des Francophonies en Limousin) founded in 1984 by Pierre Debauche, then director of the Centre Dramatique National du Limousin, to promote interaction between local people and francophone artists from around the world. One of its most important features are *African theatre teaching sessions in primary and secondary schools in Limoges, introducing young pupils to the staging of African *folk tales and traditional forms like the *kotèba of Mali and the Togolese *concert party of Senouvo *Zinsou and Kokovivina. *Street theatre by minstrels, *acrobats, drummers, and other percussionists brings Limoges alive during the festival. The regular companies invited include Zadi *Zaourou's Didiga (1984), Sony *Labou Tansi's *Rocado Zulu (1986, 1988), Théâtre de la Soif Nouvelle directed by Wole *Soyinka (1986, the year he won the Nobel Prize), Werewere *Liking's *Ki-Yi Mbock (1988–94), and Prosper Kampaoré's Atelier Burkinabé. Since 1995 an increasing number of troupes from the French *Caribbean, Québec, Louisiana, the Maghrib, and even Lebanon, *Cambodia, and *Vietnam have participated in the festival. The event also has a residence programme for writers from the francophone world, a notable recent participant being the *Paris-based Chinese Nobel laureate *Gao Xingjian.

PNN trans. JCM

LINCOLN CENTER FOR THE PERFORMING ARTS

An urban renewal project for the upper west side of Manhattan in *New York, promoted by John D. Rockefeller III and con-

structed between 1959 and 1972. Its centrepiece is the *Metropolitan Opera House. Among its many other venues for *dance, *music, *opera, theatre, and education is the New York State Theatre (capacity 2,779), designed by Philip Johnson and John Burgee, which opened in 1964 and hosted a number of important *musicals until the renovations of 1982. It is now the home of the New York City Ballet and the New York City Opera. Lincoln Center's two primary *playhouses, the Vivian Beaumont (capacity about 1,100) and the Mitzi E. Newhouse (called the Forum until 1973; capacity 299), were designed by Eero Saarinen and Jo *Mielziner and opened in 1965. The Beaumont featured a steeply raked *auditorium with a large *stage that was to be easily changed from *thrust to *proscenium. The theatres were built for the Repertory Theater of Lincoln Center, headed by Elia *Kazan and Robert Whitehead, both of whom resigned before the buildings opened. A succession of co-directors and directors—Herbert *Blau (1965–7), Jules Irving (1965–73), Joseph *Papp (1973–7), and Richmond Crinkley (1979–84)—failed to make the *repertory a success. In 1980–1 the Vivian Beaumont stage was converted to a proscenium arch and the rake of the seating was reduced. In 1985 the not-for-profit Lincoln Center Theatre corporation was established under *artistic director Gregory *Mosher, who ran it until 1992. With the motto 'Good Plays, Popular Prices', the LCT finally made the Beaumont one of the pre-eminent theatres in the country. In 1996 both theatres underwent major renovation, and LCT is currently under the direction of André *Bishop and Bernard Gersten. Lincoln Center also houses a library of performing arts (*see* MUSEUMS OF THEATRE). FJH

LINCOLN'S INN FIELDS THEATRE

William *Davenant's conversion in 1660–1 of Lisle's indoor *tennis court in Portugal Street in *London established the spatial arrangement used in British theatres for some 150 years. The *proscenium arch created two stage spaces: an upstage scenic stage with painted shutters drawn to meet in the middle, and a deep *thrust *forestage which was entered by pairs of doors on either side of the stage. Rows of side *boxes (some on the forestage itself), the pit, and gallery permitted the *audience to enjoy scenic spectacle (although many areas had limited sight lines) while retaining an intimacy with the players which was central to Restoration theatre. Davenant's Duke's Company occupied the theatre until 1671 when they moved to *Dorset Garden Theatre. The intimate 'Little Theatre' of Lincoln's Inn Fields was later home to the Players' Company managed by *Barry, *Bracegirdle, and *Betterton (1695–1705). Successfully refurbished by John *Rich in 1714, it fell into disrepair and ceased to be a regular *playhouse after 1732. *See also* SCENOGRAPHY. GBB

LINDSAY, DAVID (c.1486–1555)

Scottish dramatist and courtier. His diplomatic missions to Europe in the 1530s and 1540s probably exposed him to French dramatic forms, notably the mock sermon, which he later incorporated in his own work. Involved in *Edinburgh court theatricals from 1511, he was probably the author of a lost *allegorical play performed at Linlithgow Palace in 1540, which attacked clerical abuses; the material was later extensively reworked into his day-long epic about the government of the realm, *A Satire of the Three Estates* (1552). Its juxtaposition of trenchant social commentary with scatological *farce remained potent in several twentieth-century revivals, notably that of Tyrone *Guthrie at the *Edinburgh Festival in 1948.

MJW

LINES OF BUSINESS

A system of *character specialization within an *acting company, which enabled each member to play a large number of roles within the bounds of his or her own speciality. The Elizabethan acting company offered this kind of specialization; by the late eighteenth and early nineteenth centuries and especially the advent of *melodrama, the system was firmly established. An actor was hired to fill a vacant line of business. The *leading man and lady did not, strictly speaking, act lines of business, since each simply assumed the principal male or female part in a play. The main and well-defined lines of business were juvenile lead, female juvenile lead (or *ingénue), heavy man, character actor, low comedian, light comedian, old man, old woman, walking gentleman (a *confidant of the leading man) and utility (in America, responsible). Such a company, with additions and omissions and the extensive *doubling or trebling of parts, could handle anything in the repertory: *tragedy, *comedy, *farce, or melodrama. Almost every male line of business had its female counterpart. Dion *Boucicault lists eighteen necessary lines of business, too many for all but the largest first-class *stock companies. Each actor with a line of business built up a stock of *characters within his or her own line, fully aware of the essential characteristics of a melodramatic *villain or *heroine, but also able to handle variations in personality, manner, and social type, since all villains and heroines were not the same.

MRB

LINNEY, ROMULUS (1930–)

American playwright and director. Linney's work has the unadorned poetic quality of a testament. Reviewing *True Crimes* (1998), Vincent Canby compared their effect to the Depression-era photographs of Walker Evans. Best known for his plays about Appalachia—including *Holy Ghosts* (1976), about snake-handlers, and *Sand Mountain* (1981), based on Appalach-ian folklore—his *historical dramas include *The Sorrows of Frederick* (1967), *Childe Byron* (1978), and *2* (1990), about Hermann Goering. Adaptations include *Gint* (1998) and *A Lesson before Dying* (2000), from the novel by Ernest Gaines. The lyric southern language in Linney's plays is derived, he says, from the rhythms of the King James Bible. *Trained in acting and directing at the *Yale School of Drama, Linney often directs his own work, and teaches playwriting at the New School and at *Juilliard. *New York's Signature Theatre devoted their first season to him (1991–2).

GAO

LIN ZHAOHUA (LIN CHAO-HUA) (1936–)

Chinese director. After graduation from the Central Academy of Drama in 1961, Lin has worked regularly as an actor and then a director at the Beijing People's Art Theatre. He is the most all-round stage director in China. His productions of *Gao Xingjian's *Absolute Signal* (1982) and *Bus Stop* (1983) are considered by critics to have initiated the 'Little Theatre movement' (experimental productions in *studio theatres) on the Chinese mainland. He excels, too, in handling slice-of-life drama, which represents the mainstream tradition in *China. Celebrated productions that were also *box-office hits include Guo Shixing's *Birdmen* (1996) and *Lao She's classic *Teahouse* (1999). He is just as inspiring in directing plays with complex *characters, such as Jin Yun's *Uncle Doggie's Nirvana* (1986) and *Hamlet*, which he adapted for production in 1990. Beijing opera (*jingju) also fascinates him, and his production of *Prime Minister Liu Luoguo* (2000, co-director Tian Qinxin) opened up new possibilities of development for the form. His productions have *toured places such as *Hong Kong, Taiwan, *Singapore, *Japan, France, Italy, Germany, and England.

MPYC

LIPMAN, MAUREEN (1946–)

English actress, best known for her work in *comedies and *musicals. She was a member of the *National Theatre at the *Old Vic (1971–3) and played Celia with the *Royal Shakespeare Company (1974). *London productions have included *Shaw's *Candida* (1976), Philip King's *See How They Run* (1984), *Bernstein's *Wonderful Town* (1986), *Simon's *Lost in Yonkers* (1992), *Wasserstein's *The Sisters Rosensweig* (1994), and her *one-person celebration of the work of Joyce Grenfell, *Re: Joyce* (from 1988). She was in *Nunn's revival of *Oklahoma!* for the National (1998), took the role of Peggy Ramsay in Alan Plater's *Peggy for You* (1999), and joined the expanding list of actresses to appear in Eve Ensler's *The Vagina Monologues* (2001). Many of her *television roles were written by her husband Jack Rosenthal, including those in *The Evacuees* (1975) and *The Knowledge* (1979). She has also appeared in several sitcoms, including *Agony* (1979–81). In 1999 Lipman was awarded the CBE.

AS

LISBON

The ruins of a Roman *amphitheatre, built before AD 57, are the earliest vestiges of theatrical activity in Lisbon. In *medieval times, plays were presented in churches and the court. No information about them has survived; but the continuous prohibitions passed against performances indicate that they must have had a large and eager public. *Censorship of theatrical *texts and *performance was later exercised by the Inquisition (1536–1821), and state control lasted until 1974. On 7 June 1502 Gil *Vicente staged his first play in the Queen's chamber, in celebration of the birth of the royal prince, and many historians consider this to be the birth of Portuguese theatre (*see* EARLY MODERN PERIOD). Sixteenth-century theatre was closely connected with the court and the emerging class of wealthy merchants active in overseas trade. There were no *playhouses; performances took place in private halls where admission was restricted. However, on such occasions as royal *entries and farewell ceremonies the whole city was a stage. Theatre gradually asserted its autonomy as an art form; frequent productions were given for urban *audiences who began to recognize its cultural significance.

Venues, audiences, repertories, and the organization of the profession began to change in 1580: Philip II of Spain was crowned king of Portugal, and the theatrical atmosphere was affected by Spanish imports. Playhouses were built and their management entrusted to religious orders. The architecture of the playhouses indicated a new stratification of audiences, with class and sex divisions in the *auditorium, and also suggested the new importance of theatre to the city's economy, as in the case of the Pátio das Arcas (1594–1755), a company which held the exclusive right to present Spanish plays performed by Spanish companies. The Pátio helped introduce a style of speech that was emulated by Portuguese actors up to the 1720s. At the turn of the eighteenth century, the Spanish model was replaced by French *neoclassical drama and by *opera, introduced by Italian artists who occasionally gave recitals and staged productions at court. The first public opera was performed at the Academia da Trindade in 1735. The opera, originally an emblem and instrument of absolutism, fashioning the Portuguese court after other European models, evolved into a complex institution which was able to stage *financially secure productions, engage artists, and offer professional *training. Again wealth from overseas—Brazilian gold—made royal investment in the arts possible. Its grandest instance was the Ópera do Tejo, inaugurated in March 1755, a sumptuous opera house designed by the architect G. C. *Bibiena that collapsed on 1 November during an earthquake that devastated most of the city.

At a palace in the Bairro Alto district turned into an improvised theatre, musical *puppet shows had been presented since 1733—notably António José da *Silva's highly successful operas. The popularity of the opera was established, but it was only after 1755 that the reconstruction of the city facilitated an intense (but precarious and unrewarding) theatrical activity. Small theatres at Rua dos Condes, and in the districts of Bairro Alto and Graça, were adapted to the needs of performances and their growing popularity. The establishment of the Society for the Support of Public Theatres (1771) marked a turning point in the organization of theatrical events. This was the first governmental initiative, albeit sponsored by the bourgeoisie, aimed at regulating and managing public theatres. In 1793 civic enterprise was to supersede the sovereign's control by founding the Teatro Real de São Carlos, still the finest opera house in the country. Nevertheless, poor levels of performance and the interdiction against *women on the stage were to lead to the decline of the art until Almeida *Garrett was made responsible for reforms after the revolution of September 1836. He built a modern national theatre (Teatro *Nacional D. Maria II, 1846), founded the Conservatório Real de Lisboa for the training of professional performers, and sought to invigorate dramatic writing.

Theatre in Lisbon was to follow this model until the Revolution of April 1974. Besides the National Theatre, administered by private *managers under licence, other playhouses, run by ephemeral companies, were built during the nineteenth and twentieth centuries, all striving to gratify bourgeois tastes. They took their *realist and *naturalist repertory and aesthetics from France, and remained impervious to *avant-garde trends. The creation of actors' companies between the 1950s and 1970s gave rise to independent groups (Teatro Experimental de Cascais, A Comuna, Grupo 4). Their stability, however, was compromised by the indifference of theatregoers unused to a repertory that was so different from traditional *comedies and *revues. The Revolution of April 1974 led to deep social and political changes, including government funding of theatrical activities and the end of censorship, and sapped a commercial theatre that had been depressed since the 1960s. Despite the numerous enthusiasts of the revues in the Parque Mayer theatres, this popular *genre of *political *satire was doomed to disappear in a time of revolution and freedom.

Banned playwrights were rediscovered and performances given on unconventional stages. New companies emerged, some following the example of independent groups (Teatro da Cornucópia, A Barraca, O Bando), others operating as short-lived enterprises for the development of a single project. Audiences, too, enjoyed the new freedom of gathering together, and responded to the appeal of new artistic forms and texts, performers, and directors. It was this generation of theatre artists who moved forward from traditional standards to the experimental and multidisciplinary works that emerged in the 1990s. Discarding obsolete professional structures and models of production, they were able to exploit the growing diversity of the public and capitalize on the opportunities provided by government funding. Many theatre groups appeared at the turn of the twenty-first century, establishing production networks to support intense activity. Some favour contemporary authors (Artistas Unidos), others have opted for multidisciplinary or *multimedia performance. Initiatives like the Encontros Acarte, the Almada Festival, *acting workshops, and a significant increase in theatre courses, have enlarged the contemporary frame of reference.   MJB/JCa

LISTON, JOHN (1776–1846)

English actor, the best low comedian of the *romantic era. He played in the provinces before securing an engagement at the *Haymarket in 1805, and his breakthrough role was Caper in J. T. Allingham's *Who Wins?* (1806). He spent most of his career at *Covent Garden, acting there from 1805 to 1822 when he left for *Drury Lane. The switch was a shrewd one, for at that theatre Liston became the highest-paid comic actor. Given his great success at the established *patent houses, his move to Madame *Vestris's *Olympic Theatre in 1831 is surprising; perhaps he sought the intimacy of a smaller *playhouse. Liston specialized in buffoon roles and was physically suited to them, being corpulent and red faced. While a physically expressive performer, he was nonetheless admired for underplaying roles that others tended to exaggerate. His most memorable role was Paul Pry in John Poole's play of that name (1825). His Shakespearian roles include Ophelia in Poole's *Hamlet Travestie* (1813) and Sir Andrew Aguecheek.   MJK

LITTLE THEATRE MOVEMENT

A term describing the wave of small *amateur companies founded in the United States from 1909 to 1929, popularized with the publication of Constance D'arcy Mackay's *The Little Theatre in the United States* (1917). Professional theatre production in the USA had by 1890 been consolidated under the *Theatrical Syndicate (and later the *Shuberts) to such an extent that a handful of individuals in *New York dictated play selection and production styles for theatres around the country, where local *playhouses had been bought up and local companies liquidated. American intellectuals despaired at the standardized, industrialized condition of the theatre, as the *touring system favoured by these organizations tended toward the lowest common denominators in playwriting—obvious themes, cheap sentiment, and childish *musical comedy—and conventional *scenery selected more for ease of shipping than for artistic purpose. The Little Theatre movement arose from the desire of small groups of intellectuals and aesthetes to restore American theatre as an art form and, from a somewhat different perspective, to provide meaningful leisure activity for a middle class whose lives were being made easier through the introduction of electricity, the internal combustion engine, and consequent labour-saving devices. While organizations such as the Drama League (founded 1909) pointed to European small companies such as the *Abbey Theatre as models of socially relevant art, playwright and producer Percy *MacKaye in his book *The Civic Theatre* (1912) argued for theatre activity as a means of 'constructive leisure' by which Americans could find meaning, forge relationships, and improve their communities.

Constance Mackay traced the Little Theatre movement to 1887 with the founding in *Paris of *Antoine's Théâtre *Libre and its arrival in the USA to 1911 with the foundings of Maurice *Browne's Little Theatre in *Chicago and Mrs Lyman Gale's Toy Theatre in *Boston. Other little theatres actually pre-dated these, such as the *Hull-House Players in Chicago (1901) and the Players in Providence, Rhode Island (1909). Irene and Alice Lewisohn began their community-based theatre work with immigrants in New York in 1902 and founded the *Neighborhood Playhouse in 1912. The *Washington Square Players and *Provincetown Players (both founded 1915) propelled the Little Theatre idea to national prominence with their discoveries of provocative new American playwrights—especially Eugene *O'Neill and Susan *Glaspell—and the introduction of European staging techniques derived from *symbolism and *expressionism. Little theatres began to spring up around the country and, while no exact programme was followed, tended toward a few key characteristics: the preference for short plays, many of them European; an interest in staging new American plays, often written by members of the group; a willingness to experiment with *avant-garde staging techniques witnessed in Europe or described in such sources as *Theatre Arts* magazine (founded 1916); the preference for intimate venues seating less than 100. The outstanding little theatres founded in the 1910s tended to be attached to one charismatic individual who rallied others around an ideal. These included Samuel A. Eliot, Jr.'s Little Theatre of Indianapolis (1915); Sam *Hume's Arts and Crafts Theatre in Detroit (1915); Frederick McDonnell's Cleveland Play House (1916); and Aline Barnsdall's Little Arts Theatre of *Los Angeles (1916). While some of these groups transformed themselves into professional theatres, others continued deliberately as amateur operations, still focusing on art and constructive leisure, and formed the basis of the American *community theatre movement.   MAF

LITTLE TICH (HARRY RELPH) (1867–1928)

English *music-hall comedian. He began as a Negro *minstrel—'people thought you couldn't be funny unless you had a burnt-cork face', he said—and reputedly acquired the sobriquet 'Little Tichborne' because he resembled the stout claimant in the Tichbourne case, which was notorious at the time. Little Tich's big-boot dancing earned him success (though he regarded it as merely a grotesque novelty), and after an American debut in 1887 with Tony *Pastor's company, he returned to *London to play the *Drury Lane *pantomime under Augustus *Harris. His stage caricatures of the Tax Collector, the Spanish Señora, and the Zoo Keeper were bizarre amalgamations of patter and *dance. A considerable linguist, he was fêted in France and was made an Officier d'Académie. On his memorial in Marylebone Cemetery he is remembered as 'Le plus petit et le plus grand comique du monde'.   AF

LITTLEWOOD, JOAN (1914–2002)

English director. After rejecting the training she received at the *Royal Academy of Dramatic Art, Littlewood worked in *agit-prop theatre in Manchester with Jimmie Miller (later known as Ewan MacColl). With Theatre of Action, Theatre Union, and finally *Theatre Workshop (based at the Theatre Royal, Stratford East, *London, from 1953), Littlewood became famous for her anti-establishment, risk-taking, collaborative theatre. Her developmental approach, called 'workshopping', was applied to the classics and living authors alike. Some distressed dramatists found their plays workshopped beyond recognition, but the scripts of Brendan *Behan and Shelagh *Delaney, among others, were very successfully produced by this method. Littlewood was always opposed to what she saw as the *bourgeois theatre of *illusion; she advocated anti-*realistic theatre, often based in popular styles such as the *music hall, and she worked extensively with *physical theatre techniques derived from *Meyerhold, *Stanislavsky, and *Laban. Littlewood's irrepressible, entertaining, and yet *politically serious style was epitomized by *Oh! What a Lovely War* (1963), a *satire on the First World War, which had profound influence in Britain and abroad (her method was most unsuccessfully transferred to *film by Richard Attenborough in 1969). Theatre Workshop initially existed in conditions of great poverty and was ignored by the press. As recognition and appreciation grew, the company was persuaded to transfer several productions to the West End; this was financially rewarding but overextended the enterprise. Worn out by running several companies simultaneously, Littlewood became increasingly disenchanted and retired from active theatre work in the early 1970s. Her autobiography *Joan's Book* (1994) is a delightfully ramshackle, idiosyncratic, and mesmerizing account of her adventures.   EJS

LITURGICAL DRAMA

A term normally applied to approximately 1,000 Latin *texts, extracted from a variety of *medieval ecclesiastical service books, which modern scholars have identified as dramatic scripts. This 'drama', performed as part or in the context of the official public worship of the Christian Church, shares most of its dramatic and theatrical characteristics—symbolic gesture, movement, and *costume; antiphonal singing; role playing—with the mass itself, and it has proved difficult always to dis-

tinguish adequately between a liturgical and a dramatic performance. Any distinction must be based less on the formal qualities of a performance than on its status and function. A liturgical *ritual performance is primarily a form of worship sanctioned by ecclesiastical authority; a drama is a non-essential elaboration of the liturgy, not an essential part of it. Nevertheless, medieval liturgy and liturgical drama are formally and functionally on a performance continuum that precludes sharp distinction. We are dealing with purpose and perception as well as with formal techniques of presentation. Although the longest and most complex texts date from the twelfth and thirteenth centuries, there is no discernible pattern of development reflected in the texts and no question of more elaborate texts replacing simpler ones. Performances can, however, be roughly categorized in terms of the closeness of their connection to the liturgy proper.

1. *Mass*. Medieval observers were themselves aware of the resemblance between the celebration of the mass and a theatrical performance. Early in the twelfth century, the theologian Honorius of Autun likened the priest to a tragedian who 'represents to the Christian people in the theatre of the church, by his gestures, the struggle of Christ, and impresses upon them the victory of his redemption'.

2. *Liturgical ceremonies*. Ceremonies not essential to the liturgy but firmly based in it were common by the tenth century. During Holy Week a number of such ceremonies—the procession of a carved figure of Christ on an ass (*palmesel*), the washing of the disciples' feet (*mandatum*), the extinguishing of candles (*tenebrae*), and the *Adoratio*, *Depositio*, and *Elevatio* of the cross—enriched and intensified the commemorated events. Other ceremonies, some quite elaborate, commemorated the Annunciation, the Purification, the Assumption, and the Presentation in the Temple. These ceremonies certainly approached dramatic status and may have sometimes been detached from the liturgy altogether, as was the case of the Annunciation at the cathedral of Cividale del Friuli in the thirteenth century. In at least one instance a liturgical ceremony was the focus for a fully developed drama. Philippe de *Mézières's *Presentation in the Temple* (late fourteenth century), although firmly attached to the mass, is precise and detailed in its costume, setting, and *action.

3. *Tropes and drama*. Elaborations on the 'Te Deum', 'We praise thee, O God', at Christmas and especially Easter, are usually held to lie behind most liturgical drama. The *Quem Quaeritis* trope, dating from the tenth century, which presents the visit of the three Marys to Christ's empty tomb and their short *dialogue with the angel—both a ritual and a drama—gave rise to the *Visitatio Sepulchri*, which appears in nearly 800 texts from the tenth to the twelfth centuries. The less elaborate of these visits to the tomb should be considered liturgical ceremonies in that, though not technically part of the liturgy, they live only within it. More elaborate versions added extra *scenes—the race of

Peter and John to the tomb or the disciples' encounter with the risen Christ—and included non-biblical characters: these are clearly true liturgical plays, performances dependent for their meaning and significance on a liturgical context, but expanded dramatically through the use of non-liturgical material.

4. *Independent drama.* Approximately twenty Latin religious plays, most of them dating from the twelfth century or later, were not integral to the liturgy, and indeed were not necessarily performed in a liturgical context at all, or even in a church. They are often designated *ludus, jeu,* or *Spiele,* 'play', rather than the liturgical *Ordo* or *Officium.* Often too, the only indication of a liturgical connection is a brief reference at the end to the 'Te Deum', and even this may represent little more than an atrophied convention. The subject matter, which included material concerning Daniel, Lazarus, St Paul, and St Nicholas, also suggests that performances were not limited to Easter or Christmas. The so-called Fleury Playbook (twelfth or thirteenth century) contains ten texts that appear to have been consciously collected as pieces of drama, neither demanding nor requiring a liturgical context. Among the best known of these independent plays are two on Daniel, one by the wandering scholar Hilarius (fl. 1125), the other from Beauvais Cathedral (*c.*1180). The latter play was revived for performance at the Cloisters in *New York in 1958.

Liturgical drama used the resources of the church itself in its staging. The church building functioned as *playhouse, providing defined spaces for performers (clerics) and *audience (congregation). Dramatic costume was an augmented version of liturgical vestments; dialogue was a development of chanted antiphons; setting and scene were provided by the nave, the altar, the sepulchre, the cross, the pulpit—all of which had or could be given symbolic significance—as well as by specially constructed *mansions. The performance of these plays was formed and informed by the costumes, ceremonies, music, architecture, and iconography of medieval Christianity. This highly developed form of religious musical drama was one of the remarkable achievements of medieval civilization.

RWV

COLLINS, FLETCHER, *The Production of Medieval Church Music-Drama* (Charlottesville, Va., 1972)

SMOLDON, WILLIAM L., *The Music of the Medieval Church Dramas,* ed. Cynthia Bourgeault (London, 1980)

YOUNG, KARL, *The Drama of the Medieval Church,* 2 vols. (Oxford, 1933)

LIVANOV, BORIS (1904–72)

Russian/Soviet actor who joined the *Moscow Art Theatre in 1924, appearing in a number of contemporary Soviet plays and as Cassio in *Othello* (1930). He continued to make an important contribution to the Soviet repertoire during the 1930s and 1940s, for which he received a State Prize in 1942. Whilst committed to contemporary drama, Livanov showed another side to his talent in plays by *Beaumarchais and *Goldoni, in *Gogol's *Dead Souls* (as the gambler Nozdryov), and in *Nemirovich-Danchenko's revival of *Chekhov's *Three Sisters* (as Solyony, 1940). His production of *The Seagull* was seen in *London in 1970.

NW

LIVERPOOL PLAYHOUSE

The home of the Liverpool Repertory Company from 1911 (*see* REGIONAL REPERTORY THEATRES, UK), it was renamed the Playhouse in 1917. The ambitious repertoire of the first director, Basil *Dean, proved financially unviable and in 1914 Madge McIntosh averted collapse. Of necessity successive directors pursued a relatively conservative policy, developing actors like Michael *Redgrave and Rachel Kempson. The *Old Vic company took up wartime residence (1942–6). Following refurbishment in 1968, the new 150-seat Theatre Upstairs provided more experimental opportunities. From 1981 to 1984 Liverpudlian playwrights Alan *Bleasdale and Willy *Russell were part of a team dedicated to the promotion of popular new work, including Russell's *Blood Brothers.* Following a period under commercial impresario Bill Kenwright (1991–6), *financial crisis forced the Playhouse to close in 1998. It reopened in 2000 after the formation of the Liverpool and Merseyside Theatres Trust brought the Playhouse and the Everyman Theatre under one administration.

CEC

LIVING NEWSPAPER

A species of *documentary theatre pioneered by the *Blue Blouses and others in the Soviet Union and by *Piscator in *Berlin in the 1920s. The form was adapted in the 1930s by the *Unity Theatre and Theatre of Action in Britain and the *Federal Theatre Project in the United States. Living newspapers tend to combine live *action, often based upon actual documents such as newspaper accounts or court documents, with large-scale projections of photographs or—especially in the work of Piscator—motion pictures of actual events. The American productions were especially elaborate, intended by FTP director Hallie *Flanagan as a means of employing large numbers of theatre people and journalists as part of a government-funded works programme (1935–9). Flanagan had witnessed living newspapers in the Soviet Union and Germany in the 1920s and had experimented with the form in college productions. She and Elmer *Rice, head of the *New York FTP, along with Morris Watson, vice-president of the American Newspaper Guild, created the Living Newspaper Unit. Rice resigned when the first Living Newspaper—*Ethiopia* (1936)—was prevented from opening due to pressure from the US State Department. The unit went on to produce numerous successful works praised for their theatrical inventiveness but which were magnets for controversy in their advocacy of land redistribu-

The **Living Theatre**'s *Paradise Now*, 1968, an ecstatic celebration of youth, personal freedom, and sexuality, based on improvisation, collective creation, and audience participation. First seen at the Avignon Festival and performed throughout Europe and America for the next two years, the piece encouraged spectators to disrobe like the actors and ended with a mass exodus to the streets, where the real revolution was to begin. Julian Beck (bald and seated) is on the right.

tion (*Triple-A Plowed Under*, 1936), government ownership of utilities (*Power*, 1937), as well as housing (*One Third of a Nation*, 1938). Productions made creative use of projected silhouettes, life-sized *puppets, and *naturalistic stage effects, such as the simulated tenement fire in *One-Third of a Nation*.

MAF

LIVINGS, HENRY (1929–98)

English playwright. Before turning to writing in 1961, Livings worked as an actor in regional theatre and with Joan *Littlewood's *Theatre Workshop. Sometimes labelled as a northern farceur (many of his plays are set in his native Lancashire), Livings's plays are typical of the *absurdist style of the early 1960s and usually contain an element of despair as his 'little man' *protagonists struggle in vain against larger forces. His first play, *Stop It, Whoever You Are* (1961), was produced at the *Arts Theatre Club in *London and concerns the revenge fantasies of a lavatory attendant. Livings wrote over 30 plays, including *Big Soft Nellie* (1961), *Nil Carborundum* (1962), *Kelley's Eye* (1963), *Eh?* (1964), and *The Little Mrs Foster Show* (1966). In the early 1970s, he developed 'The Pongo Plays', a series of twelve short plays inspired by Japanese *kyogen, centred on his working-class protagonist Sam Pongo.

MDG

LIVING THEATRE

American theatre *collective. Founded in 1947 by Julian *Beck and Judith *Malina, the company was instrumental in the development of *Off-Broadway in the 1950s, promoting new

American and European drama and experimental performance techniques of collectivity, abstraction, and *improvisation. The first performances of the Living Theatre took place in small theatres throughout *New York: in a basement on Wooster Street (1948), a living room in a West End Avenue apartment (1951), the Cherry Lane Theatre in Greenwich Village (1951), and a loft on lower Broadway (1954). During this time the company produced the *avant-garde plays of Gertrude *Stein, William Carlos Williams, *Cocteau, *Brecht, and *Pirandello. In the company's first permanent home on 14th Street and Broadway, the Living Theatre gained national prominence with a series of *politically charged and aesthetically provocative productions, including *The Connection* by Jack *Gelber (1959), *A Man's a Man* by Brecht (1962), and *The Brig* by Kenneth Brown (1963). The performances developed a violent *realism inspired in part by *Artaud's notions of a theatre of *cruelty. A primary meeting place for radical artists and politics in the early 1960s, the company collaborated with John Cage to produce an evening called 'Theatre of Changes' which utilized Cage's strategies of chance operations in art creation. In 1963 the Internal Revenue Service closed the theatre for failure to pay back taxes. The company undertook a voluntary exile in Europe in 1964, where they began their experimentations in collective creation influenced by alternative lifestyles of the 1960s, including politics, drug culture, and sexual liberation. Major productions of this period included *Mysteries and Smaller Pieces* (1964), *Frankenstein* (1965), *Antigone* (1967), and *Paradise Now* (1968). Each of these works, collectively devised, attempted a marriage of radical politics with a new aesthetics of improvisation and confrontation, with a reconfigured *audience–actor relation. In *Paradise Now* audience members were engaged in direct *dialogue on issues of the day, invited to discard their identification papers and clothes, turn on to drugs, and join the performance in some manner.

During a *tour of the USA in 1968, the company decided to move away from performance for middle-class audiences to focus on a radical theatre for working-class participants in Brazil (1970) and later with steel mill workers in Pittsburgh. The company have continued to produce theatre works, although much of their influence and reputation rests on their work from the 1950s and 1960s. After Beck's death in 1985, the company continued under the direction of Malina and Hannon Reznikov.

MDC

LI YU (LI YÜ) (1611–c.1680)

*Chinese writer, author of 'southern style' *chuanqi* operas. Li Yu wrote *comedies (ten altogether) with the intent to entertain and amuse rather than instruct his *audience. He trained and directed his household troupe of actresses and *toured with them, giving performances of his plays in the homes of wealthy patrons. Several plays adapt his own stories, and in all of these

respects Li Yu broke with existing conventions for southern drama. His largest contribution was as a theorist. Two chapters in his *Xianqing ouji* (*Casual Expressions of Idle Feeling*) are the first systematic treatise on drama in Chinese (*see* THEORIES OF DRAMA). In them Li emphasized performability rather than prosodic skill, and instructed playwrights to write shorter plays (about 30 *scenes) centred on 'one *character and one *action', with equal importance given to arias and *dialogue. He found fresh subjects for his own plays. In *Lianxiang ban* (*Women in Love*), two women in love unite by marrying the same man. *Huang qiu feng* (*Woman in Pursuit of Man*) inverts a familiar *plot when three women compete for one man, and in *Naihe tian* (*You Can't Do Anything About Fate*) three beautiful women cooperate and make bearable life with an ugly husband, played by the *chou* actor (who depicts comic characters using dialect)— a first for southern drama. Li's interest in dialogue led him to write scenes wholly devoted to dramatized comment, debate, and soliloquy.

CS

LIZARRAGA, ANDRÉS (1919–)

Argentine playwright whose work commented on the political situation using *farce combined with *Brechtian methods. *Santa Juana de América* (*St Joan of America*, 1960), the second play of his *Trilogía sobre mayo* (*May Trilogy*), used rapidly changing scenes, non-linear chronology, and actors stepping out of *character as distancing devices for the *audience (*see* VERFREMDUNG). *Jack el destripador* (*Jack the Ripper*, 1967) relied on a *cabaret format in a style similar to *The Threepenny Opera*.

EJW

LLAMAS, ARMANDO (1950–)

Born in Spain and raised in Argentina, since 1973 Llamas has resided in France and written the bulk of his work for the theatre in French. With the human body and its place in history as their prime focus, such provocatively named plays as *Images de Mussolini en hiver* (*Pictures of Mussolini in Winter*, 1987), *Meurtres de la princesse juive* (*Murders of the Jewish Princess*, 1994), and *Gustave n'est pas moderne* (*Gustave Isn't Modern*, 1994) are set in hallways, galleries, and airport lounges. Llamas uses these locations as sites that underline the body's materiality and processes of change, including, in the case of *Gustave Isn't Modern*, changes of sex. He has also translated plays by *Lorca, *Valle-Inclán, and Edward *Bond.

KG

LLOYD, MARIE (MATILDA VICTORIA WOOD) (1870–1922)

English *music-hall performer. With her sisters Daisy, Alice, and Rose she began in the Fairy Bells Minstrels, *touring local mission halls with temperance songs. As Bella Delamare, her first professional engagement was at the Sebright Music Hall, Hackney. Changing her name to Marie Lloyd, her first success, as vocalist and *dancer, was with 'The Boy I Love Is up in the Gallery'. Her popularity increased with saucy songs such as George Le Brun's 'Among my Knick-Knacks' and 'What's That for, Eh?' As she said, people 'don't pay their sixpences and shillings at a music hall to hear the Salvation Army'. She played *pantomime throughout her career, notably at *Drury Lane in *Robinson Crusoe* with *Little Tich and George *Robey, and had successful *tours of America, South Africa, and Australia. Her private life was dogged by a succession of violent and miserable marriages, but she was unfailingly generous, contributing large sums to the Music Hall Strike Fund in 1907. At the Edmonton Empire, whilst singing 'It's a Bit of a Ruin That Cromwell Knocked about a Bit', she was taken ill, the *audience convinced that her staggering and swaying was part of the act. Her funeral attracted over 50,000 people. 'She had', said a mourner, 'a heart the size of Waterloo Station.' AF

LLOYDS, FREDERICK (1818–94)

English scene painter. Lloyds did significant work for Charles *Kean at the *Princess's Theatre in the 1850s, *painting scenes for *Sardanapalus, Faust and Marguerite, The Courier of Lyons*, and six Shakespeare plays. In 1865, at the same theatre, he painted the controversial treadmill scene in Charles *Reade's *It's Never Too Late to Mend*, with a *perspective of prison corridors radiating from the centre. His *Practical Guide to Scene Painting and Painting in Distemper* (1875) is the only extended monograph on the subject by a Victorian scene painter. Lloyds was also an easel painter, and exhibited. *See also* SCENOGRAPHY.

MRB

LLOYD WEBBER, ANDREW (1948–)

English composer. Raised in a musical family (his father was director of the London College of Music, his brother a world-class cellist), he developed an interest in both classical and popular music, although his formal musical education was minimal. While still in school, he teamed up with lyricist Tim *Rice to write *Joseph and the Amazing Technicolor Dreamcoat* (1968), a gentle biblical tale with a soft-rock score that attracted a good deal of attention. It was followed by the controversial *Jesus Christ Superstar*. Released as a record album in 1970, orchestrated for rock band and symphony orchestra, it effectively musicalized the difference between generations with its mix of contemporary rock and old-fashioned *music-hall turns. Subsequently staged in *New York and *London, it made Lloyd Webber a household name. Lloyd Webber and Rice's *Evita* (1978), another 'pop opera' which cemented their reputation, also marked the end of their collaboration. In subsequent years, Lloyd Webber has had varying success with *musicals on some-

times unlikely subjects. His two greatest hits, *Cats* (1981) and *The Phantom of the Opera* (1986), have achieved record-breaking *long runs in London and New York, and his roller-skating parable of trains, *Starlight Express* (1984), while a failure in New York, was still running in London in 2002. Less triumphant have been such titles as *Aspects of Love* (1989), *Sunset Boulevard* (1993), and *Whistle down the Wind* (1996). While many associate his musicals with gaudy *spectacle—dancing cats, falling chandeliers—Lloyd Webber has never shied away from smaller-scale, human-interest musicals, such as *Song and Dance* (1982) and *The Beautiful Game* (2000). While some have deplored his economy in building an entire score around a few melodies and for recycling songs, his melodic gifts, typically wrapped in lush, inventive orchestrations, have endeared him to *audiences. Musicals have made him one of the wealthiest men in England, and he now owns thirteen West End theatres. Knighted in 1992, he was made a life peer in 1997.

JD

LOA

From an old Spanish word for 'praise', *loas* were performed in the sixteenth and seventeenth centuries as brief *prologues to the main entertainment and were designed to explain the *plot of the play, seek the *audience's favour (*captatio benevolentiae*), and praise the author or performers as well as the generosity of the patron. Spoken by an actor or actors appearing in the main play, they were generally accompanied by music. The term *loa* is also used to denote a short independent piece, often *allegorical in nature, performed at the start of an entertainment to praise an illustrious personage or to commemorate an important event.

KG

LOCHHEAD, LIZ (1947–)

Scottish playwright. Born near Glasgow and educated at the Glasgow School of Art, Lochhead began writing poetry and plays while teaching art. She first received recognition as a poet, and performing her own poetry led to writing for the stage. Her first produced play, *Blood and Ice*, premièred in 1982 at the *Edinburgh Festival. In 1988 she was writer-in-residence for the *Royal Shakespeare Company. Notable plays since then are *Dracula* (1985) and *Mary Queen of Scots Got her Head Chopped Off* (1989), both of which premièred at the Lyceum in *Edinburgh, and *Perfect Days* (1998). She has also translated *Tartuffe* (1986) and the York Mystery Cycle (1992), adapted *The Tempest* as a play for children (*The Magic Island*, 1993), and written several scripts for *radio and *television. Her work addresses issues of *history, myth, and *gender, and has been praised for its strong narrative, connections with popular memory, and poetic language.

AHK

LOCUS (PLURAL: LOCI)

In *medieval staging, one of several terms used to refer to scenic structures arranged in conjunction with an 'unlocalized' playing area or *platea (place). Loci were variously arranged in a line, in a circle, or occasionally in less regular formations. Also called *sedes* (sites), *domi* (houses), or *mansions.

RWV

LOESSER, FRANK (1910–69)

American composer-lyricist. The most versatile Broadway songwriter since Irving *Berlin, Loesser began his career in Hollywood and from 1936 to 1942 wrote *film lyrics with Burton Lane, Hoagy Carmichael, Jule *Styne, and others, producing a string of hits including 'Heart and Soul', 'Two Sleepy People', and 'I Don't Want to Walk without You'. In 1942 he wrote music and lyrics to 'Praise the Lord and Pass the Ammunition', one of the Second World War's biggest hits, and thereafter wrote his own music. In 1948 he composed *Where's Charley?*, his first Broadway score, and followed it in 1950 with *Guys and Dolls*, a masterpiece of *musical comedy. The show, based on the fiction and *characters of Damon Runyon, featured a rare balance of comic and romantic elements. His other successes include *The Most Happy Fella* (1956) and *How to Succeed in Business without Really Trying* (1962), for which he and director/librettist Abe *Burrows received the Pulitzer Prize. Loesser's gift for novelty and character songs, especially the contrapuntal duet, was unsurpassed. He also founded his own publishing company, Frank Music, and nurtured the careers of emerging writers such as Meredith Wilson, Richard Adler, and Jerry Ross.

SN

LOEWE, FREDERICK See LERNER, ALAN JAY.

LOGAN, JOSHUA (1908–88)

American director and playwright. After studying with *Stanislavsky in *Moscow, Logan turned to directing and before the Second World War had directed more than a dozen Broadway plays and *musicals. His post-war success began with his direction of *Annie Get your Gun* (1946) and continued with *Mister Roberts* (1948) and *South Pacific* (1949), both of which he co-authored as well as directed, winning a Pulitzer Prize for the latter. Continuing to direct and sometimes *produce on Broadway, he began directing Hollywood *films as well, beginning in 1955 with *Mister Roberts* and *Picnic*. His success in film was not surprising, as his stage direction had been noted for its cinematic fluidity. Logan's career on both stage and screen declined following the failures of his film versions of *Paint your Wagon* (1960) and *Camelot* (1967).

JD

LOGEION

A rare term, meaning 'talking place' in Greek, referring to the high stage (*c*.2.5 m or 8 feet) of Hellenistic times, roughly equivalent to the *pulpitum* of *Roman theatre; but it might be the equivalent of *proskenion* (*see* SKENE). It was made of wood supported on stone or wood columns.

WJS

LOKADHARMI

Drawing on *loka*, which literally means 'the world', *lokadharmi* refers to that mode of representation in traditional *Indian performance that deals with the worldly activity of people. Often reductively and misleadingly translated as 'realistic', *lokadharmi* is often set in opposition to the *natyadharmi (stylized) mode of representation. These categories are better read in a relational rather than antithetical context. While *lokadharmi* does not draw on a prescribed codification of gestures (*hastas) and walks (*gatis*), among other aspects of stylized *acting, it draws on its own modes of exaggeration, emphasis, improvisation, and play, which are non-realistic in their own right. Certainly, *lokadharmi* should not be conflated with European traditions of *realistic acting, as is only too evident in its rich play of signs in traditional forms like *krishnattam and the *folk theatrical traditions of India. *See also* NATYASASTRA.

LSR/RB

LONDON *see page 758*

LONDON ACADEMY OF MUSIC AND DRAMATIC ART

One of the world's oldest drama schools, LAMDA was founded as a music academy by Henry Wilde in 1861, and by 1867 elocution had been added for the improvement of students of singing. In 1868 it offered, for five guineas a term, a year's course in *acting. Since the early 1880s generations of budding actors have grown through its famous examinations, but it was in 1935, when Wilfred Foulis took over as director, that actor *training became its main business. It adopted its current name in 1938. Then based in South Kensington, it moved to Tower House following the Second World War, and in 2003 plans to move into the former Royal Ballet School buildings. Principals have included Matthew Forsyth (1951–4), Michael MacOwen (1954–66), and Peter James (1994–), who succeeded in producing stellar alumni for a wide firmament of performance, including Diana Dors, Nigel Planer, Donald Sutherland, Harriet Walter, and Stacy *Keach.

BRK

(continued on p. 767)

LONDON

The political and financial capital of England and, variously in history, of Great Britain, the United Kingdom, and the British Empire, London has been a world theatre centre since the sixteenth century.

1. 1550–1800; 2. 1800–1900; 3. 1900–1945; 4. 1945–2001

1. 1550–1800

London owes its historical pre-eminence to the tidal River Thames, which allowed passage to seagoing vessels whilst safeguarding the citizens from casual invasion by offshore adventurers. The city wall, which determined its medieval boundary, enclosed some 133 hectares (330 acres) on the north bank. By 1550, about 60,000 people, the vast majority under 30 years of age, lived inside the ten-gated wall, and perhaps a further 10,000 immediately outside it. It was in 1550 that the city purchased the right to Southwark on the south bank. Londoners could reach Southwark by boat or, on payment of a toll, across London Bridge (constructed 1176–1209). The twenty piers of the bridge created fierce tidal currents. East of the bridge, where the big ships traded, was a different world from the western stretches, where small boats dodged and jostled for right of way. The waterman's cry of 'Eastward ho!' hailed passengers for a trip to the port area of Blackwall or the palace of Greenwich, 'Westward ho!' for Whitehall and Westminster. Villages east and north of the wall, outside the city of London's jurisdiction, displayed distinct characteristics: Wapping was the unruly haunt of seamen, Stepney, comparatively peaceful, would make its own unique contribution to the history of London theatre, Islington became a centre of milk production for the burgeoning metropolis, Hampstead and Highgate developed into salubrious hill villages for the city rich. But it is Clerkenwell that figures first in the theatrical record, in a 1301 petition from the prioress to Edward I 'to provide and order a remedy because the people of London lay waste and destroy her corn and grass by their *miracle plays and wrestling matches'. The mixing and matching of drama with sideshows and violence is common to most of the opponents of the London theatre during its first recorded centuries of existence.

In retrospect, it is the westward drift of the metropolitan theatrical centre that dominates the view, but that was not predictable whilst drama remained within the popular domain. The first purpose-built *playhouse, the *Red Lion, was erected in the grounds of a farm in Stepney in 1567. It was the speculative venture of John *Brayne, a wealthy greengrocer, who

must have calculated that something definable as a theatrical 'public' was already in existence. Despite the fact that the Red Lion's impetus was dissipated by litigation, he was probably right. Nine years later he collaborated with his brother-in-law James *Burbage in the building of the *Theatre, north of Bishopsgate, in Shoreditch, on a site that had belonged to the Holywell Priory before the English *Reformation. Burbage was a master joiner as well as an actor, and he may well have overseen the timber construction of the Theatre. It is likely that he envisaged it as a multi-purpose (wrestling, animal-*baiting, fencing, *acrobatics, as well as plays) site for entertainment. There was, after all, no dramatic repertoire to sustain a paying public. It was the building of the Theatre and its immediate successors, the *Curtain (1577), an unnamed playhouse in Newington Butts south of Southwark (before 1580), and the *Rose (1587), that enforced the creation of a repertoire and added to the population of London a distinct new breed of self-proclaimed 'players' and a smaller group of 'playwrights' eager to purvey their commodity of plays.

Brayne and Burbage were responsive to the Elizabethan ethos of economic expansion. In 1570, between the failed project of the Red Lion and the evident success of the Theatre, Thomas Gresham's Royal Exchange was completed, providing the city of London with a commercial palace to rival Elizabeth I's favoured residences of Whitehall and Greenwich. But no speculator, however bold, operates in thin air. There was, to be sure, a rapidly expanding population to cater for—it had risen to about 140,000 within the walls, about 200,000 within and without, by 1600—but there was also a well-established tradition of hostility to unruly assembly to threaten any crowd-pulling enterprise. London's government was multi-layered. The Lord Mayor, annually elected, was the figurehead of the Court of Aldermen. Aldermen were appointed for life (Roy Porter has called them 'the City's fat cats'), but they were expected to consult with the Common Council and apportion jurisdiction to guilds, wards, and parishes. Mayor and aldermen were regular and vocal opponents of plays within the city, though their regulation of playing places also raised revenues on fines for non-compliance. In 1564, the year of Shakespeare's birth and of the great Frost Fair on the frozen Thames, the bishop of London had complained to Sir William Cecil about the daily performance of plays in the city. That the London theatre should have grown so rapidly during the final quarter of the sixteenth century, in the teeth of opposition from church and civic authorities, is extraordinary. Brayne and Burbage, as guildsmen, may have counted on supporters within the Guildhall—*guilds had, within living memory, been proud to promote the great pageants of the *mystery *cycles. They may have been in close contact with some of the groups whose activities had aggravated the bishop of London in 1564. They must have been confident that there were players enough to provide the requisite quantity of bookings. Even so, they built their Theatre outside the city (it would have been suicidal to do otherwise) and sought their most powerful support at the Queen's court. It was, ironically, the desire of aristocrats to enrich their leisure that did most to preserve playgoing as a popular pastime.

London's first professional theatre companies evolved from the household troupes of Tudor and pre-Tudor regional grandees. There was prestige attached to the patron of an accomplished group of performers. Tudor and Stuart monarchs were rarely without one, and Henry VIII was not best pleased to find his troupe outshone by Cardinal Wolsey's—the four men and a boy nostalgically recalled in the Elizabethan play of *Sir Thomas More*. James Burbage may have gathered the confidence to build the Theatre from his membership of the company of players under the patronage of the showman-grandee Robert Dudley, Earl of Leicester: *Leicester's Men were probably the first stars of the Theatre. Elizabeth I enjoyed plays, and she allowed to develop—as protective cover for the London companies—the fiction that their public appearances were neither more nor less than open *rehearsals for royal command performances. A distinct city of Westminster was already growing around the Palace of Whitehall, west of the city wall, but the later playhouses of Elizabethan and early Stuart London continued to taunt the successive mayors from sites just outside the walls—the *Boar's Head in Whitechapel, the *Red Bull in Clerkenwell, the *Fortune in Finsbury—or from liberties (areas which, for historical reasons, were outside the jurisdiction of the London authorities) on the south bank—the *Rose, the *Globe, the *Swan, the *Hope. All of these were *open-air theatres, in which the social barriers of hierarchy were blurred, though not eradicated, and in which players and *audiences were necessarily affected by the weather. To play indoors at court to elite auditors, many of them with a personal investment in poetic diction, was a very different experience for the first generations of professional actors. It was there that the transformation of the English theatre from popular spectacle to minority interest took root. James Burbage was anticipating this change of tide when, in 1596, he leased a hall in the Blackfriars precinct and set about converting it into a playhouse. Boy players had been active in the Blackfriars (and at St Paul's), inside the city walls, since the 1570s, but an adult professional company was perceived as a greater threat to public order. The city fathers had no jurisdiction over the Blackfriars precinct, but they welcomed (may have conspired in) the petition from the residents that blocked Burbage's enterprise, effectively delaying for thirteen

years the establishment of an indoor playhouse for adult actors inside London's walls.

London owed its initial theatrical centrality to the proximity of the court, but there were other factors to determine the kind of centre it became. Unlike *Paris and many other Christian capitals, London sustained a port as well as a court. By 1700 it would be handling 69 per cent of the nation's exports and 80 per cent of its imports. Ports are inherently more cosmopolitan than inland conurbations. London was also a financial centre long before the foundation of the Bank of England in 1694, and it is unsurprising that the fraught negotiations between money and nobility remained a running theme of English drama from the 1590s until the primacy of capital could no longer be doubted. It was not until the 1680s that the regional rich became regular visitors to London, but eager or reluctant litigants were necessarily resident during legal terms and constituted a floating audience of some significance. Even more significant were the 1,000 young men who attended, and sometimes studied at, London's four *Inns of Court and six Inns of Chancery. It made commercial sense for theatres to cater for them during term time. It is not, then, surprising that London quickly became the theatrical magnet that it has remained, but it is a mistake to suppose that the early professional companies left the capital only when forced to by outbreaks of plague or *financial exigencies. The new *Queen Elizabeth's Men, assembled in 1584, *toured the provinces by policy, and it is mere supposition that the two great Elizabethan companies, the *Chamberlain's and the *Admiral's Men, never did so by choice. The discernible shift came when the Stuart kings, James I and Charles I, indulged their inclination to clutch the national culture to the national court. James's decision to take Shakespeare's company, the Chamberlain's Men, under his personal patronage is the theatrical emblem of that inclination. From 1603 until the closure of the city's theatres by parliamentary ordinance in 1642, the King's Men belonged essentially to London.

*Theatricality is not, of course, the preserve of theatres. What distinguishes all the great commentators on London, from John Stow in the 1590s to Pierce Egan during the Regency, is their sense of the city as a theatre in its own right. Bartholomew Fair in Smithfield was a spectacular fourteen-day August festival until reduced to three days in 1708 and ultimately sacrificed to respectability in the mid-nineteenth century. Ned Ward's alter ego in the pamphlet sequence *The London Spy*, finding the *Drury Lane playhouse closed in August 1699 because the players could make more money in Smithfield, tolerantly concluded that 'it was equally reputable to play the fool in the Fair for fifteen or twenty shillings a day as 'twas to please fools in the playhouse at so much per week'. Southwark Fair took over the south-bank streets each September until the 1760s. The Lord Mayor's Show, even when its shaping was entrusted to playwrights like *Webster or *Middleton, was a people's pageant (*see* CIVIC FESTIVALS; STATE DISPLAYS). Visitors to the Saba Tavern in Gracechurch Street in the 1570s might find themselves entertained impromptu by the landlord, Richard *Tarlton; two centuries later, and before his official stage debut, David *Garrick was also inclined to provide his drinking companions with impromptu entertainments. It is clear from the permission granted to Toussaint le Jond in 1667 to 'erect a stage or theatre in any town of England or Wales and to vend his balsams and remedies' that the Restoration of Charles II in 1660 did not immediately define the boundaries of the theatre; and who is to say that, when Mrs Salmon, in the mid-eighteenth century, established London's first exhibition of *waxworks in Fleet Street, or Alderman Boydell his Shakespeare Gallery in Pall Mall in 1786, their intentions were not theatrical? Before the nineteenth century, there was music (and especially singing) all over the city, not least on the Thames. A charming entry in *Pepys's diary for 13 July 1665 records a late-night encounter when 'there being no oars to carry me I was fain to call a skuller that had a gentleman already in it, and he proved a man of love to musique, and he and I sung together the way down with great pleasure'. Above all, though, it is the teeming life of the city streets that shines out in the work of London observers like Pepys, Evelyn, Ward, and, perhaps above all, Hogarth. Lydia Melford, up from the country in Smollett's *Humphrey Clinker* (1771), admires the three stupendous bridges (Westminster Bridge was completed in 1750, Blackfriars Bridge in 1769), 'so vast, so stately, so elegant, that they seem to be the work of the giants', but is overwhelmed by 'the crowds of people that swarm in the streets', and Charles *Lamb 'often shed tears in the motley Strand from fullness of joy at so much life'.

To reach the Strand from his office in East India House, Leadenhall Street, Lamb would walk the diameter of the old walled city—past Leadenhall Market (monument to the enterprise of Simon Eyre, the fifteenth-century Lord Mayor joyfully celebrated in *Dekker's *The Shoemaker's Holiday*), over Cornhill and past the Royal Exchange, along Poultry and Cheapside ('worthily called the beauty of London', wrote John Stow) to St Paul's, over Ludgate Hill and into Fleet Street (the bricking in of the Fleet River was not finally completed until early in the nineteenth century). Fleet Street and the Strand formed a corridor connecting the twin cities of Westminster and London, with Temple Bar as a notional frontier. High society and its aspirants preferred to live west of Temple Bar. The drift to Westminster accelerated through the seventeenth century, not least because James I and Charles I greatly enlarged the Elizabethan court of about 1,000. London was stoutly for Parliament during the Civil Wars, and equally stoutly opposed to the theatre. Few of the old playhouses survived the Interregnum in working order. In effect, then, the London theatre had to start afresh after the restoration of the monarchy in 1660, when Charles II made it clear that plays were part of his revisionist social programme. Between 1650 and 1700, the population of the city of London shrank from about 130,000 to less than 95,000

whilst the population of 'greater' London rose from 400,000 to 575,000, more than 11 per cent of the nation. The new King, unlike his father and grandfather, enjoyed mixing with his subjects—his well-advertised strolls in St James's Park drew crowds of them—and his fondness for the theatre, however inflected by an appetite for actresses, had developed during his long exile in France. Charles II's court was a volatile mixture of overt egalitarianism and cherished privilege, reflected in the theatre that grew under his patronage. The letters patent issued by Charles to his old associates-in-exile Thomas *Killigrew and William *Davenant were both permissive and restrictive: 'only the said company to be erected and set up by the said Thomas Killigrew, his heirs and assigns . . . and one other company to be erected and set up by Sir William Davenant, Knight, his heirs or assigns and none other, shall from henceforth act or represent *comedies, *tragedies, plays or entertainment of the stage within our said cities of London and Westminster and the suburbs thereof.' For the next 180 years, the story of London's theatres unfolds in the shadow of the letters patent (*see* PATENT THEATRES).

Killigrew and Davenant had first to find satisfactory sites for their indoor playhouses. After various false starts and make-shifts, the King's Men under Killigrew settled in Drury Lane, already a crowded area, and the Duke's Men under Davenant in *Lincoln's Inn Fields. Pepys thought Davenant's theatre 'the finest play-house . . . that ever was in England', but he was snob enough to be affected by the locale. A 1664 list names 21 peers and 42 gentlemen living around the Fields in properties newly built at mid-century. A year later Henry Jermyn, Earl of St Albans, began the development of the crown land of St James's Fields that would bring high society into what is now the West End of London. By the end of the eighteenth century, at much the same time as Lamb was relishing the life of the Strand, Beau Brummell tried to exonerate himself from the lapse of being there, so far east, by explaining that he had got lost. Jermyn's enterprise eclipsed the 1630s development of Covent Garden by the 4th Earl of Bedford, but Covent Garden is much more central to the early history of London's theatres. The Earl was advised by Inigo *Jones on the grand Italianate design of the piazza whose fine houses were snapped up by noblemen, some of whom were disconcerted when the 5th Earl licensed the fruit and vegetable market. Nearby streets, not least Drury Lane, were notorious for prostitution by the end of the seventeenth century, and Covent Garden's precarious reputation was further threatened in 1732, when John *Rich built his theatre there. Six years earlier, George Vertue had written of the piazza, 'inhabited by Painters [Vertue names ten]. A Credit to live there.' In the meanwhile, the phenomenal success of *Gay's *The Beggar's Opera* at Lincoln's Inn Fields in 1728 had filled Rich's purse. His grand new playhouse, the *Covent Garden Theatre, was a weapon in the unending competition with the rival patent house in Drury Lane, but it did nothing for the social standing of Covent Garden itself. Sir James Thornhill, an artist patronized by monarchs, continued to live there until his death in 1734, at which point his son-in-law William Hogarth took over the house for a while. More than anyone else, Hogarth created the link between theatre and the visual arts that is a distinct feature of eighteenth-century London, but he was no longer living in Covent Garden in 1748 when Fanny Hill, John Cleland's lady of pleasure, moved in.

The tendency to associate theatre with illicit sex was reinforced in post-Restoration London, not least by Charles II. When in 1667 he finally discarded his wayward mistress Lady Castlemaine, he replaced her successively with two actresses, Moll Davis and Nell *Gwynn, whilst she settled for Jacob Hall, a muscular rope dancer famous at Bartholomew Fair. It is a mistake, though, to suppose that Londoners condoned the King's behaviour. They liked his manners but deplored his morals. In 1670 Sir John Coventry MP proposed a tax on playhouses in defiance of Charles's protest that 'the players were the king's servants, and a part of his pleasure'. Sir John went so far as to ask the Commons 'whether did the king's pleasure lie among the men or the women that acted'. Pepys, constantly in a losing struggle with his own prurience and frequently resolving to cut down his playgoing, is a fair audience representative. Three diary entries for January 1661 give us the flavour of Restoration theatregoing. On 3 January, 'the first time that ever I saw women come upon the stage'; on 19 January, 'troubled to be seen by four of our office clerks, which sat in the half-crown *box and I in the 1s. 6d'; and on 28 January, 'I sitting behind in a dark place, a lady spit backward upon me by mistake, not seeing me [John Evelyn complained about the profusion of spitting in London]; but after seeing her to be a very pretty lady, I was not troubled at it at all' (see WOMEN IN AUDIENCES). As the century neared its end, the concern for moral welfare, exemplified by the Society for Reformation of the Manners of the Lower Orders, grew. Jeremy *Collier's polemical Short View of the Immorality and Profaneness of the English Stage (1698) highlights a latent class-based antagonism between city merchants and the court faction that would rumble on through the succeeding century, even commenting on itself in George *Lillo's inexcusably popular tragedy of 1731, The London Merchant (see ANTI-THEATRICAL POLEMIC).

The intensity of factional politics in the eighteenth century—London has never been more ferociously political—inevitably affected the theatres. Drury Lane, more or less consistently, aligned itself with the Whigs, and Covent Garden, by default, with the Tories. The first two Hanoverian kings, never eloquent in English, were more prominently patrons of *Handel and the Italian *opera than of spoken drama. This preference took them to *Vanbrugh's comparatively grandiose King's Theatre in the *Haymarket, at the eastern rim of Jermyn's West End development, but it was in the unlicensed 'Little' Theatre on the opposite side of the broad highway that political fangs were

most vividly bared. From The Beggar's Opera in 1728 to the *Licensing Act of 1737, Walpole's demonstrable venality was meat and drink to theatrical discourse, above all during Henry *Fielding's tenancy of the Little Theatre during the 1730s. The Licensing Act, astutely forced through a moribund House of Commons on the edge of its summer recess, reiterated the patent theatres' monopoly of *legitimate drama and effectively restricted the right of playwrights to comment on any subject that the *Lord Chamberlain of the day considered sensitive (see also CENSORSHIP). A socially committed drama was the victim of this repressive legislation, which was in other respects easily evaded. It was, for example, at another unlicensed theatre, near *Goodman's Fields in Stepney, that David Garrick made his sensational debut in 1741. 'From the polite ends of Westminster', wrote Arthur *Murphy, 'the most elegant company flocked to Goodman's Fields, insomuch that from Temple Bar the whole way was covered with a string of coaches.'

It is not easy to overstate Garrick's impact on eighteenth-century London. He was not only a brilliant actor but also a singularly energetic and accomplished socialite. His *management of Drury Lane (1747–76) raised, perhaps inflated, the status of London's theatres. He was a connoisseur of art, the friend of painters from Hayman and Hogarth to Reynolds and Gainsborough, a competent playwright and a play-surgeon of genius, and his circle of friends included some of the highest in the land, as well as the Drury Lane audiences whom he courted in finely turned *prologues. Stagecoaches linked the city to more than 150 towns by the 1760s, and a pilgrimage to Drury Lane to see Garrick act became the adjunct of a liberal education. The eighteenth century saw the spread of theatres to every sizeable town in England, Scotland, Wales, and Ireland, and Garrick's name was known in all of them. The quality of the provincial playhouse circuits was as various as their managers, but all aspiring actors dreamt of London. The city grew fast in the final decades of the century. Smollett's Matthew Bramble, seeing in 1771 that 'Pimlico and Knightsbridge are now almost joined to Chelsea and Kensington', feared that, within 50 years, 'the whole county of Middlesex will be covered with brick'. By 1800 the metropolitan population was close to a million, making London much the biggest city in Europe, a third again larger than its nearest rival, Paris. There were too few theatres to satisfy the public demand for dramatic entertainment, and a smouldering resentment about the restrictive practices of the patent houses.

With the barrier of Victorian England between us and the eighteenth century, we are now prone to forget just how unruly and how flimsily policed the nation was. The reading of the Riot Act, inaugurated in 1715, was frequently authority's response to the perceived ugliness of crowds. Twelve hundred Londoners were publicly hanged between 1700 and 1799 (see EXECUTIONS, PUBLIC): open-air entertainment to rival Mr Punch or promenading to the sound of music in the gardens of Ranelagh where the hugely impressive Rotunda opened to the public in 1742.

The French Revolution brought into the open the deep fissures, religious and political, in London society. The spirit of egalitarianism threatened ancient privilege. Its most virulent theatrical expression came a few years into the new century. Sporadic *riots had occurred in and around London's playhouses, some even in Garrick's Drury Lane, since the Elizabethan apprentices had created their annual Shrove Tuesday mayhem, but they were generally random, disorganized, and fairly quickly dispersed. It was altogether different when the managers of Covent Garden, on opening their rebuilt theatre in 1809, announced an increase in the price of seats. Sixty-seven nights of increasingly systematic disruption followed. It was one of 123 catalogued cases of public disorder in London between 1790 and 1810, but by far the longest-lived and most observed. In the *OP riots, as the *Examiner* commented on 24 September 1809, 'the actors had become the audience, and the audience the actors'. Some of the leaders were died-in-the-wool radicals, but for most of the rioters the issue was one of simple principle. The London theatres belonged to Londoners, not Londoners to the London theatres.
                                                                    PT

2. 1800–1900

During the nineteenth century London's function as the theatrical centre of Britain became more complex. One significant reason for this was the huge growth in population, leading to the expansion of working- and lower-middle-class districts away from the old theatrical core, and the consequent dispersal of theatres and audiences over a much wider area. The years after the battle of Waterloo saw a major shift in Britain from a rural and agricultural society to an urban and industrial society. Great cities sprang up in the north, and the population of London rose rapidly from 900,000 in 1801 to 3,000,000 in 1851 and to 6,000,000 in 1901. This growth was prompted by massive rural emigration into the cities, a rising birth rate, and, after 1840, a declining death rate. For the theatre, the immediate social consequence of this growth was the increase in the potential audience, notably in the new, densely populated working-class districts spreading east of the city of London. By 1900 the population of the East End was about 2,000,000, the biggest urban working-class centre in the world. From the 1830s theatres were built to serve this population: the City (1831), the Garrick (1831), the Standard (1835), and the City of London (1837). The Grecian, Britannia, and Effingham opened as saloons with their own theatre spaces between 1834 and 1843, and were operating in regular theatre buildings by the 1850s. These theatres underwent renovations, suffered *fires, shut down and reopened, but generally flourished until about 1870, when they began to close. They catered to a very large audience; in 1866 the capacity of six East End theatres alone amounted to 17,600 places nightly, or a third of the London total aside from the opera houses. Indeed, two-thirds of that total capacity, even excluding *music halls, was in theatres outside the West End, not only in the East but in

the working- and lower-middle-class areas on the south side of the Thames and in the northern fringes of the West End. These neighbourhood theatres, drawing their patrons largely from the surrounding streets, and tailoring their repertory specifically to that local audience, constituted a social phenomenon of great theatrical and cultural significance.

The sharp class divisions evident in Victorian *melodrama and society as a whole also manifested themselves in playhouses. Whereas in the eighteenth century the pre-industrial 'working class' was confined to the galleries and affected the choice of repertory only marginally—since the *box-office revenue they provided was itself of only marginal importance—in the nineteenth century this situation was radically altered. The neighbourhood theatres were an important development: the working classes were now dominant in their own theatres, not crowded together under the roof of the primarily middle-class theatres in the centre. They still attended these theatres, however, and made their presence felt in the pit and gallery of such melodrama theatres as Drury Lane, the *Adelphi, and, in the 1880s and 1890s, the *Princess's. They also gave their patronage to *Phelps at *Sadler's Wells. Hardening class divisions dictated a rigid class separation in middle-class West End theatres, far beyond the standard division of audience space into box, pit, and gallery that characterized eighteenth-century theatres. Mid- and late Victorian theatres guaranteed their middle-class and fashionable patrons complete freedom from contamination by lower elements. Boxes, pit, balconies, *stalls, and galleries could have separate entrances; the new *Her Majesty's in 1897 even had separate exits. The box offices, bars, and coffee rooms were similarly segregated.

The increase in London's population was not the only factor in providing a much larger audience than before. Another was the accessibility to London by rail of a potential provincial audience and an audience from the new suburbs. Theatres first noticed this phenomenon in 1851, the year of the Great Exhibition. It was believed that the great majority of those who attended the theatre during the Exhibition were country people, and as a result of the press of business many theatres extended their season instead of closing in the early summer, as was the usual practice. These spectators had come to London by train, and in 1851 they could have arrived at any one of the new termini of Euston, Paddington, London Bridge, and Waterloo. In the next 50 years six more main line termini were built. Most of these were constructed around the edges of the West End; it took a network of local omnibus services, beginning in 1829, and the licensed cab to get people from the stations to the theatres. No one with any money at all had to walk to the theatre any more; if it was unavoidable, gas street lighting and a decline in street crime from the 1860s had made the streets much safer. By the 1870s and 1880s the burgeoning suburbs were also served by rail, which made it easy for theatregoers to come into town for a show and supper and return home in good time for bed. Such improvements in public transport, binding the provinces and the suburbs closely to London, greatly increased the audience. It is not surprising that, combined with economic prosperity and a middle class with more disposable income, the theatre embarked on a West End building spree beginning in 1866 and lasting to the end of the century, whereas from 1843 to 1866, in times of economic depression and managerial bankruptcies, not a single new theatre building was erected in London. Yet this boom would not have occurred without the passage of the Theatres Regulation Bill in 1843, which abolished the patent theatres' old monopoly on the legitimate drama and allowed any theatre, anywhere, to put on what it liked, subject only to licensing and censorship restrictions. The incentive to build was there when the times were right. A new audience presence was also noted: the overseas tourist. Travel by steamship from North America in ten days was an enormous improvement on the slow and frequently perilous crossing by sail. The publication of *A London Directory for American Travellers* in 1874 is an indication of this new audience; the *Directory* lists 23 West End theatres. Finally, observers at the end of the century noticed a considerable increase in the female audience, coincident with the increase in female employment. Shopgirls, milliners, stenographers, typists, cashiers, and telephone operators were only a few of the many female occupations now represented in the audience.

The railways and steamships also served another theatrical purpose, exporting companies of actors from London to the provinces and overseas. For generations individual stars had gone into the provinces in the summer, when Drury Lane and Covent Garden were closed, as did Sarah *Siddons, *Macready, and Charles and Ellen *Kean as a husband and wife team. Large-scale touring out of London was very different, and can be dated from the 1870s, although there were several earlier tours on a small scale. In 1893, for instance, seven companies were touring the smash farce hit *Charley's Aunt*, still running in London, and by 1896 there were 158 companies touring Britain, most of them assembled in London. These included companies specializing in a repertory of melodrama or Irish drama or comedy, or major companies each touring several important productions, such as those of *Irving and *Tree, which took carloads of *scenery with them. All of this was only made possible by an efficient railway network. Such touring had the important consequence of destroying the long-established *stock company; its theatre now became merely a venue for touring companies. Overseas tours to North America and the empire—South Africa, *India, Australia, New Zealand—were also organized in London. Irving, for example, took his *Lyceum company to North America eight times between 1882 and 1903.

The increase in population, the large numbers of visitors from outside London, and the steadily growing prosperity of the theatregoing middle class meant that West End theatres could now afford to abandon their *repertory system and their programme of two or three plays an evening, and adopt a new kind of economic structure, the *long run of a single play. The eighteenth-century repertory system, which entailed the performance of perhaps 60 to 70 mainpieces and many *afterpieces during a single season, with perhaps several changes in the bill during a single week, had disappeared before 1850. The interim system that took its place was the performance of a play for a week or two, or longer if the public was enthusiastic. Even in the old repertory system managers would let a popular piece run as long as it drew audiences, as did Gay's *The Beggar's Opera* in 1728 and *Jerrold's *Black-Ey'd Susan* in 1829; sometimes these runs were interrupted briefly by other plays. But this was not the same as the long run that eventually became the settled way of doing business in the West End, and remains so today in the commercial theatre everywhere.

The manager, or syndicate of backers—an increasingly common way of financing productions late in the century—could contemplate a long run only if there was the hope that the play chosen would take in enough money at the box office to pay off the production costs in a reasonably short time and then achieve a level of revenue that would healthily exceed the running costs and thus turn a decent profit. In nineteenth-century London this began to happen as a matter of settled policy rather than happy accident in the 1860s, first with the long run of *Taylor's *The Ticket-of-Leave Man* (407 performances) at the *Olympic, beginning in 1863, and particularly with the profitable practice of the *Wilton–*Bancroft management at the *Prince of Wales's Theatre of letting each new Tom *Robertson comedy exhaust itself at the box office in a long run and then achieve a further run in the not-too-distant future. Thus *Caste* ran for 156 performances in 1867, was revived in 1871 for 195, and again in 1879 for 126. *School*, the most financially successful of the Robertson comedies, began a run of 381 performances in 1869 and was revived in 1876 for 166 more. In the 1870s 107 plays in the West End ran for over 100 performances each, including Irving's production of *The Merchant of Venice* (1879), with 250. The star long-run play of the 1870s was H. J. *Byron's *Our Boys* at the Vaudeville (1,362 performances) from 1875; this was exceeded by *Charley's Aunt* (1,466 performances) from 1892. The long run changed the face of theatre, but without substantial audience growth it would have been impossible. It also perfectly suited the system of the *actor-manager, in which a leading actor had financial and administrative authority over the theatre or company he put together for the production, and which completely dominated the West End for the last two decades of the century.

The long run profoundly changed the life of the ordinary actor as well. In London a cast was now assembled for each play and disbanded when the run was over. No longer did the novice actor learn from many parts; he or she might be stuck with five lines to speak in a play touring for a year. As a result, early in the twentieth century dramatic academies were founded to *train the actor and replace the stock company experience of self-training on the job. Thus many features of contemporary English theatre practice originated in nineteenth-century London: the middle-class ascendancy over the West End theatre, both in attendance and in the content of the drama, the development of company touring, the expansion of the audience catchment area to include the provinces (whose inhabitants now journey to the West End in coach parties) and overseas, the long run, and new conditions of actor employment and experience.　　　MRB

3. 1900–1945

The new century found the actor-managers firmly in charge, class divisions still dominating the types of entertainment on offer, and the audiences larger than ever. When Victoria died in 1901, the long period named after her did not end so much as slide into a further extension; and when her son, who reigned as Edward VII, died nine years later, the structure and qualities of mainstream theatre were not substantially different from how they had been in 1880. Historically the most important development would be the arrival of *modernist methods, though they came to London through the back door. André *Antoine's model of a free stage (Théâtre *Libre, Paris, 1887) was followed in *Berlin two years later and in London in 1891 when J. T. *Grein established the *Independent Theatre. Its first production was a single private performance of *Ibsen's *Ghosts*, which had been denied a licence by the *Lord Chamberlain because of its treatment of syphilis and sexual infidelity. The social uproar that followed, much of it engineered by Clement *Scott's scathing review, made Grein 'the best abused man in London', as he put it himself. A group of other pioneer play-producing societies appeared in the next fifteen years, the most important being the *Stage Society, introducing European *naturalism and *symbolism. The goal of these groups was to offer to subscription audiences a repertoire of plays that for reasons of commerce or censorship could not find their way on the regular stage. The Independent Theatre also produced the first play of George Bernard *Shaw (*Widowers' Houses*, 1892), starting the career of the most carefully self-promoted dramatist of the twentieth century. But Shaw's significance was established in the next decade, and its jumping-off point was a connection formed in the Stage Society with the young actor, director, and playwright Harley Granville *Barker.

Barker's major contribution in the early years of the century was to expand the audience for what became known as the 'New Drama' through the establishment of the *Vedrenne–Barker seasons at the *Royal Court Theatre (1903–7). In those three years, relying principally on the plays of *Euripides, Shaw, and a few other contemporary writers, Barker made the largest advance yet towards a modernist reform of the stage in London, emphasizing ensemble *acting, simple staging, *repertory playing, and, crucially, the idea of the *director. The enterprise was poorly funded and remained small scale; though it easily ex-

panded into regular evening performances, when Barker attempted to put it on a more permanent footing at a larger theatre in 1907, it failed almost immediately. His campaign for a *national theatre, theoretically informed by William *Archer, would lead Barker to a series of repertory experiments that culminated in three remarkable productions of Shakespeare at the Savoy Theatre in 1912 and 1914 that took substantial advantage of new forms of directing and *scenography.

The road to modernism in London went through Edward Gordon *Craig. The son of Ellen *Terry, who had been Irving's leading lady and a light of the Victorian stage, Craig was obsessively committed to creating a new form of symbolist theatre, insisting that a single designer-director must be in charge of production: theatre would become an art primarily visual in implication and the actor become the *Über-marionette, only one part of a larger unified plan. The commercial theatre was vehemently opposed to such concepts, and Craig had little success as a director in London or elsewhere. But his ideas, first given form in *The Art of the Theatre* (1905, expanded 1911), were potent and highly influential. They affected Max *Reinhardt (whose work Barker saw in Berlin), who brought large-scale productions to London in 1911. The currents of European modernism were also swept in by the *Ballets Russes the same year, by the post-Impressionist art exhibition of 1910, and the extravagant *costumes of Leon *Bakst even affected design of non-theatrical dresses. Further, the rising tide of *feminist political action, the clamours for Irish Home Rule, the rally against stage censorship, and the German military threat, made the years between 1905 and 1914 a ferment of reformist zeal—confronting an entrenched, plutocratic establishment that seemed unshakeable.

The general theatregoer might not have noticed. Though Barker and Craig would ultimately win the battle for reform, both more or less abandoned active work after the war. Meanwhile audiences were more than content with the music hall, with George *Edwardes's *musical comedies at the *Gaiety, the technological wonders of large-scale melodramas at Drury Lane, and Oscar *Asche's orientalist musical fantasy *Chu Chin Chow* (1916; *see* INTERCULTURALISM), which ran for 2,238 performances over five years. The war would finally put an end to the actor-manager system and alter the *financial structure of theatre in London, but the real threat to the theatre industry came neither from organizational change nor from modernist reform, but rather from the upstart cinema. *Film began to affect spectator habits as early as 1910, especially in the music halls and working-class theatres. The West End was not seriously disturbed until the arrival of the talkie in 1927, when the cinema could compete with spoken drama; the informality of filmgoing, considerably lower *ticket prices, and the novelty of a new form stole much of the audience for live performance and never returned it. Between the wars London production would be engaged in dialogue with film, as star actors like

Ralph *Richardson, John *Gielgud, and Laurence *Olivier balanced careers that seemed a partial return to the age of the actor-manager, based not on their business acumen but on their screen drawing power. If they spent considerable time with Shakespeare at the *Old Vic—where new directors like Tyrone *Guthrie would also make a mark—they became international names through British and American films that cast them in literary roles that capitalized on their status as classic theatre actors.

The founding of the *Abbey Theatre in *Dublin in 1904, and the development of the *regional repertory movement in Britain before and after the First World War, did not diminish London's centrality but did point up the limitations of a theatre contracting to middle-class concerns. New plays reflected this retrenchment, as dramatists like Noël *Coward wrote about the fantasy lives of the rich in country houses and ocean liners, and T. S. *Eliot and others attempted to revive the effete traditions of *verse drama. The strongest voice in opposition to *bourgeois theatre was the Dubliner Sean *O'Casey (who had moved to London in the 1920s), with some lesser support from J. B. *Priestley. But the quarter-century after 1920 was dominated not by playwrights or modernist directors, rather by great actors. In addition to the three mentioned above, they included Sybil *Thorndike, Edith *Evans, Peggy *Ashcroft, Alec *Guinness, Michael *Redgrave, and Donald *Wolfit, all of whom would grow in importance after 1945. But when the war arrived in London, and bombs destroyed the *Shaftesbury, the Queen's, and the Little theatres, and badly damaged the *Duke of York's, the Royal Court, and the Old Vic, when *audience dress codes and curtain times were altered, it was clear the capital's theatre, though it would probably survive, would undergo a substantial change.   DK

4. 1945–2001

The evolution of post-war London theatre is marked by two key facts: a series of assaults on the hegemony of the commercialized West End and the geographical spread of drama throughout the capital. But in the immediate aftermath of the Second World War, the old structures remained intact. 'The war has been the making of me,' remarked the commercial impresario Hugh (Binkie) *Beaumont who, through the profit-making H. M. Tennent Ltd. and its non-profit subsidiary Tennent Productions, enjoyed a virtual monopoly of the West End in the post-1945 period: it was Beaumont who presented native playwrights like Terence *Rattigan, Emlyn *Williams, Christopher *Fry, and N. C. *Hunter, American imports ranging from *Oklahoma!* to *A Streetcar Named Desire,* and French successes by *Anouilh and *Cocteau. Beaumont's productions, lavishly presented and graced by star names, did much to sustain the glamour of the West End in a period of economic austerity but were increasingly attacked for their preoccupation with middle-class values.

Alternatives to Beaumont's vision of the West End as a fashionable emporium certainly existed. Under the directorship of Laurence Olivier, Ralph Richardson, and John Burrell, the exiled Old Vic enjoyed legendary post-war seasons at the New Theatre (now the Albery) with *Henry IV*, *Peer Gynt*, and *Oedipus the King* before the artistic triumvirate was summarily sacked and the company returned to its Waterloo home. And, under the directorship of Alec *Clunes, the tiny *Arts Theatre fulfilled the role of a de facto national theatre, producing an extraordinary range of classic and contemporary work including Fry's *The Lady's Not for Burning* in 1948 and John *Whiting's controversial *Saint's Day* in 1951.

Significantly it was at the Arts Theatre, then under the directorship of John Fernald, that one of the landmark plays of the post-war era received its English-language première in 1955. Despite being turned down by Richardson and Alec *Guinness and being greeted with a good deal of philistine derision, *Beckett's *Waiting for Godot* instantly became a theatrical talking point: in the words of a later, Beckett-influenced dramatist, Tom *Stoppard, the play 'redefined the minima of theatrical validity' and on its transfer from the Arts to the Criterion Theatre provoked nightly displays of enthusiasm and execration. Its noisy success was the first sign of a seismic shift in theatrical taste. Of equal importance was the creation of the *English Stage Company at the *Royal Court, dedicated to unearthing new writers and hitting the jackpot in May 1956 with its third production: John *Osborne's *Look Back in Anger*. Though formally far more conservative than Beckett, Osborne articulated the baffled frustration felt by England's alienated young and restored bravura speech to a verbally anaemic theatre. Coexisting with the ESC at the Royal Court, Joan *Littlewood's itinerant *Theatre Workshop put down roots at the Victorian Theatre Royal in Stratford East and created a brilliantly collaborative style in which the writer enjoyed rough parity with the actors and director. A momentous visit by *Brecht's *Berliner Ensemble—shortly after its founder's death—to the Palace Theatre in August 1956 also had a huge influence on theatre practitioners: Brecht's episodic structure, the commitment of the ensemble, the ascetic beauty of the design, the emphasis on used *props and costumes, even the nakedly visible *lighting rig, were all imitated by a whole generation of British writers, directors, designers, and technicians. From the première of *Godot* in August 1955 to the visit by the Berliner Ensemble a year later, London experienced a series of aesthetic tremors that rearranged the theatrical landscape forever.

Foreign companies like the Berliner Ensemble and the equally acclaimed *Moscow Art Theatre, who came in 1958, showed London what it had been missing: permanence and continuity. So it was no surprise that in the early 1960s steps were taken to establish two large-scale British companies. At Stratford-on-Avon Peter *Hall created the *Royal Shakespeare Company, based on long-term actors' contracts, out of the annual ad hoc Shakespeare festival. Believing it was vital for his company to combine contemporary and classic work and to have a permanent London base, Hall took a lease on the *Aldwych Theatre despite fierce opposition from Binkie Beaumont: actors were able to bring Shakespearian disciplines to modern work and the result bore exciting fruit in Peter *Brook's version of Peter *Weiss's Marat/Sade (1964) and Hall's own production of Harold *Pinter's The Homecoming (1965). After a century of farcical procrastination, the National Theatre Company was also finally established in the expansive early 1960s (see NATIONAL THEATRE OF GREAT BRITAIN). It was created by Olivier out of summer seasons he had directed in *Chichester and it made its debut at the Old Vic in October 1963 with an unremarkable Hamlet. What followed, however, was exceptional not least because of Olivier's magpie-like gift for appropriating the best available talent: his associate directors were John *Dexter and William *Gaskill from the Royal Court, his literary manager was the *critic Kenneth *Tynan, and the lower echelons of his company included such future stars as Michael *Gambon and Anthony *Hopkins.

In every way the 1960s was a decisive decade for London theatre. The balance of power shifted away from commercial *producers towards the subsidized princes. New writing flourished with Peter *Nichols, Joe *Orton, Edward *Bond, Stoppard, Alan *Ayckbourn, David *Storey, and Caryl *Churchill among the talent to emerge. The Theatres Act of 1968 finally abolished the statutory power of the Lord Chamberlain to censor British theatre. And a whole series of concurrent events—the student revolutions of 1968, the emergence of an alternative counter-culture, the rejection of big institutions—led to a more directly *political theatre and a vast expansion in performance spaces. This new movement was covered by the blanket term of 'the *fringe' borrowed from the *Edinburgh Festival. But it was also the simultaneous presence of three expatriate Americans—Charles *Marowitz, Ed Berman, and Jim Haynes—that led to the establishment of an *Off-Broadway equivalent in London. By the beginning of the 1970s the capital was teeming with new theatres, many of which have survived the ravages of time, including the *Bush Theatre, the Orange Tree, and the *King's Head.

But even as alternative spaces multiplied, London theatre faced a mounting crisis in the 1970s for reasons beyond its control: a world economic recession and a drastic rise in oil prices led to national belt-tightening. The opening of the National Theatre complex on the South Bank in 1976 could hardly have come at a less propitious time. With housing, health, and education subsidies all being cut, a three-*auditorium national playhouse seemed to some an extravagant luxury. But under Peter Hall's directorship, the National survived economic cutbacks and internal strikes to become a popular success and a theatre that embraced new plays as diverse as Ayckbourn's Bedroom Farce (1977), *Hare's Plenty (1978), and *Shaffer's

Amadeus (1979). It was in the West End that the crisis was most visible, as it turned largely into a shop window for transfers from Broadway and the subsidized sector. But the advent of Mrs Thatcher as Conservative Prime Minister in 1979 had a decisive effect on London theatre. Suddenly private profit was respectable and public subsidy suspect. And that was reflected in the dominance of musicals throughout the 1980s. Andrew *Lloyd Webber's *dance-driven Cats in 1981 was followed by the long-running Starlight Express (1984), Les Misérables (1985), The Phantom of the Opera (1986), and Miss Saigon (1989). Significantly, Les Misérables was a co-production between Cameron *Mackintosh and the Royal Shakespeare Company and was jointly staged by two classical directors, Trevor *Nunn and John *Caird: it symbolized the marriage of art and commerce and embodied the Thatcherite belief that even subsidized institutions had to survive through self-help.

Inevitably the profit-driven ethos of the 1980s bred dissent: theatre increasingly acted as a form of political opposition through plays such as *Brenton and Hare's Pravda (1985), Churchill's anti-capitalist Serious Money (1989), and Ayckbourn's A Small Family Business (1989). The process reached its apogee when the National Theatre in 1993 staged a contemporary trilogy by Hare dealing with the erosion of British institutions. But however much the subsidized theatre itself may have been blighted by underfunding, it showed throughout the 1980s and 1990s a remarkable tenacity and resilience.

Big musicals were undeniably the commercial salvation of West End theatre in the 1980s and continue to exert popular appeal. But the long-term trend was towards diversity—not least through the emergence of groups devoted to black, *feminist, or *gay theatre—and decentralization. In the 1990s the real energy also derived from fashionable smaller venues. The success story of the decade was the *Almeida Theatre in north London which, under the direction of Jonathan Kent and Ian McDiarmid, offered an oustanding repertory of classic and contemporary work in much the same way as the Arts Theatre had in the 1940s. It was closely followed by the *Donmar Warehouse in Covent Garden: another small-scale playhouse with an eclectic policy. The Royal Court Theatre under Stephen *Daldry in the mid-1990s also played host to a wealth of new talent in a way that had not been paralleled since the George *Devine era 40 years earlier: its most exciting discoveries were the sadly short-lived Sarah *Kane, Joe *Penhall, and Jez Butterworth.

But alongside the presentation of new writing in established venues, an equally important phenomenon emerged: the realization that theatre need not be confined to special areas or designated buildings. The shift in the centre of gravity away from Shaftesbury Avenue had been going on steadily since the late 1960s: it was symbolized by the geographical expansion of the fringe, the situation of the National Theatre on the South Bank, and the RSC's tenancy of the *Barbican Centre. The process was accelerated by the opening of Shakespeare's *Globe on *Bankside in 1997 and by the Almeida's colonization of new spaces such as the former Gainsborough Film Studios in Shoreditch in 2000. Stimulated by the biennial *London International Festival of Theatre, young audiences also showed a delight in found spaces: under the festival's aegis Deborah *Warner staged extraordinary events in a disused hotel above St Pancras Station and on the top storey of a Euston Road office block. None of this invalidates the continued existence of big institutions or a busy commercial sector: it is proof, however, that the definition of 'theatre' is constantly evolving and that the post-war period has been marked not just by periodic booms in new writing or musicals but by the growing awareness that London itself is one vast performance space.

MKB

ACKROYD, PETER, *London: the biography* (London, 2000)
BILLINGTON, MICHAEL, *One Night Stands* (London, 1993)
BOOTH, MICHAEL R., et al., *The Revels History of Drama in English*, vi: *1750–1880* (London, 1975)
—— *Theatre in the Victorian Age* (London, 1991)
—— and KAPLAN, JOEL H. (eds.), *The Edwardian Theatre: essays on performance and the stage* (Cambridge, 1996)
DUFF, CHARLES, *The Lost Summer* (London, 1995)
INGRAM, WILLIAM, *The Business of Playing: the beginnings of the adult professional theater in Elizabethan London* (Ithaca, NY, 1992)
KENNEDY, DENNIS, *Granville Barker and the Dream of Theatre* (Cambridge, 1985)
PORTER, ROY, *London: a social history* (London, 1994)
SHELLARD, DOMINIC, *British Theatre since the War* (New Haven, 1999)
THOMAS, DAVID (ed.), *Restoration and Georgian England, 1660–1788* (Cambridge, 1989)
THOROLD, PETER, *The London Rich* (London, 1999)
WICKHAM, GLYNNE (ed.), *English Professional Theatre, 1530–1660* (Cambridge, 2000)

LONDON INTERNATIONAL FESTIVAL OF THEATRE (LIFT)

A biannual summer festival started in 1981 by neophyte cross-cultural impresarios Lucy Neal and Rose Fenton, which has consistently presented an eclectic mix of experimental, *alternative, and mainstream performance from all over the world. Ten companies were hosted in 1981, from as far afield as *Malaysia and Peru, and including the Polish Theatre of the Eighth Day, the Dutch *Werkteater, and a sell-out Brazilian show, *Macunaima*, at the *Lyric Theatre Hammersmith. Outdoor aesthetic extravagance was introduced in 1983: the 30-strong French group Urban Sax abseiled down Covent Garden Piazza playing wild saxophone sonics; Catalan company Els *Comediants enveloped a huge Battersea Park *audience in a firecracker frenzy in *The Devils*; the UK's *Welfare State International staged a spectacular dockside *allegory with *The Raising of the Titanic* in the East End's Limehouse Basin. Commissions and local community-based projects have also featured, alongside main-stage productions from the Katona József Theatre of *Budapest, Beijing opera (*jingju*, 1985), *St Petersburg's *Maly Theatre (1991), and the *Market Theatre of *Johannesburg with Theatre Connection's *Jozi Jozi* (1995). By the late 1990s a young people's education programme, seminars, and talks complemented a remarkable diversity of world-class performances, from Argentina's De La Guarda through the Deutsches Schauspielhaus of Hamburg to Australian-Chinese *performance artist William Yang.

BRK

LONG RUN

A system of theatrical organization whereby the play performed runs as long as there is an *audience for it. In the nineteenth century, in the largest urban centres, especially in Britain, the long run replaced the full or partial *repertory system previously operated; that is, where the play was changed daily, two or three times a week, weekly, or fortnightly. A long run was possible only if the potential audience in the city concerned was large enough for the *management to take the financial risk of letting a play run, and, crucially, if a sufficiently large audience existed outside the city with easy access of transportation to the centre and could profitably swell the local audience. In *London, a city whose population increased from 900,000 in 1800 to 6,000,000 in 1900, these conditions were met by mid-century. In the 1850s thirteen plays ran for more than 100 nights, in the 1860s 45, in the 1870s 107. From the 407 of *The Ticket-of-Leave Man* from 1863 to the 1,466 for *Charley's Aunt* from 1890 to the 50 years of *The Mousetrap* from 1952, population growth, railway transport, overseas tourists arriving by ship and then by plane, coach parties from all over the country, all combined to make the long run the preferred method of commercial presentation in the West End. *New York, slower to become a large urban centre, showed a similar development. Broadway's 3,782 performances of *Tobacco Road* from 1933 were matched by the 3,213 for *Life with Father* from 1939, and exceeded by modern *musicals like *A Chorus Line*, which ran for fifteen years, and the Andrew *Lloyd Webber mega-hits like *Cats* and *Phantom of the Opera*, which became marvels of commodified packaging.

Organizationally, the long run changed theatre. The provincial *stock company disappeared, replaced in part by companies *touring a long-run play. Actors were hired for the run of the play only, or for a year, six months, or three months. Longer *rehearsal periods than the repertory system allowed became possible. The expenses of long-run productions eventually necessitated substantial contributions from financial backers, since they were beyond the means of a single theatre or producer. And most theatres became mere venues, to be leased or rented for the run. It is important to note, however, that versions of the old repertory system still operate at the start of the twenty-first century in subsidized national and municipal theatres, especially in Central Europe, and in *opera and *ballet companies worldwide. MRB

LONG WHARF THEATRE

American *regional theatre in New Haven, Connecticut. Founded in 1965 by Jon *Jory and Harlan Kleiman, the theatre came to renown under *artistic director Arvin *Brown and executive director M. Edgar Rosenblum. They ran LWT for 30 years and gained a reputation for mounting productions that made successful transfers to nearby Broadway, including David *Storey's *The Changing Room*, David *Mamet's *American Buffalo*, David *Rabe's *Streamers*, Michael Cristofer's *The Shadow Box*, and D. L. Coburn's *The Gin Game*. In 1997 Brown was replaced by Doug Hughes, who had a similar success with Margaret Edson's *Wit*, before quitting abruptly in 2001. STC

LONSDALE, FREDERICK (LIONEL FREDERICK LEONARD) (1881–1954)

English playwright and librettist. Lonsdale began his theatrical career as a librettist for pre-First World War Ruritanian *musical comedies such as *The King of Cadonia* (1908), *The Balkan Princess* (1910), and *The Maid of the Mountains* (1917), which ran for 1,352 performances. In the 1920s he began writing the social *comedies for which he is chiefly remembered, including *Aren't We All* (1923), *The Last of Mrs Cheney* (1925), *On Approval* (1927), *Canaries Sometimes Sing* (1929), and *Once Is Enough* (1938). Lonsdale's success rests primarily on his lightly ironic style and witty *dialogue, combined with well-constructed *plots. MDG

LOOS, ANITA (c.1893–1981)

American playwright and screenwriter. Loos was a professional *film scenarist from the age of 19. The spectacle of sexually attractive young women competing to marry wealthy if unperceptive older men was presented as comic sport in her best-selling novel *Gentlemen Prefer Blondes* (1925). This material and its *protagonist Lorelei Lee came to define Loos's career, as she and her husband (John Emerson) adapted the novel for the stage in 1926, and she collaborated with Joseph Fields and composer Jule *Styne to create the 1949 *musical—a production centred upon a career-making performance by Carol *Channing. Loos's *Happy Birthday* (1946), a Helen *Hayes vehicle, and *Gigi* (1951, adapted from stories by Colette) were also commercial successes. MAF

LOPE DE RUEDA *See* RUEDA, LOPE DE.

LOPE DE VEGA *See* VEGA CARPIO, LOPE DE.

LOQUASTO, SANTO (1944–)

American designer. Moving among stage, *film, and *dance since the early 1970s, Loquasto has built a reputation for sculpturally striking and exquisitely detailed design. His work for American *regional theatre and Broadway notably includes the conceptual design for Andrei *Şerban's 1977 production of *The Cherry Orchard*, and the meticulous evocation of a 1940s Lower East Side restaurant in the 1989 revival of *Café Crown*. Since his first Broadway sets in 1972 for *Sticks and Bones* and *That Championship Season*, Loquasto's prolific output has included designs for *Bent* (1980), *Lost in Yonkers* (1991), and *Fosse* (1999), as well as Liviu *Ciulei's *Peer Gynt* (1983) at the *Guthrie Theatre. In dance, Loquasto's work for American Ballet Theatre in *New York began with *costumes for Twyla Tharp's *Push Comes to Shove* (1976), and has included collaborations with Jerome *Robbins, Agnes *de Mille, and Mark Morris. He started a longtime association with Woody Allen in 1980, receiving particular recognition for production designs in period films like *Bullets over Broadway* (1994). EW

LORAINE, ROBERT (1876–1935)

English *actor-manager. Loraine's acting career began in 1889 when he performed in the companies of Beerbohm *Tree and George *Alexander. He soon established himself as a popular star in *melodramas, from *The Three Musketeers* (1899) to *The Prisoner of Zenda* (1923). He also performed regularly in Shakespeare and *Shaw, and in 1905 he played John Tanner in *Man and Superman* in *New York. Back in *London, he appeared in several of Shaw's plays in 1907 and 1908; during the next few years he worked in plays by *Sheridan, *Goldsmith, Shakespeare, and *Maugham, and in 1911 took over the lease on the Criterion Theatre in London, reviving *Man and Superman*. During the war he served in the Royal Flying Corps and was wounded in action. In 1919 he was a success in a revival of *Cyrano de Bergerac*, then returned to actor-management in the 1920s, performing not only plays by Shaw, *Barrie, *Strindberg, *Congreve, and Shakespeare but also romantic melodramas. TP

LORANGER, FRANÇOISE (1913–95)

Québec playwright and novelist. She was one of the first to raise feminist concerns in her play *Encore cinq minutes* (*Five More Minutes*, 1967), also a success on *radio and *television, in which a middle-aged, middle-class housewife decides to abandon her smothering, patriarchal family and set out on her own. It was followed by more political works reflecting her growing nationalist convictions, notably the caricatural *Le Chemin du roy* (*The King's Highway*, 1968), dealing with conflict between Ottawa and Québec, and *Médium saignant* (*Medium Rare*, 1970), exploring the tensions caused by the predominance of English in *Montréal.   LED

LORCA, FEDERICO GARCÍA *See* García Lorca, Federico.

LORD CHAMBERLAIN

An official of the English royal household, the Lord Chamberlain included among his duties the planning of the revels and the keeping of order in the banquet hall. In practice, however, the supervision of court entertainments was delegated to the *Master of the Revels, and it was this official who exercised the Lord Chamberlain's authority over the Elizabethan and Jacobean theatre. A royal patent of 1581 gave the Master of the Revels powers to supervise, control, and censor the stage, and further edicts strengthened his position through the seventeenth century. The Stage *Licensing Act of 1737 refocused authority in theatrical matters to the Lord Chamberlain, whose powers finally received statutory recognition. Specifically, he was authorized to *license both theatres and plays. In practice dramatic *censorship was in the hands of a hired subordinate, the Examiner of Plays. The number and complexity of regulations enacted over the next 100 years meant that the severity or laxity of their interpretation depended upon the personal predilections of a given Lord Chamberlain. The Theatre Regulatory Act of 1843 consolidated the laws, and reaffirmed and strengthened the Lord Chamberlain's authority to license theatres in *London (other than *Drury Lane and *Covent Garden), and to preview and license every new play or addition 'presented for hire' in Great Britain. This statute remained in effect until the Theatres Act of 1968 abolished censorship. During the sixteenth and seventeenth centuries, authorities prohibited plays mainly on political or religious grounds; later Lords Chamberlain and Examiners of Plays tended to shape the drama as arbiters of public taste. As a consequence British drama in the eighteenth, nineteenth, and early twentieth centuries avoided serious treatment of sex, *politics, and *religion.   RWV

LORTEL, LUCILLE (1902–99)

American *producer, theatre owner, and philanthropist. Dubbed the 'Queen of *Off-Broadway', Lortel originated workshops and readings of new plays (from 1947) at her White Barn Theatre, on the grounds of her estate in Connecticut, at the Theatre de Lys (later the Lucille Lortel Theatre) in Greenwich Village in *New York from 1956, and through the *American National Theatre and Academy Matinée Series at the de Lys (1956–75). Independently wealthy, she produced over 500 works, both in fully staged and workshop productions, introducing major plays by American and European dramatists, notably *Beckett and *O'Casey.   AW

LOS ANGELES

Before the arrival of Anglo-Americans in the gold rush of 1849, Spanish-language theatre and *opera flourished in Los Angeles. New roads and railways in the following decades created a *touring circuit for *Hispanic theatre, linking Los Angeles with cities as distant as *Mexico City and San Antonio, as well as *San Francisco to the north. This system virtually collapsed after the forced repatriation of Mexican workers by the United States in the 1930s. The rise of the *Chicano movement in the 1960s led to a rebirth of Spanish-language performance and companies, of which El Teatro *Campesino (1965) and Teatro de Esperanza (1971) are the best known.

Oliver Morosco was responsible for the first flush of English-language *bourgeois drama in Los Angeles; by the early 1900s he was producing plays and *musicals throughout the city. The populism of *film began a process of converting theatres to cinemas in the 1920s that the economic crisis of the Depression only accelerated, despite the city's resurgent interest in *community theatre and the temporary presence of the *Federal Theatre Project (1935–9). By the end of the decade, the Biltmore was one of the few venues open to professional theatre, limited to touring companies. The Greek Theatre (1930), a major civic landmark, was used as a barracks during the Second World War and was largely neglected as a performance space until the 1950s.

After the war the proximity of the film industry to the theatre programme at the University of California became a magnet for attracting a national talent pool of young actors and directors. Graduates founded the *Mark Taper Forum (1959), now one of the leading *regional theatres in the country, and the Actors' Gang (1981), a theatre *collective associated with actors Tim Robbins and Annette Bening that has produced original plays and modern classics. Due to an Actors' Equity (*see* TRADE UNIONS, THEATRICAL) rule that permits contract waivers for its members performing in small non-profit houses, the city is dotted with 99-seat theatres that fulfil a variety of artistic missions, not the least of which is to showcase *acting talent for *casting directors working in *television and film.

By the late 1960s the population explosion and unchecked suburban sprawl had decentred the entertainment district (what Angelenos call the 'geography factor'). City officials and developers have supported expensive arts complexes such as the Los Angeles Theatre Center and events like the Los Angeles Festival (begun during the 1984 summer Olympics) in order to re-create locales for civic performance. The urgency of this project was underscored by the Rodney King rioting of 1992, an event that prompted the hiring of director Peter *Sellars to raise the profile of the Los Angeles Festival, a post he held until 1996. The success of these efforts continues to be debated.   JAB

LOUIS, VICTOR (1731–1800)

French architect. Louis's major contribution to eighteenth-century *playhouse architecture was the monumental Grand Théâtre at Bordeaux. Inaugurated in 1780, this was probably the first *auditorium designed upon a perfect circle actually built in France. The last decades of Louis's life were devoted to work in *Paris, largely in Louis-Philippe's Palais Royal, where, in 1781, the architect had built the galleries surrounding the gardens. In 1782–3 he designed a little *puppet theatre for these galleries, and in 1787–8 the Théâtre du Cirque du Palais Royal in the gardens. From 1786 to 1790 he built the Théâtre des Variétés-Amusantes on the rue de Richelieu (since 1799 the *Comédie-Française). It was in this *auditorium, where he reproduced the circular Bordeaux plan, that Louis made history by using cast-iron girders to support an elaborate vault. His last theatre, which opened in 1793 further along the rue de Richelieu, was the Théâtre des Arts.   JG

LOURENÇO, JOÃO (1944–   )

Portuguese actor and director. His acting career began in 1952 in *radio, includes some notable roles at the Teatro *Nacional D. Maria II, and extends to *television and *film. His discovery, during a *tour, of the new theatre in Brazil led to the foundation in 1966 of a society of actors, Grupo 4. This was a pioneering step in a movement for the creation of a Portuguese theatre independent of the commercial circuits, which was to prove instrumental in changing theatrical structures and repertoires after the 1974 Revolution. A year later Lourenço began directing, staging authors previously banned by the *censors (*Kopit, *Weiss, *Mrożek, and Dario *Fo) and promoting contemporary Portuguese playwrights. An enthusiastic director of *Brecht (his most admired production remains *Mother Courage*, 1986), Lourenço turned his attention to contemporary German and English-speaking drama in the 1990s. *Opera and *musicals also feature in his long directing career, characterized by a sober inventiveness in *scenography and a socially responsible repertoire.   MJB

LOUTHERBOURG, PHILIP JAMES DE (1740–1812)

Alsatian designer. Trained as an academic painter by Carle Van Loo, Loutherbourg established a fashionable career in Paris during the 1760s. His visit to *London in 1771 may have been part of a search for landscape alternatives to the fashionable pilgrimage to Italy. However, during this visit he met David *Garrick and, although there is no evidence of earlier theatre experience, intrigued the *actor-manager with ideas for new scenes and stage machinery. Loutherbourg's ideas suited Garrick's ambition to stage more topical and scenically extravagant 'entertainments', and the painter was employed at *Drury Lane Theatre from 1772 to 1781. His terms of employment indicate that he should have total *scenographic authority over the stage; he would prepare designs and models, personally supervise their execution, and design and supervise *costumes and *properties. He sought a harmony of scenographic elements, a visual unification of scene and performer within imagined space, and an involvement of the *audience that predicted the *romantic *realism of the following century. Loutherbourg designed scenes only for *pantomimes, spectacular *tragedies, and topical entertainments; it was assumed that his approach would not replace the traditional stock scenery used in the majority of plays, *comedies. He was noted for carefully observed detail in topography, and for the romantic wildness of his landscape scenes.

He remained at Drury Lane when Garrick retired in 1776. In 1779 he created a 'travelogue' pantomime, *The Wonders of Derbyshire*, for the new manager, R. B. *Sheridan. The surviving scenic model clearly illustrates the way in which he extended the two-dimensional vocabulary of scenic devices. He visually linked side wings (*see* FLATS AND WINGS) with top scenes to enclose the stage, and he gave a dynamic to the stage floor through the clever use of horizontal *ground rows. As a newly elected member of the Royal Academy, he left Drury Lane in 1781 to pursue his career as an easel artist. Painting tours to Derbyshire, the Lake District, and Snowdonia effectively created these districts as topics for art. Concurrently, he created a large model theatre—the *Eidophusikon*—that showed views of scenic *spectacle to small *audiences. Building upon the excitement created by Captain Cook's South Sea explorations, Loutherbourg worked with John *O'Keeffe to prepare *Omai; or, A Trip round the World* at *Covent Garden Theatre in 1785, probably his final stage work, after which he focused upon landscape, naval, and his late mystical canvases.   CLB

LOVELACE, EARL (1935–   )

Trinidadian novelist and playwright, particularly associated with theme of the clash of city and country. His first play, *The New Boss* (1962), used the metaphor of the island as an estate left to its workers after independence. *My Name Is Village* (1976), a *musical with *folk themes, followed his emergence as an accomplished novelist, and was staged as part of Trinidad's Best Village Festival, involving the whole village of Matura in the production. *Jestina's Calypso* (1978) is a witty exploration of sexism in Trinidadian culture, while *The New Hardware Store*

(1980) relies on elements of *carnival. Lovelace's celebrated novel *The Dragon Can't Dance* was dramatized by the *Trinidad Theatre Workshop in 1978, and a later novel, *The Wine of Astonishment*, was staged as a play in Trinidad a decade later.

ES

LOWIN, JOHN (c.1576–c.1659)

English actor and *manager. Lowin performed with Worcester's Men but made his career with the King's Men (*see* CHAMBERLAIN'S MEN) whom he joined by 1603 when he appeared in the cast list for *Jonson's *Sejanus*. Many other highly versatile parts for that company followed, including Bosola in *Webster's *The Duchess of Malfi*. Along with John *Heminges and Henry *Condell, Lowin ranked as one of the chief actors of the company. He also became one of the company's managers, as well as a housekeeper in the *Globe and *Blackfriars *playhouses. John *Downes claimed in 1708 that Thomas *Betterton excelled in the lead of Shakespeare's *Henry VIII* because he had been instructed in the role by *Davenant, who had, in turn, been taught by Lowin.

SPC

LUCAS, CRAIG (1951–)

American playwright. Starting his career in the *choruses of several Broadway *musicals, Lucas produced a steady stream of plays, primarily *Off-Broadway and *regionally, beginning with *Missing Persons* in 1981. Lucas's career coincided with the AIDS epidemic, and many of his plays deal with *characters—whether gay or straight—coping with cataclysmic change. He collaborated with director Norman Rene on *Reckless* (1983), *Blue Window* (1984), *Prelude to a Kiss* (South Coast Repertory, California, 1988; *Circle Repertory Company and Broadway, 1989), and *God's Heart* (*Trinity Repertory Company, 1993). After Rene's death in 1996, Lucas's work often centred more directly on AIDS, a central element in *The Dying Gaul* (1998). Individual cruelty is the subject of *Stranger* (2000). Lucas actively mentored younger writers and directors after his initial success.

AW

LUCIE, DOUG (1953–)

English playwright who holds up the illusions and delusions of Thatcherite and post-Thatcherite Britain to unflinching ridicule. Whether he is dealing with political advertising in *Fashion* (1987) or journalism in *The Shallow End* (1997), his plays are characterized by cruel humour and passionate moral polemic. He shows an indebtedness to *Osborne in his scabrous articulacy, and he has turned his fire equally on the delusions of the left in *Progress* (1984) and right-wing evangelism in *Grace* (1992). *Fashion* (1988) most precisely places his *satire within a fully worked narrative, dealing hilariously and shockingly

with the influence of advertising and spin doctors in British politics; it has seemed increasingly relevant in the early twenty-first century.

DR

LUCO CRUCHAGA, GERMÁN (1894–1936)

Chilean playwright and journalist, with Armando *Moock one of the most important playwrights of the first half of the twentieth century. Luco Cruchaga's plays are *melodramas depicting the customs of Chilean society, mainly in the countryside. His most accomplished work is *La viuda de Aplablaza* (*The Widow of Aplablaza*, 1929), considered a classic of Chilean drama. In a *realistic style it portrays an amorous relationship between a mature woman and a young man, similar to *Racine's *Phèdre*. It was staged successfully in 1956 and 1999 in *Santiago.

MAR

LUDLAM, CHARLES (1943–87)

American playwright, actor, and *manager. His youth was influenced greatly by Hollywood *film, popular *television, *puppets, and comic books, and at the age of 15 he worked as an actor in the Long Island summer *stock company the Red Barn Theatre. After attending two performances of the *Living Theatre in *New York, including *The Connection* (1959), he was inspired to form the Students' Repertory Theatre at his high school in Long Island. In 1966 Ludlum joined the company of the Playhouse of the *Ridiculous, formed by Ronald Tavel and Jon Vacarro. The *gay camp style of the Playhouse of the Ridiculous was marked by *parodies of *historical dramas and classic Hollywood formulas, sexual wordplay (primarily homosexual references), scatological humour, and allusions to popular entertainment. Ludlum developed the 'Ridiculous' aesthetic further in his own troupe, the *Ridiculous Theatrical Company, in which he was the lead actor, playwright, and director. His dramas construct a labyrinth of allusions and pastiche of earlier forms through *textual appropriations that strive to elicit a *laughter not of moral judgement but of the absurdity of action and belief. Ludlum's performances of the central women of his plays, especially Camille, won him much praise as an actor. His 29 plays include *Bluebeard* (1970), *Camille* (1973), *Stageblood* (1975), and *The Mystery of Irma Vep* (1984).

MDC

LUDLOW, NOAH (1795–1886)

American *actor-manager. A pioneer barnstorming through the American west (in his day extending to the Mississippi River in mid-continent), Ludlow built theatres and performed along the Ohio and Mississippi rivers, travelling by barge, horseback, and on foot from Pittsburgh to New Orleans in a career spanning 1815 to 1853. He was among the earliest to perform in Mobile, New Orleans (in English), and St Louis. Partnered with actor-manager Sol *Smith for some eighteen years, the two parted company acrimoniously, quarrelling over financial matters and ending in court. Ludlow felt doubly betrayed when Smith published his reminiscences in 1868, including unflattering accounts of Ludlow's performance and managerial abilities. Ludlow responded with his own memoirs, attacking Smith in often intemperate terms. His *Dramatic Life as I Found It* (1880), however, provides a detailed and richly evocative account of theatrical life under harsh conditions in the first half of the nineteenth century on the American *frontier.

AW

LUDRUK

Regional theatre popular in east Java (*Indonesia). Its origins are obscure, believed to reach as far back as the thirteenth century as *ritual *ludruk bandan* and *ludruk lyrok*. The first written evidence dates from 1822. Main features were *female impersonators (*waria*) who perform songs and *dances, and *clown characters. Since the 1920s more complex dramatic stories have been added under the influence of *bangsawan* theatre. These *melodramas and *farces feature mostly contemporary domestic stories or, less frequently, legendary or historical and political material. Scenes are *improvised based on short *scenarios, presented in a *realistic acting style in contemporary dress, and performed in local east Javanese dialects. A typical *ludruk* performance starts with a preliminary *dance (*ngremo*), followed by a comic skit (*dagelan*), and a song-and-dance number by a *female impersonator (*selingan*) leading into the main story. Between *acts of the play additional *selingan* are inserted. A *gamelan orchestra accompanies the entire performance. Clowns are central characters in *ludruk*, as they voice criticism, subvert power structures, and speak for common people. The form has become commercial entertainment popular with urban and rural working-class *audiences.

KP

LUDWIG, OTTO (1813–65)

German dramatist, novelist, and critic. Best known today as a prose writer and exponent of poetic *realism, Ludwig considered himself primarily a dramatist. The major influences on his work were the *romantic poets *Tieck and E. T. A. *Hoffmann. His *tragedies *Der Erbförster* (*The Forester*, 1850) and *Die Makkabäer* (*The Maccabeus*, 1854) demonstrated elements of psychological characterization and enjoyed successful productions, although the latter was less popular in Germany on account of its pro-Jewish tendencies. In his fragmentary *Shakespeare Studies* (1871) he developed a normative poetics of *realistic drama with Shakespeare as a model, and in opposition to *Schiller's classicist *dramaturgy (*see* WEIMAR CLASSICISM).

CBB

LUGNÉ-POE, AURÉLIEN-MARIE (1869–1940)

French actor and director who championed the *symbolist movement. His early *Paris acting career was inauspicious, in *Antoine's Théâtre *Libre and Paul *Fort's Théâtre d'*Art; but at the latter he encountered the work of Maurice *Maeterlinck, with whom he became closely associated. After the demise of Fort's theatre in 1893, Lugné-Poe set up a company which would perform the work of the great foreign dramatists as well as the plays of the young 'idealists', as the symbolists and others called themselves. He first directed Maeterlinck's *Pelléas and Mélisande* before naming this new venture the Théâtre de l'*Œuvre. The early seasons were composed of a mixture of Scandinavian drama (including *Brand* and *Rosmersholm* by *Ibsen as well the work of *Strindberg and *Bjørnson), and in this he differed little in repertoire from Antoine. But his aim was to turn actors into instruments of the *director and give precedence to poetry in 'mood plays'—in effect, to detheatricalize theatre. One notable exception to this ideal was the première of *Jarry's *Ubu roi* in 1896. A year later Lugné-Poe announced a break with symbolism to focus on the work of foreign dramatists, which angered the theatre community.

The whole project of the l'Œuvre was fraught with difficulty. He never managed to secure a permanent troupe of actors, and after a brief spell at the *Bouffes du Nord he moved to the 1,000-seat Nouveau-Théâtre, an annexe of the Casino de Paris, hardly appropriate for an *avant-garde programme. But he managed to fill the seats nonetheless, with only 10 per cent of them going to paying subscribers, 30 per cent to journalists, and the remainder given away free. The small subscription base, a reputation for trouble in the *auditorium with the 'popular' *audience, the snub to young French authors, and mounting debts led to the theatre's demise in 1899. Lugné-Poe reopened the theatre in 1912, but though he is now recognized as the champion of Maeterlinck, Belgium's greatest dramatist, and the director of some of the most influential *modernist drama, in his day these successes were not appreciated and he lived near to the breadline for most of his life.

BRS

LUKIN, VLADIMIR (1737–94)

Russian dramatist who was among the first to turn his back on *neoclassicism and embrace *bourgeois sentimentalism. His attitude to drama was also very nationalistic: he sought to eliminate foreign influence and to write a dramatic language which was close to human speech and with particular performers in mind. As a democratic advocate of an 'all-comers theatre', he anticipated the *Moscow Art Theatre by a century or more. His best plays are probably *The Spendthrift Reformed by Love* (1765) and a *one-act *comedy, *The Pedlar*, in which he attempted to capture the vividness of peasant speech.

NW

LULLY, JEAN-BAPTISTE (1632–87)

Italian composer, musician, and dancer. Giovanni Lulli was born in Florence and arrived in France in 1646 as an Italian tutor for Mlle de Montpensier. In her service he learned to *dance, compose, and play several instruments. He moved to Louis XIV's household in 1652, and by February 1653 had danced with Louis in the *Ballet de la nuit*. One month later Lulli was named Compositeur de la Musique Instrumentale du Roi. In 1656, he began conducting the royal *petits violons*. In 1661 Louis appointed him Surintendant de la Musique et Compositeur de la Musique de la Chambre, and the King granted him naturalization as Jean-Baptiste Lully. In 1662 he became Maître de la Musique de la Famille Royale, responsible for all court music. In 1672, upon his installation as director of the Académie Royale de Musique, Lully determined to bring *opera to *Paris's audiences. At a *rehearsal in 1687, he banged his big toe with a cane: a few weeks later he died of gangrene. Lully was the most influential of Louis XIV's court musicians. As a composer, his output was tremendous: eleven *comédies-ballets*, thirteen *tragédies-lyriques* (a form of opera), over 30 *ballets de cour*, instrumental music, and twenty motets. He collaborated with important figures in music, dance, and theatre, including *Molière, *Quinault, and *Corneille. By the time of his death he had established the French opera as an independent form which incorporated not only song and dance, but a unified *plot and poetic *recitative.   GES

LUNACHARSKY, ANATOLY (1875–1933)

Russian/Soviet dramatist, critic, and the Soviet Union's first cultural commissar, from 1917 to 1929. Educated at the University of Zurich, Lunacharsky's tastes were cosmopolitan and, on the whole, enlightened. In a book of critical and *theoretical essays which appeared in 1908, he rubbed shoulders with leading *symbolist theorists/practitioners of the day, including *Meyerhold, whom he appointed head of the theatrical section of the Cultural Commissariat in 1919, before growing alarmed at some of his protégé's innovative excesses and dismissing him. In 1923 he coined the slogan 'Back to *Ostrovsky', as part of an attempt to curb the tendencies of the theatrical *avant-garde to distort or pervert the classics in the name of revolutionary innovation. During the latter years of his cultural leadership, however, Lunacharsky did his best to protect theatrical practitioners such as Meyerhold and *Tairov from persecution, despite his own predilection for a specifically proletarian culture which would replace organized religion and ensure the masses a kind of collective immortality. Throughout the 1920s he polemicized at public meetings (he was a charismatic orator) and in the columns of various newspapers and journals, whilst continuing to write plays of his own. These are large scale and include some in *verse drawing on themes from Russian *folk-

lore or, like *Oliver Cromwell* and *Faust and the City*, bring together themes from the past with those of the Russian Revolution. During the Soviet period, many theatres were named after him, as was the State Institute of Theatrical Art (GITIS).   NW

LUNT, ALFRED (1892–1977) AND LYNN FONTANNE (1887–1983)

American actors. The Lunts first appeared together in 1919, married in 1922, and made an indelible impression in the *Theatre Guild production of *Molnár's *The Guardsman* in 1924. Of the opening, Alexander *Woollcott wrote that it was possible that 'we were seeing the first chapter in a partnership destined to be as distinguished as that of Henry *Irving and Ellen *Terry'. Both Lunt and Fontanne were well-known actors in their own right—Lunt having risen to stardom in Booth *Tarkington's *Clarence* in 1919 and Fontanne in *Kaufman and *Connelly's *Dulcy* in 1921—but after 1929 they declined offers to act separately. They excelled in *comedy. Plays such as Robert E. *Sherwood's *Reunion in Vienna* (1931) and *Idiot's Delight* (1935), or S. N. *Behrman's *Amphitryon 38* (1937) were specially crafted to exploit the articulate, rapid-fire overlap of their *dialogue and the precise physical collisions that appeared spontaneous. Perfectionists about their work, the Lunts were said to *rehearse almost non-stop, even taking scripts to their bed. The couple developed a close friendship with Nöel *Coward; he wrote *Point Valaine* (1934) and *Quadrille* (1952) for them, and appeared with them to complete the romantic threesome in his *Design for Living* (1933). The Lunts appeared in Sherwood's anti-totalitarian drama *There Shall Be No Night* from 1940 to 1944, performing on *tour in the USA and Britain more than 1,600 times. Their longest Broadway run was in Terence *Rattigan's *O Mistress Mine*, which had 451 performances in 1946–7. In 1958 the couple made a farewell appearance in a much heralded production of *Dürrenmatt's *The Visit* as the opening production in the former cinema on 46th Street, reclaimed as a Broadway theatre and named the Lunt-Fontanne.

MAF

LUPINO FAMILY

Perhaps the best example of dynastic English theatre history. The *family story traces origins in England to Georgius Luppino, a refugee of a wealthy family from Bologna who arrived in Plymouth in 1634, with only his marvellous but previously non-professional skills with *puppets, and goes on to tales of Bartholomew Fair performers, before arriving at George Charles Luppino (1683–1725), a *dancer. Historians cannot substantiate the romantic tales of the early Lupinos, and even the family stories of the eighteenth-century members, such as

George Richard Escourt (1710–87), traditionally supposed to have danced with John *Rich at *Lincoln's Inn Fields in 1718 and designed *scenery and *costumes for Galuppi's *opera *Enrico* in 1743, are unverifiable. Nonetheless, Lupino ancestry in the profession is deep rooted and important. The family members were leaders in traditional and innovatory stage skills—scene *painters, *acrobats, dancers, animal impersonators, singers, *music-hall comedians, *film and *television makers—hard-working stars of entertainment. In the ninth generation, George Hook Lupino (1820–1902) and Rosina Proctor, both acrobatic dancers, had sixteen theatrical children, including George (1853–1932), 'the last of the old-time clowns', Arthur (1864–1908), a famous 'skin' performer who played the dog Nana in *Peter Pan*; and Harry Charles (1865–1925), who with Arthur formed a music-hall act as the Brothers Lupino. These three had many children and grandchildren in the profession, including Lupino Lane, famous for the dance the Lambeth Walk, as well as Stanley (1893–1942), Mark, and Barry (1882–1962), all working comic actors on stage and screen. Barry Jr. was a BBC TV director, and Richard and Ida (b. 1914) went to Hollywood; Ida, 'Queen of the Bs', became a star actress, and movie and TV director. The family renewed itself in each generation by marriages to talent, often linking to other theatrical families: Violantes, Bolognas, Simonets, Websters, Glovers, Crawfords, Pooles, and Lanes were all recruited, and it was the Lupinos' boast that every boy and girl was trained to the profession, and no true Lupino ever left it.

JSB

LUPONE, PATTI (1949–)

American actress and singer. *Trained at *Juilliard, she became a member of the first *touring *Acting Company. Although she has appeared in numerous non-musical plays, she has been best known for her work in *musicals. She won Tony *awards for the title role in *Evita* in *New York and for Reno Sweeney in the 1988 revival of *Anything Goes*. In *London, she created the roles of Fantine in *Les Misérables* and Norma Desmond in *Sunset Boulevard*, although composer Andrew *Lloyd Webber controversially had her replaced in the latter. She has also performed extensively in *film and on *television.

JD

LYCEUM THEATRE (*LONDON)

Theatre situated just north of the Strand near Waterloo Bridge. The first building on this site was converted to a theatre in 1794; a new theatre, called the English Opera House, opened in 1817. Burnt down in 1830, it reopened in 1834 as the Lyceum; its portico still stands in Wellington Street. For 45 years it saw many *managements, chiefly those of the *Keeleys (1844–7), Madame *Vestris and Charles *Mathews (1847–55), Charles *Fechter (1863–7), and the *Batemans (1871–9). The Vestris-

Mathews management was notable for *comedy and extravaganza, Fechter's for French *melodrama, and the Batemans' for *Irving's *The Bells* and Irving's *Hamlet*. Under Irving from 1879 to 1899, and with a repertory of Shakespeare and *romantic drama, the Lyceum achieved years of glory, but they ended in *financial failure when Irving had to yield the theatre to a syndicate; it too failed, and the Lyceum was demolished. Rebuilt in 1904 as a *music hall, it became for nearly 30 years a melodrama and Christmas *pantomime house under the Melville brothers. After 60 years of standing empty and use as a dance hall, it has been reconstructed as a venue for *musicals.

MRB

LYCEUM THEATRE (*NEW YORK)

On West 45th Street, it opened under the name New Lyceum with *The Proud Prince* (1903). Now Broadway's oldest *playhouse, it contains the unique feature of a ten-storey backstage area equipped with dressing rooms, construction shops, and studios, allowing all the technical needs of production to be met in the same building. Its first *manager, Daniel *Frohman, could watch the stage from a private apartment. With business in the doldrums, the Lyceum barely escaped demolition in 1939 when a band of major theatre figures bought it and allowed Frohman to live there until his death in 1940. The Lyceum was sold to the *Shubert brothers in 1945. The greatest of its many hits was *Born Yesterday* (1946). A major period was from 1965 to 1969, when the Lyceum offered a classical repertory under the aegis of the *Phoenix Theatre and Ellis Raab's APA Repertory Company.

SLL

LYDGATE, JOHN (c.1370–c.1451)

Benedictine monk and court poet. Between 1427 and 1435 Lydgate composed seven *mummings, *allegorical entertainments that combined poetic recital and visual representation. The performances were perhaps similar to Lydgate's description in *The Troy Book* (1412–20) of an ancient poet reciting his tragedy while masked actors mimed the action.

RWV

LYLY, JOHN (c.1554–1606)

English dramatist. The grandson of the distinguished grammarian William Lily, he was educated at the King's School, Canterbury, and Magdalen College, Oxford, both institutions with dramatic traditions. He was already established as a writer of prose fiction when his patron, the Earl of Oxford, made him a partner in the first *Blackfriars Theatre in the early 1580s. For the rest of the decade he *managed the associated company of *boy actors and wrote many of the *comedies in their repertory, beginning with *Campaspe* (1583). The company's history was a jerky one. In 1584, the Blackfriars was repossessed (the owner felt its use as a *playhouse violated the terms of the lease), leaving Lyly with no venue for his Ovidian comedy of cross-dressing and metamorphosis, *Galatea*. The play was eventually produced several years later when he secured an alternative theatre at St Paul's; other productions there included his *Endymion* (1588) and *Midas* (1589). In the late 1580s, he was drawn into the Marprelate controversy, and wrote satirical pamphlets in support of the government; he may also have used the theatre to the same end. His company collapsed in disarray soon afterwards, perhaps closed down by the authorities in the wake of the controversy, perhaps merely edged out commercially by the new styles of adult drama developed by *Marlowe and *Kyd. For the rest of his life, Lyly hoped for court advancement, but repeatedly failed to achieve it. He died in poverty.

Performing at upmarket theatres and often at court, Lyly's boy company served a socially elevated clientele, and his plays reflect this. One feature of their courtliness is their polite self-deprecation: there is a deliberate triviality in their mythological subject matter, and where most plays of the time were written in *verse, Lyly typically uses a polished, witty prose; a recurrent comic effect is the wry acknowledgement that some of the *characters' speeches are over-long. Without ever underestimating their own artfulness, these court comedies never arrogate an undue importance to themselves: Lyly's is a drama that bows to its *audience throughout the performance rather than just at the end.   MJW

LYON MUNICIPAL THEATRE

The Lyon theatre opened in 1765 with a production of *Racine's *Britannicus*, starring Mlle *Clairon, whose new simplified *acting style was keyed to the relative intimacy of Jacques-Germain Soufflot's design. Its *auditorium was the first in France to abandon the traditional U shape, inherited from *tennis-court design, in favour of an ellipse truncated on its minor axis, as in *Alfieri's court theatre at Turin, but with three receding tiers of *boxes. Completely autonomous, the theatre offered both actors and the 2,000 spectators it could hold a degree of comfort and security unknown in *Paris *playhouses: dressing rooms, scene docks, and administration offices were all accommodated under the same timber-less, stone-vaulted roof as the *stage and *auditorium. There were two cafés, a spacious warming room on the first floor, wide evacuation corridors on all levels, and—for the first time anywhere—a fire *curtain. The theatre was demolished in 1827.   JG

LYRIC THEATRE HAMMERSMITH

This west *London theatre (seating capacity 537) arose from the ruins of an onstage *fire. Rebuilt in the Victorian rococo style by Frank Matcham, the Lyric's 1895 opening night was launched by Lillie *Langtry. Renowned for spectacular *pantomimes and *melodramas, it became Nigel *Playfair's 'Lyric Ham' in the 1920s. Fashionable West End *audiences came for Ellen *Terry's final stage appearance in *Crossings* (1925) and rising stars John *Gielgud, Edith *Evans, and Elsa Lanchester. The war and post-war years brought the Royal Navy's 1945 all-male drag *revues and the première of *Pinter's *The Birthday Party* (1958). In 1972 it was demolished to make way for a shopping centre, but public demand led to a new theatre in 1979, incorporating elements of Matcham's original *auditorium. Under Neil Bartlett's direction in the 1990s, it created adventurous in-house productions and collaborations with the *Maly Theatre of *St Petersburg, Theatre de *Complicité, and Tamasha.   RVL

LYTTELTON THEATRE *See* NATIONAL THEATRE OF GREAT BRITAIN.

LYTTON, EDWARD BULWER, LORD *See* BULWER-LYTTON, EDWARD.

LYUBIMOV, YURY (1917–)

Soviet/Russian director. After *training as an actor, Lyubimov joined the troupe of the Vakhtangov Theatre after the war. In the 1950s he taught a course at the Shchukin School, where he directed *Brecht's *The Good Person of Setzuan*, which was so successful that he was given the *artistic direction of the *Taganka Theatre, which opened in 1964 with the same play. Lyubimov developed a repertoire of prose adaptations and montages of poetry and other texts, the director effectively authoring the production. *Listen!* (1967), for example, was based on *Mayakovsky's poetry and integrated the poet's biography into the production with the presence of five Mayakovskys, each representing a different facet of his personality. Lyubimov created a genuinely synthetic theatre, drawing on *music hall, *circus, and *shadow play, and involving well-known composers and set designers such as Edison Denisov and David *Borovsky. Lyubimov largely drew on the *theories of Brecht and *Meyerhold, never formulating his own. In the 1960s his work assumed solidarity with the individual and promoted confidence in independent action in work like *Ten Days That Shook the World* (1965), where the *audience's opinion on the production was cast in a poll at the end of each performance. In the 1970s, as Lyubimov's position became more vulnerable and his productions increasingly subjected to *censorship, the tone changed to doom and despair about the individual in society. In *Hamlet* (1971) the main part was played by the bard Vladimir *Vysotsky, reciting Pasternak's unpublished poem 'Hamlet' to the guitar. Vysotsky's *costume—a black sweater and jeans—made him a man of the people rather than a prince, and his troubles of conscience could be shared by the audience.

The folk singer and poet Vladimir Vysotsky as Hamlet (right) with the King and Queen, directed by Yury **Lyubimov**, Taganka Theatre, Moscow (in repertory 1971–80). The chief feature of David Borovsky's design was a massive curtain on movable tracks that swept the dead and the dying into a pit grave, a not-so-subtle critique of Stalinist political methods.

Lyubimov was exiled in 1983 during a stay in *London, where he directed *Crime and Punishment*. He was allowed to return for a visit in 1988, and permanently in 1989; he resumed the artistic direction of the Taganka in 1991 and continued to apply the aesthetics of his early productions in work such as *Doctor Zhivago* and *Marat/Sade*. BB